THE NEW COMPREHENSIVE A–Z CROSSWORD DICTIONARY

THE NEW COMPREHENSIVE A–Z CROSSWORD DICTIONARY

Compiled by
Redentor Ma. Tuazon
and
Edy Garcia Schaffer

BARNES & NOBLE
BOOKS
NEW YORK

This edition published by Barnes & Noble, Inc.,
by arrangement with G.P. Putnam's Sons

1993 Barnes & Noble Books

ISBN 0-88029-371-3

Printed and bound in the United States of America

M 15 14 13 12 11 10 9 8 7

To Edy, whose generous material support and encouragement enabled me to finish this book, and to our children Bobby, Lynn and Ruby.

Also to Blas F. Ople, Philippine Secretary of Labor, and Rafael L. Dizon, Sr., for timely aid.

Redentor Ma. Tuazon

"Most puzzle dictionaries can be more of a riddle than the puzzle you are seeking to solve. One of the attractions of this dictionary is the alphabetical arrangement, a practical method which enables the puzzle fan to go directly to subject words on the basis of the barest clue." *Charles Preston*

Foreword

The authors and the publishers want you to know that no effort has been spared to bring to you, the serious word puzzle fan, the most comprehensive and useful crossword dictionary available on the market today.

The compiling, assembling and cross-referencing of the material for this compendium of clues and solutions took almost half a century. In recent years, special attention has been paid to updating clues, adding current material and making sure that the puzzle addict is fully equipped to do battle with today's clever and wily crossword puzzle constructors.

In the setting of the text, no less than three different types have been used so as to proffer an easy-to-read-and-understand page. Individual and initial entries are set in a clean boldface type. Subentries are indented and set in an unobtrusive lightface. (If a subentry, however, has a further indented subentry, the column's head reverts to boldface to catch the eye.) All solution words appear in small caps. A bold type runninghead allows quick location of clue words in this completely alphabetized work.

The following page lists the abbreviations used in this book. Though necessary to make manageable a work of these proportions, they have been used sparingly in the interest of readability.

The authors and the publishers hope that they have succeeded in putting together a volume that will take its place on shelves alongside more serious reference works and see practical and pleasurable use for years to come.

Listing of Abbreviations Used

abbr.	abbreviation
Austral.	Australian
Brit.	British
colloq.	colloquial
comb. form	combining form
Eng.	English
Fr.	French
Ger.	German
Gr.	Greek
Ital.	Italian
Lat.	Latin
Mex.	Mexican
myth.	mythology
N.	North
Russ.	Russian
S.	South
Scot.	Scottish
sl.	slang
Sp.	Spanish
U.S.	United States

THE NEW COMPREHENSIVE A–Z CROSSWORD DICTIONARY

A

A, Greek .... ALPHA
Hebrew .... ALEPH
aa .... LAVA
aardvark .... ANTEATER, ANTBEAR
eating place .... ANTHILL, FORMICARY
Aaron's ally .... HUR
brother .... MOSES
death mount ...... HOR
miracle worker ..... ROD
rod .... MULLEIN
sister .... MIRIAM
son ...... NADAB, ABIHU
aba .... ROBE, GARMENT
abaca .... LINAGA, LUPIS, HEMP, FIBER
product .... ROPE
aback, taken .... SURPRISED, STARTLED, CONFUSED, DISCONCERTED
Abaddon .. HELL, ABYSS, SATAN
angel .... APOLLYON
abaft .... ASTERN, AFT, BEHIND, REAR
abalone .... ORMER, SNAIL, EARSHELL, ASSEIR, MOLLUSK
abandon .... LEAVE, DISCARD, FORSAKE, DESERT, ABDICATE
abandoned .... DESOLATE, DERELICT, FORSAKEN, LEFT
abandonment .... DESERTION, DESOLATION, DEFECTION
à bas .... DOWN
abase ...... DEMEAN, LOWER, HUMBLE, DEGRADE, DISHONOR
abasement .... SHAME, HUMILIATION, DEGRADATION
abash ... EMBARRASS, SHAME, CONFOUND, DISCOMFIT, DISCONCERT, CONFUSE
abate ...... SUBSIDE, LESSEN, DECREASE, DIMINISH, LOOSEN, WANE, QUASH, EASE
abatement .... LETUP, REDUCTION, EASEMENT
abatis .... BARRICADE
abattoir .. SLAUGHTERHOUSE, SHAMBLES
abb .... YARN, WOOL
abba .... FATHER
abbe ... ABBOT, MONK, PRIEST
domain .... ABBACY, MONASTERY
abbess .... AMMA
domain ...... CONVENT, NUNNERY
who loved Abelard ..... HELOISE
abbey .. CONVENT, MONASTERY
head ..... ABBOT, ABBESS
of an .... ABBATIAL
abbot ... ABBE, ABBAS, COARB, HEGUMEN
assistant .... PRIOR
hero .... ROLLO
abbreviate .... SHORTEN, CONTRACT, CUT
ABC power ..... ARGENTINA, BRAZIL, CHILE
abdicate .. RENOUNCE, RESIGN, SURRENDER
abdication .... DEMISSION
abdomen ... BELLY, STOMACH, PAUNCH, VENTER
of the .... ALVINE
abdominal .... VENTRAL
limb, crustacean .... PLEOPOD
pain .... COLIC, COLLYWOBBLES, PYROSIS
region .... PUBES
swelling .... BLOAT
abduct .... KIDNAP
slang .... SNATCH, SHANGHAI
Abdul the Bul Bul ..... AMIR
Abel's brother .... CAIN
parent .... ADAM, EVE
Abelard's love ...... HELOISE
abele .... POPLAR, PINE
aberration ...... DEVIATION, DERANGEMENT, DELIRIUM
abet ... EGG, FOMENT, INCITE, AID, HELP, SECOND
abeyance .... SUSPENSION, PENDENCY
abhor .. DETEST, HATE, LOATHE
abhorrence .... AVERSION, ODIUM, HATRED, DETESTATION
abide .... DWELL, LIVE, STAY, REMAIN, (A)WAIT, TARRY
abiding ... ENDURING, LASTING
Abie's loved one .... ROSE
abigail .... MAID
Abigail's husband ..... NABAL, DAVID
Abijah's son .... ASA
ability .... FLAIR, POWER, PROWESS, TALENT, CALIBER, FACULTY
to borrow .... CREDIT
to feel ..... (A)ESTHESIA, SENSATION
to read and write .... LITERACY
abject .... BASE, PITIFUL, WRETCHED, SERVILE
abjectly afraid .... CRAVEN
abjure ... RECANT, REPUDIATE, DENY, RENOUNCE, DISAVOW
ablaze .... AFLAME, AFIRE, BURNING, EAGER, EXCITED
able .... HABILE, ADEPT, SKILLFUL, SKILLED, COMPETENT, QUALIFIED
to pay .... SOLVENT
to read and write .... LITERATE
to reason .... SANE
willing and .. READY, SET
ablegate .... ENVOY
abluent .... DETERGENT, SOAP
ablution .... BATH(ING), WASHING, CLEANSING
abnegation .... DENIAL
Abner epithet/character ... LIL
abnormal .... IRREGULAR, UNNATURAL, ODD
eye condition .... MYOPIA
Abo .... TURKO
abode ...... NEST, HABITAT, RESIDENCE, HABITATION, HOME
of animals ... LAIR, DEN, WARREN, HUTCH, STY
of birds ..... NIDE, NEST, AERIE, COTE, AVIARY
of gods ...... ASGARD, OLYMPUS
of humans ..... MIGARD
of paradise .... EDEN
of sinner's soul ... LIMBO, PURGATORY
of the dead ..... ARALU, ORCUS, HADES, SHEOL, PARADISE, NIRVANA
of the Muses .... PARNASSUS
abolish .... ANNUL, CANCEL, REPEAL, REVOKE, DISCARD
aboma .... SNAKE, BOA
abominable .... VILE, LOATHSOME, DETESTABLE, HATEFUL, HEINOUS
Snowman .... YETI
abominate ... DETEST, LOATHE, EXECRATE, HATE
abomination .... PLAGUE, AVERSION, HATRED, LOATHING
aboriginal .... NATAL, FIRST, INDIGENOUS
weapon .... WADDY, BOOMERANG, NULLA, BLOWPIPE, WO(O)MERA
aborigine .... NATIVE, INDIGENE
world boxing champ .... (LIONEL) ROSE
abort ...... CHECK, THWART
abortion .... MISCARRIAGE
illegal .... FETICIDE, ABORTICIDE
abortive .... FRUITLESS, UNSUCCESSFUL
abound .... TEEM, SWARM
abounding .... RIFE, PLENTIFUL, TEEMING
suffix .... FUL, ULANT
about .... OF, ANENT, RE, REGARDING, CIRCA, ALMOST, CONCERNING
face: colloq. ... REVERSAL, SOM(M)ERSAULT, TURNABOUT
above ... OVER, ALOFT, HIGHER, ATOP, UPON, PAST, SUPRA
board ..... LEGIT, OPEN, HONEST, FAIR, BLAMELESS
poetic .... O'ER
prefix ...... SUPER, SUPRA
reproach ..... INNOCENT, BLAMELESS, PURE
the ear .... EPIOTIC
zero .... PLUS

abra .... DEFILE, PASS
abracadabra .... SPELL, JARGON, GIBBERISH
abrade ... RUB, CHAFE, GRATE, RASP, SCRAPE, WEAR, ERODE
abrading tool .... FILE, RASP
abrading material .... EMERY, CORUNDUM, SAND(PAPER), ERODENT
Abraham's birthplace ..... UR
brother .... HARAN
father .... TERAH
grandfather ..... NAHOR
nephew .... LOT
son ..... ISAAC, MEDAN, SHUAH, ISHMAEL
wife ..... SARAH, SARAI
abramis ... BREAM, CARP, FISH
abrasion ..... SCRAPE, BRUISE
abrasive ... EMERY, BORT(Z), ERODENT, QUARTZ, SAND(PAPER), TRIPOLI
abraxas ... CHARM, GEM, STONE
abri ...... SHELTER, DUGOUT
abridge ... SHORTEN, CURTAIL, EDIT, DIGEST
abridgment .... SUMMARY, SYNOPSIS, DIGEST, EPITOME, COMPEND(IUM)
abroad .... OUTDOORS, OVERSEAS, AWAY
abrogate .... ANNUL, CANCEL, REPEAL, ABOLISH, RESCIND
abrogation ...... RESCISSION, CASSATION, ABOLITION
abrupt ... STEEP, RUDE, HASTY, BRUSQUE, CURT, GRUFF, SUDDEN, UNEXPECTED
abruptly ... SPANG, SUDDENLY
Absalom's captain/cousin .... AMASA
father .... DAVID
sister .... TAMAR
slayer .... JOAB
abscess ...... PUSTULE, BOIL, FESTER, ULCER
on gums ..... GUMBOIL
abscond .... ELOPE, FLEE, DECAMP, LEVANT, ESCAPE, ELOINE
absence, leave of ..... EXEAT, PERMIT, FURLOUGH
of feeling .... INSENSATE, COLD, NUMB
of hair .... ACOMIA, ALOPECIA
of motion .. REST, INERTIA
of shame .... BRAZEN
of taste .... AGEUSIA
absent ..... AWAY, OUT, GONE
minded .... LOST, ABSORBED, DISTRAIT, PREOCCUPIED
without leave ..... AWOL
absentee, a kind of .... MALINGERER, TRUANT
absinthe ... GENIPI, LIQUEUR, WORMWOOD
absolute ...... UTTER, TOTAL, SHEER, PLENARY, WHOLE, CERTAIN, DEFINITE, PURE, VERY, STARK
independence ...... ALOD
rule .... AUTARCHY, DESPOTISM
ruler ..... DESPOT, TSAR, SULTAN, SHAH, CZAR
superlative .... ELATIVE, ULTRA
absolutely .... SIMPLY, CERTAINLY, UTTERLY
absolution .... REMISSION, PARDON, FORGIVENESS, CLEARANCE
absolve ...... PARDON, REMIT, ACQUIT, CLEAR, FREE, EXONERATE
in law .... VESTED
sin .... SHRIVE
absorb ..... ENGROSS, SUCK, ENGULF, DRINK, SWALLOW, ASSIMILATE
absorbed ... (W)RAPT, ENRAPT, LOST, ENGROSSED, ASSIMILATED
absorbent .... BIBULOUS
material .... SPONGE, BLOTTER, GAUZE
abstain .... REFRAIN, DESIST, FORBEAR, DENY
from .... ESCHEW
from eating .... FAST
abstainer of a kind .... TEETOTALER, DRY
abstemious ...... TEMPERATE, MODERATE, SOBER
absterge ... PURGE, CLEAN(SE), WIPE
abstinence .. SELF-RESTRAINT, SELF-DENIAL
from alcoholic drinks .... TEETOTALISM, SOBRIETY
sexual .... CHASTITY, CONTINENCE, CELIBACY
total ...... TEMPERANCE
abstract ...... REMOVE, BRIEF, STEAL, PRECIS, COMPEND, EPITOME, SUMMARY, RESUME, DIGEST
being .... ENS, ESSE
abstraction .... NOTION, PREOCCUPATION
abstruse ... DEEP, RECONDITE, ESOTERIC, SUBTLE, HIDDEN
absurd .... RIDICULOUS, SILLY, NONSENSICAL, INEPT, FOOLISH, PREPOSTEROUS
slang ... COCKEYED, RICH
absurdity .... NONSENSE, FOOLISHNESS
abundance ...... PLENITUDE, RIFE, EXUBERANCE, WEALTH, GALORE, STORE
abundant .. AMPLE, PLENTIFUL, TEEMING, AFFLUENT, RIFE
abuse ..... REVILE, MISTREAT, RAIL, MISUSE, VIOLATE, SCOLD, MALTREAT(MENT)
a confidence .... BETRAY
abut .... ADJOIN, BORDER
abysm .... ABYSS
abysmal .... FATHOMLESS, IMMEASURABLE
abyss .... CHASM, GULF, HOLE, PIT, DEPTH
Babylonian mythology .. APSU
below Hades .. TARTARUS
Abyssinia ... ETHIOPIA, AXUM
Abyssinian .... KAF(F)A, ETHIOPIAN
banana .... ENSETE
capital .... ADDIS ABABA
city ..... HARAR, ADOWA
coin/money ..... TALARI, GIRSH, BESA
dialect ..... GEEZ, GHESE
district .... HARAR
division .... SHOA, TIGRE
drink ..... BOUSA, MESE
emperor .... NEGUS, SELASSIE, MENELIK
fly .... ZIMB
grain/plant .... TEFF
Hamite ..... AGAO, BEJA, AFAR(A)
herb .... RAMTIL
lake .... TSANA, DEMBEA
language .... SAHO, GEEZ, AMHARIC, AGOW
liquid measure .... KUBA
money .... BESA, TALARI
mountain .... AMBA
ox .... GALLA, SANGA
primate .... ABUNA
prince .... RAS
river ..... MOFER, MAREB, ABAI
rock salt money ... EMOL
tree .... KOSO, CUSSO
tribe .... AFAR
tribesman .... SHOA
wolf .... KABERU
weight ..... AKET, ALADA, KASM, NATR
acacia ...... LOCUST, BABUL, SHRUB, MIMOSA, SHITTAH, MYALL, WATTLE
astringent ..... CATECHU
academe .... GROVE
academic .... CLASSIC, SCHOLASTIC, SCHOLARLY, PEDANTIC, SPECULATIVE
achievement .... DEGREE, DOCTORATE
costume appendage ..... LIRIPIPE
degree, kind of .... LICENTIATE
paper .... THESIS
Acadia .... NOVA SCOTIA
acaleph .... JELLYFISH, SEA NETTLE
acarid .... MITE, TICK, ARACHNID
acaudal/acaudate ... TAILLESS
accede ..... CONSENT, AGREE
accelerant .... CATALYST
accelerate ... SPEED, HASTEN, RACE, STEP-UP
accelerator ... THROTTLE, GUN
accent .. TONE, STRESS, BROGUE, ICTUS, EMPHASIS, MARK
accenting syllable ...... ARSIS
accentuate .... STRESS, EMPHASIZE, HEIGHTEN
accept ..... ADMIT, SWALLOW, ALLOW, RECEIVE, GRANT
as true .... CREDIT, ADMIT
accepted standard ..... NORM, TYPE, MODEL, PAR
access ...... ENTREE, ENTRY,

INCREASE, ADMISSION, APPROACH
accessible .... OPEN APPROACHABLE
accessory .... ADJUNCT, APPURTENANT, ACCOMPLICE, ADDITIONAL, EXTRA
accident ... CASUALTY, MISHAP
accidental ...... FORTUITOUS, CASUAL, ADVENTITIOUS
accipiter ... HAWK, EAGLE, OWL
acclaim ...... LAUD, PRAISE, APPLAUD, HAIL
acclamation .... SHOUT, CRY, PRAISE, PLAUDIT
word of .... OLE, BRAVO, BANZAI, MABUHAY, RAH, HAIL, AVE, HEIL
acclimate ..... ENURE, INURE, ACCUSTOM
acclivity .... SLOPE, TALUS
accolade .... AWARD, HONOR, PRAISE, EMBRACE
accommodate ... LEND, ADAPT, OBLIGE, GRANT, ADJUST, RECONCILE, LODGE
accommodation ... LODGING, LOAN, BERTH, FAVOR
accompaniment .... VAMP
accompany .... JOIN, ESCORT, CONVOY, CHAPERON(E)
accomplish .... EFFECT, ACHIEVE, FILL UP, DO
accomplished ...... SKILLED, SKILLFUL, PROFICIENT, POLISHED
accomplishment .... ACHIEVEMENT, DEED, SKILL, TALENT
accord .... UNITY, GIVE, CONCERT, UNISON, HARMONY
according to ...... PER, ALLA, PURSUANT
good form ... DE RIGUEUR
law/rule ..... LEGAL(LY), LEGITIMATE, DE REGLE, FORMAL
morals .... ETHICAL
usage .... CUSTOMARY
accordion-like instrument .... CONCERTINA, MELODEON
accost .... HAIL, GREET, CALL, ADDRESS, SALUTE
account .... STATEMENT, EXPLAIN, COMPUTE, STORY, SCORE, TAB, SAKE, REPORT
entry ...... ITEM, CREDIT, DEBIT
accounting ..... BOOKKEEPING
form .... LEDGER
accouter ...... DRESS, EQUIP, ARRAY, OUTFIT
accouterment ... TRAPPING(S), HABILIMENT
accredit .... APPOINT, DEPUTE, AUTHORIZE, CERTIFY
Accra is its capital .... GHANA
accrue .... ENSUE, RESULT, INCREASE, ACCUMULATE, ISSUE
accumulate ... AMASS, ACCRUE, COLLECT, GATHER
accumulation ... HOARD, FUND, COLLECTION, HEAP, PILE
accuracy .... PRECISION, FAITHFULNESS
of reproduction .... FIDELITY
accusation ..... CHARGE, RAP, BLAME, ARRAIGNMENT, INDICTMENT
accuse ...... CHARGE, BLAME, INDICT, ARRAIGN, IMPEACH
accustom ...... INURE, ENURE, HABITUATE, TOUGHEN, ACCLIMATE
accustomed ... INURED, WONT, USED, USUAL, HABITUATED
ace ..... STAR, HERO, ONE(R), EXPERT, TIB, ONESPOT
of clubs .... BASTO
queen combination ..... TENACE
to ten in poker .... STRAIGHT
to ten, same suit .... (ROYAL) FLUSH
acephalous .... HEADLESS, LEADERLESS
acerate .... NEEDLELIKE
acerb .... TART, BITTER, SHARP, ACID, HARSH
acerbate .... EMBITTER, VEX, IRRITATE
aces, two .... AMBSACE, AMESACE
acetic acid .... ACETATE, VINEGAR, ESTER
acetone ... ACETOL, KEYSTONE
acetose .... ACID, SOUR
acetum .... VINEGAR
acetylene .... TOLANE, ETHIN(E)
ache ... PAIN, YEARN, THROB, PINE
Acheron ...... HADES, RIVER
tributary ...... COCYTUS
achieve .... ATTAIN, WIN, REALIZE, ACCOMPLISH, REACH
achievement .... FEAT, EXPLOIT, ACCOMPLISHMENT, ATTAINMENT
Achilles .... PELIDES
adviser .... NESTOR
captive .... BRISEIS
parent ... PELEUS, THETIS
slayer .... PARIS
teacher .... CHIRON
victim .... HECTOR
vulnerable spot .... HEEL
warriors .... MYRMIDONS
woman captive ... BRISEIS
achira .... CANNA
achromatic substance ... LININ
acicular ...... SPINY, BRISTLY
acid ..... SOUR, TART, SHARP, BITING, ACERB
base indicator .... LITMUS
etching .... MORDANT
kind of .... AMINO, BORIC, SALYCIC, NITRIC, OLEATE
neutralizer ...... ALKALI
nicotinic .... NIACIN
slang .... LSD
tanning ...... CATECHIN
acidity ..... ACOR, ACERBITY, SOURNESS
acidulous .... TART
acinus .... RASPBERRY
ack-ack fire .... FLAK
gun .... POMPOM
acknowledge ..... OWN, ADMIT, AVOW, SIGN, RECOGNIZE, CONFESS
acknowledgment ..... CREDIT
of liability .... COGNOVIT
acle .... IRONWOOD
acme ...... APEX, PINNACLE, SUMMIT, TOP
acolyte .... ALTARBOY, THURIFER
acolyte's garb .... COTTA
acomia .... BALDNESS
aconite .... ATIS, MONKSWOOD, WOLFSBANE
acor .... ACIDITY
acorn .... NUT, CAMATA, FRUIT, OVEST, MAST
barnacle .... SCUTA
cup .... VALONIA
shaped .... BALANOID
acoustic equipment .... SIRENE
vase .... ECHEA
acoustics .... PHONICS
acquaint .... APPRISE, INFORM, TELL, FAMILIARIZE
acquainted .... KNOWN, FAMILIAR, (CON)VERSANT
acquiesce .... AGREE, ACCEDE, ASSENT, CONSENT
acquire ...... GAIN, OBTAIN, REAP, EARN, GET
in advance .... PREEMPT
knowledge ...... LEARN
acquired knowledge .... EDUCATION
acquisitiveness ...... GREED, AVARICE
acquit .... ABSOLVE, EXCUSE, CLEAR, FREE, EXCULPATE
acquittance .... RELEASE, CLEARANCE
acre, ¼ of .... ROOD
acres, 2.47.......... HECTARE
acrid ... SHARP, SOUR, BITING, PUNGENT, BITTER, HARSH, MORDACIOUS
acrimonious .... BITTER, STINGING, CAUSTIC, HARSH
acrimony .... ASPERITY
acrobat .... GYMNAST, TUMBLER, DAREDEVIL, AERIALIST, STUNTMAN
high-wire ..... AERIALIST
of India .... NAT
tights of ..... FLESHINGS
acrobat's equipment .... BARS, TIGHTWIRE, TIGHTROPE, POLE, TRAMPOLINE
forte ... . STUNTS, SOM(M)ERSAULTS
net .... TRAMPOLINE
risk .... FALL, SLIP
wear .... LEOTARD, TIGHTS, FLESHINGS
acrogen .... FERN
acrolith .... STATUE
acropolis .... CADMEA, CITADEL, HILL, LARISSA
across .... OVER, TRAVERSE, ATHWART, ASTRADDLE, ASTRIDE

combining form .... TRA, TRANS, DIA
acrostic ... AGLA, TELESTIC(H)
act ...... DEED, FEAT, EMOTE, PERFORM, EDICT, BEHAVE
according to rules ...... CONFORM
helpful ..... GOOD TURN
like .... SIMULATE
of prudence .... CAUTION
over .... EMOTE
prima donna's .... TANTRUM
silly .... CLOWN
up .... PRISS
with exaggeration .. HAM, EMOTE
acting by turns ...... ALTERN
pertaining to .... HISTRIONIC, THESPIAN
trophy .... OSCAR, TONY
action ...... DEED, LAWSUIT, ACTIVITY, COMBAT, BEHAVIOR
melodramatic ... HEROICS
put into .... ACTUATE, ACTIVATE
to outwit another .. PLOY
to recover ...... TROVER, REPLEVIN
where it is .... ARENA, STAGE, TABLE, DIAMOND, COURT, OVAL, SCENE, STADIUM, (COCK)PIT
with ridiculous end ..... FIASCO
word .... VERB
activate .... SPARK
activator .... CATALYST
active ... SPRY, ABOUT, AGILE, LIVELY, BRISK, WORKING, BUSY, MOVING, ASTIR
place .... HIVE, HUB
activity .... OPERATION, STIR, ACTION
actor .... STAR, THESPIAN, MIME, HISTRIO(N), PLAYER, PERFORMER, MUMMER
last words of .... TAG
many-faced ...... MUNI, (LON) CHANEY
minor role .... WALK-ON
mythical .... SPELVIN
of a thousand faces ..... (LON) CHANEY
overacting ..... MUGGER
second-rate .... HAM, BARNSTORMER
veteran .... TROUPER
with speaking part ...... SUPER
actors' aid .... (PRESS)AGENT, STANDIN, DRESSER, PROMPTER, ZANIES
apers .... ZANIES
association ... AEA, AAAA
group .... CAST, TROUPE
hint to .... CUE
improvisation ... AD LIB
in dramatics .. AMATEURS
offstage place .... GREEN ROOM
part .... ROLE, LEAD, STAR(RING), VILLAIN, COMIC
pest .... HECKLER
actress (see actor) ...... DIVA, STAR
"blond bombshell" ..... HARLOW
from Brooklyn .... (MAE) WEST
role sometimes .. INGENUE
with "it" .. (CLARA) BOW
with "oomph" .... (ANN) SHERIDAN
actual .... REAL, FACTUAL, TRUE, VERITABLE, DE FACTO
being .... ESSE
actuality .... FACT, TRUTH, VERITY, REALITY
actually ..... REALLY, IN FACT
actuate .... ROUSE, MOVE, INCITE, STIR, MOTIVATE, ACTIVATE
acuate .... POINTED
acuity .... EDGE, WIT, KEENNESS
acumen .... INSIGHT, KEENNESS, SHREWDNESS
acute .... CUTE, SHREWD, SEVERE, CRITICAL, SHARP
A.D., part of ... ANNO, DOMINI
ad .... ADVERTISEMENT, NOTICE, INSERTION
in tennis .... ADVANTAGE
infinitum .. WITHOUT END, ENDLESSLY, FOREVER
interim ..... MEANTIME, TEMPORARY, MEANWHILE
lib .... IMPROVISE, EXTEMPORIZE, ASIDE
sum .... PRESENT
type of ..... CLASSIFIED, DISPLAY, COVER, INSIDE, COLOR(ED)
verbum ..... VERBATIM, LITERAL
verse .... JINGLE
adage .... SAW, MAXIM, PROVERB, SAYING
subject ...... TIME, TIDE
adagio .... SLOW, BALLET(DANCE)
Adam-and-Eve ..... ORCHID, PUTTYROOT
Smith is pseudonym of .. GOODMAN
Adam's mate of legend ...... LILITH
needle .... YUCCA
second mate/rib .... EVE
son ... ABEL, CAIN, SETH
adamant ... HARD, FIRM, SET, IMMOVABLE
Adamite .... NUDIST
adapt ..... ADJUST, CONFORM, FIT, SUIT, ORIENT
add carbon dioxide ... CHARGE
dash of liquor ...... LACE
details ..... EMBROIDER, ELABORATE
member to a board ...... COOPT
on ...... AFFIX, ATTACH
spirits .... LACE
sugar .... SWEETEN
up .... TOTAL, SUM, TOT, TALLY, JIBE
up to .... MEAN, SIGNIFY
adda .... LIZARD
addax .... ANTELOPE
added to .... PLUS
addendum .... ADDITION, APPENDIX
adder ..... ASP, SNAKE, VIPER, REPTILE
addict .... USER, DEVOTEE
slang .... BUG, FIEND
addicted .... PRONE
addiction ...... WONT, HABIT, INCLINATION
adding machine ... TOTALIZER
Addis Ababa is capital of .... ABYSSINIA, ETHIOPIA
Addison, poet ... CLIO, JOSEPH
addition .... ADDENDUM, ALSO, ELSE, AND, ADDEND
to a bill .... RIDER
to a building .... ELL, ANNEX
to a letter .... PS, POSTSCRIPT, NOTA BENE
additional name ...... ALIAS, PSEUDONYM
pay .... BONUS, TIP
addle .... MUDDLE(D), CONFUSE(D), EMPTY
addlebrained ..... MUDDLED, STUPID
addlepated ... STUPID, IDIOTIC
address .... SPEECH, TALK, ACCOST, BEARING, GREET, TACT
army .... APO
navy .... FPO
President's .... WHITE HOUSE
Secretary of Defense .... PENTAGON
to someone ... DEDICATE
adduce .... CITE, INFER, QUOTE, ADVANCE
adeem ..... REVOKE, CANCEL
Adelina, singer .... PATTI
Adenauer's sobriquet .... (DER) ALTE
adept .... ACE, SKILLED, EXPERT, DEFT, PROFICIENT
adequate .... EQUAL, SUFFICIENT, SUITABLE, ACCEPTABLE
Adhem ____ ..... (BEN) ABOU
adhere .... CLING, STICK, CLEAVE, GLUE
adherent .... FOLLOWER, DISCIPLE, ZEALOT, VOTARY, ITE, IST, DEVOTEE, STICKING, RETAINER, PARTISAN
adhesive ...... GLUE, PASTE, PLASTER, STICKY, GUM
adhibit .... APPLY, ADMIT
adieu .... GOODBY(E), FAREWELL, TATA
adios: Sp. .... GOODBY(E), FAREWELL
adipose ...... OBESE, FAT(TY)
adit ...... ENTRANCE, ACCESS, STULM
adjacent .... CONTIGUOUS,

NEAR, ADJOINING
adjective .... ADNOUN
ending .... ENT, IAL, INE, ITE, IST, ISH, OUS
adjoin .... TOUCH, ABUT
adjourn .... CEASE, END, PROROGUE, SUSPEND, RETIRE, RECESS
adjudge .... CONDEMN, DECIDE, SENTENCE, SETTLE, AWARD, DEEM
unfit .... CONDEMN, DISQUALIFY, RULE OUT
adjudicate .... TRY, HEAR, DECIDE
adjunct .... APPENDAGE
adjust .... FIX, ADAPT, ATTUNE, ORIENT, FIT, SUIT
adjutant .... AIDE, HELPER, ALLY, ASSISTANT
bird .... MARABOU, ARGALA, HURGILA
ad-lib .... EXTEMPORIZE, IMPROVISE, ASIDE
adman .... COPYWRITER, HUCKSTER, SPIEL, BARKER
Admetus' wife ..... ALCESTIS
administer .... MANAGE, GIVE, CONDUCT, GOVERN, HUSBAND, DEAL
administration .... RULE, MANAGEMENT, REGIME(N)
administrative body ... JUNTA, JUNTO, BOARD
admiral of fame .... BYRD, NELSON, KING, DEWEY, HALSEY, FARRAGUT
winged ..... BUTTERFLY
admire ...... ESTEEM, REGARD
admissible, in law .... LIE
admission .... ENTREE, ACCESS, ACKNOWLEDGMENT, CONCESSION, CONFESSION
ticket: sl. .... DUCAT
admit .... FESS, ALLOW, OWN, PROFESS, CONCEDE, RECEIVE, INTROMIT
admitted fact .... DATUM, TRUTH, TRUISM
admixture .... BLEND, COMPOUND, ALLOY
admonish .... ADVISE, WARN, REPROVE, CHIDE, CAUTION, SERMON(IZE)
adnoun .... ADJECTIVE
admonisher .... MONITOR, ADVISOR, MENTOR
admonition .... ADVICE, WARNING, REPRIMAND
first word of, sometimes .. DON'T
ado .... FUSS, STIR, POTHER, BUSTLE, TO-DO
adobe .... CLAY, BRICK, DOBY
adolescence .... YOUTH, TEENS, TEENAGE, NONAGE
adolescent, designating one ... BOBBYSOXER, HIPPIE, TEENAGER
Adonais, per Shelley ... KEATS
Adonis' slayer .... ARES
adopt .... ESPOUSE, TAKE ON, CHOOSE
adore ..... WORSHIP, IDOLIZE, REVERE, DOTE
adorn .... DECORATE, GRACE, ORNAMENT, BEAUTIFY, EMBELLISH, (BE)DECK, DRESS, DIGHT
with diamonds ... BEGEM
with rich clothing .... CAPARISON
adorner .... DECORATOR, EMBELLISHER
adrenal hormone ... CORTISONE
Adriana's servant ...... LUCE
Adriatic city .... TRIESTE
island .... LAGOSTA
peninsula .... ISTRIA
port .... FIUME, TRIESTE, RIJEKA, RIMINI
resort .... LIDO
seaport .... VALONA, AVLONA
wind .... BORA
adrift ...... DERELICT, LOST, ASEA, AFLOAT, UNTIED, LOOSE
adroit .... HABILE, SKILLFUL, ADEPT, CLEVER, DEFT, NEAT
adularia .... MOONSTONE, FELDSPAR
adulate ..... FLATTER, PRAISE
adulation, object of .... HERO, STAR, CONQUEROR, WINNER, VICTOR
adulator, kind of .... SYCOPHANT, BOOTLICKER, COURTIER, YESMAN, FAWNER, FLATTERER, TOADY, FAN
adulterant, common .. WATER, FIZZ
adulterate .... DEBASE, DEFILE, DENATURE, CORRUPT, ADMIX
adulterated .... IMPURE
adult .... GROWN(UP), MATURE, OF AGE
person ... MAN, WOMAN
insect .... IMAGO
tadpole .... FROG
wriggler ...... MOSQUITO
adust .... BURNT, SCORCHED, PARCHED
advance .... MARCH, PROGRESS, LEND, PROMOTE, LATEN
money .... (IM)PREST
payment ... ANTE, ARLES
slowly ..... CREEP, INCH
to prospector .... GRUBSTAKE
unit .... VAN(GUARD)
word .... TIP, WARNING
advanced .... FAR(GONE)
advancement ..... PROGRESS, PROMOTION, IMPROVEMENT
advantage ..... EDGE, PROFIT, ODDS, USE, BENEFIT, GAIN
kind of, in tennis ..... AD IN, AD OUT
take ..... TRICK, CHEAT, ABUSE
advent .... COMING, ARRIVAL, APPROACH
adventitious .... CASUAL, ACCIDENTAL, EPISODIC
lung sound .... RALE
adventure .... GEST(E), QUEST, ENTERPRISE, ESCAPADE
adventurer ...... SPECULATOR, FORTUNE HUNTER, PICAROON
of old .... KNIGHT, FREEBOOTER, MERCENARY
adventurous .... RASH
adversary ...... ENEMY, FOE, OPPONENT, PROTAGONIST
adverse .... HOSTILE, OPPOSED, UNFAVORABLE, INIMICAL
criticism: sl. .. PAN(NING)
opinion .... CENSURE
reaction, show of ... HOOT, HISS, BOO, RASPBERRY, SCOWL, POUT
adversity .... MISFORTUNE, POVERTY, CALAMITY
advertisement .... AD, INSERTION, NOTICE, ORBIT, HANDBILL, BLURB, BILLBOARD, NEON, COMMERCIAL
abbreviation ... AD, ADVT
book jacket ..... BLURB
interpolate .... PLUG
make-up ...... LAYOUT
slang .... PLUG, DODGER
advertiser .... PLUGGER, SPIELER, HAWKER
kind of .... BARKER
to an ad agency .... ACCOUNT
advertising client ... ACCOUNT
colloquial .... BALLYHOO
contract ...... ACCOUNT
handbill: sl. ..... DODGER
man: colloq. .... HUCKSTER
medium .... NEWSPAPER, RADIO, TV, BROCHURE, BILLBOARD, FLYER, MARQUEE
on book jacket .... BLURB
poster .... BILL
praise in .... PUFFERY
statuette .... CLIO
text .... COPY
advice ...... COUNSEL, REDE, REPORT, MESSAGE, AVISO, ADMONITION
in 1835 .... GO WEST
to stockholders in 1933... SELL, UNLOAD
advise .... INFORM, TELL, APPRISE, CAUTION, ACQUAINT
and ____ ...... CONSENT
adviser .... MONITOR, COUNSELOR, MENTOR, NESTOR, EGERIA
advisory .... HORTATIVE
on weather .... WARNING
advocate .... LAWYER, APOLOGIST, ABETTOR, DEFENDER, PLEAD(ER), ESPOUSE
of majority rule .... DEMOCRAT
adytum .... SANCTUARY, SHRINE, SANCTUM

adz . . . . . AX(E), CUTTING TOOL
Aeetes' daughter . . . . . MEDEA
Aegean gulf/sea . . . . . . SAROS
inhabitant . . . . . SAMIOTE, LELEGE
island . . . . MELOS, SAMOS, TENOS, IOS, NIO, PATMOS, MYTILENE, LESBOS
river . . . . STRUMA
Aegeon's wife . . . . AEMILIA
Aegir's wife . . . . RAN
aegis . . . . SHIELD, AUSPICES, SPONSORSHIP
Aello . . . . HARPY
Aeneas follower . . . . ACHATES
great grandson . . . . BRUT
parent . . . . ANCHISES, VENUS
son . . . . ASCANIUS
wife . . . . CREUSA
Aeneid author . . . . VERGIL, VIRGIL
first word of . . . . . ARMA
Aeolian lyricist . . . . . . SAPPHO
Aeolus' daughter . . . HALCYONE
aeonian . . . . ETERNAL
aerial . . . . IMAGINARY, UNREAL, ANTENNA
battle . . . . DOGFIGHT
bomb: sl. . . BREADBASKET, EGG
bombardment . . . . BLITZ
bombing, describing one . . SATURATION, CARPET
car suspended from cables TELPHER
navigation aid . . TELERAN
stunt . . . . AEROBATIC, LOOP, BARREL, ROLL, LOOP-THE-LOOP
aerialist . . . . ACROBAT, WIREWALKER, BALANCER
aerobatics . . . . . STUNTS, LOOP, ROLL, IMMELMANN TURN
aerolite . . . . METEORITE
aeronaut . . . AVIATOR, AIRMAN, PILOT, SPACEMAN
aeronautics . . . . AVIATION
aerostat . . . . BALLOON, BLIMP, DIRIGIBLE, ZEPPELIN
aerugo . . . . . RUST, VERDIGRIS
aes . . . . BRONZE, COIN
Aesculapius' teacher . . CHIRON
Aesir . . . . LOKI, ODIN, THOR, FREYA, WODEN, BALDER
Aesop . . . . . FABULIST, WRITER
story . . . . FABLE
aesthete . . . . DILETTANTE, CONNOISSEUR, VIRTUOSO
aesthetic . . . . ARTISTIC
aestival . . . . SUMMER
aestivate, opposed to . . . . HIBERNATE
Aether's father . . . . . . EREBUS
Aetolian prince . . . . TYDEUS
afar . . . . AWAY, OFF, DISTANT, HAMITE
affable . . . . POLITE, AMIABLE, SUAVE
affair . . . . . . BUSINESS, AMOUR, MATTER, ROMANCE
of honor, usually . . DUEL
of high school juniors . . . PROM
of seniors . . . . HOP
affect . . . . . . PRETEND, FEIGN, POSE, INFLUENCE, TOUCH, MOVE, IMPRESS, SWAY
affectation . . . . PRETENSE, PRETENSION, POSE, AIR
of elegance . . . FRIPPERY
affected . . . . FEIGNED, FALLAL, POSEY, AFFLICTED, MOVED, HISTRIONIC
elegance . . . . . . FROUFROU
affection . . . . FONDNESS, DISEASE, LOVE, FEELING
affectionate . . . FOND, WARM, TENDER, LOVING
afferent . . . . SENSORY
affiance . . . . TRUST, BETROTH, ENGAGE, PLEDGE, FLIGHT
affiant . . . DEPONENT, TESTATOR
affidavit addendum . . . . JURAT
maker . . . . . . DEPONENT, TESTATOR
taker . . . . NOTARY
affiliate . . . . . JOIN, ASSOCIATE, MEMBER
affinity . . . . . . RELATION(SHIP), ATTRACTION, KINSHIP, CONNECTION
affirm . . . . ASSERT, AVER, AVOW, SWEAR, POSIT, VOUCH, RATIFY
affirmation . . . CONFIRMATION, DECLARATION, ASSERTION
affirmative . . . . POSITIVE, YES, YEA, AMEN, AYE
affix . . . . APPEND, ATTACH, FASTEN, SEAL, STAMP
afflatus . . . . INSPIRATION
afflict . . . DISTRESS, TRY, VEX, TROUBLE, PAIN, GRIPE
affliction . . . . . WOE, DISTRESS, TRIAL, AILMENT, SCOURGE, PAIN, SUFFERING, MISFORTUNE
affluence . . . . WEALTH, RICHES, ABUNDANCE, OPULENCE
afflux . . . . FLOW
afford . . . . SPARE, GIVE, YIELD, SUPPLY, ENABLE
affray . . . . MELEE, BRAWL, FIGHT, RIOT
affront . . . . . INSULT, OFFEND, SLIGHT, DISPLEASE, SNUB
affright . . . . SCARE, ALARM, DAUNT, TERRIFY, HORRIFY
affy . . . . . . BETROTH, ESPOUSE
Afghan(istan) . . . . . . PATHAN, DURANI, HOUND, BLANKET, SHAWL
ameer . . . . SHERE
capital . . . . KABUL
carpet . . . . BUKHARA
city . . . . HERAT
coin . . . . AMANIA
garment . . . . CHADRI
king . . . . SHAH, ZAHIR
language . . . . . . PASHTO, PUSHTU
nomad . . . . KUCHI
parliament . . . . WOLESI JIRGA
pony . . . . YABU
prime minister . . . YUSUF
prince . . . . . AMEER, AMIR
range . . . . . . HINDU KUSH
river . . . . HARIRUD
rug . . . . BUKHARA
ruler . . . . SHER SHAH
title . . . . KHAN
town . . . . . FERAH, HERAT, KUNDUZ, KANDAHAR
tribe . . . . ULUS, SAFI
tribesman . . . . . . PATHAN
valley . . . . WAKHAN
aficionado . . . . FAN, DEVOTEE, ENTHUSIAST
aflame . . . . ABLAZE, GLOWING, BURNING
afloat . . . . . . ASEA, CURRENT, IN CIRCULATION, SEABORNE, AIRBORNE
afoot . . . . . ABROAD, MOVING, ASTIR
aforesaid . . . . PRIOR, ANTECEDENT
aforethought . . . . . PREPENSE, PREMEDITATED
afraid . . . . . SCARED, FEARFUL, FRIGHTENED, TIMOROUS, TERRIFIED
afresh . . . . ANEW, AGAIN
afreet . . . . JINNEE, DEMON, JINNI
Africa's ancient name . . LIBYA
African . . . . NEGRO, NEGROID, BLACK
antelope . . . . ASSE, ELAND, GEMSBOK, KOB, ORIBI, KUDU, IMPALA, BLESBOK, BLESBUCK, ADDAX, PEELE, BUBAL(IS), BUSHBUCK, BOS(C)HBOK, BONGO, GNU, BONTEBOK, KOODOO, DUIKER(BOK)
ape . . . . BABOON
aunt . . . . TANTA
bass . . . . IYO
bat . . . . . . HAMMERHEAD
bird . . . . TURAKOO, UMBER, UMBRETTE, COLY, LORY, LOURI
boss . . . . BAAS
burrowing animal . . . . . . SURICATE, GERBIL(LE)
bushman . . . . . NEGRILLO
bustard . . . KORI, PAAUW
caffeine tree . . KOLA, COLA
camp . . . . BOMA
cape . . . . RAS
capital . . . . DAKAR, ALGIERS, ADDIS ABABA, ANKARA, BOMA, ACCRA, LAGOS, BERBERA, CAIRO
carnivore . . . . CANNIBAL, LION, RATEL, HYENA
catfish . . . . SHAL
charm . . . . GRIGRI
civet . . . . NANDINE
city . . . . . . ORAN, DAKAR, TUNIS, HERAT, RABAT, TRIPOLI, ALGIERS, CASABLANCA, CAIRO, ANKARA
coin . . . . . . PESA, TOQUE, GIRSH, TALARI, RIAL, OKIA
colonist . . . . BOER
cony . . . . DAS, DASSIE
corn . . . . MEALIE

council ... INDABA, BAAD
country .... EGYPT, ALGERIA, ETHIOPIA, CONGO, GHANA, MALI, NIGERIA, SOMALIA, TUNISIA, GABON, UGANDA, TOGO, LIBERIA, ZAMBIA, KENYA, GUINEA, IVORY COAST, MALAWI
dance .... N'GOMA
desert .... SAHARA, KALAHARI
dialect .... TAAL
disease .... NENTA
district ... RAND, NYASSA
dog .... BASENJI
drink .... OMEIRES
explorer .... AKELEY
ferryboat .... PONT
fish .... CHARACIN
fly .... KIVU, TSETSE
fox .... ASSE, CAAMA
garment ... TOBE, KAROSS
gazelle ..... ADMI, ARIEL, CORA, NORA
giraffe-like animal ...... OKAPI
gold district ...... RAND
gorge .... KLOOF
grass .... ESPARTO, ALFA, FUNDI
grass country ... VELD(T)
grivet .... WAAG
harp .... NANGA
hartebeest .... TORA
headland .... RAS
hemp .... IFE
hill .... KOP
hog .... BOSCHVARK
hornbill .... TOCK
horse disease ..... SURRA
Hottentot .... NAMA
hunting party .... SAFARI
hut .... KRAAL
iris .... IXIA
jackal .... DIEB
lake .... NYAS(S)A, T(S)ANA, VICTORIA, CHAD
language ... TAAL, BANTU
lemur .... MACACO
lily ... ALOE, AGAPANTHUS
master .... BAAS
mint plant ...... COLEUS
money (shell) ... COWRIE, COWRY
monkey .... GRIVET, COLOBUS, MACAQUE, MONA, BASENJI, GUENON
Moslem .... BERBER
mountain .... ATLAS, CAMERON, KILIMANJARO
mountain pass ..... NEK
musical instrument ..... NANGA
native ...... ASHA, ZULU, DAMARA, ASHANTI, FULAH, MAUMAU, KOPI, IBO, WATU(T)SI
nut tree .... COLA
palm ...... DOOM, DOUM
peasant .... KOPI
pigmy ..... HOTTENTOT, NEGRILLO, ITA
pirate .... ALGERINE
plant .... IXIA, ALOE, CALABAR, COLEUS
plateau .... KAROO
poisonous tree .... SASSY
port ...... ORAN, DAKAR
Portuguese colony ...... ANGOLA
pygmy ...... [see pigmy]
race .... SOMALI
region .... CONGO, NUBIA, SUDAN, SOUDAN
rhinoceros ..... KEITLOA
river ...... GABON, NILE, CALABAR, UMO, SENEGAL, TANA, UELE, CONGO, NIGER, ABDA, SHARI, VAAL, BIA, UBANGI, BENIN, ORANGE, GABUM, CHARI
rug .... KAROSS
ruminant .... CAMEL
scrub .... BITO
seaport .... TUNIS, CASABLANCA, ORAN, DAKAR
sect .... ABELITE
snake ... ELAP, CERASTES
soldier ... ASKARI, SPAHI
songbird .... LINNET
sorcery .... OBI
spear .... ASSAGAI, ASSEGAI
squirrel .... XERUS
stockade ... BOMA, KRAAL
stork .... ARGALA, MARABOU
tableland .... KAROO
"telegraph" ... TOM TOM
title .... SIDI, AGA, AGHA, NEGUS, RAS
tree .... COLA, ARTAR, BAOBAB, TARFA, KOLA, AKEE, BAKU, SHEA, SASSY, MOLI, SAMANDURA, COPAIBA
tribal conference .... PALAVER
tribe ... BONI, KABONGA, BANTU, KREPI, KUA, GOGO, MAKA, ZULU, KAFFIR, TIBU, ABO, KALI, DOMA, ALUR, NUBA, AKAN, HABE, KETU, VACA, WARI
trip .... TREK, SAFARI
U.N. president .... (MONGI) SLIM
valley .... WADI, KLOOF
village ..... DORP, STAD, KRAAL
weasel .... ZORIL(A)
weasel-like animal ...... ICHNEUMON
whip .... KOORBASH
wild cat .... SERVAL
wild hog .... BOSCHVARK, WART(HOG), BOAR
wild sheep ...... UDAD, AOUDAD, ARUI
wind .... SIMOOM, SIMOON, SAMIEL
witchcraft ... OBEAH, OBI
wolf .... AARD
wood .... TEAK, EBONY
worm .... LOA

Afrikaans ..... BOER, TAAL

aft .... ABAFT, (A)STERN

after ... LATER, NEXT, BEHIND
a while .... ANON, SHORTLY, LATER
dinner treat .... CORDIAL
expenses .... NET
the style of .... A LA

afterbirth .... SECUNDINE

aftermath ..... CONSEQUENCE, ROWEN, RESULT, SEQUEL

afternoon nap .... SIESTA
party .... TEA
show .... MATINEE

afterpiece ..... EXODE, EPODE
of a sort .... ENCORE

aftersong .... EPODE

afterthought .... REGRET, REMORSE, RECONSIDERATION
in letter ..... POSTSCRIPT

afterward .... LATER, SUBSEQUENTLY

Agag's slayer .... SAMUEL

again .... ANEW, ENCORE, MORE, BESIDES
appear/happen ... RECUR
do/say .... REPEAT

against .... CON, ANTI, CONTRA, VERSUS
a person/thing .... UNFRIENDLY, HOSTILE
a thing, in law .... IN REM
morals .... WICKED, OBSCENE, UNETHICAL, ILLICIT
prefix .... ANTI, CONTRA
the current ... UPSTREAM
the law .... ILLEGAL, ILLICIT
the state .. TREASON(OUS), SEDITIOUS

agalite .... TALC

agalloch wood .... ALOE, AGAR, GAROO

agallochum ..... AGAL, AGAR, ALOE

agama .... LIZARD, CHAMELEON

Agamemnon rescued her ..... BRISEIS

Agamemnon's brother .... MENELAUS
children ...... IPHIGENIA, ELECTRA, ORESTES
father .... ATREUS

agamic .... ASEXUAL

Agana IS capital of..... GUAM

agaric .... FUNGUS, MUSHROOM, TOADSTOOL

agate .... MARBLE, ONYX, ACHATE, RUBY, QUARTZ, TYPE

agave .... AMOLE, ISTLE, PITA, SISAL, ALOE, DATIL, MAGUEY, PULQUE, HENEQUEN
juice drink ..... PULQUE, MESCAL

age ..... MELLOW, EON, ERA, CENTURY, RIPEN, YEARS, MATURE, TIME, EPOCH, LIFETIME
designating one ... IRON, STONE, BRONZE, ATOMIC, GOLDEN, TEEN(S),

ADOLESCENCE, PUBERTY, OLD
  of moon on June 1st .... EPACT
  old .... SENESCE, SENILITY
  pertaining to an ... ERAL, EVAL, INNOCENCE, HEYDAY
  same .... COEVAL
aged .... OLD(EN), ANILE, SENILE, RIPE
agee .... ASKEW, AWRY
Agena .... ATLAS
agency .... MEANS, HAND, MEDIUM
  news .... UPI, AP, REUTERS, TASS, DOMEI, MENA, NCNA, HAVAS
agendum .... RITUAL
Agenor's daughter .... EUROPA
agent ...... FACTOR, FACIENT, DEPUTY, ENVOY, EMISSARY, REPRESENTATIVE, PROXY, MIDDLEMAN, PROCTOR, BROKER
  foreign firm .... COMPRADOR
  insurance .... UNDERWRITER
  007 .... BOND
  007 movie .. GOLDFINGER, THUNDERBALL, DR. NO
  undercover .... SPY
  undercover work .... ESPIONAGE
agglomerate .... MASS, LUMP, HEAP, CLUSTER, GATHER
aggrandize .... INCREASE
aggravate .... WORSEN, INTENSIFY
aggregate ..... TOTAL, MASS, SUM, GATHER
  fruit of strawberry ...... ETAERIO
aggress .... ATTACK, INVADE, PROVOKE
aggressive .... MILITANT, ASSERTIVE, PUSHING
aggressor .... ATTACKER, ASSAILANT, PROVOKER, INVADER, OFFENDER
aggrieve ..... SLIGHT, OFFEND, INJURE, WRONG
aghast .... AMAZED, STUNNED, APPALLED, TERRIFIED, HORRIFIED
agialid .... BITO
agile .... NIMBLE, SPRY, LISSOM(E), ACTIVE, QUICK
aging .... SENESCENT
agio .... PREMIUM, FEE, EXCHANGE, DISCOUNT
agitate .... STIR, ALARM, CHURN, ROUSE, EXCITE, DISTURB, FLUSTER, ROLL, WORRY, F(E)AZE, FEEZE
agitation .... RUMPUS, DITHER, TUMULT, POTHER, TURMOIL, FLURRY
  state of .... SEETHING, STORMY, TUMULTUOUS, BOILING, AGOG
agitator ..... RABBLE-ROUSER, PROVOKER, INCITER, DEMAGOG(UE), PROVOCATEUR, FIREBRAND, ANARCHIST, INCENDIARY
Aglaia .... GRACE
aglet .... LACE, SPANGLE, TAG
agley .... AWRY
aglow .... ALIT, SHINING, RADIANT
agnail .... HANGNAIL
agname .... NICKNAME, PET NAME, MONICKER
agnate ...... KIN, RELATIVE, ALLIED
agnomen .... (NICK)NAME
agnostic .... ATHEIST, SKEPTIC, CYNIC, NESCIENT
Agnus Dei .... PRAYER, LAMB
ago ...... PAST, ERST, GONE, SINCE
agog .... EAGER, EXPECTANT, ASTIR
agonize ..... SUFFER, STRAIN, TORTURE, RACK, STRUGGLE
agonizing struggle .... THROES
agony ...... THROE(S), ANGUISH, DISTRESS, SUFFERING, PASSION
"agony ___" of newspaper .. COLUMN
agora .... ASSEMBLY, MARKETPLACE
  coin .... OBOL
agouti .... PACA, RODENT
Agra's pride ..... TAJ MAHAL
Agram .... ZAGREB
agree .... JIBE, CONCUR, MATCH, TALLY, ASSENT, COINCIDE, CORRESPOND, APPROVE
agreeable .... PLEASING, SUITABLE, PLEASANT, WILLING, AMENABLE
  odor .... AROMA, PERFUME, FRAGRANCE, SCENT
  taste .... SAVORY, SWEET, TOOTHSOME, PALATABLE
agreeableness of letter ...... EUTONY
agreement .... PACT, TREATY, CARTEL, ACCORD, DEAL, MISE, ENTENTE, CONCORD, CONTRACT, COVENANT
  in opinion ... CONSENSUS
  with conditions .. ESCROW
agrestic ..... RURAL, RUSTIC, PASTORAL, CRUDE
agricultural ...... AGRARIAN
  overseer .... AGRONOME
  worker .... PEASANT, OKIE, RYOT
agriculture, goddess of ...... CERES, DEMETER
Agrippa's temple .. PANTHEON
Agrippina's son .... NERO
agua .... TOAD, WATER
ague .... FEVER, CHILL
Ahab's cabin boy .... PIP
  daughter ...... ATHALIE
  father .... OMRI
  ship .... PEQUOD, WHALER
Ahasuerus' minister .. HAMAN
  wife .... ESTHER
ahead .... LEADING, FORWARD, FRONT, BEFORE
  forge .... PROGRESS, ADVANCE, LEAD
ahem sound .... COUGH
ahuehuete .... CYPRESS
ai .... SLOTH
aid .... ASSIST, HELP, SUCCOR, ABET, FURTHER
Aida's lover ..... R(H)ADAMES
  rival .... AMNERIS
aide .... ASSISTANT, ADJUTANT, SUBALTERN, LIEUTENANT
  memoire .. MEMORANDUM
aiglet .... POINT, TAG
ail .... PAIN, BOTHER
aileron part .... TAB
ailing .... SICK, ILL
ailment .... ILLNESS, DISEASE, MALADY
  minor .... PIP
aim .... INTENT, PURPOSE, END, GOAL, AMBITION, ASPIRE, POINT, OBJECT(IVE), TARGET, SIGHT
aimless .... DESULTORY, HAPHAZARD, FUTILE, POINTLESS
  scribble .... DOODLE
  wanderer of sorts .... NOMAD, TRAMP, JEW, ROVER
ain .... OWN
air .... ARIA, MEIN, TUNE, MANNER, CARRIAGE, SONG, ATMOSPHERE, MELODY
  apparatus ..... AERATOR, FAN, BLOWER, SCUBA
  bends .... AEROEMBOLISM
  boundary .... FRONT
  castle ..... (DAY)DREAM, AUTISM, FANTASY, REVERIE
  combining form .... AER(I), AERO
  current ... EDDY, STREAM
  currents, rising .... ANABATIC
  expose to ...... AERATE
  fear of ..... AEROPHOBIA
  fill with .... AERATE, GAS UP
  filled film of liquid ..... BUBBLE
  force girl ... WASP, WREN
  fresh .... OZONE
  friction ...... WINDAGE
  gauge ...... AEROMETER
  group .... WING, RAF, USAF, ESCADRILLE
  hero .... ACE
  in motion .... WIND, BREEZE, ZEPHYR
  in violent agitation ..... WHIRLWIND, STORM, TORNADO, CYCLONE, TEMPEST

mail, via ..... PAR AVION
navigation officer ....
AVIGATOR
navigation system ......
SHORAN, TELERAN
of .... AERIAL
open .... ALFRESCO
passage .... FLUE,
NOSTRIL, VENT(IDUCT)
pertaining to .... AURAL,
AERIAL
pipe .... VENTIDUCT,
FLUE
plant .... ORCHID,
EPIPHYTE
poisonous ..... MIASMA,
MALARIA
pure .... OZONE
race marker ..... PYLON
spirit ..... SYLPH, ARIEL
stream producer ....
BELLOWS, FAN, PROPELLER
tight .... HERMETIC
unwholesome .. MALARIA,
MIASMA
upper ..... OZONE, ETHER

aircraft .... AIRPLANE,
DIRIGIBLE, GLIDER,
ZEPPELIN, AUTOGIRO,
HELICOPTER
abrupt climb ....
CHANDELLE
air from propeller ......
SLIPSTREAM, DOWN-WASH
altitude controller ......
BALLAST
altitude indicator ....
ALTIMETER, STATOSCOPE
attack with gunfire ......
STRAFE
battle .... DOGFIGHT
body .... FUSELAGE
bombs .... EGGS
carried by another ......
PICKABACK
carrier .... FLAT-TOP,
AMERICA, ENTERPRISE
climb, sudden .... ZOOM
commercial ...... LINER
delivery of sold ... FERRY
designer ..... SIKORSKY,
FOKKER
detector .... RADAR
dome .... BLISTER
enclosed part ... NACELLE
engine cover ... COWLING
engineless ..... GLIDER,
SAILPLANE
flapping ...... FLUTTER,
ORTHOPTER, ORNITHOPTER
flight ... HOP, BARNSTORM
flight record .... LOG
formation .... ECHELON,
FLIGHT
front .... NOSE
fuel, antiknock ....
TRIPTANE
group ... ECHELON, WING,
SQUADRON, ESCADRILLE
gun turret shield ....
BLISTER, DOME
heavier than air ....
AERODYNE
idle propeller of ....
FEATHER
landing position ....
PANCAKE
landing/take-off strip ...
RUNWAY
launcher on ship ....
CATAPULT
lever .... (JOY)STICK
maneuver on ground ....
TAXI
manufacturer ... BOEING,
DOUGLAS, LOCKHEED,
CESSNA
military scouting ....
GRASSHOPPER
movable flap ...... GILL,
AILERON, RUDDER
navigation aid ....
SHORAN, LORAN, TELERAN,
BEACON
notice to pilots ... NOTAM
obsolete .... CANARD
opening for missile .....
BOMB BAY
pilotless .... DRONE,
GLIDER
pilot's place ... COCKPIT
position finder ... LORAN
propeller .... SCREW
recovery from a dive ....
PULLOUT
runner for landing .. SKID
shed/shelter ... HANGAR,
SHED, AIRDROME,
AERODROME
small .... FLIVVER
squadron ... ESCADRILLE
stabilizer .... FIN,
EMPENNAGE, AIRFOIL
struts arrangement .....
CABANE
stunts ..... AEROBATICS,
(BARREL) ROLL,
LOOP(-THE-LOOP),
SPIN, IMMELMAN(TURN)
tail part .... FIN,
RUDDER, STABILIZER,
ELEVATOR
towed target .... DROGUE
throttle .... GUN
trip .... FLIGHT, HOP
turn .... BANK,
BARREL ROLL, LCOP
twisting force ... TORQUE
type .... FIGHTER,
BOMBER, JET, AMPHIBIAN,
TWOSEATER, MONOPLANE,
COMMERCIAL, LINER
war .... FIGHTER,
BOMBER, MIG, SABREJET,
SUPERFORT, STUKA,
SPITFIRE, SPAD, ZERO
water landing gear ......
PONTOON
window ..... BOMB BAY
wing section for
banking .... AILERON
wing support .... STRUT,
CABANE

airdrome .... HANGAR,
AIRPORT

airedale .... TERRIER

airfoil .... PLANE, TAB

airing .... OUTING,
VENTILATION, REVEALING,
EXPRESSION

airmail, by .... PAR AVION

airman ...... AVIATOR, PILOT,
BARNSTORMER
mythological .... ICARUS
non-flying .... KIWI
would-be .... DODO

airplane (see aircraft) ....
AIRCRAFT, PLANE, AERO,
AVION

airport .... (AIR)DROME,
AERODROME
marker .... PYLON
part .... APRON,
RUNWAY, TOWER
paving .... TARMAC

air-raid shelter .... ABRI,
BUNKER, DUGOUT

airs, given to .... PRISSY,
SNOOTY

airship ..... AERO, BALLOON,
BLIMP, DIRIGIBLE, ZEPPELIN
gas-using ...... BALLOON,
BLIMP, DIRIGIBLE, ZEPPELIN

airtight .... HERMETIC

airy .... GAY, ETHEREAL,
LIGHT, JAUNTY, BREEZY

aisle ..... CORRIDOR, ALLEY,
PASSAGEWAY, NAVE
tread the middle .. MARRY
treader of the middle ...
BRIDE(GROOM)

ait ...... ISLE(T), HOLM, EYOT

Aix-la-Chapelle ..... AACHEN

Ajaccio is capital of .. CORSICA

Ajax, father of ...... TELEMON
the ____ .... LESS

akin .... SIB, AGNATE,
GERMANE, LIKE, RELATED

Al Smith character ...... JEFF,
MUTT

ala .... WING
mode .... STYLISH,
FASHIONABLE
mort .... MORTALLY,
MELANCHOLY

Alabama capital ....
MONTGOMERY
city ... SELMA, ANNISTON,
DECATUR, MOBILE, PELL
county ..... LAMAR, LEE
nickname ....
COTTON STATE,
YELLOWHAMMER
state flower ... CAMELLIA

alackaday .... ALAS

alacrity ...... WILLINGNESS,
READINESS, QUICKNESS,
CELERITY

Aladdin's servant ..... GENIE,
JINNI

alamandite .... GARNET

alameda ... PROMENADE, WALK

alamo .... POPLAR
hero ... BOWIE, CROCKETT
in Texas .... MISSION,
SHRINE

Alamogordo county .... OTERO

Alan, author .... PATON

aland .... DOG

alange .. DREARY, DRAB, DULL
alantin .... INULIN
alar .... WINGED, WINGLIKE, WINGSHAPED, PTERO
Alaric's men .... GOTHS
alarm .... SCARE, PANIC, SIREN, AROUSE, CALL, WARN(ING)
bell .... TOCSIN
poetic .... ALARUM
system for short ... DEWS
whistle .... SIREN(E), BLAST, FOGHORN
alas .... ALACK(ADAY), WOE (IS ME)
Alaska capital .... JUNEAU
former capital .... SITKA
Alaskan auk .... ARRIES
bear .... KODIAK
blizzard .... PURGA
cape .... NOME
city .... NOME, ANCHORAGE, SITKA, JUNEAU, GADSDEN
garment .... PARKA
glacier .... MUIR
highway .... ALCAN
Indian .... TLINGIT, TLINKIT
inlet .... COOK
island .... ADAK, ATKA, ATTU, ALEUTIANS, PRIBILOF, KODIAK
mining town ...... NOME
monument ...... KATMAI
mountain .... ADA, FAIRWEATHER
native .... ALEUT, ESKIMO, DENE
peak .... MCKINLEY
peninsula .... KENAI, UNGA, SEWARD
river ... YUKON, TANANA
seaport ..... KETCHIKAN
town .... FAIRBANKS, NOME
valley ...... MATANUSKA
vehicle .... SLED
volcano .... KATMAI
alb .... VESTMENT, ROBE
alba .... AUBADE, SONG
albacore .... TUNNY, BONITO, FISH, MACKEREL
Albanese, soprano ..... LICIA
Albanian .... GHEG
capital .... TIRANA
city ... SCUTARI, VALONA
coin ..... LEK, QUINTAR
dialect .. TOSK, CHAM, GEG
king .... ZOG
river .. DRIN, ARTA, MATIA
seaport .... SCUTARI, VALONA, AVLONA
soldier .... PALIKAR
spy .... CICERO
Albany is capital of .... NEW YORK
albatross ...... GONY, NELLY, MALLEMUCK
Albee's Alice .... TINY
albeit ... ALTHOUGH, EVEN IF
Alberta scenery .... BANFF
albinism .... ALPHOSIS
Albion .... ENGLAND
adjective for .. PERFIDIOUS
albite .... FELDSPAR
album .... SCRAPBOOK
albumen .... GLAIR
alburnum .... SAPWOOD
alcaide ..... JAILER, WARDEN
Alcestis' husband ... ADMETUS
alchemical .... HERMETIC
alchemist, pioneer .... THOTH
alchemy, work on .. ALMAGEST
alchitran .... TAR, PITCH
Alcides .... HERCULES
Alcinous' gardens .... SCHERIA
alcohol ... INTOXICANT, SPIRITS
crystal .... TALITOL
ingredient ...... ETHYL, AMYL, METHYL
solid .... STEROL
alcoholic .... DRUNKARD, DIPSOMANIAC
drink .... GIN, RUM, MEAD, POSSET, WINE, TOT
drink from rice/molasses ARRACK, SAKE
haunt of ...... SKIDROW
liquor .... TIPPLE, MESCAL
liquor, craving for ...... THIRST
liquor from wine .... BRANDY
liquor, fruit ..... BRANDY
liquor smuggler .... RUMRUNNER
liquor to an Indian ..... FIREWATER
sugar .... TROSSE
Alcoran .... KORAN
Alcott heroine .... AMY, BETH, JO, MEG
alcove .... RECESS, NOOK, ORIEL, BOWER, BAY, NICHE
Alda, Frances ...... SOPRANO, DIVA
aldehyde, liquid ..... CITRAL
alder .... SAGE ROSE, ALNUS, ARN
ale ... BEER, ALEGAR, LAGER, PORTER, FLIP, BOCK, MOM, STOUT, YILL, STINGO, NOG(G)
flavor .... HOPS
ingredient .... MALT, YEAST, HOPS
measure ...... NOGGIN, PINT, GILL
mug .... TOBY, STEIN
strong .... NAPPY, STINGO
sour .... ALEGAR
vinegar .... ALEGAR
alec .... (FISH)SAUCE
Alecto .... FURY
alee, opposite of .. AWEATHER, STOSS
alegar ... VINEGAR, (SOUR)ALE
alehouse .... SALOON, TAVERN, INN, PUB
alembic .... RETORT, STILL, DISTILLER
Alençon is capital of .... ORNE
product .... LACE
Aleppo native .... SYRIAN
alert .... AWAKE, AWARE, KEEN, WARNING, VIGILANT, READY, GLEG
Aleut .... UNUNGUN
Aleutian fish ..... GREENLING
isle ... ADAK, ATTU, ATKA
alewife ...... FISH, WALLEYE, POMPANO, HERRING
Alexander ____ .... POPE, FLEMING, SEROV, KING, ARCHIPELAGO, THE GREAT
Alexander the Great's battlesite GRANICUS
conquest .... ISSUS, ARBELA, PARTHIA
general ...... ANTIPATER
Alexandria, patriarch ... PAPA
Alexandrian courtesan .. THAIS
mathematician .... PTOLEMY
theologian .... ARIUS
writer .... ORIGEN
alfalfa ..... LUCERN(E), PEA, FODDER, MEDIC, SATIVA
alforja .... SADDLEBAG
alfresco .... OUTDOOR(S), OUTSIDE
alga .... NORI, DIATOM, SEAWEED, SCUM, DESMID, ANABAENA, CONFERVA, SPYROGYRA, NOSTOC
filament ...... TRICHOMA
algae genus .... ALARIA
like .... ALGOID
algarroba ..... CAROB, TREE, (HONEY) MESQUITE, CALDEN, LOCUST
Algeria, Roman name .... POMARIA
Algerian capital .... ALGIERS
cavalryman ...... SPAHI
city ...... ORAN, ALGIERS
city section ...... CASBAH
governor .... DEY
grass .... ESPARTO
guerilla chieftain .. ZBIRI
infantryman ..... TURCO
minority group .. BERBERS
native .... BERBER, KABYLE
native quarter .. KASBAH, CASBAH
port ...... ORAN, BONE, ALGIERS
president .... BELLA, BOUMEDIENNE
ruler .... BEY
soldier .... SPAHI, SPAHEE, TURCO
weight .... ROTL
algesis .... ACHE, PAIN
algia, as suffix .... PAIN
algid .... COLD, CHILLY
algolagnia .... SADISM, MASOCHISM
Algonquian Indian ..... CREE, LENAPE, OTTAWA, MIAMI, SAC, SHAWNEE, ARAPAHO(E)
friend .... NETOP
Indian money .... SE(A)WAN, SEAWANT

algor . . . . CHILL
algum . . . . ALMUG, SANDALWOOD
Ali Baba . . . . . . WOODCUTTER
brother of . . . . . . CASSIM
helper of . . . . . MORGIANA
word(s) of . . . . (OPEN) SESAME
alias . . . . PSEUDONYM, OTHERWISE KNOWN, HANDLE
letters before . . . . . . AKA
alibi . . . . PLEA, EXCUSE
alible . . . . NUTRITIVE, NOURISHING
Alice's cat . . . . DINAH
alidade . . . . DIOPTER
alien . . . . FOREIGN(ER), STRANGER, ADVERSE, METIC, OUTSIDER, EMIGRE(E), OUTLANDER
alienate . . . ESTRANGE, WEAN, TRANSFER, DISAFFECT
alienist . . . . PSYCHIATRIST
alight . . . . DISMOUNT, STEP DOWN, ROOST, LAND
align . . . . TRUE, ALINE, STRAIGHTEN
alignment . . . . LINAGE
alike . . . . SIMILAR, AKIN, SAME, MATCHED
combining form . . . . . ISO
aliment . . . FOOD, NOURISHMENT
alimentary canal . . . . ENTERON
motion . . . . . PERISTALSIS
aliped creature . . . . BAT
alit . . . . AGLOW, LANDED, DISMOUNTED, RADIANT
alive . . . . QUICK
alkali . . . . . . LYE, SALT, SODA, SALTWORT, POTASH, ANTACID
alkaline . . . . LIME, OXIDE
solution . . . . LYE
alkaloid . . . . ARICIN, CAFFEIN(E), ESERINE, ARABINE, CODEINE, DITAMIN, SINAPIN, CAPSAICIN, QUININ(E), MESCALINE, BERBERIN(E), MORPHINE
bean . . . . ESERIN
hemlock . . . . . . CONIN(E)
mushroom . . MUSCARINE
poison(ous) . . . . CURARE, CONIN, MUSCARIN(E), BRUCIN(E), TROPIN(E), THEBAINE
sedative . . . . . CODEIN(E)
tea . . . . THEINE
alkanet . . . . ANCHUSA, BUGLOSS, DYE
alkene . . . . OLEFIN
all . . . . . WHOLE, EVERY(ONE), ANY, TOTAL(ITY), ENTIRE
around . . . . VERSATILE
combining form . . . . PAN, OMNI
creating . . . . OMNIFIC
fours . . . . SEVEN UP
in . . . . TIRED, WEARY, FATIGUED
in Latin . . . . TOTO
in music . . . . TUTTI
powerful . . . OMNIPOTENT
religions, believer in . . . . OMNIST
right . . . . . HONEST, GOOD
Saints' Day, observance . . HALLOWMASS, HALLOWEEN
seed . . . . KNOTWEED, GOOSEFOOT
seed herb . . . . . RADIOLA
allan . . . . GULL
allanite . . . . . ORTHITE, CERINE
allay . . . CALM, EASE, RELIEVE, ASSUAGE, ASSURE, QUIET, MOLLIFY, SLAKE, ALLEVIATE
allegation . . . . . PLEA, CLAIM, AVERMENT, EXCUSE, ALIBI
allege . . . CLAIM, ASSERT, STATE
alleged electric force . . . ELOD
force . . . . OD, ODYLE
Allegheny city . . . . OLEAN
allegiance . . . . FEALTY, LOYALTY, DEVOTION
allegorical . . . . PARABOLIC
allegory . . . . PARABLE, FABLE
Allen, ____ . . FRED, STEVE, IRA, ETHAN
allergic reaction . . . . BASH, SNEEZE, COLD
skin condition . . . . HIVES
to firearms . . . . . GUNSHY
allergy . . . . SENSITIVENESS
medicine for . . BENADRYL
alleviate . . . . LIGHTEN, MITIGATE, EASE, ALLAY, LESSEN
alleviation . . . . RELIEF
alley . . . LANE, MIB, PASSAGE, STREET, TAW, WALK, MARBLE
blind . . . . CULDESAC, DEADEND
closed at one end . . . . DEADEND
allheal . . . . . PLANT, VALERIAN
alliance . . . . . LEAGUE, UNION, CONFEDERACY
of nations . . . UN, NATO, SEATO, OAS, AXIS, BIG FIVE
of parties . . . . COALITION
allied . . . . AKIN, SIMILAR, RELATED, UNITED, ASSOCIATED, JOINED
alligator . . . CAYMAN, CAIMAN, SAURIAN, LIZARD, LEATHER
pear . . . . AVOCADO
allium . . . . ONION, GARLIC, LEEK
allocate . . . . . . METE, ASSIGN, GRANT, GIVE, DISTRIBUTE, ALLOT, ASSIGN, SHARE
allot . . . . ALLOCATE, ASSIGN, SHARE, APPORTION, METE
allotment . . . . . . SHARE, QUOTA, PORTION, RATION
allow . . . . PERMIT, LET, ADMIT, PROVIDE, OPINE, TOLERATE
free use . . . . LEND
to become known . . LEAK
allowable variance . . . . TOLERANCE
allowance . . . . SUPPORT, REDUCTION, RATION, TOLERATION
depreciation . . . . . . AGIO
food . . . CORODY, RATION
loss of weight . . . . DRAFT
small . . . . PITTANCE
waste . . . . . TRET, DRAFT
weight . . . . TARE
alloy . . . . . . METAL, MIXTURE, AMALGAM
aluminum . . DURALUMIN, ALNICO
black . . . . NIELLO
cheap jewelry . . . . TOMBAC(K), TOMBAK
copper-nickel-zinc . . . . . . ALBATA, ELECTRUM
copper-tin . . . . . . BRONZE
copper-tin-zinc . . OROIDE
copper-zinc . . . . . . BRASS
gold-like . . . . . . AROIDE, ORMOLU
gold-silver . . . . ASEM, ELECTRUM
iron-carbon . . . . . . STEEL
lead-tin . . . . TERNE, PEWTER
mercury . . . . . AMALGAM
nickel-steel . . . . INVAR
non-ferrous . . . . TULA
pewter-like . . . . BIDRI
sulfur . . . . NIELLO
three-metal . . . TERNARY
tin-copper-antimony . . . . BABBIT, BRITANNIA
tin-copper-lead . . PEWTER
tin-zinc . . . . OROIDE
used in cheap jewelry . . . OROIDE, TOMBAC, TOMBAK, TOMBACK
with aluminum . . . . CALORIZE
yellow . . . . AICH
alloyed . . . . SPURIOUS, SHAM, MIXED, BASE, INSINCERE
allspice . . . . . PIMENTO, BERRY
allude . . . . . REFER, MENTION, CITE
allure . . . . . . ENTICE, ATTRACT, BAIT, FASCINATION, TEMPT, TOLE
allurement . . . . . FASCINATION, CHARM, ENTICEMENT
allusion . . . . . HINT, INKLING, REFERENCE
allusive . . . . . . METAPHORICAL
alluvial clay . . . . ADOBE
deposit . . . . . . MUD, SILT, PLACER
fan . . . . DELTA
matter . . . . GEEST
alluvion . . . . FLOOD, SILT
ally . . . . JOIN, ASSOCIATE, HELPER
alma . . . . . . ALME(H), DANGER
almain . . . . GERMAN
almanac . . . . CALENDAR, YEARBOOK
astronomical . . . . EPHEMERIS
almandine . . . SPINEL, GARNET
almighty . . . . OMNIPOTENT, ALL-POWERFUL
almond . . . . . TREE, LIGHT TAN,

AMYGDALA, BADAM, KANARI
emulsion ...... ORGEAT
eyed .... SLANT-EYED
flavored liquor .. RATAFIA
oil .... AMARIN
shaped ..... AMYGDALOID
almost .... NEARLY
alms .... DOLE, CHARITY
box .... ARCA
distributor .... ALMONER
almshouse ...... POORHOUSE, BEADHOUSE
almuce .... HEADDRESS, TIPPET, AMICE
alnus .... ALDER
alod .... ALODIUM, ESTATE, FREEHOLD
aloe ..... AGAVE, LILY, DRUG, MAGUEY
derivative .... ALOIN
aloft .... UP, IN THE AIR, ASOAR, OVERHEAD
aloha ...... LOVE, GREETING, FAREWELL, GOODBYE, WELCOME
alone ...... SOLITARY, SOLO, ONLY, SOLE, SINGLE
on stage ... SOLA, SOLUS
along .... LENGTHWISE, BESIDE, ON
the way ...... ENROUTE
aloof ..... APART, RESERVED, DISTANT, COLD
alopecia .... BALDNESS
aloud .... AUDIBLE
alow .... BELOW, UNDER
alp .... MOUNTAIN, PEAK
alpaca ...... WOOL, CLOTH, RUMINANT
like animal ... GUANACO, VICUNA, LLAMA
alpha ..... START, STAR, FIRST, DENEB
rays .... BETA
alphabet .... RUDIMENTS, PRIMER
character .... OGAM, RUNE, LETTER
Kashmir .... SARADA
teacher ... ABECEDARIAN
alphabetical list, kind of..... CATALOG(UE), CONCORDANCE
Alpine animal .... IBEX, CHAMOIS
dress .... DIRNDL
goat ..... IBEX, STEINBOK
herdsman .... SENN
house/hut ...... CHALET
pass ..... (MONT)CENIS, COL, SIMPLON
primrose ..... AURIOULA
river .... RHONE
wind .... FOEHN, BISE, BORA
Alps .... TIROL, TYROL, MATTERHORN, BLANC, NERNINA, JUNGFRAU
already .... PREVIOUSLY
Alsatian ...... WHITEFRIARS, POLICE DOG
alsike ...... CLOVER, FODDER
also .... LIKEWISE, TOO, BESIDES, AND

known as ... ALIAS, AKA
ran .... LOSER
alt .... ISLE(T)
Altair .... STAR
altar .... TABLE, STAND
area around ... CHANCEL
boy .... THURIFER, ACOLYTE
carpet .... PEDALE
cloth ... DOSSAL, DOSSEL, PALL, HAPLOMA, CORPORAL, VESPERAL
constellation .... ARA
curtain .... RIDDEL
enclosure .... BEMA
end of the church .. APSE
endowed ..... CHANTRY
offering ...... ALTARAGE, EUCHARIST
part .... PREDELLA, PISCINA
piece .... TRIPTYCH
rail .... SEPTUM
screen/veil .... REREDOS, ANTEPENDIUM
shelf ... GRADIN, RETABLE
slab/top .... MENSA
table .... CREDENCE
altazimuth of astronomer .... ABA
alter ... ADAPT, VARY, CHANGE, MUTATE, MODIFY, PERMUTE
ego .... SIDEKICK, FRIEND, STOOGE
alteration .... CHANGE, REVISION
altercation .... QUARREL, DISPUTE, ARGUMENT, SPAT
alternate .... ROTATE, OTHER, SUBSTITUTE, STAND-IN
alternative ...... CHOICE, OR, EITHER, AND/OR, OPTION
althorn .... SAXHORN
although .... EVEN IF, IN SPITE OF, WHILE
altogether ... IN ALL, WHOLLY, QUITE
altitude barometer .. OROMETER
Altona .... HAMBURG
altruist, one kind of .... SAMARITAN
opposite of ..... EGOIST
alum .... ASTRINGENT, EMETIC, SALT
aluminum compound .... TERMITE, BAUXITE
ore .... BAUXITE
oxide .... ALUMINA, CORUNDUM, RUBY, TOPAZ
alumnus .... GRAD(UATE)
alveary .... (BEE)HIVE
alveolar .... GINGIVAL
alveolate ..... HONEYCOMBED, HOLEY
always .... AY, E'ER, INVARIABLY, (FOR)EVER
alyssum .... MADWORT
ama .... CUP, VESSEL
amadou ..... PUNK, STYPTIC, TINDER
amah .... NURSE(MAID), SERVANT, AYAH
amain .... FORCEFULLY, HASTILY, MIGHTILY

Amakusa port .... AMUTA
Amalekite king .... AGAG
amalgam .... ALLOY, MIXTURE, BLEND, COMBINATION
amalgamate .... MIX, BLEND, FUSE, MERGE, COMBINE
amalgamating pan ...... TINA
amanuensis ...... SECRETARY, SCRIVENER
amaranth .... PIGWEED, TUMBLEWEED, FLOWER
amaranthine ..... DEATHLESS, UNFADING
amaryllis .... AGAVE, SHEPHERDESS, BULB, PLANT, BELLADONNA
mass .... HEAP, GATHER, COLLECT, PILE, ACCUMULATE
Amata's daughter ... LAVINIA, LATINIA
amateur .... DILETTANTE, TYRO, NOVICE, DABBLER, DUB, GREENHORN, NEOPHYTE
athlete's goal .. OLYMPICS
boxing championship .... GOLDEN GLOVES
colloquial ... SIMON PURE
opposite of .... PRO(FESSIONAL), EXPERT
painter .... DABBLER
radio operator ..... HAM
thief, sometime .... SHOPLIFTER
amateurish .... CLUMSY, INEPT, AWKWARD
Amati ...... VIOLIN, NICOLO
amative .... AMOROUS, EROTIC, LOVING
amatol .... EXPLOSIVE
amaze .... SURPRISE, ASTONISH, STUN
amazed .... AGHAST, PUTOUT, AWED
amazing event ..... MIRACLE
trick .... MAGIC, SLEIGHT OF HAND
Amazon ...... RIVER, WOMAN, ANT, PARROT, VIRAGO
cetacean .... INIA
estuary/mouth ..... PARA
fish .... LEPIDOSIREN
part of .... SOLIMOES
tributary .... APA, TAPAJOZ, JURUA, JAVARI, JAVARY, JAPURA
valley Indian .. TAPUYAN
ambagious .... DEVIOUS, CIRCUITOUS
ambary .... FIBER, NALITA, PLANT
ambassador .... ENVOY, DIPLOMAT, MINISTER, AGENT, EMISSARY
papal ... NUNCIO, LEGATE
amber .... RESIN, YELLOW
fish .... MEDREGAL
like .... AMBEROID, AMBROID
ambergris ...... SECRETION, PERFUMERY
ambi: comb. form ..... BOTH

ambience .... MILIEU, ENVIRONS
ambiguous .... INDEFINITE, UNCERTAIN, VAGUE, OBSCURE, DELPHIC
ambit ...... CIRCUIT, SCOPE, LIMITS, BOUNDS
ambition .... GOAL, END, DESIRE, ASPIRATION
amble: sl. .... MOSEY
ambling horse .... PADNAG
ambo .... PULPIT, STAND, LECTERN
Ambracian Gulf .... ARTA
ambrosia .... RAGWEED, BEEHEAD, NECTAR
ambrosial .... DELICIOUS, FRAGRANT
drink .... AMRITA
ambry .... CUPBOARD, LOCKER, CLOSET, NICHE, PANTRY
ambsace ...... DOUBLE ACES, BAD LUCK, TWO ACES
ambulance chaser, so-called .. SHYSTER
ambulant .... WALKING, ON FOOT
seller .... PEDDLER
ambulator ...... PEDOMETER
ambush ...... TRAP, WAYLAY, AMBUSCADE
ameliorate .... IMPROVE, BETTER, RELIEVE, ALLEVIATE
amen ...... VERILY, SO BE IT, APPROVAL
amenable .... OBEDIENT, AGREEABLE, RECEPTIVE, PERVIOUS
to reason .... BROADMINDED, OPEN-MIND(ED)
amend .... ALTER, REVISE, IMPROVE, CHANGE, MODIFY
amendment ..... CORRECTION, REVISION, CHANGE
tricky .... RIDER, JOKER
amends .... PAYMENT, ATONEMENT, REDRESS
amenities, observance of the .. PUNCTILIO
amenity .... COURTESY, CIVILITY
ament .... IDIOT, SPIKE, CATKIN, CHAT, CATTAIL
amerce .... PUNISH, FINE, PENALIZE
America, reputed discoverer .. (AMERIGO) VESPUCCI, ERIC, VOTAN
American (see U.S.) .... YANK(EE), AMERICANO, GRINGO
aborigine ...... INDIAN
admiral .... CARNEY, FARRAGUT, HALSEY, KING, SIMS, NIMITZ, KINKAID, DEWEY
aircraft carrier .... ENTERPRISE, AMERICA
antelope ...... BLESBOK, SASSABY
anthologist .... UNTERMEYER
archeologist .. ANDREWS
artist ..... KENT, FLAGG, WEST, PEALE, HOMER, HICKS, COPLEY, CADMUS, INNESS, BENTON
astronaut ...... WHITE, SCHIRRA, BORMAN, LOVELL, STAFFORD, COLLINS, ALDRIN
author ..... ASCH, AMES, HERSEY, YERBY, HARTE, BAUM, FERBER, LORING, WYLIE, POE, TARKINGTON, HEMINGWAY, SPILLANE, GARDNER
badger ...... CARCAJOU
balladeer ..... GUTHRIE
balsam .... TOLU
battle scene, Phillipines .. BATAAN, CORREGIDOR, MANILA BAY
beauty .... ROSE
bingo .... LOTTO
bird ..... GUAN, TOWHEE, RHEA, JUNCO, GROUSE, ROBIN, STARLING, BOBOLINK, SPARROW
bishop .... SHEEN
cactus .... CEREUS
capitalist .... ASTOR, BARUCH
capital lobbyist .... RAINMAKER
cardinal .... CUSHING, SPELLMAN, BRENNAN
caricaturist .... NAST
cartoonist .... CAPP, FISHER, DISNEY, ARNO, NAST, HERBLOCK, CONRAD, SANDERS, OLIPHANT, MAULDIN, HESSE, DARCY
choreographer .. FOKINE
coin ..... DIME, NICKEL, QUARTER, CENT, EAGLE
columbo ...... GENTIAN
commodore ..... PERRY
composer ...... BERLIN, PORTER, COPLAND, PAINE, NEVIN, IVES, KERN
Confederate soldier ..... REB(EL), BUTTERNUT
contralto .... ANDERSON
critic .... AYRES, HALE
dinosaur .... BRONTOSAURUS
dramatist ...... BARRY, WILLIAMS, ODETS, CROUSE, HART
diplomat .... HARRIMAN, LODGE, DULLES, BOHLEN, GREW
dog .... ALCO
duck ...... BUFFLEHEAD
editor ...... BOK, LUCE, MENCKEN, WALLACE, GREELY, DANA
educator ...... CONANT, HUME, FISK, HUTCHINS, MANN, KIRK
elk .... WAPITI
evangelist ..... GRAHAM
evergreen ..... FIR, PINE
explorer .... PEARY, BYRD, LEWIS, FREMONT, CLARK
fashion designer .. STARR, CHARLES
feminist .... CATT, PAUL, STONE, STANTON
financier .... ASTOR, MORGAN, BARUCH, GOULD
finch ..... JUNCO, SISKIN
flag .... OLD GLORY
flycatcher ...... PHOEBE
fowl ...... WYANDOTTE
frontier scout ... HICKOK
frontiersman ... CARSON, CROCKETT, BOONE
fur merchant .... ASTOR
game .... POKER, BASEBALL, FOOTBALL, BASKETBALL
general .... LEE, GRANT, RENO, BRADLEY, MACARTHUR, OTIS, MEADE, SCOTT, ORD, EISENHOWER, STILWELL, POPE, BURNSIDE, BUELL
general of the army ..... PERSHING, MACARTHUR, EISENHOWER
geologist .... DANA
girl of 1890's .... GIBSON
grapes .... NIAGARA
Great White Father ..... PRESIDENT
guitarist ...... GUTHRIE
historian .... BAILEY, HYMAN, ROBINSON, SCHLESINGER
horse .... BRONCO, PINTO, MUSTANG
humorist ..... ADE, NYE, COBB, ROGERS, NASH, BENCHLEY, TWAIN, LARDNER
illustrator ...... FLAGG, ROCKWELL, NEWELL
imaginary town .... PODUNK
Indian .. HOPI, UTE, SIOUX, ARIKARA, MIAMI, SENECA, PECOS, KIOWA, APACHE, PIMA, LENAPE, BILOXI, CROW, OTOE, OSAGE, PAWNEE, UINTA, LUMMI, POMO
and Negro descent .... SAMBO, GRIFF(E)
ax .... TOMAHAWK
baby .... PAPOOSE
beads ...... WAMPUM
dwelling ...... TEPEE, WIGWAM, LODGE
greeting .... NETOP
grunt .... UGH
language .... NA-DENE
peace offering ... PIPE
pipe .... CALUMET
pony .... CAYUSE, PINTO
trophy .... SCALP
woman's husband .... SQUAWMAN

inventor .... MORSE, HOWE, EDISON, OTIS, FULTON, WHITNEY
ivy .... WOODVINE
isthmus .... PANAMA
Japanese .... NISEI, ISSEI, KIBEI
journalist ...... BROWN, REID, BIGELOW, GUNTHER
jurist .... TANEY, MARSHALL, COOLEY, MOORE, CARDOZO, TAFT, PAINE, LANDIS
jute .... MALLOW
keno ..... BINGO, LOTTO
larch .... TAMARACK
lawyer ... DARROW, PAINE
leopard .... JAGUAR
lexicographer .. WEBSTER
light wood ...... BALSA
lion ..... COUGAR, PUMA
lizard ... ANOLE, BASILISK
lotto ...... KENO, BINGO
lynx .... BOBCAT
mammal .... OTTER, OPOSSUM
Marine .. LEATHERNECK, GYRENE
Mexican name for ...... GRINGO
monetary unit .. DOLLAR
money market .... WALL STREET
monkey .... TEETEE, SAPAJOU, TITI, CAPUCHIN
national military cemetery ARLINGTON
national military park ... SHILOH
naturalist .... SETON, BAIRD, AUDUBON, MUIR
nature writer ..... BEEBE
naval historian .. MAHAN
navy enlisted man ...... BLUEJACKET
navy gripe session .. MAST
newspaper publisher .... SCRIPPS, FIELDS, HEARST
night hawk .... PISK
nightshade ... POKEHEED, HENBANE, BELLADONNA
novelist ...... FAULKNER, BALDWIN, FERBER, STEELE
nutmeg .... CALABASH
operatic singer ... PRICE, FARRAR, CALLAS, STEVENS, ALDA
orator ..... BRYAN, OTIS, HENRY
painter .... SARGENT, BENTON, INNESS, LUKS, BELLOWS, RYDER, CURRY, HOMER, PETERS, SLOAN
painter of animals ...... SETON
paper money .... GREENBACK, LONG GREEN
patriot ... HALE, REVERE, ROSS, ALLEN, OTIS, HENRY, PAINE
"patron saint" .... TAMMANY
philanthropist .... CARNEGIE, HEARST, FORD, RIIS, BARTON, CHANNING, ROCKEFELLER
philosopher ... DURANT
pianist .... DUCHIN, CLIBURN, LEVANT
pioneer .... BOONE
pirate .... KIDD
playwright ... SAROYAN, WILLIAMS, MILLER, ODETS, KAUFMAN, ASCH
plover .... KILLDEER
poet .... POE, BENET, ELIOT, FROST, SANDBURG, LANIER, NASH, AUDEN, GUEST, TATE, WHITTIER, LINDSAY
poetess .... MILLAY, STEIN, LOWELL
political scientist .... MACGREGOR, ROSSITER, NEUSTADT
portraitist .... PEALE
President .. WASHINGTON, ADAMS, JEFFERSON, MADISON, MONROE, JACKSON, VAN BUREN, HARRISON, TYLER, POLK, TAYLOR, FILLMORE, PIERCE, BUCHANAN, LINCOLN, JOHNSON, GRANT, HAYES, GARFIELD, ARTHUR, CLEVELAND, MCKINLEY, ROOSEVELT, TAFT, WILSON, HARDING, COOLIDGE, HOOVER, TRUMAN, EISENHOWER, KENNEDY, JOHNSON, NIXON
president's wife .... FIRST LADY
prime minister of England CHURCHILL
professor of drama ...... BAKER
publisher ... MCCORMICK, HEARST, HOWARD, FIELD, NEWHOUSE, OCHS, COWLES, LUCE, KNIGHT
quail .... COLIN
railroad magnate .... HARRIMAN, REA
rebel soldier .. BUTTERNUT
Red Cross organizer .... BARTON
reformer .... RIIS
Revolution soldier ...... BUCKSKIN
river .... MISSISSIPPI, OHIO, RAPIDAN, HUDSON, WABASH, COLUMBIA
rodent .... RABBIT, SQUIRREL, BEAVER
sculptor .... SMITH, PROCTOR, CALDER
shipyard ...... GROTON
shrub ... CHICO, WAHOO
singer .... HORNE, PRESLEY, MARTIN, BAEZ, PRICE, GARLAND, TUCKER, PAGE, LANZA, STEVENS, EDDY
soldier .... YANKEE, DOGFACE, DOUGHBOY, GI, SAD SACK
songbird ..... GREENLET
songwriter ..... PORTER, RODGERS, BERLIN
soprano .... CALLAS, PONS, STEBER, ALDA, MUNSEL, STEVENS, SILLS
statesman ...... DULLES, BARUCH, BAKER, LODGE, BLAINE, JAY, STIMSON, STEVENSON, ACHESON, BENTON, LOGAN
suffragist .... CATT
surgeon .... MAYO, PARRAN
thrush .... WAGTAIL
tree .... CALABASH, MAPLE, OAK, REDWOOD, PINE, SYCAMORE, ELM, ASH, BUTTONWOOD
volcano .... SHASTA, LASSEN
weather phenomenon ... SMOG, SMAZE, POGONIP
widgeon ...... BALDPATE
wild sheep .... BIGHORN, ARGALI
winter fog ..... POGONIP
wolf .... COYOTE
woman governor, first ... ROSS
wood, light ...... BALSA
writer ...... CALDWELL, MICHENER, MEAD, PYLE, SAROYAN, HARTE
writer in Yiddish ... ASCH
writer of fables ..... ADE
yew .... HEMLOCK

Amerind .... REDSKIN, INDIAN, ESKIMO, CREE
symbol .... XAT
amethyst .... QUARTZ, CORUNDUM, PURPLE, VIOLET
ami(e): Fr. .... FRIEND
amiable ..... AFFABLE, GENIAL
amicable .... PEACEFUL, FRIENDLY
amice .... COWL, TIPPET, ALMUCE, CAPE, HOOD
amid(st) ...... AMONG, MIDST
amidine .... STARCH
Amiens river .... SOMME
amigo .... FRIEND
amino acid .... PROLIN(E), LACTAM, LEUCINE, LYSINE
amiss ...... WRONG, FAULTY
amity .... FRIENDSHIP, GOODWILL
Amman is capital of .. JORDAN
ammo .... AMMUNITION
Ammon ...... ZEUS, JUPITER
ammonia compound .. AMIN(E), DIAMINE
in water solution ...... HARTSHORN
ammoniac ...... GUM RESIN, STIMULANT, CEMENT
ammunition .... AMMO, SHOT, MEANS, SHELLS, BULLETS, GRENADES
carrier .... CAISSON
amnesia .... FUGUE
amnesty .... PARDON

amok .... KILLER, BERSERK, AMUCK
amole ..... SOAP, ROOT, AGAVE
among .... AMID(ST), IN, MID(ST)
amor .... LOVE, EROS
amoretto .... CUPID
amorous .... LOVING, EROTIC, SPOONY
amorous look .... OBLE, LEER
amorphous .... FORMLESS, SHAPELESS
amort .... LIFELESS, SPIRITLESS
Amos' partner .... ANDY
amount caught .... HAUL, CATCH
  lost by waste .... DECREMENT
  of boastful words .... MOUTHFUL
  of gossip .... EARFUL
  of stake in gambling .... MISE
  offered at auction ... BID
  possessed .... RATAL
  produced ...... OUTPUT
  used ...... CONSUMPTION
amour propre ..... SELF LOVE
ampere .... WEBER
ampersand .... AND
amphetamine ... METHEDRINE
amphibian ... ANURAN, FROG, TOAD, NEWT, BATRACHIA, SALAMANDER
  order .... ANURAN, BUFO
  tailed .... CAUDATE
  tank .... ALLIGATOR
  tree .... HYLA
  young .... TADPOLE
amphibious carnivore .. MINK, OTTER, SEAL
  vehicle .... AMTRAC, DUCK
amphibole .... ASBESTOS, MINERAL, EDENITE, URALITE, TREMOLITE
Amphion's wife .... NIOBE
amphioxus .... LANCELET
amphipod .... SAND FLEA, SHRIMP, CRUSTACEAN
amphitheater .... ARENA, GALLERY, BOWL
  entrance ..... VOMITORY
  natural .... CIRQUE
amphora ..... JAR, URN, VASE
ample .... SPACIOUS, ROOMY, ABUNDANT, FULL
  poetic .... ENOW
amplification factor ...... MU
amplify ... EXPAND, INCREASE, ELABORATE
amplifying device .... MASER, LASER
amputate ..... LOP, CUT OFF
Amu Darya .... OXUS
amuck .... BERSERK, BARESARK
amulet .... CHARM, TALISMAN, PERIAPT
  Philippine .... ANTING ANTING
Amun-Re's wife .... MUT
Amundsen, explorer .. ROALD
Amur tributary ..... SUNGARI, USSURI, ARGUN
amuse .... DIVERT, ENTERTAIN, BEGUILE, HUMOR
amusement .... FUN, DIVERSION, SPORT, GAME
amusing ...... DROLL, RISIBLE, FUNNY
amygdala .... ALMOND, TONSIL
Amy's sister ... MEG, BETH, JO
an ... ANYONE, EACH, ONE, PER
ana ..... COLLECTION, DATA, MEMOIR, ANECDOTES, BITS
anabaena .... ALGA
anaconda .... BOA, CONSTRICTOR, SNAKE
anadem ... WREATH, GARLAND
anadromous ...... EMPORIUM
an(a)esthetic .... GAS, OPIATE, SEDATIVE, ANALGESIC
anagram .... GAME, REBUS, LOGOGRIPH
  game .... LOGOMACHY
analgesic .... OPIATE, AN(A)ESTHETIC
analogy .... LIKENESS, COMPARISON
analyst, ore .... ASSAYER
analyze .... EXAMINE, ASSAY, DISSECT
  grammatically .... PARSE
anamnesis .... REMEMBRANCE
Ananias .... LIAR
  wife of .... SAPPHIRA
anarchic .... LAWLESS
anarchist .... TERRORIST, AGITATOR, REBEL, NIHILIST, RED
anarchy .... DISORDER, VIOLENCE
anasarca .... EDEMA, DROPSY
anathema .... DAMNED, CURSE
anathemize ...... (AC)CURSE, DAMN, BAN
Anatole ____ novelist .. FRANCE
Anatolia .... ASIA MINOR
Anatolian capital ... ANKARA
  goddess .... MA
anatomical model, of an ..... CLASTIC
  model of human body .. MANIKIN
  walls .... SEPTA
anatomy .... SCIENCE, SKELETON, STRUCTURE
  dealing with muscles ..... MYOLOGY
  of animals ..... ZOOTOMY
  of regions ... TOPOLOGY
ancestor .... ELDER, FOR(E)BEAR, FAMILY, STOCK, SIRE
  Irish .... MIL, MILED
ancestral ..... AVITAL, AVAL
  spirits .... LARES, MANES
ancestry .... FAMILY, LINEAGE, PEDIGREE
Anchises' son ......(A)ENEAS
anchor ... FIX, KEDGE, MOOR, TIE, BERTH, CAT, HOOK, BOWER
  chain .... CABLE
  fluke .... BILL
  heaviest of a ship .... BOWER
  lift .... CAT, WEIGH
  lifting device .. CAPSTAN, WINDLASS
  man .... ENDMAN
  part ... ARM, FLUKE, RING, CROWN, SHANK, STOCK, PALM
  place of ...... CATHEAD
  slightly raised .... ATRIP
  small .... KEDGE, GRAPNEL, KILLICK, KILLOCK
  tackle .... CAT
anchorage .... MOORAGE, RADE, MARINA, DOCKAGE, (ROAD)STEAD, HARBOR
anchoret .... RECLUSE, ASCETIC, EREMITE
anchorite .... HERMIT, RECLUSE
  opposed to .. C(O)ENOBITE
anchovy .... HERRING, SPRAT
  sauce .... ALEC
anchusa .... ALKANET, BUGLOSS
ancient .... ANTIQUE, OLD(EN), AGED, PRIMEVAL, ELD, ARCHAIC, HOARY
  Alexandrian writer ...... ORIGEN
  alphabetical character ... RUNE
  Briton ...... CELT, PICT
  Chinese .... SERES
  city .... THEBES, CORINTH, NICAEA, NINEVEH, TYRE, EUS
  country .... ELAM, GAUL, MEDEA, EOLIS, ARAM
  court .... EYRE, LEET
  drink .... MORAT
  Egyptian king .. RAMESES, PHARAOH
  Egyptian scrolls .. PAPYRI
  Greek invader .. DORIAN
  language .... LATIN, SANSKRIT, GREEK
  lyre .... ASOR
  manuscript ..... CODEX
  Mariner's victim .... ALBATROSS
  musical instrument ..... ASOR, CITHARA, LUTE, REBEC
  Persian .... MEDE
  priests .... MAGI
  sword .... ESTOC
  tax .... CRO
  temple .... NAOS
  times .... YORE
  warship ...... GALLEON, BIREME, GALLEY, LONG SHIP
  weapon .... DAG, SPEAR, PIKE, MACE, SLING, HALBERD, ARQUEBUS
  wicked city ..... SODOM, GOMORRAH, BABYLON

ancillary ...... SUBORDINATE, HELPER, AUXILIARY, SERVANT
ancon ...... ELBOW, CONSOLE
and .... ALSO, MOREOVER, PLUS, AS WELL AS, TOO, AMPERSAND
others .... ET AL
so on/so forth .... ETC(ETERA), USW
Andalusian .... SPANIARD, SPANISH, LEGHORN
port .... CADIZ
province .... JAEN
Andean .... PAMPERO
Andersen, Christian ... HANS
Anderson, singer .... MARIAN
writer .... MAXWELL, SHERWOOD
Andes .... MOUNTAIN
camel-like animal .... GUANACO, LLAMA, VICUNA, ALPACA
deer .... PUDU
grass .... ICHU
mountain ...... SORATA, CHIMBORAZO, POTOSI, HUILA, MISTI, ILLAMPU, HUASCARAN, COTOPAXI
peak ...... ACONCAGUA
plain ... PARAMO, LLANO
plateau .... PUNA
rodent ..... CHINCHILLA
ruminant ...... LLAMA, GUANACO, ALPACA
volcano .... OMATE, MISTI, CHIMBORAZO
wind .... PAMPERO
andiron ....(FIRE)DOG, HESSIAN
Andre, John, for example .... SPY
Andrew .... APOSTLE
androgen .... HORMONE
Andromache's husband ...... HECTOR
Andromeda's husband .... PERSEUS
androsterone ...... HORMONE
Andy Gump's wife ...... MIN
Andy's partner .... AMOS
anecdotage ..... TALES, ANA
anecdotes, expert in .... RACONTEUR
anele .... ANOINT, OIL
anemia .... CHLOROSIS
anemic .... PALE, BLOODLESS, WAN, COLORLESS
anemone .... PLANT, WINDFLOWER, ANIMAL, POLYP, ACTINIA, SNOWDROP
anent .... REGARDING, ABOUT, CONCERNING, INRE
anes .... ONCE
anesthesia .... NUMBNESS
anesthetic .... ETHER, PROCAINE, OPIATE, CARVACROL, COCAIN(E), STOVAIN(E)
anet .... DILL(SEED)
anew .... AGAIN, AFRESH
do .... REPEAT, RESUME
angel .... CHERUB, SERAPH(IM), MESSENGER, SPIRIT, SERAF
fallen .... LUCIFER
fish .... SHARK
gold-digger's .... SUGAR DADDY
loyal .... MICHAEL
of bottomless pit .... APOLLYON
of Broadway, etc. ...... SUGAR DADDY, FINANCIER
of death .... AZRAEL, SAMUEL, DANITE
of music .... ISRAFIL
rebel .... AZAZEL, LUCIFER
Angeli, actress .... PIER
angelic .... CHERUBIC, SAINTLY
messenger ...... GABRIEL
Angelica .... ARCHANGEL
angels collectively .... HIERARCHY
angelus .... PRAYER, VESPER
anger .... IRE, DANDER, RILE, ENRAGE, INDIGNATION, WRATH, INCENSE
fit of .... TEMPER, RAGE, PIQUE, TANTRUM, CHOLER, TIFF
give vent to .... RAGE, FUME
angina .... CROUP
Angkor relics .... RUINS, TEMPLES
temple ruins ..... BAYON
Wat (or Vat) .... TEMPLE
angle .... SLANT, ANCON, CORNER, ASPECT, POINT, FISH, TRICK, RADIAN
branch .... AXIL
formed by aircraft .. YAW
forming no ..... AGONIC
in geology .... HADE
leafstalk .... AXIL
measuring device ...... GONIOMETER
outside .... CANT
pipe .... TEE
trench .... ZIG
with no .... AGONIC
angler .... FISHER(MAN), SCHEMER, TRICKSTER
angler's basket .... CREEL
delight .... BITE, STRIKE
need .... BAIT, ROD, CREEL, LINE, HOOK
Angleterre .... LACE
Anglian kingdom ..... DEIRA
Anglican anthem ... AGNUS DEI
Anglo-Indian empire founder .. CLIVE
kingdom .... KENT
nurse ...... AMAH, AYAH
title of address ..... BABU
troop .... RESSALA
man, rich ..... NAWAB, NABOB
woman, rich ... BEGUM
Anglo-Saxon .... ENGLISH
armor .... HAUBERK
assembly ..... GEMOT(E)
coin .... ORA, SCEAT
consonant ..... ETH, EDH
court .... GEMOT(E)
folk hero ..... BEOWULF
freeman .... THANE
hunter's attendant ...... GILLY, GILLIE
king .... EDGAR
king's council .... WITAN
kingdom .... MERCIA, ESSEX
lord's attendant .. THANE, THEGN
noble/prince .. ATHELING
slave .... ESNE
warrior ... THEGN, THANE
Angola capital ...... LUANDA
port .... LUANDA, LOBITO
Angora .... ANKARA, CAT, GOAT, RABBIT
goat .... CHAMAL
goat fabric ..... MOHAIR
angostura .... BOLIVAR, BARK, TONIC, FLAVOR
angry .... INDIGNANT, SORE, IRATE, CROSS, MAD, HOT, WROTH
creature ..... SOREHEAD, WET HEN, AMOK, AMUCK, BERSERK
look .... GLOWER, SCOWL, GLARE
anguillid .... EEL
anguine .... SNAKELIKE
anguish .... PAIN, AGONY, DOLOR, PANG, DISTRESS
angular .... CORNERED, GAUNT, BONY
opposite of ..... AGONIC
anhydrous ..... DRY, PARCHED
ani .... CUCKOO
anil .... SHRUB, INDIGO
anile .... CRONE, INFIRM, WEAK
aniline, dye/red .... FUCHSIN, MAGENTA
anima ...... PRINCIPLE, SOUL
animal ...... BEAST, BESTIAL, SENSUAL, GROSS
anatomy ..... ZOOTOMY
ant-eating .... ECHIDNA, AARDVARK, TAMANDUA, PANGOLIN, ANTBEAR
antlered .... STAG, CARIBOU, ELK, MOOSE, (REIN)DEER
aquatic .... SEAL, OTTER, WHALE, SEACOW, WALRUS, MINK
arboreal ..... TARSIER, SQUIRREL, KOALA, UNAU, AI, SLOTH
armor ...... ARMATURE, CARAPACE, SHELL, PLATE
"armored" .. ARMADILLO
baggage carrier .... SUMPTER
body .... SOMA
bone-like covering ...... CARAPACE
born prematurely .. SLINK

breast .... BRISKET, THORAX
bristly .... HOG, BOAR, PORCUPINE
burrowing ..... WOMBAT, ARMADILLO, BADGER, RATEL, BROCK, MOLE, MARMOT, GROUNDHOG, GOPHER
castrated ... STAG, CAPON, OX, STEER, GELDING, BARROW
cat family .... FELID, FELINE
clumsy .... JUMBO
coat ...... PELAGE, FUR, WOOL, HAIR, PELT
collection .... ZOO, MENAGERIE
coop .... HUTCH
dam builder ..... OTTER
decay poison .... PTOMAIN(E)
disease .... ROT, ANTHRAX, GID, STAGGERS
doctor ... VET(ERINARIAN)
enclosure ... PEN, CAGE, CORRAL
fat ...... SUET, TALLOW, GREASE, LARD
fierce .... OUTLAW
flying .... BAT, LEMUR
food .... FORAGE, FODDER
footless .... APOD
footprint .... PUG
game-killer ..... VERMIN
giraffe-like .... OKAPI
handler .... TAMER, TRAINER
hibernating ...... BEAR, WOODCHUCK
hide .... FELL, PELT
homing instinct .... ORIENTATION
hornless .... POLLARD
humped .... CAMEL, ZEBU, DROMEDARY, BISON
imaginary ...... SNARK
inferior: sl. .... PLUG
innards ...... HA(R)SLET
large ...... PACHYDERM, RHINO, ELEPHANT, BEHEMOTH
lean, scrawny ..... SCRAG
leopard-like ... CHEETAH
life in a region ... FAUNA
life, study of ... ZOOLOGY
like an .... THEROID
living inside another .... ENTEZOON
magnetism .. MESMERISM
male .. BUCK, BULL, JACK
marsupial .... KOALA, TAIT, WOMBAT, KANGAROO, (O)POSSUM, PHALANGER
microscopic .... ROTIFER
mixed breed .. MONGREL, MULE, HYBRID
mouth opening .. RICTUS
multi-celled ... METAZOA
multi-segmented .... CENTIPEDE
mythical ...... GRIFFIN, GRIFFON
neck hair .... MANE
"necklace" .... TORQUES
nipple .... DUG
of an .... ZOOID
of mixed parentage ..... HYBRID, MONGREL
one-celled ...... MONAD, PROTIS, PROTOZOAN, RHIZOPOD, STENTOR
one-horned .... RHINO(CEROS), UNICORN, BADAK
pack .... SUMPTER
passage .... BURROW, TUNNEL
pen .... STY, HUTCH, CORRAL
Peruvian .... ALPACA, LLAMA
pet .... CAT, POODLE, DOG, CADE, COSSET
pictures painter .... LANDSEER
plant life .... BIOTA, BIOS
pound .... PINFOLD
scent .... FOIL
sexual excitement .. HEAT, RUT, ESTRUS
shelter .... BURROW, TUNNEL
skin .... PELT, FUR, HIDE, FELL
skin dealer .. FELLMONGER
skin disease ..... MANGE
simplest form of .... AM(O)EBA
snouted ... COATI, TAPIR
spiny .... PORCUPINE
spot on face of ... BLAZE
spotted .... PIEBALD, DAPPLE(D)
starch .... GLYCOGEN
stomach ... CRAW, MAW
stories, collection of .... BESTIARY
striped .... TIGER, ZEBRA, QUAGGA
tanned hide of .... CROP
ten-footed .... DECAPOD
thigh .... HAM
trail .... SLOT, SPOOR, SPUR, PUG, FOIL
trainer ..... LEHR (LEW)
trap .... DEADFALL
tusked .... WARTHOG, WALRUS, ELEPHANT
uncontrollable .. OUTLAW
vital organs ...... PLUCK
weasel family .... PEKAN
web-footed ..... BEAVER, PLATYPUS, DUCKBILL
with no nervous system .. ACRITA
with pouch for young .... KOALA, (KANGA)ROO
young ..... JOEY, COLT, CUB, FOAL, PIGLET, CALF, HEIFER, BULLOCK, BUNNY

animalcule .... ROTIFER
animals born at one time .... FALL, LITTER
brood of young ... TEAM
carrying their young ..... MARSUPIAL
collectively .... ZOOLOGY
driven together .. COFFLE, HERD
male of some ..... BULL, BUCK, TOM, STAG, BOAR
molt of some ... EXUVIAE
painter of .... BONHEUR, SETON
tied together .... COFFLE

animate .... QUICKEN, INSPIRE, STIMULATE, (EN)LIVEN, VIVIFY
animated-cartoon producer ... DISNEY, LANTZ
bird .... WOODPECKER
character ...... MAGOO, POPEYE
dog .... PLUTO
duck .... DONALD
person .... GRIG

animating principle ..... SOUL
animation .... VIVACITY, LIFE, BRIO, PEP, SPIRIT
anime .... RESIN, COPAL
animosity .... HATRED, ILL WILL, RANCOR, HOSTILITY, SPITE, ANIMUS, ENMITY, GRUDGE
animus .... GRUDGE, ANIMOSITY, SPIRIT, MIND, PASSION
anion, opposite of .... CATION
anise ...... ANET, DILL(SEED), FLAVOR
anisette .... CORDIAL
Ankara .... ANGORA
is capital of ..... TURKEY, ANATOLIA

ankh ... CROSS, CRUX, ANSATA
ankle .... TALUS, TARSI, CUIT, JOINT, TARSUS
bone .... TALUS, ASTRAGALUS
iron .... BASIL
joint protuberance ...... MALLEOLUS
pertaining to .... TARSAL, TALARIC

anklet .... SOCK, FETTER, CHAIN, BANGLE
anlace .... DAGGER
anlage .... PROTON
anna .... COIN
$\frac{1}{4}$ of .... PICE
16 of them .... RUPEE

"Annabel Lee" author .... POE
annals .... HISTORY, CHRONICLES, RECORD
Annamese ...... MONGOL(IAN)
capital .... HUE
coin .... QUAN
measure ...... TAO, SAO, GON, MAU

Annapolis, former name .... ANNE ARUNDEL

institution .... ACADEMY, USNA
student .... CADET, MIDSHIPMAN
annatto .... DYE
anneal .... TEMPER, BAKE, GLAZE, FUSE, FIRE
annealing oven .... LEER, KILN
annelid ...... WORM, LEECH, CHAETOPOD
annex .... ELL, WING, ATTACH(MENT), CONNECT
Annie Oakley .... PASS, (FREE)TICKET
annihilate .... DESTROY, DEMOLISH, EXTERMINATE
anniversary, 100th .... CENTENNIAL
anno —— .... DOMINI, MUNDI, REGNI
annotate .... GLOSS
annotation ... NOTE, COMMENT, REFERENCE, FOOTNOTE, APOSTIL, GLOSSARY
announce .... DECLARE, PROCLAIM, HERALD, STATE
announcement ...... NOTICE, BLURB, BULLETIN, ORBIT, AD
printed .... CARD
annoy .... FASH, IRK, VEX, TRY, TEASE, MOLEST, DISTURB, PESTER, GRATE, (BE)DEVIL
annoyance ..... HARASSMENT, VEXATION
expression of ...... BAH, OH MY, GLOWER, GRIMACE, SCOWL
annoyer .... PEST, HARASSER, HECKLER
camp .... GNAT
annual .... YEARLY, YEARBOOK, ETESIAN
bean .... URD
headache of a sort ...... INCOME TAX
income .... RENTES
movie award ..... OSCAR
plant .... OKRA
prize ... NOBEL, PULITZER
produce .... CROP
TV award .... EMMY
annually .... YEARLY, PER YEAR
annuity .... INCOME, TONTINE, RENTE
annul .... INVALIDATE, VOID, CANCEL, UNDO, REVOKE, RECALL, VACATE, QUASH
in law .... QUASH
annular .... RINGLIKE, ROUND
die .... DOD
annulate .... RINGED
annulet, in heraldry ..... VIRE
annum .... YEAR
annunciate .... ANNOUNCE
anodyne .... OPIATE, SEDATIVE, DRUG, SOOTHER, BALM
anoint .... OIL, ENOIL, ANELE, BLESS, CONSECRATE
anomalous .... ODD, IRREGULAR, ABNORMAL
anon .... SOON, SHORTLY, THENCE, IMMEDIATELY, ANONYMOUS
anonym ... PSEUDONYM, ALIAS
anonymous .... NAMELESS, UNKNOWN, INNOMINATE
anorak .... JACKET
garment like ..... PARKA
another .... DIFFERENT, ADDITIONAL, ELSE
set of clothes ... CHANGE
ansate .... HANDLED
anschluss .... UNION
anserine .... GOOSELIKE, FOOLISH, STUPID
answer .... REPLY, RESPOND, RESPONSE, REJOIN(DER), DEFENSE
in kind .... RETORT
purpose .... SERVE, DO, SATISFY
unfavorable .... REBUFF
ant .... PISMIRE, EMMET, TERMITE, ANAY, AMAZON
bear .... AARDVARK
black .... KELEP
combining form .... MYRMECO
cow .... APHID
eater .... AARDVARK, ECHIDNA, TAMANDU(A), PANGOLIN, MANIS
genus .... FORMICA
kind of .... SOLDIER
nest .... FORMICARY, HILL
thrush .... PITTA
anta .... PIER, COLUMN, PILASTER
antacid .... ALKALI, MAGNESIA
antagonism .... ENMITY, HOSTILITY, ANIMUS
antagonist ...... RIVAL, FOE, OPPONENT, ADVERSARY
antagonistic .... HOSTILE, OPPOSED, UNFRIENDLY
Antarctic —— ...... OCEAN, CONTINENT, CIRCLE, SEA, ZONE
bird .... PENGUIN
explorer .... BYRD, ROSS, AMUNDSEN
icebreaker .... ATKA
sea ...... WEDDEL, ROSS
Antares ..... RED STAR, MARS
antbear .... AARDVARK
ante .... PAY, STAKE, RAISE, PONY, PRICE
as prefix ... BEFORE, PRIOR
bellum .... PRE-WAR
antebrachium .... FOREARM
antecedence ...... PRIORITY, PRECEDENCE
antecedent .... PRIOR, ANCESTOR, PRECEDING
antecedents ...... ANCESTRY
antechamber ..... ANTEROOM, WAITING ROOM
antedate .... PREDATE, PRECEDE
antelope .... NILGAI, SASIN, SAIGA, BEIRA, OTEROP, CHIRU, GOA, GAZELLE, TAKIN, ELAND, BUBALINE, BUBALIS, CHAMOIS
African .... IMPALA, ASSE, KOB, GNU, KUDU, TORA, ELAND, ORIBI, STEINBOK, WANTO, KONZE, ADDAX, BONGO, GEMSBOK, KOODOO, DIKDIK, NAGOR, DUIKER(BOK), SASSABY, ORYX
American ..... BLESBOK, SASSABY
ancient .... PYGARG
female .... DOE
goat ... SEROW, CHAMOIS
Himalayan ..... CHIRU, GORAL
like .... BOVID
male .... BUCK
pygmy .... ORIBI
red .... PALLA(H), REEDEBOK
sheep-like .... SAIGA
striped .... OTEROP, BONGO
tawny .... ORIBI
young .... KID
antenna .... AERIAL, PALP, FEELER, ANTENNULE
part of .... LEAD IN
anterior .... PRIOR, PREVIOUS, EARLIER, FRONT, PRECEDING
anteroom .... WAITING ROOM, ANTECHAMBER, LOBBY
anthelion .... HALO, AUREOLE
anthem .... SONG, MOTET, AGNUS DEI
anther .... STAMEN
anthesis .... BLOOM
anthocyanin .... PIGMENT
anthologist .... COMPILER
anthology ...... COLLECTION, ANA, POTPOURRI, COLLECTANEA, COMPILATION
anthozoan ..... POLYP, CORAL, ANEMONE
anthracite .... COAL
pieces/refuse ..... CULM
anthrax .... BOIL, CARBUNCLE, PUSTULE
anthropoid .... APE, MANLIKE, GORILLA, GIBBON, CHIMPANZEE, ORANG(UTAN), LAR, MONKEY, SIMIAN, TROGLODYTE
anthropophagi ... CANNIBALS
anti .... CON, AGAINST, OPPOSED, OPPOSER, HOSTILE
knock fuel .... TRIPTANE
knock fuel ingredient ... BROMINE
labor union contract .... YELLOW DOG

antiaircraft artillery .... ACK-ACK, POMPOM
cannon .... BOFORS
gunfire ... FLAK, ACK-ACK
missile .... NIKE
target aiming device .... PREDICTOR
antiar ... UPAS, TREE, POISON
antibiotic .... PENICILLIN, STREPTO(MYCIN), AUREOMYCIN
antibody dissolving bacteria, etc. .... LYSIN(E)
antic .... DIDO, CAPER, PRANK, CLOWN
anticipate .... EXPECT, HOPE, FORESEE
anticipating ...... PROLEPSIS
anticlimax .... DROP, DESCENT, DECREASE
antidote ..... REMEDY, SODA, SERUM, TREACLE
for madness .... CHRYSOLITE
Antigone's parent .. OEDIPUS, JOCASTA
sister .... ISMENE
uncle .... CREON
antihemophilic factor .... GLOBULIN
Antilles, ____ ...... GREATER, LESSER
island .... CUBA
native ..... CARIB(BEAN)
antimacassar .... TIDY
antimalaria remedy .... ATABRIN(E), ATEBRIN, QUININE
antimony .... STIBIUM, REGULUS
source .... STIBNITE
Antiope's son ...... AMPHION
antipasto .... APPETIZER, RELISH
antipathy .... DISLIKE, AVERSION, REPUGNANCE, DISTASTE
antiphon ...... HYMN, PSALM
antipodean ..... AUSTRALIAN
antipodes .... OPPOSITES
antiquate .... OUTDATE
antiquated ... OLD, OBSOLETE, PASSE, OUT OF DATE, ARCHAIC, FOSSIL
antique .... ANCIENT, RELIC, OLD
antiques, where usually found MUSEUM, CURIO SHOP
antiquity .... PAST, YORE, PALEOLOGY, ELD
antiseptic .... ALCOHOL, LISTERINE, IODIN(E), EUSOL, LYSOL, SALOL, CRESOL, EGOL, EUPAD, CHLORINE, ARNICA, ARGYROL, CATECHOL, FORMALIN, TACHIOL, PICROL, BORIC, RETINOL, CARVACROL
surgery pioneer .. LISTER
antisubmarine vessel .... CORVET(TE)
antitoxin .... SERUM, ANTIVENIN
antler .... HORN
branch .... PRONG, BEZ, BAY, BROW
furry skin ...... VELVET
main shaft .... BEAM
part of .... PALM
point ..... PRONG, TINE
unbranched ...... SPIKE, DAG(UE)
antlered animal .... STAG, ELK, MOOSE, CARIBOU, (REIN)DEER
antlers of stag .... ATTIRE
antlion larva ..... DOODLEBUG
antra .... SINUSES
antre .... CAVE, CAVERN
antrum .... CAVERN
ants, pertaining to ... FORMIC
anurous .... TAILLESS, ACAUDAL, ACAUDATE
amphibian .... TOAD, FROG
Anu's husband .... ANAT
Anubis .... HERMES
anvil ..... INCUS, BLOCK, JAW, TEEST, STITHY
block .... STOCK
City .... NOME
user ..... (BLACK)SMITH
anxiety .... WORRY, MISGIVING, CARE, CONCERN
anxious .... UNEASY, TENSE, EAGER
any .... ALL, SOME, WHICHEVER
anything ..... AT ALL, AUGHT
badly matched ... CENTO
of least value .... PLACK, TRIFLE
of value .... ASSET
small .... PINHEAD
that stirs .... FILLIP
aoristic .... INDEFINITE
aorta .... ARTERY, BLOOD VESSEL
aoudad .... SHEEP, ARUI
apace .... FAST, SWIFT(LY), SPEEDY
Apache ...... INDIAN, THUG, GANGSTER, DANCE
chief .... GERONIMO, COCHISE
ap(p)anage ..... DEPENDENCY, SUPPORT, ADJUNCT, PERQUISITE
apart .... ASIDE, AWAY, SEPARATE, SPLIT
prefix .... DIS
apartment ...... ROOM, SUITE, FLAT, DUPLEX
for women ...... HAREM
house, English .. MANSION
without elevator .... WALK-UP
apathetic .... INDIFFERENT, LISTLESS, UNMOVED, COLD
apathy .... INDIFFERENCE, COOLNESS, DISINTEREST
ape ...... MONKEY, GORILLA, ORANG(UTAN), GIBBON, KRA, COPY, IMITATE, PRIMATE, SIMIAN, SIAMANG
kind of ..... MIME, MIMIC, CLOWN, JESTER
sound .... CHATTER
apeman .... ALALUS
of fiction ...... TARZAN
Apennines people .... SABINES
aper .... MIMIC, MIME, IMITATOR
apercu .... GLANCE, INSIGHT, DIGEST
aperient .... LAXATIVE
aperitif .... DRINK, APPETIZER, COCKTAIL
wine .... DUBONNET
aperture ..... VENT, ORIFICE, HOLE, SLOT, GAP, STOMA, OPENING
apery .... MIMICRY
apes .... SIMIA
apetalous .... PETALLESS
apex .... TIP, PEAK, VERTEX, CLIMAX, ZENITH, SUMMIT, PINIAL
covering .... EPI
of elbow .... ANCON
rounded .... RETUSE
aphasia .... ALALIA
aphid .... INSECT, LOUSE
sucking tube ... NECTARY
aphorism .... SAW, MAXIM, ADAGE, SAYING, PROVERB, AXIOM
aphrodisiac .... ERINGO, ERYNGO
Aphrodite .... VENUS, URANIA, GODDESS, BUTTERFLY
Aphrodite's love .... ADONIS, ARES
mother .... DIONE
priestess .... HERO
son .... EROS
temple site ..... PAPHOS
aphta .... THRUSH
apian .... BEELIKE
apiculture .... BEEKEEPING
apiece .... EACH, PER
apish .... SILLY, IMITATIVE, AFFECTED
aplomb .... ASSURANCE, POISE, AIR, FLAMBOYANCE
fellow of ..... COXCOMB, FOP, DANDY, BLUFFER, DUDE, ORATOR, BRAGGART, (PEA)COCK
apnea .... ASPHYXIA
apocalypse .... BOOK, REVELATIONS, PROPHECY
apocope .... ELISION
apocopate ... ELIDE, SHORTEN
apocryphal .... SPURIOUS, COUNTERFEIT
book ..... ESDRA, TOBIT
apodal .... FOOTLESS
apogee .... CLIMAX
Apollo ... SUNGOD, PHOEBUS, HELIOS
astronaut ...... LOVELL, ANDERS, BORMAN, ALDRIN, COLLINS
birthplace .... DELOS

festival .... DELIA
giant killed by ..... OTUS
instrument .... LUTE, LYRE, BOW
mother ... LETO, LATONA
oracle .... DELOS
oracle site ...... DELPHI
priest .... ABARIS, CALCHAS
serpent slain by .. PYTHON
sister .... ARTEMIS, DIANA
son .... ION, IAMUS
spring sacred to .... CASTALIA
temple site ...... DELOS
twin .... ARTEMIS
vale .... TEMPE

Apollyon ..... ANGEL, DEVIL, SATAN
apologia .... APOLOGY, EXCUSE, EXPLANATION
apologue .... FABLE, ALLEGORY
apomixis .... APOGAMY
apoplectic with ____ ... RAGE
apoplexy .... PARALYSIS
aport .... LEFT(SIDE), NEAR
apostasy .... BETRAYAL, DESERTION
apostate .... RENEGADE, DESERTER, RECREANT, TURNCOAT
apostil .... ANNOTATION, FOOTNOTE
apostle .... DISCIPLE, PREACHER, MISSIONARY
Biblical ...... ANDREW, BARTHOLOMEW, JAMES, JUDE (THADDEUS), PHILIP, SIMON, PETER (SIMONPETER), PAUL, JUDE (LEBBAEUS), JUDAS (ISCARIOT), MATTHEW, (LEVI), JOHN, THOMAS (DIDYMUS), MATTHIAS
of the Franks ..... REMI
of the Indians .... ELIOT
of the Goths ... ULFILAS
thirteenth .... MATTHIAS

Apostles John and James .... BOANERGES
teaching of .... DIDACHE

apostolic .... PAPAL
see ..... BISHOPRIC, ROME

apothecary .... DRUGGIST
measure .... MINIM, DRAM, OUNCE, PINT, GALLON
weight .... GRAIN, SCRUPLE, DRAM, OUNCE, POUND

apothegm .... SAYING, MAXIM, APHORISM, ADAGE, DICTUM, AXIOM
apotheosize .... DEIFY, GLORIFY, IDEALIZE
Appalachian range .. RAMAPO
appal(l) .... HORRIFY, SHOCK, DISMAY, AWE, STUN, ASTONISH, FRIGHTEN
appanage .... PREQUISITE, SUPPORT, DEPENDENCY, ENDOWMENT
apparatus .... DEVICE, MACHINE, GEAR, INSTRUMENT, TACKLE, GADGET
air blowing ... BELLOWS
air cooling .... FAN
artificial respiration ..... PULMOTOR
beauty shop .... (HAIR)DRIER
binding .... BALER
blacksmith's ..... FORGE
dentist's .... DRILL
doctor's ... STETHOSCOPE
for bacterial cultures .... INCUBATOR
hauling/hoisting .... WINDLASS, WINCH, CRANE, FORKLIFT
machine shop .... LATHE
under-water breathing ... AQUALUNG, SNORKEL, SCUBA
water drawing .... PUMP
weaver's .... LOOM

apparel .... GARMENT, CLOTHING, DRESS, ATTIRE, RAIMENT
apparent .... VISIBLE, EVIDENT, OBVIOUS, PLAIN, PATENT, CLEAR, OVERT
apparently .... SEEMINGLY, EVIDENTLY
apparition .... GHOST, PHANTOM, SPECTER, SPECTRE, WRAITH, EIDOLON
of living person ... FETCH

appassionata ... IMPASSIONED, PASSIONATE
appeal ..... CALL, PRAY, SUE, PROTEST, PLEAD, PETITION, ATTRACTION
sex: sl. ...... OOMPH, IT

appear .... SEEM, LOOK, LOOM, EMERGE
appearance .. AIR, MIEN, LOOK, SHOW, SEMBLANCE, PRESENCE
appease .... CALM, SOOTH, PLACATE, ALLAY, PACIFY, BELIEVE, SATISFY, MOLLIFY
appeasement, kind of .... SOP
appellation .... NAME, TITLE, DESIGNATION, NAMING
append ... ADD, AFFIX, ATTACH
appendage ... LEG, TAIL, ARM, ADJUNCT, LIMB
crab .... ANTENNA, FEELER
fish .... FIN, BARBEL
leaf .... STIPULE
lobster .... PALP(US)
grain ...... AWN, BEARD
threadlike ...... CIRRUS

appendix .... ADDENDUM, OUTGROWTH, CODICIL
appertain ... BELONG, RELATE
appetence .... CRAVING, APPETITE, DESIRE
appetite ... DESIRE, CRAVING, APPETENCE, STOMACH
for alcoholic drink ...... DIPSOMANIA
for food ...... HUNGER
for something ... TOOTH, TASTE
for water .... THIRST
huge ...... GARGANTUAN
insatiable .... GREED, VORACITY
pertaining to ... ORECTIC

appetizer .... CANAPE, ANTIPASTO, TIDBIT
drink .... COCKTAIL, DUBONNET, APERITIF

appetizing .... SAVORY, DELICIOUS, TASTY
applaud ..... CHEER, PRAISE, COMMEND, LAUD, EXTOL, GIVE A HAND
applauder .... CHEERER, ROOTER, FAN, CLAPPER
applauders' group .... CHEERING SQUAD, CLAQUE
applause .... APPROVAL, PRAISE, COMMENDATION, HAND, ECLAT
round of ..... OVATION
word of .... HEAR, MABUHAY, OLE, BANZAI

apple .... POME, PIPPIN, GOLDEN, LOVE, SORB, DELICIOUS, COSTARD, RUSSET, CRAB, WINESAP, MAY, GREENING, GRIMES, GRAVENSTEIN, PEARMAIN, QUEENING, JONATHAN
acid .... MALIC
butter .... JAM
center .... CORE
crushed pulp .... POMACE
custard .... ANONA
disease .... STIPPEN
elongated ..... CODLING
fall variety ... FAMEUSE, WEALTHY
fermented drink ... CIDER
for backing ..... BIFFIN
fried .... ROLPENS
inferior ..... CODLIN(G)
juice .... CIDER
kin ...... TOMATO, POME, QUINCE
love .... TOMATO
of the eye .... PET, FAVORITE
Persian .... PEACH
pie, deep-dish .... PANDOWDY
pudding ... BROWN BETTY
pulp .... POMACE
red .... MCINTOSH
red winter ..... BALDWIN
Russian ..... ASTRACHAN
sauce: colloq. .... NONSENSE, HOKUM
seed/stone .... PIP, PYRENE
seller .... COSTER
shaped fruit .... QUINCE
tosser: myth. ...... ERIS

tree . . . . SORB, SAPODILLA, WILDING
unripe . . . . CODLIN
variety . . . . NON(E)SUCH
worm . . . . MOTH
apples, pert. to . . . . MALIC
applesauce . . . . DESSERT, RELISH
colloquial . . . NONSENSE, HOKUM, BALONEY
applethorne . . . . EPIGENE
appliance, electrical . . . . IRON, RANGE, OVEN, MIXER, DISHWASHER, TOASTER, REFRIGERATOR
applicable . . . . RELEVANT, PERTINENT
application . . . . REQUEST, FORM, DILIGENCE, RELEVANCE, USE, REMEDY
applied decoration . . . . GESSO, OIL, APPLIQUE, PAINT
science . . . . TECHNOLOGY
apply . . . . . EMPLOY, USE, PUT, PLACE, DEVOTE, REQUEST
force . . . . . EXERT, PRESS
friction . . . . RUB, GRATE, RASP
pressure . . . . . INFLUENCE, COERCE
appoggiatura . . . GRACE NOTE, THANK YOU
appoint . . . . . . NAME, ASSIGN, NOMINATE, DETAIL, CHOOSE, DESIGNATE, COMMISSION
as agent . . . . DEPUTE, DELEGATE
to benefice . . . . . COLLATE
appointment . . . . TRYST, DATE, NOMINATION, ENGAGEMENT, SET, FURNITURE, EMPLOYMENT
apportion . . METE, DEAL, ALLOT, DIVIDE, DISTRIBUTE
apposite . . . . RELEVANT, APT, APPROPRIATE, PROPER
appraisal . . . . EVALUATION, RATING, ESTIMATE
appraise . . . . ASSESS, RATE, VALUATE, JUDGE, ASSAY
appraiser . . . . ASSESSOR, RATER
appreciable . . . . . NOTICEABLE, PERCEPTIBLE
appreciate . . . . . VALUE, ENJOY, ESTEEM, UNDERSTAND, NOTICE
apprehend . . . . ARREST, PERCEIVE, UNDERSTAND, NAB, HOLD, HENT
apprehension . . . . ALARM, PERCEPTION, ARREST, FEAR, ANXIETY, CAPTURE
apprehensive . . . . UNEASY, ANXIOUS, WORRIED, FEARFUL
apprentice . . . . TRAINEE, LEARNER, NOVICE, BEGINNER, DEVIL
apprenticeship contract . . . . . . INDENTURE
approach . . . . . NEAR, ACCESS, COME, APPROXIMATE, OVERTURE
stealthily . . . . STALK
approbation . . . . . APPROVAL, SANCTION, FAVOR
appropriate . . . . STEAL, SUITABLE, FIT, PROPER, APT, BECOMING, MEET, PREEMPT, ADOPT, APPOSITE, GERMANE, POCKET
improperly . . . . . USURP, STEAL
approval . . . . . ENDORSEMENT, SANCTION
kind of . . . . IMPRIMATUR
sign of . . . . NOD
word of . . OK(AY), SHOOT
approve . . . . SANCTION, CONFIRM, ENDORSE, CERTIFY, PASS, RATIFY
approving mention . . . . ACCOLADE, CITATION
approximate . . . . NEAR, CLOSE, APPROACH
approximately . . . . ABOUT, NEARLY, ROUGHLY
appurtenance . . . . . . ADJUNCT
appurtenant . . . . . PERTINENT, GERMANE
aprenaceous . . . . SANDY
apres . . . . AFTER
apricot . . . . FRUIT, TREE, DRUPE, ANSU, UME
cordial . . . . PERSICO
April Dancer's colleague . . . . . NOEL
apron . . . . PINAFORE, SHIELD, BELT
child's . . . . . . BISHOP, BIB
painter's . . . . SMOCK
apropos . . . . RELEVANT, APT, OPPORTUNELY, PAT, FITTING, BY THE WAY
apse . . . . . . APSIS, PROJECTION
dome cover . . . . . CONCHA
apt . . . . APPROPRIATE, FITTING, RELEVANT, PRONE, INCLINED, QUICK, LIKELY, DEFT, CLEVER
apteral . . . . WINGLESS
apteryx . . . . KIWI, MOA, BIRD, ROA
aptitude . . . . INCLINATION, BENT, FLAIR, TALENT, ABILITY, KNACK, GIFT
aptly chosen . . . . . . FELICITOUS
Apulia's capital . . . . BARI
aqua . . . . WATER, LIQUID, SOLUTION
fortis . . . . . . NITRIC ACID
vitae . . . . ALCOHOL, BRANDY, LIQUOR
aquamarine . . . . BERYL, PIGMENT, (BLUISH)GREEN
aquarium . . . . . (WATER)TANK
fish . . . . GUPPY
plant . . . . FANWORT
small . . . . FISHBOWL
aquatic animal . . . . OTTER, BEAVER, NEWT, MINK
bird . . . . FLAMINGO, GOOSE, GULL, DUCK, COOT, AUK, LOON, GREBE, PENGUIN, SWAN, SCAUP, PELICAN
entertainment . . . . AQUACADE
mammal . . . . . MANATEE, SEACOW, WHALE, SEAL, OTTER, DUGONG, MINK
movie character . . . . FLIPPER
performer . . . . SEAL, FLIPPER, DIVER, DOLPHIN
vertebrate . . . . FISH
aqueduct . . . . PIPE, CONDUIT, CANAL, PASSAGE
of Sylvius . . . . ITER
aqueous . . . . WATERY
solution . . . . JAVEL
Aquila . . . . EAGLE, CONSTELLATION
star . . . . ALTAIR
ara . . . . ALTAR, CONSTELLATION, MACAW
Arab . . . . SEMITE, TATAR, GAMIN, BEDOUIN, HORSE, WAIF, URCHIN, SARACEN, ANSAR
Arabia . . . . SAUDI, PENINSULA
poetic . . . . ARABY
Arabian abode . . . . DAR
antelope . . . . ADDAX
ape . . . . BABOON
beverage . . . . LEBAN, BOZA, BOSA(H)
bird of fable . . . . ROC
camel . . . . . . DROMEDARY
capital . . . . SAN'A
chief . . . . . SAYID, SHERIF
chieftain . . . AMIR, EMIR, AMEER, EMEER, REIS, SHEIK(H)
chieftain's domain . . . . . . EMIRATE
city . . . . ADEN, BEDA, CHAFRA, BERA, DAMAR, SAN'A, MEDINA, RIYADH, JIDDA, JEDDA
cloth . . . . ABA
coffee . . . . MOCHA
coin . . . . TALARI
country . . . . YEMEN, JORDAN, SAUDI ARABIA, IRAN, IRAQ, KUWAIT
demon . . . . EBLIS, GENIE, JINN(I), AFREET
dervish of story . . . . AGIB
desert . . . SAHARA, NEFUD
drink . . . LEBAN, BOSA(H), BOZA
dromedary . . . . . BELOOL, HEJEEN
evil spirit . . . . . . AFREET, AFRIT(E)
father . . . . ABOU, ABU
garment . . . ABA, HAI(C)K
gazelle . . . . ARIEL
gulf . . . . ADEN, OMAN
head cord . . . . AGAL
jasmine . . . . BELA

javelin .... JER(R)ID, JER(R)EED
judge .... CADI
kingdom .... SABA, SHEBA, JORDAN
laborer .... FELLAH
leather .... MOCHA
letter .... BA, GAF, KAF, MIM, ALIF, THA, JIM, KHA, DAL, LAM, NUN, DAD, YA, WAW, DHAL
magistrate .... CADI
measure .... COVIDO, ARDEB
measure, grain .. TOMAN, SAA
mock battle ... JER(R)ID, JER(R)EED
monarchy .... YEMEN
Moslem .... WAHABI
nomad .... SLEB
oasis .... DOUMA
palm .... DOUM
peasant .... FELLAH
peninsula .... SINAI, ADEN
prince .... SHERIF
ruler ...... EMIR, EMEER, SULTAN, SHEIK(H)
sacred territory .. HARAM
sailboat .... DHOW
Scripture ..... ALCORAN
Sea river .... INDUS
seaport ... ADEN, MOCHA
sheikhdom .... KUWAIT
spirit .... JINN(I), AFREET, AFRIT
state ..... YEMEN, OMAN
sultanate .... OMAN
sword .... SCIMITAR
system of numerals ..... ALGORISM
tambourine ...... DAIRA, DAIRE, TAAR
teacher .... ULEMA
tent village ...... DOUAR
tribal chief ..... SHEIK(H)
veil .... YASMAK
wagon .... ARABA
weight .... DIRHEM
wind .... SIMOOM, SAMIEL
woman's veil ... YASMAK

Arabic acid .... ARABIN
letter .... DAL, AYN, KAF, KHA, MIM, THA, WAW, ZAY, ALIF, DHAL, GHAYN

arabinose ... PENTOSE, SUGAR
arable .... TILLABLE
araceous .... AROID
plant .... LILY, TARO, CABBAGE, ARUM

Arachne .... SPIDER
arachnid .... MITE, SPIDER, SCORPION, TICK, ACARID
segment .... TELSON, SOMITE

arachnoid, space below ...... CISTERNA
structure .... WEB

arado .... LAND
Aram .... SYRIA
arbalest .... CROSSBOW
Arbela .... ERBIL
arbiter .... JUDGE, ARBITRATOR, MEDIATOR, OVERMAN
archaic ...... DAYSMAN
baseball ...... UMP(IRE)
boxing, basketball ...... REF(EREE)
fashion .... STYLIST, DIOR, BALMAIN

arbitrary .... CAPRICIOUS, DESPOTIC, DICTATORIAL, WHIMSICAL
arbitrator .... JUDGE, ARBITER, MIDDLEMAN, OVERMAN
arbor ..... BOWER, PERGOLA, TREE, SHAFT, BEAM, SPINDLE, AXLE, TRELLIS
vitae .... THUJA

Arboreal .... TREE-LIKE, DENDRAL
amphibian .... TREETOAD
creature .. SLOTH, UNAU, AI, KOALA, SQUIRREL, TARSIER, COLUGO

arbutus .... MAYFLOWER, PLANT, SHRUB
arc ..... CURVE, ARCH, BOW
chord .... SINE
of 90 degrees .. QUADRANT
sky .... RAINBOW

arcade .... PORTICO, ARCATURE, GALLERY, PIAZZA
Arcadian .... PEACEFUL, PASTORAL, RUSTIC, BUCOLIC, SHEPHERD
princess .... AUGE

Arcady .... ARCADIA
arcane ...... SECRET, HIDDEN
arcanum ... SECRET, MYSTERY, ELIXIR, REMEDY
arcature .... ARCADE
arch .... CHIEF, MAIN, PRINCIPAL, CURVE, SLY, CRAFTY, CLEVER, HANCE, FORNIX, ARC
as combining form ..... RULER
curve inside ... INTRADOS
fiend ..... DEVIL, SATAN
lower part ..... IMPOST, SPRINGER
of bridge .... SPAN
of heaven .... COPE
of spears over shoulders YOKE
over eye .....(EYE)BROW
pointed .... OGIVE, OGEE
side of .... HAUNCH
underside .... SOFFIT

archaic ...... ANCIENT, OLD, ANTIQUATED
command .... HEST

archangel ..... SATAN, URIEL, ANGELICA, MICHAEL, RAPHAEL
archbishop .... PRIMATE, METROPOLITAN
of Canterbury .... CRANMER, ANSELM, BECKET
subordinate of .... SUFFRAGAN

archbishopric ..... APOSTOLIC, SEE
arched .... CURVED, VAULTED, COPED
passageway .... ARCADE
way .... CLOISTER

archeological find in 1887 .... SIDON
archeologist's concern .. RUINS
archer .... BOWMAN, CONSTELLATION
angel .... CUPID
buff ...... TOXOPHILITE
of story .... ROBIN HOOD, (WILLIAM) TELL
of the sky ... SAGITTARIUS
protective band .. BRACER
target ..... CLOUT, ROVER

archery, of .... SAGITTARY
arches, row of .... ARCUATION
archetype .... MODEL, IDEAL, PROTOTYPE, EXAMPLE
archil .... LICHEN, DYE
archimage .... MAGICIAN, WIZARD
archipelago .... COLON, SULU, MALAY, PAUMOTO, BISMARCK, TUAMOTU
architect .... DESIGNER, BUILDER, CREATOR
architectural .... TECTONIC
column ...... PILASTER
concave molding .... CAVETTO
design .... SPANDREL
drawing .... EPURE
ornament ...... CORBEIL, DENTIL
pier .... ANTA
type ..... DORIC, IONIC, GOTHIC, MAYAN

archly ..... PERTLY, SAUCILY
archon ... MAGISTRATE, RULER
Arctic .... COLD, FRIGID, OVERSHOE, POLAR, NORTH(ERN)
base ...... THULE, ETAH
bird .... AUK, ROTCH(E), DOVEKIE, DOVEKEY, JUNCO, GUILLEMOT
dog ... MALEMUTE, SAMO, SAMOYEDE
explorer ... PEARY, ERIC, KANE, RAE
goose .... BRANT
gulf .... OB
gull .... XEMA, BURGOMASTER
home ..... IGLU, IGLOO
jacket ... ANORAK, PARKA
native .... ESKIMO
pinniped .... SEAL
plain .... TUNDRA
seagull ..... KITTIWAKE
tribesman .... LAPP
wasteland ..... TUNDRA

arcuate .... CURVED, ARCHED
arcubalist ..... CROSSBOWMAN
Arden, ____ .... ENOCH, EVE, ELIZABETH
ardent.......... PASSIONATE,

EAGER, ENTHUSIASTIC, FERVENT, WARM
partisan ...... DEVOTEE, FANATIC
spirits ..... GIN, WHISKY, LIQUOR
ardor .... FIRE, ZEAL, VERVE, ELAN, FERVOR, PASSION, HEAT
arduous .... LABORIOUS, ENERGETIC, DIFFICULT, HARD
area .... SCOPE, RANGE, EXTENT, DISTRICT, REGION
around moving body .... PERIPTER
between leaf veins ...... AREOLA
measure of .... ARE, ACRE, DECARE, HECTARE, CENTIAR(E)
on bird's bill .... CERE
small ..... CLOSE, AREOLA
eaway ...... YARD, COURT, PASSAGE
areca .... BETEL, PALM
arena .... FIELD, RING, SPHERE, BULLRING, STADIUM, OVAL, PIT, LISTS
kind of ..... (COCK)PIT, GRIDIRON, DIAMOND, COURT
arenaceous .... SANDY
arenose .... SANDY
areo, as combining form ..... MARS
areola ...... SPACE, HOLLOW
Ares .... MARS
parent ..... ZEUS, HERA
sister .... ERIS
arete .... RIDGE, CREST, ARISTA
Arethusa .... NYMPH, ORCHID
argal .... ERGO, HENCE, THEREFORE, TARTAR, SHEEP, ARGALI
argala .... STORK, MARABOU, ADJUTANT
argali ..... SHEEP, BIGHORN, AOUDAD
argent .... SILVER(Y)
Argentina's capital .... BUENOS AIRES
Argentine armadillo .. PELUDO
city .... SALTA, AVELLANEDA, CORDOBA, CORRIENTE, TUCUMAN
crested bird .... SERIEMA
Indian .... PAMPEAN
plain .... PAMPAS
port .... LA PLATA, ROSARIO
president .... ILLIA, ONGANIA, PERON
region ...... PATAGONIA
river .... BERMEJO, PARANA, SALADO
seaport ...... LA PLATA
"sleeping beauty" ...... (MARIA) TELLO
timber tree .... TALA
wage earner .... DESCAMISADO

argil .... CLAY
Argo ... SHIP, CONSTELLATION
argol .... TARTAR
Argolis native .... AGIVE
vale of .... NEMEA
Argonaut .... JASON, ACASTUS, MELEAGER
of the gold rush .... FORTY-NINER
ship .... ARGO
argosy ... SHIP, FLEET, VESSEL
argot ...... JARGON, SLANG, LINGO, CANT, DIALECT, PATOIS
argue ..... REASON, DISPUTE, OBJECT, DEBATE, DISCUSS, CONTEND, JAW, WRANGLE
for argument's sake ..... ARGUFY
in court .... PLEAD, PRAY
price/terms ... HAGGLE, HIGGLE, BARGAIN
argument .... DEBATE, DISCUSSION, HASSLE, TOPIC, POLEMIC
about words .... LOGOMACHY
kind of .... PRO, CON, RHUBARB
to justify .... DEFENSE
argumentation ... DIALECTICS
argumentative .. CONTENTIOUS, COMBATIVE, POLEMICAL, ERISTICAL
Argus .... GIANT, WATCHMAN
eyed .... VIGILANT, OBSERVANT
aria .... SONG, SOLO, AIR, MELODY
brilliant flourish .... CADENZA
like an .... ARIOSO
arias .... SOLI
Ariadne's father ...... MINOS
love .... THESEUS
arid .... DRY, BARREN, UNFERTILE, JEJUNE, STERILE, TORRID, ANHYDROUS
region .... DESERT
region, U.S. .. DUST BOWL
ariel ...... SPIRIT, SATELLITE, GAZELLE
Ariel's master ..... PROSPERO
Aries ... RAM, CONSTELLATION
arietta .... MELODY, ARIA, AIR, SONG
arikara .... REE
ariose .... MELODIC, SONGLIKE
arioso .... MELODIOUS
composer .... BACH
arise .... GET UP, ASCEND, EMANATE, ISSUE, ORIGINATE
arista .... AWN, BEARD, BRISTLE
aristocracy .... ELITE, NOBILITY, OLIGARCHY
aristocrat .... NOBLEMAN, HIGH BORN, SNOB

Athenian/Greek .... EUPATRID
Roman ..... PATRICIAN
Russian .... BOYAR
Spanish .... HIDALGO, GRANDEE
aristocratic .... PATRICIAN
aristocrats collectively .... NOBLESSE, NOBILITY
Aristotle .... STAGIRITE
birthplace ...... STAGIRA
follower ... PERIPATETIC
logic .... DEDUCTIVE, SYLLOGISM
teacher of .... PLATO
arithmetic, common .. LOGISTIC
arivederci .... GOODBY, SO LONG
Arizona capital .... PHOENIX
city .... TUCSON, YUMA, MESA
Cochise county seat ..... BISBEE
county .... PINAL
desert .... PAINTED
Indian .... HOPI, HANO, MOQUI, TEWA, PIMA, YUMA, APACHE, PAIUTE
nut .... PINON
river .... GILA
state flower ... SAGUARO, CACTUS
state nickname .... SUNSET LAND, APACHE
tourist's sight .... GRAND CANYON
ark .... BOAT, REFUGE
animals/birds .... PAIRS
builder ..... NOAH, NOE
landing place .... (MT) ARARAT
porter .... BEN
Arkansas capital .... LITTLE ROCK
county ..... IZARD, YELL
nickname ... BEAR STATE
river .... WASHITA
state flower .... APPLE BLOSSOM
arles .... ANTE, PREPAYMENT, TOKEN, EARNEST
arm .... LIMB, FORTIFY, FURNISH, TENTACLE, BRANCH, WEAPON
badge .... BRASSARD
band .... BRACER
bone ... HUMERUS, ULNA
bone, pert. to ... ULNAR
cover .... SLEEVE
extendible .. PANTOGRAPH
hole .... SCYE
in-arm .... OXTER
joint ..... ELBOW, WRIST
length of .... REACH
like .... BRACHIAL
of the sea .... BAY, FIRTH, FIORD, INLET, FJORD
pertaining to .. BRACHIAL
shield .... BUCKLER
armada .... FLEET
armadillo .... APAR(A), PEBA, TATOU, POYOU
Argentine ...... PELUDO

shell .... CARAPACE
6-banded ...... PELUDO
3-banded .... APAR, MATACO
12-banded ..... TATOUAY
Armageddon .. (LAST) BATTLE
author .... URIS
maybe .... MEGIDDO
armament ...... WEAPONRY, ARMS, EQUIPMENT, ORDNANCE
factory ... KRUPP, SKODA
armature .... ARMOR
armband, protective .. BRACER
armchair .... FAUTEUIL
armed band .... POSSE
conflict .... WAR, BATTLE
escort .... CONVOY, BODYGUARD
fleet .... NAVY
galley .... AESC
guard .... SENTINEL, SENTRY
Armenia's capital .... ERIVAN
mountain ...... ARARAT
armet .... HELMET
armhole .... SCYE
armiger ..... ARMOR BEARER, SQUIRE
armistice .... TRUCE, CEASE-FIRE
armlet .... BANGLE
armoire .... CUPBOARD, CABINET
armor .... MAIL, SHIELD, BARD(E), PLATE
arm .... BRASSARD, PALLETTE, BRASSART
back .... CUIRASS
bearer .... ARMIGER, SQUIRE
body ...... TACE, CULET, CUIRASS, SURCOAT LORICA, TASSE
breast .... CUIRASS
chain .... MAIL
clamp .... AGRAFFE
elbow to shoulder ...... BRASSARD
foot .... SOLLERET
hand .... GAUNTLET
head ... VISOR, BASINET, BEAVER, HAUBERK, SCONCE, ARMET, HELMET
hook .... AGRAFFE
horse .. BARD(E), TESTIERE
jacket .... JUPON, GIPON
joint .... GUSSET
leg .... JAMB(E), GREAVE
neck .... GORGET
plate ..... LAME, MASCLE
rings ...... BRIGANDINE
snail's .... SHELL
shirt cover ... CAMISADO
shoulder ...... AILETTE, PAULDRON
thigh .... TASSET, CUISH, TUILE, CUISSE
throat .... GORGET
tunic .... GIPON, JUPON
turtle's ...... CARAPACE
unworn ..... BARESARK
armored animal .. ARMADILLO
person of old ... KNIGHT
ship .... IRONCLAD, MONITOR, MERRIMAC
vehicle .... TANK
armorial .... HERALDIC
bearings/ensigns .... HERALDRY
armory .... HERALDRY, ARSENAL
orator's .... WORDS, CLICHES
armpit .... AXILLA, ALA, OXTER
swelling .... BUBO
arms .... WEAPONS, INSIGNIA, WARFARE
creature with eight ...... OCTOPOD, OCTOPUS
of the night, so-called ... DARKNESS
army .. HOST, TROOPS, HORDE, ARMED FORCES, LEGION
car .... JEEP
caterer .... SUTLER
chaplain .... PADRE
engineer .... SAPPER
follower .... SUTLER
front of ... VAN(GUARD)
group .... CORPS, REGIMENT, BRIGADE, SQUAD, PLATOON
insignia of rank ... STAR, EAGLE, LEAF, BAR, STRIPE
mascot .... MULE
meal .... MESS, CHOW
mounted sentinel .... VEDETTE, VIDETTE
of the .... MILITARY
priest .... CHAPLAIN, PADRE
rank .... GENERAL, COLONEL, CAPTAIN, LIEUTENANT, SERGEANT, CORPORAL, PRIVATE, MAJOR
vehicle ... AMTRAC, JEEP, TANK, WEAPONS CARRIER
Arndt (Felix) piece ..... NOLA
arnica ... ANTISEPTIC, PLANT
Arnold (Matthew) character .. SOHRAB, RUSTUM
aroid ..... ARUM, ARACEOUS, TARO, TANIA
aroma ... ODOR, FRAGRANCE, SMELL, SAVOR, FLAVOR
aromatic ... SPICY, PUNGENT, FRAGRANT, SAVORY, ODOROUS
bark .... ANGOSTURA, CASCARILLA
berry .... CUBEB
beverage .... COFFEE
condiment .... SPICE
fruit .... NUTMEG
gum .... MYRRH, ARALIA, BALM, BALSAM
herb ...... MINT, ANISE, THYME, CARAWAY, FLEAWORT
leaves ..... LAUREL, BAY, BUCHU
liquid .... BAYRUM
oil .... BALM
ointment .... NARD
plant ...... WORMWOOD, ARTEMISIA, NARD, BASIL, TANSY, MINT, SAGE, CARUM, ANGELICA
resin ... COPAIBA, COPALM
root .... GINSENG
seed .... ANISE, DILL, CUM(M)IN, GUAIAC, FENNEL
smoke .... FUME
spice ... CLOVE, NUTMEG, MACE
tree .... BALSAM, FIRPINE
weed .... TANSY
wood .... CEDAR, BASSWOOD
Arouet's nickname ..... ZOZO
around ..... NEARBY, ABOUT, CLOSE TO, CIRCA
arouse .... STIR, FIRE, EXCITE, ANIMATE, INCITE, SPUR, FAN, INFLAME, FOMENT, PIQUE
arpeggio .... ROULADE
arraign ..... INDICT, ACCUSE, CHARGE
arrange .... PREPARE, FIX, SORT, CLASSIFY, ADJUST, ADAPT, MARSHAL
by twos ...... PAIR, MATE
for battle .... DEPLOY
for reference ...... FILE
in advance .... PLAN, PREPARE
in files .... STACK
in threes ...... TERNATE
methodically ...... FILE
the hair .... COMB, DRESS
arrangement ... PREPARATION, PLAN, AGREEMENT, ORDER, SET-UP, ADAPTATION, SETTLEMENT
arrant .... NOTORIOUS, UNMITIGATED, OUT AND OUT, BOLD
arras .... TAPESTRY
array ...... ATTIRE, MARSHAL, ORDER, DECK, DRESS, FINERY, TURN-OUT
arrear .... BACKLOG
arrest .... STEM, CHECK, HALE, STOP, HOLD, SEIZE, NAB, NICK
slang .... PINCH
writ .... CAPLAS
arrival, scheduled: abbr. .. ETA
arrive ... REACH, ATTAIN, COME
arrogance ..... HAUGHTINESS, PRIDE, HUBRIS
arrogant ...... OVERBEARING, PROUD, HAUGHTY, CAVALIER, COCKY, LOFTY
arrow ... SHAFT, DART, BOLT, SAGITTA
ancient .... QUARREL
barb .... FLUKE
blunt .... BUTT, SHAFT
body of .... STELE
case .... QUIVER
crossbow .... BOLT
feather .... VANE
feather-fitter .... PLUMIER

feathered .... VIRE
like .... SAGITTAL
notch for bowstring ..... NOCK
poetic .... REED
poison .... CURARE, UPAS, INEE, ANTIAR(IN)
put feather on ... FLETCH, FLEDGE
user ... BOWMAN, ARCHER
arrowroot ... CANNA, TAPIOCA, PIA, ARARAO, ARUM
arrows, quiverful of ... SHEAF
Arrowsmith, Mrs. ..... LEORA
arrowwood .... WAHOO, VIBURNUM, DOGWOOD
arrowworm .... SAGITTA
arroyo .... WADI, GULLY, RIVULET, STREAMBED, PIT, HONDO
arse .... BUTTOCKS, RUMP
arsenal .... ARMORY
Arsene, Monsieur ..... LUPIN
arsenic sulfide ......REALGAR
powder ...... SALVARSAN
arsis .... UPBEAT, ICTUS
arsonist ...... PYROMANIAC, FIREBUG, INCENDIARY
art .... SKILL, ARTIFICE, CRAFT, TRICK, PAINTING, MUSIC, DRAMA, DANCE
exhibition .... SALON
gallery ..... FREER, TATE, SALON
Latin .... ARS
movement of 1920's ..... DADA
objects .... VIRTU, VERTU
of argumentation .... DIALECTICS
of bookbinding .... BIBLIOPEGY
of carving/engraving .... GLYPTICS
of devising dances ...... CHORE(O)GRAPHY
of discourse .. RHETORIC
of disputation ... ERISTIC
of dwarfing trees/plants .. BONSAI
of horsemanship .... MANEGE
of mapping .... CHOROGRAPHY
of motion pictures ...... CINEMATICS
of public speaking ...... ELOCUTION
of teaching ... DIDACTIC
style ..... GENRE, DADA, CUBISM, IMPRESSIONISM, ARABESQUE
work, inferior .... POTBOILER
artal, singular of ...... ROTL
artel .... COOPERATIVE
Artemis ...... DIANA, DELIA, PHOEBE, GODDESS
birthplace ...... DELOS
mother ... LETO, LATONA
twin .... APOLLO
victim .... ORION
artemisia .... WORMWOOD
artery .... AORTA, BLOOD VESSEL, STREET
neck .... CAROTID
pulse .... ICTUS
artful .... WILY, CRAFTY, CUNNING, DECEITFUL, ADROIT, POLITIC, SLY
arthritis ... GOUT, DROP, CLOT
treatment ... CORTISONE, ACTH, VERATRIA, VERATRIN(E)
arthropod .... ARACHNID, CRUSTACEAN, INSECT, MYRIAPOD, MILLEPEDE
segmented part .. SOMITE, TELSON
arthropoda .... PHYLA
arthrotome .... SCALPEL
Arthur (see King Arthur)
Arthur Conan ____ .... DOYLE
character .... SHERLOCK (HOLMES)
title .... SIR
Arthurian enchantress .... VIVIAN
tales compiler .. MALORY, LOOMIS
artichoke .... PLANT, SUNFLOWER, TUBER, CYNARA, CHOROGI
kin .... CARDOON
leaf stalks ...... CHARD
article .... AN, THE, ESSAY, ITEM, REPORT, THING, PAPER
in a document ... CLAUSE
of faith/belief ... CREED, CREDO
of personal property .... CHATTEL
articles, miscellaneous .... RUMMAGE
of excellence .. IMPERIALS
of virtu .... CURIO, BIBELOT
sold together ..... TIE-IN
articulate .... JOINTED, ENUNCIATE, EXPRESSIVE, VOICE
articulated joint ...... HINGE
speech sound ..... LENIS
artifice .... STRATEGEM, CRAFT, RUSE, GUILE, WILE, DODGE, DEVICE, TRICK(ERY)
artificial .... POSTICHE, SIMULATED, SYNTHETIC, SHAM, COUNTERFEIT
bait ...... LURE, DECOY
butter .... OLEO, MARGARINE
fly ..... COACHMAN, DUN, DOCTOR, NYMPH
foodstuff .... ERSATZ
ivory .... IVORIDE
jewelry .... PASTE
language .... IDO, ESPERANTO
respiration apparatus ... PULMOTOR
smile of a sort ... SIMPER
teeth .... DENTURE
waterway .... CANAL
artillery .... GUNNERY, ORDNANCE
abbreviation .... ORD
antiaircraft ... ACK ACK, POMPOM
fire angle measurement .. MIL
man .... GUNNER, CANNONER, LASCAR
type of .... MOBILE, MOUNTED
wagon .... CAMION, CAISSON
artisan .... ARTIST, CRAFTSMAN, TRADESMAN
artist .... PERFORMER, PAINTER, MINIATURIST, ETCHER, DANCER, PORTRAITIST, PIANIST, SCULPTOR
abbreviation on painting PNXT
unconventional .... BOHEMIAN
artistic style .... GUSTO
artist's colony .... TAOS, LATIN QUARTER, GREENWICH
copy .... TRACING
frock .... SMOCK
medium .... OIL, CANVAS, PASTEL, TEMPERA, MARBLE, CLAY, BRONZE
milieu .... STUDIO, ATELIER
mixing board .. PALETTE
name on painting ...... DELINEAVIT
stand .... EASEL
artless ...... NAIVE, CLUMSY, CRUDE, SIMPLE, NATURAL, INGENUOUS
woman/girl ... INGENUE
artlessness .... NAIVETE, INNOCENCE, SIMPLICITY
arts and ____ .... CRAFTS, SCIENCES, LETTERS
votary .... ESTHETE, CONNOISSEUR, PATRON
arum ..... TARO, LILY, AROID, CALLA, CALADIUM
aruspex ... SOOTHSAYER, SEER
Aryan .... MEDE, SLAV
god .... AGNI
language ...... SANSKRIT
as .... THUS, WHILE, BECAUSE, THOUGH, QUA
if .... QUASI
soon as .... ONCE
usual: music ..... SOLITO
written: music ...... STA
"As You Like It" character .. ROSALIND, JACQUES
asafetida .... RESIN, FERULA, LASER
asarum .... PLANT, GINGER
asbestos .... SILICATE, AMPHIBOLE, BOARD
ASCAP member ..... AUTHOR
ascarid ...... ROUNDWORM, HOOKWORM, (PIN)WORM
ascend ...... CLIMB, (A)RISE, SOAR, SCALE
ascendancy ..... DOMINATION,

MASTERY, RISE, PREDOMINANCE
ascent ..... RISE, ACCLIVITY, SLOPE, STIPE
ascertain ..... LEARN, VERIFY, SEE, DETERMINE
ascertainment ... ASSURANCE
ascetic .... AUSTERE, HERMIT, ESSENE, RECLUSE, MONASTIC, YOGA, FAKIR, STOIC, EREMITE, MONK, STYLITE
Asch name .... SHOLEM, SHOLOM
asci .... SPORE SAC
ascidian .... TUNICATE
Ascot ...... SCARF, (NECK)TIE
ascribe .... ATTRIBUTE, IMPUTE, CREDIT, ASSIGN
ascus .... (SPORE)SAC
aseptic .... STERILE
asexual .... SEXLESS, NEUTER, AGAMIC
reproduction .... FISSION
Asgard, bridge to .... BIFROST
watchman of .. HEIMDALL
ash ..... TREE, WOOD, EMBER, POWDER, RESIDUE, PALLOR, ARTAR
can .... DUSTBIN
can: sl. ... DEPTH BOMB, DEPTH CHARGE
fruit .... SAMARA, KEY, MAPLE
gray .... CINEREOUS
mountain .... ROWAN
pertaining to .. CINERARY
solution .... LYE
tree juice .... MANNA
Wednesday to Easter .... LENT
Ashanti capital ...... KUMASI
ashen ..... PALE, WHITE, WAN, GRAY, PALLID, LIVID
Asher's daughter ...... SERAH
mother .... ZILPAH
son .... ISUI, BERIAH
ashes, pert. to ..... CINERARY
ashlar .... BEAM, PLAN
Ashtoreth .... ASTARTE, ISHTAR
ashy .... PALE, LIVID
Asia Minor .... ANATOLIA
bishop ... (ST) NICHOLAS
city ..... MYRA, ANTIOCH, TYRE, GAZA, TROY, NICAEA, ISSUS, EPHESUS, CHALCEDON, SARDIS
country .... CARIA, CILICIA, LYCIA, MYSIA, LYDIA, PISIDIA, PHRYGIA
district ... IONIA, TROAD
Greek city ..... MILETUS
island .... SAMOS
kingdom .... PONTUS
mountain .... IDA
people .... HITTITES
province ...... GALATIA, LYCAONIA
region .... EOLIS, TROAS
river ...... CAICUS, IRIS, GRANICUS
sheep .... BROADTAIL, KARAKUL
tree .... SYCAMORE
Asiatic ancient people .. SERES
ass .... ONAGER
bean .... SOY(A)
bird .... MINA, MYNA(H), PITTA
cat .... OUNCE, SIAMESE, TIGER
cattle .... ZEBU
civet .... ZIBET(H)
coin, Annam ..... QUAN
coin, China ... LI, TAEL, TIAO, YUAN
coin, India ... ANNA, PIE, HOON, PICE, FELS, RUPEE, TARA
coin, Iran ... PUL, POUL, RIAL, DARIC, DINAR, MOHUR, LARI
coin, Iraq .... DINAR
coin, Malaya .... TRA(H)
coin, Nepal ..... MOHAR
coin, Siam/Thailand .... BAHT, TICAL, ANNA
country ... ANNAM, IRAQ, IRAN, BURMA, CHINA, VIETNAM, KOREA, SYRIA, THAILAND (SIAM), SIKKIM, NEPAL, MALAYSIA, SINGAPORE, INDIA, PAKISTAN, LAOS, CAMBODIA, TIBET, ARABIA
country, ancient .. MEDEA, EOLIA, ELAM, ACCAD
cow .... ZO(H), ZOBO
deer .... AXIS, SAMBAR, SASIN
desert .... GOBI
disease .... BERIBERI
fiber ...... RAMIE, HEMP
finch .... SISKIN
gangster .... DACOIT
gazelle ..... AHU, CORA, ARIEL
ginger ...... CARDAMOM, CARDAMUM
goat antelope .... SEROW
grass ...... CITRONELLA
grassland ...... MAIDAN
herb .... CARDAMOM, CARDAMUM
hog .... BABIRUSA
isthmus .... KRA
kingdom ... ELAM, IRAN, IRAQ, SIAM, NEPAL, AN(N)AM, KOREA
lake ...... BAIKAL, ARAL
lemur ... LORIS, MACACO
medicine man ... SHAMAN
millet .... DARI
monkey .... MACAQUE
mountain .... ALTAI
native .... MONGOL, TA(R)TAR, AN(N)AMESE, SIAMESE, TIBETAN, TAI, CHINESE, KOREAN, INNUIT, YUIT, HUN
nomad .... TATAR
palm .... ARECA, BETEL, NIPA
peninsula .... KOREA, MALAY
perennial plant ... RAMIE
plague .... CHOLERA
plain .... CHOL
plant ... RAMIE, SESAME, TAMPALA, ODAL, GINSENG, HEMP
port .... AMOY, HAIPHONG, SAIGON, SHANGHAI, MACAO
river .... MEKONG, AMUR, YALU, YANGTZE, YELLOW, OXUS, ILI, LENA, ONON, PEARL, INDUS
rodent .... MARMOT, PIKA, CONY
ruminant .... YAK, ZEBU
sardine .... LOUR
sea ... CHINA, ARAL, AZOL
sheep .... ARGALI
shrub ... TEA, THEA, TCHE
storm .... TYPHOON
snowstorm ...... BURAN
tea .... CHA, PEKOE, OOLONG
thug .... DACOIT
trade wind .... MONSOON
tree .... TEAK, ACLE, SIRIS, BANYAN, DITA, NARRA
tribe .... TAI, UZBEG, TATAR
weight .... TAEL, CATTY
wild hog ..... BABIRUSA, BOAR
wild sheep ..... ARGALI, RASSE
aside .... AWAY, APART
set .... TABLE
stage ... AD LIB, WHISPER
asinine ...... IDIOTIC, STUPID, SILLY, NUTTY, INANE
ask ...... DEMAND, INQUIRE, INVITE, QUESTION, QUIZ, SOLICIT, BEG
for a handout ... TOUCH
for a loan: sl. .... BRACE
askew ... AWRY, ALOP, AGEE, ASLANT
asleep .... DOZING, DORMANT, DEAD, INACTIVE, NAPPING
at the ____ ..... SWITCH
Asmara is capital of .. ERITREA
asor .... LYRE
asp ... VIPER, SNAKE, URAEUS
on headdress .... URAEUS
asparagus tip .... SPEAR
aspect .... VIEW, LOOK, PHASE, OUTLOOK, MIEN, APPEARANCE
general .... FACIES
aspen .... POPLAR, FLUTTERING, TREMBLING, QUIVERING
asper .... COIN
asperation .... SLUR
asperity .... HARSHNESS, ROUGHNESS, SHARPNESS, RIGOR
asperse ..... SLANDER, LIBEL, VILIFY, SLUR, REVILE

aspersion .... INNUENDO, SLANDER, SLUR
asphalt .... BITUMEN, GILSONITE, UINTAITE
like mineral ... ALBERTITE
asphyxia ... APNEA, ACROTISM
aspic ...... JELLY, LAVENDER, RELISH, MOLD
aspirant .... CONTENDER, CANDIDATE
aspiration .... BREATH, AMBITION, DESIRE, GOAL
aspire .... HOPE, LONG, SEEK, BREATHE
aspirin .... TABLET
ass .... DONKEY, BURRO, DOLT, FOOL, SIMPLETON, ONAGER
female .... JENNY
hybrid .... ZEBRASS
male .... JACK
young .... FOAL
assa .... CAAMA
assagai ...... SPEAR, JAVELIN
assai .... PALM, DRINK
assail ..... SET UPON, ATTACK, ASSAULT, BESET
assailant .... ATTACKER, AGGRESSOR
Assamese capital .. SHILLONG
dialect .... LHOTA
Mongol .... GARO, NAGA
shrub .... TEA
silkworm .... ERI(A)
tribe .... AKA, NAGA, AHOM, GARO
assassin .... MURDERER, KILLER, BRAVO, SLAYER, THUG
Abel's .... CAIN
Biblical .... CAIN
character ..... SMEARER, SLANDERER, DEFAMER, ROORBACH
Garfield's ..... GUITEAU
Kennedy's ..... OSWALD
Lincoln's .... BOOTH
origin of word .. HASHISM
assassinate .... KILL, MURDER, SLAY
assault ..... ONSET, ATTACK, CHARGE, RAPE
and battery .... BEATING
prolonged .... SIEGE
prolonged verbal .... TIRADE
assaulter .... MUGGER
assay .... TEST, ANALYZE, ANALYSIS, APPRAISE
assaying cup .... CUPEL, TEST
asse .... FOX, ANTELOPE
assemblage ... CONGREGATION, MEETING, GATHERING
assemble ..... (FOR)GATHER, COLLECT, FIT, MUSTER
assembly .... GATHERING, MEETING, SESSION, AUDIENCE, HUSTINGS, RALLY
assent .... CONSENT, COMPLY, AGREE(MENT), CONCUR(RENCE)
show .... NOD
sign of .. NOD, THUMBS UP
word of .... AMEN, OKAY, YES
assert .... AVER, STATE, SAY, DECLARE, AFFIRM
as a fact .... POSIT, CLAIM, ALLEGE
formally ..... ALLEGATE
positively .... SWEAR
assess ...... APPRAISE, RATE, TAX, LEVY, FINE, DUN
assessment ... RATAL, WORTH, ESTIMATE, TAX, VALUATION, APPRAISAL
assessor .... JUDGE, APPRAISER, RATER
asset .... PROPERTY, POSSESSION, ADVANTAGE, ESTATE, RESOURCE
personal ...... BEAUTY, WIT, TACT, CHARM, CHARISMA
assets and liabilities .. ESTATE
asseverate .... STATE, ASSERT, AVER
assiduous .... DILIGENT, BUSY
assign .... DESIGNATE, APPOINT, TRANSFER, ALLOT, RELEGATE
cause/reason .... ATTRIBUTE, ASCRIBE
parts in play ...... CAST
assignation .... TRYST, RENDEZVOUS, APPOINTMENT
assimilate .... ABSORB, DIGEST, INCORPORATE
facts .... LEARN
assimilation of learning ...... EDUCATION
assist .... HELP, AID, SUPPORT, ATTEND
assistance ... HELP, HAND, AID
in kind ...... ALMS, DOLE
to disaster victims .... RELIEF
assistant .... AIDE, DEPUTY
chairman at public dinner CROUPIER
first, of a sort .... RIGHT HAND
of bishop .. COADJUTOR, VERGER
pastor .... CURATE
to an abbot ...... PRIOR
assize ..... COURT, SESSIONS, INQUEST, OYER
associate .... ALLY, COLLEAGUE, CRONY, CONNECT, JOIN, PARTNER, CONFRERE
in crime .... ACCOMPLICE
with others ..... HOBNOB
association .... SOCIETY, LEAGUE, ORGANIZATION
business firms' .. CARTEL
football .... SOCCER
merchants' ...... HANSE
mutual aid .... ARTEL
mutual protection ...... GUILD
oldest in membership ... DEAN
scholars', etc. .. ACADEMY
workers' .... UNION
assoil .... ATONE, PARDON, ABSOLVE
assonance .... PUN
assort ..... CLASSIFY, MATCH, HARMONIZE
assorted .... VARIOUS, MISCELLANEOUS, CLASSIFIED
assortment ... VARIETY, OLIO, COLLECTION
of types .... FONTS
assuage ..... ALLAY, PACIFY, CALM, RELIEVE, MITIGATE
assume .... INFER, FEIGN, SUPPOSE, UNDERTAKE, PRETEND, AFFECT, SIMULATE, ARROGATE
a part .... IMPERSONATE, ACT
an attitude .... POSE
as a fact .... POSIT
another's personality .... IMPERSONATE
control ..... TAKE OVER
without right ..... USURP
assumed character ..... ROLE
identity for disguise ..... INCOGNITO
name .... ALIAS, PSEUDONYM
personality .... IMPERSONATION
assumer of other personality ... IMPOSTOR
assumption .... PRETENSE, PRESUMPTION
assurance ...... CONFIDENCE, CERTAINTY, GUARANTEE
assuredly .... CERTAINLY, DECIDEDLY
assurgent .... RISING
Assyrian .... AMORITE, S(H)EMITE
capital .... NINEVEH
chief deity ..... AS(S)UR, AS(S)HUR
city ..... ARBELA, HARA, OPIS, AKKAD
god ..... ASHUR, AS(S)UR, ANAT, IRA, NINIB, TAMMUS, NABO, NUSKU, HADAD, SIN
goddess ...... IS(H)TAR, ALLATU, NANA, SARPANIT
king ... PUL, SARGON (II)
mountain ...... ZAGROS
pyramid ..... ZIGGURAT, ZIKURAT
queen .... SEMIRAMIS
river ...... ZAB, ADHIAN
warrior .... SARGON
weight .... COLA
Astaire, ____ ... FRED, ADELE
dancing partner .... RITA
Astarte .... ISHTAR, ASHTORETH
astatic .... UNSTEADY, UNSTABLE
aster .. FLOWER, TANGLEFOOT, DAISY, OXEYE, TANSY, ZINNIA

asterisk .... STAR
astern ..... BACKWARD, AFT, ABAFT, REAR, BAFT
asteroid .... STARLIKE, EROS, CERES, STARFISH, PALLAS
asthenic .... FEEBLE
asthma medicine ... GRINDELIA
asthmatic breath .... WHEEZE
astigmatism ...... AMETROPIA
astir .... MOVING, ABOUT, AGOG, AWAKE
Astolat maid .... ELAINE
astonish .... AMAZE, SURPRISE, ASTOUND
Astor, Lady ....(NANCY), LANGHORNE
astound .... AMAZE, BEWILDER
astrachan .... APPLE
astrakhan ..... APPLE, PELT, KARAKUL, CLOTH
astraddle .... ASTRIDE
Astraea .... VIRGO
astragal(us) .... ANKLEBONE, TALUS
astral ..... STELLAR, STARRY, ASTER, LAMP
astray ..... LOST, OFF COURSE, AMISS
astride .... ASTRADDLE
astringent .... ALUM, STYPTIC(AL), HARSH, SEVERE, TANNIN, STERN, COTO, CASHOO, CATECHU
  fruit .... SLOE
  gum .... KINO
  material .... CATECHU
  resin .... MASTIC
  root .... BISTORT
  salt .... ALUM
astrolabe .... ALIDAD(E)
astrologer .... STARGAZER, ASTRONOMER
  ancient .... MAGUS, CHALDEAN
  French .. NOSTRADAMUS
  legendary ...... MERLIN
astrological .... CHALDEAN
  diagram .... SCHEME
  belief .... SIDERISM
astrology, work on .. ALMAGEST
astromonk .... BONNY
astronaut .... SPACEMAN, MOONMAN
  American ..... SHEPARD, WHITE, BORMAN, SCHIRRA, BEAN, CONRAD, LOVELL, STAFFORD, EISELE, GORDON, ALDRIN
  Russian ...... KOMAROV, GAGARIN
astronautic activity .... LUNAR PROBE
  vehicle .... SPUTNIK, MARINER, APOLLO, SURVEYOR
astronomer .... BRAHE, METON, PTOLEMY, STARGAZER
astronomical ... LARGE, HUGE, URANIC
  almanac ..... EPHEMERIS
  arc .... AZIMUTH
  cloud .... NEBULA
  cycle .... SAROS
  instrument ..... ORRERY
  intersecting points ...... NODES
  measure ... APSIS, PARSEC
  phenomenon .... PULSAR, QUASAR
  shadow .... UMBRA, PENUMBRA
astronomy, work on .... ALMAGEST
astute ..... SHREWD, CRAFTY, KEEN, WILY, CANNY
Astyanax's parent .. HECTOR, ANDROMACHE
Asuncion is capital of .... PARAGUAY
asunder .. APART, SEPARATED
Aswan .... DAM, SYENE
asylum .... RETREAT, HAVEN, REFUGE, SANCTUARY, HOME, SHELTER
  describing a kind of .... POLITICAL
  inmate .... LUNATIC, REFUGEE
at .... NEAR, BY, ON
  all .... ANY, AUGHT
  all times .. EVER, ALWAYS
  an angle ... ATILT, ALIST
  full length ... FLAT(LING)
  hand .... PRESENT, HERE, NEAR(BY)
  home ..... IN, RECEIVING
  large ...... LOOSE, FREE, ABROAD
  last .... FINALLY, ULTIMATELY, ENFIN
  not time .... NEVER
  odds .... HOSTILE
  once .... RIGHT NOW, PRONTO, IMMEDIATELY
  that time .... THEN
  the age of ...... AET(AT)
  the same time ... COEVAL
  variance ...... DIFFERENT
atabal .... (KETTLE)DRUM, TABOR
Atahualpa .... INCA, KING
Atalanta's victor .. HIPPOMENES
ataman .... COSSACK
atap .... NIPA, PALM
Ataturk, Kemal ..... MUSTAFA
Ate .... AVENGER
atelier ... STUDIO, WORKSHOP
  worker .... PAINTER, ARTIST, MODEL
athanasia ..... IMMORTALITY
atheist .... AGNOSTIC, INFIDEL, FREE-THINKER, NONBELIEVER
atheling .... NOBLE(MAN), PRINCE
Athena .... MINERVA, PALLAS, NIKE
  shield .... (A)EGIS
  title of .... ALEA
Athenian .... ATTIC
  aristocrat ..... EUPATRID
  astronomer ...... METON
  citadel .... ACROPOLIS
  clan .... OBE
  coin .... CHALCUS
  courtesan .... THAIS
  demagogue ...... CLEON
  general ... CLEON, CIMON, ARISTIDES, MILTIADES, NICIAS
  judge .... DICAST
  juryman .... DICAST
  law-giver .... SOLON
  magistrate ..... ARCHON
  market .... AGORA
  money .... OBOL
  political subdivision ..... PHYLE
  room ... ADYTUM, CELLA
  ruler .... ARCHON
  sculptor .... PHIDIAS
  seaport .... PIRAEUS
  statesman .... ARISTIDES, PERICLES, CIMON
  temple ..... NIKE, ZEUS, PARTHENON
  tribunal .... AREOPAGUS
Athens founder ..... CECROPS
athirst .... EAGER, AVID, PARCHED
athlete's crown ...... LAUREL
  dream ... CHAMPIONSHIP, OLYMPICS
  foot .... RINGWORM
  jump .... BROAD
  jump with pole ... VAULT
  speed event ...... DASH, SPRINT
  throw .... JAVELIN, DISCUS, PASS
  trainer .... GYMNAST, HANDLER, COACH
athletic .... BRAWNY
  contest, 5 events .... PENTATHLON
  contest, 10 events ...... DECATHLON
  exercises .. CALISTHENICS, GYMNASTIC(S)
  field ..... OVAL, DIAMOND, COURT, STADIUM
  group ...... TEAM, FIVE, NINE, CREW, ELEVEN
  prize ..... AGON, MEDAL, TROPHY
athletics ...... SPORTS, GAMES, EXERCISES, GYMNASTICS
athodyd .... RAMJET
atingle ...... EXCITED, AGOG
atis .... CONITE
Atlanta is capital of .. GEORGIA
atlantes .... TELAMON
Atlantic coast fish ... TAUTOG, RED DRUM
  tributary ...... MIN(H)O, SENEGAL
Atlas' daughter .... CALYPSO, HYAD(E), MAIA, PLEIAD
  name .... AGENA
  wife .... PLEIONE
Atli .... KING, HUN
  wife .... GUDRUN
atman ... . EGO, SOUL
atmosphere .. AIR, TONE, AURA
  in some cities ..... SMOG, SMAZE

atmospheric condition .... CLIMATE, WEATHER
gas .... ARGON
phenomenon .... STORM, TEMPEST, CYCLONE, TORNADO, TYPHOON, HAIL, RAINBOW
pressure .... BARIC
atoll .... (CORAL) ISLAND, BIKINI
pool .... LAGOON
atom .... JOT, PARTICLE, IOTA, MONAD, ION, PROTON
bomb target .. HIROSHIMA
part .... PROTON, ION
smasher ... SYNCHROTON
smashing .... FISSION
with valence of two ..... DYAD
atomic .... MOLECULAR, MINUTE
particle ..... NEUTRINO, ELECTRON, PROTON, NEUTRON
physicist .... UREY, RABI, COMPTON, MILLIKAN, FERMI, BOHR
submarine ...... SKATE, NAUTILUS, TRITON, SCORPION
atomize ... SPRAY, PULVERIZE
atomizer .... SPRAYER
atomy ...... DWARF, PYGMY, SKELETON, PIGMY
atone ...... EXPIATE, AMEND, REDEEM, ASSOIL
atonement ..... REPARATION, REDRESS, REDEMPTION
atonic sound .... SURD
atoning .... PIACULAR, EXPIATORY
atrabilious .... MOROSE
Atreus' brother ..... THYESTES
parent .... PELOPS
son .... AGAMEMNON, MENELAUS
atrium .... COURT, ROOM, HALL, ENTRANCE
atrocious .... CRUEL, BRUTAL, ABOMINABLE, BAD, HEINOUS
atrocity .... BRUTALITY, OUTRAGE, BARBARITY
a physical ...... FREAK, DWARF, GNOME, MONSTER
visual .... EYESORE
atrophy of horse's muscles ... SWEENY
Atropos .... FATE, WEIRD
attach .... ADD, AFFIX, APPEND, CONNECT, JOIN, TIE, SEIZE, TACK
attaché .... DIPLOMAT
attached .... FOND, DEVOTED, APPENDED
to branch .... SESSILE
attack ..... ASSAIL, ASSAULT, OFFENSIVE, ONSLAUGHT, ONSET, POUNCE, SIC
artillery ..... CANNONADE
diversionary ..... FEINT
for quick victory .... BLITZ(KRIEG)
in words/writing .. SQUIB, LAMPOON, LASH, BASTE
kind of .... SNEAK, SURPRISE, VERBAL, BLITZ(KRIEG), BLIND, TACTICAL, STRATEGIC
prolonged .... SIEGE
reputation ..... DEFAME, SLANDER, LIBEL, MALIGN
signal .... WARISON
swift, overwhelming ..... BLITZ(KRIEG)
swift, surprise ..... RAID
violent, intense .... ONSLAUGHT
warning of ...... ALERT, ALARM
attacker .... ASSAILANT, AGGRESSOR, OFFENDER, INVADER, RAIDER
attain .... ACHIEVE, EARN, GAIN, REACH, WIN
attainment .... SKILL, ACCOMPLISHMENT, ACHIEVEMENT, LEARNING, SUCCESS
attaint ... CONVICT, DISGRACE, DISHONOR, ATTAINDER, CONDEMN, CORRUPT
attar .... OIL, PERFUME, (ROSE)EXTRACT
attempt ... TRY, ESSAY, STAB, ENDEAVOR, ATTACK
in Scottish .... ETTLE
attend ... SERVE, ACCOMPANY, HEED, ESCORT
attendance ...... TURN-OUT, GATHERING, HOUSE
describing some ... FULL, FULL-HOUSE, STANDING ROOM, SRO
full .... PLENARY
attendant .... SERVER, CONCOMITANT, SERVANT, RETAINER, SERVITOR
bridegroom's ... BESTMAN
fact ..... CIRCUMSTANCE
hunter's .... GILLIE, GILLY, GUNBEARER
knight's .... SQUIRE
on horseback .. OUTRIDER
patient's .... NURSE
personal .... VALET
queen's .... CONSORT
attendants, group of .... RETINUE, ENTOURAGE, TRAIN, COURT
attended by all ...... PLENARY
attent .... HEEDFUL
attention .... EAR, HEED, NOTICE, CONSIDERATION
getting sound ..... AHEM, COUGH, PSST, PST, SST, WHISTLE, YELL
holding ...... GRIPPING
order of ...... PRIORITY
attentive .... OBSERVANT, ALERT, DEVOTED, THOUGHTFUL
attenuate ... DILUTE, RAREFY, LESSEN, WEAKEN
attest ...... VOUCH, CERTIFY, AFFIRM, DEMONSTRATE
in earnest ...... SWEAR
attestation, formal/solemn ... OATH
sign of official ..... SEAL, SIGNATURE
attic ... GARRET, (COCK)LOFT, ATHENIAN, MANSARD
bird ...... NIGHTINGALE
part of .... DORMER
salt .... WIT
Attica, capital of .... ATHENS
king .... CECROPS
native .... METIC
township .... DEME
valley ... . LCARIA
Attican .... ATHENIAN
Attila .... HUN, KING, ETZEL, ATLI
adjective for ... SCOURGE
attire .... GARB, ARRAY, CLOTHES, FINERY, DRESS, RIG, RAIMENT
man's complete .... SUIT
stag's .... ANTLERS
winter's .... SNOW
woman's .... GOWN
Attis' love .... CYBELE
attitude .... DISPOSITION, OPINION, POSTURE, MOOD, FEELING
strike an .... POSE
attract .... DRAW, LURE, CHARM, FASCINATE, CAPTIVATE
attractive .... FETCHING, ALLURING, PRETTY, ENGAGING, CUTE
girl, describing one ..... CURVACEOUS, SEXY, PINUP, WHISTLEBAIT
girl's body: sl. .... CHASSIS
powerfully ... MAGNETIC
price to buyer .... CHEAP, BARGAIN, CUTRATE
very .... STUNNING
attribute .... ASSIGN, ASCRIBE, QUALITY, IMPUTE
attribution ...... IMPUTATION
attrition .... EROSION, REPENTANCE
battle of .... SIEGE
attune .... HARMONIZE, RECONCILE
to the times .. MODERNIZE, UP-DATE
au .... COLD
courant .... UP-TO-DATE
fait .... EXPERT
naturel .... NAKED
revoir .... GOODBY
aubade .... MATIN, ALBA
counterpart .. SERENADE
auberge .... INN, HOSTEL(RY)
auburn ...... BROWN, TITIAN
auction .... SELL, SALE, VENDUE, ROUP
price ...... BID, UPSET
auctioneer's hammer .. GAVEL, MALLET
platform .... BLOCK
word ..... SOLD, GOING
audacious ... SAUCY, DARING, RECKLESS, BOLD, INSOLENT

audacity . . . . TEMERITY, DARING, INSOLENCE, IMPUDENCE, CRUST, CHEEK, BRASS, GALL
audience . . . . ASSEMBLY, HEARING, RECEPTION INTERVIEW
kind of . . . . . . AUDITION
official . . . . DURBAR
part of, sometimes . . . . . . STANDEES
audio-visual aid . . . . FILM, SLIDE, TAPE, MOCK-UP
audiphone . . . . . HEARING AID
audition . . . . HEARING, TRY-OUT, TEST
auditor . . . . HEARER, LISTENER, CPA
auditory . . . . OTIC, AURAL, AURICULAR
Audubon, John . . . . ORNITHOLOGIST, NATURALIST, PAINTER
auf wiedersehen . . . . . GOODBY
Augean . . . . . STABLE, FILTHY
auger, groove of . . . . POD
relative . . . . . AWL, DRILL, BORER, GIMLET, WIMBLE
augment . . . . . ENLARGE, ADD, INCREASE, EKE
augur . . . . . . BODE, PORTEND, PROPHET, SOOTHSAYER, AUSPEX
augury . . . . . . OMEN, PORTENT, PROPHECY, SIGN
august . . . . IMPOSING, MAGNIFICENT, GRAND, SUBLIME
body, so-called . . SENATE, CONGRESS, SUPREME COURT
first . . . . LAMMAS
Augustan . . . . CLASSICAL, ELEGANT
Age writer . . . . OVID
Augustinian . . . . FRIAR
Augustus title . . . . . . PRINCEPS
wife . . . . LIVIA
auk . . . ALCA, MURRE, PUFFIN, DOVEKIE, DOVEKEY, ROTCH(E)
family . . . . ALCIDINE
genus . . . . ALLE
small . . . . ROTCH(E)
aulic . . . . COURTLY, SUAVE
aunt: Fr. . . . . TANTE
S. African . . . . TANTA
Spanish . . . . TIA
Auntie of stage/movies . . MAME
aura . . . . EMANATION, ATMOSPHERE
of splendor . . . . . NIMBUS
aural . . . . . . OTIC, AURICULAR
aureate . . . . GOLDEN, GILDED, ORNATE
aureole . . . . . . HALO, GLORY, CORONA
auric . . . . GOLDEN
acid salt . . . . AURATE
auricle . . . . EAR, PINNA
auricular . . . . OTIC, AURAL
Auriga . . . . WAGONER
aurist . . . . OTOLOGIST
instrument . . . OTOSCOPE
aurochs . . . . . BISON, URUS, OX
Aurora . . . . EOS, DAWN, BOREALIS, AUSTRALIS
auroral . . . BRIGHT, RADIANT, ROSEATE, EOAN
aurum . . . . GOLD, AU
auscultation . . . . . . LISTENING
Ausonia . . . . ITALY
auspex . . . . AUGUR, SOOTHSAYER, SEER
auspice(s) . . . . OMEN, DIVINATION, PROPHECY, PATRONAGE, EGIS
auspicious . . . . FAVORABLE, PROPITIOUS, SUCCESSFUL
start in a theater . . . . FULL HOUSE, SRO SIGN
start of a speech . . . . . . LAUGHTER, APPLAUSE
austere . . . . STERN, HARSH, SEVERE, ASCETIC, RIGOROUS
austral . . . . SOUTHERLY, SOUTHERN
Australian . . . . AUSSIE, ANTIPODEAN, ANZAC
aborigine . . . . . . MAORI, MARA, MYALL, BUSHMAN
aborigine weapon . . . . . . NULLA, WO(O)MERA, BOOMERANG
acacia . . . MYALL, WATTLE
anteater . . . . ECHIDNA
arboreal animal . . KOALA
badger . . . . WOMBAT, BANDICOOT
bear-like animal . . KOALA
bee . . . . KARBI
beef-wood . . . . BELAR
bird . . . . PARDALOTE, LEIPOA, ARA, ARARA, LOWAN, MALLEE, LORY, EM(E)U, LORIKEET, MEGAPOD
boomerang . . . . . KILEY, KYLIE
brushwood . . . . . MALLEE
bushman . . . . ABO
bushranger . . . . HIGHWAYMAN
cane . . . . WADDY
cape . . . . HONE, YORK, HOWE
capital . . . . . . CANBERRA
cat-like animal . . . . LINSANG
cedar . . . . TOON(A)
chick . . . . SHEILA
city . . . . PERTH, BRISBANE, MANLY ADELAIDE, BALLARAT SYDNEY, BENDIGO
clover . . . . NARDOO
club of aborigines . . . . . . WADDY
cockatoo . . . . GALAH
cry . . . . COOEE, COOEY, CODER
dasyure . . . . YABBI
Davis Cup player . . . ROY, EMERSON, ROCHE, STOLLE, HOAD, NEWCOMBE
desert . . . . NULLARBAR
explorer . . . . . BASS, COOK
eucalyptus . . . . . . MALLEE
festival . . . . CORROBORI, CORROBOREE
fish . . . . . BARRAMUNDA, MADO
fish with lungs . . . . CERATODUS
flycatcher . . . . . FANTAIL
gale . . . . BUSTER
goldfish . . . . FANTAIL
grass . . . . SPINIFEX
gum tree . . . . TUART, KAR(R)I
harrier/hawk . . . . KAHU
highwayman . . . . BUSHRANGER
hinterland . . . . . OUTBACK
horse . . . . WALER, BRUMBY, BRUMBIE, WARRAGAL
hut . . . . . . MIMI, MIAM(IA)
island . . . . TASMANIA
kangaroo . . . . . WALLABY, WOLABA, WOLARU
kingfisher . . . . . HALCYON
lake . . . . EYRE, FROME
laughing bird . . . . KOOKABURRA, DACELO, GIGAS
lizard . . . . GOANNA, MOLOCH
marsupial . . . . KOALA, YABBI, WOMBAT, TAIT, PHALANGER, KANGAROO, BANDICOOT, DASYURE
measure of capacity . . . . . ARNA
mining refuse . . MULLOCK
mole . . . . PLATYPUS
mountain . . . . BLUE
mountain range . . . . FLINDERS
native . . . MAORI, MARA, MYALL, BUSHMAN, ABO
ostrich . . . . EM(E)U
oven . . . . UMU
parrot . . . . . . COCKATEEL, COCKATOO, PARAKEET, BUDGERIGAR, ROSELLA, GALAH, CORELLA
peninsula . . . . EYRE
pepper . . . . KAVA
pigeon . . . . WONGA
pine . . . . DAMMAR
plant . . . . WARATAN
prime minister . . . . HOLT, GORTON
"puritan" . . . . . WOWSER
river . . . . SWAN, DARLING, MURRAY
sea mile . . . . NAUT
seaport . . . . SYDNEY, BRISBANE, DARWIN, PERTH
shark . . . . MAKO
shield . . . . MULGA
shrub . . . . CORREA
soldier . . . . ANZAC
spear-throwing device . . . WO(O)MERA
territory . . . . PAPUA
traveler . . . . SWAGMAN
tree . . . . . . BILLA, BELAR,

PENDA, QUADANG, QUANDONG, ACACIA, MYALL, TODART, BOREE, MARARA
tree-dwelling animal .... KOALA
walking stick ... WADDY
wild dog .... DINGO
wild horse ..... BRUMBIES
wilderness ..... OUTBACK
Austria: Ger. ... OSTERREICH
Austrian amphibian .... OLM
capital .... VIENNA
chancellor ..... DOLLFUSS
city .... GRAZ, WEIN, VIENNA, LINZ
coin ... DUCAT, FLORIN, HELLER, GROSCHEN, KRONE, KREU(T)ZER, GULDEN, GUILDER
composer ...... MOZART, STRAUSS
country dance .. LANDLER
folk dance ...... DREHER
grass .... MARRAM
hunter ... JAGER, YAGER
liquid measure .... FASS
monetary unit ... KRONE, CROWN
name prefix .... VON
physicist .... MACH
province .... STYRIA
psychiatrist ..... ADLER, FREUD
rifleman .. JAGER, YAGER
river .... MUR, ENNS, DANUBE, DRAVE, RAAB, RABA, ISER, DRAU
ruling family .. HABSBURG
ski champ ...... SAILER, SCHRANZ
soprano .... JERITZA
violinist ...... KREISLER, MORINI
writer .... KAFKA
autarchy .... DESPOTISM
authentic .... GENUINE, ORIGINAL, REAL, VERITABLE, TRUE
authenticate ... SEAL, ATTEST
author .... ORIGINATOR, CREATOR, WRITER, FATHER
concern of .... PLOT, STYLE
of many works .... POLYGRAPH
unknown .... ANON(YMOUS)
authoritative .... MAGISTRAL, OFFICIAL
rule of law .. ORDINANCE
authority .... POWER, INFLUENCE, LICENSE, FORCE
letter of ... BREVE, BILLET
point as .... CITE, QUOTE
authorization .... FIAT, MANDATE, BILLET, LICENSE
authorize .... LICENSE, EMPOWER, COMMISSION, ACCREDIT, DEPUTE, PERMIT, ALLOW, GIVE LEAVE
auto (see automobile) .... CAR, MOTORCAR, AUTOMOBILE
clean .... SIMONIZE
colloquial .... BUS
court .... MOTEL
explosion ..... BACKFIRE
for hire ... CAB, TAXI(CAB)
obsolete .... REO, PACKARD, MODEL T, FLIVVER
old ..... JALOPY, CRATE, FLIVVER
old style .... LANDAU, CABRIOLET, VICTORIA
panel ...... DASHBOARD
prefix .... MANU
racing champion .. CLARK
shelter ... BARN, GARAGE, CARPORT
super-charged: colloq. .... HOTROD
type ..... SEDAN, COUPE, BERLIN(E), ROADSTER, HARDTOP, CONVERTIBLE, TUDOR
autobiography .... MEMOIR
autochthon .... NATIVE, ABORIGINE, INDIGENE
autocrat .... DESPOT, DICTATOR, TSAR, MOGUL, CAESAR
automat .... RESTAURANT
automatic .... SPONTANEOUS, PISTOL
action, kind of ..... TIC, REFLEX
coal stoker ..... HOPPER
clothes cleaner .... LAUNDROMAT
automaton ... ROBOT, GOLEM, ANDROID
automobile (see auto) .... (MOTOR)CAR, BUS
accessory ..... MUFFLER
baggage compartment ... BOOT
body .... BERLIN(E), TONNEAU
canvas-topped .... CONVERTIBLE
decrepit .... FLIVVER, CRATE
fast .... CLIPPER
framework ..... CHASSIS
furnishings .... TRIM
hood .... BONNET
lamp .... HEADLIGHT
like a coupe .. CABRIOLET
model .... V-EIGHT
mudguard ...... FENDER
operator .... DRIVER
panel ...... DASHBOARD
shelter .... CARPORT, GARAGE
speed .... HIGH, LOW
starter .... IGNITION
supercharged: sl. .... HOTROD
two-door .... COUPE
with folding top .... CABRIOLET
autopsy ...... POST-MORTEM, NECROPSY
autumn .... FALL
flower .... ASTER
auxiliary .... SUBSTITUTE, SUB, SUBSIDIARY, COADJUTOR, ASSISTANT, HELPER
avail ... USE, PROFIT, UTILIZE
available .... HANDY, ACCESSIBLE, ON HAND, READY, FREE, OPEN
money .... CASH
avalanche .... LAWINE, (LAND)SLIDE
Avalon .... ISLE, AVILION
avant garde ...... VANGUARD
avarice .... GREED, CUPIDITY
avaricious .... GREEDY, MISERLY, GRASPING, GRIPPLE
avast .... STOP, CEASE
avaunt ...... BEGONE, AROINT
ave .... HAIL, GREETING, FAREWELL, SALUTATION
avena .... OAT, GRASS
avenge .... RETALIATE, REVENGE, PUNISH, REQUITE
avenger .... ATE, NEMESIS
avenging spirit .... FURY, ALECTO, MEGAERA, TISIPHONE, ATE
avenue .... ROADWAY, DRIVE, PROMENADE, STREET, THOROUGHFARE, MALL
of trees .... ARCADE
aver .... ASSERT, AFFIRM, DECLARE
average ...... MEAN, USUAL, ORDINARY, NORM(AL), MEDIAN
averse ... LOATH, RELUCTANT, UNWILLING, AGAINST
aversion .... DISLIKE, ANTIPATHY, REPUGNANCE, REVULSION
avert ...... PREVENT, WARD, AVOID, THWART, PARRY, FRUSTRATE
a blow .... DUCK
a draft .... DODGE
a thrust .... PARRY
Avesta language .... ZEND
aviary .... BIRD(S)CAGE, VOLERY
aviate .... FLY
aviator .... PILOT, FLYER, AIRMAN
free lance .. BARNSTORMER
hazard .... BLACKOUT
signal .... CONTACT
with five kills ...... ACE
aviatrix, famous .... (AMELIA) EARHART
avid ... EAGER, GREEDY, KEEN
avifauna .... ORNIS
Avilion .... AVALON
avion .... AIRPLANE
avis indica .... APUS
aviso .... NOTICE, ADVICE, INFORMATION, BOAT
avital .... ANCESTRAL
avocado .... PEAR
Mexican .... COYO

avocation ... HOBBY, PASTIME
avocet .... STILT, PLOVER, COOT, STORK, GODWIT
avoid .... SHUN, SHIRK, ESCAPE, SIDESTEP
blow .... DUCK
commitment ..... HEDGE, HEM AND HAW
conscription .... DODGE
person ... DUCK, DODGE
work .... MALINGER, SHIRK, GOLDBRICK, DUCK
avoidance ...... ANNULMENT, SHUNNING
of battle .... FABIAN
avoirdupois .... WEIGHT, HEAVINESS, EMBONPOINT
$1\frac{1}{3}$ pounds .... CATTY
avouch ...... AVOW, AFFIRM, GUARANTEE
avow .... DECLARE, AVER, ADMIT, CONFESS, ACKNOWLEDGE
awa .... MILKFISH, KAVA
Scottish .... AWAY
await ... EXPECT, BIDE, ATTEND
awake ...... ROUSE, ACTIVE, ALERT, ACTIVATE, STIR
award .... ADJUDGE, GRANT, DECISION, PRIZE, MEDAL
journalism/literature .... PULITZER
kind of .... BOOBY PRIZE
movie .... OSCAR
peace/medicine ... NOBEL
TV .... EMMY
aware .... CONSCIOUS, COGNIZANT, ON TO, SENSIBLE, HIP
awash ..... FLOATING, AFLOAT
away ..... GONE, OFF, ABSENT, OUT, ABROAD
from mouth .... ABORAL
from wind .... ALEE
prefix .... AB
awe .... FEAR, REVERENCE, VENERATION, DREAD
aweather .... WINDWARD
opposite of .... ALEE
awesome .... FEARFUL, TERRIBLE
awful .... APPALLING, DREADFUL, TERRIBLE
awfully ... VERY, EXTREMELY
awkward ..... CLUMSY, INEPT, UNWIELDY, GAUCHE, MALADROIT
age .... ADOLESCENCE
boat ..... ARK, DROGHER
person .... LOUT, RUSTIC, GAWK, SIMPLETON, FOOZLE, GALOOT, DUFFER
stroke .... FOOZLE
awl .... BODKIN, GIMLET, AUGER, ELSIN
for picking typeset ...... BODKIN
shaped .... SUBULATE
type of ..... PEG, SEWING
with chisel head .... BRADAWL
awn .... BEARD, ARISTA, BARB, FIBER
awned .... ARISTATE
awning .... CANVAS, SHELTER, MARQUEE, SUNSHADE
of bed/door .... CANOPY
Roman .... VELARIUM
awry .... ASKEW, AMISS, AGEE, AGLEY, CROOKED, TIPSY
ax(e) .... ADZ, HATCHET
bonehead .. TOMAHAWK
cut of .... KERF
head, prehistoric .. CELT
Indian ..... TOMAHAWK
like tool .... ADZ(E)
stone .... TOMAHAWK
axil .... ANGLE, ALA
axilla .... ARMPIT
axillary .... ALAR
axiom .... MAXIM, PRINCIPLE
axis deer .... CHITAL
member .... JAPAN, ITALY, GERMANY, REICH
axle ... SPINDLE, ARBOR, ROD
bearing .... HOTBOX
ayah ..... AMAH, NURSEMAID
ay(e) .... YES, YEA, EVER, ALWAYS, ALAS
aye-aye .... LEMUR
ayuntamiento ..... CITY HALL, TOWN HALL
azalea .... LAUREL
Azerbaijan's capital .. TABRIZ, BAKU
azo, as combining form ...... NITROGEN
Azores island .... FLORES, PICO, FAYAL, TERCEIRA
port .... HORTA
volcano .... PICO
azote .... NITROGEN
azoth .... QUICKSILVER, MERCURY
azothic .... NITRIC
Aztec .... NAHUATLAN
country .... AZTLAN
emperor ... MONTEZUMA
god .... XIPE, EECATL
hero .... NATA
language ...... NAHUATL
spear .... ATLATL
temple .... TEOPAN
azure .... (SKY)BLUE, CERULEAN, CELESTE, CYANIC
azygous .... ODD, SINGLE, MATELESS
azym .... BREAD

B

B .... SHOT, SECONDARY, BISHOP
girl .... BARGIRL, BARMAID
Greek .... BETA
Hebrew .... BETH
in chemistry ...... BORON
in chess .... BISHOP
letter ..... BE, BEE, BETA
picture (movies): sl. ..... QUICKIE
ba .... SOUL
in chemistry .... BARIUM
baa .... BLEAT
bleater .... SHEEP, LAMB
Baal .... (SUN)GOD, IDOL
Baalist .... IDOLATER
Bab .... BABUDDIN
babbitt .... PHILISTINE, BUSINESSMAN
babble .... PRATTLE, BLAB, MURMUR, BLAT, PRATE, JABBER
babe ..... BABY, INFANT, GIRL
Ruth's forte ... HOMERUN
Babel .... TOWER, TUMULT, CONFUSION, JARGON
baby's breath .... MADDER, HYACINTH, PLANT, GYPSOPHILA
babirusa .... HOG
baboo ...... CLERK, SIR, TITLE
baboon .... APE, CHACMA, (MAN)DRILL
babu .... SIR, TITLE
babul .... ACACIA
babushka .... KERCHIEF, SCARF
baby .... PAMPER, CODDLE, INFANT, YOUNG, CHILD, GIRL, CHRISOM
ailment .... CROUP
bathing tub .. BATHINETTE
bed .... CRADLE
bedroom ..... NURSERY
boot .... BOOTEE
breechcloth ..... DIAPER
cap .... BONNET, BIGGIN
carriage .... PRAM, PERAMBULATOR, BUGGY, STROLLER, GO-CART
cloth .... DIAPER, LAYETTE, CREEPER
diaper .... NAPKIN
food .... PAP
grand .... PIANO
head's soft spot .... FONTANEL(LE)
Indian .... PAPOOSE
Italian .... BAMBINO
jacket .... SACQUE, SACK
outfit .... LAYETTE
pacifier .... NIPPLE, TEETHING RING
pants .... SOAKERS
powder .... TALC
premature ..... PREEMIE
robe, baptismal .... CHRISOM
shoes .... BOOTEES
sitter ...... AMAH, AYAH, AUNT, NURSE
sitter's problem ... BRAT, CRYBABY

sound ..... CROW, MEWL
Spanish ..... NINA, NINO, NENA
talk ...... DADA, LISP, BABBLE
teething toy ..... CORAL, PACIFIER
toy .... BAUBLE
word .... DADA
Babylonia .... SHINOR, SHINAR
founder ...... SEMIRAMIS
Babylonian .... WICKED
abode of dead ... ARALU
canal .... JESUF
chief god ... ANU, ENKI, BEL, HEA
chief goddess .. IS(H)TAR
city ... AKKAD, CUNAXA
deity ... ALALU, HEA, BEL, MERODACH, ANU
division ... SUMER, ELAM, NITUK
god .... NABU, NEBO, RAMMAN, ZU, ADDU, ADAD, TAMMUZ, UTUG, DAGAN, SIRIS, SHAMASH, ANU, EA, NANNAR, UTU, NINIB, BEL, ENLIL, MARDUK, ANSHAR
goddess .. NINA, NANA(I), AYA, ERUA, ISHTAR, GULA, BAU, ARURU
hero .... ETANA
monarch .... ALOROS
numeral .... SAR(OS)
people .... SUMERIAN
priestess .... ENTUM
river .... TIGRIS
storm god .... ADAD
temple ...... BEL, ISTAR
tower .... ZIGGURAT
weight .... MINA
bac .... VAT, CISTERN
baccarat ..... CHEMIN DE FER
baccate .... PULPY
bacchanal ... ORGY, CAROUSER
cry .... EVOE
bacchante .... M(A)ENAD, CAROUSER
Bacchus ..... GOD, DIONYSUS
devotee .... SATYR, BACCHANT, M(A)ENAD
son .... COMUS
Bach's composition ... ARIOSO
bachelor .... GRADUATE, SINGLE, CELIBATE
bachelor's button .... CORNFLOWER, KNAPWEED, TANSY
party .... STAG
back .... AID, REAR, REVERSE, SPONSOR, ABET, SUPPORT, HIND, SECOND, ENDORSE, TUB, TERGUM, DORSUM, TERGAL
ache .... LUMBAGO
and fill .... ZIGZAG
at the .... RETRAL
book's .... SPINE
call .... REVOKE, WITHDRAW
country ... HINTERLAND
cramp .... CRICK
door .... POSTERN, UNDERHAND, SURREPTITIOUS, CLANDESTINE
down/out ... WITHDRAW, YIELD
entrance .... POSTERN
flow .... EBB, RECEDE
gate .... POSTERN
in zoology ..... TERGUM
lying on .... SUPINE
near the .... RETRAL
of animal ...... DORSUM, RIDGE
of head .... POLL
of insects .... NOTUM
of neck ... NAPE, NUCHA, SCRUFF, SCRAG
of skull ..... OCCIPITAL, NION
pain .... STITCH
part .... DERRIERE
part: comb. form .. NOTO
pertaining to the .... DORSAL, TERGAL
scratcher .... TOADY
seat, carriage ... DICKEY, RUMBLE
seat driver: colloq. .. WIFE
take word ..... RECENT, RETRACT
talk: colloq. .... SASS, RETORT, LIP
toward .... RETRAL
wound .... STAB
backache .... LUMBAGO
backbite .... SLANDER, MALIGN, VILIFY
backbone ...... SPINE, RIDGE, COURAGE, VERTEBRA
having ...... VERTEBRATE
of animal .... CHINE
of fish .... GRATE
backbreaking .... HEAVY, TIRING, DIFFICULT, STRENUOUS
backdoor .... SECRET, CLANDESTINE
backdrop .... SETTING, SCENE(RY)
backer .... PATRON, SPONSOR
stage show ...... ANGEL, SUGAR DADDY
backfire .... EXPLOSION, BOOMERANG
backgammon .... TRIC(K)TRAC(K)
exposed man .... BLOT
game series ..... RUBBER
backhanded ..... SARCASTIC, EQUIVOCAL, INSINCERE
backhouse .... PRIVY
backless .... SPINELESS
dress .... DECOLLETE
person .... YELLOW, COWARD
seat .... STOOL, OTTOMAN
backlog .... RESERVE, ACCUMULATION
backside ... RUMP, BUTTOCKS
backslide .... RELAPSE
backtrack .... RETREAT
backward ..... REVERSE, SHY, BASHFUL, SLOW, RETARDED
backwater .... BAYOU
channel ...... BILLABONG
backwoodsman ...... RUSTIC, HILLBILLY
bacon, bring home the .. WIN, SUCCEED
coating .... RIND
cut .... RASHER
side of .. FLITCH, GAMMON
strip .... LARDO(O)N
bacteria culture .... AGAR, STRAIN
destroyer .... LYSIN, BACTERICIDE, ALEXIN
free of .... ASEPTIC
mass of .... CLUMP
organ of locomotion .... FLAGELLUM
s-shaped .... VIBRIO
bacterium .... FUNGUS, BACILLUS
bacteriologist's wire .... OESE
Bactria .... BALKH
bactrian .... CAMEL
bad ... EVIL, UNFIT, WICKED, DISAGREEABLE, HARMFUL, SPOILED, INFERIOR, ILL, BASE
blood .... ENMITY, RESENTMENT
breath .... HALITOSIS
combining form ... MAL
girl ...... TRAMP, HUSSY
habit .... VICE
humor ..... TIFF, TEMPER
Land mountain .. BUTTE
liquor: colloq. .... BOUSE
luck ...... MISFORTUNE, MISHAP, WANION, AMBSACE, AMESACE, CESS, HOODOO
luck man .. JONAS, JONAH
mannered person .. GOOP, BOOR, LOUT
prefix ... CACO, MAL(O), MIS
smell .... STENCH, MEPHITIS, REEK
smell of oil/fats .. RANCID
smelling ..... MEPHITIC, MALADOROUS
sport .... CRYBABY
temper .... BILE, SPLEEN
temper sign .... TANTRUM
tempered .... GRUFF, DORTY, TESTY, IRRITABLE, WASPISH, CRANKY, CRUSTY, SURLY, SPLENETIC, GRUMPY, SNAPPISH, GRUMPISH
tempered person .. FURY, SHREW, VIRAGO, HOTHEAD
woman .... FLOOZY, FLOOZIE, QUEAN, TRAMP, WHORE, TART
badak .... RHINO
badge .... EMBLEM, PIN, SIGN, MARK
Japanese .... MON
of braid .... CORDON
of honor .... MEDAL
of ribbon .... CORDON

on arm ...... BRASSARD
on hat .... COCKADE
badger .... NAG, TORMENT, PESTER, HECKLE, HARRY, TEASE, BROCK
animal .... WOMBAT, BANDICOOT, BROCK, HAWKER
Canadian ... CARCAJOU
European .... BROCK
genus .... MELES
honey .... RATEL
Java .... TELEDU
like animal .... MARMOT, PAHMI
State .... WISCONSIN
badinage .... CHATTER, BANTER, TALK
badlands .... WASTE
badly .... ILLY, POORLY
colloquial ..... GREATLY, MUCH
badminton ... (COURT) GAME, DRINK
cork ..... SHUTTLECOCK
racket ..... BATTLEDORE
Baedeker .... GUIDEBOOK
Baffin's discovery .... SEA, ISLAND
baffle .... BALK, PUZZLE, ELUDE, CONFOUND, NONPLUS, BEWILDER, FRUSTRATE, FOIL, MYSTIFY, THWART, CONFUSE
baffling .... INSCRUTABLE, ELUSIVE
problem .... POSER, DILEMMA, PUZZLE, MYSTERY
question .... RIDDLE, ENIGMA, PUZZLE, CONUNDRUM
bag ...... SAC, POUCH, POKE, LUGGAGE, SATCHEL, SUITCASE, PURSE, UDDER, CAPTURE, SEIZE, CYST
floating ...... BALLOON
for books, papers, etc. ... BRIEFCASE
grain .... SACK
kind of .... DUFFEL
making material .... SACKING, JUTE, BURLAP, FLAX, HEMP
slang .. WOMAN, CAPTURE
sleeping .... SACK
toilette .... MUSETTE
with perfumed powder ... SACHET
bagasse ...... (CANE) REFUSE, MEGASS(E)
bagatelle .... TRIFLE
baggage .... LUGGAGE
boy .... PORTER
car .... FOURGON
carrier ...... HAM(M)AL, PORTER, REDCAP
slang .... WOMAN, SAUCY, GIRL
wagon .... FOURGON
baggie ...... BELLY, STOMACH
bagging material .... JUTE, HEMP, FLAX, BURLAP
baggy .... PUFFED, UNPRESSED
bagman: Eng. ..... SALESMAN
bagnio .... BATHHOUSE, BROTHEL, PRISON, CABANA
Bagnold .... ENID
bagpipe .... MUSETTE, DRONE, DOODLESACK, LOURE
drone .... BOURDON
flute .... CHANTER
music .... PIBROCH
part .... CHANTER
play .... SKIRL
sound .... SKIRL
bagworm .... LARVA, CATERPILLAR
bah! ... ROT, TUT, PSHAW, FIE, NUTS
Bahama Islands ..... ABACO, ANDROS, ELEUTHERA, BIMINI
capital .... NASSAU
premier .... PINDLING
Bahia ...... (SAO) SALVADOR
Bahrein Islands capital ..... MANAMA, MANAMEH
bail .... BOND, RELEASE, BUCKET, PALISADES, FREE, SCOOP, FORTIFICATION, LADE
one who needs .... DETAINEE, PRISONER
out .... PARACHUTE, JUMP, RELEASE
bailiff .... TIPSTAFF, REEVE, OVERSEER, STEWARD
bailiwick ...... FIELD, SPHERE, HOMEGROUND, DOMAIN, JURISDICTION
bairn .... CHILD, SON, DAUGHTER
bait .... LURE, TORMENT, TEMPT, BADGER, RIDE, HECKLE, DECOY, TRAP, HECTOR, ENTICE(MENT), GUDGEON
drop .... DIP, DAP
fish .... CHUM, LURE
take .... BITE
baize .... DRAPE, CLOTH, DOMETT
bake .... FIRE, ROAST, COOK, DRY UP, BROIL, ANNEAL
with crumbs ... SCALLOP, ESCALOP
baked clay .... TILE
dishes, etc. ... CROCKERY
pot .... OLLA
baker bird .... HORNERO
baker's dozen ..... THIRTEEN
itch .... RASH, PSORIASIS
job .... KNEAD
kneading trough .. BRAKE
material .... FLOUR, YEAST, LEAVEN
shovel .... PEEL
tool .... PEEL
workshop .... YALE
baking chamber ...... OAST, OVEN, KILN
dish .... RAMEKIN, RAMEQUIN, CASSEROLE, SCALLOP
pit: Hawaiian ...... IMU
soda .... SALERATUS
baksheesh .... ALMS, TIP, GRATUITY
Balaam's beast .... ASS
bal ____ ... TABARIN, MASQUE
balalaika .... GUITAR
balance ...... EVEN, OFFSET, SCALES, LIBRA, REMAINDER, POISE, SYMMETRY, EQUILIBRIUM
crossbar of .... BEAM
of sales .... ATRY
state of ...... EQUIPOISE
weighing .... STEELYARD
balancer .... ACROBAT, TIGHTROPE WALKER, WIRE WALKER
of books ... ACCOUNTANT
balancing weight .... BALLAST
balas .... SPINEL
balata gum .... CHICLE
Balboa's ocean ...... PACIFIC
balcony .... TERRACE, GALLERY, GAZEBO
bald .... BARE, PLAIN, FRANK, BLUNT, HAIRLESS, GLABROUS
headed man ... PILGARLIC
baldachin .... BROCADE, CANOPY
Balder, giant victim of .. LOKI
parent ..... ODIN, FRIGG
slayer of ...... HODUR, HODER
wife .... NANNA
balderdash .... NONSENSE, PALAVER, RIGMAROLE
baldness .... ALOPECIA, ACOMIA, CALVITIES
baldpate .... WIDGEON
cover ..... TOUPEE, WIG
baldric .... BELT
Baldwin .... APPLE
cousin .... WINESAP
bale .... PACKAGE, BUNDLE, DISASTER, SORROW, BAIL, WOE
Balearic Island .... MAJORCA, MINORCA, MENORCA
capital .... PALMA
language ..... CATALAN
baleen .... WHALEBONE
balefire ...... BONFIRE, PYRE
baleful .... SINISTER, EVIL, DEADLY
baler .... BUNDLER, TIER
Bali holy day .... NJEPI
balk .... JIB, OBSTRUCT, SHY, BLUNDER, ERROR, THWART, FOIL, STOP
Balkan ..... SERB(IAN), SLAV, BULGAR(IAN), SLOVENE
balker, congenital .... ASS, DONKEY, MULE
Balkh .... BACTRIA

balky . . . . CONTRARY, RESTIVE, OBSTINATE, STUBBORN
ball . . . . GLOBE, IVORY, DANCE, SPHERE, PLANET, BULLET
and chain . . . . WIFE
batted high . . . . FLY
game . . . . KENO, SOCCER, TENNIS, BASEBALL, BOWLING, CRICKET, RUGBY, BOWL, LACROSSE
hit for practice . . FUNGO
low . . . . LINER
metal, athletics . . . . SHOTPUT, HAMMER
of electrical discharge . . . CORPOSANT
of meat/rice . . . . . PINDA
of perfume mixture . . . . . POMANDER
of yarn/thread . . . . CLEW
on the . . . . ALERT, EFFICIENT
play . . . . COOPERATE
rope missile . . . . . BOLA(S)
sign displayer . . . . PAWNSHOP
swing bat at . . . . . . SWAT
thread . . . . CLEW
throwing device . . . TRAP
tiny . . . . GLOBULE
up . . . . CONFUSE, MUDDLE
yarn . . . . CLEW
ballad . . . . SONG, POEM, LAY, DERRY, CALYPSO, CHANSON
hero . . . . LOCHINVAR
monger . . . . . . POETASTER
singer . . . . MINSTREL, TROUBADOUR
stanza, rhyme of . . ABCB
word . . . . DERRY
ballast . . . . STABILIZE(R)
ballerina . . . . DANSEUSE, TOE DANCER
descriptive word for a . . . ASOLUTA, PRIMA
famous . . . . FONTEYN, TALLCHIEF, MARKOVA, ULANOVA, SHEARER, RASCH
finale . . . . TWIRL, PIROUETTE
forte . . . . . . TOEDANCE, PIROUETTE
ballet . . . . ADAGIO, CHOREOGRAPH, MASQUE, DANCE, BEZANT
dance solo . . . . . PAS SEUL
dancer . . . . . . BALLERINA, DANSEUSE, CORYPHEE, FIGURANT
dancer's buoyancy . . . . . . BALON
dancer's skirt . . . . . TUTU
director . . . . IMPRESARIO
famous . . . . . SWAN LAKE
jump . . . . JETE, ENTRECHAT
number . . . . . TOE DANCE
number between acts . . . . INTERMEZZO
Petipa's . . . . . RAYMONDA
posture . . . . . ARABESQUE
step . . . . . PAS, GLISSADE
turn . . . . PIROUETTE, FOUETTE
wear . . . . . TUTU, TIGHTS, LEOTARD
ballista . . . . CATAPULT
ballistic missile launching . . . . BLAST-OFF
launching place . . . . PAD
storage place . . . . . . SILO
warhead . . . . . . PAYLOAD
balloon . . . . AEROSTAT, INFLATE, RUBBERBAG, BAG, SWELL
altitude controller . . . . . . BALLAST
bag . . . . ENVELOPE
ballast . . . . . . DRAGROPE
basket . . . . NACELLE, CAR
cabin . . . . GONDOLA
car . . . . NACELLE, BASKET
covering . . . . . ENVELOPE
gas . . . . HELIUM, HYDROGEN
mooring line . . DRAGROPE
pilot . . . . AERONAUT
shape of . . . . . . SAUSAGE, ROUND
trial . . . . FEELER, TEST
vine . . . . HEARTSEED
ballot . . . . VOTING, TICKET, VOTE(S), SLATE
straw . . . . POLL
ballroom dance . . . . . . WALTZ, REDOWA
balls tosser . . . . JUGGLER
ballyhoo . . . . . TALK, UPROAR, PROPAGANDA, ADVERTISE, PLUG, TOUT
balm . . . . BALSAM, OINTMENT, OIL, SALVE, FRAGRANCE, SOOTH, UNGUENT, RESIN, ANODYNE
for divorce . . . . ALIMONY
for injury . . . . . DAMAGES
of Gilead . . . . . . BALSAM, POPLAR, FIR, OINTMENT, OIL
Balmoral . . . . PETTICOAT, CAP, CASTLE
balmy . . . . FRAGRANT, SOOTHING, SOFT, MOONY, CRAZY, FOOLISH, IDIOTIC, MILD
balneal . . . . BATH(ING)
baloney . . . . . NONSENSE, ROT, BUNCOMBE, BUNK, BOLOGNA
balsa . . . . WOOD, RAFT, TREE, CORKWOOD
like wood . . . . . . BONGO
balsam . . . . RESIN, BALM, GUM, TOLU, IMPATIENS, FIR, COPAIBA, LIQUIDAMBAR
gum resin . . . . . STORAX, BALM
Swiss . . . . RIGA
tree . . . . TOLU
Balt . . . . ESTH
Baltic gulf . . . . RIGA
island . . . . . ALSEN, DAGO, OS(S)EL
port . . . . KIEL, RIGA, STETTIN, MEMEL, REVAL
river . . . . ODER
Sea city . . . LIBAU, LIEBAJA
seaport . . . . ROSTOCK
state . . . . LATVIA, LITHUANIA, ESTONIA, FINLAND
Baltimore oriole . . . HANGBIRD, GOLDENROBIN, HANGNEST
stove . . . . LATROBE
Balto-Slav . . . . LETT
Baluchistan capital . . . QUETTA
grain . . . . JOWAR
mountain . . . . HALA
race . . . . BRAHOES
river . . . . BOLAN, MOOLA
ruler . . . . KHAN, SIRDAR
town . . . . BEYLA, DADUR
tribe . . . . REKI
tribesman . . . . MARI
balustrade . . . . . BAN(N)ISTER, RAILING
Balzac's father . . . . . . GORIOT
bambino: Ital. . . . . CHILD, BABY(BOY)
bamboo . . . . CANE, GRASS, REED, TONKIN
like . . . . REEDY
shoot pickle . . . . ACHAR
stalk . . . . REED
bamboozle . . . . TRICK, CHEAT, PUZZLE, BUFFALO
ban . . . . FORBID, PROHIBIT, CURSE, TABU, TABOO, GOVERNOR, PROCLAMATION
Bana, daughter of . . . . . USHA
banal . . . . TRITE, CORNY, HACKNEYED, STALE, TRIVIAL
banality . . . . PLATITUDE, CLICHÉ
banana . . . . ENSETE, MUSA, PESANG, FEI
bunch/cluster . . . . HAND
disease . . . . MOSAIC
like fruit . . . . . . PLANTAIN
of the . . . . MUSACEOUS
oil: sl. . . . . NONSENSE
Philippine . . . . . SAGING, LATUNDAN
plant . . . . MUSA, PESANG
band . . . . BELT, STRIP, COPULA, BINDING, COLLAR, COMPANY, TAPE, FILLET, GATHER, GROUP, GIRDLE, FASCIA
across escutcheon . . FESS
brain . . . . LIGULA
deputized . . . . POSSE
head . . . CORONET, AGAL
ecclesiastical . . ORPHREY
leader . . . . JAMES, SHAW, VALLEE, CUGAT, WHITEMAN, CHORAGUS
leaders . . . . CHORAGI
mourning . . . . WEED
narrow . . . . STRIA(E), TAPE
of soldiers . . . . . COHORT
of stone on wall . . . . CORDON

ornamental .... CORONET
priest's arm .... FANO(N), FANUM, PHANO
sheriff's .... POSSE
wheel .... RIGGER
bandage ..... STUPE, LIGATE, LIGATURE, SWATH(E), GAUZE, SPICA
in surgery .... FASCIA
shaped .... LIGULATE
used as compress .. DOSSIL
bandanna .... (HAND)KERCHIEF
bandeau ...... (HAIR)RIBBON, BRASSIERE
banderilla .... DART
banderole ... FLAG, PENNANT, STREAMER, BANNEROL
bandicoot ..... RAT, BADGER
bandit .... BRIGAND, HIGHWAYMAN, ROBBER, LADRONE
more than one .. BANDITTI
banditry .... BRIGANDAGE
bandleader .... CHORAGUS
bandmaster .... SOUSA, CONDUCTOR
bandog .... MASTIFF, BLOODHOUND, WATCHDOG
bandoline .... POMADE
bandore .... PANDORA, PANDORE
bandwagon riders ... WINNERS
bandy .... EXCHANGE, GIVE-AND-TAKE, CLUB, CHAFFER, BOWED
legs .... BOWED
some are .... LEGS
bane .... POISON, RUIN, CURSE
baneful .... VENOMOUS, DEADLY, PERNICIOUS, RUINOUS, BAD
Banff National Park Lake .... LOUISE
bang .... SLAM, BEAT, STRIKE, CLOSE, EXPLOSION
slang .... PLEASURE, ENJOYMENT
up ..... BRUISE, DAMAGE
Bangalore, where it is .... MYSORE
banged-up .... EXCELLENT, WELL DONE, A-ONE
bangs ...... HAIRCUT, HAIRDO
Bangkok, capital of .... THAILAND, SIAM
coin ... BAHT, ATT, TICAL
language .... THAI
river .... MENAM
twin city .... DHONBURI
bangle .... BRACELET, ARMLET, ANKLET
banian ..... MERCHANT, SHIRT
banish .... EXILE, DISMISS, PROSCRIBE, RELEGATE, EXPATRIATE, DEPORT
banister .... BALUSTER, BALUSTRADE, HANDRAIL
banjo .... SAMISEN
string sound .... TWANG, TUM
bank .... RELY, DEPEND, RIDGE, SHOAL, SHORE
clerk .... TELLER
employee .... RUNNER
kind of .... BLOOD, EYE, POOL, DOMESTIC, PIGGY
note .... BILL
river .... RIPA
river, pert. to .. RIPARIAN
teller's window .. WICKET
vole .... MOUSE
bankbook .... PASSBOOK
banker ... LAMONT, MORGAN, GIANNINI, SHROFF, ROTHSCHILD
banking game .... FARO
bankroll .... WAD
colloquial ... CAPITALIZE
bankrupt .... INSOLVENT, FAILURE, PENNILESS, BROKE
abbreviation ...... BKPT
banner .... ENSIGN, FLAG, BANDEROLE, FOREMOST, LEADING, BLAZON, PENNON, STREAMER, GONFALON
headline ..... STREAMER
bannock .... CAKE
banquet ..... FEAST, DINNER, MEAL
rich, luxurious .... LUCULLAN
banquette .. SIDEWALK, BENCH
banshee .... SPIRIT
bant .... DIET
bantam .... SMALL, PINT-SIZE, FOWL, MIDGET
publication ... VESTBOOK, POCKETBOOK, TABLOID
banteng .... OX, TSINE
banter ... TEASE, PERSIFLAGE, RAILLERY, BADINAGE, JEST, CHAFF, JOSH, PLEASANTRY
bantling ... YOUNGSTER, BRAT
Bantu .... KAF(F)IR, JAGA
Congo .... RUA, WARUA, BAKALAI
language ..... ILA, SUTO, RONGA
lion .... SIMBA
nation .... GOGO
native ..... ZULU, YAKU, BASUTO, DUALA, SWAZI
speaking people .... BECHUANA
tribe ...... PONDO, RORI, RAVI
banzai ... CHARGE, GREETING, CHEER, CRY
baobab .... FIBER, TREE
leaves, dried/powdered .. LALO
baptism ...... PURIFICATION, RITE, INITIATION, NAMING
for example .. SACRAMENT
of fire ..... TEST, ORDEAL
baptismal basin .... FONT, LAVER, BAPTISTERY
cloth .... CHRISOM
oil .... CHRISM
robe .... CHRISOM
water .... LAVER
baptize ...... CHRISTEN, DIP, PURIFY, CLEANSE, INITIATE, NAME
bar ..... LAWYERS, BARRIER, COUNTER, STRIPE, PUB, DRAMSHOP, OBSTRUCT, BISTRO, EXCLUDE, ESTOP, OPPOSE, WINESHOP, TAPROOM, TAPHOUSE
chisel-pointed .. SPUDDER
dividing .... MULLION
door .... STANG
employee .... B-GIRL, TAPSTER
for holding hair .... BARRETTE
for mining .... GAD
habitue .... BARFLY
iron ingot .... BLOOM
legally .... ESTOP
of —— .... SOAP, CHOCOLATE, METAL, JUSTICE
of justice .... COURT
of loom .... EASER
pin .... BROOCH
room .... TAPROOM, SALOON
sinister .... BATON
slang .... GIN MILL
soap frame .... SESS
square metal .... BILLET
supporting .... FID
used with fulcrum ...... LEVER
woman employee .... B-GIRL
Bara, actress .... THEDA
barb .... BRISTLE, AWN, STING, SHARPNESS, JAG, FLUE, FLUKE, PIGEON, HORSE, SPINE
of feather ... HARL, HERL
of wit .... STING
small .... BARBULE, BARBEL
Barbados fish .... GUPPY
native ... BARBADIAN, BIM
barbarian ... BRUTE, SAVAGE, BEAST, PRIMITIVE, HUN, VANDAL, GOTH(IC)
barbarism .... SOLECISM
barbarity .... CRUELTY, BRUTALITY
barbarized term/word ...... CORRUPTION
barbarous .... GOTHIC, BRUTAL, CRUEL, PRIMITIVE
Barbary ape .... MAGOT
horse .... BARB
state .... MOROCCO, ALGIERS, TUNIS, TRIPOLI
barbate ... BEARDED, AWNED
barbecue ..... ROAST, BROIL, BURGOO, COOK OUT
bar .... SPIT, SKEWER
site ... PATIO, BACKYARD
barbed ... STINGING, CUTTING, HOOKED, UNCINATE
dart .... BANDERILLA
missile .... ARROW, DART, HARPOON, SPEAR
point .... FLUE
spear .... GAFF
tool .... HOOK
wire blaster .. BANGALORE
wire obstacle .. ABAT(T)IS

barbel . . . BARB, FISH, BARBULE
fish . . . . WATTLE
fish with . . . . . . CATFISH, MULLET
barber . . . TONSOR, SHAVE(R), HAIRCUTTER
of Seville . . . . FIGARO
work . . . . TONSORIAL
barber's call . . . . NEXT
barbet . . . . POODLE, BIRD
barbital . . . . . VERONAL, DRUG
barbiturate . . . . SEDATIVE
slang . . . . DOWNIES, UPPIES
"Barcarolle" composer . . . . . . CHOPIN
bard . . . . POET, RUNER, VERSIFIER, MINSTREL, DRUID, SCOP
of Avon . . . SHAKESPEARE
bard's river . . . . AVON
bare . . . . NAKED, EXPOSE, STARK, DIVULGE, STRIP, MERE, NUDE, BARREN
faced . . . . SHAMELESS, OPEN, UNCONCEALED, BRAZEN
foot . . . UNSHOD, SHOELESS
foot pilgrim, car-buyer . . SUCKER
footed . . . . DISCALCED
headed . . . . HATLESS, UNCOVERED
naked . . . . DENUDE
rock, standing . . . . SCAR
barely . . . . HARDLY, MERELY, SCARCELY, MEAGERLY, SCANTILY
bargain . . . CONTRACT, HIGGLE, DICKER, CHEAP, HAGGLE, TRADE, BARTER, DEAL, BUY
closed . . . . DEAL
colloquial . . . . DEAL
hunter . . . . SHOPPER
place . . . . BASEMENT
strike a . . . . AGREE
bargainer's delight . . . . SALES, CUTRATES, BUYS, DISCOUNT, REBATE
favorite spot . . BASEMENT
barge . . . . BOAT, COLLIDE, WHERRY, KEEL, LIGHTER, SCOW, PUNT, CASCO
heavy . . . . HOY
in . . . . ENTER
load of coal . . . . KEEL
river . . . . GONDOLA
baric . . . . BAROMETER
barilla . . . . SALTWORT
barite . . . . SPAR
barium monoxide . . . BARYTA
oxide . . . . BARYTA
sulphate . . . . BARITE
bark . . . . SNAP, TAN, BARQUE, (SAIL)BOAT, TREE SKIN, YAP, YELP, CORTEX, BAY, BRUISE, RIND, WOOF
aromatic . . . CASCARILLA
bitter . . . . . ANGOSTURA, NIEPA, NIOTA, CHINCHONA
buckthorn . . . . . CASCARA
cloth . . . . TAPA
drug from . . . BEBEERINE
fiber . . . . BAST
flavoring . . . . SASSAFRAS
fragrant . . . . CANELLA
inner . . . . BAST, LIBER
laxative . . . . . BEARWOOD
louse . . . . . APHID, APHIS
medicinal . . CHINCHONA, COTO, PEREIRA
mulberry . . . . TAPA
of pain/fear . . . . . . YELP
pertaining to . . CORTICAL
remover . . . . SPUDDER
shrill . . . . YELP, YIP
soap . . . . QUILLAI
spice/tonic . . . . . CANELLA
stripper . . . . SPUDDER
tree . . . . RIND, NIEPA
barkeeper . . . . . . BARTENDER, PUBLICAN, TAPSTER
barker . . . . TOUT, SPIELER
aide of . . . . SHILL
talk of . . . . PATTER, SPIEL
barking . . . . LATRANT
barley . . . BIGG, BERE, TSAMBA, CEREAL, GRASS
beard . . . . AWN
Indian . . . . PAPOOSE
liquor . . . . WHISK(E)Y
meal cake . . . . . BANNOCK
steeped . . . . MALT
water . . . . PTISAN
barm . . . . YEAST
barman . . . . BARTENDER, TAPSTER
barmy: Brit. sl. . . . . SILLY, IDIOTIC
barn . . . . . SHED, MEW, STABLE
bar . . . . BAIL
bird . . . . OWL
compartment . . . . . . BAY
cow . . . . BYRE
gallery . . . . LOFT
owl . . . . TYTO
part for hay/grain . . . . . . (HAY)LOFT, (HAY)MOW
pole . . . . BAIL
barnacle . . . . SHELLFISH, GOOSE, CIRRIPED
Bill: sl. . . . . TAR, SAILOR
of a sort . . . . BUR(R)
barnacles: Brit. colloq. . . . . EYEGLASSES
barnstorm . . . . CAMPAIGN
Barnum . . . . SHOWMAN, PHINEAS
elephant . . . . JUMBO
midget . . . . TOM THUMB
specialty . . . . CIRCUS
barnyard denizen . . ROOSTER, COCK, TURKEY, HEN, COW, GOAT
pest . . . . FOX, WEASEL
sound . . . . . MOO, BLEAT, CROW, CACKLE, BAA
barometer . . . . ANEROID, OROMETER, STATOSCOPE
barometric . . . . BARIC
line . . . . ISOBAR
baron . . . . MAGNATE, NOBLEMAN, SIRLOIN, CAPITALIST
dwelling of . . . . HALL
heir apparent of . . MASTER
wife of . . . . LADY
"Baron Munchausen" . . PEARL
compiler . . . . RASPE
baronet's addition to name . . . BART
baronial . . . . . GRAND, SHOWY
barony, Japanese . . . . HAN
baroque . . . ROCOCO, ORNATE
barque . . . . . . BARK, SAILBOAT, VESSEL
barracks . . . . CASERN, ETAPE, GARRISON
barracuda . . . . SPET, SENNET, PICUDA
barrage . . . . . DRUMFIRE, DAM, BARRIER, BOMBARD
barramunda . . . . . CERATODUS
barranca . . . . . RAVINE, GORGE
barrel . . . . . CYLINDER, CASK, TIERCE, BUTT, SPEED UP, KEG, KILDERKIN, CASK
cork . . . . BUNG
groove . . . . CROZE
house . . . . . SALOON, BAR, TAVERN
like container . . . . DRUM
maker . . . . COOPER
one part . . . . FIRKIN
part . . . . STAVE, HOOP
rim . . . . . . CHIMB, CHIME, CHINE
stave . . . . LAG
staves, set . . . . SHOOK
stopper . . . . BUNG
worker . . . . COOPER, HOOPER
barrelful . . . . CASK
barren . . . . . . STERILE, EMPTY, DEVOID, EFFETE, BORING, UNFRUITFUL, JEJUNE, ARID, STARK
land . . . . DESERT, USAR, DUSTBOWL
barret . . . . CAP, BIRETTA
barrette . . . . BAR, CLASP
barricade . . . . BARRIER, CONSTRUCT, ABAT(T)IS, PALISADE, OBSTACLE, ROADBLOCK, STOCKADE
Barrie (James) play . . . . MARY ROSE
barrier . . . . OBSTRUCTION, OBSTACLE, WALL, SCREEN
of logs . . . . BOOM
of stakes . . . . . PALISADE, STOCKADE
river . . . . BOOM
barrio . . . . SUBURB
chief . . . . DAT(T)O
barrister . . . . LAWYER, ATTORNEY, COUNSELOR
head wear . . . . WIG
barrow . . . . HANDCART, TRUCK, HILL, MOUND, TUMULUS, PIG, CITY
type of . . . . HAND, WHEEL
Barrymore, ____ . . . . . . ETHEL, JOHN, LIONEL, MAURICE
Bart . . . . BARONET
bartender . . . . BARMAN, BARKEEP(ER), TAPSTER, MIXER

barter .... SWAP, TRADE, EXCHANGE, TRUCK
bartizan .... TURRET
Bartlett .... PEAR
Baruch, statesman .. BERNARD
barytron ... MESOTRON, MESON
bas bleu ...... BLUE-STOCKING
basal .... BASIC, FUNDAMENTAL
basalt .... ROCK, POTTERY
source ... . LAVA
basaltic rock .... WHIN, TRAP, GREENSTONE
bascule .... SEESAW
base ..... FOUNDATION, BED, BASIS, HEADQUARTERS, ROOT, IGNOBLE, MENIAL, IMPURE, MEAN, ABJECT, VILE, FELON
architectural ..... SOCLE, PLINTH
attached to ..... SESSILE
baseball ..... SACK, BAG
coal tar .... ANILINE
hit in baseball ... SINGLE, TWO-BAGGER
of bird's bill ...... CERE
of column .... PEDESTAL, DADO, PLINTH
root .... RADIX
baseball abbreviation .... RBI
backstop .... CAGE
base .... SACK, PLATE
batting practice .. FUNGO
bungler in .... MUFF
catcher .... RECEIVER
catcher-pitcher combination .. BATTERY
club/team .... METS, WHITESOX, CARDINALS, TWINS, SENATORS, TIGERS, GIANTS, YANKEES, ORIOLES, INDIANS, DODGERS, ATHLETICS, PHILLIES, PIRATES, ANGELS, BRAVES, ASTROS, PADRES, REDSOX
commissioner .... CHANDLER, LANDIS, FRICK, KUHN
curve .... HOOK
event .... SERIES
field dispute .. RHUBARB
ground .... DIAMOND
"Hall of Fame" name ... SISLER, DIMAGGIO, COBB, RUTH
hit .... CLOUT
mistake .... ERROR
name ..... (CONNIE)MACK
pitch ..... SLIDER, CURVE, DROP BALL, SPITBALL
pitch aimed at batter's head ...... BEANBALL
pitcher's fault ..... BALK
pitcher's stand .. MOUND, SLAB, BOX
play .... ASSIST, SQUEEZE, DOUBLE, PUT-OUT
player of fame ... RUTH, COBB, DIMAGGIO, DEAN, MARIS, MANTLE, MAYS, KOUFAX, REESE, SPAHN, ROBINSON
player's miss at bat .. FAN, STRIKEOUT
player's shelter .. DUGOUT
Rule 8.02's concern .... SPITBALL
stadium .... PARK
team .... NINE
VIP .... UMP(IRE), PITCHER, COMMISSIONER
baseball's Dean ..... DIZZY, DAFFY
Koufax ... SANDY, LEFTY
Mel .... OTT
"Preacher" .... ROE
Ruth .... BABE
Sparky .... LYLE
"The Lip" .... DUROCHER (LEO)
Yogi .... BERRA
baseborn .... BASTARD, ILLEGITIMATE
based on 10 .... DECIMAL
baseless .... UNFOUNDED, SUPPORTED
report/rumor ... CANARD, HOAX
bash .... SMASH, STRIKE, PARTY, SPREE
Bashan King .... OG
Bashaw's title .... AGHA, PASHA, AGA, KEMAL, PACHA
bashful .... SHY, COY, SHEEPISH, RETIRING, TIMID
Bashful of fairy tale .. DWARF
Bashkir's capital .... UFA
basic .... FUNDAMENTAL, ESSENTIAL, PRIMARY, ELEMENTAL
law ..... CONSTITUTION, CHARTER
part .... ROOT, CORNERSTONE
rule .... CANON, PRINCIPLE, LAW
basics .... ABC(S)
basidiomycete ... MUSHROOM, RUST, SMUT, PUFFBALL, FUNGUS
basil .... PLANT, HERB
basilica .... COURTROOM, TEMPLE, LATERAN, PALACE
part of .... APSE
basilisk .... COCKATRICE, LIZARD
basin .... BOWL, SINK, POND, RESERVOIR, BAY, LAVER, FONT, STOUP, PAN, DOCK
altar .... PISCINA
holy water ...... STOUP, FONT, ASPER SORIUM, STOOP
in geology .... TALA
ornamental .... CUVETTE
basinet ...... BASNET, HELMET
basis ..... BASE, FOUNDATION
of argument ... PREMISE
bask ...... EXPOSE, SUN, BEAT,
basket .... POT, HAMPER, GABION, DOSSER, SCUTTLE, PANNIER, CAUL
abbreviation .... BKT
baby .... BASSINET
balloon ... CAR, NACELLE
coal ..... CORF, SCUTTLE
fiber .... RAFFIA
figs ...... CABAS, TAPNET, FRAIL
fish ..... CREEL, WICKER
fruits .... POTTLE, PUNNET, CALATHUS, SCUTTLE
grains .... SCUTTLE
hop-picker's .... BIN
material .... OSIER, WILLOW, RUSH, RAFFIA, REED, WICKER, WOOD, RATTAN, SPLINT
official papers .. HANAFER
ore .... CORF
pack animal ..... DOSSER, PANNIER
pelotari's .... CESTA
raisins .... FRAIL
rummy .... CANASTA
sculptured ..... CORBEIL
symbol of abundance ... CALATHUS
vegetables ..... SCUTTLE
wicker .... HANAFER, BASSINET, CORF
basketball basket ...... CAGE
maneuver ...... DRIBBLE, LAY-UP, FREEZE, PRESS
player .... CAGER, GUARD, CENTER, FORWARD
team ... FIVE, QUINT(ET)
basking shark ...... SAILFISH
basnet .... BASINET
basque ..... BLOUSE, BODICE, TUNIC
Basque .... IBERIAN
cap .... BERET
game .... PELOTA
land .... EUZKADI
pelota player .. PELOTARI
province ...... BISCAY, ALVA, VISCAYA, SOULE, NAVARRA, LABOURD, GUIPUZCOA
Basra native .... IRAQI
bass .... BAST, CHUB
black .... CHUB
double .... VIOL
double-reed ... BASSOON, OBOE
European .... BRASSE
horn .... TUBA
like fish .... SNAPPER
sea .... JEWFISH
stop of organ .. BOURDON
viol .... CONTRABASS
voice .... DRONE
wind instrument .... HELICON
basset .... DOG, HOUND
horn .... CLARINET
bassinet .... (BABY)BED, BASKET, CRADLE
bassoon ... OBOE, WOODWIND
basswood .... LINDEN, LIME(TREE), WAHOO
bast .... PHLOEM, RAMIE, BARK, BASS, FIBER
fiber .... CATENA
like .... LIBRIFORM

bastard .... SHAM, INFERIOR, BYBLOW, COUNTERFEIT, ILLEGITIMATE, MISBEGOT(TEN)
wing of bird ..... ALULA
baste .... SEW, MOISTEN, STRIKE, BEAT, ABUSE, THRASH, TACK
bastille .... PRISON, FORTRESS, TOWER
bastinado .... ROD, STICK, CUDGEL
bastion ... BULWARK, DEFENSE
Basutoland capital ... MASERU
bat ... CLUB, STICK, CUDGEL, CHUNK, VAMPIRE, WINK, NOCTULE, BLINK, HAMMERHEAD
an eye ..... WINK, BLINK
blood-sucking .. VAMPIRE
colloquial .... SPREE, SPEED, BLOW, WINK, BLINK, FLUTTER
flying .... KALONG
for .... DEFEND, ADVOCATE
hold on .... GRIP
like .... ALIPED
like fish ...... GURNARD, GURNET, (STING)RAY
manure .... GUANO
mining .... SHALE
pingpong .... PADDLE
tennis .... RACKET, RACQUET
wing-footed .... ALIPED
batch ...... LOT, SET, GROUP
bate ...... REDUCE, DIMINISH, SOAK
bateau .... BOAT
batfish ... GURNARD, DIABOLO, STINGRAY, SKATE, RAY, STINGAREE
bath ...... ABLUTION, WASH, SOAK, STEEP
kind of .... TURKISH, SAUNA, MILK, SHOWER
therapeutic .. WET PACK
tub .... TOSH
Bath's river .... AVON
bathe ... WASH, WET, MOISTEN, LAVE, SUFFUSE
bathhouse .... BAGNIO, CABANA, SAUNA
bathing, of .... BALNEAL
suit .... BIKINI
batho: as prefix .... DEPTH
batholite .... GRANITE
bathos .... ANTICLIMAX
bathroom .... TOILET
fixture .... TUB
baths .... THERMAE
Bathsheba's husband .. DAVID, URIA(H)
mother .... SHEBA
son .... SOLOMON
bathtub .... TOSH
Bathurst is capital of .. GAMBIA
batiste ...... LINEN, MUSLIN, CAMBRAI
batman .... SERVANT
baton .... ROD, STAFF, STICK, WAND, TRUNCHEON
fairy's .... WAND
jester's .... BAUBLE
race .... RELAY
wielder ... CONDUCTOR, TOSCANINI, BEECHAM, SOUSA, MAJOR(ETTE), MAGICIAN
batrachian ..... AMPHIBIANS, TOAD, FROG
batten .... THRIVE, OVERFEED, WOODSTRIP, FASTEN
batter ... BEAT, POUND, RAM, BATSMAN
cake .... CRUMPET, WAFFLE, PANCAKE, FLAPJACK
battering machine ...... RAM
ram of ship .... BEAK
battery ...... BEATING, CELL
compartment ...... CELL
floating .... PRAM
material .... ACID
part .... ANODE, CATHODE, PLATE
partner of ...... ASSAULT
plate .... GRID
batting, manner of .... FUNGO
order .... LINEUP
battle ...... FIGHT, CONTEST, WAR, COMBAT, CONFLICT
area .... ARENA, RING, NO-MAN'S-LAND, SECTOR
avoidance .... FABIAN
ax .... TOMAHAWK, HATCHET, TWIBIL(L), GISARME
ax: sl. .... SHREW, VIRAGO, NAG, AMAZON
cry .... BANZAI, TO HORSE, (WAR)WHOOP
dress .... ARMOR
formation ..... PHALANX, HERSE, ARRAY, ECHELON
of Hastings site .. SENLAR
of the ____ .... SEXES
of wits ...... REPARTEE, BANTER
of words ...... DEBATE, ARGUMENT
plane .... FIGHTER, BOMBER, SPITFIRE, SABREJET, SPAD, ZERO
relic ..... SCAR, TROPHY
royal .... MELEE, FEEE-FOR-ALL, BRAWL, RUMBLE
scarred fighter .... VET(ERAN)
trophy of Indian .. SCALP
victim .... CASUALTY
battledore .... PADDLE, RACKET
battlement .... RAMPART, BASTION
part of .... MERLON, EMBRASURE, CRENEL(LE)
Battles of 1429 ..... ORLEANS
battleship .... GALLEON, MAN O'WAR, DESTROYER, DREADNAUGHT, CRUISER
gun turret ..... CUPOLA
slang .... WAGON
battue ..... HUNT, MASSACRE
batty .... CRAZY, ECCENTRIC, INSANE
bauble .... TRINKET, GIMCRACK, GEWGAW, TOY, TRIVIA, BEAD, DOODAD
baudekin .... BALDACHIN, BROCADE
baudrons: Scot. .... CAT
Bauhaus school founder ...... GROPIUS
Bavaria, capital of ... MUNICH
German name ... BAYERN
Bavarian city .... HOF, BAYREUTH, NUREMBERG
river ...... ILLER, ISAR, MAIN, EGER
weight .... GRAN
bawbee ... COIN, HALF PENNY
bawd .... PROCURESS
bawdy .... INDECENT, OBSCENE
house .... BROTHEL, BAGNIO
bawl .... HOWL, SHOUT, BELLOW, YELL, WEEP, CRY
colloquial ...... SCOLD, REPRIMAND, REPROVE
bay ..... COVE, BIGHT, BARK, HOWL, INLET, WING, HORSE, ULULATE
bring to ... CORNER, TREE
color .... ROAN
horse .... ROAN, BAYARD
keep at ...... HOLD(OFF)
name of ... VOE, MANILA, BISCAY, BAFFIN, CAMPECHE
of Biscay city/resort .... BIARRITZ
of Biscay river .... LOIRE
State ... MASSACHUSETTS
sweet ...... BREWSTER
tree .... LAUREL
window .... ORIEL, MIRADOR, PAUNCH, (POT)BELLY
bayard ..... HORSE, KNIGHT,
Bayern .... BAVARIA
Baylor eleven .... BEARS
bayou .... BACKWATER, EVERGLADES, INLET, CREEK
bazaar .... SHOP, FAIR
church/club .. SALE, FAIR
bbl. .... BARREL
bdl. .... BUNDLE
be ...... ARE, EXIST, OCCUR, HAPPEN, BELONG
a match .... COPE
a success .... CLICK
at habitually .... HAUNT, FREQUENT
of use .... AVAIL, UTILE, SERVICEABLE
on one's guard .. BEWARE
overly fond ...... DOTE, ADORE
silent, in music .. TACE(T).
still ...... QUIET, HUSH, SHUT-UP, SSH
your age ...... BEHAVE
beach .... SHORE, STRAND, GROUND, COAST, SANDS
bath house ..... CABANA
bird .... SANDERLING

fixture ...... LIFESAVER, LIFEGUARD, SUNBATHER
Florida ...... POMPANO
on the: colloq. .... UNEMPLOYED
panhandler .... BEACHCOMBER
pest .... SANDFLY
walk ..... BOARDWALK, ESPLANADE
wave over ..... COMBER
beacon .... SIGNAL FIRE, LIGHTHOUSE, PHAROS, BEAM
light .... CRESSET
on summit .... PIKE
Beaconsfield, Earl of .... DISRAELI
bead .... DROP, BUBBLE, GLOBULE
draw one on .... AIM
for trimming dresses .... BUGLE
gun muzzle's ..... SIGHT
money .... PEAG
beaded moisture .... DEW
beadhouse .... ALMSHOUSE
beading .... GADROON
beadle .... MESSENGER, MACE-BEARER
of fiction .... BUMBLE
beads .... NECKLACE
Indian .... WAMPUM, PEAG(E)
of perspiration ... SWEAT
prayer .... ROSARY, CHAPLET
trimming dress ... BUGLE
beadsman .... PRAYER, BEGGAR
beagle .... DOG, HOUND
beak .... BILL, NEB, NIB, ROSTRUM
like process ..... ROSTEL
ship's ...... RAM, SPERON
slang ..... NOSE, SNOUT
trim with .... PREEN
beaked .... HOOKED, AQUILINE
beaker .... CUP, GOBLET
beam .... SIGNAL, SMILE, RAY, ASHLAR, DIRECT, RAFTER, RADIATE, SHINE, CROSSBAR, SCANTLING
architectural .. TEMPLET, TEMPLATE
on the .... ALERT, KEEN, RIGHT
off the .... WRONG, AMISS, LOST
supporting ..... GIRDER
tie .... BALK
underside .... SOFFIT
beaming .... RADIANT, SMILING, HAPPY
beamy ..... BROAD, MASSIVE, JOYOUS, BRIGHT
bean ... SEED, ARBOR, SOY(A), LEGUME, CALABAR, GOA, LIMA, TONKA, PINTO
dish .... SUCCOTASH
flour .... FARINA
fly .... MIDAS
kidney .... HARICOT, FRIJOL(E)
like plant ..... SAINFOIN
lima .... HABA
locust .... CAROB
meal .... FARINA
Mexican ...... FRIJOL(E)
mottled .... PINTO
oil .... CASTOR
poisonous ..... CALABAR
sauce .... SOY
seed .... SOY, PULSE
slang ..... HEAD, BRAIN, MIND
soy .... SOJA
stalk/stem .... HA(U)LM
yonka .... GUAIAC
tree ... CAROB, CATALPA
used for counting ...... BEANO
versatile .... SOY(A)
white .... PEA
beanie .... (SKULL)CAP
beano .... BINGO
beany .... CAP
bear .... ENDURE, CARRY, SHOW, STAND, TRANSPORT, BRUIN, TOTE, WEAR, SUFFER, SUSTAIN, TOLERATE
brown .... URSUS
down ...... PRESS, PUSH
down on .... CHARGE
honey .... KINKAJOU
in mind ..... REMEMBER
like .... URSINE, URSIFORM
like animal ..... KOALA, PANDA
out ... CONFIRM, SUPPORT
sky .... URSA
squeeze of a .... HUG
Syrian .... DUBB
variety .... BROWN, BLACK, GRIZZLY, POLAR, HONEY
which was a nymph ..... CALLISTO
with .... TOLERATE, PUT UP, ENDURE
witness .... ATTEST, TESTIFY
woolly .... WOOBUT, CATERPILLAR
young ..... CUB, WHELP
bearberry ..... HOLLY, SHRUB
bearcat .... PANDA, CIVET
beard ...... WHISKERS, BARB, BARBEL, DEFY, BURNSIDES, GOATEE, IMPERIAL
disease of the ... SYCOSIS
grain ..... AWN, ARISTA
hairlike .... CRINITE
pointed .... GOATEE, VANDYKE
red .... BARBAROSSA
short growth ... STUBBLE
the lion ... TAME, SUBDUE
bearded .... ARISTATE, BARBATE, AWNED, GOATEED
butter .... GOA
grass .... RYE
seal .... MAKLUK
beardless .... YOUNG, CALLOW
bearer in India ...... SIRDAR
of the world: myth. ..... ATLAS
bearing .... MIEN, AIR, RELATION, CARRIAGE, MANNER, DEMEANOR, PRESENCE, CARRYING
twins .... BIPAROUS
writer's name .. ONYMOUS
bearish .... RUDE, ROUGH, CROSS, SURLY
bear's breech ..... ACANTHUS, SHRUB
foot .... HELLEBORE
skin .... (FOR)CAP
bearwood .... CASCARA
beast .... BRUTE, ANIMAL, QUADRUPED
huge .... BEHEMOTH, MONSTER, MASTODON
in French .... BETE
like .... THEROID
of burden .... BURRO, ASS, CARABAO, CAMEL, MULE, LLAMA, DONKEY, YAK, ONAGER
of prey ..... LION, TIGER, WOLVERINE
beastly .... BESTIAL, THEROID, BRUTAL, DISGUSTING
British colloq. .... VERY
beat .... CANE, CADENCE, FLAIL, TROUNCE, POMMEL, PULSE, RHYTHM, DRUB, POUND, FLOG, WHIP, MIX, DEFEAT, FORGE, THRASH, PUMMEL, LAMBASTE
back ... REPEL, REPULSE
colloquial ...... WHALE, LARRUP, SHELLACK
dead ... CHEAT, WELSHER
group member .. BEATNIK
in foil .... FOLIATE
in journalism .... SCOOP, ASSIGNMENT
into plate ..... MALLEATE
it! .... SCRAM, SCAT, SHOO
off ..... REPEL, REPULSE
on the .... ATEMPO, IN TUNE, ATTUNED
police .... ROUND
repeatedly ..... CLOBBER
slang .... TIRED, EXHAUSTED, PASTE, LAM
sole of feet with stick ... BASTINADO
soundly .... ROUT, DRUB, OVERWHELM, WALLOP
thin .... MALLEATE
to softness .... MASH
up ...... THRASH, MAUL
with stick .... DRUB, CUDGEL, BASTINADO, CLUB
with whip ... FLOG, LASH
beatable .... VINCIBLE, VULNERABLE
beaten path .... TRAIL
beatific .... JOYFUL, BLISSFUL
beatify .... BLESS

beating .... DEFEAT, PULSATION, PUNISHMENT
of person ..... BATTERY
underbrush to flush game BATTING, BATTUE
Beatles, former manager of .. EPSTEIN
one of the ...... RINGO, LENNON
beatnik .... HEPCAT, HIPSTER
Beatrice's lover .... DANTE
beau ... DANDY, SWEETHEART, SUITOR, LOVER, FOP, FELLOW
colloquial ..... BF, SPARK
Brummell .. DANDY, FOP
geste .... GALLANTRY
ideal .... NERO
monde's center ... SALON
beaut .... LULU
beautician ...... MANICURIST, COIFFURIST, HAIRDRESSER
beautiful .. PRETTY, HANDSOME, COMELY, FAIR, LOVELY
eyes .... TULIPS
girl: sl. .... LULU
island .... FORMOSA
slang .... SHARP
woman .... PERI, HELEN, VENUS, HOURI, NYMPH
beauty, a .... ACE, LULU, PERFECT, HOURI, VENUS, HELEN
reigning .... BELLE
of form, etc. ..... GRACE
parlor dye .... HENNA
parlor specialty ..... SET, WAVE, PERMANENT, MASSAGE, DYE, MANICURE
parlor worker .. MASSEUR, MANICURIST, PEDICURIST
shop .... SALON
spot ...... MOLE, PATCH
beaver .... ANIMAL, (SILK)HAT, FUR
den of .... LODGE
describing one ... EAGER
eager .... DOER, HUSTLER
fur hat .... CASTOR
like animal .... NUTRIA, COYPU
of armor .... CASTOR
oily substance .... CASTOR(EUM)
skin .... PLEW
State .... OREGON
bebop .... JAZZ
because ..... SINCE, INASMUCH
beche-de-mer ...... TREPANG, SEACUCUMBER
beck ...... STREAM, SUMMON, BECKON, NOD
partner of .... CALL
beckon ...... SUMMON, CALL
becloud .... DARKEN, CONFUSE, MUDDLE
become .... BEFIT, SUIT, CHANGE, DEVELOP, GROW
cheese-like ..... CASEFY
different .... CHANGE
dull .... PALL, BORE, HEBETATE
extinct .... DIE
forfeit .... LAPSE
less stern ...... RELENT, SOFTEN, THAW
red in face ...... FLUSH, BLUSH, COLOR
shabby ...... GO TO SEED
void for cause .... LAPSE
well .... HEAL
bed .... PALLET, BOTTOM, BUNK, KIP, STRATUM, SACK
and board ... HOME, KEEP
awning .... CANOPY
baby's ... CRIB, CRADLE
British slang ...... DOSS
built-in ... BERTH, BUNK
canopy .... TESTER
clothes .... PILLOWS, BLANKETS, SHEETS, LINEN
coils .... SPRINGS
cover(ing) .... PUFF, TESTER, COVERLET, QUILT, (BED)SPREAD
curtain/drapery .... VALANCE
frame .... STEAD
hanging ..... HAMMOCK
kind of ... ROSES, OYSTER
maker ... CHAMBERMAID
of roses: colloq. .... LUXURY, EASE
ore .... REEF
pest .... BEDBUG
river .... CHANNEL
slang ... BAG, DOSS, SACK
small .... COT, BASSINET, PALLET
straw .... PALLET
stream .... DONGA, ARROYO, WADI
type .... HAMMOCK, BERTH, BUNK, MATRIMONIAL
bedaub ...... SMEAR, SMUDGE, PAINT
bedbug ..... CHINCH, CIMEX, VERMIN
bedding, straw/hay/leaves ... LITTER
Bede, ____ .. ADAM, VENERABLE
bedeck .... ADORN, TRIM, EMBELLISH
bedevil .... HARASS, PLAGUE, PESTER, WORRY, TORMENT
bedew .... MOISTEN
bedfellow .... ASSOCIATE, CO-WORKER, COMPANION
bedlam .... CONFUSION, UPROAR, MADHOUSE, TURMOIL
Bedloe island .... LIBERTY
bedmate ..... WIFE, HUSBAND
Bedouin .... ARAB, NOMAD, WANDERER, BERBER, RIFF
headband cord .... AGAL
tribe .... AMALEKITE
bedraggled .... UNKEMPT, UNTIDY, UNCOMBED
bedroom .... CUBICLE, CABIN, CHAMBER
caretaker .. CHAMBERMAID
bedside character ... DOCTOR, NURSE, (BABY)SITTER
manners, describing ..... GENTLE, SOOTHING, REASSURING
bedstead .... CHARPOY, CHARPAI, FOURPOSTER
bedtime story: colloq. .. YARN, FAIRY TALE, EXPLANATION
bee .... APIS, SOCIAL, MEETING, ANDRENID, HYMENOPTER
balm .... PLANT, (OSWEGO) TEA
bird .... FLYCATCHER
birling .... ROLEO
built structure .... HONEYCOMB
caulking substance ...... PROPOLIS
colony .... HIVE
eater .... KINGBIRD
family .... APIDAE
female ...... QUEEN
girl named after .... MELISSA
glue .... PROPOLIS
hive .... SKEP
house .... APIARY, HIVE, SKEP
keeper .... APIARIAN, APIARIST
keeping ..... APICULTURE
killer .... ROBBERFLY
kind of .... SPELLING, SEWING, DRONE, WORKER, QUEEN
like .... APIAN
male .... DRONE
martin .... KINGBIRD
nest-building ... CARDER
nose of .... LOR
of the .... APIAN
plant .... BALM, CLOVER, SPIDERFLOWER
pollen brush of ... SCOPA
scientific study of .... APIOLOGY
secretion .... WAX
sound ..... BUZZ, HUM, DRONE
tree .. LINDEN, BASSWOOD
wax .... CEROTIC
beebread .... AMBROSIA
beech .... NUT, WOOD, TREE, ROBLE
beechnuts .... MAST
beef ... COW, OX, BULL, STEER
braised ..... POT ROAST
cattle breed .. GALLOWAY, ANGUS
colloquial/slang .... MUSCLE, BRAWN, COMPLAIN(T), GRIPE
corned .... BULLY
cut .... RIB, CHUCK, SHANK, SEY, LOIN, ROAST, BRISKET, STEAK, SIRLOIN
dish .... MIROTON, PASTRAMI
double sirloin ... BARON
dried .... CHARQUI, BUCCAN

eater: Eng. ..... YEOMAN
food for explorers ...... PEM(M)ICAN
nearest shoulder .. CLOD
rolled .... PASTRAMI
State .... NEBRASKA
stew .... GOULASH, POT-AU-FEU
tea .... BROTH
tinned .... BULLY
up .... STRENGTHEN, FATTEN
beehead .... AMBROSIA
beehive .... SKEP, BEEGUM, APIARY
State .... UTAH
beekeeper .... APIARIST, SKEPPER, APIARIAN
beefwood .... TOA
beefy .... BRAWNY, FLESHY, MUSCULAR
Beelzebub ..... DEVIL, SATAN
beer ...... ALE, LAGER, SUDS, BOCK, KVAS(S), MALT, WEISS, PORTER, STOUT
cask .... TUN, KEG, PUNCHEON
cup .... STEIN, MUG, TOBY, SEIDEL
flavor ...... MULL, HOPS
foam ..... BEAD, FROTH, HEAD
glass .... SCHOONER
house .... SALOON, TAVERN, INN
ingredient .. MALT, HOPS, YEAST
inventor ..... GAMBRINUS
make .... BREW
material ... MALT, MASH, MEAL, HOPS
mug ...... SEIDEL, STEIN
party .... WASSAIL
plant ... HOPS, BREWERY
shop ..... PUB, TAVERN, FARO, INN, SALOON
slang .... SUDS
sour .... KVAS(S)
spiced/sweetened .. FLIP
strong .... STINGO, MUM
sweeten and flavor ...... MULL
weak .... SWIPES
beery .... DRUNKEN, TIPSY, MAUDLIN
bees, feeding on .. APIVOROUS
pertaining to ..... APIAN
study of ...... APIOLOGY
beet .... PLANT, ROOT, CHARD, MANGEL
crushed ..... MEGASS(E)
sugar .... SUCROSE, SACCHAROSE
Beethoven's birthplace .. BONN
composition ... MINUET, MISSA SOLEMNIS
forte .... SONATA
opera .... FIDELIO
teacher .... NEEFE, HAYDN
3rd symphony ... EROICA
beetle .... SCARAB, DOR, ELATER(ID), MELOE, WEEVIL, CLUB, CURCULIO, EARWIG, SNAPPER, MALLET, SKIPJACK, SAWYER, WHIRLIGIG
blister .... MELOID
browed ...... FROWNING, SCOWLING
click ...... ELATER, DOR, SNAPPER
dung ..... COCKCHAFER
fruit-eater ... FIG-EATER, JUNE BUG
gaudy .... LADYBUG, LADYBIRD
grain .... CADELLE
grapevine .... THRIP
ground .... AMARA
head .... BLOCKHEAD, NITWIT
larva .... BEEWOLF, CADELLE, GRUB, GRUGRU
like charm ..... SCARAB
like insect ..... EARWIG
order of .... COLEOPTERA
sacred to Egyptians ..... SCARAB
snouted ..... CURCULIO
tree .... GIRDLER
wing cover ...... SHARD, ELYTRON
with club-shaped feelers CLAVICORN
wood .... SAWYER
beetling ..... OVERHANGING, PROJECTING
befall ...... HAPPEN, OCCUR, PASS, HAP
befit .... SUIT, BECOME
befitting .... PROPER, SUITABLE, APPROPRIATE
befog ...... BLUR, OBSCURE, CONFUSE
befool .... TRICK, DUPE, DECEIVE
before .... ERE, PREVIOUS, PRECEDING, FORMERLY, PRIOR
all others .... FIRST
long ...... SOON, ANON, SHORTLY, PRESENTLY
prefix .... PRE, ANTE
befoul .... DIRTY, SOIL
befuddle .... CONFUSE, STUPEFY
beg .... IMPLORE, BESEECH, ASK, ENTREAT, IMPORTUNE, PRAY, PLEAD, PANHANDLE, MOOCH
off ... ASK OUT, DECLINE, EXCUSE
the question .... EVADE
beget .... SIRE, FATHER, PRODUCE, PROCREATE
beggar .... RASCAL, DERVISH, FAKIR, PANHANDLER, LAZZARONE, MENDICANT, LAZAR, PLEADER, RANDY, SCHNORRER
equipment of ... TINCUP
gift to .. HANDOUT, ALMS
roving .... GANGREL, GABERLUNZIE, FAKIR
speech of .... CANT
beggarly .... MEAN, PETTY
beggars' lice .... BUR(R), CLEAVERS
patron saint ...... GILES
begging, practice of .... MENDICANCY, MENDICITY
begin .... OPEN, START, INITIATE, COMMENCE, ORIGINATE
beginner ...... TYRO, NOVICE, NEOPHYTE, APPRENTICE GREENHORN, PUPIL
beginning ..... ONSET, ORIGIN, GERM, BIRTH, GENESIS, OUTSET
begone! .... SCAT, SCRAM, AVAUNT, SHOO, AROINT
begrime .... SOIL, DIRTY, SMUDGE, SMEAR
begrudge ..... GRUMBLE, ENVY
beguile .... DECEIVE, DELUDE, VAMP, CHARM, AMUSE, COZEN, MISLEAD, LURE
beguilements .... ARTS
begum, Indian ..... PRINCESS
Beguin .... BEGHARD
behalf .... INTEREST, SIDE, SAKE
behave ... CONDUCT, DEPORT, COMPORT, ACT
foolishly .... FRIBBLE
behavior .... CONDUCT, MANNERS, ACTION, ACTUATION
in polite society .... ETIQUETTE
science of ..... ETHOLOGY
behead .... DECAPITATE, DECOLLATE
behemoth .... BEAST, HIPPO(POTAMUS), ELEPHANT
behest ..... ORDER, BIDDING, COMMAND
behind .... ABAFT, LATE, ASTERN, (A)REAR
colloquial ..... BUTTOCKS
time(s) .... PASSE, OUTMODED, LATE, OVERDUE, TARDY
behold! .... SEE, LO, VOILA
Latin .... ECCE
beholden .... INDEBTED, OBLIGED
behoove .... INCUMBENT
beige .... ECRU, GRAYISH TAN
being .... LIFE, EXISTENCE, CREATURE, ENTITY
abstract ...... ENS, ENTIA
actual .... ESSE
essential .... ENS
individual .... MONAD
Beirut is capital of .. LEBANON
bejewel .... BEGEM
Bela Lugosi's pet .... BAT
belabor .... BEAT, WHIP, ATTACK, POUND
belated .... TARDY
belay ... SECURE, HOLD, STOP
belaying cleat ...... BOLLARD, KEVEL
belch ..... EMIT, ERUCT(ATE), VOMIT, BURP

beldam . . . . HAG, CRONE, ALECTO, MEGAER, ERINYES
beleaguer . . . . BESIEGE, SURROUND
beleaguerment . . . . SEIGE
Belem is capital of . . . . . . PARA
belemite . . . . . THUNDERSTONE
belfry . . . . BELL TOWER
dweller . . . . BAT
Belgian . . . . WALLOON, FLEMING, FLEMISH
canal . . . . YSER
capital . . . . BRUSSELS
city . . . . MONS, GHENT, LOUVAIN, MALINES, TOURNAI, ARLON, YPRES, SPA, ALOST, JEMAPPES, ROULERS, HUY, LIEGE, BRUGES
commune . . . . TAMINES, NAMUR, JETTE, VORST, SPA, LEDE, ROUX, ANS, ATH, NIEL
Congo river . . . . . . UELE
currency unit . . . . . BELGA
dog . . . . SCHIPPERKE
fascist party . . . . REX
hare . . . . LEPORID
king, former . . BAUDOUIN, ALBERT, LEOPOLD
marble . . . RANCE, RANSE
police . . . . GENDARME
port . . . . OSTEND
possession, former . . . . . . CONGO
province . . . . LIEGE, NAMUR, LIMBOURGE
queen . . . . ASTRID
reclaimed land . . . POLDER
resort . . . . . . SPA, OSTEND
river . . . . LYS, YSER, SENNE, MEUSE, SAMBRE, SCHELDE, OISE
rodent . . . . LEPORID
seaport . . . . OSTEND, ZEBRUGGE
statesman . . . . SPAAK
textile center . . . . GHENT
town . . . . YPRES
violinist . . . . YSAYE
watering place . . . . . SPA
Belgrade . . . . BEOGRAD
is capital of . . YUGOSLAVIA
Belial . . . . ANGEL, SATAN
belie . . . . DENY, DISPROVE, DISGUISE
belief . . . . CONVICTION, FAITH, TRUST, OPINION, CREED, ISM, DOCTRINE, CREDENCE
based on . . . . DOXIC
beyond . . . . . INCREDIBLE
in ghosts . . . . . . EODOLISM
in one god . . . . . . THEISM
beliefs, set of . . CREDO, CREED
believe . . . . SUPPOSE, EXPECT, TRUST, ASSUME, CREDIT
believer . . . . IST, DEIST
easy . . . . GULLIBLE, CREDULOUS
in god . . . . . THEIST, DEIST
in spirits . . . . ANIMIST
of all religions . . . OMNIST
believing . . . . CREANT
belittle . . . . SLIGHT, DEPRECIATE, DISPARAGE, DEMEAN, KNOCK
Belize is capital of . . . . HONDURAS
bell . . . . CAMPANA, CARILLON, GONG, BELLOW, ROAR
alarm . . . . TOCSIN
call to prayer . . . ANGELUS
clapper . . . . TONGUE
flower . . . . . CAMPANULA, RAMPION
jar . . . . CLOCHE
man . . . . RINGER, (TOWN)CRIER
ring by hammer . . CHIME
ringer . . . . SEXTON
ringing device . . . . CHIME
striker . . . . HAMMER, CLAPPER
sound . . . . DONG, PEAL, TING, CLANG, RING, TING-A-LING, KNELL, TOLL
shaped glass jar . . CLOCHE
tongue . . . . CLAPPER
tower . . . . BELFRY, COMPANILE
town in story . . . . ADANO
belladonna . . . . NIGHTSHADE, MANICON
alkaloid . . . . ATROPIN(E)
drug . . . . ATROPIN(E)
lily . . . . AMARYLLIS
bellboy . . . . . PAGE, BELLHOP, BUTTONS
call to . . . . FRONT
colloquial . . . . . . BUTTONS
belle . . . . BEAUTY
of the West . . . . . . STARR
belles-lettres . . . . . LITERATURE
bellhop . . . . BELLBOY, CALLBOY, BUTTONS
call . . . . FRONT, BELL
bellicose . . . . HOSTILE, WARLIKE, BELLIGERENT
belligerence . . . . WAR, BELLICOSITY
belligerent . . . . WARLIKE, BELLICOSE, PUGNACIOUS, PROTAGONIST, CONTENTIOUS, AGGRESSIVE, QUARRELSOME
right of a . . . . ANGARY
Bellini . . . . PAINTER
pupil . . . . TITIAN
son . . . . GENTILE, GIOVANNI
Bellini's (Vincenzo) opera . . . . NORMA
Bellona's brother . . . . MARS
bellow . . . . ROAR, WAIL, BELL
bellows . . . . BLOWER
bells, set of . . . . CARILLON, CHIME(S)
bellwether . . . . SHEEP, LEADER
belly . . . . . . ABDOMEN, BAGGIE, WOMB, STOMACH, BULGE, WAME, VENTER
laugh . . . . GUFFAW, ROAR, CHORTLE
near/on the . . . . VENTRAL
protruding . . . . . PAUNCH, BAY WINDOW
bellyache: colloq. . . . . . GRIPE, COMPLAIN
bellyband . . . . . . GIRTH, CINCH
bellybutton . . . . NAVEL
bellyful . . . . SURFEIT
belong . . . . APPERTAIN, PERTAIN
belonging to certain people . . . NATIVE, ENDEMIC, INDIGENOUS
belongings . . . . POSSESSION, PROPERTY, CHATTEL
beloved . . . . DARLING, LIEF
physician . . . . LUKE
below . . . . (BE)NEATH, (UNDER)NEATH, ALOW
combining form . . HYP(O)
the belt . . . . FOUL
belt . . . . BAND, GIRDLE, AREA, BLOW, CUFF, CORDON, SASH, STRAP, CESTUS, OBI, BALDRIC, CINGULUM, CINCTURE, ZOSTER
below the . . FOUL, UNFAIR
case . . . . HOLSTER
fancy . . . . SASH
imaginary, heavenly . . . . . ZODIAC
tighten . . . . . ECONOMIZE, RETRENCH
sword . . . . BALDRIC
Beltane . . . . MAYDAY
beluga . . . . STURGEON, DOLPHIN, WHALE, WHITEFISH
roe/eggs . . . . CAVIAR
belvedere . . . . SUMMERHOUSE, GALLERY, PAVILION
bema . . . . PLATFORM, CHANCEL
bemoan . . . . LAMENT, DEPLORE, WAIL,
bemuse . . . . MUDDLE, CONFUSE, STUPEFY
ben . . . . . . SON, PEAK, PARLOR
relative . . . . IBN
bench . . . . SEAT, GALLERY, SETTEE, WORKTABLE, COURT, EXEDRA, PEW
judges' . . . . BANC
in sports . . . . . . SIDELINE
the . . . . JUDICIARY
tool . . . . VISE
bend . . . . CROOK, CROFT, FLEX(URE), ARCH, BOW, STOOP, YIELD, WALE, KINK
and bob . . . . NID
as of light, heat . . . . REFRACT
back . . . . REFLEX
in adoration . . . . . . KNEEL
in stream . . . . HOOK
in timber . . . . SNY
inward . . . . . INTROVERT
knee in worship . . . . . . GENUFLECT
light wave . . . . . . REFRACT
sinister . . . . BATON
the arm . . . . FLEX
bender . . . . SPREE, ORGY, WASSAIL

bending ... BIGHT, FLECTION, FLEXION
bends, having two ..... BIFLEX
the .... CRAMPS
bendy .... OKRA
bene .... (WILD)HOG, PRAYER, BOON
vale .... FAREWELL
beneath ...... BELOW, UNDER
combining form .. HYP(O)
benedict, former ... BACHELOR, CELIBATE
Benedictine .... LIQUEUR, MONK, NUN
benediction .... BLESSING, INVOCATION, GRACE, BENISON
benefaction .... BOON
benefactor .... PATRON
benefic .... KINDLY, CHARITABLE
benefice, appoint to a .... COLLATE
first income of .... ANNAT
holder ... APPROPRIATOR
of a sort ...... SINECURE
revenue ...... ANNAT(E)S
temporary .. COMMENDAM
beneficial .... BENIGN
benefit ...... FAVOR, PROFIT, AVAIL, SAKE, HELP
benevolent .... KIND, HUMANE, CHARITABLE
order .... ELKS
Bengal bison .... GAUR
capital .... CALCUTTA
city .... PATNA
cotton .... ADATI
grass .... MILLET
groom .... SAICE
light .... FIREWORK
native .... BENGALI, KOL, BANIAN
benighted .... LOST
benign .... KIND(LY), FAVORABLE, BENEFICIAL
benison .... BLESSING, BENEDICTION
benjamin .... GUM, BENZOIN, FAVORITE SON
Benjamin's father ..... JACOB
son ...... ROSH, ARD, EHI
Benjamin Franklin's musical instrument .... HARMONICA
benne .... SESAME
bennet ... VALERIAN, HEMLOCK
bent .... INCLINATION, GRASS, TASTE, CROOKED, SET, CURVED, BOUND, FLAIR, APTITUDE, PROPENSITY
backward ..... RETRORSE
like a knee .. GENICULATE
Bentley's sleuth .... TRENT
benumb .... HEBETATE
benzedrine .... INHALANT, STIMULANT
benzene .... BENZOL, SOLVENT
Beograd .... BELGRADE
Beowulf, monster slain by .... GRENDEL
bequeath .. WILL, HAND DOWN, ENDOW, LEAVE
bequest .... LEGACY, INHERITANCE, HERITAGE, ENDOWMENT
berate ...... SCOLD, REBUKE, UPBRAID
Berber .... MOSLEM, RIFF, HAMITE, TUAREG, KABYLE
chief .... CAID
dialect .... TUAREG
hermit .... MARABOUT
tribe .... RIFF, DAZA
tribesman ..... KABYLE
berceuse .... LULLABY
bereave ...... DEPRIVE, STRIP, ROB
bereavement .... LOSS, DEPRIVATION
expression of .... CONDOLENCE
bereft ..... LORN, DEPRIVED, LONELY
beret .... CAP, BIRETTA
berg .... ICE
bergamot .... PEAR, HORSEMINT, MONARDA
Bergen's Mortimer .... SNERD
Berger, singer .... ERNA
Bergerac's sore point ... NOSE
Bergman, Miss ...... INGRID
beriberi .... DROPSY
Japanese .... KAKKE
medicine ..... THIAMIN(E)
Bering Sea river ...... YUKON
Berkshire .... HOG
county seat ..... READING
race course .... ASCOT
Berlin ...... CARRIAGE, CITY, CAPITAL, SONGWRITER
district .... SPANDAU
hit .... REMEMBER
prison .... SPANDAU
river .... SPREE
sight .... WALL
songwriter ...... IRVING
berm .... LEDGE, TERRACE
Bermuda capital ... HAMILTON
arrowroot ...... ARARAO
grass ...... DOOB, DOUB
product .... ONION
to pleasure seekers ...... PLAYGROUND
Bern is capital of .... SWITZERLAND
Bernese Alps mountain ...... WETTERHORN
bernicle .... GOOSE
berry ...... TOMATO, GRAPE, BANANA, CURRANT, BOCCA, ACINUS, ALLSPICE, MADRONA
branch .... CANE
cigarette .... CUBEB
combining form ... BACCI
fragrant .... MYRTLE
grape .... ACINUS
like .... BACCATE
slang .... DOLLAR
bersagliere .... RIFLEMAN, SHARPSHOOTER
berserk .... AMOK, AMUCK, BARESARK
berseem .... CLOVER
Bert ____ ..... LAHR, PARKS
berth .... ANCHORAGE, BED, BUNK, PLACE
Pullman car ..... LOWER, UPPER
Bertha .... COLLAR
"Big" .... CANNON
beryl .... EMERALD, AQUAMARINE, MINERAL, MORGANITE
beseech ...... PRAY, ENTREAT, PLEAD, IMPLORE, BEG, SOLICIT
beset ...... ATTACK, HARRY, HARASS, STUD, PESTER, OBSESS
beshow .... SABLEFISH
beshrew: archaic ..... CURSE
beside ..... NEAR, CLOSE, BY
prefix .... PARA, PAR
oneself ... MAD, ANGRY, SORE
besides ..... MOREOVER, ELSE, EXCEPT, ALSO, TOO
besiege .... OVERWHELM, BESET, CROWD, HARASS, BELEAGUER, INVEST
besiegers' explosive ... PETARD
protective cover .... MANT(E)LET
besmirch .... STAIN, TARNISH, SULLY, SOIL, DIRTY, DEFAME
besom .... BROOM
bespangle .... STUD, DECORATE, STAR
bespatter ...... SOIL, SMEAR, SPLASH
bespeak ..... RESERVE, SHOW
Bessemer process product .... STEEL
best .... EXCELLENT, UTMOST, DEFEAT, OUTWIT
colloquial .... TOPFLIGHT
combining form .. ARISTO
man at wedding .... PARANYMPH
part ..... ELITE, CREAM, MEAT, FLOWER
seller .... HIT
bestial .... BRUTISH, BRUTAL, SAVAGE, VILE, ANIMAL
bestiary book author .. BORGES
bestow .... GIVE, AWARD, CONFER, DEVOTE
bestrew .... SCATTER
bestride .... STRADDLE
bet .... WAGER, STAKE, PROPOSITION, GAMBLE, PARLAY
against card dealer ..... PUNT
colloquial ... CANDIDATE, ENTRY
fail to pay .... WELSH
in an election .... CANDIDATE
in roulette .... BAS
sure win ..... IN THE BAG
to win in horse race .... ON THE NOSE

without odds ...... ITOI
you! .... CERTAINLY, YES INDEED
betake .... GO, JOURNEY, REPAIR
Betancourt .... MONK, CURATE
bete noire .... OUTCAST, PARIAH, LEPER, BUGBEAR
of nursery .... CROUP
betel ..... SIRI, PEPPER, PLANT
leaf .... BUYO, PAN
nut ..... SERI, CATECHU
palm ... ARECA, PINANG
pepper ..... ITMO, IKMO
Betelgeuse .... STAR
bethel ...... CHURCH, CHAPEL
betide ..... HAPPEN, BEFALL, OCCUR
betimes .... EARLY, QUICKLY, PROMPTLY, SOON
betoken .... DENOTE, FORESHOW, AUGUR, INDICATE
beton .... CONCRETE
betray ..... DECEIVE, REVEAL, SELL, VICTIMIZE
betrayal .... PERFIDY
betrayer .... TRAITOR, SEDUCER, DECEIVER
Biblical .... JUDAS (ISCARIOT)
betroth .... AFFIANCE, ENGAGE, PLIGHT, AFFY
betrothed person ..... FIANCE, FIANCEE
Betsy: sl. .... GUN, GAT, EQUALIZER
better ...... IMPROVE, OUTDO, AMEND, SURPASS
half: colloq. .... WIFE
looking .... CUTER, HANDSOMER
betting system ..... PARLAY, PARI-MUTUEL
another way: colloq. .... ROLL
loser's ... MARTINGAL(E)
between .... MIDDLE, INTERMEDIATE, BETWIXT
in law .... MESNE
meals treat .. SNACK, SODA
prefix .. INTER, DIA, META
betwixt and between .. MIDDLE
Bevan's nickname .... NYE
bevel ... EDGE, BEZEL, SLANT, CANT
out .... REAM
ship timber ...... SNAPE
to join ..... MITER, MITRE
beveled angle/surface .. SPLAY
beverage ..... DRINK, COFFEE, ADE, ALE, TEA, SOUR, WINE, TOKAY, SAKE, MATE, KAVA, BOZA, LEBAN, NOG(G), EGGNOG
add liquor to ...... LACE
almond flavored .... RATAFIA
beer-lemonade .. SHANDY
brandy, sugar, spice ..... TODDY
carbonated ... POP, SODA
Christmas ..... EGGNOG
fermented .. SAKE, MEAD
from leaves .... TEA
from meat extract ...... BEEF TEA
from molasses ..... RUM
fruit (crushed) ... SMASH
hot milk .... POSSET
palm sap .... TODDY
sour ... LIME, LEMONADE
vermouth, etc. ... BRONX
wine .... VERMOUTH, NEGUS, BISHOP
with anise ...... KUMMEL
beverages, place for .... CELLAR(ET), BAR
bevy .... FLOCK, COVEY
bewail ..... MOURN, LAMENT, COMPLAIN, GRIEVE, DEPLORE
beware ...... GUARD, WATCH
bewilder ... PUZZLE, MYSTIFY, CONFUSE, STUMP, PERPLEX, DAZE
bewildering .... MAZY
bewitch .... ENCHANT, FASCINATE, CHARM, HEX, ENTRANCE
bewitchment .... SPELL
bey .... DEY, GOVERNOR
Beyoglu .... PERA
beyond .... PAST, YONDER, EXCEEDING, LATER
combining form .. ULTRA, META, SUR, PARA
compare .... PEERLESS
reach ... UNATTAINABLE, INACCESSIBLE
Beyrouth .... BEIRUT
bezant .... COIN, BALLET
bezel .... FACET, FLANGE, TEMPLATE, RIM
bhang .... HEMP
Bhutan capital (summer) ..... TASHI-CHHO
capital (winter) .... PUNAKHA
people .... BHOTIYA
pine .... KAIL
ruler ...... MAHARAJA(H)
Bialystok .... BELOSTOK
Biafran leader ...... OJUKWU
biannual .... BIENNIAL, SEMIANNUAL
bias .. PARTIALITY, PREJUDICE, INFLUENCE, TENDENCY
biased ... PARTIAL, ONE-SIDED, UNFAIR, NARROW-MINDED, PREJUDICED
person .... BIGOT
bib ... DRINK, IMBIBE, TIPPLE, APRON, NAPKIN, DICKEY
and tucker ..... CLOTHES
companion of ... TUCKER
bibb .... BIBCOCK
bibber ...... DRINKER, TOPER, TIPPLER
bibcock .... BIBB, FAUCET
bibelot .. CURIO, BRIC-A-BRAC, VIRTU, ARTIFACT, VERTU
Bible books of New Testament MATTHEW, MARK, LUKE, JOHN, ACTS, ROMANS, CORINTHIANS, GALATIANS, EPHESIANS, PHILIPPIANS, COLOSSIANS, TIMOTHY, THESSALONIANS, TITUS, PHILEMON, HEBREWS, JAMES, PETER, JUDE, REVELATION
books of Old Testament GENESIS, EXODUS, LEVITICUS, NUMBERS, JOSHUA, JUDGES, RUTH, DEUTERONOMY, SAMUEL, KINGS, CHRONICLES, EZRA, ESTHER, JOB, PSALMS, PROVERBS, ISAIAH, AMOS, JEREMIAH, LAMENTATIONS, EZEKIEL, DANIEL, JOEL, HOSEA, OBADIAH, JONAH, MICAH, NAHUM, HAGGAI, ZECHARIAH, MALACHI, NEHEMIAH, ZEPHANIAH
reading .... PSALM
the .... HOLY WRIT, SCRIPTURES
translator ..... ULFILA(S)
version ...... VULGATE, PESHITO, DOUAY, APOCRYPHA, DOUAI
biblical .... SCRIPTURAL
armies .... SABAOTH
ascetic order ..... ESSENE
boat .... ARK
character ... BOAZ, ESAU, EZRA, NOAH, AMOS, HEROD, HAGAR, AARON, NAOMI, RUTH, PILATE, ABEL, CAIN, JONAH, ELIAS, ENOS, HAMAN, PELEG, LEAH, JOSIAH, TOBIT, LABAN
charioteer .... JEHU
city ...... GOLM, BABEL, DAN, AVEN, EKRON, RESEN, GATH, GAZA, SODOM, HEBRON, ZOAR
coin ... TALENT, SHEKEL
cony .... HYRAX
country .... CANAAN, CHALDEA, EDOM, SHEBA, SEIR, PUL, ENON, SEBA
curser .... BALAAM
desert .... PARAN
expression .... SELAH
flight .... EXODUS
food .... MANNA
giant .... GOLIATH, ANAK, ENIM
gift-bearer(s) ..... MAGI, GASPAR, MELCHOR
Hades .... SHEOL
hill .... ZION
hosts .... SABAOTH
hunter ... ESAU, NIMROD
judge .... HEROD, ELI, GIDEON, ELON, SOLOMON
king ... SAUL, OMRI, OG, AGAG, ASA, AHAB, HEROD, BERA, NADAB, ELAH, AMON
kingdom ... ELAM, MOAB, SAMARIA, SHEBA
land ..... NOD, GOSHEN, EDOM, TOB
language .... ARAMIC

length measure ..... REED
liar .... ANANIAS, SAPPHIRA
lion .... ARI
lyrelike instrument ...... SACKBUT
mass migration .. EXODUS
measure ... OMER, CUBIT, EPHA(H), SHEKEL, KOR, GERAH, BEKA
merchant .... TUBAL
mount ...... ABLA, HOR, EBAL, NAIN, PEOR, HOREB, NEBO, SIER, SINAI, TABOR, ARARAT, GILEAD, OLIVET
name ...... ARAM, AROM, EBAL, EBED, GADDI, ONO, ANIM, REBA, ASOM, IVAH, REBA, AMASA, AHIRA, ABIAM, MAGOG, ISHMAEL, VASHTI, UR, MERAB, HELI, IRAD, IRA, ELAH
ornament .... URIM
passage used .... TEXT
patriarch ... ADAM, ENOS, NOAH, SETH, SHEM, ABRAM, JOB, ISAAC, JACOB, PELEG, TERAH, LAMECH, JARED, REU
place .... ENDOR, ENON, SHILOH, JORDAN
place of torment .... GEHENNA
pool .... SILOAM
precious stone .. JACINTH, LIGURE
priest .... ELI, LEVI, AARON, ANNAS
promised land .. CANAAN
prophet ... AMOS, EZRA, JOEL, HOSEA, JONAH, MICAH, MOSES, ELISHA, ISAIAH, DANIEL, JEREMIAH, EZEKIEL
queen .... SHEBA, ESTHER, VASHTI
rich man .... DIVES
river ..... JORDAN, NILE, ABANA, ARNON
sacred objects .... URIM
scribe .... BARUCH
serpent ..... NEHUSHTAN
sheep-owner ..... NABAL
shepherd .... ABEL
skipper .... NOAH
spice .... STACTE
spring .... AIN, ESEC, SILOAM
spy .... CALEB
stopping place ... MARAH
tax collector ... MATTHEW
temptress .... EVE, DELILAH
thief .... BARABBAS
timber .... ALMUG
tower ...... BABEL, EDAR
town ..... ENDOR, CANA, NAIN, BETHEL
tree ..... ALGUM, ALMUG
tribe .... AMON
valley .... NEMEA, BACA, SIDDIM, ELAH
verb ending .... ETH
vineyard owner .. NABOTH
wanderer .... CAIN
weed .... TARE
well ..... AIN, ESEK, ESEC
wild ox .... REEM
wise men .... MAGI
word .... SELAH, MENE, RACA

bibliographer's abbr. .... OBED
bibliotheca .... LIBRARY, CATALOG(UE)
bibulous .... DRUNK, ABSORBENT, ALCOHOLIC
festival .... ALE, BACCHANALIA
party .... WASSAIL
person .... SOT, TIPPLER, DRUNKARD, BACCHANT, TOPER
bicarbonate ... SODA, BICARB
bice .... PIGMENT, BLUE, VERDITER
bicephalous .... TWO-HEADED
bicker .... CAVIL, ARGUE, WRANGLE, QUARREL, SQUABBLE, GURGLE, DISPUTE
bicuspid .... TOOTH
bicycle .... BIKE, VELOCIPEDE
rider's seat ..... SADDLE
two-seater ...... TANDEM
bid .... TENDER, ASK, COMMAND, OFFER OVERTURE
in bridge .. DECLARATION
return .... RECALL
bidarka .... CANOE
bidding .... COMMAND, REQUEST, SUMMONS, INVITATION, (BE)HEST
biddy .... HEN, CHICKEN
bide .... STAY, CONTINUE, WAIT, DWELL, RESIDE
bield .... SHELTER
bienvenue .... WELCOME
bier ... COFFIN, CATAFALQUE, PYRE, FERETORY, HEARSE, LITTER
bifacial ... TWO-FACED, JANUS
biff ... CUFF, HIT, STRIKE, BOX
biffin .... APPLES
bifid .... FORKED, CLEFTED
bifurcate .... FORKED, BRANCHED
big .... LARGE, LOUD, IMPRESSIVE, POMPOUS, HUGE, NOBLE, SIZABLE, MAN-SIZE
and clumsy .. LUBBER(LY), HULKING
and strong ...... BURLY, BRAWNY, HUSKY
Ben .... CLOCK
Ben's place ...... TOWER, LONDON
Bertha .... CANNON
Bertha, where cast ...... ESSEN
casino .... TEN
Dipper ..... URSA MAJOR
Five member, WWI ..... JAPAN, ITALY, FRANCE
Five member, WWII .... CHINA, FRANCE, RUSSIA
Horn .... MOUNTAIN, RIVER
house: sl. .... PRISON
shot: sl. .... BIGWIG, BRASS, VIP, FATCAT
show: sl. .... THREE RING CIRCUS
teethed .... MACRODONT
toe .... HALLUX
toe ailment .... GOUT, BURSITIS
top .... CIRCUS, TENT(ROOF)
tree .... SEQUOIA, REDWOOD
with child .... PREGNANT

bighead .... CONCEIT, EGOTISM
biggin: Brit. ..... CAP, HOOD
bighorn ...... SHEEP, ARGALI
bight ... LOOP, GULF, CORNER, HOLLOW, FORK, CURVE, BAY
bignonia tree ..... CALABASH
bigot .... ZEALOT
bigwig: colloq. ..... TOPBRASS, VIP, FATCAT
Oriental .... AGA
Bihar's capital .... PATNA
bijou .... TRINKET, JEWEL
bike: colloq. .... BICYCLE
Bikini .... ATOLL
on the beach .. SWIMSUIT
bilateral .... RECIPROCAL, TWO-SIDED
bilbo ..... SHACKLES, RAPIER
bile ... GALL, CHOLER, ANGER, BITTERNESS, TEMPER
black ..... MELANCHOLY
combining form .... CHOL(O), CHOLE
yellow .... CHOLER
bilestone .... GALLSTONE
bilge .... BULGE, SWELL
slang .... NONSENSE
bilingual .... DIGLOT
bilious ...... CROSS, LIVERISH, BITTER, BAD-TEMPERED, GREEN
bilk .... SWINDLE(R), DEFRAUD, CHEAT(ER), DECEIVE, GYP
bill .... DUN, NEB, BEAK, TAB, STATEMENT, POSTER, HALBERD, LIST, ROAR, BELLOW, WILLIAM
and coo .... KISS, PET
fill the .... QUALIFY, SUIT
five-dollar .... VEE
foot the .... PAY
joker in a .... RIDER
of exchange ..... DRAFT
of exchange dealer ...... CAMBIST
of fare .... MENU, CARTE
of lading ... CARGO LIST
of Rights .... MAGNA CHARTA
part of .... NEB, CERE
pass thru mutual aid .... LOGROLL
stroke with ...... PECK, PREEN

one dollar .... BUCK
two dollar ...... DEUCE
ten dollar .... SAWBUCK, TENNER
100 dollar ...... C-NOTE CENTURY
1000 dollar ..... GRAND
billboard .... SIGNBOARD, HOARDING, POSTER
billet .... QUARTER(S), LODGING, POSITION
doux ..... (LOVE)LETTER
billfish .... GAR, SKIPPER, SAILFISH, SPEARFISH
billfold ...... WALLET, CASE, POCKETBOOK
billhead .... LETTERHEAD
billiards ball .... IVORY
red ball ..... CARAMBOLA
shot ..... CAROM, MASSE
stick .... CUE
billing .... LISTING, DUNNING
billingsgate lingo ...... FOUL, VULGAR, ABUSIVE
billion .... MILLIARD
billow ... WAVE, SHELL, DORE, EAGRE, SURGE, ROLL
billy ...... CLUB, TRUNCHEON, STICK, CAN, KETTLE
billycock .... HAT, DERBY
bilsted ..... TREE, SWEET GUM
Bimini legend .... FOUNTAIN OF YOUTH
bimonthly .... BIMENSAL
bin .... BOX, RECEPTACLE
fish .... KENCH
fodder .... CRATCH
for ship's coal, fuel oil ... BUNKER
storage .... HUTCH
binal .... TWOFOLD
binate .... DOUBLE
binaural .... STEREO
bind ..... TIE, ATTACH, TAPE, ROPE, HOLD, GIRD, SECURE
matrimonially .. MARRY, WED
mouth .... GAG
together by rope ... FRAP
wound .... BANDAGE
binder ... BAND, CORD, ROPE, BALER
binding .... OBLIGATORY, BANDAGE, BAND
device .... CONTRACT
machine .... BALER
substance .... TAR, GLUE, PASTE
bindle stiff ..... HOBO, TRAMP
bine .... STEM, HOP
binge .... SPREE, BENDER, LARK, ORGY, WASSAIL
bingo ... LOTTO, BEANO, KENO
binocle .... TELESCOPE, FIELD GLASS, OPERA GLASS
biocatalyst .... VITAMIN, HORMONE
biographical sketch .. PROFILE
biography .... LIFE STORY, MEMOIR
biological .... BIOTIC(AL)
change .... MUTATION
division .... GENERA
factor .... GENE
group .... SPECIES
reproductive cell .... GAMETE
biology, branch of .... GENETICS
of behavior .. ETHOLOGY
Bion .... POET
opposed to ... MORPHON
bionomics .... ECOLOGY
biped ...... MAN, TWO-FOOTED
birch .... BETULA, HORNBEAM, IRONWOOD, HAZELNUT, WHIP, BIRK, CANE, ALDER
bird .... FLYER, CROW, DOVE, PARROT, MYNA, RAIL, SHRIKE, KIWI, SWAN
adjutant .... STORK, MARABOU, ARGALA
African .... COLY, LORY, LOURI, TURAKOO, UMBER, UMBRETTE
air route .... FLYWAY
albatross .... NELLY
American .... JUNCO, TOWHEE, RHEA
Andean .... CONDOR
apteryx ...... IAO, KIWI
aquatic .... LOON, AUK, GOOSE, DUCK, PELICAN, SWAN, GULL, SCAUP, PENGUIN
Arctic .... FULMAR, XEMA, LONGSPUR
Asiatic ..... MINA, MYNA, PITTA, PITA
attack ... POUNCE, SWOOP
auk family ..... PUFFIN, ALCA, DOVEKIE, ROTCH(E)
Australian ... EMU, KOEL, COOEE, EMEW, PARDALOTE, ARARA, ARA, KAHU, LEIPOA, COCKATOO
baker .... HORNERO
bastard wing ..... ALULA
beach ...... SANDERLING
beak ... LORA, NEB, NIB, BILL
beak part ..... MANDIBLE
beaky .... TOUCAN
bell .... MAKO
big-footed ..... MEGAPOD
bill .... NEB, BEAK
bittern .... HERON
black .... CROW, ANI, RAVEN, ROOK, MERL(E), AMSEL, OUSEL, THRUSH, GRACKLE
blue .... JAY, IRENA
blue-footed .... TITI
bobolink ...... ORTALAN
bobwhite .... QUAIL, COLIN, PARTRIDGE
Brazilian ..... CARIAMA, SERIEMA, TOUCAN
bright-colored .. HOOPOE, TOURACO, TOUCAN
bristle-billed ..... BARBET
broad-billed .... SCAUP, DUCK, SPOONBILL
brood ..... COVEY, NIDE
butcher .... SHRIKE
call .... PIPE
caress .... BILL
carrion .... VULTURE, URUBU, CROW
catcher .... FOWLER
catching at night .... BATFOWL
chameleonic .... PTARMIGAN
chatterer .... JAY, (MAG)PIE, WAXWING, WHEAT-EATER, STONECHAT, COTINGA
class of .... AVES
claw-winged .... HOA(C)TZIN
cockateel .... PARROT
cockatoo .... ARARA
colin .... BOBWHITE
"collar" .. RUFF, TORQUES
colloquial ...... PERSON
colored beak .... PUFFIN
cormorant ..... GUANAY
corvine .... CROW, DAW, RAVEN
courlan .... JACAMAR, TINAMOU
crane ...... DEMOISELLE, SERIEMA
craw .... MAW
crest ... TUFT, CALOT(TE), COP, HOOD
crested ...... QUE(T)ZAL, COCKATOO, BLUEJAY, HOA(C)TZIN
crocodile ... TROCHILUS
crop ...... CRAW, MAW
crow .... CHOUGH, CORBIE, CORBY
crow-like ...... MAGPIE, CORVINE, ROOK
cry .... CAW, SHRIEK, ROAR, WEEP, BELLOW
cuckoo ...... KOEL, ANI, ANO
disease .... GAPES
diving ..... AUK, GREBE, DUCKER, DIDAPPER, LOON, SMEW, ALCIDINE, PUFFIN, LOOM, OSPREY
dodo .... GEESE
dog .... POINTER, SETTER
duck family .... MERGANSER, SMEW
duck-like ... COOT, GOOSE
dunlin .... STIB, SANDPIPER
eagle, sea .... ERN(E)
eagle's nest ...... AERIE, EYRIE
East Indies ..... SHAMA, BESRA, PEREGRINE, REDPOOL, SHAHIN
Egyptian sacred .... IBIS
emu-like .... CASSOWARY
European .... REED, OUSEL, GLEDE, TEREK, SEDGE, AMSEL, REDSTART, WOODCOCK
extinct ..... DODO, MOA, MAMO, GREAT AUK, NOTORNIS
eye tissue ...... PECTEN

fabulous .. ROC, PHOENIX
falcon .... MERLIN, SAKER, TERCEL, BESRA, PEREGRINE, REDPOOL
feather .... PENNA
feather-legged ... GROUSE
feather under the wing .. AXILLAR
feathers .... PLUMAGE
feathers near mouth ..... VIBRISSA
feet for perching .... ENSESSO
fighting ...... AMADAVAT
finch ... SISKIN, TOWHEE, MORO, SERIN, BUNTING, CANARY, CARDINAL, LINNET, SPARROW
finch-like .... GROSBEAK, CHEWINK
fish-eating .... ERN, KINGFISHER, OSPREY, GOOSANDER, LOON, MERGANSER
fish-hawk ...... OSPREY
flightless .... DODO, MOA, OSTRICH, PENGUIN, KAGU, KIWI, AUK, CASSOWARY, RATITE, APTERYX, WEKA, RHEA, EM(E)U, NOTORNIS
flock ...... CONVEY, POD
fluid spraying .. HOUBARA
flycatcher .... OSCINE, PEWEE, KINGBIRD, PHOEBE
footless: heraldry .... MARTLET
for food .... CAPON
forelimb .... WING
fork-tailed ...... PETREL
frigate .... IWA
fruit-eating ..... TOUCAN, PARROT
fulmar .... NELLY
game bird ...... GROUSE, SNIPE, TURNIX
game-killer ..... VERMIN
gluttonous .. CORMORANT
goatsucker ... GUACHARO
gold finch ...... REDCAP
goose .... GANDER
greedy ...... CORMORANT
grouse .... BLACKCOCK, GORCOCK
guan .... ORTALIS
gull-like .... TERN, JAEGER, SKUA
gull, pert. to .... LARINE
gull, sea ..... KITTIWAKE, MEW, TERN
harsh-voiced ... MACAW
Hawaiian ... MAMO, IWA, IIWI, OOAA, ALALA
hawk .... CARACARA, GOSHAWK, KITE, EYAS, KAHU
hawk-like .... OSPREY
heron ...... EGRET, IBIS, BITTERN, SOCO
hind toe .... HALLUX
homing instinct .... ORIENTATION
honey-eating .... TUI, MANUAO, MOHO, IAO
hood-like crest .... CALOT(TE)
house ..... COTE, AVIARY, NEST, NIDE, VOLERY
humming ..... COLIBRI, SYLPH, TROCHILUS, AVE
hunter .... FOWLER
hunting .... FALCON, HAWK
Indian ...... AMADAVIT, SHAMA, SARUS, ARGALA, JACANA
insectivorous ..... VIREO, TODY, HARRIER
jackdaw ..... COE, KAE, DAW
jay-like .... PIET, MOTMOT
killing of .... AVACIDE
kite .... GLEDE
lake .... LOON
lamellirostral ..... DUCK, SWAN, GOOSE
lapwing .... WEEP, PEWIT, PLOVER
laughing .. LOON, DACELO GIGAS, KOOKABURRA
large .... EMU, OSTRICH, GUAN, MOA, KITE, JABIRU
large-footed ... MEGAPOD
Latin for .... AVIS
leaf-walker ...... JACANA
leg outgrowth ..... SPUR, CALCAR
leg strap .... JESS
life .... ORNIS
like in appearance ...... ORNITHOID
limicoline ...... AVOCET
long-billed .. NUTHATCH, CREEPER
long-legged ..... AGAMI, STILT, HERON, BUSTARD, EGRET, CRANE, WADER, FLAMINGO, SERIEMA, IBIS
long-necked ...... SWAN, FLAMINGO, CRANE, HERON, EGRET
loon-like .... GREBE
love-making .... BILL AND COO
lyre .... MENURA
magpie .... PIET
male ... COCK, ROOSTER, TOM, GOBBLER, GANDER, BANTAM
marsh .... STILT, RAIL, SORA, BITTERN, COOT, GALLINULE
martin .... MARTLET
meadow .... LARK, BOBOLINK
migratory ...... PLOVER, WHEATEATER, KNOT, SANDPIPER, BOBOLINK, WHIN, WOODCOCK
mina .... STARLING
morepork .... RURU
mound-building .. LEIPOA, MEGAPOD
mouth opening .. RICTUS
mythical ... ROC, PHOENIX
nail of .... CLAW
national .... EAGLE
nest-collector .. OOLOGIST
nocturnal .... OWL, GOATSUCKER, GUACHARO
noisy .... BLUEJAY
non-flying (see flightless bird)
non-passerine ... HOOPOE, TODY, KINGFISHER, HORNBILL
note ..... TWEET, CHIRP, PIPE
ocean .... FULMAR, PETREL, ALBATROSS, MALEMUCK
of Jove .... EAGLE
of Paradise .... APUS
of peace .... DOVE
of prey .... EAGLE, BUZZARD, ACCIPETER, GLEDE, ERN(E), HAWK, KITE, OWL, KESTREL, ELANET, GOSHAWK, VULTURE
one-year-old .. ANNOTINE
orange-colored .. ORIOLE
order of .... RASORES
oscine .... CROW, TANAGER, VIREO, CHAT, ORIOLE, LARK, SHRIKE, BUNTING
ostrich-like ..... EM(E)U, RATITE, RHEA, TINAMOU
owl: Samoan ...... LULU
parakeet .... BUDGIE
parrot .... KAKAM, KAKAPOS, KEA, COCKATOO, LORY
parson .... POE, TUI
partridge .... SEESEE, BOBTAIL, QUAIL
partridge-like .. TINAMOU, TINAMIDA
passerine ..... SPARROW, PITA, STARLING, TANAGER
patch on throat .. GORGET
pelican-like ...... SOLAN
perching .... LARK, BUNTING, SHRIKE, FINCH, OSCINE
Persian .... BULBUL
pertaining to .... AVIAN, ORNITHIC, AVINE
Peruvian .... GUANAY
petrel ..... TITI, FULMAR
pewee .... PHOEBE
phoebe ... PEWIT, PEWEE
plover-like .... LAPWING, KILLDEER
protuberance ..... SPUR, CALCAR
quail .... BOBWHITE, PARTRIDGE
queer: colloq. .... ECCENTRIC, IDIOT(IC), LOCO
rail .... CRAKE, MOHO, SORA, COOT, GALLINULE, SCOTER, SULTANA
rail-like .... COURLAN
rain .... PLOVER
razor-billed .... AUK, MURRE
rear young ..... FLEDGE

red-eyed .... VIREO
reed .... BOBOLINK
ring-dove .... CUSHAT
robber .... SKUA, JA(E)GER, DAW
ruffed .... SANDPIPER, REEVE, GROUSE, PIGEON, PARTRIDGE
running, swift .. COURSER
sacred .... IBIS
Samoan ..... IAO, LULU
sandpiper .. REEVE, KNOT, DUNLIN, GREENSHANK
scaup duck .. BLACKHEAD
screamer .... CHAJA
sea ..... ERN(E), GANNET, GULL, MURRE(LET), SCAUP, ALBATROSS, TERN, PETREL, PUFFIN, SCOTER, SKUA, JAEGER, CORMORANT
seed-eating ...... JUNCO, GROSBEAK, CHICKADEE, CANARY, FINCH, CARDINAL, SPARROW, BUNTING
sheep-killer .... KEA
shore .... AVOCET, SORA, STILT, WILLET, RAIL, SNIPE, PLOVER, SANDPIPER, PRATINCOLE
short-tailed ...... BREVE, PLOVER
singing .... OSCINE
skin around eye ... ORBIT
small .... TIT, PIPIT, WREN, TODY, TITMOUSE, BLUET, CHICKADEE, COSTA, BIRDIE, FINCH, SYLPH, PEWEE, VIREO, TOMTIT, SERIN, VERDIN, COLIBRI, MANAKIN, SAPPHO
snake .... ANHINGA
snipe .... CURLEW, DOWITCHER, GODWIT
snipe-like ...... WILLET
song ..... LARK, SHAMA, BOBOLINK, ROBIN, LINNET, PIPE, BLUEBIRD, OUZEL
sorrel .... OCA
sound ...... COO, CHIRP, PEEP, TWEET, SHRIEK, CROW, HONK, ROAR, BELLOW, CAW, WEEP, CHATTER, SCREECH, TIRALEE, WHOOP, TWITTER, QUACK
South American .... TOUCAN, GUAN, WARRIOR, JACANA, SYLPH, TURCO, SERIEMA, JACU, TINAMOU, GUACHARO
space on head ..... LORE
sparrow .... TOWHEE, BUNTING, PEABODY
starling .... MINA, MYNA, MINAH
stib .... DUNLIN
stitch .... IHI
stupid .... NODDY, GOOSE, DODO
swallow .... MARTLET
swallow-like .... HIRUNDINE, MARTIN, SWIFT
swan .... WHOOPER
swimming .... SWAN, DUCK, GREBE, LOON, PHALAROPE
symbolic .... EAGLE, OWL, STORK, DOVE
tail feathers ..... TRAIN, RECTRIX
tail hump ... UROPYGIUM
talking .... PARROT, MINA, MYNA(H)
thief ...... DAW, SKUA, JA(E)GER, ROOK
three-toed .... STILT, TURNIX
thrush .... THROSTLE
titmouse ..... BLUECAP, VERDIN, CHICKADEE
toe .... HALLUX
top of its head ... PILEUM
towhee ...... CHEWINK, SPARROW
trill .... TIRALEE
tropical ... ANI, BARBET, JACANA, TROGON, JACAMAR, TOUCAN, JABIRU
trumpeter .... AGAMI, (BLACK)SWAN
turkey ... TOM, GOBBLER
turkey-like ... CURASSOW
unfledged .... SQUAB
vulture .... URUBU, CONDOR
wading .... COOT, CURLEW, HERON, IBIS, JACANA, RAIL, WILLET, CRANE, SORA, AVOCET, STORK, FLAMINGO, GALLINULE, STILT, EGRET, UMBER, BOATBILL, JABIRU, KILLDEER, SNIPE, UMBRETTE
wag-tail .... PIPIT
warbler ..... REDSTART, TROCHILUS, BLACKPOLL, CHICKADEE
water .... HYACINTH, PELICAN
water-carrier .. ALBATROSS
weaver ... MUNIA, TAHA
web-footed .... DUCK, LOON, GOOSE, COOT, AUK
whiskered ...... BULBUL
white-plumed ... EGRET, SHRIKE
white-tailed ...... ERN(E)
whooper .... SWAN
wing .... PINION
wing-outgrowth .... CALCAR
wing quills .... FLAG
wing part .... ALULA, CALCAR, SPUR
with changing color ..... PTARMIGAN
with irregular flight ..... LAPWING, PEWIT
with scalelike feathers ... PENGUIN
woman .... AVIATRIX
woodpigeon .. RINGDOVE
yellowhammer ... FINCH, CUCKOO, FLICKER
young ..... FLEDGLING, OWLET, EAGLET, EYAS, CHICK, GOSLING, NESTLING

birds .... AVES
breeding place .... ROOKERY, HERONRY
care of ..... AVICULTURE
eggs, study of ... OOLOGY
flight south ... MIGRATION
foot plant .... FERN, TREFOIL, VIOLET
of a region .... ORNIS
of singing .... OSCINE
pertaining to ..... AVIAN, AVINE, ORNITHIC
raising of ... AVICULTURE
reservation .. SANCTUARY
study of ... ORNITHOLOGY

biretta .... BARRET, CAP, BER(R)ET(T)A
birk .... BIRCH
birl .... REVOLVE, WHIRR, SPIN
birling .... LOGROLLING
bee .... ROLEO
object of ...... BALANCE
what lumberjacks use for LOGS
birr .... ENERGY, FORCE, ONRUSH, SPEECH
birth .... NATIVITY, GENESIS, ORIGIN, DESCENT, BEGINNING
before .... PRENATAL
control advocate ...... SANGER
control device .... CONTRACEPTIVE, PILL
Jesus' .... NATIVITY
of high .... NOBLE
of one's .... NATAL
of two .... BIPAROUS
pains .... LABOR
rate .... NATALITY
root .... TRILLIUM
birthmark ... MOLE, N(A)EVUS
birthright .... HERITAGE, INHERITANCE, PATRIMONY
birthstone, January ... GARNET
February ..... AMETHYST
March .... JASPER, AQUAMARINE, BLOODSTONE
April .... DIAMOND
May ... EMERALD, AGATE
June .. PEARL, MOONSTONE
July .... ONYX, RUBY
August ...... SARDONYX, CARNELIAN
September .... SAPPHIRE
October .... OPAL
November .... TOPAZ
December ... TURQUOISE, ZIRCON
birthwort .... CLEMATITE, ARISTOLOCHIA
bis ...... TWICE, REPEAT, BI, ENCORE
Biscay .... BASQUE
island .... YEU
biscuit ..... WAFER, CRACKER, COOKY, SNAP, SCONE, POPOVER, RUSK, PANAL, BUN, RATAFEE, SIMNEL, ZWIEBACK, MACAROON
in ceramics ...... BISQUE

knotted .... PRETZEL
sweetened .... RUSK
bisect .... DIVIDE, FORK
bishop .... PRELATE, CHESSMAN, PONTIFF, EPARCH
in chess .... ALFIN
of Rome .... POPE
vestment ..... DALMATIC
weed ...... AMMI, GOUT
bishop's assistant .... COAD(JUTOR), VERGER
cap ...... HURA, MITRE, MITER, MITERWORT
deputy .... VICAR
first year's revenue ...... ANNAT
lap cloth .... GREMIAL
letter .... PASTORAL
robe .... CHIMER(E), CHIMAR
seat .... BEMA, CATHEDRA, SEE
see .... EPISCOPATE
skullcap .... ZUCCHETTO
staff .... CROSIER, CROZIER, CROOK
staff bearer ..... VERGER
throne .... CATHEDRA
title ..... PRIMATE, ABBA
vestment .... ROCHET, GREMIAL, COPE, SURPLICE
bishopric .... SEE, DIOCESE
bishops collectively .... EPISCOPACY
bison .... BUFFALO, AUROCHS, BOVINE
crossed with cattle ...... CATALO
bisque ..... SOUP, ICE CREAM, BISCUIT
bissextile .... LEAP YEAR
bistort .... ASTRINGENT
bistro .... WINESHOP, BAR, NIGHTCLUB, RESTAURANT, CAFE
habitue .... BARFLY
bit ..... CHECK, CURB, SPECK, PIECE, COIN, MOMENT, SMALL, BLADE, NIPPED, MOTE, WHIT, MORSEL, GOBBET
by bit ...... GRADUALLY
colloquial ...... STITCH
holder .... BRACE
least .... WHIT
of comic business ... GAG
of gossip .... TIDBIT
player .... EXTRA
small .... NIP
bitch .... SHREW, BRACH
of Buchenwald .... (ILSE) KOCH
slang .... COMPLAIN, BOTCH, SPOIL
bite ... STING, GRIP, CORRODE, MOUTHFUL, HOLD, NIP, SNACK, MORSEL, NIBBLE
bit by bit .. GNAW, CHEW, MASTICATE
colloquial .... LUNCH
down hard ..... CHAMP
impatiently .... FRET
off .... CROP
sharply ..... KNAP, SNAP
suddenly .... SNAP
the dust ..... LOSE, FALL
biting .... CUTTING, MORDACIOUS, STINGING, SHARP, CAUSTIC, NIPPY
Bitolj .... MONASTIR
bits .... ANA
bitstock .... BRACE
bitt .... DECK POST
bitte .... PLEASE
bitter .... ACERB, ACRID, GRIEVOUS, HARSH, SEVERE, VIRULENT, PAINFUL
apple ...... COLOCYNTH
bark .... ANGOSTURA
cassava product .... TAPIOCA
combining form .. PICRO
compound ..... AMARINE
cynic .... TIMON
drug .... ALOE
feeling ...... ACRIMONY, HATE, GRUDGE, RANCOR
flavoring agent .. ASARUM
herb .... ALOE
liquid from brine .... BITTERN
nut .... KOLA
plant substance ... ALUM, LUPULIN, ALOIN
vetch .... ERS
bittern .... SOCO, BIRD
bitterness .... ILL WILL, RANCOR, HATE, ACERBITY, VILE
bitters: Fr. .... AIGRE
bitterweed .... RAGWEED
bitumen .... PITCH, ASPHALT, MALTHA
bivalent .... DIATOMIC
bivalve .... MOLLUSK, CLAM, MUSSEL, SCALLOP, OYSTER, QUAHOG, PIDDOCK
bivouac ..... ENCAMP(MENT), ETAPE, CAMP
bizarre .... ODD, GROTESQUE, QUEER, FANTASTIC, OUTRE, LURID
Bizet opera .... CARMEN
blab ..... CHATTER, PRATTLE, GOSSIP
blabber ..... GOSSIP(MONGER), TATTLER
black ..... EBON, SABLE, JET, INKY, WICKED, RAVEN, COLLY, JET(TY)
alder .... WINTERBERRY, SHRUB
alloy .... NIELLO
and-blue .... BRUISED, LIVID
and-tan ...... TERRIER, DOG, RAT TERRIER
and-white .... WRITING, PRINT, PHOTOGRAPH
art ..... MAGIC, SORCERY
bass .... (GAME)FISH
beer .... DANTZIC
bile, having .... MOROSE, MELANCHOLY
bird .... CROW, DAW, RAVEN
bread ingredient .... RYE
buck .... SASIN
chimney product .. SOOT
coal .... ATROUS
coffee .... CAFE NOIR
combining form ... ATRO, MELAN(O)
country ..... MIDLANDS
cuckoo .... ANI
Death .... (BUBONIC) PLAGUE
diamonds .... COAL
Earth area .... OREL
eye: colloq. ...... SHAME, SHINER, DISHONOR, MOUSE
eyed nymph ..... HOURI
eyed pea ...... COWPEA
eyed Susan .... KETMIE, (YELLOW) DAISY, RUDBECKIA
fever .... KALA-AZAR
fin snapper .... SESI
flag .... JOLLY ROGER
Forest ... SCHWARZWALD
Friar .... DOMINICAN
garnet .... MELANITE
gold .... OIL
gum .... TUPELO, NYSSA, PEPPERIDGE
hair and eyes .... BRUNET(TE)
Hand .... CAMMORA, MAF(F)IA, BLACKMAILERS
haw .... VIBURNUM, SHEEPBERRY
hole .... DUNGEON
ink item .... ASSET
knot .... FUNGUS
lead .... GRAPHITE
letter .... UNLUCKY, UNFORTUNATE
letter type ..... CAXTON
lustrous .... RAVEN
magic .... SORCERY, WITCHCRAFT, VOODOO
make .... NIGRIFY
Maria .. (POLICE)WAGON, PATROL WAGON, PADDY WAGON
mark .... DISREPUTE
mineral ..... IRIDE, JET, COAL
Monk ..... BENEDICTINE
nightshade .... MOREL
pepper ...... SEASONING
Plague .... BUBONIC
Power leader ... BROWN, NEWTON, CARMICHAEL
Prince .... EDWARD
race .... NEGRO
rhinoceros ..... BORELE
Rod .... USHER
rot .... FUNGUS
rust .... FUNGUS
saltwort .... GLAUX
Sea .... EUXINE
Sea city .... ODESSA, YALTA
Sea empire .. TREBIZOND
Sea fish .... HAUSEN
Sea inlet .... AZOV

Sea, of the ...... PONTIC
Sea peninsula ... CRIMEA
Sea port .... VARNA, ANAPA, ODESSA
Sea resort .... YALTA
sheep: colloq. .... PRODIGAL, BAD ONE
Shirt ..... FASCIST, NAZI
silver ...... STEPHANITE
snake .... RACER
suit cards .... SPADES, CLUBS
swan .... TRUMPETER
tea .... BOHEA
tern .... DARR
tie .... BOW, (DINNER)JACKET
very .... JETTY
vomit ... YELLOW FEVER
water .... PYROSIS
widow .... SPIDER
wood .... EBONY

blackamoor .... NEGRO
Blackbeard .... PIRATE, TEACH, PRIVATEER
blackbeetle ..... COCKROACH
blackberry ... BRAMBLE, BUSH, VINE
blackbird ...... RAVEN, ANI, MERL(E), CROW, GRACKLE, COWBIRD, THRUSH, STARLING, JACKDAW
European .. OUSEL, OUZEL
blackboard .... SLATE
blackboy .. GRASS TREE, PLANT
blackcap ... BIRD, CHICKADEE, RASPBERRY
blackcock .... GROUSE
blackdamp .... GAS
blacken ..... JAPAN, SMEAR, TAR, INK, SLANDER, DARKEN, NIGRIFY, DENIGRATE, SOIL
blackened with soot .. COLLIED
blackface ...... BOLD, NEGRO, MINSTREL
Blackfeet .... INDIAN
blackfellow: Austral. .. MAORI
blackfin snapper .... SESI
blackfish .... TAUTOG, WHALE, SWART
blackguard ..... SCOUNDREL, CAD, VILLAIN, VULGAR, ABUSIVE
blackhead .... DUCK, PIMPLE, PLUG, COMEDO
blackheart .... CHERRY
blackhearted .... WICKED, MALEVOLENT, CRUEL
blacking .... SHOE POLISH
blackjack .... BLUDGEON, MUG, OAK, CARD GAME, TWENTY-ONE
blackleg .... FUNGUS
British .. STRIKEBREAKER, SCAB, GAMBLER, CROOK, CHEAT
blacklist .... OSTRACIZE
blackly .... ANGRILY, GLOOMILY, MENACINGLY
blackmail .... TRIBUTE, EXTORTION, COERCE, CHANTAGE
blackmailer .... VAMPIRE, MAF(F)IA, CAMMORA
blackness .... NIGRITUDE
blackout .... PASS OUT
kind of .... FAINT, SWOON
news ...... CENSORSHIP
blackpoll .... WARBLER, CHICKADEE, REDSTART
blacksmith ... FARRIER, LOHAR
block .... ANVIL
chisel .... HARDY
furnace .... FORGE
shop .... SMITHY, STITHY
tool .... FULLER
blacksnake .. RACER, COLUBER
blacktail .... MULEDEER
fish .... DASSY
blackthorn .. SLOE, HAW, CANE
blacktop ...... TAR, ASPHALT
blackwood ...... BITI, EBONY
blackwort .... COMFREY
bladder .... BAG, AIR SAC, VESICA
combining form .. VISICO
deposit ...... CALCULUS
bladdernose .. (HOODED) SEAL
bladderworm ...... HYDATID, CYSTICERCUS
blade ... VANE, RUNNER, LEAF, OAR, SWORD(SMAN), TOLEDO
grass .... SPEAR
in botany .... LAMINA
leaf .... LAMINA
sword .... TOLEDO, DAMASCUS
bladebone .... SCAPULA
blah: sl. ..... NONSENSE, ROT
blain ...... BLISTER, PUSTULE, SORE, BULLA
Blake's symbol .... ZOA
blame .... ACCUSE, RAP, CONDEMN, FAULT, CENSURE, CRITICIZE, ACCUSATION, REPROACH
blamed: colloq. ..... DAMNED
blameless .... SPOTLESS, CLEAN, INNOCENT
blanch ..... WHITEN, BLEACH, SCALD, PALE, ETIOLATE
blancmange .... FLUMMERY
bland .... SUAVE, SMOOTH, SOOTHING, MILD, TEMPERATE, SOFT, GENTLE, AFFABLE
blandation .... FLATTERY, BLARNEY
blandish .... FLATTER, CAJOLE, COAX
blank ..... MARKLESS, EMPTY, WHITE, BARREN, UNWRITTEN
check of a sort .... CARTE BLANCHE
draw a .... FAIL, LOSE, ZERO
in baseball .... SHUTOUT
in printing .... QUAD
look .... POKER FACE
look, describing one .... VACANT
sheet in book ... FLYLEAF
space ..... HIATUS, GAP, VOID
blanket .... COVER, SHEET, OVERSPREAD, AFGHAN
authority .... FULL POWER(S)
horse .... MANTA
Mexican .... SERAPE
worn as cloak .. PONCHO
blankety-blank ..... DAMNED, EXPLETIVE
blare .... BLAZON
trumpet's ..... FANFARE, TANTARA
blarney .... FLATTERY, WHEEDLE, COAX, SOFT TALK, FLAM
blase .... BORED, WEARY, SATED, SATIATED
blaspheme .... PROFANE, CURSE, REVILE
blasphemous ..... IRREVERENT
blasphemy ...... PROFANITY, IRREVERENCE
blast ..... GUST, EXPLOSION, EXPLODE, BLOW-UP, ATTACK, ERUPTION, SEAR, BLIGHT
furnace .... FORGE, SMELTER
furnace part ...... BOSH, TROMPE, TUYERE, MANTLE
of horn .... TOOT
off step ... COUNT DOWN
sluice .... SOW
blastie: Scot. .... DWARF
blat ..... BLEAT, BLURT, BLAB
blatant .... BOISTEROUS, NOISY, FLASHY, SHOWY, GAUDY, VOCIFEROUS, LOUDMOUTHED
blather .... NONSENSE, FOOLISH TALK
blaubok .... ANTELOPE, ETAAC
blaze ... FLARE, FLAME, FIRE, OUTBURST, FLASH, SHINE
away .... SHOOT, (RAPID)FIRE
on animal's face ... SPOT
star .... NOVA
blazer .... JACKET
blazes, go to ..... BE DAMNED, HELL
blazing star .... COMET, TORCH LILY
blazon ...... COAT OF ARMS, DISPLAY, PROCLAIM, EMBLEM, BLARE
bleach .... WHITEN, BLANCH, ETIOLATE, CHLORE, DECOLORIZE
by sunning .... INSOLATE
bleaching powder .. CHLORIDE
vat .... KEIR, KIER
bleak .... TREELESS, BARE, STARK, PALE, COLD, DESOLATE, RAW, GLOOMY, DREAR
blear .... MISTY, BLURRED, BLUR, DIM

eyed .... RHEUMY, DULL-WITTED, TEARY
bleat .... BLAT, MAA, BAA, WHINE
bleater .... SHEEP, LAMB, CRYBABY, GOAT, CALF, WHINER
bleb .... BLISTER, VESICLE, BUBBLE, BULLA
bleed .... SUFFER, OOZE, EXTORT, SUCK
certain way ...... LEECH
white ...... IMPOVERISH
bleeder .. LEECH, HEMOPHILIAC
bleeding, stoppage of .... HEMOSTASIS
stopper ...... HEMOSTAT
uncontrollable .... HEMOPHILIA
bleffert .... SQUALL
blemish ..... DEFECT, FAULT, STAIN, FLAW, MAR, BLOT, MACULATE, TARNISH
cloth .... AMPER
on reputation .. DISHONOR
skin .... NEVUS, NAEVUS, SCAR
blench ...... SHRINK, QUAIL, FLINCH, WHITEN, PALE
blend .... MERGE, FUSE, HARMONIZE, MIX(TURE), MELD
colors .... FONDU
blende ..... SPHALERITE, ORE
blenny .... GUNNEL, SHANNY
blesbok .... ANTELOPE, NUNNI
bless .... HALLOW, CONSECRATE, BEATIFY, ENDOW, GLORIFY, SANCTIFY
against evil .... SAIN
blessed .... HOLY, SACRED, BLISSFUL, BEATIFIED
event .... BIRTH
French .... SACRE
Sacrament ... EUCHARIST
blessing .... BENEDICTION, GRACE, APPROVAL, BOON, SAIN, BENISON
at meal .... GRACE
blet .... FRUIT DECAY
blight .... DESTROY, FRUSTRATE, SEAR, RUST, SMUT, MILDEW, NIP, BLAST, RUIN
blighter: Brit. sl. ..... RASCAL, FELLOW, CHAP
blighty: Brit. sl. ..... ENGLAND, HOME
blimp: colloq. .... AIRSHIP
blind .... EYELESS, SIGHTLESS, DAZZLE, SEEL, SHUTTER, COVER, RECKLESS
a hawk .... SEEL
alley .... DEADEND, IMPASSE, CUL-DE-SAC
as a ____ .... BAT
bargain ... PIG-IN-A-POKE
daters .... STRANGERS
dolphin .... SUSU
fear .... PANIC
flower-girl .... NIDIA
god ...... HODER, HOTH
impulse .... ATE
love, usually .... INFATUATION
pig: sl. ...... SPEAKEASY
shot .... HIT OR MISS
slang: .... DRUNK
spot .... SCOTOMA
spot: colloq. .. WEAKNESS, IGNORANCE
staggers ... GID, MEGRIM, VERTIGO
tiger: sl. ..... SPEAKEASY
blindage .... CAMOUFLAGE
blinder .... BLINKER, SEEL, WINKER
blinders .... GOGGLES
blindfold .... HOODWINK, MISLEAD, SEEL
blinding light .... GLARE
blindman: Sp. .... CIEGO
blindness .. CECITY, TYPHLOSIS
blindpig .... SPEAKEASY
blinds .... PERSIENNES
blindstory .... GALLERY
blindworm .... ORVET
blink .... TWINKLE, WINK, IGNORE, BAT, FLUTTER, NICTATE
blinker .... BLINDER, EYE
bliss .... JOY, RAPTURE, ECSTASY, FELICITY
blissful ..... ELYSIAN, JOYOUS
blister ... BULLA, BLEB, BLAIN, VESICATE, VESICLE
beetle ...... SPANISH FLY
causing ...... VESICANT
cloth .... YAW
on neck .... MALANDERS
blistering agent ... SPISPASTIC, VESICANT
blithe ...... GAY, CHEERFUL, AIRY, MERRY, CHEERFUL
spirit, Shakespearean ... ARIEL
blitz ..... ATTACK, DESTROY, OVERWHELM
blitzkrieg of a sort ..... COUP, COUP D'ETAT, COUP DE MAIN
blizzard .... SNOWSTORM, WINDSTORM
in Alaska .... PURGA
blk. .... BLACK, BLOCK, BULK
bloat .... SWELL, PUFF, DRUNKARD
bloated .... TURGID
blob .... SPLOTCH, DROP, SPLASH
block .... MOLD, OCCLUDE, SPRAG, IMPEDE, HINDER, DAM
casks' .... QUOIN
for nails on wall .... NOG
go to the ... UP FOR SALE, AUCTION
hawser .... BITT
house .... FORT
ice .... SERAC
mechanical ..... PULLEY
metal .... NUT
of type metal ..... QUAD
of wood .... NOG, DEADEYE, CHUMP
set against wheel ... TRIG
small .... TESSERA
up .... BLOCKADE, STEM, OBSTRUCT, DAM, CHOKE, CLOG
wedge-shaped .... QUOIN
blockade .... ISOLATE, BOTTLE-UP, ROADBLOCK
runner of a sort .... SMUGGLER, CONTRABANDIST
blockhead ..... IDIOT, STOCK, ASS, FOOL, NITWIT, MUTT, NUMSKULL
blocky ..... STOCKY, CHUNKY
bloke: sl. .... FELLOW, OAF
blond(e) .... FLAXEN(HAIRED), LACE, WOMAN, TOWHEAD
kind of .... PEROXIDE, PLATINUM
Blonde Bombshell of movies .. HARLOW
blood .... GORE, LIFE, LIFE-FLUID, LINEAGE, KINSHIP, PEDIGREE
accumulation in body .... CONGESTION
bad .... ANIMOSITY, ANGEL, ANTAGONISM
bath ... MASSACRE, PURGE
cancer .... LEUKEMIA
cell .... MONOCYTE
clot ..... GRUME, CRUOR, GORE
clot formation .... THROMBOSIS
clotted .... GORE
carrying .. SANGUIFEROUS
clotting remedy .... HISTONE
color ... RED, SANGUINE
colored .... HEMATIC
coloring matter .. CRUOR, HEMOGLOBIN
combining form .. HEMA, HEM(O), HEMATO, SANGUI, HEMAT, HAEMATO, HAEMO
condition ...... LITHEMIA
congestion .. HYPEREMIA
corpuscle ... MACROYTE, MICROCYTE
corpuscle structure ...... STROMA
coughing ... HEMOPTYSIS
covered/filled with ...... HEMATOSE, GORY
disease ...... LEUKEMIA
emulsion .... CHYLE
escaping from its vessel .. HEMORRHAGE
excess of ..... PLETHORA
feud .... VENDETTA
flow, stoppage of .. STASIS
flowing from wound .... CRUOR, GORE
fluid part of .... PLASMA
formation .... HEMATOSIS
from wound ...... GORE
having to do with ...... H(A)EMIC, H(A)EMAL
kin ..... GENS, RELATIVE
like .... HEMATOID, HEMOID

money . . . . CRO, WER(E)GILD
movement . . . . CIRCULATION
of gods . . . . ICHOR
of the . . . . HEMIC
oxygen-carrier . . . . HEMOGLOBIN
particles in . . CORPUSCLES
pertaining to . . . HEMATIC
poisoning . . SEPTICEMIA, PY(A)EMIA, SAPR(A)EMIA, SEPSIS, TOXEMIA, COPR(A)EMIA
pressure drug . . . . ADRENALIN, HISTAMINE
pressure hormone . . . . . . ADRENALIN
pressure instrument . . . . . MANOMETER
pudding . . . . SAUSAGE
red . . . . CRIMSON, SANGUINE
relation . . KIN, RELATIVE, FAMILY, SIB
shed from wound . . GORE
solvent . . . . LYSIN(E)
spitting . . . . HEMOPTYSIS
stream foreign matter . . . CLOT, (AIR)BUBBLE, EMBOLUS
study of . . . HEMATOLOGY
substance in . . . . OPSONIN
sucker . . . LEECH, VAMPIRE
sucking insect . . . . CONENOSE, TABANID, HORSEFLY, GADFLY, MOSQUITO, FLEA, LOUSE, BEDBUG
sucking monster . . LAMIA
thirsty one . . . . LEECH, VAMPIRE, LOMIA
transferred to another person . . . TRANSFUSION
vessel . . . AORTA, ARTERY, VEIN, CAPILLARY
vessel, dilated . . . . VARIX
vessel obstruction . . . . EMBOLISM
vessels network . . . . RETE
watery part of . . . SERUM, SERA
with reduced corpuscles . . AN(A)EMIA

bloodbath . . . . PURGE, MASSACRE
bloodcurdling . . . . FRIGHTFUL, TERRIBLE, HORRIFYING, DREADFUL
blooded . . . . . THOROUGHBRED
bloodhound . . . . SLEUTH, HUNTING DOG, MANHUNTER
bloodied . . . . GORY
bloodily . . . . SAVAGELY, CRUELLY
bloodless . . . PALE, AN(A)EMIC
bloodletting . . . . . LEECHING, BLEEDING, BLOODSHED
art of . . . . . PHLEBOTOMY
bloodline . . . . LINEAGE, PEDIGREE, DESCENT, ANCESTRY
bloodroot . . . . PUCCOON, POPPY, SANGUINARIA
bloodshed . . . . KILLING, SLAUGHTER, CARNAGE
much . . . . GORY
bloodshot . . . . RED
bloodstone . . . . . BIRTHSTONE, HELIOTROPE, HEMATITE
bloodsucker . . . . LEECH, TICK, MITE, VAMPIRE, EXTORTER, PARASITE, FLEA, DEERFLY
bloodthirsty . . . . CRUEL, MURDEROUS, PITILESS, SANGUINARY
bloody . . . . GORY, CRIMSON
Brit. slang . . . . . CURSED, DAMNED, VERY
bloom . . . . FLOWER, BLOSSOM, PRIME, FLOURISH
life's . . . . HEYDAY
bloomers . . . . TROUSERS
bloomery . . . FURNACE, FORGE, HEARTH
blooming . . . . THRIVING, FLOURISHING
colloquial . . . . UTTER, CONFOUNDED
too early . . . . RATH(E)
blossom . . . . . FLOWER, BLOOM, FLOURISH
blot . . . . STAIN, SPOT, DISGRACE, EXPUNGE, SULLY, MACKLE
in printing . . . . . MACKLE
out . . . . . ERASE, DELETE, DESTROY, WIPE OFF
blotch . . . . STAIN, SMEAR, MARK, MACULA, MOTTLE
blotter . . . . RECORD
usual keeper of . . POLICE
blotto: sl. . . . . DRUNK, UNCONSCIOUS
blouse . . . . MIDDY, WAIST
Korean silk . . . . . CHIMA
under pinafore . . GUIMPE
with tight waist . . BASQUE
blow . . . . . . SWAT, THUD, PUFF, STORM, SHOCK, BRAG, BUFF, BLAST, MISFORTUNE, WALLOP, HUFF
colloq. . . . SPEND, TREAT, FETE
dull-sounding . . . . . DUNT
for blow . . . TIT FOR TAT, RETALIATION
gently . . . . WAFT
horn . . . . TOOT
horn: colloq. . . . . . BRAG, BOAST
hot and cold . . . . WAVER, HESITATE, VACILLATE
in: colloq. . . . . . . ARRIVE
off . . . . . ERUPT, EXPLODE, TALK, RANT
off chaff . . . . WINNOW
on the head . . . NOB, CONK
on the knuckles . . . . . RAP
one's top off: colloq. . . . . EXPLODE, RAVE, RAGE
over . . . . PASS, COOL, DISSIPATE
resounding . . . . . WHACK
Scottish . . . BLAW, DEVEL
sharp and quick . . . CLIP
slang . . . . . SCRAM, LEAVE, FLEE
stormily . . . . . . BLUSTER
unexpected . . . . SNEAKPUNCH, BOLT
up . . . . EXPLODE, ENLARGE, INFLATE, ERUPT
whistle . . . TOOT, BLAST, SIREN
with club . . . . DRUB, CUDGEL
with fist: sl. . . POKE, PASTE

blower . . . . BELLOWS, FAN
blowgun . . . . SPRAYER, SUMPITAN
missile . . . . DART, PELLET
blowhole . . . . BREATHER, FLUE, SPIRACLE
of whale . . . . . . SPIRACLE
blowing mammal . . . . WHALE
blowoff: sl. . . . . BOASTER
blowout . . . . PARTY, BANQUET, CELEBRATION, TREAT, FEAST
one result of a . . FLAT TIRE
blowpipe . . . . BLOWGUN
blowup: colloq. . . . EXPLOSION, OUTBURST
blowy . . . . WINDY, GUSTY, BLUSTERY
blowzy . . . SLOVENLY, FROWZY
woman . . . . SLATTERN, SLUT
blubber . . . . CRY, WEEP, (WHALE)FAT
piece of . . . . LIPPER
strip . . . . FLENSE
blucher . . . (HALF)BOOT, SHOE
bludgeon . . . . . CLUB, COERCE, BULLY, CUDGEL, BAT
blue . . . . ANIL, COBALT, LIVID, GLOOMY, SAD, AZURE, PERSE, SMALT, CELESTE
back . . . . TROUT
bird . . . . JAY
blood . . . . . ARISTOCRAT, NOBLE, NOBILITY, ROYALTY, (SOCIAL)REGISTER
chip . . . . STOCK
chips: colloq. . . . . VALUABLE, EXCELLENT
combining form . . . CYAN
days . . . . MONDAYS
deep . . . . . ULTRAMARINE
devils . . . . DELIRIUM
dyestuff . . . . WOAD, INDIGO, ANIL
Eagle of New Deal . . NRA
fin . . . . . . TUNA, HERRING
flag . . . . IRIS, FLOWER
flower . . . . LARKSPUR
gas . . . . OZONE
grass . . . . POA
grayish . . . . SLATE, BICE, TEAL, PERSE, AZURINE
Grotto home . . . . . CAPRI
jeans . . . . . LEVIS, DENIMS
mineral . . . . IOLITE
Nile country . . ETHIOPIA
peacock . . . . PAON
pencil . . . . EDIT, CUT, CORRECT
pigment . . . BICE, SMALT

pill . . . . LAXATIVE
pointer shark . . . . . MAKO
print . . . . CYANOTYPE
racer . . . . SNAKE
river, so-called . . DANUBE
ribbon . . . . FIRST(PRIZE), AWARD, BADGE, DECORATION
shade . . . . . ALICE, AZURE
star . . . . VEGA
the . . . . SKY, SEA
wing teal . . . . GARGANEY
Bluebeard, latest . . . . LANDRU
Bluebeard's wife . . . . . FATIMA
bluebell . . . . HYACINTH, HAREBELL, COWSLIP
bluebonnet . . SCOTS(MAN), CAP, LUPINE
bluebottle . . . . BLOWFLY, FLY, CORNFLOWER
bly larva . . . . GENTLE
bluecap . . . . TITMOUSE
bluecoat . . . . POLICEMAN
bluegill . . . . SUNFISH
bluegrass State . . . . KENTUCKY
bluejack . . . . VITRIOL
bluejacket . . . . SOLDIER, SAILOR, ENLISTED MAN
bluenose: colloq. . . . . PURITAN, NOVA-SCOTIAN
bluepoint . . . . OYSTER
blueprint . . . . CYANOTYPE
blues . . . . DOLDRUMS, MEGRIM, DUMPS
bluestone . . . . VITRIOL
bluet . . . . INNOCENCE
blueweed . . . . BUGLOSS
blueprint . . . . . PLAN, OUTLINE
bluish gray . . . . CESIOUS, MERL(E), PEARL, SLATE, BICE
green . . . . . AQUAMARINE
red . . . . MALLOW
white metallic element . . . ZINC
bluff . . . . . . MISLEAD, BLUSTER, BLUNT, BRAVADO, BRUSQUE, SCARE, BAMBOOZLE, FOURFLUSH(ER)
in poker . . . . RAISE, COUNTER-RAISE
rounded . . . . MORRO
bluffer . . . FOURFLUSHER, LIAR, IMPOSTOR
bluing material . . . . . . INDIGO
bluish green . . . . AQUA
blunder . . . . STUMBLE, FLOUNDER, ERR(OR), MISTAKE, BUNGLE, SLIP, GAFFE
in social etiquette . . . . FAUX PAS, SOLECISM
stupid: sl. . . . . BONER
blunderbore . . . . OGRE
blunderbuss . . . . GUN
blunt . . . . CURT, TERSE, DULL, BLUFF, OBTUSE, BRUSQUE, OUTSPOKEN, GRUFF, OBTUND
arrow . . . . BUTTSHAFT
end . . . . CHUMP
end of hammer . . . . POLL
headed bullet . . . DUMDUM
refusal . . . . REBUFF

blur . . . . . . BLOT, STAIN, DIM, HAZE, MACULATE, MACKLE
on film/photo . . . . . . FOG
blurb . . . . ANNOUNCEMENT, AD(VERTISEMENT)
blurt . . . . BLABBER
blush . . . . REDDEN, FLUSH, COLOR
at first . . . . . . INITIALLY, OFFHAND
cause of . . DISCOMFITURE, EMBARRASSMENT, ANGER, SHAME
bluster . . . BULLY, THREATEN, STORM, RANT, BRAVADO
blustering . . . . SWASH
blustery . . . . . WINDY, GUSTY
blvd. . . . . BOULEVARD
bo: slang . . . HOBO, VAGRANT, TRAMP
tree . . . . PIPAL
boa . . . . ANACONDA, CONSTRICTOR, PYTHON, SCARF, SNAKE
ringed . . . . ABOMA
boar . . . . . HOG, PIG, BARROW, SUS, SWINE
flesh, picked . . . . . BRAWN
for example . . . . . TUSKER
tooth . . . . TUSK
board . . . . PLANT, TABLE, FOOD, COUNCIL, CLOSE UP, GET ON, PLANCH(E)
and lodging . . . . KEEP
artist's . . . . PALETTE
for holding mortar . . . . . . HAWK
from sugarcane residue . . CELOTEX
game . . . . DARTS, BACKGAMMON, PA(R)CHISI, CHECKERS, CHESS
member . . . . . . TRUSTEE, DIRECTOR, REGENT
boarding house . . . DORMITORY, DORM, PENSION
house lodger . . . . . GUEST
school pupil . . . . . . SCUM
boards, the . . . STAGE, THEATER
boarish . . . . SWINISH
boast . . . BRAG, VAUNT, CROW, GASCONADE
empty . . . . BLUFF
boaster . . . . BRAGGART, BRAGGADOCIO, BLOWOFF
of one's patriotism . . . . . JINGO
boastful . . . . THRASONICAL
air . . . . BRAVADO, SWAGGER
talk . . . . GASCONADE, BRAG, GAS, FANFARONADE
walk . . . STRUT, SWAGGER
boasting . . . . . BRAGGADOCIO, RODOMONTADE
boat . . . . STEAMER, WATERCRAFT, GIG, VESSEL, TUB, SHIP
African . . . . DHOW
American river . . . CANOE
ancient . . . . BIREME, TRIREME, CORACLE, GALLEY, GALLEON

awkward . . . . . DROGHER, ARK
basin . . . . MARINA
Bolivian . . . . BALSA
Canadian . . . . BATEAU
canoe-like . . . . . . PIROGUE
captain . . . . SKIPPER
captain of story . . . AHAB, NEMO, BLIGH
Ceylon/E. Indies . . DONI, DHONI, DINGEY
Chinese . . . . SAMPAN, JUNK
clumsy . . . . . TUB, HULK, ARK, DROGHER, HOOKER
dispatch . . . AVISO, OOLAK
Dutch Indies . . . PRAAM, HOOKER
Egyptian . . . . . . SANDAL, BARIS
English . . . . COBLE
Eskimo . . . . UMIAK, KAYAK, KYAK, OOMIAK, BIDARKA, BIDARKEE
ferry . . . . BAC
fishing . . . . DOGGER, TRAWLER, COBLE, CORACLE, SMACK, DORY
flatbottomed . . . . . DORY, PUNT, COBLE, BARGE, PONTOON, BATEU, KEEL
for gathering shellfish . . . DREDGER
freight . . . . WHERRY, LIGHTER, BARGE, SCOW, TRAMP
French . . . . . CARAVELLE
front . . PROW, FORE, BOW
helm . . . . TILLER
Indian . . DHOW, MASOOLA
Indian river . . . ALMADIA
Italian . . . . GONDOLA
landing . . . . LST
Levantine . . . . SAIC, XEBEC, BUM, KETCH
mail . . . . PACKET
Malayan . . . PROA, PRAU, PAHI, PRAO, PRAH, TOUP
marker . . . . BUOY
Mediterranean . . SET(T)EE
merchant . . . . ARGOSY
Netherlands . . . BILANDER
Nile river . . . . . . SANDAL
North Sea . . . . . . DOGGER
of classified words . . . . . . THESAURUS, DICTIONARY, GLOSSARY
old . . . . . HOOKER, HULK
on vessel . . . . JOLLY, PINNACE
on warship . . . . . DINGHY, LAUNCH
Philippine . . . . CASCO, BANCA, BATEL
pole-propelled . . . PUNT, CASCO, GONDOLA
propeller . . . . OAR, POLE, SCULL, PADDLE, POLE, SAIL
race . . . . REGATTA
racing . . . SCULL, SHELL, YACHT
raft . . . . CATAMARAN

rear end of .. AFT, STERN
river ... BARGE, WHERRY, SAMPAN, FERRY, PACKET, CANOE
row .... DINGHY, WHERRY, SKIFF, COBLE, SHELL
rudder ... TILLER, WHEEL
sail .... SKIFF, SMACK
scout .... VEDETTE, VIDETTE
shallow, small ... COCKLE
shaped ..... NAVICULAR, SCAPHOID
shaped ornament .... NEF
ship's ... PINNACE, YAWL
sink deliberately .... SCUTTLE
small ... DINGHY, DORY, SHALLOP, COG, SKIFF, COCKLE, JIGGER
slow .... DROGHER, BUCKET, ARK, TRAMP
steering part .... WHEEL, RUDDER, TILLER
tender .... HOY
tiller .... WHEEL, RUDDER
timber .... KEEL
towing .... TUG
three-oared ..... RANDAN
two-masted ... PIRAGUA, PIROGUE, DOGGER

boating ... ROWING, SAILING, CRUISING
boatman .... OARSMAN, POLER, GONDOLIER, PADDLER, VOYAGEUR
on styx .... CHARON
boats, small fleet of .. FLOTILLA
boatswain .... BOSUN
whistle .... PIPE
Boaz' son .... OBED
wife .... RUTH
bob .... RAP, CURTSY, PENDANT, HAIRCUT, FLOAT, SLED, DOCK, REFRAIN, SHILLING
bait .... DIB
British slang ... SHILLING
bobbery .... ROW, HUBBUB
bobbin ... REEL, SPOOL, PIRN, PIN
lace .... CLUNY
of weaver's shuttle .. PIRN
bobbins holder ...... SPINDLE, CREEL
bobby .... POLICEMAN
soxer: colloq. .... TEENAGER
station of a ...... POINT
bobcat .... LYNX, WILDCAT
bobolink .... ORTALAN, SONGBIRD, SORA, RICEBIRD
bobsled .... TOBOGGAN
bobwhite .... COLIN, PARTRIDGE, QUAIL
bocaccio ...... ROCKFISH, COD
bocca .... BERRY
Boccaccio's work .... DECAMERON
Boche .... GERMAN, SQUAREHEAD, HUN, JERRY

bock .... BEER
bode .... PRESAGE, OMEN, AUGUR, PORTEND
bodega: Sp. .... CELLAR, WAREHOUSE
bodice .... VEST, BASQUE, CHOLL, WAIST, CORSAGE
front piece .... JABOT
posy .... CORSAGE
bodily .... SOMATIC
bodkin .... HAIRPIN, NEEDLE, DAGGER, STILETTO, EYELETEER
body ... SOMA, TRUNK, TORSO, CORPSE, PERSON, CARCASS
animal .... SOMA
appetite .... LUST
beautiful, adjective for .. SEXY
coldness .... CHILL
combining form .... SOMAT(O)
dead .... CORSE, CORPSE, CADAVER, CARCASS
duct .... MEATUS
heavenly .... SUN, STAR, PLANET, MOON, COMET
injury .... TRAUMA
internal organs ... VITALS, INNARDS
joint ...... KNEE, ELBOW, WRIST
main .... TRUNK, TORSO
odor: colloq. .... BO
of advisers ..... CABINET
of assistants ...... STAFF
of horse .... BARREL
of laws .... CODE
of learning .... LORE
of men .... POSSE, ARMY, TROOP
of nobility ...... PEERAGE
of retainers ... RETINUE, ENTOURAGE, SUITE
of the .... SOMATIC, CORPOR(E)AL
of troops ..... COMPANY
of vertebra .... CENTRUM
of writing .... TEXT
opening .... FORAMEN
orbiting around planet .. SATELLITE
orbiting around sun ..... PLANET
pertaining to the .... CORPOREAL
plant .... SOMA
politic ..... WEAL, STATE
servant .... VALET
slang .... CHASSIS
trunk of .... TORSO
weakness ..... DEBILITY
bodyguard .... ESCORT, PROTECTOR
slang .... TORPEDO
Boeotia's capital ..... THEBES
Boer dialect .... TAAL
general .... BOTHA, HERTZOG
statesman ..... HERTZOG
War town besieged ..... MAFEKING
troops ...... COMMANDO

Boers' victim ...... MATABELE
bog .... QUAG, MIRE, FEN, MARSH, OOZE, QUAGMIRE, SWAMP, MUSKEG
orchid .... CALYPSO
peat .... MOSS
product .... PEAT
trotter .... IRISH(MAN)
bogey .... BUGABOO, BOGY, BUGBEAR, BOGIE, PAR
bogged down .... STALLED
boggle .... EQUIVOCATE, BUNGLE, BOTCH, SCRUPLE, HESITATE
boggy .... MIRY, SWAMPY, MARSHY, QUAGGY
tract .... MORASS
bogie: Brit. .... CART, TRUCK
bogus .... SPURIOUS, COUNTERFEIT, SHAM
bogy .... (HOB)GOBLIN, BUGBEAR, BOGIE, BUGABOO
bohea .... (BLACK) TEA
Bohemia .... CECHY
Bohemian .... GYPSY, ARTIST, DILETTANTE, ARTY
city ..... PRAHA, PILSEN
composer ...... MAHLER
dance .... TALIAN, POLKA, REDOWA
garnet .... PYROPE
general ... ZIZKA, ZISKA
Girl .... ARLINE
hotsprings site .... CARLSBAD, KARLSBAD
martyr .... HUS(s)
mountain .... ERZ
patron saint .... WENCESLAUS
reformer .... HUS(s)
river ... ISER, EGER, OHRE
town .... CARLSBAD
Bohr, physicist .... NIELS
boil .... SEETHE, CHURN, BUBBLE, SIMMER, STEW, ANGER, PUSTULE, STY, ANTHRAX, CARBUNCLE, FURUNCLE
eyelid .... STY
slow ..... SIMMER, STEW
boiled rice: Philippines .... KANIN
rice with meat, spiced .... PILAU
shirt: sl. ..... BRAGGART, POPINJAY
boiler .... COPPER, CA(U)LDRON
coating inside of .. SCALE
covering ..... LAG(GING)
safety device .... HYDROSTAT
tend .... STOKE
vent .... TUE
boiling point ...... HIGH-TEST
boisterous .... ROUGH, VIOLENT, TURBULENT, VOCIFEROUS, JINK(S)
bola: Span. .... BALL
bolar .... CLAYEY
bold ..... DARING, FEARLESS, FRESH, BRAVE, AUDACIOUS, PROMINENT

and resolute ..... HARDY
faced .... FORWARD, IMPUDENT, SAUCY, PERT
front .... BLUFF
girl .... TOMBOY, HOYDEN
bole ..... TRUNK, CLAY, TREE
bolero .... DANCE, VEST
composer of ...... RAVEL
boletus .... TOADSTOOL
bolide .... METEOR, FIREBALL
Bolivar .... COIN, (THE) LIBERATOR
Bolivian boat .... BALSA
capital .... LA PAZ
capital, nominal .. SUCRE
city .... ORURO
Indian .... URO, ITEN, AYMARA
lake .... POOPO
llama .... ALPACA
money ...... BOLIVIANO, TOMINE
mountain ...... POTOSI, SORATA, ILLAMPU
plains .... GRAND CHACO
river ..... BENI, MAMORE, MADEIRA, IVARI, PIRAY
seat of government ..... LA PAZ
boll .... POD, CAPSULE
weevil .... PICUDO, BEETLE
bollard ... COLT, HORSE, BEAM
bollix: sl. ... BUNGLE, BOTCH
bolo .... MACHETE, KNIFE
bologna .... SAUSAGE
slang .... BALONEY
Bolshevik ... LENIN, TROTSKY
secret police ...... OGPU, NKVD
bolster .... CUSHION, PAD, PILLOW, PROP, SUPPORT
bolt .... ARROW, COTTER, SHAFT, RIVET, PAWL, ROLL, LIGHTNING, ROD, DECAMP, DEFECT, RUN, PIN, PINTLE
fastener .... NUT
pivot .... PINTLE
turner .... SPANNER
bolter .... SIEVE, SIFTER, DEFECTOR, DESERTER, RUNAWAY
bolthead ..... FLASH, ALEMBIC
bolus ...... PILL, LUMP, MASS
boma .... BOA, PYTHON
bomb ...... MISSILE, ATTACK, EXPLOSIVE, GRENADE, ATOM, SHELL, TEAR
aerial: sl. .. BREADBASKET, EGG
defective .... DUD
kind of .... TEAR, INCENDIARY, ATOM, HYDROGEN, MOLOTOV
pit .... CRATER
powerful .. BLOCKBUSTER
shelter .... DUGOUT, ABRI, BUNKER
small .... GRENADE
sound on way ... WHINE, BUZZ
underwater .... DEPTHCHARGE, ASHCAN
bombard ..... SHELL, BATTER, STRAFE
bombardment ..... BARRAGE, DRUMFIRE, CANNONADE, SHELLFIRE
bombardon .... BASSOON, TUBA, ORGAN, OBOE
bombast .... RANT, BLUSTER, FUSTIAN
bombastic .... TURGID, POMPOUS, TUMID, FLOWERY, OROTUND, GRANDIOSE, FLAMBOYANT, PLETHORIC
style .... TUMID
Bombay city ... POONA, SURAT
native .... MARATHA, MAHRATTA
bomber .... AIR-RAIDER, LIBERATOR
approach of .... RUN
crewman ...... GUNNER, NAVIGATOR, BOMBARDIER
famed .... ENOLA GAY
German .... STUKA
gunner's place in .... TURRET
bombing, describing a kind of CARPET, SATURATION, STRATEGIC
raid starting place .... SHANGRI-LA
victim .... EVACUEE, REFUGEE
bombproof shelter .. CASEMATE, BUNKER, DUGOUT
bombshell, sort of .. SCANDAL, SENSATION
bombycid ... MOTH, EGGER, IO
bombyx ... ERI(A), SILKWORM
bon ami .... FRIEND
mot .... WITTICISM, QUIP, (APT)SAYING
vivant .... GOURMET, EPICURE, GOURMAND
bona fide .... AUTHENTIC, FEAL, GENUINE
fides .... HONESTY, GOOD FAITH
bonanza .... PROSPERITY, WINDFALL, MINE
Bonaparte .... EMPEROR, CORSICAN, NAPOLEON, LUCIEN, JEROME, LOUIS
bonbon ... CANDY, SUGARPLUM
bonbonniere ..... CANDYBOX
bond ..... TIE, VOW, PLEDGE, LINK, COVENANT, GUARANTEE, DUTY, AGREEMENT, SLAVE
marriage .... KNOT
part of .... COUPON
bondage .... SERFDOM, SLAVERY, SERVITUDE, YOKE
bondman ... SERF, ESNE, SLAVE, VASSAL, CHURL, CARL, VILLEIN
bondsman ... SURETY, SLAVE, ESNE, HELOT
bone .... OS, DICE, CUBE, SKULL, STERNUM, RIB, FEMUR, VERTEBRA, CLAVICLE, SCAPULA
ankle .... TARSUS
arched .... RIB
arm .... ULNA HUMERUS
break .... FRACTURE
breast .... STERNUM
canals, of .... HAVERSIAN
cavity ... ANTRUM, SINUS
change to .... OSSIFY
cheek .... MALAR
colloquial .... DICE
combining form .... OSTE(O)
decay .... CARIES, OSITE
disease ...... RACHITIS, RICKETS
ear ...... ANVIL, INCUS, TYMPANIC, HAMMER, STAPES
elevation, knoblike ..... TUBERCLE
face .... MAXILLA
finger .... PHALANGE
flat .... BLADE
forelimb ..... HUMERUS
formation .... OSTOSIS
growth on ..... EXOTOSIS
inflammation .. OSTEITIS
joint inflammation ...... ARTHRITIS
leg ..... FEMUR, PATELLA, TIBIA, FIBULA
like .... OSTEOID, OSSEOUS
marrow, of the .... MYELOID
of contention, literally ... WOMAN
of leg ..... FIBULA, TIBIA
of sorts .... FUNNY
of sternum ..... STERNAL
of thigh .... FEMUR
of wrist .... CARPUS, CARPAL(E)
opening .... FORAMEN
organic basis .... OSSEIN
pelvic .... ILIUM
pertaining to .... OSTEAL
sac between joints ...... BURSA
scraper .... XYSTER
skull .... PARIETAL, TEMPORAL, FRONTAL, MANDIBULA
small .... OSSICLE
spine .... SACRUM, VERTEBRA
tissue .... MARROW
turn into .... OSSIFY
U-shaped .... HYOID
boner ...... ERROR, BLUNDER, GOOF
bonehead ..... FOOL, NITWIT, DOLT
boneless fish/meat ... FIL(L)ET
bones .... OSSA, DICE
as in song .... DRY
combining form .... OSTE(O)
container for .. OSSUARY
boneset .... AGUEWEED
bonfire .... BALEFIRE
kind of .... CAMPFIRE

bongo ..... ANTELOPE, DRUM
bonhomie .... PLEASANT, AFFABLE, GOOD NATURE
boniface .... INNKEEPER, LANDLORD, HOST
Bonin Island ..... OGASAWARA
bonito .... FISH, MACKEREL
bonne .... MAIDSERVANT, NURSEMAID
foi: Fr. .... HONESTY
bonnet ..... CAP, HEADDRESS, HAT, POKE, HOOD
folding .... CALECHE, CALASH
projecting rim ..... BRIM
woman's .... CAPOTE
bonnie/bonny .... BEAUTIFUL, HANDSOME, PRETTY, FINE
bonnyclabber .... (CURDLED) MILK
bonus .... GIFT, BOUNTY, PREMIUM, DIVIDEND, TIP
bony ... SCLEROUS, SCRAGGY, ANGULAR, OSTEAL, THIN, EMACIATED, OSSEAN, OSSEOUS
part of nose ..... BRIDGE
plate/scale .... SCUTE
tissue inflammation ..... OSTEITIS
bonze .... MONK
boo .... HOOT, JEER, HISS
boob: sl. .. FOOL, IDIOT, DUNCE
booboo .... SNAFU
booby .... NITWIT
prize scores ...... LOWS
trap .... PITFALL
trap, lethal .... MINE
boodle .... CROWD, MOB, BRIBE, LOOT
boohoo ...... WEEP(ING), CRY
boojum .... SNARK
book .... PRIMER, TEXT, READER, REGISTER, RECORD, ENTER, SCHEDULE, TOME, ENGAGE, VOLUME, LIBER
about saints .. PASSIONAL
announcement ... BLURB
Bible ...... SCRIPTURES
back of .... SPINE
blank sheet of ... FLYLEAF
case for ... FOREL, FORRIL
circulating agency ...... LIBRARY
collection .. BIBLIOTHECA, LIBRARY
collector ... BIBLIOPHILE
combining form .. BIBLIO
cover fastener ..... HASP
division .... CHAPTER
end .... FINIS
first page ... FRONTISPIECE
foreign exchange .... CAMBIST
installment ..... FASCICLE
introduction ... ISAGOGE, PREFACE, FOREWORD
jacket ad .... BLURB
large ... TOME, VOLUME, FOLIO
leaf .... PAGE
leaf turned down .... DOG-EAR
left-hand page ... VERSO
lining .... DOUBLURE
make-up .... FORMAT, LAYOUT
map .... ATLAS
marginal comment ...... MARGENT
of account ..... LEDGER
of charts, etc...... ATLAS
of church service forms .. ORDINAL, ORDINARY
of devotions .... MISSAL
of feasts .... ORDO
of fiction .... NOVEL
of gospel .... MARK
of hours .... HORA(E)
of Jewish law ... TALMUD
of knowledge .... (EN)CYCLOPEDIA
of listings ... DIRECTORY
of loose leaves ... CAHIER
of nobility ..... PEERAGE
of psalms ... PSALTER(Y)
of public records .. LIBER
of rolled script ... SCROLL
of synonyms/antonyms .. THESAURUS
of stories of same author OMNIBUS
on nobles ..... PEERAGE
on plants .... HERBAL
on saints' lives .... HAGIOLOGY
on strange subjects ...... CURIOSA
operatic ...... LIBRETTO
page size ... DUODECIMO
palm .... TARA, TALIERA
paper cover ..... JACKET
part .... FLYLEAF, FRONTISPIECE, PREFACE, FOREWORD, GLOSSARY, CHAPTER, PAGE, JACKET, COVER
sampler .... BROWSER
school .... TEXT
section ..... LEAF, PAGE, CHAPTER
shape and size ... FORMAT
shelves, set of .... STACK
size .... QUARTO
technical description of .. COLLATION
the .... BIBLE
title page .. FRONTISPIECE
unbound .... PAMPHLET
boogie-woogie .... JAZZ
bookbinding ..... BIBLIOPEGY
material ...... BUCKRAM, SUPER, MOROCCO, VELLUM, SKIVER
style ... . GROLIER
bookie: sl. .... BET TAKER
booking .... ENGAGEMENT
bookish .... LITERARY, PEDANTIC, STODGY, SCHOLARLY, ERUDITE, LEARNED
bookkeeper .... ACCOUNTANT
book of .... LEDGER
mentor of ..... AUDITOR
bookkeeping book ... LEDGER
column ... DEBIT, CREDIT
item .... RENTAL, INTEREST, INCOME, DISBURSEMENTS, PROFIT, LOSS
booklet .... PAPERBACK, BANTAM, POCKETBOOK
unstitched ...... FOLDER
bookmaker ...... PUBLISHER, COMPILER
slang .... BOOKIE
bookmakers collectively .. RING
bookplate .... EX LIBRIS
books .... LIBRI
collection of .... LIBRARY
bookseller .... BIBLIOPOLE, STATIONER
catalogue of .... BIBLIOTHECA
bookselling ...... BIBLIOPOLY
bookstall .... NEWS-STAND
bookstore reading .. BROWSING
boom .... RESOUND, SPAR, SPRIT, JIB, BARRIER, ROAR, FLOURISH, PROSPERITY, BOOST, GROW
Boomer State ..... OKLAHOMA
boomerang .... KILEY, KYLIE
in a way ...... REBOUND, RICOCHET, KICKBACK, BACKFIRE
boon ..... BLESSING, BENEFIT, FAVOR, REQUEST, MERRY, PLEASANT, GAY, BENE
boondocks ..... WILDERNESS, HINTERLAND
Boone, ____ .... PAT, DANIEL
boor ...... OAF, LOUT, CHURL, CLOD, CLOWN, PLEASANT, TYKE, CHUFF
boorish .... RUDE, AWKWARD, UNCOUTH, ILL-MANNERED
boost: colloq. ...... PUSH UP, LIFT, RAISE, INCREASE
booster .. SHOPLIFTER, ROOTER
boot ..... BUSKIN, GALOSH(E), STOGIE, STOG(E)Y, KICK, DISMISS, RECRUIT, PAC(K), BROGAN
Eskimo .... KAMIK
kind of .... ZIPPER
named after German fieldmarshal .. BLUCHER
of Europe, so-called ..... ITALY
part of .... VAMP
slang ...... DISCHARGE, DISMISS
to .... BESIDES, IN ADDITION
brightest star .. ARCTURUS
Bootes .... HERDSMAN
bootblack .... SHOESHINER
booth .... STALL, SHED, KIOSK(O), STAND
Oriental market ... SOOK
bootlace .... LACET
tip .... AGLET

bootleg .... SMUGGLE
whisky maker ....
MOONSHINER
bootlegger ..... MOONSHINER, SMUGGLER, RUMRUNNER
bootlegger's ware ..... ALKY, POTEEN, MOONSHINE, WHISKY
bootless ... HOPELESS, USELESS, VAIN, FUTILE
bootlick .... FLATTER, FAWN, PANDER
bootlicker ... YESMAN, TOADY, SYCOPHANT
boots .... SHOES
and saddles .. BUGLE CALL
high, waterproof ....
WADERS
booty .... LOOT, PRIZE, SPOILS, SWAG, PELF
booze ..... LIQUOR, WHISKY, DRINK
bop .... JAZZ
slang .... BLOW, STRIKE, PUNCH
borax .... TINCAL, FLUX
Bordeaux ..... CLARET, WIND
bordel(lo) .... BROTHEL
border ..... EDGE, SIDE, RIM, FRONTIER, FRINGE, BRIM, BRINK, RAND, LIMBUS, MARGE
customs gate ... BARRIER
design .... GUILLOCHE
land is dispute ... MARCH
on .... ABUT
on stamps ..... TRESSURE
raise and ridge .... MILL
river ..... YALU, MEKONG
wall .... DADO
bordered .... FLANKED, HEMMED
borderland disputed .. MARCH
borderline .... INDEFINITE, DOUBTFUL
bore ... TIRE, DRILL, WEARY, HOLE, CALIBER, EAGRE, WAVE, ENDURED
gun ... GAUGE, CALIBER, CALIBRE, CHASE
mine shaft ..... TREPAN
river .... EAGRE
slang .... DRAG
boreal .... NORTHERN, NORTHWIND
bored .... BLASE, FED UP
boredelaise .... SAUCE
boredom ..... ENNUI, TEDIUM
sign of .... YAWN
borele .... RHINO(CEROS)
borer ... AWL, AUGER, GIMLET, DRILL, BEETLE
Borge's (Victor) forte .. PIANO
Borges' (Jorge) forte ....
BESTIARY
Borgia, ____ .... CESARE, LUCREZIA
boric acid salts ...... BORATE
boring ... TIRESOME, TEDIOUS, DULL
tool .... AWL, DRILL, AUGER, WIMBLE, GIMLET, JUMPER
borings .... CHIPS
born .... NEE
being .... NASCENT
borne .... CARRIED
Borneo .... KALIMANTAN
apartment ... LONGHOUSE
ape .... ORANG
burrowing animal ....
TELEDU
capital .... BRUNEI
hornbill .... KENYALANG
mountain .... KINABALU
native .... DYAK
pepper plant .... ARA
port .... MIRI, JESSELTON
squirrel .... PENTAIL
tribe ..... DAYAK, IBAN, KAYAN, KENYAH, DELABIT, MELANAUS
Borodin's prince .... IGOR
boron and one other element ...
BORIDE
borough .... BURG, TOWN
citizen .... BURGESS
borrow .... BRACE
bort ..... DIAMOND, ABRASIVE
borzoi .... DOG, WOLFHOUND
bos(s) .... BEEF, COW
bosc .... PEAR
boscage .... GROVE, SHRUBBERY, THICKET
bosh: colloq. ..... NONSENSE, ROT
bosk .... GROVE, THICKET
bos's'n .... BOATSWAIN
bosom ..... BREAST, INTIMATE, MIDST
Bosporus rowboat .... CAIQUE
boss ...... MASTER, SACHEM, FOREMAN, EMPLOYER, CHIEF, KNOB, STUD
on shield .... UMBO
bossy .... DOMINEERING, STUDDED
Boston ... CARD GAME, WALTZ
basketball team .. CELTICS
Brahmin .... SNOB
city near .... MALDEN
name ... CABOT, FILENE, LOWELL
symbol of ..... CODFISH
Bostonian .... HUBBITE
bosun .... BOATSWAIN
bot(t) .... LARVA, MAGGOT
botanical angle .... AXIL
sac .... THECA
botanist ..... MENDEL, BROWN
botany .... PHYTOLOGY
botch ... FLUB, BUNGLE, FAIL, MESS, SPOIL, GOOF, MUFF, FUMBLE, LOUSE(UP)
both .... TOGETHER, EQUALLY, ALIKE
prefix .... AMBI
bother .... ANNOY, WORRY, MOLEST, TROUBLE, PESTER, FUSS, ADO, AIL
Bothnia .... ALAND
botryose .... RACEMOSE
bottle .... VIAL, PHIAL, CARAFE, DECANTER, CARBOY, COSTREL, FLASK, CRUET, FLAGON, MAGNUM
containing garden ......
TERRARIUM
earthenware ... DEMIJOHN
for acids .... CARBOY
for condiments .. CASTER, CRUET
for liquids ..... CARBOY
hit the .... BOOZE
indentation at bottom ...
KICK
medicine .... TENREC
perfume .... FLACON
shaped vessel .... FLASK
stopper .... CORK
top .... CAP, CROWN
two-quart ..... MAGNUM
vinegar .... CRUET
water .... CARAFE, DECANTER
bottleneck .... HINDRANCE, SNAG
bottlenose .... PORPOISE, DOLPHIN
bottom ..... BED, BASE, ROOT, SHIP, SOURCE, LOWEST, LAST
colloquial ..... BUTTOCKS
of ship .... KEEL
bottomless .... ABYSMAL
pit/gulf ... ABYSS, HELL, UNDERWORLD, ABADDON
bottoms .... HOLM
boudoir .... BOWER, DRESSING ROOM
bouffant ...... PUFFED, FULL
bouffe .... COMIC OPERA
bough ... BRANCH, TWIG, LIMB
of tree .... RAMAGE
boughpot .... JARDINIERE, BOUQUET, BOWPOT
bougie .... WAX, CANDLE
boullabaisse .... CHOWDER, SOUP
bouillon .... BROTH, CUBE
Boulder Dam designer ....
SAVAGE
boulevard ... STREET, AVENUE, CONCOURSE, PROMENADE
Boumedienne, Algerian president ..... HOUARI
bounce ...... BUMP, THUMP, BOUND, EXPEL, DISMISS, SPRING, JUMP, REBOUND, DASH, SPIRIT
British ..... IMPUDENCE, BLUSTER
on water surface .... DAD
slang ..... SPIRIT, DASH, DISMISS
bouncing ... LUSTY, HEALTHY, BUXOM, BIG
bound .... LEAP, SWORN, PLEDGED, JUMP, TIED, DESTINED, OBLIGED, HEADED
horse's .. VAULT, CURVET
boundaries, mark off ....
DEMARCATE
boundary .... BORDER, BUTTING, VERGE, LIMIT, METE, MERE, LINE, AMBIT
common .. CONTERMINAL, CONTERMINOUS

combining form .... ORI
outer .... PERIMETER
bounden .... OBLIGATORY, INDEBTED, OBLIGED
bounder .... CAD, BOOR, SCOUNDREL
Bounding Main .. (OPEN)SEA, OCEAN
boundless .... VAST, INFINITE, UNLIMITED
bounds .. AMBIT, SCOPE, LIMITS
out of ..... OFF LIMITS, PROHIBITED
bounteous .... GENEROUS, ABUNDANT, PLENTIFUL, AMPLE
bounty .... BONUS, TIP, REWARD, PREMIUM, ALLOWANCE, GENEROSITY, LARGESSE
bouquet .... CORSAGE, AROMA, SPRAY, FRAGRANCE, NOSEGAY, ODOR, SCENT, POSY
Bourbon ...... REACTIONARY, REUNION, WHISKY
bourg .... TOWN, VILLAGE
bourgeois ...... SHOPKEEPER, MIDDLECLASS, SMUG RESPECTABLE, COMMONPLACE
bourgeoisie ..... CAPITALISTS, MIDDLECLASS
bourn(e) ..... BROOK, STREAM, DOMAIN, GOAL, OBJECTIVE
bourse .... (STOCK)EXCHANGE
bouse .... LIQUOR, BOOZE, HOIST, DRINK, CAROUSE
boutique .... STORE, SHOP
Bovary, Mme. .... EMMA
bovid .... OX, CATTLE, SHEEP, GOAT, ANTELOPE
bovine .... OX, SLOW, STOLID, PATIENT, BULL, TAURINE, CATTLE, COW
Asiatic .... YAK
Celebes .... ANOA
male .... BULL, STEER
tuberculosis ..... GRAPE
bow .... STOOP, SUBMIT, CURVE, NOD, YIELD
and arrow art .. ARCHERY
maker .... BOWYER
of eyeglasses .... BRIDGE
of ship ..... PROW, FORE
of woman's dress .... BUSTLE
of wood .... YEW
Oriental .... SALAAM
ornamental/ribbon ..... KNOT
shaped .... ARCUATE
bowdlerize ..... EXPURGATE, PURIFY
bowed .... ARCHED, BENT, SURRENDERED
bowel .... INTESTINE, GUT, ENTRAIL, INTERIOR, COLON
movement stimulant .... CATHARTIC, LAXATIVE
pains .... GRIPES
bowels .... GUTS
clearer .... LAXATIVE, PURGATIVE, CATHARTIC
purge of ...... CATHARSIS
bower ...... ARBOR, RETREAT, COTTAGE, ANCHOR, ALCOVE, PERGOLA
bowery ... FARM, PLANTATION, LEAFY
"Bowery Boys" member ...... GORCEY
bowfin .... MUDFISH, AMIA, DOGFISH, GANOID
bowhead .... WHALE
bowie .... HUNTING KNIFE
bowl .... STADIUM, CUP, ROLL, DISH, BASIN, CRATER
drinking .... MAZER, MAZARD
flower .... JARDINIERE
for pounding substance .. MORTAR
name of U.S. athletic .... ORANGE, SUGAR, SUN, ROSE, COTTON, TANGERINE
over .... OVERWHELM, ASTONISH, STAGGER
punch .... MONTEITH
sound ...... BOOLA, RAH, BOO, YELL, CHEERS
toilet .... CLOACA
bowleg ...... VARUS, TALIPES
bowler .... DERBY, KEGLER
bowling .... TENPINS, DUCKPINS
alley .... LANE
alley track ..... RUNWAY
center mark ...... JACK
first-ball target .. KINGPIN
game division .... FRAME
green .... RINK
seven/ten pins .... CORNERS
term .... SPARE, STRIKE, BREAK
widest split .. GOALPOSTS
bowls .... TENPINS, NINEPINS, SKITTLES
bowman ... ARCHER, OARSMAN
bowse .... DRINK
bowstring .... CORD, GARROTE
sound .... TWANG
bowwow .... BARK
box ... CASE, BIN, SPAR, CHEST, CARTON, CUFF, BIFF
cash ..... REGISTER, TILL
fish .... KENCH
for fodder .... CRIB
for money .... KIST
for relics ..... RELIQUARY
for tea, etc. ... CANISTER
like sleigh .... PUNG
of explosives ... CAISSON
office receipts: colloq. ... TAKE
office window ... WICKET
score item ... RUNS, HITS, ERRORS
seat .... LOGE
small .... CASKET
specimen coins .. PYX, PIX
strong .... SAFE
tea ... CANISTER, CADDY
tool .... KIT, CHEST
boxcar, in dice ..... TWELVE, CRAP
boxer .... PUG(ILIST), PRIZEFIGHTER, DOG, RINGSTER
colloquial .. MITTSLINGER, BEAKBUSTER, BRUISER, PUG, MAULER
boxer's arm length ... REACH
hands: colloq. .... MITTS
savior, sometimes .. GONG
second .... HANDLER
trade mark .... CAULIFLOWER EARS
trainer .... HANDLER
boxing bouts collectively ..... CARD
champion ... CLAY, BAER, CARNERA, DEMPSEY, LOUIS, TUNNEY, WILLARD, VILLA, WALCOTT, ORTIZ, CORBETT, HARADA, COKES, GRIFFITH, SCHMELING
decision ... DRAW, TKO, KO, NO CONTEST
glove .... CESTUS
match ..... SETTO, BOUT, GO, FISTICUFFS
of .... FISTIC
official .... REF(EREE)
period .... ROUND
pertaining to ..... FISTIC
pre-bout need .. WEIGH-IN
promoter .... (TEX) RICHARD
science of .... FISTICUFFS
wrestling contest .... PANCRATIUM
boxwood ..... SERON, SHRUB, TREE
boy .... LAD, YOUTH, MAN-CHILD, YOUNGSTER, STRIPLING, SPRIG, TAD, NIPPER, GOSOON
age of .... PUBERTY
assistant .... JACK
attendant .... PAGE
colloquial .... BUB, SON(NY), SHAVER, KID, BUSTER
friend: colloq. ..... BEAU, LOVER, SWEETHEART ESCORT
Scottish ..... GALLAN(T)
Boy Scout assembly .... JAMBOREE, CAMPOREE
daily object .. GOOD TURN
founder .. BADEN-POWELL
gathering .... JAMBOREE, CAMPOREE
group .... TROOP, PATROL, DEN, PACK
hiking gear .. HAVERSACK
motto ..... BE PREPARED
new .... TENDERFOOT
popular image of ...... DO-GOODER
boycott, in a way .. OSTRACIZE, STRIKE
Boz, pseudonym ..... DICKENS
BPOE .... ELKS
bra .... BRASSIERE
Brabant's capital ... BRUSSELS
princess .... ELSA

brabble .... QUARREL, SQUABBLE, CHATTER
brace ... BIND, TIGHTEN, PROP, STIMULATE, BIT, PAIR, COUPLE, FASTENER, BITSTOCK, SPLINT
bracelet ... ARMIL, WRISTLET, BAND, CHAIN, BANGLE, HANDCUFF
bracer ... STIMULANT, TONIC, DRINK
braces .... GALLUSES
Brit. slang .. SUSPENDERS
brachial .... ARMLIKE
brachyuran .... CRAB, CRUSTACEAN
bracing .... INVIGORATING, REFRESHING
bracken .... BRAKE, FERN
bracket ... CONSOLE, CORBEL, CLASSIFICATION, GROUP, ANCON
brackish ...... SALTY, BRINY, NAUSEOUS
bract .. GLUME, SPATHE, PALEA
cluster .... COMA
grass .... GLUME
brad ..... (WIRE)NAIL, SPRIG
brae: Scot. ... BANK, HILLSIDE
brag .... BOAST(ER), BRAGGART, VAUNT, GASCONADE, CROW
braggadocio ...... BRAGGART, BOASTING
braggart .... BOASTER, BRAGGER
slang .... BLOW
Bragi's parent .. ODIN, FRIGGA
Brahma ... CREATOR, CATTLE, FOWL
Brahman bull .... ZEBU
rule .... SUTRA, SUTTA
title .... AYA
wiseman .... PUNDIT
Brahmin: Hindu ..... PRIEST
braid ... TRESS, BAND, PLAIT, QUEUE, LACET, PLAT
decoration ..... CORDON
of gold thread .. GALLOON
trimming ..... RICKRACK, GALLOON, SOUTACHE
zigzag .... RICKRACK
braided material ..... SENNIT
brain .... MIND, INTELLECT
action ..... CEREBRATION, COGITATION
canal .... ITER
child: colloq. ..... IDEA, PLAN
colloquial .. GRAY MATTER
covering .... MATER
disease .... PARESIS, APHASIA, KURU
fever ..... ENCEPHALITIS
"food" .... FISH
groove .... SULCUS
layer of gray matter ..... CORTEX
membrane .. PIA(MATER), DURA(MATER), ARACHNOID, EPENDYMA
of the .... CEREBRAL, CEREBRIC
opening .... PYLA
part .... CEREBRUM, CEREBELLUM, MEDULLA
passage .... ITER
pertaining to the .... CEREBRAL
ridge ..... HIPPOCAMPUS
storm: colloq. .... (BRIGHT) IDEA, INSPIRATION, PLAN, CEREBRATION
structure of nerve fibers .. FORNIS
surgery ...... LOBOTOMY
tissue .... TELA
truster: sl. ..... EGGHEAD, ADVISER, EXPERT
tumor .... GLIOMA
brainless ... STUPID, FOOLISH, IDIOTIC
brainpan ... CRANIUM, SKULL
brains .... INTELLIGENCE, INTELLECT
colloquial/slang .... MASTERMIND, IDEAMAN, KNOWHOW
brainwash ..... INDOCTRINATE
brainy .... INTELLIGENT, SHARP, SMART, WISE, INTELLECTUAL
brake .... FERN, BRACKEN, KNEADER, HARROW, SLOWDOWN, CLUMP, THICKET, CURB
for woman's tongue ..... BRANKS
part .... SHOE
Bram Stoker's thriller .... DRACULA
bramble .... RASPBERRY, DEWBERRY, BLACKBERRY, SHRUB, BRIER
brambling .... FINCH
brambly ... PRICKLY, THORNY
bran .... HUSK, SKIN
meal, etc., mixture ...... MASH
branch ... BOUGH, TWIG, LIMB, BROOK, RIVULET, OFFSHOOT, DIVISION, RAMIFY, ARM, RAMUS, FURCATE, SPRIG, FURCATION
angle .... AXIL
in biology .... RAMUS
like .... RAMOUS
of family .... STIRPS
of learning ...... ART(S), SCIENCE, DISCIPLINE, OLOGY
off ...... FORK, DIVERGE
railroad ... SPUR, SIDING
trim .... LOP
branched ... RAMOSE, RAMOUS, RAMIFORM
branches, bearing many ...... RAMOSE
branchiae .... GILLS
branching ..... ARBORESCENT
brand ... MARK, STIGMA(TIZE), LABEL, TRADEMARK, STAMP, SEAR, DISGRACE
goose .... BRANT
new .... UNUSED, FRESH
brandish ...... WAVE, SHAKE, FOURISH, SWING
brandling ... WORM, FISHBAIT
brandy ...... MARK, COGNAC, AQUA VITAE
and soda .... PEG
cordial .... ROSOLIO
branks .... BIT, BRIDLE
brant .... GOOSE
brantail ..... REDSTART, BIRD
brash .... RASH, HASTY, BRITTLE, INSOLENT, FRAGILE, IMPUDENT, SHOWER, PYROSIS
Brasilia is capital of ... BRAZIL
designer of ... NIEMEYER
brass .... METAL, ALLOY
as imitation gold .... ORMOLU
colloquial ... IMPUDENCE
color .... AENEOUS
combining form .... CHALCO
knuckles ... BLACKJACK
like alloy .... LATTEN
mythical man of ... TALOS
plate, kind of .... CYMBAL
slang .... MONEY
tacks .... FACTS, PARTICULARS
brassard ... CABBAGE, TURNIP, BROCCOLI, COLE
brassica .... CABBAGE, TURNIP, BROCCOLI, COLE
brassie, for example .... GULF CLUB
brassiere ... BANDEAU, UPLIFT
slang .... FALSY
brassworker .... BRASIER
brassy .... IMPUDENT, LOUD, INSOLENT, SHOWY, BOLD
brat ...... IMP, CHILD, RAG, CLOTH, BANTLING
brattice .... PARAPET, BREASTWORK
brattle ..... RATTLE, CLATTER, SCAMPER
brave ... COURAGEOUS, BOLD, PLUCKY, VALIANT, MANLY, HEROIC, DEFY, STOUT
front, usually .... BLUFF
Indian .... WARRIOR
bravery .... VALOR
bravo .... WELL DONE, EXCELLENT, OLE, VERY GOOD, ASSASSIN, DESPERADO, CHEER, EUGE
bravado ..... BLUSTER, BLUFF
bravura ... DASH, TECHNIQUE, BRILLIANCE
braw .... FINE, EXCELLENT
brawl .... MELEE, FRAY, RIOT, ROW, FREE-FOR-ALL, UPROAR, BROIL, FRACAS
brawler .... HECTOR HOOLIGAN, HOODLUM
brawn .... MUSCLE(S), STRENGTH
colloquial .... BEEF
brawny .... MUSCULAR, STRONG, STRAPPING
bray ..... HEEHAW, GUFFAW, LAUGH, TRITURATE,

SPREAD, CRUSH, POUND
brayer, in printing .... ROLLER
braze .... SOLDER
brazen ..... IMPUDENT, BOLD, SHAMELESS, HARSH
brazier and grill ..... HIBACHI
Brazilian aborigine ... CARIB, ANDOA, AMIRANHA
armadillo .... TATOUAY, TATU
bird ...... ARA, AGAMI, SERIEMA, JABIRU
"Black Pearl" ..... PELE
capital .... BRASILIA
capital, former ...... RIO
cape .... FRIO
city ...... RIO, CUYABA, MACEIO, MANAOS, BELEM, PARA, CEARA, FORTALEZA
coin .... CENTAVO, MOIDORE, (MIL)REI
crested bird .... SERIEMA
dance .... SAMBA
drink .... ASSAI
estate .... PAZENDA
estuary .... PARA
fiber .... IMBE
footballer .... PELE, TOSTAO
forest ... MATTA, MATTO
heron .... SOCO
holly .... MATE
Indian ... ARARA, CARIB, TUPI, GUANA, ZAPARO, MURA, PURU, ACROA, TAPUYAN
ipecac .... EVEA
island .... MARAJO
killers .... JAGUNCOS
long-legged bird .... SERIEMA
macaw .... ARARA
measure, dry ..... MOIO
measure, liquid .... PIPA
medicinal plant .... AYAPANA
money .... (MIL)REI, CONTO, CRUZEIRO
mountain ... CORCOVADO
nut ..... PARA, COQUILLA
orchid .... DICHEA
palm .... ASSAI, PIAS(S)AVA, BABASSU, JUPATI, CARNAUBA
parrot .... ARA(RA), MACAW, TIRBA
plant .... MANIHOT, MANIOC
port ...... RECIFE, PARA, BELEM, NATAL, PELOTAS, BAHIA, CEARA
quartz .... CACO
river ..... APA, JAPURA, JAVARY, MADEIRA, TAPAJOZ, PARA, PUTUMAYO, ARAGUAYA, IGUASSU, PARNARIBA, PARANA, JAVARI, JURUA, ICA, ACARA, ACAMEA
rubber tree ... ULE, HULE, SERINGA
seaport ... NATAL, SANTOS
state ... CEARA, PARANA, PARA, BAHIA
stork .... JABIRU
tapir .... ANTA
tea plant .... MATE
title of respect ..... DOM
tree .... APA, ANDA, MURURE, ARAROBA
tree bark ...... PEREIRA
tree powder .... ARAROBA
waterfall ...... IGUASSU
weight ... ONCA, ARROBA
wood .... BRASIL, SATINE
breach ..... GAP, RIFT, BREAK, HERNIA, RUPTURE, BREAKTHROUGH, OPENING
of etiquette ... SOLECISM, FAUX PAS, IMPROPRIETY
of the peace ...... RIOT, BRAWL
of relations .... RENT
of trust .... BETRAYAL
bread ... LOAF, GLUTEN, FOOD, PONE, RUSK, CRUST, AZYM, MUFFIN, BROTCHEN
and-butter .. LIVELIHOOD, YOUTHFUL, COMMONPLACE, EVERYDAY
and-butter letter .... GRACENOTE
blessed ... EULOGIA, HOST
boiled and flavored ..... CUSH, PANADA
break .... EAT, DINE
crisp coating .... CRUST, RIND
from heaven ..... MANNA
dough .... SPONGE
Eucharist .... HOST
garnish .... SIPPET
hard .... HARDTACK
Hebrew .... AZYM
in one baking ... BATCH
ingredient .... FLOUR, YEAST, LEAVEN
maker .... BAKER
part ..... CRUST, CRUMB, RIND
roll .... BAGEL
St. John's .... CAROB
soaked in beef broth ..... BREWIS
soaked in milk ..... SOP
soaked in soup/gravy ... SIPPET
spread .... OLEO, MARGARINE, BUTTER, JAM, JELLY
sweet, raised ...... RUSK
toasted/fried ..... SIPPET
white .... MANCHET
unleavened ... HARDTACK
breadbasket ...... GRANARY
slang ... BELLY, STOMACH, (AERIAL)BOMB
breadfruit .... RIMA(S)
like tree .... JACK
breadwinner: colloq. .. DADDY, PAPA, EARNER
break ..... GAP, C(A)ESURA, PAUSE, HIATUS, BUST, SNAP, RUPTURE, SMASH, CRACK, SHATTER, DEMOTE, RUIN, FRACTURE, SURPASS, DISCLOSE, QUARREL
away .... ESCAPE, SEPARATE, BOLT
colloquial ...... ESCAPE
down .... ANALYZE, ITEMIZE, CRUSH, DEMOLISH, GIVE WAY
from habit .... WEAN
in .... TRAIN, INTERRUPT, INTRUDE, ENTER
in rock strata .... FAULT
in the dike .... CREVASSE
into parts ..... DIFFRACT
of day .... DAWN, MORN, DAYBREAK
off ..... STOP, SEPARATE, SEVER
off connection ... SECEDE
out ...... ERUPT, ESCAPE
moral principle ..... SIN
popular to workers ...... COFFEE, REST
religious law .... SIN
through .... PIERCE
thru eggshell .... PIP
up .... DISPERSE, SEPARATE
up marriage .... DIVORCE
breakable .... BRITTLE, FRAGILE
breakbone fever ..... DENGUE
breakdown .... COLLAPSE, FAILURE, CRACKUP
breaker .... WAVE, KEG, COMBER, EAGRE
breakers .... SURF
breakfast and lunch .. BRUNCH
food .... OATMEAL, CEREAL, FARINA
last .... DEJEUNER
nook .... ALCOVE
breaking of waves .... BREACH
breakneck .. FAST, DANGEROUS
breakthrough .... BREACH, INFILTRATION
breakup .... COLLAPSE, DISPERSION, SEPARATION, END, STOPPAGE, DISBAND(MENT)
breakwater ...... MOLE, PIER, JETTY, DIKE, BULWARK
bream ..... SPAROID, PORGY, CHAD, SUNFISH, ABRAMIS
Japanese .... TAI
breast .... BOSOM, BUST, CHEST, OPPOSE, PETTO
animal's .... BRISKET
feed ..... SUCKLE, NURSE
inflammation .. MASTITIS
meat cut .... BRISKET
of the .... PECTORAL
plate .... CUIRASS
shaped .... MASTOID
surgical removal of ..... MASTECTOMY
breastbone .... STERNUM
flat .... RATITE
of the .... STERNAL
breastpin .... BROOCH
breastplate .... URIM, PLASTRON, (A)EGIS

breastwork .... REDOUBT, BARRICADE, BARRIER, BRATTICE
breath ... ODOR, WHIFF, PUFF, LIFE, AIR, WHISPER, HALITUS, RESPIRATION, MOMENT
asthmatic ...... WHEEZE
bad .... HALITOSIS
catch one's .... GASP, PANT, PAUSE, GULP
forced noisily .... SNORT
odorous ..... HALITOSIS
of life .... PNEUMA
of wind .... FLATUS
out of .... WINDED
save one's ..... SHUT UP, STOP, REST
sweetener .... LOZENGE, CACHOU
taking ...... THRILLING, EXCITING
whistling .... WHEEZE
breathe .... INHALE, EXHALE, MURMUR, RESPIRE, BLOW
hard ...... PANT, HEAVE, GASP
in .... SUCK, INHALE
noisily .... HAZZLE, HASSEL, SNORE
one's last .... DIE
out .... EXHALE, SUSPIRE
out noisily .... SNORT, SNORE
tentatively, as it were .... SNIFF
with whistling sound .... WHEEZE
breather .. NOSE, NARES, GILL
of fish .... GILL
of whale ... BLOWHOLE, SPIRACLE
slang ..... REST, PAUSE, BREAK
breathing ...... RESPIRATION, LIVING, ALIVE
abnormal .... HYPERPNEA
device ..... RESPIRATOR
device, under water ..... SNORKEL
difficult .... DYSPNEA, DYSPNOEA
harsh ..... RALE, SNORE
hole ..... SPIRACLE, NOSE
rapid .... HYPERPNEA
smooth .... LENE
sound ..... RALE, SNORE, STRIDOR, RHONEUS
space: colloq. .... ROOM, REST, RESPITE
breathless ... DEAD, GASPING, PANTING, STIFLING
bree: Scot. .... BROTH
breech ...... BUTTOCKS, RUMP
loading rifle .. CHASSEPOT
breechblock signature, ballistics .... IDENTIFICATION
breechcloth ..... LOIN(CLOTH)
Polynesian .... MALO
breechclout .... G-STRING
breeches .... TROUSERS, TRUNKS, SLOPS
riding .... JODHPURS
Scot. .... TREWS
too big for one's .... SWELL-HEAD(ED), PROUD, OVERBEARING
breed .... HATCH, RAISE, ORIGINATE, REPRODUCE, RACE, STOCK, KIND, REAR
cattle .... DEVON
breeding ...... UPBRINGING, REARING
place ...... NIDUS, NEST, STUD FARM, ROOKERY
breeze .... GENTLE WIND, AIR, ZEPHYR
colloquial .. COMMOTION, DISTURBANCE
refreshing ...... CALLER
slight .... BREATH, ZEPHYR
water rippling .... CAT'S PAW
breezing horse in a race ...... EASY WINNER
breezy .... LIVELY, CAREFREE, BRISK, AIRY
Bremen's river .... WESER
Brenner ____ .... PASS
Breslau river ..... OSAR, ODER
Breton .... CELT
breve .... BILLET, ORDER, WRIT, LETTER
brevet .... COMMISSION
breviary ... PORTAS, COMPEND
brevity .... BRIEFNESS, CONCISENESS, TERSENESS, SHORTNESS
is the soul of ____ .. WIT
of expression .. LACONISM
brew .. ALE, BEER, TEA, PUNCH, PLOT, CONCOCT, LAGER
brewer's ferment ..... LOB(B)
grain .... BARLEY
tub .... KEEVE
yeast .... BARM
vat .... TUN
brewery .... DISTILLERY
refuse ...... LEES, DREGS, DRAFF
brewing, one .... GYLE
brewis .... (BEEF)BROTH, BREAD
Briareus, what it had many of HANDS
bribe ... SOP, BOODLE, SUBORN
collector ...... BAGMAN
money .... SLUSH(FUND), BOODLE
slang .... SQUARE, GREASE, PAYOLA
bric-a-brac ... KNICKKNACK, CURIO, BIBELOT, VIRTU
brick ..... BLOCK, NOG, TILE, (A)DOBE
burned partly ..... BAT, BUR(R), CLINKER
carrier .... HOD
colloquial .. FINE FELLOW
compressed coal dust .... BRIQUET
cracked .... CHUFF
hard .... CLINKER
making material .. MARL, PUG
masonry ..... NOGGING
pile .... HACK
refuse .... SAMEL
sun dried .... ADOBE
trough for .... HOD
worker .... MASON
bricklayer .... MASON
helper of .... HODMAN
tool of .... TROWEL
bricks, pile of .... HACK
brickwork .... MASONRY
bricole .... CATAPULT
bridal ... WEDDING, MARITAL
path .... AISLE
wreath ... SPIREA, SHRUB
Bridalveil .... WATERFALL
bride .... BETROTHED
in needle-work .... LOOP, TIE
bridesmaid ...... PARANYMPH
bridewell .. GAOL, JAIL, PRISON
bridge .... SPAN, PONTOON, BAILEY, CARD GAME, CANTILEVER, VIADUCT, RIALTO
bid .... SLAM
builder .... EADS
calls .... BIDS
card game ..... AUCTION, CONTRACT
card game position ..... NORTH, EAST, SOUTH, WEST
declaration .... BID
defeat .... SET
expert .... GOREN
floating ...... PONTOON
game series ..... RUBBER
hand without trumps .... CHICANE
holding .... TENACE
Midgard to Asgard ...... BIFROST
move/maneuver .. FINESSE
"no game" .... NIL
of bow instrument ...... PONTICELLO
of musical instrument ... MAGAS
over gorge, etc... VIADUCT
part .... TRESTLE, SPAN, GIRDER, WALK
pathway ..... CATWALK
railroad .... TRESTLE
support .... TRUSS, GIRDER, ABUTMENT, PIER, PONTOON
term ... SLAM, GOBY, BID, PASS, TENACE, BOOK, RUFF, NIL
to Paradise .... ALSIRAT
tricks .... BOOK
type .... BASCULE, DRAW, SUSPENSION
bridle .... HARNESS, RESTRAIN, CURB, REIN
part ... HEADSTALL, BIT, REINS, NOSE BAND
wise animal ..... HORSE
brief ... SHORT, TERSE, CURT, PITHY, CONCISE, SUMMARY
biography .... VITA

case .... BAG, PORTFOLIO
in expression .. LACONIC, TERSE, BLUNT, CURT
in law .... BREVE
note .... JOT, MEMO
sleep .... NAP, DOZE, SNOOZE
summary ..... EPITOME, RESUME, GIST, FILL-IN
telegraphic message ..... FLASH
time .... MOMENT, SECOND, FLASH
briefly .... IN SUM, IN SHORT, MOMENTARILY
briefs .... UNDERSHORTS
brier ... BUSH, BRAMBLE, PIPE, HEATH, THORN
briery ..... PRICKLY, THORNY, SPINY
brig .... SHIP, PRISON, GUARDHOUSE
brigade need .... BUCKET
brigadier general, rank below .. COLONEL
brigand ..... BANDIT, PIRATE, HIGHWAYMAN, LADRONE
bright .... SHINING, CHEERFUL, LIVELY, QUICK, CLEVER, LUSTROUS, LUMINOUS, SMART, RELUCENT, ROSY, ROSEATE
and cheerful .... SUNNY
colored bird ... TANAGER, ORIOLE
colored fish ...... OPAH, WRASSE, CATALINA
combining form .. HELI(O)
idea: colloq. .... BRAINSTORM, INSPIRATION, BRAINCHILD
saying .... BON MOT, WITTICISM
star .... NOVA
youngster ..... PRODIGY
youngster: slang .... WHIZ KID
Bright's disease .... NEPHRITIS
brighten .... GLADDEN, CHEER(UP), FURBISH, POLISH
brightness .... LUMINOSITY, SHEEN, LUSTER, RADIANCE, GLOSS
brill .... FLATFISH, TURBOT
brilliance .... SPLENDOR, GLITTER, ECLAT
brilliant .... VIVID, PRISMATIC, GAY, EMINENT, TALENTED, GEM, MAGNIFICENT
array .... GALAXY
facet of .... CULET
gathering .... SALON
stroke/strategem ... COUP
tennis stroke .... ACE
brim ... EDGE, RIM, BRINK, LIP
of bonnet .... POKE
of cap .... BILL
brimless cap ...... TAM, FEZ, BIRETTA, BARRET, BERET
brimmer .... BUMPER
brimming ... FULL, SUFFUSED
brimstone .... SULPHUR, SULFUR
brindled .... TABBY
brine ..... SEA, OCEAN, TEARS, SALT WATER, SOUSE
shrimp .... ARTEMIA
to salt residue ... BITTERN
bring .... FETCH, PRESENT
about ..... ACCOMPLISH, CAUSE
around ..... CONVINCE, PERSUADE
back ... RETURN, RESTORE
down .... LOWER
foot down ...... STAMP
forth .... ENGENDER, EAN, PRODUCE, SPAWN
forth young ..... HATCH, YEAN, WHELP
forward .... SHOW, INTRODUCE, CARRY OVER
home the bacon: colloq... WIN, EARN
in ...... IMPORT, ARREST, CAPTURE
in as price .... FETCH
into court ..... ARRAIGN, SUE, HALE
on oneself .... INCUR
out .... REVEAL, EXPOSE, DISPLAY, PUBLISH, INTRODUCE
to .... REVIVE
to bay .... TREE, CORNER
to bear .... EXERT, PRESS
to completion .. FINALIZE, FINISH
to light .... UNEARTH, DISCLOSE, REVEAL
to mind .... REMIND, RECALL, REMEMBER, RECOLLECT
to naught .... UNDO, NULLIFY, DESTROY, RUIN
to standstill .. STALEMATE, STALL
together ..... ASSEMBLE, GATHER, AMASS
up .... REAR, INTRODUCE, BROACH
up the ___ .... REAR
upon oneself ..... INCUR
bringer of bad luck ..... JINX
bringing to central point ...... AFFERENT
brink .... EDGE, VERGE
brinkmanship, exponent of .... DULLES
briny .... SALTY
deep .... SEA, OCEAN
brio .... ANIMATION, ZEST, VIVACITY
brioche .... ROLL
briquet .... BRICK
brisk ... LIVELY, ZIPPY, SHARP, SPRY, ACTIVE, ENERGETIC
in music .... ALLEGRO
brisket ... BREAST, MEAT CUT
brisling .... SPRAT, FISH, SARDINE
bristle ..... HAIR, TRICHOME, STIFFEN, SETA, CHAETA
combining form ... SETI
hooked .... BARB
like growth .... AWN, ARISTA, BARBEL, SETA
pertaining to ..... SETAL
ruffed animal ..... BOAR
shaped .... SETIFORM
surgical .... SETON
bristles, covered with .. HISPID
having .... SETOSE, STRIGOSE, SETACEOUS
tuft of .... PAPPUS
bristletail ...... THYSANURAN
bristling ..... ECHINATE, IRATE
bristly ..... HORRENT, HAIRY, HIRSUTE, SHAGGY, SETOSE, HISPID, PRICKLY, SCOPATE, ACICULAR
animal ...... PORCUPINE, HOG, BOAR
Bristol paper ..... PASTEBOARD
Britain ... BRITANNIA, ALBION
ancients ... PICT, SILURES
mythical king ..... BRAN, BRUT
part of .... WALES, ENGLAND, SCOTLAND
B'rith, ___ .... BNAI
British .... BRITON, ENGLISH, BLIGHTY, SAXON, LIMEY
ache .... STOUND
active .... NIPPY
actor ... OLIVIER, EVANS, MARSHALL, AHERNE, RATHBONE, ARLISS, COWARD, GRANGER
actress .... NEAGLE, GARSON, KERR, OBERON, GWYN, ANDREWS
admiral .... BEATTY, NELSON
airforce .... RAF
ale .... NOG(G)
altogether .... JOLLY
anger .... WAX
apartment house .... MANSION
architect ... ADAM, WREN, SCOTT
armor bearer .... SQUIRE, ARMIGER
army bugle call .... POST
army fur hat ..... BUSBY
army staff officer: sl. ..... BRASSHAT
assurer ... UNDERWRITER
author ..... MEE, MORE, ARLEN, SHUTE, CAINE, BACON, LANDOR, ROGET, WAUGH, OPIE, AUSTEN, DEFOE, ELIOT, READE, BARRIE, BELLOC, MILNE, STERNE, DORAN
authoress ...... BRONTE, AUSTEN, ELIOT, WAUGH
baby carriage ..... PRAM
baby hood ..... BIGGIN
bagman ...... SALESMAN
bailiff ... REEVE, STEWARD
ballerina ..... FONTEYN
bar .... PUB
bard, ancient ...... SCOP
barge .... WHERRY

baseball-like game ...... ROUNDERS
basket .... CORF
bathe .... TUB
beak .... MAGISTRATE, SCHOOLMASTER
bed .... DOSS
beer .... SWIPES
bit .... SPOT
blackbird ...... THRUSH
boat, ancient .. CORACLE
boatman .... BARGEE
boon on the aristocracy .. BRETT'S
borough .... BURGH, LEEDS
bottoms .... HOLM
boy .... NIPPER
boys' school ...... ETON, RUGBY
brandy soda .... PEG
bread .... MANCHET
bulrush .... CATTAIL
bunk .... DOSS
buttercup ... CROWTREE
buttocks: sl. ...... BUM
canal laborer .... NAVVY
captain's boat ... GALLEY
car name .... ROVER, AUSTIN
carbine .... STEN
card game .... PATIENCE
card sharp .... BLACKLEG
carol singer ...... WAIT
cascade .... LADORE
cash: sl. .... RHINO
cask .... KILDERKIN
cat-boat .... UNA
cathedral city ...... ELY, YORK, TRURO
cavalry ...... YEOMANRY
certainly .... RATHER
channel .... SOLENT
Channel isle .... WIGHT
Channel, river to .. SEINE, RANCE, ORNE, SOMME
chap .... COVE
chase .... CHEVY
chemist ...... FARADAY
chief, ancient .... PENDRAGON
cheese .... STILTON
china .... SPODE
cigarette: sl. .... GASPER
circuit court ...... EYRE
city .... COVENTRY, LEEDS, BATH, LONDON, MANCHESTER, DOVER, HASTINGS, YORK, ELY
clown .... GRIMALDI
cluster .... PLUMP
coachman ...... JARVEY
coal carrier .... CORF
coin ... GEORGE, SOVRAN, SOV(EREIGN), GUINEA, PENNY, FARTHING, PENCE, SHILLING
coin, old ..... CAROLUS, GROAT, ANGEL
college ... ETON, BALLIOL
college servant ..... GYP
college steward .... MANCIPLE
colonial official .... PROCONSUL
Columbia capital .... VICTORIA
Columbia Indian .. HAIDA
comedian .... TOOLE
composer .... ARNE, ELGAR, DELIUS, COATES
conductor .... BEECHAM, BARBIROLI, SARGENT
conservative party .. TORY
coronation rite .... UNCTION
country festival ..... ALE
country gentleman ...... SQUIRE
county ..... CORNWALL SHIRE, SUSSEX, DORSET, ESSEX, WILTS, SURREY, HANTS, KENT, YORK, OXON, DERBY, BUCKS
courage .... PECKER
court ...... LEET, EYRE, SOC, HUSTINGS
cow .... RUNT
crazy .... POTTY
crook .... BLACKLEG
crow .... BRAN
crown jewel .. KOHINOOR, KOHINUR
cue ball .... MASSE
dance, ancient ... MORRIS
dandy .... TOFF, (BEAU)BRUMMEL
dealer .... MONGER
derby hat ...... BOWLER
dessert .... FLAN
diarist ... EVELYN, PEPYS, BURNEY
diplomat .. EDEN, LLOYD
divine ..... INGE, DONNE
dramatist .. SHAW, READE, PINERO, TOBIN, PEELE, SITWELL, MARLOWE
drunk: sl. ..... SCREWED
dump truck ..... TIPPER
dupe .... MUGGINS
dynasty .. STUART, TUDOR
early conqueror .. HORSA, HENGIST, NORMANS
elevator .... LIFT
emblem .... ROSE
emperor of India .... PADISHAU
entry .... CLOSE
essayist ...... LAMB, ELIA
estuary .... HUMBER
exam for honors .. TRIPOS
explorer ... SCOTT, ROSS, STANLEY, CABOT, HUDSON, RALEIGH, STEELE, LANG, BAFFIN, BURTON, FROBISHER
expression .... ISAY, BULLY, CHEERIO
fashion model .. TWIGGY
fell ... MOOR, HILL, DOWN
fellow .... COVE
field marshal ..... HAIG
field marshal at Arlington .... DILL
financier ...... GRESHAM, RHODES
first overlord ... EGBERT
fishing boat ..... COBLE, HOOKER
flashlight .... TORCH
food .... TUCK
fool .... MUGGINS
foolish ...... SPOON(E)Y
forest .... ARDEN, SHERWOOD
fox hunter .... PINK
franchise .... SOC
free tenant ...... DRENG
freeman .... THANE, CHURL, CEORL
gambler who cheats ..... BLACKLEG
gasoline .... PETROL
general ...... BRADDOCK
geologist .... LYELL
good-by .... PIPPIP
good time .... BASH
government .. WHITEHALL
grove .... SPINNEY
Guiana's capital .... GEORGETOWN
gum .... DEXTRIN
gumshoe: sl. .... TEC
gun ...... ENFIELD, STEN
hackney driver .. JARVEY
hamlet .... DORP
handball .... FIVES
handbook on peers ...... BRETT'S
hare .... PUSS
hawker .... CHAPMAN
hayfork .... PIKEL
head .... CONK
headland .... NAZE
hedgerow .... REW
highball .... STINGER
highwayman .... TURPIN
historian .... BEDE, ACTON, GIBBON, GROTE
holm .... BOTTOMS
Honduras' capital/seaport BELIZE
hooligan .... SPIV
horse .... PRAD, GARRON, SCREW
horse dealer ..... COPER
house-dress ... OVERALL
humorist .... STERNE
hunt .... CHEVY
hunting cry ...... CHEVY, YOICKS
hunting dog ... LURCHER
hut .... NISSEN
hymnodist ...... NEALE, LYTE
ID mark .. BROAD ARROW
India emperor .... PADISHAH
India, founder of ... IVAN
Indian coin .... ANNA
Indian monetary unit ... RUPEE, ANNA
Indian nursemaid ...... AYAH, AMAH
Indian province ... SIND, ASSAM
informer ..... NARK, SPY, NOSE
innkeeper ..... PUBLICAN

island in Atlantic .... ASCENSION
island in Indian Ocean ... MAURITIUS
island near Borneo ...... LABUAN
isle ... ELY, MAN, IRELAND
king ... EDWARD, GEORGE, JAMES, HAL, HAROLD
king, ancient .... A(E)THELSTAN
king, legendary ... BRUT, KNUT, ARTHUR, LUD, CANUTE, BELI, BRAN
labor strike(r) .... TURN-OUT
laborer ... PROLE, NAVVY
landowner ...... SQUIRE, THANE
language, ancient .... CYMRIC
lecturer .... READER
legislator .... COMMONER
legislature .. PARLIAMENT
lexicographer .. FOWLER, GOWERS
liberal party ...... WHIG
loan money .... PREST
lodgings .... DIGS
lunch .... TIFFIN
machine-gun ..... BREN
mail .... POST
malt liquor ..... PORTER
marine: sl. .... JOLLY
mark on gov't property .. BROAD ARROW
martyr .... ALBAN
meal .... (HIGH) TEA
measure .... ELL
measure, former ... INCH
measure, liquid .... KILDERKIN
mendicant order .. FRIARS
merry-making .... RANT
military police .. REDCAP
military school .... SANDHURST
mine wagon .... ROLLEY, CORF
minister of state ... PITT, PEEL, WALPOLE
mint box .... PYX
miser .... SCREW
model .... TWIGGY
molasses .... TREACLE
money ...... STERLING, POUND, PENCE, SHILLING, FARTHING
money advanced to enlisted men .... PREST
money: sl. .... RHINO
monk .... B(A)EDA
monk historian .... BEDE
mop .... MALKIN
murderer .... ARAM
naturalist ...... SLOANE
navigator .... DRAKE
navy enlisted man .... BLUEJACKET
nimble .... NIPPY
noble ...... DUKE, EARL, LORD, BARON, PRINCE, VISCOUNT
nonsense! ...... HAVERS
North America .. CANADA
novelist .. READE, RAMEE, ARTHUR, CRONIN, CAINE, MACHEN, BRONTE, HUXLEY, STERNE, DICKENS
nurse .... SISTER
oak .... ROBUR
oatmeal pudding .. MUSH
odd .... RUM
officer's servant .. BATMAN
orator ... PITT, WILLIAM, BURKE
order .... GARTER
ore carrier .... CORF
outcry of blame .. DIRDUM
outlet .... POINT
ox .... RUNT
Pacific protectorate ..... TONGA
pain .... STOUND
painter .... ORPEN, TURNER, CONSTABLE, ROMNEY, PAYNTER, OPIE
parish official .. OVERSEER
parliament member ..... BURGESS
parliamentary record .... HANSARD
party ..... TORY, WHIG, LABOR
passageway ..... SMOOT, CLOSE
path .... PAD
patron saint .. (ST)GEORGE
peddler .... CHAPMAN
people, ancient ... ICENI
petrol ... GAS, GASOLINE
petty .... POTTY
philosopher .... RUSSELL, BACON, HUME, JOAD, SPENCER
physician .... ROSS
physicist .... FARADAY
pianist .... BAUER
pickpocket .... PRIG
playwright .... SHAW, PEELE
pluck .... PECKER
pocket .... SACK
poet .... AUDEN, HUGH, GRAY, KEATS, SPENCER, BLAKE, MASEFIELD, AUSTIN, BYRON, SITWELL, DONNE, ELIOT, LANG
poet, earliest .. CAEDMON, SCOP
poet laureate .... MASEFIELD, CIBBER, AUSTIN, DAY-LEWIS
poetess .... SITWELL, BROWNING
policeman ...... BOBBY, PEELER
policeman's station ..... POINT
political party ..... TORY, CONSERVATIVE, LABOR
political philosopher .... BURKE
Pope .... ADRIAN(IV)
port ..... HULL, DOVER, POOLE, LIVERPOOL, PRESTON, COWES, BRISTOL
pot herb .... CLARY
pottery/porcelain .. SPODE
prefab shelter ... NISSEN
prig .. THIEF, PICKPOCKET
prime minister .. WILSON, ASQUITH, CHURCHILL, PITT, BALDWIN, PEEL, ATTLEE, BALFOUR, HOME, LAW, MACMILLAN, CANNING
prime minister called Ironside .... PITT
prime minister with the cigar ..... CHURCHILL
prime minister with the umbrella .... CHAMBERLAIN
prince .... ANDREW, CHARLES
princess ..... MARGARET, ANNE, URSULA
printer .... CAXTON
prison ..... DARTMOOR, LEADS
printing tyre ...... RUBY
prison: sl. ... QUOD, QUAD
property tax ...... RATE
psychologist ...... ELLIS
publisher .. BEAVERBROOK
pudding .... MUSH, ROLY-POLY
pupil: sl. .... SCUM
Quaker .... PENN
queen .... ANNE, MARY, ELIZABETH, VICTORIA
queen, ancient .... BOADICEA
queer .... RUM
quick .... NIPPY
race course ...... ASCOT, EPSOM(DOWNS)
RAF fighter .. SPITFIRE
rage .... WAX
raincoat ... WATERPROOF
range ...... KITCHENER
ratable .... TAXABLE
Reformation leader ..... SEYMOUR
reformer .... SPENCE
resort ...... BLACKPOOL, BATH, MARGATE
retail store .. WAREHOUSE
river .... AVON, MERSEY, THAMES, ALN, CAM, WYE, EXE, URE, OUSE, TEES, AIRE, TEE, TRENT, TYNE, USK, NENE, NEN, SEVERN, DEE, YARE
river lowland .. BOTTOMS, HOLM
road .... PAD
rock singer .... (MICK) JAGGER
routine .... ROTA
royal family ..... TUDOR, STUART
royal guard officer .. EXON
royal house ..... TUDOR, YORK, HANOVER, WINDSOR, STUART
royal household official .. GROOM
royal stables ...... MEWS

rubbish! .... HAVERS
ruler, early .. EGBERT, OFFA
ruling family .. WINDSOR, TUDOR
sailor .... LIMEY
saint .... ALBAN, AARON
salary .... SCREW
salesman ...... BAGMAN
saloon-keeper .. PUBLICAN
sandhill .... DENE
scarecrow ...... MALKIN
school boy servant .. FAG
school, prep ...... ETON, HARROW, RUGBY
school teacher ... MASTER, MISTRESS
schoolmaster .... ARAM, BEAK
scientist .... DARWIN
seaman .... RATING
seaport .... BOOTLE, DOVER, MARGATE, GRIMSBY, WHITBY
sedan .... SALOON
sentimental ...... SOPPY
serf ...... ESNE, THRALL
sergeant-at-law cap ..... BIGGIN
sheriff's aid ... BULLDOG
sidewalk artist .... SCREEVER
silly .... SPOON(E)Y
slaughterhouse .... KNACKER
sleep: sl. .... DOSS
smart .... STOUND
smack .... HOOKER
smock ...... OVERALL
snarl .... GIRN
social event ...... ASCOT
socialist .... FABIAN
soldier .. REDCOAT, LIMEY, TOMMY, ATKINS
soldier's furlough/leave .. BLIGHTY
solitaire .... PATIENCE
songbird .... BULBUL, BULLFINCH
spa ..... BATH, MARGATE
spark .... SPUNK
spot .... BIT
spy .. ANDRE, NOSE, NARK
stage .... PLATEAU
statesman .. PITT, BURKE, GREY, HOARE, EDEN, CLIVE
steal .... PRIG
stool pigeon: sl. .... NARK
stove .... KITCHENER
strange .... RUM
streetcar .... TRAM
student, senior .... PREPOS(I)TOR
surgeon .... LISTER
swell dresser .... TOFF
symbol .... (JOHN) BULL
tax ... SESS, GELD, EXCISE
tea .... ELM
tent .... MARQUEE
thanks .... TAS
theologian ..... ALCUIN
theorist .... LASKI
thicket .... SPINNEY
thief .... PRIG
tin mine ..... STANNARY
title ..... DUKE, PRINCE, BARON, EARL
toast .... CHEERS
tobacco bit ...... SCREW
tourist .... TRIPPER
trader .... MONGER
traveler .... TRIPPER
trout .... SEWIN, SEWEN
truck .... LORRY
tutor .... MASTER
25 pounds: sl. ..... PONY
unit of measure ... STACK
university disciplinarian .. BULLDOG
university official .... BEADLE
university student .... SOPHISTER
very .... JOLLY
village ... BOURG, ARAWE, DORP
wage earner ..... PROLE
waiter .... POTMAN
warrior .... CNUT
Wave .... WREN
weight ..... STONE, MAST, KEEL
weight for wool ..... TOD
whisky-soda .... STINGER
willow herb ... ROSEBAY
with the umbrella ...... CHAMBERLAIN
woman politician .... (LADY) ASTOR
woman servant .. SLAVEY
woman, slovenly .... MALKIN
wood pigeon ... CULVER
woodland area ... WEALD
work horse ..... GARRAN
World War I commander HAIG
wrap .... RUG

Briton, early ... ANGLE, JUTE, PICT, CELT, ICENI
Brittany .... BRETAGNE, ARMORICA
brittle ...... CRISP, FRAGILE, CRACKLY, BRASH
Brno name ..... (JOSIP) TITO
bro. .... BROTHER
broach ..... BRING UP, AWL, CHISEL, RIMER, HOLE, REAMER, SPIT, SKEWER, INTRODUCE
broad ...... WIDE, SPACIOUS, EXTENSIVE, GENERAL, CLEAR
band: heraldry ..... FESS
slang .... WOMAN
broadbill ...... SCAUP, DUCK, SPOONBILL, GAPER, RAYA
broadbrim: colloq. .... FRIEND, QUAKER, HAT
broadcast .. SPREAD, SCATTER TELECAST, SOW
broadcasting system ..... NBC, CBS, ABC
broadcloth .... PIMA
broaden .... WIDEN, EXPAND, SPREAD
broadleaf .... TOBACCO
broadminded ..... TOLERANT, LIBERAL, UNDERSTANDING
broadside ..... ABUSE, SALVO, ATTACK
broadsword ..... CLAYMORE, CUTLASS, BILL, GLA(I)VE
broadtail ... SHEEP, KARAKUL, ASTRAKHAN
Broadway character ... ANGEL, SUGAR DADDY, PRESS AGENT, HOOFER
girls, former .... FLORADORA
impresario .... MERRICK
(nick)name .... FLO ZIEGFELD, COHAN, BILLY ROSE
restaurateur ..... SARDI
square .... HERALD
venture ... PLAY, REVUE, MUSICAL(E)
Brobdingnagian ..... GIANT, GIGANTIC
brocade .... BALDACHIN, BAUDEKIN, BROCHE
gold .... KINCOB
Japanese .... NISHIKI
broccoli .... CAULIFLOWER
brochette .... SKEWER
brochure .... PAMPHLET
brock .... BADGER
brocket .... DEER, PITA, SPITTER
brogan ... BROGUE, BOOT, SHOE
brogue .... ACCENT, PRONUNCIATION, SHOE
Scotch .... TRICK, DECEPTION
broil ..... ROAST, BARBECUE, BRAWL, GRILL, BAKE, BRAISE
broiled meat ...... BARBECUE
broiler ..... CHICKEN, CAPON, PAN, GRIDIRON
broke: sl. .... PENNILESS, BANKRUPT
broken ... TAMED, SPLINTERED, VIOLATED, INTERRUPTED, SMASHED
colloquial .... DISMISSED
down ... RUINED, USELESS, CHATTERED, DECREPIT
grain husk .... BRAN
ice .... BRASH
mass of clouds .... RACK
piece .... FRAGMENT
pieces of pottery .... SHARDS
pieces of masonry .... RUBBLE
spike of grain .... CHOB
stone debris .... RUBBLE
wind .... HEAVES
broker ..... AGENT, FACTOR, MIDDLEMAN
business of .... AGIOTAGE
order to ..... BUY, SELL, UNLOAD
real estate ..... REALTOR
brokerage .... AGIO
fee .... BROKAGE
Brom Bones' lack ...... HEAD
broma .... COCOA
bromide .... SEDATIVE, PLATITUDE, SOP
bromine .... HALOGEN

bronchial tube ..... TRACHEA, WINDPIPE
bronchitis remedy .... GRINDELIA
bronc(h)o ..... HORSE, PONY, MUSTANG
buster .. COWBOY, TAMER
Bronte biographer ..... GERIN
brother ...... BRANWELL
family's native village ... HAWORTH
husband of Charlotte .... NICHOLLS
pseudonym of Anne ..... ACTON BELL
pseudonym of Charlotte CURRER BELL
pseudonym of Emily .... ELLIS BELL
work .... JANE EYRE, WUTHERING HEIGHTS
bronto as combining form ..... THUNDER, HUGENESS
brontosaurus ...... DINOSAUR
Bronx ... BOROUGH, COCKTAIL
cheerer's feeling .... DERISION, DISGUST, SCORN
bronze .... ALLOY, TAN, COPPER, AENEOUS, LATTEN
coating/crust of .. PATINA
coin .... AES
component ..... COPPER (AND) TIN
"gold" .... ORMOLU, VERMEIL
green coating ..... VERD, PATINA VERDIGRIS, ANTIQUE
Roman .... AES
tool .... CELT
broo: Scot. ..... BROTH, BREE
brooch ... PIN, OUCH, CLASP, CLIP, CAMEO
brood .... MOPE, THINK, COGITATE, HATCH, PONDER, SULK, HOVER, SIT, FLOCK
of birds .... COVEY
of chicks .... CLUTCH
of family .... CHILDREN
of eaglets .... AERIE
of goats/sheep ... FLOCK
of pheasants ...... NIDE
of sucks/pigs ..... TEAM
brooder ...... HEN, WORRIER
brooding hen's sound .. CLUCK, CACKLE
brook .... STREAM, BEAR, RILL(ET), RIVULET, RUNNEL, ENDURE, GILL
brooklime .... VERONICA
Brooklyn Dodgers' nickname SUPERBAS
institute .... PRATT
island .... CONEY
brookweed ...... PIMPERNEL
broom .... BRUSH, SWEEP, SHRUB, BESOM, CLEANER, WHISK
grass/material .. ZACATON
plant .... BESOM
broomcorn grain ...... HIRSE
broth ...... SOUP, CONSOMME, POTAGE, BROO, BREE, GRUEL
cabbage/greens ... KALE
brothel .... BORDEL(LO), BAGNIO, WASTE, KIP, BAWDYHOUSE
keeper .... BAWD, PROCURESS, MADAM
brother .... FRA, FRIAR, FRATER, PEER, FELLOW, MONK
colloquial ... BROD, BUB
brotherhood .... ELKS, SODALITY, ORDER, FRATERNITY, ASSOCIATION, UNION
brotherly .... FRATERNAL
brougham .... CARRIAGE, AUTOMOBILE, LIMOUSINE
brought up ... BRED, REARED, BROACHED, INTRODUCED
by hand .... CADE
brouhaha .... UPROAR, COMMOTION, HUBBUB, STIR
brow ...... FOREHEAD, BRAE, EYEBROW, EDGE
browbeat ... BULLY, INTIMATE, BAMBOOZLE, HECTOR
brown ... TAN, SEPIA, UMBER, BISTER, RUSSET, SORREL, SIENNA, TOAST, ROAST, DUN, BEIGE
actress .... VANESSA
apple .... RUSSET
betty ... (APPLE)PUDDING
coal .... LIGNITE
dark .... BURNET
kiwi .... ROA
light .... PONGEE
paper .... KRAFT
pigment .... BISTER, BISTRE, UMBER
reddish .... AUBURN
seaweed .... KELP
Shirt ... NAZI, HITLERITE
shoes .... TANS
skinned people .... MALAY(IANS), FILIPINOS, INDONS
study .... REVERIE
thrasher ..... SONGBIRD
yellow .... PABLO
brownie .... ELF, GOBLIN, GIRL SCOUT, CAKE, GNOME, NIS, PIXIE, KOBOLD, CAMERA
Browning's home in Italy ..... ASOLO
brownish .... DUN
purple .... PUCE
red .... TERRA-COTTA, RUFOUS, MAROON
yellow .... TAWNY, BUFF
brownout .. DIMOUT, DIMMING
brownstone front ..... STOOP, FACADE
sign ..... ROOMS, TO LET
browntail .... MOTH
browse .... NIBBLE, GRAZE, FEED, GLANCE
Broz, Josip .... TITO
brucine .... ALKALOID
bruin .... BEAR
bruise ...... CONTUSE, CRUSH, DISCOLORATION, JAM
application for .. ARNICA
bruiser .... BOXER, BULLY
bruising implement ... PESTLE
bruit ....CLAMOR, RUMOR, SPREAD, GOSSIP, TELL, REPORT
brumal .... WINTRY, SLEETY, HIEMAL
brume ..... FOG, MIST, VAPOR
brummagem: colloq. ... CHEAP, GAUDY, FAKE
brumous .... FOGGY, MISTY
Brunhild's husband .... GUNTHER, GUNNAR
Brunn .... BRNO
Brunnhilde (see Brynhild) ..... VALKYRIE
fate of .... SLEEP
mother of .... ERDA
savior .... SIEGFRIED
brunt .... IMPACT, SHOCK
brush .... TOUCH, CLEAN, POLISH, PAINT, FITCH, GRAZE, SKIRMISH, BROSSE, DUSTER, BROOM, SWEEP
aside .... IGNORE, SWEEP(OUT)
for sweeping ..... BROOM
lightly .... SCUFF
like .... SCOPULATE
material ...... ZACATON
off .... DISMISS(AL), SNUB
up ... NEATEN, CLEAN UP
brushwood .... COPSE, COPPICE, SCRUB, BRAKE
fence .... WEIR
brushwork .... PAINTING
brushy ...... BRISTLY, BUSHY
brusque ..... ABRUPT, BLUNT, CURT, SHORT, BLUFF, GRUFF
Brussels, capital of .. BELGIUM
carpet .... TOURNAI
sprouts .... CABBAGE
brut .... DRY
brutal ...... SAVAGE, CRUEL, COARSE, RUDE, FERAL, FERINE
behavior .... BARBARISM
soldier .... PANDOUR
brute ..... INSENSATE, STUPID, BEAST, ANIMAL, GROSS
Brynhild's brother-in-law .... SIGURD
husband ...... GUNNAR, GUNTHER
mother .... ERDA
sister-in-law ... GUDRUN, GUTHRUN
bryophyte .. MOSS, LIVERWORT
bryozoan ..... POLYP, HYDRA, CORAL, SEAPEN, SEA ANEMONE, POLYZOAN
Brythonic sea-god .... LER
bskt. .... BASKET
bub: colloq. ... BROTHER, BOY
bubaline .... ANTELOPES, HARTEBEESTS
bubble ...... BLEB, GLOBULE, BEAD, BOIL, FOAM
air .... BLEB
Archaic .... CHEAT, SWINDLE
fragrantly .... PERK
maker .... GUM

over .. OVERFLOW, EXULT
up . . . . BOIL
with excitement/joy . . . . . GUSH
bubbler of a sort . . . FOUNTAIN, BROOK
bubbling . . . . FIZZY, EFFERVESCENT
bubbles, full of . . . . . HUBBLY
bubonic plague carrier . . . FLEA, RAT
buccal . . . . MALAR
buccaneer . . . . PIRATE, SEA ROBBER, CORSAIR, GRILL
ancient . . . . VIKING
Bucephalus . . . . . (WAR)HORSE, STEED
Buceresti . . . . BUCHAREST
Bucharest, capital of . . . . ROMANIA
buck . . . . DEER, GOAT, SAWHORSE, DANDY
and wing . . . . . TAPDANCE
antler of . . . . . ADVANCER
black . . . . SASIN
colloquial . . . . RESIST
four-year old . . . . . . SORE
Indian . . . . SASIN
novelist . . . . PEARL
red . . . . PALLAH
slang . . . . DOLLAR
up: colloq. .. CHEER(UP), BRACE(UP)
water . . . . KOB
young . . . INDIAN, NEGRO, LAD
buckaroo . . . . COWBOY
bucket . . . . PAIL, SKEEL, BAIL, CANNIKIN
butter . . . . KIT
coal . . . . . SCUTTLE, TUB
fish . . . . KIT
handle . . . . BAIL
kick the . . . . DIE
make of a . . . . OAKEN
mining . . . . TUB
Scot. . . . . STOUP
Buckeye State . . . . OHIO
buckish . . . . FOPPISH
buckle . . . CLASP, CATCH, JOIN, GRAPPLE, WARP, KINK, OUCH
ancient . . . . FIBULA
under . . . YIELD, SUBMIT, COLLAPSE, GIVE IN
buckler .. (ARM)SHIELD, TARGE
bucko . . . . BULLY
buckra, in Africa .. WHITEMAN
buckthorn .. CASCARA, WAHOO
buckwheat tree .. TITI, TEETEE
weed . . . . . . DOCK, JUNK, TARE, LOCO
bucolic . . . ARCADIAN, RURAL, RUSTIC, AGRESTIC, PASTORAL, GEOPONIC
sound . . . MOO, LOW, BAA, BLEAT, CROW, CACKLE
bud . . . BULB(IL), PULLULATE, (S)CION, GÉMMA, BURGEON, SPROUT, GERM
dried . . . . CLOVE
Fisher's creation .. MUTT, JEFF, CICERO
for grafting . . . . . (S)CION
large and compact .. HEAD
like outgrowth . . . GEMMA
nip in the .. CHECK, STOP
of society . . . . DEB
on a flower stalk .. BULBIL
potato . . . . EYE
scale . . . . CATAPHYLL
variation . . . . SPORT
Budapest is capital of . . . . HUNGARY
Buddha . . . . GAUTAMA, FO
cousin of . . . . . . ANANDA
Japanese . . . . AMIDA, AMITA
mother of . . . . MAYA
tree of . . . . PIPAL
Buddhism, fate in . . . . KARMA
form of . . . . LAMAISM
founder of . . . . GAUTAMA
hatred . . . . DOSA
perfect blessedness . . . . . . NIRVANA
religious language .. PALI
Buddhist angel . . . . DEVA
column . . . . LAT
church . . . TERA, PAGODA
dialect . . . . PALI
fate . . . . KARMA
festival . . . . BON
final release . . . . NIRVANA
gateway . . . . TORAN
hell . . . . NARAKA
holy city . . . LHASA, LASSA
holy man . . . . MAHATMA
language . . . . PALI
lierature . . . . SUTRA
monastery . . . . TERA
monk . . . . TALAPOIN, BONZE, BO, LAMA
mound . . . . STUPA
novice . . . . GOYIN
paradise . . . . JODO
pillar . . . . LAT
priest . . . . LAMA, BONZE, MAHATMA, BO
religious observances . . . . DHARMA
saint . . . . AR(A)HAT
scripture .. SUTRA, SUTTA
sect, Japanese . . . . . . ZEN
shrine . . . . DAGOBA, STUPA, TOPE
Siamese . . . . LAO
temple . . . . PAGODA, VIHARA
title of respect . . . . MAHATMA
buddle . . . . . TROUGH, DRAIN
buddy . . . . COMPANION, PAL, COMRADE, BOY, CRONY
British slang . . . . . CULLY
budge . . . . MOVE, FUR, LAMBSKIN, POMPOUS
budgerigar . . . . PARAKEET, BUDGIE
budget . . . BAG, POUCH, STOCK, SCHEDULE, APPROPRIATION
anything . . . . . APPORTION
plan . . . . INSTALLMENT
buds, pickled . . . . CAPERS
put forth . . . . . . SPROUT, SHOOT, BURGEON
bueno: Sp. . . GOOD, VERY WELL
Buenos Aires is capital of . . . . ARGENTINA
buenos dias: Sp. . . . . GOOD MORNING, GOOD DAY, GREETING
buff . . . . . . LEATHER, POLISH, SPINDLE, BLOW
colloquial . . . . . DEVOTEE, FAN, AFICIONADO
buffalo . . . . OX, BISON
Bill . . . . CODY
bird . . . . COWBIRD
bug . . . . BEETLE
Celebes . . . . ANOA
crossed with cattle . . . . . . CAT(T)ALO
female . . . . COW
hybrid . . . . . . CAT(T)ALO
Philippine . . . . CARABAO, TIMARAW, TIMARAU
skin . . . . BUFF
slang . . . . BAMBOOZLE, BULLY
S. African . . . . NIARE
buffer . . . . CUSHION, SOCK ABSORBER
buffet . . . . . CREDENZA, BLOW, PUNCH, SLAP, COUNTER, TOSS, TABLE, SIDEBOARD
meals . . . . SPREADS
buffeted: poetic . . . . TOST
bufflehead . . . . . BUTTERBALL, DUCK
buffo . . . . COMIC, OPERA SINGER, CLOWN
voice of a . . . . BASS
buffoon . . . . CLOWN, PRANKSTER, DROLL, ZANY, JESTER, MIME(R), (MERRY) ANDREW, FOOL, HARLEQUIN, PUNCHINELLO
buffoonery . . . . . . CLOWNING, DROLLERY
bufo: Latin . . . . TOAD
bug . . . . . . CONENOSE, CIMEX, GERM, ANNOY, HOBGOBLIN, BEETLE, INSECT
living on other insects . . . ASSASSIN
river . . . . NAREW
slang . . . . . . MICROPHONE, ADDICT, DEFECT, ANGER, ANNOY
with sucking beak . . . . ASSASSIN
with built-in light . . . . FIREFLY
bugaboo . . . . . . MUMBO JUMBO, BUGBEAR, SCARECROW
African . . . GOGO, BOGIE
bugbear . . . (HOB)GOBLIN, BOGY
of a kind . . . . OGRE
bugger . . . . . SODOMITE, CHAP, FELLOW
buggy . . . . PRAM, PERAMBULATOR, CARRIAGE, CHAISE, SHAY

bughouse: sl. ..... NUTHOUSE, INSANE, CRAZY
bugle .... HORN, PLANT, BEAD
call .... RETREAT, TANTARA, TAT(T)OO, TAPS, REVEILLE, ASSEMBLY
carabao horn .. TAMBULI
note .... TIRALEE
signal .... TATTOO
yellow .... IVA
bugloss .... ANCHUSA
bugs: sl. ..... INSANE, CRAZY
buhr .... WHETSTONE
build .... REAR, ERECT, CONSTRUCT, RAISE, STATURE, PHYSIQUE
up: colloq. ... PUBLICITY, PRAISE, PLUG
builder's knot ... CLOVEHITCH
building ... . EDIFICE, STRUCTURE, PILE
caretaker ...... JANITOR
crowded .... WARREN
behind a big one .... BACKHOUSE
external corner of .... QUOIN
for bowling ..... ALLEYS
for exhibits ... PAVILION
for famous dead persons PANTHEON
for fodder .... SILO
for fruit-growing .... GRAPERY
for gambling ... CASINO
for grains .... GRANARY, ELEVATOR
for musical performances OPERA HOUSE, AUDITORIUM
inscription on .. EPIGRAPH
material .... ADOBE, MORTAR, CONCRETE, WOOD, STONE, STAFF
projecting ornament .... GARGOYLE
projection .... BAY
round .... ROTUNDA
site ..... LOT, STEADING
wing ... ELL, ANNEX, BAY
built-in bed .... BUNK, BERTH
Bukhara product .... RUG
bulb .... BUD, ONION, HYACINTH, GARLIC, LEEK, SEGO
edible .... CAMAS(S)
glass .... AMPOULE
like root ..... TUBEROSE
like stem, plant with ..... CORM, TUBER, CROCUS
lily .... CAMAS, SEGO
lily, dried ...... SQUILL
plant ...... SEGO, TULIP
segment .... CLOVE
bulbous plant .... GARLIC, TUBEROSE
bulbul .... SONGBIRD, NIGHTINGALE
Bulgarian ... SLAV, CHUVASH
capital .... SOFIA
coin ... LEV, LEW, DINAR, STOTINKA
czar/tsar ... ... BORIS
king .... SIMEON
moslem .... POMAK
queen ...... MARGARITA
seaport .... VARNA
weight .... OKA, OKE
bulge .... SWELLING, PROTRUDE, FLARE, PROTUBERANCE, PROJECTION
of belly: sl. .... BAY WINDOW
of skull .... INION
bulging ..... GIBBOUS, TUMID, TOROUS, TOROSE
bulimia, in medicine .. HUNGER
bulk .... SIZE, MASS, VOLUME, TOTAL, WHOLE, MAJORITY
bulkhead .... WALL, EMBANKMENT
bulky .... LARGE, MASSIVE, BIG, MASSY, HEFTY
bull ..... TORO, TAURUS, MALE, SEAL, LIE
castrated ..... BULLOCK
cry .... BELLOW
John .... ENGLAND
of/like a ..... TAURIN(E)
of Hercules .... CRETAN
of myth ..... MINATOUR
sacred: Egyptian ... APIS
slang .... NONSENSE, POLICEMAN, COP
young ... STOT, BULLOCK
bull's eye, circle next to ...... INNER
bulla ...... BLISTER, VESICLE, BLAIN, BLEB, PUSTULE
bullace .... PLUM, TREE
bullbat .... NIGHTHAWK
bulldog ...... PUG, MASTIFF, REVOLVER
color .... BRINDLE
soft-nosed .... DUMDUM
trait .... COURAGE, STUBBORNNESS, TENACITY
bulldogging place ..... RODEO
"Bulldogs" .... ELIS
bulldoze .... COERCE, BROWBEAT, FORCE, BULLY, FRIGHTEN
bullet ... PELLET, SHOT, SLUG, MISSILE, BALL
charge container .... CARTRIDGE
kind of .... DUMDUM, TRACER
metal covering .. JACKET
size .... CALIBER
bulletin .... STATEMENT, PUBLICATION, NEWS(LETTER), REPORT
kind of .... WEATHER, MEDICAL
bulletproof shield .... MANT(E)LET
bullfight cheer .... OLE
bullfighter .... MATADOR, TOREADOR, PICADOR
assistant .... PICADOR
mantle .... CAPA
on foot .... TORERO
queue of .... COLETA
bullfighting dart .... BANDERILLA
participant .... BANDERILLERO
bullfinch .. SONGBIRD, HEDGE OLP, REDBIRD
bullfrog's cry .... BOOM
bullhead ...... FISH, CATFISH, SCULPIN
bullheaded .... STUBBORN, HEADSTRONG
animal, of a sort ... MULE
bullion before coinage .. INGOT, BAR, GOLD, SILVER, BILLOT
bullock ..... OX, STEER, STIRK
bully ... BUCKO, PIMP, THUG, BRUISER, CORNED BEEF, HUFF, BROWBEAT, HECTOR, BULLDOZE, BAMBOOZLE
colloquial ... FINE, GOOD, WELL DONE
tree .... BALATA
bulrush ...... PAPYRUS, TULE
British .... CATTAIL
bulwark .... EARTHWORK, WALL, RAMPART, BREAKWATER, SCONCE, DEFENSE, PROTECTION
bum .... IDLER, LOAFER, SPREE, SPONGER, LOAF, BOAT
a ride ..... HITCH(HIKE)
ambulant ..... VAGRANT
British slang .. BUTTOCKS
check, describing one .... BOUNCING
bumble .... BLUNDER
bumblebee .... DOR
bump .... COLLIDE, JOLT, SWELLING, LUMP, JOSTLE
off: sl. .... MURDER, KILL
slang .... REPLACE
bumper ... LARGE, ABUNDANT, TOAST, BRIMMER
auto .... GUARD
bum(p)kin ...... LOUT, YOKEL, CLOD, RUBE, YAHOO
ship's .... BOOM, SPAR
bumpkins .... CAVES
bumptious .... CONCEITED, ARROGANT, PUSHING
bumpy ..... ROUGH, JOLTING, JERKY
bun .... ROLL, LOAF, KNOT
bunch ...... CYME, CLUSTER, TUFT, COLLECTION, LOT, BUNDLE
grass .... STIPA
of branches ...... COMA
of grapes ..... BOTRYOID
of sheaves ...... SHOCK, SHOOK
small .... WISP
bunchberry .... DOGWOOD
bunco: colloq. .... SWINDLE, CHEAT
buncombe .... HUMBUG, BOMBAST, BUNK, TWADDLE, MALARKEY
bund .. LEAGUE, CONFEDERATION
Oriental .... QUAY, EMBANKMENT

bundle ... PACKAGE, PARCEL, BUNCH, BALE, PACK, SHEAF, TRUSS
of fibers .... FASCICLE
of hay .... WASE
of joy: colloq. ..... BABY
of rods .... FASCES
of sticks/twigs ... FAGOT, FASCINE
of straw .... WASE
small .... FASCICLE
of sheaves of grain ...... STOOK
bundling device .... BALER
bung .... CORK, STOPPER, CLOSE
slang ... BRUISE, DAMAGE
bungalow .... COTTAGE
bungle .... BOTCH, LOUSE(UP), SPOIL, MESS, MUFF, FOOZLE, FUMBLE
a golf stroke .... DUB
a play .... MUFF
slang .... BOLLIX
bungling .... MALADROIT
bunion .... BURSITIS
bunk ...... BED, COT, BERTH, SLEEP
British slang ...... DOSS
slang .... HOKUM, BUNCOMBE, NONSENSE, TWADDLE, HOOEY
bunker .... BIN, TANK, SANDTRAP
bunko ...... CHEAT, SWINDLE
bunny .... RABBIT
playboy's .... HOSTESS
tail .... SCUT
time .... EASTER
bunt ...... SHOVE, BAT, SMUT
with horn: Brit. ... BUTT, STRIKE
bunting .... FLAGS, BIRD, ORTOLAN, ETAMINE, FINCH
migratory ... DICKCISSEL
Bunyan's ox .... BABE
buoy .. DAN, FLOAT, MAKEFAST
for mooring boat .... DOLPHIN
type .... CAN, NUN, WHISTLE, BELL, SPAR
up ... ENCOURAGE, BOOST
buoyancy ... GAIETY, LEVITY, FLOTAGE, RESILIENCE, CHEERFULNESS
bur .... SEEDCASE, WEED
buran .... WINDSTORM
burble ...... GURGLE, BUBBLE
burbot ... LING, MARIA, CUSK
burd: obsolete .... LADY
burden .... LOAD, OPPRESS, ONUS, CUMBER, WEIGH DOWN, INCUBUS
bearer .... AMASA, ATLAS, PORTER
beast of ..... MULE, ASS, BURRO, CAMEL, DONKEY
squaw's .... PAPOOSE
burdensome .... HEAVY, OPPRESSIVE, ONEROUS
burdock .... BURR, CLITE, COCKLEBUR

bureau .... DRESSER, DESK, CHEST, OFFICE, CHIFFONIER, HIGHBOY
top cover .... SCARF
bureaucracy ...... OFFICIALS, OFFICIALDOM
petty ...... BEADLEDOM
bureaucratic failing: colloq. ... RED TAPE
burg ... TOWN, CITY, VILLAGE
lord of .... BURGRAVE
burgeon .... SPROUT, BUD
burgess .... CITIZEN, FREEMAN
burgess' invention ..... GOOP
burgh ..... BOROUGH, TOWN
burglar .. THIEF, ROBBER, YEGG
hazard of ... ALARM BELL
loot of .... SWAG
burgomaster ... MAYOR, GULL
burgonet ... HELMET, MORION
burgoo .... PORRIDGE, GRUEL, SCUP, BARBECUE
Burgundy wine ...... CHABLIS
kingdom of .... ARLES
burial .... INTERMENT, SEPULTURE, INHUMATION
box ..... CASKET, COFFIN, BIER
clothes ..... CERECLOTH, CEREMENT, SHROUD
ground for the poor ..... POTTER'S FIELD
heap/mound .. TUMULUS, BARROW
pertaining to ... FUNERAL, FUNERARY
pile .... PYRE
place .. TOMB, CATACOMB, SEPULCHER, CRYPT, CEMETERY, GRAVE(YARD)
vault .... SEPULTURE
burin .... GRAVER
like tool .... CHISEL
burke .... MURDER, SUFFOCATE, SUPPRESS
Burke's subject ..... PEERAGE
Burkitt's tumor .. LUMPHOMA
burl .... KNOT, VENEER
burlesque .... PARODY, CARICATURE, COMEDY, VAUDEVILLE
number .... STRIP TEASE, SKIT
burley .... TOBACCO
burly .... MUSCULAR, HUSKY, GROSS
Burma Road's other name .... (THE) HUMP
terminus .... LASHIO
Burmese Buddhist ..... MON, PROME
capital .... RANGOON
capital, former ..... AVA
chief ....BO(H)
city .... MANDALAY, RANGOON, MAULMAIN, MOULMEIN
dagger .... DOW, DAH
demon .... NAT
district .... PROME
division .... PEGU, ARAKAN, YEU

ethnic group ..... MONS, CHINS, KARENS, NAGAS, KACHINS
gibbon .... LAR
garment .... LONGYI
gate .... TORAN
girl .... MIMA
governor .. WOON, WUN
hill .... NAGA, CHIN, KACHIN
hillman .... LAI
knife ... KAH, KHAO, DOW
language .... LAI, PEGU, CHIN, KUKI, WA, KACHIN
measure ..... DHA, SEIT, BYEE
Mongol .... LAI
monk .... BO
mountain range .... ARAKAN
musical instrument ...... TORAN, TURR
native ... PEGUAN, KADU, KUKI, LAI, WA, WAS
pagoda .... PHAYA
peasant .... TAO
premier .... U NU
river .... IRRAWADDY, TAPING
robber .... DACOIT
sarong .... LONGYI
shelter .... ZAYAT
shrimp .... NAPEE
spirit .... NAT
town .... LASHIO
tree .... ACLE
tribe .... TAI, SHAN
weight ..... VIS(S), RUAY, KYAT, TICAL
burn .... FIRE, SCORCH, GLOW, SEAR, CHAR
down .... RAZE
hair ends .... SINGE
incense .... CENSE
mark .... ESCHAR
mark of sun .... TAN, SUNTAN
mark with hot iron ... BRAND
nap of cloth ...... SINGE
Scot. .... STREAM
slightly .... SINGE
the midnight oil .... LUCUBRATE, BONE, CRAM
the road .... RACE, SPEED(UP), BARREL
to stop infection .... CAUTERIZE
unsteadily ...... FLICKER
up: colloq. ...... ANGER, ENRAGE, IRRITATE
with hot fluid .... SCALD
with hot iron/needle .... CAUTERIZE, BRAND
without flame .... SMO(U)LDER
burned up: sl. ... SORE, ANGRY
burner .... BUNSEN, CREMATORY, INCINERATOR, ARGAND
burning ..... AFIRE, AFLAME, ABLAZE, EAGER, FEVERISH

bush .... WAHOO, FRAXINELLA
coal container .. BRASIER, BRAZIER
glass .... LENS
malicious .... ARSON
process .... COMBUSTION
sensation ... CAUSALGIA, HEAT
stick .... BRAND
woodpile outdoors ...... BONFIRE
burnish ...... POLISH, GLOSS, SHINE, FURBISH
an error/fault .... GLOSS
Burns' sweetheart .... (HIGHLAND) MARY
burnsides .... WHISKERS, BEARD, MUTTON CHOPS
burnt .... ADUST
sugar .... CARAMEL
burp: sl. .... BELCH
burr .... SEEDCASE, ROUGH EDGE, DRILL, POD
plant/weed ... BURDOCK, COCKLEBUR, THISTLE, TEASEL
Burr's daughter .... THEO
burro .... DONKEY, ASS
female .... MARE
burrow ... HOLE, TUNNEL, DIG
burrowing animal .... ARMADILLO, BADGER, HARE, WOMBAT, MOLE, BROCK, RATEL, GOPHER, GERBIL(LE), TELEDU
crustacean ... SQUILL(A)
mammal of S. Africa .... SURICATE
mollusk .... PIDDOCK
rodent .... VOLE
tortoise .... GOPHER
burry .... PRICKLY
bursa .... SAC, POUCH
inflammation of a ...... BURSITIS
bursal .... FISCAL
bursar .... TREASURER
burse .... PURSE
Scot. ..... SCHOLARSHIP
bursitis .... BUNION
burst .... EXPLODE, BREAK OPEN, BULGE, RUPTURE, BUST, BREACH, SPLIT, SALVO
forth .... ERUPT
of anger .... HUFF
of cheers ..... OVATION, APPLAUSE, SALVO
of energy .... SPURT, RALLY
open .... POP
pod, open ..... DEHISCE
sudden .... GUST
bursting tire .... BLOW-OUT
Burundi capital .. BUJUMBURA
king .... (MWAMI) MWAMBUTSA
native .... WATUSI, BAHUTU
tribe .... BAHUTU, WATUTSI

bury .... INTER, INHUME, INURN, SINK, IMMERSE, SEPULCHER
the hatchet ... RECONCILE
to hoard/hide ... CACHE
bus ... (MOTOR)COACH, JITNEY
colloquial .... AUTO(MOBILE), FAMILY CAR
for excursion .... CHARABANC
busby .... HAT
wearer .... HUSSAR
bush .... SHRUB, BRIER, THICKET, TAIL, TOD
burning .... WAHOO
league .... MINORS
leaguer .. SECOND RATER
bushbuck .... ANTELOPE
bushel, in tailoring ... ALTER, MEND
$\frac{1}{8}$ of .... GALLON
$\frac{1}{4}$ of .... PECK
bushelman .... TAILOR
bushels, $11\frac{2}{3}$ .... HOMER
32 or 36 ...... CHALDRON
bushes, stunted ...... SCRUB
bushing .... LINING
bushman ... PIGMY, NEGRILLO
bushmaster .... VIPER, SNAKE
bushranger .... HIGHWAYMAN
bushwhacker .... (BACK)WOODSMAN, GUERRILLA, RAIDER
bushy clump .... TOD
tail .... BRUSH
business .... PROFESSION, OCCUPATION, AFFAIR, COMMERCE, TRADE, STORE
agent .... SYNDIC, COMPRADOR, SALESMAN
association ... SYNDICATE
cartel .... TRUST, MONOPOLY
connection ..... CONTACT
cycle, part of ..... BOOM, SLUMP, PROSPERITY, DEPRESSION
establishment ..... FIRM, COMPANY, STORE
event .... MERGER, RECESSION, SLUMP, BOOM, STRIKE, DEAL
firm .... HOUSE
location .... STAND, SITE
monopoly ..... CARTEL, CORNER
schedule .... AGENDA
secrets, spy on .... KEEK
slump ...... RECESSION, DEPRESSION
solicitor ...... RUNNER, BARKER
transaction ...... DEAL
upsurge .... BOOM
businessman ...... MERCHANT, TRADER
conventional ... BABBITT
Latin of .... INRE
one kind of .... ENTREPRENEUR
busk .... READY, OUTFIT

buskin .... BOOT, DRAMA
busline, end of ..... TERMINUS
buss .... KISS
colloquial .. PECK, SMACK
bust .... BOSOM, BREAST, BREAK, BURST
form/shape ..... TAILLE
slang ... SPREE, FAILURE, HIT, PUNCH, DEMOTE, BLOW
bustard ... BIRD, OTIS, TARDA
buster of a kind .... TRUST BREAKER
slang .... BOY
bustle .... TO-DO, ADO, POTHER, STIR, HURRY
colloquial ..... HOOPLA
companion of ... HUSTLE
of woman's dress .... PADDING, BOW
busy .... DILIGENT, ASSIDUOUS, ACTIVE, INDUSTRIOUS, OCCUPY
creature .... ANT, BEE, OTTER
place .... HIVE
sound .... HUM
busybody .... MEDDLER, GOSSIP, SNOOP(ER), QUIDNUNC
but .... EXCEPT, SAVE, YET, STILL, HOWEVER, MERELY
Scottish .... OUTER, OUTSIDE, OUTER ROOM
butcher .... MEAT-SELLER, KILL, SLAUGHTER
bird .... SHRIKE
hook of ...... GAMBREL, GAFF
meat cutter ..... CLEAVER
shop of .... SHAMBLES
butler .... MAJORDOMO, STEWARD, MAITRE D'HOTEL
concern of ...... CELLAR, PANTRY, SILVER(WARE)
butt .... TARGET, BARREL, CASK, FISH, ABUT, TUP
in ... MEDDLE, INTERFERE, INTERVENE, INTRUDE
of cigar(ette) ...... STUB
of criticism usually ..... SCAPEGOAT
of goat .... RAM
of joke, figuratively ..... GOAT
of tree .... STUMP
of whip .... CROP
slang ..... CIGARET(TE), BUTTOCKS
butte .... HILL, MESA
butter .... SPREAD, OIL, FLATTER(Y), GHEE
and-eggs .... PLANT, TOADFLAX
and-flour mix ..... ROUX
bucket .... KIT
buffalo milk .... GHEE
color for .... ANATTO, AN(N)ATTO
India .... GHEE, GHI
like ... OLEO, MARGARINE, BUTYRACEOUS, BUTTERINE

lump .... PAT
making contrivance ..... CHURN
piece of .... PAT
roll .... BRIOCHE
substitute .. MARGARINE, OLEO, BUTTERINE, SUINE
tree .... SHEA
tub .. CHURN, FIRKIN, KIT
butterball .... BUFFLEHEAD
slang ...... FATSO, FATTY
butterbean .... LIMA
buttercup ...... GOLDILOCKS, CROWTOE
buttered crumbs/crust .... GRATIN
butterfish .... GUNNEL
butterflies, order of .... LEPIDOPTERA
butterfly .... ADMIRAL, FRITILLARY, VANESSA, IO, GRAYLING, SATYR, KIHO, SWALLOWTAIL, SKIPPER, VICEROY, MONARCH, TROILUS, NYMPHALID
admiral ...... ATALANTA
combining form .. CALIGO
fish ...... BLENNY, PARU
large .... IDALIA
larva ..... CATERPILLAR
lily .... SEGO
named after goddess .... APHRODITE, DIANA
peacock .... IO
proboscis .... LINGUA
small .... BLUE
tongue-like organ .... LINGUA
butternut .... SOUARI
buttery .... STOREROOM, PANTRY, SPENCE
butting animal ... GOAT, RAM, CARABAO
buttinsky .... MEDDLER
buttocks ..... RUMP, BREECH, ARSE, DERRIERE, FUNDAMENT, BEHIND, BUTT, PRAT, ASS, NATES, BUM, SEAT, POSTERIOR
button .... EMBLEM, KNOB, FASTEN, STUD, KNOP
cover .... FLY, FLAP
fencing sword ..... FOIL
the lips .... SHUT UP
buttonhole ..... HOLD, DETAIN
flower .... GARDENIA
buttons .... BELLBOY, (HOTEL)PAGE
and .... BOWS
buttonwood .... SYCAMORE
buttress ...... SUPPORT, PROP, PIER, REINFORCE, BOLSTER, STAY
butts and bounds .... BOUNDARIES
buxom ..... PLUMP, COMELY, OBEDIENT, HEALTHY, JOLLY
buy .... PURCHASE, BRIBE, BARGAIN
at one's risk .... CAVEAT EMPTOR
back .... REDEEM
good: colloq. .... CHEAP, BARGAIN
off .... BRIBE
buyer .... PURCHASER, CONSUMER, VENDEE, EMPTOR
and seller ..... DEALER, JOBBER
of office ..... BARRATER
of old horses .. KNACKER
buyers' strike ...... BOYCOTT
buying to gain monopoly .... COEMPTION
buzz ... HUM, GOSSIP, SIGNAL, DRONE, WHIRR
bomb: Ger. V1
colloquial ... TELEPHONE
buzzard ..... HAWK, BUTEO, HARRIER, FALCON, TESA, OSPREY, COCKCHAFER, DUCKHAWK
honey .... BEEHAWK
moor .... HARPY
turkey ... VULTURE, JOHN
buzzer signal .... CALL
buzzing sound ... DRONE, HUM
by .... PER, NEAR, AT, BESIDE, THROUGH, ASIDE
and by ... SOON, SHORTLY, ANON
birth .... NEE, NATAL
blow .... BASTARD
hand .... PERSONAL
hand: prefix ...... MANU
pass ..... AVOID, SHUNT, DETOUR
right .... DEJURE
the day .... PERDIEM
way of .... VIA
word of mouth .... ORAL, VERBAL, PAROL
work .... SIDELINE, HOBBY, AVOCATION
byblow .... BASTARD
bye ...... RUN, INCIDENTAL, ODD MAN
bye .... GOODBY
Byelorussian city .... MOGILEV
bygone .... PAST
byname .... SURNAME, NICKNAME
byplay .... ADLIB
byre .... COWBARN
Byron, name of .... NOEL
poem by .... BEPPO
Byronic ... ROMANTIC, PROUD, CYNICAL, IRONIC
byssus .... FLAX, LINEN
bystander .... ONLOOKER
bystreet .... ALLEY
byway ..... ALLEY, SIDEROAD, SIDESTREET
byword .... PROVERB, PROVERBIAL
Byzantine coin ...... BEZANT
emperor .... ALEXIUS, HERACLIUS
emperor's scepter .... FERULA
empress .... ZOE
logothete, so-called .... (WOODROW) WILSON
works of art ..... ICONS
Byzantium capital .. ISTANBUL, CONSTANTINOPLE

C

C, Greek .... GAMMA
letter .... CEE
mark under .... CEDILLA
Roman numeral .... HUNDRED, 100
symbol for ... CONSTANT
Ca, in chemistry ... CALCIUM
Caaba .... SHRINE
site .... MECCA
caama .... ASSE, FOX
cab .... TAXI, HACK, HANSOM, CARRIAGE, FIACRE, CALASH
driver .. HACK, CABETTE
CAB subjects ..... AIRLINES
cabal .... PLOT, FACTION, INTRIGUE, JUNTO, CLIQUE, JUNTA
cabala .. OCCULTISM, MYSTERY
cabalist .... MYSTIC
cabalistic ... SECRET, MYSTIC
caballero .... GENTLEMAN, CAVALIER, KNIGHT, HORSEMAN
cabana ... BATHHOUSE, CABIN, HUT, COTTAGE, BAGNIO
cabaret .... BARROOM, RESTAURANT, HONKY-TONK
cabbage ... SAVOY, OXHEART, KOHLRABI, COLE(WORT), KALE, KAIL, CAULIFLOWER
broth .... KALE
fermented .. SAUERKRAUT
garden .... KALEYARD
plant like .... COLE
salad/shredded ... SLAW
tree .... YABA
cabby ... TAXI-DRIVER, HACK
caber .... POLE, BEAM
cabin .. COTTAGE, HUT, SHACK, CABANA, SHED, LOGHOUSE
balloon/dirigible .... GONDOLA
ship's main ..... SALON
Swiss .... CHALET
cabinet ...... CASE, PRIVATE, SECRET, CONSOLE, ALMIRAH, BUHL, ARMOIRE
composition ... ADVISERS
describing one .. KITCHEN
for wines, etc. .. CELLARET
wood ...... ROSEWOOD, CEDAR, KOA, WALNUT
cable .. ROPE, CHAIN, MESSAGE, WIRE
car ...... TELFER, ELPHER
old .... JUNK
used as brace ..... STAY

cabob .... (ROAST) MEAT
holder .... SPIT, SKEWER
cabochon .... STONE
caboodle .... LOT, GROUP
companion of ..... KIT
caboose .... CAB
ship's .. GALLEY, KITCHEN
cabrilla ...... GROUPER, FISH, REDHIND
cacao alkaloid .. THEOBROMINE
product .... COCOA, CHOCOLATE
seed powder .... BROMA
cachalot ...... SPERM, WHALE, PHYSETER
cache ..... CONCEAL, HOARD, STORE, SECRETE
cachet .... CAPSULE, SEAL, STAMP
cachou ... LOZENGE, CATECHU
cacique .... LORD, PRINCE, ORIOLE, CHIEF, TROUPIAL
cackle ..... LAUGH, CHATTER, PRATTLE, CLACK
cackler .... HEN, GOOSE
cacoethes ..... ITCH, MANIA
cacophonous .... DISCORDANT
cactus ..... CHOLLA, CEREUS, PRICKLY PEAR, MESCAL, SAGUARO, PEYOTE, NOPAL, OPUNTIA
fruit ...... COCHAL, FIG
like plant ...... SPURGE, EUPHORBIA, STAPELIA
plant .... TUNA
plant process ..... SPINE
spineless .... CHAUTE
cad ... BOUNDER, SCOUNDREL, HEEL, MUCKER
cadaver ... COR(P)se, CARCASS, BODY, REMAINS
preserved .... MUMMY
slang .... STIFF
cadaverous .... PALE, GAUNT, GHASTLY
caddis worm .... CADEW
caddish .. ILL-BRED, LOUTISH
caddy .... (TEA)BOX
Caddoan Indian .... REE, PAWNEE
cade .... JUNIPER
cadence ...... MODULATION, CADENZA, LILT, METER, BEAT, INFLECTION, RHYTHM
recite in .... CHIME
cadet .... STUDENT, SON
designating one ... PLEBE, DODO, MILITARY, AIR, NAVAL
mark against .. DEMERIT
naval ...... MIDSHIPMAN, MIDDY
cadge .. BEG, PEDDLE, MOOCH, SPONGE
cadgy ..... LEWD, WANTON, MERRY
cadi .... JUDGE, MAGISTRATE
Cadmean-like victory .... PYRRHIC
Cadmus' daughter .. SEMELE, INO
parent .... AGENOR
sister .... EUROPA
wife .... HARMONIA
cadre .... FRAMEWORK, NUCLEUS, CELL
caduceus .... STAFF, SCEPTER, WAND
bearer .... MERCURY, HERMES
Caen river .... ORNE
Caesar .... SALAD, SID, EMPEROR, DICTATOR, JULIUS
augur who warned ..... SPURINNA
assassin of .... CASSIUS, BRUTUS, CASCA
love of .... SERVILIA
mistress of ...... EUNOE, CLEO(PATRA)
Pompey battle site ..... THAPSUS
wife .... POMPEIA
Caesarian operation .... HYSTEROTOMY
Caesars, one of the ... JULIUS, AUGUSTUS, TIBERIUS, GAIUS, CLAUDIUS, NERO, GALBA, OTHO, VITELLIUS, VESPASIAN, TITUS, DOMITIAN
caesura .. REST, BREAK, PAUSE
cafe .... COFFEE, SALOON, CABARET, DIVAN, ESTAMINET, BISTRO, RESTAURANT
card .... MENU
owner ... RESTAURATEUR
society member .... PLAYBOY
caffein source .. COFFEE, COLA, KOLA, TEA
tea .... THEIN(E)
caftan .... ROBE
cage ..... CONFINE, PEN, GIG, JAIL
elevator .... CAR
hauling .... MEW
hawks' .... MEW
poultry .... COOP
occupant .... BIRD, PET, ANIMAL, PRISONER, TELLER, CASHIER
cagey .. SLY, TRICKY, CUNNING
cahier .... NOTEBOOK, REPORT
cahoots, in .... LEAGUE, PARTNERSHIP, CONNIVANCE, CONSPIRACY
caiman .... ALLIGATOR
Cain, ... MURDERER
brother of .... ABEL
descendant of .... JUBAL
land of .... NOD
parent of .... ADAM, EVE
son of .... ENOCH
caique ... ROWBOAT, SAILBOAT
caird ...... TINKER, VAGRANT, GYPSY
cairngorm .... QUARTZ
Cairene .... EGYPTIAN
Cairo is capital of .... EGYPT
shopping district .... MOUSSKY
caisson .... WAGON, BOX, CHEST, TUMBREL, TUMBRIL
content of .. AMMUNITION, EXPLOSIVES, AMMO
disease .... BENDS
man in a ...... SANDHOG
occasional use of ...... HEARSE
caitiff .. EVIL, MEAN, CRAVEN, POLTROON
cajeput .... LAUREL
cajole ...... FLATTER, COAX, WHEEDLE, BLANDISH
cajolery .... PALAVER
cake ...... HARDEN, CIMBAL, RUSK, TORTE, MERINGUE
barley meal ... BANNOCK
batter .... CRUMPET, CRULLER, FRITTER
chocolate ..... BROWNIE
corn .... PONE
covering ..... MERINGUE, FROSTING, ICING
fish .... PATTY
in pipe bowl ... DOTTLE
kind of ... BATTER, LAYER
meat .... PATTY
oatmeal .... BANNOCK
porous .... SPONGE
pressed tobacco ... PLUG
ring-shaped .. DOUGHNUT
rum .... BABA
seed .... WIG
small ...... COOKY, BUN
takes the .. WINS, EXCELS, OVERDONE
tea .... SCONE
thin ... JUMBLE, WAFER, FARL
without flour .... TORTE
cakes and ale, life of .... HEDONISM
cakewalk ...... DANCE, STEP, STRUT
calabash ...... GOURD, SHELL
calaber ...... FUR, SQUIRREL
calaboose .. JAIL, PRISON, GAOL
Calais' English neighbor ..... DOVER
calamary .... SQUID
calamine .... OINTMENT
calamitous .. FATAL, TRAGIC, DISASTROUS
calamity ... MISERY, REVERSE, WOE, DISASTER, CATASTROPHE, BLOW
calamus .. QUILL, PALM(TREE), SWEET FLAG
calcar .... SPUR
calced .... SHOD
calcine ...... BURN, OXIDIZE
calcined metal/residue .. CALX
calcium carbonate .. CALCITE, TUFA, CALICHE
carbonate, of .... CALCAREOUS
crust .... SINTER
gypsum .... PLASTER
oxide ...... (QUICK)LIME
phosphate .... APATITE
sulphate ...... GYPSUM, PLASTER, HEPAR
calculate .. COUNT, COMPUTE, ESTIMATE, RECKON, FIGURE, THINK, SUPPOSE, GUESS
calculating ...... CUNNING, SHREWD, CAUTIOUS

device ... ABACUS, TABLE, COMPUTER
calculation, of ..... LOGISTIC
calculi, of .... LITHIC
calculus .... (GALL)STONE, GRAVEL
combining form .. LITHO
Calcutta is capital of .. BENGAL
calderite .... GARNET
caldron ...... BOILER, KETTLE
Caleb's companion ... JOSHUA
Caledonia .... SCOTLAND
calefy .... WARM, HEAT
calendar ..... REGISTER, LIST, SCHEDULE, ALMANAC, DOCKET, MENOLOGY
church .... ORDO
of business ..... AGENDA
calender ... DERVISH, MANGLE
calenture .... FEVER
calesa .... CALASH, CALECHE, CAB
calf .... BOSS
cry .... BL(E)AT
for slaughter ... FATLING
front .... SHIN
hide .... KIP
leather .... ELK
leg .... SURAL
like a .... VITULINE
meat .... VEAL
motherless ... MAVERICK, DOGIE, DOGY
skin .... KIP
skin parchment .. VELLUM
stray ... DOGIE, MAVERICK
suckling .... BOB
unbranded ... MAVERICK
Caliban's master .. PROSPERO
mother .... SYCORAX
caliber ...... BORE, QUALITY, ABILITY, GAUGE, METTLE
calico ...... (COTTON)CLOTH, DOWLAS
East Indies ..... SALLOO
horse .. PINTO, PIEBALD, PONY
loin cloth .. LAVA-LAVA
printing .... LAPIS, TEER
printing material .... TRAGACANTH, LACTARENE
California .... EL DORADO
army base .... ORD
bay .... MONTEREY
bulrush .... TULE
cape ...... MENDOCINO
capital .... SACRAMENTO
capital, former .... MONTEREY
city .... ALAMEDA, PALOMAR, MORAGA, NAPA, CHINO, LODI, POMONA, FRESNO, GLENDALE, LONGBEACH, LYNWOOD, VALLEJO, BUENA PARK, DOWNY, PALO ALTO, PASADENA, TORRANCE
college .... NAIROBI
county .... NAPA, KERN, LAKE, MONO, YOLO
fish .. CABEZON, GRUNION
gold rusher .. ARGONAUT
grape picker .. BRACERO
grape pickers' strike .... HUELGA
herb .... AMOLE
holly .... TOYON
Indian ... PAIUTE, HUPA
kingfish .... OPAH, PINTADO, WHITING
lake .... TAHOE, BUENA, OWENS
laurel .... CAJEPUT, CAJUPUT, MYRTLE
motto .... EUREKA
mountain ..... PALOMAR, SIERRAS, MUIR
mountain peak .. SHASTA
nickname ...... GOLDEN
oak ..... ROBLE, ENCINA
observatory ... PALOMAR
pass .... SONORA
pioneer .... SUTTER
river .... TRINITY, SACRAMENTO
rockfish .... RE(I)NA
shrub .. SALAL, KUMQUAT
state flower ... (GOLDEN) POPPY
town .. ASTI, MONTEREY
valley .... YOSEMITE
volcano .... SHASTA
Caligula .... BOOTIKIN
caliph .... IMAM, ALI, OMAR, OMMIAD
calisthenics .... GYMNASTICS, EXERCISES
system ...... DEL SARTE
calix .... CUP, CHALICE
calk .... CHINSE, SEAL, CLOSE, STOP
calker .... STAVER
calking material .. OAKUM, TAR
call .. DUB, CRY, DIAL, SHOUT, ANNOUNCE, SUMMON, CONVOKE, (TELE)PHONE, NAME, PAGE, VISIT, RING
army .... DRAFT
auction .... BID
baseball ..... OUT, SAFE, STRIKE
boy ..... PAGE, BELLHOP
creditor's .... DUN
down .. SCOLD, REBUKE, UPBRAID
for .... DEMAND, ASK
for aid .... APPEAL
for hogs .... SOOK
for repetition ..... ENCORE
forth .. EVOKE, SUMMON, ELICIT, EXCITE
girl .. PROSTITUTE, HOSTESS
greeting ..... HAIL, AVE
hotel lobby .... PAGE
in .... SUMMON
in poker .... SEE
in question ..... IMPUGN
off .... CANCEL
on ...... SEE, VISIT, TAP
out .... SHOUT, SUMMON, ANNOUNCE
prayer ..... ADAN, AZAN
to account .... ARRAIGN, CHARGE
to arms, medieval .. BAN
to attract attention ..... HEY, PSST, HIST
to mind .... REMINISCE, REMEMBER, RECALL
to witness ...... OBTEST
together ..... CONVOKE, ASSEMBLE
up .... (TELE)PHONE, SUMMON, DIAL, RING UP
within ... CLOSE, NEARBY
calla .... ARUM, LILY
callboy ..... BELLHOP, PAGE, BUTTONS
called .... YCLEPT, NAMED
caller .... VISITOR, GUEST
from minaret .. MUEZZIN
midnight .... CRIER
persistent .... DUTY
calligrapher .... COPYIST, PENMAN
calligraphy .. HANDWRITING, SCRIPT
calling ... METIER, VOCATION, PROFESSION, OCCUPATION, PURSUIT, TRADE, MISSION
Calliope .... MUSE
Callisto .... NYMPH, CONSTELLATION
callous ... UNFEELING, HARD, PITILESS, HARD-BOILED, TOUGH
growth .... CORN
render ... HARDEN, SEAR, NUMB
calloused .... HORNY
callow .... IMMATURE, UNFLEDGED, YOUNG, GREEN
person .... YOUTH
callus, horse's ..... CHESTNUT
on toe .... CORN
calm .. SOBER, PACIFY, PACIFIC, IMPASSIVE, COOL, LULL, ABATE, PLACATE, STILL, SERENE, SMOOTH, SOOTHE, ALLAY
before the ____ ... STORM
calmness, mental/emotional .. ATARAXIA
calmative ... OPIATE, SEDATIVE, DRUG, BALM
calomel .. POWDER, CATHARTIC
caloric ...... HEAT, THERMAL
calorie .... THERM(E)
counter .. DIETER, MILADY
counter's standby .... CYCLAMATE, SACCHARIN
calories, count(ing) .... DIET(ING)
pertaining to .. THERM(AL)
calotte .. (SKULL)CAP, CREST
Calpurnia's husband .... (JULIUS) CAESAR
caltrop .... THISTLE
calumet .... (PEACE)PIPE
user of .. INDIAN, REDSKIN
calumniate .. MALIGN, ASPERSE, SLUR, LIBEL, SLANDER, DEFAME
calumny ..... SLANDER, LIBEL
Calvary ...... ARAM, SKULL
Calve, soprano .... EMMA, ROQUER
Calvinist of Toulouse .. CALAS
Calvinist(ic) ...... GENEVAN,

GENEVESE, DOGMATIC
calvities .... BALDNESS
Calydonian boar killer .... MELEAGER
Calypso ..... NYMPH, ORCHID, FLOWER, DANCE, BALLAD, SONG, MUSIC
island of ...... OGYGIA
calypster .... ALULA
calyx leaf ..... SEPAL, PETAL
cam .... TAPPET, TRIPPET, COG(WHEEL), CATCH, TRIPPER, WIPER
wheel projection .. LOBE
camaraderie .... COMRADESHIP
camalig .... GRANARY, WAREHOUSE, HUT
camarilla .... CABAL, CLIQUE
camass ... LOBELIA, QUAMASH
Cambodia ...... CAMBODGE, CAMBOJA
capital ...... PNOM PENH
capital, ancient .. ANGKOR
city .... ANGKOR
lake .... TONLE SAP
native of .... KHMER
neighbor .... LAOS, VIETNAM, THAILAND
premier .... NOL
river .... MEKONG
ruins .... ANGKOR
seaport .... KAMPOT
skirt .... SAMPORT
cambogia ...... (GUM)RESIN
cambrai ...... BATISTE, LINEN
cambric ... PERCALE, COTTON, LINEN, LAWN
Cambridge U. college servant GYP
exam for honors .. TRIPOS
head/fellow ...... DON
student ... SIZAR, SIZER, OPTIME
came about ..... HAPPENED, AROSE
down ...... DESCENDED, (A)LIT
camel .. DELOUL, RUMINANT, ARABIAN, GUANACO, DROMEDARY, BELOOL, HEJEEN, BACTRIAN
back breaker ... STRAW
driver .... SARWAN
feature .... HUMP
hair cloth .. ABA, CAMLET, CAMLOT, CASHMERE
hair robe .... ABA
keeper .... OBIL
like animal ..... LLAMA, GUANACO
load .... FARDEL
milk, fermented .... KOUMIS(S), KUMISS
rawhide ...... SHAGREEN
seat on .... HOUDAH, HOWDAH
ship of the ____ .. DESERT
camellia .... JAPONICA
camelopard .... GIRAFFE
Camelot's source of fame .... ARTHUR, ROUND TABLE, KNIGHTS
lady .... ENID

sport ..... TILT, JOUST, TOURNEY
Camenas .... NYMPHS
cameo ..... ANAGLYPH, GEM, CARVING
cutting tool ..... SPADE
opposed to .... INTAGLIO
stone .... ONYX
camera .. POLAROID, LUCIDA, BROWNIE, BOX, CHAMBER, KODAK
film protector .... CARTRIDGE
holder .... TRIPOD
kind of .... CANDID
opening ...... APERTURE
part ..... FINDER, LENS, SHUTTER
platform .... DOLLY
portable .... KODAK
shot .... STILL
stand .... TRIPOD
camerlingo ... CHAMBERLAIN, CARDINAL
Cameroon capital .. YAOUNDE
native .... ABO
Camille author ..... DUMAS
role actress ..... GARBO
camion ..... WAGON, TRUCK, DRAY
camise .... SHIRT, SMOCK
camisole .... JACKET
camlet ...... PONCHO, CLOTH
camomile .... MAYWEED
Camorra .. (SECRET) SOCIETY
like group ..... MAF(F)IA
member's specialty ..... MURDER, TERRORISM, EXTORTION, BLACKMAIL
camouflage ..... DECEPTION, DISGUISE
expert .... CAMOUFLEUR
camouflaging material .... SMOKE, PAINT, LEAVES
camp ...... BIVOUAC, ETAPE, TABOR
barricaded by wagons ... LA(A)GER
besiegers' ..... LEAGUER
facility .. LATRINE, TENT
follower ...... SUTLER, VIVANDIERE, DOXY
kind of .... INTERNMENT, CONCENTRATION
military .... BASE
out .... MAROON
pertaining to .. CASTRAL
privy/toilet ... LATRINE
campagna .... PLAIN
campaign .. CRUSADE, DRIVE, BARNSTORM
against an idea .. JIHAD
goal .... ELECTION
matters .... ISSUES
motive .... CAUSE
campanile ..... (BELL)TOWER, BELFRY
campanula ...... HAREBELL, RAMPION
camper's kit/equipment ...... DUFFLE, DUFFEL
campesino .... PEASANT
camphol .... BORNEOL

camphor-like ...... BORNEOL
oil .... SAFROL(E)
campo .... PLAIN
campstool-shaped chair ...... CURULE
campus .. QUAD, FIELD, YARD
building .... GYM, DORM
group .. FRAT, SORORITY
VIP .... DEAN, ATHLETE, PREXY
can ... CONSERVE, CONTAINER, PAIL, TIN, JUG
slang .... PRISON, BUTTOCKS, TOILET, DISMISS, DISCHARGE
Canada, Lower ..... QUEBEC
Canadian .... CANUCK
airport .... GANDER
boatman .... VOYAGEUR
capital .... OTTAWA
city .... LEVIS, BANFF
crookneck .... CUSHAW
canal .... WELLAND
emblem .... MAPLE
farmer ...... HABITAN(T)
folk singer .. LIGHTFOOT
football .... ROUGE
game .... LACROSSE
game preserve .. JASPER
gannet .... MARGOT
gold field .... KLONDIKE
goose .... OUTARDE
grape .... ISABELA
humorist ...... LEACOCK
Indian .... CREE, SIOUX, MICMAC
lake ...... TESLIN, CREE, LOUISE
land measure .. ARPENT
lynx .. CARCAJOU, PISHU
mountain ...... LEWIS, LUCANIA
national park .. JASPER, YOHO, BANFF
official .... REEVE
park ..... BANFF, JASPER
peak .... LOGAN
peninsula .... GASPE
policeman ..... MOUNTIE
porcupine .... URSON
prime minister .... TRUDEAU, PEARSON, LAURIER
province .... ALBERTA, ONTARIO, QUEBEC, MANITOBA, YUKON, NOVA SCOTIA, NORTHWEST
provincial capital .... TORONTO, EDMONTON, QUEBEC, HALIFAX, REGINA, VICTORIA, WINNIPEG, ST. JOHNS
resort .... GASPE
river ... OTTAWA, YUKON, NELSON, BATEAU, LIARD, MACKENZIE
rodent .... LEMMING
scenic region .... GASPE
settler ...... SOURDOUGH
squaw .... MAHALA
summer resort ... BANFF
territory .... YUKON
town president .. REEVE

woodsman ... VOYAGEUR
canaille .... MOB, RABBLE, RIFFRAFF
canal ..... WATERWAY, ERIE, CONDUIT, SUEZ, WELLAND, PANAMA, KIEL, PASSAGE, ACEQUIA
bank .... BERM(E)
boat .... GONDOLA
boat tower .... MULE
ear .... SCALA
enclosed part ..... LOCK
from mouth to anus .... ALIMENTARY, ENTERON
in anatomy/zoology .... DUCT, TUBE, VAS
lock gate .... WICKET
Suez: colloq. ...... SOO
worker .... NAVVY
zone seaport .... BALBOA
zone town ..... GATUN, ANCON
canape ..... DIVAN, COUCH, APPETIZER
spread .. CAVIAR, CHEESE, SARDINE
canard .... RUMOR, HOAX, DUCK, HUMBUG, AIRPLANE
Canary ...... DANCE, WINE, MADEIRA, SONGBIRD, ROLLER, FINCH
hybrid .... MULE
island .... PALMA, TENERIF(FE)
island mount .... TEIDE, TEYDE
island seaport .... LAS PALMAS
island wine ...... SACK
kin .... SERIN
seed .... ALPIST
yellow .... MELINE
canasta play/score .... MELD
Canaveral, Cape .. KENNEDY
Canberra is capital of .... AUSTRALIA
cancel .. ANNUL, ERASE, REMIT, RESCIND, REVOKE, RECALL
deletion made ..... STET
in printing ... DELE(TE), KILL
cancellation mark on mail .... CACHET, STAMP
cancer .. CARCINOMA, TUMOR, SCIRRHUS, LEUKEMIA, CRAB
describing .... BENIGN, MALIGNANT
like .... CANCROID
non-malignant .. BENIGN
of the jaw .... LYMPHONA
producing substance..... CARCINOGEN
surgery .... MASTECTOMY
treatment ..... RADIUM, RADON
candelabrum .. CANDLESTICK, CANDELABRA
candent .... GLOWING, (WHITE)HOT
candescent .... GLOWING
Candia .. CRETE, HERAKLEION
candid ..... OPEN, HONEST, IMPARTIAL, FRANK, OUTSPOKEN, GUILELESS, BLUNT
"Candida" author .... SHAW
candidate .. NOMINEE, ASPIRANT
for graduation .. SENIOR
for knighthood .. ESQUIRE
kind of ...... OFFICIAL, REBEL, INDEPENDENT
candidates' list ..... TICKET, SLATE, BALLOT
platform ...... HUSTINGS
staple ...... PROMISES, PLEDGES
winning score .... MAJORITY, PLURALITY
candied .... GLACE
fruit .... COMFIT, SWEETMEAT
rind .... CITRON
candies, imitation of .... CONFETTI
Candiot .... CRETAN
candle ... DIP, TAPER, CIERGE, SERGE, RUSH, GLIM
holder .. SCONCE, HEARST, CANDELABRA, CHANDELIER, GIRANDOLE
lighter .... TAPER
maker .... CHANDLER
material .... CARNAUBA, WAX, TALLOW, WICK, OZOCERITE
part .... WICK, SNAST
seller .... CHANDLER
slang .... GLIM
spike .... PRICKET
wax .... TAPER, BOUGIE, CARNAUBA
wick's end .... SNUFF
candlelight .... EVENING, TWILIGHT
candlenut .... AMA
candlestick .. PRICKET, CRUSIE, LAMPAD, SCONCE
branched .. GIRANDOLE, CANDELABRA, JESSE, CANDELABRUM
ornamental .. FLAMBEAU, LUSTRE
shelf .... GRADIN(E)
candlewick's charred end .... SNUFF
candor .... SINCERITY, FRANKNESS
candy .. BONBON, LOLLYPOP, COMFIT, SWEETMEAT, SWEET, DRAGEE, KISS, LOZENGE
chewy .. CARAMEL, TAFFY, TOFFEE, TOFFY
crisp .... BRITTLE
filler .... FONDANT
flavor .... LIME
fudge-like ... PANOCHA, PENUCHE
gelatinous ... JELLYBEAN
hard: sl. ... JAWBREAKER
jelly-like .... PASTE
nutty .. PRALINE, NOUGAT
on a stick .... LOLLIPOP, LOLLYPOP
piece .. DROP, LOLLYPOP, WAFER, GOODY
pull .... PARTY
seller .... BUCHER
soft .... FUDGE
candytuft .... MUSTARD
cane .... BEAT, STEM, (WALKING)STICK, FLOG, FLAY, RAT(T)AN, HICKORY, WADDY
flogging .... SWISH
like a ..... FERULACEOUS
metal cap .... SHOE, PERRULE
plant .... BAMBOO, RATTAN
strip .... SPLINT
sugar .... SACROSE, SACCHAROSE
walking .... MALACCA
canella .... CINNAMON
Canfield (D.) play .... SOLO
cangue-like device ... PILLORY
canicula .. DOG STAR, SIRIUS
canine (see dog) .. DOG, WOLF, JACKAL, FOX
disease .. RABIES, MANGE, DISTEMPER
mongrel .... CUR, TYKE
tooth ..... TUSH, FANG, LANIARY
canister .... BOX, CAN
canker .. INFECT, ROT, DECAY, SORE
canna .... ACHIRA
cannabin .... RESIN
cannabis .... HEMP, HASHISH
canned ... PRESERVED, TINNED
beef .... BULLY
food toxin .... BOTULIN
food poisoning .... BOTULISM
slang ...... DISMISSED, CASHIERED
Cannes .... RESORT
cannibal .... SAVAGE, MAN-EATER, CARNIVORE
human food of .... LONG PIG
cannikin .. CUP, CAN, BUCKET, PAIL
cannon .. MORTAR, HOWITZER, (CRACK)GUN, ORDNANCE
ball .... MISSILE, PROJECTILE
collectively ... ARTILLERY
dummy .... QUAKER
firing material .... LANIARD, LANYARD, LINSTOCK
fodder, so-called .... SOLDIERS
harness for men .... BRICOLE
in billiards ..... CAROM
kick of .... RECOIL
mounted .... JINGAL, GINGAL
old ..... DRAKE, ASPIC, CULVERIN, FALCON
pivot .... TRUNNION
oriental .... LANTAKA
platform .... TERREPLEIN
shot .... PROJECTILE
cannonade .... BOMBARDMENT, BARRAGE, SALVO

cannoneer .... GUNNER, ARTILLERYMAN
cannonry .... ARTILLERY, ORDNANCE
cannular .... TUBULAR
canny .. CAREFUL, CAUTIOUS, WARY, SHREWD
canoe ...... BOAT, DUGOUT, PITPAN
African .... BONGO, ALMADIA
air chamber .. SPONSON
dugout .... PIRAGUA, PIROGUE
Arctic .... KAYAK
Eskimo .. KAYAK, KAIAK, UMIAK, BIDARKA
Hawaii .... WAAPA
Malabar .... TONEE
Malay .... PROA, PAHI, PRAU, PRAH(O)
Maori .... WAKA
Philippine ..... BANCA, BANKA, CASCO
propeller .. PADDLE, POLE
with outrigger/sail ...... PROA
canon .... RULE, LAW, CRITERION
in music .... ROUND
law expert .... DECRETIST
of the Mass prayer ..... MEMENTO
canonical ... AUTHORITATIVE, ACCEPTED
hour ..... PRIME, SEXT, COMPLIN, NONES, VESPERS, LAUDS, MATIN, TIERCE
law, Moslem .... SHERI
canonicals .... ALB, COPE, STOLE, AMICE, SURPLICE, MANIPLE
canonize .... SAINT, GLORIFY, DEIFY
canonized person .... SAINT
canons, group of ... CHAPTER
canopy .. COPE, AWNING, CIEL, DAIS, TILT, COVER
altar ...... BALDACHIN, CIBORIUM
bed/tomb .... TESTER
boat/cart .... TILT
support .... BAIL
canorous ...... MELODIOUS, MUSICAL, CLEAR
cant ...... DIALECT, ARGOT, LINGO, TRITE, SLANG, PATOIS, JARGON, TILT, TOSS, TURN, SLANT, PATTER
hook .... PEAV(E)Y
cantabile .... SONGLIKE
cantaloup(e) .. (MUSK)MELON
cantankerous ...... ORNERY, BAD-TEMPERED, CONTENTIOUS, PERVERSE, QUARRELSOME
fellow .... CURMUDGEON
cantata .... VOCAL SOLOS, CHORUSES, ARIA, PASTORAL
dramatic/pastoral ...... SERENATA
canteen ... POST EXCHANGE, SHOP, PX, FLASK
canter .. LOPE, GALLOP, GAIT

Canterbury, archbishop of ... DUNSTAN
bell .... CAMPANULA
Tales' author .. CHAUCER
Tales' heroine .... GRISELDA
Tales' inn ...... TABARD
cantharides ...... IRRITANT, STIMULANT
cantharis .... FLY
canticle .. ODE, CHANT, PSALM, HYMN, BRAVURA, SONG
canticles .... SONG OF SONGS
cantina .... SALOON
cantle .... PIECE, SLICE
canto .... PASSUS, STANZA
Archaic .... FIT
obsolete .. SONG, BALLAD
Canton .. DISTRICT, QUARTER, BILLET, QUADRANS
capital of .. KWANGTUNG
city ...... KWANGCHOW
flannel .... NAP
river .... PEARL
river island ...... MACAO
cantor .... PRECENTOR, CHAZ(Z)AN
cantrip ...... (MAGIC)SPELL, PRANK
cantus ...... SONG, MELODY
Canuck .... CANADIAN
canvas ..... SAIL(S), TENT(S), PAINTING, CLOTH, DUCK
boat .... CANOE
cover .... TILT, AWNING
like fabric .... WIGAN
shelter .... TENT
ship's .. JIB, FOREROYAL, STUDDING, MIZZEN, SPANKER
waterproofed .... TARP(AULIN)
canvasback .... DUCK
relative .... SCAUP, REDHEAD
canvass ... SOLICIT, EXAMINE, DISCUSS
voters .... ELECTIONEER, POLL, SURVEY
canyon ..... VALLEY, RAVINE
entrance .... JAWS
mouth .... ABRA
wall .... CLIFF
canzone ... MADRIGAL, POEM
canzonet ... SONG, MATIN(S), CENTO, LILT
caoutchouc .... RUBBER, ELATERITE
source ...... CEARA, ULE, LATEX
cap ...... HEADGEAR, COVER, COIL, COIF, FEZ, TAM, SURPASS, BERET, BEANY
a-pie .... ENTIRELY, HEAD TO FOOT
academic .. MORTARBOARD
and bells wearer .... (COURT) JESTER
bottle .. CAPSULE, CROWN
brim .... VISOR
brimless .... CALOT(TE), PILEUS, BERET, TAM, BALMORAL, TARBOOSH, FEZ, BIRETTA
child's .... BIGGIN
children's ..... BONNET
close/fitting ...... COIF, TOQUE
decoration ... COCKADE, POMPON, FEATHER
ecclesiastical ... BARRET, BERET, BIRET(TA)
jester's ...... COCKSCOMB
Jewish priest's .. MITER, MITRE
kind of .. MORTARBOARD, PERCUSSION
knitted .... THRUM
lawyer's .... COIF
military ...... PERSHING, BUSBY, SHAKO, KEPI, HAVELOCK
mushroom's ... PILEUS
Oriental .. CALPAC, FEZ, TURBAN, KALPAK
part .. BRIM, VISOR, BILL
Scottish ..... BALMORAL, TAM
shaped .... PILEATE
sheepskin ..... CALPAC, KALPAK
skull ..... COIF, PILEUS, CALOT(TE)
slang .... LID
square .... BIRETTA
tube .... CAPSULE
turned up front .... COCKUP
visor .... BILL
winter .... TUQUE
with flap ..... MONTERO
capable .... COMPETENT, SKILLED, EFFICIENT, ABLE
of defense .... TENABLE
of following advice ..... AMENABLE
of motion ...... MOTILE
capacious .. AMPLE, SPACIOUS, ROOMY
capacitor .... CONDENSER
capacity .. CONTENT, VOLUME, APTITUDE, POSITION, STATUS, FUNCTION
for feeling ... SENTIENCE
caparison .... OUTFIT, TRAP(PINGS)
cape .... HEADLAND, PROMONTORY, MANTLE, NESS, TALMA, MANTILLA, FORELAND, MANTELET, MANTA
cod food fish .... CERO
cotton .... MANTA
Dutch ..... AFRIKAANS, TAAL
ecclesiastical ... AMICE, COPE
fur .. PALATINE, ERMINE, PELERINE, COLLARET(TE)
hanging part ... TIPPET
hooded .. AMICE, ALMUCE, MOZ(Z)ETTA
land's .... RAS
like garment .. DOLMAN
Mexican .... SERAPE
muslin .... FICHU

papal ... ORALE, FANON, FANUM, PHANO
sleeveless ..... INVERNESS
3-cornered ...... FICHU
vestment resembling .... COPE
Cape Verde Islands capital ... PRAIA
native .... SERER
Capek (Karel) character ..... ROBOT
play .... RUR
capelin .... SMELT
Capella .... GOAT, STAR, KID
caper ... ANTIC, DIDO, JUMP, FRISK, GAMBOL, CAPRIOLE, CURLICUE, LEAP, TITTUP, ROLLICK, OATCAKE
capillary .. HAIRLIKE, MINUTE
action .... ATTRACTION, REPULSION
capital ... RESOURCES, CHIEF, PRINCIPAL, ASSETS, METROPOLIS
business .... STOCK
colloquial .. FIRST RATE, EXCELLENT
make .... EXPLOIT
letter ...... UPPER-CASE, INITIAL, MAJUSCULE
punishment .... DEATH, EXECUTION, HANGING
ship .... BATTLESHIP, CRUISER, DREADNAUGHT
capitalist .... BARON
capitate ...... HEAD-SHAPED
capitulary .... ORDINANCES
capitulate ...... SURRENDER, YIELD, SUBMIT
capon .... ROOSTER, CHICKEN
caporal .... TOBACCO
capote .. BONNET, TOP, COVER, HOOD
capouch .... HOOD, CAPUCHE
capra .... SHE-GOAT
Capri .... ISLE
capriccio ..... PRANK, WHIM
caprice .... WHIM(SY), FANCY, VAGARY, FREAK, HUMORESQUE
capricious ...... WHIMSICAL, ECCENTRIC, ERRATIC, FLIGHTY, MOONISH, FANCY, HOITY-TOITY, FANTASY, WAYWARD, FICKLE
Capricorn .... GOAT, CONSTELLATION
capriole .... CAPER, LEAP
capsize .... KEEL, TIP, OVERTURN, UPSET, TURN TURTLE
capsicum .. PEPPER, CAYENNE, PAPRIKA, PAPRICA
capstan ..... WINDLASS, WHIM
drum .... RUNDLE
top .... DRUMHEAD
capsule .... CAP, SEAL, CONTAINER, POD, PILL, WAFER, CACHET, AMPULE
egg .... OVISAC
plant .... BOLL
spore .... THECA
captain ..... CHIEF, LEAD(ER), HEAD
Absalom's ...... AMASA
allowance of ... PRIMAGE
boat of the .... GIG
Cook's discovery .... SANDWICH(ISLAND)
dialectic .... CAP'N
in a restaurant .... HEADWAITER
of ship, fiction ... AHAB, NEMO, BLIGH, QUEEG
ship's .. SKIPPER, MASTER
caption .. LEGEND, HEADING, (SUB)TITLE
subject of .... PICTURE, EXHIBIT
captious ... TRICKY, CRITICAL, FAULT-FINDING
captivate .. ENAMOR, CHARM, FASCINATE, ATTRACT, ENTHRALL, ENCHANT
captive .... PRISONER
bail of .... RANSOM
burden of .... YOKE
captivity ..... IMPRISONMENT, BONDAGE
capture ... BAG, CATCH, NAB, NET, SEIZE, COP, SEIZURE
captured object ...... PRIZE
capuche .... HOOD, CAPOUCH
Capuchin ..... MONK, CLOAK, MONKEY, SAPAJOU
monkey .... SAI
caput .... HEAD, DOOMED
capybara ..... RODENT, CAVY, HOG
car ..... SEDAN, AUTOMOBILE, CAGE
baggage ..... FOURGON
balloon .... NACELLE
battered .... HEAP
bubble of .... BLISTER
checkup, repair .... OVERHAUL
closed .... SEDAN
compartment ... TRUNK
decrepit .. CRATE, JALOPY, HEAP
dome .... BLISTER
for hire .. TAXICAB, CAB, TAXI
hyped-up ..... MACH(I), MUSTANG, HOTROD
in a building .. ELEVATOR, LIFT
kind of .... USED, SECONDHAND, MOTOR, RACER, UTILITY, RAILROAD, TOWN, ARMORED, CLOSED, SEDAN, COUPE
mine .... HUTCH
old-make .. REO, T-MODEL
part .. FENDER, RADIATOR, TIRE, WINDSHIELD, WHEEL, HEADLIGHT, BUMPER, MUFFLER
suspended .... TELPHER, TELFER, MONORAIL, ELEVATOR, LIFT
tassle .... TOGGLE
touring .... PHAETON
train's last ..... CABOOSE
versatile .... JEEP
carabao .... BUFFALO, TAMARAW, TAMARAU
horn bugle .... TAMBULI
carabineer ..... CAVALRYMAN, HORSEMAN
carabinieri .... POLICE
caracal .... LYNX, FUR
caracara ..... HAWK, FALCON
Caracas is capital of .... VENEZUELA
coin .... BOLIVAR
carack .... GALLEON
caracole ...... TURN, WHEEL
caracul .... SHEEP, FUR
carafe ... BOTTLE, DECANTER
caramel ...... (BURNT)SUGAR, CANDY
carangoid ... FISH, CAVALLA, CERO, POMPANO, YELLOWTAIL, YELLOWJACK
carapace .... LORICA, SHELL
animal with .... TURTLE, TORTOISE, ARMADILLO, CRAB, TERRAPIN
material .... CHITIN
under part of .. PLASTRON
caravan .... VAN, TRAIN
Arabian .... CAFILA
of a kind .... SAFARI
stopping place .... CARAVANSARY, SERAI, OASIS
caravansary ... KHAN, SERAI, IMARET, INN
caravel .... BEETLE, SHIP, VESSEL
of history ... NINA, PINTA
caraway .... SEED, PLANT
cooky ...... SEED CAKE
carbide, tungsten .. CARBOLOY
carbine ..... MUSKET, RIFLE, ESCOPET, STEN
firearm resembling ...... PETRONEL
carbohydrate ...... STARCH, SUGAR, CELLULOSE, PECTIN, LICHENIN, LEVULIN
suffix .... OSE
carbolic acid .... PHENOL
carbon ... LEAD, SOOT, COKE, CRAYON
combine chemically with.. CARBURET
copy: colloq. .... LOOK ALIKE, (SPITTING)IMAGE, DUPLICATE
iron alloy ..... PEARLITE
pencil .... CHARCOAL
precious/pure .. DIAMOND
product .... SOOT
carbonado ... MEAT, DIAMOND, SLASH, HACK
carbonate of lime .... STALAGMITE, STALACTITE, CALCITE
carborundum ..... ABRASIVE, EMERY
tool .... GRINDSTONE
carboy .... BOTTLE
carbuncle .. PIMPLE, ANTHRAX
carburetant ...... GASOLINE, BENZENE
carcajou .. WOLVERINE, LYNX, BADGER, COUGAR
carcass .. BODY, FRAMEWORK, SKELETON

carcinoma surgery .... MASTECTOMY
card .. ACE, PASTEBOARD, LIST, DEUCE, JACK, KING, TREY, KNAVE, COMB, BRUSH, CARTE, PAM
cheat .... SHARPER, BLACKLEG
combination ... TENACE, MELD
dealer .... TALLIER
dealer's leftovers .... STOCK, TALON
file .... CATALOG(UE)
fortune-telling ... TAROT
French .... CARTE
game ... BACCARAT, LOO, FARO, MONTE, WHIST, SOLITAIRE, MUGGINS, BEZIQUE, CRIBBAGE, HEARTS, PEDRO, CASINO, SLAPJACK, FANTAN, CANASTA, BRIDGE, PINOCHLE, NULLO, POKER, ECARTE, BRAG, QUADRILLE, SEVEN-UP
game "adviser" .... KIBITZER
game dealer ... TALLIER
game extra hand .... KITTY, WIDOW
game for one .. SOLITAIRE
game for two ... PIQUET, COONCAN, CONQUIAN
game holding .... HAND
game like bridge .. VINT
game like rummy .... CONQUIAN, COONCAN
game shuffler .... DEALER
game, solitaire .... CANFIELD
game, 3-hand ..... SKAT
game win ... GIN, VOLE, SLAM
games, authority on .... HOYLE
holding .. HAND, TENACE
in faro .... SODA
kind of ...... COMPASS, CALLING, POST(AL), WEDDING, PLAYING, PASTE, BUSINESS
playing .... PASTEBOARD
sharp .... BLACKLEG
suit, same ...... FLUSH
three-spot .... TREY
two-spot .... DEUCE
with four spots .. QUATRE
wool ..... TEASE, COMB, ROVE
cardamom ..... HERB, SEED, GINGER
cardboard box ..... CARTON
cardialgin ...... HEARTBURN
cardigan ... JACKET, SWEATER, WAMPUS, WAM(M)US
cardinal .. CHIEF, PRINCIPAL, FUNDAMENTAL, BIRD, CLOAK, RED, PIVOTAL, FINCH
American ...... REDBIRD
chair of .... THRONE
is one .... PRINCE
office of ...... DATARIA, PURPLE
rank of .... PURPLE
sign of rank .. RED HAT
skullcap of .. ZUCCHETTO
title of honor .. EMINENCE
vestment .... DALMATIC
cardinals' meeting room ..... CONCLAVE
carding machine cylinder ..... SWIFT
cards, fortune-telling .... TAROTS
held .... HAND
highest .... HONORS
left after dealing .... TALON, CAT, STOCK
care ...... WORRY, ANXIETY, CUSTODY, CHARGE, MIND, CONCERN, CAUTION, TUTELAGE
for ..... PROVIDE, LOVE, (AT)TEND, NURSE, MIND
of the aged .. MEDICARE
careen .... TIP, LURCH, LIST, LEAN, TILT, HEEL
career .... LIFEWORK, PROFESSION, OCCUPATION, VOCATION
careful ..... WARY, PRUDENT, DISCREET, CAUTIOUS, CHARY, FINICAL, METICULOUS
careless .... ARTLESS, NEGLIGENT, LAX, SLIPSHOD, SLOPPY
caress ..... FONDLE, DANDLE, EMBRACE, KISS, CUDDLE, BILL, PET
bear's .... HUG
bird's .... PECK, BILL
dove's .. BILL (AND COO)
Scottish ... DAUT, DAWT
slang .... NECK
caretaker .... CUSTODIAN, KEEPER
apartment .. CONCIERGE
house of .... LODGE
museum/library .... CURATOR
of government, temporary .... REGENT
property .... TRUSTEE
careworn .. HAGGARD, WEARY
cargo ...... FREIGHT, LOAD, PORTAGE, LADING
boat ... OILER, TANKER, SCOW, TRADER, FREIGHTER
cast overboard ship ..... JETSAM
from wrecked ship ..... FLOTSAM
hot ...... CONTRABAND
put on .... LADE, LOAD
ship's .... BULK
space in ship ..... HOLD
carhop .... WAITRESS, WAITER
Carib .... GALIBI, INDIAN
Caribbean island .... ARUBA, AVES, BONAIRE
port .... COLON
caribe .... PIRAYA
caribou .... REINDEER
Algonquian ... KALEBOO
male .... STAG
caricature .... PARODY, TRAVESTY, SATIRE, DISTORTION, BURLESQUE, TAKE-OFF
means of expression .... CARTOON, LAMPOON, BURLESQUE
caricaturist ..... CARTOONIST, SATIRIST
carinate .... KEEL-SHAPED
carillon .... PEAL
cariole ..... CART, CARRIAGE
cark .... WORRY, ANNOY
carl ...... CHURL, BONDMAN, VILLEIN
carline .. HAG, WITCH, WOMAN
Carlton's (hotel) partner ..... RITZ
Carmelite .... (WHITE)FRIAR
"Carmen" composer .... BIZET
Carmichael (Hoagy) songhit .. STARDUST
carminative seeds .. CARAWAY
carmine ...... CRIMSON, RED
carnage .... SLAUGHTER, MASSACRE, BLOODSHED, BUTCHERY
carnal .... SENSUAL, SEXUAL, BODILY, FLESHY, MUNDANE, WORLDLY
carnation .. DIANTHUS, PINK, RED, FLOWER, PICOTEE
carnauba .... PALM
product .... WAX
carnelian .... QUARTZ, CHALCEDONY
carnival .... GALA, FESTIVAL, FESTIVITY, MERRYMAKING, FAIR, EXHIBITION
character ..... BARKER, SHILL, GRIFTER
famous .... MARDI GRAS
feature ...... CONFETTI, PARADE, PAGEANT, SIDESHOWS, RIDES
gambling operator ..... GRIFTER
hawker's spot ... PITCH
carnivore ...... MINK, URSUS, OTTER, DOG, PUMA, WOLF, LION, SEAL, (POLE)CAT, FOUMART, BEAR, TIGER, GENET, HYENA, RATEL, SERVAL
diet ...... MEAT, FLESH
opposed to .. HERBIVORE
carnivorous insect ... MANTIS
reptile .... TUATARA, CROCODILE, MONITOR
carnotite .. MINERAL, URANIUM
carob ... LOCUST, POD, TREE, ALGAROBA
carol .... TRILL, SING
Christmas .... NOEL
singer .... WAIT
Caroline, diminutive of ...... CARRIE
island .. PALU, TRUK, YAP
Carolinian .... TARHEEL
carom .. RICOCHET, REBOUND
carotid .... ARTERY
carousal ...... BINGE, SPREE, ORGY, REVELRY, WASSAIL, TEAR
carouse .. BOUSE, SPREE, REVEL

carousel ... MERRY-GO-ROUND, WHIRLIGIG, LILIOM
carp ...... CRITICIZE, CAVIL, BLEAK, TENCH, LOACH
Japanese .... KOI
kin .... MINNOW
like fish .... DACE, GOLDFISH, IDE
minnow .... SHINER
red-eye .... RUDD
carpal joint .... KNEE
Carpatho-Ukraine .. RUTHENIA
carpel .... ACHENE
carpels, united ...... PISTIL
carpenter .. WRIGHT, JOINER, WOODWORKER, ANT
joint of .. MITER, MORTISE
tool of .... CHISEL, PLANE, BEVEL, SAW, ADZE
carpet .... MAT, COVER, RUG, TAPETE, TAPIS, MOQUETTE, FOOTCLOTH, WILTON
Afghan .... HERAT
city ..... TOURNAI, AGRA
India .... AGRA
material .... DRUGGET, MOQUETTE
on the .... CHARGED, ACCUSED
Persian .... KALI
carpetbagger .. ADVENTURER, POLITICIAN, PROMOTER
carping .. CAPTIOUS, CRITICAL
carport .... GARAGE
carpus .... WRIST
bone .... CARPAL(E)
carrack ... GALLEON, VESSEL
carrageen ...... IRISH, MOSS, SEAWEED
carreta .... CART
carriage .... POISE, BEARING, CONVEYANCE, CARIOLE, GIG, CHAISE, VOITURE, SULKY, LANDAU, PHAETON, SHAY, AIR, SURREY, PORTANCE, RIG, ROCKAWAY, STANHOPE
attendant .... FLUNKEY, OUTRUNNER, OUTRIDER
baby ... PERAMBULATOR, BUGGY, GO-CART, PRAM, CLARENCE
berlin(e) .... BAROUCHE
closed .... COUPE
dog .... DALMATIAN
driver ..... HACK(MAN), COACH(MAN)
driver's seat .. DICK(E)Y
folding top .... CALASH, CALECHE, PHAETON
for hire .... FIACRE, HANSOM, HACK
for state occasions ...... CAROCHE
four-wheeled .... DEARBORN, LANDAU, CLARENCE, BERLIN(E), PHAETON, BAROUCHE, BUCKBOARD, TARANTAS, CHAISE, VICTORIA
French .... FIACRE
hackney .... FLY
hood .... CAPOTE
Java .... SADO
low-wheeled .. TARANTAS, CALASH
luggage space .. RUMBLE
man-drawn .. JINRIKSHA, RICKSHA(W)
one-horse .... TRAP, CARRYALL, CARIOLE, SHAY, CHAISE, CALESIN
Philippine ..... CALESA, CARROMATA, TARTANILLA, CALESIN
pole ..... THILL, SHAFT
Russian ... TARANTAS(S), TROIKA
seat .... RUMBLE
servant's seat in .... DICKEY, RUMBLE
single-seat ... STANHOPE
top .... CAPOTE
two-wheeled ..... SULKY, TRAP, TILBURY, CURRICLE, CALESA, CALECHE, CALASH, CHAISE, HERDIC
with collapsible top ..... CHAISE, CALASH, CALECHE, BRITSKA
with liveried attendants .. EQUIPAGE
carried ...... TRANSPORTED, BORNE, TOTED, SWAYED
away .... RAPT, OVERWHELMED
carrier .. REDCAP, MESSENGER, PORTER, BEARER, TOTER, PORTER
air .... AIRPLANE
armor .. ARMIGER, SQUIRE
bad luck .... JINX
coal/brick/mortar .. HOD, CORF
in a depot ..... PORTER
of disease virus .. VECTOR
Oriental .... HAMAL
Spanish ..... CARGADOR
water .... BHEESTEE
carrion .. FILTHY, DECAYING, ROTTEN
crow .... VULTURE
Carroll (Lewis) heroine ...... ALICE
forte .... PARODY
carron oil .... LINIMENT
carrot ...... FENNEL, PLANT
like plant ...... PARSNIP
oil tube .... VITTA
carroty .. ORANGE, RED-HAIRED
car(r)ousel ... TOURNAMENT, MERRY-GO-ROUND, WHIRLIGIG
carry .. TRANSPORT, CONVEY, LEAD, WIN, TRANSMIT, CART, SWAY, LUG, BEAR, TOTE, SUSTAIN, FETCH
across water .... FERRY
away .... EXCITE
off .... ABDUCT, KIDNAP
on ... CONTINUE, WAGE, CONDUCT, PROSECUTE
on person .... WEAR
out ...... ACCOMPLISH, EFFECT, OBEY, EXECUTE
over .... POSTPONE
too far .... OVERDO
weight .... COUNT
carryall ...... BAG, BASKET, CARRIAGE
kind of .... BUS
carrying away .... EFFERENT
unborn child .... PREGNANT, ENCEINTE
Carson City is capital of ..... NEVADA
cart .... WAIN, VAN, LORRY, CARRY, WAGON, HAUL, DRAY, CARIOLE, BOGY, TRUNDLE
ammunition ... TUMBREL, TUMBRIL, CAISSON
hand .... PRAM
racing .... CHARIOT
carte ... MENU, BILL OF FARE, QUART(E), CARD
blanche of a sort .... BLANK CHECK
cartel .... CHALLENGE, AGREEMENT, MONOPOLY
of a sort .... TRUST, SYNDICATE
Carter Dickson pseudonym ... CARR
Carthage, capital of .... CARALIS
destroyer of ... ROMANS, SCIPIO
foe of .... CATO
founder of .... DIDO
god of .... MOLOCH
goddess .... TANIT
of .... PUNIC
queen of .... DIDO
Roman idea of .... TREACHEROUS, FAITHLESS
wars of .... PUNIC
Carthaginian conqueror ..... HANNIBAL
general ..... HAMILCAR, HANNIBAL, HASDRUBAL
Carthusian .. EREMITE, MONK, NUN
order founder .... (SAINT) BRUNO
cartilage .... PLAIT, GRISTLE
combining form .... CHONDRO
dog tongue's .... LYTTA
cartograph ..... MAP, CHART, PLAT
cartographer ..... MERCATOR
cartographical half .... HEMI
carton .... (CARDBOARD) BOX
cartoon .... DRAWING, COMIC STRIP, SKETCH
kind of .... CARICATURE, EDITORIAL
vocals .... BALLOONS
cartoonist .... DRAWER, SKETCHER, (DAVID) LOW, (PETER) ARNO, ADDAMS, CAPP, DISNEY, NAST, KIRBY, SOGLOW, OLIPHANT, SCHULTZ
cartoons .... STRIPS
cartridge .... SHOT, SHELL
box .... CARTOUCH(E)
container .... CLIP
cartwheel .. HAT, HANDSPRING
slang .... COIN

caruncle .... COMB, WATTLE, GILL
Caruso, opera singer .. ENRICO
carvacrol .... ANTISEPTIC, ANESTHETIC
carve ...... CUT, (EN)GRAVE, CHISEL, SLICE, INCISE, SCULPT
carved ..... GRAVEN, GLYPHIC
figure .... GLYPH
gem .... CAMEO
image .... STATUE
carver .... SCULPTOR, GRAVER
carving .... SCULPTURE
art .... GLYPTICS
in low relief .... ANAGLYPHY
stone .... CAMEO
tool .... CHISEL
Cary Grant .. (ARCHIE) LEACH
casaba .... (MUSK)MELON
fruit like ... CANTALOUPE
Casal's (Pablo) instrument ... CELLO
cascade .. WATERFALL, LINN, SHOWER, FALL
cascara .... BUCKTHORN, BEARWOOD, WAHOO
case ...... MATTER, INSTANCE, AFFAIR, EXAMPLE, SITUATION, EVENT, CAPSULE, CONTAINER, CRATE, SHEATH, BOX, QUESTION, LOOK OVER
armadillo's ... CARAPACE
auto tire .... SHOE
book .... FOREL
bullet ...... CARTRIDGE
chalice linen ..... BURSE
egg .... SHELL
for arnica ...... BRUISE
for liquor bottles .... CELLARET
fruit .... RIND
grammatical .... DATIVE, NOMINATIVE, ABLATIVE, ACCUSATIVE, GENITIVE
hospital ...... PATIENT
in any .... ANYHOW
in: sl. .... DIE
insect larva's .. INDUSIUM
of explosives ... PETARD
pea .... POD
portrait .... LOCKET
pupa .... COCOON
sausage ..... INTESTINE
seed .... POD
ship .... HULL
slang ...... LOOK OVER, EXAMINE
small ... CAPSULE, ETUI, ETWEE, PYXIS
toilet ... ETUI, COMPACT, ETWEE
trial site .... VENUE
turtle .... CARAPACE
casein preparation .... LACTARENE
synthetic fabric .... LANITAL
casemate .... ENCLOSURE
describing a .... SHELLPROOF, ARMORED
casement ... WINDOW, FRAME
casern .... BARRACKS
cash .. (READY) MONEY, COINS, BILLS, CURRENCY, SPECIE
advance .. IMPREST, ARLES
box ..... TILL, REGISTER
note .... VOUCHER
note of sorts .... IOU
on delivery .... COD
ready .... TILL
receipts/payments handler ...... CASHIER, TELLER
register sign ... NO SALE
cashaw .... CUSHAW, SQUASH
cashbook .... LEDGER
cashew .... ANACARD, PISTACHIO, MANGO
French .... (A)CAJOU
oil .... CARDOL
cashier .. TELLER, DISCHARGE, DISCARD, BURSAR, PURSER, DISMISS
cashmere ... WOOL, KASHMIR
cashoo .... CATECHU
Cashin, dress designer .... BONNIE
casing .... HULL, COVER, SHEATH(ING), FRAME
casino ...... SUMMERHOUSE, CARD GAME
cask ..... KEG, BARREL, VAT, TUN, BARECA, TIERCE, BUTT, FIRKIN, PUNCHEON
bulge .... BILGE
content measurer .... GA(U)GER
cork .... BUNG
forty-two-gallon .. TIERCE
four-gallon .... TUB
groove .... CROZE
maker .. COOPER, HOOPER
rim ..... CHIMB, CHIME, CHINE
small .... RUN(D)LET
stave .... LAG
staves, set ...... SHOOK
stopper .... BUNG
casket .. BOX, CHEST, COFFIN, PIX
carrier ..... PALLBEARER
for sacred relics .. CIST, KIST, RELIQUARY
for valuables .... COFFER
Caspary (Vera) play .. LAURA
Caspian Sea fish .. STURGEON, BELUGA
tributary .. URAL, VOLGA, KURA
casque .... HELMET
cassaba .... (MUSK)MELON
Cassandra .... SEERESS, PROPHETESS
descriptive of ..... LIAR
parent of .... PRIAM, HECUBA
cassava .... JUCA, MANIOC, MANIHOT
product .... STARCH, BREAD, TAPIOCA
casserite .... TINSTONE
casserole .... STEW, RAGOUT, DISH, (SAUCE) PAN, (FRYING) PAN
dish .... GRATIN
cassia ...... CINNAMON, BARK
cathartic drug ... SENNA
cassimere .... CASHMERE, CLOTH
Cassini, designer ...... OLEG
Cassiopeia's chair .... STARS, CONSTELLATION
daughter ... ANDROMEDA
husband .... CEPHEUS
cassock .. VESTMENT, SOUTANE, CLERGYMAN
belt .... SURCINGLE
cassowary ..... BIRD, RATITE
bird like ...... OSTRICH, RHEA, EMU
cast .. FLING, THROW, HURL, SHED, MOLD, TOSS, FOUND
about ... SEARCH, LOOK, DEVISE
amorous glances .. OGLE
aside .... DISCARD, ABANDON
away .... DISCARD
ballot .... VOTE
blame on ...... REFLECT
down .. REJECT, DISOWN, HURL
founded ...... FUSIL(E)
horn .... MEW
in printing .. STEREOTYPE, ELECTROTYPE
iron ...... HARD, RIGID
metal mass .. PIG, INGOT
of characters .. PERSONAE
off .... EXUVIATE, SHED, DISCARD, SLOUGH
off by animal .... MOLT
out .. EXPEL, EJECT, EVICT
thing ..... VOTE, BALLOT, BAIT, DICE, FLY, NET, ANCHOR
up .... VOMIT
with matrix ...... MOLD
Castalia .... SPRING
castanea .... CHESTNUT
castaway ... WAIF, OUTCAST, PARIAH
a kind of .... LEPER
merchants' .... TELI
shipwreck's .... DERELICT
caste .. SOCIAL SYSTEM, CLASS
castellan .... WARDEN, GOVERNOR, CHATELAIN
caster ...... CRUET, ROLLER, BOTTLE, STAND, TRUNDLE, TRUCKLE
castigate .. CHASTISE, REBUKE, PUNISH, CRITICIZE
Castile .... SOAP
designating part of ..... NUEVA, VIEJA
province .... AVILA
river .... EBRO
casting mold .... DIE, MATRICE
place .... FOUNDRY
castle .... STRONGHOLD, CHESSPIECE, ROOK, KEEP, HOME
attackers' explosive ..... PETARD
court .... BAILEY
ditch .... MOAT
entrance ...... POSTERN
French .... CHATEAU

governor/warden .... CASTELLAN
in the air ... DAYDREAM, REVERIE
keep .... DONJON
keeper ..... CASTELLAN, CHATELAIN
lady of the .. CHATELAINE
open space .... WARD
tower .... DONJON, BARRICAN, KEEP
underground cell .... DUNGEON
VIP ...... KING, KNIGHT
wall .... BAIL(EY)
warden ...... CONSTABLE
Castles' dance .... WALK, BUNNY HUG
castoff .... DISCHARGED, DISOWNED, ABANDONED, SHED
Castor .. CRUET, BEAVER, HAT, BEAN, STAR
and Pollux ..... GEMINI, TWIN, DIOSCURI
bean protein ..... RICIN
father of .... ZEUS
killer of .... IDAS
mother of .... LEDA
oil poison .... RICIN
silk .... ERI(A)
twin brother of .. POLLUX
castrate .. EMASCULATE, GELD, MUTILATE, CAPONIZE, UNMAN, SPAY, STERILIZE, ALTER
castrated .... GIBBED
animal .. NEUTER, STAG, GIB
boar .... HOG
bull .... OX
cat .... GIB
cattle .... STEER
horse .... GELDING
man .... EUNUCH
pig .... BARROW
rooster/cock ..... CAPON
sheep .... WETHER
casual .... CHANCE, IDLE, OFFHAND, INCIDENTAL, AIMLESS, CURSORY, RANDOM, PASSING
casualty .. ACCIDENT, VICTIM, FATALITY
casuist .... QUIBBLER
alleged .... JESUIT
of a sort .... SOPHIST
casuistic .... SPECIOUS
casus .... HAPPENING, EVENT, CASE
belli result .... WAR
cat .. FELINE, TIGER, ANGORA, LION, COUGAR, LEOPARD, PUMA, CIVET, GENET(TE), FELID, BAUDRONS, LYNX, MALKIN, MAWKIN, OCELOT, MARGAY, PANTHER, PUSS(Y)
brier .... SMILAX
castrated ...... GIB(BED)
colloquial .. KITTY, PUSSY
domestic .... MANX
drinking way of .... LAP
epithet ...... BAUDRONS
eyed animal ...... LYNX
family ...... FELI(DAE), FELINE
female .... TABBY, GRIMALKIN, QUEEN
grinning, proverbial .... CHESHIRE
like animal .... ZIBET(H), GENET(TE), LINSANG
mice-hunting .... MOUSER
move like a .. PUSSYFOOT
musk-yielding .... CIVET
nap .... DOZE
o-nine-tails .... WHIP
of the .... FELINE
pet ... SIAMESE, PERSIAN, MALTESE, ANGORA
ring-tailed ...... SERVAL
sound ..... PURR, ROAR, MIAOW, MIAUL, MEW, MEOW, CATERWAUL
spotted .... JAGUAR, SERVAL, MARGAY, OCELOT
striped .... TIGER
young .... KITTEN
cats'-eye ..... GEM, QUARTZ, CHATOYANT, CHRYSOBERYL
paw .. PAD, DUPE, TOOL, STOOGE, PAWN, KNOT
whisker(s) .. VIBRISSA(E)
cata, as prefix .... DOWN, AWAY, AGAINST, THROUGH, BACKWARD
catachresis, victim of .... (MRS.) MALAPROP
cataclysm ... FLOOD, DELUGE, DISASTER, UPHEAVAL
kind of .... WAR, EARTHQUAKE
catacomb .. CRYPT, CEMETERY, LOCULUS
catafalque .... BIER
catalase .... ENZYME
catalo ...... BUFFALO, BISON, BOVINE
catalogue ..... LIST, RECORD, SCHEDULE, REGISTER, CLASSIFY, ROLL, INDEX
bookseller's .... BIBLIOTHECA
box .... CARD FILE
of goods, etc. .... INVENTORY
of saints ..... HAGIOLOGY
official .... CANON
Catalonian poet-musician .... TROUBADOR
catalyst .... ACTIVATOR, REAGENT
catamaran ..... RAFT, BALSA, BOAT, FLOAT
catamenia .... MENSTRUATION
catamite .... PUNK
catamount ... PUMA, COUGAR, LYNX
cataplasm .... POULTICE
catapult ..... BRICOLE, HURL, ONAGER, BALLISTA, TREBUCHET
kin of ...... MANGONEL
projectile .... PELLET
cataract ...... (WATER)FALL, DELUGE, DOWNPOUR, LINN, CASCADE
catarrh .... RHEUM, COLD
cigarette for ...... CUBEB
nasal .... CORYZA
catastasis .... EXORDIUM
catastrophe .. RUIN, DISASTER, MISFORTUNE, CALAMITY
in geology ... CATACLYSM
Catawba ...... GRAPE, WINE
catch ..... NAB, SEIZE, HOOK, CAPTURE, NAIL, RATCHET TRAP, PAWL
breath ..... GASP, PANT
fish .... HAUL
in a bill .. RIDER, JOKER
of clock .... DETENT
on .... GET IT, CLICK, UNDERSTAND
phrase .... SLOGAN, WARCRY, MOTTO
releaser .. PAWL, TRIPPER, DETENT
sight of .... ESPY, SPOT, DESCRY
up .... OVERTAKE, OVERHAUL
with the ___ .... GOODS
catchall .. (RAG)BAG, BASKET, HANDBAG, ET AL, ETC(ETERA)
one kind of ..... ATTIC, CLOSET
catcher ..... CAPTOR, NABBER
catching .... CONTAGIOUS, INFECTIOUS, ATTRACTIVE, FETCHING
catchment, kind of .... RESERVOIR, CISTERN
catchpenny .... CHEAP, WORTHLESS
catchpole ..... TAXGATHERER, CHICKEN CHASER
catchup ... KETCHUP, CATSUP
catchword ..... SLOGAN, CUE, MOTTO
catchy ...... TRICKY, FITFUL, DECEIVING
cate ..... DELICACY, DAINTY
catechism .... HANDBOOK
catechu ... CASHOO, GAMBLER, CUTCH
like gum .... KINO
catechumen .... PUPIL
categorical .... ABSOLUTE, POSITIVE, DIRECT, EXPLICIT
category ... DIVISION, SPECIES, CLASS, GENRE
catena .... CHAIN
cater .... PANDER, SERVE, PURVEY, PROVIDE
cornered .. DIAGONAL(LY)
cateran .... ROBBER
caterer, army .... SUTLER
kind of ..... PANDERER, PROCURER, PIMP
caterpillar .... LARVA, WERI, WOOLLYBEAR, SLUG, CUTWORM, WOOBUT, LOOPER, WEBWORM
disease .... WILT
hair .... SETA
treaded vehicle ... TANK, HALF-TRACK, AMTRAC, TRACTOR, CAT
caterwaul .... MIAUL, HOWL, SCREECH, WAIL, SCREAM

catfish .... TANDAN, (BULL)POUT, BULLHEAD, DORAD, SILURID, SCULPIN, SHAL
electric .... RAAD
Row resident ... PORGY, BESS
catgut ..... CATLING, VIOLIN, WHIPCORD
cathartic .... CALOMEL, CASTOR OIL, LAXATIVE, PURGING, ALOIN, GAMBOGS, ALOE, EVACUANT, EMETIC, CASSIA, PHYSIC
drug .... SENNA
from flax .... LININ
resin .... SCAMMONY
Cathay .... CHINA
cathedra .... THRONE, SEE
cathedral .... AUTHORITATIVE, OFFICIAL, DUOMO, MINSTER
city .... ELY, AMIENS, CHARTRES, R(H)EIMS
clergyman ...... CANON
famous ..... NOTRE DAME
passage .... SLYPE
presiding official ... DEAN
private land of ... CLOSE
Cather, novelist ..... SIBERT, WILLA
Catherine, mother of 3 kings .. MEDICI
Catherine the Great .. TSARINA
favorite ...... POTEMKIN
Catholic .... UNIVERSAL, LIBERAL
lay society .... SODALITY
tribunal .... ROTA
tribunal member .... AUDITOR
catholicon .... PANACEA, CURE-ALL, ELIXIR
cation .... ION
catkin ... AMENT(A), CATTAIL, PUSSY, CHAT
tree .... BIRCH, WILLOW, POPLAR
catlike .. NOISELESS, STEALTHY
animal .... LINSANG
catling ...... CATGUT, KNIFE
catnap .... DOZE
catnip .... NEP
catouse .... UPROAR
catsup ..... KETCHUP, SAUCE, CATCHUP
Catt, American suffragist .... CARRIE
cattail .... CATKIN, TULE, (BUL)RUSH, DODD, REED(MACE), RAUPO
cattiness .... MEANNESS
cattle .. BOVINE, KINE, BOVID, OXEN, NOWT
beef ... STEER, HOLSTEIN
black .... KERRY
boat .... TARTAN
breed .... DEVON, KERRY, DURHAM, LONGHORN
castrated .... STEER
catcher .... HAYWARD
catching rope ..... BOLA
crossed with bison/buffalo CAT(T)ALO
dairy .. KERRY, GUERNSEY
dealer .... DROVER
dewlap .... JOWL
disease ...... BOTS, GID, STAGGERS, ANTHRAX, NAGANA, GARGET, TEXAS FEVER, LUMPY JAW, LOCO, MURRAIN, MEASLES, SCOURS, SHAKES
dwarf .... DEVON, NIATA
dysentery .... SCOURS
enclosure ...... RODEO, KRAAL, CORRAL
epidemic ... RINDERPEST
farm ... RANCH, ESTANCIA
farm manager .. RANCHER
fat .... SUET, TALLOW
feed for hire ...... GIST
feed from linseed .... OIL CAKE
fodder .... FARRAGO
foot of .... HOOF
frenzied run .. STAMPEDE
grazing land .... RANGE, PASTURE
herdsman ..... VAQUERO
hybrid ...... CAT(T)ALO
nervous ailment .... STAGGERS
parasitic larva .. WARBLE
pen .... KRAAL, CORRAL, YARD
plague ...... RINDERPEST
polled .... MUL(L)EY
ranch .... ESTANCIA
ranch man .... COWBOY, VAQUERO
raiser .... STOCKMAN, RANCHER
round-up .... WRANGLE, RODEO
short-horned ... DURHAM
stall .... CRIB
stealer .... RUSTLER
stealing .... RUSTLING
tender .... COWHEAD, VAQUERO
tormentor .... GNAT
urine .... STALE
vertigo .... MEGRIM
cattleman .. RANCHER, DROVER, HERDER
catty .... MEAN, SPITEFUL, MALICIOUS
catwalk .... PATHWAY, PLATFORM, BRIDGE
Caucasian .. IRANIAN, ARYAN, TATAR, WHITE MAN
carpet ..... KUBA, BAKU
goat .... TUR
language .... GEORGIAN, SEMITIC, CIRCASSIAN
race .... SEMITE
rug .... BAKU
Caucasus inhabitant .... OSSET(IAN)
region .... OSSETIA
river .... KUBAN
wild goat .... TUR
caucho tree .... ULE
caucus .... MEETING, CONFAB
caudad, opposed to .... CEPHALAD
caudal appendage ...... TAIL
caudillo .... LEADER, COMMANDER
El .... FRANCO
caudle .... DRINK, GRUEL
caul .... VEIL
cauld .... COLD
cauldron ... KETTLE, COPPER, POT
caulicle .... STEM
cauliflower .... CABBAGE, BROCCOLI
eared one .. BOXER, PUG
row character ... BOXER, PUG
caulis .... STEM, STALK
caulk .. STOP UP, SEAL, CHINSE
caulking material ...... TAR, OAKUM
causal connective ..... SINCE, THEREFORE, FOR
cause ...... REASON, MOTIVE, GROUND, MOVEMENT, EFFECT, INDUCE, OCCASION
bad luck .... HEX, JINX
celebre, usual .... CASE, TRIAL, SCANDAL
for divorce .. GROUND(S)
for war ..... CASUS BELLI
in law ...... (LAW) SUIT
impelling ... MAINSPRING
spasm .... CONVULSE
to arch .... ROACH
to do unwillingly .... COERCE, PRESS
to fight .... EMBROIL
to happen ...... BRING, EFFECTUATE
causerie .... PLEAD, PARLEY, DEBATE, CHAT, DISPUTE, TALK
causes, science of .... (A)ETIOLOGY
causeuse .. SOFA, TETE-A-TETE
causeway ..... ROAD, CAUSEY
causing abortion ... ECBOLIC
disaster .... MALEFIC
no pain ..... INDOLENT
sneezing ...... ERRHINE
caustic .. CORROSIVE, CUTTING, SNAPPISH, VITRIOLIC, MORDACIOUS, SARDONIC, MORDANT, BITING, TART, STINGING, LIME, SARCASTIC
agent .. ERODENT, ACID, LYE
solution .... LYE
substance, burn with .... CAUTERIZE
temper .. SNAPPISH, TESTY
cauterant .... MOXA
cauterize .. BURN, SEAR, CHAR
cauterizing agent ...... MOXA
cautery .... MOXA
caution .... WARN(ING), BAIL, PRUDENCE, CARE, ALERT, ADMONITION, ADMONISH
cautious ..... WARY, CHARY, CAREFUL, CIRCUMSPECT, WARE
general .... FABIUS
cavalcade .... PARADE, PROCESSION, PAGEANT
cavalier .... KNIGHT, GENTLEMAN, GAY, ARROGANT, PROUD

cavalla ... CARANGOID, HORES, CERO, FISH
cavalry .... TROOPS, HORSE
attack obstacle .... CALTRAP, CALTROP
command ... TO HORSE, DISMOUNT, CHARGE
commander .. HIPPARCH
flag .... CORNET
horse .. TROOPER, WALER
men's hazard .. CALTRAP, CALTROP
soldier .. LANCE(R), SPAHI
standard ..... LABARUM
sword .... SABER
unit .... SQUADRON
cavalryman .... DRAGOON, TROOP(ER), LANCER
Algerian .... SPAHI
French .... CARABINEER, CARABINIER, CHASSEUR
German .... U(H)LAN
horse .... WALER
Hungarian/Croatian .... HUSSAR
mount of Algerian ...... CAMEL
Russian .... COSSACK
Turkish .. SPAHI, SPAHEE
weapon of ..... LANCE, SABER
cavatina ..... SONG, MELODY
cave .. DEN, HOLLOW, CRYPT, GROT(TO), ANTRE, ANTRUM, LAIR
dweller ... TROGLODYTE, BAT, BEAR, LION, HERMIT, TROLL
dweller ..... SPEL(A)EAN
explorer .... SPELUNKER
formation .. STALACTITE, STALAGMITE
in ...... COLLAPSE, SINK, YIELD, SUBMIT
man ...... TROGLODYTE, HERMIT
man-made ...... CRYPT
man's time .. STONE AGE
of a .... SPELEAN
poetic ..... GROT, ANTRE
caveat .... WARNING, NOTICE
Cavell, nurse .... EDITH
cavern ...... GROT(TO), LAIR, ANTRE
Hebrides Island .... FINGAL'S CAVE
caves, inhabiting .. SPELEAN
science of .. SPELEOLOGY
caviar .... RELISH, ROE
connoisseur ... GOURMET, RUSSIAN, GOURMAND
fish .. STERLET, STURGEON
material .... (FISH)EGGS, ROE
source of ..... STERLET, SALMON, STURGEON, SHAD
cavil .. CARP, QUIBBLE, OBJECT, BICKER
cavities, full of ... CAVERNOUS
cavity ...... ANTRUM, HOLE, HOLLOW, CELL, PIT, SINUS, FOSSA, FOLLICLE
animal tissue .. LOCULUS
combining form .... C(O)ELE
crystal-lined .... GEODIC
crystal-lined rock .... GEODE, VOOG, VUGG, VUGH
embryonic .. COELOM(E)
eye .... ORBIT
heart .... ATRIUM
honeycomb .... CELL, ALVEOLUS
in anatomy ..... FOSSA, BURSA, ANTRUM, LACUNA, SINUS, ALVEOLUS
in biology ...... LACUNA
in zoology ..... CLOACA, ALVEOLUS
membrane ..... VESICLE
nose .... ANTRUM, SINUS
of abdominal .. COELIAC
opening/outlet .. ORIFICE
plant tissue .... LOCULUS
stone with crystal-lined .. GEODE
cavort .. CAPER, PRANCE, LEAP
cavy .... RODENT, PACA, CAPYBARA, GUINEA PIG
caw sounder ... CROW, RAVEN
Cawdor castle site .... NAIRN
cay .... (CORAL)REEF, (SAND)BANK, KEY
cayenne ... PEPPER, CAPSICUM, CHILIES, CANARY
cayman .... ALLIGATOR, YAKI
cayuse .... PONY
cowpoke's .... HOSS
Ceara .... FORTALEZA
cease ..... END, DESIST, STOP, DISCONTINUE, REFRAIN, HALT
nautical .... AVAST
ceaseless .... CONTINUAL, ENDLESS, CONTINUOUS
Cechy .... BOHEMIA
Cecrops .. KING, MAN-DRAGON
daughter of ...... HERSE
cecum .... POUCH
cedar ...... JUNIPER, THUJA, WOOD, SAVIN(E), TOON(A), DEODAR, CONIFER
Himalayan ...... DEODAR
cedarbird .... WAXWING
cede ..... GRANT, TRANSFER, YIELD
Cedric .... (WAR) CHIEF
ward of .... ROWENA
cedula .. CERTIFICATE, PERMIT
ceiba .. KAPOK, SILK-COTTON
ceil .... LINE, COVER
ceiling, decorated ... PLAFOND
division .... TRAVE
hit the: colloq. ... RAGE, ERUPT
mine .... ASTEL
of sunken panels .... LACUNAR
picture .... MURAL
plasterwork .... PARGET(ING)
rounded .. CUPOLA, DOME
section .... PANEL
Celaeno .... HARPY
celandine .... PILEWORT
celanese .... RAYON
Celebes .... SULAWESI
city .... MACASSAR
ox .... ANOA
celebrant at mass ..... PRIEST
celebrate .... SOLEMNIZE, COMMEMORATE, OBSERVE, FETE
in song .... CAROL
celebrated .. OBSERVED, NOTED, FAMOUS, RENOWN, SOLEMNIZED, EMINENT
celebration, gala ..... FIESTA
with much drinking .... CAROUSAL, WASSAIL
celebrities' meeting place ..... SALON
celebrity .. IDOL, LION, FAME, RENOWN, STAR, HERO
treat like a ..... LIONIZE
celerity .... QUICKNESS, DISPATCH, HASTE, SPEED, SWIFTNESS
celery ... PLANT, VEGETABLE, SMALLAGE
like plant .... UDO
celesta for example .... IDIOPHONE
celeste .... BLUE, AZURE
celestial .. HEAVENLY, DIVINE, URANIC, HOLY, ETHEREAL, SUPERNAL, OLYMPIAN
being ... ANGEL, CHERUB, SERAPH
body .. SUN, STAR, MOON, COMET
circle .... COLURE, HALO
empire .... CHINA
happiness .... BLISS, ECSTASY
phenomenon .... COMET, ECLIPSE, RAINBOW
slang .... CHINAMAN
vault .... EMPYREAN
celibacy ..... BACHELORHOOD, SINGLE LIFE
celibate .. BACHELOR, SINGLE, UNMARRIED
former .... BENEDICT
one kind of ...... MONK, PRIEST
cell ... EGG, GERM, CONVENT, MONASTERY, CADRE, BATTERY
cavity .... VACUOLE
center .... NUCLEUS
combining form ... CYTO, CYTE
destruction .. (CYTO)LYSIS
division .... SPIREME, (A)MITOSIS
formation .. CYTOGENESIS
formed by two gametes .. ZYGOTE
framework ..... STROMA
honeycomb ... ALVEOLUS
nerve .... NEURON(E)
nucleus ...... MESOPLAST
small .. CELLULE, PAPILLA
stinging .... NEMATOCYST
study of the .. CYTOLOGY
wall .... PARIES
wall rib .... RAPHE
cella .... NAOS, TEMPLE
cellar .. WINE-STOCK, PANTRY, STOREROOM
location of .... BASEMENT

man in charge of .... BUTLER
room .... VAULT
wine .... VAULT, BUTTERY
celled structure ..... PRISON, CONVENT, MONASTERY, HONEYCOMB
cells, consisting of .... LOCULAR, CELLULAR
change in ... CATAPLASIA
form into .... CELLULATE
mass of .... MORULA
ovum-formed mass of ... MORULA
union of .... ZYGOSIS
water-conducting .... TRACHEID
cellular .... ALVEOLATE, LOCULAR
celluloid: colloq. .... (MOVIE) FILM, MOVIES
cellulose fiber .... RAYON, CELANESE
wrapping material ...... CELLOPHANE
Celt ... BRETON, IRISH, GAEL, WELSH, SCOT, CHISEL
Celtic .... ERSE, IRISH
chief's heir ...... TANIST
dart .... COLP
god .... AENGUS, LER
island of paradise ...... AVALON
judge .... DRUID
king .... BELI
language .... WELSH, BRETON, MANX, CYMRIC
lord .... TANIST
people of Wales .... CYMRIC
priest .... DRUID
religious order ... DRUID
sea god .... LER
sea robber ...... FOMOR
cement .. GLUE, JOIN, SOLDER, MALTHA, MASTIC
ingredient .. LIME, CLAY, WATER
like substance .... PASTE, GLUE
material .... MARL
mixture .... MORTAR, SLURRY, PUTTY
patch with .... SLUSH
pipe joints .... LUTE
sealing .... LUTE
smoothing tool .. TROWEL
wall .... STUCCO
cemetery .... GRAVEYARD, BONEYARD, ACROPOLIS, NECROPOLIS, GOD'S ACRE
underground .... CATACOMB(S)
cenobite .... MONK, RECLUSE, ESSENE
dwelling ..... CONVENT, MONASTERY
opposed to .. ANCHORITE
cenotaph ... TOMB, MONUMENT
cense .... THURIFY
censer .... THURIBLE
censor .. CRITIC, FAULTFINDER, REVIEWER
kind of .... EDITOR
tool of movie .. SCISSORS
censorious .... CRITICAL
censorship of speech .... GAG
movie scenes ...... CUTS
censure .... CHIDE, LASH, CONDEMN(ATION), ASPERSE, DECRY, CRITICIZE, BLAME, IMPEACH, RAP, OBLOQUY
census, literally .... HEAD COUNTING, NOSE COUNTING
taker ...... ENUMERATOR
cent ... COIN, COPPER, PENNY
one hundred of them ... DOLLAR
one tenth of ...... MILL
per .... HUNDRED
twenty-five of them ..... QUARTER
centaur .... CHIRON, NESSUS, SAGITTARY
father of .... IXION
killed by Hercules ...... NESSUS
centavo ...... COIN, CENTIMO
centenary .... CENTURY
center .... CORE, MID, FOCUS, HUB, PIVOT, NUCLEUS, MIDDLE, HEART
at, in or near .. CENTRIC
farthest from .... DISTAL
having common .... CONCENTRIC
line of verse .... CESURA
moving from .... CENTRIFUGAL
moving toward .... CENTRIPETAL
nearest the ... PROXIMAL
non-revolving .... DEAD POINT
of activity .... HIVE, HUB, GANGLION, FOCUS
of attention ...... FOCUS
of attraction .. CYNOSURE
of command .... HEADQUARTERS
of energy/force .... GANGLION
of mass ...... CENTROID
of operations .. THEATER
of target .... BULL'S-EYE, EYE
toward .... MESIAL
wheel's .... HUB
centerpiece .. EPERGNE, DOILY
centesimal ...... HUNDREDTH
unit .... GRADE
centesimo, 100 of them .. LIRA, BALBOA, PESO
centiare, 100 of them .... ARE
centimes, five .... SOU
100 .... FRANC
centipede .... MYRIAPOD, CHILOPOD, EARWIG, ARTHROPOD
le s, front pair .. FANGS
relative ...... MILLIPEDE
cento .... PATCHWORK
central .... BASIC, PRINCIPAL, HUB, CHIEF, FOCAL, MAIN, MID(DLE)
Central African capital ...... BANGUI
president .... DACKO, BOKASSA
Central American bird ...... CACIQUE, CURASSOW, URUBU, ATRATA, JUNCO, MANAKIN, QUE(T)ZAL
city .... BAMBARI, BERBERATI
country .. (EL)SALVADOR, GUATEMALA, NICARAGUA, COSTA RICA, PANAMA, HONDURAS
ethnic group .... BANDA, AZANDE, MBAKA
fiber plant .... MAGUEY, HENEQUEN
hat .... JIPIJAPA
monkey ..... MARMOSET
parrot .. MACAW, AMAZON
plant .... JIPIJAPA
president .... DACKO, BOKASSA, ROBLES, LOPEZ(ARELLANO), SOMOZA, TREJOS, SANCHEZ, MENDEZ
rodent .... PACA, AGOUTI
sash .... TOBE
stinging ant ..... KELEP
tortoise .... HICATEE
tree ...... EBO(E), AMATE
vulture .. URUBU, ATRATA
wildcat .. EYRA, MARGAY
central and guiding ... POLAR
figure ...... STAR, HERO, HEROINE
line .... AXIS
mark of target .... BULL'S-EYE
part .... CORE, NUCLEUS
point(s) ... FOCUS, FOCI, PIVOT, NODE
centrifugal force, cause of ... INERTIA
in physiology .. EFFERENT
centripetal, in physiology .... AFFERENT
century ..... AGE, HUNDRED, SIECLE
plant (fiber) ..... AGAVE, ALOE, TEQUILA, PITA, MAGUEY
ceorl ...... FREEMAN, CHURL
cephalad, opposed to .... CAUDAD
cephalopod .... MOLLUSK, OCTOPUS, CUTTLE(FISH), SQUID
Cepheus' daughter .... ANDROMEDA
wife .... CASSIOPEIA
ceraceous .... WAXY, WAXLIKE
Ceram .... SERANG
ceramic .... FICTILE
mixes .... FRITS
pigment ..... SMALTINE
plaque .... TILE
ceramics, of .... FICTILE
product .... POTTERY, EARTHENWARE, TILE, PORCELAIN
ceramist .... POTTER

cerate . . . . . . WAX, OINTMENT, SALVE
ceratodus . . . . . BARRAMUNDA
ceratin product . . . HAIR, NAIL, HORN, CORN
ceratoid/ceratose . . . . . HORNY
cerberus . . . . DOG
  concern of . . . . HADES
  descriptive of . . . . THREE-HEADED
cere . . . . WAX, MEMBRANE
cereal . . . . GRAIN, GRASS
  flour . . . . FARINA
  food . . . . RICE, OATMEAL, HOMINY, SAMP
  grain . . OAT, RYE, MILLET, WHEAT, CORN, MAIZE
  grass . . . . . . RYE, WHEAT, RAGGY, MILLET, OAT, RAG(G)I, RAGGEE
  ground . . HOMINY, GRITS
  husk . . . . BRAN
  meal . . . . FARINA
  spike . . . . EAR, COB
  stem . . . STALK, HA(U)LM
cerebral . . . . INTELLECTUAL
  vitamin, so-called . . . LSD
cerebrate . . THINK, COGITATE, PONDER
cerebrum, cortex of . . MANTLE
cerecloth . . SHROUD, CEREMENT
ceremonial . . RITUAL, FORMAL
  bow . . . . CURTSY, SALAAM
  dance . . . . PAVAN(E)
  drink . . . . TOAST
  entrance/exit signal . . . . . SENNET
  procession . . . . . PARADE, CAVALCADE, CORTEGE
  trumpet call . . . . . SENNET
ceremonious . . FORMAL, PRIM
  act . . . . . SALUTE, SALAAM, FLOURISH
  display . . . . FANFARE
  leave-taking . . CONGE(E)
  motion . . . . FLOURISH
  show of homage . . . . KOWTOW, SALAAM
ceremony . . FORMALITY, RITE, RITUAL, POMP
  hypocritical . . . MUMMERY
Ceres . . . . DEMETER, PLANET, ASTEROID, GODDESS
  parent of . . OPS, SATURN
cereus . . . . CACTUS
Cerigo Island . . . . . . KYTHERA
cerise . . . . RED
cerium dioxide . . . . CERIA
  silicate . . . . CERITE
cero . . . . CAVALLA
  combining form . . . . WAX
  fish resembling . . . . MACKEREL
certain . . . . . FIXED, APODITIC, SURE, TRUE, RELIABLE, POSITIVE
certainly . . SURELY, OF COURSE
  archaic . . . . IWIS
certainty . . . . CERTITUDE, ASSURANCE
certificate, graduation . . . . DIPLOMA
  money . . . . SCRIP
  Spanish . . . . CEDULA
certification . . . ATTESTATION, OK
certify . . . . . . VOUCH, VERIFY, DEPOSE, ASSURE, TESTIFY, NOTARIZE, ATTEST
certitude . . . . ASSURANCE, CERTAINTY
cerulean . . AZURE, (SKY) BLUE
cerumen . . . . EARWAX
ceruse . . . . (WHITE)LEAD, COSMETIC
Cervantes, author . . . MIGUEL
cervine . . DEER, STAG, CERVID
Cesare, basso . . . . SIEPI
cespitose . . MATTED, TURF-LIKE
cess . . . . TAX, ASSESSMENT
cessation . . END, STOP(PAGE), PAUSE, CEASING, LET-UP, SURCEASE
  of activity, temporary . . . LULL, BREAK, RESPITE
  of war, temporary . . . . . . TRUCE, CEASEFIRE
cession . . . YIELDING, CEDING
cessionary . . . . ASSIGNEE
cesspool . . . . SUMP
cestode . . . . TAPEWORM
cestus . . . . GIRDLE, BELT
cesura . . . . PAUSE
cetacean . . . . . DOLPHIN, INIA, GRAMPUS, WHALE, PORPOISE, SUSU
  Arctic . . . . NARWHAL(E), NARWAL
  tusked . . . . NARWHAL
Cetus . . . . WHALE, CONSTELLATION
Ceylon . . . . SINHALA
Ceylon(ese) . . . . TAMIL, SIN(G)HALESE, CINGALESE
  aborigine . . . . VEDDA(H), TODA
  ape . . . . MAHA
  Buddhist temple site . . . . KANDY
  capital . . . . COLOMBO
  city . . . . KANDY
  export . . . . TEA
  fortress town . . . . GALLE
  garment . . . . SARONG
  grass . . . PATANA, CHENA
  hill dweller . . . . TODA
  language . . TELUGU, PALI, MALAYALAM, KANARESE, TAMIL, INDIO
  lotus . . . . NELUMBO
  monkey . . . . LANGUR, WANDEROO, MAHA, TOQUE
  moss . . . AGAR, GULAMAN
  moss derivative . . . . ALEC
  native . . . . SIN(G)HALESE, DRAVIDIAN, CINGALESE, VEDDA(H), TODA, TAMIL
  palm . . . . TALIPOT
  policeman . . . . PEON
  rat . . . . BANDICOOT
  seaport . . GALLE, JAFFNA
  snake . . . . . . ANACONDA
  strait . . . . PALK
  tea . . . . PEKOE
  temple site . . . . . . KANDY
  trading vessel . . D(H)ONI
  tree . . . . PALMYRA
  water lily . . . . . NELUMBO
CGS, part of . . CENTIMETER, GRAM, SECOND
  unit . . . . ERG, DYNE
cha . . . . TEA
chablis . . . . WINE
chabouk . . . . HORSEWHIP
chacma . . . . BABOON
Chad . . . . .BREAM
  capital of . . . FORT LAMY
  city . . . . MOUNDOU
  ethnic group . . . . MASSA, SARA, KANEMBOU
  president . . TOMBALBAYE
chaeta . . SETA, SPINE, BRISTLE
chaetopod . . . . ANNELID
chafe . . . . . ANNOY, IRRITATE, RUB, EXCORIATE, GALL, ABRADE
  at the bit . . . . FRET
chafer . . . . . BEETLE, SCARAB, ROSE BUG
chaff . . . . . . BANTER, TEASING, HUSK, BRAN
  like . . . . ACEROSE
  like bract . . . . PALEA
  mixed with . . . . ACEROSE
chaffer . . . . . HIGGLE, BANDY, HAGGLE, BARGAIN(ING)
chaffinch . . . . (SONG) BIRD
chaffy . . . WORTHLESS, ACEROSE
chafing . . . . GALLING
  result of . . . SORE, FROTH
chagrin . . . . . MORTIFICATION, DISCOMFITURE
chain . . . . . FETTER, SHACKLE, CATENA, IRON, LINKWORK
  ball and . . . . WIFE
  decorative . . CHATELAINE
  form into a . . . CATENATE
  mail . . HAUBERK, BYRNIE
  mail, like . . . . . . ARMURE
  mountain . . CORDILLERA, RANGE
  of reasoning . . . . CONSECUTION
  part . . . . LINK
  pulling . . . . TUG
  smoker for example . . . . ADDICT
  TV-radio . . . . NETWORK
chair . . . . SEAT, OFFICE, POSITION, BENCH, CENTER, PLACE, ROCKER
  arrangement . . . . SEATING
  back part . . . . SPLAT
  backless . . . . STOOL, OTTOMAN
  bar connecting legs . . . . . ROUND
  bowlegged . . . . . CURULE
  cover . . . . TIDY
  covered . . . . SEDAN
  litter-like . . . . KAGO
  making material . . SPLAT
  of authority . . . . . THRONE
  on elephant's back . . . . . HOWDAH, HOUDAH
  on poles . . . . SEDAN
  part . . SEAT, RUNG, ARM, SPLAT, LEG, BOTTOM, ROUND

portable .. SEDAN, LITTER, PALANQUIN
state .... THRONE
take the .... PRESIDE
chaise .... CARRIAGE, BUGGY, SHAY, SHANDRYDAN
longue .... CHAIR
chalaza .... TREAD
chalcedony .. QUARTZ, ONYX, JASPER, CARNELIAN, AGATE, (CHRYSO)PRASE, CAT'S-EYE, SARD(INE), CHERT
Chaldean .... ASTROLOGER, SORCERER
astronomical cycle ..... SAROS
capital .... BABYLON
city .... UR
chalet .. HUT, CABIN, COTTAGE
chalice .... AMA, GOBLET, CUP, GRAIL, CALIX
cloth .... PALL
flower .... DAFFODIL
chalk .... LIMESTONE, TALLY, CRAYON, CALCITE, WHITING
composition .. SEASHELLS
linseed oil mixture ...... PUTTY
up .... SCORE
chalkstone .... TOPHUS
chalky silicate .... TALC
challenge .... DEMAND, EXCEPTION, QUESTION, DARE, DEFY
as false .... IMPUGN
hurled ..... DEFI, GAGE
means of ... SLAP, GAGE
to duel .... CARTEL
written .... CARTEL
challenging .... DEFIANT, BELLICOSE, BELLIGERENT
Cham .... KHAN
chamber .... (BED)ROOM, COUNCIL, CAMERA, CAMARILLA
for dead .... VAULT
judge's .... CAMERA
of a .... CAMERAL
pot .... JORDAN
underground .... VAULT
chambered creature of poetry .. NAUTILUS
chamberlain ...... STEWARD, TREASURER
Oriental potentate's ..... EUNUCH
chambers, legislature of two .. BICAMERAL
chambray .... GINGHAM
chameleon .... LIZARD, LACERT(IL)IAN
like .... FICKLE, CHANGEABLE
like creature ..... AGAMA
chamfer ..... BEVEL, GROOVE, FLUTING
chamois .. ANTELOPE, AOUDAD, SHAMMY
animal like ...... GORAL, KLIPSPRINGER
habitat .... ALPS
champ .... CHEW, MUNCH
colloquial ... CHAMPION
champagne .... WINE
bottle .... JEROBOAM
brand .... POMMERY
capital of ...... TROYES
for example ..... FIZ(Z)
of teas, so-called ...... DARJEELING
champignon ..... MUSHROOM
champion ...... ADVOCATE, PALADIN, ESPOUSE, WINNER, DEFEND(ER), PROTECTOR
auto racing ...... MOSS, CLARK
boxer .... CLAY, HARADA, DEMPSEY, LOUIS, GRIFFITH, ELORDE, VILLA
golf .. NICKLAUS, PALMER, HOGAN, PLAYER, SNEAD, JONES
heroic .... PALADIN, KNIGHT
marathon .... BIKILA
pole vault ..... SEAGREN, BIZZARRO
soccer football ..... PELE
tennis .... NEWCOMBE, ASHE, TILDEN, HOAD, KING, GONZALES, SANTANA, LAVER
wrestling .... TAKTI
yacht racing .. INTREPID
chance ... CASUAL, FORTUITY, HAP, RISK, GAMBLE, LUCK, RANDOM, HAZARD
betting .... ODDS
big .... OPPORTUNITY
by ..... ACCIDENTAL(LY)
goddess of ..... TYCHE, FORTUNA
on ... MEET, ENCOUNTER
chancel .... SACRARIUM
part ..... BEMA, RAILING
part surrounded by ..... ALTAR
screen .... JUBE
seats .... SEDILIA
chances .... ODDS
chancre .. SORE, LESION, ULCER
chandelier .... CORONA, GASELIER, LUSTER
pendant .... LUSTER
change .... ADAPT, ALTER, AMEND, MODIFY, MUTATE, VARY, SWITCH, MUTATION
color .... FADE
course ..... HAUL, TACK, VEER
current flow .... RECTIFY
direction ... CANT, TACK, TURN, VEER, DEVIATE
in form, nature .... MUTATION
in linguistics ... UMLAUT
in religion .. CONVERSION
into liquid .... LIQUEFY
into steel ..... ACIERATE
of mind, feeling .... CAPRICE
opinion .... HAUL
party ...... DEFECT, BOLT
policy ...... DEMARCHE, TACK
residence .... MOVE
sentence ..... COMMUTE
small .... COINS
tack .... JIBE
to direct current .... RECTIFY
changeable .... FICKLE, CAPRICIOUS, MOBILE, PROTEAN, MUTABLE, VOLATILE, FLUID
person ...... CHAMELEON
changeling ..... DOLT, IDIOT, CHILD, TURNCOAT, OAF
Changsa is capital of .. HUNAN
channel ..... STRAIT, COURSE, MEDIUM, CHUTE, RUNNEL, RUNWAY, NECK, KILL, SHOOT
artificial .. FLUME, CANAL, SLUICE(WAY)
between cliffs ...... GAT
cutting sandbank .... SWASH
direct .... PIPELINE
English .... (THE) SOLENT
entrance .... CHOPS
excess water .. SPILLWAY
fence .... WEIR
inland .... GAT
island .... JERSEY, ALDERNEY, GUERNSEY, SARK
Island, official ... JURAT
marker .... BUOY
narrow .... STRIA
obstruction ...... WEIR
of unpredictable currents EURIPUS
principal .... ARTERY
vertical .... GLYPH
water ...... RACE(WAY)
channeled .... GROOVED, FLUTED, COURSED, ROUTED
channels .... MEDIA
chanson ...... SONG, BALLAD, LYRIC
chant .... SINGSONG, MELODY, INTONE, INTONATION
poetic .... WARBLE
chantage .... BLACKMAIL
chanterelle .... MUSHROOM
chanteuse .... SINGER
chantey ...... (SAILOR) SONG
chanticleer ... ROOSTER, COCK
chantilly .... LACE
chantry ..... ALTAR, CHAPEL
chaos .... DISORDER, CONFUSION, MESS
Archaic .. ABYSS, CHASM
in language ...... BABEL
in printing .... PI
chaotic .... MUDDLED, DISORDERLY
chap .. JAW, CHEEK, BUGGER, ROUGHEN, KIBE, SKATE, GUY
colloquial .... MAN, BOY, FELLOW
chapeau .... HAT, HEADGEAR
chapel ... CHANTRY, GALILEE, VESTRY
clergyman ... CHAPLAIN
Egyptian mortuary's .... MASTABA(H)
medieval church .... GALILEE

private .... ORATORY
sailors' .... BETHEL
small .... ORATORY, CHANTRY
Vatican .... SISTINE
chaperon .... DUEN(N)A, ACCOMPANY, ESCORT
strict .... DRAGON
chaplain .... CLERGYMAN, PADRE, ORDINARY
chaplet ... WREATH, GARLAND
poetic .... ANADEM
chapman .. TRADER, DEALER, PEDDLER, HAWKER
chaps .. CHOPS, CHAPAREJOS, CHEEK, JAW
of hound .... FLEWS
chapter .... EPISODE, SECTION, LOCAL
fraternity .... LODGE
of a .... CAPITULAR
char .... BURN (UP), SCORCH, CINDERS, TROUT
charabanc .... BUS
character .... CODE, CIPHER, KIND, NATURE, ROLE, TRAIT, REPUTE
ancient alphabetical .... OGHAM, RUNE
assassination .. SLANDER, LIBEL
element in .... ETHOS
giver .... TONER
ill-tempered ... VINEGAR
in .... APPROPRIATE
in a play .... ACTOR
musical ..... CLEF, REST, NOTE
odd .. ECCENTRIC, CRANK
of community ... ETHOS
police ...... CRIMINAL, LAW-BREAKER, MALEFACTOR
quality of .... METTLE
representing a word ..... LOGOGRAM
sour .... VINEGAR
strength of .... GRISTLE
characteristic .... TRAIT, TYPICAL, DISTINCTIVE, PECULIARITY
expression .... IDIOM
marks .... INDICIA
taste .... FLAVOR
characters, drama/play ...... PERSONAE
of slums .... DEAD-END
characterize .. DESCRIBE, MARK
charade .... PUZZLE, WORD GAME
charcoal .. CARBON, LIGNITE, BONEBLACK
burning brazier .... HIBACHI
combining form .... CARB(O)
pencil .... FUSAIN
powdered ...... POUNCE
residue .... BREEZE
use of .... FILTER
chard ...... LEAFSTALK, BEET
chare .... CHORE
charge .... INDICT(MENT), DEBIT, PRICE, INSTRUCT, ATTRIBUTE, COMMAND, FEE, ACCUSATION, COST, IMPUTE, RUSH, DASH
in court .... ARRAIGN
kind of .... CAVALRY
mail .... POSTAGE
of the Light ____ .... BRIGADE
on property .. LIEN, TAX
restaurant/tavern .... COVER, CORKAGE, TIP
road .... TOLL
school .... TUITION
solemnly .... ADJURE
to expense/loss ... DEBIT
to experience .... WRITE OFF
with crime ...... INDICT
charged .... FRAUGHT
particle .... ION
water .... SODA
charger ... STEED, WARHORSE
Archaic ...... PLATTER, DESTRIER
chariot .. ESSED(E), QUADRIGA
race .... AGON
race course .... HIPPODROME
race site, ancient .... CIRCUS, COLOSSEUM
charioteer .... WAGONER
constellation ... AURIGA
furious .... JEHU
of fiction ..... BEN HUR
charisma ... CHARM, APPEAL, GIFT, GRACE
Charisse, dancer .... CYD
charitable institution .. MISSION
charity .. ALMS, BENEVOLENCE, BENEFACTION, DOLE
fair .... KERMIS, KERMESS
sale .... RUMMAGE, BAZA(A)R
charivari .... SERENADE
charlatan .. IMPOSTOR, QUACK, EMPIRIC, FAKER, PHON(E)Y, SCIOLIST
Charlemagne .. CARLO MAGNO, EMPEROR
father of .... PEPIN (THE SHORT)
gift to Rinaldo .. BAYARD
grandfather of ... MARTEL
knight(s) of ... PALADIN, DOUZEPERS, TWELVE
nephew of .... ORLANDO, ROLAND
peer ... OLIVER, ROLAND, ORLANDO
soubriquet .. (THE) GREAT
Charles Dickens' pseudonym .. BOZ
Charles' Wain ... BIG DIPPER, URSA MAJOR, AURIGA
charleyhorse .... CRAMP
charlock ... MUSTARD, WEED
charlotte .. PUDDING, DESSERT, LOTTA, LOTTIE, LOTTY
charm ... ENAMOR, ENCHANT, INCANTATION, FASCINATE, ATTRACT, GRACE, FETISH, SPELL
African .... OBEAH, OBI, JUJU
against evil/injury ...... AMULET
bracelet disc ... BANGLE
good luck .... TALISMAN
jewel .... SCARAB
magic .... JUJU
charmer .... MAGICIAN, ENCHANTER, SORCERER, EXORCIST
female .... SIREN
of German legend ...... LORELEI
charming .... WINSOME, WINNING
charnel house ...... OSSUARY, TOMB
of a sort ..... PANTHEON, MORTUARY
Charon .... FERRYMAN
fee .... OBOL
river .... STYX
charpoy (charpai) .. BEDSTEAD, COT
charqui .... BEEF
char(r) .... TROUT
chart ... MAP, LAYOUT, PLOT, GRAPH, OUTLINE
charter ..... HIRE, FRANCHISE, LEASE
fundamental .... CONSTITUTION
Charteris (Leslie) detective ... (THE) SAINT
forte of ..... WHODUNITS
Chartres river .... EURE
Chartreuse .... LIQUEUR
chary .. CAREFUL, CAUTIOUS, SHY
Charybdis .... WHIRLPOOL
rock opposite ... SCYLLA
chase ..... PURSUE, FOLLOW, CHEVY, FRET, HUNT, PURSUIT, ENGRAVE
continually ..... HOUND
object of .... HARE, FOX, RAINBOW, ESCAPEE, GAME
the .... VENERY
chaser ..... HUNTER, DRINK, CHISEL, GRAVER, WASH
ambulance ..... SHYSTER
chasing tool .. CHISEL, TRACER
chasm .. GAP, ABYSS, HIATUS, RIFT
in a glacier ... CREVASSE
chasseur .... HUNTER, HUNTSMAN, SERVANT
chassis .... FRAME
slang .... BODY
chaste ..... PURE, VIRTUOUS, MODEST, VESTAL, DECENT
woman .... VIRGIN
chatelaine .... PIN, CLASP
chasten ... PUNISH, CHASTISE, SUBDUE, HUMBLE
chastise ..... SPANK, PUNISH
physically ... WHIP, FLOG
verbally .. SCOLD, BERATE
chastity .... CELIBACY, VIRGINITY, DECENCY
vower of .. MONK, NUN, PRIEST, VESTAL

chat ... TALK, CONVERSATION, CONVERSE
colloquial ...... CONFAB
French .... CAUSERIE
friendly ..... COZE, COSE
hippie's slang ...... RAP
of maple ...... SAMARA
of plantain .... SPIKE
of willow .... AMENT, CATKIN
chateau .... CASTLE
entrance .... PORTE
mistress of .. CHATELAINE
chatelain .... CASTELLAN
chatelaine .. CHAIN, BROOCH, ETUI
chatoyant ... GEM, CAT'S-EYE
chattel .... CHOSE, GOODS
Archaic .... SLAVE
chatter .... BLAB, PRATE, CACKLE, CLACK, PRATTLE, BABBLE, GAS, GIBBER
Aussie colloq. .. YABBER
colloquial .... GAB
gossipy .... TATTLE
incoherent ...... JABBER
slang .... CHIN
unintelligible ... GIBBER
chatterbox ..... MAGPIE, JAY
chatterer, bird ..... MAGPIE, COTINGA, WAXWING, JAY, PIET
Chaucer, poet .... GEOFFREY
pilgrim .... REEVE
songs .... CHAUNTS
title .... DAN
work .... CANTERBURY TALES
chauffer ...... STOVE, HEATER
chauffeur .... DRIVER
chaussure ... FOOTWEAR, SHOE, BOOT, SLIPPER
chauvinist .... JINGO
chazan .... CANTOR
cheap .. COMMON, INEXPENSIVE, MEAN, PICAYUNE, RAFFISH
and showy ..... TINHORN
colloquial .. BRUMMAGEN, DIME-A-DOZEN
in Spanish ...... BARATO
jewelry .... TRINKET
jewelry peddler .. DUFFER
price .... BARGAIN
race horse ...... PLATER
slang .... TWO-BIT
cheapest theater seats .... GALLERY
cheapskate .... MISER, TIGHTWAD, PIKER, NIGGARD
cheat .... SWINDLE(R), SHAM, FOIL, (DE)FRAUD, GYP, BILK, COZE, GAFF, HUMBUG, FUB, FOB, FINAGLE, NICK, WELSH(ER), MUMP
colloquial ..... DIDDLE, CHISEL, BUNCO
by fraud .... FLEECE
easy to ...... GULLIBLE
in schoolwork .... CRIB
slang ..... MUMP, STICK, CLIP
through trickery .... COZEN, GOUGE
cheated, person easily .. GULL, DUPE
cheater in school ... CRIBBER
mean .... JACKAL
cheaters: sl. .... FALSIES, (EYE)GLASSES
chebec .... FLYCATCHER
Checchi, Signora ...... DUSE
check ..... NIP, RESTRAIN(T), CURB, CONTROL, REIN, VERIFY, REBUFF, ASCERTAIN
accounts .... AUDIT
bad ...... RUBBER, KITE
bleeding .. STANCH, STEM
colloquial ..... CORRECT, RIGHT
completely .... STOP
describing bad one ..... RUBBER, BOUNCING
flow ..... STEM, STANCH, DAM
growth/development .... NIP, STUNT
in .... REGISTER, REPORT
infection by burning .... CAUTERIZE
mark .... TICK
out place ...... COUNTER
rain .... STUB
restaurant .... TAB, CHIT
speed .... BRAKE
up .... PROBE
checker ...... CASHIER, DICE
Archaic .... CHESSBOARD
checkerberry .. WINTERGREEN
checkered .... VARIED, TATTERSALL
cloth .... PLAID, TARTAN
checkers ... GAME, DRAUGHTS
checking block .... SPRAG
checkmate ...... FRUSTRATE, STYMIE, BAFFLE, DEFEAT, CORNER, STOP
Cheddar .... CHEESE
cheddite .... EXPLOSIVE
cheek ..... JOWL, TEMERITY, JAW, CHOP, CHAP
by jowl .... CLOSE, FAMILIAR, INTIMATE
bone .... MALAR
colloquial .. SAUCE, GALL, INSOLENCE, NERVE, BRASH, SAUCINESS, IMPUDENCE
glow of .... BLOOM
hair growth ... SIDEBURN
hollow .... DIMPLE
muscle ..... BUCCINATOR
of the .. MALAR, BUCCAL, GENAL, JUGAL
pouch .... ALFORJA
to cheek .... CLOSE, CHUMMY
tongue in .... INSINCERE
cheeks and mouth .... CHOPS
cheeky: colloq. .... SAUCY
cheep .... CHIRP, PEEP
cheer .. GLADDEN, COMFORT, APPLAUD, ROOT, INCITE, ELATE, ENCOURAGE, (EN)LIVEN
approving ..... ATTABOY
bullring .... OLE
college .... RAH
English .... HEAR
French .... VIVE
Italian .... VIVA, BRAVO
Japanese .... BANZAI
kind of .... BRONX
Mexican .... VIVA
Nazi .... HEIL
Philippine ..... MABUHAY
Spanish .... OLE
up .. (EN)LIVEN, COMFORT
cheerer .... ROOTER, FAN
cheerful ..... JOLLY, BLITHE, GAY, MERRY, RIANT, SUNNY
cheerfully bright ..... SUNNY
cheerio: Brit. .... HELLO, GOODBYE
cheerless ..... DRAB, DREARY, SAD
cheery .... GAY, LIVELY
cheese ..... MYSOST, STILTON, SAPSAGO
and toast dish .. RABBIT, RAREBIT
basis of .... CASEIN
American .... BRIE
Belgian ... LIMBURG(ER)
brick ...... LIMBURG(ER)
crust .... GRATIN
dish .. SOUFFLE, FONDUE, RAREBIT
drying frame ..... HACK
Dutch .. EDAM, COTTAGE
English .... STILTON, CHEDDAR
enthusiast ...... MOUSE
French .... CAMEMBERT, BRIE, ROQUEFORT
from curds ...... GOUDA
goat's/ewe's milk .... ROQUEFORT
Italian .... PARMESAN
like .... CASEOUS
making substance ...... RENNET
place for drying .. HACK
Scottish ...... KEBBOCK
Swiss .... COTTAGE, SAPSAGO, GRUYERE
tang .... NIP
whole milk ..... DUNLOP
cheesecake: sl. .... PIN-UP
cheesy .... CASEOUS
slang .... INFERIOR, POOR
cheetah .... GUEPARD
chef .... (CHIEF) COOK
Chek(h)ov, writer ..... ANTON
chela ..... CLAW, PINC(H)ERS
India .. NOVICE, DISCIPLE
cheloid .... TUMOR
chelonian .. TORTOISE, TURTLE
chemical catalyst ... REAGENT
change ...... REACTION
combining capacity ..... VALENCE
compound ..... AMIDE, AMINE, ESTER, BORIDE, CERIA, IODINE, ISOMER, TOULENE, ELATERIN
compounds, describing .. LABILE
element .... ARGON, HALOGEN
element 43 ... MASURIUM

ink remover .... ERADICATOR
prefix ..... OXA, AMIDO, ACETO, AMINO
radical ... TOLYL, BUTYL
reaction ..... CATALYSIS
reagent ...... CATALYST, CATALYSER
salt .. SAL, IODATE, ESTER, NITRE, BORATE
substance ...... LININ
suffix .. OSE, YLENE, ANE, YL, OLIC
unit ...... TITER, TITRE
word ending ... OL, INE, ENOL
chemin de fer .... RAILROAD, BACCARAT
chemise ...... CYMAR, SARK, LINGERIE, SLIP
colloquial ..... UNDIES, SHIMMY
chemisette .... TUCKER
chemist .... ANALYST, PHARMACIST, DRUGGIST
flask of ...... BOLTHEAD
pot of .... ALUDEL
chemistry, suffix in ...... OLE, ENE, INE
Chemulpo .. INCHON, JINSEN
chenille .... CORD, DOG
Chenpao to Russians .... DAMANSKY
Cheops .... KHUFU
edifice built by .... PYRAMID
cherish .... NURTURE, APPRECIATE, VALUE, ADORE, FOSTER, PRIZE, TREASURE
companion in marriage VOW .... LOVE, OBEY
Cherokee sage .... SEQUOYAH
cheroot .... CIGAR
cherry .... MARASCA, DRUPE, OXHEART, MORELLO, BIGAROON, AMARELLE, CAPULIN, BLACKHEART, RUDDY
disease .... BLACKKNOT
product ...... PIE, JAM
red .... CERISE
sour .... EGRIOT
stone .... NUTLET
sweet/wild ... MAZZARD, GEAN, BIGAROON
cherrystone .. CLAM, QUAHOG, NUTLET
chersonese .... PENINSULA
cherub .... ANGEL, AMOR, SERAPH
cherubic .... ANGELIC
chess castle .... ROOK
certain defeat in .... CHECKMATE
champion .. BOTVINNIK, SPASSKY, CAPABLANCA, PETROSIAN, FISHER
corner piece ...... ROOK
expert .... HOYLE
opening .... GAMBIT, CHASSE
piece ..... PAWN, ROOK, CASTLE, KING, QUEEN, BISHOP, KNIGHT
sacrifice .... GAMBIT
term ...... CHECKMATE, EN PASSANT
chest .... TREASURY, BOX, BUREAU, LOCKER, ARCA, BOSOM, THORAX, KIST, COFFERS
a kind of ..... CAMPHOR, MEDICINE, TOOL, COMMUNITY
animal .... BRISKET
bone .... RIB
cavity membrane .... PLEURA
clothes .... TRUNK
combining form .... STETH(O)
for money/valuables .... COFFER, CASKET
for storage ..... HUTCH
for supplies ... WANIGAN
human .... THORAX
located on the .... PECTORAL
of drawers .. CHIFFONIER, COMMODE, TALLBOY, HIGHBOY, LOWBOY
of sacred utensils .. CIST
sacred ...... ARCA, ARK
Scottish .... KIST
small .... CASKET
sound .... RALE
tool .... KIT
vibration ..... FREMITUS
Chesterfield .. SOFA, TOPCOAT, LORD
Chesterfieldian ...... SUAVE, ELEGANT, URBANE
chessman .... PAWN
chestnut ...... HORSE, TREE, MARRON, BUCKEYE, MAST, OLDIE
Chinese .... LING
colloquial .. JOKE, CLICHE
Polynesian .... RATA
preserved in syrup ...... MARRONS
tree .... CHINCAPIN, CHINQUAPIN
water .... LING
chevalier ... GALLANT, NOBLE
Archaic .... KNIGHT
Cheviot .... OVINE, SHEEP
chevron .... BAR, STRIPE
shape .... VEE
symbol of ...... SERVICE, RANK
chevrotain ... NAPU, DEERLET
chevy .... HUNT, CHASE, FRET
chew .... MASTICATE, GRIND, CHAMP, GNAW, MUNCH, CUD, (S)CRUNCH, MANDUCATE, MUMBLE
cud .... RUMINATE
inability to ... AMOSESIS
leaf to .... BETEL
chewing gum ingredient ..... CHICLE, MASTIC
gum tree .... SAPODILLA
tobacco piece ..... PLUG
chewink ..... TOWHEE, FINCH
chewy confection .. CARAMEL, GUM
Chiang Kai-shek .... GISSIMO
party of .. KUOMINTANG
wife of .... MEI-LING
Chianti .... (RED) WINE
Chiapas, capital of .. TUXTLA
chiaus: Turkish ... EMISSARY, SERGEANT
chibouk ..... (TOBACCO) PIPE
chic .... SMART, STYLISH, ELEGANT, FASHIONABLE, JAUNTY
Chicago .... WINDY CITY
airport .... O'HARE
ball team .... WHITESOX
business/theater area ... LOOP
feature ..... STOCKYARDS
football team .... BEARS
personage .... SANDBURG
"Wall Street" .. LA SALLE
chicalote .... POPPY
chicane .... TRICK(ERY)
chicanery .... TRICKERY, DECEPTION
chick .. PEEPER, CHILD, SHEILA
pea .... PLANT, GRAM, FODDER
chickadee .. TITMOUSE, BIRD, TOMTIT
chickaree .... SQUIRREL
chicken .... FOWL, BIDDY, SHANGHAI, HAMBURG
breast, cause of .... RICKETS
breed .... (WHITE) LEGHORN, PLYMOUTH, CANTONESE, SULTAN, JAVA, MINORCA
castrated .... CAPON
chaser ...... CATCHPOLE
dish .... GALANTINE
feed: sl. .. COINS, CHEAP, NEGLIGIBLE, PIDDLING, DIMES, PEANUTS
female .... HEN
five-toed .... HOUDAN
hearted ..... COWARDLY, TIMID, YELLOW
livered .... TIMID, COWARDLY, YELLOW
male .... ROOSTER, COCK
meat course .. GALANTINE
pen/cage .... COOP, RUNWAY
pox .... VARICELLA
resting place ... PERCH, ROOST
slang .. TIMID, COWARDLY
small .... BANTAM
snake .... BOBA
sound .... CACKLE
young ... FRYER, CHICK, POULT, PEEPER
chickens, collectively .... POULTRY
enclosure for ... RUNWAY
chickweed .... ALSINE, SPURR(E)Y, STITCHWORT, ALSONE
chicle .... SAPOTA
product .. CHEWING GUM, BALATA
source ...... SAPODILLA

chico .. SHRUB, GREASEWOOD
chicory .... ENDIVE, SUCCORY
use for .... COFFEE
chide ...... SCOLD, UPBRAID, REBUKE, BERATE, BLAME, REPROVE
chief .. LEADER, ARCH, HEAD, PRINCIPAL, MAIN, FOREMOST, CAPTAIN, STELLAR, PREMIER
actor .. STAR, LEAD, HERO
barrio ...... DATO, DATU
Canaan .... SISERA
character .... HERO
colloquial .... BOSS
commander-in ..... CINC
commodity ..... STAPLE
Cossack ...... ATAMAN, HETMAN
excellence ...... FORTE, STRONG, POINT, TALENT
executive .... PRESIDENT
Indian ...... TECUMSEH, GERONIMO, COCHISE, SACHEM, BRANT, POWHATAN, SITTING BULL
ingredient .... BASE
Italian .... DUCE
Justice, U.S. ... WARREN, MARSHALL, TANEY
Moslem .... REIS
of foreign mission ...... AMBASSADOR, NUNCIO
of state ...... PRESIDENT, KING
of workmen ... FOREMAN, OVERSEER
official .... PREMIER, PRIME MINISTER
product .... STAPLE
singer .... CANTOR
Spanish .... JEFE
chiefly ..... MAINLY, MOSTLY, ESPECIALLY
chieftain .... LEADER
Scandinavian ..... JARL
Indian .... SACHEM
political .... BOSS
chield .... YOUTH
chiffon .... SILK
chigger ...... FLEA, CHIGOE, LARVA
chigoe .... LARVA, FLEA, CHIGGER
Chihli .... HOPEI
Chihuahua .... (TOY)DOG
chilblain .... SORE, KIBE
child .... BABY, INFANT, TAD, PRODUCT, TOT, BABE, MOPPET, ISSUE, CHIT, KIDDY, KIDDIE
abnormal .... OAF
bastard .... BY-BLOW
bad-tempered .... CHANGELING
beggar's employer ...... PADRONE
bib .... DICKEY
cap of .... BIGGIN
colloquial .. TYKE, TIKE, TODDLER, CHIT, CHICK, LAMBKIN
combining form .... P(A)EDO
dirty, ragged .... RAGAMUFFIN
feet of ...... PETTITOES
game of ...... PEEKABOO
hand of .... PUD
homeless .... WAIF
hood of .... BIGGIN
impudent .... BRAT
like .... NAIVE
little .... MOPPET
milk source .. WET NURSE
mischievous .. ELF, BRAT, LIMB, IMP, JACKANAPES
murder of .. PROLICIDE, FILICIDE
noble born ..... CHILDE
of .... FILIAL
of light and day, so-called EROS
of mixed blood .. MUSTEE, MESTEE, MESTIZO, HALF-BREED, MULATTO, HALF-CASTE, GRIFFE
of the street ...... ARAB, WAIF, GAMIN
of the Sun .... INCA
Philippine .. BATA, ANAK
pinafore .. DICKEY, TIER, SLIP
playroom ..... NURSERY
pretty .... DOLL
ragged ..... RAGAMUFFIN
relation to parent ...... FILIATION
savings bank of .... SAVE-ALL
Scottish .... BAIRN
spoiled .. COCKNEY, BRAT
substitute .. CHANGELING
teacher/trainer .... GOVERNESS
toy of .... PEG TOP
ugly .... CHANGELING
undershirt ..... WAIST
unruly .... BRAT
unweaned .... SUCKLING
walk of .... TODDLE, WADDLE, PADDLE
childbearing ... PARTURATION
primitive custom .... COUVADE
childbirth .... DELIVERY, PARTURATION
confinement ... LYING-IN
discharge after .. LOCHIA
pains .. TRAVAIL, LABOR
childhood writings, etc. ...... JUVENALIA
childing .... PREGNANT
childish ... IMMATURE, SILLY, ASININE, FOOLISH, PUERILE, INFANTILE, ANILE
state due to age .... DOTAGE
walk .. TODDLE, WADDLE
childhood disease .... MUMPS
childlike .... INNOCENT, TRUSTING, NAIVE, NAIF
adult .... MORON, IDIOT
speech .... LISP
children .... PROGENY, OFFSPRING
book for ..... JUVENILE
colloquial ... (SMALL)FRY
of family ...... BROOD, FLOCK
of heaven and earth, alleged .... TITANS
of Israel .... JEWS, HEBREWS
of the mist ... NIBELUNG
study of ..... PEDOLOGY
without .... NONPAROUS
children's book author ...... MILNE, OUIDA, RAMEE
book, doll in .... GOLLIWOG
disease .... RICKETS, MUMPS, RACHITIS
game .. TAG, JACKSTONE
doctor ...... PEDIATRIST, PEDIATRICIAN
jacket .... PALETOT
mouth disease .. APHTHA, THRUSH
patron saint .... SANTA (CLAUS)
pinafore .... TIER
playroom ...... NURSERY
playsuit .... ROMPERS
wasting condition ...... MARASMUS
Chile, meaning of ..... SNOW
Chilean aborigine ...... INCA
beech tree ...... ROBLE
capital .... SANTIAGO
city/town .... SANTIAGO, VALPARAISO, ARICA, CONCEPCION, LOTA, TALCA, VINA DEL MAR, IQUIQUE, ANGOL, ANTOFAGASTA
coastal wind ..... SURES
coin ... COLON, CENTAVO, ESCUDO
court dance ..... CUECA
deer .... PUDU
department ..... ARICA
desert .... ATACAMA
evergreen .... MAQUI
island .... HOSTE
language ...... SPANISH
monetary unit .. ESCUDO
mountain ..... JUNCAL, MAIPU, ANDES
palm tree ..... COQUITO
pianist .... ARAU
president ..... ALLENDE
province ...... ATACAMA, TACNA, MAULE, TARAPACA
region ..... PATAGONIA
river .... BUENO, BIOBIO, LOA, ITATA
saltpeter .... NITER
seaport ... ARICA, LOTA
shrub .... MAQUI
tree .... PELU, RAULI, ROBLE, ULMO, QUILLAI
volcano .... ANTUCO, CALBUCO
wind .... SURES
chili con ____ .... CARNE
flavored dish .... ENCHILADA
chiliad .... THOUSAND
chill .. COOL, DEPRESS, FROST, DISPIRIT, COLD(NESS), AGUE, ALGOR

chilling device .... ICER, REFRIGERATOR
material .... ICE
chills and fever ...... AGUE, MALARIA
chilly ... COLD, RAW, ALGID, BLEAK
chilopod .... CENTIPEDE
chimar .... ROBE
chimb .... RIM
chime .. HARMONY, RIM, BELL, PEAL
in ... INTERRUPT, AGREE, JOIN
chimer .... ROBE
chimera ... FANCY, MONSTER
desert traveler's ... OASIS, WATER
sailor's .... LAND
chimerical ...... IMAGINARY, FANTASTIC, VISIONARY
chimney ..... (SMOKE)STACK, TEWEL, FUNNEL
bird .... SWIFT, SWALLOW
carbon .... SOOT
corner .... FIRESIDE, INGLE(NOOK)
cover ..... MITER, COWL, MITRE
lining .... PARGET
of volcano .... VENT
piece ... MANTEL, PAREL
pipe .... FLUE
pot .... TALLBOY
screen .... BONNET
swallow .... SWIFT
chimpanzee ...... APE, JOCKO, TROGLODYTE
relative .... GORILLA, ORANGUTAN, GIBBON
chin flesh .... GILL
hairy growth ... GOATEE, BEARD
hollow .... DIMPLE
pertaining to .... GENIAL, MENTAL
slang .. CHATTER, TALK, GAB
China .... CATHAY, SPODE
capital .... PEKING
made with clay ... BONE
chinaware ...... PORCELAIN, DRESDEN, DISHES, CROCKERY
chincapin .... CHESTNUT
chinch .... BEDBUG
chinche .... SKUNK
chinchilla ...... RODENT, FUR
relative ...... VISCACHA
chine ..... BACKBONE, SPINE, RAVINE, RIDGE, SILK
Chinese .... SINIC, ORIENTAL, MIAO, SERIC
A-bomb site ... LOP NOR
alimentary paste .... WANTON, WONTON
American dish .... CHOWMEIN, CHOP SUEY, SUBGUM
arithmetical device ..... ABACUS
aromatic root .. GINSENG
art/customs expert ..... SINOLOGUE
artichoke ..... CHOROGI
association .... TONG
autumn .... CH'IU
bamboo stick .. WHANGEE
bean .... ADSUKI
boat .... JUNK, SAMPAN, TONGKANG
brand on goods .. CHOP
Buddhism .... FOISM
Buddhist monk/priest ... LAMA
bugaboo .. YELLOW PERIL
capital .... PEKING
capital, former .... CHUNGKING
card game .... FAN TAN
Caucasian tribesman .... LOLO
cauterizing agent .. MOXA
characters in Japanese .. MANA
chestnut .... LING
city ...... SIAN, CANTON, PEKING, SOCHE, CHEFOO, SHANGHAI, TIENTSIN, WUHAN, SHUFU, TSINAN, MUKDEN, FATSHAN, NINGPO, NANKING, SWATOW, SOOCHOW, PEIPING, HANKOW, JEHOL, KOTIEN, MINHOW, KALGAN, KHOTAN, FOOCHOW, ICHANG, KWEILIN, YENAN, WUSIH, WUHU
club .... TONG
coat .... MANDARIN
coin .. TAEL, LIANG, TIAO, YUAN, LI
coin with hole .... CASH
combining form .. CHINO, SINO
Communist leader ...... MAO, CHOU, PING, PIAO
custom peculiar to ...... SINICISM
dependency ...... TIBET
dialect ...... CANTONESE, PEKIN(G)ESE
dialect, official .... MANDARIN
dictator .... MAO (TSE-TUNG)
dog .. CHOW, PEKIN(G)ESE
duck eggs, preserved .... PIDAN
dynasty .. MANCHU, WEI, CHOU, YIN, MONGOL, HSIA, T'ANG, MING, SUNG, HAN, SHANG, LIAO, TA CHING
dynasty, first ...... HSIA
dynasty, last ... MANCHU
eating implement .... CHOPSTICKS
emperor ...... KUBLAI, HUANG
emperor, last .... PU-YI
empress .... HOU
empress, last ... TZU-HSI
eyes describing .... ALMOND, SLIT
factory .... HONG
feudal state .... WEI
fiber plant ...... RAMIE
fish .... TREPANG
flute .... TCHE
fruit .... LOQUAT
gambling game .... FAN-TAN
game with tiles .... MAHJONG(G)
gateway .... PAILOU
gelatin .... AGAR
glue .... AGAR
god .... JOSS, SHEN
gong .... TAM-TAM, TOM-TOM
grape .... WAMPEE
guild .... TONG
hairdo .... PIGTAIL
Han city ...... HANKOW, HANYANG, WUCHANG
harbor craft .... SAMPAN
herb .. GINGER, GINSENG
ideograph .... KANJI
idol .... JOSS
import duties .. HAIKWAN
incense ..... JOSS STICK
indigo .... ISATIS
invention ... GUNPOWDER
island .. TAIWAN, AMOY, MATSU, FORMOSA, QUEMOY
kingdom, old ...... WEI
laborer .... COOLIE
lake .... POYANG, KOKO NOR
language .... SHAN, MANDARIN
language/customs, study of .... SINOLOGY
license .... CHOP
lord of lower world ..... YENLO
magnolia .... YULAN
Manchu dynasty .... TA CHING
mandarin's residence .... YAMEN
measure .. CHANG, TSUN, CHIH, LI
medicinal herb .... GINSENG
metropolis ...... WUHAN
mile LI
military academy .... WHAMPOA
monetary unit ... YUAN
money ...... TAEL, SYCEE
Mongol ...... MANCHU
Mongol dynasty .. YUAN
Mongol dynasty founder....... KUBLAI
monk .... BONZE, LAMA
mountain ...... LUSHAN
Nationalist party .... KUOMINTANG
noodles .... MEIN
nuclear center .... LOP NOR, LANCHOW
numeral, 1 to 10 .... YIH, URH, SAN, SZE, WOO, LUH, TSIEH, PA, KEW, SHIH
nurse .... AMAH
official ...... MANDARIN, KUAN, KWAN
official seal .... CHOP

oil tree .... TUNG
omelet .... FOOYONG
orange ...... MANDARIN
ounce .... TAEL
pagoda .... TAA
pear .... PYRUS
peninsula ..... LIAOTUNG
peony .... MOUTAN
permit .... CHOP
philosopher ....
CONFUCIUS, YUTANG,
MENCIUS, MENG-TSE
phoenix .. FENG, HUANG
pickles ..... CHOWCHOW
pine .... MATSU
plant .. GINSENG, MOXA,
RAMIE
poet .... LI PO
political party .... TONG,
KUOMINTANG
porcelain material ....
PETUNTSE
port .. CANTON, TIENTSIN,
AMOY, ICHANG, SHANGHAI
pottery .... MING
pound .... CATTY
president .. SUN (YAT-SEN)
priest .... LAMA
principle .... YIN, YANG
province .. HOPEI, CHIHLI,
SHAN(G)TUNG, HUNAN,
SHANSI, KIANGSI,
SINKIANG, HONAN,
CHINGHAI, CHEKIANG,
SHENSI, KANSU, YUNNAN,
KWANGSI, HOPEH,
HUPEH, HUPEI
provincial tax ..... LIKIN
punishment .... CANGUE
puzzle .... TANGRAM
race designation ....
YELLOW
rebellion of 1900 .. BOXER
religion .... TAOISM,
BUDDHISM
river ..... YUAN, PEARL,
HAN, ILI, LIAO, TARIM,
WEI, SIKIANG, YUEN
river boat ...... SAMPAN
sacred tree ... WU TUNG
salutation .... KOWTOW
satin .... PEKIN
sauce .... SOY
sea cucumber :. TREPANG
seal .... CHOP
seaport .... DAIREN,
TSINGTAO
season .... CH'UN, HSIA,
CH'IU, TUNG
secret society ..... TONG
sedge .... MATI
servant .... AMAH
shark fins .... YU CHI
silk ..... PONGEE, PEKIN,
SHA, SHANTUNG, TUSSER,
TUSSA(H)
silkworm .. SINA, TASAR
silver ingot ...... SYCEE
silver money ..... SYCEE
sky .... TIEN
slang .... CHINK
soapberry ...... LICHEE,
LITCHI
society ..... BOXER, HUI,
TONG
son .... TAI
soup material .. TREPANG,
BIRD'S NEST
spring .... CH'UN
squash .... CUSHAW,
CASHAW
stamp .... CHOP
statesman .... KOO
string money ...... TIAO
summer .... HSIA
tax .... LIKIN
tea ...... CHA, OOLONG,
CONGO(U), TSIA, BOHEA,
HYSON, SOUCHONG
team work ... GUNG HO
temple ..... JOSSHOUSE,
TAA, PAGODA
trading boat ....
TONGKANG
treaty port .... AMOY,
SHANGHAI
tree .... GINK(G)O,
WUTUNG, LOQUAT
truth .... TAO
unicorn ... CHLLIN, LIN
walking stick .. WHANGEE
warehouse .... HONG
wax .... PELA
weight .. CATTY, PICUL,
TAEL, LI, HAO, FAN
wine vessel .... TSUN
winter .... TUNG
wood oil .... TUNG
work together ....
GUNG HO
wormwood .... MOXA
yellow .... SIL
chink .. FISSURE, RIMA, CRACK,
SLIT, CRANNY, CREVICE
filler .... GROUT
slang .... CHINESE
chinks, full of ...... RIMOSE,
RIMOUS
chinky .... RIMOUS
Chinook ..... WIND, INDIAN,
SALMON
Indian .... FLATHEAD
powwow .... WAWA
lily/bulb ...... QUAMASH
chinquapin ..... (CHEST)NUT,
TREE
chinse .... CLOSE, CALK
chintz .... CLOTH
chip ...... NICK, CUT, CHOP,
SLICE, SCRAP, BIT, FLAKE
in .... CONTRIBUTE
of stone .. SPALL, GALLET
off the old block ....
SON(NY), JUNIOR
on one's shoulder ......
GRUDGE, RANCOR
chipmunk .. SQUIRREL, CHIPPY,
TRACKEE
cheek pouch .. ALFORJA
chippendale furniture leg .....
CABRIOLE
chipper .... PERT, LIVELY,
CHISEL, ADZ, CHIRP, TWITTER
colloquial ...... BABBLE,
CHATTER
Chippewa .. OJIBWA(Y), INDIAN
chippy .. SPARROW, CHIPMUNK,
PROSTITUTE
chirk ..... LIVELY, CHEERFUL
chiro, as combining form ....
HAND
chirographer .... PENMAN
chiromancer .... PALMIST
Chiron .... CENTAUR
forte of ...... MEDICINE
pupil of ...... ACHILLES,
HERCULES
chiropodist .... PEDICURE
advice of ..... FOOTBATH
chiropter .... ALIPED, BAT
chirp .. CHEEP, PEEP, TWITTER,
TWEET
chirper .... NESTLING,
FLEDGLING, BIRD, CICADA
chirrup .... CHIRP, TWEET
chisel .. CUT, GOUGE, ENGRAVE,
BURIN, HARDY, SCULP(T),
BROACH, FIRMER, GRAVER,
CHASER, TOOLER
bar .... SPUDDER
broad-faced ..... DROVE
colloquial ...... CHEAT,
SWINDLE
mason's .... POMMEL
part .... TANG
polishing .... SLICK
primitive/stone .... CELT
stonemason's .. QUARREL
chiseled profile .... CLASSICAL,
ROMAN
chiseler .... SWINDLER,
CHEAT(ER)
chit .... NOTE, SHOOT, SPROUT
colloquial .... TAB, IOU,
CHILD, GIRL
of a kind ..... VOUCHER,
MEMO
chitchat .... TALK, GOSSIP
chiton .. MOLLUSK, GARMENT,
LIMPET
chitter ..... TWITTER, SHIVER
chive .... ONION, FLAVOR,
GARLIC
chiv(v)y .... HARRY, HUNT,
CHASE, FRET
chlamys .... MANTLE. CLOAK
Chloe and others ..... AUNTS
love of .... DAPHNIS
chloride .... MURIATE
chlorine ... BROMINE, IODINE,
HALOGEN
chloroform, for one ....
ANESTHETIC, SOLVENT
chlorophyll .... ETIOLIN
chock .... BLOCK, WEDGE,
CLEAT, TRIG, SPRAG
chockablock .... CROWDED
chocolate .... DRINK, CANDY
cake .... BROWNIE
candy filling .. FONDANT
flavored .... MOCHA
mixer .... MOLINET
powder .... COCOA
source .... CACAO
tree .... CACAO
choice .... PREFERENCE,
SELECTION, ELITE, CREAM
between two evils ......
DILEMMA

food .... DELICACY
make a .... OPT
morsel .... TIDBIT
object .... PLUM
of words ...... DICTION
other ...... ALTERNATIVE
part ...... CREAM, MEAT, MARROW
choir boys' collar ...... ETON
leader .... CHORAGUS
leader's aide .... SUCCENTOR
of a .... CHORAL
place in church .... LOFT, GALLERY
section ..... ALTO, TENOR
vestment .... COTTA, SURPLICE
choke .. SMOTHER, SUFFOCATE, STIFLE, THROTTLE
by squeezing throat ..... STRANGLE
by stuffing mouth .. GAG
to death .... BURKE
up .... CLOG
with iron collar .... GARROTE
choked up: colloq. .... SPEECHLESS
choker .. NECKLACE, NECKTIE, FUR(PIECE), COLLAR
cholecyst .... (GALL)BLADDER
choler ...... BILE, RAGE, IRE, ANGER, FIT, WRATH
cholera bacillus ...... COMMA
type of ...... NOSTRAS, INFANTUM, MORBUS
choleric ... IRASCIBLE, ANGRY, IRATE, TESTY, IRRITABLE
cholesterol product .... GALLSTONE
cholla .... CACTUS
chololith .... GALLSTONE
Chomo-lungma ..... EVEREST
chondroma .... TUMOR
choose .. SELECT, CULL, PICK, OPT, PREFER, WALE
for office .... ELECT
your ____ ... EXIT, WILD, PARTNER
choosing, right of .... OPTION
choosy .... FASTIDIOUS, FUSSY
chop .. CUT, LOP, AXE, CHEEK, HEW, JAW, DICE, FELL, HACK, MINCE
chop-chop .... QUICKLY, AT ONCE
in China, India .. PERMIT, SEAL, LICENSE
stroke, in tennis .. SLICE
tool ..... AX(E), CLEAVER
chophouse, Chinese .... CUSTOMHOUSE, RESTAURANT
specialty .... STEAK
Chopin's (Frederic) country .. POLAND
love ..... (GEORGE) SAND
chopine .... SHOE, PATTEN
chopper .... AX(E)
meat .... CLEAVER
slang .... HELICOPTER
chopping blows with hand .... KARATE
chops .... JAWS, JOWL, MOUTH
choral music ...... ORATORIO, CANTATA
chord .... STRING
dissonance .... WOLF
3-tone .... TRIAND
chordate .... VERTEBRATE
example of a ...... MAN
chore .... CHARE, TASK, (ODD)JOB, STINT
choreographer of note .... ANTON, BALANCHINE
choreography ...... DANCING, BALLET
chorine .... CHORUS GIRL, STEPPER
chorister's garment .. CASSOCK
chorography .... MAP
choroid membrane .. TAPETUM
chortle ..... CHUCKLE, SNORT
chorus .... UNISON, REFRAIN
girl: colloq. .... CHORINE
leader .... CHORAGUS
of a ... CHORAL, CHORIC
of song .... BURDEN, REFRAIN
chose .... CHATTEL
Chosen .... KOREA
Chou ____, Chinese bigwig ... EN-LAI
chough .... CROW
chouse .. CHEAT, SWINDLE(R), DUPE
chow ...... DOG, FOOD, MEAL
chowchow .... PICKLES, OLIO, MIXED, ASSORTED
chowder ingredient .... CLAM
christen ..... BAPTIZE, NAME
Christian .... DECENT, HUMAN
abbreviation ..... XTIAN
bishop of the Goths .... ULFILA(S)
church .. ORANT, BASILICA
church as a whole ...... CATHOLIC
church of Egypt .. COPT
church, the .... HERITAGE
love feast .... AGAPE
non .... PAYNIM, PAGAN, HEATHEN
Oriental .... UNIAT
pulpit .... AMBO
religion founder .. JESUS
Science founder .. BAKER
Science healer .... PRACTITIONER
theologian ...... ORIGEN
traitor .... TRADITOR
Christiania .... OSLO
was capital of .. NORWAY
Christians, all ...... CHURCH
Christmas .. YULE(TIDE), NOEL
abbreviation ..... XMAS
bonanza .... GIFTS
cake .... SIMNEL
carol ...... NOEL, NOWEL
crib .... CRECHE
day .... NATIVITY
decorative item .... MISTLETOE
drink .... EGGNOG
favorite figure .... SANTA (CLAUS)
fruitcake .... SIMNEL
gift container .. STOCKING
masked funster .... MUMMER
mock-up of Nativity .... CRECHE
musician .... WAIT
pantomime .... MUMMER, GUISER
season ...... YULE(TIDE)
song ...... CAROL, NOEL
street singer ...... WAIT, CAROLER
time entertainment ..... PANTOMIME
tree .... HOLLY, PINE
vehicle .... SLED, SLEIGH
chromosome load ..... GENES
chronic .... RECURRING, HABITUAL, CONFIRMED
chronicle .... ACCOUNT, HISTORY, RECORD, DIARY, ANNAL(S)
chronicler .... HISTORIAN, ANNALIST, RECORDER
chronometer .... WATCH
chrysalis ..... PUPA, COCOON
chrysanthemum .. MUM, KIKU, POMPON, DAISY, COSTMARY, MARGUERITE
badge: Jap. .... MON
chrysolite .. PERIDOT, OLIVINE
chub .... (BLACK) BASS
chubby ..... ROTUND, PLUMP
chuck .... TOSS, THROW, DISCARD
slang .... FOOD
chuckle ..... LAUGH, CLUCK, GIGGLE
chucklehead .... DOLT, IDIOT
chuckleheaded ...... STUPID
chuddar .... SHAWL
Chudskoe lake ...... PEIPUS
chuff ... BRICK, BOOR, CHURL
chum .... ROOMMATE, FRIEND, CRONY, PAL
in fishing .... BAIT
chummy .... INTIMATE, FRIENDLY
chump .... BOOB, FOOL
chunk ...... PORTION, PIECE, GOBBET, HUNCH, BAT
chunky .. CORPULENT, STOUT, THICKSET, STOCKY, SQUAT
church .. DENOMINATION, SECT, TEMPLE, CHAPEL, BETHEL, KIRK, FOLD, FANE, MINSTER
altar offerings .... ALTARAGE
archaic .... FANE
basin .... LAVABO, FONT, PISCINA, STOUP
bell/ringer ..... SEXTON
bell tower ...... BELFRY
bench .... PEW
benefice .... LIVING
benefice, holding of ..... INCUMBENCY
benefit sale ..... BAZAAR
bishop's .... CATHEDRAL
body of .... NAVE
Buddhist .... PAGODA
building ...... ECCLESIA

calendar .... ORDO
caretaker ...... SEXTON, VERGER
chancel .... BEMA
cathedral ...... MINSTER
chandelier ..... CORONA
chapel .... CHANTRY, ORATORY
ceremony .. (HIGH) MASS, TE DEUM
choir leader .. CHORAGUS, CHORISTER, PRECENTOR
contribution to ... TITHE
council .... SYNOD, CONSISTORY
court ..... ROTA, CLASSIS, CONSISTORY
cup .... CHALICE
dignitary .. POPE, DEAN, LEGATE, NUNCIO, PRELATE, CARDINAL, PRIMATE, BISHOP
director .... PRECENTOR, CHORAGUS
dish .... PATEN
dissenter .... APOSTATE, SECTARY
district .. PARISH, DIOCESE
division in a .... SCHISM
doorkeeper .... OSTIARY
elder .... PRESBYTER
endowment to a .... PATRIMONY
festival .... EASTER
fund-raising sale .... BAZA(A)R
gallery ...... JUBE, LOFT
governing group .... CLASSIS
government .. HIERARCHY
grave-digger .... SEXTON
grounds .... PRECINCT
guard .... OSTIARY
head .... PONTIFF
jurisdiction .. OBEDIENCE
land .... GLEBE
law .... CANON
lay leader .... ELDER
leader .... HIERARCH
lectern .... AMBO
living .... BENEFICE
loft .... JUBE
main part .... NAVE
members .... ECCLESIA, FOLD, FLOCK
monastery's ... MINSTER
morning service .. LAUD, MATIN
Moslem .... MOSQUE
of Latter Day Saints .... MORMON
office .... BENEFICE
office, sale of .... SIMONY
officer ...... PRESBYTER, SACRIST(AN), SEXTON, BEADLE, ORDINARY, ELDER, VERGER
part .... APSE, PEW, STEEPLE, TRANSEPT, ALTAR, CHANCEL, SACRISTY, BEMA, ORATORY, VESTRY
place for shrines .... FERETORY
poetic .... FANE
porch .. GALILEE, PARVIS
practice of peace .... IRENICS
property .... GLEBE
reader .... LECTOR
reading stand .... AMBO, LECTERN
recess .... APSE
revenue ...... BENEFICE, TITHE
rite .... BAPTISM, COMMUNION, BENEDICTION, MASS
Roman .... BASILICA
room for sacred vessels .. VESTRY, SACRISTY
sale of offices, etc. ...... SIMONY, BARRATRY
sanctuary ... SACRARIUM
Scottish .... KIRK
screen ..... ICONASTASIS
seamen's .... BETHEL
seat .... PEW, STALL
seat for clergy .. SEDILIA
separation from .. SCHISM
service .. TE DEUM, MASS, NONES, LAUD
service clothes .... CANONICALS
service invocation ...... BENEDICTION
service reader ... LECTOR
service reading .. LECTION
shrine's place .. FERETORY
singers' group .... CHOIR
tax .... TITHE
tower .. STEEPLE, BELFRY
tower top .... SPIRE
tribunal .... ROTA
vault .... CRYPT
vestibule ..... NARTHEX
vestment room .... SACRISTY, VESTRY
washbowl ...... LAVABO
wine cup ...... CHALICE
woman assistant .... DEACONESS
yard .... PARVIS

Churchill Downs event .... DERBY, RACE

Churchill's (W.) daughter .... SARAH
forte .... PROSE
lady .... CLEMENTINE
nickname ...... WINNIE
son .... RANDOLPH
son-in-law ..... SOAMES
trademark ...... CIGAR, VEE SIGN

churchman .. MINISTER, PRIEST, ECCLESIASTIC, ELDER, PASTOR, CARDINAL, BISHOP, CLERGY

churchyard .... PARVIS

churl ...... BOOR, OAF, HIND, PEASANT, LOUT, CEORL, KNAVE, FREEMAN, VILLEIN, CARL(E)

churlish ...... RUSTIC, SURLY, BOORISH, DOUR, SULLEN

churn ..... STIR, BEAT, SHAKE
rotator .... DASHER

chute ... WATERFALL, RAPIDS, TROUGH, RUNWAY, ROLLWAY, SHOOT, SLIDE
for logs .... FLUME

chutney .... RELISH

Chuvash .... BULGARIAN

cibol .... ONION

ciborium .. CUP, PYX, CANOPY

cicada .... LOCUST
vibrating membrane of .. TIMBAL

cicatricle .... TREAD

cicatrix .... SCAR

Cicero ...... MARCUS, TULLY
target of ..... CATILINE

cicerone .. DRAGOMAN, GUIDE

Cid .... LEADER
play, author of .... CORNEILLE
name of .... RUY, (RODRIGO) DIAZ
sword of ...... COLADA

cider .... (APPLE) JUICE, VINEGAR, SYTHER, PERKIN
pear juice .... PERRY
spiced/sweetened .. FLIP
sweeten .... MULL

ci-devant ..... FORMER, LATE, RECENT

cigar ..... HAVANA, LONDRES, SMOKE, CULEBRA, CORONA, COLORADO, CHEROOT, TOBACCO, PANATEL(L)A, MANILA, TOBY, WEED, CLARO, PERFECTO
box .... HUMIDOR
butt .... STUB, SNIPE
cheap .. STOGIE, STOG(E)Y, TOBY
descriptive of a .... MADURO
Philippine ...... MANILA
puff .... DRAG
self-lighting .. LOCOFOCO
Spanish .. CIGARRO, PURO
stub .... BUTT

cigarette, berry ...... CUBEB
brand .... SALEM, CAMEL, PALL MALL, PIEDMONT, KENT, MARLBORO, WINSTON, TRUE, CHESTER(FIELD)
butt .... STUB, SNIPE
ingredient .... TOBACCO
kind of .... FILTER
lighter .... VESUVIAN
marijuana ...... REEFER
material .... MAKINGS
non-tobacco .... REEFER, CUBEB, MARIJUANA
piece .... STICK
product .. NICOTINE, TAR
puff .... DRAG
slang .... FAG, BUTT, GASPER, NAIL
smoke cleaner ... FILTER
smoke cooler .. MENTHOL
smoking aid ...... PIPE
stub .... BUTT

cigarfish .... SCAD

cilia .... EYELASHES

cilice .... HAIRCLOTH

cilium .... EYELASH

cimex .... BEDBUG

Cimmerian .... DARK, BLACK, GLOOMY
cinch .... GIRTH, FASTEN
slang ...... SURE THING
cinchona .. BARK, TREE, QUILL
alkaloid ...... QUININE, QUINIDINE
Cincinnati ball club .... REDS, REDLEGS
family .... TAFT(S)
cincture ... BELT, ENCLOSURE, GIRDLE, WAISTBAND
cinder .... SLAG, ASH(ES)
like lava .... SCORIA
sifter .... RIDDLE
Cinderella of Pop ... HOPKIN
cinema ..... MOVIE, THEATER, MOTION PICTURE
cinerarium .... URN
cinerator .... CREMATORY, FURNACE
cingulum ...... BELT, GIRDLE
cinnabar ..... ORE, PIGMENT, VERMILION, SINOPLE
cinnamon .... SPICE, BARK, CANELLA
adulterant .... CASSIA
roll .... QUILL
stone .. GARNET, ESSONITE
cinquefoil .... CLOVER, FIVE-FINGER, POTENTILLA
cion ..... GRAFT, SHOOT, BUD
Cipango .... JAPAN
cipher .... NONENTITY, CODE, NAUGHT, MONOGRAM, ZERO, OUGHT
system .... CODE
cipolin .... MARBLE
circa .... ABOUT
Circe .... ENCHANTRESS, TEMPTRESS
home of .... AEAEA
circle .... COTERIE, CIRQUE, GROUP, ORBIT, LOOP, RING, CLIQUE, WHIRL, ZODIAC
angle/arc .... RADIAN
describing one .. VICIOUS
half a ...... HEMICYCLE
imaginary celestial ...... COLURE
of guards ...... CORDON
of light .. CORONA, NIMB, HALO
part ...... ARC, SECTOR, RADIUS, SECANT
poetic .... RONDURE
quarter section .. OVOLO, QUADRANT
circuit .... AMBIT, LAP, TOUR, CYCLE, DISTRICT, ORBIT, LOOP
court .... EYRE
in radio .... HOOKUP
judges' .... EYRE
track .... LAP
circuitous .... DEVIOUS, ROUNDABOUT
circular .... ROUND, BILL, ADVERTISEMENT
band .... RING, HOOP
course ...... RACETRACK, OVAL
cross section ... TERETE
figure/line .... RING
form .... GYRE
letter, papal .... ENCYCLICAL
motion .... EDDY, GYRATION, SPIN, GYRE
plate ... DISH, DISC, DISK
saw .... EDGER
space .... CIRQUE
step .... AMBIT
turn .... LOOP
wall of dome ..... DRUM
circulate .... SPREAD, MOVE AROUND, DIFFUSE
circumference .... PERIPHERY, AMBIT, GIRTH
circumlocution ..... AMBAGE, PERIPHRASE, VERBIAGE, PERIPHRASIS
circumnavigator, first .... MAGELLAN
circumscribe ...... ENCIRCLE, CONFINE, ENCOMPASS, LIMIT
circumspect .... WARY, CAUTIOUS, CAREFUL, PRUDENT
circumspection .... PRUDENCE
circumstance .. STATE, DETAIL, CONDITION, FACT
circumvent ... SKIRT, OUTWIT
circus ...... ARENA, CIRQUE, (TENT) SHOW
animal ..... LION, BEAR, ELEPHANT, SEAL
arena .... RING, HIPPODROME
colloquial ..... BIG TOP
director .... RINGMASTER
horse .... GRAY
laborer ...... ROUSTER, ROUSTABOUT
minor attraction .... SIDE SHOW
name, bigtime .... RINGLING, BARNUM, BAILEY
net ...... TRAMPOLIN(E)
perennial ...... CLOWN
performer .. FLEA, SEAL, EQUESTRIEN(NE), CLOWN, UNICYCLIST, AERIALIST, TUMBLER, ACROBAT
ring cover .... TANBARK
swing .... TRAPEZE
vehicle .... CARAVAN
cirque .... CIRCLE, RING, AMPHITHEATER, CIRCUS
cirriped .... BARNACLE, CRUSTACEAN
cirrus .... FEELERS, TENDRIL, CLOUDS
cloud ...... MARE'S-TAIL
cirsoid ..... VARICOSE, VARIX
cisco .. (WHITE)FISH, HERRING
cist .... TOMB, CHEST
cistern .... (RAIN) TANK, BAC, VAT
in anatomy .. SAC, CAVITY
natural ..... RESERVOIR
citadel .... FORT, CASTLE, REFUGE, TOWER, STRONGHOLD, FORTRESS, ACROPOLIS
of justice, so-called ..... COURT
Russian ...... KREMLIN
cital .... SUMMONS
citation .... SUMMONS, QUOTATION, REFERENCE
favorable .... ACCOLADE
cite .... SUMMON, QUOTE, MENTION, CALL
cithern .... CITOLE
cities, between .. INTERURBAN
citified: colloq. .... URBAN
citizen .. NATIVE, INHABITANT, FREEMAN, BURGESS, RESIDENT, SUBJECT, NATIONAL, DENIZEN
army .... MILITIA
French .... CITOYEN
of the world .... COSMOPOLITE
citizens, assembly of .... ECCLESIA
of .... CIVIC, CIVIL
citole .... CITHERN
citron .. LEMON, LIME, ETROG
citrus drink .... (LEMON)ADE, (ORANGE)ADE, (LIME)ADE
citrus fruit .. MANDARIN, LIME, GRAPEFRUIT, BERGAMOT, LEMON, ORANGE, CITRON
disease .... PSOROSIS
membrane .... RAG
oil .... BERGAMOT
skin .... ZEST
city ... TOWN, MUNICIPALITY
bishop's .... SEE
business section .... DOWNTOWN
cathedral ... YORK, ELY, R(H)EIMS, CHARTRES
colloquial ... BURG, BURH
district .... WARD
father ...... ALDERMAN, COUNCILOR
fellow: sl. .... DUDE
gangster ... PLUG-UGLY
great ...... MEGALOPOLIS
hall .... AYUNTAMIENTO
heavenly .... SION, ZION
main ...... METROPOLIS
of a ...... CIVIC, URBAN, MUNICIPAL
of Angels .... BANGKOK
of Bridges ..... BRUGES
of Kings .... LIMA
of lights .... PARIS
of masts .... LONDON
of Pillars .... IREM
of Refuge ...... MEDINA
of Saints ..... MONTREAL
of Seven Hills .... ROME
of sin .... SODOM, GOMORRAH, BABYLON
of the dead .. NECROPOLIS
of the Gods ... ASGARD
of the leaning tower .... PISA
of the Rhine ..... MAINZ
of vice .... BABYLON
official .... MAYOR, COUNCILOR, ALDERMAN
on the sea .... PORT
Pearl of the Orient ..... MANILA
pertaining to .... CIVIC, URBAN
square .... PARK

state .... VATICAN, SINGAPORE
subdivision ...... WARD, PRECINCT
vice center .. TENDERLOIN
wicked ...... BABYLON, SODOM, GOMORRAH
civet .... FUR, CAT, NANDINE, RASSE, FOSSA, DEDES, MUSANG, ZIBET
like animal .. GENET(TE), SURICATE
odor .... MUSK(LIKE)
of the .... VIVERINE
civil .... POLITE, URBANE, COURTEOUS, TEMPORAL
magistrate ..... SYNDIC
marriage performer ..... JUDGE
wrong .... TORT
Civil War admiral .... FARRAGUT
battlefield ... ANTIETAM, GETTYSBURG, SHILOH, ATLANTA, BULL RUN
before the .. ANTEBELLUM
cartoonist .... NAST
general .... FREMONT, GRANT, LEE, HOOD, POPE, SHERMAN, SCOTT, BUELL, HOOKER, EWELL, MEADE, SHERIDAN, BRAGG, MCCLELLAN
soldier ... YANKEE, REB
vet .... GAR
volunteer ..... ZOUAVE
civilian .... NONMILITARY, CIV(V)IES
clothes .... MUFTI
civilization .... CULTURE
cradle of .... ASIA
civilize .... EDUCATE, REFINE
clabber ...... MILK, CURDLE
clack .. BLAB, PRATE, CHATTER
clad ...... DRESSED, ROBED, CLOTHED, ATTIRED
claim .. RIGHT, TITLE, ASSERT, ALLEGE
legal .... DEMAND, LIEN
mining .... STAKE
on property ...... LIEN
without right .. ARROGATE
claimant, kind of .. PRETENDER
clairvoyance .... INSIGHT
clairvoyant .... SEER
clam .... MOLLUSK, MYA
hard-shell ..... QUAHOG, QUAHAUG
joint of .... HINGE
killer .... WINKLE
razor .... SOLEN
shell ...... TEST, SHUCK
shell opening ..... GAPE
soft-shell ..... STEAMER
young ...... LITTLENECK
clamant ...... NOISY, URGENT
clambake ... PICNIC, OUTING, COOKOUT
clamber ...... CLIMB, SCALE
clamor .. RIOT, NOISE, UPROAR, OUTCRY, DIN, YAMMER
clamorous .... NOISY, VOCIFEROUS, LOUD
clamp .... VISE, FASTENER
like device ...... CHUCK
clan ..... TRIBE, SET, CLIQUE, FAMILY, GENS
leader ...... CHIEFTAIN, TANIST, THANE
of a .... GENTILE
pattern .... TARTAN
quarrel .... FEUD
symbol .... TOTEM
clandestine .. SECRET, FURTIVE, HIDDEN, UNDERHAND, SURREPTITIOUS
meeting, usually .. TRYST, RENDEZVOUS
clang ..... DING, RING, PEAL
clangor .. PEAL, JANGLE, DIN
clannish .... TRIBAL
clans, quarrel between .. FEUD
clap .... SLAP, BLOW
clapboard .... SIDING
clapper, bell .... TONGUE
claptrap ...... DRIVEL, BOSH, HEROICS, HOKUM
clare .... MINT
clarence .... CARRIAGE
claret ...... WINE, BORDEAU
clarify .. EXPLAIN, ELUCIDATE, PURIFY, CLEAR, DEFINE, EXPOUND
lard .... RENDER
clarinet .... REED
forerunner .. CHALUMEAU
socket .... BIRN
clarinetist, bandleader .... (ARTIE) SHAW
clarion .... TRUMPET
clarity .. CLEARNESS, LUCIDITY
claro .... CIGAR
clarry .... MINT
clash ..... COLLIDE, CONFLICT, DISAGREE
clasp ...... EMBRACE, TASSEL, HUG, HASP, HOOK, BUCKLE, FASTENING, ENFOLD, CINCH, FIBULA, OUCH
hair .... BARRETTE
ornamental .... BROOCH
class ...... KIND, CASTE, ILK, CATEGORY, ORDER, SPECIES, KIDNEY
first .... BEST
of animal/plant .. GENUS
of ruling deities .... THEARCHY
scientific .... GENUS, GENERA
slang ...... EXCELLENCE, QUALITY
classical language .... LATIN, GREEK
music .... CONCERTO, SYMPHONY, SONATA
non .. MODERN, POPULAR, ROMANTIC
classics annotator .. SCHOLIAST
classification .... LABEL
of diseases .... NOSOLOGY
science of ... TAXONOMY
classified (information) ...... SECRET
classify .... LIST, SORT, CATALOGUE, TYPE, LABEL, RATE
classis .... ROTA
classy ..... ELEGANT, STYLISH
clatter .... HUBBUB, RATTLE, BRATTLE, HURTLE
claudicant .... LAME, LIMPING
clavichord .... SPINET
clavicle .... COLLARBONE
clavier .... KEYBOARD
common .... PIANO
claviform .... CLAVATE, CLUB-SHAPED
claw ...... SCRATCH, TALON, UNGUIS, UNGULA, HOOK, POUNCE, NAIL, NIPPER
having/like a ... UNGUAL
like process .... CALCAR
of crustacean ... CHELA, PINCER
pincer-like .. CHELIFORM
retract .... SHEATHE
claws .... UNCI
clay .... LOESS, ARGIL, MARL, LOAM, LATERITE, LUTE, SAGGER, SAGGAR, LITHOMARGE, KAOLIN(E), FIGULINE
baked ... ADOBE, BRICK, TILE, BOLE
case .. SAGGER, SAGGAR, SEGGAR
chunk .... BAT
clump of .... CLOD
desert .... ADOBE
earthy ... OCHER, OCHRE
formation .... SHALE
granite .... PETUNTSE
layer .... SLOAM
like .... BOLAR
lump .... BAT
mixture .. LOAM, PUDDLE, CEMENT
molded .... PUG
ore-bearing ..... OCHER, OCHRE
paste .... PATE
pertaining to ..... BOLAR
pigeon .... TARGET
pigeon shoot .... SKEET
plastic .... PUG
porcelain ...... KAOLIN, PASTE
potter's .... ARGIL, FIGULINE, PASTE
rock .... MUDSTONE
sieve .... LAUN
thinned .... SLIP
tobacco pipe ... DUDEEN
wad .... BAT
water mixture ... SLURRY
white .... PETUNTSE
clayey .... BOLAR, LUTOSE
cement .... LUTE
soil .... MARL, LOAM, MALM, LOESS, BOLE
claymore .... (BROAD) SWORD
clean ...... PURE, ABSTERGE, SINLESS, UNSOILED, SPOTLESS
and draw fowl ... DRESS
breast, make a .. CONFESS
by rubbing ...... SCOUR, SCRUB
clothes .... LAUNDER
copy .... LEGIBLE, READABLE

hands .... INNOCENT
of impurities .... PURGE, PURIFY
ship's bottom .. BREAM, GRAVE
slate ...... TABULA RASA
up .... FINISH
with abrasive ... SCRAPE, SCOUR
with broom ..... SWEEP
with mop .... SWAB
cleaner ..... SOAP, SWEEPER, CHARWOMAN
cleaning cloth .... RAG
powder ... PUMICE, ARIEL
cleanse .... PURGE, DETERGE, PURIFY
cleansing substance .... ABSTERGENT, SOAP, BORAX, DETERGENT, PURGATIVE, ARIEL
clear .... APPARENT, OBVIOUS, CLARIFY, LIMPID, LUCULENT, RID, EVIDENT, LIQUID, (PEL)LUCID, HURDLE, FREE
conscience ... INNOCENT
cut .... DISTINCT, SHARP, TRENCHANT
day .... SUNNY
of charges ..... ABSOLVE, ACQUIT, EXONERATE
out .. LEAVE, DEPART, GO, DECAMP
perfectly .. LUCID, LIMPID
profit .... NET
sky .... ETHER
the way! ..... GANGWAY
throat audibly ... HAWK, HEM
title .... UNENCUMBERED
to the mind ... PALPABLE
up .. EXPLAIN, CLARIFY, STRAIGHTEN
clearance .... MARGIN, ADJUSTMENT
sale .... RUMMAGE
cleareyed .... PERCEPTIVE
clearing, wood ...... GLADE
cleat .. KEVEL, BATTEN, PITON
make secure around .... BELAY
cleavage .... CLEFT, RIFT, DIVISION, FISSION, GULF
cleave .. SPLIT, DIVIDE, SEVER, REND, RIVE, CLING, SUNDER
cleaver .... FROE, FROW, CHOPPER
sky .... LIGHTNING
cleek .... HOOK
cleft ... SPLIT, DIVIDED, GAP, FISSURE, RIFT, SCISSURE, FORKED
easily .... FISSILE
Clemenceau's soubriquet ..... TIGRE, TIGER
clemency .... GRACE, MERCY, LENIENCY
Clemens' pen name .... (MARK) TWAIN
clement ..... MILD, LENIENT, MERCIFUL
clench .... CLINCH, GRIP
clenched hand .... FIST

Cleopatra's domain .. EGYPT, NILE
killer .... ASP
lover .... ANTONY, (JULIUS) CAESAR
maid .... IRAS
Needle .... OBELISK
river .... NILE
son .... CAESARION
clepe .... CALL, NAME
clepsydra ... (WATER)CLOCK, WATERGLASS
clergy .. CLOTH, FIRST ESTATE, MINISTRY
clergyman .. MINISTER, PRIEST, CURATE, CLERIC, ABBE, PARSON, PASTOR, CANON, DIVINE
and author ...... SHEEN
church service vestment .. CANONICALS
colloquial ..... DOMINIE
degree of .... STB
position/garment .... CASSOCK, FROCK
residence of ...... MANSE, PARSONAGE, RECTORY
salary of .... PREBEND
with the military .... CHAPLAIN, PADRE
clerical cap .... BIRETTA
collar .. RABATO, REBATO
vestment ... AMICE, ALB, SURPLICE, FANON, ORALE
clerisy .... INTELLECTUALS
clerk .... SALESMAN, OFFICE WORKER, SCRIBE, SCRIVENER
"Clerk's Tale" heroine ...... GRISELDA
Cleveland waterfront ... ERIE
clever .... ADEPT, ADROIT, TALENTED, BRIGHT, CUTE, CUNNING, SMART, HABILE, SLICK
as a fox .... VULPINE
remark: sl. ...... NIFTY, CRACK
retort .. REPARTEE, SALLY, BON MOT, RIPOST(E), WITTICISM
cleverly done/said ..... NEAT
clew .... THREAD, CLUE, KEY, TIP, BALL
cliche ... BANALITY, PLATITUDE
click .. PAWL, CATCH, AGREE, SUCCEED, PALLET, SNICK
beetle .. ELATER, DOR(R)
clicking sound .... TICK
client .. DEPENDENT, CUSTOMER
without ...... BRIEFLESS
clientele .... PATRONAGE, PATRONS, TRADE, CUSTOMERS
cliff .. ESCARPMENT, PRECIPICE, BLUFF
debris .... TALUS
edge .... BROW
fissure .... CHINE
fissure for climbing ..... CHIMNEY
rock pile .... TALUS
cliffs, channel between ... GAT
line of .... PALISADES

climacteric .... CRUCIAL
woman's .... MENOPAUSE
climate ...... SKY, WEATHER
study of ... METEOROLOGY
climax ...... SUMMIT, ACME, CULMINATION, APOGEE
climb .. ASCEND, MOUNT, RISE, ASCENT, SCALE, CLAMBER
a rope/pole .... SHIN
down .... DESCEND
climbers .... VINES
social .... PARVENU
climbing .... SCALING
adapted for .. SCANSORIAL
by attachment .... SCANDENT
iron .... CRAMPON, SPUR
means of ...... LADDER
palm .... RATTAN
plant process ... TENDRIL
vine .. IVY, BINE, BRYONY, LIANA, LIANE, HOP, PEA
wall by ladder .... ESCALADE
clime ...... CLIMATE, REALM, REGION, COUNTRY
clinch ... FASTEN, NAIL, GRIP, GRAPPLE, HUG, CLOSE
argument .... SETTLE
breaker .... REFEREE
nautical .. KNOT, NOOSE, CLENCH
slang .... EMBRACE
cling .... ADHERE, STICK, COHERE
clingfish .... REMORA, TESTAR
clinic .... DISPENSARY
clink ..... PRISON, JAIL, RING
clinker .... SLAG, BRICK
built .... LAPSTRAKE
clinking sound ...... TINKLE
clinquant .... TINSEL(ED)
"Clinton's ditch" .... ERIE (CANAL)
Clio's field .... HISTORY
clip ..... CUT, FASTEN, GRIP, MOW, SCAR
colloquial .... PACE, HIT, PUNCH, SPEED, CHEAT, SWINDLE
ornamental .... BROOCH
Scottish .... COLL
clipper ...... SHIP, AIRPLANE, SHEARER
barber's ...... SCISSORS
clippings .... SCRAPS
clique ...... CIRCLE, COTERIE, SET, RING, FACTION
advisers' .... CAMARILLA, CABAL
cloaca .... SEWER, PRIVY
cloak ... DISGUISE, GARMENT, CONCEAL, MANTUA, WRAP, CHLAMYS, PALL, GREGO
and-dagger group .. CIA, OSS, OGPU
blanket-like ... PONCHO, SERAPE
fur-lined .... PELISSE
hood of .... COWL
hooded .... CAPOTE, BURNOOSE, BURNOUS, CAMAIL, CARDINAL

over armor ... SURCOAT, TABARD
room .. VESTIARY, CLOSET
short ...... MANT(E)LET, GREGO, MANTILLA
Spanish .. MANTA, CAPA
used as raincoat .... PONCHO
woman's ..... MANTEAU, CARDINAL
clobber .... BEAT, HIT, MAUL, DEFEAT
cloche ..... (GLASS) JAR, HAT
clock .... TIME(PIECE), HOROLOGE
face of .... DIAL
inhabitant ..... CUCKOO
London's famed .... BIG BEN
part .. CHIME, PENDULUM, HAND, PALLET, CLICK, PAWL
shaped .... NEF
sound ..... TICK(TOCK), CHIME
water .... CLEPSYDRA
work device .... METRONOME
clocklike .. PRECISE, REGULAR
clockwise .... SUNWISE
clod .... DOLT, LUMP, EARTH, SOIL, GALOSH(E)
clodhopper .. PLOWMAN, BOOR, SHOE
clodpate .. BLOCKHEAD, FOOL
clodpoll .. BLOCKHEAD, DOLT
clog ... SABOT, SHOE, IMPEDE, BLOCK, PATTEN, DANCE, HAMPER, CHOKE, CHOPINE
cloisonne finish ..... ENAMEL
cloister ..... NUNNERY, STOA, ABBEY, MONASTERY, CONVENT, PRIORY, FRIARY
dweller .... MONK, NUN, ABBOT, ABBESS
cloistered .... SECLUDED, RETIRED
close ... SHUT(IN), CONCLUDE, FINISH, COMPACT, FINALE, END, SEAL, LOCK, OCCLUDE, INTIMATE, NIGH, SULTRY, STINGY
British .. ENTRY, PASSAGE
building ...... PADLOCK
by ...... (A)NEAR, NIGH
conclusively .... CLINCH
down/up .... STOP
fist .... CLENCH
fitting .... (SKIN)TIGHT, SNUG
hermetically .... SEAL
in .... SURROUND
in music .... CODA
mouthed ..... TACITURN
mouthed one ..... CLAM
of day .... EVENTIDE
poetic .... ANEAR, NIGH
tightly ...... SEAL, CORK
to the wind .... LUFF
violently .... SLAM
closed at one end ..... BLIND
closefisted .. STINGY, MISERLY, NIGGARD
closet .... TOILET, CUPBOARD, ROOM, CUDDY, PRIVY, AMBRY, LOCKER
closing passage in music ..... CODA
word .... AMEN
closure .... CONCLUSION, END, CLOTURE, STOPPAGE
clot .... GRUME, COAGULATE, CRUOR, JELL, GOUT
preventing substance .... HEPARIN
cloth ...... FABRIC, DRAPERY, BRAT, SERGE, TWEED, DENIM, MUSLIN, TABARET, TRICOT, TEXTILE, TWILL, GOODS, RATTEEN, WOOF
altar .... PALL, VESPERAL
baptismal ...... CHRISOM
bark .... TAPA
buff-colored ... NANKIN, NANKEEN
calico .... DOWLAS
camel's hair .... ABA, CAMLET
chalice .... PALL
checkered ...... PLAID, TARTAN
corded .... DIMITY, BENGALI
cotton ... MUSLIN, JEAN, MANTA, CALICO, DRILL, CHINTZ, NANKEEN, HOLLAND, GINGHAM, CHINO, DENIM, CANVAS, CRASH, MADRAS
cover ...... DRAPE, TILT
cretonne .... TOILE
crinkled .. CRAPE, CREPE
curtain .... TAPIS
damask-like .... LAMPAS
dealer .... DRAPER, CLOTHIER
diagonal weave .. TWILL
dressing .. STUPE, GAUZE
drying .... TOWEL
drying frame ... TENTER
edge .... SELVAGE
end part of .... FAG
equal to $2\frac{1}{4}$ inches .. NAIL
fiber .... COTTON, RAMIE, LINEN, FLAX, NAP, SILK
figured ...... BROCADE, BROCATEL(LE)
finishing machine .... BEETLE, CALENDER
flaxen .... LINEN
flaw .... RIP, TEAR, SNAG
floor covering ...... RUG
for face sweat .... VERONICA, SUDARIUM
for sheets, pillowcases ... MUSLIN
frieze-like ..... RATTEEN
gauzy .. BAREGE, ILLUSION
glazed .... CHINTZ, JACONET
glossy ... SATIN, SATEEN, SILK, LUSTRING, LUTESTRING, CALAMANCO
goat's hair .... ABA
gold .. CYPRUS, CYPRESS
hairy surface .... NAP
handwoven .. TAPESTRY
hanging in folds .... DRAPERY
heavy .... MACE
hemp .... CANVAS
jute .... GUNNY
knot .... BURL
lightweight .... DELAINE
linen ..... DRILL, TOILE, DOWLAS, HOLLAND
loin .... LAVA-LAVA
make of .... WOVEN, KNITTED, PRESSED
maker .... DRAPER
making spy ...... KEEK
material .... COTTON, WOOL, SILK, HAIR, RAYON, SKIN, FIBER, FLAX
measure ..... ELL, NAIL
medicated .... STUPE
metallic .... LAME
mix-colored .... MOTLEY
mulberry bark .... TAPA
mummy .... BYSSUS
nautical .. CANVAS, SAIL
needlework ..... CANVAS
ornamentally designed .. LAMPAS
penitent's ... SACKCLOTH
plaid .... TARTAN
plush-like ...... BOLIVIA
powder .... SACHET
rib .... CORD
ribbed .... CORDUROY
ridge .... RIB
sample .... SWATCH
selvage .... LIST
sheer .... TOILE
silk .. CHIFFON, SARCENET, LUSTRING, LEVANTINE, CHARMEUSE
soft .... SATIN, SILK, GOSSAMER
stiffening .... WIGAN
strip .... LIST
strips for decoration .... BUNTING
surface .... NAP
symbol of penitence .... SACKCLOTH
synthetic .... RAYON, DACRON, NYLON
table .... NAPKIN
tapestry .... TAPIS
texture .... WALE
the .... CLERGY
to wrap dead person in .. CEREMENT, SHROUD, BYSSUS
triangular .... GORE
twilled .... JEAN, SERGE, DENIM, CHINO, PLAID, LEVANTINE
umbrella .... GLORIA
upholstering .... BROCATEL(LE), TABARET
veil .... BAREGE
velvet-like ...... PANNE
wall hanging .. TAPESTRY
waste .... RAG
waterproof ... GOSSAMER
waxed .... CEREMENT
wiping .. NAPKIN, TOWEL

with decorative pictures .. TAPESTRY
with diagonal weave .... DRILL
with raised design ...... BROCADE, BROCHE
with satin strips .... TABARET
with uncut loops .. TERRY
wool(en) .... SEE "WOOL(EN)"
worn like a scarf .. STOLE
clothe .. DRESS, GARB, INVEST, ROBE, RIG
clothed ..... CLAD, INVESTED
clothes ..... RAIMENT, DRESS, APPAREL, ATTIRE, TOGGERY
basket .... HAMPER
bride's ...... TROUSSEAU
cheap .... SLOPS
chest .. BUREAU, DRESSER
closet .... WARDROBE
collection of .... WARDROBE, ENSEMBLE
colloquial .. TOGS, DUDS, RAGS
fancier ..... DUDE, FOP, DANDY
gaudy .... FRIPPERY
moth .... TINEA
party ..... (GLAD)RAGS
pertaining to .. VESTIARY
place for ...... CLOSET, BUREAU, DRESSER, WARDROBE
powder .... SACHET
press .... IRON, ARMOIRE
ragged .... TATTERS
set of .. SUIT, ENSEMBLE
splendid .... REGALIA
stand ...... TREE, RACK
to be washed .. LAUNDRY
work .. DENIM, COVERALL, JEANS, SMOCK, DUNGAREES, APRON
clotheshorse: colloq. .... FOP, DANDY, COXCOMB, DUDE
famed .. (BEAU) BRUMMEL
clothespress .... ARMOIRE
clothing .... RAIMENT, ATTIRE
of men's ..... SARTORIAL
ready-made ...... SLOPS
store .... TOGGERY
Clotho .... FATE, WEIRD
clotting protein ... GLOBULIN
cloture .... CLOSURE, CLOSING
cloud .... DARKEN, OBSCURE, SULLY
combining form .. NEPHO
composition ..... DUST, SMOKE, STEAM, GAS
formation ...... CIRRUS, CUMULUS, STRATUS, NIMBUS
like mass .... COMA, NEBULA
of dust/smoke/gas .. MIST
photo of .... NEPHOGRAM
surrounding gods .... NIMBUS
cloudburst .. RAIN, DOWNPOUR
cloudless .... BRIGHT, CLEAR, SUNNY
clouds, fleecy .... CIRRUS
broken mass of .... (W)RACK
combining form .. NEPHO
cumulus ..... WOOLPACK
in the .... IMPRACTICAL, FANCIFUL
study of .... NEPHOLOGY
wind-driven .... SCUD
cloudy .. NUBILOUS, OVERCAST, DIM, HAZY, LOWERING, NEBULOUS, TURBID
clough ...... RAVINE, GORGE
clout ..... SWAT, RAP, BLOW, KNOCK, HIT, CUFF, SLAP
clove .. SPICE, BUD, CARNATION
cloven .. CLEFT, SPLIT, DIVIDED
footed .... DEVILISH, SATANIC, FISSIPED
hoofed ...... BISULCATE
clover ..... TREFOIL, NARDOO, SHAMROCK, LADINO, BERSEEM, ALSIKE, MELILOT, MEDIC, ALFALFA, FOUR-LEAF
plan resembling .. MEDIC
clown .. BOOR, BUFFOON, LOUT, ZANY, APER, JESTER, COMIC, BUFFO, MIME, CUTUP, HARLEQUIN, PUNCHINELLO
forte of a .... (TOM)FOOLERY, JOKES, TRICKS, ANTICS
garment of .... MOTLEY
of a sort: sl. .... CUTUP
Shakespearean play ..... FESTE, LAVACHE
woman .... BUFFA
clownish ..... BOORISH, RUDE, CLUMSY
cloy .. SURFEIT, SATIATE, PALL, SATE, GLUT
cloying .... LUSCIOUS
club .... STICK, CUDGEL, TRUNCHEON, MAUL, BAT
aborigine's ...... WADDY
armor-breaking ... MACE
baseball .... BAT
benefit sale .... BAZAAR, RUMMAGE
billiards ..... MACE, CUE
college ...... SORORITY, FRAT(ERNITY)
for beating cloth .... BEETLE
for sandtraps .... WEDGE
golf ...... CLEEK, IRON, DRIVER, PUTTER
hockey .... BANDY
hold on .... GRIP
local division .. CHAPTER
manager ...... STEWARD
metal-headed .... MACE
military service ..... USO
moss .... LYCOPOD
policeman's ..... BILLY, TRUNCHEON
polo .... MALLET
service .... KIWANIS, ROTARY, LIONS, JAYCEES
shaped .... CLAVATE, CLAVIFORM
social .... COTERIE, SORORITY
women's ...... SOROSIS, ZONTA, SORORITY
wooden .... MAUL
clubfoot .... TALIPES
clubfooted .... TALIPED
clubman .. ROTARIAN, JAYCEE, LION, KIWANIAN
clucking sound ...... CLACK
clue .... CLEW, TIP, HINT, POINTER
clumber ...... DOG, SPANIEL
clump .... MASS, CLUSTER, THICKET
bushy .... TOD
of bushes .... SHAW
of earth .... CLOD
of ivy, etc. .... TOD
of trees .. BOSK, MOTT(E), TUFT
clumps, growing in .. CEPITOSE
clumsy .... AWKWARD, INEPT, INELEGANT, GAUCHE, OAFISH, UNGAINLY, GAWKY, LUMPY, MALADROIT
and stupid ..... LOUTISH
boat ... ARK, DROGHER, BARGE
person .... OAF, JUMBO, LUBBER, OX, LUMMOX
player .... DUB
thing .... JUMBO
worker .... COBBLER, DABSTER, DABBLER, BUNGLER
Cluny product .... LACE
clupeid .. HERRING, SARDINE, SHAD
cluster ..... BUNCH, CLUMP, TUFT, SORUS, GLOMERATION, KNOT
arranged in ... AGMINATE
banana .... HAND
bracts .... COMA
compact .... GLOMERULE
fibers .... FASCICLE
flowers .. CYME, RACEME, PANICLE
fruits .... BUNCH
leaves .... FASCICLE
of seven stars .. PLEIADES
of shrubs .... CLUMP
of spore cases .... SORUS
of trees .... CLUMP
clustered .... GLOMERATE
clusters, growing in .... ACERVATE
clutch .. GRASP, SNATCH, SEIZE, GRIP, HOLD
clutches ... POWER, CONTROL, GRIP
clutter ..... JUMBLE, LITTER, BUSTLE, LUMBER
clyster .... ENEMA
Clytemnestra's husband ..... AGAMEMNON
lover .... AEGISTHUS
mother .... LEDA
son .... ORESTES
coach .. CARRIAGE, BUS, TUTOR
athletic .... TRAINER
dog .... DALMATIAN
for hire .. HACK, HANSOM, FIACRE

for state occasions ...... CAROCHE
four-horse drawn .... TALLYHO
roof/top of ... IMPERIAL
coachman ..... DRIVER, LURE, HACK, JEHU, FLY
coaction ... FORCE, COERCION, COMPULSION
coagulate .... CURDLE, CAKE, CLOT, CONGEAL, JELL, SET, CRUD
coagulated mass ...... CLOT
coagulating substance .... RENNET, RENNIN, STYPTIC, COAGULIN, PRECIPITIN
coagulation, blood ..... CLOT, THROMBOSIS
coal .... CARBON, COKE, ANTHRACITE, BITUMINOUS, LIGNITE
barge load of ..... KEEL
bin .... BUNKER
box ..... HOD, BIN, DAN, SCUTTLE
bucket .... SCUTTLE
burner .... BRASIER
container of live .... BRAZIER
deposit .... SEAM
digger .. PITMAN, COLLIER
distillate .... TAR
dust .. CULM, DUFF, SMUT, ASH, SLACK
feeder .... STOKER
glowing piece of .. EMBER, GLEED
grade of ..... WALLSEND
hod .... SCUTTLE
impurities .... CLINKER, CULM
leavings .... SLACK
like substance .... JET
live ...... EMBER, GLEED
lump/mass .... COB
measure .... CHALDRON, PEA
mine ..... COLLIERY, PIT
bed .... WINNING
carrier .... TUB, TRAM
gas .... METHANE, FIREDAMP
roof prop ..... SPRAG
shaft ... PIT, WINNING
wagon .... CORF
miner .. COLLIER, PITMAN
miner's consumption .... ANTHRACOSIS
oil .... KEROSENE, PETROLEUM
partially burned .... CINDER
pieced .... LUMP
region ..... SAAR, RUHR
screening device .... TROMMEL
scuttle .... HOD
ship .... COLLIER
shovel .... SCOOP
sieve .... TROMMEL
size of .. PEA, EGG, NUT, WALLSEND
stoker .... HOPPER
tar compound .... SACCHARIN
tar derivative .. TOLUENE, PITCH, CRESOL, BITUMEN, CREOSOTE, TOLUOL(E)
tar dye .. EOSIN, ALIZARIN
truck .... CORF
wagon ..... CORF, TRAM
waste .. CULM, CLINKER
coalesce .. MIX, MERGE, UNITE
coalescence .. MERGER, UNION
coalfish .... POLLACK, CUDDY
coalition ... UNION, ALLIANCE, FUSION, MERGER, ENTENTE
coals, rake over the .... CRITICIZE, CENSURE
coarse .. CRUDE, INDELICATE, RIBALD, ROUGH, GROSS, VULGAR, OBSCENE, CRASS, HARSH, LOWBRED
cloth .. DENIM, BURLAP, SCRIM, JUTE, LENO
corn meal .... SAMP, HOMINY
fiber .... TOW
flour .... MEAL
hominy ... GRITS, SAMP
lace .... MACRAME
meal .... GROUT
coast .. (SEA) SHORE, SEASIDE, GLIDE, BEACH, RIVAGE
Guard boat ..... CUTTER
Guard girl .... SPAR
line curve .... BIGHT
of the .... LITTORAL
on aircraft ... VOLPLANE
coastal .... LITTORAL
coaster ..... SLED, TOBOGGAN
coasting vehicle .... SLED, TOBOGGAN, SKI, SURFBOARD
coat .... JACKET, LAYER, COVERING, GARMENT, PLATE, TOG, KIRTLE
animal ...... FUR, SKIN, WOOL
arm-pinning .... STRAIGHTJACKET
close-fitting .... COATEE, NEW MARKET
daytime ...... CUTAWAY
double-breasted .... REEFER, MACKINAW
formal .. CUTAWAY, TAILS
fur-lined .... PELISSE
icy ... RIME, (HOAR)FROST
kind of ... TRENCH, TOP, DUSTER
leather .... JACK
long .... REDINGOTE
long-sleeved ... KAFTAN, CAFTAN
loose .... SACK, PALETOT
madman's .... STRAITJACKET
of a mammal .. PELAGE, HAIR, FUR
of alloy .... PATINA
of armor .. BRIGANDINE
of arms ...... BLAZON, SHIELD, CREST, HERALDRY
of arms band .... BATON, TRESSURE
of arms edge .. BORDURE
of gold ..... GILD, GILT
of icing .... GLACE
of mail .... ARMOR, HAUBERK, BYRNIE
of metal .... PLATE
person in white .. DOCTOR
slang .... TOG
sleeveless .... JACK
slit .... VENT
soldier's .... TUNIC
thin .... VENEER
waterproof .... SLICKER, MACKINTOSH
with aluminum .... CALORIZE
with brass .... BRAZE
with gold ... GILD, GILT
with metal .... PLATE
with tar .... PAY
woman's .... REDINGOTE, REEFER, DOLMAN
worn as armor .... GAMBESON
coati-like animal .. RACCOON
coating ..... COVERING, FILM, VENEER
boiler's inside ...... FUR
for photographic plates .. COLLODION
for wounds .. COLLODION
fruit .... BLOOM
glossy .. ENAMEL, GLAZE
icy ... SLEET, (HOAR)FROST
metal ... PATINA, PATINE
on ceiling ...... PARGET
on copper, bronze .... PATINA, PATINE
on eyes .... GLAZE
pottery .. GLAZE, ENAMEL
wall .... PARGET
coax ..... CAJOLE, WHEEDLE, PERSUADE, TEASE, BLARNEY, BLANDISH
cob .... SWAN, HORSE, (SEA)GULL
coal .... COBBLES
cobalt .... BLUE
Cobb, baseball player ..... TY
cobble .. PAVE, MEND, PATCH
cobbler .... SOLER, (SHOE)MENDER, CRISPIN
block of .... LAST
tool of .... AWL
coble .... ROWBOAT, (FISHING)BOAT
cobra .. SNAKE, NAGA, VIPER, MAMBA, ELAPINE
fighter ...... MONGOOSE
headdress ..... URAEUS
cobweb ..... GOSSAMER, TRAP
describing a .... FLIMSY, GAUZY, FILMY
material .... FIBROID
Coca-Cola product ..... TAB, FRESCA
Coca, comedienne .. IMOGENE
cocaine .... NARCOTIC, ALKALOID, ANESTHETIC
addict .... SNOWBIRD
slang .... SNOW
source .... COCA, CUCA
Cochin-China capital .... SAIGON

cochineal .... DYE
pigment .... LAKE
cochleate .... SPIRAL
cock .... ROOSTER, CROW, LEADER, FAUCET, TAP
-a-hoop ..... CONCEITED, ELATED
-and-bull story .... CANARD, HOAX, YARN
comb of ..... CARUNCLE
fighting .... HEELER
young .... COCKEREL
cockade ..... KNOT, ROSETTE
cockateel .... PARROT
cockatoo .... PARROT, ARARA
cockatrice .... SERPENT, BASILISK
cockboat ...... COG, TENDER
cockchafer ..... DOR, BEETLE, BUZZARD
cockcrow ..... DAWN, MORN
cocker .... SPANIEL, PAMPER, CODDLE, PET, FONDLE
cockerel .... ROOSTER
cockeyed: sl. ..... CROOKED, AWRY, ABSURD, SCREWY, DRUNK
cockfight .... SPAR
cockiness .... CONCEIT
cockle ... DARNEL, WRINKLE, WEED, SHELLFISH, BOAT, PUCKER
cocklebur .... BURDOCK, RAGWEED
cockloft ...... ATTIC, GARRET
cockney .... EGG, CHILD, DIALECT
famous ...... HORNSBY
cockpit .... ARENA, CABIN
occupant .... PILOT
of Europe, so-called .... BELGIUM
cockroach .... WATERBUG
cockscomb .. CAP, FOP, DANDY
cockspur ...... (HAW)THORN
cocktail .... DRINK, MARTINI, APPETIZER, BRONX, MANHATTAN
fruit .... MACEDOINE
ingredient ...... BITTERS
lethal .... MOLOTOV
measure .... SPLIT
mixer ...... BARTENDER, SHAKER
room .... LOUNGE
rum .. DAIQUIRI, ZOMBI(E)
tidbit .... OLIVE
with legs .... HORSE
cocky ..... CONCEITED, VAIN, SAUCY
coco .... PALM(TREE)
cocoa .... CHOCOLATE, BROMA
bean, crushed ...... NIBS
coconut .... PALM
husk fiber .... COIR
liquid .... MILK
meat, dried .. COPRA(H), COPPERAH
oil source ...... COPRA
cocoon .... POD, CASE, THECA
covering .... FLOSS
fiber .... SILK
in zoology .... FOLLICLE
occupant .... PUPA
silkworm .... CLEW
Cocos Islands ..... KEELING
cod .... LING, BURBOT, BOCACCIO, CUSK, GADID, GLASHAN, WHITING
Archaic .... BAG
fishing bait .. CAP(E)LIN
kin .... HAKE
COD, part of ..... CASH, ON, DELIVERY, COLLECT
coda .... FINALE
coddle .... PET, PAMPER, PARBOIL, SPOONFEED, BABY
code .. SALIC, CODEX, CIPHER, LAW
church .... CANON
emperor's .... NAPOLEON
message in .... CRYPTOGRAM
moral .... ETHICS
of a kind ..... PASSWORD
of laws .... HAMMURABI
word, GI's radio .. ABLE, BAKER, ROGER
codfish .... TORSK, CUSK, GADOID, GLASHAN, BURBOT, LING, GADID
young .... SCROD
codger .. FELLOW, ECCENTRIC, MISER, CHURL
codicil ..... APPENDIX, RIDER
codling ...... SCROD, APPLE
Cody, American plainsman ... (BUFFALO) BILL
coelenterate .... HYDRA, JELLYFISH, ANEMONE, ACALEPH(E)
larva of .... PLANULA
coenurus .... LARVA
host of .... SHEEP
coerce ...... COMPEL, FORCE, CONSTRAIN, COW
colloquial .... BULLDOZE, BULLY
coercion .... COMPULSION, DURESS
slang ... HEAT, PRESSURE
coercive indoctrination .... BRAINWASHING
coetaneous .... COEVAL
Coeur d'Alene Indian .... SALISHAN
de Lion .... RICHARD (I)
coeval .... CONTEMPORARY, COETANEOUS
coffee .. JAVA, MOCHA, SHRUB, CAFE, BRAZIL, SUMATRA, MADDER
alcoholic addition .. LACE
alkaloid ..... CAFFEIN(E)
bean .... NIBS
box .... CANISTER
break .. RESPITE, TIME-OFF
brewer ..... URN, SILEX
cake .... KUCHEN
can .... CANISTER
cup .... DEMITASSE
cup stand .... ZARF
extract .... CAFFEIN(E)
grinder .... MILL
house .... CAFE
making container .. URN, SILEX, PERCOLATOR
mixture ...... SUCCORY, CHICORY
plantation ...... FINCA
pot .. URN, DRIPOLATOR, BIGGIN, PERCOLATOR
room .... DIVAN
substitute ..... CHICORY, SUCCORY
tree .... CHICOT
coffer ... CHEST, STRONGBOX, LOCK, ARK
coffers .... TREASURY, FUNDS, CHEST
coffin .. CASKET, (BURIAL) BOX, BIER, LITTER
carrier .... PALLBEARER, HEARSE, CAISSON
cover .... PALL
nail: sl. ..... CIGARETTE
stand .. CATAFALQUE, BIER
stone .... SARCOPHAGUS
cog .... GEAR, TOOTH, WHEEL, (COCK)BOAT, PAWL, SWINDLE, CHEAT
cogent .... CONVINCING, COMPELLING, VALID
cogitate ... THINK, CONSIDER, PONDER, MULL, CEREBRATE, CHEW
cognac .... BRANDY
cognate ...... RELATED, AKIN
cognition .... NOESIS, PERCEPTION
cognizance .... NOTICE, PERCEPTION
cognizant .... ON TO, AWARE, HEP
cognize .... KNOW, PERCEIVE, NOTICE
cognomen ...... (SUR)NAME, NICKNAME
cognoscente ... CONNOISSEUR
cogon .... GRASS
cogwheel ...... GEAR, PINION
Cohan's song .... OVER THERE
coheir .... PARCENER
cohere .... ADHERE, STICK
coherent .... CONSISTENT
cohort .... ALLY, BAND
one third of ... MANIPLE
cohune .... PALM
coif .... (SKULL)CAP
coiffeur .... HAIRDRESSER
coiffure .. HAIRDO, HEADDRESS
pad .... RAT
quickie .... WIG, TOUPEE
style .... CHAR
coign .... CORNER
coil .. WIND, CURL, CONVOLVE, TWIST, LOOP, WHORL, FAKE
cable/rope .... FAKE
in a ball .... CLEW
yarn .... SKEIN
coiled .. CONVOLUTE, TORTILE, SPIRY, HELICOID
coiling creature .. SNAKE, BOA, CONSTRICTOR, PYTHON
coin .. MINT, INVENT, DEVISE, SPECIE
Abyssinian .. GIRSH, BESA
Afghanistan ... AMANIA
Albanian .. LEK, QUINTAR
American (U.S.) .. CENT, DIME, DOLLAR, EAGLE, NICKEL, QUARTER

Anglo-Saxon ...... ORA, SCEAT
Annam .... QUAN
Arabian .... TALARI
Argentine ..... CENTAVO
Austrian .... DUCAT, KRONE, GULDEN
back of .... VERSO
Biblical .... TALENT, SHEKEL
box .... PYX, PIX
Brazilian ..... (MIL)REI, MOIDORE, CENTAVO
Bulgarian .. DINAR, LEV, LEW, STOTINKA
Chilean .... COLON, ESCUDO, CENTAVO, PESO
Chinese ... TIAO, LIANG, TAEL
coating .... BLOOM
collector .. NUMISMATIST
Colombian .... PESO
Costa Rican ..... COLON
counterfeit ... RAP, SLUG
cross-figured .... KREU(T)ZER
cut edges of .... NIG
Czech .. DUCAT, KRONEN
Danish .... ORA, KRONE, CROWN, ORAS
design .... INCUSE
drop .... SLOT
Dutch .. GULDEN, STIVER, GUILDER, FLORIN
Dutch East Indies .. DUIT
Ecuadorian ..... SUCRE
edge .... NIG
Egyptian ..... PIASTRE, PIASTER
El Salvador ..... COLON
English .. GROAT, PENCE, GUINEA, UNITE, ORA, TESTON, CAROLUS, FLORIN
Ethiopian ...... TALARI
expert .... NUMISMATIST
French ..... ECU, LOUIS, BESANT, SOU, PISTOLE
front of .... OBVERSE
German .. KRONE, MARK, T(H)ALER
Greek .. OBOL, DRACHMA
Hebrew .. GERAH, SHEKEL
hole .... SLOT
Hungarian ...... PENGO, GARA, FORINT, FILLER
Icelandic ...... AURAR, KRONA
imitation .... SLUG
India ...... ANNA, PICE, RUPEE, PIE
into money .. MONETIZE, MINT
Iranian .... RIAL, DARIC, DINAR, MOHUR, PAHLAVI
Iraqi .... DINAR
Italian .... LIRA, SCUDO, SOLDO
Japanese .. RIN, SEN, YEN
Jewish .. GERAH, SHEKEL
large ...... CARTWHEEL
Latvian .... LAT(U)
Lithuanian ..... LIT(AS), RUBLE
making metal .... FLAN
metal .. FLAN, PLANCHET
metallic .... SPECIE
Mexican ...... CUARTO, CENTAVO, PESO
money .... MINT
Moroccan .... RIAL
Nepalese .... MOHAR
Norwegian ..... KRONE, ORE, CROWN
Oman .... GAZ, GOZ
Oriental .... DINAR
Persian .. DINAR, DARIC
Peruvian ...... CENTAVO, SOL, DINERO, PESETA
pewter .... TRA
plant .... MINT
Polish ... DUCAT, ZLOTY
Portuguese ..... (MIL)REI
reverse side ...... VERSO
ridges .... KNURL
Roman ... SOLIDUS, AES, SESTERCE, DENARIUS
Rumanian .... LEU, LEY
Russian .... RUBLE, CHERVONETS, KOPE(C)K
Scandinavian ... KRONAR
Serbian .... DINAR
shaped ..... NUMMULAR
Sicilian .... SCUDO
side .... OBVERSE, VERSO
slang .... INVENT
small value ... PICAYUNE, MITE
South American .... CONDOR
space for date, etc. ..... EXERGUE
Spanish ... PESETA, REAL, PESO, DOBLA, DURO, PISTOLE
Spanish colonial .... PISTAREEN
Swedish .... KRONA, ORE, KRONER
Swiss ...... FRANC, BATZ
tester .... SHROFF
Thailand .... ATT, BAHT, CATTY, TICAL
tin .... TRA
Turkish .... LIRA, ASPER, ALTUN, PIASTER, PIASTRE
Venetian .... DUCAT
Venezuelan .... PESO
Yugoslav .... DINAR

coincide .... AGREE
coiner of words ... NEOLOGIST
coins, collection of .... NUMISMATICS
collector of .... NUMISMATIST
pertaining to .... NUMISMATICS
roll of .... ROULEAU
small .... CHANGE
sound of .... JINGLE
study of .. NUMISMATICS

coke .... COAL, FUEL
measure .... CHALDRON
residue .... BREEZE
slang .... COCAIN(E)

col .... GAP, PASS
colander .... PAN, SIEVE, STRAINER
Colchis princess ..... MEDEA
cold .. BLEAK, CATARRH, ICY, ALGID, RHEUM, GELID, MARBLY, CHILLY
blooded ...... CALLOUS, PITILESS
blooded creature .. FISH
congeal by ..... FREEZE
dish .... SALAD, SLAW
extremely .... GELID, FRIGID
head .... CORYZA
hearted .... UNKIND
leave out in the ... SNUB, IGNORE, NEGLECT, ABANDON
Scottish .... CAULD
season .... WINTER
shoulder .. SNUB, REBUFF, BRUSH-OFF
sore .... HERPES, LABIALIS
steel .... BLADE, SWORD
stinging .... NIP
tableland .... PUNA
very .. FRIGID, FREEZING, GELID, HYPERBOREAN
War weapon .... PROPAGANDA
weather wear .. ANORAK, PARKA, EARMUFFS, EARFLAPS

coldness of body ...... CHILL
cole ... CABBAGE, RAPE, KALE
coleopter .... BEETLE, WEEVIL
coleslaw .... SALAD
colewort .... KALE, CABBAGE, COLLARD
colic .... ILEUS
stone .... JADE
colima .... IRONWOOD
colin ...... BOBWHITE, QUAIL
coliseum .... STADIUM
collaborator .... LAVAL, QUISLING
what he gives enemy .... AID, COMFORT
collage of a sort ..... MOSAIC
collapse ... CAVE IN, FALL IN, FAIL, BREAKDOWN, FOLD UP, DEFLATE, SLUMP
collapsible hat .... GIBUS
collar .. NECKWEAR, CAPTURE, RUFF, PARRAL, PARREL, GORGET, CARCANET
ancient metal ... TORQUE
bird with feathered ..... GROUSE, PARTRIDGE
bird's .... FLANGE
bone .... CLAVICLE
clerical .... RABATO
colloquial ...... CHOKER
detachable ...... TUCKER
English schoolboy's .... ETON
fastener .... STUD
frilled .... RUFF
high .... FRAISE
ornamental .. CARCANET
pleated/frilled ..... RUFF
projecting ..... FLANGE
strangling .... GAROTTE, GARROTE
turned down ... RABATO, FALL

woman's ...... BERTHA, DICKEY
collard .... KALE
collared .... TORQUATE
collate ... COMPILE, COMPARE
collateral .... PARALLEL
collation .... MEAL, TEA
colleague .... ASSOCIATE, CONFRERE
collect .... PRAYER, COMPILE, GATHER, ASSEMBLE, AMASS, ACCUMULATE, REAP, GARNER, SCRAPE
grain leftovers .. GLEAN
collectanea ...... ANTHOLOGY, CORPUS
collected .... COOL, CALM, SERENE, AMASSED
collection ... GROUP, BUNCH, REPERTORY, HEAP, LUMP, KIT, PACK, GALAXY, BEVY
a .... SET
anecdotes .... ANA
animal fables .. BESTIARY
animals .... MENAGERIE, ZOO, HERD, DROVE
art works ...... GALLERY
assorted .. MISCELLANEA, MISCELLANY
books .... LIBRARY, BIBLIOTHECA
Brahman maxims .... SUTRA
bridal clothes .... TROUSSEAU
coins ...... NUMISMATICS
commentaries .... GLOSSARY
documents ...... PAPERS
dried plants .. HERBARIUM
essays ...... SYMPOSIUM
explanatory notes ...... GLOSSARY
facts .... ANA, DATA
information about person DOSSIER
large .... RAFT, RAFF
laws .... CORPUS, JURIS, CODE
literary ...... ANALECTA, ANALECTS
logs on river .... DRIVE
Norse poetry ..... EDDA
of writings ..... PAPERS
operas, songs, etc. ...... REPERTOIRE
opinions .... SYMPOSIUM
paintings ...... GALLERY
piano pieces ... GRADUS
poems, etc. .. ANTHOLOGY
postage stamps .... PHILATELY
prayers for mass .. MISSAL
precious ..... TREASURE
reminiscences .. MEMOIRS, ANA
saints' lives .... HAGIOLOGY, LEGENDARY
sayings .... ANA
statues .... GALLERY
things .... CONGERIES
tools .... KIT
types .... PI(E)

collective bargaining result ... CONTRACT
farm .... KOL(K)HOZ
security group ... NATO, SEATO
collectivism ...... SOCIALISM
collector, art ...... VIRTUOSO
bank .... RUNNER
birds' eggs .... OOLOGIST
book .... BIBLIOPHILE
coin ...... NUMISMATIST
curios .... VIRTUOSO
excise tax ..... GA(U)GER
fare .... CONDUCTOR
gem .... LAPIDARY
item for a .... CURIO, RELIC, BIBELOT, MASTER, FIRST ISSUE
jokes .... CERF
Munchausen's tales ..... RASPE
phonograph record ..... DISCOPHILE
plants ...... HERBALIST
shell .... CONCHOLOGIST
stamp ..... PHILATELIST
colleen .... GIRL, LASS
college .. UNIVERSITY, SCHOOL, ACADEMY
athletic team ... VARSITY
building ...... LAB, GYM, DORM(ITORY)
campus .... QUAD
cheer .. YELL, RAH(RAH)
cheerleader: Japan ...... OENDAN
course: abbr. .... ANAT, MATH, ECON, TRIG, BIOL, BOT, ARCH, MED, ZOOL, ENG
dance ...... HOP, PROM
dining hall .. REFECTORY
exams ...... MIDTERMS
fellow .... DON
freshman .... FROSH
get-together ... REUNION
girl .... COED
graduate(s) .. ALUMNUS, ALUMNI
grounds .. QUAD(RANGLE), CAMPUS
group .... FRAT(ERNITY), SORORITY
half year ..... SEMESTER
hall .... AULA
honor society .... ARISTA
league symbol .... IVY(LEAF)
lecturer ..... PRELECTOR
living quarters .... DORM(ITORY), HALL
of attendance .... ALMA MATER
official .. DEAN, REGENT, REGISTRAR, PROVOST
optional subject .... ELECTIVE
organization .... FRATERNITY, SORORITY, CLUB
permit for absence ...... EXEAT
president .... PREXY

publication .... ANNUAL, YEARBOOK
rank .... DEGREE
scholars' .... ULEMA
servant .... GYP
student ..... FRESHMAN, SOPHOMORE, JUNIOR, SENIOR
students' revelry .... GAUDEAMUS
teacher ..... PROF(ESSOR)
treasurer ...... BURSAR
colleges' sports group .... IVY LEAGUE
collegiate .... VARSITY
collide .... CLASH, CRASH, HURTLE, BUMP
collie .... (SHEEP) DOG
of book ..... LASSIE, LAD
of movies .... LASSIE
collier .... (COAL)MINER, PITMAN, SHIP, TENDER
colliery .... (COAL)MINE
tunnel .... ADIT
collinsia .... FIGWORT
collision .... SMASHUP
force of .... IMPACT
colloidal dispersion in fluid ... SOL
collop .... PIECE, SLICE
colloquial .. CONVERSATIONAL
affirmative ... YEP, YEAH
colloquialism .. IDIOM, SLANG, PATOIS
"Colloquies" author .... ERASMUS
colloquy ..... CONVERSATION, PARLEY, CONFERENCE
collude .... CONSPIRE
colly .. BLACKEN, SOOT, GRIME
collyrium .... EYEWASH, EYEWATER
collywobbles .... COLIC
colocynth ...... VINE, BITTER, APPLE
cologne ...... TOILET WATER
Colombia, capital of .... BOGOTA
city .. CARTAGENA, CALI, PASTO, MEDELLIN
Indian .... MIRANA
mountain .... HUILA
river ...... MAGDALENA, CAUCA, JAPURA
volcano .... PASTO
colon, surgical removal of .... COLECTOMY
colonel's command .... REGIMENT
insigne .... EAGLE
navy counterpart .... CAPTAIN
colonial senate member ...... DECURION
colonist ... SETTLER, PLANTER
Indian greeting to ...... NETOP
colonize .... SETTLE
colonizing insect ... ANT, BEE
colonnade .... GALLERY, PORTICO
colony .... PLANTATION, SETTLEMENT

bees .... SWARM
of insects .... NEST
colophony .... ROSIN
color .... BLUSH, FLUSH, DYE, PIGMENT, PAINT, STAIN, HUE, BICE, SEPIA, BLUE, RED, WHITE, YELLOW, GREEN, EBONY, COBALT, CORAL, TINCT
animal .. ROAN, TAWNY, DAPPLE, FAWN, TAUPE, BRINDLE, PINTO
band .... FASCIA
blindness .... DALTONISM
change ... BLUSH, FLUSH
changing substance ..... ALTERANT
combining form .... CHROMAT(O)
expert .... DYER
fixer .... FIXATIVE, MORDANT
fixer, in dyeing .... BASE
flesh .... INCARNATE
for French victory ...... MAGENTA
gradation .. TINT, SHADE
in music .... TIMBRE
intensity .... CHROMA
lack of .... PALLOR
lacking .... ALBINO
lightly ...... TINGE, TINT
lose .... FADE, PALE
neutral .... GREGE
pale .... PASTEL
patch of .... FLECK
pertaining to .... CHROMATIC
primary/prismatic .. RED, ORANGE, GREEN, VIOLET, YELLOW, BLUE, INDIGO
purity of .... CHROMA
small amount of .. TINGE, TINT
splash .... BLOB
streak .... FLECK, LACE
with red ocher .... RADDLE, REDDLE
Colorado capital ..... DENVER
city .. ALAMOSA, LAMAR, PUEBLO, AURORA, BOULDER
county .. LARIMER, OTERO
feature .... MESA
Indian ... ARAPAHOE, UTE
mountain .... RATON, OWEN, ANTERO, SAGUACHE, SAWATCH
nickname .... ROVER, CENTENNIAL
park .... ESTES
peak ...... ESTES, EOLUS
phenomenon .. RAINBOW
Pittsburgh of ... PUEBLO
resort .... MANITOU
river ..... GILA, LARAMIE
River lake .... MEAD
state flower .. COLUMBINE
colored chalk .... PASTEL, CRAYON
glass .... SMALTO
highly .... PRISMAL
many .... PRISMATIC
colorful bird .... TANAGER
life, describing a .... CHECKERED
spectacle .. PAGEANT(RY), EXTRAVAGANZA
coloring matter .. DYE, STAIN, PIGMENT, MORIN, RUDDLE
for crayon ...... PASTEL
colorless .... WAN
combining form .. LEUKO
person .... ALBINO, NONENTITY
colors, artist's ...... PALETTE
having three ... TRICHOIC
the .... FLAG
colossal .... HUGE, GIGANTIC, ENORMOUS, LARGE
beast .... BEHEMOTH, LEVIATHAN, WHALE
Colossi of Memnon, actually .. AMUNHOTEP
colossus ...... STATUE, GIANT
sculptor of the .. CHARES
colt .... HORSE, REVOLVER, BOLLARD, FOAL
revolver: sl. .... PEACEMAKER, HOG-LEG
coltish .... FRISKY
columbary .... DOVECOTE
Columbia eleven ..... LIONS
River catch ..... SALMON
columbine .... AQUILEGIA
columbite .... DIANITE
columbium .... NIOBIUM
columbo .... GENTIAN
Columbus' birthplace .. GENOA
discovery ..... AMERICA, CUBA, COSTA RICA
navigator of ... PINZON
ship ...... NINA, PINTA, SANTA MARIA
starting point .... PALOS
column .... PILLAR, PILASTER, SHAFT
base .... PLINTH
Buddhist .... LAT
capital of ..... CHAPITER
convex swelling .. ENTASIS
designating a ..... IONIC, DORIC
figure, female .. CARYATID
figure, male .. TELAMON, ATLANTES
ornament .... GRIFFE
shaft .... SCAPE
square .... ANTA, PIER
substitute for .... ATLANTES, ATLAS
support of .... BASE, PEDESTAL, PLINTH
top of .... CAPITAL
columnist .... WINCHELL, LIPPMANN, WESTON, PEARSON, ALSOP
columns, row of .. PERISTYLE, COLONNADE
colza .. COLE(SEED), RAPESEED
coma ... STUPOR, CATALEPSY, TRANCE
having a ..... COMATOSE
comate, in botany .... HAIRY, TUFTED
comatose .... TORPID
comb .... CARUNCLE
horse .... CURRY
like implement .. RIPPER
of fowl ..... CARUNCLE, CREST
the hair .... DRESS
wool ...... TEASE, CARD
combat ...... BATTLE, FIGHT, STOUR, STRIFE, JOUST, TILT, DUEL
challenge to ..... CARTEL
end of mortal .... DEATH
mortal .... AMORT
operation ...... MISSION
place .... LISTS
to decide issue .. DERAIGN
troops .... CAVALRY, INFANTRY
with lances .. JOUST, TILT
combatant .... FIGHTER
combative ...... PUGNACIOUS, QUARRELSOME, MILITANT
comber .... WAVE
combination .. ALLOY, BLEND, AMALGAM, MIXTURE, UNION
combine .... UNITE, JOIN, MERGE(R), COMPOUND
kind of ...... SYNDICATE, COALITION
resources .... POOL
combining form for:
alike .... ISO
among .... INTER
another .... HETERO
angle .... GONIO
asunder .... DICH(O)
bad .... CAC(O), MAL
below .... INFERO
between .... INTER
bile .... CHOL(O), CHOLE
body fluid .... SERO
both .... AMBI
brass .... CHALCO
bright .... HELI(O)
bristles .... CHAET(O)
broad .... EURY, PLAT(Y)
cartilage ...... CHONDRO
cavity .... C(O)ELE
cell .... CYTE
circular .... CYCL(O)
cold .... CRY(O)
color ...... CHROMAT(O)
copper .... CUPRI
corpse .... NECR(O)
curl .... CIRRI
cutter .... TOME
death .... NECR(O)
depth .... BATHO
different ..... HETER(O)
digit .... DACTYL(O)
double .... DIPL(O)
drawing .... GRAPHO
dreadful .... DINO
dung .... COPR(O)
earth .... GEO
end .... TEL(O)
English .... ANGLO
entire .... HOLO
equal .... ISO, EQUI, PARI
external .... ECT(O)
eye defect .... OPIA
far .... TELE
fatty .... LIP(O)

feather .... PTERO
feces .... COPR(O)
feet .... PED(E), PEDI
female .. GYN(O), GYNOUS
fermentation ...... ZYMO
fever .... FEBRI
fine .... LEPT(O)
finger .... DACTYL(O)
firm .... STERE(O)
fish .... PISCI
flat .... PLAT(Y)
flesh .... SARC(O)
flow .... RHEO
foot ...... PED(E), PED(I)
freezing .... CRY(O)
French .... GALLO
fruit .... CARP(O)
fungus .... MYC(O)
gall ..... CHOL(O), CHOLE
gaseous .... AERI
glass .... HYALO
grain .... GRANI
gyrating .... GYRO
hair .... CHAET(O)
hand .... CHIRO, CHEIRO
hatred .... MIS(O)
height .... HYPSO
hidden .... CRYPT(O)
hide .... DERMAT(O)
horn .. CERAT(O), KERATO
horse .... HIPPO
hundred .... CENTI, HECT(O)
identical .... ISO
inner .... END(O)
insect(s) ...... ENTOMO
inside .... INTRA, INTRO
intestine ...... ENTER(O)
iron .... FERRO
latest .... CENE, NEO
liking .... PHIL(E)
lime .... CALCI
lip .... CHIL(O)
little .... MICR(O)
liver .... HEPAT(O)
male/man ...... ANDR(O)
many .... POLY
Mars .... AREO
masculine ...... ANDR(O)
milky .... GALACT(O)
minute .... MICR(O)
moon .... LUNI
moving .... KINETO
much .... POLY
nitrogen .... AZO
one and a half .. SESQUI
one tenth of ...... DECI
other .... HETER(O)
outside .... ECT(O)
people .... ETHN(O)
personal .... IDIO
pointed .... STYL(O)
poor .... CAC(O)
prickly .... ECHIN(O)
race .... ETHN(O)
radiant .... HELI(O)
red .... ERYTHR(O)
rib(s) .... COST(O)
secondary ... DEUTER(O), DEUT(O)
secret .... CRYPT(O)
self .... AUTO
seven .. SEPTEM, HEPT(A)
shaft .... SCAPI
sham .... PSEUD(O)
sharp .... STYL(O)
short .... BRACHY
similar .... ISO
simple .... HAPL(O)
single .... HAPL(O)
skin .... DERMAT(O), DERM(O)
sleep .... HYPN(O)
slender .... LEPT(O)
small .... MICR(O)
solid .... STERE(O)
spiny .... ECHIN(O)
spiral .. GYRO, HELIC(O)
stalk .... SCAPI
stationary .... STAT
stomach ...... GASTR(O)
stone .. LITH, LITE, LYTE
sun .... HELI(O)
swelling .... CELE
tallow .... SEBI
teeth .. ODONT(O), DENT(I)
ten .... DEC(A)
terrible .... DINO
thin .... LEPT(O)
tissue .... HIST(O)
tooth .. DENTI, ODONT(O)
transparent ..... HYAL(O)
tree .. DENDRO, DENDR(I), DENDRON
tumor .... CELE
twin .... DIPL(O)
two .... DIPL(O)
universe ...... COSM(O)
water .... HYDR(O)
wave .... CYMO
wax .... CERO, SEBI
weight .... BARO
whole .... HOLO
wing .... PTERO
within .. END(O), INTRA, INTRO
woman .... GYN(E)O, GYNOUS
wood .... HYL(O)
wool .... LANI
world .... COSM(O)
worship .... LATRY
writing .... GRAPHO
yellow(ish) ...... LUTEO

combustible .... IMFLAMMABLE, EXCITABLE, FIERY

combustion ... BURNING, FIRE

come ...... ARRIVE, APPEAR, OCCUR, RESULT
about ... OCCUR, HAPPEN
across .... GIVE, PAY UP, MEET
afterwards ...... ENSUE
around .. REVIVE, YIELD, VISIT
back .... RETURN, RECUR
before .... PRECEDE
between .... DIVIDE, INTERVENE
by ...... GAIN, ACQUIRE
down .... ALIGHT, LAND
forth .... APPROACH, EMERSE
forward .... VOLUNTEER, ADVANCE
into ... INHERIT, ACQUIRE
into view .. LOOM, PEER, PEEP
on! .... HURRY(UP)
ons .... LURES, BAITS
out .... EMERGE
out even .... DRAW, TIE
to grips with ... TANGLE
to mind .... OCCUR
to pass .. HAPPEN, OCCUR, TRANSPIRE
to rest .... SETTLE
to terms .... AGREE
to view .. APPEAR, LOOM
together .... GATHER
up .... ARISE
up to .... EQUAL
upon .... CHANCE, MEET

comeback .... RETORT, REPARTEE, REJOINDER, RIPOSTE

comedian ..... BUFFO, COMIC, ZANY, JESTER, PIERROT
circus .... CLOWN
deadpan .... KEATON
foil of .... STOOGE, STRAIGHTMAN
forte ...... JOKES, GAGS, CRACKS, TOMFOOLERY, HORSEPLAY
missile of .... PIE
of note .... (BOB) HOPE, (ED)WYNN, FERNANDEL, (JERRY) LEWIS, (JACK) BENNY, (BUSTER) KEATON, (RED) SKELTON, (STAN) LAUREL, (OLIVER) HARDY, (BERT) LAHR

comedienne .. (FANNY) BRICE, (ZAZU) PITTS, (LUCY) BALL

comedo .... BLACKHEAD

comedy .. FARCE, SLAPSTICK, BURLESQUE, HORSEPLAY
character ...... PIERROT, ZANY
symbol .... SOCK

comely .... HANDSOME, DECOROUS, PRETTY, FAIR, GAINLY
woman .... BUXOM

comensal .... INQUILINE

comestible(s) ...... EATABLE, EDIBLE, VICTUAL, FOOD

comet .... BIELA'S, HALLEY'S, HOLMES', SWIFT'S, ALCOCK'S
envelope .... COMA
head's part .... NUCLEUS
nucleus and coma ...... HEAD
part ...... TAIL, TRAIN

comeuppance: sl. .... PUNISHMENT

comfit .... CONFECTION, PRALINE, CANDY, SWEETMEAT

comfort .. CONSOLE, SOOTHE, SOLACE, EASE

comfortable .... SNUG, COSE, COZY
chair .... ROCKER

comic .... COMEDIAN, FUNNY, HUMOROUS, AMUSING, DROLL, LAUGHABLE
afterpiece .... EXODE

element in play .. HOKUM
opera .. BOUFFE, BUFFO, BUFFA
relief .. SKIT, AFTERPIECE
strip .... CARTOONS
strip brat .. HANS, FRITZ
strip character .... MILQUETOAST, LULU, SLUGGO, NANCY, MUTT, JEFF, (LIL) ABNER, (ETTA) KETT, JIGGS
strip vocals .. BALLOON(s)
theatrical sketch ... SKIT
with wooden sword ..... HARLEQUIN
comical ..... FUNNY, DROLL, HUMOROUS, ZANY
very .... KILLING
coming .. ADVENT, APPROACH
early in the day .... RATH(E)
from outside .. ENTHETIC, EXTRANEOUS
of tide .... FLUX
out party .... DEBUT
to an end ... MORIBUND
comity .... COURTESY, POLITENESS
comma .... PAUSE, MARK
shaped organism .... VIBRIO
command .. DICTATE, CHARGE, DIRECT, BID(DING), BEHEST, ORDER, ENJOIN
authoritative .. MANDATE
level of .... ECHELON
market .... CORNER, MONOPOLIZE
station .... POST
to helmsman ... STEADY
to horse .... GEE, WHOA, HAW
to huskies .... MUSH
commander .... LEADER
Egyptian .... SIRDAR
in-chief, U.S. .... PRESIDENT
of 1000 men: Roman .... CHILIARCH
rod/staff of .... WARDER
commanding .... DOMINATING, IMPRESSIVE
commandment ..... PRECEPT, ORDER, LAW
in Judaism .... MITZVAH
Commandments, the Ten .... DECALOG(UE)
commando .... RAIDER
assignment .... MISSION
specialty .... SABOTAGE, RAID, DEMOLITION
comme il faut ...... PROPER, FITTING
commemorate .... CELEBRATE, OBSERVE
commemorative ... MEMORIAL
piece .... MEDAL
commence .... BEGIN, START, OPEN
commencement .... START, BEGINNING
address .... VALEDICTORY
exercise .... GRADUATION

commend ..... EXTOL, LAUD, ENTRUST, PRAISE, CITE
commensurate .... PROPORTIONATE, EVEN
comment ...... ANNOTATION, REMARK, TALK, DESCANT
adverse ...... CRITICISM
at bottom of page ...... FOOTNOTE
derisive .... JEER
favorable .. PRAISE, RAVE
marginal ...... MARGENT
on disapprovingly ...... ANIMADVERT
commentary .... MEMOIR, REMARK, OBSERVATION, CRITIQUE
commentator .... CRITIC, ANNOTATOR
newspaper ...... EDITOR, COLUMNIST
commerce .. TRADE, BUSINESS, TRAFFIC
commercial ...... MERCANTILE
agent .... CONSUL
paper, worthless .... KITE
spy .... KEEK
comminate ...... CURSE, BAN
commingle .... BLEND, (INTER)MIX
comminute ...... PULVERIZE, GRIND, MILL, CRUSH
comminution, product of ..... POWDER, TALC, DUST
commiseration .... PITY, EMPATHY, COMPASSION
commissary .. DEPUTY, STORE, CANTEEN
colloquial .... PX
commission .... ORDER, EMPOWER, AUTHORITY, DOING, AUTHORIZE
grafter's ..... KICKBACK
slang .... RAKE-OFF
commissure .... JOINT, SEAM
commit ..... CONSIGN, BIND, ENGAGE, ENTRUST
in mind ...... MEMORIZE
perjury .... FORSWEAR
to paper .... RECORD
commitment .... PLEDGE, PROMISE, UNDERTAKING
commix .... BLEND
commode ... CHEST, BUREAU, CHIFFONIER, WASHSTAND, TOILET
commodious .... ROOMY, SPACIOUS
commodity .. WARE, ARTICLE, STAPLE
control of ... OLIGOPOLY
common ..... PUBLIC, USUAL, GENERAL, LOW, AVERAGE, ORDINARY, MUTUAL
arithmetic ..... LOGISTIC
carrier ..... BUS, TRAIN, COACH
footing .... PAR
people .... MASSES, POPULACE, DEMOS, PLEBS, PLEBE, FOLKS, HOI POLLOI
people, of the .... GRASS ROOTS

run .... RUCK
saying ..... SAW, ADAGE, PROVERB
sense .. SAVVY, GUMPTION
talk .. RUMOR, HEARSAY, GOSSIP
to both sexes ... EPICENE
commoner .... LOWBORN, ROTURIER
commonly accepted .... VULGATE
supposed ..... PUTATIVE
commonplace ..... ORDINARY, USUAL, TRITE, PROSAIC, BANAL, HUMDRUM, BOURGEOIS
expression .... BROMIDE, CLICHE, PLATITUDE, TRUISM
commonsense .... SAVVY, GUMPTION
commotion .. TURMOIL, STIR, TO-DO, HUBBUB, ADO, BROUHAHA, FUSS, POTHER, UPROAR, SHINDY, FLURRY, MUSS
commove .... EXCITE
communal .... PUBLIC
marriage .... HETAERISM
commune .... CONVERSE, MIR, KIBBUTZ, ANS, ATH, EDE, EPE
communicable .. CONTAGIOUS
communicate .... IMPART, TRANSMIT
communication .... INFORMATION, MESSAGE
form of .... SIGNAL, LETTER, TALK, ORAL, CODE
means of .... TELEPHONE, TELEGRAPH, RADIO, WORD, SIGN, CABLE
communications satellite ..... TELSTAR
signal set .... CODE
communicative ... TALKATIVE
communion .... SHARING
cloth .... CORPORAL
cup .... AMA
Holy ...... EUCHARIST, SACRAMENT
plate .... PATEN
table .... CREDENCE
communique .... STATEMENT, BULLETIN
communism, exponent of ..... MARX, ENGELS
Communist curtain .... IRON, BAMBOO
Party member .... COMRADE
policy body .. POLITBURO
spy .. BURGESS, MACLEAN, PHILBY
youth league .. COMSOMOL
community .. PUBLIC, SOCIETY, SIMILARITY, TOWN
of creatures .... COLONY
of Greek monks/hermits .... SKETE
of peasants: Russ. .. MIR
commutator ...... RHEOTROPE
commute .. EXCHANGE, TRAVEL

Comoro Islands capital ...... MORONI
island .... MAYOTTE
comose .... HAIRY
compact .... BRIEF, TERSE, DENSE, SOLID, AGREEMENT, THICK, SERRIED
between nations .... TREATY
mass .... WAD
companion .... COMRADE, ASSOCIATE, MATE, FERE
at meals .... COMMENSAL
close .. COMRADE, BUDDY
colloquial .... SIDEKICK
constant .... ALTER EGO, SHADOW
of back .... FORTH
of bill .... COO
of black .. WHITE, BLUE
of blue .... RED, WHITE
of bolts .... NUTS
of bread .... BUTTER
of cease .... DESIST
of fits .... STARTS
of hook .. CROOK, LINE, SINKER
of huff .... PUFF
of kit .... CABOODLE
of mortise ...... TENON
of oro .... PLATA
of snick .... SNEE
of stars .... STRIPES
of Tom .... DICK, HARRY
of turn .... TOSS
of wrack .... RUIN
companionway .. STAIR, WALK
companionship ...... SOCIETY
company .... SOCIETY, BAND, FIRM, TROOP
amusing .... CAST
colloquial .... GUEST(S), VISITOR(S)
commander ... CAPTAIN
French .... CIE
of hunters ...... SAFARI
of players ..... TROUPE, TEAM
of soldiers ..... TROOPS
of ten soldiers .... DECURION
of travelers ... CARAVAN, CARAVANSARY
part .... SEPARATE
comparable .... SIMILAR
compare .... COLLATE, CONTRAST, LIKEN
beyond ...... PEERLESS, NONPAREIL
critically ...... COLLATE
compartment .. STALL, BOOTH, LOCKER
grain/hay .... BAY
in aircraft ..... CAPSULE
small/sleeping .. CUBICLE
compass .. UNDERSTAND, GAIN, SCOPE, SURROUND, REACH
beam .... TRAMMEL
cardinal point .... EAST, NORTH, WEST, SOUTH
case .... BINNACLE
dial .... CARD
face of .... DIAL
plant .... ROSINWEED
point .... QUARTER, R(H)UMB
sight .... VANE
zero of .... NORTH
compassion .... PITY, MERCY, GRACE, EMPATHY
compatible ...... CONGRUOUS
compeer .... EQUAL, COMRADE
compel .. FORCE, CONSTRAIN, OBLIGE, DRIVE, INTIMIDATE, COERCE
compelling .... COGENT
influence .... PRESSURE, DURESS
compend .... BREVIARY
compendium ...... SUMMARY, DIGEST, SYLLABUS, PRECIS
compensation ...... PAY, FEE
for loss ..... INDEMNITY, DAMAGES
for service ..... SALARY, WAGE, STIPEND
compete ...... CONTEND, VIE
competence .. SKILL, ABILITY, CAPACITY
competent ... CAPABLE, ABLE, FIT
mentally .... SANE
competition .... RIVALRY, STRIFE, MATCH, CONTEST, OPPOSITION
competitor ..... (COR)RIVAL, CONTENDER, ENTRANT, ENTRY
Compiegne river .... OISE
compilation .... COLLECTION, SELECTION
of anecdotes .. MEMOIRS
of stories, poems .... ANTHOLOGY
compiler ...... ANTHOLOGIST, ENCYCLOPEDIST, CERF, RILEY, GLOSSARIST
Arthurian tales .. MALORY
English words ... ROGET
population data .... CENSUS TAKER
quotations .... BARTLETT
complain ..... GRIPE, ACCUSE, CARP, GROUSE, BEEF, GRUMBLE, BELLYACHE, CRAB, KICK, YAMMER
complainer, habitual .. GROUSE
complainant .... ACCUSER, PLAINTIFF, LITIGANT
complaining ...... QUERULOUS
cry .... WHINE
complaint .... GRIEVANCE, CLAMOR, SQUAWK, GROUSE, AILMENT, ILLNESS, CHARGE, PROTEST, KICK, WHINE
muttered ..... MURMUR
part of ...... GRAVAMEN
complaisant ...... OBLIGING, POLITE
complete ...... FULL, ENTIRE, WHOLE, TOTAL, INTACT, OUTRIGHT, RANK, UTTER
attendance .... PLENARY
disorder .... CHAOS
entity .... INTEGER
consumption .... EXHAUSTION
not .... PARTIAL
completed ..... DONE, ENDED, FINISHED, OVER
completely .... UTTERLY
occupied .... RAPT, ENGROSSED, BUSY
united .... SOLIDARY
complex .... INTRICATE, INVOLVED, MIXED UP, NETWORK
get .... THICKEN
kind of .... INFERIORITY, OEDIPUS
complexion .... TEMPERAMENT, COLOR, ASPECT
complexity .... INTRICACY
compliant .... SUBMISSIVE, OBEDIENT, WEAK, TRACTABLE
complicated ...... INVOLVED, COMPLEX, KNOTTY
complication ... MESS, NODUS, SNAG
compliment .. PRAISE, TOAST, CONGRATULATE, LAUD
exaggerated ... FLATTERY
kind of .... LEFT-HANDED
complot .... CONSPIRE, CONSPIRACY
comply .... OBEY, ACCEDE
compo .... PLASTER, MORTAR
component .. PART, ELEMENT, INGREDIENT, CONSTITUENT, UNIT
of atom .... PROTON
comport .... BEHAVE, ACT
comportment ...... CONDUCT, BEHAVIOR
compos mentis .... SANE
non .... MAD, CRAZY, INSANE
compose .... CONSTITUTE, FRAME, CREATE, ADJUST, WRITE
differences ... RECONCILE
in printing .... TYPE
composed .... COOL, WROTE, CALM
composer ...... SONGWRITER, DEBUSSY, PUCCINI, HAYDN, CHOPIN, BACH, TUNESMITH, HARMONIST, WEBER, BIZET, RAVEL, WAGNER
great .... MAESTRO
in printing shop .... TYPESETTER, LINOTYPIST
of marches ...... SOUSA
of poems .... BARD, RHYMER, VERSIFIER
opera .. BIZET, WAGNER, VERDI, LEHAR, DONIZETTI
of *Thais* ...... MASSENET
composers' group ..... ASCAP
composite .... COMPOUND, INTEGRAL
composition .. ESSAY, THEME, OPUS
artistic .... PIECE
for nine instruments .... NONET
for organ ..... TOCCATA
for piano ..... BALLADE, STUDE, TOCCATA
for practice ..... ETUDE

for seven ... SEPTET(TE)
for three .... TRIO
for two .... DUET
hodgepodge musical .... MEDLEY, CENTO
musical .. OPUS, SONATA, CONCERTO, ORATORIO, ETUDE, MOTET, RONDO, SUITE, FANTASIA, SERENADE, NOCTURNE
operatic .... SCENA
sacred .... MOTET
compositor ...... LINOTYPIST, TYPESETTER
guide of .... JIGGER
compost heap part .... HUMUS
composure .... CALMNESS, EQUANIMITY, POISE, AIR, SANG-FROID
compound .... COMBINE, MIX, CONCOCT
carbon .... CARBIDE
of silica .... GLASS
raceme .... PANICLE
words' separation of parts TMESIS
comprador .... BUYER
comprehend .... UNDERSTAND, INCLUDE, GRASP, SEE
comprehensible .... INTELLIGIBLE, EXOTERIC
comprehension .... GRASP
thru intellect .... NOESIS
compress ... PAD, CONTRACT, DOSSIL, WRING, SQUEEZE
comprise .. INCLUDE, CONTAIN
compromise ... TRIM, ADJUST, ENDANGER
compulsion .. FORCE, DURESS, CONSTRAINT, COACTION
compulsive craze, obsession, etc. .. MANIA
petty thievery .... KLEPTOMANIA
compulsory .... COERCIVE, OBLIGATORY, MANDATORY
military service .. DRAFT, CONSCRIPTION, LEVY
compunction ...... PENITENCE, SCRUPLE, QUALM, REMORSE
compurgation .... CLEARANCE
computation ... CALCULATION
compute ... RECKON, FIGURE, CALCULATE
computer, type of ... ANALOG, DIGITAL, IBM
computerize ...... AUTOMATE
computing device .... COMPTOMETER, ABACUS, SLIDE RULE
comrade .... FRIEND, PAL, COMPANION, PARTNER, BUDDY, TOVARISCH, FRATER, KAMERAD
comte .... COUNT
con .... STUDY, READ, ANTI, AGAINST, PERUSE
amore .... TENDERLY, WITH LOVE
man .. SWINDLER, SHILL, GRIFTER, STEEPER
over .... SCAN
slang ..... CONFIDENCE, SWINDLE
vessel .... STEER
concatenate .... LINK(ED)
concave molding ... CAVETTO, SCOTIA
conceal ...... HIDE, SECRETE, CLOAK
goods .. CACHE, HOARD, ELOI(G)N
in law .... ELOIN
concealed ...... CLANDESTINE, HIDDEN, COVERT, PERDUE
sharpshooter .... SNIPER
concealment, attack from .... AMBUSH, AMBUSCADE, SNIPE
concede ...... YIELD, GRANT, ADMIT
conceit ...... VANITY, PRIDE, EGO(ISM), TYMPANY
colloquial ...... BIGHEAD
conceited .. VAIN(GLORIOUS), PROUD, EGO(T)ISTIC, STUCK-UP
person .... PEACOCK, EGO(T)IST
conceive ..... THINK, IDEATE, IMAGINE
concenter .. CONVERGE, FOCUS
concentrate .. FOCUS, COLLECT
concentration camp, German .. STALAG, DACHAU
concept .... IDEA, NOTION
conception ...... IDEA, HENT, IDEATION
product of .... EMBRYO, BRAINCHILD
concern ...... AFFAIR, CARE, WORRY, SOLICITUDE, LOOKOUT
concerned .. UNEASY, ANXIOUS
concerning .... ABOUT, ANENT, INRE
concert .... CONCORD
hall .... AUDITORIUM, ODEUM
in .... TOGETHER
master's instrument ..... VIOLIN
organizer .... IMPRESARIO
outdoor platform .... BANDSHELL
concertina kin ... ACCORDION
concession ... GRANT, RIGHT, PRIVILEGE, FRANCHISE
kind of .... SOP
conch .... SHELL
concha .... APSE
Conchobar's intended .... DEIRDRE
concierge ..... DOORKEEPER, JANITOR, CARETAKER
conciliate .. PLACATE, PACIFY, APPEASE, SOOTHE, MOLLIFY
conciliatory theology .... IRENICS
concise .. BRIEF, TERSE, PITHY, SUCCINCT, LACONIC
conclave .... MEETING
conclude .... CLOSE, END, DEDUCE, INFER, FINISH, TERMINATE
a speech ...... PERORATE
concluding passage in music .. CODA, STRETTO, STRETTA, FINALE
conclusion .... OUTCOME, END, RESULT, DECISION, JUDGMENT, FINIS(H), FINDING
in .... LASTLY
judge's .... FINDING
conclusive ... DECISIVE, FINAL
blow: sl. .. SOCKDOLOGER, HAYMAKER
point .... CLINCHER
concoct .. DEVISE, PLAN, BREW, HATCH, MIX, COOK-UP, COMPOUND
concoction, liquid ... COFFEE, TEA, COCKTAIL
concomitant .... ATTENDANT
concord .. ONENESS, HARMONY, GRAPE, UNISON, TREATY
concordant ..... HARMONIOUS
concordat .... COMPACT, COVENANT, AGREEMENT, ENTENTE
concourse .. CROWD, THRONG
concrete ..... REAL, ACTUAL, SPECIFIC, BETON
being .... ENS
concubinage ..... HETAERISM, HETAIRISM
concubine in harem .. ODALISK, ODALISQUE
concupiscence .... LUST
concur ...... ACCEDE, AGREE, ASSENT, CONSENT, COINCIDE
concurrence .... ACCORD, AGREEMENT
concussion .. SHOCK, SHAKING
condemn ... CENSURE, DOOM, CONVICT, DENOUNCE, DECRY
condemnation .... DECRIAL
condemned heretic's garment .... SANBENITO
condense .... COMPRESS, CONTRACT, ABRIDGE, INSPISSATE
condensed form .... CAPSULE
moisture .... DEW
condenser .... CAPACITOR
condescend .... DEIGN, STOOP
condescending .. PATRONIZING, HOITY-TOITY
condign .. DESERVED, FITTING, SUITABLE
condiment .. SPICE, VINEGAR, SEASONING, RELISH, SAUCE, MACE, MUSTARD, PEPPER, PAPRIKA, PAPRICA
bottle/container .... CASTER, CRUST
condition ..... IF, PROVISION, STATE, STATUS, ACCUSTOM, CASE, FIG, FETTLE
contract ... STIPULATION, TERM, PROVISO
of body .... HEALTH
of decline ... DECADENCE
of great vitality .... STHENIA
of oblivion ...... LIMBO
of payment ..... TERMS
of servitude .. BONDAGE, SLAVERY

of stupor .... COMA, NARCOSIS
conditional surrender .... CAPITULATION
conditions of possession ..... TENURE
condole .... COMMISERATE
condone .... FORGIVE, OVERLOOK, PARDON
condor .... VULTURE
conduce .... TEND, LEAD, CONTRIBUTE
conduct .... WAGE, BEHAVIOR, ESCORT, MANAGE
in polite society .... ETIQUETTE
under guard .... CONVOY, ESCORT
conductor .... GUIDE, LEADER, MAESTRO
orchestra .... TOSCANINI, BEECHAM, BERNSTEIN, BARBIROLLI, MEHTA, BOULEZ, ORMANDY
platform of .... PODIUM
stick .... BATON
tourists' ..... CICERONE, GUIDE, DRAGOMAN
woman .... QUACH
conduit .. MAIN, PIPE, SEWER, DRAIN
cone .... STROBILE
bearing tree .. PINE, FIR, SPRUCE, CYPRESS, PINASTER, LARCH, CEDAR, YEW, CONIFER, JUNIPER, ZAMIA
seed-bearing .. STROBIL(E)
shaped .... CONOID, PINEAL, CONIC(AL), TURBINATE
shaped paper container .. CORNUCOPIA
shaped pile ...... COCK
shaped yarn roll .... COP
spiral .... HELIX
conepate .... SKUNK
coney ...... RODENT, RABBIT, DAMAN, HYRAX
confab .... TALK, CHAT, POWWOW
confection .... PRALINE, BONBON, CONFITURE, SWEETMEAT, COMFIT
almond .... NOUGAT, MARZIPAN, MARCHPANE
cold .... ICE CREAM
flavor .... VANILLA
sugar .... CANDY
Turkish .... HALVAH
confederacy ...... ALLIANCE
confederate .... ACCOMPLICE, ALLY
general .... LEE, BRAGG, HAMPTON, LONGSTREET
president .... DAVIS
soldier, Civil War .. REB
confederation .... BUND
confer ... BESTOW, CONVERSE, AWARD, ENDOW
privately .... COLLOGUE
conference .... MEETING, CONFAB, PALAVER, POWWOW, HUDDLE, CAUCUS, PARLEY, JUNTA
Indian .... POWWOW
private .... HUDDLE, CAUCUS, TETE-A-TETE
site of 1945 ...... YALTA
site of 1943 ...... CAIRO, TEHERAN
conferred, thing ..... HONOR, FAVOR, TITLE, RIGHT, DEGREE
conferring respect .... HONORIFIC
confess .. ADMIT, OWN, AVOW
slang ..... SING, SQUEAL, PEACH
confession ...... ADMISSION, REVELATION, AVOWAL
of faith .. CREED, CREDO
"Confessions" author .... ROUSSEAU
confetti .. CANDIES, PAPER BITS
confidant .... FRIEND
confide ...... ENTRUST, TELL
confidence .... TRUST, SECRET, ASSURANCE
game .... SWINDLE, THIMBLERIG, SHELL GAME, BUNCO, BUNKO
game item .. SEED, CUP, NUTSHELL
man .... CON, SWINDLER, STEEPER, SHILL, GRIFTER
show of .... BRAVADO
confident .... ASSURED, SURE, CERTAIN, BOLD, SECURE
confidential .... ESOTERIC, SECRET, PRIVATE
advisers' group .... CAMARILLA, CABAL
disclosure/warning ..... TIP-OFF
confiding .... TRUSTFUL
confine ..... RESTRICT, LIMIT, IMMURE, BOX, PEN, CAGE, FETTER, HEM
to a place ..... LOCALIZE
confined .... PENT(UP)
in circulation .... CLOSE
confinement, place of .... PRISON, HOSPITAL, ASYLUM
cause of .... ILLNESS, CONVICTION
confirm .... VERIFY, VALIDATE, RATIFY, ATTEST, SUBSTANTIATE
confirmation .. RITE, EVIDENCE, VERIFICATION, SACRAMENT
confirmed ...... INVETERATE, ARRANT, CHRONIC, HABITUAL
confiscate .... SEIZE, ESCHEAT APPROPRIATE,
confiture .. PRESERVE, CANDY, SWEETMEAT,
conflict .... CLASH, DISCORD, STRUGGLE, CONTEST, FIGHT, STOUR, STRIFE, JAR
armed .... WAR
of characters in drama .. AGON
confluence .... CROWD
conform ..... ADAPT, AGREE
conforming to morals .... ETHICAL
conformist .... ASSENTER
kind of .... YESMAN
confound .. STUMP, CONFUSE, BEWILDER, PUZZLE
confraternity .. BROTHERHOOD
confrere .... COLLEAGUE, ASSOCIATE
confront .. FACE, STAND, MEET
confuse .... DISCONCERT, PUZZLE, FLUMMOX, ABASH, PERPLEX, FLABBERGAST, BEWILDER, CONFOUND
confused .. ADDLED, HAYWIRE, MUZZY
confusion .... CHAOS, MESS, DISORDER, DISARRAY, JUMBLE, MOIL, MUDDLE, RUCKUS, WELTER, TANGLE, MIX-UP
of tongues .... BABEL
sudden .... FLURRY
conge .. DISMISSAL, FAREWELL
congeal .... GEL, FREEZE, SET, SOLIDIFY, JELL, CURDLE
congealed water (vapor) .. ICE, SNOW
congealer, wound ... COMFREY
congenial .. BOON, FRIENDLY, AGREEABLE
congenital .. INBORN, INNATE, CONNATE
mark .... MOLE
conger .... EEL
trap .... EELPOT
congeries .... HEAP, PILE, COLLECTION
congest .... OVERCROWD
Congo .. EEL, TEA, DYE, RIVER
capital ... BRAZZAVILLE, KINSHASA
city ...... POINTE-NOIRE, KISANGANI
dwarf .... AKKA, ACHUAS
ethnic group ... BALALI, BAVILI, BATEKE, HAMITE, BANTU
language .... BANTU, SWAHILI, LINGALA
peanut .... NGUBA
premier .... ADOULA, LUMUMBA, TSHOMBE
president .... KASAVUBU, YOULOU, MOBUTU
province .. KWILU, KIVA, KATANGA
red .... SALT
river tributary .. UBANGI
tribesman .... SIMBA
congou .... TEA
congratulate .... FELICITATE, HAIL, SALUTE, COMMEND
congratulatory ... GRATULANT
congregate .... COLLECT, GATHER, ASSEMBLE
congregation ...... ASSEMBLY, ASSEMBLAGE, FLOCK, FOLD, PARISH
congress .. MEETING, ASSEMBLY, LEGISLATURE
attendant .... PAGE
concern of ...... BILLS, RESOLUTIONS, BUDGET
time off .... RECESS

congressman not reelected .... LAMEDUCK
congruence ...... AGREEMENT
congruity .. FITNESS, HARMONY
congruous .... FIT(TING), SUITABLE
conic section .... CURVE, ELLIPSE, PARABOLA
conical roll of yarn ..... COP
conifer .... PINE, CEDAR, SPRUCE, YEW, FIR, LARCH
coniferous forest ...... TAIGA
conium .... HEMLOCK
conjecture .... SURMISE, GUESS(WORK), THEORY
conjoin ..... UNITE, CONNECT
conjoint .... UNITED
conjugal ...... MATRIMONIAL, CONNUBIAL, MARITAL
conjugate ..... UNITE, COUPLE
conjugation .... SYNGAMY
conjunction ..... UNION, AND, COINCIDENCE, OR, BUT, SINCE
in biology ...... ZYGOSIS
conjunctivitis ..... TRACHOMA
conjuration .. MAGIC, SORCERY
conjure .... SUMMON, INVOKE, CALL UPON
conjuror ... MAGICIAN, MAGE, SORCERER, WARLOCK, WIZARD
stick of .... WAND, ROD
words of .. HOCUS-POCUS
conk .... KNOCK
British slang ...... NOSE, HEAD, BLOW
out .... FAIL
connate .... INBORN, INNATE, CONGENITAL
connect ...... JOIN, COUPLE, ASSOCIATE, LINK
secretly .... TAP
Connecticut, capital of ...... HARTFORD
city .... DANBURY, STAMFORD, MERIDEN, HARTFORD
nickname ...... NUTMEG
official, borough .... WARDEN
state flower .... (MOUNTAIN) LAUREL
town .... LYME, HAMDEN, GREENWICH
connecting body of water .... STRAIT
part .... LINK
pipe .... TEE
strip of land ... ISTHMUS
connection .... UNION, RELATION, CONTACT, NEXUS, KINSHIP
connective .... SYNDETIC
tissue ... TENDON, FASCIA
word .... AND, (N)OR, (N)EITHER
Connelly, playwright .... MARC(US)
Connie Mack's ballpark ..... SHIBE
conning tower adjunct .... PERISCOPE
conniption .... TANTRUM
connive .... CONSPIRE, COOPERATE
connoisseur ...... (A)ESTHETE, CO(G)NOSCENTE, JUDGE
art .... VIRTUOSO
fine foods/drinks .... GO(U)RMAND, GOURMET, EPICURE
connubial .... CONJUGAL, MARITAL
conquer .... OVERCOME, DEFEAT, SUBDUE, VANQUISH, SUBJUGATE
conquerable .... VINCIBLE
conqueror .... VICTOR
conquistador .... CORTEZ, PIZARRO, CONQUEROR
Conrad (Joseph) character ... SEAMAN, MARINER, LENA, AXEL
novel .... VICTORY
consanguinity ...... KINSHIP, AFFINITY
conscience, twinge of .... SCRUPLE, QUALM, REMORSE
conscientious objector .... CONCHY
conscious ... (A)WARE, AWAKE, COGNIZANT, SENTIENT
consciousness, lose .... PASS OUT, FAINT, SWOON
conscript .... ENROLL, DRAFT(EE), FORCE, RECRUIT, MUSTER, LEVY
conscripted person ... DRAFTEE
consecrate .. DEVOTE, ANOINT, DEDICATE, HALLOW, BLESS, SANCTIFY
consecrated bread .... SACRAMENT
Host's receptacle .... MONSTRANCE
oil .... CHRISM
consecration .... BLESSING
of the bread ... SACRING
consecutive ...... SUCCESSIVE
consensus .... AGREEMENT, OPINION, SYMPOSIUM
consent ..... AGREE, CONCUR, ACCEDE, AGREEMENT
consenting .... WILLING
consequence .... RESULT, EFFECT, OUTCOME, IMPORTANCE, SEQUEL
person of ..... BIGSHOT, BIGWIG, NABOB, TYCOON, VIP
consequently .. THUS, HENCE, THEREFORE, ERGO
conservative ..... MODERATE, PRUDENT, RIGHT(IST), REACTIONARY, TORY, STANDPAT
person .... FOG(E)Y
conservatory .. MUSIC SCHOOL, GREENHOUSE
conserve .... SAVE(UP)
fruit .... JAM
consider ..... HEED, PONDER, STUDY, WEIGH, ENTERTAIN
kindly .... FAVOR
considerable .. MUCH, LARGE, GREAT DEAL
colloquial ...... PRETTY, TIDY, GOODLY
consideration .... ESTEEM, REFLECTION, FEE
consign .. ENTRUST, RELEGATE, DELIVER
to hell .. DAMN, CONDEMN
consistency .... FIRMNESS, HARMONY, AGREEMENT
consistent .... UNIFORM, COHERENT
consisting of 100 degrees ..... CENTIGRADE
consolation .... SOLACE, COMFORT, SOP
console .... COMFORT, CHEER, BRACKET, ANCON
like bracket .... CORBEL
the bereaved ... CONDOLE
consolidate ... UNITE, MERGE, COMBINE, STRENGTHEN, STABILIZE
consomme ..... SOUP, BROTH
consonant, aspirated ... SURD
hard .... FORTIS
unaspirated ...... LENE
voiceless .... ATONIC
consonantal sound ... SPIRANT
consort ...... SPOUSE, MATE, HUSBAND, WIFE
Queen Juliana's .... BERNHARD
Queen Victoria's .... ALBERT
Siva's .... DEVI
conspicuous .... OBVIOUS, NOTICEABLE, SALIENT, OVERT
success ..... ECLAT, HIT
conspiracy .. PLOT, INTRIGUE, CONNIVANCE, CABAL
to defraud ...... COVIN
conspire .... (COM)PLOT, COLLUDE, CONNIVE, SCHEME
constable .. WARDEN, BAILIFF, POLICE(MAN), BULL, TIPSTAFF
constabulary .. (STATE)POLICE
constancy ...... CONSISTENCY, STEADINESS
constant .... CONTINUAL, FAITHFUL, CHRONIC, LOYAL, STEADY, STABLE
visitor ..... FREQUENTER
Constantinople ... ISTANBUL, ISTAMBOUL
foreign quarter ... PERA, BEYOGLU
inn ...... IMARET, SERAI, CARAVANSARY
constellate .... CLUSTER
constellation ...... CLUSTER, GATHERING, NORMA
altar .... ARA
arrow .... SAGITTA
balance .... LIBRA
bear .... URSA
bird of paradise ... APUS
box .... PYXIS
brightest star ...... COR
bull .... TAURUS
centaur .... SAGITTARIUS
charioteer ...... AURIGA
crab .... CANCER
crane .... GRUS

cross .... CRUX
dog .... CANIS
dragon .... DRACO
eagle .... AQUILA
equatorial .... CETUS, ORION
fish .... PISCES
fly .... MUSCA
foot .... RIGEL
goat .... CAPRICORN
hare .... LEPUS
harp .... LYRA
hunter .... ORION
in the Zodiac .... ARIES, TAURUS, GEMINI, CANCER, LEO, VIRGO, LIBRA, SCORPIO, SAGITTARIUS, CAPRICORN(US), AQUARIUS, PISCES
lion .... LEO
Northern ...... SAGITTA, CYGNUS, AURIGA, BOOTES, PERSEUS, DRACO, DELPHINUS, CASSIOPEIA, LEO MINOR, LYRA, POLARIS, CEPHEUS, PEGASUS, ARIES, SERPENS, AQUILA, HERCULES, ANDROMEDA, LACERTA, HYDRA, VULPECULA, URSA, SCUTUM
painter .... PICTOR
peacock .... PAVO
ram .... ARIES
raven .... CORVUS
scales .... LIBRA
scorpion ...... SCORPIO, SCORPIUS
serpent .... HYDRA
snake .... SERPENS
Southern .. ARA, ORION, CANIS, LUPUS, PICTOR, LEPUS, CETUS, CIRCINUS, DORADO, CRUX, CRATER, FORNAX, CENTAURUS, INDUS, VELA, PAVO, TUCANA, ERIDANUS, GRUS, HYDRUS, MENSA, MONOCEROS, NORMA, PHOENIX, APUS, MUSCA, ANTLIA, CAELUM, CARINA, PUPPIS, OCTANS, PYXIS, SEXTANS, VOLANS, SCULPTOR, CORVUS, COLUMBA
swan .... CYGNUS
twins .... GEMINI
veil .... VELA
water carrier .. AQUARIUS
whale .... CETUS
wolf .... LUPUS
woman .... VIRGO

consternation .... DISMAY, ALARM, TERROR, AMAZEMENT
constipated .... COSTIVE
constituent .... ELECTOR, COMPONENT, ELEMENT, INTEGRANT
constitution ...... STRUCTURE, COMPOSITION, MAKE-UP, BASIC LAW, CHARTER
addition to .. AMENDMENT
composition of .... ARTICLES, BY-LAWS, PREAMBLE
constitutional .... BASIC, ESSENTIAL, ORGANIC
colloquial ...... WALK, EXERCISE
constrain .... FORCE, COMPEL, OBLIGE, IMPEL
constraint ..... COMPULSION, COERCION, REPRESSION
constrict .... CONTRACT, SQUEEZE, COMPRESS
constriction of duct, etc. ..... STENOSIS
constrictor .. BOA, ANACONDA, PYTHON, SPHINCTER, CRUSHER
construct ..... ERECT, BUILD, FORM, DEVISE, MAKE
construction ...... BUILDING, STRUCTURE, INTERPRETATION
battalion member ...... SEABEE
constructive .... POSITIVE, HELPFUL
arts .... TECTONICS
construe .. EXPLAIN, ANALYZE, PARSE, READ, INFER, INTERPRET
consuetude .. HABIT, CUSTOM, USAGE
consul's authority .... EXEQUATUR
consult ... CONFER, REFER TO
consultant, common .... DOCTOR, LAWYER, ENGINEER, EXPERT, TECHNICIAN
consume ..... EAT, DESTROY, USE UP, WASTE
consumer .... USER, EATER
goods .. FOOD, CLOTHING
opposed to .. PRODUCER
consummate .. END, COMPLETE, PERFECT, FINISH
is what some are .... ARTISTS, LIARS
skill .... FINESSE
consummation .... OUTCOME, FULFILLMENT
consumption .... WASTE, USE, DESTRUCTION
lung .... TABES, PHTHISIS, TUBERCULOSIS
consumptive .... HECTIC, LUNGER
contact .... TOUCH, MEET, CONNECTION, TACTION
in physical .. CONTIGUOUS
contagion .. POISON, MEASLES, INFECTION, (SMALL)POX, VECTION
contagious .... CATCHING, INFECTIOUS, COMMUNICABLE
contain ..... HOLD, ENCLOSE, EMBODY, CHECK
container .... TIN, JAR, PAIL, BOX, CRATE, CAN, BAG, POUCH, KEG, BASKET
cardboard ...... CARTON
dose of medicine .... CAPSULE
animal food .... TROUGH
burning oil .... CRESSET
documents ..... HANAFER
for relics .... RELIQUARY, CUSTODIAL
for the sacred host ..... TABERNACLE
glass .... CARBOY
half-gallon ..... POTTLE
material for making .... OSIER, JUTE, FLAX, TIN, ALUMINUM, PLASTIC, BURLAP, STAVE
metal .... COPPER
of assorted things ...... HANDBAG, ATTIC, CATCHALL
oil .... AMPULLA
pasteboard .... CARTON
perforated .... DREDGER
sealed .... CAN, TIN, ENVELOPE
water .. TROUGH, TANK, CISTERN, RESERVOIR
wine .... AMPULLA
containing defects ... FAULTY
perforations .... FENESTRATE
contaminate ...... POLLUTE, TAINT, DEFILE, SULLY, CORRUPT, SPOIL
contaminator, air ...... SMOG, SMAZE
conte .... TALE, SHORT STORY
contemn ...... DESPISE, SCORN
contemplate .. GAZE AT, MUSE, CONSIDER, MEDITATE
contemporaneous ... COEVAL, SIMULTANEOUS, CURRENT
contemporary ...... COEVAL, COETANEOUS
contempt ..... DISDAIN, SCORN
show of ... SNIFF, SNEER, SNORT, FLEER
contemptible .... MEAN, BASE, VILE, LOW, ABJECT, PALTRY, SCURVY, LOW(DOWN)
fellow .... HEEL, RASCAL, BLOKE, SCOUNDREL, CULLION, SKATE, CAD
contend ...... FIGHT, ARGUE, COPE, COMPETE, VIE
contender ...... COMPETITOR, CONTESTANT, RIVAL
contending parties .... SIDES, OPPONENTS, PROTAGONISTS
contendre, ____ (not contested) NOLO
content .. SATISFIED, CAPACITY
contention ...... ARGUMENT, DISPUTE, STRIFE
in words only .... LOGOMACHY
contest .. TOURNAMENT, AGON, DISPUTE, FIGHT, TOURNEY
armed .... WAR
boxing .... BOUT
endurance .. MARATHON
for two, armed .... DUEL
in court .... LITIGATION, LITIGATE
in law .... LITIGATE
judges .... PANEL, JURY

long distance .... MARATHON
of knights ... TOURNEY, TILT, JOUST, DUEL
participant ..... ENTRY, ENTRANT
second placer .... RUNNER UP
winner ...... CHAMPION
with lances .. JOUST, TILT
contestant .. ENTRY, ENTRANT, COMPETITOR, CONTENDER
mercenary ...... POTHUNTER
contestants as a whole .. FIELD
contiguous .. NEXT, ADJACENT, TOUCHING
continence ...... MODERATION
continent .... TEMPERATE, CHASTE, MAINLAND, AFRICA, ASIA, AUSTRALIA, EUROPE, NORTH AMERICA, SOUTH AMERICA
hypothetical .. CASCADIA, LEMURIA
icy .... ANTARCTICA
legendary .... ATLANTIS
Continental Congress president HANCOCK
contingency ..... POSSIBILITY, CHANCE, EVENT, EMERGENCY
contingent ...... DEPENDENT, FORTUITOUS, PROVISORY, GROUP, SUBJECT
continual .... CONSTANT, INCESSANT
change/movement ...... FLUX(ION)
continually ..... REPEATEDLY, CONSTANTLY, NEVER-ENDING
continuance in time .... DURATION
continuation .... SEQUEL, RESUMPTION
continue .. PERSIST, KEEP-UP, GO ON, STAY, LAST
obsolete .... DURE
tediously .... DRAG
continued story/movie .... SERIAL
continuous ...... UNBROKEN, NONSTOP
series .... STREAM
contort ...... TWIST, DEFORM, WARP
contortionist ...... HOUDINI
contour .... (OUT)LINE
of head .... PROFILE
of region .. TOPOGRAPHY
contra .... OPPOSITE
contraband ...... HOT GOODS
of a sort ..... BOOTLEG
contrabandist .... SMUGGLER, (RUM)RUNNER
contrabass .... VIOL(ONE)
contract .. INCUR, (COM)PACT, NARROW, AGREEMENT, SHRINK, FLEX
betrothal .... HANDFAST
bridge bid .... SLAM
brow(s) .... KNIT, FROWN
illegal labor .... YELLOW DOG
of agency .... MANDATE
rental .... LEASE
work .... INDENTURE
contraction of muscles .... SPASM, CRAMPS
contradict ..... DENY, BELIE, REBUT, REFUTE, GAINSAY
contradiction ...... DENIAL, INCONSISTENCY
in terms ...... ANTILOGY
contraption .... GADGET, CONTRIVANCE
contrary ... BALKY, OPPOSED, OBSTINATE, PERVERSE, REVERSE, WRY
to rules .... FOUL
contrast .... COMPARE
contravene .... OPPOSE, DISAGREE, VIOLATE
contribute .... GIVE, DONATE
contribution .. DONATION, GIFT
form of .... CASH, KIND
small .... MITE
to the Pope .... (PETER'S) PENCE
contrite .. REPENTANT, SORRY, REGRETFUL, PENITENT
contrition .... PENITENCE, REMORSE
contrivance ... CONTRAPTION, INVENTION, DEVICE, GADGET, GIMMICK
contrive .... DEVISE, PLAN, SCHEME
control .... DIRECT, MANAGE, RESTRAIN(T), CHECK, RULE, GRASP, GRIP, MASTERY
firm, severe .. IRON HAND
controversial ..... DEBATABLE, MOOT, ERISTIC(AL), POLEMIC(AL)
area .... SAAR, RUHR, KASHMIR, SABAH, CHACO, DAMANSKY
city .... DANZIG
theorist .... DARWIN
theory ...... EVOLUTION
controversialist ...... ERISTIC
controversy .... DEBATE, DISPUTE, QUARREL
controvert .... DISCUSS, DENY, DISPUTE, ARGUE, DEBATE, OPPUGN
contumacious .... INSUBORDINATE, DISOBEDIENT
contumely .... INSOLENCE, RUDENESS
contusion .... BRUISE, INJURY
conundrum .. RIDDLE, PUZZLE, QUESTION, ENIGMA, MYSTERY
convalescent, diet of .. GRUEL, SOUP, LIQUIDS
convene .. ASSEMBLE, SIT, CALL, SUMMON, MEET, CONVOKE
convenience .... ADVANTAGE, COMFORT, ACCOMMODATION, FACILITY
convenient .. HANDY, EXPEDIENT
convent .... NUNNERY, MONASTERY, CLOISTER
cubicle .... CELL
dining hall .. REFECTORY
head .... SUPERIOR
inmate .. CENOBITE, NUN, MONK
member, new .... NEOPHYTE
convention .... ASSEMBLY, CUSTOM, USAGE
man .... DELEGATE
conventional .... CUSTOMARY, USUAL, SET, BOURGEOIS, ORTHODOX
act .... FORMALITY
measure of length .. PACE
conversant .... FAMILIAR, HEP
conversation .... CHAT, DIALOGUE, COLLOQUY
between two .. DUOLOGUE
private ..... TETE-A-TETE
witty .... REPARTEE
conversational comeback .... RETORT, RIPOSTE
event .... GABFEST
expert of a sort .... WIT
form of writing .... COLLOQUY
style, writing in .... CAUSERIE
converse .... TALK, OPPOSITE, COMMUNE, CHAT
convert .... (EX)CHANGE, TRANSFORM, PROSELYTE
fat into soap .. SAPONIZE, SAPONIFY
into money .... REALIZE, LIQUIDATE
new .. NOVICE, NEOPHYTE
convertible into cash .. LIQUID
vehicle .... LANDAU
convertite .... MAGDALEN
convex curve .... CAMBER
molding .. OVOLO, TORUS, TORE, ASTRAGAL
swelling in column ...... ENTASIS
convey .. CEDE, CARRY, DEED, TRANSPORT, TRANSMIT, TRANSFER, BRING
beyond jurisdiction....... ELOIN
by deed .... REMISE
conveyance .. CARRIAGE, CAR, CARRIER, VEHICLE, CESSION
for dead .... HEARSE
instrument .... DEED
conveying away from center .. EFFERENT
toward center .. AFFERENT
conveyor basket/car ... TRAM
convict .... FELON, CONDEMN, PRISONER, CULPRIT
privileged ...... TRUSTY
slang .... TERMER, LIFER, LOSER, JAILBIRD, LAG
convicts, squad of .... GANG
conviction .. OPINION, BELIEF
convince .... PERSUADE
convincing .. VALID, COGENT, PERSUASIVE
convivial .. GAY, BOON, JOVIAL, FESTIVE, SOCIABLE, JOLLY, MERRY
drinking .... BOWL, WASSAIL

convocation ...... ASSEMBLY
convoke .... CALL, CONVENE, ASSEMBLE
convolute .... COIL
convoy .. ESCORT, ACCOMPANY, CONDUCT
convulse .... SHAKE, AGITATE
convulsion .... SPASM, FIT, UPHEAVAL, PAROXYSM
attacks of .... ECLAMPSIA
of rage, etc. .. PAROXYSM
cony .. DAMAN, HYRAX, DUPE, PIKA, RABBIT, FUR, DAS(SIE), GANAM
coo .... CURR, MURMUR
companion of .... BILL
cooer .. DOVE, PIGEON, LOVER
cooing sound .... CURR
cook by dry heat ...... BAKE
chief .... CHEF
colloquial ...... FALSIFY
galley of .... CUDDY
gently .... CODDLE
in cream ...... SHIR(R)
in oil/fat .... FRY
in oven .... BAKE, ROAST
specialty of .... POTPIE, POT ROAST
up ... CONCOCT, DEVISE, PLOT
cook's domain aboard ship ... GALLEY, CUDDY
cookbook item .... RECIPE
cooked meat shop .... DELICATESSEN
partially .... RARE
cookhouse, ship's ..... GALLEY
cookies .. SNAPS, BUNS, CAKES, MACAROON
cooking aid .... SPICE, CONDIMENT
art of .... CULINARY, CUISINE
directions .... RECIPE
formula .... RECIPE
glassware .... PYREX
means of .... BOILING, FRYING, BAKING, ROASTING
odor .... NIDOR
outfit .... KITCHEN
pot .... OLLA
stove .... RANGE
style .... CUISINE
vessel .... PAN
cooky ..... MACAROON, BUN, (GINGER)SNAP, JUMBLE, LADYFINGER, HERMIT
cool .. COMPOSED, CALM, FAN, QUENCH
calm and .... COLLECTED
color ...... BLUE, GREEN, GRAY
hot liquid .... KEEL
make .... CHILL, ICE
cooled .... FRAPPE
cooler: sl. .... JAIL, CLINK
Coolidge Dam river .... GILA
alma mater .... AMHERST
coolie .... LABORER
woman ...... CHANGAR
coomb .... RAVINE
coon .... RACCOON
coop ...... COTE, HUTCH, PEN
fly the .. ESCAPE, DECAMP, ABSCOND
cooper .. HOOPER, CASKMAKER
actor ..... GARY, JACKIE
Mohican hero of .... UNCAS
cooperate .... HELP
secretly .... CONNIVE, COLLUDE
coordinate ...... HARMONIZE, ADJUST
Coorg's capital .... MERCARA
coot ... SCOTER, FOOL, DUCK, SIMPLETON, AVOCET, SHUFFLER, MUDHEN, NOTORNIS, WATERHEN
cootie .... LOUSE
cop .... TOP, CREST, HEAD
club of .... BILLY, STICK, TRUNCHEON
slang .. POLICEMAN, SEIZE, STEAL, BULL, FLATFOOT
copaiba .... RESIN, TUPI
copal .... RESIN, ANIME
copalm .... RESIN, TREE
cope .... VESTMENT, CANOPY, VAULT, SKY, CONTEND
Copenhagen is capital of ..... DENMARK
copier .... IMITATOR
copious ...... PROFUSE, LUSH, PLENTIFUL, AMPLE
Copland, composer ... AARON
copper .... COIN, METAL, AES, CA(U)LDRON, CUPRUM
alchemist's .... VENUS
alloy .. AROIDE, TOMBAK, TOMBAC(K)
alloy coin .... CASH
and tin alloy .... ORMOLU
coating .... PATINA, VERDIGRIS, VERD ANTIQUE
coin .... PENNY
color ... REDDISH BROWN
combining form .... CHALCO
gilded .... VERMEIL
nickel .... NICCOLITE
nickel, zinc alloy .... ALBATA
ore .... CUPRITE, CHALCOCITE
skin .... INDIAN
sulphate ...... VITRIOL
tin, zinc alloy .. OROIDE
zinc alloy .... PINCHBECK
copperah .... COPRA
copperhead .... SNAKE, NORTHERNER, VIPER
coppice ..... COPSE, THICKET
copra .... COPPERAH
copse ..... COPPICE, THICKET, BOSCAGE, BOSK, HOLT, SHAW
Coptic bishop's title .... ABBA
copula .... BAND, LINK
copy .... MODEL, DUPLICATE, FACSIMILE, IMITATE, APE, ECTYPE, RESCRIPT
closely .... MIMIC
court record .... ESTREAT
document's ..... TENOR
of original ...... REPLICA
photographic .... PHOTOSTAT, PRINT
read .... EDIT
copycat ..... APER, IMITATOR, MIMIC
copyist .... TRANSCRIBER, COPIER, SCRIVENER
copyread .... EDIT
copyright .... PATENT
coquet .. FLIRT, DALLY, TRIFLE
coquette .... FLIRT
coquina .... LIMESTONE
coquito .... PALM
cora .... GAZELLE
coracle ..... BOAT, CURRACH, CURRAGH
coral ...... POLYP, RED, ROE, SPAWN, ZOOID, POLYPITE
cavity .... CALICLE
formation .. REEF, SHELF, ATOLL
group ...... MADREPORE
island .. KEY, ATOLL, REEF
lobster's .... ROE
part .... STOLON
reef .... CAY, KEY, MADREPORE
source .... POLYPS
corbel .... BRACKET, CONSOLE, ANCON
corbeling .... SQUINCH
corbie .... CROW, RAVEN
Corcyra .... CORFU
cord ... STRING, ROPE, TWINE, FUNICLE
braided .... SENNIT
cable end's ... MARLINE
cattle catching ..... BOLA
drapery .... TORSADE
head .... AGAL
knob/lump .... KNOT
rope end's ..... MARLINE
strangling .... GAROTTE, GARROTE
tip .... TAG, A(I)GLET
trimming .... CHENILLE
umbilical .... FUNICULUS
cordage fiber .. AGAVE, SISAL, FERU, HEMP, IMBE, MAGUEY, JUTE, ABACA, COIR, ISTLE
grass .... ESPARTO
corded cloth .... REP, POPLIN, CORDUROY
Cordelia's father .... LEAR
sister .... REGAN
cordelle .... TASSEL
cordial .... LIQUEUR, GENIAL, ROSOLIO, RATAFIA, HEARTY, AMIABLE, ANISETTE, HIPPOCRAS, MARASCHINO
apricot .... PERSICO
cordierite .... IOLITE
cordite .... EXPLOSIVE
cordon .. CIRCLE, BRAID, RING, CORD, RIBBON, BELT
corduroy .... FUSTIAN
ridge .... WALE
core .... HEART, CENTER
bone/feather ...... PITH
corn ear .... COB
coreopsis .... TICKSEED
corf ... BASKET, MINEWAGON, TRUCK

corfu .... CORCYRA, KERKYRA
corium ..... DERMA, DERMIS, SKIN, CUTIS
Corinthian capital's scroll .... VOLUTE
volute .... HELIX
cork .... TAP, PLUG, STOPPER, BARK, STOPPLE, BUNG, SPILE
barrel's .... BUNG
bottle .... SHIVE
change into ... SUBERIZE
county port ...... COBH
famous feature of ...... BLARNEY STONE
helmet ..... TOPI, TOPEE
like .... SUBEROSE
noise .... POP
of a .... SUBERIC, SUBEREOUS
shallow .... SHIVE
waxy substance .... SUBERIN(E)
corker .. LIE, LULU, CLINCHER
corking .... EXCELLENT
corkwood .... BALSA
corm .... BULB, TUBER
plant with ... GLADIOLUS, CROCUS
cormorant .... BIRD, GREEDY, GLUTTON(OUS), SHAG, GUANAY, GORMAW
corn .. KERNEL, MAIZE, GRAIN, CALLUS, SALT, PAPILLOMA, FLINT, PICKLE
and beans dish .... SUCCOTASH
belt (per J. Luzzatto) ... BOURBON
bin .... CRIB
bread .. PONE, TORTILLA
cake .... TORTILLA
covering .... HUSK
crake .. RAIL, DAKER HEN
flour .... PINOLE
flower .... BLUENOSE
green ear ...... TUCKET
ground .. HOMINY, GRITS, MEAL, FLOUR
grower .... IOWAN
hair .... TASSEL
hulled .... HOMINY
husk .... SHUCK
imperfect .... NUBBIN
Indian .... MAIZE
lily .... IXIA
liquor .... WHISK(E)Y
meal ...... MASA, SAMP, HOMINY
meal, baked/fried ...... HOECAKE
meal bread/cake .... DODGER, PONE
meal dish ..... SCRAPPLE
meal dough .... HUSH PUPPY
meal mush .... ATOLE
meal porridge .... MUSH, STIRABOUT, POLENTA
meal pudding ..... MUSH
mill .... QUERN
porridge .... SAMP
slang .... MUSH
small .... NUBBIN
stalk .... STOVER
state .... IOWA
stump ...... STUBBLE
toe .... CALLUS
variety .... FLINT
cornea inflammation .... KERATITIS
leucoma of the .... WALLEYE
opacity on .... NEBULA, LEUCOMA
corned .... SALTED
beef .... BULLY
beef connoisseur .. JIGGS
beef's partner .. CABBAGE
cornel .... DOGWOOD
Cornelia Otis ____ .. SKINNER
corneous .. HORNY, HORNLIKE
corner .. BIGHT, REGION, TRAP, ANGLE, COIGN, NOOK, NICHE, TREE
angle .... CANT
chimney .... INGLENOOK
cozy .... NOOK, ALCOVE
fireplace .... INGLENOOK
of building .... CANT, QUOIN
of sail .... CLEW
projecting .... COIGN(E)
support .... CORBELING, LINTEL, ARCH, SQUINCH
cornerstone ... FOUNDATION, COIGN(E), QUOIN
cornet .... CAVALRY FLAG
Cornhusker state .. NEBRASKA
cornice .... MOLDING
projection .... DRIP, CORONA
support .... ANCON
corniculate .... HORNED
Cornish patron saint .. COLIN
town .... ST. IVES
cornu(copia) .... HORN
Cornwall county seat .... BODMIN
islands .... SCILLY
corny .... TRITE, BANAL, SENTIMENTAL, MUSHY
corolla ... PETALS, PERIANTH, LIGULE
cuplike part .... CORONA
heraldic .... GALEA
corollary, a ...... INFERENCE, DEDUCTION
geometrical ...... PORISM
corona .. AURA, HALO, CROWN, AUREOLE, CIGAR
Australis .... WREATH
coronach .. DIRGE, THRENODY
coronal .... CROWN, DIADEM, GARLAND
coronet .... ANADEM, CROWN, DIADEM, TIARA
wearer .... DUKE
corporal .. BODILY, PERSONAL
famous ...... NAPOLEON
for short .... NCO
infamous .... HITLER
Little .... NAPOLEON
punishment .. FLOGGING, WHIPPING
rank after ... SERGEANT
tobacco of .... COPORAL
corporate .. UNITED, COMMON, JOINT
corporation manager .. SYNDIC
corporeal .. SOMAL, MATERIAL, PHYSICAL, BODILY, SOMATIC
corpse .... CADAVER, CARCASS, CARCASE, LICH
animated ..... ZOMBI(E)
dissection .. NECROTOMY
embalmed ..... MUMMY
platform for ...... BIER
prefix .... NECR(O)
slang .... STIFF
corpsman .... MEDIC
corpulent .... FAT, OBESE, FLESHY, STOUT, GROSS, PURSY
corpuscles, lack of red .... AN(A)EMIA
corral ... ROUND UP, POUND, PEN, STOCK(ADE)
correct .... CURE, PROPER, ACCURATE, PRIM, RIGHT, EDIT, EMEND
one's fault ...... REFORM
correctional house .... BRIDEWELL, REFORMATORY
correlative .. (N)EITHER, (N)OR
correspond .. MATCH, AGREE, EQUAL, SUIT, TALLY, WRITE, COINCIDE
correspondence .. AGREEMENT, COMMUNICATION
kind of ...... BUSINESS, OFFICIAL
correspondent, kind of .... PENPAL, STRINGER, FOREIGN
corrida cry .... OLE
corridor .. PASSAGEWAY, AISLE, GALLERY, HALL(WAY)
corrival .... COMPETITOR
corroborant .... TONIC
corroborate .... SUPPORT, CONFIRM
corrode .. WEAR AWAY, RUST, EAT INTO, ERODE, GNAW
corroded .... CARIOUS
corrosive ... ACID, MORDANT, CAUSTIC, ESCHAROTIC
corrugate ... FURROW, PLEAT WRINKLE
corrugated .... RUGATE, RUGOUS, RUGOSE
corrupt .. ROTTEN, SPOIL, EVIL, VITIATE, VENAL, DEBASE, DEFILE, PERVERT, INFECT
morally .... PUTRID
one way .. BRIBE, SUBORN
official .... GRAFTER
corruption, trace of ... TAINT
corsage .. BOUQUET, BODICE, NOSEGAY
corsair .... FREEBOOTER, PRIVATEER, PIRATE
ship .... XEBEC
corselet .... LORICA, CUIRASS
corset .... BODICE, LORICA, LORLEA
bone .... BUSK
stiffener .... STAY, BUSK, WHALEBONE
Corsican capital .... AJACCIO
famous ...... NAPOLEON

seaport .... BASTIA
sheep .... MOUFLON
cortege ..... TRAIN, RETINUE, PROCESSION
cortex .... BARK, RIND
corundum ..... RUBY, TOPAZ, AMETHYST, SAPPHIRE, EMERY
coruscate .. SPARKLE, GLITTER
corvine bird .. RAVEN, CROW, ROOK
Corvus .... RAVEN
coryza ...... COLD, CATARRH
sign of .. SNIFFLE, SNEEZE
cos .... COAN, LETTUCE, ROMAINE
cosher .... PAMPER
cosmetic .... CERUSE
base for ..... LANOLIN(E)
cheek/lip .... ROUGE
eyelid/eyelash .... MASCARA, KOHL
hair .... HENNA
paste .... PACK
skin .... LOTION
use/decorate with ...... PAINT
cosmetics: sl. ..... WARPAINT
cosmic ..... GRANDIOSE, VAST
cycle .... EON
ray particle ...... MESON
cosmography, branch of ..... GEOGRAPHY, ASTRONOMY, GEOLOGY
cosmonaut ...... ASTRONAUT, SPACEMAN, ROCKETMAN
American .... SHEPARD, COLLINS, ALDRIN, BORMAN, BEAN
Russian ...... GAGARIN, KOMAROV
cosmos .... UNIVERSE, REALM, EARTH, GLOBE, HARMONY, ORDER, WORLD, THISTLE
god of the ..... VARUNA
opposed to ...... CHAOS
Cossack ...... CAVALRYMAN, RUSSIAN, TATAR
chief .. ATAMAN, HETMAN
fame of the .... HORSEMANSHIP
whip .... KNOUT
cosset .. PET, PAMPER, FONDLE, LAMB
cost .... PRICE, SACRIFICE
colloquial ..... DAMAGE
exceeding contract price . OVERRUN
costa .... RIB
Costa Rica capital .. SAN JOSE
coin .... COLON
discoverer of .. COLUMBUS
mountain .... IRAZU
port .... LIMON
president .... TREJOS
costard .... HEAD, APPLE
costly ..... EXPENSIVE, DEAR, PRECIOUS
costmary .. CHRYSANTHEMUM
costrel ...... FLASK, BOTTLE
costume .... DRESS, HABIT, GET-UP
colloquial ..... RIG, TOG
jewelry .... TRINKET, GEWGAW, BAUBLE, BROOCH
jewelry material .... STRASS, PASTE, OROIDE, ORMOLU
masquerade .... DOMINO
matching parts .... ENSEMBLE
riding .... HABIT
silk material .... SENDAL
wear one in fun .... MUM(M)
cot .. BED, SHELTER, CHARPAI, CHARPOY
poetic .... COTTAGE
cote .... SHELTER, SHED
coterie .. CIRCLE, CLIQUE, SET, CAMARILLA, JUNTO
cotillion .... DANCE
cotinga .... CHATTERER
Cotswold .... SHEEP
cotta .... SURPLICE
cottage .... CASINO, CHALET, VILLA, CABANA, BUNGALOW, HUT, BOWER
cheese ...... SMEARCASE
cotter .... BOLT, WEDGE
pin .... FORELOCK
cotton ..... THREAD, CLOTH, JEAN, MADRAS, PIMA, ROVE, NAINSOOK, JACONET, MALLOW
and wool cloth .... SATINET(TE), LINSEY
batting fibers ... LINTERS
Bengal .... ADATI
canvaslike .... WIGAN
cleaning machine ...... WILLOW, GIN, LINTER
cloth .... KHAKI, CHINO, CRASH, CHINTZ, CALICO, ETAMINE, GALATEA, NANKEEN, NANKIN, PIMA, MULL, DUCKS, MANTA, MADRAS, REPP, REP(S), OXFORD, SEERSUCKER, MUSLIN, JEAN, GRENADINE, ORGANDY
cloth, canvaslike .... WIGAN
cloth for curtains, etc. .. SCRIM, DIMITY, LAWN
cloth for handkerchiefs, blouse, etc. .... LAWN
cloth for linings .... PERCALINE, SILESIA
cloth for sheets .... PERCALE, MUSLIN
cloth, glazed .. JACONET, CHINTZ
cloth, glossy .... SATEEN
comb .... CARD
fiber .... LINT(ER), BATTING
fiber knot .... NEP
gauze .... LENO
gum tree ...... TUPELO
machine .... GIN, BALER, MULE, LINTER, WILLOW(ER)
measure .... HANK, LEA
pad .... SPONGE
pod .... BOLL
seed cleaner .... LINTER, GIN
seed fiber .... LINTER
sheer .... VOILE
spinning wheel .... CHARK(H)A
stainer .... BUG
State .... ALABAMA
thread .... LISLE
tuft .... LOCK
twilled .... JEAN, DENIM, CHINO
twisted .... ROVE
waste .... FLOCK
with glazed/water finish . PERCALINE
cottonmouth .... SNAKE
cottontail .... HARE, LEVERET, RABBIT
cottonwood .. ALAMO, POPLAR
cottony ..... FLUFFY, DOWNY
couch .. DIVAN, LAIR, CANAPE, DAVENPORT, SETTEE, SOFA, STATE, SQUAB, LOUNGE, RECLINE, OTTOMAN
hanging ...... HAMMOCK
like chair .... CHAISE LONGUE
poetic .... BED
to carry wounded ...... LITTER
cougar ..... PUMA, PANTHER, CATAMOUNT, CARCAJOU, PAINTER
cough .... TUSSIS, HACK
candy .... HOARHOUND, HOREHOUND
drop .... LOZENGE, TROCHE, PASTILLE
medicine .... GRINDELIA
of a .... TUSSIVE, TUSSAL
sound like a .... HICCUP
to attract attention ..... AHEM
up .... HAND OVER, EJECT
whooping .... PERTUSSIS
coughing up pus ..... VOMICA
coulee .. RAVINE, GULCH, LAVA
couloir ...... GORGE, GULLY
coulter .... (PLOW)SHARE
council .... BOARD, JUNTA
African tribe's .. INDABA
chamber .... CAMARILLA, DIVAN, CABINET
church .... SYNOD, CONSISTORY
of deacons .. CONSISTORY
table .... BOARD
counsel ..... ADVICE, ADVISE, REDE
legal .... LAWYER
counselor .. ADVISER, LAWYER, MENTOR
woman .... EGERIA
count .. TALLY, RELY, RECKON, ADD, (E)NUMERATE, FIGURE
down purpose .... BLAST-OFF, LAUNCHING
French .... COMTE
German .... GRAF
in .... INCLUDE
in law .... CHARGE
of Monte Cristo .... DANTES
of population ... CENSUS

of Vienne ...... DAUPHIN
out .... DISREGARD, OMIT
palatine ..... PALSGRAVE
countenance ..... ABET, FACE, VISAGE, SUPPORT
counter ...... OPPOSITE, BAR, COMPUTER, BUFFET, CONTRARY
in cards .... MILLE
irritant .... SALVE, DEMULCENT, OINTMENT, CALAMINE, MOXA, SETON, LOTION, MUSTARD
kind of .... GEIGER
sale .... RETAIL
counteract ...... NEUTRALIZE
counterbalance ... EQUIPOISE
counterfeit .. FALSE, FORGE(D), POSTICHE, IMITATION, SHAM, BOGUS, PHON(E)Y
coin .... SLUG
countermand .... CANCEL, OVERRULE, REVOKE, CALL BACK
counterpane .... COVERLET
counterpart ..... COPY, LIKE, DUPLICATE, TWIN, REPLICA, PARALLEL
counterpoint .... DESCANT
of ...... CONTRAPUNTAL
countersign .... PASSWORD
countersink .... REAM
counterweight .... TARE
countess' title of respect ...... LADY
counting frame .... ABAC(US)
sheep purpose ... SLEEP
ten purpose .. COOL OFF, STALL
countless .... MYRIAD
countrified .. RUSTIC, RURAL, CORNFED, HODDEN
country ...... REGION, LAND, REALM
ancient .. ILLYRIA, PERSIA
bumpkin .. HICK, RUBE, YOKEL, RUSTIC, CHURL, YAHOO
dance ...... REEL, HAY
dance: Brit. ... COVERLEY
fellow .... CORYDON
French .... PAYS
gallant .... SWAIN
gentleman .... COVERLEY, ESQUIRE
girl ... PHILLIS, PHYLLIS, WENCH
house .... VILLA, CASINO, HACIENDA
house, of a .... VILLATIC
in law .... PAIS
in the city .. RUS IN URBE
lad .... SWAIN
live in the ... RUSTICATE
middle region .... MIDLAND, INTERIOR, INLAND
of fable .... EL DORADO
of the .... RURAL
on 38th parallel .. KOREA
open, flat ... CHAMPAIGN
open, wild ...... WEALD
poetical .... CLIME
social .. BEE, BARNDANCE
Spanish .... PAIS
ways .... PATHS
countryman .... RUSTIC, COMPATRIOT
Spanish .... PAISANO
countryside, of the .. BUCOLIC
county .. SHIRE, DISTRICT, AMT
law officer ..... SHERIFF
coup .... BLOW, (MASTER) STROKE
d' ____ .... ETAT
de grace ... DEATH BLOW
de grace dagger .... MISERICORD(E)
reporter's .. SCOOP, BEAT
couple .... DUO, PAIR, BRACE, LINK, DUAD, YOKE, FEW, SEVERAL, TWO (SOME)
coupled .. GEMINATED, LINKED, PAIRED, TEAMED
"Couples" author .... UPDIKE
couplet .... DISTICH
coupling for electric fixtures .. HICKEY
courage ...... PLUCK, HEART, GUTS, NERVE, GALL, FACE, CHEEK, VALOR, METTLE, GRIT, SPUNK, SAND, FORTITUDE
loss of .... COLDFEET
pretended .... BRAVADO
symbol of ..... BULLDOG
courageous ... BRAVE, SANDY, STOUT, SPUNKY
courier ..... MESSENGER, POST, ESTAFETTE
courlan .... LIMPKIN
course ... PATH, WAY, ROUTE, DIRECTION, LANGLAUF, PROCESS, DISH
athletics .... GYMNASTICS
meal .... VIAND, SALAD, ENTREE, DISH
of action .. PROCEDURE, PROCEEDING, TACK
of official papers .... CHANNELS
of study ... CURRICULUM, LESSONS
of travel ..... ITINERARY, ROUTE
court .. WOO, ASSIZE, BENCH, PERISTYLE, ROMANCE, TRIBUNAL, SPARK
action .... SUIT
aggressively ..... RUSH
assembly .... LEVEE
case .... CAUSE
castle's .... BAILEY
central .... ATRIUM
challenge .... RECUSE
church ..... CONSISTORY, ROTA
crier .... BEADLE
crier's call .. OYEZ, OYES
criminal .... ASSIZE
decree .... ARRET
enclosed .... PARVIS
entrance .... ATRIUM
equity ...... CHANCERY
favorite ...... GRACIOSO
game .... TENNIS, HANDBALL, BASKETBALL, BADMINTON, SQUASH
hearing .... OYER
inner .... PATIO
jurisdiction .... SOKE
manorial .... LEET
martial defendant ...... MUTINEER, AWOL, TRAITOR, DESERTER
martial in the field ...... DRUMHEAD
messenger ...... BEADLE
minutes .... ACTA
of a .... AULIC
of justice ... BAR, BENCH
of law .... FORUM
official ...... ATTORNEY, BAILIFF, FISCAL, REFEREE, DA
order .... WRIT, ARRET, MANDAMUS, SUBPOENA
order extract ... ESTREAT
panel .... JURY
pertaining to .... AULIC
proceeding .... TRIAL, HEARING
ruling, plea for .. MOTION
session .. ASSIZE, HEARING
summons .... CITATION, SUBPOENA
writ .... OYER, SUBPOENA, SUMMONS
yard .... PATIO
courteous .... URBANE, CIVIL, POLITE
regard .... RESPECT, DEFERENCE
courtesan .. PROSTITUTE, THAIS
courtesy .. FAVOR, POLITENESS
courtly ..... SUAVE, ELEGANT, POLISHED, AULIC
courtship ..... WOOING, SUIT, PLIGHT
dance .... CUECA
of Miles ____ .. STANDISH
result of, usually .... WEDDING, MARRIAGE
courtyard .... PATIO, QUADRANGLE
sunken ...... AREAWAY
cousin .... COS
couteau .... DAGGER
couturier ...... DRESSMAKER, STYLIST
fabric of .... SOIE, LAME
famed .. DIOR, BALMAIN, ST. LAURENT, GIVENCHY, NORELL, MAINBOCHER, GERNREICH, BALENCIAGA
cove ...... HOLE, BAY, INLET, NOOK
British .. FELLOW, CHAP, BOY
covenant .. AGREEMENT, PACT, TESTAMENT, BOND
Coventry, goddess of .. GODIVA
cover ... TOP, LID, CAP, HIDE, COAT, SHEATHE, ENVELOP(E), ROOF, CANOPY, WHELM
bottle ...... CROWN, CAP
break .... EMERGE
detachable ...... BINDER
face .... VEIL, MASK
girl ..... PIN UP, MODEL

hard ..... SHELL, PLATE, CARAPACE
inner surface .. LINE, PAD
lap .... RUG
leg .. PUTTEE, CHAUSSES, LEGGING
nipa .... THATCH
ornamental ...... SHAM
pie's ...... CRUST, RIND
protective ...... ARMOR, SHELL, CARAPACE
superficial ...... VENEER
thickly .... SMOTHER
thin .... VENEER
thinly .... SKIM
top wall .. CEIL, COPING, CAPSTONE
under .. HIDDEN, SECRET
up ...... CONCEAL, HIDE
with asphalt ...... PAVE
with cloth .... DRAPE
with feathers ... FLEDGE
with jewels ...... BEGEM
with plaster .... CEIL
with trappings .... CAPARISON

coverage, insurance ..... RISK

covered colonnade .... STOA
entrance .... PORCH
garden ...... HOTHOUSE
portico .... GALLERY
vehicle .... VAN
wagon .... SCHOONER, CONESTOGA
walk ...... STOA, MALL, CLOISTER, PORTICO, ARCADE, GALLERY
with blood ... HEMATOSE, GORY
with bristles .... HISPID
with fine feathers .... DOWNY
with flakes .... SCURFY, LEPIDOTE
with hair .... PILOSE, HISPID, TOMENTOSE
with leaves ..... FOLIOSE

covering .. SHEATHE, TEGUMEN, INTEGUMENT, TEGMEN
for concealment .... CAMOUFLAGE, BLINDAGE
gloomy .... PALL
glossy .... SHEEN
material .... PATCH
membrane of ovary ..... TUNICA
of clouds ..... OVERCAST
protective ...... LORICA, ARMOR, SHELL, MAIL
shiny .... SHEEN
teeth .... DENTINE

coverlet .. BEDSPREAD, QUILT, COUNTERPANE, PALL

covert .. SECRET, CONCEALED, VEILED, HIDDEN

covet .... DESIRE, CRAVE, ENVY

covetous .... GREEDY, AVARICIOUS

covey .. FLOCK, BROOD, BEVY

cow ..... DAUNT, (OVER)AWE, BOVINE, BULLY, KINE, THREATEN, VACA, BEEF, BOSS, CRUMMIE, CRUMMY
ad .... ELSIE
barn ..... STABLE, BYRE
breed .... ANGUS, KERRY, JERSEY
call .... MOO, LOW
cud .... RUMEN
dewlap of .... LAPPET
dialectic .... CRITTER, CRITTUR
fat ...... TALLOW, SUET
fish .... TORO
genus .... BOS
gland .... UDDER
headed deity .... ISIS
hornless ..... MUL(L)EY
killer .... WASP
mammary gland .. UDDER
milking .... MILCH
pilot .... PINTANO
polled .... MUL(L)EY
sea .. MANATEE, DUGONG
sound .... LOW, MOO
tuberculosis of ... GRAPE
udder inflammation ..... GARGET
unbranded ... MAVERICK
young .... HEIFER, CALF, STIRK

coward ..... CRAVEN, SNEAK, POLTROON, DASTARD
colloquial ..... YELLOW, CHICKEN
descriptive of a .... YELLOW
(Noel) show .... BITTER-SWEET
(Noel) song ...... NINA

cowardice, symbol of .... WHITE FEATHER

cowardly .... CRAVEN, DASTARDLY
animal ...... HY(A)ENA
knight of story .... FALSTAFF
person .. CUR, POLTROON, CAITIFF
slang .. CHICKEN, YELLOW

cowbird .... TROUPIAL

cowboy .... BUCKAROO, VAQUERO, HERDER, LLANERO, RANCHER, WRANGLER, BRONCOBUSTER, BUCKAYRO
Australian .. STOCKMAN, RINGER
bed .... BUNK
big day of ...... RODEO, ROUNDUP
breeches .... CHAPS
concern of ...... CATTLE
friend of ..... PARD(NER)
habitat .. RANGE, RANCH, PAMPAS
jacket .... CHAQUETA
kind of ...... PUNCHER
original ...... PECOS BILL
overalls .... LEVIS
pampas .... GAUCHO
rope ..... LASSO, REATA, RIATA, LARIAT
saddlebag ...... ALFORJA
show .... RODEO
South American .... GAUCHO
trousers .... CHAPS, CHAPARAJOS

cowcatcher .... FENDER

cower .... CRINGE, QUAIL, SHRINK, CROUCH

cowering thru fear .... FUNK

Cowes, sight in ...... YACHTS

cowfish ..... TORO, MANATEE, DUGONG, GRAMPUS

cowl ... HOOD, CLOAK, AMICE
like headdress .. ALMUCE, COUS

cowpox .... VACCINIA

cows .... KINE
roundup of .. WRANGLE

cowslip .... BLUEBELL, MAYFLOWER

coxa .... HIP

coxcomb ..... DANDY, DUDE, POP, TOFF

coy ...... BASHFUL, DEMURE, TIMID, RETIRING, SHY, DIFFIDENT

coyo .... AVOCADO

coyote .... WOLF

coypu ...... RODENT, NUTRIA

coze .... CHAT, TALK

cozen ...... DECEIVE, CHEAT, TRICK

cozy .... SNUG, COMFORTABLE, HOM(E)Y
retreat .. NEST, NOOK, DEN

crab .. SHELLFISH, NAG, CARP, MALACOSTRACAN
apple .... SCRAB
claw .... CHELA, NIPPER PINC(H)ER
constellation .... CANCER
feeler .... ANTENNA
front of .... METOPE
kind of .... FIDDLER
king .... LIMULUS, LIMULOID
larva .... ZOEA
like a .... CANCROID
mantis .... SQUILLA
Scottish .... PARTAN
shell .... TEST
upper shell of .... CARAPACE
walk of .... SIDLE, SIDEWISE

crabbed .... CRAMP

crabfish .... GRAMPLE

crack ... BREAK, SPLIT, SNAP, CREVICE, CHINK, FIRST RATE CHAP, RIFT, JOKE, FRACTURE, QUIP
deep .... CREVASSE
filler .... GROUT
glacier .... CREVASSE
open .... CHAP
seal .... CA(U)LK
up ... COLLAPSE, CRASH, BREAK DOWN

crackbrained .... NUTTY, CRAZY, INSANE, IDIOTIC

cracked wheat/oats .. GROATS

cracker ..... BISCUIT, WAFER, SALTINE

crackerjack .... NAILER

crackers, dish of ... PANADA

crackle .... CREPITATE

cracklings .. SCRAPS, GREAVES
crackly .... CRISP
cracknel .... GREAVES
crackpot ...... CRANK, NUT
cracks, full of ...... CHOPPY, CHAPPED
cracksman .. BURGLAR, YEGG
cradle .... CRATE, CRIB
in mining ...... ROCKER
period .... INFANCY
song .... LULLABY
craft .... ART, TRADE, SKILL, TALENT, GUILE, OCCUPATION, CUNNING, ARTIFICE
air .... AIRPLANE, HELICOPTER, DIRIGIBLE
union of old .... GUILD
water ...... BOAT, SHIP, VESSEL
craftsman .. ARTIST, ARTISAN, ARTIFICER
chief .... MAESTRO
metal .... SMITH
crafty .. SLY, CUNNING, WILY, ARTFUL, FOXY, FELINE, INSIDIOUS
crag .. CLIFF, TOR, PRECIPICE
crake .... RAIL
cram .... BONE, PACK, STUFF, TUCK
cramp .... HAMPER
neck ...... KINK, CRICK
crampfish .... TORPEDO
crampon .. GRAPLIN, GRAPNEL
cranberry disease ..... SCALD
crane .... HERON, STORK, DEMOISELLE, RUBBERNECK
arm .... JIB
framework ..... GANTRY
genus .... GRUS
Ichabod, rival of .... (BROM) BONES
like bird .... CHUNGA, SERIEMA
pertaining to .... GRUINE
relative .... BUSTARD
ship's .... DAVIT
sound .... CLANG
cranesbill .... GERANIUM
cranial nerve .... VAGUS
cranium .... SKULL
crank .... WHIM, TWIST, CAPRICE
case reservoir ... OILPAN
colloquial .... CRACKPOT, QUEER, ECCENTRIC
cranky .... CROSS, IRRITABLE, QUEER, GROUCHY
cranny ...... CREVICE, CHINK
crap, in dice .... BOXCAR
shooter's "four" .... CATER, JOE
crape .... WEED, WEEPER
crapehanger ...... PESSIMIST
crappie .... SUNFISH
craps throw .... DIE
crash .. FALL, COLLIDE, BREAK, COLLAPSE, SMASH
crass .. GROSS, STUPID, CRUDE, COARSE
Cratchit's job .... CLERK
crate .. BASKET, HAMPER, BOX
slang .... JALOPY

crater .... PIT, CAVITY, HOLE, CALDERA
lunar .... LINNE
one with ...... VOLCANO
cravat ..... SCARF, (NECK)TIE, ASCOT, OVERLAY
fabric .... REP
hangman's ...... NOOSE
ornament ..... STICKPIN
crave .. BEG, HANKER, YEARN, COVET
craven .... COWARD(LY)
person ...... POLTROON, CAITIFF
craving .. APPETITE, HUNGER, APPETENCE, MANIA, OBSESSION
craw .... CROP, MAW
crawl .. CREEP, SLITHER, INCH, GROVEL
crawler .... BABY, WORM, REPTILE
crawling ... REPENT, REPTANT
crayfish egg .... BERRY
segment ...... METAMERE
crayon .. CHARCOAL, CHALK, PASTEL
pastel .... PASTILLE
picture .... PASTEL
craze .. FUROR, FASHION, FAD, MANIA
women's style .... MINISKIRT, PANTSUIT
crazed ... INSANE, DEMENTED, MAD(DENED)
crazy ... INSANE, MAD, DAFT, WACKY, CRACKED, DOTTY, LOCO, BUGS, NUTS, POTTY, CUCKOO, KOOKY, KOOKIE, LOONY, LUNY
person .... MANIAC
to kill .... AMUCK, AMOK, BERSERK
creak ...... SQUEAK, SCROOP, GRATE
cream .. ELITE, BEST, COSMETIC
color .... ECRU
French .... CREME
separator ... CENTRIFUGE
creamy white .. IVORY, MILKY
crease ... RIDGE, FOLD, MUSS, WRINKLE, RUCK, RIMPLE, RUMPLE, RUCK, RUGA
creased .... RUGATE
create .... MAKE, ORIGINATE, PRODUCE
creation .. INVENTION, COSMOS, GENESIS
God's .... UNIVERSE
creative .... INVENTIVE
writing .. FICTION, NOVEL, POEM, POETRY
creator, the .... GOD
creature, small, imaginary ... GREMLIN
creche figure .. JOSEPH, MARY, INFANT, LAMB, MAGI, SHEPHERD
part .... MANGER
crecopia .... MYTH
credence .... BELIEF, CREDENTIAL
credential ...... CERTIFICATE, CREDENCE

credenza .... BUFFET
credible .... RELIABLE, PLAUSIBLE, BELIEVABLE, LIKELY
credit .. BELIEVE, ATTRIBUTE, ASCRIBE, TRUST, HONOR, REBATE
British .... TICK
card organization ...... DINER'S(CLUB)
for achievement .. KUDOS
creditor .... LENDER, NOTE HOLDER
avaricious ..... USURER, LOAN SHARK
exacting ...... SHYLOCK
credo .. BELIEF, CREED, TENET
credulous .... GULLIBLE
creed, one such ..... NICENE
political .... ISM, DOXY
creek ...... INLET, BAY, RIA, INDIAN, STREAM, BAYOU, KILL
creel .... BASKET
user .... FISHERMAN, ANGLER
creep .... CRINGE, FAWN, CRAWL, SLINK, SLITHER
slang .... DRIP
creeper .. VINE, IVY, SNAKE
creeping .... REPENT, REPTANT
charlie, for one ... WEED
plant .. VINE, BINE, LIANA
creeps, the .... FEAR, REPUGNANCE, REVULSION
creepy ...... EERIE, CRAWLY
creese ... KRIS, CRIS, DAGGER
cremate .. BURN, INCINERATE
crematory .... CINERATOR
Cremona .... AMATI, VIOLIN, STRAD(IVARIUS)
river .... ADDA
violin maker .. GUARNERI, AMATI
crenate .... SCALLOPED, NOTCHED
crenel .... EMBRASURE
Creole ancestry .... SPANISH, FRENCH
and Indian ...... MESTIZO
milieu .... NEW ORLEANS
patois ... GUMBO, GOMBO
rice cake .... CALA
state .... LOUISIANA
creosol .... ANTISEPTIC
crepe suzette .... PANCAKE, FLAPJACK
crepitate .. CRACKLE, RATTLE
crepuscle .... DUSK, TWILIGHT
crescent .... SEMILUNAR, DEMILUNE, MENISCUS
moons .... MENISCI
of a ...... BICORN, HORN
point of .... CUSP
shape figure ...... LUNE, LUNULE, LUNULA, MENISCUS
shaped .. LUNATE, LUNE, BICORN, LUNULAR (SEMI)LUNAR
cress .... SALAD, HERB
cresset .... LANTERN
crest ..... CAP, HELMET, TOP, CROWN, RIDGE, PEAK

cock's .. COMB, CARUNCLE
mountain .... ARETE
of bird/fowl ..... COMB, CALOT(TE), CARUNCLE
wave's .... COMB
crested .. CROWNED, PILEATE, CRISTATE
crestfallen .... DEJECTED
Cretan ... CANDIAN, MINOAN
Crete .... CANDIA
born painter/sculptor ... EL GRECO, DOMENICO
capital/seaport ... CANEA
city ... KNOSSOS, KHANIA
guard of .... TALOS
king .... MINOS
mountain .... IDA
mythical beast .... MINOTAUR
mythical structure ...... LABYRINTH
princess ...... ARIADNE
cretin .... IDIOT
cretonne .... TOILE
crevasse .... CHASM, FISSURE
crevice .... CHINK, CLEFT, FISSURE
crevices, full of ..... RIMOSE
crew .. GANG, COMPANY, MOB, CROWD, TEAM
of ship .... COMPLEMENT
relief .... RELAY
crewel .... YARN
crib .... RACK, TROUGH, BIN, STALL, MANGER, PLAGIARIZE, PONY
baby's .... CRADLE
colloquial .... STEAL
content of ...... FODDER
in writing ... PLAGIARISM
cribbage .... CARD GAME
game lost .... LURCH
score ...... PEGS, NOBS
crick .... CRAMP, KINK
cricket .. GRASSHOPPER, GRIG, FOOTSTOOL, HOOP
bowled ball .... YORKER
club .... BAT
colloquial .... FAIR PLAY
equipment .. BALL, BAT, WICKET
inning unplayed .... WICKET
like insect ...... LOCUST
score .... BYE
sound .... CHIRP
team .... ELEVEN
term .... (TICE)BYE
crier .... MUEZZIN
crime .... SIN, WRONGDOING, FELONY, GUILT, MISDEED, MALEFACTION
against king .... LESE MAJESTE
high .... TREASON
major .... FELONY
syndicate .. COSA NOSTRA, MAFIA
syndicate member ...... MAFIOSO
where committed .. VENUE
Crimea Conference (1945) site YALTA
Crimean city .... SEVASTOPOL, YALTA
lamb's fur ... CRIMMER, KRIMMER
river .... ALMA
sea .... AZOF
seaport .. YALTA, KERCH
strait .... KERCH
criminal .. IMMORAL, CONVICT, FELON, CULPRIT, YEGG, MALEFACTOR, OUTLAW, MISCREANT, MALFEASANT
act .... JOB
colloquial .... LOSER
conditional release of ... PROBATION
dangerous ... DESPERADO
habitual .... RECIDIVIST, ROUNDER
lawyer: sl. .. MOUTHPIECE
mark of a ...... STIGMA
unreconstructed .... RECIDIVIST
criminals collectively .... FELONRY
crimp .. PLEAT, WAVE, CURL, CRINKLE, FOLD, FLUTE, GOFFER
crimple .... WRINKLE
crimson ...... RED, CARMINE, BLOODY, MADDER
Crimson's rival .... YALE
cringe .... QUAIL, COWER, SHRINK, CROUCH
crinkled paper/cloth ... CREPE
crinkly .... WAVY
crinoid .... SEA LILY
crinoline .... PETTICOAT, (HOOP)SKIRT
cripple .. LAME, DISABLE, MAIM, HAMSTRING
a horse .... HOCK
walking aid .... CRUTCH, CANE
cripples .... (THE) HALT
patron saint of .... (ST.) GILES
crisis ...... TURNING POINT, EMERGENCY
of disease ..... SOLUTION
crisp ...... WAVY, ANIMATED, BRITTLE, CURT, CRUMP
biscuit ... CRACKER, SNAP
crisper .... CURLER
cristate .... CRESTED
criterion .. RULE, TEST, NORM, STANDARD, CANON
critic ...... SLATER, CARPER, FAULTFINDER, CENSOR, REVIEWER
disapproval of a .... PAN(NING)
inferior ..... CRITICASTER
literary .... REVIEWER
"missile" of, literally .... TOMATO, EGG
uninhibited ...... BOOER, HISSER
work of .... REVIEW(ER), CRITIQUE
critical .... CAPTIOUS, ACUTE, DECISIVE, CENSORIOUS, EXIGENT
analysis .... EXEGESIS
mark .... OBELUS
moment .. CRUX, CRISIS, ZERO HOUR
situation ...... CLUTCH
writing .... LAMPOON, SATIRE
criticism .. REVIEW, DESCANT, CRITIQUE
abusive ...... DIATRIBE
adverse: colloq. .... PAN
criticize .... FLAY, BLAME, CENSURE, DENOUNCE, SLASH, SLAM, SLATE, DAMN, CONDEMN, ANIMADVERT, SCORE, OPPUGN
colloquial .. PAN, ROAST, RAKE
critique .... REVIEW, EPICRISIS COMMENTARY
croak ..... CROUP, GRUMBLE
slang .... DIE
croaker ...... FROG, RAVEN, CROW, SQUETEAGUE
croaking .... RAUCOUS
Croat .... SLAV
Croatian capital .... ZAGREB
soldier .... PANDOUR
croc .... CROCODILE
crochet .... KNIT(TING), KINK
crock .. SMUT, SOOT, POT, JAR, SHARD, POTSHERD
crockery ..... CHINA(WARE), POTS, JARS, DISHES
Crockett, frontiersman ...... DAVID, DAVEY
place of heroism .... ALAMO
crocodile .. REPTILE, SAURIAN, YACARE
bird .... PLOVER, TROCHILUS
for short .... CROC
India .. GAVIAL, MUGGER, MUGGAR, MUGGUR
relative .... CAYMAN, CAIMAN, ALLIGATOR
Malaysia ...... MUGGAR, MUGGER, MUGGUR
Philippine .... BUAYA
River .... LIMPOPO
teeth picker .. TROCHILUS
crocus .... IRIS
bulb .... CORM
color .... SAFFRON
croft .... FARM
cromlech .... DOLMEN, TOMB, MONUMENT, MEGALITH
Cromwell (Oliver), army of .. IRONSIDES
soubriquet ... IRONSIDES
title ... LORD PROTECTOR
victory site ..... NASEBY
crone ...... HAG, BELDAM(E), CARLINE, ANILE, WITCH
Cronus ...... TITAN, SATURN
parent .... URANUS, GAEA
sister of .... TETHYS
son of .... ZEUS
crony .... PAL, CHUM
Cronyn, actor .... HUME
crook ... BEND, HOOK, CURVE
bishop's .... CROSIER

branch's .... KNEE
colloquial ...... THIEF, SWINDLER, CHEAT(ER)
in tree branch .... KNEE
crooked ...... AGEE, CURVED, ASKEW, DISHONEST, TIPSY, AWRY, BENT, TORTUOUS
slang .... COCKEYED
crop .. GIZZARD, CRAW, MAW, CLIP, PRODUCE
animal feed ..... FODDER
riding .... WHIP
up again .... RECUR
cropper .. FAILURE, SHEARER, FARMER
croquet .... ROQUE
handicap .... BISQUE
kind of .... ROQUE
wicket .... ARCH
croquette .... CUTLET
Crosby, ____ .... BING, BOB, GARY
crooner's soubriquet .... (THE) GROANER
crosier .... STAFF, CROOK, PASTORAL
cross .... ROOD, TESTY, EDGY, SURLY, INTERSECT, CRANKY, SPAN, FRACTIOUS, LIVERIZE, HYBRIDIZE, CRUCIFIX
bar .... RUNG
bearer .... CRUCIFER
breed .... HYBRIDIZE
by wading .... FORD
carrier .... CRUCIFER
church .... ROOD
country runner .... HARRIER
country skiing .... LANGLAUF
current ...... RIP(TIDE)
cut .... SAWN
decoration ... VICTORIA, IRON
Egyptian .... ANKH
examination, of .... ELENCTIC
examine .. INTERROGATE, GRILL
eye(d) ..... STRABISMUS, SQUINT, STRABISMAL
fertilization .. XENOGAMY
horizontal beam .... TRANSOM
in heraldry .... CRUX
off .... CANCEL
out ... DELE(TE), CANCEL
question ...... EXAMINE
river .... FORD
shaped .... CRUCIAL, CRUCIFORM
Southern .... CRUX
stroke .... SERIF
crossbar .... RUNG
crossbeam .... TRAVE, TREVE, TRANSOM
crossbill genus .... LOXIA
crossbow .... ARBALEST
missile .. BOLT, QUARREL
crossbreed .... HYBRID, MONGREL
crossed .. THWARTED, OPPOSED FRUSTRATED
star .. ILLFATED, TRAGIC
crossette .... ANCON
crosspiece ...... RUNG, SPAR, CLEAT, TRANSOM, LINTEL, SILL
crossruff in whist ..... SEESAW
crossthreads .... WOOF
crosswise .... TRANSVERSE
crotchet ..... HOOK, CAPRICE
half of a .... QUAVER
crotchety person ..... CRANK, CURMUDGEON, GROUCH
croton bug ...... COCKROACH
crouch .... BOW, CRINGE, COWER, STOOP
crouching position .... SQUAT
croup .... CATARRH, ANGINA, CRUPPER
horse's .... RUMP
crouse .... BOLD, PERT
crouton .... SIPPET
crow .... CRAKE, (JACK)DAW, CAW, BOAST, EXULT, BRAG, ROOK, CHOUGH, NUTCRACKER
constellation .... CORVUS
cry .... CAW
eat .... RECANT
hooded ...... GRAYBACK
Indian .... SIOUX
kin .... JAY
like a .... CORVINE
like bird .. ORIOLE, ROOK, RAVEN
of .... CORVINE
crow's-nest .... LOOKOUT
crowbar .. PRY, LEVER, JIMMY, JEMMY
crowd ...... HORDE, CLIQUE, PRESS, JAM, FLOCK, CRAM, THRONG, MOB, SHOVE, DROVE, CONCOURSE, SWARM, GATHERING
busy .... HIVE
close together .. HUDDLE, HERD
every which way ... MILL
fancier ..... ACTOR, DIP
moving .... SWARM
crower ...... COCK, ROOSTER, BABY, BOASTER
crowfoot flower ...... PEONY
crown .... DIADEM, TREE TOP, CREST
bottle .... CAP
cock's .... COMB
Egyptian .... ATEF
head's .... POLL
in botany ...... CORONA
in zoology ...... CREST
jewel .... TIARA
prince .... HEIR (APPARENT), DAUPHIN
Prince, English .... CHARLES
Prince, Japanese .... AKIHITO
slang .... CONK
small .... CORONET
crowtoe .... BUTTERCUP
crucial .... SEVERE, DECISIVE, CRITICAL
point ...... CRUX, CRISIS
crucible ...... CRUSET, TEST, TRIAL, FIREPOT, MELTING POT
crucifix .... CROSS, ROOD
crucifixion, place of Jesus' ... CALVARY
crude ... ROUGH, RAW, BARE, COARSE, UNREFINED, AGRESTIC, UNCOUTH, LOWBRED
metal .... ORE
Scottish .... RANDY
sugar .... MELADA, PANOCHA
cruel ...... BRUTAL, PITILESS, HEARTLESS, MEAN, BESTIAL, SAVAGE, HARSH
ruler ... DESPOT, TYRANT
cruet .... VIAL, CASTER, AMPULLA, CASTOR
cruller .. DOUGHNUT, DONUT, (FRIED)CAKE
crumb .. BIT, SCRAP, PARTICLE, ORT
ore .... SPALL
crumble ...... DISINTEGRATE, DECAY, MO(U)LDER
easy to .... FRIABLE
crummy ..... LOW, INFERIOR, SHABBY
crumple .... CRUSH, WRINKLE, RUCK, COLLAPSE, BUCKLE
crunch .... CHEW, CHAMP, MUNCH
cruor .... BLOOD, GORE
crus .... SHANK
crusade .... CAMPAIGN, MOVEMENT, MISSION
Moslem .. JIHAD, JEHAD
crusader .... REFORMER, TEMPLAR, PILGRIM, TANCRED
crusaders' foe ..... SALADIN, SARACENS
leader .... TANCRED
objective ..... REFORM(S)
port .... ACRE
crush ... GRIND, BRAY, MASH, SUBDUE, SUPPRESS, PRESS, QUASH, BRUISE, JAM, (OVER)WHELM, TRITURATE, SQUASH, SQUEEZE
colloquial .... INFATUATION, LOVE
to softness .... MASH
underfoot .... TRAMPLE
with mortar, pestle ..... BRUISE
with teeth .... CHEW
crushed sugarcane refuse ..... BAGASSE, MEGASS(E)
crust .... SCAB, BREAD, LOAF, RIND
fruit-filled ... DUMPLING
metal .... PATINA
slang .... AUDACITY, INSOLENCE
crustacean .. LOBSTER, CRAB, SHRIMP, LIMULUS, PRAWN, COPEPOD, ISOPOD, PAGURID, SCHIZOPOD, PAGURIAN
burrowing ..... SQUILLA, MANTIS CRAB

claw .... CHELA
covering .... SHELL
eggs .... ROE, CORAL
feeler .... ANTENNA
horny substance .. CHITIN
limb of .... PLEOPOD
parasitic ...... CIRRIPED, BARNACLE
segment .... SOMITE, TELSON
skin secretion .... CHITIN
spawn ...... ROE, CORAL
10-legged ...... PRAWN, MACRURAN, LOBSTER, SHRIMP, DECAPOD
walking and swimming ... AMPHIPOD, SANDFLEA, SHRIMP
crusty .... HARSH, SURLY, ILL-TEMPERED
spot .... SCAB
crutch ...... PROP, SUPPORT
crux .... PUZZLE, CROSS
ansata .... ANKH
cry .... SHOUT, SOB, BEG, EXCLAIM, ENTREATY, CLAMOR, WEEP, PULE, YELP, WAIL
animal's .... BRAY
Australian .... COOEE, COOEY
baby .... MEWL
companion of ..... HUE
harsh, loud .... SQUAWK
high-pitched/shrill .... SQUEAL, SQUALL
hunter's ...... TALLYHO
like crazy .... BAWL
mournful ...... YOWL
of Bacchantes .... EVOE
of calf .... BLEAT
of child ... MEWL, PULE, WHIMPER
of disapproval ..... BOO, HISS, CATCALL, HOOT
of goat .... BLEAT
of pain .... OUCH
of surrender, 1918 ...... KAMERAD
out ..... ULULATE, YELL, EXCLAIM
party ...... SHIBBOLETH, WATCHWORD, SLOGAN
to the hounds ... YOICKS
crybaby .... POOR LOSER, POOR SPORT
crypt .... VAULT
cryptic ..... SECRET, OCCULT, OBSCURE, ENIGMATIC
cryptogram .... CODE, CIPHER
crystal .... CLEAR, GLASS, HEMITROPE
clear .... LUCID
gazer .... SEER
crystalline .... PELLUCID
alcohol .... CALCIFEROL
alkaloid ...... ATROPINE, AMARINE
and granular .... SACCHAROID
biblical ...... BDELLIUM
compound ... BORAZON, SERINE, CATECHOL, CELESTINE
lined stone ...... GEODE
moisture .... DEW
resin .... CANNABIN
salt .... BORAX
substance ... CARBAZOLE, UREA
crystallite .... JELL, SOLIDIFY, (TAKE)FORM
crystallize .... JELL
crystallized sugar/syrup ..... CANDY
ctenophores .... NUDA
cub ...... NOVICE, BEGINNER, LIONET
kind of ...... REPORTER
Scout group .... DEN
Cuba, U.S. base in .... GUANTANAMO
cubage .... VOLUME
Cuban .... HABANERO
bearded one .... (FIDEL) CASTRO
capital .... HAVANA
castle .... MORRO
chess champ .... CAPABLANCA
cigar .... HAVANA
city .. MARIANO, HOLGUIN, CAMAGUEY
dance .... R(H)UMBA, HABANERA
dictator .... BATISTA, CASTRO
discoverer ... COLUMBUS
drum .... BONGO
food fish .... PINTADO
measure .... TAREA
monetary unit ..... PESO
music .... MAMBO
palm leaf .... CHIP
premier .... CASTRO
president .... DORTICOS, MACHADO
province .... ORIENTE
rum .... BACARDI
seaport .... MANZANILLO, MATANZAS
secret police ...... PORRA
snake .... JUBA
tempest ...... BAYAMO
tobacco .... VUELTA
cubbyhole of a sort .... DEN
cube .... DIE, DICE
cubeb ...... BERRY, CIGARETTE
cubic capacity, ship's ...... TONNAGE
content ...... CUBATURE, VOLUME
decimeter .. LITER, LITRE
foot per second ... CUSEC
meter .... STERE
cubicle .. DEN, BEDROOM, CELL, COMPARTMENT
cuckoo .... ANI, BIRD, GOWK, KOEL, TOURACO
of the ..... CUCULIFORM
slang ..... CRAZY, SILLY, FOOLISH
cuckoopint .... ARUM
cucullate .. COWLED, HOODED
cucumber .... GHERKIN, PEPO, GOURD, PICKLE
cool as a .. CALM, POISED, COMPOSED
pickled .... MANGO
relish .... PICKLES
Spanish .... PEPINO
cucurbit ...... GOURD, FLASK
cucurbitaceous herb .. GOURD, SQUASH, MELON, CUCUMBER
cud .... RUMEN, CHEW
chew the .... RUMINATE, PONDER
chewer's stomach .... PAUNCH, RUMEN
chewing animal ... COW, RUMINANT, CATTLE, BUFFALO, BISON, DEER, CAMEL, GOAT, LLAMA, GIRAFFE, CARABAO
variant of .... QUID
cudbear .... DYE, LICHEN
cuddle .... HUG, CARESS, EMBRACE, SNUGGLE, NESTLE, CURL UP
cuddy .... CUPBOARD, CLOSET
Scottish ...... DONKEY, COALFISH
cudgel .... CLUB, SHILLALAH, DRUB, STICK, TRUNCHEON, BASTINADO, BAT
one's brains ...... RACK
cudgels, take up the .. DEFEND
cue .. HINT, SIGNAL, ROD, TIP, TAIL
actor's ..... CATCHWORD
bridge of .... JIGGER
in music .... PRESA
of hair .. PIGTAIL, QUEUE, BRAID
substitute, billiards ..... MACE
cuff ... BOX, SLAP, BIFF, BELT, CLOUT, WRISTBAND
Cugat, bandleader ... XAVIER
cuirass .. BREASTPLATE, MAIL, LORIC(A), ARMOR, CORSELET, LORLEA
cuisine .... KITCHEN
of the .... CULINARY
cuisinier .... CHEF, COOK
cul-de-sac ...... BLIND ALLEY
Culbertson, card expert .. ELY
culex pipiens ..... MOSQUITO
cull ...... SELECT, PICK OUT, GLEAN
cullis .... GUTTER
cully .... DUPE
British: sl. .. PAL, BUDDY
culm ... COAL, DUST, HA(U)LM
culminating point .. HIGH TIDE, CRISIS
culmination ... ACME, CLIMAX
sun's ..... NOON, ZENITH
culpa .... FAULT, GUILT
culpability .... GUILT
culprit .. OFFENDER, CRIMINAL
cult .... SECT, FAD, ISM
artistic .... DADA
naked .... NUDISM
cultivate .. GROW, FARM, TILL, FOSTER, DEVELOP, NURSE
cultivated .. REFINED, TILLED, CULTURED, HIGHBROW
land ...... ARADA, FARM
plot .... GARDEN
cultivation of soil ... CULTURE, TILTH

cultivator .... TILLER
cultural studies .... ARTS
culture .. CIVILIZATION, ARTS, REFINEMENT, POLISH
  medium .... AGAR
cultured person .... LADY, GENTLEMAN, SCHOLAR
culver .... DOVE, PIGEON
culvert .. WATERWAY, DRAIN
  opening .... INLET
cum .... WITH
cumber .... HINDER, HAMPER, BURDEN, LOAD
cumbersome .. HEAVY, CLUMSY
cumin .... ANISE
cummer .... GODMOTHER
cummerbund .... SASH
cumshaw .... GRATUITY, TIP
cunner .... GILTHEAD
cunning .. CLEVER, SLY, WILY, ARTFUL, CRAFT(Y), FOXY, GUILE
  as a fox .... VULPINE
cuon .... DHOLE
cup .. BOWL, CHALICE, CALIX, CANNIKIN, BEAKER
  assaying .... CUPEL, TEST
  ceremonial .... AMA
  drinking .. MUG, GOBLET, TASS, TANKARD, NOGGIN, CRUSE, STOUP, CYLIX, RUMMER, TAZZA
  druggist's .... BEAKER
  flower .... CALYX
  gem-cutting .... DOP
  holder .... ZARF
  knight's quest .... GRAIL
  like .... CALICULAR
  like spoon .... LADLE
  like vessel .. CUPEL, TEST
  metal .... PANNIKIN
  of tea: Brit. colloq. .... HOBBY, AVOCATION
  sports championship .... DAVIS, RYDER, WIGHTMAN, AMERICA'S
  to measure liquid .... JIGGER
  wine .... BEAKER
cupbearer of the gods .. HEBE, GANYMEDE
cupboard .. ARMOIRE, CUDDY, AMBRY, CLOSET, CABINET
Cupid .... EROS, AMOR
  infant .... AMORETTO, AMORINO
  mother of .... VENUS
  sweetheart of .... PSYCHE
  title of .... DAN
cupidity .... AVARICE, GREED
cupola .... DOME
  battleship's .... TURRET
cuprous oxide .... CHALCOCITE
cuprum .... COPPER
cur .... MONGREL, TIKE, TYKE, MUTT
curable .... MEDICABLE
curacao, orange-flavored .... COINTREAU
curare .... POISON, URARI, OURALI, WOURALI, WOORALI, URALI
curate .. CLERGYMAN, PRIEST
curative .... THERAPEUTIC, SANATIVE, SANATORY, HEALING, REMEDIAL
curator .... GUARDIAN
  concern of .... ARCHIVES, MUSEUM, LIBRARY, RELICS
curb .. CHECK, REIN, RESTRAIN, MARKET
  colloquial .... LID
  for woman's tongue .... BRANKS
  market item .... STOCK, BOND
curbing inward .... ADUNC
curch .... KERCHIEF
curculio .... BEETLE
curcuma .. TURMERIC, GINGER
curd .... CASEIN
  soybean .... TAHO, TOFU, TOKUA
curdle .... COAGULATE, CLABBER, CONGEAL
curdled milk .... CLABBER
curdling material .... RENNET, RENNIN
curds with cream .... JUNKET
cure .... HEAL, REMEDY, THERAPY, PRESERVE
  all .... ELIXIR, PANACEA, CATHOLICON, NOSTRUM
  by salting .... CORN
  French .... PRIEST
  kind of .... REST, WATER
curfew feature .. LIGHTS OUT
  man .... TOWN(CRIER)
curia official, Catholic .... DATARY
curio(s) .... BIBELOT, VIRTU
  collector .... VIRTUOSO
curiosa .... NOVELTIES
curious .... ODD, PRYING, INQUISITIVE, NOS(E)Y
  one .. PRY, SNOOP(ER), BUSYBODY, CAT
curl .. COIL, RINGLET, FRIZ(ZLE)
  hair .... MARCEL
  snugly .... ENSCONCE, CUDDLE
  the lip .... SNEER
curled .... CRISPATE, SPIRY, CRIMPED
  lip .... SNEER
curlew .... SNIPE, WHAUP, GODWIT
  bird resembling .... WHIMBREL
"Curlew River" character .... FERRYMAN
curlicue .... FLOURISH, CURVE
curling iron .... CRISPER
  mark/target .... TEE
  match .... BONSPIEL
  place .... RINK
curlpaper .... PAPILLOTE
curly .... KINKY, WAVY
curmudgeon .... CRAB
curn .... GRAIN, FEW
curr .... MURMUR, COO
currach .... CORACLE
currant .... GRAPE, BERRY, SHRUB, RISSEL
  syrup .... CASSIS
currency .... CIRCULATION, PREVALENCE, MONEY, CASH
  value of .... VALUTA
current .... GOING(ON), TIDE, IN VOGUE, STREAM
  air .... DRAFT
  beneath surf .... UNDERTOW
  combining form .. RHEO
  expenses .... OVERHEAD
  opposite .... SETBACK
currently .. NOW, PRESENTLY, AT PRESENT
currier .... COMBER
Currier and Ives .... PRINTS
curry .... STEW, BEAT, COMB, DRESS, FLOG, DRUB
  favor .... FAWN, FLATTER
  ingredient .... CUMIN
curse .... DAMN, ANATHEMA, BAN, OATH, REVILE, IMPRECATION, EXECRATE, SWEAR, BANE, SWEARWORD, MARANATHA, MALISON, MALEDICTION
  Archaic .... WANION, MALISON
  colloquial .... CUSS
cursed .. EVIL, WICKED, ODIOUS
curser, Biblical .... BALAAM
cursillo founder .... HERVAS
cursive .... RUNNING
cursory .... RANDOM, CASUAL, SUPERFICIAL
  look .. GLANCE, GLIMPSE
curt .... BLUFF, BRIEF, TERSE, BLUNT, SHORT, BRUSQUE
  dismissal .... CONGE
curtail .... REDUCE, SHORTEN
curtain .... DRAPE, SCREEN, COVER, VALANCE, VEILING
  behind stage .. BACKDROP
  Cold War .... IRON, BAMBOO
  color .... ECRU
  holder .... ROD
  material .. GAUZE, SCRIM, NINON, TAPIS, LENO, GRENADINE
  of gun fire .... BARRAGE
  raiser .... SKIT, PRELIMINARY
  rod band .... CORNICE
  sash .... TIEBACK
  shade .... ECRU
  woman's apartment .... PURDAH
curtains: sl. .... END, DEATH
curtsy .. SALUTATION, SALUTE, BOB, LOUT
curvature .... ARC(H)
curve .... ARC, BEND, OGEE, ARCH, SINUS, FLEXURE, HYPERBOLA
  baseball pitch .... HOOK
  double .... ESS
  handwriting .. CURLICUE, FLOURISH
  inward .... INFLECT
  mark over vowel .. BREVE
  of a column .... ENTASIS
  of river .... BEND
  path of missile .... TRAJECTORY

pitcher's .... HOOK
plane .... PARABOLA
S-shaped .... OGEE
curved ... ARCUATE, ARCHED, BENT, ADUNC, FALCATE, FALCIFORM
in .... CONCAVE
molding .... OGEE
out .... CONVEX
plank, ship's ...... SNY
surface of arch .... EXTRADOS
sword .... SCIMITAR
curves, having two ... BIFLEX
curvet .... LEAP, FROLIC, GAMBOL, VAULT
curving inward ...... ADUNC
cushat ...... (WOOD)PIGEON, (RING)DOVE
cushaw .... SQUASH
cushion .. PILLOW, PAD, MAT, ABSORB, HASSOCK, BOLSTER, SQUAB
Cush's father .... HAM
son .... NIMROD
cushy: sl. .... EASY
cusk .... BURBOT
relative .... COD
cusp of moon .... HORN
cuspid .... TOOTH, FANG
cuspidor .... SPITTOON
cussed: colloq. .... STUBBORN, SWORE
custard .... PIE
apple .... PA(W)PAW
cake .... ECLAIR
dish .... FLAN
like dish .... TIMBALE
Custer's battle site .... LITTLE BIG HORN
nemesis .. SITTING BULL
custodian .... CARETAKER, CONCIERGE, KEEPER, CUSTOS, GUARDIAN, JANITOR, WARDEN, WARDER
museum ...... CURATOR
of funds .... TREASURER
of minors ... GUARDIAN
custody ...... CHARGE, CARE, GUARDIANSHIP, TRUST, WARDSHIP
take into .... ARREST, DETAIN, HOLD
custom ...... HABIT, USAGE, WONT, PRACTICE, PRAXIS
built ... MADE-TO-ORDER
with force of law .... MORES, MOS
customary .. WONTED, USUAL, HABITUAL, RULE
extras .... ETCETERAS
requirement .. FORMALITY
usage .... MODE
customer .... PATRON, BUYER, USER
credit record .. PASSBOOK
present to a .... LAGN(I)APPE
customers .. TRADE, CLIENTELE
customs .... MORES
charge .... IMPOST, DUTY
collector: biblical .... MATTHEW

municipal ...... OCTROI
official ...... SURVEYOR
cut .. SHEAR, LOP, SEVER, SAW, SNIP, NIP, KERF, DOCK, TRENCH, HEW
across .... TRANSECT, INTERSECT
beef .... CHUCK
blubber .... FLENSE
and dried .... DULL, BORING, ROUTINE
close .. SHAVE, CROP, CLIP
colloquial .... SNUB, IGNORE
companion of .... DRIED
crop .... REAP
crudely .... HACKLE, HAGGLE
dead: colloq. ..... SNUB, COLD SHOULDER, REBUFF
deep .... GASH
down ...... FELL, MOW
down trees .... LUMBER
edge of coin .... NIG
ends .. SHEAR, TRIM, LOP
expenses .... ECONOMIZE, RETRENCH
glass .... CRYSTAL
grass .... MOW
hair .... BARBER
horse's tail .... DOCK
in .... INTERRUPT
in cubes .... DICE
in half ... BISECT, HALVE
into ...... INCISE, LANCE
into small pieces .... MINCE, DICE, HASH
leather .... SKIVE
lengthwise .... SLIT
meat .... CARVE
neck .... BEHEAD, DECAPITATE
notch ..... NICK, SNICK
of ax .... KERF
of meat ...... SPARERIB, SIRLOIN, CHINE, LOIN, T-BONE, CHOP, CHUCK, STEAK
off .... BOB, DOCK, CLIP, POLL, KERF, LOP, ROACH, INTERCEPT, INTERRUPT
off head .... DECAPITATE
off piece/slice ... CANTLE
off wool ... SHEAR, POLL
out ...... EXCISE, ELIDE, EXCIDE, EXSCIND, EXSECT
out disk .... TREPAN
rind .... PARE, PEEL
roast .... CARVE
roughly .. HACKLE, HACK
saw-toothed edge .. PINK
short .. BOB, CROP, STOP, POLL, CLIP
skin .... PARE, PEEL
slang .... SHARE
slight ..... NICK, SNICK
spiral grooves .... RIFLE
thin ...... SLICE, SLIVER, SKIVE

thru water .... PLOUGH, PLOW
to pieces .. SHRED, MINCE
to requirement .. TAILOR
V-shaped .... NOTCH
way thru .... PLOW
with axe ... HACK, HEW, CHOP
with scissors ...... SNIP
with sweeping stroke .... SLASH
cutaneous .... DERMAL
cutch .... CATECHU
cute .... CLEVER, SHARP, SHREWD, PRETTY
cuticle ....EPIDERMIS, SKIN
cutis .... DERMA, DERMIS, CORIUM
cutlass ...... (BROAD)SWORD, CURTLE AX
cutlery item .. KNIFE, SPOON, FORK
cutlet, veal .... SCHNITZEL
cutout pattern ...... STENCIL
cutpurse .. THIEF, PICKPOCKET
cutter .. VESSEL, SLED, YACHT, SLEIGH, SLOOP
leaf .... ANT
of life's thread .. ATROPOS
of precious stones ...... LAPIDARY
cutthroat .... ASSASSIN, THUG, MURDERER
cutting .... TART, EDGED, SHARP, INCISIVE, (S)CION, KERF, TRENCHANT, KEEN
British .... CLIPPING
edge .... LIP
off last letter of word ... APOCOPE
off vowel .... ELISION
part of tool .... BIT
remarks ...... RAP, DIG, INSULT, SARCASM
tool .... AX(E), BOLO, MACHETE, ADZ(E), RAZOR, KNIFE, BUR, SHEARS, MOWER, SCISSORS, SICKLE, SCYTHE, SAW
tool, engraver's .. BURIN, GRAVER, CHISEL, CHASER
tool holder ...... ARBOR
tool seller .... CUTLER
tools .... CUTLERY
tooth .... INCISOR
cuttlefish ...... SEPIA, SQUID, BELEMNITE
bone .... POUNCE
ejecting organ .. SIPHON
fluid/secretion ...... INK
fossil .... THUNDERSTONE, BELEMNITE
kin .... SPIRULA
cutup .... PRANKSTER, CLOWN
Cuzco Indian .... INCA
location of .... PERU
Cy Young awardee .. MCLAIN, GIBSON, SEAVER
cyanic .... BLUE
cyanotype .... BLUEPRINT

Cybele .... RHEA
beloved of .... ATTIS
Cyclades ... IOS, MILO, NAXOS, PAROS, TINOS, DELOS, ZEA, KEOS, MELOS
cycle .... AGE, SAROS
of 15 years ... INDICTION
of heavenly body .. ORBIT
of years .... EPOCH, EON
cycloid .... CIRCULAR
cyclone .... TORNADO, HURRICANE, WINDSTORM, TWISTER
Cyclops .... GIANT
Odysseus' captor .... POLYPHEMUS
cyclostome .... LAMPREY, HAGFISH
cyesis .... GESTATION, PREGNANCY
cygnet .... SWAN
Cygnus .... SWAN, CONSTELLATION
star in .... DENEB
cylinder ..... TUBE, BARREL
covering .... LAG(GING)
in a cylinder ..... PISTON
part .... PISTON
spiral .... HELIX
water marker .... DANDY ROLL(ER)
cylindrical .. TOROSE, TOROUS, TERETE
cyma ...... MOLDING, GOLA
cymar .... CHEMISE
cymbals .... TAL, ZEL
cyme .... PHLOX
Cymric ..... WELSH, BRETON, CELTIC
cynic, look of ... LEER, SNEER, COLD
of sorts .... SKEPTIC
cynosure .... POLESTAR, LODESTAR, NORTH STAR
Cynthia .... LUNA, MOON, ARTEMIS, DIANA
diminutive of .... CINDY
cypress .. TREE, CLOTH, SATIN, SILK
cyprinoid ... CARP, GOLDFISH, BARBEL, IDE, DACE, CHUB
Cyprus, capital of .. NICOSIA, LIMASSOL
city ... SALAMIS, PAPHOS, FAMUGUSTA
leader .... MAKARIOS
union with Greece ...... ENOSIS
Cyrano's shame .... NOSE
Cyrenaica .... BARCA
capital .... CYRENE
Cytherea .. VENUS, APHRODITE
cyst .. SAC, WEN, POUCH, BAG, VESICLE
with worm larvae .... HYDATID
czar .... TSAR, EMPEROR, DESPOT, NICHOLAS
daughter of .. CZAREVNA, TSAREVNA
heir of ..... CZAREVITCH
wife of .... CZARINA, TSARINA, CZARITZA
Czechoslovakian .... SLOVAK, BOHEMIAN, MORAVIAN, SLAV, SILESIAN
brandy ...... SLIVOVITZ
capital .. PRAGUE (PRAHA)
castle .... HRADCANY
city ...... BRNO, PILSEN, BUDWEIS, BRUNN, BRATISLAVA, OSTRAVA, KOSICE, OLOMOUC
coin .. DUCAT, KRONEN, HELLER, KORUNA
composer .... (RUDOLF) FRIML, SMETANA, JANACEK
folk hero ..... SCHWEIK
hero .... (JAN)HUS
historian ...... PALACKY
leader .. DUBCHEK, HUSAK
monetary unit .. KORUNA
munition works .. SKODA
news agency .... CETEKA
patriot ...... MASARYK, STEFANIK
premier .... LENART, CERNI(C)K
president .... NOVOTNY, BENES, MASARYK, GOTTWALD, SVOBODA
public square .... WENCESLAS
rail center ...... ZILINA
region .. CECHY, BOHEMIA
river .. ISER, IPOLY, OHRE, MOLDAU, VLTAVA, MORAVA, EGER
steel works .... SKODA
town .. CARLSBAD, LIDICE

D

D, Greek .... DELTA
Hebrew ..... DALETH, DALEDH
letter .... DEE, DELTA
dab .... PECK, PAT, TAP, FLATFISH, FLOUNDER, TOUCH, STRIKE, PAINT
colloquial ...... EXPERT
dabble .... DIP, WET
in .... SMATTER
dabbler ...... DILETTANTE, AMATEUR, TYRO, DUFFER
dabchick .... GREBE, DUCKER, DIDAPPER, DIPPER, HELL-DIVER
dabster ..... EXPERT, DABBLER
dace .... CARP
dachshund .... DOG
dacoit ...... ROBBER, BANDIT
dacron .... FIBER
dactyl, in zoology ... FINGER, TOE
dactylogram .... FINGERPRINT
dad .... FATHER
daddy ..... FATHER, DAD, POP, PAPPY
longlegs .... CRANE, FLY, SPINNER, HARVESTMAN
dado .... DIE, WAINSCOT, SOLIDUM
daedal .... INGENIOUS, INTRICATE, ELABORATE, VARIED
Daedalus' son .... ICARUS
victim/nephew .. TALOS
daemon .... DEVIL
daffodil .... NARCISSUS
plant resembling .... JONQUIL
Daffy, baseball player .. DEAN
colloquial ...... CRAZY, SILLY, IDIOTIC, FOOLISH
daft .... SILLY, FOOLISH, INSANE, IDIOTIC
dagger ...... DIRK, BODKIN, PONIARD, SNEE, STILETTO, CREESE, SKEAN
attached to gun .... BAYONET
Burmese .... DAH
double .... DIESIS
handle .... HILT, HAFT
hilt .... DUDGEON
mark, in printing .... DIESIS, OBELUS
Malay ..... KRIS, CRIS(S)
medieval .... ANLACE
of mercy .. MISERICORD(E)
signs in printing ... OBELI
stroke ..... LUNGE, STAB, THRUST, STOCCADO
two-edged ..... COUTEAU
wound .... STAB
Dahomey capital .... PORTO NOVO
chief of state ..... SOGLO
city .... COTONOU
ethnic group ...... FON, ADJA, BORIBA, MAHI, YORUBA
native .... FON
seaport ...... WHIDAH
Dai Nippon .... JAPAN
daily .... NEWSPAPER, DIURNAL, EVERYDAY, QUOTIDIAN, PER DIEM
delivery ...... MAIL, MILK
dozen ...... EXERCISES, CONSTITUTIONAL
fare .... DIET
feature article ... COLUMN
newspaper ..... JOURNAL
record .... DIARY, JOURNAL
daimio .... NOBLEMAN
retainer of ..... SAMURAI
dainties .. DELICACIES, TIDBITS
dainty .... FINE, NICE, FASTIDIOUS, DELICATE,

MIGNON, CHOICE, TAFFETA
archaic .... CATE
daiquiri .... COCKTAIL
ingredient .... RUM, LIME
Dairen .... TALIEN, DALNY
dairy .... LACTARY, LACTARIUM
cattle .... JERSEY
farm area MILKSHED
maid ...... DEY, GOWAN
product .... BUTTER, CHEESE, MILK
shop .... CREAMERY
dais ...... PODIUM, PLATFORM, ROSTRUM, STAGE, ESTRADE, TRIBUNE
daisy .... OXEYE, SHASTA, CHRYSANTHEMUM, GOWAN, MARGUERITE
cutter, baseball .... GROUNDER
English .... GOWAN
dak .... MAIL
Dakar, capital of ... SENEGAL
Daker hen ..... CORN CRAKE
Dakota Indian .... SIOUX, REE
dale .... DELL, DINGLE, GLEN, VALE, VALLEY
Dali, painter ..... SURREALIST, SALVADOR
dalles .... RAPIDS
dalliance .... FLIRTATION
dally ...... LOITER, TRIFLE, FLIRT, TOY
Dalmatian ...... DOG, SLAV
decor .... SPOTS
dog's name .... SPOT
dam ..... BARRAGE, BARRIER, MILLPOND, KEEP BACK, STEM, DIKE
archaic .... MOTHER
builder, animal ... OTTER
designer .... SAVAGE
Egyptian .... ASWAN, SADD
horse .... MARE
in the U.S. ..... HOOVER, SHASTA, BOULDER, COULEE
river .... WEIR
damage ...... LOSS, INJURE, INJURY, HARM
colloquial .... COST, EXPENSE
slang .... BUNG
suit .... TROVER
damages, claim for ... TROVER
daman .... HYRAX, CONY, CONEY, MAMMAL
Damansky to the Chinese ..... CHEN PAO
Damascene .... PLUM
Damascus caliph .... OMMIAD
is capital of ..... SYRIA
damask .... ROSE, LINEN, STEEL
for hangings ... DORNICK
for vestments, etc. .... DORNICK, DORNOCK
like cloth ...... LAMPAS
dame .... LADY, MATRON
equivalent title of .... SIR

slang .... GIRL, WOMAN, GAL
dammar .... RESIN
damn ...... CONDEMN, CURSE, DOOM
damnation .... PERDITION
damned .... OUTRAGEOUS
dialectic .... TARNATION, TARNAL
Damocles, word associated with SWORD
damoiselle ..... DAMSEL, MISS
Damon and ____ .... PYTHIAS
damp .... HUMID, DANK, MOIST, WET(NESS)
become .... JIG
dampen .... DEPRESS, WET, DISHEARTEN, MOISTEN
damsel .... GIRL, MAIDEN
fly .... DRAGONFLY
damson .... PLUM
Dan ...... MASTER, SIR, BUOY
Cupid .... EROS
Dane .... JUTLANDER
dance .... BALL, CLOG, CAPER, BALLET, JIG, POLKA, HOOF, GALOP, TRIPPING
attendance ..... WAIT ON
Bohemian ..... REDOWA
child on knee ... DANDLE
college ...... HOP, PROM
colloquial ...... SHINDIG, DRAG
country ..... REEL, BARN, ALTHEA, LANDLER, HAY
crazed person .... TARANTIST
Cuban .... R(H)UMBA, CONGA, HABANERA
English .... MORRIS
folk .... DREHER, HORA
for two .... TANGO, WALTZ, FOXTROT
French .... BAL, MINUET, FARANDOLA, RIGADOON, GAVOT, GALLIARD
hall ......CABARET, GAFF, CASINO
hall girl .... HOSTESS
Hawaiian .. HULA (HULA)
Hungarian ..... CZARDAS
Israeli .... HORA
Italian .... COURANTE
kind of .... FOXTROT, TOE, WALTZ, BALLET, TAP, BELLY
lively ...... REEL, JUBA, FANDANGO, GALOP, COURANTE, CONGA, GALLOPADE, COTILLION, HORNPIPE, TAMBOURIN, CORANTO, FLING, SALTARELLO
made to castanets ...... BOLERO, FLAMENCO
modern .... SHAG, FRUG, ROCK N'ROLL
music .... VALSE, WALTZ, FOXTROT, TANGO, RAGTIME
Negro .... JUBA
of death .... DANSE MACABRE

of 1930 .... SHAG
of 1929 .... CHARLESTON
old .... PAVAN(E), PAVIN, CAROLE
on knee .... DANDLE
Polish .... POLONAISE
polka like .. MAZ(O)URKA
sailor's ...... HORNPIPE
school .... PROM, HOP
Scottish .... REEL
slang .... HOOF
slow, graceful ... ADAGIO, MINUET
South American .... TANGO, CARIOCA
Southwest ...... BAILE
Spanish ..... FANDANGO, FLAMENCO, BOLERO, TANGO
square ...... DOSADOS, LANC(I)ERS, HOEDOWN
stately .... MINUET, SARABAND
step .... CURTSY, PAS, GLISSADE, CHASSE, SHAG
triple time .... JIG
two-fourth time ... GALOP
Virginia .... REEL
war .... PYRRHIC
watcher ... WALLFLOWER
white-tie .... FORMAL
with castanets .... FLAMENCO, BOLERO
with handclapping .. JUBA
with high kicking .... CANCAN
with wooden shoes ..... CLOG
dancer ...... ALME(H), ALMA, CHORINE, DANSEUSE, ASTAIRE, CASTLE, ZORINA, STEPPER
ballet ...... DANSEUSE, FIGURANT, BALLERINA, CORYPHEE, FONTEYN, SHEARER, PAVLOVA, RASCH, ULANOVA, NUREYEV
co-worker of ..... COMET
concern of .... RHYTHM, CHOREOGRAPHY, STEPS
dress of .... TUTU
jazz music .... JITTERBUG
kind of ...... TOE, BELLY, TAP, BALLET, TANGO, FLAMENCO, APACHE, STRIPTEASE
professional ..... HOOFER
shoe of .... CLOG
swing .... HEPCAT
tap .... HOOFER
wear of ...... LEOTARD, TUTU, TIGHTS
dancing ..... CHOREOGRAPHY, SALTANT, SALTATION
craze for .... TARENTISM, TARANTISM
girl, Egyptian .... ALME(H), ALMA
girl, India .... BAYADERE, BAYADEER, ALME(H)
girl, Japanese .... GEISHA
girls .... CHORINE
horses .... LIPPIZAN

kind of .... TOE, BELLY, TAP
master .... MURRAY, ASTAIRE
muse of .... TERPSICHORE
partner, professional .... GIGOLO
place also .... CASINO
shoes .... PUMPS
dandelion .... WEED, KOK-SAGYZ
stalk .... SCAPE
tuft .... PUFFBALL
dander ...... ANGER, TEMPER, IRE
dandify .... SPRUCE, DRESS UP
dandle .... FONDLE, DANCE, PET, CARESS
dandruff .... FURFUR, SCURF
dandy .... PRIG, COXCOMB, TOFF, NATTY, BUCK, FOP, DUDE, BEAU
fever .... DENGUE
roll impression .... WATER MARK
slang .... FIRST CLASS, FINE, JOHNNY, JOHNNIE
dandyish .... BUCKISH
danger ...... PERIL, HAZARD, JEOPARDY, RISK
hidden .... PITFALL
signal .... RED, ALARM, SIREN
dangerous .... PERILOUS, UNSAFE, CRITICAL, RISKY
dangle .... LOLL, HANG
dangling .... ALOP
Daniel ____ .... BOONE, WEBSTER
Danish .... DANE
astronomer ...... BRAHE
capital .... COPENHAGEN
cheese ..... DANBO, ELBO, FYNBO, TYBO, MOLBO, MARIBO, BRIE, MYCELLA, CAMEMBERT
chieftain .... JARL
coin .... RIGSDALER, KRONE
composer ...... NIELSEN
district .... AMT
duchy .... HOLSTEIN
"farmer prince" .. INGOLF
historian .... SAXO
horse .... ZAIN
island ..... AERO, FAROE, LOLLAND, GREENLAND, ALS, FUNEN, FYN, SEELAND
king ..... CANUTE, CNUT, FREDERIK, WALDEMAR, KNUT
king, Shakespearean .... HAMLET
land measure ... MORGEN
legislature .... RIGSDAG, FOLKETING
monetary unit .... KRONE
native .... DANE
navigator ...... BERING
noble .... JARL
novelist .... NEXO
parliament .... RIGSDAG
peninsula ...... JUTLAND
physicist .... BOHR, OERSTED
pianist .... BORGE
queen .... INGRID
seaport ...... HELSINGOR, AARHUS
toast .... SKOAL
weight .... LOD
dank .... DAMP, MOIST, WET, HUMID
"Danse ____" ...... MACABRE
danseuse .... DANCER, BALLERINA, CORYPHEE, FIGURANT
Dante's beloved ..... BEATRICE
deathplace ..... RAVENNA
work .... INFERNO, DIVINE COMEDY
Danube city ...... LINZ, ULM
in German ...... DONAU
in Hungarian ..... DUNA
in Romanian .. DUNAREA
river .... ULM, SAVA, SAU, MORAVA, ISAR
Danzig .... GDANSK
dap .... DIP, BOUNCE, DIB, SKIP
Daphne ..... NYMPH, LAUREL, SHRUB
Dapnis' lover .... CHLOE
dapper ...... NEAT, SPRUCE, SMART, TRIM, NATTY
dapple .... MOTTLED, SPOTTED, PIEBALD, FLECK(ED), PIED
poetic .... FREAK
Dar es Salaam is capital of .... TANZANIA
darb .... DILLY, DART
Darcy's forte .... PRIDE
Dardan .... TROJAN
Dardanelles ..... HELLESPONT, STRAIT
dare .... RISK, VENTURE, FACE, DEFY, DAST, CHALLENGE, OPPOSE, DEFI
daredevil .... STUNTMAN, RECKLESS, BOLD, FOOLHARDY
Darien ...... GULF, ISTHMUS
daring .... BOLD, INTREPID, BRAVE, RISQUE, HARDY, ICARIAN
action ...... DERRING-DO
Darius scene of defeat .. ISSUS
dark .... EVIL, SINISTER, BLACK, DIM, EBON, HIDDEN, DUSKY, MIRK, RAYLESS, SABLE, TENEBROUS, MURK(Y), TENEBRIFIC
and dull .... SOMBER, SOMBRE
area of vision ... SCOTOMA
brown ...... BRUNET(TE), SEPIA, BISTRE, BISTER
complexion ..... BRUNET, SWARTHY
Continent .... AFRICA
haired .... MELANOUS
horse: colloq. ... SLEEPER, LONG-SHOT
hue ..... SOMBRE, SWART
in the .... IGNORANT, UNAWARE
marking in marble ...... CLOUD
portending rain .... LOWERING
red .... LAKY
skinned ...... MELANOUS, SWARTHY
skinned person ... DAGO, WOP
wood .... EBONY
darkey .... NEGRO
darkness .... NIGHT
combining form .. SCOTO
darling ...... FAVORITE, PET, BELOVED, CHERI(E), MINIKIN
colloquial ...... DEARIE, DEARY, TOOTS
darn .... MEND
colloquial .... DAMN
darnel .... COCKLE, WEED, TARE
darning needle ... DRAGONFLY
dart ...... FLIT, DASH, SCOOT, MISSILE, ARROW, BARB, BOLT, SPURT
darter .... SNAKEBIRD
darts, bullfighter's .... BANDERILLA
Dartmoor ...... GAOL, PRISON
Darwinian theory .... EVOLUTION, PANGENESIS
dash .... SMASH, SPLASH, WRITE, VERVE, BIT, ELAN, ARDOR, DART, SPRINT, THROW
against .... LASH
colloquial .... DAM
mark .... HYPHEN
opposed to .... DOT
dashboard .... PANEL
dasheen ...... SPROUTS, TARO
dasher .... DOLLY
of a churn ..... PLUNGER
dashing ..... SHOWY, SPIRITED
manner .... PANACHE, DEVIL-MAY-CARE
dastard ...... COWARD, CAD, CRAVEN, POLTROON
dastardly .... COWARDLY, MEAN
dasyure .... MARSUPIAL
data .... FACTS, FIGURES
computer's .... INPUT
date .... APPOINTMENT, PERIOD, FRUIT, CALENDS, TRYST, RENDEZVOUS
abbreviation ...... APPT
approximate ...... CIRCA
fruit like .... JUJUBE
go on a .... STEP OUT
plum .... KAKI, PERSIMMON
out of .... PASSE, OLD-FASHIONED
sugar .... GHOOR
tree .... PALM

up to .... MODERN, FASHIONABLE, AS YET, UNTIL NOW
dated .... OLD-FASHIONED, PASSE, DECLASSE
datum plane example .... SEA LEVEL
datura .... JIMSON
daub .... PLASTER, SMEAR, PAINT, GREASE, SLUBBER
daughter .... FILLE, HIJA
daughter(s) of Atlas and Pleione PLEIAD(ES)
daunt .... DISMAY, COW, INTIMIDATE, AWE, FAZE
dauntless .... BRAVE, INTREPID
davenport ...... COUCH, SOFA, DESK
David's (King) captain .. JOAB
commander ..... AMASA, JOAB
daughter .... TAMAR
father .... JESSE
rebuker .... NATHAN
son .... SOLOMON
wife .... BATHSHEBA
Davidoff's subject ..... CIGARS
Davis, actress .... BETTE
Davis, Jr. .... SAMMY
davit .... CRANE
Davy Jones' seabottom ...... LOCKER
daw .... CROW
dawdle .... LOITER, IDLE, LOAF, LINGER, PIDDLE, PUTTER, POTTER
dawn .... DAYBREAK, SUNRISE, AURORA, MORN, SUNUP
goddess of .... EOS
herald of .... COCK, ROOSTER, LARK
pertaining to ...... EOAN
to noon .... MORNING
to sunset ...... DAYTIME
day .... AGE, EPOCH, ERA
and night of equal length .... EQUINOX
bed .... SOFA, COUCH
before .... EVE
every .... DAILY
in court .... HEARING, CHANCE, OPPORTUNITY
Latin .... DIES
letter .... TELEGRAM
march .... ETAPE
of greatest vigor .... HEYDAY
Roman ..... IDES, NONES
scholar .... EXTERN
star .... SUN
daybook .... DIARY, JOURNAL
daybreak .... DAWN, SUNRISE, AURORA, MORN
daydream .... REVERY, REVERIE, FANCY
daydreaming .... AUTISM, REVERIE
dayfly .... MAY FLY
daylight .... DAWN, PUBLICITY
slang .... EYES
dayspring .... DAWN
daytime, pertaining to .... DIURNAL
days, describing youthful ..... SALAD
Dayton suburb .... KETTERING
daze .... STUPEFY, TRANCE, DAZZLE, STUN, BEWILDER(MENT)
dazzle .... BLIND, IMPRESS
dazzling .... BLINDING, PRISMATIC
momentarily .... METEORIC
DDT .... INSECTICIDE, PESTICIDE
de facto .... ACTUAL, IN FACT
jure .... BY RIGHT
luxe .... ELEGANT, SUMPTUOUS
deacon .... CLERGYMAN, ADULTERATE
clergyman above .. PRIEST
deactivate ...... DEMOBILIZE
dead ..... DECEASED, LIFELESS, (A)MORT, INANIMATE, DEPARTED, EXTINCT
animal pretending to be .. POSSUM
beat: colloquial .... TIRED, EXHAUSTED
beat, slang ..... SPONGE, WELSHER, LOAFER
bodies on battlefield .... CARNAGE
body .... CADAVER, CORPSE, CARCASS, CARCASE, CORPUS, STIFF, LICH
calm .... DOLDRUMS
combining form ... SAPRO
end .... IMPASSE
End Kids' member ..... GORCEY
end place .... SLUM, GHETTO
flesh .... CARRION
hand .... MORTMAIN
heat .... TIE
house .... CHARNEL, OSSARIUM, MORTUARY
pan .... POKERFACE
pan comedian .... KEATON
person .... DECEDENT, DECEASED
point .... CENTER
recently .... LATE
Sea find .... SCROLLS
Sea kingdom ...... MOAB
Sea river .... JORDAN
Sea scrolls location ..... QUMRAN
set .... DETERMINED, FIRM
species .... EXTINCT
when delivered .... STILLBORN
word preceding name of .. LATE
deaden .... DULL, NUMB, DAMPEN, OBTUND
sound .... MUFFLE, MUTE
deadener, pain ...... OPIATE, AN(A)ESTHETIC, ANALGESIC, DEMEROL
deadline .... TIME LIMIT
deadlock .... STALEMATE, IMPASSE, STANDSTILL
jury .... HANG
deadly ...... FATAL, MORTAL, LETHAL, DANGEROUS, FERAL, BANEFUL, VIRULENT, VITAL
Archaic .... FELL
enemy .... NEMESIS
plant ...... NIGHTSHADE, BELLADONNA
poison ... STRYCHNINE(E)
sin .... PRIDE, LUST, ANGER, COVETOUSNESS, GLUTTONY, ENVY, SLOTH
snake .... COBRA, ASP
to both sides .... INTERNECINE
deadpan .... MASK
deaf ... UNHEARING, HEEDLESS
and ___ .... DUMB
deafen .... SOUNDPROOF
Scottish .... DEAVE
deafening .... NOISY
deal ...... DISTRIBUTE, SALE, TRADE, FIR WOOD, GIVE, ADMINISTER, NEGOTIATE, TREAT
colloquial ..... BARGAIN, AGREEMENT
crookedly ...... PALTER
give-and-take .... (HORSE)TRADE
out .... DOLE, ISSUE
dealer .... DISTRIBUTOR, BUYER, SELLER, TRADER, CHAPMAN, MONGER
cattle .... DROVER
cloth .... CLOTHIER, DRAPER, MERCER
cutting tools .... CUTLER
foodstuff .... GROCER
gem .... LAPIDARY
in bonds .... (STOCK)BROKER
in houses/lots .. REALTOR
in skins .... FURRIER
right of .... PONE
scrap .... JUNKMAN, RAGMAN
dealings ...... TRANSACTIONS, RELATIONS
dean .... DOYEN
baseball player .... DIZZY, DAFFY
ecclesiastical .... PREFECT
feminine ...... DOYENNE
of a .... DECANAL
residence of .... DEANERY
deanery .... DECANAL
dear ...... BELOVED, COSTLY, DARLING, EXPENSIVE
slang .... TOOTS
dearie .... DARLING
dearth ..... PAUCITY, FAMINE, SCARCITY, LACK
death ...... DEMISE, PASSING, DECEASE, MORT
by burning ..... SUTTEE

by hanging .... ROPE
causing .... FATAL, LETHAL, MORTAL
combining form .... NECR(O)
cup .... MUSHROOM
herald of ..... BANSHEE, BANSHIE
march .... DIRGE
march scene .... BATAAN
mercy ...... EUTHANASIA
near .... DYING
noise .... RATTLE
notice ...... OBIT(UARY), NECROLOGY
of .... LETHAL, MORTUARY
painless, easy .... EUTHANASIA
put to ...... KILL, HANG, EXECUTE, SLAY
rate .... MORTALITY
rattle .... RALE
ring announcing .. TOLL, KNELL
symbol .... SKULL
toll .... KNELL
view of .... THANATOPSIS
deathblow .... COUP DE GRACE
deathless .... IMMORTAL
deathlessness ..... ATHANASIA
death's-head .... SKULL
deathsman ...... EXECUTIONER
deathwatch ..... VIGIL, BEETLE
deave .... DEAFEN
deb .... DEBUTANTE, BUD
debacle ...... ROUT, DISASTER
debar ...... HINDER, EXCLUDE
debark .... LAND, UNLOAD, ALIGHT
debase ..... CORRUPT, DEFILE, DEGRADE, DEMEAN, LOWER, PERVERT, VITIATE, PROFANE
liquid .... DILUTE
metal .... ALLOY
morally .... DEPRAVE, DEBAUCH
debatable .... MOOT, CONTROVERSIAL
debate ...... ARGUE, DISPUTE, CAUSERIE, CANVASS, DISCUSS, REASON, PALAVER, PLEAD
ending device .. CLOTURE
pertaining to ... FORENSIC
debauch .... CORRUPT, DEPRAVE, DEBASE, ORGY
prolonged .. HELLBENDER
debauchee ...... RAKE, SATYR, ROUE, LIBERTINE, LECHER
debilitate .... WEAKEN, ENERVATE, ENFEEBLE
debilitated .... RUN-DOWN
debility .... ATONY
debit .... CHARGE
debonair .... GENIAL, GAY, SUAVE, URBANE
debouch .... EMERGE
debris ...... RUBBLE, RUBBISH, SCREE, RUINS, DETRITUS, TRASH, LITTER
tree prunings ..... BRASH
debt .... LIABILITY, ACCOUNT, OBLIGATION
evader .... DEADBEAT
in theology .... SIN
note .... IOU
overdue .... ARREAR
relating to .... DEBIT
debtor .... OWER
debtor's prison .... FLEET
debunk ..... EXPOSE, UNMASK, REFUTE
Debussy, composer .... ACHILLE CLAUDE
composition .... REVERIE
debut .... INTRODUCTION, PRESENTATION
debutant(e) .... BUD, DEB
ball .... COTILLION
delight of ..... STAGLINE
party for .... COMING OUT
decade ..... TEN, DECENNIUM
decadence ... DECLINE, DECAY, DETERIORATION
decalogue, part of .... COMMANDMENT
Decameron tales author ...... BOCCACCIO
decamp .... BOLT, FLEE, ABSCOND, RUN AWAY, VAMO(O)SE, CLEAR OUT
decanal .... DEANERY
decant ..... POUR, ELUTRIATE
decanter .... CARAFE
stand .... TANTALUS
decapitate .... BEHEAD, DECOLLATE
decapitation ...... EXECUTION
decapod .... CRAB, SQUID, LOBSTER, SHRIMP, PRAWN
decay .... ROT, SPOIL, DECOMPOSE, PUTREFY, GANGRENE
bone .... CARIES
dental .... CARIES
fruit .... BLET, ROT
slow, crumbling .... MO(U)LDER
teeth .... CARIES
decayed .... PUTRID, ROTTEN, CARIOUS
in botany .... DOTY
in fruit .... BLET
decaying .... ROTTING
combining form ... SAPRO
dead body ..... CARRION
from age .... DOTING
vegetable matter ... DUFF
decease .... DEATH, DIE, DEMISE
deceased .... DECEDENT, DEAD, DEPARTED, LATE
deceit ..... LIE, WILE, FRAUD, COZENAGE, DECEPTION, IMPOSTURE, GUILE
archaic .... COVIN
deceitful .... FALSE, DISHONEST, DECEPTIVE, ARTFUL, WILY, TRICKY, CRAFTY
face .... MASK
sight .... MIRAGE, ILLUSION, HALLUCINATION
words .... LIES
deceive ...... DUPE, MISLEAD, DELUDE, LIE, HOODWINK, BEGUILE, FOOL, BETRAY, SPOOF, FOB, FUB, COZEN, ENTRAP
by flattery .... FLAM
deceiver .... BETRAYER, LIAR, FAKER, IMPOSTOR
decelerate .... SLOW DOWN
December decoration .... MISTLETOE, TINSEL
perennial .... SNOW
symbol ... SANTA (CLAUS)
28th........ CHILDERMAS
decenary .... TITHING
decency .... PROPRIETY, GOOD TASTE, DECORUM
decennium .... DECADE
decent ..... CHASTE, MODEST, RESPECTABLE, FAIR, PROPER, KIND
decentralize .... DISPERSE
deception .... LIE, FRAUD, HOAX, IMPOSTURE, CHICANERY, JAPE, TRICKERY, SPOOF, RUSE, FLIMFLAM
deceptive .... ILLUSORY, TRICKY, AMBIGUOUS, MISLEADING, DELUSIVE
trick .... FLAM
decide .... SETTLE, JUDGE, RESOLVE, CONCLUDE
issue by combat .... DERAIGN
judicially ...... ADJUDGE
decided ..... DEFINITE, SET, CLEAR CUT, SETTLED
decidedly .... CERTAINLY, DEFINITELY
decider of right or wrong ..... CASUIST
deciding game when tied ..... RUN-OFF
vote .... CASTING
deciduous .... TEMPORARY
opposed to ... EVERGREEN
decimal ...... TENTH, DENARY
point .... DOT
point system inventor ... STEVIN
system of counting ..... ALGORISM
decimate .... SLAUGHTER, MASSACRE
decipher ...... READ, DECODE, TRANSLATE
decipherable .... LEGIBLE, READABLE
decision .... JUDGMENT, SENTENCE, VERDICT, DECREE
await .... PEND
good for the future ..... PRECEDENT
decisive .... CONCLUSIVE, FINAL, FATEFUL
argument ..... CLINCHER
point/moment .. CLIMAX CRISIS, CRUCIAL, ZERO HOUR
deck .... ADORN, TRIM,

CLOTHE, PLATFORM, COVER, ARRAY
hand .... SAILOR, ROUSTABOUT
hit the ..... GET UP, RISE
lowest .... ORLOP
on ..... READY, ON HAND
out .... (BE)DIZEN, ARRAY, ADORN, CAPARISON
Scottish .... DINK
ship's ...... ORLOP, POOP
declaim .... ORATE, RANT, RECITE, PERORATE
declaimer .... RANTER, ORATOR
declamation ...... HARANGUE, ORATORY, ORATION
declaration ...... STATEMENT, PROCLAMATION
in bridge .... BID
of aims .... CHARTER, MANIFESTO
Declaration of Independence signer .... HANCOCK, WYTHE
declare ..... ASSERT, ALLEGE, PROFESS, AVER, STATE, PUBLISH
guilty .... CONDEMN
in cards .... MELD
innocent .... ACQUIT, CLEAR
untrue .... DENY
declasse .... DATED, PASSE
decline .... SPURN, ABATE, REFUSE, SLUMP, WANE, DIP, EBB, REJECT
declivity .... SLOPE, SCARP
decoct ..... EXTRACT, DISTILL
decoction .... TISANE, PTISAN, TEA
decode .... DECIPHER
decollate .... BEHEAD, DECAPITATE
decollete .... LOW-CUT, LOW-NECKED
decolorize .... BLEACH
decompose ...... DECAY, ROT, PUTREFY, SPOIL
decomposed .... PUTRID
decompression sickness .... BENDS
decontaminate .... PURIFY, CLEAR
decontrol ..... FREE, LIBERATE
decor .... DECORATION
decorate .... TRIM, DECK, DRESS, ADORN, EMBELLISH
in showy way .... BEDIZEN
with jewels ...... BEGEM, ENCRUST
decorated wall .... DADO
decoration ...... ADORNMENT, TRIMMING, RIBBON, ORNAMENT
as sign of honor .... MEDAL, BADGE
furniture .... BUHL
hat .... COCKADE
military ... PURPLE HEART
style of .... ROCOCO
decorative ...... ORNAMENTAL
anklet/armlet ... BANGLE
band .... SASH
border design .... GUILLOCHE
braid .... CORDON
curve .... ESCALOP, SCALLOP
garland .... FESTOON
line in writing .. FLOURISH
plant .... HERB
ribbon .... RIBAND, CORDON
stroke .... TAG, FLOURISH
decorous ...... PRIM, PROPER, DIGNIFIED
person .... PRIG
decorticate ...... STRIP, PARE, PEEL, BARK
decorum .... DECENCY, PROPRIETY, DIGNITY, ETIQUETTE
decoy .... LURE, BAIT, ENTICE, PLANT, BLIND
barker's .... SHILL
dog .... TOLLER
gambler's .... SHILL, CAPPER
object of .... GAME
police ..... STOOLPIGEON
songbird, use .... CAJOLE
decrease ...... ABATE, LESSEN, DIMINISH, REDUCE, TAPER
decree .. ORDER, LAW, ARRET, ACT, DECISION, EDICT, ORDAIN, MANDATE, FIAT, DECIDE, FIRMAN, CANON, RESCRIPT
by judicial sentence ..... DECERN
by the Pope .. DECRETAL
judicial .... WRIT
Moslem ruler's .... IRADE
of outlawry .... BAN
papal .... BULL
Russian .... UKASE
decrees, collection of papal ... DECRETAL
decrement .... WASTE, LOSS
opposed to ... INCREMENT
decrepit .... OLD, WEAK, BROKEN DOWN, WORN
airplane .... CRATE
automobile ..... JALOPY, CRATE
decresent .... WANING
decretal .... DECREE
decrier .... DEPLORER
decry .... CENSURE, CONDEMN, DISPARAGE, DISCREDIT, DENOUNCE
decumbent .... TRAILING, PROSTRATE, PRONE
opposed to ...... SUPINE
decuple .... TENFOLD
dedicate ..... DEVOTE, APPLY, INSCRIBE
dedication ...... INSCRIPTION, ENVOY, ENVOI
deduce .... INFER, CONCLUDE, DERIVE
deduct .... SUBTRACT
deductible tax item .... EXPENSES, DONATIONS
deduction .... INFERENCE
for loss of weight .... DRAFT
for waste .... DRAFT
kind of .... TARE
opposed to .. INDUCTION
union dues .... CHECKOFF
deed ...... ACT, FEAT, ACTION, GEST(E), EXPLOIT
in ...... REALLY, IN FACT
kind of .... SALE, TRANSFER
ownership .... TITLE
deeds .... ACTA
of chivalry .... ERRANTRY
deejay's concern .... DISKS
deem ...... CONSIDER, JUDGE, BELIEVE
deep .... ABSTRUSE, WISE, PROFOUND, OCEAN
bow .... OBEISANCE, SALAAM
crack .... CREVASSE
dish, covered .... TUREEN
dish, fruit pie .. COBBLER
dish pudding .... PANDOWDY
gorge .... GULLY, RAVINE
hole .... PIT
low .... CURTSY, NOD
red .... CARNATION
seated .... ROOTED
sleep .... SOPOR, STUPOR, LETHARGY
sound .... RUMBLE, BOOM
the .... SEA, OCEAN
valley .... CANYON, CANON
deepfreeze ..... REFRIGERATOR
deeply .... INLY
deepset .... CAVERNOUS
deer .... WHITETAIL, ROE, RUMINANT, BROCKET, MUNTJAK, MUNTJAC
American ..... CARIBOU, WAPITI, MOOSE
Andean .... PUDU
antler .... TAG
antler branch ..... POINT
antler shaft .... BEAM
antler, type ...... RUSINE
Asiatic .... ROE, SAMBAR, SAMBUR, AHU
axis .... CHITAL
barking .... KAKAR
entrails .... UMBLES
feeding place ...... YARD
female ...... DOE, HIND, ROE
flesh .... VENISON
foot .... HOOF
forest cover .... VERT
genus .... RUSA
green cover .... VERT
hart .... STAG
hog .... AXIS, RUSA
horn .... ANTLER
hornless .... POLLARD
horn's second branch ... BEZ ANTLER

large ...... MOOSE, ELK, REINDEER, CARIBOU
like a .... CERVINE
like giraffe ...... OKAPI
male .... (ROE)BUCK, STAG, HART
maned .... RUSA, SAMBAR
moose-like .... ELK
mouse .... NAPUS
mouse-like .. CHEVROTAIN
mule .... BLACKTAIL
of a .... CERVINE
of India ...... AXIS, RUSA
Persian .... MARAL
red ..... ELAPHINE, HART, STAG
secretion .... MUSK
sexual excitement .. RUT, ESTRUS
short tail of .... SCUT
small ..... MUNTJAC, ROE, NAPUS, BROCKET, CHEVROTAIN
spotted .... CHITAL
tail .... FLAG, SCUT
Tibet .... SHOU
track .... SLOT
three-year-old ..... SOREL
two-year-old .... BROCK(ET), TEG, PRICKET
vital organs .... NUMBLES, NOMBLES, HUMBLE PIE
young .... FAWN, SPITTER
deerlet .... NAPU, CHEVROTAIN
deerlike .... CERVINE
deface ...... MAR, MUTILATE, DISFIGURE
defalcate .... EMBEZZLE
defamation ... LIBEL, SLANDER, CALUMNY
defamatory .... LIBELOUS
remarks .... MUD
defame .... LIBEL, SLANDER, CALUMNIATE, MALIGN, VILIFY
default ..... FORFEIT, FAILURE, WELSH
defaulter .... EMBEZZLER DEFALCATOR
defeat .... WIN, BEAT, OVERCOME, REVERSE, BEST, WORST, LICK, LOSS, WHIP, TROUNCE
by small margin .... NOSE
chess .... MATE
decisively ...... CLOBBER, DRUB, WALLOP, ROUT
disorderly .... ROUT
easy to .... PUSHOVER
incumbent ...... UNSEAT
overwhelming .... ROUT, SHELLACKING, MASSACRE, LACING
scoreless .... WHITEWASH
soundly .... DRUB, LACE, SKUNK
two ways ..... WHIPSAW
unexpectedly ..... UPSET
defeated: slang .... KAPUT
defeatist, kind of.... PESSIMIST
defecate ...... PURIFY, REFINE, EXCRETE
defect .... SHORTCOMING, BOLT, IMPERFECTION, BLEMISH, FLAW, FAULT, SNAG, FLEE, DEMERIT, SPOT, FAILING
in fabric .... SCOB
in machine .... BUG
in weave .... SCOB
labial .... HAIRLIP
slang .... BUG
defection .... DESERTION
defective .... FAULTY, FLAWED, IMPERFECT, MANQUE
bomb .... DUD
defector ...... BOLTER, RAT, TURNCOAT, RENEGADE
defend ..... GUARD, PROTECT, JUSTIFY, SHIELD
defendable .... TENABLE
defendant .... ACCUSED, CULPRIT
opposed to ... PLAINTIFF, COMPLAINANT
place of .... DOCK
plea of .... NOLO
statement of .... PLEA
who refuses to plead .... MUTE
defender .... CHAMPION, PROTECTOR, ADVOCATE
defense .... JUSTIFICATION, PROTECTION, BULWARK
defendant's .... ALIBI
kind of .... ORAL, LEGAL, ATTACK
line: Ger. .... LIMES
means of .... ARMOR, ABATIS, SPINE, SHELL, PALISADE, SMOKESCREEN, BARRICADE, MUNIMENT
defenseless .... HELPLESS
defensible .... TENABLE, JUSTIFIABLE
defensive covering .... ARMOR, MAIL, SHIELD, EGIS, HELMET
ditch .... MOAT
embankment .... EARTHWORK, GABIONADE
structure .... FORT, STOCKADE, ABATIS
outwork ..... FORTALICE
wall .... BULWARK
defer ...... DELAY, POSTPONE, PEND, YIELD, SHELVE
deference .... RESPECT, YIELDING, OBEISANCE
deferment .... DELAY
defi .... CHALLENGE, DARE, CARTEL
defiance .... CHALLENGE, RESISTANCE
defiant .... CHALLENGING, BELLIGERENT
confidence .... BRAVADO
one .... REB, REBEL, CHALLENGER
deficiency .... SHORTAGE, LACK, DEFECT, DEFICIT, WANT, ULLAGE
disease .... BERIBERI, DROPSY, RICKETS, SCURVY, PELLAGRA
in supply ..... SHORTAGE
of oxygen in body ...... ANOXIA
deficient .... DEFECTIVE, INCOMPLETE, WANTING, SHORT
deficit ...... SHORTAGE, LACK
defile ...... TAINT, POLLUTE, CORRUPT, PASS, SULLY, DIRTY, VALLEY, PROFANE
define ...... OUTLINE, EXPLAIN
definite ... EXPLICIT, CERTAIN, POSITIVE
definitive ..... FINAL, DECISIVE, CONCLUSIVE
deflate .... COLLAPSE
deflated tire .... FLAT
deflect .... BEND, TURN, SWERVE, DIVERT, FEND
Defoe, novelist ...... DANIEL
character ...... CRUSOE, FRIDAY
deform .... CONTORT, WARP, MISSHAPE
deformed person .... HUNCHBACK, CRIPPLE, FREAK
deformity, back...... HUNCH, HUMP
buccal .... HARELIP
foot ..... TALIPES, VARUS, CLUBFOOT
of lower limbs .... BOWLEGS, VARUS
defraud ...... SWINDLE, GYP, CHEAT, BILK, COZEN, STICK, NICK
defray ...... PAY, COVER COST
defrost .... MELT, DEICE
deft ...... SKILLFUL, ADROIT, DEXTEROUS, CLEVER, APT
defunct ...... EXTINCT, DEAD
defy .... DARE, RESIST, OPPOSE, CHALLENGE, FLOUT
degrade .... ABASE, HUMILIATE, DEBASE, HUMBLE, DEMEAN
degraded .... DISGRACED, SHAMED
degrading .... MENIAL
degree .... STEP, STAGE, RANK, PEG
of occurrence .... INCIDENCE
suffix .... NESS
to a .... SOMEWHAT
dehydrate ...... DRY, PARCH
deictic ...... DEMONSTRATIVE
opposed to .... ELENCTIC
deific .... GODLIKE
deiform ..... DIVINE, GODLIKE
deify .... IDEALIZE, ADORE, WORSHIP, EXALT, APOTHEOSIZE
deign .... CONDESCEND, STOOP
deil: Scot. .... DEVIL
Deirdre's guardian .... CONCHOBAR
deity .... GOD(HOOD), GODDESS
Buddhist .... DEVA
Japanese .... AMIDA, AMITA
minor .... DEMIGOD

of music/poetry .... APOLLO
of flocks .... FAUN
secondary ..... DEMIURGE
underworld ...... OSIRIS
woodland .... FAUN, PAN, SATYR, ZEPHYRUS
deject ...... SADDEN, DEPRESS
dejected .... SAD, DOWNCAST, CRESTFALLEN, DEPRESSED
dejection, lowest point .... NADIR
dejeuner .... BREAKFAST, LUNCHEON
delate: Scot. .... ACCUSE, DENOUNCE, ANNOUNCE
delator .... INFORMER
Delaware ...... LENI, LENAPE, GRAPE
Bay discoverer .... HUDSON
capital .... DOVER
city .... ELSMERE, NEWARK, MILFORD, TRENTON
Indian .... LANAPE
River city ..... TRENTON
settlers .... SWEDES
delay .... SLOW, HINDER, DEFER(MENT), IMPEDE, DETAIN, STALL, RETARD, LINGER, PEND
in law .... MORA, LACHES
inexcusable ..... LACHES
delaying action .... STALL
in Congress ... FILIBUSTER
in law .... MORATORY
dele .... DELETE, REMOVE, ERASE
delectable .... YUMMY
delectation .... DELIGHT, AMUSEMENT
delegate ... DEPUTE, DEPUTY, REPRESENTATIVE, ENVOY, DEPUTIZE
kind of .... ACCREDITED, ALTERNATE
unofficial ...... OBSERVER
delete ...... ERASE, EXPUNGE, DELE, CROSS OUT
deleterious .... HARMFUL, BAD, PERNICIOUS
deletion of word's last letter .. APOCOPE
cancel .... STET
Delia .... ARTEMIS
deliberate .... PONDER, PREMEDITATED, UNHURRIED, SLOW, CONSIDER, KNOWING
discourtesy .... SNUB, REBUFF, CUT
Delibes, composer .... LEO
ballet .... NAILA
opera .... LAKME
delicacy .... FRAILTY, FINENESS, FINESSE, CAVIAR, CATE, TIDBIT, KICKSAW
of performance .... FINESSE
delicate ..... DAINTY, TENDER, EXQUISITE, FRAIL, NICE, FINE(SPUN), FRAGILE, TICKLISH, TAFFETA
delicately pretty ..... DAINTY, MIGNON
delicatessen .... FOODSHOP
delicious .... DELIGHTFUL, AMBROSIAL, SWEET, TASTY, APPETIZING, LUSCIOUS
fruit .... APPLE
delict .... OFFENSE, MISDEMEANOR
delight ...... ENTRANCE, JOY, PLEASE, PLEASURE
delightful .... PLEASING, CHARMING
Delilah ... TEMPTRESS, HARLOT
victim of .... SAMSON
delimit .... DEMARCATE
delineate ...... DRAW, DEPICT, DESCRIBE, OUTLINE
delineation .... SKETCH, PORTRAIT, DRAWING
delinquency ... GUILT, MISDEED
record/report ...... GIG
delinquent .... GUILTY, OVERDUE
a .... JUVENILE
alleged other .... PARENT
likely home of .... REFORMATORY, BOYS' TOWN
deliquesce .... MELT
delirious .... EXCITED, RAVING
delirium ...... MANIA, FRENZY
tremens .... JIMJAMS
delitescent ... LATENT, HIDDEN, INACTIVE
deliver .... FREE, RESCUE, SAVE, HAND OVER, RID, UTTER, TRANSFER, DISTRIBUTE
goods for sale ... CONSIGN
prematurely ..... SLINK
sermon .... PREACH
deliverance .. RESCUE, RELEASE, OPINION
deliverer .... LIBERATOR, REDEEMER, COURIER
delivery .... TRANSFER, DISTRIBUTION, CHILDBIRTH, UTTERANCE, PARTURITION
boy .... JUMPER
of property ...... LIVERY
dell .... VALE, GLEN, DALE, VALLEY, RAVINE, DINGLE, SLACK
dells .... RAPIDS
Delmar, novelist .... VINA
Delos inhabitant ...... DELIAN
Delphic .... ORACULAR
priestess .... PYTHIA, PYTHONESS
seer .... ORACLE
delphinium .... LARKSPUR
delude .... MISLEAD, DUPE, BEGUILE, DECEIVE, KID
deluge ..... FLOOD, INUNDATE, INUNDATION, CATACLYSM, CATARACT
of words .... SPATE
delul ..... CAMEL, DROMEDARY
delusion .... MIRAGE, ILLUSION, VISION, FANCY, PARANOIA
of grandeur .... MEGALOMANIA
delve ...... DIG, INVESTIGATE, SEARCH, FATHOM, PROBE
demagogue ... RABBLE ROUSER, MOUNTEBANK, AGITATOR, QUACK
demand ...... REQUIRE, CLAIM, EXACT, CRY, NEED
final .... ULTIMATUM
for identification .... CHALLENGE
in .... SOUGHT
noisy .... CLAMOR
payment of debt .... DUN
repetition .... ENCORE
demandant .... PLAINTIFF
demanding .... CLAIMANT, EXACTING, CLAMOROUS, EXIGENT
demarcate .... DELIMIT
demarcation .... LINE
deme .... TOWNSHIP
demean ..... DEGRADE, ABASE, HUMBLE
demeanor ..... MANNER, AIR, CONDUCT, BEARING, MIEN, CARRIAGE, PORTANCE
having dignified .... PORTLY
dement .... DERANGE
demented ...... MAD, CRAZY, INSANE, FLIGHTY, LOONY, LUNY, LOCO
dementia .... INSANITY
demerit .... FAULT, DEFECT
slang .... GIG
demerol .... ANALGESIC, DRUG, SEDATIVE
demesne ..... DOMAIN, REALM, REGION
Demeter .... CERES
demigod .... HERO, DEITY, IDOL
demilune .... CRESCENT
demise ...... DEATH, DECEASE, BEQUEST
demit ...... RESIGN, ABDICATE
demitasse ...... (COFFEE) CUP
demobilize .... DISBAND, DISMISS
democracy, a ...... REPUBLIC
world's largest .... INDIA
world's smallest .... SAN MARINO
Democrat, any ..... LOCOFOCO
Democratic Party faction .... LOCOFOCO
demode ...... OLD-FASHIONED, PASSE
demographic item ..... BIRTH, DEATHS, MARRIAGES
demoiselle .... CRANE, DAMSEL, DRAGONFLY
demolish ...... RAZE, DESTROY
demon .... FIEND, DEVIL, OGRE, ANITO, D(A)EDAL, GHOUL, NAT
Arabian ... AFREET, EBLIS, JINN(I), GENIE, AFRIT, DAITYA
female .... LAMIA
little .... IMP
demoness .... LILITH, SUCCUBA, SUCCUBUS
demoniac .... DEVILISH, FRANTIC

demons, abode of all .... PANDEMONIUM
demonstrable ..... APODICTIC
demonstrate .... PROVE, SHOW, EVINCE, EXHIBIT
demonstrative .. ILLUSTRATIVE, D(E)ICTIC
in grammar .... D(E)ICTIC
demoralize ...... DISHEARTEN, CONFUSE, WEAKEN, DISCOURAGE
demos .... PEOPLE, DEME, MASSES, POPULACE
demote ..... DEGRADE, LOWER
opposed to ..... PROMOTE
slang ...... BUST, BREAK
demotics .... SOCIOLOGY
Dempsey, Jack, soubriquet ... (MANASSA) MAULER
demulcent .. SOOTHING, SALVE, OINTMENT
demur ..... OBJECT, HESITATE, PROTEST
demure ...... PRIM, COY, SHY, SEDATE, MODEST, MIM, SOBER
demurrer .... OBJECTION, OBJECTOR
den ...... DIVE, STUDY, LAIR, CAVE, ROOM, HAUNT, RETREAT, HANGOUT
secret .... MEW, HIDEOUT
wild animal's .... LODGE, LAIR
denarii, 12 .... SOLIDUS
denary .... DECIMAL, TENFOLD
dendritic .... TREELIKE
dendroid .... TREELIKE
dene .... DUNE
dengue .... DANDY FEVER
denial .... REFUSAL, ABSTINENCE, REPUDIATION
in diplomacy ... DEMENTI
official .... DEMENTI
opposed to .... COMPLIANCE, AFFIRMATIVE
statement of .... DENEGATION
denier .... DISOWNER, DISCLAIMER, COIN
denigrate .... BLACKEN, DEFAME
denim ...... (COTTON) CLOTH
use for .... (C)OVERALLS, UNIFORMS
denizen .... INHABITANT, CIT(IZEN), OCCUPANT
Denmark (see Danish)
island .... FALSTER
Dennis ____ .... DAY
Dennis the ____ ..... MENACE
denominate ..... NAME, TITLE, CALL
denomination .... CLASS, SECT, NAME
denominational .... SECTARIAN
denote ...... MARK, INDICATE, SIGNIFY, MEAN
denouement .... OUTCOME
denounce ..... ASSAIL, ACCUSE, EXCORIATE, CONDEMN, CRITICIZE, DECRY
dense .... THICK, STUPID, PACKED, POPULOUS, CLOSE, GROSS
growth of trees .... FOREST, WOODS, JUNGLE
dent .... DINT, HOLLOW
dental drill .... BURR
paste .... DENTIFRICE, ZIRCATE
dentate ... SERRATE, TOOTHED, NOTCHED
dented .... TOOTHED
denticle .... TOOTH
dentine .... IVORY
dentist: colloq. .... TOOTH PULLER
drill of .... BURR
pincers of ...... FORCEPS
dentistry .... ODONTOLOGY
dentifrice .... ZIRCATE
denture .... PLATE, TEETH, BRIDGE
denude .... STRIP
denunciation .... ACCUSATION, THREAT, DIATRIBE
Denver is capital of .... COLORADO
deny .... NEGATE, ABJURE, GAINSAY, REFUSE, DISAVOW, CONTRADICT, DISOWN, REPUDIATE, FORSWEAR
denying .... DENEGATION
deodar .... CEDAR
deodorant ..... MUM, PASTILLE
deontology .... ETHICS
depart ...... GO (AWAY), DIE, SET OUT, LEAVE
from script ...... AD LIB
secretly .... DECAMP, ABSCOND
slang .... MOSEY
departed .... PAST, LEFT, (BY)GONE
the .... DEAD
department store, designating a FIVE-AND-TEN
stairway ..... ESCALATOR
departure .... DEVIATION, LEAVING, DEATH, EXIT
mass .... EXODUS
of Israelites from Egypt .. EXODUS
depend .... RELY, BANK
dependable .... RELIABLE
dependency .... COLONY, AP(P)ANAGE
dependent .... CONTINGENT, SUBORDINATE, WARD, SUBJECT, PENSIONARY
kind of .... SATELLITE
depict .... PICTURE, PAINT, PORTRAY, DRAW, RENDER
in words ..... DELINEATE, DESCRIBE
depilate .... SHAVE, PLUCK
depelation .... ELECTROLYSIS
deplete ...... EXHAUST, DRAIN
deplorable .... GRIEVOUS
deplore .... LAMENT, BEWAIL, RUE, DECRY
deploy .... SPREAD (OUT)
deplume .... PLUCK
depone ...... TESTIFY, DEPOSE
deponent's statement .... AFFIDAVIT, TESTIMONY
deport ...... BANISH, BEHAVE, EXPEL, EXILE
deportment .... BEHAVIOR, BEARING, CONDUCT
depose ...... TESTIFY, REMOVE, OUST, DEPONE, DETHRONE
deposit, alluvial ...... DELTA, GEEST
body .... CALCULUS
clayey .... MARL
geyser .... SINTER
glacial .... MORAINE, PLACER
mineral .... LODE
on teeth .... TARTAR
sediment .... SILT
waste .... SLUDGE
water-borne ..... PLACER
wine cask ...... TARTAR
depositary .... TRUSTEE, BANK, SAFE, VAULT
deposition .... TESTIMONY
form of .... AFFIDAVIT
depot .... STOREHOUSE, WAREHOUSE, STATION, ENTREPOT
arms .. ARMORY, ARSENAL
French .... GARE
military ...... MAGAZINE, ARSENAL
deprave .... DEBASE, PERVERT, DEBAUCH
depraved ..... EVIL, CORRUPT, VILE, PUTRID, DISSOLUTE
depravity .... TURPITUDE
deprecate ... DEPLORE, BEWAIL
depreciate ...... DISPARAGE, BELITTLE, LESSEN
money officially .. DECRY
depredate ..... PLUNDER, ROB, PILLAGE
depress ..... SADDEN, LOWER, DAMPEN, DISHEARTEN, DEJECT
depressant .... SEDATIVE
depressed .... DEJECTED, BLUE, FLATTENED, SAD, GLUM, MOODY
depression .... SADNESS, DENT, HOLLOW
between hills ...... GLEN
between mountains .. COL
in economics .. RECESSION
small .... FOVEA
deprivation ...... LOSS, DENIAL
deprive .... DISPOSSESS, DIVEST, TAKE (AWAY)
of ownership .... EXPROPRIATE
of power to reproduce ... GELD, CASTRATE, STERILIZE, EMASCULATE
of sunlight ..... ETIOLATE
deprived ..... (BE)REFT, SHORN
depth ... LOWNESS, OCEAN, SEA
bomb .... ASHCAN
charge .... ASHCAN
combining form .. BATHO
of water displaced by ship DRAFT
depurate .... PURIFY
deputation ...... DELEGATION

depute .... APPOINT, SEND, DELEGATE
deputies' group .... POSSE
deputy ... AGENT, (DE)LEGATE, SURROGATE, PROXY, ENVOY, VICAR, VICEGERENT, LIEUTENANT
Der Alte .... ADENAUER, SCHRANZ
Fuehrer .... HITLER
deracinate .... UPROOT
derange .... UPSET, DISORDER, MESS UP
deranged ...... INSANE, CRAZY
Derby .... HAT, BOWLER, HORSE RACE
English colloquial ...... BILLYCOCK
site .... EPSOM, KENTUCKY
winner ..... KAUAI KING, CITATION, BUCKPASSER, ZEV, TWENTY GRAND, WAR ADMIRAL, ASSAULT, WHIRLAWAY, SWAPS, TIM TAM, SECRETARIAT
derelict .... FLOTSAM, WRECK, TRAMP, FORSAKEN, REMISS, CASTAWAY
deride ...... RIDICULE, SCORN, JEER, MOCK, GIBE, SCOFF, TAUNT
derisive .... SCORNFUL, CONTEMPTUOUS
cry ..... CATCALL, HOOT, BOO, HISS, RAZZ
derivation .... DESCENT
word .... ETYMOLOGY
derive ...... DRAW, (D)EDUCE, INFER, GET
derived from oil .... OLEIC
derm, as suffix .... SKIN, COVERING
dermatoid .... SKINLIKE
dermis .... SKIN, CUTIS
dernier .... LAST, FINAL
cri .... LAST WORD, LATEST(STYLE)
derogate .... DECRY, DETRACT, DISPARAGE
derogatory .... ADVERSE, CRITICAL, DETRACTING
remark .... SLUR
derrick .... CRANE, STEEVE, HOIST, RIG, DAVIT
part of ..... BOOM, SPAR, BEAM, PULLEY, JIB
derriere ...... REAR, BEHIND, BUTTOCKS
derringer .... PISTOL, GUN
derris extraction ... ROTENONE
derry .... BALLAD
dervish .... FAKIR, BEGGAR
headgear .... TAJ
Moslem .... SADITE
practice ...... WHIRLING, HOWLING
wandering .... CALENDER
Des Moines is capital of ..... IOWA
descant .... MELODY, SING, COMMENT
descend .... COME DOWN, STEP DOWN
descendant .... SCION, OFFSPRING, PROGENY, BREED
female .... DAUGHTER
male .... SON
descent .... DERIVATION, BIRTH, EXTRACTION, ORIGIN, DECLINE, FALL, LINEAGE
sudden, swift .... SWOOP, POUNCE
describe ...... DEPICT, PAINT, PICTURE, LIMN, LABEL
exactly .... DEFINE
grammatically .... PARSE
graphically .... PORTRAY
description ...... KIND, SORT
descriptive name/title .... EPITHET
word .... LABEL
descry .... ESPY, SEE, KEN, DETECT, SIGHT, SPOT
Desdemona's husband .... OTHELLO
slanderer .... IAGO
desecrate .... PROFANE, DEFILE, VIOLATE, POLLUTE
desecration .... SACRILEGE
deseret .... HONEYBEE
desert ...... ABANDON, LEAVE, FORSAKE, WASTE, MERIT, QUIT, COLORADO
African .... SAHARA, KALAHARI
Arabian .... NEFUD, DAHNA
Asiatic .... GOBI, SHAMO, THAR, KARA KUM, QARA QUM
Australian ... NULLABAR, GIBSON
animal .... CAMEL
Arctic .... TUNDRA
Chilean .... ATACAMA
China .... TAKLA MAKAN
dweller ...... ARAB(IAN), BEDOUIN
dwelling .... TENT
fertile spot .... OASIS
Fox .... ROMMEL
horse .... ARAB
India .... THAR
Iran .... LUT
like .... ARID
Mongolian .... GOBI
pertaining to .... EREMIC
plant .... CACTUS, AGAVE, OCOTILLO
plant, tree like .... SOTOL
Russian ...... KIZIL DUM
shrub .... RETEM
train .... CARAVAN, CARAVANSARY
Turkestan ... KARA KUM, KIZIL KUM
U.S. .... MOHAVE, PAINTED (DESERT)
valley .... BOLSON
wind .... SIMOOM, SIROCCO, SIMOON
deserted .... DESOLATE, SOLITARY, ABANDONED, FORLORN
by owner ...... DERELICT
deserter ... RENEGADE, BOLTER, TURNCOAT, RUNAGATE, APOSTATE, RUNAWAY, RATTER, FUGITIVE
army .... AWOL
describing a .... RAT
desertion .... DEFECTION, ABANDONMENT
deserts .... DUE
deserve .... EARN, MERIT
deserved reward/punishment .. DESERT(S)
deservedly .... JUSTLY
deserving .... MERITORIOUS
punishment ..... GUILTY, CULPABLE
desiccant .... DRIER
desiccate .... DRY
desiccated coconut meat ...... COPRA
design .... IDEA, PATTERN, CONTRIVE, PURPOSE, SCHEME, AIM, PLAN
having .... FIGURED
highlight .... MOTIF
on a page ..... VIGNETTE
ornamental ...... DEVICE
sinister, usually .... PLOT
designate ...... MARK, ASSIGN, ENTITLE, SPECIFY, NAME, APPOINT
designation ..... APPOINTMENT
designer .... STYLIST
designing .... ARTFUL, CRAFTY, SCHEMING
desil .... DEIL
desinence .... SUFFIX
desirable part ... MEAT, CREAM
desire .... WISH, CRAVE, WILL, WANT, COVET
characterized by .... ORECTIC
for sleep .... NARCOLEPSY
overwhelming ..... ESTRUS
seat of .... LIVER
strong .... HUNGER
weakest .... VELLEITY
desirous .... FAIN
desist .... STOP, ABSTAIN, CEASE, FORBEAR
desk .... TABLE, PULPIT, POST, ROLLTOP
for prayer ..... PRIE DIEU
reading .. LECTERN, AMBO
use of .... WRITING, DRAWING, READING
writing ..... DAVENPORT, ESCRITOIRE, SECRETARY
desman .... MUSK
desmid .... ALGA
desolate ...... BLEAK, LONELY, SOLITARY, DESERTED, (FOR)LORN, FORSAKEN, STARK
desolation ...... WASTE, RUIN, MISERY
despair .... MISERY, DESPERATION, DESPOND
desperado ... BRAVO, OUTLAW, CRIMINAL
hunters .... POSSE
desperate ... HOPELESS, RASH, RECKLESS

appeal .... SOS
criminal .... BRAVO, DESPERADO
despicable .... CONTEMPTIBLE, CONDEMNABLE, VILE, LOW-DOWN
person ..... CAD, SKUNK, SCOUNDREL, COWARD
slang .... SCALY
despise ...... SCORN, DISDAIN, CONTEMN, HATE, ABHOR, DETEST
despite ... NOTWITHSTANDING, INSULT, MALICE, (AL)THOUGH
despoil .... ROB, RUIN, PILLAGE, PLUNDER, LOOT, RAVAGE
despoiled: archaic .... REFT
despond .... DESPAIR
despondency ...... DEJECTION, DESPAIR
despot .... AUTOCRAT, DICTATOR, TYRANT, CZAR, TSAR
Persian .... SATRAP
despotic ruler .... TSAR, SHAH, CZAR
despotism .... TYRANNY, AUTOCRACY, AUTARCHY
despumate .... SKIM
desquamate .... PEEL (OFF)
dessert ..... FLAN, SWEET, ICE, MOUSSE, PARFAIT, SILLABUB, SUNDAE
fruit juices .... FRAPPE
fruit, gelatin .... CHARLOTTE
item ..... PUDDING, PIE, ICE CREAM, FRUITS
kind of .... SASS
melon .... BOMBE
milk and starchy substance BLANC MANGE
rum .... BABA
spongecake ...... TRIFLE
desserts .... DUE
destiny ..... FATE, LOT, DOOM
Oriental .... KISMET
destitute ...... POOR, NEEDY, DEVOID, LACKING
destitution .... POVERTY, NEED, PENURY
destrier ..... CHARGER, STEED, WARHORSE
destroy .... RAZE, RUIN, WRECK, ERADICATE, SACK, SLAY, RAVAGE, LAY WASTE, OBLITERATE
by fire .... GUT
entirely .... EXTERMINATE
machinery to force agreement .... RATTEN
slowly .... ERODE, WASTE
destroyer, crop ...... BLIGHT, DROUGHT, LOCUST
historical .... ATTILA
kind of .... VANDAL
of monster ...... HERMES, ST. GEORGE
of vermin .... EXTERMINATOR
of wood .... TERMITE
destruction ..... HAVOC, RUIN, WRECKAGE, WRACK
by fire .... HOLOCAUST
malicious .... VANDALISM
mass .... SLAUGHTER, MASSACRE, DECIMATION, GENOCIDE
of nation ..... GENOCIDE
widespread .. HOLOCAUST
destructive insect ..... LOCUST, TERMITE, MOTH
liquid .... ACID
natural phenomenon .... STORM, TORNADO, TYPHOON, EARTHQUAKE, CYCLONE
to metal .... RUST
destructor .... FURNACE, INCINERATOR
desuetude .... DISUSE
desultory .... RANDOM, HAPHAZARD, AIMLESS, EXCURSIVE
detach ...... SEVER, SEPARATE, UNFASTEN
detached .... ALOOF, SEPARATE, INDIFFERENT
in music ...... SPICCATO
detachment .... UNIT, ALOOFNESS, ISOLATION
detail ..... PARTICULAR, ITEM, ASSIGN(MENT), SPECIFY
attentive to .. METICULOUS
detailed .... ITEMIZED, ELABORATE, ASSIGNED
account .... EXPLICATION
explanation .. EXPOSITION
list ...... ENUMERATION, DIRECTORY, INVENTORY, ROSTER
details, small and unimportant MINUTIAE
detain .... HOLD, DELAY, CONFINE
ship in port ..... INTERN
detect .... DISCOVER, SPOT, SENSE, ESPY, DESCRY
detecting device ...... RADAR, BUG DOWSER, SONAR, ANTENNA, FEELER, TENTACLE
detection ... DISCOVERY, ESPIAL
detective ...... SLEUTH, TEC, DICK, OPERATIVE, HAWKSHAW, GUMSHOE, SPOTTER
Conan Doyle's .. HOLMES
describing one .. SHADOW, PRIVATE EYE, TAIL
of fiction/movie .. TRENT, NERO, CHAN, MOTO, HOLMES, DRAKE, POIROT, SAINT
orchid-loving ...... NERO
story .... MAIGRET
story character .... CORONER, SHERIFF, GOON, HATCHETMAN, INFORMER
detector of sorts .... BUG, ANTENNA, FEELER, NOSE, SONAR, RADAR
detent ... CATCH, CLICK, PAWL
detente .... COOLING OFF
of a sort .... RAPPROCHEMENT
deter .. DISCOURAGE, PREVENT
deterge .... CLEAN(SE)
detergent .... ABLUENT, CLEANSER, SAPONIN, SOAP, ARIEL
deteriorate .. DECAY, CORRUPT, DEBASE, WORSEN, DEPRECIATE
determinant .... CAUSE
determinate .... FIXED, DEFINITE, SPECIFIC
determination .... WILL
determine .... JUDGE, DECIDE, DEFINE, ASCERTAIN
issue by combat .... DERAIGN
quotient .... DIVIDE
worth of ..... EVALUATE, APPRAISE
determined .... SET, RESOLUTE, FIRM, DEAD SET
deterrent of a kind ..... FEAR, SHAME, DOUBT
war .... A-BOMB
detest ...... DISLIKE, ABHOR, HATE, LOATHE, EXECRATE
detestable .... ODIOUS, HATEFUL, EXECRABLE
person ...... BOOR, LOUT, COWARD, POLTROON
detestation .. HATRED, DISLIKE, LOATHING
dethrone .... DEPOSE
dethronement, object of ..... KING, EMPEROR, CHAMPION
detonate .... EXPLODE, FULMINATE
detonating device ...... FUSE, PERCUSSION, CAP, PIN, TRIGGER
object ..... FIRECRACKER, SQUIB, BOMB, GRENADE, BULLET, SHELL, DYNAMITE
detour ..... TURN, DEVIATION, DIVERT
detract .... DEROGATE, DISPARAGE, TAKE AWAY, DEPRECIATE
d'etre, ____ .... RAISON
detriment ..... HARM, INJURY, DAMAGE
detritus .... DEBRIS
Detroit (Michigan) product ... AUTOMOBILE, CAR
of Italy .... TURIN
suburb .... ECORSE
deuce .... TWO (SPOT)
Deus .... GOD
deus ex ____ .... MACHINA
Deutschland .... GERMANY
devastate ...... SACK, RAVAGE, DESTROY, LAY WASTE, RAZE, LEVEL
devastation ..... HAVOC, RUIN, DESTRUCTION
devel .... BLOW
develop ...... GROW, EVOLVE, RIPEN, ELABORATE
development .... EVENT, GROWTH, PROGRESS
of fetus .... FETATION, PREGNANCY

Devi .... SAKTI, MAYA
consort of .... SIVA
father of .... HIMAVAT
deviate ...... STRAY, DIVERGE, SHEER
from course .... DETOUR, YAW, VEER, SWERVE
from main topic .... DIGRESS
device .... PLAN, SCHEME, HICK(E)Y, TRICK, INVENTION, DESIGN, GADGET
air moistening .. HUMIDOR
any: sl. .... DINGUS
deceptive ...... GIMMICK
for catching criminals/fish DRAGNET
for hearing sound .... STETHOSCOPE
for holding stone in jewel cutting .... DIAL
for raising bucket .... WINDLASS
for secret listening .. BUG
gripping .... VISE, CLAMP
ingenious .... GADGET
light wave amplifying .... LASER
measuring .... TAPE, RULE(R)
secret .... GIMMICK
sound amplifying .... MASER
time beating .... METRONOME
to check vibration ...... DAMPER
tone muffling .... PEDAL, MUTE
trick .... GIMMICK
devil .... DEMON, SATAN, BELIAL, AZAZEL, LUCIFER, FIEND, SHAITAN, MAHOUND, OLD NICK, OLD HARRY, SCRATCH
dog .... MARINE, LEATHERNECK
little .... IMP, BRAT
may-care ... INSOUCIANT, RECKLESS
Moslem .... SHAITAN
of the .... DIABOLIC
worshipper .... DIABOLIST
devilfish .... RAY, MANTA, OCTOPUS, SKATE, SEABAT
devilish .... INFERNAL, WICKED, CRUEL, DIABOLIC(AL), DEMONIAC
devilkin .... IMP
devil's bones .... DICE
name ...... NICK, SATAN, LUCIFER
deviltry .... MISCHIEF
devious .... ROUNDABOUT, CROOKED, WINDING, CIRCUITOUS, TORTUOUS
devise .... PLAN, WILL, CONCOCT, INVENT, SCHEME, CONTRIVE, GIFT
devised, not .... INTESTATE
devisor .... TESTATOR
devitalize .... WEAKEN, SAP
devotee .... FAN, BUFF, ZEALOT, AFICIONADO
of beauty .... (A)ESTHETE, CONNOISSEUR
of the fine arts .... DILETTANTE
devoid ... DESTITUTE, LACKING
devoir .... DUTY
devolve .... PASS (ON)
devote .... CONSECRATE, DEDICATE, APPLY
devoted ..... LOYAL, FAITHFUL
devotee ..... ZEALOT, IST, FAN, FOLLOWER, VOTARY, PARTISAN, BUFF
devotion ...... PIETY, FEALTY, ZEAL, LOYALTY, ARDOR, FIDELITY
nine-day .... NOVENA
devotions .... PRAYERS
devour .... EAT, CONSUME, DESTROY
greedily .... WOLF, GORGE
devout .... PIOUS, EARNEST, RELIGIOUS
devoutness .... PIETY
dew .... MOISTURE
frozen .... RIME, (HOAR)FROST
dewclaw .... DIGIT
dewlap .... JOWL, WATTLE, PALEA, LAPPET
DEWS, part of ..... DISTANT, EARLY, WARNING, SYSTEM
dexter .... RIGHT-HAND
opposed to ..... SINISTER
dexterity ...... KNACK, SKILL, ADROITNESS, CLEVERNESS
special .... CRAFT
dexterous .... HANDY, ADROIT, SKILLFUL, ADEPT, DEFT
dextral ...... RIGHT(HANDED)
dextrose .... SUGAR, GLUCOSE
dhole .... CUON
di, as prefix .... TWICE, DOUBLE, TWOFOLD
dia, as prefix .... ACROSS, THROUGH
diabetes remedy ..... INSULIN
diabetics' bread ..... GLUTEN
remedy .... INSULIN
diablerie .... SORCERY, MISCHIEF, DEVIL(T)RY
diablerie .. SORCERY, MISCHIEF, DEVIL(T)RY
diabolic .... SATANIC, DEVILISH, FIENDISH, WICKED, INFERNAL
diabolism .... SORCERY
diacritical mark .... TILDE, UMLAUT, DIERESIS
diadem .... CROWN, TIARA, HEADBAND
diagnose .... EXAMINE
diagnostic in medicine .... SYMPTOM, DIACRITIC
rap .... PERCUSS
diagonal .... OBLIQUE, SLANTING
line .... BIAS
line between words ..... VIRGULE
diagram ..... SKETCH, CHART, DRAWING, GRAPH, PLAN, PLOT, SCHEMA, SCHEME
dial .... TUNE IN, CALL
compass .... CARD
miner's .... COMPASS
dialect .... LANGUE, IDIOM, LINGO, SPEECH, SLANG, ARGOT, CANT, PATOIS, VERNACULAR, JARGON, TONGUE
dialects, mixture of .... LINGUA FRANCA
dialectician .... LOGICIAN
dialectics .... ARGUMENTATION
dialogue ...... CONVERSATION, INTERLOCUTION
dialogues of Buddha .... SUTRA
diamagnetic substance .... BISMUTH, ZINC
diameter ... WIDTH, THICKNESS
measuring device .... CALIPER
of tube/gun .... CALIBER, BORE
diametrical .... DIRECT, CONTRARY, OPPOSITE
diamond .... STONE, GEM, PLAYGROUND, LOZENGE
base .... CULET
base, baseball ...... SACK
center, ancient .... GOLCONDA
circular, flat .... RONDEL
crystal .... MACLE
cup .... DOP, DOBB
cut .... FACET, BRIOLETTE
drill .... CARBONADO
facet .... CULET
holder .... DOP
in baseball ...... INFIELD
industrial use .. ABRASIVE, DRILLING, CUTTING
inferior .... BORT
native .... CARBON
official, baseball .... UMP(IRE)
perfect .... PARAGON
rough .... BRAIT
shaped armor plate ..... MASCLE
figure .. LOZENGE, MASCLE
shaped pattern ... DIAPER
slang ..... ICE, SPARKLER
State .... DELAWARE
synthetic ..... FABULITE
twin crystal ...... MACLE
diamondback ... SNAKE, MOTH, TERRAPIN, RATTLER
diamonds or hearts .... RED SUIT
Diana .... DELIA, ARTEMIS
parent of .... JUPITER, LATONA
poetic .... MOON
dianthus .... CARNATION
diapason .... (ORGAN)STOP, TUNING FORK
diaper .. TOWEL, NAPKIN, DIDY
diaphanous ...... SHEER, THIN, TRANSPARENT, GAUZY, TRANSLUCENT
diaphoresis .... SWEAT, PERSPIRATION
diaphragm .... MIDRIFF
pertaining to.... PHRENIC

sound . . . . HICCUP, HICCOUGH
diarist . . . . PEPYS, BURNEY, NICOLSON, JOURNALIST
diarrhea . . . . LIENTERY
medicine . . . . . PAREGORIC
diary . . . . . RECORD, DIURNAL, JOURNAL, DAYBOOK, EPHEMERIS
ship's . . . . LOG(BOOK)
diastase . . . . ENZYME, AMYLASE
diatomic . . . . BIVALENT
shell . . . . FRUSTULE
diatonic, opposed to . . . . CHROMATIC
scale . . . . GAMUT
diatribe . . . . . . DENUNCIATION, PHILIPPIC, TIRADE
Diaz, Mexican president . . . . . PORFIRIO
Rodrigo . . . . (EL) CID
dib . . . . BOB, DIP, DAP
dibble . . . . DIB, DAP
dice . . . . BONES, CUT, CRAP, CHOP, CUBE, GAME, CHECKER, IVORY
cater of . . . . FOUR
five on . . . . CINQUE
game . . . . NOVUM, HAZARD
game losing throw . . CRAP
six in . . . . SICE
spot . . . . PIP
term . . . . COME, NATURAL, CRAPS, AMBSACE, ELEVEN
three spots . . . . TREY
throw . . . . DIE, CHAPS, ROLL, RAILROAD, BOXCAR, CATER, JOE
throw natural . . . . . SEVEN
trick . . . . COG
diced . . . . CUBED
dichroite . . . . IOLITE
Dick: sl. . . . . DETECTIVE
Dickens (Charles) beadle . . . . . (MR.) BUMBLE
character . . . ROSA, DORA, DORRIT, PICKWICK, GAMP, TIM, FAGIN, (OLIVER) TWIST, HEEP, (JENNY) WREN, PIP, BUMBLE
colloquial . . . . DEVIL, DEUCE
hero . . . . CARTON
pen name . . . . BOZ
pickpocket . . . . FAGIN
dicker . . . . . BARTER, BARGAIN, TRADE
dickey . . . . BIB, PINAFORE, DONKEY, COLLAR, PLASTRON, (BACK)SEAT, RUMBLE
dicotyledon . . . . EXOGEN
dictate . . . . COMMAND, ORDER, BID
dictator . . . DESPOT, AUTOCRAT, TYRANT
propaganda of. . . BIG LIE
dictatorial . . . BOSSY, DESPOTIC, IMPERIOUS, ARBITRARY
diction . . . . ENUNCIATION
poor . . . . CACOLOGY
dictionary . . . . LEXICON, THESAURUS
prosody . . . . GRADUS
dictum . . . . SAYING, SAY-SO, PRONOUNCEMENT
didactic . . . . PEDANTIC
didactics . . . . PEDAGOGY
didapper . . . . GREBE, DABCHICK
diddle . . . . . . CHEAT, SWINDLE, JIGGLE
Diderot, Fr. philosopher . . . . . . DENIS
dido . . . . ANTIC, PRANK, CAPER
love of . . . . AENEAS
realm of . . . . . . CARTHAGE
didy . . . . DIAPER
didymous . . . . . . TWIN, DOUBLE
die . . . . . . DADO, DICE, MATRIX, MOLD, STAMP, CUBE, PERISH, EXPIRE, SUCCUMB, DECEASE, PASS AWAY, CROAK
due to cold . . WINTERKILL
diehard . . . . STUBBORN
dieresis . . . . UMLAUT
Dics Irac . . . . HYMN, JUDGMENT DAY
diet . . . . ASSEMBLY, FAST, (DAILY)FARE
course of . . . . . . REGIMEN
faulty . . . . DISTROPHY
old style . . . . BANT
dietetics . . . . SITOLOGY
differ . . . . EXCEPT, TAKE ISSUE, VARY, DISAGREE, DISSENT
difference . . . . . DISAGREEMENT, DISPUTE, QUARREL, VARIANCE
lunar and solar year . . . . EPACT
different . . . . ELSE, OTHER, DIVERSE(E), (AN)OTHER, UNLIKE
ones . . . . OTHERS
difficult . . . . HARD
problem . . . . POSER, DILEMMA, GORDIAN(KNOT)
to please . . . . QUEASY
difficulty . . . . SNAG, JAM, HARDSHIP, FIX, TROUBLE, PROBLEM, PICKLE, SCRAPE, RIGOR, STRAITS
without solution . . . . STALEMATE
diffident . . . . . . COY, TIMID, SHY
diffuse . . . . . . WORDY, SPREAD, SCATTER, RADIATE, PERMEATE
diffusion . . . . SPREADING, DISSEMINATION
thru a membrane . . . . OSMOSIS
dig . . . . DELVE, JAB, EXCAVATE, UNEARTH, PROD, POKE, NUDGE, SPUD
colloquial . . . TAUNT, JEER
for metal . . . . MINE
out . . . . GOUGE, MINE, SCOOP, EXHUME
slang . . . . . . UNDERSTAND, SEE
up . . . . DELVE
with snout . . . ROOT, ROUT
digest . . . ABSTRACT, SUMMARY, ASSIMILATE, SYNOPSIS, SUMMARIZE, APERCU
the . . . . PANDECT
digestion, good . . . . . EUPEPSIA
impaired . . . . . DYSPEPSIA
of . . . . PEPTIC
digestive enzyme . . . . . . PEPSIN, PAPAIN
digger . . . . . MINER, TRENCHER, SAPPER, SPADER, HOER, SANDHOG
digging tool . . . . . . SPADE, HOE, TROWEL, PICKAX(E), MATTOCK, SPUD
dight . . . . ADORN, EQUIP
digit . . . . FINGER, TOE, CIPHER, NUMBER, INTEGER
useless . . . . DEWCLAW
digital infection . . . . FELON
digitalis . . . . FOXGLOVE
digits . . . . HALLUCES
diglot . . . . BILINGUAL
dignified . . . . DECOROUS, STATELY, SEDATE
grace/richness . . . . ELEGANCE
dignify . . . . . HONOR, ENNOBLE, EXALT
dignitary . . . . PERSONAGE
dignity . . . . . NOBILITY, HONOR, STATELINESS, DECORUM, MAJESTY
steeped in . . . . STAID, DECOROUS, PRIM, PRIGGISH
digress . . . . . RAMBLE, DEVIATE, DIVAGATE
digressions of a sort . . . ASIDES, AD LIBS
dik-dik . . . . ANTELOPE
dike . . . . . . DITCH, LEVEE, DAM, CAUSEWAY, EMBANKMENT
break in a . . . . . CREVASSE
protective mat . . . . MATTRESS
dilantin, users of . . EPILEPTICS
dilapidated . . . . BROKEN DOWN, RUINED, RAMSHACKLE, RUN-DOWN, RATTY
dilapidation . . . . RUIN
dilate . . . . SWELL, EXPAND, WIDEN, DISTEND
dilation . . . . ENLARGEMENT, EXPANSION
cause of eyes' . . . . SURPRISE, WONDER, INCREDULITY
heart's . . . . DIASTOLE
pupil's . . . . MYDRIASIS
dilatory . . . . DELAYING
tactic in Congress . . . . . . FILIBUSTER
dilemma . . . . . . PREDICAMENT, FIX, JAM
horn of . . . . ALTERNATIVE, CHOICE
play's . . . . NODE
dilettante . . . . TRIFLER, AMATEUR, DABBLER, (A)ESTHETE
of a sort . . . . AFICIONADO, BOHEMIAN
diligence . . . . STAGECOACH, APPLICATION, INDUSTRY, PERSEVERANCE

diligent .... ACTIVE, SEDULOUS, HARDWORKING, BUSY
dill(seed) .... ANET, ANISE
dilly .... BARB
colloquial .. BEAUT, LULU
dillydally ..... LOITER, TRIFLE, HESITATE, VACILLATE, WAVER
diluent .... SOLVENT
dilute .... WATER, THIN
diluted .... THIN, WASHY
diluting substance .... DILUENT
dim ..... VAGUE, DARK, FAINT, UNCLEAR, OBSCURE, DULL, MIRK(Y), MURK(Y)
dime .... TEN CENTS, COIN
novel detective .... (NICK) CARTER
dime-a-dozen .... CHEAP
dimension ..... EXTENT, SCOPE, MEASUREMENT, SIZE, BREADTH
dimensions, of three .... CUBIC
diminish ..... REDUCE, LESSEN, (A)BATE, DECREASE, PETER, TAPER, WANE
diminutive ...... PETITE, WEE, TINY, SMALL, MINIKIN
animal .... RUNT
fowl .... BANTAM
suffix .... KIN, ETTE, ULE, IE, LET, LING
dimple .... HOLLOW, FOSSETTE
dimwit .. IDIOT, SIMPLETON, SAP
din .... NOISE, UPROAR
dinar .... COIN
dindle .... TINGLE, THRILL, VIBRATE
diner .... RESTAURANT
ding .... RING
dingbat......... STONE, STICK
dinghy .... (ROW)BOAT, SHALLOP, SABOT
dingle .... DALE, DELL, VALLEY, GLEN
dingus .... DEVICE, GADGET
dingy .... GRIMY, DISMAL, SHABBY
dining alcove .... DINETTE
car .... DINER
hall .... REFECTORY, MESS
room .... GRILL, DINETTE
table .... BOARD
table companion .... MESSMATE
table ornament .... EPERGNE
dink .... TRIM, DECK
dinkey .... TROLLEY, LOCOMOTIVE
dinky .... SMALL
dinner course .... ENTREE
jacket .... TUX(EDO)
of .... PRANDIAL
treat .... POTROAST
wagon .... TEACART
with toasting, etc. ...... BANQUET
dinosaur .... DIPLODOCUS, ORNITHOPOD, SAURIAN, SAUROPOD

dint .... FORCE, EXERTION, DENT
diocese .... SEE, BISHOPRIC, EPARCHY
Diomedes' father ..... TYDEUS
Dionysus' attendant .... NYMPH, M(A)ENAD
son .... PRIAPUS
staff .... THYRSUS
diopter .... ALIDADE
Dioscuri ..... TWINS, CASTOR, POLLUX
dip ...... IMMERSE, SINK, DAP, CANDLE, LADE
a doughnut .... DUNK
bait .... DAP, DIB(BLE)
in liquid ...... (IM)MERSE, DOUSE
lightly .... DIB, DAP
slang .... PICKPOCKET
the colors .... SALUTE
diplo, as combining form ..... TWO, TWIN, DOUBLE
diploma .... CHARTER, CERTIFICATE
colloquial .... SHEEPSKIN
diplomacy .... TACT
way of .... PROTOCOL
diplomat ..... ENVOY, LEGATE, AMBASSADOR, MINISTER, CONSUL
papal .... NUNCIO
diplomatic .... POLITIC, TACTFUL, ARTFUL, SUAVE
agreements ... PROTOCOL
ceremonial forms .... PROTOCOL
change of policy .... DEMARCHE
corps, dean of .... DOYEN
denial .... DEMENTI
dispatch container ...... POUCH
immunity .... DIPPLE
paper .... MEMORIAL
privilege ...... IMMUNITY
staff member .... ATTACHE
diplopia ...... DOUBLE VISION
dipody .... SYZYGY, VERSE, DIMETER
dipper .... SCOOP, PIGGIN, URSA, GREBE, LADLE
dipsomaniac ..... DRUNKARD, SOT, TOPER
dipsomaniacs, society of ...... ANONYMOUS
dipterous insect .... GNAT, HOUSEFLY, MOSQUITO
dire ...... FEARFUL, TERRIBLE, DREADFUL, HORRIBLE
direct ...... STRAIGHT, FRANK, CONDUCT, MANAGE, IMMEDIATE, FIRST HAND
attention to .... REFER
hit .... BULL'S EYE, ON TARGET
proceedings .... PRESIDE
direction ..... COURSE, ORDER, ADDRESS, GUIDANCE, TREND, MANAGEMENT
without fixed ... AIMLESS, MEANDERING, ERRATIC

directions, in all ...... ABOUT
directive .... ORDER, INSTRUCTION
directly .... SOON, INSTANTLY, AS SOON AS
colloquial .... SPANG
opposite ... DIAMETRICAL
director .... SUPERVISOR, MANAGER
in music .... CONDUCTOR
directory .... REGISTER
enter in .... LIST
dirge .... HYMN, MASS, THRENODY, CORONACH, LAMENT, GRIEF, SONG, EPICEDIUM
for dead .... REQUIEM
dirigible .... BALLOON, BLIMP, ZEPPELIN
bag/covering .. ENVELOPE
cabin .... GONDOLA
gas .... HELIUM
pilot .... AERONAUT
diriment .... NULLIFYING, VOIDING
dirk ...... DAGGER, PONIARD, SNEE
dirl .... TINGLE, VIBRATE
dirt ...... FILTH, SOIL, GRIME, GOSSIP, MUCK
dirty .... FOUL, UNCLEAN, OBSCENE, FILTHY, DEFILE, POLLUTE, SORDID
Dis .... PLUTO, HADES, UNDERWORLD, ORCUS
disability .... INCAPACITY
disable .... CRIPPLE, MAIM, DISQUALIFY, LAME, HAMSTRING
disadvantage ..... DRAWBACK, HANDICAP, DETRIMENT
disaffect .. ESTRANGE, ALIENATE
disagee .... DIFFER, DISPUTE
disagreeable .... CROSS, UNPLEASANT, OFFENSIVE
situation .... SCRAPE, FIX, JAM, SCOUR
smell .... FETOR
disagreement .... DISPUTE, DIFFERENCE, QUARREL
result of couple's .... DIVORCE, SEPARATION, SPAT
disallow .... REJECT, DENY
disappear ... VANISH, GO, PASS, EVANESCE, FLEE, ESCAPE
disappoint ... FAIL, LET DOWN, DISPLEASE
disappointment .... LET DOWN
disapproval .... REJECTION, DISLIKE
show of ...... BOO, HISS, SNEER, SNORT, HOOT
disapprove .... REJECT, TURN DOWN, CONDEMN, DENY
disarrange ...... MUSS, MIXUP, RUMPLE, MESS, UNSETTLE
disarray ... UPSET, CONFUSION, DISORDER
disarticulate ...... AMPUTATE, DISJOINT
disaster ...... EVIL, CALAMITY, MISFORTUNE

sudden and great .... DEBACLE
disavow .... ABJURE, DISCLAIM, DISOWN, REPUDIATE, DENY
disband .. BREAK UP, DISPERSE, DEMOBILIZE, SCATTER
disbar .... EXCLUDE
disbelief in God ..... ATHEISM
disbeliever .. SKEPTIC, DOUBTER
disburse ...... EXPEND, SPEND, PAY OUT
disc ...... DISH, PLATE, PATEN
discalced .... BAREFOOTED
discard ..... SCRAP, SHED, RID, JUNK, DROP, CAST OFF, CHUCK
card from hand .. THROW
discarded cargo .... JETSAM
discern .... SEE, PERCEIVE, NOTICE
beforehand ..... FORESEE
discerning .. ASTUTE, SHREWD, APPRECIATIVE, SAGACIOUS, SAPIENT
discernment ..... TASTE, SENSE, ACUMEN, APPRECIATION, UNDERSTANDING, FLAIR, KNACK
discharge .. RELIEVE, EMISSION, RELEASE, UNLOAD, FREE, DISMISS, EMIT, FIRE, FLUXION, SACK, CASHIER
a debt .... QUIT
morbid .... GLEET
of pus ..... SANIES, ISSUE
projectile .... FIRE
pus .... MATURATE, SUPPURATE
disciple .... PUPIL, ADHERENT, FOLLOWER, APOSTLE
India .... CHELA
disciplinarian ...... MARTINET, STICKLER
British university .... BULLDOG
stick of a .... FERULE
disciplinary mark .... DEMERIT
discipline .... TRAIN, CONTROL, PUNISH, DRILL
fellow student ..... HAZE
disclaim ..... DISAVOW, DENY, DISOWN, REPUDIATE
disclaimer .... DENIAL
disclose .... REVEAL, TELL, OPEN, BARE, DIVULGE
disclosure .... REVELATION, EXPOSE
confidential ..... TIP-OFF
discolor .... STAIN
discolored by bruise .... LIVID
discomfit .... CONFUSE, UPSET, DISCONCERT, JAR, EMBARRASS, ABASH, RUFFLE
discomfort .... ACHE, DISTRESS, UNEASINESS, PAIN
physical .... MALAISE
discommode .. INCONVENIENCE, DISTURB
discompose ... UPSET, AGITATE, DISTURB, DISCONCERT, RUFFLE
disconcert .... ABASH, RATTLE, DISTURB, UPSET, JAR, EMBARRASS, CONFUSE, FLABBERGAST, F(E)AZE, FEEZE
disconnect .... UNCOUPLE, SEPARATE, DETACH, SEVER
disconsolate .... SAD, GLOOMY
discontent, feeling of .... DYSPHORIA
discontented one .... WHINER, GRIPER
discontinue .... STOP, QUIT, HALT, CEASE, SUSPEND
discord .... DISSENSION, CONFLICT, CLASH, DIN
discordant .... JARRING, DISSONANT, HARSH, CACOPHONOUS
ringing .... JANGLE
discotheque .... CAFE
discount .... REBATE, AGIO, SUBTRACT, SET ASIDE, DEDUCT(ION)
discourage ... DETER, DAMPEN, DISHEARTEN, DEPRESS, DEMORALIZE, DAUNT
discourse ..... CONVERSATION, TALK, LECTURE, SERMON, TREATISE, DISSERT(ATION), HOMILY, DESCANT
art of .... RHETORIC
combining form .. LOG(O)
discourteous .. RUDE, IMPOLITE
discover ...... LEARN, DETECT, FIND(OUT), ESPY, DESCRY
discovery .. DETECTION, ESPIAL, FIND(ING)
discredit ... DISGRACE, DOUBT, DISHONOR, DISPARAGE, SLUR
discreet... PRUDENT, CAREFUL
discrepancy ... GAP, VARIANCE, DIFFERENCE
discrete ... SEPARATE, DISTINCT
discretion .... PRUDENCE, OPTION, JUDGMENT
discriminate ... DIFFERENTIATE, SECERN, DISTINGUISH, DEMARCATE
discrimination .. DISCERNMENT, TASTE, PERCEPTION
discursive .... PROLIX
discus .... DISK, QUOIT
thrower's statue .... DISCOBOLUS
discus ...... DISPUTE, DISSERT, DELIBERATE, DEBATE, ARGUE
in detail .... CANVASS
discussed publicly .. NOTORIOUS
discussion ..... DELIBERATION, DEBATE
group .... FORUM, PANEL, SEMINAR
heated ... HASSLE, HASSEL, RHUBARB
secret: sl. .... HUDDLE
disdain .... SNEER, DESPISE, CONTEMPT, SCORN, SPURN
disdainful one ...... SNEERER, SCORNER, SNOB
disease ..... ILLNESS, AILMENT, MALADY, AFFECTION, DISORDER
animal .... ANTHRAX, MANGE, GID, SPAVIN, NAGANA
bone .... RACHITIS, RICKETS
carried by mosquito ..... MALARIA
carried by tsetse .... NAGANA
carrier ...... TSETSE, RAT, MOSQUITO, ANOPHELES, FLY, VECTOR
cause of .... GERM, MICROBE, BACILLUS, VIRUS, PATHOGEN
causing .... PECCANT, MORBIFIC
combining form .. NOS(O)
contagious ..... MEASLES, TUBERCULOSIS, PLAGUE, PESTILENCE
chronic tropical ... SPRUE
cranberry .... SCALD
deficiency .... PELLAGRA, BERIBERI, RICKETS, SCURVY, MARASMUS, KWASHIORKOR
dust-caused .... SILICOSIS
epidemic .... PESTILENCE, PLAGUE, BUBONIC
eye .... CATARACT
fowl .... PIP, ROUP
from Anopheles mosquito MALARIA
germ killer .. ANTIBIOTIC, ANTIBODY
gradual end of ..... LYSIS
imaginary .... CRUD
indigenous ..... ENDEMIC
infectious ..... MALARIA, NAGANA, FAVUS
intestinal ...... CHOLERA
leading to ..... MORBIFIC
liver .... CIRRHOSIS, PORPHYRIA
malignant ...... PLAGUE, PESTILENCE, TUMOR, CANCER, FEVER
muscles ...... MYOPATHY
nervous .. PELLAGRA, TIC, CHOREA, EPILEPSY
of .... MORBID
of beard .... SYCOSIS
of chills and fever .. AGUE, MALARIA
of hip .... COXALGIA
of horses .... SPAVIN, GLANDERS, LAMPERS, LAMPAS
of kings so-called ...... HEMOPHILIA
of rye .... ERGOT
of wheat .... RUST
origin of ...... ETIOLOGY
passage into body ...... ATRIUM
pig .... BULL NOSE
plant .... SMUT
poultry .... ROUP, PIP
recurrence of ... RELAPSE
recurring ...... CHRONIC
scratchy .... ITCH
sheep .... ROT, GID
skin ..... ECZEMA, TINEA,

RINGWORM, TETTER, ACNE, LUPUS
source .... NIDUS
spreader .... CARRIER
study of causes .... ETIOLOGY
swine .... GARGET
tropical .... YAWS, SPRUE
virus .... FLU, COLD, RUBELLA, INFLUENZA, VARIOLA, RABIES, POX, VIROSIS, MEASLES, VARICELLA
warning symptom ...... PRODROME
wasting .... TABES, CONSUMPTION
diseased .... SICK, ILL, MORBID, PATHIC
beggar .... LEPER, LAZAR
diseases, classification of ..... NOSOLOGY
disembark .... DETRAIN, LAND
disembodied spirit ...... SOUL
disembowel ...... EVISCERATE, GUT, DRAW
disembowelment, suicide by ... HARAKIRI
disenchant .... DISILLUSION
disencumber .... RID, RELIEVE, FREE
disengage ..... DETACH, FREE, UNFASTEN, RELEASE
disentangle .... RAVEL, EXTRICATE
disfigure ...... DEFACE, SCAR, DEFORM, MAR, UGLIFY, MUTILATE, MANGLE
disfigurement .. BLEMISH, SCAR
disgorge .... VOMIT, EMPTY
disgrace .... BLOT, ODIUM, INFAMY, IGNOMINY, OBLOQUY, SHAME, DISHONOR, SCANDAL
disgraceful .... INDIGN
disgruntle .... DISPLEASE
disgruntled one .... SOREHEAD, CRYBABY, AX-GRINDER
disguise .. MASK, CAMOUFLAGE, CLOAK, VEIL
assumed ..... INCOGNITO
in .... INCOGNITO
wearer .... MUMMER
disgust .... DISTASTE, REPUGNANCE
disgusting .. FULSOME, ODIOUS, LOUSY
matter .... FILTH
dish .. PLATE, PLATTER, PATEN, VIAND, COURSE, RAMEKIN, RAMEQUIN, SAUCER, TUREEN
between courses .... ENTREE, ENTREMETS
boiled bread/cracker .... PANADA
candy .... COMPOTE, COMPOTIER
cheese .... RAREBIT
choice .... VIAND
colloquial ...... SERVING, TREAT, FOOD
cooking .... BLAZER
eggs, cheese, etc .... SOUFFLE
fancy .... KICKSHAW
for cookies, etc. .... EPERGNE
for cooking ... CASSEROLE
for cooking over coal ... BLAZER
for evaporating liquid .... CAPSULE
fruit .... COMPOTE, COMPOTIER, EPERGNE
highly spiced ...... OLIO
Hungarian ..... GOULASH
main .... ENTREE
maize and pepper .... TAMALE
make of a ... PORCELAIN, GLASS, PLASTIC, METAL, EARTHENWARE
meat ..... STEW, RAGOUT
Mexican .... CHILI CON CARNE, TAMALE
served before the roast ... ENTREE
serving .. NAPPY, NAPPIE, TRAY
soup .... TUREEN
tasty .... MORSEL
type ..... SAUCER, PLATE, BOWL, CUP
vegetable .... SALAD
dishearten .... DAUNT, DEJECT, DISCOURAGE, DAMPEN
dishes .... WARE
dishevel .... TOUSLE, MUSS, RUMPLE
disheveled .... BLOWZY, UNKEMPT
dishonest ... DECEITFUL, LYING
card player .... SHARPER, CHEAT, BLACKLEG
lawyer .... PETTIFOGGER, SHYSTER
person ... LIAR, CHEATER, STEALER, DECEIVER
dishonor .... SHAME, DISGRACE, DISCREDIT, ABUSE
dishonorable .... BASE
disillusion .... DISENCHANT
disinclined .. AVERSE, AGAINST, UNWILLING, RELUCTANT
disinfect .... STERILIZE, FUMIGATE
disinfectant ... LYSOL, CRESOL, CHLORINE, IODINE
disingenuous ... SLY, INSINCERE
disintegrate .... DECAY, CRUMBLE, BREAKUP, ERODE, MELT
by acid .... CORRODE
by water/wind .... ERODE
disinter .... EXHUME, DIG UP
disinterested .... UNBIASED, IMPARTIAL
disjoint .... DISLOCATE, DISMEMBER
disk ... PATEN, PATINA, PLATE
bright surrounding saints .... NIMBUS
for breaking soil .... HARROW
gem-cutting .... LAP
hockey .... PUCK
ice hockey .... PUCK
jockey ..... ANNOUNCER, DEEJAY
like ..... DISCOID, DISCAL
metal .... PATEN
obsolete .... DISCUS
on radio/telephone ..... DIAL
phonograph .... RECORD
poker .... CHIP
sealing .... WAFER
shaped .... DISCOID
throwing device .... TRAP
to seal joints .... GASKET
dislike .... ANTIPATHY, AVERSION, DISTASTE
intense .... HATRED, DETESTATION
dislocate .... SPLAY, UPSET, DISARRANGE, LUXATE, DISJOINT
dislodge ...... EJECT, REMOVE
disloyal .... FAITHLESS, UNFAITHFUL, RECREANT
person, kind of .... TRAITOR, TURNCOAT, RENEGADE, INGRATE
dismal .... DREARY, DINGY, BLEAK
dismantle .... STRIP
dismay ...... DAUNT, TERRIFY, DISCONCERT, ALARM, ABASH, APPAL(L)
dismember .... DISJOINT
dismiss ...... REMOVE, DEMIT, EXPEL, CASHIER, OUST, DISCHARGE, FIRE
archaic .... DEMIT
colloquial ... SACK, BOOT, BRUSH OFF
from command .. CASHIER
in disgrace ...... CASHIER
troops ...... DEMOBILIZE
dismissal ... OUSTER, REMOVAL, MITTIMUS
curt .... CONGE
dismount .. ALIGHT, GET DOWN, STEP DOWN
Disney, movie producer ..... WALT
artist ...... CARTOONIST, ANIMATOR
dog .... PLUTO
duck .... DONALD, DAISY
duckling .. HUEY, DEWEY, LOUIE
goldfish .... CLEO
middle name of .... ELIAS
mouse ... MICKEY, MINNIE
pachyderm ...... DUMBO
puppet .... PINOCCHIO
disobedient ... INSUBORDINATE
disorder .. CONFUSION, JUMBLE, CLUTTER, RIOT, MESS, CHAOS, UPSET, MUSS, LITTER
vague: sl. .... CRUD
disorderly ... CHAOTIC, MESSY, RIOTOUS, UNRULY, UNTIDY, PELLMELL
flight ... ROUT, STAMPEDE

disorganized .... DISORDERLY, HAYWIRE
disown ...... DISCLAIM, DENY, DISAVOW, REPUDIATE
disparage ... PEJORATE, DECRY, DEMEAN, DEPRECIATE, BELITTLE, LESSEN, SLUR, DISCREDIT, VILIPEND
disparaging remark ... SMEAR, SLUR, ASPERSION
disparate .. UNLIKE, DIFFERENT
dispassionate ..... FAIR, CALM, COOL
dispatch ... NEWS STORY, KILL, SEND(OFF), SPEED, HASTE, MESSAGE, POST
  bearer .... COURIER, MESSENGER
  boat .... AVISO
dispel ...... DISPERSE, SCATTER
dispensary .... CLINIC, INFIRMARY
dispensation ... DISTRIBUTION, EXEMPTION, MANAGEMENT
dispense ... EXCUSE, DEAL OUT, DISTRIBUTE
dispenser of alms ... ALMONER
disperse .... SCATTER
displace .... DISCHARGE, SUPPLANT, SUPERSEDE
displaced person .... DP, EVACUEE, REFUGEE
display .... EXHIBIT(ION), SHOW (OFF), UNFOLD, REVEAL, EXPOSE, SPORT
  brilliant .... RIOT, POMP, SPECTACLE, PARADE
  case .... COUNTER
  empty .... PAGEANT
  frame ..... EASEL, SHELF, SHELVE
  means of ..... SHOWCASE, (FASHION) SHOW
  of temper ..... TANTRUM
  ostentatiously .. FLAUNT, PARADE
  pretentious: colloq. ..... SPREAD
  showy .... FANFARE, SPLURGE, BLAZON
  superficial ...... VENEER
displease ...... ROIL, OFFEND, VEX, PIQUE, ANNOY, ANGER, MIFF
disport .... PLAY, FROLIC
dispose .... POSIT
  of .... SETTLE, SELL, GIVE AWAY, LIQUIDATE
disposed ...... APT, INCLINED, PRONE, BENT, WILLING, MINDED
  to agree ...... AMENABLE
  to fight .... BELLIGERENT, PUGNACIOUS
disposition ...... BENT, MOOD, ARRANGEMENT, TENDENCY, TEMPER(AMENT), MORALE, NATURE
  of mean .... ORNERY
  sour ... TESTY, GROUCHY, CRANKY, VINEGARY
dispossess ...... DIVEST, OUST, EJECT, DEPRIVE, EVICT, EXPROPRIATE
disproof .... REFUTATION
disprove ... GAINSAY, CONFUTE, REFUTE, REBUT
disputable .... MOOT
  at law .... LITIGIOUS
disputant .... ERISTIC
disputation ... DEBATE, POLEMIC
  art of .. POLEMICS, ERISTIC
disputatious .... CONTENTIOUS
dispute ..... ARGUE, DEBATE, CONTEST, CAUSERIE, BICKER, QUARREL, DOUBT, SQUABBLE, DOUBT, DISCUSS, ARGUMENT, FLITE, POLEMICS
  angrily ...... ALTERCATE
  beyond .... SETTLED
  noisy .. FRACAS, WRANGLE
  petty .... SPAT
disputer ... ARGUER, DEBATER, OPPOSER, DISSENTER
disqualified .... INELIGIBLE
disqualify .... RULE OUT
disquiet .... UNEASE, FRET, ANXIETY, UNREST
disquisition .... DISCOURSE
disregard .. IGNORE, OVERRIDE, OVERRULE
disregarding rule .... PECCANT
disreputable .... SHADY, UNSAVORY, ODOROUS, RAFFISH
  shrewish woman .... HARRIDAN, DEMIREP
disrespectful .. RUDE, IMPOLITE
disrupt .. REND, BREAK APART, SPLIT
dissatisfied (one) .... MALCONTENT
dissatisfy .... DISPLEASE
dissect .... CUT APART
dissemble .... FEIGN, PRETEND, SIMULATE, LIE
dissembler, alleged ..... JESUIT
disseminate ..... SPREAD, SOW, SCATTER, PROPAGATE, STREW
  by word of mouth ...... BROADCAST
  through the press .... PUBLICIZE
  through the radio .... BROADCAST
  through TV .... TELECAST
dissension .. DISCORD, QUARREL
dissent .... DISAGREE, PROTEST
dissenter ... PROTESTANT, ANTI, OPPOSER, OBJECTOR, SECTARY
dissepiment .... SEPTUM
dissert .... ARGUE
dissertation .. THESIS, TREATISE, DISCOURSE, PAPER
dissident .... ANTI, REBEL, OPPOSER, INTRANSIGENT, MALCONTENT
disservice .... INJURY
dissimilar .... DIFFERENT, DISPARATE, UNLIKE
dissipate ... DISPEL, SQUANDER, SPEND, WASTE
dissipated man ... ROUE, RAKE, DEBAUCHEE
dissociate .... SEPARATE, DISENGAGE
dissolute .... LAX, PROFLIGATE, RAKISH, LICENTIOUS
  person ...... RAKE, ROUE
dissolution .... DIALYSIS
  combining form ... LYSIS
dissolve .... LIQUEFY, MELT, THAW
  and wash away ... LEACH
dissolved substance .... SOLUTE
dissonance from violin group .. WOLF
dissonant .... ATONAL
dissuade .... DEHORT
  opposed to ... PERSUADE, EXHORT
distaff ..... WOMAN, WOMEN
distal .... TERMINAL
  opposed to .... PROXIMAL
distance .... REMOTENESS
  around .. CIRCUMFERENCE
  between ends ...... SPAN
  from equator .. LATITUDE
  in radio .... DX
  in the .... AFAR
  shortest .... BEELINE, STRAIGHTLINE
  three miles ...... LEAGUE
  traveled recorder .... ODOGRAPH
distant ..... AWAY, RESERVED, ALOOF, REMOTE, A(FAR), OFF
  past .... EARLY
  prefix .... TEL(E)
distaste .... DISLIKE, AVERSION
distemper ..... DISEASE, PAINT, DISORDER
distend ...... DILATE, EXPAND, STRETCH, INFLATE, SWELL
distended .... TURGID
  condition ..... TYMPANY
distich .... COUPLET
distill .... DRIP, TRICKLE, DECOCT, BREW
  several times .. COHOBATE
distillery ..... BREWERY, STILL
  mash .... SLOPS
  waste .... POTASH
distilling apparatus .. ALEMBIC, STILL
  refuse .... TAILING
  vessel .. RETORT, MATRASS
distinct .... DIFFERENT, CLEAR, SEPARATE, PLAIN
  part .... FEATURE
distinction .... HONOR
distinctive air .... AURA, ATMOSPHERE
  nature .... FLAVOR, TRAIT
  taste ..... SAVOR, PALATE
distinctly .... CLEARLY
distinguish ..... DISCRIMINATE, DISCERN, KNOW, LABEL, DIFFERENTIATE, SECERN
distinguished .... FAMOUS, EMINENT
  man .... DON
distinguishing feature .. TRAIT, CHARACTERISTIC

distort .... DEFORM, TWIST, MISREPRESENT, WARP
distorted ...... WRY, WARPED
distortion, ludicrous .... TRAVESTY
distract ..... DIVERT, CONFUSE, HARASS
distraction ...... AMUSEMENT, DIVERSION
frenzied .... TIZZY
distraint .... POIND
distraught ..... CRAZED, MAD, CONFUSED, HARASSED
distress ..... AGONY, AFFLICT, TROUBLE, PAIN, GRIEF, GRIPE, UPSET, STRAITS
signal ...... SOS, MAYDAY
distribute .. DOLE, METE, ALLOT
cards .... DEAL
distributor .... DEALER
district .. AREA, ZONE, CIRCUIT, SECTOR, WARD, PRECINCT
distrust .... DOUBT, SUSPICION
disturb .... ANNOY, PESTER, AGITATE, PERTURB, ROIL, MOLEST, FEEZE, F(E)AZE, UPSET
disturbance .... DISORDER, COMMOTION, HUBBUB, RUMPUS, UPROAR
disunion ... SCHISM, BREAK-UP, SEPARATION, DISCORD
disunite .. SEPARATE, BREAK UP
disuse .... DESUETUDE
ditch .. CHANNEL, DIKE, FOSS(E)
a suitor .... JILT
castle .... MOAT
digger .... TRENCHER
filling sticks ..... FASCINE
for defense ...... TRENCH
road .... GUTTER
slang ... DESERT, DISCARD
dither, in a ... EXCITED, AGOG
dithyramb ..... SONG, SPEECH, POEM, ODE, HYMN
dittany .... MINT, FRAXINELLA
ditto ... SAME, LIKEWISE, COPY
ditty .... SONG, REFRAIN
diuretic ..... URETIC, URINARY
stimulant .. CANTHARIDES
diurnal ...... DAILY, JOURNAL, DIARY
opposed to .. NOCTURNAL
diva .... PRIMA DONNA, SINGER
forte of ..... ARIA, OPERA
divagate .... DIGRESS
divan ..... CAFE, SOFA, COUCH, SETTEE, CANAPE, OTTOMAN, LOUNGE
divaricate ..... FORK, BRANCH
dive .... PLUNGE, DEN, HONKY-TONK
bomber .... STUKA
colloquial .... SALOON
fancy .... SWAN, GAINER, BACKFLIP
into water .... SUBMERGE
diver, breathing aid of .. SCUBA
from airplane .... PARACHUTIST
gear of .... FLIPPERS, AQUALUNG, SPEARGUN, (PARA)CHUTE
diverge .... DIFFER, VARY, DEVIATE
divergent strabismus .... WALLEYE
divergence .... VARIANCE
divers ...... VARIOUS, SUNDRY
diverse .... VARIED, DIFFERENT, SEVERAL
prefix .... POLY
diversify .... VARY
diversion .... AMUSEMENT, PASTIME, DISTRACTION
diversionary tactic ...... FEINT
divert ...... AMUSE, ESTRANGE, DISTRACT, DEFLECT, ENTERTAIN
divertissement ..... DIVERSION, ENTR'ACTE, INTERMEZZO, BALLET
divest ...... STRIP, DISPOSSESS, DEPRIVE
divide ..... SUNDER, SEPARATE, BISECT, SPLIT, APPORTION, ALIENATE, HALVE, TRANSECT
grammatically .... PUNCTUATE
into feet .... SCAN
into four parts .. QUARTER
into layers ...... FOLIATE
into three .... TRISECT
into two .... BISECT, HALF
voting area .... GERRYMANDER
divided .... CLEFT
into 100 degrees .... CENTIGRADE
dividend .... BONUS
dividing line .... SOLIDUS
wall .... SEPTUM
divination .... AUGURY, PROPHECY, NUMEROLOGY, HYDROMANCY
by communication with the dead .... NECROMANCY
by figures .... GEOMANCY
by lots .... SORTILEGE
by the stars .. ASTROLOGY
combining form .. MANCY
having powers of ...... MANTIC
pertaining to .... FATIDIC
powers of .... MANTIC
divine .. HOLY, SACRED, GUESS, GODLIKE, CONJECTURE, SUPERNAL
bread .... MANNA
Comedy author ... DANTE
Comedy setting .... HELL, PURGATORY, PARADISE
communication .. ORACLE
favor ... GRACE, BLESSING
food .... MANNA
intervention ... THEURGY
love .... AGAPE
presence ...... SHEKINAH
punishment ..... PLAGUE
spirit .... GHOST
tree .... DEVA
word .... LOGOS
work .... MIRACLE
diviner ...... SEER, CONJUROR
divining rod .... WAND
search water with .... DOWSE
user .... AARON
diving aid .... AQUALUNG
apparatus .. BATHYSCAPH
bell inventor .... EADS
bird .... LOON, GREBE, DUCKER
boat .... SUBMARINE
hazard .... BENDS
divinity .... DEITY, NUMEN, THEOLOGY, CANDY, GOD(HEAD), GODHOOD
division .... PART, SECTION, SEPARATION, FISSION, PARTITION, SCISSION, SCHISM
book .... CHAPTER
cell .... MITOSIS
city .... ZONE, WARD, PRECINCT
game .... HALF, SET, INNING, QUARTER, CHUKKER
in a group .... SCHISM
mankind .... RACE
mark of .... OBELUS
opera .... SCENA
play .... ACT, SCENE
poem ... CANTO, STANZA, VERSE
race .... LAP, HEAT
road .... LANE
society .... CASTE
religious .... SCHISM
result of .... QUOTIENT
divorce allowance ... ALIMONY
ground for ... ADULTERY, MENTAL CRUELTY, INCOMPATIBILITY
suit defendant .... CORRESPONDENT
suit subject .... ALIMONY, SETTLEMENT
divorcee .... FEME SOLE
divorcee's alimony .. ESTOVERS
divot .... TURF
divulge ... TELL, REVEAL, SPILL, DISCLOSE
divvy: sl. ..... SHARE, PORTION
Dixie-land ...... (THE) SOUTH
suffix used with .... CRAT
dixit, ____ .... IPSE
Dixon's partner .... MASON
dizen .... DECK
dizziness .. VERTIGO, GIDDINESS
attack of .... FAINT
dizzy .... GIDDY, GROGGY, VERTIGINOUS
colloquial .... SILLY, FOOLISH
of baseball fame ... DEAN
person: colloq. .... DAME
djebel .... HILL
do ..... CARRY OUT, PERFORM
alone .... SOLO
away with .... KILL, ABOLISH
in .... KILL, SLAY
it-yourself set .... KIT
make .... EKE
over .... REDECORATE

superficially ..... DABBLE
without ... SPARE, FOREGO
dobbin .... HORSE
dobson fly .... SIALID(AN)
doby: colloq. .... ADOBE
doc ...... DOCTOR, DOCUMENT
docile ...... GENTLE, PLIANT, TRACTABLE, OBEDIENT, TAME
dock .... JETTY, PIER, CLIP, BOB, WHARF, BANG, QUAY, LAND
area .... MARINA
post .... BOLLARD
worker ...... STEVEDORE, LONGSHOREMAN, LUMPER
docked tail .... BOB
docket .... AGENDA, LABEL, TICKET
docking space .... SLIP
doctor .. SURGEON, PHYSICIAN, OSTEOPATH, CHIROPRACTOR, MEDICINEMAN, TAMPER, FALSIFY, TREAT
assistant of ... INTERN(E), NURSE
colloquial ... MEDICO, VET
fake .... QUACK
herb .... QUACK
hospital .... INTERN
inquest .... CORONER
kind of ... QUACK, WITCH
Moslem .. HAKEEM, HAKIM
of animals .... VET(ERINARIAN)
of foot/hand diseases ... CHIROPODIST
teeth .... DENTIST
doctors' association ..... AMA
rap .... PERCUSS
doctrinaire .... VISIONARY, DICTATORIAL
doctrine ...... BELIEF, DOGMA, CULT, ISM, THEORY, TENET, PRINCIPLE, PRECEPT
mystical .... CABALA
of salvation ... LEGALISM
religious .. DOGMA, DOXY, CREED
widespread ..... GOSPEL
doctrines to be believed .... CREDENDA
document .. PAPER, CONTRACT, DEED
container ...... HANAPER
draft .... PROTOCOL
formal ..... INSTRUMENT
handwritten by signer .... HOLOGRAPH
legal .... WRIT
part of .... SEAL
ribbon of .... LAPEL
written .... SCRIPT
documents, collection of ..... PAPERS
dodder ...... SHAKE, TREMBLE, TOTTER
doddering person ..... DOTARD
Dodecanese island ... COS, KOS, PATMOS, RHODES, COAN, LERO, SIMI, CASO
dodge ... EVADE, RUSE, PARRY, DUCK
dodger ...... EVADER, ELUDER, RASCAL
Dodgers' (baseball) "preacher" ROE
dodo in flying school ... CADET
doe .... DEER
in its 2nd year ...... TEG
doff .... REMOVE, GET RID, TAKE OFF, VAIL
dog ...... FOLLOW, CLUMBER, CANINE, TYKE, PUG, HOUND, HUNT, DANE, SLUT, SPANIEL, BOXER, LAP, BEAGLE, CHENILLE, MASTIFF, RATTER
Alaskan ..... MALEMUTE, MALAMUTE, MALEMIUT
Arctic .... HUSKY, MALEMUTE
ape .... BABOON
Australian .... DINGO
Chinese breed .... CHOW, PEKIN(G)ESE
chops .... FLEWS
coach .... DALMATIAN
collar ring .... TERRET
combining form ... CYNO
command to ...... MUSH
constellation ...... CANIS
cry .... HOWL
cur .... TYKE
curly-haired .... POODLE, BARBET
disease ...... DISTEMPER, RABIES, MANGE
drinking way of ..... LAP
eat-dog affair .. RAT RACE
Eskimo .... HUSKY
face of .... MASK
family .... CANIDAE
FDR's .... FALA
female ..... BITCH, SLUT, BRACH(ET)
fennel .... HOGWEED, MAYWEED
ferocious ...... BANDOG, BLOODHOUND
foxhound-like .. HARRIER
genus .... CANIS
German ...... SHEPHERD
gone! ...... DARN, DAMN
greyhound ...... SALUKI
guard of the underworld CERBERUS
hair on neck ... HACKLES
hell .... CERBERUS
hound .... BEAGLE, BRACH(ET)
house .... KENNEL
howl of .. ULULATION, BAY
hunting .... BASSET, RETRIEVER, BRACH(ET), POINTER, SETTER, BEAGLE, HARRIER
hybrid ... CUR, MONGREL
in meteorology .... PARHELION
large .... MASTIFF
LBJ's .... YUKI
like animal ...... JACKAL
long-bodied .... DACHSHUND
loss of scent ...... FAULT
mongrel ...... TYKE, CUR
mongrel in White House YUKI
movie ...... ASTA, LASSIE, RIN TIN TIN, KELLY, NEIL
mythological .. CERBERUS
name of ..... ASTA, FALA, LASSIE, FIDO, ROVER, SPOTTY
neck hair ...... HACKLES
of hell .... CERBERUS
on India .... DHOLE
of mixed breed ..... CUR, MONGREL
pack .... KENNEL
parasite .... HEARTWORM
pet .... LAP, PEKINESE, POMERANIAN, CHIHUAHUA
Philippine .... ASO
police ... DANE, ALSATIAN
pound ... MONGREL, CUR, STRAY
pug-nosed ... PEKIN(G)ESE
rabbit/hare hunter ...... HARRIER
racing .... WHIPPET
Russian .... SAMOYED
short-legged ..... BEAGLE
Siberian .... SAMOYED
slang .... POOCH
sled .... HUSKY
small .... ALCO, CHIHUAHUA, POMERANIAN, PUG, BEAGLE, WHIFFET, POM
"space" .... LAIKA
spaniel .... COCKER
Star ... SIRIUS, CANICULA, PROCYON
Star, of the ...... SOTHIC
swift .... WHIPPET
tail of .... FLAG
tailless ..... SCHIPPERKE
team leader .. OUTRUNNER
television .. LASSIE, CLEO, LAD-A-DOG
terrier ...... SCHNAUZER, SEALYHAM
tongue cartilage .. LYTTA
tooth ..... FANG, CUSPID, LANIARY
toy ..... POM, PEKE, PUG, CHIHUAHUA
three-headed .. CERBERUS
Wales .... SEALYHAM
wild ..... DINGO, JACKAL, TANATE, DHOLE
wire-haired .... GRIFFON, GRIFFIN, PINSCHER, SCHNAUZER
with foxlike head .. CORGI
young ... PUP(PY), WHELP
dogcart .... TRAP
dogface: sl. .... G.I., INFANTRYMAN
dogfish .... BOWFIN, SHARK
skin .... SHAGREEN
dogged .... STUBBORN
dogger .... BOAT
doggerel .... JINGLE, VERSE
dogie .... CALF, MAVERICK

dogma ..... DOCTRINE, TENET, BELIEF, ISM
dogmatic .... DICTATORIAL
principle .... DICTA
saying .... DICTUM
dogmatist, a .... CALVINIST
dogs: sl. .... FEET
dogwood ..... CORNEL, OSIER, ASSEGAI, ASSAGAI, CORNUS, TUPELO
doilies .... NAPERY
doily .... MAT, NAPKIN
doited: Scot. .. SENILE, FOOLISH
doldrums ..... CALM, TEDIUM, LISTLESSNESS, BLUES, DUMPS
dole .. ALMS, DISTRIBUTE, METE
archaic .. SORROW, DOLOR
out .... RATION, METE
doleful .... DISMAL, SAD, MOURNFUL, LUGUBRIOUS
dolerite .... BASALT
doll ..... CHILD, TOY, PUPPET, MARIONETTE, MAUMET, MAMMET
real .... LULU
slang ...... GIRL, WOMAN
dollar bill, five: sl. .. FIN, FIVER
bill, one: sl. .... BUCK
bill, 100: sl. ... CENTURY, C-NOTE
bill, 1000: sl. ..... GRAND
bill, ten: sl. ... SAWBUCK, TENNER
bill, two: sl. ...... DEUCE
coin part .. NICKEL, DIME, CENT, QUARTER, EAGLE
coin: sl. ..... CARTWHEEL
Mexican .... PESO
quarter: sl. .... TWO BITS
slang .. SIMOLEON, BERRY, BUCK, PLUNK
Spanish .... DURO
dolly .... DASHER, LOCOMOTIVE
Indian .... TRAY
Varden ..... TROUT, HAT
what it holds ..... RIVET
dolman .. ROBE, JACKET, COAT, WRAP, MANTLE
dolmen stone ...... MEGALITH
Dolomites peak .. MARMOLADA
dolor .. SORROW, GRIEF, PANG, ANGUISH, AGONY
dolorous .... SAD
dolphin .... INIA, SOOSOO, PORPOISE, BELUGA, SUSU, BUOY, CETACEAN
frolic of .... GAMBOL
musician saved by ...... ORION
Spanish .... DORADO
striker .... SPAR, MARTINGAL(E)
whale .... ORC
dolt ...... CLOD, DUNCE, OAF, FOOL, ZANY, BLOCKHEAD, NUMSKULL, NITWIT, NINNY, HALFWIT, SAP
domain ..... REALM, DEMESNE, DEMENE, ESTATE, FIELD, SPHERE, BAILIWICK
poetic .... BOURN(E)
dome .... ROOF, CUPOLA
apse's .... CONCHA
building/hall with ...... ROTUNDA
poetic .... MANSION
slang .... HEAD
with cupola .... TOPE
Domenico, painter .. EL GRECO
domestic ... ENCHORIAL, TAME, NATIVE, ENCHORIC, SERVANT, MENIAL, LOCAL, SLAVEY
animal: dialectic .... CRITTER, CRITTUR
establishment ... MENAGE, HOUSEHOLD, DOMICILE
fowl .. DORKING, POULTRY
servant ..... (HOUSE)MAID
type of .... SLEEP-IN
worker .. SERVANT, COOK, MAID, BUTLER
domesticate ... TAME, CIVILIZE, BREAK
domicile ...... HOME, MENAGE, RESIDENCE, HOUSE(HOLD)
dominance .... CONTROL, MASTERY, SUPREMACY
dominant .... RULING, PREVAILING, PRE-EMINENT, IN CONTROL
dominate .... RULE, CONTROL, MASTER, HECTOR
dominated .... RIDDEN
domineer .. LORD OVER, BULLY
husband ...... HENPECK
Dominican .... FRIAR
dominie .... PASTOR, SCHOOLMASTER, CLERGYMAN
dominion ..... DOMAIN, SWAY, RULE, REIGN, REALM, EMPERY, EMPIRE, LORDSHIP
domino .. CLOAK, (HALF) MASK, TILE, LUMP
spot .... PIP
with four spots .. QUATRE
variant .... MUGGINS
dominoes not dealt .... STOCK
don .... WEAR, PUT ON, INVEST
Cambridge college ...... HEAD, TUTOR, FELLOW
Juan .... RAKE, PHILANDERER
Juan, greatest .... (ANTOINE) DUBOIS
Juan's mother ...... INEZ
opposed to .... DOFF
Quixote, author .... CERVANTES
Quixote's horse .... ROSINANTE
Quixote's ladylove ...... DULCINEA
river .... DUNA
Spanish .... GENTLEMAN, NOBLEMAN
dona .... LADY, MADAM
Donar, god of thunder .. THOR
donate ..... GIVE, CONTRIBUTE
Donau river .. DUNAREA, DUNA, DANUBE
done for ...... KAPUT, KILLED
with .... OVER
with hands ..... MANUAL
Donetsk .... STALINO
donjon .... TOWER, KEEP, DUNGEON
donkey ..... BURRO, DICK(E)Y, ONAGER, JENNET, CUDDY, (JACK)ASS
and horse offspring ..... HINNY, MULE
animal like a ... QUAGGA
cry .... BRAY
female .... MARE
male .... JACK
man rebuked by .... BALAAM
pet name of .... MOKE
young .... COLT, FOAL
donna: Ital. .... LADY, MADAM
donnybrook .... FREE-FOR-ALL
donor .... GIVER
doodad ... BAUBLE, GIMCRACK, GADGET, TRINKET, GEWGAW
doodle ..... DAWDLE, SCRAWL
doodlebug .... LARVA
doodlesack .... BAGPIPE
doohickey ... DINGUS, DEVICE, GADGET, DINGBAT
doom .. DESTINY, FATE, DEATH, CONDEMN
doomed .. KAPUT, CONDEMNED, FATED
to death .... FEY
to eternal punishment ... DAMNED
Doone, heroine .... LORNA
husband of .... RIDD
door ...... PASSAGE, ACCESS, PORTAL, ENTRY, WICKET
back .... POSTERN
catch .... LATCH
cover .. CANOPY, AWNING
crosspiece ...... LINTEL, TRANSOM
fastener .... LATCH, HASP
frame piece .... TILE
frame(work) .... GRATE, GRATING, SASH
grating .... GRILLE
handle .... KNOB
joint .... HINGE
knocker .... RAPPER
lock .... LATCH
lower half of .... HATCH
part .. STILE, SILL, LINTEL, PANEL, KNOB, LATCH, HASP, JAMB, RAIL
rooflike projection ..... CANOPY
doorkeeper .. PORTER, OSTIARY, CONCIERGE, USHER
Masonic .... TILER
doorman .... CONCIERGE, JANITOR, PORTER
doorsill .... THRESHOLD
doorway .. PORTAL, ENTRANCE
curtain .... PORTIERE
drapery .... LAMBREQUIN
out .... EXIT
sidepost .... JAMB(E)
dope .... DRUG, NARCOTIC
addict .... FIEND, JUNKIE, JUNKY
seller .... PUSHER
slang ..... INFORMATION,

FIGURE OUT, STUPID, INFO, LOW-DOWN
dor .... BEETLE, BUMBLEBEE
dorado .... DOLPHIN
dorbeetle ...... COCKCHAFER
Dorcas .... TABITHA
Doric cornice block .. MUTULE
droplike ornaments ..... GUTTA
Dorlcote Mill site ...... FLOSS
dormancy .... TORPOR
dormant ..... ASLEEP, QUIET, STILL, INACTIVE, TORPID, LATENT, QUIESCENT, RESTING
dormer .. LUTHERN, SKYLIGHT, WINDOW
dormitory ... BOARDINGHOUSE, HALL
dormouse ..... LEROT, RODENT
dornick ...... DAMASK, STONE
dorp .... VILLAGE, HAMLET
dorsal .... BACK, TERGAL
opposed to ..... VENTRAL
dorsum .... TERGUM, BACK
dorty .... SULLEN
dory .... (FISHING)BOAT
dos-a-dos .... SOFA, SEAT
Dos Passos' trilogy ...... USA
dose .... POTION
doss .... BED, BUNK, SLEEP
dosser .... PANNIER
dossier .... RECORD, FILE
dossil .. TENT, PLEDGET, STUPE, COMPRESS
dot .. POINT, SPOT, IOTA, MARK, PERIOD, DOWRY, STIPPLE, SPECK
dotage .... SENILITY
dotard .... OCTOGENARIAN
describing a ...... SENILE
dote .... ADORE
doting ...... DECAYING, FOND
dotted ..... MOTTLED, DAPPLE, STIPPLED, PIED
in heraldry .... SEME
dotterel .... DUPE, GULL, PLOVER
dotty .... FEEBLE, CRAZY
double ...... BINATE, DUPLEX, TWIN, TWOFOLD, PAIRED, DUAL, TWICE, DUPLE
aces .. AMBSACE, AMESACE
bass .... VIOLONE
chromosome ...... DYAD
cross: sl. .... TREACHERY, BETRAY, CHEAT
curve .... ESS
dagger mark ...... DIESIS
dealer .... CHEATER
dealing .... DUPLICITY
decker: colloq. .... SANDWICH
door part .... SWING
faced .... INSINCERE
faced god .... JANUS
faced person .... HYPOCRITE
meaning .... EQUIVOQUE, EQUIVOKE
moldboard plow .. LISTER
on the .... QUICKLY
prefix .... DI(S)
reed instrument ... OBOE, SHAWN, BASSOON
ripper/runner ...... SLED
ring .... GEMEL
sirloin beef ...... BARON
talk .... GIBBERISH
tongued ...... DECEITFUL
tongued creature .. SNAKE
tooth .... MOLAR
tripod .... CAT
up .... CLENCH, FOLD
vision .... DIPLOPIA
doublet .... POURPOINT
doubletree .... CROSSBAR
doubly .... TWICE
doubt .... FEAR, UNCERTAINTY, MISTRUST
beyond ... SURE, CERTAIN
cause/feel ...... MISGIVE
doubter ..... SKEPTIC, THOMAS
doubtful .... UNSURE, DUBIOUS
doubting Thomas .... SKEPTIC
douce: Scot. .... PLEASANT
douceur .... TIP, BRIBE
dough .... PASTE, BATTER
dry strip of ..... NOODLE
fermenting ...... LEAVEN
slang .... MONEY
toughener ...... GLUTEN
doughboy ..... INFANTRYMAN, DUMPLING
doughnut ... CRULLER, DONUT, FRIEDCAKE
colloquial .... SINKER
doughty .... BOLD, BRAVE, VALIANT
doughy .... PASTY, SOFT
doum .... PALM
dour .... STERN, SEVERE, GRIM, SULLEN
Douro .... DUERO
douse .... EXTINGUISH, DUCK, HIT, DRENCH
dove ... NUN, CULVER, PIGEON
describing a ..... GENTLE
genus .... COLUMBA
kind of .... HOMING, POUTER, TUMBLER
like .... COLUMBINE
make sound of .. MOURN, COO
shelter .... COTE, COLUMBARY
symbol ..... HOLY SPIRIT, PEACE
dovecote .... COLUMBARY
dovekie ...... AUK, ROTCH(E), GUILLEMOT, ALLE
Dover is capital of .. DELAWARE
dovetail .... JOINT, FIT
dowager .... WIDOW
dowdy .... SLOVENLY, SHABBY, FRUMP, TACKY
woman .... FRUMP
dowel .... PIN
like ...... TENON, PINTLE
dower ...... BEQUEST, TALENT, INHERITANCE, GIFT, ENDOW, DOWRY
dowlas .... LINEN, CALICO
down ..... FLOOR, BELOW, ILL, FEATHERS, HAIR, FLUFF, FUR, PILE, FELL
a mound like ..... DUNE
and out .... HELPLESS, HOPELESS
combining form .. CAT(A), KATA, CATH
covered with .... PUBESCENT, LANUGINOSE, LANUGINOUS
duck's .... EIDER
east .... MAINE, NEW ENGLAND
facing .. PRONE, PRONATE
feather .... PLUMULE
in baseball .... (PUT)OUT
in the mouth .... SAD
loose particles of ... FUZZ
plant .... VILLUS
prefix ..... CAT(A), KATA, CATH
source of .... EIDER
Under ...... AUSTRALIA, NEW ZEALAND, ANZAC
downcast ..... DEJECTED, SAD, GLOOMY
downfall .. RUIN, LABEFACTION
downhearted .. SAD, DEJECTED, DESPONDENT
downhill, go .... DECLINE
downpour ...... RAIN(STORM), SPATE, TORRENT, SHOWER
downright ... BLUNT, UTTERLY, ABSOLUTE, PLAIN, FRANK, SHEER, STARK
Downs, the .... ROADSTEAD
downtrodden ...... OPPRESSED
downy .... FLUFFY, FUZZY, NAPPY, VILLOUS, FLOSSY, FEATHERY, SERICEOUS
feather .... PLUMULE
growth ... LANUGO, MOLD
mass .... FLUE
surface/fiber .... NAP
dowry .... GIFT, TALENT, ENDOWMENT
of a .... DOTAL
doxology .... KADDISH
first word ...... GLORIA
doxy ... DOCTRINE, ISM, CREED
slang ..... HUSSY, WENCH
doyen .... DEAN
doze ..... (CAT)NAP, DROWSE, SNOOZE, SLEEP
dozen .... TWELVE
baker's .... THIRTEEN
long .... THIRTEEN
dozy .... SLEEPY, DROWSY
Dr. No's nemesis .... BOND
drab .... DULL, SLUT, LACKLUSTER
drabbet .... LINEN
drach .... DRAM
drachma .... COIN
1/100 of .... LEPTON
drachmas (1,700) in 1949 ...... DOLLAR
Draco .... DRAGON
Draconian ..... CRUEL, SEVERE
draff .... DREGS, LEES, REFUSE, SEDIMENT

draft ..... SKETCH, CONSCRIPT, DRAWING, POTATION, DRINK(ING), TASS, CHECK, DRAIN, POTION
animal ... OX, ELEPHANT, CARABAO, MULE
animal and its vehicle ... TEAM
card burner ... OBJECTOR, DODGER
deep .... SWIG
military service .. IMPRESS
draftee .. CONSCRIPT, RECRUIT
drafts .... CHECKERS
draftsman .... SCRIVENER
drag .... HAUL, HALE, LUG, TOW, TUG, DREDGE, CONTINUE, TRAIL, PULL, SWEEP, GRAPNEL
feet .... SCUFF(LE)
slang .. INFLUENCE, PUFF, DANCE
dragee .... CANDY, PILL
draggletail ... SLUT, SLATTERN
dragnet .... TRAWL, WEB
dragoman ...... INTERPRETER, CICERONE, GUIDE
dragon .. MONSTER, FIREDRAKE
archaic .. SNAKE, SERPENT, DRAKE
breath of .... FIRE
deb's .... DUENNA
giant .... FAFNIR
Greek .... LADON
in astronomy .... DRACO
mythical .... BASILISK
slayer ...... (ST.)GEORGE, CADMUS
two-legged ...... WIVERN
dragoon .... CAVALRYMAN, HARASS
drain .... EMPTY, SEWER, EXHAUST, DEPLETE, BUDDLE, FILTER, DRAW OFF, PIPE, DRAFT
liquid from ..... TAP, SAP
open ... KENNEL, GUTTER
road .... CULVERT
drainage hole ...... CESSPOOL, SUMP
pit .... SUMP
drake .... DUCK, CANNON, MAY FLY, MALLARD
archaic .... DRAGON
dram .. NIP, SLUG, SIP, DRINK, DRAFT
in assaying ..... CENTNER
drama .... (STAGE)PLAY, BUSKIN
climax ..... CATASTROPHE
colloquial .... LEGIT
comic scenes ..... RELIEF
conflict of character ..... AGON
Japanese .... KABUKI
main character .... PROTAGONIST
opening .... PROTASIS
outdoor .... PAGEANT
pertaining to ... THESPIAN
staging place ... THEATER
tragic .... BUSKIN
wordless ..... PANTOMIME

dramatic ..... VIVID, EXCITING
art .... THEATER
impersonator .... DISEUSE
dramatics .... HISTRIONICS
dramatis personae ...... CAST, CHARACTERS
dramatist .... PLAYWRIGHT
dramshop .... BAR, SALOON
drape .. CURTAIN, BAIZE, FOLD
draper .... CLOTHIER
drapery ... ARRAS, CURTAIN, CLOTH, FABRIC, TEXTILE, VALANCE
bed .... CANOPY
cloth ... MOREEN, MADRAS
cord .. TORSADE, TIEBACK
material ...... VELOURS, VELURE
shelf/door/window ..... LAMBREQUIN
drapes .... CURTAIN
drastic .... SEVERE, HARSH, EXTREME
drat .... EXPLETIVE
draught .... DRAFT
draughts: Brit. ..... CHECKERS
Dravidian ... TELEGU, TELUGU
draw .. DRAFT, LIMN, TIE, TUG, STALEMATE, DEPICT, DELINEATE, DRAG, PULL, SKETCH, HAUL, ATTRACT, DISEMBOWEL, EXTRACT
after .... TOW
as conclusion ..... INFER, DEDUCE
at a cigar(ette) ..... PUFF, DRAG
away ..... DIVERT, DRAFT
back .... RECOIL, RECEDE, QUAIL
back in fear .... QUAIL, COWER, CRINGE
close ... APPROACH, NEAR
forth ..... ELICIT, EDUCE, EVOKE
in dots .... STIPPLE
lots .... CAST
off .... DRAFT, SIPHON
off from dregs ..... RACK
out .... PROTRACT, CONTINUE, PROLONG, LENGTHEN, EXTRACT
sap .... BLEED
tight ..... TAUTEN, TENSE, FRAP
to scale ...... PROTRACT
drawback ... DEFECT, REFUND, REBATE, SHORTCOMING
drawbridge .... BASCULE, PONTLEVIS
drawer .... DRAFTSMAN
for money .... TILL
handle of .... KNOB
drawers .... SHORTS
women's .... PANTIES, PANTALET(TE)S
drawing ..... DESIGN, SKETCH, DIAGRAM, LOTTERY, TRACTION
architectural ..... EPURES
carbon pencil .... CHARCOAL
charcoal .... FUSAIN

in dots .... STIPPLE
of load/vehicle ... DRAFT
on walls, etc. .. GRAFFITO
paper .... ATLAS
power .... PULL
room .... PARLOR, SALON, SALA
with crayons .... CALCOGRAPHY
with lead-pointed instrument .... PLUMBAGO
drawn ...... TIRED, HAGGARD, EVEN, TENSE, TAUT
out .... LENGTHY
dray .... CART
dread .... AWE, FEAR
dreaded disease ...... CANCER, CHOLERA, TUBERCULOSIS, LEUKEMIA, SMALLPOX
dreadful ..... DIRE, AWESOME, TERRIBLE, HORRID, HIDEOUS
dreadfully: colloq. ...... VERY, EXTREMELY
dreadnaught ..... BATTLESHIP, WARSHIP
dream .. FANCY, VISION, HOPE, ILLUSION, FANTASY
day .... REVERIE
French .... REVE
goal .... IDEAL
up ... CONCEIVE, IMAGINE
world .... UTOPIA
dreamer .. FANTAST, VISIONARY
dreamland .... SLEEP
dreams, forecast based on .... ONEIROMANCY
interpret .... REDE
interpretation of .... ONEIROLOGY
interpreter .... ONEIROCRITIC
dreamy .... FANCIFUL, VISIONARY, IMPRACTICAL, VAGUE, MISTY
from dope smoking .. KEF
person .... POET, IDEALIST
dreary .... DISMAL, DULL, GLOOMY, CHEERLESS
Scottish .... DREE
dredge ... SIFT, DEEPEN, DRAG, SPRINKLE
bucket ...... CLAMSHELL
shovel .... SCOOP
dree .... ENDURE, DREARY, TEDIOUS, SUFFER
dregs ... RESIDUE, SILT, DRAFF, MAGMA, LEES, REFUSE, SEDIMENT, SCUM, FECES, GROUT
Dreiser (Theodore) character .. CARRIE
drench ...... SOP, WET, SOAK, SATURATE, SOUSE, DOUSE
drenched ...... ASOP, SOAKED, WET, SOPPING
Dresden .... PORCELAIN, CHINAWARE
dress .. ATTIRE, DECK, CLOTHE, FROCK, GARB, DECORATE, ACCOUTERMENTS, ADORN, TRIM, APPAREL, RAIMENT, RIG

a horse .... CURRY
by rubbing .... DUB
characteristic .... LIVERY
colloquial .... TOG(S), FIG
designer .... STYLIST
down .... SCOLD, REPRIMAND
external .... COAT, CLOAK, CAPE
fashion designer .... NORELL, GALANOS, SARMI, BALMAIN, BLASS, CASHIN, BEENE, TIFFEAU, GERNREICH
feathers .... PREEN
formal .. GOWN, TUXEDO, CUTAWAY
flax .... TED
gaudily .... BEDIZEN
hat .... SHAKO
in fine array .... DINK
leather .... CURRY, TAN, DUB
man's full .... TAILS
manner of .... GUISE
material .. VOILE, MUSLIN, SILK, PONGEE, WOOL
odd .... TOG
ornamental slit .... SLASH
pertaining to .. SARTORIAL
riding .... HABIT
showily .... FIG
spangle .... SEQUIN
stone .... NIG
style, men's .... NEHRU
style, women's .... MINISKIRT, SEE-THROUGH, TOPLESS, PANTSUIT, MUU-MUU, PALAZZO, CHEONGSAM
suit .... TUX(EDO)
to the ____ .... NINES
trimming .. RUCHE, GIMP, PIPING
up .... DANDIFY, PRANK, PRIMP, PRINK, PRUNE
with beak .... PREEN
with tails .... CUTAWAY
dressed .... CLOTHED, CLAD, GARBED, ARRAYED
shabbily .... POK(E)Y, DOWDY
smartly .... CHIC
to ____ .... KILL
to the ____ .... NINES
dresser ... BUREAU, CUPBOARD, CHEST
flashy .... SPIFF
of another person .... VALET
stylish .. TOFF, DUDE, FOP, DANDY
dressing .... SAUCE, STUFFING, PLEDGET
down .... SCOLDING
gown ... KIMONO, CAMISE, CAMISOLE, ROBE
medicated .... STUPE
soil .... MANURE
table .... TOILET, VANITY
wound .... BANDAGE, DOSSIL, STUPE, LINT
dressmaker .... MODISTE, SEAMSTRESS, COUTURIER(E), TAILOR, SARTOR
dressmaking term .... GORE, FACE, HEM
dressy .... STYLISH, ELEGANT, CHIC
Dreyfus' champion .... (EMILE) ZOLA
dribble .... TRICKLE, DROOL, SLAVER, DROP
in basketball .... BOUNCE
in football .... KICKS
dried coconut meat .... COPRA
flower bud .... CLOVE
grape .... RAISIN
grass .... HAY
orchid tuber .... SALEP
plum .... PRUNE
up ....SERE
drier .... DESICCATOR, KILN, OVEN, OAST, BLOWER, DESSICANT
natural .... SUN, FIRE
drift .... TENOR, INTENT, PILE, TREND, TENDENCY, INCLINATION, MEANING
ice .... SLUDGE, FLOE
in mining .... HEADING
in nautical usage .... SAG
drifter .. HOBO, TRAMP, CLOUD, DERELICT, NOMAD, VAGABOND
drill .... AWL, BORE, PIERCE, AUGER, BABOON, TRAIN, CLOTH, GIMLET, PRACTICE, DISCIPLINE
dentist's .... BURR
hall .... ARMORY
team .... SQUAD
drilling equipment .... RIG
machinery support .... DERRICK
drink .... SWALLOW, ABSORB, RICKEY, IMBIBE, QUAFF, TIFF, POTATION, LAP, TIPPLE, BOUSE, TEA, BEVERAGE, TODDY, ADE, ALE, BIB, AMRITA, DRAFT
a certain way .... LAP
addicted to alcoholic .... BIBULOUS
admiral's .... GROG
agave juice .... PULQUE
alcoholic .... LIBATION, RUM, GROG, GIN, SAKE, PEG, WHISKY, MEAD, BRANDY, BOOZE, TOT, LIQUOR, SWIZZLE
ancient .... MEAD, MORAT
another's health ... TOAST
appetizer .... COCKTAIL, BRACER
aromatic .. COFFEE, JULEP
barley .... PTISAN
beer and lemonade .... SHANDY
beerlike, sour .... KVAS(S)
before meal .... APERITIF
brandy .... COGNAC, SANGAREE
brandy and soda .... PEG
Brazilian .... ASSAI
Christmas .... NOG
claret, soda and sugar ... BADMINTON
cocktail .... MARTINI, HIGHBALL
cold .... JULEP, COBBLER
crushed fruit .... SMASH
deep .... SWILL
drug a .... HOCUS
East Indies .. NIPA, SOMA, TODDY
effervescent .... FIZ(Z)
excessively .. TOPE, BOUSE
fermented .... MEAD, ALE, BEER, RUM, SAKE, PERRY
for invalids .... CAUDLE
for fermented molasses .. RUM
for fermented rice .. SAKE
fruit juice .. BRANDY, ADE
gin .... RICKEY
granting immortality .... AMRITA
greedily .... SWILL, GULP, GUZZLE
habitually .. TIPPLE, TOPE
heartily/heavily .... CAROUSE
honey .... MORAT, MEAD
hot .... TODDY
iced .... COBBLER, SLING
in great gulps .... SWIG
in large quantities .... QUAFF, SWILL
insipid .... WISH-WASH
Japanese alcoholic .. SAKE
Mexican .... TEQUILA
mint, etc. .. JULEP, SMASH
mixed ... COCKTAIL, NOG, HIGHBALL
named after admiral .... GROG
of beverage with shaved ice .... FRAPPE
of forgetfulness .... NEPENTHE
of poison/medicine .... POTION
of rum .... GROG, BUMBO
of sarsaparilla sirup .... MEAD
of spiced, sugared gruel .. CAUDLE
of the gods .... NECTAR
palm .... TUBA, NIPA
rice .... SAKE
Russian .... VODKA
short .... DRAM
single .... SLUG, SHOT
slang .. OCEAN, SEA, LUSH
slowly .... SIP, NURSE
sly .... NIP
small .. DRAM, SIP, SNORT, SNIFTER, TIFF, (S)NIP
soft .... ADE, POP
spiced .... BISHOP, FLIP, PUNCH
spiced ale .... WASSAIL
stimulant .... BRACER
stirring stick ... MUDDLER
sweet sap .... TODDY
sweetened .. POSSET, FLIP, BISHOP, ORGEAT, NEGUS, PUNCH

teenage ... SODA, MALTED
to .... TOAST, SALUTE
to excess ... TOPE, SWILL, CAROUSE
together .... HOBNOB
weak .... WISH-WASH
whisky-soda ... HIGHBALL
wine and honey .... OENOMEL
wine, spices and water .. SANGAREE
drinkable .... POTABLE
drinker .. TOPER, SOT, IMBIBER, TIPPLER, TOSSPOT, BIBBER
insatiable alcoholic ..... DIPSOMANIAC
drinking .... TIFFIN, POTATION
bout .... WASSAIL, SPREE, COMPOTATION, BENDER, BAT
bowl ... MAZER, MAZARD, JORUM
convivial .... BOWL, WASSAIL
cup ..... RUMMER, TOBY, BEAKER, TASS, NOGGIN, MUG, TANKARD, STEIN
excessive ..... POTATION, WASSAIL, CRAPULOUS, CRAPULENT
fountain ...... BUBBLER, SCUTTLEBUTT
glass .. TUMBLER, GOBLET, RUMMER
mug, leather .... JACK
party .. CAROUSAL, ORGY, WASSAIL
salutation ..... WASSAIL, TOAST
song .... WASSAIL
spree ..... BOUSE, BOOZE, CAROUSAL, WASSAIL, BENDER
toast .. MABUHAY, PROSIT, SALUD, SKOAL
drip .... TRICKLE, LEAK, DROP, SEEP
slang .... CREEP
dripping .... ASOP, TRICKLING
drive ... AVENUE, URGE, GOAD, FORCE, IMPEL, RIDE, PROPEL, PRESSURE, FEEZE, PROD, CAMPAIGN, PUSH, ENERGY, RUSH, CHARGE
away .... SHOO
back .... REPEL, REPULSE, REBUFF
colloquial .... HUSTLE
from cover .... FLUSH
head first ..... BUTT, RAM
in offering .. FOOD, DRINK, MOVIE
in waiter .... CARHOP
nail obliquely .... TOE
out .... ROUT, ROUST
out by incantation ...... EXORCISE
reformer's ..... CRUSADE
tree-lined .... AVENUE
drivel .... DROOL, SLOBBER, TWADDLE, SALIVA, NONSENSE, MAUNDER, SLUSH
driven obliquely .... TOED
driver .. JEHU, WHIP, MOTORIST, CHAUFFEUR, MOTORMAN
animal .... MAHOUT, MULETEER, SKINNER
backseat, usual .. WIFE(Y)
camel .... SARWAN
carriage ..... COACHMAN, HACK
coach .... JARVEY
elephant .... MAHOUT
gear of ... CRASH HELMET
kind of .... PILE, MALLET, HAMMER, TAMP
mule .... MULETEER
reckless .... JEHU
seat of .... BOX
slave ...... TASKMASTER, MARTINET
driving, a .... DRIFT
ambition .... GET-UP
desire .... OBSESSION
force, human ..... LIBIDO
line .... REIN
drizzle .... MIZZLE, RAIN
drogher .... SAILBOAT
droghiere .... GROCER
droit .... (LEGAL) RIGHT
droll .. BUFFOON, COMIC, JESTER, AMUSING, WAG, ODD, HUMOROUS
drome, as suffix .... RUNNING, RACECOURSE
dromedary ... DELUL, MEHARI, CAMEL
dromon(d) .... SHIP
drone .... HUM, IDLER, (HONEY)BEE, LOAF(ER), AIRPLANE, BAGPIPE
drool .... DRIVEL, SLAVER, SLOBBER, TWADDLE, NONSENSE
droop ..... LOP, WEAKEN, SAG, NUTATE, WILT, FLAG, PEAK, LANGUISH, LOLL
drooping .... NUTANT, LOPPY, LANGUID, SLOUCH
on one side .... ALOP
drop .... BLOB, FALL, OMIT, GUTTA, GLOBULE, DECREASE, SLUMP, GOUT, DISMISS, LOWER, PLOP, FLUNK, FLUMP, PLUMP
below surface ...... SINK
fish line .... DAP
gently .... DAP, DIP, PLOP
heavily .... FLUMP
in trickles .... DRIP
one .... MINIM
sharp .... NOSE DIVE
straight down .. PLUMMET
sudden ..... SLUMP, DIVE, CRASH
viscous substance .. BLOB
droplike ornaments .... GUTTA
dropout, for one ..... QUITTER
dropper .... PIPET(TE)
droppings .... DUNG, MANURE, GUANO
dropsical .... EDEMIC
dropsy ... (O)EDEMA, BERIBERI, ANASARCA
drosophila .... (FRUIT)FLY
dross .... SCORIA, SCUM, SLAG, WASTE, REFUSE, RUBBISH
drought .... DRYNESS
plant .... XEROPHYTE, GUAR, CACTUS
droughty .... DRY, ARID
drove .... CROWD, FLOCK, HORDE, HERD
composition of .. CATTLE, HOGS, SHEEP
drover .... CATTLE DEALER
drown ..... INUNDATE, FLOOD, DEADEN, MUFFLE
drowning, execution by ...... NOYADE
drowse ...... DOZE, NOD, NAP
drowsiness .... OSCITANCY, LETHARGY
drowsy .... SLEEPY, HEAVY-LIDDED, LETHARGIC
from using drug ..... KEF
drub .. BEAT, CUDGEL, THRASH, DEFEAT
drubbing .... DEFEAT
drudge ... PLOD, HOUSEKEEPER, SLAVE, TOIL(ER), CHORE, MOIL, GRUB, SCRUB
literary .... HACK
drudgery .. FAG, MOIL, CHORE, TASKWORK, RUT, GRIND, SWEAT
drug ..... COCAIN(E), HEROIN, OPIUM, MARIJUANA, NARCOTIC, MEDICINE, STUPEFY, HOCUS
addict .... JUNKIE, HOPHEAD, SNOWBIRD
bitter .... QUASSIA
causing vomit .... EMETIC
cocain .... COKE
compressed form ...... TABLOID
eye .. NEOMYCIN, MYOTIC, MYDRIATIC
for addicts ... METHADON
for blood pressure ...... ADRENALIN
for drying .... DESSICANT
for epileptic attacks ..... DILANTIN
for forgetfulness .... NEPENTHE
for perspiration .... BONESET
grinder .... MULLER
heroin: sl. .... SMACK
intoxicating ..... PEYOTE
laxative .... ALOE
LSD: sl. .... ACID
marijuana: sl. .... POT
plant .... ALOE, POPPY
slang .... DOPE
"speed" .... LSD, METHEDRINE, AMPHETAMINE
drugget .... RUG, MAT
druggist .... PHARMACIST, CHEMIST
container of ... GALLIPOT
drugs, action of ..... SYNERGY
drugstore ...... APOTHECARY, PHARMACY
soap .... SAPO

drum .. TUM, TAMBOUR, BONGO, TAMBOURIN(E), TYMPAN
beat ..... DUB, RUBADUB, RATAPLAN
call .... TATTOO, DIAN
capstan's .... RUNDLE
continuously .... TATTOO
hand ... TIMBREL, TABOR, TAMBOURINE
head .... TYMPANUM
jungle .... TOMTOM
like a .... TYMPANIC
long .... TAMBOURIN
low continuous beating of RUFFLE
major's rod ...... BATON
Moorish .... ATABAL
of a .... TYMPANIC
Oriental .... TOMTOM
played with hands ...... BONGO
played with stick .... TABORIN(E)
player .... TYMPANIST
primitive ...... TOM-TOM, TAM-TAM
signal ... CHAMADE, TAPS, TATTOO
small .. TABORET, TABOUR, TABORIN(E), TABRET
sound .... ROLL, BEAT
string across ...... SNARE
with fingers ...... THRUM
drumbeat ...... DUB, TATTOO, FLAM, RATAPLAN, RUFFLE, RUB-A-DUB-DUB
continuous ...... ROLL, RUFFLE
drumfire .... BARRAGE
drumfish .... WHITING
drumlin .... HILL, RIDGE
drummer .... SALESMAN
famed ..... (GENE) KRUPA
kind of .... SALESMAN
drumming, continuous .... TATTOO
drunk(ard) ..... INTOXICATED, INEBRIATE(D), TIPSY, BOUSY, BOOZY, BIBULOUS, GROGGY, TIGHT, BLIND, COCKEYED, FRIED, STEWED, HIGH, BLOAT, RUMMY, DIPSOMANIAC, SOT, TOSSPOT, TOPER, BLOTTO, WALLEYED, LOADED, NAPPY, SOAK, PLASTERED, TIPPLER, SOUSE, POTTED, BARFLY, MALTY, ROUNDER
drunken .... SOUSED, BACCHIC, INTOXICATED
carouser ... BACCHANT(E)
celebration .... JAG
party ...... BACCHANAL, WASSAIL
spree .... BINGE, SOAK
drunkenness ..... INTOXICATION
drupe ..... APRICOT, CHERRY, PLUM
drupelet ..... TRYMA, ACINUS, NUTLET
drupelets, fruit of many ...... (BLACK)BERRY, LOGANBERRY, RASPBERRY, GRAPE
dry .. SERE, BRUT, DEHYDRATE, ARID, DULL, BORING, WITHERED, MATTER-OF-FACT, (DE)SICCATE, JEJUNE, ANHYDROUS
as wine .... SEC, BRUT
cleaning solvent .... GASOLINE, NAPHTHA, BENZINE
colloquial .... PROHIBITIONIST
combining form ... XERO
fly .... LURE
French ....SEC
goods dealer .... DRAPER
lake basin .... PLAYA
moderately ..... SUBARID
opposed to .... WET
run .... REHEARSAL
spell .... DROUGHT
story, describing .. JEJUNE
throat .... HUSKY
to .... BLOT, SUN
tongue, sign of ... THIRST
up ..... WITHER, PARCH, WIZEN
with cloth/mop .... WIPE
with heat .... SUN, BAKE, TORREFY, TORRIFY
dryad .... NYMPH
dryer .... BLOWER, DESICCANT, SUN, OAST, KILN
dryfly .... LURE
drying cloth .... TOWEL
machine .... TEDDER
drying, spread for .... TED
dryness from lack of rain .... DROU(G)HT
of skin/eyeball .. XEROSIS
DST, part of ..... DAYLIGHT, SAVING, TIME
Du Barry's title ..... MADAME, COMTESSE
duad ...... DUAL, TWO, PAIR, COUPLE
dual ...... DOUBLE, TWOFOLD
channel audio .... STEREO
dualism, element of .... MIND, MATTER, GOOD, EVIL, PHYSICAL, SPIRITUAL
dub ... POKE, THRUST, KNIGHT, DUFFER, HIT, (NICK)NAME, DRUMBEAT
dubiety .... UNCERTAINTY
dubious ...... SHADY, VAGUE, SKEPTICAL, DOUBTFUL, QUESTIONABLE, LEERY
dubitation .... DOUBT
Dublin is capital of .. IRELAND
ducal .... DUKEDOM
ducat: sl. .. (ADMISSION) TICKET
duce: Ital. ..... LEADER, CHIEF
Italian ...... MUSSOLINI
Duchess of Windsor .... (WALLIS) WARFIELD
title of respect .... GRACE
duck .... AVOID, BUFFLEHEAD, CLOTH, BIRD, DOUSE, TERN, SMEE, PINTAIL, EIDER, MALLARD, DODGE, PEKIN, COOT, SCO(O)TER
Asiatic .... MANDARIN
colloquial ...... DARLING
color on wing .... SPECULUM
cry of .... QUACK
decoyer .... TOLLER
diving .. REDHEAD, SMEW, MERGANSER, POCHARD
downy .... EIDER
fabric .... COTTON, LINEN
fish-eating .. MERGANSER, GOOSANDER
foot membrane ..... WEB
genus ...... ANSER, ANAS
handsome ... WOODLUCK
Hawaiian .... NENE
hawk .. FALCON, HARRIER
hunter's screen .... BLIND
large .... MUSCOVY
like .... COOT
lure .... DECOY
male .... DRAKE
merganser .... SMEW
non-quacking .. MUSCOVY
pintail .... SMEE
river .... TEAL
sea .. EIDER, SCAUP, COOT, SCO(O)TER
shooting boat ..... SKAG
slang ..... PERSON, QUEER
small .... SMEW
use of man-made .. DECOY
walk .... WADDLE
wild .... MALLARD, CANVASBACK, SHELDRAKE, SCAUP, DRAKE, WIDGEON, GADWALL, GOLDEN-EYE
young .... DUCKLING
duckbill .... PLATYPUS, MONOTREME
ducker ..... DABCHICK, GREBE
duckpins .... BOWLING
ducks, brood of .... TEAM
duct ...... CANAL, PIPE, TUBE, CHANNEL, CONDUIT, VAS
body .... MEATUS
narrowing of ... STENOSIS
ductile ..... TENSILE, ELASTIC, PLASTIC, PLIANT, PLIABLE, TRACTILE
ductless gland, of a .. THYROID, ADRENAL, PITUITARY, ENDOCRINE
glandlike body .. THYMUS
ducts, of or having .. VASCULAR
dud .... FLOP, FAILURE
duddy: Scot. .... RAGGED
dude .. COXCOMB, FOP, DANDY
one kind of ..... TOURIST
ranch's use ...... RESORT
dudeen ...... (TOBACCO)PIPE
Dudevant, Baronne .... (GEORGE) SAND
dudgeon ... RESENTMENT, HILT, PIQUE, ANGER
duds .... CLOTHES, TRAPPINGS
due ... DEBT, RIGHT, PAYABLE, OWING, FITTING, PROPER
one's .... DES(S)ERTS
duel .... CONTEST, COMBAT
challenge .... CARTEL
mock .... TILT, JOUST
principal of famous ..... BURR, HAMILTON

victim of ..... HAMILTON
dueling code/art ..... DUELLO
position ...... EN GARDE
duenna .... CHAPERON, GOVERNESS
Duero .... DOURO
dues .... FEE, TAX
duet .... DUO
duff ... PUDDING, (COAL)DUST, SLACK
duffel .... BAG
duffer .... PEDDLER, DUB, FUMBLER
dug .... NIPPLE, TEAT
dugong .... COWFISH, SEACOW, HALICORE, MANATEE
dugout .. BOAT, CANOE, BANCA, PIROGUE, (BOMB)SHELTER, FOXHOLE, PIRAGUA
French .... ABRI
India .... DONGA
duke, of a .... DUCAL
son eldest, of .. MARQUIS
title of respect .... GRACE
wife of .... DUCHESS
dukedom .... DUCHY
dukes: sl. .... FISTS, HANDS
dulcet .... SWEET, MELODIOUS, ARIOSO, ORGAN STOP
dulcimer ...... CITOLE, SITAR, PSALTERY, HARP
Dulcinea .... SWEETHEART
dull .. STODGY, STUPID, TEDIOUS, BORING, SLACK, INSIPID, VAPID, BLUNT, LACKLUSTER, DRAB, JEJUNE, PROSY, FLAT, FISHY, MAT(TE), CRASS, GROSS, OBTUSE, LOGY, HUMDRUM, HEBETATE
and fat .... JEJUNE
color ...... MATTE, DUN, TERNE, DRAB
edge/point .... BLUNT
finish .... MAT(TE)
grayish brown ..... DUN
make .... OBTUND, BLUNT
mentally .... STUPID
period ..... SLACK, LULL, SLUMP
person, describing one ... BORE, DULLARD, DUNCE
sound .... THUD
dullard .... DUNCE, OAF, LOUT, BOOR, SIMPLETON, DOLT, NUMSKULL
dulse .... SEAWEED
duly .... PROPERLY, FITTINGLY, AS DUE
Dumas character .... ARAMIS, PORTHOS, ATHOS, BONIFACE, D'ARTAGNAN
novel .... CAMILLE
dumb .... MUTE, SILENT, RETICENT
clucks .... OXEN
clucks, per J. Luzzatto .. OXES
colloquial .... STUPID
show figure ..... PUPPET, MARIONETTE, PANTOMIME
waiter .... ELEVATOR
dumbbell ...... MORON, IDIOT
dum(b)found .... AMAZE, ASTONISH
dumdum .... BULLET
dummy .... STRAWMAN, DUPE, MUTE, MANNEQUIN, TOOL
cannon .... QUAKER
colloquial .... FRONT
field .... SCARECROW
in railroading .... LOCOMOTIVE
kind of ..... FIGUREHEAD
ventriloquist's .... SNERD
dump .... LUMP, UNLOAD, EMPTY OUT, CHUCK, PILE, HEAP
archaic ..... TUNE, SONG
dumpling .... PIE
boiled .... DOUGHBOY
dumps, the .... BLUES, GLOOM, DOLDRUMS
dumpy .. SQUAT, MELANCHOLY, PUDGY
dun ..... ASK, ARTIFICIAL FLY, MAY FLY, BROWN
Duna, in German ..... DVINA
in Hungarian ... DANUBE
in Russian .... DON
Duncan, dancer ..... ISADORA
dunce .. COOT, OAF, NUMSKULL, DOLT, NANNY, SIMPLETON, MORON
dunderhead .... DUNCE, DOLT, IDIOT, NUMSKULL
dune ...... HILL, RIDGE, DENE
dung .. DROPPING(S), MANURE, FILTH, EXCREMENT, ORDURE
beetle .. CHAFER, SCARAB, DOR
piece .... CHIP
dungeon .... DUNJON, PRISON, TOWER, OUBLIETTE
dungy .... FILTHY
dunk .... DIP, SOUSE
dunker .... SOPPER
dunlin .... SANDPIPER
dunnage .... BAGGAGE
Dunne, actress .... IRENE
dunnite .... EXPLOSIVE
duo .... DUET, PAIR
as combining form ...... TWO, DOUBLE
duomo .... CATHEDRAL
dupe .... CHEAT, FOOL, TRICK, VICTIM, GULL, CON(E)Y, GREENHORN, HOCUS, MUGGINS, HUMBUG
kind of .. TOOL, CATSPAW, DUMMY
rare .... CULLY
duple ..... DOUBLE, TWOFOLD
duplex ... APARTMENT, HOUSE, DOUBLE
duplicate ..... COPY, REPLICA, DOUBLE, FACSIMILE
copy .... ESTREAT
duplicating machine ... RONEO, (XEROX) COPIER, MIMEOGRAPH, MULTIGRAPH
duplication .... COPY, REPLICA
duplicity .. FRAUD, DECEPTION, DOUBLE-DEALING, FALSENESS
durable ..... STABLE, LASTING
stage performer .... (MAE) WEST, (MARLENE) DIETRICH
duramen .... HEARTWOOD
durance .... IMPRISONMENT
duration .. PERIOD, TIME, TERM
durbar: India ..... RECEPTION, AUDIENCE, HALL
dure .... LAST, ENDURE
duress .... IMPRISONMENT, CONSTRAINT, COERCION, COMPULSION
during .... PENDING
durmast .... OAK
duro: Sp. ...... PESO, DOLLAR
Duroc-Jersey .... HOG
Durocher, baseball manager .. (THE)LIP, LEO
durra ...... SORGHUM, MILLET
durum .... WHEAT, FLOUR
Duse, actress ..... ELEONORA, CHECCHI
burial place ...... ASOLO
dusk ...... GLOOM, TWILIGHT, EVENFALL, GLOAMING, CREPUSCLE, NIGHTFALL
dusky ..... DARK, SWART(HY), TAWNY
dust .... POLLEN, EARTH, POWDER, SPRINKLE, ASH, STOUR
bite the .... LOSE
British ... ASHES, RUBBISH
filter .... INHALER
lick the .... LOSE, GROVEL
of flower .... POLLEN
slang .... MONEY
windblown .... STOUR
dustbin .... ASHCAN
duster .. COAT, BRUSH, WIPER, RAG, WIND, BROOM
dusting powder .... TALC
Dutch (see Netherlands)
admiral .... RUYTER
Antilles .... ARUBA
apple, fried ..... ROLPENS
astronomer .... HUYGENS
beef .... HUTSPOT
botanist .... VRIES
cheese ..... EDAM, GOUDA
city .... EDE
coin .... DOIT, STIVER
colonist .... BOER
colonizer ...... PATROON
cupboard .... KAS
dialect in Africa ... TAAL, AFRIKAANS
donkey .... EZEL
East Indies island ...... TIMOR, JAVA
engraver .... LEYDEN
farm .... BOWERY
fishing boat ..... HOOKER
Guiana .... SURINAM
gypsy .... BAZIGAR
Hottentot breed .... GRIQUA
housewife ..... VROU(W)
humanist ...... ERASMUS
measure .... AAM, ANKER
metal .... TOMBAC
mistress, in S. Afr. .. NOI

Mrs. . . . . VROUW
navigator . . . . TASMAN
New Guinea negrito . . . . TAPIRO
news agency . . . . . ANETA
painter . . . . . HALS, STEEN, REMBRANDT, LELY, GOGH, BORCH, CUYP, MEER, LEYDEN
philosopher . . . . SPINOZA
physicist . . . . . . HUYGENS, LORENTZ
river . . . . MAAS
settler's farm . . . BOWERY
ship . . . . GAL(L)IOT, GALLOT
slang . . . . GERMAN
South African statesman KRUGER
South African . . . . . BOER
statesman . . . . . . GROTIUS
theologian . . . . . ERASMUS, JANSEN
title of address . . . . HEER, MYNHEER
town . . . . STAD
uncle . . . . OOM
vessel, flatbottomed . . . . . FLYBOAT
village . . . . DOORN
West Indies . . . . ANTILLES
woman . . . . FROU(W), VROUW

Dutchman . . . . . . HOLLANDER, MYNHEER
slang . . . . GERMAN

dutiful . . . . OBEDIENT

duty . . . . . . TASK, EXCISE, TAX, RESPONSIBILITY, TOLL, IMPOST, OBLIGATION
burdensome . . . . ONUS
turn of . . . . TRICK

duumvir . . . . MAGISTRATE

Dvina river . . DAUGAVA, DUNA

Dvorak, composer . . . . ANTON
symphony . . NEW WORLD

dwarf . . . . . . ATOMY, MANIKIN, BANTAM, MANAKIN, RUNT, MIDGET, STUNT, OUTSHINE, HOMUNCULUS
African/Asiatic . . PYGMY, PIGMY
animal . . . . RUNT
antelope . . . . ORIBI
cattle . . . . . NIATA, DEVON
chestnut . . . . CHINQUAPIN
kind of . . . . FREAK, GRIG, ELF, GNOME, PEE WEE
like . . . . GNOMISH
misshapen . . . . GNOME
Norse mythology . . . . ANDVARI
Philippine . . . . . NEGRITO, AETA
plant . . . . ALYSSUM
Scandinavian folklore . . . TROLL
Scottish . . . . BLASTIE
shrub/tree . . . . BONSAI
storybook . . TOM THUMB, LILLIPUTIAN, DOPEY, DOC, BASHFUL
underground . . . . . GNOME

dwarfish deer . . . . CHEVROTAIN
dog . . . . CHIHUAHUA
horse . . . . PONY

dwarfism . . . . NANSOMA

dwarfs, fairy tale . . . BASHFUL, DOC, DOPEY, GRUMPY, HAPPY, SLEEPY, SNEEZY
king of . . . . ALBERICH

dwell . . . (A)BIDE, LIVE, LODGE, RESIDE
on . . . . HARP

dweller . . . . TENANT, RESIDENT, INHABITANT

dwelling . . . RESIDENCE, HOUSE, ABODE, HOME
house . . . . TENEMENT
instant . . . . PREFAB
bear's . . . . CAVE, DEN
bird's . . . . NEST
high . . . . AERIE, EYRIE
imposing . . . . . . MANSION
lion's . . . . LAIR, DEN
miserable . . . . HOVEL
mobile . . . . TRAILER
on artificial island . . . . . . CRANNOG
on wheels . . . . . . TRAILER
place, kind of . . . . . FLAT, APARTMENT
royal . . . . PALACE
rude . . . . HOVEL, HUT
slum . . . . TENEMENT

dwindle . . . . . SHRINK, LESSEN, DIMINISH, PETER, DECREASE, ABATE

DX, in radio . . . . DISTANT, DISTANCE

dyad . . . . PAIR

Dyak blowgun . . . . . SUMPITAN
knife . . . . PARANG

dye . . COLOR, STAIN, TINT, HUE, BRASIL, FUCUS, CASHOO, ANNATTO, WELD, TAINT
aniline . . . . MAGENTA, FUCHSIN, SAFRANINE
azo . . . . CROCEIN(E)
base . . . ANILINE, FLAVONE
blue . . . . . . WOAD, PASTEL
butter coloring . . . . ANNATTO
coat tar . . EOSIN, MADDER, MAUVE
from whelks . . . . . MUREX
gum . . . . KINO
hair . . . . HENNA
Hindu . . . . ALTA
indigo . . . . . . ANIL, ISATIN
ingredient . . ALAZARIN(E), TANNIN
insect body's . . . . KERMES
lichen . . . . ARCHIL
mustard plant . . . . WOAD
orange . . . . MANDARIN
plant . . . . CHAY, ANIL, SUMAC(H), ALKANET, ANCHUSA, BUGLOSS, PUCCOON, AMIL, BLOODROOT
purple . . MUREX, ARCHIL, ORCHAL, ORCHIL, TURNSOLE
red . . . . . EOSIN(E), AURIN, COCHINEAL, CERISE, RHODAMINE, ALKANET, ANCHUSA, MADDER, KERMES, FUCHSIN, SOLFERINO
reddish-brown . . . . HEMAT(E)IN
source . . . . LICHEN, CUDBEAR
substance . . . . TANNIN
synthetic . . . . RHODAMINE
yellow . . . . FUSTIC

dyeing astringent . . . . GAMBIER
color fixer . . . . . MORDANT
liquid container . . . . . VAT
method . . . . BAT(T)IK
solution . . . . VAT
substance . . . . . MORDANT

dyer . . . . . . STAINER, COLORIST

dyestuff . . CATECHU, MAGENTA, ANIL, INDIGO, WOAD, CASHOO

dyeweed . . . . . . WOODWAXEN

dying . . . . MORIBUND

dyke . . . . DAM, DIKE

dyna as combining form . . . . . . POWER

dynamic . . . . ENERGETIC, VIGOROUS
opposed to . . . . . . STATIC, ORGANIC

dynamics . . KINETICS, STATICS, FORCES

dynamite . . . . EXPLOSIVE
kind of . . . . TNT
ingredient . . . . NITROGLYCERIN(E)
inventor of . . . . NOBEL

dynamo . . . . GENERATOR, MAGNETO
combining form . . POWER
part . . . . STATOR, COMMUTATOR, ARMATURE, WINDING, BRUSH

dynast . . . . RULER

dynasty, Chinese . . MING, SUNG

dys as prefix . . . . ILL, BAD

dysgenic, opposed to . . . . EUGENIC

dyspepsia . . . . INDIGESTION
medicine . . . . HYDRASTINE

dyspeptic . . GLOOMY, GROUCHY

dysphoria . . . . ANXIETY, DISCONTENT, DISCOMFORT

Dzhugashvili . . . . STALIN

E

E, Greek .... EPSILON
each ...... PER, EVERY(ONE), APIECE, ALL, ANA
Eads (James) invention ...... DIVING BELL
eager .... FAIN, AGOG, ARDENT, AVID, KEEN, ANXIOUS, AFIRE, IMPATIENT, EARNEST, DESIROUS
eagle .. BIRD, COIN, ACCIPITER
beaked .... AQUILINE
biblical .... GIER
brood .... AERIE
constellation .... AQUILA
double-crested ... HARPY
family .... FALCON
Latin .... AQUILA
like/of an ..... AQUILINE
like bird .... VULTURE, CONDOR
nest of .... AERIE, EYRIE, AERY
passenger of ..... ETANA
sea .... ERN(E)
young ..... EYRIE, EYRY, AIGLETTE
eaglestone .... ETITE
eagre ... BORE, (TIDAL) WAVE
Eamon de Valera .... DEV
eanling .... LAMB, KID
ear .... HEARING, LUG
anvil .... INCUS
auricle .... PINNA, PAVILION
bone ... STAPES, STIRRUP, INCUS, ANVIL, HAMMER, TEGMEN, AMBOS, OCCICLE
canal .... SCALA
cartilage .... HELIX
cavity .... COCHLEA, UTRICLE, SACCULE
doctor ...... OTOLOGIST, AURIST
drum .... TYMPANUM
external .... AURICLE, CONCHA, PINNA
give ...... LISTEN, HEED, HEARKEN
gland below .... PAROTID
hammer .... MALLEUS
hollow .... CONCHA
in Latin .... AURIS
inflammation .... OTITIS
inner .... LABYRINTH
instrument .... OTOSCOPE
labyrinth ...... SACCULE
lend an .... LIST(EN), HEED, HEARKEN
like part .... LUG
lobe ...... EARLAP, LUG, ALA, LAPPET
middle ...... TYMPANUM
near the ...... PAROTIC, PAROTID
of corn .... MEALIE
of grain ..... SPIKE, SPICA
opening ...... FENESTRA
outer rim .... HELIX
pain .... OTALGIA
part .... LOBE, AURICLE, PINNA, COCHLEA, TYMPANUM, ANVIL, HAMMER, STIRRUP
pertaining to ..... AURIC, OTIC, AURAL
play by the ... IMPROVISE
prefix .... OTO
projection .. LUG, TRAGUS
science of the .. OTOLOGY
secretion .... WAX, CERUMEN
shaped .... AURIFORM
shaped mollusk .. ORMER, ABALONE
shell .... ABALONE, MOLLUSK, ORMER
specialist .... AURIST, OTOLOGIST
stirrup-shaped bone ..... STAPES
wax .... CERUMEN
wheat .... SPICA
earache .... OTALGIA
eardrum .... TYMPANUM
of the .... TYMPANIC
prominence ...... UMBO
eared .... AURICULATE
seal .... OTARY
earful ..... SCOLDING, NEWS, GOSSIP
earl .... NOBLEMAN
Biggers' sleuth .... (CHARLIE) CHAN
deputy of an .. VISCOUNT
wife of .... COUNTESS
earliest .... PREMIER
early .... FORWARD
bird's victim ...... WORM
in the day/season .... RATH(E)
earmark ...... BRAND, SIGN, IDENTIFY, RESERVE
earn ...... MERIT, GAIN, WIN
difficultly .... EKE
earnest .... ASSURANCE, SERIOUS, AVID, SINCERE, FERVENT, EAGER, TOKEN, PLEDGE
money .... HANDSEL, ARLES, TOKEN, ADVANCE
earnings ... WAGES, SALARIES, PROFITS
earphone .... RECEIVER
earpiece .... FLAP
earring .... GIRANDOLE, HOOP, PENDANT
ears .... ANTENNA
all .... ATTENTIVE
having two ... BINAURAL
earsplitting .... LOUD, DEAFENING
earth ... LAND, DIRT, GLOBE, TERRA, DUST, TERRENE, GROUND, UNIVERSE, WORLD
combining form .... GEO
crust ...... LITHOSPHERE
deposit ..... MARL, SILT
division .... ZONE
down to ..... REALISTIC, PRACTICAL
eating of ..... GEOPHAGY
goddess ...... DEMETER, SEMELE, ERDA, CERES
greenish ... TERRE-VERTE
hypothetical figure ...... GEOID
inhabitant ... TELLURIAN
line .... EQUATOR
lump of .... CLOD
of the .... TELLURIAN
pertaining to the .... GEOGRAPHICAL, TERRENE
pigment .... UMBEL
poetic ...... VALE, MARL
satellite ..... EXPLORER, ATLAS, PIONEER, MIDAS, ECHO, TIROS, MARINER, SPUTNIK, LUNIK, SKYLAB, VOSTOK
tamping implement ..... BEETLE
volcanic .... TRASS
white ...... TERRE ALBA, GYPSUM, KAOLIN, MAGNESIA
earth's treasure guardian ..... GNOME
earthborn ...... LOW, HUMAN, MORTAL, VULGAR
earthdrake .... DRAGON
earthen cup .... MUG
jar .... OLLA
earthenware .... DELFT, POTTERY, PORCELAIN, CROCK(ERY), JUG, POT
cooking ...... CASSEROLE
jar .... CROCK
maker .... POTTER
making material .... PUG
pertaining to ... CERAMIC
pot .... PIPKIN
unglazed .. TERRA COTTA
water container .... GOGLET, GURGLET
earthly .... WORLDLY, TEMPORAL, SECULAR, MUNDANE, TERRESTRIAL, TERRENE, TELLURIAN, TELLURIC
not .... CELESTIAL, ETHEREAL
opposed to .... SPIRITUAL
earthnut .... TUBER, POD, PEANUT, TRUFFLE, FUNGUS
earthquake ... SEISM, TEMBLOR, TREMOR
combining form .... S(E)ISMO
focus of ..... EPICENTER
over center of disturbance EPIFOCAL
pertaining to ... SEISMAL, SEISMIC
recorder .... RICHTER
slight .... MICROSEISM
starting point .... FOCUS
earthquakes, pertaining to .... SEISMIC
phenomena of .. SEISMISM
study of ..... SEISMOLOGY

earthwork .... TUMP, FORTIFICATION, DIKE, MOUND, AGGER, VALLATION
earthworm .... ESS
like an ..... LUMBRICOID
earthy ..... NATURAL, SIMPLE, COARSE, GROSS, TEMPORAL, TERRENE
pigment .... SIENNA
earwax .... CERUMEN
earwig ... CENTIPEDE, BEETLE
ease ...... RELIEVE, COMFORT, POISE, FACILITY, REST, LEISURE, LOOSEN, PALLIATE
take one's .... RELAX
easel .... CANVAS HOLDER
easement ... RELIEF, COMFORT
in law .... SERVITUDE
easily .... DEXTEROUSLY, BY FAR, READILY
affected .... SENSITIVE
angered .... IRACUND, IRASCIBLE, IRRITABLE, TESTY
bent ... FLEXIBLE, LIMBER, PLIANT
broken .... FRAGILE
cheated .... GULLIBLE, CREDULOUS
frightened .... SCARY
handled ... TAME, GENTLE
mixed .... MISCIBLE
offended .... TOUCHY, SENSITIVE
remembered ... CATCHY
set on fire .... FIERY, FLAMMABLE
tempted .... FRAIL
tricked .... GULLIBLE, CREDULOUS
easiness .... FACILITY
east ... ORIENT, LEVANT, ASIA
East Indies .... INDONESIA
animal, small .... TARSIER
ape .... GIBBON
arboreal mammal .... COLUGO
bark .... NIEPA
bird ... LORIKEET, ARGUS
boatman .... SERANG
calico .... SALLOO
cat-like animal .. LINSANG
cedar ..... TOON, DEODAR
cereal grass ..... RAGEE, RAG(G)
chief .... RAJA(H)
civet .... MUSANG
coin .... CASH
cuckoo .... KOEL
deer .... MUNTJAC
dye .... CHAY
elephant driver .. MAHOUT
fiber (plant) .. JUTE, SUNN
fish .... DORAB
fruit ... DURIAN, DURION, MANGOSTEEN
garment .... SARONG
grass ... GLAGA, VETIVER
harvest .... RABO
hemp .... SUNN
herb ... SESAME, ROSELLE, PIA, CHOY, CHAY, SOLA, GINGER
honeybee .... DINGAR
island ... BALI, SUMATRA
lemur .... COLUGO
litter .... DOOLEE, DOOLI(E), DOOL(E)Y
mail .... DAK
medicinal root .. ZEDOARY
mint plant ...... COLEUS
monkey ...... ENTELLUS
musical instrument ..... RUANA, BINA
myrtle .... CAJEPUT, CAJUPUT
oil plant .... BENNE, SESAME
palm tree ...... TALIPOT
parrot .... COCKATOO
peacock-like bird .... ARGUS
perfume .... PATCHOULI
persimmon ...... GA(U)B
plant ... DERRIS, COLEUS, SESAME, BEN(NE), CHAY, AMBARY, JUTE, TURMERIC, SUNN, AMIL, PATCHOULI
prince .... RAJA(H)
rat .... KOK
relish .... PICALILI
root .... CHOY, CHAY
sailor .... LASCAR
sauce .... CURRY
seaweed product .... AGAR-AGAR
shrub .... CUBEB
snake .... KUPPER
spice .... CINNAMON
squirrel .... TAGUAN
tree .... CAJUPUT, CALAMANDER, TOON, CHAULMOOGRA, TEAK, JACK, DEODAR, POON, SAJ, CINCHONA, BANYAN, ACANA, SIRIS, MEE, SAPANWOOD, PINEY, KAMALA
vessel .... PATAMAR
warrior .... SINGH
weight .... CATTY
wood ...... TOON, TEAK, LIGNALOES, KOKRA, ENG
Easter .... PASCH(A)
feast of .... PASCH
fruitcake .... SIMNEL
Island .... RAPANUI
of .... PASCHAL
souvenirs ..... BUNNIES, EGGS
third Sunday after ...... JUBILATE
eastern .... ORIENTAL, ASIATIC
Christian .... UNIAT
Orthodox church prayers .... EKTENE
Orthodox church monk .. CALOYER
palace .... SERAI, SERAGLIO
ruler .... EMEER, EMIR
easy .... SOFT, FACILE, MODERATE, SMOOTH, SIMPLE, EFFORTLESS
chair .... ROCKER
course: sl. .... PIPE
gait ...... LOPE, CANTER
job .... SNAP, SINECURE, CINCH
mark ...... DUPE, GULL, PUSHOVER
opposed to ..... TIGHT, HARD
slang .... CUSHY
take it ...... RELAX, REST
to convince ... GULLIBLE, CREDULOUS
to understand .... PELLUCID, SIMPLE
eat ... SUP, GNAW, CONSUME, DINE, GRUB
away ... GNAW, CORRODE, CANKER, ERODE, FRET
greedily .... DEVOUR, GORGE, GAMP, WOLF, GOBBLE, GULP, GUTTLE, GORMANDIZE
immoderately ..... GLUT, GORGE
into .... CORRODE
one's word ... RETRACT, RECANT
eatable ... ESCULENT, EDIBLE, FOOD, COMESTIBLE
eater, heavy ... TRENCHERMAN, GLUTTON
eating capacity, huge .... EDACITY
implement .... CUTLERY, CHOPSTICK
hall ... MESS, REFECTORY
of .... DIETARY
place ... AUTOMAT, DINER, CAFE, RESTAURANT
regulated .... DIET, REGIMEN
eats: colloq. .... FOOD, MEALS
eau .... DEVIE, WATER
de vie .... BRANDY
designating one kind .... COLOGNE, JAVELLE
eaves, trough under ... GUTTER
eavesdrop .... LISTEN
Eban, Israeli diplomat .. ABBA
ebb ...... SUBSIDE, RECEDE, DECLINE, FLOW BACK, REFLUX, WANE
and flow .... TIDE
tide .... NEAP
tide, opposed to .. FLOOD
ebbing .... REFLUX, REFLUENT, REFLUENCE
Eber's father .... MILED
Eblis .... SATAN
ebon .... BLACK, DARK
ebonite .... VULCANITE
ebonize .... BLACKEN
ebony .... WOOD, BLACK
ebullience .... ELAN, EXUBERANCE
ebullient .... BUBBLING, BOILING, EXUBERANT
ecarte .... CARD GAME
ecce ...... LO, SEE, BEHOLD
eccentric ...... ODD, OUTRE, OFF CENTER, CAPRICIOUS, PECULIAR, QUEER, CRANK(Y), W(H)ACKY

person ..... NUT, GEEZER
slang ... KOOKIE, KOOKY, BATTY
wheel part .... CAM
eccentricity .... ODDITY, IDIOSYNCRASY, KINK
Ecclesiastes, book of .... KOHELETH
ecclesiastic .... PRIEST, CLERGYMAN, PRELATE, FRA
ecclesiastical attendant ...... ACOLYTE
benefice .... GLEBE
cape .... ORALE, MOZ(Z)ETTA
council .... SYNOD
court ..... CLASSIS, ROTA
dean .... PREFECT
headdress .... MITER, BIRETTA
hood .... AMICE
office, trading of .... BARRATRY
proceedings ...... ACTA
residence .... MANSE, ABBEY, PRIORY
seat .... SEDILE
skullcap .... BIRETTA
vestment .... AMICE, ALB, STOLE, ORALE, COPE
eccrinology, subject of .... SECRETION, EXCRETION
ecdysis .... MO(U)LT
echidna .... ANTEATER, MONOTREME
echinate .... BRISTLY, SPINY, PRICKLY
animal ..... PORCUPINE, HEDGEHOG
echinoderm .... STARFISH, SEA URCHIN, TREPANG
echinus .... SEA URCHIN
echo ...... REPEAT, RESOUND, OREAD, NYMPH, REVERBERATE, PARROT
echoing .... RESOUNDING, RESONANT
eclair .... PASTRY
eclat ... RENOWN, SPLENDOR, PRAISE, ACCLAIM, FAME, NOTORIETY, GLORY
eclectic .... CHOOSING
eclipse ... OBSCURE, SURPASS, STAIN, DARKEN, OVERSHADOW, SURPASS
kind of .... LUNAR, TOTAL, PARTIAL, SOLAR, STELLAR
part .... PENUMBRA
eclogue .... POEM, PASTORAL, IDYL(L)
ecole .... SCHOOL
economic policy, kind of ..... AUTARKY
system .... COMMUNISM, CAPITALISM
economical .... THRIFTY, FRUGAL, SPARING
economize .... SCRIMP, SAVE, RETRENCH, SKIMP
ecru .... TAN, YELLOW, BEIGE
ecstasy ... RAPTURE, BLISS, JOY
ectad, opposed to ..... ENTAD
ectoparasite .... REMORA, LEECH
ectype .... COPY
ecu .... COIN, SHIELD
Ecuador, capital of .... QUITO
city/town ...... AMATO, CUENCA, IBARRA, LOJA, MANTO, NAPO
Indian .... CARA, KECHUA, QUECHUA
monetary unit .... SUCRE
mountain ..... COTOPAXI
province .... ORO
seaport .... MANTA, GUAYAQUIL
volcano ..... ANTISANA, COTOPAXI, CHIMBORAZO
ecumenical .... UNIVERSAL, GENERAL
council site .... TRENT
eczema ...... HERPES, TETTER
horse's ... MAL(L)ANDERS
edacious .... VORACIOUS, DEVOURING, CONSUMING, RAVENOUS
edacity .... GREED, VORACITY
eddo .... TARO, ROOT
eddy .... SWIRL, VORTEX, WHIRLPOOL, BORE, (WHIRL)WIND
edema ... DROPSY, ANASARCA
edemic .... SWOLLEN, EDEMATOUS
Eden .... HEAVEN, PARADISE, GARDEN
resident ...... EVE, ADAM
river .... PISON
edentate ... TOOTHLESS, SLOTH, ANTEATER, ECHIDNA, AARDVARK
edge .... BRIM, PICOT, VERGE, MARGE, RIM,MARGIN, BLADE, LEDGE, SKIRT, BRINK, BORDER, SIDLE
beveled .... CANT
cliff's .... BROW
colloquial ... ADVANTAGE
crater's .... LIP
garment's .... HEM
hat's .... BRIM
keen ...... ZEST, SHARP
on ... IMPATIENT, EAGER, IRRITABLE
roof's .... EAVE
tool .... CHISEL
with loops .. PURL, PICOT
edged ...... CUTTING, KEEN, SHARP
object ... SWORD, RAZOR, BLADE, SABER, KNIFE, BOLO, CUTLASS, AX(E)
rough .... EROSE
edgewise, move .... SIDLE
walker .... CRAB
edging ..... RUCHE, TATTING, FRINGE, TRIMMING, PICOT, LIMBUS
edgy ...... NERVOUS, TENSE, IRRITABLE
edible .... COMESTIBLE, ESCULENT, EATABLE, FOOD
bulb .... CAMAS(S), QUAMASH
fungus ... MOREL, CEPE, MUSHROOM
grain .... CEREAL
plant .... VEGETABLE
root ..... YAM, CASSAVA, TARO, GARLIC, CARROT, BEET, MANIOC
seed ..... BEAN, PEANUT, PEA, LENTIL, PINON
shoot .... UDO, BAMBOO
tuber ...... TARO, YAM, OCA, POTATO, SALEP
edict .... DECREE, FIAT, MANDATE, PROCLAMATION
Pope's .... BULL
sultan's .... IRADE
tsar's .... UKASE
edifice .... BUILDING
edify ... INSTRUCT, ENNOBLE
Edinburgh is capital of .... SCOTLAND
poetic .... EDINA
Edirne .... ADRIANOPLE
Edison, inventor .... THOMAS (ALVA)
edit .... REVISE, CORRECT, REDACT
edition ...... ISSUE, NUMBER, COPY, PRINTING
collector's .... FIRST
early morning newspaper .... BULLDOG
six versions ... HEXAPLA
special .... EXTRA
editor .... REDACTOR, JOURNALIST
editorial .... ARTICLE, COMMENT, OPINION
main .... LEADER
Edmonton is capital of .... ALBERTA
Edna Ferber novel ... SO BIG, SARATOGA
Edo .... TOKYO
Edom ..... ESAU, IDUM(A)EA
mountain .... HOR
Edson de Arantes Nacimento .. PELE, NEGRAO
educate ...... TRAIN, TEACH, INSTRUCT
educated .... LITERATE, LEARNED
education .... TRAINING, KNOWLEDGE, TEACHING
educational institution ...... COLLEGE, SCHOOL, ACADEMY, SEMINARY, UNIVERSITY, CONSERVATORY
group .... NEA
educator ... TUTOR, MENTOR, TEACHER, PROFESSOR, INSTRUCTOR
educe ...... ELICIT, DEDUCE, INFER, EXTRACT, EVOKE, DRAW, EVOLVE
Edward Kennedy Ellington ... DUKE
specialty .... JAZZ
eel .... MORAY, LAMPREY, CARAPO, GRIG, ANGUILLID
fish for .... SNIGGLE
fried .... SPITCHCOCK
young ... ELVER, CONGER

eelpout ..... BURBOT, LING
eelworm .... NEMA
eely .... SLIPPERY, ELUSIVE
eerie (eery) .... UNCANNY, WEIRD, MACABRE, ELDRITCH
efface ...... EXPUNGE, ERASE, ODIC, RUB OUT, BLOT OUT, OBLITERATE, WIPE OUT, BLUR
effect ..... ACHIEVE, RESULT, EFFICACY, TENOR, MEANING, IMPRESSION, ACCOMPLISH, OUTCOME, ISSUE
  in .... VIRTUALLY, ACTUALLY
effective .... ACTIVE, EFFICIENT, OPERATIVE
effects .... PROPERTY, BELONGINGS
effectual ... VALID, EFFECTIVE
effectuate ...... ACCOMPLISH
effeminate .... UNMANLY, WEAK, SOFT, WOMANISH, FEMININE, LYDIAN
  boy ..... SISSY, MILKSOP
  person, in a way ... FOP, DANDY
effendi ... SIR, MASTER, TITLE
effervesce ..... BUBBLE, BOIL, FOAM, FIZZ, FROTH, SPARKLE
effervescence ..... VIVACITY, EXUBERANCE, FOAMING, LIVELINESS, EBULLIENCE
effervescent ...... BUBBLING, FIZZY
effete .... BARREN, ARID, STERILE, SPENT, EXHAUSTED, WORN OUT
efficacious .... EFFECTIVE
efficient .... COMPETENT, CAPABLE, ABLE, EFFECTIVE
effigy .... ICON, LIKENESS, STATUE, PORTRAIT, IMAGE
  fate of, sometimes ...... HANGED, BURNED
effloresce .... FLOWER, BLOSSOM (OUT)
effluence .... EMANATION
effluvia .... RAIN
effluvium ..... AURA, VAPOR, ODOR, REEK, FLATUS, MIASM(A)
efflux .... OUTFLOW
effluxion .... EMANATION, STREAM
effort ... NISUS, TRY, EXERTION, ENDEAVOR, PAINS, ATTEMPT, CONATUS
effortless .... EASY
effrontery ..... BRASS, CHEEK, GALL, TEMERITY, IMPUDENCE, PRESUMPTION, GUTS
effulge .... SHINE
effulgence ... GLORY, LUSTER, RADIANCE, SPLENDOR
effuse .... SPREAD
effusive .... EXUBERANT, OVERFLOWING, GUSHY, DEMONSTRATIVE, GUSHING
eft .... LIZARD, NEWT
eftsoon: archaic ...... AGAIN, FORTHWITH, OFTEN
e.g., part of ...... EXEMPLI, GRATIA
egad .... EXPLETIVE, OATH
Egeria ...... NYMPH, ADVISER
egest ... DISCHARGE, EXCRETE
egesta .... FECES, SWEAT, PERSPIRATION
egg ..... OVUM, URGE, INCITE
  capsule .... OVISAC, OOTHECA
  case .... OVISAC
  collector ..... OOLOGIST
  combining form .... OO, OVI
  constituent .... YOLK, GLAIR, ALBUMEN
  dish ...... OMELET(TE)
  drink .... NOG(G)
  fertilized ..... OOSPERM, OOSPORE
  immature .... OOCYTE
  insect .... NIT
  laying animals .. OVIPARA
  laying mammal .... PLATYPUS, DUCKBILL, ECHIDNA, MONOTREME, ANTEATER
  lobster .... BERRY
  louse .... NIT
  mollusk's ..... OOTHECA
  on ... PROD, GOAD, URGE, SPUR
  part .... YOLK, SHELL
  protoplasm .... ARCHIBLAST
  relish .... CAVIAR(E)
  shaped ... OVATE, OVOID, OVAL, OVIFORM, OBOVOID
  shaped, longitudinal section ...... OBOVATE
  slang .... PERSON
  small .... OVULE
  tester .... CANDLER
  unfertilized .... OOSPHERE
  white ... GLAIR, ALBUMEN
  yolk .... VITELLUS, VITELLINE
  yolk pigment ... LUTEIN
  yolk substance .. LECITHIN
egger ...... MOTH, BOMBYCID
egghead ...... INTELLECTUAL
eggheads collectively .... CLERISY
eggs .. URGES, NIT, OVA, PRODS
  fish .... ROE, BERRIES
  nest of .... CLUTCH
eggshell color ... ECRU, IVORY
egis .... SHIELD, BREASTPLATE, AUSPICES, SPONSORSHIP, PROTECTION
eglantine .... SWEETBRIER
ego ... ATMAN, SELF, CONCEIT
egocentric ... SELF-CENTERED
egoism .... CONCEIT, SELFISHNESS, VANITY
  opposed to ... ALTRUISM
egoist, opposite of ... ALTRUIST
egotism ..... PRIDE, VANITY, BIGHEAD
egregious .... FLAGRANT, BAD, GROSS, PRECIOUS
egress .... OUTLET, EXIT, WAY OUT, EMERGENCY
egret .... HERON, PLUME
Egypt .... MIZRAIM
Egyptian .... NILOT, COPT
  alloy .... ASEM
  amulet .... MENAT
  antelope .... BUBALIS
  ape: myth. .... AANI
  archaeologist .... RAZEK, SALEH, SAAD
  Asiatic conquerors ...... HYKSOS
  asp on headdress .... URAEUS
  astronomer ... IMHOTEP
  boat .... FELUCCA
  bird .... IBIS, TROCHILUS
  bull: myth. .... APIS
  capital .... CAIRO
  capital, ancient .... AMARNA, TANIS, SAIS, MEMPHIS
  captain ...... RAIS, REIS
  captor of Jerusalem ..... SALADIN
  Christian .... COPT
  city ... ASWAN, DUMYAT, TANTA, DAMIETTA, FA(I)YUM, TANIS, ZOAN, FAYUM, SYENE, THEBES, HELIOPOLIS, EL GIZA
  cobra .... HAJE, URAEUS
  coin .... BEDIDLIK, PIASTRE
  commander ..... SIRDAR
  conquerors ... LYBIANS, NUBIANS, PTOLEMY, NAPOLEON, AMRU
  cosmetic .... KOHL
  cowheaded goddess ..... HATHOR
  creator god .... ATUM
  crocodile god .... SOBEK
  cross ..... ANKH, CRUX, ANSATA
  dancing girl ... ALMA(H), ALME(H), GHAWAZI
  dead body, preserved .... MUMMY
  desert .... SKETIS
  division ...... PATHROS, MAZOR, FAIYUM
  dry measure ..... ARDEB
  dynasty .... NARMER, MENES, CHEOPS, PEPI, UNAS, AHMOSE, SETI, RAMSES, NECHO, DARIUS, PTOLEMY
  dynasty founder .... MENES
  elf .... OUPHE
  embalmed dead body .... MUMMY
  fabled monster .. SPHINX
  falcon-headed god ...... HORUS, MENTU
  fertile land ..... GOSHEN
  gate .... PYLON
  god ...... SETH, ANUBIS, HORUS, GEB, ATEN, MNEVIS, THOTH, ATMU, WAPUET, KHENSU, AMEN-RA, MIN, HAPI

god bearer of the ankh ... PTAH
god judge of the dead ... OSIRIS
god-king ...... RAMSES, KHAFRE, THUTMOSE, SENUSERT, PEPI, MENKAURE
god of creation .... PTAH
god of evil .... SET(H)
god of lower world ...... SERAPIS
god of medicine .... IMHOTEP
god of pleasure ..... BES
goddess ...... BAST, NUT, (H)ATHOR, SESHAT, DOR, MAAT, SATI, ISIS, APET, MUT, SEKHET
governor ... BEY, MUDIR
hairstyle ...... SIDELOCK
hare-like animal .. HYRAX
hawk-headed god .... RA
heart .... HATI
heaven ..... AARU, AALU, LALU
high priest ..... RANOFER
ibis-headed god .. THOTH
jackal-headed god ...... WAPUET
khedive's domain .... DAIRA
king .... PTOLEMY, MENES, CHEOPS, TUT, FUAD, FAROUK
king of underworld ..... OSIRIS
laborer .... FELLAH
language .... COPTIC
lighthouse ...... PHAROS
lizard .... ADDA
lord of sky .... HORUS
lute .... NABLA
magician .... IMHOTEP
measure .... ARDES
money ... MINA, PIASTRE, TALENT, DRACHMA
money of account .. ASPER
month ..... APAP, TOTH, MECHIR, MESORE
monument figure .... CARTOUCH(E)
moon god .... THOTH
mortuary chapel .... MASTABA(H)
mouse .... JERBOA
mullet .... BOURI
mummy cloth ... BYSSUS
native .... NILOT
oasis .... DAKHLA
obsolete .... GYPSY
opium .... THEBAINE
party .... WAFD
patron of artists .. PTAH
peasant .... FELLAH
peninsula ...... PHAROS, SINAT
Pharaoh .... RAM(E)SES, AKHENATON
phoenix .... BENU
police .... GHAFIR
port .... SAID
pound .... ROTL
premier .... SAAD
queen ..... CLEOPATRA, NEFERTARI, NEFERTITI, HATSHEPSUT
queen of gods ...... SATI
Rameses ..... PHARAOH
rattle .... SISTRUM
reed .... PAPYRUS
relic, kind of ... MUMMY
river .... NILE
rock .... PORPHYRY
royal tomb .... PYRAMID
ruler .... KHEDIVE, MAMELUKE, PHARAOH
sacred beetle ... SCARAB
sacred bird ... IBIS, BENU
sacred bull .... APIS
scribe .... ANI
seaport .... PORT SAID
serpent: myth. .... APEPI
"shepherd kings" .... HYKSOS
singing girl ...... ALMA, GHAWAZI
site of ruins ...... LUXOR, AMARNA, KARNAK, THEBES, SAKKARA, ABYDOS
skink .... ADDA
slave-soldier .. MAMELUKE
snake .... ASP
solar deity .... SHU
solar disk .... ATEN
soul .... KA
spirit .... HAPI
statue, kind of ... SPHINX
structure .... PYLON, PYRAMID
sultan .... SALADIN
sun .... ATEN
sun god ...... RA, AMON, HORUS, AMEN-RA
sycamore fig tree .. DAROO
symbol of fertility .... SERAPIS
symbol of life .... ANKH
tambourin .... RIKK
Tanis .... ZOAN
temple gate ...... PYLON
temple site ..... KARNAK
Thebes .... LUXOR
thorn ..... BABUL, KIKAR
title ..... CALIPH, PASHA
tomb .... MASTABA(H)
tree .... SYCAMORE
unit of currency .. GERSH, PIASTRE
verbal shrug .. MA'ALESH
viceroy .... KHEDIVE
waterway .... SUEZ
weight ..... OCHA, KET, KANTAR, MINA, OKA, OKE, KAT
whip .... KURBASH
wind .... K(H)AMSIN, KHAMSEEN
woman pharaoh .... HATSHEPSUT
woman singer .... (OM)KALTHUM
writing form .. DEMOTIC, HIERATIC, HIEROGLYPHIC
writing material .... PAPYRUS
Zeus .... AMMON

Egyptologist ... EMERY, LAUER, NIMS, EADY
eider ...... DOWN, (SEA)DUCK
eidolon .... IMAGE, ICON, PHANTOM
eight ball, behind the .... FIX, DILEMMA, PREDICAMENT, SPOT
combining form .. OCT(O), OCT(A)
group of .... OCTAD, OCTET(TE), OCTAVE, OCTONARY
hundred forty yards of cotton .... HANK
multiply by ... OCTUPLE
of .... OCTONARY
performers ... OCTET(TE)
series of .... OCTAD
sided figure ... OCTAGON
stringed instrument ..... OCTACHORD
eighteen XVIII
eightfold .... OCTUPLE
eighth day, every ..... OCTAN
note .... QUAVER
part of circle .... OCTANT
eighty .... FOURSCORE
Einstein's birthplace ..... ULM
Eire legislature .... DAIL
president .... HYDE
river .... SHANNON
Eisenhower, Gen. .... IKE, DWIGHT
middle name ..... DAVID
wife of ... MAMIE (DOUD)
ejaculate .... EXCLAIM, DISCHARGE, EJECT
eject ..... EMIT, EXPEL, EVICT, OUST, DISLODGE, VOID, DISMISS, ERUPT, SPEW, SQUIRT, EJACULATE, CAST OUT
ejecta .... REFUSE
eke .... ADD, INCREASE,
out .... SUPPLEMENT
el .... WING, EXTENSION, RAILWAY, THE
Cid ..... (RODRIGO) DIAZ, RUY
Salvador coin ... COLON
elaborate .. DETAILED, ORNATE, PAINSTAKING, FANCY, EXPATIATE
decoration ...... FINERY
elaborately made ... EXQUISITE
Elam's capital .... SUSA, SHUSHAN
elan ... ARDOR, VIGOR, DASH, SPIRIT
eland .... ANTELOPE
elanet .... HAWK, KITE
elapine .... COBRA, MAMBA
elapse ... DIE, PASS, SLIP (BY), EXPIRE
elastic .... FLEXIBLE, SPRINGY, SUPPLE, RESILIENT, BUOYANT, ADAPTABLE
band/strap ..... GARTER
wood .... YEW
elasticity .... RESILIENCE

muscular .... TONUS
elate .... EXALT, GLADDEN
elated ..... GLEEFUL, JOYFUL
elater ... (CLICK) BEETLE, DOR
Elba's important inhabitant ... NAPOLEON
Elbe .... LABE
city on the ..... MEISSEN
tributary ..... EGER, ISER, OHRE, MOLDAU
elbow ...... CROWD, ANCON, NUDGE, BEND, JOINT, JOSTLE, SHOVE
jab with the ..... NUDGE
of the .... ULNAR
elder ...... IVA, SIRE, SENIOR, ANCIENT, ANCESTOR, EARLIER, FORMER
church .... PRESBYTER
elder statesman .. GENRO, ITO
elderly ...... OLD, VETERAN, AGED, SENILE
eldest ... FIRST-BORN, SENIOR, AINE
Eldorado's riches ...... GOLD, DIAMONDS
eldritch .... EERIE, EERY, WEIRD, GHASTLY
Eleanor, diminutive of ...... NORA, ELLA, NELL
variant .... ELINOR
Eleanora ____, actress ... DUSE
elecampane roots ..... INULA
elect .... CHOOSE, ELITE, CHOSEN, SELECT, OPT
election .... POLL
casualty ..... LAME DUCK
platform ..... HUSTINGS, PLANK
proceedings ... HUSTINGS
report .... RETURNS
tour .... STUMP
electioneer .... STUMP
elective .... OPTIONAL, ELECTORAL
elector .... VOTER, ELISOR
Electra .... PLEIAD
brother of ..... ORESTES
parent of .... CLYTEMNESTRA, AGAMEMNON
electric .... MAGNETIC, EXCITING
bell part ..... ARMATURE
bulb .... GLOBE
catfish .... RAAD
chair .... HOT SEAT
circuit .... LOOP
circuit switch .... TOGGLE
company employe ...... READER
current regulator .... RHEOSTAT
engine for towing .. MULE
generator ...... DYNAMO
insulating material ...... EBONITE
light .... BULB, LAMP
light bulb ...... MAZDA, GLOBE
particle ... ... (AN)ION, CATION
potential .... TENSION
railway, underground ... SUBWAY, METRO
ray .... NUMBFISH, TORPEDO
unit ... AMP(ERE), DYNE, ELOD, OHM, VOLT, WATT, REL, FARAD, PERM
wires tube ..... RACEWAY
electrical appliance ... RANGE, (FLAT)IRON, TOASTER, FRYPAN, BLENDER
atom .... ELECTRON
circuit regulator .... BOOSTER
failure .... SHORT
force .... ELOD
particle .... CATION, (AN)ION
phenomenon .... ARC
system .... WIRING
terminal ... ELECTRODE, ANODE
unit ...... VOLT, JOULE, WATT
unit of measurement .... FARAD, BARAD, FARADAY, REL
electrician .... WIRE MAN
electricity: sl. .... JUICE
unit of ... AMPERE, OHM, MHO
electrified particle .... ION
electrify ..... THRILL, EXCITE, SHOCK
electrode .. ANODE, CATHODE, GRID, THERMION
electrograph .... WIRE PHOTO
electromagnet ...... SOLENOID
electromotive force .... PRESSURE, TENSION, VOLT(AGE)
electron .... MESON
tube .... TRIODE, STROBOTRON, KLYSTRON
electronic "brain" .... CALCULATOR, COMPUTER
detector ... RADAR, SONAR
device .... MASER, LASER
electrum .... ALLOY
eleemosynary ... CHARITABLE, FREE, GRATUITOUS
elegance ..... GRACE, POLISH, REFINEMENT, LUXE
affected/excessive .... FROUFROU
of manners .... PANACHE
elegant .... DIGNIFIED, DE LUXE, REFINED, FINE, COURTLY, POSH, PLUSH, SUPERB, GENTEEL, POLISHED, FLOSSY
elegiac ..... SAD, PLAINTIVE, MOURNFUL
elegist .... GRAY, SHELLEY
elegy .... DIRGE, NENIA, REQUIEM
Shelley's .... ADONAIS
eleme .... FIG
element ... COMPONENT, PART, INGREDIENT, FACTOR, SILICON
an ..... EARTH, AIR, FIRE, WATER
inert gas .... NEON
number 10 .... NEON
of air .... ARGON
similar to another .... ISOTOPE
with valence six .. HEXAD
with valence two .. DYAD
worthless .... SCUM
elemental .... PRIMARY, SIMPLE, HYPOSTATIC
elementary .... PRIMARY, BASIC, PRIMAL, SIMPLE
elemi .... RESIN, ANIME
elenctic .... REFUTING
opposed to ... D(E)ICTIC
elephant .... PACHYDERM, HATHI, JUMBO, TUSKER
boy .... SABU
driver .... MAHOUT
extinct ...... MASTODON, MAMMOTH
female .... COW
frenzy of .... MUST
goal .... ANKUS
keeper .... MAHOUT
male .... BULL
maverick .... ROGUE
nose .... SNOUT
outlaw .... ROGUE
seat on ...... HOWDAH, HOUDAH
sound .... TRUMPET, BELLOW
tooth .... TUSK
tower on .... CASTLE
trap .... KEDDAH, KHEDAH
tusk .... IVORY
white .... ALBINO
young .... CALF
elephants ear ...... BEGONIA, TARO
elevate ... RAISE, LIFT, EXALT
elevated .... LOFTY, EDIFYING, HIGH
railway ... EL, MONORAIL
roadway ..... OVERPASS
elevating muscle .... LEVATOR
elevation .. EMINENCE, HEIGHT, ALTITUDE, PLATEAU, MOUNT
elevator .... WAREHOUSE, GRANARY, HOIST
aircraft .... AIRFOIL
British .... LIFT
car .... CAGE
kind of ... DUMB-WAITER
passage for ...... SHAFT
pawnbroker's ..... SPOUT
elf .... GNOME, HOB, IMP, GOBLIN, PERI, PUCK, FAY, NIX, SPRITE, PIXY, BROWNIE, FAIRY, PIXIE
elfin .... FEY
shelter ...... TOADSTOOL
Eli .... HIGH PRIEST
pupil of .... SAMUEL
Elia .... LAMB
elicit .... EDUCE, EXTRACT, DRAW, EVOKE, FETCH
elide .... SUPPRESS, SLUR, LEAVE OUT, OMIT
eligibility .... QUALIFICATION, ACCEPTANCE

eligible ..... COMPETENT, FIT, QUALIFIED, SUITABLE
eliminate .... RID, REMOVE, OMIT, EXPEL, ERASE, EXCRETE, EXCLUDE
Elijah ... ELIA, ELIAS, PROPHET
diminutive .... LIGE
successor of ..... ELISHA
Eliot, George .... EVANS
hero ..... MARNER, BEDE
heroine .... ROMOLA
Elisheba's husband ... AARON
elision ... SYNCOPE, OMISSION
victim of .... VOWEL, SYLLABLE
elite ... SELECT, PICK, CREAM
assemblage ..... GALAXY, SALON
elixir ... PANACEA, CURE-ALL, ARCANUM, NOSTRUM, CATHOLICON
Elizabeth ___ .... TAYLOR
diminutive of ... LIZ(ZIE), LISSET(T)E, BETH, BETTY
Elizabeth I adviser ..... CECIL
parent .... BOLEYN, HENRY (VIII)
tutor .... ASCHAM
elk .... MOOSE, SAMBAR, WAPITI, ALCE, LOSH
male .... BULL
ell .... WING, EXTENSION
Elfen's lake .... KATRINE
Ellice Islands' old name ...... LAGOON
ellipse .... CURVE, OVATE
ellipsoidal .... OVAL
elliptical ...... OVAL, OVATE, OVOID, OBLONG
elm .... WAHOO
fruit .... SAMARA
Elman, violinist ..... MISCHA
Elmo's (St.) fire .. CORPOSANT
Elohim .... GOD
elongate .... STRETCH, LENGTHEN, EXTEND
elongated .... PROLATE, OBLONG
combining form .... MACR(O)
elope .... RUN AWAY, ESCAPE, ABSCOND
elopers, usual .... LOVERS
eloquent .... ORATORICAL, FLUENT, EXPRESSIVE, ARTICULATE
else .... OTHER(WISE), DIFFERENT, IF NOT, BESIDES
elt .... PORKER
elucidate .... CLEAR, CLARIFY, EXPLAIN
elude .... SHUN, AVOID, EVADE, ESCAPE, BAFFLE, DODGE
elusive .... EVASIVE, EELY, BAFFLING, SLIPPERY
eleuthera yield ... CASCARILLA
elsin .... AWL
elusion ... EVASION, AVOIDANCE
elusive ... SLIPPERY, BAFFLING
thing ..... FUGITIVE, EEL
elutriate .... DECANT, PURIFY
elver .... CONGER, EEL
Elwin, anthropologist .... VERRIER
Ely's famed building .... CATHEDRAL
Elysian ..... HAPPY, BLISSFUL
Elysium .... PARADISE, EDEN
em: colloq. .... THEM
half an .... EN
emaciated .... THIN, BONY, GAUNT, SKINNY, WASTED
emaciation ... TABES, WASTE, ATROPHY, MARASMUS
emanate .... ISSUE, RISE, COME FORTH, EMIT
emanation(s) .... NITON, VAPOR, EFFLUX, EXHALATION, AURA(E)
flower ... AROMA, SCENT
invisible ... AURA, VAPOR
subtle .... AURA
emancipate ... FREE, MANUMIT, RELEASE, LIBERATE
emancipation .. MANUMISSION
emasculate .... CASTRATE, WEAKEN, GELD, STERILIZE
embalm .. PRESERVE, MUMMIFY
embalmed body ..... MUMMY
embalming fluid ... FORMALIN
embankment .... DIKE, LEVEE, DAM, BUND, STAITH
castle .... RAMPART
protective mat .... MATTRESS
embar .... ARREST, STOP, CONFINE
embargo .... RESTRAINT, RESTRICTION
embark .... ENGAGE
embarrass ...... DISCONCERT, FLUSTER, ABASH, DISCOMFIT, FAZE
a speaker ...... GRAVEL, HECKLE
embarrassed .... QUEASY
embarrassing situation .... SCRAPE
embarrassment ..... PUDENCY
embassy ... LEGATION, MISSION
official .... ATTACHE
embellish ...... PINK, ADORN, GILD, EMBOSS, EMBROIDER, POLISH, DECK, DECORATE, TOUCH UP, ORNAMENT
embellishment .... FILLIP, TRAPPING, ADORNMENT
ember ... ASH, CINDER, SPARK, GLEED, IZLE, COAL
embezzle .. STEAL, DEFALCATE, PECULATE
embezzlement .... THEFT
embezzler .... PECULATOR
embitter .... ACERBATE, ENVENOM, FESTER, RANKLE
emblaze .... KINDLE
emblazon .... ADORN, EXTOL, DECORATE
emblem (see symbol) .. BADGE, SYMBOL, SIGN, INSIGNE
authority .... MACE, ENSIGN, BADGE, FASCES, GAVEL, CROWN
Christianity's .... CROSS
clan .... TOTEM
heraldic .... DEVICE
international .. RED CROSS
national .... FLAG
of royalty ...... PURPLE
shield .... IMPRESA
Turkish .... CRESCENT
U.S.A. .... EAGLE
emblematic .. HIEROGLYPH(IC)
embodiment .... AVATAR, EPITOME, INCARNATION, IMAGE
embody ...... INCORPORATE, INCARNATE
embolden .... ENCOURAGE
embolism .... INTERCALATION
embonpoint ..... CORPULENCE, STOUTNESS
embowel .... EVISCERATE
embrace ...... CARESS, HUG, INCLUDE, ENCLASP, ENFOLD, ADOPT, ENCLOSE, COMPRISE, INARM, CUDDLE
affectionate ... BEARHUG
slang .... CLINCH
embracer .... ARM
embrasure ...... CRENEL(LE)
embrocation .... LOTION, LINIMENT
embroider .... TAT, DECORATE, PURL, ORNAMENT, EMBELLISH, EXAGGERATE, COUCH
embroidery ...... LACEWORK, NEEDLEWORK
design .... BREDE
frame ..... TABO(U)RET, TAMBOUR
loop .... PICOT
piece of .... BREDE
embroil ... MIX UP, MUDDLE, INVOLVE, ENTANGLE
embrown .... TAN
embrue .... WET
embryo .... CELL, GERM
developed .... FETUS
food for ..... ENDOSPERM
outer cells ..... EPIBLAST
membrane ..... AMNION
middle layer .. MESODERM, MESOBLAST
emend ...... CORRECT, EDIT, REVISE
emerald ...... BERYL, GREEN, STONE, SMARAGD
Isle ...... IRELAND, ERIN
emerge .... ISSUE, RISE
emergence .... EGRESS
emergency man .... PINCH-HITTER, TROUBLE-SHOOTER
situation ...... CLUTCH
treatment ..... FIRST AID
emeritus .... RETIRED
emery .... CORUNDUM, ABRASIVE
use for .... GRINDING, POLISHING, BRASIVE
emesis .... VOMITING
emetic .... ALUM, ALOIN, CATHARTIC, EVACUANT, IPECAC, EXPECTORANT, VOMIT
plant .... TURPETH

emetine .... EXPECTORANT
source .... IPECAC
emigrant ..... EMIGRE, ALIEN
emigre, kind of ..... REFUGEE, EVACUEE
Emil ____, author ... LUDWIG
Emile Herzog's pen name .... MAUROIS
Zola book .... NANA
eminence .... DIGNITY, REPUTE, FAME, NOTE
eminent .... RENOWNED, EXALTED, DISTINGUISHED, FAMOUS, NOTED
emir's domain .... EMIRATE
emissary .. AGENT, MESSENGER, ENVOY, (DE)LEGATE
emission .... DISCHARGE, ISSUANCE
of urine, involuntary .... ENURESIS
emit .... ERUCT, EXHALE, DISCHARGE, ISSUE, REEK
air .... ELOW
Emma ____, poet ... LAZARUS
emmet .... ANT, PISMIRE
Emmy .... STATUETTE, AWARD
brother of .... OSCAR
emodin shade .... ORANGE
emolument ... GAIN, SALARY, WAGE(S), FEE(S), STIPEND
emote .... ACT, PERFORM
emotion ...... PATHOS, ENVY, PASSION, FEELING, ANGER, FEAR, LOVE, HATE
seat of ... SPLEEN, LIVER
strong .. FLAME, PASSION
turn of .... CAPRICE
emotional excitement .... HYSTERIA
illness .... PSYCHOSE, NEUROSE
emotionless ...... UNFEELING, STOICAL, NUMB, DEAF, INSENSATE
emperor .... PADISHAH, IMPERATOR, BUTTERFLY, DESPOT, AUTOCRAT, CAESAR
Constantine's standard .. LABARUM
decree of ...... RESCRIPT
German .... KAISER
Japanese ...... MIKADO, TENNO
Russian .... CZAR, TSAR
sovereignty of ... EMPERY, EMPIRE
emphasis ... STRESS, WEIGHT, ACCENT
emphasize .... STRESS
emphatic .... FORCIBLE, STRIKING
speech .... BIRR
emphysema .... HEAVES
empire ..... DOMINION, REALM
state .... NEW YORK
empiric .... CHARLATAN, QUACK, MOUNTEBANK
employ .... HIRE, USE, AVAIL, OCCUPY, DEVOTE, ENGAGE, PLACE
employees .... PERSONNEL
employer .... HIRER, BOSS, USER
employment .... WORK, OCCUPATION, JOB, PROFESSION, EXERCISE
contract, illegal .... YELLOW-DOG
emporium ..... STORE, MART, MARKET(PLACE)
empower .... ENABLE, AUTHORIZE, DEPUTE, PERMIT, VEST
empress .... ZITA
emprize .... DARING, PROWESS
emptiness .... VACUITY
empty .... IDLE, INANE, BLANK, DEPLETE, (DE)VOID, VACUOUS, DRAIN, VACANT, BARE, WORTHLESS, VAIN, TEEM, LACKING, WITHOUT, FLUSH
colloquial ..... HUNGRY
headed ... SILLY, STUPID
of thought ...... VACANT
talk .... FUDGE
wind from sail .... SPILL
empyema .... PUS
empyreal .... CELESTIAL, SUBLIME, HEAVENLY
empyrean .... ETHER, SKY, FIRMAMENT
EMs .... RANKS
emu-like bird .... OSTRICH, CASSOWARY
emulate ..... COMPETE, RIVAL, VIE, APE, EQUAL
emulsifier .... GELATIN, GUM ARABIC
emunctory ... LUNGS, KIDNEYS, SKIN
enable .... EMPOWER
enact .... ORDAIN, DECREE, PORTRAY, PASS, ACT OUT, LEGISLATE, PERFORM, PLAY
enactment .... DECREE, LEGISLATION, PASSAGE, EDICT, LAW, ORDINANCE
enamel ... COATING, LACQUER, PAINT, VARNISH, GLAZE, NAIL POLISH, SMALTO
enamelware .... LIMOGES, CLOISONNE, CERAMICS, PORCELAIN, DISHES, UTENSILS
enamor ... CAPTIVATE, CHARM
encamp ..... BIVOUAC, TENT, PITCH
enceinte .... PREGNANT
enchain .... FETTER, BIND
enchant ... BEWITCH, CHARM, ATTRACT, DELIGHT, ENTHRAL(L)
enchanting .... MAGIC
enchantment ... CHARM, SPELL
enchantress ... SIREN, WITCH, SORCERESS, MEDEA, HAG
in Odyssey .... CIRCE
enchiridion .... HANDBOOK
enchorial ... NATIVE, POPULAR
encina .... (LIVE) OAK
encircle .... GIRD, RING, CORDON, ENCOMPASS, ENLACE, ENVIRON, WREATHE, GIRT, SURROUND, HEM
encircling, an ..... CINCTURE
enclasp ...... EMBRACE, HUG
enclave .... GOA
enclose .... HEM, FENCE (IN), SURROUND, ENCYST, ENVIRON
enclosed area .... CORRAL, RING, STOCKADE, SEPT, YARD, COMPOUND
part of aircraft .. NACELLE
space .... COMPOUND
enclosing line .... VERGE
membrane ...... TUNICA
enclosure ... STOCKADE, YARD, PEN, CAGE, FENCE, WALL, CORRAL, COTE, WRAPPER, ENVELOPE, COCOON, COOP, CINCTURE, TERRARIUM
animal .... VIVARIUM, TERRARIUM
cattle ... CORRAL, KRAAL, ATAJO
for grazing ...... WALK
for stray animals .... POUND
in water .... CRAWL
of wagons for defense ... CORRAL
race track .... PADDOCK
encomiast .... EULOGIST
encomium .... TRIBUTE, PANEGYRIC, PRAISE, ELOGE, EULOGY, COMMENDATION
encompass .... ENCIRCLE, SURROUND, INCLUDE, RING, GIRD
encore .... AGAIN, OVER, REPETITION, BIS, REPEAT
encounter .. MEET, COME UPON, BATTLE, FIGHT
encourage ..... ABET, BOOST, EMBOLDEN, HEARTEN, FOSTER, CHEER
encroach .... INVADE, TRESPASS, INTRUDE, IMPINGE
encroachment ..... INTRUSION
encumber ..... LOAD, SADDLE, BURDEN, HAMPER
encumbrance .... BURDEN
in law ..... CLAIM, LIEN
kind of ...... MORTGAGE
encyclopedist ..... COMPILER, DIDEROT, D'ALEMBERT
end ...... AIM, FINALE, CLOSE, TAIL, FINIS(H), CONCLUSION, TIP, PURPOSE, LAST, OBJECT, RESULT, UPSHOT, STOP, TERMINATE, OMEGA, SAKE
combining form .. TEL(O)
in music .... FINE
thick .... BUTT
toward an ...... TELIC
up .... LAND
endanger .... IMPERIL, JEOPARDIZE
endearment .... CARESS, AFFECTION
endeavor ..... STRIVE, ESSAY,

VIE, NISUS, TRY, ATTEMPT, EFFORT
endemic .... INDIGENOUS, NATIVE
ending .... CONCLUSION, FINIS(H), FINALE
have same .... CONTERMINAL
in grammar ... DESINENCE
endive ... CHICORY, ESCAROLE
endless .... ETERN(AL), INFINITE, LASTING, PERPETUAL, INTERMINABLE
endmost ..... LAST, FARTHEST
endocrine .... GLAND
designating one .... ADRENAL, THYROID, PITUITARY
endogamy .... INBREEDING
endoparasite ..... HOOKWORM, ENDAMEBA
endorse .... SANCTION, APPROVE, BACK
endorsement .. VISA, BACKING
endow .... VEST, BESTOW, BEQUEATH, ENDUE
endowment ..... GIFT, BOON, GRANT, TALENT, BEQUEST, (WITH)STAND, DONATION
for graduate student ..... FELLOWSHIP
natural .. DOWER, DOWRY
endue .... DIGEST, CLOTHE, COVER, ENDOW, DOWER
endurable .... TOLERABLE
endurance ...... FORTITUDE, STAMINA, PATIENCE
endure .... BEAR, LAST, LIVE, BROOK, HOLD OUT, STAND, UNDERGO, TOLERATE, CONTINUE
enduring .... LASTING, PERMANENT
endways .... UPRIGHT, LENGTHWISE
Endymion .... SHEPHERD
lover of .... SELENE
enema .... CLYSTER
enemy .... FOE, RIVAL, ADVERSARY, OPPONENT, ANTAGONIST
alien detained .. INTERNEE
energetic .... ACTIVE, FORCEFUL, LIVE
activity .... EXERTION
one .... DYNAMO, HUSTLER, GO-GETTER
energize ... FORTIFY, ACTIVATE
energy ...... PEP, VIGOR, ERG, VIM, STEAM, BIRR, FORCE, ZIP
and initiative .... ENTERPRISE
luminous .... LIGHT
measure of .... ENTROPY
potential .... ERGAL
slang .... STINGO
unit of ...... ERG, JOULE
enervate ..... DRAIN, WEAKEN, SAP, DEBILITATE
enfeeble .... WEAKEN
enfilade ..... BARRAGE, RAKE, GUNFIRE
enfin ...... AT LAST, FINALLY
enfold .... EMBRACE, ENLACE, WRAP
enforce ...... COMPEL, IMPOSE
enfranchise .. FREE, LIBERATE, EMANCIPATE
engage .... BIND, PLEDGE, BETROTH, HIRE, EMPLOY, RESERVE, AFFIANCE, BOOK, MESH, OCCUPY, UNDERTAKE
engaged .... BUSY, OCCUPIED, BETROTHED
engagement .... DATE, APPOINTMENT, TROTH
engaging .... SAPID, WINSOME
engender ..... BEGET, BREED, CAUSE, PRODUCE, GENERATE, PROMOTE
engine ...... MOTOR, MOGUL, TURBINE, LOCOMOTIVE, APPARATUS, MACHINE, GIN, DIESEL
compressed air .. RAMJET
cylinder .... PISTON
exhaust noise ..... CHUG
of war .... ONAGER, CATAPULT, RAM, MANGONEL, TREBUCHET
on wheels ... LOCOMOTIVE
platform .... WALK
puff .... PANT
engineer's aid .... STOKER, OILER
place .... CAB
engineless airplane .... GLIDER
England (see British) .... ANGLIA, ALBION, EGBERT
personified ... JOHN BULL
English ... ANGLE, ANGELICAN, SILURES
East India company ship INDIAMAN
Englishman ...... SASSENACH, LIMEY
engram .... TRACE
engrave ... CHISEL, CUT, ETCH, CHASE, CARVE, INCISE, HATCH
engraver ... ETCHER, CHASER, LAPIDARY
mark of ..... REMARQUE
tool of .... BURIN
engraving .... PRINT, CUT
art of .... GLYPTICS, GLYPTOGRAPHY
by dots .... STIPPLE
means of ...... GRAVURE
method ...... MEZZOTINT
on metal .... CHALCOGRAPHY
pertaining to ... GLYPTIC
process ...... CEROTYPE, ELECTROTYPE
stone .... INTAGLIO
tool ..... STYLE, CHISEL, BURIN
wood .... XYLOGRAPH
engross ..... ABSORB, OCCUPY
engrossed .... RAPT, ABSORBED
engulf .... (OVER)WHELM, SWALLOW
enhance .... INCREASE, AUGMENT, INTENSIFY, HEIGHTEN
Enid .... BAGNOLD
husband of: legendary ... GERAINT
enigma ...... REBUS, PUZZLE, RIDDLE, MYSTERY, CONUNDRUM
enigmatic .... OBSCURE, BAFFLING, INSCRUTABLE, MYSTIC(AL), CRYPTIC
person .... SPHINX
saying .... PARABLE
enisle ... (SET) APART, ISOLATE
enjoin ...... URGE, (FOR)BID, DIRECT, ORDER, EXHORT
enjoy with others ..... SHARE
enjoyment .... PLEASURE, RELISH, GRATIFICATION, GUSTO, ZEST, FUN
enlarge .... DILATE, EXPAND, INCREASE, DISTEND, MAGNIFY, BLOW UP, EXPATIATE, REAM
hole/bore .... REAM
on .... EXPATIATE, ELABORATE
enlarged thyroid gland ..... GOITER
picture: colloq. .. BLOWUP
enlarger .... REAMER
enlighten ... INFORM, CLARIFY, ILLUMINE
enlist ...... ENROLL, RECRUIT, JOIN(UP), VOLUNTEER
enlistment, compulsory ...... DRAFT, LEVY, CONSCRIPTION
period .... HITCH
enliven .... ANIMATE, REFRESH, BRIGHTEN
enmesh .... KNOT, SNARL, (EN)TANGLE, ENGAGE
enmity .... HATRED, ANTAGONISM, ANIMOSITY, ANIMUS, RANCOR, FEUD, DISCORD, HOSTILITY, MALICE
ennead .... NINE
ennoble ...... DIGNIFY, EXALT
ennui ... LANGUOR, BOREDOM, WEARINESS
enormous ...... HUGE, VAST, IMMENSE, GIGANTIC, MAMMOTH
animal ...... MASTODON, BEHEMOTH
number .... GOOGOL
Enos' cousin .... ENOCH
father .... SETH
grandparent .. EVE, ADAM
uncle .... ABEL, CAIN
enough ... QUITE, SUFFICIENT, ADEQUATE
archaic .... ENOW
enrage .... ANGER, INFURIATE, INCENSE
enrapture .. DELIGHT, RAVISH, ENTRANCE, ENCHANT
enrich .... LARD
enroll ...... ENLIST, JOIN UP, ENTER, IMPANEL, INSCRIBE, RECORD, REGISTER

enroot ..... IMPLANT, EMBED
ens .... BEING, ENTITY, EXISTENCE
ensconce .... HIDE, CONCEAL, SHELTER
ensemble .... SUIT
ensiform .... XIPHOID
ensign .... FLAG, BANNER, ORIFLAMME, STANDARD, GONFALON
ensilage ... FODDER, STORAGE
ensile .... STORE
enslave .... DOMINATE, SUBJUGATE, ENTHRAL(L)
enslavement .... BONDAGE
ensnare ... SNIGGLE, TREPAN, TRICK, (EN)TRAP, NET
ensue ..... FOLLOW, RESULT, SUPERVENE
entablature, part of .. CORNICE, ATLANTES, FRIEZE, ARCHITRAVE
support .... ATLAS, ATLANTES, COLUMN
entail .. INVOLVE, NECESSITATE
entangle .... WEB, ENLACE, MAT, ENMESH, ENSNARE, FOUL, RAVEL, MESH, EMBROIL, COMPLICATE, CONFUSE, KNOT
entanglement .... KNOT
Entebbe is capital of .. UGANDA
entellus .... MONKEY
entente .... AGREEMENT, UNDERSTANDING
enter .... RECORD, START, ENROLL, INSERT, PIERCE, INSERT, JOIN, POST
clumsily .... BARGE
into conflict ... ENGAGE, WAR, AGGRESS
enteric fever .... TYPHOID
enterprise ..... UNDERTAKING, PROJECT, VENTURE, GUMPTION
entertain ... DIVERT, REGALE, AMUSE, TREAT, FETE, CONSIDER
entertainer ... COMIC, AMUSER, DISEUSE, HOST(ESS), ARTISTE
entertaining .... AMUSING, HOSPITABLE
entertainment ... AMUSEMENT, HOSPITALITY, FETE
between acts .... INTERLUDE, INTERMEZZO, RELIEF
enthrall .... ENSLAVE, ENCHANT, CAPTIVATE, FASCINATE
enthrone .... SEAT, EXALT
enthuse .... RAVE, REVEL
enthusiasm ... ARDOR, VERVE, PEP, SPIRIT, CRAZE, MANIA, ZEAL, ELAN, FERVOR, PASSION
enthusiast .... IST, ZEALOT, BUG, AFICIONADO, FAN, BUFF, DEVOTEE, FANATIC, ADDICT
enthusiastic ..... AVID, WARM, HOT, EAGER, ARDENT, RABID, KEEN
appreciation ..... GUSTO
entice .... BAIT, TEMPT, CAJOLE, LURE, ATTRACT, COAX, INVEIGH, TOLE, INVEIGLE
enticer ..... SEDUCER, DECOY, TEMPTRESS
entire ..... LIVELONG, TOTAL, ALL, WHOLE, COMPLETE
combining form .. HOLO
prefix .... HOLO
range .... GAMUT
entirely .... UTTERLY
entitle .... NAME, DUB, CALL, QUALIFY
entity ..... THING, UNIT, ENS, BEING, EXISTENCE
entoblast .... ENDODERM
entomb .... BURY, INTER, INURN
entomo, as prefix .. INSECT(S)
entourage ...... ATTENDANTS, ROUT, RETINUE, TRAIN
entozoon .... PARASITE, TAPEWORM, HOOKWORM
entr'acte ...... INTERMISSION, INTERLUDE
entrails ... INTESTINES, GUTS, VISCERA, INNARDS, BOWELS, OFFAL, UMBLES
entrance ...... PORTAL, ADIT, GATE, DELIGHT, CHARM, DEBUT, INGRESS, ENCHANT, DOOR, ADMISSION, GATE
back .... POSTERN
court .... ATRIUM
hall ..... LOBBY, FOYER, ATRIUM
with evil intent ... ENTRY
entrant .. ENTRY, CONTESTANT, COMPETITOR
entrants collectively .... FIELD
entreat ... BESEECH, IMPLORE, PRAY, BEG, PLEAD
entreaty ...... PRAYER, PLEA, SUPPLICATION
entrechat .... LEAP, JUMP
entree .... ADMISSION, ACCESS, DISH
entrench .... TRESPASS, ENCROACH, INFRINGE, SECURE
entrepot .... DEPOT, WAREHOUSE, STOREHOUSE
entrepreneur ...... PROMOTER
entresol .... MEZZANINE
entrust .... CONFIDE, TURN OVER, CONSIGN
entry ...... POST, ENTRANCE, DOOR, INGRESS, ACCESS
British .... CLOSE
illegal ...... INTRUSION, TRESPASS
in ledger ... ITEM, DEBIT, CREDIT, RENT(AL), INTEREST
permit .... VISA, PASS, PRATIQUE
entwine .... (EN)LACE, WEAVE, TWIST
enumerate .... COUNT, TICK OFF, NUMBER
enumeration .... CENSUS, LIST
enumerator, kind of .... NOSE COUNTER
enunciate ...... UTTER, STATE, ANNOUNCE, DECLARE, PROCLAIM
enunciation .... DICTION
enure ... HARDEN, ACCUSTOM, HABITUATE
enuresis .... URINATION
envelop ..... SHROUD, COVER, HIDE, CONCEAL, ENFOLD, WRAP, INVEST
envelope ...... CASE, SHROUD, WRAPPER, COVER(ING), SHEATHE
fetus .... CAUL
silky .... COCOON
turtle's ...... CARAPACE, SHELL
envenom ... POISON, EMBITTER
environ .... PURLIEU, OUTSKIRT, ENCIRCLE, ENCLOSE, SURROUND, LOCALE
environment .... HABITAT, AMBIENCE, MILIEU, SETTING
environs .... PRECINCTS, VICINITY, SUBURBS, NEIGHBORHOOD, SURROUNDING, PERIPHERY, PURLIEU
envoy .... LEGATE, AMBASSADOR, MESSENGER, AGENT, EMISSARY
originally ... DEDICATION, POSTSCRIPT
papal .... NUNCIO
envy .... COVET, (BE)GRUDGE, JEALOUSY, SPITE
enzyme .... DIASTASE, MUTASE, RENNIN, CASEASE, ASE, MALTASE, CATALASE, OLEASE, EREPSIN, AMYLASE, OXIDASE, INVERTASE, INULASE, PECTASE, PROTEASE, RENNET, ZYMASE, ZYME
action of .... ZYMOLYSIS
blood .... THROMBIN
digestive ...... TRYPSIN, PEPSIN(E), LIPASE
in saliva .... PTYALIN
in yeast .... LACTASE
producing ... ZYMOLYSIS
protein-splitting .. PAPAIN
eolith .... AX
eon ...... AGE, EPOCH, OLAM
eonic .... ERAL
Eos .... GODDESS, AURORA, DAWN
eosin .... NOPALIN, DYE
eparch ... GOVERNOR, BISHOP
eparchy .... DIOCESE
epaulet .... KNOT
epee .... SWORD
epergne ... CENTERPIECE, DISH
ephah, one tenth of ..... OMER
ephemera .... MAY FLY
ephemeral ...... TRANSITORY, TRANSIENT, EVANESCENT, MOMENTARY
ephemeris .... ALMANAC, DIARY, CALENDAR

ephemeron .... MAY FLY
epic ...... POEM, EPOS, SAGA, GRAND, HEROIC, MAJESTIC
events, series of .... EPOS
poem .... EPOPEE, (A)ENEID, ILIAD, ODYSSEY, BEOWULF, EPOS
poetry .... EPOPEE, EPOPOEIA, EPOS
epicarp .... HUSK, RIND
epicedium .... DIRGE
epicene .... NEUTER
epicrisis ... CRITIQUE, REVIEW, CRITICISM
epicure .. GOURMET, SYBARITE, GOURMAND, GASTRONOME
of a kind ..... GLUTTON
epicurean .... APICIAN, LUXURIOUS, SENSUOUS
epicurism ...... GASTRONOMY, HEDONISM
epidemic .... PLAGUE, WIDESPREAD
among plants .... EPIPHYTOTIC
epidermal tissue .... KERATIN
epidermis .... CUTICLE, SKIN, BARK, INTEGUMENT, SCARFSKIN
epigram .... ADAGE, MOT, SAYING, POEM, MONOSTICH
epigraph .... INSCRIPTION, MOTTO, QUOTATION
epilepsy ...... CATALEPSY, FIT, SEIZURE
attack of ... GRAND MAL, PETIT MAL
epileptic attack, feeling before AURA
treatment ...... DILANTIN
Epimetheus .... TITAN
brother ..... PROMETHEUS
wife .... PANDORA
epinephrin(e) ..... ADRENALIN, HORMONE
epinette .... LARCH
epiphyte ...... ORCHID, MOSS, LICHEN, FUNGUS
episcopacy .... BISHOPS
episcopal minister .. PRESBYTER
see .... CATHEDRA
episcopate .... SEE
episode .... INCIDENT, INSTALLMENT, EVENT
epispastic .... VISICANT
episperm .... TESTA
epistaxis .... NOSEBLEED
epistle .... LETTER, NOTE, BILLET(DOUX), MISSIVE
epitaph .... INSCRIPTION, HIC JACET, HERE LIES
epithem .... POULTICE
epithet .... AGNOMEN, (BY)NAME, OATH, MISNOMER
for Alexander .... (THE) GREAT
Clemenceau .... TIGER
Eric .... (THE) RED
Ivan ... (THE) TERRIBLE
Jackson ... STONEWALL
Pitt .... IRONSIDE
epitome ...... BRIEF, DIGEST, ABSTRACT, SUMMARY, GIST

epoch .. EON, AGE, ERA, PERIOD
epode .... (LYRIC) POEM, AFTERSONG
epopee .... EPIC (POEM), EPOS
epoptic .... MYSTIC
epos .... EPIC
Epsom ____ .. DOWNS, SALT(S)
event .... DERBY
equable .... TRANQUIL, EVEN, STEADY, UNIFORM, SERENE
equal .... EVEN, TIE, PARALLEL, RIVAL, SAME, (COM)PEER, ALIKE, MATCH
angled figure ..... ISOGON
combining form .... ISO, PARI, EQUI
distribution of weight ... EQUIPOISE
footing .... PAR
make .... EQUATE
quantity .... IDENTIC
Rights party .. LOCOFOCO
without ..... NONPAREIL, PEERLESS
equalitarian of a kind .... DEMOCRAT
equality .... PARITY
French .... EGALITE
of laws .... ISONOMY
of rights, laws .. ISONOMY
state .... WYOMING
equanimity .... POISE, COMPOSURE, SERENITY, SANG-FROID
colloquial .... COOL
equator crosser ... SHELLBACK
equatorial .... TORRID, TROPICAL, SUBSOLAR
Equatorial Guinea capital ... BATA
native .... BUBI, FANG
president .... MACIAS
equestrian .... HORSEMAN, RIDER
order of knights .. EQUITES
equilateral figure .... RHOMB, TRIANGLE
equilibrist .... BALANCER, ROPE WALKER
equilibrium ...... (EQUI)POISE
lacking .... ASTASIA
equine .... HORSE
cry ..... NEIGH, WHINNY
disease .... FARCY, GLANDERS, LAMPAS, LAMPERS, SPAVIN
equip .... RIG, GIRD, FIT, TRAIN, FURNISH, DIGHT
for military service ...... ACCOUTER, ACCOUTRE
equipage .... CARRIAGE, RETINUE, TRAIN, FOLLOWING, TURN-OUT
equipment .... GEAR, OUTFIT, RIG, TURN-OUT, TACKLE
equipoise .... BALANCE, EQUILIBRIUM
equisetum .... HORSETAIL
equitable .. HONEST, FAIR, JUST
equitant .... OVERLAPPING
equitation ..... RIDE, MANEGE, HORSEMANSHIP

equity .... JUSTICE, FAIR
Equity initials .... AEA
member .... ACTOR, ACTRESS, PLAYER
equivalent ..... TANTAMOUNT
equivocal .... ENIGMATIC, UNCERTAIN, DOUBTFUL, UNDECIDED, AMBIGUOUS, MISLEADING, EVASIVE
equivocate ... FENCE, PALTER, LIE, HEDGE, EVADE
equivoke .... PUN, AMBIGUITY
era ... AGE, EON, TIME, EPOCH, PERIOD
eradicate ... EPILATE, ANNUL, (UP)ROOT, DESTROY, WIPE OUT, EXTERMINATE
erase ..... DELE(TE), EFFACE, EXPUNGE, OBLITERATE, CANCEL
slang ..... KILL, RUB OUT
erased, can't be ... INDELIBLE
eraser .... RUBBER
Erbil .... ARBELA
ere .... RATHER, BEFORE, IN TIME, SOONER THAN
Erebus, place after ... HADES
erect .... REAR, RAISE, UPRIGHT, VERTICAL, BUILD, PITCH, CONSTRUCT, STIFF, ASSEMBLE
erelong .... ANON, SOON
eremite ..... HERMIT, RECLUSE
erenow .... HERETOFORE
ergo ..... HENCE, THEREFORE
ergon .... WORK, ERG
ergot .... FUNGUS
of rye .... SPUR
eri .... SILKWORM
eria .... BOMBYX
erica .... HEATH(ER)
Erie port .... SANDUSKY
Erin .... EIRE, HIBERNIA, IRELAND, IERNE, OLD SOD
erinaceous animal .. HEDGEHOG
Erinyes .... MEGAERA, TISIPHONE, FURIES, ALECTO, EUMENIDES
eristic .... DISPUTANT, ARGUMENTATIVE, CONTROVERSIAL
Eritrea's capital ..... ASMARA
seaport .... MASSAUA, MASSAWA
ermine ... STOAT, WEASEL, FUR
fur ... MINIVER, MINEVER
ern .... (SEA)EAGLE
erode .... EAT INTO, DISINTEGRATE
erodent .... CAUSTIC
"Eroica" composer ... LISZT
Eros ..... CUPID, AMOR, GOD
erose .... GNAWED, IRREGULAR, UNEVEN
erosion .... CORROSION
erotic ... AMATIVE, AMOROUS, AMATORY, SEXY, PAPHIAN, LESBIAN
err ... TRIP, SLIP, SIN, BLUNDER
errand .... MISSION
boy ..... PAGE, BELLHOP, CADDIE, RUNNER, BUTTONS
errant .... WANDERING,

ITINERANT, WRONG, TRUANT
erratic .... VAGRANT, IRREGULAR, QUEER, ECCENTRIC, WAYWARD, UNSTEADY, CAPRICIOUS
erring .... SINNING
erroneous .... WRONG, MISTAKEN, FALSE
error ...... ERRATUM, LAPSE, SIN, SLIP, GAFFE, GOOF, FALLACY, LAPSUS, BONER, MISCUE, MISTAKE, BLUNDER, FAULT, WRONGDOING, FAUX PAS
in etiquette ... FAUX PAS
in naming .... MISNOMER
error(s) in printing .. ERRATUM, ERRATA
ersatz .... SUBSTITUTE, ARTIFICIAL
Erse ..... CELT, GAEL, GAELIC
erst ... FORMERLY, LONG AGO, FIRST
erstwhile ...... FORMER, ONCE
erubescent .... REDDISH, BLUSHING
eruct .... BELCH
erudite .... LEARNED, SCHOLARLY, WISE
person .... PUNDIT
erudition ..... WISDOM, LORE, LEARNING, SCHOLARSHIP
erupt ...... EJECT, EXPLODE, BURST, EMIT
eruption ... RASH, OUTBURST, EXPLOSION, OUTBREAK
eryngo .... SEA HOLLY
erysipelas ... ROSE, WILDFIRE
Esau .... EDOM
brother .... JACOB
descendant of .. EDOMITE
father-in-law ..... ELON
grandson ...... AMALEK
parent ... ISAAC, REBEKAH
wife .... ADAH
escadrille .... SQUADRON
escalade .... SCALE
escalate .... EXPAND
escalator .... STAIRWAY
escalop .... MOLLUSK
escapade ...... CAPER, DIDO, PRANK, ADVENTURE
escape ... ELOPE, EVADE, FLEE, AVOID, LAM, LEAK, DISAPPEAR, KEEP AWAY, ELUDE, VENT, GET AWAY
narrow .... CLOSE SHAVE
escapee .... RUNAWAY
escargot .... SNAIL
escarole .... ENDIVE
escarpment ...... SLOPE, CLIFF
eschalot .... SHALLOT, ONION, SCALLION
eschar(a) ... SCAB, BRYOZOAN
escharotic .... CAUSTIC, CORROSIVE
eschatology subject ... DEATH, RESURRECTION, IMMORTALITY, JUDGMENT
escheat .... CONFISCATE
eschew .... AVOID, SHUN
escort .... ACCOMPANY, RETINUE, (E)SQUIRE, BEAU, CONDUCT, CHAPERON(E)
armed .... CONVOY
kind of ..... BODYGUARD, USHER, CONVOY, OUTRIDER
lady's .... CAVALIER, CABALLERO
woman .... DUENNA, CHAPERONE
escritoire ... DESK, SECRETARY, TABLE
escrow .... BOND, DEED, AGREEMENT, CONTRACT
escudo .... COIN
1/100 of .... CENTAVO
esculent .... EDIBLE, EATABLE, COMESTIBLE
escutcheon ..... ARMS, CREST, SHIELD
band .... FESS(E)
center .... FESSPOINT
point on .... NOMBRIL
vertical stripe ... PALLET
voided .... ORLE
Esdras .... APOCRYPHA, EZRA, NEHEMIAH
esker (eskar) .... OS, OSAR, RIDGE
Eskimo .... ALASKAN, ALEUT, INNUIT, ESQUIMAU, ITA, YUIT, HUSKY
boat ..... UMIAK, OOMIAC
boot .... MUKLUK
canoe .... KAYAK, BIDARKA, OOMIAK, BAIDAR
dog ... HUSKY, MALEMUTE
garment .... PARKA, TEMIAK
house ..... IGLOO, IGLU, TOPEK
jacket .... ANORAK
knife .... ULU
language .... HUSKY
medicine man .. ANGEKOK
memorial post ...... XAT
settlement .... ETAH
esne .... SERF, SLAVE
esophagus .... GULLET, WEASAND, GULA
pain .... CARDIALGIA
rod for clearing .... PROBANG
esoteric .... PRIVATE, CONFIDENTIAL, MYSTIC, ARCANE, OCCULT
doctrine .... CABALA
opposed to ... EXOTERIC
espalier .... TRELLIS, LATTICE, PALISADE
España .... SPAIN
esparto .... GRASS
especial .... PARTICULAR, EXCEPTIONAL, OUTSTANDING
Esperanto .... IDO
deviser ...... ZAMENHOF
espionage .... SPYING
esplanade ..... WALK, GLACIS, ROADWAY
espousal .... BETROTHAL, MARRIAGE, WEDDING, ADVOCACY
espouse ..... MARRY, ADOPT, ADVOCATE, ABET, AFFY
esprit de corps ...... MORALE, SPIRIT, CAMARADERIE
espy .... SPOT, DESCRY, SIGHT, SEE
Esquimau .... ESKIMO
esquire ...... SHIELDBEARER, ATTENDANT, ESCORT, GENTLEMAN
ess .... CURVE
essay .... TOY, ATTEMPT, THEME, PAPER, TRACT, TREATISE, THESIS
esse .... ESSENCE, BEING, EXISTENCE
essence .... ATTAR, GIST, ENS, PITH, NATURE, CORE, KERNEL, ESSE, PERFUME, INBEING, FLAVOR, EXTRACT
of anything ...... JUICE
Essene ...... MYSTIC, ASCETIC
essential .... INHERENT, INTRINSIC, HYPOSTATIC, BASIC, NECESSARY, VITAL, MUST, BASAL, REQUISITE, INDISPENSABLE
element .... PART
oil .... ESSENCE
oil liquid ...... CINEOLE
part ..... PITH, MEMBER
thing .... KEY
Essex city .... ILFORD
essonite .... GARNET
establish .... FOUND, FIX, SETTLE, INSTITUTE, PROVE, VERIFY, SET
securely ..... ENTRENCH, PLANT, EMBED, RIVET
established value .... PAR
establishment, domestic ...... MENAGE
estafet .... COURIER
estaminet .... CAFE
estancia .... RANCH(O)
estate .... ASSETS, PLANTATION, CAPITAL, HACIENDA, ALOD, DEMESNE, PROPERTY
country ...... HACIENDA
first .... CLERGY
fourth .... PRESS, JOURNALISM
holder .... TERMOR
in expectancy .... REMAINDER
landed .. DOMAIN, MANOR
overseer .... BAILIFF
second .... NOBILITY
Spanish-America .... ESTANCIA
third ...... BOURGEOISIE
under feudal lord .. FIEF, FEOD
esteem ..... ADMIRE, HONOR, PRIDE, VALUE, PRIZE, RESPECT, REGARD, APPRECIATE
ester .... OLEATE, SILICATE, STEARIN, ACETIN, IODIDE, MALATE, PICRATE
esthesia .... SENSATE
esthete .... CONNOISSEUR
esthetic .... ARTISTIC
esthetics .... ARTS

estimate .... MEASURE, APPRAISE, GAUGE, CALCULATE, EVALUATE
in advance ... FORECAST
estivate .... SUMMER
opposed to ... HIBERNATE
Estonia, capital of ... TALLINN
city of ... TARTU, YUREV
Estonian island .... OESEL
monetary unit .... KROON
estop .... PREVENT, BAR, OBSTRUCT
estovers .... NECESSARIES
allowed divorcee .... ALIMONY
estrange ... ALIENATE, WEAN, DIVERT, SEPARATE, DISAFFECT
estray .... WAIF
estrol ..... HORMONE, THEELOL
estrone ... THEELIN, HORMONE
estrus .... FRENZY, HEAT
estuary ... RIA, LOCH, FRITH, BAY, FIRTH, INLET, FIORD
tidal wave .. EAGRE, BORE
esurient ... GREEDY, HUNGRY, VORACIOUS
et .... AND
al .... OTHERS
etagere .... WHATNOT
etamine .... CLOTH, VOILE
Etanin .... DRACONIS
etape .... STOREHOUSE, ENCAMPMENT
Etats ____ .... UNIS
etch .... CUT, ENGRAVE, CHISEL
etching acid .... MORDANT
Eteocles, brother of .... POLYNICES
kingdom .... THEBES
parent of ...... JOCASTA, OEDIPUS
eternal .... AGELESS, (A)EONIAN, EVERLASTING, TIMELESS, FOREVER, PERPETUAL
City .... ROME
The .... GOD
eternity .... (A)EON, TIME, INFINITY, IMMORTALITY, OLAM
etesian .... PERIODIC, ANNUAL, SEASONAL
Ethan Frome's wife .... ZEENA
Ethanim .... TISHRI
Ethel ____, performer .... MERMAN, BARRYMORE
ether .... AIR, SKY, SPACE
compound .... ESTER
use of ..... ANESTHETIC, SOLVENT
ethereal ..... AIRY, DELICATE, HEAVENLY, CELESTIAL, SUPERNAL
fluid .... ICHOR
salt .... ESTER
ethical ... VIRTUOUS, MORAL, RIGHT
ethics .... MORALS
Ethiopia .... ABYSSINIA
Biblical ..... CUSH, KUSH
capital .... ADDIS ABABA
Ethiopian antelope ... DIKDIK
ape .... GELADA
Black Jews ..... FALASHA
capital, ancient .. MEROE
city ...... ADOWA, ADUA, HAR(R)AR
coin .... TALARI
cotton toga ..... SHAMMA
district .. AMHARA, HARAR
fly .... ZIMB
Hamite ... GALLA, AFAR
Hamitic tribe member ... FALASHA
ibex .... SAOL, WALIE
king ... NEGUS, MEMNON
kingdom, former .... AMHARA
lake ... T(S)ANA, DEMBEA
language ..... AMHARIC, GEEZ
native .... NEGRO
prince .... RAS
province ... SHOA, TIGRE
queen .... CANDACE
river ...... OMO, ATBARA, TANA
seaport .... MASSAUA
table-mountain ... AMBA
title .... RAS, NEGUS
tribesman ...... FALASHA
walled city ..... GONDAR
wolf .... KABERU
ethnarch .... GOVERNOR
ethnic ...... HEATHEN, RACIAL
group ...... FOLK, RACE
ethologist .... LORENZ
ethos ...... CHARACTERISTICS
opposed to ..... PATHOS
ethyl .... GASOLINE
alcohol .... ETHANOL
derivative .... ETHER
etiolate ..... BLANCH, BLEACH
etiquette .... DECORUM, PROPRIETY
breach of ..... SOLECISM, FAUX PAS
required by ... DE RIGUER
Etna .... VOLCANO, LAMP
Eton .... TOWN, SCHOOL
article of wear .. COLLAR, JACKET, COAT
rival of .... HARROW
student .... OPPIDAN
Etruscan god .... LAR(ES), PENATES, TINIA, TURMS
goddess ... UNI, MENFRA, TURAN
king .... PORSENA
Minerva .... MENFRA
Etta of comic strips .... KETT
etude .... STUDY
etui .... CASE
etwee .... CASE
etymological .... LITERAL
etymon .... RADIX, ROOT
Etzel .... ATTILA
eucalyptol .... CINEOLE
eucalyptus .... MALLEE, YATE, IRONBARK
Eucharist .... EULOGIA, HOUSEL, SACRAMENT
box .... PIX, PYX
bread ... HOST, OBLATION, WAFER
cloth .... FANON
to dying person .... VIATICUM
vessel .... PATEN, AMA
wafer .... HOST
wine of the ... OBLATION
eucharistic plate ...... PATEN
service .... LITURGY
vestment ..... MANIPLE, FANON
Euclid ...... MATHEMATICIAN
forte of .... GEOMETRY
work on geometry ...... ELEMENTS
eudaemonia ...... HAPPINESS
euge .... BRAVO
eugenics, pioneer in .. GALTON
subject of .... RACES, BREEDS
eulogia .... EUCHARIST
eulogistic .... ELOGE, LAUDATORY, MAGNIFIC
eulogize ...... EXTOL, LAUD, PRAISE
eulogy .... ENCOMIUM, PANEGYRIC, TRIBUTE, PRAISE, ELOGE
Eumenides .... FURIES, ERINYES
eunuch .... CHAMBERLAIN, GELDING
euphemism for hell ..... HECK
euphonium, like .... TUBA
euphony ..... MELODY, METER
euphorbia .... SPURGE, POINSETTIA
euphoria ..... COMPLACENCY, SMUGNESS
Euphrosyne .... JOY
euphuism .... BOMBAST
Eurasian in India ... FERINGI, FERINGHEE
range .... URAL
eureka .... AHA, SEE, EXCLAMATION
state .... CALIFORNIA
euripus ...... STRAIT, CHANNEL
Europa's father ..... OGENOR
lover .... ZEUS
European ..... LAPP, FRENCH, BOHUNK, FRANK, DANE, FINN, LETT, BALT
antelope ...... CHAMOIS
apple tree .... SORB
aromatic herb .... FLEAWORT
ash tree juice .... MANNA
beetle .... DORBUG, COCKCHAFER
bellflower ...... RAMPION
bird ... HOOPOE, TURNIX, REEDLING, ROLLER, WHIMBREL
bison .... AUROCHS
blackbird .... MERLE, OUSEL, OUZEL
blenny .... SHANNY
brantail ...... REDSTART
buttercup .. GOLDILOCKS
butterfly ... RED ADMIRAL
canal .... KIEL

carp .... BLEAK
catfish .... SILURID
cavalryman ... U(H)LAN, HUSSAR
cereal grass ..... MILLET
chestnut .... MARRON
chicken .... HAMBURG
coal region .... SAAR
commercial weight ...... CENTNER
country, ancient .... HELVETIA
crow .... CHOUGH, NUTCRACKER
deer ..... FALLOW, STAG
diving duck ... POCHARD
dog .... GRIFFON
dormouse .... LEROT
dotterel .... PLOVER
duck ... WIDGEON, SMEW, POCHARD
falcon .... HOBBY, LANNER(ET), MERLIN
finch ...... SERIN, SISKIN
fish .... RUDD, BOCE, BARBEL, PLAICE, GUDGEON
flatfish .... BRILL
fly .... FRIT
food fish ... SAUREL, SCAD
food seed .... LUPINE
gamebird .... TURNIX
garlic .... MOLY
grosbeak ..... HAWFINCH
hawk .... PUTTOCK
haybird ...... BLACKCAP
health resort .... BADEN, EMS
herb ..... LOVAGE, RUTA, ELECAMPANE, TARRAGON
herring .... SPRAT
holly .... ACEBO
in India .... FERINGI
iris .... ORRIS
juniper .... CADE
kite .... GLED(E)
lake ..... ONEGA, GENEVA
mignonette ...... WELD, WOLD
mint .... CLAR(R)Y, CLARE, HYSSOP
news agency ...... HAVAS
nomad .... LAPP
oak .... HOLM, DURMAST
oriole .... LORIOT
pea .... LICORICE
plant .... ALFILARIA, COMFREY, LAVENDER, LICORICE
plover ...... DOTT(E)REL
polecat .... FITCH, FOUMART
principality ... MONACO, ORANGE, WALACHIA
range .... URAL
ratlike animal .. HAMSTER
ray .... THORNBACK
redstart ...... BRANTAIL
river .... ISAR
robin .... RUDDOCK
rodent .... DORMOUSE
rose tree .... MEDLAR
shad .... ALOSE
shark .... TOPE
shore bird ... WHIMBREL
shrub ...... MEZEREON, OLEASTER
slang .... BOHUNK
smelt .... SPARLING
songbird ...... LINNET, OUSEL, REDWING, THROSTLE, THRUSH, WHITETHROAT, MAVIS
squirrel .... SUSLIK
sumac .... TEREBINTH
swallow ...... MARTLET, MARTIN
thrush ... OUSEL, MISSEL, MAVIS, FIELDFARE
tree .... DURMAST, HOLM
vulture ... LAMMERGEI(E)R
water bird ... GARGANEY
wheat .... SPELT
wild duck ... WI(D)GEON, SHELDRAKE
wild goose .... GRAYLAG, GREYLAG
woodpigeon ... CUSHAT, RINGDOVE
wormwood .. SANTONICA

Eustachian tube ..... SYRINX, SALPINX
euthenics subject ..... RACES, BREEDS
evacuant .... CATHARTIC, EMETIC
evacuate .... VOID, EMIT, (RE)MOVE, WITHDRAW, EMPTY
evacuee .... REFUGEE
evade .... AVOID, ESCAPE, ELUDE, DODGE, GEE
payment .... BILK
work .. SHIRK, MALINGER, GOLDBRICK
evaginate .... EVERT
evaluate ... APPRAISE, ASSAY, GAUGE, ESTIMATE, RATE, ASSESS
evanesce ...... FADE, VANISH, DISAPPEAR
evanescent ...... EPHEMERAL, TRANSIENT, FLEETING
evangel .... GOSPEL
evangelist ... MARK, MATTHEW, LUKE, JOHN, PREACHER, REVIVALIST, MISSIONARY
Mormon .... PATRIARCH
"Evangeline" locale .... GRAND PRE
Evans, Mary Ann ..... ELIOT
evaporate ...... DRY, VANISH
evaporating quickly .. VOLATILE
evasion .... ELUSION, EQUIVOCATION, SALVO, SUBTERFUGE
evasive ..... TRICKY, ELUSIVE, EQUIVOCAL, SHIFTY
eve .... EVENING
of festival .... VIGIL
even ... EQUABLE, PLANE, TIED, LEVEL, FLAT, SMOOTH, UNIFORM, CALM, SERENE, STILL, TOSSUP, STEADY, PLACID
if .... THO(UGH)
minded ...... EQUABLE, PLACID
slang .... HUNKY
evenfall ..... TWILIGHT, DUSK
evenhanded .... FAIR, IMPARTIAL, JUST
evening .... DUSK, GLOAMING
affair .... SOIREE
dress .... TUXEDO
glory .... SUNSET
love song ..... SERENADE
of .... VESPERTINE
poetic .... EVE
prayer .... VESPER(S), EVENSONG
service .... VESPER
star ..... VENUS, MOON, HESPER(US), VESPER
evensong .... VESPERS
event .... INCIDENT, OCCURRENCE, RESULT, HAPPENING, CASUS, OCCASION
causing war .. CASUS BELLI
of June 1953 .... CORONATION
eventful .... MOMENTOUS
eventide ...... VESPER, DUSK, TWILIGHT
eventual ... FINAL, ULTIMATE
eventuality ..... CONTINGENCY
eventually .... FINALLY, ULTIMATELY
eventuate ..... RESULT, TURN, HAPPEN
ever ... ALWAYS, REPEATEDLY, AYE
Everest conqueror .. HILLARY, TENZING
peak .... LHOTSE
rival ...... ANNAPURNA
everglade .... SWAMPLAND
denizen .... (ALLI)GATOR
evergreen ... SPRUCE, CASHEW, CAROB, YEW, CEDAR, TITI, CALABA, BALSAM, MADRONA, PINE, FIR, CONIFER, DEODAR, OLIVE
bean .... CAROB
genus .... ABIES
giant .... REDWOOD, SEQUOIA
herb .... GALAX
oak .... ILEX, HOLM
opposed to .. DECIDUOUS
shrub .... OLEANDER, ROSEMARY
tree .... HEMLOCK
tree bark .... CASSIA
tree fruit .... CONE
everlasting .... AGELONG, ETERNAL, ETERN(E), ETERNITY, DURABLE
every .... EACH, ALL
combining form .... PANT(O)
everyday ... USUAL, COMMON, DAILY
everything .... ALL
everywhere ... HIGH AND LOW, UBIQUE
combining form ... OMNI

evict .... OUST, EJECT, EXPEL, REMOVE
evidence .... INDICATION, SIGN, PROOF
evident .... APPARENT, CLEAR, MANIFEST, OBVIOUS, PLAIN, PALPABLE, PATENT
evil .... WICKED, BAD, SIN, DEPRAVITY, BASE, VILE, MAL, MALEFIC(ENT)
act .... CRIME
child .... IMP
combining form .... MAL
deed .... SIN
doer .... MISCREANT, CRIMINAL, MALEFACTOR
eye ...... JINX, WHAMMY
for evil .... RETALIATION
habit .... VICE
intent ... DOLUS, MALICE
minded ..... MALICIOUS, WICKED, SALACIOUS, PRURIENT
motivation ..... MALICE, SPITE
person .... CAITIFF
smelling .. MALODOROUS, STINKING
spirit, taken by .... POSSESSED
spirit, woman ..... HAG
wishing ..... MALIGNANT
evince ... INDICATE, MANIFEST, SHOW
eviscerate ... DISEMBOWEL, GUT
evitable .... AVOIDABLE
evocation .... SUMMONS, CALLING
evoke .... EDUCE, CALL, REMIND, RECALL, ELICIT, DRAW, SUMMON
evolution ..... DEVELOPMENT, GROWTH, MUTATION
theorist on ..... DARWIN, LAMARK
evolutionary development of plant/animal ... PHYLOGENY
evolve ... UNFOLD, WORKOUT, DEVELOP, DERIVE
ewe .... SHEEP
mate of .... RAM
necked animal ... HORSE
udder inflammation ..... GARGET
ewer .... PITCHER, JUG
ex ____ ... CATHEDRA, PARTE
libris .... BOOKPLATE
parte .... ONE-SIDED
preposition ... WITHOUT
exacerbate ... EMBITTER, IRK, ANNOY, IRRITATE
exact .... LITERAL, LEVY, BLEED, STRICT, ACCURATE, CORRECT, PRECISE, DEMAND, SEVERE, EXTORT
copy .... DUPLICATE
moment .... POINT
money .... LUG
thoroughly ... RIGOROUS
exaction ... EXTORTION, TAX, TOLL
ancient .... TRIBUTE
exactitude .... ACCURACY, PRECISION
exaggerate ...... EMBROIDER, OVERSTATE, MAGNIFY
tendency to ... MYTHOMIA
exaggerated .... OUTRE
comedy .... FARCE
pious feeling .... PIETISM
praise .... PUFFERY, FLATTERY
exaggeration .... OVERSTATEMENT
for effect .... HYPERBOLE
exalt ...... ELEVATE, EXTOL, RAISE, PRAISE, GLORIFY, ELATE
exaltation .. ELATION, RAPTURE
exalted .... SUBLIME, HIGH, NOBLE, STRONG, TIPSY
examination ...... SCRUTINY, INQUIRY, INSPECTION, TEST(ING), QUIZ, TRIAL
of dead body .. AUTOPSY, NECROPSY
examine .... TRY, TEST, EXPLORE, SCRUTINIZE, INSPECT
accounts .... AUDIT
by touching ... PALPATE
examiner .... CENSOR, INSPECTOR, EYER, TESTER
example ... PARADIGM, MODEL, CASE, SAMPLE, INSTANCE, PATTERN, SPECIMEN
examples, set of ...... PRAXIS
exasperate .... INFURIATE, INCENSE, IRK, ENRAGE, TRY, IRRITATE, ANNOY, VEX, ANGER
exasperation .... DISGUST
excaudate .... TAILLESS
excavate ...... DIG, UNEARTH, HOLLOW OUT, DREDGE, EXHUME, HOE, SCOOP
excavation .... MINE, PIT, HOLE, HOLLOW, STOPE
mining .... STOPE
excavator .... DREDGE(R), DIGGER, SCOOP(ER)
exceed ... SURPASS, OUTDO, EXCEL, OUTREACH
exceedingly .... UNCO
excel .... BEST, OUTDO, STAR, EXCEED, SURPASS, TRANSCEND
excellence .... MERIT, SUPERIORITY, VIRTU(E), GOODNESS
excellent .... CAPITAL, AONE, RARE, PEACHY, TOPS, OUTSTANDING, SUPERB, RIPPING, SUPER
except ...... SAVE, BUT, BAR, EXCLUDE, OMIT, OBJECT
exception .... EXCLUSION, OMISSION, OBJECTION, RESERVATION, CHALLENGE
in law .... SAVING
take .... DEMUR, RESENT, OBJECT
exceptional .... ESPECIAL, OUTSTANDING, UNUSUAL
excerpt ..... EXTRACT, QUOTE, PASSAGE, SELECT
excess ... (SUR)PLUS, NIMIETY, PLETHORA, OVER(AGE), INTEMPERANCE, EXTRA, SURFEIT
of solar over lunar year .. EPACT
excessive .... UNDUE, IMMODERATE, EXTRAVAGANT, EXORBITANT, INORDINATE, ULTRA
affection .... DOTAGE
combining form .. HYPER
demand ..... EXACTION, EXTORTION
in belief .... RABID
joy .... RAPTURE, EXALTATION
saliva secretion .... PTYALISM
zeal .... FANATICISM
excessively .... UNDULY, EXTREMELY, OVERLY
fond .... DOTING
exchange .. BANDY, COMMUTE, SWAP, TRADE, BARTER, TRUCK, SWITCH, RIALTO
business ... AGIO, BONDS, SHARES, CURRENCY
discount .... AGIO
fee .... AGIO
medium .... SYCEE
of shots .... GUNPLAY
premium .... AGIO
Scottish .... NIFFER
stock .... BOURSE
visit .... GAM
exchequer ... FISC, TREASURY, FUNDS, FINANCES
excide .... CUT OUT, REMOVE, EXCISE
excise .... TOLL, DUTY, CUT OUT, IMPOST, REMOVE, EXSCIND, TAX
tax collector .. GA(U)GER
excitable .... FIERY, HOT
excite ... STARTLE, TITILLATE, FLUSTER, PIQUE, STIR(UP), (A)ROUSE, PROVOKE, AGITATE, ROIL
interest/curiosity ...... INTRIGUE
excited .... ASTIR, AGOG, (A)DITHER, HET UP, AGITATED
greatly .... FRANTIC, FRENZIED
state .... FEY
exciting .... ELECTRIC
excitement ..... FUROR, TIZZY, FEVER, STIR, HEAT, FLUTTER
pleasurable .... KICK
reducer .... SEDATIVE
exclaim .. EJACULATE, CRY OUT
exclamation ... OUTCRY, POOH, AH, ALAS, BAH, FIE, PUGH, SHUCKS, RATS, NUTS, PSHAW, OH MY, GEE, GOSH
German ..... ACH, HOCH
of joy .... WHOOPEE
of pain ..... YOW, OUCH
of praise ...... HOSANNA, ADORATION
of triumph ..... EUREKA
point .... SCREAMER

to attract attention .. HEY
exclave, example of .. PRUSSIA
exclude ...... OMIT, EXCEPT, EXPEL, ELIMINATE, (DE)BAR, REJECT, BAR
by general consent ...... OSTRACIZE
exclusive .... SOLE, SINGLE, POSH, ONLY, SELECT
control ..... MONOPOLY
of .... EX
set .... ELITE
excommunicate .... BAN, CONDEMN, DAMN
excommunication .. EXCISION, CONDEMNATION, BAN, ANATHEMA
excoriate ..... ABRADE, FLAY, CHAFE, DENOUNCE
excoriation ... SORE, ABRASION
excrement .... FECES, REFUSE, MANURE, DUNG
excrescence .... STUD, OUTGROWTH, APPENDAGE, WART
example of .. FINGERNAIL, BUNION, HAIR
excreta .... URINE, SWEAT
excrete .... EGEST, EXUDE
excretion .... SWEAT, PERSPIRATION, URINE
excruciate ... TORTURE, PAIN, TORMENT, AGONIZE
exculpate .... ACQUIT, CLEAR, EXONERATE, ABSOLVE
excursion .... JAUNT, TOUR, SIDE TRIP, OUTING, JUNKET
coach ...... CHARABANC
excursive .... RAMBLING, WANDERING
excusable .... VENIAL
excuse .... ALIBI, PLEA, PRETEXT, OVERLOOK, JUSTIFY, ABSOLVE, APOLOGY, RELEASE, SALVO
for absence ..... ESSOIN
partial ..... EXTENUATION
execrable .... DETESTABLE, HATEFUL, ABOMINABLE
execrate ..... DETEST, CURSE, HATE, LOATHE, ABHOR
execute .... HANG, DO, PERFORM, FULFILL, KILL
unlawfully ...... LYNCH
execution by burning .. STAKE
by drowning .... NOYADE
by hanging ..... HALTER, SWING, STRETCH
executioner ...... HANGMAN, HEADSMAN, DEATHSMAN, HANGER
gangland's .... HATCHETMAN
Executive Mansion .... WHITE HOUSE
exegesis .... EXPLANATION
exemplar ... MODEL, PATTERN, EXAMPLE, (ARCHE)TYPE, SPECIMEN
exempt .... IMMUNE, FREE, EXCUSE(D), RELEASE
exemption from punishment .. IMPUNITY, IMMUNITY
temporary .... GRACE
exequies .... FUNERAL, OBSEQUIES
exercise .... USE, EMPLOY(MENT), PRACTICE, PROBLEM, TRAIN, DRILL, PRAXIS, LESSON, EXERT, PERPLEX, WORRY, HARASS
exercises, athletic .... CALISTHENICS
set of .... PRAXIS
trained .... MANEGE
exert .... EXERCISE
exertion .... EFFORT
exeunt .... EXIT
exfoliate ..... CAST OFF, PEEL
exhalation ... HALITUS, AURA, FUME, BREATH, EXPIRATION, EVAPORATION, EMANATION
exhale ... EXPIRE, EVAPORATE, BREATHE OUT
exhaust .... TIRE, FAG, DRAIN, DEPLETE, USE UP, SPEND
exhausted ..... TIRED, DONE, SPENT, USED UP, ALL IN, EFFETE
exhibit .... STAGE, SHOW, DISPLAY, PRESENTATION, EXPOSE
in law ...... DOCUMENT, EVIDENCE, PROOF
exhibition ..... PRESENTATION, DISPLAY, FAIR
international .... EXPOSITION
of art works ...... SALON
place ... GALLERY, SALON
exhilarate ... ELATE, ENLIVEN, ANIMATE, STIMULATE
exhilaration ..... ANIMATION, LIVELINESS
exhort .... URGE, PROD, EGG, ADMONISH
exhume .... DISINTER, UNEARTH, DIG OUT
exigency .... NEED, URGENCY, EMERGENCY, DEMAND
exigent .... URGENT, CRITICAL, EXACTING, PRESSING
exiguous ... SMALL, MEAGER, LITTLE, SCANTY
exile ..... RELEGATE, DEPORT, EXPATRIATE, BANISH(MENT)
exist .... (A)LIVE, BE, IS
existence ... ESSE, BEING, ENS, LIFE, LIVING
coming into ... NASCENT
existent ..... ALIVE, PRESENT
existing ...... REAL, EXTANT, ALIVE
exit .... EGRESS, ISSUE, OUTLET, DEPART(URE), WAY OUT, LEAVE
exocarp .... RIND
exodus ..... HEGIRA, FLIGHT, DEPARTURE, EMIGRATION
hero .... ARI
leader .... MOSES
scene .... RED SEA
exogen .... DICOTYLEDON
exogenous .... ENTHETIC
exonerate .... ACQUIT, CLEAR, EXCULPATE, ABSOLVE
exorbitant .... EXCESSIVE, IMMODERATE, UNDUE
interest .... USURY
exorcism .... EXPULSION
exordial ...... INTRODUCTORY
exordium .... PROEM, OVERTURE, OPENING, BEGINNING
exoteric .... EXTERNAL, POPULAR, PUBLIC
opposed to .... ESOTERIC
exotic ...... ALIEN, FOREIGN, IMPORTED, STRANGE
expand .... INFLATE, INTUMESCE, DILATE, FLAN, ENLARGE, SWELL, DISTEND
expanse .... SEA, OCEAN, BREADTH, AREA, REACH, SPREAD
expatiate .. ENLARGE, DESCANT, ELABORATE
expatriate ..... EXILE, BANISH
expect ... HOPE, ANTICIPATE, PRESUME, AWAIT
expectation .... HOPE, ANTICIPATION, PROSPECT, OUTLOOK
expecting .... PREGNANT
expectorant .. EMETIN(E), EMETIC
expectorate .... SPIT
expedient ...... CONVENIENT, ADVISABLE, POLITIC
expedite ...... EASY, HASTEN, FACILITATE, SPEED(UP), HURRY
expediter: colloq. ... TICKLER
expedition .... CRUSADE, SAFARI, SPEED, DISPATCH, TRIP, MARCH
heroic .... QUEST
hunting .... SAFARI
military .... ANABASIS
purpose .. EXPLORATION, BATTLE, HUNT(ING)
religious ...... CRUSADE
expeditious .... PROMPT, SPEEDY
expel ..... EJECT, DRIVE OUT
from country .... EXILE, BANISH, DEPORT, EXPATRIATE
expend .... USE, CONSUME, SPEND
expendable ..... REPLACEABLE
expenditure .. OUTGO, OUTLAY
expense .... COST, FEE, CHARGE, SACRIFICE
colloquial ..... DAMAGE
expensive ..... COSTLY, DEAR
experience .... FEEL, UNDERGO
trying .... ORDEAL
experiment ...... TEST, TRIAL, TRY
experimental .... TENTATIVE, TESTING
workshop .... LAB(ORATORY)
expert ... ACE, VIRTUOSO, PRO, SKILLFUL, DEFT, ADEPT, MASTER, DAB(STER), SHARP
in canon law .. DISCRETIST
on anecdotes/stories .... RACONTEUR

on coins .... SHROFF
expiate ..... ATONE, REPAIR, SATISFY
expiation ...... ATONEMENT, AMENDS, REPARATION
place of ..... PURGATORY
expiatory .... PIACULAR
expire ...... DIE, PERISH, END, STOP, CEASE, TERMINATE
explain ... EXPLICATE, DEFINE, CLEAR, ELUCIDATE, CLARIFY, EXPOUND, INTERPRET
explanation .. INTERPRETATION, CLARIFICATION, ELUCIDATION
of Biblical passage ...... EXEGESIS
explanatory .... EXEGETIC
expletive ...... OATH, CURSE, EXCLAMATION
explicate .... EXPLAIN
explicit ... DEFINITE, EXPRESS, EXACT, PRECISE, SPECIFIC, CLEAR
explode .... POP, BURST, DISCREDIT, DETONATE, BLOW UP, FIRE, CRUMP
exploding meteor ..... BOLIDE, BOLIS
exploit ... ACT, FEAT, GEST(E), PROMOTE, DEED, HEROISM, ACTION, UTILIZE
explore .... INVESTIGATE, EXAMINE, PROBE
explorer ... ERIC, RAE, BYRD, AMUNDSEN, BALBOA, DE SOTO, CORTES, PERRY, LEWIS
explosion .... BLOWUP, DETONATION, OUTBURST
explosive ... DYNAMITE, TNT, MINE, GUNPOWDER, CORDITE, SOUP, TONITE, BOMB, DUNNITE, LIGNOSE, CHEDDITE, ROBURITE, LYDDITE, AMYTOL, PETARD
charge, part of .... WARHEAD
sound ..... DETONATION, CHUG, POP, BOOM, CLAP
explosives box ...... CAISSON
material .... CELLULOSE
storage place .. MAGAZINE
exponent ... SYMBOL, EXAMPLE, ADVOCATE
in mathematics ... INDEX
expose ...... BARE, DISCLOSE, REVEAL, UNMASK, DISPLAY, EXHIBIT, SHOW
as false .... EXPLODE, DEBUNK
to danger .... IMPERIL
exposition .... EXHIBITION, SHOW, FAIR
expository .... EXEGETIC, EXPLANATORY
expostulate .... OBJECT, REMONSTRATE, PROTEST
exposure .... AIRING
expound .... EXPLAIN, ELUCIDATE, CLARIFY, INTERPRET
express ...... STATE, REVEAL, SIGNIFY, EXPLICIT, UTTER, EXTORT
dissatisfaction .... COMPLAIN, GRIPE, BEEF, HOOT
in numbers ... EVALUATE
expression .... TERM, REPRESENTATION, LOCUTION, SAYING, ARTICULATION
local .... IDIOM
of contempt ...... SNIFF, SNORT, GRUNT, SNEER
of reproach .... FIE
of sympathy .... CONDOLENCE
expressionless mien .... DEADPAN, POKERFACE
expressive .... ELOQUENT
action .... GESTURE
expressly .... DEFINITELY, PLAINLY, ESPECIALLY, EXPLICITLY
expropriate ...... DISPOSSESS
expulsion ... EJECTION, OUSTER
kind of .... DEPORTATION
expunge ... DELE(TE), EFFACE, ERASE, CANCEL, WIPE(OUT)
expurgate ... CENSOR, PURGE, CLEANSE, PURIFY
exquisite .... DELICATE, FASTIDIOUS, RARE
exsanguine .... ANEMIC
exscind .... EXCISE, CUT(OUT)
exsert ... THRUST, PROTRUDE
exsiccate .... DRY, PARCH
extant .... EXISTING
extemporaneous ... OFFHAND, IMPROMPTU, IMPROVISED
extemporize ...... IMPROVISE
extend .... PROTRACT, OUTREACH, RENEW, STRETCH, JUT, CONTINUE, PROLONG, SPREAD
across .... SPAN
extension .... RENEWAL, ADDITION, CONTINUATION
building ...... ELL, WING
extent ...... LENGTH, SCOPE, COVERAGE, MAGNITUDE, LATITUDE
of precedence ..... LEAD
extenuate .... WEAKEN, LESSEN, DIMINISH, MITIGATE, PALLIATE
exterior ... ECTAL, EXTRINSIC, OUTER, OUTSIDE, FOREIGN, EXTERNAL
toward the .... ECTAD
exterminate ...... EXTIRPATE, ERADICATE, DESTROY, ANNIHILATE
extermination, mass .... GENOCIDE
external ... OUTER, EXOTERIC, EXTERIOR, SUPERFICIAL
combining form .. ECT(O)
covering ..... HIDE, PELT, COAT, SKIN, CRUST, SHEATHE
cover of flower .... PERIANTH
world .... NONEGO
extinct ...... EXTINGUISHED, DEAD, DEFUNCT, NON-EXISTENT
animal .... MASTODON
bird .... DODO, MOA, MAMO, KIWI
elephant ..... MAMMOTH
elephantlike animal ..... DINOTHERE
mammal ... GLYPTODONT
ox .... URUS
reptile .... DINOSAUR, DINOCERAS
extinguish .... PUT OUT, DESTROY, SMOTHER, QUENCH, ECLIPSE, DOUSE, DOWSE, SNUFF
in law .... NULLIFY
extirpate .... EXSCIND, DESTROY, ABOLISH, RAZE, UPROOT, ERADICATE
extol ... PRAISE, LAUD, EXALT, GLORIFY
extort .. WRING, MILK, SCREW, EXTRACT, EXACT, WREST, SQUEEZE, BLEED, MULCT
extortioner ..... BLACKMAILER
extra ... SPARE, ODD, EXCESS, SURPLUS, ADDITIONAL, OVER
actor .... SUPER, SUPERNUMERARY, FIGURANT(E)
pay .... BONUS
Scottish .... ORRA
extract .... DISTIL, ELICIT, ESTREAT, EXCERPT, PULL OUT, QUOTATION, WRING, EDUCE, EVOKE, EXTORT, ATTAR, DRAW
by boiling ..... DECOCT
by dissolving ..... LEACH
forcibly .... EVULSE
from balsam ... TOLUENE
of court record .. ESTREAT
extraction .... LINEAGE, ORIGIN, BIRTH, DESCENT
extracurricular activity ...... DEBATING, DRAMATICS, ATHLETICS
extradite .... REPATRIATE
extraneous ... EXOTIC, OUTER, FOREIGN, EXTRINSIC, ALIEN
extraordinary ...... UNIQUE, GREAT, UNUSUAL, EXCEPTIONAL, UNCO, REMARKABLE, MARVELOUS
extrasensory perception ... ESP
extravagant .... BAROQUE, PROFUSE, EXCESSIVE, EXORBITANT, WASTEFUL, LAVISH, PRODIGAL, ULTRA
spending .... LAVISH
extravaganza ..... SPECTACLE, REVUE
extreme ... RADICAL, ULTRA, SEVERE, SUPERLATIVE, FINAL, EXCESSIVE, IMMODERATE, DRASTIC, RANK, LAST
limit .... OUTRANCE
opposed to .... MEAN

unction ..... SACRAMENT
unction, give ..... ANELE
extremely ...... VERY, UNCO, HIGHLY
fine .... SUPERB
wicked .... HEINOUS
extremist .... RADICAL, NIHILIST
extremity .... POLE, TIP, TOE, END, DYING
extremities .... LIMBS
extricate ...... RELEASE, FREE
extrinsic ...... EXTRANEOUS, FOREIGN, ALIEN
extrude ...... EXPEL, PROJECT
extrusive .... VOLCANIC
exuberant .... EFFUSIVE, LAVISH
exudate, plant ... GUM, RESIN, LAC
exudation .... SUDOR, EMANATION, SWEAT, PERSPIRATION, RESIN, GUM
exude .... EMIT, REEK, DISCHARGE, FLOW, OOZE
water .... WEEP
exult ..... REJOICE, GLORIFY, JUBILATE, GLORY
exultant .... JUBILANT
exults ..... CROWS, REJOICES, GLORIES
exuviae .... MOLTS, SHELLS
exuviate ..... MOLT, CAST OFF
eyas .... HAWK, NESTLING
eye ... OPTIC, OCELLUS, OGLE, BUD, ORB, GLIM, SIGHT, VISION, GLANCE, LOOK, SEE
bean's ..... HILUM, HILA
black ... SHINER, MOUSE
bruise under .... MOUSE
cavity .... ORBIT
coating .... GLAZE
colloquial .... OPTIC
combining form .... OCUL(O)
contraction of pupil .... MYOSIS
cover .... PATCH
defect .... DIPLOPIA, MYOPIA, OXYOPIA
dirt .... MOTE
discharge .... RHEUM
disease ...... GLAUCOMA, CATARACT
disorder .... SQUINT, STRABISMUS
doctor .... OCULIST, OPHTHALMOLOGIST
dropper .... PIPETTE
filler .... BEAUTY
filling .... BEAUTIFUL
film .... GLAZE
for-an-eye .. TIT FOR TAT, TALION
for only one.. MONOCULAR
German .... AUGE
glass .... PINCENEZ, MONOCLE, LENS, SPECTACLES, LORGNETTE, LORGNON
glass maker/seller ...... OPTICIAN
inflammation ...... STY, IRITIS
instrument .. ORTHOSCOPE
lashes .... CILIA
layer .... UVEA
magic ... RADAR, SONAR
membrane .... IRIS
of the .... OPTIC, OCULAR
opening .... PUPIL
part ...... UVEA, RETINA, LENS, CHOROID, PUPIL, CORNEA, HUMOR
pus .... HYPOPYON
shield .... PATCH, BLINDER, VISOR, BLINKER
simple .... OCELLUS
slang ... PEEPER, WINKER
socket .... ORBIT
Spanish .... OJO
thing with ...... POTATO, STORM, NEEDLE, TARGET, HURRICANE
wash .... EYEMO, MURINE
worm .... LOA
eyeball dryness ..... XEROSIS
outer coat ..... CORNEA
eyebrow .... BREE
cosmetic ..... MASCARA
marker .... PENCIL
Spanish .... CEJA
eyebrows, space between ..... GLABELLA
eyedrop drug .... ESERINE, MURINE
eyeful .... ATTRACTIVE, STRIKING
eyeglasses .... PINCE NEZ, SPECS, MONOCLE, LORGNETTE, SPECTACLES, HARLEQUIN
maker/seller of .... OPTICIAN
slang .... CHEATERS
eyelash ..... CILIUM, WINKER
cosmetic ..... MASCARA
eyelashes .... CILIA
of .... CILIARY
eyeless .... BLIND
"Eyeless In Gaza" author .... HUXLEY
eyelet ... GROMMET, GRUMMET, PEEPHOLE, LOOPHOLE, OCELLUS
making tool ... BODKIN, STILETTO
eyeleteer ... BODKIN, STILETTO
eyelid, corner of ... CANTHUS
cosmetic .... KOHL
drooping .... PTOSIS
inflammation .... STY, BLEPHARITIS
eyes: colloq. ...... SPARKLERS
cover the .... SEEL, BLINDFOLD, HOODWINK
deep-set .... CAVERNOUS
slang .... DAYLIGHT
describing some .... DEEPSET, GREEN, SOULFUL, DOE, EVIL, SHIFTY, SQUINT(Y)
inflammation ...... STY, HAW
of the .... OCULAR
poetic .... ORBS
slang .... LAMPS
swelling ...... MOUS(I)E
third .... HAW
tissue .... TARSUS
trouble ...... TRICHOMA
eyelids, of the ..... PALPEBRAL
eyesight .... VISION
by .... OCULAR
eyesore .... UGLY
eyetooth ..... CUSPID, FANG, CANINE
eyewash ...... COLLYRIUM, EXCUSE, MURINE, EYEMO, NONSENSE, FLATTERY
eyewink ...... INSTANT, HINT, SIGNAL
eyot .... AIT, ILE, ISLE(T)
eyra .... WILD CAT
eyre .... TOUR, CIRCUIT
eyrie .... NEST, EAGLET
Ezida frequenter .... NEBO
Ezra, book about .... ESDRAS

F

F, letter .... EF
fabaceous plant .... PEA
Fabian strategy ...... DELAY, AVOIDANCE
Fabius, soubriquet .... CUNCTATOR, (THE) DELAYER
victim of ..... HANNIBAL
fable ... LEGEND, APOLOG(UE), MYTH, FALSEHOOD, FICTION, ALLEGORY, PARABLE, STORY
writer .... (A)ESOP, MORALIST, ADE, PHAEDRUS
fabled being .... TROLL, GNOME, DWARF, MINOTAUR, SIREN, OGRE, TITAN, CENTAUR
bird .... ROC
fish .... MAH
fables have one .... MORAL, LESSON
fabric .... DRAPERY, FELT, SATEEN, SOIE, ORLON, STRUCTURE, CREPE, LENO, ETOILE, TULLE, VOILE, SILK, ATLAS, FAILLE, NINON, TEXTURE, CLOTH, RAYON, MOIRE, MOHAIR, CANVAS, TAPA, WOOF, WEB, RAS
Angora .... MOHAIR, CAMLET
carpet .... MOQUETTE
coarse ... ORLON, CRASH, MAT, DOWLAS, RATINE
corded .... REP(P), PIQUE, PADUASOY, REPS

cotton .... MOREEN, PENANG, PIQUE, MADRAS, DENIM, SCRIM, CALICO, NANKIN, NANKEEN, CRETON(NE), MULL, MANTA, LENO
cravat/tie .... REP
creased ...... KORATRON
crinkled .... CREPE, CRAPE
curtain ..... NET, SCRIM
drapery .... MOREEN
edge .... SELVAGE
felt-like .... BAIZE
filling .... WEFT
floor cover ..... CARPET
glazed .... CAMBRIC
glossy .... SATIN, ETOILE
heavy .... BROCADE
kind of ... KNIT, PRINT, WOOLEN, WORSTED
knitted .... TRICOT
hempen .... BURLAP
light wool ..... ALPACA
linen .... SCRIM, DOWLAS
lining ... FLEECE, SATEEN
metallic .... LAME
mourning .... CRAPE, ALMA
napped .... FLEECE
net ..... TULLE, MALINE
plaid .... TARTAN
printed .... PERCALE, CHALLIS, BAT(T)IK
protector ..... CAMPHOR
puckered .... PLISSE
reversible ...... DAMASK
rib .... WALE
ribbed ... TWILL, PIQUE, REP(P), CORD, REPS
rugs .... CHENILLE
satin ..... ETOILE, PEKIN
sheer .... ORGANZA, GAUZE, VOILE, BATISTE
shiny .... SATEEN, POPLIN, SILK
silk ..... SURAH, FAILLE, PONGEE, SAMITE, TOBINE
silk and gold .... SAMITE
stiff .... WIGAN
stretcher .... TENTER
striped .... GALATEA, DORIA, MADRAS, ZENANA, DO(O)REA, BAYADEER, BAYADERE
towel .... TERRY
twilled .... SERGE
upholstery .... BROCATEL, MOREEN
velvet-like .... TERRY
wastes .... MUNGO
watered silk ..... MOIRE
wavy patterned ... MOIRE
wax-coated ... BAT(T)IK
window shades .... HOLLAND
woolen ... BEIGE, ALPACA, SERGE, MERINO, VICUNA, TAMIS, TARTAN, ESTAMIN(E), ETAMINE
worsted .... SERGE, ETAMINE
woven silk ..... TRICOT

fabricate ... CONCOCT, COIN, DEVISE, INVENT, MAKE(UP), CONSTRUCT, LIE
fabrication .... LIE, WEB, DECEIT, MANUFACTURE, FALSEHOOD
fabricator .... FORGER, INVENTOR, LIAR, MAKER
fabrics dealer .... MERCER
fabulist .... (A)ESOP, ADE, LIAR, GRIMM, LA FONTAINE
fabulous .... MYTHICAL, IMAGINARY, LEGENDARY, INCREDIBLE
animal .... UNICORN, CENTAUR
bankers ... ROTHSCHILD
monster .... CHIMERA
place .... EL DORADO
serpent .... BASILISK, COCKATRICE
tale .... LEGEND
facade .... FRONT, FACE
main ..... FRONTISPIECE
face .... MEET, ANSWER, (CON)FRONT, FACADE, VISAGE, COUNTENANCE,
card ..... KING, QUEEN, JACK
coin's .... HEAD
colloquial ... AUDACITY, MUG, MAP, PUSS, SNOOT
crease ... WRINKLE, LINE
down .... LIE, PRONE
expressionless .... DEAD PAN, POKER
gem's .... FACET
guard ... BEAVER, VISOR
hair .... BEARD
obsolete .... MAZARD
of rock ..... BROW, CLIFF
powder .... TALCUM
slang .... PAN, PUSS, KISSER, PHIZ, MAP, MUG
spot .... FRECKLE
to face .... VIS-A-VIS, TETE-A-TETE
value .... PAR
with stone .... REVET
facet .... BEZEL, CULET, PHASE, COLLET, BEZIL, FLANGE
facetious ... COMICAL, DROLL, WITTY, JOCOSE, JOCULAR
person ...... HUMORIST, WAG, JESTER
facial adornment .... GOATEE, MUSTACHIO, BEARD, VANDYKE, MUSTACHE, IMPERIAL
expression ...... SMILE, GRIMACE, POUT, LEER, GRIN, PHIZ, SMIRK, SCOWL
facile .... EASY, FLUENT, AFFABLE, DEFT, ADROIT
facilitate ..... FURTHER, HELP, QUICKEN
facility .... MEANS, EASE, DEXTERITY, FLUENCY, SKILL, CONVENIENCE, KNACK
facing ... LINING, TRIMMING, FORNENT, TOWARD

glacier .... STOSS
inward .... INTRORSE
facsimile .... COPY, LIKENESS, REPLICA, REPRODUCTION
fact ... FIAT, DATUM, TRUTH, REALITY, ACTUALITY
of knowing .... KNOWLEDGE
state as a ... POSIT, AVER
faction ... BLOC, JUNTO, SIDE, CLIQUE, CABAL
factional .... PARTISAN
division .... SCHISM, SPLIT, SPLINTER
factious ...... CONTENTIOUS, PARTISAN
factitious .... ARTIFICIAL, FORCED
factor ...... AGENT, BROKER, ELEMENT, GENE
biological .... GENE
Scottish ...... STEWARD, BAILIFF
factory .... PLANT, MILL
country ...... HACIENDA
factotum .... SERVANT, AGENT, HANDYMAN
facts ..... DATA, LOW-DOWN
factual .... REAL, ACTUAL
facultative ...... CONTINGENT, OPTIONAL
faculty .... TALENT, SENSE, POWER, ABILITY, KNACK, APTITUDE
of apt expression .... FELICITY
fad .... CRAZE, HOBBY, FASHION, MODE, STYLE, MEGRIM
fade .... PEAK, WILT, LANGUISH, WITHER, DIM, DROOP, WANE, DIE(OUT)
from sight ... EVANESCE, DISAPPEAR
out ...... END, DISSOLVE
faded ... DULL, WORN, DRAB
fading .... FUGITIVE
fado .... FOLKSONG
"Faerie Queen" ... MAB, UNA
character ...... AMORET, ALMA, TALUS, ACRASIA
Fafnir's brother ...... REGIN
slayer .... SIGURD
fag .... EXHAUST, SLAVE, TIRE, DRUDGE(RY), FATIGUE, HOMOSEXUAL, WEARY
end .... RUCK, STUB, REMNANT, RUMP
slang .... CIGARETTE
fagaceous plant ... BEECH, OAK
fagot ... SEW, FASCINE, ESCINE
faience .... POTTERY, PORCELAIN
fail .... PETER, EBB, COLLAPSE, MISCARRY, DEFAULT, MISS, FIZZLE, FLOP, FLUNK
as a motor ... CONK OUT
in duty .... SHIRK, REMISS
in health ..... LANGUISH
to catch ... FUMBLE, MUFF

to follow suit ..... RENIG, RENEGE, FAINAIGUE
failing ...... DEFECT, FAULT, WEAKNESS
failure .... DUD, FIASCO, OMISSION, BUST, FLOP, TURKEY
complete ..... WASHOUT, FIASCO
to pay .... DEFAULT
to prosecute ... DEFAULT
fain ...... GLAD(LY), READY, EAGER
faineant .... OTIOSE, LAZY, IDLE
faint .... WAN, DIM, SWOON, WEAK, FEEBLE, TIMID, UNCLEAR, SWOUND
fainthearted .... TIMID, COWARDLY
fainting .... SYNCOPATION
fit ..... SYNCOPE, SWOON
fair .... EVEN, JUST, COMELY, CLEAR, FESTIVAL, KERMIS, CARNIVAL, BAZA(A)R, EXHIBITION, IMPARTIAL, LOVELY, BEAUTIFUL, UNBIASED, DECENT, SO-SO, BLOND, EXPOSITION
haired .... FAVORITE, BLOND(E), PET
place ..... STALL, BOOTH, PAVILION
portion .... CHUNK
sex .... WOMAN
spoken .... POLITE, BLAND
to middling ... PASSABLE, SO-SO
Fairbanks native .... ALASKAN
fairies' queen ... MAB, TITANIA, UNA
fairy ...... LEPRECHAUN, ELF, PIXIE, PIXY, SPRITE, ELVE, FAY, PERI, TINKERBELL
air .... SYLPH
fort .... SHEE, LIS(S)
king .... OBERON
lake dweller .... MORGAN(LE FAY)
like .... ELFIN
queen ... TITANIA, UNA, MAB
story .... MARCHEN, ALLEGORY, FABLE, TALE, MYTH, LIE
tale character .. SANDMAN
wood .... NYMPH
faith ... BELIEF, CREED, TROTH, DOXY, RELIGION, TRUST, LOYALTY, CULT, DOGMA
archaic .... FAY
article of .... TENET
bad .... DUPLICITY, DISHONESTY
good .... SINCERITY
healer, kind of ... QUACK
matters of ... CREDENDA
of .... PISTIC
faithful ...... FAST, DEVOTED, LOYAL, HONEST, STA(U)NCH, CONSTANT, RELIABLE, EXACT, TRUE, TRIED
friend .... ACHATES, DAMON, PYTHIAS
poetic .... LEAL
faithless ... FALSE, DISLOYAL, PERFIDIOUS, TRAITOROUS
faitour .... ROGUE
fake .... CHEAT, TRICK, PHONEY, SHAM, COUNTERFEIT, FRAUD, COIL
attack .... FEINT
colloquial .. BRUMMAGEN
faker ..... SWINDLER, FRAUD, QUACK
kind of ..... MALINGERER
fakir .... MENDICANT, MONK, YOGI, SWAMI, BEGGAR
falbala ..... FRILL, FLOUNCE, FURBELOW, RUFFLE
falcate .... CURVED, HOOKED
falchion .... SWORD
falcon ..... HAWK, CANNON, LANNER(ET), PEREGRINE, MERLIN, LUGGER, WINDHOVER, SAKER
Asian .... LAGGAR
close eyes of .... SEEL
E. Indian .... BESRA
European .... SAKER, KESTREL, HOBBY
eye-blinder .. SEEL, HOOD
female .... LANNAR
headed deity .... RA, MENT(U)
India ... SHAHIN, LAGGER
leg-strap .... JESS
male .... TERCEL, LANNERET
peregrine .. DUCK HAWK
repair wing of ...... IMP
small .... MERLIN, KESTREL
swoop of .... SOUSE
use of .... HUNTING
falconer .... HAWKER
falconer's decoy .... LURE
falconry .... HAWKING
falderal .... NONSENSE, TRIFLE, GEWGAW
fall ..... DROP, SLIP, LITTER, SPILL, PLOP, RUIN, CASCADE, PLUNGE, AUTUMN, SLUMP, DESCEND, TUMBLE, PLUMMET, COLLAPSE, TOPPLE, PLUNK
back ... RECEDE, RETREAT, RELAPSE
behind .... LAG
forward .... TOPPLE
guy: sl. .... PATSY, SCAPEGOAT, DUPE
headlong .... PITCH
in .... AGREE
in drops .... DRIP, DRIB(BLE), TRICKLE
in line .... FILE
out ..... QUARREL, SHED
through .... FAIL
to .... START
to pieces ..... CRUMBLE, DISINTEGRATE
fallacious ...... ERRONEOUS, DECEPTIVE
notion .... IDOLISM
fallacy .... ERROR, IDOLA, IDOLUM, DECEPTION, MISTAKE
fallal ...... FINERY, FRIPPERY
fallen .. DROPPED, PROSTRATE, DEGRADED, DEAD
falling .... CADENT
out .... QUARREL
over .... TOPPLE
sickness ...... EPILEPSY
star .... METEOR
Fallopian tube ...... OVIDUCT, SALPINX
fallout particles .... SLEET, SNOW
fallow deer .... TEG, DAMA
false .... SPURIOUS, UNTRUE, MENDACIOUS, PSEUDO, SHAM, FORGED, INCORRECT, FAKE, BOGUS, WRONG, MISTAKEN, ARTIFICIAL, FAITHLESS
belief .... DELUSION
entry .... RINGER
excuse ...... SUBTERFUGE
face .... MASK
friend ... TRAITOR, JUDAS, IAGO
front ..... BLUFF, DUMMY
god .... BAAL, IDOL
hair .... PERUKE, (PERI)WIG, TOUPEE
jewelry .... PASTE
move ...... MISSTEP, SLIP
name ... ANONYM, ALIAS
prefix .... PSEUDO
pretense ... AFFECTATION
reasoning ...... IDOLISM
report ... CANARD, HOAX
seed cover .... ARILLODE
show ..... MASQUERADE
show, make ...... FEIGN
show to be ..... DEBUNK, DISPROVE
step ..... TRIP, STUMBLE
story ... CANARD, HOAX, FUDGE
swearing ...... PURJURY
teeth .... DENTURE
wing .... ALULA
witness .. PERJURER, LIAR
falsehood ... LIE, TALE, FLAM, FABLE, CANARD, INVENTION, PERJURY, DECEPTION, LYING, FIB
falsies: colloq. .... PADS
falsify .... FORGE, FAKE, (BE)LIE, GARBLE, DISTORT, ALTER
Falstaff's man .... PETO
falter .... HAW, WAVER, TOTTER, STUMBLE, STAMMER, FLINCH, HESITATE
fama .... RUMOR
fame ...... KUDOS, RENOWN, GLORY, REPUTE, REPUTATION, NAME, ECLAT
kind of ...... NOTORIETY
famed .. EMINENT, NOTORIOUS, REPUTED, CELEBRATED
Fameuse .... APPLE
familiar ..... CLOSE, INTIMATE, FRIENDLY, COMMON,

ORDINARY, BOLD, VERSANT
saying ..... SAW, ADAGE, MOT, MOTTO, TAG
familiarize .... ACQUAINT
families, quarrel between ..... FEUD
family .... LINE, HOUSEHOLD, STIRPS, TRIBE, CLAN, KIN, RACE, LINEAGE, STOCK, KINSFOLK, ILK, BREED
ancient ... ESTE, MEDICI, DORIA
branch ..... STIRPS, STEM
car .... SEDAN
car: colloq. .... BUS
diagram .... TREE
famous ... ESTE, SOONG, ROTHSCHILD, MEDICI, KENNEDY
life .... FIRESIDE
meal .... POTLUCK
name .... SURNAME, COGNOMEN, PATRONYMIC
next door .... NEIGHBOR
pertaining to ... LINEAGE, FAMILIAL, DOMESTIC
tree .... PEDIGREE
famine .. STARVATION, HUNGER
famish .... STARVE
famous ..... NOTED, EMINENT, CELEBRATED, NOTORIOUS, RENOWNED
aunt .... MAME
friend .. DAMON, PYTHIAS
murderer .... CAIN, BOOTH, ARAM, OSWALD
trio member ..... ATHOS, ARAMIS, PORTHOS
fan ... COOL, FOMENT, VOTARY, EXCITE, AFICIONADO, BLOW, ROOTER, BUFF, ZEALOT, DEVOTEE
form .... PLICATE
of leaves .... TALIPOT
oriental ..... PUNKA(H)
palm .... PALMETTO
Pope's ...... FLABELLUM
shaped ..... FLABELLATE
fanatic .... BIGOT, NUT, ZEALOT, PHRENETIC, PARTISAN, RABID, JINGO
murderous .... THUG, AMOK, BERSERK
fanatical .... RABID, RADICAL
fanaticism ...... ZEAL(OTRY)
fancied .... IMAGINED, IMAGINARY
fear ... BUGABOO, BOG(E)Y
fancier, kind of .... CONNOISSEUR, GOURMET, GOURMAND
fanciful .... IMAGINATIVE, WHIMSICAL, ODD, IMAGINARY, QUAINT, UNREAL
fancy ..... DREAM, DELUSION, FAD, IDEA, MEGRIM, ILLUSION, NOTION, WHIM, VISION, WEEN, CAPRICE, CHIMERA
dive ..... SWAN, GAINER, ISANDER
foolish .... CHIMERA
fandango ... . DANCE
fane .... TEMPLE, SANCTUARY, CHURCH, SHRINE
fanfare ... TANTARA, FLOURISH
fanfaron .... BRAGGART
fang .... CUSPID, CLAW, TALON, TUSK, CANINE TOOTH
fanlight .... TRANSOM
Fannie ____, writer ... HURST
fanny: sl. .... BUTTOCKS
fanon ...... MANIPLE, ORALE, VANE
fantail .... PIGEON, GOLDFISH
fantasia .... MEDLEY
fantast .. VISIONARY, DREAMER
fantastic ...... OUTLANDISH, UNREAL, BIZARRE, GROTESQUE, ODD, ECCENTRIC
imitation ...... PARODY, TRAVESTY
style ... OUTRE, BAROQUE, ROCOCO
fantasy ..... DREAM, FANCY, ILLUSION, CAPRICE, PHANTASM
far .... REMOTE, DISTANT, ADVANCED, AWAY
and near ... EVERYWHERE
and wide .... ABROAD
apart .... DISPARATE
combining form .... TELE
cry .... LONG WAY
down .... DEEP
go .... LAST LONG
off ..... DISTANT, REMOTE
farce .... COMEDY, SKIT, TRAVESTY, MOCKERY, PARODY, EXODE, BURLESQUE, MIME
farceur ... JOKER, HUMORIST, WAG, CLOWN
farcical .. FUNNY, LUDICROUS, RIDICULOUS, ABSURD
farcy .... GLANDERS
fardel .... BURDEN, PACK, BUNDLE
fare ..... FOOD, DIET, MENU, PAY, RESULT, GET ON, PASSENGER
farewell ...... CONGE, VALE, ADIOS, GOODBY, PARTING, LAST, AVE, VALEDICTION
appearance .. SWANSONG
drink ..... STIRRUP CUP
French .... ADIEU
Hawaiian .... ALOHA
Japanese ..... SAYONARA
Latin .... AVE
Spanish .... ADIOS
farfetched .... FORCED, STRAINED, REMOTE
farflung .... REMOTE
farina ... FLOUR, MEAL, STARCH
farinaceous .... STARCHY, MEALY
drink .... PTISAN
farinose .... MEALY
farm .... TORP, GRANGE, HACIENDA, CULTIVATE, RANCH, BARTON, TILL
building .... BARN, SILO, SHED
grazing .... RANCH(O)
implement .... HARROW, FLAIL, PLOW
kind of ... DAIRY, OYSTER
machine .... REAPER, CHURN, TRACTOR, SCARIFIER, TEDDER
of a .... VILLATIC
small .... CROFT
Spanish ..... HACIENDA
Swedish .... TORP
tenant .... COTTER, CROFTER
worked by renter .. CROFT
worker .... HIND, CAMPESINO, ORRAMAN, PLOWMAN
yard .... BARTON
farmer ..... PLANTER, RYOT, SOWER, GRANGER, TILLER, HUSBANDMAN, PEASANT, CROPPER, HABITAN(T)
migrant .... OKIE
peasant .... CROFTER
Philippine ... MAGSASAKA
Russian .... KULAK
S. African ... BOER, WERF
farmhouse, land nearest ...... INFIELD
farming .... HUSBANDRY, AGRICULTURE
farmyard .... BARTON
faro card .... SODA
form of .... MONTE
Faroes whirlwinds .... OES
farrago .... JUMBLE, MEDLEY, MIXTURE
Farrar, soprano .. GERALDINE
farrier .... BLACKSMITH, VETERINARY
farrow .... LITTER, PIG
farseeing .... PROVIDENT
farsighted ... HYPERMETROPIC
farsightedness ... HYPEROPIA
farther .... REMOTER
India .... INDO-CHINA
farthest .... ENDMOST, ULTIMATE
back .... HINDMOST, REAR
fasces carrier .... LICTOR
fascia .... STRIP, BAND(AGE), FILLET
fascicle .... CLUSTER
fascinate .... ALLURE, CAPTIVATE, ENCHANT, ATTRACT, CHARM, INTRIGUE, BEWITCH
fascination .. CHARM, ALLURE, ENCHANTMENT
Fascist .... NAZI, FALANGIST
leader ..... MUSSO(LINI), FRANCO, HITLER, RAS
mayor .... PODESTA
organization in Spain .... FALANGE
theoretician ..... PARETO
fash: Scot. ..... VEX, ANNOY, TROUBLE
fashion ... RAGE, VOGUE, CUT, FAD, STYLE, CRAZE, KIND, SORT, MODE, MANNER, MOLD, SHAPE, DESIGN
designer .. SCHIAPARELLI,

ST. LAURENT, GIVENCHY, BALENCIAGA, NORELL, BALMAIN, DIOR, MAINBOCHER, GALITZINE, GERNREICH
figure .... MODEL, MODISTE, DESIGNER, TAILOR, CUTTER
model .... TWIGGY
news .... HEMLINE, NECKLINE, MINI, MAXI
plate .. BEAU(BRUMMELL), DANDY, DUDE
fashionable ... RITZY, TONEY, NEW, SMART, SLEEK, CHIC, STYLISH, POSH, ALAMODE, KNOBBY
gathering .... SALON
society .... BONTON
Fashoda, Sudan town .. KODOK
fast .... APACE, FIRM, RAMADAN, SECURE, TANTIVY, PRESTO, DEVOTED, FIRM, SPEEDY, SWIFT, RAPID, FLEET, HASTY, QUICK
combining form .. TACHY
fasten .... TETHER, ROPE, ATTACH, CONNECT, FIX, TIE, BATTEN, RIVET, LASH
boat .... BERTH
firmly ...... RIVET, NAIL, SECURE, CHAIN, INFIX
nautical .. BATTEN, BELAY
fastener ... PEG, CLAMP, SNAP, STRAP, PIN, HASP, CLASP, STAPLE, CLEAT, CLIP, BITT
slide .... ZIPPER
wire .... STAPLE
wood .... PEG, NOG, PIN
fastening .... BOLT, LOCK, BUTTON, HOOK, CLASP, LATCH, TACH(E)
fastidious .... PRECISE, CRITICAL, NICE, QUEASY, REFINED, DAINTY, FINICAL, FINICKY, FUSSY, PER(S)NICKETY
fastigiate .... CONELIKE
fasting period .... LENT, RAMADAN, RAMAZAN
fastness .... STRONGHOLD
fat ...... OILY, PORTLY, SUET, ESTER, STOUT, PORKY, PUDGY, DUMPY, PUFFY, OBESE, PINGUID, GROSS, PURSY, FLESHY, PLUMP, CORPULENT, THICK, TALLOW
and squat .... FUBSY
animal .... ADIPOSE, GREASE, TALLOW, LARD, ALEPS
beef .... SUET
chance: sl. .... HOPELESS
chew the ..... CHAT, GAB
combining form .... STEAT(O)
decomposition of .... LIPOLYSIS
hog .... LARD
in butter .... OLEO
like .... LIPAROID, LIPOID, LIPIDE, UNGUINOUS, STEARIC
liquid part .... OLEIN
lot .... NOTHING
of .... UNGUINOUS, STEARIC, ADIPIC
refuse .... SLUSH
roasting meat .. DRIPPING
solid part of .. STEARIN(E)
Tuesday ... MARDI GRAS
wool ... SUINT, LANOLIN
yielding tree .... SHEA
Fata Morgana .... MIRAGE, FAIRY
fatal .... VITAL, FUNEST, FATEFUL, LETHAL, RUINOUS, DEADLY, MORTAL, FERAL
fatality .... DEATH, DEADLINESS, CASUALTY
fate .... DOOM, DESTINY, KISMET, LOT
Buddhism/Hinduism .... KARMA
mythological .. ATROPOS, CLOTHO, LACHESIS, PARCA
twist of .... IRONY
fated .... DOOMED, FEY, ORDAINED, DESTINED
fateful .... PROPHETIC, DECISIVE, OMINOUS, DIRE
Fates, one of the ..... PARCA, CLOTHO, ATROPOS, LACHESIS, NONA, MORTA, DECUMA
whichever one ... WEIRD
fathead ...... DUNCE, IDIOT, STUPID
fatheaded .... DULL, OBTUSE, STUPID
father ..... SIRE, PAPA, ABBA, PARENT, PROTECTOR, ANCESTOR, FOREBEAR, CREATOR, BEGET, PRIEST, PATER
Arabic ...... ABU, ABOU
brother of .... UNCLE
colloquial ..... OLDMAN, DAD, PA, POP, PAPPY
combining form .. PATRO, PATRI
dialectic .... PAW
disciples' .... ZEBEDEE
French .... PERE
Hebrew .... ABBA
of all .... JUBAL
of American football .... CAMP
of gods .... ZEUS
of History ... HERODOTUS
of Medicine .... HIPPOCRATES
of Waters .... MISSISSIPPI
pertaining to a .. AGNATE, PATERNAL
relative on side of .... AGNATE
Spanish ... PADRE, PAPA
superior .... ABBOT
fatherhood ...... PATERNITY
fatherless .... ORBATE
fathom .... DELVE, PROBE, PLUMB, SOUND
one fourth of .. QUARTER
fatigue ... WEARY, FAG, JADE, WEARINESS, EXHAUST, TIRE, BORE
clothes .... DENIM
Fatima descendant .. SAY(Y)ID
descended from .... FATIMID, FATIMITE
father of ..... MOHAMMED
husband of ... BLUEBEARD
sister ..... ANNE, JINNAH
step-brother .... ALI
fatling ..... CALF, LAMB, KID, PIG
fats, solvent for ...... ETHER
fatten .... BATTEN, ENRICH
land .... FERTILIZE
fatty .... GREASY, OILY, ADIPOSE, LIPAROID, ALIPHATIC
acid ... ADIPIC, VALERIC
combining form .. LIP(O)
comedian ..... ARBUCKLE
secretion of gland .... SEBUM
substance from sheep's wool .... SUINT
tumor .... LIPOMA
fatuity ...... FOLLY, IDIOCY, STUPIDITY, IMBECILITY
fatuous ..... SAPPY, IDIOTIC, SILLY, FOOLISH, INANE, ASININE
faubourg .... SUBURB
fauces ..... GULLET, THROAT
faucet .... BIBB, TAP, (BIB)COCK, SPIGOT, PETCOCK, STOPCOCK
fault .... CAVIL, LAPSE, MISTAKE, WEAKNESS, LACK, FLAW, FAILING, DEFECT, ERROR, MISDEED, IMPERFECTION
amusing .... FOIBLE
antonym of ..... VIRTUE
find ..... CARP, CENSURE, COMPLAIN, NAG, CAVIL
finder .... NAG(GER), CENSOR, SCOLD(ER), CRITIC, KNOCKER
finding .... CRITICAL, CAPTIOUS, CARPING, QUERULOUS
moral .... VICE
slight .... PECCADILLO
faultfinder .... KNOCKER, NAG(GER), CRITIC, MOMUS
faultless ..... IDEAL, PERFECT, MODEL, PARAGON, IMPECCABLE
faulty .... PECCANT
faun .... SATYR, DEITY
Fauntleroy .... CEDRIC, ERROL
mother of ..... DEAREST
Faunus .... PAN
son .... ACIS
Faure, essayist .... ELIE
"Faust," composer of .... GOUNOD
poem, writer of .. GOETHE
fauteuil .... ARMCHAIR
faux pas ..... ERROR, MISSTEP, SOCIAL BLUNDER, GAFFE,

BONER, SLIP
faveolate .... CELLED, HONEYCOMBED, ALVEOLATE
favonian .... GENTLE
favor ..... LETTER, RESEMBLE, LIKING, LEAVE, GRACE, LEAN, HELP, NOTE, BOON
favorable .... AUSPICIOUS, PRO, PROPITIOUS
in astrology .... TRINE
most .... OPTIMUM
opinion .... ESTEEM
favored ... TALENTED, GIFTED
favoring .... PRO, FOR
favorite .... PET, PREFERRED, MINION, DEAR
activity .... HOBBY
activity: Brit. .... CUP OF TEA
son .... BENJAMIN
favoritism .... NEPOTISM
favors from public office .. PAP
fawn ...... CRINGE, FLATTER, DEER, GROVEL, DOE
fawning .... SERVILE
fay .. ELF, JOIN, FAIRY, SPRITE
archaic .... FAITH
faze .... ANNOY, DAUNT, DISTURB, AGITATE, WORRY, DISCONCERT, EMBARRASS
FBI director, former .. HOOVER
FDR's burial place .... HYDE PARK
fe .... IRON
fealty ... LOYALTY, FIDELITY, ALLEGIANCE, DUTY
fear .... AWE, PANIC, MISGIVING, FRIGHT, APPREHENSION, DISMAY, PHOBIA
excessive .... PHOBIA
frantic, unreasoning ..... PANIC
from sudden danger ..... ALARM
intensely .... DREAD
of animals .. ZOOPHOBIA
of becoming insane ..... LYSSOPHOBIA
of being alone .... MONOPHOBIA
of being poisoned .... TOXIPHOBIA
of fire ..... PYROPHOBIA
of food ..... SITOPHOBIA
of heights .. ACROPHOBIA
of lightning .. TROPHOBIA
of pain .... ALGOPHOBIA
of law .... METUS
of strangers .. XENOPHOBIA
overwhelming .. TERROR
sudden, shocking .... FRIGHT, CHILL
fearful .... NERVOUS, DIRE, AFRAID, TERRIFYING, TREPID, PAVID
fearless .... BRAVE, BOLD, DARING, HEROIC, IMPAVID, INTREPID
fearsome .... DREADFUL, FRIGHTFUL, TIMID, TIMOROUS
one .... OGRE
feasible ... POSSIBLE, LIKELY, PRACTICABLE
feast .... FESTIVAL, BANQUET, REGALE, FETE
after harvest .... FOY
day: comb. form ... MAS
describing one .... LUCULLAN
for departing person .... FOY
Hawaiian .... LUAU
list .... ORDO
of Lots .... PURIM
of the Nativity .... YULE
outdoor .... PICNIC
feastless day .... FERIA
feat ..... DEED, EXPLOIT, ACT, STUNT, ACCOMPLISHMENT
feather .... PENNA, PINNA, PLUMAGE, PLUME, QUILL, PINION, DOWN
arrow ... FLETCH, FLEDGE
barb .... HARL, HERL
cloak .... MAMO
combining form .. PENNI
fine .... EGRET
grass .... STIPA
helmet .... PANACHE
like .... PINNATE, PLUMOSE, PENNIFORM
neckwear .... BOA
part of ..... VANE, WEB
prefix .... PTERO
quill .... BARREL, CALAMUS
resembling a .. PINNATE, PLUMATE
shaft .... SCAPE
shed: archaic ..... MEW, MOLT
small .... PLUMULE, PLUMELET
submarine's ...... WAKE
under wing ..... AXILIAR
vane of .... VEXILLUM
wing .... PINION
featherbed .... MATTRESS
featherbrained .... IDIOT, FOOLISH, SIMPLE, SILLY, FRIVOLOUS
feathered .... PENNATED, PLUMOSE, PLUMY, FLEDGED, PLUMED, WINGED
neckpiece ... . BOA
featherer of arrows .. PLUMIER
featherless .... CALLOW
feathers .... DOWN, PLUMAGE
adorn with ... (IM)PLUME
bunch of .... TUFT
bird's wing ..... ALULA, COVERTS
for flying ...... REMIGES
grow .... FLEDGE
plume of ..... PANACHE
pull out the ... DEPLUME, PLUCK
quill ... CALAMI, BARRELS, COVERTS
smooth the ...... PLUME
soft ...... DOWN, EIDER
tail .... RECTRIX
trim the .... PREEN
featherweight .... LIGHT, TRIVIAL, NONENTITY, BOXER, WRESTLER
feathery .... DOWNY, FLUFFY
feature .... PART, CHARACTERISTIC, TRAIT, MOTIF, FORM
double .... CHIN
salient ...... HIGHLIGHT, MOTIF
feaze .... UNRAVEL, FAZE, FEEZE
febrile .... FEVERISH
feces ...... DREGS, SEDIMENT, EGESTA
feckless ..... WEAK, CARELESS
feculence ...... FILTH, DREGS
feculent ...... FILTHY, FOUL
fecund ... FERTILE, FRUITFUL, PROLIFIC, PRODUCTIVE
fecundate .... POLLINATE
fecundity .... FERTILITY
fed up: sl. .... BORED, DISGUSTED, SURFEITED
fedayeen leader .... HABASH, ARAFAT
federate .... UNITE
federation .... ALLIANCE, LEAGUE, UNION
fedora .... HAT
author of play ... SARDOU
fee ...... FIEF, HONORARIUM, TIP, AGIO, DUES, TOLL, CHARGE, GRATUITY, FEOD
for settling accounts ..... EXCHANGE
hold in ... OWN, POSSESS
lawyer's ...... RETAINER
feeble .... DOTTY, PUNY, WASHY, WEAK, FRAIL, FLABBY, FLACCID, RICKETY
minded .... DOTTY
mindedness ... AMENTIA
minded person .... IMBECILE, IDIOT, MORON, DOTARD, AMENT, HALF-WIT, DOLT, FOOL
feed .... OATS, EAT, NOURISH, SUBSIST, PROVIDE, BROWSE, COSHER
animal .... FORAGE, FODDER
breast .... NURSE
cattle .... AGIST
colloquial ... MEAL, CHOW
fuel to .... STOKE
well at other's expense ... BATTEN
feeder .... TRIBUTARY, SUBSIDIARY
of furnace .... STOKER
of lines .... STOOGE, STRAIGHTMAN
feeding box .... TROUGH, MANGER
feel ..... PALP, SENSE, SUFFER, TOUCH
ability to ... (A)ESTHESIA
able to .... PASSIBLE, SENSIBLE
about .... GROPE
absence .... MISS
like .... INCLINED
out .... SOUND

regret ..... RUE, REPENT
feeler .... TENTACLE, PALP(US), BARBEL, ANTENNA, SMELLER
kind of .... TRIAL, BALLOON, CIRRUS
small .... ANTENNULE
feelers, having .... LONGICORN
feeling .... SENSITIVITY, SENSATION, AWARENESS, EMOTION, PITY, OPINION, PREMONITION, PASSION, SENTIMENT, SENTIENCE
affect the .... MOVE
capable of .... SENTIENT
impatient ...... RESTIVE
of illbeing .... DYSPHORIA
of regret ..... REMORSE, REPENTANCE
of weariness ..... ENNUI, LASSITUDE
of wellbeing ... EUPHORIA
show .... EMOTE, REACT
strong .... HEAT
sudden, violent .. SPASM
turn of .... CAPRICE, WHIM
feet, care of ...... PODIATRY
combining form .. PED(E), PED(I)
having .... PEDATE
having many .... MULTIPED(E)
having three .. TRIPEDAL, TRIPODIC, TRIPODAL
of two syllables ... IAMBI
pertaining to the .. PODAL, PEDARY, PEDAL
pig's .... PETTITOES
slang .... DOGS
three .... YARD
verse of two .... DIPODY
without .... APOD
feeze .... DISTURB, AGITATE, DRIVE, DISCONCERT
feign .... FAKE, DISSEMBLE, INVENT, FABRICATE, PRETEND, SIMULATE, ACT, ASSUME
sickness ...... MALINGER
feigned .... FICTIVE, SIMULAR
feint ...... BLIND, DIVERSION, SHAM, PRETENSE
in fencing .... APPEL
feldspar .... ANORTHITE, ALBITE, ADULARIA, MOONSTONE, KAOLIN, ODINITE, SILICATE, LABRADORITE
felicitate .... BLESS, CONGRATULATE
felicitous .... APPROPRIATE
felicity .... BLISS, HAPPINESS
felid .... CAT, FELINE
feline .... OUNCE, TIGER, CRAFTY, SLY, JAGUAR, PUSS, CAT(LIKE), LEOPARD, LION, PUMA, PANTHER, LYNX
fell .... TERRIBLE, CRUEL, CUTDOWN, FIERCE, PELT
archaic .... DEADLY
British ..... HILL, MOOR, DOWN
of animal ... SKIN, HIDE, PELT
fellah: Egyptian ... PEASANT, LABORER
feller: sl. .... FELLOW
felling .... HAG
fellow (see person/man) ...... CHAP, EGG, PARTNER, ASSOCIATE, PEER, MATE, BUGGER, SIRRAH, BLOKE, CORYDON, JACK, TRUMP
archaic .... SIRRAH
big, clumsy ...... LOOBY
British: colloq. ... CULLY
brutish .... YAHOO
clumsy ... LOUT, LOOBY, OAF
colloquial .... MAN, BOY, BEAU, SUITOR, GUY
conceited ..... COXCOMB
contemptible ...... CAD, SCAB, BLOKE, SCOUNDREL
countryman .... COMPATRIOT
feeling .... SYMPATHY
fine .... TRUMP
flashy .... SPORT
little .... BUB
member .... CONFRERE, ASSOCIATE, COLLEAGUE
nicknamed Hi ... HIRAM
queer ... GEEZER, CODGER
Scottish .... WAT, CALLAN(T)
slang .... FELLER, BOZO, GUY, HOMBRE, GINK
stupid .... LUG, LOOBY, OAF, GANDER, CLOD, LOGGERHEAD
traveler ... SYMPATHIZER
unprincipled .... SCAPEGRACE
worthless ... CAD, SCAMP, ROGUE, RASCAL
young .. CHAP, BLADE, CALLAN(T), SPRIG
fellowship .... SODALITY, BROTHERHOOD, COMPANY, ENDOWMENT
felly .... CRUELLY, WHEEL RIM, DEADLY
felo-de-se .... SUICIDE
felon .... VILLAIN, CRIMINAL, BASE, WICKED, CON, WHITLOW
felonious .... BASE, CRIMINAL
felony ...... CRIME, MURDER, ARSON, RAPE
felt .... SENSED, FABRIC
obliged .... COMPELLED, HAD TO
felucca .... SHIP
felwort ... GENTIAN, MULLEIN
female ..... GIRL, FEMININE, WOMAN(LY)
animal ..... JENNY, SOW, JILL, BITCH, DAM, COW, SHE, VIXEN
animal's teat .... DUG
buffalo .... ARNEE
camel .... NAGA
cat .... TABBY
change of life .... MENOPAUSE, CLIMATERIC
combining form .... GYNE
deer .... DOE, ROE, HIND
demon .... HAG
dog ...... BITCH, SLUT
donkey .... JENNET
elephant .... COW
ferret .... JILL
figure, sculptured .... ORANT, CARYATID
fox .... VIXEN
gossip .... TABBY
insect .... GYNE
kangaroo .... GIN
mythical .... FURY
pig .... SOW, GILT
praying figure ... ORANT
prophet .... SEERESS, CASSANDRA
rabbit .... DOE
reproductive organ ...... OVARY
ruff .... REEVE, REE
sandpiper .... REE
servant ... MAID, WENCH
sex .... DISTAFF
sex hormone ... ESTRIOL, ESTRONE
sheep .... EWE
slave ..... ODALISK, DASI
sovereign .... QUEEN, EMPRESS
warrior .... AMAZON
wolf .... BITCH
feme .... WIFE
sole ... SPINSTER, WIDOW
feminine .... PETTICOAT, FEMALE, WOMANLY, EFFEMINATE
suffix ...... ETTE, STRESS, INE, ESS, TRIX
feminity .... MULIEBRITY
femme .... WOMAN, WIFE
fatale ... LORELEI, SIREN, MATA HARI, DELILAH
femur .... THIGH(BONE)
fen ... MORASS, MOOR, MARSH, SWAMP, BOG
fence .... PALE, BARRIER, PARRY, EVADE, PALISADE, RAIL(ING), ENCLOSE, DEFENSE, SWORDPLAY, RADDLE
construction site .... HOARDING
crossing .... STILE
material ... TITE, PICKET, PALE
of shrubs .... HEDGE
of stakes ...... PALISADE
of woven work .. WATTLE, RADDLE
part .... PALING, BARBED WIRE
stake ...... PALE, PICKET
step .... STILE
sunken .... (H)AHA
temporary ..... HURDLE, HOARDING
to .... SCRIME

fenced enclosure for cattle/ sheep .... KRAAL
grounds ..... CURTILAGE
fencer .... SWORDSMAN
cry of .... SASA, HAI, ON GUARD
opening position .... EN GARDE
fencing attack ...... REPRISE
breastplate ... PLASTROM
dummy for .... PEL
foil guard ...... BUTTON
leap .... VOLT
mask .... HELMET
movement .... APPEL
point .... FOIL
position .... CARTE, TIERCE, SECONDE, SEPTIME, SIXTE, QUARTE, QUINTE
score .... PUNTO
stroke ..... BUTT, APPEL, LUNGE, RIPOSTE
sword ..... EPEE, RAPIER, FOIL
term .... TIERCE, EN GARDE, TOUCHE, SECONDE
thrust .... REPRISE, BUTT, REMISE, LUNGE, RIPOSTE, PUNTO
fend .... AVERT, WARD, SHIFT, RESIST, PARRY
off ...... REPEL, REPULSE
fender .... MUDGUARD, COWCATCHER
fenestra .. WINDOW, OPENING
fennec .... FOX
fennel .... ANISE, HERB
fenny .... BOGGY
feod .... FEE, FIEF
feracious .... FRUITFUL
feral .... DEADLY, FERINE, UNTAMED, WILD, SAVAGE, BRUTAL, FATAL
Ferber (Edna) heroine .... SELINA
novel .... SO BIG
Ferde, composer ...... GROPE
fer de lance .... SNAKE
Ferdinand .... BULL, TORO
fere ...... COMPANION, MATE, PEER, WIFE, HUSBAND
feretory .... SHRINE, BIER
feria .... FESTIVAL, HOLIDAYS
ferine .... FERAL, WILD
fermata .... PAUSE, HOLD
ferment ... FRET, SACCHARIZE, YEAST, LEAVEN, BREW, BACTERIA, (EN)ZYME, AGITATION, UNREST, COMMOTION, SEETHE
fermented drink ... ALE, BEER, MEAD, SAKE, WINE, KUMISS
fermentation .... ZYMOSIS
chemistry of ... ZYMURGY
fermenting agent ..... YEAST, ENZYME, LEAVEN
fern .... WOODSIA, BRACKEN, MULEWORT, BRAKE, MAIDENHAIR, MOONWORT
coarse .... BRAKE
edible .... TARA
filaments .... RHIZOID
flowering ...... OSMUND
leaf .... FROND
like plant ...... ACROGEN
patches .... SORI
perennial stemmed ...... ACROGEN
petiole .... STIPE
rootstock .... ROI
seed .... SPORE
spore .... SORUS
ferocious .... SAVAGE, FERAL, BEASTLY, FIERCE, WILD
Ferrer, actor .... JOSE
ferret ...... WEASEL, SEARCH, INVESTIGATE
female .... JILL
like animal ..... TAYRA, MONGOOS(E)
ferric oxide, anhydrous ...... HEMATITE
powder .... ROUGE
ferrotype .... TINTYPE
ferrous sulfate .... COPPERAS
ferrule ... TIP, RING, BUSHING
ferrum .... IRON
ferry ...... PONT, TRANSPORT, CROSS
ferryboat ...... BAC, TENDER, PONT
ferryman .... CHARON
fertile ... PINGUID, FRUITFUL, FECUND, RANK, FAT, PROLIFIC, PRODUCTIVE
area .... OASIS
become .... BATTEN
land's surface ... TOPSOIL
fertilize .... ENRICH, POLLINATE, FRUCTIFY
fertilizer ... COMPOST, MARL, MANURE, AMMONITE, GUANO, ALINIT
ferule ...... STICK, TIP, ROD, RULER, HERB, SCEPTER
fervency ...... ARDOR, ZEAL
fervent .... HOT, EARNEST, ARDENT, PASSIONATE, GLOWING
fervid .... FIERY, HOT, BURNING, FERVENT, IMPASSIONED, INTENSE
fervor ... ZEST, ARDOR, ZEAL, PASSION
Fescennine .... OBSCENE, VULGAR
fescue .. GRASS, STICK, STRAW
festal .... GALA, JOYOUS, GAY
fester .... RANKLE, PUSTULE, ULCERATE, ABSCESS, SUPPURATE, DECAY, EMBITTER
festering condition .... ULCER
festival .... FAIR, ALE, FIESTA, FEAST, FERIA, FETE, GALA, CARNIVAL, CELEBRATION, MERRYMAKING
Apollo .... DELIA
Dutch .... KERMIS
Greek ...... DELIA, AGON
New Orleans .... MARDI GRAS
paper shower .. CONFETTI
religious .... FIESTA
festive .... GAY, MERRY, JOYOUS, JOVIAL
festivity .... JOY, PARTY, MIRTH, GAIETY, REVELRY
festoon ... GARLAND, WREATH, LEI
feta .... CHEESE
fetation .... PREGNANCY
fetch ... GET, RETRIEVE, BRING, PRODUCE, ELICIT, INFER, WRAITH, CHARM, SELL FOR
fetching .... ATTRACTIVE, CHARMING
fete .... ENTERTAIN(MENT), FESTIVAL
feterita .... SORGHUM
fetial .... PRIESTS
fetid .... OLID, RANCID, STINKING, ODOROUS, RANK, FOUL, PUTRID
fetiparous animal .... MARSUPIAL, KANGAROO, BANDICOOT, OPOSSUM, WOMBAT
fetish .... JUJU, AMULET, TALISMAN, WEAKNESS, CHARM, ANITO, VOODOO, OBEAH, GRIGRI, TOTEM
fetlock .... TUFT
fetor .... STENCH, STINK
fetter ... CHAIN, BOND, IRON, GYVE, SHACKLE, HAMPER, HOBBLE, MANACLE, HANDCUFF
fettle .... TRIM, STATE, CONDITION
fetus, hair of .... LANUGO
malformed ... TERATISM
membrane .... CHORION, CAUL
premature birth of ...... MISCARRIAGE
feu .... FEE
feud ... QUARREL, VENDETTA, FEE, FIEF, FEOD, STRIFE
feudal .... FEOD
baron .... THANE
benefice .... FIEF, FEU
estate .... FEU, FIEF
estate head .... LORD
jurisdiction ... SOC, SOKE
land .... BENEFICE, FEOD
lord .... SEIGNEUR
retainers .... MEINIE, MEINY
service .... AVERA
slave .... SERF
tax .... TALLAGE, TAIL(L)AGE
tenant .... SOCAGER, VASSAL, COTTER
tenant's payment .... HERIOT
title .... BARON, EARL
feudatory ...... FIEF, VASSAL
fever .... AGUE, PYREXIA, CAUMA, BRUCELLOSIS, HEAT
blister ..... COLD (SORE), HERPES
causing .... PYRETIC
characterized by .... FEBRILE

chill .... ALGOR, AGUE
intermittent ..... OCTAN, QUARTAN, TERTIAN
kind of .... DENGUE, MALARIA, DANDY, BREAKBONE, TROPICAL, JUNGLE, YELLOWJACK, TERTIAN, QUINTAN, QUARTAN
pertaining to ... PYRETIC
recurring .... QUOTIDIAN
reducer ...... FEBRIFUGE, ANTIPYRETIC, PIPERINE
sore .... HERPES
tropical .... CALENTURE, DENGUE
undulant .... MALTA

fevered .... HECTIC
feverish ... FEBRILE, PYRETIC, HECTIC
few .... CURN
and far between .. SPARSE
the .... MINORITY
fewer .... LESS
fewest .... LEAST
fey .... FATED, DOOMED
fez-like cap .... TURBAN, TARBOOSH
wearer .... SHRINER, EGYPTIAN
fiacre .... CARRIAGE, CAB
fiance .... BETROTHED
fiasco .... FAILURE, WASHOUT, FIZZLE, TURKEY
fiat ...... SANCTION, DECREE, ORDER
fib .... LIE
fibber .... LIAR
fiber ...... NATURE, QUALITY, FILAMENT, FUNICLE, DATIL
bark .... TAPA
century plant ...... PITA, AGAVE
cleaning tool ... HATCHEL
coconut .... COIR
combing ...... CARDING
cordage .... HEMP, ABACA, MAGUEY, SISAL, IMBE, PIÑA, FILASSE, AMBARY, AMBARI, RAFFIA, SUNN
East Indies plant .. RAMIE
knot .... NEP
palm .... ERUC
phloegm .... BAST
plant .... COTTON, ISTLE, FLAX, IXLE, MAGUEY, ALOE, RAMIE, SISAL, HEMP, ABACA, AMBARY
roll of .... SLUB
small .... FIBRIL
strand .... YARN
synthetic .... DACRON, ORLON
tree .... BASS, BAST, BAOBAB
waste ...... NOIL, FLOSS
wool ...... STAPLE, PILE
woven fabric .. MAT(TING)
fibers, fine .... FUZZ
to clean .... SCUTCH
twist .... ROVE

fibril ... FILAMENT, ROOT HAIR
fibrin .... GLUTEN
fibrous texture ..... DESMOID
fibula .... PIN, CLASP, BUCKLE, BONE
of the .... PERONEAL
fichu .... CAPE, LACE
fickle .... VOLATILE, FLIGHTY, GIDDY, MOONISH, INCONSTANT, CAPRICIOUS, CHANGEABLE
girl .... FLIRT, COQUETTE
fico .... TRIFLE, SNAP, FIG
fictile ..... PLASTIC, CERAMIC
fiction ... TALE, YARN, NOVEL
kingdom of .... OZ
fictitious ... FALSE, FABULOUS, MYTHICAL, ASSUMED, IMAGINARY, UNREAL
name ... ALIAS, JOHN DOE
story .... PIGMENT
fictive .... SHAM, FEIGNED, IMAGINARY
fid .... BAR, PIN
fiddle ..... VIOLIN, KIT, VIOL, FIDGET, GIGA
bow of .... ARCO
faddle ... FUSS, NONSENSE
fit as a .... HALE
fiddledeedee ...... NONSENSE
fiddler .... VIOLINIST
crab .... UCA
fiddlestick .... TRIFLE
fiddlesticks .... NONSENSE
fiddling ..... PETTY, USELESS, TRIFLING
"Fidelio" character .... LENORE, FLORESTAN
fidelity ... LOYALTY, FEALTY, FAITHFULNESS, DEVOTION, ALLEGIANCE
fidget ... FRET, FIDDLE, JITTER
fidgety .... RESTIVE, UNEASY, NERVOUS, RESTLESS
fie .... SHAME
fief .... FEE, FEUD, FEOD, BENEFICE
give or sell .... FEOFF
holder .... FEOFFEE
person granting .... FEOFFER, FEOFFOR
field .... ACRE, GLEBE, PLAIN, SAVANNA
border .... RAND
combat .... ARENA
enclosed ... AGER, CROFT
glacial ...... NEVE, FIRN
glass .... BINOCLE
grassy ..... LEA, PASTURE
hospital ..... AMBULANCE
mouse .... VOLE
of honor .... BATTLEGROUND
of work .... METIER, CAREER, LINE
officer .. COLONEL, MAJOR
open .... CAMPUS
tent .... MARQUEE
unplowed strip ... RAND
fieldfare .... THRUSH
fiend ..... SHAITAN, SHEITAN, DEMON, DEVIL, ADDICT, SATAN

fiendish .... HELLISH, DEMONIC, CRUEL, WICKED, DEVILISH
fierce .... WILD, SAVAGE, VIOLENT, INTENSE, LUPINE, FEROCIOUS
fiery .. ARDENT, INFLAMMABLE, HOT, IGNEOUS, SPIRITED, EXCITABLE, GLARING, RED, SULTRY
fiesta ... GALA, FETE, FESTIVAL, FERIA, HOLIDAY, CELEBRATION
fife .... FLUTE
Fifth Avenue jewelry shop .... CARTIER
columnist .... COLLABORATOR, QUISLING
finger ..... PINKY, PINKIE
fiftieth anniversary .. JUBILEE
fifty-fifty ...... EQUAL, EVEN
fig ...... TRIFLING, BIT, FICO, DRESS, SHAPE, RETUND, SYCONIUM, ELEME
basket .... CABAS
don't care a .... INDIFFERENT
dried .... CARICA
Italian .... FICO
like .... CARICOUS
marigold .... SAMH
parrot .... LORILET
Smyrna ... ELEME, ELEMI
tree .... UPAS, PIPAL, BO TREE
figeater ... BEETLE, JUNE BUG
fight .... ROW, SCRAP, STRIFE, FRAY, TUSSLE, WARFARE, CONTEST, QUARREL, STRUGGLE, CONTEND, OPPOSE, COMBAT, CONFLICT, BATTLE, BRUSH, MELEE, RUN-IN
close quarters .... HAND TO HAND
colloquial .... MIX-UP
desire to .... ANIMUS
fond of .... SCRAPPY
free-for-all ..... MELEE, RIOT, RUMBLE
program .... CARD
with feet and fists .... SAVATE
fighter .... PUGILIST
frenzied .... AMOK, AMUCK, BARESARK
kind of ...... AIRPLANE
Fighting Bob, soubriquet ..... EVANS
chance of a sort ... ODDS
policy ...... MILITANCY
figment of the mind .. FANTASM, PHANTASM(A)
figuline .... STATUE, CLAY, POTTERY, PORCELAIN
figurant ... (BALLET)DANCER, SUPERNUMERARY, EXTRA
figuration .... ADORNING, SHAPING, FORM(ING), APPEARANCE
figurative .... ALLEGORIC(AL), SYMBOLIC, METAPHORICAL

language ...... IMAGERY, TROPE
not .... LITERAL
figure ... SYMBOL, DIGIT, FORM, DIAGRAM, PICTURE, RECKON, IMAGINE, COMPUTE, SOLID
architectural .. CARYATID, TELAMON
carved .... GLYPHIC
crescent shaped ... LUNE, LUNULA
8-sided .... OCTAGON, OCTANGLE
equal-angled .... ISOGON
4-sided ...... TETRAGON, QUADRANGLE, SQUARE
of speech .... TROPE, SIMILE, LITOTES, HYPERBOLE, HENDIADYS, ZEUGMA, OXYMORON, METAPHOR, METONYMY, IMAGERY
on .... RELY, DEPEND
ornamental ..... DEVICE
out ... SOLVE, COMPUTE, UNDERSTAND, REASON, DOPE
oval .... ELLIPSE
part of human ..... BUST, TORSO, TRUNK
10-sided ... DECAGON(AL)
up .... ADD, TOTAL, COMPUTE
used as support ... ATLAS, TELEMON, CARYATID, ATLANTES
figurehead .... DUMMY
figures .... DATA, STATISTICS, ADDS UP
figurine .... STATUETTE, TANAGRA
well-known ..... OSCAR, EMMY
figurines, Gr. town known for .. TANAGRA
figwort .... MULLE(I)N, FOXGLOVE, SNAPDRAGON
Fiji island .... VITI
capital .... SUVA
chestnut .... RATA
dependency .... ROTUMA
tree .... BURI
filament ...... STRAND, HERL, HAIR, THREAD, FIBER, FILUM, HARL(E)
spun .... YARN
filature .... REEL
filbert .... HAZEL(NUT)
filch .... NIM, PURLOIN, PILFER, STEAL, ROB
file ...... DOSSIER, ROW, RASP, CARLET, ENTER, RECORD, CABINET, FOLDER
flat .... QUANNET
rough .... RASP
filet .... NET, LACE
filial duty ...... HONOR, OBEY
filibeg .... KILT
filibuster .... FREEBOOTER, ADVENTURER, MERCENARY
filigree .... LACE
filings .... SCRAPINGS

Filipino (see Philippines) ..... MORO, TAGALOG
aborigine ...... NEGRITO
boat .... BATEL
canoe .... BANCA
canoe, big .... CASCO
child .... BATA
food staple .... RICE
knife .... BOLO, ITAK
language ...... TAGALOG, ENGLISH, SPANISH
Muslim leader .... DATO, DATU, HADJI
native ... MORO, NEGRITO, IGOROT, ATA, IFUGAO, ITA
nursemaid .... YAYA
peasant ... TAO, KASAMA
sailboat .... KUMPIT
soldier .... KAWAL
fill .... PAD, STUFF, SATE, OCCUPY, PLUG, SUPPLY, PERVADE, LOAD
in .... SUBSTITUTE, BRIEF
to excess .... HEAP, CONGEST
with hate ..... EMBITTER, ENVENOM
with wrath ..... INCENSE
fille ... GIRL, MAID, SPINSTER, DAUGHTER
de joie ..... PROSTITUTE
filled gold .... BRASS
to capacity ...... SATED, CHOCKFUL
filler .... SHIM, STUFFING
fillet .... RIBBON, BONE, BAND, STRIP, FACIA, LABEL, T(A)ENIA
architectural .. ORLE, ORLO
hair ...... SNOOD, BAND
narrow .... ANADEM, ORIE, STRIA
filling .... WOOF
dentist's ...... AMALGAM, GOLD
material .... PUTTY
fillip ..... EXCITE, TAP, TONIC, STIMULUS, SNAP
fillister .... GROOVE
filly .... FOAL, MARE
colloquial .... GIRL, WOMAN
film .... COATING, MOVIE, PHOTOGRAPH, NEGATIVE, SHOOT
green .... PATINA
part .... REEL
filmy .... GAUZY, HAZY, BLURRED
cloth .... GOSSAMER
filose .... THREADLIKE, FILAMENTOUS
fils .... SON, YOUTH
English equivalent ...... JUNIOR
filter ...... PERCOLATE, SIEVE, SIFT, COLATURE, OOZE, STRAIN, FILTRATE
screen .... RESEAU
substance ... SAND, FELT, CHARCOAL
through .... SEEP

filth .... SQUALOR, MUCK, DIRT, LUCRE, FECULENCE, OBSCENITY, INDECENCY, ORDURE
filthy ..... FOUL, LUCRE, RICH, DIRTY, SQUALID
animal .... PIG
smelly place ... CESSPOOL, STY
filtrate .... STRAIN, FILTER
fin .... FLIPPER, PINNA, PINNULE, VEE, FIVER
de ____ .... SIECLE
describing one .. DORSAL, VENTRAL, CAUDAL
footed animal .. PINNIPED
in aeronautics .. AIRFOIL, RUDDER
slang .... HAND
finagle ...... CHEAT, RENEGE, WANGLE
final ... DERNIER, END, TELIC, LAST, DECIDING, CONCLUSIVE, ULTIMATE
discharge .... QUIETUS
judgment .... DOOM
finale .... CODA, END, SWAN SONG, CONCLUSION
finally ...... AT LAST, EN FIN, IN THE END, EVENTUALLY
finances ... PURSE, ACCOUNTS, FUNDS
financial .... PECUNIARY, MONETARY, FISCAL
gain, unexpected .... WINDFALL
financially sound ... SOLVENT
financier .... CAPITALIST, BANKER, TYCOON
finback ...... WHALE, GRASO, RORQUAL, RAZORBACK
finch ...... REDPOOL, SISKIN, CANARY, SPINK, CHEWINK, GROSBEAK, SERIN, SONGBIRD, MORO, BUNTING, CARDINAL, SPARROW, OSCINE
African ..... MORO, FINK
American ..... CHEWINK, TOWHEE, LINNET, BURION, JUNCO
canary-like .... SERIN
kin .... CARDINAL
like bird ...... TANAGER
small .... SERIN
yellow .... SERIN
find ...... DISCOVER, LEARN, DECIDE
fault .... BEEF, CARP, COMPLAIN
out ...... LEARN, SOLVE
finding .... DISCOVERY, CONCLUSION
fine .... AMERCE, BULLY, SCONCE, EXCELLENT, THIN, KEEN, SUBTLE, MULCT
and ____ ...... DANDY
arts .... PAINTING, SCULPTURE, CERAMICS, MUSIC, DANCING, LITERATURE
arts buff ..... DILETTANTE
bearing .... BEL AIR

drawn .... SUBTLE
feather .... EGRET
for misconduct .. SCONCE
gravel .... SAND
in law .... CRO
line of letter ...... SERIF
point .... NICETY
porcelain ...... LIMOGES
powder ..... SOOT, DUST
rain .... DRIZZLE
record of .... ESTREAT
thread .... LISLE
fineness .... DELICACY, RARITY, TENUITY
finery ... DECORATION, FRILL, FRIPPERY, FALDERAL, REGALIA, GAUD(ERY)
useless .... FALLAL
finespun .... DELICATE, FRAGILE, SUBTLE
finesse ..... SKILL, CUNNING, CRAFT, ART
finest part .... FLOWER
Fingal's Cave island .. STAFFA
finger .... DIGIT, STEAL, HANDLE, DACTYL(US), TOUCH
covering/sheath .... COT
cymbals ..... CASTANETS
fifth/smallest .... PINKIE, PINKY
fore .... INDEX, POINTER
game .... MORA
hole of instrument ...... VENTAGE
infection .... AGNAIL, FELON, WHITLOW
joint .... KNUCKLE
like .... DIGITATE
little .... PINKIE
middle .... MEDIUS
nail half-moon .. LUNULE
pertaining to ... DIGITAL
protective cover .. STALL, COT
ring .... HOOF
slang .... IDENTIFY, POINT TO, INDICATE
snap of .... FILLIP
stall .... COT
stroke .... FLIP
fingerless glove .... MITT
fingerling ... PARR, FISH, FRY, SAMLET
fingernail, care of .. MANICURE
mark .... LUNULE
fingerprint ... DACTYLOGRAM
mark .... ARCH, LUNULE, WHORL, LOOP
fingers, membrane uniting .... WEB(BING)
finial .... APEX, PEAK, TIP, SUMMIT, EPI
finical .... PRUDISH, METICULOUS, FASTIDIOUS, FUSSY, PARTICULAR, EXACTING
finicky ... PRECISE, OVERNICE
finis ...... END, CONCLUSION
finish ..... END, ACCOMPLISH, POLISH, STOP, TERMINATE, PERFECTION, CLOSE
colloquial .... KILL

dull .... MATTE
line .... TAPE, WIRE
off ...... DESTROY, KILL
finished, for short ...... THRU
finisher ..... REAMER, EDGER, SOCKDOLAGER
finishing school product ..... LADY
tool ..... REAMER, LATHE
fink .... SPY, STRIKEBREAKER, INFORMER
Finland .... SUOMI
finnan haddie ...... HADDOCK
Finnish .... SUOMI
bath(house) ..... SAUNA
canto .... RUNE
capital .... HELSINKI
city ... TURKU, TAMPERE
coin ..... MARKKA, PENNI
composer ..... SIBELIUS
dialect .... KARELIAN
epic poem ... KALEVALA
field marshal .... MANNERHEIM
god .... JUMALA
inlet .... FIORD
island .... ALAND
lake ..... ENARA, ENARE, SAIMA
language .... SUOMI
monetary unit .. MARKKA
native .... LAPP, LAPLANDER, KARELIAN
poem .... RUNE
seaport .... ABO, TURKU
finnikin .... PIGEON
Finno-Ugric language .. LAPP, FINNISH, ESTONIAN, MAGYAR, HUNGARIAN
Finns .... SUOMI
fiord .... INLET
fipple .... PLUG
fir ...... BALSAM, EVERGREEN
board wood .... DEAL
pole .... UFER
fire ... KINDLE, HURL, DISMISS, INGLE, IGNITE, ARDOR, BURN, EXCITE, (IN)FLAME, ANNEAL
alarm ...... BELL, SIREN, WHISTLE, PYROSTAT
artillery ...... BARRAGE, SALVO
away .... START
back .... REREDOS
basket ... CRESSET, GRATE
big, destructive .... CONFLAGRATION
catching .... IGNITION
clay ..... BRICK, SAGGER
combining form .. PYRO, IGNI
cracker .... PETARD
damp .... METHANE
Dance composer .... DE FALLA
department head .... MARSHAL
feeder .... STOKER
god ...... VULCAN, AGNI, SIVA, KAMA
irons ... POKER, SHOVEL, TONGS

of .... IGNEOUS
opal .... GIRASOL(E)
pot .... CRUCIBLE
principle of .. PHLOGISTON
produced by ... IGNEOUS
put out .... DOUSE
stir up .... STOKE
worshiper .. PYROLATER, PARSEE, GHEBRE, GHEBER, PARSI
firearm (see gun) ..... PISTOL, RIFLE, DERRINGER, REVOLVER, GUN, GAT, PETRONEL, IRON
barrel's end .... MUZZLE
charge .... LOAD
hammer .... COCK
firearms protective coating .... COSMOLINE
fireball ..... METEOR, BOLIDE
firebrand .... AGITATOR, HOTHEAD
firebug .... ARSONIST, INCENDIARY, PYROMANIAC
firecracker .... PETARD
box for .... MARROON
broken .... SQUIB
fired clay .... TILE, BRICK
firedamp ..... METHANE, GAS
firedog .... ANDIRON
firedrake .... DRAGON
firefly .... BUG, BEETLE, GLOWWORM
lighting substance ...... LUCIFERIN
fireman ...... STOKER, VAMP, HAGBUT, HACKBUT
hat of .... HELMET
Firenze .... FLORENCE
fireplace ..... INGLE, GRATE, HEARTH
guard .... FENDER
ledge .... HOB
log holder ..... FIREDOG, ANDIRON
part ...... MANTEL, SPIT, HOB, JAMB(E), CHIMNEY, SHELF
screen .... FENDER
Spanish .... FOGON
tool .... TONGS
fireplug .... HYDRANT
fireside ...... HEARTH, HOME
firewater ...... WHISKY, RUM
firewood ... FAG(G)OT, BARIN, BILLET
fireworks ... PETARD, RIPRAP, PYROTECHNICS, ROCKETS, GERB(E)
cluster ...... GIRANDOLE
hissing ... SQUIB, FIZGIGS
material .... REALGAR
firkin .... TUB
firm .... FIXED, HARD, SOLID, RESOLUTE, FINAL, STEADY, STIFF, COMPANY, STA(U)NCH
firmament ..... HEAVEN, SKY, VAULT, ARCH
revolving ..... PINWHEEL, TOURBILLION
firman ..... DECREE, SANCTION
firmer .... CHISEL
firmly set ..... ROOTED, FIXED,

EMBEDDED, PINNED, RIVETED
united .... SOLID
firmness, lacking .... FLABBY, LOOSE, LAX, LIMP, SOFT
firn .... SNOW, NEVE, ICE
first .... INITIAL, ORIGINAL, MAIDEN, CHIEF, FOREMOST, EARLIEST, PRINCIPAL
abbreviation ...... ORIG.
appearance ...... DEBUT, MAIDEN
born ...... HEIR, OLDEST, EIGNE
cause .... SOURCE
circumnavigator .... MAGELLAN
class ... QUALITY, AONE, TOPS, DANDY
day of Quakers .. SUNDAY
day of Roman month ... CALENDS
estate .... CLERGY
finger .... INDEX
game .... OPENER
in rank .... PREMIER
in time .... PRIMAL
Lady's husband .... PRESIDENT
letter .... INITIAL
move .... OVERTURE, INITIATIVE
night .... PREMIERE
nighter ...... REVIEWER, CRITIC
officer: nautical ... MATE
performance ... PREMIERE
Pope .... PETER
prefix .... PROTO
principles .... ABCS
rate ... SUPER, ACE, AONE, ONER, TOPS, EXCELLENT, NOBBY, TOPFLIGHT, CAPITAL, TOPNOTCH
rate: Anglo-Indian ...... PUCKA, PUKKA
sergeant ...... TOPKICK
showing .... PREMIERE
sight ...... PRIMA FACIE
space traveler .. GAGARIN
speech, describing ...... MAIDEN
stage .... INCIPIENCE
valuable .... EDITION
year's revenue of benefice ANNAT
year student ..... FROSH, FRESHMAN, PLEB(E)
year West Pointer .. PLEBE
firsthand .... ORIGINAL, DIRECT, BRAND NEW
firth .... KYLE, ARM, INLET, ESTUARY, FIORD
fisc .... TREASURY, EXCHEQUER
fiscal .... FINANCIAL, PROSECUTOR, BURSAL
fish ...... ANGLE, BRAINFOOD, TROLL, TRAWL, SABALO, GAR, RAY, BASS, SHAD, OPAH, LING, CHUB, HAKE, CARP, DACE, DARTER, SCROD, PERCH, SNAPPER, TARPON, EELPOUT, WRASSE, STURGEON, SCULPIN, MACKEREL, BULLHEAD, LABROID
African ...... CHARACIN
air bladder .... MAW
air-swallowing .. PUFFER, SWELLFISH, GLOBEFISH
appendage .... FIN, FLIPPER, BARBEL
aquarium .... MOLLY, SWORDTAIL
ascending river .... ANADROM
Atlantic .... TAUTOG
bait ..... LIMPET, HOLA, LURE, SHINER, CHUM, CAP(E)LIN, LUGWORM, MENBRADEN, MINNOW
ball .... RISSOLE
barbel .... WATTLE
barracuda .... SPET
basket .... WEEL, CREEL, CAWL
batlike ...... GURNARD, GURNET, (STING)RAY
beaked .... SAURY
beard .... BARB(EL)
bin for salting .... KENCH
boat ... COBLE, TRAWLER, WHALER, DORY
boneless .... FIL(L)ET
bony .... TELEOST
box .... KENCH
bright-colored ... OPAH, WRASSE, PINTANO, COWPILOT, DRAGONET, MORAY, MOLLY
bucket .... KIT
burbot ...... LING, CUSK, EELPOUT
butter .... GUNNEL
butterfly .... PARU, BLENNY
capelin .... SMELT
carangoid ...... CAVALLA, YELLOWTAIL, POMPANO, YELLOWJACK
caribe .... PIRAYA, PIRANHA
carp family ...... ROACH, BLEAK, IDE, LOACH, MINNOW, DACE, CHUB, TENCH, REDFIN, ROUD, RUD(D)
cat .... RAAD
catch .... HAUL
char(r) .... TROUT
chopped .... CHUM
cigar .... SCAD
cleaner .... SCALER
climbing .... ANABAS
clinging ...... REMORA, TESTAR
coal .... POLLACK, POLLOCK
cod family .... CUSK, GADID, BACALAO, HADDOCK, POLLACK, HAKE, LING, BURBOT
combining form ... PISCI
cow .... MANATEE, DUGONG, GRAMPUS
crab and fiddler .... UCA
creature: legendary ..... MERMAN, MERMAID
Cuban .... DIABLO
cure .... BLOAT
cusk .... BURBOT
cuttle ...... SEPIA, SQUID
cyprinoid ...... BARBEL, CARP, LOACH, ROUD, BREAM, DACE, GOLDFISH, BLEAK, ORF(E)
deep sea .... WEEVER
delicacy .... ROE
devil ...... MANTA, RAY, SKATE
dog .... SHARK, BOWFIN
dolphin .... INIA, CETACEAN, PORPOISE
drying frame ..... HACK
East Indies ...... DORAB, GOURAMI
eating ...... PISCIVOROUS
eating animal .... OTTER, SEAL
eating bird ..... OSPREY, PELICAN, ERN(E)
eating fish ..... ANGLER
edible ...... BASS, TROUT, DORY, BRISLING, HADDOCK, LOACH, SPRAT, BARRACUDA, PIKE, MACKEREL, TAUTOG, IDE, ARAPAIMA, WRASSE, COD
eel .... CONGER, LAMPREY, ELVER, MORAY, LING
eel-like .... APOD
eelpout .... BURBOT
eel-shaped .. LEPIDOSIREN
eggs .... ROE, SPAWN
eggs relish .... CAVIAR(E)
elasmobranch .. SAWFISH, RAY, MANTA, SKATE, SHARK
elongated .... EEL, PIKE, GAR
European ...... BARBEL, PLAICE, BRISLING, BREAM, UMBER, WRASSE, BRASSE, BLEAK, SENNET, TENCH, DACE, SPRAT
eyed on head's top ..... STARGAZER
fabled .... MAH
feeler .... BARBEL
fence ..... WEIR, CRAWL,
fierce ... PIKE, PIRANHA, BARRACUDA, BLENNY, PICKEREL, SEABASS, SHARK
flat .. TURBOT, FLOUNDER, SKATE, DAB, BRILL, PLAICE, HALIBUT, BUTT, SOLE, RAY, FLUKE
Florida .... TARPON, BONACI
flying .... SAURY, GURNARD

food ... SNAPPER, JUREL, POLLACK, MORAY, TUNA, SCUP, HAKE, CERO, CARP, GROUPER, MULLET, COD, LING, PLAICE, POMPANO, SMELT, SARDINE, SHAD, TROUT, BONITO
fork-tailed .. CARANGOID, CAVALLA, POMPANO, JUREL
fresh-water ..... ANABAS, IDE, DACE, CRAPPIE, BASS, TENCH, LOACH, DARTER, REDEYE, ARAPAIMA
frog .... ANGLER
from boat .... TROLL
full of: poetic ..... FINNY
game .... MARLIN, TARPON, SWORDFISH, SALMON, TROUT, (BLACK)BASS
ganoid .... GAR, BOWFIN, STURGEON
garth .... WEIR
genus .... AMIA
gig .... SPEAR, HOOK
gobioid .... GOBY
goby-like ..... DRAGONET
grampus .... ORC, DOLPHIN
grasping-tailed .... HIPPOCAMPUS
green ... SHANNY, PLAICE
grouper ..... (SEA)BASS, MERO
grunting ..... CROAKER, PIGFISH, GURNARD
gurnard family .... SEA ROBIN
Hawaiian .... AKU
hawk .... OSPREY
head of .... JOWL
herring .... CISCO, MENHADEN, SPRAT, PILCHARD, PILCHER, CLUPE(O)ID, SARDINE, ANCHOVY, TARPON, OLDWIFE
herring-like ...... SHAD, ALEWIFE
herring, young .... BRIT
hook .... GAFF, GIG
illegally .... POACH
Japanese ..... TAI, FUGU
jelly .... MEDUSA, ACALEPH
jew ...... MERO, TARPON, (SEA)BASS
jurel .... RUNNER
king ... OPAH, WHITING, PINTADO
lacking pelvic fins .. APOD
lake .... POLLAN
land-walking ... ANABAS
largest freshwater .... ARAPAIMA
like animal ... LANCELET
line ...... SNELL, TROT, TROLL, TRAWL
line cork .... BOB
ling .... BURBOT
little .. MINNOW, SARDINE, SMELT
lizard .... ULAE
loach .... SMERLIN
long-beaked ..... SAURY, GAR
lure .... SPINNER
mackerel .. TUNA, TUNNY, ALBACORE, BONITO
mackerel-like ..... CERO, TINKER
male .... MILTER
man-eating ...... SHARK
marine ... SCUP, BONITO, WRASSE, CUSK, LING, TARPON, ROBALO, BLENNY, MENHADEN
maskonge .... PIKE
measure .... MEASE
meat, broiled .... CARBONADO
migration .... RUN
milk .... SABALO
mollusk ...... OCTOPUS, SQUID
mucous coating ... SLIME
mythological .... MAH
nest-building .... ACARA
net .... SEINE, TRAWL, FYKE, GILL, FLUE, FLEW
New Zealand .... IHI
ocean bed ...... WEEVER
of .... PISCINE, PISCATORY, PISCATORIAL
organ of touch ... BARBEL
parasite .... REMORA
parrot ..... LANIA, LORO
pen ...... CRAWL, WEIR
perch family .... RUFF(E)
perch-like ...... ANABAS, DARTER, CABRILLA
pertaining to ... PISCINE, PISCATORY, FINNY, TELEOST
pickle .... ALEC
piece .... FIL(L)ET
pike .... LUCE, PICKEREL
pike-like .... GAR, BARRACUDA, ROBALO
place for drying ... HACK
pond .... PISCINA
poor .... SIMP
porgy .... SCUP, TAI
Polynesian .... ISDA
porpoise ..... DOLPHIN, INIA, CETACEAN
primitive ... COELACANTH
ray ...... MANTA, SKATE
red-eyed .... RUDD
relish .... BOTARGO
reproductive glands ..... MILT
resembling ..... PISCINE
river ascending .. SALMON, SHAD, ANADROM
rock .... RE(I)NA, BASS, GROUPER, COD
runner .... JUREL
Russian .... STERLET, STURGEON
salmon, young .... PARR, SAMLET
salmonoid .. NAMAYCUSH, TROUT, STEELHEAD
salt-water ... DORY, SHAD, TUNA, CYCLOTOME, HAKE
salting box ...... KENCH
sardine ..... PILCHARD, HERRING, SPRAT, CLUPEID
sardine-like ... BRISLING, ANCHOVY, CISCO
sauce ... ALEC, ANCHOVY
saurel .... SCAD
scabbard .... HIKU
scad .... SAUREL
scale .... GANOID
scaleless .... BULLHEAD, SCULPIN, CATFISH
sculpin family .. CABEZON, BULLHEAD
sea .... TUNA, SAURY, SCULPIN
sergeant .... ROBALO
shad-like .... ALEWIFE
shark ..... MAKO, TOPE, ANGELFISH
shark family .. CHIMAERA
shark's pilot .... REMORA
shell ... CLAM, ABALONE, WHELK, LIMPET, SLUG, SCALLOP, OCTOPUS
sign of zodiac .... PISCES
silver-bellied .. MACKEREL
silvery .... PINTADO, MULLET, SMELT, OPAH
skeleton ... ARETE, ARISTA
slimy .... BLENNY
small .... FRY, ID(E), SMELT, FINGERLING, DARTER, SPELT, MINNOW, DACE, SPRAT, SAMLET
smelt .... CAP(E)LIN
snouted ... SAURY, GAR, BOARFISH, PORPOISE, DOLPHIN, PICKEREL, STURGEON
South American .... CARIBE, ARAPAIMA, PIRANHA, PIRAYA
spawning movement .... CATADROMOUS, ANADROMOUS
spear ..... GIG, LEISTER
sperm .... MILT, ROE
spiny ... GOBY, SCULPIN
spotted .... OPAH
stewed ..... MATELOT(TE)
story .... YARN, EXAGGERATION
sturgeon .... STERLET, BELUGA
sucking .... REMORA, HAMMERHEAD
swimming bladder ...... SOUND
tank ... STEW, AQUARIUM
teleost .... EEL
that recently spawned ... SHOTTEN
to .... ANGLE, TROLL
toad .... SAPO
trap ..... KELONG, WEIR,

TRAWL, EELPOT, HATCH, FYKE, CRAWL, SEINE, GILL, CREEL
tropical ... BARRACUDA, SARGO, SALEMA, ROBALO, SNAPPER
trout .... CHAR(R)
tub .... KIT
ugly-looking .... CATFISH
unicorn .... UNIE
upholding universe .. MAH
voracious ...... CARIBE, SHARK, PIRANHA, CATFISH
wahoo .... ONO
wall-eyed ..... BLOWFISH
West Indies ..... TESTAR
whale ...... CETACEAN, CACHALOT, NARWHAL, GRAMPUS, ORC(A)
whisker .... BARBEL
whiskered ..... CATFISH
whiting ..... MENHADEN, HAKE
with a spoon ...... SPIN
with lungs/gills .... CERATODUS, DIPNOAN, BARRAMUNDA
with staring eyes ... PIKE, PERCH, POLLACK, ALEWIFE
with sucking mouth ..... LAMPREY, CYCLOSTOME, HAGFISH, REMORA
with suction disk ... GOBY
with whiplike tail ...... SKATE, STINGAREE, (STING)RAY
young .... BRIT, ALEVIN, FRY, PARR, FINGERLING, ELVER, SAMLET

fishbait .... LUGWORM, CHUM
fishbowl .... AQUARIUM
fisher ...... WEJACK, PEKAN, MARTEN, SEAL
fisherman .... WALTON, EELER, ANGLER, PISCATOR
basket .... CREEL
line of .... SNELL
fisherman's bend .... KNOT
hut .... SKEO
fishes, characteristic of .... ICHTHYIC
fishgig .... SPEAR
fishhook ... GAFF, DRAIL, GIG
line .... SNELL
fishing .... ANGLING
bait .... DRAKE, MAYFLY
basket .... CREEL
boat ... DORY, TRAWLER, SMACK, CORACLE, DOGGER, SHARPIE
device .... EELPOT
float .... BOB
fly .... HACKLE
fly, artificial ..... NYMPH
fly trimmer .... HERL
ground .... FISHERY, PISCINA, PISCARY, POUND
line float .... BOB
line with hooks .... BOULTER
net .... FLUE, FLEW, SEINE, FYKE, TRAWL, GILL, TRAMMEL
pertaining to .... PISCATORIAL
place ... PISCARY, POUND
pole ...... ROD, TONKIN
reel .... PIRN
right .... PISCARY
season, feast after ... FOY
smack .... DOGGER
spear ... HARPOON, GAFF

fishline leader .... SNELL
fishnet sagging part ..... BUNT
fishpond .... WEIR
fishskin disease .. ICHTHYOSIS
fishwife .... NAG(GER)
fishworm: Jap. ..... ANISAKIS
fishy .... FUNNY, INCREDIBLE, SHADY, DOUBTFUL, DULL, SUSPICIOUS
fission .... SCISSION
fissure ... RIFT, CRACK, SPLIT, CLEFT, CRANNY, RENT, CHINK, CREVICE, RIME
in glacier ..... CREVASSE
fissures, full of ...... RIMOUS, RIMOSE
fist .... NIEVE
blow .... PUNCH, PASTE
fight .... MILL
fistic .... PUGILISTIC, BOXING
fisticuffs ..... BOUT, PUNCHES, SETTO, BOXING
fists: sl. .... DUKES
fistula .... CAVITY, PIPE, TUBE
fistulous .... TUBULAR
fit ...... APT, SPASM, ADAPT, MEET, TRIG, ELIGIBLE, KOSHER, KASHER, SUIT(ABLE), EQUIP, PAT, ATTACK, APOPLEXY, PAROXYSM, CONVULSION, PROPER, RIGHT, READY
arrow on string ... NOCK
closely/exactly ..... FAY
for cultivation .. ARABLE
gamecock with spurs .... HEEL
of shivers .... AGUE
of temper ... ANGER, IRE, OUTBURST, HUFF, RAGE, TANTRUM, TIFF, CONNIPTION, MIFF, PIQUE
out .... EQUIP
to be ____ .... TIED
to drink .... POTABLE
to eat .... EDIBLE, EATABLE, ESCULENT, KOSHER
to live in ..... HABITABLE
to requirement ... TAILOR
to work .... ABLE
together .... MESH

fitchew .... POLECAT
fitful .... IRREGULAR, SPASMODIC
fitly .... DULY, SUITABLY, SPASMODIC
fitness ... APTNESS, PROPRIETY
fits and ____ .... STARTS
fitting ... APT, MEET, PROPER
fittingly .... DULY
fittings .... FIXTURES, DECORATIONS, FURNISHINGS
Fitzgerald, singer ...... ELLA
Fiume .... RIJEKA
Five Civilized Nations member CHEROKEE, CREEK, CHOCTAW, CHICKASAW, SEMINOLE
cent coin .... NICKEL, JITNEY
collection of .... QUINTUPLET
combining form .... PENT(A)
consisting of .... QUINTUPLE
day duel protagonist .... ROLAND, OLIVER
dollar bill ..... FIN, VEE, FIVER
finger .... OXLIP, CINQUEFOIL, STARFISH, POTENTILLA
fold .... QUINTUPLE
group of .... PENTAD
hundred, card game ..... EUCHRE
in cards .... PEDRO
lined nonsensical poem .. LIMERICK
Nations member .... CAYUGAS, ONEIDAS, MOHAWKS, SENECAS, ONONDAGAS, TUSCARORAS
of trumps in 7-up .. PEDRO
on the dice ...... CINQUE
set of .... QUINARY, QUINTET(TE)
sided figure ... PENTAGON
year period ... LUSTRUM, PENTAD

fiver .... FIN
fives .... HANDBALL
fix ...... (A)MEND, SPOT, SET, DEFINE, RIVET, REPAIR, DILEMMA, LIMIT, FASTEN, ESTABLISH, FREEZE
colloquial .... PREDICAMENT, SCRAPE, SPOT, DILEMMA
in memory .... CON, REMEMBER
jewel in setting .. MOUNT
fixation .... OBSESSION, PREOCCUPATION
fixative .... MORDANT
fixed ..... FIRM, IMMOVABLE, RIGID, SET, RESOLUTE, STATIONARY, STABILE
charge item ...... RENT, INTEREST, TAX
fixings .... ACCESSORIES
fixture hanging from ceiling ... CHANDELIER
fixtures .... FITTINGS, FURNITURE
fizgig .... FIREWORK, FLIRT
fizz ...... DRINK, CHAMPAGNE
fizzle ...... FIASCO, FLOP, FAIL
fizzwater .... SODA
fizzy .... BUBBLING, EFFERVESCENT

fjeld .... PLATEAU
fjord .... INLET
passage .... GAT
flabbergast .... SURPRISE, ASTONISH, STUN, ABASH, DISCONCERT
flabellum .... FAN
flabby ...... FLACCID, WEAK, FEEBLE
flaccid ... LIMP, WEAK, FLABBY
flacon .... FLASK
flag ..... GONFALON, ENSIGN, WEAKEN, BUNTING, BLACKJACK, SIGN, BANNER, DROOP, TIRE, COLORS, STANDARD, GUIDON
background ...... FIELD
bearer .... CORNET
cloth .... BUNTING
corner .... CANTON
deer's .... TAIL
flower .... IRIS
identifying ...... BURGEE
little .... PENNANT, BANDEROLE, BANNERET, BANNEROL
military .... GUIDON, ENSIGN
officer .... ADMIRAL, CAPTAIN
over tomb .. BANDEROL(E)
pirate's .... ROGER
plant .... IRIS
pole ...... STAFF, SHAFT
position .... FANION
rope .... HALYARD
ship's .... BURGEE
signal .... ENSIGN
swallow-tailed .... BURGEE, PENNON
sweet .... CALAMUS
triangular ...... PENNON, BURGEE
flagellant .... ALBI
flagellate .... WHIP, FLOG
flagellum .... WHIP, SHOOT, RUNNER
flageolet ... FLUTE, RECORDER, PIPE
flagitious .... HEINOUS, WICKED, VILE
flagon ... JUG, EWER, CARAFE, STOUR, STOUP
flagrant .... EGREGIOUS, OUTRAGEOUS, SCANDALOUS, NOTORIOUS, GLARING, GROSS, RANK
flagrante delicto .... RED-HANDED
flagship official launch .. BARGE
flags collectively .... BUNTING
flagstone .... SLAB, BRICK
Flaherty movie film ... MOANA
flail ..... THRESH, WHIP, BEAT
part .... SWIP(P)LE, SWINGLE
flair .... BENT, TALENT, APTITUDE, KNACK, ABILITY, DISCERNMENT
flak .... ACK-ACK
flake ... CHIP, SPALL, LAMINA, CARNATION, RACK, SCALE, FLECK
flakes, covered with .. LEPIDOTE
flaky ...... SCALY, SQUAMOSE
flam ..... HUMBUG, BLARNEY, LIE, TRICK, DECEPTION
flambeau ... CRESSET, TORCH, CANDLESTICK
flamboyance ...... PANACHE
flamboyant .... ORNATE, SHOWY, FLOWERY, BOMBASTIC
flame ..... BEAM, BLAZE, FIRE, SPUNK
long, narrow .... TONGUE
slang ..... SWEETHEART
flamen .... PRIEST
flamenco dancer .... GRECO
flan .... TART, BLANK
Flanders battlesite .... YPRES
native .... FLEMING
river .... YSER
flanerie .... LOAFING
flaneur ... STROLLER, LOAFER, TRIFLER, ROAMER, GADABOUT
flank .... SIDE, LOIN
combining form .... LAPAR(O)
flannel .... LANA
flannelmouth .... CATFISH
flannels: colloq. .. UNDERWEAR
flap ..... TAB, SWING, SLAP, BEAT, FLUTTER, FLY, LAPPET, WHIP, SLAT
airplane ...... AILERON, AIRFOIL
of flesh .. GILL, WATTLE, DEWLAP
vigorously .... SLAT
wings .... FLICKER
flapjack .... PANCAKE, GRIDDLECAKE
flapper .... FIN
flare .... BLAZE, FUZEE, FLICKER, GLARE, FLECK, FLASH, BULGE, OUTBURST
signal .... FUSEE
flaring .... LURID, GAUDY
edge .... FLANGE
flash .... GLINT, GLEAM, GLIMMER, SPARK, FLARE, SPARKLE, BLAZE, MOMENT, SCINTILLATE, GLITTER
of lightning .... BOLT
out .... EFFULGE
flasher .... BEACON
flashy .... GAUDY, SHOWY, RAFFISH
flask ..... CANTEEN, MATARA, CRUSE, COSTREL, CARAFE, THERMOS, MATRASS, CUCURBITE, FLAGON, FLACON
flat ..... LEVEL, APARTMENT, EVEN, TABULAR, SUITE, INSIPID, PLANE, STALE, VAPID, ABSOLUTE, DULL
and circular ...... DISCOUS
and even ... HORIZONTAL
boat .... DORY, SCOW, BARGE, PUNT, RAFT
bottle .... FLASK
bottom boat ..... BARGE, SCOW, PUNT, BATEAU, DORY
canopy .... TESTER
colloquial ... PENNILESS, BROKE
dish .... PLATTER
fish ... SKATE, SOLE, DAB, RAY, TURBOT, FLOUNDER, FLUKE
headed Indian .. CHINOOK
headed nail .... TACK
hill .... MESA
land .... PLAIN
nosed .... SNUB, PUG, SIMOUS
on one's back ... SUPINE
stick .... FERULE
stone .... SLAB
surface .... AREA, TABULAR, PLANE, PLAIN
taste .... INSIPID
flatboat .... BARGE, PUNT, SCOW
flatfish ..... FLOUNDER, SOLE, HALIBUT, FLUKE, BUT(T), BRILL, TURBOT, PLAICE, RAY, (SAND)DAB
flatfoot: sl. ...... POLICEMAN, COP
Flathead ... CHINOOK, SALISH
flatiron .... SADIRON
flatten .... KNOCK DOWN, LEVEL OFF, PROSTRATE
flatter .... PRAISE, PLEASE, COMPLIMENT, TOADY, FAWN, BLANDISH, ADULATE, OIL
flatterer, servile .. FLUNK(E)Y, TOADY, SYCOPHANT, COURTIER, LICKSPIT(TLE)
flattery .... SOFT SOAP, BLARNEY, PALAVER, TAFFY, BLANDISHMENT, FLUMMERY, SUGAR
flattop: sl. .... (AIRCRAFT)CARRIER
flatulence .... VANITY, GAS
flatulent .... POMPOUS, VAIN, WINDY
flatus .... GAS, PUFF
flatwork ..... SHEETS, NAPKIN
flatworm .... TREMATODE, FLUKE
Flaubert heroine .... EMMA
novelist .... GUSTAVE
flaunt .... FLUTTER, WAVE, SHOW(OFF), DISPLAY
flavescent .... YELLOWISH
flavin .... PIGMENT
flavor .... SMACK, SAUCE, AROMA, ODOR, SMELL, GUST, SAPOR, SAVOR, SALT, TASTE, ESSENCE, RELISH, TANG, LACE, SEASON
drinks .... MULL
keeping substance ..... ESSENCE
of .... SAPOROUS
spicy .... GINGER
with spice .... MULL
flavoring .. EXTRACT, LICORICE, ESSENCE, VANILLIN, VANILLA
bulb .... SHALLOT

plant ...... ANISE, MINT, LAUREL, LEEK, BASIL, SAGE
root .... LICORICE
seed ... ANISE, CARAWAY
flavorless .... VAPID
flavorsome .... SAPID
flaw .... CRACK, BLEMISH, DEFECT, FAULT, ERROR
flawless ... PERFECT, POLISHED
flax .... LINEN, FIBER, BYSSUS
capsule .... BOLL
clean and dress .. HECKLE
cloth .... CANVAS, SACKING, STUPE
comber .... HATCHEL, HACKLE, CARD
dresser .... HATCHEL, HECKLE
fabric .... LINEN
fiber .... TOW, SILVER
filament .... HARL
husk .... SHIVE
like .... TOWY
pod .... BOLL
prepare .... RET
refuse of .... HARDS, HURDS, TOW
remove seeds from ...... RIPPLE
seed .... LINSEED
soak .... RET
weed .... TOADFLY
flaxen color .... GOLDEN, BLOND(E)
flaxseed .... LINSEED
flay .... EXCORIATE, BEAT, CANE, WHIP, SCOLD, CRITICIZE, ROB, FLEECE, PILLAGE
flea .... JIGGER, CHIGOE, REDBUG, CHIGGER
bitten .... DECREPIT, WRETCHED
fleam ... LANCET, PHLEBOTOME
fleawort .... HERB, PLANTAIN
fleche .... SPIRE
fleck ... SPOT, SPECK, FREAK, PARTICLE, FLAKE, SPECKLE
flection ... BEND(ING), FLEXING
"Fledermaus" character ...... ADELE
fledgling .... NESTLING
flee ... SKIP, DECAMP, ELOPE, RUN, BOLT, DESERT, LAM, ABSCOND, VANISH
fleece .... FELL, PILE, ABB, FLAY, MULCT, WOOL, CHEAT, SWINDLE, STEAL, SHEAR
cloth .... HODDEN
fleeced .... SHORN
fleecy .... LANIFEROUS
fleer ..... GIBE, MOCK, SNEER, RUNAGATE, RUNAWAY, JEER, SCOFF
fleet ..... FLOTILLA, MARINE, RAPID, FAST, NAVY, FLIT, FLY, SWIFT
commander's vessel ..... FLAGSHIP
front of .... VAN
merchant .... ARGOSY
small .... FLOTILLA
Spanish .... ARMADA
unit .... SQUADRON
fleeting .... TRANSIENT, EPHEMERAL, TRANSITORY
Flemish geographer .... MERCATOR
mathematician .. STEVIN
painter ...... MEMLING, RUBENS, VANDYKE, VAN DYCK
flense .... SKIN
flesh .... MEAT, MANKIND
become .... CARNIFY
calf .... VEAL
cattle .... BEEF
deer .... VENISON
eating ... CARNIVOROUS, CANNIBAL(ISTIC), CARNIVORE
eating plant .. CARNIVORE
eating raw .. OMAPHAGIA
fly .... BLOWFLY
fold of .... COLLOP
game animal .. VENISON
of dead body ... CARRION
outgrowth ... CARUNCLE, COMB, WATTLE
pertaining to .. SARCOUS, CARNAL
sheep .... MUTTON
swine .... PORK
fleshings .... TIGHTS
fleshly .. CARNAL, CORPOREAL, SENSUAL
fleshpot .... LUXURY
fleshy ..... FAT, OBESE, PLUMP, ADIPOSE, PULPY, STOUT
fruit .... APPLE, QUINCE, DRUPE, BERRY, TOMATO, BANANA, PEAR, POME, SARCOCARP, CHERRY, PLUM
fleur-de-lis ... COAT-OF-ARMS, IRIS, LILY
flex .... BEND, CURVE, CONTRACT
flexible .... SUPPLE, LITHE, LIMBER, TENSILE, DUCTILE, LISSOM(E), PLIANT, TRACTABLE, ELASTIC, PLASTIC
flexile .... MOBILE, PLIANT
flexing .... FLECTION
flexor .... MUSCLE
flexure .... FOLD, CURVE, BEND(ING)
flibbertigibbet .. CHATTERBOX
flick ...... FLIP, SNAP, DASH, STREAK, FLUTTER, FLECK
"Flicka" creator ..... OHARA
flicker ...... YELLOWHAMMER, FLUTTER, FLAP, BLAZE, WOODPECKER
dialect ..... HIGH-HOLE, WOODPECKER
flickering .... LAMBENT
flick: sl. .... MOTION PICTURE, MOVIE, FILM
flier ..... WINGMAN, AVIATOR, STEP, HANDBILL
on an eagle ...... ETANA
slang .... GAMBLE, SPECULATION
flight ...... EXODUS, HEGIRA, HEJIRA, VOLITATION, FLEEING, MIGRATION
capable of .... VOLITANT
disorderly .... ROUT
hasty .... SCUTTLE
headlong .... LAM, STAMPEDE
organ .... WING
short .... HOP
slang .... LAM
type of ... TEST, NONSTOP, MAIDEN, SOLO
flightless bird .... RATITE, CASSOWARY, OSTRICH, WEKA, EMU, RHEA, PENGUIN, KIWI, APTERYX, MOA, DODO
flighty ... FICKLE, FRIVOLOUS, BARMY, FANCIFUL, HOITY-TOITY, GIDDY, CAPRICIOUS
one .... BIRDBRAIN
flimflam ..... TRICK, HUMBUG, NONSENSE, HOCUS, RUBBISH
flimsy .... FRAGILE, FRAIL, TRIVIAL, THIN, SHEER, WEAK, SLIGHT, TENUOUS
flinch .... QUAIL, WINCE, RECOIL, COWER, BLENCH, CRINGE
flinder ... FRAGMENT, SPLINTER
fling ... TOSS, HURL, THROW, CAST, EMIT, RUSH, DASH, SLING
flint ... SILICA, CORN, CHERT, QUARTZ, SILEX
rock like ... HORNSTONE
flintlock .... MUSKET
Flint's outfit .... ZOWIE
flip ... TOSS, FILLIP, JERK, TAP, DRINK, PERT, SAUCY, FLIPPANT, SNAP
flippancy .... LEVITY
flippant ... GLIB, PERT, SAUCY, SASSY, AIRY
flipper .... FIN, PADDLE
relative .... PAW
slang .... HAND
flippered mammal .... SEAL, WALRUS
flirt ..... COQUET(TE), TRIFLE, PLAY, TOY, DALLY, VAMP
in the theater .... SOUBRETTE
male .... WOLF
flirting .... DALLIANCE
flit .... HOVER, FLUTTER, FLY, DART
flittermouse .... BAT
flivver ...... AUTO(MOBILE), AIRPLANE, FAIL, CRATE
float ...... BUOY, BOB, RIDE, RAFT, CORK, WAFT, PONTOON, DRIFT, SELL
fishing line ..... DOBBER, BOB
floating .... NATANT, ADRIFT, AWASH
debris .... FLOTAGE
ice .... FLOE, BERG,

GROWLERS, CLUMPERS
island ingredient ... EGGS
leaf .... LILYPAD
plant .... WATERLILY
power of....... FLOTAGE
wreckage ..... FLOTSAM
flocculent .. FLUFFY, WOOLLY
flock .... SWARM, DROVE, PACK, HERD, CROWD, BROOD, CONGREGATION, GROUP
of a .... GAGGLE
of birds .... COVEY, BEVY, POD
of cattle ... HERD, DROVE
of partridges/quail ...... COVEY
of seals .... POD
of sheep ... HERD, DROVE, FOLD
of whales .... POD
pertaining to a .... GREGARIOUS
wild fowl .... SKEIN
flog .... LARRUP, LASH, TAN, FLAGELLATE, SHELLACK, LAM, SWISH, HIDE, BEAT, WHIP, TROUNCE
flogging rod .. SWISH, SWITCH
whip ...... CHAB(O)UK, KURBASH
flood ... CATARACT, TORRENT, SPATE, SWAMP, INUNDATE, INUNDATION, OVERFLOW, DELUGE, OUTPOURING
gate ..... SLUICE, HATCH
great .... DELUGE, CATACLYSM
light .... KLIEG
tidal .... EAGRE
flooded condition ..... SPATE
floor .... PLANCH(E), KNOCK DOWN, STORY, PUZZLE, DALLE
above street floor .... ENTRESOL, MEZZANINE
chateau .... ETAGE
cover ..... RUG, CARPET, LINOLEUM, MAT(TING)
covering, fabric for ..... DRUGGET
raised border .. COAMING
floorcloth .... LINOLEUM
flooring chip/slab .... DALLE, TERRAZZO, PARQUET
floorleader .... WHIP
flop .... DROP, FALL, FAIL
colloquial ...... FAILURE
slang .... SLEEP
flora .... PLANTS
and fauna .... BIOTA
floral arrangement, art of .... IKEBANA
envelope ..... PERIANTH
leaf ...... SEPAL, BRACT
Florence .. FIRENZE, FIORENZA
Florentine friar ...... SERVITE
name .... MEDICI
painter .. CIMABUE, LIPPI, SARTO
florid .... ORNATE, FLOWERY, TAFFETA, RUDDY, ROSY, GAUDY, SHOWY
style .... ARABESQUE, ROCOCO
Florida bay .... TAMPA
bird .... LIMPKIN, COURLAN
cape .... SABLE
capital of .. TALLAHASSEE
city .... OCALA, NAPLES, TAMPA, ORLANDO, MIAMI, HIALEAH, PALATKA, LAKELAND
fish ...... TETARD, MERO, BONACI, PINTADO, CABRILLA, SALEMA
grouper .... BONACI
Indian .... SEMINOLE
perchlike fish .. CABRILLA
plant .... COONTIE
resort .... MIAMI, PALM BEACH
river .... S(U)WANEE
sapodilla .... BUSTIC
seaport ..... PENSACOLA, TAMPA
scenic road .... TAMIAMI
tortoise .... GOPHER
tree .... BUSTIC
wood oil .... TUNG
florist's specialty ... CORSAGE, BOUQUET
floss .... SLEAVE, SILK
flossy ...... FLUFFY, DOWNY, FANCY, ELEGANT, LA-DI-DA
flotage .... FLOTSAM
Flotow opera ...... MART(H)A
flotsam ... FLOTAGE, FLOATAGE
and jetsam ... VAGRANTS, DRIFTERS
flounce .... FALBALA, JERK, TWIST, RUFFLE, FURBELOW
flounder .. SOLE, DAB, TURBOT, FLUKE, PLAICE, WALLOW, WALLOP, TOSS, FLATFISH, HALIBUT
flour .... FARINA, DURUM, BUCKWHEAT
bean .... PINOLE
boiled, thick .. FLUMMERY
cereal .... FARINA
corn .... PINOLE
making product .... SEMOLINA
mixture .... PASTE, DOUGH, ROUX
pudding .... DUFF
sieve .... BOLTER
Spanish .... HARINA
flourish ..... BRANDISH, WAVE, ROULADE, TWIRL, PROSPER, FLAUNT, TANTARA, BOOM, SWING, THRIVE, FANFARE, SUCCEED
in an aria ..... CADENZA
in music .... ROULADE
in signature ..... PARAPH
in writing .... TAG
flout ..... MOCK, JEER, SCOFF, FLEER
flow ... RISE, FLUX, RUN, OOZE, SPOUT, ISSUE, WELL, STREAM, GLIDE, CURRENT
against/along ..... LAVE
and spread .... FLUSH
back ...... EBB, RECEDE, REGORGE
combining form .. RHEO
in drops .... DRIBBLE
of tide ...... EBB, FLUX, NEAP, RISE
out ...... POUR, EXUDE, ISSUE, SPILL, STREAM
stop ..... STANCH, STEM
that can .... FLUID
through .... SEEP
flower ...... BLOSSOM, BLOOM, MAGNOLIA
amaranth ..... PIGWEED
annual .... ASTER
arrangement .. VERTICIL, IKEBANA
aster ...... TANGLEFOOT
balsam ...... IMPATIENS
bell-shaped ... HYACINTH
bending downward ..... CERNUOUS
biennial ..... FOXGLOVE
bloom .... ANTHESIS
blue .... VIOLET, HYDRANGEA
bract .... PALEA
bud .... BULBIL, KNOT
buds for seasoning ...... CAPERS
butterfly-like .... MARIPOSA(LILY)
children, so-called ...... HIPPIES
cluster ... UMBEL, CYME, CORYMB, PANICLE, CAPITULUM, LILAC, TRUSS, THYRSUS, RACEME
cover of .... SPATHE
cormus ..... GLADIOLUS, CROCUS
covering .... CALYPTRA, SPATHE
cowslip ..... MARIGOLD, PRIMROSE
cup-shaped ..... CHALICE
daisy .... OX-EYE
Dutch .... TULIP
envelope ...... PERIANTH
erica .... HEATH
ericaceous ...... LAUREL, AZALEA
extract .... AT(T)AR
fadeless ..... AMARANTH, EVERLASTING
fall .... ASTER
field ..... DAISY, GOWAN
form of .... PELORIA
fragrant .... ROSE, HONEYSUCKLE, HYACINTH, AZALEA, LILAC, JASMIN(E), JESSAMINE
full bloomed .. ANTHESIS
garden .... ROSARY, GREENERY
genus ..... ROSA, HEATH
goddess .... FLORA
growing, art of .... HORTICULTURE
having only one .... MONANTHOUS

head .... PANICLE, CAPITULUM
heath .... AZALEA
honeysuckle .... ELDER, CLOVER
imaginary ... AMARANTH
iris ...... ORRIS, ORRICE
leaf ...... BRACT, PALEA, SEPAL, COROLLA
like .... ANTHOID
like animal .... ANEMONE
like ornament .. ROSETTE
lily .... LOTUS, SEGO, CALLA, MARIPOSA
marigold ...... COWSLIP
moon .... ACHETE
musk-odored .... MOSCHATEL
nightblooming .. CEREUS
nightshade ... HENBANE, BELLADONNA
of .... FLORAL
of forgetfulness .... LOTUS
orchid .... ARETHUSA, WALING-WALING
pansy .... HEARTSEASE
part ...... STEM, STYLE, POLLEN, ANTHER, BRACT, PISTIL, SEPAL, PETAL, OVULE, STAMEN, SPADIX, AMENT, CALYX, COROLLA, OVARY, STIGMA
perennial ...... DAHLIA, AMARANTH
petals .... COROLLA
pigweed ..... AMARANTH
pink .... TITI, RHODORA, ELDER, HYDRANGEA
pistil .... CARPEL
plot .... BED
pollen-bearing part ..... STAMEN
primrose ...... COWSLIP
receptacled ...... TORUS, THALAMUS
red .... MARIGOLD, CAMELLIA, OXALIS
rootstock .... TARO, ORRIS, ORRICE
rose of Sharon .. ALTHEA
seed .... OVULE
seed bearing part .. PISTIL
sex cells .... POLLEN
shaped .... FLEURON
small .... FLORET
spike ... SPICULE, SPICA, MIGNONETTE, AMENT, CATKIN
spring .... TULIP, HYACINTH
stalk .... PETIOLE, PEDUNCLE
stalk bud/bulb ... BULBIL
stand .... EPERGNE, JARDINIERE
sun prone .. HELIOTROPE
support ..... PEDUNCLE
symbol of luxury .... ORCHID
syringa .... LILAC
tanglefoot .... ASTER
the .... ELITE
three-petaled .... ORCHID
turban-like ...... TULIP
unfading .... AMARANTH, EVERLASTING
velvety .... PANSY
waterlily......... LOTUS
white ..... TITI, CROCUS, CAMELLIA, OXALIS, LILAC, GENTIAN, ELDER, HYDRANGEA, TRILLIUM
wild .... THISTLE
wind .... ANEMONE
windowbox .... PETUNIA
wood sorrel ..... OXALIS
yellow .... BENNET, GOWAN, MARIGOLD, COWSLIP

flowering grass .... STIPA
herb .... HEPATICA
more than once a season REMONTANT
plant ..... FERN, AVENS, ARUM, CANNA, YUCCA, POINSETTIA, LOBELIA, ROSE, VALERIAN, GERANIUM, SPIREA, LUPIN(E), ORCHID
shrub ... LILAC, SUMAC, AZALEA, SPIREA
vine .... WISTERIA

flowerless plant .... AGAMOUS, FERN, LICHEN, GENTIAN

flowers, bunch of ... BOUQUET, CORSAGE, POSY, NOSEGAY
in a spathe ...... SPADIX
of .... FLORAL
on woman's shoulder .... CORSAGE
sculptured ..... CORBEIL

flowery .... BOMBASTIC, FLAMBOYANT, ORNATE
girl .... ROSA

flowing ... (AF)FLUX, CURSIVE, EMANATING, FLUXION
and ebbing .... TIDAL
back .... REFLUX, REFLUENT
out .... EFFLUX
together ...... CONFLUX, CONFLUENCE

flown ..... EXCITED, FLUSHED

flu .... INFLUENZA
drug for .... SYMMETREL, AMANTADINE

flub .... ERROR, FAILURE

fluctuant .... VARYING, UNDULATING

fluctuate .... SWING, VEER, VARY

flue .... CHIMNEY, PIPE, FUNNEL, SHAFT, FLUKE, FLUFF
dust .... POTASH

fluency .... ELOQUENCE, GLIBNESS

fluent ... FACILE, EXPRESSIVE, ELOQUENT, GLIB

fluff ... ERROR, BONER, FLUE, DOWN, LINT, FLOSS, NAP

fluffy .... FLOSSY, LINTY, DOWNY, FEATHERY, FLOCCULENT

fluid .... SERUM, LIQUID, GAS, SAP, MOBILE, PLASTIC
aeriform .... GAS
body ...... LYMPH, BILE
colloidal system ..... SOL
life-saving ...... BLOOD
matter .... FLUX
rock .... LAVA

fluke ..... BARB, TREMATODE, CLEEK, HOOK, FLOUNDER, FLATFISH, (FLAT)WORM, FLUE

flume ..... CHANNEL, CHUTE, TROUGH, GORGE, RAVINE, SLUICE, SHUTE

flummery .... OATMEAL, CUSTARD, FLATTERY

flummox: sl. ...... CONFUSE, PERPLEX

flump .... DROP

flunk ..... GIVE UP, RETREAT, FAIL(URE)

flunk(e)y .... TOADY, YES-MAN, FOOTMAN

flunks at Annapolis ... BILGES

fluorite .... JADE

flurry .... STIR, HURRY, ADO, GUST, COMMOTION, CONFUSION, AGITATION

flush .... BLUSH, REDDEN, GLOW, EXCITE, LAVISH, PROFUSE, FULL, EMPTY, EXHILARATE
with water .... WASH

flushed .... RED, AGLOW, FLORID, RUDDY, HECTIC

fluster ..... POTHER, FUDDLE, CONFUSE, EXCITE, UNSETTLE, EMBARRASS

flute .... PIPE, GROOVE, PIPING, FIFE, PICCOLO
ancient .... HEMIOPE, TIBIA
bagpipe ...... CHANTER
Chinese .... (T)CHE
early form ... RECORDER
India .... MATALAN
like instrument .... FLAGEOLET
player .... TOOTLER, FL(A)UTIST
stop .... VENTAGE

fluted .... SULCATE

fluting .... GROOVE(S), GAUFFER, GOFFER
architectural .. GODROON, GADROON
wavelike .... STRIGIL

flutter .. WAVE(R), TREMBLE, QUIVER, PALPITATE, BUSTLE, HOVER, FLIP, FLICKER, FLIT, FLAP, VIBRATE, FLY
of eyes .... BLINK

flux ..... FLOW(ING), PURGE, SOLDER, ROSIN, BORAX, FUSE

fluxion .... FLOWING, DISCHARGE

fly ...... MUSCA, SOAR, SCUD, WING, FLEE, FLAP, AVIATE, FLIT, HOVER, FLUTTER, GNAT, MOSQUITO, MIDGE, WHIR, TACHINA

able to .... VOLANT, VOLITANT
African .... TSETSE
after game .... RAKE
agaric ..... MUSHROOM, AMANITA
amanita ..... MUSHROOM
artificial ... HARL, HERL, CAHILL, DUN, ZULU, HACKLE
at .... ATTACK
before the wind .... SCUD
block .... PULLEY
bloodsucking .. TABANID, GADFLY
case .... ELYTRON
catcher .. PEEWEE, PEWIT, PHOEBE, TODY
close to the ground ...... HEDGEHOP
experimental .... DROSOPHILA
hit .... SWAT
insect resembling .... CICADA
Latin .... MUSCA
let .... THROW
of the .... MUSCID
sheet .... PAMPHLET
slang ..... SHARP, AGILE, NIMBLE
small ..... MITE, PUNKIE
to and fro .... VOLITANT
wheel .... WHORL
wing cover ... ELYTRON, ELYTRUM

flyaway .... STREAMING, FLIGHTY, ESCAPEE
flyblow ... LARVA, SPOIL, TAINT
flycatcher .. PEWEE, KINGBIRD, PHOEBE, TODY, ALDER, CHEBEC, FANTAIL, PEWIT
flyer of myth .... ICARUS
flyer's stunt ..... LOOP, ROLL
flying .... VOLANT, VOLITANT
act of ...... VOLITATION
air mattress ... PARAFOIL
colors .... VICTORY, SUCCESS
Dutchman ..... SAILOR, SHIP
Dutchman maid ... SENTA
Finn .... NURMI
fish ... SAURY, GURNARD, GURNET
Fortress .... BOMBER
fox .... BAT, KALONG
gurnard .... GURNET
island, fictional .. LAPUTA
jib .... SAIL
lemur .... COLUGO
lizard's skin fold .... PARACHUTE, PATAGIUM
machine .... AERO, (AIR)PLANE, AIRCRAFT
marsupial ... PHALANGER
saucer, for short .... UFO
signal .... ROGER
spindrift .... SCUD
squirrel's skin fold ...... PATAGIUM
water .... SPRAY

Flynn, actor .... ERROL
flyspeck .... DOT, SPOT
flywheel .... WHORL, WHARVE
foal .... FILLY, COLT
foam ... SCUM, LATHER, YEAST, FROTH, SPUME, SUD(S), BUBBLE, FIZZ
of ..... SPUMY, SPUMOUS
poetic .... SEA
foaming .... NAPPY
foamy ..... SPUMOUS, FROTHY
yeast .... BARN
fob .... CHEAT, TRICK, (WATCH)POCKET, DECEIVE, PENDANT
off .... FOIST, PALM
focal point ...... EPICENTER, CYNOSURE, HUB
focus .... CONCENTRATE, SPOTLIGHT
in ..... CLEAR, DISTINCT
fodder .... BERSEEM, PROVENDER, SILAGE, OATS, GRASS, ALFALFA, VETCH, ALFILARIA, RAPE, CORNSTALK, HAY, STRAW, FORAGE, ALSIKE
bin .... CRATCH
grain .... KAFFIR
pertaining to .... FORAGE
pit .... SILO
plant .. GRAM, CHICKPEA, CLOVER, ALSIKE, ALFALFA, STOVER, SAINFOIN
preservation ... ENSILAGE
rack .... CRATCH
storage place ...... SILO
straw .... STOVER
tower .... SILO
tree pod .... CAROB
trough .... MANGER

foe .... ENEMY, RIVAL, ADVERSARY, OPPONENT
of shams ... ICONOCLAST
fog .... HAZE, BRUME, MURK, VAPOR, CONFUSE, MIST
and smoke ...... SMOG
fog(e)y .... MOSSBACK
fogeyish .... FUSTY
foggy ... CLOUDY, BRUMOUS, NUBILOUS, MISTY, MURKY, DIM, CONFUSED
foghorn .... SIREN(E)
foible .... FAULT, WEAKNESS, FRAILTY
opposed to ...... FORTE
foil .... BALK, STOOGE, BAFFLE, EPEE, FRUSTRATE, THWART, STUMP
comedian's .... STOOGE, STRAIGHTMAN
foilsman .... FENCER
foist .... PALM(OFF), FOB
Fokine, choreographer ...... MICHEL
fold ...... CRIMP, LAP, PLY, WRAP, CLASP, RUCK, REEF, RUGA, DRAPE, PLAIT, FLOCK, PLEAT, EMBRACE, FLEXURE, ENVELOP, CREASE, LAYER, PLICA(TION)
animal's throat .. DEWLAP
coat .... LAPEL
mark .... CREASE
sail .... REEF
sheep .... PEN
skin .... PLICA
slang .... FAIL
stitched .... TUCK
up .... FAIL, CLOSE, COLLAPSE

folded .... DOUBLED, PLEATED, PLICATE, RUGATE
folder .... PAMPHLET, BOOKLET, LEAFLET
folding bed .... COT
hood .... CALASH
leaves, plant with .... MIMOSA
foliage ..... LEAVES, LEAFAGE, UMBRAGE
mass of .... SPRAY, BOUQUET
folio ... PAGE, BOOK, NUMBER
foliose .... LEAFY
folium .... LOOP
folk .... PEOPLE, RACE, NATION, TRIBE, PERSONS, KOLO
dance .... HORA, MORRIS, DREHER
tale .... MARCHEN
tale tiny hero .... TOM THUMB
folklore .... LEGEND, BELIEFS, SAYINGS
character .... OGRE, DWARF, FAIRY, TROLL, GIANT, SANDMAN
folksinger .... IVES, BAEZ
folksong .... LULLABY
folkways .... MORES
follicle .... SAC, CAVITY, GLAND, POD, CAPSULE, COCOON
follies .... REVUE
follow ... HEED, ENSUE, CHASE, PURSUE, TAG, ATTEND, ACCOMPANY, IMITATE, RESULT, OBEY, TRAIL, TAIL, TRACK
continually .... DOG, HOUND
stealthily .... TAIL, SHADOW, STAG
follower .... PARTISAN, VOTARY, HENCHMAN, IST, ITE, BUFF, ADHERENT, FAN, MINION, SUPPORTER, DISCIPLE, SERVITOR
faithful .... FRIDAY, MYRMIDON
kind of .... SERVANT, ATTENDANT, SATELLITE, HANGER-ON
followers, group of ..... CULT
following .... TRADE, EQUIPAGE, ENSUING, RETINUE, SECT, AFTER
this .... HEREAFTER, HENCEFORTH
folly .... FOOLISHNESS, FATUITY, LUNACY
foment ..... BREW, AROUSE,

INSTIGATE, INCITE, ABET, SPUR
fond .... ATTACHED, TENDER, LOVING, AFFECTIONATE, DOTING
of arguing .. DISPUTATIVE
of fighting .. COMBATIVE, PUGNACIOUS
of, foolishly ... UXORIOUS, DOTING
of luxury, etc. .... EPICUREAN
fondant .... CANDY
fondle ... COSSET, PET, CARESS, STROKE, DANDLE
fondling .... PET, FOOL, NINNY, SIMPLETON
fondness ..... TASTE, LIKING, PENCHANT, FLAIR
font .... BOWL, BASIN, FOUNTAIN, SPRING, ORIGIN, LAVER, STOUP, SOURCE, STOOP
rite .... BAPTISM
fontal .... ORIGINAL, BAPTISMAL
fontanel(le) .... OPENING, OUTLET
food .... NOURISHMENT, NUTRIMENT, ALIMENT, FARE, VICTUAL, PABALUM, DIET, VIAND, MESS, REFECTION, COMESTIBLE, TABLE, BOARD, PEMMICAN
allowance ..... CORODY, RATION
and shelter ...... KEEP, BOARD
animal .... FORAGE, FODDER
being digested ... CHYME
between meals ... SNACK
bits .... SCRAPS, ORTS
cereal ..... OAT, WHEAT, RICE, CORN
chewed, solid ... BROMA
choice: archaic .... CATE
colloquial ...... CHOW, GRUB, EATS
dealer .... GROCER
desire for ...... HUNGER
diet ..... REGIMEN, FARE
disk-shaped ..... PATTY
drying platform ... FLAKE
fancy .... KICKSAW
fish ...... TROUT, SHAD, BASS, SALMON, SARDINE, SCROD, TUNA, CERO, COD, MACKEREL, PERCH
from heaven .... MANNA
Hawaiian .... POI
liquid .... SLOP, BROTH, SOUP
look for ..... SCAVENGE
Maori .... KAI
need for .... HUNGER
non-flesh .... MAIGRE
of the gods ... AMBROSIA, AMRITA
place for .... LARDER, PANTRY, SPENCE, SPENSE, CUPBOARD
plant ..... TARO, MANIOC, CASSAVA
poisoning .... BOTULISM, PTOMAIN(E)
provider .... CATERER
rack .... FLAKE
regimen .... DIET
scrap .... ORT
served .... HELPING
shavings .... CHIPS
shop ..... DELICATESSEN
slang ...... CHOW, EATS, GRUB, CHUCK
slices .... CHIPS
soft .... PAP, FLUMMERY
solid in medicine .. BROMA
spoiler ... YEAST, MOLD, ENZYME, BACTERIA
stock of ..... PROVISIONS, VICTUAL
supplier .... CATERER
supply place .... LARDER
foods, study of ... SITOLOGY, DIETETICS
fool .... IDIOT, CLOWN, SIMP, OAF, DUPE, ZANY, DOTARD, DUNCE, NINNY, JAPE, SAP(HEAD), GABY, SIMPLETON, CHUMP, BOOB, JESTER, DECEIVE, TRICK, ASS, DOLT, MUGGINS, MOONCALF, NOODLE, NODDY
around .... TRIFLE
hen .... GROUSE
play the .... CLOWN
professional ..... JESTER
foolhardy .. ICARIAN, DARING, BOLD, RASH, RECKLESS, BRASH
person ..... DAREDEVIL
foolish .... SILLY, BALMY, ANSERINE, SAPPY, ABSURD, RIDICULOUS, UNWISE, DAFT, ASININE, IMPRUDENT, INANE, PUERILE, SILAGE, ZANY, LUNATIC, CUCKOO
action ... (TOM)FOOLERY, FOLLY
affection .... DOTAGE
blunder .... HOWLER
fancy .... CHIMERA
from overdrinking ...... SCOTTISH
from old age ... DOITED, SENILE
talk ...... FLAPDOODLE, BABBLE, CHATTER
undertaking ..... FOLLY
foolishly loving .... FOND
foolishness .... FOLLY, NONSENSE, FATUITY, LUNACY
fool's bauble ...... MAROTTE
gold .... PYRITE
foot ... HOOF, BASE, BOTTOM, WALK, TREAD
animal ...... PAW, PAD
and-mouth disease ...... MURRAIN
child's .... TOOTSY
colloquial ..... PAY, PEG
combining form .. PED(I), PED(E), POD(E)
deformity ...... TALIPES
disease ...... PODAGRA, GOUT
disorders, specialist in ... PODIATRIST
lever ... PEDAL, TREADLE
like part .... PES
loose .... FREE, WANDERING
of 4 syllables .... TETRABRACH
on .... STANDING
part ... INCH, SOLE, SHIN, ARCH, TOE
pedal .... TREADLE
pertaining to a .... PEDAL
poetic .... ANAPEST, IAMB(IC), SPONDEE, DACTYL
prefix .... PED
race ...... STEEPLECHASE
shaped .... PEDIFORM
soldier ... INFANTRYMAN, KERN(E)
soldier's coat ..... JACK
sole of .... VOLAR, THENAR, PLANTAR
sore .... CHILBLAIN
study of ...... PODIATRY
swelling .... BUNION
three-syllable ... ANAPEST
traveler .... HIKER, TRAMP, PEDESTRIAN
with .... PEDATE
woman's .... TOOTSY
football ...... ELEVEN, RUGBY
association ..... SOCCER
colloquial ..... PIGSKIN
conference ..... BIG TEN
field .... GRID(IRON)
name in .... ROCKNE, STAGG, THORPE
official ...... LINEMAN
player .... UNITAS, NAMATH, BLANDA, GABRIEL, OJ, TITTLE
position .... END, GUARD, TACKLE, CENTER, KICKER
score ...... TOUCHDOWN
slang .... GRID
team .... JETS, RAMS, DOLPHINS, CHIEFS, COLTS, PACKERS, BROWNS, COWBOYS, VIKINGS
term .... PUNT, PASS, CUTBACK, HUDDLE
footboy .... PAGE
footcloth ..... RUG, CARPET
footed, large ...... MEGAPOD
single .... MONOPODE
footfall .... TREAD, STEP
foothold, for example .... BEACHHEAD, LODG(E)MENT
footing ...... BASIS, POSITION, FOOTHOLD, TOEHOLD
footless .... APOD(AL)
footlights .... THEATER, STAGE, KLIEG, FLOAT(S)
footlike .... PEDATE
footloose ..... FREE, ROVING
footman .... FLUNK(E)Y, LACKEY, PEON

footnote .... COMMENTARY, REFERENCE, APOSTIL, ANNOTATION
marker ...... ASTERISK, OBELUS
footpad .... HIGHWAYMAN, ROBBER, HOLDUPPER, THUG, BRIGAND, BANDIT
footprint .... CLUE, PAD, STEP, TRACK, TREAD, PUG
animal .... PUG
combining form .. ICHNO
mold ... MOULAGE, CAST
study of .... ICHNOLOGY
footrest .... STOOL, OTTOMAN
foots ...... DREGS, SEDIMENT
footstalk ... SHANK, PEDICEL
footstep sound ... PAD, CLUM
footstool .... OTTOMAN, CRICKET, HASSOCK
footway .... SIDEWALK, PATH
ship .... CATWALK
footwear ..... SHOES, SPATS, SABOTS, RUBBERS, CLOGS, SKATES, BOOTS, SLIPPERS
foozle .... BUNGLE
fop .... DUDE, DANDY, COXCOMB, POPINJAY, JOHNNIE, JOHNNY
foppish ... BUCKISH, LADIDA, LADEDA
for .... PRO, IN FAVOR
aye ...... ALWAYS, EVER
each .... PER, EVERY
example ...... VIDE, E.G.
fear that .... LEST
shame .... FIE
the most part ... MAINLY, LARGELY
the time being .... PRO TEM, NONCE, MEANWHILE
this reason ...... HENCE, THEREFORE
forage .... FOOD, PROG, FODDER, FEED, RAVAGE, PLUNDER, MARAUD
crop ... MILO, SORGHUM
plant .... ALFALFA, LUCERN(E), ALSIKE, GUAR
foramen ...... OPENING, PORE, MEATUS
foray .... RAID, MARAUD, INROAD, PILLAGE, PLUNDER
forbear .. ANCESTOR, ABSTAIN, PARENT, ENDURE, TOLERATE, AVOID, REFRAIN
forbearance ..... RESTRAINT, PATIENCE, TOLERANCE
forbearing .... TOLERANT, PATIENT
forbears, of ..... ANCESTRAL, AVITAL
Forbes, novelist ...... ESTHER
forbid .... TABOO, STOP, BAN, INHIBIT, PREVENT, INTERDICT, ENJOIN, PROSCRIBE, PROHIBIT, VETO
forbidden ..... TABU, TABOO, BANNED, VERBOTEN
city .... LHASA, LASSA
fruit .... APPLE
forbidding ...... STERN, GRIM, UGLY, REPELLANT, DISAGREEABLE
force .... DURESS, ODYL, COMPEL, DINT, STRAIN, COERCE, CONSTRAIN, IMPEL, DRIVE, IMPETUS, STRENGTH, POWER, VIGOR, ENERGY, BIRR, VIS, SINEW
armed .... POSSE
back ... REPEL, REPULSE
by .... AMAIN
colloquial .... STEAM
down ... DETRUDE, RAM
driving ..... MAINSPRING
hypothetical .... OD, ODYLE, OG, ELOD
into service .... LEVY, COMMANDEER, DRAFT, CONSCRIPT
Latin .... VIS
military ... ARMY, NAVY
of blow .. IMPACT, BRUNT
of expression/feeling .... EMPHASIS
one's way in .... MUSCLE
out .... EXCLUDE, OUST, ROUT, EJECT, EVICT, EXPEL
rotating .... TORQUE
side of .... FLANK
unit of .... DYNE
forced .... COMPULSORY
journey .... FLIGHT, HEGIRA
labor .... CORVEE
forceful .. COGENT, EFFECTIVE, VIGOROUS, STRONG, ENERGETIC, STOUT
forceps ..... TONGS, PINCERS, NIPPER
forcible .... VIOLENT
ford .... CROSS, WADE
fore, opposite of .... AFT
forearm bone .... ULNA
forebode .... PREDICT, PORTEND, FORETELL
foreboding ... AUGURY, DARK, OMINOUS, OMEN PRESENTIMENT, PORTENT
forecast ... FORESEE, PREDICT, PROPHESY, PROGNOSIS, PREVISE
forecaster ... SEER, DOPESTER
racetrack ...... TIPSTER, TOUT
forefather ..... PROGENITOR, ANCESTOR
forefinger ... INDEX, POINTER
forefoot .... PAW
part of .... MANUS
forefront ...... VAN(GUARD), FOREMOST
forego ...... WAIVE, ABSTAIN
foregoing .... ABOVE, PRECEDING, PREVIOUS
forehead ... SINCIPUT, BROW
animal/bird ... FRONTLET
bone .... FRONTAL
hairy point .... WIDOW'S PEAK
of the .... METOPIC
foreign ... OVERSEAS, EXOTIC, ALIEN, PEREGRINE, ECDEMIC, STRANGE
bill period of payment ... USANCE
exchange .... VALUTA
exchange dealer .... CAMBIST
lands .... OUTREMER
mission ...... LEGATION, EMBASSY
opposed to .... DOMESTIC
origin .... EXOTIC
quarter ... ENCLAVE, PERA
trade discount ..... AGIO
foreigner .... ALIEN, OUTLANDER, TRAMONTANE, OUTSIDER, STRANGER
in Japan .... GAIJIN
in South Africa .... UITLANDER
foreknowledge ... PRESCIENCE
foreland .... CAPE
forelimb part .... MANUS
forelock .... COTTER PIN, LINCHPIN
foreman .... GAFFER
foremost .... FIRST, PREMIER, LEADING, CHIEF
part ... VAN, FRONT, BOW
forenoon .... MORNING
foreordain ..... (PRE)DESTINE
forerun .. PRECEDE, ANTECEDE, FORESHADOW, HERALD
forerunner .... HERALD, PROGNOSTIC, ANCESTOR, PREDECESSOR, HARBINGER, PRECURSOR
foreshadow .... ADUMBRATE, PRESAGE, PREFIGURE
foresight .... VISION
foreskin .... PREPUCE
forest ... WOODLAND, WOODS, WEALD
clearing .... GLADE
cutting right in the ..... VERT
debris .... SLASH
decaying matter ... DUFF
deity ..... NYMPH, FAUN, PAN
fire locator .... ALIDADE
floor layer .... LITTER
glade .... CLEARING
green growth ..... VERT
humus .... MOR
keeper .... RANGER
kind of .... PINERY
of the .... SYLVAN
open space ...... SLASH, CLEARING, GLADE
outlying part ... PURLIEU
ox .... ANOA
pertaining to ... SYLVAN
Philippine .... GUBAT
soil .... PODZOL
trees of certain area ..... SILVA
trees, the .... SYLVA
warden .... RANGER
forestall .... ANTICIPATE, PREVENT, AVERT
Forester's opera ...... LORLE
forests, coniferous .... TAIGA

foretell .... PREDICT, FORECAST, PROPHESY, AUGUR, VATICINATE, PROGNOSTICATE, PRESAGE, (FORE)BODE
foretoken .... OMEN, PROGNOSTIC, AUGURY
foretooth .... INCISOR
forever ... ETERN(E), ALWAYS, ETERNALLY, AY(E)
forewarning .... AUGURY, OMEN, PORTENT
foreword .... PREFACE, INTRODUCTION, FRONTISPIECE
Forfar .... ANGUS
forfeit .... FINE, PENALTY, GIVE, DEFAULT, LOSE
for pious purpose .... DEODAND
forfeiture .... FINE, PENALTY, LOSS
of right for cause .. LAPSE
for(e)gather ...... ASSEMBLE, MEET, ENCOUNTER
forge .... BLOOMERY, STITHY, IMITATE, SMITHY, FURNACE, FORM, COUNTERFEIT, SHAPE, FALSIFY
apparatus ...... TROMPE
fireplace of .... HEARTH
forget ..... LAPSE, OVERLOOK, NEGLECT
me-not ..... MOUSE-EAR, PLANT, MYOSOTIS
forgetful one ..... AMNESIAC, LOTUS-EATER, PROF(ESSOR)
forgetfulness ..... OBLIVION, AMNESIA
drug .... NEPENTHE
fruit of .... LOTUS
river of .... LETHE
forgive ...... EXCUSE, REMIT, PARDON, OVERLOOK, ABSOLVE
forgiving .... PLACABLE
forgo .. ABSTAIN, DO WITHOUT, WAIVE
fork .... BISECT, (BI)FURCATE, PRONG, TINE, BIGHT, BRANCH
forked .... CLEFT, PRONGED, ZIGZAG, FURCATE, BIFID
organ/part ... FURCULUM
forlorn .... DESERTED, MISERABLE, WRETCHED, BEREFT
form .... CAST, BLANK, CONTOUR, MOLD, FIGURE, PATTERN, RITUAL, FORMALITY, SHAPE, OUTLINE, ORGANIZE, CEREMONY, FASHION, CREATE
into fabric ...... WEAVE, KNIT
of bust .... TAILLE
of government ... POLITY
of obeisance .... BOW, SALAAM, GENUFLECTION, KOWTOW
oval .... OVOID
take .... MATERIALIZE
formal .... CEREMONIOUS, PRIM, STIFF, METHODICAL, FRIGID
artificially ...... STILTED
ceremony .... FUNCTION, RITE
choice .... VOTE
dance .... BALL
entrance .... DEBUT
march .... PROCESSION
talk ... ADDRESS, LECTURE
formality .... CEREMONY, PROPRIETY
formation .... ARRANGEMENT, ORDER
battle ... HERSE, PHALANX
military .... ECHELON
panlike .... PATELLA
side of .... FLANK
formative ending of word ..... DESINENCE
formed on earth's surface ..... EPIGENE
former .... QUONDAM, ERST(WHILE), EX, ONE-TIME, WHILOM, EARLIER, PREVIOUS
days/times .... PAST, YORE, AGO, ELD
emperor .... KAISER, TSAR, CZAR
opposed to ...... LATTER
formerly ...... ERST(WHILE), NEE, ONCE, ONE-TIME, WHILOM
prefix .... EX
formic acid source .... ANT
formicary .... ANTHILL
formicid .... ANT
formidable .... MEAN, DREADFUL, DIFFICULT, AWESOME, FEARFUL
formless .... AMORPHOUS, ARUPA
void .... CHAOS
Formosa .... TAIWAN
capital .... TAIPEI
strait port .... AMOY
tea .... OOLONG
formula ..... CREED, RECIPE, SOLUTION, PRESCRIPTION
fornent .... FACING, OPPOSITE
forsake ... ABANDON, DESERT, RENOUNCE, LEAVE
forsaken ... LORN, DESOLATE, LEFT
forsooth ... INDEED, NO DOUBT
forswear ... RENOUNCE, DENY, PERJURE
fort ..... KEEP, (ARMY)POST, COTTA, CITADEL, GARRISON, PRESIDIO
coastal .... MARTELLO
of Moros .... COTTA
small .... FORTALICE, SCONCE
U.S. ... DIX, DONELSON, DUQUESNE, (MC)HENRY, SUMTER, ORD
wall .... PARAPET
wooden ... BLOCKHOUSE
Fortaleza .... CEARA
forte .... SPECIALTY, STRONG POINT, LOUD
opposed to ...... FOIBLE
forth .... ONWARD, OUT, FORWARD
forthright .... DIRECT, FRANK
forthwith ... EFTSOON, ANON, AT ONCE, IMMEDIATELY, NOW
fortification .... EARTHWORK, REDAN, OUTWORK, STRONGHOLD, FORTRESS, ABAT(T)IS, PALISADE, BAIL, BASTION, RAVELIN, REDOUBT, BULWARK, FORT
ditch/moat ..... FOSS(E)
material .... GABION
outwork .... TENAIL(LE), FLECHE, DEMILUNE
part of .... PARAPET, RAMPART, EMBRASURE, BATTLEMENT, BREASTWORK, BAIL
sloping embankment .... GLACIS, SCARP
wall .... TALUS
fortified .... ARMED, STRENGTHENED
hill .... MERLIN
house .... PEEL
line .... MAGINOT, SIEGFRIED, WESTWALL
place .... FORTRESS, CASTLE, PILLBOX, CITADEL, REDAN, GARRISON, PRESIDIO
rampart ..... BULWARK
tower .... DONJON, DUNGEON, PEEL
town .... BURG
fortify .... ARM, MAN, STRENGTHEN
fortis .... SPEECH SOUND
opposed to .... LENIS
fortitude .... ENDURANCE, PATIENCE, GRIT, GUTS, PLUCK, COURAGE
fortnight .... TWO WEEKS
fortnightly ...... PERIODICAL
fortress .... GIBRALTAR, CITADEL, FORT, BASTILLE, STRONGHOLD
flying .... SUPERFORT
impregnable, so-called ... GIBRALTAR, CORREGIDOR, SINGAPORE
mobile .... TANK
fortuitous ..... (BY)CHANCE, ACCIDENTAL
Fortuna, Roman ...... TYCHE
fortunate .... FAVORABLE, BLESSED, HAPPY, LUCKY, AUSPICIOUS
fortunately .... HAPLY, HAPPILY
fortune ..... RICHES, CHANCE, STARS, LUCK, LOT, FATE, WEALTH
hunter ..... ADVENTURER
hunter's prize ..... HEIR
slang .... PILE
teller ..... ORACLE, SEER, GYPSY, PALMIST,

AUGUR, SIBIL, SIBYL, HARUSPEX
teller's cards ...... TAROT
telling .... TAROT
forty days fast .... CARENE, LENT
five degree angle .... OCTANT
inches .... ELL
niner .... MINER, ARGONAUT
rods .... FURLONG
winks ... DOZE, (CAT)NAP
winks of Spaniard ...... SIESTA
forum .... ASSEMBLY, (LAW)COURT, MARKET(PLACE), SQUARE
forward ... PERT, PRECOCIOUS, FRONT, AHEAD, EAGER, ADVANCE(D), EARLY, TRANSMIT, BOLD, DISPATCH, SEND
part ...... FORE, FRONT, BOW, ANTERIOR
fossa .. PIT, HOLLOW, CAVITY
fosse .... DITCH, MOAT
fossette .... DIMPLE, HOLLOW
fossil .... ROCK, MINERAL, ANTIQUATED, PINITE
crinoid .... CRINITE
mollusk .... DOLITE
plants .... CALAMITE
resin ... AMBER, RETINITE
fossilize .... PETRIFY
foster .... REAR, SUCKLE, NOURISH, PROMOTE, CHERISH
child .... STEPSON, FOUNDLING, FOSTERLING
songwriter ..... STEPHEN
foul ... FECULENT, STINKING, LOATHSOME, PUTRID, ROTTEN, OBSCENE, INDECENT, UNFAIR, ENTANGLE, UNCLEAN, SQUALID
dirt .... FILTH
smelling .... FETID, OLID, NOISOME, ROTTEN
smelling fruit ... DURIAN
smelling plant .. HENBANE
up ... BUNGLE, ENTANGLE
foulard .... (NECK)TIE, SCARF
foumart .... POLECAT
found ...... BASE, ESTABLISH, CAST
on earth's surface .... EPIGENE
thing .. TROVE, DISCOVERY
foundation .... CORSET, BASIS, BASE, ENDOWMENT, FUND, BED(ROCK), RIPRAP
garment .... CORSET, GIRDLE
founded .... FUSIL
abbreviation .... ESTAB, EST
founder ...... STUMBLE, FALL, FAIL, COLLAPSE, LAMINITIS, CASTER
foundling ...... WAIF, EPPIE
place for .... CRECHE
foundry .... CASTING(S)
fount .... SOURCE, SPRING, WELL
fountain ...... WELL, SPRING, FONT, SOURCE
drink .... SODA, POP
drinking ...... BUBBLER
Mt. Helicon .... HIPPOCRENE
nymph .... EGERIA, NAIAD
of youth .... BIMINI
poetic .... FONT
fountainpen .... STYLOGRAPH
tube .... BARREL
four-bagger ..... HOMER(UN)
combining form ... TETRA
dollar gold piece .. STELLA
flush ...... BLUFF, BRAG
footed .... TETRAPOD, QUADRUPED
group of ..... TETRAD, H-CLUB
H club's concern .... HEART, HANDS, HEAD, HEALTH
hundred, the ..... ELITE
in hand item ..... ASCOT, TEAM, COACH, NECKTIE
inch measure ..... HAND
o'clock, the .... MARVEL-OF-PERU, PLANT
pecks .... BUSHEL
poster ...... BED(STEAD)
set of .... TETRAD
fourchette .... WISHBONE
fourflusher .... BLUFFER, PHONY, HUMBUG, BRAGGART
game of a .... POKER
fourfold .... QUADRUPLE
fourgon .... WAGON, CAR, TUMBRIL, VAN
fourpence ..... GROAT, COIN
fourscore .... EIGHTY
foursome .... QUARTET
gathering place of ... TEE
foursquare ..... FIRM, FRANK
14 days .... FORTNIGHT
pounds .... STONE
1492 ship .... NINA, PINTA
fourth .... QUARTER
dimension .... TIME
estate .... PRESS
foussa .... CIVET
fouter .... FIG
foveola .... VARIOLE
fowl .... PHEASANT, TURKEY, COCK, HEN, CHICKEN, GOOSE, DUCK
castrated .... CAPON
comb of .... CARUNCLE
dealer .... POULT(ER)
disease .... PIP
dish stewed in wine ..... SALMI(S)
domestic ..... DORKING, LEGHORN, MINORCA, COCHIN, POULTRY
flesh below beak .... WATTLE
forelimb .... WING
leg joint .... HOCK
meat, broiled .... CARBONADO
outgrowth ..... WATTLE, JOWL, SPUR
small .... BANTAM
stuffing for .... FARCE
table .... CAPON
wattle .... JOWL
young .... POULT
fowling piece .... GUN
fowls, domestic .... POULTRY
fox .... TOD, RE(Y)NARD
African .... CAAMA, ASSE, FENNEC
face of .... MASK
female ..... VIXEN, BITCH
flying .... KALONG
head of .... MASK
hunter .... PINK
hunter's coat ..... PINK
hunter's cry ... TALLYHO
killer .... VULPECIDE
like .... VULPINE, VULPECULAR
male .... DOG
tail .... BRUSH
terrier .... WIREHAIR
terrier, RCA's ... NIPPER
young .... CUB
foxglove .. DIGITALIS, FIGWORT
foxtail .... GRASS
foxy ... CUNNING, CUTE, SLY, CRAFTY, SOUR, VULPINE
foy .... FEAST, PRESENT
foyer ..... VESTIBULE, LOBBY
fra ... MONK, BROTHER, ABBE
title of .... MONK, FRIAR
fracas ..... BRAWL, QUARREL, MELEE, RUMBLE
fraction .... FRAGMENT, DECIMAL, SCRAP, PART
fractious ..... UNRULY, CROSS, PEEVISH, FRETFUL
fracture ..... BREAK, CRACK, SPLIT
fragile .... FRAIL, BRASH, FINESPUN, FLIMSY, TENDER, DELICATE, FRANGIBLE, WEAK, BRITTLE
fragment ... PIECE, PART, BIT, FLINDER, MORCEAU, SHRED, FRACTION, CHIP, SIPPET, SHIVER
cloth ..... RAG, TATTER
pottery ... SHARD, SHERD
fragrance .... SCENT, AROMA, INCENSE, ODOR
of wine/brandy .... BOUQUET
fragrances: rare .... AROMATA
fragrant .... REDOLENT, ODOROUS, BALMY, OLENT, AROMATIC, SWEET, SPICY
bark .... CANELLA
flower ... ROSE, JASMINE, LILAC
gum resin .... MYRRH
oil ..... BALSAM, ATTAR
ointment ... (SPIKE)NARD
plant .... PINESAP, LAVENDER

rootstock .... ORRIS
seed .... ANISE, DILL, ANISEED
shrub .... TIARA
wood .... CEDAR
frail .... DELICATE, WEAK, BASKET, FLIMSY, SLIGHT, FEEBLE, FRAGILE, SLENDER, TENDER
slang ..... GIRL, WOMAN
frailty .... WEAKNESS, FAILING, FAULT, DEFECT
fraise .... RUFF, COLLAR
framb(o)esia .... YAWS
frame ...... DEVISE, COMPOSE, RACK, SHAPE, FORM, FASHION, DESIGN, CONSTRUCT
automobile ..... CHASSIS
bobbins' .... CREEL
body .... BUILD
building's boarding ..... SIDING
carriage .... CHASSIS
cloth-stretching .. TENTER
counting .... ABACUS
display .... EASEL
drying .... HERSE, RACK, TENTER
for embroidery .... TABO(U)RET
for feeding animals ...... HAYRACK
for holding things .. RACK
in baseball ..... INNING
of mind .... MOOD, MORALE, TEMPER
of ship .... HULL
openwork .... CAGE
set with spikes .... HERSE, PORTCULLIS
soap bar .... SESS
stand ..... RACK, EASEL
spiked .... HERSE
supporting ..... TRESTLE
torch .... CRESSET
framework ... FABRIC, SHELL, TRUSS, CADRE
bridge support ... TRUSS
for carrying person ..... LITTER
for traveling crane ...... GANTRY
of animal body .... SKELETON
of rods, sticks, etc. .... WATTLE
on which to dry skins .... HERSE
over oil well .... DERRICK
roof support ..... TRUSS
franc, 1/100 of ...... CENTIME
France (see French) .. GALLIA, GAUL
novelist ...... ANATOLE
Southern .... MIDI
symbol of .... COCK
franchise ..... RIGHT, LICENSE, CHARTER, SUFFRAGE, PRIVILEGE, SOC
Franciscan .... MINORITE, FRIAR, CAPUCHIN
friar .... MINORITE
mission .... ALAMO
Franck, composer .... CESAR
Franco (dictator) title .... (EL) CAUDILLO
francolin .... TITAR, PARTRIDGE
francs, 20 .... LOUIS
frangible .... BREAKABLE, FRAGILE
frangipani .... JASMIN(E)
neckwear .... LEI
frank .... BLUNT, OPEN, CANDID, PLAIN, EXEMPT, OUTSPOKEN, HONEST, RIPUARIAN
Frankenstein novel authoress .. SHELLEY
frankfurter .... SAUSAGE, WIENER, WEENIE, HOTDOG, WEENY
jurist .... FELIX
frankincense ..... OLIBANUM, GUM RESIN
Frankish king .... CLOVIS
law .... SALIC
peasant .... LITUS
franklin .... FREEHOLDER
frankness .... CANDOR, CANDIDNESS
Franks, ruler of ...... PEPIN, MARTEL
frantic .... FRENZIED, EXCITED, FRENETIC, FURIOUS
make ... PANIC, FRENZY, MADDEN
person .... FRENETIC
frap .... TIGHTEN
frappe .... DESSERT, ICED, DRINK
frater .... FRIAR, BROTHER, COMRADE
fraternity ..... BROTHERHOOD
local .... CHAPTER
meeting place .... LODGE
to-do .. RUSH, INITIATION
fraternize .... ASSOCIATE
frau .... WIFE
fraud ..... DECEIT, DECEPTION, JAPE, IMPOSTOR, IMPOSTURE, HOAX, TRICK(ERY), ARTIFICE, SHAM, BUNCO, HUMBUG
conspiracy to commit ... COVIN
fraudulent ... FAKE, DECEITFUL
fraught .... FILLED, BESET, CHARGED, LOADED, LADEN
fraxinella .... DITTANY
fray ...... FIGHT, CONFLICT, FRAZZLE, RAVEL, RAG, MELEE, BRAWL, RUMBLE
fraying, cord to stop .... MARLINE, MARLING
frazzle .... FRAY, SHRED
freak ..... CAPRICE, DAPPLE, WHIM, MONSTROSITY, QUEER, ABNORMAL, STREAK, FLECK, ATROCITY
of nature .. SIAMESE TWIN, HUNCHBACK, BEARDED LADY
freckle .... LENTIGO
Frederick I of Germany ...... BARBAROSSA
the Great's palace ...... SANS SOUCI
free .... ABSOLVE, LOOSE, GRATIS, CLEAR, OPEN, DISENGAGE, LIBERATE, LIBRE, RID, MANUMIT, RELEASE, FOOTLOOSE, EMANCIPATE, AT LARGE
and easy ..... INFORMAL
for-all ..... MELEE, FRAY, BRAWL, RHUBARB, CLEM, RUMBLE, BATTLE ROYAL
from infection .. ASEPTIC
lance .... MERCENARY
speech restraint .... GAG
swimming organism ..... PROTOZOA
ticket .... PASS
ticket holder .. DEADHEAD
freebooter .... CATERAN, PIRATE, FILIBUSTER, BUCCANEER, PLUNDERER
freedman .. TIRO, LAET, THANE
freedom .... LIBERTY, EXEMPTION, INDEPENDENCE, FRANCHISE, LICENSE
from doubt .. CERTITUDE, CERTAINTY
from punishment .... IMMUNITY, IMPUNITY
kind of .... LICENSE
to enter .... ENTRY
freehanded ...... GENEROUS
freehold ..... ESTATE, OFFICE
freeholder .... YEOMAN, FRANKLIN
freeman .... CITIZEN, CHURL, THANE, CEORL, VILLEIN, BURGESS
actress .... MONA
freemen's assembly ..... MOOT
freestone ...... PLUM, PEACH
freethinker .... ATHEIST, LIBERTINE
freewill .... VOLUNTARY
freeze .. ICE, CONGEAL, CHILL, GELATE, NIP
freezer .... REFRIGERATOR
freight .... CARGO, LADING
boat ...... SCOW, BARGE
car dumping apparatus .. TIPPLE
steamer ... WHALEBACK
surcharge ..... PRIMAGE
train car .... CABOOSE
freighter ... TANKER, SHIPPER, LIGHTER, TRAMP
fremd .... FOREIGN, STRANGE, ALIEN
fremitus .... VIBRATION
French .... GALLIC
abbe .... ABBOT
according to .... A LA
actor ...... FERNANDEL, CHEVALIER, BOYER
administrative department INTENDANCE
afoot .... A PIED
African lake .... (T)CHAD
after .... APRES

again .... ENCORE
airplane ... SPAD, AVION
airship .... AERONAT
Algerian soldier .. TURCO
all .... TOUT(E)
Alp top .... PIC
Alpine sight ... ADROITE
among .... ENTRE
angel .... ANGE
annual income ... RENTE
anxiety .... SOUCI
aperitif .... PERNOD
April .... AVRIL
architectural ornament .. OVE
arm .... BRAS
army sharpshooter ...... TIRAILLEUR
art center ..... BARBIZON
art show .... SALON
article ...... LA, LE, DES, LES, UN(E), UNES, DE
artist ... MONET, MATISSE, CHAGALL, DORE, DERAIN, DEGAS, COROT, RENOIR, MANET
astronomer ... LAGRANGE
aunt .... TANTE
author ... CAMUS, ZOLA, GIDE, COCTEAU, STAEL, FRANCE, RENAN, DUMAS, HUGO, VERNE, SARTRE, LOTI
awl .... ALENE
axe .... HACHE
baby .... ENFANT
back .... DOS
bacteriologist ... PASTEUR
ballet member .. DANSEUR
banner .... FANION
basis .... FOND
bath .... BAIN
beach .... PLAGE, RIVAGE
bean ..... FEVE, PHASEL, HARICOT
beast .... BETE
beauty .... NINON
bed .... LIT, COUCHE
beef .... BOEUF
behold .... VOILA
being .... ETRE
Belgian river ...... YSER
bench .... BANC
between .... ENTRE
bicycle .... VELO
biologist .... CARREL
bitter ...... AMER, ACRE
black .... NOIR(E)
blessed .... SACRE
blue .... BLEU
"Bluebeard" .... LANDRU
boarding house/school .. PENSION
bodice .... GILET
bonds .... RENTES
book .... LIVRE
box .... BOITE
bread .... PAIN
broken .... CASSE
broth .... POTAGE
brown .... BRUN
but .... MAIS

cabbage .... CHOU
cafe .... ESTAMINET
cafe noir .... COFFEE
cake ... GATEAU, CIERGE
Canadian: sl. .. CANUCK
cap's decoration .... POMPOM, COCKADE
car .... RENAULT
card .... CARTE
care .... SOIN
carriage .... FIACRE, VOITURE
castle .... CHATEAU
cathedral city .. R(H)EIMS
cavalryman .. CARABINIER
chain .... SAUTOIR
chalk .... TALC
challenge .... DEFI
cheese .... BRIE
chemist .... PASTEUR, RAOULT
chestnut .... MARRON
chicken .... POULE, HOUDAN
child .... ENFANT
citizen .... CITOYEN
city .... RIOM, LILLE, AMIENS, CALAIS, CLICHY, BLOIS, CAMBRAI, CANNES, CASTRES, CHARTRES, NANTES, AVIGNON, NIMES, CAEN, COLMAR, CHAUMONT, PARIS, AGEN, ARLES, LIMOGES, DOUAY, DOUAI, BELFORT, DIJON, NANCY, ORLEANS, LYON(S), LISLE, VERDUN, VICHY, TROYES, TOURS, TOULON, SOISSONS, SEDAN, NEUILLY, PAU, R(H)EIMS, RENNES, METZ, ROUEN
cleric .... ABBE, PERE
cloth .... TOILE
clothes .... DRAP
cloud .... NUAGE
coach for hire .... FIACRE
cognac .... MARTELL
coin ... OBOLE, ECU, SOU, FRANC, DENIER, CENTIME, LIVRE, TESTON, LOUIS (D'OR)
colony .... (T)CHAD
combining form .. GALLO
comfort .... AISE
company .... CIE
composer ...... RAVEL, BIZET, BERLIOZ, LALO, (D)INDY, RAMEAU
concrete .... BETON
conqueror ...... CLOVIS
corn .... BLE
count .... COMTE
country dance ... BRAWL
couturier .... DIOR, BALMAIN
critic .... TAINE
crown princess .... DAUPHINE

crude .... CRU
crusader ..... MONTFORT
cry for help .... AMOI
cup .... TASSE
curse .... ANATHEMA
dance .. GAVOT, CANCAN, APACHE, BAL, BRAWL, COURANTE, QUADRILLE, RONDE, GALLIARD, COTILL(I)ON
daughter .... FILLE
dear .... CHER(I)
decree .... ARRET
deed .... FAIT
delightful ... CHARMANT
department ..... ARLES, OISE, ORNE, NORD, VENDEE, HAUT-RHIN, EURE, ARIEGE, SOMME, GIRONDE
department head .... PREFECT
depot .... GARE
detective force ... SURETE
devil .... DIABLE
dialect .... PATOIS, LANGUE D'OC
district .... PERCHE
diversion .... JEU
donkey .... ANE
down .... BAS
down with .... ABAS
dramatist ..... MOLIERE, ETIENNE, COCTEAU, DUMAS, LESAGE, VOLTAIRE, RACINE
dream .... REVE
droghiere ...... GROCER
dry .... SEC
duchy ...... AQUITAINE, ANJOU, VALOIS
dugout .... ABRI
duke .... DUC
dungeon .... CACHOT
east .... EST
edict .... ARRET
egg ... OEUF, OVALE, OVE
elder .... AINE
eleven .... ONZE
emblem .... LILY
emperor .... LOUIS, NAPOLEON
empress ...... EUGENIE, JOSEPHINE
enamel .... EMAIL
enamelware .... LIMOGES
end .... FIN
entertainer ..... DISEUSE
equal ..... EGAL, PAREIL
equality .... EGALITE
evening .... SOIR
exist .... ETRE
explorer ..... CADILLAC, LA SALLE
eye .... OEIL
fabric .... GROS, ETOILE, DRAP, LAME
fabulist ... (LA) FONTAINE
fascist organization ..... CAGOULARD
fat .... GRAS
father .... PERE
"FBI" .... DST

fear .... PEUR
feudal tax .... TAILLE
fighter plane .... SPAD
finally .... ENFIN
fine bearing .... BEL AIR
fire .... FEU
five .... CINQ
flag .... TRICOLOR
flax .... LIN
forest .... BOIS
fortification ... PARADOS
foundation .... FOND
fox .... REYNARD
friar .... FRERE
fried potatoes .... CHIPS
friend .... AMI(E)
from .... DES
froth .... BAVE
fund .... FOND
game .... JEU(X)
gauze .... LISSE
general .... KLEBER
geologist ..... CORDIER
gift .... CADEAU
gingerbread ....
PAIN D'APICE
girl .... FILLE
glance .... APERCU
glass .... VERRE
glove .... GANT
go .... ALLER
god .... DIEU
good .... BON
goodby .... ADIEU,
AU REVOIR
gopher .... GAUFRE
gossip .... ONDIT
grape-growing area .....
MEDOC
gravy .... JUS
gray .... GRIS
ground .... TERRE
guerrillas ...... MAQUIS
Guiana capital ....
CAYENNE
hack .... FIACRE
hair style .... GOULUE
hairdresser .... MARCEL,
FRISEUR
half .... DEMI
half-mask .... LOUP
hall .... SALLE
handle .... ANSE
hat designer ...... DACHE
head .... TETE
headache ... MAL DE TETE
health .... SANTE
heaven .... CIEL
heavenly being ... ANGE
heir to throne .. DAUPHIN
helmet .... HEAUME
here ICI
hero in romance .....
AMADIS, BAYARD
heroic verse ....
ALEXANDRINE
hidden ... SECRE, PERDU
high society ....
HAUT MONDE
hill .... PUY
hillock .... MOTTE
his .... ALUI, SES
historian ...... MERIMEE,
RENAN, TAINE
holy .... SACRE
horn .... BRASSE
house .... MAISON
hunting match ..... TIR
husband .... MARI
in .... DANS
income .... RENTE
infantryman .. CHASSEUR,
ZOUAVE
infinitive .... AVOIR
ink .... ENCRE
inn .... AUBERGE
is .... EST
island .... ILE
island in Indian Ocean ...
REUNION
island off Newfoundland
MIQUELON
join .... UNIR
juice .... JUS
kind .... SORTE
king .... ROI
king's heir .... DAUPHIN
kingdom .... ARLES
lace ... ALENCON, CLUNY,
FAL
lamb .... AGNEAU
land .... TERRE
land measure ... ARPENT
landscape artist .. COROT
language .... LANGUE
laugh .... RIRE
law .... LOI
lawyer .... AVOCAT
leather .... CUIR
leave .... CONGE
Legion of Honor member
CHEVALIER
legislature .... SENAT
Lenten season .. CAREME
lexicographer .. LAROUSSE
life .... VIE
likewise .... DEMEME
liking .... GRE
lily .... LYS
little ...... PETIT(E), PEU
lodging place ...... GITE
love .... AIMER
loving .... TENDRE
maid (servant) ... BONNE,
FILLE
mail .... POSTE
Manche capital .. ST. LO
mansion .... HOTEL
marshal .... FOCH,
BAZAINE, VENDOME,
MURAT, NEY, SAXE,
RUEL, JOFFRE,
MASSENA, TURENNE
mask .... LOUP
matchless .... SAN EGAL
matin lay ...... AUBADE
May .... MAI
meager .... MAICRE
measure .... MINOT
meat dish .... SALMI
merry .... GAI
military ensign ....
ORIFLAMME
milk .... LAIT
minstrel ..... JONGLEUR
mirth .... GAITE
misdemeanor ..... DELIT
money of account .. LIVRE
month ... MAI, MOIS, JUIN
morning .... MATIN
Morocco capital ....
MEKNES
mother .... MERE
mountain .... MONT
municipal official .. JURAT
museum .... MUSEE,
CLUNY, RODIN, GUIMET,
CARNAVALET, LOUVRE
muslin ..... MOUSSELINE
my .... MON
my dear ..... MA CHERE
nail .... CLOU
name .... NOM, RENE,
HENRI, JACQUES,
MICHEL(LE), PIERRE, JEAN
national ...... CITOYEN
national anthem ....
MARSEILLAISE
naturalist ..... LAMARCK
naval base .... BREST
navigator ..... CARTIER
near .... PRES
neat .... SOIGNE(E)
negative .... PAS
nerve .... NERF
news .... NOUVELLES
night .... NUIT
no .... NON
nobleman ... COMTE, DUC
noon .... MIDI
nose .... NEZ
nothing .... RIEN
notion .... IDEE
novelist .... LESAGE,
MALRAUX, GARD,
MAUROIS, SAGAN,
LOTI, ROMAINS
nursemaid .... BONNE
oath .... VOIRE DIRE
obsession ..... IDEE FIXE
ogre .... HUGON
on .... ADROITE
on foot .... A PIED
one .... UN(E)
our .... NOUS
out .... HORS
over .... SUR
Pacific islands ....
MARQUESAS
painter .... RENOIR,
SEURAT, MANET,
CEZANNE, MONET,
INGRES, PISSARRO,
DEGAS, COROT
pancake .... CREPE
pantomimist ... PIERROT
paper-maker .. PAPETIER
parent ...... PERE, MERE
parliament ...... SENAT
pastry .. BABA, NAPOLEON
patron saint ...... DENIS
petticoat .... COTTE
philosopher ..... SARTRE,
PASCAL, DIDEROT
phonetician ...... PASSY
physicist .... PERRIN,
AMPERE
pilgrimage town ....
LOURDES

plumcake .... BABA
pocket .... POCHE
poem ...... VERS, DIT, VILLANELLE
poet ...... LAMARTINE, TROUVEUR, TROUVERE, RACINE, RONSARD
police .... GENDARME
police official .... COMMISSARY
pond/pool ...... MARE
porcelain .... SEVRES, LIMOGES
pork .... SALE
port ..... BREST, DIEPPE, CAEN, HAVRE, ROUEN, SETE
porter .... SUISSE, CONCIERGE
possessive ..... MES, SES, NOUS
pot au feu .... STEW
pout .... MOUE
premier .... TARDIEU, HERRIOT
president .... BLUM, (DE) GAULLE, CARNOT, POMPIDOU
president's residence .... ELYSEE
pretty .... JOLI(E)
priest .. ABBE, CURE, PERE
prize for literature ...... GONCOURT
profession ...... METIER
pronoun ... MOI, TOI, TU, VOTRE, JE, ILS, UNE, ELLE, MES, CES, VOUS
Protestant ... HUGUENOT
Protestant leader .... MORNAY
Protestant reformer ..... CALVIN
Provencal poet .. MISTRAL
province ... LANGUEDOC, LYON(N)AIS, PICARDY, PROVENCE
punishment ...... PEINE
pupil .... ELEVE
queen .... REINE
rabbit .... LAPIN
racecourse ..... AUTEUIL
railroad station ... GARE
read .... LIRE
ready .... PRET
rebel .... JACOBIN
receipt .... RECU
refugee .... EMIGRE
relative ..... MERE, PERE, TANTE
Republic personified .... MARIANNE
resort .... ANTIBES, BIARRITZ, BAIN, CANNES, MENTON
revenue .... RENTE
Revolution refrain ...... CAIRA
revolutionist ... DANTON, MARAT, CARMAGNOLE
ribbon .... SAUTOIR
rifle .... CHASSEPOT
river ...... RHONE, SEINE, ISERE, DOUBS, SAONE, AIRE, VESLE, LOIRE, OISE, SOMME, MARNE, MEUSE, ORNE, SAAR, YSER, LOT, AISNE
roast .... ROTI
Roman Catholic .... GALLICAN
room .... SALLE
royal edict .... ARRET
royal family ..... CAPET, VALOIS
royal standard .... ORIFLAMME
ruling family .... VALOIS
rumor .... ON DIT
sad(ness) .... TRISTE(SSE)
salt .... SEL
salt tax .... GABELLE
satin fabric ..... ETOILE
satirist .... VOLTAIRE, RABELAIS
saying .... DIT
school ..... ECOLE, LYCEE
sculptor .... HOUDON, RODIN
sea .... MER
seaport .... CALAIS, CHERBOURG, (LE)HAVRE, MARSEILLE(S), TOULON
seasoning .... SEL
secondary school .. LYCEE
secret intelligence .. SDECE
security .... RENTE
senior .... AINE
servant .... BONNE
she .... ELLE
sheep .... MOUTON
shelter ... ABRI, COUVERT, GITE
shepherd .... PATRE
shield ..... EGIDE, ECU, TARGE
shoot .... TIRER
shooting match ..... TIR
shoulder .... EPAULE
shrine .... LOURDES
sickness .... MALAISE
silk .... SOIE, GROS
silk center .... LYON
singer .... PIAF
sir .... SIEUR
site of Roman ruins ..... ORANGE
skater .... PATINEUR
ski champ .... KILLY
slang .... FROG
small .... PETIT(E)
smoking-room .... ESTAMINET
soap .... SAVIN
society .... MONDE
soldier ... POILU, SOLDAT, LEGIONNAIRE, CHASSEUR
soldier hero ..... BAYARD
Somaliland capital ...... DJIBOUTI, JIBUTI
son .... FILS
song .... CHANSON
soprano .... PONS
soul .... AME
soup .... POTAGE
south .... MIDI, SUD
spinster .... FILLE
spirit .. AME, ELAN, ESPRIT
square .... CARRE
star .... ETOILE
state .... ETAT
statesman ...... BRIAND, MAZARIN, CARNOT, REYNAUD
stock exchange .. BOURSE
stoneware .... GRES
storehouse .... ETAPE
storm .... ORAGE
street .... RUE
student .... ELEVE
style .... TON
stylist .... DIOR
Sudan .... MALI
summer .... ETE
supply .... FOND
sweetbread .... RIS
sweetmeat ..... DRAGEE
taste .... GRE
tawny .... TANNE
tea .... THE
their .... LEUR
then ...... ALORS, DONC
there! .... VOILA
they .... ILS
think .... PENSER
thirty .... TRENTE
tidy .... SOIGNE(E)
tire .... PNEU
title of respect ..... SIEUR
tobacco .... TABAC
too .... TROP
town ..... AGEN, ST. CYR, CRECY, VALENCE, VIMY, NESLE, RIOM
true .... VRAI
Tuesday .... MARDI
twelve peers .. DOUZEPERS
uncle .... ONCLE
under .... SOUS
underground fighters .... MAQUIS
upon .... SUR
verse .... RONDEL, VIRELAY, ALBA
very .... TRES
vest .... GILET
vineyard .... VIGNE, CLOS
vogue .... TON
voucher .... RECU
wagon .... VOITURE
wall .... MUR
warehouse ... ENTREPOT
wartime capital .. VICHY
water .... EAU
watered silk ..... MOIRE
wave .... ONDE
wax .... CIRE
we .... NOUS
weapon .... ARME
weight ..... LIVRE, SOL, GRAMME
well .... BIEN
well groomed .. SOIGNE(E)
wheat .... BLE
wind .... MISTRAL
wine .... MEDOC, HERMITAGE, BORDEAUX, BURGUNDY, PINARD, VIN

wing .... AILE
winter .... HIVER
with .... AVEC
without .... SANS
wood .... BOIS
woodland .... FORET
world .... MONDE
World War I plane ...... NIEUPORT
writer .... MAUROIS, RENAN, HUGO, STAEL, DUMAS, VERNE, FRANCE, VOLTAIRE, HEINE, VILLON
yesterday .... HIER
your .... VOTRE
youth .... FILS
Frenchman .... GAUL, HUGUENOT
frenzied ..... BERSERK, AMOK, FRANTIC, RAVING, ENRAGED, MADDING
fighter ... AMUCK, AMOK, BERSERK, BARESARK
frenzy ...... FUROR, ORGASM, MANIA, RAGE
freon ..... GAS, REFRIGERANT
frequent .... HAUNT, OFT, CONSTANT, HABITUAL, OFTEN
frequenter of a kind .. HABITUE
frequently .... OFTEN
frere .... BROTHER, FRIAR
fresh ...... NEW, SASSY, PERT, CLEAN, RECENT, BRISK, DRUNK, TIPSY, RAW
clothes .... CHANGE
colloquial ... PERT, BOLD, SAUCY, IMPUDENT
talk .... LIP
water alga ...... DESMID
water worm ...... NAID
freshener, skin .... LOTION
freshet .... FLOOD, SPATE, TORRENT
freshman .... NOVICE, BEGINNER, NEWCOMER
Annapolis .... PLEBE
slang .... FROSH
West Point .... PLEBE
fret .... FUME, NAG, STEW, FUSS, VEX, CHAFE, CHAMP, GNAW, WORRY
British .... CHEVY
fretful ... PEEVISH, IRRITABLE, PETULANT
Freud, psychiatrist .. SIGMUND
Freya's dwelling ... FOLKVANG
friable ..... BRITTLE, MEALY, FRAGILE, FRAIL, CRISP, SHORT
friar ...... MONASTIC, LISTER, ABBOT, FRATER, FRA, MONK, CARMELITE, DOMINICAN, AUGUSTINIAN
beggar .... SERVITE
bird .... PIMLICO
head covering .... COWL, CAPUCHE
of fiction .... TUCK
robe of .... FROCK
friar's lantern .. IGNIS FATUUS
friary .... MONASTERY
fricative ...... SPIRANT, HISS
friction .... ERASURE, RUB(BING), DISAGREEMENT, ABRASION
air .... WINDAGE
match .... FUSEE
fried lightly .... SAUTE(E)D
slang .... DRUNK
friedcake .... CRULLER, DOUGHNUT
friend ... ALLY, QUAKER, PAL, AMIGO, SUPPORTER, SYMPATHIZER, BUDDY, CHUM, CRONY
boy's best ...... MOTHER, MAMA
close .... SIDEKICK
faithful .... ACHATES, DAMON, PYTHIAS
false .... IAGO
French .... AMI(E)
lion's ...... ANDROCLES, ANDROCLUS
man's best .... DOG
friendly .... AMICABLE, KIND(LY), AMIABLE
dwarf .... TROLL, LEPRECHAUN
hint .... TIP
Islands .... TONGA
relations .... AMITY
understanding .. ENTENTE
friendship .... AMITY
Friesian .... FRIESE
frieze square .... METOPE
frigate .... WARSHIP
bird .... IWA, ATAFA
Frigg's husband .... ODIN
fright ... PANIC, ALARM, AWE, FEAR, TERROR
frighten ... DAUNT, STARTLE, FEEZE, SCARE, TERRIFY, ALARM, TERRORIZE
frightened ... AFEAR, AFRAID, SCARED, ALARMED
frigid .... COLD, FORMAL, STIFF, HYPERBOREAN
zone subsoil .... PERMAFROST
frijol .... BEAN
frill .... RUFF(LE), JABOT FURBELOW, ADORNMENT, FALBALA, RUCHE
Friml (Rudolf) forte .... OPERETTA
fringe ..... THRUM, BORDER, MARGIN, EDGE, LOMA, SKIRT
benefit ..... INSURANCE, VACATION, BONUS
hairs, etc. ...... FIMBRIA
of Jew's scarf ..... ZIZITH
frippery .... FINERY
useless .... FALLAL
friseur .... HAIRDRESSER
frisk .... FROLIC, CAPER, GAMBOL, TITTUP
slang .... SEARCH
frisky ...... SPRY, KITTENISH
animal ..... GOAT, COLT, KITTEN
Frisson of horror ...... GRUE
frith .... INLET, ESTUARY
fritter .... SHRED, PIECE, CAKE, DALLY, DAWDLE, WASTE
frivolity .... LEVITY
frivolous ... PALTRY, TRIVIAL, GIDDY, TRIFLING, LIGHT, PETTY, SILLY, FLIGHTY, FLIPPANT
frizz .... SIZZLE, FRY
frizzed .... CRAPED, CRIMPED
fro ..... AWAY, BACK(WARD)
frock ... ROBE, TUNIC, GOWN, MANTLE, SOUTANE, COAT, SMOCK, OVERALL, JERSEY, DRESS
froe .... CLEAVER
frog ...... POLLYWOG, TOAD, ANURAN, PEEPER, FROSH, RANA, PADDOCK, SALIENTIAN
farm .... RANARIA
fish .... ANGLER
genus .... RANA
larva .... TADPOLE
like .... RANINE
slang .... FRENCHMAN
sound .... CROAK
young .... TADPOLE
froggery .... RANARIA
frolic ...... GAY, FUN, MERRY, MERRIMENT, GAIETY, GAMBOL, PLAY, ROMP, (SKY)LARK, PRANK, CAPER, FRISK, CAVORT, SPREE
from head to foot .. CAP-A-PIE
here .... HENCE
now on ..... HENCEFORTH
that time .... THENCE
there .... THENCE
where? .... WHENCE
fromenty .... PUDDING
Frome's (Ethan) wife ..... ITU, ZEENA
frond .... LEAF
front .... OBVERSE, VAN, FOREHEAD, FACE, FORE
boat .... PROW, BOW
hoof .... TOE
of building ...... FACADE
of coin/medal .. OBVERSE
page box .... EAR
page news .... CRIME, SCANDAL, DISASTER, CALAMITY
position .... FIRING LINE
slang ... DUMMY, STOOGE
frontage .... FACADE
frontal .... METOPIC
frontier .... BOUNDARY
settlement ..... OUTPOST
frontiersman ... BOONE, EARP, CODY, CARSON, LOGAN, BOWIE, HICKOK
frontlet ... FOREHEAD, FILLET, HEADBAND
frontispiece .... PREFACE, FOREWORD
fronton .... JAI ALAI
frosh ...... FRESHMAN, FROG
Frost, Robert ____, poet .. LEE
frost .... ICE, RIME, HOAR, CHILL, NIP
frosting .... ICING

equipment .... ICER, FREEZER, REFRIGERATOR
frosty .... HOARY, ICY, FREEZING, AUSTERE, FRORE, RIMY
froth ..... SCUM, SUDS, FOAM, YEAST, LATHER, SPUME
drink's .... HEAD
frothy ...... SPUMY, FOAMY, TRIFLING
froufrou ..... RUSTLE, SWISH
frounce ... CREASE, WRINKLE, CURL
frow .... WIFE, WOMAN
frown ...... (G)LOWER, LOUR, SCOWL, GRIMACE
frowzy ...... MUSTY, UNTIDY, DIRTY
woman .... DOWD, SLATTERN
frozen .... CHILLY, ICY, FRAPPE, GLACE, GELID, CONGEALED
dessert ..... FRAPPE, ICE, MOUSSE, SHERBET
dew .... RIME
partly .... FRAPPE
rain .... SLEET, SNOW(FLAKES)
vapor .... FROST
fructify .... FERTILIZE
fructose ... SUGAR, LEVULOSE
fructuous .... FRUITFUL, PRODUCTIVE
frugal .... ECONOMIC(AL), THRIFTY, SPARING, SAVING, CHARY
frugality ..... THRIFT(INESS), PARSIMONY, ECONOMY
fruit ... DRUPE, YIELD, CROP, PRODUCT, RESULT, CONSEQUENCE, BERRY
aggregate ...... ETAERIO
apple-shaped .... QUINCE
basket .... POTTLE
bat .... PECA
bear .... FRUCTIFY
bearing no .... ACARPOUS
beech tree .... MAST
boat .... ORANGER
cactus .... FIG
cake .... SIMNEL
carbohydrate ... PECTIN
citrus ..... LIME, LEMON, ORANGE
coating .... BLOOM
cocktail ..... MACEDOINE
collective ..... SYNCARP
combining form .... CARP(O)
cordial .... RATAFIA
course .... DESSERT
covering.......... RIND, EPICARP, CALYPTRA
cultivation, study of ..... POMOLOGY
date-like .... JUJUBE
dealer .... COSTER
decay .... BLET, ROT
dish .... COMPOTE, COMPOTIER
dot(s) ...... SORI, SORUS
downy bristles ... PAPPUS
dried .... PRUNE, RAISIN
drink .... ADE
dry .... ACHENE
eating ..... FRUGIVOROUS
eating bat .. FLYING FOX, HAMMERHEAD, KALONG
elm .... SAMARA
enzyme .... PECTASE
filled crust ... DUMPLING
fir .... CONE
flesh .... PULP
fly .... DROSOPHILA
foul-smelling ... DURIAN
gourd ...... PEPO, SETON
growing, science of ...... POMOLOGY, HORTICULTURE
hard-shelled ...... NUT, GOURD
hawthorn .... HAW
hybrid .... POMA
injury .... BRUISE
inner layer ... ENDOCARP
juice .... MUST, STUM
juice, distilled ... BRANDY
juice drink ..... BRANDY, LEMONADE, ADE, SHRUB, SHERBET, SQUASH
juice squeezer ... REAMER
juicy part .... PULP
key .... SAMARA
knife .... CORER
lemon-like ...... CITRON
liquid .... JUICE
maple .... SAMARA
multiple .... SOROSIS
oak .... ACORN
of discord .... APPLE
of forgetfulness ... LOTUS
oil tube .... VITTA
one-seeded .... NUT
palm ... DATE, COCONUT, BETEL NUT
part .... RIND, PULP, CORE, PIT
peel .... ZEST, RIND
picker .... OKIE, BRACER
pie ...... TART, COBBLER
pine .... CONE
plant stem .... CANE
plum-like .... SLOE, PERSIMMON
preserve ..... COMPOTE, JAM
prune-like ... MYROBALAN
pulp ...... POMACE, PAP
pulpy ...... DRUPE, UVA
refuse .... MARC
rind ..... PEEL, EXOCARP, EPICARP, CALYPTRA
rosebush .... HIP
salad .... MACEDOINE
sculptured ..... CORBEIL
seed .... PIP, KERNEL
seller .. COSTER(MONGER)
ship .... FRUITER, ORANGER
skin ..... EPICARP, PEEL, RIND
small .... HAW, ACHENE, AKENE
sour .... LIME, LEMON
stew .... SASS, SAUCE
stone ... PIT, PIP, PYRENE, PUTAMEN, NUTLET
sugar .... FRUCTOSE, LEVULOSE
tomato-like .... POMATO
trees collectively .... ORCHARD
tropical ... MANGO, DATE, BANANA, AVOCADO, PAPAYA, PA(W)PAW
undeveloped .... NUBBIN
vineyard .... GRAPE
winged .... SAMARA
fruitcake .... SIMNEL
fruiter ...... SHIP, ORANGER
fruiterer .... COSTER
fruitful .... FERACIOUS, FRUCTUOUS, PRODUCTIVE, PROLIFIC, FERTILE, FECUND
make .... FRUCTIFY
fruitless ... STERILE, BARREN, FUTILE, VAIN
undertaking ...... FOLLY
fruits, study of .. CARPOLOGY
frustrate ...... DEFEAT, DASH, HINDER, NULLIFY, FOIL, THWART, BAFFLE, BALK
frustration .... DEFEAT
frutescent .... SHRUBBY
fruticose .... SHRUBBY
fry ..... FRIZZ, FINGERLING, CHILDREN, YOUNG, FISH
lightly/quickly ... SAUTE
frying-pan .. SKILLET, SPIDER
fub .... TRICK
fubsy .... PLUMP, SQUAT
fuchsia red .... MAGENTA
fuchsin .... MAGENTA, DYE, SOLFERINO
fucoid .. SEAWEED, ROCKWEED
fucus ... PAINT, DYE, SEAWEED
fuddy-duddy .... DODO
fudge ..... NONSENSE, CANDY, FAKE
Fuego island native ...... ONA
Fu(e)hrer .... HITLER, LEADER
fuel ..... COMBUSTIBLE, PEAT, PEET, COKE, WOOD, (CHAR)COAL
brick .... BRIQUET
carrying vessel .. TENDER, OILER, TANKER
dung .... CHIP
liquid .. OIL, PETROL(EUM) ALCOHOL, GAS
oil .... KEROSENE
ship ...... OILER, TANKER
turf .... PEAT
fugacious .... FLEETING, TRANSIENT, EPHEMERAL
fugitive ...... EXILE, FLEEING, FLEETING, ESCAPEE, ABSCONDER, RUNAGATE, RUNAWAY, DESERTER, REFUGEE
Negro slave .... MAROON
fugue .... TONAL
concluding passage ..... STRETTA, STRETTO
fulcrum .... PROP, THOLE
oar .... THOLE
Fulda river .... EDER

fulfill .... OBEY, ACCOMPLISH, SATISFY, COMPLETE, PERFORM, IMPLEMENT, REDEEM
fulfillment .... FRUITION
fulgent .... RADIANT
full ...... FILLED, COMPLETE, CROWDED, OROTUND, REPLETE, SATED
and rounded ..... PLUMP
as a skirt ... BOUFFANT(E)
attendance ..... PLENARY
blooded .... THOROUGHBRED, PEDIGREED
blooded horse .... ARAB
blown .... OPEN, MATURE(D)
dress ..... FORMAL, TAILS
flavored .... MELLOW
grown .... ADULT
house: colloq. ...... SRO
measure ..... AMPLITUDE
meeting .... PLENARY
of cracks .... RIMOSE
of holes .... PITTED, POCKMARKED
of life ...... LUSTY, SPRY
of: suffix ..... ITOUS, OSE, ULENT
of ups and downs .... CHECKERED
stop .... PERIOD
fullness .... PLENUM, PLENITUDE, SATIETY, SURFEIT, REPLETION
fulmar ... PETREL, MALDUCK, NELLY, MALLEMUCK
fulminate .... DETONATE, EXPLODE, THUNDER
fulsome .... COARSE
Fulton's (Robert) invention ... STEAMBOAT
boat .... CLERMONT
fumarole .... HORNITO
fumble ..... GROPE, BUNGLE
fume ... STEAM, VAPOR, RAGE, REEK, GAS, SMOKE, FRET, RAVE
fumigant .... PASTILLE
fumigate .... DISINFECT
fuming .... RAGING
fumy .... VAPOROUS
fun .... SPORT, JEST, JOLLITY, PLAY, AMUSEMENT, MERRIMENT, JINKS
Island seaport .. ODENSE
of, make .... MOCK, RIDICULE
Funafuti .... ATOLL
funambulist .... TIGHTROPE WALKER
kind of .... ACROBAT, AERIALIST
function .... OFFICE, DUTY, RITE, USE, PARTY, ROLE, WORK
trigonometry ..... SINE, COSINE, TANGENT
functionary .... OFFICIAL
fund ... STOCK, STORE, SUPPLY, OUTLAY, COPPERS
kind of ... SLUSH, TRUST
raiser .... TAGGER
fundament ... BUTTOCKS, ANUS
fundamental .... BASAL, ELEMENTAL, VITAL, ORGANIC, CARDINAL, BASIC, ESSENTIAL
funeral .. EXEQUIES, OBSEQUIES
announcement .... OBIT(UARY)
attendants .... CORTEGE, PALLBEARERS
bell .... KNELL
box ..... COFFIN, CASKET
"casket team" .... PALLBEARERS
coach .... HEARSE
director ..... MORTICIAN, UNDERTAKER
fire .... PYRE
hymn ...... EPICEDIUM, DIRGE
music .. DIRGE, REQUIEM
notice ...... OBIT(UARY)
ode .... EPICEDIUM
oration .. ELOGE, EULOGY
pile .... PYRE
procession ..... CORTEGE, EXEQUY
pyre .... PILE, SUTTEE
rite(s) .... EXEQUY, OBSEQUY, OBSEQUIES
song ... LAMENT, ELEGY, DIRGE, NENIA, REQUIEM, THRENODY
funereal .... SAD, FERAL, DISMAL, LUGUBRIOUS, GLOOMY, MOURNFUL
fungi .... SPORE, BOLETUS, YEAST
native to region .... MYCOLOGY
parasitic .... ERGOT
pertaining to .... AGARIC
spongy material .... AMADOU
study of ..... MYCOLOGY
tissue .... TRAMA
fungous .... SPONGY
fungus ..... SMUT, PUFFBALL, MILDEW, MOLD, AGARIC, EPIPHYTE, YEAST, (BLACK)KNOT, BLACKRUST, AMANITA, WART, RHIZOPUS, TUCKAHOE, LICHEN, MUSHROOM, RUST, TOADSTOOL
cells/sacs .... ASCI
combining form .. MYC(O)
disease ..... ERGOT, SCAB, BRAND, ROT, MYCOSIS
dots .... TELIA
edible ...... EARTHNUT, TRUFFLE
foul-smelling .... STINKHORN
growth ... ERGOT, MOLD, MILDEW
growth in body .. MYCOSIS
parasitic on animal ..... EPIPHYTE
plant .... MOREL, MUSHROOM, UREDO, AMANITA
poisonous ... TOADSTOOL, AMANITINE
smut .... BUNT
spores cluster .... SORUS
thallus of .... MYCELIUM
funicle .... FIBER, CORD
funk ...... FEAR, FRIGHT(EN), PANIC, SHIRK, COWARD
funnel .... FLUE, CHIMNEY, SMOKESTACK
funny ..... DROLL, AMUSING, COMIC(AL), ABSURD, FARCICAL, HUMOROUS
bone .... HUMERUS
bone site .... ELBOW
colloquial ..... KILLING
fur .... BUDGE, FITCH(ET), FITCHEW, CARACAL, KARAKUL, CARACUL, MINK, PELAGE, CRIMMER, VAIR, GRIS, SKIN, PELT, MINEVER, CALABER
bearing animal ... MINK, COYPU, GENET, VAIR(E), MARTEN, OTTER, SABLE, LYNX, WEASEL, POLECAT, RABBIT, CALABAR, SEAL, ERMINE, FITCH(ET), FITCHEW, CHINCHILLA
bearing skins collectively PELTRY
cape .... PELERINE
coypu's .... NUTRIA
garment .... WRAP, PARKA, ANORAK
hat ...... BUSBY, CASTOR
kid pelt .... GALYAK
lamb pelt ...... GALYAC
lynx .... CARACAL
matted .... DAGLOCK
neckpiece ... STOLE, BOA, CHOKER
pertaining to ... PELISSE
piece .. MUFF, BOA, STOLE
rabbit .... LAPIN
royal .... ERMINE
scarf .... TIPPET
seal .... SEECATCH
squirrel ... VAIR, CALABER
furbelow .... FRILL, FALBALA, JABOT, FLOUNCE, RUFFLE
furbish .... BRIGHTEN, POLISH, BURNISH, RENOVATE
furcate ... FORK(ED), BRANCH
furculum .... WISHBONE
furfur .... DANDRUFF, SCURF
Furies, one of the ... ERINY(E)S, ALECTO, EUMENIDES, TISIPHONE, MEGAERA
furious ... FRANTIC, VIOLENT, MAD, FRENZIED
furl .... ROLL UP
furlough .... LEAVE
furnace ... SMELTER, SMITHY, STITHY, CRESSET, BLOOMERY, CUPOLA, BLAST, FORGE, OVEN, CREMATORY, KILN, CREMATORIUM, BELLOW
air pipe of ..... TUYERE
feed the .... STOKE
for cremation .... (IN)CINERATOR

opening ..... STOKEHOLE
part ... BOSH, CRUCIBLE
tender .... STOKER
vent .... TUE
furnish ..... CATER, ENDOW, SUPPLY, PROVIDE, EQUIP, OUTFIT, PLENISH
furnishings ..... GEAR, DECOR
furniture .... GOODS, FIXTURE
decoration .... BUHL
inlaid wood .... BUHL
lace decoration .... MACRAME
leg, kind of ... CABRIOLE
set .... SUITE
wood ..... KOA, WALNUT
furor ..... FLURRY, TUMULT, FURY, RAGE, CRAZE, FRENZY
furrow ... GROOVE, WRINKLE, RUT, CHASE, PLOW, SEAM, STRIA, TRENCH, SULCUS, RILL(E)
for seeds .... DRILL
for sugarcane planting ... WINDROW
of wheel .... RUT
furrowed .. SEAMED, RUTTED, SULCATE
furry growth .... MOLD
tail .... SCUT
furs collectively ...... PELTRY
further ...... AID, MOREOVER, PROMOTE, ADVANCE, AND, ABET
furtive .... SURREPTITIOUS, SECRET, STEALTHY, COVERT, SLY, SNEAKY, SHIFTY, WARY
furuncle ...... BOIL, ABSCESS
fury ... RAGE, ANGER, WRATH, IRE
furze ... GORSE, WHIN, GORST, WHUN
fusain .... PENCIL
fuse .... ANNEAL, (S)MELT, SOLDER, BLEND, WELD, MIX, MERGE
kind of .... CHEMICAL, ELECTRICAL, PERCUSSION
partly .... FRIT
fused .... FUSIL
fusee .... FLARE, MATCH, VESUVIAN
fuselage .... NACELLE
fusiform .... ROUNDED
fusil .... FUSED, MELTED, MUSKET
fusillade .... BARRAGE, DRUMFIRE, SALVO, BURST
fusing .... SYMPHYSIS
fusion .... COALITION, MERGER
fuss .... ADO, PREEN, FIDGET, FRET, TINKER, KICKUP, BUSTLE, TO-DO, STIR, POTHER, BOTHER
fussy ... FINICAL, FASTIDIOUS, FINICKY, PER(S)NICKETY, PRISSY, HOITY-TOITY
fustian .... CORDUROY, VELVETEEN, POMPOUS, BOMBAST
fustic .... DYE
fusty ... STALE, STUFFY, MOLDY
futile .... VAIN, IDLE, OTIOSE, USELESS, FRUITLESS
future .... POSTERITY
kind of ...... HEREAFTER
futurity .... RACE
fuzz .... LINT, DOWN
fuzzball .... PUFFBALL
fuzzy ..... BLURRED, UNCLEAR
dog .... RAGS
fyke .... (FISH)NET
fylfot ..... SWASTIKA, CROSS, EMBLEM
Fyn .... FUNEN, ISLAND

G

G, Greek .... GAMMA
Hebrew .... GIMEL
letter .... GEE
slang .... GRAND
string ...... LOINCLOTH, BREECHCLOUT
gab ...... CHATTER, GABBLE, TALK
gift of .... GLIBNESS, ELOQUENCE, FLUENCY
gabble ..... JABBER, CHATTER
gabby .... TALKATIVE
gaberlunzie .... BEGGER
gabion .... CYLINDER
gable .... PEDIMENT, AILERON, PINION
ornament .... FINIAL
Gabon capital .... LIBREVILLE
city .... PORT GENTIL
ethnic group .. PONG-WE, CHIRA, PAHOUIN, PUNU, ADOUNA, LUMBU
Gabriel .... ARCHANGEL
what he sounded .... TRUMPET
gaby .... FOOL, SIMPLETON
gad ..... OATH, EXCLAMATION, SPIKE, PROWL, RAMBLE, GALLIVANT, TRAIPSE, ROAM, ROVE, GOAD
parent of .... JACOB, ZILPAH
son of .... ERI, ARELI
gadabout .... ROAMER, FLANEUR, PLAYBOY
gadfly .... PEST, TORMENTOR, ANNOYER, TABANID
gadget .... DOODAD, DINGUS, JIGGER, HICKEY, THINGUMBAOB, DEVICE, CONTRIVANCE, GIMMICK, JIMJAM
gadid .... COD, POLLACK, HADDOCK, FISH, HAKE
gadoid, a .... CODFISH, HAKE, HADDOCK, POLLACK
gadroon ... BEADING, REEDING, FLUTING
gadwall .... DUCK
Gadzooks ... OATH, EXPLETIVE
Gaea .... TELLUS, MOTHER EARTH, GODDESS, GE
son ..... URANUS, TITAN
Gael .... CELT, SCOT
Gaelic .... ERSE, SCOT(CH), CELT(IC), MANX, IRISH, KELTIC
bard .... OSSIAN
game pole .... CABER
god .... LER, MIDER, DAGDA
poem .... DUAN
sea god .... LER
spirit .... BANSHEE
warrior .... DAGDA
Gaels, of the ..... GOIDELIC, GADHELIC
gaff ..... SPAR, HOAX, HOOK, SPEAR, FLEECE, SPUR, DANCEHALL
rope .... VANG
slang ..... HOAX, TRICK, CHEAT
gaffe ... BLUNDER, FAUX PAS
gaffer .... FOREMAN, OLD MAN
gag ..... CHOKE, QUIP, HOAX, SILENCE, JOKE, MUZZLE, WISECRACK, MUFFLE, SCOB, RETCH
overworked .... WHEEZE
gage .... SECURITY, CHALLENGE, PLEDGE, WAGER, ESTIMATE, PLUM
Gahlee native ...... GALILEAN
gaiety .... FESTIVITY, FINERY, JOLLITY
Gaillard Cut, formerly .... CULEBRA
gain .... EARN, REALIZE, NET, WIN, GET, ATTAIN, LUCRE, REAP, PROFIT
control .... MASTER
extra .... PERQUISITE
knowledge ...... LEARN
slang .... VELVET
strength .... RALLY
gainly ..... COMELY, SHAPELY, GRACEFUL
gainsay ...... DENY, REFUTE, OPPOSE, CONTRADICT, FORBID, IMPUGN
Gainsborough's forte .... PORTRAITS
gait .... PACE, RUN, LOPE, WALK, RACK, STRIDE, CANTER, GALLOP, STEP
circular .... AMBIT
easy/slow ... TROT, LOPE, CANTER, ROMP
fastest .... GALLOP
gaiter .... PUTTEE, SPAT, LEGGING, SHOE, GAMBADE
gal .... GIRL
gala .... FIESTA, FESTIVAL, CELEBRATION, FESTAL, FESTIVE

galactic .... LACTIC
galacto: comb. form ... MILKY,
Galahad, describing .... PURE, NOBLE
parent ...... LANCELOT, ELAINE
quest of ... (HOLY) GRAIL
Galatea's beloved ...... ACIS
lover .... PYGMALION
galaxy ... MILKY WAY, BEVY, COLLECTION
Galcha .... PAMIR(I)
gale .... BREEZE, SHRUB, OUTBURST, WIND GUST
Gale (Zona), novelist .. BREESE
galena .... LEAD
Galilean .... CHRISTIAN
sea .... TIBERIAS
the .... JESUS
town ... MAGDALA, CANA, NAZARETH
galilee ...... PORCH, PORTICO
galimatias .... GIBBERISH
galingale ...... SEDGE, ROOT
galiot .... GALLEY, MERCHANT SHIP
galipot .... TURPENTINE, OLEORESIN
gall .... NERVE, BILE, AUDACITY, IMPUDENCE, SORE, IRRITATION, ANNOY, VEX, CHEEK, EFFRONTERY, TEMERITY, FELL
bladder ..... CHOLECYST
bladder fluid .... GALL, BILE
bladder, of the ... CYSTIC
bladder part ... CERVIX
combining form .... CHOL(O), CHOLE
gallant ... STATELY, IMPOSING, GRAND, CAVALIER, SQUIRE, BRAVE, HERO, NOBLE, LOVER, CIVIL, KNIGHT, BULLY
galleon .... CAR(R)ACK, ARGOSY, (WAR)SHIP, TRADER
gallery .... BELVEDERE, ARCADE, VERANDA, LOGGIA, POY, SOLLAR, PIAZZA, MUSEUM, LOFT, ART-ROOM, CORRIDOR, PORCH, PORTICO, COLONNADE, BALCONY, SALON
art .... SALON
bench .... BANK
church .... JUBE
French .... LOUVRE
in mining ...... HEADING
Italian .... UFFIZI
London .... TATE, GUILDHALL
gallet .... CHIP, SPALL
galley ... KITCHEN, ROWBOAT
armed ... AESC, DROMOND
Mediterranean .... GAL(L)IOT
Roman ...... UNIREME, BIREME, TRIREME
ship's .... CABOOSE
slave .... DRUDGE
work on .... EDIT, PROOFREAD
Galli-Curci, soprano .... AMELITA
Gallia .... GAUL
Gallic .... FRENCH
chariot .... ESSED
gallimaufry ..... HASH, OLIO, HODGEPODGE, ASSORTMENT
gallinaceous .... RASORIAL
bird .... TURKEY, PEAFOWL, PHEASANT, QUAIL
galling .... VEXING, CHAFING, IRRITATING, BITTER
gallinipper .... MOSQUITO
gallinule .... RAIL, (MUD)HEN
gallipot .... JAR
gallivant .... GAD
galliwasp .... LIZARD
gallon, half .... POTTLE
gallons, 8 .... BUSHEL
31½ .... BARREL
galloon ...... BRAID, RIBBON
gallop ... GAIT, LOPE, HURRY, TANTIVY, AUBIN, CANTER
Galloway ..... CATTLE, HORSE
gallstone .... CHOLOLITH
galluses .... BRACES, SUSPENDERS
gallows ... SCAFFOLD, GIBBET, YARDARM, TREE
galop .... DANCE
galore .... PLENTIFULLY, ABUNDANCE
galosh ... CLOD, (OVER)SHOE, BOOT
galumph ..... PRANCE, STRUT
galvanize ... EXCITE, STARTLE
Galway Bay island ..... ARAN
gam ..... HERD, VISIT, CALL, POD, SCHOOL
slang .... LEG
gamb(e) .... LEG, SHANK
gambado .... GAITER, PRANK, LEAP, LEGGING
Gambia's capital .. BATHURST
Gambier island ... MANGAREVA
gambit .... MANEUVER
gamble ... BET, STAKE, WAGER, RISK
reckless ... FLIER, FLYER
gambler ..... DICER, BETTOR, GAMESTER, GAMER, PLAYER
confederate of .... SHILL
kind of .... TINHORN, PLUNGER, SPECULATOR, PUNTER
gambler's accomplice ... SHILL
capital .... STAKE
concern .... ODDS
note .... IOU
gambling center .. LAS VEGAS, CASINO, MONACO, MONTE CARLO, RENO
table character .. BETTOR, CROUPIER, DEALER, RAKER, KIBITZER
gamboge .... GUM RESIN, PIGMENT
gambol .... DIDO, CAPER, ROMP, FRISK, FROLIC, PLAY, CURVET
gambrel .... HOCK, ROOF
Gambrinus' invention ... BEER
game .... POLO, GOLF, LAME, BINGO, BADMINTON, TAROT, PLOY, FUN, CRICKET, FOOTBALL, BEANO, AMUSEMENT, SPORT, PLAY, FROLIC, RECREATION, PLUCKY, SCHEME
anagrams ... LOGOMACHY
animal .... FOX
animal flesh ... VENISON
Basque .... PELOTA, JAI ALAI
big ... ELEPHANT, TIGER, LION, GORILLA, RHINO, BEAR
board .... CHESS, DARTS, HALMA, CHECKERS, PACHISI, PARCHESI
breeding place .. WARREN
card ... MONTE, BRIDGE, CASINO, TAROT, CANASTA, OMBER, FARO, POKER, WHIST, PAM, LOO, ECARTE
children's .... TAG, JACKSTONE
court .... TENNIS, BASKETBALL
dice .... CRAPS, LUDO
fish ..... SALMON, TROUT, MARLIN, BARRACUDA, BASS, TARPON
follow ... STALK, TRACK
guessing ..... CHARADE, MORA
handball: Eng. ..... FIVES
hockey ...... SHINN(E)Y
hold scoreless in .. BLANK, SKUNK
like billiards .. BAGATELLE
lottery number ... POLICY
military tactics .... KRIEGSPIEL
ninepins-like ... SKITTLES
of chance .... BINGO, FARO, LOO, KENO, LOTTERY, LOTTO, RAFFLE, HAZARD
of forfeits ..... FILLIPEEN
of marbles ... TAW, MIGS, MIGGLES
of skill .... TENNIS, CHESS, POKER, DARTS, BOWLING, POOL
oriental .... FANTAN
parlor .... LOTTO
period ...... CHUKKER, QUARTER, SET
piece ... ROOK, KNIGHT, QUEEN, TILE, MAN, DOMINO, KING, PIN, DIE
pin .... BOWLING
point .... GOAL, RUN
pointed missiles .. DARTS
preserve ..... SANCTUARY
rhyming .... CRAMBO
Scotch .... SHINTY
snare .... GIN
Spanish .... PELOTA, MONTE, OMBER

start of .... KICKOFF, TOSS UP
tennis-like .... FIVES
tossing .... DIABOLO
trail .... TRACK
trap .... GIN
with plastic disk .... FRISBIE
gamecock .... ROOSTER
spur of .... GAFF
gamekeeper .... WARDEN, RANGER
gamete, female, immature .... OOCYTE
gametes' union ...... ZYGOSIS, SYNGAMY
gamic .... SEXUAL
gamin .... ARAB, URCHIN, WAIF, TAD
gaming cube .... DICE, BONES
tile .... DOMINO
gamma .... MICROGRAM
gammon .... NONSENSE, BACON, HAM, HUMBUG
gamp .... UMBRELLA
gamut .... RANGE, SCALE
gamy .... PLUCKY
Gand .... GHENT
gander ...... GANNET, GOOSE
take a .... LOOK
Gandhi .... MAHATMA, MOHANDAS
political doctrine .... SATYAGRAHA
ganef .... THIEF, GANOV
gang ..... CREW, SQUAD, SET, MOB, WALK
criminals' ... MOB, RING
fight .... RUMBLE
head of ...... FOREMAN, RINGLEADER
member .... MOBSTER
Ganges boat .... PUTELEE
city on the .... VARANASI
fish .... SOOSOO
gangland ..... UNDERWORLD
gangling .... LANKY
gangplank ... RAMP, CATWALK
gangrel .... BEGGAR
gangrene .... DECAY, MORTIFICATION
gangrenous state .... NECROSIS
gangster ... GOON, HOOD(LUM), TOUGH(IE), THUG, GORILLA, MUG, YEGG, MOBSTER, HIGHBINDER
bodyguard .... TORPEDO
chief ...... RINGLEADER
girl of .... MOLL
gun: sl. .... GAT, ROD, ROSCOE, EQUALIZER
gangue .... MATRIX
gangway's handrail .. MANROPE
gannet ...... SOLAN, GANDER, MARGOT, GOOSE
ganoid ..... GAR, STURGEON, BOWFIN, AMIA
gantlet .... GLOVE
Ganymede ...... CUPBEARER
gaol .... JAIL, BRIDEWELL
gap .... GULF, HIATUS, CHASM, LACUNA, CLEFT, SHARD, HOLE, OPENING, BREACH
between peaks ..... COL
credibility .... DISTRUST
gape .... STARE, DEHISCE, OGLE, GAWK, YAWP, YAUP, YAWN, LOOK
gapes, the .... RICTUS
gaping ..... RINGENT, RICTUS
gar ..... NEEDLEFISH, GANOID, SNOOK, STURGEON
garage .... MEW, CARPORT
way to ...... BREEZEWAY
Garand .... RIFLE
Garapan Island's capital ...... SAIPAN
garb ..... CLOTHING, STYLE, ATTIRE, DRESS, GUISE
garbage ...... TRASH, SWILL, REFUSE, OFFAL
collect .... SCAVENGE
garble .... CONFUSE, FALSIFY, DISTORT, MIX UP, MUDDLE, JUMBLE
Garbo, actress .... GRETA
garcon .... BOY, YOUTH, WAITER, SERVANT
garden ...... PITCH, HERBARY, PLEASANCE, ARBOR, ORCHARD, GARTH
bed .... PLOT
Biblical ... GETHSEMANE
cultivation of .... HORTICULTURE
fence .... HAHA
first .... EDEN
kind of ...... HOTHOUSE, GREENHOUSE, TERRARIUM
kitchen .... OLITORY
miniature ... TERRARIUM
of golden apples .... HESPERIDES
pest .... APHID, WEED
plant .... ORACH(E)
rock .... ROCKERY
section .... BED, PLOT
soprano .... MARY
tool ...... HOE, TROWEL, RAKE, DIBBLE
vegetable .... SASS, KAILYARD, KALEYARD
wall .... HAHA
gardener's asset .... GREENTHUMB
handtool ...... TROWEL, DIBBLE
plague ...... CUTWORM, WEED, APHID, BORER
gardenia ... FLOWER, MADDER
Gardner, Erle ____ .. STANLEY
garfish .... SNOOK
Gargantua ..... GIANT, KING
creator of .... RABELAIS
son .... PANTAGRUEL
gargantuan .... HUGE, GIGANTIC
gargle ...... RINSE, LISTERINE, WASH
garibaldi .... BLOUSE
garish ...... GAUDY, SHOWY, GLARING
garland ... FILLET, CHAPLET, LEI, FESTOON, WREATH, ANADEM
garlic .... ALLIUM, MOLY, RAMSON
part .... CLOVE
garment ... CLOTHING, DRESS, RAIMENT, COAT, VESTMENT, HABILIMENT, CLOTH(E), COVERING, WRAP, BLOUSE, ROBE, TEDDY
Arabian .... AB(B)A
bishop's ..... CHIMER(E), CHIMAR
breast .... HALTER
clergyman's .... CASSOCK
corsetlike .... GIRDLE
East Indies .... SARI
Eskimo .... PARKA
fastener .... PATTE, AUTOMATIC
flap/fold of ..... LAPPET
Greek .... CHITON
hooded .... ALMUCE, PARKA
India ...... SARI, SAREE, BANIAN, BANYAN
knight's .... TABARD
knitted .... JERSEY
leg .... CHAUSSES
loose .... KIMONO, BLOUSE, ROBE, TOGA, CAMISE, DOLMAN, CYMAR
Malay ... SARONG, BATIK, PAREUS
Moslem .... IZAR
outer ... CAPOTE, TOGA, SCAPULAR, SURTOUT, COAT, PALETOT, KIMONO, SMOCK
patchwork .... CENTO
Polynesian .... PAREU(S)
priest's ... COPE, STOLE, AMICE, ALB, EPHOD
rain .... PONCHO
Roman ... ROBE, TOGA, STOLA, TUNIC
scarflike .... TIPPET
sleeveless .... CAPE, SCAPULAR
tentlike .... CHADRI
trade spy .... KEEK
trimming ..... BEADING
tunic-like ...... TABARD, CHITON
Turkish .... DOLMAN
under ... CHEMISE, SHIRT
garments .... COSTUME
garner ... GRANARY, GATHER, STORE, HOARD
garnet ..... RED, ALMANDITE, OLIVINE, CARBUNCLE, TACKLE, RHODOLITE, MELANITE, UVAROVITE, PYROPE, ESSONITE, GEM, TOPAZOLITE
garnish .... TRIM, RELISH, EMBELLISH, DECORATE, ADORN, DECK, OLIVE, ORNAMENT, LARD
garnishee .... TRUSTEE
garnishment .... LIEN

Garonne river tributary ... LOT
garret ... ATTIC, (COCK)LOFT, ATELIER, MANSARD
Garrick, actor .... DAVID
garrison .... (MILITARY)POST, PRESIDIO
garrote .... STRANGLE, STRANGULATION, SCRAG
garrulous .... TALKATIVE, VOLUBLE, LOQUACIOUS, GASSY
garter snake .... ELAP(S)
garth .... GARDEN, YARD
gas ... VAPOR, RADON, DRUG, BRAG, FREON, NEON, ARGON, ETHYL, FUEL, BUTANE, ETHER, FLATUS, STIBINE, PROPANE
balloon .... HELIUM
blue .... OZONE
burner .... BUNSEN, WELSBACH
charger .... AERATOR
cigaret lighter .. BUTANE
colorless .... OXAN(E), STIBINE, KETENE, ETHENE
combining form .. AER(O)
container .... TANK
dirigible .... HELIUM
engine .... PETROL
fill with .... AERATE, INFLATE
fitter .... PLUMBER
garlic-odored ..... ARSINE
in stomach/intestine .... FLATUS, FLATULENCE
inert .... ARGON
jet .... LAMP
marsh .... METHANE
mask part .... CANISTER
mine .... DAMP
non-inflammable .... HELIUM
pipe .... FLUE
radioactive ...... RADON, NITON
step on the ...... HURRY, ACCELERATE, GUN
gasconade ..... BRAG, BOAST, BLUSTER
gaseous .... AERIFORM
cloud .... NEBULA
combining form ... AERI
gash ...... CUT, HEW, HACK, SLASH
gasket .... LINING
gasoline .... PETROL
air mixer ... CARBURETOR
jellied .... NAPALM
slang .... JUICE
gasp .... HEAVE, PANT
gast(e)ropod ...... W(H)ELK, MOLLUSK, SLUG, SNAIL, LIMPET
marine .... MUREX
mollusk ...... ABALONE, TRITON, WHELK
gastric digestion product ..... CHYM
gastrin .... HISTAMINE, HORMONE
gastronome .... EPICURE, GOURMET, GOURMAND
gastronomy .... EPICURISM
gat .... CHANNEL
gata .... SHARK
gate .. DOOR, WICKET, PORTAL
bar .... PORTCULLIS
give the .... DISMISS, SACK, DISCHARGE
in metallurgy ... RUNNER
joint .... HINGE
keeper's dwelling .. LODGE
rear .... POSTERN
receipts: colloq. ... TAKE
revolving ..... TURNSTILE
tower .... BARBICAN
trellised .... LATTICE
water .... SLUICE, PENSTOCK
gatehouse .... LODGE
gatekeeper .... PORTER
gateway ... TORAN(A), PYLON
bar .... PORTCULLIS
Egyptian temple .. PYLON
Persian .... DAR
Shinto temple ..... TORII
gather .... REAP, (A)MASS, ACCUMULATE, CULL, COLLECT, INFER, ASSEMBLE, MUSTER, SHEAVE, FOLD, GLEAN, PUCKER, HARVEST, GARNER, SHIRR
gathering .... MEET(ING), RALLY, CROWD, BOIL, CONCOURSE, ASSEMBLAGE, ASSEMBLY
of people ...... TURNOUT
social ...... BEE, PARTY
gauche .. AWKWARD, CLUMSY, TACTLESS
gaucho ... COWBOY, LLANERO
knife .... MACHETE
milieu ... PAMPAS, LLANO
place .... RANCHO
rope of .... REATA
weapon ...... MACHETE, BOLA(S)
gaud ...... FINERY, TRINKET, ADORN, BAUBLE, ORNAMENT
gaudy ...... GARISH, SHOWY, FLASHY, TAWDRY, FLORID, GINGERBREAD, TAFFETA
ornament .... TINSEL
gauffer ... CRIMP, PLEAT, FLUTE
gauge ... VALUE, RATE, TYPE, EXTENT, CAPACITY, FEE, MEASURE, APPRAISE, ESTIMATE
face of .... DIAL
rain .... UDOMETER, PLUVIOMETER
Gauguin's island home .. TAHITI
Gaul ... GALLIA, FRENCHMAN
metal collar ..... TORQUE
gaunt ..... HAGGARD, SPARE, LANK, LEAN, EMACIATED, GRIM, SICKLY, BONY, THIN
gauntlet .. GLOVE, CUFF, GAGE
throw down the .... CHALLENGE, DEFY
Gautama .... BUDDHA
gauze .... BAREGE, CREPE, HAZE, MIST, TISSUE, LENO
silk .... TIFFANY
gauzy .... FILMY, SHEER, DIAPHANOUS
fabric ... CHIFFON, LACE, TULLE
film in wine ... BEESWING
gavel .... HAMMER, MALLET
gavial .... CROCODILE
gawk .... STARE, GAPE, CUCKOO, SIMPLETON
gawky ... CLUMSY, AWKWARD, UNGAINLY
gay .... MERRY, LIVELY, WANTON, BRIGHT, BOON, PERKY, RIANT, FESTAL, FESTIVE, JOLLY, JOVIAL, JOCUND, HILARIOUS
and swaggering .. JAUNTY
rake .... LOTHARIO
tune .... LILT, JAZZ
Gay-Pay-Oo ...... GPU, OGPU
successor .... NKVD
gaze ..... GAPE, STARE, LEER, GAWK, GLARE
gazebo .... BALCONY, TURRET
gazelle ..... ANTELOPE, GOA, CORINNE, KUDU, CORA, ADDRA, SPRINGBOK, KORIN, MOHR, KEVEL, CHIKARA, ARIEL
African ... ADMI, MOHR, SPRINGBOK, ORYX, KORIN, CORA
Asiatic .... AHU
black-tailed .... GOA
Sudan .... DAMA
Tibetan .... GOA
gazette .... NEWSPAPER
Gaziantep .... AINTAB
Gdansk .... DANZIG
Ge .. GAEA, GAIA, GERMANIUM
gear ..... CAM, KIT, TACKLE, COG, OUTFIT, OVERDRIVE, TOOLS, RIG(GING), HARNESS, BAGGAGE, GARB
gecko .... LIZARD, LACERT(IL)IAN, TARENTE
gee ... EXCLAMATION, EVADE, TURN RIGHT, GO AHEAD, JESUS
opposed to .... HAW
geese, domestic ...... EMDENS
fat .... AXUNGE
flock ..... RAFT, GAGGLE
genus .... ANSER
geest .... ALLUVIUM
geetas .... STINGY
Gehenna .... HELL
geisha ..... DANCER, HOSTESS, DANCING GIRL
gel .... JELLIFY
opposed to .... SOL
gelatin(e) ... ASPIC, COLLOID, AGAR, JELLY, GLUTIN
case .... CAPSULE
copying pad .... POLYGRAPH
fish bladder ... ISINGLASS
gelatinous ... VISCOUS, VISCID
geld ... STERILIZE, CASTRATE, EMASCULATE
gelding .... EUNUCH
gelid .... COLD, FROSTY, FROZEN, ICY

gem . . . . STONE, JEWEL, CAT'S-EYE, OPAL, CHATOYANT, MUFFIN, LIGURE, TOPAZ, AGATE, EMERALD, AMETHYST, SARDONYX, BERYL, JADE, GARNET, RUBY, PERIDOT, SPINEL, SARD, ONYX, PEARL, DIAMOND
artificial . . . . . . PASTE, RHINESTONE
Biblical . . . . LIGURE
blue . . . . HYACINTH
carnelian . . . . . SARD(INE)
carved . . . . CAMEO
carving . . . . GLYPTICS
cut . . . . BRIOLETTE
cutter . . . . LAPIDARY
cutting device . . . . . . LAP
dealer . . . . LAPIDARY, CARTIER, BEERS
Egyptian . . . . SCARAB
engraver . . . . . . LAPIDARY
engraving . . . . . GLYPTICS
expert . . . . LAPIDARY
facet . . . . . CULET, BEZEL, BEZIL
flaw . . . . FEATHER
green . . . . BERYL, EMERALD, AQUAMARINE
green-like . . . PERIDOTIC
merchant . . . . . LAPIDARY
polisher . . . . . . LAPIDARY
red . . . . CARBUNCLE
relief . . . . CAMEO
rim of . . . . GIRDLE
ruby spinel . . . . BALAS
setting . . . BEZEL, CHATON
simulated . . . . . DOUBLET
slang . . . . . SPARKLER, ICE
State . . . . IDAHO
weight . . . . CARAT, KARAT
gemel . . . . HINGE
part of . . . . . HOOK, LOOP
Gemini . . . . TWINS
star . . . . CASTOR, POLLUX
geminate . . . . COUPLED, DOUBLE, PAIRED
gemma . . . . BUD
gems collector/dealer . . . . LAPIDARY
gemsbok . . . . ANTELOPE, CHAMOIS, ORYX
gemstone . . . . IOLITE
gendarme(rie) . . . POLICE(MAN)
gender . . . . MASCULINE, BEGET, SEX, FEMININE, BREED, NEUTER
classification . . . . MASCULINE, FEMININE, NEUTER, NATURAL, GRAMMATICAL
common . . . . EPICENE
gene . . . . FACTOR
genealogical record . . . . . TREE
genealogy . . . HERALDRY, TREE, LINEAGE, PEDIGREE, DESCENT
general . . . . GENERIC, INCLUSIVE, ECUMENICAL, PANDEMIC, USUAL, COMMON, WIDESPREAD, UNIVERSAL
arrangement . . . GET-UP, FORMAT
aspect . . . . TENOR
Civil War . . . . GRANT, LEE, BRAGG, MEADE, SCOTT, SHERIDAN
direction . . . . DRIFT, TREND
man of a . . . . AIDE
of the Armies . . PERSHING
of the Army . . . . MACARTHUR, EISENHOWER
opinion . . . . . CONSENSUS
opposed to . . . . PARTICULAR, SPECIFIC, DETAILED
paralysis . . . . PARESIS
pardon . . . . AMNESTY
welfare . . . COMMONWEAL
Generalissimo . . . . CHIANG (KAI CHEK), SHOGUN, FRANCO
generate . . BEGET, PROCREATE, ORIGINATE, PRODUCE
generation . . . . AGE
generator . . . . DYNAMO
generic . . . . GENERAL, INCLUSIVE, UNIVERSAL
generous . . . . LIBERAL, LAVISH, AMPLE, OPEN-HANDED, GRACIOUS, UNSELFISH
giving . . . . . . LARGESS(E)
genesis . . . . . . ORIGIN, BIRTH, CREATION, BEGINNING
genet . . . . JENNET, CIVET
genetic . . . . GENIC
genetics, subject of . . . . HEREDITY
geneva . . . . GIN
lake . . . . LEMAN
genial . . . . . . WARM, AMIABLE, DEBONAIR(E), JOCUND, JOVIAL
geniculate . . . . BENT
genie . . . . JINNI, DEMON, SPIRIT, JINNEE
genius . . . . . ABILITY, TALENT, DEMON, SPIRIT
Genoese city . . . . LIGURIA
magistrate . . . . DOGE
genre . . . . . . TYPE, KIND, SORT, STYLE
gens . . . . CLAN, TRIBE
gent . . . . PRETTY, GUY, GENTLE(MAN)
genteel . . . . REFINED, WELL-BRED, POLITE, ELEGANT, NICE
gentian . . . . ROOT, FLOWER, COLUMBO, AGUEWEED
gentile . . . . PAGAN, HEATHEN, GOY, NON-JEW
gentle . . . . . . REFINED, POLITE, TAME, PLACID, TENDER, KINDLY, MILD, SOFT, DOCILE, LENIENT, LAMBLIKE
breeze . . . . ZEPHYR
craft, the . . . . . . FISHING, SHOEMAKING
heat . . . . TEPOR
push . . . . NUDGE
sex . . . . WOMAN, WOMANKIND
gentleman . . . . YOUNKER, CAVALIER, GENT, COURTIER, SIR, GALLANT, MILORD, SIGNOR, RYE
amateur in sports . . . . CORINTHIAN
attendant . . . . DONZEL
from Indiana . . . . TARKINGTON
in waiting . . . . . COURTIER
of fortune . . ADVENTURER, PIRATE
Spanish . . . . . CABALLERO
gentleman's gentleman . . . . VALET
"Gentlemen Prefer Blondes" author . . . . . (ANITA) LOOS
gentlewoman . . . . . (MI)LADY, MILADI
Gentoo . . . . HINDU
gentry . . . . NOBLE
genu . . . . KNEE
genuflect . . . . . . KNEEL, BEND, CURTSY
genuine . . . . REAL, TRUE, AUTHENTIC, HONEST, LEGIT, PUREBRED, SIMON PURE, PUCKA
genus . . . . CLASS, VARIETY, SORT, ORDER, KIND
birds . . . . CORVUS
cats . . . . FELIS
cattle . . . . BOS
cetaceans . . . . INIA
chestnuts . . . . . CASTANEA
cows . . . . BOS
dogs . . . . CANIS
ducks . . . . . . ANAS, ANSER
eels . . . . CONGER
fishes . . . . ANABAS
foxes . . . . VULPES
frogs . . . . . RANA, ANURA
gannet . . . . SULA
gastropods . . . . . . HARPA, NERITA, OLIVA, TRITON
grapes . . . . VITIS
geese . . . . ANSER
ginseng . . . . ARALIA
goats . . . . CAPRIA
goose barnacles . . LEPAS, ANATIFA
gooseberry . . . . RIBES
goshawks . . . . ASTUR, BUTEO
grasses . . . . . POA, AVENA, STIPA, AIRA
griffon . . . . GYPS
gulls . . . . LARI, XEMA, LARUS
herbs . . . RUTA, TOVERIA, ANEMONE, ARUM, RULAC, MANIHOT, ACARUM, CICER, NOLANA
herring . . . . ALOSA
hogs . . . . SUS
honeybee . . . . APIS
housefly . . . . MUSCA, FANNIA
insects . . . . CICADA
lemurs . . . . GALAGO
lily . . . . ALOE
man . . . . HOMO
maples . . . . ACER
mints . . . . NEPETA

mollusks .... NERITA, ANOMIA, TEREDO
monkeys .... ATELES
moose .... ALCES
nettles .... URTICA
oats .... AVENA
olives .... OLEA
oysters .... OSTREA
palms .... ARECA
peacocks .... PAVO
pigs .... SUS
primates .... HOMO
shads .... ALOSA
sheep .... BOS
shrubs ... FUCHSIA, ITEA, RHUS, OLEA, ERICA
swans .... OLOR
swine .... SUS
terns .... STERNA
thistles .... CARLINA
thrushes .... TURDUS
trees ... CORNUS, CELTIS, SAPOTA
turtles .... EMY
wasp .... VESPA
whales .... INIA
wrens .... NANNUS

geode ...... CAVITY, VUG(H), DRUSE, VUGG, VOOG

geographer ...... MERCATOR, PTOLEMY, VAREN

geography, work on .... ALMAGEST

geological age .... PLIOCENE, CENOZOIC
angle .... HADE
division ...... EON, LYAS, LIAS, ERA
epoch ..... UINTA, ECCA, PLEISTOCENE, PLIOCENE, MIOCENE, OLIGOCENE, EOCENE, PALEOCENE, DRIFT
era .... PALEOZOIC, MESOZOIC, CENOZOIC
formation ..... TERRANE, TRIASSIC, TERRENE, IONE, TERRAIN
recent epoch .. HOLOCENE
ridge .... OSAR
system .... TERTIARY, CRETACEOUS, JURASSIC, PERMIAN, CAMBRIAN, DEVONIAN, SILURIAN

geology on land structure ..... TECTONICS

geomancy .... DIVINATION

geometrical body ...... LUNE, PRISM
curve .... PARABOLA
figure ... ELLIPSE, CONE, RHOMB, CUBE, CIRCLE, SQUARE, ANGLE, PRISM, POLYGON, HELICOID
line ..... LOCUS, SECANT
point relating to curve ... ACNODE
premise ...... POSTULATE
principle ..... THEOREM
ratio .... SINE, PI
solid ... CUBE, PYRAMID, SPHERE, LUNE, PRISM, CONE
study .... CONICS
term ..... SINE, TANGENT, VERSOR, LOCUS, SECANT, THEOREM

geometrid moth larva .. LOOPER

geometry, branch of ... CONICS
subject of ... POINT, LINE, SOLID, PLANE
type ...... PLANE, SOLID

geoponic ... RURAL, BUCOLIC, PASTORAL, RUSTIC, AGRICULTURAL

George Eliot .... EVANS

georgette .... CREPE

Georgia, capital of .. ATLANTA
city ...... ROME, MACON
Negro .... GULLAH
peak .... KENNESAW
pine .... LONG-LEAF
river .... S(U)WANEE
seaport ...... SAVANNAH

Georgian seaport (Soviet) ..... BATUM

georgic .... POEM, RURAL, AGRICULTURAL

Geraint .... KNIGHT
wife of .... ENID

geranium .... CRANESBILL

gerbil(l)e .... JERBOA

gerent ..... MANAGER, RULER

geriatrics .... NOSTOLOGY

germ ..... MICROBE, BACTERIA, SPORE, ORIGIN, VIRUS, BUG, SEED
fermenting .... ZYME
free .... ASEPTIC

German .... HUN, BOCHE, TEUTON(IC), ALMAIN, COTILLION, JERRY, ALEMAN, JUNKER
above .... UBER
admiral .... SPEE, RAEDER, TIRPITZ
adventurer .... MUNCHAUSEN
again .... UBER
air .... LUFT
aircraft manufacturer ... DORNIER
airplane ... STUKA, TAUBE
alas .... ACH
already .... SCHON
and .... UND
army ..... REICHSWEHR
art songs .... LIEDER
article .... DAS, EIN, DER
ass .... ESEL
at no time .... NIE
bacteriologist ..... KOCH, LOFFLER
bank .... UFER
battleship ... BISMARCK, TIRPITZ, (GRAF)SPEE
beautiful .... SCHON
because .... WEIL
bed .... BETT
beer ...... BIER, LAGER
blood .... BLUT
blue .... BLAU
bomber .... STUKA
bread ... BROT, BROTCHEN
but .... ABER
cake .... KUCHEN, TORTE, STOLLEN, SPRINGERLE
camp .... STALAG
canal .... KIEL
cathedral site ..... ESSEN, COLOGNE
chancellor ... ADENAUER, ERHARD, BRANDT, BISMARCK
chap .... KERL
cheese .... KASE
chemist .... LIEBIG, BUNSEN
city ..... HAMELIN, JENA, EMDEN, EMS, CASSEL, COLOGNE, COBLENZ, SPEYER, TREVES, BONN, KOLN, KREFELD, MAINZ, HALLE, ESSEN, TRIER, HANOVER, DRESDEN, LEIPZIG, STUTTGART, GOTHA, WEIMAR, DESSAU, LUBECK, KARLSRUHE, ROSTOCK, ULM, MUNSTER, MEISSEN, MANNHEIM, MARBURG
coal region .... SAAR, AACHEN, RUHR
coffee cake ..... KUCHEN
coin .... T(H)ALER, GROSCHEN, GUILDER, GULDEN, PFENNIG, KRONE, KREU(T)ZER, MARK, HELLER
cold .... KALT
composer ...... BRAHMS, BACH, FLORIO, WAGNER, WEBER, STRAUSS
councillor .... RAT
count .... GRAF, LANDGRAVE
criminologist .... SAUER
critic .... LESSING
cry of surrender .... KAMERAD
dam .... EDER
dance .... COTILLION
day .... TAG
dear .... LIEB
defense force .... LANDSTURM
defense line .. SIEGFRIED, LIMES
dessert .... STREUSEL
district ..... SAAR, RUHR
dog .... HUND
dollar .... TALER
donkey .... ESEL
dramatist .... LESSING
dream .... TRAUM
drinking toast ... PROSIT
duchy .... HESSE, BADEN, LIPPE
east .... OST(EN)
eat .... ESSEN
eight .... ACHT
emperor .... KAISER, WILHELM, OTTO
evening .... ABEND
everything .... ALLES
exclamation .... ACH,

HOCH, HIMMEL
explorer .... BARTH
eye .... AUGE
fairytale writer .. GRIMM
far .... WEIT
fascist .... NAZI
fellow .... KERL
field .... FELD
five .... FUNF
folksong ..... VOLKSLIED
forest .... WALD
forest keep .. WALDGRAVE
four .... VIER
from .... VON
fruit .... OBST
full .... VOLL
gentleman .... HERR(EN)
Gestapo chief .. HIMMLER
girl .... FRAULEIN
glad .... FROH
god ..... WODEN, WODAN
good .... GUT(EN)
government ...... REICH
governor .... MARGRAVE
gypsy .... ZIGUENER
hair .... HAAR
hall .... AULA, SAAL
head .... KOPF
heart .... HERZ
heir .... ERBE
hero, legendary ....
SIEGFRIED
high .... HOCH
highway ..... AUTOBAHN
historian .... RANKE
home ..... HAUS, HEIM
hot .... HEISS
housewife ... HAUSFRAU
hunter .... JAGER
hypnotist ...... MESMER
ice .... EIS
iron .... EISEN
island ..... HELGOLAND,
ALSEN
Kantian philosopher ....
FICHTE
king .... KONIG
kingdom .... SAXONY,
HANOVER, HESSE,
PRUSSIA
knight ..... TANNHAUSER
leaf .... BLATT
league .... BUND
legend's site ... HAMELIN
legislative assembly .....
LANDTAG
letter .... RUNE
love .... LIEBE
lyric .... LIED
lyric poem .... LIEDER
married woman .... FRAU
master race ....
HERRENVOLK
mathematician .... HESSE
measles .... RUBELLA,
ROSEOLA, RUBEOLA
mercenary soldier ....
LANSQUENET, HESSIAN
military governor ....
MARGRAVE
military reserve ....
LANDWEHR
mimist.. .... SCHARRE
minnesinger ....
TANNHAUSER
mister .... HERR
money .... MARK
money, Soviet zone .....
OSTMARK
moon .... MOND
morning ...... MORGEN
mountain .... HARZ
mouth .... MUND
musician, legendary .....
PIED PIPER
name prefix .... VON
nation .... VOLK
naval base ...... EMDEN,
KIEL
Nazi ideology ....
HERRENVOLK
negative .... NEIN
new .... NEUE
night .... NACHT
nine .... NEUN
no .... NEIN
number .... DREI, ZWEI,
FUNF, SECHS, NEUN,
ZEHN, EIN(E), VIER
ocean .. MEER, NORTH SEA
one .... EIN(E)
only .... NUR
operatic soprano ....
LEHMANN
painter .... HOLBEIN,
GROSZ
parliament ... REICHSTAG
part .... TEIL
people .... VOLK
philosopher ...... KANT,
HEGEL, FICHTE, HERDER,
HERBART
physicist .... HERTZ,
PLANCK
playwright-cobbler ......
SACHS
please .... BITTE
poet ...... RILKE, ARNDT,
HEINE, SCHILLER
port .... BREMEN
POW camp ..... STALAG
president .... LUBKE,
EBERT, TALER, HEUSS
prince's title ....
LANDGRAVE, MARGRAVE
principality .... LIPPE
printer ...... GUTENBERG
prison camp .... STALAG,
DACHAU
pronoun ...... DU, ICH,
SIE, UNS, WIR
republic .... LIPPE,
WEIMAR
resort .... EMS, BADEN
rifleman .... YAGER,
JA(E)GER
river ..... RHINE, RUHR,
EDER, AAR, ISER,
WESER, ODER, HUNTE,
WERRA, ELBE, ALLE
roll .... BROTCHEN
robbery .... RAUB
roof .... DACH
royal family member ....
GUELPH, GUELF
sacred place .... HIERON,
ABATON
sausage .... WURST
scientist .... MACH
seaport ... KIEL, EMDEN,
WISMAR
shore .... UFER
Sigurd .... SIEGFRIED
silver .... ELECTRUM
siren .... LORELEI,
LURLEI
six .... SECHS
sky .... TIU
slang ... JERRY, DUTCH
Slavic people .... WEND
snare .... SPRINGE
socialist .... LASSALLE
society .... VEREIN
soldier ... KRAUT, UHLAN,
HEINIE, BOCHE
song .... LIED(ER)
spa .... EMS, BADEN
spirit .... GEIST
sprite .... NIX
state ..... BADEN, HESSE,
STAAT
state police ..... GESTAPO
steel .... STAHL
steeple .... TURM
street .... STRASSE
student, freshman ......
FROSH
students' hall .... BURSE
submarine ....
UNTERSEEBOOT
sun .... SONNE
superior .... OBER
tank, armored .. PANZER
ten .... ZEHN
the .... DER, DAS
three .... DREI
time .... ZEIT
title of nobility ... GRAF,
PRINZ, VON
title of respect .... GRAF,
HERR
toast .... PROSIT
today .... HEUTE
town .... STADT
train .... ZUG
true .... WAHR
two .... ZWEI
U-boat ... UNTERSEEBOOT
upper .... OBER
village .... DORF
water sprite .... NIX
watering place ..... EMS
weight .... LOTE
wheat .... SPELT
white .... WEISS
whole .... GANZ
wife .... FRAU, FROW
wine .... HOCK
with .... MIT
without .... OHNE
woman, unmarried .....
FRAULEIN
WWI plane ..... TAUBE
year .... JAHR
yellow .... GELB
yes .... JA
young .... JUNG
your .... DEIN, EUER

germane .... RELEVANT, PERTINENT, AKIN
Germanic people .... CIMBRI
tribesman .... JUTE
germanium .... GE
Germany .... REICH
germinate .... SPROUT, PULLULATE
Gernreich, fashion designer ... RUDI
Geronimo .... APACHE
Gershwin, composer ..... IRA, GEORGE
gesso ...... GYPSUM, PLASTER
Gestapo chief .... HIMMLER
gestation ...... PREGNANCY, CYESIS
gest(e) ...... DEED, EXPLOIT, ADVENTURE, BEARING
gesture .... MOTION, ACTION, TOKEN, GESTE, MOVEMENT
of contempt .. FICO, FIG
of indifference .... SHRUG
of respect ... OBEISANCE, BOW, CURTSY
get .... OBTAIN, SECURE, GAIN, ACQUIRE
aboard .... EMBARK
about ...... CIRCULATE
ahead .... PROSPER, SUCCEED
along ... MAKE OUT, FARE
along well .... CLICK, PROSPER, THRIVE
around .... GAD, EVADE, OUTWIT, CIRCULATE, CIRCUMVENT
away .... LEAVE, ESCAPE
by ... MANAGE, SURVIVE
by trickery .... FINAGLE
in touch .... CONTACT
in uninvited ...... CRASH
on ____ .... BOARD
rid of .... LIQUIDATE, DISPOSE
the idea .... SAVVY, GRASP, SEE
to the bottom of .... FATHOM
together .... AMASS, REUNION, BEE
up ... COSTUME, OUTFIT, WEAR
well .... HEAL
getaway .... ESCAPE
Gettysburg general ... MEADE, LEE
gewgaw ... BAUBLE, TRINKET, GIMCRACK, GAUD, FALDEROL, FOLDEROL, DOODAD, KICKSHAW
geyser .... (HOT)SPRING
mouth of .... CRATER
Ghana, capital of ..... ACCRA
junta leader ..... ANKRAH
"redeemer" ... NKRUMAH
region .... ASHANTI
ghastly ..... MACABRE, PALE, GRIM, LURID, GRIS(T)LY, GRUESOME, PALLID
gha(u)t .... PASS, RANGE
ghee .... BUTTER
gherkin .... CUCUMBER
ghetto .... JEWRY
ghost ...... SPIRIT, INKLING, MANES, EIDOLON, KER, SHADE, LEMUR, SPOOK, WRAITH, PHANTOM, HANT, APPARITION, SPECTRE, SHADOW, LARVA, WAFF
place of .... HAUNT
ghostly .... SPECTRAL, SPIRITUAL, EERIE, SPOOKY
ghoulish .... FIENDISH, LOATHSOME, VAMPIRIC, HORRIBLE
GI .. YANK, GOVERNMENT ISSUE
address .... APO
bed .... SACK
ID .... DOGTAG
insect repellent ..... DDT
Joe ... DOGFACE, PRIVATE
rifle ..... BAR, GARAND, ARMALITE
giant .... BANA, GOLIATH, BALDER, TROLL, TITAN, ANTAEUS, ASTERIUS, LOKI, ETEN, OGRE, JUMBO, GARGANTUA, PANTAGRUEL, MIMIR, BALDER, YMER, FAFNIR, JOTUN(N)
Biblical .... ANAK
fairy tale .... OGRE
killer ...... DAVID, JACK
legendary .... ATLAS
one-eyed .... ARGES, CYCLOPS, ALEC
100-armed ... ENCELADUS
100-eyed .... ARGUS
Philistine ...... GOLIATH
rime-cold .... YMER
underground .... TROLL
giantess ...... NORN, SKULD, GROA, URTH, NATT
giaour .... CHRISTIAN, UNBELIEVER
gib ...... (TOM)CAT, GILBERT, SALMON, GUT
gibbed .... CASTRATED
gibber ...... CHATTER, JABBER
gibberish .. JARGON, CHATTER, MUMBO-JUMBO, JABBER
gibbet ... GALLOWS, SCAFFOLD
gibbon ... APE, LAR, PRIMATE, WAUWAU, WOUWOU
Sumatran ...... SIAMANG
Gibbons, composer .. ORLANDO
gibbous .... HUMPBACKED, ROUNDED
gibe ..... JEER, TEASE, SNEER, HECKLE, JAPE, FLEER, SCOFF, RIB, TAUNT, GIRD, DERIDE
giblet .... GIZZARD
Gibraltar, cape ... TRAFALGAR
founder of .... GEBIR
Gibson, Charles ____ .. DANA
girl .... MODEL
tennis champ .... ALTHEA
gibus .... OPERA HAT
gid ...... STAGGERS, STURDY
giddiness .... VERTIGO
giddy ..... DIZZY, WHIRLING, FICKLE, HOITY-TOITY, QUEER
Gide, critic .... ANDRE
gift .... PRESENT, TALENT, ABILITY, BOUNTY, TIP, DONATION, BENEFICENCE, INSTINCT, LARGESS(E), BONUS, DOLE, GRANT, LEGACY, BOON, ALMS, SOP, HANDOUT
giver .... DONOR
of gab .... GLIB, ELOQUENCE
of money ..... GRATUITY
recipient .... DONEE
to bride .. DOWER, DOWRY
to employee ..... BONUS
gifted .... TALENTED
gig ... CARRIAGE, (ROW)BOAT, DEMERIT, NAP, CHAISE
gigantic .... COLOSSAL, HUGE, TITANIC, ENORMOUS, IMMENSE, MAMMOTH
statue .... COLOSSUS
giggle ...... LAUGH, TITTER, SNICKER, CHUCKLE
gigot .... MUTTON, VEAL, SLEEVE
gigue .... JIG
Gil, writer .... BLAS
gila monster .... LIZARD
Gilbert and Sullivan actor/fan SAVOYARD
island .... MAKIN, BERU, TARAWA
gild ... AUREATE, GILT, ADORN
gill ... WATTLE, SWEETHEART, GIRL, CHOLLER, BRANCHIA, GLEN, BROOK, NOGGIN, QUARTERN
fungus .... AGARIC
gillie ... SERVANT, ATTENDANT
gills, 4 .... PINT
gillyflower .... STOCK
gilsonite .. UINTAITE, ASPHALT
gilt .... GILDING, DORE, SOW, PIG
gilthead ... CUNNER, SPAROID, PORGY, SCUP, BREAM
gimcrack ... CHEAP, DOODAD, SHOWY, GAUD(Y), (K)NICK(K)NACK, GEWGAW, BAUBLE, TRINKET, NOVELTY
gimlet .... WIMBLE
gimmick .... GADGET
gimp .... ORRIS, FABRIC, NOTCH, GUIPURE
gin ... RUM(MY), TRAP, SLOE, SNARE, BEGIN, NET, GENEVA, WHETHER, IF, TOILS
liquor .... SCHNAPPS
mill .... SALOON
rummy debacle ... BLITZ
ginger .... SPICE, ROOTSTALK, PEP, ENLIVEN, CARDAMON, ASARIUM, CURCUMA
ale-beer ... SHANDYGAFF
colloquial .... VIGOR, SPIRIT
cookies .... SNAPS
wild .... ASARUM
gingerbread .... GAUDY, TAWDRY, CAKE
gingerly .... TIMIDLY, CAUTIOUSLY

gingersnap .... COOKY
gingery ..... SPICY, PUNGENT
gingham ... CHAMBRAY, CLOTH
gingili .... SESAME
gingival .... ALVEOLAR
gingko ... ICHO, MAIDENHAIR
ginseng .... HERB, ROOT
genus .... ARALIA
"Gioconda, La" .. MONA LISA, OPERA, PORTRAIT
composer ... PONCHIELLI
painter .... DA VINCI
gip ...... CHEAT, SWINDLE(R)
gipon .... TUNIC, JACKET
gipsy (see gypsy) .... ROM
giraffe .... CAMELOPARD
like animal ...... OKAPI
long feature of .... NECK
girandole .... FIREWORKS, CANDLEHOLDER, PENDANT, EARRING
girasol ..... OPAL, SUNFLOWER
gird ...... GIBE, JEER, SCOFF, ENCIRCLE, FASTEN, ENCLOSE, EQUIP, CLOTHE, ENDUE
girder ... TBAR, IBEAM, TRUSS, IBAR
girdle ..... SASH, BELT, GIRT, SURCINGLE, CEST(US), ZODIAC, ZONE, CINCTURE, CORSET, SASH, RING, CINGULUM, ZOSTER
India ..... CUMMERBUND
Japanese .... OBI
girdler .... BEETLER
world .... TOURIST, CIRCUMNAVIGATOR
girl ... MISS, SIS, MINX, BELLE, MADCAP, LASS(IE), TIT, JILL, DAMSEL, FILLE, MAID(EN), CHIT
age of .... PUBERTY
beautiful ...... STUNNER
bold .... HOYDEN, TOMBOY, QUEAN, SLUT
colloquial .. SWEETHEART, FILLY
flirtatious .... FIZGIG
giddy .... FIZGIG
graceful .. NYMPH, SYLPH
group .... GSA
haircut ..... BOB, BANGS, PAGEBOY
impudent ... QUEAN, SLUT
in uniform ...... NURSE, WAC, MAJORETTE, SPAR, WREN
in white .... NURSE
introduced to society .... DEB(UTANTE)
lively ... FILLY, HOYDEN
name meaning .. COLLEEN
happiness .. FELICITAS
hospitable ..... ZENIA
joyful .... ADA
noble .... ADELA
of song .... KATE, IRENE, DAISY, LOLA, ADELINE, IDA, LILI MARLENE, FANNY, EADIE, SALLY, RIO RITA
pert, saucy ..... HUSSY, CHIT, MINX, FRAIL
Scouts founder .... LOW
slang ... FLOSSY, FLOSSIE, TIT, SKIRT, BABE, TOMATO
society .... SORORITY
student .... COED
sulky look ... MOUE, POUT
young .... MOPPET
girls' group ... GSA, SORORITY
girth ...... ENCIRCLE, GIRDLE, STRAP, BAND, CINCH
saddle .... CINCH
gisarme .... BATTLE-AX, HALBERD
gist ... CORE, NUB, ESSENCE, SUMMARY, CRUX, PITH, KERNEL, POINT
gitano .... GYPSY, NOMAD
gittern ..... CITHER, CITHARA
Giuba .... JUBA
give .... YIELD, CONCEDE, IMPART, HAND OVER, PAY, CONFER, GRANT, (EN)DOW
and take ..... EXCHANGE, BANTER, REPARTEE, BANDY, HORSE-TRADE
away ... DONATE, BETRAY, EXPOSE, REVEAL, BESTOW
back ... RESTORE, RETURN
birth .... KINDLE, FARROW, DELIVER, WHELP
birth prematurely .. SLINK
ear .... HEED, LISTEN, HEARKEN
expression .... VOICE, ARTICULATE
forth ...... EMIT, ISSUE, SPOUT, EXUDE
in ...... YIELD, CONCEDE, GRATIFY
in law .... REMISE
occasion .... INVITE
off/out .... EMIT
party .... THROW
pleasure to ..... GRATIFY, SATISFY
Scottish .... GIE
sparingly ... DOLE, STINT
up ... CEASE, QUIT, CEDE, YIELD, SURRENDER, CAPITULATE, FORSAKE, LET GO, RENOUNCE
way ...... BEND, YIELD, LET PASS
with reluctance .. GRUDGE
given .... PRONE, STATED, SPECIFIED, ASSUMED
orally .... PAROL
to fighting .. PUGNACIOUS, QUARRELSOME, COMBATIVE
giving attention ..... AUDIENT
milk .... MILCH
offense ...... INVIDIOUS
satisfaction ..... HUNKY
gizzard ...... CROP, STOMACH, GIBLET
glabrous .... HAIRLESS, BALD, SMOOTH
glace ...... CANDIED, FROZEN, ICED
glacial .... ICY, FRIGID, COLD
deposit .... ESKER, MORAINE, OSAR, ESKAR, ASAR, DILUVIUM, PLACER
drift ..... TILL, DRUMLIN
epoch ..... PLEISTOCENE
fissure .... CREVASSE
formation ..... DRUMLIN, SERAC
hill .... KAME, PAHA
ice ... NEVE, FIRN, SERAC
ice block .... SERAC
period .... ICE AGE
ridge ..... ESKAR, ASAR, DRUMLIN, OSAR, ARETE, ESKER, KAME, OS
snowfield ... NEVE, FIRN
glaciate .... FREEZE
glacier .... ICECAP
deposit of ...... MORAINE
facing .... STOSS
fissure .... CREVASSE
ridge .... OS
shaft .... MOULIN
glacis ... SLOPE, EMBANKMENT
glad .... FAIN, WILLING, PLEASED, HAPPY
eye: slang .... OGLE
rags: slang ..... FINERY, CLOTHES
slang .... GLADIOUS
tidings .... EVANGEL, GOSPEL
glade .... LAUND, DELL, VALLEY, LAWN
combining form ... NEMO
gladiator .... RETIARIUS, LANISTA, WARRIOR
school for .... LUDI
gladiolus ..... LILY, IRIS, IRID
bulb .... CORM
gladly .... FAIN, READILY, WILLINGLY, LIEF
glair .... ALBUMEN
glaive .... (BROAD)SWORD, HALBERD
glamor ...... CHARM, ALLURE
colloquial ... OOMPH, IT
glamorous .... ALLURING
glance .... GLIMPSE, LEER, OGLE, FLASH, APERCU, ONCE-OVER
amorous ...... OEILLADE
at book .... BROWSE
off .... GRAZE
quick ... SCAN, LOOK-IN, SKIM
sideways .... SKEW, SQUINT
glancing blow .... SNICK
gland .... CAROTID, THYROID, PAROTID, PANCREAS, SPLEEN, PINEAL, FOLLICLE
combining form .... ADEN(O)
describing one .... DUCTLESS
hormone, adrenal .... CORTISONE
milk .... MAMMA
organ .... THYROID, LIVER, KIDNEY

reproductive cell .... GONAD
secretion ..... HORMONE, ADRENALIN(E), BILE, URINE, SALIVA, GALL, SEBUM, CERUMEN
surgical removal .... ADENECTOMY
glanders .... FARCY
glandlike .... ADENOID
glands inflammation .... ADENITIS
study of .... ADENOLOGY
glandular ...... ADENOID(AL)
disease .... GOITER, CRETINISM
inflammation .. ADENITIS
organ .... LIVER
tumor .... ADENOMA
glare .... STARE, BLAZE, LOOK
glaring ... GARISH, FLAGRANT
Glasgow river .... CLYDE
glass ..... MIRROR, CRYSTAL, CALX, SMALTO, VERRE, MOUSSELINE, TACHYLITE, LENS, TUMBLER, CULLET, SMALT, LALIQUE, RUMMER
artificial jewelry .. STRASS
baking dish .. CASSEROLE
bead .... BUGLE
beer .... SCHOONER
blowpipe ..... MATRASS
blue .... SMALT
bottle ... CRUET, CASTOR, CARBOY, CASTER, PHIAL, VIAL
bowl .... AQUARIUM
bubble .... BLEB
coloring pigment .... SMALTINE, MAT(T)RASS
combining form .. VITRO, HYAL(O)
container .. PHIAL, VIAL, BEAKER, AMP(O)ULE
container for distilling ... BALLOON, MATRASS
cutter .... GLAZIER
cutting tool .... LAP, DIAMOND
drinking ..... TUMBLER, GOBLET
for drinking toasts ...... RUMMER
fused .... FRIT(T)
gem .... STRASS
ground .... FRIT
heat-resistant ..... SILEX
jar ..... BOCAL, CLOCHE
lead .... STRASS
liqueur .... PONY
liquor .... SNIFFER
like ... VITRIC, VITREOUS
made of ...... VITREOUS
maker .... GLAZIER
making material .. SILICA, SAND, POTASH, SILICON, ZAFFRE, ZAFFER, FRIT(T)
making, rod used in ..... PUNTY, PONTIL
molten .... PARISON
mosaic(work) .. TESSERA, SMALTO
piece ..... PANE, SLIVER
polishing disk ...... LAP
roof .... BULL'S-EYE
scraps .... CULLET
Senator .... CARTER
set .... GLAZING
spangled ... AVENTURINE
toast-drinking .. RUMMER
translucent ..... OPALINE
tube, graduated .... BURET(TE)
vial .... AMP(O)ULE
waste .... CULLET
window .... PANE
Glassboro "summit" figure ... JOHNSON, KOSYGIN
glasses: colloq. .... SPECS, GOGGLES
glassmaker .... GLAZIER
glassware articles .... VITRICS
cooking .... PYREX
glassworker .... GLAZIER
glasswort .... KALI, SAMPHIRE
glassy .... TRANSPARENT, SMOOTH, LIFELESS, VITREOUS, HYALOID, VITRIC, HYALINE
eyed ... DAZED, STUNNED
sea .... HYALIN(E)
substance ...... ENAMEL, FEL(D)SPAR
volcanic rock .. OBSIDIAN
glaze ...... COAT(ING), FILM, ENAMEL, VENEER, GLOSS, POLISH
metallic .... REFLECT
with stickum .... SIZE
glazier .... PUTTIER
glazing machine ... CALENDER
gleed .... COAL
gleam .... GLINT, FLASH, GLISTEN, GLOZE
glean .... REAP, COLLECT, GATHER
glebe ... LAND, EARTH, LUMP, FIELD, SOIL, CLOD, TURF
glede .... KITE
glee .... MIRTH, GAIETY, MERRIMENT
gleed .... COAL, EMBER
Gleek .... TIB
gleeman .... MINSTREL
gleet .... OOZE
gleg .... KEEN, SHARP, ALERT
glen .... DINGLE, VALLEY, VALE, DALE, DELL, GILL
Glengaries .... TAMS, CAPS
Glengary man .... SCOT
glib .... FACILE, BLAND, FLUENT, OILY, SMOOTH, VOLUBLE
glide ...... FLOW, SKIM, SLIP, SKIP, SCUD, SKATE, SLIDE, SASHAY
in music .... SLUR
on aircraft .... VOLPLANE
snake's .... SLITHER
gliding across .... LABILE
step .... GLISSADE
glim ... CANDLE, LAMP, LIGHT, EYE
glimmer ..... GLEAM, BLINK, FLICKER
glimpse ..... GLANCE, FLASH, INKLING
glint ... FLASH, DART, GLEAM, GLIMPSE
glioma .... TUMOR
glissade .... SLIDE, GLIDE
glisten ... SPARKLE, GLITTER, FLASH, GLEAM, SHINE
glitter .... CORUSCATE, GLISTEN, SPARKLE, FLASH, BRILLIANCE
glittering .... RUTILANT, BRILLIANT
glitters, it .... GOLD
gloaming ... DUSK, TWILIGHT
global .... WORLD-WIDE, ROUND, SPHERAL
globe ... EARTH, ORB, SPHERE, CLEW, BALL
king's .... MOUND
trotter .... TOURIST
globefish .... PUFFER
globin .... HISTONE
globular ... SPHERICAL, ROUND
globule .. BLOB, PILL, SPHERULE
liquid ...... DROP, BEAD
glockenspiel, instrument like a XYLOPHONE, MARIMBA
glomerate .... CLUSTERED
glonoin ...... NITROGLYCERIN
gloom ..... DARKNESS, BLUES, SADNESS, DUMPS, DIMNESS, MIRK, MURK
gloomy ... DREAR(Y), MOROSE, GLUM, DISMAL, BLUE, SATURNINE, RAYLESS, MOODY, SAD, DARK, MELANCHOLY, DOUR, FERAL, STYGIAN
gloria .... PRAISE, HALO
glorify ...... EXALT, HONOR, PRAISE, BLESS
gloriole .... HALO
glorious .... SPLENDID, MAGNIFICENT
glory .... FAME, RENOWN, SPLENDOR, RADIANCE, EXULT, HALO, HONOR, REJOICE, KUDOS, ECLAT
cloud of .... NIMBUS
head's ... CORONA, HALO, LAUREL, HAIR, TOP, CROWN, TIARA
light .... HALO
gloss .... LUSTER, SHEEN, SHINE, ANNOTATE, POLISH
over .... EXCUSE
glossary ..... LEXICON, CLAVIS
glossing machine .. CALENDER
glossy ... SPECIOUS, LUSTROUS, GLACE, SHINY, SILKEN, SLICK, SLEEK
colloquial .. PHOTOGRAPH
fabric ... SATIN, SATEEN, SILK
material .... ENAMEL
glot: comb. form .. LANGUAGES
glottal stop .... STOSS
glove .... MITT, CUFF, CESTUS, SUEDE, GA(U)NTLET
fabric ..... LISLE, SUEDE
leather ...... SUEDE, KID, MOCHA

triangular piece of ...... GUSSET
glow .... RADIATE, FLUSH, FLASH, GLEAM, BLAZE, ARDOR, RUTILATE
glower ...... GLARE, SCOWL, FROWN, GRIMACE, GAZE, STARE
glowing ... ARDENT, LAMBENT, CANDENT, LUMINOUS, FLUSHED
thru/haze .... LURID
glowworm .... FIREFLY
Gluck, composer .. CHRISTOPH
opera .... ARMIDA
soprano .... ALMA, (REBA) FIERSOHN
glucose .... DEXTROSE, SUGAR, RUTIN, SIRUP
glucoside ... SALICIN, RUTIN, GEIN, INDICAN, SAPONIN, SINIGRIN, SINALBIN
glue .... GELATIN, GOO, GUM, MUCILAGE, AGAR, CEMENT, PASTE
gluey .... STICKY, PASTY
glum ... LONG-FACED, SULLEN, SULKY, GLOOMY, MOROSE
glume .... HUSK, BRACT
glut ... SURFEIT, GORGE, CLOY, FILL, SATIATE, SATE, PAMPER
gluten ... LOAF, BREAD, FIBRIN
glutenous material .... FLOUR
glutin .... GELATIN
glutinous ...... VISCID, GLUEY, SIZY, ROPY, STICKY
glutton .... WOLVERINE, EPICURE, GO(U)RMAND, CORMORANT, GARGANTUAN
gluttonous .... GREEDY, VORACIOUS, PIGGISH
animal .... PIG, HOG, MARTEN, WEASEL
appetite/meal ... GORGE
gluttony .... VORACITY, EDACITY, GREEDINESS
glyph .... CARVING
gnarl ...... CONTORT, TWIST, SNARL, GROWL, SNAG, KNOT, NURR
gnash ... BITE, GRIND, GRATE
gnat ..... MOSQUITO, STINGER, MIDGE, PEST
gnaw .. CHEW, BITE, CORRODE, TORMENT, HARASS, NIBBLE, FRET
gnawed, appear .... EROSE
gnawer ...... RODENT, MOUSE
gnome ..... ELF, NIS, KOBOLD, BROWNIE, DWARF, GOBLIN, SAYING, GREMLIN, BOGIE, MAXIM, IMP
gnomon of sundial .. COLUMN, PIN, STYLE
gnosis: comb. form .... KNOWLEDGE
Gnostic sect member .... MANDEAN
GNP, part of .... GROSS, NATIONAL, PRODUCT
gnu ... ANTELOPE, WILDEBEST
go .... TRAVEL, PROCEED, OPERATE, DEPART, DIE, QUIT, RETIRE
about ...... TACK, GAD, CIRCULATE
after .... PURSUE, CHASE, FOLLOW
against .... OPPOSE
ahead .... GEE, PROCEED
along .... AGREE, COOPERATE, ACCOMPANY
around ... CIRCUMVENT, CIRCULATE, SKIRT
astray .... ERR, SIN, DEVIATE, ABERRATE
at high speed .... BARREL
away! ..... SCAT, SCRAM, SHOO
away suddenly .. DECAMP
back ... REGRESS, REVERT, RECEDE, RETURN, RETREAT, RETROCEDE
between ...... MEDIATOR, AGENT, MIDDLEMAN, ARBITRATOR, INTERMEDIARY
by .... PASS
by plane .... FLY
cart .... PRAM, STROLLER
devil .... SLED
down ... LOSE, SET, SINK
for ..... SUPPORT, LIKE, ADVOCATE
forth .... SALLY, FARE
getter ... HUSTLER, DOER, SALESMAN
off ... EXPLODE, HAPPEN, DEPART, DETONATE
on ____ .... AND ON
one better .... EXCEL, OUTDO, SURPASS
over the wall .... BREAK JAIL, ESCAPE
Scottish .... GAE
to bed .... RETIRE
to bed: colloq. .... HIT THE SACK, HIT THE HAY
wrong ... MISCARRY, SIN
goa ...... GAZELLE, COLONY, ANTELOPE
capital of .... PANJIM
language ..... KONKANI
powder .... ARAROBA
goad ..... SPUR, PROD, GAD, EGG, URGE, INCITE, NEEDLE, PRICK, STING, STICK, ANKUS
goal ...... INTENTION, POST, AIM, END, THULE, OBJECT, BOURN(E)
falls short of .... MANQUE
goat ...... ANGORA, PASANG, BEZOAR
Alpine .... IBEX
animal related to .... GORAL, SHEEP
antelope .... SEROW, GORAL
constellation .... CAPRICORN
cry .... MAA
deity .... PAN
female ... NANNY, CAPRA
genus .... CAPRIA
get one's ... RILE, ANNOY, ANGER, IRK, IRRITATE
hair of .... MOHAIR
hair cloth ...... CAMLET, TIBET, CILICE, ABA, SACKCLOTH
hair cord .... AGAL
Himalayan ...... GORAL, TAHR
horn of ..... CORNUCOPIA
leap .... CAPRIOLE
leather ...... MOCHA, KID
like ... CAPRINE, HIRCINE
like animal ...... GORAL, CHAMOIS
male .... BUCK
man deity .... FAUN
mountain .... TAHR, IBEX, GORAL
pertaining to .... CAPRIC
seller .... BUTCHER
sexual excitement ... RUT, HEAT, ESTRUS
shaped constellation .... CAPRICORN
sucker .... POTOO
wild ... TAIR, TEHR, IBEX, TUR, THAR, KRAS
willow .... SALLOW
wool .... CASHMERE
goatee ..... BEARD, VANDYKE, IMPERIAL
goatfish .... MULLET
goatish ... HIRCINE, CAPRINE
goatman .... FAUN
goats, group of .... FLOCK
goatskin .... MOROCCO
bag .... MUSSUCK
goatsucker ..... NIGHTHAWK, WHIPPOORWILL, POTOO
gob .. MASS, LUMP, TAR, SAILOR
gobbet .... BIT, LUMP, CHUNK, MASS, FRAGMENT
gobble .... EAT, SEIZE
gobbledygook .... TALK
coiner of word .... MAVERICK
gobbler .... TURKEY, TOM
Gobbo .... LAUNCELOT
Gobi .. SHAMO, LAKE, DESERT
gobioid fish .... LOTER
goblet ...... GLASS, CHALICE, CRYSTAL, TASS, BOCAL, CUP, HANAP
drinking ...... MAZARD, MAZER
Eucharist ...... CHALICE
goblin .... ELF, SPIRIT, BOGIE, NIS(SE), POOK, GNOME, PUCK, PUCA, OUPHE, KOBOLD, HOB, BOGY, BROWNIE
doglike .... BARHEST
Egyptian .... OUPHE
friendly .... NIS(SE)
habitat .... CAVE
helpful .... BROWNIE
Norse .... NIS(SE), KOBOLD
goby .... MAPO, FISH

god ... DEITY, IDOL, CREATOR, ALMIGHTY, BRAHMA, SIVA, JEHOVAH, DEVI, ALLAH
agriculture .... SATURN, FAUNUS, THOR, NEBO, OSIRIS
air .... SHU
alcoholic drinks ... SIRIS
altar fire .... AGNI
appearance of .... THEOPHANY
Arcadian .... PAN
avarice .... MAMMON
baboon-faced ... THOTH
beauty .... APOLLO
belief in (one) .... (MONO)THEISM
caduceus-carrying ...... HERMES
combining form ... THEO
commerce ... MERCURY, HERMES
cosmos .... VARUNA
creator .... ATUM
darkness ..... SETH, SIN
day .. JANUS, HORUS, HOR
dead .... YAMA, ANUBIS, ORCUS, OSIRIS
defender .... ANSEL
discord ...... LOKI, LOKE
dog-headed ..... THOTH
dreams ...... MORPHEUS
earth ... BEL, DAGAN, GEB
east wind .... EURUS
elephant-headed .... GANESHA
euphemism for .,... GAD, GOSH, GOLLY
falcon-headed ... HORUS
false ..... BAAL, MOLOCH, MAMMON
fearing ... PIOUS, DEVOUT
fertility ... OSIRIS, DAGAN, FREY
fields .... PAN, FAUN
fire .... AGNI, GIRRU, VULCAN
fish .... DAGAN
flocks .... PAN
force .... PTAH, SHU
forest .... FAUN, PAN
given food ...... MANNA
goat .... PAN
guide to Hades .. HERMES
Hades .. PLUTO, HERMES, DIS, ORCUS
half man, half fish ...... DAGON
happiness .... EBISU, HOTEI
harvest .... CRONUS
health .... OSIRIS
heaven .... BEL, ANU
herds .... PAN
horses .... POSEIDON
ibis-headed ...... THOTH
image conveyance .. RATH
jackal-headed .. ANUBIS, WAPUET
justice .... RAMMAN
killer .... DEICIDE
learning .... THOHT
light ... BALDER, BALDUR, OSIRIS, SHU
like .... DEIFIC
light .... BALDER
lightning .... AGNI, JUPITER
love .... AMOR, EROS, KAMA, POTHOS, CUPID
lower world .... SERAPIS, PLUTO, HADES, DIS
marriage .... HYMEN
medicine ...... IMHOTEP, ASCLEPIUS
Memphis .... PTAH
mirth ..... COMUS, KOMOS
mischief .... LOKI
moon ... THOTH, NANNAR
mountains .... ATLAS, OLYMPUS
music ...... APOLLO, BES
north wind ..... BOREAS
offering to ...... CORBAN
one-eyed .... ODIN
peace ... BALDER, FREY, FORSETI
pleasure .... BES(A)
poetry .... APOLLO
praise to ...... HOSANNA
prosperity .... FREY
rain .. FREY, INDRA, ESUS, JUPITER
revelry .... COMUS, BACCHUS, KOMOS
river .... ALPHEUS
Saturday .... SAETER
science .... HERMES
sea ...... DYLAN, ATLAS, POSEIDON, NEPTUNE, NEREUS, TRITON, PONTUS, AEGER, YMIR
seven-armed ...... AGNI
shepherds .... PALES
sky ..... ANU, NUT, TYR, YMIR, JUPITER, DYAUS, TIU
sleep .... SOMNUS, MORPHEUS, HYPNOS
southeast wind ... EURUS
study of ...... THEOLOGY
sun ..... RA, SOL, FREY, NINIB, BELI, SHAMASH, AMEN-RA, PHOEBUS, APOLLO, AMON, BAAL, BALDER, HELIOS, HORUS, MITHRAS
thieves ...... MERCURY, HERMES
thunder ... THOR, DONAR, ZEUS, JUPITER
two-faced .... JANUS, AGNI
underworld ...... PLUTO, ORCUS
vegetation ... ESUS, ATTIS
victory ...... ODIN, ZEUS
visible appearance of .... THEOPHANY
war ..... THOR, AS(S)UR, TYR(R), ER, ODIN, MARS, MENT, ARES, COEL, QUIRINUS, WODEN, IR(R)A, TIU
waters ... NEA, FONTUS, VARUNA
wealth .... PLUTUS
winds ... ADAD, AEOLUS, BOREAS, ADDU, EURUS, VAYU
wing-shod ..... HERMES, MERCURY
wisdom .... NEBO, ODIN, EA, GANESA, SABU, THOTH
woods ...... SYLVANUS, SILVANUS
youth .... APOLLO

God's acre .... CEMETERY
chosen people .... ISRAELITE(S)
Little Acre ... CALDWELL

Godden .... RUMER

goddess ...... DEA, BEAUTY, DEVI, SHRI, LACHESIS
abundance .... SRI
agriculture ... DEMETER, CERES, ISIS, OPS
air .... HERA
arts and sciences .... ATHENA, MUSE, CLIO, CALLIOPE, EUTERPE, ERATO, THALIA, URANIA, MELPOMENE
astronomy ..... URANIA
avenging .. NEMESIS, FURY
beauty ... VENUS, FREYA
birth .... PARCA
cat-headed ...... PACHT
chance .... TYCHE
chase .. ARTEMIS, DIAN(A)
childbirth .... LUCINA
comedy .... THALIA
crops .... ANNONA
dawn .... EOS, AURORA, US(H)AS
death ..... DANU, HEL(A)
destiny ..... URD, URTH, MOIRA, NORN
destruction .. KALI, ARA
discord .... ERIS, ATE
doom ..... URTH, WYRD
earth ...... TELLUS, TARI, GAIA, TERRA, CERES, ARURU, ISHTAR, LUA, GAEA, GE, ERDA, OPS, SEB
faith .... FIDES
fate .... PARCA, NORN, NONA
fertility .... ASTARTE, FAUNA, ANNONA, ISIS, ISHTAR
fields ..... TELLUS, FAUNA
fire .. VESTA, HESTIA, PELE
flowers .... CHLORIS, NANNA, FLORA
fortune .... TYCHE
fountains ...... FERONIA
fruits .... POMONA
ghosts .... HECATE
giant .... NORN, URTH
grains .... CERES
harvest ...... OPS, CARPO
healing .... EIR, GULA
health ... SALUS, HYGEIA, HESTIA
hearth .... HESTIA, VESTA
heaven .... NUT

history ...... CLIO, SAGA
hope .... SPES
horses .... EPONA
hunting .... DIAN(A), VACUNA
invention ...... MINERVA
justice .... THEMIS, ASTRAEA, MAAT
life ...... ISIS, LACHESIS
light .... LUCINA
love ... HATHOR, ASTARTE, SELENE, ARTEMIS, FREYA, APHRODITE, IS(H)TAR, VENUS
magic .... HECATE
marriage ...... GAEA, GE, JUNO, HERA
minor .... NYMPH
mischief ...... ATE, ERIS
moon .... CYNTHIA, SELENE, LUNA, DIANA, ARTEMIS, LUCINA, PHOEBE, HECATE, ISIS
music .... EUTERPE
nature .... ARTEMIS, CYBELE, NYMPH
night .... LETO, NOX, NYX
peace ...... PAX, IRENE, MINERVA, EIR
persons drowning ... RAN
plenty .... OPS
poetry .... ERATO, CALLIOPE
prosperity .... SALUS
rainbow .... IRIS
retribution ... ARA, ATE, NEMESIS
revenge .... NEMESIS
science .... MUSE
seas ..... DORIS, RAN(A), INO, SALACIA, AMPHITRITE
seasons ... HORA, HOUR
sky .... NUT, FRIGG
splendor .... UMA
spring .... VENUS, IDUN, ITHUN(N)
strife .... ERIS
trees .... POMONA
truth .... MAAT, MA
underworld .... HEL, HECATE, LARUNA, GAEA
vegetation .... CORA, CERES, FLORA, KORE
vengeance .... ARA, NEMESIS
victory .... NIKE
virtue .... FIDES
volcano .... PELE
war ... MINERVA, ANATU, ALEA, ATHENA, ENYO, BELLONA, ISHTAR, VACUNA
waters .... ERUA
welfare .... SALUS
wisdom ...... MINERVA, PALLAS, ATHENA
womanhood ...... MUT, SATI, JUNO
woods .... DIAN(A), ARTEMIS
youth ...... HEBE, IDUN, ITHUN(N)

goddesses of beauty/charm ... GRACES
destiny .... FATES
fate ..... NORNS, MOERAE
nature .... HORAE
seasons ... HOURS, HORAE

godfather .... SPONSOR
godforsaken .... WICKED, DESOLATE, FORLORN, DEPRAVED
godhead .... DIVINITY
godless .... PAGAN, WICKED, IMPIOUS, ATHEISTIC
godlike ...... HOLY, DIVINE, OLYMPIAN
godliness .... PIETY
godly ...... PIOUS, RELIGIOUS, DEVOUT
person .... SAINT
godmother .... CUMMER
godparent .... SPONSOR
godown .... WAREHOUSE
gods' abode ... ASGARD, MERU
battle against the .... THEOMACHY
"blood" .... ICHOR
cupbearer ... GANYMEDE, HEBE
drink .... NECTAR
king of .... WODEN
messenger ...... HERMES, MERCURY, IRIS
mother of .... RHEA
origin of .... THEOGONY
queen of ..... SATI, HERA, JUNO
race of .... VANIR
strife among .... THEOMACHY

godsend .... MANNA
godspeed .... SUCCESS
Godwin Austen, Mount ...... DAPSANG
godwit .... SNIPE
Goebbels' (Joseph) forte ...... PROPAGANDA, BIG LIE
Goethe's hero .... FAUST, WERTHER
heroine .... MIGNON
goffer ... CRIMP, PLEAT, FLUTE
Gog and ____ .... MAGOG
goggle ... STARE, BULGE, ROLL
goggler ..... CICHARRA, SCAD
goggles .... SPECTACLES, SUNGLASSES
Gogol hero .... (TARAS) BULBA
Goidelic language ..... ERSE, MANX
going ..... EXIT, DEPARTURE, WORKING, AVAILABLE, LEAVING
get .... BEGIN, START
in .... ENTRY, ENTRANCE
on .... NEARLY, NEARING
out ...... EXIT, EXODUS, EGRESS(ION)
goings on .... BEHAVIOR, CONDUCT
goiter .... STRUMA
Golconda .... MINE
gold ...... GILT, ORO, CYME, MONEY, RICHES, WEALTH, AU(RUM), SOL
alchemist's .... SOL
alloy .... ASEM
assaying cup ..... CUPEL
band .... CARCANET
black .... OIL
braid .... ORRIS
brick .... SHIRK(ER), LOAF(ER)
Bug author .... POE
cast .... INGOT
Coast .... GHANA
Coast languages ... TSHI
Coast river ...... VOLTA
coat with .... GILD
coating ... GILT, GILDING
coin ..... DUCAT, KRONE, GUINEA, ANGEL, MOHUR, LOUIS, OBANG, LIRA, SCUDO, TOMAN, DARIC, LION, PISTOLE, IMPERIAL, DOUBLOON, BEDIDLIK, EAGLE
collar .... CARCANET
color .... YELLOW
colored metal ... ORMOLU
colored ore ..... PYRITE
content ... CARAT, KARAT
cover .... GILT
deposit .... PLACER
district, African ... RAND
fineness ... CARAT, KARAT
imitation ...... ORMOLU, PINCHBECK
in alchemy .... SOL
lace .... FILIGREE
land .... OPHIR
leaf .... FOIL
leaf, imitation .... CLINQUANT, ORMOLU
like .... AUREATE
like alloy .... ASEM, OROIDE, ORMOLU
lump .... NUGGET
miner of 1849 .... FORTY-NINER
miner' camp: sl. .... DIGGINGS
mines region .. KLONDIKE
mosaic .... ORMOLU
native .... NUGGET
necklace ..... CARCANET
paint .... GILT
pertaining to ..... AURIC
product ... COIN, ALLOY, JEWELRY
rush partaker .... ARGONAUT
rush site .... YUKON
seeker .... MINER, ARGONAUT
separate gravel from .... PAN
sheet ..... FOIL, LATTEN
Spanish .... ORO
symbol .... AU
tinge .... GILD, GILT
vein .... LODE
wire work ..... FILIGREE

goldbrick .... LOAF, SHIRK
golden ...... AURIC, YELLOW, AUREATE
Age .... SATURNIAN, MILLENIUM

apples, guardian of ..... IDUN, ITHUN, HESPERID
ball, king's ..... MOUND
ball, small .... GLOBE
calf .... IDOL
color ..... YELLOW, DORE
combining form .... CHRYS(O)
Fleece keeper ... AEETES
Fleece location .. COLCHIS
Fleece maiden .... HELLE
Fleece searcher ... JASON, ARGONAUTS
Fleece ship .... ARGO
Horn location .... BOSPORUS, ISTANBUL
king, legendary ... MIDAS
oriole ..... PIROL, LORIOT
robin .... ORIOLE
shiner ..... ROACH, DACE
Treasury item ...... ODE, SONNET, POEM
goldeneye ... BIRD, WHISTLER
goldenrod .... SOLIDAGO, YELLOWWEED
"Goldfinger" hero ..... BOND
goldfinch .... REDCAP, (YELLOW)BIRD
goldfinny .... CUNNER
goldfish ..... FANTAIL, COMET
goldilocks ...... BUTTERCUP
Goldsmith, poet ..... OLIVER
golem .... ROBOT, AUTOMATON
golf aid ...... CADDY, CADDIE
ball material .... BALATA
ball's position ...... LIE
championship cup ...... RYDER
club ..... CLEEK, IRONS, (MID)IRON, BRASSIE, NIBLICK, JIGGER, WOOD, PUTTER, SPOON, BULGER, MASHIE, DRIVER
club part .... NECK, HOSEL, TOE, HEAD
course .... GREEN, LINKS
course hazard .... (SAND)TRAP, STYMIE, POND, BUNKER
feat ..... EAGLE, BIRDIE, HOLE-IN-ONE
hole ...... CUP, DOGLEG
holes unplayed ..... BYE
partner, imaginary ...... BOGEY
position .... STANCE
problem .... STYMIE
score ...... PAR, BOGEY, BIRDIE, EAGLE
stroke ...... PUTT, BAFF, SCLAFF, DRIVE, LOFT
stroke, awkward .... FOOZLE
stroke over par ... BOGEY
term ... LIE, LOFT, BOGEY, TRAP, FORE, BIRDIE, EAGLE, BONE, BAFF, DIVOT, DORMIE, BISQUE, PUTT, FAIRWAY, GREEN, HOLE, HAZARD, ROUGH, SLICE, HOOK
tourney .... PRO-AM, OPEN
turf .... DIVOT
golfer .... HOGAN, SNEAD, TEER, CASPER, LITTLER, PALMER, PLAYER, NICKLAUS, SANDERS, OUIMET, MANGRUM, DIVOT DIGGER, JONES
adviser of, sometimes .... CADDIE
attire of ... PLUS FOURS, KNICKERS
cry of .... FORE
goal of .... CUP
poor .... DUBBER
Golgotha .... CALVARY
goliard ..... JESTER, MINSTREL
Goliath ... GIANT, PHILISTINE
home of .... GATH
slayer of .... DAVID
golliwogg .... DOLL
gomeral ... SIMPLETON, DOLT, FOOL
gomuti ... SAGO, EJOO, PALM, ARENGA
palm .... ARENG(A)
product ... SUGAR, WINE, ROPE
gonad .... OVARY, TESTIS, SPERMARY
gonagra .... GOUT
gondola ...... (CANAL)BOAT, BARGE, CABIN
man ... POLER, BOATMAN
place of .... VENICE
race .... REGATTA
gondolier's song .. BARCAROLE
work ... ROWING, POLING
gone ...... LOST, DEAD, AGO, OUT, USED, UP, CONSUMED, OFF, AWAY
by .... PAST
"Gone with the Wind" character .... MELANIE, (RHETT)BUTLER, (SCARLETT) O'HARA, ASHLEY
Goneril's father .... LEAR
sister .. REGAN, CORDELIA
gonfalon ..... FLAG, ENSIGN, BANNER
gong .... BELL, TAMTAM, TOM-TOM
Philippine .. KULINTANG
striker .... HAMMER
gonof/gonoph .... THIEF
gonorrhea .... CLAP
goo .... GLUE
goober .... PEANUT
good ... SUITABLE, EFFICIENT, UNSPOILED, VALID, GENUINE, REAL, SOUND, MORAL, BON, KIND, PUCKA, PUKKA
arrangement .... EUTAXY
Book .... BIBLE
by .... ADIEU, TATA, FAREWELL, AU REVOIR
cheer .... REVELRY, FEASTING
digestion ..... EUPEPSIA
fellow (Robin) ... SPRITE
for-nothing fellow .... IDLER, LOAFER, WASTREL, VAGABOND, NE'ER-DO-WELL
harvest: archaic .. FOISON
health .... PEART
humored ..... CHEERFUL, JOLLY, AGREEABLE
looking .... COMELY, FAIR, BEAUTIFUL, HANDSOME
luck bringer .... MASCOT
luck present .... HANDSEL
management .... EUTAXY
natured .... AMIABLE, PLEASANT
news ... EVANGEL, GOSPEL
order .... EUTAXY
point! .... TOUCHE
sense ... JUDGMENT, WIT
Shepherd .... JESUS
taste, of ...... ESTHETIC
time ...... BASH, SPREE
turn .... FAVOR
will .... GREE
"Goodbye, Columbus" author ROTH
player ... (ALI) MCGRAW
goodly ..... READILY, AMPLE, FINE, PLEASING
goodman ... HUSBAND, MASTER
title equivalent to .... MISTER
goodness ... VIRTUE, KINDNESS
goods .... FEE, STOCK, MERCHANDISE, WARES
British .... FREIGHT
cast overboard .. JETSAM, LIGAN, LAGAN, JETTISON, LAGEND
deliver the .... COME ACROSS, PRODUCE, FULFILL
movable .... CHATTEL
on hand ..... INVENTORY, STOCK
sold together .... TIE-IN
goody .... CANDY
gooey .... STICKY
goof ...... BONER, BLUNDER, FAIL, DOLT, ERR(OR)
on diamond ... FUMBLE, MUFF
goofy .... STUPID, SILLY
gook ..... KOREAN, JAPANESE, ORIENTAL, VIETCONG
goon .... THUG, HOOD(LUM), RUFFIAN, ROUGH(NECK)
goop's inventor ..... BURGESS
goosander ...... MERGANSER, DUCK
goose .... SOLAN, BARNACLE, GRAYLAG, BERNICLE, BRANT, IDIOT
berry .... FABES
colloquial ... DUPE, GULL
cry ..... YANG, CACKLE, HONK
domestic, large .. EMDEN
eggs .... 000, ZERO(s)
European wild .... GRAYLAG

foot membrane .... WEB(BING)
footless .... GANNET
genus .... ANSER
grease .... AXUNGE
Hawaiian .... NENE, NENI
male .... GANDER
of a .... ANSERINE
pygmy .... GOSLET
sea .... SOLAN
sound ..... HISS, CACKLE
stepper .... GERMAN
wild ... BERNICLE, BRANT
young .... GOSLING
gooseberry ...... FABES, POHA
goosefoot ..... BEET, SPINACH
gooseneck .... LAMP
gopher ... RODENT, SQUIRREL, TORTOISE, MINNESOTAN, SUSLIK, SPERMOPHILE
Mexican .... TUCAN
slang .... BURGLAR
state .... MINNESOTA
tortoise ...... MUNGOFA
gorcock .... GROUSE
Gordian knot cutter .... ALEXANDER
tier .... GORDIUS
gore .... PIERCE, CRUOR, BLOOD, GUSSET, STAB, HOOK
gorge ..... CLOUGH, CANYON, RAVINE, GULLET, PASS, GORMANDIZE, BARRANCA, GULLY, CHASM, FLUME, GLUT, POUCH, CLOY, STUFF, COULOIR, KLOOF
gorged .... REPLETE
gorgeous .... BEAUTIFUL, RESPLENDENT, MAGNIFICENT, SPLENDID
"Gorgeous Gussie" .. MORAN
gorget .... COLLAR
Gorgon ... MEDUSA, JEZEBEL, EURYALE, STHENO
Gorgons, watchers for the .... GRAEAE, GRAIAE
gorilla ..... APE, TROGLODYTE
slang .. THUG, GANGSTER, GOON
Gorki, novelist .... MAXIM
gormandize .. GORGE, GUTTLE
gorse .. FURZE, WHIN, SHRUB
gory .... BLOODY
goshawk .... BUTEO
Goshen race .... TROT
gosling .... GOOSE
gospel ..... EVANGEL, TRUTH, DOCTRINE, EVANGILE
preaching of .... EVANGELISM
writer .... MARK, MATTHEW, JOHN, LUKE
gossamer .... (COB)WEB, FILM(Y)
gossamery ..... DIAPHANOUS, GAUZY, THIN, FILMY
gossip .... TATTLE(R), CAT, BLAB(BER), TIDBIT, TITBIT, BUSYBODY, HEARSAY, SCUTTLEBUTT, CHAT(TER), ONDIT, EME, QUIDNUNC, TALK, BUZZ, CHITCHAT, TALE(BEARER)
choice: colloq. .. EARFUL, TIDBIT
female ...... TABBY, CAT
malicious ..... SCANDAL
gossipy morsel .... TIDBIT
gossoon .... BOY
Goth .... BARBARIAN, ALARIC
Gothic .... MEDIEVAL, BARBAROUS
arch .... OGIVE
bard .... RUNER
vault's groin ..... OGIVE
Goths' Christian bishop ...... ULFILA(S)
Gotland seaport .... VISBY
Gouda .... CHEESE
gouge .... ROUT, CHEAT, CHISEL, BENT, GROOVE, SWINDLE(R), (DE)FRAUD, IMPOSTOR
goulash ...... RAGOUT, STEW
Gounod opera .... FAUST
opera hero ...... ROMEO
gourd ...... MELON, SQUASH, CALABASH, PUMPKIN, PEPO, CURCURBIT(E)
pod's substance .. LOOFAH
rattle .... MARACA
shaped rattle ... MARACA
shell .... CALABASH
gourmand .... GLUTTON, GOURMET, EPICURE
gourmet ... TASTER, EPICURE, GASTRONOME, GO(U)RMAND
gout .... CLOT, BURSITIS, ARTHRITIS, PODAGRA, GONAGRA
French .... TASTE
remedy .... GUACO
govern .... DIRECT, RULE, REIGN, MANAGE, CURB, RUN
governess ... DUENNA, NANNY
government ... CONTROL, RULE, DIRECTION, STATE, REGIME(N), POLITY
business .... OFFICIAL
by gods ..... THEARCHY
by men .... PATRIARCHY
by military .... STRATOCRACY
by priests ... THEOCRACY, HAGIARCHY, HIERARCHY, HIEROCRACY
by saints ... HAGIARCHY
by ten .... DECARCHY
by three rulers .... TRIARCHY, TRIUMVIRATE
declaration .. MANIFESTO
fiscal problem ... BUDGET
grant .... SUBSIDY, FRANCHISE
mob's .... OCHLOCRACY
of 2 rulers ...... DIARCHY
report ..... WHITE PAPER, BLUE BOOK
seat .... CAPITAL
without .... ACRACY
women's .... GYNARCHY, GYNECOCRACY
governor .... RULER, REGULATOR, BAN, REGENT, PILOT, NOMARCH, VICEROY, EPARCH, EXARCH, ETHNARCH
Algerian .... DEY
military ..... MARGRAVE
Moslem .... HAKIM
Persian .... SATRAP
Roman ..... PROCONSUL
subordinate ... TETRARCH
Turkish .... BEY
gowan .... DAISY
gowk ... SIMPLETON, CUCKOO
gown .... DRESS, ROBE, NEGLIGEE, MANTUA, FROCK
like garment ..... TUNIC, TOGA
outer .... SURCOAT
skirt of .... LAP
goy .... GENTILE
Graafian follicle ..... OVISAC
grab .... SEIZE, SNATCH, TAKE, SHIP, HOG
grabble ...... SEIZE, GROPE, SPRAWL
Gracchus' brother ...... GAIUS
grace ...... BEAUTY, FAVOR, CHARM, DECENCY, PRAYER, DIGNIFY, TACT, ATTEND, ADORN, CHARISMA, HONOR, MERCY, TITLE
Aglaia ..... BRILLIANCE
Euphrosyne .... JOY
kind of .... REPRIEVE, RESPITE, MORATORIUM
note .... INCIDENTAL
Thalia .... BLOOM
graceful .... BEAUTIFUL, WILLOWY
animal .... GAZELLE
bird .... SWAN
dance ... BALLET, WALTZ
graceless .... CLUMSY, AWKWARD, INELEGANT
Graces, one of the ... THALIA, EUPHROSYNE, AGLAIA, JOY
mother of .... AEGLE
gracile .... SLENDER, SLIM
gracious ... BENIGN, URBANE, POLITE, MERCIFUL
grackle ... BLACKBIRD, MINA, MYNA(H), DAW, TINKLING, TROUPIAL
gradate .... BLEND
gradation ... ABLAUT, STAGE, DEGREE, NUANCE, STEP, TRANSITION
grade ... STEP, DEGREE, MARK, RATING, INCLINE, CLASS, LEVEL, RANK, SORT
"failure" .... FLUNK
grader .... PUPIL
gradient ..... WALKING, SLOPE
gradin ..... SHELF, STEP, SEAT
gradual fall .... DECLINE
graduate ... ALUMNUS, GRAD
graduated glass tube .. BURETTE
graduation ceremony .... COMMENCEMENT
certificate ..... DIPLOMA
gradus .... DICTIONARY
Graeae, one of the .... DEINO

concern of the .. GORGONS
describing the .. ONE-EYED
parent of ..... PHORCUS
Graf .... EARL, COUNT
battleship .... SPEE
graffiti .... SCRAWLS
graft ... CLAVE, TRANSPLANT, (S)CION, IMP, INARCH
grafted, in heraldry .... ENTE
grafter, petty .... GRIFTER
grail .... AMA, PLATTER, CHALICE, CUP
Holy .... SANGREAL, SANGRAAL
grain ... SEED, CEREAL, WHEAT, RICE, OAT, RYE, BIT, KERMES, WALE, MEAL, SPELT, CORN, CURN, MILLET, KERNEL
basket .... SCUTTLE
batch of .... GRIST
beard ..... AWN, ARISTA
beetle .... CADELLE
black .... URD
bract .... GLUME
building ..... GRANARY
chaff .... BRAN
combining form .. GRANI
cracked .... GROATS
cutter .... SCYTHE
disease .... SMUT, ERGOT
elevator .... SILO
exchange .... PIT
fungus .... ERGOT
grindstone .... MANO
ground .... GRITS, GRIST, SAMP
hand mill .... QUERN
hulled .... GROATS, GRITS
husk ...... GLUME, BRAN
in kernels .... CORN, MAIZE, MEALIES
Indian ..... MAIZE, CORN
loss thru spillage .... ULLAGE
measure .... BUSHEL, QUARTER, MOY, CAVAN, GANTA, CHUPA, SACK
mill .... QUERN
outer covering .... HUSK
pest .... CADELLE
refuse .... SCOURINGS
row, drying ... WINDROW
shelter .... HUTCH
skin .... BRAN
small .... GRANULE
sorghum ...... KAF(F)IR
stack .... MOW
storehouse .. ELEVATOR, SILO, GARNER, GRANARY
stumps .... STUBBLE
grains .... SPEAR
3.17 .... CARAT
grainy .... GRANULAR
gram ..... PLANT, CHICK-PEA
molecule .... MOL(E)
grama .... GRASS
gramary .... MAGIC
gramercy .... THANKS
gramineous .... GRASSY
grammar causal connective .... FOR, SINCE, THEREFORE
grammarian .... PROSODIST
grammatical case ..... DATIVE
construction ... SYNESIS, SYNTAX
description ...... PARSE
error .... SOLECISM
mark .... ASPER
term ..... CASE, GENDER, MOOD, PARSE, SUBJECT, TENSE
gramophone .... PHONOGRAPH, VICTROLA
grampus ... SPRINGER, ORC(A), WHALE, COWFISH
relative .... DOLPHIN
Granada, king of ... BOADBIL
granary ..... SILO, ELEVATOR, GRANGE, CRIB, GARNER, STOREHOUSE, BIN, GOLA
grand ... GREAT, CHIEF, MAIN, MAGNIFICENT, IMPOSING, STATELY, AUGUST, NOBLE, PIANO, MAJESTIC
Canal bridge .... RIALTO
Coulee .... DAM
Coulee designer .. SAVAGE
duchess' relative .... TSARINA
jury's word .. IGNORAMUS
mal .... FIT, EPILEPSY
National site .... AINTREE
Old Party member ...... REPUBLICAN
Pre heroine .. EVANGELINE
slam .... JACKPOT, VOLE
grandam .... CRONE
grandchild .... OYE
Grande and others ...... RIOS
grandee ..... NOBLEMAN, PEER
grandeur ... GLORY, MAJESTY, EMINENCE, DIGNITY, NOBILITY, SPLENDOR
grandfather ...... PATRIARCH
pertaining to .... AVITAL, AVAL
grandfatherly .... KINDLY, BENIGNANT
grandiloquence ...... BOMBAST
grandiloquent ..... MAGNIFIC, TURGID
grandiose ...... COSMIC, EPIC, IMPOSING, GRAND, HOMERIC, POMPOUS, IMPRESSIVE
Grandma Moses ...... ANNA
grandmother .... BELDAM(E), GRANDAM
grandmotherly .... FUSSY, INDULGENT
grandparents, having same ... GERMAN
of .... AVAL
grandson .... NEPOTE
grandstand .... BLEACHERS
play .... STUNT
grange ..... GRANARY, FARM
granger .... FARMER
granite .... ROCK, PORPHYRY, APLITE, MUSCOVITE, BIOTITE
constituent .. FEL(D)SPAR, MICA, QUARTZ
imitation ... SCAGLIOLA
rock resembling .. GNEISS
granny ..... KNOT, GRANDMA
grant ..... APPANAGE, ADMIT, CONFER, ASSENT, AGREE, (CON)CEDE, AWARD, PATENT, (RE)MISE
by will .... DEMISE
of money ...... SUBSIDY, ENDOWMENT
U.S. president .. ULYSSES
granted without obligation .... GRATUITIOUS, GRATIS, FREE
grantee .... RECIPIENT
grantor .... DONOR
granular .... GRAINY
mineral ...... CORUNDUM
mow .... NEVE, FIRN
grape .... MUSCADINE, DELAWARE, CONCORD, CATAWBA, NIAGARA, ISABELLA, MALMSEY, MUSCAT, UVA, BERRY, TOKAY, ACINUS, MALAGA, SCUPPERNONG, WAMPEE, MALVASIA
acid, of ...... GLYCOLIC
coating, powdery .... BLOOM
conserve .... UVATE
crushed pulp ...... RAPE, POMACE
disease ...... COULURE, ESCA, ERINOSE
dried ..... RAISIN, PASA
fruit .... SHADDOCK, POMELO
fruit, dried .... CURRANT
jelly .... SAPA
juice ... DIBS, SAPA, STUM, MUST
juice deposit .... TARTAR
juice, in pharmacy .. SAPA
juice liquor ...... RAKI, RAKEE
like ...... POKE, UVA(L), UVIC
preserve .... UVATE
product .... WINE
pulp ..... POMACE, RAPE
refuse ... BAGASSE, MARC
seed .... ACINUS
Spanish .... UVA
sugar .... MALTOSE, DEXTROSE, GLUCOSE
unfermented ...... STUM
wine .... CATAWBA
grapefruit .... POMELO, PUMELO, SHADDOCK
grapes, bunch .... BOB, BOTRYOID
of/like .... VINACEOUS
powdery coating .. BLOOM
pulp ..... RAPE, POMACE
where grown .. VINEYARD
grapevine ... RUMOR, HEARSAY
disease .... ERINOSE
item ..... RUMOR, GOSSIP
graph ..... DIAGRAM, CHART
meteorological event .... ISOPLETH
graphic .... CLEAR, VIVID, LIFELIKE, PICTORIAL
art .... PAINTING,

DRAWING, ETCHING, PHOTOGRAPHY, DRYPOINT, OFFSET
description ...... IMAGE
granite....... PEGMATITE
graphite ... LEAD, PLUMBAGO, CARBON, KISH
graplin ... GRAPNEL, CRAMPON
grapnel .... GRAPLIN(E), ANCHOR, CREEPER, DRAG
grapple ...... WRESTLE, BIND, GRIP, HOLD, CLUTCH, LOCK
grappler ... WRESTLER, HAND
grappling iron ..... GRAPNEL, GRAPLIN, CRAMPON
grasp ... SEIZE, UNDERSTAND, HOLD, CONTROL, REACH, HENT, GRIP, GRAB, CLUTCH
grasping .... GREEDY, AVARICIOUS, FELL, SORDID, HENT, MISERLY
grass ..... POA, DARNEL, RIE, ZACATON, GRAMA, SORGO, HERB(AGE), BROME, REED, BAMBOO, LAWN, PASTURE, GRAZE, RYE, WHEAT, BARLEY, OAT, AVENA, QUITCH, FESCUE, VETIVER, NARD, FOXTAIL
African .... ALFA
Algerian ...... ESPARTO
Andean .... ICHU
Asiatic .... MILLET, CITRONELLA
basketry .... OTATE, REED, ESPARTO
blade .... SPEAR
blue .... POA
bract .... GLUME
brooms .... ZACATON
bunch .... TUFT
carpet ..... CHICKWEED
cereal ..... RICE, MILLET, SORGHUM, RAGGEE, RAG(G)I, OAT, RYE
Ceylon .. PATANA, CHENA
chafflike bract ... GLUME
cloth material .... RAMIE
clump .... HASSOCK, TUSSOCK
coarse .... SEDGE, REED, ESPARTO, COUCH, SACATON
cordage .... ESPARTO
corn .... KAF(F)IR
country .... VELD(T)
covered soil .... TURF, SWARD
cutter ... (LAWN)MOWER, REAPER, SCYTHE
dried .... HAY
East Indies ...... GLAGA
family, of the .. POACEOUS
flower part ...... PALEA, BENT
fodder .... TEOSINTE
for thatch ... NETI, ALANG
forage ... GAMA, MILLET, REDTOP, SORGHUM, SORGO, TEOSINTE
genus .... AVENA, STIPA, POD
grain-yielding .. FETERITA
grapevine .... MESQUITE
growth, new .... FOG
hay .... TIMOTHY
husk .... GLUME
Indian cereal ..... RAGEE, CORN
jointed stem ...... CULM
Kentucky .... POA
killer .. DOWPON, ESTERON
lawn .... REDTOP
leaf ...... BLADE, SPEAR
like Indian corn .... TEOSINTE
marsh ... SPART, SEDGE, REED, FESCUE
meadow ... POA, FESCUE
mesquite .... GRAMA
millet .... PANIC
moor .... HEATH
new growth .... FOG
oat .... AVENA
ornamental ... EULALIA
paper-making ... ESPARTO
pasture .. GRAMA, FESCUE, REDTOP
pertaining to .. POACEOUS
Philippine ...... COGON, TALAHIB
plant like .... SEDGE
plot .... LAWN
poisonous ...... DARNEL
quaking .... BRIZA
reedy .... BENT, DISS
rope-making ..... MUNG
rope: Sp. .... SOGA
rug .... MAT
rye ... MARCITE, DARNEL
scale .... PALEA
second crop ..... ROWEN
seed weight measure ..... CARAT
shoot .... SPEAR
snipe .... SANDPIPER
sorghum .... SORGO
sour .... SORREL
Spanish .... ESPARTO
stem .... CULM
stemmy .... REED
swamp ..... SEDGE, REED
tuft .. TUSSOCK, HASSOCK
uncut/ungrazed .... FOG
wheat-like ...... CHEAT, CHESS
widow .... DIVORCEE
wiry .... BENT, POA, ZACATON
grasshopper .. GRIG, LOCUST, KATYDID, CRICKET
military ..... AIRPLANE, SCOUTER
grassland ... SWARD, PASTURE, RANGE, LEA, CAMPO, SAVANNA(H), VELD(T), PRAIRIE, MEAD, PAMPA
grassy .... TURFY
plain .... CAMPO
grate ..... RUB, RASP, GRIND, ANNOY, FRET, CREAK, FIREPLACE, GRIDE, ABRADE, SCRAPE, IRRITATE, CHARK, JAR, SCROOP
grateful .... APPRECIATIVE, WELCOME, PLEASING, THANKFUL
grater ..... ANNOYER, VEXER, PEST
gratification ..... GRATUITY, SATISFACTION
gratify ..... SATISFY, HUMOR, INDULGE, REWARD, PLEASE, SATE
vanity .... FLATTER
gratin .... CRUST
grating .. GRATE, IRRITATING, HOARSE, ANNOYING, RASPING, GRID(IRON), RASPY, GRILL(E), LATTICE(WORK), STRIDENT
gratis ..... FREE, GRATUITOUS
gratitude ...... APPRECIATION
gratuitous ..... FREE, GRATIS
gratuity .... TIP, PRESENT, BOON, CUMSHAW, VAIL, LAGN(I)APPE, PERQUISITE, FEE, GIFT
gratulation .... JOY
graupel .... SLEET, HAIL
gravamen .... GRIEVANCE, COMPLAINT, CHARGE, ACCUSATION
grave .... WEIGHTY, OMINOUS, MOUND, TOMB, SOLEMN, SOMBER, SCULPTURE, BARROW, SOBER, ETCH, SEDATE, DULL, SERIOUS, STAID, CARVE, SEPULCHER, SATURNINE
cloth .... CEREMENT, SHROUD
digger .... SEXTON
heap of earth/stone ..... BARROW, TUMULUS, MOUND
marker .... BARROW, STELE, HEADSTONE
robber .... GHOUL
gravel ..... CALCULUS, BEACH, SAND, HECKLE, GRIT
a boat .. BEACH, GROUND
between road ties .... BALLAST
colloquial ..... IRRITATE, ANNOY
deposit .... GEEST
mound .... OS
shifter .... RIDDLE
graven .... CARVED, SCULPTURED, FIXED
image .. IDOL, ICON, IKON
Gravenstein .... APPLE
graver .... BURIN, ETCHER, SCULPTOR, CARVER, CHASER, CHISEL
Graves' disease .... GOITER
gravestone ... MARKER, STELE, STELA, MEMORIAL, BARROW, SLAB
graveyard .... CEMETERY
gravid .... PREGNANT
graving tool .... STYLET, CHISEL, BURIN
gravitate .... DROP, FALL, SINK, SETTLE
gravity .... SOLEMNITY,

SERIOUSNESS, WEIGHT
gravy ..... SAUCE, PROFIT, JUS
thickener .... ROUX
gray .... DULL, DREARY, DISMAL, OLD, ASHEN, GRIZZLE, HOAR(Y)
brownish .... TAUPE
Friar .... FRANCISCAN
hair .... GRIZZLE
matter .... BRAINS, THALAMUS
mole .... TAUPE
mottled ...... GRISEOUS
parrot .... JAKO
rock .... SLATE
grayfish .... DOGFISH
grayish blue ..... TEAL, BICE, AZURINE, PERSE, LIVID
brown ...... TAUPE, DUN
tan .... BEIGE
white .... HOARY
graylag .... GOOSE
grayling .... UMBER, BUTTERFLY, FISH, TROUT
graze .... PASTURE, RUB, SCRAPE, SCRATCH, TOUCH, GLANCE(OFF), FEED, BRUSH, SHAVE, NICK, BROWSE, AGIST
livestock .... PASTURE
with bullet .... CREASE
grazing land ...... (G)RANGE, RANCH(O), PASTURE
rope ... LARIAT, TETHER
grease .... FAT, LARD, LUBRICANT, LUBRICATE, BRIBE, TIP, AXUNGE, DAUB, OIL, COOM
cosmetics ... COSMOLINE
monkey ..... MECHANIC
refuse .... SLUSH
sheep's wool ..... SUINT
greasewood .... ORACHE, CHICO
greasy ... UNCTUOUS, SLIPPERY, PINGUID, FATTY, OILY
great ...... HUGE, EMINENT, SUPER(IOR), IMPOSING, CLEVER, EXPERT, FINE, NOBLE, UNCO, MAGNA, BIG, TITANIC
amount .... BARREL, LOADS
artist .... MASTER
artistic work .... MASTER(PIECE)
Barrier reef .... OTEA
Bear .... URSA
care .... PAINS
combining form .. MAGNI, MEGA(LO)
Commoner ..... BRYAN, CLAY, PITT, STEVENS
Dane .... DOG
deal: colloq. .... HEAP, LOT
Desert .... SAHARA
Divide ... DEATH, CRISIS
Emancipator ... LINCOLN
grandchild .... IER
Lakes ... ERIE, ST. CLAIR, ONTARIO, HURON, SUPERIOR, MICHIGAN
Lakes boat ... MACKINAW
Lakes fish .... TULLIBEE, CISCO, PIKE, MASKALONGE
Lakes steamer .... WHALEBACK
Mogul ..... NABOB, VIP
northern diver .... LOON
number ... HORDE, LOTS, HOST, LEGION, GALAXY, HEAP, LAKH
omentum .... CAUL
Profile ...... BARRYMORE
Pyramid builder .. CHEOPS
Pyramid dweller .... PHARAOH, KHUFU, KHAFRE, MENKAURE
Pyramid site .... GIZA
Spirit, Indian ... MANITO
Tom of Oxford .... BELL
toe .... HALLUX
White Father .. PRESIDENT
White Way .. BROADWAY, RIALTO
greatcoat .... PALETOT
Greater Antilles island .. CUBA, PUERTO RICO, JAMAICA, HISPANIOLA
greatest .... UTMOST, VERIEST
greatly .... HIGHLY
greaves .... CRACKLINGS, ARMOR, CRACKNEL
grebe ..... DABCHICK, LOON, DUCKER, DIPPER, DIDAPPER
Grecian ... GREEK, HELLENIC, GRECO
Grecism .... HELLENISM
Greco-Egyptian deity .... SERAPIS
Turkish dispute, object of CYPRUS
gree .... GOOD WILL
Greece .... ATTICA, (H)ELLAS, ACHAEA, ELIS
of modern ...... ROMAIC
greed(iness) .... EDACITY, CUPIDITY, AVARICE, GLUTTONY, AVIDITY
greedy .... GRASPING, AVARICIOUS, ACQUISITIVE, VORACIOUS, GRIPPLE, RAVENOUS, ESURIENT, AVID, COVETOUS, INSATIABLE
person ... PIG, GLUTTON, GO(U)RMAND, HARPY, CORMORANT
Greek ..... CRETAN, ARGIVE, HELLENE, AEOLIAN, ATTIC, ACHAEAN, IONIAN, HELLENIC
abbess .... AMMA
actor's boot ..... BUSKIN
after piece .... EXODE
alphabet ... MU, PI, TAU, RHO, ALPHA, BETA, ETA, NU, XI, KAPPA, THETA, ZETA, OMEGA, IOTA
alphabet first letter ...... ALPHA
alphabet last letter ...... OMEGA
apartment ..... ANDRON
architect .... ICTINUS
aristocrat ..... EUPATRID
assembly .. AGORA, BOULE
athlete .... MILO
athletic contest ... AGON
author ... AESOP, HOMER, PINDAR, ZENO, SAPPHO, PLATO, PLUTARCH, TIMON
avenging spirit .. ERINYS, ATE, FURY
basket of fruits .... CALATHUS
bee .... MELISSA
belt .... ZOSTER
bestman ... PARANYMPH
beverage ..... OENOMEL
bishop .... EPARCH
boatman .... PHAON
bottle .... AMPULLA
boxing-wrestling bout ... PANCRATIUM
bridesmaid .. PARANYMPH
buckle .... FIBULA
cape ... PAPAS, MATAPAN, ARAXOS, MALEA
capital .... ATHENS
Catholic .... UNIAT(E)
centaur .... NESSUS
channel .... EURIPUS
choral dance movement .. STROPHE
church diocese .... EPARCHY
Church, father of .... GREGORY, ORIGEN
Church hermits' community .... SKETE
circus arena .... HIPPODROME
citadel .... ACROPOLIS
city ..... NEMEA, SPARTA, ARGOS, SALONIKA, CORINTH, CHALCIS, PIRAEUS, MYCENAE, JANINA, THERMA, LARISSA, ELIS, ARTA, ERETRIA, SICYON, ELEUSIS
city in Asia Minor ...... MELETUS
city in Italy .... SYBARIS
city in Turkey .... PERGAMUM
clan .... OBE
clasp .... FIBULA
classical name ... DANAI
coin ... OBOL, DRACHMA, OBOLUS, LEPTON, STATER
colony ..... ELEA, IONIA
column ... DORIC, IONIC
comic poet ... MENANDER
commander ... NAVARCH, HIPPARCH, CHILIARCH
concubine ..... HETAERA, HETAIRA
commonalty ..... DEME, DEMOS
concert hall ...... ODEUM
contest .... AGON
counselor .... NESTOR

country .... ELIS, EPIRUS
courtesan .... THAIS, HETAERA
cross, design like .... SWASTIKA
cry of sorrow ..... AI AI
cup .... SCYPHUS, DEPAS
dance .... PYRRHIC
devoted wife: myth. ..... BAUCIS
dialect .... (A)EOLIC, DORIC, IONIC
dirge .... LINOS
district ... AONIA, ATTICA, ARGOLIS, LOCRIS, MEGARIS
drink .... NECTAR
earth .... GEOS
enchantress ...... CIRCE, MEDEA
epic poem ..... ODYSSEY, ILIAD, RHAPSODY
fabulist .... AESOP
faction .. ELAS, EAM, EDES
farce .... MIME
fate .... LACHESIS
feather .... PTERON
female worshipper ...... ORANT
festival ... DELIA, AGON, DIONYSIA
fillet .... TAENIA
flask .... OLPE
galley .... BIREME, TRIREME
garden: myth. .... HESPERIDES
garment .... PEPLOS, CHITON, CHLAMYS
geographer ..... STRABO
geometer .... HERON
ghost .... KER
giant ..... ARGUS, ORION, CYCLOPS, BRIAREUS, ARGES, TITAN, CACUS
giant wrestler .. ANTAEUS
girdle .... ZOSTER
god ..... APOLLO, ARES, ARTEMIS, EOS, CHAOS, ONIROS, HYMEN, BACCHUS, LETO, EROS, ZEUS, HELIOS
  earth .... BEL
  festivity ...... COMUS
  fire .... VULCAN
  flocks .... PAN
  heaven(s) .... URANUS, ZEUS, BEL
  hunter .... ORION
  love .... EROS
  marriage ..... HYMEN
  medicine ... ASCLEPIUS
  mockery ..... MOMUS
  north wind ... BOREAS
  rain .... ZEUS
  revelry ..... BACCHUS, COMUS
  river .... ERIDANUS
  sea .... NEREUS, POSEIDON
  sky ..... ARGUS, ZEUS
  sleep .... HYPNOS, HYPNUS
  sun ... HELIOS, APOLLO, PHOEBUS
  supreme .... ZEUS
  vegetation .. DIONYSUS
  wealth .... PLUTUS
  winds .. AEOLUS, EURUS
  wine .... DIONYSUS
  war .... ARES
goddess .... DEA
  agriculture ... ARTEMIS, DEMETER
  air .... HERA
  arts .... ATHENA
  beauty ..... APHRODITE
  chance .... TYCHE
  chase .... ARTEMIS
  dawn .... EOS
  destruction .... ARA
  discord .... ERIS
  earth .... GAEA, GAIA, HECATE
  fate .... MOERA
  flowers .... CHLORIS
  ghosts .... HECATE
  goblins ...... ARTEMIS
  health .... HYGEIA
  hearth .... HESTIA
  heavens .... HERA
  hunting ...... ARTEMIS
  justice .... THEMIS
  love .... APHRODITE
  marriage ... DEMETER, GAIA, HERA
  memory ... MNEMOSYNE
  mischief ..... ATE, ERIS
  moon .... SELENE, HECATE, ARTEMIS, ASTARTE
  nature .... ARTEMIS
  night ...... LETO, NYX, LEDA
  peace .... IRENE
  retribution ... ARA, ATE
  seas ...... INO, DORIS
  sky .... INO
  sorcery ...... HECATE
  strife .... ERIS
  vegetation ...... CORA, COTYS
  vengeance ... NEMESIS, ARA
  victory .... NIKE
  war .... ATHENA, BELLONA
  weaving ...... ERGANE
  wisdom ...... ATHENA, PALLAS
  witchcraft .... HECATE
  women .... HERA
  youth .... HEBE
gods, queen of ..... HERA
governor .... EPARCH, NOMARCH
grave marker ..... STELE
guerrilla ..... ELAS, EDES, EAM, KLEPHT
guest .... XENOS
gulf .... AEGINA, SALONIKA, CORINTH, PATRAS
gymnasium .... XYST, PAL(A)ESTRA
half man, half dragon ... CECROPS
hat ... PETASUS, PETASOS
headband .... TAENIA, MITER
headland .... ACTIUM
heart .... KARDIA
hedgehog ...... ECHINOS
hemp .... KANNABIS
herald .... STENTOR
hermit .... GILES
hero .... AJAX, IDAS, THESEUS, JASON, ALCINOUS
historian .... XENOPHON, DIONYSIUS, HERODOTUS
"holy hill" .... ATHOS
Hours .... HORAE
hunter: myth. ..... ORION
huntress ..... ATALANTA
hymn .... PAEAN
immigrant .... METIC
initiate .... EPOPT(A)
island ..... CHIOS, DELOS, SALAMIS, LEMNOS, LEUCADE, CRETE, ELIS, KOS, RHODES, NAXOS, MILO, NIO, MELOS, PELION, SKORPIOS, MYTILENE, SAMOS, IOS, THASOS, SPORADES, PATMOS, EVVOIA, PAROS
isthmus ...... CORINTH
jar ... CRATER, AMPHORA
jump .... HALMO
king ...... CONSTANTINE
king of Arcadia .. LYCAON
king of Corinth .... SISYPHUS
king of Crete .... IDOMENEUS
king of Mycenae .... ATREUS
language .... KOINE
language, pertaining to .. ROMAIC
legislative assembly ..... BOULE
leper .... LEPRA
leprosy .... ALPHOS
letter ...... ALPHA, BETA, CHI, DELTA, ETA, EPSILON, GAMMA, IOTA, KAPPA, PHI, LAMBDA, MU, NU, OMICRON, PSI, RHO, SIGMA, TAU, THETA, UPSILON, XI, ZETA, OMEGA
liqueur .... OUZO
love feast .... AGAPE
lyric poet .... PINDAR, ANACREON, ALCAEUS
magistrate .... DIMIURGE, ARCHON, EPHOR
mantle ...... CHLAMYS, PALLIUM, PALLA, HIMATION
market place .... AGORA
marriage .... GAMOS, HYMEN
masses .... DEMOS
mathematician .. EUCLID
measure .... BEMA

memorial of victory ..... TROPHY
metropolitan .... EPARCH
milestone .... HERMA
military organization .... EAM, ELAS, EDES
militia .... PALIKAR
Modern .... ROMAIC
monks' community ..... SKETE
money ... MINA, TALENT, DRACHMA
monster: myth. .. SPHINX, HYDRA, CHIMERA, HARPY, LAMIA, TYPHON
moralist ..... PLUTARCH
mountain ...... PELION, PARNASSUS, ATHOS, OLYMPUS, HELICON, HYMETTUS, IDA, OSSA
mountain chain .... OETA, PINDUS
mouse .... HYRAX
Muse .... CLIO, EUTERPE, ERATO, URANIA, CALLIOPE, POLYMNIA, THALIA
Muses' home: myth. .... AONIA
musician .... ARION
mythical flier ... ICARUS
mythical princess .... EUROPA
native ... SCIOT, CYPRIOT
note in music ...... NETE
nymph ...... M(A)ENAD, (HAMA)DRYAD, SALMACIS, HESTIA, NEMERTES, ARETHUSA, OENONE
official .... EPHOR
orator .... DEMOSTHENES
order of architecture .... CORINTHIAN, IONIC, DORIC
overseer .... EPHOR
painter .. GRECO, ZEUXIS
parliament .... BOULE
pastoral district .... ARCADIA
pastoral poet ..... BION, THEOCRITUS
patriarch .... ARIUS
patriot .... BOZZARIS
peasant-poet .... HESIOD
people .... DEMOS
peninsula .... MOREA, PELOPONNESUS
philosopher ...... ZENO, PLATO, DIOGENES, EPICTETUS, HERACLITUS, THALES, ARISTOTLE
physician .... GALEN
pillar .... HERMA
pitcher .... OLPE
place for discussions .... EXEDRA
plain .... OLYMPIA
platform .... BEMA
poem ...... EPIC, EPODE, ILIAD, ODYSSEY
poet ..... HOMER, ARION, HESIOD, MENANDER, PINDAR, ANACREON, THESPIS, ALCAEUS
poetess .... SAPPHO
poetry in strophes .... MELIC
populace .... DEMOS
port .... AULIS
portico ...... STOA, XYST
premier........ PAPAGOS
priest's helper .. PARASITE
priestess .... HERO
princess .... IRENE
province .... NOME
queen ...... ANNE-MARIE
queen-mother .... FREDERIKA
race .... GENOS
racing course .... HIPPODROME
regent .... ZOETAKIS
region .... DORIS, THESSALY
resistance group .. EDES, ELAS, EAM
retreat to the sea .... KATABASIS
revolutionary leader ...... YPSILANTI
river .... PENEIOS, SALAMBRIA
rose .... CAMPION
sacred grove ...... ALTIS
satirist .... LUCIAN
scarf .... PEPLOS, PEPLUS, PEPLUM
scholar's specialty ...... ILIAD
sculptor .... MYRON, PHIDIAS, LYSIPPUS
seagod .... TRITON
seaport .... ENOS, SALONIKA, PATRAS
senate .... BOULE
serf .... PENEST
serpent: myth. .. PYTHON
seven .... ZETA
shawl ... PEPLOS, PEPLUM
shepherd, legendary ..... ENDYMION
shield .... PELTA
shipping tycoon .... ONASSIS, NIARCHOS, VERGOTTIS
signpost .... HERMA
skeptic .... PYRRHO
skirt for men .... FUSTANELLA
slab .... STELE
slaughter of cattle ...... HECATOMB
slave .... PENEST, HETAERA, HIERODULE
soldier .... PELTAST, PALIKAR, HOPLITE
song .... MELOS
soothsayer ..... TIRESIAS, CALCHAS
sorceress .. CIRCE, MEDEA
soul .... PNEUMA
speaker's platform ...... BEMA
spider .... ARACHNE
spirit .... PNEUMA
stage ...... PROSCENIUM
star .... ASTER
statesman ..... METAXAS, PERICLES
stoa .... PORTICO
Stoic philosopher .... EPICTETUS
street dress .... HIMATION
sungod .... HELIOS
sylvan deity ...... SATYR
symbol .... ORANT
symbol of abundance ... CALATHUS
talking horse .... ARION
temple part .... NAOS, CELLA
theater .... ODEON
theologian .... ARIUS
thread, legendary .. CLEW
time .... CHRONOS
titan .. CRONUS, OCEANUS
town .... SERES
township .... DEME
tragedian ...... THESPIS
tragedy, father of .... THESPIS
tragic hero ..... ORESTE
tribe .... PHYLE
tribe subdivision .... PHRATRY
troop unit .... TAXIS
trumpet .... SALPINX
tunic .... CHITON
underground army ...... ELAS, EAM, EDES
uterus .... METRA
valley .... TEMPE, NEMEA
vase ..... PELIKE, PYXIS
verb tenses ..... AORISTS
village, battlesite .... MARATHON
war cry .... ALALA
war dance ...... PYRRHIC
warrior ..... DIOMEDES, AJAX, ACHILLES, ACAMAS, ODYSSEUS
wedding song/poem .... HYMEN(EAL)
weight ... MINA, OBOL(US)
wine .... OENOMEL
wing .... PTERON
wise man .... THALES
woman .... GYNE
women's headband ..... MITER
word .... LOGOS
wrestling school .... PAL(A)ESTRA

green .... NEW, LEAFY, MILD, ACTIVE, BILIOUS, UNRIPE, VERT, SIMPLE, RAW, NILE, CALLOW, BICE, FRESH, NAIVE, VERDANT, OLIVE, EMERALD, RESEDA, JADE
becoming .... VIRESCENT
bright .... EMERALD
chalcedony ..... JASPER
cheese .... SAPSAGO
colloquial ...... JEALOUS
color .. JADE, VERT, BICE, OLIVE, EMERALD
eyed .... JEALOUS, ENVIOUS

film on copper .. PATINA
fly .... APHID
gage .... PLUM
garnet .... OLIVINE
golden .... AENEOUS
growing plants .... VERDURE
Hat author ...... ARLEN
heraldic .... VERT
land .... ERIN
light: colloq. .... PERMISSION, PERMIT, AUTHORIZATION
Mansions character ..... ABEL, RIMA
manure .... CLOVER
monkey .... GRIVET, VERVET, GUENON
mountain state .... VERMONT
onion .... SCALLION
room .... FOYER
room occupant ... ACTOR
sand .... MARL
shade ... LIME, OLIVE, PEA
sickness ..... CHLOROSIS
stamp name .... EIRE
stone .... PERIDOT, JADE
tail .... GRANNOM
tea .... HYSON
vegetation .... VERDURE
vitriol .... COPPERAS
greenery .... VERDURE, HOTHOUSE
greenfinch .... LINNET, GROSBEAK, SPARROW
greenheart ... WOOD, BEBEERU, TREE
greenhorn .... NOVICE, BEGINNER, DUPE, ROOKIE, GULL, TYRO
greenhouse .... HOTHOUSE, VINERY, VIVARIUM
vine .... SMILAX
greening .... APPLE
greenish .... VIRIDISCENT, VIRESCENT
blue .... TORQUOISE
white .... RESEDA
yellow ... OLIVE, SULPHUR
Greenland base .... ETAH
capital .... GODTHAAB
discoverer .... ERIC
fish ...... LING, BURBOT
native .... ITA
town .... ETAH
greenlet .... SONGBIRD, VIREO
greenness .... VIRIDITY, VERDANCY, VERDURE
greens ..... VEGETABLES, KALE
greenshank ...... SANDPIPER
greensickness .... ANEMIA, CHLOROSIS
greenstone ..... JADE, WHIN, DIORITE
greensward .... TURF
greet ..... ACCOST, WELCOME, MEET, HAIL, ADDRESS
greeting ... AVE, SALUTATION, WELCOME, SALUTE, ALOHA, HAIL
card .... VALENTINE

Indian .... NETOP
Oriental .... SALAAM
gregarious .... SOCIABLE, OUTGOING
grego .... CLOAK
Gregory of ____, Saint .... NYSSA, TOURS
gremlin ... MEDDLER, GNOME
grenade .... SHELL, BOMB
grenadier ..... INFANTRYMAN, FISH
grenadine ..... SIRUP, CLOTH
Grendel .... MONSTER
Grenoble river .... ISERE
Gretchen .... MARGARET
Gretna Green arrivals .... ELOPERS, SWEETHEARTS
Grey, author .... ZANE
greyhound ... DOG, STEAMSHIP, BUS, WHIPPET, SALUKI
gribble .... BORER
grid ... GRATING, ELECTRODE, FOOTBALL
slang .... FOOTBALL
griddle .... PLATE, PAN
cake ... SCONE, FLAPJACK
gride .... SCRAPE, RASP, GRATE, JAR
gridiron ... GRILL(E), GRATING, FOOTBALL FIELD
scores, briefly .... TDS
grief ... TEEN, WOE, SORROW, PAIN, SADNESS, MISERY, DOLOR
grievance .... GRAVAMEN, COMPLAINT, RESENTMENT, SCORE
colloquial .. BEEF, GRIPE
grieve .... RUE, DISTRESS, SADDEN, LAMENT, MOURN, CRY
grievous .... SEVERE, ATROCIOUS, SAD, HEINOUS, LAMENTABLE
griff(e) .... MULATTO, SPUR
griffon .... DOG, GYPS
grifter .... CONMAN
assistant .... SHILL
grig ...... EEL, GRASSHOPPER, CRICKET
grill .... RESTAURANT, BROIL, GRID(IRON), QUIZ, RACK, INTERROGATE, HIBACHI
meat-roasting .... BUCCANEER
grilse .... SALMON, FISH
grim .... FIERCE, SAVAGE, CRUEL, STERN, DOUR, MACABRE, RESOLUTE, SINISTER, GHASTLY, MERCILESS
Reaper .... DEATH
grimace ...... SCOWL, FLEER, POUT, MOUE, MOP, FROWN, GLOWER, MOW(E), MOUTH, MUG, SNOOT
grimalkin ..... CAT, WOMAN
grime ..... SOOT, DIRT, COLLY
Grimes (Golden) ...... APPLE
grimy .... DINGY
grin .... SMILE
grind ..... MASTICATE, GRATE, PULVERIZE, CRUSH, MULL, CHEW, GRIT, BRAY, MILL, TRITURATE, CRUNCH, LEVIGATE, SHARPEN, HONE, RUB, SAND, DRUDGERY, TASK, WHET
harshly .... GRIDE
the teeth ... GNASH, GRIT
grinder ...... MOLAR, HONER, TOOTH, CRUSHER, MILL
grinding device .... MILL, MOLAR, MULLER, MORTAR, PESTLE, MILLSTONE, WHETSTONE, METATE
substance .... SAND, EMERY, ABRASIVE
grindstone ..... HONE, MANO, METATE
gringo .... AMERICANO, FOREIGNER
grinning .... RIDENT
grip ..... HOLD, GRASP, CLASP, CLUTCH, CLAMP, CONTROL, HANDLE, BAG, VALISE, STAGEHAND
gripe ...... PINCH, DISTRESS, CLUTCH, AFFLICT, CONTROL, HANDLE
slang ..... COMPLAIN(T), GRUMBLE, BEEF
grip(pe) .... COLD, FLU, INFLUENZA
gripping device .... VISE, VICE, CLAMP, DOG, CLUTCH
gripple .... AVARICIOUS, MISERLY
gripsack .... VALISE
Griqua .... MULATTO
Griselda, like .... PATIENT, MEEK
griseous .... GRAY
grisette .... SHOPGIRL
griskin .... LOIN
grisly .... HORRIBLE, MORBID, GHASTLY, GRUESOME
grist ... MEAL, LOT, QUANTITY
for the ____ ...... MILL
gristle .... CARTILAGE
grit .... PLUCK, SAND(STONE), NERVE, COURAGE, FORTITUDE, GRAVEL
grith ..... SANCTUARY, PEACE, SECURITY
grits ... MEAL, HOMINY, KASHA
gritty ..... SANDY, PLUCKY, BRAVE, SABULOUS
grivet ..... GUENON, WAAG, TOTA, MONKEY
kin .... VERVET
grizzle ... GRAY, FRET, WORRY, COMPLAIN
grizzly ...... GRAYISH, BEAR
groan .... MOAN
groat .... COIN
grocer .... STOREKEEPER
grog .... RUM, RUMBO
groggery/grogshop ... SALOON
groggy ...... TIPSY, DRUNK, DIZZY
groin, of or near ... INGUINAL
swelling .... BUBO
grommet ...... EYELET, RING, BECKET
gromwell .... FLOWER

Gromyko, Soviet diplomat .... ANDREI
groom .... MANSERVANT, DEVELOP, CURRY, NEATEN, (H)OSTLER, TRAIN, ATTENDANT, BRUSH, TIDY(UP), EQUERRY, SICE
horse ... COISTREL, SYCE
grooming process ... TOILETTE
groove .... CULLIS, ROUTINE, FLUTING, FURROW, FLUTE, RUT, CREASE, CHASE, STRIA(E), SCARF, FILLISTER, SULCUS
barrel .... RIFLING, CROZE
in architecture ... GLYPH
in iron .... FULLER
made by plow ... FURROW
masonry .... RAGLET, RAGGLE
minute .... STRIA
grooved ..... LIRATE, STRIATE, SULCATE, STRIGOSE
grooves ..... RIFLINGS, SCORES, SPLINES
grope ..... PROBE, FEEL, TAY, FERDE, FUMBLE
for words .... HAW
Gropius .... GROPE
architectural school ..... BAUHAUS
grosbeak .... MORO, (HAW)FINCH
gross ... COARSE, FAT, BURLY, CORPULENT, GLARING, FLAGRANT, DENSE, THICK, RANK, ENTIRE, CRASS, VULGAR, RUDE, CRUDE
1/12 of .... DOZEN
opposed to .... NET
grot .... CAVE, SHRINE
grotesque .... BIZARRE, FANTASTIC, ABSURD, BAROQUE
Groton product ... SUBMARINE
grotto .... CAVE, SHRINE, SUMMERHOUSE
grouch ... SULK, GRUMBLE(R)
Groucho ____ .... MARX
ground .... EARTH, LAND, SUBJECT, TOPIC, BASIS, FOUNDATION, CAUSE, MOTIVE, REASON, TERRAIN
above .... ALIVE
beam .... SLEEPER
break .... START, DIG
corn .... MEAL, SAMP, FARINA
cover .... TRAVERSE, TRAVEL
dig in the .... GRUB
elevation .... RISE
gain .... PROGRESS
give .... YIELD, RETREAT
grain ...... MEAL, SAMP, GRIST
hog ...... WOODCHUCK, MARMOT
hog day .... CANDLEMAS
meal .... FARINA
nut ..... GOBBE, PEANUT
parcel of .... SOLUM
pulverizer ...... SPIDER
rising .... HURST
squirrel ..... CHIPMUNK, HACKEE, GOPHER, SUSLIK, SPERMOPHILE
unplowed, solid .... HARDPAN
grounder ...... DAISY CUTTER
groundhog .... MARMOT, WOODCHUCK
groundless .... BASELESS, IDLE, UNJUSTIFIED
groundling .... CREEPER
grounds ... DREGS, SEDIMENT, BASIS, REASON, LAWNS, GARDENS, LEES, RESIDUE, GROUT
around building .. CLOSE, COMPOUND
college .... CAMPUS
groundsel .... RAGWORT
groundwork ..... BASIS, BASE, FOUNDATION
group ... UNIT, BAND, CREW, MASS, CLUSTER, SCHOOL, SWARM, BLOC, BODY, HERD, FLOCK, DROVE, BEVY, COVEY, GENUS, CADRE, CLASS, CORPS, NYE
advisers' ... BRAINTRUST, CAMARILLA
discussion .. BULL SESSION
of admirers ..... CLAQUE
animals/plants .... GENUS
buildings .... PILE
buses, etc. .... FLEET
eight .... OCTAD, OCTET(TE)
families .... CLAN
fishes .... SCHOOL
five .... PENTAD, QUINTET(TE), QUINARY
fliers .... FLIGHT
flora or fauna .. GENUS
girls .... BEVY
houses, country ...... HAMLET
lions .... PRIDE
modeled figures .... DIORAMA
nine .... ENNEAD, NONUPLET
paid applauders .... CLAQUE
performers ...... CAST, TROUPE
seven .... HEPTAD, SEPTET(TE)
ships .... FLEET, FLOTILLA
speech sounds .... PHONEME, DIAPHONE
ten .... DECADE
trees ... GROVE, WOODS, FOREST
20 priests ..... FETIAL
singing ... HOOTENANNY, CHOIR, TRIO, CHORUS
slang .... CABOODLE
small .... KNOT
grouped .. AGMINATE, BANDED
grouper .... MERO, BONACI, SEABASS, WARSAW
grouse .... HEATHBIRD, PTARMIGAN, SAGE HEN, PINTAIL, PHEASANT, BLACKCOCK
female .... GORHEN
male .... GORCOCK, BLACKCOCK
red .... MOOR COCK, MUIRFOWL
slang ...... COMPLAIN(T), GRUMBLE, CRAB
grout ...... MEAL, GROUNDS, LEES, SEDIMENT, DREGS, PORRIDGE
grove ...... BOSCAGE, COPSE, TOPE, NEMUS, BOSK(ET), WOOD(S), HOLT, SPINNEY
near Athens .. ACADEME
pines .... PINETUM
prairie .... MOTT(E)
sacred .... NEMUS
where Aristotle taught ... LYCEUM
grovel .... CRAWL, CREEP, CRINGE, FAWN
grow ... SPROUT, CULTIVATE, ACCRUE, DEVELOP, BREED, FLOURISH, RAISE, ACCRETE, THRIVE, WAX, MATURE
dim/faint .... WANE
hot/red .... FLAME
rapidly ..... MUSHROOM, BOOM
tired ...... FLAG, WEARY
grower .... FARMER
growing in couples ... BINATE
in high altitude .. ALPINE, ALPESTRINE
in pairs ..... GEMINATE, DIDYMOUS
on .... EPIGEOUS
one side only .... SECUND
out .... ENATE
together ...... ACCRETE
under water .. IMMERSED
growl .. RUMBLE, COMPLAIN(T), GRUMBLE, YAR(R), GNAR, SNARL, GIRN
growler .... DOG, BEAR
growler's content ...... BEER
grown .... MATURE
up .... ADULT
growth ...... DEVELOPMENT, CORN, SHOOT, WATTLE, POLYP, WEN, SPUR, ACCRETION
abnormal body .. TUMOR, CANCER
body ...... WART, MOLE
facial ... BEARD, WHISKER
new .... SHOOT
place of rapid ... HOTBED
process .... NACENCY
skin ... WEN, WART, MOLE
stunted in ..... SCRUBBY, RUNTY
together ..... SYMPHYSIS
grub .... DIG, DRUDGE, RUMMAGE, ASSART, UPROOT, LARVA, MAGGOT
axe .... MATTOCK

slang ..... EAT(S), FEED, FOOD
street .... MILTON
street habitues ... HACKS
to ... SLAVE, MOIL, SPUD
grubble .... FEEL, GROPE
grubby .... DIRTY, UNTIDY, MESSY
Gruber, composer .... FRANZ
grubstake recipient .... PROSPECTOR
grudge .... ILLWILL, MALICE, ENVY, SPITE, ANIMUS, PIQUE, PEEVE
grue .... SNOW, ICE
gruel .... BROTH, ATOLE, EXHAUST, CAUDLE, PORRIDGE, BURGOO, LOBLOLLY
grueling .... EXHAUSTING
gruesome .... MORBID, GRISLY, GHASTLY, FEARSOME, MACABRE, HORRIFYING, GRIM
gruff .... HOARSE, BLUNT, HARSH, RUDE, SURLY
throat sound .... GRUNT
grugru .... PALM, LARVA
grume .... CLOT
grumble ... GRIPE, COMPLAIN, GROUCH, GROUSE, GROWL, RUMBLE, MUTTER, FRET, REPINE, KICK
grumbler .... GROUCH, COMPLAINER
grumpy ..... SURLY, PEEVISH
Grundy, Mrs. .... PRUDE
grunion .... SILVERSIDE
grunt and groaner .. WRESTLER
sound .... OINK
grunter .... PIG, HOG
former .... INDIAN
Grus .. CRANE, CONSTELLATION
Gruyere .... CHEESE
g-string .... LOINCLOTH
guacharo ...... GOATSUCKER, (OIL)BIRD
Guadalcanal town ..... AOLA
guaiac .... TONKA BEAN, SEED
Guam capital .... AGANA
governor ..... GUERRERO
illness ...... GUHA, GUJA
native/tribe .. CHAMORRO
tree .... IPIL
guama .... INGA, GUAVA
guana .... MAJAGUA
guanaco-like animal ... LLAMA, CAMEL
guanay .... CORMORANT
droppings .... GUANO
guano .... TUATARA, MANURE, FERTILIZER
source of .. BATS, GUANAY
Guarani .... TUPI
guarantee ... VOUCH, PLEDGE, ASSURANCE, ASSURE, ENDORSE, WARRANT(Y), AFFIRM, SURETY, BOND
guarantor .... SURETY
guaranty .... SECURITY
guard ...... DEFEND, SHIELD, PROTECT(OR), WATCH, SHIELD, OSTIARY, PATROL, PICKET, CONVOY
armed .... SENTRY, SENTINEL
Asgard's ...... HEIMDALL
car's .... FENDER
Freemason's ...... TILER
Hades .... CERBERUS
Io's .... ARGUS
night .... BIVOUAC
of the bed ..... EUNUCH
on ..... ALERT, VIGILANT
post .... WATCH
ship .... CONVOY, CORVET(TE)
troops' .... PICKET
guarded .. CAUTIOUS, CAREFUL
guardhouse .. BRIG, HOOSEGOW
guardian .... CUSTODIAN, TRUSTEE, CUSTOS, KEEPER, WARDEN, TUTELAR, DRAGON
concern of .... WARD, INCOMPETENT
function of .... TUTELAGE
legendary .... ARGUS, CERBERUS
minor's .... CURATOR, TUTOR
of an incompetent ...... CURATOR
of portals .... JANUS
spirit ... GENIUS, DAEMON, LARES
guardianship ..... TUTELAGE, TUITION
guarding against attack ...... DEFENSE
Guatemala grass ... TEOSINTE
Indian .... MAYA
insect .... KELEP
money .... QUE(T)ZAL
plain .... PETEN
president .... MENDEZ, ARBENZ, AREVALO, PONCE
volcano .... FUEGO, ATITLAN
guava .... ARACA
guayule .... SHRUB
gude .... GOOD
gudgeon .... MINNOW, TRICK, GULL, BAIT, DUPE, GOBY, TRUNNION
Gudrun, brother of .. GUNNAR
husband of ..... SIGURD, ATLI
rival of .... BRYNHILD
guenon .... TALAPOIN, MONKEY, GRIVET, MONA
guerdon .... REWARD, RECOMPENSE, CROWN, PRIZE
Guernsey ..... CATTLE, SHIRT, SWEATER
guerrilla ... MAQUI, PARTISAN, REBEL, RAIDER, BUSHWACKER, FEDAYEEN, CHETNIK
Philippine .... HUK
Serbian .... CHETNIK
Vietnamese ... VIETCONG
guess ...... SURMISE, THEORY, CONJECTURE, ESTIMATE
guessing game ..... CHARADE
guesswork .... SURMISE
guest ..... VISITOR, COMPANY, CALLER, LODGER
paying .... BOARDER
guff .... NONSENSE
guffaw ...... HEEHAW, BRAY, LAUGH(TER), HORSELAUGH
Guiana hut .... BENAB
native .... BONI
tree .... MORA
guide ... KEY, MARON, PILOT, COURIER, SCOUT, CLUE, CLEW, STEER, LEAD, CONDUCT, TRAIN, CONVOY, MERCURY
to solution ... CLUE, KEY, HINT
tourist's ..... CICERONE, DRAGOMAN
traveler's .... DRAGOMAN
guidebook .... BAEDEKER, MANUAL, ITINERARY
guided missile ... IRBM, ICBM
guiding ... DIRIGENT, POLAR, LEADING
example ..... PRECEDENT
ideal .... LODESTAR
light .... BEACON, LODESTAR, NORTH STAR
rule ... MOTTO, PRINCIPLE
star .... LODESTAR
guidon .... FLAG, PENNANT
Guido, musical note of ... UT, ELAMI
highest note .... ELA
guild ... CRAFT, UNION, HANSE
Hall statue .. GOG, MAGOG
in plant ecology .... PARASITES, LIANAS, EPIPHYTES
guilder .... COIN, GULDEN
guile ...... CUNNING, DECEIT, WILE, CRAFT
guileful .... TRICKY
guileless .... NAIVE, CANDID, ARTLESS, FRANK, OPEN, HONEST, SINCERE
guillemot ... BIRD, COOT, AUK, MURR(E), DOVEKIE, DOVEKEY
guillotine ... BEHEAD, MAIDEN
wagon .... TUMBREL, TUMBRIL
guilt ... CULPABILITY, CULPA, CRIME, SIN
guiltless .... INNOCENT, PURE, CLEAR
guilty .... CULPABLE, NOCENT
guimpe .... BLOUSE, CHEMISETTE
Guinea .... COIN, FOWL
capital .... CONAKRY
city .... KANKAN
corn ..... DURRA, MILLET
fowl .... PINTADO
native .... SUSU, FULANI, MALINKE
pig .... RAT, CAVY, PACA
pig, animal like .... PIKA
pig kin .... AGOUTI
pig, male .... BOAR
president .... TOURE
seaport .... CONAKRY

squash .... EGGPLANT
young .... KEET
Guinevere's husband .... (KING) ARTHUR
lover .... LANCELOT
guipure .... LACE, GIMP
guise .... CLOAK, GARB, SEMBLANCE, PRETENSE, MIEN, APPEARANCE
guitar, ancient .... LUTE
Hawaiian .... UKE(LELE)
India .... VINA
Japanese .... KOTO
like instrument .. CITOLE, BANDORE, BALALAIKA, PANDORE, SAMISEN, GITTERN, CITHER(N), CITTERN, ROTE
oriental .... SITAR
plucking implement ..... PLECTRUM, PLECTRON
small .... UKE(LELE)
strumming tool .... PLECTRUM
guitarist, famed .... SEGOVIA
guitguit .... BIRD, HONEY CREEPER
Guitry, playwright .... SACHA
gula .... GULLET, THROAT
gulch .... RAVINE, VALLEY, ARROYO, CANYON, COULEE
gulden .... COIN, GUILDER
gules .... RED
gulf .... BIGHT, GAP, CLEAVAGE, EDDY, WHIRLPOOL, ABYSS
Greek .... AEGINA
Lepanto .... CORINTH
of Bothnia ...... ALAND
of Finland (sea)port ..... LENINGRAD, KRONSTADT
state .... FLORIDA, TEXAS, LOUSIANA, ALABAMA
weed .... SARGASSO, SARGASSUM
gull .... DUPE, CHEAT, GUDGEON, CULLY, KITTIWAKE, PEWEE, PEWIT, ALLAN, MEDRICK, GOSLING, BURGOMASTER, COB(B), XEMA
bird like .... TERN
like a .... LARINE
of a .... LARINE
robber .... JA(E)GER
sea .... COB, MEW, SKUA, KITTIWAKE
gullet .... MAW, FAUCES, GORGE, NECK, CRAW, ESOPHAGUS, THROAT
gullible ... CREDULOUS, NAIVE
person .... GULL, DUPE, CONY
"Gulliver's Travels" author ... (LEMUEL) SWIFT
dwarf ...... LILLIPUTIAN
land .. LAPUTA, LILLIPUT, BROBDINGNAG
people ... LILLIPUTIANS, YAHOOS
gully ..... RAVINE, CHANNEL, DONGA, GUT, ARROYO, COULOIR, SIKE, WADI, NULLAH
gulp ..... SWALLOW, REPRESS, SWIG
down .... BOLT
gum ... CAROB, LATEX, RESIN, ADHESIVE, CHICLE, KINO, MATTI, ASA, STORAX, GLUE, MUCILAGE, RUBBER, BALATA, BENJAMIN, CAMPHOR, KAURI
arabic .... ACACIA, ACACIN(E)
astringent .... KINO
benzoin .... BENJAMIN
elastic .... RUBBER
for golf balls ... BALATA
leaves eater ..... KOALA
pharmacy .. TRAGACANTH
plant .... ULE
resin .... AMMONIAC, CAMBOGE, OLIBANUM, FRANKINCENSE, TACAMAHAC, ASAFETIDA, CAMBOGIA, BALM, BALSAM, MYRRH, STORAX, TACMAHACK, BDELLIUM, GALBAN, LOBAN, ELEMI, COPAL, COPALM
resin, bad-smelling ...... GALBANUM
resin in alcohol .... LACQUER
resin narcotic .. HASHISH
resin poison ..... ANTIAR
resin solvent ... HEXOME
tree .... EUCALYPTUS, ACACIA, KARRI, XYLAN, NYSSA, TUPELO, TUART, BALATA, COPALM
gumbo ... PATOIS, OKRA, SOUP, SOIL, OCRA, GOMART
gumboil ... ABSCESS, PARULIS
gumma .... TUMOR
gummed paper ...... STICKER
gummy ...... STICKY, VISCID
substance ...... GUTTA, DEXTRIN(E)
gumption .... COURAGE, ENTERPRISE, COMMON SENSE
gums, abscess ...... GUMBOIL
inflammation of .... GINGIVITIS
pertaining to .. GINGIVAL, ULETIC
source .... FERULA
the .... ULA
gumshoe .... RUBBER
slang ... TEC, DETECTIVE, SNEAK
gun ... COLT, MAUSER, LUGER, MAXIM, CARBINE, GATLING, JINGAL, JEZAIL, PISTOL, REVOLVER, BAZOOKA, AUTOMATIC, RIFLE, CANNON, FIREARM, MORTAR
ancient .... MUSKET, HARQUEBUS(E), BLUNDERBUSS, BLUNDERBORE
attachment ... SILENCER
barrel sight .... BEAD
barrel's end .... MUZZLE
British ..... STEN, BREN
brush .... SWAB
butt .... STOCK
caliber .... BORE
carriage .... CAISSON, GALLOP
carriage part ... LIMBER, RACER
carriage rope .. PROLONGE
case .... HOLSTER
chamber .... GOMER
crew's shield .... MANT(E)LET, TURRET
dog ... POINTER, SETTER, RETRIEVER
emplacement ... PILLBOX
for .. HUNT, SEEK, ATTACK
house on warship .... TURRET
make ... COLT, MAGNUM, HARRINGTON, MAUSER, WINCHESTER, LUGER
muzzle plug ... TAMPION, TOMPION
part ... BORE, BUTT, BOLT, COCK, LOCK, HAMMER, GOMER, STOCK, BARREL, BREECH, CYLINDER, TRIGGER, PIN, SIGHT, CHAMBER, MAGAZINE
pointer ... SIGHT, DOTTER
position of .... EMPLACEMENT
ship's .... CHASER
sight .... BEAD
slang ... THROTTLE, GAT, ROD, IRON, BARKER, ROSCOE, BETSY
small .... DERRINGER
strap .... SLING
tube .... BARREL
turret ... BLISTER, CUPOLA
gunboat .... TINCLAD
guncock .... NAB
guncotton plus picric acid ..... MELINITE
gunfire ...... VOLLEY, SALVO, DRUMBEAT, FUSILLADE
gung ho ... WORK TOGETHER, SLOGAN
gunlock catch .... SEAR
tumbler .... NUT
gunman ... THUG, GANGSTER
female accomplice ...... MOLL
Gunnar's brother-in-law ..... SIGURD
sister .... GUDRUN, GUTHRUN
wife .... BRYNHILD
gunnel .... FISH, BLENNY, GUNWALE
gunners' platform .... BANQUETTE
gunnery .... ARTILLERY, CANNONS
gunny .... BAG, SACK
gunpowder ...... TEA, NITER
"Gunpowder Plot" figure ..... FAWKES
gunrunner .... SMUGGLER
guns .... WEAPONS, ARMS,

FIREARMS, ARTILLERY, ORDNANCE
set of heavy ... BATTERY
warship's .... BATTERY
gunstock .... BUTT
Gunther's wife .... BRUNHILD
gunwale .... GUNNEL
guppy .... MINNOW
gurgitation ...... WHIRLING, SURGING
gurgle ..... BICKER, BUBBLE, BURBLE
gurglet .... GOBLET
gurgling sound producer ...... BABY, BROOK
gurnard ... GURNET, ROCHET, BATFISH
gurnet .... GURNARD
gush ..... POUR(OUT), SPOUT, OUTFLOW, SPURT, JET, SLOP OVER
gusher, kind of ... OIL WELL, GEYSER
sometimes ...... CRITIC, REVIEWER, VOLCANO, WRITER
gushing ... EFFUSIVE, POURING
gushy .... EFFUSIVE, SENTIMENTAL
gusset .... GORE
gust ...... WIND, OUTBURST, RUSH, SAPOR, FLURRY, BLAST, SAVOR, FLAVOR, TANG, RELISH
gusto .... TASTE, LIKING, RELISH, ZEST, ENJOYMENT, PALATE, ELAN
gusty ..... WINDY, BLUSTERY
gut ...... INTESTINE, GULLY, EVISCERATE, DESTROY, CATGUT, SNELL
guts ..... ENTRAILS, BOWELS, INTESTINES, PLUCK, COURAGE, IMPUDENCE
gutta .... DROP, MINIM
gutter .... TROUGH, SLUM, VALLEY, CULLIS, DITCH, KENNEL
guttersnipe ... URCHIN, ARAB, GAMIN
guttle ... GORMANDIZE, GORGE
guttural ... GULAR, RASPING, VELAR, DRY, HUSKY, THROATY
guy ... ROPE, CHAIN, FELLOW, CHAP, JOSH, TEASE
rope ... STAY, VANG, STAT
guzzle ... DRINK, SWIG, SWILL
guzzler .... TOPER, SOT
Gwyn, king's mistress .. NELL, ELEANOR
gymkhana performer .. RIDER, ATHLETE, EQUESTRIAN
gymnast ... ACROBAT, TURNER, TUMBLER, ATHLETE
club of ..... TURNVEREIN
feat of ..... HANDSPRING
suit .... MAILLOT
gymnastics ...... ATHLETICS, CALISTHENICS, TUMBLING
apparatus .... BUCK
gymnosophist .... NUDIST
gynoecium .... PISTIL(S)
gyp .... SWINDLE(R), CHEAT, SERVANT
gypsum .... SELENITE, ALABASTER, GESSO, TERRE ALBA, YESO
gypsy ..... ROAMER, NOMAD, BAZIGAR, CALO, BOHEMIAN, ROMANY, ZINGARA, ZINGARO, TSIGANE
book LIL
boy/husband ...... ROM
devil .... BENG
Dutch .... BAZIGAR
French .... BOHEMIAN
gentleman .... RYE, ROM
German ...... ZIGEUNER
girl .... CHAI
Hindu .... KARACHEE
horse .. GRI, GRY, GRASNI
Italian .... ZINGABI
language ...... ROMANY
non .... GAJO
opera .... MANERICO
Persian .... SISECH
Rose ___ .... LEE
Scottish .... CAIRD
sea .... BADJAO
Spanish .... GITANO, ZINCALO
thief .... CHOR
tongue .... CHIB
village .... GAV
wagon .... CARAVAN
winch .... CRAB
woman .... ZINGARA, RANI, ROMI
gyrate ...... ROTATE, WHIRL, SPIN
gyrating toy .... TOP
gyrator .... PILOT
gyratory .... WHIRLING, SPIRALLING
gyre .... WHIRL, VORTEX
gyrene: sl. .... MARINE, LEATHERNECK
gyve ..... FETTER, SHACKLE, IRON

H

H, letter .... AITCH
-shaped ... AITCH, ZYGAL
sound of ...... ASPIRATE
habanera .... DANCE
habeas corpus ... WRIT, ORDER
habergeon .. JACKET, HAUBERK
haberdashery .... TOGGERY
habile ... APT, DEXTEROUS, FIT, ABLE, CLEVER, HANDY, ROBE
habiliment ..... ATTIRE, DRESS, GARMENT, CLOTHING
habilitate ...... EQUIP, OUTFIT
habit .... COSTUME, DRESS, DISPOSITION, PRACTICE, CUSTOM, USAGE, GARB, WONT, ROUTINE, ATTIRE, RUT
prefix .... ECO
riding .... JOSEPH, JODHPURS
habitable .... LIV(E)ABLE
habitant .. RESIDENT, DWELLER
habitation · · · · HOME, LAIR, DWELLING, ABODE
habitual .... WONTED, USUAL, CUSTOMARY, STEADY, CHRONIC
habitually silent ... TACITURN, RETICENT, RESERVE
habituate ... FREQUENT, INURE, ENURE, ACCUSTOM, DRILL
to weather ... ACCLIMATE
habituated .... USED
habitue .... FREQUENTER, USER
tavern .... BARFLY
hachure .... LINES
hacienda ...... FARM, ESTATE, RANCH, PLANTATION, MINE
hack .. CHOP, AX, HOE, COUGH, MATTOCK, GASH, TAXI(CAB), TRITE, STALE, DRUDGE
driver .... CABBIE
literary .... DEVIL, SCRIBBLER, POETASTER
worker .... JOBBER
hackbut .... HARQUEBUS
hackle .... HATCHEL, HAGGLE, FEATHERS, MANGLE, CUT, COMB
hackmatack .. LARCH, JUNIPER, TAMARACK
hackney .... FIACRE, FLY
driver .... JARVEY
hackneyed ...... STALE, TRITE, BANAL, DRAB, STOCK
expression ...... CLICHE, COMMONPLACE, PLATITUDE
haddock ... COD, FISH, GADID, GADOID
Hades .. ABADDON, DIS, ORCUS, PIT, HELL, PLUTO, SHEOL, ARALU, TARTARUS, AVERNUS
abyss below ... TARTARUS
guard of ...... CERBERUS
related to .. LIMBO, ABYSS
river .... ACHERON, STYX, PHLEGETHON, LETHE
way place to ..... EREBUS
wheel-turner in .... IXION
hadj .... PILGRIMAGE
Hadrian's favorite .. ANTINOUS
haft .... HILT, DUDGEON, BAIL, HANDLE
hag .... WITCH, ENCHANTRESS, DEMON, MARSH, HARPY, VIRAGO, CARLINE, FURY, HARRIDAN, VIXEN, FELLING, CRONE, JEZEBEL, BELDAM(E)
haggard ..... GAUNT, DRAWN, WILD, UNRULY, WAN, HAWK
novel of .... SHE
hagfish .... CYCLOSTOME
haggle .... CHOP, HACK, MANGLE, WRANGLE, CAVIL,

BARGAIN, QUIBBLE, PRIG, CHAFFER
haha .... FENCE, WALL, LAUGH
haiku .... POEM
hail .. GREET(ING), SLEET, AVE, AHOY, GRAUPEL, SALVE, METEOR, SIGNAL, CHEER, SALUTE, SHOWER, POUR, RAINDROPS
Hailey novel .... HOTEL, AIRPORT, WHEELS
hair .. TRESS, DOWN, FUR, NAP, THATCH, SHAG, PILE, ROACH, CRINE, FILAMENT
arrange .... COIF
band .... FIL(L)ET
braid .... CUE, PLAIT, QUEUE, PIGTAIL, TRESS
bunch of .... WHISK
caterpillar .... SETA
cheek .... BURNSIDES, SIDEBURNS
cloth .... ABA, CILICE
coarse .... SETA
coat .... MELOTE
comb the .... COIF
combining form .. PIL(O), CHAET(O), PILI, TRICHO
covered with ..... PILOSE, TOMENTOSE, LANATE, SHAGGY, FLOCCOSE
curl of ... LOCK, RINGLET
curlylike .... CIRROSE
cut short .... CROP
disease .. MANGE, XERASIA, TRICHOSIS, SYCOSIS
diseased condition of .... PLICA
do the ..... MARCEL, SET, COIF
dresser .... FRISEUR, COIFFEUR, CURLER
dresser's term .... PERM(ANENT), SET, MARCEL, COIF, (COLD)WAVE, RINSE
dressing .... POMADE, BANDOLINE
dressing style ..... CHAR
dye .... HENNA
dyer .... ANCIETTE
face .. BEARD, MUSTACHE, WHISKER
falling out of .... PSILOSIS
false .. PERUKE, JANE, RAT, TOUPEE, WIG
feeler .... PALP(US)
fetus .... LANUGO
fillet .... SNOOD
fine .... FUZZ, PILE
follicles disease .. SYCOSIS
girl's .... TRESS
head .... CRINE, MOP
hooked .... BARB
knot ..... CHIGNON, BUN, BOB
lock ... TRESS, CURL, TAG
mass of .... SHOCK
matted .. SHAG, DAGLOCK
matted condition .... TRICHOMA
neck ..... MANE, HACKLE
net .... LINT, SNOOD
nostril .... VIBRISSA
not curly .... LANK
of head .... LOCK, POLL, THATCH
ointment .... POMADE
on abdomen ...... PUBES
ornament .. RIBBON, CLIP, COMB, BOW
pad .... RAT
piece .... RUG
pigment .... MELANIN
pin .... BODKIN
plait .... BRAID, PIGTAIL, QUEUE, TRESS
plant ...... PILUS, VILLUS
prefix .... CRINI
raising ..... HORRIFYING, EERIE, FEARSOME
remove .. EPILATE, BOB, DEPILATE, TRIM, TONSURE
ribbon .... BANDEAU
rigid .... SETA
ringlet .... CURL
roll ..... PUFF, CHIGNON, RAT, BUN, WATERFALL
rough .... SHAG
sensitive ...... TENTACLE
shedding of ..... ECDYSIS
sheep's .... WOOL
shirt .... CILICE
shreds .... NOIL
soft, fine .... PILE, FUZZ, DOWN
standing .... ROACH
strip .... EPILATE, DEPILITATE
substance ...... KERATIN
tuft .... FLOCCUS
unruly .... COWLICK
wash the ...... SHAMPOO
wave .... MARCEL, PERMANENT
hairbreadth .. CLOSE, NARROW
haircloth .... CILICE, ABA
haircut .... SHINGLE
hairdo ..... COIFFURE, BANGS, POMPADOUR, PAGEBOY, POODLE, TETE
hairdresser .... COIFFEUR, FRISEUR, CURLER, COIFFUSE
haired .... PILIFEROUS
hairiness .... VILLOSITY, PILOSITY
hairless ..... GLABROUS, BALD, PELON
state .... ALOPECIA
hairlike .... TRICHOID
process .... CILIA, CILIUM
hairline point .... PEAK
hairpiece .... WIG, TOUPEE, PERUKE
hairpin .... BODKIN
hairs, bunch of .. TUFT, PINICIL
covered with stiff .. HISPID
hairsplitter .... QUIBBLER
hairy .... PILOSE, BARBATE, COMATE, COMOSE, HIRSUTE, PILAR(Y), CILIATE, PILEOUS, NAPPY, CRINITE, VILLOSE, VILLOUS
Ape .... YANK
covering, having .... LANATE
tuft .... FLOCCUS
Haiti .... HISPANIOLA
Haitian bandit .... CACO
capital .. PORT-AU-PRINCE
city .... GONAIVES, LES CAYES
coin .... GOURDE
dictator ...... MAGLOIRE
evil spirit .... BAKA, BOKO
hunter (ox) .. BUCCANEER
king .... CHRISTOPHE
liberator ..... DESSALINES
lord .... CACIQUE
monetary unit ... GOURDE
president ..... DUVALIER, ESTIME, MAGLOIRE
rebel .... TOUSSAINT
seaport .... CAYES
sweet potato .... BATATA
voodoo deity ... ZOMBI(E)
voodoo priest ... PAPALOI
voodoo priestess .... MAMALOI
hake .... WHITING, GADID, GADOID
kin of .... COD
hakeem/hakim ...... DOCTOR, PHYSICIAN
halberd ... SPEAR, (BATTLE)AX, PARTISAN, PARTIZAN, GLA(I)VE, GISARME, POLE-AX(E), SPONTOON
halcyon .... HAPPY, TRANQUIL, PEACEFUL
hale .... WELL, HEARTY, HAUL, HEALTHY, ROBUST, DRAG
half .. HEMI, MOIETY, DEMI, SEMI
an em .... EN
and half part .... ALE
baked ..... AMATEURISH, SOPHOMORIC
boot ...... BUSKIN, PAC
breed .. METIS(SE), MESTEE, GRIFF(E), MESTIZO, HYBRID, LADINO, MESTIF(F), MULATTO, MULE, MUSTEE
caste .... METIS
farthing .... MITE
gainer .... (BACK)DIVE
hearted ..... RELUCTANT, UNWILLING, SPIRITLESS, LUKEWARM
hitch .... KNOT
man, half bull .... BUCENTAUR
man, half dragon .... CECROPS
man, half fish .. MERMAN, DAGON
man, half goat ..... PAN, FAUNUS
man, half horse .... CENTAUR
mask ..... LOUP, DOMINO
moon .... CRESCENT, ARC, LUNE
note, in music .... MINIM
one's better ... HUSBAND, WIFE
penny .... MAG
prefix ... HEMI, SEMI, DEMI
step, in music .. SEMITONE
turn of horse .... CARACOL(E)

way . . . . MID
wit . . DOLT, FOOL, IDIOT
witted . . SILLY, IMBECILIC, MORONIC, STUPID
year's income . . . . ANNAT
halfway . . . . PARTIAL, INCOMPLETE
meet . . . . . . COMPROMISE
halibut . . SOLE, FLATFISH, BUTT
Halicarnassus' wonder . . . . MAUSOLEUM
halicore . . . DUGONG, SEACOW, MANATEE
halidom(e) . . . . HOLINESS, SANCTUARY
halite . . . . (ROCK)SALT
halitus . . . EXHALATION, AURA, BREATH, VAPOR
hall . . . . VESTIBULE, CORRIDOR, DORM, SAAL, SALLE, AULA, ATRIUM, SALA, LYCEUM
concert . . . . ODEUM
heroes' . . . . VALHALLA
hotel . . . . . . FOYER, LOBBY
Odin's . . . . VALHALLA
reception . . COURT, SALON
round . . . . ROTUNDA
Halley, astronomer . . EDMUND
discovery . . . . COMET
halloo . . . . SHOUT, YELL
hallow . . . . . . SANCTIFY, HOLY, CONSECRATE, BLESS
hallowed . . . . . . HOLY, SACRED
place . . . . SHRINE
Hall's (C. F.) concern . . ARCTIC
halluces . . . . DIGITS
hallucination . . . . . . DELUSION, ALUSIA, FANTASY, CHIMERA, AUTISM
kind of . . . . VISUAL, AUDITORY
product of . . . . . . MIRAGE
hallucinogen . . LSD, MESCALINE, AMPHETAMINE, SEDATIVE
drug: sl. . . . . ACID
source . . . PEYOTE, FUNGI, CAAPI
hallux . . . . (GREAT) TOE
hallway . . . . CORRIDOR
Halmahera . . . . GILOLO
halo . . . . AURA, NIMB(US), AUREOLE, CORONA, GLORIA, AUREOLA, GLORY, GLORIOLE
halogen . . . . IODINE, ASTATINE, BROMINE, CHLORINE, FLUORINE
compound . . . . . . HALIDE
Hals, painter . . . . FRANS
halt . . . . PAUSE, STOP, LIMP, HOBBLE, WAVER, LAME
the . . . . CRIPPLES
halter . . . . NOOSE, STRAP
halting place . . . . . ETAPE, INN, OASIS, CARAVANSARY
halve . . DIVIDE, BISECT, DISSECT
ham . . . . . MEAT, HOCK, ACTOR
hog's . . . . GAMMON
it up . . . EMOTE, OVER-ACT
parent of, Biblical . . NOAH
slang . . . . AMATEUR, OVERACT
slice for frying . . . RASHER
son of . . . . CUSH

hamal . . . . PORTER, (HOUSE)SERVANT
Hambletonian . . . . . . TROTTER, HORSE
gait . . . . TROT
race, site of . . . . . GOSHEN
hamburg . . . . CHICKEN
hamburg(er) . . . STEAK, PATTY, SANDWICH
Hamilcar's son . . . . HANNIBAL
Hamite . . . . . BERBER, LIBYAN, SOMAL(I), MASAI, AFAR
Hamitic language . . NUMIDIAN
hamlet . . . . VILLAGE, TRAGEDY, TREF, BURG, DORP, MIR, THORP(E), CLACHAN, WICH
and others . . . . DANES
home of . . . . ELSINORE
locale of . . . . . . ELSINORE, ELSINGOR
uncle of . . . . . . CLAUDIUS
Hammarskjold, UN secretary . . DAG
hammer . . . . MALLET, BEAT, MALLEATE, BANG, KEVEL, FULLER, BEETLE, MAUL, POUND(ER), SLEDGE, OLIVER
auctioner's . . . . GAVEL
and sickle flag . . . . SOVIET
blow . . . . POUND
chairman's . . . . GAVEL
companion of . . . . TONGS
ear . . . . MALLEUS
end . . . . PEEN, POLL
firearm's . . . . COCK
head of . . . . . . PEEN, POLL
heavy . . . . . SLEDGE, MAUL
kind of . . . . . CLAW, TRIP, BALL PEEN, DROP
large . . . . SLEDGE
lead . . . . MADGE
lock . . . . HOLD
part . . PEEN, CLAW, HEAD
percussion . . . . . . PLEXOR, PLESSOR
piano . . . . MALLET
presiding officer's . . . . GAVEL
soft-headed . . . . . PLEXOR, PLESSOR
stone-breaking . . . . KEVEL
striking part . . . . TUP
to . . . . MALLEATE
trip . . . . OLIVER
hammerhead . . . . SHARK, FISH, BAT, BIRD, UMBRETTE
hammock . . . . BED, COUCH
lines . . . . CLEWS
hamper . . . HINDER, ENCUMBER, IMPEDE, FETTER, MANACLE, HANAPER, CRATE, MAUND, TRAMMEL, HOBBLE, SEROON, CRAMP, BASKET
Hampshire . . . . HANTS
Hampton Roads protagonist . . MONITOR, MERRIMAC
hamster . . . . RODENT
hamstring . . TENDON, CRIPPLE, DISABLE, LAME, MAIM
Hamsun, novelist . . . . . . KNUT
hamulus . . . . HOOK
Han . . . . DYNASTY
cities . . WUHAN, HANKOW, HANYANG, WUCHANG

hanaper . . . . . BASKET, HAMPER
hand . . . . NIEVE, MANUS, PAW, PUD, DEAL, HOLDING, FIST, GIVE, SIGNATURE, APPLAUSE, AID, HELP, POINTER, WORKER
at . . . . READY, NEAR
baby's . . . . PUD
below full house . . FLUSH
by . . . . MANUAL
care . . . . MANICURE
cart . . . . BARROW
clapping to music . . . TAL
clenched . . . . FIST
clock . . . . POINTER
combining form . . CHIRO
done by . . . . MANUAL
down . . . . DELIVER, BEQUEATH
drum . . . . . . TAMBOURINE, TOMTOM
first . . . . . NEW, ORIGINAL
give a . . . . APPLAUD
glass . . . . MIRROR
grenade . . EGG, PINEAPPLE
grinding device . . MULLER
in . . . . GIVE, SUBMIT, PRESENT
in hand . . . . COOPERATION
jurist . . . . LEARNED
me-down . . SECONDHAND, USED, CHEAP, READY-MADE
measure . . . . SPAN
mill . . . . QUERN, MANO
on . . . . PASS, READY, TRANSMIT, AVAILABLE, PRESENT
organ . . . . HURDY-GURDY
out . . . . DEAL, DISTRIBUTE
over . . . . SHELL, DELIVER, CONSIGN
palm of . . . . VOLAR, LOOF, THENAR
pick . . . . SELECT, CHOOSE
reared by . . . . CADE
screw . . . . JACK
second . . . . USED
slang . . . . PAW, HAM, FIN, FLIPPER, MITT, GRAPPLER
sore on . . . . . . CHILBLAIN
terminal part . . . . MANUS
upper . . . . ADVANTAGE
whist . . . . TENACE
without trumps . . . . CHICANE
written . . . . MANUSCRIPT
handbag . . . ETUI, PURSE, GRIP, VALISE, RETIC(U)LE, SATCHEL, CASE
handball . . . . . . FIVES, PELOTA
handbill . . . . . DODGER, FLYER, FLIER, THROWAWAY, POSER, NOTICE, LEAF
handbook . . CATECHISM, TOME, MANUAL, ENCHIRIDION
kind of . . . . . . BAEDEKER
handcar . . . . VELOCIPEDE
handcart . . . . BARROW
handclasp . . . . SHAKE
handcuffs . . . . BRACELETS, NIPPERS, DARBY, FETTER, MANACLE, WRISTLET

Handel opus . . MESSIAH, LARGO, NERO, BERENICE
birthplace of . . . . HALLE
handful . . . . PLENTY, FEW, FISTFUL
of hay/straw . . . . . . WISP
handicap . . ODDS, HINDRANCE, (DIS)ADVANTAGE, HINDER, IMPEDE, RACE
handily . . . . . . DEFTLY, EASILY
handkerchief . . . . . . VERONICA, MALABAR, SCARF, FOULARD, SUDARY, SUDARIUM, MOUCHOIR
colloquial . . . . . . HANKIE, WIPE(R)
large . . . . . . BANDAN(N)A, MADRAS
handle . . . . HELVE, HAFT, HILT, WIELD, EAR, GRIP, HANK, TAKE CARE, ANSE, MANAGE, OPERATE, DIRECT, MANIPULATE, PLY, DEAL, LUG, HEFT, ANSA, TREAT, SWIPE
as middleman . . . . . . JOB
awkwardly/clumsily . . . . PAW, FUMBLE
bar: colloq. . . MUSTACHE
boat's . . . . TILLER
clumsily . . . . PAW
colloquial . . NAME, TITLE
cup's . . . . EAR
door . . . . KNOB
having . . . . ANSATE
hoop-shaped . . . . . . BAIL
pail . . . . BAIL
printing press . . . ROUNCE
roughly . . . . MAUL, PAW
rudder . . . . TILLER
scythe . . SNATH(E), SNEAD
slang . . NAME, MONICKER
sword . . . . HILT
whip's . . . . CROP
with . . . . ANSATE
handled . . . . PALMED, ANSATE, MANAGED
handmade . . . . MANUAL
handmaiden . . . . . ATTENDANT, SERVANT
handout . . . . GIFT, DOLE
handrail, kind of . . . MANROPE
hands, clean: colloq. . . . . INNOCENT, CLEAR
expertness with . . . . HANDICRAFT
having two . . . . BIMANOUS
join . . . . COOPERATE
on hips . . . . AKIMBO
pertaining to . . . . MANUAL
warmer . . . . MUFF
without . . . . AMANOUS
handsel . . . . PRESENT, EARNEST, TOKEN
handsome . . . . LARGE, COMELY, IMPRESSIVE, BONNY, SHARP
man . . . . APOLLO, ADONIS
handspring . . . . TUMBLE
handstone . . . . MANO
handwriter, wall . . . . AGITPROP
handwriting . . . . . SCRIPT, FIST, PENMANSHIP
bad . . . . CACOGRAPHY
expert . . . CHIROGRAPHER
on the wall . . . . MENE, TEKEL, UPHARSIN, GRAFFITI
pertaining to . . . GRAPHIC
study of . . . GRAPHOLOGY
style . . . . CHARACTER
handwritten document/will . . . HOLOGRAPH
handy . . . CONVENIENT, READY, DEFT, ADROIT, DEXTEROUS, HABILE
man . . . . . . JACK-OF-ALL-TRADES, MOZO
hang . . . . . . SUSPEND, EXECUTE, EXHIBIT, HOVER, DANGLE, DRAPE, SWAG, DROOP, (IM)PEND, LOLL, STRING
around: colloq. . . LOITER, LINGER, HOVER, LOAF
back . . . . LAG
down . . . . LAVE, PERPEND, DROOP, LOP, SAG
fire . . . . PEND
jury . . . . DEADLOCK
loosely . . . . LOP, LOLL, DANGLE, DRAPE
on . . . . WAIT, HOLD, PERSEVERE
out . . . . HAUNT
over . . . . HOVER
slang . . . . . SCRAG, STRING
hangar . . . . (AIR)DROME, SHED, SHELTER
area . . . . APRON
hangbird . . . . ORIOLE
hangdog . . . . MEAN
hanger . . . . EXECUTIONER
on . . . . . . TOADY, HEELER, TRENCHER, SYCOPHANT, PARASITE, FAVOR-SEEKER, HABITUE, LEECH, HENCHMAN
hanging . . . . SUSPENDED, PENDULOUS, UNSETTLED, PENDENT, PENSILE, SESSILE
apparatus . . . . . . GIBBET, GALLOWS
cloth cover . . . . DRAPE
crookedly . . . . ALOP
down(ward) . . . . CERNOUS
nest maker . . . . . . ORIOLE
piece/rag . . . . TAG
unevenly . . . . ALOP
hangings . . . . . ARRAS, DRAPES, DRAPERY, TAPESTRY, WASH
hangman's noose . . . . . HALTER
rope . . . . HEMP
hangnail . . . . WHITLOW
hangnest . . . . ORIOLE
hangout . . . . HAUNT, DEN, RETREAT
hangover feeling . . . . . NAUSEA, HEADACHE
hank . . SKEIN, LOOP, COIL, RAN
hanker . . . ITCH, CRAVE, LONG, YEARN
hankering . . . . ITCH
hanky-panky . . . . TRICKY, DECEPTIVE, TRICKERY, JUGGLERY
Hannibal's conqueror . . SCIPIO
father . . . . HAMILCAR
defeat . . . . ZAMA
surname . . . . BARCA
victory site . . . . . CANNAE
Hanover beer . . . . BOCK
hanse . . . . GUILD, LEAGUE
Hanseatic League . . . . . HANSE
member . . . . BREMEN, LUBECK, HAMBURG
Hansen's disease . . . . LEPROSY
hansom . . . . . . CARRIAGE, CAB, HACK
handspring . . . . . . CARTWHEEL
hap . . CHANCE, LUCK, FORTUNE
haphazard . . RANDOM, CASUAL, HIT-OR-MISS, AIMLESS
hapless . . LUCKLESS, UNLUCKY
happen . . . TRANSPIRE, BEFALL, FARE, OCCUR, CHANCE, BETIDE, EVENTUATE
again . . . . RECUR
in the end . . . EVENTUATE
together . . . . . . COINCIDE, CONCUR
happening . . EVENT, INCIDENT, OCCURRENCE, TIDING, OCCASION, CASUS
before due . . PREMATURE, RATH(E)
by chance . . . FORTUITOUS
happiness . . . . . BLISS, FELICITY
happy . . JOYOUS, GLAD, COSH, LUCKY, BLITHE, FAUST
go-lucky . . . . . EASYGOING
medium . . AVERAGE, MEAN
hara-kiri . . . SUICIDE, SEPPUKU
harangue . . . TIRADE, DIATRIBE, EXHORT(ATION), SPIEL, PERORATE, RANT, ORATE, SCREED
Haran's brother . . . . ABRAHAM
daughter . . . . MILCAH
father . . . . TERAH
harass . . . . TORMENT, RIDE, TROUBLE, HARRY, HECKLE, NAG, BOTHER, ANNOY, VEX, IRK, MOLEST, BESET, TEASE, OBSESS, PESTER, JADE, PLAGUE
harbinger . . . FORETELL, OMEN, USHER, HERALD, PRECURSOR, FORERUNNER
harbor . . . . . . SHELTER, HAVEN, ANCHORAGE, CONCEAL, CHERISH, COVE, PIER, PORT, BAY
boat . . . . TUG
city . . . . SEAPORT
laborer . . . . STEVEDORE
small . . . . MARINA
sound . . . . . CHUG(CHUG), TOOT, (FOG)HORN, CHURN, BELL
wall . . . . JETTY
hard . . . . . . FIRM, RIGID, SOLID, VIOLENT, DIFFICULT, HARSH, CALLOUS, NEAR, PETROUS, STERN, ARDUOUS, ADAMANT, DOUR, PETROSAL, SCLEROID, SCLEROUS, MARBLY
bed . . . . PALLET
biscuit . . TACK, CRACKNEL
bitten . . . TOUGH, DOGGED
boiled . . TOUGH, CALLOUS
cash . . . . SPECIE

coal .... ANTHRACITE
covering .. SHELL, ARMOR
drawn ...... TAUT, TENSE
fat .... SUET
hearted .. CRUEL, PITILESS
heartwood .... DURA
prefix .... DIS
problem .... POSER, DILEMMA
roll .... BAGEL
rubber .... EBONITE
shell .. LORICA, CARAPACE
to bear .... GRIEVOUS
to grasp .... ELUSIVE
to understand ..... DEEP, OBTUSE
very .... STEEL, CASTIRON
water .... ICE
working .... INDUSTRIOUS
harden ... STIFFEN, INURE, GEL, ENURE, TEMPER, STEEL, PETRIFY, SEAR, OSSIFY, SET, INDURATE
by heat .... BAKE
hardfisted ... STINGY, MISERLY
hardhack .... SPIR(A)EA, ROSE, SHRUB
hardhanded .... SEVERE, RUTHLESS
hardhead .... MENHADEN, SCULPIN
hardheaded ...... PRACTICAL, STUBBORN, SHREWD
animal .... MULE, ASS, DONKEY
hardihood .... DARING, INSOLENCE
hardly ..... BARELY, SCARCELY
hardship .... RIGOR, TRIAL
hardtack ..... BREAD, WAFER, TOMMY, PANTILE
hardware dealer .... IRONMONGER
hardwood .... TEAK, OAK, ASH, ELM, EBONY, YAKAL, HICKORY, MAHOGANY
hardy ... DARING, BOLD, RASH, ROBUST, CHISEL, DURABLE, TOUGH
Hardy novel character ... TESS, JUDE
locale .... WESSEX
hare .. CONY, RODENT, RABBIT, LEPUS, LEPORIDE, PIKA, MALKIN, PUSS, LAGOMORPH
dialect .... WAT
family .... LEPORID
female .... DOE
genus .... LEPUS
hunting dog .... HARRIER
like .... LEPORINE
like animal ..... AGOUTI, HYRAX
male .... BUCK
rabbit hybrid .. LEPORIDE
Scottish .... MALKIN
tail .... SCUT
track .... SLOT, SPOOR
young .... LEVERET
harebrained ... STUPID, GIDDY, RASH
harem ...... SERAGLIO, SERAI, ZENANA
dweller/slave .... ODALISQUE, ODALISK
room .... ODA
hari-kari ... SUICIDE, SEPPUKU
haricot .. STEW, (KIDNEY) BEAN
hark .... LISTEN, HEAR
back .... REVERT
harl .... FILAMENT(S), BARB
harlequin .... CLOWN(ISH), COMIC, LUDICROUS, COLORFUL, (PANTO)MIME, BUFFOON
girl of .... COLUMBINE
Harlem painter .... HALS
harlot .... RAHAB, STRUMPET
harm ... SCATHE, EVIL, INJURY, DAMAGE, HURT, WRONG, MALEFIC, INJURE, MAR, BALE, BANE, MALIGNANT
harmattan .... WIND
harmful .... ILL, NOXAL, INJURIOUS, NOXIOUS, NOCENT, BANEFUL, NOISOME, NOCUOUS
gas in mine .... DAMP
harmless .... INNOCUOUS, INOFFENSIVE, INNOCENT, NAIVE
harmonic .... CONSONANT, AGREEING
harmonica ..... MOUTH ORGAN
harmonious ..... CONSONANT, CONGRUOUS, IN ACCORD, ORDERLY
harmonist .... MUSICIAN, POET, COMPOSER
harmonium .... ORGAN, MELODEON
harmonize .... ATTUNE, AGREE
harmony .. AGREEMENT, MUSIC, TUNE, PEACE, CHORD, UNISON, RAPPORT, TONE, BALANCE, CHIME, CONCORD, CONSONANCE, COSMOS, ORGANUM, SYMMETRY
of voices ...... CONCENT
harness ... GEAR, INSPAN, RIG, EQUIP, GRAITH, DRAFT
bull .... COP
course site ...... GOSHEN
horse .... HEADGEAR, TACKLE
men's .... BRICOLE
part ..... BLIND(ER), BIT, COLLAR, TRACE, HAME, HALTER, TERRET, REIN, SADDLE, TUG, BILLET, BRIDLE
ring .... TERRET
strap .... CRUPPER, MARTINGAL(E)
harnessed horses .. TEAM, SPAN
Harold, diminutive of .... HAL
harp .... LYRE, KOTO, NANGA, TRIGON
constellation ...... LYRA
like instrument .... DULCIMER, SAMBUKE, PSALTERY
slang .... IRISHMAN
Harper's Ferry event ... RAID, BATTLE
Harpies, one of the ... AELLO, CELAENO, OCYPETE
harpoon ...... SPEAR, JAVELIN
barb .... FLUKE
missile like a .. HURLBAT
harpsichord .... SPINET, VIRGINAL
Harpy .. WITCH, EAGLE, AELLO, MONSTER, BUZZARD, OCYPETE, CELAENO
harquebus .... HACKBUT, HAGBUT, FIREARM
fork .... CROC
harridan .. SHREW, FURY, NAG, VIRAGO, HAG, JEZEBEL
harrier .. FALCON, DOG, HAWK
Harriet, diminutive of .. HATTIE
harrow .... DRAG, BRAKE, WOUND, LACERATE, VEX, TORMENT
rival of .... ETON
harry .... RAID, HARASS, TORMENT, PILLAGE, PESTER, PLUNDER
Old .... DEVIL, SATAN
harsh .... STERN, DISCORDANT, BITTER, COARSE, CRUDE, ROUGH, SEVERE, CRUEL, RASPING, DRASTIC
and dry .... HACKING
critic .... SLATER
sound ... STRIDOR, ROAR, GRUFF
sounding ...... STRIDENT
taste ..... ACERB, BITTER
voiced person ... STENTOR
harshness .... ASPERITY
hart .... DEER, STAG
Harte, author .... BRET(T)
character .... AH SIN
hartebeest ... ANTELOPE, ASSE, BONTEBOK, CAAMA, TORA, LECAMA
kin of .... SASSABY
hartshorn .... ANTLERS
hartstongue .... FERN
harum-scarum ... WILD, RASH, RECKLESS, AMOK
haruspex .... SOOTHSAYER, PRIEST
Harvard educator ..... PUSEY, CONANT, LOWELL
newspaper ..... CRIMSON
harvest ... CROP, REAP, YIELD, RABI, KIRN
bug ...... CHIGGER, TICK, MITE
feast .... KIRN
festival .... LAMMAS
fly .... CICADA
home .... KIRN
last sheaf .... KIRN
leftover .. STUBBLE, STUMP
harvestman .... DADDY-LONGLEGS
hash ... CHOP, MINCE, BUNGLE, MIXTURE, HODGEPODGE, RAMEKIN, RAMEQUIN, MULLIGAN
house: sl. .. RESTAURANT, JOINT
mark: military .... STRIPE
hashish .. B(H)ANG, NARCOTIC, MARIJUANA, CANNABIS

source .... HEMP
hasp .... SKEIN, CATCH
hassle .... FRAY, MELEE, SQUABBLE, DISCUSSION, RUCKUS, BRAWL
Hasso, actress .... SIGNE
hassock .. SEAT, MAT, CUSHION, KNEELER, FOOTSTOOL, TUSSOCK
haste .... SPEED, HURRY
hasten ..... HURRY, DISPATCH, SPEED(UP), ACCELERATE, APACE, HIE, SCAMP
hasty .. QUICK, HURRIED, FAST, IMPETUOUS, IMPATIENT, IMPULSIVE, CURSORY, RASH, ABRUPT, BRASH, TEARING
pudding ... MUSH, SEPON, HASH
hat ... SCONCE, TOQUE, BERET, HEADGEAR, CAP, CAUBEEN, PETASOS, PETASUS, FELT, TAM, TOPPER, CHAPEAU, BONNET
beaver fur .... CASTOR
brimless ..... TOQUE, FEZ
collapsible .... GIBUS
crown .... POLL
cylindrical .... SHAKO
decoration .... COCKADE, POMPON
ecclesiastic ...... BIRETTA
felt ... HOMBURG, FEDORA
fur .... CONEY
high .... TILE, BEAVER
holder .... BANDBOX
hunter's .... TERAI
lining leather .... SKIVER
maker .... MILLINER
making fiber ... BUNTAL, RAFFIA
man's silk .... BEAVER
material ..... VELOUR(S), FELT
opera .... GIBUS
part .. BRIM, BAND, LINING
pith .... TOPEE, TOPI, HELMET
plant .... SOLA
rabbit fur .... CASTOR
silk .... BEAVER
slang .... LID
small .... COIF
soft .... FEDORA, PORKPIE
soldier's ..... HAVELOCK, SHAKO, KEPI, BUSBY, BERET
straw .... PANAMA, LEGHORN
take off ...... DOFF, VAIL
tasseled .... FEZ
three-cornered .. TRICORN
trimming ...... ROULEAU
turned up brim .... COCKUP, BRETON
under one's ..... SECRET, CONFIDENTIAL
woman's .... PILLBOX, CLOCHE, TURBAN
hatch ...... CONCOCT, DEVISE, PLAN, PLOT, TRAPDOOR, FLOODGATE, FISHTRAP, ENGRAVE
hatchel .... HECKLE, TEASE
hatchery .... INCUBATOR
hatchet ...... AX, TOMAHAWK
handle .... HELVE
man .... GOON
stone .... MOGO
type ... CLAW, SHINGUNG, LATHING
hatchway .... SCUTTLE
hate .... DETEST, LOATHE, DESPISE, DISLIKE, ABHOR, ABOMINATE, AVERSION, PHOBIA, MALICE, ODIUM
combining form ... MIS(O)
of foreigners .... XENOPHOBIA
hateful ... EXECRABLE, ODIOUS, REPUGNANT, OBNOXIOUS, LOATHSOME, REPULSIVE, ABOMINABLE, HEINOUS
person ...... CAD, TOAD
Hatfield enemy .... MCCOY
hating, combining form ...... MIS(O)
hatred ...... ODIUM, ENMITY, AVERSION, ILL WILL, HATE, ANIMOSITY, DISLIKE
combining form .. MIS(O)
of change .. MISONEISM
of debate/argument ..... MISOLOGY
of mankind .... MISANTHROPY
of marriage ... MISOGAMY
of women .... MISOGYNY
hats, women's ..... MILLINERY
hatrack .... TREE
hatter, woman ...... MILLINER
hauberk .. ARMOR, HABERGEON
haughtiness .... HAUTEUR, ARROGANCE
haughty .. ARROGANT, PROUD, SNOOTY, STUCK-UP, SNOTTY, CAVALIER, SUPERCILIOUS, PROUD, LOFTY
haul ...... PULL, DRAG, TUG, CATCH, BOOTY, TRICE, LUG, BOUSE, ROUSE, DRAW, HALE, SWAG, TOW, CART, DRAG, HEAVE, TOTE
haulage ... CARTAGE, PORTAGE
hauling car .... VAN
haulm ... STALK, STEM, STRAW, HAY, CULM
haunch .. HIP, HANCE, HUCKLE
bone .... ILIUM
part ...... HIP, BUTTOCK, THIGH, LOIN, LEG
haunt .. HANG-OUT, FREQUENT, PERVADE, DEN, RETREAT, OBSESS, LAIR, NEST, LIE, RESORT, SPOOK, PURLIEU
animal ...... LAIR, DEN
dialect .... GHOST
in mind .... OBSESS
low .... DEN, DIVE
of literary hacks .... GRUB STREET
hausfrau .... HOUSEWIFE
haustellum .... PROBOSCIS
haustorium .... SUCKER
hautboy .... OBOE
haute monde ... HIGH SOCIETY
hauteur ..... SNOBBERY, PRIDE, ARROGANCE
Havana .... CIGAR, (LA) PARASITA
castle .... MORRO
have at .... ATTACK
done .... FINISH, STOP
effect .... TELL
feeling .... SENTIENT
feet .... PEDATE
flavor ...... TASTY, SAPID
limits .... FINITE
no worries .... CAREFREE
offensive smell ..... OLID
ribs .... COSTATE
rough edges ..... EROSE, RAGGED
same origin ... CONNATE, COGNATE
Scot. .... HAE
scruples .... DEMUR
spikes .... SPINED, TINED, PRONGED
strong desire for .... HUNGER, COVET
title to .... OWN
haven ...... REFUGE, SHELTER, ASYLUM, SANCTUARY, PORT, HARBOR, HITHE, LEE
animal's .... PRESERVE
ship's ...... ANCHORAGE
haversack ...... (CANVAS)BAG
havoc .... DESTRUCTION, DEVASTATION
haw ..... BERRY, HOI, EYELID, SLOE, FRUIT, COMMAND, FALTER
companion of ...... HEM
inflammation .... STY
opposed to .... GEE
Hawaii .... OWYHEE
author of book .... MICHENER
Hawaiian .... POLYNESIAN, KANAKA
acacia .... KOA
apple .... MAILE
association .... HUI
bathing resort ... WAIKIKI
bird ...... IO, OOAA, IIWI, MAMO, KOAE, NOIO, OMAO, NUKUPUU
blueberry .... OHELO
bonito .... AKU
breech cloth ...... MALO
bush .... OLONA
canoe .... WAPA
capital ...... HONOLULU
chant .... MELE
city .... HONOLULU, HILO
cliff .... PALI
club .... HUI
cloak .... MAMO
cloth .... TAPA, KAPA
coffee .... KONA
crater .... KILAUEA
dance .... HULA
dancer .... WAHINE
dress .... MUUMUU
drink .... KAVA
emblem .... LEHUA

farewell .... ALOHA
feast .... LUAU
fern .... IWAIWA, HEII
fiber .... WAUKE
fish .. ULUA, LANIA, AKU, PALANI, AHI
floral emblem .... LEHUA
floral wreath .... LEI
flower .. LEHUA, HIBISCUS
food .... POI, TARO
food fish ... ULUA, LANIA, UKU
foreman .... LUNA
frigate bird .... IWA
fruit .... POHA
game .... HEI
garland .... LEI
god .... KANE, KUPO
goddess of fire/volcano .. PELE
goggler .... AKULE
goose .... NENE, NENI
grass .... HILO
greeting .... ALOHA
harbor .... PEARL
herb .... NOLA
honeyeater .... OO
hula dancer ..... WAHINE
island ... MAUI, MOLOKAI, NIIHAU, HAWAII, KAUAI, LANAI, OAHU, KAHOOLAWE
Islands ..... SANDWICH
Islands discoverer ...... GAETANO
language .... POLYNESIAN
lava .... AA
like bird .... KITE
liquor ...... AWA, KAWA
lizard fish .... ULAE
loincloth .... PAU, MARO, MALO
love .... ALOHA
mountain ...... KEA, LOA
mulberry bark ..... TAPA
musical instrument ..... UKE(LELE), PUA
national park .... HALEAKALA
native .... KANAKA
neckpiece .... LAI, LEI
newcomer ...... MALHINI
noble .... ALII
noddy .... NOIO
nut .... LITCHI
octopus .... HEE
papercloth .... OLONA
party .... LUAU
pepper .... AVA
pit for baking ...... IMU
plant ...... KALO, OLONA
plantation boss .... LUNA
porch .... LANA(I)
port .... HILO
precipice .... PALI
press .... LOMILOMI
range .... KOOLAU
raven .... ALALA
royal chief .... ALII
rub .... LOMILOMI
salutation .... ALOHA
seaweed .... LIMU
shampoo ...... LOMILOMI
shrub .... AKIA
song .... MELE
starch .... APII
state flower .... HIBISCUS
taro, fermented .... MOD
taro paste .... POI
tern .... NOIO
thrush .... (OL)OMAO
town .... HILO
tree ...... LEHUA, AALII, AULU, ALANI, KOA, ILIAHI, OHIA
tree fern .... PULU, AMAU
valley .... MANOA
volcano ... KILAUEA, LOA, MAUNA, HALEAKALA
windstorm .... KONA
woman .... WAHINE
wood .... MILO, KOU
wreath .... LEI
yam .... HOI

hawfinch .... GROSBEAK
Hawhaw of WWII ..... LORD
hawk ...... CHEATER, SPREAD, SWINDLER, PEDDLE, ELANET, HARRIER, FALCON, KITE, BUZZARD, CARACARA, IO, MORTARBOARD, HAGGARD, ACCIPITER, MERLIN, OSSIFRAGE
Australian .... KAHU
bill of .... PAWL
blind .... SEEL
cage .... MEW
carrier .... CAD
claw .... TALON
European .... FALCON
eyed ...... KEEN-SIGHTED
falconry .... BATER
fish .... OSPREY
genus .. BUTEO, ACCIPITER
head cover .... SEEL
headed god ... HORUS, RA
hunt with .... FLY
leash of ...... LUNE, JESS
leg's feather .... FLAG
like bird ... OSPREY, KITE
male .... TERCEL
moth .... SPHINX
moth caterpillar .... HORNWORM
nemesis of the .. HOUBARA
nest .... AERIE, AERY
parrot .... HIA
small .... EYAS, KITE, ELANET
sparrow .... NISUS
stomach of ...... PANNEL
swoop of .... SOUSE
vulture-like ... CARACARA
weed .... MOUSE-EAR
young ..... AERIE, EYRIE, EYAS

hawker .. PEDDLER, HUCKSTER, COSTER, CADGER, CHAPMAN, FALCONER, PEDLAR
route of .... WALK
spot/talk of ...... PITCH

Hawkeye .... IOWAN
state .... IOWA

Hawkshaw .. DETECTIVE, DICK, SLEUTH
hawkweed .... DINDLE
hawser frame .. BITT, BOLLARD
iron .... CALKING
knot .... BEND
post .... BOLLARD

hawthorn ...... MAY(FLOWER), COCKSPUR, AZAROLE
fruit .... HAW, BERRY

Hawthorne's birthplace ...... SALEM
hay .. GRASS, CLOVER, ALFALFA, DANCE, FODDER, TIMOTHY
bale of .... TRUSS
bird .... BLACKCAP
box .... MANGER
bundle of .... TRUSS
fever .... POLLINOSIS, ROSE COLD
fever, cause of ... POLLEN
fever characteristic ..... SNEEZING, ASTHMA
fever remedy .. BENADRYL
fine cut .... CHAFF
fodder .... CHAFF
for thatching ... HA(U)LM
grass .... REDTOP
hit the ..... RETIRE, SLEEP
lifting implement .... PITCHFORK
pile .... COCK
plant .... SAINFOIN
row, drying ... WINDROW
second crop ..... ROWEN
spread the .... TED
stack of ...... RICK, MOW
storage place ...... MOW, LOFT

haycock .... RACK, COB, RICK
Hayden, ballerina .... MELISSA
haying job .... TED
hayseed .... RUSTIC, HICK
haystack .... RICK, MOW, COB, COIL, PIKE, GOAF
haywire ...... CRAZY, AMOK, DISORDERLY, CONFUSED
Hayworth, actress ...... RITA
role ... SADIE (THOMPSON)

hazard .... RISK, CHANCE, JEOPARDY, DANGER, STAKE, VENTURE, PERIL, JUMP
hazardous ... RISKY, PERILOUS, DANGEROUS, UNSAFE
haze .. FILM, FOG, BRUME, MIST, SMOG, VAPOR, SMAZE, GLIN, PALL
composition of ..... FOG, SMOKE, DUST
fellow student .. INITIATE
thin .... GAUZE

hazel ...... TREE, SHRUB, NUT, WOOD, BIRCH
hazelnut .... FILBERT
hazy .... VAGUE, OBSCURE
hd. .... HEAD
he .... PERSON, ANYONE
carved it ...... SCULPSIT
combining form ... MALE
in chemistry ..... HELIUM
Latin .... IPSE
man, describing a .... VIRILE
painted it .. PNXT, PINXIT
speaks .... LOQUITUR
wrote it .... SCRIPSIT

head .. PATE, TETE, MIND, VAN,

POLL, LEAD(ER), CAPITA, PASH, NOB, MAZARD, WITS, CAPUT, CONK, SKULL, TOP, APTITUDE, FRONT, CHIEF
  and shoulders ..... BUST
  and shoulders cover .... NUBIA
  armor .... MORION
  back part ...... OCCIPUT, POLL
  band .... FILLET
  beer .... FROTH
  cold ... CORYZA, SNIFFLES
  colloquial ...... NODDLE, PATE, WITS, SCONCE
  combining form .... CEPHAL(O)
  convent .... ABBESS
  cord .... AGAL
  counting .... CENSUS, CAPITATION
  cover .. HAT, CAP, SHAWL, HELMET, COWL, HOOD, HAIR, WIMPLE, TURBAN, BURNOOSE
  crown of ... PATE, VERTEX
  effervescent beverage .... FROTH
  enlarged at the .... CAPITATE
  garland .... CHAPLET
  gear ...... WIMPLE, HAT, BERET, BEANIE, MITRE, CAP, HELMET
  hair of .... POLL
  like structure ..... CAPUT
  membrane covering ..... CAUL, OMENTUM
  money .... POLL TAX
  monastery .... ABBOT
  nautical slang .... TOILET
  newspaper ..... CAPTION
  of foreign mission ...... NUNCIO, AMBASSADOR
  of the .... PARIETAL, CEPHALIC
  off .... INTERCEPT, AVERT, BLANCH
  pain .... HEMIALGIA, HEMICRANIA
  protective covering ..... HELMET, MASK, MORION
  shaped like .... CAPITATE
  shaved .... TONSURE
  ship's .... BOW
  shrinker .... ANALYST
  side of .... MALAR
  skin of .... SCALP
  skull .... SCONCE
  slang ..... BEAN, NOGGIN, NOB, DOME, NUT
  start .... LEAD
  to foot .... CAP-A-PIE
  to shave .... TONSURE
  top of .... PATE, CROWN, VERTEX
  wrap .. BURNOOSE, NUBIA, TURBAN, TARBOOSH, SHAWL
  wreath .... CHAPLET, LAUREL

headache .... MEGRIM, HEMIALGIA, MIGRAINE
  colloquial ...... WORRY, TROUBLE, PROBLEM

headband ...... AGAL, FILLET, TAENIA

headcheese .... BRAWN

headdress .. COIFFURE, DIADEM, MITER, MITRE, BIRETTA, WIG, COMMODE, TIAR(A), POUF, TOUPEE
  bishop's .... MITER, MITRE
  capelike .... PINNER
  cobra .... URAEUS
  cowl-like .... ALMUCE
  Indian .... BONNET
  maker .... MILLINER
  military ... SHAKO, BUSBY
  nun's ... CORNET, WIMPLE
  of feathers ..... TOPKNOT
  Sister of Carmelite's .... CORNET
  widow's .... BANDORE
  women's .... POUF, POMPADOUR, MILLINERY

header .... DIVE

headgear .. HAT, CAP, HELMET, HARNESS, HOOD, TOQUE, TAJ, SHAKO, TIAR(A), TOPI, FEZ

headhunter .... DAYAK

heading ...... TITLE, CAPTION, GALLERY, DRIFT
  of subject matter .. TROPE

headland .. CAPE, NESS, BLUFF, PROMONTORY, HOOK

headless .. ACEPHALOUS, ETETE, LEADERLESS
  man of fiction .... (BROM)BONES

headline .. BANNER, SCREAMER, STREAMER, TITLE

headliner .... STAR
  of 1898 .... MAINE
  of 1909 .... PEARY
  of 1914 ..... WORLD WAR
  of 1917 .. AEF, DOUGHBOY, ARMISTICE
  of 1934 .... DIONNE
  of 1945 .... A-BOMB, HIROSHIMA
  of 1950 .... BRINKS
  of 1957 .... SPUTNIK
  of 1959 .... CASTRO
  of 1969 ... MAN ON MOON

headlong ..... RECKLESS(LY), RASH(LY), PELLMELL, TANTIVY
  fall .... CROPPER
  flight .... LAM

headman .... CHIEF, BOSS, LEADER, HETMAN, RINGLEADER

headmaster .... PRINCIPAL, RECTOR

headpiece .... CAP, HELMET

headquarters .... MAIN OFFICE, BASE

headrest .... PILLOW

headset part ..... EARPHONE

headsman ..... EXECUTIONER, LEADER

headspring ... SOURCE, ORIGIN, FOUNTAIN

headstone ..... STELE, BARROW

headstrong ..... SELF-WILLED, RASH, WILLFUL, WAYWARD, STUBBORN

headwaiter .... CAPTAIN

headway .... PROGRESS

heady .... RASH, NAPPY

heal .... CURE, REMEDY, GET WELL, RECONCILE, RECUPERATE, MEND

healer ..... DOCTOR, SHAMAN, PHYSICIAN
  kind of ... FAITH, QUACK, MEDICINE MAN

healing .. CURATIVE, REMEDIAL, MEDICINAL, THERAPEUTIC
  substance ..... MEDICINE, PANACEA, BALM, NOSTRUM, DRUG, OINTMENT, BALSAM

health .... WELL-BEING, SOUNDNESS
  condition ...... WELFARE
  drinking toast ... PROSIT, SALUD, MABUHAY
  in good .... FIT, HALE
  resort .... SPA
  science of ..... HYGIENE, HYGIENICS

healthful .... SALUTARY, SALUBRIOUS, WHOLESOME

healthy .. SOUND, WELL, HALE, ROBUST

heap ..... MOW, RUCK, STACK, PILE, MOUND, (A)MASS, COB, RAFT, CONGERIES, RAFF
  colloquial .... LOTS, GREAT DEAL
  of a .... ACERVAL
  of rock fragments .... DEBRIS
  piled by wind ..... DRIFT
  slang .... CAR
  stone ..... MOUND, SCREE, CAIRN

hear .... LISTEN, LEARN, HEARKEN, HARK(EN), HEED
  ye .... OYEZ, OYES

hearer .... AUDITOR, LISTENER

hearing ..... OYER, AUDITION, AUDIENCE, INTERVIEW, TRIAL, INQUEST
  act/sense of ... AUDITION
  aid .... AUDIPHONE, EAR(PHONE)
  hard of .... DEAF
  in court .... TRIAL
  instrument .... AUDIOMETER, STETHOSCOPE
  keen ...... HYPERACUSIA, HYPERACUSIS
  of .... AURAL, OTIC, AUDITORY, ACOUSTIC
  organ .... OTOCYST
  range .... EARSHOT
  science of .... AUDIOLOGY

hearken ...... LIST(EN), HEED, HEAR, HIST, ATTEND

Hearn, writer ...... YAKUMO, LAFCADIO

hearsay ..... REPORT, RUMOR, GOSSIP, TALK
  means of spreading ..... GRAPEVINE

hearse . . . . BIER
cover . . . . PALL
heart . . . . . . GIST, PITH, COR(E), BREAST, BOSOM, ESSENCE, CARDIA, SPIRIT
action record . . . . CARDIOGRAM
ailment . . . . ANGINA, CARDITIS
attack . . . . . . OCCLUSION, STROKE, SHUTDOWN
attack cause . . . . THROMBOSIS
auricle . . . . ATRIUM
beat . . . . . . PULSE, STROKE
beat condition . . FLUTTER, PALPITATION, ARRHYTHMIA
beat regulator . . . . PACEMAKER
bleeding . . . . . . DICENTRA
blood vessel . . . . . . AORTA
booster . . . . . . PACER, LVB
cavity . . . . AURICLE, CAMERA, ATRIUM
colloquial . . . . TICKER
contraction . . . . . SYSTOLE
deposit . . . . PLAQUE, CHOLESTEROL
enlargement . . . . MEGALOCARDIA
inflammation . . . CARDITIS
leaf . . . . MEDIC
muscular substance . . . . . MYOCARDIUM
of the . . . . CARDIAC
part . . . . AURICLE, VENTRICLE
point . . . . FESS
shaped . . . . CORDATE, CARDIOID, CORDIFORM
sound . . . . MURMUR
stimulant . . . . SPARTEIN(E), DIGITALIS, CORDIAL, HELLEBOREIN
study of . . . . CARDIOLOGY
transplant patient . . . . . . BLAIBERG, BLOCK, KASPERAK, WASHKANSKY
transplant surgeon . . . . . . WADA, COOLEY, SHUMWAY, BARNARD
trouble . . . . ANGINA, CONDITION
heartache . . . . . GRIEF, SORROW
heartbeat . . . . . . PULSE, THROB, TACHYCARDIA, PALPITATION, PULSATION
condition . . . . . . FLUTTER
heartburn . . . . . PYROSIS, ENVY, JEALOUSY, CARDIALGIA, WATER BRASH
hearten . . . . ENCOURAGE, CHEER (UP)
heartfelt . . . . GENUINE, SINCERE
hearth . . FIRESIDE, HOME, LING
goddess of the . . . . VESTA, HESTIA
heartless . . . . . CRUEL, PITILESS, SARDONIC, MERCILESS
heartdeaf . . . . MEDIC
hearts/diamonds . . . (RED)SUIT
heartsease . . . . PANSY, PERSICARY, WALLFLOWER
heartsick . . . DESPONDENT, SAD
heartwood . . . . DURA(MEN)
heartworm . . . . NEMATODE
hearty . . . . HALE, SINCERE, CORDIAL, GENIAL, LUSTY, VIGOROUS, FELLOW, COMRADE, ROBUST, SAILOR
heat . . CALOR, HOTNESS, FEVER, WARM(TH), EXCITEMENT, ANGER, TEPOR, ARDOR, FIRE, ZEAL, CAUMA, INTENSITY, INFLAME
animal . . . . . RUT, ESTRUS
bubble up with . . . . INTUMESCE
caused by . . . . . . THERMIC
combining form . . . . THERMO, THERMY
decomposition by . . . . PYROLYSIS
exhaustion . . . SUNSTROKE
gentle . . . . TEPOR
great . . . . BROIL
lightning . . . . . . WILDFIRE
liquify with . . . . MELT
measuring device . . . . CALORIMETER
oppressive . . . . . SWELTER
pertaining to . . . . CALEFY, CALORIC, THERMAL, THERMIC
pervious to . . . . TRANSCALENT
production of . . . . DIATHERMY
prostration . . . SUNSTROKE
rash . . . . MILIARIA
resistant . . . . STABILE
resistant material . . . . ASBESTOS, COPPER
sexual . . . . . . ESTRUS, RUT
source . . . . SUN, FUEL
to liquid state . . . . . MELT
unit . . THERM(E), CALORIE, CALORY, BTU
heated . . . . HOT, ANGRY
chamber . . . . STOVE
to whiteness . . . CANDENT
wine . . . . REGUS
heater . . ETNA, BURNER, BUNSEN, OVEN, STOVE, CHAUFFER
hot-water/gas . . . GEYSER
portable . . . . . . CHAUFFER
slang. . . . . . . GUN, PISTOL
heath . . . . . MOOR, BENT, ERICA, AZALEA, WASTELAND, PIPE
heathbird . . . . GROUSE, BLACKCOCK
heathen . . . . . PAGAN, INFIDEL, GENTILE, ETHNIC, PAYNIM, IRRELIGIOUS
deity . . . . IDOL
heather . . . GORSE, ERICA, LING, BILBERRY, CROWBERRY
heating . . . . CALEFICIENT, CALEFACTION
device . . . . RETORT, ETNA, BOILER, STOVE, OVEN, BURNER
heaume . . . . HELMET
heave . . . . . HEFT, CAST, FLING, KECK, HURL, RAISE, LIFT, HAUL, SWELL, BULGE, PANT, GASP
heaven . . PROVIDENCE, GLORY, CIEL, WELKIN, ZION, EDEN, ELYSIUM, SKY, FIRMAMENT, OLYMPUS
arch of . . . . SKY
combining form . . URANO
edge of . . . . HORIZON
flier to . . . . ETANA
personified . . . . . URANUS
heavenly . . EDENIC, CELESTIAL, ETHEREAL, SUPERNAL, HOLY, URANIC, DIVINE
being . . . . ANGEL, CHERUB, SERAPH(IM)
city . . . . SION, ZION
body . . . . . COMET, MOON, STAR, SUN, PLANET, METEOR
bread . . . . MANNA
path . . . . ORBIT
heavens, imaginary belt of . . . ZODIAC
description of the . . . . URANOLOGY
heaves . . . . BROKEN WIND
heavily . . . . CLUMSILY, SLOWLY
heavy . . . . GRAVE, SERIOUS, BURDENSOME, PONDEROUS, SAD, LEADEN, GLOOMY, WEIGHTY, ROUGH, THICK, MASSIVE
blow . . . ONER, HAYMAKER
boat . . . . . STOGY, BROGAN
demand . . . . DRAFT
duty . . . . TOUGH
earth . . . . BARYTA
footed . . . . PLODDING
hammer . . . . SLEDGE
handed . . . . CRUEL, ARBITRARY, OPPRESSIVE
hang . . . . DRAG
hearted . . . . SAD
hydrogen . . . . DEUTERIUM
load . . . . BURDEN
nail . . . . SPIKE
role . . . . VILLAIN
spar . . . . BARITE, BARYTES
step/walk . . . TROD, SLOG, CLUMP
wire . . . . CABLE
with child . . . . PREGNANT
hebdomad . . . . . . WEEK, SEVEN
hebephrenia . . . . DEMENTIA
hebetate . . . . DULL, STUPID, BLUNT
Hebraism . . . . JUDAISM
Hebrew . . . . . ZION, ISRAELITE, S(H)EMITE
acrostic . . . . AGLA
alien resident . . . . GER
alphabet . . . ALEPH, ALEF, AIN, NUN, MEM, JOD, VAU, WAW, PE, TAV, TAW, RESH, TETH, CHETH, BETH, GIMEL, DALETH, ZAYIN, YODH, CAPH, KAPH, LAMED(H), SAMEKH, AYIN, SADHE, KOPH, SHIN
ancestor . . . . EBER

ascetic .... ESSENE, NAZARITE
bible books ...... NEBIIM
bread .... AZYM
bride .... KALLAH
brotherhood ..... ESSENE
canonical lawbook ...... TALMUD
city .... KIRJATH
coin ..... GERAH, SHEKEL
day .... YOM
deity .... BAAL
divine presence .... SHEKINAH
drum .... TOPH
dry measure .. EPHA, KAB
ear of corn .... ABIB
father .... ABRAM
festival .... PURIM, SEDER
first month .... TISHRI
flute .... NEHILOTH
god ....EL, ELOHIM, JEHOVAH
greeting .... SHALOM
Hades .... SHEOL
healer .... ASA
hello .... SHALOM
herdsman .... AMOS
high priest .... ELI, EZRA
high priest, first .. AARON
horn ... SHOFAR, SHOPHAR
household idols .... TERAPHIM
hymn .... KADDISH
instrument .... ASOR
judge ..... HALAKIST, ELI, HALACHIST, ELON
king .... DAVID, SAUL
kind of demons .... ASMODEUS
kingdom .... ISRAEL
language ...... RABBINIC
law of Moses ... TORA(H)
letter .. PE, DALETH, MEM, AYIN, RESH, TETH, YOD, VAU
lyre .... ASOR
marriage custom .... LEVERATE
measure ...... KOR, KAB, (H)OMER, EPHA(H), HIN
month ..... TISHRI, ELUL, ADAR, BUL, AB, ZIV, ABIB, SEBAT, KISLEV, NISAN, TEBET, SHEBAT, VEADAR, IYAR, SIVAN, TAMMUZ
name for God .... EL, ADONAI, ELOHIM
name for Syria .... ARAM
order .... ESSENE
Passover month .... ABIB
precept .... TORA
psalms of praise .. HALLEL
priest .... LEVITE
princess .... SARAH
prophet .. HOSEA, DANIEL, ELIAS, ISAIAH, NAHUM, JOEL, HAGGAI, NASI, MALACHI, JEREMIAH, AMOS, ELISHA, EZRA, MICAH, JONAH
prophetess ..... DEBORAH
psalms of praise .. HALLEL
quarter .... GHETTO
religion .... JUDAISM, HEBRAISM
sanctuary .... BAMAH
scarf .... ABNET, TALLITH
scholar .... HALAKIST, HALACHIST
scripture marginal notes .. MASORA
seer ..... BALAAM, ISAAC, MOSES
son .... BEN
songs of praise ... BALLEL
stringed instrument ..... ASOR
sun god .... BAAL
teacher .... RAB
ten .... YOD(H)
trader .... BANIAN
tribe .... DAN, LEVITES
universe .... OLAM
weight .... GERAH, OMER, SHEKEL
word .... SELAH

Hebrides Island .. LEWIS, UIST, HARRIS, MULL, IONA, SKYE
hecatomb .... SACRIFICE, SLAUGHTER
heck! .... HELL, INTERJECTION
heckle ..... HATCHEL, ANNOY, TAUNT, BAIT, NEEDLE
heckler .... TAUNTER, HOOTER, HISSER, BOOER, TEASER
hectic .... CONSUMPTIVE, HOT, FEVERED, FEVERISH, FLUSHED, FEBRILE
hector ..... BULLY, BRAWLER, TEASE, PESTER, BROWBEAT, BAIT, HUFF
parent of .... PRIAM, HECUBA
wife of .... ANDROMACHE
Hecuba's children ... HECTOR, TROILUS, CASSANDRA, PARIS
husband .... PRIAM
heddle .... CAAM
hedge ..... TEMPORIZE, HAW, HEM, REW, BUSH, THICKET, BOMA, EQUIVOCATE, QUICKSET, SHILLY-SHALLY, FENCE, BARRIER, WAVER, HEM AND HAW, ROW
debris .... BRASH
form a .... PLASH
laurel .... TARATA
pant .... PRIVET
trimmer .... PLASHER, SHEAR
hedgehog .... PORCUPINE, URCHIN
Greek .... ECHINOS
like animal ..... TENREC, TENDRAC
spine of .... QUILL
hedgerow .... REW
Hedin, explorer .... SVEN(ANDERS)
hedonist .... VOLUPTUARY
heebie-jeebies .... JITTERS, NERVOUSNESS
heed .. HEAR(KEN), OBEY, CARE, ATTENTION, NOTE, LISTEN, MIND, RECK, NOTICE
heedful .... VIGILANT, ATTENT(IVE)
heehaw ...... BRAY, GUFFAW, LAUGH(TER)
heel ... LOUSE, TAP, BOUNDER, CAD, CHASE, LIST, SLANT, TILT, LEAN, CAREEN, CANT, CALX
boot's .... DUCE
bone .... CALCANEUS, FIBULA
combining form ... TALO
down at the ...... SEEDY, SHABBY
over .. TIP, CAREEN, TILT, CAPSIZE
heeled: sl. .... MONEYED, RICH, ARMED
heeler ..... COCK, HANGER-ON
heeling .... ALIST, ATILT
Heflin, actor .... VAN
heft ... INFLUENCE, PULL, LIFE, WEIGHT, HEAVE, BULK
hefty ...... HEAVY, WEIGHTY, POWERFUL
Hegel, philosopher .... GEORG
hegemonic .. RULING, LEADING
hegira ...... FLIGHT, JOURNEY
destination ...... MEDINA
hegumen .... ABBOT
Hehe crop ..... MAIZE, MILLET
Heidelberg memento .... SCAR
heifer .... COW, STIRK
maid changed to ..... IO
height ..... EXTREME, CLIMAX, ALTITUDE, ELEVATION, ACME, PINNACLE, TOP, SUMMIT, STATURE, EMINENCE, APEX
of great .... SKYEY
of play's action .... CATASTASIS, CLIMAX, DENOUEMENT
heighten .... INTENSIFY, INCREASE, ENHANCE
heinous .. ODIOUS, ABOMINABLE, WICKED, HATEFUL
heir .... LEGATEE, (IN)HERITOR, SCION, SON, HERES
joint .... PARCENER
kind of ...... APPARENT, PRESUMPTIVE, FORCED, LEGAL
legal .... HERES
to a throne .... CROWN PRINCE
heist: sl. ... HOLDUP, ROBBERY
Hejaz capital .... MECCA
holy city .... MECCA, MEDINA
Hel .. GODDESS, UNDERWORLD
held ...... DETAINED, GRIPPED
capable of being .... TENABLE
in music .... TENUTO
in trust ...... FIDUCIARY
Helen .. EILEEN, ELAINE, ELENA, AILEEN
dimunitive of ... NELL(Y), LENA
Mitchell Armstrong ..... MELBA

of Troy's abductor ...... PARIS
daughter .... HERMIONE
husband .... MENELAUS
mother .... LEDA
son .... DORUS
suitor ..... PARIS, AJAX
heliacal .... SOLAR
helianthus .... SUNFLOWER
helical .... SPIRAL, TORSE
helico: comb. form .... SPIRAL
helicoid ...... COILED, SPIRAL
Helicon ..... MOUNTAIN, TUBA
dweller .... MUSE
helicopter: colloq. ....
WHIRLYBIRD, GIRO, CHOPPER
kin .... AUTOGIRO, GYROPLANE
Heliopolis ...... BAALBEK, ON
Helios ..... APOLLO, SUN GOD, HYPERION
daughter of .... CIRCE
father of ...... HYPERION
sister of .... ARTEMIS
heliotrope ...... BLOODSTONE, (SUN)FLOWER, TURNSOLE
hell ..... INFERNO, TOPHET(H), SHEOL
border of .... LIMBO
capital of .. PANDEMONIUM
hellbender ... SPREE, DEBAUCH, SALAMANDER
hellbent .... DETERMINED, SET, RESOLVED
helix .. SPIRAL, MOLLUSK, SNAIL
hell .. HADES, SHEOL, ABADDON, TARTARUS, ABYSS, PIT, INFERNO, GEHENNA, AVERNUS
diver .... DABCHICK
euphemism for .... HECK
in New Testament ...... GEHENNA
Hellas .... GREECE
hellcat ...... VIRAGO, SHREW, WITCH, VIXEN
Hellene .... GREEK
Hellenism .... GRECISM
Hellespont ..... DARDANELLES
nightly swimmer .... LEANDER
victim .... LEANDER
hellhound .... CERBERUS, FIEND
hellish .... FIENDISH, STYGIAN, INFERNAL
helm .. RUDDER, WHEEL, STEER, TILLER
Helmer, Mrs. .... NORA
helmet .. HAT, ARMET, SALLET, BAS(I)NET, CASQUE, MORION, BURGONET, SCONCE, HEAUME
crested, hatlike .. MORION
decoration ..... PANACHE
eye cover .... VISOR
faceguard .... VISOR
front .... VENTAIL
lower part ...... BEAVER
nosepiece .... NASAL
opening .... VUE
part ...... BEAVER, VISOR
pith .... TOPI, TOPEE
plume .... PANACHE
Roman .... GALEA
shaped .... GALEATE
shaped part ...... GALEA
visored .... ARMET
helminth .... (TAPE)WORM, (ROUND)WORM, PARASITE
helmsman ... TILLER, CONNER, PILOT, STEERSMAN, COX(ON), COXSWAIN
Heloise, husband of .. ABELARD
helot .... SERF, ESNE, SLAVE
help .. ASSIST, WAIT ON, HAND, SERVANT, EMPLOYEES, STAFF, SUCCO(U)R, AID, SECOND, ABET
me signal .. SOS, MAYDAY
of any kind .... LIFT
over .... TIDE
helpless .... WEAK, FEEBLE, SPINELESS, IMPOTENT, LOST
helpmate .... WIFE, HUSBAND, SPOUSE
Helsingfors .... HELSINKI
Helsingor .... ELSINORE
helter-skelter .... HURRIED, DISORDERLY
helve .... HANDLE, HAFT, ANSE, HILT
Helvetia .... SWITZERLAND
hem .. BORDER, MARGIN, EDGE, SEW, SHUT, ENCIRCLE
and haw .. HEDGE, FALTER
in .. FENCE, CROWD, BESET, INVEST
stiffening cloth ... WIGAN
hematin .... HEME
hematite .. LIMONITE, IRON ORE
hematoma .... TUMOR
heme .... HEMATIN
Hemingway, author ... ERNEST
character ... PILAR, BRETT
soubriquet .... PAPA
hemiplegia .... PARALYSIS
hemipterous insect ... BEDBUG, LICK, APHID
hemlock .. YEW, WEED, POISON, VALERIAN, CONIUM
alkaloid .... CONIN(E)
poison .... BENNET
hemoglobin product .... BILIRUBIN
hemophiliac .... BLEEDER
hemorrhage .... BLEEDING
hemorrhoid ..... PILES, TUMOR
hemostatic .... STYPTIC
hemp ...... PITA, TOW, FIBER, PLANT, RAMIE, IFE, RINE, HASHISH
African .... IFE
cleaning tool .. SWINGLE, HATCHEL
cloth .. CANVAS, SACKING
dampen .... RET
drug .... HASHISH
E. Indies .... SUNN
fabric ... BURLAP, GUNNY
fiber .. TOW, AGAVE, SISAL
fiber from ropes .. OAKUM
filament .... HARL
Greek .... KANNABIS
Indian .. B(H)ANG, K(I)EF, RAMIE, DAGGA
leaves .. KEF, KIEF, BHANG
Manila .... ABACA
narcotic .... HASHISH, CHARAS, MARIJUANA
plant .. MARIJUANA, SUNN
refuse ..... TOW, HURDS, HARDS
resin ... CHARAS, HASHISH
sisal .... HENEQUEN, HENEQUIN
shrub .... PUA
soak .... RET
source .... CANNABIS
hempen cloth .... HESSIAN
hen ...... CHICKEN, CACKLER, LAYER, PULLET
brooding .... SITTER
chickens of ...... BROOD
cry of .. SQUAWK, CACKLE
extinct .... HEATH
hawk .... REDTAIL
mud .... RAIL
roost .... PERCH
slang .... WOMAN
sound .. CACKLE, CLUCK, CHUCK(LE), SQUAWK
spayed .... POULARD
young .... POULARD, CHICKEN
henbane .... NIGHTSHADE, HYOSCYAMUS
henbit .... PLANT, MINT
hence .... THUS, ERGO, AWAY, THEREFORE, OFF, THEN, SO
henchman .... ADHERENT, SQUIRE, ATTENDANT, FOLLOWER, HANGER-ON, PAGE
henequen ...... FIBER, AGAVE, (SISAL)HEMP
Hengist's brother ..... HORSA
kingdom .... KENT
henhouse .... COOP
henna ... ALCANA, DYE, SHRUB
henpeck ...... NAG, DOMINEER
Henrietta, diminutive of ...... ETTA, NETTY, NETTIE, HETTY
Henry, diminutive of ... HAL, HENNY, HANK
IV's family ... LANCASTER
Kaiser .... NOAH
VIII's wife ..... ARAGON, BOLEYN, SEYMOUR, CLEVES, HOWARD, PARR
hent .... GRASP(ING), PURPOSE, APPREHEND, CONCEPTION
hep: sl. .... ON TO, INFORMED, FAMILIAR, CONVERSANT, AWARE
hepatic(a) .... LIVERWORT, LIVER-SHAPED
hepcat ...... (SWING)DANCER, HIPSTER, BEATNIK
cry of .... SOLID
Hephaestus .... VULCAN
heptachord .... LYRE
Hera, husband of ...... ZEUS, JUPITER
mother of .... RHEA
of Romans .... JUNO
rival of .. LETO, IO, LEDA, EURODA, THEMIS
son of .... ARES
Herakleion .... CANDIA
Herakles .... HERCULES

herald . . . . . MESSENGER, CRIER, FORERUNNER, HARBINGER, USHER, PROCLAIM, BLAZON, ANNOUNCE(R), FORETELL
coat of . . . . TABARD
god . . . HERMES, MERCURY
morning . . . . COCK, LARK
of good news . . . GABRIEL
staff of . . . . CADUCEUS
heraldic . . . . . . ARMORIAL, BAY
band . . . . . . FESS(E), ORLE, TRESSURE, FILLET
bearing . . . . FESS(E), ORLE, GIRON, GYRON, ENTE, BEND, SALTIRE, PHEON, LAVER
cross . . . . . . PATTE, PATEE
design . . . . SEME
device . . . . CREST
fillet . . . . ORLE
mastiff . . . . ALAN
shield border . . . . . . ORLE, BORDURE
shield boss . . . . UMBO
shield division . . . . . ENTE, CANTON
shield horizontal band . . . FESS
shield side segments . . . . . FLANCH
shield stripe . . . . PALE
star . . . . ESTOILE
term . . . . PATTE, SEME
triangle . . . . GIRON
wreath . . . . . TORSE, ORLE
heraldry . . . . . . ENTE, ARMORY
animal partly visible . . . . ISSUANT
bar, horizontal . . . . LABEL
bastardy mark . . . . BATON
bear . . . . GRISE
bearing . . . ORLE, SALTIRE, TRESSURE
bend . . . . COTISE
bird . . . . MARTLET
black tincture . . . . . SABLE
blood-red . . . . . . MURREY
blue . . . . AZURE
chaplet . . . . ORLE
checkered . . . . VAIR
cherub . . . . SERAPH
circle . . ANNULET, BEZANT
colter . . . . LAVER
creature . . . . . LION, BISSE, CANNET, GRIFFON, PARD, MARTLET, WYVERN, WYVER
crest . . . . MARTLET
cross . . . SALTIRE, SALTIER, CRUX
diamond-shaped figure . . MASCLE
division . . . . . . PALE, PALY
dog . . . . ALANT
duck . . . . CANNET(TE)
face-to-face . . . AFFRONTE
fillet . . . . ORLE
flower strewn . . . . . . SEME
flying in air . . . . FLOTANT
footless bird . . . . MARTLET
foreleg of beast . . . GAMB
fur tincture . . . . PEAN, VAIR(E)
grafted . . . . ENTE
green tincture . . . . . VERT
headless . . . . ETETE
horizontal band . . . . FESS, FILLET
iris . . . . LIS
laver . . . . COLTER
leaves, having . . . . POINTE
left side . . . . SINISTER
line . . UNDE, URDY, UNDY, NEBULY, DEXTER, SINISTER
lozenge . . . MASCLE, FUSIL
manacle . . . . TIRRET
orange tincture . . . . TENNE
ornament of headpiece . . CREST
pointed . . . . URDE
position of animal . . . . . . GARDANT, SEJANT, PASSANT
purple tincture . . . . PURPURE
red tincture . . . . GULES
row of squares . . . . COMPONY
running . . . . COURANT
sheaf of grain . . . GERB(E)
shield . . . . PAVIS
shield bar . . . . GEMEL
shield-shaped . . . PELTATE
shield's center . . . . . . FESS
shield's corner . . CANTON
silver . . . . ARGENT
sitting . . . . . SEJANT, ASSIS
sleeping position . . . . DORMANT
snake . . . . BISSE
spangled . . . . SEME
standing . . . . STATANT
strewn . . . . SEME
subject of . . COAT OF ARMS, ARMORY, GENEALOGY
triangle . . . GYRON, GIRON
two-winged . . . . VOL
vertical division . . . . PALY
voided escutcheon . . ORLE
walking . . . . PASSING
wavy . . . . ONDE, UNDE(E), NEBULE
winged . . . . AILE, VOL
wreath . . . . . . ORLE, TORSE
herb . . . . SAGE, GRASS, CATNIP, RUE, MOLY, WORT, RUTA, GALAX, CARAWAY, OREGANO, THYME, SEDGE, PARSLEY, PARSNIP, SEDUM, CHERVIL, QUINOA, TARRAGON, YARROW, CLINTONIA
aromatic . . GINGER, MINT, GINSENG, BERGAMOT, ROSEMARY, ANISE, DILL, ANET, BASIL, DITTANY, FLEAWORT
aromatic root . . . . NONDO
aster family . . . . . ARNICA
bean family . . PEA, LOTUS
bennet . . . . AVENS
bitter . . ALOE, RUE, TANSY, GENTIAN
bulbous . . . . GARLIC
carrot family . . . LOVAGE, PARSLEY, ERINGO, ERYNGO, FENNEL, DILL
chicory family . . . ENDIVE
cloverlike . . . . MEDIC, LUCERNE
coarse . . . . . ELECAMPANE, IVA, ERYNGO
concoction . . . . . . TISANE
crowfoot family . . . . CLEMATIS, COHOSH
decoction . . . . PTISAN, TISANE
dill . . . . ANET
eve . . . . IVA
evergreen . . . . GALAX
fabulous . . MOLY, PANACE
flowering . . . . . . HEPATICA
forage . . . . SULLA
fragrant . . . . BALM
genus . . . . . . RUTA, GEUM, ALETRIS
ginger . . . . ALPINIA, CARDAMOM, CARDAMUM
goose foot family . . BLITE
gourd family . . . . . MELON, SQUASH
Himalayan . . . . ATIS
laxative . . . . SENNA
lily family . . . . COLICROOT
magic . . . . MOLY
medicinal . . . . . ALOE, RUE, BONESET, TANSY, FENNEL
mint family . . . . . . BALM, CATNIP, BASIL, HYSSOP
mustard family . . . . CRESS
mythical . . . . MOLY
nettle family . . . . . . HEMP
nightshade . . . . HENBANE, TOMATO
of grace . . . . RUE
onion . . . . CHIVE
parsley family . . . . CICELY
pea family . . . . . . MIMOSA, CASSIA, LOTUS, LOTOS, FENUGREEK
perennial . . . SEDUM, SEGO
pink family . . . . CAMPION
pod . . . . OKRA, OCRA
purslane family . . . . CLAYTONIA
root . . . . GINSENG, CHOY, CHAY, NONDO
scented . . . . CATNIP
seasoning . . . . . . PARSLEY, SAGE, THYME, BASIL
snake charm . . . . MUNGO
spinach-like . . . . . ORACHE
starch yielding . . . . . . PIA
strong smelling . . . . YARROW, RUE
symbol of grief . . . . . RUE
tonic . . . . BONESET, CORIANDER
tropical . . . . GINSENG, GINGER, LOOFA
use of . . . MEDICINE, FOOD, SEASONING
with aromatic seeds . . . . . ANISE
with stinging hairs . . . . . . NETTLE
woolly . . . . POLY
herbage . . . . GRASS
herbivore . . VEGETARIAN, TAPIR

Hercules . . . . HERAKLES, STRONG MAN, ALCIDES, CONSTELLATION
captive . . . . IOLE
monster slain by . . HYDRA
parent of . . . . . ALCMENE, ZEUS
queen served by . . . . OMPHALE
tutor . . . . CHIRON
victim of . . . . NESSUS
wife of . . . HEBE, DEIANIRA
woman saved by . . . . HESIONE
herd . . CROWD, PUBLIC, FLOCK, SHOAL, DROVE, RABBLE, POD, CORRAL
animals together . . . . POD
of horses . . . . . . CAVIYA, HARRAS
of whales . . . . . GAM, POD
herd's grass . . . . REDTOP, TIMOTHY
herds, living in . . . GREGARIOUS
herdsman . . . . VAQUERO, SHEPHERD, COWBOY, RANCHERO, GAUCHO, DROVER
constellation . . . . . BOOTES
stick of . . . . GOAD
here . . . . ICI, HITHER, NOW, EXCLAMATION, PRESENT
and ____ . . . NOW, THERE
and there . . . . ABOUT
lies: inscription . . . . HIC JACET
opposed to . . . . . . THERE
hereafter . . . . FUTURE
heredes . . . . HEIRS
singular of . . . . . . HERES
hereditary . . . . . . ANCESTRAL, LINEAL, INNATE, GENETIC
factor . . . . GENE
right . . . . UDAL
ruler . . . . DYNAST
heredity . . . . GEN(E), GENETICS
theoretician on . . MENDEL
Hereford . . . . CATTLE
heres . . . . HEIR
plural of . . . . HEREDES
heresy . . . . HERETODOXY
heretic . . . . . DISSENTER, ARIUS
garment of . . . SANBENITO
public burning of . . . . AUTODAFE
heretofore . . . . ERENOW
heritable land . . . . ODAL
heritage . . . . PATRIMONY, LOT, LEGACY, BIRTHRIGHT, ISRAELITES
heritor . . . . HEIR
herl . . . . FLY, BARB
herma . . . MILESTONE, SIGNPOST
hermaphroditic . . . EFFEMINATE
hermaphroditism . . GYNANDRY
hermeneutic . . . . INTERPRETIVE
Hermes . . . . . . GOD, MERCURY, HERALD, MESSENGER
footwear . . . . TALARIA
gift to Odysseus . . . MOLY
hat, winged . . . . PETASOS, PETASUS
parent of . . . . MAIA, ZEUS
son of . . . . PAN
staff of . . . . CADUCEUS
hermetic . . MAGICAL, AIRTIGHT, ALCHEMICAL, SEALED
Hermione's brother . . . DORUS
husband . . . . ORESTES
parent . . . . HELEN, MENELAUS
hermit . . ANCHORITE, EREMITE, RECLUSE, TROGLODYTE, SOLITAIRE, ASCETIC, SANTON, ANCHORET, MARABOUT, COOKY, HUMMINGBIRD, CRAB, THRUSH
crab . . PAGURIAN, PAGURID
hermitage . . . . RETREAT, WINE, CLOISTER, MONASTERY
Russia's . . . . MUSEUM
hermitic . . SECLUDED, SOLITARY
hern . . . . HERON
hernia . . . . . RUPTURE, BREACH, CYSTOCELE
support . . . . TRUSS
Hero . . . IDOL, STAR, DEMIGOD, PALADIN, DEFENDER, CHAMPION, PRIESTESS, LION, PROTAGONIST
animal . . . . AKELA, RIN TIN TIN
Crusades . . . . . . TANCRED
Filipino . . . RIZAL, MABINI
legendary . . . . . TRISTRAM, TRISTAN, AMADIS, PALADIN, LEONIDAS, (EL)CID
lover of . . . . LEANDER
of old . . . . KNIGHT
opposed to . . . . . VILLAIN
Persian . . . . RUSTUM
Spartan . . . . LEONIDAS
Herodias' daughter . . . SALOME
husband . . . . ANTIPAS
heroic . . . . BOLD, BRAVE, VALIANT, GALLANT, SPARTAN, EXALTED, DARING, EPIC(AL)
events . . . . EPOS
narrative . . SAGA, ODYSSEY
poem . . . . . . EPIC, EPOPEE, EPOS, ILIAD
verse . . . . . . ALEXANDRINE
heroics . . . . CLAPTRAP
heroin . . . . . . NARCOTIC, HORSE
addict . . . . SNOWBIRD
slang . . . . . . SNOW, SMACK
heroine . . . . JOAN OF ARC
heron . . . . BITTERN, RAIL, SOCO, AIGRET(TE), EGRET, HERN, CRANE, BOATBILL, SHOEBILL
brood . . . . EDGE
green . . . . POKE
kin . . . . HAMMERHEAD
night . . . . . QUA, SQUAWK
herpes . . SHINGLES, COLD SORE, TETTER
designating one . . ZOSTER, LABIALIS
herpetology subject . . . REPTILE
herring . . . . . SPRAT, PILCHARD, CISCO, BLUEFIN, ANCHOVY, PILCHER, SARDINE
canned . . . . SARDINE
cured . . . . BLOATER
keg . . . . CADE
kin . . . . SHAD
lake . . . . MELBA, CISCO
like fish . . . . SPRAT, SHAD, ANCHOVY, ALEWIFE, CISCO
measure . . . . CRAN
pertaining to . . CLUPEOID
pond . . . . OCEAN
red . . . . BAIT
sauce . . . . ALEC
slang . . . . ALEWIFE
that recently spawned . . . SHOTTEN
tub . . . . CADE
young . . SMELT, SPARLING, BRIT
Herriot, premier . . . . EDOUARD
Herschel's discovery . . URANUS
herse . . . . PORTCULLIS
Hersey novel town . . . . ADANO
hesitant . . . . RELUCTANT, WAVERING, VACILLATING, TIMID, UNCERTAIN, CHARY
hesitate . . . WAVER, VACILLATE, FALTER, HAW, HEM, PAUSE, DEMUR, TEETER
in speaking . . . . STUTTER, STAMMER, HEM
hesitation . . . . INDECISION, RELUCTANCE
sound of . . . . ER, UM
Hesperia . . BUTTERFLY, ITALY, SPAIN, WESTERN LAND
Hesperian . . . . WESTERN, OCCIDENTAL
Hesperides . . . . AEGLE, HESTIA, NYMPHS, GARDEN
treasure . . . . (GOLDEN) APPLES
Hesperus . . . . (EVENING) STAR, VENUS
fate of . . . . WRECK
parent . . . . EOS, ASTRAEUS
Hess, a Nazi . . . . RUDOLF
pianist . . . . MYRA
Hessian . . . . MERCENARY, GERMAN
hessite . . . . TELLURIDE
hest . . . . ORDER, PLEDGE, BID(DING)
Hestia . . . . . . VESTA, GODDESS, NYMPH
parent of . . RHEA, CRONUS
Hesychast . . . . MYSTIC
het up: sl. . . . . EXCITED, AGOG
hetaera . . . COURTESAN, SLAVE, CONCUBINE, THAIS
hetaerism . . . . . . CONCUBINAGE
hetero: comb. form . . . . (AN)OTHER, DIFFERENT
opposed to . . . . HOMO
heterodox . . . . HERETICAL
opposed . . . . . ORTHODOX
heterogeneous . . . . . . FOREIGN, VARIED, DISSIMILAR, MOTLEY
heterogynous insect . . ANT, BEE
hetman . . . . ATAMAN, COSSACK, COMMANDER, CHIEF
hew . . . CHOP, CUT, HACK, AX, GASH
hex . . . . (BE)WITCH, JINX, SORCERER, HOODOO

hexad ..... SESTET, SEXTET(TE)
Hexham's river .... TYNE
hexapod .... SIX-FOOTED
hexapody .... HEXAMETER
hexastich ...... STANZA, POEM
hexose .... SUGAR
heyday .... PRIME, MAY
hiatus .. GAP, LACUNA, BREAK, PAUSE, COL, OPENING
Hiawatha's bark ...... CANOE
hibachi .... GRILL, BRAZIER
hibernal .... WINTRY, HIEMAL, BRUMAL
hibernate .... SHACK, WINTER, SLEEP
  opposed to ... GESTIVATE
hibernating animal ..... BEAR, WOODCHUCK, LEMMING
Hibernia ...... ERIN, IRELAND
hibiscus .. PLANT, SHRUB, TREE, MALLOW, GUMAMELA
hic jacet .. HERE LIES, EPITAPH, INSCRIPTION
hick .... RUSTIC, HAYSEED
hickey ...... GADGET, DEVICE
hickory .. PECAN, WOOD, CANE, SWITCH, TREE, (WAL)NUT
  fruit .... PIGNUT
  nut ...... PECAN, TRYMA
  tree .... SHAGBARK, SHELLBARK
  wattle .... ACACIA
hidalgo .... NOBLEMAN
  state capital ... PACHUCA
hidden ...... LATENT, COVERT, INNATE, ARCANE, CRYPTIC, OBSCURE, SECRET, INNER, PERDU
  provision .. JOKER, RIDER
hide ...... SECRETE, CONCEAL, COVER, BURY, FLOG, PELT, SKIN, THRASH, VEIL, MASK, FELL, CLOAK, STOW, SCREEN
  behind words .... HEDGE
  calf/lamb .... KIP
  for safekeeping ... CACHE
  raw ...... KIP, SHAGREEN
  softening solution .. BATE
hideaway .. LAIR, DEN, RETREAT
hideous ..... SCABROUS, UGLY, GRUESOME, REVOLTING, AWFUL, GRIM, REPULSIVE
  monster .... MEDUSA, GORGON
hideout ... LAIR, DEN, RETREAT
hiding, in .... PERDU
hidrosis .... SWEATING, PERSPIRATION
hidrotic .... SUDORIFIC
hie .... HASTEN, HURRY, SPEED
hiemal .... WINTRY, HIBERNAL, BRUMAL
hierarch .... HIGH PRIEST
hierarchy .... ANGELS
hieratic .... PRIESTLY, SACERDOTAL
hiero: comb. form .... SACRED, HOLY
hieroglyph ...... PICTOGRAPH
hieroglyphic ..... EMBLEMATIC, SYMBOLICAL
hieroglyphics, pillar with ..... OBELISK
hierophant .... HIGH PRIEST
higgle .... CHAFFER, WRANGLE, BARGAIN
higgledy-piggledy .. DISORDER, JUMBLE
high .... TOWERING, LOFTY, TALL, SUPERIOR, EXPENSIVE, SHRILL, DRUNK, ALT, DEAR, ALOFT
  abode ...... AERIE, AYRIE
  and dry ...... STRANDED
  and low ...... EVERYWHERE
  and mighty ... HAUGHTY, ARROGANT
  and piping ...... TREBLE
  blood pressure .... HYPERTENSION
  brow .... INTELLECTUAL, CULTURED, CULTIVATED, CIVILIZED
  class .... QUALITY, TONY, PLUSH, RITZY, SUPERIOR
  colloquial .... STIFF
  colored .... VIVID, LURID, FLORID
  combining form .... ALTI
  crime .... TREASON
  explosive .... TNT
  flown .... EUPHUISM, BOMBASTIC
  hat .... SNOB(BISH), SNUB, STYLISH, STOVEPIPE, SNOOTY
  hole .... FLICKER, WOODPECKER
  jinks ... PRANKS, CAPERS, REVELRY, MERRIMENT
  Mass celebrant .. DEACON
  pitched ... SHRILL, TREBLE
  priest .... ELI, AARON, ANNAS, HIERARCH, PONTIFF, HIEROPHANT
  sign .... SIGNAL, CUE
  society .... HAUTE MONDE
  sounding ..... SONOROUS
  spirited .... FIERY, PROUD
  strung .... EXCITABLE, TENSE, SENSITIVE, NERVOUS
  tail .... SCURRY, RUSH
  time ..... NONE TOO SOON
  toned .. STYLISH, MODISH, LUXURIOUS, LOFTY, QUALITY
  waters .... FLOOD
  wind .... GALE
highball ...... DRINK, STINGER
highbinder .... GANGSTER, HOODLUM, RUFFIAN
highboy ...... BUREAU, CHEST
highbrow .... LONGHAIR, INTELLECTUAL
highest ...... SUPREME, SUMMA
  combining form ... ACRO
  heaven .... EMPYREAN
  mountain .... EVEREST
  note, in music ...... ELA
  number of die ...... SISE
  point ..... FINIAL, NOON, APOGEE, PEAK, CLIMAX, APEX, ZENITH, VERTEX, PINNACLE
  possible .... MAXIMAL, MAXIMUM
highfalutin ..... HIGH-FLOWN, POMPOUS, PRETENTIOUS, FLIGHTY
highhanded .... OVERBEARING, ARBITRARY
highland rock ... MONADNOCK
highlander ..... TARTAN, SCOT, GAEL, PLAIDMAN
  breeches .... TREWS
  pouch .... SPORRAN
  sword of ..... CLAYMORE
  wear of .... KILT
Highlands robber ... CATERAN
highly ...... EXTREMELY, VERY
  colored .. FLORID, LURID, VIVID
  decorated .... GAUDY
  wrought ...... D(A)EDAL
highway ...... ROAD, AVENUE, THOROUGHFARE, ITER, FREEWAY, (TURN)PIKE
  Alaska–Canada .. ALCAN
  German ...... AUTOBAHN
  pest .... ROADHOG
  Roman ..... ITER, AVIAN
highwayman ... PAD, BRIGAND, HIJACKER, LADRONE
Hiiumaa .... DAGO
hijack(er) ...... HOLDUP(PER)
hike ... WALK, TRAMP, MARCH, RAISE, BOOST
hiker's bag ...... HAVERSACK, KNAPSACK
hilarious .... GAY, MERRY
hilarity .. GAIETY, MIRTH, GLEE, MERRIMENT
hilding .... WRETCH
hill ... MOUND, PILE, BARROW, BUTTE, DJEBEL, FELL, CUESTA, KOP(JE), MOUNT, MONTICULE, HEAP
  builder .... ANT
  cone-shaped .... BRAE
  dugout .... ABRI
  flat-topped .... MESA
  fortified .... MERLIN
  glacial .... KAME
  go over the .... DIE
  in a plain .... BUTTE
  isolated .... INCH
  of glacial drift .. DRUMLIN
  pointed .... TOR
  Rome .... PALATINE, AVENTINE
  rounded .. MORRO, KNOB, HUMMOCK
  sand .... DENE, DUNE
  signal .... BEACON
  small .... MOUND, DOWN, HILLOCK, DUNE
  South African ..... KOP, BULT
  top ... TOR, KNAP, CREST, COP, BROW
  U.S. ...... LOMA, LOMITA
  wood .... HOLT
Hillary's conquest ... EVEREST
  other work .. APICULTURE
hillbilly ..... BACKWOODSMAN, RUSTIC
  food .... TATERS

hillock .. MOUND, TOFT, TUMP, KNOLL, KOPJE
hills, land between .... INTERVALE
range of .... SIERRA
hillside .... BRAE, SLOPE
hollow ... CORRIE, SLACK
rubble .... SCREE
hilltop .... KNAP, TOR
hilt .... HAFT, HANDLE, HELVE
wooden .... DUDGEON
Himalayan animal .... OUNCE, PANDA
antelope .. GORAL, SEROW
bearcat .... PANDA
broadmouth ...... RAYA
capital .... GANGTOK, KATMANDU
cedar .... DEODAR
country ... SIKKIM, NEPAL
forest .... BHABAR
goat .. KYL, GORAL, TAHR, KRAS, TAIR
grassland .... TARAI
herb .... ATIS
marmot .... PIA
massif ...... ANNAPURNA
monkshood .... ATIS
mountains, personification of .... HIMAVAT
Mts. state ...... BHUTAN
peak .... NEPAL, EVEREST, MASHARBRUM, HUMP, API
river .... INDUS
sheep .... NAHOOR
tea .... AUCUBA
tree ...... DEODAR, TOON
walnut .... CORYLUS
wild goat .... KYL, THAR, TAHR, TAIR, KRAS
Himalayas: sl. ... (THE) HUMP
himself: Lat. .... IPSE
hind .. BACK, POSTERIOR, REAR, DEER, ROE, PEASANT, TAIL, RUSTIC
brain .... CEREBELLUM
leg of animal .... HAM
red .... CABRILLA
hinder .... IMPEDE, BLOCK, OBSTRUCT, PREVENT, DETER, DELAY, EMBAR, HAMPER, RETARD, CUMBER
hindmost .... LAST
hindquarter .... HAUNCH
hindrance .... RUB, CLOG, LET, OBSTACLE, IMPEDIMENT, HITCH, BAR
Hindu .. GENTOO, JAIN(A), SER, KOLI, TAMIL, SIKH, BABU, BANA
acrobat .... NAT
age of the world ... YUGA
ancestor .... MANU
Anglicized .... BABU
ascetic .. YATI, YOGI, JOGI, FAKIR, SADHU, MUNI
avatar .... RAMA
bandit .... DACOIT
banker .... SOWCAR, SOUCAR
barber .... NAPIT
bear .... BHALU
beggar .... NAGA
betelnut .... SUPARI
bible .... VEDA
boat .... YARAHA
brook .... NALA
bulbul .... KALA
butter .... GHI
call to prayer ..... AZAN
caste .. PASI, SUDRA, TELI, JAT, MAL, KORI, RAJPUT
caste, military .... KSHATRIYA
caste, priestly .. BRAHMAN
cavalry .... RISALA
charitable gift ..... ENAM
city .... ABAD
city, holy ..... BENARES
congregation ..... SAMAJ
cottage .... BARI
court officer ..... AMALA
cremation of a widow ... SATI
cultured .... BRAHMIN
cultured person .... BRAHMAN
cymbal .... TAL, DAL
dance drama ...... RASA
dancing girl .. BAYADERE, BAYADEER
deity .... KRISHNA, DEVA, UMA, KAMA, VARUNA, AGNI, DEWA, VAYU, YAMA, BHAGA, SIVA, VISHNU, MANU, RAMA, AKAL
demon ..... ASURA, RAHU
destiny .... KARMA
Devi .... MAYA
Devi's father ... HIMAVAT
disciple .... SIKH
divorce law ...... TALAK
drinking pot ...... LOTA
ejaculation .... OM
epic .... RAMAYAMA
epic hero .... ARJUNA
essence .... AMRITA
exchange rate ..... BATTA
evil spirit .. ASURA, MARA
fair .... MELA
fate .... KARMA
female slave .... DASI
festival ... PUJA, DEWALI, HOLI
flying beings ... GARUDAS
gardener .... MALI
garment .... DHOTI, SARI, SAREE
gentleman .. BABOO, BABU
giant: myth. .... BANA
gnome .... YAKSHA
god .. DEVI, BRAHMA, SIVA, AKAL, INDRA, KA, JAGANNATH
cosmos ...... VARUNA
elephant-headed ...... GANESHA
fire .... AGNI
heaven .... DYAUS
love ... KAMA, BHAGA
nature .... DEVA
rain .... INDRA
sky .... DYAUS
supreme .. SIVA, VISHNU
trinity ...... TRIMURTI, BRAHMA, SIVA, VISHNU
underworld ..... YAMA
goddess ...... UMA, VAC, USHAS, MAYA, SAKTI, LAKSHMI
beauty/luck .... SHREE, S(H)RI
dawn .... US(H)AS
destruction/evil .. KALI
mothers .... MATRIS
speech .... VAC(H)
splendor .... UMA
wealth .... SRI
gods' abode .... MERU
groom .... SYCE
guitar .. SITAR, VINA, BINA
gypsy .... KARACHEE
handkerchief ... MALABAR
hell .... HARAKA
hero .... RAMA, NALA, ARJUNA
holy book .. SASTRA, VEDA
holy city .... BENARES
holy destination .... HARDWAR, VARANASI
holy man ...... SADH(U)
idol .... SWAMI
illusion .... MAYA
immortality ..... AMRITA
incarnation ..... AVATAR
kingdom, last ..... NEPAL
kismet .... KARMA
kneeling rug .... ASAN
land grant .. INAM, ENAM, SASAN
language ...... SANSKRIT
lawgiver .... MANU
leader ... GANDHI, SIRDAR
loincloth ...... DHO(O)TI
lord .... SWAMI
low-caste ..... MAL, KORI
magic .... MAYA
margosa .... NEEM
master .... SAHIB, SWAMI, SWAMY, MIAN
Maya .... SAKTI, DEVI
meal .... ATA
measure ..... KOS, RYOTS
mendicant .... NAGA
merchant .... BANIAN
military caste .... RAJPUT
monastic philosophy .... VEDANTA
money .... ANNA
month ...... SA(RA)WAN, ASIN, BAISAKH, JETH, KUAR, KA(R)TIK, AGHAN, MAGH, CHAIT, PHA(L)GUN
mountain .... MERU
mountain pass ... GHAUT
mountaineer .... BHIL
musical instrument ..... SITAR, VINA, SAROD
mystic word .... OM
Nobel Prize winner ..... TAGORE
noble .... RAJAH
nursemaid .... AYAH
patriarch .... PITRI
peasant .... RYOT

philosophy .... YOGA, SANKHYA, VEDANTA
pillar .... LAT
poet .. TAGORE, KALIDASA
police station .... THANA
policeman .... SEPOY
pot .... LOTA
prayer carpet/rug .. ASAN
priestly caste .. BRAHMAN
prince .... MAHARAJA, RAJA(H), RANA
princess ..... MAHARANI, RANEE, RANI
private apartment ...... MAHAL
puce .... UDA
pundit .... SWAMI
queen ...... RANEE, RANI
ravine .... NALA
religious book ... SASTRA
religious creed ... JAINISM
religious observances ... DHARMA
religious devotee .. MUND
religious sect .... SIKHISM
religious teacher .... PIR, SWAMI, GURU
rites .... ACHAR
rug for prayer ..... ASAN
ruling caste ..... RAJPUT
sacred literature ... VEDA
sacred river ..... GANGA, GANGES
sacred tree .... PIPAL, BO
sacred word .... OM
sage .... GAUTAMA, MAHATMA
Sakti .... MAYA
Sanskrit school ..... TOL
savant .... PANDIT
scarf .... SAREE
school of philosophy .... MIMANSA, VEDANTA
scripture .... AGAMA, TANTRA, SASTRA
seclusion of women ..... PURDAH
sect .... JAINA
sect member .. SIKH, SEIK, SADH
serpent .... NAGA
servant .... CELA
social class .... CASTE
soldier .... SEPOY
sorceress .... USHA
soul .... ATMA(N)
spirit .... MARA
summer house ... MAHAL
supreme deity ... VARUNA
swan .... HANSA
teacher ... MULLA(H), PIR, GURU
temple .... DEUL
temple tower .... SIKHRA
timber tree .... DAR
title .... MIR, SIDI, SRI, RAJA(H), NAIK, SAHIB, RAO
title for European ...... SAHIB
title of respect ... SWAMI, SWAMY, SAHIB, MIAN, BAHADUR
trader .. BANIAN, BANYAN
tree .... DAR
trinity .... BRAHMA, SIVA, TRIMURTI, VISHNU
turban .... PAGRI
turban cloth ..... LUNGI, LUNGEE
underworld king ... YAMA
veranda .... PYAL
water nymph ...... APAS
weaver .... TANTI
weight .... TAEL, MAUND, SER, TOLA
widow ..... SATI, SUTTEE
woman personified ...... MAYA
woman's dress.... SAREE, SARI
writings .... VEDA

Hinduism .... ANIMISM
cosmic principle .. KARMA
ego ..... ATMAN, JIVATMA
elixir .. AMRITA, AMREETA
fate .... KARMA
pilgrim's city .. VARANASI
sacred literature ... VEDA
universal soul .... ATMAN

Hindustan hillman ..... TODA
magic .... JADU
Mogul emperor .. AKBAR, AURANGZEB
state .... PUNJAB

Hindustani ...... HINDI, URDU

hinge ..... JOINT, AXIS, PIVOT, KNEE, ELBOW, DEPEND, GIMMER
type of .... BUTT, SPRING, STRAP

hinny .. MULE, WHINNY, NEIGH
parent of .... HORSE, DONKEY

hint ... INTIMATION, INTIMATE, SUGGEST, ALLUDE, CUE, IMPLY, INKLING, POINTER, INNUENDO, CLEW, CLUE, ALLUSION, TIP(OFF)
kind of .... WINK, NUDGE

hinterland .... BOONDOCKS, BACK COUNTRY, INLAND, BACKWOODS

hip .... FRUIT, COXA, HUCKLE, HAUNCH, ILIA
boots .... WADERS
bone .. ILIA, PELVIS, ILIUM
joint .... COXA
joint disease ... COXALGIA
pains .... SCIATICA
pertaining to the .... SCIATIC, ILIAC
slang .. INFORMED, ON TO, AWARE
width of: sl. .... BEAM

hipbone .... ILIUM
part of ... PUBIS, ISCHIUM

hippo: comb. form ..... HORSE

hippocampus .... SEA HORSE

hippocras ..... CORDIAL, WINE

Hippocrates' birthplace ... COS

Hippocratic ____, doctors' .... OATH

hippodrome .... ARENA, (RACING) COURSE

hippopotamus ..... BEHEMOTH, PACHYDERM, SEACOW

hips supporter .... GIRDLE
width .... BEAM

hipster ..... HEPCAT, BEATNIK

hircine .... GOATLIKE

hire ... EMPLOY, ENGAGE, LET, RENT, CHARTER, LEASE, FEE

hired assassin/killer .... HIGHBINDER, BRAVO, CUTTHROAT

hireling .... MERCENARY, PENSIONARY

hirsute .... PILOSE, HAIRY, SHAGGY, BRISTLY

Hispania .... SPAIN
former part of .... PORTUGAL

Hispanic .... SPANISH

Hispaniola .... HAITI

hispid .... STRIGOSE, SPINY, HAIRY

hiss .... SIBILATE, SISS
sign of .... DISAPPROVAL, HATRED

hisser .... GOOSE, SNAKE, HECKLER

hissing ... SIBILANT, SIBILANCE, FIZZY, FIZ(Z)
drink ...... SODA WATER, CHAMPAGNE, FIZ(Z)
sound .. SIBILATION, PSST, FIZZLE, SSH, SIZZLE, WHIZ(Z), SWISH

hist .... SHUSH

histamine .... GASTRIN

histone ...... PROTEIN, GLOBIN

historian .... ANNALIST, CHRONICLER, RECORDER

historical ..... FACTUAL, REAL, AUTHENTIC
period .... ERA
records ..... CHRONICLES, ANNALS

history .... ANNALS, PAST, RECORD, CHRONICLE, STORY, NARRATIVE, TALE, ACCOUNT, LORE, MEMOIRS
famous in ...... STORIED
Muse of .... CLIO
person's life .. BIOGRAPHY

histrionic .... THEATRICAL, ARTIFICIAL, AFFECTED, OVERACTING

histrionics .... DRAMATICS, THEATRICALS, AFFECTATIONS

hit ... BOP, ACE, STRIKE, SMITE, SOCK, CUFF, BIFF, KNOCK, BUMP, SUCCESS, CLOUT, SLUG, POMMEL
aloft .... LOB
baseball ... SINGLE, BUNT, HOMERUN
colloquial .. WED, MARRY, SUCCESS
direct .... BULL'S-EYE
hard .... SLUG, SLOG
lightly .... TAP
on the head .. CONK, BOP, BEAN
or miss .... AIMLESS, HAPHAZARD, RANDOM
sign .... SRO

hitch .... HOBBLE, LIMP, JERK,

HINDRANCE, FASTEN, TIE, TUG, SNAG
hitchhike ...... THUMB A RIDE
hitchpost .... PICKET
hither .... HERE, NEARER
hitherto .... UNTIL NOW, TO NOW, HERETOFORE
Hitler's occupation .... HOUSE PAINTER
  rank .... CORPORAL
  title ..... (DER)FU(E)HRER
  wife .... (EVA) BRAUN
Hitlerite .... NAZI
Hittite .... SYRIAN
hive .. SWARM, BOX, GUM, SKEP, APIARY
hives .... URTICARIA
  cement for ..... PROPOLIS
  characteristic of ... ITCH, WHEAL
  nettle .... UREDO
  remedy for ... BENADRYL
"Hizzoner": sl. ...... MAYOR, HIS HONOR
"HMS Pinafore" character ... BUTTERCUP
ho! .... WHOA, HALT, STOP
hoactzin .... BIRD
hoar .... WHITE, GRAY
hoard ... AMASS, ACCUMULATE, RESERVE, CACHE, STORE(UP), SUPPLY
hoarder ..... MISER, SQUIRREL, ANT, BEE
hoarding ... BILLBOARD, FENCE
  time, usually .. SHORTAGE
hoarfrost .... RAG, RIME
hoarse ..... HUSKY, GRATING, RAUCOUS, GRUFF, THROATY, ROUPY
hoarseness .... ROUP
hoary .. WHITE, GRAY, FROSTY, OLD, CANESCENT, ANCIENT
hoatzin .... BIRD
hoax ..... BAM, HOCUS, SPOOF, SHAM, GAFF, KID, CANARD, TRICK, FRAUD, JOKE, RUSE
hob ..... RUSTIC, LOUT, PUCK, ELF, GOBLIN, PEG
hobble .... LIMP, HAMPER, HINDER, FETTER, ROPE, HITCH
hobbledehoy ..... YOUTH, BOY, ADOLESCENT
hobby .... HORSE, AVOCATION, PASTIME, FALCON, FAD
  British colloquial .... CUP OF TEA
  of kings, alleged .... PHILATELY
hobgoblin .... PUCK, BUGBEAR, SPRITE, ELVE, ELF, BOG(E)Y, IMP
hobnail .... RUSTIC
hobnob ... ASSOCIATE, MINGLE, RUB ELBOWS, PAL
hobo ..... STIFF, VAGRANT, BO, TRAMP
  bundle/bedding of ...... BINDLE
  camp .... JUNGLE
  stew .... MULLIGAN
hobo's city hangout .... SKID ROW
Hobson's choice .. TAKE-IT-OR-LEAVE-IT
hock ...... HAM, HOX, PAWN, JOINT, WINE
  joint ailment ..... SPAVIN
  of humans .... ANKLE
  slang .... PAWN
hockey .... SHINNY
  cup .... STANLEY
  disk .... PUCK
  field .... BANDY
  goal .... CAGE
  player .... GOALIE
  stick ....CAMAN
hockshop .... PAWNSHOP
  sign .... BALL
hocus .... DRUG, DUPE, HOAX, FRAUD, CHEAT
  pocus .... TRICK(ERY), LEGERDEMAIN, GIBBERISH
hod .... TROUGH, SCUTTLE
hodgepodge .. STEW, POTTAGE, HASH, FARRAGO, MESS, CENTO, MEDLEY, MELANGE, OLIO, MISHMASH
hoe .... TILL, HACK
hog .... PIG, SWINE, GRUNTER, BABIRUSA, PORK(ER), GRAB
  British dialect ...... SHEEP
  cholera .... ROUGET
  cured side .... FLITCH
  deer .... AXIS
  disease .... MEASLES
  fat .... LARD, ADEPS
  female .... SOW, GILT
  food .... MAST
  ground .... MARMOT
  hind leg .... HAM
  kind of .... ROAD
  leg: sl. .. REVOLVER, COLT
  like animal ...... TAPIR
  male .... BOAR
  peanut .... EARTHPEA
  plum ....AMRA
  salted side .... FLITCH
  thigh .... HAM
  uncastrated .... BOAR
  vital organ ...... HASLET
  wild .... BOAR, PECCARY, BENE, BOSCHVARK, RAZORBACK
  young ...... GILT, SHOAT, SHOTE
hogback .... RIDGE
hogfish .... PORPOISE
hoggish ...... FILTHY, GREEDY
hognose .... SAND VIPER
hognut .... PIGNUT
hogs genus .... SUS
hogshead ...... BARREL, CASK
  content of .... BEER
hogtie .... TRUSS
hogwash .... SWILL, BALONEY, REFUSE
hoi polloi .... MASSES, COMMON PEOPLE
hoiden .... TOMBOY
hoist .... RAISE, PULL UP, ELEVATOR, TACKLE, REAR, JACK, HEAVE, LIFT, CAT, WINCH, BOUSE
  anchor .... WEIGH
hoisted just off bottom .. ATRIP
hoisting device .... CRANE, WINCH, WINDLASS, BOOM, FORKLIFT, DERRICK, SLING, DAVIT, PARBUCKLE, GIN, CAPSTAN, SHEER LEGS
hoity-toity ..... GIDDY, FUSSY, PETULANT, CAPRICIOUS, ARROGANT, PATRONIZING, SNOOTY, HUFFY
  person .... SNOB
hokeypokey ...... TRICK(ERY), ICECREAM, HOCUS-POCUS
Hokkaido, capital of .... SAPPORO, YEZO
  city .... OTARU
  native .... AINU
Hoko Gunto ..... PESCADORES
hokum ..... BUNK, NONSENSE, HUMBUG, CLAPTRAP, BALONEY, APPLESAUCE
hold .... GRASP, CLUTCH, SUSTAIN, KEEP BACK, BIND, OCCUPY, CONTAIN, REGARD, PRISON, MAINTAIN, RESTRAIN, DAM, STAY, DETAIN, GRIP
  attention ...... INTEREST
  back .. RESTRAIN, DETAIN, DAM, DETER, STEM
  dear .... CHERISH
  due to war ...... INTERN
  fast .. GRIP, CLING, BELAY
  forth .... OFFER, PREACH, LECTURE
  in custody ...... DETAIN, IMPOUND
  in law .... DECIDE, ADJUDGE, BIND
  off .... AVERT
  on .... PERSIST, CONTINUE
  out .. LAST, ENDURE, OFFER
  over ... DELAY, POSTPONE
  scoreless ... BLANK, BLITZ
  session .... SIT
  ship's .... HATCH
  up ... HIJACK, ROB(BERY), DELAY, STOPPAGE
holder .... OWNER, PAYEE, POSSESSOR, CONTAINER, DOP
  benefice ..... INCUMBENT
  lease .... LESSEE, TENANT, RENTER
holding ... TENURE, PROPERTY, CLASP
  device ...... CLAMP, VISE, TONGS
holdings ... PROPERTY, BONDS, STOCKS, POSSESSIONS
holdout .... RESISTER
holdup: sl. .... HEIST
holdup man .... FOOTPAD, BRIGAND, BANDIT, HIJACKER
hole .... CAVITY, EXCAVATION, COVE, BAY, INLET, GAP, HOLLOW, BORE, ORIFICE, OPENING, LILL, DEFECT, FLAW, PREDICAMENT, WELL, PIT, EYE, VENT(AGE), APERTURE
  ace in the .... CLINCHER, ADVANTAGE
  air .... SPIRACLE
  animal's ..... LAIR, DEN, BURROW

automat's .... SLOT
cloth .... EYELET
coin .... SLOT
embankment ...... GIME
enlarger tool ...... REAM
for cable .... HAWSE
for molten metal .. SPRUE
gangster's ...... HIDEOUT
golf game .... CUP
in garment ... TEAR, RENT
in-one, golf .... ACE
in mold .... GEAT
of tube, etc. .... BORE
skin .... PORE
sleeve's .... SCYE
stopper ..... PLUG, SPILE, SPILL, CORK
up ... HIBERNATE, DIG IN, HIDE
water .... POND, POOL
holed up .... ENSCONCED
holes, full of .... PERFORATED
holiday .. FESTIVAL, VACATION, RECESS, FERIA, FIESTA
kind of .. ROMAN, EASTER, WEEKEND
of a .... FERIAL
Roman .... FERIA
holiness .... SANCTITY
Holland ...... DUTCH, CLOTH, NETHERLANDS
capital ..... (THE) HAGUE
capital (North) .... HAARLEM
city ...... EDE, ARNHEIM, (THE) HAGUE, LEYDEN
dialect .... FRANKISH, FRISIAN
gin .. GENEVA, SCHNAP(P)S
merchants' league .... HANSE
painter ..... (VAN) EYCK
province .... ZEELAND
river ...... EMS, SCHELDT
seaport .... EDAM
village .... EDE
Hollandia .... KOTABARU
hollands .... GIN
holler .... YELL, SHOUT
hollow .... CONCAVE, SUNKEN, EMPTY, CAVITY, HOLE, VALLEY, FOSSA, FOVEA, FOSSETTE, BIGHT, FALSE, CAVERNOUS, CAPSULAR
boggy .... SLAK
cheek/chin's ..... DIMPLE
circular .... CORRIE
cylinder .... TUBE
formed by curve ... SINUS
long, narrow ... TROUGH
narrow .... DINGLE
opposed to .... SOLID
pipe's .... BORE
sound .... HOOT
tile .... KEY
holly .. HOLM, ILEX, INKBERRY, WINTERBERRY, YAUPON, ACEBO, ASSI, ERYNGO
hollyhock .... ALTH(A)EA, MALLOW
Hollywood award ..... OSCAR
columnist ..... GRAHAME, LOUELLA, (HEDDA) HOPPER, RONA
industry .... MOVIE
landmark .... CIRO'S
name .... GABLE, GARBO, HARLOW, KEATON, BARA, NEGRI, MENJOU, PICKFORD, SWANSON, DEMILLE, FORD, FONDA, COOPER
street ...... VINE, SUNSET
writer .... SCENARIST
holm .. HOLLY, OAK, AIT, ISLET, BOTTOMS
oak .... ILEX
Holmes, Sherlock .. DETECTIVE
alter ego .... WATSON
brother of ..... MYCROFT
creator of .... (CONAN) DOYLE
favorite word .... ELEMENTARY
holograph .... HANDWRITTEN, (MANU)SCRIPT
holothurian .... TREPANG
Holstein .... CATTLE
holt ..... COPSE, GROVE, HILL, COPPICE, WOODS, WILLOWS
holy .. SANTA, CHASTE, BLESSED, SACRED, SINLESS, SAINTLY, HALLOW(ED), DIVINE
city ...... ROME, MECCA, JERUSALEM, LHASA, VARANASI, HARDWAR
communion .. EUCHARIST
cross .... ROOD
Father .... POPE
Grail ...... SANGR(E)AL, CHALICE, SANGRAAL
Grail finder ... GALAHAD
Grail knight ..... BORS, PERCIVAL, PARSIPAL, AMFORTAS
Grail knights' enemy .... KLINGSOR
Innocents' Day .... CHILDERMAS
Land .... PALESTINE
Land Pilgrim's badge ... SCALLOP
Land visitor ....PILGRIM, PALMER
man .. FAKIR, MARABOUT, MAHATMA
of holies ...... SANCTUM SANCTORUM
office .... INQUISITION
oil .... CHRISM
person .... SAINT
picture .... ICON
place .... SANCTUARY, CHURCH, TEMPLE, SANCTUM, SHRINE, HALIDOM(E)
prefix ..... HAGIO, HIERO
Scriptures .... BIBLE
Sepulcher visitor .. HADJI, PILGRIM
Spirit .... PNEUMA, PARACLETE
Thursday island .... ASCENCION
War: Moslem ..... JIHAD
water container ... FONT, CRUET, STOUP, STOOP
water sprinkling .... ASPERGES
Writ .... BIBLE
homage ..... TRIBUTE, HONOR, REVERENCE
to saints .... DULIA
hombre ... OMBER, CARD GAME
slang ..... FELLOW, MAN, GUY
Homburg .... (FELT) HAT
home .... RESIDENCE, HOUSEHOLD, INSTITUTION, DWELLING, DOMICILE, ABODE, HEARTH, ROOF
animal's ..... DEN, LAIR, HABITAT
base, baseball .... PLATE, PLATTER
bird's .... NEST, AERIE
bred .. DOMESTIC, NATIVE, CRUDE
figuratively .... ROOF
grown .... NATIVE, LOCAL
for poor/sick ... HOSPICE
in a jiffy/instant .. PREFAB
Indian .. TEPEE, WIGWAM
of gods .. OLYMPUS, MERU, ASGARD
of Golden Fleece .... COLCHIS
of mentally ill ... ASYLUM
of the .... DOMESTIC
screen .. TV, VIDEO, TELLY, TELEVISION
Sweet Home" composer .. PAYNE
homecoming, alumni .... REUNION
homeground .. BAILIWICK, BASE
homeless child .... WAIF, ARAB
homelike ..... COZY, FAMILIAR
homely .. PLAIN, SIMPLE, UGLY, CRUDE, INTIMATE
homemaker .... HOUSEWIFE
Homer .... KOR, HOMERUN
enchantress .... CIRCE
epic of ... ILIAD, ODYSSEY
sea nymph ..... CALYPSO
swineherd of ... GUMAEUS
translator of ... CHAPMAN
writings of .. EPICS, SAGAS, NARRATIVES
Homeric .... EPIC(AL)
homerun with bases full ...... GRAND SLAM
homesickness ..... NOSTALGIA
excessive ... NOSTOMANIA
homespun .... PLAIN, HOMELY, UNPRETENTIOUS, SIMPLE
cloth .... RUSSET
homestead ... MESSUAGE, TOFT
outbuildings ... STEADING
single farm ..... ONSTEAD
site .... TOFT
homesteader .... SOONER
homestretch .... LAST LAP
homework .... LESSONS
homey ...... COZY, FRIENDLY, FAMILIAR
homicidal .... MURDEROUS
homily .... SERMON, LECTURE, TALK

homing faculty .. ORIENTATION
hominy .... SAMP, GRITS
homo .... MAN, PRIMATE
combining form ... SAME, LIKE, EQUAL
sapiens .... MAN
homologate .. CONFIRM, AGREE, RATIFY
homonym .... NAMESAKE
homopterous insect ... CICADA, APHID
homosexual .... INVERT, LESBIAN
homunculus .... DWARF
Honan's capital ..... KAIFENG
Hondo .... HONSHU
Honduras capital .... TEGUCIGALPA
hero .... LEMPIRA
monetary unit .. LEMPIRA
seaport ... TELA, LA CEIBA
hone .. SHARPEN, WHET(STONE), MOAN, STROP, OILSTONE, GRUMBLE, YEARN, GRIND(ER)
honest ...... FAIR, TRUTHFUL, PURE, UPRIGHT, VERACIOUS, WHITE
honesty ..... HONOR, PROBITY, INTEGRITY, PLANT, MOONWORT, VERACITY
honewort .... PARSLEY
honey .. DEAR, DARLING, SWEET
and water mixture ...... MEAD, HYDROMEL
and mulberry juice ...... MORAT
badger .... RATEL
bear .... KINKAJOU
bee ...... APIS, DINGAR, DESERET
buzzard ..... KITE, PERN
container ... COMB, CRUSE
creeper .... GUITGUIT
drink ..... MEAD, MORAT
eater ... IAO, MOHO, BEAR, MANUAO
fermented .... MEAD, METHEGLIN
pharmacy .... MEL
plant .... FIGWORT
pollen mix .... BEEBREAD
prefix .... MELI
producing .. MELLIFEROUS
source .. NECTAR, FLOWER
weasel .... RATEL
honeybee genus .... APIS
honeycomb eater .... BEEMOTH
material .... BEESWAX
part .... CELL
honeycombed .... FAVOSE, ALVEOLATE, FAVEOLATE
honeydew .... NECTAR
honeyed ...... MELLIFLUOUS, SWEET, SACCHARINE, SUGARY
drink ...... MEAD, MORAT
words .... FLATTERY
honeysuckle .... AZALEA, VINE, CLOVER, WOODBINE, EGLANTINE
hong ... FACTORY, WAREHOUSE
Hongkong capital ... VICTORIA
peninsula ..... KOWLOON

honk .... YANG
honky-tonk: sl. .... DIVE, SALOON, CABARET
Honolulu airbase ... HICKHAM
exclusive section .... KAHALA
greeting .... ALOHA
native dancer ... WAHINE
swimming resort .... WAIKIKI
honor .. GLORY, FAME, CREDIT, CHASTITY, DIGNITY, DECORATION, AWARD, ESTEEM, VENERATE, EXALT, RESPECT, ENNOBLE, HOMAGE, REVERE(NCE)
mark of ...... CHAPLET, LAUREL
honorable .... UPRIGHT
mention .... CITATION
honorarium .... TIP
honorary commission, military BREVET
honors ..... DIGNITIES, TITLES, TRIBUTES, COMPLIMENTS, ACCOLADE, AWARDS
Honshu .... HONDO
bay .... ISE, TOYAMA
city .... HIMEJI, KURE, KYOTO, SENDAI, KOBE, OKAYAMA
historical city .... HIROSHIMA
port .... KOBE
hooch ..... WHISKEY, LIQUOR, BOOTLEG
hood .... BIGGIN, CAMAIL
airplane's ...... NACELLE
bird's .. CREST, CALOT(TE)
carriage's .... CAPOTE
cloak .... CAPOTE
folding .... CALASH, CALECHE
hanging part ..... TIPPET
monk's .... AMICE, COWL, CAPOUCH, CAPUCHE
movable .... CAPOTE
part .... CAMAIL
slang ... GANGSTER, THUG
tail of .... LIRIPIPE
woman's folding .... CALASH
hooded .. CUCULLATE, COWLED
garment ... PARKA, CAPE, CAPOTE
seal .... BLADDERNOSE
snake .. COBRA, PUFFING, ADDER
woman's cloak .... CAPUCHIN
hoodlum .. HOOLIGAN, ROWDY, PUNK, GANGSTER, LARRIKIN
hoodoo ... BAD LUCK, VOODOO, BEWITCH, JINX, HEX
hoodwink .. BLINDFOLD, DUPE, DECEIVE, CHEAT, SEEL
hooey .... NONSENSE, BUNK
hoof .... FOOT, PAW, UNGULA
colloquial .... TRAMP, WALK
like a .... UNGUAL
on the .... ALIVE
paring tool .... BUTTERIS

shaped .... UNGULATE
slang .... DANCE
hoofbeat .... CLIP-CLOP
hoofed ... UNGUAL, UNGULATE
hoofer: sl. ..... (TAP) DANCER
hook ... BEND, CROOK, CLEEK, HAMULUS, CLEVIS, GAFF, HEADLAND, GRAMPON, TACH(E), SWINDLE, GORE, GRAPNEL, JIGGER
and eye .... FASTENER
and loop .. GEMEL, HINGE
colloquial .. LAND, CATCH
engine .... GAB
in baseball .... CURVE
like .. FALCATE, UNCINAL, UNCINATE
like mark ...... CEDILLA
longshoreman's .. BALING
money .... LARI(N)
on a pole .... GAFF
part .... BARB
pot .... CLEEK
shaped .... UNCINAL, UNCIFORM, HAMULATE
stretcher .... TENTER
hooka(h) ..... NARGILEH, PIPE, NARG(H)ILE, HUBBLE-BUBBLE
hooked .... UNSCINATE, AQUILINE, ADUNC(OUS), GAFFED, FALCATE
nose, describing a ...... AQUILINE
hookey player .... TRUANT
hooklike .. UNCINATE, FALCATE
process .... UNCUS
hookup .... TIE-UP
hooligan .... RUFFIAN, ROWDY, HOODLUM, SPIV
hoop .... [EAR)RING
shaped handle .... BAIL
hooper .... COOPER, SWAN
hoopla .. EXCITEMENT, BUSTLE, FUROR
hoosegow: sl. ... JAIL, PRISON, CLINK
Hoosier humorist .... ADE
novelist .... TARKINGTON
poet .... RILEY
State .... INDIANA
hoot ... SHOUT, EXCLAMATION, SASS, WHOOP, BOO, CRY, ULULATE
sign of a .... SCORN, DISAPPROVAL
hooter ... FAN, OWL, HECKLER
Hoover, ____ .... JOHN, DAM, HERBERT
blankets" ... NEWSPAPERS
Dam lake .... MEAD
flag" .... (EMPTY) POCKET
hop ... CAPER, SPRING, DANCE, LEAP, VINE, FRISK
airplane .... FLIGHT
kiln .... O(A)ST
of ball/stone .... DAP
o'-my-thumb .... DWARF
plant .... LUPULUS
stem .... BINE
hope ...... LOOK FOR, DESIRE, ASPIRE, ANTICIPATION, LONG
hopeful .... OPTIMISTIC, EXPECTANT, SANGUINE,

ASPIRANT, CONTENDER, CANDIDATE
Hopei .... HOPEH, CHIHLI
capital of ...... TIENTSIN
hopeless .. DESPERATE, FUTILE, VAIN
position .... CHECKMATE, RATTRAP
hophead .... ADDICT
Hopi .... MOKI, MOQUI
room of .... KIVA
hoplite weapon .... SPEAR
hopped up ...... STIMULATED, CHARGED
hopper .. TOAD, FROG, LOCUST, FLEA, CRICKET, CICADA, KANGAROO
columnist .... HEDDA
short for a .... ROO
hops drier .... OAST
kiln .... O(A)ST
mellowed .... OLDS
resinous powder .... LUPULIN
stem .... BINE
hora .... FOLKDANCE
Horae ...... EIRENE, EUNOMIA, HOURS
horary .... HOURLY
horde .. SWARM, HOST, SWARM, LEGION, CROWD, DROVE, THRONG, ARMY, PACK
Horeb .. (MT.) SINAI, MOUNTAIN
horizon .... LIMIT, SKYLINE
arc of the ...... AZIMUTH
designating kind of ..... APPARENT, TRUE, VISIBLE, SENSIBLE, CELESTIAL
horizontal ..... LEVEL, PLANE, FLUSH, FLAT
band: heraldic .... FRIEZE
position .... PRONE
rudder .... HYDROFOIL
hormone .. ESTRADIOL, PROLON, ESTRONE, ADRENALIN, CORTISONE, ESTROGEN, ESTRIOL, INSULIN, SECRETIN, GASTRIN, THEELIN, THEELOL, PROLACTIN, ANDROGEN, PROGESTIN
for blood pressure ...... ADRENALIN
horn ..... BUGLE, SIREN, TUBA, CORNU, PRONG, DAG, CROCKET
bell-like part ..... FLARE
bird beak's .... EPITHEMA
blare .... FANFARE, TOOT, TANTARA
blow one's: colloq. ..... BOAST
crescent .... CUSP
deer .... CROCHE, ANTLER
hollow .... CAVICORN
hunting .... BUGLE
in ... MEDDLE, INTERVENE
insect's .... ANTENNA
Jewish .... SHOPHAR, SHOFAR
like ... CORNEOUS, CORNU
moon's .... CUSP
musical .. CORNET, TUBA, TRUMPET
of a ____ ...... DILEMMA
of plenty ... CORNUCOPIA
part of .... MUTE
pierce with .. GORE, HOOK
pout .... CATFISH, BULLHEAD
quicksilver ..... CALOMEL
rani's .... SHOFAR
shaped thing ..... CORNU
snail's .... TENTACLE
sound ...... MORT, BLARE
stag's .... ANTLER
tissue .... KERATIN, SCUR
tone .... MOT
unbranched .... DAG
hornbeam .... IRONWOOD
hornbill .... TOCK, HOMARI
Hornblower of fiction .... HORATIO
hornbook .... PRIMER
Horne, singer .... LENA
horneblende .... EDENITE
horned .. CORNICULATE, GORED
animal .. GNU, RAM, STAG, RHINO, DEER, BUFFALO, BULL, IBEX
animal, fabled .. UNICORN
devil .... SATAN
horse .... UNICORN
pout .... BULLHEAD, CATFISH
problem .... DILEMMA
toad .... LIZARD
viper ..... ASP, CERASTES
hornet .... WASP, STINGER, VESPID, YELLOW JACKET
Hornie .... SATAN
hornless .... POLLED, ACEROUS
animal .... POLLARD
cow .... MUL(L)EY
dialect .... NOT
stag .... POLLARD
hornlike .... CERATOID, KERATOID, CORNEOUS, CORNU
hornpipe-like ...... MATELOTE
horns of a deer ...... BALCON
hornswoggle: sl. .... HUMBUG, SWINDLE
horntail ...... SAWFLY, INSECT
hornworm ...... CATERPILLAR
horny ... CORNEOUS, CALLOUS, CERATOID, KERATOID
growth .... WART, CORN, KERATOSIS, NAIL
scale .... NAIL, SCUTE, SCUTUM
plate ..... SCUTUM, SCUTE
plates, covered by ...... SCUTATE
skin ...... CORN, CALLUS
substance ..... KERATOSE, KERATODE
tissue .... CERATIN
horologe ..... CLOCK, WATCH, SUNDIAL, HOURGLASS, TIMEPIECE
horologist ..... WATCHMAKER
horrendous .... HORRIBLE, FRIGHTFUL
horrent .... BRISTLING
horrible .... DIRE, GRIM, TERRIBLE, DREADFUL, HIDEOUS, GRIS(T)LY
colloquial .... UGLY, SHOCKING
horrid ..... UGLY, REVOLTING, REPULSIVE, HATEFUL, DREADFUL
horrified .. AGHAST, APPALLED
horrify ...... DISMAY, SHOCK, FRIGHTEN, APPAL(L), SCARE
horrifying .... GRUESOME
horror .... TERROR, AVERSION, DREAD, LOATHING
hors de combat ..... DISABLED
d'oeuvre ..... APPETIZER, OLIVE, CANAPE
horse .... BIDET, ARAB, BEAST, EQUINE, PADNAG, SORREL, BOLLARD, ZAIN, TURK, MOUNT, DOBBIN, PRAD, COB, STEED, JENNET, BAYARD, CAVALIA
Alexander the Great's ... BUCEPHALUS
ambling .... PADNAG
ancestor of .... EOHIPPUS
ankle .... HOCK
armor .... BARD(E)
Australian ...... WALER, BRUMBIE
back of .... WITHERS
back tumor ..... WARBLE
backward movement .... PASSADE
baggage .... SUMPTER
Barbary .... BARB
belly band .... GIRTH
blacksmith ..... FARRIER
blanket .... MANTA, HOUSING, TRAPPING
blinder .... WINKER
body .... BARREL
breaking rope .... HACKAMORE
box of .... STALL
breaker .... ROUGHRIDER
breed .... MORGAN
broken-winded .... WHISTLER
brown .... SORREL, ROAN, BAY
buyer .... KNACKER
callus, foreleg .... CHESTNUT
care for pay of ... LIVERY
caretaker ...... HOSTLER, GROOM
castrated ...... GELDING
cavalry .... WALER
chestnut .... BUCKEYE
clean coat of .... CURRY
colloquial .... BANGTAIL, RIP
color .. PIED, PINTO, ROAN, DAPPLE, BAY, SORREL
comber .... CURRIER, GROOM
combining form .... HIPP(O), KERAT(O), HIPPUS
command to .. GEE, HAW, WHOA, GIDDAP
covering, ornamental .... TRAPPINGS

curvetting .... GAMBADE, GAMBADO
dancing .... LIPPIZAN
dealer .. KNACKER, COPER
desert .... ARAB
dialect .... HOBBY
disease .... HEAVES, BOTS, MAL(L)ANDERS, GID, LAMPERS, ROARING, SPAVIN, SURRA(H), LAMPAS, NAGANA, LOCO, FARCY, DISTEMPER, STRANGLES, DOURINE, EMPHYSEMA, STAGGERS, WHISTLING, QUITTOR, THRUSH, VIVES
dishonestly entered in race RINGER
dock-tailed ..... CURTAL
doctor ..... FARRIER, VET
donkey offspring .. HINNY
Don Quixote's .... ROSINANTE
draft .... SHIRE, SUFFOLK, PERCHERON, CLYDESDALE
dried intestine ...... GUT
easy paced .... PAD
eczema ...... MALANDERS
exercise before race ..... SWEAT
exercise place .. PADDOCK
eye cover ...... BLINDER, WINKER
eyelid inflamation .. HAW
famous .... TRIGGER, CHAMPION, TRAVELLER, MAN O' WAR, BUCEPHALUS, CITATION, SEA BISCUIT, WHIRLAWAY
farm .... RANCH
feed ...... FODDER, OATS
feeder .... GROOM
feeding for a fee .. LIVERY
female ...... MARE, DAM
fictional ..... ROSINANTE, BAYARD
fetlock growth .... GRAGE
fetlock inflammation .... GREASE
foot disease .... QUITTOR, THRUSH, FOUNDER, LAMINITIS, GREASE
foot pad .... FROG
for hire .... HACK
forehead of ... CHANFRIN
fresh .... REMOUNT
from Medusa's body .... PEGASUS
gait of ...... RACK, LOPE, (FOX) TROT, GALLOP, CANTER, WINDING
gentian ...... FEVERROOT
genus .... EQUUS
glandular inflammation .. VIVES
goader .... SPUR
golden .... PALOMINO
graceful .. ARAB, COURSER
growth .... GRAGE, FUSSE
guide rope .... LONGE
Gulliver's Travels .... HOUYHNHNM
gypsy .... GRAS, GRI, GRY
habit .... VICE
hair .... SETON
half turn ..... CARACOLE, DEMIVOLT
halter ...... HACKAMORE
herd of stud .... HARRAS
hock .... GAMBREL
hoof's hollow .... COFFIN
hoof's inflammation .... LAMINITIS
horned .... UNICORN
hybrid .... ZEBRULA
incisor .... NIPPER
Indian ... PINTO, CAYUSE, PAWNEE, MUSTANG, PONY
inferior .... NAG, PLATER, SLEEPER, PLUG, COCKTAIL
joint ... HOUGH, FETLOCK
lame a .... GRAVEL
laugh .... GUFFAW
lead .... PACER
leap .. CURVET, CARACOLE, GAMBADO, GAMBADE, BUCK, VAULT, CAPRIOLE
leg eczema .... MAL(L)ANDERS
leg growth .... FUSSE
leg part ... HOUGH, HOOF, FETLOCK, PASTERN, SHANK, HOCK, GASKIN
longshot ...... OUTSIDER, SLEEPER
mackerel .. SAUREL, CERO, SCAD, TUNA, TUNNY, CAVALLY
magic .... BAYARD
male .... GELDING, COLT, STALLION, STEED
man: myth. .... CENTAUR
mane of .... CREST
master of the . MARSHAL
mettle .... PRIDE
mint .... MONARDA
mouth disease .. LAMPAS, LAMPERS
muscles atrophy .... SWEENY
nearest wheels .... POLER
nervous condition ...... STAGGERS
nettle .... WEED
old .... JADE, SKATE, RIP, PADNAG, PLUG, HACK
opera .. WESTERN, MOVIE, OATER
ornamental covering .... CAPARISON
pack .. SUMPTER, DRUDGE
parasitic larva .. BOTFLY, WARBLE
pedigreed .... THOROUGHBRED
pen .... CORRAL
piebald ... CALICO, PINTO
position of ..... PESANTE
race ... PLATER, TROTTER, PACER, STEEPLECHASE
race board .... TOTE
race, fixed .... BUILDER PLAY
race "triple crown" winner OMAHA, CITATION, GALLANT FOX, COUNT FLEET, WHIRLAWAY, SECRETARIAT, WAR ADMIRAL
racing .... TURF
bet .... FORECAST, QUINELLA
course ... HIPPODROME
fan .... TURFMAN
meet .... DERBY, ASCOT
official ...... STEWARD
radish tree .... BEHEN
rawhide ...... SHAGREEN
rearing of .... PESADE
reddish brown ..... BAY, SORREL, CHESTNUT
relief .... RELAY
rider .... EQUESTRIAN, CAVALRYMAN
rider's fall .... SPILL
rider's seat ...... SADDLE
riding ... STEED, PALFREY, MOUNT, STEED
river .... HIPPO
round-up .... RODEO
rump ... CROUP, CRUPPER
runaway .... BOLTER
saddle .. MOUNT, PALFREY, NAG
seat on .... SADDLE
shackle .... TRAMMEL
shelter .... STALL, STABLE
shoer .... FARRIER
short .... COB
side .... FRANK
sideways step of ... VOLT
skin disease ..... CALORIS
slang .... SKATE
small .... BRONCO, BIDET, PONY, COB, GEN(N)ET, GENET(TE), SHETLAND, GALLOWAY, JENNET, TIT
sound .... NEIGH, SNORT, WHINNY, NIE
spirited .. STEED, COURSER
spotted ...... APPALOOSA
stall .... BOX
stand on hind legs .. REAR
stocky .... COB
sweat ..... FOAM, LATHER
swift ..... PACER, RACER, ARAB, CLIPPER, SPANKER
talking .... ARION
tamer ...... ROUGHRIDER
tender .... GROOM
tooth ...... TUSH, NIPPER
toy ..... SHETLAND, PONY
training rope/place ..... LONGE
trappings ...... HARNESS
trotting .... MORGAN
tumor ... WARBLE, SPLINT
turn of .... MANEGE, CARACOLE, (DEMI)VOLT
upward leap ... CAPRIOLE
urine .... STALE
useless .... WEED
vertigo ..... GID, MEGRIM
war .. CHARGER, COURSER, BUCEPHALUS

whip . . . . CROP
white-flecked . . . . . . ROAN
wild . . MUSTANG, TARPAN, BRUMBIE, BRONC(H)O
winged . . . . PEGASUS
winless . . . . MAIDEN
winning gait . . . . . . ROMP
woman's . . . . . . PALFFREY
work . . . . GARRAN, HACK
worn out: sl. . . . . . SKATE, JADE, YAUD, PLUG, SCREW, HACK
worthless . . . WEED, JADE, NAG, RIP
young . . . . . . COLT, FOAL, FILLY, YEARLING
horseback . . . . HOGBACK
on . . . . A CHEVAL
horsefly . . . . . GADFLY, BOTFLY, TABANID
horsehair . . . . SETON, SNELL
horsehide ball . . . . . . BASEBALL
leather . . . . ELK
horselaugh . . . . GUFFAW
horseman . . EQUESTRIAN, RIDER, CAVAL(I)ERO, CABALLERO
armed . . . . CAVALIER
in bullfighting . . PICADOR
horsemanship . . . . MANEGE, EQUESTRIAN, EQUITATION
movement in . . . . PIAFFER
horsemen . . . . CAVALRY
horsemen's parade . . . . CAVALCADE
horsemint . . . . MONARDA
horseplay . . . PRANK, COMEDY, FUN, JINKS
horses, art of riding . . MANEGE, EQUITATION
collection of . . . . . . STUD, STABLE
herd of . . . . HARRAS
left behind in race . . RUCK
of . . . . EQUESTRIAN
of one owner . . . . STABLE, STRING
pertaining to . . . . . EQUINE
relief . . . . RELAY
school for . . . . . . MANEGE
string of . . . . STABLE
troops on . . . . . . CAVALRY
horseshoe . . . . RINGER
gripper . . . . CALK
points . . . . LEANERS
horseshoeing enclosure . . . . TRAVE
horsetail . . . . EQUISETUM
leaves . . . . STROBIL(E)
to a pasha . . . . STANDARD
horsewhip . . LASH, CROP, FLOG, CHAB(O)UK
horsewoman . . . EQUESTRIENNE
hortatory . . URGING, ADVISING, ADVISORY
horticultural lot . . . . . . GARDEN
hortus siccus . . . . . HERBARIUM
Horus . . . . RA, SUN GOD
head of . . . . HAWK
parent of . . . . . OSIRIS, ISIS
hosanna . . . . . . SHOUT, PRAISE, EXCLAMATION
hose . . . . SOCKS, STOCKINGS
spout . . . . NOZZLE
Hosea . . . . OSSE
wife of . . . . GOMER
hosiery . . . . STOCKINGS, SOCKS
hospice . . POORHOUSE, REFUGE, ASYLUM, INN
oriental . . . . IMARET
hospitable . . . . RECEPTIVE, ENTERTAINING
hospital . . . . INFIRMARY, LAZARETTO
attendant . . . . . . ORDERLY
dispensary . . . . CLINIC
division . . WARD, CLINIC, PAVILION
for foundlings . . . CRECHE
for mentally sick . . . . . . BUGHOUSE, BOOBY HATCH
for the poor . . . . . SPITAL, LAZARET(TE)
kind of . . . . LYING-IN, MENTAL, MATERNITY, SANATORIUM
vehicle . . . . . . AMBULANCE
hospitality for all . . . . OPEN HOUSE, OPEN HAND(ED)
hospitium . . . . INN, HOSPICE
host . . . . . MULTITUDE, HORDE, THRONG, ARMY, BREAD, ENTERTAINER, LANDLORD, INNKEEPER, LEGION
heavenly . . . . ANGEL
receptacle . . . PYX, PATEN, TABERNACLE
hostage . . . . PLEDGE, PAWN
hostel . . . . INN, TAVERN
hostelry . . . . INN, HOTEL
hostess . . . . ENTERTAINER
famed . . . . (PERLE) MESTA, HOWAR
hostile . . . . ANTAGONISTIC, WARLIKE, ADVERSE, INIMICAL, BELLICOSE
feeling . . . . ANIMUS, GRUDGE, RANCOR
hostilities . . . . WAR(FARE), CONFLICT
hostility . . . . . ANIMUS, ENMITY, BELLICOSITY, ANTAGONISM, ILL-WILL
hostler . . . . GROOM
hot . . THERMAL, HEATED, FIERY, EXCITABLE, HECTIC, ANGRY, VIOLENT, ARDENT, TORRID, SULTRY, PEPPERY
air . . . . HUMBUG, BOMBAST
and bothered . . . . UNEASY
and damp . . . . MUGGY
baths . . . . THERME
blooded . . . . ARDENT, LUSTY, PASSIONATE, RECKLESS
cargo . . . . . . CONTRABAND
dog . . WIENER, SANDWICH, FRANKFURTER
foot . . . . PRANK
goods . . . . . CONTRABAND, SWAG
iron treatment . . CAUTERY
plate . . . . STOVE
property, literally . . . . . . GOLDMINE
rod: sl. . . . JALOPY, RACER
rods' race . . . . DRAG
slang . . NEW, FRESH, GOOD
spring . . . GEYSER, THERME
springs deposit . . . . GEYSERITE
springs, of . . . . . THERMAL
taste . . . . PEPPERY
tempered . . . . TESTY, IRRITABLE, IRACUND, PEPPERY
water: colloq. . . TROUBLE, FIX, JAM
wind . . . . SIROCCO
hotchpotch . . . . STEW, MESS, JUMBLE
hotel . . . . SUITE, PUB, TAVERN, HOSTEL, INN
boy . . . . . . PAGE, BUTTONS
chain . . . . HILTON, SHERATON
cheap . . . . FLOPHOUSE
dining room . . . . . . GRILL
employee . . . . VALET
entrance hall . . . . . FOYER, LOBBY
floor . . . . MEZZANINE, ENTRESOL
foyer . . . . LOBBY
guest . . . . TRANSIENT, TRAVELER
keeper . . . BONIFACE, HOST
page . . . . BUTTONS
public room . . . . LOUNGE
reception center . . . . DESK
resident . . . . GUEST
hotfoot: colloq. . . HURRY, HIE, HASTEN
hothead . . . . YANIGAN, FIREBRAND
hotheaded . . . . . . RASH, HASTY, TESTY, IMPETUOUS
hothouse . . . STOVE, GREENERY, VIVARIUM
hotrod . . . . RACER, JALOPY
hotrods, race of . . . . DRAG
Hottentot . . . . . . NAMA, NEGRO
land . . . . NAMAQUA
language . . . . NAMA, BUSHMAN
race . . . . NEGROID
tribe . . . . NAMA
village . . . . KRAAL
Houdini, magician . . . . HARRY, (EHRICH) WEISS
hound . . . . NAG, FOLLOW, CERBERUS, (HUNTING) DOG, HUNT, CHASE, AFGHAN, BRACHET
female . . . . BRACH
hunting . . . . HARRIER, SETTER, BEAGLE, BASSET
wolf . . . . ALAN
hour . . . . MATIN
hourglass . . . . HOROLOGE
houri . . . . NYMPH
hourly . . FREQUENT(LY), OFTEN, HORAL, CONTINUAL
Hours . . . . PRAYERBOOK
house . . . . . DWELLING, HOTEL, INN, FAMILY, THEATER, CHURCH, TEMPLE, LODGE, PALACE, CASINO, COTTAGE, HOME, ROOF, APARTMENT, DOMICILE, AERIE

bees' . . . . HIVE
bird's . . . . NEST, AERIE
correctional . . . . BRIDEWELL, REFORMATORY
country . . . . . . HACIENDA, VILLA, CASINO
Eskimo . . . . . IGLOO, IGLU
flat roof of . . . . . TERRACE
fortified . . . . PEEL
French . . . . MAISON
ground around . . . . CURTILAGE
ice . . . . IGLOO, IGLU
instant . . . . PREFAB
Indian . . . . TEPEE, HOGAN, WIGWAM, LODGE
kind of . . . . . PENT, POOR, HASH
legislative . . . . CONGRESS, DIET, PARLIAMENT
log . . . . IZBA, CABIN
mud . . . . TEMBE
of the . . . . DOMESTIC
of two family units . . . . . DUPLEX
organ . . . . PERIODICAL
pertaining to a . . . DOMAL
pigeon . . . . COTE
plant . . . . FERN
poor man's . . . . . . SHACK, HUT, HOVEL
portable . . . . TENT, TEPEE, WIGWAM
porter . . . . JANITOR
ranch . . . CASITA, GRANGE, HACIENDA
side covering . . . SHINGLE, SIDING
slang . . . . . . JOINT, HOLE
slippers . . . . SCUFF
small, dingy . . . . . . HOLE
Spanish . . . . CASA
state visitor's (U.S.) . . . . . BLAIR
stately . . PALACE, MANSION
summer . . . . CASINO, GAZEBO, RANCH, VILLA, MAHAL
with its outbuildings . . . . MESSUAGE
work for pay . . . CHAR(E)
houseboat . . . . BARGE
housebreak . . . . TAME, SUBDUE
housebreaker . . . . BURGLAR
housefly genus . . . . FANNIA, MUSCA
of the . . . . MUSCID
household . . . MENAGE, FAMILY, DOMESTIC, HOME, MAINPOST
animal . . . . PET
feudal . . . . MEINIE, MEINY
food supply . . . . LARDER, PROVISIONS
gods . . . . . LARES, PENATES
linen . . . . NAPERY
mallet . . . . BEETLE
sprite . . . . KOBOLD
task . . . . . CHORE, CHAR(E)
things, discarded . . . . LUMBER
housekeeping . . . . MENAGE
housel . . . . EUCHARIST
houses, buyer of old . . . . KNACKER
housesite . . . . TOFT
housetop . . . . ROOF
housewarming . . PARTY, INFARE
housewife . . HAUSFRAU, HUSSY, SEWING KIT, VROUN
concern of . . . SOOT, DIRT, WASH, MENU
housing . . . . PAD, SHELTER, COVERING, LODGING
engine . . . . NACELLE
horse's . . . . BLANKET, TRAPPING(S)
hovel . . . . SHELTER, DWELLING, SHED, HUT, SHACK, HUTCH
hover . . FLUTTER, LINGER, FLY, WAVER, LIBRATE
how . . . . METHOD, MANNER
-de-do . . . . MESS
howdah . . . . SEAT
howdy . . . . . GREETING, HELLO
however . . YET, NEVERTHELESS, BUT, THO(UGH)
howitzer . . . . CANNON
howl . . WAIL, ULULATE, WAUL, YIPE
howler . . . . OWL, MONKEY
colloquial . . . . . BLUNDER
howling monkey . . . . . . ARABA
slang . . . . . . GREAT, HUGE
howly . . . . HORARY
hoy . . . . BARGE
hoyden . . . . TOMBOY
hr., part of . . . . MIN, SEC
huaraches . . . . SANDALS
hub . . . . NAVE, CENTER
the . . . . BOSTON
Hubbard . . . . SQUASH
hubble . . . . HUMP
bubble . . . PIPE, HOOKAH, UPROAR, HUBBUB
hubbly . . . . . . ROUGH, UNEVEN
hubbub . . . UPROAR, DIN, ADO, TURMOIL, STIR, BROUHAHA, NOISE, TUMULT
hubby . . . . HUSBAND
hubris . . . . ARROGANCE, INSOLENCE
huckle . . . . HAUNCH, HIP
"Huckleberry Finn" composer GROPE
hucklebone . . HIPBONE, TALUS, ANKLEBONE
huckster . . . . TRADESMAN, PEDLAR, PEDDLER, HAWKER
colloquial . . . . ADMAN
huddle . . JUMBLE, CONFERENCE, CAUCUS
"Hudibras" author . . . BUTLER
Hudson cliffs . . . . . . PALISADES
River city . . . . . YONKERS, TROY
hue . . . . . COLOR, SHADE, TINT, TINGE, CRY, DYE
and cry . . . . SHOUTING
Huey P., the kingfish . . . LONG
huff . . BULLY, OFFEND, HECTOR, PUFF, MIFF, TIFF, TANTRUM
huffy . . . . TOUCHY, PETULANT
hug . . . . EMBRACE, CUDDLE, CLASP
kind of . . . . BEAR, BUNNY
me-tight . . . . VEST
huge . . GIGANTIC, VAST, LARGE, ENORM(OUS), IMMENSE, MAMMOTH, OUTSIZE, TITANIC, LEVIATHAN
huggermugger . . . . JUMBLE, SECRET, MUDDLE
Hugo, novelist . . . . VICTOR
Huguenot . . . . PROTESTANT
leader . . . ADRETS, CONDE
hula hula . . . . DANCE
dancer . . . . WAHINE
hull . . . . . HUSK, POD, SHUCK, SHELL, CALYX
hullabaloo . . UPROAR, HUBBUB, CLAMOR
hulled grain . . . . . SAMP, GROAT
hum . . . DRONE, CROON, BUZZ, WHIR(R)
human . . HOMO, ADAMITE, MAN, BIPED, MORTAL, PERSON, WIGHT
body . . . CARCASS, CORPUS
body model . . . MANIKIN, MANAKIN
flesh eater . . . . . CANNIBAL
limb . . . . ARM, LEG
race . . . . MANKIND
soul . . . . PSYCHE
trunk . . . . TORSO
humane . . . . . KIND, MERCIFUL, TENDER
humanities . . . . . LANGUAGES, LITERATURE, (FINE)ARTS
humanity . . MANKIND, PEOPLE, MERCY, KINDNESS
humanize . . . . REFINE, CIVILIZE
humankind . . . . PEOPLE
humble . . . . MODEST, LOW(LY), UNPRETENTIOUS, DEGRADE, STOOP, SUBMISS, ABASE, CHASTISE, MEEK, DEMEAN
pie . . . . . NUMBLES, CROW, NOMBLES
humbug . . FRAUD, HOAX, SHAM, IMPOSTOR, DUPE, DECEIVE, CHEAT, GAMMON, BOSH, FLAM, HOKUM, SLAVER, HORNSWOGGLE
humdinger: sl. . . . ONER, AONE, LULU, EXCELLENT, SNORTER
humdrum . . . . DULL, DRAB, COMMONPLACE, ROUTINE, MONOTONOUS
humerus . . . . BONE
humid . . . DAMP, MOIST, DANK, WET, SULTRY
humidity measuring device . . . . HYGROMETER
humiliate . . . DEGRADE, ABASE, MORTIFY, SHAME, ABASH
humility . . MODESTY, MEEKNESS
humming . . . . BUZZING, BRISK, DRONING, ACTIVE
sound . . WHIR(R), CHIRM, DRONE
hummingbird . . HERMIT, TOPAZ, SYLPH, RACKETTAIL, TROCHILUS, SWORDBILL, COLIBRI, COSTA, SAPPHO, STAR, AVA, BLUET
hummock . . . KNOLL, HILLOCK, HILL, MOUND, HUMP

humor .. CAPRICE, BLOOD, BILE, CHOLER, PHLEGM, TEMPERAMENT, DISPOSITION, FANCY, WHIM, LYMPH, INDULGE, BABY, GRATIFY, CODDLE, SALT, MOOD, WIT
bad .... TIFF
body .... BILE
out of .. CROSS, IRRITABLE, MOODY
quaint .... DROLLERY
slang .... CORN
humoresque .... CAPRICE
humorist ... WIT, WAG, JOKER, RABELAIS, COBB, ROGERS, BENCHLEY, NASH, ADE, FARCEUR
humorous .... FUNNY, JOCOSE, DROLL, COMICAL, JOCULAR, WITTY, AMUSING
play ..... COMEDY, FARCE
slang suffix .... EROO
hump .... HUBBLE, HUMMOCK, ARCH, HUNCH, BULGE
animal with ...... CAMEL
of a humpback .. KYPHOS
the .... HIMALAYAS
humpback .. WHALE, KYPHOSIS
humpbacked .... GIBBOUS
humped animal .. CAMEL, ZEBU, DROMEDARY
Humpty Dumpty, describing .. SQUAT
personification ..... EGG
humus .... MULCH, MOLD, SOIL
Hun ...... GERMAN, VANDAL, SAVAGE, ATTILA, ATLI, BOCHE, ETZEL
hunch .. HUMP, LUMP, CHUNK, HUNK, PREMONITION
hunchback of Notre Dame .... QUASIMODO
hundred .... CENTUM
combining form .. HECTO, CENTI
dollar bill: sl. ... C-NOTE, CENTURY
lacs .... CRORE
years .... CENTURY
hundredfold .... CENTUPLE
hundredth .... 100TH, CENTISIMAL
abbreviation of ..... PCT
hundredweight ..... CENTNER, CENTAL, QUINTAL, KANTAR
Hungarian .... MAGYAR
capital .... BUDAPEST
cavalryman ..... HUSSAR
city ..... BUDAPEST, PECS, MISKOLC, DEBRECEN, SZEGED
chocolate party ... DOBOS
coin ...... FILLER, PENGO
composer .. LISZT, LEHAR, BARTOK
Communist leader ...... KADAR, (BELA)KUN
dance .... CZARDAS
designer .... BALAZS
dessert .... STRUDEL
dog .... PULI
dramatist .... MOLNAR
dynasty .... ARPAD
gypsy .... TZIGANE
hero .... HUNYADI, NAGY
king .... BELA
kingdom .... SERBIA
lake .... BALATON
language .... MAGYAR
leader .... (BELA)KUN
legislator ...... MAGNATE
monetary unit ... FORINT, GULDEN, PENGO
patriot .... KOSSUTH
pianist .... LISZT
plain .... PUSZTA
premier ... KALLAI, FOCK
president ..... LOSONCZI, DOBI
Red leader ... (BELA)KUN
regent .... HORTHY
river .... PECS, DRAVE, THEISS, TISZA, DRAVA, DRAU
shepherd's food .... GOULASH
slang .... HUNKY, HUNKIE
violinist .... AUER
wine .... TOKAY
writer .... JOKAI
hunger ... APPETITE, CRAVING, DESIRE, STARVE, PINE, YEN, ACORIA, ESURIENCE
continuous ..... BULIMIA
for home/country ...... NOSTALGIA
greedy .... RAVENOUS
politician's ... PUBLICITY, PRAISE
striker, famous .. GANDHI
hungry ... FAMISHED, STARVED, RAVENOUS, ESURIENT, AVID
go .... FAST
hunk ...... LUMP, SLICE, SLAB, PIECE, CHIP, HUNCH
hunks ...... MISER, TIGHTWAD
hunky .... SQUARE, WELL, HUNGARIAN
Huns, king of the ..... ETZEL, ATTILA, ATLI
hunt .... SEARCH, PURSUE, HOUND, HARRY, SEEK, CHEVY, FERRET, QUEST, BATTUE, CHASE, SCOUR, TRAIL, SHIKAR
actress .... MARSHA
African .. SAFARI, SHIKAR
critic, poet .... LEIGH
for lost scent ...... CAST
goddess of the ... DIANA, ARTEMIS
illegally .... POACH
on private property ..... POACH
with hawk .... FLY
hunted animals .... GAME
hunter ...... TRAPPER, YAGER, FOWLER, CHASSEUR, JAGER, NIMROD, ORION, PREDATOR, STALKER, SHIKARI
actor .... TAB
actress .... KIM
aid of .... RETRIEVER
bait of .... DECOY
cap of .... MONTERO, DEERSTALKER
clue to ... SPOOR, TRACKS
cry of .... TALLYHOO
kind of .... TREASURE, FORTUNE
screen of .... BLIND
sea .... WHALER
hunters, collectively ... CHASE
help to .... BATTUE
hunting, art of .... CHASE, VENERY
bird .... FALCON
call .. HALLOO, TALLYHOO, YOICK, CHEVY, TANTIVY
dog .... BASSET, ALAN(D), SETTER, BEAGLE, HOUND, POINTER
dog's chase .... RAKE
dog's clue .... SCENT
dog's cry .... TONGUE
dog's stance ... DEADSET, POINT
dogs, set of .... PACK
event .... MEET
expedition ...... SHIKAR, SAFARI
fond of .... VENATIC
ground .... PRESERVE
hat .... TERAI
horn .... BUGLE
horn note .... MORT
hounds, set of ..... PACK
knife .... BOWIE
living by .... VENATIC
party member ... BEATER, GUN-BEARER
pertaining to .... VENATIC(AL)
preserve, royal .... PARK
sport .... CHASE, VENERY
huntress: myth. ... ATALANTA, DIANA, ARTEMIS
hup, sergeant's .... ONE
hurdle .... BARRIER, SLED, OBSTACLE, SURMOUNT, WATTLE
fence on horseback ..... LARK
hurds .... TOW
hurdy-gurdy .. (BARREL) ORGAN
hurl .... LAUNCH, HURTLE, THROW, FLING, CAST DOWN, TOSS, PITCH, CATAPULT
in baseball .... PITCH
hurlbat .... HARPOON, JAVELIN
hurly-burly .... HUBBUB, DISORDERLY, TUMULT, UPROAR, TURMOIL, CONFUSION
Hurok, impresario .... SOL
Huron .... WYANDO(TE), LAKE, IROQUOIS
hurrah ..... VIVA, OLE, CHEER, SHOUT, APPLAUSE
hurricane ... STORM, CYCLONE, TORNADO, TYPHOON
center .... EYE
hurried .... HASTY, SPED
in music .... AGITATO
hurry .. RUSH, URGENCY, DASH, HUSTLE, FLURRY, SPEED, HIE, HASTE(N), ACCELERATE, BRUSH
colloquial ...... HOTFOOT
Hurst, novelist .... FANNIE

hurt . . . . . . WOUND, DAMAGE, OFFEND, INJURE, ACHE, HARM, PAIN(ED), DERE
hurtful . . . . MALEFIC
hurtle . . CLASH, COLLIDE, DASH, FLING, CAST, HURL
husband . . . SPOUSE, HELPMEET, CONSERVE, GROOM, CONSORT, GOODMAN, HELPMATE, LORD, FERE, YOKEFELLOW
and wife . . . . COUPLE
authority of . . . . . . MANUS
bereaved . . . . . . WIDOWER
brother of . . . . LEVIR, IN-LAW
having one . . MONANDRY
prospective: colloq. . . . . . INTENDED
husbandman . . . . GRANGER, FARMER
husbandry . . THRIFT, FARMING, FRUGALITY, TILLAGE, GEOPONICS
hush . . SILENCE, CALM, SOOTHE, LULL, QUIET, SHUSH
up . . . . SILENCE, SUPPRESS
husk . . . . HULL, SHELL, CHAFF, BRAN, SHUCK
of grain . . . BRAN, GLUME
rice in the . . . . PADDY
husky . . . . . . HOARSE, ESKIMO, HOARSE, BURLY, ROBUST, DOG
command to a . . . . MUSH
hussar . . . . CAVALRYMAN
jacket . . . . DOLMAN
monkey . . . . PATAS
Hussites' leader . . . . ZIZKA
hussy . . . MINX, WOMAN, GIRL, ETUI, TART, SLUT, DOXY, QUEAN, CASE, SEWING KIT, HOUSEWIFE
hustings . . . ASSEMBLY, COURT, PLATFORM, BOONDOCKS
hustle . . JOSTLE, SHOVE, HURRY, DRIVE, PUSH
hustler . . . . GO-GETTER
hut . . . . BARI, CABANA, (COTE), SHANTY, SHACK, CABIN, HOVEL, LEANTO, JACAL, MIMI, MIAM(IA)
army . . . . QUONSET
dome-shaped . . . . . . IGLOO
icy . . . . IGLOO, IGLU
kind of . . QUONSET, NISSEN
leanto . . . . SHED
prefab . . NISSEN, QUONSET
Swiss . . . . CHALET
hutch . . BIN, CHEST, HUT, PEN, TROUGH, COOP, WARREN
Huxley, writer . . . . . . ALDOUS, JULIAN
huzza . . . . CHEER, SHOUT, HURRAH
Hwang Hai . . . . . . YELLOW SEA
hyacinth . . GEM, MUSK, STONE, FLOWER, BULB, BIRD
gem . . . ZIRCON, GARNET, TOPAZ, JACINTH
wild . . . . CAMAS
hyaline . . . . GLASSY, TRANSLUCENT
hyalite . . . . OPAL
hyaloid . . . . GLASSY, VITREOUS
hybrid . . . . CROSS, MULE, HALFBREED
animal . . . HINNY, CATALO
cattle . . . . CATTABU
citrus tree . . . . . . TANGELO
dog . . . . MONGREL
language . . . . JARGON
sterile . . . . MULE
hybridize . . . . CROSS
hydatid . . . . CYST
Hyderabad city . . . GOLCONDA
ruler . . . . NIZAM
hydra . . . . POLYP, SERPENT, CONSTELLATION, HYDROZOAN, COELENTERATE
hydrangea . . . . SHRUB
hydrant . . . . FIREPLUG
attachment . . . . HOSE
hydranth . . . . ZOOID
hydrargyrum . . . . MERCURY
hydrate . . . . SLAKE
of aluminum . . . DIASPORE
hydraulic device . . RAM, TREMIE
hydrocarbon . . . . BENZENE, (M)ETHANE, BUTANE, OCTANE, TOLANE, CYMENE, PROPANE, MELENE, PINENE, TERPENE, RETENE
aromatic . . . . CARANE, CHRYSENE
coal tar . . . . PYRENE
compound . . . . IMINE
gaseous . . . . . . FLUORINE, ETHANE
inflammable . . . . BUTANE
isotrope . . . . PROTIUM
liquid . . . . TOLUENE
mixture . . . . MALTHA, OZOCERITE
oily . . . . ETHERIN, OCTANE
pine tar . . . . RETENE
radical . . . . . ETHYL, AMYL
resins . . . . RETENE
wax . . . . MONTAN
hydrocephalus victim . . . . WATERHEAD
hydroid . . . . POLYP
colony branch . . . ZOOID, HYDRANT
hydromedusa . . . . . . JELLYFISH
hydromel, fermented . . . MEAD
hydrometer . . . . SPINDLE
scale . . . . BAUME
hydropathy . . . . . . WATER CURE
hydrophobia . . . LYSSA, RABIES, LYTTA
hydroponics . . . TANK FARMING
hydrous . . . . WATERY
silicate . . . . TALC
wool fat . . . . LANOLIN
hydrozoan . . . . POLYP, HYDRA, JELLYFISH, MILLEPORE
covering of . . . . PERISARC
stinging cell . . . . NEMATOCYST
hyena-like animal . . . . . WOLF
hygienic . . . . SANITARY, HEALTHFUL
Hyksos . . . . HIQ SHASU
hyla . . . . TREETOAD
hylophagous . . . WOOD-EATING
hymen . . . . . MARRIAGE, POEM, SONG, MAIDENHEAD
hymenopter . . . BEE, WASP, ANT
hymeneal . . . . NUPTIAL
hymn . . . . PSALM, PAEAN, ODE, CANTICLE, CHORALE, INTROIT, TE DEUM, ASPERGES
book . . PSALTER, HYMNAL, GRADUAL
for the dead . . . . REQUIEM
in God's praise . . . . KADDISH
of praise . . . . ANTHEM, LAUD, MAGNIFICAT
praising God . . . . GLORIA, ALLELUIA, ALLELUJAH
sacred . . . . ANTHEM
thanksgiving . . . . . PAEAN
tune . . . . CHORAL
hymnist . . . . . . NEALE, WATTS, WESTLEY, HEBER, DOONE
hymnoptera . . . . BEES
hyoscyamus . . . . HENBANE
hyp . . . . MELANCHOLIA, HYPOCHONDRIA
hypaethral . . . . ROOFLESS
hyperbole . . . . EXAGGERATION, AUXESIS, ELAS
hyperbolic function . . . . . COSH
hyperborean . . . . FRIGID, COLD, GELID
Hyperion . . . . TITAN
daughter of . . . . EOS
parent of . . . . . . URANUS, GAEA
son of . . . . HELIOS
hyperpnea . . . . PANTING
hypethral . . . . ROOFLESS
hyphen . . . . DASH
hypnosis . . . . TRANCE
hypnotic . . SOPORIFIC, ACETAL, LUMINAL, ECTENIC, URETHAN(E), MESMERIC
compound . . . . . . AMYTAL
drug . . . . VERENOL, TRIONAL NEMBUTAL
force . . . . . . OD, ODYL(E)
state . . . . TRANCE
hypnotism . . . . MESMERISM
founder of . . . . . . MESMER
hypnotist . . . . MESMERIST
hypnotize . . ENTRANCE, CHARM
hypochondria . . HYP, ANXIETY, MELANCHOLY
hypochondriac . . . . VALETUDINARIAN, NOSOMANIA
hypocrisy . . . . PHARISAISM, PRETENSE, INSINCERITY
example of . . . . CROCODILE TEARS
hypocrite . . PRETENDER, SHAM, PHARISEE, TARTUF(F)E
hypostasis . . . . SEDIMENT, DEPOSIT, ESSENCE
hypothecate . . . . PLEDGE, MORTGAGE
hypothermal . . . . TEPID, LUKEWARM
hypothesis . . . . . THEORY, ISM, PROPOSITION, SUPPOSITION, ASSUMPTION
hypothesize . . SUPPOSE, ASSUME
hypothetical . . . . ASSUMED, CONDITIONAL

force ... IDANT, OD, ELOD, ODYL, BIOD
primordial substance .... PROTYLE
hyrax ... RABBIT, HYRACOID, CONY, DAMAN
hyson .... TEA
hyssop .... MINT, THISTLE
hysteria .... EXCITABILITY, ANXIETY, JITTERS, PANIC, FIT, FRENZY, TARASSIS
symptom ... AEROPHAGIA, AURA
hystricomorphic animal ...... RODENT, CAVY, AGOUTI, PORCUPINE

I

I .... EGO, SELF
am to blame .. MEA CULPA
big .... EGO
don't care pose .... INSOUCIANT
excessive use of .... IOTACISM
have found it! .. EUREKA
letter .... IOTA
pray thee .... PRITHEE
used in wires .... AYE
Iago's master ...... OTHELLO
wife .... EMILIA
iamb ...... (METRICAL) FOOT
Iasi .... JASSY
coin .... LEU
iatric .... MEDICINAL, MEDICAL
Ibanez, novelist ...... BLASCO, VICENTE
Iberia ...... SPAIN, PENINSULA
author of ..... MICHENER
Iberian region .... LUSITANIA
ibex .... GOAT, TUR, ZAC, KAIL, WALIE, TEK, SAKEEN
habitat ..... MOUNTAIN, ALPS, APENNINES, PYRENEES
ibid(em) .... SAME
ibis .... HERON, JABIRU
Ibo .... NIGERIAN
Ibsen, dramatist ... HENDRICK
character .... (A)ASE, HEDDA, GYNT, NORA, ELLIDA
Icarian ...... RASH, DARING, FOOLHARDY
Icarus's daughter ... ERIGONE
parent .... DAEDALUS
ice ..... DESSERT, FROST(ING), FREEZE, SHERBET, GRUE, CHILL, FIRN
breaker ...... PICK, ATKA
breaking in water .... DEBACLE
coat .... RIME
cream ... BISQUE, SUNDAE
cream freezer rotator .... DASHER
cream holder ...... CONE
cream treat .... SODA
crosser .... ELIZA
field bump .... HUMMOCK
flakes .... SNOW
floe .... PACK, PAN
fragments .... BRASH
hockey disc .... PUCK
mass ... SERAC, GLACIER, FLOE, BERG, PACK
of .... GLACIAL
partly melted .... SLUSH
pinnacle .... SERAC
rain .... SLEET, HAIL
runner .... SKI, SKATE
sheet .... GLACIER
slang ...... DIAMOND(S)
iceberg .... FLOE, LETTUCE
piece from .... CALF
small .... GROWLER
iceboat .... SKIFF
equipment ... RUNNERS, SAIL
icebox .... REFRIGERATOR
items .... LEFTOVERS
iced .... GLACE, FRAPPE
Iceland bay .... FAXA
capital ...... REYKJAVIK
city .... VIK
epic .... EDDA
god ... LOKI, THOR, AESIR, WODEN, BALDER, ODIN HEIMDALL
hot spring ...... GEYSIR
king .... ATLI
language .... NORSE
literature .... EDDA
measure ...... FET, ALEN, KORNTUNNA
monetary unit ... KRONA
narrative ... SAGA, EDDA
parliament ..... ALTHING
poet .... SKALD
queen of story .... BRUNHILD
volcano .... HECKLA, ASKJA
Iceni, queen of ..... BOADICEA
Ichabod Crane's rival .. BROM
work ...... PEDAGOGUE
ichneumon ... FLY, MONGOOSE
ichnology subject .. FOOTPRINTS
ichthyic .... PISCINE
ichthyosis ...... XERODERMA
icing .... FROSTING
icon .... IMAGE, FIGURE, PICTURE
Ictalurus punctatus ... CATFISH
icterus .... JAUNDICE
ictus ... FIT, STROKE, ACCENT, UPBEAT, ARSIS
icy .... COLD, GLACIAL, GELID, FRIGID, ALOOF
coating .... RIME, HOARFROST
id. .. SAME, IDAHO, IDEM, EGO
Idaho .... POTATO STATE
capital .... BOISE
city ...... POCATELLO, NAMPA, TWIN FALLS, BOISE
county .... ADA
nickname ... GEM STATE
state bird ...... BLUEBIRD
state flower .... SYRINGA
state gem .... GARNET
town .... MOSCOW
idant .... CHROMOSOME
idea ...... THOUGHT, IMAGE, NOTION, OPINION, PLAN, AIM, INKLING, FANCY, EIDOS, IMPRESSION, CONCEPT(ION)
combining form .... IDEO
main .... MOTIF
utopian .... BUBBLE
worthless .... BILGE
ideal ... MODEL, ARCHETYPE, VISIONARY, PERFECT, PARAGON, HERO, FAULTLESS, UTOPIAN
guiding ...... LOADSTAR
state ... UTOPIA, OCEANA
idealist .... DREAMER, VISIONARY
idealize .... DEIFY
ideals of citizenship ... CIVISM
ideas, sentimental ..... CORN
worthless .... BILGE
ideate ...... IMAGINE, FANCY, CONCEIVE, THINK
idee fixe .... OBSESSION
idem .... (THE) SAME
identical ..... ALIKE, EQUAL, ONE, (SELF)SAME
identification, means of ...... CHECK, LABEL, BRAND, (DOG)TAG, NOTCH, MARKER
identify .... EARMARK
identity .... ONENESS, INDIVIDUALITY
of origin .... ISOGENY
ideologist .... VISIONARY, THEORIST, DREAMER
ideology ..... DOCTRINE, ISM, PRINCIPLE, THEORY, DOGMA
Ides, date before ..... NONES
of March victim .. CAESAR
idiocy .... STUPIDITY, AMENTIA, FOLLY, ANOESIA, MONGOLISM, FATUITY
idiom ... DIALECT, LOCUTION, CANT, SLANG, ARGOT, PARLANCE
idiophone ... CELESTA, CHIMES, TRIANGLE
idiosyncrasy .. ECCENTRICITY, ODDITY
idiot .... DULLARD, OAF, AMENT, SIMPLETON, NITWIT, DUNDERHEAD, CRETIN, CHANGELING, MOONCALF
better than an .. IMBECILE, MORON
idle .... USELESS, FUTILE, VAIN, POINTLESS, BASELESS,

INACTIVE, LAZE, LOITER, OTIANT, LOAF, OTIOSE, LAZY
talk .... GOSSIP, GAB, PATTER, CHITCHAT, GAS
idleness ... INDOLENCE, SLOTH, LAZINESS
idler ... LOAFER, LAZYBONES, ROUNDER, SPIV, BUM, DRONE, LOUNGER
ido, creator of .... JESPERSEN
idocrase .... VESUVIANITE
idol ..... IMAGE, ICON, EFFIGY, LION, EIDOLON, CELEBRITY
Chinese .... JOSS
household god .... TERAPHIM
in logic .... FALLACY
social .... LION
idolater ... ADORER, ADMIRER, PAGAN
idolism .... SOPHISM, SOPHISTRY
idolize .... ADORE, ADMIRE
idolatry, object of ...... GOD, HERO
Idum(a)ea .... EDOM
Idun .... ITHURN(N)
idyl(l) ...... POEM, PASTORAL, ECLOGUE
idyllic .... PASTORAL, PICTURESQUE
i.e. .... ID EST, THAT IS
Ieperen .... YPRES
if .... SUPPOSITION, PROVIDED
not ... NISI, UNLESS, ELSE
ign. ..... UNKNOWN, IGNITION
igneous ..... FIERY, PLUTONIC
rock .... DIABASE, BASALT, BOSS, LAPILLUS, MARGARITE, MONZONITE, MELAPHYRE
rock formation .... LACCOLITH
ignis fatuus .... DELUSION, WILL-O'-THE-WISP
ignite ... LIGHT, KINDLE, FIRE, BURN, EXCITE
igniter ..... FUSE, DETONATOR
ignoble ..... HUMBLE, LOW, BASE, MEAN
ignominious ..... DEGRADING, SHAMEFUL, DISGRACEFUL
ignominy .... INFAMY, SHAME, DISGRACE
ignoramus ... DUNCE, NITWIT, KNOW-NOTHING
ignorance .... TAMAS, INNOCENCE, NESCIENCE
ignorant .... UNLETTERED, ILLITERATE, UNTUTORED, UNAWARE, NESCIENT
ignore .... DISREGARD, NEGLECT, OMIT, ELIDE, SNUB, OVERLOOK, CUT
Igraine's husband ..... UTHER
iguana ..... LIZARD, GOANNA
"Il Trovatore" gypsy .... MANRICO
ileus .... COLIC
cause of .. CONSTIPATION
ilex .... HOLLY, OAK

"Iliad," ascribed author of ... HOMER
character ..... STENTOR, ACHILLES, AJAX, CALCHAS, HECTOR
Ilion .... TROY
ilium .... HIPBONE
ilk .... KIND, SORT, CLASS, FAMILY, BREED, STRIPE
ill .... BAD, SICK, EVIL, ADVERSE, INDISPOSED, QUEER
advised .... UNWISE
at ease .... UNEASY, RESTIVE
bred ... RUDE, IMPOLITE, LOUT, BOOR, CARL(E)
combining form .... MAL
considered ..... UNWISE
disposed .... HOSTILE, UNFRIENDLY
fated .... UNLUCKY, UNFORTUNATE, STAR-CROSSED
favored .... UGLY
gotten gain .... LOOT, LUCRE
humored .... CROSS, SULLEN
mannered .... RUDE, CADDISH, LOW-BRED
prefix .... MAL
starred .... UNLUCKY
temper .... BILE, SPLEEN, PET
tempered .... CROSS, PEEVISH, SULLEN, SURLY, CRANKY, VINEGARY, WASPISH
tempered person .... CURMUDGEON
use ... ABUSE, MALTREAT
will ...... ENMITY, HATE, MALICE, DISLIKE, GRUDGE, RANCOR, SPITE, ANIMUS, HATRED
illation .... INFERENCE, CONCLUSION
illative word ..... THEREFORE
illegal ..... FOUL, UNLAWFUL, ILLICIT
blow in boxing ... FOUL
liquor .... BOOTLEG
illegible .... UNREADABLE
illegitimate .... BASTARD, ILLEGAL, MISBEGOT(TEN)
Illinois, capital ... SPRINGFIELD
city ... CHICAGO, PEORIA, ROCKFORD, ALTON, ELGIN, DECATUR, CAIRO, PEKIN, GRANITE, JOLIET, MOLINE, QUINCY, URBANA
greatest son .... LINCOLN
river ... SPOON, WABASH
state bird .... CARDINAL
state flower ..... VIOLET
state tree .... OAK
illiterate .... IGNORANT, UNLETTERED, UNEDUCATED
illness .... DISEASE, INDISPOSITION, MALADY

feign .... MALINGER
illume .... LIGHT
illuminant .... LIGROIN(E)
illuminate ...... ENLIGHTEN, LIGHT(UP) ELUCIDATE, EXPLAIN
illumination .... LIGHT, INSTRUCTION
unit .... LUX
illusion .... DELUSION, HALLUCINATION, TULLE, FANTASY, CHIMERA, MIRAGE, FANCY
illusionist, kind of .. MAGICIAN
illusive ... DECEPTIVE, UNREAL
illustrate ..... CITE, PICTURE, EXEMPLIFY, EXPLAIN, DRAW, ADORN
illustration .... DRAWING, DIAGRAM, GRAPH, EXEMPLUM, SAMPLE, INSTANCE, EXAMPLE
illustrious .... EMINENT, CELEBRATED, NOBLE, FAMOUS, DISTINGUISHED, NOTED
illy .... BADLY
image ...... COPY, LIKENESS, IDEA, EMBODIMENT, (E)IDOLON, ICON, IDOL, STATUE, EIKON, REPLICA, SIGIL, EFFIGY
deceptive ...... CHIMERA, ILLUSION
destroyer ... ICONOCLAST
mental ... RECEPT, IDEA, CONCEPT(ION)
imagery .... STATUES
imaginary .... UNREAL, VISIONARY, FANCIFUL, MYTHICAL, FICTIVE
ailment .... CRUD
land of sleep .... NOD
imagination .... DREAM, FANCY, NOTION, IDEA
imagine ..... GUESS, SUPPOSE, SURMISE, WEEN, CONCEIVE, FANCY, IDEATE, WIS, VISUALIZE
imagist ...... POET, DREAMER, VISIONARY
imam .... PRIEST, CALIPH
imaret .... INN, SERAI
imbecile .... CRETIN, FOOL, ANILE, MORON, FEEBLE-MINDED, STUPID, AMENT, DOTARD
imbecility .... STUPIDITY, FATUITY, IDIOCY
imbibe ...... DRINK, INHALE, ABSORB, SIP, BIB
imbricate .... OVERLAP
imbroglio ... ENTANGLEMENT, CONFUSION, PLOT DISAGREEMENT
imbrue ... WET, STAIN, SOAK, STEEP
imbue .... TINCT, INGRAIN, STAIN, INSPIRE, PERVADE, DYE, SATURATE, INFUSE, PERMEATE, TINGE
imitate ..... DUPLICATE, ECHO, EMULATE, SIMULATE,

MIMIC, APE, MIME, COPY, MOCK
imitation . . . . COPY, COUNTERFEIT, MIMICRY, BOGUS, SHAM, MIMESIS, PARODY
gem . . . . PASTE
gold . . . OROIDE, ORMOLU
gold leaf . . . . . CLINQUANT
ludicrous . . . . TRAVESTY, CARICATURE
of behavior/speech . . . . . . MIMESIS
pearl . . . . OLIVET
imitative . . . . . MIMETIC, APISH
animal . . . . . APE, MONKEY
imitativeness . . . . APERY
imitator . . . . . . COPIER, APER, MIMIC
immaculate . . . . . . UNSOILED, CLEAN, PRISTINE, SPOTLESS, PURE, SINLESS, INNOCENT
immanent . . . . INHERENT OMNIPRESENT, UBIQUITOUS
immaterial . . . . SPIRITUAL
immature . . . . . . YOUNG, RAW, CALLOW, GREEN, UNRIPE, PUERILE
immaturity, period of . . . . NONAGE
immeasurable . . . . VAST, BOUNDLESS
immediate . . . . NEAR(EST), CLOSE(ST), ADJACENT, INSTANT, DIRECT
immediately . . . . AT ONCE, FORTHWITH, INSTANTLY, AS SOON AS, PROMPTLY
slang . . . . PDQ
immemorial . . . . ANCIENT, (AGE)OLD
immense . . . LIMITLESS, HUGE, ENORM(OUS), INFINITE
immensity . . . . VASTNESS, INFINITY
immerse . . . . ABSORB, DOUSE, DUNK, SUBMERGE, ENGROSS, DIP, PLUNGE, BAPTIZE, DUCK, STEEP
immersed . . . ABSORBED, RAPT, BAPTIZED
immersion . . . . BAPTISM
immigrant . . . . ALIEN
describing one . . . . ALIEN, STRANGER, FOREIGNER
illegal . . . . WETBACK
newly arrived . . . GRIFFIN, GREENHORN
immobile . . . . FIXED, FIRM, STABLE, MOTIONLESS, SET, STILL, SESSILE
immoderate . . . . . . EXCESSIVE, UNDUE, EXTRAVAGANT
immodest . . . . IMPUDENT, FORWARD, BOLD, INDECENT, BRAZEN
immolate . . . . SACRIFICE
immoral . . . INDECENT, LEWD, WICKED, OBSCENE, WANTON
immorality . . . . VICE
immortal . . . . DEATHLESS, DIVINE, ENDURING, PERPETUAL, AMBROSIAL
immortality . . . . . ATHANASIA, AMRITA
immortelle . . . . . EVERLASTING
immovable . . . . . . STATIONARY, SET, IMPASSIVE, FIXED
immune . . EXEMPT, PROTECTED
render . . . . . . VACCINATE, INOCULATE
immunity . . . . EXEMPTION, PROTECTION
kind of . . . . . DIPLOMATIC, CONGRESSIONAL
immunization method . . . . INOCULATION
immunizer . . . . SERUM
immunizing substance . . . . TOXOID, SERUM, ANTITOXIN, VACCINE, HAPTEN(E)
immure . . . CONFINE, IMPRISON, ISOLATE, SECLUDE, SHUT UP
immutable . . . . . UNCHANGING, CHANGELESS, ETERNAL
imp . . . . . . CHILD, DEMON, ELF, PUCK, SPRITE, BRAT, TROLL
impact . . . . WEDGE, COLLISION, SHOCK, PACK, DINT, FORCE, CONTACT
main . . . . BRUNT
impair . . . . . INJURE, REDUCE, DAMAGE, MAR, VITIATE, SPOIL
impairment . . . . INJURY, DETERIORATION
speech . . . . DYSPHASIA
impale . . . . FENCE IN, TRANSFIX, PIERCE, SPIT
impalpable . . . . SUBTLE, INTANGIBLE
impart . . . GIVE, REVEAL, TELL, SHARE, COMMUNICATE, CONVEY, LEND, BESTOW
impartial . . . JUST, UNBIASED, FAIR, EVEN(HANDED)
impasse . . . . DEADLOCK, STALEMATE, BLIND ALLEY
impassioned . . . FIERY, ARDENT
impassive . . . . . CALM, SERENE, PLACID, STOIC, STOLID, APATHETIC, INSENSIBLE, PHLEGMATIC
impasto . . . . PAINTING
impatience . . . . . RESTLESSNESS, EAGERNESS
impatiens . . . . . . JEWELWEED, TOUCH-ME-NOT
impatient . . . . EAGER, RESTIVE, INTOLERANT
impeach . . . . DISCREDIT, CHALLENGE, IMPUGN, INDICT, ACCUSE
impeccable . . . . . . FAULTLESS, FLAWLESS, BLAMELESS
impecunious . . . POOR, BROKE
impede . . . . . BLOCK, RETARD, HINDER, OBSTRUCT, DELAY, HAMPER, STYMIE
legally . . . . ESTOP
impediment . . . . . . OBSTACLE, BARRIER, HITCH, HINDRANCE
speech . . . LISP, STAMMER, STUTTER
impedimenta . . . . . . BAGGAGE, ENCUMBRANCE
impel . . . PUSH, PROPEL, FORCE, INCITE, COMPEL, CONSTRAIN, ACTUATE, MOVE, MOTIVATE, DRIVE, URGE
impending . . . . IMMINENT, OVERHANGING
impenetrable . . . . . IMPERVIOUS, DENSE
impennate bird . . . . . . PENGUIN
imperative . . . . URGENT, ORDER, COMPELLING
imperator . . . . EMPEROR
imperceptible . . . . UNSEEN, INVISIBLE
imperfect . . . . FLAWED, DEFECTIVE, FAULTY
imperfection . . . FLAW, FAULT, DEFECT, BLEMISH, VICE
imperial . . . . MAJESTIC, SOVEREIGN, AUGUST, MAGNIFICENT, BEARD, REGAL, GOATEE
color . . . . PURPLE
decree . . . . RESCRIPT
palace officer . . PALATINE
domain . . . . EMPIRE, EMPERY
imperil . . . . ENDANGER, JEOPARDIZE
imperious . . . . ARROGANT, DICTATORIAL, URGENT, MAGISTRAL
impersonal . . . . . . DETACHED, OBJECTIVE
impersonate . . . . EMBODY, MIMIC, IMITATE, ACT
impersonator . . . . . IMPOSTOR, ACTOR
impertinence . . . . . INSOLENCE, IRRELEVANCE, IMPUDENCE
impertinent . . . . SAUCY, PERT, FLIP(PANT), INSOLENT, IMPUDENT, SASSY, MALAPERT
talk . . . . LIP, SASS
impetuous . . . . RUSHING, IMPULSIVE, RASH, TEARING, HOT, HASTY
impetus . . INCENTIVE, IMPULSE, MOTIVE, DRIVE, FORCE, MOMENTUM
impi . . . . ZULU, KAFFIR, WARRIOR
impiety . . . . IRREVERENCE
impinge . . . . ENCROACH, TRESPASS
impious . . . GODLESS, PROFANE, IRREVERENT
impish . . . . MISCHIEVOUS, ELVAN
implacable . . . . . . RELENTLESS, INEXORABLE, INFLEXIBLE, PITILESS, MORTAL
implant . . . . . EMBED, INSTILL, INCULCATE, GRAFT, (EN)ROOT
implement . . . . FULFILL, ACCOMPLISH, ENFORCE, UTENSIL, KIT, TOOL, EFFECTUATE, INSTRUMENT, DEVICE

hay spreading .. MULCHER
household .... APPLIANCE
kitchen .... UTENSIL
pounding .... PESTLE
threshing .... FLAIL
implicate .... INVOLVE, ENTANGLE, INCLUDE, INCRIMINATE
implication .... OVERTONE
implicit .... TACIT, ABSOLUTE, IMPLIED, INHERENT
implied ..... TACIT, IMPLICIT
implore ..... PLEAD, BESEECH, ENTREAT, BEG, PRAY
imply .... HINT, SUGGEST, INTIMATE, CONNOTE
impolite .... RUDE, DISCOURTEOUS
impolitic ... UNWISE, TACTLESS
impone ...... WAGER, STAKE
import .... INTRODUCE, SIGNIFY, TENOR, DRIFT, INTENT, SENSE, MEANING
tax .... TARIFF
important .... VITAL, MOMENTOUS
importance .... WEIGHT, MOMENT, VALUE, CONSEQUENCE, HEFT
importune ... ENTREAT, PRAY, URGE, ASK, PLEAD, BESEECH, PRESS
impose ...... INFLICT, FORCE, FOIST, ENTAIL, PALM OFF, FOB, LEVY
by fraud .... FOIST
imposing .... IMPRESSIVE, NOBLE, GRAND(IOSE), AUGUST, MAGNIFIC
imposition .... OBTRUSION, INFLICTION
impost .... DUTY, LEVY, TAX, SPRINGER
impostor ..... FRAUD, CHEAT, QUACK, IMPERSONATOR, CHARLATAN, SHAM, FAKER, GOUGE, HUMBUG, PHON(E)Y
imposture .... FRAUD, SHAM, DECEPTION
impotent .... POWERLESS, STERILE, HELPLESS
impound .... POIND
impractical one ... DREAMER, IDEALIST
imprecation ..... CURSE, OATH
impregnable .. INVULNERABLE, FIRM
impregnate .... FERTILIZE, FILL, FECUNDATE, SATURATE
impresario .... ENTREPRENEUR, PROMOTER
Sol .... HUROK
impress .... DRAFT, LEVY, STAMP, (IM)PRINT, AFFECT, MARK
impressed clearly .... GRAVEN
impression .. EFFECT, INKLING, PRINTING, MARK, STAMP, IMPRINT, IDEA
on coin .... MINTAGE
trial .... PROOF
impressionist composer ...... DEBUSSY, RAVEL, FAURE
painter .... MONET, MANET, DEGAS, RENOIR, PISSARRO
imprest .... LOAN, (CASH)ADVANCE, LENT
imprimatur ...... SANCTION, LICENSE, APPROVAL
imprint .... PRESS, STAMP, MARK
imprison ...... IMMURE, JAIL, CONFINE, INCARCERATE, CAGE
imprisonment .... LIMBO, INCARCERATION
improbable .... UNLIKELY
impromptu ...... EXTEMPORE, EXTEMPORANEOUS, OFFHAND, IMPROVISED
improper .... UNFIT, INDECOROUS, UNSEEMLY, UNBECOMING, INDECENT, AMISS, WRONG, UNDUE
improperly .... UNDULY
impropriety ... MISBEHAVIOR, MISCONDUCT
improve ..... BETTER, EMEND, REVISE
improvisation on stage .... AD LIB, ASIDE
improvise ...... EXTEMPORIZE, MAKE-DO, AD LIB, INVENT, VAMP, CONTRIVE
in music .... VAMP, RIDE
improvised .... OFFHAND, IMPROMPTU
imprudent .... CARELESS, INDISCREET, RASH
impudence .... CHEEK, NERVE, GALL, BRASS, INSOLENCE, LIP
impudent .... INSOLENT, SAUCY, BOLD, IMPERTINENT, SASSY, IMMODEST, BRASH, RUDE, MALAPERT, PERT, FORWARD, SNOTTY, FRESH, AUDACIOUS
impugn .... CRITICIZE, CHALLENGE, ASPERSE, BLAME, DENY, ATTACK
impulse ...... PUSH, IMPETUS, THRUST, URGE, FORCE, MOTIVE, ESTRO, NISUS
to steal ... KLEPTOMANIA
impulsive ... RASH, IMPETUOUS, CAPRICIOUS, SNAP
impunity .... EXEMPTION, FREEDOM
impure ...... DIRTY, DEFILED, MIXED, ADULTERATED
impute .... ATTRIBUTE, ASCRIBE, CHARGE
in ... AMIDST, WITH, ENCLOSE, AMONG, AT, AT HOME
a body ...... EN MASSE, ALTOGETHER
a group ...... EN MASSE
a hurry ..... POSTHASTE
a manner of speaking .... SO TO SAY
a series .... EN SUITE
abundance ..... GALORE, TEEMING
accord .... EN RAPPORT
accordance with .... PURSUANT
addition ...... ALSO, TOO
agreement .... UNITED
any case .... AT ALL
as-much-as .... SINCE
bad faith ..... MALA FIDE
bad taste ...... COARSE, RANK
circulation ..... ABROAD, ABOUT
clover ...... PROSPEROUS
due manner ...... DULY, ACCORDINGLY, REALLY, TRULY
fact .... DE FACTO
favor of .... FOR, PRO
good time .. EARLY, SOON
high spirits .. EBULLIENT
hoc signo ____ .. VINCES
line .... AROW
love .. GAGA, INFATUATED
name only ..... NOMINAL, TITULAR
no manner ..... NOWISE
one's element .. AT HOME
place of ...... FOR, LIEU, (IN)STEAD, ELSE, VICE
progress ..... (ON)GOING, CURRENT
re ... CONCERNING, ANENT
row ... ALINED, ALIGNED
spite of .... MAUGER, MAUGRE, DESPITE, NOTWITHSTANDING
status quo .... AS IS
that case .... THEN
the capacity of ..... QUA
the course of ... DURING
the end .... FINALLY, EVENTUALLY, ULTIMATELY
the name of Allah .... BISMILLAH
the same place .. IBID(EM)
the whole ...... IN TOTO
time, musically, ... ATEMPO
Ina, actress .... CLAIRE
inaction ... IDLENESS, INERTIA
inactive .... IDLE, INERT, PASSIVE, DORMANT, LATENT, STATIC
inadequate .... MEAGER, SCANTY, NOT ENOUGH, LACKING
inadvertence ...... OVERSIGHT
inamorata .... MISTRESS, SWEETHEART
inane ..... PUERILE, FATUOUS, INEPT, SILLY, EMPTY, VACANT, FOOLISH, VACUOUS
inanimate .... DEAD, SPIRITLESS, DULL, LIFELESS
inanity .... VACUITY
inappropriate .... MALAPROPOS
inapt .... INEPT, UNSUITABLE, AWKWARD
inarch .... GRAFT
inarm .... EMBRACE
inarticulate ..... DUMB, MUTE, VOICELESS, APHONIC

inasmuch ..... SINCE, BECAUSE
as .... SEEING
inattention ..... NEGLIGENCE
inattentive .... LOST
inaugurate .... INDUCT, BEGIN, DEDICATE, OPEN
inauspicious ...... UNLUCKY, ILL-OMENED, UNFAVORABLE, ILL, ADVERSE, UNTIMELY
inbeing .... ESSENCE
inborn .... NATURAL, INNATE, INBRED, INDIGENOUS, INHERENT, NATIVE, ORGANIC, CONGENITAL, CONNATE
character .... NATURE
inbreeding ...... ENDOGAMY
incalculable .... UNTOLD
Incan .. QUECHUA(N), PERUVIAN
empire capital ... CUSCO, CU(Z)CO
king .... ATABALIPA, ATAHUALPA, HUASCAR
incandescence .... GLOW
incandescent ...... RED-HOT, WHITE-HOT, GLOWING
incantation ...... CHANTING, MAGIC, SORCERY, CONJURATION, INVOCATION
incapacitate .... DISABLE, DISQUALIFY
incarcerate .... IMPRISON, CONFINE, JAIL
incarnadine .... PINK, RED
incarnate .... RED, ROSY, PERSONIFIED
incarnation ..... EMBODIMENT, PERSONIFICATION, AVATAR
incendiary .... ARSONIST, FIREBUG, AGITATOR, PYROMANIAC
bomb material .... THERMIT(E)
incense ..... ENRAGE, ANGER, IRK, ODOR, PERFUME, OLIBANUM, GUM, STACTE, MATTI, MASTIC, SANDARAC, BENZOIN
burner .... THURIBLE
Chinese ..... JOSS STICK
incensed ...... IRATE, ANGRY, WROTH
incentive .... ENCOURAGEMENT, INDUCEMENT, IMPULSE, MOTIVE, STIMULUS
incept .... INGEST
inception ..... ORIGIN, START
inceptive .... INITIAL
incertitude .... DOUBT, INSECURITY
incessant .... CONTINUAL, CONSTANT
inch ...... TRIFLE, BIT, HILL, ISLAND
.001 of an .... MIL
1/12 .... LINE
inches, eighteen .... CUBIT
nine .... SPAN
thirty .... PACE, STEP
twelve .... FOOT
inchoate .... INCIPIENT, RUDIMENTARY

Inchon .... CHEMULP(H)O
incident .... OCCURRENCE, HAPPENING, EPISODE, EVENT, ATTENDANT(ON)
incidental .... MINOR, SECONDARY, BYE, ODD, CASUAL, CHANCE, RANDOM, PASSING
in music ... GRACE NOTE
opinion .. OBITER DICTUM
incidentally .... OBITER
incinerate .... CREMATE, BURN (UP)
incinerator ..... CREMATORY, CREMATORIUM, FURNACE, DESTRUCTOR
incipient ... INCHOATE, INITIAL
incise .. ENGRAVE, CARVE, CUT
incision ..... CUT, GASH, SLIT
incisive .... KEEN, SHARP, PIERCING, ACUTE, CUTTING, BITING, TRENCHANT
incisor .... TOOTH
incite .... INSTIGATE, FOMENT, INDUCE, EXHORT, GOAD, EGG, AGITATE, SPUR, ABET
inciter .... INSTIGATOR, PROVOCATEUR, AGITATOR, EGGER
inclement .... SEVERE, ROUGH, HARSH, STORMY, PITILESS
inclination ... GRADE, SLANT, BEND(ING), LEAN(ING), SLOPE, BIAS, TASTE
incline ... SLOPE, SLANT, BEND, GRADE, CANT, TEND, LEAN
downward .... DIP
inclined ... WILLING, DISPOSED, ALIST, PRONE, PRONATE, APT, OBLIQUE, MINDED
chute/trough .... FLUME
walk .... RAMP
inclose ... HEM(IN), SURROUND, SHUT IN
inclosure ..... FENCE, YARD, CORRAL, WALL, PEN
include ... INVOLVE, ENCLOSE, COMPRISE, EMBRACE, CONTAIN
inclusive .... GENERIC
incognito .... DISGUISE
incoherent .... RAMBLING, DISJOINTED
income ... EARNING, REVENUE, ANNUITY, RENTE, USANCE
from lease ..... RENT(AL)
incommode .... BOTHER, PUT OUT, INCONVENIENCE
incomparable ...... PEERLESS, MATCHLESS
incomplete ... LACKING, PART
incomprehensible: slang .. GREE
inconclusive ...... UNCERTAIN, DOUBTFUL
incondite .... CRUDE, UNPOLISHED
incongruous ... INCOMPATIBLE, UNFIT, INAPPROPRIATE, INCONSISTENT
inconsequential ..... TRIVIAL
inconsiderable ...... TRIVIAL, SMALL

inconstant .... UNSTABLE, VOLATILE, FICKLE, CAPRICIOUS, MUTABLE
inconvenience .... BOTHER, TROUBLE, INCOMMODE
incorporate .... INCLUDE, EMBODY, MIX, MERGE
incorporeal right .. COPYRIGHT, PATENT
incorrect .... INACCURATE, UNTRUE, FAULTY, WRONG, ERRONEOUS
incorrect epithet/naming ..... MISNOMER
incorruptible .... HONEST
increase ... GROW, MULTIPLY, ENLARGE, AUGMENT, ACCRETE
bet on .... RAISE
incredible .... UNBELIEVABLE
incredulity .... DOUBT, SKEPTICISM, UNBELIEF
cry of .... WHAT, OH NO
incredulous ...... SKEPTICAL
increment .... ACCRUAL, INCREASE, GROWTH, GAIN
incretion, product of .... HORMONE
incriminate .... INVOLVE, CHARGE, IMPLICATE, ACCUSE
incrustation .... SCAB
incubate ... BREED, HATCH, SIT, BROOD
incubator .... HATCHERY
incubus ..... SPIRIT, BURDEN, DEMON, NIGHTMARE
inculcate .. INSTIL(L), IMPRESS, IMBUE
incumbency ... TENURE, DUTY
incumbent .... IMMINENT
incumbrance ... LIEN, BURDEN
incunabula .... INFANCY
incur .... RUN
incurable ..... IRREMEDIABLE
incursion .... INVASION, INTRUSION, INROAD, FORAY, RAID
incus .... ANVIL
indecency .... FILTH
indecent .... OBSCENE, IMMODEST, IMMORAL, FOUL, COARSE, RANK, LEWD, RACY, OFF-COLOR, RISQUE
indecision ...... VACILLATION, HESITATION
indecisive ..... VACILLATING, WAVERING
indecorous .... IMPROPER, UNSEEMLY
indeed ... TRULY, CERTAINLY, FORSOOTH, REALLY
indefatigable ..... UNTIRING, TIRELESS
indefensible ..... UNTENABLE, UNJUSTIFIABLE
indefinite .... UNSURE, HAZY, NEBULOUS, OBSCURE, AMBIGUOUS, VAGUE, INDISTINCT, NUBILOUS
amount ..... ANY, SOME
article .... AN
pronoun ..... (ANY)ONE

indelible .... LASTING, PERMANENT
indelicate ... COARSE, ROUGH, CRUDE, GROSS
indemnify ..... PAY, INSURE, REDEEM, REIMBURSE
indent ...... NOTCH, IMPRESS, REQUISITION
indentation .... NOTCH, DINGE, JAG, CUT, MARGIN, CRENELET
  on a blade .... CHOIL
  on glass bottle .... KICK
independent, an ...... LONER, MUGWUMP
indescribable .... UNTOLD
indeterminate .... VAGUE, UNDECIDED, INDEFINITE
  in botany ..... RACEMOSE
index .... FOREFINGER, POINTER, INDICATOR, SIGN, LIST, CATALOG(UE), EXPONENT, MARK
India .... BHARAT, TAMIL, HINDUSTAN
  aborigine ...... BENGALI
  acrobat .... NAT
  adjutant ...... MARABOU, ARGALA
  alcoholic drink .. ARRACK
  animal ..... DHOLE, ZEBU
  antelope ..... NILG(H)AI, CHIRU, SASIN, NILG(H)AU
  ape .... GIBBON
  army officer .... JEMADAR
  army servant .... LASCAR
  artilleryman ..... LASCAR
  astrologer .... JOSHI
  attendant ... AYAH, PEON
  audience .... DURBAR
  banker .... SOWCAR, SARAF, SHROFF, SOUCAR
  bear .... BALOO
  bearer .... SIRDAR
  bedstead ...... CHARPOY
  Bihar capital ..... PATNA
  bird .... ARGALA, MARABOU, JACANA, SHAMA, KOEL, AMADAVAT, RAYA
  bison ...... GAUR, TSINE, GAYAL
  black buck .... SASIN
  boat ..... DONGA, DUNGA
  bodice .... CHOLI
  bond .... ANDI
  boycott of foreign goods SWADESHI
  bread .... CHAPATI
  bride's neck wear .. TALIS
  buck .... SASIN
  buffalo ... ARNA, ARNEE
  building .... MAHAL
  bulbul .... KALA
  burrowing animal ...... RATEL
  bush .... KANHER
  business suspension ..... HARTAL
  butter .... GHEE
  cake .... CHAPATI
  calico .... SAL(I)OO
  canoe .... TANEE
  cap .... TOPEE, TOPI
  cape ..... COMORIN, DIVI
  capital .... (NEW) DELHI
  capital, summer .. SIMLA
  carpet .... AGRA
  carriage .... RATH, GHARRY, TONGA
  cashmere .... ULWAN
  caste ...... JAT, GADDI, MEO, PARIAH, SUDRA, MAL(I), SHIR, LOHANA, RAJPUT
  caste mark .... TILKA
  caterpillar .... SUGA
  cattle ... BRAHMA, ZEBU, GAUR, GOUR
  cavalryman ..... SOWAR
  cedar .... DEODAR
  chamois .... SARAU
  chief ... RAJA(H), SIRDAR
  cigarette .... BIRI
  church .... SAMAJ
  city ... GOLCONDA, GAYA, SHOLAPUR, MUTTRA, LUCKNOW, MEERUT, BENARES, SURAT, BANGALORE, SIBI, SIMLA, SALEM, AGRA, HYDERABAD, HOWRAH, PATNA, PATIALA, MORADABAD, LASHKAR, LAHORE, BARODA, MADURA
  civet .... ZIBET(H)
  clerk ..... BABOO, BABU
  cloth ... SALU, SAL(L)OO, SURAT, ULWAN
  cloth strip .... PATA
  coin ...... MOHUR, HOON, FELS, FANAM, ANNA, PICE, PI(E), RUPEE
  combining form ... INDO
  condiment .... CURCUMA
  corporal .... NAIK
  cot .... CHARPOY
  cotton cloth ..... CALICO
  courthouse .. CUTCHERRY
  cow .... GAEKWAR
  crane .... SARUS
  crocodile ...... GAVIAL, MUGGER, MUGGAR
  cuckoo .... KOEL
  curtain .... PURDAH
  custom .... DASTUR
  dancing girl .. BAYADEER, BAYADERE
  dancing girl's act .... NAUTCH
  deer ...... CHITAL, AXIS
  desert .... THAR
  devil's tree .... DITA
  dialect .... PUSHTU
  diamond cutting center .. GOLCONDA
  diamond, famous ...... KOHINOOR, KOHINUR
  dill .... SOYA
  disciple .... CHELA
  district .. AGRA, MALABAR
  district ruler ..... NABOB, NAWAB
  division .... OUDH
  dog ..... DHOLE, KOLSUN
  dormitory ..... GHOTUL
  drama .... NATAKA
  Dravidian ..... GOND(I)
  Dravidian language ..... TELUGU, TELEGU
  drink .... SOMA
  drug .... BHANG
  dugout .... DUNGA
  dust storm ..... PEESASH
  dye .... CURCUMA
  elephant .... HATHI
  elephant driver .. MAHOUT
  elk .... SAMBAR
  emperor ... BABER, ASOKA
  empress of .... VICTORIA
  entertainment .. TAMASHA
  epic .... RAMAYAMA, MAHABHARATA
  estate, inherited ... TALUK
  Eurasian in .... FERINGI, SAHIB, FERINGHEE
  European lady in .... MEMSAHIB
  extra pay .... BATTA
  falcon .... BAS(A)RA, SHASHIN, SHAHEEN
  fan .... PUNKA(H)
  farmer .... RYOT, MEO
  feathered headdress ..... BONNET
  festival .... DEWALI
  fiber tree .... BAOBAB
  fig tree ... PIPAL, BO TREE
  fighter bird .. AMADAVAT
  flute ... PUNGI, MATALAN
  foot soldier .... PEON
  footman .... PEON
  footstool .... MORA
  forage plant .... GUAR
  founder .... IVAN
  fowl .... BRAHMA
  fruit .... BEL
  game .... PACHISI
  garment .... BANIAN, DHOTI, KURTA
  gateway .... TORAN
  gazelle .... CHIKARA
  ghost .... BUHT
  girl leader ...... BELOSA
  goat, wild .... TAHR
  gold coin .... MOHUR
  gorge .... TANGI
  gossip .... GUP
  government estates ..... AMANI
  government official ..... DEWAN, DIWAN
  granary ... GOLA, GUNJ, GUNGE
  grant .... ENAM
  greeting ...... NAMASTE
  groom .... SYCE, SICE
  guide .... SHIKARI, SHIKAREE
  guitar .... VINA
  gully .... NULLAH
  guru .... MAHARISHI
  harem .... ZENANA
  harvest .... RAB(B)I
  hat .... TOPEE, TOPI

hawk .... SHIKRA, BADIUS
headman .... PATEL, MOKADDAM
head servant .... SIRDAR
helmet ...... TOPI, TOPEE
hemp .... B(H)ANG, KEF, GANJA, RAMIE, KEEF
hemp drug ..... HASHISH
hemp shrub .... PUA, POOA(H)
hill dweller ...... DOGRA
hill .... GARO
Hindu banker ... SOUCAR
hog deer ... AXIS, ATLAS
holy city ..... HARDWAR, NASIK, BENARES
holy man .... FAKIR, SADHU, YOGI
home rule ..... SWARAJ
horse disease .... SURRA
hunter .... SHIKAR(I), SHIKAREE
hunt(ing) ...... SHIKAR
hunting guide .... SHIKARI
hut .... BARI
inheritance ...... TALUK
intoxicant .... SOMA
island .... CEYLON, MAURITIUS, NICOBAR, ANDAMAN
islands near .... MALDIVE
jacket .... KOLA
Jesuit in .... PAULIST
jungle .... SHOLA
kingdom .... NEPAL
knife .... DAO
laborer .... PALLI
lace .... GOTA
lacs, 100 .... CRORE
lady ...... BEGUM, BIBI, MEMSAHIB
lady's maid ...... AYAH
land grant .... SASAN
land grant tenant .... ENAMDAR
landing place ..... GHAT
landowner ... ZAMINDAR
language ...... SANSKRIT, ASSAMESE, BENGALI, BIHARI, GUJARATI
learned man ... PUNDIT, PANDIT
leguminous plant .. GUAR
levee .... DURBAR
license .... CHOP
licorice .... ABRIN, JEQUIRITY
lieutenant governor ..... NAIB
litter .... MUNCHEEL, DOOLEE, DOLY
litter bearer ..... SIRDAR
loam .... REGUR
loincloth .... LUNGI, LUNGEE
low class .... BHAT
lunch .... TIFFIN
macaque .... RHESUS
magnolia tree .... CHAMPAC, CHAMPAK
mahogany .... TOON
mail .... DA(W)K
marijuana .... GANJA
market .... PASAR
master ..... SAHIB, MIAN
matting .... TATTA
meal .... AT(T)A
measure of distance ..... KOS, GUZ
merchant ..... SOUDAGUR
midwife .... DHAI
military caste ... RAJPUT
military post .... CANTONMENT
millet ... DHOOR, DURRA, DOURA(H), JOAR, CHENA
minstrel .... BHAT
mistress ...... MEMSAHIB
mogul dynasty founder .. BABER, BABAR, BABUR
monetary unit ... RUPEE, LAC, LAKH
money lender .. MAHAJAN
monkey .... RHESUS, WANDEROO
Moslem .... SWAT
Moslem princess .. BEGUM
Moslem language .... URDU, HINDUSTANI
mountain .... ABIL, DAPSANG, NILGIRI
mountain chain .... GHA(U)T, MUSTAGH, KARAKORAM, GHATS
mountain pass .. GHA(U)T
mulberry ... (A)AL, ACH
murder .... THUGGEE
musical instrument ...... RUANA, SAROD, SARON, VINA
musket ball .... GOLI
muslin .... GURRAH, DOREA
mystic .... GURU
Naga capital ... KOHIMA
narcotic .... BHANG, HASHISH
national mourning ...... HARTAL
native .... BENGALI
native cavalryman ...... SOWAR
native chief ..... SIRDAR
native clerk, in English .. BABOO, BABU
native's inheritance ..... TALUK
Negro .... HUBSHI
news by relays ..... DAK, DAWK
Nilgiri .... BADAGA
northern ..... HINDUSTAN
novice .... CHELA
nurse ...... AMAH, AYAH
Occidental just arrived in GRIFFIN
official ... DEWAN, NAZIR
official seal .... CHOP
oil plant .... RAMTIL
oil tree .... BEN
100 lacs .... CRORE
ox .... GAUR
oxlike animal ..... ZEBU
pageant ...... TAMASHA
pagoda .... CHORTEN
palanquin ...... PALKEE
palm .... NIPA
palm sap .... TODDY
panda .... WAH
parliament lower house .. LOK SABHA
part of .... DECCAN
partridge .... KYAH
paymaster .... BUXY
peasant .... RYOT
peninsula ... HINDUSTAN
people in Bombay ...... MARATHA, MAHRATTA
pepper plant ..... BETEL
permit .... CHOP
physicist ... BOSE, RAMAN
pigeon .... TRERON
pillar .... LAT
plum .... AMRA
poetic .... IND
poison ...... BISH, BIKH
police station .... THANA
policeman .... PEON, SEPOY
political party .. SWARAJ, SWATANTRA
political protest .. HARTAL
Portuguese district ..... DAMAO
powder .... ABIR
prayerlike gesture ...... NAMASTE
president .... PRASAD
priest .... SHAMAN
priest's garment .. DHOTI
prime minister .. NEHRU, GANDHI, SHASTRI
prince .... RAJA(H), MAHARAJA(H)
princess ... RANI, BEGUM, RANEE, MAHARANEE, MAHARANI
property .... DHAN
protectorate .... SIKKIM
province .... PUNJAB
queen .... BEGUM, RANI, RANEE, MAHARANI
queen mother .. RAJMATA
race .... TAMIL, JAT
rat .... BANDICOOT
ravine .... NULLAH
reception (hall) .. DURBAR
region .... CARNATIC, MALABAR, CANARA
religious fanatic ... THUG
religious sect .... SAMAJ
republic .... BHARAT
resort .... SIMLA
revenue collector .... ZAMINDAR
rice .... BORO
rich man .... NABOB, NAWAB
rifle pit .... SANGAR
river ..... INDUS, GUMTI, JUMNA, GANGES, GODOVARI, KISTNA, JAMUNA, NARBADA, NERBUDDA
river landing place ...... GHAT
road .... PRAYA

roast meat ...... CABOBS, KABOBS
robber ... THUG, DACOIT
robe of distinction ...... SEERPAW
root .... ATIS
rope dancer .... NAT
rug .... DRUGGET
rule .... RAJ
ruler .... NAWAB, NABOB, NIZAM, RAJA(H), RANI, RANEE, RAO
ruling caste ..... RAJPUT
sacred city .... BENARES, NASIK, HARDWAR
sacred word .... OM
sacrificial victim .. TRAGA
sailor .... LASCAR
salute with palms .... NAMASTE
salvation ...... MOKSHA
sash ...... CUMMERBUND
savant .... PUNDIT
scholar .. PANDIT, PUNDIT
screen ... PURDAH, TATTY
seal .... CHOP
seaport .... SURAT
servant .... AMAH, MATY, AYAH, HAM(M)AL, HAMAUL
shawl .... CHUDDAR, CHUDDER
sheep ...... OORIAL, SHA, URIAL, SNA
shell money ...... ULO, UHLLO
shirt .... BANIAN
show .... TAMASHA
shrine .... DAGOBA
shrub ..... MADAR, ODAL
silk ..... MUGA, ROMAL, RUMAL, CABECA, ERI
silk cloth .... PONGEE
sir .... SAHIB
skipper .... SERANG
snake ... KRAIT, DABOIA, BONGAR, KATUKA, COBRA
snake fighter .... MONGOOS(E)
soldier .... PEON, SEPOY, GURKHA
songbird .... SHAMA, WHITE EYE, KOEL, AMADAVAT
sorghum .... CUSH
sovereign(ty) .... RAJ
spectacle ..... TAMASHA
spinning wheel .... CHARK(H)A
spittoon .... PIGDAN
stairs to river landing .... GHAT
stamp .... CHOP
state ... SIKKIM, MYSORE, ASSAM, BOMBAY, GUJARAT, KERALA, BENGAL, MADRAS, COORG, TRIPURA, ORISSA, MARWAR, MANIPUR JODHPUR, BIHAR, KASHMIR, AJMER, PUNJAB, JAIPUR
state capital ..... PATNA, IMPHAL, CALCUTTA, MERCARA
state revenue lands ...... AMANI
stone .... LINGAM
storehouse .... GOLA
stork .... ARGALA, ADJUTANT
sugar .... GUR
sun helmet .. TOPI, TOPEE
suspension of work, etc... HARTAL
tax collector .. TAHSILDAR, ZAMINDAR
tax collection area ...... TALUK
tea .. PEKOE, DARJEELING, ASSAM, NILGIRI
teacher .... GURU
temple .... PAGODA
temple girl ... BAYADERE, BAYADEER
temple tower .. SHIKARA
tenant .... ENAMDAR
tenant farmer ..... RYOT
term of address ... SAHIB
territory ... GOA, DAMAN, DIU, ANDAMAN, NICOBAR, TRIPURA, MANIPUR
timber tree .... DAR, SAL
title ...... AYA, NAWAB, SAHIB, RAJA(H)
title of respect .. PANDIT, S(H)RI, SHREE, SAHIB, HUZOOR
tower ... SHIKARA, MINAR
tracker ... PUGGE, PUGGI
tree .... NEEM, BEL, DAR, AMRA, SAL, CHAMPAC, CHAMPAK, BANYAN, PIPAL, ENG, GORAN, SAJ, MYXA, AMLA, RAMTIL, PALMYRA, MARGOSA
tree bark .... NIEPA
tribal community .... MURIA
tribesman .... NAGA, KHOND
turban ..... PUG(G)REE, PUGGRY
turban cloth ..... LUNGI, LUNGEE
turmeric ..... CURCUMA
twilled cotton .... SALOO, SALU
two-wheeled carriage .... TONGA
umbrella .... CHATTA
valley .... DHOON
vehicle ... GHARRY, RATH, TONGA
veranda .... PYAL
vernacular .... PRAKRIT
vessel .... LOTA(H), PATAMAR
vetch .... AKRA
viceroy .... CURZON
village .... ABADI
vine .... ODAL, SOMA
viol .... RUANA
violin ... SAROD, RUANA
waistband .... CUMMERBUND
warrior .... SINGH, GURKHA
watchman .... MINA
water carrier .. BHEESTY, BHEESTIE
water course .... NULLAH
wayside stop ..... PARAO
weasellike animal .... MONGOOSE, ICHNEUMON
weight ...... TOLA, PICE, POLLAM, CHITTAK, MAUND, RAT(TI), SER
Westerner in ... GRIFFIN
wheat .... SUJI
wild cat .... CHAUS
wild dog .... DHOLE, BUANSU
wild hog ..... BABIRUSA
wild sheep ..... OORIAL, SHA, NAROOR, SHABO
woman's house .. ZENANA
xylophone .... SARON
yellow .... P(I)URI, PURREE
Zoroastrian ..... PARSEE, PARSI

Indian ...... HOPI, MOHAWK, OTOE, UTE, INCA(N), ERIE, AMERIND, CREE, CHIPPEWA, KIOWA, PEQUOT, SAC, SEMINOLE, REDSKIN, ONEIDA, DELAWARE, SIOUX, APACHE, MAYAN, IROQUOIS
Alabama .... CREEK
Alaska .... ALEUT, TLINGIT, TLINKIT
Aleutian island .. AKKHAS
Algonquian .. CHIPPEWA, ARAPAHO(E), OJIBWA(Y), MAHICAN, MOHEGAN, DELAWARE, CREE, MOHICAN, KICKAPOO, SAC, SAUK, SANNUP, MICMAC, FOX, PEQUOT
Antilles .... CARIB
Argentine .... ARAUCAN(IAN)
Arikara .... REE
Arizona .... APACHE, HOPI, YUMA, NAVAJO, PIMA, PAPAGO
arrow poison ... CURARE
Athapascan .... APACHE, TAKU, DENE, NAVAHO, NAVAJO
ax .... TOMAHAWK, HATCHET
baby .... PAPOOSE
ball game .... LACROSSE
battle-ax ... TOMAHAWK
bead money ... WAMPUM
blanket ...... MACKINAW
boat .... CANOE
Bolivia .... AYMARA, CHARCA, MOXO, MAROPA, OTUKE
brave, young .... TENDERFOOT

Brazil ... GUARANI, TUPI, CARIB, TAPUYA
bread ... TUCKAHOE
British Columbia .. HAIDA
British Honduras .... MAYA(N)
Caddoan ...... PAWNEE, ARIKARA, REE
California ... SERI, YUKI
Canadian .... HAIDA, DENE, CREE
ceremonial pipe .... CALUMET
ceremony .... POWWOW
challenge sign .... SCALP LOCK
chick pea .... GRAM
chief ... COCHISE, LOGAN, SACHEM, TECUMTHA, TECUMSEH, HIAWATHA, PONTIAC, SAGAMORE, BRANT, GERONIMO, MASSASOIT, POWHATAN
chief, Apache .... GERONIMO, COCHISE
chief, Delaware .... TAMMANY
chief, Seminole .. OSCEOLA
Chile .... ARAUCAN
Chippewa .... OJIBWA(Y)
clan symbol ..... TOTEM
Colorado .... UTE
communal home .... LONG HOUSE
conference ... POWWOW
corn ... MAIZE, MANDAN, KANGA, ZEA, SAMP, MEALIES, MEALY, NUBBIN, FLINT
council hall .... LONG HOUSE
council room ...... KIVA
Creek .... ALABAMA, MUSKHOGEAN
Dakota .... SIOUX, ARIKAREE, REE
Delaware .... LENAPE
dwelling .. HOGAN, TEPEE, WIGWAM, LODGE, WI(C)KIUP
Ecuador .... CANELO, CARA
Eskimo .... AMERIND
feast .... POTLATCH
female .... MAHALY, PURIS
fetish .... TOTEM
Flathead .... SALISH(AN)
Florida ...... SEMINOLE, CALUSA
food .... PEMICAN
footwear ..... MOCCASIN
Georgia .... CREEK
Gila River .... PIMA
girl in poem .... MINNEHAHA
god .... MANITOU
great spirit ... MANITO(U), MANITU
greeting .... NETOP, HOW
Guatemala .... MAYA(N)
halfbreed ..... METIF(F)
headdress .. WAR BONNET
hero in poem .... HIAWATHA
Hopi ...... MOKI, MOQUI
horse .... MUSTANG, CAYUSE, PINTO
Huron .... WYANDOT
hut ... LODGE, WI(C)KIUP, HOGAN, TEPEE
Illinois ...... KICKAPOO
Iowa .... SAC, SAUK
Iroquoian ..... MOHAWK, WYANDOT, ERIE, CAYUGA, CHEROKEE, ONEIDA, HURON, SENECA, MINGO, TUSCARORA, ONONDAGA
Kansas ... PANI, PAWNEE
Lake Erie .... CHIPPEWA
maize .... CORN
male, married .. SANNUP
Manitoba .... CREE
medicine man .. POWWOW
memorial post ... TOTEM, XAT, XYST
mestizo .... GRIFF(E), HALF-BREED, METIF(F)
Mexican .... APACHE, OTOMI, YAQUI, AZTEC, MAYA(N)
Michigan .... SAC, SAUK
Missouri ...... MANDAN
mixed blood .. METIF(F), METISSE, HALF-BREED
moccasin .... PAC
money .... PEAG(E), SE(A)WANT(T), WAMPUM, PIMAN
mystic symbol .... SWASTIKA
Nebraska ..... PAWNEE, OMAHA, PONCA
Negro .... ZAMBO
New Mexico ... PUEBLO, ZUNI, TANO
New York ..... CAYUGA, IROQUOIS, SENECA
nomadic .... APACHE
North Dakota .... CHIPPEWA, PAWNEE, CADDOAN
Ocean continent .... LEMURIA
Ocean vessel ..... DHOW
Oklahoma .... CREEK, PONCA, ARAPAHO(E), SAC, SAUK
Oregon .. YANAN, CAYUSE
Panama .... CUNA
peace pipe ..... CALUMET
Penutian ...... CHINOOK, CHINUK
Peru .... PANO, INCA, CANA, AYMARA, CHANCA
pierced nose .. NEZ PERCE
poison .... CURARE
pole .... TOTEM
pony .... CAYUSE, PINTO
prayer stick .. BAHO, PAHO
priest .... POWWOW
princess ... POCAHONTAS
Pueblo ..... HOPI, ZUNI, TANO
Quechuan .... INCA
room for religious service KIVA
Salishan ...... TULALIP, FLATHEAD
seafaring .... TLINGIT
Seneca Lake ... CAYUGA
Shoshonean .... HOPI, COMANCHE, PAIUTE, UTE
Sioux ... PONCA, DAKOTA, MANDAN, OMAHA, SAPONI, KAW, OTOE, OSAGE, TETON
sled dog .... HUSKY
sledge ...... TRAVOIS(E)
slipper .... MOCCASIN
South American .... GUARANI, TUPI, CARIB, OTA, TAPUYA(N), AYMARA, ONA, ARAWAK, ANETO, ARAUCAN(IAN)
Sonora ..... YAQUI, SERI
spirit .... MANITOU
supplanted by Incan ..... AYMARA
tepee ... WIGWAM, LODGE
tent .... TE(E)PEE, LODGE, WIGWAM
Tierra del Fuego .... ONA
trophy .... SCALP
unit of money .... PIMAN
Utah .... UTE
Uto-Aztecan .... YAQUI
village .... PUEBLO
wampum ... SE(A)WAN(T)
war ceremony .... POWWOW
war cry .... WHOOP
war trophy ...... SCALP
warrior .... BRAVE
weapon ..... TOMAHAWK
West Indies ...... CARIB
Western ..... UTE, ZUNI, OTO(E), HOPI
whisky to an .. FIREWATER
white person to an ...... PALEFACE
wife .... SQUAW
wigwam ...... TE(E)PEE, LODGE
winter festival .... POTLATCH
Wisconsin ... SAC, SAUK, KICKAPOO
woman .... SQUAW
yell .... WHOOP
"yes" of .... UGH
young .... BUCK
Yucatan .... MAYA(N)

Indiana capital .. INDIANAPOLIS
city ... GARY, EVANSVILLE, KOKOMO, MUNCIE, MARION, MISHAWAKA
county .... OWEN, CASS, CLAY, WELLS, KNOX, PIKE
native .... HOOSIER
river .... MAUMEE, TIPPECANOE, WABASH
state bird .... CARDINAL
state flower ...... PEONY

state nickname .. HOOSIER
state tree .... TULIP
university .... PURDUE
village ..... SANTA CLAUS
Indic dialect .... PALI
Indica(avis) .... APUS
indican .... GLUCOSIDE, UROXANTHIN
indicate ...... SHOW, POINT, INTIMATE, SIGNIFY, EVINCE
indication(s) .. SIGNS, INDICIA, TOKEN
indicator ... GAUGE, REGISTER, POINTER, INDEX, ARROW, DIAL, CLUE, SIGN
wind .... VANE
indict ... IMPEACH, ARRAIGN, ACCUSE, CHARGE
indictment .... CHARGE, ACCUSATION
indifference .... APATHY, LETHARGY
indifferent ...... APATHETIC, FAIR, AVERAGE, UNCONCERNED, DETACHED, COOL, ALOOF, SOSO, LANGUID, COLD
to pain/hardship .... STOIC(AL)
indigence ... POVERTY, NEED, WANT, PENURY
indigenous .... INHERENT, INBORN, ENDEMIC, INNATE, NATIVE, EDAPHIC
indigent ... POOR, DESTITUTE, NEEDY
indigestion .... DYSPEPSIA, APEPSIA
indignant ..... ANGRY, IRATE, WROTH
indignation ... ANGER, SCORN, IRE, WRATH
indignity ... INSULT, AFFRONT, HUMILIATION
indigo ...... DYE, BLUE, ANIL
bale of .... SEROON
berry .... RANDIA
blue .... INDIGOTIN
Chinese .... ISATIS
compound .... ISATIN
derivative ..... KETOLE, INDOL(E), ISATIN
dye .... ISATIN
forming substance ...... INDICAN
plant .... ANIL
oxidized .... ISATIN
source of .... ANIL
wild .... BAPTISIA
indirect ...... ROUNDABOUT, SECONDARY, DEVIATING, OBLIQUE
expression .... CIRCUMLOCUTION, AMBAGE, PERIPHRASIS, PERIPHRASE
indiscreet .... UNWISE, IMPRUDENT
indiscrete .... COMPACT
indispensable ..... NECESSARY, VITAL, ESSENTIAL
one .... KEYMAN
indisposed .... SICK, ILL, UNWILLING, AVERSE
indisposition .... MALAISE, AVERSION, ILLNESS, AILMENT, PIP
indisputable .... UNQUESTIONABLE, APOD(E)ICTIC
indistinct ... FAINT, OBSCURE, DIM, VAGUE, HAZY
indite .... COMPOSE, PEN, WRITE, INSCRIBE
individual ...... PARTICULAR, PERSON, SELF, ONE, SINGLE, SOLE
biological development .. ONTOGENY
combining form .... IDIO
performance .... SOLO
individualism .... EGOISM
Indo-China, part of ... BURMA, MALAYA, THAILAND, CAMBODIA, LAOS, VIETNAM
Chinese .. LAO, TAI, SHAN
European .... ARYAN, CROAT
European language ..... AVESTAN, HITTITE
Iranian .... KAF(F)IR
indoctrinate .... TEACH, BRAINWASH, INSTRUCT, BRIEF
indolence .... IDLENESS, LAZINESS, INERTIA, SLOTH
indolent .... IDLE, LAZY, LISTLESS, SUPINE, SLOTHFUL, OTIOSE
Indonesia .... EAST INDIES
capital of ...... JAKARTA
part of ... JAVA, BORNEO, SUMATRA, CELEBES, WEST IRIAN
Indonesian ... BATTAK, DYAK, LAMPONG, ATTA
bird .... PEAFOWL, HORNBILL, BULBUL
city .... JAKARTA, SURABAJA, BANDUNG, MACASSAR
island ... JAVA, MADURA, MOLUCCAS, BANGKA, TIMOR, BALI, LOMBOK, BORNEO, CELEBES, SUMATRA, CERAM, MADOERA
knife .... PARANG
language ..... JAVANESE, SUNDANESE, MADURESE, MALAY
monetary unit ... RUPIAH
news agency .... ANTARA
ox .... BANTENG
premier .... HATTA
president ..... SUKARNO
puppeteer .. (TO)DALANG
rhino .... BADAK
shadow-play .... WAYANG PURWA
vulcano ...... TAMBORA, KRAKATAO
xylophone ...... GENDER, GAMBANG
indorse ... ATTEST, SANCTION, APPROVE
indri .... LEMUR
indubitable .... SURE, EVIDENT, DOUBTLESS, UNQUESTIONABLE, CERTAIN
induce .... PERSUADE, CAUSE, EFFECT, DRAW, URGE, PREVAIL, LEAD
inducement .... INCENTIVE, MOTIVE
induct ... INSTALL, INTRODUCE, INITIATE
inductance, measure of ...... HENRY
induction ceremony .... INAUGURAL
indulge .... HUMOR, SPOIL, BABY, GRATIFY, CODDLE, PET, PAMPER, YIELD, SATISFY
indulgence .... FAVOR, PRIVILEGE
indulgent .... LENIENT, KIND, TOLERANT
indurate .... HARDEN
Indus .... CONSTELLATION
River tributary ... SUTLEJ
tribesman .... GOR
industrial giant .... MAGNATE, TYCOON
spy .... KEEK
Workers of the World member ..... WOBBLY
industrialist .... TYCOON
industrious ... DILIGENT, BUSY, HARD-WORKING, ASSIDUOUS, OPEROSE
inearth .... INTER, BURY
inebriate .... INTOXICATE(D), EXCITE, DRUNK(ARD), SOT, TOPER
ineffectual .... IDLE, VAIN, FUTILE
inelastic .... STIFF, RIGID, INFLEXIBLE
inelegant ..... CRUDE, COARSE
ineligible ...... UNSUITABLE, UNQUALIFIED
ineluctable .... CERTAIN, INEVITABLE, UNAVOIDABLE, DOOM, FATE
inept .... ABSURD, FOOLISH, CLUMSY, AWKWARD, PUERILE, UNFIT
inerrant .... INFALLIBLE
inert .... DULL, SLOW, INACTIVE, NEUTRAL, LATENT, SUPINE, TORPID
inescapable ...... INEVITABLE
inevitable ...... DUE, CERTAIN
inexorable ..... HARD, STERN, UNYIELDING
inexperienced ... RAW, GREEN
inflexible .... INERRANT
infamous .... NOTORIOUS, OUTRAGEOUS, SCANDALOUS, VICIOUS
infamy .... DISGRACE, NOTORIETY, ODIUM, SHAME, OBLOQUY
infancy .... BABYHOOD, MINORITY, INCUNABULA
to puberty .. CHILDHOOD
infant ... MINOR, BABY, CHILD,

TOT, BABE, BAIRN, CHRISOM
doctor of .... PEDIATRIST
room of .... NURSERY
infanta .... PRINCESS
infante .... PRINCE
infantile .... CHILDISH
paralysis .... POLIO(MYELITIS)
infantryman .. (FOOT)SOLDIER, DOUGHBOY, DOGFACE, TURCO
firearm of .... MUSKET
mounted ...... DRAGOON
infantrymen's formation ...... PHALANX
infatuate .... CHARM, ENAMOR
infatuated .... FOOLISH, GAGA, ENAMORED
infatuation ... PASSION, FOLLY, CRUSH, RAVE
infect .... CONTAMINATE, CORRUPT, IMBUE, TAINT, AFFECT
infected ... DISEASED, TAINTED
infection ..... DISEASE, TAINT
source .... NIDUS
infectious ..... CONTAGIOUS, CATCHING
infecund .... BARREN
infer ...... DEDUCE, GATHER, CONCLUDE, PRESUME, DERIVE
inference ...... COROLLARY, DEDUCTION, CONCLUSION, ILLATION
inferior ...... SUBORDINATE, MEDIOCRE, LOW(ER), POOR, LESS, MINOR, PETTY, LOUSY, EXECRABLE, SHODDY
diamonds .... BORTS
horse .. PLATER, TIT, NAG
lawyer .... SHYSTER, PETTIFOGGER
poet .... RHYMESTER, RIMESTER, VERSIFIER, POETASTER
writer .... HACK
infernal ... HELLISH, FIENDISH, DIABOLICAL, HATEFUL, DEVILISH, SATANIC
abyss .... TARTARUS
region .... AVERNUS
inferno ... HELL, ABYSS, HADES, GEHENNA
Hebrew .... SHEOL
infertile .... BARREN
infest ...... OVERRUN, SWARM
infidel ...... PAGAN, ATHEIST, HEATHEN, SARACEN, MISCREANT
infielder .... SHORTSTOP, BASEMAN
infiltrate .... FILTER
infinite .... ENDLESS, ETERNAL, VAST, BOUNDLESS, IMMENSE
infinitesimal .... MINUTE
infirm .... WEAK, FEEBLE, DECREPIT, UNSTABLE, LAME, SENILE, ANILE
infirmary .... HOSPITAL, DISPENSARY
infirmity .... DEFECT, FRAILTY, WEAKNESS
inflame .... EXCITE, FIRE, IGNITE, FAN, RANKLE, MADDEN
inflammable ... COMBUSTIBLE, PICEOUS, FIERY
material .. TINDER, PUNK, AMADOU, ACETONE
inflammation .... ITIS, ANGINA
bone .... OSTEITIS, ARTHRITIS
bone marrow .. MYELITIS
breast .... MASTITIS
cornea .... KERATITIS
eyelid .... STY
glandular ...... ADENITIS
intestinal .... COLITIS, ENTERITIS
iris ..... IRITIS, UVEITIS
respiratory passages ..... CROUP
throat .... CATARRH
tissue .... CELLULITIS
udders of cow .. GARGET
urinary bladder .... CYSTITIS
inflate ...... DILATE, EXPAND, INCREASE, DISTEND, SWELL, PUFF, AERATE
inflated .... BOMBASTIC, POMPOUS, HIGHFLOWN, TUMID, SWOLLEN, BLOATED, TURGID
condition ..... TYMPANY
in finance ..... WATERED
inflect ... TURN, BEND, CURVE, MODULATE
inflection .... CADENCE
inflexible ... FIRM, ADAMANT, UNSHAKABLE, FIXED, SET, UNALTERABLE, IRON, RIGID, STIFF, OBDURATE
inflict .... DEAL, IMPOSE, WREAK
inflorescence ...... FLOWER(S), FLOWERING, CYME, RACEME, WHORL
influence ... WEIGHT, EFFECT, AUTHORITY, POWER, INDUCE, AFFECT, DRAG, HOLD, PULL, IMPEL, SWAY, HEFT
in electricity .. INDUCTION
influential .... EFFECTIVE, POWERFUL
influenza .... GRIPPE, FLU, CATARRH, CORYZA
influx .... INFLOW
inform .... APPRISE, TELL, ACQUAINT, NOTIFY, ADVISE, WARN, ALERT
against .... DELATE, BETRAY, DENOUNCE
slang .. RAT, SQUEAL, SING
informal .... CASUAL
talk .... CHAT, CAUSERIE
information ... NEWS, WORD, INTELLIGENCE, DATA, FACTS, LEARNING, AVISO
bit of .... ITEM
file .... DOSSIER
in law ...... ACCUSATION
slang .. DOPE, LOW-DOWN
informative ..... INSTRUCTIVE, EDUCATIONAL, NEWSY, FACT-FULL
informant .... REPORTER, APPRISER
informed .... HEP, WISE, AWARE, ON TO, HIP, CONVERSANT
informer ..... STOOL(PIGEON), SQUEALER, REPORTER, RAT, NARK, SPY, DELATOR, SNITCH, BIRDIE, FINK, NOSE
turn ...... PEACH, SING, STOOL, SQUEAL
infract .... VIOLATE
infrequent ..... RARE, SELDOM
infringe .... VIOLATE, ENCROACH, BREAK, TRESPASS
infringement, copyright/patent PIRACY
infuriate ... ENRAGE, MADDEN
infuse .... INSTILL, SOAK, IMPART, IMBUE, FILL, STEEP, INGRAIN
infusion .... TINCTURE, ADMIXTURE, TEA
infusoria .... PROTOZOA, VORTICELLA
infusorian's stinger .... TRICHOCYST
ingenious .... CLEVER, INVENTIVE, ORIGINAL, D(A)EDAL
ingenue ... ACTRESS, STARLET
ingenuity .. SKILL, CLEVERNESS
ingenuous ...... NOBLE, OPEN, CANDID, ARTLESS, INNOCENT, GUILELESS, FRANK, NAIVE
ingest ... INCEPT, SWALLOW, EAT
ingle .... BLAZE, FIRE(PLACE)
ingot ...... PIG, (METAL)BAR, BULLION
silver .... SYCEE
zinc .... SPELTER
ingrain ... DYE, INFUSE, IMBUE
ingratiate .... INSINUATE
ingredient .... ELEMENT, COMPONENT, CONSTITUENT
ingress .... ENTRY, ACCESS, ENTRANCE
ingressive, in grammar .... INCEPTIVE
ingrown ..... INNATE, NATIVE, INBORN
inhabit .. LIVE, DWELL, PEOPLE
inhabitant ..... RESIDENT, ITE, DENIZEN, CIT(IZEN), INMATE
castle's ...... CASTELLAN
inhabiting the shore .... LIMICOLINE
inhalant .... BENZEDRINE, VICKS
inhale .... BREATHE, DRAW, INSPIRE, SUCK, RESPIRE
sharply .... SNIFF
inhere .... STICK, CLEAVE
inherence .... IMMANENCE
inherent .. INDIGENOUS, BASIC, IMMANENT, INNATE,

INBORN, INTRINSIC, ORGANIC
inheritance .... LEGACY, HERITAGE, BEQUEST, BIRTHRIGHT, PATRIMONY, PARCENARY
law .... SALIC
tax .... DEATH DUTY
unit of .... GENE
inheritor ...... DEVISEE, HEIR, LEGATEE
inhibit ...... FORBID, CHECK, WITHHOLD, RESTRAIN, PROHIBIT, SUPPRESS, ENJOIN, BAR
inhospitable .... HOSTILE, FORBIDDING
inhuman ..... BESTIAL, CRUEL
inhume .... INTER, BURY
inimical .... UNFRIENDLY, ADVERSE, HOSTILE, UNFAVORABLE
inimitable ...... MATCHLESS, PEERLESS
iniquitous .... WICKED, VICIOUS, UNJUST
iniquity ... EVIL, WICKEDNESS, SIN, INJUSTICE
initial ..... INCEPTIVE, FIRST, INTRODUCTORY
ornamental letter .... PARAPH
initials .... MONOGRAM
woven together .. CIPHER
initiate ...... INDUCT, START, INTRODUCE, ADMIT, OPEN, BEGIN, INSTITUTE, FOUND, HAZE
initiative ... ENTERPRISE, LEAD
inject .. INTERJECT, INOCULATE
injector .... SYRINGE
injection .... CONGESTION, INOCULATION, SHOT
set .... SYRETTE
injunction .. ORDER, COMMAND, ENJOINING, MANDATE
injure ...... HURT, DAMAGE, HARM, SPOIL, IMPAIR, SCATHE, MAR, WRONG, TEEN
injurious ... NOXIOUS, NOISOME, DAMAGING
injury ..... OFFENSE, DAMAGE, TRAUMA, HARM, WOUND, TEEN
compensation for .... DAMAGES, SOLATIUM
done in retaliation ...... REPRISAL
injustice ... WRONG, INEQUITY
ink ... BLACKEN, DAUB, SIGN, COLOR
berry .... POKEWEED
fish .... CUTTLE
ingredient ...... TANNIN
spreader .... BRAYER, ROLLER
inker ... ROLLER, DABBER, PAD
inking pad, printer's .. DABBER
inkle ... TAPE, YARN, THREAD
inkling ... IDEA, HINT, NOTION, SUSPICION, INDICATION, INTIMATION
inky .... DARK, BLACK
inlaid work ... MOSAIC, BUHL, TARSIA, NIELLO, MARQUETRY, PARQUETRY
inland .... INTERIOR
body of water ..... LAKE
sea ..... ARAL, CASPIAN
Sea island ...... KYUSHU, HONSHU, SHIKOKU
inlay ... FILLING, INSERT, INSET
material .... NIELLO, TILE
inlet ...... CREEK, BAY, ZEE, FIORD, ARM, RIA, BAYOU, BIGHT, COVE, FIRTH, FJORD, ESTUARY
inmate .... OCCUPANT, INHABITANT, PRISONER
inmost .... DEEPEST
part ...... CORE, HEART, DEPTHS
inn ... LODGING, RESTAURANT, KHAN, SERAI, CARAVANSARY, AUBERGE, IMARET, HOSPITIUM, TAMBO, POTHOUSE, PUB, TAVERN, HOTEL, MOTEL, HOSTEL, HOSPICE, FONDA, ROADHOUSE
Canterbury Tales' .... TABARD
worker .... POTBOY, TAPSTER, BARMAID
innards .... ENTRAILS, NUMBLES, VISCERA, GUTS
innate .... INDIGENOUS, INBORN, INHERENT, INBRED, HEREDITARY, CONGENITAL, NATIVE, NATURAL
inner ... INTERIOR, INTERNAL, ENTAL, BEN
bark .... BAST
coat of eye ...... RETINA, UVEA
combining form ... ENTO
man .... SOUL, STOMACH, PALATE
Mongolian province .... JEHOL, CHAHAR, NINGSIA
parts .... INNARDS
sole .... RAND
wheel member .... (ROTARY)ANN
Innisfail .... ERIN, EIRE, IRELAND
innkeeper .... BONIFACE, PADRONE, PUBLICAN, (H)OSTLER, HOST(ELER), LANDLORD
wife of .... HOSTESS
innocence .... SIMPLICITY, BLUET, NAIVETE
innocent .... GUILTLESS, ARTLESS, SIMPLE, NAIVE, IGNORANT, FOOL, PURE
innocuous .... HARMLESS
innominate ...... ANONYMOUS
bone ... HIPBONE, ILIUM, ISCHIUM, PUBIS
innovation .... CHANGE, IMPROVEMENT
innuendo .. HINT, INSINUATION, SLUR, ASPERSION
innumerable ..... COUNTLESS, MANY, MYRIAD
Innuit's home ... IGLOO, IGLU
inoculate .... INJECT, VARIOLATE, INFECT
Inonu, Turkish president ..... ISMET
inopportune .... UNTIMELY, INAUSPICIOUS, MALAPROPOS
inordinate .... EXCESSIVE, IMMODERATE, UNDUE
inordinately .... OVERLY
input, computer's ...... DATA
inquest .... INQUIRY, INVESTIGATION, ASSIZE
official .... CORONER
inquiline .... COMENSAL
inquiry .... EXAMINATION, INVESTIGATION, QUERY, QUESTION
inquisition ... INVESTIGATION, HOLY OFFICE, INQUIRY
inquisitive .... CURIOUS, PRYING, SNOOPY, NOS(E)Y
inroad ...... RAID, INVASION, ENCROACHMENT
insane .. DEMENTED, SENSELESS, FOOLISH, DAFT, BUGS, PHRENETIC, BATTY, MAD, CRAZY
asylum ..... BUGHOUSE, MADHOUSE
make .... DERANGE, DEMENT
person .... LUNATIC, MADMAN, NUT
insanity ... MADNESS, LUNACY, DEMENTIA, PSYCHOSIS, MANIA
near .... FRENZY
insatiable .... GREEDY, VORACIOUS
inscribe ...... MARK, ENROLL, DEDICATE, ENGRAVE, WRITE
inscription ..... DEDICATION, LETTERING, RUNE, GRAFFITO
bookplate .... EX LIBRIS
on book .... ENVOY, COLOPHON
on coin .... LEGEND, EXERGUE
tomb's .... EPITAPH
inscrutable ...... ENIGMATIC, MYSTERIOUS, ABSTRUSE, INCOMPREHENSIBLE
expression .. POKERFACE, IMPASSIVE, DEADPAN
one .... SPHINX
insect ... BEETLE, BEE, WASP, FLY, MOSQUITO, SPIDER, TICK, MITE, NIT, ANTLION, APHID, COCCID, CHALCID, BUG, EARWIG
adult .... IMAGO
eating animal .... AARDVARK, MOLE, HEDGEHOG, SHREW, DESMAN
back of .... NOTUM
blood-sucking .... CONENOSE

bodies, dried ... KERMES
body part ..... THORAX, CLAVA, COXA, NOTUM, ACRON
burrow of .... MINE
colonists .... BEES, ANTS
combining form .... ENTOMO
dipterous ..... MOSQUITO, GNAT
eating animal .. TENREC, TENDRAC
egg ...... NIT, OOTHECA
exudation .... LAC
eyes .... OCELLI
feeding ant ...... KELEP
feeler .... PALP(US), ANTENNA
flylike ... CICADA, CICALA
form between molts ...... INSTAR
four-winged .... BEETLE
guest of another .... INQUILINE
hard covering .... CHITIN
immature .... LARVA, PUPA
jaw .... MANDIBLE
larva .... MAGGOT, GRUB
leaping ... FLEA, LOCUST, CRICKET, GRASSHOPPER, FROGHOPPER, SPRINGTAIL
leg part .... TARSUS
leg segment ...... COXA, TIBIA
lepidopterous..... MOTH, BUTTERFLY
life stage ... PUPA, LARVA, IMAGO, MAGGOT, EGG, INSTAR
like .... ENTOMOID
limb .... PROLOG
lip ..... LABIUM, LABRUM
migratory ...... LOCUST
molting .... ECDYSIS
nest .... NIDUS
noisy .... CICADA
order of .... ACARID, LOCUST, DIPTERA
plant juice sucker .... THRIPS, APHID
poison .... VENOM
poison remedy .... SABADILLA
powder ..... PYRETHRUM
resin .... LAC
scale .... COCCID
segment .... SOMITE, TELSON
shieldlike process .... CLYPEUS
slim-waisted ...... WASP
small .... CHALCID
smelly ...... STINK BUG
social .... ANT, BEE, TERMITE
sound ... CHIRP, CHIRR, DRONE, HUM, BUZZ, STRIDOR
stick .... EMESA
stinger of .... DART
stinging ... GADFLY, BEE, WASP, HORNET, GNAT
sucking .... SAPPER
sucking organ .... HAUSTELLUM, PROBOSCIS
tree .... KATYDID
twig-like .... WALKING STICK
wing cover .... ELYTRON, ELYTRUM
wing, rib in .... NERVURE, NERVE
wing spot .... ISLE
winged ... WASP, GNAT, BEE, HORNET, MOSQUITO, COCKROACH
wingless .... APTERA
with incomplete metamorphosis .... NYMPH
young .... NIT

insecticide ... DDT, PESTICIDE, ROTENONE
insectivore ..... SHREW, MOLE, VIREO, HEDGEHOG, DESMAN, TENREC
insects, kind of .... LACEWING
moving mass of .. SWARM
pertaining to ... ENTOMIC
swarm of .... NEST
insecure .... UNRELIABLE, UNSTABLE, UNSAFE, UNCERTAIN, RISKY
inseminate ..... IMPREGNATE, SOW
insensate ...... COLD, STUPID, FOOLISH, UNFEELING
insensibility ...... ANALGESIA, COMA
insensible .. NUMB, UNFEELING, IMPASSIVE, STOIC
insert ... PUT IN, INTRODUCE, INTROMIT, INGRAFT, INSET, IMMIT
slyly .... FOIST
insertion ... AD(VERTISEMENT), INSET, INTRODUCTION
sign .... CARET
inset .... INSERT, INFLUX, INLAY, PANEL
inside ... INTERIOR, INTERNAL, INDOOR(S), SECRET, WITHIN
clinch .... KNOT
colloquial ..... STOMACH, INTESTINES
combining form ... INTRA
out, turn .... EVERT
insidiate .... PLOT, SCHEME
insidious .... WILY, SLY, CUNNING, CRAFTY
insight .... ACUMEN, KEN, DISCERNMENT, INTUITION
insigne .... STAR
insignia .... EMBLEM, REGALIA, BADGE, CROWN, SCEPTER
insignificant .... TRIVIAL, SMALL, PALTRY, PUNY, MINOR, PETTY
person ..... INSECT, SNIP, SHRIMP
insincere ...... HYPOCRITICAL, UNTRUE
insinuate ...... IMPLY, HINT, INTIMATE, SUGGEST, FOIST
insinuation .... INNUENDO, HINT
insipid ..... BANAL, TASTELESS, DULL, LIFELESS, DRY, STALE, VAPID, FLAT, JEJUNE, TAME, WASHY
insipient ..... STUPID, UNWISE
insist ...... URGE, MAINTAIN, DEMAND, AFFIRM, PERSIST, PRESS
insolation .... SUNSTROKE
insolence .... ARROGANCE, HUBRIS, IMPUDENCE, IMPERTINENCE
insolent .... AUDACIOUS
insolvent .... BANKRUPT
insomnia .... VIGILANCE
insouciant ...... COOL, CALM, CAREFREE, INDIFFERENT
inspan ...... YOKE, HARNESS
inspect .... EXAMINE, SCRUTINIZE, PRY, SCAN
inspection, brief ... LOOK-SEE
inspector .... OVERSEER, EXAMINER
inspiration .... INHALING, IDEA, STIMULUS, INHALATION
inspire .. BREATHE, INFLUENCE, AROUSE, CAUSE, STIR, ANIMATE, INHALE, IMBUE, EXCITE, UPLIFT
inspired .... DEMONIC
inspirit .... CHEER
inspissate .... THICKEN, CONDENSE
instability .... INCONSTANCY, INSECURITY
install ...... INSTATE, INVEST, INDUCT, FIX, SET UP, ESTABLISH
instance .... INSTIGATION, OCCASION, SUIT, ILLUSTRATION, PLEA, SOLICITATION, EXAMPLE, CASE, BEHEST, REQUEST
instant ... URGENT, PRESSING, IMMEDIATE, IMMINENT, TRICE, QUICK, WINK, TIME, MOMENT, JIFFY, TICK
drink .... COFFEE, TEA, COCOA, ADE
instar ... LARVA, PUPA, IMAGO, MAGGOT
instead .... ELSE, LIEU, RATHER, VICE
instigate ...... URGE, FOMENT, CAUSE, EGG, PROMPT, ABET, INCITE, SPUR
instigation .... INSTANCE
instigator, kind of ... PLOTTER, AGITATOR, DEMAGOGUE, PROVOCATEUR
instill ..... INFIX, INCULCATE, INFUSE, IMPLANT
instinct .... BENT, GIFT, TALENT, KNACK
institute ...... SET UP, FOUND, ESTABLISH, INITIATE, START, SCHOOL
institution .. SCHOOL, CHURCH,

ESTABLISHMENT, HOME, REFORMATORY
instruct ...... COACH, TEACH, BRIEF, EDUCATE, EDIFY, TUTOR
instruction ...... EDUCATION, LESSON, ORDER, TUTORSHIP, TUTELAGE, TUITION
art of .... DIDACTICS
in teaching methods ..... PEDAGOGY
instructive .... DIDACTIC
instructor ... TEACHER, COACH, MENTOR, PEDAGOGUE, LECTOR
instrument ... AGENT, MEANS, TOOL, IMPLEMENT, DEVICE, DEED, AGENCY
board .... PANEL
boring .... JUMPER, AUGER, GIMLET
Hebrew .... TIMBREL
in law ...... DOCUMENT, DEED, CONTRACT
lutelike .... BANDORE
measuring ...... OCTANT
nautical .... SECTANT
of punishment ... STOCKS
stringed musical .... GUITAR, UKE, MANDOLIN, BANJO, LYRE, VIOLIN, VIOLA, SAMISEN, CITTERN, REBEC, KOTO
surveyor's ...... TRANSIT, ALIDADE
torture ... WHEEL, RACK, STRAPPADO
instrumental introduction ..... INTRADA
instrumentality ...... AGENCY, MEANS, MEDIUM
instruments, for all .... TUTTI
insubordinate ... DISOBEDIENT, REBELLIOUS
insufferable ..... UNBEARABLE, INTOLERABLE
insufficient .... LACKING, INADEQUATE, SCANTY
insular .... NARROW-MINDED, DETACHED
insulate .... SET APART, SEGREGATE, ISOLATE
insulating material .. ASBESTOS, BAGASSE, CELOTEX, KERITE, OKONITE
insulin discoverer ...... BEST, BANTING
disease treated with ..... DIABETES
insult ... AFFRONT, INDIGNITY, ASSAIL, OFFEND, FLOUT, SLUR, RUFFLE, OUTRAGE
insurance agent .... UNDERWRITER
contract .... POLICY
protection ... COVERAGE
term .... TONTINE, RISK, ANNUITY, POLICY
insure .... GUARANTEE, SECURE, PROTECT, UNDERWRITE
insurer .... UNDERWRITER
insurgence .... UPRISING, INSURRECTION
insurgent .... MUTINEER, REVOLTER, REBEL, REBELLIOUS, RISER
insurrection ..... REBELLION, UPRISING, REVOLT
intact ..... COMPLETE, WHOLE
intaglio ...... DIE, ENGRAVE, GEM
opposed to ...... CAMEO
intangible .... VAGUE, INCORPOREAL
asset .... GOOD WILL, PRESTIGE
intarsia .... MOSAIC
integer ...... ENTITY, WHOLE
odd .... GNOMEN
integral .... ESSENTIAL, NECESSARY, COMPOSITE, WHOLE, ENTIRE
integrate .... UNIFY
integrity .... SINCERITY, UPRIGHTNESS, VIRTUE, SOUNDNESS, HONESTY, HONOR
integument ..... SHELL, HIDE, RIND, HUSK, TESTA, COAT, DERM, SKIN, ARIL
intellect ...... INTELLIGENCE, INWIT, BRAIN, MENTALITY, NOUS
of the .... NOETIC
intellectual .... MENTAL, INTELLIGENT, EGGHEAD, HIGHBROW, NOETIC
identification ... EMPATHY
liking .... PALATE
intellectuals, collectively ...... CLERISY, INTELLIGENTSIA
intelligence ... NEWS, TIDINGS, INFORMATION, REPORT, INTELLECT, MIND, WIT, SENSE, ACUMEN, BRAINS
lively .... ESPRIT
intelligencer ..... INFORMANT, SPY, NEWSLETTER
intelligent .... SMART, BRILLIANT, CLEVER, SHARP, ASTUTE, APT, BRIGHT, SENSIBLE
intelligentsia .. INTELLECTUALS
intelligible .... CLEAR, UNDERSTANDABLE
intemerate .... PURE
intemperance .. DEBAUCHERY, EXCESS, CRAPULENCE
intemperate ...... EXCESSIVE, SEVERE, VIOLENT, IMMODERATE
intend .... PLAN, MEAN, PROPOSE, CONSTRUE
intended .... MEANT
colloquial .... FIANCE(E), BETROTHED
intensify .... HEIGHTEN, DEEPEN, ENHANCE
intensity .... DEPTH, VEHEMENCE
intent ... EARNEST, ENGROSSED, SET, PURPOSE, OBJECT, EAGER, DETERMINED
intention .... PURPOSE, GOAL, OBJECT(IVE), AIM, END
intentional ...... DELIBERATE, VOLUNTARY
inter .... BURY, INHUME, INURN, ENTOMB
companion of .... ALIA, ALIOS
interbreed .... CROSS
intercalation ...... EMBOLISM
intercede .... INTERVENE, MEDIATE, INTERPOSE
intercept ..... CUT OFF, STOP, PREVENT
intercessor .... MEDIATOR, PLEADER, ADVOCATE, BISHOP, PARACLETE
interchange ... SWAP, TRADE, EXCHANGE, ALTERNATE
intercom .... TALKBACK
interdict ... BAN, PROSCRIBE, FORBID, PROHIBIT, RESTRAIN, ENJOIN, VETO, BAR
in Scottish law .... INJUNCTION
interest .... CLAIM, RIGHT, BENEFIT, CONCERN, BEHALF, SHARE, WEAL, ZEAL, STAKE, PIQUE, USANCE
excessive .. USURY, MANIA
interested ...... CONCERNED, BIASED
interfere .... COLLIDE, INTERVENE, MEDDLE, INTERPOSE, MOLEST
interim .... MEANWHILE, PROVISIONAL, TEMPORARY, INTERVAL, MEANTIME, DIASTEM
interior ...... INSIDE, INNER, INLAND
interject ... INTERPOSE, INSERT
interjection ... EXCLAMATION, OH, AH, EGAD, AW, OUTCRY, HECK, GEE, GOSH
interlace ..... WEAVE, BRAID, PLEACH, TWINE
interlard .... DIVERSIFY
interlock ... KNIT, LINK, MESH
interlocution ..... DIALOGUE, CONVERSATION
interlope(r) ..... MEDDLE(R), INTRUDE(R)
interlude .... OVERTURE, INTERMISSION, EPISODE, INTERVAL, VERSET
intermediary ... GO-BETWEEN, MEDIATOR, MEANS, AGENCY, MEDIUM, MIDDLEMAN
intermediate .... MESNE, MIDDLE, BETWEEN, MEDIAN
interment .... BURIAL, SEPULTURE
intermezzo .... INTERLUDE
interminable .... ENDLESS, CEASELESS, LASTING
intermingle ..... MIX, BLEND
intermission ... RECESS, PAUSE, INTERLUDE, INTERRUPTION, ENTR'ACTE, INTERVAL
intermittent ..... RECURRENT, PERIODIC, OFF AND ON, FITFUL, SPASMODIC
intermix .... BLEND

intern .... DOCTOR, CONFINE, DETAIN
internal ... DOMESTIC, INNER, INTERIOR, INWARD, INTRINSIC
combustion apparatus ... CARBURETOR
fruit decay .... BLET
organs .... VISCERA, VITALS
international agreement ...... TREATY, PACT, ENTENTE
business combine .... CARTEL
exhibition ... EXPOSITION
language ...... IDO, RO, ESPERANTO, VOLAPUK
sports .... OLYMPICS
writers' group ..... PEN
"Internationale" author ...... POTTIER
internecine .... DEADLY, DESTRUCTIVE
interoffice note .... MEMO
interpolate .. INSERT, CORRUPT, FOIST
interpose .... INSERT, INTRODUCE, INTERVENE, INTERCEDE, MEDIATE, INTERRUPT
interpret .... EXPLAIN, ELUCIDATE, CONSTRUE, TRANSLATE, READ, REDE, RENDER
dreams .... REDE
falsely .... GLOSS
interpretation .. EXPLANATION, EXPOSITION, TRANSLATION, CONSTRUCTION, RENDITION, READING, REDE
Biblical .... EXEGESIS
false .... WRENCH
interpretative .. EXPLANATORY, HERMENEUTIC
interpretation, science of ..... HERMENEUTICS
interpreter ...... TRANSLATOR, EXEGETE
of sacred mysteries ...... HIEROPHANT, MYSTAGOGUE
travelers' ... DRAGOMAN
interred .... BURIED
interregnum .... PAUSE, INTERVAL
interrex .... REGENT
interrogate ... ASK, QUESTION, EXAMINE, QUIZ
interrogation mark .. EROTEME
interrogative word, usually .... WHAT, HOW, WHEN, WHERE, WHO
interrogator .... PROBER, QUESTIONER, INQUIRER, QUERIST
interrupt .... BREAK INTO, CUT OFF, OBSTRUCT
interruption ... INTERMISSION, BREAK, OUTAGE
intersect ... DECUSSATE, CROSS, CUT, MEET, JOIN
intersecting lines .... SECANTS
interstice .... CHINK, SLIT, AREOLA, CREVICE, PORE
intertwine ..... LACE, PLEACH, WEAVE, TANGLE
interval .... GAP, INTERLUDE, BREAK, LACUNA, HIATUS, CAESURA, INTERREGNUM, INTERIM
intervene .... INTERPOSE, INTERFERE, MEDDLE, BUTT IN
intervening .. MESNE, BETWEEN
period .... INTERVAL
intervention ... INTERFERENCE
interweave ..... (INTER)LACE, BLEND, ENTWINE, PLAIT, PLAT, SPLICE, RADDLE
interwoven ... LACED, NETTED, RETICULAR
intestinal .... ENTERIC
deposit .... BEZOAR
fortitude ... GRIT, GUTS, PLUCK
griping .... CRAMPS
not .... PARENTERAL
pains ... CRAMPS, COLIC
parasite ..... TRICHINA, PINWORM, NEMATODE, ASCARIS, TRICHURIS, HOOKWORM, TAPEWORM
pouch .... C(A)ECUM
worm purgative .... SANTANIN(E)
intestine(s) .... COLON, BOWEL(S), GUTS, ENTRAILS, VISCERA
combining form .. ENTERO
inflammation of .... ENTERITIS, (ENTERO)COLITIS
membrane .... CAUL, PERITONEUM
obstruction of .... ILEUS, VOLVULUS
of the ... ENTERIC, ALVINE
part ... ILEUM, ENTERON, COLON, DUODENUM, JEJUNUM
process, hairlike .. VILLUS
intimacy ...... FAMILIARITY, CLOSENESS
intimate ..... HINT, PRIVATE, CLOSE, IMPLY, CRONY, FRIEND, SUGGEST
wear .... STEP-IN(S), PANTY, SLIP-IN
intimately ..... INLY, CLOSELY
intimation .... NOTICE, SUGGESTION, DECLARATION, INKLING, CUE, HINT, ANNOUNCEMENT
intimidate ... COERCE, DAUNT, BULLY, COW, (OVER)AWE, FRIGHTEN, BUFFALO, BAMBOOZLE
intolerable .... UNBEARABLE, UNENDURABLE
intolerance .... BIGOTRY
intolerant .... IMPATIENT, BIGOTED
person ... BIGOT, ZEALOT
intone .. CHANT, RECITE, SING
intort .... TWINE, COIL, CURL, TWIST
intoxicant ..... LIQUOR, GROG, RUM, GIN, WHISKY , SOMA
intoxicate .... INEBRIATE, ELATE, EXCITE, SOUSE
in medicine ..... POISON
intoxicated .. LIT, DRUNK(EN), SOUSED, POTTED, FRIED, GROGGY, NAPPY, PLASTERED, LOADED, JAG
intoxicating .... HEADY
effect .... KICK
intractable .... UNRULY, STUBBORN, UNMANAGEABLE, WILD
intransigent ...... STUBBORN, UNCOMPROMISING
intrepid .... BOLD, BRAVE, FEARLESS
intrepidity .. COURAGE, NERVE, VALOR
intricacy .... COMPLEXITY
intricate .... INVOLVED, COMPLICATED, INVOLUTE, KNOTTY, KNOTTED, DA(E)DAL, MAZY, COMPLEX, TRICKY
knot .... GORDIAN
points/plots, etc. .. NODI
intrigue ..... CABAL, SCHEME, FASCINATE, PERPLEX, PLOT, CONSPIRACY, AMOUR, AFFAIR, BRIGUE
intriguer ...... MACHINATOR, SCHEMER
intrinsic .... INTERNAL, ESSENTIAL, INHERENT, TRUE, REAL
intrinsically .... PER SE
introduce ... INDUCT, INITIATE, INSTITUTE, INSERT, PRESENT, OPEN, INTERPOLATE, USHER, INFUSE, BEGIN, BROACH, LAUNCH, IMMIT, INTERJECT
introducer, kind of ... EMCEE, USHER, TOASTMASTER
introduction .... FOREWORD, PRESENTATION, PRELUDE, PREFACE, PROEM
musical ...... OVERTURE
to branch of study ...... ISAGOGE
to constitution .... PREAMBLE
to play/poem .... PROLOGUE
to society .... DEBUT
introductory .... PRELIMINARY, INITIAL, EXORDIAL, PREFATORY
remark .... PREFACE, FOREWORD
study .... ISAGOGICS
introit .... PSALM, HYMN
intromit ..... ADMIT, LET IN, INSERT, ENTER
intrude .... INTERLOPE, BUTT IN, TRESPASS, ENCROACH
intuition ... HUNCH, INSIGHT, PERCEPTION
intuitive .... INSTINCTIVE, NOUMENAL

intumesce ... SWELL, EXPAND, BUBBLE, ENLARGE
inulase .... ENZYME
inulin .... ALANTIN
hydrolyzed ... LEVULOSE
inundant ...... OVERFLOWING
inundate .. FLOOD, OVERFLOW, DELUGE, OVERWHELM, SWAMP
inundation .... DELUGE, SPATHE, FLOOD, OVERFLOW
inure .. HABITUATE, ACCUSTOM
inurn .. BURY, ENTOMB, INTER
inutile .... USELESS, UNPROFITABLE, IDLE
invade ... INTRUDE, VIOLATE, RAID, TRESPASS, CROWD, THRONG
invaders' foothold .... BEACHHEAD
invalid ....INFIRM, WEAK, SICKLY, NULL, VOID, SICK, NUGATORY
invalidate .... NULLIFY, VOID, ANNUL, VITIATE, OUTLAW
invaluable .... PRICELESS, PRECIOUS, COSTLY, DEAR
invar, for one .... ALLOY
invariable .... UNIFORM, CONSTANT, UNCHANGING
invariably .... ALWAYS
invasion .... INTRUSION, INFRINGEMENT, TRESPASS, INROAD, INCURSION
craft .... LST
invective ...... VITUPERATION, DENUNCIATION, CURSE, ABUSE
inveigh ..... RAIL, DENOUNCE, CENSURE
inveigle .... LURE, TRICK, ENTICE, LEAD ON, CAJOLE, COAX, SEDUCE, TEMPT
invent .... FABRICATE, ORIGINATE, DEVISE, CONCOCT, COIN
new word .... COIN, NEOLOGIZE
invention .... FIGMENT, FABRICATION, INGENUITY, FALSEHOOD, DEVICE, CONCOCTION
kind of ...... FALSEHOOD, LIE
inventor .... ARTIFICER
automobile ..... DAIMLER
camera .... EASTMAN
celluloid .... HYATT
cotton gin ..... WHITNEY
decimal measurement ... STEVIN
dynamite ...... NOBEL
dynamo ...... FARADAY, GRAMME
elevator .... OTIS
escape-lung .... MOMSEN
fountain pen .... WATTERMAN
harp .... JUBAL
machine gun ... GATLING
motion pictures .. EDISON
motor .... TESLA
new words ... NEOLOGIST
phonograph .... EDISON
protection of .... PATENT
radar ...... TUVE, BREIT
radio .... MARCONI
revolver .... COLT
sewing machine .. HOWE
steam engine ..... WATT
steamboat ..... FULTON
tank (military) .. SWINTON
telegraph .... MORSE
telephone .... BELL
thermometer ... GALILEI
tractor .... HOLT
training airplane ... LINK
transistor ..... BARDEEN, BRATTAIN
typewriter ...... SHOLES
safety lamp .... DAVY
inventory ..... STOCK, STORE, CATALOG(UE), LIST
official ...... INDENTURE
Inverness .... OVERCOAT, CAPE
inverse .... OPPOSITE
opposed to ..... DIRECT
inversion .... REVERSAL
invert .... REVERSE, HOMOSEXUAL
invertebrate .... SPINELESS
covering of .. TEST, SHELL
hearing organ of .... OTOCYST
sense organ of .... STATOCYST
inverted state .. TOPSY-TURVY
invest ...... CLOTHE, ADORN, ENVELOP, COVER, INSTALL, DON, BESIEGE, ARRAY, ENDOW, ENDUE, SPEND, BELEAGUER, ORDAIN, SURROUND
investigate ... EXAMINE, PROBE
investigation .... PROBE, RESEARCH, INQUEST
investigator .... PROBER, TRACER, INQUISITOR, EXAMINER
investiture .... INDUCTION, INSTALLATION, VESTURE
investment .... COVERING, SIEGE, CLOTHING, CAPITAL
kind of .... CAPITAL, EBOND, BLUE CHIPS
rash .... PLUNGE
investor .... CAPITALIST
list/securities of .... PORTFOLIO
inveteracy ..... FEUD, ENMITY
inveterate .... CHRONIC, DEEP-ROOTED, HABITUAL, OBSTINATE
invidious .... OFFENSIVE
invigorate .... ENLIVEN, ANIMATE, STRENGTHEN, BRACE
invigorating .. TONIC, BRACING
invincible ... UNCONQUERABLE
inviolable .... SACRED, SACROSANCT
inviolate .. UNBROKEN, SACRED
invisible .... UNSEEN, IMPERCEPTIBLE
emanation .... AURA
invitation .... BID, CARD
invite ..... BEG, ASK, REQUEST, ENTICE, CALL, ALLURE, BID
inviting .. TEMPTING, ENTICING
invocation ..... INCANTATION, PRAYER, CONJURATION, MARANATHA
opening ..... AGNUS DEI
invoke ... CONJURE, ENTREAT, BEG, PRAY, IMPLORE
involucre .... BRACTS
secondary .... INVOLUCEL
involuntary ..... ACCIDENTAL, AUTOMATIC, UNINTENTIONAL
action .... REFLEX
involute .... INVOLVED, INTRICATE, ROLLED UP
involve ... ENTAIL, IMPLICATE, INCLUDE, EMBROIL, COMPLICATE, REQUIRE
involved .... INVOLUTE, COMPLICATED, COMPLEX, INTRICATE, IMPLICATED
get .... THICKEN
invulnerable ... UNASSAILABLE
inward ..... INTERNAL, ENTAD
Io, lover of .... ZEUS
rival of .... HERA
watcher of .... ARGUS
iodine antiseptic ...... IODOL, IATROL
source .... KELP
Iolanthe .... PERI
iolite .... CORDIERITE
ion, negative .... ANION
positively charged ...... CATION
Ionian gulf .... PATRAS
island ... ITHACA, CERIGO, CORFU, CORCYRA, KAI, LAUT, LET(T)I, PAXOS, ZANTE
Ionic capital's volute ... HELIX
iota... JOT, WHIT, DOT, TITTLE
IOU, part of ...... OWE, YOU
Iowa, capital of ... DES MOINES
college .... COE
city .... WATERLOO, DAVENPORT, SIOUX, DUBUQUE, CLINTON, KEOKUK
college city .... AMES
county .... POLK, TAMA, ADAIR, CASS, LINN, LYON
native .... HAWKEYE
religious society .. AMANA
state bird ... GOLDFINCH
ipecac .... EVEA, MADDER
product .... EMETINE
Iphigenia's brother .. ORESTES
sister .... ELECTRA
ipse ____ .... DIXIT
ipsissima ____ .... VERBA
ipso ____ ...... FACTO, JURE
IQ, part of .... INTELLIGENCE, QUOTIENT
iracund .... CHOLERIC, IRASCIBLE, TESTY
irade .... DECREE

Iran ... PERSIA
Iranian ... TUDAH, PERSIAN, KURD, SOGDIAN
angel ... MAH
bird ... BULBUL
capital ... TEHERAN
carpet .. HAMADAN, KALI
chief ... MIR
city ... ISFAHAN, MESHED, TABRIZ, TEHERAN, AMOL, HAMADAN, RESHT, KERMAN, YEZD, PERSEPOLIS, SHUSHAN, SUSA, SHIRAZ
coin ... RIAL, LARI, P(O)UL, DINAR, DARIC, MOHUR
desert ... LUT, KAVIR
empress ... FARAH (DIBA)
evil spirit ... AHRIMAN
fairy ... PERI
gate ... DAR
gazelle ... CORA
governor ... SATRAP
hero ... RUSTAM, YIMA
in Russia ... TA(D)JIK, TADZHIK
island ... QUISHM
lake ... URMIA
language ... KURDISH, AFGHAN, PUSHTU, PERSIAN, PASHTO, ARYAN, AVESTAN, PAHLAVI, GALCHA, PAMIR
lower house ... MAJLIS
monetary unit ... RIAL
moon ... MAHI
mystic ... SUFI
official ... KHAN
oil center ... ABADAN
poet ... OMAR
port ... ABADAN
premier ... HOVEIDA, RAZMARA, MOSSADEGH, ZAHEDI
province ... FARS
queen ... SORAYA
river .. KARUN, TAB, ZAB, SAFID RUD
rug ... SENNA, KURDISTAN
ruler ... SHAH, PAHLEVI
sacred cord ... KUSTI
sacred writings .. AVESTA
screen ... PURDAH, PARDAH
shah ... PAHLEVI
sir ... AZAM
tiara ... CIDARIS
tile ... KAS(H)I
trading center ... ISPAHA
Turk ... SART
water vessel ... AFTABA
water wheel ... NORIA
weight ... MAUND
Iraq ... MESOPOTAMIA
capital ... BAGDAD
city ... BAGHDAD, MOSUL, BASRA
district ... AMARA
gnostic ... MANDEAN
king ... FAISAL, GHAZI
monetary unit ... DINAR
president ... ARIF
prime minister .. YAHYA
province ... AMARA
seaport ... BASRA, MOSQUES
irascible ... IRACUND, IRRITABLE, WRATHFUL, CROSS, BRASH, TESTY
irate ... ANGRY, INCENSED, WROTH, MAD
IRBM, part of ... INTERMEDIATE, RANGE, BALLISTIC, MISSILE
ire .. WRATH, ANGER, CHOLER, RAGE, FURY, DISPLEASURE
Ireland ... IRENA, EIRE, ERIN, EIRANN, HIBERNIA, IRISH FREE STATE, ERSE, IERNA
capital of North ... BELFAST
emblem of ... SHAMROCK
patron saint ... PATRICK
settlers in ... OSTMEN
Spenser's ... IRENA
Irene ... PAX
actress ... DUNNE, RICH
parent of .. ZEUS, THEMIS
irenic ... PEACEFUL, PACIFIC, SERENE
iridescent ... RAINBOWLIKE, OPALESCENT, LUSTROUS, PAVONINE, VERSICOLOR, NACREOUS
gem ... OPAL
iridiscence ... REFLET
iris ... IXIA, GODDESS, ORRICE, FLEUR-DE-LIS, EYE, RAINBOW, (BLUE)FLAG
combining form .. IRIDO
inflammation of ... UVEITIS, IRITIS
layer of ... UVEA
plant ... TILEROOT, FLAG, IXIA, ORRIS
plural of ... IRIDES
root ... ORRIS
Irish ... ERSE, MILESIAN, CELTIC, HIBERNIAN
accent ... BROGUE
alas ... OCHONE
alphabet ... OGUM, OG(H)AM
ancestor, legendary ... MILESIAN
assembly signal .. SLOGAN
assessment ... CESS
ballad hero ... RORY
battle cry ... ABU, SLOGAN
bay ... GALWAY, SLIGO
beauty: legendary .. EMER
buxom ... SONSIE
capital ... DUBLIN
capital (former) ... TARA
castle ... TARA
cattle ... KERRY
cheese ... KEBBOK
chieftain's follower ... GALLO(W)GLASS
chisel ... CELT
city ... DUBLIN, BELFAST, CORK, LIMERICK, TARA, COBH, SLIGO
church ... KIL
clan ... SEPT, SIOL
clansman ... AIRE
club/cudgel .. SHILLELAH, SHILLALA, ALPEEN
coin, fake ... RAP
colloquial ... TEMPER
county ... DONEGAL, MONAGHAN, GALWAY, KERRY, KILKENNY, CORK, MAYO, SLIGO, CLARE, KILDARE
cudgel ... ALPEEN
dagger ... SKENE
dandy ... BUCKEEN
dialect ... OGHAM
dirge ... KEEN
doctor ... OLLAM
dissident ... FENIAN
district ... BIRR
dramatist ... O'CASEY, SHAW, YEATS, STEELE, BEHAN
early kingdom .. MUNSTER
emblem ... SHAMROCK
endearment term ... MACHREE
epic ... TANA
essayist ... LECKY
exclamation ... ARRA(H), AROO
export ... LINEN
fairy ... LEPRECHAUN, SHEE
family ... CINEL
farmer ... COTTAR, COTTIER
fish ... POLLAN
fishing boat ... HOOKER
floral emblem ... SHAMROCK
folklore character .. LIMER
foot soldier ... KERN
fortification ... LIS
Free State ... IRELAND, SAORSTAT
freebooter ... RAPPAREE
freeman ... AIRE
garment ... INAR, LENN
general ... SHEA
girdle ... CRISS
girl ... COLLEEN, LASSIE
god ... DAGDA, LER
god of poetry ... OGMA
handsome ... SONSIE, SONSY
hero ... FINN, FIONN, RORY, FENIAN, FERGUS
heroine ... EMER
hill ... INCH
historian ... LECKY
hockey ... HURLING
hood ... COCHULL
initials ... IRA
island ... ACHILL, INCH
island group ... ARANN
jargon ... SHELTA
John ... SEAN, EOIN
king ... ENNA, AED, BRIAN, BORU
laborers ... AIRE
lake ... KILLARNEY, LOCH,

REE, DERG, CONN, LOUGH, NEAGH, CORRIB
lake dwelling .. CRANNOG
lament .... KEEN, CORONACH, WIRRA
landholding system ..... RUNDALE
legislature .... DAIL, EIREANN
lighthouse rock .. FASTNET
limestone .... CALP
lord .... TANIST
love .... GRA
lower house .... DAIL
Lowlander .. SASSENACH
luck .... CESS
lucky ..... SONSIE, SONSY
moss ..... CARRAG(H)EEN
mountain ..... DONEGAL, SPERRIN, WICKLOW
musical festival .... FEIS
musical instrument ...... CRUT, TIMPAN
nationalist ...... EMMET, PARNELL
novelist ... REID, SHAW, MOORE
outlaw .... PAPIST
Papist .... TORY
parliament .. OIREACHTAS
party .... SINN FEIN
patriot .... EMMET, PARNELL
patriotic group ..... IRA
patron saint .... PATRICK
peasant .... KERN(E), COTTAR, COTTIER
pipe (tobacco) .. DUDEEN
playwright .... SHAW, MOORE
poet .... YEATS, COLUM, JOYCE, WILDE
policeman .... PEELER
potato .... YAM
pretender ...... BUCKEEN
priest .... DRUID
prime minister ... LYNCH, LEMASS, DE VALERA
princess .... ISEULT, ISOLDE, DEIRDRE
proprietor ...... TANIST
province ...... MUNSTER, LEINSTER, CONNAUGHT, ULSTER
rascal .... SPALPEEN
rebel ... FENIAN, FIANNA
river .. SHANNON, CAVAN, NORE, LAGAN, BOYNE, SUIR, FOYLE
Royalist .... TORY
saint ... AIDAN, PATRICK
saloon .... SHEBEEN
Saxon .... SASSENACH
scamp .... SPALPEEN
sea god .... LER
seaport .... CORK, LIMERICK, DUBLIN, TRALEE, COBH, BELFAST
secret organization .. IRA, MOLLY MAGUIRES
secret society member ... ORANGEMAN
shield .... SCIATH
shillaly .... LAH
shoe .... BROGUE
slang .... MICK
smack .... HOOKER
society ...... FEINN, AOH
soldier .... KERN(E), GALLOGLASS, RAPPAREE
song .... RANN
sorrow .... WIRRA
spirit .... BANSHEE
sprite .... SHEE
statesman .... GRATTAN
steward ...... ERENACH
sweetheart .... GRA
symbol .... DEIRDRE
tax .... CESS
tenant .... SAER
tobacco pipe .... DUDEEN
tobacco pouch .... SPLEUCHAN
tribe ... CINEL, SIOL, SEPT
Ulster county ..... DOWN
verse .... RANN
wail .... KEEN
whiskey ... USQUEBAUGH, POT(H)EEN
white .... BAWN
woman revolutionary ... GONNE
young man ... BUCKEEN

Irishman ... MICK, HIBERNIAN, PADDY, CELT, PAT, MILESIAN, TEAGUE, HARP

irk .... ANNOY, DISGUST, TIRE, IRRITATE, VEX, TROUBLE, NETTLE, BOTHER

irksome ... TEDIOUS, TIRESOME

iron .... PRESS, POWER, FIRM, FERRITE, FERRUM, SMOOTH, MANGLE
alloy .... STEEL
bar .... BLOOM, JOINTER
chancellor: sobriquet .... BISMARK
coated .... TERNE
collar .... GARROTE
combining form .... SIDER(O)
disulfide .... PYRITE
hand .... CONTROL
horse ...... LOCOMOTIVE, BICYCLE, TRICYCLE
in golf ... CLUB, MASHIE, NIBLICK
lung .... RESPIRATOR
meteorite ..... SIDERITE
ore .... HEMATITE, SIDERITE, MAGNETITE, TURGITE, TACONITE, LIMONITE
out .... SMOOTHEN, STRAIGHTEN, ELIMINATE
oxide .... MAGNETITE
oxide powder ... CROCUS
oxidized .... RUST
peg used in quoits .. HOB
pertaining to ... FERROUS, FERRIC
pig .... SPIEGEL
prefix .... FERRO
pyrite .... MARCASITE
ready for rolling .... LARGET
sheet ...... TERNEPLATE
slang .... FIREARM
sulfide .... PYRITE
symbol for .... FE
weed genus .... VERNONIA
wood ...... ACLE, HELE, COLIMA

ironbark .... EUCALYPTUS

ironclad .... MONITOR, MERRIMAC, WARSHIP, UNBREAKABLE, FOOLPROOF, IRONSIDES

ironer .... MANGLE

ironic(al) .... SATIRIC(AL), SARCASTIC
writing .... LAMPOON

irons ..... CHAINS, SHACKLES, FETTERS, GYVE

Ironsides .... CROMWELL

ironwood ..... TITI, COLIMA, ACLE, HORNBEAM

ironworks .... SMELTERY

irony ...... MOCKERY, SATIRE, SARCASM

Iroquoian .... HURON, SENECA, WYANDOT, ONEIDA, MOHAWK, CAYUGA, TUSCARORA, CHEROKEE, ONONDAGA, ERIE

irrational .... SENSELESS, INANE, ABSURD, W(H)ACKY
number .... SURD

Irrawaddy tributary .... CHINDWIN

irreconcilable .. CONFLICTING, INCOMPATIBLE

irredenta ...... UNREDEEMED

irrefragable ... INDISPUTABLE

irregular ...... ANOMALOUS, DISORDERLY, UNEVEN, ABNORMAL, ATYPIC(AL), DESULTORY, SPOTTY, ERRATIC, EROSE, FITFUL, SPORADIC
in shape ...... BAROQUE

irregularity .... ANOMALY

irregularly edged ..... EROSE

irreligious .... PROFANE, IMPIOUS, GODLESS, PAGAN

irreproachable .... FAULTLESS, BLAMELESS, IMPECCABLE, ABOVEBOARD

irresistible ..... COMPELLING, OVERPOWERING

irresolute .... HESITANT, UNDECIDED, INDECISIVE

irrespective ..... REGARDLESS

irreverence .... DISRESPECT

irrevocable .... FINAL, UNALTERABLE

irrigate ...... WATER, FLUSH

irrigation ditch ...... SLUICE, ACEQUIA

irritability .... ERETHISM, IMPATIENCE

irritable .. IRASCIBLE, TOUCHY, TESTY, CROSS, CRANKY, EDGY, TE(T)CHY, GRUMPY, IRACUND, SPLENETIC

irritable person ..... TARTAR, CURMUDGEON, GROUCH, CRANK

irritate ..... NETTLE, PEEVE,

EXASPERATE, PROVOKE, VEX, CHAFE, RANKLE, PIQUE, RASP, ANNOY, IRK, ITCH, NEEDLE, TEASE, GRATE, GRAVEL, RILE, GALL

irritation .. ITCH, ANNOYANCE, PIQUE

irruption .... BURSTING, INVASION

is .... EXISTS

Isaac .... PATRIARCH
- parent of ..... ABRAHAM, SARAH
- son of ...... ESAU, EDOM, GAD, JACOB

Isadora, dancer ..... DUNCAN

isagoge ...... INTRODUCTION

Isaye's pupil ...... MENUHIN

Iscariot ..... JUDAS, TRAITOR

ischemia .... ANEMIA

Iseult .... ISOLDE
- husband of .... MARK
- love of ..... TRIST(R)AM

Ishmael ... OUTCAST, PARIAH
- parent of ..... ABRAHAM, HAGAR
- son of .... DUMAH

Isidore, diminutive of ... IZZY

isinglass .... GELATIN, AGAR, CARLOCK, MICA
- source of ..... STURGEON

Isis' brother/husband .. OSIRIS
- sister .... NEPHTHYS

Islam adherent ...... MOSLEM, MUSLIM, MUSLEM
- canonical law .... SHARIA
- convert .. ANSAR, MURED
- founder/prophet .... MOHAMMED
- school .... MADARA
- supreme deity ... ALLAH

Islamic teacher ..... MULLAH, ALIM

island .... ISLE, AIT, ALT
- Alaskan ... KISKA, ATTU, PRIBILOF, ALEUT
- at earth's center ... MERU
- Beautiful ...... FORMOSA
- Caroline .... YAP
- city .... AMOY
- coral .... ATOLL
- country ... JAPAN, ERIN
- Danish .... AERO
- empire .... JAPAN
- enchanted .... BALI
- French .... ILE
- Greek .... CRETE
- Hebrides .... IONA
- in a lake .... HOLM
- isolated .... INCH
- Italian ..... ELBA, CAPRI, SICILY
- largest (world's) .... GREENLAND
- legendary ...... ATLANTIS
- low .... KEY
- mythical .... NAXOS
- near bigger one .... CALF
- Philippine .... PANAY, SAMAR, MINDANAO, LUZON, MINDORO, PALAWAN, SULU
- river ... AIT, EYOT, HOLM
- small ..... AIT, CAY, KEY, ISLE, ISLET
- Spanish .... ISLA

islands, group of .... ARCHIPELAGO
- of Langerhans secretion INSULIN

isle .... AIT, KEY
- of Man capital .. DOUGLAS
- of Man judge .. DEEMSTER
- of Wight channel .... SOLENT
- of Wight town ... COWES

islet ..... CAY, KEY, AIT, ALT, HOLM

ism .... DOCTRINE, SYSTEM, THEORY, BELIEF, DOGMA, TENET, DOXY

isolate .... SET APART, SEGREGATE, ENISLE, INSULATE, IMMURE, SECLUDE

isolated ...... QUARANTINED, (EN)ISLED, SEGREGATED
- rock .... SCAR

isolation........... SOLITUDE

Isolde .... ISEULT
- love of .... TRISTRAM

isomer .... METAMER, MALEIC

isomeric terpene ..... PINENE

isometric .... CUBIC

isopiestic .... ISOBAR

isopod .... CRUSTACEAN

isopyre .... OPAL

Israel(i) ... SION, ZION, JACOB
- ancient capital .. SAMARIA
- ancient city .... SAMARIA, TIRZAH
- battlesite .... ESDRAELON
- camp .... ETHAM
- capital ...... JERUSALEM, TEL AVIV
- city ...... HAIFA, JAFFA, TEL AVIV, JOPPA
- coin .... MIL
- dance .... HORA
- defense line ..... BARLEV
- desert .... NEGEV
- foreign minister ... EBAN
- general .... DAYAN
- hero .... GIDEON
- high priest .... ELI
- king .. AHAB, OMRI, SAUL, ELAH, NADAB, SOLOMON, JEHU, JEROBOAM
- lake .... HULEH
- legislature ..... KNESSET
- peace .... SHALOM
- plain .... SHARON, ESDRAELON, JEZREEL
- political party ... MAPAM
- port ...... ELATH, ACRE, HAIFA, JAFFA
- premier .... ESHKOL, BEN GURION, (GOLDA) MEIR
- president .... SHAZAR, WEIZMANN
- prophet of ...... ELISHA, ELIJAH, ELIAS
- region .... NEGEV
- seaport ... JAFFA, JOPPA
- strip .... GAZA
- town .... EILAT

Israelite ..... JEW(ISH), SION, HEBREW, ZION
- judge .... ELON
- king .... DAVID
- land in Egypt ... GOSHEN
- leader ... JOSHUA, JOSUE
- paid curser ..... BALAAM
- strong man .... SAMSON
- tribe ... GAD, LEVI, DAN, AS(H)ER, GAD, MANASSEH, NAPHTALI

Israelites, biblical .. HERITAGE

issei's kin of a sort .... NISEI, KIBEI

issue .... EXIT, OUTFLOW, OUTLET, RESULT, UPSHOT, OFFSPRING, CHILD, POINT, QUESTION, EMANATE, EMIT, ARISE, EDITION, EMERGE, DEAL OUT, PUBLISH, PROGENY, OUTCOME
- minor point of .... TECHNICALITY
- take ... DIFFER, DISAGREE

Istanbul .... STAMBOUL, BYZANTIUM, CONSTANTINOPLE
- foreign quarter .... PERA, FANAR, BEYOGLU
- inn .... SERAI, IMARET
- section .... BEYOGLU, SCUTARI, USKUDAR, STAMBOUL
- suburb .... GALATA

isthmus .... STRAIT, PANAMA, BALK, NECK, KRA
- Corinth .... MEGARIS
- Panama .... DARIEN

istle .... FIBER, PITA, PITO

ita .... NEGRITO

itacolumite ...... SANDSTONE

it doesn't pay .... CRIME
- is legal .... LICET
- is silent, in music .. TACET
- reads same both ways ... PALINDROME

Italian ...... ROMAN, LATIN, PICENE, SABINE
- actress .... ANGELI, MAGNANI, LOREN, DUSE, LOLLOBRIGIDA
- adventurer ... CASANOVA
- anatomist ..... FALOPIUS
- ancient .... ROMAN, PICENE, SABINE, OSCAN
- ancient city ...... CAPUA, CANNAE
- anew .... DE NOVO
- art period ..... SEICENTO, TRECENTO
- astronomer ...... GALILEO
- author .... DANTE, PETRARCH
- baby .... BAMBINO
- baked shrimp ... SCAMPI
- bandit .. BRIGANTE, CACO
- bathhouse ...... BAGNIO
- bell .... CAMPANA
- bell town .... ATRI
- bowl .... TAZZA
- breed of cattle .. MODICA, PADOLIAN

capital ..... ROME, ROMA
car .... FIAT
cathedral .... DUOMO
cathedral city .... MILAN
Celt .... SENONE
cheer .... VIVA
cheese .... GRANA, GORGONZOLA, PARMESAN
chest .... CASSO(NE)
chief .... DUCE
city .... MILAN, NAPLES, GENOA, PALERMO, SIENA, TARANTO, TRIESTE, ASTI, RIMINI, RAVENNA, PERUGIA, LUCCA, PAVIA, MODENA, MONZA, FOGGIA, FORLI, LODI, TORINO, NOVARA, UDINE, PISA, MASSA, GORIZIA, OSTIA, ANCONA, CREMONA, TRENT(O), ROME, SPEZIA, PARMA, PADUA, BRESCIA, CARRARA, LEGHORN, BARI, VENICE, TURIN, FERRARA, VERONA
civil government .... QUIRINAL
coin ..... LIRA, SOLDOS, LIRE, SOLDI, ZECHIN, ZECCHINO, SCUDO, SEQUIN
comedy character .... SCARAMOUCH(E), PANTALOON
commune .... MEDA, ESTE, TRIEA, ASOLA, ALBA
composer .... GUIDO, ROSSINI, TOSTI, MENOTTI, LULLY, MASCAGNI, PAGANINI, VERDI
condiment ..... TAMARA
conductor ... MANTOVANI, TOSCANINI
country, ancient .... LATIUM, ETRURIA
countryside .. CAMPAGNA
cup .... TAZZA
cupid .... AMORINO, AMORETTO
customs house .. DOGANA
dance .. PAVIN, PAVAN(E), CALATA, VOLTA, TARANTELLA, SALTARELLO
dear .... CARO, CARA
department ... LIGURIA, CALABRIA, PIEDMONT, UMBRIA, EMILIA, LOMBARDY, LUCANIA, APULIA
dessert .... SPUMONI, SPUMONE
"Detroit" .... TURIN
dialect .... LIGURIAN
dictator ... MUSSO(LINI)
dish ... PIZZA, RISOTTO, PASTA
dough .... PASTA
dramatist ...... ALFIERI
drink .... BEVERE
duchy .... PARMA
dynasty .... SAVOY
eight .... OTTO
enclave, Swiss .... CAMPIONE
enough .... BASTA
evening .... SERA
faction ... BIANCHI, NERI
family ...... ASTI, DORIA, ESTE, DONATI, MEDICI, CENCI
farewell .... ADDIO
Fascist gangster .... DUMINI
Fascist leader ...... RAS, MUSSO(LINI)
feast .... FESTINO, FESTA
festival .... RIDOTTO
field .... CAMPO
first .... PRIMO
flower .... FIORE
fortress .... ROCA
fountain, famous .. TREVI
gallery .... UFFIZI
game .... BOCCE, MORA
gentleman ... SIGNOR(E), SIGNORINO, SER
goodby .... ADDIO
good morning .... BUON GIORNO
goose .... OCA
governor ...... PODESTA
Greek city .... PAESTUM (PESTO)
Greek colony ..... ELEA
guessing game .... MORA
gulf ... GENOA, SALERNO, TARANTO, VENICE
gypsy .... ZINGABI
hair .... PELO
hamlet .... BORGO, CASAL(E)
hammer ...... MARTELLO
hand .... MANO
harbor .... PORTO
harp .... ARPA
hat .... LEGHORN
hate .... ODIO
headland .... SCILLA
health resort ... AGNONE
helmet .... ELME
historian .... CANTU
holiday .... FESTE, FESTA
house .... CASA
innkeeper ..... PADRONE, OSTE
island ... CAPRI, CORSICA, ELBA, LINOSA, PANTELLERIA, LAMPEDUSA, LIDO, LIPARI, SARDINIA, SICILY, COS
islander .... SARD
judge .... PODESTA
king .... EMMANUEL, HUMBERT(O)
kiss .... BACIO
labor contractor .... PADRONE
lady ... DONNA, SIGNORA, SIGNORINA
lake ...... COMO, LAGO, MAGGIORE, AVERNO, VICO, AVERNUS, GARDA, ALBANO
language .... TUSCAN, OSCAN, LADIN
leader .... DUCE
little .... POCO
love .... AMORE
lover .... AMOROSO
magistrate .... PODESTA, DOGE
man .... SIGNOR(E)
marble .... CIPOLIN, CAR(R)ARA
marshy land .. PONTINE, MAREMMA
mayor .... PODESTA
measure .... BRACCIO
meat balls ...... RAVIOLI
millet ...... BUDA, MOHA, TENAI
miss .... SIGNORINA
mister .... SIGNOR
mother .... MADRE
mountain ..... ALBANITA, CENIS, APENNINES, CAVO, CHIANTI
movie director .... (DE)SICCA
music ..... TARANTELLA
musical suite .... PARTITA
musical theorist .. GUIDO
musician .... GUIDO
muslin ..... MUSSOLINO
name .... ESTE
name for Italy ... ITALIA
nationalist .... MAZZINI
naval base ... TARANTO, POLA, BRINDISI
night .... SERA
nine .... NOVE
noblewoman .... MARCHESA, CONTESSA, MARCHIONESS, MARQUIS, MARCHESE
not only .... NONCHE
novelist .... MANZONI
one .... UNO
opera ..... NORMA, AIDA
opera house ..... SCALA
opera singer .... CARUSO, PATTI, TEBALDI, ALDANESE, CORELLI, PINZA, AMATO, GIGLI
otto in French ..... HUIT
painter .... LIPPI, VINCI, GIOTTO, SPADA, TITIAN, RENI, ANDREA, VASARI, RAPHAEL, ROSSI
patriot ...... GARIBALDI, MAZZINI, CAVOUR
patriotic organization ... RISORGIMENTO, CARBONARI
peak .. CIMA, MARMOLADA
people .... OSCAN, SARDS, SABINES
philosopher ..... BRUNO, DION
physicist .... ROSSI, VOLTA, MARCONI

pie .... PIZZA
plague .... PELLAGRA
plain .... CAMPAGNA
plateau .... SILA
poet .... LEOPARDI, PETRARCH, MANZONI, DANTE, ARIOSTO, TASSO, REDI
police ..... CARABINIERI
political party .... IRREDENTIST
political party member .. GUELF, GUELPH
porridge ...... POLENTA
port ...... BARI, GENOA, TRIESTE
pottery .... FAENZA, MAJOLICA
premier .... MORO, CRISPI, CAVOUR, PARRI, RUMOR, ORLANDO
prima donna ...... DIVA, TEBALDI
province ... ESTE, COMO, PISA, PARMA, MANTUA
public entertainment .... RIDOTTO
public square ... PIAZZA
region ...... CALABRIA, VENETO, SICILIA, LIGURIA, (LE)MARCHE, LUCANIA, PIEMONTE
republic .... GENOA
resort ..... CAPRI, LIDO, COMO, SORRENTO, SAN REMO
restaurant .... PIZZERIA
rifleman ... BERSAGLIERE
river ... ORCO, PO, ARNO, RENO, TEVERE, TREBBIA, LIVENZA, PIAVE, ADIGE, TIBER
Romance language ..... LADIN
sausage .... SALAMI
sculptor .... CANOVA, DUPRE, CELLINI, LEONI, PISANO
seacoast .... MARINA
seaport .... GENOA, NAPLES, PALERMO, VENICE, (LA)SPEZIA, POLA, SAN REMO, TRANI, SALERNO, TRIESTE, GENOVA
seashore .... RIVA
secret society ..... MAFIA, CAMORRA, CARBONARI
ship .... POLACCA
shrimp dish ..... SCAMPI
sign .... SEGNO
silk .... SETA
sir .... SIGNOR(E)
sky .... CIELO
slang .... GUINEA
somewhat .... POCO
song .... VILLANELLA, CANZONE
songbird ..... BECCAFICO
soprano ..... ALBANESE, TEBALDI, PATTI
spa .... AGNONE, ABANO
spider .... TARANTULA
strait .... MESSINA
street .... CALLE, VIA, CORSO
tender .... PIA
tenor .... CORELLI, CARUSO, SCHIPA
that .... CHE
the .... GLI
three .... TRE
time .... TEMPO
title ... CONTE, MARCHE, MARQUIS, DONNA, SIGNOR, CONTESSA
tobacco ..... CAPORALE
today .... OGGI
town .... CASAL(E), CASSINO, MEDA, ELEA, ITRI, ASTI, POLA, ATRI
tractor ...... PICCOLINO
tribe .... SABINE
under .... SOTTO
university city .. PADUA, PISA, BARI
valley .... SACCO
vase .... TAZZA
verse .... RANN
violin .... CREMONA, STRAD(IVARIUS), AMATI
violin maker .... GUARNERI, AMATI STRADIVARI
violinist ...... TARTINI, PAGANINI
voice .... VOCE
volcano .... ETNA, STROMBOLI, VESUVIUS
waterway .... CANALE
weight ..... LIBRA, ONCIA
well .... BENE
what .... CHE
wind ..... ANDAR, SOVER, SIROC(CO)
wine .... ASTI
wine measure ...... ASTI, ORNA, ORNE
winter .... INVERNO
woman's title .. MADONNA
woods .... PINETOS
woodwork ...... TARSIA
you .... TU

Italic type inventor .. MANUTIUS
Italy ..... AUSONIA, HESPERIA
barbarian ruler of .... ODOVACAR, ODOACER
itch ...... PRURITUS, PSORA, SCABIES, HANKERING, URGE, CRAVE, RIFF
barber's .... SYCOSIS
item ..... UNIT, PARTICULAR, THING, ENTRY, ARTICLE, DETAIL
itemize .... LIST
iterate .... REPEAT
Ithunn .... IDUN
itinerant .... TRAVELER, NOMADIC, VAGRANT, HOBO, TRAMP
vendor .... PEDDLER
itineration .... CIRCUIT, TOUR, JOURNEY
itinerary .. ROUTE, ROADBOOK, GUIDEBOOK
itself .... PER SE
iva .... YELLOW BUGLE
"Ivanhoe" author ..... SCOTT
character ...... ROWENA, CEDRIC, GURTH, WAMBA, ULRICA, ISAAC, CRONE, BOUEF
Ives, actor .... BURL
composer ..... CHARLES
partner of ..... CURRIER
ivied .... VINY
ivories .... DICE, KEYS, TEETH
ivorine .... WHITE
ivory ... DENTINE, TUSK, TUSH
animal with ... ELEPHANT, WALRUS, WARTHOG
Coast capital .. ABIDJAN
Latin .... EBUR
like .... DENTINE
source .. NARWHAL, TUSK, ELEPHANT
synthetic .... IVORIDE
tickler .... PIANIST
time-beaters .. CASTANETS
ivy .... VINE
clump .... TOD
of the .... HEDERAL
istle .... IXTLE, PITA
Iwo ____ .... JIMA
Jima mount .. SURIBACHI
ixia .... IRIS
Ixion offspring ..... CENTAUR
Izmir .... SMYRNA

J

J, in physics .... JOULE
letter .... JAY
ja .... YES
jab .... THRUST, POKE, BLOW, DIG, PUNCH
jabber .... BABBLE, PRATE, GIBBER(ISH), CHATTER, SPUTTER, YAP
jabberwocky .... RIGMAROLE
jabiru ..... STORK, IBIS, BIRD
jabot .... FRILL, RUFFLE, STONE, LIGURE
jack .... JUG, HOIST, OPENER, RABBIT, CLOWN, KNAVE, NOB, FELLOW, SAILOR, DONKEY, SALMON, TORCH, MULE, BOWER, MUG
and ____ .... JILL
Benny's stock in trade ... VIOLIN, GAGS
Ketch .... HANGMAN
in cribbage .... NOB
in-the-pulpit ...... ARAD,

AROID, WAKEROBIN
Leonard's forte .. INSULT
of-all-trades .... TINKER
of clubs .... PAM
part of .... DETENT
slang .... MONEY
Sprat's favorite .... LEAN
pudding ...... BUFFOON, FOOL
rabbit .... HARE
tar .... SAILOR
tree .... JACA
up .... RAISE, HIKE
jackal .... DIEB, KOLA, THOS, CHEAT(ER), SWINDLER, (WILD)DOG, SCAVENGER
headed deity .... ANUBIS
jackanapes .... MONKEY, UPSTART, IMP
jackass ...... DONKEY, FOOL, NITWIT, DOLT
and mare offspring ..... MULE
rarely one ... WISE GUY, SMART ALECK
jackdaw, bird like ..... CROW
jacket ... ETON, REEFER, RIND, BOLERO, SACK, SPENCER, SACQUE, DOUBLET, CASING, WRAPPER, JERKIN, SKIN, NORFOLK, ROUNDABOUT, COAT(EE), JUPE
ad on book ...... BLURB
Arctic region ... ANORAK
armor ... ACTON, JUPON, GIPON
children's ..... PALETOT
cold wear .... PARKA, ANORAK
cowboy's ..... CHAQUETA
dinner .... TUX(EDO)
Eskimo .... PARKA
fur .... PARKA
hooded .... JUMPER, ANORAK, PARKA
knitted .... JERSEY
leather .... ANORAK
Levant .... GREGO
life-saving ..... MAE WEST
mail .... HAUBERK, HABERGEON
Malay .... BAJU
outer .... WAM(M)US, WAMPUS
sailor's .... PEACOAT
sleeveless .... VEST, BOLERO, TABARD, WAISTCOAT
sports... WINDBREAKER
women's ... JUPE, JUPON, CAMISOLE, PALETOT
woolen ...... CARDIGAN, LUMBERJACK
jackknife ..... (FANCY) DIVE, STAB
jacksnipe .... SANDPIPER
Jackson, Andrew .... OLD HICKORY, ANDY
Jacob .... ISRAEL
brother of .. EDOM, ESAU
diminutive of ..... JAKE, JACK
father of .... ISAAC
father-in-law ..... LABAN
in French ...... JACQUES
son of ... JUDAH, ASHER, DAN, GAD, LEVI, REUBEN, JOSEPH, BENJAMIN
twin .... ESAU
variant of .... JAMES
wife of ... LEAH, RACHEL
Jacobin .... DOMINICAN, FRIAR, RADICAL, PIGEON
jaconet ... NAINSOOK, COTTON
jac(ti)tation ...... BRAGGING, BOAST
jade ... TIT, NEPHRITE, MARE, YAUD, MURRHINE, PLUG, GREEN, WOMAN, WEARY, ROSINANTE, TIRE, HUSSY, SLUT, HARASS, STONE, NAG
jaeger .... SHOOI, TEASER, ALLAN, SKUA, SEABIRD
Jaffa .... JOPPA
jag ..... BARB, NOTCH, PINK, TEAR, SPREE, SNAG
Jaga .... BANTU
jager .... RIFLEMAN
jagged .... EROSE, SERRATED, RAGGED, ROUGH, CLEFT, NOTCHED
jaguar .. PANTHER, TIGER, CAR
Jahve(h) .... JEHOVAH
jai-alai .... PELOTA
court .... FRONTON
game like .... HANDBALL
player .... PELOTARI
racquet .... CESTA
stroke .... REBOTE
jail ...... BRIDEWELL, LIMBO, LOCK UP, CELL, (IM)PRISON, GAOL, CAGE, COOP, PEN, QUOD
not in ..... FREE, LOOSE, AT LARGE
official .... WARDER, WARDEN
ship's .... BRIG
slang ..... JUG, COOLER, CALABOOSE, STIR, CLINK(ER), POK(E)Y
jailbird .. PRISONER, CONVICT, LAWBREAKER
with privileges ... TRUSTY
jailer ..... PROVOST, WARDEN, TURNKEY, GAOLER
Jakarta .... BATAVIA
jake .... SATISFACTORY
jakes .... PRIVY, TOILET
jalap .... ROOT, PLANT
jalopy .... CRATE, HOTROD
jalousie ..... BLIND, SCREEN, SHADE
jam ... BLOCK, CRAM, WEDGE, SQUEEZE, SHOVE, CROWD, PRESERVES
colloquial .... PREDICAMENT, SPOT, FIX
like preparation .... PRESERVE(S), JELLY
material .... CURRANT
jama .... TUNIC
Jamaican bird .... TODY, TINKLING, GRACKLE
capital .... KINGSTON
export .... RUM
grackle ...... TINKLING
island .... CAYMAN
jamb(e) .... (SIDE) POST, JAMBEAU
James Bond's creator .... FLEMING
direction normally given.. HOME
father of disciple .... ZEBEDEE
the outlaw .... JESSE
the Second supporter .... JACOBITE
Jamshid subjects .... PERIS
Jane, mate of ...... TARZAN, ROCHESTER
of history .... GREY
singer .... FROMAN
jangle ..... QUARREL, BICKER
Janis ____, popsinger .. JOPLIN
janitor ... PORTER, DOORMAN, CONCIERGE, SUPER, SEXTON
Janus, describing .... TWO-FACED, DECEITFUL
Japan ..... ENAMEL, VARNISH, LACQUER, NIPPON, NIHON, CIPANGO, ZIPANGU
foreigner in ..... GAIJIN
Japanese .... NIPPONESE
aborigine .... AINO, AINU
admiral ...... ITO, TOGO, YAMAMOTO, NOMURA
adviser .... GENRO
alien to a .... GAIJIN
American .... ISSEI, SANSEI, KIBEI, NISSEI
apricot .... UME
army reserve ..... HOJU
automobile ..... TAJURI, DATSUN, TOYOTA
badge .... (KIRI)MON
bamboo ..... WHANGEE
banjo .... SAMISEN
baron .... HAN
battle cry .... BANZAI
bay .... OSAKA, ISE, YED(D)O
bean .... ADSUKI
beer ... SAKE, SAKI, ASAHI
beriberi .... KAKKE
board game ... GOBAN(G)
boat .... SAMPAN
box .... INRO
brazier .... HIBACHI
bream .... TAI
Buddha .... AMIDA
Buddhism .... ZEN
Buddhist festival .... BON
Buddhist monastery ..... TERA
camellia .... JAPONICA
cape ... OKI, MINO, SUZU, MELA, OMA, SADA, DAIO, NOMO
capital ... TOKIO, TOKYO, YED(D)O
capital, former .... NARA, KYOTO
carp .... KOI
carriage .... SADOS, RICKSHA(W)
caste .... SAMURAI

cedar .... SUGI
charcoal stove .. NIBACHI
cheer .... BANZAI
cheer leader .... OENDAN
cherry .... FUJI
chest .... TANSU
chicken dish ... YAKATORI
chinaware ...... KUTANI, IMARI
church .... TERA
city ... OTARU, OKAYAMA, MOJI, IWAKUNI, MIYAJIMA, OSAKA, TOKYO, NAGOYA, KYOTO, SENDAI, YOKOHAMA, NAGASAKI, NARA, FUKUOKA, KAWASAKI, HIMEJI, SASEBO, KOBE
clan .... GEN, HEI, TOKUGAWA
clogs .... GETA
clover .... HAGI
coin ..... SEN, YEN, RIN, OBAN(G), ITZEBU
commoner ..... HEIMIN
confection .... AME
conveyance .... KAGO
councilor .... KARO
court .... DAIRI
crash pilot ... KAMIKAZE
crest .... MON
Crown Prince .. AKIHITO
dancing girl ..... GEISHA
date plum .... KAKI
deer .... SIKA
deity ...... AMIDA, AMITA
dish .... SUKIYAKI, TERIYAKI, YAKATORI, SUSHI
divine wind .. KAMIKAZE
dog .... TANATE
door .... FUSUMA
drama .... KABUKI, NOGAKU, NOH
drink .... SAKE
earthquake, 1923 .. KANTO
eating tool .. CHOPSTICKS
emperor .... MIKADO, HIROHITO, JIMMU, TENNO, YOSHIHITO, MUTSUHITO
emperor's reign .. MEIJI, SHOWA, TAISHO
Empire .... EDO
empress .... NAGAKO
engraver ...... HOKUSAI
"Enlightened Peace" era.. MEIJI
factory .... HONG
family .... BATSU
family emblem .... MON
fan .... OGI
festival .... BON
fighter plane ...... ZERO
fish ..... FUGU, TILAPIA, TAI, AYU, GOURAMI
flag .... RISING SUN
flower arrangement ..... IKEBANA
foreign ministry .... GAIMUSHO
foreigner to a .... GAIJIN
game .... GOBAN(G)
garment .... KIMONO
gateway .... TORII
general ... ARAKI, TOJO, YAMASHITA
generalissimo .. SHOGUN
gift .... OMIYAGE
glue .... AME
god .... KAMI
god of happiness .. EBISU, HOTEI
goldfish .... FUNA
government system ..... SHOGUNATE
grill .... HIBACHI
guitar .... KOTO
hanging ..... KAKEMONO
heart transplant surgeon.. WADA
herb .... UDO
house .... MITSUI, MITSUBISHI, SUMITOMO
immigrant .... ISSEI, NISSEI
imperial badge .. KIRIMON
industrial family .... ZAIBATSU, MITSUI, YASUDA
Inland sea ..... NAIKAI, SETO
island .... HONSHU, SAISHU, HONDU, IZU, KURIL(E), KYUSHU, SADO, HOKKAIDO, SHIKOKU
Kurile islands .. CHISHIMA
legislature .... DIET
lily .... AURATUM
litter .... NORIMONO
lord .... DAIMIO
lute .... BIWA
measure ... RIN, CHO, RI, MO, SHO
mile .... RI
military caste .. SAMURAI
military code .. BUSHIDO
military governor .... SHOGUN
military service .... YOBI
monastery .... TERA
money .... SEN, YEN
monk .... BONZE
monopolies ... ZAIBATSU
mountain ... FUJI(YAMA), USU, WASHU
musical instrument ...... SAMISEN, KOTO
mystic symbol .... SWASTIKA
naval base .... KURE, SASEBO
news agency ..... DOMEI, KYODO, JIJI
newspaper ... SHIMBUN, MAINICHI, YOMIURI
nobility .... SAMURAI, HATAMOTO
nobleman .... KUGE, DAIMIO, DAIMYO, KAMI
opera .... YUZURU
outcast .... RONIN, A(E)TA, YETA
outer garment .. KIMONO, HAORI, MINO
outlaw .... RONIN
pagoda .... TAA
painter .... HIROSHIGE
painting school .... TOSA, KANO, SESSHU, SHIJO
palanquin .... KAGO, NORIMONO
paper art ...... ORIGAMI
parliament .... DIET
paste .... AME
peach .... MOMO
peninsula .... IZU
persimmon .... KAKI
pine .... MATSU
"Pittsburgh" .. YAWATA
plant ..... AUCUBA, UDO
play .... NOH, KABUKI
plum ..... KELSEY, KAKI, SUMOMO
plumlike fruit .. LOQUAT
poem .... HAIKU
porgy .... TAI
pottery .... AWATA, SATSUMA
prefecture .... FU, MINO, KEN, OWARI
premier .... KISHI, KONOYE, TOJO, SATO, IKEDA
primitive ... AINU, AINO
province ...... KUNI, ISE, UGO
puppet emperor of ...... PU-YI
puppet show .. BUNRAKU
puppet state .... MANCHU(O)KUO
quince .... JAPONICA
radish .... DAIKON
raincoat .... MINO
rattle-trap ... GATAKURI
religion .... SHINTO(ISM), BUDDHISM
religious dance ...... NO
religious festival ... BON
resort area .... NIKKO, HAKONE
rice beer ..... SAKE, SAKI
rice paste .... AME
river boat ...... SAMPAN
robe .... KIMONO
room-divider .... SHOVI
rose .... AINO
sake-like wine ... SHOCHU
salmon .... MASU
salad plant .... UDO
samurai's code .. BUSHIDO
sash .... OBI
sauce .... UDO
screen .... SHOVI, BYOBU
scroll ...... KAKEMONO
sculptress ... (YOKO) ONO
seal, business .... HANKO
seaport .... KOBE, MOJI, SAKATA, NAGASKI, KURE, TOYAMA, YOKOHAMA, OTARU
seaweed .... NORI
seaweed food .... KOMBU, KOBU
sect .... ZEN

self-defense forces ...... JIEITAI
self-defense system ...... JUDO, KARATE, JUJITSU, JUJUTSU
ship .... MARU
shoe .... GETA
shogun .. GENERALISSIMO, TYCOON
shoot, edible ...... UDO
shrine ..... OYAMA-ZUMI
shrub .... QUINCE, JAPONICA
signature stamp .. HANKO
slang .... NIP
sliding door .... FUSUMA
social reformer .... KAGAWA
sock .... TABO, TABI
song .... UTA
spirit .... GANBARO
spruce .... YEDDO
stamp .... HANKO
statesman .... GENRO, ITO, TANAKA
stew .... CHANKO
strait .... TSUSHIMA
straw cape .... MINO
street, famed ..... GINZA
style of painting ... KANO
suicide .... SEPPUKU, HARAKIRI, HARI-KARI
suicide attack .... KAMIKAZE
sun tree .... HINOKI
sword .... CAT(T)AN, KATANA
syndicate ...... ZAIBATSU
temple gate .... TORII
tidal wave ...... TSUNAMI
teacher .... SENSEI
temple .... PAGODA
10,000 years .... BANZAI
title .... KAMI
town .... TOI, MACHI
tree .... KIRI, LOQUAT, GINGKO, SUGI, HINOKI
umbrella ..... AMA-GASA
varnish .... RHUS
vegetable ... UDO, GOBO
vehicle, man-drawn ..... RICKSHA
verse ..... HOKKU, HAIKU
village .... MURA
volcano .... ASOSAN, FUJI(YAMA), ASAMA(YAMA), ADZUMAYAMA
walking stick .. WHANGEE
warehouse .... HONG
warplane .... ZERO
warrior .... SAMURAI
watermelon ..... SUIKA
way of the warrior ...... BUSHIDO
weight .... RIN, SHI, MO, CATTY
whisky .... SUNTORY, NIKKA
wild dog .... TANATE
wind .... MONSOON
wine ..... SHOCHU, SAKE
wisteria .... FUJI
wood oil .... TUNG
wooden shoes ..... GETA
wrestler's foot exercise ... SHIKO
wrestling .... SUMO
wrestling champion ..... YOKOZUNA
writer .... KAGAWA
writing .... KANA, KATAKANA
yeast .... KOJI
zaibatsu .... MITSUI, SUMITOMO, YASUDA
zither .... KOTO

jape ...... JOKE, JEST, MOCK, FOOL, TRICK, JEER, FRAUD, GIBE

japery .... RIBALDRY

Japheth's father .... NOAH
son .... GOMER

japonica .. QUINCE, CAMELLIA, SHRUB

jar .... GRATE, SHAKE, VIBRATE, BANGA, EWER, JUG, PELIKE, HYDRIA, RATTLE, SHOCK, JOG, JOLT, CLOCHE, DISCORD, CLASH, TURN, URN, CRUSE, AMPHORA, DISCONCERT, OLLA
bell-shaped ..... CLOCHE
clay stone .... STEEN
druggist's ..... GALLIPOT
earlike projection .. LUG
earthenware ... TERRINE, CROCK, GOGLET
like glass container ...... BEAKER
long-necked .... GOGLET, GURGLET
porcelain ...... POTICHE
table .... TERRINE
wide-mouthed ... OLLA, EWER
with moist sponge ...... HUMIDOR

jara .... PALM

jardiniere ... POT, URN, VASE, BOWL, STAND

jargon .... LINGO, SLANG, SHELTA, CANT, PATOIS, PATTER, ABRACADABRA, ZIRCON, DRIVEL, ARGOT, GIBBERISH, DIALECT

jargonel(le) .... PEAL

jarl .... EARL, CHIEFTAIN, NOBLEMAN

jarovize .... VERNALIZE

jasmine .... JESSAMY, JESSAMINE, BELA

Jason, father of ...... AESON
men of ..... ARGONAUTS
quest of .. GOLDEN FLEECE
ship of .... ARGO
sorceress who helped .... MEDEA
uncle of .... PELIAS
wife of .. CREUSA, MEDEA

jasper .. MICA, QUARTZ, PARK

jaundice .... ICTERUS, PREJUDICE
cause of .... ENVY, JEALOUSY
remedy .... ICTERIC

jaundiced ... YELLOW, BIASED, PREJUDICED

jaunt .... EXCURSION, (SIDE) TRIP, SALLY

jaunty .... AIRY, DAPPER, SPRUCE, RAKISH, DEBONAIR(E), STYLISH, CHIC, PERKY, COCKY, MODISH

Java .... CHICKEN, COFFEE, ISLAND, HOOD
capital of ..... JAKARTA

Javanese ...... INDONESIAN, SUNDANESE
almond .... KANARI
badger ... RATEL, TELEDU
bat .... KALON
burrowing animal ...... TELEDU
carriage .... SADO
city .... SEMARANG, BANDUNG, BANDOENG
civet ..... RASSE, DEDES
cotton .... KAPOK
language ... KAWI, KAVI
man .. PITHECANTHROPUS
measure .... PALEN
mountain .... AMAT
ox .... BANTENG
pepper .... CUBEB
plum .. JAMAN, JAMBOOL, LOMBOY
port .... TEGAL
resin .... BENZOIN
rhinoceros ...... BADAK
silk .... IKAT
skunk .... TELEDU
sparrow ...... RICEBIRD
tree ...... UPAS, KAPOK, ANTIAR(IN)
upas .... ANTIAR
village .... DESSA
volcano .... SEMERU, RAUN, GEDE
weight ..... TALI, AMAT

javelin .... LANCE, DART, ASSEGAI, SPEAR, SHAFT, JER(R)EED, JER(R)ID, PILUM
throwing device .... AMENTA
with a line .... HURLBAT, HARPOON

jaw ... MAW, CHAP, MANDIBLE, JOWL, CHOP, CHAT
angle of .... GONION
combining form .... GNATHOUS
cover .... GUM(s)
device with .... VISE
flesh .... GILL
lower .... MANDIBLE, GONION, CHIN
muscle .... MASSETER
of the .... GNATHIC
slang ..... TALK, SCOLD
upper .... MAXILLA
without ..... AGNATHIC

jawbone ..... JOWL, MAXILLA

jawbreaker .... CANDY
in boxing .... HAYMAKER

jay ..... CROW, PIE, JACKSON, JOIN, CHATTERBOX

bird like a ..... MOTMOT
talk .... CHATTER
Jayhawk state .... KANSAS
jazz ..... SWING, RAG(TIME), BOOGIEWOOGIE (BE)POP
composer .... (DUKE) ELLINGTON
dance .... SHIMMY
ensemble .... COMBO
fan .. HEPCAT, JITTERBUG, HIPSTER
fan jargon .... JIVE
melodic phrase .... RIFF, LICK
music .... SWING
up .... ENLIVEN
jealous .... ENVIOUS, GREEN(EYED)
Jeanneret, architect .... (LE) CORBUSIER
jeans .... OVERALLS, TROUSERS, LEVIS, DENIMS
jeep .... PEEP
jeer ... TAUNT, FLOUT, SNEER, SARCASM, GIRD, JIBE, MOCK, SCOFF, GIBE, JEST, BOO, JAPE, DERIDE
jeers .... TACKLE
Jeeves, creator of .... WODEHOUSE
position of ..... BUTLER
Jefferson's (President) home .. MONTICELLO
Jeffries, prize-fighter .... JIM
Jehol .... CHENGTEH
Jehovah .... (THE) LORD, YAHWE(H), GOD, JAH, YAHVE(H)
prophet of .... ELIAS
Jehovah's Witnesses founder .. RUSSELL
jejune ..... ARID, BANAL, DRY, STALE, BARREN, DULL, FLAT, INSIPID
Jekyll's (Dr.) alter ego .... (MR.) HYDE
jell ...... CRYSTALLIZE, SET, CONGEAL, SOLIDIFY
jellied gasoline ...... NAPALM
jelly ...... ASPIC, PRESERVES, JAM, DESSERT, SPREAD
animal .... GELATINE
bean .... CANDY
delicacy .... ASPIC
fruit .... JAM, GUAVA
ingredient .... PECTIN
like candy .... PASTE
like substance ...... GEL, GELATIN, COLLOID
material .... CURRANT
meat juice .... ASPIC
petroleum .... VASELINE
tomato juice ...... ASPIC
vegetable .... PECTIN
jellybean .... CANDY
jellyfish .... HYDROZOAN, MEDUSA, PLANOBLAST, QUARL, ACALEPH(E)
disk .... PILEUS
like a .... MEDUOID
stinging cell .... NEMATOCYST
jellyroll .... CAKE
jennet ....ASS, DONKEY, HORSE
Jenny, singer .... LIND, WREN
jeopardize .... IMPERIL, ENDANGER
jeopardy ...... HAZARD, RISK, PERIL, DANGER
jerboa ... GERBIL(LE), RODENT
jeremiad .... TALE, WOE, LAMENT(ATION)
Jeremiah's scribe .... BARUCH
Jerez .... XERES
Jericho's betrayer .... RAHAB
jerk ... TWITCH, FLIP, TWEAK, TWIST, PUSH, SODA MAN, MEAT, YANK, BOB, HITCH, BEEF
jerked beef .... CHARQUI
jerkin .... JACKET, VEST, (WAIST)COAT
jerkwater ...... TRAIN, SMALL
Jerry .... GERMAN, HUN
Jersey ..... CATTLE, SWEATER, CLOTH, SHIRT, SINGLET
Jerusalem ...... (HOLY) CITY, ARIEL
artichoke ... SUNFLOWER, TUBER, GIROSOL, GIRASOL(E)
captor of .... SALADIN
hill .... ZION, SION
mosque .... OMAR
oak .... AMBROSE
pool .... BETHESDA
ravine .... KEDRON
ridge .... OLIVET
spring .... SILOAM
stream .... KEDRON
theater .... KHAN
thorn tree .... RETAMA
Jespersen's language ..... IDO
jess .... STRAP, LEASH
user of ...... FALCON(ER)
jessamine .... JASMINE
jest .... JAPE, WAGGERY, BADINAGE, RAILLERY, QUIP, TRIFLE, WIT, JIBE, TAUNT, JOKE, WITTICISM, RIDICULE, FUN, JEER, MOCK, BANTER, SALLY
jester ..... BUFFOON, CLOWN, MIME, WAG, ZANY, JOKER, FOOL
ancient .... GOLIARD
cap of .... COXCOMB, COCKSCOMB
garment of ..... MOTLEY
wandering ..... GOLIARD
Jesuit .... CASUIST, SCHEMER
order, founder of .... LOYOLA
saint .... REGIS
Jesus ..... SAVIO(U)R, LOGOS
agony and sufferings .... PASSION
brother of .. JUDAS, JAMES
Christ, ____ SUPERSTAR
life's event ..... MYSTERY
monogram .... IHS
of ____ ..... NAZARETH
sayings of ...... LOGIA
jet ... SPURT, EBON(Y), SQUIRT, RAVEN, STREAM, GUSH, SPOUT, NOZZLE, BLACK, LIGNITE, SPRAY
engine ...... ATHODYD, TURBO PROP
fuel .... HYDRAZINE
plane ... SABRE, SCORPION
jetsam .... LIGAN, LAGAN, LAGEND, JETTISON
jettison .... JETSAM, DISCARD
jetty .... MOLE, BLACK, STARLING, PIER, WHARF
jeu .... DIVERSION, GAME
de mots .... PUN
d'esprit ..... WITTICISM
jeune fille .... GIRL
Jew ..... ISRAELITE, HEBREW, JUDEAN, TOBIT, SEMITE
born in Israel ..... SABRA
bread .... MATZOS, MATZOTH
legendary .... GOLEM
not a .... GENTILE, GOY(IM), GOI
Portuguese.. SHEPHARDIM
pseudo-christian .... MARRANO
Shakespearean ... TUBAL, ISAAC
Spanish .... SHEPHARDIM
jewel .... BRILLIANT, GEM, NAIF, STONE, BIJOU, OPAL, TRINKET
Biblical ...... BDELLIUM
setting ..... BEZEL, PAVE, MOUNT(ING)
jeweler's magnifying glass .... LOUPE
weight .... KARAT, CARAT
jewelry .... BROOCH, PIN, QUOIN, JEWELS, BIJOUTERIE
artificial .... PASTE, STRASS
cheap .... PASTE
expert .... APPRAISER
item ..... PIN, (EAR)RING, PENDANT, BROOCH, DIADEM, TIARA, NECKLACE, BRACELET, TRINKET
making material .... TOMBAC(K), OROIDE, ORMOLU, CORUNDUM, TOPAZ, AMETHYST
set of .... PARURE
jewels, adorn with ..... BEGEM
jewelweed .... CELANDINE, IMPATIENS
Jewett, writer .... SARAH (ORNE)
jewfish ..... (SEA)BASS, MERO, TARPON
Jewish ... HEBREW, YIDDISH, JUDEAN, JUDAIC
ascetic .... ESSENE
battle trumpet .. SHOFAR, SHOPHAR
benediction ..... SHEMA
bread .... MATZOS, MATZOTH
breastplate gem .. LIGURE, SARDIUS
bride .... KALLAH
calendar month .. TISHRI,

CHESHVAN, KISLEV, TEBET, SHEBAT, ADAR, NISAN, IYAR, (ZIF), SIVAN, TAMMUZ, AB, ELUL, ABIB
cantor ...... CHAZ(Z)AN
captive .... MESHACH, ABEDNEGO, SHADRACH
Christians .... DIASPORA
commentaries on Scriptures ... MIDRASH
council/court .... SANHEDRIN
day .... YOM
Day of Atonement ...... YOM KIPPUR
demon ...... ASMODEUS
evil spirit .... ASMODEUS
family of patriots .... MACCABEES
Feast of Lots ..... PURIM
festival ... SEDER, PURIM
Festival of lights .... HANUKKAH
high priest ... ELI, EZRA
holiday .... YOM KIPPUR, PASSOVER, SUKKOTH, HANUKKAH, PURIM, PESACH, SABUOTH, CHANUKAH, SUCCOS
holy of holies ... ORACLE
language ...... YIDDISH
law .... TALMUD, TORAH
liturgy's first word ...... SHEMA
living place ..... GHETTO
marriage broker .... SCHATCHEN
month, extra .... VEADAR
mystic .... ESSENE
New Year .... ROSH HASHANA
occult philosophy .... CABALA
Passover .... PESACH
Pentecost ..... SABUOTH
people .... ZION, ISRAEL, SION
place for worship .... SYNAGOGUE
prayer book ... MAHZOR, SIDDUR
priest's girdle ..... ABNET
priest's headdress .... MITRE, MITER
priest's vestment .. EPHOD
quarter .... GHETTO
ram's horn ...... SHOFAR
rebel in Jerusalem .... ZEALOT
religion .... JUDAISM
religious philosophy ..... CABALA
religious service .. HALLEL
scarf .... ZIZITH
scholar .... RAB(BI)
school .... YESHIVA, CHEDER
scribe .... MASORITE, MASORETE
sect member .. PHARISEE, SADDUCEE
seminary ...... YESHIVA
shawl .... ZIZITH
skullcap .... YAMILKE
slang .... YIDDISH
tabernacle wood .... SHITTIM
tassels .... ZIZITH
teacher .... RAB(BI), SCRIBE
temple builder ... MICAH
title of honor ..... GAON, RAB
trumpet ...... SHOPHAR, SHOFAR
undergarment .. TALLITH
vestment .... EPHOD
weight .... GERAH, OMER

Jews' dispersion ... DIASPORA
cloak .... GABERDINE
evensong ...... MINHAN
harp ...... CREMBALUM
massacre .... POGROM
of the........... JUDAIC
parchment on doorpost .. MEZUZA(H)
savior .... MORDECAI
section of city ... GHETTO

Jezebel .... VIRAGO
describing .... EVIL, WICKED
husband of ...... AHAB
victim of .... NABOTH

jib .... BALK, BOOM, SAIL, SIDLE, SHY, START, SPAR
boom's stay .... MARTINGAL(E)

jibe ..... AGREE, HARMONIZE, JEST, JEER, SCOFF, TAUNT, FIT, RIB

jiffy .... INSTANT, TRICE, MOMENT, SECOND

jig .... DANCE, FISHHOOK, GIGUE

jigger ... FLEA, CHIGOE, TICK, CUP, GADGET, SAIL, TACKLE

jiggle ... ROCK, JERK, TEETER

jihad ... CRUSADE, HOLY WAR, DEFENSE

jill .... SWEETHEART, WOMAN, GIRL

Jim Crow .... NEGRO

jimjams .... DELIRIUM, JITTERS

jimmy ..... (CROW)BAR, PRY, LEVER, JACK
Valentine, of fiction ..... THIEF, SAFE-CRACKER

jimson weed .... DATURA, STINKWEED, THORN APPLE

jingal ..... CANNON, MUSKET

jingle .... CLINK, VERSE, TINKLE, DOGGEREL

jingo .... CHAUVINIST, RADICAL, (SUPER)PATRIOT, MILITARIST, WARRIOR

jingoism .... MILITARISM

jink .... ELUDING

jinks .... HORSEPLAY, PRANKS

jinn(i) ....GENIE, DEMON

jinrikisha .... RICKSHA(W)

Jinsen .... CHEMULPHO, SEAPORT

jinx .... HEX, HOODOO, EVIL EYE, BAD LUCK

personification of .... JONAH

jipjapa hat .... PANAMA

jitney .... NICKEL, BUS

jitter .... FIDGET

jitters ...... DITHERS, NERVES, NERVOUSNESS, HYSTERIA
the ... JIMJAMS, FIDGETS, (BIG)SCARE, WILLIES, CREEPS

jittery .... EDGY, JUMPY, NERVOUS, HECTIC, SCARED

jiujutsu .... JUDO

jivatma .... ATMAN, EGO

jive .... JAZZ

jo(e) .... SWEETHEART

Joan of Arc, name for .... PUCELLE
place of execution ...... ROUEN
scene of triumph .... ORLEANS

Joan's spouse (in a song) ...... DARBY

job .... CHORE, CHARE, DUTY, WORK, POSITION, STINT, TASK
do inferior ...... SCAMP
easy ..... SNAP, WHISTLE, SINECURE
kind of .... SINECURE, PARTTIME
opening ...... VACANCY

Job's comforter ..... BILDAD, ELIHU, ELIPHAZ, ZOPHAR
tears .... GRASS, COIX

jockette .... TESTA, RUBIN, CRUMP, KUSNER

jockey ..... SLOAN, ARCARO, DODSON, HARTACK, BAEZA, SHOEMAKER, BROOKS, SANDE, CHEAT, SWINDLE, RIDER, MANEUVER
uniform .... SILKS, COLORS
woman .... KUSNER, RUBIN, CRUMP

jocko .... CHIMP(ANZEE), MONKEY

jocose .... MERRY, DROLL, PLAYFUL, FACETIOUS, HUMOROUS, WITTY

jocular ... JESTING, WAGGISH, WITTY, HUMOROUS, FACETIOUS

jocund ... GAY, GENIAL, AIRY, MERRY

Jodhpur .... MARWAR

jodhpurs .... BREECHES

Joe .... SWEETHEART
pye weed ... EUPATORIUM

joey .... PAL, KANGAROO

jog .... REMIND, TROT, PROJECTION

John ____, actor .... BARRYMORE, GILBERT PAYNE, IRELAND
Birch society founder .... WELCH
Brown's Body" author ... BENET
Bull .... ENGLAND, ENGLISHMAN

Dory .... FISH
Dos ___ .... PASSOS
father of disciple ....
ZEBEDEE
Hancock ..... SIGNATURE
Irish .... IAN
Mannering ...... BARON
Smith's savior ....
POCAHONTAS
johnnie ... LOTHARIO, DANDY, FOP, MAN, BOY
Johnny jumper ...... VIOLET, PANSY
johnnycake .... HOECAKE, PONE, CORN BREAD
Johnson, (Mrs.) hunter .. OSA
Samuel birthplace ...... LICHFIELD
U.S. President .. ANDREW, LYNDON
join ... YOKE, MERGE, RABBET, ENROLL, ENLIST, MORTISE, LOCK, COALESCE, MEET, WELD, SPLICE, SOLDER, CONNECT, FASTEN, UNITE, ACCOMPANY, COMBINE, LINK, MELD
corners ... MITER, MITRE
in marriage ...... SPLICE
the colors .... ENLIST
joiner ... FOLLOWER, ENLISTEE
joint ...... TENON, HIP, SEAM, LINK, HINGE, TOGGLE, SCARF, RABBET, ELBOW, CONCURRENT, NEXUS, JUNCTURE, MUTUAL
arm's .... WRIST, ELBOW
carpal .... KNEE
carpenter's ...... MITER, MITRE
cavity .... BURSA
deposit .... TOPHUS
door's .... HINGE
finger .... KNUCKLE
fluid .... SEROSITY
grass .... CULM
in marriage ...... SPLICE
L-shaped .... ELL
leg's .... KNEE
mutton .... HAUNCH
of stem ..... KNOT, NODE
out of ...... DISLOCATED
piping .... ELL
put out of .... LUXATE, DISLOCATE
rheumatic pain ....
LUMBAGO
right angled .... ELL
rule .... CONDOMINIUM
slang ... SALOON, HOUSE, RESTAURANT, REEFER, DIVE
stem .... NODE
tighten .... STEM
tubing .... ELL
venison .... HAUNCH
jointly .... TOGETHER, HAND IN HAND
joke ... JOSH, QUIP, SALLY, JAPE, TWIT, PUN, PRANK, WHEEZE, JEST, WAGGERY, WISECRACK, GAG, DIDO, SPOOF, KID, WITTICISM, RIB, HOAX
said as a .... JOCULAR
joker .... CLOWN, JESTER, FLOP, GAG, CUTUP, CARD, WAG, WIT, BUFFOON, FARCEUR
in a bill, etc. .... RIDER
joking ..... JOCOSE, JESTING, FACETIOUS
jollity ... FUN, GAIETY, MIRTH
jolly .... BUXOM, GAY, MERRY, CONVIVIAL, VERY, JOVIAL, BOAT, YAWL
Jolson, Al .... ASA
jolt ...... SHAKE, JAR, JERK, SHOCK, SURPRISE, BUMP, JOUNCE, BOUNCE
Jonah (Jonas) ..... PROPHET
dislikers of ..... SAILORS
swallower of .... WHALE
to all people .. BAD LUCK, JINX
Jonathan .... APPLE
father of .... SAUL
Jones, bandleader ..... SPIKE
spirit of sea ...... DAVY
jongleur .... MINSTREL
jonquil .... NARCISSUS
plant like ..... DAFFODIL
Joplin, pop singer ..... JANIS
Joppa .... JAPPA
Jordan .... POT, RIVER, KINGDOM
ancient name .... EDOM, MOAB
capital of .... AMMAN
city .... AMMAN, JERUSALEM, PETRA, JERICHO
king .... HUSSEIN
language .... ARABIC
monetary unit ... DINAR
mountain .... GILEAD
port .... AQABA
prime minister ... JUMAA
valley .... GHOR
village .... JERICHN
Joseph .... HABIT
native place of ....
ARIMATHEA
parent of .... JACOB
son of .... MANASSEH
wife of .... MARY
josh .... JEST, BADINAGE, BANTER, KID, RIDICULE, TEASE, RIB, RAG
Joshua, people of .. ISRAELITES
predecessor of .... MOSES
tree .... YUCCA
Josip Broz ... TITO, DICTATOR
joss .... IDOL
house .... TEMPLE
jostle .. ELBOW, RUSH, NUDGE, SHOVE, PUSH, BUFFET, HUSTLE, MAUL
jot .... BIT, NOTE, TITTLE, MINIM, MITE, PARTICLE, MOTE, POINT, WHIT, SPECK, IOTA
jota .... DANCE
jotting .... MEMO, NOTE
Jotun(n) .... GIANT
joule, part of .... ERG
jounce .... JOLT, BOUNCE, SHAKE
journal ..... RECORD, DIARY, EPHEMERIS, REGISTER, PAPER, LOGBOOK, MAGAZINE, PERIODICAL, NEWSPAPER, DAYBOOK, ANNALS, TRUNNION
journalism .... PRESS
journalist .... EDITOR, REPORTER, CORRESPONDENT, DIARIST, NEWSPAPERMAN, PUBLICIST, SCRIBE, NEWSMAN
budding ...... COPY BOY, CUB (REPORTER)
kind of .... LEGMAN, STRINGER
journey ... TREK, FARE, TOUR, TRIP, TRAVEL, HIKE, JUNKET, SAFARI, RUN
extended ..... ODYSSEY, TOUR
for adventure .... QUEST
forced .... HEGIRA, FLIGHT, EXODUS
in circuit .... EYRE
of a .... VIATIC(AL)
of solon abroad .. JUNKET
on foot .... HIKE, TRAMP
over snow .... MUSH
stage of .... LEG
stopping place ... STAGE, INN
to shrine ... PILGRIMAGE
water .... VOYAGE, PASSAGE
journeyman .... WORKER, JOBBER
joust .... COMBAT, TILT, TOURNAMENT, TOURNEY, BOUT
Jove .... JUPITER
jovial ... GAY, GENIAL, JOLLY, MERRY
friar .... TUCK
jowl .... CHAP, CHEEK, JAW(BONE), CHOP, DEWLAP, WATTLE
joy .... BLISS, ECSTASY, GLEE, DELIGHT, PLEASURE, RAPTURE
ride, of a sort ...... SPIN
song of .. CAROL, P(A)EAN
joyful and triumphant ....
JUBILANT
joyous .... MERRY, BLITHE, ELATED, GAY, GLAD, FESTAL, FESTIVE, RIANT
JP, part of .. JUSTICE, PEACE, JET, PROPULSION
jube .... LOFT, GALLERY
jubilate .... EXULT
juca ...... CASSAVA, MANIOC
Judah, city of .... AMAM, ENAM, ADAR
king of ... ADAD, AMON, AHAZ, OBIJAH, JOSIAH, JOSIAS, ASA, MANASSEH
parent of .... JACOB
son ..... ONAM, ER, ZARA
tree .... REDBUD
Judaism .... HEBRAISM

commandment .... MITSVAH, MITZVAH
convert to .... GER
hymn of praise .. KADDISH
mourners' prayer .... KADDISH
scriptures ...... TORA(H)
Judas ... BETRAYER, TRAITOR, ISCARIOT
brother of .. JESUS, JAMES
replacement .. MATTHIAS
tree .... REDBUD
Judea procurator .... PILATE
judge ..... (A)EDILE, CRITIC, TRY, ARBITRATOR, SETTLE, ARBITER, UMPIRE, DEEM, RATE, REFEREE, CRITICIZE
Athenian .... DICAST
of lower world .. AEACUS, MINOS, RHADAMANTHUS
quality/worth .. APPRAISE, EVALUATE, RATE
judge's assistant ... ASSESSOR, MASTER
bench ... BANC, TRIBUNAL
challenge .... RECUSE
chamber .... CAMERA
court .... BENCH
decision ...... VERDICT, SENTENCE
entry after verdict .... POSTEA
jurisdiction .. JUDICATURE
lower rank ...... PUISNE
Moslem .... CADI, HAKIM
order ... WRIT, SUBPOENA, INJUNCTION
position/rank ... ERMINE
robe .... GOWN
room .... CHAMBER
seat ...... BENCH, BANC
Spanish .... ALCALDE
symbol of authority ..... MACE, GAVEL
judges collectively .... BENCH
said of .... PUISNE
judgment ...... DOOM, SENSE, ARRET, DECISION, OPINION, SENTENCE, VERDICT, AWARD, VIEW
against person .... IN PERSONAM
against property .. IN REM
await .... PEND
Day .... DOOM(SDAY)
suspension of ... EPOCHE
judicatory .. COURT, TRIBUNAL
judicial assembly ..... COURT
inquiry .... INQUEST
order .... WRIT
judicious ..... WISE, POLITIC, PRUDENT, WISE
judo ..... JUJITSU, J(I)UJUTSU
Judy, (puppet) husband of .... PUNCH
jug .. RANTER, EWER, FLAGON, THERMOS, TOBY
slang .... JAIL
jugal .... MALAR
jugate .... PAIRED
Juggernaut .... KRISHNA
incarnation .... VISHNU
juggle .... MANIPULATE, WANGLE, RIG
juggler .... MANIPULATOR, CHEATER
jugulate .... STRANGLE
juice .... ESSENCE, LIQUID, FLUID, JUS, SAP, SURA, MUST, STUM, RHOB, LIQUOR, WINE, AL
meat ... GRAVY, DRIPPING
plant/tree .. SAP, MANNA, CHICLE, LATEX
slang ...... ELECTRICITY, GAS(OLINE), OIL
juicy .... PIQUANT, RACY, SUCCULENT, SPICY
Juilliard school degree: abbr. .. DMUS
specialty .... MUSIC
jujitsu (jiujutsu) .... JUDO
juju ... FETISH, TABOO, CHARM
jujube ..... LOZENGE, JELLY, ELB, BER
juke box ...... PHONOGRAPH
julep .... DRINK
ingredient ...... BRANDY, MINT, SIRUP
Jules Verne's captain .. NEMO
vessel .... NAUTILUS
Juliana's (Queen) domain .... NETHERLANDS
house .... ORANGE
mother .... WILHELMINA
people .... DUTCH
spouse ...... BERNHARD
julienne .... SOUP
Juliet's confessor .... (FRIAR) LAURENCE
cousin .... TYBALT
family .... CAPULET
love .... ROMEO
suitor .... PARIS
July 15, Roman calendar ..... IDES, IDIBUS, IDUS
4th day ... INDEPENDENCE
7th day of ...... NONES, NONAS, NONIS
jumble ... MEDLEY, MIX, MESS, FARRAGO, MISHMASH, CLUTTER, LITTER, HASH, COOKY, MUDDLE, CONFUSION, PI(E)
jumbled type .... PI(E)
jumbo .... LARGE, ELEPHANT
jump ..... HOP, LEAP, START, VAULT, BUCK, SPRING, BOUNCE, BOB, BOUND, SKIP
about ... FRISK, PRANCE
in music .... SALTO
playful .... CAVORT, CAPER, PRANCE, FRISK
jumper .... SLED, PAWL, DELIVERY BOY, JACKET, ROMPER, BLOUSE
jumping ... SALTANT, LEAPING, SALTATION
amphibian .... FROG, TOAD
animal ...... KANGAROO, JERBOA, GOAT
bean dweller ..... LARVA
dance .... JIG
insect .... FLEA, LOCUST, GRASSHOPPER
stick .... POGO
jumpy ...... EDGY, NERVOUS, TENSE, SKITTISH
junco ..... FINCH, SNOWBIRD
junction .... CROSSING, UNION, MEETING
line .... SEAM
juncture ...... CRISIS, POINT, JOINT
June bug ...... DOR, BEETLE, FIGEATER
event .... WEDDING, MARRIAGE
13, Roman calendar ..... IDES
21 .... SOLSTICE
juneberry .... SHADBLOW, SHADBUSH
jungfrau .... ALPS
jungle .... WILDERNESS
Book's wolf ...... AKELA
fever .... MALARIA
junior .... CADET, PUISNE, YOUNGER
French .... FILS
leaguer .... DEB
weekly "take" of .... ALLOWANCE
juniper ...... CEDAR, RETEM, GORSE, SAVIN(E), SHRUB, EZEL, CADE, HACKMATAK
junk ... CABLE, ROPE, TRASH, RUBBISH, DISCARD, SCRAP, SHIP, SOMA
junker .... PRUSSIAN, GERMAN
junket .... FEAST, PICNIC, EXCURSION
junkie: sl. .... ADDICT, (DOPE) FIEND
junkman .... SCRAPPER
Juno .... HERA, GODDESS
husband of .... JUPITER
messenger of .... IRIS
junta .... COUNCIL, MEETING, ASSEMBLY
junto ...... FACTION, CLIQUE, CABAL
Jupiter ... ZEUS, PLANET, JOVE
consort of ... JUNO, HERA
daughter of ... MINERVA, HEBE
Egyptian .... AMMON
giver of rain .... PLUVIUS
moon of ... IO, EUROPA, CALLISTO, GANYMEDE
nurse of .... GOAT
son of ... ARCAS, CASTER, TANTALUS, HERMES, HEPHAETUS
temple .... CAPITOL
jupon .... JACKET, TUNIC
jura .... LAW
jural .... LEGAL
jurant .... SWEARING
Jurassic, strata below .. TRIAS
system strata ...... LIAS
jurel .... FISH, RUNNER
jurisdiction ...... SOKE, SOC, VENUE, SPHERE, DOMAIN
bishop's .... SEE
jurisprudence .... LAW
jurist .... TANEY, HAND
juror ... TALESMAN, VENIREMAN

challenge a ...... RECUSE
guard of .... BAILIFF
jurors collectively ..... PANEL
one of the .... POLL
jury .... PANEL
finding of ...... VERDICT
head .... FOREMAN
illegally influence ....
EMBRACE
kind of .... GRAND
member ..... TALESMAN
summons to .... VENIRE
juryman ... JUROR, TALESMAN
jus ...... JUICE, GRAVY, LAW
just .... FAIR, RIGHTEOUS,
EQUITABLE, IMPARTIAL,
UPRIGHT, ONLY, BARELY,
MORAL, SIMPLY
begun .... INCHOATE
clear of bottom ....
AWEIGH, ATRIP
right .... JAKE
think! .... IMAGINE
justice .... DOOM, EQUITY,
RIGHT, FAIRNESS, JUDGE
Supreme Court ... CHASE,
VINSON, WARREN,
FORTAS, STONE,
HUGHES, MARSHALL,
TAFT, TANEY,
CARDOZO, JAY
justification .... DEFENSE,
VINDICATION, EXCUSE,
EXPLANATION, WARRANT
justify ... EXCUSE, WARRANT,
ACQUIT, ABSOLVE,
VINDICATE
jut .... ABUT, PROJECT,
PROTRUDE, STICK OUT,
OVERHANG
jute .... FIBER, PLANT
chief .... HENGIST
cloth .... SACKING,
GUNNY
product .... BURLAP,
(GUNNY)SACK, MAT,
ROPE
refuse ..... HURDS, TOW
Jutland seaport ..... AARHUS
Jutlander .... DANE
jutting land ..... HEADLAND,
PROMONTORY, NESS, CAPE
rock .... CRAG, TOR
jutty ..... JETTY, PIER, MOLE
Juvenal .... POET, SATIRIST
juvenile ... YOUTHFUL, YOUNG,
CHILD, INFANTILE
hero .... ROLLO
story writer ..... MILNE,
OUIDA, RAMEE, SEUSS

K

K, Greek .... KAPPA
Hebrew .... KAPH
in assaying ...... CARAT,
KARAT
chemistry .... KALIUM,
POTASSIUM
chess .... KING
electricity .... CAPACITY
mathematics ....
CONSTANT
meteorology .... SMOKE
nautical usage .... KNOT
ka .... SOUL
kabobs .... (ROAST)MEAT
kaddish .... DOXOLOGY,
HYMN, PRAYER
kadi ..... JUDGE, MAGISTRATE
Kaffir ...... INFIDEL, BANTU,
SORGHUM, FODDER, CORN
language .... XOSA
tribe .... ZULU
war club .... KIRI
warriors .... IMPI
kago ..... PALANQUIN, LITTER
kail .... KALE, COLE
kailyard .... GARDEN
kaiser ... WILHELM, EMPEROR
Biblical .... NOAH
kaka(po) .... PARROT
kakemono .... SCROLL,
HANGING
kaki .... PERSIMMON
kala-azar ...... BLACKFEVER
Kalahari ... DESERT, PLATEAU
nomad .... BUSHMAN
kale ... BORECOLE, CABBAGE,
COLE(WORT), BROCCOLI,
COLLARD, GREENS, BROTH
slang .... MONEY
kaleyard .... GARDEN
kali ... GLASSWORT, SALTWORT
by-product .... SODA ASH
Kalinin .... TVER
Kaliningrad .... KONIGSBERG
kalinite .... ALUM
Kallikaks, the .... JUKES
kalmuck .. MONGOL, ELEUT(H)
kalong .... BAT
kalpak .... CAP
kamala .... POWDER
kame .... HILL, RIDGE
kamerad .... COMRADE
kamsin .... WIND
kanae .... MULLET
kanaka .... HAWAIIAN
kanari .... ALMOND
kangaroo .... WALLAROO,
MACROPODIAN, MARSUPIAL,
ROO, WOLABA, WOLARU,
WALLABY
female .... DOE, GIN
male .... BOOMER
pouch .... MARSUPIUM
rat .... POTOROO
young .... JOEY
Kansan .... JAYHAWKER
famous ..... EISENHOWER
Kansas, capital of ... TOPEKA
city ... TOPEKA, SALINA,
WICHITA, EMPORIA,
ABILENE
guerrilla .... JAYHAWKER
native ...... JAYHAWKER
river .... OSAGE
state animal ... BUFFALO
state bird .... LARK
state flower .. SUNFLOWER
state tree .. COTTONWOOD
Kansu, capital of ... LANCHOW
kantar ..... HUNDREDWEIGHT
kaoliang .... SORGHUM
kaolin(e) .. CLAY, LITHOMARGE
kaph in Greek .... KAPPA
kapok .... CEIBA, COTTON
kaput ..... RUINED, DEFEATED,
LOST, DONE FOR
Kara Kum .... DESERT
Karachi is its capital .... SIND
Karafuto .... SAKHALIN
karakul ... SHEEP, FUR, OVINE
Karelian .... FINN
lake ..... SEG, LADOGA
Karloff, actor .... BORIS
Karlovy Vary ..... KARLSBAD,
CARLSBAD
karma .... DESTINY, FATE
Karnak city .... THEBES
feature .... TEMPLE
kar(r)oo .... TABLELAND
karyo, as comb. form ... NUT,
KERNEL
karyotin .... CHROMATIC
Kashmir, capital of ....
SRINAGAR
claimant of .... INDIA,
PAKISTAN
district .... LADAKH
pagoda .... CHORTEN
river .... JHELUM
wool .... CASHMERE
katabasis .... RETREAT
Katanga leader .... TSHOMBE
katchung .... PEANUT
Katherine, diminutive of ......
KIT(TY), KAY, KATE
Katmandu is capital of ....
NEPAL
native .... NEPALI
katydid kin..... GRASSHOPPER
kauri ..... PINE, WOOD, RESIN,
GUM
kava .... SHRUB, PEPPER,
DRINK, AVA
kayak .... CANOE, UMIAK
kayo .... KNOCKOUT
Kazak(h) .... KIRGHIZ
Kazan, movieman ...... ELIA
kea .... PARROT
favorite prey of ... SHEEP
Keats' name by Shelley ....
ADONAIS
keck .... RETCH, HEAVE,
BELCH, VOMIT
keddah .... TRAP
kèdge .... ANCHOR
keek .... PEEP, SPY
keel .... SHIP, RUDDLE,
LIGHTER, BARGE, CAREEN,
TILT, LIST, CARINA
like .... CARINAL
like structure .... CARINA
over ..... CAPSIZE, UPSET,
TURN OVER
part .... SKEG

shaped ...... CARINATE
without .... RATITE
Keeling Islands .... COCOS
keen .... ASTUTE, INCISIVE, SMART, TART, SNELL, GARE, GLEG, SUBTLE, SHARP, CUTTING, PIERCING, ACUTE, WAIL, DIRGE, EAGER, PUNGENT, PENETRATING, PERCEPTIVE, SHREWD, TRENCHANT
eyed animal .. LYNX, CAT
keenness .... ACIES, EDGE, ACUITY
of mind .... ACUMEN
keep ... TEND, GUARD, SAVE, DONJON, DETAIN, RETAIN, DEFEND, PRESERVE, (WITH)HOLD, CONCEAL, CUSTODY, FORT, STRONGHOLD, CASTLE, LIVELIHOOD, RESERVE
close to .... HUG
company ..... CONSORT, HOBNOB
from flying ..... GROUND
house for oneself .. BACH
out ..... EXCLUDE, BAR
tally ..... SCORE, RECORD
up .... CONTINUE, MAINTAIN
keeper .... GUARD(IAN), PROTECTOR, CUSTODIAN, CARETAKER
castle .... CONSTABLE
forest .. RANGER, WARDEN
fortress ...... CONSTABLE
game .... WARDEN
jail .. TURNKEY, WARDEN
museum ...... CURATOR
keepers, usually .... FINDERS, BROTHERS
keeping .... CUSTODY, CARE, CHARGE, OBSERVANCE
horses for hire ... LIVERY
keeps course .... CAPES
keepsake ...... RELIC, TOKEN, SOUVENIR, MEMENTO
keeve ..... TUB, VAT, KIVER, KEIR
kef .... HEMP, NARCOTIC
Kefauver, senator ..... ESTES
keg .... CADE, CASK, FIRKIN, TUN, VAT, BARREL
cork .... BUNG
of beer .... GROWLER
open a .... UNHEAD
stopper .... BUNG
water .... BREAKER
kegler .... BOWLER
Keijo .... SEOUL
keir .... VAT
keitloa .... RHINO(CEROS)
Kelantan capital .... KOTA BHARU
kelep .... ANT
Keller, Miss .... HELEN
keloid .... TUMOR
Kelly, performer .... EMMETT, GENE, PATSY
kelp ..... SEAWEED, WRACK, VARIC, ASH
derivative ...... IODINE
kelpie .... (WATER) SPIRIT
kelter ..... CONDITION, ORDER
Kemal, Turkish leader ...... ATATURK
Kemble, actress ...... FANNY
ken .... LORE, PRESCIENCE, DESCRY, SEE, RECOGNIZE, SIGHT
kench .... BOX, BIN
content of ... FISH, SKIN
Kennedy Space Center site ... CANAVERAL
kennel ..... DOGHOUSE, PACK, GUTTER, SEWER, DRAIN
sound ... YIP, BARK, YELP
keno, game like .... LOTTO, BINGO, BEANO
Kent county seat .. MAIDSTONE
resort/seaport .. MARGATE
Kentuckian .... LINCOLN
Kentucky capital .. FRANKFORT
city .... PADUCAH, COVINGTON, LEXINGTON, OWENSBORO
college .... BEREA
county .... OWEN, BOYD, TODD, LYON, HART, KNOX, PIKE
event .... DERBY
explorer .. JOLIET, BOONE
honorary title .. COLONEL
personage ..... COLONEL
pride of .... HORSES, WHISKY
state bird ..... CARDINAL
state flower .. GOLDENROD
state nickname .... BLUEGRASS
tobacco .... BURLEY
tourist attraction .... MAMMOTH CAVE
tree .... CHICOT
Kenya capital ...... NAIROBI
city... MOMBASA, NAIROBI
language .... HINDU, BANTU, SWAHILI
monetary unit .. SHILLING
Olympic champ .. KEINO, TEMU, BIWOTT
president ..... KENYATTA
seaport .... MOMBASA
secret society .. MAUMAU
Kenyatta, Kenya president .... JOMO
Keos .... ZEA
kepi .... CAP
Kepler, astronomer .... JOHANNES
keratinous .... HORNY
formation .. HAIR, HORN, NAIL
keratoid .. HORNY, HORNLIKE
keratosis .... WART
kerchief .... BABUSHKA, BANDAN(N)A, SCARF, MADRAS, CURCH
kerf ...... CUT(TING), NOTCH
Kerkyra .... CORFU
kermes .... DYE, OAK
kermess .... FAIR, CARNIVAL
kern(e) .... PEASANT, (FOOT)SOLDIER
kernel .... GIST, SEED, GRAIN, PIT, NUT(MEAT), NUCLEUS, BARREL, CORE, HEART, PITH, ESSENCE, CORN
combining form .. KARYO, CARYO
having .... NUCLEATE
kerosene .... OIL
source of .... COAL, PETROLEUM
Kerry ..... CATTLE, COUNTY
blue .... TERRIER
kersey .... CLOTH
kestrel .. FALCON, WINDHOVER
ketch .. JACK, SHIP, HANGMAN, YAWL
Levantine .... SAIC
ketchup ..... CATSUP, SAUCE
ketone .. ACETONE, BUTYRONE, IRONE, CARONE
ketosis, cause of ... DIABETES MELLITUS
Kett, comic strip's ..... ETTA
kettle ... BILLY, CA(U)LDRON, POT(HOLE), BOILER
coating inside .... SCALE
handle .... BAIL
in the South ...... SIROP
repairer .... TINKER
stand .... TRIVET
kettledrum .... TIMPANO, TIMPANI, AT(T)ABAL, NAKER, TIMBAL
cavalry .... ANACARA
player .... TIMPANIST
kevel .... CLEAT, PEG
key .... COTTER, CLAVIS, PIN, BOLT, WEDGE, PITCH, TONE, REEF, ISLE(T), CLEW, CODE, CAY, ISLAND, SOLUTION
blade of .... WEB
emergency .... PICK
false .... GLUT
filler .... ULLER
fruit .... SAMARA
instrument ..... MANUAL
locksmithing ..... WARD
part ..... BIT, PIN, STEM
pertaining to ..... TONAL
repairer ..... LOCKSMITH
shaped ... URDE, CLECHE
signature in music ...... SHARP, FLAT
substitute .... PICK
telegraph .... TAPPER
keyboard .... CLAVIER
instrument (musical) ... CELESTA, PIANO, ORGAN, SPINET, HARMONIUM, MELODEON, CLAVIER, CLAVICHORD, HARPSICHORD, VIRGINAL
machine ... LINO(TYPE), TYPEWRITER, TELETYPE, TELEX
shaped .... URDE
keyed up ...... AGOG, EAGER, EXCITED, TENSE
keyhole guard ...... TAPPET
ridge .... WARD

keynote ...... TONIC, THEME
sign .... ISON
keystone .. SAGITTA, SUPPORT, WEDGE
characters .... COPS
prop .... PIE
State ..... PENNSYLVANIA
state founder ...... PENN
keyway .... SLOT
khaki color .... DUN
khamsin .... WIND
khan .... INN, ALY, CARAVANSARY, AGA, CHAM
Khania .... CANEA
Khartoum is capital of .. SUDAN
khedah .... TRAP
khedive's estate .... DAIRA
Khmer .... CAMBODIAN
emperor ... JAYAVARMAN
temple ..... ANGKOR VAT
Khotan .... HOTIEN
Khrushchev, USSR premier ... NIKITA
Khufu .... CHEOPS
Kiangsi, capital of .... NANCHANG
Kiangsu, capital of .. NANKING
city .... SOOCHOW
kibblings .... BAIT
kibbutz .... SETTLEMENT
kibe .... CHILBLAIN
kibitz ..... MEDDLE, HORN IN
kibitzer .... SPECTATOR, MEDDLER, ONLOOKER
kibosh ...... NONSENSE, VETO, SQUELCH
kick ..... BOOT, CALCITRATE, KEVEL, RECOIL, GRUMBLE, COMPLAIN(T), SPURN, EXCITEMENT, OBJECT(ION), THRILL
in .... DIE, PAY
in football .. PUNT, HACK
off .... DIE, START
Kickapoo ...... ALGONQUIAN, INDIAN
kickback, usually ..... BRIBE, PAYOLA, REBATE
kickshaw .... TIDBIT, TRIFLE, TRINKET, GEWGAW, DELICACY, BAUBLE, TOY, FOOD
kickup .... ROW, FUSS
kid ..... BANTER, JOSH, JOKE, RIB, (Y)EANLING, GOAT, SUEDE, ANTELOPE, LEATHER, TEASE, DECEIVE, LAD
colloquial .... CHILD
prepared for slaughter ... FATLING
sailor's .... TUB
slang .... HOAX
undressed .... SUEDE
Kidd, Captain .... PIRATE, PRIVATEER
kidder .... TEASER
kidderminster .... CARPET
kiddy: colloq. .... CHILD
wear .... ROMPER
kidnap ..... ABDUCT, SNATCH, SHANGHAI
kidney ...... GLAND, CLASS, SORT, NEER
ailment remedy .... NEPHRITE
bean .... BON, HARICOT, PHASEL
combining form ... RENI, RENO, NEPHRO
concretion ...... GRAVEL
condition ..... NEPHRISM, NEPHROSIS
duct .... URETER
external layer ... CORTEX
of the .... RENAL, NEPHRITIC, NEPHRIC
protein .... RENIN
shaped .... RENIFORM
shaped fruit ... CASHEW
stone .... JADE, NEPHRITE
substance .... MEDULLA
tube .... URETER
kidskin parchment ... VELLUM
kier .... VAT
Kilauea, goddess of .... PELE
kilderkin ..... CASK, BARREL
Kilimanjaro peak ...... KIBO
kill .... BLAST, DISPATCH, LIQUIDATE, SLAY, DESTROY, RUIN, CANCEL, CHANNEL, STREAM, CREEK
bill .... VETO
by drowning ... NOYADE
by hanging .. STRING UP
by mob action ... LYNCH
by stoning ..... LAPIDATE
by suffocation ... BURKE
in printing ..... DELE(TE), CANCEL
in tennis .... SMASH
joy ...... WET BLANKET, SPOILSPORT
legally .... EXECUTE
unlawfully ..... MURDER, ASSASSINATE
Killarney land .... ERIN
killdeer ...... PLOVER, BIRD
killer .... SLAYER, MURDERER
hired ... BRAVO, ASSASSIN
of a god .... DEICIDE
political .... ASSASSIN
whale .... ORC(A), DOLPHIN, GRAMPUS
killick .... ANCHOR
killing .... CARNAGE, FATAL, DEADLY, SLAUGHTER
deliberate ...... MURDER
mass .... MASSACRE, BATTUE, PURGE, CARNAGE, POGROM, GENOCIDE, BUTCHERY
of fetus .... ABORTICIDE
of a king ..... REGICIDE
of old men ..... SENICIDE
political .... PURGE, ASSASSINATION
killock .... ANCHOR
Kilmer poem .... TREES
poet .... JOYCE
kiln .... O(A)ST, STOVE, OVEN, TILER(Y), FURNACE, DRYER, DRIER, LEER
kilograms, 100 ...... QUINTAL, CENTAL, CENTNER
1,000 .... MILLIER
kiloliter .... STERE
kilt ...... FILIBEG, PHILIBEG, TUCK, PLEAT, SKIRT
undergarment ... TREWS
kilting .... PLEATS
kiltie .... SCOT(SMAN)
Kim ____ .... O'HARA, NOVAK, HUNTER
friend of .... LAMA
kimono ...... DRESSING GOWN
sash .... OBI
kin .... FOLKS, FAMILY, RELATIVE(S), RELATED, SIB(S)
kind .... RACE, VARIETY, GENTLE, GENEROUS, BENIGN, ILK, SPECIES, CLASS, SORT, GENUS
in ...... GOODS, PRODUCE
of ... SOMEWHAT, ALMOST
of a ... ALIKE, MEDIOCRE
of this/that ... SUCH(LIKE)
kindergarten .. SCHOOL, CLASS
activity .... GAMES, EXERCISES
pioneer .... FROEBEL
kindle .... BURN, ROUSE, IGNITE, LIGHT, EXCITE, TIND, FIRE, SPUNK, LUNT
kindled .... LIT
kindling ..... PUNK, AMADOU
kindling brick .... BRIQUET(TE)
kindly ..... BENIGN, GENIAL, PLEASE
kindness .... GOOD WILL, LENITY, GRACE
kindred ... COGNATE, ALLIED, AKIN, BLOOD, KITH, TIE, SIB, KINSHIP, RELATIVES, FAMILY
kine .... CATTLE, COWS
king .... SOVEREIGN, ROI, REGULUS, PADISHAH, RANK, REX, MONARCH, RULER, SIRE
and jack .... TENACE
Albanian .... ZOG
Ammonite ..... HANUN
Arthur's birthplace ...... TINTAGEL HEAD
capital ..... CAMELOT
chronicler .. GEOFFREY
clown .... DAGONET
court .... CAMELOT
death place ... CAMLAN
fairy sister .... MORGAN LE FAY
father .... UTHER
father-in-law .... LEOGADAN
fictitious visitor ...... YANKEE
fool/jester ... DAGONET
foster brother .... KAY
half-sister .... MORGAN (LE FAY)
knight (see round table) GARETH, GAWAIN, GALAHAD, LANCELOT, MODRED
knights .. ROUNDTABLE
lance .... RON(E)
magician ..... MERLIN

mother ..... IGRAINE, YGERNE, IGERNE, IGERNA
nephew ..... GAWAIN, KAY, GARETH, MO(R)DRED
place .... ASTOLAT
queen ..... GUINEVERE
realm .... BRITAIN
resting place .. AVALON
seneschal .... KAY
shield name .. PRIDWIN
step-sister .... MORGAN (LE FAY)
sword ..... EXCALIBUR
wife .... GUINEVERE
Canute's consort .. EMMA
changed to mountain .... ATLAS
Cole .... NAT, OLD
crab .... LIMULOID, LIMULUS, XIPHOSURAN
David's daughter .. TAMAR
faithful friend ... ITAI
father .... JESSE
general .... REI, IGAL, ABNER, AMASA, ABIGAIL, SHAMAH
son .. ABSALOM, AMNON
during Christ's time ..... HEROD
Egyptian ...... PHARAOH
fairyland .... OBERON
Ferdinand ...... BOMBA
Gath .... ACHISH
great .... PADISHA
Iranian .... SHAH
killer .... REGICIDE
Lear's daughter .... GONERIL, REGAN, CORDELIA
dog .... TRAY
legendary .... MIDAS
maned .... LION
Midian .... REBA
Mongkut's country ..... SIAM
morning reception of .... LEVEE
of a ...... ROYAL, REGAL
of Amalek .... AGAG
Arcadia ..... LYCAON
Argos .... DANAUS
Assyria .... PUL, SENACHERIB
Athens ...... THESEUS, CODRUS
Attica .... CECROPS
Babylon .. HAMMURABI, BELSHAZZAR, SELEACUS
Bashan .... OG
beasts .... LION
Belgium ... BAUDOIN, LEOPOLD
birds .... EAGLE
Bohemia ..... WENZEL, WENCESLAUS
Britain ..... ARTHUR, UTHER, LEAR, ARTEGAL, BELINUS, LUD
Bulgaria .... BORIS
Burgundy ... GUNTHER
Bythinia ... NICOMEDES
Colon .... GASPAR
Corinth ..... POLYBUS
Crete .... MINOS
Cyprus ... PYGMALION
Damascus ... ARETUS
Denmark .. VALDEMAR, WALDEMAR
dwarfs ...... ALBERICH
Egypt .. FUAD, FAROUK
elves .... ERLKING
England .... STEPHEN, ETHELRED
England and Denmark KNUT, CNUT
Epirus ..... PYRRHUS
Ethiopia .... CEPHEUS
fairies .... OBERON
Franks .... PEPIN
"golden touch" ...... MIDAS
hobbies, alleged ...... PHILATELY
Huns ... ATLI, ATTILA, ETZEL
Ioclus .... AESON
Iran .... XERXES
Iraq .... FIESAL
Israel .... AHAB, JEROBOAM, NADAB, HOSHEA, JEHU, ELAH, OMRI, SAUL, SOLOMON, DAVID
Israel, last .... HOSHEA
Jews .... HEROD
Judah/Judea .. ABIJAH, AHAZ, MANASSEH, HEROD, ASA, UZZIAH, JOSIAH, JOSIAS
Kent .... ETHELBERT
Langobards .. ALBOIN
Ligurians .... CYGNUS
Lydia .... CROESUS
Moab .... EGLON
Mycenae ..... ATREUS
Myrmidons ... PELEUS
Naples .... MURAT
Norway .... OLAF, OLAV, HAAKON
Numidia ... JUGURTHA, MASINISSA, SYPHAX
Peris .... JAMSHID
Persia .... CYRUS, XERXES, DARIUS
Phrygia .... MIDAS, GORDIUS
Pontus .. MITHRIDATES
Rome ...... TARQUIN
Salem ... MELCHIZEDEK
Scotland ...... BRUCE
Siam .... ANANDA, MONGKUT
Sodom .... BERA
Spain .... REY, ALFONSO, JUAN
Sparta .... MENELAUS, LEONIDAS
Syria .... HAZAL
Thebes .. LAIUS, CREON
Thessaly ... ADMETUS, PELIAS
Thrace .... TEREUS, LYSIMACHUS
Troy .... PRIAM
Tyre .... HIRAM
Ulster ... CONCHOBAR
Visigoths ..... ALARIC
Volsunga .... ATLI
Zulus ..... CETEWAYO
Saul's commander ...... ABNER
sculptor ..... PYGMALION
snake .... COBRA
Solomon's country ...... OPHIR
with ass' ears ..... MIDAS
with eternal thirst, hunger TANTALUS
kingbird ...... FLYCATCHER, BEE MARTIN, PIPIRI
kingcup .... MARIGOLD
kingdom ... REALM, REGALITY, ESTATE, DOMAIN, MONARCHY, EMPIRE, LESOTHO
African .... NUBIA, NUMIDIA
ancient .... EDOM, CROATIA, IDUMEA, ELAM, MACEDONIA
Asiatic .... SIAM, THAILAND, KOREA, NEPAL
Caspian .... PARTHIA
cause of loss of .... NAIL, HORSE
come .... HEREAFTER, HEAVEN
kind of .... ANIMAL, PLANT, VEGETABLE
kingfish .... BARB, OPAH, PINTADO, WHITING, HAKU, SIERRA, CERO
kingfisher .... HALCYON, KOOKABURRA
kingfisher's kin ...... MOTMOT
kinglet ..... WREN, SONGBIRD
kingly ..... LEONINE, ROYAL, AUGUST, REGAL, MAJESTIC, NOBLE
authority/power.. ...... DIADEM
kingmaker: soubriquet ...... WARWICK
King's chamber ... CAMARILLA
clover .... MELILOT
color .. ORPIMENT, PURPLE
evil .... SCROFULA
Peak range ...... UINTA
robe .... DALMATIC
rod .... WARDER
steward ... CHAMBERLAIN
symbol ... ORB, MOUND
kingship ... ROYALTY, MAJESTY
kink .. BUCKLE, KNOT, SNARL, CURL, CRICK, TWIST, CROTCHET, QUIRK, WHIM
thread .... BURL
kinkajou ... POTT(O), MAMMAL
animal like a .. RACCOON
kinky .... CURLY
kino ..... GUM, ASTRINGENT
kinsfolk ... RELATIVES, FAMILY
kinship ... AFFINITY, ENATION, AGNATION
kinsman ..... RELATIVE, SIB, RELATION

kiosk .... PAVILION, SUMMERHOUSE, BANDSTAND, NEWSSTAND
kip .... HIDE, BED, ROOMING HOUSE
Kipling's heroine ..... MAISIE
novel .... KIM
"Shere Khan" .... TIGER
title .... SAHIB
wolf .... AKELA
Kirghiz ... KAZAK(H), MONGOL
mountains .... ALAI
tent .... YURT
kirk .... CHURCH
Kirman .... RUG
kirmess ...... FAIR, CARNIVAL
kirn .... FEAST
kirtle ... SKIRT, COAT, TUNIC
Kish's father .... NER
son .... SAUL
kismet .... DESTINY, FATE, DOOM
kiss ...... OSCULATE, CANDY, BUSS, SMACK, CARESS, SUGARPLUM, PECK
and ___ .... TELL
"Kiss" sculptor .... RODIN
kisser: sl. ...... MOUTH, LIPS, FACE
kissing game .... POST OFFICE
kist ..... BOX, LOCKER, CHEST, TOMB
kit ...... TUB, BUCKET, PACK, SET, LOT, COLLECTION, GEAR, VIOLIN, OUTFIT
and ___ ..... CABOODLE
kitchen .... CUISINE, COOKERY, SCULLERY
chief .... CHEF
garden .... OLITORY
help .... SCULLION
leftovers ..... PEELINGS
of the ...... CULINARY
police for short ...... KP
ship's .... GALLEY, CABOOSE
table .... DRESSER
tool ..... CORER, DICER, GRATER, SIEVE
waste .... SLOPS
wear .... APRON
worker .... SCULLION
Kitchener ..... STOVE, RANGE
statesman ...... HORATIO
kitchenware ...... POTS, PANS, UTENSILS
kite .... MILAN, ELANET, GLED(E), HAWK, BIRD, ROGUE, SHARPER, SOAR, FALCON
kith and kin ...... RELATIVES
kitsch .... TRASH
kittenish ... FRISKY, PLAYFUL
kittens: colloq: ... HYSTERICS
kittiwake .... GULL, WAEG
kittle .... PUZZLE, TICKLE
kitty ...... CAT, ANTE, POOL, STAKES, POT, WIDOW
kiva ...... DWELLING, ROOM
kiwi ..... ROA, MOA, APTERYX
Klausenburg .... CLUJ
klaxon .... HORN
klepht .... BRIGAND
kleptomaniac .... THIEF, FILCHER, SHOPLIFTER
Klingsor .... MAGICIAN
klipspringer .... ANTELOPE
Klondike road .... ALCAN
kloop .... GORGE, VALLEY
knack ... HANG, FLAIR, SKILL, ART, TALENT, APTITUDE, INSTINCT, DEVICE, TRICK, DEXTERITY, TRINKET, FEAT
knaggy ..... ROUGH, KNOTTY
knap ..... HILL, KNOCK, RAP, NIBBLE, SNAP, BITE, SUMMIT
knapsack ...... (DUFFLE)BAG, PACK, KIT, MOCHILA
knar .... KNOT
knarl .... NODE
knave ...... SERVANT, SCAMP, COISTREL, VARLET, LOREL, LOSEL, ROGUE, RASCAL, CHURL
game cards' .... JACK
in cribbage .... NOBS
of clubs .... PAM
playing cards' ..... JACK
knead .... MALAX, MOLD, PETRIE, MASSAGE, ELT
kneading material .... DOUGH, CLAY
knee .... JOINT, GENU
ailment ..... GONAGRA
bend the .... GENUFLECT
bone .... DIB
flexure .... GENU
inflammation ... GONITIS
joint ... HOCK, KNUCKLE
like part .... GENU
tendon ..... HAMSTRING
kneecap ... PATELLA, ROTULA
kneel .. GENUFLECT, KOWTOW
kneeling, act of .... KOWTOW
desk .... PRIE DIEU
kneepan .... PATELLA
knell ...... TOLL, RING, OMEN
knickerbocker(s) .... NEW YORKER, TROUSERS, PLUS FOURS
knickknack ...... GIMCRACK, TOY, DOODAD, NOVELTY, TRIFLE, TRINKET, GEWGAW, GAUD, BAUBLE
knife ..... CUT, STAB, BLADE, CHIV, SNEE, SNY, MACHET(T)E, BARLOW, PARANG, BOWIE, BOLO, GENEFE
Burmese ..... DAH, DOW
combining form ... DORI
cord .... LANYARD, LANIARD
dealer .... CUTLER
Dyak .... PARANG
Eskimo woman's ... ULU
for opening veins .... LANCET, FLEAM
handle .... HAFT
Hindu .... KURRI
Irish .... SKEAN
kind of .... PEN, BOWIE, FAN, SWITCHBLADE, TRIVET, TREVET
large .... COUTEAU
like tool .... SLITTER
Malay ..... CREESE, KRIS
Maori .... PATU
Moro .... KRIS
part .... TANG, HAFT
Philippine .. ITAK, BOLO
sharpener .... STEEL
surgical .... SCALPEL, CATLIN, LANCET
thrust ... STAB, STOCCADO
tosser .... JUGGLER
knight .... SIR, CAVALIER, BAYARD, EQUITE, EQUES, PALADIN, TEMPLAR, CHAMPION, EREC, RITTER
arena of the ...... LISTS
armor bearer of .... ARMIGER
attendant .... SQUIRE, ARMIGER, PAGE, DONZEL
challenge .... GAGE
cloak of .... TABARD
Crusader ...... TEMPLAR
ensign .... PENNON
errand of a ...... QUEST
errant .... PALADIN
fight of a ... TILT, JOUST, TOURNEY
groom of ..... COISTREL
in chess .... HORSE
lance target ... QUINTAIN
mantle of .... TABARD
medieval .... BEVIS
of the road .... HOBO, TRAMP
of the "Round Table" ... BORS, GARETH, BALAN, BALIN, BORT, GALAHAD, LANCELOT, KAY, GERAINT, GAWAIN, PELLEAS, MO(R)DRED, BEDIVERE, TRISTAN, MORGA(I)N, PERCIVAL, TRISTRAM
page of .... VARLET
pledge .... GAGE
protective cover of ...... ARMOR
Templar .... MASON
title of .... SIR
to .... DUB
vocation ..... CHIVALRY
weapon of ..... LANCE
without armor .... BARESARK
knighthood ... CHIVALRY, HOST
knightliness .... CHIVALRY
knightly .... CHIVALROUS
knit .... PURSE, PUCKER, INTERLOCK, COUPLE, SEAM, UNITE, JOIN
knitted goods dealer .. HOSIER
knitting ... BROCADE, CROCHET
machine guide ..... SLEY
stitch .... PURL
knives, seller of ..... CUTLER
tosser of .... JUGGLER
knob ..... NUB(BLE), KNURL, NODE, UMBO, HILL, KNOLL, HANDLE, KNOP, STUD, FINIAL

like .... NOPAL
like ornament .... KNOP
medical .... TUBERCLE
ornamental .. BOSS, STUD
pertaining to a .... ORLET
projecting .... BOSS
knobbed .... TOROSE, NODOSE, TOROUS
knobby .... TUBEROSE, TUBEROUS, NUBB(L)Y
knobkerrie .... CLUB, KIR(R)I, KERRI
knobs, decorate with .... BOSS
knobstick .... RAT, SNOB
knock ... RAP, BLOW, CLASH, BUMP, HIT, CRITICIZE, STRIKE, KNAP
about ... ROAM, HUSTLE, WANDER
down .. FLATTEN, FLOOR
kneed ...... BOWLEGGED, WOBBLY, VALGUS
lightly .... RAP, TAP
out ... KAYO, DEFEAT, KO
knockabout ... YACHT, NOISY, ROUGH, HUSTLE
knocker .... RAPPER, FAULTFINDER, NAGGER, CRITIC
knockout blow .... HAYMAKER
knoll ... HILLOCK, HUMMOCK, TOFT, MOUND, KNAP
Knossos .... CRETE
knot .... NODE, JOINT, TUFT, NODUS, HITCH, TIE, SNAG, COCKADE, NODULE, NUB, BOW, EPAULET, CLUSTER, BOND, KNUR, SANDPIPER, PROBLEM, LUMP, ENTANGLE
cloth .... BURL
fiber .... NOIL, NEP
fibrous .... NEP
hair ..... NOIL, CHIGNON
kind of ...... OVERHAND, THIEF, LOOP, REEF, BOWLINE, GRANNY, PROLONGE, TREFOIL, CAT'S-PAW, SHEEPSHANK, MOUSE
lace .... TAT(T)
loose .... GRANNY
nautical .... MILE
pertaining to a .... NODAL
rope .... CLINCH
running .... NOOSE
silk .... NOIL
thread .... BURL
tree .... GNARL
wood ...... BURL, KNAR, NURL, GNARL, KNOR
wool .... NOIL
yarn .... SKEIN
knots, full of .... NODOUS
rid of .... ENODATE
knotted .... NODATED, TANGLED, INTRICATE, NODED
knotty .... KNAGGY, NODOSE, NODOUS
knotweed ...... PERSICARY, ALLSEEDS
knout .... WHIP, FLOG
know ...... REGARD, REVEAL, KEN, WOT, AWARE, WIS(T)
all: colloq. ... WISEACRE, SMART ALECK, QUIDNUNC
beforehand .... FORESEE
how .... SKILL
it-all .... WISEGUY, WISEACRE
long ago .... WOT
nothing ..... IGNORAMUS, AGNOSTIC
knowing .... HEP, SCIENT, GNOSTIC, SHREWD, CLEVER, DELIBERATE
knowledge ...... LORE, KITH, NOESIS, EXPERTISE, KEN, COGNITION, WISDOM, SCIENTIA, AWARENESS, INFORMATION
branch of ...... OLOGY
has .... AWARE
lack of ...... IGNORANCE
means to ..... ORGANON
of .... GNOSTIC
source of .... LAMP
spiritual .... GNOSIS
surface .... SCIOLISM, SMATTER(ING)
universal ... PANTOLOGY, PANSOPHY
knowledgeable ...... HEP, HIP, WISE, INTELLIGENT, SAPIENT, INFORMED
known as ... YCLEPT, YCLEPED
knuckle .... JOINT
down under ..... YIELD, GIVE IN
knucklebone ...... KNOB, BIB
knur .... KNOT
knurl .... RIDGE, KNOT, KNOB, NODULE
KO: sl. .... KNOCKOUT
koa .... ACACIA
koala .... BEAR
Kobenhavn ..... COPENHAGEN
kobold .. GNOME, (HOB)GOBLIN, BROWNIE, SPRITE, NIS(SE)
kodak .... CAMERA
kodok .... FASHODA
koel .... CUCKOO
Koheleth .... SOLOMON
Kohinoor .... DIAMOND, (CROWN) JEWEL
kohl .... COSMETIC
kohlrabi .... CABBAGE
kok-sagyz ...... DANDELION
Kok's (Adam) settlers .... GRIQUA
kokama .... GEMSBOOK
Koko's weapon .... SNEE
kokoon .... GNU
Kol dialect .... MUNDARI
kola .... NUT
nut content .. CAFFEIN(E)
kolinsky .... MINK, FUR
koodoo .... KUDU
kook .... CUCKOO
kookaburra ..... KINGFISHER
kooky .... CRAZY, SILLY, ECCENTRIC
kop .... HILL, MOUNTAIN
kopje .... HILL(OCK)
kor .... HOMER
Koran chapter ..... ALCORAN, SURA(H), SURO
interpreter ...... ULEMA
memorizer ...... HAFIZ
paradise bridge .... AL SIRAT
scholar .... ULEMA
supplement to the .... SUNNA(H), SHIITE
teacher of ...... ALFAQUI
Korea .... CHOSEN
founder of ..... TANGUN
Korean capital, North .... PYONGYANG
capital, South ... SEOUL, KEIJO
city ..... FUSAN, TAEGU, GENSAN, WONSAN
coin .... WON
dynasty .... SILLA
kingdom .... SILLA
island .... KOJE
monetary unit ..... WON, HWAN
mount .... SORAK
port ..... GENSAN, FUSAN
premier .... KIM IL SUNG (NORTH), CHUNG IL KWON (SOUTH)
president .... (CHUNG HEE) PARK, RHEE
river .... YALU, HAN
seaport .... JINSEN, CHEMULP(H)O, INCHON, WONSAN, PUSAN
soldier .... ROK
stockade .... JKOJE
true faith ..... AL SIRAT
weight .... KON
women's blouse .. CHIMA
women's skirt .. CHOGORI
Korina wood .... AFARA
koruna, 1/100 of ...... HELLER
kosher ... CLEAN, FIT, PROPER
opposed to .... TREF
Kosygin, Russian premier .... ALEKSEI
Kotabaru .... HOLLANDIA
Kovno .... KAUNAS
kowtow .... SALUTATION, HOMAGE, RESPECT
kr. .... KRONA, KRONOR, KRONER, KRONE(N), KRYPTON, KREUTZER
kraal ... ENCLOSURE, VILLAGE, PEN
kraft ..... WRAPPING PAPER
Kreisler, violinist ...... FRITZ
Kremlin .... CITADEL
Kriemhild's husband .... SIEGFRIED, ETZEL, ATTILA
krimmer .... LAMBSKIN
kris .... CREESE, DAGGER
Kriss Kringle .. SANTA (CLAUS)
krona .... CROWN
Kronos' wife .... RHEA
Kronstadt ..... BRASOV, PORT
Kropotkin, anarchist .... PETR
Kruger, Transvaal president .. OOM PAUL

Ku Klux Klan official .... KLEAGLE
Kublai Khan dynasty ... YUAN
kuchen .... COFFEECAKE
kudos .... FAME, GLORY, CREDIT, PRAISE, PRESTIGE
kudu ..... ANTELOPE, KOODOO
kulak .... FARMER
kulun .... ULAN BATOR
Kumasi is capital of .. ASHANTI
is in .... GHANA
kumiss .... OMEIRIS
kummel .... LIQUEUR
Kung Fu-tse ...... CONFUCIUS
Kuomintang .... YUAN
founder ... SUN YAT-SEN
leader .. CHIANG KAI-SHEK
kurrajong .... CALOOL
Kurdistan .. .. RUG
Kuril(e) island .... ITURUP, CHISHIMA, ETORO
kust .... NODE
Kuwait .... SHEIKDOM
export .... OIL
monetary unit .... DINAR
kvass .... BEER
Kwangchow .... CANTON
Kwangsi capital ... NANNING
Kwantung capital ... CANTON
city .... SWATOW
seaport .... DAIREN
kyack .... PACKSACK
Kymric .... WELSH
kyphos .... HUMP
kyphosis .... HUMPBACK
Kyser, bandleader .... KAY
Kyushu base .... SASEBO
city .... KUMAMOTO, NAGASAKI, SASEBO, MOJI
volcano .... ASO(SAN)

L

L, Greek .... LAMBDA
in chemistry .... LANTHANUM
in geodesy ... LONGITUDE
letter .... ELL, EL
shaped .... ELL
"La Boheme" character ...... MIMI, MUSETTA, RODOLPHO
"La Gioconda" ... MONA LISA
La Guardia, Mayor .... FIORELLO
La Rochefoucauld's forte ..... MAXIMS
laager .... CAMP
Laban's daughter ...... LEAH, RACHEL
labarum .... STANDARD
labdanum .... RESIN
Labe .... ELBE
labefaction ...... DOWNFALL
label ... FILLET, TAG, LAPPET, CLASSIFICATION, STICKER, TAB, NAME, TALLY, PASTER, DESCRIBE, MARK, STAMP, BRAND, DOCKET
labellum .... LIP, PETAL
flower with ..... ORCHID
labia .... LIPS
minora ...... NYMPHA(E)
labial .... (ORGAN) PIPE
labiate .... LIPPED
labile ... UNSTABLE, SKIMMING
labium ...... LIP, LABELLUM
labor .... WORK, TRAVAIL, TOIL, PARTURATION, STRIVE, CHILDBIRTH, TASK, MOIL
group .... UNION
leader ... LEWIS, GREEN, MEANY, HOFFA, PETRILLO, REUTHER
omnia ____ ...... VINCIT
organization, international ILO
throes, pains ... TRAVAIL
resources .... MANPOWER
spy recruiter ... HOOKER
strike placard carrier .... PICKET
union .... CIO, AFL, ILGWU, ARTEL
union branch .... LOCAL
union negotiation ...... COLLECTIVE BARGAINING
laboratory burner ..... ETNA, BUNSEN
need ... ACIDS, OLEATES, TEST TUBES
labored ... OPEROSE, DIFFICULT
breath ...... PANT, GASP
laborer .... WORKER, NAVVY, PROLE, TOTY, HAND, SERF, SEGGON
Chinese .. COOLIE, COOLY
Egyptian .... FELLAH
India .... TOTY
Mexican .... PEON, BRACERO
migratory .... OKIE
oriental .... COOLIE
Spanish .... OBRERO, PEON, TRABAJADOR
underground .. SANDHOG
unskilled .... NAVVY, BOHUNK
transient .. ROUSTABOUT, FLOATER
laborious .... DIFFICULT, INDUSTRIOUS, TOILSOME
labra .... LIPS
Labrador .... PENINSULA
tea .... LEDUM
labradorite .... FELDSPAR
labroid fish .... WRASS
labrum .... LIP
laburnum ... SHRUB, PEA TREE, SANDALWOOD
labyrinth .... MAZE
builder of .... DAEDALUS
dweller, legendary ...... MINOTAUR
labyrinthine ..... INTRICATE, MEANDROUS
lace .... MACRAME, GIN, EDGING, EMBROIDER, WEAVE, NOOSE, SNARE, GUIPURE, LACIS, WHIP, THRASH, BEAT, ADORN, FILET, TATTING, MALINES, VAL, STRING, RIBBON, BRAID, NETTING, INTERTWINE, FILIGREE, LASH
cape .... MANTILLA
collar .... BERTHA
edging .... FRILL
French .... ALENCON, CLUNY
frilled .... R(O)UCHE
into .... ATTACK, ASSAIL, SCOLD, CRITICIZE
loop(s) .... PURL
make .... TAT
metal tip of ... A(I)GLET, TAG
opening .... EYELET
pattern .... TOILE
shoe/sandal ..... LATCHET
silk bobbin ..... BLONDE
three-cornered ... FICHU
thread .... MACRAME
trimming .. JABOT, FRILL
Lacedaemon .... SPARTA
lacer .... TIER
lacerate .... RIP, TEAR, MANGLE, DISTRESS, REND, HURT, TORN, CUT
lacert(il)ian .... LIZARD, CHAMELEON, GECKO
lacet .... BRAID
Lachesis .... FATE, GODDESS, WEIRD
companion of .. ATROPOS, CLOTHO
lachrymose .... TEARFUL, MOURNFUL, TEARY
lady .... NIOBE
lacing .... THRASHING, CORD, TRIMMING, BRAID, BEATING
laciniate .... FRINGED
lack .... REQUIRE, DEARTH, NEED, SHORTAGE, DEFICIENCY, WANT(ING)
desire ..... INAPPETENCE
of stress .... ATONY
lackadaisical .... LISTLESS, SPIRITLESS, LANGUID, INDOLENT
lackey .... FLUNK(E)Y, FOOTMAN, SLAVE, TOADY, (MAN)SERVANT, FOLLOWER, ATTENDANT
uniform of ...... LIVERY
lacking .... (DE)VOID, SHORT, DESTITUTE, IN NEED, DEFICIENT, SHY
brightness .. LACKLUSTER
enthusiasm .. LUKEWARM
grace .... CLUMSY, AWKWARD, CRUDE, GAUCHE
refinement ...... COARSE,

GROSS, CRUDE, INCONDITE
reverence .... IMPIOUS
lackluster .... DULL, DRAB
Laconia, capital of .... SPARTA
people of .... SPARTAN(S)
laconic ...... CONCISE, TERSE, BRIEF, PITHY
answer .... UGH
person .... INDIAN
lacquer ...... DUCO, VARNISH, JAPAN, ENAMEL, LAC
plus pigment ... ENAMEL
lacs, 100 .... CRORE
lactary .... DAIRY
lactase .... ENZYME
lactate .... SUCKLE
lacteal .... MILKY
lactescent .... MILKY
lactose .... SUGAR
lacuna ... GAP, HIATUS, SPACE, CAVITY
lad ..... STRIPLING, SHAVER, YOUTH, SONNY, YOUNGSTER
ladanum .... RESIN
ladder .... STEE, SCALADE, SCALE
accommodation .... GANGWAY
attack using ... ESCALADE
part ..... RUNG, STAVE, SPOKE, STEP, ROUND, RUNDLE
lade .... LOAD, BAIL, LADLE, DIP, BURDEN
ladida: sl. .... FLOSSY, FOP(PISH)
ladies' man .... SHEIK(H)
Ladin .... ROMANSH
Ladino .... MESTIZO, DIALECT
ladle ... DIPPER, BOWL, SCOOP, SPOON, BAIL, DIP
dip/pour with ..... LAVE
spout .... GEAT
ladore .... CASCADE
ladrone ...... THIEF, ROBBER, BANDIT
Island(s) .... GUAM, MARIANAS
lady ... MADAM, FEMALE, BIBI, BURD, MISTRESS, WIFE, SWEETHEART, (GENTLE)WOMAN, DAME
Churchill .. CLEMENTINE
Godiva, he saw .... PEEPING TOM
Hamilton .... EMMA
Italian .... DONNA, SIGNORA, SIGNORINA
killer: sl. ..... DON JUAN, CASANOVA
of the Lake ...... ELLEN, VIVIAN, NIMUE
silk habit .... PELISSE
Spanish .. DONA, SENORA, SENORITA
ladybird .... BEETLE, VEDALIA
ladybug .... BEETLE
ladyfinger .... COOKIE, COOKY
ladylike .... WELL-BRED, REFINED
ladylove .... SWEETHEART
lady's maid .... ABIGAIL, SOUBRETTE
slipper .... ORCHID
smock .... CRESS, CUCKOOFLOWER
tresses .... ORCHID
Laertes' sister ...... OPHELIA
son .... ODYSSEUS
lag ...... DELAY, TRAIL, IDLE, LOITER, LINGER, STAVE, DRAG, FALTER, ARREST, CONVICT, DALLY, TARRY
lagan ...... JETSAM, FLOTSAM
lager .... BEER, CAMP
Lagerlof .... SELMA
laggard .... LOITERER, BACKWARD, SLOWFOOT
lagn(i)appe .... GRATUITY, PRESENT
lagomorph ...... HARE, PIKA, RABBIT, RODENT
lagoon .... LAKE, POND, LIMAN, HAFF
islands .... ELLICE
site of ..... CORAL REEF, ATOLL
Lahr, comedian .... BERT
laic .... CIVIL, TEMPORAL, LAY(MAN), SECULAR
lair ... CAVE, DEN, LIE, HAUNT, HANGOUT
hare's .... FORM
laity .... LAYMEN, PEOPLE
Laius's son .... OEDIPUS
lake .... LOCH, ERIE, LAGOON, POOL, PIGMENT, SHAT, SHOTT, SALINA
African .. NYASSA, CHAD, VICTORIA
artificial ...... RESERVOIR
Australian .. EYRE, FROME
basin .... PLAYA
bird .... LOON
Blue Nile .... TANA
Chad tributary .... SHARI
city .... ERIE
Erie city .... LORAIN, LACKAWANNA
Erie port .... TOLEDO
Erie tributary .. MAUMEE
fish .... POLLAN
Geneva .... LEMAN
Great ... ERIE, ONTARIO, SUPERIOR, MICHIGAN, HURON
herring .... CISCO
Hoover Dam ..... MEAD
in an atoll ...... LAGOON
Irish .... LOUGH
island in a ...... HOLM
Maggiore town .... LOCARNO
Michigan city .... MILWAUKEE, GARY, KENOSHA
mountain .... TARN
Nyassa country .. MALAWI
of a ...... LACUSTRINE, LACUSTRAL
of Constance .... BODENSEE
outlet .... BAYOU
poet .... COLERIDGE, SOUTHEY, WORDSWORTH
resort .... TAHOE
salt .... SALINA
Scottish .... LOCH
shallow .... LAGOON
small .... MERE, POND
trout .... POGY, SALMON, NAMAYCUSH
world's lowest .. DEAD SEA
lakes, found in/on .... LACUSTRINE
study of .... LIMNOLOGY
lakh .... LAC
laky .... DARK-RED
Lal Bahadur ___ ... SHASTRI
lalique .... GLASS
lallation ...... LAMBDACISM
Lalo, composer .... EDOUARD
lam .... BEAT, FLOG, FLEE, VAMO(O)SE, THRASH, FLIGHT, ESCAPE
lama ... MONK, PRIEST, NUN, TESHU
chief ..... DALAI, BLAMA
lamasery .... MONASTERY
lamb .... (Y)EAN, SHEEP, CHILD, COSSET, (Y)EANLING, FATLING
breast .... CARRE
Charles .... ELIA
fur .... KARAKUL
hide .... KIP
holy .... AGNUS
leg of .... GIGOT
like a .... TIMID(LY), MEEK(LY), INNOCENT
mother of .... EWE
of God .... JESUS
pet ...... CADE, COSSET
skin .... BUDGE
slice .... CHOP
stew .... HARICOT
lambast(e) .... THRASH, BEAT, SCOLD
lambda in Hebrew .. LAMED(H)
lambdacism ..... LALLATION
lambent .... GLOWING, FLICKERING
lambkin .... CHILD
lamblike ..... MEEK, GENTLE, INNOCENT
lambrequin .... DRAPERY
lambskin .... BUDGE, VELLUM
lame ..... CRIPPLE(D), HALT, MAIM, DISABLE(D), CLAUDICANT, SPAVINED, HALTING, PLATE, FEEBLE
duck, kind of .... SPECULATOR
Lamech, son of ...... JABAL, JUBAL, NOAH
wife of .... ADAH
lamed(h) ...... ELL, LAMBDA
lamelli as prefix ...... PLATE, SCALE, LAYER, LEAF
lamellibranch ...... MOLLUSK, OYSTER, CLAM
lamelliform ..... PLATELIKE, SCALELIKE
lamellirostral bird ..... DUCK, SWAN, GOOSE
lament ... DEPLORE, (RE)PINE, GRIEVE, ELEGIZE, RUE,

MOURN, ELEGY, DIRGE, (BE)WAIL, I(BE)MOAN
lamentable ..... DEPLORABLE, WRETCHED
lamentation ...... JEREMIAD, WAILING, PLAINT
lamia .... SORCERESS, VAMPIRE, DEMON(ESS), WITCH
lamiaceous plant .... MINT, BERGAMOT, ROSEMARY
lamina .... FLAKE, SCALE, BLADE, LAYER, PLY, LEAF, PLATE
brain .... OBEX
laminated .... LAYERED, SHEETED
material ..... PLYWOOD
rock .... SHALE
lamination ...... PLY, LAYER
laminitis .... FOUNDER
Lammas .... FESTIVAL
lammergeier ...... VULTURE, OSSIFRAGE
lamp .... ETNA, LUCERNA, GEORDIE, ARGAND, TORCH, GOOSENECK, LANTERN, BULB, GAS JET, GLIM, LUMINAIRE
automobile .. TAIL LIGHT
black .... SOOT
chain .... PENDANT
cord/tape .... WICK
decorative ..... LAMPION
fuel .... KEROSENE, PETROLEUM
heating .... ETNA
holder .... CRESSET
lighter ..... SPILL, TAPER
miner's .... DAVY
oil .... LAMPION
part .... WICK, BURNER, CRESSET
poetic .... SUN, STAR, MOON
slang .... EYES, GLIM
waving .... ARATI
lampas ..... LAMPERS, CLOTH
lampblack ..... GRIME, SOOT, PIGMENT
lamper eel .... LAMPREY
lampers .... LAMPAS
lampoon ...... PASQUINADE, LIBEL, SATIRE, CARICATURE, SQUIB, RIDICULE, SKIT
lamprey ... EEL, CYCLOSTOME
lanai .... PORCH
lanate .... WOOL(L)Y
Lancashire city .... WIGAN
county seat ... LANCASTER
seaport ...... LIVERPOOL, MANCHESTER
Lancaster, actor .... BURT
lance .... JAVELIN, SPEAR, DART, CUT, (SEA)FISH, PIERCE
barb .... FLUKE
corporal in reality .... PRIVATE
flag of ..... BANDEROL(E)
part ...... REST, MORNE
lancelet .... AMPHIOXUS
Lancelot .... KNIGHT
liege of .... ARTHUR
love of .... ELAINE
mistress of .. GUINEVERE
uncle of .... BORS
lancer ...... HUSSAR, U(H)LAN
lancers ..... (SQUARE)DANCE, QUADRILLE
lancet .... (SURGICAL) KNIFE, SCALPEL, FLEAM, PHLEBOTOME
point .... NEB
lancewood .... YAYA
Lanchester, actress ..... ELSA
lancinate .... STAB, TEAR, PIERCE
land ..... COUNTRY, REGION, SOIL, GROUND, ESTATE, CATCH, DISEMBARK, ALIGHT, EARTH, TERRA, DEBARK, TRACT, TERRENE
along river .... HOLM, BOTTOMS, INTERVALE
and sea fighter ... MARINE
barren .... DESERT, WASTE, GALL
between hills .. INTERVALE
border .... RAND
church ... GLEBE, CLOSE
cleared .... FIELD, ASSART, CUTOVER
close .... GARTH
colloquial .... WIN, GET, SECURE, HOOK
conveyance .... DEED
cultivated .... ARADO, TILLAGE, TILTH, ARADA
disputed .... MARCH
east of Eden .... NOD
ecclesiastical benefice ... GLEBE
eroded ...... PENEPLAIN, PENEPLANE
grabber of a sort .... STAKE JUMPER
grant .... HOMESTEAD
grassy ... DOWN, VELDT
held in fee simple .. ALOD, ODAL
holder ... THANE, THEGN
holdings, record of ...... TERRIER
irrigated to excess .... WATER-SICK
marshy ...... MAREMMA
meadow .... LEA
measure ... ACRE, AR(E), HECTARE, RO(O)D, MORGEN, VIRGATE
mine .... CLAYMORE
of dwarfs ...... LILLIPUT
of leprechauns .... EIRE
of Office Machines, alleged .... SWEDEN
of plenty .... GOSHEN
of shrubs, etc. .. BARRENS
of song .... ARABY
owner of adjacent ...... ABUTTER
ownership, restricted .... FEE TAIL
ownership, unrestricted .. FEE SIMPLE
pertaining to .. GEOPONIC, AGRARIAN
piece of ... PARCEL, LOT, PLAT
plaster .... GYPSUM
pledged as security ...... WADSET
plowed ... ARADA, ARADO
point of low .... SPIT
power ..... (RED) CHINA
promised ...... CANAAN
reverting to the state .... ESCHEAT
reclaimed ...... POLDER, INNINGS
relating to ... AGRARIAN
rental .... FEU
rented .... HOLDING
strip of .... NECK
tenure ...... LEASEHOLD
tenure system ... SOCAGE
tilled .... ARADO, ARADA
title .... PATENT
treeless .... TUNDRA, SAVANNA(H), STEPPE
triangular piece .. DELTA, GORE
turtle .... TORTOISE
valued for taxes .... CADASTRE
wet ..... SWAMP, MARSH, MAREMMA
with heaviest rainfall .... ASSAM
with hardwoods .... HAMMOCK
landau .... CARRIAGE, AUTOMOBILE
landed ... TITHES, PRAEDIAL, ALIT, ALIGHTED
estate ... DOMAIN, MANOR
property .... ESTATE
landfall .... ISLE
landgrave .... COUNT
landing ground, aircraft ...... STRIP, RUNWAY
passage .... GANGPLANK, RAMP
place .... AIRPORT, PIER, HELIPORT, DOCK, GHAT, LEVEE, QUAY, JETTY, TARMAC, WHARF, QUAI
place of the Ark .... ARARAT
Landis, baseball czar .... KENESAW
landloper .... VAGABOND, VAGRANT, TRAMP
landlord .... BONIFACE, HOST, LAIRD
landmark .... MOUNTAIN, MONUMENT, MILESTONE, CAIRN, SENAL
landowner .... LAIRD
landscape .... PAYSAGE, SCENE(RY)
landscapist .... TOPIARIST
landslide .... VICTORY, AVALANCHE
landsman .... SAILOR
landtag ..... DIET, ASSEMBLY
lane .... PATH, COURSE,

STREET, ALLEY, WYND
langrage .... SHOT
Langtry, actress .... LILY
language ...... LIP, TONGUE, SPEECH, DIALECT, IDIOM, DICTION, PARLANCE
artificial .... ESPERANTO, VOLAPUK, IDO, RO
beggars' .. ARGOT, LINGO
classical ... LATIN, GREEK
colloquial ...... SLANG
dead .... LATIN
dialect .... LINGO, IDIOM
difficulty of understanding DYSPHASIA
gypsy .... ROMANY
hybrid .... JARGON, LINGUA FRANCA
hypothetical .... URSPRACHE
kind of .. GESTURE, SIGN
mixed .... PIDGIN
of .... LINGUISTIC, LINGUAL
of special vocabulary .... LINGO, ARGOT
of the soul, so-called .... MUSIC
of the street ..... SLANG
ordinary .... PROSE, DIALECT
outlandish ..... JARGON
pompous .. HIGHFALUTIN
pretentious ... CLAPTRAP
Romance ...... SPANISH, FRENCH, CATALAN, PROVENCAL, ITALIAN, ROMANIAN, PORTUGUESE
science/study of .... LINGUISTICS
slang .... ARGOT
thieves' ... ARGOT, FLASH
using click sounds .... NAMA
languages, he speaks/writes several .... POLYGLOT, LINGUIST
Languedoc's capital .... TOULOUSE
languid ... DROOPING, WEAK, LISTLESS, DULL, SLOW, LACKADAISICAL, WAN, DREAMY
languish .... WASTE, PINE(AWAY), FLAG, FADE, SWOON
languor .... LASSITUDE, KAIF, WILT, WEAKNESS, INDIFFERENCE, DULLNESS, BLUES, HEAVINESS, LETHARGY, STILLNESS, ENNUI
langur .... MONKEY, MAHA, WANDEROO, SIMPAI
laniard .... CORD
laniary .... CANINE
Lanier, poet .... SIDNEY
laniferous .... FLEECY
lank(y) .... LEAN, GANGLY, SLENDER, SPINDLING, GANGLING
lanner(et) .... FALCON
lanose .... WOOL(L)Y
lansquenet .... SOLDIER, MERCENARY
lantana .... VIBURNUM, MAJORANA
lantern ... LAMP, LANTHORN, CRESSET
feast .... BON
roof's .... LOUVER
wheel .... TRUNDLE
lanthorn .... LANTERN
Lantsang .... MEKONG
lanuginose .... DOWNY
lanugo .... DOWN, HAIR
lanyard ...... THONG, CORD, ROPE
Lanza, singer .... MARIO
Laocoon .. PRIEST, SCULPTURE
Laodicea .... LATAKIA
Laomedon's kingdom ... TROY
son .... PRIAM
Laos .... KINGDOM
capital (administrative) .. VIENTIANE
capital (royal) .... LUANG PRABANG
fortress town .. NAM BAC
king of .... (SAVANG) VATHANA
monetary unit ...... KIP
language .... FRENCH, LAOTIAN
rebels ..... PATHET LAO
lap .... WRAP, (EN)FOLD, CIRCUIT, LICK
dog .... PET, POM
robe .... RUG
lapel ...... REVER(S), FACING, FOLD, FLAP
stiffener .... WIGAN
thing pinned on .... BUTTON, BADGE, BOUTONNIERE
lapidary .... ENGRAVER, JEWEL(L)ER, GEM-CUTTER, ARTIFICER
lapidate .... STONE
lapidify .... PETRIFY
lapillus .... ROCK
lapin .... RABBIT, FUR
lapis .... STONE
lazuli ...... SAPPHIRUS, AZURE-BLUE
lazuli pigment .... ULTRAMARINE
Laplander .... LAPP
sledge of ...... PULK(H)A
lapper .... DOG, CAT
lappet .... FLAP, WATTLE, FOLD, LOBE, DEWLAP, LABEL
lapse .... ERR(OR), FALL, LAPSUS, INTERVAL, MISSTEP, SLIP, FAULT
lapsus .... SLIP, LAPSE, ERROR
lapwing ... PLOVER, TREUTERO, PEWIT, PEWEE, WEEP
lar .... SPIRIT
larboard ... PORT(SIDE,) APORT
larceny .... THEFT
describing kind of ..... PETTY, GRAND
larch .... TAMARAC(K), TREE, PINE, SPRUCE, HACKMATACK
lard .... FAT, GREASE, GARNISH, ENRICH
tub for .... FIRKIN
larder ..... BUTTERY, SPENCE, PROVISIONS, PANTRY, CUPBOARD
Lardner, humorist ..... RING
large ..... OUTSIZE, MAN-SIZE
amount .. OODLES, SCADS,
at .... LOOSE, FREE, ABROAD
prefix .... MEGA, MACRO, MAGNI
scale .... EXTENSIVE
very .... DECUMAN
largely .... MAINLY
largess(e) ... GIFT(S), BOUNTY
lariat .... LASSO, ROPE, TETHER, RIATA, REATA, NOOSE
eye of ... HONDA, HONDO
larine bird .... GULL
lark .... ADVENTURE, PRANK, SONGBIRD, WAGTAIL, PIPIT, FROLIC, TEASE, HURDLE, SPREE, OSCINE, LAVEROCK
genus .... ALAUDA
larkspur .. PLANT, DELPHINIUM
larrigan .... MOCCASIN
larrikin ... HOODLUM, ROWDY
larrup .... FLOG, BEAT, WHIP, THRASH
larva .... PLANULA, GRUB, MAGGOT, CATERPILLAR, LOA, BOT(T)
butterfly ... CATERPILLAR
beetle's .... GRUB, CADELLE, WOLF
botfly .... WABBLE
case enclosing .. INDUSIUM
final stage of .. CHRYSALIS
flea's .... CHIGOE, CHIGGER
fly .... GENTLE
frog's .... TADPOLE
mite's ... JIGGER, LEPTUS
moth's .... EGGER, CATERPILLAR, WOLF
next form of ...... PUPA
of antlion ... DOODLEBUG
of horsefly .... BOT
of tapeworm .. COENURUS
of trematode .. CERCARIA
six-legged .... LEPTUS
weevil's .... GRUGRU
wingless .... CREEPER
larval tapeworms ..... MEASLES
laryngeal clearing sound ...... AHEM
larynx, rod for clearing ...... PROBANG
lasagna .... MACARONI
lascar .... SAILOR, ARTILLERYMAN
lascivious .... LEWD, WANTON, LUSTFUL, LIBIDINOUS, LICENTIOUS
laser inventor .... TOWNEE
lash ... QUIRT, SPLICE, STROKE, FASTEN, DASH, SCOURGE, WHIP, SWITCH, FLOG, CENSURE, REBUKE, BIND, SMITE, WALE, TIE

with words ..... BLISTER
lashing ... REBUKE, SCOLDING, WHIPPING, ROPE, TYING
lashings .... LOADS
lass ...... GIRL, SWEETHEART, MAID, SERVANT
lassie .... COLLEEN, GIRL, SWEETHEART
of the movies .... COLLIE
lassitude .... LANGUOR, LETHARGY, WEARINESS
lasso ... LARIAT, REATA, LASH, ROPE, NOOSE, THONG, RIATA
last .. END, ENDURE, ENDMOST, OMEGA, HINDMOST, FINAL(E), LATEST, NEWEST, ULTIMATE, GO ON, CONTINUE, DURE, REARMOST
act .... FINALE
at .... FINALLY
chance of ___ .... MONTANA
but one .. PENULT(IMATE)
Goth .... RODERICK
in succession .... LATTERMOST
Judgment ... DOOMSDAY
mentioned of two ...... LATTER
Mohican .... UNCAS
month .... ULTIMO
resort .... PIS ALLER
will and ___ .... TESTAMENT
person in a race .... TAILENDER
supper .... CENA
supper cup/platter ...... GRAIL
syllable of word .. ULTIMA
word of comedian ...... PUNCHLINE
word, usually ..... AMEN
lastex .... THREAD
lasting ... DURABLE, LIFELONG
effect .... SCAR
lastly .... ENFIN, FINALLY
Latakia .... LAODICEA, TOBACCO
latch .... HOOK, FASTEN(ING), (SPRING)LOCK, LASKET
latchkey notch .... WARD
latchet ... STRAP, LACE(T), TAP
late ...... OVERDUE, RECENT, NEW, FORMER, DEAD, TARDY, NEO
lateen .... VESSEL, DHOW
latent .... DORMANT, QUIESCENT, POTENTIAL, CONCEALED, HIDDEN, DELITESCENT
later ... AFTER, SUBSEQUENTLY
lateral .... SIDEWAYS, SIDEWISE
opposed to ..... MEDIAL
laterally .... SIDEWISE
laterite .... CLAY
latest .... LAST
combining form ... CENE, NEO
latex, plant's .... MILK
plural of .... LATICES
source of .... POPPY, MILKWEED, RUBBER TREE
lath ..... SLAT, SPLINT, SPALE
lathe clamp .... CHUCK
operator .... TURNER
lather ... FOAM, FROTH, SWEAT, FLOG, SUDS, FRENZY, SCUM, SPUME
lathing shop .... TURNERY
Latin ...... ROMAN, ITALIAN, SPANIARD, LANGUAGE
abbot .... ABBAS
above .... SUPRA
after .... POST
alas .... VAE, EHEU
all .... TOTO
alone .... SOLUS
always .... SEMPER
am present ..... AD SUM
America, foreigner in ... GRINGO
American measure ...... VARA
and .... ET
and others .... ET AL
anger .... IRA
art .... ARS
band .... FASCIA
bear ..... URSA, URSULA
before .... ANTE
behold .... ECCE
being .... ESSE
between .... INTER
bird .... AVIS
blessed .... BEATA
book .... LIBER
born .... NATUS
both .... AMBI
bronze .... AES
brother .... FRATER
bug .... CIMEX
but .... SED
city .... URBIS
copper .... CUPRUM
day .... DIEM, DIES
day of wrath .. DIES IRAE
discourse .... SERMO
dog .... CANIS
duct .... VAS
earth .... TERRA
earth exhalation .... MEPHITIS
egg .... OVUM, OVA
epic .... AENEID
equal .... PAR
error .... LAPSUS
everywhere ..... UBIQUE
evil ...... MALA, MALUM
fate .... NONA
fillet .... FASCIA
fire .... IGNIS
fish .... PISCES
fly .... MUSCA
force .... VIS
gentle .... LENIS
god .... DEUS
god willing .... DEO VOLENTE
goddess .... DEA
gold .... AURUM
good .... BONUM
grape .... UVA
great .... MAGNA
he .... ILLE, IPSE
head .... CAPUT
heat .... CALOR
hence .... ERGO
highest .... SUMMA
himself .... IPSE
holidays .... FERIA
holy .... SANCTUS
honey .... MEL
hour .... HORA
house .... DOMUS
hut .... TABERNA
in passing ...... OBITER
is .... EST
itself .... IPSO
knee .... GENU
lamb .... AGNUS
laughter .... RISUS
law ..... JUS, LEX, JURA
leisure .... OTIUM
light .... LUX, LUMEN
magpie .... PICA
man .... HOMO
mass .... MISSA
members .... SOCII
mine .... MEUM
mint .... MONETA
month .... MENSIS
mountain .... MONS
name .... NOMEN
needle .... ACUS
net .... RETE
not .... NON
number .... UNUS
observe .... NOTA
onion .... CEPA
order .... ORDO
other .... ALIA
our .... NOSTER
peace .... PAX
peacock .... PAVO
people .... POPULI
place(s) .... LOCUS, LOCI
poet .... OVID
power .... VIS
quarter site .... PARIS
quarter dwellers .... ARTISTS, STUDENTS
same .... IDEM
sash .... FASCIA
see .... VIDE
shed .... TABERNA
sister .... SOROR
skin .... CUTIS
snow .... NIVIS
soft .... LENIS
star .... STELLA
stone .... LAPIS
strength .... VIS
table .... MENSA
that is .... ID EST
thing .... RES
this .... HOC
thread .... FILUM
throat .... GULA
throughout ..... PASSIM
thus .... SIC
tile .... TEGULA
time ... TEMPUS, TEMPORA
toad .... BUFO
total .... SUMMA

twice .... BIS
under .... SUB
unless .... NISI
voice .... VOX
wasp .... VESPA
waste away ..... TABERE
water .... AQUA
wax .... CERA
we .... NOS
well .... BENE
where .... UBI
wife .... UXOR
within .... INTRA
without .... SINE
wolf .... LUPUS
wool .... LANA
yawn .... HIARE
year ...... ANNO, ANNUS
latite .... LAVA
latitude ... WIDTH, BREADTH, EXTENT, SCOPE
latitudinarian of a sort .... DEMOCRAT
Latium people .... VOLSCI
Latona .... LETO
progeny of ...... APOLLO, DIANA
latria .... WORSHIP
latrine .... TOILET, PRIVY
latten .... BRASS
latter, opposed to ..... FORMER
Latter-day Saint ... MORMON
lattice .... ESPALIER, GRILLE, TRELLIS, SCREEN
latticework .... ESPALIER, TRELLIS, PERGOLA
Latvian .... LETT(IC)
capital .... RIGA
city ..... RIGA, LIEPAJA, LIBAU
coin .... LAT
monetary unit .... LAT(U)
river .... DVINA
rulers .... RUSSIANS
seaport .... LIEPAJA
state, ancient .. LIVONIA, COURLAND
laud .... EXTOL, PRAISE, HYMN, GLORIFY, EXALT
laudable ..... PRAISEWORTHY, COMMENDABLE
laudanum .... RESIN
laudation .... PRAISE, EULOGY,
laudatory .... EULOGISTIC, PRAISING
laugh ..... CHORTLE, DERIDE, CHUCKLE, GIGGLE, TITTER, FLEER, SNICKER, GUFFAW, TE-HEE, HAW-HAW, CACKLE, HEEHAW, BRAY, NICKER, ROAR
able to .... RISIBLE
at .... RIDICULE, DISREGARD, MOCK
coarse .... FLEER
down .... SILENCE, EMBARRASS
off ...... SCORN, REJECT
too much ... CACHINNATE
laughable ... DROLL, RISIBLE, FUNNY, COMICAL, AMUSING, RIDICULOUS, ABSURD
laughing ...... RIANT, RIDENT
gas ..... NITROUS OXIDE
jackass .... KINGFISHER, KOOKABURRA, BIRD
laughingstock .... BUTT
laughs, he never ..... AGELAST
laughter (see laugh)
causing .... RISIBLE
pertaining to ... GELASTIC
sound of .... PEAL
la(u)nce .... EEL
Launcelot, the clown .. GOBBO
Launce's dog .... CRAB
launch ... HURL, START, BEGIN, MOTORBOAT, DISCHARGE, SEND OFF
Malay .... LANCA
Spanish/Portuguese ..... LANCHA
launder .... WASH
laundress .... WASHERWOMAN
lauraceous tree .... AVOCADO, NUTMEG, LAUREL, CAMPHOR
laurel .... BAY, DAPHNE, IVY, SHRUB, TREE, AZALEA, RHODODENDRON, CAJEPUT
actor .... STAN
bark .... COTO
bay .... MAGNOLIA
California ..... CAJEPUT, CAJUPUT
family .... HEATH, KALMIA
mountain ...... CALICO, BUSH
woven sprigs of .... LAUREATE
laurels .... HONOR, FAME
Lausanne canton ...... VAUD
La(u)wine .... AVALANCHE
lava .... TAXITE, MAGMA, COULEE, LATITE, OBSIDIAN, ASH
cinder .... SCORIA
cooled .... AA
fragment ..... LAPILLUS
lava .... LOINCLOTH, WAISTCLOTH
pieces of .. SLAG, SCORIA
stream of .... COULEE
lavabo ... WASHBOWL, BASIN, TOWEL, LAVATORY
lavage .... WASHING,
Laval, premier .... PIERRE
lavalier(e) .... PENDANT
lavatory .... (WASH)BOWL, BASIN, LAVABO, RESTROOM
lave ...... ABSTERGE, BATHE, WASH, FLOW, DIP, POUR, REMAINDER
lavender .... ASPIC, MINT, PURPLE
product ... OIL, PERFUME
laver ... BASIN, FONT, SEAWEED
laverock .... LARK
lavish .... PRODIGAL, MUNIFICENT, WANTON, UNSPARING, UNSTINTED, GENEROUS, LIBERAL, PROFUSE
law .... CANON, CODE, ORDINANCE, REGULATION, STATUTE, RULE, PRINCIPLE, LEX, JUS, EDICT, ACT
and order .... PEACE
appendix, in .... CODICIL
break the ...... INFRACT
breaker .... FELON, SINNER, CRIMINAL, JAILBIRD
court .... FORUM, BENCH
courts of ..... JUDICIARY
decree having force of ... UKASE
degree .... LLB
denying throne to women SALIC
expert .... JURIST
fictitious name in .... (JOHN) DOE
imperial .... UKASE
intervening ...... MESNE
kind of .... STATUTE, COMMON, (UN)WRITTEN
like for like ...... TALION
making ..... LEGISLATION
municipal ... ORDINANCE
not enforced .... DEAD LETTER
of Moses ...... TORA(H), PENTATEUCH
of Moses book .. GENESIS, NUMBERS, EXODUS
of the place ... LEX LOCI
offenses against ... MALA
pertaining to .. FORENSIC, CANONIC, LEGAL, JURAL
points in .... LIS, RES
Roman .... LEX, JUS
the: colloq. .... POLICE(MAN)
unwritten ..... COMMON
usance .... USAGE
violate the ..... INFRACT
volume .... CODEX
written .... STATUTE
lawful ... LEGITIMATE, LEGAL, LICIT, JUST
lawgiver ..... SOLON, DRACO, MINOS, MOSES
Lawine .... AVALANCHE
lawless .... UNRULY
lawlessness .... ANARCHY, LICENSE
lawmaker .... LEGISLATOR, SOLON, SENATOR, COUNCILOR
lawmaking ..... LEGISLATION, ENACTMENT, LEGISLATIVE
lawn ...... CAMBRIC, GLADE, GRASS PLOT, BATISTE
Lawman .... LAYAMON
Lawrence of ____ .... ARABIA
laws, body of .... CODE, PANDECTS, DECALOG(UE)
describing some .... DEAD LETTER, ARCHAIC
what some lack ... TEETH
lawsuit .... CASE, LITIGATION, ACTION
expenses .... COSTS
grounds .... GIST
party to ...... LITIGANT, LITIGATOR, SUER
lawsuits, habitual .. BARRATRY
prone to ...... LITIGIOUS

lawyer .... BARRISTER, COUNSEL(OR), ATTORNEY, SOLICITOR, LEGIST, ADVOCATE, LEGALIST, MOUTHPIECE, JURIST
cap of .... COIF
fee of .... RETAINER
of fiction .... TUTT, PERRY MASON
profession of .... BAR
stock objection of .... LEADING, IRRELEVANT, INCOMPETENT
unscrupulous .. SHYSTER
woman .... PORTIA
lawyers' bag ...... BRIEFCASE
Bible .... BLACKSTONE
concern ... BRIEF, CASE, TRIAL, HEARING, EVIDENCE
patron saint .... IVES
lax .... LOOSE, SLACK, CARELESS
laxative ... PHYSIC, APERIENT, PURGATIVE, CATHARTIC, BLUE PILL, ALOIN, CASSIA, MAGNESIA
drug .... ALOES
leaf .... SENNA
pulp .... CASSIA
lay ..... DITTY, BET, BALLAD, PLACE, LAIC, SECULAR, DEPOSIT, SET, ASCRIBE, RECLINE, POEM, SONG, MELODY
aside .... SAVE, PEND, TABLE
down ...... BET, WAGER
down arms .. SURRENDER, CAPITULATE
figure ... PUPPET, DUMMY
into .... BEAT, SCOLD
it on .... EXAGGERATE, FLATTER
off ... DISCHARGE, STOP, CEASE
open .... EXPOSE
out .... SPEND
siege .... INVEST
up ...... STORE, HOARD, PILE, HEAP
waste .... RAVAGE, DEVASTATE
Layamon's verse chronicle .... BRUT
layer .... COAT, VENEER, LAMINA, TIER, THICKNESS, FOLD, STRATUM, SHOOT, TWIG, DESS, PATINA, PLY
feathered .... BIRD, HEN
of iris .... UVEA
product of .... EGG
layers, form in ...... STRATIFY
layette, part of ...... BOOTEE, BEDDING
layman ...... LAIC, AMATEUR
layout .... ARRANGEMENT, MAKE-UP, FORMAT
lazar .... LEPER, BEGGAR
Lazarus ...... BEGGAR, LEPER
poet and essayist .. EMMA
sister of .. MARTHA, MARY
laze .... LOAF, LOUNGE

laziness ... SLOTH, INDOLENCE
lazy ... INDOLENT, SLOTHFUL, IDLE, SLUGGISH, OTIOSE
fellow ... DRONE, IDLER, LOAFER, DEADBEAT
Susan ..... TURNTABLE, TRAY
lazybones .... IDLER, LOAFER, BUM, DRONE
lazzarone .... BEGGAR
Le Gallienne, actress .... EVA
lea ..... MEAD(OW), PASTURE, GRASSLAND
measure of .... YARN
leach ..... LIXIVIATE, EXTRACT
leaching product .... LYE
leachy .... POROUS
lead ...... GUIDE, CONDUCT, PLUMBUM, PROMPT, HEAD, MINIUM, CLUE, HINT, CUE, GALENA, BULLET, PILOT, CONDUCE
astray .... MISGUIDE
black .... GRAPHITE, PLUMBAGO
color .... LIVID
glass for gem making .... STRASS, PASTE
in alchemy ..... SATURN
off .... BEGIN
on ... ENCOURAGE, LURE
ore ... GALENA, SULPHIDE
oxide .... LITHARGE
pellets .... SHOT
poisoning ... PLUMBISM, SATURNISM
red .... MINIUM
rope .... LONGE
shot .... PELLET
up to .... PAVE
white .... CERUSE
writing implement ...... PENCIL
leaden ..... DULL, SLUGGISH, HEAVY, GLOOMY
sky .... CLOUDY
leader .... CHIEF, HEAD, COMMANDER, OVERMAN
Argonauts' .... JASON
chorus .... CANTOR, CORYPHEUS
in music .... CONDUCTOR
in printing .... DOTS, DASHES
Italian .... DUCE
of Israelites ..... MOSES, JOSHUA
racing contest early ...... PACER, PACESETTER
sheep ...... BELLWETHER
Spanish ...... CAUDILLO
leadership quality, special .... CHARISMA
leading ...... CHIEF, AHEAD, PRINCIPAL, FOREMOST, STELLAR, MAIN
actor/actress ..... STAR
lady .... PREMIERE
leads .... BULLETS
leaf ... PHYLLOME, LAMELLA, PAGE, TENDRIL, FROND, SPATHE, PETAL, LAMINA
attachment .... STEM, PETIOLE, STIPEL, TWIG
beverage .... TEA
book .... FOLIO, PAGE
bud .... GEMMA
central vein ...... MIDRIB
combining form .... PHYLL(O)
cutter .... ATTA, ANT
disease ... MOSAIC, RUST
division of calyx .. SEPAL
drug ... HEMP, HASHISH, MARIJUANA
fern .... FROND
floating .... PAD
flower ..... SEPAL, BRACT
fodder .... RAPE
form ... SIMPLE, PINNATE, PALMATE, DENTATE, CRENATE, SERRATE, UNDULATE, LOBED
front side of ..... RECTO
gland .... LENTICEL
grass .... BLADE
large .... FROND
like .... PHYLLOID
like part .... STIPULE, BRACT
lily .... PAD
metal .... FOIL
miner beetle ..... HISPA
modified .... BRACT, PALEA, CARPEL, PISTIL
of calyx .... SEPAL
palm ...... OLA, FROND
part ... STOMA, LAMINA, STIPEL, STIPULES, BLADE, PETIOLE, STALK, VEIN, (MID)RIB
pitcher-like ... ASCIDIUM
poetic .... FROND
point .... MUCRO
pores .... STOMA
rib ...... VEIN, NERVURE
rudimentary .... CATAPHYLL
side of ... VERSO, RECTO
stalk .. PETIOLE, RHUBARB
stem angle .... AXIL
through book ... RIFFLE
tip .... MUCRO
tissue .... MESOPHYLL
tobacco ..... CAVENDISH
type .... LILYPAD
vein ..... RIB, NERVURE
water lily .... PAD
leafage .... FOLIAGE
leafless .... APHYLLOUS
plant .... CACTUS
leaflet ...... PINNA, FOLDER, TRACT, HANDBILL, PINNULE, THROWAWAY
leaflets, ring of ...... BRACTE, EPICALYX
leaflike design in windows ... FOIL
part .... SPATHE
leafstalk ... PETIOLE, CHARD, PHYLLODE, RHUBARB
leafy .... FOLIOSE
shelter .... BOWER
league ... FEDERATION, BUND, ALLIANCE, ASSOCIATION, BLOC

in ... ALLIED
merchants' ... HANSE
leaguer ... (BE)SIEGE
Leah's father ... LABAN
husband ... JACOB
sister ... RACHEL
son ... LEVI
leak ... LET, SEEP, OOZE, DRIP
leal ... LOYAL, TRUE
lean ... SPARE, LANK(Y), POOR, BONY, CANT, TILT, SCRAGGY, HEEL, SLIM, INCLINE, TEND, SLANT, GAUNT, SCRAWNY, SKINNY, THIN, MEAGER
make ... EMACIATE
pocket ... POOR
sideways ... CAREEN
to ... SHED, SHACK, ROOF
Leander's love ... HERO
leaning ... PENCHANT, INCLINATION, BENT
tower of ___ ... PISA
leap ... SPANG, LOUP, DIVE, LUNGE, SPRING, JUMP, BOUND, VAULT, HOP
ballet ... ENTRECHAT
goat's ... CAPRIOLE
horse's ... CURVET, CAPRIOLE
over ... SKIP
playful ... GAMBOL, CAPER, CAVORT
year ... BISSEXTILE
year gainer ... FEBRUARY
year hope ... PROPOSAL
leapfrog ... GAME
leaping ... SALIENT, SALTANT, SALTATION
Lear, daughter of ... REGAN, GONERIL, CORDELIA
dog of ... TRAY
forte of Edward ... LIMERICK
learn ... KNOW, ASCERTAIN, DISCOVER, UNEARTH, HEAR
by heart ... MEMORIZE
superficially ... SMATTER
learned ... ERUDITE, LETTERED, WISE, EDUCATED, INFORMED, LITERATE
man ... PANDIT(A), PUNDIT, SCHOLAR, INTELLECTUAL, SAGE, PEDANT, SAVANT, MULLA(H)
people ... LITERATI, CLERISY
learning ... WISDOM, ERUDITION, KNOWLEDGE, LORE, CULTURE, EDUCATION
branch of ... OLOGY, SCIENCE
shallow ... SCIOLISM
lease ... DEMISE, REMISE, LET, CONTRACT, HIRE, RENT, CHARTER, TENURE
consideration ... RENT(AL)
grant ... DEMISE
party to a ... LESSOR, LESSEE, LANDLORD, TENANT
leaseholder ... LESSEE
leash ... CONTROL, ROPE, CURB, BRACE, JESS, SLIP, THONG, REIN, LUNG, LONGE, TETHER
hound ... LIMER
ring ... TERRET
least ... SMALLEST, SLIGHTEST, MINIMUM, FEWEST
likely ... LAST, MINIMAL
leastwise ... ANYWAY
leather ... SUEDE, KID, CALF
armor ... GAMBESON
bag ... POUCH
bookbinding ... SKIVER
bottle ... MATARA
convert into ... TAW, TAN
cordovan ... CORDWAIN
cutter ... SKIVER
decorated ... DICING
factory ... TANNERY
fine ... VELLUM, CALFSKIN
flask ... OLPE, MATARA
glove ... NAPA, SUEDE, KID, MOCHA, MITTEN
heel (shoe) ... RAND
kind of ... CHAMOIS, MOCHA, SHAGREEN, KIP, CALF, OXHIDE, LEVANT, NAPA, ROAN, COWHIDE, ELK
like ... CORIACEOUS
maker ... TANNER
pouch, Highlanders' ... SPORRAN
prepare ... TAN, TAW
saddle ... MOCHILA
sheepskin ... ROAN
shoe repair ... FOXING
soft ... CHAMOIS, SUEDE, NAPA, ROAN, MOCHA
softener ... DUBBIN(G)
strap ... THONG
strip ... RAND, WELT, STRAP, THONG
thong ... BRAIL
velvety ... MOCHA
waterproofer ... DUBBIN(G)
worker ... CORDWAINER, TANNER
worker's tool ... GRINDERY
leatherback ... TURTLE
leatherette ... MOROCCO
leatherfish ... LIJA
leatherneck ... MARINE, GYRENE
leatherwood ... WICOPY
leave ... BEQUEATH, ENTRUST, COMMIT, FORSAKE, SET OUT, DEPART, PERMISSION, RETIRE, EXEAT, VAMOSE, QUIT, SKIDDOO
hurriedly ... HIGHTAIL, DECAMP, LAM, SKIDDOO
kind of ... SABBATICAL
military ... FURLOUGH
off ... DESIST, CEASE, STOP
out ... OMIT, IGNORE, ELIDE, EXCEPT
port ... OUTSTAND
secretly ... DECAMP
stage ... EXIT, EXEUNT
taking ... CONGE, ADIEU, FAREWELL
leaven ... BARM, YEAST, (EN)ZYME, SOURDOUGH
leaves ... FOLIAGE, PAGES, DEPARTS
circular arrangement of ... VERTICIL
cluster ... ROSETTE
collectively ... FOLIAGE
covered with ... FOLIOSE
fragrant ... THYME
having ... FOLIACEOUS, FOLIAGED, PETALED
having two ... BIFOLIATE
laxative ... SENNA
numbering of ... FOLIATION
of ... FOLIAR
seasoning ... LAUREL, THYME
spread around plant ... MULCH
vegetable ... SLAW
leaving(s) ... CHAFF, REFUSE, WASTE, RESIDUE, DRAFF, DREGS, REST, ORTS, REMNANTS, OFFAL
pick up ... GLEAN
Lebanon capital ... BEIRUT
city/town ... HERMEL, BAALBEK, ZAHLE, TRIPOLI, BEIRUT, SAIDA
monetary unit ... POUND
native ... LEVANTINE
premier ... KARAME
president ... HELOU
seaport ... TYRE, SAIDA, TRIPOLI
Valley river ... ORONTES
lebensraum ... LIVING SPACE
lebistes ... GUPPY
lecher ... SATYR, DEBAUCHEE
lecherous ... LUSTFUL, RANDY, SENSUAL
lechery ... LEWDNESS
lectern ... AMBO, PULPIT, (READING) DESK, STAND
lection ... READING
lector ... READER, LECTURER
lecture ... SCOLD(ING), TALK, PRELECT(ION)
hall ... LYCEUM
kind of ... SERMON
moralizing ... SERMON, HOMILY
lecturer ... DOCENT, (PRE)LECTOR, READER
foreign ... LECTOR
stand of ... LECTERN
Leda's daughter ... HELEN, CLYTEMNESTRA
husband ... TYNDAREUS
lover: mythology ... SWAN, ZEUS
son ... CASTOR, POLLUX
ledge ... LODE, BERM(E), RIDGE, SHELF, SILL
altar ... RETABLE
ledger entry ... CREDIT, DEBIT, LOSS, RENT, INTEREST
lee ... SHELTER, PROTECTION
opposed to ... STOSS, WEATHER, WINDWARD
leech ... ANNELID, PARASITE,

WORM, BLEED, PHYSICIAN, HEAL
like .... HIRUDINOID
sucker of .. ACETABULUM
leek .... ALLIUM, VEGETABLE, BULB, ROCAMBOLE, SCALLION
relation .... ONION, GARLIC
leer ...... SCOFF, SNEER, EYE, OGLE, STARE, MOCK
leery ..... WARY, SUSPICIOUS, DUBIOUS
lees .... DRAFF, DREGS, GROUNDS, RESIDUE
leet .... COURT
Leeward islands .... NEVIS, ANTIGUA, ST. KITTS, MONTSERRAT
leeway ... MARGIN, SAG, ROOM
left ... LARBOARD, DEPARTED, WENT, PORT, GONE, SINISTER
after expenses ...... NET
aground .... NEAPED, BEACHED, STRANDED
combining form .... L(A)EVO
hand ..... LEVO, SINISTER
hand of page ..... VERSO, LEVO
handed ..... SOUTHPAW, CLUMSY, AWKWARD, DUBIOUS, INSINCERE, SINISTRAL, MORGANATIC
lonely .... BEREFT
on the .... NIGH
opposed to ...... RIGHT
over .... REMNANT
political .... LIBERAL, RADICAL
side of bow ... LARBOARD
side, on the ..... APORT, NEAR
turn .... HAW
leftist .... RED, RADICAL, LIBERAL
leftover ... ORT, MANAVELIN, MORSEL, SCRAP
lefty .... SOUTHPAW
leg .... LIMB, PROP, PIN, GAMB(E), SHANK
armor .... GREAVES, JAMB(EAU)
bone ..... FIBULA, TIBIA
colloquial .. PIN, STUMP, GAM, PEG
covering ..... LEGGINGS, PUTTEE, PEDULE, CHAUSSES, GAITER, PUTTY
fleshy part .... CALF
fowl's ...... DRUMSTICK
front of .... SHIN
from knee to ankle ..... CRUS, SHANK
in heraldry .... GAMB
irons .... NIPPERS
joint ...... KNEE, ANKLE, HOCK
journey's .... TREK
lamb's, cooked .. GIGOT
mutton .... GIGOT, AVINE
part .. SHIN, SHANK, HAM, CALF, CRUS
pertaining to ... CRURAL, SURAL
protuberance, bird's .... SPUR, CALCAR
shake a .... HURRY, DANCE
thigh .... FEMUR
triangle's .. HYPOTENUSE
vein .... SAPHENA
wooden .... STUMP
work .... WALK(ING)
legacy .... BEQUEST, INHERITANCE, GIFT, PATRIMONY
receiver of ..... LEGATEE, HEIR(ESS)
legal .... LAWFUL, VALID, LEGITIMATE, LICIT, LICET, JURAL
abstract .... PRECIS
action ...... (LAW)SUIT, CASE, LITIGATION, RES, REPLEVIN
arrest .... CAPTION
attachment .... LIEN
charge .... FEE
claim .... LIEN, DEMAND
code .... PANDECT
contestant .... LITIGANT
defense .... ALIBI
delay .... MORA
fee ..... DUE, RETAINER
force, lose .... STALE
hearing .... OYER, TRIAL
instrument .... DEED
matter .... RES
notice .... MONITION
offense ... DELICT, DELIT, CRIME
order .... WRIT
paper .... DEED
point .... RES
possession ..... SEIZIN, SIESIN
profession .... BAR, LAW
record ... ESTREAT, ACTA
redress .... REMEDY
right .... DROIT
site .... VENUE
substitute .... SURROGATE
summons ..... SUBPOENA
tender .... MONEY
thing .... RES
warning .... CAVEAT
wrong .... TORT
legalism in relation ... NOMISM
legalist .... LAWYER
legalize .... SIGN
legally bound .... LIABLE
competent ... SUI JURIS
legate ... ENVOY, AMBASSADOR
Papal .... NUNCIO
Roman .... GOVERNOR
legatee .... HEIR, INHERITOR
legation ... MISSION, EMBASSY
legato, opposed to .. STACCATO
legend ... MYTH, FABLE, SAGA, MOTTO, TALE, CAPTION, STORY, INSCRIPTION, TITLE
legendary ..... TRADITIONAL, FABULOUS, FICTITIOUS, EPIC, STORIED
bird .... ROC
leger .... LIGHT
legerdemain .... DECEIT, SLEIGHT OF HAND, TRICKS, MAGIC, HOCUS-POCUS
practice .... CONJURE
leges, singular of .... LEX
legging(s) .... GAITER, GAMBADO, PUTTIE, GAMBADE, PUTTEE
leggy .... LONG LIMBED
Leghorn .... LIVORNO, CHICKEN, HAT
legible .... READABLE, DECIPHERABLE
legion .... ARMY, HORDE, MULTITUDE
unit ... COHORT, MANIPLE
legislate .... ENACT
legislation .... LAW(S)
legislative body .... DIET, HOUSE, SENATE, CONGRESS, CORTES, DAIL, FOLKETING, BUNDESTAG, STORTING, PARLIAMENT, ASSEMBLY, COUNCIL
building .... CAPITOL
legislator .... LAWMAKER, SOLON, SENATOR
legislature .... DIET, PARLIAMENT, CONGRESS, SENATOR
lameduck .... RUMP
two-chambered .... BICAMERAL
legist .... LAWYER
legit: sl. ..... THEATER, STAGE
legitimate .... LAWFUL, LICIT, LEGAL, ALLOWED, REASONABLE
legless amphibian .. CAECILIAN
legree ..... MASTER, OVERSEER
fictional .... SIMON
legume ..... POD, BEAN, PEA, PLANT, SEED, LOMENT, LENTIL, SOY
legumin .... GLOBULIN, CONGLUTIN
leguminous seed ..... LOMENT, PULSE, PEA, BEAN
Lehar, composer ..... FRANZ
Lehmann, soprano ..... LILLI, LOTTE
lehua .... TREE, MYRTLE
lei ...... GARLAND, WREATH
singular .... LEU
Leicester .... SHEEP
leister ...... SPEAR, TRIDENT
leisure .... EASE, OTIOSE
leisurely .... SLOW(LY), UNHURRIED
leman .... MISTRESS, SWEETHEART, LOVER
Lemberg ...... LWOW, LVOV
lemming ...... RODENT, RAT
lemon .... CITRUS, FRUIT
juice squeezer ... REAMER
juice vitamin ..... CITRIN

like fruit .... LIME, CITRON
peel .... RELISH
yellow .... CITRINE, CITREOUS
lemons, of .... CITRIC
lemur ...... AYEAYE, MONKEY, POTTO, MACACO, SIFAKA
arboreal .... LORIS
Asiatic .... LORI(S)
Ceylon .... LORI
flying .. COLUGO, GALAGO
kin of .... TARSIER
Madagascar ...... INDRI
nocturnal .... LORIS
Lemuria .... CONTINENT
lemuroid .... POTTO
Lena, singer .... HORNE
tributary .... ALDAN
lenard .... LINNET
Lenape .... INDIAN
lend .... LET OUT, IMPART
length .... EXTENT
abbreviation ..... LGTH
at .... FINALLY
finger to elbow ... CUBIT
great .... LONG
having .... LINEAR
in time .... DURATION
of day's march ... ETAPE
unit ...... MICRON, MIL, METER, YARD
lengthen ... STRETCH, EXTEND, PROLONG, ELONGATE, DISTEND, PROTRACT
lengthwise .... LONGWAYS
lengthy ...... PROLIX, LONG, DRAWN OUT, EXTENDED
colloquial .... TALL
lenient .... GENTLE, CLEMENT, MILD, MERCIFUL, AUDIENT
Lenin, premier .... NIKOLAI (ULIANOV)
Leningrad .... PETROGRAD
river .... NEVA
lenis ..... SMOOTH, SOFT, MILD
opposed to ...... FORTIS
lenitive .... SOOTHING, SOFTENING, LAXATIVE
lenity ..... MILDNESS, MERCY
leno .... WEAVE, FABRIC
lens .... MENISCUS
hand .... READER
kind of ...... CONCAVE, CONVEX
shaped .... LENTOID, LENTICULAR
type of .... MENISCUS, TORIC
lent .... IMPREST
observance ... PENITENCE, FASTING
revelry before .. CARNIVAL
Lenten ... MEAGER, CHEERLESS, QUADRAGESIMAL
lentiginous .... FRECKLY
lentigo .... FRECKLE
lentil .... PEA, SEED, PLANT, ERVUM, LEGUME, PULSE
l'envoi ... POSTSCRIPT, STANZA, VERSE, DEDICATION, INSCRIPTION
Leonard's (Jack) forte .... INSULT
Leonardo da ____ ..... VINCI
Leoncavallo, composer ...... RUGGIERO
opera by ... PAGLIACCI, ZAZA
Leonidas' scene of defeat ..... THERMOPYLAE
leopard .... OCELOT, CAT, PANTHER, OUNCE
like animal ..... JAGUAR
pet .... CHEETAH
young .... WHELP
leotard .... TIGHTS
leper ...... OUTCAST, LAZAR, LAZARUS, PARIAH
colony .... LEPROSARIUM
hospital .... SPITAL
patron saint of .... GILES
lepidolite .... MICA
lepidopteron .... MOTH, BUTTERFLY
lepidosiren .... DOKO
lepidate ...... SCALY, FLAKY, SCURFY
Lepontine Alps peak .. LEONE
leporid (leporine) animal ..... HARE, RABBIT
leprechaun ..... ELF, GOBLIN, FAIRY
leprose ...... SCALY, SCURFY
leprosy .... LEPRA
leprous .... UNCLEAN
beggar .... LAZAR(US)
leptons, 100 .... DRACHMA
leptus .... LARVA, MITE
lepus ... HARE, CONSTELLATION
lerot .... DORMOUSE
"Les Miserables" author ..... HUGO
character ..... FANTINE, JAVERT, VALJEAN
Lesage, novelist ...... ALAIN, RENE
lesbian .... EROTIC, HOMOSEXUAL, SAPPHO
Lesbos .... MYTILENE
poet ... ARION, LESCHES, ALCAEUS, SAPPHO
lese majeste .... TREASON
lesion ..... INJURY, DAMAGE, HURT
less .... MINOR, MINUS, FEW(ER), SMALLER
in music .... MENO
lessee .... TENANT, LEASEHOLDER, RENTER
lessen ...... (A)BATE, REDUCE, MINIFY, MITIGATE, THIN, DIMINISH, TAPER, DECREASE, DISPARAGE, MINIMIZE
lesser ...... SMALLER, MINOR
Antilles islands .... LEEWARD
Bear ..... URSA (MINOR)
lesson .... INSTRUCTION, EXERCISE, ASSIGNMENT
from fable .... MORAL
music .... ETUDE
lessor .... LANDLORD
let ... ALLOW, LEASE, PERMIT, RENT, LEAVE, ABANDON, FORSAKE, HIRE (OUT), ASSIGN, OBSTACLE, SUFFER
bait drop .... DAP
down ..... DISAPPOINT, RELAX, SLACKEN, LOWER
fall .... DROP
go .... UNHAND, RELEASE, LOOSE
in ..... ADMIT, INTROMIT
it be given .... DETUR
it stand ...... STET, STA
on ...... PRETEND, HINT,
out ..... RELEASE, EMIT, LEASE, DISMISS
sink .... VAIL
up .... CEASE, RELAX, SLACKEN, ABATE, EASE
letdown ..... DISAPPOINTMENT
lethal .... FATAL, DEADLY
lethargic ..... INERT, TORPID, COMATOSE, DULL, SLUGGISH
sleep .... SOPOR
lethargy .... TORPOR, STUPOR, LANGUOR, LASSITUDE, INERTNESS, DROWSINESS, INERTIA, APATHY, INDIFFERENCE, COMA
Lethe .... OBLIVION, FORGETFULNESS, RIVER
lethiferous .... DEADLY
Leto .... LATONA
daughter of .... ARTEMIS, DIANA
son of .... APOLLO
Lett ..... LATVIAN, LIVONIAN
letter ...... MESSAGE, EPISTLE, MISSIVE, INSCRIBE, BREVE, CREDENCE
addresser of ..... MAILER
airmail ...... AEROGRAM
beginning a word .... INITIAL
bishop's ...... PASTORAL
capital, in printing ...... UPPER CASE
carrier .... POSTMAN, MAILMAN, POSTBOY, COURIER
cross stroke ...... SERIF
cut off last ..... APOCOPE
for letter ..... LITERATIM, LITERALLY
illuminated ... MINIATURE
large .... MAJUSCULE, CAPITAL, UNCIAL
main stroke .... STEM
of challenge ..... CARTEL
of credence .. CREDENTIAL
official .... BULL
opener .... CENSOR, MADAM, SIR
Papal .... BULL
perfect .... CORRECT
representing a word ..... LOGOGRAM
resignation ...... DEMIT
short ... MISSIVE, MEMO, NOTE, LINE
silent .... MUTE
small, in printing .... LOWER CASE, MINISCULE

to ____ .... GARCIA
to host .... GRACENOTE, BREAD-AND-BUTTER
to the .... EXACTLY, PRECISELY, LITERAL
lettered .... LEARNED, EDUCATED, LITERATE
letterhead detail .... ADDRESS, NAME
letterpress .... TEXT
letters ..... LITERATURE, MAIL
capital, in printing ...... UPPER CASE
collection/delivery of .... MAIL, PAPERS
men of .... LITERATI, INTELLECTUALS, SCHOLARS
of credence .. CREDENTIAL
slanting up ..... ITALICS
woven in design .... MONOGRAM
lettuce .... MINION, ROMAINE, SALAD, COS, BIBB
slang .... (PAPER)MONEY
letup .... LESSENING, ABATEMENT, STOP, PAUSE, CEASE
leucorrhea .... WHITES
leukemia ..... TUMOR, CANCER
Levantine .... SILK, SHIP
garment .... CAFTAN, GREGO
ketch ...... XEBEC, SAIC, SETTEE
land .... ISRAEL
port ...... ACRE, ELATH
region .. SYRIA, LEBANON, PALESTINE
state ... SYRIA, LEBANON
levee .... DIKE, DURBAR, LANDING, QUAY, EMBANKMENT, RECEPTION
break in ...... CREVASSE
level .... RASE, EVEN, GRADE, RAZE, HEIGHT, ALTITUDE, DEMOLISH, LAY LOW, AIM, PLANE, SMOOTH, FLAT(TEN)
combining form ... PLANI
headed .... SENSIBLE
on the .... FAIR, HONEST
plot .... TERRACE
leveling slip .... SHIM
lever ... SWIPE, TAPPET, PEDAL, CRANK, PRISE, PRY, (CROW)BAR, SAMSON, PRIZE, PEAV(E)Y, PEEV(E)Y, LAM
foot .... TREADLE
leveret .... HARE
Levi's parent .... JACOB, LEAH
leviathan ..... WHALE, HUGE, MONSTER
author of ...... HOBBES
levigate .... MIX, GRIND
levin ..... LIGHT, LIGHTNING
levis .... OVERALLS
levitate ... FLOAT, RISE, SOAR
levity .. BUOYANCY, FRIVOLITY, FICKLENESS
levulin .... CARBOHYDRATE
levulose .... FRUCTOSE
levy .... COLLECT, ASSESS, TAX, IMPRESS, IMPOSITION, DRAFT, IMPOSE, TRIBUTE, FINE, IMPOST, ENLIST, WAGE, CESS, MUSTER, TITHE, SCOT
en masse, for example ... MOBILIZE
Lew Wallace hero .. (BEN) HUR
lewd ...... LUSTFUL, CADGY, INDECENT, UNCHASTE, LASCIVIOUS, LIBIDINOUS
Lewis Carroll character ...... MADHATTER, ALICE, SNARK
companion-explorer .... CLARK
Gantry of Sinclair ...... ELMER
lex .... LAW
lexicographer .... WORDMAN, COMPILER, ROGET
lexicographic work ..... DICTIONARY, THESAURUS
lexicon .... DICTIONARY, VOCABULARY, WORDBOOK
Leyte, capital of .. TACLOBAN
Lhasa holy man .... (DALAI) LAMA
is capital of ...... TIBET
liability ... OBLIGATION, DEBT, DUTY, HANDICAP, RESPONSIBILITY
opposed to ...... ASSET
liable .... APT, OPEN, BOUND, SUBJECT, RESPONSIBLE, ANSWERABLE, LIKELY
liaison .... LINKING (UP), LOVE AFFAIR, AMOUR, SANDHI
officer ... COORDINATOR
liana ... CIPO, VIBURNUM, SIPO
liang .... TAEL, WEIGHT
liar........ FIBSTER, CHEAT, FIBBER, SAPPHIRA, ANANIAS, DISSEMBLER, PREVARICATOR
tall ...... MUNCHAUSEN, ANGLER
lias .... ROCK
libation .... DRINK
Libau .... LIEBAJA
libel ... ROORBACK, SLANDER, MALIGN, DEFAME, CALUMNY, MUD
libelous .... VILLIFYING, DEFAMATORY, SLANDEROUS
liber .... BOOK
diminutive of ...... LIBEL
plural of .... LIBRI
liberal ... LEFTIST, FRANK, AMPLE, GENEROUS, ABUNDANT, FREE, BROADMINDED, LICENTIOUS, PROGRESSIVE, RADICAL
arts subject ... HISTORY, LITERATURE, LOGIC, RHETORIC
liberate ...... FREE, REDEEM, RANSOM, RELEASE, UNTIE, MANUMIT
military slang ..... LOOT
slang .... DEPRIVE
Liberian capital .. MONROVIA
coast .... KRU
native .... VAI, TOMA
president ...... TUBMAN
tribe .... KRA, KRU, GOLA, GORA
"Uncle Shad" .. TUBMAN
libertine ..... RAKE, SKEPTIC, LICENTIOUS, DEBAUCHEE, ROUE
liberty .... FREEDOM, EXEMPTION, FAMILIARITY, PERMISSION
abuse of .... LICENSE
at .... FREE, ALLOWED
Island .... BEDLOE'S
libidinous .... LEWD, LASCIVIOUS, LUSTFUL
libido .... SEX
library .... BIBLIOTHECA
newspaper ..... MORGUE
reading place .. CARREL(L)
supervisor ..... CURATOR
librate .... OSCILLATE, HOVER, POISE
libretto ... BOOK, TEXT, WORDS
libri .... BOOKS
Lybia .... KINGDOM
Libyan capital (joint) .... TRIPOLI, BENGASI
city .... BENGASI
gulf .... SIDRA
king .... IDRIS
premier ...... (EL) BADRI
port .... TRIPOLI
strongman ..... GADAFFI
lice .... VERMIN
infested .... LOUSY
of .... PEDICULAR
license .... PATENT, AUTHORIZATION, PERMIT, FREEDOM, AUTHORIZE, FRANCHISE, PERMISSION, LIBERTY
licentious .... LIBERTINE, DISSOLUTE, LASCIVIOUS, LEWD
licet .... LEGAL
lich .... CORPSE
lichee .... LITCHI, NUT
lichen .... PARELLA, ALGA, FUNGUS, MOSS, PARELLE, RATMARA, ORCHIL, ARCHIL, ORCHAL, EPIPHYTE, LUNGWORT
bearded .... USNEA
genus ... EVERNIA, USNEA
product .... LITMUS, CUDBEAR, ORCIN(OL)
licht .... LIGHT
licit .... LAWFUL, LEGAL, DUE, JUST, PERMITTED
lick ... LAP, WHIP, THRASH, BEAT, VANQUISH, BLOW, CLIP
plural: sl. ...... CHANCE, TURN
licking: colloq. ..... BEATING, DRUBBING, WHIPPING
lickspittle .... TOADY, FLATTERER
licorice ... ABRIN, JEQUIRITY, PEA
seed .... GOONCH, JEQUIRITY

lid ... CAP, CASE, COVER, TOP
colloquial .... CURB, RESTRAINT
joint .... HINGE
slang .... HAT, CAP
lie .... FLAM, PERJURE, PLUMPER, NESTLE, SPRAWL, TALE, FIB, MENDACITY, RECLINE, STRETCH, EXIST, ENTOMB, FALSEHOOD, EQUIVOCATE, ADMISSIBLE, LAY, LAIR, CORKER, REST, LIGE, PREVARICATE, FABRICATE
anchored ...... MOORED
at anchor .... RIDE
big: colloq. ... WHOPPER
describing one ... WHITE
detector ..... POLYGRAPH
in warmth .... BASK
U.N. Secretary General .. TRYGVE
waiting .... LURK, SKULK
Liechtenstein's capital .... VADUZ
king .... JOZEF II
peak .... FALKAIS
premier .... BATLINER
lied .... LYRIC, SONG
lief .... GLADLY, DEAR, WILLING(LY), VALUED, BELOVED
Liege .... LUIK, LOYAL, FAITHFUL, LORD, SOVEREIGN, VASSAL, SUBJECT, DEVOTED
liegeman .... VASSAL
lien .... CLAIM
lienectomy, objective of ...... SPLEEN
lientery .... DIARRHEA
Liepaja .... LIBAU
lier .... RECLINER
lierne .... RIB
lieu .... PLACE, STEAD
lieutenant ..... AIDE, DEPUTY
command of ... PLATOON
slang ..... LOOIE, LOOEY, SHAVETAIL
life ...... DAYS, ANIMATION, BIOTA, EXISTENCE, BREATH
account of one's .... BIOGRAPHY, MEMOIRS
after death .. HEREAFTER
belt, kind of .. MAE WEST
destruction of .. BIOLYSIS
French .... VIE
insurance ...... TONTINE
Latin ...... VITA, ANIMA
long ...... LONGEVITY
of ____ .... RILEY
of the party ...... CUTUP
pertaining to .. BIOTIC(AL)
plant and animal .. BIOTA
prefix .... BIO
preserver ..... MAE WEST
principle .... ATMAN, PRANA, JIVA, SPIRIT
prolonger, alleged ...... ELIXIR
relating to .... BIOTIC(AL)
saving fluid ..... PLASMA
saving jacket .. MAE WEST
size, larger than .. HEROIC
without .... AZOIC, AMORT, DEAD
work .... CAREER
lifeless .... DEAD, DULL, LISTLESS, AMORT, INERT, AZOIC, VAPID
lifelike .... NATURAL, GRAPHIC
lifesaver .... LIFEGUARD
lifetime .... AGE, DAYS
lift ..... HEFT, SWIPE, PERK, RAISE, HOLD UP, ELEVATE, EXALT, PLAGIARIZE, STEAL, HOIST, BOOST
British ...... ELEVATOR
colloquial ... PLAGIARIZE
slang .... STEAL
with effort .... HEAVE
lifting muscle ...... ERECTOR, LEVATOR
ligament .... TENDON, TAENIA
combining form .. DESMO
like a .... DESMOID
twist a .... SPRAIN
ligan ...... FLOTSAM, JETSAM
ligate .... BANDAGE
ligature .... TAENIA, TIE, BANDAGE, BOND, THREAD
light ... LAND, ILLUME, AIRY, SLEAZY, GLIM, LEGER, (IL)LUMINE, ILLUMINATION, NEON, MILD, IGNATE, FAIR, ASPECT, LAMP, KLIEG, TAPER, WHERRY
again .... RELUME
amplifier .... LASER
anchor .... KEDGE
around sun .... AUREOLA
beacon .... FANAL
burning .. TORCH, CRESSET
carrying case ... LANTERN
celestial .... CORONA, HALO, NIMBUS
circle of ...... AUREOLA, HALO, NIMB(US), AUREOLE, CORONA
feeble .... TAPER
fingered gentry member .. DIP, PICKPOCKET
flooded with .. LUMINOUS
footed ... NIMBLE, SPRY
fuse .... SPIT
game luring ...... JACK
giving device .... TORCH, LAMP, LANTERN
giving of ...... LUCENT, LUMINOUS
giving substance .... PHOSPHOR
guiding .... BEACON
handed .... DEFT
headed ..... GAY, SILLY
holding case ... LANTERN
Horse Harry ...... LEE
measure .... LUMENS
of reflected ... CATOPTRIC
opera .... OPERETTA
pertaining to .... PHOTIC
providing ... LUCIFEROUS
put out .... DOUSE
reflecting ..... RELUCENT
ring of .... CORONA
science of ...... OPTICS, PHOTICS
source of .... SUN, LAMP
streak in sky ... METEOR
surrounding saint .... NIMBUS
touch .... TAP, PAT
type of ..... KLIEG, ARC, NEON
unit .... LUX, PHOT, LUMEN, PYR, HEFNER
up .... KINDLE
very .... ETHEREAL
without ...... APHOTIC
wood ... BALSA, POPLAR
lighted: poetic ...... LITTEN
lighten .. ILLUMINATE, FLASH, GLADDEN, RELIEVE, EASE
lighter ... KEEL, SCOW, BARGE, BOAT, HOY
lamp .... SPILL
than-air craft .. AEROSTAT
lightfingered person .... PICKPOCKET, DIP
lightheaded ... GIDDY, DIZZY, FRIVOLOUS, FLIGHTY, DELIRIOUS
lighthearted ... GAY, CAREFREE
lighthouse ... BEACON, PHARE, FANAL, PHAROS
appurtenance .... BEACON (LIGHT)
lighting fixture ...... SCONCE
means of ... SPILL, MATCH
lightly .... AIRILY
lightning ... LEVIN, IGNITION, FLASH, FIREBALL
bug .... FIREFLY
flash of .... BOLT
rod .... ARRESTER
without thunder .... WILDFIRE
lights .... LUNGS
out signal .... TAPS, CURFEW
lightsome ..... NIMBLE, GAY, LIVELY, LUMINOUS, BRIGHT
lignaloes .... ALOES
ligneous ..... WOODY, XYLOID
lignite ...... JET, (CHAR)COAL
lignose .... EXPLOSIVE
ligulate ..... LORATE, THONG
ligule .... COROLLA
ligure .... JACINTH, STONE
Ligurian Sea city ..... GENOA, LEGHORN, LIVORNO, LA SPEZIA
like ...... SIMILAR, AS, COPY, ENJOY, COGNATE, RESEMBLING, CHOOSE, AKIN, RELISH
bear .... URSINE
better .... PREFER
combining form .... HOME(O), OID, INE
hare .... LEPORINE
ladder .... SCALAR
tail .... CAUDAL
wing .... PTERIC
likelihood ..... PROBABILITY, CHANCE

likely .... APT, LIABLE, PROBABLE, CREDIBLE, PRONE, SEEMLY
liken .... COMPARE
likeness .... EFFIGY, ICON, IMAGE, GUISE, SIMILARITY, (RE)SEMBLANCE
bad .... CARICATURE
show .... MIRROR
likes ... TASTES, PREFERENCES
likewise ... ALSO, DITTO, TOO, MOREOVER, BESIDES
not .... NOR
likin: Chinese .... TAX
liking ..... FONDNESS, GUSTO, TASTE, PREFERENCE, PALATE, AFFECTION, FANCY, PENCHANT
lilac ...... FLOWER, SYRINGA, SHRUB
lilaceous plant ... ALOE, ONION, LEEK
Liliom .... CAROUSEL
Lilith ..... DEMON, VAMPIRE, WITCH
husband of .... ADAM
Lillie, Miss .... BEA(TRICE)
Lilliputian .... MIDGET, TINY, DWARF(ISH), SMALL
republic ... SAN MARINO
lilt ... RHYTHM, SONG, SWING
lily .... ARUM, ALOE, IXIA, LOTUS, YUCCA, LIS, CALLA, SEGO, TULIP, ONION, LYS
bulb .... SQUILL
butterfly ..... MARIPOSA, SEGO
calla .... ARUM
family .... ALOE, SQUILL, GARLIC, CAMAS(S), QUAMASH
family, of the .... LILACEOUS
leaf .... PAD
"Maid of Astolat" ...... ELAIN(E)
palm .... TI
plant .. CAMAS(S), CAMMAS
livered .... COWARDLY
relative .... ONION
sand .... SOAPROOT
sea .... CRINOID
shaped .... CRINOID
water .. LOTUS, NELUMBO, LOTOS, NYMPHAEA
Lima, money in .... SOL
limacine mollusk .. SLUG, SNAIL
limax/limacis .... SLUG
limb ...... BRANCH, LEG, FIN, BOUGH, ARM, WING, IMP, DISJOINT, MEMBER, EDGE, MARGIN, BORDER
joint ..... KNEE, ELBOW
muscle .... FLEXOR, LEVATOR
limber .... PLIANT, AGILE, FLEXIBLE, LITHE, SUPPLE, LISSOM(E)
limbo .... JAIL, PRISON, IMPRISONMENT
Limburg(er) .... CHEESE
limbus ..... EDGING, BORDER
lime ... CALX, CATCH, CEMENT, LINDEN, CITRON, FRUIT
bush .... SNARE
combining form ... CALCI
fruit like .... CITRON
harden with ... CALCIFY
mixture .... CEMENT
powder .... CONITE, KONITE
product .... APATITE, CALCIC
remove ..... DECALCIFY
sulfur, use of ..... SPRAY
tree ...... LINDEN, TEIL, BASS(WOOD), TUPELO
limelight .... SPOTLIGHT
limen .... THRESHOLD, STIMULATION
limerick man .... LEAR
limes .... DEFENSES, FORTIFICATION
limestone .... TUFA, PISOLITE, TRAVERTIN(E), DOLOMITE, CALCITE, MALM, LIAS, CHALK, CALP, OOLITE, COQUINA
crystallized .... MARBLE
limey .... SAILOR, SOLDIER, ENGLISHMAN
limicoline bird ...... CURLEW, PLOVER, SNIPE, SANDPIPER, KILLDEER
limit ..... MARGIN, BOURN(E), TERM, BOUND(ARY), RESTRICT, CURB, CONFINE, DEMARCATION, BUTTING, PALE, SPAN, FIX, CIRCUMSCRIBE, METE, STINT, STENT
limitation to inheritance .. TAIL
limited ..... SCANT, NARROW, CIRCUMSCRIBED, FINITE
limitless ...... VAST, INFINITE, UNBOUNDED, BOUNDLESS, IMMENSE
limits .... BOUNDS
limn ... DEPICT, DRAW, PAINT, PORTRAY, DESCRIBE, SKETCH
Limoges .... PORCELAIN, CHINAWARE
limonene .... TERPENE
limousine ..... AUTO(MOBILE), SEDAN
limp ... HITCH, FLABBY, HALT, SOFT, LAX, WILTED, HOBBLE, FLIMSY, FLACCID
limpet ... SHELLFISH, LAMPREY
limpid .... CLEAR, PELLUCID, TRANSPARENT
limpkin .... COURLAN
limuloid .... KING CRAB, LIMULUS
limulus .... KING CRAB
limy .... STICKY
linage .... ALIGNMENT
linchpin .... FORELOCK
Lincoln's hat ..... STOVEPIPE
sobriquet .. RAILSPLITTER, (HONEST) ABE
son ..... WILLIE, ROBERT
wife ...... (MARY) TODD
Lind, soprano .... JENNY
soubriquet .... NIGHTINGALE
linden .... TEIL
tree ... LIME, BASSWOOD, LINN
Lindsay, poet .... VACHEL
line .... ROUTE, CORD, CERIF, ROW, ROPE, STRING, WIRE, REIN, DEMARCATION, CORDON, OCCUPATION, TRADE, BUSINESS, VECTOR, FILE, PATTER, QUEUE, RANK, SERIF
ancestral .... LINEAGE
battle .... FRONT
control .... REIN
cutting .... SECANT
draw the .... LIMIT
family .... ANCESTRY, BLOOD, TREE
fine ... SERIF, CERIF, STRIA
hair ...... CERIPH, SERIF
imaginary....... VECTOR
in .... AROW
in prosody .... STICH
in trigonometry .... SECANT, SINE, TANGENT
inside of .... CEIL
intersecting .... SECANT, VECTOR
joining barometric points ISOBAR
junction .... SEAM
nautical .... MARLINE, EARING
of action ..... DEMARCHE
of color .... STREAK
of persons ...... QUEUE
pertaining to .... LINEAL, LINEAR
reference .... AXIS
roof .... CEIL
ship side ..... PLIMSOLL
the inside .... CEIL
threadlike .... STRIA
toe the .. OBEY, CONFORM
waiting ..... CUE, QUEUE
walls of .... CEIL
with bricks ...... REVET
with stone ..... STEAN(E)
without angle ... AGONE
lineage ... STEM, GENEALOGY, BLOOD, STRAIN, DESCENT, ANCESTRY, FAMILY, PEDIGREE, STOCK
lineal .... HEREDITARY
lineament ... FEATURE, MARK, (OUT)LINE, CHARACTERISTIC
lineate .... STREAKED
lined ...... RULED, STRIATE(D)
linen .... CRASH, TOILE, LINGERIE, STATIONERY, FLAXEN, NAPERY, BYSSUS, HOLLAND, BATISTE
and wool cloth ... LINSEY
articles of ...... LINGERIE
closet item ...... TOWEL, SHEET, NAPKIN
cloth .... SEERSUCKER, DUCK
cloth for bookbinding ... BUCKRAM
cloth, mummy's .. BYSSUS
coarse .... DOWLAS, DRABBET

fabric .... VELOUR(S), SCRIM, CRASH
fiber .... FLAX
fine ... BATISTE, CAMBRIC, DAMAS, LAWN, TOILE
household ...... NAPERY
measure .... CUT
plant .... FLAXEN
room .... EWERY
scraped/softened .. LINT
sheer .... TOILE
source of .... FLAX
tape .... INKLE
table ... NAPERY, RUNNER
vestment ... ALB, AMICE
liner .... STEAMER, VESSEL, (STEAM)SHIP
lines on map .... HACHURE
on optical lens .. RETICLE
ling .... BURBOT
linger .... DELAY, DWELL, DALLY, HOVER, LAG, TARRY, LOITER, WAIT, DAWDLE
lingerie ... UNDERWEAR, SLIP, LINEN, UNDIES
lingo .... CANT, JARGON, PATOIS, LANGUAGE, DIALECT
lingua ... TONGUE, PROBOSCIS, GLOSSA
linguiform .... LINGULATE
linguist .... POLYGLOT
linguistic form .... PHRASE, WORD, SENTENCE
linguistics branch .... MORPHOLOGY, SYNTAX, SEMANTICS, PHONOLOGY, PHILOLOGY
liniment .... LOTION, INUNCTION, ARNICA
linin .... CATHARTIC
lining ..... GASKET, BUSHING, BUCKRAM, DOUBLURE
link ... NEXUS, TORCH, YOKE, CONNECT(ION), JOIN, LOOP, RING, TIE, COPULA, ATTACH, CATENATE, CHAIN
train cars .... COUPLE
linked series .. CHAIN, CATENA
Linkletter, TV man ...... ART
links .... GOLF COURSE, CAT(ENA)
connect in series .... CATENATE
man ... CADDY, CADDIE
linn ...... LINDEN, CASCADE, WATERFALL, RAVINE, POOL
linne .... CRATER
linnet ..... SONGBIRD, FINCH, LINTWHITE
linotypist .... COMPOSITOR, TYPESETTER
linseed oil, hardened .... LINOLEUM
mixture ..... MEGILP(H)
source .... FLAX
refuse ...... MILKCAKE
lint ...... FLAX, FLUFF, FIBER, LINEN, NAP, RAVELINGS, FUZZ
lintel ... CROSSPIECE, SQUINCH, TRANSOM, SUMMER
counterpart of ..... SILL
lintwhite .... LINNET
linty .... FLUFFY
liny .... THIN
lion .... LEO, CAT, FELINE, CELEBRITY, SIMBA, IDOL
female .... LIONESS
group .... PRIDE
mane of .... CREST
mountain .... PUMA, COUGAR, PANTHER
neck hair .... MANE
of God .... ARIEL
of Judah .... SELASSIE
pride of .... MANE, CREST
young of a ...... WHELP, LIONET, CUB
lioness of story/movie ... ELSA
lionet .... CUB
lionheart .... RICHARD I
lionhearted .... BRAVE
lip .... LABIUM, LABRUM, LABELLUM, KISS, LABIAL, SUPERFICIAL, IMPERTINENCE
adornment ..... PELELE, LABRET
combining form .. CHIL(O)
cup's .... BRIM
ladle .... GEAT
like edge .... LABRUM
like organ ...... LABIUM
of the .... LABIAL
ornament ..... PELELE, LABRET, M(O)USTACHE
service, of sorts .... MALARK(E)Y, HYPOCRISY
slang .... INSOLENCE, IMPERTINENCE
sound .... LABIAL
touch with .... KISS, OSCULATE
liparoid .... FATTY, FAT-LIKE
lipase .... ENZYME
lipide .... FATS, LIPOID
lipoid .... FAT-LIKE
lipoma .... TUMOR
Lippe, capital of .... DETMOLD
lipped .... LABIATE
lipper .... SPRAY, RIPPLE, BLUBBER
Lippi, painter ...... FILIPPO, FILIPPINO
lips .... LABRA, LABIA, KISSER
combining form ... LABIO
of the .... LABIAL
lipstick ..... ROUGE, POMADE
liquefied .... FUSIL(E)
liquefy ... FUSE, MELT, THAW
opposed to ..... SOLIDIFY
liquescent .... MELTING
liqueur ... RATAFIA, KUMMEL, CORDIAL, POUSSE, CURACAO, COGNAC, CREME, ABSINTH(E), CHARTREUSE
glass .... PONY
sweet .... GENEPI, ANISETTE, CURACAO, MARASCHINO
liquid .... FLUID, CLEAR, TRANSPARENT
becoming ... LIQUESCENT
body tissue ...... LYMPH
change into ..... LIQUEFY
fatty oil .... OLEIN
fire substance ... NAPALM
food ...... SOUP, BROTH
in pharmacy ...... AQUA
made .... FUSIL(E)
measure ... PINT, QUART, GALLON, GILL, BARREL, HOGSHEAD, MINIM, TUN
measuring device .... DOSIMETER, JIGGER
medicated, for sores ..... LINIMENT
mouthful of .... SUP
oily .... FURFURAL
opposite .... SOLID
oxygen .... LOX
pickling .... BRINE, SOUSE
rock .... MAGMA
solvent .... MENSTRUUM
strained .... FILTRATE
thick .... DOPE, TAR
waste .... SLOPS
liquidambar ... BALSAM, TREE, SWEETGUM
liquidate ...... CASH, SETTLE, PAY, KILL, DISPOSE (OF)
liquify by heat .... MELT
liquor ... TIFF, RAKI, MASTIC, RUM, RYE, JUICE, DRINK, MEAD, BITTERS, CREME, WHISKY, GIN, GROG, POTATION, TAP, RAKEE, POTTLE, ALE, ANISETTE
alcoholic .... LUSH, MESCAL
bad ..... BOUSE, BOWSE
bitter .... ABSINTH(E)
bottle .... MAGNUM
cabinet .... CELLARET
cheap .... SLIPSLOP
colloquial .... BOOZE
drink .... DRAM, TIFF
drink, drugged .... MICKEY (FINN)
fruit juice ...... BRANDY
glass .... SNIFTER
intoxicating ..... TODDY
leftover in glass .... HEELTAP
loss thru leakage, etc. .... ULLAGE
malt .... STOUT, ALE, PORTER
measure ..... NIP, DRAM, GILL, PINT, NOGGIN
Oriental .... ARRACK
pick-me-up .... STIM
rice .... SAKE
sap .... NIPA
sold here ...... SALOON, BARROOM, CANTINA
sugarcane ..... TAF(F)IA
tonic .... BITTERS
weak .... SLIPSLOP
lira, 1/20 of .... SOLDO
liriodendron .... TULIP, MAGNOLIA, WHITEWOOD
liripipe .... TIPPET
Lisbon river .... TAGUS
Lisle .... LILLE, THREAD, FABRIC, GLOVES, STOCKINGS
lissom(e) ...... LITHE, SUPPLE, NIMBLE, SVELTE, LIMBER
list ... CALENDAR, HEEL, TIP,

CANT, TABLE, CAREEN, LEAN, ITEMIZE, SCROLL, SELVAGE, BOUNDARY, INVENTORY, SLATE, CATALOG(UE), ROLL, PLOW, REGISTER, TILT, ROTA, TARIFF, TABULATE, INDENTURE, INDEX, SCHEDULE
actors' .... CAST
ancestors' ..... PEDIGREE
business meeting .... AGENDA
candidates' ...... SLATE, TICKET
jury .... PANEL
of bonds, etc. .... PORTFOLIO
details .... TABLE
goods .... INVOICE
legal decisions .... DOCKET
officers .... ROSTER
persons ...... ROSTER, ROLL
saints .... HAGIOLOGY, CANON
the dead .... BEADROLL
titles .... CATALOG(UE)
team players' ... LINEUP
listen ...... HIST, EAVESDROP, HARK(EN), OBEY, HEARKEN, HEED, HEAR
listener .... AUDITOR
surreptitious .... EAVESDROPPER, BUGGER
listening .... AUDIENT
device ... BUG, MONITOR
post, usually ... EMBASSY
lister .... PLOW
listing .... TABLE, SELVAGE
listless ...... LACKADAISICAL, LANGUID, SPIRITLESS
listlessness ... ENNUI, APATHY
lists ... ARENA, TOURNAMENT, TILTS, ROLLS
Liszt, pianist .... FRANZ
lit .... LANDED, ALIGHTED
litany .... PRAYER
litas .... LIT
litchi ..... LICHEE, TREE, NUT
literal .... WORD-FOR-WORD, ETYMOLOGICAL, TEXTUAL, PROSAIC, REAL, MATTER-OF-FACT, ACCURATE, UNVARNISHED, VIRTUAL, PLAIN, EXACT
quotation, indication of .. SIC
translation .. METAPHRASE
literally .... VIRTUALLY, LITERATIM
literary ... LETTERED, LEARNED
bits .... ANA, ANALECTA
collection .... ANA, MISCELLANEA, MISCELLANY
composition .... PARODY, VIGNETTE
criticism ..... EPICRISIS, REVIEW, CRITIQUE
drudge .... HACK
effort .... LUCUBRATION
extracts ..... ANALECTA, ANALECTS
form ..... POEM, VERSE, ESSAY
hack .... GRUB
hacks, of ... GRUBSTREET
initials .... RLS, GBS
invention ...... FORGERY
man .... LITTERATEUR
movement leaders ...... AVANT GARDE
patchwork .... CENTO
pseudonym ... ELIA, SAKI
quotation, brief .. SNIPPET
review .... CRITIQUE
scholar ...... HARMONIST
scraps ... ANA, ANALECTS
society .... LYCEUM
study .... GRAMMAR
style ..... PEN, ROCOCO
work, inferior .. SCRIBBLE, POTBOILER
literate .... LEARNED, EDUCATED, CULTURED, LETTERED
literati ..... MEN OF LETTERS, SCHOLARS, INTELLECTUALS
literatim .... LITERALLY, LETTER FOR LETTER
literature .... WRITINGS
lithe .... SLIM, LISSOM(E), SVELTE, LIMBER, SUPPLE, FLEXIBLE, AGILE
lithograph ... PRINT, CHROMO
lithoid .... STONELIKE
lithology, subject of ... ROCKS
lithomarge .... CLAY, KAOLIN
lithophyte ..... CORAL, PLANT
lithopone .... PIGMENT
Lithuanian .... BALT, LETT
capital .... KAUNAS, KOVNO, VILNA
city ... VILNIUS (WILNO)
coin ...... LIT(AS), RUBLE
river port .... KAUNAS
seaport .... MEMEL
territory .... MEMEL
litigant ... SUER, DEFENDANT, COMPLAINANT
litigate .... SUE
litigation .... LAWSUIT
litigious .... QUARRELSOME
litotes .... MEIOSIS
litten .... LIGHTED
litter ... BIER, COFFIN, DOOLI, FALL, PALANQUIN, PALANKEEN, DOOLEE, STREW, MULCH, SCATTER, JUMBLE, DISORDER, MESS, STRETCHER, RUBBISH, CLUTTER
bearer ... PIG, CAT, DOG
last-born of .... WALLYDRAG
of pigs .... FARROW
litterateur ... MAN OF LETTERS, WRITER, AUTHOR
little ... PUNY, WEE, PALTRY, SMALL, BRIEF, TRIVIAL, YOUNG, MINUTE, TINY, POCO
Bear .... URSA MINOR
Big Horn protagonist .... SITTING BULL, CUSTER
"big" man .... COCKALORUM
bit .... MORSEL, FIG
Boy Blue" author .. FIELD
by little ..... PIECEMEAL
combining form .... MICR(O)
Corporal .... NAPOLEON
fellow .... BUB
Flower, mayor .... LA GUARDIA
Fox .... VULPECULA, CONSTELLATION
hours ..... SEXT, TIERCE, PRIME, NONE
Miss Muffet's food ...... WHEY
people .... FAIRIES
piece .... FLINDER
ring .... ANNULET
Russia .... UKRAINE
Tibet .... LADAKH
littleneck .... QUAHOG, CLAM
littoral ..... SHORE, COAST(AL)
litu, singular of .... LITAS
liturgical singer ..... CANTOR
vestment .... AMICE, ALB
liturgy ... RITE, RITUAL, MASS
litus .... SERF
Litvinov, Russ. statesman ..... MAXIM
livable .... HABITABLE, ENDURABLE
live .... INHABIT, BREATHE, DWELL, EXIST, ENDURE, SUBSIST, RESIDE, ENERGETIC, VIVID
able to .... VIABLE
alone .... BACH
coal .... EMBER
it ____ .... UP
oak .... ENCINA
together .... COHABIT
under false pretenses .... MASQUERADE
wire: colloq. ... HUSTLER, GO-GETTER
livelihood ...... SUBSISTENCE, SUPPORT, SUSTENANCE, LIVING, KEEP, (DAILY)BREAD, MAINTENANCE
liveliness .... VIVACITY
livelong ...... ENTIRE, WHOLE
lively ..... SPRY, AGILE, GAY, CANTY, BRISK, SPIRITED, VIVID, KEEN, ANIMATED, SPRIGHTLY, VIVACIOUS, ACTIVE, PE(A)RT, PERKY
air .... LILT
dance .... REEL
music ... ANIMATO, VIVO
person .... GRIG
liven .... CHEER(UP)
liver .... HEPAR
disease ..... CIRRHOSIS, PORPHYRIA
function of .. METABOLISM
inflamation ... HEPATITIS
is supposed seat of ...... DESIRE, EMOTION
lobster's ...... TOMALLEY

pertaining to .. HEPATIC, VISCERA
secretion .... BILE, GALL
shaped like .... HEPATIC
substance in ... HEPARIN
livered, yellow .... COWARDLY
liveried servant .... FLUNK(E)Y
liverish ...... BILIOUS, CROSS, PEEVISH
liverwort .... AGRIMONY, HEPATICA, BRYOPHYTE
genus .... RICCIA
lettuce .... PYROLA
liverwurst .... SAUSAGE
livery ..... UNIFORM, STABLE
wearer of ...... SERVANT, RETAINER, LACKEY, FLUNK(E)Y
liveryman .... RETAINER, LACKEY
livestock ..... CATTLE, COWS, STEERS
farm .... RANCH
round up ...... WRANGLE
livid ...... BLACK-AND-BLUE, WAN, PALE, ASHEN, DISCOLORED
living .... BEING, QUICK, EXTANT, ALIVE, LIVELIHOOD, ANIMATE
capable of ...... VIABLE
close to ground .... EPIGEAL
corpse .... ZOMBI(E)
ecclesiastical ... BENEFICE
inside animals .... ENTOZOIC, ENTOPHYTIC
on land or in water ...... AMPHIBIAN
on river bank .. RIPARIAN
picture .. TABLEAU VIVANT
prefix LIVI
room ..... SALA, PARLOR
space ..... LEBENSRAUM
thing .... ORGANISM
wild, loose .... RIOT
within ...... IMMANENT
Livonian .. ESTH(ONIAN), LETT
Livorno .... LEGHORN
livre, replacement of .. FRANC
lixiviate .... LEACH
lixivium .... LYE, LEACH
lizard ...... AGAMA, GUANA, BASILISK, ADDA, GECKO, SAURIAN, LACERT(IL)IAN, MONITOR, EFT, SKINK, GILA, NEWT, SWIFT, UTA, GALLIWASP, MOLOCH, SEPS, IGUANA, REPTILE, CHAMELEON
amphibious ...... NEWT, SALAMANDER
chameleon-like ... AGAMA
climbing ...... IGUANA
color-changing .. AGAMA, CHAMELEON
combining form .. SAURO, SAURUS
crested .... BASILISK
fish .... SAURY, ULAE
genus ..... AGAMA, UMA
legless ..... BLINDWORM, SLOWWORM
like .... SAURIAN
monitor ... URAN, VARAN
Old World .... SEPS, AGAMA
wall .... GECKO
with winglike membranes DRAGON
Lizette of poetry ...... REESE
llama ... VICUNA, RUMINANT, ALPACA
habitat .... ANDES
hair of .... WOOL
relative .... CAMEL, GUANACO
llanero's weapon .... BOLA
llano .... PLAIN, STEPPE
lo ... ECCE, SEE, BEHOLD, LOOK
companion of .. BEHOLD
loa .... LARVA
loach .... CARP
load ..... ENCUMBER, LADING, FILL, FREIGHT, ONUS, SADDLE, CARGO, BURDEN, WEIGHT, LADE
a gun .... CHARGE
transported ...... HAUL
loaded .... WEIGHTED
slang ..... INTOXICATED, DRUNK, IN THE MONEY, MONEYED
loader, dock ..... STEVEDORE
loadstar ... POLARIS, LODESTAR
loadstone .... MAGNET(ITE)
loaf .... IDLE, LOUNGE, LOLL, BREAD, LOITER, BAP, CAKE, GOLDBRICK
white bread .. MANCHET
loafer ..... IDLER, LOUNGER, SHOE, DRONE, BUM
loam ..... MARL, SOIL, LOESS, REGUR, EARTH, DIRT, MALM
constituent .. CLAY, SAND
loan .... PREST, TOUCH
ask for a .. BRACE, TOUCH
of money ...... IMPREST
note: colloq. .... IOU
privilege .... CREDIT
shark .... USURER
loath .... AVERSE, HOSTILE, UNWILLING, RELUCTANT, HESITANT
loathe ...... ABHOR, DETEST, HATE, ABOMINATE
loathsome ..... CLOYING, VILE, DETESTABLE, DISGUSTING, FOUL, REPULSIVE, ABHORRENT
lob .... COP, LOP, LOFT
lobby ...... HALL, ANTEROOM, VESTIBULE, FOYER, LOUNGE
lobbyist .... RAINMAKER
lobe .... LOBULE, LAPPET
ear .... EARLOP
whale tail's .... FLUKE
lobelia .... CAMAS(S)
loblolly .... PINE, GRUEL, MUDHOLE, PUDDLE, BROTH
lobo .... WOLF
lobscou(r)se .... STEW
lobster .... CRUSTACEAN, MALACOSTRACAN, MACRURAN
appendage ..... UROPOD
claw .... NIPPER, CHELA, PINCER
coral .... ROE
egg(s) ..... ROE, SPAWN, BERRY
feeler of ..... PALP(US), ANTENNA
first legs of ..... PINCERS
liver .... TOMALLEY
ovaries of .... CORAL
part of a ...... THORAX, TELSON, CHELA
protective covering ..... MAIL
spawn of .... CORAL
trap for .... POT
lobworm .... LUGWORM
local ... RESTRICTED, BRANCH, CHAPTER, TOPICAL, WAY TRAIN, REGIONAL, VICINAL
relationship ..... UBIETY
locale .... SCENE, VENUE, PLACE, LOCALITY, SITE
locality .... AREA, PLACE, SITUS, SPOT, LOCUS, HABITAT, LOCALE, DISTRICT, NEIGHBORHOOD, VENUE
restricted to a .. ENDEMIC, INDIGENOUS
locate .... MARK OFF, SETTLE, SPOT, PLACE, FIND
location .. POSITION, SITUATION, SITE, SPOT, PLACE(MENT)
person's ... WHEREABOUTS
loch .... LAKE, POND, BAY
loci, singular of .... LOCUS
lock .... TRESS, DETENT, COTTER, CURL, JAM, HASP, CONFINE, LINK, RINGLET
away .... STORE
brand .... YALE
hair ...... CURL, TRESS, RINGLET, TAG
mechanism ..... DETENT
of wool .... FLOCK
out .... BAR
part ..... BOLT, TUMBLER, CYLINDER, STUMP
ship .... COFFER
up .... JAIL
locker .... CHEST, CLOSET, COMPARTMENT, AMBRY, KIST
locket's content .... PICTURE, HAIR, MINIATURE
lockjaw ... TETANUS, TRISMUS
lockup ...... CALABOOSE, STIR, JUG, JAIL, PEN
loco ...... CRAZE, DEMENTED, CRAZY
locofoco ...... CIGAR, MATCH
locomotion, form of .... WALKING
locomotive .... MOGUL, SWITCHER, DOLLY, DINKEY, DUMMY, IRON HORSE
coal car .... TENDER
cowcatcher ..... FENDER
driver .... ENGINEER, MOTORMAN
driver's place ...... CAB

on a mission ... WILDCAT
pulling power .. TRACTION
safety device ..... PILOT, COW-CATCHER
stopping place .... TANKTOWN
sound ..... CHOO, CHUFF
locoweed .... PLANT
locum tenens ..... SUBSTITUTE
locus .... PLACE, POINT
locust ...... CICADA, CICALA, TREE, INSECT, ACACIA
kin .... CRICKET, GRASSHOPPER
tree ..... ACACIA, CAROB, HONEY
locution ... EXPRESSION, WORD, PHRASE, IDIOM
lode ...... VEIN, ORE DEPOSIT
cavity ... VUG(G), VUGH
mining .. VUG, VEIN, REEF
lodestar .... POLARIS
lodge ...... HOUSE, CHAPTER, DEN, HUT, BILLET, BOARD, QUARTER, ROOM, CABIN
Indian ..... TENT, TEPEE, WIGWAM
lodger .... ROOMER, GUEST
temporary ... TRANSIENT
lodging .... QUARTERS, ABODE, BILLET, PIED-A-TERRE
house ...... HOTEL, INN, HOSTEL(RY)
house bed .... DOSS
loess .... LOAM
loft .... ATTIC, GALLERY, JUBE, LOB, GARRET, MANSARD
lofty .... HIGH, GRAND, ARROGANT, HAUGHTY, NOBLE, SUBLIME, SKYEY
dwelling .... AERIE, AERY
log .... DIARY, RECORD, TIMBER
barrier .... BOOM
birling contest ... ROLEO
float .. RAFT, CATAMARAN
holder .... PEAV(E)Y, CANT HOOK
house .... CABIN
measure ...... SCALAGE
roller .... DECKER
sling .... PARBUCKLE
spin a .... BIRL
splitter .... WEDGE
turner .... PEAV(E)Y
loganberry .... BRAMBLE
logarithm decimal part .... MANTISSA
inventor .... NAPIER
unit .... BEL
loge..... BOX, COMPARTMENT, STALL
logger .... LUMBERJACK, WOODCUTTER
boots of .... PACS
sled of .... TODE, GO-DEVIL, TRAVOIS
loggerhead .. TURTLE, DUNCE
bird .... SHRIKE
loggia ..... ARCADE, GALLERY, PORTICO
logging, evade work in .. SNIB
sled .... GO-DEVIL, TODE, TRAVOIS
tool .... PEAV(E)Y
logia ...... MAXIMS, SAYINGS
logic .... REASONING
deductive .... SYLLOGISM
major premise .... SUMPTION
logical .... REASONABLE
logically connected .... COHERENT
logion .... MAXIM, SAYING
plural of .... LOGIA
logistic .... ARITHMETIC, CALCULATIVE
logistics, concern of .... TRANSPORTATION, SUPPLY, QUARTERS
logogriph .... ANAGRAM, WORD PUZZLE
Logos .... REASON, WORD
logroller ... DECKER, BIRLER, POLITICIAN
logrolling .... BIRLING
subject of .... BILL
logs floating in mass .. DRIVE
passage down slope ..... SLUICE, FLUME
pile of .... ROLLWAY
logy .... DULL, SLUGGISH
Lohengrin's bride ...... ELSA
composer ..... WAGNER
father .... PARSIFAL
opera character .... ELSA, ORTRUD, TELRAMUND
loin .... CHUMP, RACK, BEEFCUT
combining form .... LUMB(O)
muscle .... PSOAS
section of ...... GRISKIN
loincloth ..... MARO, LUNGI, LUNGEE, MALO, DHOTI, PAGNE, LAVA-LAVA, SARONG, G-STRING
loins .... HIPS
pertaining to the .... LUMBAR
Loire River city ..... ORLEANS, BLOIS, NANTES
loiter .... LOUNGE, LOAF, LINGER, DAWDLE, IDLE, DALLY, LAG, TARRY, SAUNTER
loiterer ...... LAGGER, IDLER, LAGGARD
Loki's daughter ...... HEL(A)
son .... NARE
victim .... BALDER
wife .... SIGYN
loll ... DROOP, LOUNGE, HANG, LOP, LAZE
lollapaloosa .... LULU, KNOCKOUT
Lollard leader .... WYCLIFFE
lollipop ..... SUCKER, CANDY
Lollobrigida, actress ... GINA
Lombard capital ...... PAVIA
Lombardy capital .... MILAN
city .... PAVIA
ruler .... ALBOIN
Lome, location of ..... TOGO
loment .... LEGUME
London, ancient name of ..... AGUSTA
art gallery .... TATE
barrister .... TEMPLAR
bobby's beat .... POINT
borough ... KENSINGTON, GREENWICH, STEPNEY, CHELSEA, BATTERSEA, ISLINGTON, WESTMINSTER, LAMBETH
botanical gardens site ... KEW
city company member ... LIVERYMAN
cleaning woman ... CHAR
club .... KITCAT
coach builder .. TILBURY
court .... HUSTINGS, MARSHALSEA
dialect .... COCKNEY
district .... SOHO, LAMBETH, MAYFAIR, CHELSEA, ADELPHI, BANKSIDE, LIMEHOUSE, WHITEFRIARS, WHITECHAPEL
fashionable section ...... MAYFAIR, BELGRAVIA
foreign quarter ... SOHO
hair style .... ONION
hawker .... COSTER, MUN
hooligan .... SPIV
horse market .... TATTERSALL'S
landmark ...... BRIDGE, TOWER
mental hospital .. BEDLAM
native .... COCKNEY
park .... HYDE
place of execution .... TYBURN
prison .... NEWGATE, MARSHALSEA
ship of Jack ..... SNARK
royal stables ..... MEWS
ruffian .... MOHOCK, MOHAWK
statue ..... MAGOG, GOG
street .... SOHO, STRAND, FLEET, PALLMALL, LOMBARD
streetcar .... TRAM
student of law .. TEMPLAR
suburb .... EALING, WEMBLEY, KEW
subway .... TUBE
theatre .... DRURY LANE
underwriters ... LLOYD'S
West End .... SOHO
writer .... JACK
Londoner .... COCKNEY
Londres .... CIGAR
lone .... SOLITARY, ISOLATED, SOLO, SOLE
Ranger's pal .... TONTO
Star State .... TEXAS
loneliness ..... MELANCHOLIA
kind of ...... NOSTALGIA
lonely ..... DESOLATE, LORN, SOLITARY, ISOLATED
loner, kind of .... HERMIT, MUGWUMP
lonesome .... DESOLATE

long .... HANKER, PROLIX, EXTENDED, SLOW, PINE, CRAVE, YEARN, LENGTHY, ASPIRE, ACHE
ago .... LANG SYNE
before .... SOON
cut .... SLASH, GASH
discourse ..... DESCANT
distance contest .... MARATHON
dozen .... THIRTEEN
drawn ..... PROLONGED, EXTENDED
faced ...... GLUM, SAD, DISCONSOLATE
fish .... GAR, EEL
for ...... HANKER, PINE, CRAVE
green: sl. .. (PAPER)MONEY
headed .... SHREWD
Island county .. QUEENS, KINGS, NASSAU, SUFFOLK
Island racetrack .... BELMONT
journey ... ODYSSEY, TREK
knife .... YATAGAN
leaf .... PINE
legged bird .... HERON, EGRET, STORK, STILT, RAIL, CRANE, CURLEW
life .... LONGEVITY
limbed .... RANGY, LEGGY
live! .... VIVE, VIVA
necked animal .. GIRAFFE
necked bird ...... SWAN, STORK, HERON
opposite of ...... BRIEF, SHORT
seat ...... SETTEE, BENCH
since .... LANG SYNE
shot race horse .. SLEEPER, PLATER
shot, what it isn't .... FAVORITE
spear .... LANCE
step .... STRIDE
suffering .... PATIENT, MEEK
tongued .... TALKATIVE, GOSSIPY
tooth .... FANG, TUSK
tramp .... TREK
winded .... PROLIX, WORDY, VERBOSE

longanimity ... FORBEARANCE, PATIENCE
longeron .... SPAR
longevity .... LONG LIFE
Longfellow bell town .... ATRI
longhair ...... INTELLECTUAL, HIGHBROW
longhand reporting .... LOGOGRAPHY
writing .... SCRIPT
longhorn .... CATTLE
longing ..... YEN, YEARNING
longshoreman ...... DOCKER, STEVEDORE, DOCKHAND, LUMPER
longshot winner ..... SLEEPER
longspur .... BIRD, FINCH, SPARROW
longways ...... LENGTHWISE
loo .... PAM, CARD GAME
looby .... LUBBER, LOUT
loofah .... SPONGE
looie (looey) ..... LIEUTENANT
look .... CON, PORE, HIST, MIEN, GANDER, PRY, SEE, SEARCH, SEEM, APPEAR(ANCE), GLANCE, SEEK, ASPECT, GAZE, GAPE, PEER, EYE, SKEW, SCAN
alike .... RINGER
amorous .... OGLE
askance .... LEER
back .... RECOLLECT, RECALL
dagger .... GLARE
forward to .. ANTICIPATE, EXPECT
frowning .... LOUR, SCOWL, (G)LOWER
in .... VISIT
into ...... INVESTIGATE, PROBE, INQUIRE
obliquely .. SKEW, SQUINT
over .... INSPECT, EXAMINE
over: sl. .... CASE
prying ..... PEEK, KEEK, PEEP, SPY
quick ... PEEK, GLIMPSE, GLANCE
scornful .... SNEER
see: sl. ... GLANCE, PEEK
sly .... LEER, PEEK
steady ..... GAZE, STARE, GAPE
threatening ..... LOWER
up to .... ADMIRE

looker-on .... SPECTATOR, OBSERVER, BYSTANDER
looking glass .... MIRROR
lookout .... CONCERN, PROSPECT, WORRY, WATCHER, ESPIER, GUARD, OBSERVER, SPOTTER
nautical usage .... CROW'S NEST
ship's .... CONNER
turret .... BARTIZAN, BARTISAN

loom .... APPEAR, LOON, TAKE SHAPE, WEAVE
frame .... BATTEN
part ..... HEDDLE, PIRN, SHUTTLE, REED, TREADLE, WARP, PICKER, HARNESS, BEAM, ROLLER, SLEY, CAAM, EASER, BATTEN, HEALD
remnant .... THRUM

loon .... DIVER, GREBE, (DIVING)BIRD, LOUT, DOLT
archaic .... SERVANT, SCAMP, ROGUE
Scottish .... BOY

loony .... CRAZY, LUNY, DEMENTED, DAFT
loop ..... TAB, BRIDE, TERRY, CIRCUIT, EYE(LET), RING, NOOSE, PICOT, LAP, FOLIUM, GROMMET
edging .... PICOT
in electricity .... CIRCUIT
in lace .... PICOT
in lariat .... HONDOO
in physics ..... ANTINODE
like structure ..... ANSA
of rope, nautical .... PARREL, PARRAL
on boot/garment .. TAG
on lace's edge ...... PURL
rope ...... BIGHT, NOOSE
running .... NOOSE
thread's .... EYE

looper ... (MEASURING)WORM, LARVA
loophole ...... PLEA, ESCAPE, EYELET, JOKER, M(E)USE
loops, edge with .... PURL
Loos, writer .... ANITA
loose ...... FREE, AT LARGE, UNBOUND, INEXACT, LEWD, UNBIND, (RE)LAX, RELEASE
cut .... FREE, UNTIE, ESCAPE
end .... TAGRAG
jointed .... LIMBER, LANKY
let .... RELEASE
set/turn ... RELEASE, FREE
tongued .... TALKATIVE
woman .... WANTON

loosen ..... SLACKEN, UNTIE, RELEASE, FREE, RELAX, EASE, UNDO
loot .... PLUNDER, RIFLE, SPOILS, DESPOIL, PILLAGE, BOOTY, (RAN)SACK
lop .... TRIM, CUT OFF, SNIP, HANG, LOLL, PRUNE, POLL, CHOP, SNED, SNATHE
lope of sorts .... CANTER
lopobranch .... SEA HORSE
loppy .... DROOPING
lopsided .... UNEVEN, UNBALANCED, ASKEW, ALIST, ALOP
loquacious ...... TALKATIVE, GARRULOUS, VOLUBLE
bird ...... JAY, MAGPIE
opposite .... TACITURN, RETICENT

loquacity .... GARRULITY, LERESIS, TALKATIVENESS
loquitur ...... HE/SHE SPEAKS
loran, part of ... LONG, RANGE, NAVIGATION
lord ..... SEIGNOR, SEIGNEUR, LIEGE, PEER, EARL, RULER, MASTER, NOBLEMAN, DOMINEER, BARON, RULE, BISHOP, VISCOUNT, MARQUIS
companion of ... MASTER
humorous usage .... HUSBAND
Marmion's horse ... BEVIS
of Hosts .. JEHOVAH, GOD
privileged ..... PALATINE
Scottish .... LAIRD
the .... GOD
wife of .... LADY

Lord's Day .... SUNDAY
land ... DEMESNE, MANOR
manor .... DEMESNE

Prayer, first word(s) ..... PATERNOSTER, OUR FATHER
Supper .... HOLY COMMUNION, EUCHARIST
lordly .... OVERBEARING, HAUGHTY, NOBLE
lordship ..... RULE, DOMINION
lore .... WISDOM, ERUDITION, LEARNING, KNOWLEDGE
creature with ..... BIRD, SNAKE
Lorelei .... SIREN, LURLEI
golden possession of .... COMB
victims of ...... SAILORS, MARINERS
Lorenz, ethologist ... KONRAD
lorgnette .... LORGNON, EYEGLASSES, OPERA GLASS
lorgnon .... MONOCLE, PINCENEZ, LORGNETTE
lorica ... CARAPACE, LORLEA, SHELL, CORSELET, CUIRASS
lorikeet .... PARROT, LORY
loris .... LEMUR
lorn .... FORSAKEN, DESOLATE, BEREFT
Lorna, heroine ...... DOONE
Doone author .... BLACKMORE
Doone character ... RIDD
lorry .... TRUCK, WAGON
lory ...... PARROT, LORIKEET
Lortzing's opera .... UNDINE
Los Angeles football team .... RAMS
suburb ...... TORRANCE, LYNWOOD
lose .... MISPLACE, MISS, FORFEIT, MISLAY, WASTE, SQUANDER
ardor .... PALL
color .... FADE, PALE, WHITEN
footing .... SLIP
forward speed .... STALL
one's head .... PANIC
one's way ...... WILDER
purposely .... THROW
loser, poor/bad .... CRYBABY, SOREHEAD
loss .... FORFEITURE, DEPRIVATION, DEFEAT, DECREMENT, PERDITION
at a .... PUZZLED, BEWILDERED
cause of, sometimes ..... LEAKAGE, SPILLAGE
compensation for .... SOLATIUM
describing one .... IRREPARABLE
from container .... SPILLAGE, LEAKAGE
gambling, ultimate ...... SHIRT
of consciousness .... SYNCOPE, SYNCOPATION
of feeling .... INSENSATE, ANESTHESIA
of hair .... ALOPECIA
of memory ...... AMNESIA
of mental power .... DEMENTIA
of reading ability .... ALEXIA
of sense of smell .... ANOSMIA
of speech ..... APHASIA, ALALIA
of the soul ... PERDITION
of voice .... APHONIA
of will power .. AB(O)ULIA
unexpected ...... UPSET
lost .. MISLAID, GONE, MISSING, WASTED, BEWILDERED, RUINED, ENGROSSED
animal .... STRAY
Horizon author .. HILTON
Horizon, site of .... SHANGRI-LA
often, figuratively .. SHIRT
lot ..... SHARE, BUNCH, FATE, PARCEL, SCAD, RAFT, SLEW, SLUE, CABOODLE, DESTINY, FORTUNE, PORTION, PLOT, GRIST
city of .... ZOAR
colloquial .... SORT
father of .... HARAN
feast of .... PURIM
uncle of ...... ABRAHAM
sister of .... MILCAH
son of .... MOAB
loth ... HATE, DETEST, ABHOR
Lothario .... RAKE, SEDUCER
Loti, Pierre .... VIAUD
lotion ... COLOGNE, OINTMENT, FRESHENER, CALAMINE
lots .... MUCH, PLENTY
divination by .. SORTILEGE
of something .. HEAP, PILE
lottery ...... GAME, CHANCE, TOMBOLA, DRAWING,
kin ...... RAFFLE, KENO, NUMBERS, BINGO, LOTTO
ticket .... BLANK
winning ... PRIZE, TERN
lotto kin .... BINGO, KENO
lotus ...... NELUMBO, SHRUB, HERB, WATER LILY, CHINQUAPIN, LOTE, SADR
enzyme .... LOTASE
tree ...... JUJUBE, SADR
loud ...... NOISY, CLAMOROUS, INSISTENT, VIVID, FLASHY, SHOWY
colloquial ...... VULGAR, UNREFINED
in music .... FORTE
speaker ...... AMPLIFIER, WOOFER, TWEETER, MONITOR
loudmouthed ... THERSITICAL, BLATANT, STENTORIAN
person .... STENTOR, THERSITES
lough .... LAKE
Louis of trumpet fame .... PRIMA
XIII's minister .... RICHELIEU
Louiseville event ...... DERBY
Louisiana ... PELICAN (STATE)
boat .... BATEAU
capital of .. BATON ROUGE
city ...... SHREVEPORT, MONROE, NEW ORLEANS
county .... PARISH, WINN, CADDO, ACADIA
farmer ...... HABITAN(T)
land measure ... ARPENT
native .... CREOLE, ACADIAN, CAJUN, CAIJAN
Negro patois ..... GUMBO
nickname ..... PELICAN, CREOLE, SUGAR
patois .... CREOLE
parish .... ACADIA
river .... AMITE
state bird ...... PELICAN
state flower .. MAGNOLIA
tobacco .... PERIQUE
lounge ... LOAF, LOITER, LOLL, COUCH, SOFA, DIVAN, SETTEE, LAZE, LOBBY
lounger .... IDLER, LOAFER
lounging suit .... PAJAMAS
loup .... (HALF)MASK
garou .... WEREWOLF
lour .. LOWER, FROWN, SCOWL
Lourdes miracle .... CURE
Lourenco ____, Mozambique capital .... MARQUES
louse .... NIT, APHID, INSECT, PARASITE, COOTIE, SLATER, RAT
plural of .... LICE
up ...... BUNGLE, SPOIL, BOTCH
lousy .... DIRTY, DISGUSTING, INFERIOR, POOR, PEDICULAR, PEDICULOUS
lout .... GAWK, APE, HOB, LOOBY, BOOR, LOB, LOON, BUMPKIN
archaic ... CURTSY, BOW, STOOP, BEND
louver ..... LANTERN, TURRET, WINDOW, SLAT, TRANSOM
lovage .... PARSLEY
love .... AMO(R), GRA, AFFECTION, LIKING, SWEETHEART, ATTACHMENT, DOTE, WOO, ENAMOR
affair ... AMOUR, LIAISON, INTRIGUE, ROMANCE
apple .... TOMATO
feast .... AGAPE
foolish .... INFATUATION
foolishly .... DOTE
full of .. EROTIC, AMATIVE
god of ... AMOR, CUPID, EROS
goddess of ...... FREYA, VENUS
in .... ENAMORED
in tennis .... ZERO
knot .... AMORET
letter ..... BILLET-DOUX
lies-bleeding ..... PLANT, AMARANTH
lightly ...... PHILANDER
make ..... WOO, COURT
note .... VALENTINE
of country .. PATRIOTISM

of fine arts ...... VIRTU
potion .... PHILTER, PHILTRE
pertaining to ... EROTIC, AMATORY
seat .... SOFA
set, in tennis ... SIX-ZERO
song .. SERENA, SERENADE
story .... ROMANCE
lovebird .... PARROT
lover ... BEAU, SWAIN, ROMEO, LEMAN, SPARK, SWEETHEART, FLAME, MINION, PARAMOUR
boy .... AMORIST
silly .... SPOONER
lovers' lane frequenters ...... SWEETHEARTS, TRYSTERS
meeting .... TRYST
song .. SERENADE, SERENA
loving ... AMOROUS, AMATIVE, EROTIC, DOTING, FOND, DEVOTED, AMATORY
combining form .. PHILE
cup .... TIG, TROPHY
low .... MENIAL, SCURVY, SCALY, MOO, ORRA, SHALLOW, DEEP, WEAK, HUMBLE, COARSE, VULGAR, INFERIOR, VILE, BASE, POOR
birth-weight infant ...... PREEMIE
bow .... CURTSY
brow .... PLEBEIAN
comedy ..... HORSEPLAY, FARCE, BURLESQUE, SLAPSTICK
country .... BELGIUM, NETHERLANDS, LUXEMBURG
down: colloq. .... MEAN, DESPICABLE
down: sl. .... FACTS, DOPE, INFO(RMATION)
lay .... KILL, HIDE
necked ..... DECOLLETE
lowan .... LEIPOA, MALLEE
lowbred .... COARSE, VULGAR, CRUDE, ILL-MANNERED, BASE
Lowell, poet ... AMY, ROBERT
lower ... DIP, DEBASE, DEMIT, NETHER, DEMOTE, SCOWL, LOUR, GLOWER, FROWN, VAIL, LOOM, INFERIOR, REDUCE, WEAKEN, ABASE
Alsace .... BAS-RHIN
California capital ...... LAPAZ, MEXICALI
Canada .... QUEBEC
classman .... FRESHMAN, SOPHOMORE
House member .... REPRESENTATIVE
in architecture ..... VAIL
in geology ..... EARLIER
in rank .. JUNIOR, PUISNE
in value .... DEBASE, DEPRECIATE
on one side ... LOPSIDED
World ..... HELL, SHEOL, HADES, EARTH, DIS
World gods ..... MANES
lowering .. OVERCAST, CLOUDY, FROWNING

lowery ... OVERCAST, CLOUDY
lowest .... LOWERMOST, MEANEST, LAST
animal life ..... AM(O)EBA
deck .... ORLOP
form of wit .... PUN
part .... BOTTOM
point .... NADIR, NETHERMOST, BOTTOM
point of planet's orbit ... PERIGEE
Lowin role .... HAMLET
lowland .... HOLM, PLAIN
Lowlander ...... SASSENACH
Lowlands dialect ..... LALLAN
lowly .... HUMBLE, MEEK(LY), HUMBLY
lox .... SALMON, OXYGEN
loxia .... WRYNECK
loyal ...... LEAL, STA(U)NCH, TRUE, FAITHFUL, DEVOTED
friend .... ACHATES, DAMON
wife .... PENELOPE
loyalty ..... FIDELITY, FEALTY, HOMAGE, ALLEGIANCE, TROTH
lozenge ... CATECHU, CACHOU, JUJUBE, MASCLE, PEPPERMINT, PASTIL(LE), TROCHE, DIAMOND, CANDY, COUGH DROP, RHOMB
LP .... LONG PLAY(ING)
LSD source .... ERGOT
term .... ACID, TRIP, TURN ON
lu, in chemistry ... LUTETIUM
Luanda is capital of .. ANGOLA
luau .... FEAST
dish .... POI
lubber ... LOOBY, LOB, SAILOR
lube .... OIL, LUBRICANT
Lublin extermination camp ... MAIDENEK
lubricating oil .... LUBE
lubricant .. OIL, GREASE, DOPE, CASTOR, VASELINE
lubricate .... OIL, GREASE, SMOOTHEN
lubricator ...... OILER, DOPER
lubricous .... SLIPPERY
Lucan's work .... PHARSALIA
luce .... PIKE, FISH
Luce (Clare Booth) estate ..... HALENAIA
lucent .... SHINING
Lucern(e) .. FODDER, ALFALFA, CANTON, LAKE, MEDIC
luces .... LIGHTS
singular of .... LUX
Lucian the ____ ..... SKEPTIC
lucid .... BRIGHT, SANE, CLEAR(HEADED), SHINING, RATIONAL, TRANSPARENT, LUCULENT
lucida .... STAR
lucidity ... SANITY, CLARITY, CLEARNESS, TRANSPARENCY
Lucifer .. DEVIL, MATCH, SATAN
poetic .... VENUS
lucite .... RESIN
luck .... FORTUITY, HAP, LOT, FORTUNE, FATE, CHANCE

bad .... DEUCE, WANION, HOODOO, JINX, CESS, ACE
of .... ALEATORY
of Roaring Camp .. HARTE
luckily .... HAPLY, FORTUNATELY
lucky .... CANNY, WITCH, FORTUNATE
piece .... AMULET
stroke .... FLUKE
lucrative .... FAT, PAYING, PROFITABLE, GAINFUL, REMUNERATIVE
lucre ..... PELF, EMOLUMENT, PROFIT, MONEY, RICHES
descriptive word for ..... FILTHY
Lucrezia ____, poisoner ..... BORGIA
lucule .... SUNSPOT
luculent .... LUCID, CLEAR
ludicrous .... FARCICAL, ABSURD, RIDICULOUS, COMIC(AL), LAUGHABLE
Ludwig, biographer .... EMIL
lues .... SYPHILIS
luetic .... SYPHILITIC
Luftwaffe divebomber .... STUKA
leader .... GOERING
lug ...... EAR, DRAG, CARRY, PULL, HAUL, TOW
luggage ...... BAGGAGE, TAN, BAGS, TRAPS
carrier .... PORTER
item .... SUITCASE, VALISE, TRUNK
lugger .... VESSEL, TOTER, FALCON
lugubrious ... SAD, MOURNFUL, DOLEFUL, DISMAL
lugworm .... ANNELID
Luik .... LIEGE
Luish .... LUWIAN
Luke .... EVANGELIST
lukewarm .... TEPID, INDIFFERENT
lull .... MITIGATE, CALM, SOOTHE, ALLAY, QUIET, RESPITE, ROCK, HUSH, SLACK
lullaby ...... (CRADLE)SONG, BERCEUSE
lulu: sl. .. ONER, OUTSTANDING, WHIZ
lumbago .... BACKACHE, RHEUMATISM
lumber ... CLUTTER, BOARDS, RUMBLE, WOOD
British .... TIMBER
dressing machine .... TRIMMER
marker .... KEEL
lumberjack .... LOGGER, WOODCUTTER, JACKET, SAWYER
blanket of ... MACKINAW
climbing iron of .... SPUR
warning cry .... TIMBER
lumberman .... LOGGER, SAWYER, GIRDLER, HEWER
boot of ..... PAC, OVER, LARRIGAN

hook of .... PEAV(E)Y, PEEV(E)Y
lodging of .... CAMP
tool of .. AXE, ADZE, SAW
sled .... TRAVOIS
lumbricoid ..... ROUNDWORM
lumen .... LUX
luminal .... SEDATIVE, HYPNOTIC, PHENOBARBITAL
luminary ... STAR, SUN, MOON
luminescence ... COLD LIGHT
luminous .... BRIGHT
energy .... LIGHT
radiation .... AURA
lummox .... LOUT, LOON, LOOBY, LUBBER, DUNCE, LUNKHEAD, DUMBBELL
lump ... WAD, CLOT, NUB(BIN), MASS, NODE, SWAD, HUNK, BURL, HUNCH, KNOT, GOB(BET), BAT, NODULE, DOMINO, SWELLING, COLLECTION, NUGGET, NUBBLE
butter .... PAT
clay .... CLOD
of earth .... CLOD
round, small ..... BOLUS, KNOB
lumper .... STEVEDORE, DOCKER
lumpish ...... DULL, STUPID, HEAVY
lumpy ..... CLUMSY, KNOBBY
Lumumba, Congo premier .... PATRICE
Luna .... SELENE, MOON
in alchemy .... SILVER
lunacy ..... MADNESS, MANIA, INSANITY
lunar .... PALLID, PALE, CRESCENT-SHAPED
crater .... LINNE
month ...... LUNATION, MOON
phenomenon ... ECLIPSE
spaceship .... APOLLO
lunate .... CRESCENT-SHAPED, LUNAR
lunatic ..... INSANE, MADMAN
lunch(eon) .... SNACK, DEJEUNER, BITE, REFECTION, TIFFIN, MEAL
lune .... LEASH, LUNULA
lung disease .. TUBERCULOSIS, CONSUMPTION, PHTHISIS, SILICOSIS, TB, SIDEROSIS
membrane ...... PLEURA
pus-filled cavity .. VOMICA
sound .... RALE
lunge .... THRUST, LONGE, LEAP, FOIN, PASSADO
lungee ... LUNGI, LOINCLOTH
lunger .... TUBERCULAR, CONSUMPTIVE
lungfish .... DIPNOAN, MUDFISH
lungi .... LOINCLOTH
lungs used as food ..... LIGHTS
lungwort .... LICHEN
lunkhead ... DUMBBELL, LOON, DUNCE, LUMMOX
lunt .... MATCH, KINDLE, TORCH, SMOKE
lunula .... LUNE, LUNULE
lunule ..... LUNE, HALFMOON
luny .... LOONY
Lupercus .... FAUNUS
Lupin, thief .... ARSENE
lupine .... WOLFLIKE, PLANTRAVENOUS, WOLFISH
animal .... WOLF
Lupino, actress .... IDA
Lupus .. WOLF, CONSTELLATION
lurch ... ROLL, PITCH, SWAY, CHEAT, LURK
lurcher ..... THIEF, POACHER, (HUNTING)DOG
lure .... ATTRACT, TEMPT, ENTICE, DECOY, INVEIGLE, BEGUILE, BAIT, FLY, SPINNER, TREPAN, SEDUCE, INDUCE(MENT)
lurer .... SIREN, SEDUCER, BAITER, DECOY, TEMPTRESS
lurid ..... RED, SENSATIONAL, STARTLING, GLOWING, GARISH, VIVID
lurk .... SKULK, SNEAK, PROWL
Lurlei .... LORELEI, SIREN
luscious ... DELICIOUS, TASTY, SWEET, CLOYING
lush ..... JUICY, SUCCULENT, LUXURIANT
Lusitania, now .... PORTUGAL
lust .... DESIRE, APPETITE
luster ..... SCHILLER, SHEEN, GLORY, GLOSS, RADIANCE, BRILLIANCE, LUSTRUM, REFLET, NAIF, SHINE, GLAZE, POLISH
lusterless ...... DULL, WAN, DRAB, MAT(TE)
lustful ..... LEWD, SENSUAL, RANDY
lustrate .... PURIFY
lustring .... LUTESTRING, SILK CLOTH
lustrous ... NACREOUS, NITID, SILKY, SHINING, RADIANT, SATINY, GLOSSY, BRILLIANT
lustrum ... FIVE-YEAR(PERIOD), LUSTER
lusty .... ROBUST, STURDY, STRONG, VIGOROUS
lute ..... CEMENT, SEAL, CLAY, INSTRUMENT
composer for the .... LUTANIST, LUTENIST
obsolete ...... THEORBO
oriental .... TAR
relative of ...... GUITAR, MANDOLIN, ASOR, PANDORE, UKELELE
lutestring .... LUSTRING
Lutetia .... PARIS
Luther, theologian ... MARTIN
Lutheran .... PROTESTANT
luthern .... DORMER, WINDOW
Luwian .... LUISH
luting .... CEMENT
lux .... LUMEN, LIGHT
luxate .. DISLOCATE, DISJOINT
luxe .... ELEGANCE, RICHNESS
Luxemb(o)urg capital .. ARLON
luxuriant .... RANK, FERTILE, LUSH, PROFUSE
luxuriate .... BASK, WALLOW
luxurious ...... TONY, RICH, PLUSH, POSH
luxury-lover ...... SYBARITE, LUCULLUS
Luzon battlesite ..... BATAAN, MANILA BAY, CORREGIDOR
city ... PASAY, CALOOCAN, DAGUPAN, QUEZON, MANILA, CAVITE, ANGELES, LAOAG, OLONGAPO
island .... MINDORO, CORREGIDOR, LUBANG
falls .... PAGSANJAN
mountain ...... ARAYAT, CORDILLERA, CARBALLO, ZAMBALES
mountain capital .... BAGUIO
mountain people .... IGOROTS
native ... NEGRITO, AETA
peninsula ..... BONDOC, BICOL
people of .... BICOLANOS, PAMPANGOS, TAGALOGS ILOCANOS, ZAMBALENOS
province .... TARLAC, PAMPANGA, QUEZON, BULACAN, PANGASINAN, BATAAN, ABRA, CAGAYAN, BATANGAS
rare animal .... TAMARAU
volcano ... TAAL, MAYON
walled city .. INTRAMUROS
water buffalo .. CARABAO
wild buffalo ... TAMARAU
world wonder .... RICE TERRACES
Lwow .... LVOV, LEMBERG
lycanthrope ..... WEREWOLF
lycanthropy, product of ...... WOLF
lycee .... (SECONDARY)SCHOOL
lyceum ...... LECTURE HALL, LYCEE
Lycian city .... MYRA
king .... SARPEDON
leader .... PANDARUS
lycopod .... CLUB MOSS
Lydia, capital of ..... SARDIS
Lydian .... EFFEMINATE, GENTLE, SENSUAL, VOLUPTUOUS
king .... CROESUS
language ..... ANATOLIC
lye .. LIXIVIUM, BUCK, CAUSTIC
soak in ..... BATE, BUCK
source of ... (WOOD)ASHES
lying .... MENDACIOUS, DECUMBENT, FALSE, DISHONEST, RECLINING, RECUMBENT
downward ..... PRONE, PRONATED, ACUMBENT, DECUMBENT
flat .... PROSTRATE
on one's back ... SUPINE
under oath ..... PERJURY
lymph ...... HUMOR, SERUM,

SPRING, WATER
and fats .... CHYLE
gland swelling ..... BUBO
vessel .... VARIX
lymphatic .... PLASMIC, SLUGGISH
glands tuberculosis ...... SCROFULA
vessels .... LACTEAL
lymphoid tissue back of mouth TONSIL
lyncean .... KEEN-EYED
animal .... LYNX
lynching, usual end of .... HANGING
lynx .... CARACAL, WILDCAT, BOBCAT, CONSTELLATION, CARCAJOU, CATAMOUNT, PISHU
fur .... CARACAL
of a .... LYNCEAN
Lyra ... HARP, CONSTELLATION
lyre .... HARP, TRIGON
like instrument .... ASOR, CITHARA, SACKBUT
shaped .... LYRATE, LYRIFORM
player .... LYRIST
lyrebird .... MENURA
lyric .... LIED, SONGLIKE, MELIC, ALBA
muse .... ERATO
ode .... EPODE
poem .... MELIC, RONDEAU, SONNET, ELEGY, HYMN, ODE, RONDEL, CANZONE, EPODE
poet ..... ODIST, LYRIST, SAPPHO, MINSTREL
solo .... MONODY
lyrics of opera/oratorio ...... LIBRETTO
lyriform .... LYRATE
lysin .... ANTIBODY
of .... LYTIC
lysol .... ANTISEPTIC, DISINFECTANT
constituent .... SOAP, CRESOL
lytic .... LYSIN
lytta .... WORM

M

M, Greek .... MU
letter .... EM(MA)
ma .... MOTHER, MAMMA
chere .... MY DEAR
Maas .... MEUSE
mabolo .... PLUM
macabre .... GHASTLY, GRIM, LURID, GRUESOME, HORRIBLE, EERIE
part of a title .... DANSE
macaco .... LEMUR, MONKEY, MACAQUE
macadam ..... ROAD, STONES
material .. TAR, ASPHALT
Macao coin .... AVO
island .. TAIPA, COLOANE
MacArthur, general .... ARTHUR, DOUGLAS
macaque ...... KRA, RHESUS, MACACO, MONKEY, WANDEROO
macaroni .... DANDY
flour paste like .... SPAGHETTI
ingredient .... SEMOLINA, DURUM
strip .... LASAGNA
macaroon .. COOKY, RATAFIA, BISCUIT
Macassar .... MALAYAN
Macau island .... TAIPA, COLOANE
macaw .. ARA(RA), MARACAN, PARROT
"Macbeth" character .... DUNCAN, ROSS, BANQUO, HECATE, MACDUFF
maccaboy .... SNUFF
mace .. STAFF, STICK, CLUB, SPICE, MAUL
bearer .. BEADLE, MACER
reed .... DOD
royal .... SCEPTRE
source of ...... NUTMEG
wielder .... KNIGHT
macedoine .. SALAD, MEDLEY
Macedonia capital .... PELIA, SKOPJE
city ..... BEREA, EDESSA, PYDNA
region .... PIERIA
seaport ...... SALONIKA
macer .... BEADLE
macerate .... STEEP, SOFTEN, RET, TORMENT, WASTE AWAY, SOAK
Mach, physicist ...... ERNST
machete .... KNIFE, BOLO
Machiavelli, Florentine ...... NICCOLO
Machiavellian ...... CRAFTY, DECEITFUL
machina, ___ .... DEUS EX
machinate ...... PLOT, PLAN, SCHEME, DEVISE
machination(s) ...... DESIGN, ARTIFICE, INTRIGUE, CABAL, PLOT, SCHEME
machine ...... MOTOR, TOOL, AUTOMATON, ENGINE, MECHANISM, DEVICE, GADGET
cloth smoothing .... MANGLE
cotton-cleaning .... GIN
crushing .... PRESS, MILL
cutting .... CROPPER
duplicating ..... RONEO, XEROX
finishing .... EDGER
flying .... AIRPLANE, AIRCRAFT
glazing ...... CALENDER
grass-cutting ...... MOW
grass-spreading .. TEDDER
grinding .... MILL
gun .... GATLING, BREN, STEN, MAXIM, POM POM
gunner .... MITRAILLEUR
gunner's post ..... NEST
hoisting ..... GIN, CRAB
nap-raising .. TEASEL(LER)
ore-dressing .... VANNER
part .. CRANK, SOLENOID, GEAR, COG, CAM, ROTOR, PISTON, VALVE, PAWL
parts adjusting device ... TRAMMEL
political .... PARTY
printing .... PRESS
repairer ...... MECHANIC
shearing ...... CROPPER
spinning .... MULE
threshing ..... COMBINE
tool .... LATHE
weaving .... LOOM
weighing .... TRONE
wood-turning .... LATHE
machinist's groove .... TSLOT
machree .... MY HEART
Mack, of baseball .... CONNIE
Mackenzie river tributary .... LIARD
mackerel .... TUNA, FISH, SCOMBROID, SAUREL, BONITO, ALBACORE
cured .... BLOATER
like fish .... CERO, SCAD, SIERRA, PINTADO, PLAINTAIL, TUNNY, CAVALLA, BESHOW
net .... SPILLER
of the ...... SCOMBROID
young .... SPIKE, TINKER
Mackinaw .. BLANKET, COAT, BOAT
trout .... NAMAYCUSH
Mackintosh .... RAINCOAT
mackle .. BLUR, MACULE, BLOT
MacLeish, poet .. ARCHIBALD
macrocosm .... UNIVERSE, WORLD
macrural crustacean .. PRAWN, SHRIMP, LOBSTER
maculate ..... STAIN, DEFILE, IMPURE, SPECKLE, SPOT(TED), BLOTCH
macule .... BLUR, BLOT
mad ... INSANE, SORE, RABID, CRAZY, FRANTIC, FRENZIED, IRATE, FRENETIC, SENSELESS, ANGRY, FURIOUS
monk .... RASPUTIN
Madagascar animal .. LEMUR, TENREC, TENDRAC, AYEAYE, TEMEE
civet .... FOSSA
fiber .... RAFFIA
lemur .. INDRI(S), AYEAYE
native .... HOVA

palm tree ...... RAFFIA
tribe .. HOVA, MALAGASY
madam ...... LADY, WOMAN, MISTRESS, MILADY
Italian .... MADONNA
"Madame Butterfly" composer PUCCINI
name of .. CIO-CIO (SAN)
madame, English equivalent .. MRS
Spanish .... SENORA, SRA
madcap .... RASH, IMPULSIVE, RECKLESS, HOTSPUR
madden ... INCENSE, ENRAGE, ANGER
madder ...... VINE, CRIMSON, PLANT, DYE, ALIZARIN(E), COFFEE, RUBIA, GARDENIA, IPECAC, EVEA, CHINCHONA
made .... SUCCESSFUL, INVENTED, CONSTRUCTED
of wood .... XYLOID
to order .. CUSTOM-BUILT
up ... INVENTED, FALSE, FABRICATED, COSMETIZED
Madeira ..... WINE, ISLAND, RIVER
capital .... FUNCHAL
Island wind ...... LESTE
town .... FUNCHAL
wine .... TINTA
mademoiselle .... LADY, MISS, WOMAN, GIRL
abbreviation .... MLLE
madhouse .. BEDLAM, CHAOS, BABEL, ASYLUM
madman .. LUNATIC, MANIAC
madness .. FRENZY, DEMENTIA, FURY, MANIA, DELIRATION, FOLLY, RABIES, RAGE, LUNACY
fits of .... LUNES
kind of .... INFATUATION
Madonna .... MARY
madras .... KERCHIEF, CLOTH
city .... CALICUT, SALEM
state .... COCHIN, TRAVANCORE
state, part of .. CARNATIC
weight .... POLLAM
madre .... MOTHER
madrepore .... CORAL
formation .. ATOLL, REEF
Madrid boulevard/park/ museum ...... PRADO
madrigal .. POEM, SONG, GLEE
Madrileno .... SPANIARD
madrona .. EVERGREEN, BERRY
madwort .... ALYSSUM, SHRUB
Mae West .... LIFEBELT, LIFE-PRESERVER
maelstrom .... WHIRLPOOL
maenad .. NYMPH, BACCHANTE
maestro .... TEACHER, CONDUCTOR, COMPOSER, MASTER
Mafeking native .... BOER
Maffei work .... MEROPE
maf(f)ia ..... BLACK HAND
nemesis of .. FEDS, NARCO
magazine ..... STORE(HOUSE), WAREHOUSE, DEPOT, PUBLICATION, PERIODICAL, JOURNAL
classy .... SLICK
content .... MUNITION(S), AMMO
inferior .... PULP
leaves .... SHEETS
part of .... SPREAD
work .... JOURNALISM
Magdalen college scholar .... DEMY
mage .... WIZARD, MAGICIAN
Magellan, navigator .... FERDINAND
ship of .... VICTORIA, TRINIDAD, SANTIAGO
magenta .. FUCHSIN, DYE, RED
maggot .. GRUB, LARVA, WHIM, NOTION, MAWK, BOT(T)
bluebottle fly ... GENTLE
Magi ... BALTHASAR, MAGUS, MELCHIOR, GASPAR
magic .... OBEAH, ART, GRAMARY(E), WITCHCRAFT, WIZARDRY, THEURGY, THEURGIC, RUNE, JUJU, CONJURATION
black .. VOODOO, SORCERY
formula .. ABRACADABRA
hammer, owner of ...... THOR
horse .... BAYARD
image .... SIGIL
lamp finder ... ALADDIN
Mountain author ... MANN
potion .... PHILTER, PHILTRE
practice .... CONJURE
sign .... SIGIL
spell ..... CONJURATION, ABRACADABRA, CANTRIP
symbol .... PENTACLE
word .... SESAME
magical .... RUNIC, HERMETIC
herb .... MOLY
piece ... CHARM, AMULET
magician .. WARLOCK, MAGE, MERLIN, HOUDINI, MAGUS, MEDICINE MAN, SHAMAN, MAGI(AN), WIZARD, SORCERER, THEURGIST, KLINGSOR, CONJURER, ARCHIMAGE
device of ..... GIMMICK
skill of .... SLEIGHT OF HAND, LEGERDEMAIN
stick of .... WAND
talk of .... PATTER
tricks of .. LEGERDEMAIN, HOCUS-POCUS
word of .... PRESTO
Magindanao .... MORO
Maginot line, opposed to .... LIMES, SIEGFRIED
magisterial ..... MASTERFUL, POMPOUS
magistral .... IMPERIOUS
magistrate .. JUDGE, JUSTICE, CADI
Athenian .... ARCHON
civil .... SYNDIC
Genoese/Venetian ...... DOGE
Greek .... EPHOR
Roman ...... DUUMVIR, PR(A)ETOR
Spanish .. ALCALDE, JUEZ
town .... REEVE
magnanimous ...... GENEROUS
magnate ... BIGWIG, TYCOON, MOGUL, NABOB
magnesia .... ANTACID, LAXATIVE
magnesium silicate .... TALC
magnet .... LOADSTONE, LODESTONE
alloy .... ALNICO
end .... POLE
magnetic .... ATTRACTIVE, MESMERIC, ELECTRIC
direction .. NORTH, SOUTH
flux, unit of .. MAXWELL, WEBER
force .... OD, ODYL(E)
resistance ... RELUCTANCE
magnetism ...... MESMERISM, ATTRACTION, ALLURE
magnetite .... LOADSTONE
magneto .... DYNAMO
magnific .... POMPOUS, GRANDILOQUENT, IMPOSING
magnificat ...... HYMN, SONG, POEM
magnificence .. STATE, POMP, SPLENDOR, GLORY, GRANDEUR
magnificent .. GRAND, STATELY
array .... PANOPLY
magnify .... ENLARGE, EXALT, EXAGGERATE
magnifying instrument .... TELESCOPE, MICROSCOPE
magniloquent ...... POMPOUS, LOFTY, GRANDIOSE, BOMBASTIC
magnitude ..... SIZE, EXTENT
magnolia .... SHRUB, FLOWER, SWEET BAY
state .... MISSISSIPPI
magnum .... BOTTLE
opus .... WORK, MASTERPIECE
magnus hitch .... KNOT
magpie .. PIET, CROW, MAG(G), PICA
kin .... JAY
Latin .... PICA
maguey .. ALOE, AGAVE, FIBER
magus .. SORCERER, MAGICIAN, ASTROLOGER
Magyar .... HUNGARIAN
Magyarorszag ..... HUNGARY
maharaja's wife .. MAHARANI, MAHARANEE
Mahatma, famous ... GANDHI
Mahdi follower ..... DERVISH
Mahican .... MOHEGAN
mahjongg playing piece ...... TILE
wind ..... NORTH, EAST, SOUTH, WEST
mahogany ..... (HARD)WOOD, TOON, TREE, CAOBA, BAYWOOD, NARRA

of the ...... MELIACEOUS
pine .... TOTARA
Mahomet ...... MOHAMMED, PROPHET
burial place of .. MEDINA
Mahound .. DEVIL, MOHAMMED
Mahren .... MORAVIA
Maia .... PLEIADE, MAY
maid ... VIRGIN, FILLE, LASS, WENCH, GIRL, DOMESTIC, SLAVEY
lady's .... ABIGAIL
of Astolat ...... ELAINE
of Orleans .... JOAN OF ARC
old .... SPINSTER, TABBY
servant .... BONNE, SOUBRETTE
maiden .. VIRGIN, GUILLOTINE, UNMARRIED, NEW, FRESH, FIRST, DAMOSEL, NYMPH, DAMSEL, LASS, COLLEEN
appearance ...... DEBUT, INTRODUCTION
changed to heifer .... IO
changed to spider ...... ARACHNE
in song .... CHLOE
name .... NEE
maidenhair .... FERN, GINKO
maidenhead ..... VIRGINITY, HYMEN
maidenly .... GENTLE, MODEST
mail .. POST, LETTERS, ARMOR, DAWK, SEND, DA(U)K
bag .... POUCH
boat .... PACKET
carrier .... POSTMAN, PONY EXPRESS
coat of .... ARMOR, HAUBERK, BYRNIE
examine .... CENSOR
India .... DA(W)K
mark .. CACHET, STAMP, INDICIA
pertaining to .... POSTAL
Mailer, author ..... NORMAN
mailing charge ..... POSTAGE
right .... FRANK
maillot ...... SWIMMING SUIT
mailman .... POSTMAN, LETTER CARRIER
maim .... LAME, CRIPPLE, MANGLE, MUTILATE, DISABLE, SCOTCH
main ...... CHIEF, FOREMOST, DUCT, FORCE, POWER, PRINCIPAL, LEADING
action of drama .... EPITASIS
body .... TRUNK
bounding ... SEA, OCEAN
course .... ENTREE
in the .. MOSTLY, CHIEFLY
part ...... BODY, TRUNK
point .. GIST, CRUX, NUB
stress .... BRUNT, ACCENT
Maine admiral ..... SIGSBEE
bay .... CASCO
capital .... AUGUSTA
city .. BANGOR, LEWISTON, AUBURN, SACO, BATH
college .... BATES, COLBY
lake .... SEBAGO
motto .. DIRIGO, I GUIDE
mountain .... KATAHDIN
native .... DOWN-EASTER
peak .... KATAHDIN
river .... SACO
state bird .... CHICKADEE
state symbol ...... PINE
town ..... MILO, ORONO, BANGOR
trout .... OQUASSA
Mainland .... POMONA
mainly .... CHIEFLY, MOSTLY, LARGELY
mainspring ...... INCENTIVE, MOTIVATION
maintain .. CARRY ON, KEEP, CONTINUE, PRESERVE, DEFEND, (UP)HOLD, AFFIRM, CLAIM
maintenance .... UPKEEP, SUPPORT, LIVELIHOOD
divorcee's ..... ALIMONY
Mainz .... MAYENCE
maison de sante .... SANITARIUM, HOSPITAL
maitre d'hotel .... BUTLER, STEWARD, MAJOR-DOMO, HEADWAITER
maize .... CORN, CEREAL, YELLOW, MEALIE, MEALY
ground .... GRITS, SAMP, HOMINY
majestic .... AUGUST, NOBLE, GRAND, STATELY, EPIC, IMPERIAL, KINGLY
majesty .... DIGNITY, GRANDEUR, NOBILITY
majolica .... POTTERY
major .. MAIN, CHIEF, OF AGE, SPECIALIZE
Barbara author .... SHAW
domo ..... SENESCHAL, STEWARD, BUTLER, MAITRE D'HOTEL
opposed to ...... MINOR
premise ...... SUMPTION
suit, in bridge ... SPADES, HEARTS
Majorca .... MAJOLICA, MALLORCA, ISLAND
city .... PALMA
majority .... AGE, BULK, SENIORITY, PLURALITY
age .... ADULTHOOD
opposed to ... MINORITY
rule .... DEMOCRACY
majuscule .. CAPITAL, UNCIAL
make .. CREATE, BUILD, STYLE, DEVISE, BRAND, FASHION
airtight ..... SEAL, LUTE
believe ..... ACT, FEIGN, PRETEND, PRETENSE, SHAM, MIMETIC
black .... NEGRIFY
capable ...... ACTIVATE
capital of ..... EXPLOIT
cheeselike ...... CASEFY
choice .... OPT
cross sign .... SAIN
dainty .... PRETTIFY
do .... EKE
eyes at ...... OGLE, FLIRT
fast .... SECURE, BELAY, TIGHTEN
for .... ATTACK
haste ...... HIE, HURRY
hit .... CLICK
indistinct .... BLUR
insane .... DEMENT, DERANGE
into law .... ENACT, LEGISLATE
into leather ... TAN, TAW
intricate .... COMPLICATE
it .... SUCCEED, ACHIEVE
laws .... LEGISLATE
less .... (DI)MINISH, DECREASE
level ...... EVEN, PLANE
like .... IMITATE, IMPERSONATE
member .... ENROLL
merry .... REVEL
nervous .... FLUSTER
out ...... FARE, DESCRY, ESPY, DISCERN
out the meaning .... DECIPHER
over .. RE-DO, RENOVATE, REVAMP, CHANGE
position secure .... ENTRENCH
possible .... ENABLE
public .... AIR, BARE, ANNOUNCE, VENTILATE
quiet .... (S)HUSH, MUTE, MUFFLE
ragged .... FRAY
ready .. PRIME, PREPARE
resentful ..... EMBITTER
room ...... MOVE OVER
safe .... SECURE
selection .. PICK, CHOOSE, OPT
sense .... ADD UP
small(er) ...... MINIFY, MICRIFY, MINISH
smooth ...... SLICK(EN), POLISH, PREEN
stupid .... HEBETATE
unfriendly ... DISAFFECT, ANTAGONIZE
unnecessary .... OBVIATE
up ... INVENT, COMPOSE, FORM, RECONCILE, COSMETICS, LAYOUT, NATURE
up material ..... ROUGE, COSMETICS, LIPSTICK, MASCARA
use of .. AVAIL, EXERCISE, UTILIZE
watertight .... CALK
whole ..... MEND, HEAL, INTEGRATE
wine .... VINT
young ...... REJUVENATE
maker: archaic .... POET
makeshift .... STOPGAP, PROVISIONAL, EXPEDIENT
makeup, newspaper .. FORMAT
mako .... SHARK
makua .... KUA
mal de mer .... SEASICKNESS
Malabar monkey .. WANDEROO

Malacca ...... CANE, STRAIT
malachite .... BICE, VERDITER
maladroit .... CLUMSY, AWKWARD
malady .... ILLNESS, DISEASE, AILMENT, SICKNESS
Malaga .... GRAPE, WINE
Malagasy capital .... TANANARIVE
city .... TAMATAVE, MAJUNGA
ethnic group ... MERINA, BETSILEO, SAKALAVA
French ...... MALGACHE
president ... TSIRANANA
seaport ...... TAMATAVE
malaise .... DISCOMFORT
malamute ...... HUSKY, DOG
malanders .... ECZEMA, PUSTULES
malapert ...... BOLD, SAUCY, IMPUDENT
Malaprop's (Mrs.) creator ... SHERIDAN
malapropos .. INAPPROPRIATE, INOPPORTUNE
malar .... CHEEKBONE
malaria .. MIASM(A), QUARTAN, PALUDISM
carrier ...... MOSQUITO, ANOPHELES
characteristic .... CHILLS
drug ...... PLASMOCHIN, ATABRINE, ATEBRIN
organism ... SPOROZOAN
malarial .... PALUDAL
malark(e)y .... NONSENSE, BALONEY, LIP SERVICE, BUNCOMBE
Malawi .... NYASALAND
capital .... ZOMBA, LILONGWE
city .. LILONGWE, ZOMBA
language .... BANTU
president .... BANDA
Malay ape .... LAR, MIAS
apple .... OHIA
archipelago .. INDONESIA
beverage .... TAFIA
bird .... MEGAPOD
canoe ..... PRAH, PRAU, PROA, PRAO
chief .... DATO, DATU
cloth .... BAT(T)IK
coin .... TAMPANG, ORA, TRA(H)
dagger ...... KRIS, CRIS, CREESE
dish .... SATAY
dress .... SARONG
dyeing method .... BAT(T)IK
English trade language .. BECHE-DE-MER
fiber .... TERAP
fruit .... KANARI
garment .... SARONG
gibbon .... LAR
island ..... JAVA, TIMOR, BORNEO, SABAH, SUMATRA
isthmus .... KRA
jacket .... BAJU
jumping disease ... LATA
knife .... PARANG
law .... ADAT
leather .... KULIT
measure .... PAU
motorcar ...... MOTOKAR
mountain .... TAHAN
negrito ..... A(E)TA, ITA
nervous disease ... LATA
nut .... KANARI
orangutan .... MIAS
outrigger .... PROA
palm .. ARENG, GOMUTI, ARECA, BETEL, GEBANG
Peninsula city .... KUALA LUMPUR
puppeteer .. (TO)DALANG
rattan .... SEGA
sea cucumber .. TRIPANG
seaweed product .... AGAR(AGAR)
self-defense art .... KURIPAN
shadow play .. WAYANG
sir .... TUAN
stage .... PANGGONG
state .... KEDAH, PERAK, PAHANG, SELANGER, KELANTAN, PENANG, TRENGGANU, PERLIS, JOHORE
station .... STESHEN
telephone ...... TALIPON
tic .... LATA
title .... TUAN
tree .. TERAP, RAMBUTAN, DURIAN, UPAS
tribe .... ARIPAS
tribesman .... MACASSAR, MAKASSAR
ungulate .... TAPIR
verse form ...... PANTUN
village .... KAMPONG
warehouse ...... GODON
warrior ...... KURIPAN
weapon .... PARANG
weight .... KATI, CADDY
wild ox .... BANTENG
xylophone .... GAMBANG, GENDER
yam .... UBI
Malayan .... TAGALOG
Malaysia capital .... KUALA LUMPUR
city ..... IPOH, KLUANG, MALACCA
crocodile ...... MUGGER
flower ...... GUMAMELA, HIBISCUS
flying bat ...... KALONG
head of state .... NASIRUDDIN SHAH
plant .... RAFFLESIA
prime minister .. RAHMAN
river .... PERAK
seaport .. GEORGE TOWN, MALACCA
shadow play ... WAYANG
state .. MALAYA, SABAH, SARAWAK
title for man ...... TUN
title for woman .... TOH PUAN
malcontent .... REB(EL), REBELLIOUS, DISSIDENT
Maldive Islands .. SULTANATE
capital .... MALE
prime minister .... NASIR
sultan .... FARID DIDI
male .... HE, MANLY, VIRILE, MASCULINE
animal ..... STAG, RAM, BULL, BOAR
attendant .... HENCHMAN
bee .... DRONE
bird ...... TERCEL, TOM, LANNERET, COCK
castrated human .... EUNUCH
cat .... TOM, GIB
chicken .. ROOSTER, COCK
deer .... STAG, PRICKET, BUCK, HART
donkey ...... JACK(ASS)
duck, wild ... MALLARD, DRAKE
ferret .... HOB
figure of column .... TELAMON, ATLANTES
fish .... MILTER
fish reproductive gland .. MILT
hog .... BOAR
horse .... STALLION
kangaroo .... BOOMER
line of family .... SPEAR SIDE
plant .... MAS
salmon .... JACK
seal .... SEECATCH
servant .... VALET, MAN, BOY, KNAVE, LACKEY
sex .... MANKIND
sex hormone .... ANDROGEN
sheep .... TUP, RAM, WETHER
swan .... COB
swine .... BOAR
turkey .... TOM
young .... BUCK
maledict .... ACCURSED
malediction .... CURSE, ANATHEMA, MARANATHA, MALISON, SLANDER, DAMNATION
malefaction .... CRIME
malefactor .... CRIMINAL, FELON, EVILDOERS
malefic ...... EVIL, HARMFUL
malevolence ...... ILL WILL, MALICE
malevolent .. EVIL, MALICIOUS, SPITEFUL, VICIOUS
malfeasance .... MISCONDUCT, WRONGDOING
malformed .... MISSHAPEN
human ..... HUNCHBACK
Mali capital .... BAMAKO
city ...... SEGOU, KAYES
ethnic group ..... PEULS, BAMBARA, TOUAREG, MALINKES, MARKAS
president .... (MODIBO) KEITA
malic acid salt ...... MALATE

malice ...... RANCOR, SPITE, ILL WILL, ENVY, SPLEEN, VENOM, MALEVOLENCE, GRUDGE
malicious .. SPITEFUL, CATTY, VINDICTIVE, NASTY, VICIOUS
burning .... ARSON
malign .... DEFAME, ASPERSE, BALEFUL, ABUSE, VILIFY, TRADUCE, SLANDER, SINISTER, LIBEL, REVILE
malignant .. DANGEROUS, EVIL, VICIOUS, HARMFUL, VIRULENT
opposed to ..... BENIGN
spirit .... KER
tumor .... CANCER
Malines ...... MECHLIN, LACE
malinger ...... SHIRK, SKULK
malison .. CURSE, MALEDICTION
malkin .. DOWDY, MOP, HARE, SCARECROW, CAT
mall ..... LANE, PROMENADE, WALK, AVENUE, ALLEE
mallard .... DRAKE, (WILD)DUCK
genus .... ANAS
malleable .. PLIABLE, DUCTILE, AMENABLE, TENSILE, SOFT
malleate .... POUND
mallee .... EUCALYPTUS
mallemuck .. PETREL, FULMAR, ALBATROSS
mallet .... GAVEL, MAUL, HAMMER, BEETLE, PESTLE, TUP, MADGE
game played with .... CROQUET, POLO
presiding officer's .... GAVEL
striking part of .... TUP
tamping .... BEETLE
malleus .... HAMMER
Mallorca .... MAJORCA
mallow ... ALTHEA, HIBISCUS, COTTON, OKRA, (HOLLY)HOCK
malm ..... LIMESTONE, LOAM, MARL
Malmo man .... SWEDE
malmsey .... MADEIRA, WINE, GRAPE, MALVOISIE
grape .... MALVASIA, MALVOISIE
malodorous .. FETID, STINKING
malt .... BARLEY, LIQUOR
liquor .... ALE, BEER, PORTER, STOUT
liquor's yeast ..... BARM
product ...... ALE, BEER, VINEGAR, ALEGAR
sugar .... MALTOSE
Malta capital ...... VALETTA
defender .... GORT
island .... GOZO, COMINO
prime minister .. OLIVIER
wind .... GREGALE
Maltese .... CAT, DOG, CROSS
maltha .. CEMENT, OZOCERITE, BITUMEN, TAR
maltose .... SUGAR
maltreat(ment) .... ABUSE
malty .... DRUNK
malvasia .... GRAPE
product ...... MALMSEY

mama .... MOTHER, MAW, MOM(MY)
mamba ..... COBRA, ELAPINE, SNAKE
mambo .... RIFF, DANCE
mameluke .... SLAVE
mamey .. MAMMEE, SAPODILLA
Mamie's maiden name .. DOUD
mammal .. SUCKLER, PRIMATE
aquatic .... DESMAN, MANATEE, OTTER, SEAL, DUGONG, SEACOW, WHALE, DOLPHIN, PORPOISE
"armored" .. ARMADILLO
cetacean ...... DOLPHIN, WHALE, NARWHAL, PORPOISE
egg-laying .... PLATYPUS, DUCKBILL
extinct ...... MASTODON
flesh-eating .... MINK, OTTER, WEASEL
fur .... PELAGE
hairless water ... WHALE, CETACEAN, DOLPHIN, PORPOISE
lowest order .... MONOTREME
mouselike .... SHREW
nocturnal ... LEMUR, BAT
plant-eating .... RHINO(CEROS)
ring-tailed .... RACCOON
snouted ...... DOLPHIN, DESMAN, PORPOISE
two-handed .... BIMANE
mammals, of certain .... MUSTELINE
mammary gland ...... UDDER
inflammation .. MASTITIS
gland secretion .... COLOSTRUM
mammee .. SAPODILLA, MAMEY, MARMALADE
mammet .. DOLL, IDOL, PUPPET
mammilla ...... NIPPLE, TEAT
mammock ..... SCRAP, SHRED, FRAGMENT
mammoth .. ELEPHANT, HUGE, ENORMOUS, GIGANTIC
like animal ... MASTODON
mammy ..... MAMA, MOTHER, NEGRESS
man (see person/fellow) ...... FORTIFY, PERSON, HUSBAND, BRACE, MALE, OPERATE, HOMO SAPIENS, BIPED, STAFF, SERVANT, HOMBRE, GEEZER, GUY, FELLER, RUN
among men ...... HERO
and ___ .... WIFE
at-arms .... SOLDIER
bald-headed .. PILGARLIC
child .... BOY
country, old ... GAMMER, GAFFER
dashing, gay .... SPARK
eater .. CANNIBAL, SHARK, CROCODILE, LION, TIGER, LAMIA
elderly .... CRONE, FOGY, DOTARD

Friday .... SERVANT, FOLLOWER
Genesis .... ONAN
gentleman's ...... VALET
handsome ...... ADONIS, APOLLO
handy ...... FACTOTUM
hideous .... OGRE
Isle of, capital of .... DOUGLAS
kind of .... STRAW
lanky .... BEANPOLE
Latin .... HOMO
lecherous .... SATYR
like .... ANDROID
little .... MANIKIN
long-suffering ...... JOB
nautical usage ...... SHIP
newly-married .... BENEDICT
of brass.......... TALOS
of Destiny, alleged ..... NAPOLEON
of figures .... CPA, BOOKKEEPER
of Galilee .... JESUS
of God .. SAINT, HERMIT, PRIEST, RABBI
of learning ..... SAVANT, PUNDIT
of letters .... SAVANT, SCHOLAR, LITTERATEUR
of the world .... SOPHISTICATE
old .. GEEZER, GRAYBEARD
on a beat .... COP, REPORTER
patient .... JOB
prehistoric .... ZINJANTHROPUS
recently married .... BENEDICT
sea .... SAILOR, TAR, MARINER
servant .. VALET, LACKEY
single .... BACHELOR
strong .. SAMSON, ATLAS
to a .... ALL, EVERYONE
unmanly ...... MILKSOP, SISSY
unmarried .... CELIBATE, BACHELOR
wise .... SOLON, NESTOR
without a country ...... NOLAN, STATELESS
who annoys women ..... MASHER
young, gay ...... SPARK
manacle .. FETTER, HANDCUFF, SHACKLE, HAMPER
manage .... WIELD, HANDLE, CONTROL, CONDUCT, TEND, ADMINISTER, CONTRIVE, OPERATE, RUN
frugally ...... HUSBAND, NURSE
to live .... SCRAPE
manageable .. DOCILE, RULY, TRACTABLE, GENTLE, TAME, WIELDY
management of household .... MENAGE
manager .. GERENT, DIRECTOR,

STEWARD, OPERATOR, SYNDIC
opera ...... IMPRESARIO
Managua is capital of .... NICARAGUA
manakin .... DWARF, MODEL, BIRD
manana .... TOMORROW
manatee .. DUGONG, SEA COW, HALICORE, SIRENIAN, COWFISH
manavelins .. LEFTOVERS, ORTS, ODDS AND ENDS
Manchester native .... MANCUNIAN
manchet .... BREAD
Manchu .... MONGOLIAN, TUNGUS
dynasty ...... TA CH'ING
dynasty, revolt against .. TAIPING
Manchukuo .... MANCHURIA
emperor of .... PU-YI
Manchuria capital .... FENG-TIEN, M(O)UKDEN
city .. JEHOL, CHENGTEH, TALIEN, DAIREN
port of .... HARBIN, ANTUNG
river .... SUNGARI
manciple .... SLAVE, STEWARD
mandamus .... WRIT, ORDER
Mandan ...... SIOUX, INDIAN
mandarin .... ORANGE, COAT, TANGERINE, DUCK
residence of .... YAMEN, YAMUN
tea .... CHA
mandate .. ORDER, COMMAND, COMMISSION
mandatory ...... OBLIGATORY
mandible .... BEAK, JAW
Mandingo .... NEGRO
mandolin strumming piece ... PLECTRUM
mandragora ...... MANDRAKE
mandrake ..... MANDRAGORA, MAY APPLE
mandrel ..... LATHE, SPINDLE
mandrill ...... BABOON, APE
manducate .... CHEW, MASTICATE
mane .... JUBA, CREST
maned ..... LEONINE, JUBATE
king .... LION
manege ...... HORSEMANSHIP
manes .... SOUL
maneuver .... PLOY, ARTIFICE, TRICK, STRATAGEM, JOCKEY, MANIPULATE
manganese spar .. RHODONITE
mange .... SCAB
cause of .... MITE
loss caused by .... HAIR
mangel .... BEET
manger ..... BIN, CRIB, RACK, TROUGH, CRATCH, STALL
mangle .... GARBLE, MAR, HACKLE, HAGGLE, MUTILATE, DISFIGURE, LACERATE, CALENDER
mangler .... MUTILATOR
mango .... MUSKMELON, FRUIT
mangonel kin ...... CATAPULT
mangy ...... SCURVY, MEAN, SORDID, SQUALID, SCURFY, SCALY, SCABBY, SCABROUS
manhandle .... MAUL
Manhattan hotel .... CHELSEA, AMERICANA, DELMONICO'S, WALDORF, WARWICK, PLAZA
purchaser of ... MINUIT, MINNEWIT
manhunters' group .... POSSE
mania .... CRAZE, OBSESSION, DELIRIUM
for dancing .. TARANTISM
maniac ... MADMAN, LUNATIC
maniacal ...... MAD, RAVING
manifest ..... SHOW, ATTEST, SIGNIFY, PATENT, LIST, OVERT, TESTIFY, WAYBILL, APPARENT, EVIDENT, OBVIOUS, CLEAR, PLAIN, EVINCE, REVEAL, OPEN
manifestant .. DEMONSTRATOR
manifesto ..... DECLARATION, PROCLAMATION, EDICT
manifold .... MULTIFARIOUS, MANY, VARIED, MULTIPLE
manihot .... CASSAVA, MANIOC
manikin .. PHANTOM, DWARF, MODEL, MANNEQUIN
Manila .... PAPER, HEMP, CIGAR, CITY
Acapulco trading ship .. GALLEON
Bay hero .... DEWEY
Bay island .. CORREGIDOR
hemp source .... ABACA
manioc .. CASSAVA, MANIHOT, STARCH, YUCA, JUCA
maniple .... ORALE, FANO(N), FANUM
maniples, three ...... COHORT
manipulate .... HANDLE, MANEUVER, JUGGLE, RIG
manipulator .... JUGGLER
Manipur capital .... IMPHAL
Manitoba capital .. WINNEPEG
mankind .... HUMANITY
manlike .... MASCULINE
manly .... VIRILE, MASCULINE
manna .. FOOD, SUSTENANCE, LERP
mannequin .... MODEL, MAN(N)IKIN
manner ..... AIR, MIEN, SORT, MODE, FASHION, BEHAVIOR, BEARING, HABIT, DEPORTMENT, METHOD
of dress .... GUISE
of running .. LOPE, JOG, CANTER, TROT
of speaking .... DICTION
of walking .... GAIT, WADDLE, SWAGGER
mannerism .... POSE, AFFECTATION
mannerist .... STYLIST
mannerly .... POLITE, COURTEOUS
manners .. MORES, BEHAVIOR, CONDUCT
study of ...... ETHOLOGY
mannish .. MASCULINE, VIRILE, MANLY
manor .. MANSION, DEMESNE, ESTATE
manorial court .... LEET
manque .... DEFECTIVE
manrope .... HANDRAIL
mansard .... GARRET, ATTIC, ROOF
manse .... PARSONAGE
manservant .. FOOTBOY, VALET, YEOMAN, LACKEY, FLUNK(E)Y
mansion ...... HOUSE, DOME, MANOR
manslaughter ..... HOMICIDE
premeditated .. MURDER
mansuetude ...... TAMENESS, GENTLENESS
manta .... SHAWL, CAPE, RAY, DEVILFISH, BLANKET
manteau .... CLOAK, MANTLE
mantel .... SHELF, LEDGE, LINTEL
ornamental band .... FRIEZE
mantelet .. SHELTER, SCREEN, CAPE, CLOAK
mantic .... PROPHETIC
mantilla .. SCARF, VEIL, CAPE, CLOAK
user .. SENORITA, SENORA
mantis crab/shrimp .. SQUILLA
mantle .. CAPE, CLOAK, COVER, PALLIUM, COPE, CHLAMYS, FROCK
armor .... TABARD
having a ...... TUNICATE
Mantua .. MANTOVA, CLOAK, MANTLE
Mantuan, the .... VIRGIL
manual .... HANDBOOK, GUIDEBOOK, TEXTBOOK
art .... CRAFT
training .... SLOYD, SLOID
workers, all ..... LABOR
manufacture ...... PRODUCE, INVENT, CONCOCT, MAKE, FABRICATE
manufacturing left-overs ..... SHORTS
manumission .... LIBERATION, EMANCIPATION
manumit .... FREE, LIBERATE, EMANCIPATE
manure .. FERTILIZE, GUANO, DUNG, MUCK, ORDURE
manuscript .... MS., HANDWRITTEN
copier .... SCRIBE
leaf of .... FOLIO
mark, ancient ... OBELUS
rolled .... SCROLL
to be set in type .. COPY
volume .... CODEX
manx ...... CAT, CELT, GAEL
many .. NUMEROUS, MANIFOLD, MULTIFARIOUS, LOADS, INNUMERABLE, LOTS, MYRIAD, SCORES
a time .... OFT(EN)
combining form .. POLY, MYRIA
headed monster .. HYDRA
manyplies .... OMASUM
Mao Tse ____ .... TUNG

daughter of ..... LI-NA, MAU-MAU
son .... AN-YING
wife .... CHIANG CHING
Maori canoe .... WAKA
clan .... HAPU
club .... MARREE
human flesh .. LONG PIG
parrot .... TUI
raft .... MOKI
tattoo .... MOKO
village .... KAIK(A)
wages .... UTU
weapon .... PATU
wood .... RATA
map .. CHART, CARTE, ORRERY, PLAT, COROGRAPHY, PLAN, GRAPH
book .... ATLAS
extra in a .... INSET
line(s) .... HACHURE, ISOBAR, OSOCHEIM, ISOTHERM, ISOTHERE
maker .... MERCATOR, CARTOGRAPHER
maker's abbreviation ... ISL, RD, RTE
maker's machine .... OROGRAPH
marker .... PUSHPIN
of lines ..... CARTOGRAM
slang .... FACE
maple .. TREE, SIRUP, SUGAR, WOOD, ACER, BOX ELDER
chat of .... SAMARA
fruit ...... SCHIZOCARP
leaf land ...... CANADA
samara of .... CHAT
seed .... SAMARA
tree .... BOX ELDER, SYCAMORE
tree tap/spout .... SPILE
maps .... ATLAS
maquis .... GUER(R)ILLA
mar .. BLEMISH, SCAR, INJURE, DAMAGE, SPOIL, IMPAIR, DISFIGURE, DEFACE
marabou .... ARGALA, STORK, ADJUTANT
marabout .... HERMIT, TOMB, HOLY MAN
maraca .... RATTLE
Maracanda ...... SAMARKAND
maranatha .... CURSE, MALEDICTION, INVOCATION
marasca .... CHERRY
product .. MARASCHINO, LIQUEUR, CORDIAL
marasmus .... WASTING
Marat, (Jean) killer of ...... CORDAY
marathon .... FOOTRACE, NONSTOP
victorious general at .... MILTIADES
maraud .. PLUNDER, PILLAGE, RAID, FORAY
marauder .... RAIDER
marble ...... AGATE, RANCE, SHOOTER, ALLEY, RANSE, ALAY, CARRARA, DOLOMITE, MIB, LIMESTONE, MIG(GLE), TAW, COLD, CALCITE, CIPOLIN, AGGIE, HARD
flooring ...... TERAZZO
game .... TAW, MIGS, MIGGLES
glass, small, square ..... TESSERA
imitation .... SCAGLIOLA
like/of .... MARMOREAL, MARMOREAN
players' line .... TAW
stone resembling .... SODALITE
worker's tool .... BURIN
marc ...... BRANDY, REFUSE
marcel .... HAIRDRESSER
March .. FILE, ADVANCE, HIKE, PROGRESS, WALK, BORDER, FRONTIER, BORDERLAND
date ....IDES
day's .... ETAPE
for dead .... DIRGE
organized ...... PARADE
style .... GOOSESTEP
triumphantly .. GALUMPH
marchen .... TALE, STORY
marches, king of ..... SOUSA
marchese .... MARQUIS
marchioness ...... MARQUISE, LADY, MARCHESA
Marco ____, traveler ... POLO
Marconi, physicist .... GUGLIELMO
marconigram .... RADIOGRAM
Mardi Gras ...... CARNIVAL, FESTIVAL
day .... TUESDAY
home of .. NEW ORLEANS
king .... REX
scene of .... PARIS, NEW ORLEANS
mare .... YAUD, HORSE, SEA, JADE
milk of ...... KOUMIS(S), KUMISS
nostrum ...... OUR SEA, MEDITERRANEAN
tail of .... CLOUD
young .... FILLY
Margaret, diminutive of ..... MEG, PEG, GRETA, MARGE, PEGGY, MAGGIE, MADGE
margarin(e) .... OLEO
margarite .... PEARL
margay .... CAT, OCELOT
marge ..... MARGIN, BORDER, EDGE, SHORE
margin .... MARGE, RAND, LEEWAY, MARGENT, EDGE, BRINK, BORDER, VERGE, LIMIT, LIP
marginal note .... SCHOLIUM, MARGENT, APOSTIL(LE)
notes of Old Testament .. MASORA(H)
margrave .... GOVERNOR
territory of .... BORDERLAND, MARCH, MARQUISATE
marguerite .... DAISY, CHRYSANTHEMUM
Maria .... LING
Marian, contralto .. ANDERSON
Marianas Island .... ROTA, LADRONES, GUAM, TINIAN, PAGAN, AGUIJAN, AGRIHAN, GUGUAN, SAIPAN
Marie Antoinette ...... REINE
Wilson role ...... IRMA
marigold ... ASTER, COWSLIP, (MAY)FLOWER, KINGCUP, CAPER
marijuana .. HEMP, NARCOTIC, CIGARETTE, WEED, GANZA, POT, HASHEESH
cigarette .... REEFER
cigarette holder .... ROACH CLIP
form of .... HASH
marimba-like instrument ..... XYLOPHONE
marina .. HARBOR, BOAT BASIN, DOCK
marinade .... VINEGAR, WINE, SALT, PICKLE
marinate .... PICKLE
marine ... NAVAL, NAUTICAL, MARITIME, FLEET, LEATHERNECK, THALASSIC, GYRENE
British: sl. .... JOLLY
glow .... SEAFIRE
organism, phosphorescent NOCTILUCA
plant .... SEAWEED
plant cast ashore .... WRACK
plant group .... BENTHOS
worm .... SYLLID, NEMERTIAN, NEMERTEAN
mariner .... SAILOR, SEAMAN, JACK-TAR, GOB
colloquial .... TAR, SALT
domain of .... SEA, SPACE
victim of (fictional) ..... ALBATROSS
Marion, actress ..... DAVIES
Civil War general ...... FRANCIS, SWAMP FOX
marionette .... PUPPET, DOLL
man ...... (TONY) SARG
mariposa flower .. LILY, TULIP
marish .... SWAMP(Y)
marjoram ..... ORIGAN, MINT, OREGANO
mark .. VESTIGE, STAIN, SIGN, TOKEN, BRAND, SCAR, MACRON, DENOTE, EVANGELIST, SYMBOL, SCRIBE
adverse .... DEMERIT
aimed at by throw ...... COCKSHY
Antony's wife .. OCTAVIA
authentication .... SEAL, CACHET
black .... STIGMA
cattle .... BRAND
critical .... OBELUS
diacritical ...... BREVE, TILDE, ACCENT, CEDILLA, UMLAUT, ABLAUT
dirty .... SMUT, SMUTCH, SMUDGE, BLOT
down .... RECORD, NOTE
footnote ..... ASTERISK,

STAR, OBELISK, DAGGER
for identification .... DAGGER, DOGTAG, MOLE, LABEL, BRAND
for doubtful passages ... OBELUS
kind of ...... DOT, SPOT, LINE, STAIN, SCRATCH, BLEMISH, DENT, BRUISE, PUNCTUATION
missile's .... TARGET
of bondage ...... YOKE, BRAND
of disgrace ..... STIGMA, BRAND
of omission ... ELLIPSIS, DELE, CARET
of word addition .. CARET
of wound .... SCAR
one hundredth of ...... PFENIG
over syllable ..... BREVE
over vowel .... MACRON, BREVE, TILDE, UMLAUT
postal .. STAMP, CACHET
pronunciation .... TILDE, UMLAUT, CEDILLA, BREVE, MACRON
proofreader's .... CARET, DELE, STET
question .... QUERY
reference .... OBELUS, ASTERISK, OBELI, DIESIS, DAGGER
VI .... TIGER, TANK
skin ...... MOLE, NEVUS
skin with color .. TATTOO
thin .... LINE
Twain .... CLEMENS
up .... HIKE, RAISE
with line ...... STRIATE
with spots ...... MOTTLE, DOT, DAPPLE, SPECKLE

markdown .... DISCOUNT
marked .. DISTINCT, OBVIOUS, NOTICEABLE
marker .. MONUMENT, SCORER, GRAVESTONE, MILESTONE, LINER, STELE, PEG, PICKET
air-race .... PYLON
channel .... BUOY
grave .... BARROW
slang ...... IOU, PLEDGE
stone .... CAIRN, MONUMENT

market .. MART, STORE, SHOP, SELL, BAZA(A)R
bond ... CURB, EXCHANGE
place ... FORUM, AGORA, EMPORIUM, PLAZA, RIALTO
stock .. EXCHANGE, CURB
town .... BOURG

marking instrument ... SCRIBE
marksman .. SHARPSHOOTER, SHOT
hangout ..... GALLERY, RANGE
hidden .... SNIPER
target of .... BULL'S-EYE

marl .... MALM, EARTH, STRATUM
marlin .... SPEARFISH
kin .... SAILFISH, SWORDFISH

marlinspike .... FID
marmalade ..... CONFECTION, PRESERVE, JAM
material .... RIND, PEEL(ING)
tree .... SAPODILLA, MAMMEE, SAPOTA, MAMEY, CHICO

"Marmion" character .... LOCHINVAR
marmoreal ..... MARBLELIKE, COLD, SMOOTH
marmoset .... MONKEY, MICO, TAMARIN
marmot .... RODENT, WOODCHUCK, PRAIRIE DOG, WHISTLER
Maroc .... MOROCCO
maroon ..... SLAVE, ISOLATE, CHESTNUT, STRAND, LOITER, LOAF, ENISLE
Marpessa's abductor .... IDAS
Marquand's sleuth .... (MR.) MOTO
marque .... REPRISAL
marquee .. AWNING, MARQUISE, TENT, CANOPY, SHELTER
marquetry .... MOSAIC, PARQUETRY
material .. TILE, PARQUET, IVORY, WOOD

Marquette, explorer .... JACQUES, PERE
Marquis, humorist ...... DON
Marquisate, ruler of .... MARGRAVE
marquise .... MARQUEE, RING
British equivalent ...... MARCHIONESS

Marrakech .... MOROCCO
marriage .... WEDLOCK, MATRIMONY, WEDDING, HYMEN, NUPTIALS
bond .... KNOT
broker ..... SCHATCHEN
contract ..... HANDFAST
dowry .... DOT
gift .... DOWRY
hater of .... MISOGAMIST
hatred of .... MISOGAMY
kind of .... MORGANATIC, CONVENIENCE, MONOGAMY
notice .... BAN(N)S
obstacle annulling ...... DIRIMENT
outside the tribe .... EXOGAMY
pertaining to ... MARITAL
proclamation ... BAN(N)S
second .... DIGAMY
settlement .. DOWRY, DOS
song .... NUPTIAL, HYMNEAL
unsuitable .. MISALLIANCE
vow .... TROTH
with one of lesser status . MESALLIANCE
within the tribe .... ENDOGAMY

marriageable woman .. NUBILE
married .... CONJUGAL, CONNUBIAL
marron .... CHESTNUT
marrow ...... PITH, ESSENCE, MEDULLA
bones .... KNEES
fat .... PEA

Marruecos .... MOROCCO
marry .. WED, UNITE, ESPOUSE, WIVE, ADOPT, HITCH
Mars .... ARES, WAR, PLANET
combining form ... AREO
in alchemy .... IRON
moon of ..... PHOBOS, DEIMOS
of .... MARTIAN
sister of ...... BELLONA
son of .... REMUS

"Marseillaise" composer .... (DE) LISLE
marsh .. SLUE, LERNA, MOOR, BOG, SLOUGH, OOZE, WETLAND, MORASS, SALINA, QUAG, SWAMP, MUSKEG, FEN
bird .. RAIL, COOT, SORA
danger spot ... QUAGMIRE
elder ..... RAGWEED, IVA, GUELDER-ROSE
fever .... HELODES
gas .... METHANE
grass ...... REED, SEDGE
hen .... RAIL, COOT
hollow .... SWALE
mallow .... ALTHEA
marigold .... COWSLIP, MAYFLOWER, CAPER
plant .. BULRUSH, TULE, MOORWORT, CATTAIL, FESCUE
salt .... SALINA

marshal .... GUIDE, ARRANGE, ARRAY, ASSEMBLE
famous ..... NEY, FOCH, PETAIN, MONTGOMERY, GORT, ROMMEL

Marshall Islands group ...... RALIK, RATAK
island .... MILI, MAJURO, WOTJE, MALOELAP, LIKIEP, JALUIT, WOTHO, BIKINI, KWAJALEIN, ENIWETOK

marshmallow .. CONFECTION, CANDY
marshy .. PALUDINE, PALUDAL, PALUDIC, FENNY, BOGGY
ground hollow .... WALE
inlet/outlet ..... BAYOU
land .... MAREMMA

marsupial ..... KOALA, TAIT, (O)POSSUM, DASYURE, YABBI, PHALANGER, POUCHLIKE, BANDICOOT, WOMBAT, KANGAROO
marsupium formation .. POUCH
Marta, actress .... TOREN
Martell .... COGNAC
marten ..... SABLE, MAMMAL
describing a .. MUSTELINE
fur .... BAUM
kin .... GLUTTON
like animal .... WEASEL

martial .. WARLIKE, MILITARY, SOLDIERLY
opposed to .. CIVIL(IAN)
martin ...... BIRD, MARTLET, SWALLOW
martinet .... DISCIPLINARIAN
martini .... COCKTAIL
extra .... OLIVE
ingredient .... GIN, VERMOUTH
Martinique capital .... FORT-DE-FRANCE
music .... BEGUINE
volcano .... PELEE
Martinmas to X'mas .... ADVENT
martlet .... MARTIN
marvel ... PRODIGY, WONDER, MIRACLE
of-Peru .... PLANT, FOUR-O'CLOCK
marvelous ..... MIRACULOUS, SPLENDID
Marwar .... JODHPUR
Marx .... CHICO, HARPO, GROUCHO, KARL
co-worker of Karl ...... ENGELS
Marxism .... SOCIALISM, COMMUNISM
Mary, mother of Jesus ...... MADONNA
picture/statue of .... MADONNA
Maryland capital .. ANNAPOLIS
city .... BALTIMORE, CUMBERLAND, ROCKVILLE
founder .... CALVERT
governor .... AGNEW
seaport ...... BALTIMORE
state bird ...... ORIOLE
state fish ..... ROCKFISH
state sport .... JOUSTING
swamp .... POCOSON
symbol .... ORIOLE
Mascagni, composer .. PIETRO
mascara .... COSMETIC
mascle ..... LOZENGE VOIDED
masculine ..... MALE, VIRILE, MAN(LY), MANNISH
Masefield work ...... ODTAA
mash .... PAP, CRUSH
masjid .... MOSQUE, MOSK
mask .... VISOR, VIZARD, VISARD, HELMET, SCREEN, LOUP, LARVE, DISGUISE, MASQUE, CONCEAL, CAMOUFLAGE
grotesque .... MASCARON
half ...... DOMINO, LOUP
lacy .... VEIL
wearer ...... MASQUER, MUMMER, KLANSMAN
maskalonge ...... FISH, PIKE
masked .... DISGUISED
ball .... MASQUE, MASQUERADE
in botany .... PERSONATE
masker .... MUMMER
masochism .... SADISM
mason .... STONECUTTER
bench .... BANKER
chisel of ...... BROACH TOOLER
companion of .... DIXON
hammer of ...... GAVEL
mortar board .... HAWK
Masonic doorkeeper .... TILER
masonry .... BRICKWORK, STONEWORK
broken pieces ... RUBBLE
wedge .... SHIM
Masqat .... MUSCAT
masque .. MASQUERADE, BALL, COMUS
masquerade .... DISGUISE, RIDOTTO, MUM(M), MASQUE, BALL
costume .... DOMINO
mass ...... SQUASH, BOLUS, GOB(BET), FLAKE, CLOT, LUMP, BULL, MAGNITUDE, MAJORITY, LARGE-SCALE, WAD, LITURGY, ASSEMBLE, GATHER, MUSH
book .... MISSAL
for the dead ... REQUIEM
killing ...... MASSACRE, CARNAGE, BATTUE
loose, downy ..... FLUE
meeting .... RALLY
movement, kind of ..... STAMPEDE, MIGRATION, EXODUS
of bacteria ...... CLUMP
of dusts, etc. .... CLOUD, FOG
of inferior things .. RUCK
shapeless .... LUMP
solidified ... CONCRETION
Massachusetts cape .... ANN, COD
capital .... BOSTON
city .... CHICOPEE, CHELSEA, TAUNTON, LYNN, MALDEN, QUINCY, REVERE, MELROSE, SALEM, CAMBRIDGE, SPRINGFIELD, ATHOL, WORCESTER, HOLYOKE
county .. DUKES, SUFFOLK
famous hall .... FANEUIL
nickname .... BAY STATE
state bird .... CHICKADEE
state flower . ARBUTUS, MAYFLOWER
state tree .... ELM
massacre .... CARNAGE, POGROM, SLAUGHTER
organized .... POGROM
massage ... KNEAD, SHAMPOO, RUB(DOWN)
massager, man ...... MASSEUR
woman ...... MASSEUSE
Massenet, composer .. JULES
opera by .. MANON, THAIS
masses, the .. PLEBS, PEOPLE, HOI POLLOI, MULTITUDE
masseur ... RUBBER, MASSAGER
Massey, performer ... ILONA, RAYMOND
Massine, ballet dancer .... LEONIDE
massive .. PONDEROUS, BULKY, SOLID, IMPOSING, HEAVY, HUGE
mast .... ACORNS, SPAR, POLE, (CHEST)NUTS, BEECHNUTS
iron band of ...... TRUSS
platform ..... MAINTOP, LOOKOUT, CROW'S NEST
support .... BIBB
mastaba(h) ... TOMB, CHAPEL
master .... MAIN, CHIEF, CONTROL, SUBDUE, DOM, BOY, EFFENDI, SAHIB, PADRONE, EMPLOYER, TUTOR, EXPERT
builder ...... ARCHITECT
cruel .... LEGREE
hand .... EXPERT
in any art ..... MAESTRO
music .... MAESTRO
of ceremonies ...... MC, EMCEE, COMPERE
of household .. GOODMAN
pertaining to a .. HERILE
race ideology .... HERRENVOLK
ship's .. SKIPPER, CAPTAIN
stroke .... COUP
workman ...... ARTIST, CRAFTSMAN, FOREMAN, OWERSEER
masterly .... EXPERT(LY)
mastermind .... PLANNER, DIRECTOR
masterpiece .. CHEF-D'OEUVRE, MAGNUM OPUS
mastership .. RULE, CONTROL, DOMINION
mastery .. GRIP, SWAY, SKILL, ASCENDANCY, CONTROL, UPPER HAND
masthead .... LOOKOUT
mastic .... CEMENT, RESIN, LIQUOR
tree .... ACOMA
masticate ..... CHEW, GRIND, CRUNCH, MANDUCATE
masticating animal .... GOAT, CAMEL, CATTLE, RUMINANT, DEER, LLAMA, ANTELOPE, GIRAFFE, BISON
mastication product ..... CUD
mastiff .. (WATCH)DOG, ALAN, BULLDOG
mastodon, animal resembling .. ELEPHANT, MAMMOTH
mat ...... SHAG, DOILY, PAD, DULL, CUSHION, SNARL, MATRIX, INTERWEAVE, CARPET
leaf .... YAPA
making material .. RUSH, REED, BAST, VETIVER
protecting dike or embankment .... MATTRESS
sleeping .... PETATE
Mata Hari .... SPY
Matabele .... ZULU
matador ...... BULLFIGHTER, TOREADOR, TORERO
dart with flag of .... BANDERILLA
garment of .... CAPE

queue of .... COLETA
red cloth used by .... MULETA, MULETILLA
sweet sounds to a .. OLES
sword of .... ESTOQUE
match ..... LUNT, VESUVIAN, MATE, TEAM, EQUAL, FIT, TALLY, PARALLEL, MARRIAGE, CONTEST, COUNTERPART, PAIR, SUIT
boxing ..... SETTO, BOUT
cockfighting ...... MAIN
friction .. FUSEE, LUCIFER, FUZEE, LOCOFOCO
in dice .... MAIN
stick .... LINSTOCK
tycoon .... KREUGER
wax .... VESTA
wooden .... VESTA
matching piece .... MATE
matchless .... PEERLESS, UNEQUALED, INIMITABLE
matchmaker ..... SCHATCHEN
indefatigable ...... EROS, CUPID
matchwood .... SPLINTERS
mate .... MARRY, MATCH, COMRADE, HUSBAND, WIFE, FERE, HOLLY, TEA, COUPLE, SPOUSE
mateless .... AZYGOUS
mater .... MOTHER
dolorosa .. VIRGIN MARY
material .. MATTER, PHYSICAL, SUBSTANCE, PERTINENT, ESSENTIAL, CORPOREAL, SENSUAL, WORLDLY, DATA
inner surface .... LINING
maternal .... MOTHERLY
relationship .... ENATION
maternity ...... MOTHERHOOD
hospital ...... LYING-IN
matey .. CHUM(MY), FRIENDLY
matgrass .... MARRAM, NARD
mathematical ...... PRECISE, EXACT, ACCURATE
arbitrary number .... RADIX
arc .... RADIAN
figure ..... GRAPH, CONE, DIAGRAM
formula .... LAW
function ...... (CO)SINE
instrument .... VERNIER, CALCULATOR, COMPUTER
line .... VECTOR
proposition .... THEOREM
ratio .... SINE
symbol ... DIGIT, POINT, DOT, FACIEND, OPERAND, MULTIPLICAND
term ..... FACIEND, COSH, CONSTANT, FACIENT, SURD, (CO)SINE
mathematician ...... EUCLID, NEWTON, DESCARTES, PASCAL, PTOLEMY, GAUSS, VERNIER
of the earth .... GEODETE
mathematics subject .... TRIGONOMETRY, ARITHMETIC, ALGEBRA, GEOMETRY, CALCULUS
matin ...... MORNING(SONG), (CANONICAL)HOUR, AUBADE
canticle .... VENITE
singer .... LARK
matinee ...... LEVEE, SOIREE, RECEPTION, PERFORMANCE
idol of old .. VALENTINO, GABLE, BARRYMORE
matrass .... BOLTHEAD, FLASK
matriculate .... ENTER, ENROL(L), REGISTER
matriculation fee ... TUITION
matrimonial ..... CONJUGAL, NUPTIAL, MARITAL
matrimony .... MARRIAGE
matrix ...... MO(U)LD, CAST, UTERUS, WOMB, MAT, DIE, GANG(UE)
matron .... WIFE, WIDOW
matronly .. SEDATE, DIGNIFIED
matted .... CESPITOSE
matter ..... COPY, PUS, PITH, SUBSTANCE, CONTENT, AFFAIR
classification of .... ANIMAL, MINERAL, VEGETABLE, ORGANIC
in law .... RES
of course ...... ROUTINE
of fact .... LITERAL, CASUAL, PROSAIC, DRY, PRACTICAL
of opinion ...... MOOT, DEBATABLE
Matterhorn ... MONT CERVIN, MOUNTAIN
matters of faith ... CREDENDA
Matthew .... EVANGELIST, APOSTLE
Matto Grosso capital .... CUYABA
mattock .... PICK(AX), HACK TWIBIL(L)
like tool ...... ADZ, AXE
mattress .. PALLET, PAILLASE
case .... TICK
stuffing material .... KAPOK, FLOCK, CEIBA
maturate .. RIPEN, SUPPURATE
maturation .... MEIOSIS
mature .... AGE, RIPE(N), FULL-GROWN, DEVELOPED
note ..... DUE, PAYABLE
Mau Mau land ...... KENYA
maud .. RUG, SHAWL, PLAID, WRAP
wearer of .... SHEPHERD
maudlin ..... SENTIMENTAL, TEARFUL, MUSHY, WEEPY, TEARY
sentiment .... MUSH
Maugham (W. Somerset)
heroine .... SADIE (THOMPSON)
play .... RAIN
maul .... BEETLE, MALLET, MANGLE, HAMMER, MACE, CLUB, CLOBBER, BRUISE, PAW
mauler .... WRESTLER, BOXER
Manassas: soubriquet ... (JACK) DEMPSEY
maumet .. IDOL, DOLL, PUPPET
Mauna Loa crater .. KILAUEA
volcano ...... LOA, KEA
maund ..... BASKET, HAMPER
maunder .... DRIVEL
Maurer, Rumanian premier .. ION
Mauriac, Fr. novelist .... FRANCOIS
Maurois, novelist .... ANDRE, HERZOG
work on George Sand .. LELIA
work on Shelley ... ARIEL
Mauritania capital .... NOUAKCHOTT
city .... ATAR, KAEDI
ethnic group ..... MOOR, NEGRO, BERBER
president ...... DADDAH
Mauser .... RIFLE, PISTOL
mauve .... MALLOW, DYE, PIGMENT, PURPLE
maverick .. CALF, DOGIE, WAIF
mavis .... THRUSH, BIRD
maw .... CRAW, STOMACH, GULLET, THROAT, CROP
dialect ..... MA, MAMMA, MOTHER
mawkish .... SPOON(E)Y, SICKENING, NAUSEATING, SENTIMENTAL
max., opposite of .... MIN
maxilla .... JAW(BONE)
segment of ...... STIPES
maxim .... MOTTO, PROVERB, ADAGE, REDE, TRUISM, APHORISM, MORAL, SAW, AXIOM, PRINCIPLE, PRECEPT, SAYING, GNOME
invention of .... EXPLOSIVES, (MACHINE)GUN
Maximalist ...... BOLSHEVIK
maxims, collection of .. SUTRA
religious leader's .. LOGIA
Maxwell .... ELSA, WEBER
May .. HEYDAY, SPRINGTIME, PRIME, MAIDEN
apple ...... MANDRAKE, PLANT
Day folk dance .. MORRIS
Day signal .... SOS, M'AIDEZ
fifteen .... IDES
first .... BELTANE
fly .... DUN, EPHEMERID, EPHEMERA, DRAKE, EPHEMERON
tree .... HAWTHORN
VIPs .... MOTHERS
Maya .. SAKTI, DEVI, GODDESS, INDIAN
consort of .... SIVA
Mayan .... INDIAN
city .. CALAKMUL, UXMAL
maybe .. PERHAPS, PERCHANCE, MAYHAP, POSSIBLY
Mayday .... SOS, M'AIDEZ, SIGNAL
Mayence .... MAINZ
Mayflower .... ARBUTUS, HAWTHORN, COWSLIP, ANEMONE, MARIGOLD

passengers of the .... PILGRIMS
mayor ...... BURGOMASTER, HIZZONER
mayor's domain ...... TOWN, CITY, MUNICIPALITY
title of address: sl. ...... HIZZONER
mazard .. HEAD, SKULL, FACE, MAZER
Mazarin, statesman ... JULES, CARDINAL
maze .... STUPEFY, BEWILDER, LABYRINTH
exit aid .... CLEW
mazed .... MEANDERED
mazer .. MAZARD, CUP, BOWL, GOBLET
mazurka ...... DANCE, POLKA
mazzard .... CHERRY
MC's asset .... WIT
McCambridge, actress ...... MERCEDES
McCoy, the real .... GENUINE
McIntosh .... APPLE
McLaglen's role .. INFORMER
mdse. .... MERCHANDISE
mead .... LEA, HYDROMEL
meadow .... LEA, GRASSLAND, MEAD
barley .... RIE
bird ... BOBOLINK, LARK
grass .... POA, FESCUE
lark .... TROUPIAL
mouse .... VOLE
plant .... INNOCENCE
poetic .... MEAD
rue .... CROWFOOT
meadowsweet ...... SPIR(A)EA
meager .. BARE, SPARE, LEAN, THIN, LENTEN, SPARING, POOR, INADEQUATE, SPARSE, SCANT(Y), EMACIATED
meal .. FARINA, MESS, SPREAD, SUPPER, DINNER, BREAKFAST, CHOW, FOOD, CORN, GRIST, FEED, REPAST, FARE, FLOUR, BRAN, PINOLE, AGAPE, MASH
boiled in milk .... MUSH
boxed, field ... K RATION
coarse .... GROUT, SAMP, GRITS, HOMINY, GROATS
corn ...... SAMP, HOMINY
end's serving .... DESSERT
family .... POTLUCK
light .... SNACK, LUNCH, COLLATION, REFECTION
main course .... ENTREE
noon ...... LUNCH(EON)
oat .... GROATS
part of .... HELPING, SERVING
table .... BOARD
wheat .... GROATS
mealies .... MAIZE, CORN
meals .... BOARD
mealy .. FARINACEOUS, PALE, POWDERY, SPOTTY, FARINOSE
mouthed .. EUPHEMISTIC
mean .. LOW-DOWN, AVERAGE, CAITIFF, PITIFUL, PITIABLE, SCALY, NASTY, BASE, CRUEL, SNIDE, CATTY, SIGNIFY, DENOTE, POOR, INFERIOR, HUMBLE, PALTRY, IGNOBLE, INTEND, PETTY, MISERLY, VICIOUS, MEDIUM, MIDDLING, EVIL
person .... CAITIFF
meander .. RAMBLE, WANDER, ROAM
meandrous .... WINDING, TORTUOUS, LABYRINTHINE
meaning ...... SENSE, IMPORT, PURPORT, SIGNIFICANCE, INTENT
ambiguous in .. CRYPTIC
meaningless .... IDLE, FUTILE
means ..... AGENCY, RICHES, WEALTH, RESOURCES, WAY, METHOD, TOOL, WHEREWITHAL
by all ...... CERTAINLY, OF COURSE
by any ...... SOMEHOW
for communicating knowledge .... ORGANON
of defense .... MUNIMENT
of entry .... DOOR, GATE, PORTAL, INGRESS
of escape .... LOOPHOLE
of expression ... OUTLET, MEDIUM
of living .... LIVELIHOOD
meantime ... INTERIM, WHILST
measles .. RUBELLA, MORBILLI, RUBEOLA, ROSEOLA, (ROSE)RASH
mark .... SPOT
measly ..... SCANTY, SKIMPY, MISERLY
measure .. LITER, STEP, METE, CRITERION, POLE, PERCH, GAUGE, STANDARD, INCH, YARD, BUSHEL, FOOT, LAW, STATUTE, APPRAISE
cloth .... ELL
combining form .. METRO
depth of .... FATHOM
distance .... MILE, KILOMETER
dry .... ROTL, BUSHEL
equality of ... ISOMETRY
grain .... BUSHEL, PECK
land .... MORGEN, ACRE, AR(E), HECTARE
length ..... CUBIT, YARD, FOOT, ROD, METER, STEP, ELL
liquid .. QUART, TIERCE, LITER, TUN, GALLON, PINT, GILL, DRAM
medicine .... DOSE
metric .... MICRON, TON, STERE
metrical foot .... ANAP(A)EST
nautical .... KNOT
of .... MENSURAL
of astronomical distance .. SECPAR, PARSEC
of capacity .. CASK, PINT, PECK, BUSHEL, QUART, STERE, BARREL, TUN
of earth ...... GEODESY
of energy ...... ENTROPY
of length, ancient .... CUBIT
of wood .... CORD
of work, in physics ..... ERGON
out .... METE
paper ...... REAM, QUIRE
poetry .... SCAN
sound volume .. DECIBEL
speed .... KNOT
swords .. DUEL, CONTEND
time .... CLOCK
type .... EM, EN
weight .... GRAIN, GRAM, METAGE, CARAT
wine .... BUTT
wire .... MIL
yard .... VERGE
yarn ...... LEA, SPINDLE
measured medicine .... DOSE, DOSAGE
measurement .. MENSURATION, DIMENSION, METERAGE
contents/weight .... METAGE
end to end .... LENGTH
standard/unit of .... MODULE
measurer .... METER, GAUGER
measuring instrument .... TRANSIT, STADIA, CAL(L)IPER, STADIOMETER, GA(U)GE, METER, SEXTANT
standard .... YARDSTICK
stick .... RULE, ROD
unit, sound volume ..... DECIBEL
worm .... LOOPER, LARVA
meat .... PORK, FOOD, FLESH, BEEF, MUTTON, VEAL, STEAK, VENISON, TRIPE
and vegetable dish ...... RAGOUT, OLLA, HASH
ball ..... RISSOLE, PINDA
carving board .... TRENCHER
covering, jellylike .... GLAZE
cured .... HAM
cut ..... CHOP, BRISKET, RUMP, FIL(L)ET, RIB, CHUCK, LOIN, STEAK, ICEBONE, HAM
dish .... RAVIOLI, SALMAGUNDI, RISSOLE, STEW
dried .... BILTONG, JERK, PEM(M)ICAN, CHARQUI
eater .... CARNIVORE
hard, salted ...... JUNK
in gravy .... AU JUS
jelly .... ASPIC
juice .... GRAVY
leg .... CUTLET
paste ...... PEM(M)ICAN
pie ...... RISSOLE, PATE, PASTY
piece ..... COLP, CHUNK, FIL(L)ET, COLLOP
pickle .... CORN
pickled ...... MARINADE
pig .... PORK

product .... HAM
restaurant .. ROTISSERIE
rib .... CUTLET
roast .. CABOBS, KABOBS, BAR, FRICANDO, FRICANDEAU
roasting device .... SKEWER, GRILL, SPIT, BUCCANEER, BROACH
roll ... RISSOLE, ROULADE
salted, smoked .. BACON, HAM
seasoned .. BAR, CABOBS
seller .... BUTCHER, KNACKER
shop .... SHAMBLES, ROTISSERIE
slice .... COLLOP
spiced .... BOLOGNA, SALAMI, SAUSAGE
stew .. HARICOT, RAGOUT, GOULASH, FRICASSEE, OLLA
strips .... BILTONG
stuffed .... SAUSAGE
thick piece ..... CHUNK
meatball ..... PINDA, RISSOLE
meatless .... MAIGRE
meatman .... BUTCHER
meatus ... OPENING, PASSAGE, FORAMEN, DUCT
mechanical contrivance ...... DEVICE, GADGET
game .... PINBALL
Mecca black stone location .. KIBLAH
chief magistrate .. SHERIF
Moslem who visited .... HADJI
pilgrimage .... HADJ
pilgrim's dress ... IHRAM
shrine ... KAABA, CAABA
son of ...... MOHAMMED, MAHOMET
to Medina journey .... HEJIRA, HEGIRA
mechanic, military .... ARTIFICER
mechanical .... INVOLUNTARY, AUTOMATIC, SPONTANEOUS
bar .... LEVER
man .... ROBOT, AUTOMATON
mechanics .... DYNAMICS, STATICS, WORKINGS
Mechlin ...... MALINES, LACE
medal .... BADGE, MEDALLION
back of .... VERSO
face of .... OBVERSE
give .. DECORATE, AWARD
space .... EXERGUE
medallion .... CAMEO
medals, collector of .... NUMISMATIST
of .... NUMISMATIC
meddle .. TAMPER, INTERFERE, INTERVENE, INTRUDE, PRY, BUTT IN, INTERLOPE, MELL
meddler .... BUSYBODY, KIBITZER, GREMLIN
meddlesome .... CURIOUS, OFFICIOUS, INTERFERING
man .... PAUL PRY

Medea .... SORCERESS
consort of .... JASON
father of .... AEETES
victim of .... CREUSA, CREON, GLAUCE
Medean king of Persia ...... CAMBYSES
Medes' language .... AVESTAN
media, part of mass .. PRESS, TELEVISION, RADIO
medial .... MIDDLE, AVERAGE, ORDINARY
median .... AVERAGE, MIDDLE, MESAL, MEAN, MESNE, MESIAL
priests .... MAGI
mediate .... INTERVENE, CONCILIATE
mediator ...... INTERCESSOR, ARBITER, ARBITRATOR, REFEREE
medic ...... DOC, CORPSMAN, SURGEON, PHYSICIAN, ALFALFA
medicable .... CURABLE, CURATIVE
medical .... IATRIC, CURATIVE
assistant ...... INTERN(E)
combining form .. IATRO
examiner ...... CORONER
group .... AMA
profession symbol ...... CADUCEUS
science branch .... GERIATRICS, THERAPY, NEUROLOGY
student ...... MEDIC(O), INTERN(E)
suffix .... ITIS, OMA
treatment ...... THERAPY
treatment: comb. form .. IATRY
medicate .... TREAT
medicated candy .. LOZENGE, COUGH DROP
cloth .... STUPE
liquid .... LOTION
medication .... DOSAGE
medicinal .... IATRIC
bark .... PEREIRA, VIBURNUM, CINCHONA
capsule .... CACHET
cigarette .... CUBEB
gum .... KINO
herb .... SENNA, ARNICA, ALOE
lozenge .... TROCHE
plant ..... RUE, COHOSH, ALOE, HERB, TANSY, SPURGE, SIMPLE, URENA, BONESET, IPECAC
root .. ZEDOARY, JALAP, ARTAR, GINSENG
shrub .... ALEM
tablet .... LOZENGE, TROCHE, TABLOID
medicine .... DRUG, REMEDY, CURE
capsule .... CACHET
chest .... CABINET
cure-all .... ELIXIR, PANACEA
dropper .... PIPETTE

drugs with syrup .... ELECTUARY
man .... SHAMAN, (WITCH)DOCTOR, MAGICIAN, ANGEKOK, MUMBOJUMBO, PEAI, QUACK
measure .... DOSE
mock .... PLACEBO
patent/quack .. NOSTRUM
pertaining to .... IATRIC
science of .... IATROLOGY
treat with .... MEDICATE
vomit .... EMETIC
medieval catapult ... ONAGER, MANGONEL, TREBUCHET
coat .... GAMBESON
empire ...... TREBIZOND
fortification .... CASTLE
galley .... AESC, BIREME, GALIOT
household official ...... SENESCHAL
judicial council ... CURIA
knight .... PENNON
lyric .... ALBA
lyric poet .... MINSTREL
musical instrument ..... ROT(T)E, LUTE, LYRE, REBEC(K)
servant .... SEWER
shield ...... ECU, PAVIS
ship .... DROMON
singer .... MINSTREL, TROUBADOUR
sport ...... TILT, JOUST, TOURNEY
town .... BOURG
trading vessel ..... NEF
tunic ..... JUPON, GIPON
vassal .... VAVASOR
village .... BOURG
war engine .... BOAR, TREBUCHET
warship .... DROMON
weapon .... MACE, ONCIN
wind instrument .... SACKBUT
mediocre .... SO SO, INFERIOR, ORDINARY, AVERAGE, MIDDLING
meditate ..... MUSE, BROOD, PORE, PONDER, REFLECT, CONTEMPLATE, RUMINATE, MULL
meditative .. PENSIVE, MUSING
Mediterranean ...... INLAND, LANDLOCKED
bush .... CAPER
city .... ORAN
country .... TUNISIA
evergreen .. LAURUSTINE
fish .... OMBER
galley .. BIREME, TRIREME, GAL(L)IOT
grass .... DISS
gulf .... TARANTO, TUNIS
island ..... CAPRI, LIDO, ELBA, RODI, SICILY, GOZO, MALTA, CRETE, SARDINIA
pine .... PINASTER
pirate .... XEBEC

plant .... MANDRAKE, TURNSOLE
principality ..... MONACO
raisin .... SULTANA
regions .... LEVANT
resin .... MASTIC
resort ...... NICE, LIDO, RIVIERA, MENTON
river to the .. EBRO, NILE, RHONE
sailboat .... LATEEN, CAIQUE
seaport .... TETUAN, TOULON, TRIPOLI, PORT SAID
ship ...... XEBEC, SETEE, FELUCCA, SAIC, TARTAN, LATEEN, ZEBEC(K), POLACRE
ship master ... PADRONE
shrub ...... LAURUSTINE
sparoid ...... GILTHEAD
trading ship ... PADRONE
tree .... CAROB
tributary .... TIBER, TEVERE, ORONTES
vessel .... FELUCCA, LATEEN, GALLEASS
volcanic island .. LIPARI
WARSHIP .... BIREME, TRIREME
wind .... LEVANTER, MISTRAL, PTESIAN, SOLANO, SIROCCO

medium .. AGENCY, MEAN(S), AVERAGE
artist's .... CANVAS, OIL, CLAY, BRONZE, MUSIC, PAINTING, STONE, VIOLIN, PIANO
exchange ...... MONEY, CURRENCY
in music .... MEZZO
response of a .... ORACLE
session with a ... SEANCE
size .... MIDDLING
spiritualistic .... PSYCHIC
with deities ..... ORACLE

medley .. MIXTURE, FANTASIA, MACEDOINE, FARRAGO, OLIO, POTPOURRI, MELANGE, PASTICHE, CENTO, SALMAGUNDI, HODGEPODGE, PASTICCIO
race .... RELAY

medulla ...... MARROW, PITH
oblongata .... BULB

medullary sheath .... MYELIN

Medusa .. GORGON, JELLYFISH
hair of .... SNAKE(S)
sister of .... STHENO, EURYALE
slayer of ...... PERSEUS

medusan .... JELLYFISH

meed .. REWARD, RECOMPENSE

meek .. SPINELESS, LAMBLIKE, HUMBLE, LOWLY, SUBMISSIVE

meerschaum .... SEPIOLITE, PIPE, MINERAL, SEAFOAM

meet ...... EQUAL, CONVENE, RENDEZVOUS, MATCH, SEEMLY, ENCOUNTER, CONFRONT, FACE, ASSEMBLE, FIT(TING), SIT
by appointment ... DATE, RENDEZVOUS
companion of ... PROPER
face to face ... CONFRONT

meeting .... RALLY, HUDDLE, CAUCUS, DATE, SESSION, ASSEMBLY, GATHERING, BEE, CONFERENCE, CONCLAVE, SYMPOSIUM
clandestine .... RENDEZVOUS, TRYST
full attendance .... PLENARY
hostile .... DUEL, RENCONTRE, RENCOUNTER
lovers' .... TRYST, RENDEZVOUS
place of "Big Three" ... POTSDAM, YALTA, CASABLANCA
point .... JUNCTION
room .... CAMARILLA
to elect Pope .. CONCLAVE

megalomania ...... DELUSION

megalomaniac's delusion ..... POWER, GRANDEUR, WEALTH

megapod .... MALEO
mound-building .. LEIPOA

megalith ..... STONE, MENHIR
structure using .... DOLMEN, CROMLECH, MONUMENT, TOMB

megaphone of a kind .... LOUDSPEAKER

megass(e) .... BAGASSE

Megiddo ..... ARMAGEDDON

megrim(s) .. VERTIGO, WHIM, HEADACHE, MIGRAINE, FANCY, FAD, BLUES

Mehitabel .... CAT

Mehta, conductor .... ZUBIN

Meiji emperor .... MUTSUHITO

"Mein Kampf" author .... HITLER

meinie (meiny) .... RETINUE, RETAINERS, HOUSEHOLD

meiosis .... LITOTES, MATURATION, REDUCTION

Meir, Israeli premier .. GOLDA

Mekong .... LANTSANG

mel .... HONEY
actor .... FERRER
baseballer .... OTT
singer .... TORME

melancholia .... GLOOM, DEPRESSION

melancholic spell ...... HUMP

melancholy .... DREAR, SAD(NESS), ATRABILIOUS, GLOOMY, PENSIVE, BLUE, HIPPED, SOMBER
fit of .... HYP(S), HUMP, HYPOCHONDRIA

Melanesian islands .... FIJI, SOLOMON, ADMIRALTY
native .... FIJI

melange ...... MIXTURE, OLIO, HODGEPODGE

melanin .... PIGMENT

melanite .... GARNET

melanoma .... TUMOR

melanous, opposed to .... XANTHOUS

Melba, soprano ..... NELLIE

Melchior, tenor ..... LAURITZ

meld .. BLEND, MERGE, UNITE

Meleager .... ARGONAUT
animal killed by ... BOAR
mother of ...... ALTHEA

melee .... FREE-FOR-ALL, RUMBLE, MIX-UP, SCUFFLE, BRAWL, (AF)FRAY, RUCKUS, HASSLE, SKIRMISH

melic .... LYRIC

melicocca .... GENIP

melilot .... CLOVER

melinite .. LYDDITE, EXPLOSIVE

mell .... MEDDLE, MIX

melli: comb. form .... HONEY

mellifluous .... HONEYED

mellow .... RIPE(N), SOFT, MATURE, LOAMY, TIPSY, GOOD, AGE

melodeon .... ACCORDION
like .... HARMONIUM

melodic .... LYRICAL, ARIOSE
embellishment .... GRACE NOTE, CADENZA
phrase .... OSTINATO

melodious .... CANOROUS, DULCET, ORPHEAN, TUNEFUL, ARIOSO, MUSICAL

melodrama ..... HISTRIONICS

melodramatic ... HISTRIONIC

melody .. ARIA, LAY, STRAIN, CAVATINA, ARIETTA, AIR, TUNE, SONG
counterpoint to main ... DESCANT

meloid .... BEETLE

melon .. PEPO, CANTALOUP(E), GOURD, CAS(S)ABA
dessert .... BOMB
pear .... PEPINO
slang .... PROFITS

Melpomene .... MUSE

melt ... RUN, FUSE, DISSOLVE, SOFTEN, THAW, LIQUEFY, FUZE, VANISH
fat .... RENDER
into mold ...... FOUND
ore .... SMELT

melted .... FUSIL(E)

melting pot .... CRUCIBLE, AMERICA

Melville, novelist ... HERMAN
character .... AHAB, WHALE, MOBY DICK, BILLY BUDD
novel ..... TYPEE, OMOO, MOBY DICK

member .. ORGAN, LIMB, LEG, ARM, AFFILIATE, PART
academy .... FELLOW
club ... ROTARIAN, LION, JAYCEE
embassy staff .. ATTACHE
fraternity ...... BROTHER
sorority .... SISTER

membership .... AFFILIATION, SEAT
charge .... DUE

membrane .... PIA, WEB, COVERING, VELUM, VELAMEN,

PELLICLE, TELA
animal eye .... TAPETUM
bird's beak .... CERE
brain .... MENINGES, PIA MATER, DURA MATER, ARACHNOID
combining form .... HYMEN(O)
diffusion thru .. OSMOSIS
egg yolk .... VITELLINE
embryo's sac ... AMNION
enclosing .... CAUL
eye ...... UVEA, CORNEA
eyeball .... SCLERA
fetus .... CHORION, CAUL
fold of mucous ... PLICA
lining abdominal cavity .. PERITONEUM
nictitating .... HAW
uniting toes/fingers ..... WEB(BING)
membranous covering .... INVOLUCRE
layer .... TAPETUM
Memel River city ..... TILSIT
Memmon, killer of .. ACHILLES
memento .. RELIC, KEEPSAKE, TOKEN, PRAYER, SOUVENIR, REMEMBRANCE, TROPHY
memo .... NOTE, CHIT
memoir ...... REMINISCENCE, BIOGRAPHY, MONOGRAPH
memorabilia .... ANA
memorable .... NOTABLE
period ...... EPOCH, ERA
memorandum .... CHIT, NOTE, BRIEF, MINUTE
pad .... TICKLER
memorial .... SHRINE, STATUE, COMMEMORATIVE, MONUMENT, TROPHY
of a sort ...... PETITION
post .. XAT, TOTEM, XYST
memory ...... REMINISCENCE, REMEMBRANCE, RECOLLECTION
book ... DIARY, MEMOIR, ALBUM
helping the .. MNEMONIC
loss of .... AMNESIA
of .. MNESIC, MNEMONIC
pertaining to .... MNESIC
pill .... CYCLERT, RIBAMINOL
science to improve ...... MNEMONICS
testing device .... TACHISTOSCOPE
Memphis god .... PTAH
high priest .... RANOFER
river .... NILE
ruler .... PHARAOH
men in blue suits .. UMP(IRES)
in white ...... DOCTORS
of .... MASCULINE
of letters ..... LITERATI
party for .... STAG, SMOKER
men's affair ... STAG, SMOKER
menace .... THREAT(EN)
menacing .... MINATORY, MINACIOUS

menad .. NYMPH, BACCHANTE
menage .... HOUSEHOLD, HOUSEKEEPING, DOMICILE
menagerie .... ZOO
mend .... COBBLE, PATCH, DARN, REPAIR, IMPROVE, FIX
in tailoring ..... BUSHEL
mendacious .... FALSE, LYING
mendacity ... LIE, FALSEHOOD
Mendel, botanist .... GREGOR
forte of ...... GENETICS, HEREDITY
Mendelssohn, composer ...... FELIX
mender .... REPAIRER
pots/pans ...... TINKER
shoe .... COBBLER
socks .... DARNER
tear .... DARNER
mendicant .. BEGGAR, BEGGING
kind of .... FRIAR
Moslem .... FAKIR
Menelaus' brother .... AGAMEMNON
daughter .... HERMIONE
father .... ATREUS
wife .... HELEN
menhaden ..... YELLOWTAIL, FISH, HERRING, WHITING, POGY, MOSSBUNKER, HARDHEAD, OLDWIFE
menhir .... MEGALITH, MONUMENT
menial .... SERVILE, SERVANT, DOMESTIC
meninges .... ARACHNOID, PIA MATER
meniscus .... LENS, CRESCENT
Menlo Park inventor .. EDISON
Mennonite .... AMISH
menopause ...... CLIMATERIC
Menotti, composer .... GIAN-CARLO
heroine .... AMELIA
mensal .... MONTHLY
menstrual .... MONTHLY
discharge .... CATAMENIA
mental .... INTELLECTUAL, PHRENIC
attitude ..... VIEWPOINT
bias .... WARP
communication .... TELEPATHY
concept .... IDEA
condition .... DEMENTIA
deficiency ...... IDIOCY, IMBECILITY, AMENTIA, MORONITY, MONGOLISM
discipline .... YOGA
disorder ..... PARANOIA, SCHIZOPHRENIA, NEUROSIS, DISTEMPER
drug .... METRAZOL
effort ...... HEADWORK, CEREBRATION
hospital ..... BUGHOUSE, BEDLAM
patient ...... BEDLAMITE
perception .... KEN
picture ..... IDEA, VISTA, PHANTASM, FANTASM, RECEPT, VISION, FANCY
quirk .... WARP

reservation .... QUALIFICATION
reservation, dishonest ... SALVO
state .... MORALE, MOOD, DISPOSITION
strain .... TENSION
training .... EDUCATION
view .... OUTLOOK
mentality .. MIND, ATTITUDE, DISPOSITION
mentally alert .... ACUTE
deficient person .. IDIOT, IMBECILE, MORON
sound ..... LUCID, SANE
wandering ... DELIRIOUS
mention .... CITE, ALLUDE, SPECIFY, REFER(ENCE), NAME
mentor ... ADVISER, TEACHER, COACH
mentum .... CHIN
menu .. CARTE, BILL (OF FARE)
item .... ENTREE
Menuhin, violinist .. YEHUDI
teacher of ...... ENESCO
Mephisto(pheles), debtor of .. FAUST(US)
Mephistophelean .... CRAFTY, DIABOLICAL, FIENDISH
mephitic .... NOXIOUS, POISONOUS
mephitis ..... MIASMA, DAMP, STENCH
mercantile ...... COMMERCIAL
paper .... DRAFT, CHECK
mercaptan .... THIOL
Mercator ... CARTOGRAPHER, GEOGRAPHER, MAPMAKER
mercenary .... HIRED, VENAL, GREEDY, HIRELING, SORDID, POTHUNTER
soldier .... HESSIAN, CONDOTTIERE, SWISSER
mercery .... TEXTILES
merchandise .. COMMODITIES, WARE(S), GOODS
merchant .. TRADER, COSTER, SHOPKEEPER, DEALER
fleet captain .... COMMODORE
of .... MERCANTILE
of Venice character ..... ANTONIO, SHYLOCK, TUBAL, PORTIA, JESSICA, NERISSA, BASSANIO, SOLANIO, GOBBO, SALERIO
ship ... TRADER, ARGOSY, GAL(L)IOT
ship captain ... MASTER
ship, India-England ..... INDIAMAN
ships collectively .... MARINE
merchants, guild of ... HANSE
merci .... THANKS
merciless .... GRIM
Mercouri, actress ... MELINA
mercurial .. VOLATILE, FICKLE, SWIFT
mercuric chloride ... CALOMEL
sulfide .... CINNABAR, VERMILION

Mercury ... HERMES, PLANET, QUICKSILVER, MESSENGER, AZOTH
cap of .... PETASUS
ore .... CINNABAR
shoes of .... TALARIA
staff of ...... CADUCEUS
mercy .... HUMANITY, GRACE, CHARITY, CLEMENCY, COMPASSION, LENITY
grant .... SPARE
in military usage .... QUARTER
killing ..... EUTHANASIA
mere .. ONLY, NOTHING MORE, LAKE, SEA, MARSH, POND, BOUNDARY, SIMPLE
nonsense .... FALDERAL
nothing .... FIDDLESTICK
merely .. ONLY, PURELY, JUST, SIMPLY
meretricious .... TAWDRY
merganser ..... HARLE, SMEE, GOOSANDER, SMEW, DUCK, SHELDRAKE
merge .. MELD, MELT, UNITE, MIX, FUSE, BLEND, ABSORB
merger ..... FUSION, COMBINE
Merida is capital of .... YUCATAN
meridian .... NOON, APEX, ZENITH, PRIME
merino .. WOOL, SHEEP, YARN
merit .... VIRTUE, EARN, WORTH, DESERT, VALUE, EXCELLENCE, DESERVE, MEED
merits .... QUALITIES
Merkel, actress .... UNA
merl(e) .... BLACKBIRD
actress .... OBERON
Merlin ..... SEER, MAGICIAN, FALCON, PIGEON-HAWK
mistress of ..... VIVIAN
Mermaid Tavern habitue ..... (BEN) JONSON, SHAKESPEARE
Meroe's location ...... NILE, ETHIOPIA
meros ...... THIGH, SURFACE
Merovingian king .... CLOVIS
Merrimac .... IRONCLAD, FRIGATE
merriment ... MIRTH, GAIETY, GLEE, FROLIC
merry .. JOCOSE, GAY, FESTIVE, MIRTHFUL, JOLLY, FESTAL
Andrew .. JOKER, JESTER, MIME, CLOWN, BUFFOON
go-round .... WHIRLIGIG, TURNABOUT, WHIRL, CAR(R)OUSEL, CAR(R)OUSAL
maker ...... REVEL(L)ER
making, riotous ... ORGY
making time .. CARNIVAL, FESTIVAL
monarch .... COLE
person .... ANDREW
thought ..... WISHBONE
Widow composer .... LEHAR
mesa .. PLATEAU, TABLELAND, BUTTE
mescal ...... CACTUS, AGAVE, LIQUOR, PEYOTE
mescaline .... ALKALOID
mesh ...... NET(WORK), WEB, INTERLOCK, TISSUE, ENTANGLE, ENGAGE, NETTING
knot ...... SHEET BEND
meshed ..... SHRINE, GEARED
fabric .... NET, LACE
is in ____ .... IRAN
mesial plane .... MESON
mesmeric .... MAGNETIC, HYPNOTIC
force .... OD
mesmerism ...... MAGNETISM, HYPNOTISM
mesmerist .... HYPNOTIST
mesne .... MIDDLE, INTERMEDIATE
meson .... TETRACHORD, BARYTRON, PENETRON
Mesopotamia .... IRAQ, IRAK
boat .... GUFA
city .... EDESSA, URFA, NIPPUR
wind .... SHAMAL
mesquit(e) ...... ALGARROBA, SCREWBEAN
bean flour .... PINOLE
mess .. FOOD, MEAL, JUMBLE, MUDDLE, BOTCH, BUNGLE, CHOW, HODGEPODGE, HASH, MEDDLE, PUTTER, MUSS
message .... COMMUNICATION, REPORT, WORD
messenger .. NUNCIO, ENVOY, ERRAND BOY, HARBINGER, HERALD, PAGE
of the gods ... MERCURY, HERMES
Messiah ... JESUS, DELIVERER
composer ...... HANDEL
Messina, rock in the Straits of SCYLLA
Messrs. .. MESSIEURS, MISTERS
messuage .. TOFT, HOMESTEAD
messy ...... UNTIDY, DIRTY
mestee .... MUSTEE
mestizo .... METIS, LADINO
metabolism .. METAMORPHOSIS, TRANSFORMATION, METASTASIS
metal ...... IRON, TIN, LEAD, ALUMINUM
alloy .... BRONZE, BRASS, MONEL(L), NIELLO, STEEL, SOLDER
assaying vessel .... TEST, CUPEL
band .... COLLET
bar .. OFFSET, INGOT, FID
block .... DIE
bolt .... RIVET
casting(s) ... PIG, INGOT, FOUNDRY
coat with .... PLATE, TERNE
coating ... PATINA, RUST
"coin," slot machine .... SLUG
comb .... CARD
cutting tool ... HACKSAW
decorative alloy .. NIELLO
disk ..... MEDAL, PATEN, MEDALLION, SEQUIN
dross .... SLAG
extracting apparatus .... SMELTER
eyelet .... GROMMET
fabric .... LAME
fastener .... TNUT
filings .... LEMEL
for coinage .... FLAN, PLANCHET
hard-tipped end .... TAG
heavy .... LEAD
in furnace, molten ...... BATH
leaf .... FOIL
lightest .... LITHIUM
line of type .... SLUG
lining .... BUSH(ING)
loop of .... EYE
marker ..... DIE, STAMP, SWAGE
mass from outer space .. METEOR(ITE)
mixture .... ALLOY
patching/joining alloy .. SOLDER
peg/pin .... SPILL, BOLT, GUDGEON
piece .... SHIM
plate .. PATEN, PATIN(A), HORSESHOE
plate, cut ...... TREPAN
plate on scabbard ...... CHAPE
plate, thin .. SHIM, LAME
purify .... SMELT
rare-earth .. LANTHANUM
rattle .... SISTRUM
refine .... SMELT
refuse ..... SLAG, DROSS, SCORIA, SCUM
ring ..... BEE, GROMMET
rod .... BOLT
scum .... DROSS
shaped for coinage ..... FLAN
shaper ..... SWAGE, DIE, STAMP, LATHE
shavings .... WOOL
sheet cutter ...... SHEAR
sheet of .. FOIL, LAMINA, TAGGERS, LATTEN
spacer, in printing ...... SLUG
strip ...... SLAT, SPLINT
suit ...... MAIL, ARMOR, HAUBERK
thread ..... WIRE, LAME
threads, cloth made of .. LAME
waste ..... SPRUE, SLAG, CALX, CALCES
welding .... SOLDER
white .. ALUMINUM, TIN
worker .. SMITH, WELDER
works .... FOUNDRY, SMITHY
Metalious, novelist ... GRACE
work .... PEYTON PLACE
metallic rock .... ORE
sound .. CLASH, CLANK, CLINK

sulfide .... PYRITE
wire .... LAME
metalloid .. SILICON, ARSENIC
metals, melting and molding of FOUNDRY, CASTING
metalware, enameled ... TOLE
metalworker .... WELDER, (TIN)SMITH, RIVETER
metamer .... ISOMER
metamere .. SOMITE, SEGMENT
metamerism .. SEGMENTATION
metamorphose ... TRANSFORM
"Metamorphoses" author .... OVID
character ...... THISBE, PYRAMUS
metamorphosis .... TRANSFORMATION, CHANGE, METASTASIS
metaphorlike figure of speech .. TROPE, SIMILE
mixed ...... CATACHRESIS
metaphorical ..... FIGURATIVE
metaphrase .... TRANSLATION, TRANSLATE
metaphysical ...... ABSTRACT, SUBTLE, ABSTRUSE
poet .. DONNE, CRASHAW, COWLEY
metastasis ...... METABOLISM, TRANSFORMATION
metathesis .... TRANSPOSITION
Metaxas, Gr. general .... JOANNES
mete .. DOLE, ALLOT, MEASURE, APPORTION, LIMIT, BOUNDARY
metencephalon .... HINDBRAIN
meteoric .... DAZZLING, SWIFT
phenomenon ..... HAIL
shower .. LEONID, PERSEID
meteor .... BIELID, FIREBALL, SHOOTING STAR, HAIL, RAINBOW, LEONID, PERSEID
exploding .. BOLIDE, BOLIS
train of .... TAIL
meteorite .... AEROLITH, AEROLITE, SIDERITE, ANIGHITO, TEKTITE, WILLIAMETTE
meteorologic prefix ... STRATO
meteorologist's concern ...... CLIMATE, WEATHER
meteors, shower of .... ANDROMID, LEONID, PERSEID
meter .... RHYTHM, CADENCE
cubic .... STERE
face of .... DIAL
millionth part of .... MICRON, MIKRON
meters, 100 square ..... AR(E)
10,000 square ... HECTARE
methane .... PARAFFIN, HYDROCARBON
metheglin ..... MEAD, LIQUOR
material .... HONEY
method ...... SYST(EM), WAY, PROCEDURE, PROCESS, MANNER, MODE, TECHNIQUE
of making ..... FACTURE
of procedure .... TECHNIQUE
methodical .... ORDERLY, SYSTEMATIC, FORMAL
Methodism, founder of ...... WESLEY
Methodist Church, of the .... WESLEYAN
preacher ..... ROUNDER
Methuselah's claim to fame .. AGE
father .... ENOCH
grandson .... NOAH
meticulous .... FINICAL, CAREFUL, SCRUPULOUS
metier .. TRADE, OCCUPATION, PROFESSION, FORTE, WORK, SPECIALTY
metif(f) .. HALFBREED, MESTEE
metis .... MULATTO
metopic .... FRONTAL
metric measure .... HECTARE, DECIARE, DECASTRE, AR(E), LITER, STERE, KILO, DECARE, GRAM
ton .... MILLIER
metrical accent .... ICTUS
beat .... ICTUS
composition ..... POEM, VERSE
foot .. ANAPEST, DACTYL, IAMB(US), TROCHEE, CHORIAMB(US), TRIBRACH, PYRRHIC
stress .... ICTUS
time unit .... MORA
writing .. VERSE, POETRY
metrify .... VERSIFY
metro .... SUBWAY
metropolis .... CITY, CAPITAL, SEE, SEAT
metropolitan .. (ARCH)BISHOP, URBAN, EPARCH
Opera man .... BING, MEHTA
mettle ..... COURAGE, SPIRIT, ARDOR, SPUNK, PLUCK
mettlesome .. BRAVE, SPUNKY, COURAGEOUS, GAME
Metz's river .... MOSELLE
Meuse .... MAAS, LESSE
River city .... SEDAN
mew .. GARAGE, BARN, SHED, CAGE, STABLE, (SEA)GULL, MOLT, DEN
cat's .... MIAOW, MEOW, MIAU
mewl ...... WHIMPER, WHINE
mews .... STABLES
Mexican .... NAHUATL
agave .... PULQUE
alcoholic drink .... PULQUE, MESCAL, TEQUILA
American to a .. GRINGO, YANQUI
Aztec emperor .... MONTEZUMA
bandit .... LADRONE, BANDIDO
basket grass ...... ISTLE
battlesite .. BUENAVISTA
bean beetle .... LADYBUG
beverage .... OCTLI, PULQUE, TEQUILA, MESCAL
beverage seed ..... CHIA
bird .. TINAMOU, VERDIN
blanket .... SERAPE
bread .... TORTILLA
brick .... ADOBE
cactus .. MESCAL, PEYOTE, CHAUTE
cake .... TORTILLA
cat, wild, spotted .... MARGAY, EYRA
city .... MONTERREY, PUEBLA, JUAREZ, COLIMA, TAMPICO, JALAPA, OAXACA, PACHUCA, ORIZABA, GUADALAJARA
coin ..... PESO, CENTAVO
conqueror ...... CORTEZ
corn cake ..... TORTILLA
corn mush ...... ATOLE, AMOLE
cottonwood ..... ALAMO
cypress .... AHUEHUETE
dance .... RASPA
dish .... TAMALE, TACOS, ENCHILADA
district .... TEQUILA
dog .... CHIHUAHUA
dollar .... PESO
drink .. TEQUILA, PULQUE, MESCAL
emperor .. MAXIMILIAN, MONTEZUMA
fascist movement .... SINARCHISM, SINARQUISM
fiber plant .. DATIL, PITA, ISTLE, IXTLE, SISAL
food .... TAMALE
gopher .... TUZA
grass .... OTATE, TUCAN, TEOSINTE, ZACATON
grinding stone .. METATE
gruel .... ATOLE
handyman .... MOZO
hut .... JACAL
illegal migrant .... WETBACK
Indian .... OTOMI, ZUNI, SERI, TOLTEC, OPATA, MAYAN, AZTEC, LIPAN, YAQUI, ALAIS
Indian craft .... OJOS
intoxicating drink ...... MESCAL, PULQUE, TEQUILA
laborer .. PEON, BRACERO
liquor .... TEQUILA, PULQUE, MESCAL
man .... HOMBRE
mat .... PETATE
mescal .... PEYOTE
minnow ...... MOONFISH
mix-blood ...... MESTIZO
monetary unit ..... PESO
mountain .... PARICUTIN, TOLUCA, ORIZABA, COLIMA
mullet .... BOBO, LISITA
muralist .... RIVERA, OROZCO
mush .... ATOLE
musical instrument ..... CLARIN

native .. AZTEC, MAYA(N)
noble .... HIDALGO
onyx .... TECALI
painter .... OROZCO, RIVERA
patriot .... JUAREZ
peasant .... PEON
peninsula .... YUCATAN
persimmon .... CHAPOTE
pine .... OCOTE
plant .... CHIA, MAGUEY, SOTOL, AGAVE, PULQUE, MESCAL, OCOTILLO, CACTUS, JALAP, DATIL, AMOLE
plantation .... HACIENDA
policemen ..... RURALES
poppy .... CHICALOTE
president ..... MADERO, ALEMAN, DIAZ, CALLES, MATEOS, GIL, HUERTA, CARDENAS, CAMACHO, JUAREZ, ORDAZ, CARRANZA, OBREGON
pyramid ..... TEOCALLI
raccoonlike animal ..... CACOMISTLE
race ..... MAYA, TOLTEC, AZTEC
ranch .... HACIENDA
reed .... OTATE
resin tree .... DRAGO
revolutionary .... (PANCHO) VILLA
river .. RIO BRAVO, FUERTE, SALADO, YAQUI
robber .... BANDIDO
rodent .... TUCAN
rubber tree ... (GUAY)ULE
ruins, site of .. PALENQUE
salamander ... AXOLOTL
saloon .... CANTINA
sandals ..... HUARACHES
sauce .... TABASCO
scarf .... TAPALO
scorpion .. VINEGARROON
seaport ...... ACAPULCO, TAMPICO, MATAMOROS
shawl .... SERAPE
shrub .... GUAYULE
"spitfire" actress .... (LUPE) VELEZ
state .... SINALOA, VERACRUZ, CHIAPAS, CHIHUAHUA, COLIMA, HIDALGO, PUEBLA, ZACATECAS, DURANGO, JALISCO, SONORA, TABASCO, YUCATAN
state capital ..... JALAPA, OAXACA, CULIACAN, TOLUCA, TUXTLA, MERIDA, GUADALAJARA, HERMOSILLO
statesman .... JUAREZ
sugar .... PANOCHA, PENUCHI, PENUCHE, PANOCHE
tea .... APASOTE
temple .... TEOCALLI
tennis star .... OSUNA
thong .... ROMAL
tree ... ABETO, GUAYULE, DRAGO, RETAMA, MESQUIT(E), AHUEHUETE, ULE
volcano .... ORIZABA, PARICUTIN, COLIMA, POPOCATEPETL, BOQUERON, TOLUCA
weight .... ARROBA
wild cat .... EYRA
wind instrument .... CLARIN
wood .... LINALOA

Mexico City district .... TACUBAYA
empress of ... CARLO(T)TA

Meyerbeer, composer .... GIACOMO, JAKOB
opera by .... L'AFRICAINE

mezereon .... DAPHNE
mezuzah, name on .. SHADDAI
mezzanine .... ENTRESOL
mezzo .... HALF, MEDIUM, MODERATE, SOMEWHAT
mho, reciprocal of ...... OHM
Miami county .... DADE
miasma .... METHANE
disease .... MALARIA
mib(s) .... MARBLE(S)
mica ..... BIOTITE, NACRITE, TALC, SILICATE, MINERAL, MUSCOVITE, PARAGONITE, LEPIDOLITE
transparent .... ISINGLASS
Micah .... PROPHET, MICHEAS
Micawber, Dickens' .... WILKINS
what he has plenty of ... OPTIMISM
mice .... VERMIN
of .... MURINE
Michael ...... (ARCH)ANGEL, ORANGE
Michaelmas daisy .... ASTER
miche .... PILFER, SKULK
Micheas .... MICAH, PROPHET
Michener (James) novel ...... HAWAII, IBERIA
Michigan capital ... LANSING
city .... DETROIT, FLINT, DEARBORN, LANSING, GRAND RAPIDS, IONIA, KALAMAZOO, SAGINAW, PONTIAC
county .... ALGER, CASS, CLARE, IOSCO
lake city .... MILWAUKEE, MUSKEGON
lake port .... RACINE
nickname .... WOLVERINE STATE
river .... CASS
state animal .... WOLVERINE
state bird .... ROBIN
state fish .... TROUT

Mick of "Rolling Stones" .... JAGGER
Mickey ____ .... FINN, MOUSE, ROONEY
mickle .... MUCH
micra, singular of ... MICRON
miscrastur .... HAWK
micrify .... MINIMIZE
microbe .. BACTERIUM, GERM, MICROORGANISM, VIRUS, PATHOGEN
microcosm .... WORLD, MAN, UNIVERSE
microgram .... GAMMA
Micronesia island .... NAURU, PONAPE
microorganism(s) ..... VIRUS, PROTOZOA, BACTERIA, AM(O)EBA
microphone .... MIKE
range of .... BEAM
microscope glass plate .. SLIDE
microscopic .... MINUTE
microspores .... POLLEN
Midas' touch, product of .... GOLD
midday .... NOON
middle ..... MESIAL, MEDIAN, MESNE, MEDIAL, MID, MEAN, WAIST, CENTER, MIDST, HUB
Ages, of the .. MEDIEVAL
Ages, the .... MOYEN AGE
class .... BOURGEOIS(IE), BOURGEOISE
combining form .... MEDI(O)
ear ... TYMPANUM, DRUM
East country ..... IRAN, IRAQ, INDIA, TIBET, BURMA
in law .... MESNE
kingdom .... CHINA
part .... DEEP
toward the .... MESAD
way .... VIA MEDIA
West product ..... CORN

middlebreaker .... LISTER
middleman .... BROKER, INTERMEDIARY, GO-BETWEEN
middling .... AVERAGE, SOSO, MEDIOCRE, ORDINARY, MEDIUM, PORK
middy .. MIDSHIPMAN, BLOUSE
Midgard .... EARTH
to Asgard .... BIFROST
midge .. FLY, GNAT, MIDGET, BANTAM, DWARF, PUNKIE
midget ...... MIDGE, DWARF, MINIATURE
Midianite king ... HUR, REBA
midland .... INTERIOR
dialects .... MERCIAN
midmorning .... TEN, ELEVEN
midnight sun, land of .... NORWAY
midriff .... DIAPHRAGM
midshipman .. REEFER, MIDDY, PLEBE
"Midsummer Night's Dream" character .... THISBE, PUCK, OBERON, HERMIA, TITANIA
tinker .... SNOUT
midterm event ...... EXAM(S)
midway features .. SIDESHOWS
island .. SAND, EASTERN
Islands discoverer ...... BROOKS
midweek .... WEDNESDAY
midwifery ...... OBSTETRICS, TOCOLOGY
mien ... LOOK, AIR, BEARING,

APPEARANCE, MANNER
miff ..... HUFF, TIFF, OFFEND
miggle ..... TAW, MIBS, MIGS
might .. POWER, VIGOR, FORCE, STRENGTH
and ____ .... MAIN
mightily .... AMAIN
mighty .... VERY, POWERFUL, PUISSANT, EXTREMELY, STRONG, GREAT, HUGE, POTENT
mignon ..... DAINTY, PRETTY
mignonette .. RESEDA, PLANT, WELD, WOLD
migraine .. HEADACHE, MEGRIM
migrate .... MOVE, TREK
migration ..... EXODUS, TREK
birds/animals' .... VISITATION
migratory .... NOMADIC, ROVING, WANDERING, PEREGRINE
bird .. TERN, WI(D)GEON, SHOVELER, KUTSARA
butterfly ..... MONARCH
creature ...... LEMMING, LOCUST
horde .... SWARM
worker .. JOAD, BRACERO, OKIE, PEON, WETBACK, ARKIE, HOBO
Mikado ... EMPEROR, OPERA
character .... YUM YUM, KOKO
court of the ..... DAIRI, DAIRO
mike ..... LOAF, MICROPHONE
milady's concern .... HAIRDO, FIGURE, DIET, WEIGHT, WAISTLINE
Milan opera house .... (LA) SCALA
mild .. PLACID, SOFT, GENTLE, TEMPERATE, MODERATE, BLAND, LENIENT
drink after hard one .... CHASER
oath .. EGAD, DRAT, GEE, GOSH
mildew .... BLIGHT, MOLD, FUNGUS, RUST
mile, nautical .... KNOT
$\frac{1}{8}$ of .... FURLONG
$\frac{1}{3}$ of LI
Miled, son of .... EBER
Milesian .... IRISH
milestone ... STELE, LANDMARK, PILLAR, EVENT, HERMA
milfoil ..... YARROW, PLANT
miliaria .... HEAT RASH, STROPHULUS
milieu ...... ENVIRON(MENT), SURROUNDINGS, AMBIENCE
militant .... WARLIKE, COMBATIVE, AGGRESSIVE, FIGHTING
militarist .... JINGO
military .. MARTIAL, SOLDIERS, ARMY
academy site .... WEST POINT
address ...... FPO, APO
assistant .... AIDE
banner .... ENSIGN, STANDARD
cap .... KEPI, SHAKO, BUSBY, PERSHING
chaplain .... PADRE
coat, buffalo skin .. BUFF
depot .... ARSENAL, MAGAZINE
engine .. ONAGER, TANK, CATAPULT
engineer ...... PIONEER, PONTONIER
equipment, heavy .... HARDWARE
expedition .... ANABASIS, CRUSADE
force .... ARMY, LEGION, MILITIA
formation .... PHALANX
governor .... MARGRAVE
greeting .... SALUTE
group .... ARMY, CORPS, DIVISION
guardhouse ...... BRIG
headdress ...... SHAKO, BUSBY
horn .... BUGLE
landing point .... BEACHHEAD
messenger ..... ESTAFET
movement .... DEPLOYMENT, MARCH, MANEUVER
occupation, lift .... EVACUATE
officer .... BRASSHAT
police ...... MP, REDCAP
post ... GARRISON, BASE, STATION, PRESIDIO, FORT
prisoner .... POW
punishment .... GA(U)NTLET
rank, temporary .... BREVET
roll .... MUSTER
salute .... SALVO
school .... ACADEMY
school site .. WEST POINT, ANNAPOLIS
school student ... CADET
science .... SOLDIERY
science subjects .... TACTICS, STRATEGY, BALLISTICS, LOGISTICS
signal for parley/retreat .. CHAMADE
station .... GARRISON
store .... EXCHANGE, CANTEEN, PX
storehouse ...... ETAPE, ARSENAL, ARMORY, DEPOT, MAGAZINE
student ... CADET, PLEBE
supplies ..... MUNITIONS
tactical exercises .... WAR GAMES
truck .. CAMION, AMTRAC
unit .. SQUAD, PLATOON, CADRE, COMPANY
unit roll .... MUSTER
weapons ..... ORDNANCE
militate .... FIGHT
militia .. SOLDIERY, RESERVES, (CITIZEN)ARMY
member ...... RESERVIST
milk .... LAC, EMULSION, EXTRACT, LACTOSE, BLEED, SUCK
beverage .... SHAKE
camel .... KUMISS
coagulated part ... CURD
coagulating enzyme ..... RENNIN
combining form .... LACT(O)
constituent ..... CASEIN
cow's .... KOUMIS(S), KUMISS
curd .... CASEIN
curdled .... (BONNY)CLABBER
curdler .... RENNET
curdling substance ...... RENNET, RENNIN
curds .... LACTARENE
farm ... DAIRY, LACTARY
fermented ... K(O)UMISS
food from fermented .... YOG(H)URT
giving .... MILCH
gland .... MAMMA
like .... LACTEOUS
mare's .... KUMISS
not giving .... YELD
obtained from ... LACTIC
part of .... CURD, WHEY, CASEIN, PLASMA, SERUM, LECITHIN
pertaining to ... LACTIC, LACTARY, LACTEAL
protein .... CASEIN
run .... AVERAGE, ORDINARY
secrete .... LACTATE
secreting ... LACTESCENT
separator .. CENTRIFUGE
shake .... FRAPPE
sickness .... SHAKES
sour ... CURD, CLABBER, WHIG
store .... DAIRY
sugar .... LACTOSE
synthetic fabric .... LANITAL
watery part ...... WHEY
with .... AU LAIT
yielding .... LACTIFEROUS
milkfish .... SABALO, TARPON, AWA
milking, kept for ...... MILCH
milkless .... YELD
milksop .. SISSY, MOLLYCODDLE
milkweed .. SPURGE, STAPELIA
juice .... LATEX
milkwort .... SENEGA
milky .. LACTEAL, LACTEOUS, LACTESCENT
liquid .... LATEX
way .... GALAXY
Way black area .... COALSACK
Way, of the ... GALACTIC
mill ..... GRIND(ER), FACTORY
dam .... WEIR
hand .... QUERN

owner's fee ... MULTURE
slang ... FIST FIGHT, BOX
Millay, Edna ____ ST. VINCENT
milldam ... WEIR
millenary ... THOUSAND
millepore ... CORAL, HYDROZOAN
miller ... MOTH
Miller's salesman ... LOMAN
millesimal ... THOUSANDTH
millet .. PANIC, JUAR, GRAIN, GRASS, PEARL, HIRSE, DURRA, DOURA(H)
seed(s) like ... MILIARY
sorghum-like ... MILO
milliard ... BILLION
milliner ... HATTER
millinery .. HATS, HEADDRESSES
milling charge ... TOLL, THIRLAGE, MULTURE
refuse ... TAILING
millimeter, 1/1,000 of a ... MICRON, MIKRON
million electron volts ... MEV
hardest to earn ... FIRST
times: comb. form ... MEGA
ton explosive force ... MEGATON
millipede ... MYRIAPOD, ARTHROPOD, WIREWORM
it has plenty of ... LEGS
millpond ... DAM, DIKE
Mills bomb ... GRENADE
millstone ... BURDEN
part ... RYND, INK
Milo ... MELOS, SORGHUM
milord ... NOBLEMAN, GENTLEMAN
Milquetoast ... CASPAR
creator of ... WEBSTER
where he appears ... COMIC STRIP
milreis, antecedent of ... ESCUDO, CRUZEIRO
milt ... SPLEEN, ROE
mim ... QUIET, SHY, DEMURE
mime ... IMITATE, FARCE, CLOWN, JESTER, BUFFOON, MIMIC
mimeograph ... STENCIL, DUPLICATE
mimesis ... IMITATION, REPRESENTATION, MIMICRY
mimetic ... IMITATIVE, MAKE-BELIEVE
mimic ... MIME, IMITATIVE, MAKE-BELIEVE, MOCK, COPY, SIMULATE(D), IMITATE, APE(Y)
female ... MIMA
mimicking ... APERY
mimicry .. MIMESIS, IMITATION
mimosa ... HERB, SHRUB, ACACIA, SOAPBARK
descriptive word for ... SHRINKING
mimosaceous tree ... SIRIS
mina ... STARLING
New Testament .. POUND
minacious ... MENACING
minaret ... TOWER
caller from a ... MUEZZIN
part of ... MOSQUE
minatory ... MENACING
mince ... HASH, DICE, CHOP, SUBDIVIDE
minced meat ... RISSOLE
oath .. GEE, GAD, DRAT, EGAD, HECK
mincing ... MINIKIN
bite ... NIBBLE
mind ... REASON, HEED, LOOK AFTER, PURPOSE, CARE, NOUS, MOOD, MENTALITY, TEND, MEMORY, OPINION, INTELLECT, PSYCHE
bear in ... REMEMBER
call to ... RECOLLECT
drug .. LSD, MESCALINE, SEDATIVE, AMPHETAMINE
of the ... MENTAL, PHRENIC
vagueness of ... HAZE
Mindanao city ... DAVAO, ZAMBOANGA, BUTUAN
inhabitant ... MUSLIM, MORO
province ... AGUSAN, DAVAO, SURIGAO, COTABATO
volcano ... APO
minded .. INCLINED, DISPOSED
mindful ... AWARE, CAREFUL
mine ... PIT, DIG, EXPLOSIVE, TUNNEL, SOURCE
arch ... OVERCAST
car ... HUTCH
ceiling ... ASTEL
channel ... TAILRACE
claim ... STAKE
coal ... PIT
compartment ... PANEL
drain pit ... SUMP
entrance ... ADIT
excavation, steplike ... STOPE
gas ... DAMP, MEPHITIS
gold ... BONANZA
gunpowder ... NITER
kind ... COAL, GOLD, DIAMOND, SILVER
partition ... SOLLAR
passage .. STULM, WINZE
pit/pool .. STOPE, SUMP, ARROYO
product ... ORE
prop ... STULL, SPRAG, NOG
railway car ... TRAM
refuse ... MULLOCK, TAILING
rich ... BONANZA
rubbish ... ATTLE
shaft ... WINZE, ARROYO, DOWNCAST
shaft lining ... TUB
sieve ... JIG(GER)
step ... LOB
support against cave-ins . STULL, SPRAG, NOG
sweeper ... PARAVANE
thrower ... MORTAR
truck ... HUTCH
tunnel ... ADIT
vein ... LODE
ventilating shaft ... DOWNCAST
wall ... ASTEL
waste ... TAILING
waterway ... TAILRACE
winch ... WHIM
worker ... COLLIER, PITMAN
miner ... PITMAN, COLLIER, GOLDDIGGER, SAPPER
compass of ... DIAL
disease of ... SILICOSIS
safety lamp of ... DAVY
mineral ... TALC, GYPSUM, CALCITE, DIAMOND, ORE, TRONA, EPIDOTE, APATITE, SPALT, SPINEL(LE), QUARTZ, TOPAZ, FLUORITE, URALITE, ELATERITE, SPINEL, PYRITE, LEUCITE, BARITE
amorphous ... PINITE
black .. COAL, GRAPHITE
blue .. IOLITE, LAZULITE
concretion ... CALCULUS
crystalline .. SPAR, MICA, FELDSPAR
deposit .. PLACER, LODE, SINTER, MASS, VEIN, BED
glassy ... SILICA
hard ... SPINEL(LE)
hardest ... DIAMOND
jelly ... PETROLEUM, VASELINE
luster of ... SCHILLER
lustrous ... RUTILE
magnetite ... LOADSTAR, LODESTAR
mixture ... MAGMA
native ... ORE
oil ... KEROSENE, PETROLEUM
pitch ... ASPHALT, TAR, BITUMEN
radioactive ... CARNOTITE
salt ... ALUM
silicate ... MICA
softest ... TALC
spot in a ... MACLE
spring ... SPA
tar .. MALTHA, BITUMEN, ASPHALT, BREA
truck/wagon ... CORF
vein ... LODE
water ... SELTZER, VICHY
wax ... OZOCERITE
worthless ... GANGUE
miners' group: abbr. ... UMW, MFD
Minerva ... ATHENA, AZALEA, GODDESS
shield of ... (A)EGIS
minestrone ... SOUP, TUREEN
minesweeper ... TRAWLER
minever ... FUR, ERMINE
mingle ... MELL, MIX, BLEND, COMBINE, JOIN
Minhow ... FOOCHOW
miniature .. MODEL, PAINTING, PORTRAIT, SMALL, DIMINUTIVE
aquarium .. TANK, BOWL
garden ... TERRARIUM

tree .... BONSAI
minify .. REDUCE, MINIATURIZE
opposed to .... MAGNIFY
minikin .... DIMUNITIVE, DARLING
minim .. DROP, TINIEST, DASH, SMALLEST
in music .... HALF NOTE
minimal .... LEAST
minimize .... LESSEN
minimum .. LEAST, SMALLEST, LOWEST
mining bar .... GAD
basket .... CORF
bed of ore .... REEF
car .... TRAM, HUTCH
chisel .... GAD
claim .... STAKE
excavation .... STOPE
kind of .... PLACER
nail .... SPAD
refuse .... MULLOCK, ATTLE, TAILING
tool ...... GAD, JUMPER
trough .... HUTCH
minion ..... FAVORITE, TYPE, FOLLOWER, DAINTY, MISTRESS
of the law .. POLICEMAN
minister .. SHEPHERD, CURATE, SERVE, REVEREND, CATER, AGENT, DIPLOMAT, VIZIER, (AT)TEND, CLERGYMAN, PASTOR
assistant of ..... DEACON
home of .... MANSE, RECTORY, PARSONAGE
title of ...... REVEREND
ministry .... CLERGY, PULPIT
admit to the .... ORDAIN
minium .... VERMILION
miniver .... FUR, ERMINE
mink .. FUR, MAMMAL, VISON, KOLINSKY
kin of .... SKUNK
like animal ..... WEASEL
Minnehaha's love .. HIAWATHA
minnesinger ...... MINSTREL, TROUBADOUR
Minnesota capital .. ST. PAUL
city ...... DULUTH, ELY, WINONA, MINNEAPOLIS, ST. PAUL, MANKATO, HIBBING
lake .... ITASCA
native .... GOPHER
nickname .... GOPHER STATE
state bird .... LOON
Minnesotan .... GOPHER
minnow .... MINNY, GUDGEON, SILVERSIDE(S), MOONFISH
minor ...... PETTY, YOUTH, LESS(ER), UNDER-AGE
details .... MINUTIAE
in law .... PUPIL
offense .... MISDEMEANOR
planet ..... AMOR, CERES, EROS, HERMES
suit .. DIAMONDS, CLUBS
minorate .... CURTAIL
Minorca ... CHICKEN, ISLAND
minoress .... CLARE

Minorite .. FRIAR, FRANCISCAN
minority .. NONAGE, PUPILAGE
group's persecution ..... POGROM
Minos' co-judge .... AEACUS
daughter ...... ARIADNE
kingdom .... CRETE
monster ...... MINOTAUR
parent .... ZEUS, EUROPA
structure .... LABYRINTH
wife .... PASIPHAE
Minotaur's dwelling .... LABYRINTH
killer .... THESEUS
minster .... CHURCH, CATHEDRAL
minstrel ... BARD, MUSICIAN, RIMER, SKALD, TROUBADOUR, (MINNE)SINGER
musical instrument ..... HARP, LUTE
show end man ... BONES
show entertainer .... INTERLOCUTOR
song .... LAY
wandering .... GLEEMAN, GOLIARD, JONGLEUR
mint .... BASIL, COIN, HYSSOP, STAMP, INVENT, FABRICATE, PLANT, CANDY, THYME, MARJORAM, DITTANY, CLARY, SAGE, CATNIP, SAVORY, HERB
charge .... BRASSAGE
drink .... JULEP
genus .... MENTHA
plant .... BASIL, CATNIP, OREGANO
product .... COIN(S)
mintage .... COINAGE
minuet .... DANCE
Minuit's bargain .... MANHATTAN
minus .... LESS, NEGATIVE, WITHOUT
minuscule ...... SMALL, TINY, MINUTE
minute .... WEE, NOTE, MICROSCOPIC, MINUSCLE, MOMENT, INSTANT, SMALL, TINY, MEMORANDUM, PETTY
account .... DETAIL
combining form .. MICRO
distinction ...... NICETY
groove .... STRIA
organism ...... MICROBE, GERM, AM(O)EBA, BACTERIUM
orifice .... STOMA, PORE
minutiae .... DETAILS
minutes ...... ACTA, RECORD
15 .... QUARTER
minx .... HUSSY, GIRL, TART, MALAPERT, JADE
play the .... FLIRT
miracle .... MARVEL, WONDER
bread .... MANNA
scene of .... LOURDES, CANA
worker .. THAUMATURGE
miracles, study of .... THAUMATOLOGY
miraculous .. SUPERNATURAL, MARVELOUS, WONDERFUL

mirage .... ILLUSION, VISION, DELUSION
mire .... OOZE, MUD, BOG, SLUSH, MUCK
Miriam's brother ..... MOSES, AARON
mirror ..... (LOOKING)GLASS, REFLECT, CRYSTAL, SPECULUM
back coating .... SILVER
star .... SIDEROSTAT
tinfoil of .... TAIN
mirrors, of .... CATOPTRIC
mirth ..... GLEE, MERRIMENT, HILARITY, JOLLITY, GAIETY
mirthless .... HUMORLESS, SAD
miry .. OOZY, BOGGY, MUDDY, SWAMPY
misadventure .... MISHAP, BAD LUCK, ACCIDENT
misalliance .... MISMATCH
misanthrope .... (MAN)HATER
of a sort .... CYNIC
misbegotten .... BASTARD, ILLEGITIMATE
misbehavior ..... MISCONDUCT
miscarriage .... ABORTION
miscarry .... FAIL, ABORT
miscegenation, product of .... MESTIZO, MULATTO, HYBRID, MESTEE
miscellanea .... ANA, MISCELLANY
miscellaneous .... VARIED, MIXED, ASSORTED, SUNDRY
miscellany .. OLIO, POTPOURRI, MELANGE, MIXTURE
mischief ... DEVILTRY, HARM, INJURY, PRANK, TRICK, DIDO, WRACK
maker .. ERIS, LOKI, IMP, DEVIL, PEST, PRANKSTER, PUCK, INTRIGUER, PLOTTER
mischievous .. IMPISH, PESKY, NAUGHTY, TROUBLESOME, PRANKISH, ELFIN, DEVILISH, PUCKISH, ROGUISH, ARCH
miscreant .. VILLAIN, INFIDEL, CRIMINAL, HERETIC
miscue ..... MISTAKE, ERROR
misdeed .. CRIME, SIN, FAULT
misdemeanor .... OFFENSE, MISCONDUCT, DELICT
mise ..... PACT, AGREEMENT
miser .... NIGGARD, WRETCH, MUCKWORM, HOARDER, HUNKS, SKINFLINT, TIGHTWAD
of fiction ..... MARNER, SCROOGE
miserable .. FORLORN, ABJECT, PITIABLE, WRETCHED, UNHAPPY
misericord .... DAGGER
place of a .. MONASTERY
miserly .... SORDID, CRIPPLE, TIGHT, STINGY, GREEDY, NIGGARD(LY), PENURIOUS
person ..... TIGHTWAD, SKINFLINT, CHURL, NIGGARD
misery .... GRIEF, DISTRESS,

PAIN, AGONY, DOLOR, WOE
misfortune . . . . FARDEL, BAD LUCK, ADVERSITY, WOE, MISHAP, AFFLICTION
misgiving . . . . . . DOUBT, FEAR, QUALM, APPREHENSION, SCRUPLE
misguided . . . . MISLED
mishandle . . ABUSE, MALTREAT
mishap . . BAD LUCK, ACCIDENT
awkward . . CONTRETEMPS
mishmash . . . . OLIO, JUMBLE, HODGEPODGE, MELANGE
misinform . . LIE, MISREPRESENT
mislay . . . . LOSE, MISPLACE
misle . . MIST, MIZZLE, DRIZZLE
mislead . . . . DELUDE, DECEIVE
mismanage . . . BUNGLE, BOTCH
mismatch . . . . . . MISALLIANCE
misogynist . . . WOMAN-HATER
misplace . . . . MISLAY, LOSE
misplay . . . . ERR(OR)
misrepresent . . . . LIE, DISTORT, GARBLE
miss . . . . FAIL, OVERLOOK, AVOID, ESCAPE, GIRL, LADY
a catch . . . . MUFF
intentionally . . . . BALK
something . . . . MUFF
the bus . . . . FAIL
"Missa Solemnis" composer . . BEETHOVEN
missal . . . . PRAYERBOOK
missel . . . . THRUSH
misshape . . DEFORM, CONTORT, DISTORT
misshapen . . . . . . MALFORMED, DEFORMED
missile . . . . . ARROW, BULLET, LANCE, SHELL, PROJECTILE, SHAFT, DART, ICBM, MIRV, SPEAR, ROCKET, GRENADE
detecting device . . RADAR
guided . . IRBM, ROCKET, SAM, TALOS, NIKE
part of . . . . . . WARHEAD
pit . . . . SILO
returning . . . BOOMERANG
square-headed . . QUARREL
tip of . . . . WARNOSE
type . . . . BALLISTIC
whaler's . . . . HARPOON
missing . . . . ABSENT, LOST, LACKING
mission . . . EMBASSY, ERRAND, CALLING
missionary . . . . . . EVANGELIST, APOSTLE
Mississippi capital . . JACKSON
city . . MERIDIAN, BILOXI, JACKSON, HATTIESBURG
county . . . CLAY, LAMAR, YAZOO
explorer . . . . JOLIET
nickname . . . . BAYOU
river . . . . . YAZOO, PEARL
steamboat quarters . . . . . TEXAS
Valley pike . . . . MUSKELLUNGE, MASKALONGE
Mississippian, any . . TADPOLE
missive . . . . . LETTER, MESSAGE
Missouri caverns . . . MERAMEC
city . . . . ST. LOUIS, SPRINGFIELD, SEDALIA, INDEPENDENCE, JOPLIN, KANSAS
county . . . . KNOX, LINN, OZARK, ADAIR, DADE, HOLT
guerrilla . . . JAWHAWKER
mountains . . . . OZARK
notable . . . . . . PERSHING
river . . . . OSAGE
state flower . . HAWTHORN
state tree . . . . DOGWOOD
tributary . . . . PLATTE
misspelling . . . . . CACOGRAPHY
misspend . . . WASTE, SQUANDER
misstep . . . . ERROR, FAUX PAS, TRIP
missy: colloq. . . . . GIRL
mist . . . . BRUME, MISLE, SMOG, SEREIN, SMUR, GAUZE, VAPOR, HAZE, FOG
rain like . . . . DRIZZLE
mistake . . . . . . BONER, FAULT, MISCUE, ERROR, BLUNDER, LAPSE, SLIP, SOLECISM
in conduct . . . . . FAUX PAS
in printing . . . . ERRATUM
mistaken . . . . ERRONEOUS, INCORRECT, WRONG
mister . . SIR, HERR, MONSIEUR, SENOR, SIGNOR, GOSPODIN, GOODMAN
mistletoe berry eater . . MISSEL
mistral . . . . WIND
poet . . . . FREDERIC
mistreat . . . . ABUSE
mistress . . . . . LEMAN, MINION, MISSUS, INAMORATA, MOLL, MRS., MADAM, MISSIS, PARAMOUR
mistrial, cause of, sometimes . . TECHNICALITY
mistrust . . . DOUBT, SUSPICION
misty . . NUBILOUS, BRUMOUS, NEBULOUS
rain . . . . SEREIN, MIZZLE
misunderstanding . . . QUARREL, IMBROGLIO
misuse . . . . . . ABUSE, MISTREAT
of words, ridiculous . . . . MALAPROPISM
Mitchell (Helen) singer . . . . . . MELBA
mite . . SPIDER, ACARID, MOTE, ACARUS, TICK, ARACHNID, ATOMY
larva . . JIGGER, CHIGOE, CHIGGER, LEPTUS
miter . . . . TIARA, HEADDRESS, HEADBAND, BISHOPRIC
mithridate . . . . ANTIDOTE
mitigate . . . . EXTENUATE, TEMPER, SOFTEN, MODERATE, ASSUAGE, EASE
mitosis . . . . CELL DIVISION
stage of . . . . . . ANAPHASE, PROPHASE, TELOPHASE
mitrailleur . . MACHINE GUNNER
mitt . . . . GLOVE
slang . . . . HAND
mitten . . . . GLOVE
mittimus . . . DISMISSAL, WRIT, WARRANT
mitzvah . . . . . COMMANDMENT, PRECEPT
mix . . . . . . LEVIGATE, JUMBLE, BLEND, SCRAMBLE, ADDLE, STIR, COMBINE, MINGLE, MERGE, FUSE, COALESCE
up . . . . . FIGHT, TANGLE, SNAFU, EMBROIL, GARBLE, COMPOUND
mixed, capable of being . . . . . MISCIBLE
language . . . . PIDGIN, JARGON
type . . . . PI
mixer, drink . . . . SHAKER, BARTENDER
mixture . . . . . . HODGEPODGE, FARRAGO, POTPOURRI, COMPOUND, (MISH)MASH, HASH, AMALGAM, MELANGE, OLIO, BLEND
flour, milk, etc. . . BATTER
jumbled . . . HODGEPODGE
musical . . . . MEDLEY
Mizar . . . . ALCOR
Mize, baseball player . . . . BIG JAWN
mizzen . . . . SAIL
mizzle . . . . DRIZZLE, RAIN
mnemonic subject . . . MEMORY
Mnemosyne's daughter(s) . . . . MUSE(S)
concern . . . . MEMORY
moa . . . . RATITE
relative . . APTERYX, KIWI, OSTRICH
Moab . . . . KINGDOM
father of . . . . LOT
giant . . . . . EMIM, ZUZIM
king . . . . MESHA
mountain . . . . NEBO
Moabite stone, name on . . . . . AMRI
moan . . CRY, LAMENT, GRIEVE, COMPLAIN, (BE)WAIL
sound like . . . . . . GROAN
moat . . . . FOSS(E), DITCH
structure surrounded by . . FORTRESS, CASTLE
mob . . . . THRONG, CANAILLE, GANG, BOODLE, RIFFRAFF, RABBLE, CROWD, MASSES
mobile . . . . . MOVABLE, FLUID, VARIABLE, FLEXIBLE
field hospital . . . . AMBULANCE
mobilize . . ORGANIZE, MUSTER
mobster: sl. . . . . . . GANGSTER, GOON
girl . . . . MOLL
Moby Dick . . . . PELEG, WHALE
author of . . . . MELVILLE
hunter of . . . . AHAB
moccasin . . . . SLIPPER, SNAKE, LARRIGAN, FLOWER, PAC
flower . . . . ORCHID
sport shoe like . . LOAFER
mocha . . . . . . COFFEE, LEATHER
mochila . . . . KNAPSACK
mock . . DERIDE, FLEER, JAPE, FLOUT, TAUNT, JEST, MIMIC,

SCOFF, IMITATION, JEER, RIDICULE, DEFY, IMITATE, COUNTERFEIT, SNEER, JIBE
attack .... FEINT
combat .... JOUST
orange .. SERINGA, SHRUB, SYRINGA
sea battle ... NAUMACHY, NAUMACHIA
sun .... PARHELION
up ..... MODEL, DUMMY
mockery .. TRAVESTY, FARCE, BURLESQUE, JOKE
god of .... MOMUS
modal auxiliary verb ... MAY, MIGHT, WOULD, MUST, SHOULD
mode .... FAD, VOGUE, STYLE, METHOD, MOOD, WAY, FASHION
model .... SIT(TER), PATTERN, EXAMPLE, (ARCHE)TYPE, STANDARD, MANIKIN, MOCK-UP, DESIGN, POSE, PARADIGM, EXEMPLAR, MANNEQUIN
for imitation .. LODESTAR
of human being .... HOMUNCULUS
of perfection .. PARAGON, IDEAL
original .... ARCHETYPE, PROTOTYPE
small scale .. MINIATURE
moderate ... MITIGATE, MILD, TEMPERATE, RESTRAIN, BATE, PRESIDE
in music .... MEZZO
moderation ..... TEMPERANCE
modern ... NEO, NEW, LATEST, UP-TO-DATE
city sight ... SKYSCRAPER
person .... NEOTERIC
modernize .... RENOVATE, RETOOL, UPDATE
modest .. SHY, DEMURE, COY, VERECUND, UNASSUMING, RESERVED, DECENT, HUMBLE
modicum .... BIT
modified leaf .... BRACT
modifier .. ADVERB, ADJECTIVE
modify ..... ALTER, QUALIFY, CHANGE, AMEND, ENODATE, VARY
modish .. FASHIONABLE, CHIC, STYLISH
modiste .... DRESSMAKER
modulate .... ADJUST, ADAPT, ATTUNE, INFLECT, (IN)TONE
modulation .... CADENCE
modus operandi .. PROCEDURE
vivendi .... COMPROMISE
moguey .... RAFT
mogul .. NABOB, MONGOL(IAN), LOCOMOTIVE, VIP
dynasty founder .. BABER, BABUR, BABAR
emperor .. BABER, AKBAR, HUMAYUN, JEHAN, BABAR, BABUR
ruler .... NAWAB
mohair .... FABRIC, GARMENT, MOREEN
source of ...... ANGORA
Mohammed ...... MAHOMET, MAHOUND, MUHAMMAD, PROPHET
birthplace of .... MECCA
burial place of .. MEDINA
daughter of ..... FATIMA
descendant of .. SHERIF, SAYID, SEID
destination ...... MEDINA
flight of .. HEGIRA, HEJIRA
follower of ..... ISLAM, MUSLIM, MOHAMMEDAN
religion founded by ..... MOSLEM, ISLAM
sister of .... JINNAH
son-in-law .... ALI
successor of ..... CALIF, CALIPH, K(H)ALIF
wife of .... AISHA, AYESHA(H)
Mohammedan angel .. AZRAIL, AZRAEL
beggar/ascetic ... FAKIR
bible .. KORAN, ALCORAN
bier .... TABUT
blacksmith ...... LOHAR
call to prayer ..... AZAN, ADAN
canonical law ... SHARIA
caravansary ..... IMARET
crusade .. JIHAD, JEHAD
cup .... LOTAH
day of fasting ... ASHURA
demon .... JINNI(E)
devil .... EBLIS, SHAITAN, SHEITAN
fasting period .... RAMADAN, ASHURA
festival .... BAIRAM
Filipino .... MORO
god .... ALLAH
hermit .... SANTON
holy war .. JEHAD, JIHAD
infidel .... KAFIR
inn .... IMARET, CARAVANSARY
judge .... CADI
law .... SUNNA(H)
leader .... IMAM
magistrate .... CADI
Malay .... MORO
messiah .... MAHDI
monk .... SANTON
month .. RAJAB, JUMADA, RABIA, RAMADAN, SAFAR, SHABAN, SHAWWAL
mystic .... SUFI, SUNNITE
mysticism .... SUFISM
noble ...... AMIR, EMIR, AMEER, SHERIF, EMEER
non .... KAF(F)IR
nymph .... HOURI
orthodox ...... SUNNITE
prayer hour ...... AZAN
priest .... IMAM
prince .... AMIR, AMEER
prince's title ..... NAWAB
principle .... IJMA
religion .... ISLAM
ruler .. SULTAN, CALIPH, AMIR, AMEER
ruler's decree .... IRADE
sacred book .. ALCORAN, KORAN
saint .... PIR
salutation ...... SALAAM
Satan .... EBLIS, SHAITAN
savior .... MAHDI
scholars .... ULEMA
sect member .. SUNNITE, SHIITE, SHIAH, SUFI
shrine .... KAABA
slave .... MAMELUKE
teacher .... MOLLAH, MULLA(H)
title .. EMIR, EMEER, AMIR, AGA, NAWAB, CALIPH, SAY(Y)ID
unbeliever ..... KAF(F)IR
uncle .... ABBAS
veil .. YASHMAK, YASHMAC
woman's clothing .. IZAR, ISAR
Mohave .... YUMA(N)
Mohawk ..... INDIAN, RIVER, IROQUOIAN
chief .. HIAWATHA, BRANT
city on the .... UTICA
mohur, 1/15 of .... RUPEE
moiety ... HALF, PART, SHARE
moil .... DRUDGE(RY), CONFUSION
and ___ .... TOIL
moire .. FABRIC, SILK, TABBY, TAFFETA
moist .... WET, DANK, DAMP, HUMID, IRRIGUOUS
to the touch ... CLAMMY
moisten .. (BE)DEW, DAMPEN, WET, WASH, BATHE
with oil .... EMBROCATE
moisture .... DEW
combining form .... HYGR(O)
condensed ... MIST, DEW
moke .. DONKEY, IDIOT, DOLT
Moki .... HOPI
molar ... GRINDER, CHOPPER, TOOTH
molasses ...... SIRUP, SYRUP, THERIACA, TREACLE
beverage ... RUM, TAFIA, ARRACK
candy ... TOFFEE, TAFFY
rum .... TAF(F)IA
source .... SORGO
tobacco leaf mixture .... CAVENDISH
molave ... VITEX, TREE, WOOD
mold .. CAST, MILDEW, KNEAD, SOIL, MOULAGE, MATTER, SHAPE, FORM, FUNGUS, MATRIX, PATTERN
core .... NOWEL
opening for molten metal SPRUE, GEAT, GIT
poetic .... EARTH
product .... CASTING
slime ..... MYXOMYCETE
Moldavia, capital of .... KISHINEV
prince's title .. HOSPODAR
town .... JASSY
molded, can be ..... FICTILE

molder .... DECAY, CRUMBLE, DIE, STAMP
molding .. SHAPING, CORNICE, CYMA, REGLET, CONGE, OGEE, LISTEL, FILLET
building's ..... CORNICE
concave .... COVING, SCOTIA, CAVETTO, COVE
convex .... REEDING, OVOLO, TORUS, BAGUET(TE)
cornice .... CYMA
curved .... NEBULE
decoration .... GADROON
edge .... ARRIS
egg-shaped ...... OVOLO
material .... ORMOLU
narrow .... TRINGLE
ogee .... TALON
rounded .... REED
S-shaped .... OGEE
square .... LISTEL
wall .... CORNICE
moldy .. MUSTY, STALE, MUCID, FUSTY, HOAR
mole .... JUTTY, PIER, QUAY, MAMMAL, STAR NOSE, N(A)EVUS, BREAKWATER, ANCHORAGE, HARBOR, TALPA, PLATYPUS
animal resembling ...... DESMAN
gray .... TAUPE
molecular film ... MONOLAYER
molecule .... PARTICLE
component ...... ATOM, (AN)ION
moleskins .... TROUSERS
molest .... ANNOY, TROUBLE, DISTURB, PESTER
molestation ..... ANNOYANCE
Moliere character .... TARTUF(FE), ALCESTE
moll's friend ..... GANGSTER, MOBSTER
mollifier, baby's ..... SUCKER, RATTLE(R), PACIFIER, THUMB
mollify .... PLACATE, PACIFY, CONCILIATE, APPEASE, SOOTHE
mollusca .... MOLLUSKS, SLUG
molluscoid .... BRYOZOAN, BRACHIOPOD
by-product .... PEARL
mollusk .. CLAM, SNAIL, SLUG, MUSSEL, MUREX, CHITON, ABALONE, WENTLETRAP, RETEPORE, OCTOPUS, SQUID, WHELK, LIMPET, COCKLE, OYSTER, SCALLOP, HELIX, NAUTILUS, PTEROPOD, TRITON
arm of .... TENTACLE
beaked .... OCTOPUS, SQUID, CEPHALOPOD, CUTTLEFISH
bivalve .. CLAM, PIDDOCK, CHAMA, MUSSEL
borer .... TEREDO, SHIPWORM
burrowing ..... PIDDOCK
counterfeit .... SLUG, QUEER
edible part ..... SCALLOP
egg(s) of .... SPAWN, OOTHECA
genus .... MUREX, OLIVA
gills .... CERATA
light producing substance LUCIFERIN
muscle of ..... SCALLOP
shell .... CONCH, COWRY, COWRIE
study of .. CONCHOLOGY
sucking organ .... PROBOSCIS
teeth .... RADULA
tentacled .... SQUID, OCTOPUS
two-gilled ..... SPIRULA
molly .... FISH
where seen usually ...... AQUARIUM
mollycoddle .. MILKSOP, PET, PAMPER
Molnar, dramatist .. FERENC
work .... LILIOM
Moloch .... GOD, LIZARD
sacrificial site ... TOPHET
Molotov .... PERM
cocktail: sl. ...... BOMB, GRENADE
molt .. SHED, CAST(OFF), MEW, EXUVIA(T)E
molten ... MELTED, LIQUEFIED
rock ...... LAVA, MAGMA
waste ..... SPRUE, SCUM, DROSS, SCORIA
Molucca island .... MALUKU, BANDA, CERAM, SERANG, TERNATE, HALMAHERA, GILOLO
moly .. GARLIC, MOLYBDENUM
mom: colloq. .... MOTHER
moment .. SEC, TRICE, FLASH, JIFF(Y), POINT, TICK, INSTANT, IMPORT(ANCE), CONSEQUENCE
of truth .... CRISIS
momentarily .. SHORTLY, SOON
momentary ...... TRANSIENT, PASSING, TRANSITORY
momentum .. IMPETUS, FORCE, SPEED
Momus .... FAULTFINDER
Mona Lisa .. (LA) GIOCONDA, PORTRAIT
painter .... DA VINCI
smile of ..... ENIGMATIC, CRYPTIC
monacero .... UNICORN
monachal .... MONASTIC
Monaco playground .... MONTE CARLO
ruler .... RAINIER
monad .... ATOM, UNIT, ELEMENT, RADICAL, MICROCOSM, MONATOMIC
monarch .. SHAH, CZAR, TSAR, KAISER, ROI, REY, REX, POTENTATE, EMPEROR, KING, BUTTERFLY
golden ball of .. MOUND
jungle ...... LION, TIGER
of the sky .... EAGLE
monarchist .... ROYALIST
monarchy, type of .... ABSOLUTE, DESPOTIC, LIMITED, CONSTITUTIONAL
monarda .... HORSEMINT, OSWEGOTEA, BERGAMOT
monastery .. FRIARY, CLOISTER, HERMITAGE, MONKERY, PRIORY, HOSPICE, LAMASERY, ABBEY, NUNNERY
buyer of provisions ..... MANCIPLE
church of ...... MINSTER
dining hall ...... FRATER, REFECTORY
head of .. ABBOT, PRIOR, MANDRA, HEGUMEN, ARCHIMANDRITE
resident .... MONK, CENOBITE
room .... LOCUTORY, LAVABO
small .... CELL
subsidiary ... SUCCURSAL
monastic ...... OBLATE, MONK, ASCETIC, SELF-DENYING, MONACHAL
brother .... FRA
haircut .... TONSURE
life .... CLOISTER
monde ..... SOCIETY, WORLD
Monegasque territory .... MONACO
Monet, painter ...... CLAUDE
monetary ...... PECUNIARY, FINANCIAL
unit for calculation ..... MILL
money .... FUND, ORA, CASH, COWRY, TENDER, LUCRE, WAD, SPENSE, SILVER, COIN(S), BILLS, BANKNOTES
advance .... EARNEST, IMPREST, ARLES
bead .. WAMPUM, PEAG(E)
box .... ARCA, KIST, TILL
bribe .. SOAP, SLUSH FUND
bronze .... AES
certificate .. BOND, SCRIP, TENDER
changer .... SHROFF, CAMBIST
coin .... MINT
coined .... SPECIE
drawer for .... TILL
earnest ... ARLES, TOKEN, ADVANCE
exchange fee ...... AGIO
fishhook .... LARI(N)
for political purposes ... LUG
from public office .. PAP
function of .. EXCHANGE, MEASURE
handler .... CASHIER, TELLER
Indian .. WAMPUM, BEAD, PEAG(E), SEWAN
left by will ..... LEGACY
legalize as ... MONETIZE
lender .... SHYLOCK, USURER
making .... PROFITABLE, LUCRATIVE

manual .... CAMBIST
market .... BOURSE
metal .. SPECIE, COIN(AGE)
of .... PECUNIARY, FINANCIAL
on hand .... CASH
paid for injury .. DAMAGE
paid to slain man's kin .. WER(E)GILD
payer/receiver ... TELLER, CASHIER
political patronage .. PAP
pouch .... SPLEUCHAN
premium .... AGIO
project .... FUND
ready ...... CASH, FUND
received: sl. ...... TAKE
reserve .... FUND
resources .... FINANCES, FUNDS
roll of .. ROULEAU, WAD
sent by mail .... REMITTANCE
shell .. SE(A)WAN, COWRY, COWRIE
slang .. BOODLE, CABBAGE, MOOLA, DOUGH, LETTUCE, MAZUMA, SHEKEL, KALE, JACK, SCRATCH, SUGAR, WAMPUM, ROLL, DUST
small amount .. PITTANCE
stone .... FEI
substitute ..... COUPON, SCRIP
token .. EARNEST, ARLES, ADVANCE
tray .... TILL

moneyed .... RICH, WEALTHY
monger ..... TRADER, DEALER
Mongol ..... BURIAT, ESKIMO, INDIAN, ASIATIC, TA(R)TAR, ELEUT(H), MOGUL
conqueror .. TAMERLANE, TIMURLENK, GENGHIS(KHAN)
dynasty .... YUAN
emperor .. KUBLAI KHAN

Mongolian .... KALMUCK, KALMYK, TUNGUS
capital ..... ULAN BATOR
conqueror ...... KUBLAI, GENGHIS(KHAN)
desert .... GOBI, SHAMO
dynasty .... YUAN
monetary unit .. TUGRIK
monk .... LAMA
People's Republic capital KULUN, ULAN BATOR
premier ..... TSEDENBAL
presidium chairman ..... SAMBU
priest .... SHAMAN, LAMA
tent .... YURT
tribesman ...... BURYAT
weight .... LAN

Mongolism .... IDIOCY
Mongoloid .... LAI, DURBAN, TURK, SHAN, SHAR(R)A, LAPP
Mongols, clan/tribe of ...... HORDE
mongoos(e) ..... ICHNEUMON, URVA
prey of .... SNAKE, RAT, COBRA

mongrel .. CUR, HYBRID, DOG, MUTT, TYKE
relative .... SURICATE

mongst .... MIDST
moni(c)ker ...... (NICK)NAME
monition .. WARNING, NOTICE, CAUTION, SUMMONS
monitor .. IRONCLAD, LIZARD, REMINDER, WARSHIP, RECEIVER, LOUDSPEAKER, CHECK, MENTOR
builder of the .. ERICSSON
lizard .... URAN

monk .. LAMA, SANTON, FRIAR, BONZE, FRA, PRIOR, BEDE, TALAPOIN, FRANCISCAN, AUGUSTINIAN, CARMELITE, CENOBITE, VOTARY, DOMINICAN
ascetic .... FAKIR
Buddhist .... BONZE, AR(A)HAT
cloak of .... COWL
Eastern Orthodox Church CALOYER
ever silent .... TRAPPIST
Franciscan ... CAPUCHIN
head .... ABBOT
head cover ...... HOOD, COWL, CAPUCHE, CAPOUCH, AMICE
hermit ...... ANCHORET
hood .. COWL, CAPUCHE, CAPOUCH, AMICE
room for conversation .. LOCUTORY
room of .... CELL
settlement .... SCETE
title .... FRA

monkey .. PRIMATE, TITI, ZATI, CAPUCHIN, HOWLER, TAMARIN, SIMIAN, JACKANAPES, WANDEROO, MONA, RHESUS, MARMOSET, VERVET, TARSIER, JOCKO, TOTA, FUR, RAM, TRIFLE, FOOL, PLAY, LANGUR, MACAQUE, NISNAS, MACHIN, TALAPOIN
arboreal .... POTTO, TARSIER, GRIVET, TITI, SIME, TOTO
Asiatic .... LANGUR
astronaut .... BONNY
bearded ...... ENTELLUS
bonnet ..... SATI, TOQUE
bread .. BAOBAB, FRUIT, TREE
business ... FOOLISHNESS, MISCHIEF
capuchin .. SAPAJOU, SAI
flower .... FIGWORT
green .... GUENON
green-haired .... GRIVET, VERVET
grivet .... TOTA, VERVET
howling .. ARABA, MONO, STENTOR
marmoset .... TAMARIN
puzzle .... PINON
red .... PATAS
sacred .... RHESUS
space traveler .... ASTROMONK, BONNY
spider .... ATELES, QUATA
squirrel .... SAMIRI
suit .... UNIFORM
wrench part .... JAW

monkeyshine ... PRANK, JOKE, MISCHIEF
monkish .... MONASTIC
title .... DOM

monkshood ... ATIS, ACONITE, ATEES, WOLFSBANE
monochord .... SONOMETER
monocle .. EYEGLASS, LORGNON
monocotyledon plant .... LILY, PALM, ORCHID
monody .. LYRIC SOLO, DIRGE, ELEGY, THRENODY, MONOPHONY
monogram .... CIPHER
composition of .... INITIALS, LETTERS

monograph .. MEMOIR, PAPER, TREATISE, THESIS
monolith ... PILLAR, OBELISK, COLUMN, MENHIR, MEGALITH, DOLMEN
monolithic ..... SOLID, SINGLE
monologue .... SOLILOQUY
monologuist of a sort .... SOLILOQUIST
monomachy .... DUEL
monomania .... CRAZE, OBSESSION
monopolize .... CONTROL, CORNER
monopoly .... CARTEL, TRUST, SYNDICATE, POOL
maneuver ... COEMPTION

monosaccharide .. SUGAR, OSE, GLUCOSE, PENTOSE
monosodium glutamate ...... AJINOMOTO, MSG
monostich .. VERSE, EPIGRAM, POEM
monotone .... DRONE
monotonous .. TEDIOUS, DRAB, FLAT, HUMDRUM, TIRESOME, DREARY
talk .... DRONE

monotony .... TEDIUM
monotreme .... DUCKBILL, ECHIDNA, ANTEATER
Monroe ____ ...... DOCTRINE
actress .... MARILYN
poet .... HARRIET

mons ____ .... PUBIS, VENERIS
language .... PEGU

monsieur ... (GENTLE)MAN, SIR, MR
monsoon ...... (TRADE)WIND
weather .... RAINY

monster .... CERBERUS, UNICORN, CENTAUR, ENORMOUS, HUGE, OGRE, GILA, TERATISM, FREAK, MONSTROSITY
combining form .... TERAT(O)
fabulous .... MINOTAUR, CHIMERA, BASILISK, COCKATRICE, HARPY

female ...... GORGON, MEDUSA, HARPY, CHARYBDIS, CHIMERA
fire-breathing .. CHIMERA, DRAGON
hundred-eyed .... ARGUS
hundred-handed .... BRIAREUS
hundred-headed .... TYPHOEUS
many-headed .... HYDRA
mythical ... BUCENTAUR, CENTAUR, SPHINX, HARPY, DRAGON, CHIMERA, HIPPOGRIFF, MINOTAUR, GRIFFIN, GRYPHON, GRIFFON, CHARYBDIS
resembling a .. TERATOID
sea ..... KRAKEN, WHALE
snake-haired ... MEDUSA
tiger-bodied .... SU
winged .... GERYON
monstrosity .... FREAK, TERATISM, MONSTER
monstrous .. TERATOID, HUGE, ENORMOUS, HIDEOUS, ATROCIOUS, HORRIBLE
Mont Cervin .... MATTERHORN
montage .... ASSEMBLAGE
Montague Barstow.... ORCZY
scion of .... ROMEO
Montaigne "Essays" translator FLORIO
Montana capital ..... HELENA
city .. HELENA, MISSOULA, BUTTE, GREAT FALLS, BILLINGS
county .. BLAINE, CARTER
lake .... FLATHEAD
motto .... ORO Y PLATA
national park .. GLACIER
river .... TETON, LITTLE HORN
state flower .. BITTERROOT
Monte Carlo location .... MONACO
Cristo author .... DUMAS
castle .... D'IF
hero .... DANTES
monteith .... PUNCHBOWL
Montenegro's former capital .. CETINJE
montero .... CAP
Montezuma's conqueror ...... CORTES
month, by the ... PERMENSEM
excess of calendar over lunar .... EPACT
first day ..... KALENDS, CALEND(I)S
last .... ULT(IMO)
named after pleiad .. MAY
monthly .... MENSAL, MENSES, PERIODICAL, MENSTRUAL
monticule .. HILL, MOUNTAIN
monument .... STATUE, CAIRN, CENOTAPH, DOLMEN, SHRINE, TABLET, OBELISK, STELE, (CROM)LECH, PILLAR, PANTHEON, MAUSOLEUM, TOMB, MENHIR, MEMORIAL, MILESTONE
honoring the dead ...... CENOTAPH
inscription .... EPIGRAPH
of stone(s) ..... CAIRN, MEGALITH, MENHIR, DOLMEN
monumental .... GREAT, COLOSSAL
moo .... LOW
mooch .. SNEAK, SKULK, LOAF, LOITER, PILFER, STEAL, CADGE, BEG
mood .. VEIN, HUMOR, TEMPER, MORALE, SPIRIT(S)
describing a .... INDICATIVE, IMPERATIVE, SUBJUNCTIVE
in logic .... MODE
moody .... SULLEN, GLOOMY, DEPRESSED
moon .... MONTH, ORB, LUNA, SATELLITE, DIANA, LUMINARY
apogee/perigree .. APSIS
between half and full ... GIBBOUS
crater .... COPERNICUS, TYCHO, COLOMBO, LANGENUS, GUTENBERG
dark area on ..... MARE
erratic movement .... LIBRATION
first on .. USA, ARMSTRONG
flower .. MORNING-GLORY, ACHETE
goddess .. LUNA, PHOEBE, SELENE, ASTARTE, ARTEMIS, DIAN(A), CYNTHIA, LUCINA, HECATE
half-lighted ... QUARTER
hole .... CRATER
horn .... CUSP
inhabitant ... LUNARIAN
motion's variation .... EVECTION
mountain ..... PYRENESS
of the .. LUNAR, SELENIC
on the wane .... DECRESCENT
orbit closest to .... PERILUNE
orbiter .. APOLLO, COLLINS, GORDON, ROOSA, WORDEN
personified .... LUNA
pertaining to the .... LUNAR, SELENIC
phase ...... NEW, FULL, GIBBOUS
poetic .... LAMP
point ...... CUSP, HORN
point farthest from earth APOGEE
point nearest earth ..... PERIGREE
satellite .... ORBITER, SURVEYOR
science dealing with the .. SELENOLOGY, ASTROLOGY, ASTRONOMY
sea .... RAINS, SERENITY, CRISES, NECTAR, FERTILITY
shadow .... UMBRA
shaped .... ROUND, CRESCENT, LUNATE
sun relationship .... LUNISOLAR
trench .... RILL(E)
valley .... RILL(E)
vehicle .... ROVER
walker ..... ARMSTRONG, ALDRIN, CONRAD, BEAN, SHEPARD, MITCHELL, SCOTT, IRWIN, YOUNG, DUKE, CERNAN, SHIMITT
watcher ... ASTROLOGER, ASTRONOMER
mooncalf .... IDIOT, FOOL, IMBECILE
moonling, fictional ... SQUAPS
moonshine .. FUSTIAN, WHISKY, NONSENSE
moonshiner ..... BOOTLEGGER
moonstone .... FELDSPAR, ADULARIA
moonstruck .... CRAZED, LUNATIC
moonwort .... FERN, HONESTY
moor ...... SECURE, ANCHOR, HEATH, FEN, DOCK, MORISCO, MOSLEM, LANDE, BENT, FELL
cock/fowl ..... GROUSE, GORCOCK
grass .... NARD
grouse .... GORHEN
hen .. GROUSE, GALLINULE
moorage .. DOCK, ANCHORAGE
mooring buoy/spar .. DOLPHIN
fee .... WHARFAGE
place ...... ANCHORAGE, DOCK, BERTH, MARINA, PORT
rope .... PAINTER
Moorish .... MORESQUE, MORISCAN
cloak .... BURNOUS, BURNOOSE
coin .... MARAVEDI
fabric .... TIRAZ
fortress .... ALCAZAR
garment .... JUPON
hermit ...... MARABOUT
kettledrum .. AT(T)ABAL
king of Granada .... BOABDIL
palace/fortress .... ALCAZAR, ALHAMBRA
sailboat .... SAPIT
tabor .... AT(T)ABAL
moose ..... ALCES, ELK, DEER
feeding place ..... YARD
kin .. REINDEER, CARIBOU
male .... BULL
pouch .... BEL
territory .... MAINE
moot .. ASSEMBLY, DEBATABLE
place of .. LAW SCHOOL, MOCK COURT
mop ...... WIPE, WASH, RUB, SWAB, GRIMACE, SWOB, MALKIN, MAUKIN
cannon .... SWAB
mope .... MOON, SULK
moppet .. CHILD, DOLL, GIRL, (SMALL)FRY
Moqui .... HOPI

mora, in law .... DEFAULT, DELAY
moraceous tree ... MULBERRY
moral ..... CHASTE, ETHICAL, VIRTUOUS, MAXIM, LESSON, RIGHTEOUS, DECENT
allegorical story with ... FABLE, APOLOGUE
constitution .... CHARACTER
decay .... DRY ROT
distinction ...... RIGHT, WRONG
fault .... VICE
law .... DECALOG(UE)
obligation .... DUTY
philosophy ...... ETHICS
poem .... DIT
slip .... LAPSE
talk .... HOMILY, SERMON
teachings .... PRECEPTS
weakness ...... FRAILTY
morale ...... MOOD, TEMPER, SPIRIT
morality .... ETHICS, RIGHT CONDUCT
talk on .... HOMILY, SERMON
moralized tale .... EXEMPLUM
morally corrupt .... PUTRID, ROTTEN, VENAL
instruct .... EDIFY
instructive ... DIDACTIC
unrestrained .... LICENTIOUS, LIBERTINE
weak .... FRAIL
morals, pertaining to .. ETHICS
supervisor .... CENSOR
morass .... SLACK, FEN, BOG, MARSH, SWAMP, QUAGMIRE
moratorium .... GRACE
Morava river .... MARCH
Moravia .... MAHREN
capital .... BRNO
writer .... ALBERTO
moray .. CONGER, EEL, ELGIN
morbid .... DISEASED, UNHEALTHY, PATHOLOGICAL, GRISLY, GRUESOME
morbilli .... MEASLES
morceau .... BIT, MORSEL, FRAGMENT
mordant .... EROSIVE, BITING, CAUSTIC, CUTTING, ACRID, ACID, SARCASTIC, CORROSIVE
Mordecai's cousin .... ESTHER
mordent .... TRILL
more .. AGAIN, PLUS, GREATER, FURTHER
cry for .... ENCORE
in music .... PIU
than enough .... AMPLE, SURPLUS, EXCESS
than one/once .... MULTIPLE
work .... UTOPIA
moreen .... FABRIC, TABBY
morel .... MUSHROOM, NIGHTSHADE
morello .... CHERRY
moreover .... AND, ALSO, BESIDES, ELSE, LIKEWISE, FURTHER
morepork .... RURU
mores .. FOLKWAYS, CUSTOMS
singular of .... MOS
Moresque .... MOORISH
Morgan .. STALLION, TROTTER, BUCCANEER
morganatic union .... MESALLIANCE
morganite .... BERYL
morgue .... MORTUARY, LIBRARY
moribund .... DYING
moringa .... BEN
morion ..... HELMET, QUARTZ
Morisco .... MOOR
Mormon .... DANITE
church founder .. SMITH
church head, U.S. ...... YOUNG
not a .... GENTILE
priest .... ELDER
sacred instrument .. URIM
state .... DESERET
Mormonite .... DANITE
morning ...... EOS, AURORA, MATIN, DAYBREAK, DAWN, MORROW
canticle .... VENITE
delivery .... MAIL, MILK, (NEWS)PAPER
glory .. SUNRISE, PLANT, IPOMEA
music .. AUBADE, MATIN
of .... MATUTINAL, MATIN(AL)
poetic .... MORN
prayer .... MATINS
reception .... LEVEE
song .. MATIN, MATTINS, ALBA
star .... PLANT, PLANET, SATURN, VENUS, PHOSPHOR
Moro cannon ...... LANTAKA
chief ...... DATO, DATU, MAGINDANAO
island ...... MINDANAO
Ital. premier ...... ALDO
musical instrument ..... KULINTANG
priest .... PANDITA
sailboat .... VINTA
Moroccan ..... BERBER, RIFF, MOOR
soldier .... ASKAR
wife .... SHERIFA
Morocco ...... MARRAKECH, LEATHER, MAROC, KINGDOM
capital .... RABAT
city ...... CASABLANCA, MARAKECH, RABAT, FEZ
coin .... RIAL
district .... RIFF
dynasty founder ..... ALI
French name .... MAROC
hat .... FEZ
international zone ...... TANGIER
leather, imitation .. ROAN
monetary unit .. DIRHAM
mountain .. JEBEL MUSA
mountainous region .... RIF
native ..... BERBER, RIF, CLEUH, MOOR
premier .... BENHIMA (MOHAMED)
region ..... TAFILET, RIF
ruler .. SULTAN, HASSAN, KING
seaport .. RABAT, CEUTA, MOGADOR, TETUAN, CASABLANCA, TANGIER
Spanish name .... MARRUECOS
moron ...... IDIOT, IMBECILE, NITWIT, AMENT
morose .. GLUM, BLUE, SOUR, DOUR, SATURNINE, GLOOMY, SULLEN, SURLY
Morpheus, god of ____ ...... DREAMS
morphine addicts' analgesic drug ..... METHADONE
refined .... HEROIN
morro ..... HILL(OCK), BLUFF
morrow .. MORNING, NEXT DAY
Mors .... THANATOS
Morse invention .. TELEGRAPH
morsel .. TIDBIT, BIT(E), PIECE, MORCEAU, DISH, SCRAP, ORT
mort .... DEAD, DEATH
mortal ...... FATAL, DEADLY, IMPLACABLE, EXTREME, PERSON, LETHAL, HUMAN
opposed to ...... VENIAL
remains .. CORPSE, DUST, CADAVER
mortality ...... DEATH(RATE)
mortar ...... BOWL, CANNON, PLASTER, CEMENT, COMPO
and ____ .... PESTLE
crush in a .... BRAY
for filling .... GROUT
mixer .... RAB
patch with ...... SLUSH
sound-proofing .... PUGGING
tray .... HOD
mortarboard .... HAWK, CAP
part .... TASSEL
mortgage ..... PLEDGE, DEED, LIEN, WADSET
mortgagee .... LIENOR
mortician ...... UNDERTAKER
mortification ..... GANGRENE, CHAGRIN, SHAME, HUMILIATION
example of ... FAST(ING), SELF-DENIAL, FLAGELLATION
mortify .. HUMILIATE, SHAME, EMBARRASS, DECAY, ABASH
Mortimer, the dummy ...... SNERD
mortise .... JOIN, FASTEN
mortmain ...... DEAD HAND
mortuary .... CINERARIUM, MORGUE, CREMATORY, CHARNEL
morvin .... MALLEIN
mos, plural of .... MORES
mosaic ...... INLAY, COLLAGE
gold .. ORMOLU, PIGMENT
law .... TORA(H), PENTATEUCH

law reading .. PARASHAH
material .. TESSERA, TILE, SMALTO
work .... TESSERA, INTARSIA
moschate .... MUSKY
Moscow .... MOSKVA
chief rabbi ...... LEVIN
citadel .... KREMLIN
square .... PUSHKIN
Moselle .... WINE
city on .. METZ, TREVES, TRIER
tributary .... SAAR
Moses ... LAWGIVER, LEADER
brother of ...... AARON
death place .... NEBO
father-in-law of .. JETHRO
people led by .... ISRAELITES
saw Canaan there ...... NEBO, PISGAH
sister of .... MIRIAM
spy of .... CALEB, NAHBI
successor of .... JOSHUA, JOSUE
wife of ...... ZIPPORAH
mosey: sl. .... AMBLE, STROLL, SHUFFLE(ALONG), MOVE
mosk .... MOSQUE
Moslem (see Muslim) .... SARACEN, PAYNIM, ISLAM(IC), MOHAMMEDAN, BERBER, PATHAN, MUSLIM, MUSSULMAN
beggar .. FAKIR, DERVISH
bridge to paradise ...... ALSIRAT
caliph .... OMMIAD
call to prayer .... AZAN, ADAN
cap ..... FEZ, TARBOOSH
Christian to a ... GIAOUR
chronicle ...... SARSILA, TARSILA
coin .... DINAR
college .... ULEMA
converts .... ANSAR
crier .... MUEZZIN
decree .... IRADE
devil .... EBLIS
doctor .. HAKIM, HAKEEM
drinking cup .... LOTAH
Egyptian .... FULA(H)
era, start of .... HEGIRA, HEJIRA
fasting period .... RAMADAN, RAMAZAN
festival .... BAIRAM
garment .... JUBBAH
governor .... HAKIM
head .... RAIS, REIS
headgear ...... FEZ, TAJ, TARBUSH, TARBOUCHE, TARBOOSH
hermit .... SANTON, MARABOUT
hero .... GHAZI
holy book .... KORAN
holy city .... MECCA, MEDINA, KAIROUAN
holy man .... IMAM, MARABOUT
holy war .. JIHAD, JEHAD
idol .... MAUMET
interpreter of religious laws .. MOLLAH, MUFTI, MULLA(H)
judge ...... CADI, KADI, HAKIM, CAZI, KAZI
lady .... BEGUM
language .... URDU
law .... SUNNA(H)
lawyer .... MUFTI
leader .... AGA, CALIPH, IMA(U)M
marriage .... MUTA
measure .... ARDEB
mendicant ...... FAKIR, DERVISH
messiah .... MAHDI
minister .... VIZI(E)R
"miracle" performer .... FAKIR
monk .... SANTON
month .... SAFAR, RABIA, RAMADAN, RAJAB, SHABAN, JUMADA, RAMAZAN
mosque .. MASJID, MUSJID
mystic .... SUNI
noble ..... SHERIF, EMIR, EMEER, AMEER
nomad .... KURD
non ...... RAIA, RAYAH. KAF(F)IR, GIAOU, ZENDIK
nymph .... HOURI
official .... HAJIB
people .... PATHAN
Philippine .... MORO
philosopher .. AVICENNA, AVERROES
physician ...... HAKIM, HAKEEM
pilgrim .. HA(D)JI, IHRAM
pilgrimage .... HADJ
pilgrim's costume . IHRAM
place for prayer .... MOSQUE
power emblem .... CRESCENT
prayer .... SALAT
prayer caller .. MUEZZIN
prayer's direction .... KIBLAH, KAABA
priest .... IMA(U)M
prince .... AMIR, AMEER, EMIR, EMEER, NAWAB
princess .... BEGUM
principle .... IJMA
prophet .... MAHDI
religion .... ISLAM
religious brotherhood ... SENUS(S)I
religious duty ..... HADJ
religious festival .... BAIRAM
religious person .. IMAM, HATIB, PAKIL, HADJI
rosary .... TASBIH
ruler ... SULTAN, HAKIM, CALIPH, CALIF
sacred book ..... KORAN
saint .... PIR, SANTON
Satan .... EBLIS
scholars .... ULEMA
school .... MADRASA
sect founder .. WAHHAB(I)
sect member .. SUNNITE, SUFI, WAHABI, WAHABEE
shrine .. KAABA, CAABA, MESHED
slave .... MAMELUKE
spirit .... JIN(N), JINNEE, GENIE, GENII, JINN(I)
summons to prayer ..... AZAN
sword ..... (Y)ATAGHAN, SCIMITAR
teacher .. ALIM, MULLA(H), MOLLAH
temple .... MOSQUE
theologian ...... ULAMA
title .... SHERIF, NAWAB, MULLA(H), MOLLA, AGA, HAFIZ, MAHDI, HADJI
title of respect .. SAYYID, AG(H)A, SA(I)YID, NAWAB
tomb .... TABUT
tribe .... BASHKIR
tunic .... JAMA(H)
Turkestan .... SALAR
Turko-Tartar ... BASHKIR
unbeliever ...... GIAOUR, KAF(F)IR
viceroy .. NAWAB, NABOB
weight .... ROTL
who memorized Koran .. HAFIZ
woman's dress .... IZAR
Moslems collectively .. ISLAM
mosque ...... TEMPLE, MOSK, MASJID, MUSJID
tower .... JAMI, MINARET
mosquito ... CULEX, CULICID, STEGOMYIA, GALLINIPPER, INSECT
bite injection .. ALLERGEN
carried disease .. DENGUE, MALARIA
genus .... CULEX, AEDES
hawk ...... DRAGONFLY
larva ...... W(R)IGGLER
yellow fever .. STEGOMYIA
moss .... LICHEN, BRYOPHYTE, CARRAGEEN, EPIPHYTE
filaments ...... RHIZOID
mossbunker ...... MENHADEN, POGY
mosstrooper .... RAIDER, MARAUDER
most .... GREATEST
is superlative of .. MANY, MUCH
mostly .... CHIEFLY
mot .... WITTICISM, REPARTEE
mote .... SPECK
motel .... INN
motet .... SONG, ANTHEM
moth ..... EGGER, FORESTER, INSECT, IO, BROWNTAIL, GYPSY, LUNA, BOMBYCID, MILLER, ARRINDA, CECROPIA, CLEARWING, SATURNIID, PYRALIDID, AGLOOSA
clothes .... TINEA
destroying apples .... CODLIN(G)

eaten .... WORN OUT, PASSE, GNAWED
hawk .... SPHINX
kin .... BUTTERFLY
larva .... LOOPER
proboscis ...... LINGUA
night-flying ... NOCTUID
repellent ..... CAMPHOR
spot in wing of .... FENESTRA

mother ...... ABBESS, MATER, DREGS, AMMA
Carey's chicken .. PETREL
colloquial .. MAMA, MUM, MOM(S), MOMMY, MUMMY, MAMMY, MOMSY
combining form .. MATRI
country ...... HOMELAND
earth .... GAEA
Goose creator .... PERRAULT
Hubbard .... CRONE
killer .... MATRICIDE
nursery rhyme's .. GOOSE, HUBBARD
of Cities .... KIEV
of gods .. RHEA, CYBELE
of horse .... DAM
of many children .... MULTIPARA
of pearl .... NACRE
of presidents .. VIRGINIA
of quintets ...... ZAHRA
of the Gracchi .... CORNELIA
superior .... ABBESS
who rules family/tribe .. MATRIARCH
wit ..... COMMON SENSE, INTELLIGENCE

motherhood ...... MATERNITY
motherly .... MATERNAL
moths, of a group of .... TORTRICID
motif ...... THEME, SUBJECT, FEATURE, IDEA
motion .. MOVEMENT, GESTURE, PROPOSAL, SUGGESTION
imparting ...... MOTOR, KINETIC
in .. MOVING, TRAVELING
neurosis .... TIC
pertaining to ... KINETIC, MOTIVE
picture .. CINEMA, MOVIE, PHOTOPLAY, FLICKER, FILM
picture, cheap .. QUICKIE
picture first prints ...... RUSHES
picture word .. FINIS, END
pictures collectively ..... SCREEN
producing ...... MOTILE
rolling/swelling .. SURGE
toward the left .... LEVODUCTION

motionless ...... INERT, STILL
motivate ...... IMPEL, INCITE
motivation ...... MAINSPRING
motive .. REASON, IMPELLENT, GROUND, INCENTIVE, CAUSE, GOAL, INDUCEMENT, SPUR
in art, music ...... MOTIF
power .... STEAM, ELECTRICITY

motley .... VARICOLORED, HETEROGENEOUS
motor ..... ENGINE, TURBINE
fuel substance ... BORON, ETHYL, OCTANE
speed up ..... REV, RACE
vehicle frame ... CHASSIS

motorboat .. LAUNCH, SCOOTER
motorcar ...... AUTOMOBILE
motorcyclist ...... HAILWOOD
motorman, what he drives .... LOCOMOTIVE, STREETCAR
mott(e) .... GROVE
mottle .... DAPPLE, SPOT, STREAK, BLOTCH
mottled .... PIED, PINTO, DAPPLED, VARIEGATED, PIEBALD
gray .... GRISEOUS

motto .... DEVICE, ADAGE, GNOME, SAYING, MAXIM, CATCHWORD, SLOGAN, SAW
in a book .... EPIGRAPH
in a ring .... POSY

mouchoir .... HANDKERCHIEF
moue .... GRIMACE, POUT
mouflon .... SHEEP
mould .... FORM, KNEAD, MATRIX, FASHION
moulding (see molding)
moulin .... SHAFT
Moulmein is in .... BURMA
mound .. TELL, DENE, GLOBE, TERP, HILLOCK, HUMMOCK, KNOLL, DUNE, TUMULUS, PILE, HEAP, BARROW, HUMP, HILL
domelike .... STUPA
formed by wind .. DOWN
golfer's .... TEE
of a burrowing animal .. MOLEHILL

mounds, full of ... TUMULOSE
mount .. HILL, CLIMB, ASCEND, HORSE, POST, FIX
by ladder ..... ESCALADE, SCALE
Cook .... AORANGI
Etna town .... ENNA
Hood's range .. CASCADES
of Olives .... OLIVET
Rainier .... TACOMA

mountain .... HEAP, PILE, MOUND, BUTTE, BARROW, MONTICULE, KOP
antelope .. KLIPSPRINGER
Apollo's .... PARNASSUS
ash .... ROWAN, SORB
ash, tree-like ... SERVICE
Asia Minor .... IDA
base .... PIEDMONT
Biblical .... NEBO, SINAI, ARARAT, HOREB
cat ...... COUGAR, PUMA
chain .... RANGE, SIERRA
climber ...... ALPINIST
climber's aid ..... PITON, CRAMPON
climber's slider .... GLISSADE
climber's staff .... ALPENSTOCK
combining form .... ORO
crest ...... ARETE, SPUR
defile .... PASS, COL
dew .... WHISKY
feature .... ARETE, SPUR, CRATER, SNOWCAP
formation .... OROGENY, RIDGE, ARETE, SPUR
gap .. PASS, DEFILE, COL, GATE
goat .... IBEX, TAHR
gorge/gully ... COULOIR
high .... ALP
highest .... EVEREST
lake .... TARN
legendary .... MERU
lion .... COUGAR, PUMA, PANTHER, PAINTER
main mass ..... MASSIF
measuring instrument ... OROMETER
movable .... OSSA
of light, so-called ...... KOHINUR
pass .. COL, GHAT, GAP, DEFILE
pass, historical .... THERMOPYLAE
peak .. CONE, HORN, BEN
Pennine Alps .... MATTERHORN, MONT CERVIN
pool .... TARN
prefix .... ORO
range .... SIERRA, CORDILLERA
ridge .. SAWBACK, SIERRA, ARETE
ridge central mass ...... MASSIF
ridge notch .. WIND GAP
road's bend .... LOOP
rocky .... TETON
rounded .... KNOB
rubble .... SCREE
sheep. . BIGHORN, MOUFLON
sickness ..... PUNA, VETA
slope .... VERSANT
small ...... MONTICULE
spinach .... ORACH
spur .... ARETE
State .... MONTANA
sunrise/sunset light ..... ALPENGLOW
system ..... CORDILLERA
system in Europe .. ALPS
Tagalog .... BUNDOK
top .... PEAK
top cover .... SNOWCAP, ICECAP
top light ... ALPENGLOW
trail marker ..... KARN
way .... TUNNEL
where Moses saw Canaan NEBO, PISGAH
youngest .... PARICUTIN

mountaineer .... ALPINIST, CLIMBER, SHERPA
climbing aid of ... PITON

mountains, formation of ..... OROGENY

range of .... SIERRA
study of .... OROGRAPHY, OROLOGY
mountebank .... QUACK, CHARLATAN, EMPIRIC
mounted sentinel .... VEDETTE
traveler .... RIDER
Mountie .... POLICE, TROOPER
outfit of .... RCMP
mourn .... RUE, GRIEVE, LAMENT, (BE)WAIL
in sympathy ... CONDOLE
mourner, hired .... MUTE, WEEPER
revivalist church .... PENITENT
mourners' bench occupant .... PENITENT
mournful .. LUGUBRIOUS, SAD, MELANCHOLY, LACRIMOSE, GRIEVOUS
mourning band .... CRAPE, CREPE
cloak .... BUTTERFLY
clothes .. SABLES, WEEDS, SACKCLOTH, BOMBASINE
song .... DIRGE
mouse ..... GIRL, BLACK EYE, RODENT
bird .... COLY
deer .... NAPUS, CHEVROTAIN
ear .. PLANT, HAWKWEED, FORGET-ME-NOT
he's not one .... MAN
like animal ...... SHREW, SORICINE
meadow .... VOLE
relative .... JERBOA, GERBIL(LE)
mousse .... DESSERT
mousseline .... MUSLIN, GLASS
mousy .... TIMID, QUIET
mouth ...... LIPS, STOMA, OS, GRIMACE, OPENING, SAY, DECLAIM, ORIFICE
and lower cheeks .. CHOPS
away from ..... ABORAL
by word of ...... ORAL, VERBAL
channel's .... CHOPS
combining form .... ORI, STOME
condition .... NOMA
gag .... MUZZLE
gaping .... RICTUS
inflammation .... STOMATITIS
Latin .... ORIS, OS
of the .. BUCCAL, ORAL, STOMATIC, OSCULAR
opening .... RICTUS
opening measurement ... GAPE
organ ...... HARMONICA, (PAN)PIPE, OCARINA, BAGPIPE
part ...... TONGUE, LIP, UVULA, VELUM
pertaining to .. STOMATIC, BUCCAL
river .. DELTA, ESTUARY, FRITH
slang .. MUG, KISSER, YAP, PUSS, TRAP
spoken by the ..... ORAL
strap .... MUZZLE
study of the .... STOMATOLOGY
thru the .... ORAL
to pharynx passage ..... FAUCES
toward the .... ORAD
ulcerous condition ...... NOMA
volcano .... CRATER
wash .... GARGLE, LISTERINE
mouthed, loud .. STENTOR(IAN)
open .... AGAPE
mouthful .... GOBBET
small .... MORSEL
mouthlike opening .... STOMA
mouthpiece ...... SPOKESMAN, BOCAL, REED, NOZZLE
slang .... LAWYER
mouths .... ORA
mouthy .... BOMBASTIC, TALKATIVE
mouton .... FUR
movable .. MOBILE, PORTABLE
defense structure .... BASTIL(L)E
mountain .... OSSA
shelter in siege ..... CAT
support .... TRESTLE
move .... TOUCH, AFFECT, PROMPT, PROPOSE, EVACUATE, TRANSFER, STIR, BUDGE, (A)ROUSE, SHIFT, PUSH, CARRY
able to .... MOTILE
about slyly ..... SLINK, PROWL, LURK
aimlessly ...... DOODLE, MAUNDER
along .... MOSEY, SASHAY
back .. RETREAT, REGRESS, JIB
back and forth .. SEESAW, SHUTTLE, DIDDLE
clumsily .. LOB, LUMBER, LUMP, WALLOP
confusedly .... MILL
forward ...... ADVANCE, FORGE, NOSE
furtively .. SNEAK, LURK, SKULK
gradually .. EDGE, INCH
heavily ... LOB, LUMBER, LUG, WALLOP
in a line .... FILE
in and out ...... WEAVE
in circles .. PURL, EDDY, CIRCULATE, SWIRL, GYRATE, CURL, MILL
in little waves ..... LAP
like a bird/butterfly ..... FLIT
movie camera ..... PAN
nimbly .... WHISK, FRISK
on casters .... TRUCKLE, TRUNDLE
on wheels .... ROLL
over .... TRANSFER
side to side ..... WEAVE
sidewise .... EDGE, SIDLE, SKEW, SLUE, JIB
slightly .... BUDGE
slowly .... INCH, WORM, FILTER, CRAWL, CREEP
smoothly .... GLIDE
suddenly, fast .... DART
to and fro .... WAG, SHUTTLE, OSCILLATE, VIBRATE
toward something .... GRAVITATE
TV camera .... PAN
uneasily .... FIDGET
unsteadily ...... WAMBLE
up and down ..... WAVE, SEESAW
with sudden turn .. JINK
movement .. MOTION, ACTION, TEMPO
in music .... TEMPO, RHYTHM
in prosody .... CADENCE
of charged particles ..... CATAPHORESIS
of organism ...... TAXIS
of the sea .... TIDE
mover, slow .. SNAIL, TURTLE
movie .. CINEMA, PHOTOPLAY, MOTION PICTURE
award .... OSCAR
camera platform .. DOLLY
combining form .. CINE
early heroine ... PAULINE
fare .. WESTERN, MYSTERY, MELODRAMA, MUSICAL, CARTOON
film, 1,000 ft. ..... REEL
full length ..... FEATURE
immortal star .... VALENTINO
last word of a ..... END
low budget .... QUICKIE
operator .... EXHIBITOR
part .... ROLE, LEAD, INGENUE
part of a .. REEL, SCENE, CREDITS
process .. TECHNICOLOR, CINEMASCOPE
projector ..... BIOSCOPE
role, small .... BIT
script .... SCENARIO
short .... NEWSREEL, CARTOON
shot .. CLOSE-UP, CLINCH
studio worker .... GRIP, STAGEHAND
term for sound adjustment SYNC
theaterowner .. EXHIBITOR
with sound ...... TALKIE
moving .. STIRRING, PATHETIC, MOTILE, IMPELLING, TOUCHING, POIGNANT, AFFECTING
about .... AMBULANT
area around body .... PERIPHERY
combining form .. KINETO
engine .... LOCOMOTIVE
in circular path .. GYRAL, GYRATORY

picture award .... OSCAR
staircase ..... ESCALATOR
vehicle .... VAN
mow ...... CUT DOWN, DESS, DESTROY, MATH, REAP, HAYSTACK, (HAY)LOFT, GRIMACE
'em down ..... KILL 'EM
Mowgli, friend of ..... BEAR, AKELA, BALOO
tiger of .... SHERE KHAN
mowing implement .. SCYTHE, SICKLE, REAPER
Mowrer, Edgar ___ .. ANSEL
moxa .. CAUTERANT, CAUTERY, PLANT
Mozambique native .. BANTU, YAO
port .... BEIRA
Mozart, composer .... WOLFGANG
opera .... SERAGLIO (ABDUCTION FROM), MAGIC FLUTE, MARRIAGE OF FIGARO, DON GIOVANNI. COSI FAN TUTTI
Mozart's city .... SALZBURG
mozetta .... CAPE
wearer of .... POPE
Mr. Catastrophe, sobriquet .. TRIPP
Europe, sobriquet ...... MONNET
Mrs. .... MISTRESS
Grundy .... PRUDE
Montagu Barstow ...... ORCZY
Sairey or her umbrella .. GAMP
Ms. ...... MANUSCRIPT, MIZZ, MISS, MRS
much ... LOT, MANY, ALMOST, NEARLY
in music .... MOLTO
mucid .... MUSTY, MOLDY
mucilage ..... ARABIN, PASTE, GLUE, ADHESIVE, GUM
mucilaginous .. STICKY, SLIMY
muck .. MANURE, DIRT, MIRE, FILTH, FERTILIZER
mucker .... CAD
muckle .... MUCH
muckworm .... MISER
mucous: comb. form .. MYX(O)
membrane disease ...... LUPUS
membrane fold ... PLICA
membrane inflammation.. CATARRH
membrane secretion .... MUCIN
membrane tumor .... PAPILLOMA
membrane watery discharge ..... RHEUM
mud ..... MIRE, SLIME, WASH, WARP, SLUDGE, MURGEON, OOZE, LIBEL, SLANDER, SLUSH, MUCK, SLOP
animal living in .. SIREN
bath .... WALLOW
dauber .... WASP
hen .... RAIL, COOT, GALLINULE
living in .... LIMICOLOUS
puppy .... SALAMANDER
river .... SILT
volcano .... SALSE
muddle ...... EMBROIL, MESS, ADDLE, HASH, JUMBLE, BUNGLE, MIX UP, CONFUSE, SNAFU
headed .... STUPID, CONFUSED
muddled .... WOOZY
muddy .. ROILY, RILE, SLUDGY, CLOUDY, DULL, VAGUE, SLOPPY, TURBID
mudfish .... DIPNOAN, BOWFIN
mudguard .... FENDER
mudhole .... LOBLOLLY, WALLOW
mudslinger ...... MUCKRAKER
mudworm .... IPO
muezzin .... CRIER
call of .... AZAN
place of ...... MINARET
muff .... BUNGLE(R), FUMBLE, BOTCH
muffin .... GEM, BREAD, COB, POPOVER
muffle .. MUTE, OVEN, STIFLE, DEADEN, WRAP
muffler .... SCARF, BAFFLE, MUTE, SILENCER
mufti .... ULEMA
slang .... CIV(V)IES
mug ..... SEIDEL, TOBY. CUP, NOGGIN, STEIN, MUNGO
leather .... JACK
slang ... FACE, GRIMACE, PHOTOGRAPH, ASSAULT
mugger .. CROC(ODILE), GOA, ROBBER, ACTOR
muggins ..... DOMINO, DUPE, CARD GAME, FOOL
muggy ..... HUMID, SULTRY
mugwump ...... REPUBLICAN, INDEPENDENT
Muhammad Ali .... (CASSIUS) CLAY
Mukden is capital of .... MANCHURIA
mulatto .... CREOLE, GRIQUA, METIS, GRIFF(E)
mulberry .... MURREY, TREE, AAL, FUSTIC, SYCAMINE
bark .... TAPA
tree genus .... CECROPIA, MORUS
mulct .... FINE, DEFRAUD, AMERCE, BILK, PENALIZE
mule ..... SHAVETAIL, HINNY, HYBRID, TRACTOR, SLIPPER
cry .... BRAY
disease .... DOURINE
driver .... SKINNER
female .... MARE
pack .... SUMPTER
parent .. MARE, DONKEY
skinner .... DRIVER
young .... FOAL
muliebrity ..... WOMANHOOD, FEMININITY
opposed to ... VIRILITY
mulish .. STUBBORN, STERILE, OBSTINATE
mull ...... PONDER, SWEETEN, COGITATE, MUSLIN, FLAVOR, THINK, CONSIDER
mulla(h) .... INTERPRETER, TEACHER
mulle(i)n .. FIGWORT, PLANT, FOXGLOVE
muller ...... GRINDER, PESTLE
mullet ...... LIZA, (GOAT)FISH
mulley .... POLLED COW
mulligan .... STEW, HASH
mulligatawny, for example SOUP
multifarious .... DIVERSE, MANIFOLD, MANY, VARIED
multiflora .... ROSE
multiped creature .. CENTIPEDE
multiple .... MANIFOLD
multiplicand .... FACIEND
multiplication result .... PRODUCT
multiply number by itself .... SQUARE
multitude ..... SWARM, HOST, LEGION, RUCK, CROWD, THRONG, MYRIAD, HORDE, GALAXY
multitudinous .... MANY, NUMEROUS, MANIFOLD, CROWDED
mum ..... BEER, DEODORANT, CHRYSANTHEMUM, MOTHER, SILENT, ALE
is the ___ .... WORD
mumble ..... MUMP, MUTTER, MURMUR, CHEW
mumbojumbo .. FETISH, IDOL, MEDICINE MAN, GIBBERISH
mummer .... ACTOR, GUISER, MASKER, MASQUER, PARADER
mummify ...... DRY, SHRIVEL
mummy .... CORPSE
cloth .... BYSSUS
mump .... MUMBLE, MUTTER, CHEAT, BEG
mumps .... PAROTITIS
munch .... CHEW, CHAMP
Munchausen, specialty of .... YARNS
tales, collector of .... RASPE
title of .... BARON
weakness of .... MYTHOMANIA
Munchen .... MUNICH
mundane .... TERRENE, TERRESTIAL, TEMPORAL, WORLDLY, EARTHLY
mundungo .... TOBACCO
Mundy work .... OM
mungo cloth ... SHODDY, MUG
Munich .... MUNCHEN
municipal tax .... OCTROI
municipality .... CITY, TOWN, PUEBLO
munificent .... LAVISH, GENEROUS
muniment .... DEFENSE, FORTIFICATION
munitions manufacturer ..... KRUPP, SKODA

plant/storehouse .... ARSENAL
Munro, H. H. .... SAKI
Munsel, singer ..... PATRICE
muntjac .... RATWA, DEER
mural .. WALL-LIKE, PAINTING
painter .... RIVERA
Murat, Fr. marshal .. JOACHIM,
murder ..... HOMICIDE, SLAY, KILL, BUMP OFF
by drowning .... NOYADE
by suffocation ... BURKE
king's .... REGICIDE
parent's .... MATRICIDE, PATRICIDE
murderer .... MANSLAYER, PARRICIDE, PATRICIDE, MATRICIDE, ASSASSIN
Biblical .... CAIN
murderous frenzy .... AMOK, BERSERK
murex .... WHELK
murid .... DISCIPLE, RAT
murine .. RODENT, RATS, MICE
murk ... GLOOM, DARK(NESS), DIM
murmur .. HUM, CURR, PURL, COMPLAINT, MUMBLE, MUTTER
cat's .... PURR
dove's .... COO
wind's .... SOUGH
murmuring sound .. SUSSURUS
murphy .... POTATO
murrain .. ANTHRAX, PLAGUE, PESTILENCE
murre ..... AUK, GUILLEMOT
murrelet .... (SEA)BIRD
murrey .... MULBERRY
murrhine substance ... STONE, JADE, FLUORITE
mus .... RAT, RODENT
musaceous plant ..... BANANA
musca .. FLY, CONSTELLATION
muscadine ..... GRAPE, WINE
Muscat .... GRAPE, WINE
and ____ .... OMAN
natives .... OMANI
muscatel .... WINE
muscid insect ..... HOUSEFLY
muscle ..... BRAWN, LACERT, LEVATOR, TERES, TENSOR, RECTUS, SPHINCTER, SINEW, TISSUE, STRENGTH, ERECTOR, TRICEPS, BICEPS
attachment ..... TENDON
bending .... FLEXOR
buttocks ...... GLUTEUS
combining form ... MY(O)
contraction .. TIC, SPASM, CRAMPS
disease ...... MYOPATHY
injury .... SPRAIN
jaw .... MASSETER
like .... MYOID
loin .... PSOAS
of .... SARCOUS
pain .... MYALGIA
part of .. HEAD, T(A)ENIA
protuberance .... VENTER
spasm(s) ..... CLONUS, CLONOS, CRAMP(S), CRICK
tension .... TONUS
muscles ..... THEWS, BRAWN, PSOAS
science dealing with .... MYOLOGY
wasting of ... DYSTROPHY
muscovado .... SUGAR
Muscovite ... RUSSIAN, MICA, SERICITE, GRANITE
Muscovy ..... RUSSIA, DUCK
muscular .. BRAWNY, THEWY, BURLY, STRONG, TOROSE
contraction .. TIC, CRAMP
contraction, childbearing LABOR
elasticity .... TONUS
fatigue .... MYASTHENIA
impotence ..... ATAXIA
power .... THEWS, SINEW
strength .... BRAWN
tissue tumor ..... MYOMA
muse .... PONDER, MULL, GODDESS, MEDITATE, THINK, MEDITATION, PIERIS
astronomy .... URANIA
chief .... CALLIOPE
comedy .... THALIA
dance .... TERPSICHORE
eloquence .... CALLIOPE
epic poetry .... CALLIOPE
history .... CLIO
love .... ERATO
lyric poetry ... EUTERPE, ERATO
music .... EUTERPE
pastoral poetry .. THALIA
poetry .... ERATO
sacred poetry .... POLYMNIA, POLYHYMNIA
tragedy .... MELPOMENE
Muses, domain of the .... PARNASSUS, AONIA
fountain of the .... HIPPOCRENE
home of the .... HELICON
mountain of the .... PARNASSUS, HELICON
of the .... PIERIAN
one of the .... CALLIOPE, CLIO, ERATO, EUTERPE, MELPOMENE, POLYMNIA, URANIA, THALIA
place where worshipped .. PIERIA
spring of the .. CASTALIA
musette ... BAGPIPE, MELODY, OBOE
museum .... GALLERY
custodian ..... CURATOR
part of .... COURT
mush .. ATOLE, PAP, PORRIDGE, SENTIMENTALITY, JOURNEY, SAMP
to whom addressed ..... (SLED)DOG, MALEMUTE, HUSKY, MALAMUTE
mushroom .. FUNGUS, AGARIC, MORIL, DEATH CUP, MOREL, CHAMPIGNON, CHANTERELLE, AMANITA
alkaloid ... MUSCARIN(E)
cap .... PILEUS
cap's part ...... LAMELLA
covering .... VOLVA
immature ...... BUTTON
leaflike plates ... PILEUS
poisonous ... TOADSTOOL, AMANITA, AGARIC
stalk .... STIPE
sugar extract .... TREHALOSE
underground .. TRUFFLE
mushy .. SENTIMENTAL, PAPPY, SOFT
Musial, baseball player ...... STAN, THE MAN
music .. HARMONY, AIR, TUNE, LAY
adapter ..... ARRANGER
aftersong .... EPODE
appropriate to night .... SERENADE, NOCTURNE
arranger ...... ADAPTER
as is .... STA
canto .... PASSUS
clef .... TREBLE
concluding passage ..... CODA
cradlesong .... LULLABY
excerpt .... MORCEAU
for nine .... NONET
for practice ... ETUDE
for two .... DUET
grace note ..... SANGLOT
hall ...... ODEUM, GAFF, AUDITORIUM, ODEON, ODEA
high in .... ALT
high part ...... TREBLE
highest singing voice .... SOPRANO
interval in ...... OCTAVE, TRITONE
lead in .... PRESA
leap in .... SALTO
lively .. GIOCOSO, GALOP
major scale ..... GAMUT
man .... PRESTON
mark in .... SLUR, SEGNO
measured beat ... PULSE, TEMPO, MOTO
melodious .... ARIOSO
moderately, slow .... ANDANTE
mute .... SORDINO
night .... NOCTURNE, SERENADE
note in Guido's scale ... ALT, ELA, ELAMI
nursery .... LULLABY
played on bells .. CHIMB, CHIMES, CARILLON
played outdoors .... SERENADE
playful .... SCHERZANDO
rate of speed .... TEMPO, ANDANTE, ALLEGRO, LENTO
sacred ...... CHORAL(E)
sentimental ...... CORN, SCHMALTZ
short song .... ODE
silent: direction .. TACET
sign ...... SEGNO, PRESA
slow in .. TARDO, LARGO, LENTO

smooth style in .. LEGATO
so much .... TANTO
soft in .... PIANO
solo .... ETUDE
stately .. MINUET, LARGO
sustained .... TENUTO
teacher .... MAESTRO
tempo .... ANDANTE, ALLEGRO, PRESTO, LENTO
theme .... MOTIV
time in .... TEMPO
timing device .... METRONOME
together in .... ADUE
too much .... TANTO
twice in .... BIS
unaccented ...... ARSIS
whole note .. SEMIBREVE

musical .. MELODIOUS, MELIC, LYRIC(AL), CANOROUS
accompaniment .... OB(B)LIGATO
ballad .... DERRY
beginning .... INTRO
bells .. CARILLON, CHIMES
burlesque .. COMIC OPERA
character .... CLEF, KEY, REST, SHARP
chord ... TRIAD, CATGUT
combination .... CHORD
comedy .... REVUE, EXTRAVAGANZA, BURLESQUE
comedy music ... SCORE
comedy that fails .... TURKEY
composition ..... FUGUE, ARIOSO, NOCTURNE, CONCERTO, MOTET, OPERA, SONATA, SYMPHONY, CANTATA, ORATORIO, MINUET, OCTET(TE), SERENADE, SERENATA, RONDO, ETUDE, BAGATELLE, CAPRICCIO, HUMORESQUE
concord .... CONCENT
consonance .... CONCERT
direction ..... STA, SOLI, TACET
disability ...... AMUSIA
drama .... OPERA
ending .... CODA
entertainment between acts INTERMEZZO
excerpt .... MORCEAU
exercise .... ETUDE
flourish .... FANFARE, CADENZA
group .... TRIO, CHORUS, CHOIR, GLEE CLUB, BAND, COMBO, ORCHESTRA, MAZURKA, SERENADE, QUARTET, OCTET, DUET
half step ..... SEMITONE
horn, comic ... BAZOOKA
instrument .... CALLIOPE, REED, OCARINA, PIANO, LYRE, LUTE, FLUTE, VIOL(IN), ROTTE, SPINET, SITAR, CORNET, MANDOLIN, GUITAR, CITHERN, CLAVICHORD
brass-wind ... CORNET, TROMBONE, TRUMPET, BUGLE
fingerboard .... VINA
flute-like ... FLAGEOLET
guitar-like ...... LUTE, GITTERN, UKULELE, MANDOLIN, BANJO
harp-like ... SAMEBUKE
inventor ...... JUBAL
keyboard .... CLAVIER, SPINET, PIANO, CLAVICHORD, ORGAN, CELESTA
lute-like ..... THEORBO
lyre-like .... CITHARA
muffler .... MUTE
organ-like .. CALLIOPE
player ...... HARPIST, PIANIST(E), VIOLINIST, GUITARIST, FLUTIST
range of .... DIAPASON
soundboard ... ZITHER
string .... CHORD, CATGUT
stringed ... DULCIMER, BANDORE, VINA, LUTE, GUITAR, REBEC, CLAVIER, LYRE, ROTE, BANJO, ASOR, CITOLE, ZITHER, CITHER(N), SAMEBUKE, SAMISEN, MANDOLIN, UKULELE, VIOLA, VIOL
thread .... CATGUT
tone/volume changer .. PEDAL
toy .... KAZOO
trumpet-like .... CLARION, TUBA
violin-like .. REBEC(K), CELLO, VIOL, VIOLA
wind ..... FLAGEOLET, FLUTE, OCARINA, CLARINET, REED, TUBA, SAXOPHONE, ORGAN
with finger holes ..... OCARINA, FLUTE, PIPE
instruments, collectively . STRINGS, TRAPS, BRASS, WINDS, PERCUSSION
interlude, short .. VERSET
interval .... TRITONE, OCTAVE, REST
introduction .. OVERTURE
lines ...... STEM, STAFF
medley .... CENTO, OLIO, PASTICCIO, PASTICHE
movement .... SCHERZO
notation .... TABLATURE
note of old .... ELK, UT, ARE, FE
ornament .... ROULADE
passage ...... CADENZA, MORCEAU
passage, brilliant .... BRAVURA
passage performed in fast tempo .... PRESTO
patchwork ...... CENTO, MEDLEY
percussion instrument ... MARIMBA, XYLOPHONE, DRUM, CYMBAL
performance .. CONCERT, RECITAL, REVUE
phrase ...... LEITMOTIF
pipe .. OAT, REED, OBOE, CLARINET, FLAGEOLET, FLUTE
pitch .... TONE
play .... OPERETTA
range .... GAMUT
reed .... PIPE, FLUTE
rhythm, unit of ... BEAT
show .... REVUE, EXTRAVAGANZA, VAUDEVILLE
show that fails .. TURKEY
sign .... ISON, PRESA, SEGNO, CLEF, REST, DOT
signature .... THEME
sound .... TONE
sound, make ..... SING, YODEL, WARBLE, TRILL
sounds, science of ...... HARMONICS
study .... ETUDE
syllable .. DO, RE, MI, FA, SOL, LA, TI
symbol .... CLEF
trill .... TREMOLO
vibrato .... TRILL
work .... OPUS

musician ... ORPHEUS, JUBAL, HARMONIST

musicians' patron saint ...... CECILIA
stand .... DESK

musing .... MEDITATION, REFLECTIVE, REVERIE

musk cat .... CIVET
have smell of .... MOSCHATE
product .... PERFUME

muskeg .... MARSH, BOG

muskellunge .... PIKE

musket ... FIREARM, DRAGON, CULVERIN, JINGAL, GINGAL(L)
flintlock .... FUSIL

musketeer of fiction .. ARAMIS, ATHOS, PORTHOS, D'ARTAGNAN

Muskhogean Indian .... CHICKASAW

muskmelon .... ATIMON, CANTALOUPE, CAS(S)ABA, MANGO

muskrat .... MUSQUASH
kin .... VOLE

musky .... MOSCHATE

Muslim (see Moslem) .... MOSLEM, MUSSULMAN
cap .... KOPIA
chronicle ..... TARSILA, SARSILA
court .... AGAMA
fasting month .... RAMADAN
maid .... HOURI
religious person .. HADJI,

IMAM, HATIB, PAKIL
muslin ...... BATISTE, MOSAL, TARLETAN, MULL, ADATI, TARLATAN, SHELA, NAINSOOK
bag .... TILLOT
gauze .... TIFFANY
striped .... DORIA
musquash .... MUSKRAT
muss .... DISHEVEL, ROW, CREASE, RUMPLE, MESS, TOUSLE, DISORDER, COMMOTION
mussel .... MOLLUSK, UNIO
product .... PEARL
Mussolini, dictator .. BENITO
nickname .... MUSSO
son-in-law ...... CIANO
title of .... (IL)DUCE
Mussulman .... MOSLEM, SARACEN
must...... JUICE, SAPA, STUM, NECESSARY, MILDEW, ALBA, MAUN, ESSENTIAL, WINE, MOLD
elephant's ..... FRENZY
mustache ...... HANDLE BAR, BEARD, WHISKERS
mustached sea animal .... WALRUS
Mustafa Kemal ____ .... ATATURK
mustang .... HORSE, BRONCO, PONY
mustard .. CONDIMENT, WEED, WOAD, SEASONING, TURNIP, CRESS, RADISH
application ... POULTICE
container ...... CASTER
dye .... WOAD
gas .. YPERITE, VESICANT
glucoside ..... SINALBIN
plaster .... SINAPISM
pod .... SILIQUE
seed glucoside .... SINALBIN, SINIGRIN
wild .... CHARLOCK
mustee .. OCTOROON, MESTIZO
musteline animal ...... MINK, MARTEN, POLECAT, WEASEL, WOLVERINE, RATEL, OTTER
muster .... GATHER, SUMMON, ASSEMBLE, LEVY, COLLECT, ROLL, LIST
in .... ENLIST
out .... DISBAND
musty .. FUSTY, STALE, DULL, SMELLY, TRITE, ANTIQUATED, FETID, HOAR, RANCID, RANK, MUCID, MOLDY
mutable .... FICKLE, INCONSTANT, CHANGEABLE, VOLATILE
mutant .... SPORT
mutate ...... VARY, CHANGE
mutation .... EVOLUTION, CHANGE, SALTATION
in linguistics .... UMLAUT
mute .. MUFFLE, DUMB, MUM, DEADEN, DUMMY, VOICELESS, SURD
consonant .... LENE
for trumpet ... SOURDINE
in linguistics .... SILENT
mutilate ..... DAMAGE, MAIM, DISFIGURE, MAR, DEFORM, MANGLE
mutineer .... REBEL
mutiny .... RISE, REVOLT, REBELLION
Mutsuhito's realm .... JAPAN
reign .... MEIJI
son .... HIROHITO
mutt .... MONGREL, DOG, CUR
mutter .. MUMBLE, GRUMBLE, COMPLAIN, MURMUR
mutton .... SHEEP, FLESH, CABOB, (RED)MEAT
bird .... OII
cut .... SADDLE
chop .... CABOBS, KABOBS
chops .... WHISKERS, SIDEBURNS, BURNSIDES
fish .... SAMA
head ...... DOLT, DUNCE
neck .... SCRAG
stew .... HARICOT
mutual .. JOINT, RECIPROCAL, COMMON
aid, solons'............ LOG-ROLLING
mutually destructive .... INTERCINE
muzhik .... PEASANT
muzzle .... NOSE, GAG, SNOUT
muzzy .... CONFUSED, DAZED, BEFUDDLED
my faith, literally .... MA FOI
fault .... MEA CULPA
Gal ____" .... SAL
heart, literally .. MACHREE
Sweetness .... NAOMI
mycelium of fungi .... SPAWN
myelencephalon .. AFTERBRAIN
myna(h) .... BIRD
kin of .... STARLING
Mynheer .... SIR, DUTCHMAN
myopic ...... NEARSIGHTED, SHORTSIGHTED
Myra Breckinridge personified (RAQUEL) WELCH
pianist .... HESS
myriad .... MULTITUDE, COUNTLESS, TEN THOUSAND
myriapod .... CENTIPEDE, MILLIPEDE, ARTHROPOD
segment .. TELSON, SOMITE
myrmicid .... ANT
Myrmidon ...... FOLLOWER, ADHERENT, SUBORDINATE
myrrh .... CICELY
myrtle .. PERIWINKLE, GUAVA, CAJEPUT, SHRUB, CAJUPUT
berry .... ALLSPICE
Mysore, capital of .... BANGALORE
mysterious .. WEIRD, CRYPTIC, ORACULAR, ARCANE, SECRET, ENIGMATIC, INSCRUTABLE, OCCULT, MYSTIC(AL), RUNIC, UNKNOWN, ESOTERIC
mystery ..... RIDDLE, CRAFT, CONUNDRUM, ARCANUM, ENIGMA, SECRECY, PUZZLE, RUNE
in Christianity .... MASS, SACRAMENT, EUCHARIST
story .... WHODUNIT, MAIGRET
mystic ..... ESSENE, EPOPT(IC), ORPHIC, OCCULT, MYSTERIOUS, ESOTERIC, ENIGMATIC, SUFIST, YOGA, YOGI(N), CABALIST
art ..... CABALA, MAGIC, ASTROLOGY, ALCHEMY, OCCULTISM, VOODOO, SORCERY, WITCHCRAFT
cry .... EVOE, OM
Mt. Athos ... HESYCHAST
practice .... YOGA
symbol ...... CHARACTER
union with God .... THEOCRASY
word .... ABRAXAS, ABRACADABRA
writing .... RUNE
mystical .... OCCULT, ALLEGORICAL, ENIGMATIC, MYSTERIOUS
doctrine .... CAB(B)ALA, KABALA
ecstasy ..... THEOPATHY
interpretation .. ANAGOGE
mystify .. OBFUSCATE, PUZZLE, PERPLEX, BEWILDER, HOAX
myth .. FABLE, LEGEND, STORY
mythical .... IMAGINARY, LEGENDARY, FICTITIOUS, FABULOUS
animal .... GRIFFIN, GRYPHON, GRIFFON
antelope .... YALE
being .... CENTAUR
bird .... ROC
ferryman ...... CHARON
flyer .... ICARUS
giant ... CYCLOPS, YMIR, YMER, JOTUN, FAFNIR
hero .... EGIL(E)
horse .... UNICORN, PEGASUS
hunter .... ORION
island/continent .... ATLANTIS
king .... OLAF, ATLI
land .... LEMURIA
maiden ...... IO, DANAE
man of brass ..... TALOS
monster .... DRAGON, CHIMERA, SPHINX, MINOTAUR, GRIFFIN
mountain .... OSSA, HELICON, PARNASSUS
musician ...... ORPHEUS
river .... STYX
serpent .. APEPI, MIDGARD
sisters .... GORGONS
trio .... FATES, GORGONS
watchdog .... GARM, CERBERUS
wolf .... FENRIR
woman .... IDUN
mythologist .... MULLER
mythomania, victim of .. LIAR, MUNCHAUSEN, ANANIAS
Mytilene .... LESBOS

N

N.B. .... NOTA BENE
  Greek .... NU
  Hebrew .... NUN
  letter .... EN
na .... NO, NOT, NOR, SODIUM
NAACP, part of .. NATIONAL, COLORED, PEOPLE
nab .. SEIZE, SNATCH, CATCH, ARREST, NICK, SNAG, CAPTURE
Nabal's wife .... ABIGAIL
nabob .... NAWAB, RICH MAN, DIVES
nacelle .... BASKET, CAR, FUSELAGE
nacl .... SALT
nacre .... SHELLFISH, MOTHER-OF-PEARL
nacreous .... LUSTROUS
nacrite .... MICA
nadir .... DEPTHS, LOW POINT
  opposite of ..... ZENITH
nae .... NO, NOT
naevus .... FRECKLED
nag .. BADGER, ANNOY, PONY, HORSE, SHREW, VIRAGO, TERMAGANT, PESTER, TEASE, RIDE, SCOLD, HECTOR, TIT, HENPECK, PLAGUE
naga .... COBRA, SNAKE
nagana disease carrier .... TSETSE
Nagasaki, destroyer of ...... A(TOM)BOMB
nagger .. SCOLD, TERMAGANT, SHREW, VIRAGO
Nagoya's bay .... ISE
Naha is capital of .. OKINAWA
nahoor .. SHEEP, BHARAL, SNA
Nahor's wife .... MILCAH
naiad ..... NYMPH, SWIMMER, OREAD
naif .... NAIVE, ARTLESS
nail .. BRAD, PIN, SPAD, SPRIG, TACK, SPIKE, UNGUIS, TENTER, TACH(E), CLAW, FASTEN, SECURE, FIX, CATCH, UNGULA
  biting .... PHANEROMANIA
  finishing .... BRAD
  having .... UNGUAL
  headless ..... SPARABLE, SPRIG
  horseshoe .... STUB
  like a .... UNGUAL
  polish .. ENAMEL, CUTEX
  shoemaker's .. SPARABLE
  short .... TACK
  size .... TENPENNY
  slang .... CIGARETTE
  slantingly .... TOE
  substance ...... KERATIN
  3-inch .... TENPENNY
  unit of weight ..... KEG
  wooden .... PEG
nailhead .... STUD
nails, 100 lbs. .... KEG
nainsook .... MUSLIN, COTTON
naive .... ARTLESS, INNOCENT, GUILELESS, GREEN, SIMPLE, INGENUOUS, CHILDLIKE
  girl .. INGENUE, INNOCENT
naivete .... INNOCENCE
naked .. BARE, NUDE, EXPOSED, STARK, PLAIN
  in law .... INVALID
namaycush .. TROUT, TOGUE, SALMONOID
namby-pamby .. INSIPID, SILLY, VAPID, WISHY-WASHY
  person nicknamed ...... PHILIPS
name ..... DUB, COGNOMEN, NOMINATE, TERM, LABEL, EPITHET, APPELLATION, CITE, MENTION, (EN)TITLE, APPOINT, DESIGNATE, REPUTATION
  announcer .... NOMENCLATOR
  assumed .... ALIAS, PSEUDONYM, SOBRIQUET, INCOG
  bad .... NOTORIETY, ILL-REPUTE, CACONYM
  characteristic .. EPITHET, SOBRIQUET
  derivation of ... EPONYM
  fake .... ALIAS
  false .... ANONYM
  give a .... ENTITLE
  meaning beauty ..... ADA
    bright .... BERTA
    comfort .... NOAH
    daughter ...... INGA
    girl .... COLLEEN
    healer .... ASA
    high .... ELI
    holy .... OLGA
    life .... EVA
    little .... ETTA
    moon goddess .. DELIA
    noble ...... PATRICK
    peace .... IRENE
    pleasure .... EDNA
    princess .... SARA
    rose .... RHODA
    serving .... OBED
    spring born ... VERNA
    weary .... LEAH
  of a place .... TOPONYM
  of thing, etc. ..... NOUN
  of two same terms ...... TAUTONYM
  one by one .. ENUMERATE
  plate .... FACIA
  slang ...... MONI(C)KER, HANDLE
  substitute ...... DINGUS
  to an office ... NOMINATE
named ...... CITED, YCLEPT, YCLEPED, MENTIONED, APPOINTED
nameless ...... ANONYMOUS, UNKNOWN, UNIDENTIFIED, OBSCURE
  person .... ANONYM
namely .. SILICET, TO WIT, VIZ, VIDELICET
names list .... BEADROLL
namesake .... HOMONYM, EPONYM
nana .. AMAH, NURSE, NANNY
Nancy .... NARCISSUS
nankin .... BUFF, COTTON
nanny .... NURSE
  vehicle of .... PRAM, BUGGY, STROLLER
Naomi .... MARA
  daughter-in-law of ...... RUTH
naos .... TEMPLE, CELLA
nap ...... SIESTA, SLEEP, PILE, SHAG, SNOOZE, DOZE, WINK, RAS
  of a sort .. FORTY WINKS, SIESTA
  raising device .. TEASEL, TEAZEL, GIG, CARD
  shearer .... CROPPER
napalm inventor ...... FIESER
nape .. SCRAG, SCRUFF, PALL, NUCHA, NUQUE
napery ...... LINEN, DOILIES, NAPKINS, DAMASK
Napier's invention .... LOGARITHMS
napkin ..... DIAPER, NAPERY, SERVIETTE, TOWEL, BIB, DOILY
Naples .... NAPOLI
  beggar in ... LAZZARONE
  bay island .... CAPRI
  king of .... MURAT
  lake near ...... AVERNUS
  native of ... NEOPOLITAN
  patron saint .. JANUARIUS
Napoleon .. COIN, CARD GAME, PASTRY
  birthplace of ... AJACCIO
  brother of ...... LUCIEN, JEROME
  conqueror of .... WELLINGTON, KUTUZOV
  downfall of ... WATERLOO
  game like .... PAM
  isle identified with ...... ELBA, CORSICA, HELENA
  marshal of .. NEY, MURAT
  scene of defeat .... WATERLOO
  scene of victory ... JENA, MARENGO, AUSTERLITZ, WAGRAM
  sister of .... ELISA, CAROLINE
  wife of .... JOSEPHINE
Napoli .... NAPLES
nappy ..... WOOLLY, DOWNY, HAIRY, DISH, ALE, FOAMING
Naraka, Hindu .... HELL
narcissism .... SELF-LOVE
narcissus .. JONQUIL, FLOWER, DAFFODIL, EGOIST, NANCY
  composer .... NEVIN

love of .... SELF
nymph who loved .. ECHO
narcosis ...... SLEEP, STUPOR
narcotic .. OPIATE, SEDATIVE, DOPE, MORPHINE, CODEINE, ANODYNE, HASHISH, OPIUM, HEROIN, COCAINE, DRUG, JUNK
beechnut .... FAGINE
cigarette .. REEFER, KEF, MARIJUANA
dreamy tranquillity .. KEF
drug, inject .. MAINLINE
plant ..... HEMP, POPPY, BHANG, MARIJUANA, K(H)AT, MANDRAKE, DUTRA, CUCA
slang .. DOPE, SNOW, POT
smoking effect ...... KEF
under influence of ...... DOPEY, STONED
user .... DOPE, ADDICT, FIEND, POT-HEAD
nard ...... SALVE, OINTMENT, PLANT
nares .... NOSTRILS
narghile ..... HOOKA(N), PIPE
narial .... RHINAL
narine .... NASAL
nark .... SPY, INFORMER, STOOL PIGEON
narrate .... RECITE, RECOUNT, RELATE, TELL
narration .. STORY, ACCOUNT, RECITAL
narrative .... TALE, ACCOUNT, STORY, SAGA, NOVELLA, CONTE
poem ...... EPIC, ILIAD, ODYSSEY, BEOWULF, EPOS, LAY
narrow ... CONTRACT, CLOSE, LIMIT, ANGUST, STRAIT(EN)
band .... FANON
combining form .. STENO
escape ...... CLOSE CALL
minded .... BIGOTED, BIASED, PEDANTIC, SECTARIAN, PETTY
opening .... SLOT
street ..... ALLEY, LANE
narrower at the base .. OBTUSE
narrows ..... STRAIT, SOUND
narthex .... VESTIBULE
narwhal .. WHALE, CETACEAN
nary .... NO, NOT ANY
nasal .... RHINAL, NARINE
catarrh .... CORYZA
hemorrhage .. EPISTAXIS
intonation ...... TWANG
mucous ... SNOT, SNIVEL
noise .... SNORT
passage .. NARES, NOSTRIL
nascency .. BEGINNING, BIRTH, GENESIS, FORMATION
naseberry .... SAPODILLA
Nash, humorist .... OGDEN
Nasser, UAR president ...... GAMAL (ABDEL)
nasty ... MEAN, FOUL, FILTHY, OBSCENE
natal .... INNATE, INBORN, NATIVE
natant .. SWIMMING, FLOATING
natatorium .... POOL
nates .... BUTTOCKS
Nathan, George ____ .. JEAN
nation ..... STATE, COUNTRY, PEOPLE
extermination of .... GENOCIDE
temperance leader ...... CARRY
national .... CITIZEN
character .... ETHOS
Guard .... MILITIA
hymn .... ANTHEM
native .. INDIGENOUS, NATAL, ENDEMIC, SON, INBORN, AUTOCHTHON, ABORIGINE, ENCHORIC, NATURAL, ENCHORIAL
ability .... TALENT, GIFT, APTITUDE
agent ...... COMPRADOR
animal .... INDIGENE
chief .... CACIQUE, DATU
inhabitant .... DENIZEN
metal .... ORE
original .... ABORIGINE, ABORIGINAL
plant .... INDIGENE
salt .... HALITE
suffix .... ITE
nativity .... BIRTH
natrium .... SODIUM
natty .. SMART, SHARP, CHIC, TRIM, SPRUCE
natural .. WILD, INNATE, REAL, INBORN, NORMAL, UNPOSED
ability .. APTITUDE, GIFT, KNACK, TALENT, FLAIR, GENIUS
abode .... HABITAT
philosophy .... PHYSICS
science branch .. BOTANY, PHYSICS, GEOLOGY, ZOOLOGY, CHEMISTRY
naturalist ...... BEEBE, MUIR, BIOLOGIST, ANIMIST, AUDUBON, BURBANK, DARWIN, ANDREWS
naturalize .... DENIZEN
naturalized plant/animal ..... DENIZEN
naturally .... OF COURSE
nature .. ESSENCE, KIND, SORT, TYPE, CHARACTER
naught .. NOTHING, NIL, ZERO
bring to .. VOID, NULLIFY, UNDO, CANCEL
naughty .. MISCHIEVOUS, BAD, IMPISH, OBSCENE
nausea ..... QUALM, DISGUST, PALL, WAMBLE
affected with ... QUEASY
nauseate .... SICKEN
nauseous .... SICKENING
Nausicaa's find ..... ULYSSES
parent .... ALCINOUS
nautical .... MARINE, NAVAL, MARITIME, OCEANIC
call .... AHOY
chain .... TYE
command .... AVAST
dick .... DEADEYE
fly .... BURGEE
mile .... KNOT
rope .. RATLINE, HAWSER, MARLINE, NETTLE
term .. ALEE, AWEATHER, ABEAM, ASTERN, ABAFT, AFORE, ATRY
nautilus .... ARGONAUT, MOLLUSK
Verne's commander of .. NEMO
Nauvoo, formerly .. COMMERCE
Navaho .... ATHAPASCAN, INDIAN
hut .... HOGAN
naval .... NAUTICAL, MARINE, MARITIME
academy .... ANNAPOLIS
cadet ..... MIDSHIPMAN, MIDDY
commander ... CAPTAIN, ADMIRAL, SKIPPER
force .... FLEET, ARMADA
hero .... NELSON, DEWEY, FARRAGUT
officer .. ENSIGN, YEOMAN, MATE
pass of a sort .. NAVICERT
protective/offensive device PARAVANE
Reserve woman ... WAVE
ships collectively .... MARINE
title .... ADMIRAL, COMMODORE
unit list/roll .... MUSTER
vessel ...... DESTROYER, CORVETTE, FLATTOP, WARSHIP, UBOAT, CRUISER, TENDER
War College site .... NEWPORT
nave .... HUB
navel .... UMBILICUS
of Sicily .... ENNA
point .... NOMBRIL
navigate .... AVIATE, SAIL, STEER, CRUISE
navigation detecting system .. LORAN, SONAR
navigator .... NAVVY, BERING, ERIC, TASMAN, COOK, MAGELLAN, BAFFIN
Navigators Island .... SAMOA
navvy .... LABORER
navy ...... FLEET, WARSHIPS, SEA FORCE
bed .... SACK
color .... BLUE
group .... FLOTILLA, SQUADRON, ARMADA, TASKFORCE
mascot of .... GOAT
pharmacist ... CORPSMAN
ration .... HARDTACK
recruit .... BOOT
scout boat .... VEDETTE, VIDETTE
nawab .... NABOB, TITLE
nay ...... DENIAL, NO, VOTE
Nazarene .... JESUS
Nazarite, he was one .. .. SAMSON

Nazi ...... FASCIST, HITLERITE
airforce ..... LUFTWAFFE
collaborator .. QUISLING, LAVAL
concentration camp ..... DACHAU, NORDHAUSEN, BUCHENWALD, BELSEN
defector .... HESS
district .... GAU
district leader .... GAULEITER
emblem ...... SWASTIKA, FYLFOT
extermination center .... BELSEN
greeting .... HEIL
ideology ... HERRENVOLK
leader .... HITLER, GOERING, HIMMLER, GOEBELS, HESS, LEY, FUEHRER
organization, U.S. ...... BUND
salute ..... HEIL HITLER
state police ... GESTAPO
symbol ...... SWASTIKA
Nazimova, actress ...... ALLA
NB .... NOTA BENE
NCO ..... SERGEANT, SARGE, CORPORAL
neap .... TIDE
near .. CLOSE, NIGH, ALMOST, APPROACH, INTIMATE, ABOUT
by .. VICINAL, CLOSE TO, AROUND
East country ..... SYRIA, LEBANON, TURKEY, ISRAEL, JORDAN, EGYPT
sighted .... MYOPIC
sightedness ..... MYOPIA
sighted person ... MYOPE
nearby .... NIGH, CLOSE, AROUND
nearest .... NEXT
nearly ...... ABOUT, ALMOST, ALL BUT
neat .... NATTY, TRIG, SPIFFY, PURE, TAUT, SPRUCE, NET, TIDY, SOIGNE, ADROIT, CLEAN
neatherd .... COWHERD
neb ...... BEAK, BILL, SNOUT, NOSE, TIP, NIB
Nebraska capital ... LINCOLN
city .. OMAHA, FREMONT, HASTINGS, ORD
county .... KNOX, POLK, YORK, CASS
Indian .... OMAHA, OTOE, PAWNEE
river ... PLATTE, NEMAHA
state flower .... GOLDENROD
Nebraskan ..... CORNHUSKER
nebulous .... CLOUDY, MISTY, HAZY, VAGUE, INDEFINITE
necessaries .... ESTOVERS
necessarily .... PERFORCE
necessary .. MUST, ESSENTIAL, MANDATORY, REQUISITE, VITAL, REQUIRED
necessitate .. COMPEL, ENTAIL, REQUIRE, OBLIGE
necessity .. FATE, COMPULSION, NEED, WANT
of .... PERFORCE
neck ...... CHANNEL, CARESS, GULLET, STRAIT, KISS, PET, SPOON, CERVIX, SCRAG
and neck .... CLOSE
and shoulder covering .. SHAWL, TUCKER
animal with long .... GIRAFFE
armor .... GORGET
artery .... CAROTID
back of .. NAPE, CERVIX, NUCHA, SCRUFF
covering .. MANE, RUFF, PARTLET
cramp .... CRICK
hair .... MANE
human .... SCRAG
ligament ...... PAXWAX
muscle .... SPLENIUS
of beef .... CLOD
of land ... ISTHMUS, SPIT
of the .... JUGULAR, CERVICAL
part of horse ... WITHERS
piece .. BOA, STOLE, TIE, CRAVAT, SCARF, COLLAR, FICHU
scarf .... ASCOT, TIPPET
neckcloth .... CRAVAT
neckerchief .... SCARF
necklace .. STRAND, CHAPLET, CARCANET, BEAD
appendage ..... LOCKET, LAVALIER
colloquial ...... CHOKER
metal .... TORQUE
of several strands .... RIVIERE
ornament ... LAVALIER(E)
neckline, having low .... DECOLLETE
shape .... VEE
necktie .. ASCOT, BOW, SCARF, CRAVAT, CHOKER, FOULARD
ornament .... STICKPIN
party .... HANGING
neckwear ...... COLLAR, RUFF
necrology .... OBIT(UARY)
necromancer ...... DIVINER, WIZARD, SORCERER, CONJURER
necromancy ... (BLACK)MAGIC
necropolis .... CEMETERY, GRAVEYARD
necropsy .... AUTOPSY, POST MORTEM
nectar .... DRINK, BEVERAGE, HONEYDEW
of the gods .... AMBROSIA
product .... HONEY
nectarine .... PEACH
nee .... BORN
need ...... LACK, NECESSITY, OBLIGATION, WANT, EXIGENCY, REQUISITE
needle .. POINTER, INDICATOR, GOAD, PROVOKE, PROD, PRICK, TEASE, HECKLE
blunt, thick .... BODKIN
bug .... NEPA
case .... ETUI, ETWEE
crystal like .... ACICULA
etching .... STYLE
like spine ..... ACICULA
pushing disk ...... PALM
shaped .... SPICULE, ACERATE, ACICULAR, ACEROSE, SPICULAR, ACUATE, ACIFORM
threading hole ...... EYE
needlefish ..... GAR, PIPEFISH
needlelike .... SPICULATE
crystal .... ACICULA
needlewoman ... SEAMSTRESS, SEMPSTRESS
needlework ..... EMBROIDERY, SEWING
beginner's .... SAMPLER
needy ..... POOR, DESTITUTE, INDIGENT
neep .... TURNIP
nefarious ... WICKED, VICIOUS
Nefertiti's husband .... AKHENATON, PHARAOH
negate .. NULLIFY, DENY, VOID, COUNTERACT, NEUTRALIZE, ANNUL
negation .. DENIAL, NULLITY, NONENTITY
act of ..... VETO, REJECT
negative .... MINUS, NO
connective .... NEITHER, NOR
emphatic .... NEVER
ion .... ANION
opposite of .... AFFIRMATIVE, POSITIVE
prefix .... NON
quality .... MINUS
slangy ...... NOPE, NIX, NO DICE, NO SOAP
terminal ...... CATHODE
vote .... NAY
neglect .. SHIRK, OMIT, IGNORE, DISREGARD, OVERLOOK, SLIGHT, FORGET
neglectful .. REMISS, DERELICT
negligee .... GOWN, PEIGNOR
negligence .... CULPA
negligent .... LAX, REMISS, CARELESS, DERELICT
negligible .. TRIFLING, TRIVIAL
amount .... PEANUTS, CHICKEN FEED
negotiate .. TREAT, BARGAIN, DEAL, DISCUSS, PARLEY, TRANSACT
Negrillo .... BUSHMAN
Negrito ...... ITA, NEGROID, A(E)TA, TAPIRO, BALUGA
Negro ... BLACK, HOTTENTOT, BANTU, NUBIAN, IBO, HAUS(S)A, KAFFIR, SWAHILI, DAHOMAN, ETHIOP(IAN), NUBA, JIM CROW, KROO, YORUBA, MANDINGO
and white offspring ..... MESTEE, MUSTEE, MULATTO
black magic .... VOODOO

colloquial ...... DARKIE, DARK(E)Y
dance ..... JUBA, SAMBA, CAKEWALK
family servant .. MAMMY
fugitive .... MAROON
hairdo .... NATURAL
magic ...... OBEAH, OBI
mulatto offspring .... GRIFF(E)
pigmy .... AKKA
religious folk song ...... SPIRITUAL
tribe ...... TEMBU, SERER
witchcraft ... OBI, OBEAH
woman servant .. MAMMY
young male ...... BUCK
Negroes, discrimination against JIM CROW
Negroid .... NUBIAN, KAFFIR, TEMBU, ETHIOP(IAN), PAPUAN, BANTU
negus, Ethiopia's .... (HAILE)SELASSIE
Nehru, India prime minister .. JAWAHARLAL
neigh ..... (S)NICKER, HINNY, WHINNY
neighborhood ..... VICINAGE, VICINITY, LOCALITY, PRECINCTS, PURLIEU, COMMUNITY
neighboring .... NEARBY, ADJACENT
neighbors' gathering ...... BEE
neither, companion of ... NOR
Nejd, capital of ..... RIYADH
robe .... ABA
Nellie ____, journalist ... BLY
Nelson, Admiral .... HORATIO
scene of victory .... TRAFALGAR
"Nelson's blood" ...... RUM, GROG
nelumbo .... LOTUS, (WATER)LILY
Neman .... NIEMEN, NEMUNAS
nemathelminth ... NEMATODE, (HOOK)WORM
nemato: as comb. form ...... THREAD
nematode ..... (HOOK)WORM, PINWORM, ASCARID, ROUNDWORM
nembutal .... SEDATIVE, HYPNOTIC
nemesis .. AVENGER, GODDESS, RETRIBUTION
nemoral .... SYLVAN
neon .... LIGHT
neophyte .... CONVERT, TYRO, BEGINNER, NOVICE, AMATEUR
neoplasm .... TUMOR
Neopolitan secret society ..... CAMORRA
neoteric ...... NEW, MODERN, RECENT
Nepal, capital of .... KATMANDU
coin of .... MOHAR
inhabitant ...... MAGAR, GURUNG, NEWAR, GURKHA, KHA
king .... MAHENDRA, PRITHWI
language ...... NEWARI, BHUTIA
Mongoloid .. RAIS, LAPP, LAI
mount .. EVEREST, LHOTSE
mountaineers ... SHERPAS
neighbor .. TIBET, INDIA, CHINA
people ...... GURKHA
premier ... RANA, SURYA
sect .... ACHAR(A)
warrior .... GURKHA, RAJPUT
Nephele, daughter of .. HELLE
nephew ...... NEPOTE, NEVE
nephric .... RENAL
nephrism, organ affected by .. KIDNEY
nephrite .... JADE
nephritic .... RENAL
nepotism .... FAVORITISM
beneficiary of .. RELATIVE
subject of .. EMPLOYMENT
nepotists, first ..... PRELATES
beneficiaries .. NEPHEWS
Neptune .. LER, POSEIDON, SEA, PLANET
discoverer of .... GALLE
scepter of ..... TRIDENT
son of .... TRITON
nereid .. (SEA)NYMPH, THETIS, AMPHITRITE
Nereus' daughter ... NEREID, THETIS
Nero ...... TYRANT, DESPOT, EMPEROR
band leader .... PETER
mother of .... AGRIPPINA
Poppaea of ..... SABINA
start of his reign LIV
wife of ...... OCTAVIA, POPPAEA
Wolfe's creator ... STOUT
nerol .... ALCOHOL
neroli .... OIL
nervation .... VENATION
nerve ...... TENDON, SINEW, COURAGE, BOLDNESS, TEMERITY, PLUCK
block ...... ANESTHESIA
cell .... NEURON(E)
cell branch ... DENDRON, DENDRITE
cell process ... DENDRITE, AXON, NEURITE
colloquial .. GUTS, GALL, FACE, AUDACITY, CHEEK, CRUST, GALL
combining form .... NEUR(O)
connective tissue .... NEUROGLIA
fiber, sheath of .. MYELIN
fibers, bundle of .... TRACT, PEDUNCLE
fibers network .... RETE
inflammation .. NEURITIS
layer .... ALVEUS
network .... RETIA
of a .... NEURAL
pain .... NEURALGIA
passage for ...... HILUM
sending impulses .... MOTOR
sensory ...... AFFERENT, EFFERENT
substance .... ALBA
surgical cutting of ...... NEUROTOMY
tissue substance .... LECITHIN
tonic .... NERVINE, SEDATIVE
(w)racking ..... TRYING
nerves .... HYSTERIA, FIT, JITTERS
network of ..... PLEXUS
pertaining to .... NEURO, NEURAL, NERVINE
nervous .... EDGY, TENSE, JITTERY, SKITTISH, FEARFUL, TIMOROUS
condition ... NEURALGIA
disease ..... TARANTISM, NEURITIS
disorder ..... PARALYSIS, NEUROSIS, CHOREA, TIC
feeling .. JITTERS, JIMJAMS
prostration .... NEURASTHENIA
seizure ...... ANEURIA, EPILEPSY, FRENZY, JITTERS, PANIC
state .... TIZZY
strain .... TENSION
twitch .... TIC
nescience .... IGNORANCE, AGNOSTICISM
ness ...... CAPE, HEADLAND, PROMONTORY
Nessus .... CENTAUR
slayer of ...... HERCULES
nest .. DEN, NIDUS, RETREAT, HAUNT, RESORT, NIDE
ants' .... FORMICARY
build a .... NIDIFY
eagle's .... AERIE, EYRIE, AERY, EYRY
egg .... MONEY, SAVINGS
of eggs .... CLUTCH
pheasant's .... NIDE
squirrel's .... DRAY
nestle .... SNUGGLE, SHELTER, CUDDLE, NUZZLE, SETTLE
nestling .... EYAS, OWLET, FLEDGLING, POULT, SQUAB, EAGLET
Nestor .... SAGE, COUNSELOR, WISE MAN
net ..... MESH, SAGENE, GAIN, BALANCE, LEFT-OVER, CLEAR, RETICLE, FILET, GIN, (EN)TRAP, (EN)SNARE, TULLE
armed with a ... RETIARY
fishing .. SEINE, TRAMMEL, TRAWL
hair .... SNOOD
like a .... RETIFORM, RETICULATE, RETICULAR
making of ..... RETIARY
ornamental .... FRET
silk .... MALINE(S)
trapping .... TOIL
nether .. DOWN, LOWER, UNDER

world ...... HELL, HADES
Netherlands (see Dutch) ...... HOLLAND
anatomist .... RAU
Antilles capital .... WILLEMSTAD
Antilles island ... ARUBA, CURACAO
botanist ..... (DE)VRIES
capital (commercial) .... AMSTERDAM
capital (political) .... (THE) HAGUE
carnival .... KERMIS, KERMESS
cheese market .... EDAM
city .... GOUDA, LEIDEN, UTRECHT, ROTTERDAM, HAARLEM, EINDHOVEN, ARNHEM, BREDA
coin .. GULDEN, GUILDER, RYDER
colonist .... BOER
commune .... EPE, EDE
cupboard .... KAS
duchy .... BRABANT
fair .... KERMIS
governor .... STAD(T)HOLDER
Guiana .... SURINAM
measure .... ROEDE, STREEP, MORGEN
merchants' league ...... HANSE
monetary unit .. GUILDER
of the .... DUTCH
painter ..... HALS, EYCK, LELY
premier ...... (DE)JONG, ZIJLSTRA
province ...... DRENTE, FRIESLAND, UTRECHT, ZEELAND, LIMBURG
queen of ..... JULIANA, WILHELMINA
queen's consort .... BERNHARD
regime ...... MONARCHY
river .... EMS, MAAS, SCHELDE, RHINE, MEUSE, IJSSEL
ruling family ... NASSAU
seaport .... ROTTERDAM
ship .... GAL(L)IOT
theologian ..... ERASMUS
tulip center ... HAARLEM
uncle .... EME
viceroy .... STADHOLDER
weight .... WIGT(JE)
woman .... FROW
youth gangs ..... PROVOS
nethermost .... LOWEST
netted .... GAINED
netting knot .... SHEET BEND
nettle .. WEED, STING, ANNOY, VEX, IRRITATE
Latin .... URTICA
plant ..... RAMIE, RAMEE
rash .. HIVES, URTICARIA, UREDO
sting with .... URTICATE
network .. WEB, RETE, PLEXUS, RETICULUM, MESH, LACE, TISSUE, TRELLIS, LATTICE, RESEAU
of blood vessels, etc. .... PLEXUS
ornamental .... FRET
Neufchatel .... CHEESE
neuk .... CORNER, NOOK
neurad, opposed to .. HAEMAD
neuralgia medicine .... VERATRIN(E)
neuralgic pain .... HEMIALGIA
neurasthenia ...... NEUROSIS
neurite .... AXONE
neurons' contact point .... SYNAPSE
neuropteron .... ANT LION
neurotic .... PSYCHIC, NEURAL
neuter ..... GENDER, ASEXUAL
verbal noun .... GERUND
neutral .. INDIFFERENT, ALOOF, NEUTER, NONPARTISAN
neutralize ...... COUNTERACT
magnetic field .. DEGAUSS
Nevada capital .. CARSON CITY
city .... ELKO, RENO, LAS VEGAS, SPARKS
county .. ELKO, WASHOE, LYON
Indian .... PAIUTE
lake .... TAHOE
state flower .. SAGEBRUSH
state tree .... PINON
neve .... SNOW, FIRN, ICE
never .... AT NO TIME
failing ...... FOOLPROOF
nevertheless .. YET, HOWEVER, STILL
Nevin's song ...... ROSARY, NARCISSUS
nevus ..... MOLE, BIRTHMARK
new .... NEOTERIC, DIFFERENT, FRESH, MODERN, LATE, NEO, ORIGINAL, NOVEL, RECENT, CENE
combining form .... NEO
Deal agency .. NRA, CCC, TVA
Deal president .... ROOSEVELT, FDR
England boat .. SHARPIE
England state ... MAINE, VERMONT
Englander .... YANK(EE), DOWN EASTER
New Britain city ..... RABAUL
New Caledonia capital ...... NOUMEA
New Guinea .... PAPUA
bird .... CASSOWARY
brain disease ...... KURU
capital .... RABAUL
city .... LAE
hog .... BENE
island .... ARU
kingfisher .. KOOKABURRA
native .. PAPUAN, KARON
Negroid .... PAPUAN
port .... DARU, LAE
"Stone Age" tribe ...... FORE
wild hog .... BENE
New Hampshire capital ...... CONCORD
city .... NASHUA, DOVER, KEENE, BERLIN
county .... COOS
lake .... SUNAPEE
river .... SACO
state bird .... FINCH
state flower ...... LILAC
state tree .... BIRCH
New Hebrides capital .. VILA
island .... TANA
New Jersey capital .. TRENTON
city .. NEWARK, CAMDEN, PATERSON, NUTLEY, BAYONNE, HOBOKEN, LINDEN, VINELAND, MONTCLAIR
colonizer ...... PATROON
county ... BERGEN, SALEM, MORRIS, MERCER, SUSSEX
river .... PASSAIC
state bird ... GOLDFINCH
state flower ..... VIOLET
town .... LAKEHURST
New Mexico artists' colony .. TAOS
canyon .... CHACO
capital .... SANTA FE
caverns .... CARLSBAD
city ... ROSWELL, HOBBS, LAS CRUCES
county ..... OTERO, TAOS
Indian .... NAVAJO, UTE, APACHE, MESCALERO, SIA, ZUNI, NAVAHO
Indian pueblo .... ACOMA
resort town .... TAOS
river .... GILA, CIMARRON, PECOS
state .... YUCCA
state flower ..... YUCCA
state tree .... PINON
town ...... TAOS, RATON
New Orleans festival .... MARDI GRAS
music .... RAGTIME
native .... CREOLE
New South Wales capital .... SYDNEY
New Testament book ... LUKE
hell .... GEHENNA
in Syriac ...... PESHITO
language of ...... KOINE
New York capital ... ALBANY
city ...... OLEAN, UTICA, AUBURN, GOTHAM, TROY, ROME, ELMIRA, YONKERS, ITHACA, OSWEGO
City borough ... QUEENS, MANHATTAN, RICHMOND, BRONX, BROOKLYN
political machine ..... TAMMANY
prison .... TOMBS
section ...... HARLEM
street .... BOWERY
subway .. IRT, IND, BMT
colonizer ..... PATROON
county .. TIOGA, GREENE, ESSEX, YATES, SARATOGA
fictitious name .... JUKES

Indian .... ONEIDA
island .... ELLIS
lake .. SARANAC, ONEIDA, SENECA, PLACID, CAYUGA
military post .... WEST POINT
motto .... EXCELSIOR
planetarium .... HAYDEN
river .. MOHAWK, GENESEE
state prison .. SING SING
team .. METS, JETS, KNICKS
town .... OSSINING

New Zealand aborigine ..... MAORI
bird .. MOA, MIRO, KIWI, LOWAN, TUI, KEA, MOREPORK, PEHO, NOTORNIS, APTERYX, WEKA
capital ..... WELLINGTON
caterpillar ...... AWETO, WERI
cattail .... RAUPO
city .... AUCKLAND, DUNEDIN
corn .... KANGA
demon .... TAIPO
discoverer ...... TASMAN
explorer .... COOK
fish .... IHI, HIKU, SCHNAPPER
governor general .... PORRITT
harbor .... OTAGO
hen .... WEKAS
island .... STEWART, CHATHAM, ANTIPODES, NIUE
lake .... TAUPA
locust .... WETA
mollusk .... PIPI
morepork .. RURU, PEHO
mountain climber ...... HILLARY
mulberry .... AUTE
myrtle ...... RAMARAMA
native .... M(A)ORI
owl .... RURU
palm .... NIKAU
parrot .... KEA, KAKAPO, KAKA
pigeon .... KUKU
pine tree .. KAURI, KAURY
plant .... KARO
prime minister .... HOLYOAKE, COATES
raft .... MOKI
rail .... WEKA
robin .... MIRO
sandalwood ..... MAIRE
seaport ...... AUCKLAND
shark .... MAKO
sheep ...... CORRIEDALE
shrub ...... RAMARAMA, KARO, TUTU
smelt .... INANGA
soldier .... ANZAC
tree .. AUTE, MIRO PUKA, TOTARA, PELU, HINO(U), NAPAU, RATA, KAIKAKA, TATARA, GOAI, HINAU, MAIRE, WHAU, AKE, KOPI, TORU, TARATA, RAMARAMA
tribe .... RINGATU
volcano ...... RUAPEHU
wages .... UTU
war club .... MERI
weapon .... PATU
wild hog .... BENE
wineberry .... MAKO
wood hen .... WEKA

newborn .... YEANLING
Newcastle river .... TYNE
newcomer ...... TENDERFOOT
newel .... POST
Newfoundland airport ...... GANDER
capital .... ST. JOHN'S
cod-fisher ...... BANKER
companion island ...... LABRADOR
fishing grounds .. BANKS
floating ice ... CLUMPERS, CROWLERS
Indian .... MICMAC
seal .... MOTHER
seal hunter ..... SWILER
tea .... SWITCHEL

newlywed .... BRIDE(GROOM), BENEDICT
serenade to .. CHARIVARI, SHIVAREE

newmarket .... COAT
newness .... NOVELTY
news ...... TIDINGS, WORD, REPORT, INFORMATION
agency .. WIRE SERVICE, UPI, TASS, REUTERS, ANETA, INS, DOMEI, KYODO, JIJI, HAVAS, CETEKA
beat .... SCOOP
bit .... ITEM
commentator .... BRINKLEY, CRONKITE, KALB, LAWRENCE, DOWNS, HUNTLEY
item .... OBIT
last minute ..... FUDGE, BREAK, FLASH
maker, (*Time* says) ..... NAME
medium ..... BULLETIN, RADIO, GRAVEVINE, GOSSIP
report .. FLASH, BULLETIN
source .... PIPELINE
stand .... KIOSK

newsboy's territory .... ROUTE
newsletter .... BULLETIN, INTELLIGENCER
newsman .. REPORTER, SCRIBE, JOURNALIST
newsmonger .... GOSSIP, TATTLER
newspaper .. GAZETTE, SHEET, JOURNAL, DAILY, TABLOID
bit .... FILLER, ITEM
columnist ...... RESTON, ALSOP, WINCHELL
extra leaf .... INSERT
feature ...... HEADLINE, COLUMN, COMICS, SCOOP, ROTO(GRAVURE)
headline ..... STREAMER, BANNER
item .... FILLER, PARAGRAPH
issue ... EDITION, EXTRA, STARFINAL
makeup of ..... FORMAT, LAYOUT
official .... REDACTOR, EDITOR
page insert ...... FUDGE
stand .... KIOSK
style of writing .... JOURNALESE
two facing pages .... SPREAD
work ...... JOURNALISM

newspaperman .... REPORTER, CUB, JOURNALIST, COLUMNIST, SCRIBE, INKSLINGER
achievement of ... SCOOP, BEAT
report of ..... DISPATCH, COPY, STORY
source of ..... CONTACT, PIPELINE
territory of .... BEAT

newspapers in general .. PRESS
newsprint .... PAPER
roll of .... WEB

newsstand .... KIOSK
newt .... EFT, SWIFT, TRITON, SALAMANDER
Newton, mathematician ..... ISAAC
next .. NEAREST, THEN, BESIDE
door resident .. NEIGHBOR
to last ... PENULT(IMATE)

nexus .... LINK, TIE, CONNECTION
Ney, Marshal .... MICHEL
Nez Perce .... INDIAN
Niagara .... FALLS
Falls .... HORSESHOE

nib ...... BEAK, BILL, POINT, PRONG
nibble .... KNAP, PECK, BITE, NIP, MORSEL, BROWSE
Nibelung .... DWARFS
guard .... FAFNIR
leader .... ALBERICH

Nibelungenlied king .. ETZEL
knight ..... HILDEBRAND

niblick .... IRON, (GOLF)CLUB
Nicaragua capital .. MANAGUA
city .... LEON, GRANADA
coin .... CORDOBA
monetary unit .... CORDOBA
president ...... SOMOZA
river .... TIPITAPA

nice ..... FINE, NEAT, NICAEA, REFINED, FASTIDIOUS, DELICATE, SUBTLE, PLEASANT, DAINTY, PRETTY, FINICAL
discernment .... ACUMEN, INSIGHT
figure .. LISSOM(E), SVELT
Nelly .... PRUDE

nicety .. DELICACY, SUBTLETY, AMENITY
niche .... RECESS, NOOK, SLOT,

TABERNACLE, CORNER, AMBRY, APSE
nick .... CHEAT, DEFRAUD, SCORE, TALLY, NOTCH, TRICK, ARREST, SLIT, CUT
actor .... ADAMS
Charles' dog ...... ASTA
Old ...... SATAN, DEVIL
the detective .... CARTER
nickel .. COIN, FIVE CENTS, NI
alloy .... INVAR
like metal ...... MONEL
silver .... ELECTRUM
slang .... JITNEY
sulfide .... MILLERITE
nicker .... NEIGH, LAUGH
nickname .... SO(U)BRIQUET, MONI(C)KER, AGNOMEN, COGNOMEN, AGNAME
feminine or masculine ... LOU
Nicosia is capital of .. CYPRUS
nicotine .... TAR
nicotine acid .... NIACIN
nictitate .... BLINK, WINK
nide .... NEST
nidus .... NEST
Niemen ..... MEMEL, NEMAN, NEMUNAS
river .... RUSS
Nietzsche, philosopher ...... FRIEDRICH
superman of .... UBERMENSCH
nieve .... FIST, HAND
niffer .... BARTER, TRADE, EXCHANGE
nifty .... STYLISH, SMART
Niger, capital of .... NIAMEY
city .... ZINDER, NIAMEY
people .... HAUSA, PEUL, TOUAREG, IJO
president .... DIORI
river mouth .... NUN
Nigerian capital ...... LAGOS
city .... IBADAN, EDE, KANO, OGBOMOSHO
dissident region .. BIAFRA
division .... SOKOTO
native .... IBO, HAUS(S)A, EDO, ARO, BENI(N)
prime minister .... BALEWA, IRONSI
seaport .. BONNY, LAGOS
secessionist state .... BIAFRA
state ..... BIAFRA, NUPE
tribal chief .... OBA
tribe ...... YORUBA, IBO, HAUSA, FULANI, BENIN, ARO, EBOE, EDO
niggard .. STINGY, SKINFLINT, CHURL, MISER(LY)
niggardly ..... MISERLY, FEW, SCANTY, STINGY
niggle .... PUTTER
nigh ..... NEAR(LY), ALMOST, ANEAR, CLOSE(BY)
night .. DARK(NESS), EVENING
attack .... CAMISADO
before .... EVE
blindness .. NYCTALOPIA
clothes .... PAJAMAS, NIGHTIE, NIGHTY
club ...... ROADHOUSE, BISTRO, CABARET
combining form .... NOCT(I)
flyer .. BAT, OWL, MOTH, FIREFLY
letter .... TELEGRAM
moth .... NOCTUID
noise-maker .. ALLEYCAT
of the ...... NOCTURNAL
nightcap .... DRINK
nightfall .... DUSK
occurring at .... ACRONICAL, ACRONYCAL
nighthawk ..... GOATSUCKER, BULLBAT
nightingale .... PHILOMEL BULBUL, THRUSH, SONGBIRD
note of .... JUG
so-called ... (JENNY)LIND
nightjar .... POTOO, BIRD, GOATSUCKER
nightmare ... DREAM, INCUBUS
demon .... MARA
nightrider .... VIGILANTE, TERRORIST
nightshade .. MOREL, DATURA, BELLADONNA, HENBANE, PLANT, MORIL, MANDRAKE, TOBACCO, SOLANUM, PETUNIA
relative .... TOMATO, POTATO
nightsight ...... NYCTALOPIA
nightstick .. TRUNCHEON, CLUB
user .. POLICE(MAN), COP
nightwalker .... THIEF
nigrescence ...... BLACKNESS
nihil .... NOTHING
Nihon .... JAPAN
Nike .... GODDESS, VICTORIA, ATHENA
nil .... NOTHING, NULL
Nile .... NILUS, HAPI
bird ..... IBIS, SHOEBILL
boat ... BARIS, DAHABEAH
catfish .... BAGRE
city .... ASWAN, THEBES, MEROE, KHARTOUM, TANTA, TANIS, SAIS, OMDURMAN
dam .... ASWAN
floating weeds .... SUDD
goddess .... ISIS
heron .... IBIS
island .... RODA
native .... NILOT
negro .... SUK, JUR
of the .... NILOTIC
passenger boat .... DAHABEAH
plant .... PAPYRUS
queen of the .... CLEO(PATRA)
reeds .... SUDD
sailboat .... CANGIA
ship's captain .... RAIS, REIS
source of .... TSANA
town .. ROSETTA, LUXOR
tributary .... KAGERA
valley hollow ...... KORE
village on the ... KARNAK
weeds .... SUDD
nilgai .... ANTELOPE
Nilus .... NILE
nim .... STEAL
nimble ...... DEFT, LISSOM(E), VOLANT, LIGHT, ALERT, AGILE, SPRY, QUICK
nimbus .... CLOUD, AUREOLA, HALO, AURA, GLORIA
nimiety ... EXCESS, PLEONASM, REDUNDANCY
Nimitz, admiral ..... CHESTER
Nimrod .... HUNTER
parent of .... CUSH
nincompoop ...... SIMPLETON, FOOL, DOLT, SOFTHEAD, NITWIT, IDIOT
nine: comb. form ..... ENNE
days' devotion .. NOVENA
group of .... ENNEAD
headed serpent.... HYDRA
inches .... SPAN
"ladies" .... MUSES
number .... ENNEA
part composition .... NONET
sided plane .. NONAGON, ENNEAGON
team of ...... BASEBALL
the .... MUSES
ninefold .... NENARY
ninepins ...... SKITTLE, GAME
nineteen XIX
nineteenth hole: colloq. ...... LOCKER ROOM, BAR
ninetieth ..... NONAGESIMAL
Nineveh founder ..... NINUS
ninny ... DOLT, FOOL, DUNCE, SIMPLETON, ASS, IDIOT
ninth day before the ides ..... NONES
Ninus .... NINEVEH
Niobe, brother of .... PELOPS
fate of .... STONE
father of ..... TANTALUS
husband of .... AMPHION
Niobean .... WEEPING, WEEPY
nip .. BITE, PINCH, SEVER, CUT, CHECK, BLIGHT, DRAM, DRINK, SIP
and tuck .... CLOSE, NECK AND NECK
slang .. JAPANESE, CATCH, STEAL
nipa .... PALM, AT(T)AP
liquor .... TUBA
nipper ...... PLIERS, PINCERS, FORCEPS, CLAW, TWEEZERS
nippers .... HANDCUFFS, LEG IRONS
nipping ...... BITING, SHARP
nipple .... PAPILLA, TIT, PAP, TEAT, DUG, MAMMILLA
baby's toy .... PACIFIER
inflammation .. THELITIS
shaped like a .. MASTOID
Nippon .... JAPAN
nippy .. SHARP, BITING, NIMBLE
nis .... KOBOLD
Nishapur's famous son ...... OMAR(KHAYYAM)
nisi .... UNLESS

Nissen .... PREFAB
nisus ..... EFFORT, ENDEAVOR
nit .... EGG, INSECT
niter .... SALTPETER, NITRATE, SALT
niton .... RADON
nitrate .... NITER, SALTPETER, FERTILIZER, SALT, ESTER
nitric .... AZOTIC
acid ..... AQUA FORTIS
nitrogen .. AZOTE, NONMETAL
containing .... AZO(TIC)
nitrogenize .... AZOTIZE
nitroglycerine ... GLONOIN(E), TNT, EXPLOSIVE
nitrohydrochloric acid .... AQUA REGIA
nitrous acid salt .... NITRITE
nitrous oxide .. LAUGHING GAS
nitwit .... JACKASS, FOOL, IDIOT, MORON, BOOB(Y)
Niven, actor .... DAVID
niveous .... SNOWY, SNOWLIKE
nix(ie) .... NO, SPRITE, FAIRY
slang .. NO, NOT AT ALL
Nizam .... NABOB
domain ..... HYDERABAD
Njorth .... VANIR
parent of ...... FREY(A)
no .... NAY, NOT SO
gentleman he .... BRUTE, BOOR, LOUT
longer existing .... EXTINCT, DEAD
more .... ENOUGH
more than .. MERE, ONLY
one .... NONE
slangy .. NOPE, NIX, NAW
Noah, boat of .... ARK
father of .... LAMECH
grandson of ...... ARAM
landing place of .... ARARAT
pertaining to .... NOETIC
son of .. JAPHETH, SHEM, HAM
nob .... HEAD, JACK
nobble .... CHEAT, BRIBE
nobby .. STYLISH, FIRST-RATE
Nobel, industrialist .. ALFRED
invention of .. DYNAMITE
laureate .... UREY
Prize winner, chemistry .. UREY, CURIE, SANGER, LANGMUIR, SEABORG, PAULING, WERNER, BAEYER, HAHN, ADLER
literature ...... MANN, CAMUS, STEINBECK, PASTERNAK, JENSEN, FAULKNER, SARTRE, SACHS, SHAW, ELIOT
medicine ..... BURNET, KOCH, RICHET, KREBS, GOLGI, ECCLES, LYNEN
peace .... ORR, MOTT, BUNCHE, WILSON, DUNANT, LANGE
physics ...... RAMAN, FERMI, CURIE, BOHR, TAMM, BRAUN, DALEN, YANG
nobility .... PEERAGE, GRANDEUR, ARISTOCRACY, NOBLESSE
rank just below .... GENTRY
noble ..... KINGLY, MAJESTIC, PATRICIAN, GRAND, LOFTY, STATELY, PEER, SUBLIME, BLUEBLOOD
birth .... HIGHBORN, EUGENY
nobleman ..... PRINCE, PEER, BARON, THANE, LORD, DUKE, EARL, HIDALGO, JARL, COUNT, MILORD, GRANDEE, YOUNKER, MARQUIS, MAGNIFICO
noblesse .... ARISTOCRATS
noblewoman .. LADY, PEERESS, DUCHESS, CONTESSA, MILADY
nobody ... NONENTITY, NONE, NO ONE
nocent .. INJURIOUS, HURTFUL, GUILTY
nock .... NOTCH
noctambulist ... SLEEPWALKER
nocti, as combining form ..... NIGHT
noctuid .... MOTH
noctule .... BAT
nocturnal bird .. OWL, KAKAPO
creature .... BAT, COON, LEMUR, RATEL, WEASEL, JACKAL, TAPIR, TARSIER, RAC(C)OON, (O)POSSUM
parrot .... KAKAPO
nocturne .... SERENADE
nocuous .. NOXIOUS, HARMFUL
nod .... BOW, BECK, DROWSE, DOZE, NUTATE
land of .... SLEEP
sign of .. YES, APPROVAL, AGREEMENT, ASSENT
nodding .. NUTANT, ANNUENT
noddle .... PATE, HEAD, GULL
noddy ..... FOOL, SIMPLETON
node .. DILEMMA, KNOT, KNOB, FOCUS, SWELLING, JOINT
nodose ..... KNOTTY, KNOBBY
nodous .... KNOTTY
nodule .. KNOT, LUMP, JOINT
cartilaginous .. SESAMOID
tone's .... GEODE
nodus .... COMPLICATION
noel ...... CAROL, CHRISTMAS
Coward's song .... NINA
noesis .... PERCEPTION, COGNITION
noetic .... SCHOLAR
nog .... PIN, ALE, BRICK
noggin .... MUG, CUP, HEAD, GILL, PATE
noise .. CLAMOR, DIN, SOUND, BRUIT, (UP)ROAR, RACKET, STRIDOR, HUBBUB
maker at night .... ALLEYCAT
surf .... ROTE
noiseless ..... SILENT, QUIET, STILL, CATLIKE
noisome .... FETID, NOXIOUS, STINKING, HARMFUL
noisy .... BLATANT, LOUD, CLAMOROUS, CLAMANT
bird ..... (MAG)PIE, JAY
merry making .... REVELRY, CAROUSAL
revelry .... JAMBOREE
nom de plume (see pen name) .. PEN NAME, PSEUDONYM
nomad .. WANDERER, GYPSY, ITINERANT, LAPP, ROVER, TRAMP, ROAMER
Afghan .... KUCHI
desert .. ARAB, BEDOUIN, SLEB, BUSHMAN, KURD
nomadic .... ITINERANT
tribe .... HORDE
nome .... NOMARCHY
is in .... ALASKA
nominal .... TOKEN, TITULAR, SLIGHT, SMALL
value .... PAR
nominate .... NAME, APPOINT, DESIGNATE, CALL
nomination .... NAMING, APPOINTMENT
nominee .... CANDIDATE, APPOINTEE
nomology, subject of .... LAWMAKING, LEGISLATION
non-believer .... PAGAN, INFIDEL, AGNOSTIC, ATHEIST
Christian .... PAGAN, PAYNIM
Jew .... GENTILE
member ..... OUTSIDER, MAVERICK
Mormon .... GENTILE
Moslem .... GIAOUR
nonage .... MINORITY
nonce .... MEANWHILE, MEANTIME
noncom ..... NCO, SERGEANT, SARGE, CPL
nonchalant .... INDIFFERENT, COOL, INSOUCIANT
nonconformist ...... SECTARY, DISSENTER, HERETIC, REB(EL), RECUSANT, DISSIDENT
none .... NARY, NO ONE, NOT ANY, NOTHING
too soon .... HIGH TIME
nonentity .. NOBODY, CIPHER, STRAWMAN, UNPERSON
nonesuch . PARAGON, APPLE, ONER, NONPAREIL
nonmetal .. CARBON, OXYGEN, FLUORINE, NITROGEN
nonmetallic element ... BORON, SILICON, IODINE, ASTATINE, FLUORINE
nonpareil .... UNRIVALED, SUPREME, NON(E)SUCH, PEERLESS
nonpartisan .... NEUTRAL
nonplus .... MYSTIFY, STUMP, PERPLEX, PUZZLE, CONFUSE, CONFOUND
nonprofit organization ...... FOUNDATION
nonsense .. TWADDLE, BUNK, (TOMMY)ROT, SLAVER, DRIVEL, TRUMPERY, BLAH, TOSH, FLIMFLAM, BLATHER, FALDEROL, FOLDEROL,

MALARK(E)Y, FUDGE, BILGE, FLAPDOODLE, HOKUM, POPPYCOCK, RUBBISH, BOSH, BAH, BALONEY, TRASH, HOOEY, BULL, RIG(A)MAROLE, BALDERDASH, KIBOSH, TOMFOOLERY
deceitful .... GAMMON
high-sounding .. FUSTIAN
nonsensical .. ABSURD, SILLY, FOOLISH, INANE, RIDICULOUS
creature .. GOOP, SNARK, SMOO, NOIO, GOOF
poem .... LIMERICK
nonstop .... MARATHON, CONTINUOUS
nonsuch .... PARAGON
noodle .. HEAD, FOOL, PASTA, FARFEL, FERFEL
dish .... CHOW MEIN
nook ..... CORNER, RETREAT, RECESS, DEN, (AL)COVE
and ____ ...... CORNER, CRANNY
noon ..... MIDDAY, MERIDIAN
rest .... SIESTA
noose .. LOOP, TRAP, HALTER, (EN)SNARE
trap .... SPRINGE
nopal .... CACTUS
nope .... NO, NIX
opposite of .... YEP
Nordic .... TEUTON(IC), CAUCASIAN
Norfolk .... JACKET
Norge .... NORWAY
noria .... (WATER)WHEEL
norm ...... STANDARD, RULE, MODEL, PATTERN, AVERAGE
normal .. NATURAL, REGULAR, USUAL, ORDINARY, MEAN, STANDARD, TYPICAL, AVERAGE
breathing ... EUPN(O)EA
school grad ... TEACHER
Norman crusade leader ...... TANCRED
Normand, actress .... MABEL
Normandy capital .... ROUEN
conqueror of ..... ROLLO
department .. EURE, ORNE, MANCHE
duke of ... ROLLO, HROLF
Norn .... SKULD, URTH, VERTHANDI, GODDESS
Norris, novelist ..... FRANK, KATHLEEN
Norse .... SCANDINAVIAN
Adam .... ASKR
chieftain .. JARL, ROLLO, YARL
deities' home ... ASGARD
deity .. ODIN, THOR, EIR
destiny .... NORN
earth: myth. ... MIDGARD
epic .... EDDA
explorer .. ERIC, ERICSSON
galley .... AESC
giant ..... ATLI, FAFNIR, YMER, MIMIR, EGIL, (H)YMIR, WATE, TROLL, JOTUN(N)
giantess .... NORN, GROA
goat .... HEIDRUN
god ... HEIMDALL, ODIN, HODER, HODUR, DONAR, ULL, LOKI, VALI, FREY, FORSETI, BALDER, AEGER, THOR, BRAGI, TYR, VANIR, AESIR, HOENIR
goddess .. FREYA, NORN, IDUN, ITHUN(N), URTH, SKULD, VERTHANDI, HEL(A), MOIRA, EIR, RANA, WYRD, SIF, FRIGG(A)
gods, abode of the ...... ASGARD
gods, king of .. WODEN, ODIN
hall of heroes .... VALHALLA
hero .... EGIL(L)
home of gods .. ASGARD
king .... ATLI, OLAF
letter .... RUNE
lore .... RUNE
minstrel .... SCALD
mythology, summary of .. EDDA
navigator .... ERIC
Nibelung dwarf .... ALBERICH
nobleman .... JARL
plateau .... FJELD
poem .... RUNE
poet ...... SCALD, SKALD
poetry .. RUNE(S), EDDA
race of gods ...... VANIR
rainbow bridge .. BIFROST
river .... KLAR
saga .... EDDA
saint .... OLAF
serpent ...... MIDGARD
tale .... SAGA, EDDA
underworld .... HEL
viking .... ROLLO
watchdog .... GARM
watchman of Asgard .... HEIMDALL
wolf .... FENRIR
woman, first .... EMBLA
world's destruction ..... RAGNAROK
Norseman .... VIKING
north .... ARCTIC, BOREAL
of the far .... HYPERBOREAN
North African city .. ALGIERS
garment .... HAIK
region .... SUDAN
seaport .... ORAN
sheep .... AOUDAD
North Atlantic fish .... LING, BURBOT, CAP(E)LIN, MACKEREL
North Borneo .... SABAH
North Carolina cape .. FEAR, HATTERAS, LOOKOUT
capital .... RALEIGH
city ...... GREENSBORO, DURHAM, CHARLOTTE
college .... ELON
county ..... ASHE, HOKE, NASK
native/nickname .... TARHEEL
resort town ..... TRYON
river .... NEUSE, PEE DEE
state bird .... CARDINAL
state flower ... DOGWOOD
university .... DUKE
North Dakota capital .... BISMARK
city ..... MINOT, FARGO, JAMESTOWN
county ..... CASS, DUNN
mining town ...... ZAP
nickname .. FLICKERTAIL
North Pole discoverer .... PEARY
North Sea port ..... BERGEN, KIEL, BREMEN, EMDEN
serpent .... KRAKEN
tributary .. THAMES, TEES, RHINE, ELBE, MEUSE, TYNE, SCHELDE, YSER, TAY, WESER, MAAS
water .... KATTEGAT
North Star .... LODESTAR, POLARIS
state .... MINNESOTA
Northern .... BOREAL
Bear .... RUSSIA
Cross .... CYGNUS
Rhodesia .... ZAMBIA
sea bird .. SKUA, JAEGER, PUFFIN
Spy .... (WINTER)APPLE
Northerner .... YANKEE, COPPERHEAD
Northampton landmark ..... MT. TOM
Northman .. NORMAN, THULE, NORSE(MAN),
Northumberland river .. TYNE
Northwest Territory settlement MARIETTA
Norway (see Norse, Norwegian) NORGE
Norwegian (see Norse) ..... NORSE(MAN)
capital .... OSLO
city .... BERGEN, TRONDHEIM, STAVANGER, NARVIK, ALESUND
coin ...... KRONA, ORA
composer .. GRIEG, OLSEN
dramatist .... IBSEN
explorer ...... NANSEN, AMUNDSEN
fish ...... LING, BURBOT
goblin .. NIS(SE), KOBOLD
haddock ..... ROSEFISH
inlet ..... FIORD, FJORD
king .... OLAV, HAAKON, OLAF
language .... RIKSMAAL, LANDSMAAL
measure .. ALEN, MORGEN
monetary unit ... KRONE
mountain .... KJOLEN
native .... LAPP, LAPLANDER
noble .... JARL
novelist .... NOJER, HAMSUN

parliament .. LAGT(H)ING, STORT(H)ING
poetry .... EDDA
port .... HAMMERFEST
prime minister .. BORTEN
region .... LAPLAND
river .... NAMSEN, KLAR, GLOMMEN, TANA
rodent .... LEMMING
saint .... OLAF
sea monster .... KRAKEN
seaport .... BERGEN, TRONDHEIM, STAVANGER, HAMMERFEST
soprano ...... FLAGSTAD
Storthing section .... LAGTING, ODELSTING
territorial subdivision ... AMT
toast .... SKOAL
traitor .... QUISLING
whirlpool .. MAELSTROM
writer .... IBSEN, NOJER
nose .... CONK, BEAK, SCENT, SNOUT, MUZZLE, SPOUT, SMELL, NOZZLE, DEFEAT, NEB, PROBOSCIS, PRY, SNIFF, SNOOP
ailment .... CORYZA, CATARRH
bone .... VOMER
combining form .... RHIN(O)
counting .. CENSUS, POLL
describing one ..... PUG, SNUB, AQUILINE, ROMAN, TILTED, SHARP, SIMOUS
discharge .... RHEUM
dive .... PLUNGE
elephant's ...... TRUNK
inflammation .. RHINITIS
Latin .... NASUS
long .. SNOUT, PROBOSCIS
of the ... NASAL, RHINAL
opening .. NARE, NOSTRIL, NARIS
person with famous ..... CYRANO (BERGERAC), DURANTE
point on .... ALARE
slang .... SPY, INFORMER, SCHNOZZLE, SNOOT, NOZZLE
turned up .... RETROUSE
nosebleed .... EPISTAXIS
nosegay ..... POSY, BOUQUET, CORSAGE
nos(e)y .. INQUISITIVE, PRYING
nostalgia ...... NOSTOMANIA, HOMESICKNESS, LONGING
nostology .... GERIATRICS
subject of ..... OLD AGE
nostomania ...... NOSTALGIA, HOMESICKNESS
Nostradamus .... SEER, ASTROLOGER
nostril .... NARE
hairs .... VIBRISSA
of the .. NARIAL, NARINE
nostrum .. REMEDY, PANACEA
nosy .... PRYING, INQUISITIVE, CURIOUS
not any .... NARY, NONE
appropriate ...... INAPT, INEPT, IMPROPER, UNFIT
at home .. OUT, ABROAD
cautious .... RASH, RECKLESS
complex .. SIMPLE, EASY
compulsory ... OPTIONAL
divided .... WHOLE
handsome ..... HOMELY, PLAIN
in jail anyway .... AT LARGE, LOOSE
in style .... PASSE
mature .... GREEN
moving .... STILL, INERT, STATIC
now .... LATER
occupied .. IDLE, VACANT
often .. SELDOM, RARELY
one or the other .... NEITHER
planned .... CASUAL, HAPHAZARD, RANDOM
prefix ..... NON, MIS, DIS
pronounced ...... MUTE, ELIDED
quite .. HARDLY, BARELY
real .. SHAM, FICTITIOUS, IMAGINARY, FAKE
ripe .... GREEN
speaking .... MUM, MUTE
specific .... GENERAL, INDEFINITE
suitable .... UNFIT, INAPT
nota bene .... NOTE WELL
notable ...... UNCO, SIGNAL, EMINENT, STRIKING
act .. DEED, FEAT, GEST(E), HEROISM, EXPLOIT
personage .... LION, VIP, CELEBRITY, HERO
notarize .... ATTEST, CERTIFY
notary .... SCRIVENER
notch .. JAG, INDENTURE, PEG, NICK, DEGREE, TALLY, MARK, (IN)DENT, DEFILE, GAP, SCORE, RECORD
key .... WARD
made by ax/saw .. KERF
notched .... EROSE, CRENATE, SERRATE, DENTATE
bar .... RATCH
part .... JOG
wheel .... RATCHET
note .. DISTINCTION, EMINENCE, HEED, BILLET, OBSERVE, REMARK
an eighth .... QUAVER
equal to two others ..... BREVE
explanatory .. SCHOLIUM, POSTIL
Guido's .... GAMUT
half .... MINIM
highest .... ELA
marginal .... (A)POSTIL, APOSTIL(LE)
musical, accented .... THESIS
of comment ...... GLOSS
part of .... STEM
promissory .... IOU
short .. CHIT, MEMO, LINE
signaling attack .... WARISON
stem of .... TAIL
well .... NOTA BENE
notebook .... CAHIER
noted .. FAMOUS, RENOWNED, EMINENT
notes in Guido's scale ... ALT, ELA, ELAMI
noteworthy .... NOTABLE, SPECIAL, EMINENT
nothing .. NAUGHT, NIHIL, NIL, ZERO, NONE, NOUGHT
but ..... ONLY, MERELY
doing! .... NO, NO DICE, NO SOAP
for .... FREE, GRATIS
notice .... HEED, REGARD, DISCERN, SEE, BILLING, REVIEW, WARNING, OBSERVE, ADVICE
death .... OBIT
of payment due .... PROMPT
official ...... BULLETIN, MONITION
to desist .... CAVEAT
to end treaty .... DENUNCIATION
notification .... AVISO, ADVICE
notify ...... APPRISE, ADVISE, WARN, INFORM, TELL, ACQUAINT
notion .. VIEW, BELIEF, FANCY, DESIRE, IDEA, CURIO, WHIM, INKLING, OPINION
counter item .. SHOELACE, SAFETY PIN, THREAD
fallacious ...... IDOLISM
foolish ...... MOONSHINE
notions .... ARTICLES
notoriety .... REPUTE, ECLAT, REPUTATION
notorious .... WELL KNOWN, FAMED, INFAMOUS, ARRANT
notornis, relative of ... COOT, RAIL
Notre Dame ...... OUR LADY, CATHEDRAL
notwithstanding .... MAUGRE, YET, INSPITE, MAUGER, THO, (AL)THOUGH
nougat .. CANDY, CONFECTION
nought ...... NOTHING, ZERO, CIPHER, USELESS
bring to .. NULLIFY, VOID
nomenal .... INTUITIVE
noun .... SUBSTANTIVE
form .... CASE
kind of .... APTOTE, TRIPTOTE
of common gender ..... EPICENE
suffix .. ULE, ERY, ENCE, IER, FER, ISE, ITE, ITIS
verbal .... GERUND
nourish .... FOSTER, SUSTAIN, FEED, SUPPORT, ALIMENT
nourishing .... ALIBLE, NUTRITIOUS, ALIMENTAL, ALIMENTARY, NUTRIENT
nourishment .... ALIMENT,

NUTRIMENT, PABULUM, FOOD
baby's ...... MILK, PAP
nous ...... MIND, INTELLECT, REASON
nouveau riche ...... UPSTART, PARVENU
nouveaute .... NOVELTY
nouvelles .... NEWS
nova .... STAR
Nova Scotia(n) ... ACADIA(N), BLUENOSE
bay .... FUNDY
cape .... CANSO, BRETON, SABLE
capital .... HALIFAX
inhabitant .... BLUENOSE, ACADIAN
seaport .... TRURO
village ...... GRAND PRE
Novarro, actor .... RAMON
movie role .... BEN HUR
novel .... FRESH, SIMENON, ROMANCE, NEW, STRANGE, RARE, UNUSUAL
novella .... NARRATIVE
novelty ...... WRINKLE, FAD, NEWNESS, INNOVATION, TRINKET, BRIC-A-BRAC, GIMCRACK
November 11 .... MARTINMAS
13, Roman calendar .... IDES
novena .... DEVOTIONS
novice .... TENDERFOOT, NEOPHYTE, CONVERT, BEGINNER, ACOLYTE, CHELA, TYRO, AMATEUR, TIRO, APPRENTICE, GREENHORN
novitiate ... NOVICE, TRAINEE, NEOPHYTE
novocaine ...... ANESTHETIC, PROCAINE
Novotna .... JARMILA
now .... AT ONCE, HERE
nowadays .... PRESENTLY, AT PRESENT
noway .. NOWISE, NOT AT ALL
nowt .... OXEN, CATTLE
Nox .... NYX, GODDESS
brother of ...... EREBUS
husband of ...... CHAOS
is goddess of .... NIGHT
noxious ...... EVIL, NOCENT, BANEFUL, NOISOME, PERNICIOUS, HARMFUL, MEPHITIC, MIASMIC, MIASMAL
air .... MIASMA, MALARIA
vapor ..... FUME, REEK, SMOG
Noyes, poet .... ALFRED
nozzle .. NOSE, SNOUT, SPOUT, JET, ROSE
furnace .... TUYERE
thing with .. HOSE, PIPE, TEAPOT, BELLOWS, WHALE
nuance .... SHADE, VARIATION
nub .. KNOB, SNAG, LUMP, GIST
nubbin .... LUMP, CORN
nubble .... KNOB, LUMP
nubia .... WRAP
Nubian .... NEGRO(ID)
harp .... NANGA
nubilous .... CLOUDY, FOGGY, MISTY, VAPOROUS, OBSCURE
nucellus .... NUCLEUS
nucha .... NAPE, SCRUFF
nuclear device ...... REACTOR
division in germ cells .... MEIOSIS
missile ..... ICBM, MIRV, A-BOMB, H-BOMB
scientist .... BRAUN
nucleus ..... KERNEL, CENTER, NUCELLUS
atom's ..... DEUT(E)RON, PROTON
cell .... MESOPLAST
military unit's .... CADRE
nude .... BARE, NAKED, UNCLOTHED
nudge ... POKE, ELBOW, PUSH, JOG, JOSTLE, PROD
nudibranchiate .... SNAIL, MOLLUSK
nudist .... ADAMITE, GYMNOSOPHIST
Nuevo Leon capital .... MONTERREY
nugatory .... TRIFLING, TRIVIAL, INVALID
nugget .... LUMP
nuisance .... BANE, BORE, ANNOYANCE, TROUBLE, PLAGUE
colloquial .. TERROR, PEST
insect .... GNAT
null .... VOID, INVALID, NIL
nullah ...... RAVINE, GORGE, GULLY, WATERCOURSE
nullify ... INVALIDATE, UNDO, VOID, CANCEL, ABROGATE, NEGATE, REPEAL, OVERRIDE
nulliparous .... BARREN
nullipore .... SEAWEED
numb ... INSENSIBLE, DEADEN, UNFEELING
number .... TOTAL, COMPANY, COUNT, DIGIT, ENUMERATE
added .... ADDEND
astronomic .... GOOGOL
countless .... MYRIAD, HORDE, SWARM
dividing evenly .. ALIQUOT
8 iron .... NIBLICK
5 iron ... MASHIE, MASHY
four .... TETRAD
irrational .... SURD
large .... LEGION, RAFT, RAFF, SLEW
leaves of book .. FOLIATE
less than ten ...... DIGIT
lost .... TOLL, CASUALTY
magazine .... ISSUE
nine .... ENNEAD
one plus 100 zeros .... GOOGOL
page .... FOLIO
part of .... FRACTION
six .... SEXTET
subtracted .. SUBTRAHEND
without ..... NUMEROUS, COUNTLESS
whole .... INTEGER
numbers .... COLLECTION, QUANTITY, BOOK
game .... LOTTO, LOTTERY
in music ..... MEASURES, RHYTHM
in poetry ... VERSES, FEET
racket .... LOTTERY, POLICY GAME
numbfish .... TORPEDO, (ELECTRIC)RAY
numbles .... INNARDS
numen ...... DIVINITY, SPIRIT
numerate .... COUNT, READ
numerous .. MANY, MANIFOLD, MYRIAD
combining form .. MYRIA
Numidian crane .. DEMOISELLE
king .... MASINISSA
town .... ZAMA
numismatic object ..... COIN, MEDAL
numismatist ..... COLLECTOR
concern of .... COINS, MEDALS
nummular ..... COIN-SHAPED
numskull .. DOLT, BLOCKHEAD, DUNDERHEAD, NITWIT, MORON, DUNCE
nun .... VIRGIN, SISTER, PIGEON, SMEW, TITMOUSE, MONASA, CLARE, CARMELITE, VESTAL, VOTARY
abode of ..... CONVENT, MONASTERY
dress of .... HABIT
head covering .. WIMPLE
moth .... TUSSOCK
throat cover ...... BARB
nunbird .... MONASE
nuncio .. AMBASSADOR, LEGATE
nuncupative .... ORAL, UNWRITTEN, VERBAL
nunnery ... CONVENT, ABBEY, CLOISTER, PRIORY
head of a .... ABBESS, SUPERIOR, PRIORESS
nuns, descriptive of some ..... CONTEMPLATIVE
of .... MONASTIC
nuptial(s) .... WEDDING, MARRIAGE, MATRIMONIAL, HYMENEAL, BRIDAL, SPOUSAL
participant .... RINGBEARER, BESTMAN, BRIDESMAID
poem ... EPITHALAMION
principal .. BRIDE(GROOM)
yes .... I DO
nuque .... NAPE, SCRUFF
Nuremberg war crimes defendant ..... GOERING, KEITEL, HESS, RIBBENTROP
nurse .... AMAH, AYAH, SUCKLE(R), TEND, FOSTER, CARE, NANNY
headcovering of .. WIMPLE
part time .... SITTER
shark .... GATA
nursemaid .... BONNE
nursery .... PLAYROOM, HOTHOUSE, GREENHOUSE, ASYLUM

furniture ..... PLAYPEN
public/day ..... CRECHE
rhyme character ... SPRAT
rhyme opening words .... PAT-A-CAKE
VIP .... BABY
worker, part time .... (BABY)SITTER
nurture ... FOOD, NUTRIMENT, FEED, NOURISH, FOSTER, REAR
nut ... BETEL, BRAZIL, PECAN, FRUIT, ACORN, KOLA, COCO, KERNEL, CASHEW, PILI, PROBLEM, ALMOND, PINON, LI(T)CHI, LICHEE, HICKORY, TRYMA, PARA
bearing ..... NUCIFEROUS
combining form .. NUCI, CARYO, KARYO
confection ..... PRALINE, MARZIPAN, NOUGAT
covering .... SHELL,
meat .... KERNEL
off one's .... CRAZY
of a sort .... FANATIC
ridges .... KNURL
slang ... HEAD, FOOLISH, QUEER, ECCENTRIC
three-cornered .... BEECH
turner .... SPANNER, WRENCH
nutant .. DROOPING, NODDING
nutcracker ..... BIRD, CROW, NUTHATCH
nuthatch ...... NUTCRACKER, BIRD, TITMOUSE, CREEPER
nutlet ... PYRENE, STONE, PIT
nutmeat .... KERNEL
nutmeg .. SPICE, KERNEL, MACE
nutria .. COYPU, RODENT, FUR
animal like ..... BEAVER
nutrient .... NUTRITIOUS, NOURISHING
nutriment ... FOOD, ALIMENT, NOURISHMENT, MILK
nutrition, faulty ... DYSTROPHY
of .... TROPHIC
study of ...... DIETETICS, SITOLOGY
nutritionist .... DIETITIAN, DIETICIAN
nutritive .... ALIBLE
nuts .... CRAZY, FOOL, QUEER, ENTHUSIASTIC, GAGA
collectively .... MAST
pertaining to ..... NUCAL
nutty ... ENTHUSIASTIC, GAGA, QUEER, FOOLISH, CRAZY
nux vomica ..... SEED, PLANT
product ... STRYCHNIN(E)
nuzzle .. PUSH, RUB, SNUGGLE, NESTLE
Nyasaland .... MALAWI
capital .... (ZOMBA), LILONGWE
president .... BANDA
nylghai .... ANTELOPE
nylon ...... THREAD, BRISTLE, HOSE
flow of ..... RUN, SNAG
thread weight of .. DENIER
nylons ..... STOCKINGS, HOSE
nymph ..... SYLPH, GODDESS, MAIDEN, WOMAN, LARVA, EGERIA, OENONE, PUPA, HOURI, OCEANID, ONDINE, SALMACIS, SYRINX, DAPHNE, MAENAD, AEGLE, HESTIA
adviser .... EGERIA
changed into bear .... CALLISTO
changed into laurel tree .. DAPHNE
changed into a rock ..... ECHO
changed into a stream ... ARETHUSA
fountain .... NAIAD
guards ..... HESPERIDES
mountain .... OREAD
pursuer of .... SATYR
river .... NAIAD, NAIS
sea ... NEREID, NEMERTES, SIREN
spring .... NAIAD
tree ..... (HAMA)DRYAD
water .... APAS
woodland ... ARETHUSA, (HAMA)DRYAD
nymphaea .. NUPAR, CASTALIA
nymphalid .... BUTTERFLY
nymphet .... LOLITA
nymphs, father of 50 .. NEREUS
spring/fountain .... CAMENAE
nyssa .... TUPELO
nystagmus, thing affected by .. EYEBALL
Nyx .... NOX
daughter of .... ERIS
is goddess of .... NIGHT

O

O .... CIPHER, ZERO, EXCLAMATION
Greek .... OMEGA, OMICRON
in baseball .. (PUT)OUTS
in chemistry .... OXYGEN
in pharmacy ...... PINT
in physics .... OHM
oaf ...... DULLHEAD, CHILD, BOOR, GAWK, RUSTIC, LOUT, DOLT, RUBE, DUNCE
variant of .... OUPHE
Oahu city .... HONOLULU
oak .... WOOD, TREE, HOLM, WOOD(WORK), ROBLE, ENCINA, CERRIS, BLACKJACK, ALDER, BLUEJACK, DURMAS, ROBUR, EMORY
bark .. TAN, EMORY, CRUT
bark infusion ..... OOZE
black ...... QUERCITRON
British slang ...... DOOR
California .... ROBLE, ENCINA
evergreen .... ILEX
fruit ...... ACORN, MAST, CAMATA
genus .... QUERCUS
holm .... ILEX
Jerusalem ..... AMBROSE
live .... ENCINA
moss .... EVERNIA
of the .... QUERCINE
pin .... THOLE
Ridge work .... NUCLEAR
thicket ...... CHAPARRAL
white .... ROBLE
Oakley, rifle expert ... ANNIE
slang .... PASS
oaks, thicket of ... CHAPARRAL
oakum .... FIBER
seal with .... CALK
oar .... PADDLE, SCULL, SWEEP, BLADE, PROPEL, ROW(ER), SPOON
blade ..... PALM, WASH
fulcrum .... THOLE
lock .... THOLE
part of .... LOOM, PALM, PEEL
shaped .... REMIPED
oarlock support ...... POPPET
oars, row of .... BANK
oarsman .... ROWER, STROKE
oasis .... WADI, WADY, SPRING, DOUMA
oast .... KILN, OVEN
oat ..... GRASS, CEREAL, REED
genus .... AVENA
grass, of the .. AVENACEOUS
rental .... AVENAGE
oatcake .... CAPER
oater .... HORSE OPERA
Oates of the Popish Plot ..... TITUS
oath .... VOW, CURSE, SWEARWORD, PLEDGE, PLIGHT
breaking of ... PERJURY
mild ...... EGAD, DRAT, GOSH, ZOUNDS
solemn ...... SACRAMENT
strong ... DAMN(ATION), HELL
take .... SWEAR, PROMISE
taker .... JURANT
testify under .... DEPOSE
oatmeal .... PORRIDGE
cake ...... SCONE, PONE
porridge .... BURGOO, STIRABOUT
oats .... FEED, AVENA
hulled, cracked .. GROATS
Oaxaca is in .... MEXICO
Ob river is in .... SIBERIA
Obadiah ... ABDIAS, PROPHET
obbligato ... ACCOMPANIMENT
obdurate .... STUBBORN, OBSTINATE, INFLEXIBLE,

MULISH, BULLHEADED, DOGGED
obeah ... MAGIC, WITCHCRAFT, FETISH, TALISMAN
obedience .... SUBMISSION
obedient .... AMENABLE, DOCILE, TRACTABLE, COMPLIANT, DUTIFUL
obeisance .... HOMAGE, DEFERENCE, CONGE(E), REVERENCE, CURTSY, BOW, SALAAM, GENUFLECTION
obelisk ...... OBELUS, PILLAR, NEEDLE, PYLON, SHAFT, MONOLITH
characters on .... HIEROGLYPH(IC)S
obelus ...... OBELISK, MARK, DAGGER
Oberammergau is in .... BAVARIA
religious play .. PASSION
Oberon .... FAIRY, KING
actress .... MERLE
domain of ... FAIRYLAND
wife of .... TITANIA
obese .... STOUT, CORPULENT, PUFFY, FAT, ADIPOSE, LIPAROUS, PURSY, FLESHY, PORTLY
obey ... MIND, HEED, SUBMIT, COMPLY, CARRY OUT, FOLLOW
obfuscate .... OBSCURE, DARKEN, BEWILDER, STUPEFY, CONFUSE
obi .... SASH, CHARM, OBEAH, FETISH, MAGIC, TALISMAN
obit .... (DEATH)NOTICE
obiter dictum .... ASIDE, COMMENT, REMARK
obituary .... NECROLOGY, (DEATH)NOTICE
words ..... IN MEMORIAM
object ... AIM, OPPOSE, THING, PURPOSE, PROTEST, TARGET, INTENT, END, MIND, KICK, GOAL, DEMUR, DISSENT
art ...... CURIO, BIBELOT
frivolously .... CAVIL
of attack .... TARGET
of manipulation .... PUPPET, MARIONETTE
of pursuit .... GAME, QUARRY
objection .. PROTEST, QUARREL, OPPOSITION, CAVIL, DEMURRER, KICK
objective ..... REAL, ACTUAL, DETACHED, GOAL, AIM, FAIR, PURPOSE, TARGET
objector ... DISSENTER, REBEL, DISSIDENT, OPPOSER
objet d'art ... FIGURINE, VASE
collector ..... VIRTUOSO
objurgate ... CHIDE, REBUKE, REPROVE, BERATE, UPBRAID
oblate .. MONK, NUN, ASCETIC
opposite of ..... PROLATE
oblation .... OFFERING
obligate .... BIND, OWE
obligated .... BOUND, INDEBTED
obligation .. DEBT, DUE, ONUS, BURDEN, DUTY, BOND, MUST
evade an .... WELSH
obligatory .... BINDING, BOUNDEN
oblige ... COMPEL, CONSTRAIN, FORCE
obliging ... HELPFUL, AMIABLE
oblique ... ASLANT, INCLINED, INDIRECT, EVASIVE, SKEW, AWRY, CANT
glance .... SQUINT
line .... BIAS
obliquely .... SIDEWAYS, SIDEWISE
obliterate .... EFFACE, EXPUNGE, RAZE, ERASE, SPONGE, BLOT OUT, DESTROY
oblivion .... PARDON, FORGETFULNESS, LETHE
drug of .... NEPENTHE
place of .... LIMBO
river of .... LETHE
oblivious .... FORGETFUL, HEEDLESS
oblong .... ELONGATED, ELLIPTICAL
obloquy ... CENSURE, INFAMY
obnoxious .... ODIOUS, UNPLEASANT, OFFENSIVE, HATEFUL, REPULSIVE
oboe ..... WOOD WIND, REED, BASSOON, BOMBARDON, SHAWN, HAUTBOY
oboli, six .... DRACHMA
obol(us) .... COIN
Obote, Uganda president ..... APOLO
Obregon, Mex. president ..... ALVARO
obscene ... LEWD, NAUGHTY, FILTHY, REPULSIVE, INDECENT, COARSE, FESCENNINE, SMUTTY, RAW, FOUL, GROSS
obscure ... NUBILOUS, DARK, MURKY, AMBIGUOUS, HIDDEN, OBFUSCATE, FOG, NAMELESS, ECLIPSE, GLOOMY, VAGUE, RECONDITE, OVERSHADOW, DIM, CRYPTIC, UNKNOWN
obscurity .... ANONYMITY
obsecration .... ENTREATY, PRAYER, PETITION
obsequies .... EXEQUY
obsequious .... SERVILE, SUBMISSIVE, FAWNING
observance .... CUSTOM, PRACTICE, RULE, RITE
for a dead .... WAKE
of formalities .. PUNCTILIO
observant .... WATCHFUL, ALERT, PERCEPTIVE, KEEN-EYED, ATTENTIVE
observation ...... ASSERTION, REMARK, COMMENT, ESPIAL
aircraft .... SCOUT
work .... SURVEY, RECONNAISSANCE
observatory, California ...... PALOMAR
concern of an ... PLANETS, STARS, WEATHER, MOON
observe .... NOTICE, SEE, CELEBRATE, ABIDE, REMARK, NOTE, DISCERN, EYE
secretly ..... SPY, STAG, STALK
observer .. LOOKOUT, WATCHER
turned toward .. OBVERSE
obsess .... HAUNT, BESET, PREOCCUPY, HARASS
obsessed ... RIDDEN, HIPPED
obsession ..... (MONO)MANIA, IDEE FIXE, FIXATION
subject of .. IDEA, DESIRE, EMOTION
obsidian .... LAVA, ROCK, PERLITE, TEKTITE
obsolete .... DISCARDED, PASSE, OUTMODED, ARCHAIC, OUT OF DATE, OLD, DISUSED, DATED
obstacle .... HITCH, IMPEDIMENT, HINDRANCE, LET, SNAG, BARRIER, BAR, HURDLE
course .... GANTLET
obstetrician .... ACCOUCHEUR
obstetrics, subject of .... CHILDBIRTH, MIDWIFERY, TOCOLOGY
obstinate .... STUBBORN, MULISH, HARD(HEADED), DOUR, WILLFUL, PIGHEADED, DOGGED, BULLHEADED, UNBENDING, ORNERY
obstreperous .... NOISY, UNRULY, VOCIFEROUS, BOISTEROUS
obstruct .. DAM, BLOCK, CLOG, IMPEDE, STOP UP, HINDER, BAR, CHECK, OPPILATE, CHOKE
obstruction ...... HINDRANCE, OBSTACLE, BARRIER
obstructionist's trick .... FILIBUSTER
obtain .... EARN, WIN, PROCURE, PREVAIL, GET, FANG, DERIVE, GAIN, SECURE
obtainable .... AVAILABLE
obtected thing .... PUPA
obtest .... BEG(FOR), BESEECH, ENTREAT
obtrude ..... MEDDLE, EJECT, IMPOSE
obtund .... BLUNT, DULL, DEADEN
obturate ...... STOP UP, PLUG, CLOSE
obtuse ... BLUNT, DULL, DENSE
obverse ...... COUNTERPART, FRONT
opposite of ..... REVERSE, VERSO
obviate .... PREVENT
obvious ..... EVIDENT, PLAIN, PATENT, PALPABLE
not .... SUBTLE, SUBTILE

oca .... OXALIS
ocarina, shape of .... POTATO
O'Casey, Irish dramatist .... SEAN
occasion .... EVENT, OPPORTUNITY, TIME, HAPPENING, CAUSE, NONCE
occasional ... CASUAL, RARE, IRREGULAR, ODD, ORRA, SPORADIC
occasionally ...... SOMETIMES, NOW AND THEN
occident .... WEST
  opposite of ..... ORIENT
occidental .... HESPERIAN, WESTERN, PONENT
occipital protuberances .. INIA
occlude .... CLOSE, SHUT, BLOCK, ABSORB
occlusion .... SHUTDOWN
occult ..... CRYPTIC, MYSTIC, ORPHIC, ESOTERIC, HIDDEN, SECRET, MYSTERIOUS
  art ... MAGIC, ASTROLOGY, ALCHEMY
  knowledge .. GRAMARY(E)
  religious philosophy ..... CABALA
occultation ..... ECLIPSE, LOST
occultism .... CAB(B)ALA, KABALA, MAGIC, NUMEROLOGY
occupancy ... TENANCY, TERM
occupant .... TENANT, INMATE, HABITANT
occupation .... PURSUIT, BUSINESS, METIER, TRADE, EMPLOYMENT, TENURE, WORK, CALL(ING)
occupational disease, miner's .. SILICOSIS
occupied ... BUSY, ENGROSSED
occupier .... TENANT
occupy .... ENGAGE, FILL, POSSESS, LIVE IN, USE, EMPLOY, INVEST
  attention wholely .... ENGROSS
  the whole of .... MONOPOLIZE
occur ... BEFALL, LIGHT, EXIST, HAPPEN, COME, BETIDE, PASS
  again ... RECUR, REPEAT
  at the same time .... COINCIDE
  irregularly ... SPORADIC
  yearly .... ANNUAL
occurrence .... OCCASION, EVENT, HAPPENING, INCIDENT, CASE
  degree/extent of .... INCIDENCE
occurring every 8th day .... OCTAN
  5th day .... QUINTAN
  4th day .... QUARTAN
  3rd day .... TERTIAN
ocean ... EXPANSE, SEA, DEEP, BRINE, MAIN, ATLANTIC, INDIAN, ARCTIC, ANTARCTIC, PACIFIC
  current ..... UNDERTOW
  depression .... DEEP
  depth finder ...... SONAR
  fish ..... OPAH, SUNFISH, SHAD
  greyhound .. STEAMSHIP, LINER
  of the .... MARINE, THALASSIC
  of Storms' location ...... MOON
Oceania island .. MICRONESIA, MELANESIA, POLYNESIA
oceanic ...... VAST, PELAGIC
oceanid .... NYMPH
Oceanus .... TITAN, GOD
  domain of .... SEA
ocellated .... SPOTTED
ocellus .... SPOT, EYE(LET)
ocelot .... CAT
  cat like .... MARGAY
ocher .... CLAY, PIGMENT, YELLOW, SIL
  red ..... RUBRIC, TIVER, REDDLE, RADDLE
ochone .... ALAS
ochre .... ALMAGRA
Ochs, newspaper publisher .... ADOLPH
  folksinger .... PHIL
ocotillo .... PINE, PLANT
  ocrea .... SHEATH
octa, as combining form ...... EIGHT
octan .... FEVER
octave ..... EIGHT, OCTONARY, UTAS
Octavia's husband .. ANTHONY
octet(te) .... EIGHT
octo, combining form .. EIGHT
October 15 .... IDES
  flower .... COSMOS, CALENDULA
  Revolution leader .... LENIN, TROTSKY
octogenarian .... DOTARD
  age of .... EIGHTIES
octonary .... EIGHT, OGDOAD, OCTAVE
octopod .... OCTOPUS
octopus .... SQUID, OCTOPOD, DEVILFISH, MOLLUSK, POULPE
  arm of .... TENTACLE
  sucker of ... ACETABULUM
octoroon ..... METIS, MUSTEE, MESTEE
octroi .... TAX
octuple .... EIGHTFOLD
ocular .... VISUAL, LENS, EYESIGHT, OPTIC(AL)
oculi .... EYES
oculist's concern .... EYE
Ocypete .... HARPY
od, manifestation of .... MAGNETISM, HYPNOTISM
odalisque .... SLAVE, CONCUBINE
  place of .. ADA, ODA, IDA
odd .... EXTRA, OCCASIONAL, INCIDENTAL, AZYGOUS, QUAINT, SINGULAR, PECULIAR, RUM, DROLL, ORRA, QUEER, ECCENTRIC, STRANGE
  notion .... FREAK
  job .... CHAR(E)
  job man .... JACK
  slang ... BATTY, SCREWY
oddity ... FREAK, QUEERNESS, QUIRK, VAGARY
oddment ... SCRAP, LEFTOVER, REMNANT
odds .... ADVANTAGE
  and ends .... SCRAPS, REMNANTS, RUMMAGE, ETCETERAS, MANAVELINS
  companion of .... ENDS
ode .... POEM, HYMN
  division of .... STROPHE
odeon .... HALL, THEATRE
Oder, city on the ... BRESLAU, STETTIN
  tributary ...... WARTHE
odeum .... HALL
Odin ... WODEN, WOTAN, GOD
  concern of .. WAR, DEAD
  horse of .... SLEIPNER
  maiden of ... VALKYR(IE)
  parent of .... BOR
  son of ..... TIU, BALDER, TYR, THOR, VALI
  wife of .. FRIGG(A), JORD, FRIA
  wolf of ...... GERE, GERI
odious .... HATEFUL, OFFENSIVE, DISGUSTING, REPULSIVE, DETESTABLE, HEINOUS
odium ... HATRED, DISGRACE, INFAMY, APPROBIUM
odograph, kind of .... TAXIMETER
  record .... DISTANCE
odometer .... TAXIMETER
odontoid .... TOOTHLIKE
odontology .... DENTISTRY
  subject of .... TEETH
odontophore .... RADULA
odor .... SCENT, SMELL, AROMA, FRAGRANCE, NOSE
  disagreeable .... STENCH, STINK, F(O)ETOR
  musty .... FUNK
  pleasant .... INCENSE, FRAGRANCE
odorless .... AOSMIC
odorous .... AROMATIC, REDOLENT, FRAGRANT, FETID
Odysseus ..... ULYSSES, KING
  captor of ... POLYPHEMUS
  father of .... LAERTES
  protection against Circe .. MOLY
  realm of .... ITHACA
  wife of ...... PENELOPE
Odyssey ...... WANDERING, JOURNEY
  author of .... HOMER
  enchantress in .... CIRCE
  nymph .... CALYPSO
  queen in ..... PENELOPE
Oedipus, daughter of .... ANTIGONE
  father .... LAIUS
  mother of ...... JOCASTA
  son of ...... POLYNICES, ETEOCLES

wife of .... JOCASTA
oeil-de-boeuf ..... BULL'S-EYE, WINDOW
oeillade .... OGLE
oenology, subject of ... WINES
Oenone .... NYMPH
husband of ...... PARIS
rival of .... HELEN
oeuvres .... WORKS
of ...... FROM, THROUGH, BY, HAVING, ABOUT
a reign .. REGIME, REGNAL
autumn .... FALL
course: sl. ...... NATCH
each .... PER
no ___ ...... MOMENT, ACCOUNT, USE
old age ...... GERIATRICS
summer ...... (A)ESTIVAL
the world .... MUNDANE
off .... AGEE, AWAY, ABSENT, WRONG, IN ERROR
color .... RISQUE, INDECENT, OBSCENE
in nautical usage .... SEAWARD
Offenbach, composer .... JACQUES
offend ..... INSULT, OUTRAGE, AFFRONT, SLIGHT, MORTIFY, MIFF, HURT, PIQUE, HUFF
offender .... CULPRIT
offense .... CRIME, TRANSGRESSION, OUTRAGE, FELONY, SIN, UMBRAGE, RESENTMENT, DELICT
in law .... DELICT
minor .... MISDEMEANOR
official overlooking of ... OBLIVION
offensive .... UNSAVORY, NOISOME, UGLY, ODIOUS, REPULSIVE, ATTACK, FULSOME
for quick victory .... BLITZ(KRIEG)
to morals ...... OBSCENE, INDECENT
offer .... BID, PROFFER, TENDER, PRESENT, PROPOSE, SUGGEST(ION), PROPOSAL
final .... ULTIMATUM
offering ..... OBLATION, GIFT, CONTRIBUTION, TRIBUTE
burnt .... HOLOCAUST
in performance of vow ... CORBAN
to God .... CORBAN
offhand ... CASUAL, SLAPDASH, EXTEMPORE, IMPROMPTU, INFORMAL, CURT, AT ONCE
office ... SERVICE, DUTY, POST, ROLE, FUNCTION, POSITION, STAFF
holder ...... INCUMBENT
resign an .... DEMIT
wall sign .... THINK
officeholder .... IN
officer .... POLICEMAN, CONSTABLE
abbreviation .... NCO, COL, CAPT, MAJ, GEN, LT, LIEUT, ADM
assistant to an ..... AIDE
kind of .... WARRANT, TRUANT
medical .... CORONER
military .... LIEUTENANT, CAPTAIN, MAJOR, COLONEL, GENERAL, ADMIRAL
military police .. PROVOST
subordinate ...... AIDE, DEPUTY
officer's insignia .... INSIGNE, EAGLE, BAR
official .... AUTHORIZED, FORMAL, BUREAUCRAT
approval ... IMPRIMATUR, VISA
course ...... CHANNEL(S)
decree .... UKASE, IRADE, EDICT, RESCRIPT
denial .... DEMENTI
family, President's ...... CABINET
list .... CANON
notice .... MONITION
paper .... DOCUMENT
paper container .... HANAPER, HAMPER
routine ...... RED TAPE
seal .... SIGNET
self-important .. BASHAW, PANJANDRUM
snafu .... RED TAPE
statement .... BULLETIN, COMMUNIQUE
officialdom ... BUREAUCRACY
officiate ... PRESIDE, PERFORM
officious .... OBLIGING, MEDDLESOME, PUSHING, INFORMAL, GRATUITOUS, PRAGMATIC
offish .... ALOOF
offscouring .... FILTH, GARBAGE, REFUSE, RUBBISH
offset .... SPUR, BRANCH, BALANCE, COMPENSATE, (OFF)SHOOT
offshoot ..... BRANCH, SCION, STEM, ISSUE
offshore .... SEAWARD
O'Flaherty, author ..... LIAM
offspring ...... CHILD(REN), PROGENY, ISSUE, RESULT, PRODUCT
in womb .... FETUS
of mixed parentage ...... MUSTEE, MESTEE, MESTIZO, MULATTO, OCTOROON
oft .... OFTEN
Ogasawara island .... BONIN
Ogden ___ .... NASH
ogdoad ... EIGHT, OCTONARY
ogee .... MOLDING
molding .... TALON
ogle ... OEILLADE, EYE, LEER, GLAD EYE
Ogpu .... GAYPAY-OO
predecessor of ... CHEKA
ogre .... MONSTER, GIANT, BLUNDERBORE
Ohio capital ..... COLUMBUS
city ... TOLEDO, AKRON, CLEVELAND, ELYRIA, CINCINNATI, PARMA, BEREA, LIMA, LORAIN, NEWARK, DAYTON, CANTON, MARION
native .... BUCKEYE
river ..... SCIOTO, MIAMI, WABASH
state bird ..... CARDINAL
state flower .. CARNATION
state gem stone ... FLINT
state nickname .... BUCKEYE
Ohm, physicist .... GEORG
oikology expert .... HOUSEKEEPER
oil ... IRONE, ACEITE, LUBE, PETROLEUM, PAINTING, ANOINT, ASARUM, LUBRICANT, SMEAR, SAFROL(E), LUBRICATE, BRIBE, BENNE, TUNG
antiseptic ... CARVACROL
aromatic .... BALSAM, ATTAR, LAVENDER
baptismal ...... CHRISM
billionaire ...... GETTY
bottle ... CRUET, CRUSE, CASTOR, AMPULLA
burner .... LAMP, CRESSET, CRAMMER
butter .... GHEE
colloquial .. FLATTER(Y)
combining form ... OLEO
container .. DRUM, CRUSE
country ... IRAN, KUWAIT
driller ..... WILDCATTER
drilling setup ...... RIG
essential .... ESSENCE
flask .... OLPE
flower ... ATTAR, NEROLI, ILANG-ILANG
fragrant .... ATTAR, NARD, ILANG-ILANG
fruit rind ..... BERGAMOT
king, so-called ... GETTY
lamp .... LUCIGEN
lubricating .... LUBE
of/obtained from .. OLEIC, UNGUINOUS
orange .... NEROLI
painting .... CANVAS
painting, board for ...... PANEL
pan .... SUMP
perfume-making ... BEN, ATTAR, BERGAMOT
plant ...... PATCHOULI, RAMTIL
refining waste ... SLUDGE
resinous .... BALSAM
rich country ...... IRAN, KUWAIT
rub with .... ANOINT
seed ... TIL, SESAME, RAPE, POON, RAMTIL, BEN(NE)
ship .... TANKER
skin .... SEBUM
solvent .... ACETONE
source .... OLIVE, COD, PEANUT, BLUBBER
trap of engine ..... SUMP
tree ...... TUNG, EBO(E)

well ... GUSHER, GASSER
oilbird .... GUACHARO
oiler .... TANKER, SHIP
oilseed ...... SESAME, TIL, BEN
oily ... SOAPY, GREASY, SLEEK, SLICK, SMOOTH, OLEAGINOUS, SEBACEOUS, UNCTUOUS, SLIPPERY, FATTY, PINGUID
hair liquid .... BRILLIANTINE
ointment ...... SALVE, NARD, POMADE, BALM, CALAMINE, SALVE, VASELINE, INUNCTION
base for .... LANOLIN(E)
Oise tributary .... AISNE
Ojibway .. CHIPPEWA, INDIAN
OK ... CORRECT, ALL RIGHT, ROGER, APPROVAL
Oka city .... OREL
okapi relative .... GIRAFFE
Okie is from ..... OKLAHOMA
Okinawa capital .... NAHA
Oklahama city .. ENID, TULSA, LAWTON, MUSKOGEE, ADA, CATOOSA
emigrant .... OKIE
Indian .... PONCA, PAWNEE, CHEROKEE
migratory worker .. OKIE
mountain .... OZARK
native .... SOONER, OKIE
part of ..... PANHANDLE
product .... OIL
state flower ... MISTLETOE
state nickname .. SOONER
state tree ...... REDBUD
Oklahoman ... OKIE, SOONER
okra ... GUMBO, PLANT, POD, SOUP, BENDY, MALLOW
old ..... WISE, AGED, SHABBY, YORE, ANTIQUE, ARCHAIC, DATED, SENILE, GRAY, WORN, ANCIENT, AULD
age .... SENILITY
age, study of .... NOSTOLOGY, GERIATRICS
campaigner .. WARHORSE, VET
car's noise ...... RATTLE
cloth measure ...... ELL
colloquial .... DEAR
country ... NATIVE LAND, MOTHERLAND
Dominion ..... VIRGINIA
dress .... RAG
fashioned .... PASSE, DATED, COCKTAIL, SQUARE, DEMODE, FUSTY
fashioned person .... FUDDY-DUDDY
Glory .... FLAG, STARS AND STRIPES
growing ..... SENESCENT, AGING
hand .... EXPERT, VET(ERAN), STAGER
Harry .... SATAN, DEVIL
Hickory .... (ANDREW) JACKSON
lady: sl. ... WIFE, MOTHER
maid .... SPINSTER
man .... GAFFER, GEEZER, FATHER, HUSBAND, BOSS
movies .... SILENTS
salt .... TAR
Nick ...... DEVIL, SATAN
Saxon poem ... HELIAND
Scratch ... SATAN, DEVIL
Sod .... ERIN
Testament addenda ...... APOCRYPHA
book .... JOB, JEREMIAH, PROVERBS, MICAH, TOBIT, JONAH, JUDGES, JOSHUA, ISAIAH
in Syriac .... PESHITO, PESHITTA
marginal notes .... MASORA(H)
Origen's edition ...... HEXAPLA
translation ... TARGUM
writer .... ELOHIST
timer .... VET(ERAN)
very ... HOARY, ANCIENT
woman .... CRONE, GAMMER, HAG
womanish .... ANILE
World lizard ...... SEPS
World, part of ..... ASIA, EUROPE, AFRICA
World plover .... PEWIT, LAPWING
World swan .. WHOOPER
olden .... ANCIENT
older .... SENIOR
oldest member .... DEAN
of course .... FIRST BORN
son .... HEIR, SCION
oldtimer .... VET(ERAN)
oldwife .... MENHADEN, TRIGGERFISH
oleaceous tree ... LILAC, ASH, FORSYTHIA, OLIVE
oleaginous .. OILY, UNCTUOUS, GREASY
oleander ... SHRUB, ROSEBAY
oleate .... ESTER, SALT
olefine .... ALKENE
olent .... FRAGRANT
oleo .... SPREAD, MARGARINE
oleoresin ...... ANIME, ELEMI, BALSAM, TOLU
olfaction .... SMELLING
olfactory organ .... NOSE
olibanum .... FRANKINCENSE, GUM RESIN, INCENSE
Oligocene epoch animal ...... MASTODON
olio .... STEW, MEDLEY, MISCELLANY, OLLA, MELANGE, MESS, SALMAGUNDI, HODGEPODGE
olive ... WREATH, OLEA(STER), TREE, RELISH
branch offering ... PEACE
drabs .... UNIFORM
genus .... OLEA
pimiento-stuffed .... PIMOLA
refuse .... BAGASSE
"Oliver Twist" character ..... FAGIN, BUMBLE, SIKES, DODGER, NANCY
olivine .... CHRYSOLITE, GARNET, PERIDOT
olla .... POT, JAR, STEW, JUG
ollapodrida ..... HASH, STEW, OLIO, MEDLEY, ASSORTMENT
ology .... SCIENCE
oloroso .... SHERRY
olvinic .... PERIDOTIC
Olympian .... EXALTED, GODLIKE, CELESTIAL, MAJESTIC, GOD
cupbearer .... GANYMEDE
queen .... HERA
Olympus ...... SKY, HEAVEN, MOUNT
mountain piled on ...... PELION, OSSA
Oman, capital ...... MUSCAT, MASQAT
companion of ... MUSCAT
sultan .... TAIMUR
Omar ____, general .... BRADLEY
Khayyam's birthplace .... NISHAPUR
country .... IRAN
work .... RUBAIYAT
omasum .... PSALTERIUM, MANYPLIES
omber ... CARD GAME, HOMBRE
ombre, trump in ..... MANILLA
omega .... END
omelet(te) .... EGG DISH
omen .... SIGN, PORTENT, AUGUR(Y), PRESAGE, AUSPICE, PRECURSOR
death's .... KNELL
omers, ten .... EPHA
ominous .... SINISTER, MENACING, FATEFUL, PORTENTOUS, GRAVE
omission .... OVERSIGHT, NEGLECT
sign of .... CARET
syllable .... APOCOPE
vowel .... ELISION
word .... ELLIPSIS
omit ...... SKIP, LEAVE OUT, NEGLECT, IGNORE, DELETE, PRETERMIT, ELIDE
Ommiad .... CALIPH
omnia vincit ____ ..... AMOR
omnibus .... (MOTOR)COACH, BUS
omnipotence .... GOD
omnipresent ...... IMMANENT, UBIQUITOUS
Omphale's domain .... LYDIA
servant .... HERCULES
Omri's son .... AHAB
on ..... UPON, ABOVE, ABOUT
dit ...... RUMOR, GOSSIP, REPORT
Egyptian .... HELIOPOLIS
one's guard ..... ALERT, WARY
right hand ...... DEXTER
tap .... NEXT
the blue .... ASEA
the face of document .... EX FACIE

the other hand ... AGAIN
the way ...... PREGNANT, EN ROUTE, OFF, IN TRANSIT
time ... DULY, PUNCTUAL
to .... AWARE, HEP
windward side .... AWEATHER, LEE
your way! .. SCRAM, SCAT

onager ...... ASS, CATAPULT, DONKEY

Onassis, (A.) nickname of .... ARI, DADDY-O
wife of .... JACKIE
yacht of ...... CHRISTINA

once .... ANES, ONE TIME, FORMER(LY), QUONDAM, WHILOM, ERST(WHILE)
all at .... SUDDENLY
more ... AGAIN, ENCORE
over .... GLANCE

oncoming ...... IMPENDING, APPROACH(ING)

one .... UNITED, UNDIVIDED, SAME, ACE, UNIT, SINGLE
against .... ANTI
and the other ...... BOTH
base hit .... SINGLE
behind another .. TANDEM
celled creature .... INFUSORIA, PROTOZOA, STENTOR, AM(O)EBA
combining form .. MONO, UNI
eyed giant ...... CYCLOPS
eyed god .... ODIN
footed .... UNIPED
god, belief in .... THEISM
horned animal .... UNICORN, BADAK, RHINO
horse .... PETTY
horse town ..... PODUNK
hundred: comb. form .... HECTO
hundred pounds .... CENTAL, CENTNER
hundred thousand, in India .... LAC
hundred years .... CENTURY, CENTENARY
legged .... UNIPOD
make ...... UNITE, WED
next to the last .. PENULT
of a trio ..... TOM, DICK, HARRY, CALM, COOL, COLLECTED, ATHOS, PORTHOS, ARAMIS
of mixed blood .... MESTIZO, METIS, QUADRON
of two .... EITHER
or another .... ANY
pound sterling .... QUID
prefix .... MONO, UNI
self: comb. form ... AUTO
sided .... EX PARTE, UNILATERAL, PARTIAL, PREJUDICIAL, BIASED, ROUT
spot .... ACE
square meter .... CENT(I)ARE
tenth are ...... DECIARE
thousand .... MIL
time .... FORMER
way sign ...... ARROW
eyed .... MONOCULAR
eyed giant ..... CYCLOPS

one's public ...... AUDIENCE, FOLLOWING
strong point ..... FORTE

Oneida .... INDIAN, IROQUOIS

oneirocritic's forte .. DREAMS

oneness ... UNITY, IDENTITY, SAMENESS

oner .... LONER

onerous .... OPPRESSIVE, BURDENSOME

onion .... SHALLOT, BULB, CIBOL, ALLIUM, ESCHALOT, LEEK, SCALLION, CEPA
plant ...... CHIVE, LEEK
sea .... SQUILL

onions, prepared with .... LYONNAISE

onionskin .... PAPER

onlooker .... SPECTATOR, BYSTANDER

only .... LONE, SINGLY, SOLE(LY), MERE(LY), BUT, SIMPLY

onomasticon ..... DICTIONARY

onomatoeia .... ECHOISM

onomatopoeic .... ECHOIC

Onondaga .... INDIAN, IROQUOIS, LAKE

onrush .... FLOW, DASH, STAMPEDE, BIRR

onset ..... ASSAULT, ATTACK, START, BEGINNING

onslaught ..... ATTACK, RUSH, CHARGE, ONSET, ASSAULT

Ontario ..... LAKE, PROVINCE
capital of ...... TORONTO
city .... KINGSTON, LONDON
lake on .... OSWEGO

onto ... AWARE, COGNIZANT, HEP, CONVERSANT

onus .... BURDEN, DUTY, RESPONSIBILITY

onward ... ADVANCING, FORTH

onyx ... AGATE, GEM, NICOLO

oocyte .... GAMETE, EGG

oodles ... SCADS, LOTS, MANY, SLEWS

oolite .... LIMESTONE

oology, subject of .... (BIRD'S) EGGS

oolong .... TEA

Oom Paul .... KRUGER

oomiak ..... UMIAK, KAYAK, CANOE

oomph .. SEX APPEAL, VIGOR

oorial .... SHA

oosperm ... ZYGOTE, OOSPORE

ootheca ... EGG CASE, OVISAC

ooze ...... LEAK, SLIME, BOG, MARSH, TRANSUDE, EXUDE, SLUDGE, MUD, PERMEATE, FLOW, PERCOLATE, GLEET, SWEAT, SEEP, SEDIMENT, EXUDATE, SOP, BLEED

oozy .... SLIMY, SLUDGY

opah .. SOKO, FISH, MOONFISH

opal ..... SILICA, GEM, RESIN, PITCH, HARLEQUIN, HYALITE, GIRASOL(E), ISOPYRE
fire .. GIRASOL(E), GIROSOL

opalescent ...... IRIDESCENT

opaline .... GLASS

opaque .... DARK, DULL, OBSCURE, OBTUSE

open ..... CLEAR, UNSEAL(ED), BARE, FREE, LIBERAL, GENEROUS, FRANK, CANDID, AVAILABLE, PUBLIC, UNFOLD, UNDO, BEGIN, START, DISCLOSE, EXPOSE(D), UNLOCK
air .... ALFRESCO, OUTDOOR(S)
and shut ...... OBVIOUS, SIMPLE
car .... PHAETON
country .... VELDT
eyed .... AWARE, AWAKE, WATCHFUL
handed .... LIBERAL, GENEROUS
hearted .... CANDID, KIND(LY), GENEROUS
minded .... PERVIOUS, AMENABLE
mouthed .... AGAPE
partly .... AJAR
sea .... MAIN
sesame .... PASSWORD
space in park .... CONCOURSE
to attack ... VULNERABLE
to choice ...... OPTIONAL
to debate .... MOOT
to the sky .... HYP(A)ETHRAL
wound .... SORE

opening ...... INAUGURATION, GAP, APERTURE, CHANCE, START, ORIFICE, VACANCY, PORE, SLOT, HOLE, MOUTH
in chess .... GAMBIT
small ..... OSTIOLE, PORE, ORIFICE, CRANNY

openings, in zoology .. STOMATA

opera .... NORMA, AIDA, LA BOHEME, MIKADO, RIENZI, THAIS, FIDELIO, FAUST, MANON, TOSCA, SALOME, ERNANI, CARMEN
box .... LOGE
comic .... BOUFFE
comic singer ..... BUFFO
company director .... IMPRESARIO
composer ...... WAGNER, PUCCINI, VERDI, ROSSINI, BIZET, MENOTTI, MASSENET, GOUNOD, MOZART, HANDEL
describing an ... COMIC, HORSE, SOAP
glass .... LORGNETTE, BINOCULARS
hat ...... GIBUS, TOPPER
heroine .... ISOLDE,

SENTA, ELSA, MIMI, CIO CIO SAN, AIDA, PAMINA
highlight .... ARIA
horse .... OATER
house ...... MET, SCALA
singer .... CALLAS, NILSSON, PONS, CHALIAPIN, PINZA, TUCKER, STEVENS, MELBA, EAMES, ALDA, STEBER, GARDEN, TEBALDI, CABALLE
singular of .... OPUS
solo ..... ARIA, CAVATINA
star .. DIVA, PRIMA DONNA
text of .... LIBRETTO
operate ... RUN, TEND, WORK, ACT, CONDUCT, MANAGE
against .... MILITATE
operatic character .... BUFFO
prince .... IGOR
slave .... AIDA
operation ... PROJECT, ACTION
operative .... EFFECTIVE, DETECTIVE, SPY, WORKER
operator .... AGENT
operculum .... FLAP, LID
operose ...... LABORED, BUSY
operetta composer ..... FRIML
Ophelia's love ...... HAMLET
parent .... POLONIUS
ophidian ..... REPTILE, SNAKE, SERPENT, COBRA, ASP
Ophir's wealth .... GOLD
ophthalmologist ..... OCULIST
ophthalmology, subject of .... EYE, VISION, SIGHT
opinion ...... BELIEF, NOTION, CONVICTION, SENTIMENT, TENET, DOOM, JUDGMENT, IMPRESSION, EVALUATION, THOUGHT, PERSUASION
general ..... CONSENSUS
man .... POLLSTER, POLL-TAKER
opposing .... HERESY
united in ... CONSENTIENT
opinionated ...... DOGMATIC, RABID
opium ..... DRUG, NARCOTIC, AFYON
addict .... (DOPE)FIEND, JUNKY, NOSCAPINE, PARAVERINE
alkaloid .... CODEINE, MORPHINE, CODEA
derivative ...... HEROIN, MORPHINE, CODEINE
seed .... MAW
seller .... PUSHER
source .... POPPY
tincture of .. LA(U)DANUM, PAREGORIC
opossum .... YAPO(C)K, MARSUPIAL, QUICA
place of young of .... POUCH
play .... DEAD, FEIGN
oppidan .... URBAN
oppilate ... OBSTRUCT, BLOCK
opponent .... ADVERSARY, ANTAGONIST, FOE, ENEMY
opportune .... TIMELY, PROPITIOUS, APROPOS, SEASONABLE, WELL-TIMED, APT
opportunist .... TRIMMER, TIME-SERVER
opportunity .... CHANCE, OCCASION
oppose ...... RESIST, FACE, WITHSTAND, OBJECT, OPPUGN, DEFY, DARE, REPUGN
opposed ..... AGAINST, ANTI, CONTRARY
opposite .... FRONTING, ANTITHETIC, CONTRARY, REVERSE, ANTIPODE, VIS-A-VIS, FORNENT
belief .... HERESY
directly .. DIAMETRIC(AL), INVERSE
extremity .... POLE
number ... COUNTERPART
opposition ..... COMPETITION, RESISTANCE, HOSTILITY, CONTRAST
in ... ANTI, AGAINST, CON
party .... MINORITY
oppress .. PERSECUTE, BURDEN, TYRANNIZE, DISTRESS, GRIPE
oppressive ...... TYRANNICAL, ONEROUS
anything .... INCUBUS
oppressor .... TYRANT
opprobrious .... ABUSIVE, INFAMOUS
opprobrium ... INFAMY, SCORN, DISGRACE, ODIUM, SHAME
oppugn ... DISPUTE, CRITICIZE, CONTROVERT, OPPOSE
Ops .... RHEA, GODDESS
concern of ..... HARVEST
daughter of ...... CERES
husband of ..... SATURN
opt .... CHOOSE, SELECT, DECIDE
optic .... EYE
branch of ... CATOPTRICS
optical ...... OCULAR, VISUAL
aid .... MONOCLE, LORGNETTE, LORGNON, PINCENEZ
glass ... LENS, CONTACT
illusion .... MIRAGE
instrument .... ALIDADE, PERISCOPE, MICROSCOPE, TELESCOPE
instrument eyepiece ..... OCULAR
instrument lines .... RETICLE
optician .... OPTOMETRIST
optimistic .... HOPEFUL, ROSY, EXPECTANT, SANGUINE, ROSEATE
optimum .... BEST
option .... CHOICE
optional .... ELECTIVE
optometrist .... OPTICIAN
opulence .... RICHES, WEALTH
opulent ..... RICH, WEALTHY
opuntia .... TUNA, CACTUS
opus ...... WORK, SYMPHONY, OPERA, COMPOSITION
plural of .... OPERA
oquassa .... TROUT
or ...... CONJUNCTION, GOLD, YELLOW
ora .... MOUTHS, COIN
orach(e) .... SPINACH, GOOSEFOOT
oracle .. SEER, HOLY OF HOLIES, DELOS, AUGUR
giver .... FAUNUS
modern ..... COMPUTER
seat .... DODONA
site of .... DELPHI
woman ..... SYBIL, SIBYL
oracular .... SYBILLINE, ORPHIC, PYTHONIC, PROPHETIC, MYSTERIOUS, WISE, VATIC
oral ...... STOMATIC, SPOKEN, VERBAL, VOCAL
pledge ... PAROLE, WORD
orale .... FANON
orally .. .. PAROL, VIVA VOCE
Oran is in .... ALGERIA
orange .... TANGERINE, CITRUS, MANDARIN
flower oil .... NEROLI
genus .... CITRUS
juice squeezer .. REAMER
mock .... SYRINGA
of an .... CITRIC
peel .... ZEST
pekoe .... TEA
preserve .... MARMALADE
River tributary .... VAAL
seed .... PIP
variety .... MICHAEL
yellow .... LUTEOUS, CROCUS, SAFFRON
orangewood .... HEDGE
orangutan .... APE, MIAS
habitat .... BORNEO, SUMATRA
orate ... DECLAIM, SPEECHIFY, MOUTH, PERORATE
oration ..... SPEECH, ADDRESS
orator ..... SPEAKER, CICERO, OTIS, BRYAN, RHETOR
in law ...... PETITIONER, PLAINTIFF
oratorio lyrics ...... LIBRETTO
part of ...... ARIA, DUET, TRIO, CAVATINA
oratory ... CHAPEL, CHANTRY
fathers, founder of .. NERI
master of ..... RHETOR
orb ..... SPHERE, GLOBE, EYE, SUN, MOON
orbit ...... PATH, EYE SOCKET
heavenly body's .. CYCLE
orbital point ... APSIS, APOGEE, APSE, PERIGEE
orc .... GRAMPUS, WHALE
kind of .... DOLPHIN
orchard .... GARDEN
orchal .... LICHEN
orchestra .... BAND, PARQUET
circle .... PARTERRE
leader .... CUGAT, DUCHIN, JAMES, VALLEE, SHAW

platform .... BANDSTAND
section ... BRASS, WINDS, TRAPS, STRINGS, PERCUSSION
space for .... PIT
theater's ... MAIN FLOOR
orchestral section .... WINDS, STRINGS, BRASS, TRAPS, PERCUSSION
orchid ..... SATYR, EPIPHYTE, MOCCASIN, PUTTYROOT, FLOWER, ORCHIS, POGONIA, DICHEA, BUTTERFLY
climbing ...... VANILLA
genus .... DISA
petal .... LABELLUM
Philippine .... WALING-WALING
symbol of an .... LUXURY
third petal of .... LIP
tuber .... SALEP
orchil .... DYE, LICHEN
orchis .... ORCHID
Orcus ..... HADES, DIS, PLUTO
ordain ...... DECREE, ORDER, ENACT, PRESCRIBE, APPOINT
ordeal ... TRIAL, TRIBULATION, HARDSHIP, CRUCIBLE, EXPERIENCE
order .. SERIES, SYSTEM, CLASS, METHOD, DIRECT(ION), BID, INSTRUCT(ION), HEST, COMMISSION, LODGE, PRESCRIPT, PRESCRIBE, COSMOS, MANDATE, COMMAND
good .... EUTAXY
orderly .... TIDY, NEAT, PEACEABLY, SYSTEMATIC, ATTENDANT, AIDE, TRIM, METHODICAL
orders, military .... ANNOUNCEMENTS
ordinal .... NUMBER
number .... FIRST, SECOND, THIRD, FOURTH, FIFTH
suffix .... (E)TH
ordinance ..... LAW, STATUTE, CUSTOM, PRACTICE, RITE, COMMAND
ordinary .... TAVERN, CHAPLAIN, USUAL, NORMAL, REGULAR, COMMON, ROUTINE, VULGATE, BICYCLE, CUSTOMARY, MEDIAL, MEDIOCRE, MILL-RUN, AVERAGE
ordnance ...... ARMOR, GUNS, ARTILLERY, WEAPONRY
piece .... CANNON, MORTAR
ordure .... FILTH, DUNG, MANURE
ore .... MINERAL
analyze .... ASSAY
assaying ... CUPEL, TEST
bearing rock layer ...... LEDGE
bed of .... REEF
crushing machine . . STAMP
deposit ... LODE, POCKET
digger .... MINER
extract/refine ..... SMELT
fusing/extracting place .. SMELTERY
ground .... PULP
iron ...... OCHER, OCHRE
layer .... SEAM, STOPE
mercury ..... CINNABAR
refiner .... SMELTER
screening sieve .... TROMMEL
shovel for washing .. VAN
smelting product .. SPEISS
stratum of .... SEAM
test .... ASSAY
truck .... CORF
vein ...... LODE, STREAK
wagon .... CORF
washing container .. PAN
washing device ... DOLLY
washing trough .. STRAKE
worthless .... MATTE
oread .... NYMPH, NAIAD
oregano .... PLANT, MINT, MARJORAM
Oregon capital .... SALEM
city .... MEDFORD, PORTLAND, CORVALLIS, EUGENE
dam .... BONEVILLE, MCNARY
Indian .. KUSAN, CAYUSE, NEZ PERCE
mountain ..... CASCADE
river .... COLUMBIA, WILLAMETTE, KLAMATH
seaport .... ASTORIA
state nickname .. BEAVER
Trail users .... PIONEERS, SETTLERS
Orestes, parent of .... AGAMEMNON, CLYTEMNESTRA
sister of .... ELECTRA
wife of ...... HERMIONE
organ .... INSTRUMENT, PERIODICAL, MEANS, BOMBARDON, HARMONIUM
atrophied ...... VESTIGE
barrel ... HURDY-GURDY
bass stop ...... BOURDON
connecting tissue .. PONS
device .... STOP, PIPE, REED, TREMOLO
dislocation ... PROLAPSE
falling of ..... PROLAPSE, PTOSIS
grinder's assistant ...... MONKEY
keyboard ... MELODEON, HARMONIUM, ACCORDION, CLAVIER
loft .... GALLERY
matrix of .... STROMA
mouth ..... HARMONICA
of speech .... TONGUE
outgrowth ... APPENDIX
part ..... PIPE, CONSOLE, REED, PALLET, STOP
pipe .... FLUE, REED, MONTRE, LABIAL
pipe plug ...... TAMPION
place in church .... LOFT, GALLERY
point .... MUCRO
seed-bearing ..... PISTIL
stop ..... MELODIA, OBOE, DIAPASON, VIOLONE, CLARABELLA, LARIGOT, MONTRE, SEXT, QUINT, TREMOLO, GEMSHORN, CARILLON, CELESTA, GAMBE, BOMBARDE, VIOLA, BOURDON, DOLCAN, BASSOON, DULCIANA, DULCET, OCTAVE, TUBA, FLUTE
tip .... MUCRO
touch .. BARBEL, PALP(US)
transplantation pioneer .. BARNARD, DEBAKEY
vital .... HEART, LUNG, LIVER, KIDNEY, EYE
voice .... LARYNX
organic .. INHERENT, INBORN, CONSTITUTIONAL, FUNDAMENTAL
basis of bone .... OSSEIN
body .... ZOOID
compound ...... AMINE
in law ... FUNDAMENTAL
law .... CHARTER, CONSTITUTION
substance of ... MEDULLA
organism ... ANIMAL, PLANT, MONAD, MONAS
animal .... ZOOID
ductless .... SPLEEN
life cycle of ... ONTOGENY
living on another .... PARASITE
mode of formation ...... MORPHOSIS
one-celled .... AM(O)EBA, PARAMECIUM
reaction to stimulus ..... TAXIS
sea .... NEKTON
with parasite ..... HOST
organist .... BIGGS
organization .... CLUB, SOCIETY, UNION, CADRE, OUTFIT, SETUP
organize .... SYSTEMATIZE, INSTITUTE, ARRANGE, SET UP, FORM
organized movement ... DRIVE, CAMPAIGN, CRUSADE
orgeat .... SIRUP
orgy .... BINGE, REVELRY, CAROUSAL, BASH
oribi .... ANTELOPE
oriel .... (BAY)WINDOW
orient ..... ASIA, (FAR)EAST, PEARL, ADJUST, ADAPT
oriental ... EASTERN, BRIGHT, ASIAN, ASIATIC, CHINESE, JAPANESE
alcoholic drink .... SAKE, ARRACK
banker .... SHROFF
beverage ...... TEA, CHA
bow .... SALAAM
caravansary ... IMARET, SERAI, KHAN
cloth .... CAMLET
coin ... SEN, PICE, ANNA,

DINAR, RIN
decree .... FIRMAN
destiny .... KISMET
drink ... ARRACK, SAKE, TUBA
dwelling .... DAR
gate .... TORII
greeting .... SALAAM
inn .... SERAI, CARAVANSARY, IMARET, KHAN
laborer .... COOLIE, SACADA
litter .... KAGO, DOOLEE, PALANQUIN
market ..... SOOK, SOUK
money-changer .. SHROFF
name .... ALI, OMAR
nurse ..... AMA(H), AYAH, EYAH
opposite of .... OCCIDENTAL, WESTERN
palanquin ...... DOOLEE
porter .. HAMAL, HAMAUL
potentate .... AGA
potentate's chamberlain .... EUNUCH
prince .... AMEER
prison .... BAGNIO
punishment .. BASTINADO
rice dish .... PILAU
ruler ...... SHAH, KHAN, SULTAN, RAJAH, NAWAB
ruler's decree ... FIRMAN
salute .... SALAAM, KOWTOW
seed .... SESAME
serai .... IMARET, INN, KHAN
ship .... GRAB
tambourine ..... DAIRA
taxi .... RICKSHA
title ...... BABA, RAJAH
topaz ...... CORUNDUM
trousers ...... PAJAMAS, PYJAMAS
weight ..... CATTY, TAEL, ROTL, PICUL
wind .... MONSOON

orientate .... ADJUST, FAMILIARIZE
orientation of sorts .. BRIEFING
orifice ...... PORE, SPIRACLE, STOMA, OPENING, MOUTH, OUTLET, VENT, HOLE, OSTIOLE
oriflamme .... STANDARD, ENSIGN, BANNER
origan .... MARJORAM
Origen, for one .. THEOLOGIAN
origin .... SOURCE, BIRTH, PARENTAGE, ANCESTRY, LINEAGE, SEED, BEGINNING, ROOT, CAUSE, GERM, GENESIS
having single .... MONOGENIC
of the .... GENETIC
original ..... FIRST, EARLIEST, NOVEL, NEW, INITIAL, NATIVE, PRISTINE
native ...... ABORIGINE
sin .... REBELLION
sinner, alleged .... ADAM, EVE
originally .. CHIEFLY, INITIALLY
originate ... CREATE, INVENT, START, BEGIN, (A)RISE
Orinoco River tributary ...... APURE
oriole ...... TROUPIAL, BIRD, LORIOT, HANGBIRD, HANGNEST, GOLDENROBIN
kin of .... STARLING
Orion .... HUNTER, CONSTELLATION
lover/killer of ... DIANA
star ... RIGEL, BETELGEUSE
orison(s) .... PRAYER
Orkney county seat .... KIRKWALL
fishing waters ..... HAAF
inlet .... VOE
island .... POMONA
Islands channel .... SCAPA FLOW
Orlando .... ROLAND
servant of, in *As You Like It* .... ADAM
orle .... BEARING
Orleans heroine .. JOAN OF ARC
orlon .... FIBER, FABRIC
orlop .... DECK
ormer .... (EAR)SHELL
ormolu .... GOLD MOSAIC, ALLOY
ornament .... ADORN(MENT), DECORATION, SPANGLE, EMBOSS, DECOR(ATE), BEAUTIFY
by engraving .... CHASE
cheap .. GAUD, GEWGAW, BAUBLE, TRINKET
drop-like .... GUTTA
in low relief ... ANAGLYPH
metal .... CHASE, EMBOSS, ETCH, ENGRAVE
perforated .... PINK
showy ... GAUD, BAUBLE, GEWGAW
with needlework .... EMBROIDER
ornamental ..... DECORATIVE, FANCY
altar cloth ..... DOSSAL, DOSSEL
article, small .... KNICKNACK
band .... SASH
belt .... SASH
border .... DADO
bracket .... CONSOLE
braid .... LACE
button .... STUD
clasp ...... CHATELAINE
collar .... CARCANET
dish .... EPERGNE
garden area ... PARTERRE
lacing .... PICOT
metal foil .... TINSEL
needlework .... EMBROIDERY
plasterwork .... PARGET
ribbon .... SASH
shrub .... HENNA
tuft of cords .... TASSEL
tuft of silk ..... POMPON
upholstery ..... DOSSAL, DOSSEL
vessel .... VASE
ornate .. SHOWY, ELABORATE, BAROQUE, FLAMBOYANT, FLORID, FLOWERY, FANCY, PURPLE, AUREATE
ornery .... OBSTINATE, ORDINARY, STUBBORN, MULISH, TESTY, BASE, QUARRELSOME
person .... CURMUDGEON
ornis .... AVIFAUNA, BIRDS
ornithologist .... AUDUBON
ornithology, subject of .. BIRDS
ornithopod .... DINOSAUR
ornithorhynchus ... PLATYPUS, DUCKBILL
oro .... GOLD
as combining form ...... MOUNTAIN
de ____ .... PLATA
orogeny, result of .. MOUNTAIN
orographical subject .... MOUNTAINS
oroide .... ALLOY
orology, subject of .... MOUNTAINS
orotund .... RESONANT, BOMBASTIC, POMPOUS, MELLOW, SHOWY
orphan .... WAIF
Jane's family .... EYRIA
orphanage .... ASYLUM
Orpheus, for one .. MUSICIAN
instrument of ..... LYRE
wife of .... EURYDICE
orphic ... OCCULT, ORACULAR, MYSTIC
orpiment .... PIGMENT
orpin(e) .... STONECROP
orra .... ODD, EXTRA
orrery .... PLANETARIUM
sight ...... PLANET, STAR, MOON, COMET
orris, orrice ..... PLANT, IRIS
Orson, actor .... WELLES
ort ..... CRUMB, FRAGMENT, LEFTOVER, SCRAP, REMNANT
orthodox ... CONVENTIONAL, PROPER
Eastern church diocese .. EPARCHY
opposite of .. HETERODOX
orthoepy .... PHONOLOGY
orthographer .... SPELLER
orthopedist's concern .. BONES
orthopteron .... INSECT, COCKROACH, CRICKET
ortolan ..... BUNTING, SORA, BOBOLINK
oryx .... ANTELOPE, GEMSBOK
os ... BONE, MOUTH, OPENING, ESKER
Osage .... INDIAN, SIOUX
Osaka Bay port .... KOBE
location of ..... HONSHU
Oscar .... STATUETTE, AWARD
sister of ... EMMY, TONY
Osceola's tribe .... SEMINOLE
oscillate ..... VIBRATE, SWING, SWAY, WAVE, LIBRATE, WAG

oscillating device .... ELECTRIC FAN
oscillation transformer .... JIGGER
oscine .... FINCH, LARK, BUNTING, SHRIKE, TANAGER, CROW
oscitancy ... APATHY, STUPOR, DROWSINESS
oscitate .... YAWN, GAPE
osculate ... KISS, TOUCH, BUSS, SMACK
osculation .... KISS(ING), CONTACT
osier ..... SALLOW, WILLOW, DOGWOOD, ROD, WAND
twig .... WITHE
Osiris' brother ..... ISIS, SET
emblem .... APIS
husband .... ISIS
son .... HORUS
Oslo .... CHRISTIANIA
Osman soubriquet .... CONQUEROR
empire founded by ...... OTTOMAN
Osmanli ..... OTTOMAN, TURK
osmund .... FERN
osprey ..... HAWK, OSSIFRAGE
Ossa's companion .... PELION
osseous .... BONY, OSTEAL
ossicle .... (EAR)BONE
ossifrage ..... OSPREY, HAWK, LAMMERGEIER
Ossining institution .... SING SING
ossuary .... URN, VAULT
content of .... BONES
osteal .... BONY, OSSEOUS
ostensible .... SEEMING, APPARENT
ostentation .... POMP, SHOWINESS, GLOSS, PARADE, SPLURGE, EXHIBITION, DISPLAY
ostentatious .... SHOWY, PRETENTIOUS, ARTY, GAUDY
show ..... POMP, PARADE
osteo: comb. form ... BONE(S)
osteoid .... BONE-LIKE
ostiole .... STOMA, PORE, ORIFICE, OPENING
osteoma .... TUMOR
Osterreich .... AUSTRIA
ostiary .... GUARD
ostler .... STABLEMAN
ostracism .. EXILE, EXCLUSION, REJECTION
ostracize .... REJECT, BANISH, EXCLUDE, BAR, SHUT OUT
ostrich .... RHEA, RATITE, NANDU
bird like .... EM(E)U, CASSOWARY
kin of .... TINAMOU
Oswego .... TEA
tea .... MONARDA, BEE BALM
Otaheite .... TAHITI
otalgia .... EARACHE
Ot(h)ello ... MOOR, TRAGEDY, OPERA
opera composer .. VERDI
tormentor of ...... IAGO
wife of ...... DESDEMONA
other ..... ELSE, ADDITIONAL, DIFFERENT
combining form .... HETER(O), ALLO
others, and ..... ET AL, REST
otherwise .. ELSE, DIFFERENTLY
Othin .... ODIN
Othman .... OTTOMAN, OSMAN
otic ...... AURAL, AUDITORY
otiose .... IDLE, USELESS, FUTILE, INDOLENT, VAIN, STERILE
Otis ____, Cornelia .. SKINNER
otological subject .... EAR
otologist .... AURIST
concern of ... EAR(ACHE)
Ottawa .. INDIAN, ALGONQUIN
Ottawan chief ..... PONTIAC
otter .... FUR, MAMMAL, BROADTAIL
genus .... LUTRA
relative of ..... WEASEL, MINK, SKUNK
ottoman ..... OTHMAN, TURK, POUF, (FOOT)STOOL, SEAT, DIVAN, COUCH, FABRIC, SILK
court .... PORTE
Empire capital .... CONSTANTINOPLE
Empire founder .. OSMAN
leader .... OSMAN
non-Moslem ...... RAIA
official .... PASHA
standard .... ALEM
sultan .... SULEIMAN
Turkish government .... PORTE
Ouachita River .... WASHITA
ouananiche .... SALMON
oubliette .... DUNGEON
ouch .... BROOCH, EXCLAMATION, BUCKLE, CLASP
ought ... ANYTHING, AT ALL, CIPHER, NAUGHT, ZERO
oui .... YES
ouija equipment .. PLANCHETTE, BOARD
user of .... SPIRITUALIST
ounce ..... (SNOW) LEOPARD, WEIGHT, ONS
ouphe .... ELF, GOBLIN
Our Lady .... MARY, NOTRE DAME
ourari .... CURARE
oust .... EXPEL, EJECT, EVICT, DISPOSSESS, FORCE OUT, BOUNCE
ouster ... EVICTOR, DISMISSAL
out ..... EXTERNAL, BEGONE, NOT IN, NOT AT HOME, AWAY
and-out .... ARRANT, COMPLETE, RANK, CONFIRMED, UTTER, SHEER
of bed .... UP
of .... BEYOND
of date .... DEMODE
of gear .... CRANKY
of place .... INEPT
of practice ...... RUSTY
of sight .... PERDU(E)
of sort .... MOODY, INDISPOSED
of-the-way ... SECLUDED, REMOTE
of-town play opening ... PREVIEW
slang .... EXCUSE
way ...... EXIT, EGRESS
outage .... INTERRUPTION
outbreak .... ERUPTION, OCCURRENCE, RIOT, RASH
outbreeding .... EXOGAMY
outbuilding .... GARAGE, BARN, SHED
outburst ... STORM, TANTRUM, ERUPTION, FLAREUP, GUST
outcast ...... PARIAH, LEPER, WRETCH, EXILE
Biblical .... HAGAR, ISHMAEL(ITE)
outclass .... BEST, EXCEL, SURPASS
outcry .... SHOUT
outcome .... RESULT, UPSHOT, AFTERMATH, ISSUE, CONSEQUENCE, EFFECT
outcropping .... BASSET
outcry .... PROTEST, OBJECTION, CLAMOR, DIRDUM
outdated .... PASSE
outdo .... EXCEL, SURPASS, EXCEED
outdoor .... OPEN-AIR, ALFRESCO, ABROAD
bench .... EXEDRA
party ...... PICNIC, FETE
set .... LOCATION
stairs .... PERRON
theatre/restaurant ...... DRIVE-IN
time .... SUMMER
outer ..... EXTERNAL, ECTAL, EXTERIOR
covering ... TESTA, SKIN, COAT, HUSK, SHELL, CRUST, RIND, WRAP, COCOON
edge .... RIM, LIP
garment .... DOLMAN, KIMONO, SURTOUT, PALETOT, ROBE, (OVER)COAT, WRAP
layer of cells .. ECTODERM
Mongolia, capital of .... ULAN BATOR, URGA
space explorer .... ASTRONAUT, COSMONAUT
outfit .... SUIT, GARB, TURN-OUT, CAPARISON, RIG, GEAR, PARAPHERNALIA, GETUP, EQUIP(MENT), ORGANIZATION
bride's .... TROUSSEAU
to .... ACCOUTER, ACCOUTRE
outflank ... OUTWIT, THWART

outflow .... EFFLUX
outgo .... EXPENDITURE
outgoing .... GREGARIOUS, SOCIABLE
outgrowth .... RESULT, OFFSHOOT
outhouse .... PRIVY
outing ... AIRING, CLAMBAKE, TRIP, PICNIC, EXCURSION
outlander .... ALIEN, FOREIGNER, STRANGER
outlandish .. STRANGE, ALIEN, ABSURD, PECULIAR, BIZARRE, FANTASTIC
outlaw ... FUGITIVE, CRIMINAL, BRIGAND, PROSCRIBE, BANDIT, DESPERADO, HIGHWAYMAN, BAN, PRESCRIBE
outlay ...... APPROPRIATION, FUND
outlet ... EXIT, VENT, PASSAGE, MARKET, AGENCY
outline ... SCHEMA, DELINEATE, SKETCH, DRAW, ADUMBRATE, SUMMARY, RUN-DOWN
outlive ..... SURVIVE, OUTLAST
outlook .. VISTA, VIEW(POINT), PROSPECT, EXPECTATION
outlying .... REMOTE, OFF-CENTER
district .... SUBURB, PURLIEU
outmoded .... PASSE, OBSOLETE, DESUETE
outplay .... BEST, DEFEAT
outpost guard .... PICKET
outpour ..... RAIN, TORRENT
outpouring ... SPATE, TORRENT
output .... YIELD, PRODUCT(ION)
outrage ..... OFFENSE, INSULT, OFFEND, SCANDAL, ATROCITY
outrageous ...... ATROCIOUS, HEINOUS, FLAGRANT, DAMNED, MONSTROUS
outre ... BIZARRE, ECCENTRIC
outrigger ..... PROA, CANOE, PRAO, PRAU
outright ..... TOTAL, WHOLE, OPENLY, AT ONCE, COMPLETE
outrival .... ECLIPSE, SURPASS, EXCEL
outset ..... START, BEGINNING
outshine ...... EXCEL, ECLIPSE
outside: prefix .... ECTO
outsider ... ALIEN, STRANGER, NON-MEMBER
outsize .... LARGE
outskirts .... SUBURBS
outsmart .... OUTWIT
outspoken ... BLUNT, FRANK, OPEN, CANDID, ARTICULATE
outspread ... EXTEND, EXPAND
outstand .... SAIL
outstanding ..... PROMINENT, UNPAID, UNSETTLED, NOTABLE, (F)SPECIAL, EXCEPTIONAL
outstrip ...... BEST, EXCEL, SURPASS
outward ...... OUTER, VISIBLE, EXTERIOR, ECTAD
outwit ... OUTSMART, EUCHRE, FOIL, OVERCOME
outwork ... TRENCH, RAVELIN, FORTIFICATION, TENAIL(LE)
between bastions .... TENAIL(LE)
ouzel ... BLACKBIRD, THRUSH
water .... PIET
ova .... EGGS
oval .... EGG-SHAPED, ELLIPSOIDAL, ELLIPTIC(AL)
figure .... ELLIPSE
ovary .... GONAD
wall .... PERICARP, EPICARP, ENDOCARP, MESOCARP
ovate .... EGG-SHAPED
ovation ... APPLAUSE, PLAUDIT
oven ... OAST, KILN, FURNACE, LEER, MUFFLE
part of .... BROILER
portable .... BAKER
over ..... ABOVE, ATOP, UPON, MORE THAN, SURPLUS, FINISHED, ENDED, BEYOND, AGAIN, ACROSS
a ____ .... BARREL
again ... ENCORE, ANEW
combining form ... SUR, SUPRA, SUPER, HYPER
expose film ... SOLARIZE
nice .... FINICAL
the hill: colloq. ... AWOL
there: poetic .. YON(DER)
overabundance .... PLETHORA
overact .... EMOTE, HAM(FAT)
overacting .... HISTRIONIC
overadorned .... ORNATE
overage ..... SURPLUS, EXCESS
overall(s) .... SMOCK, DUNGAREES, LEVIS, JEANS
shirtlike .... FROCK
overawe ...... COW, SUBDUE, OVERCOME, DAUNT, BUFFALO
overbearing ...... ARROGANT, PROUD, CAVALIER, DOMINEERING, IMPERIOUS
overbold ..... RASH, RECKLESS
overcast .. LOWERING, CLOUDY, DARK, SEW
overcharge .. GOUGE, HOLD UP
overcoat .... PALETOT, INVERNESS, BENNY, ULSTER, SURTOUT, RAGLAN, CAPOTE
double-breasted .... REDINGOTE
loose .... BALMACAAN
overcome .. SUBDUE, CONQUER, MASTER, OVERWHELM, WIN, BEST, SURMOUNT, DEFEAT, BEAT
overconfident ...... COCKSURE
overcrowd .... CONGEST
overdue .... LATE, TARDY, BELATED
instalment ...... ARREAR
overfeed ..... GLUT, SURFEIT, SATIATE, GORGE, PAMPER, BATTEN
overfed .... GROSS
overflow ...... SPILL, FLOOD, RUN OVER, SPATE, DELUGE
overflowing ...... INUNDANT
with good spirits .... EXUBERANT
overhang ...... PROJECT, JUT, BEETLE
overhanging part of roof ...... EAVES
overhaul ... REPAIR, GAIN ON, OVERTAKE
overhead .... UPKEEP, ALOFT, COSTS, ABOVE
conveyor's car ..... TRAM
item .... RENT
overheat .... PARBOIL
overindulge ... SURFEIT, SATE, GLUT
overindulgence .... EXCESS
overjoy ...... ELATE, DELIGHT
overlap ...... EXTEND(OVER), IMBRICATE
overlapping ...... IMBRICATE, EQUITANT
overlay ...... CEIL, COVERING, PAVE
overleap ... PASS OVER, OMIT, SKIP
overlook ... IGNORE, NEGLECT, CONDONE, MISS, PRETERMIT
overlord .... LIEGE, BAN
overly .... TOO MUCH, EXCESSIVELY, INORDINATELY
overman ... LEADER, REFEREE, ARBITRATOR, ARBITER
overmatch ... CRUSH, EXCEED, SURPASS
overnice .... PRECISE, FASTIDIOUS, FINICKY
overpass ...... BRIDGE, SPAN, EXCEED
overpower .... BEAT, MASTER, SUBDUE, CONQUER, CONTROL
with light .... DAZZLE
overproud .... LOFTY
override .... NULLIFY, DISREGARD
overrule ... SET ASIDE, ANNUL, COUNTERMAND
overrun ...... INFEST, SWARM
overseas .... ABROAD, FOREIGN
oversee ...... WATCH, STEER, SUPERVISE, SUPERINTEND, SURVEY
overseer .... SUPERVISOR, TASKMASTER, REEVE, BAILIFF, BOSS, STEWARD, LEGREE
overshadow ... OBSCURE, DIM, ECLIPSE, DOMINATE
overshoe ... SANDAL, PATTEN, ZIPPER, ARCTIC, GALOSH(E), GOLOSH(E), RUBBERS
overshoes, rubber ...... GUMS
overshoot .... EXCEED
oversight ... LAPSE, SLIP(UP), MISTAKE
oversize .... LARGE, HUGE
overspend .... EXHAUST
overstate .... EXAGGERATE
overstrung ... TENSE, JITTERY, TAUT

overt .... OPEN, PUBLIC, OBSERVABLE
overtake .... CATCH UP, OVERHAUL
overthrow .... UPSET, OVERCOME, CONQUER, DEPOSE, DOWN, WORST, END, RUIN, TOPPLE, UNSEAT
overtones ..... IMPLICATIONS, SUGGESTIONS
overtop ..... EXCEL, SURPASS, TOWER
overtrained .... STALE
overture .... OFFER, PROPOSAL, PRELUDE
overturn ..... UPSET, CAPSIZE, TIP OVER
overweening ...... CONCEITED, ARROGANT
overwhelm ....CRUSH, DEFEAT, SWAMP, DELUGE
overwhelming desire ... ESTRUS
overwrought ...... FATIGUED, NERVOUS, EXCITED, ORNATE, ELABORATE
Ovid .... NASO
 work of .... METAMORPHOSES, ART OF LOVE
oviform .. EGG-SHAPED, OVOID, OVATE
ovine .... SHEEP(LIKE)
ovisac .... OOTHECA
ovoid ... EGG-SHAPED, OVATE, OVIFORM
ovolo ...... THUMB, MOLDING
ovule .... EGG, EMBRYO, SEED
 center of ...... NUCELLUS
 covering .... PRIMINE
 inner coat .... SECUNDINE
 stalk .... FUNICULUS
ovum .... EGG
 content .... YOLK
owed as a debt .... DUE
owing .... UNPAID, DUE
owl ..... MOMO, RURU, BIRD, UTUM
 barn .... MADGE
 horned .... BUBO
 leg feathers .... FLAG
 nocturnal ...... KAKAPO
 sound .... HOOT, ULULATION, WHOOP
 young .... OWLET
owlish appearance .... SOLEMN
own ... POSSESS, HOLD, HAVE, CONFESS, ADMIT, RECOGNIZE
owner .... PROPRIETOR, TITLEHOLDER, POSSESSOR
ownership .. TITLE, POSSESSION
 yield .... CEDE
ox .... BEEF, BULL(OCK), BOVINE, ANOA, STEER, BUFFALO, BANTENG
 Bunyan's .... BABE
 castrated ...... BULLOCK
 command to .. HAW, GEE
 disease .... GRAPE
 extinct ... URUS, AUROCHS
 eye .... DAISY
 eyed goddess ...... HERA
 hide thong ... RIEM, REIM
 hornless ...... POLLARD
 joint .... HOUGH
 like .... BOVINE
 like animal .... ZEBU
 meat, sun-dried .... BILTONG
 Paul Bunyan's ..... BABE
 stomach .... TRIPE
 tuberculosis ..... GRAPE
 wagon journey ..... TREK
 wild ... YAK, URUS, GAUR, GAYAL, REEM, ANOA, BUFFALO, AUROCHS, BISON
 young ..... STEER, STIRK
oxalis .... OCA
oxen .... KINE, NOWT
 stall .... CRIB
oxeye .. PLANT, DAISY, DUNLIN
oxeyed goddess .... HERA
oxford .... SHOE, COTTON, BROGAN
 bell .... GREAT TOM
 fellow .... DON
 grad .... AUNT
 movement .. BUCHMANISM
 movement leader .... BUCHMAN, KEBLE
 officer .... BEDEL(L), BEADLE
 scholar ..... DEMY, DON
 University fine .. SCONCE
 University Day .... ENCAENIA
 University student ...... OXONIAN
oxheart ... CHERRY, CABBAGE
oxide .... CALX
 cobalt .... ZAFFER
 lead .... MASSICOT, LITHARGE
oxidize .... CALCINE, RUST
oxlip ..... PRIMROSE, PLANT, FIVE-FINGER
oxpecker .... STARLING
oxter .... ARMPIT
oxtongue ... BUGLOSS, PLANT
oxygen, allotropic form ...... OZONE
 compound ...... OXIDE
 lack .... ANOXIA
 liquid .... LOX
oxygenate .... OXIDIZE, AERATE
oyez ... HEAR(YE), ATTENTION
oyster ... BIVALVE, MOLLUSK, SCALLOP, BLUEPOINT
 bed .... LAYER
 bed material .... CUTCH, CULCH
 delicacy .... STEW
 fish .... TAUTOG
 gatherer ..... TONGMAN
 grounds .... BED
 joint .... HINGE
 killing snail ...... DRILL
 plant .... SALSIFY, LUNGWORT
 product .... PEARL, NACRE
 root .... SALSIFY
 shell .... SHUCK, TEST
 spawn ... SPAT, CULTCH
 species ...... MOLLUSCA
 tank of .... STEW
 young .... SPAT
Oz, creator of .... BAUM
ozocerite ..... WAX, MALTHA
ozone .... AIR, OXYGEN, BLUE GAS
ozoniferous substance .. ETHER

P

P, Greek .... PI, RHO
 Hebrew .... PEH
 letter .... PEE
 38 .... (WAR)PLANE, LIGHTNING
pa .... FATHER
pabulum .. FOOD, SUSTENANCE
paca .... AGOUTI, CAVY, RODENT
pace ... STRIDE, RATE, SPEED, WALK, TEMPO, GAIT, STEP
 kind of ...... LOPE, TROT, AMBLE, RUN, SPRINT
 setter .... LEADER
Pacelli, Eugenio ... PIUS, POPE
pachyderm ...... ELEPHANT, RHINO(CEROS), HIPPO(POTAMUS)
 trap for .... KEDDAH, KHEDAH
Pacific .... OCEAN, CALM, TRANQUIL, PEACEFUL, IRENIC
 archipelago .... SULU
 coast evergreen .... REDWOOD, SEQUOIA, MADRONA
 discoverer ...... BALBOA
 island .... PALMYRA, YAP, TUTUILA, OAHU, TAHITI
 island group ..... SAMOA, SOLOMON, CAROLINE, PALAU, PELEW, HAWAII, RYUKYU, SAIPAN, PALAU, TUAMOTU, PAUMOTO OCEANIA, OCEANICA, MICRONESIA
 island tree .... LEHUA
 shrub .... SALAL
pacifier .... NIPPLE, SOP, (TEETHING) RING, APPEASER
pacifist: colloq. .... DOVE
pacify .... PLACATE, MOLLIFY, APPEASE, ALLAY, CONCILIATE, SOOTHE
pack .... STOW, WAD, GANG, TRUSS, LOAD, (EM)BALE, CRAM, BUNDLE, PRESS, SEND OFF, CROWD, MASS, BURDEN, GROUP,

COLLECTION, FARDEL, TAMP
animal .... MULE, ASS, BURRO, DONKEY, CAMEL, SUMPTER, LLAMA
animal cover ..... MANTA
animal basket ... DOSSER, PANNIER
animal belly band .... GIRTH
dishonestly ..... DEACON
girth .... CINCH
horse .... SUMPTER, DRUDGE
mule .... SUMPTER
of ___ .... LIES
of cards .... DECK
of dogs ...... CANAILLE, KENNEL
package .. PARCEL, BALE, BOX, CASE, CEROON, WRAP, BUNDLE, CARTON
packed tightly .... DENSE
packer .... CANNER
packet .... PARCEL, BOAT
boat .... PAQUEBOAT
packing .... CANNING
box .... CRATE
house .... CANNERY
material .. OAKUM, LUTE
packman .... PEDDLER
packsack .... KYACK
packsaddle .... APAREJO
pact ..... AGREEMENT, MISE, COVENANT, TREATY, COMPACT
Atlantic .... NATO
pad .... MAT, TABLET, WALK, HIGHWAYMAN, ROAD, WAY, PATH, PILLOW, SADDLE, CUSHION, FOOT(PRINT), STUFF
for dabbing powder ..... PUFF
gauze .... SPONGE
hippie's .. BED, APARTMENT
ink .... DABBER
medicated cloth .... COMPRESS
of hay .... WASE
silk .... VELURE
slang .... BED, APARTMENT
with powder ..... SACHET
padded cell inmate .. PRISONER, MADMAN
padding ...... COTTON, WAD, KAPOK, DOWN, FELT, STRAW
hair .... RAT
paddle ...... ROW, PROPEL, SPANK, SPOON, BAT, TODDLE, WADE, SCULL, OAR
pingpong .. BAT, RACKET
paddlefish .... SPOONBILL, GANOID
paddock .. PARK, FIELD, TOAD, FROG
paddy .... IRISH(MAN), RICE(FIELD)
wagon ... BLACK MARIA
paddywack ... RAGE, BEATING
Paderewski .... PIANIST, IGNACE
padishah ..... EMPEROR, KING, SULTAN
padlock .... CLOSE
padnag .... HORSE
Padova .... PADUA
padre ...... FATHER, PRIEST, CHAPLAIN
padrone ... MASTER, PATRON, INNKEEPER
Padua .... PADOVA
Padus .... PO(RIVER)
paean .... HYMN, SONG
Paestum .... PESTO
pagan ... ETHNIC, IDOLATOR, PAYNIM, INFIDEL, HEATHEN, GENTILE, NON-MOSLEM
Paganini, violinist .... NICOLO
page ... LEAF, FOLIO, EPISODE, RECORD, (FOOT)BOY, HENCHMAN, ATTENDANT, SERVANT, SUMMON
boy .... BUTTONS
left hand .... VERSO
ledger .... FOLIO
lineson .... LINAGE
number .... FOLIO
ornamental design ...... VIGNETTE
person served by .... KNIGHT, NOBLE
place of employment .... HOTEL, CONGRESS
right hand ...... RECTO
singer .... PATTI
size .... OCTAVO
slang .... BUTTONS
title .... RUBRIC
pageant ... EXHIBITION, POMP, SHOW, SPECTACLE, PARADE
pageantry .. SHOW, SPECTACLE, DISPLAY
pages .... RECORD
of history ...... ANNALS, CHRONICLES
set of 24 .... QUIRE
Paget, actress .... DEBRA
Pagliacci character, .. NEDDA, TONIO, CANIO, BEPPO, SILVIO
word .... RIDI
Pago Pago is in ...... SAMOA, TUTUILA
pagoda .... TAA, TEMPLE
pagurian ..... CRUSTACEAN, (HERMIT)CRAB, PAGURID
pah ..... EXCLAMATION, TUT, POOH
paid .... SETTLED, DISBURSED, DISCHARGED
pail .. BUCKET, PIGGIN, SKEEL, CANNIKIN, STOUP
paillasse .... MATTRESS
paillette .... SPANGLE
pain .... DISTRESS, ACHE, THROE, AIL, PANG, PENALTY, HURT, AGONY
abdominal .... COLIC
in the side .... STITCH
minor .... FLEABITE
sharp ..... TWINGE, ACHE
pained ...... OFFENDED, HURT
painful ...... SORE, IRKSOME, ACHY, BITTER
painkiller .... TONIC, OPIATE, NARCOTIC, DEMEROL, SEDATIVE, ANALGESIC, ANODYNE, ANESTHESIA, PAREGORIC
pains, great ... CARE, EFFORT
partner of .... ACHES
painstaking ..... ELABORATE, DILIGENT, CAREFUL
paint ..... ADORN, LIPSTICK, ROUGE, PIGMENT, DAUB, LIMN, FUCUS, STAIN, DEPICT, PORTRAY, COLOR, PICTURE, STIPPLE
badly .... DAUB
by machine ...... SPRAY
drier .... JAPAN
face ... ROUGE, COSMETIC, FARD
finishing oil ...... TUNG
first coat of .... PRIMING, BASE
grinder .... MULLER
ingredient ...... BARITE, TUNG
in dots .... STIPPLE
laid on thickly .. IMPASTO
remover ...... ACETONE
spreader .... SPATULA
wall .... PARGET
painted bunting .. NONPAREIL
painter .... STIPPLER, ARTIST, COUGAR, PANTHER, DALI, DEGAS, CEZANNE, VAN GOGH, MONET, PICASSO, TITIAN, RUBENS, GOYA, MIRO, REMBRANDT
designating one .. SUNDAY
handrest of .. MAULSTICK
mediocre .... DAUBER
of animals ... BONHEUR, LANDSEER
of presidents ... STUART
painting .... CANVAS, OIL, IMPASTO, PORTRAIT, LANDSCAPE,
board .... PALETTE, PALLET
cult .... DADA(ISM)
frame .... EASEL
genre .... ABSTRACT, CUBISTIC, ORIENTAL, SURREALISTIC
material .. DYE, PIGMENT, COSMETIC, ROUGE, CANVAS
medium .... OIL, PASTE, WATER COLOR
night scene ... NOCTURNE
on a board .... PANEL
on ceiling .... MURAL
plaster ... FRESCO, SECCO
small .... MINIATURE
stand .... EASEL
style ... GENRE, CLASSIC, DADAIST, ABSTRACT, GRISAILLE, GROTESQUE
technique ..... TEMPERA, IMPASTO, SECCO, FRESCO
tool .... BRUSH, ROLLER, SPRAY GUN
wall .... MURAL
water color .. AQUARELLE
paintings, collection of .... GALLERY

pair ... SPAN, BRACE, COUPLE, MATE, YOKE, TEAM, DUO, DUET, DUAD, DYAD
of harnessed animals .... YOKE
one of a ... MATE, MATCH
paired ..... TEAMED, COUPLED, MATED, GEMEL, JUGATE, MATCHED
paisley .... SHAWL
Paiute .... INDIAN
pajamas .... TROUSERS
Pakistan capital .... RAWALPINDI, ISLAMABAD
capital (East) .... DACCA
capital (West) ... LAHORE
city .... KARACHI, MULTAN, LAHORE, DACCA, SIALKOT, HYDERABAD, PESHAWAR
disputed territory .... KASHMIR
district .... SWAT
language ..... BENGALI, PUNJABI, URDU, HINDI
native ... SIKH, PATHAN, BENGALI
president .. AYUB, MIRZA JINNAH
province .. PUNJAB, SIND
river ... CHENAB, SUTLEJ
Pakistani .... PATHAN
U.N. president ... SHAHI
pal .... CULLY, HOBNOB
palace ...... COURT, VATICAN, MALACANANG, TUILERIES, SERAGLIO, EL PARDO, BUCKINGHAM
of a .... PALATIAL, PALATINATE
resident .. EMPEROR, KING, BISHOP, QUEEN, PRINCE(SS)
paladin .... PEER, KNIGHT, CHAMPION
paladins, Charlemagne's 12 ... DOUZEPERS
palaestra .... GYMNASIUM
pupil .... WRESTLER
palanquin ..... LITTER, JAUN, DOOLEE, KAGO
bearer .... SIRDAR, HAMA(U)L
palatable .... TASTY, FLAVORFUL, SAVORY, TOOTHSOME, SAPID, AGREEABLE
palatalized, in phonetics ...... MOUILLE
palate .... TASTE, LIKING, VELUM, UVULA
covering .... VELUM
palatial .... STATELY
Palatinate .... PFALZ
palatine .... CAPE, ROYAL
Palau Islands .... PELEW
palaver .... TALK, PARLEY, CHAT, CAJOLERY, WHEEDLE, FLATTER(Y), CONFERENCE, CHATTER
pale ... WAN, PALLID, FAINT, FEEBLE, STAKE, PICKET, FENCE, WHITE, BLANCH, SALLOW, ASHEN, LIVID, DIM, ORDINARY
face .... AMERICAN, WHITE MAN
yellow .... FLAXEN
palea .... DEWLAP, FOLD, BRACT, SCALE
paleface .... AMERICAN, WHITE(MAN)
paleness .... PALLOR
Paleolithic Age division ...... CHELLEAN
Palermo is in ____ .... SICILY
Palestine .... CANAAN, HOLY LAND, ISRAEL
animal .... DAMAN
capital .... JERUSALEM
city .... HAIFA, ACRE, SAMARIA, CANA, CAPERNAUM, MEGIDDO, GAZA, HEBRON
coin .... MIL
district ...... DECAPOLIS
division .... PERAEA, GALILEE, GILEAD
guerrilla ..... FEDAYEEN
guerrilla leader .. ARAFAT
guerrilla outfit .... EL FATAH, AL FATEH
inhabitants .... JEWS
kingdom ...... SAMARIA
mountain ...... GILEAD, NEBO, CARMEL, EBAL
plain .... SHARON
port ...... ACRE, JAFFA, HAIFA
tiger cub .... ASHBAL
town ...... SILOH, CANA
tribesman ..... ADANITE
village .... BETHEL
palestra .. SCHOOL, GYMNASIUM
trainee .... WRESTLER
paletot ... JACKET, OVERCOAT, GREATCOAT
palette ...... BOARD, COLORS
knife .... SPATULA
palfrey .... (SADDLE)HORSE
palimpsest .... TABLET, PARCHMENT
paling .... FENCING
palinode ... POEM, RETRACTION
palisade .... FENCE BAIL, ESPALIER
composition of ... STAKES
pall ... SATE, SATIATE, CLOAK, CLOY, WEARY, DISGUST, BORE, COVERING
Palladium of Rome ... ANCILE
Pallas ..... ATHENA, ASTEROID
statue .... PALLADIUM
pallbearer .... MOURNER
concern of ...... COFFIN
pallet ... BED, PATE, PALETTE, PLATFORM, PAWL, CLICK, MATTRESS
palliate .. ALLEVIATE, SOOTHE, EXCUSE, TEMPER, SALVE, EASE, EXTENUATE, MITIGATE
palliative .... BROMIDE, SEDATIVE, OPIATE
pallid ..... PALE, WAN, FAINT, SALLOW
pallium ... MANTLE, HIMATION
pallor .... PALENESS
palm ...... SAGO, NIPA, TREE, GOMUTI, TALIPOT, GRIGRI, ENG, ASSAI, COHUNE, PRIZE, VICTORY, TRIUMPH, COCO, NIKAU, COQUITO, JARA
African .... D(O)UM
Asiatic .. NIPA, PALMYRA, BETEL, CALAMI
betel ..... ARECA, BONGA
Brazilian .... ASSAI, BABASSU, JUPATI, CARNAUBA
bud .... CABBAGE
cabbage ...... PALMETTO
climbing .... RATTAN
cockatoo .... ARARA
coconut .... NIOG
crease .... LINE
drink ...... ASSAI, TUBA, NIPA, TODDY
fiber ...... GOMUTI, DOH, DATIL, BURI, RAFFIA
fruit .... DATE, DOUM, SASA, COCONUT
grease the .... BRIBE
leaf ... FROND, OLA, PAN, ATAP, NIPA
leaf fan .... TALIPOT, PUNKA(H)
leaf mat ... PETATE, YAPA
leaf's symbol ... VICTORY, TRIUMPH
leaves, plaited ... SENNIT
like plant .. CYCAD, ZAMIA
lily .... TI
liquor ..... TODDY, NIPA, BINO
Madagascar ..... RAFFIA
Malayan .... ARENG, GOMUTI
muscle ..... LUMBRICALIS
nipa .... AT(T)AP
nut .... COCO
of the hand ..... THENAR
of the hand's ..... VOLAR
off .... FOIST, FOB
palmyra .... TAL
pest .... GRUGRU
pith product ...... SAGO
plant resembling .. CYCAD
raised part of ... MOUNT
reader .... PALMIST, CHIROMANCER
sago .... GOMUTI, ARENG
sap liquor .. NIPA, TODDY
sap sugar ..... JAGGERY
shrub like .... ZAMIA
starch .... SAGO
stem ... CANE, RAT(T)AN, CAUDEX
stroke on the .... PANDY
sugar .... JAGGERY
tree .... PALMETTO, PALMYRA, DATE, TODDY, SAGO, RAFFIA, ARENG, GRIGRI, TALIPOT, ROYAL, DOUM, CALAMUS
tree bud .... CABBAGE
wax .... CARNAUBA
wine ..... TUBA, TODDY, GOMUTI, TAREE

Palma, capital of .... SANTA CRUZ
palmate .... WEB-FOOTED
palmer .... PILGRIM
palmetto .... SABAL, SERENOA
palmistry ...... CHIROMANCY
Palmyra .... TADMOR
leaf .... TAL, OLA(Y)
leaf fan ...... PUNKA(H)
queen of ...... ZENOBIA
palomino ..... HORSE, EQUINE
palp(us) .... FEELER, ANTENNA
palpable .... TANGIBLE, EVIDENT, OBVIOUS, MANIFEST
palpitate .... QUIVER, THROB, TREMBLE, FLUTTER, BEAT
palpitation .... THROB, SALTATION, BEATING
palpus ..... FEELER, ANTENNA
palsgrave .... COUNT
palsied .... PARALYZED, SHAKING
palsy ... PARALYSIS, PARALYZE
palter ... TRIFLE, QUIBBLE, LIE
paltry ... TRIVIAL, PICAYUNE, TRIFLING, PETTY, MEAN, SMALL
paludal .... MARSHY, BOGGY, SWAMPY, MALARIAL
paludism .... MALARIA
pam .... JACK, GAME
game like .... NAPOLEON
Pamir .... GALCHA
pampas .... PLAIN
country of ... ARGENTINA
native .... GAUCHO
weapon .... BOLAS
pampean .... INDIAN
pamper ..... COSHER, CODDLE, GRATIFY, FONDLE, PET, HUMOR, COSSET, SPOIL, GLUT, INDULGE
pampered .... SPOONFED
pampero .... WIND
pamphlet ... TRACT, FLYSHEET, TREATISE, BROCHURE
of poems .... CHAPBOOK
unstitched ..... FOLDER
Pamplona animal ...... TORO
Pan .... FAUNUS, SKILLET, DISH, GOD, GRIDDLE, ROTATE, (ICE)FLOE
concern of .. SHEPHERDS, FLOCKS
oil .... SUMP
out .... TRANSPIRE
slang .... FACE, CRITICIZE, RIB, ROAST
small .... PANNIKIN, PATELLA
warming .. CALEFACTORY
with perforated bottom .. COLANDER
panacea .... CURE-ALL, REMEDY, NOSTRUM, ELIXIR, CATHOLICON, MEDICINE, CURE
panache .... PLUME, FLAMBOYANCE, APLOMB
Panama ... HAT, CANAL, GULF, ISTHMUS, DAIREN
Canal locks ..... GATUN, MIRAFLORES
city ..... COLON, ANCON
coin .... BALBOA
explorer of ...... BALBOA
hat material ... JIPIJAPA
monetary unit ... BALBOA
port .... COLON
president .... ROBLES
river .... CHAGRES
town .... GATUN
tree ...... COPA, CATIVO
Panamanian jockey ... ICAZA
panatella .... CIGAR
Panay city .... ILOILO
pancake .... SLAPJACK, FLAPJACK, FRITTER
mix .... BATTER
Tuesday ..... MARDIGRAS
turner .... SPATULA
pancreas .... GLAND, SWEETBREAD
pancreatic enzyme .. AMYLASE, STEAPSIN
secretion .... INSULIN
panda .... BEARCAT, WAH
animal resembling the ... RACCOON
pandanus ... SCREW PINE, TREE
pandects .... LEGAL CODE
pandemic .... GENERAL, PREVALENT
pandemonium ... HELL, CHAOS, DISORDER, CONFUSION
dweller of .... DEMON
pander .... PIMP, CATER, PROCURER
Pandora .... BANDORE
pandour .... SOLDIER
pandowdy .... APPLE PIE, PUDDING
pane, glass .... QUARREL
round .... ROUNDEL
panegyric .... ELOGE, ENCOMIUM, PRAISE, EULOGY, TRIBUTE, LAUDATION
panegyrist ...... ENCOMIAST, EULOGIST
panel ...... SADDLE, VENIRE, JURY, JURORS
sunken .... COFFER
panelist .... JUROR
panes, frame for .... SASH
panetella .... CIGAR
pang .... DOLOR, THROE, TWINGE, PAIN, AGONY, ACHE
pangolin ... ANTEATER, MANIS
pangs of childbirth ... THROES
panhandle .... BEG
panhandler .... BEGGAR
panic ... FEAR, SCARE, FUNK, TERROR, GRASS, MILLET, BUTTON
result of ..... STAMPEDE, HYSTERICS
slang .... DELIGHT
panicle ..... RACEME, CLUSTER
pannier ..... BASKET, DOSSER
panocha ..... CANDY, SUGAR
panoply .... ARRAY
panorama .... VISTA, VIEW
Panpipe .... SYRINX
pansy ... VIOLA, HEARTSEASE, PENSE
slang .... QUEER
pant .... GASP, THROB, PULSATE, PUFF, HEAVE, HUFF
Pantagruel .... GIANT
companion of .. PANURGE
father of ... GARGANTUA
pantalets .... DRAWERS
pantaloons .... TROUSERS
Pantelleria .... COSYRA
pantheon ..... TEMPLE, TOMB
panther ... COUGAR, LEOPARD, JAGUAR, PARD, PUMA, PAINTER
panties .... DRAWERS, UNDERPANTS
raid for example .. PRANK
panting .... GASPING, HYPERPNEA, PUFFY
pantofle .... SLIPPER
pantomime .... MIMIST
game .... CHARADE
pantry .. BUTTERY, CUPBOARD, EWERY, AMBRY, CLOSET, SPENCE, SPENSE, LARDER
shelf item ... TEA CADDY
pants ... TROUSERS, DRAWERS, SLACKS
baby's .... SOAKERS
work .... LEVIS
pantywaist .... SISSY, WEAKLING
Panza, Don Quixote's squire .. SANCHO
panzer .... ARMORED
pap ..... NIPPLE, TEAT, MASH, PULP
papa ..... PAW, POP, FATHER, DAD(DY), PA
papain .... ENZYME
papal (see Pope) ... APOSTOLIC
ambassador ... NUNCIO, LEGATE
authority .... TIARA
bodyguards ...... SWISS
book of decrees .... DECRETALE
cape .... ORALE, FANO(N), FANUM, FANNEL, MOZ(Z)ETTA
chamberlain .... CAMERLINGO
Court .... CURIA, SEE
decree .... DECRETAL, BULL, RESCRIPT
envoy .... LEGATE
envoy, special .... ABLEGATE
letter .. ENCYCLICAL, BRIEF, BULL(A), BREVE, TOME
order .... RESCRIPT
palace .... VATICAN
rescript ...... MANDATE
scarf veil .... FANO(N), ORALE, FANNEL, FANUM
seal .... BULI(A)
skullcap ..... ZUCCHETTO
papaveraceous plant ... POPPY
papaverine .... OPIATE
papaw .... PAPAYA

papaya .... PA(W)PAW
enzyme .... PAPAIN
Papeete's location .... TAHITI
paper ...... ESSAY, WRITING, TREATISE, MONOGRAPH, WRAPPER, PASS, DAILY, SHEET, PELURE, CASSE, PAPIER, TAPA, THESIS, TRACT
ancient .... PAPYRUS
box for .... PAPETERIE
candy holder ... CORNET
cutter .... SLITTER, GUILLOTINE
damaged .... CASSE, RETREE
drawing .... ATLAS
fastener ... STAPLER, CLIP
filler .... KAOLIN(E)
for curling hair .... PAPILLOTE
gummed .... PASTER
hanging .... COLLAGE
holder .... FOLDER
kind of .... PAPYRUS, BOND, LINEN, FOOLSCAP, MANILA, TISSUE, CREPE
making material ... PULP, CELLULOSE, ESPARTO
match .... SPILL
measure ... REAM, QUIRE
money ..... BILL, SCRIP, NOTE, KALE, LETTUCE
nautilus ..... ARGONAUT, MOLLUSK
official ...... DOCUMENT
on .... THEORETICAL, IN THEORY
once folded ...... FOLIO
pulp, pressed .... PASTEBOARD
quantity of ...... REAM, BUNDLE, QUIRE
roll of .... BOLT
scrap of, sometimes ..... TREATY
seller .... NEWSBOY, STATIONER
shell .... MARRON
size .... ATLAS, FOOLSCAP, ROYAL, CAP, POTT, POST, FOLIO, CROWN, DEMY, IMPERIAL
small town ..... WEEKLY
spoiled .... SALLE, CASS(I)E, RETREE
sugar holder .... CORNET
untrimmed edge .... DECKLE, DECKEL
waterproofing substance .. PARAFFIN
white .... REPORT
wrapping .... KRAFT
writing ..... STATIONERY
papers .... CREDENTIALS, WRITINGS
Paphian .... EROTIC
papilla .... NIPPLE
papilloma .... TUMOR, WART, CORN
papillon .... SPANIEL
papillote .... CURLPAPER
pappy .... FATHER, DADDY, MUSHY, SOFT
paprika .... CONDIMENT, PIMIENTO
vitamin .... CITRIN
papule ...... BLISTER, PIMPLE
papyrus ..... SEDGE, BULRUSH
par ...... NORMAL, AVERAGE, STANDARD
avion ..... (BY) AIR MAIL
in golf .... BOGEY
one under .... BIRDIE
two under .... EAGLE
Para, capital of ...... BELEM
parable ... FABLE, SIMILITUDE, ALLEGORY, STORY, APOLOGUE
Talmud ... HAGGADA(H)
parabolic .... ALLEGORICAL
Paracelsus' remedy .... AZOTH
parachute ...... PATAGUIUM, PARAFOIL
gear .... HARNESS
jumper .... PARAMEDIC, STUNTMAN, PARATROOPER
release device .. RIP CORD
shape of ..... UMBRELLA
paraclete .... PLEADER, ADVOCATE, HOLY SPIRIT
parade .. MARCH, SHOW(OFF), REVIEW, FLAUNT, STRUT, CAVALCADE, WALK, DISPLAY, PROCESSION, PROMENADE
feature .... FLOAT
item .... FLOAT
march ...... GOOSESTEP
of cars ..... MOTORCADE
official .... MARSHAL
prefix .... CADE
parader .... MUMMER, MODEL
paradigm ... MODEL, PATTERN, EXAMPLE
paradisiac .... EDENIC
Paradise ..... HEAVEN, EDEN, ELYSIUM, UTOPIA
imaginary .. SHANGRILA
Lost character .... (ITH)URIEL, ADAM, EVE
paraffin .... WAX
parafoil .... PARACHUTE
inventor of ..... JALBERT
paragon ...... IDEAL, MODEL, PATTERN, DIAMOND, NON(E)SUCH
paragonite .... MICA
paragraph ...... ITEM, NOTE, CLAUSE
Paraguay capital ... ASUNCION
city .... VILLARICA, CONCEPCION
explorer of ...... CABOT
language .... GUARANI
monetary unit .. GUARANI
plains .... GRAN CHACO
president .... STROESSNER
river ...... PARANA, APA
tea .... MATE, YERBA
territory .... CHACO
wood .... QUEBRACHO
parakeet ...... BUDGERIGAR, PARROT, PAROQUET, BUDGIE
parallel .... COUNTERPART, MATCH, EQUAL
parallelogram ... RHOMB(US), RHOMBOID
remains of a .... GNOMON
paralysis ... PARESIS, STROKE, PARAPLEGIA, PTOSIS, PALSY, HEMIPLEGIA
combining form .. PLEGIA, PLEGY
infantile .... POLIO
partial, local .... CRAMPS
paralytic stroke ...... SHOCK
paralyze ...... NUMB, PALSY, SHOCK
Paramaribo is capital of ..... SURINAM
paramo .... PLAIN
paramount .... CHIEF, DOMINANT, SUPREME
paramour .... LOVER, MISTRESS, SWEETHEART, LEMAN, INAMORATA, MINION
Parana river tributary .... IGUASSU, IGUAZU
parang .... KNIFE
paranymph .... BEST MAN, BRIDESMAID
parapet ..... RAILING, WALL, BRATTICE
opening .... EMBRASURE
part .... MERLON
paraph .... FLOURISH
paraphernalia .... OUTFIT, GEAR, BELONGINGS, TRAPPINGS, EQUIPMENT
paraphrase .... REWORD(ING)
paraplegic .... PARALYTIC
paraquet .... PARROT
parasite .. TOADY, HANGER-ON, LEECH, DRONE, MOOCHER, SPONGE(R), WABBLE, TRENCHER, SYCOPHANT
animal .... ENTOZOON
blood .... TRYP
concern of a ...... HOST, MEAL TICKET
feeder of .... HOST
fish .... REMORA
fungus .... LICHEN
intestinal ..... HELMINTH, TAPEWORM
living inside plant/animal ENTOPHYTE, ENTEZOON
one-celled ... SPOROZOAN
outside body ... EPIZOON
plant ... LICHEN, APHID, MISTLETOE, BINE
root .... PINESAP
parasite's find .... HOST, MEAL TICKET
parasitic insect .... FLEA, MOSQUITO, LICE, GNAT, MITE, ACARID, CHIGOE, CHIGGER, APHID, LOUSE
fungus .... LICHEN
plant ... ORCHID, DODDER
worm .... LEECH, TRICHINA, NEMATODE, TREMATODS, FLUKE
parasol .... UMBRELLA, SUNSHADE

ant .... ATTA
paravane .... OTTER
parboil .... OVERHEAT, SCALD, CODDLE
Parcae .... FATES
parcel .... PACKAGE, LOT, BUNDLE, BUNCH, PART, (AP)PORTION, PACK(ET), PLAT
out .... METE, ALLOT
parch .... DRY, TORRIFY, TORREFY, HEAT
parched ...... TORRID, ARID, DRY, THIRSTY, ADUST, ANHYDROUS
parchment .... VELLUM, DIPLOMA, PAPYRUS, SHEEPSKIN, KIDSKIN, FOR(R)EL
inscribed twice .... PALIMPSEST
roll ...... SCROLL, PELL
scroll, Pentateuch .... TORA(H)
pard ... PANTHER, COMPANION, PARTNER
pardon ...... REMIT, EXCUSE, FORGIVE, OVERLOOK, ASSOIL, CONDONE, SPARE, INDULGENCE, ABSOLVE
general .... AMNESTY
kind of .... OBLIVION
pardonable .... VENIAL, EXCUSABLE
pare ..... CUT, REDUCE, SKIN, WHITTLE, SKIVE, TRIM, PEEL, SHAVE
Fr. surgeon ... AMBROISE
paregoric .... SOOTHING, SEDATIVE
parent ...... SIRE, ANCESTOR, MATER, SOURCE, DAM, PATER, MOTHER, FATHER
child murderer .. FILICIDE
parentage ..... BIRTH, ORIGIN, ANCESTRY, PATERNITY
person of mixed .... MESTEE, MUSTEE, OCTOROON, MULATTO, MESTIZO, GRIFF
parenthesis .... EPISODE, INTERLUDE
parenthetical remark .. ASIDE
parents, having same .. GERMAN
paresis .... PARALYSIS
paretic .... PARALYTIC
pareu .... SKIRT
parfait .... DESSERT
parfleche .... RAWHIDE
parget .... PLASTER
parhelic circle's halo .. SUNDOG
parhelion .... (MOCK)SUN, SUNDOG
pariah ...... OUTCAST, LEPER, EXILE, WRETCH
paries .... WALL
parietal .... SOMATIC
Paris .... PAREE, LUTETIA
airport near .... ORLY
cathedral .. NOTRE DAME
chief of police .. PREFECT
district in ..... AUTEUIL
father of .... PRIAM
museum .... CLUNY, LOUVRE
palace .... TUILERIES
parent of .... PRIAM, HECUBA
patron saint .. GENEVIEVE
police inspector, fictional MAIGRET
rival of .... ROMEO
river .... SEINE
section .... MONTMARTRE
suburb .... CLICHY, ISSY
subway .... METRO
thug .... APACHE
university .... SORBONNE
victim of ..... ACHILLES
war caused by ... TROJAN
wife .... OENONE
woman kidnapped by ... HELEN
parish .... CONGREGATION
head of .... PARSON, PASTOR, RECTOR
official .... OVERSEER
parity .... EQUALITY, PAR
park .... STADIUM, DEPOSIT, SQUARE
fence/wall .... HAHA
parka .... JACKET, SHIRT
Parkinson's disease ... PALSY
drug for .... L-DOPA
patient's lack .. DOPAMINE
researcher ...... COTZIAS
parlance .... SPEECH, LANGUAGE, IDIOM
parlay .. BET, WAGER, EXPLOIT
parley .... PALAVER, CONFER(ENCE), TALK, NEGOTIATE, WAGER, CONVERSE, TREAT, DISCUSSION, POWWOW
trumpet signal .... CHAMADE
parliament ..... LEGISLATURE, DIET, SEJM
report .... HANSARD
parliamentary move .... CLOTURE, CLOSURE
parlor ... SALON, SHOP, SALA, LIVING ROOM, BEN
Parnassus dweller ..... MUSE
spring .... CASTALIA
parochial ...... PROVINCIAL, NARROW
parodist ... APER, IMITATOR
parody .... SATIRE, CARICATURE, SKIT, BURLESQUE
parol(e) ..... ORAL, PROMISE, (PASS)WORD
paronomasia .... PUN
paronymous .... COGNATE
parotitis .... MUMPS
paroxysm .... FIT, SPASM, ATTACK, CONVULSION, OUTBURST
parquet .... ORCHESTRA, FLOORING
circle .... PARTERRE
parr .... SALMON
parrot ..... COCKATOO, LORO, KEA, LORIKEET, LORY, VASA, PARAKEET, REPEAT, IMITATE, MACAW, KAKA, ARA(RA), JAKO, ECHO, POLLY, POPINJAY, BUGIE, KAKAPO, AMAZON
cry of .... SQUAWK
fever .... PSITTACOSIS
fish ... SHANNY, COTORO, SCARID, LANIA
hawk .... HIA
like .... ARINE
sheep-killing .... KEA
parry ...... DEFLECT, WARD, VOID, FEND, EVADE
fencing .... SEPTIME
parse .... ANALYZE
Parsee .... ZOROASTRIAN
priest .... MOBED
sacred writings .. AVESTA
Parsi "baptismal" rite ...... NAVJOT
fried rice .... PULLAO
language ...... GUJARATI
"towers of silence" ...... DAKMAS
undershirt .... SUDRA
"Parsifal" composer .... WAGNER
magican ..... KLINGSOR
person healed by .... AMFORTAS
priest .... MOBED
son of .... LOHENGRIN
woman in ...... KUNDRY
parsimonious .... MISERLY, STINGY, CLOSE, NIGGARDLY
parsley ... SANICLE, LOVAGE, GARNISH, PLANT, POTHERB, DILL
parsnip .... PLANT
parson .... MINISTER, CLERGYMAN, PASTOR
assistant of ..... CURATE
bird .... TUI, POE, KOKO
concern of a ..... PARISH
parsonage .. MANSE, RECTORY
part .... ROLE, DIVIDE, SEPARATE, LEAVE, SECTION, SEGMENT, PORTION, PIECE, SHARE, DUTY, SEVER
main .... KEYSTONE
of speech ..... (AD)VERB, (PRO)NOUN, ADJECTIVE
payment .... DEPOSIT, INSTAL(L)MENT
song ... GLEE, MADRIGAL
stage .... ROLE
that separates .. SEPTUM, DIVIDER
partake ... PARTICIPATE, EAT, SHARE
partan .... CRAB
parted .... SPLIT, DIVIDED
Parthenon .... TEMPLE
designer .... ICTINUS
sculptor of ..... PHIDIAS
site of ...... ACROPOLIS, ATHENS
Parthenope .... SIREN
Parthenos .... VIRGIN
partial ... BIASED, PREJUDICED
partiality ... BIAS, FONDNESS, LIKING, PREJUDICE

participant .... PARTAKER, PLAYER
in quarrel ...... FEUDIST
participate .... SHARE, PARTAKE, SIT IN
particle .... SPECK, SHRED, TITTLE, GRAIN, MOTE, MITE, WHIT, IOTA, JOT, SCINTILLA, FLECK, GRANULE
atom .... PROTON, NEUTRON
glowing ...... SPARK(LE)
particular .... DISTINCT, SPECIFIC, SPECIAL, DETAIL(ED), ITEM, FASTIDIOUS, EXACTING, FINICAL, FUSSY
moment ..... JUNCTURE
particularize .... ITEMIZE, SPECIFY
parties, fast round of .. WHIRL
partisan .... FOLLOWER, ADHERENT, GUERRILLA, ZEALOT, STALWART, FANATIC, MAQUI, FACTIONAL, DEVOTEE, HALBERD, PIKE
combining form .. CRAT
group .... CAMP, SIDE
partite .... PARTED
partition ... DIVIDE(R), ALLOT, DIVISION, (AP)PORTION, WALL, SEPTUM, SCREEN
partlet .... BIDDY, COLLAR, RUFF, HEN
partly open .... AJAR
partner ... SHARER, ASSOCIATE, TEAMMATE
in crime .... ACCOMPLICE
slang .... PARD
partnership .... CAHOOTS, ASSOCIATION
partridge .... GROUSE, PHEASANT, YUTU, SEESEE, FRANCOLIN, QUAIL, TINAMOU, TITAR, BIRD
call .... JUCK
flock .... BEVY, COVEY
parturition ..... CHILDBIRTH, DELIVERY, LABOR
party .... SOCIAL, GROUP, GATHERING, SHINDIG, TEA, BASH, FACTION, CLIQUE, PERSON, SOIREE
conservative section of ... RIGHT WING
declaration .. MANIFESTO
didoes ...... HIGHJINKS
disciplinarian ..... WHIP
drinking .... CAROUSAL, WASSAIL
for bride-to-be .. SHOWER
giver ... HOST(ESS), MESTA
goer .... GUEST
kind of ...... TEA, STAG, SEND-OFF, DESPEDIDA, SHOWER, HEN, SOCIAL, BRIDAL, CAROUSAL, PARTISAN, ADHERENT, POLITICIAN
organization .. MACHINE
wild .... ORGY
withdraw from .... BOLT

parvenu .... UPSTART, SNOB(BISH), CLIMBER
parvis ..... PORTICO, COURT, YARD
pas .... STEP, DANCE, PRECEDENCE
de Calais .... DOVER
Pascal, Fr. mathematician .... BLAISE
Pasch ..... PASSOVER, EASTER
paschal lamb .... JESUS
pash .... HURL, HEAD
pasha .... DEY, DOWLAH
Pasiphae's husband ... MINOS
son .... MINOTAUR
pasquinade .... LAMPOON, SATIRE, SQUIB
pass ... GAP, END, ELAPSE, MOVE, CONDITION, OCCUR, ABRA, STRAIT, GHAT, OUTSTRIP, PROCEED, DEPART, GO, NACIVERT, GORGE, BRENNER, KHYBER
away .. DIE, CEASE, LEAVE, (E)LAPSE
come to .... HAPPEN, TRANSPIRE, OCCUR
holder .... DEADHEAD
in .... REEVE
in sports .... BYE
lightly .... FLIT
matador's .... FAENA
mountain .... GHAT, DEFILE, COL
off .... FOIST, FOB, PALM
out ...... FAINT, SWOON
over .... OMIT, SKIP, SKIM, IGNORE
pretty .... FIX, JAM
slang .... ANNIE OAKLEY
through .... REEVE
tongue over .. LICK, LAP
up ...... REJECT, LET GO
word carelessly .. BANDY
passable .... FAIR, SOSO, TOLERABLE
passado ..... LUNGE, THRUST
passage ... ROAD, PATH, WAY, TRAVEL, CROSSING, OPENING, VENT, MIGRATION, TRANSIT(ION), JOURNEY, CLOSE, VOYAGE, CORRIDOR, AISLES
between cliffs ...... GAT, DEFILE
between house and garage BREEZEWAY
between traincars .... VESTIBULE
body .... MEATUS
closed at one end .... IMPASSE, BLIND ALLEY, COURT, DEAD END
covered .... ARCADE, SLYPE, CLOISTER
in(to) .... ENTRY, ENTRANCE
means of ..... CHANNEL, DUCT
mine .... ADIT
mouth to anus .. ENTERO
open to ..... PERMEABLE
organ .... LUMEN

out .... EXIT
performed by all .. TUTTI
repeat a .... CITE
reproduce one ... QUOTE
sloping .... RAMP
smoke .... CHIMNEY, STACK, FUNNEL
passageway .... HALL, CORRIDOR, ALLEY, ARCADE, CLOISTER, ADIT, CANAL, GANGPLANK, RAMP, AISLE, DUCT, CATWALK, CHANNEL, SLYPE
underground ... TUNNEL, SAP, TUBE, BURROW, SUBWAY
passbook .... BANKBOOK
passe .... PAST, OBSOLETE, OUT-OF-DATE
passed .... QUALIFIED
passenger ... FARE, TRAVELER, RIDER
kind of .... TENDER, CHANCE, STEERAGE
passerine .... SPARROW, OVENBIRD, SONGBIRD
passible .... SENSIBLE
passing .... FLEETING, MOMENTARY, CURSORY, CASUAL, DEATH, TRANSIENT
away .... LAPSE
fancy .... FAD, WHIM
over .... LABILE
through .... VIA
passion ...... ARDOR, FERVOR, ZEAL, FEELING, ANGER, AGONY, EMOTION, HATE, LOVE, FEAR, LUST, GRIEF, JOY, RAGE, FURY
flower ..... GRANADILLA, MAYPOP
for big things .... MEGALOMANIA
fruit .... MAYPOP
passionate .... INTENSE, ARDENT, AMOROUS, FERVENT, TORRID
passionflower .... MAYPOP
passive .... QUIET, PATHIC, INACTIVE, PATIENT, INERT, DORMANT
resistance exponent ..... GANDHI
Passover ..... PASCH, PESACH, SEDER
bread .... MATZOS, MATZOTH
meal .... SEDAR
of the .... PASCHAL
passport .... SAFE-CONDUCT
endorsement ...... VISA, VISE
passus .... CANTO
password ..... COUNTERSIGN, OPEN SESAME, SIBBOLETH, PAROLE
use of a .. IDENTIFICATION
past .... AGO, SINCE, PRETERITE, YORE, BEYOND, AGONE, OVER, ENDED, GONE BY, BYGONE
master .... EXPERT
middle age .... ELDERLY

pasta product .... MACARONI, SPAGHETTI, DOUGH
ingredient .... FLOUR
paste ... GLUE, PAP, PUNCH, MUCILAGE, BLOW, HIT, FASTEN, MASH, DOUGH, CANDY, ADHESIVE, GEM, STICK
alimentary ..... WANTON, ZITONI
clay .... PATE
food ... POI, PEM(M)ICAN
jewelry .... STRASS
mineral matter .. MAGMA
pellet of aromatic .... PASTILLE
pasteboard .... BRISTOL, TICKET, (PLAYING)CARD
container .... CARTON
pastel .. DYE, WOAD, PASTILLE, PLANT, TINT, CRAYON, DRAWING
Pasteur treatment, object of ... RABIES
pasteurize .... STERILIZE
pasticcio ..... CENTO, MEDLEY, POTPOURRI, PASTICHE
pastiche ... MEDLEY, PASTICCIO
pastille .... TABLET, LOZENGE
pastime .... DIVERSION, SPORT, RECREATION, HOBBY, AMUSEMENT
pastor ... SHEPHERD, DOMINIE, CLERGYMAN, PRIEST, PARSON, MINISTER
pastoral ..... RURAL, CROSIER, RUSTIC, BUCOLIC, IDYLLIC, ARCADIAN
cantata ...... SERENATA
god .... PAN, FAUNUS
melody .... MUSETTE
pipe .... REED, OAT
place .... ARCADIA
poem .... IDYL(L), ECLOGUE, BUCOLIC
poem name ... CORYDON, AMARYLLIS
poetry, symbol of .. REED
sound .... LOW, MOO, BLEAT, CANTATA
staff ..... CROSIER, PEDA
pastrami .... BEEF
pastry .... CAKE, ECLAIR, FLAN, TORTE, PIE, STRUDEL, TART(LET)
cook .... ICER, BAKER
fried .... TIMBALE
shell ...... PUFF, CRUST, ECLAIR
pasture ... GRASS, GRAZE, LEA
for pay .... AGIST
grass ... GRAMA, REDTOP, SACATON
land ...... LEA, LLANO, ESTANCIA, RANCH
pasty ...... (MEAT)PIE, PATE, DOUGHY
pat .... APT, OPPORTUNE, TIMELY, DAB, FIT, TOUCH, TAP, STROKE
patagium .... PARACHUTE
Patagonia is in .... CHILE, ARGENTINA
Patagonian ...... TEHUELCHE, INDIAN
rodent ..... MARA, CAVY
patch ...... SCRAP, REMNANT, DARN, COBBLE, COVERING, DRESSING, REPAIR, VAMP, PIECE, PLOT
of color .... FLECK
up ...... MEND, SETTLE, RECONCILE, REVAMP, TINKER
patcher .... MENDER
patchouli.... PERFUME, PLANT, MINT
patchwork .... MOSAIC, JUMBLE, CENTO, QUILT, VAMP
composition .... CENTO, MEDLEY
pate .... HEAD, NODDLE, PASTE
de foie ____ ...... GRAS
patella .... KNEECAP, PAN, ROTULA, KNEEPAN
patellar reflex .... KNEE JERK
paten .... DISC, HOST, PLATE, DISH, DISK, PATIN(A), ARCA
patent ...... PLAIN, OBVIOUS, EVIDENT, OPEN, PATULOUS, LICENSE, TITLE, MANIFEST
patentee, usually ... INVENTOR
pater ...... FATHER, OLD MAN
companion of ... NOSTER, FAMILIA
paternal .... FATHERLY
paternity .... PARENTAGE, FATHERHOOD, ORIGIN, AUTHORSHIP
paternoster .... PRAYER, ROSARY
path ... COURSE, TRAIL, LANE, TRACK, WAY, WALK, ORBIT, ROUTE, FOOTWAY
finder .... PIONEER, TRAILBLAZER
heavenly .... ORBIT
winding .... AMBAGE
Pathan ... PAKISTANI, MOSLEM
pathetic .... MOVING, PITIFUL
fallacy .... EMPATHY
pathogen .... VIRUS, MICROBE, GERM
pathological .... MORBID
subject .... DISEASE
pathos .... SUFFERING, POIGNANCY
false .... BATHOS
opposite of ...... ETHOS
pathway, winding .... AMBAGE
patience .... SOLITAIRE, ENDURANCE, FORBEARANCE, STOICISM
patient .... INVALID, CASE, FORBEARING, TOLERANT, STEADY
man .... JOB, STOIC
patina .... PLATE, PATEN, CRUST, VERDIGRIS, FILM, COATING, VERD ANTIQUE
patio .... TERRACE, COURT(YARD)
patisserie .... BAKERY
patois ...... SPEECH, DIALECT, LANGUAGE, GUMBO, GOMBO
patriarch ... NASI, NESTORIUS, FATHER, PATER, BISHOP, ELDER
Biblical .... ISAAC, ABRAHAM, JACOB
patrician .... NOBLE, ARISTOCRAT(IC)
patrimony ..... INHERITANCE, HERITAGE
patriot, kind of .... JINGO, CHAUVINIST, NATIONALIST
patriotism, fanatical .... CHAUVINISM, JINGOISM
patrol ... SCOUT, RECONNOITER
wagon .... BLACK MARIA
patrolman .... (BEAT)COP, POLICEMAN
patron .... PADRONE, BENEFACTOR, PROTECTOR, SPONSOR, CUSTOMER, SAINT
animals' ... PAN, FAUNUS
art .... MASCENAS
beggars' .... GILES
Broadway .... ANGEL
Cornish .... COLIN
cripples' .... GILES
England's ..... GEORGE
husbandry ..... GRANGE
Irish .... PATRICK
largesse of a .... PENSION
lawyers' .... IVES
lepers' .... GILES
literature ..... MAECENAS
music .... CECILIA
Russia's ...... NICHOLAS
sailors' .... ELMO, NICHOLAS
shoemakers' ... CRISPIN
wine-growers' .. VINCENT
youths' .... NICHOLAS
patronage ... FAVOR, SUPPORT, SPONSORSHIP, CLIENTELE, (A)EGIS, AUSPICES
solicitor .... RUNNER
patronize .... SPONSOR, SUPPORT, FAVOR
patronizing .... HOITY-TOITY, CONDESCENDING
patrons collectively .... CLIENTELE
patronymic .... SURNAME
patsy ... FALLGUY, SCAPEGOAT
patten .... CLOG, SANDAL, OVERSHOE, WOODEN SHOE, CHOPINE
patter .... TAPS, TALK, CANT, JARGON, CHATTER, GURGLE, BICKER
pattern ... PARADIGM, MODEL, SAMPLE, EXAMPLE, TEMPLATE, FORMAT, GUIDE, DESIGN, DIAGRAM
of flow movement .... RHYTHM, TREND
Patti, singer ... ADELINA, PAGE
patty .... PIE, CAKE
patulous ... OPEN, SPREADING, PATENT
paucity ... DEARTH, FEWNESS, SCARCITY
Paul Bunyan ... LUMBERJACK

Bunyan's ox .... BABE
pry .... SNOOP(ER)
the saint's birthplace .... TARSUS
the singer ..... ROBESON, ANKA, MCCARTNEY
paunch .... ABDOMEN, (POT)BELLY, RUMEN, BAY WINDOW, STOMACH
paunchy .... POTBELLIED
pauper .... BEGGAR
paupers' institution .... POORHOUSE
pause ...... RESPITE, LET UP, BREAK, REST, STOP, HESITATE, HESITATION, LULL
in music ...... FERMETA
in pronunciation .... HIATUS
in prosody ... C(A)ESURA
vocalized .... ER
pave ...... COVER, OVERLAY, STUD, TILE, ASPHALT, COBBLE
pavement ...... (SIDE)WALK, FLAGGING
pounder ... PATROLMAN, BEAT COP
walker ..... PEDESTRIAN
paver .... TUP
of a sort .... PIONEER
pavid .... AFRAID, TIMID, FEARFUL
pavilion .... MARQUEE, BELVEDERE, TENT, KIOSK, SUMMERHOUSE, AURICLE, GALLERY
paving material ..... ASPHALT, MACADAM, TAR, CEMENT, TILE, FLAG(STONE), SETT, SLAB
pavis .... SHIELD
Pavlova, ballet dancer ... ANNA
pavo .... PEACOCK, CONSTELLATION
pavonine .... IRIDESCENT
paw ..... MAUL, FOOT, HAND, GAUM, PUD, FATHER, OLD MAN, PAPA, TOUCH
pawl ...... PALLET, TRIPPER, RATCHET, CLICK, DETENT, BOLT
pawn ..... HOSTAGE, WAGER, TOOL, DUPE, PIGNUS, GAGE, SPOUT, HOCK, PLEDGE, GUARANTY, STAKE, CHESSMAN
queened .... FERS
receipt .... TICKET
pawnbroker .. (MONEY)LENDER
shop of .... SPOUT
slang .... UNCLE
Pawnee .... INDIAN, CHAUI
pawnshop: sl. .... SPOUT
pawpaw .... PAPAYA
pax .... PEACE, GODDESS, TABLET
pay .... FEE, REMUNERATE, RECOMPENSE, REMIT, COMPENSATE, DEFRAY, SETTLE, WAGE, SALARY, LIQUIDATE, STIPEND
attention .... HEED, LISTEN
back .... REIMBURSE
dirt .... ORE
for injury suffered .... DAMAGES
for loss incurred .... INDEMNIFY
homage .... HONOR
load .... CARGO
one's share .... ANTE
off .... RECKONING, REDEEM
something additional to .. PERQUISITE
up .... PONY, ANTE, COME ACROSS
payable .... DUE
paying guest .... BOARDER
paymaster .. PURSER, CASHIER
payment, advance ..... ANTES, HANDSEL, HERIOT
back .... REBATE
call for .... DUN
death .... CRO
forced .. EXACTION, LEVY
per capita .. CAPITATION
to atone for killing ...... WER(E)GILD, BLOOD MONEY
token ... ARLES, HANDSEL
paynim ... HEATHEN, PAGAN, MOSLEM
payola .... BRIBE
Pb in chemistry .... LEAD, PLUMBUM
pea .... LEGUME, PEASE, SENNA, LICORICE
chick .... CICER
covering .... POD
heath .... CARMELE
pod .... PEASECOD
seed .... PULSE
soup .... FOG
stalk/stem ..... HA(U)LM
tree ... AGATI, LABURNUM
peabody bird ...... SPARROW
peace .... GRITH, SHALOM, CONCORD, HARMONY, CALM, QUIET, SERENITY
agreement ...... TREATY
goddess of .. IRENE, PAX
officer .... SHERIFF, CONSTABLE
pipe .... CALUMET
Prize winner .. ORR, ROOT, BUNCHE, KING
symbol of .... DOVE
peaceable ... HENOTIC, IRENIC, SOLOMON
peaceful .. CALM, IRENIC(AL), PACIFIC, SERENE, HALCYON
person .... PACIFICO
peacemaker ..... ARBITRATOR, MEDIATOR
slang .... COLT
peach .... FREESTONE, CLINGSTONE, NECTARINE, VICTORINE, TREE, PAVY, FRUIT, BRANDY
kind of .... CLING
slang .. BETRAY, SQUEAL, SING, SNITCH
state .... GEORGIA
stone .... PUTAMEN, NUTLET
peacoat .... JACKET
peacock ... PAVO, BIRD, PAON, MAO
bird resembling .. ARGUS
butterfly .... IO
eyelike spot ... OCELLUS
feather's spot ... OCELLUS
female .... PEAHEN, PEAFOWL
fish .... WRASSE
like a .... VAIN
neck feathers ... HACKLE
of a .... PAVONINE
ore .... BORNITE
symbol of the ... VANITY
walk .... STRUT
peag(e) .... WAMPUM
peak .... CREST, SUMMIT, HEIGHT, MAXIMUM, PITON, ALP, CROWN, DROOP, FADE
of rock .... AIGUILLE
volcano's .... CONE
peaked .... POINTED
peal ...... CLAP, CHIME, RING, RESOUND, CARILLON, TOLL
peanut .... EARTHNUT, GOOBER, MANI
pear .... JARGONEL(LE), SECKEL, BOSC, TREE, FRUIT, BERGAMOT, POME, ANJOU, BARTLETT, OPUNTA, NOPAL
autumn .... BOSC
fruit like ..... AVOCADO
juice drink .... PERRY
prickly ... TUNA, NOPAL, OPUNTIA
prince's ...... BERGAMOT
seed .... PYRENE
shaped .... PEG-TOP, PYRIFORM
shaped fruit .... FIG, AVOCADO, SHADDOCK
stone .... PYRENE
pearl ...... GEM, MARGARITE, PURL, BEAD, OLIVET
biblical .... BDELLIUM
Buck heroine ...... OLAN
Harbor is in ...... OAHU
high quality ..... ORIENT
imitation .... OLIVET
mother-of .... NACRE
Mosque city ...... AGRA
of the Orient .... MANILA
producer ...... OYSTER, NACRE, MOLLUSK
quality of a ..... LUSTER
river .... CHU-KIANG
singer .... BAILEY
pearlweed .... SEALWORT, SAGINA
pearmain .... APPLE
Pearson, Canadian premier ... LESTER
peart ... CLEVER, PERT, LIVELY
Peary's discovery .... NORTH POLE
peas and beans ..... LEGUMES
peasant .... FARMER, RUSTIC, RYOT, FELLAH, HIND,

CEORL, COTTAR, TAO, SERF, TILLER, CHURL, PEON, CARL(E), CAMPESINO, VILLEIN, KASAMA, MUZHIK
farmer .... CROFTER
peasants' revolt ... JACQUERIE
pease .... PEAS
peat .... FUEL, TURF
bog .... MOSS
land .... TURBARY
moss .... SPHAGNUM
spade .... SLADE
peav(e)y .... CANTHOOK
pebble .... STONE, QUARTZ, SCREE
pecan ... NUT, TREE, HICKORY, NOGAL
tree related to .. HICKORY
peccadillo .... FAULT
peccant ..... SINFUL, SINNING
peccary .... JAVALI, BOAR
peck .... NAG, DAB, KISS, NIBBLE, PICK
1/4 of .... QUARTERN
pecker .... PICK
pecks, 4 .... BUSHEL
pectin .... CARBOHYDRATE
pectinoid bivalve ..... SCALLOP
peculate .... EMBEZZLE
peculiar .... ODD, UNIQUE, STRANGE, SPECIAL, DISTINCTIVE, SINGULAR, QUEER, SCREWY, EXCLUSIVE
to locality ..... ENDEMIC
peculiarity ... TRAIT, ODDITY, CHARACTERISTIC
pecuniary .... FINANCIAL, MONETARY
pedagogue ... TUTOR, TEACHER
pedagoguy .... TEACHING, DIDACTICS
pedal .. TREADLE, (FOOT)LEVER
digit .... TOE
pedant ... TEACHER, SCHOLAR, TUTOR, EDUCATOR
pedantic .... ACADEMIC, DIDACTIC
pedate ..... FOOTLIKE, FOOTED
peddle ... HAWK, SELL, VEND
peddler .... HAWKER, HUCKSTER, PACKMAN, PEDLAR, COSTER, CHAPMAN
cheap jewelry .... DUFFER
clandestine/illegal ...... PUSHER
confederate of .... SHILL
trinket .... FAKER
vehicle of ..... PUSHCART
peddle .... HAWK, VEND, SELL
pederasty .... SODOMY
boy used in .... CATAMITE
pedestal ...... BASE, SUPPORT
part of ..... DADO, SOCLE, PLINTH
put on a .... IDOLIZE
pedestrian .... WALKING, PROSAIC, DULL, WALKER
pediatrist, concern of .... INFANTS, CHILDREN
pedicel .... PEDUNCLE, STEM, STALK, RAY
without .... SESSILE
pedicular .... LOUSY
pedicure .... CHIROPODIST, CHIROPODY
subject of ...... TOENAILS
pedigree .... LINEAGE, ANCESTRY, GENEALOGY, BLOODLINE
pedometer .... ODOGRAPH
pedro .. SEVEN UP, CARD GAME
peduncle .... STALK, PEDICEL, STEM, PEDICLE, STIPE(S), PETIOLE, SCAPE
without .... SESSILE
Pee Dee ..... YADKIN, RIVER
Pee Wee of baseball ... REESE
peek ... PEEP, PEER, GLANCE, LOOK
peel ...... RIND, STRIP, PARE, TRIM, SHED, SKIN, UNDRESS, TOWER, EXOCARP, EPICARP, FLAY
for flavoring ...... ZEST
skin off ...... EXCORIATE
peen, tool with ..... HAMMER
peep .... PEER, CHIRP, LOOK, PULE, GLIMPSE, PEEK, KEEK, JEEP, CHEEP, PRY
military slang ..... JEEP
show .... RAREE
peeper ...... SNOOP(ER), PRY, TOM, FROG, NESTLING, CHICK, EYE
peephole ... EYELET, KEYHOLE, LOOPHOLE
Peeping Tom .... VOYEUR, PEEKER
lady looked at by .... GODIVA
peer .... NOBLE, DUKE, VISCOUNT, MARQUIS, BARON, SQUINT, EARL, EQUAL, PALADIN, LOOK, PEEP
Gynt's mother ..... ASE
peerage .... NOBILITY
Peerce, operatic singer .. JAN
peeress ... DUCHESS, BARONESS, LADY, MARQUISE
peerless .... UNRIVALED, NONPAREIL
peetweet .... SANDPIPER
peeve .... GRUDGE, ANNOY(ANCE), IRRITATE
peevish .... GRUMPY, FRACTIOUS, CROSS, SPLENETIC, TESTY, TE(T)CHY, SOUR, QUERULOUS, FRETFUL, IRRITABLE, PET
peewee ...... DWARF, RUNT, LAPWING
peg .... NOG, PIN, TRE(E)NAIL SPILL, SPIGOT, DOWEL, PLUG, BOLT, STEP, THOLE, KEVEL, HOB
and rings game .. QUOITS
colloquial ... LEG, FOOT, TOOTH
golf .... TEE
joining timbers .... TRE(E)NAIL, TRUNNEL
quoits .... HOB
pega .... REMORA
Pegasus .... HORSE
Peggy .... MARGARET
pegs, set of .... SPILIKIN
Pegu is capital of .. RANGOON
ironwood .... ACLE
peignor .... NEGLIGEE
Peiping .... PEKING
pekan ..... WEJACK, WEASEL
pekin .... SILK, SATIN
Peking .... PEIPING
Pekingese .... DOG
pekoe .... TEA
pelage .... FUR, HAIR
pelagic ..... MARINE, OCEANIC
Pele, football star ..... EDSON, NEGRAO
Peleg's father .... EBER
son .... REU
pelerine .... CAPE
Peleus, descendant of .... ACHILLES
wife of .... THETIS
Pelew .... PALAU
pelf .... BOOTY, WEALTH
Pelias' nephew .... JASON
son .... ACASTUS
Pelides .... ACHILLES
Pelion, companion of ... OSSA
pelisse .... COAT, CLOAK
pelite .... SHALE
pellagra treatment ... NIACIN
pellet ...... PILL, BALL, SHOT, BULLET
of medicine .... PILL, PILULE
pellicle ..... FILM, MEMBRANE, SCUM
pellmell .... HEADLONG, JUMBLED, DISORDER(LY)
pellucid .... CLEAR, TRANSPARENT, LIMPID, SHEER
Pelop's father .... TANTALUS
son ... ATREUS, THYESTES
Peloponnesus city ... MESSENE
country .... LACONIA
promontory .. MATAPAN
Peloponnesian seaport .... PATRAS
pelota .... JAI ALAI
basket .... CESTA
court .... FRONTON
player .... PELOTARI
pelt .... HIDE, FELL, BEAT, POUND, CAST, SKIN, PEPPER, STONE
peltry .... FURS, SKINS
pelvic .... ILIAC, PUBIC
pemmican .... MEAT
pen ...... ENCLOSURE, YARD, WRITE(R), INDITE, CORRAL, BALLPOINT, QUILL, HUTCH, KRAAL, COTE
name ... See PSEUDONYM, NOM DE PLUME
pig .... STY
point .... NIB, NEB
poultry ... COOP, HUTCH
slang .... PENITENTIARY, PRISON, JAIL
penal .... PUNITIVE
penalize .... PUNISH, FINE
penalty ...... FINE, FORFEIT, HANDICAP, PUNISHMENT

penance .... PUNISHMENT
for example .. SACRAMENT
penates .... LARES
penchant ...... FLAIR, TASTE, INCLINATION, LIKING, FONDNESS, LEANING
pencil lead .... GRAPHITE
pend .... HANG
pendant .... TASSEL, GIRANDOLE, EARRING, LAVALIER(E), FOB
pendent .... HANGING, SUSPENDED, UNDECIDED, PENDING, PENSILE
pending .... UNDECIDED, DURING, UNTIL
pendulous .... SWINGING, HANGING
pendulum, device with inverted METRONOME
weight .... BOB
Peneios .... SALAMBRIA
Penelope .... WEAVER
father .... ICARIUS
husband of ... ODYSSEUS, ULYSSES
son of ..... TELEMACHUS
penetrable .... PERVIOUS
penetralia .... SECRETS, CONFIDENCES
penetrate .... PIERCE, ENTER, PERMEATE, IMBUE, REACH
penetrating .... ACUTE, INCISIVE, TRENCHANT, DEEP, KEEN, SHARP, PUNGENT
penetration .... INSIGHT, INTRUSION
open to ..... PERMEABLE
penetron .... MESON
pengo, replacement of .... FORINT
penguin ... AUK, BIRD, JOHNNY
breeding place .. ROOKERY
describing a .. IMPENNATE
peninsula ...... CHERSONESE, BONDOC, NECK, IBERIA, SINAI, KOLA, KOWLOON, ISTRIA, LABRADOR, MALAY, KAMCHATKA
penitence .... ATTRITION, CONTRITION, REMORSE, REGRET, REPENTANCE
penitent ... CONTRITE, SORRY, REPENTANT, REMORSEFUL
wear of ..... SACKCLOTH, SANBENITO
penitential period .... LENT
penitentiary .... PRISON
penman ..... SCRIBE, WRITER, CHIROGRAPHER, AUTHOR
penmanship .. HAND(WRITING), SCRIPT
Penn, William ...... QUAKER
penna .... FEATHER
pennant .... BANNER, BURGEE, ENSIGN, FLAG, PENNON, STREAMER
pennies .... PENCE
penniless .. POOR, BROKE, FLAT
Pennine Alps peak ...... ROSA
pennon ...... FLAG, PENNANT, WING, PINION, ENSIGN
Pennsylvania capital .... HARRISBURG
city ... YORK, BRADFORD, SHARON, PHILADELPHIA, SCRANTON, LANCASTER, ERIE, ALLENTOWN, LEBANON, PITTSBURGH, ALTOONA
insurrection, cause of ... WHISKY
river .... LEHIGH
sect .... AMISH
state nickname .... KEYSTONE
state tree ...... HEMLOCK
town .... ONO
penny ...... COPPER, SALTEE, COIN, (RED)CENT, GROAT
a-liner ... HACK(WRITER)
candy .... LICORICE
dreadful ... DIME NOVEL
wise .... THRIFTY, ECONOMICAL
penpoint .... NIB, NEB
pensile .... HANGING, PENDENT
pension .... STIPEND, SUBSIDY
pensionary .... PUPPET, HIRELING, DEPENDENT
pensive .... MEDITATIVE
penstock ... TROUGH, SLUICE
pent ...... PENNED, CONFINED
pentacle ..... STAR, SYMBOL, PENTAGRAM
pentad .... FIVE, QUINTET
pentagram .... PENTACLE
Pentateuch .... TORA(H)
lesson read from .... PARASHAH
Pentecost .... SHABUOTH, WHITSUNDAY
penthouse ...... APARTMENT, LEANTO
pentobarbital sodium .... NEMBUTAL
pentosan .... XYLAN
pentose ... SUGAR, ARABINOSE
penurious ..... POOR, STINGY, MISERLY
penury .... POVERTY, INDIGENCE
peon .... LABORER, FOOTMAN, SERF
peony .... MOUTAN
flower .... PIP
people ...... FOLK, POPULATE, DEMOS, RACE, PERSONS, MORTALS, NATION, CITIZENS, HUMANS, PUBLIC
characteristics of .. ETHOS
common ..... POPULACE, MASSES, PLEBE
dark-skinned ..... NEGRO
full of .... POPULOUS
mass killing of .... GENOCIDE, NOYADE, HOLOCAUST, POGROM
non-clerical ...... LAITY
of all the ..... PANDEMIC
prehistoric ..... PELASGI
unimportant .. SMALL FRY
pep .... SNAP, VERVE
drug ... ELAVIL, TRIAVIL, TOFRANIL
pill in short ... LSD, DMT, STP
peplos .... SCARF, SHAWL, PEPLUM
peplum .... SKIRT, PEPLOS
pepo .... MELON, SQUASH, PUMPKIN, GOURD
pepper .... PIM(I)ENTO, SPRINKLE, BEAT, KAVA, CAYENNE, ARA, SPICE, CONDIMENT, PELT, BETEL, STRAFE, RIDDLE, CHILIES, CAPSICUM
and-salt .... GRAY
berry .... CUBEB
beverage .... KAVA
fruit .... PAPRIKA
picker .... PIPER
plant ..... BETEL, KAVA, PAPRIKA
pod .... CHILI
pot .... STEW
sauce .... TABASCO
shrub ..... KAVA, KAWA, CAVA
pepperidge .... TUPELO
peppermint .... CANDY, LOZENGE, PLANT, OIL
oil product .... MENTHOL
peppery ... HOT, FIERY, TESTY, SPICY, SHARP, IRRITABLE, PUNGENT
peppy .... BRISK, SPIRITED
pepsin .... ENZYME
Pepys, Samuel ...... DIARIST
Pequod .... WHALER, WHALEBOAT
captain of .... AHAB
per ..... BY, THROUGH, EACH
annum .... ANNUALLY
diem .... DAILY
hundred ...... PER CENT
Pera .... BEYOGLU
peradventure .... PERHAPS, MAYBE, POSSIBLY
perambulate ... WALK, STROLL
perambulator ... PRAM, BUGGY
percale .... COTTON
perceive ..... DISCERN, GRASP, OBSERVE, RECOGNIZE, NOTE, SENSE
percentage .... PORTION
perceptible .... PALPABLE, VISIBLE, SENSIBLE, TANGIBLE, TACTILE
perception .... NOESIS, COGNITION, INSIGHT, GRASP, EAR
perceptive ...... ACUTE, KEEN
perch ...... SIT, SEAT, ROOST, FISH, SAUGER, PERCOID, RUFF(E)
high .... AERIE, AERY
fish like .... ANABAS, DARTER, CABRILLA
perchance .... POSSIBLY, PERHAPS, MAYBE, MAYHAP
perched .... SAT, (A)LIT
percher .... BIRD
percheron .... HORSE
percoid .... FISH, PERCH
percolate ...... PERK, LEACH, BREW, FILTER, DRAIN,

OOZE, PERMEATE, SEEP
percolator .... COFFEEPOT
percuss .... RAP
percussion ... IMPACT, SHOCK
cap .... PRIMER
hammer .... PLEXOR, PLESSOR
instrument ...... TRAPS, DRUM, CYMBALS, BELL, PIANO, MARACA
section .... TRAPS
Percy, Sir Henry .... HOTSPUR
perdition .... RUIN, LOSS, DAMNATION, HELL
perdu(e) .... CONCEALED
pere .... FATHER, SENIOR
peregrinate .... TRAVEL, JOURNEY
peregrinator ..... TRAVELER, PILGRIM
peregrine .... FOREIGN, MIGRATORY, ALIEN, FALCON
falcon .... DUCK HAWK, TERCEL
peremptory .... FINAL, DECISIVE, DOGMATIC, IMPERIOUS, ABSOLUTE
perennial .... LASTING, PERPETUAL
plant .... DAHLIA
perfect .... FLAWLESS, FAULTLESS, UTTER, CONSUMMATE, IDEAL, EXACT, PRECISE, PURE, POLISH, REFINE, MODEL
blessedness .... NIRVANA
diamond ..... PARAGON
model .... IDEAL
perfection, model of .... PARAGON, PRECISION
perfectly .... FULLY
perfecto .... CIGAR
perfidious .... FAITHLESS
perfidy .... BETRAYAL, TREACHERY
perforate ..... PUNCH, BORE, DRILL, PIERCE, RIDDLE, PINK(Y), PINKIE
perforated .... FENESTRATE
thing ... SIEVE, STRAINER
perforator .... PUNCHEON
perforation ..... HOLE, PUNCH
perforce .... NECESSARILY
perform .... EXECUTE, FULFILL, EFFECT, DO, RENDER, (EN)ACT
performance .... SHOW, EXHIBITION, RENDITION
between acts .. INTERLUDE
in person .... LIVE
performer ... ACTOR, PLAYER, ARTIST(E), TALENT, DOER, TROUPER
actuated by wires .... PUPPET, MARIONETTE
balancing trick .... EQUILIBRIST
stock of .... REPERTOIRE, REPERTORY
performers, group of .... TROUPE, CAST
perfume .. SCENT, FRAGRANCE, ESSENCE, (IN)CENSE, BOUQUET, AROMA, A(T)TAR
bag .... SATCHET
base .... MUSK
box/case ..... POMANDER
flask .... FLACON
making process .... ENFLEURAGE
making substance ...... MUSK, MYRRH, BERGAMOT, CASTOR(EUM), IRONE, ATTAR, VERDIGRIS, ORRIS, ORRICE, AMBERGRIS, COUMARIN, IONONE, SAFROL(E)
oil .... ATTAR, CITRONELLA, BEN, NEROLI
old .... MUSK
pad .... SACHET
perfumer, room ..... INCENSE
perfunctory ..... SUPERFICIAL
pergola .... TRELLISWORK, ARBOR
perhaps .. HAPLY, PERCHANCE, POSSIBLY, MAYBE, MAYHAP
peri .... ELF, FAIRY
cousin of a .... NISSE
perianth .... CALYX
periapt .... AMULET
Pericles' mistress .... ASPASIA
peridot .... OLIVINE, CHRYSOLITE
peril .... JEOPARDY, RISK, HAZARD, DANGER, MENACE
perimeter .... BORDER, BOUNDARY
period ..... INTERVAL, STAGE, DOT, STREAK, POINT, TERM, TIME, SPELL
brief .... SEC, SNATCH, SNAP, SPELL
geological ...... EOCENE, ERIAN, MIOCENE, JURA, UINTA
inactive ..... LULL, REST, RESPITE, DORMANCY
of extension ..... GRACE
of quiet .... LULL
of seclusion .... RETREAT
of time .... (A)EON, ERA, EPOCH, AGE, DECADE, CENTURY, TRACT
of trial ...... PROBATION
of unemployment .... LAYOFF
of year .... SEASON
short ...... SNAP, SPELL
unbroken ...... STRETCH
woman's .... MENSES
periodic ..... INTERMITTENT, RECURRENT, ETESIAN, REGULAR
periodical .... GAZETTE, PICTORIAL, JOURNAL, MAG(AZINE)
peripatetic .... WALKER, ITINERANT
peripheral .... DISTAL, EXTERNAL, OUTER
periphery .... PERIMETER, ENVIRONS, RIM, AMBIT, CIRCUMFERENCE
periphrasis .... AMBAGE, CIRCUMLOCUTION
periphrastic .... VERBOSE
perique .... TOBACCO
periscope trail ...... FEATHER, WAKE
perish ...... DIE, END, EXPIRE
peristyle .. COLONNADE, COURT
peritoneum, fold of .... OMENTUM
periwig .... PERUKE
periwinkle ... MYRTLE, SNAIL, MUSSEL, SHELL
perjure .... LIE
perjury, induce to commit ..... SUBORN
perk .... PERCOLATE, BUBBLE, RAISE, LIFT
perky .... JAUNTY, GAY, SAUCY, SPIRITED
Perle, society hostess .. MESTA
perlite ...... ROCK, OBSIDIAN
permanence .... FIXITY
permanent.... LASTING, FIXED, PERPETUAL
permeable .... PERVIOUS
permeate .. IMBUE, PERCOLATE, PENETRATE, DIFFUSE, PERVADE
permissible ...... ALLOWABLE
permission ... LEAVE, LICENSE, CONSENT, GRACE
to enter .... ENTREE
permissive .... LENIENT, ALLOWING
permit .... ALLOW, SANCTION, LET, LEAVE, LICENSE, AUTHORIZE, WARRANT, CEDULA
reluctantly .... BEAR, SUFFER, BROOK, TOLERATE
to leave .... EXCUSE
permitted .... LICIT
permutation .... CHANGE
permute ... ALTER, REARRANGE
Pernambuco .... RECIPE
pernicious .. NOISOME, VICIOUS, NOXIOUS, BANEFUL, DEADLY, FATAL, WICKED, EVIL
pernickety .... FUSSY, FASTIDIOUS
Peron's lady ..... EVA, EVITA
slogan .... CUMPLE
perorate .... HARANGUE, SPEECHIFY, ORATE
perpend .... PONDER
perpendicular ...... VERTICAL, SINE, UPRIGHT, STRAIGHT UP, PLUMB
perpetrate ...... DO, COMMIT
perpetual .... LASTING, PERMANENT, CONSTANT, CONTINUAL, INCESSANT
perpetuate .... PRESERVE
perpetuity .... ETERNITY, SERIAL
in .... FOREVER
perplex .. NONPLUS, INTRIGUE, BAFFLE, ELUDE, CONFUSE, PUZZLE, STUMP, MYSTIFY, FLUMMOX

perquisite .... APPANAGE, TIP, GRATUITY, BONUS
perron .... STAIRCASE
perry .... DRINK
perse .... BLUE
persecute ... HARASS, AFFLICT, OPPRESS, ANNOY
persecution, victim of .... REFUGEE, MARTYR, JEW
of minority group ...... POGROM
persecutor, kind of ... TYRANT, OPPRESSOR
Perseid .... METEOR
Persephone ..... PROSERPINA, CORA
husband/abductor of .... HADES, PLUTO
parent of .... ZEUS, DEMETER
Perseus, daughter of .. PERSEIS
mother of .... DANAE
victim of .... MEDUSA
wife of ..... ANDROMEDA
perseverance ...... TENACITY, PERSISTENCE, PERTINACITY
persevere .... PERSIST
Pershing's command .... AEF
Persia .... IRAN
conqueror of ..... CYRUS
Persian ...... MEDE, ELAMITE, IRANI(AN), PARTHIAN, PAHLAVI
ally .... MEDE
almond .... BADAM
angel .... MAH
apartment ...... ZENANA
bird .... BULBUL
blinds ...... PERSIENNES
capital ...... PERSEPOLIS, ISFAHAN
carpet .... HAMADAN, SENNA, KALI
city ... ARBELA, TABRIZ, TEH(E)RAN, ERBIL
coin ...... TOMAN, ASAR, PAHLAVI, DARIC, DINAR, ASHRAFI, PUL, STATER
dance .... SARABAND
deity, supreme .. ORMAZD
dynasty ...... SASSANID, SELJUK
elf .... PERI
emigrees .... PARSIS, PARSEES
empire, destroyer of .... ALEXANDER
empire founder .. CYRUS
empire province .. EGYPT
evil spirit ...... AHRIMAN
fairy .... ELF, PERI
father .... BABA
fire worshipper ... PARSI
Gate of Faith ...... BAB
god of light .. MITHRA(s)
governor .... SATRAP
Gulf region ... CHALDEA
gypsy .... SISECH
hemp .... KANAB
hook money .... LARI
inn .... SERAI, SARAI
javelin .... JERID
judge .... CADI
king .... DARIUS, (ARTA)XERXES, CAMBYSES, CYRUS
king of peris .... JAMSHID
king's headdress .. TIARA, DIADEM
language .... ZEND, PAHLAVI, AVESTAN
lynx .... CARACAL
measure ...... PARASANG
monk .... DERVISH
mystic .... SUFI
mystic symbol .... SWASTIKA
native .... LUR
nightingale ..... BULBUL
official .... HAMAN
pavilion .... KIOSK
people .... MEDES, ELAMITES
plant .... POPPY
poet ... HAFIZ, FIRD(A)USI, OMAR(KHAYYAM)
potentate .... SHAH
pottery ...... GOMBROON
potion .... SOMA PULARI
priestly caste ..... MAGI
prophet .... MANES
refugee ... PARSI, PARSEE
religion .... BABISM, MITHRAISM
rice dish ... PILAU, PILAW
ruby spinel .... BALAS
rug .... KALI, SENNA, HAMADAN
ruler .... SHAH, SULTAN, DARIUS, XERXES
sect .... BABI(SM)
screen .... PARDAH
servant .... BACHA
songbird .... BULBUL
spinel .... BALAS
sprite .... PERI
summerhouse .... KIOSK
teacher ...... MULLA(H)
tiger .... SHER
title .... MIR(ZA), SHAH, BAB, AZAM, KHAN
turban cloth ..... LUNGI
veil .... PARDAH
weight ...... ABBAS, SER
writings ... AVESTA, ZEND
persicary .... KNOTWEED, HEARTSEASE
persiennes .. SHUTTERS, BLINDS
persiflage .... BANTER, BADINAGE, RAILLERY
persimmon .... EBONY
persist ...... INSIST, ENDURE, PERSEVERE, CONTINUE, REMAIN
persistence .... TENACITY
persistent .... DOGGED, TENACIOUS, STUBBORN, CONTINUED
persnickety .... FUSSY, FASTIDIOUS
person (see fellow/man) ...... INDIVIDUAL, SELF, FELLOW, WIGHT, ONE, EGG, BEING
abject ... WORM, WRETCH
alert .... LIVEWIRE
Anglo-Indian .. WALLA(H)
angry .... SOREHEAD
annoying ... CUSS, PEST, HUNKS
argumentative .. POLEMIST
authorized to practice ... LICENTIATE
awkward ..... GAL(L)OT, GALOOT, FOOZLE, DUFFER
bad luck .... JONAH, JONAS, HOODOO
beastly .... YAHOO
boastful .... GASCON
boorish .... LOUT, GOOP
burdensome .. DEADWOOD
called for jury service .... TALES
callow .... CALF
club-footed .... TALIPED
clumsy .... CHUMP, CHUKKER, DUB, JUMBO, LUMMOX, LOB, LUBBER, LOON, SWAB, SLOB, HULK
coarse ...... BOOR, LOUT, MUCKER, MUG
colorless .... ALBINO
comical .... WAG
common ..... PLEBEIAN
complaining ...... CRAB, CRANK, GROUSE, GROUCH
contemptible ..... TOAD, CAD, SCOUNDREL, LOUSE, WORM, SKUNK, BUGGER, ROTTER, SWINE, STINKER, INSECT, CUR, SNOT
courageous .... LION
cowardly .... CUR, POLTROON, CAITIFF
cowering in fear ... FUNK
crafty .... FOX
cunning .... WEASEL
dance-maniac .... TARANTIST
dark-skinned ..... NEGRO
defeated in contest ...... ALSO-RAN
demented ... NUT, LOCO
diabolical ...... FIEND, MEPHISTO, HELLION
disgruntled ... SOREHEAD
disorderly ..... LARRIKIN
dissatisfied .... MALCONTENT
dissolute ..... RAKE, RIP
drunken.......... LUSH, HELLBENDER
dull ... BORE, DULLARD, DUNCE, LUMP, LURDAN(E), JERK, MOKE, PLODDER, FOOZLE
easily cheated .... GULL, DUPE
eccentric .... KOOK, CRANK, NUT, JERK
eminent .... VIP, NOTABLE, LUMINARY
energetic .... LIVEWIRE,

HUSTLER, DYNAMO, RUSTLER
entertaining .... SCREAM
evil .... MISCREANT, YAHOO, CAITIFF
extraordinary .. PRODIGY, ONER
famous ...... NOTABLE, CELEBRITY
feeble-minded ... IDIOT, AMENT
fiendish .... HELLKITE
fleeing from justice ...... FUGITIVE
fond of fighting .... SCRAPPER
foolish .... GABY, JAY, COOT, BOOB(Y)
foppish .... LADIDA
formal .... STIFF
freed from slavery ...... LIBERTINE
frenzied for a fight ...... AMOK, AMUCK, BERSERK(ER).
fuzzy ...... HOITY-TOITY, FUDDY-DUDDY
gifted ..... WIZ, TALENT
greedy ... VULTURE, KITE, PIG, HARPY
gullible .... BABE
handsome ...... LOOKER, ADONIS
head of .... COSTARD
high in society ..... NOB
high-born .... NOBLE, PRINCE
high-ranking .. MAGNIFICO
holy .... MAHATMA
humorous .... WAG
ill-mannered ..... BOOR, LOUT, GOOP, CRAB, YAHOO
imaginary .... MYTH
important .... NIBS, VIP, MAGNIFICO, MOGUL, BASHAW
impractical .... DREAMER, VISIONARY, IDEALIST, FANTAST
impudent ... MALAPERT, UPSTART, HUSSY
impulsive ...... MADCAP
ineffectual .... DUD
inquisitive ...... MOUSER, BUSYBODY, SNOOP
insignificant ..... SHRIMP, SQUIRT, NONENTITY, SNIP
intellectual ... EGGHEAD, SAVANT, NOETIC, SCHOLAR, PUNDIT
lazy .... POKE, DRONE, LOAFER, IDLER, LURDAN(E)
learned .... PUNDIT, SCHOLAR, SAVANT, SAGE, SOPHIST, ORACLE
lively .... GRIG
living by his wits ... SPIV
living in town .. OPPIDAN
loud-voiced ... STENTOR, THERSITES
maladjusted ..... MISFIT
mean ...... LOUSE, CAD, CAITIFF
meddling .... BUTTINSKY
mentally deficient .... MORON, IDIOT, IMBECILE
miserly .... CHURL, NIGGARD, TIGHTWAD, SKINFLINT
mix-blooded ... MESTEE, HALFBREED, HALF-CASTE, MUSTEE, CREOLE, METIF(F), GRIFF(E), LADINO, MULATTO, METIS, MESTIZO
modern .... NEOTERIC
much-admired .. PIP(PIN)
mythical ...... SANDMAN
naive ...... BABE, LAMB
name of .... HANDLE, MONICKER
nameless ...... ANONYM
nearsighted ..... MYOPE
Negro-Indian .. GRIFF(E)
nice .... TRUMP
noble .... GENTLEMAN
noble born ..... CHILDE
noisy .. YAP, JAY, MAGPIE
not of noble rank .... COMMONER, ROTURIER
obnoxious .. FINK, HUNKS
obstinate ..... ASS, MULE
odd .. ECCENTRIC, QUEER
oddly dressed ...... GUY
of equal status .... COMPEER, CONGENER
of great energy ... DEMON
old-fashioned .... MOSSBACK, FOG(E)Y, FOSSIL
100-year-old .... CENTENARIAN
optimistic ... POLLYANNA
out of place ..... ESTRAY
overnice .... PRIG
overweight .... FATSO
pale-looking .. WHEYFACE
partly paralyzed .... PARETIC
pedantic .... PRIG
pledged .... HOSTAGE, BETROTHED
poor ... BEGGAR, PAUPER
popular .... LION, CELEBRITY
powerful .... MOGUL, TITAN, POTENTATE, GIANT, PARAMOUNT
pretending to knowledge SCIOLIST
prying ...... BUSYBODY, MOUSER
promising ...... COMER
prone to argue .. POLEMIC, POLEMIST
pugnacious .. SCRAPPER, BANTAM
puritanical .... BLUENOSE
quarrelsome .. SCRAPPER
queer ..... CHARACTER, CODGER, DUCK, GOOSE, CRANK, NUT
quick-tempered .... HOTSPUR
rebellious .. MALCONTENT, DISSIDENT
reckless ..... DAREDEVIL, MADCAP, HOTSPUR, PLUNGER
regarded with contempt .. SKATE
resembling another ..... RINGER
rich .... MONEYBAG, CROESUS, NABOB
rough ... LARRIKIN, MUG
sanctimonious ... GOODY
saucy .... MALAPERT
savage .... HUN, VANDAL
second .... YOU
self-centered .... EGOIST, EGOTIST, EGOMANIAC
self-important .... NIBS, BASHAW
servile ..... FLUNK(E)Y, SPANIEL
short, fat .... DUMPLING, SQUAB
sickly .... INVALID
silly ...... GOOSE, GOOP, GOOF, KOOK, PINHEAD, TOMFOOL
slovenly .... SLOP
slow-moving ..... POKE, SNAIL, DAWDLER, LAGGARD
sly ...... WEASEL, SNEAK, FOX
small .... DWARF, RUNT, PYGMY, BANTAM, SHRIMP, LILLIPUTIAN, INSECT, BUB, PIPSQUEAK, SNIP(PET), HALFPINT, SQUIRT, MIDGE(T), AGATE
small-teethed .... MICRODONT
stateless .... REFUGEE
stingy .... MISER, NIGGARD, SKINFLINT, HUNKS
stubborn .... MULE
stupid .... CHUKKER, DIMWIT, DULLARD, PINHEAD, DUFFER, SIMPLETON, DOLT, GABY, MUTT, OAF, NUMSKULL, LUMMOX, BOOB(Y), DUNDERHEAD, DUMBBELL, MOKE, SAP, ZOMBI(E), MUTTONHEAD, LOON, SOFTHEAD, LUNKHEAD, JACKASS, SLOB
stylish ...... DUDE, FOP, SWELL
surly .... HUNKS
sweet-faced .... CHERUB
sworn legally .... JURAT
syphilitic .... LUETIC
talkative ... (POPIN)JAY, MAGPIE
third ... SHE, THEY, HE, IT
timid ..... LAMB, MOUSE
tireless .... DYNAMO

tongue of ..... CLAPPER
tricky ..... FOX, SLICKER
tuberculous .... LUNGER, CONSUMPTIVE
ugly ... ZOMBI(E), GOON, OGRE, GOLLIWOG, FRIGHT, GAL(L)OT, SOURPUSS
under patronage .... PROTEGE, WARD
ungrateful ..... INGRATE
unreasonable .... MISOLOGIST
unwanted ..... OUTCAST, PARIAH, LEPER
used as tool ..... PAWN, FRONT, STOOGE
vain .... POPINJAY, PEACOCK
verging on insanity ...... MATTOID
vulgar ..... BOOR, LOUT, MUCKER
waist measure of .. GIRTH
weak .... GOODY
wealthy .... NABOB, CROESUS, PLUTOCRAT
white .... CAUCASIAN
who destroys maliciously VANDAL
who makes kids sleepy ... SANDMAN
who never laughs .... AGELAST, DEADPAN, POKERFACE
who sells on installment .. TALLYMAN
wise .... SOLON, SAGE, MAHATMA
with free ticket .... DEADHEAD
with insatiable thirst, etc. TANTALUS
with poor eyesight ...... MYOPE
withered, thin ... MUMMY
working off a debt .. PEON
worthless .... BUM, LOSEL
young .... LAMBKIN, TEENAGER, CALF, SLIP

personable .... COMELY, HANDSOME
personage ... NOTABLE, NIBS, BIGWIG, DIGNITARY, MAGNIFICO
personal .... INDIVIDUAL, PRIVATE, INTIMATE, CORPORAL
appearance .... MIEN, BEARING, PRESENCE
aura .... MYSTIQUE, CHARISMA
belongings .... TRAPS
characteristic ..... TRAIT
charm .... CHARISMA
combining form ... IDIO
well-being .. CONVENIENCE
personality .... PRESENCE, SELF, CHARACTER, EGO
test .... RORSCHACH
personate .... PORTRAY, MASKED
personator .... IMPOSTOR
personified .... INCARNATE
personify .... EMBODY
personnel ...... EMPLOYE(E)S, CREW, STAFF
persons .... FOLK
perspective .... VISTA, POINT OF VIEW, STANDPOINT
perspicacious .... KEEN, SHREWD, PERCEPTIVE
perspicacity .... ACUMEN, INSIGHT
perspicuous .... LUCID
perspiration .... SWEAT, HIDROSIS, SUDOR, EGESTA
stimulator ..... BONESET
perspire .... SWEAT, EGEST
persuade .... INDUCE, CONVINCE, PREVAIL ON, URGE, COAX
persuasible .... AMENABLE
persuasion .... BELIEF, CONVICTION, OPINION
art of .... SOFT SELL
persuasive .... COGENT, CONVINCING
pert ..... BRASH, FLIP, ARCH, SAUCY, FORWARD, BOLD, IMPUDENT, SASSY
girl .... MINX, CHIT
language .... SASS
pertain ..... BELONG, RELATE
Perth river .... TAY
pertinacious ...... STUBBORN
pertinence .... RELEVANT
pertinent .... RELEVANT, GERMANE, APT
perturb .... DISTURB, ALARM, UPSET, DISTRESS, RUFFLE, AGITATE
perturbation .... FEEZE
pertussis .. (WHOOPING)COUGH
Peru, capital of .... LIMA
conqueror of .. PIZARRO
peruke ...... HAIR, (PERI)WIG
peruse ... READ, SCRUTINIZE, STUDY, CON, SCAN
Peruvian, ancient .... INCA(N)
animal .... LLAMA, VICUNA, ALPACA
bark .... CINCHONA
beef .... CHARQUI
bird .... YUTU, TINAMOU
city .... CALLAO, AREQUIPA, TRUJILLO, ICA, PUNO, AYACUCHO, CUSCO
coin ..... LIBRA, PESETA, SOL
cormorant ..... GUANAY
current .... EL NINO
dance .... CUECA
department ..... TACNA
fox .... ATOC
goddess .... MAMA
hill ..... LOMA, MEDANO
Indian .... AYMARA, COLLA, QUECHUA, CHUNCHO, ANDE, INCA
inn .... TAMBO
junta leader .... VELASCO
king .. INCA, ATAHUALPA, ATABALIPA
language ...... QUECHUA, AYMARA
llama ..... PACO, ALPACA
monetary unit ...... SOL
mountain .... ANDES, MISTI, HUASCARAN
plant .... OCA, TOLA
plateau .... TABLAZO
port .... CALLAO
president .... BELAUNDE
recording device .. QUIPU
river .... APURIMAC, UCAYALI, ACARI, RIMAC, MARANON, JAVARI
seaport .... CALLAO
singer .... SUMAC
tanager .... YENI
tobacco .... SANA
tree .... CINCHONA
volcano ... MISTI, OMATE
wind .... PUNA, SURES
pervade .... FILL, PERMEATE, IMBUE, DIFFUSE
perverse ... WRY, UNTOWARD, WICKED, CONTRARY, DIFFICULT
pervert ... VITIATE, CORRUPT, MISLEAD, MISUSE, DISTORT, TWIST, DEBASE, WARP
pervious .... PERMEABLE, PENETRABLE, AMENABLE
Pesach .... PASSOVER
pesade .... REAR
Pescadores Islands .... HOKO GUNTO
pesky .... MISCHIEVOUS, ANNOYING, BOTHERSOME
peso .... DURO
1/100 of ...... CENTAVO, CENTIMO
pessimism, opposite of ...... OPTIMISM
pessimist .... WORRIER
slang .... CRAPEHANGER
pessimistic .... WORRISOME
pest ..... IMP, BANE, PLAGUE, NUISANCE, VERMIN
colloquial ...... TERROR
pester .... HECTOR, VEX, BADGER, HARASS, ANNOY, BOTHER, HARRY, DUN
pesticide .... DDT
pestiferous .... NOXIOUS, ANNOYING
pestilence .... SCOURGE, EPIDEMIC, PLAGUE, MURRAIN
pestle .... MULLER, BRAY, POUNDER, BEETLE
companion of ... MORTAR
pet ...... CODDLE, FAVORITE, DARLING, DANDLE, FONDLE, SULK, COSSET
lamb ..... COSSET, CADE
name .... NICKNAME, SOBRIQUET
Petain, Marshal ...... HENRI
petal .... LEAF, LABELLUM
base .... UNGUIS
protuberance ... CALCAR
spurred .... LABELLUM
petals, arrangement of ....

WHORL, ROSETTE
without ..... APETALOUS
petard .... FIRECRACKER, EXPLOSIVE
petasus .... CUPALO, (WINGED)HAT
petcock ...... VALVE, FAUCET
peter .... DWINDLE, WANE
actor ...... FALK, FONDA, OTOOLE, USTINOV
Bull's subject .... TEDDYBEAR, TEDDIES
Pan's author .... BARRIE
captain .... HOOK
dog .... NANA
loss .... SHADOW
pirate .... SMEE
Peter's tribute to Pope .. PENCE
petiole .... (LEAF)STALK, PEDUNCLE, STIPE
petit .... PETTY
mal .... EPILEPSY
petite .... SMALL, DIMINUTIVE
petition ...... ASK, ENTREATY, PLEA, REQUEST, PRAY(ER), SOLICIT, APPEAL, SUIT, APPLY
petitioner, in law ..... ORATOR
petits fours .... CAKES
Petrarch's lady .... LAURA
petrel ..... TITI, MALLEMUCK, STINKER, FULMAR
describing one .. STORMY
petrified goddess ...... NIOBE
petrified substance .... FOSSIL, COAL
petrify .... FOSSILIZE, HARDEN, DEADEN, STUN
Petrograd .... LENINGRAD
petrol .... GAS(OLINE), GASOLENE
petrolatum .... VASELINE
petroleum, jelly .... PETROLATUM, VASELINE
product ..... NAPHTHA, COKE, BUTANE, LIGROIN(E), CYMOGENE, GASOLINE, KEROSENE, BENZENE, PARAFFIN, PITCH, BITUMEN
Petrosian, chess champ .... TIGRAN
Petruchio's wife ...... KATIE, SHREW
petticoat ... BALMORAL, SLIP, SKIRT, WOMAN, GIRL, CRINOLINE
pettifogger .... SHYSTER
pettish ...... PEEVISH, CROSS
pettitoes .... FEET, TOES
petto .... BREAST
petty ...... PALTRY, TRIVIAL, MINOR, PICAYUNE, TRIFLING, MEAN, FIDDLING
fault ...... PECCADILLO
officer ... MATE, YEOMAN, BOSUN
petulant .... FRETFUL, HOITY-TOITY, IRRITABLE, PEEVISH, CROSS, TESTY, SHORT
petunia .... FLOWER, NIGHTSHADE

pew .... STALL, BENCHES, SLIP
end carving .. POPPYHEAD
pewee .. PHOEBE, FLYCATCHER, PEWIT
pewit ..... LAPWING, PEWEE, PHOEBE, GULL
pewter .... TRIFLE
peyote ...... CACTUS, MESCAL
"Peyton Place" author .... METALIOUS
pfennig, 1/2 of .... HELLER
100 .... MARK
Phaedra's husband .. THESEUS
parent .... MINOS
Phaedrus' forte ...... FABLES
phagedena .... ULCER, GANGRENE
phalanger ...... TAPOA, ARIEL
phantasm .... SPECTER, GHOST, EIDOLON
phantom ... VISION, SPECTER, ILLUSION, IDOL, (E)IDOLON, GHOST
Pharaoh .... RAM(E)SES, CHEOPS, SETI
residence ...... MEMPHIS
Pharisaic ...... HYPOCRITICAL
pharmacist ...... DRUGGIST, APOTHECARY
pharmaceutical concoction .... TISANE
pharmacology, subject of ..... DRUGS
pharmacy .... DRUGSTORE
pharos .. BEACON, LIGHTHOUSE
builder .... SOSTRATUS
phase ... ASPECT, SIDE, PART, FACET, STAGE, ANGLE, PHASIS
pheasant .... TRAGOPAN, LEIPOA, CHIR, GROUSE, POULT, MONAL, RING-NECK
brood .... NID(E), NYE
nest .... NIDE
phenobarbital .... LUMINOL
phenomenon .... EVENT
phial .... VIAL, BOTTLE
philabeg .... KILT
philanderer: sl. .... WOLF
philanthropic .... CHARITABLE, ALTRUISTIC
philatelist's delight ... STAMP
Philip II's naval fleet .. ARMADA
philippic .... TIRADE, HARANGUE, DIATRIBE, SCREED, ORATION, INVECTIVE
Philippine aborigine ... AETA, ATA, NEGRITO
alum .... TAWAS
animal .... TAMARAW, CARABAO, TARSIER
ant .... ANAY
archipelago .... SULU
barge .... CASCO
battlesite .... BATAAN, CORREGIDOR
boat ...... BATEL, CASCO
breadfruit .... RIMA
buffalo .... TIMARAU, CARABAO, TAMARAW
cannon .... LANTAKA

canoe .... BANCA
cape .... BOLINAO
capital .... MANILA, QUEZON CITY
child .... BATA
Chinese invader .... LIMAHONG
citizen .... FILIPINO, TAGALOG
city .... CAVITE, ILIGAN, DAGUPAN, MANILA, CEBU, DAVAO, ZAMBOANGA
civet .... MUSANG
coconut toddy ..... TUBA
coin ...... PESO, PESETA, CENTIMO
deer .... USA
dialect ...... PAMPANGO, TAGAL(OG), ILOCANO, BICOL, WARAY-WARAY
discoverer ... MAGELLAN
dissident .... HUK
drink .... VINO, TUBA, LUMBANOG
duck .... ITIK, PATO
dwarf ... NEGRITO, AETA
eggplant .... TALONG
expeditionary force ..... PEFTOK, PHILCAG
fabric .... PINA, JUSI
farmer .... KASAMA
fetish .... ANITO
fiber ... MAGUEY, HEMP, ABACA, PINA, JUSI
flag .... WATAWAT
food staple .... RICE, BIGAS, CORN
fort .... COTTA
fruit, foul-smelling ..... DURIAN
fruit tree ..... LANZONES, IBA, GUAVA, SANTOL
gourd .... UPO
governor general .. TAFT, IDE, WOOD, MURPHY, STIMSON
grapes .... UBAS
grass ... COGON, TALAHIB
guerrilla .... HUK
hardwood .... NARRA, YAKAL, IPIL, MOLAVE
heart .... PUSO
hemp .... ABACA
hero ...... AGUINALDO, LAPU LAPU, ABAD SANTOS, RIZAL, BONIFACIO
house .... BAHAY
island ..... SAMAR, CEBU, LEYTE, LUZON, MINDANAO, CORREGIDOR, PANAY, MASBATE, PALAWAN, MINDORO
jar .... BANGA
knife .... BOLO, ITAK
lamb .... TUPA
language ..... TAGALOG
leper colony .... CULION, TALA
liver .... ATAY
lungs .... BAGA
mahogany ...... NARRA

maid .... ALILA
mallard .... DUMARA
meat dried, salted .. TAPA
midwife .... HILOT
monetary unit ..... PESO
Moro boat ..... VINTA, LIPA, KUMPIT
Moro chief .. DATU, DATO
Moslem .... MORO, MUSLIM, MARANAW
mountain .... ARAYAT, CORDILLERA, APO, ZAMBALES, BANAHAW
municipality .... PUEBLO
native ... MORO, IGOROT, DUMAGAT, TAGALOG
negrito ... AETA, ATA, ITA
number ... ISA, DALAWA, TATLO, APAT, LIMA, ANIM
nut .... PILI
omelet .... TORTA
overskirt .... SAYA
oyster .... TALABA
palm .... NIPA, ANAHAW
peasant .., TAO, KASAMA
plum .... DUHAT
president .... QUEZON, OSMENA, ROXAS, QUIRINO, MAGSAYSAY, GARCIA, MACAPAGAL, MARCOS
province ... LANAO, CEBU, SAMAR, BULACAN, ILOILO, RIZAL, ALBAY, ISABELA, LEYTE, LAGUNA, ABRA
rebel .... INSURRECTO, KATIPUNAN, HUK
rice .... MACAN, WAGWAG, PAGA
river ...... PASIG, CHICO
sailboat ... VINTA, BATEL
sapodilla .... CHICO
sarong ..... PATADIONG
sea .... SULU
secret society .... KATIPUNAN
servant .... ALILA
sheep .... TUPA
shirt .... BARO
skirt .... SAYA
slave .... ALIPIN
soy sauce .... TOYO
soybean cake .... TAUSI, TAHURE
soybean curd ... TOKUA, TAHO, TOFU
spinach .... TALINUM
spleen .... LAPAY
statesman...... ROMULO, QUEZON, RECTO, OSMENA
sultanate .... SULU
summer capital .. BAGUIO
sweet potato ... CAMOTE
tail .... BUNTOT
taro .... GABI
territorial claim .. SABAH
thatch .... NIPA, COGON
tongue .... DILA
town .... PUEBLO
tree ... MOLAVE, YAKAL, IPIL, DAO, LANETE, LIGAS, SAMPALOC
tribesman .... KALINGA, IGOROT, TINGGIAN, BADJAO, TAUSUG, MARANAW, NEGRITO
tripe .... GOTO
tuna .... TULINGAN
village .... SITIO
volcano ..... APO, TAAL, MAYON, HIBOK HIBOK
water chestnut .. APULID
water buffalo .. CARABAO
weapon ..... BOLO, KRIS, KAMPILAN
weasel .... MUSANG
yam .... GABI, TUGI, UBI

Philippines, discoverer of the .. MAGELLAN
philistine .... BABBIT
city .. GAZA, GATH, GAYA
giant .... GOLIATH
Philo ____, dick ...... VANCE
philology ..... SCHOLARSHIP, LINGUISTICS
philomel ...... NIGHTINGALE
Philomela, sister of ... PROCNE
philopena .... NUT
philosopher ..... SAGE, CYNIC, SKEPTIC, HEGEL, KANT, HUME, PLATO, LOCKE, ZENO, SPINOZA
stone of .... ELIXIR
philosophy .... EGOISM, MONISM
philter .... POTION, CHARM
phiz .... FACE
phlebotome .. LANCET, FLEAM
phlegm is one .... HUMOR
phlegmatic .. DULL, IMPASSIVE, SLUGGISH, COOL
phloem ... BAST, TISSUE, BARK
phlogistic .... INFLAMMATORY
phlogosis .... ERYSIPELAS
phobia .... FEAR, HATRED, AGORA
Phoebe .... DIANA, MOON, PEWEE, PEWIT, SELENE, ARTEMIS, GODDESS
Phoebus ... SUN, APOLLO, SOL
Phoenician capital .... TYRE, SIDON
founder of Thebes ...... CADMUS
god ..... BAAL, DAGON, MOLOCH
goddess .... ASTARTE
port ...... SIDON, TYRE
princess .... EUROPA
Phoenix .... BENU
phonate .... VOCALIZE
phone call ...... BUZZ, RING
cubicle .... BOOTH
emergency .... HOTLINE
system .... INTERCOM
phonetics, smooth ...... LENE
phonics .... ACOUSTICS
phonograph .... VICTROLA, GRAMOPHONE
needle .. STYLUS, STYLE
record ... PLATTER, DISC, LONG PLAY
record mold ..... MASTER
with coin slot .. JUKE BOX

phonolite .... CLINKSTONE
phonology ...... PHONETICS, PHONEMICS, ORTHOEPY
phony .... FAKE, SHAM, FALSE, SPURIOUS, IMPOSTOR, CHARLATAN
phosphate .... APATITE
phosphor .... STAR, VENUS
photo ..... PIC(TURE), SNAP, MUG, PIX, SHOT
finish .... DEAD HEAT
solution ...... REDUCER, HYPO
photograph ... STILL, PICTURE, SHOT, PRINT, FILM
book .... ALBUM
enlarge a ...... BLOW UP
photographer's place .... DARKROOM
photographic camera .. KODAK, LEICA, CANNON, GRAFLEX
developing powder ...... METOL
equipment ..... CAMERA
material ... FILM, ORTOL, TONER
solution .... HYPO, FIXER, DEVELOPER, TONER, REDUCER
photographs pieced together ... MOSAIC, MONTAGE
photoplay .... MOVIE
phrase .... EXPRESSION, LOCUTION
in liturgy .... PARSE
in song .... REFRAIN
phraseology ...... PARLANCE, WORDING, DICTION, EXPRESSION
phratry .... PHYLE, CLAN
phrenetic ..... WILD, INSANE, EXCITED, FANATIC, DELIRIOUS
phrenic .... MENTAL
Phrygian king .... MIDAS
phthisis .... CONSUMPTION
phylactery .... CHARM, REMINDER
phyletic .... RACIAL
Phillis .... SWEETHEART
phylloid .... LEAFLIKE
physic .... LAXATIVE, CATHARTIC, APERIENT, PURGATIVE
physical .. SOMATIC, NATURAL, MATERIAL, BODILY, SOMAL
discomfort .. DYSPHORIA
exercise .... DRILL
science ...... GEOLOGY, CHEMISTRY
vigor .... VITALITY
physician ... DOC(TOR), GALEN, MAYO, LISTER, MEDIC(O), MESMER
former .... LEECH
symbol ...... CADUCEUS
physicist .... MACH, OHM, AMPERE, BOYLE, HAHN, EINSTEIN, CURLE, RABI
physics, branch of .. KINETICS, MECHANICS, OPTICS,

ACOUSTICS, STATICS, DYNAMICS
theory in .... RELATIVITY
physiognomy .... FACE
phytology .... BOTANY
pi .. JUMBLE, MIXTURE, MIX UP
piacular .... ATONING, EXPIATORY
pianist ..... CLIBURN, ITURBI, HESS, ANDA, LEVANT
White House .... NIXON, TRUMAN
piano .... SPINET
favorite .... NOLA
forerunner of .... CLAVICHORD, HARPSICHORD
in music .... SOFT
key .... IVORY
keyboard ...... CLAVIER
piece ...... BAGATELLE, BALLADE, NOLA
white key ...... NATURAL
pianolike instrument ... SPINET, CELESTA, CLAVICHORD
piaster, 1/120 of ...... ASPER
piazza ..... SQUARE, ARCADE, GALLERY, PORCH, VERANDA(H)
pibroch, instrument for a ..... BAGPIPE
pica .... TYPE
picador's prey ... BULL, TORO
picaresque character .... VAGABOND
picaroon .... ROGUE, ADVENTURER, THIEF, PIRATE
Picasso, painter .... PABLO
picayune ..... PALTRY, PETTY, TRIVIAL, CHEAP
Piccadilly in London .. STREET
piccolo .... FLUTE
pick ..... PECKER, MATTOCK, GLEAN, PLECTRUM, CULL, PROBE, PLUCK, ELITE, SELECT, CHOOSE, BEST, MANDREL, CHOICE(ST), NIBBLE
at .... NAG, FINGER
on .... ANNOY, TEASE
the .... ELITE
up ..... LEARN, IMPROVE
pickax ..... GURLET, MATTOCK
pickerel .... PIKE
picket ...... FENCE, GUARD, TETHER, PALE, STAKE, POST
station of a ..... OUTPOST
pickings ..... SCRAPS, SPOILS
pickle .... MESS, ACHAR, GHERKIN, JAM, FIX, SOUSE, MARINATE, ALEC, CORN, DILL
pickled .... DRUNK
food .... SOUSE
meat .... SOUSE
pickles .... RELISH
pickling solution .. MARINADE, BRINE, SOUSE
pickpocket .... DIP, PRIG, CUTPURSE
trainer .... FAGIN
picnic ... OUTING, CLAMBAKE, COOKOUT, JUNKET
author of .... INGE
several days' ... MAROON
picot .... PURL
picotee .... CARNATION
pictograph ..... HIEROGLYPH
pictorial ..... GRAPHIC, VIVID
picture ...... IMAGE, IMAGINE, DEPICT, LIKENESS, IMPRESSION, SLIDE, STILL, CANVAS, PROFILE, PHOTO, REFLECT, PORTRAY, SCENE(RY), TABLEAU, PRINT
composite .... MONTAGE
frame .... EASEL
girl .... PIN-UP, CHEESECAKE
in words ..... DESCRIBE, DELINEATE
life .... STILL
longer than wider .... PANEL
moving .... CINEMA, FILM, MOVIE
person's ...... PORTRAIT, BUST
poorly painted .... DAUB
pretty girl's ..... PIN-UP
puzzle .... REBUS
section .... ROTO
tube .... KINESCOPE
wall .... MURAL
writing .... PICTOGRAPH, HIEROGLYPH(IC)
pictograph .... GLYPH
picturesque .... SCENIC, GRAPHIC, QUAINT, IDYLLIC, STRIKING, VIVID
piddle ..... TRIFLE, DAWDLE, URINATE
piddling .... USELESS
pidgin .... JARGON, CHINOOK
pie .... PASTY, PATE, PASTRY, PATTY, DUMPLING, MIXTURE, JUMBLE, COBBLER, JAY
covering .... CRUST, MERINGUE
cut, shape of .... WEDGE
deer's vitals .... HUMBLE
filling .... MINCE MEAT
piebald .... HORSE, PIED, PINTO, MOTTLED, DAPPLED, CALICO
piece ... UNIT, COIN, FIREARM, BIT, PART, CHIP, SLIVER, SPLINTER, FRAGMENT, SLICE, CANTLE, SCRAP, HUNK, MORSEL, COLLOP, CHUNK, EKE, PORTION
cut off .... CHIP, KERF
de resistance .... ENTREE, MAIN EVENT
of eight .... REAL
of paper .... SLIP
of part music ... DESCANT
of soap .... CAKE
of turf ...... SOD, DIVOT
out .... EKE
together .... PATCH
worker .... JOBBER
pied ...... SPOTTED, PIEBALD, MOTTLED, VARIEGATED
a-terre .... LODGING
Piper's river ..... WESER
Piper's town ... HAMELIN
Piedmont .... PIEMONTE
city ... TURIN, OSTI, TRINO
ruling family .... SAVOY, SAVOIE
village .... MARENGO
pieplant .... RHUBARB
pier .. BUTTRESS, WHARF, DOCK, ANTA, QUAY, MOLE, SLIP, PILASTER, LANDING, JETTY, JUTTY
landing ... DOCK, JETTY
space .... SLIP
pierce ... THIRL, THRUST, STAB, PRICK, LANCE, BORE, PUNCH, GOUGE, IMPALE, SPEAR, GORE, GRIDE, PENETRATE, PUNCTURE, STICK, LANCINATE
piercing ...... SHARP, KEEN, SHRILL, INCISIVE
pieridine .... BUTTERFLY
Pierre .... PETER, PIETRO
piers, space between .... SLIP
piet ... MAGPIE, OUZEL, OUSEL
pig ..... SOW, SHOTE, DUROC, JACOBIN, SWINE, HOG, GRUNTER, PORK(ER)
animal like ..... PECCARY
castrated .... BARROW
dig like a .... ROOT
disease ...... BULLNOSE
feet of .... TROTTERS
female ...... SOW, GILT
for slaughter ... FATLING
intestines .. CHITTERLINGS
iron .... INGOT
litter .... FARROW
male .... BOAR
pen .... STY
uncastrated .... BOAR
vital organs of .... HA(R)SLET
weed .... GOOSEFOOT
wild .... BOAR
young ..... GILT, SHOAT, PIGLET, ELT, GRICE, SHOTE
pigboat .... SUBMARINE
pigeon .... PIDGIN, TURBIT, DOVE, NUN, TUMBLER, POUTER, RUFF, PIPER, FANTAIL, CULVER, BARB
Barbary .... BARB
call .... COO
carrier .... HOMING
crested ..... TRUMPETER
hawk .... MERLIN
hearted .... TIMID, COWARDLY
house ..... COLUMBARY, (DOVE)COTE
ID tag .... LEGBAND
neck feathers ... HACKLE
pea .... DAL
slang .... DUPE
tumbler .... ROLLER
wood .... CUSHAT, RINGDOVE
young .... SQUAB

pigeonhole .... SHELVE
pigeonholes, row of ..... RACK
pigfish .... GRUNTER
piggery .... STY
piggin .... PAIL, PIPKIN
piggish .... FILTHY
piggyback .... PICKABACK
pigheaded .... STUBBORN, OBSTINATE
piglet .... GILT
piglike animal ..... PECCARY
pigment .. DYE, ANTHOCYANIN, AQUAMARINE, CINNABAR, ZAFFRE, ETIOLIN, UMBER, BICE, STAINER, SMALT, ZAFFER, LITHOPONE, GAMBOGE, ORPIMENT
absence of .... ALBINISM, ALPHOSIS
being without ... ALBINO
black .... MELANIN
blood's .... HEMACHROME
blue ...... SMALT, BICE, ULTRAMARINE
bluish green ... VIRIDIAN
board .... PALETTE
brown ... UMBER, SEPIA, BISTER, BISTRE
calico printing .. CANARIN
cochineal .... LAKE
coal tar .... MAUVE, ANILIN(E), ALIZARIN, MADDER
cuttlefish .... SEPIA
dark brown .... BISTER, SEPIA
earth ... SIENNA, UMBER
grayish-blue ...... BICE
green .... BICE
iron ore .... OCHRE
lack of ... LEUCODERMA, ALPHOSIS, ALBINISM
red .... CARMINE, VERMILION, CINNABAR
reddish brown ... SIENNA
skin tissue ..... MELANIN
soot .... BISTER, BISTRE, LAMPBLACK
without .... ALBINO
yellow ... OCHRE, OCHER, ETIOLIN, FLAVIN(E), QUERCETIN, RETINENE
pigmentation: comb. form .... CHROMAT(O)
dark .... MELANISM
lack of .... LEUCODERMA, ALPHOSIS
pigmented black ... MELANOID
pigmentless creature .. ALBINO
pigmy .... (See PYGMY)
pignus .... PAWN, PLEDGE
pigpen .... STY
sound .... OINK, GRUNT(LE)
pigs' feet .... PETTITOES, TROTTERS
litter of ... FARROW, TEAM
pigskin ... FOOTBALL, SADDLE
pigtail ...... QUEUE, BRAID, TOBACCO, PLAIT, CUE, COLETA
pigweed .... AMARANTH
pika .... CONY, RODENT, LAGOMORPH
pike .... PICK, MOUNTAIN, PARTIZAN, GATE, TOLL ROAD, PIERCE, SPONTOON, FISH, LUCE(T), SPEARHEAD, PICKEREL
American explorer ...... ZEBULON
collection .... TOLL
like fish ..... ARAPAIMA, ROBALO, GAR
perch .... SAUGER
piker: sl. ...... CHEAPSKATE, TIGHTWAD
pilaf(f) .... PILAU
pilaster .... ANTA, PIER, COLUMN, ALETTE
groove .... STRIA
top of .... CAPITAL
Pilate, Rom. governor .... PONTIUS
pilau/pilaw .... PILAF(F)
pilchard .... SARDINE, HERRING, PILCHER, FUMADO
pilcher .... PILCHARD, SCABBARD
pile ... CONGERIES, HEAP, RICK, STACK, HOARD, NAP, ACCUMULATE, BUILDING, MASS, SPILE
driver .... MAUL, RAM, TUP, OLIVER
hay .. RICK, STACK, MOW
slang .... FORTUNE
velvet .... NAP
pileous .... HAIRY
piles .... HEMORROIDS
wood for .... ALDER
pileus .... (SKULL)CAP
pilewort .... CELANDINE
pilfer .... STEAL, SWIPE, ROB, THIEVE, MICHE, MOOCH
pilferer .... THIEF
pilgrim .... WAYFARER, SOJOURNER, WANDERER, PALMER, IHRAM, ALDEN
badge of ...... SCALLOP
destination of ... MECCA, SHRINE, ROME, JERUSALEM
garment of .... IHRAM
Holy Land ..... PALMER
"Pilgrim's Progress" author .. BUNYAN
protector ...... TEMPLAR, CRUSADER
pilgrimage .... HADJ
pilgrims, Indian friend of ..... MASSASOIT, WAMPANOAG
settlement ... PLYMOUTH
ship of ..... MAYFLOWER
traveling together .... CARAVAN
pill .... PELLET, PILULE, (BASE)BALL, BOLUS, DRAGEE
like a .... PILULAR
slang .... BORE
sugar coated ... DRAGEE
vet's .... BOLUS
pillage ... SACK, FLAY, LOOT, SPOIL, RIFLE, FORAY, MARAUD, RAPINE, RAVAGE, PLUNDER, HARRY
pillar ..... COLUMN, SUPPORT, STELE, POST, LAT, PIER, MONUMENT, OBELISK
bottom support .... PEDESTAL
drawing on ... GRAFFITO
of ____ .... SMOKE, STRENGTH
of Hercules .. GIBRALTAR, JEBEL MUSA
projecting ring .... CINCTURE
top inhabitant .. STYLITE
top of .... IMPOST
with figure ... CARYATID, ATLANTES, TELAMON
writing on .... GRAFFITO
pillbox .... HAT
pillory .... STOCKS, YOKE, CANGUE, EXPOSE, GIBBET
pillow ... BOLSTER, HEADREST, CUSHION, PAD
covering ..... SLIP, TICK
fight .... ROMP
stuffing .... CEIBA, KAPOK, COTTON
pilose .... HAIRY, HIRSUTE
pilot .... AVIATOR, FLYER, GUIDE, STEER(SMAN), LEAD, CONDUCT
biscuit ...... HARDTACK
boat .... HELMSMAN
cow .... PINTANO
fish .... REMORA
lifesaver for .. PARAFOIL, CHUTE
place of .... COCKPIT
test flight .... SOLO
pilotless plane .... DRONE, GLIDER
pilous .... HAIRY
Pilsudski, Polish president .... JOZEF
pilule .... PILL
Pima ...... INDIAN, COTTON
pimento .... (ALL)SPICE
pimiento ... PEPPER, PAPRIKA, RELISH
pimola .... OLIVE
pimp ... PANDER, PROCURER, RELISH
pimpernel .... PRIMROSE
pimple .... POCK, PAPULE, WHEAL, WHELK, PUSTULE, CARBUNCLE
scar .... POCK
pin ... DOWEL, TOGGLE, PEG, TRIFLE, FASTEN, ACUS, TACK, FID, RIVET, NAIL, FASTENER, COAG, NOG, LILL, BADGE, BOLT, BROOCH, COTTER
buckle's .... TONGUE
colloquial .... LEG
down ...... HOLD, NAIL
firing .... TIGE
flatheaded .... TACK
gunwale .... THOLE
in bowling .... CLUB
meat-cooking .. SKEWER, SPIT, BROACH
metal .... RIVET

money ..... ALLOWANCE
oar .... THOLE
pivot .... PINTLE
supporting .... FID
up .... CHEESECAKE
pina .... PINEAPPLE
pinaceous tree ... PINE, CEDAR, FIR
pinafore .... DICKEY, SLIP, APRON, SAVE-ALL, TIER
children's ..... TIER, SLIP
pince nez .... EYEGLASSES, LORGNON
pincer ...... NIPPER, GRIPPER, CLAW, TWEEZER, FORCEPS, TONGS, PLIERS, CHELA
pinch .... STEAL, FILFER, NIP, FILCH, DISTRESS, RAID, PUGIL, GRIPE, SQUEEZE, ARREST, CRAMP
and twist .... TWEAK
hit .... SUBSTITUTE
of something ..... DASH
pindaric .... ODE
pine .... CONIFER, CEDAR, LONG, KAURY, KAURI, LANGUISH, PONDEROSA, MOPE, PINON, WASTE, YEARN, LOBLOLLY, OCOTE
board/wood .... DEAL
colloquial ... PINEAPPLE
cone .... STROBILE
fruit .... CONE
nut .... PINON
product .... RESIN, GALIPOT
seed .... PINON
tar extract ...... RETENE
tree disease .... BLISTER, RUST
tree resin ...... DAMMER, DAMMAR
Tree state .... MAINE
wild .... PINASTER
wood .... DEAL
pineal body .... SPIPHYSIS
pineapple .... PINE, PINA, ANANA
plantation .... PINERY
slang .... BOMB, (HAND)GRENADE
topknot .... COMA
pinfold .... POUND
ping pong ..... TABLE TENNIS
racket ..... PADDLE, BAT
pinquid .... FAT, OILY, GREASY, UNCTUOUS, FERTILE
pinion ... COGWHEEL, PENNON, WING, FEATHER, SHACKLE
pink ..... SALMON, RADICAL, FOXHUNTER, STAB, PRICK, SHIP
color ... SALMON, ROSY, DAMASK, CORAL
Pinkerton .... DETECTIVE, PRIVATE EYE
pinkie .... SHIP, FINGER
Pinkster .... WHITSUNTIDE
flower .... AZALEA
pinna .... AURICLE, FEATHER, FIN, WING, LEAFLET, EAR
pinnace .... BOAT
pinnacle .... PEAK, ACME, SUMMIT, SPIRE
of ice .... SERAC
pinner .... HEADDRESS
pinniped ..... SEAL, WALRUS, SEALION
pinnule .... LEAFLET
pinochle .... (CARD)GAME
game like ...... BEZIQUE
lowest cards ..... NINES
score .... DIX
term ...... MELD, KITTY, DIX
pinole .... FLOUR
pinon .... PINE
pinpoint .... DOT, LOCATE
pins and needles .... PARESTHESIA
pint, 1/4 .... NOGGIN, QUARTERN
1/2 .... SPLIT
pintado .... CERO, SIERRA, KINGFISH
pintail .... DUCK, GROUSE, SMEE
pintano ..... COWPILOT, FISH
pintle .... BOLT
pinto ..... SPOTTED, PIEBALD, MOTTLED, PONY
pinworm ... ASCARIS, ASCARID
Pinza, operatic singer ... EZIO
pioneer ..... PAVER, PLANTER
pious ...... SACRED, DEVOUT, RELIGIOUS, GODLY, SAINTLY
feeling .... PIETISM
person .... PIETIST
pip ... SEED, ROUP, SPOT, PEEP, CHIRP, HIT
pipa .... TOAD
pipal ..... (BO)TREE, FIG TREE
pipe ... TUBE, WHISTLE, FLUE, HUB(B), BRIER, BRIAR, CALUMET
air .... VENTIDUCT
bending tool .... HICKEY
bowl leaving ... DOTTEL, DOTTLE
clay ... DUDEEN, CHALAM
collar of .... FLANGE
curve of .... OFFSET
down .... SHUT UP
fitting .... TEE
gas .... FLUE
hashish smoking .... CHALAM
joint .... ELL
joint ring ...... GASKET
line: colloq. .. CONTACT, SOURCE
musical ..... OAT, FLUTE, FIFE
nozzled .... HOSE
oriental ... NARG(H)ILE, HOOKAH, REED
part .... STEM, BOWL
peace .... CALUMET
player .... FLUTIST
principal .... MAIN
shaped .... TUBULAR, FISTULOUS
shepherd's .... OAT, LARIGOT, REED
small .... TUBULE, PIPETTE
smoke .. TEWEL, DUDEEN, CALUMET, HOOKAH, NARGILE
tobacco ...... CHIBOUK, DUDEEN
tobacco bag .... POUCH
pipefish .... GAR
pipelike .... TUBATE
piper .... TRILLER
piping .... HISSING, SIZZLING, FOLD, REEDY
joint .... ELL
pipit .... (TIT)LARK
pipkin .... PIGGIN, POT
pippin .... APPLE, SEED
pipsqueak .... SNIP
pipy .... SHRILL
piquancy .... NIP, ZEST
piquant ..... PUNGENT, SPICY, SALTY, SHARP, BITING, RACY
pique ... RESENTMENT, PEEVE, OFFENSE, EXCITE, NETTLE, PROVOKE, COTTON, OFFEND, FABRIC
piracy .... ROBBERY
literary .... PLAGIARISM, PLAGIARY
piragua .... CANOE, PIROGUE, BOAT
Pirandello, Italian dramatist .. LUIGI
piranha ..... CARIBE, PIRAYA, FISH
pirate ..... PICAROON, XEBEC, FREEBOOTER, CORSAIR, SEAWOLF, (SEA)ROVER, PRIVATEER
famed ... ROGERS, DRAKE, KIDD, MORGAN, CORNISH
flag .... ROGER
literary ..... PLAGIARIST
of old ..... KIDD, TEACH, MORGAN
ship .... PICAROON, BRIGANTINE, PRIVATEER, FRIGATE
state .... TUNISIA
pirn .... SPOOL, BOBBIN
pirogue ..... CANOE, PIRAGUA
Pisa feature .... TOWER
Pisces .... FISH
piscine lore name .... WALTON
Pisgah's biblical climber ..... MOSES
summit .... NEBO
pishu .... LYNX
pismire .... ANT, EMMET
pisolite .... LIMESTONE
piss .... URINE, URINATE
Pissarro, Fr. painter .. CAMILLE
pistachio .... CASHEW, NUT
pistil, part of ... OVARY, STIPE, STIGMA, CARPEL, STYLE
pistol .... DERRINGER, (SIDE)ARM, ZIP GUN, MAUSER, LUGER, REPEATER, FIREARM, REVOLVER, AUTOMATIC, DAG(G)
case .... HOLSTER
chamber ..... MAGAZINE
slang .... GAT, ROD,

HEATER, EQUALIZER, PEACEMAKER
pistole .... COIN
piston ...... PLUNGER, VALVE
pit ..... CAVITY, ABYSS, HELL WELL, POCK(MARK), SEED, GRAVE, ARROYO, STONE, SNARE, TRAP, ARENA, FOVEA, (POT)HOLE
bottomless ...... ABYSS
in anatomy ...... FOSSA
mine .... SUMP
peach/plum ... PUTAMEN, ENDOCARP
theater .... PARQUET
pita .. AGAVE, FIBER, BROCKET
pitch ... BITUMEN, ASPHALTUM, RESIN, ERECT, SET UP, HURL, CAST, TOSS, FLING, TAR, ALCHITRAN, THROW, DIP, ENCAMP, PLUNGE, LURCH, SWAY, ROLL, REEL, KEY, CANT
black .... PICEOUS
in baseball ...... TWIRL
pipe .... DIAPASON
salesman's ...... PATTER, LINE, SPIEL, PLUG
uncompleted ..... BALK
pitchblende ingredient .... URANIUM
pitcher ...... EWER, HURLER, OLLA, TOSSER, JUG, TOBY
and the catcher .... BATTERY
leaf .... ASCIDIUM
left-handed ... SOUTHPAW
pitch of .. TWIRL, SPITTER, SPITBALL, BEANBALL, CURVE
plant .... FLYTRAP
plate of the ...... SLAB, BOX, MOUND
preparatory motion of ... WINDUP
shaped ..... URCEOLATE
water .... CARAFE
pitchman .... HAWKER
pitchy .... BLACK
piteous .... PITIFUL, PATHETIC
pitfall .... TRAP, SNARE
pith ...... GIST, SUBSTANCE, MEDULIA, PULP, MARROW, CORE
helmet ..... TOPEE, TOPI
Pithecanthropus erectus ...... JAVA MAN
pithy ...... LACONIC, TERSE, CONCISE, FORCEFUL
pitiable .... MEAN
pitiful ... PATHETIC, PITEOUS, MEAN
pitman .... MINER
pittance .. DOLE, ALLOWANCE
pitted ..... FOVEATE, STONED, POCKMARKED
pitter patter .... PITAPAT, DRUMBEAT
pituitary hormone .. PROLACTIN
secretion .... MUCUS, HORMONE
pity ..... MERCY, COMPASSION, SYMPATHY

pivot .... PINTLE, WHEEL, SWIVEL, TURN, HINGE, STATOR
City .... GEELONG
pivotal .... CARDINAL
pixilated .... DRUNK
pixy ..... FAIRY, ELF, SPRITE, PIXIE
Pizzaro's conquest ..... PERU
pizzicato .... PLUCKED
placard ... BILL, POSTER, SIGN
placate .... MOLLIFY, APPEASE, PACIFY, SOOTHE
place ... SPACE, ROOM, REGION, APPOINT, PUT, SET, STEAD, LOCALE, LOCUS, POSITION, STANDING, SPOT, LIEU
accurately .... TRUE
apart .. ENISLE, ISOLATE, SEGREGATE
between ...... INTERPOSE
camping .... ETAPE, BIVOUAC
city's ... SQUARE, PLAZA
dancing .... CASINO, CABARET, BALLROOM
for athletics .. GYMKHANA
for relics ..... SEPULCHER
for rubbish .... DUMP
frequented ... HANGOUT, HAUNT, PURLIEU
give .... YIELD
hiding .... LAIR, DEN, HANGOUT, HIDEOUT, MEW, CACHE
in a benefice .... INDUCT, INSTALL
in a row .... ALIGN, ALINE, LINE UP
mat .... DOILY
meeting .... TRYST, RENDEZVOUS
near .... APPOSE
noisy .... MADHOUSE
of .... LIEU, STEAD
abode .... RESIDENCE, DWELLING, HOUSE, HOME
accused in court ...... DOCK
agony ..... GOLGOTHA
confusion .. MADHOUSE
honor .... HEADTABLE, PEDESTAL
oblivion ...... LIMBO
rapid growth .. HOTBED
religious seclusion .... CONVENT, ABBEY, NUNNERY, MONASTERY, PRIORY, CLOISTER
safety .... REFUGE, HAVEN, SANCTUARY, HARBOR
torment ..... GEHENNA
trial .... VENUE
secret .... MEW, DEN, HIDEOUT
set in .... POSIT, SITUATE
side by side .. COLLOCATE
snugly .... ENSCONCE
storage .... WAREHOUSE, CRIB, DEPOT, CACHE, SILO, CELLAR, CLOSET

take ... OCCUR, HAPPEN, TRANSPIRE
to stand on .... POU STO
trading .. MART, MARKET, EXCHANGE
under water ... IMMERSE, SUBMERGE
placid .... CALM, QUIET, SERENE, TRANQUIL, PEACEFUL, IMPASSIVE
placket .... POCKET
plagiarism ...... CRIB, PIRACY
plagiarist .... THIEF
plagiarize .... CRIB, STEAL, LIFT, PIRATE
plague ... SCOURGE, CALAMITY, VEX, TORMENT, PEST(ER), HARRY, MURRAIN, TEASE, HECTOR, WANION, NUISANCE, HARASS, ANNOY
plagues, one of the ... LOCUST
plaice .... (FLAT)FISH, FLOUNDER, SOLE
plaid .... MAUD, TARTAN
plaidman .... TARTAN, HIGHLANDER
plain ...... CAMPAGNA, FLAT, LEVEL, BARE, CLEAR, MERE, CAMPO, LLANO, PALPABLE, EVIDENT, SIMPLE, PATENT, HOMELY, OPEN, OBVIOUS
Arctic .... TUNDRA
barren, high .... PARAMO
dweller .... LLANERO, GAUCHO, LOWLANDER
grassy .... CAMPO, SAVANNA(H), LLANO, VELD(T), PRAIRIE
high ..... PARAMO, MESA, WOLD, WEALD
hill on a .... BUTTE
spoken ... BLUNT, FRANK, CANDID
treeless .... STEPPE, TUNDRA, VELD(T), WOLD, PAMPAS, SAVANNA(H)
plains Indian ...... PAWNEE
plainsman ...... WESTERNER
plaint .. LAMENT(ATION), GRIPE
plaintiff .... DEMANDANT, SUER, ACCUSER, ORATOR, COMPLAINANT, SUITOR
answer of .. REPLICATION
list of wrongs suffered ... LIBEL
withdrawal of case ...... NONSUIT
plaintive ... MOURNFUL, SAD, WISTFUL
plait .... PLEAT, BRAID, PIGTAIL, QUEUE, PLAT, PLEX, PLY, TRESS, WIMPLE, PLEACH
plaited .... PLICATE, BRAIDED
grass/leaves .... SENNIT
trimming .... RUCHE
plan .. OUTLINE, MAP, SCHEMA, SCHEME, ETTLE, PLAT, DRAFT, DESIGN, PROJECT
artfully ..... MACHINATE
of journey .... ITINERARY
spoiler .... MARPLOT

townsite .... PLAT
planch(e) ..... FLOOR, BOARD
plancher .... PALLET
plane .... FLAT, LEVEL, EVEN, SURFACE, AIRFOIL, TROWEL
geometry .. PLANIMETRY
inclined .... RAMP
smoothing ..... TROWEL
10-sided ...... DECAGON
tree ... PLATAN, CHINAR
war ..... SPAD, SPITFIRE, STUKA, ZERO, NAPIER, SUPERFORT, SABREJET, MIG
planet .... VENUS, MARS, SATURN, JUPITER, MERCURY, PLUTO, URANUS, EARTH, NEPTUNE
between Jupiter and Mars PALLAS
erratic movement of ..... LIBRATION
largest .... JUPITER
minor .... ASTEROID
satellite .... MOON, RHEA, DIONE, MIMAS, HESTIA, NEREID, UMBRIEL, PHOBOS, DEIMOS
shadow of ...... UMBRA, PENUMBRA
planetoid .... ASTEROID
planetarium .... ORRERY
planing tool ..... SPOKESHAVE
plank ..... BOARD, PRINCIPLE, SLATE, DECK
curve of .... SNY
down .... PAY
planks above keel .. DEADWOOD
planoblast .... JELLYFISH, HYDROID
plant (see shrub) .. PLANTAIN, HYSSOP, MILL, BUGLE, WORT, AROID, SOW, TREE, SHRUB, HERB, FACTORY, STOCK, CLOVER, FREESIA
aconite ... MONKSWOOD, WOLFSBANE
agave .... PITA
air ... EPIPHYTE, ORCHID, MOSS, LICHEN
Alpine .... EDELWEISS
amaranth family .... COCKSCOMB
amaryllis family .... EUCHARIS, CRINUM
and animal classification LINNEAN
and animal life ... BIOTA, BIOS
apiaceous ...... CARROT, PARSNIP, ANISE
appendage ..... STIPULE, TENDRIL, STIPEL
artichoke's kin .... CARDOON
aromatic .... LAUREL, MINT, GUACO, ANISE, LAVENDER, THYME, MONARDA
arum family ..... AROID, TARO
aster family ..... DAISY, C(H)AMOMILE, TARRAGON, TIDYTIPS, ZINNIA, FEVERFEW
axis .... STALK, CAUDEX
banana .... CANNA, PLANTAIN
base ... CAUDEX, CAULIS
beanlike ...... SAINFOIN
beech family .... OAK
beetle ... (COCK)CHAFER, SCARAB, ROSEBUG
berry .... CURRANT
Biblical ... HYSSOP, TARE
bitter .... RUE
blue-flowered ... BLUET, LUPINE
body .... THALLUS
borage family .. COMFREY, HELIOTROPE, LUNGWORT
branch ... SPRAY, SPRIG, TWIG
brassicaceous ..... COLE, TURNIP, CABBAGE, BROCCOLI
breathing pore ... STOMA
broom .... SPART
bryophytic .... MOSS
bud .... (S)CION
bug .... CHINCH
bulb ... NARCISSUS, SEGO, ATAMASCO, SQUILL, JONQUIL, GARLIC
burning bush ... WAHOO
bursting ..... PUFFBALL
cactus .... MESCAL, CEREUS, SAGUARO
caper family .... CLEOME
capsule .... POD
carbohydrate .... PENTOSAN(E)
carrot family ... ERINGO, ERYNGO, CHERVIL, HEMLOCK, CONIUM, CORIANDER, COWBANE, DILL, ANISE, CUM(M)IN
celery family ..... CARROT
century .. AGAVE, MAGUEY
chili .... CAPSICUM
chrysanthemum .... PYRETHRUM
climbing .... SCAMMONY, RUNNER, LIANA, LIANE, VINE, RATTAN, YAM
clinging part of .. TENDRIL
clover-like ..... MELILOT, MEDIC
composite family .... MILFOIL, YARROW, COSMOS, COREOPSIS, ASTER, DAHLIA, DAISY, DANDELION, SUNFLOWER
covering ..... ARMATURE, PEAT, TUNIC
creeping ...... IPOMOEA, GROUNDLING, PYXIE, PERIWINKLE
cross-bred ..... HYBRID
crow family .... COLUMBINE, HELLEBORE
crowfoot family .... HEPATICA, MOUSETAIL
cruciferous ...... CRESS, MUSTARD
cutting .... SLIP
cycad family ... COONTIE
cyperaceous ..... SEDGE
daisylike .... OXEYE
decay .... ROT, NECROSIS
disease .... SCAB, MOSAIC, RUST, SMUT, ESCA, BRAND, BLET, ERGOT, PSOROSIS, NECROSIS, CLUBROOT, CANKER, ERINOSE, GALL, WILT, ICTERUS, (BLACK)ROT, SCALD, YELLOW, MILDEW, BLIGHT, CURL, BUNT
dodder .... AMIL
dry climate .. XEROPHYTE, CACTUS
dwarf .... ALYSSUM
dye .... AMIL
eating animal .... HERBIVORE
eating aquatic mammal .. DUGONG, MANATEE
emetic .... IPECAC
environment ... HABITAT
experimental garden .... NURSERY
exudation .... RESIN, GUM, COPAL
fiber ..... HEMP, ABACA, RAMIE, JUSI, SUNN, FLAX, ISTLE, SISAL, MAGUEY, AGAVE, PITA
figwort family .... COLLINSIA
floating .... WATER LILY, LOTUS
flowering ... ACANTHUS, ROSE, RHODORA, CALLA, ORCHID
flowerless ..... LYCOPOD, FERN, LICHEN
fluid ... SAP, MILK, LATEX
fodder .... VETCH, SAINFOIN
forage .... GUAR
fossil .... CALAMITE, HORSETAIL
fragrant .... BASIL, ANGELICA, THYME, MARJORAM, (SPEAR)MINT, HYSSOP
fragrant-leafed .... TARRAGON, CAMOMILE
fragrant seed ...... ANISE
garden .... ORACH(E)
gentian family .... CENTAURY
genus ..... ARUM, AGAVE, ERINGO
geranium family .... ALFILARIA
ginger family .. CURCUMA, TURMERIC
goosefoot .... BEET, SPINACH
gourd family .... (MUSK)MELON, CANTALOUPE
gout medicine ... GUACO
grass .... AVENA
grasslike .... RUSH

growing from inside ..... ENDOGEN
growing in solutions ..... HYDROPHONICS
growing within another .. ENDOPHYTE, ENTOPHYTE
grown flat .... ESPALIER
growth on a ...... GALL
hair .... VILLUS
hairlike growth .... TRICHOME, BRISTLE, PRICKLE
hairy-leafed ... ANCHUSA
heath family .... AZALEA, LAUREL
hemp .... CANNABIS
herbaceous .... LOBELIA
honeysuckle family ...... ELDER
insect ..... SCALE, APHID
insect-catching .. FLYTRAP
insect-eating .. CARNIVORE
interior chaff ..... PALEA
iris family ..... CROCUS, ORRIS, ORRICE, FREESIA, IXIA
juice .... MILK, SAP
kind of .... ANNUAL
kingdom, part of .... PHYLUM
knotweed family .... PERSICARY
leaf, poisonous .... JABORANDI
leaves for salad .... ESCAROLE
leguminous ..... DERRIS, GUAR, LENTIL, PEA
lice genus .... APHIS
life .... FLORA, VEGETATION
lilaceous ... SEGO, LEEK, ONION, TULIP
lily family ... SABADILLA, CAMAS(S), GARLIC, ONION, LEEK, ALLIUM, ALOE, LOTUS, YUCCA, SQUILL, ASPHODEL, HELLEBORE
liquid ...... SAP, JUICE, MILK, LATEX
louse ..... APHID, APHIS
madder family .. COFFEE, HOUSTONIA, IPECAC, CINCHONA, GARDENIA, CHAY
main axis ... STALK, STEM
male .... MAS
mallow family .... CHECKERBLOOM, HIBISCUS, HOLLYHOCK
marigold ...... KINGCUP, ASTER, CAPER
marsh .... CATTAIL
material spread around .. MULCH
matter, decaying ... PEAT
meadow ..... INNOCENCE
medicinal ..... GENTIAN, SENNA, HERB, ALOE, BONESET, ARNICA, IPECAC, LOBELIA, SIMPLE
milkweed family .... STAPELIA
milkwort family .. SENEGA
milky liquid ..... LATEX
mint family ..... COLEUS, BASIL, BETONY, DITTANY, OREGANO, HENBIT, MAJORAM, CATNIP, SAGE, THYME, SALVIA, HYSSOP, BERGAMOT, LAVENDER, ROSEMARY, BUGLE, GERMANDER, PATCHOULI, MONARDA, FRAXINELLA
moor .... HEATHER
mosslike ... TILLANDSIA, LIVERWORT, LICHEN
mulberry family .... CONTRAYERVA
mushroom-like .... PUFFBALL
musky smelling .... MOSCHATEL
mustard family .... COLE, CABBAGE, WOAD, STOCK, CRUCIFER, CRESS, RAPE, KALE, ALYSSUM, CHARLOCK, RADISH, MADWORT
narcotic ... HEMP, POPPY, MARIJUANA, HASHISH
nettle family ...... HEMP, PELLITORY
nightshade family .... SOLANUM, TOBACCO, POTATO, PETUNIA
non-flowering ..... FERN
not native ...... EXOTIC
noxious .... WEED
odorous .... BUGBANE
oil ..... RAPE, RAMTIL, BENNE
one-celled ..... PROTIST
one-seeded .... PSORALEA
onion family ..... CHIVE
ornamental .... BEGONIA, CLARY
palmlike .... CYCAD
parasite .... LICHEN, BLIGHT, APHID
parasitic .... DODDER, ORCHID, MISTLETOE
parsley family ... CICELY, SANICLE
pea family ..... LICORICE, SENNA, GRAM, COCKSHEAD, VETCH, ALFALFA, LOCOWEED, LENTIGO, LEGUME, INDIGO, LUPINE
pepper .... KAVA, CAPSICUM, CAYENNE, BETEL
perennial .... IRIS, CROCUS, SEDUM, COLUMBINE, THYME, DOGBANE
pest .... CHINCH
pink family .... CAMPION, CARNATION, DIANTHUS, CAMPO
pith .... PULP
pithy .... SOLA
poisonous ..... ACONITE, LOCO, HENBANE, HEMLOCK, WOLFSBANE
poppy family .... CELANDINE, CHICALOTE, BLOODROOT
pore ... LENTICEL, STOMA
potato family ... DATURA
prickly .... BRAMBLE, THISTLE, NETTLE, CACTUS, TEASEL, BRIER
primrose family .... FUCHSIA, COWSLIP, CYCLAMEN, OXLIP
product .... FRUIT
ragweed ..... BURDOCK, COCKLEBUR
receptacle .... TORUS
red-sapped .. BLOODROOT
rheumatism medicine .... GUACO
rock ...... LICHEN, MOSS, STONECROP, LITHOPHYTE
root .... RADIX, EDDO
root, edible ..... MANIOC, CASSAVA
root, fragrant .... ORRIS
root ointment ..... NARD
root purgative ... JALAP
rose family ..... BURNET, DROPWORT, SHADBUSH, BENNET, AVENS, POTENTILLA, CINQUEFOIL, FIVE-FINGER
rue family .. FRAXINELLA, LIME, LEMON, ORANGE
runner .... STOLON
rushlike .... SEDGE
sacred .... RAGTREE
sage family ...... CLARY
salad .... CHICORY, (WATER)CRESS, ENDIVE
salty soil ... HALOPHYTE
saxifrage family .... MITERWORT
scale .... PALEA, SQUAMA
sea .... ENALID
sea animal resembling ... SPONGE
sea-bottom .... BENTHOS
secretion ... GUM, RESIN
sedge .... PAPYRUS
seed .... HERB
seed case .... POD
seed organ ...... PISTIL
seed yielding oil .. SESAME, BENNE
sensitive .... MIMOSA
sesame .... TIL
shoot ... (S)CION, LAYER
shoots ...... ASPARAGUS
single-seeded .. PSORALEA
slang ... SWINDLE, TRAP, TRICK, DECOY
smelly .... BURDOCK, TANSY, STINKWEED, HENBANE, RUE, FIGWORT, BUGBANE, YARROW, MILFOIL, MULLE(I)N, RAFFLESIA
soap .... AMOLE
spiny .... CACTUS
sprout .... SPIRE

stalk ... HA(U)LM, STEM, CAULIS, SPIRE
stand .... JARDINIERE
starch .... POTATO, TARO, CASSAVA, MANIOC, CORN
stem .... CAUDEX, CORM, BINE, CAULIS, HA(U)LM, AXIS
stem joint .... NODE
stem spongy center ...... PITH, MEDULLA
stunted .... SCRAG
stunter ...... HERBICIDE
suckers .... APHID
sun-turning .. HELIOTROPE
swamp ...... MARIGOLD, DIONAEA, COWSLIP
swelling on .... BLEB
tendril .... CIRRUS
thistle-like ... ARTICHOKE
thorny ... BRIAR, BRIER, BRAMBLE, WAIT-A-BIT
tissue .... XYLEM
tissue cavity ... LOCULUS
trifoliate .... SHAMROCK
tropical .... PALM, TARO, CASSAVA, UDO, BANANA, LANTANA, CYCAD, MANGROVE, PLANTAIN, PAPAYA, QUASSIA, RAMTIL, CLEOME
trumpet ...... BIGNONIA
tumor .... GALL
twining .... IPOMOEA
underwater .. HORNWORT, BENTHOS
vegetable .... CELERY, CAULIFLOWER, ARTICHOKE
verbena family .. VERVAIN
violet family ..... PANSY
water .... FANWORT, PAPYRUS, HYDROPHYTE
with aromatic seeds ..... ANISE, CUMIN
bulblike root .... TUBEROSE
edible root .... SKIRRET
edible stalk .. CARDOON
fragrant seed .... ANISE
fruit .... BEARER
heart-shaped flowers .. DICENTRA
no seeds .... FERN
perennial stem .... ACROGEN
pungent pods .... CAPSICUM
sun-turning flowers ... HELIOTROPE, TURNSOLE
trumpet-shaped flower.. SEGO
underground buds .... GEOPHYTE
woody .... BUSH
woody tissue .... XYLEM
yielding hashish .... CANNABIS
young .... SAPLING

plantain .... FLEAWORT, WEED, RIBWORT
fruit .... BANANA
spike .... CHAT

plantation ... COLONY, ESTATE, BOWERY, HACIENDA
cacti .... NOPALRIE
coffee .... FINCA
Scarlett O'Hara's .. TARA

planter ... COLONIST, SOWER, PIONEER, SEEDER

planting tool .. DIBBLE, SEEDER

plantlike animal ...... CORAL, SPONGE, ZOOPHYTE

plants, book on ..... HERBAL
collector of ... HERBALIST
of .... VEGETAL
scourge of ..... BLIGHT, LOCUSTS
stand for .... JARDINIERE
study of ..... PHYTOLOGY
where sold ..... NURSERY

plaque ..... BROOCH, TABLET, BADGE

plash .... POOL, PUDDLE

plasma ..... QUARTZ, WHEY, PROTOPLASM

plaster ..... PARGET, COVER, OVERLAY, GROUT, SMEAR, STUCCO, DAUB, COMPO
bandage .... SPICA
cement .... PUTTY
cover with .... CEIL
first coat .... RENDER
for broken limb ... CAST
mustard .... SINAPISM
of ____ .... PARIS
of Paris .. GESSO, STUCCO, GYPSUM, YESO, HYDRATE
smoothing tool .. TROWEL
wall .... STUCCO

plastered: sl. .... DRUNK

plasterwork .... PARGET, SCAGLIOLA

plastic .... FICTILE, FLEXIBLE, PLIABLE
art .... MODELING, CERAMICS, SCULPTURE
clay .... PUG
material ...... FORMICA, LIGNIN, LUCITE
synthetic .... LUCITE, BAKELITE, FORMICA, BUNA, NYLON

plastid .... CELL

plastron ...... BREASTPLATE, DICKEY, SHIRT FRONT

plat .... BRAID, PLAIT, PLAN, MAP

Plata river, city on .... MONTEVIDEO

plate ..... DISC, SHARD, DISK, DISH, SCUTE, COAT, PLATTER, PATIN(A), LAMINA, OVERLAY, LAMELLA
armor .... TASSE
baseball .... (HOME)BASE
battery .... GRID
bony ... SCUTE, SCUTUM
Eucharist .... PATEN
horny ... SCUTE, SCUTUM
hurler's .... DISCUS
metal .... LAME
metal cooking .. GRIDDLE
ship-shaped .... NEF
with brass .... BRAZE
with zinc ... GALVANIZE

plateau ... MESA, TABLELAND, PUNA, ALTIPLANO, KAROO
top cover .... ICECAP

plated .... COATED, ARMORED

platelet .... SCUTUM

platelike organ ..... LAMELLA

platen .... ROLLER

plater .... HORSE, NAG

platform ... STAGE, BALCONY, GALLERY, BEMA, ESTRADE, SOLLAR, DOLLY
article .... PLANK
car .... FLATCAR
election .... HUSTINGS
engineroom ... CATWALK
floating .... RAFT
food-drying ..... FLAKE
for execution .. SCAFFOLD
fort's gun ..... BARBETTE
house painter's .... SCAFFOLD
kind of ... SKID, ALTAR, HUSTINGS
on wheels ...... TRUCK
politician's ... HUSTINGS
portable .... PALLET
principle .... PLANK
raised .... TRIBUNE, DAIS, PODIUM, STAND, PULPIT
revolving .... TURNTABLE
ship's .... MAINTOP, CROW'S-NEST, DECK
speaker's ..... ROSTRUM, TRIBUNE
streetcar ...... VESTIBULE

platina .... PLATINUM

platinum .... PLATINA
blonde actress .. HARLOW

platitude ... TRUISM, CLICHE, BROMIDE

platitudinous ... TRITE, DULL

Plato's school ..... ACADEME
work .... DIALOGUES, APOLOGY, CRITO, PHAEDO, SYMPOSIUM, REPUBLIC

platoon commander .... LIEUTENANT
unit .... SQUAD

platter ... PLATE, (HOME)BASE, RECORD, DISH, SALVER, TRENCHER

platyhelminth ... FLATWORM, FLUKE, TREMATODE, PLANARIAN

platypus .... DUCKBILL

plaudit ... OVATION, APPLAUSE, PRAISE

plausible .... SPECIOUS, CREDIBLE

play .... FRISK, GAMBOL, GAMBLE, PERFORM, ACT, (MELO)DRAMA, SPORT, TRIFLE, BET(ON), FROLIC
actors in a .... CAST, PERSONAE
amateurs' ... DRAMATICS
around .... GAD
at love .... FLIRT, DALLY
backer of .... ANGEL
between acts .. INTERLUDE
boisterously ...... LARK
bridge .... FINESSE

dilemma in a ...... NODE, NODUS
down .... MINIMIZE
fast and loose .... DALLY, TRIFLE
first performance .... PREMIERE
for one actor .... MONOLOGUE
for stakes ...... GAMBLE
grandstand ...... STUNT
ground .... PARK, SANDLOT, OVAL, DIAMOND
heroine .... PREMIERE
instrument carelessly .... TWEEDLE
introduction to a .... PROLOGUE
joke on .... RAG
jokes .... CLOWN
on words .... PUN, QUIBBLE
part in a ...... ROLE, BIT
part of a ..... SCENE, ACT
possum ... DEAD, FEIGN, PRETEND
practical joke on ... RAG
silent .... PANTOMINE
that fails .... TURKEY
the beau .... GALLIVANT
the violin .... FIDDLE
tricks on .... JAPE
truant .... MICHE
unsuccessful .... TURKEY
up .... ADVERTISE
wrong card .... RENIG
playa .... BASIN, BEACH
playboy .... GADABOUT
bunny .... HOSTESS
club founder ... HEFNER
player ... THESPIAN, MUMMER, ACTOR, PERFORMER, GAMBLER
at dealer's right ... PONE
dishonestly entered in race RINGER
incompetent .... DUB, PALOOKA
piano .... NICKELODEON
unwilling to sign .... HOLDOUT
who cuts the cards .. PONE
with lowest score .. BOOBY
players' position ...... LINEUP
playful ... SPORTIVE, SKITTISH, FRISKY, MERRY, JOCOSE, KITTENISH
playground item ...... SWING, SLIDE
playing card(s) extra .. JOKER
spot .... PIP
shuffle .... RIFFLE
suit .. HEARTS, DIAMONDS, SPADES, CLUBS
playing field .... OVAL, ARENA, DIAMOND
playlet .... SKIT, SKETCH
plays collectively ..... DRAMA
performed by amateurs .. DRAMATICS
plaything ...... BAUBLE, TOY, PAWN
playwright ...... DRAMATIST
plaza ...... SQUARE, MARKET
plea .... EXCUSE, APPEAL, REQUEST, ENTREATY, ALLEGATION, PETITION, PRAYER
for dismissal .. DEMURRER
pleach ... PLAIT, INTERTWINE, INTERLACE
plead ... ARGUE, APPEAL, BEG, IMPLORE, ENTREAT
in law .... SHOW
pleader .... PARACLETE, ADVOCATE
pleading, act of .... SUIT
pleasant ... GENIAL, AMIABLE, GAY, MERRY, ENJOYABLE, AGREEABLE
Island .... NAURU
pleasantries .... AMENITIES, CIVILITIES
pleasantry .... JOKE, BANTER
please ...... GRATIFY, ELATE, DELIGHT, SUIT, SATISFY, WILL, WISH, GLADDEN, PRITHEE
"Please Please Me" singers ... BEATLES
pleased .... GLAD
pleasing ..... NICE, PLEASANT, AGREEABLE
pleasure ... JOY, ENJOYMENT, RELISH, LIKING, GRACE, DELIGHT, WISH, WILL, CHOICE
boat .... YACHT, BARGE, CRUISER
craft harbor .... MARINA
ground ..... PLEASANCE, RESORT
seeker .... HEDONIST, SYBARITE
trip ... JUNKET, OUTING
voyage .... CRUISE
pleat .... PLAIT, FOLD, SHIRR, PLICATE, RUFFLE
pleated .... PLICATE
pleating ... GOFFER, GAUFFER
plebe ..... FRESHMAN, FROSH
plebeian ... COMMON, COARSE, VULGAR
plebiscite .... REFERENDUM
plebs .... MASSES
plectron .... PLECTRUM
plectrum ... PICK, PLECTRON, QUILL
pledge .... PAWN, SWEAR, PROMISE, PLIGHT, SPONSION, EARNEST, TOKEN, TOAST, GAGE, ENGAGE, VOW, PIGNUS, BOND, DEPOSIT, HEST, PAROLE
pledged ..... SWORN, BOUND
pledget .... SWAB, DRESSING, WAD, DOSSIL
pledgor .... PAWNER
pleiades, one of the ... MAIA, STEROPE, TAYGETA, MEROPE, ELECTRA, ALCYONE, CELAENO
parent of ...... PLEIONE, ATLAS
Pleione's daughter ... PLEIAD, MAIA, TAYGETA, STEROPE
husband .... ATLAS
plenary ..... FULL, ABSOLUTE, COMPLETE
plenipotentiary .... FULL, PLENARY, AMBASSADOR, ENVOY
plenitude .... FULLNESS
plenteous .... ABUNDANT, COPIOUS
plentiful ...... COPIOUS, FULL, REPLETE, BOUNTIFUL, ABUNDANT, AMPLE, RIFE
plenty ...... AMPLE, ENOUGH, OPULENCE
plenum .... FULL(NESS)
opposite of ..... VACUUM
pleon .... TELSON
pleonasm ...... TAUTOLOGY, NIMIETY, VERBOSITY, REDUNDANCY
pleonastic .... REDUNDANT
plessor ..... PLEXOR, HAMMER
plethora .... EXCESS
plexor .... PLESSOR
plexus ..... NETWORK, RETE, RETIA
pliable .... FLEXIBLE, SUPPLE, PLASTIC, MALLEABLE, PLIANT
pliant .... SUPPLE, LIMBER, LITHE, FLEXIBLE
pliers .... PINCERS
plight .... SITUATION, CONDITION, PLEDGE, ENGAGE, BETROTH
plinth .... ORLO, BASE, BLOCK
plod ..... DRUDGE, TRUDGE, SLOG, WALK, STEP
plop .... DROP, PLUMP
plot ... PATCH, PLAT, CHART, SCHEME, CONSPIRACY, CONSPIRE, LOT, CABAL, DRAW, MAP, INTRIGUE, MACHINATE
of story/play ..... NODE, SCENARIO
plotter .... SCHEMER, INTRIGANT(E), INTRIGUER, MACHINATOR
plough .... PLOW
ploughshare .... CO(U)LTER
plover ...... KILLDEER, STILT, SANDPIPER, PEWIT, LAPWING, SURFBIRD, DOTT(E)REL
bird like .... TURNIX
kin of .... BUSTARD, COURSER
plow ... LIST(ER), ROVE, TILL, PLOUGH, FURROW
blade .... SHARE, CO(U)LTER
land .... ARABLE
part ...... SLADE, SHARE, SOLE, CLEVIS, SHE(A)TH
plowed land ..... ARADO, ERD, FURROW
plowman ..... TILLER, RUSTIC
shoe of ..... CLODHOPPER
plowshare part .. MOLDBOARD
ploy .... MANEUVER, STRATEGY, STRATEGEM

pluck .... FORTITUDE, SPUNK, STRUM, TWEEZE, VELLICATE, AVULSE, COURAGE, SPIRIT, GRIT, PICK, PULL(OUT), SWINDLE, GUTS, DEPLUME, NERVE, TUG
plucky .. GAME, BRAVE, SPUNKY
plug ..... TAP, NAG, PLATER, ADVERTISEMENT, PUBLICIZE, PLOD, SLOG, SPILE, SPIGOT, BUNG, STOPPER, STOP UP, SHOOT, DOSSIL
absorbent ..... TAMPON
colloquial ... PITCH, LINE
for wound ...... DOSSIL
gun .. TAMPION, TOMPION
in radio/TV .... COMMERCIAL
of dirt .... COMEDO
organ pipe ..... TAMPION, TOMPION
slang .. RECOMMENDATION
tobacco .... PERIQUE
ugly ..... ROWDY, GOON, GANGSTER, RUFFIAN, THUG
wind instrument .. FIPPLE
plugger, kind of .... PRESS AGENT, BARKER
plum .... DAMSON, PRIZE, FRUIT, RAISIN, SLOE, DAMASCENE, DRUPE, GAGE, DAMASKEEN, KAKI, FREESTONE
brandy ...... SLIVOVITZ
cake .... BABA
disease ..... BLACKKNOT, BLACKRUST
fruit like ... PERSIMMON, LOQUAT
Java .... LOMBOY
pit of .... PUTAMEN, ENDOCARP
powdery coating .. BLOOM
stone .... NUTLET
wild ..... SLOE, BULLACE
plumage .... FEATHERS
plumb ... VERTICAL, WHOLLY, SOUND, FATHOM, PLUMMET
bob .... PLUMMET
plumbago ... GRAPHITE, LEAD
plumbeous .... LEADEN
plumber .... (GAS)FITTER, PIPEFITTER
tool of .... SNAKE
plumbum .... LEAD
plume ...... EGRET, MARABOU, PANACHE, PLUMAGE, AIGRET, CREST, FEATHER, DOWN
helmet .... PANACHE
heron's ...... AIGRET(TE)
plummet .. PLUMB, FALL, DROP
plumose .... FEATHERED
plump ...... FUBSY, FAT, PLOP, CHUBBY, BLUNT(LY), PLUNK, ROTUND, BUXOM
and short ... ROLY-POLY
plumule ...... BUD, FEATHER, PLUMELET
plunder ...... LOOT, RAVAGE, BOOTY, PREY, MARAUD, PILLAGE, (DE)SPOIL, STEAL, PROG, HARRY, RIFLE, SWAG, RAPINE, (RAN)SACK, FORAY, FORAGE
search for ...... RAVEN, RAVIN
plunderer .... RAPPAREE, FREEBOOTER
plunge ...... DIP, DIVE, SWIM, LUNGE, DUNK
headlong .... PITCH
into a liquid ... IMMERSE, DUNK, DOUSE, SOUSE
plunger ..... DIVER, GAMBLER, PISTON, DASHER
plunk ... BLOW, PLUCK, STRUM, PLUMP
slang .... DOLLAR
sound ... TWANG, THUD
plural marriage ... POLYGAMY, POLYANDRY
plurality .... MAJORITY
plus value .... ASSET
plush .... LUXURIOUS
cloth like ...... BOLIVIA
Plutarch's forte ... BIOGRAPHY
Pluto ... DIS, HADES, PLANET, GOD, DOG, ORCUS
domain of ...... HADES, LOWER WORLD, SHEOL, HELL, INFERNO
voice of .... COLVIG
plutocrat ... CROESUS, NABOB
plutonic .... IGNEOUS
pluvial .... RAINY, SOPPY
ply ...... LAMINATION, FOLD, HANDLE, TWIST, LAYER
plywood layer .... VENEER
Plymouth Colony governor .... BRADFORD, CARVER, WINSLOW
pneuma .... SOUL, SPIRIT, HOLY SPIRIT
pneumogastric nerve ... VAGUS
Po, city on the .... TURIN, TORINO
river ... PADUS, ERIDANUS
tributary .... TICINO, TREBBIA, TESSIN, ADDA
valley tribesman .... LOMBARD
poach .... MIX, SHIRR, TRESPASS, TRAMPLE, STEAL
poacher .... LURCHER
dog of .... LURCHER
poachy .... SODDEN, SOGGY
Pocahontas' father .... POWHATAN
husband .... ROLFE
pochard .... DUCK, SMEE
kin of .... REDHEAD, WIDGEON
pock ... PIMPLE, PUSTULE, PIT, SCAR
pocket .... CAVITY, SACK, POUCH, BAG, SAC, SMALL, FOB, POKE
billiards .... POOL
money .... CASH
shape of .... U-CUT
pocketbook .... WALLET, BILLFOLD, PURSE
pockmark .... PIT
poco .... LITTLE
pod ... SHELL, COCOON, GAM, SCHOOL, FLOCK, ARIL, BOLL, BURR, GROOVE, CHIL(L)I, SHUCK, SEEDCASE, ACHENE, CYPSELA, POUCH, BENDY, LEGUME, CAPSULE
edible ...... OKRA, OCRA
fodder .... CAROB
gastric stimulant .... CAPSICUM
like fruit bearers .. CAROB, CATALPA
mustard plant .. SILIQUE
tree .... LOCUST
podagra .... GOUT
podesta ..... MAYOR, JUDGE, GOVERNOR
Podgorny, USSR president ... NIKOLAI
podium ..... DAIS, PLATFORM
Poe, ___ Allan ...... EDGAR
bird .... RAVEN
character .... PYM
foster father of ... ALLAN
girl in poem .... ANNABEL(LEE), LENORE
gold bug .... SCARAB
work of .... RAVEN, TAMERLANE
poem ... VERSE, ODE, SESTINA, RONDEL, BALLAD(E), LAI, VIRELAY, RUNES, PALINODE
concluding stanza ...... ENVOY, (L)ENVOI
dirgelike ...... REQUIEM
division .... CANTO, STANZA, FIT, FYTTE
epic .... ILIAD, ODYSSEY, EPOPEE, EPOS, EPODE
four-line ..... QUATRAIN
14-line .... SONNET
handed down orally ..... EPOS
Icelandic .... EDDA
introduction to a .... PROLOGUE
love .... MADRIGAL
lyric ... EPODE, CANZONE, ODE, RONDEAU, MADRIGAL, RONDEL
mourning ...... MONODY
narrative .... IDYL(L), EPIC, LAY, ILIAD, ODYSSEY
nonsense ..... LIMERICK
of lament .... ELEGY
of praise ... MAGNIFICAT
of rural life .... GEORGIC
one-line .... MONOSTICH
oral .... EPOS
part of ... CANTO, PASSUS
pastoral........ IDYL(L), BUCOLIC, ECLOGUE, GEORGIC
play's .... PROLOGUE, EPILOGUE
postscript .... (L)ENVOY, (L)ENVOI
sacred .... PSALM
said at play's end .... EPILOGUE
satirical .... IAMBIC, EPIGRAM

short ..... TELESTICH(E), VIRELAY, VILLANELLE
with witty point .... EPIGRAM
poems collection .... ANTHOLOGY, GARLAND
poet .... ODIST, MINSTREL, MINNESINGER, ELEGIST, TROUBADOUR, LYRIST, BARD, RHYMER, METRIST
and Peasant composer ... (VON)SUPPE
inferior...... POETASTER, RHYMESTER, VERSIFIER, RHYMER, RIMER, SONNETEER
inspiration of ..... MUSE
old English .... SCOP
singer ... BARD, MINSTREL
unknown .... ANON
poetess ..... SAPPHO, MILLAY, PARKER, LOWELL
poetic foot .... DACTYL, IAMB(US), SPONDEE, CHORIAMB, TROCHEE
inspiration .... PEGASUS
measure .... METER
pronoun .... THINE, THOU, THEE
retraction ..... PALINODE
trio .... NOD
verb .. DOST, HATH, HAST
poetry, epic .... EPOPEE
incomplete line of .... HEMISTICH
line of .... STICH
muse of ...... CALLIOPE, ERATO, THALIA
of .... MELIC
short-excerpt .. MORCEAU
poets, collectively .. PARNASSUS
Pogo's friend .... OWL
pogonia .... ORCHID
pogonip .... FOG
pogrom .... MASSACRE, SLAUGHTER
pogy .... MENHADEN, FISH
poi source .... TARO
poignancy .... PATHOS
poignant ... KEEN, TOUCHING, MOVING, TART, PIQUANT
poilu .... SOLDIER
poind ... DISTRAINT, IMPOUND
point ... DOT, AIM, JOT, SPECK, PERIOD, CAPE, PRICK, PUNTO, ISSUE, PEAK, USE, OBJECT
antler's .... SNAG
beside the ... IRRELEVANT
barbed .... FLUE
blank .... STRAIGHT, BLUNT, PLAIN
central ..... FOCUS, CRUX
compass .... AIRT(H), RHUMB
culmination ... SOLSTICE
earthquake's starting .... FOCUS
ending in a .. MUCRONATE
essential .... CRUX
farthest .... APOGEE, SOLSTICE
having .... ACUATE, HEBETATE
highest .... ZENITH, ACME, PEAK, CLIMAX, APEX, SUMMIT
in ...... APT, PERTINENT
in game .... SCORE
in law .... RES
joint .... JUNCTURE
land ... SPIT, CAPE, NESS, PROMONTORY
lowest ..... NADIR, ZERO
magnet .... POLE
make a .... SCORE
meeting .... FOCUS
of a curve ...... ACNODE
of concentration ... NODE
of debate .... ISSUE
of difference ..... LIMEN
of land .... MORRO
of law: sl. ...... BUTTON
of time .... JUNCTURE
of view .... OPINION, ANGLE, SLANT
orbital ... APSIS, APOGEE
pen .... NIB
spear .... PIKE, GAD
starting .... POST
to the ... APT, PERTINENT
turning ... PIVOT, HINGE
won .... SCORE, GOAL
pointed ... CONICAL, INCISIVE, PIKED, ACUATE, PEAKED, SHARP, TAPERING
arch ..... OGIVE, GOTHIC
dull .. HEBETATE, ACUATE
missile ... SPEAR, LANCE, DART, HARPOON, BOLT
stick .... GOAD
pointer .... DIAL, ARROW, SETTER, VANE, INDICATOR, WAND, HAND, INDEX, RETRIEVER, (GUN)DOG
colloquial ... TIP, CLUE, HINT
dial's .... STYLE
printer's .... FIST
sundial .... GNOMON
teacher's .... FESCUE
pointing out .... INDICANT
pointless .... INANE, SILLY, SENSELESS, DULL
poise ..... BALANCE, BEARING, SUSPEND, HOVER, STABILITY, CARRIAGE, APLOMB, LIBRATE
poison .... TOXIN, DRUG, HEMLOCK, GALL, ARSENIC, CORRUPT, DATURA, VENOM, TOXICANT, BANE
antidote ... MITHRIDATE, TREACLE
arrow ...... INEE, UPAS, CURARE, (C)URARI, (W)OURALI, WOORALI
castor bean ...... RICIN
caused by .... TOXIC
deadly .... ARSENIC, CYANIDE, STRYCHNIN(E)
food .... BOTULIN
gas .. LEWISITE, MUSTARD
hemlock ...... CONIN(E), BENNET, CONIUM
ivy .... SUMAC
ivy irritant .... URUSHIOL
remedy for ..... TREACLE
snake ..... VENOM, VIRUS
weed ... LOCO, HEMLOCK, CONIUM
poisoner, alleged ..... BORGIA
poisoning .... BOTULISM, TOXICATION
blood .... TOXEMIA
poisonous .... VENOMOUS, TOXIC(ANT), VIRULENT, VIPERINE, MEPHITIC, NOCUOUS
air .... MALARIA
alkaloid .... CONINE, TROPIN(E), NICOTINE
bark .... UPAS, SASSY
compound ..... TOXIN(E)
fungus .... AMANITA
lizard .... GILA
oil .... TUNG
plant .... CONIUM, HEMLOCK, HENBANE, NUX VOMICA, TUTU, MANDRAKE, BELLADONA, NIGHTSHADE
protein .... RICIN(E)
resin .... CANNABIN
seed .... CALABAR
shrub .... TUTU
snake ...... COBRA, ASP, VIPER, ADDER, KRAIT, COPPERHEAD, BUSHMASTER, FER-DE-LANCE
spider ...... TARANTULA
vine ...... BITTERSWEET
weed ... LOCO, HEMLOCK
poke .... JAB, PROD, PRY, DAWDLE(R), SACK, POCKET, BAG, JOG, DUB, PUSH, THRUST, INTRUDE, GOAD, PUNCH
with elbow ...... NUDGE
poker counter ..... CHIP, DIB
deal .... DRAW, STUD
face .... DEAD PAN
faced comedian .. KEATON
game like .... BRAG
hand ... STRAIGHT, PAIR, TRIO, FULL HOUSE, (ROYAL)FLUSH
player ..... FOURFLUSHER
stake ... ANTE, POT, KITTY
term ... PIGEON, KICKER, HOLE, FOLD, BOBTAIL
to call in .... SEE
variety of ... STUD, DRAW
pokerface .... DEADPAN
pokeweed ... POCAN, INKBERRY
pok(e)y .... DULL, SLOW, STUFFY, DOWDY, JAIL
slang .... JAIL
Pola .... PULJ
movie actress ..... NEGRI
Poland ... SARMATIA, POLSKA
capital of ..... WARSAW
dictator ..... GOMULKA
Mrs. in .... PANI
native of .. POLE, POLACK
weight .... LUT

Polaris .... POLESTAR, NORTH STAR
pole ..... MAST, SHAFT, THILL, CABER, POST, PUNT, STILT, ROD, CABER, SLAV
boat .... QUANT
carriage .... SHAFT
fir .... UFER
fish .... GAFF
in Gaelic game ... CABER
memorial .... XAT
metal cap .... SHOE
positive .... ANODE
propelled watercraft ..... CASCO, PUNT, GONDOLA
symbolic .... TOTEM
to pole .... AXIAL
tribal .... TOTEM
vertical .... MAST
with decoy bird ... STOOL
with footrest ..... STILT
wagon ..... THILL, SHAFT
wooden .... TREE
poleax(e) .... HALBERD, HALBERT
polecat .... FITCH(ET), FITCHEW, MUSANG, SKUNK, FOUMART, CARNIVORE
animal like ... ZORIL(A), WEASEL, FERRET
polemic .... CONTROVERSIAL, MOOT, DEBATABLE, ARGUMENT
polemics .... DISPUTE
polenta .... PORRIDGE
poler .... GONDOLIER, OARSMAN, HORSE
poles, walking .... STILTS
polestar .... POLARIS, NORTH STAR
police ...... CONSTABULARY, CARABINIERI
inspector, fictional ...... MAIGRET
line .... CORDON
military .... REDCAP, MP
record book .... BLOTTER
record, letters in .... AKA
state .... TROOPER
test .... PARAFFIN, POLYGRAPH
vehicle .... WAGON, BLACK MARIA
policeman .... MINION, BULL, FLATFOOT, COP, TROOPER, ZAPTIAH, BLUECOAT, BOBBY, PEELER, CONSTABLE, DICK, BULL, GENDARME, PEON, REDCAP
baton/club of .... TRUNCHEON, STICK, BILLY, MACE
mounted ...... TROOPER
policewoman .... MATRON
policy .... PRINCIPLE, PLATFORM, PLAN
polio vaccine man ..... SALK
treatment method .... KENNY
polish .... GLOSS, BUFF, LEVIGATE, FINISH, SLEEK, BURNISH, VENEER, FURBISH, GLAZE, WAX, LUSTRE, BRIGHTEN, REFINE, PERFECT, SHINE, SAND, SCOUR, GRACE, SHEEN, RUB
by hammering .. PLANISH
up ...... EDIT, IMPROVE
polished .... ELEGANT, SLEEK, POLITE, SUAVE, GLOSSY, REFINED, URBANE
polishing material .... EMERY, PUMICE, BUFF, WAX, RABAT, RUBIGO, CROCUS, LUSTER, ABRASIVE
Polish carriage ..... BRITSKA
city .... LODZ, BRESLAU, WROCLAW, POZNAN, LUBLIN, POSEN, TORUN, TARNOW, CRACOW, BROMBERG, LWOW, KALISZ, STETTIN, GDYNIA, KATOWICE, LIGNICA, LEMBERG
coin .... GROSZ
commander .... BOR, ANDERS, HETMA
dance ...... POLONAISE, MAZURKA
dictator ..... PILSUDSKI, GOMULKA
diet member ... MAGNATE
dress .... POLONAISE
king .. SOBIESKI, CONTI
legislator ...... MAGNATE
marshy region ... PRIPET
monetary unit .... ZLOTY
music .... POLONAISE, MAZURKA
parliament .... SEJM
pianist .... RUBINSTEIN, PADEREWSKI
port .... GDYNIA
premier .... PADEREWSKI, SIKORSKI, PILSUDSKI
president .... PILSUDSKI
region .... MASURIA
river .. PRIPET, VISTULA, BUG, NAREW, SAN NAREV, SERET, WARTHE
seaport .... DANZIG
slang .... POLACK
soldier .... UHLAN
soup .... ZUPA
title of address .... PANI
polite .... CIVIL, REFINED, GRACIOUS, MANNERLY, GENTEEL, URBANE, COURTEOUS, POLISHED, CORRECT
act .... CIVILITY
politic .... DIPLOMATIC, PRUDENT, TACTFUL, EXPEDIENT, SHREWD
political casualty .. LAMEDUCK
division ...... HUNDRED
faction ..... BLOC, RUMP, JUNTA
gathering ...... CAUCUS, POWWOW
henchman .... (WARD)HEELER
organization ..... STATE, PARTY
patronage .... PAP, PORK(BARREL)
radical .... JACOBIN
rostrum .... STUMP
science .... CIVICS, POLITICS, GOVERNMENT
spoils .... MELON, PATRONAGE
system .... REGIME
politician ... POLITICO, HEELER
not reelected .. LAMEDUCK
politics of a ...... RIGHT, LEFT, CENTER, LIBERAL
unattached ... MAVERICK
polity .... STATE
polka-like dance ..... REDOWA, MAZURKA
poll ...... HEAD, JUROR, CUT, CROP, VOTE, SURVEY, CANVASS(ING)
taker ... HARRIS, GALLUP, ROPER
pollack ... COALFISH, GADID, SEY
pollard .... DEER, GOAT
polled .... HORNLESS, CANVASSED, MUL(L)EY
pollen ... DUST, MICROSPORES
bearing organ .. STAMEN
brush .... SCOPA
sac .... ANTHER
pollex .... THUMB, DIGIT
polling place .... BOOTH
pollinosis .... HAYFEVER
polliwog .... TADPOLE
pollock .... CODFISH
pollster .... GALLUP, HARRIS, ROPER
pollute .... DEFILE, DIRTY
Pollux and Castor ..... ANAX, DIOSCURI, GEMINI
Pollyanna for example .... OPTIMIST
Pollywog .... TADPOLE
polo play period .. CHUKKER, CHUKKAR
stick .... MALLET
Venetian traveler .... MARCO
Polonius' daughter .. OPHELIA
servant ..... REYNALDO
son .... LAERTES
Polska .... POLAND
poltergeist .... GHOST
poltroon ... CRAVEN, DASTARD, COWARD, CAITIFF
polyanthus .... OXLIP, PRIMROSE, NARCISSUS
polyglot .... LINGUIST
polygon .... NONAGON, HEXAGON, ISAGON, TETRAGON
polygraph, they swear by the .. POLICE
Polynesian ... MAORI, SAMOAN, TAHITIAN, KANAKA, HAWAIIAN, NUKUORO
apple .... HEVI
baking pit .... UMU
beverage ... KAVA, KAWA
chestnut .... RATA

cloth ... TAPA
dress ... MALO
drink ... KAVA
god ... PELE, ATUA, TANE
herb ... PIA
hero ... MAUI
human food .. LONG PIG
island ... PITCAIRN, FIJI, SAMOA, TOKELAU
kingdom ... TONGA
language ... TONGAN
louse ... KUTU
mound ... AHU
mulberry bark ... TAPA
oven ... UMU
sky ... LANGI
spirit ... ATUA
supernatural force ... MANA
tree ... IPIL
wages ... UTU
yam ... UBE, UBI

polyp ... HYDRA, SEA PEN, CORAL, SEA ANEMONE, HYDROZOAN
like a ... HYDROID

Polyphemus ... CYCLOPS, MOTH
captive ... ODYSSEUS, ULYSSES

polyzoan ... BRYOZOAN, HYDRA, SEA ANEMONE, POLYP, SEA PEN

pomace ... PULP

pomaceous fruit ... APPLE, POME

pomade ... OINTMENT, COSMETIC, BANDOLINE, POMATUM

pomatum ... POMADE

pome ... PEAR, APPLE, QUINCE
disease ... BROWN ROT
like fruit ... AZAROLE

pomelo ... GRAPEFRUIT, SHADDOCK, SUHA

pomegranate flower ... BALUSTER
syrup ... GRENADINE

Pomeranian ... SPITZ DOG

pommel ... KNOB, BEAT

pomp ... STATE, SPLENDOR, PAGEANTRY, SHOW
and Circumstance composer ... ELGAR
empty ... PAGEANT

pompadour ... HAIRDO, POISSON
base ... RAT

pompano ... ALEWIFE, SAUREL, CARANGOID

Pompey's scene of defeat ... THAPSUS

pompom fire .. ACK-ACK, FLAK

pomposity ... WIND

pompous ... STATELY, BOMBASTIC, GRANDIOSE, MAGNIFIC, HIGHFALUTIN, TUMID, OROTUND, TURGID
speech ... BOMBAST
walk ... STRUT, SWAGGER

Ponca ... SIOUX, SIOUAN

Ponce de Leon's discovery ... FLORIDA

Ponchielli opera ... (LA)GIOCONDA

poncho ... RAINCOAT, CLOAK, CAMLET

pond ... LAGOON, POOL, MERE, TARN, SALINA, LAGUNE, WATER HOLE
kind of ... STEW

ponder .. PERPEND, MEDITATE, PORE, REFLECT, MULL, RUMINATE, WEIGH, CONSIDER, MUSE

ponderosa ... PINE

ponderous ... DULL, LABORED, HEAVY, MASSIVE, BULKY, WEIGHTY

ponds, study of .. LIMNOLOGY

pone ... BREAD, LOAF, MERE

poniard ... DAGGER

Pons, operatic singer ... LILY

pontiff ... BISHOP, POPE, PONTIFEX, HIGH PRIEST

pontifical ... EPISCOPAL, PAPAL

pontil ... PUNTY

Pontius ___, Roman governor PILATE

pontlevis ... DRAWBRIDGE

pontoon ... FLOAT

pony .. BRONCO, NAG, CAYUSE, HORSE, CRIB, PINTO, SHELTY, SHELTIE
tail ... HAIRDO
up ... PAY

pooch ... DOG

poodle ... BARBET, DOG

pooh ... TIRE, EXHAUST, EXCLAMATION
pooh ... DISMISS, DISREGARD

pool ... POND, PUDDLE, PLASH, POT, BILLIARDS, MONOPOLY, CARR, MERE, LINN, WATER HOLE
artificial ... TANK
ball ... RINGER
bettors' ... POT, KITTY
business firms' ... MONOPOLY, TRUST
mine ... SUMP
mountain ... TARN
pouch ... POCKET
rod ... CUE
table pouch ... POCKET
triangle ... RACK
waterfall ... LINN

poon ... TELUGU, TREE, DOMBA, DILO

poor ... DESTITUTE, NEEDY, PALTRY, INFERIOR, INDIGENT, PENNILESS
player ... DUB, HAM
slang ... LOUSY
sport ... SOREHEAD

poorhouse ... HOSPICE

poorly ... ILL
born ... LOWBRED
done literary work ... INCONDITE

pop ... CRACK, BURST, SODA, SHOT, SHOOT, SNAP, FATHER
art ... FUNK
conductor ... WHITEMAN
singer ... JOPLIN
the question ... PROPOSE

Pope (see Papal) ... PONTIFF, LEO, PIUS, JOHN, VICAR, ADRIAN, PAUL, URBAN
cape of ... MOZ(Z)ETTA
cathedral of the ... LATERAN
collar of the ... ORALE
crown of the ... TIARA
decree of the ... BULL, DECRETAL, RESCRIPT
envoy ... (AB)LEGATE
first ... PETER
headdress of ... MITRE, MITER
meeting to elect ... CONCLAVE
of Video ... SULLIVAN
palace of ... VATICAN
pertaining to the .. PAPAL
see of the ... ROME
tenure of the ... PAPACY
the ... PAPA
title of ... HOLINESS, HOLY FATHER
vestment of ... FANO(N), FANUM

Pope's (Alexander) love ... GONNE

popes collectively ... PAPACY

Popeye sweetheart of ... OLIVE(OYL)
rival of ... BRUTO
the ___ ... SAILOR

popinjay ... FOP, PARROT, WOODPECKER

poplar ... ABELE, LIARD, ASPEN, ALAMO, COTTONWOOD
balsam ... TACMAHACK
glucoside from .. SALICIN
spike ... CATKIN, AMENT

popover ... MUFFIN

Poppaea, Nero's wife .. SABINA

poppy ... CHICALOTE, CELANDINE, PAPAVER, OPIUM, BLOODROOT, SANGUINARIA, PLANT
sap ... LATEX
seed ... MAW

poppycock ... BOSH, NONSENSE, ROT, BALONEY

populace ... DEMOS, PEOPLE, MASSES

popular ... COMMON, PREVALENT, VULGATE, ENCHORIAL, EXOTERIC, DEMOTIC
beauty ... BELLE
no more ... HAS BEEN
opinion ... CONSENSUS
social figure ... LION, CELEBRITY
success ... HIT

popularity ... FAME

populate ... INHABIT, PEOPLE

population count ... CENSUS

Poquelin, Fr. writer .. MOLIERE

porbeagle ... SHARK

porcelain ... EARTHENWARE, CHINA, SPODE, LIMOGES, MING, CELADON, SEVRES,

FIGULINE, FAIENCE
art of making .. CERAMICS
clay ... CHINA, KAOLIN(E), PATE
fine .... CHINA
of .... CERAMIC
worker .... POTTER
porch .... STOA, PORTICO, PIAZZA, GALILEE, STOOP, PARVIS, VERANDA(H), GALLERY, LAN(A)I
church .... GALILEE
seat .... GLIDER
porcine animal ..... HOG, PIG
disease .... BULLNOSE
porcupine .... HEDGEHOG
anteater ...... ECHIDNA
Canadian .... URSON
spine .... QUILL
pore .... STUDY, PONDER, OSTIOLE, READ, MEDITATE, CON, FORAMEN, CHANNEL, OPENING
breathing .... STOMA
plant ... LENTICEL, STOMA
pores, block the .... OPPILATE
porgy .... FISH, PARGO, SCUP, BREAM, SPAROID, TAI
poriferan .... SPONGE
pork ... PIG, HOG, LARDO(O)N
cut .. CHOP, BACON, LOIN, HAM
loin .... GRISKIN
pie .... HAT
sausage .... BOLOGNA
shoulder .... CALA
porker .... ELT, HOG
porky .... FAT
pornographic ..... SALACIOUS, OBSCENE
porous ...... LEAKY, LEACHY
porpoise .... DOLPHIN, CETACEAN, SEA HOG, INIA, HOGFISH
porridge ... GRUEL, OATMEAL, POTTAGE, GROUT, ATOLE, SAMP, STIRABOUT, POLENTA, BROSE, MUSH, BURGOO
bowl .... PORRINGER
oat husks ...... SOWENS
Porsena, king .... LARS
Tarquin's ..... AVENGER
port .... HARBOR, LARBOARD, WINE, GATEWAY, HAVEN, ANCHORAGE
facilities ..... WHARFAGE
portable bridge ...... BAILEY, PONTOON
chair .... SEDAN
float .... PONTOON
hut .... QUONSET
kitchen cart .... CHUCK WAGON
lamp .... LANTERN
oven .... BAKER
sanctuary ... TABERNACLE
serving stand .... DUMB WAITER
shelter .... TENT
stove .... CHAUFFER
portal ..... DOORWAY, GATE, ENTRANCE, POSTERN
portance .. CONDUCT, BEARING
portas .... BREVIARY
portcullis .... HERSE, BAR
portend .... BODE, WARN, PRESAGE, FORESHADOW, AUGUR
portent ..... OMEN, PRODIGY, MARVEL, WARNING, SIGN
portentous .... OMINOUS, SINISTER
porter .... JANITOR, BEER, HAMAL, ALE, CARRIER, STOUT, CONCIERGE, GATEKEEPER, DOORMAN, REDCAP
musical .... ROSALIE
songwriter .... COLE
porterhouse .... STEAK, T-BONE, BEEF
portfolio ... BRIEFCASE, OFFICE
porthole .... EMBRASURE
Portia's maid .... NERISSA
portico .. VERANDA(H), PORCH, PARVIS, LOGGIA, COLONNADE, STOA, PROSTYLE, ARCADE, PIAZZA
portion .... SHARE, PART, DESTINY, BIT, LOT
marriage .... DOWRY
meal .... SERVING, HELPING
out .... DEAL, METE
slang .... DIVVY
tiny ... MINIM, MODICUM
portly .... OBESE, STOUT, FAT
portmanteau ...... SUITCASE, VALISE
Porto Rico (see Puerto Rico)
portrait ..... EFFIGY, PICTURE
portray .. PERSONATE, DEPICT, DELINEATE, LIMN, PICTURE, ENACT, REPRESENT, DESCRIBE
Portugal .... LUSITANIA
capital of .... LISBON
Portuguese cape .... ROCA
city ...... LISBON, EVORA, BRAGA, FARO, LAGOS, COIMBRA, SANTAREM
coin .... CENTAVO, CRUSADO, REI, MOIDORE, ESCUDO, JOHANNES
colony .... ANGOLA, MACAU, MACAO, TIMOR, MOZAMBIQUE, CAPE VERDE
colony, former ..... GOA
dictator .... SALAZAR
East Africa .... MOZAMBIQUE
folk song .... FADO
gentleman ...... SENHOR
governess .... AIA
Guinea capital ... BISSAU
India district .... DAMAO
Indian .... FERINGI, FERINGHEE
islands .... MADEIRA, AZORES, TERCEIRA
lady .... DONA
legislature ...... CORTES
measure .... VARA
molasses ...... MELACO
monetary unit .. ESCUDO
mountain ranges .. SERRAS
navigator .... MAGELLAN, (DA)GAMA, DIAZ
nobleman .... GRANDEE
overseas territory .... ANGOLA, MOZAMBIQUE, CAPE VERDE, MACAO, TIMOR, SAO TOME
poet .... CAMOES
premier ...... SALAZAR, CAETANO
river ...... SADO, SABOR, DUERO, MINHO, TAGUS, DOURO, TEJO
sail .... LATEEN
seaport .... OPORTO
ship .... CARVEL, CARAVEL(LE)
Timor capital ..... DILI
title .... DOM, DONNA, SENHOR
weight ..... LIBRA, ONCA
West Africa .... ANGOLA
wine ... MADEIRA, PORTO
pose .... SIT, MANNERISM, PRETENSE, PROPOUND, PROPOSE, ATTITUDE, POSTURE, PUZZLE
Poseidon ..... NEPTUNE, GOD
attendant of ... PROTEUS
realm of .... SEA
scepter .... TRIDENT
wife of ..... AMPHITRITE
Posen .... POSNAN
poser .... FACER, POSEUR, TEASER, MODEL, SITTER, IMPOSTOR, PROBLEM
posh .... ELEGANT, RITZY, LUXURIOUS
posit ..... SITUATE, ASSUME, POSTULATE
position .... POST(URE), ATTITUDE, SITUATION, STAND, STATUS, OFFICE, SITUS, STANCE, PLACE, LOCATION, SITE, STATION, JOB, LIE
secure .... FOOTING, FOOTHOLD
positive .... CERTAIN, ABSOLUTE, OUT-AND-OUT, SURE, PLUS, PRECISE, EXPRESS, SPECIFIC
answer ... AYE, YES, YEA
electrode .... ANODE
pole .... ANODE
sign .... PLUS
positively .... QUITE
positivism .... ASSURANCE, DOGMATISM, CERTAINTY, COMTISM
possess .... OWN, HAVE, DOMINATE
possessed ..... CRAZED, MAD, CHARMED
possession .... PROPERTY, WEALTH, OWNERSHIP
in law ... SEISIN, MANUAL
possessor ... OWNER, HOLDER
posset .... DRINK
possible .... POTENTIAL,

FEASIBLE, PROBABLE
possibly .... MAYBE, PERHAPS
possum .... COON
play .... FEIGN, PRETEND
post ... MAIL, INFORM, ENTER, DA(W)K, BOLLARD, MARKER, PILLAR, STAKE, POLE, STATION, PLACE, COURIER, POSITION, ASSIGN, GARRISON, JOB
box device ...... USMAIL
chaise .... COACH, CARRIAGE
doorway .... JAMB(E)
exchange .. PX, CANTEEN
memorial .... XAT
mortem .... AUTOPSY, NECROPSY
mortem conductor ...... AUTOPSIST, CORONER
office bank .... GIRO
staircase .... NEWEL
window frame .. JAMB(E)
wooden framework ..... PUNCHEON
postage stamp country .... SAN MARINO
postal stamp .... CACHET
system .... MAIL
poster ... STICKER, PLACARD, BILL(BOARD)
posterior ..... HIND, RETRAL, REAR, DORSAL, BUTTOCK, LATER
opposed to ... ANTERIOR, PRIOR
posterity .... FUTURE
postern .... BACKDOOR, BACKGATE, ENTRANCE
postfree mail .... FRANK
postiche .... ARTIFICIAL, PRETENSE
postmark .... CACHET
substitute ...... INDICIA
postmeridian ... AFTERNOON, PM
"postoffice" delivery .... KISS
postpone ... ADJOURN, TABLE, DELAY, DEFER, PUT OFF, SHELVE
postponing, in law .. MORATORY
postrider .... COURIER
postscript of poem ... LENVOY, LIENVOI
postulant .... CANDIDATE, PETITIONER
postulate ...... POSIT, AXIOM, THESIS, CLAIM, ASSUME, PRESUME, PREMISE
posture .... POSITION, ATTITUDE, STANCE, CARRIAGE, BEARING, POSE
posy .... NOSEGAY, BOUQUET, FLOWER, SPRAY, CORSAGE
pot .. PIPKIN, CRUSE, LOTA(H), JARDINIERE, OLLA, POOL, KITTY, SHOOT, ALUDEL, KETTLE
au-feu .... (BEEF)STEW
coffee .... URN
go to .. ROT, DETERIORATE
herb .... CLARY
marigold ... CALENDULA
mender .... TINKER
slang .... MARIJUANA
stand .... TRIVET
tea .... SAMOVAR
user .... HIPPIE
user's feeling ..... HIGH
potable .... DRINKABLE
potage .... SOUP, BROTH
potash source .... SUINT
potassium .... ALUM
bitartrate ...... TARTAR
carbonate ...... POTASH
chloride .... SYLVITE, MURIATE
nitrate ..... SALTPETER, NITER, GROUGH
potation ..... DRINK, LIQUOR, DRAFT
potato ... SPUD, TUBER, OCA, IDAHO, TATER
bud .... EYE
disease .... CURL
flour .... FARINA
fried .... CHIP
meal .... FARINA
skin .... JACKET
slang .... MURPHY
starch .... FARINA
sweet ..... CAMOTE, YAM, BATATA
potatoes with onions .... LYONNAISE
potbelly .... PAUNCH, BAY WINDOW
potboiler .... LITERARY
poteen .... WHISKY
potency ... STRENGTH, POWER, VIS
potent ... STRONG, POWERFUL,
potentate .... RULER, MONARCH, (MAJA)RAJAH
potential ... LATENT, POSSIBLE
difference .... TENSION
potentilla ...... FIVE FINGER, ROSE
potheen .... WHISKY
pother .... STIR, WORRY, UPROAR, FUSS, ADO, BUSTLE
potherb .... PARSLEY, CLARY, CHIVES
pothole .... PIT
pothook .... SCRAWL
user .... STENO
pothouse ...... INN, TAVERN
potiche .... VASE, JAR
potion .... DOSE, DRINK, NEPENTHE
love ... PHILTER, PHILTRE
potman .... WAITER
potpie .... STEW
potpourri ..... MEDLEY, STEW, MIXTURE, OLIO, ANTHOLOGY
Potsdam conference member .. STALIN, ATTLEE, TRUMAN
potsherd ..... SHARD, CROCK
potshot .... SNIPE
pottage ... PORRIDGE, BROSE, HODGEPODGE, SOUP, STEW
potted .... DRUNK
potter's clay .... ARGIL, SAGGER, SEGGAR, PATE
field .... CEMETERY, GRAVEYARD
field of Judas .... ACELDAMA
tool .... PALLET
wheel .... LATHE
pottery ...... EARTHENWARE, DELFT(WARE), GOMBROON, MAJOLICA, WARE, CERAMICS, BASALT, FAIENCE, FIGULINE
before glazing ... BISCUIT
clay ..... KAOLIN, PATE, ARGIL
fragment .... SHARD, SHERD, CROCK
glaze on .... REFLET
glazed .... DELF(T)
making ...... CERAMICS
making device .. SAGGER
of .... CERAMIC, FICTILE
pottle .... TANKARD
potto ..... LEMUR, KINKAJOU
potty .... PETTY
pouch .... SPORRAN, SPLEUCHAN, SAC, BURSA, POD, BAG, POCKET, CECUM
intestinal ..... C(A)ECUM
like a .... SACCATE, MARSUPIAL
pouf ... OTTOMAN, HEADDRESS
poulard .. HEN, FRYER, PULLET
poult .... PULLET, CHICKEN
poultice .... APPLICATION, CATAPLASM
poultry ...... FOWLS, DUCKS, GEESE, TURKEYS
breeding place .. HENNERY
disease .. PIP, ROUP, POX, GAPES
man .... POULTER
pen .... HUTCH
shelter ...... HENHOUSE, HENNERY
pounce .. TALON, CLAW, SWOOP
pound .... TAMP, THUMP, PULVERIZE, CRUSH, NETTON, SOV, BRAY, QUID, THROB, BEAT, THUD, ENCLOSURE, CORRAL, PEN, MALLEATE, LIBRA
dog .... MONGREL
dweller .... STRAY
poet ...... EZRA(LOOMIS)
pounder .... CANNON, WAVE, TAMPER
pounds, 100 .... CENTAL, CENTNER
pounding implement .. PESTLE, GAVEL, HAMMER, MALLET
pour ... FLOW, RAIN, SWARM, TEEM, SERVE, GUSH, DECANT, EFFUSE
forth .... WELL
metal into mold ... CAST, FOUND
pourboire .... TIP, GRATUITY
pouring hole .... SPRUE
pourpoint ... DOUBLET, JUPON
pout ...... MOUE, SULK, FISH, GRIMACE, MOPE
pouter .... PIGEON
poverty .... WANT, SCARCITY, NEED, INDIGENCE, PAUCITY, PENURY, LACK
stricken .... POOR

pow .... POLL, HEAD
powder .... TALC, POUNCE, PICRA, DUST, SPRINKLE, PULVERIZE, CRUSH
burn to .... CALCINE
clothes scenting .... SATCHET
crush into .... BRAY
dried fly ... CANTHARIDES
explosive ...... CORDITE, TETRYL
grind to .... BRAY, TRITURATE
insect ...... PYRETHRUM
perfumed .... SACHET
polishing .... ROUGE
pound into .... BRAY
room .... LAVATORY
skin .... TALC
stain removing .. PUMICE
powdery .... FRIABLE, DUSTY
power ..... SWAY, AUTHORITY, MIGHT, VIS, CONTROL, ABILITY, CAPACITY, FORCE, VIGOR
colloquial .... STEAM
kind of ... STEAM, SOLAR, MOTIVE, ELECTRIC
loom inventor .... CARTWRIGHT
source of ..... SUN, FUEL
symbol of .... FASCES
theoretical .... ODYL
to survive ...... VITALITY
unit .... VOLT, WATT
world ..... RUSSIA, USA, AMERICA
powerful ... POTENT, MIGHTY, STRONG, PUISSANT
powerless .... IMPOTENT
Powhatan's daughter .... POCAHONTAS
powwow ..... MEDICINE MAN, CONFERENCE
Zuluans' .... INDABA
pox .... SYPHILIS
Poznan .... POSEN
practicable .... FEASIBLE, USEFUL, POSSIBLE
practical .... PRAGMATIC(AL), UTILE, USEFUL, WORKABLE
joke ...... HOAX, PRANK, TRICK
person .... REALIST
practice .... DRILL, USAGE, USE, WORKOUT, CUSTOM, HABIT, EXERCISE, PRAXIS, REHEARSE
composition ..... ETUDE
dishonest .... RACKET
established ...... PRAXIS, USAGE, CUSTOM
firearms with blanks ..... DRY RUN
joke ...... PRANK, HOAX
performance ... REHEARSE
systematic ..... EXERCISE
practiced ..... SKILLED, DEFT
pragmatic .... PRACTICAL, OFFICIOUS
Prague .... PRAHA
castle .... HRADCANY
square ...... WENCESLAS

prairie ...... PLAIN, SAVANNA, GRASSLAND, PAMPA(S)
dog .... MARMOT
grove .... MOTT(E)
hen .... GROUSE
soil .... GUMBO
squirrel .... GOPHER
state .... NEBRASKA
vehicle ...... SCHOONER
wolf .... COYOTE
praise .... TOUT, PANEGYRIC, LAUD, EXTOL, EXALT, EULOGIZE, KUDOS, ACCLAIM, ENCOMIUM, TRIBUTE, ELOGE, COMMEND, BLESS, EULOGY, GLORIFY, GLORIA
song of .... CAROL
too much ...... FLATTER
undue .... PUFF
praiseworthy ..... LAUDABLE
praline ... CONFECTION, CANDY
pram .... BUGGY, PERAMBULATOR
prance .... CAVORT, CAPER, STRUT, SWAGGER
prandial meal .... DINNER, SUPPER
prank ...... ANTIC, DRESS UP, MISCHIEF, ESCAPADE, CANTRIP, LARK, GAMBADO, JAPE, JOKE, HOAX, TRICK, CAPER, DIDO, FROLIC
with lighted match ...... HOTFOOT
pranks .... (HIGH)JINKS
prankster .... BUFFOON
prase .. CHALCEDONY, QUARTZ
prat .... BUTTOCKS
prate ... CHATTER, YAP, BLAB, TATTLE, PRATTLE, BABBLE, GAB
prattle ...... BABBLE, BLAB, PRATE, CHATTER
prawn .... SCAMP, CRUSTACEAN, MACRURAN
praxis .... PRACTICE, CUSTOM
pray ..... ENTREAT, IMPLORE, BESEECH, BEG, APPEAL, ORA
prayer ... LITANY, ROGATION, ORISON, PLEA, AVE, BENE, SUIT, ENTREATY, REQUEST, PETITION, GRACE, NOVENA
bead .... ROSARY
bones .... KNEES
book .... PORTAS(S), BREVIARY, MISSAL, PRIMER, ORDO, HOURS
desk .... PRIEDIEU
ending .... AMEN
evening .... VESPER
for another .. BEADSMAN, INTERCESSION
hour ..... VESPER, MATIN
hour, Moslem ..... AZAN
in gibberish .. GLOSSOLIA
last of the day .... COMPLIN(E)
meal .... GRACE
morning .... MATIN
nine-day .... NOVENA
of supplication .... SUFFRAGE

protect by .... SAIN
rug .... ASAN
shawl .... TALLITH
short .... GRACE
wheel user ... BUDDHIST, LAMA
prayerful .... DEVOUT
prayers, endowment for ...... CHANTRY
praying figure .... ORANT
Indians .... NATICKS
preach .... SERMONIZE, LECTURE, ADVOCATE
preacher .... PULPITEER, CLERGYMAN, EVANGELIST, HOMILIST, PREDICANT, MINISTER
circuit .... ROUNDER
talk of .... SERMON, HOMILY
traveling .. EVANGEL(IST), MISSIONARY
preachers collectively .. PULPIT
preaching .... SERMON, PREDICANT
preamble .... PREFACE
precarious .... INSECURE, UNCERTAIN, RISKY
state .... TOUCH-AND-GO
precede ..... FORERUN, HEAD
precedence .... LEAD, PRIORITY
precedent .... EXAMPLE
preceding .... PREVIOUS
all others ..... FOREMOST, FIRST
precentor .... CANTOR
precept .... MAXIM, RULE, DOCTRINE, APHORISM, DICTUM
Brahmanism ..... SUTRA
in law ... WRIT, WARRANT
preceptor .... TEACHER
precepts, collection of .. SUTRA
precinct(s) .... ENVIRONS, NEIGHBORHOOD
precious ..... DEAR, COSTLY, BELOVED, ARRANT
colloquial .... VERY
stone .... CABOCHON, OPAL, TOPAZ, GARNET, RUBY, SARD, GEM, DIAMOND, BRILLIANT
stone cutter ... LAPIDARY
precipice ...... CRAG, BLUFF, CLIFF
precipitate .... ABRUPT, SUDDEN, HASTEN, HASTY, HEADY, RASH, BRING ON, CONDENSE
precipitation .... SNOW, SLEET, RAIN, DEW, HASTE, RUSH, MIST
precipitator .... REAGENT, CATALYST, CATALYZER
precipitous .... SHEER, STEEP, RASH, HASTY
rock .... SCAR, CRAG, CLIFF, BLUFF
precis .... DIGEST, RESUME, SYNOPSIS, ABSTRACT, SUMMARY
precise ...... PRIM, SPECIFIC,

DEFINITE, EXACT, FORMAL, PARTICULAR, CORRECT, EXPLICIT, PRISSY
precisely .... EXACTLY
precision .... ACCURACY
preclude .. PREVENT, SHUT OUT, HINDER, ESTOP, INHIBIT, BAR
precocious child ..... PRODIGY
precursor .... HARBINGER, HERALD, OMEN, FORERUNNER
predatory .... PREYING, PREDACIOUS
bird ...... EAGLE, OWL, VULTURE
predecessor ..... PRECURSOR, ANCESTOR
predestination .... FATE, ELECTION, DESTINY
predicament .... PLIGHT, FIX, DILEMMA, JAM, SPOT, PICKLE, PASS, SCRAPE, RATTRAP, QUANDARY
predicant .... PREACHER
predicate .... BASE
predict ..... PORTEND, AUGUR, FORETELL, PROPHESY, FORECAST, (FORE)BODE
prediction .... PROPHECY, FORECAST
predictor .... SEER(ESS), PROPHET(ESS), FORECASTER
predilection .... PREFERENCE, TASTE, LIKING, FONDNESS, PREJUDICE, PARTIALITY, LEANING
predisposed .... PARTIAL, PREJUDICED, BIASED, INCLINED, PRONE
predominant .... REGNANT
preempt ...... APPROPRIATE, SEIZE
preen ... DRESS, PRIMP, PRINK
prefab .... QUONSET(HUT), NISSEN
preface .... PREAMBLE, FOREWORD, INTRODUCTION, FRONTISPIECE, PROEM, PRELUDE, BEGIN, START
prefatory note ..... FOREWORD
prefect .... DEAN
prefer ...... CHOOSE, PRESENT, FAVOR
preferably .... RATHER
preference .... CHOICE, LIKING
prefix .... BEFORE
about .... PERI
across .... TRANS
against .... ANTI
backward .... RETRO
bad .... MAL
before .... PRE, ANTE
between .... META
blood .... HEMO
both .... AMBI
distant .... TEL(E)
eight .... OCT(O)
equal .... ISO
false .... PSEUDO
far .... TEL(E)
fire .... PYR(O)
half ... SEMI, DEMI, HEMI
many .... MULT(I)
mountain .... ORO
outer ...... EXO, ECT(O)
over .... SUPRA
single .... MONO
thought .... IDEO
under .... SUB
with .... SYN
within .... ENDO
wrong .... MIS
pregnable .... VULNERABLE
pregnancy .... CYESIS, FETATION, GESTATION
outside uterus ... ECTOPIC
pregnant .... CHILDING, EXPECTING, ABOUNDING, ENCEINTE, GRAVID
prehistoric: comb. form ...... PALE(O)
human .... CAVEMAN
upright stone ... MENHIR
prejudice .... HARM, BIAS, PARTIALITY, OPINION, IMPERIL, ENDANGER
prejudiced ... PARTIAL, BIASED
prelate ... BISHOP, CARDINAL, PRIMATE
prelect .... LECTURE
preliminary ..... PREFATORY
meeting .... CAUCUS
race .... HEAT
statement ... PREAMBLE, FOREWORD, PREFACE
prelude .... PREFACE, OPENING, OVERTURE, PROEM
of fugue .... TOCCATA
premature .... UNTIMELY, EARLY, INOPPORTUNE
baby .... PREEMIE
development .. PRECOCITY
premeditated ...... PREPENSE, DELIBERATE
premier ..... FOREMOST, CHIEF
Preminger, movie director .... OTTO
premise .... PROPOSITION, BASIS, PREFACE
premises, series of ... SORITES
premium .... REWARD, PRIZE, BONUS, AGIO, FEE
premonition .... FOREBODING, HUNCH
preoccupation ..... OBSESSION, FIXATION
with sex .... EROT(IC)ISM
preoccupied ...... ENGROSSED, ABSORBED, RAPT
preoccupy .... OBSESS, ENGROSS, ABSORB
preparation ...... READINESS
prepare .... FIT(OUT), PRIME, GIRD, TRAIN, READY, ADAPT, DISPOSE, ACCUSTOM
copy ..... EDIT, REDACT
for action .... UNLIMBER, GIRD
prepared ...... READY, YARE
preponderant ...... DOMINANT
preposition ...... FOR, ONTO, INTO, UNTO, FROM, OUT, AFTER
prepossessing .... ATTRACTIVE, PLEASING
prepossession .... BIAS
preposterous .... ABSURD, SENSELESS, RIDICULOUS
prerogative .... RIGHT, PRIVILEGE
king's .... REGALIA
presage .... BODE, OMEN, PORTEND, SIGN, WARNING, PORTENT, FORETELL, AUGUR(Y)
presbyter .... ELDER, MINISTER, PRIEST, PRESTER
prescience .... FORESIGHT
prescribe ... ORDAIN, ORDER, SET(DOWN), DIRECT, OUTLAW
prescribed .... THETIC
prescript ...... RULE, ORDER
prescription .... RECIPE
presence .... GHOST, ATTENDANCE, COMPANY, APPEARANCE
of mind .... WIT
present .... BESTOW, TENDER, AT HAND, GIFT, BOON, DISPLAY, NONCE, INTRODUCE, SHOW, DONATION
at .... NOW
charges against .. PREFER
good luck ..... HANDSEL
to departing person .. FOY
presentation ... PERFORMANCE, GIFT, OFFERING, EXHIBIT, SHOW, DISPLAY
presentiment ... FOREBODING, HUNCH
presently .. NOW, ANON, SOON, SHORTLY, NOWADAYS
preservative .. VINEGAR, BRINE
preserve ... CURE, SMOKE, SASS, JAM, SAVE, PROTECT, SALT, CORN, PICKLE, PERPETUATE, CONFITURE, CAN, MARMALADE
by drying .... DESSICATE, DEHYDRATE
game ...... SANCTUARY
with salt .... CORN
preserved dead body .. MUMMY
preshrink cloth .... SANFORIZE
preside .. MODERATE, CONDUCT
president, college ..... PREXY
yacht club .. COMMODORE
presidential monogram .. HST, FDR, LBJ, JFK, DDE
nickname ..... IKE, ABE, TEDDY, CAL, JACK, ANDY
disapproval ...... VETO
reception .... LEVEE
presiding officer .. MODERATOR, SPEAKER, CHAIRMAN, PRINCIPAL
officer's vote ... CASTING
presidio ..... FORT, GARRISON
press .... WEDGE, SQUEEZE, CROWD, SQUASH, PUSH, IRON, COMPEL, JOURNALISM, DRIVE, URGE, WRING, CRAM, FORCE

agency (see news agency)
agent ...... PUBLICIST, JOURNALIST
agentry ... PROPAGANDA, PUBLICITY, BALLYHOO
dough .... KNEAD
down .... TAMP
with hands ..... MASSAGE
presser .... IRONER
pressing ... URGENT, EXIGENT
iron .... GOOSE
pressure .... STRESS, INFLUENCE, URGENCY, FORCE, DEMANDS, DURESS
group ..... LOBBY, BLOC
measuring device .... MANOMETER
unit .... BARIE, BARAD
prest .... LOAN
prester ... PRIEST, PRESBYTER
prestidigitator ..... MAGICIAN
prestige .... REPUTATION, RENOWN, FAME, KUDOS
presto .... QUICKLY
he says this word .... MAGICIAN
Preston's milieu ...... YUKON
presume ..... VENTURE, DARE, SUPPOSE, ASSUME
presumption ...... TEMERITY, INFERENCE
presumptive .... BRASH, ARROGANT
presumptuous .... FORWARD, BOLD, ARROGANT
pretend ..... CLAIM, ALLEGE, PROFESS, FEIGN, SIMULATE, DISSEMBLE
pretended courage .. BRAVADO, BLUFF
pretender .... IMPOSTOR, IMPERSONATOR, CLAIMANT, ASPIRANT, FAKER, SHAM
to knowledge ... QUACK, CHARLATAN, SCIOLIST
pretense ..... ACT, AIR, RUSE, GUISE, PRETEXT, SHAM, CLAIM, FEINT
of virtue ..... HYPOCRISY
pretension ... CLAIM, PRETEXT, AIR, BLUFF
pretentious .... POMPOUS, ASSUMING, ARTY
art .... KITSCH
preterition .... OMISSION
pretermit .... NEGLECT, OMIT, OVERLOOK
pretext ... PRETENSE, EXCUSE, COVER
for war ..... CASUS BELLI
pretty ... COMELY, FAIR, NICE, BONNY, BONNIE
and delicately formed ... DAINTY, MIGNON
girl .... CUTEY
pretzel .... BISCUIT
Preussen .... PRUSSIA
prevail ..... DOMINATE, WIN, TRIUMPH, SUCCEED
on ... PERSUADE, INDUCE
prevalent .... GENERAL, PANDEMIC, REGNANT, RIFE, PREVAILING, CURRENT, WIDESPREAD, COMMON, RAMPANT
prevaricate ..... LIE, QUIBBLE, PALTER, EQUIVOCATE
prevarication .. LIE, FALSEHOOD
prevaricator .... LIAR
prevent ..... AVERT, OBVIATE, PRECLUDE, HINDER, DETER, STOP, THWART, BLOCK, BALK, FORESTALL, FRUSTRATE
legally .... ESTOP
prevention, legal ... ESTOPPEL
preventive court order .... INJUNCTION
medicine ... ANTIBIOTIC
previous ... PRIOR, PRECEDING, FORMER
previse ... FORECAST, FORESEE, WARN
prexy .... PRESIDENT
prey ...... VICTIM, QUARRY, PLUNDER, ROB, GAME
high sea .... PRIZE
search for .... HUNT, RAVEN, RAVIN
Priam's children .. CASSANDRA, PARIS, CREUSA, HECTOR, TROILUS
domain .... TROY
father .... LAOMEDON
wife .... HECUBA
price ... CHARGE, RATE, COST, VALUE, WORTH, FEE
go up in .... BULL
list .... CATALOG(UE)
of ride .... FARE
prick .. STING, PIERCE, TINGLE, SPUR, DOT, PUNCTURE, PROD, GOAD, PINK, QUALM
pricket .... BUCK, DEER, CANDLESTICK
prickle .... SPINE, THORN, STING, TINGLE, BARB, BUR(R), SETA, ACULEUS, TRICHOME, BRIAR
prickly ..... THORNY, BURRY, ECHINATE, SMARTING, TINGLING, STINGING, BRIERY, SPINY
bush ...... BRIER, ROSE, BRIAR
heat .. LICHEN, MILIARIA
pear .... TUNA, CACTUS, NOPAL, OPUNTIA
seed coat .... BUR(R)
shrub .... BRAMBLE, DEWBERRY, RASPBERRY
weed .... NETTLE
pride .. ARROGANCE, CONCEIT, VANITY, VAINGLORY, SELF-ESTEEM
disdainful ..... HAUTEUR
lion's ...... LITTER, MANE
ruffled .... PIQUE
priest ... PRESBYTER, PRESTER, SHAMAN, FRA, FLAMEN, CLERGYMAN, MINISTER, CURE
armband .... FANON
army .... PADRE, CHAPLAIN
assistant of ... ACOLYTE, SACRISTAN
Buddhist .... LAMA
gift of ...... MORTUARY
high .... PONTIFF, AARON, ELI
house of a ... PRESBYTERY
Indian .... SHAMAN, MEDICINE MAN
neckpiece of ..... AMICE
newly ordained .... NEOPHYTE
office of .. FROCK, MATINS
salaried .... VICAR
shaven head of .. TONSURE
skullcap ..... ZUCCHETTO
vestment ... ORALE, ALB, SURPLICE, COPE
priestess .... AUGE, HERO
priestly .... SACERDOTAL, HIERATIC
priests group of 20 .... FETIAL
prig .... PRUDE, PEDANT, STUFFED SHIRT, PICKPOCKET, THIEF
prim ...... DEMURE, FORMAL, PROPER, PRIGGISH, PRISSY, MODEST, PRUDISH
prima .... FACIE
donna .... DIVA, CALLAS, ALDA, STEBER, MELBA, PONS, TEBALDI
primary .... ULTIMATE, ORIGINAL, CHIEF, PRINCIPAL, FIRST
primate .... APE, BONOBO, GIBBON, (ARCH)BISHOP, MONKEY, LEMUR, ORANG, GORILLA, SIAMANG
prime ... FIRST(RATE), CREAM, PICK, PREPARE, MAY
in music .... UNISON
minister .... PREMIER
of life .... HEYDAY
primer .... HORNBOOK, (TEXT)BOOK, READER
primitive ..... WILD, CRUDE, BASIC, ANCIENT, BARBARIC
combining form .... PALE(O)
fish .... COELACANTH
tribesman's ornament ... LABRET
primogenitor ...... ANCESTOR
primordial .... ORIGINAL
primp .... PREEN, PRINK, PRUNE
primrose .... PRIMULA, FAIRYCUP, SPINK, COWSLIP, OXLIP
primula .... PRIMROSE
prince ..... KING, MONARCH, RAIA, PRINCIPE, RAS
consort's wife ... QUEEN, EMPRESS
ecclesiastical .. CARDINAL
Ethiopian .... RAS
in India .. (MAHA)RAJAH, RANA
look-alike of .... PAUPER
Monaco's reigning ...... RAINIER
Moslem .. NAWAB, IMAM

Norodom, Cambodian .. SIHANOUK
of darkness ...... SATAN
of Peace ... JESUS(CHRIST)
of the church .. CARDINAL
of Wales' motto .... ICH DIEN, I SERVE
operatic .... IGOR
princeling .... SATRAP
princely ...... REGAL, ROYAL, LAVISH, LIBERAL
princess .... INFANTA
carried by bull .. EUROPA
principal ... CHIEF, PRIMARY, ARCH, MAIN, PREMIER
actor .... STAR, LEAD
crop .... STAPLE
principle ... DOCTRINE, RULE, MAXIM, THEOREM, TENET, POSTULATE, PRECEPT, IDEAL
first .... RUDIMENTS
main .... KEYSTONE
principles of citizenship ...... CIVISM
princox ...... FOP, COXCOMB
prink .... PRIMP, PREEN, DRESS UP, PRUNE
print .... IMPRESSION, PICTURE, ETCHING, STAMP, PUBLISH
blurred/double .. MACKLE
in red letters .. RUBRICATE
printed books, early .... INCUNABULA
printer .... PUBLISHER, TYPESETTER
printer's apprentice .... DEVIL
direction .... STET, DELE(TE), RESET
helper .... DEVIL
ink pad .... DABBER
lock .... QUOIN
mark ... DAGGER, CARET, ASTERISK, DIESIS
measure ... EN, EM, PICA
metal block ...... QUAD
proof .... GALLEY
roller .... BRAY
shop spirit ...... RALPH
printing .... EDITION
art of .... PRESS
error(s) ...... ERRATUM, ERRATA
establishment .... PRESS
form ... DIE, MOLD, MAT
mark ...... FIST, DIESIS, DASH
process .... OFFSET
system for the blind ..... BRAILLE
term ... RESET, DELE(TE), CLOSE, STONE
trial impression .. PROOF
type channel .... NICK
prior ..... PREVIOUS, EARLIER, FORMER
superior of a .... ABBOT
to .... BEFORE
priority .... PRECEDENCE
priory .... MONASTERY, NUNNERY, ABBEY
Priscilla's husband .... ALDEN
suitor .. (MILES)STANDISH

prison .... PENITENTIARY, BRIDEWELL, BASTIL(L)E, GAOL, QUOD, QUAD, JAIL, CAGE, LIMBO
cell .... HOLE
chaplain ..... ORDINARY
colloquial/slang ... STIR, CLINK, JUG, PEN, CAN, HOOSEGOW, CALABOOSE
cubicle .... CELL
division .... WARD
employee ..... TURNKEY, JAILER, WARDER
federal ...... ALCATRAZ, SING SING
guard: sl. .... SCREW
head of a .... WARDEN
London ..... NEWGATE
priest .... CHAPLAIN, ORDINARY
sentence ...... STRETCH
ship's ...... HULK, BRIG
spy .... MOUTON
term .... RAP
underground .. DUNGEON
prisoner ... CAPTIVE, TERMER, CONVICT, JAILBIRD
at bar .... CULPRIT
bond of ... BAIL, PAROLE
guard of .... BAILIFF
privileged .... TRUSTY
redeem a .... RANSOM
shackles of ...... BILBO
prissy .... PRECISE, PRIM, FUSSY, OVERNICE
pristine .... NEW, UNSPOILED, ORIGINAL, PURE, FIRST
prithee ... PLEASE, I PRAY THEE
privacy .... SECLUSION, SECRECY
private ... PERSONAL, SECRET, CONFIDENTIAL, INTIMATE
apartment ...... MAHAL
army .... PFC
entrance .... POSTERN
eye ...... DETECTIVE, TEC
information .... TIP
remarks .... ASIDES, AD LIBS
road .... DRIVEWAY
room .... CLOSET
teacher .. TUTOR, COACH,
wrong .... TORT
privateer ..... KIDD, CORSAIR, PIRATE, CORNISH, DRAKE, CAVENDISH, ANSON, ROGERS, SWAN
privilege ...... FAVOR, RIGHT
corporation's .... FRANCHISE
king's .... REGALITY
privileges, equality of .... ISONOMY
privy .... LATRINE, JAKES, OUTHOUSE, PRIVATE, TOILET, STOOL, CLOACA
council ..... CAMARILLA
to .... INFORMED
prize .... STAKE, AWARD, VALUE, ESTEEM, TROPHY, LEVER, PRY, TREASURE
award since 1917 .... PULITZER

donor .... NOBEL, PULITZER
fighter .... BOXER, PUG(ILIST), SLUGGER, BEAKBUSTER, RINGSTER
fighter's wear ..... SILKS
fighting program .. CARD
kind of .... BOOBY
money .... PURSE
pro ...... FOR, PROFESSIONAL
bono ____ ..... PUBLICO
tempore ..... TEMPORARY
proa .... CANOE, PRAU
probability ...... LIKELIHOOD, ODD
probable .... LIKELY, POSSIBLE
probate court's concern ...... WILLS, ESTATES
judge .... SURROGATE
probation ..... TRIAL, TESTING
probe ...... SEARCH, EXPLORE
for examining wounds .. STYLET
surgical .... STYLET
probity .... INTEGRITY, HONESTY
problem .... KNOT, QUESTION, DIFFICULTY, TICKLER, CRUX, PUZZLE, DILEMMA, POSER, TASK
proboscidian ...... ELEPHANT, MASTODON
proboscis .... SNOUT, TRUNK, NOSE
butterfly/moth's .... LINGUA
insect ..... HAUSTELLUM
proceed ..... ISSUE, GO ON, ADVANCE, MARCH, CONTINUE
at great speed .. HIGHBALL
without power ... COAST
proceedings .... ACTA, TRANSACTIONS, ACTS
last part of .... TAG
proceeds ... PROFITS, INCOME, ISSUE
process .... COURSE, OUTGROWTH, APPENDAGE, TUBERCLE
fish .... BARBEL
in law .... SUIT, ACTION, WRIT, PROSECUTE
of decline ... DECADENCE
of knowing ..... NOESIS, COGNITION
server .... SHERIFF
steel-making .. BESSEMER
procession .. TRAIN, RETINUE, CORTEGE, FILE, PARADE, CAVALCADE
of cars ..... MOTORCADE
official .... MARSHAL
staff .... VERGE
staff bearer ..... VERGER
processional .... HYMN
prochein, in law ..... NEAREST
proclaim .... ANNOUNCE, DECLARE, HERALD, ENOUNCE, TRUMPET, SING, CRY
proclamation .... MANIFESTO, BAN, EDICT, NOTICE,

UKASE, BAN(N)S
proclivity ...... INCLINATION
Procne, husband of .. TEREUS
parent of ...... PANDION
sister of ..... PHILOMELA
transformation of .... SWALLOW
procrastinate ..... POSTPONE, DEFER, DELAY, DILLY DALLY
procreate ... BEGET, PRODUCE
proctor .... AGENT
procumbent .... PRONE
procurator .. PROCTOR, PILATE
procure .... GET, OBTAIN, SECURE
procurer ...... PIMP, PANDER
prod ...... GOAD, DIG, POKE, THRUST, JAB, URGE, ROUSE, EGG, DRIVE, PUNCH
prodder, elephant ... MAHOUT
prodigal ... LAVISH, WASTEFUL, WASTREL, SPENDER, GENEROUS, PROFUSE, SPENDTHRIFT
prodigious .... HUGE, ENORMOUS, AMAZING
prodigy ... WONDER, MARVEL
prodrome .... SYMPTOM
produce .... CAUSE, ENGENDER, GENERATE, BEAR, YIELD, CREATE, BEGET, FETCH, ISSUE
produced on earth's surface ... EPIGENE
producing abundantly .... FERACIOUS
vinegar .... ACETIC
product .... OUTGROWTH, FRUIT, RESULT, CROP, YIELD
production .... OUTPUT
productive .... FERTILE, PROLIFIC, RICH, FECUND, FRUCTUOUS
source .... MINE
proem .... PREFACE, INTRODUCTION, PRELUDE
prof .... PROFESSOR
profanation .... SACRILEGE
profane .... DEFILE, IRREVERENT, BLASPHEME, DEBASE, VIOLATE
profess ...... AFFIRM, CLAIM
profession ... CAREER, METIER, AVOWAL, VOCATION, CALLING, PURSUIT, LINE, TRADE
professed .... AVOWED, PRETENDED
professional .... PRO
non .... LAY, LAIC, AMATEUR
professor .... TEACHER
assistant of ..... READER
proffer .... OFFER, GIVE, TENDER, PRESENT
proficient .... ADEPT, APT, SKILLED, EXPERT, DEFT
profile .... SIDE VIEW, OUTLINE, BIO-DATA, SKETCH, SILHOUETTE
profit .... AVAIL, GAIN, ADVANTAGE, BENEFIT, BOOT
clear ...... NET, VELVET
easy .... GRAVY
kind of extra .. PERQUISITE
sudden, great ... KILLING
profitable .. GAINFUL, PAYING, LUCRATIVE
profiteer .... SCALPER
profits .... RETURNS, PROCEEDS
for distribution .. MELON
from lands, etc. .... ISSUE
profligate .... DISSOLUTE, WASTEFUL
person .... ROUE
profound ..... INTENSE, DEEP, ABYSS
profundity .... DEPTH
profuse ... PRODIGAL, LAVISH, LUSH, GENEROUS
prog ..... FORAGE, PLUNDER
progenitor .. ANCESTOR, PARENT
progeny ..... SEED, OFFSPRING, CHILDREN, ISSUE, SCION, BREED
prognosis ..... FORECAST(ING)
prognosticate .... PREDICT, FORETELL, PROPHESY
prognosticator ... PREDICTOR, DIVINER, SEER, PROPHET, FORECASTER
program ... CARD, SYLLABUS, PROSPECTUS, PLAN
progress .... ADVANCE, IMPROVE(MENT), GAIN
planned .... TELESIS
progressing by tens .. DECIMAL
Progressive of 1912 .... BULLMOOSE
prohibit .... FORBID, HINDER, BAN, VETO, TABOO, (DE)BAR, TABU, ENJOIN
prohibited ..... TABOO, TABU
prohibiting .... VETITIVE
prohibition ...... TABOO, BAN
trade .... EMBARGO
prohibitionist .... DRY
prohibitive price .... DEAR, COSTLY
project .... PROTRUDE, PROPOSAL, SCHEME, PLAN, JUT, IDEA, ENTERPRISE
projectile ... BULLET, ROCKET, BOMB, MISSILE, SHELL, JAVELIN
part of .... WARHEAD, WAR NOSE
path of ..... TRAJECTORY
projecting corner ... COIGN(E)
edge .... BRIM, EAVE
knob .... BOSS
part .... JOG, SOCLE
point .... NEB
projection ...... EAR, BULGE, LOBE, LEDGE, FIN, NOB, TORUS, JOB, SOCLE, JAG
prolapse .... PTOSIS
prolegomenon .... FOREWORD
proletarian .... WORKER
proliferate .... MULTIPLY
prolific ... FRUITFUL, FERTILE, FECUND, PRODUCTIVE
prolix .... LONG-WINDED, WORDY, VERBOSE, DISCURSIVE
prolocutor ..... MOUTHPIECE, CHAIRMAN, SPOKESMAN
prologue reciter ..... CHORUS
prolong ..... NURSE, STRETCH, EXTEND, LENGTHEN, PROTRACT
prolonged dry weather .... DROUGHT
prom ..... BALL, DANCE, HOP
organizers ..... JUNIORS
promenade ... WALK, AVENUE, BALL, PARADE, MALL, ESPLANADE, ALAMEDA, GALLERY, STROLL, PASEO
along coast ...... FRONT
Prometheus' boon to man ..... FIRE
prominence .... EMINENCE
between eyebrows ...... GLABELLA
give .... HIGHLIGHT, SPOTLIGHT
promiscuous .... CASUAL
woman .... COCOTTE
promise .... VOW, ENGAGE, PAROLE, PLEDGE, WORD, GUARANTEE, SPONSION
in marriage .... BETROTH
Promised Land ..... CANAAN, ZION, SION
promising ...... ROSY, BRIGHT
promissory note .... IOU
signer .... MAKER
promontory .... CAPE, HEADLAND, SKAW, TOR, NESS
promote .... RAISE, ADVANCE, BOOST, FOSTER
promoter .... IMPRESARIO
promotion ..... ADVANCEMENT
prompt ... QUICK, URGE, EGG, INSPIRE, CUE, ADVISE, MOVE, LEAD, YARE, RATH(E)
prompter .... CUER
promptly ... PRONTO, AT ONCE
promulgate .... PUBLISH
prone ... SUPINE, RECUMBENT, PROSTRATE, INCLINED, APT
pronephros .... KIDNEY
prong ... NIB, TINE, TIP, PIERCE
pronged thing .. FORK, ANTLER, TRIDENT, RAKE
pronounce .... DECLARE, ARTICULATE, UTTER
imperfectly .... LAMBDACISM
indistinctly .... SLUR
pronounced using tongue ..... LINGUAL
pronto ..... AT ONCE, QUICKLY
pronunciamento .. MANIFESTO
pronunciation of r like l ...... LALLATION
pause .... HIATUS
poor .... CACOLOGY
rough .... BURR
standard ..... ORTHOEPY
study of ..... PHONOLOGY
unit of .... SYLLABLE
proof .... EVIDENCE, EXHIBIT, TRIAL
proofreader's mark .... DELE, CARET, STET

prop ... BRACE, SUPPORT, GIB, BUTTRESS, STAY, CRUTCH, SHORE, HOLD UP, SUSTAIN
one-legged ..... UNIPOD
propaganda .... BALLYHOO
propagate ...... RAISE, BREED, MULTIPLY, SPREAD
propel ... PUSH, IMPEL, DRIVE
with a pole .... PUNT
propeller ..... DRIVER, SCREW, BLADE, ROTOR
driving force of .. THRUST
part of .... BLADE
propensity .... BENT, INCLINATION, TENDENCY, PENCHANT, FLAIR
proper ...... MEET, DECOROUS, SUITABLE, CORRECT, FIT(TING), SEEMLY, PRIM, DECENT
order .... EUTAXY
slang .... KOSHER
properly .... DULY
property .... ATTRIBUTE, CHATTEL, REALTY, HOLDINGS, OWNERSHIP, POSSESSION, ESTATE, ASSET
absolute .... AL(L)OD
act to regain ... REPLEVIN
captured at sea ... PRIZE
claim to .... LIEN
delivery of ...... LIVERY
endowed .... PATRIMONY
illegal detention of ...... DETINUE
landed .... ESTATE
legally held ..... SEISIN, SEIZIN
movie-making .... PROP
personal ..... CHATTEL, CHOSE
reverted ...... ESCHEAT
stationary ..... PRAEDIAL
willed to someone ..... LEGACY
prophecy .... PREDICTION, FORECAST
by lots .... SORTILEGE
prophesy ... AUGUR, PRESAGE, PREDICT, FORETELL, FORECAST, DIVINE
prophet .... AMOS, HOSEA, ISAIAH, JEREMIAH, EZEKIEL, DANIEL, JONAH, JOEL, ORACLE, SEER
Moslem ..... MOHAMMED
of disaster ..... ALARMIST
prophetess .... SEERESS, SIBYL, PYTHONESS
discredited .. CASSANDRA
prophetic....... VATIC(INAL), SYBILLINE, PYTHONIC, VATIC(AL), MANTIC, FATIDIC
prophets, book of the .. NEBIIM
propinquity .... NEARNESS, KINSHIP, AFFINITY
propitiate ... APPEASE, PACIFY
propitious .... GRACIOUS, FAVORABLE, AUSPICIOUS
proponent .... PROPOSER, ADVOCATE, STALWART
proportion ...... RATIO, RATE, QUOTA, BALANCE, SYMMETRY
proportions ...... DIMENSIONS
proposal ..... OFFER, TENDER, SUGGESTION, BID, MOVE, MOTION
legislative .... BILL
tentative .... FEELER
propose .... MOVE
for office ..... NOMINATE
proposed international language IDO, ESPERANTO
proposition ... THEORY, PLAN, PROPOSAL, OFFER, THEOREM, PROJECT, PREMISE, (HYPO)THESIS
secondary ...... LEMMA
propound ..... POSE, PROPOSE, SET FORTH
proprietor .... OWNER, TITLEHOLDER
propriety .... FITNESS
prorogue .... ADJOURN
prosaic .... DULL, LITERAL, UNPOETIC
proscribe ...... FORBID, BAN, OUTLAW, INTERDICT, BANISH, EXILE
prosecute .... CARRY ON, FOLLOW UP, SUE
prosecuting attorney ..... DA, FISCAL
proselyte .... CONVERT
Proserpina .... CORA, PERSEPHONE
husband of .... PLUTO
mother of .... CERES
prosit .... TOAST
prosody .... SCANSION
verse .... STICH
prospect .. SCENE, VIEW, HOPE, OUTLOOK, SEARCH
prospective .. LIKELY, FUTURE
prospector ...... SOURDOUGH
advance to ... GRUBSTAKE
prospectus .... PROGRAM
prosper ... SUCCEED, THRIVE, FLOURISH, BATTEN
prosperity .. BOOM, BONANZA
Prospero's slave ..... CALIBAN
sprite .... ARIEL
prosperous .... WEALTHY, WELL-OFF, WELL-TO-DO, FAT, PALMY
prostitute ... TART, TROLLOP, TRULL, TRAMP, WHORE, HARLOT, CHIPPY, FILLE, DRAB
kind of ...... COURTESAN
prostrate .... PRONE, FALLEN, SUPINE, LAY LOW
prosy .... DULL, JEJUNE
protagonist ..... HERO, STAR, RIVAL, CONTENDER
protect ..... GUARD, SHIELD, DEFEND
protection .... PASS(PORT), TUTELAGE, DEFENSE, (A)EGIS
against loss .. INSURANCE
means of ... SPINE, QUILL, ARMOR, PAINT, MOAT, HELMET, CAMOUFLAGE
protective band, fencing ...... BRACER
cover ... ARMOR, SHELL, SHIELD, SCREEN, CAMOUFLAGE
protector .... PATRON, GUARDIAN, DEFENDER, KEEPER
protege .... WARD
proteid(e) ... AMINE, PROTEIN
protein ... PROTEID(E), FIBRIN, AMINE, ALBUMIN, ALEURONE, RICIN, CASEIN, RICINE, GLOBULIN, HISTONE
egg yolk .... VITELLIN
muscle tissue .... MYOSIN
proteose .... ELASTOSE, ALBUMOSE
protest ..... ASSERT, OUTCRY, COMPLAINT, SQUAWK, OBJECT(ION), DISSENT
Protestant .... ANGLICAN, LUTHERAN, OBJECTOR
Anglo-Saxon ..... WASP
non-conformist .... SECTARY
proton .... ANLAGE
accelerator .. COSMOTRON
protoplasm .. PLASMA, COLLOID
granule in .... MICROSOME
unit of .... PLASTID
prototype ... PATTERN, MODEL, ORIGINAL
protozoan .... AM(O)EBA, PROTIST, MONAD, EUGLENA
organ of locomotion .... FLAGELLUM
protract .... STRETCH, LENGTHEN, PROLONG, EXTEND
protrude ... BULGE, PROJECT, JUT(OUT), EXSERT
protrusion of organ .. HERNIA
protuberance ... KNOB, HUMP, VENTER, LOBE, NODE, BULGE, SWELLING, UMBO, NUB, SNAG, EAR, INION
protuberant .... TOROSE, TOROUS, BULGING
proud .... ARROGANT, HAUGHTY, SPIRITED, BYRONIC
Proust, F. novelist ... MARCEL
prove .... TEST, TRY(OUT), VERIFY, DEMONSTRATE
false ... REFUTE, DEBUNK
provenance .... ORIGIN, DERIVATION
Provencal poet ...... MISTRAL
provender ..... FODDER, HAY, OATS, CORN, FORAGE, FOOD, FEED
proverb .... ADAGE, PARABLE, APHORISM, AXIOM, SAYING, MAXIM, SAW, BY-WORD
provide .. FURNISH, STIPULATE, PURVEY, SUPPLY, CATER, AFFORD
food .... CATER
with means ..... ENABLE
providence .... PRUDENCE
provident ... THRIFTY, FRUGAL, PRUDENT
providential .... LUCKY, FORTUNATE

province .... REGION, TERRITORY, SPHERE
ruler of ..... GOVERNOR, ETHNARCH
provincial .... RUSTIC, LOCAL, NARROW
speech .... PATOIS, DIALECT, IDIOM
proving directly ..... D(E)ICTIC
provision .... VICTUALS, CONDITION, FOOD STORE
provisional ...... TENTATIVE, INTERIM, TEMPORARY
provisioner ... SUTLER, GROCER
provisions .... LARDER, GROCERIES, CATES
search for ...... FORAGE
storage place .... CELLAR
proviso ... CLAUSE, CONDITION, STIPULATION
provisory ...... CONDITIONAL
provocation ...... INCITEMENT
provoke .... ANGER, IRRITATE, PIQUE, ANNOY, GOAD, BAIT, STIR, INCITE, EXCITE, NEEDLE, RILE
provost .... JAILER
prow .... BOW, NOSE
prowess .... VALOR, SKILL, ABILITY
prowl .... LURK, SKULK
proximal ..... NEXT, NEAREST
opposed to ..... DISTAL
proximity .... NEARNESS
proxy .... AGENT, DEPUTY
prude .... PRIG
prudent ... CAREFUL, SENSIBLE, DISCREET, CAUTIOUS
prudery personified .. GRUNDY
prudish .... PRISSY
prune ... PLUM, SHEAR, TRIM, CLIP, SNED, LOP
prunella .... TEXTILE
prurient ...... LUSTFUL, LEWD
pruritus .... ITCHING
Prussian .... JUNKER, GERMAN
cavalryman ..... U(H)LAN
city ..... AACHEN, ESSEN, EMDEN
district .... STADE
land measure ... MORGEN
legislature ..... LANDTAG
province .... SAXONY
resort .... EMS
river .... RUHR
seaport ... EMDEN, KIEL, STETTIN
prussiate .... CYANIDE
pry ...... LOOK, PEER, LEVER, PRIZE, SNOOP(ER), NOSE, CROWBAR, JIMMY, INSPECT
prying .. CURIOUS, INQUISITIVE
person .. SNOOP, PEEPER, PEEPING TOM, GOSSIP
psalm .... HYMN, SONG, CONTICLE, INTROIT, VENITE, LAUD, CANTATE
word .... SELAH
psalterium .... MANYPLIES, OMASUM
psaltery .... DULCIMER
psammite .... SANDSTONE
pseudo .. BOGUS, COUNTERFEIT, SPURIOUS, SHAM, FALSE
intellectual ..... PUNDIT, CHARLATAN, SCIOLIST
pseudonym .... ANONYM, PEN NAME, NOM DE PLUME, ALIAS, INCOGNITO
Arouet .... VOLTAIRE
Athorton .... LIN
Austen .... DAPSANG
Bronte .... (CURRER)BELL
Clemens .. (MARK) TWAIN
Dickens .... BOZ
Dodgson .... (LEWIS) CARROLL
Dudevant .... (GEORGE) SAND
Evans .. (GEORGE) ELIOT
Gardner, E. S. ..... FAIR
Goodman ... ADAM SMITH
Herzog .... (ANDRE) MAUROIS
Lamb .... ELIA
Millay ... (NANCY) BOYD
Moir .... DELTA
Mrs. Humphrey ... RITA
Munro .... SAKI
Poquelin .... MOLIERE
Porter .... (O)HENRY
Pyeshkov, Aleksei ...... (MAXIM) GORKI
Ramee, M. L. ... OUIDA
Rosegger .... PK
Stein ... (ALICE) TOKLAS
Thibault .... (ANATOLE) FRANCE
Viaud, L. M. .... (PIERRE) LOTI
Wright .. (S.S.) VAN DINE
pshaw .... POOH, TUT
Psiloriti, Mount .... IDA
location of ...... CRETE
psilosis .... SPRUE
psoas .... MUSCLE, LOIN
psora .... SCABIES
psychasthenia ..... NEUROSIS
Psyche .... SOUL, MIND
love of .... CUPID
psychedelic experience ... LSD
psychiatrist .... ALIENIST, MESMER, FREUD, ADLER
psyches, parts of ... IDS, EGOS
psychic disorder .... NEUROSIS
energy .... LIBIDO
person .... MEDIUM
psycho .... NEUROTIC
psychological .... MENTAL
psychologist .... BINET
psychopathic .... LOCO
psychosis .... INSANITY
psychotic .... CRAZY
Pt, in chemistry ... PLATINUM
ptarmigan ..... GROUSE, RIPA
pteric .... ALAR
pteridophyte .... FERN
pteris rootstock .... ROI
pterodactyl .... PTEROSAUB
pteropod ... MOLLUSK, CLIONE
pterygoid .... WINGLIKE
ptisan ... TEA, TISANE, DRINK, DECOCTION
ptomaine, liquid .... CHOLINE
ptosis .... PROLAPSE
ptyalin .... ENZYME
pub .... TAVERN, INN, HOTEL, BAR
serving ...... BEER, ALE, PORTER
worker .... TAPSTER, BARMAID
puberty, of .... HEBETIC
pubescence .... DOWN
public ... OVERT, COMMUNITY, PEOPLE, OPEN, COMMON, COMMUNAL
announcer .... CRIER
auction .... VENDUE
baths .... THERMAE
disclosure ...... EXPOSE
enemy .... CRIMINAL, GANGSTER, RACKETEER
funds, steal .... PECULATE
good ..... COMMONWEAL
house ...... INN, HOTEL, TAVERN, BAR
land .... AGER
life .... CAREER
notice ... AD, BULLETIN, PUBLICITY, SPOTLIGHT
opinion .... CONSENSUS
opinion-taker ... GALLUP, HARRIS, ROPER
prosecutor ... DA, FISCAL
recreation spot .... PARK
square ... PLAZA, PIAZZA, FORUM
utility ... BUS, (TAXI)CAB
walk .... ESPLANADE
welcome, enthusiastic ... OVATION
worship, science of ...... LITURGIES
publican ...... BARKEEP(ER), TAXMAN
publication .. BOOK, ARTICLE, PERIODICAL, MAGAZINE, BULLETIN, JOURNAL
publicist .... WRITER, (PRESS)AGENT, JOURNALIST
publicity ... NOTICE, RECLAME
exaggerated ... PUFFERY
publicize .... PLUG
publish ... BLAZON, PUT OUT, ISSUE, NOISE
publisher .. OCHS, SULZBERGER, FIELDS, HEARST, MERRIAM, MCKAY
publisher's announcement .... BLURB
trademark .... COLOPHON
Puccini, composer .. GIACOMO
heroine .... MIMI, TOSCA
opera ... TOSCA, BOHEME, MANON LESCAUT, TURANDOT
puccoon .... BLOODROOT, DYE
puce .... PURPLE
puck ...... DISK, SPRITE, ELF, IMP, (HOB)GOBLIN
pucka ... REAL, GENUINE, GOOD
pucker .... PURSE, POUT, WRINKLE, KNIT, FOLD, CREASE, COCKLE, RUCK, TUCK
puckered .... BULLATE
puckish .. IMPISH, MISCHIEVOUS, ELFIN

pudding .... CUSTARD, FROMENTY, ROLY-POLY, CHARLOTTE, MUSH, SPONGE, SAUSAGE, DUFF, HOY
flour .... DUFF
ingredient .... SUET, TAPIOCA, SAGO, SEMOLINA
sailor .... DUFF
puddle ..... PLASH(ET), POOL, MUDDY, WALLOW, LOBLOLLY
puddling tool .... RABBLE
pudency .... MODESTY
pudendum .... VULVA
pudgy ... DUMPY, FAT, STOCK, ROLY-POLY
Pueblo ..... VILLAGE, TOWN, INDIAN
council room ...... KIVA
Indian ..... HOPI, MOQUI, PIRO, ZUNI, TANO
Indian dwelling ... KIVA
puerile ... INFANTILE, YOUNG, CHILDISH, SILLY, TRIVIAL
Puerto Rico beverage ... MABI
capital .... SAN JUAN
city .... PONCE, CAGUAS, ARECIBO
conqueror .... MILES
discoverer of .. COLUMBUS
governor ...... MUNOZ, ALBERTO, SANCHEZ, MAYAGUEZ
porkfish .... SISI
seaport .... ARECIBO
puff ..... PAD, GUST, PRAISE, FLAM, WHIFF, WAFF, BREATH, SWELL(ING), PANT, INFLATE, BLOW
adder .... SNAKE
at a cigarette ...... DRAG
ball .... FUNGUS
bird ... BARBET, MONASA
headdress .... POUF
of wind .... FLATUS
out .... BOUFFANT
small .... WHIFFET
up ...... ELATE, BLOW, BLOAT, INFLATE, SWELL
puffed .... BAGGY
puffer .... (GLOBE)FISH
puffin .... BIRD
kin of .... AUK
puffy ... OBESE, FAT, PANTING, SWOLLEN
pug ...... BOXER, (BULL)DOG, PUGILIST, FOOTPRINT, TRAIL, TRACK, CLAY
Puget Sound seaport .. TACOMA
pugging ...... CLAY, MORTAR, SAWDUST
puggree .... SCARF
pugh .... EXCLAMATION, BAH, PAH, PISH
pugilist .... PUG, BOXER, BEAKBUSTER, RINGSTER
assistant of ..... SECOND, HANDLER
encounter .... MILL
pugnacious .... QUARRELSOME, COMBATIVE, BELLIGERENT, BELLICOSE
man .... BRUISER
puisne .... JUDGE, JUNIOR
puissant .... MIGHTY, STRONG
puke ...... VOMIT, THROW UP
pukka .... REAL, GENUINE
pulchritude .... BEAUTY
pulchritudinous ... BEAUTIFUL
one ..... PIN-UP, VENUS
pule .... WHIMPER, WHINE
pulex .... FLEA
Pulj, former name of ... POLA
pull ... DO, (RE)STRAIN, MOVE, PLUCK, TOW, HAUL, DRAG, TUG, DRAW, PERFORM
apart ... PAN, CRITICIZE, TEAR, REND, RIP
back .... RETREAT, WITHDRAW
by the root .... STUB
down ... HUMBLE, REDUCE
for .... CHEER, ROOT
forcibly .. WRENCH, YANK
off .... EFFECT, ACCOMPLISH, DOUSE
over .... SWEATER
slang .... INFLUENCE
up .... STOP, HIKE, REIN
up stake .. LEAVE, DEPART
pullet .... HEN, POULARD
pulley ...... WHEEL, TACKLE, SHEAVE
pullman ...... SLEEPER, BERTH
pullulate ... BUD, GERMINATE, BREED, TEEM
pulmonary disease .. PHTHISIS
pulp ...... CHYME, PAP, PITH
apple/fruit ..... POMACE
grape .... RAPE
in mining .... SLIME
product .... PAPER
slang .... MAGAZINE
pulpit ...... ROSTRUM, BEMA, PLATFORM, MINISTRY, DESK, AMBO
preachings .... SERMONS, HOMILIES
pulpiteer .... PREACHER
pulpy .... FLESHY
pulpy fruit .. GRAPE, FIG, UVA, DRUPE, POMEGRANATE
pulque .... MESCAL, AGAVE
pulsate .... QUIVER, VIBRATE, BEAT, THROB, THRILL
pulsation ... THROB, BEAT(ING)
pulse .... BEAT, THROB, FEELING, SEED, SPHYGMUS
beat absence ... ACROTISM
of the .... SPHYGMIC
plant .... PEA, BEAN, LENTIL, SOY
split .... DAL
pulverize .... BRAY, POWDER, TRITURATE, GRIND, MILL, LEVIGATE, ATOMIZE, MULL, POUND, CRUSH
pulverized material .. POWDER, DUST
pulverizing device .... SPIDER
pulverulent .. DUSTY, POWDERY
puma ... CAT, COUGAR, FUR, (MOUNTAIN)LION, CATAMOUNT
pumice .... ROCK, POLISH
pummel .... BEAT
pump .... QUIZ, INFLATE, DRAW(OUT), QUESTION, SHOE
handle .... SWIPE
kind of .... SUCTION, PRESSURE, CHAIN, LIFT, FORCE, RAM
part .... RAM, VALVE
plunger of .... RAM
pumpernickel ... BROT, BREAD
pumpkin ...... PEPO, GOURD, MELON, FRUIT
pumpkinseed ...... (SUN)FISH
pun ... QUIBBLE, PARANOMASIA, EQUIVOKE
puna .... PLATEAU
punch ... DRINK, PERFORATE, PASTE, JAB, FORCE, BOP, DOUSE, PUPPET, PIERCE, BOX, POKE, PROD, GAD, BUFFET, BLOW, STAMP
and ____ .... JUDY
and Judy character ...... PUPPET
and Judy dog ...... TOBY
bowl .... MONTEITH
drunk .... DAZED, DIZZY
engraver's ..... MATTOIR
weak .... TIFF
puncheon .... CASK, POST, TIMBER, DIE, PERFORATOR, AWL
punchinello .... CLOWN, BUFFOON
punctate ... DOTTED, SPOTTED
punctation .... DOT
punctilio .... NICETY
punctilious ... EXACT, STRICT, PRIM, SCRUPULOUS
person ..... PRIG, PRUDE
punctual ... PROMPT, ON TIME, MINUTE
punctuate ... MARK, INTERRUPT
punctuation mark .... (SEMI)COLON, DASH, COLA, PERIOD, COMMA, HYPHEN, BRACKETS, DOT
puncture .... PERFORATE, PRICK, PIERCE, HOLE
pundit ... SAVANT, AUTHORITY, SCHOLAR
pung .... SLED, SLEIGH
pungent ... RACY, SPICY, TART, ACRID, TANGY, GINGERY, PEPPERY, PIQUANT, SALTY, SHARP, BITING, KEEN
bulb ... ONION, GARLIC, SHALLOT, LEEK, SCALLION
Punic citizen .. CARTHAGINIAN
War battlesite ..... ZAMA
War belligerent ... ROME, CARTHAGE
War general ..... SCIPIO
punish .... DISCIPLINE, CHASTISE, WREAK, FRAP, CASTIGATE, CHASTEN, CORRECT, AVENGE, PENALIZE, FINE
by fine .... AMERCE
to correct .... CHASTISE, CHASTEN
punishment ... PENALTY, RAP,

BASTINADO, FINE, TALION
divine .... PLAGUE
eye for an eye ... TALION
endless ..... DAMNATION
instrument of ... STOCKS, PILLORY, RACK, GARROTE, FERULE
of ..... PENAL, PUNITIVE
voluntary ...... PENANCE
punitive .... PENAL
Punjab, capital (India) .... CHANDIGARH
capital (Pakistan) .... LAHORE
city ..... PATIALA, SIMLA, AMBALA, JULLUNDUR, SIALKOT
native .... JAT, SIKH
warrior .... SIKH
punk .... TOUCHWOOD, TINDER, HOODLUM, CATAMITE, AMADOU, ASTRINGENT
punka(h) .... FAN
punkie ..... FLY, MIDGE, GNAT
punster .... WIT, WAG
punt .... KICK, PROPEL, GAMBLE, KENT, QUANT
punty .... POINTIL
puny ... SLIGHT, WEAK, SMALL, FRAIL
pup .... DOG, SEAL
name of .... FIDO
pupa ..... CHRYSALIS, NYMPH
covering of ..... THECA, COCOON
pupil ...... GRADER, DISCIPLE, TRAINEE, TYRO, STUDENT
contraction of ... MYOSIS
dilatation of .. MYDRIASIS
dilator .... ATROPINE
French .... ECOLIER, ELEVE
organ with .... EYE
pupilage .... NONAGE
puppet .... MARIONETTE, PAWN, TOOL, DOLL, DUPE, PENSIONARY, MAUMET, MAMMET
maker .... SARG
show .... GALANTY
show character ... JUDY, PUNCH(INELLO)
show dog .... TOBY
puppeteer .... SARG
puppy ... WHELP, DOG, SHARK
purchasable .... VENAL
purchase .... ORDER
or sale of office .... BARRATRY
purdah .... SCREEN, CURTAIN
pure .... VIRGIN, CHASTE, SHEER, NEAT, ABSOLUTE, CLEAR, SIMPLE, MERE, UTTER, PERFECT
puree .... SOUP
purfle ... BORDER, TRIMMING, PURL
purgation .... CATHARSIS
purgative .... CATHARTIC, JALAP, PHYSIC, LAXATIVE, CALOMEL, APERIENT, CASTOR OIL, HELLEBORIN
rectal .... ENEMA
purgatory ..... LIMBO, EREBUS
purge ... FLUX, EXORCISE, SOIL, PHYSIC, CLEANSE, RID, PURIFY, ABSTERGE
purification ...... CATHARSIS
by holy water .. BAPTISM
purified, capable of being ..... FINABLE
purify ... CLEANSE, DISTIL(L), DEPURATE, SANCTIFY, PURGE, SUBLIMATE, REFINE
by distillation ... RECTIFY
by holy water .. BAPTIZE
Puritan .... BLUENOSE, ROUNDHEAD
of a sort ...... WOWSER
purity ... SANCTITY, CHASTITY, INNOCENCE
of color .... CHROMA
purl ...... SWIRL, LOOP, RIB, EDDY, MURMUR, PEARL, RIPPLE, PURFLE
purlieu ... HAUNT, ENVIRONS, HANGOUT
purloin .... STEAL, FILCH
purple ..... ROYAL, IMPERIAL, ORNATE, AMARANTHINE, REGAL, MAUVE, AMETHYST
brown .... PUCE
Heart .... MEDAL, DECORATION, ORDER
medic .... ALFALFA
red .. CARMINE, CRIMSON
shade ... LILAC, MODENA, AMARANTH, MAUVE
purplish red .... CLARET, MAGENTA, MURREY, MULBERRY
purport .... SENSE, OBJECT INTENTION, TENOR, PROFESS, CLAIM, MEANING
purpose .... AIM, SAKE, INTENT(ION), END, DESIGN. GOAL
purposeful .... TELIC
purse .... MONEY, PRIZE FINANCES, PUCKER, KNIT, BILLFOLD, SPORRAN, HANDBAG, POUCH, BURSE
purser .... BURSAR
purslane .... WEED
pursuant .... FOLLOWING
pursue ..... CHASE, FOLLOW, SEEK, CARRY ON, CONTINUE, DOG, HOUND, TRAIL
pursuit .. QUEST, OCCUPATION, CHASE
pursy ... FAT, OBESE, PUDGY
purulence .... PUS
purulent .... PYIC
purvey ... CATER, PROVISION, FURNISH
pus .... MATTER, SANIES
accumulation .. EMPYEMA
filled cavity ..... VOMICA
formation of ..... PYOSIS
form .... FESTER, SUPPURATE, MATURATE
of .... PYIC, PYOID
substance .... PYIN
push ... FORCE, IMPEL, PROPEL, CLIQUE, THRUST, SHOVE, PRESS, DRIVE, NUDGE, HUSTLE, JOSTLE, ELBOW
along .... PLOD
off ...... LEAVE, DEPART
on .... PROCEED
over: sl. .... SETUP
with nose .... NUZZLE
pushcart operator ... PEDDLER, VENDER
pusher .... PEDDLER
commodity of ..... DOPE, HEROIN, NARCOTIC, LSD, POT, MARIJUANA
pushing .... ARROGANT, CONCEITED, BUMPTIOUS
pusillanimous .... COWARDLY, IRRESOLUTE
puss .... CAT, GIRL, FACE, MOUTH, HARE
pussy .... CATKIN, CAT
pustule ..... WHELK, FESTER, WHEAL, PIMPLE, BLISTER, BLAIN
on neck ..... MALANDERS
scar .... POCK
put ...... IMPEL, DRIVE, PUSH, SET, LAY, PLACE, IMPOSE, APPLY, STATE, EXPRESS, WAGER
aside ..... DISCARD, DAFF
away ... KILL, CONSUME, STORE, STOW
down .... PLUMP, CRUSH, HUMBLE, RECORD, QUASH
effort .... EXERT
forward .... PRESENT, PROPOSE
film in camera .... LOAD
in .... INSERT, FOIST, INTROMIT
in-Bay hero ...... PERRY
in irons ...... SHACKLE, FETTER, MANACLE
off .... DOFF, POSTPONE, DELAY, EVADE, DIVERT, STALL, DEFER
off position .... LUXATE
on .. CLOTHE, DON, STAGE
on the block .... SELL, AUCTION
out ..... DISMISS, EXPEL, INCOMMODE, EVICT, PUBLISH, OUST, DOUSE, QUENCH
side by side .. JUXTAPOSE
to flight ..... ROUT(ED), FEEZE
to work .... HARNESS
up ... POST, ERECT, SHOW, BUILD, LODGE
up with .... BEAR, TOLERATE, ENDURE
putamen .... STONE, PIT
putative .. REPUTED, SUPPOSED
Putnam, Revolutionary general ISRAEL
putrefaction .... DECAY, ROT(TING)
putrefy ... DECAY, DECOMPOSE, ROT
putrescent .... DECAYING, ROTTING

putrid ... ROTTEN, STINKING, DECAYED, FOUL
putsch .... REBELLION, UPRISING
puttee ...... GAITER, PUTTY, LEGGING
putter ..... NIGGLE, DAWDLE, TINKER
puttier .... GLAZIER
putting area .... GREEN
putty .... CEMENT
puttyroot .... ORCHID
Putumayo river .... ICA
puzzle .... STUMP, DUM(B)FOUND, NONPLUS, CONFUSE, BEWILDER, BAFFLE, REBUS, PERPLEX, MYSTIFY, QUESTION, RIDDLE, ENIGMA, KITTLE, MYSTERY
  word .... LOGOGRAPH
puzzled .... STUCK
puzzler .... CRUX, POSER
puzzling ..... KNOTTING, ODD, ENIGMATIC
  thing .... CRUX
pygarg .... ADDAX
Pygmalion's statue .. GALATEA
pygmy ... DWARF, NEGRILLO, ATOMY, NEGRITO, RUNT, MININ
  antelope .... ORIBI
Pyle, newspaperman ... ERNIE
pylon .... GATEWAY, TOWER, MARKER, POST, PYRAMID
pyralidid .... MOTH
pyramid, builder of largest ... KHUFU, CHEOPS
  builders ..... EGYPTIANS
  dweller ... DJOSER, UNAS
  site of .... EL GIZA
  Step, builder ... IMHOTEP
  terraced ..... ZIGGURAT, ZIKURAT
  truncated .... PYLON
pyre .... PILE
pyrene .... NUTLET, SEED, STONE
Pyrenees goat .... IBEX
  highest point .. ANETHOU, ANETO
  mammal .... DESMAN
  republic ...... ANDORRA
pyretic .... FEVERISH
pyrexia .... FEVER
pyriform ...... PEAR-SHAPED
pyrite .... FOOL'S GOLD
pyrogenic .... IGNEOUS
pyromaniac .... FIREBUG, ARSONIST, INCENDIARY
pyrope .... GARNET
pyrosis ... HEARTBURN, BRASH
pyrotechnics ..... FIREWORKS
pyrrhic .... WAR DANCE
  like victory ... CADMEAN
  victory site .... ASCULUM
Pyrrhonism ..... SKEPTICISM
Pythagoras' birthplace .... SAMOS
  forte ..... MATHEMATICS
Pythias' friend ...... DAMON
python .... SERPENT, ANACONDA, BOA, SNAKE
  diety .... ZOMBI(E)
pythoness ...... SOOTHSAYER, PROPHETESS, PRIESTESS
pythonic .... ORACULAR, PROPHETIC
pyx .... BOX, CIBORIUM
pyxis .... CASE, BOX, VASE

Q

Q, Greek .... KAPPA
  in chess .... QUEEN
Qara Qum's capital .... DOHA
Qatar's capital .... DOHA
QED, part of .... QUOD, ERAT
quack .... CHARLATAN, MOUNTEBANK, DEMAGOGUE, CROCUS, EMPIRIC(IST), SCIOLIST, WISEACRE, IMPOSTOR, FAKER, CRY
  crier .... DUCK
  doctor's aide .... TOADY, TOADEATER
  medicine ...... NOSTRUM, HERB
quad .... QUOD, PRISON, JAIL
quadragesima .... LENT
quadragenarian .... FORTYISH
quadragesimal .... FORTY, LENTEN
quadrangle ..... COURTYARD, SQUARE, TETRAGON
quadrant ..... ARC, FOURTH, SEXTANT, ALTIMETER
  graduated edge of .. LIMB
quadrate ..... SQUARE, AGREE, QUARTER, RECTANGULAR, RECTANGLE, CONFORM
quadriga .... CHARIOT
quadrille ..... (SQUARE)DANCE, LANC(I)ERS
  card .... MATADOR
  second highest trump .... MANILLA
  sight .... VANE
quadrivium, part of ... MUSIC, GEOMETRY, ASTRONOMY
quadroon .... MULATTO, HYBRID
quadrumane ... BABOON, APE, MONKEY, PRIMATE
quadruped .... MAMMAL, FOUR-FOOTED, RHINO, HIPPO, CAMEL, ZEBRA, ASS, DONKEY, GIRAFFE, TAPIR
quadruple .... FOURFOLD
quaff ...... DRINK, SWALLOW, GULP
quagga-like animal ... ZEBRA, DONKEY
quaggy ... BOGGY, MIRY, SOFT
quagmire .... BOG, FEN
quahaug .... CLAM
quahog .... CLAM
  young ...... LITTLENECK
quail .... RECOIL, COWER, WINCE, COLIN, CRINGE, BOBWHITE, PARTRIDGE, BIRD, WILT
  flock .... COVEY, BEVY
quaint .. SINGULAR, FANCIFUL, STRANGE, CURIOUS, ANTIQUE, UNUSUAL
  humor ...... DROLLERY
quake ...... SHAKE, QUIVER, SHIVER, DIVER, SHUDDER, TEMBLOR, TREMBLE
Quaker .... FRIEND
  colonist .... PENN
  gray .... ACIER
  ladies ... BLUET, FLOWER
  midweek of a .... WEDNESDAY
quaking tree ... ASPEN, POPLAR
quaky .... SHAKY
qualification ..... CONDITION, ABILITY
qualified .... ABLE, FIT, COMPETENT, LIMITED
qualify ..... LIMIT, DESCRIBE, FIT, PASS, ENTITLE
qualifying word ..... ADVERB ADJECTIVE
quality ..... NATURE, CALIBER, ATTRIBUTE, KIND, AURA, FEATURE, TRAIT, GRADE, PROPERTY, CHARACTER
  bad/poor .... PUNK, INFERIOR, BUM
  colloquial .... CLASS
  distinguishing ..... TRAIT
  of high ..... TONY, PLUSH
  of sound ... TIMBRE, TONE
  special .... (DE)LUXE
qualm ...... NAUSEA, DOUBT, UNEASINESS, TWINGE, MISGIVING, SCRUPLE, COMPUNCTION
qualmish .... QUEASY, QUEER
quamash ..... CAMAS(S), LILY
quandary .... DILEMMA, PREDICAMENT, STRAIT
quant ... POLE, PROPEL, PUNT
quantity ... DOSE, MASS, GRIST, LOT, PORTION, AMOUNT
  indefinite ..... SOME, ANY
  large .... RAFT, RAFF, SLEW, BUSHEL
  small .... LICK, SCRUPLE, SCANTLING
Quantrill's men ..... RAIDERS
quantum ... AMOUNT, PORTION
  of heat energy .. PHOTON
quarantine .... ISOLATE
  building/ship .... LAZARETTO
  signal ..... YELLOW JACK
quarrel .... SPAT, ROW, SQUABBLE, PANE, CHISEL, DISPUTE, WRANGLE, FEUD, BICKER, BRUSH, MIFF, JAR, ALTERCATION, FLITE,

RUN-IN, RUCTION, BRABBLE, AFFRAY, STRIFE, BROIL, MISSILE
quarrelsome ...... LITIGIOUS, BELLIGERENT, PUGNACIOUS
quarry .... GAME, PREY, EXCAVATE, VICTIM
quarrying tool .... TREPAN, TRAPAN
quarryman .... STONECUTTER
quart(e) .... CARTE
quarter ..... FOURTH, SPAN, DISTRICT, MERCY, LODGE, BILLET, CANTON
note .... CROTCHET
of a circle .... QUADRANT
phase .... DIPHASE
round .... OVOLO
quartern .... GILL
quarters ..... BILLET, ABODE, LODGINGS, ROOMS
slang .... DIGGINGS
quarts, 4 .... GALLON
quartz ...... ONYX, SINOPLE, MORION, CRYSTAL, CACO, AVENTURINE, SILICA, SILEX, FLINT, PLASMA, CHALCEDONY, SARD(INE), CAIRNGORM, RUBASSE, AGATE, JASPER, TOPAZ, AMETHYST, CITRINE, PRASE, CHRYSOPRASE, CHERT, CARNELIAN
quartzite .... SANDSTONE
quash .... ANNUL, VOID, SET ASIDE, QUELL, SUPPRESS
in law .... ABATE
quasi .... AS IF, SEEMINGLY
quass .... KVASS
quaternion .... TETRAD
quatrain ...... STANZA, POEM
quaver ...... TREMOLO, SHAKE, TREMBLE, TRILL
quavery .... TREMULOUS
quay ... LEVEE, PIER, WHARF, LANDING
queachy .... SWAMPY, BOGGY
quean ..... JADE, SLUT, MINX, HUSSY
queasy .... QUALMISH, FASTIDIOUS
Quebec acre .... ARPENT
city .... HULL, MONTREAL, VERDUN
part of .... UNGAVA
river .... SAGUENAY
Quechuan ... INDIAN, INCA(N), PERUVIAN
Queen .... REGINA, REINA
ace combination .... TENACE
Anne's lace .... CARROT
beheaded ... ANTOINETTE
Charlotte Island Indian .. HAIDA
English .. VICTORIA, BESS, ANNE
fairy ..... TITANIA, MAB, UNA
Greek gods' .... HERA
it .... DOMINEER
legendary .... DIDO
Mab" author ... SHELLEY
Moslem .... BEGUM
of Calydon ..... ALTHEA
of gods ..... JUNO, HERA, SATI
of Ithaca ..... PENELOPE
of Iceland .... BRUN(N)HILD(E)
of Lydia ...... OMPHALE
of Palmyra ..... ZENOBIA
of the Antilles ..... CUBA
of the jungle .... SHEENA
of the Nile .. CLEO(PATRA)
of the nymphs ..... MAB
of Thebes .... JOCASTA
Olympian .... HERA
Roman gods' ..... JUNO
Sheba .... BALKIS
widowed ..... DOWAGER
queening .... APPLE
queen(ly) ... REGINA(L), REGAL
Queens .... BOROUGH
Queensland's capital .... BRISBANE
Queenstown .... COBH
queer ... FUNNY, ODD, GIDDY, BIZARRE, SINGULAR, STRANGE, ECCENTRIC, RUM, WEIRD, ERRATIC, CRANKY
bird .... NUT, CRANK
notion .... KINK
person .... NUT
slang ..... COUNTERFEIT, HOMOSEXUAL, SPOIL
quell .. ALLAY, QUIET, SUBDUE, CRUSH, QUASH, END, SUPPRESS
quelque chose .... TRIFLE
quench .... COOL, SLAKE, SATISFY, EXTINGUISH, DOUSE, PUT OUT
quercetin ..... DYE, FLAVIN(E)
quercitron .... OAK, DYE
quercus genus .... OAKS
querist .... ASKER
quern .... MILL, GRINDER
querulous .... PEEVISH, FRETFUL, PETULANT
query ... INQUIRY, QUESTION, ASK
quest .... SEARCH, HUNT, SEEK(ING), PURSUIT
question ... DOUBT, PROBLEM, INTERROGATE, DISPUTE, POINT, POSE, ISSUE, QUERY, QUIZ, INQUIRY, ASK, GRILL
and answer teaching ..... CATECHESIS
baffling .... POSER, DILEMMA
questionable .... MOOT, DEBATABLE, SHADY, DUBIOUS, DOUBTFUL, SUSPICIOUS, SUSPECT, FISHY
questioning .... ROGATORY
quetzal .... TROGON, BIRD
queue ...... LINE, (PIG)TAIL, FILE, CUE, BRAID, PLAIT, TRESS
torero's .... COLETA
Quezon, Philippine president .. MANUEL
qui vive ... ALERT, CHALLENGE
quibble .... CAVIL, PUN, EVASION, QUIP, EVADE, CARP
quick ... READY, FAST, AGILE, FLEET, ALIVE, SNAPPY, YARE, VOLANT, APT, SWIFT, RAPID, PROMPT, PREGNANT
assets .... CASH
bread .... MUFFIN
in learning .... APT
look ... EYEBEAM, GLANCE
response to helm .. YARE
tempered ...... IRACUND, IRASCIBLE
witticism .... SALLY
quicken ..... ANIMATE, SPEED, REVIVE, STIR, HASTEN, ROUSE
quickie, movie .... B-PICTURE
quickly .... SOON, PRESTO, PRONTO, FAST, ANON, PDQ
in music .... SUBITO
quicksand .... MORASS, SYRT(IS)
quickset ... HEDGE, CUTTING, SLIP
quicksilver .... MERCURY, AZOTH
quid ...... PLUG, SOVEREIGN, POUND, CUD
pro quo ..... SUBSTITUTE
quidnunc .. GOSSIP, BUSYBODY, SNOOP
quien ____, who knows? .. SABE
quiescent ...... STILL, QUIET, LATENT, DORMANT
quiet .. STILL, CALM, HUSH(ED), SILENT, PACIFY, MUM, ALLAY, MIM, SILENCE, STILLNESS
interval .... LULL
quietism, teacher of .. MOLINOS
quietude .... CALMNESS, STILLNESS, REST
quietus ... DEATH, DISCHARGE, RELEASE
quill ...... REMEX, FEATHER, CALAMUS, SPINE, PEN, PLECTRUM, BARREL
feathers .... REMIGES, CALAMI
quillai .... SOAPBARK
quilt .... PATCHWORK, BEDCOVER, STITCH, CADDOW, DUVET
quilting party .... BEE
quince .... POME, BEL
quinia .... QUININ(E)
quinine .... KINA
source ...... CINCHONA
water .... TONIC
quinnat salmon .... CHINOOK
quint .... ORGAN STOP
quintessence .... CREAM, ELIXIR
quintuple .... FIVEFOLD
quintuplets ... DIONNE, FISHER
quip .... JEST, QUIBBLE, JOKE, WITTICISM, SALLY, MOT, (WISE)CRACK, GIBE

quire .... CHOIR
quirk ... PECULIARITY, TWIST, TURN, STROKE, ODDITY, KINK
quirt .... WHIP, ROMAL
quisling ..... COLLABORATOR, TRAITOR
fifth columnist .. VIDKUN
quit .... RESIGN, LEAVE, RETIRE, FREE, STOP, REPAY, DISCHARGE, GIVE UP
quitch .... GRASS, WEED
quitclaim .... RELEASE
quite ...... ENTIRELY, TRULY, REALLY, WHOLELY, VERY, ALL, ENOUGH
Quito is capital of .. ECUADOR
quits .... EVEN
quittance .. RECEIPT, REPRISAL
quiver ..... SHAKE, SHUDDER, TREMOR, NIMBLE, QUAKE, FLUTTER, THRILL, TREMBLE, VIBRATE
content of ..... ARROWS
quivering tree .... ASPEN, PALPITANT
Quixote's giant .... WINDMILL
horse .... ROSINANTE
love .... DULCINEA
squire .. SANCHO (PANZA)
title .... DON
quixotic .... CHIVALROUS, ROMANTIC, VISIONARY, ABSURD
quiz .... HOAX, JOKE, EXAM(INATION), ASK, TEST, PROBE
kid .... PRODIGY
quizzical ...... ODD, COMICAL
quod .... JAIL, PRISON
quoin ... CORNER, KEYSTONE, LOCK, BLOCK
quoit .... DISCUS, RINGER
quoits pin .... HOB, PEG
target .... HOB, PEG, TEE
quondam .... ONCE, ONETIME, FORMER, ERSTWHILE, WHILOM
quonset hut .... PREFAB
British kind ..... NISSEN
quorum .... COMPANY
quota .... SHARE, ALLOTMENT
quotation ... CITATION, CITAL, EXCERPT, PRICE, EXTRACT
ending speech/story ..... TAG
opening chapter .... EPIGRAPH
reader .... STOCKHOLDER, SPECULATOR
quote ... CITE, REFER, REPEAT, ADDUCE
quoth .... SPOKE, SAID
quotidian .... DAILY

R

R, Greek .... RHO
Hebrew .... RESH
in chemistry ... RADICAL
in chess .... ROOK
in mathematics ... RATIO, RADIUS
pronunciation like l ..... LALLATION
Ra .... SUN GOD
crown of .... ATEN
in chemistry ... RADIUM
symbol of ...... SUNDISK
wife of .... MUT
raad .... CATFISH
Rabat is capital of .. MOROCCO
rabato .... RUFF, COLLAR
Rabbat Ammon ..... AMMAN
rabbet .... JOINT, REBATE
rabbi .... TEACHER, AMORA
seminary ...... YESHIVA
teachings .... MISHNA(H)
rabbit ... CONY, LAGOMORPH, HARE, ANGORA, RODENT, LEPORID, COTTONTAIL
breeding place .. WARREN
ears .... ANTENNA
family .... LEPORID
female .... DOE
fever .... TULAR(A)EMIA
foot ... CHARM, TALISMAN
fur ..... CON(E)Y, LAPIN
fur hat .... CASTOR
hunting dog ... HARRIER
hybrid .... LEPORIDE
like rodent ..... MARMOT
male .... BUCK
pen .... HUTCH
pet name .... BUNNY
rock .... HYRAX
tail of .... SCUT
variety .... LOP
young .... BUNNY
rabbitry .... WARREN, HUTCH
rabble .... CROWD, DOGGERY, CANAILLE, MOB, (RIFF)RAFF, RAGTAG
rouser .... AGITATOR, RIOTER, DEMAGOGUE
the .... MASSES
Rabelais, Fr. satirist .... FRANCOIS
Rabelaisian .... EARTHY
rabid ..... VIOLENT, RAGING, FANATICAL, ZEALOUS
rabies .... MADNESS, HYDROPHOBIA, LYSSA
RCA trademark ..... NIPPER
raccoon-like animal .. PANDA, COATI
race ...... LINEAGE, FAMILY, PEDIGREE, STIRPS, FOLK, CONTEST, CHANNEL, MANKIND
black .... NEGROID
channel .... FLUME
contestant .... ENTRANT, ENTRY
division .... NEGROID, CAUCASIAN, MONGOLOID
easily won .... RUNAWAY
engine .... REV
hotrods' .... DRAG
kind of .... SWEEPSTAKE, SWEEPS, RAT, TROT
of dwarfs .... NIBELUNG
pertaining to .... ETHNIC
prelims .... HEATS
short ...... DASH, SPRINT
start of ..... BREAKAWAY
track ..... HIPPODROME, TURF, CINDER PATH, OVAL
water .... ARROYO
white .... CAUCASIAN
yellow ...... MONGOLOID
racecourse .... CIRCUS, HIPPODROME, TRACK, OVAL, TURF
circuit .... LAP
combining form .. DROME
marker ... PYLON, LANE
name/site of ..... EPSOM, HIALEAH, PIMLICO, SARATOGA, ASCOT, JAMAICA
official .... STARTER
section ... STRETCH, BEND
racehorse .... TROTTER
disability .... GLANDERS, SPAVIN, STRINGHALT
enclosure ..... PADDOCK
exercise area ... PADDOCK
inferior .... PLATER, SLEEPER
kind of .. MUDDER, PLATER
winless .... MAIDEN
raceme ... CLUSTER, PANICLE
racer .... HOTROD, (BLACK)SNAKE, SPRINTER, TRACKMAN
course of .... LANE
racetrack .... OVAL, HIPPODROME, TURF
character ..... DOPESTER, TOUT, TIPSTER
cover .... TANBARK
fence .... RAIL
raceway .... CHANNEL
Rachel's father .... LABAN
husband .... JACOB
son ... JOSEPH, BENJAMIN
rachis ..... SPINE, BACKBONE, STEM
rachitis .... RICKETS
Rachmaninoff, composer/ pianist .... SERGEI
racial division, of .... ETHNIC
origin .... ETHNOGENY
Racine (Jean), Fr. poet ..... BAPTISTE
masterpiece .... PHEDRE
racing colors .... SILKS
course .... CAREER, HIPPODROME
program ... CARD, FORM
scull .... WHERRY
racists, latest .... NAZIS
rack ... GIN, GRATING, FRAME, TORMENT, UPHEAVAL, TORTURE, WRECKAGE,

CLOUDS, STAND, SCORE
corn .... CRIB
display .... EASEL
fodder ..... CRIB, HACK, CRATCH
food .... FLAKE
hat .... TREE
horse's ..... PACE, GAIT
racket ... BAT, NOISE, PADDLE, SNOWSHOE, BABEL, DIN, UPROAR, REVEL(RY)
hold on .... GRIP
slang .... BUSINESS, PROFESSION, LINE
string .... CATGUT
rackets .... TENNIS
raconteur's forte .. ANECDOTES, STORIES
racy .... PIQUANT, FRESH, PUNGENT, RISQUE, LIVELY, SPIRITED
Radames' love .... AIDA
radar device, for short ... TFR
image .... BLIP
like device .... SONAR
screen flash .... BLIP
part of word ..... RADIO, DETECTING, RANGING
sound ..... BEEP, RACON
system .... SHORAN
raddle ... INTERWEAVE, OCHER
Radek, Soviet writer .... KARL
radian .... ARC
radiance .... GLORY, REFULGENCE, BRIGHTNESS, LIGHT
radiant ... BRIGHT, BEAMING, AGLOW
combining form .. HELI(O)
look .... BEAM
radiate .... SHINE, EMIT, CAST
radiation measure .. ROENTGEN
radical ... BASIC, FIREBRAND, JINGO, RED, PINK, EXTREME, ULTRA, LEFTIST, JACOBIN
with valence of two ..... DYAD
radicel .... ROOT(LET)
radicle .... ROOT, RADIX
radio .... WIRELESS
active shower .. FALLOUT
ad .... COMMERCIAL
aerial .... ANTENNA
broadcasting outfit .. VOA
cabinet .... CONSOLE
dash in .... DAH
detector .... RADAR
frequency band .... CHANNEL
gear ... ANTENNA, AERIAL
interference ..... STATIC
news, brief ...... FLASH
newscaster ... MURROW, HEATTER, SWING
operator, amateur .. HAM
performer ..... TALENT
receiver ... CRYSTAL, SET, TRANSISTOR
reception disturbance ... STATIC, STRAYS
signal for aviators .. BEAM
signoff .... ROGER
station ID .. CALL LETTERS
term .... ROGER
tube .... GRID
radioactive matter .. NOBELIUM, CARNOTITE, RADON, NITON
particles .... GEIGERS
radioactivity, measure of ..... CURIE
radiotelephony term ... ROGER
radium F .... POLONIUM
discoverer .... CURIE
disease treated with ..... CANCER
emanation ...... NITON, RADON
source of .. PITCHBLENDE, URANITE
radius ...... SPOKE, EXTENT, RAY, SCOPE, RANGE
radix .... BASE, ROOT, RADICAL, ETYMON
radon .... NITON
RAF, part of .... ROYAL, AIR, FORCE
raff .... RABBLE, TRASH
companion .... RIFF
raffish ...... VULGAR, CHEAP, TAWDRY, LOW, DISREPUTABLE, FLASHY
raffle .... LOTTERY
ticket .... BLANK
raft ....BALSA, LOT, CATAMARAN, COLLECTION
component of ..... LOGS, BARRELS, BOARDS
log .... CATAMARAN
rafter .... SPAR, BEAM
rag ... TATTER, TEASE, SCOLD, SLATE, SHRED, REMNANT, BRAT, JOSH, RIB
baby .... DOLL
chew the ..... CONVERSE, CHAT
ragamuffin .. TATTERDEMALION
rage .... FAD, FASHION, SPREAD, VOGUE, CRAZE, WRATH, FRENZY, RAVE, FUROR, FURY, FUME, ANGER
ragged ..... UNEVEN, ROUGH, RAMPAGE, FRAYED, TATTERED, JAGGED, SHAGGY, UNKEMPT, SHABBY
raggee .... GRASS, RAGI
ragger .... TEASER
Raggedy doll ... ANNE, ANDY
raging .... RAMPANT, RAMPAGING
raglan ... TOPCOAT, OVERCOAT
ragman .... JUNKMAN
ragout .... HARICOT, HASH, TUCKET, STEW, GOULASH, SALMI
ragpicker .... JUNKMAN
rags .... CLOTHES
ragtag .... RABBLE
ragtime .... JAZZ
ragwort .... JACOBY, GROUNDSEL
ragweed .... COCKLEBUR, AMBROSIA
rah .... CHEER, HURRAH
raia .... NON-MOSLEM, RAYAH
raid ..... INVADE, INCURSION, FORAY, ASSAULT, FORAGE, SORTIE, ATTACK, INVASION, MARAUD
slang .... PINCH
raider ... COMMANDO, UBOAT, RANGER
rail ..... COOT, CRAKE, SORA, FENCE, BIRD, COMPLAIN, WEKA, BAR, HERON, ORTOLAN, SCOFF, RANT, MUDHEN
bird like .... COURLAN
collar of .... FLANGE
kin of .... NOTORNIS
railing .. FENCE, BALUSTRADE, PARAPET
bridge .... PARAPET
raillery ..... SATIRE, BANTER, PERSIFLAGE, RIDICULE, BADINAGE
railroad .... RUSH
baggage car .... VAN
bridge .... TRESTLE
car ..... COACH, DINER, CABOOSE, SLEEPER, SMOKER, PULLMAN
car compartment .... DUPLEX
center .... YARD
crossing .... GATE
elevated .... EL, MONORAIL
engine ..... LOCOMOTIVE
engine serviceman ...... HOSTLER
flare ...... FUSEE, FUZEE
freight car ..... GONDOLA
handcar .... VELOCIPEDE
industrial ..... TAPLINE
line end ...... TERMINUS
side track .... SPUR
siding .... TURN-OUT
signal .... HIGHBALL, SEMAPHORE
single track ... MONORAIL
sleeping car .. WAGON-LIT
station .... DEPOT
stop for locomotives .... TANK TOWN
supply car ...... TENDER
switch device ... SHUNT, FROG
tie .... SLEEPER
track section .. GANTLET
trunkline .... MAIN
underground ... SUBWAY, METRO
workers' vehicle .... HANDCAR
raiment ... ATTIRE, CLOTHING, APPAREL, DRESS
rails, of the .... RALLINE
support .... ROADBED
railway, amusement .. COASTER
car .... TRAM
railways .... ROADS
rain ... SEREIN, SHOWER, FALL, (OUT)POUR, FLURRY, DOWNPOUR
briefly .... SPIT
character .... SADIE

forest .... SELVA
fine mist .... MIZZLE, SEREIN
formed by ..... PLUVIAL
frozen ..... SLEET, HAIL
gauge .... UDOMETER
heavy .... TORRENT
mist .... SCUD
shower .... BRASH
sudden ... SPATE, BRASH
sunset .... SEREIN
tree ...... ZAMIA, SAMAN
rainbow .... IRIS, ARC(H), METEOR
bridge .... BIFROST
color like ..... PAVONINE
trout .... STEELHEAD
raincheck .... STUB
raincoat ...... MACKINTOSH, SLICKER, PONCHO, TRENCH COAT
raindrops, frozen ...... HAIL
Rainer, actress .... LUISE
Maria ____, Ger. poet .... RILKE
rainfall .... SHOWER
heavy .... DELUGE
place of heaviest .. ASSAM
Rainier (Mount) site .... TACOMA
rainmaker: sl. ..... LOBBYIST
rainproof canvas ... TARPAULIN
rainy .... WET, PLUVIOUS, PLUVIAL, SOPPY
raise .... BREED, HIKE, HOIST, EXALT, REAR, (UP)LIFT, AROUSE, STIR, NURTURE, COLLECT, EAN, BOOST, ELEVATE, ERECT, INCITE, PULL UP
in relief .... EMBOSS
nap .... TEASE(L)
rents exorbitantly .. RACK
to third power ..... CUBE
raised .... EMBOSSED
road .... CAUSEWAY
raisin ...... SULTANA, GRAPE
in pudding .... PLUM
raisins drink .... CORDIAL, ROSOLIO
raison ____ .... D'ETAT, D'ETRE
raj .... RULE
rajah's wife ..... RANEE, RANI
Rajasthan's capital ... JAIPUR
rake .... SCRAPE, SCOUR, DEBAUCHEE, SLANT, RANSACK, COMB, LOTHARIO, LECHER, ROUE, LIBERTINE
off .... REBATE, COMMISSION, KICKBACK
with gunfire ... ENFILADE, STRAFE
rakish ... DISSOLUTE, DASHING, JAUNTY
rale ..... RHONCHUS, RATTLE
ralline bird .... RAIL
rally ... COLLECT, GATHERING, ASSEMBLY, REVIVE, RESURGE, MEET, BANTER
ram ..... PRESS, DRIVE, STUFF, CRAM, POUND, TUP, SHEEP, PUMP, BATTER, TAMP
constellation ..... ARIES
headed god ...... AMMON
horn ... SHOPHAR, SHOFAR
kind of ... (BELL)WETHER
ship's .... BEAK
Rama .... KRISHNA
Ramadan .... FASTING
ramage .... BOUGH
Ramayam character .... SITA, HANUMAN
Ramazan .... FASTING
ramble ..... MEANDER, ROVE, SPREAD, GAD, SAUNTER, STROLL, ROAM
rambler ...... ROSE, TRUANT, TRAMP, NOMAD, ROVER
Rambouillet .. (MERINO) SHEEP
rambunctious .... WILD, UNRULY, DISORDERLY
ramekin/ramequin ..... HASH
Rameses .... PHARAOH
ramie .... FIBER, HEMP
ramification .... BRANCH, OFFSHOOT, RESULT
ramify ...... DIVIDE, SPREAD
ramjet ..... ATHODYD, ENGINE
rammer ...... BEAK, RAMROD
ramose .... BRANCHED
ramp ...... REAR, HELICLINE, RAGE, STORM, RUSH, PASSAGE, ROADWAY, STAND
rampage .... RAGE, RUSH, OUTBREAK
rampaging person ..... AMOK, BERSERK, JURAMENTADO
rampant ... RIFE, WIDESPREAD
rampart ... RAVELIN, PARAPET, BULWARK, VALLATION, EMBANKMENT, REDAN
rampion .... CAMPANULA, BELLFLOWER
Ramses .. PHAROAH, MONARCH
domain .... EGYPT
ramshackle .... RICKETY, SHAKY, RUN-DOWN
ramson .... GARLIC, ROOT
ramus .... BRANCH
ran, also ... COMPETED, LOST
rana .... FROG
rance .... MARBLE
ranch ..... FARM, ESTANCIA, HACIENDA, GRAZE, PLANTATION
event .. RODEO, ROUNDUP
hand .... COWBOY, COWPOKE
tyro .... DUDE
rancher .. COWBOY, STOCKMAN
rancho .... HUT
rancid ..... RANK, STINKING, SPOILED, SMELLY
rancor ...... ILL-WILL, GALL, SPITE, MALICE, HATRED, ENMITY
rand .... MARGIN, EDGE, BORDER
random .... HAPHAZARD, AIMLESS, CASUAL, CHANCE, DESULTORY, HIT-OR-MISS
randy .... CRUDE, COARSE, LUSTFUL, BEGGAR, VULGAR
range .... ROW, RANK, GRASSLAND, SCOPE, STOVE, SIERRA, TRAIN, ROAM, REACH, GAMUT, LATITUDE, SWEEP
finder ...... TELEMETER, STADIA
of emotion ..... GAMUT
of hills .... RIDGE
of vision .... SCAN, EYESHOT, EYESIGHT, SCOPE
over .... SCOUR
Rocky Mountains ...... UINTA, TETON
sighting for .... ZERO
ranger ... WARDEN, FORESTER, SOLDIER
concern of a .... FOREST
Rangoon is capital of .. BURMA
weight .... CATTY
rangy .... LANKY
rani/ranee .... QUEEN
husband of ..... RAJA(H)
Ranier's domain, Prince ...... MONACO
ranine .... FROGLIKE
rank ... EMINENCE, POSITION, FERTILE, RANCID, INDECENT, UTTER, FLAGRANT, GRADE, TIER, RANGE, ROW, LINE, COARSE, ARRANT, STANDING, REEKY
and file ...... SOLDIERS, FOLLOWERS
having .... GENETIC
of lower .... PUISNE
rankle .... FESTER
ranks .... ARMY
ransack ...... RIFLE, SEARCH, PILLAGE, RUMMAGE
ransom ...... RESCUE, REDEEM, BLOODMONEY
person held for .. HOSTAGE
rant ...... HARANGUE, BOAST, RAVE, DECLAIM, RAIL, TIRADE, BLUSTER, RAGE
ranunculaceous plant .. PEONY, ANEMONE, LARKSPUR
ranunculus ...... CROWFOOT, BUTTERCUP
rap .... TAP, PUNISHMENT, CUFF, KNAP, (TH)WACK, BOP, CLOUT, PERCUSS, KNOCK, BLAME, SENTENCE, BLOW
rapacious .... GREEDY, RAVENOUS, AVARICIOUS, VORACIOUS
bird .... SHRIKE
fish .... PIRANHA
rapacity ... VORACITY, GREED
rape ...... VIOLATE, RAVISH, PLUNDER, ASSAULT, PULP, CABBAGE, COLE, FODDER
soil .... COLZA
rapeseed .... COLZA
mass of crushed .... OIL CAKE
rapid .... SWIFT, ABRUPT, QUICK, FLEET, FAST, RIPPLE
combining form .. TACHY
fire .... STACCATO, FUSILLADE

rapidity ..... VELOCITY, SPEED
rapidly .... APACE
rapids .... DALLES, DELLS, CHUTE
rapier .. SWORD, BILBO, TUCK
rapine ... PILLAGE, PLUNDER, RAVIN
rapparee .... VAGABOND, ROBBER, PLUNDERER
rappee .... SNUFF
rapper ...... DOOR KNOCKER
rapping .... TATTOO
rapport .... HARMONY, AGREEMENT, RELATIONSHIP
rapscallion ... ROGUE, RASCAL
rapt ...... ABSORBED, INTENT, ENGROSSED
raptorial bird ... EAGLE, OWL, HAWK, VULTURE, FALCON
rapture ...... ECSTASY, BLISS, TRANSPORT
rapturous .... ECSTATIC
Raquel Welch's pet name ..... BIRDLEGS
soubriquet ... SEX QUEEN
rara avis .. RARITY, ONER, BIRD
rare ... UNDERDONE, TENUOUS, UNCOMMON, UNUSUAL, SCARCE, THIN, ODD
rarebit .... RABBIT
raree .... (PEEP)SHOW
rarefy .... THIN, REFINE
rarely .... SELDOM
rareripe fruit .... PEACH
rarity ... TENUITY, SCARCITY, THINNESS
rascal ... SCAMP, SCOUNDREL, BEGGAR, SCALAWAG, YAP, CAD, VARLET, SCAPEGRACE, SPALPEEN, ROGUE
rascally .... BASE, MEAN, DISHONEST
rase .... LEVEL, DESTROY
rash ... RECKLESS, ERUPTION, FOOLHARDY, WILD, WANTON, HASTY, ROSEOLA, EXANTHEMA, MEASLES
person .... HOTSPUR, PLUNGER
rasher .... HAM, BACON
rashness .... TEMERITY
Rasmussen, Arctic explorer ... KNUD
rasorial .... GALLINACEOUS
bird ...... HEN, CHICKEN
rasp ... GRATE, FILE, SCRAPE, RUB, IRRITATE, ABRADE
raspberry .... ACINUS, SHRUB, SASS, FRUIT
Raspe's character .... MUNCHAUSEN
Rasputin, Russian monk ...... GRIGORI
raspy ..... IRRITABLE, ROUGH, GRATING
rasse .... CIVET
rassle .... WRESTLE
rat ... GNAWER, VERMIN, VOLE, APOSTATE, RODENT
domesticated .... GUINEA PIG
genus .... MUS
hair .... PAD
kind of .... MOLE
poison .... RATSBANE
race .... SCURRY, SCRAMBLE
rodent resembling ...... MOUSE, HAMSTER
slang .... DESERTER, INFORMER, STOOL(PIGEON)
ratable .... TAXABLE
ratal .... ASSESSMENT
ratafia ..... COOKY, LIQUEUR, MACAROON
rataplan .... DRUMBEAT
ratchet .... PAWL, CLICK, CATCH, WHEEL, DETENT
rate ..... RATIO, PROPORTION, PRICE, CLASS, APPRAISE, ESTEEM, DESERVE, SCOLD, CHIDE
at any .... ANYWAY
exchange .... AGIO
of mass to volume ...... DENSITY
rated .... VALUED, TAXED, RANKED
ratel-like animal ..... BADGER
Rathbone, actor .... BASIL
rathe .... QUICK, EAGER, EARLY, PROMPT
rather .... SOMEWHAT, CERTAINLY, SOONER, PREFERABLY
than .... ERE
Ratibor river .... ODER
ratification .... SANCTION, APPROVAL
ratify .. SEAL, PASS, SANCTION, CONFIRM, APPROVE, ENDORSE
rating .... RANK, CLASS, GRADE, SCORE, MARK, REPRIMAND
ratio .... PROPORTION, QUOTIENT
ratiocinate .... REASON
ration ... ALLOWANCE, SHARE, ALLOTMENT, DISTRIBUTE, METE
rational ...... SANE, SENSIBLE, REASONABLE, SOUND, LUCID
rationale ...... REASON, BASIS
rationalize .... EXPLAIN
rations .... FOOD
bag .... HAVERSACK
ratite .... MOA, EM(E)U, OSTRICH, CASSOWARY, RHEA
ratoon .... SHOOT, SPROUT
rats, of .... MURINE
rattail .... GRENADIER
rattan ... PALM, CANE, REED, SEGA
ratter ... DESERTER, BETRAYER, DOG
rattle .... CHATTER, DISCONCERT, UPSET, CLACK, CLAPPER, NOISE, SISTRUM, UPROAR, MARACA, CREPITATE, RALE
rattlebrain .... IDIOT, ASS, FOOL
rattlebrained .... SILLY, FRIVOLOUS
rattlepate .... ASS, FOOL
rattlesnake .... VIPER, CASCABEL, SIDEWINDER, MASSASAUGA
plantain .... ORCHID
without rattle .... COPPERHEAD
rattletrap ... MOUTH, JALOPY
rattling .... CREPITANT
rattrap .. JAM, PREDICAMENT, FIX
ratwa .... MUNTJAC
raucous ..... HARSH, HOARSE
ravage .... DEVASTATE, SACK, PLUNDER, HAVOC, DESPOIL, PILLAGE, RUIN
rave ...... RAGE, RANT, ROAR
ravel ..... INVOLVE, UNTWIST, UNDO, SLEAVE, FRAY, (EN)TANGLE
stocking's .... RUN
ravelin .... OUTWORK, FORTIFICATION, REDAN
raveling .... LINT
raven .... DEVOUR, PREY, PLUNDER, CROW, BLACK(BIRD), CORBY, CORBIE
Barnaby Rudge's .. GRIP
cry of .... CAW
like a .... CORVINE
of a .... CORVINE
quote of ..... NEVERMORE
ravenous .... VORACIOUS, HUNGRY, RAPACIOUS, LUPINE
ravin ...... RAPINE, PLUNDER, PREY
ravine ...... CLOUGH, CHINE, WADI, WADY, GULCH, CANYON, BARRANCA, GILL, NULLAH, COOMB, COMB(E), GORGE, GULLY, DELL, LINN, FLUME, COULEE
raving .... DELIRIOUS, NOTABLE, FRENZIED
ravish ..... RAPE, ENRAPTURE, DELIGHT
ravishment .... ECSTASY, RAPTURE
raw .... SORE, UNCOOKED, BLEAK, BAWDY
cotton .... LINT
in the ..... NUDE, NAKED
material .... STAPLE, STOCK, STUFF
slang .... UNFAIR
rawboned ..... GAUNT, LEAN
Rawalpindi is capital of ...... PAKISTAN
rawhide ... WHIP, PARFLECHE
kind of .... SHAGREEN
whip ... THONG, KNOUT, QUIRT
ray ... BEAM, SKATE, TRACE, THORNBACK, BETA, GAMMA, ALPHA, GLEAM, STINGAREE, PETAL, MANTA, LASER, SAWFISH
actor .... ALDO
eagle .... OBISPO
flower .... FLORET
kind of ... BETA, GAMMA, LASER

like part .... RADIUS
rayah .... RAIA, NON-MOSLEM
Rayburn, Speaker ...... SAM
rayless ...... DARK, GLOOMY
"Raymonda" ballet composer .. PETIPA
rayon ...... ACETATE, RATINE, FIBER, VISCOSE, JERSEY
cellulose acetate .... CELANESE
corded/ribbed .. REP(S), REPP, OTTOMAN
making material .... CELLULOSE
sheer .... VOILE
twilled .... SERGE
raze ... SCRAPE, SHAVE, LEVEL, DEMOLISH, ERASE, DESTROY
razee .... SHIP
razor .... SHAVE(R)
billed bird .... ALCA
clam .... SOLEN
seller .... CUTLER
sharpen .... HONE, STROP
razorback .... HOG, FINBACK, (RORQUAL)WHALE
razz ..... HECKLE, RIDICULE, TEASE, DERIDE, SASS
razzle-dazzle ..... CONFUSION
Rb, in chemistry ... RUBIDIUM
re ..... ANENT, CONCERNING, REGARDING, ABOUT
echoing .... REBOANT
in chemistry .. RHENIUM
rea .... TURMERIC
reach ..... EXTEND, STRETCH, RANGE, SPAN, ATTAIN, ACHIEVE, GAIN, HEIGHT, GRASP
react ..... RESPOND, REDOUND
reacting easily/readily .... RESPONSIVE
reaction .. RESPONSE, TROPISM, REFLEX
reactionary .... TORY, CONSERVATIVE, RIGHT(IST)
read ..... PERUSE, INTERPRET, CONSTRUE, FORETELL, UNDERSTAND, DECIPHER, PORE, CON, STUDY, REGISTER
inability to ...... ALEXIA
metrically .... SCAN
numbers ..... NUMERATE
out of ... EXPEL, DISMISS
readable .... LEGIBLE
reader ..... PRIMER, RECITER, LECTURER, BOOK, PERUSER
meter .... RECORDER
scripture .... LECTOR
readily .... EASILY, WILLINGLY, QUICKLY
readiness .... ALACRITY
reading ... LECTION, PERUSAL, RECORD(ING)
desk/stand ... LECTERN, PRIE-DIEU, AMBO
of Scriptures ... LECTION
reads alike forward or backward ..... PALINDROME
ready .... PREPARE(D), WILLING, LIKELY, APT, INCLINED, AVAILABLE, FAIN, SET, YARE, HANDY, QUICK, OPEN, WARE, PROMPT
artillery ..... UNLIMBER
made .... STOCK
money .... CASH
real .... PUCKA, PUKKA, ACTUAL, GENUINE, SIMON PURE, FACTUAL, COIN, CONCRETE
estate ..... REALTY, LAND
estate broker ... REALTOR
plural of .... REIS
thing .... MCCOY
realgar .... SANDARAC, MINERAL
realism, opposite of .. IDEALISM
realistic .... PRACTICAL
opposite of ... VISIONARY
reality .. VERITY, TRUTH, FACT
realize ... GAIN, UNDERSTAND, ACHIEVE, APPREHEND, OBTAIN
really ...... TRULY, INDEED, ACTUALLY, QUITE
realm ..... KINGDOM, SPHERE, DOMAIN, REGION, DEMESNE, CLIME
ream .... ENLARGE
reamer ..... BORER, BROACH, ENLARGER
reams .... LOTS
reanimate .... REVIVE
reap .... HARVEST, GAIN, GATHER, MOW
reaper .... MOWER
Grim .... DEATH
reaping tool .... SICKLE, SCYTHE, TWIBIL(L)
rear ..... RAISE, RAMP, ERECT, BUILD, GROW, RISE, SUCKLE, BACK(PART), (BE)HIND, BREED, NURSE, ARRIERE, AFT
horse's .... PESADE
young bird ...... FLEDGE
reared by hand .... CADE
rearmost .... LAST
rearrange .... PERMUTE
reason .... SANITY, ARGUE, DISCUSS, JUSTIFY, NOUS, LOGOS, GROUND, RATIOCINATE, MOTIVE, CAUSE, EXPLANATION, BASIS
against .... OPPUGN
deprive of ...... DEMENT
for being .... END, RAISON D'ETRE
for ill-will ...... GRUDGE
with .... RIGHTLY
reasonable ... RATIONAL, SANE, SENSIBLE, JUST, LOGICAL
reasoning, correct .. LOGIC(AL)
false .... IDOLISM, SOPHISM
faulty ..... PARALOGISM, SYLLOGISM
subtle, difficult .... METAPHYSICS
reata ... LARIAT, LASSO, NOOSE
reave .... SEIZE, TEAR
rebate ... KICKBACK RAKE-OFF, DEDUCTION, RABBET
rebec(k) ..... VIOLIN, FIDDLE
Rebecca's brother ..... LABAN
diminutive of ..... REBA, BECKY
father .... ISAAC
husband .... ISAAC
son .... ESAU, JACOB
rebel .. DISSENTER, DISSIDENT, OPPOSE(R), REVOLT(ER), MUTINEER, RELUCT, RISE, RESIST, INSURGENT, INSURRECTO, DEFIER, RECUSANT, MALCONTENT
angel .... BELIAL
rebellion .... REVOLUTION, SEDITION, MUTINY, REVOLT, INSURGENCE, INSURRECTION, UPRISING
minor .... PUTSCH
rebellious .... DEFIANT
rebirth .... REVIVAL
rebound .... RICOCHET, RECOIL, CAROM, RESILE, BOUNCE
rebuff ...... REFUSE, REPULSE, REPEL, SPURN, SLAP, SNUB, REJECT
rebuke .... REPRIMAND, REPREHEND, SLAP, UPBRAID, DERIDE, CENSURE, REPROVE
rebus for example .... PUZZLE
rebut ...... REFUTE, DISPROVE, CONTRADICT
recalcitrant ...... RESISTANT, DEFIANT, UNRULY, REBEL, RENITENT
recall ... REMEMBER, CANCEL, REVIVE, RECOLLECT, REPEAL, ANNUL, REVOKE, WITHDRAW
recant ... RENOUNCE, ABJURE, RETRACT, WITHDRAW
recap .... RETREAD
recapitulate .... REPEAT, SUMMARIZE, SUM UP
recapitulation ...... SUMMARY, REPRISE
recede ..... EBB, DRAW BACK
receipt ... QUITTANCE, RECIPE
receivable .... DUE
receive ...... HOLD, ACCEPT, ADMIT, ACQUIRE, TAKE
received, in radio ...... ROGER
receiver .... TREASURER, COLLECTOR, RECIPIENT
in baseball ..... CATCHER
stolen goods ..... FENCE
trust property ... BAILEE, TRUSTEE
receiving callers .... IN, AT HOME
recent .... NEW, MODERN, NEOTERIC
combining form ... NEO
recently ... LATELY, OF LATE, LATTERLY
receptacle ...... CONTAINER, VESSEL, BIN, BOX, BASKET, FONT, BASIN, CAN
flower .... TORUS
holy water ...... STOUP, FONT
reception ... WELCOME, LEVEE,

SOIREE, AT HOME, DURBAR
receptive .. AMENDABLE, OPEN
receptor ..... EYE, EAR, NOSE
recess ... NICHE, BREAK, NOOK, HOLLOW, VACATION
recession ... RECEDING, SLUMP
business .... SLUMP
recessional .... HYMN
Recife .... PERNAMBUCO
recipe ... FORMULA, REMEDY, PRESCRIPTION, RECEIPT
recipient ... DONEE, RECEIVER
reciprocal .... MUTUAL
reciprocate .... EXCHANGE, RETURN
recital ... NARRATION, STORY, ACCOUNT, CONCERT, MUSICALE
recitation ... STORY, ACCOUNT
recite ..... NARRATE, RELATE, REPEAT, ENUMERATE
loudly .... DECLAIM
mechanically ... PATTER
monotonously ... CHANT, DRONE
reciter of literary works ...... READER
reck .... HEED
reckless ... MADCAP, WANTON, WILD, RASH, HEEDLESS, CARELESS, AUDACIOUS
courage ... DERRING-DO
person .... HOTSPUR, MADCAP, PLUNGER, DAREDEVIL
reckon .... FIGURE(UP), COUNT, CALCULATE, COMPUTE, CONSIDER, JUDGE, SUPPOSE
reckoning .... GUESS, CALCULATION, TAB, COUNT
reclaim ... RECOVER, RESTORE, REFORM
reclaimed land ...... POLDER
reclame .... PUBLICITY
recline ... LIE, REST, LAY, LEAN
reclining .... RECUMBENT
recluse ..... HERMIT, EREMITE, TROGLODYTE, SOLITAIRE, MONK, SOLITARY, ANCHORITE, ANCHORESS
recognition ...... ADMISSION, NOTICE, AWARENESS, GREETING
recognizance ... BOND, BADGE, TOKEN
recognize ... IDENTIFY, ADMIT, ACCEPT, OWN, PERCEIVE
recoil .... RESILE, COWER, RETREAT, REACT(ION), SHRINK, QUAIL, KICK, DRAW BACK, REDOUND
recollect .... RECALL, REMEMBER
recollection ..... ANAMNESIS, MEMORY, REMEMBRANCE
recommend .... TOUT, ENTRUST, COMMIT, ADVISE, COUNSEL
recommendation .... PLUG
recompense .... REPAY, REWARD, COMPENSATE
reconcile ... ATONE, COMPOSE, ADJUST, HARMONIZE, SYNCRETIZE
recondite .... ABSTRUSE, OBSCURE, DEEP, PROFOUND
reconnaisance .... SURVEY
reconnoiter .... SCOUT, SURVEY, EXPLORE
record .... TAB, ENTER, SET DOWN, ENTRY, TAPE, ACTA, FILE, NOTATE, PLATTER, POST, ENROLL
copy of .... ESTREAT
formal .... MINUTES, REGISTER, DOCUMENT
historical .... ANNALS
of arrests ...... BLOTTER
of past events ... HISTORY
of travel ..... ITINERARY
personal .... DIARY, DOSSIER
police .... BLOTTER
ship .... LOG
recorded proceedings ... ACTA
recorder .... REGISTRAR, FLUTE, SECRETARY, TAPER
recording device .... TAPE, METER
records, place for public ...... ARCHIVES
recount ... RELATE, NARRATE, TELL, RECITE
recoup .... REIMBURSE, RECOVER, WIN BACK
recourse .... RESORT
recover .... RALLY, RETRIEVE, REGAIN, RECOUP, RECLAIM, RECUPERATE
from illness .. CONVALESCE
one's spirit ... PERK(UP), RALLY
recreant .... CRAVEN, COWARD(LY), TRAITOR(OUS), DISLOYAL
recreation ..... AMUSEMENT, PASTIME, PLAY
recrement .... REFUSE, WASTE, DROSS
recruit .... DRAFT(EE), CONSCRIPT, ENLIST(EE), ROOKIE, MUSTER
rectangle .... QUADRATE
rectangular .... QUADRATE
rectifier .... ADJUSTER
tube .... DIODE
rectify .... AMEND, CORRECT, ADJUST, REFINE, PURIFY, REMEDY
rectitude .... HONESTY, INTEGRITY
recto, opposed to ..... VERSO
rector .... MINISTER
assistant of ..... CURATE
dwelling of ...... MANSE
recumbent .... PRONE, RESTING, LEANING
recuperate .... RECOVER
recuperation ...... RECOVERY
recur ... RETURN, COME BACK
recurrence .... RETURN, REPETITION
recurring period ...... CYCLE
recuse .... CHALLENGE
red ... CERISE, CORAL, GARNET, COLOR, RUBIOUS, RUBY, RADICAL, COMMUNIST
admiral ...... BUTTERFLY
and blue color ... PURPLE
apple .... DELICIOUS
bird .... CARDINAL, TANAGER, BULLFINCH
breast .... ROBIN, SANDPIPER
breasted bream .. SUNFISH
bright .... MADDER, CARDINAL, CERISE, SCARLET
bug .... CHIGGER
cedar .... JUNIPER, SAVIN(E)
cent .... PENNY
corundum .... RUBY
country .... USSR
Cross' concern .... DISASTER, CALAMITY
Cross fund raiser .... TAGGER
deep ..... GARNET, RUBY, CARNATION
deer ...... STAG(GARD), STAGGART
Desert ... NEFUD, NEFUF
dye ...... AURINE, EOSIN, HENNA
eyed fish ... RUDD, CARP
flag signal ..... DANGER
fushcia .... MAGENTA
haired .... CARROTY
hat .... BIRETTA
hat wearer ... CARDINAL
hind .... CABRILLA
hot ..... INCANDESCENT, SIZZLING
in heraldry .... GULES
in the .... LOSING, INDEBTED
hue ...... ROSE, BLOOD, PINK
inscribed in ...... RUBRIC
lattice ..... TAVERN, INN
lead .... MINIUM
letter ...... MEMORABLE
light signal ..... DANGER
man .... INDIAN
meat ..... BEEF, MUTTON
mineral .... RUTILE, GARNET
ocher .... REDDLE, RADDLE, RUBRIC, RUDDLE
pigment ... CHICA, ROSET
osier .... DOGWOOD
pepper .... CAYENNE
planet .... MARS
Polled .... CATTLE
purplish ...... CARMINE, AMARANTH, MAGENTA
River .... SONGKOI
Sea city ... JIDDA, JEDDA
Sea kingdom .... YEMEN
Sea seaport ...... MOCHA
Sea ship .... DHOW
shade .... TOMATO
Square figure ..... LENIN
Square landmark .... KREMLIN
squirrel ..... CHICKAREE

star ..... ANTARES, MARS
stone ...... RUBY, SARD
suit ... HEARTS, DIAMONDS
wine .... CLARET
yellow .... ORANGE, TITIAN
redact .... REVISE, EDIT
redbreast ...... ROBIN, KNOT, BREAM
redbug ...... FLEA, CHIGGER
redcap .... PORTER, GOLDFINCH
redd .... TIDY-UP
redden .... BLUSH, FLUSH, COLOR
reddish .... RUFESCENT, RUFOUS, ERUBESCENT
brown .... AUBURN, MAHOGANY, BAY, CHOCOLATE, HAZEL, LUGGAGE, TITIAN, RUSSET, SORREL
yellow .... SANDY, AMBER, LUTEOUS, ORANGE, TANGERINE, TITIAN
rede ..... ADVISE, PLAN, TALE, COUNSEL, STORY, SCHEME
redeem ... RECOVER, RANSOM, RESCUE, FULFILL, ATONE, DELIVER
Redeemer ..... JESUS CHRIST, SAVIOR, GOEL
redemption ...... SALVATION
Redemptorist founder .... LIGUORI
redeye .... VIREO, RUDD
redfin .... FISH, CARP
redhead .... DUCK, WOODPECKER, CARROT TOP
kin of .... POCHARD, WIDGEON
redingote .... OVERCOAT
redness, excessive .. ERYTHRISM
of skin ..... RUBEFACTION
redo .... REVAMP
redolence ...... SCENT, ODOR
redolent .... SMELLING, SCENTED, FRAGRANT
redouble ... (RE)ECHO, REPEAT, INCREASE, REFOLD
redoubt ...... BREASTWORK, STRONGHOLD
redoubtable .... FEARSOME, DREAD
redound ...... REACT, RECOIL
redowa-like dance .... POLKA, WALTZ
redpoll .... FINCH
redress ... REMEDY, CORRECT
redskin .... INDIAN
trophy of .... SCALP
redstart ..... BIRD, WARBLER, BRANTAIL
redtop .... GRASS
reduce .... LOWER, THIN, LESSEN, DIMINISH, CHANGE, DEGRADE, SUBDUE, CONQUER, DECREASE, SLASH
reduction .... CUTBACK
in biology ...... MEIOSIS
redundancy .... NIMIETY, PLEONASM, TAUTOLOGY
redundant ...... PLEONASTIC, REPETITIOUS, EXCESS(IVE), WORDY
reduplicate, in botany .... VALVATE
redware .... SEAWEED
redwing .. SONGBIRD, THRUSH
redwood .... SEQUOIA
ree .... ARIKARA
reecho .... RESOUND
reechoing .... REBOANT
reed .... OAT, GRASS, RATTAN
bird .... BOBOLINK
buck .... NAGOR, ANTELOPE
in architecture .. MOLDING
instrument with .... CLARINET, OBOE, SAXOPHONE, BASSOON, ORGAN
like .... FERULACEOUS
loom .... SLEY
mace .... CATTAIL
poetic .... ARROW
weaver's .... SLEY
reeding .... GADROON
reedy .... PIPING, THIN
reef ..... SHELF, KEY, SHOAL, RIDGE, LEDGE
coral .... CAY, KEY
mining ..... LODE, VEIN
reefer ... COAT, MIDSHIPMAN, MIDDY, CIGARETTE
prototype of ..... JOINT
reek ... FUME, VAPOR, EXUDE, SMOKE, STINK
reel ..... SWING, FALL BACK, WHIRL, DANCE, SWAY, SWIFT, SPOOL, WAMBLE, TEETER, STAGGER, LURCH, TOTTER, WIND, WINCE
for thread ..... FILATURE
reeling of cocoon silk .... FILATURE
reem .... UNICORN
Reese, baseball player .... PEEWEE
Tears author ... LIZETTE
reeve ..... OVERSEER, BAILIFF, STEWARD, SLIP, PASS IN, SANDPIPER, THREAD
refection ..... REPAST, LUNCH, MEAL
refectory .... FRATER, DINING HALL, MESS(HALL)
refer ...... ASSIGN, ADVERT, ASCRIBE, ALLUDE, SUBMIT, POINT
to .... VIDE
referee ... JUDGE, MODERATOR, UMPIRE, OVERMAN, ARBITER
reference .... REGARD, ALLUSION, MENTION, TESTIMONIAL
book .. ATLAS, ALMANAC, MANUAL
mark .... ASTERISK, DAGGER, OBELUS, DIESIS, STAR
to a law .... CITATION
referendum ...... PLEBISCITE
refine .... POLISH, PURIFY, SUBLIMATE, CLARIFY, IMPROVE, PERFECT
by distillation .. RECTIFY
by melting .... SMELT
refined .... GENTEEL
refinement .... GENTILITY, POLISH, DELICACY, ELEGANCE
refinery .... SMELTERY
refining vessel .... CUPEL
reflect ...... MIRROR, PONDER, THINK, IMAGE
reflection ..... IMAGE, REFLEX, LIKENESS, MUSING, BLAME, DISCREDIT
reflective .... PENSIVE
reflet .... LUSTER
refluent ...... EBBING, REFLUX
reform ..... CORRECT, BETTER
reformer .... MORALIST, CRUSADER, RIIS
religious .... LUTHER
reformatory ..... MAGDALENE
refract .... BEND
refractory .... OBSTINATE, UNRULY, STUBBORN, RESTIVE
refrain ... FORBEAR, ABSTAIN, CHORUS, HOLD BACK, VERSE, PHRASE, SONG, WHEEL, BURDEN, REPETEND
short .... BOB
song .... BURDEN
syllable .... TRA
refresh .... COOL, REVIVE, RENEW
with food/drink .. REFECT
refreshment ...... REFECTION, DRINK, SNACK
refrigerant ..... ICE, ETHANE, CRYOGEN, FREON
refrigerate ..... CHILL, COOL, FREEZE
refrigerator .... FREEZER, ICEBOX, FRIGIDAIRE
reft .... ROBBED
refuge ...... HAVEN, HARBOR, SANCTUARY, ASYLUM, SHELTER, RETREAT, CITADEL
refugee .... EVACUEE, ESCAPEE
organization .... IRO
refulgent .... RADIANT, SHINING, GLOWING
refund .... REBATE, REIMBURSE, REPAY(MENT)
refurbish .... RENOVATE
refusal ...... OPTION, DENIAL, REJECTION
refuse .... NAYSAY, NILL, SPURN, REJECT, WASTE, RUBBISH, TRASH, OFFAL, SCUM, BALK, DECLINE, DRAFF, EJECTA, REBUFF
cane .... BAGASSE
consent to .... VETO
grape .... MARC
metal ..... DROSS, SCUM
table ...... ORT, SCRAPS
wine .... LEES
refusing to plead in court ..... MUTE
refutation .... DISPROOF
refute ...... REBUT, DISPROVE
regain ..... RECOVER, RECOUP

regal ..... QUEENLY, KINGLY, ROYAL, STATELY
regale .... ENTERTAIN, FEAST, TREAT
regalia .... FINERY, DECORATIONS, INSIGNIA
king's .... SCEPTER, CROWN
Regan's father .... LEAR
sister .... CORDELIA, GONERIL
regard ..... CONSIDER, LOOK, ESTEEM, GAZE, CONCERN, REFERENCE, RESPECT, OBSERVE
regarding ..... CONCERNING, IN RE, ABOUT
regards ..... EYES, AFFECTION
regatta .... BOAT RACE
boat ..... YACHT, SCULL, SHELL
sights .... CATBOATS
regent .... INTERREX
of the sun .... URIEL
regicide's victim .... KING
regime .... GOVERNMENT
regimen ... DIET, SYSTEM, RULE
regiment commander .... COLONEL
part of .... BATTALION
regimental flag ...... PENNON
Regin, son of .... SIGURD, SIEGFRIED
Regina ____, monastery ...... LAUDIS
regina(l) .... QUEEN(LY)
region .... REALM, AREA, SPACE, PLACE, SPHERE, CLIME, TERRITORY
regional ... LOCAL, SECTIONAL
register ..... (EN)ROLL, LIST, RECORD, ENTER, METER, CALENDAR
death .... NECROLOGY
regma ... SCHIZOCARP, MAPLE
regnant ... RULING, REIGNING, PREVALENT
regorge .... VOMIT
regress .... RETURN
regret .... RUE, REPENT, DEPLORE, PENITENCE, MOURN, REMORSE
regular ..... STABLE, STEADY, ORDERLY, USUAL, CUSTOMARY, UNIFORM, PROPER
patronage ..... CUSTOM
regulate ..... ADJUST, DIRECT, CONTROL
regulation .... RULE, LAW
regulator ... GOVERNOR, VALVE
temperature .. CRYOSTAT
rehash .... REVISE
rehearsal .... PROLUSION, PRACTICE
kind of .... DRYRUN, DRESS
rehearse ...... RECITE, DRILL, PRACTICE, TRAIN
Reich .... GERMANY
reign ... RULE, SWAY, PREVAIL, REGIME
of a family ..... DYNASTY

reigning .... REGNANT
reimburse .... REFUND, PAY BACK, REPAY
rein .... CHECK, CONTROL, RESTRAIN, LEASH
draw .... STOP
reindeer .... CARIBOU
man .... LAPP
reine's husband .... ROI
reinstate ... RESTORE, REVEST
reiterate .... SAY AGAIN, REPEAT
reject .... VOMIT, REBUFF, DISCARD, REPEL, SPURN, DECLINE, REFUSE
bill .... VETO
rejoice ... DELIGHT, GLADDEN, GLORY
rejoin .... ANSWER
rejoinder ..... REPLY, ANSWER
relapse .... BACKSLIDE, SLIP BACK, FALL BACK
relate .... TELL, PERTAIN, RECOUNT, NARRATE
related ... TOLD, CONNECTED, COGNATE, GERMANE, AKIN, ALLIED
by blood .. SIB, KIN(DRED)
on father's side .. AGNATE, AGNATIC
on mother's side .. ENATE, ENATIVE
relation .... ACCOUNT, RECITAL, KIN(SHIP), KINSMAN
relationship .... CONNECTION, RELEVANCE, KINSHIP
sympathetic .... RAPPORT
relative .... RELEVANT, PERTINENT, KINSMAN, SIB, KIN(FOLK)
for short ...... BROD, SIS
relatives, employment of ...... NEPOTISM
relator .... NARRATOR, COMPLAINANT
relax .... LOOSEN, EASE, REST, SOFTEN, REDUCE, SLACKEN
relaxation ...... RECREATION, AMUSEMENT, DIVERSION
relay .... SHIFT, REMOUNT
release .... FREE, RELIEVE, CLEAR, DISCHARGE, UNTIE, UNDO, LIBERATE, EXEMPT, LOOSE, LET GO, QUITCLAIM, RELIEF
air .... DEFLATE
claim ... REMISE, WAIVER
hold .... DROP
mass of ice .... CALVE
relegate ...... EXILE, ASSIGN, CONSIGN, BANISH, COMMIT
relent ... SOFTEN, THAW, YIELD
relentless ..... PITILESS, GRIM, HARSH
relevant .... PERTINENT, GERMANE, RELATED, APPLICABLE, APT, APROPOS, APPOSITE
reliable .... DEPENDABLE, TESTED, TRIED, WORTHY, TRUSTY, SOLID
reliance .. TRUST, DEPENDENCE

relic ...... CURIO, SOUVENIR, RUIN
sacred .... HALIDOM
relics .... RUINS
relict ..... WIDOW, WIDOWED, SURVIVOR
relief ..... RELEASE, REMEDY, RELIEVO, RILIEVO, SUCCOR, EASING, AID
relieve .... EASE, LIGHTEN, REDUCE, FREE, REMOVE, ALLAY, COMFORT, ALLEVIATE, RID
by talking ..... ABREACT
thirst .... SLAKE
relievo .... RELIEF
religieuse .... NUN, SISTER
religieux .... MONK, PIOUS
religion .... BELIEF, FAITH
religionist .... FANATIC
religious ..... PIOUS, DEVOUT, GODLY, SCRUPULOUS, MONK, NUN, DIVINE
beggar ... FAKIR, SERVITE
belief .... CREED
belief, antagonistic ...... HERESY
brotherhood .. SODALITY, ORDER
devotee .... FAKIR
devotion .... NOVENA
emotion ..... THEOPATHY
expedition .... CRUSADE
festival .... HOLIDAY
group chief ... HIERARCH
journey ..... PILGRIMAGE
lay society .... SODALITY
leader .... SHEPHERD
leader's saying .... LOGIA
lore .... HIEROLOGY
man ...... MONK, LAMA
military order member ... TEMPLAR
mysticism .... QUIETISM
observance ... FAST, LENT
offering ...... OBLATION, SACRIFICE
order .... DOMINICAN, JESUIT, TEMPLAR, FRANCISCAN, MARIST
period .... LENT
person .. PIETIST, OBLATE
reformer .. LUTHER, HUSS
rites, of .... SACRAL
ritual .... CULT
school head ..... RECTOR
sect ...... DENOMINATION
vigil .... WATCH
war .... CRUSADE
worship, system of .. CULT
relinquish ... RELEASE, YIELD, FOREGO, WAIVE, ABANDON, LET GO, SURRENDER, RESIGN, RENOUNCE
reliquary ...... SEPULCHER, CASKET, SHRINE
relish ... CONDIMENT, FLAVOR, PICKLES, ENJOY, GUSTO, ACHAR, SAVOR, ZEST, SAUCE, RADISH, TASTE, PLEASURE, CHUTNEY, CHUTNEE, SAPOR
fish egg .... CAVIAR(E)

meat juice .... ASPIC
relucent .... BRIGHT
reluct .... REVOLT
reluctant ... AVERSE, LO(A)TH, UNWILLING, HESITANT
rely ...... COUNT(ON), BANK, DEPEND, TRUST, RECKON, LEAN
relying on experience .... EMPIRICAL
remain ... STAY, LAST, ENDURE
balanced .... LIBRATE
firm .... STAND(PAT)
undecided .... PEND, HANG FIRE
remainder .... REMNANT, BALANCE, REST, RESIDUUM, LEFT-OVER, RESIDUE, RESIDUAL
remains .. CADAVER, VESTIGES, RUINS, REMNANT, TRACES
remand .. SEND BACK, RETURN
remark .... NOTE, WORD, OBSERVE, NOTICE, COMMENT(ARY), REMARQUE
correct: sl. .... MOUTHFUL
cutting ... SARCASM, NIP
indirect, derogatory ..... INNUENDO
clever ... NIFTY, BON MOT, WITTICISM, CRACK, SALLY
mocking .... JEST
unfavorable ... BRICKBAT
remarkable .... UNCO, SIGNAL, UNUSUAL, NOTABLE
Remarque, Ger. novelist ..... ERICH (MARIA)
Rembrandt, Dutch painter .... (VAN) RIJN, RYN
work .... TITUS
remedy ...... CURE, RECIPE, REDRESS, RELIEF, HEAL, CORRECT, ANTIDOTE, REPAIR
any .... TREACLE
cure-all .... ELIXIR, PANACEA
in coinage ... TOLERANCE
quack .... NOSTRUM
secret .... ARCANUM, ELIXIR
soothing .... LOTION, BALM, BALSAM, SALVE, UNGUENT, DEMULCENT
remember .... RECALL, RECOLLECT, REMIND, REMINISCE
remembrance ...... SOUVENIR, KEEPSAKE, MEMENTO, TOKEN, MEMORY
remex ... FEATHER, OARSMAN
remiges .... FEATHERS
reminder .... MEMENTO, SOUVENIR, TICKLER, MEMO
reminiscence .... MEMORY
reminiscent ...... SUGGESTIVE
remiss ...... LAX, NEGLIGENT, DERELICT
remission .... PARDON
remit .... PARDON, SEND, FORGIVE, CANCEL, SLACKEN, PAY
remnant .... RAG, TRACE, FRAGMENT, REMAINDER, RESIDUE, LEAVING, ODDMENT, (TAG)END, LEFT-OVER
remodel .... RECAST
remo(u)lade .... SAUCE
remonstrance ...... PROTEST, COMPLAINT
remonstrate .... PLEAD, PROTEST, OBJECT
remora ...... PEGA, SUCKFISH
favorite host of .. SHARK
remorse ...... REGRET, PITY, PENITENCE, COMPASSION
remorseless .... CRUEL, MERCILESS, PITILESS
remote ...... ALOOF, SLIGHT, FAR(OFF), SECLUDED, DISTANT, ULTERIOR
remount ...... RELAY, HORSE
removal ... OUSTER, DISMISSAL
of diseased tissue .... ERASION
surgical ...... ABLATION
remove ... OUST, EJECT, EXPEL, DEPOSE, TAKE OFF, KILL, DISMISS, DELE
bark ...... DECORTICATE
clothes ... STRIP, UNDRESS
by popular vote .. RECALL
from grave ..... DISINTER
from office .... OUST, DEPOSE
ice .... DEFROST
impurities ...... FILTER, REFINE, RECTIFY, SMELT
in law .... ELOIGN, ELOIN
juice .... REAM
marks .... ERASE
tumor .... EXCISE
to another place .... TRANSFER
water ..... DEHYDRATE
remunerate .... REWARD, RECOMPENSE, PAY
remuneration .... EMOLUMENT, PAY, REWARD
remunerative .... PAYING, LUCRATIVE, GAINFUL
Remus' brother .... ROMULUS
parent ..... MARS, RHEA
renaissance .... REBIRTH, REVIVAL
humanist ..... ERASMUS
sword .... ESTOC
renal .... NEPHRIC, NEPHRITIC
Renard .... FOX
renascence .... REVIVAL, REBIRTH
rend ... RIP, RIVE, TEAR, PULL, SPLIT
render .... DEPICT, RECITE, PERFORM, PLAY, ACT(OUT), TRANSLATE, CONSTRUE, DELIVER, SUBMIT, PRESENT, HAND OVER
fluid ..... FUSE, LIQUEFY
rendezvous ..... DATE, TRYST, MEET(ING), APPOINTMENT, ASSEMBLE
rendition ...... PERFORMANCE, VERSION, TRANSLATION
renegade .... APOSTATE, DESERTER, TURNCOAT, TRAITOR, RAT
renege .... FINAGLE
renew ...... RESUME, REPEAT, REFRESH, RENOVATE, RESTORE
Reni, Ital. painter .... GUIDO
rennet .... RENNIN
Reno is in .... NEVADA
Renoir, painter ...... PIERRE
renounce ... RECANT, GIVE UP, ABJURE, ABDICATE, FORSWEAR, REJECT, DENY, DISOWN, RELINQUISH
throne .... ABDICATE
renovate ... FURBISH, RENEW, REPAIR, REVIVE, REDO
renown ... FAME, REPUTATION, ECLAT, NAME, REPUTE
person of ..... CELEBRITY
renowned .... FAMOUS
rensselaerite .... TALC
rent ... RIP, TEAR, LEASE, LET, HIRE, SCHISM, HOLE, GAP
rente ..... REVENUE, ANNUITY
renunciation ..... ABDICATION, WAIVER
reopen .... RESUME
reorganization ...... REVAMP, SHAKE-UP
rep .... FABRIC
repair .... GO, MEND, FIX, RESTORE, REMEDY, BETAKE
hole/tear .... DARN
repairman .... COBBLER, MECHANIC
reparable .... MENDABLE
reparation .... REDRESS, ATONEMENT, REPAIRS, SALLY
repartee ...... MOT, RETORT, GIVE-AND-TAKE, RIPOSTE, REJOINDER, DIALOGUE, BANTER
engage in .... FENCE
skilled in .... WITTY
repast ...... REFECTION, MEAL
repatriate .... RETURN, SEND BACK
repay .... RECOMPENSE, REIMBURSE, REFUND, REWARD
repeal ..... REVOKE, CANCEL, ABROGATE, RESCIND, ANNUL, ABOLISH, REVOCATION
repeat ...... RECITE, PARROT, BIS, RECUR, (RE)ITERATE
gossip .... RETAIL
performance ... ENCORE
repeatedly .... OFT(EN), FREQUENTLY
repeater ...... ECHO, PARROT, RIFLE, PISTOL, WATCH, CLOCK
repeating rifle inventor .... MAUSER
repel ...... REPULSE, SPURN, REJECT, REFUSE
repellent .... REPULSIVE, WATERPROOF

repent .. RUE, GRIEVE, REGRET, CREEPING, CRAWLING
repentance ...... PENITENCE, REMORSE, REGRET, CONTRITION, ATTRITION
repercussion .... RECOIL, REBOUND, ECHO, REACTION
repertoire .... STOCK
repertory .... STOCK, COLLECTION, STOREHOUSE
repetend .... REFRAIN
repetition ...... RECITATION COPY, ROTE, RECURRENCE
in music .... REPRISE
mechanical .... ROTE
of performance .. ENCORE, REPLAY
repine ...... FRET, COMPLAIN
replace ... SUPPLANT, RETURN, RESTORE
replenish .... RESTOCK
replete .... FULL, STUFFED
repletion .... FULLNESS
replica .... REPRODUCTION, COPY, FACSIMILE
replicate .... FOLD
replication ..... FOLD, REPLY, ECHO, COPY(ING), ANSWER
reply ...... RETORT, ANSWER, RETURN, RESPONSE, RESPOND, COMEBACK, REJOIN(DER)
repondez s'il vous plait .. RSVP
report .... RUMOR, GOSSIP, BRUIT, SAY, DENOUNCE, TALK, HEARSAY, ACCOUNT, BROADCAST, CAHIER, HANSARD, TELL, BULLETIN, NOISE
card entry .... MARK, GRADE
slanderous ..... SCANDAL
reporter .... JOURNALIST, SCRIBE, NEWSMAN, CRIER
concern of ...... SCOOP, BEAT, FACTS, DATA, CONTACTS, DEADLINE, ACCURACY
delight of .... BY-LINE
paper of .... FLIMSY
routine of .... LEGWORK
repose .... SLEEP, PEACE, (EN)TRUST, PLACE, RELY, REST, LAY, LIE, CALM
repository .... CHEST, CLOSET, VAULT, SAFE, CONFIDANT, MUSEUM, WAREHOUSE, SEPULCHER
reprehend .... CENSURE, REBUKE, REPROVE, BLAME
reprehensible .... CENSURABLE
represent .. EXHIBIT, PORTRAY, DEPICT, DESCRIBE, DENOTE, ENACT, TYPIFY, SYMBOLIZE
graphically .... PLOT
representation .... IMAGE, LIKENESS, ALLEGATION, ALLEGORY, MIMESIS
of heavenly bodies ...... ORRERY
ridiculous ..... TRAVESTY
representative .... AGENT, DEPUTY, DELEGATE, ENVOY, AMBASSADOR, PROXY, TYPICAL, SOLON
repress .... CURB, STIFLE, RESTRAIN, SUBDUE, HOLD BACK
reprieve ... DEFER, POSTPONE, GRACE, RESPITE
reprimand .. SCOLD, CENSURE, BAWL, REBUKE, RATING, REPROVE
reprint .... REISSUE
reprisal .... QUITTANCE, RETALIATION, VENGEANCE, MARQUE, REVENGE, RETORTION
reprise .. REPETITION, SUMMARY
reproach ... CHIDE, REPROVE, REBUKE, CENSURE, UPBRAID, BLAME
reprobate .... VICIOUS, DEPRAVED, ROGUE, SCOUNDREL, ROUE, RAKE
reproduce .... REFLECT
reproduction .... COPY
reproductive cell .... GAMETE, GONAD
organ .... OVARY, TESTIS
reproof ... CENSURE, REBUKE
reprove .... REBUKE, CENSURE, UPBRAID, CHIDE
reptant .... CREEPING, CRAWLING, REPENT
reptile .... LIZARD, SAURIAN, OPHIDIAN, SNAKE, ALLIGATOR, TURTLE, CROCODILE, LACERT(IL)IAN
carnivorous ... TUATARA
extinct ...... PTEROSAUR
eye tissue .... PECTEN
footless ... APOD, SNAKE
fossil ..... STEGOSAURUS
movement of ..... CREEP, CRAWL, SLITHER
mythical ... SALAMANDER
Nile .... CROC
scale .. SCUTUM, PLATELET
reptiles, study of .... HERPETOLOGY
republic .... DEMOCRACY
author .... PLATO
not quite one ... BANANA
of letters ...... LITERATI
Republican .... WHIG
mascot ...... ELEPHANT
Mr., soubriquet .... TAFT
Party .... GOP
recalcitrant ... MUGWUMP
repudiate ... RECANT, REJECT, DISOWN, DENY
repugnance .... AVERSION, DISTASTE, HATE
repugnant .... OFFENSIVE, HATEFUL
repulse .... REPEL, REBUFF, REJECT, REFUSE, DRIVE BACK
repulsion .... AVERSION, DISLIKE, DISTASTE
repulsive ...... UGLY, ODIOUS, COARSE, LOATHSOME, REVOLTING, DISGUSTING, OFFENSIVE
reputation ..... REPUTE, NAME, FAME
repute .... ESTEEM, ODOR
reputed .... SUPPOSED, PUTATIVE, KNOWN
request .... APPEAL, SUIT, PRAY, PETITION, ASK, BEG, INSTANCE, ENTREAT(Y)
requiem ... MASS, DIRGE, HYMN
requiescat in ____ ...... PACE
require ..... DEMAND, COMPEL, NEED, ORDER, INVOLVE
requirement .... NEED, IMPOSITION
requisite ... NEED, ESSENTIAL, REQUIRED
requite ...... PAY, RETALIATE, ATONE, COMPENSATE
reredos ... SCREEN, PARTITION
reroute .... DETOUR
rerun ...... REPLAY, RESHOW
rescind ..... RECALL, REPEAL, ABOLISH, CANCEL, ANNUL, ABROGATE
rescript ...... DECREE, ORDER, COPY
rescue .... RANSOM, SAVE, DELIVER(ANCE), REDEEM, SALVATION
research .... STUDY
center .... LAB(ORATORY)
reseau .... NETWORK
resect .... EXCISE
reseda .... MIGNONETTE
resemblance .... LIKENESS, SIMILARITY
resentment .. HUFF, DUDGEON, INDIGNATION, UMBRAGE, OFFENSE, BAD BLOOD
reservation, in law ... SAYING, SALVO
without .... OUTRIGHT
reserve ..... KEEP, SET ASIDE, EARMARK, BACKLOG, STORE, STOCK, RETICENCE, SILENCE, CASH, RETAIN
reserved .... TACITURN, RETICENT, QUIET, RETIRING, SHY, ALOOF, DISTANT
reserves, armed forces .... MILITIA
reservoir .... SUMP, STORE, SUPPLY, CISTERN
overflow of ..... SPILTH
reset gem .... REMOUNT
reside ... DWELL, LODGE, LIVE
residence .... DOMICILE, DWELLING, ABODE, MANSION
king's .... PALACE
minister's .... MANSE, PARSONAGE, RECTORY
papal.......... VATICAN
place of .... ADDRESS
rural .... BOWER
stately .... MANSION
resident ...... (IN)HABITANT, INHERENT
doctor .... INTERN(E)
residential street .... TERRACE
residual .... REMAINDER
residue .... ASH, DREG, REMAINDER, REST,

LEFT-OVER, REMANENT, SHIFTINGS, BITTERN
resign .... QUIT, RELINQUISH, ABDICATE, DEMIT
resignation ...... ABDICATION, DEMISSION, SUBMISSION
resile .... REBOUND
resiliency .... ELASTICITY, BUOYANCY
resilient .... ELASTIC, FLEXIBLE, SUPPLE, BUOYANT
resin .... MASTIC, SHELLAC(K), PITCH, ROSIN, ELATERITE, AMBER, ANIME, COPAL, ASAFETIDA, ALKYD, COPAIBA, COPALM, TUPI, GUM, KAURI, LA(B)DANUM
aromatic .... COPAIBA
cathartic ..... SCAMMONY
fossil ... RETINITE, AMBER
fragrant .... MYRRH, ELEMI, FRANKINCENSE
gum .. MYRRH, RESINOID, COPAL, MASTIC, BDELLIUM, GAMBOGE, AMMONIAC
hemp .... CHARAS, HASHISH
incense ..... SANDARAC, MYRRH
perfume making .... BENZOIN
pine .. DAMMAR, DANAMER
poisonous ... CANNABIN
solvent for ...... ETHER
synthetic ..... BAKELITE, CATALIN, SILICONE, LUCITE
thermoplastic ... SARAN
varnish ... COPAL, ANIME, DAMMAR, DAMMER
resinous juice ..... LAUDANUM
powder, hops ... LUPULIN
secretion .... LAC
resist ... FIGHT, DEFY, BUCK, FEND, OPPOSE, REPUGN, WITHSTAND
resistance .... OPPOSITION, DEFIANCE
fighter .... PARTISAN, MAQUI, ELAS, EDES, GUERRILLA, ACTIVIST
to authority .... MUTINY
resolute .... DETERMINED, RESOLVED, GRIM
resolve ..... ANALYZE, DECIDE
resonance .... SONORITY, SYNTONY, VIBRANCY
resonant .... SONOROUS, REECHOING, VIBRANT, OROTUND
resort .... RECOURSE, SPA
Riviera .... CANNES
resound ..... (RE)ECHO, PEAL, EXTOL, RING, BOOM, VIBRATE, REVERBERATE
resource(s) .... WEALTH, CAPITAL, MEANS, ASSETS, RESORT, EXPEDIENT
resourceful ... QUICK-WITTED
respect ..... ESTEEM, HONOR, REGARD
respectable .... DECENT
respectful .... OBEISANT
Respighi, composer .. OTTORINO
respiration .... EUPN(O)EA, BREATHING, DYSPN(O)EA
combining form .. SPIRO
stimulant .... METRAZOL
respirator .... GAS MASK, IRON LUNG
respiratory disease ... HEAVES
organ .... LUNG
respire .... BREATHE, INHALE, EXHALE
respite .... DELAY, LULL, REPRIEVE, GRACE
resplendent .... DAZZLING, SHINING, GRAND, SPLENDID, BRILLIANT, GORGEOUS
respond ..... REACT, ANSWER, REPLY, RETURN
respondent .... DEFENDANT
response ... REACTION, REPLY, ANSWER
responsibility ... DUTY, ONUS, LIABILITY, OBLIGATION
responsible .... LIABLE, ACCOUNTABLE, RELIABLE
responsive .... SENSITIVE
rest ... REMAINDER, BALANCE, SEAT, RECLINE, SLEEP, REPOSE, EASE, SUPPORT, STOP, OTHERS
colloquial ... BREATHER, BREAK
eternal .... DEATH
in prosody ... C(A)ESURA
midday .... SIESTA
restaurant ..... CAFE(TERIA), AUTOMAT, DINER, CABARET, EATERY, BISTRO
bench .... BANQUETTE
compartment .... BOOTH
restful ..... QUIET, PEACEFUL
resting .... DORMANT
restive ... BALKY, IMPATIENT, UNRULY, NERVOUS, RESTLESS, FRETFUL
restless .... RESTIVE, UNEASY, FRETFUL, AGITATO
restock .... REPLENISH
restorative .... ANODYNE
restore ...... RETURN, RENEW, REPAIR, REBUILD, RETROCEDE
to health .... RECUPERATE
restrain ...... INHIBIT, STAY, BRIDLE, DETER, CHECK, HOLD, SUPPRESS, CURB
restraint ... CURB, LID, REIN, RESERVE, CONTROL
restrict .... LIMIT, CONFINE
restroom .... CLOSET, LAVATORY
result ... EFFECT, EVENTUATE, ISSUE, ENSUE, UPSHOT, OUTCOME, ANSWER, AFTERMATH
resume .. SUMMARY, ABSTRACT, REOPEN, REPRISE, PRECIS, RENEW, CONTINUE
resurge ...... RALLY, REVIVE
resurrect ... REVIVE, RESTORE
resurrection .... REVIVAL
he experienced .... JESUS, LAZARUS
resuscitate .... REVIVE
resuscitation ...... ANABIOSIS
ret ...... SOAK, STEEP, DAMP, MACERATE
retable .... SHELF
retailer ...... DEALER, CLERK
retain .... HOLD, KEEP
retainer .... ATTENDANT, ADHERENT, FEE
retainers, body of ... RETINUE
retaining wall .... REVETMENT
retake .... RECAPTURE
retaliate .... REQUITE
retaliation .... TALION, REPRISAL, RETORTION, RETORSION, TIT-FOR-TAT
retard ...... HINDER, DELAY, IMPEDE, SLOW
retch ..... KECK, VOMIT, GAG
rete ...... NETWORK, PLEXUS
retem .... JUNIPER
retention .... MEMORY
retentive .... TENACIOUS
retepore .... MOLLUSK
retiarius .... GLADIATOR
retiary .... NETLIKE
reticence .... RESERVE
reticent .... TACITURN, RESERVED, SILENT
reticular .... NETLIKE
reticule .... (HAND)BAG, RETICLE
reticulum .... NETWORK
retinue ... TRAIN, ENTOURAGE, CORTEGE, ROUT, ESCORT, SUITE, RETAINERS, MEINIE, MEINY
retire ... WITHDRAW, RETREAT, REST, REMOVE
retired ..... ABED, SECLUDED, ASLEEP, EMERITUS
retiring .... SHY, MODEST, RESERVED
retort .... REPARTEE, WITTICISM, RIPOSTE, REJOIN(DER), SQUELCH, ALEMBIC, QUIP, SALLY, REPLY
retortion .... REPRISAL
retract ... DISAVOW, REVOKE, RENEGE, RECANT, ABJURE, UNSAY, WITHDRAW
retraction .... PALINODE
retral .... POSTERIOR
retread .... RECAP
retreat .... ASYLUM, NEST, WITHDRAW, BACK DOWN, HIDEOUT, SHELTER, LAIR, RETIRE, SANCTUM, REFUGE, STUDY, PULLOUT, ARBOR, KATABASIS
cozy .... DEN, NOOK, ALCOVE
disorderly .... ROUT, FLIGHT
kind of ..... MONASTERY, CONVENT, HERMITAGE, NUNNERY
shaded .... BOWER
signal .... CHAMADE
retrench ... CURTAIL, LESSEN,

REDUCE, DECREASE, CUT-DOWN, ECONOMIZE
retrenchment ...... RAMPART
retribution .... REQUITAL, NEMESIS, REWARD
retributive justice .... NEMESIS
retrieve ... RECOVER, RESTORE, REGAIN, REVIVE, SET RIGHT, MAKE UP
retriever ... (GUN)DOG, SETTER, POINTER
retrocede .... RESTORE
retrograde .... DECLINE, REVERSE, INVERSE
retrogress .... DECLINE, DEGENERATE
return ..... REPLY, RESPOND, REPLACE, REQUITE, REELECT, REPORT, RECUR, COME BACK, RESTORE, YIELD, RESPONSE, REVERT
in kind .... RECIPROCATE
returns ...... YIELD, REVENUE, PROFIT
Reuben's father ...... JACOB
reunion .... GET-TOGETHER, BOURBON
capital .... ST. DENIS
with Brahma ... NIRVANA
rev ...... ACCELERATE, RACE
Reval .... TALLINN
revamp .... REDO, PATCH, RENOVATE, SHAKE-UP
reveal .... EXHIBIT, MANIFEST, TELL, BETRAY, JAMB, BARE, DIVULGE, DISCLOSE, DISPLAY
reveille .. CALL, SIGNAL, ROUSE
revel ... DELIGHT, CAROUSAL, FESTIVITY, ROISTER
revelation ...... DISCLOSURE, ORACLE
revelations ...... APOCALYPSE
revel(l)er ..... MERRYMAKER, CORYBANT
exclamation of a .... WHOOPEE
revelry ...... FESTIVITY, RIOT, SATURNALIA
revenant ..... EIDOLON, GHOST
revenge ... RETALIATE, AVENGE, VENGEANCE, TALION
revenue .... INCOME
bishop's .... ANNAT
reverberate .... (RE)ECHO, REFLECT, RESOUND, REBOUND, RECOIL
revere .. VENERATE, WORSHIP, ADORE, RESPECT
reverence .... OBEISANCE, AWE, WORSHIP, VENERATION, BOW, CURTSY, ADORATION
gesture of .... OBEISANCE
lacking .... IMPIOUS
reverie .... MUSING, FANTASY, (DAY)DREAM, NOTION
revers .... LAPEL
reversal .... ABOUT-FACE, VOLTE-FACE, TURNABOUT, ANNULMENT
reverse .... OPPOSITE, CONTRARY, BACK, REVOKE, ANNUL, INVERT
reversion .... RETURN
of property .... ESCHEAT
to primitive type .... ATAVISM, THROWBACK
revert .... RETURN
revest .... REINSTATE
revet .... FACE
review ..... REPORT, ACCOUNT, SURVEY, NOTICE, REVUE, INSPECT, CRITICISM, CRITIQUE, PARADE, EPICRISIS
adverse .... PAN
enthusiastic .... RAVE
reviewer .... CRITIC
revile .... VILIFY, ABUSE, ASPERSE, VILIPEND, SCOLD
revise .... EDIT, AMEND, REWRITE, REHASH
revival .... REBIRTH, RENEWAL
revivalist .... EVANGELIST
revive ...... RALLY, RESURGE, RESUSCITATE
memory .... REFRESH, REMIND, JOG, RECALL
revocation ..... ANNULMENT, REPEAL
revoke ..... ABJURE, REPEAL, CANCEL, RESCIND, RENEGE, ANNUL, RENIG, ADEEM
revolt .... UPRISING, REBEL(LION), MUTINY, DISGUST, RISE
revolting .... OFFENSIVE, LOATHSOME, HORRID
revolution .... CYCLE, ROTATION, REBELLION, GYRE
fighter ...... MINUTEMAN
general of the ..... ASHE, GATES, ARNOLD, GREENE, LINCOLN, SULLIVAN
revolutionary .... RADICAL, REBEL
revolutionist .... ANARCH, REB(EL)
revolve .... ROTATE, CIRCLE, GYRATE, SPIN, TURN, ORBIT
revolver .... PISTOL, COLT, GAT, ROD, BULLDOG
revolving part .... ROTOR
revue .... SHOW, FOLLIES
revulsion .... AVERSION
reward ... TIP, PAY, GUERDON, BONUS, RETURN, PRIZE, AWARD
of a sort ..... SOP, WAGES
rewrite .... REVISE
rewriting .... RESCRIPT
rex .... KING
Reynard .... FOX
Rh factor .... RHESUS
rhabdomancy ...... DOWSING, DIVINATION
rhapsodical .... ECSTATIC
rhea .... NANDU, EMU, OSTRICH, CYBELE, OPS
husband of ..... CRONUS
parent of .... URANUS, GAEA
progeny of .... ZEUS, HADES, HERA, HESTIA, POSEIDON, DEMETER
rheotrope ...... COMMUTATOR
rhesus .... MACAQUE, MONKEY
rhetor .... ORATOR
rhetorical device .. ANAPHORA
figure .... LITOTES
rheum ... RHINITIS, CATARRH, COLD
rheumatic pain ..... LUMBAGO
person .... ACHER
rheumatism of back/loins .... LUMBAGO
remedy .... GUACO
rhinal .... NASAL
Rhine .... RHEIN, RIJN, RIVER
branch .... WAAL
city on the ... MANNHEIM, MAINZ, MAYENCE, KOLN
siren ... LORELEI, LURLEI
tributary .... MAIN
wine ..... HOCK, MOSELLE
rhinitis .... RHEUM
rhino(ceros) ... ABADA, MONEY, CASH, BORELE
for one ..... PACHYDERM
one-horned ..... BADAK
two-horned .... KEITLOA
rhinology, subject of .... NOSE
rhizoid .... ROOTLIKE
rhizome ..... STOLON, TUBER, STEM, ROOTSTALK (ROOT)STOCK
rhizopod .... TESTACEAN
rhizopus .... FUNGUS
Rhode Island capital .... PROVIDENCE
city .... PAWTUCKET, WARWICK, CRANSTON
founder ...... WILLIAMS
state flower ..... VIOLET
Rhodes .... RODI
ancient wonder .. COLOSSUS
Rhodesia capital ... SALISBURY
city ... GWELO, UMTAIL, BULAWAYO
language .. BANTU, SHONA
port .... BEIRA
premier .... SMITH
tribe .... ILAS
rhododendron ..... ROSEBAY, LAUREL
kin of .... AZALEA
rhodolite .... GARNET
rhomb ...... PARALLELOGRAM, LOZENGE
rhombencephalon .. HINDBRAIN
part .. PONS, CEREBELLUM
rhombus .... LOZENGE
rhonchus ...... RALE, SNORE, RATTLE
Rhone tributary ...... ISERE, SAONE
rhubarb .... (PIE)PLANT, ARGUMENT, DISCUSSION
rhyme ...... VERSE, CRAMBO
and reason ...... SENSE
rhymer .... VERSIFIER, POET(ASTER)
rhymester .... VERSIFIER, POET(ASTER)
rhyming .... CRAMBO
rhythm .. TEMPO, BEAT, SWING,

CADENCE, METER, MEASURE, LILT, TIME
rhythmic rise and fall .. HEAVE
rhythmical accent ..... ICTUS
ria .... INLET
rial .... COIN
rialto .... BRIDGE, MART, MARKET
riant .... GAY, BLITHE, CHEERFUL, LAUGHING, SMILING
riata .... LARIAT
rib ... COSTA, VEIN, KID, WIFE, TEASE, TWIT, RIDGE
in architecture ... LIERNE
leaf .... NERVURE
of a .... COSTAL
ribald ..... COARSE, VULGAR
ribaldry .... JAPERY
riband .... RIBBON
ribbed ..... COSTATE, RIDGED, TEASED, KIDDED
ribbon .... DECORATION, BADGE, STRIP, BAND
cutting, for example ..... CEREMONY
decorative ...... RIBAND
document's ...... LABEL
hair .... BANDEAU
knot .... COCKADE
like part ...... T(A)ENIA
of cotton, etc. ... FERRET
paper ..... TICKER TAPE
seal .... LABEL
trimming ...... GALLOON
worsted .... CADDIS
ribbons .... TATTERS
ribs, having .... COSTATE
ribwort .... PLANTAIN
rice ... CEREAL, PADDY, GRASS, GRAIN
alcoholic drink .. ARRACK, SAKE
boiled with meat .. PILAU, PILAF(F)
cooked with gravy ...... RISOTTO
dish, spicy .... PILAU
field .... PADDY
husk .... BRAN
in husk .... PADDY
playwright ...... ELMER
wine .... SAKE
riceball .... PINDA
ricebird .. SPARROW, BOBOLINK
rich ... WEALTHY, ABOUNDING, VALUABLE, OPULENT, WELL-TO-DO, LUXURIOUS, ABSURD, AFFLUENT
man .... CROESUS, NABOB, PLUTO, MIDAS, DIVES
Richard I of England .... LIONHEART, COEUR DE LION
unknown .... ROE
riches ... OPULENCE, WEALTH, LUCRE
richest part ..... CREAM, FAT
richly .... FULLY, AMPLY
richness .... LUXE, MEANS
ricin .... PROTEIN
rick .... STACK
Rickenbacker, American ace .. EDDIE
rickets .... RACHITIS
rickety ...... FEEBLE, SHAKY
rickey .... DRINK
Rickover, Adm. ...... HYMAN
rickrack ... BRAID, TRIMMING
ricksha(w) .... JINRIKISHA
ricochet ..... SKIP, REBOUND, CAR(R)OM
rictus ..... GAPING, RINGENT
rid .... FREE, CLEAR, DISENCUMBER, RELIEVE
of defect .... REAM
of false ideas .. DISABUSE
Ridd's heroine .... LORNA (DOONE)
ridden .... OBSESSED
riddle ...... ENIGMA, PEPPER, SIEVE, PERFORATE, PUZZLE, PROBLEM, CONUNDRUM, MYSTERY
bandleader ...... NELSON
picture .... REBUS
ride .... TEASE, HARASS, BAIT, MOUNT
pay for ... FARE, PASSAGE
take for a ...... DECEIVE, KILL
to hounds .... HUNT
rider .... CLAUSE, JOKER, AMENDMENT, EQUESTRIAN, PASSENGER, FARE
ridge .... RUGA, WALE, BACK, CREST, RANGE, CHINE, ARETE, RAND, CUESTA, ARISTA
between furrows ... LIST
between peaks ... SADDLE
glacial ... OSAR, DRUMLIN
like part ... KEEL, CARINA
of earth ..... HOGBACK, HORSEBACK
sand .... DUNE, DENE
sandy .... LANDE
ridgepole .... ROOFTREE
ridicule .... DERISION, MOCK, DERIDE, TAUNT, JEER, SCOFF, SCOUT, JEST, ROAST, TWIT
playfully .... KID
ridiculous .... ABSURD, GROTESQUE, LUDICROUS, FOOLISH
riding boot .... JEMMY
breeches ..... JODHPURS
academy .... MANEGE
costume .... HABIT
horse .... PALFREY, MOUNT, ROADSTER
school .... MANEGE
whip ...... QUIRT, CROP
Rieka .... FIUME
"Rienzi" composer .. WAGNER
rife ... CURRENT, PREVALENT, PREVAILING, WIDESPREAD
Riff .... BERBER
riffle .... SHOAL, REEF, SHUFFLE
riffraff .... MOB, DOGGERY, TRASH
rifle ... CARBINE, CHASSEPOT, BROWNING, PILLAGE, PLUNDER, ROB, MAUSER, REPEATER, FIREARM, GROOVE, RANSACK, BAR, GARAND
bullet ..... MINIE(BALL)
chamber ..... MAGAZINE
pin .... TIGE
position .... READY
rifleman .... JA(E)GER, YAGER
rating of .... EXPERT, MARKSMAN, SHARPSHOOTER
rifler .... ROBBER
rift ..... CLEFT, CRACK, GAP, SPLIT, FISSURE, BREACH
rig ...... FIT, DRESS, CLOTHE, ATTIRE, EQUIP(MENT), CARRIAGE, COSTUME, DRESS, GEAR, MANIPULATE, TACKLE, CART
Riga gulf island ...... OESEL
native .... LATVIAN
Rigg's disease ..... PYORRHEA
Rigel .... STAR
rigger .... SCAFFOLD
rigging ..... EQUIPMENT, GEAR
part ..... ROPES, CHAINS, SPAR, SAILS, SHROUDS, YARDS
right ...... TITLE, STRAIGHT, VIRTUOUS, CORRECT, SUITABLE, REDRESS, LICENSE, SOUND, NORMAL, FITTING, DEXTRAL
and wrong decider ...... CASUIST
by .... PROPERLY
combining form .. RECT(I)
exclusive .... PATENT
hand side .... DEXTER
hand page .... RECTO
king's .... REGALITY
legal ...... TITLE, DROIT
now ... PRONTO, AT ONCE, IMMEDIATELY
of expression ..... VOICE
of way .... EASEMENT
on the .... OFF
side .... DEXTER
slang .... ROGER
special ...... FRANCHISE, CHARTER
to choose ..... OPTION
to decide .... SAY-SO
to enter .... ENTREE, INGRESS
to mail free ...... FRANK
turn .... GEE
word .... MOTJUSTE
righteous ... VIRTUOUS, MORAL
rightfully .... DULY
righto .... YES, CERTAINLY
rights, equality of ... ISONOMY
relating to .... JURAL
rigid ...... STRICT, STIFF, SET, SEVERE, RIGOROUS, AUSTERE
rigmarole .... NONSENSE, BLATHER
"Rigoletto" author ..... VERDI
rigor ... SEVERITY, HARDSHIP, RIGIDITY
companion of ... MORTIS
rigorous .. STERN, STIFF, RIGID, HARSH, SEVERE, PRECISE, STRICT

Rigsdag, part of .. LANDSTING, FOLKETING
Riis, social reformer .. JACOB
Rijeka .... FIUME
Rijn .... RHINE
rile .... ANGER, IRRITATE, ROIL, VEX
rilievo .... RELIEF
Rilke, Ger. poet ..... RAINER
rill .... RIVULET, BROOK, TRENCH, VALLEY, FURROW
rim .... BORDER, LIP, BRINK, VERGE, MARGIN, BRIM, EDGE
cap's projecting ... VISOR
cask's ..... CHINE, CHIMB
rail/pipe's ...... FLANGE
roof's .... EAVE
wheel ..... FELLY, FELLOE
rime ... RHYME, (HOAR)FROST
rimer ..... BROACH, MINSTREL
rimple ..... CREASE, WRINKLE
rimy .... FROSTY
Rinaldo's magic horse .... BAYARD, BAJARDO
rind ... BARK, COATING, SKIN, CRUST, PEEL, CORTEX, EPICARP, EXOCARP
candied .... CITRON
ring ... RESOUND, KNELL, RIM, ANNULET, SET, (EN)CIRCLE, SET, ARENA, DING, SIGNAL, CALL(UP), CLIQUE, CIRQUE
bell .... PEAL, TOLL, CHIME, KNELL
give a .... CALL, (TELE)PHONE
harness .... TERRET
jeweled ...... MARQUISE
metal .... BEE
neck .... PHEASANT
of guards .... CORDON
of leaves ... INVOLUCEL, INVOLUCRE
of light .... HALO
of neck feathers ... RUFF, TORQUES
of rope .... GROMMET
of rubber ...... GASKET
shaped .... ANNULAR
shaped cake .. DOUGHNUT
single gem of .. SOLITAIRE
stone setting ..... COLLET
tailed animal ..... COON
up ... (TELE)PHONE, CALL, DIAL
ringdove .... CUSHAT
ringent ..... GAPING, RICTUS
ringer .... QUOIT, HORSESHOE, LOOK-ALIKE
ringing, persistent .. CLANGOR
sound in ear ... TINNITUS
ringlet ... CURL, TRESS, LOCK
ringworm .... TINEA, SERPIGO
rinse .... WASH, LAVE
rinsings .... DREGS
Rio —— .... BRAVO, GRANDE, NEGRO, MUNI
de —— ... ORO, JANEIRO
Grande, city on .. LAREDO
Grande tributary .. PECOS
Muni city .... BATA
seaport ...... MATAMOROS
riot ...... UPROAR, DISORDER, HUBBUB, ORGY, HIT, EMEUTE
riotous ..... WILD, DISSOLUTE, WANTON, LUXURIANT, NOISY, DISORDERLY
rip ... CUT, SPLIT, REND, TEAR, RIVE
colloquial ... NAG, HORSE
into .... ATTACK
roaring .... NOISY, BOISTEROUS
van Winkle author ...... IRVING
riparian .... RIVERINE
ripe .... MATURE, READY, MELLOW, ADULT, DEVELOPED
ripen .... MATURE, AGE
ripening early .... RATH(E), RARERIPE
ripost(e) .... RETORT, THRUST, RETURN
ripping .... FINE, EXCELLENT, SPLENDID
ripple ..... WAVE(LET), PURL, RAPID, LAP, UNDULATION, LIPPER
riptide .... UNDERTOW
Ripuarian .... FRANK
ris de veau ..... SWEETBREAD
rise .... OCCUR, HAPPEN, ASCENT, HILL, REBEL, STAND, GET UP, REVOLT, ASCEND, SOAR
again .... RESURGE
and fall .... WELTER, FLUCTUATE
and float in the air ...... LEVITATE
from the dead .... RESURRECT
in the ground .... LIFT
of the tide .... FLOOD
soprano .... STEVENS
risible .. AMUSING, LUDICROUS, LAUGHABLE, FUNNY
rising .. ANABATIC, MONTANT, BOIL, MOUNTING
risk .... HAZARD, CHANCE, (EN)DANGER, PERIL, JEOPARDY
risque ..... RACY, OFF-COLOR, DARING, SCABROUS
rissole .... MEATBALL
rite ..... CEREMONY, LITURGY
meaningless .... MUMBO-JUMBO
public worship .. LITURGY
washing .... LAVABO
Ritz, Swiss hotelman .. CESAR
ritzy ... ELEGANT, LUXURIOUS, TONY, CLASSY, POSH
rivage ... SHORE, COAST, BANK
rival ..... EMULATE, VIE, FOE, MATCH, COMPETITOR, EQUAL, OPPONENT, COMPETE
rivalry .... EMULATION, COMPETITION
rive ... REND, SPLIT, CLEAVE, TEAR
riven ..... RENT, SPLIT, TORN
river .... STREAM
Avignon's ...... RHONE
bank ...... RIPA, LEVEE
bank, of a .... RIPARIAN
barge .... GONDOLA
barrier ..... WEIR, BOOM, BARRAGE
"beautiful" ...... OHIO
bed .... CHANNEL
bend .... OXBOW
blue, poetically .. DANUBE
boat ..... FERRY, BARGE, PACKET, SAMPAN
bottom .... BED
branch .... ARM
channel .... FAIRWAY
cross a ..... FORD, FERRY
crossed by Caesar .... RUBICON
curve in .... BEN, BIGHT
dam .... WEIR
deep, still spot of .. POOL
deposit .... LOESS
duck .... TEAL, SHOVEL(L)ER
edge ...... BANK, LEVEE
elbow .... BEND
embankment .... LEVEE
falls .... SAULTS
famous ... NILE, RUBICON, AVON, DANUBE
horse ... HIPPO(POTAMUS)
inlet ... SLOUGH, BAYOU
island .... HOLM
isle .... HOLM, AIT
land near ...... HOLM, BOTTOMS
landing ... LEVEE, GHAT
large ..... AMAZON, NILE
mouth ... EMBOUCHURE, ESTUARY, DELTA, BOCA
nymph .... NAIAD
of song ... VOLGA, OHIO, SWANEE, DANUBE
of wailing ..... COCYTUS
outlet .... BAYOU
rapid .... SAULT
sacred ... GANGES, ALPH
sell down the .... BETRAY
siren .... LORELEI
soil .... DELTA
source .... HEAD
underworld .... STYX
valley ..... DALE, STRATH
wade across ...... FORD
widened part ..... LAKE
winding of .... ESS
Rivera, Mex. painter .. DIEGO
painting .... MURAL
Riviera beach .... PLAGE
resort .... CANNES
riviere .... NECKLACE
riverine .... RIPARIAN
rivet .... BOLT, FASTEN
holder .... DOLLY
washer of ...... BURR
riveter, female .... ROSIE
rivulet .... RILL, ARROYO, BROOK, STREAM, RUN(D)LET, RUNNEL
Riyadh is capital of ..... NEJD
riyal, where used ..... YEMEN
Rizal, Filipino patriot ... JOSE
Rn, in chemistry ...... RADON
roach .... CARP, SUNFISH
movie producer ..... HAL

road .... MACADAM, PATH, CAUSEWAY, (HIGH)WAY, ITER, COURSE
agent .... HIGHWAYMAN
along embankment ..... STAITH
Canada to Key West .. USI
character ... HOBO, HOG, TRAMP, (HITCH)HIKER
charge .... TOLL
curve .... ESS
fast .... SPEEDWAY
for locomotive .. RAILWAY
ledge .... BERM(E)
map abbreviation ... RTE
of a .... VIATIC(AL)
on the ..... TRAVELING, ON TOUR
pavement ..... TELFORD
private ...... DRIVEWAY
runner ..... COCK, BIRD, CUCKOO
shoulder ...... BERM(E)
sign ...... ESS, MILEPOST, MILESTONE
surface .. TAR, MACADAM, ASPHALT
toll .... (TURN)PIKE
worker .... NAVVY, CAMINERO
roadblock .... BLOCKADE
roadhouse ..... INN, TAVERN, NIGHT CLUB
roadside sign ... EATS, MOTEL
weed ...... DOG, FENNEL
roadster ... RUNABOUT, HORSE, TWO-SEATER
seat .... RUMBLE
roadway, sloping ...... RAMP
roam .... ROVE, MEANDER, RANGE, WANDER, RAMBLE, GAD
roan .. HORSE, SHEEPSKIN, BAY
roar .... BELLOW, LAUGHTER, GROWL, DIN, RUMBLE, ROLL, BELL
roaring .... BRISK, NOISY
Twenties dance .... CHARLESTON
roast .. BAKE, BROWN, PICNIC, BARBECUE, BROIL, PARCH, HEAT, PAN, CRITICIZE
meat ... CABOBS, KABOBS
turner .... JACK
roaster ... BROILER, CHICKEN, PIG
roasting device/tool .... SPIT, GRIDIRON, OVEN, PAN, GRILL, BUCCANEER
rob ... PLUNDER, CLIP, FLAY, LOOT, RIFLE, REAVE
a truck .... HIJACK
robalo .... FISH, SNOOK
robbed ...... REFT, DEPRIVED
robber .... RIFLER, THIEF, SPOLIATOR, (FOOT)PAD, YEGG, CATERAN, BANDIT, RAPPAREE, BANDIDO, LADRONE, BRIGAND
bird .... DAW, JA(E)GER, SKUA, SHOOI
cattle .... RUSTLER
den of ... LAIR, HIDEOUT
highway ..... HIJACKER
sea .... PRIVATEER, CORSAIR, PIRATE
robbery ..... THEFT, STICKUP, HOLD-UP
robe .. TOGA, (DRESSING)GOWN, WRAP, VESTMENT, CHIMAR, CHIMER
bishop's .... CHIMER, CHIMAR
girdle .... CAFTAN
long-sleeved ... CAFTAN, KAFTAN
loose .... SIMAR
monk's .... FROCK
plural .... COSTUME, APPAREL, CLOTHES
woman's .... SIMAR
robed .... VESTED
robin ... THRUSH, REDBREAST, RUDDOCK
Goodfellow .... HOB(GOBLIN), PUCK, ELF, FAIRY, SPRITE
Hood .... OUTLAW
Hood's companion ..... WILL (SCARLET), (FRIAR) TUCK
Hood's sweetheart ...... (MAID) MARIAN
Hood's weapon .... LONGBOW
Robinson Crusoe's man ...... FRIDAY
model .... SELKIRK
Ray .... SUGAR
roble ...... OAK, BEECH, TREE
roborant .... TONIC
robot .... AUTOMATON, GOLEM
robots, play about .... RUR
robust ...... HARDY, STURDY, HEALTHY, ROUGH, HALE, SOUND, MUSCULAR, LUSTY, WALLY, HUSKY
roc .... SIMURG, BIRD
passenger of the .... SIN(D)BAD
rocambole .... LEEK
rochet ... VESTMENT, SURPLICE
rock .... SHAKE, STONE, CANDY, TOTTER, TEETER, SWAY, JIGGLE, GNEISS, PSEPHITE, GANISTER, DOLOMITE
above a plain .... MONADOCK
basaltic .... WHIN(STONE)
bass .... SUNFISH
black .... BASALT
boring tool ..... TREPAN, TRAPAN
bottom .... LOWEST
carving .... PETROGLYPH
cavity ... GEODE, VUG(G), VUGH
combining form ... SAXI, PETR(O), LITH(O)
conglomerate .... GRAYWACKE
containing gem, fossil, etc. MATRIC
crushed .... BALLAST
decomposed .. SAPROLITE
dug out .... FOSSIL
easily split ...... SCHIST
ejected by volcano ...... LAPILLUS
eroded .... BOSS
face .... PRECIPICE
fine-grained ..... SHALE, SLATE
finely broken ..... SAND
formed by geyser .. SINTER
fragment(s) ...... SPALL, BRASH, DETRITUS
garden .... ROCKERY
granite-like ...... GNEISS
green .... OPHITE, VERD ANTIQUE
growths on ...... LICHEN
igneous .... BASALT, PORPHYRY, TRAP, SYENITE, DIORITE, PERIDOT(ITE), PEGMATITE, PICRITE, GRANITE, PHONOLITE
in another rock .... XENOLITH
isolated .... SCAR
like .... PETROUS
like fish roe ..... OOLITE
mass .... HORST
metamorphic .... GNEISS
mica and quartz .. GREIN
molten.......... MAGMA
mottled .... OPHITE
of .... PETROUS
oil .... PETROLEUM, NAP(H)THA
pinnacle .... NEEDLE
plural: sl. ..... DIAMOND, GEM
porous ...... TUFA, TUFF, TOPH(E)
projecting .. SCAR, LEDGE
rabbit .... HYRAX
ribbed ..... RIGID, FIRM
rose product .... LA(B)DANUM
salt .... HALITE
salt money .... EMOL
sedimentary ..... PELITE, MUDSTONE
siliceous ...... GANISTER
steep .... CLIFF
stratified .... SHALE
volcanic .. LAVA, BASALT, WACK, LATITE, PERLITE
weed ..... SEA OAK, TANG
rockaway .... CARRIAGE
Rockefeller, John ____ ...... DAVISON
one other .... EDSEL, NELSON
rocker .... CHAIR, CRADLE, SKATE
rockery .... GARDEN
rocket ... PROJECTILE, ASROC
firing platform .... LAUNCHING PAD
fuel ... LOX, HYDRAZINE
gun .... BAZOOKA
launcher ...... BAZOOKA
load .... WARHEAD

part of .... CAPSULE, (NOSE)CONE
to get astronaut back .... RETRO
rockfish ..... BASS, GROUPER, RE(I)NA, BOCACCIO, YELLOWTAIL
rockfoil .... SAXIFRAGE
Rockies' range ...... TETON, UINTA
Rockne, football coach .... KNUTE
rocks at foot of cliff ... TALUS
bluish .... LIAS
living on ..... SAXATILE, SAXICOLINE
of the oldest .. ARCHEAN
on the .... BANKRUPT
pile of ... TALUS, DEBRIS
slang ..... MONEY, GEM, DIAMOND
study of ..... PETROLOGY, LITHOLOGY
rockweed .... FUCOID
rocky .... UNSTEADY, SHAKY, WEAK, CRAGGY, DIZZY
cliff .... SCAR
hill .... TOR
mountain sheep .... BIGHORN
mountain wind .... CHINOOK
Mountains ..... ROCKIES
pinnacle .... SCAR, TOR, ARETE
rococo .... FLORID, TASTELESS, BAROQUE
rod ... POLE, TOGGLE, WAND, PERCH, TWIG, WATTLE, FERULE, VERGE, SHOOT, SHAFT, BAR, STAFF, STICK, SWITCH, SCEPTER
Biblical use ...... STOCK, RACE, OFFSHOOT
billiards .... CUE
connecting ...... PITMAN
divination ..... DOWSING, RHABDOMANCY
flogging .... SWISH
king's .... WARDER
royal .... WARDER, SCEPTER
shaped .... BACILLAR, VIRG(UL)ATE
slang ..... GAT, PISTOL, REVOLVER, GUN
steadying .... GUY
rodent ...... GNAWING, RAT, MOUSE, BEAVER, SQUIRREL, PIKA, CON(E)Y, MURINE, RABBIT, LEPORID, CAVY, HARE
aquatic .... BEAVER, MUSKRAT
Belgian ...... LEPORIDE
burrowing ... VISCACHA, CHIPMUNK, MARMOT, GOPHER, VOLE, GERBIL(LE), SUSLIK
eight-toothed .. OCTODON
largest extant .... CAPYBARA
leaping .... JERBOA
Patsy winner .... BEN
pet .... HAMSTER
squirrel-like .. DORMOUSE, GOPHER, SUSLIK, CHIPMUNK
suicidal .... LEMMING
tailless .... PACA
water .. COYPU, MUSKRAT, NUTRIA
rodents' disease .... TULAR(A)EMIA
enemy .... RATTER
of .... MURINE
rodeo .... ROUNDUP
Rodi .... RHODES
Rodin, Fr. sculptor .... AUGUSTE
work of .... THINKER
rodomontade ... BOAST(ING), BRAG(GING)
Rodrigo Diaz de Bivar .... (EL) CID
rods, 40 .... FURLONG
roe .. MILT, OVA, DEER, SPAWN, CORAL, (FISH)EGGS
roebuck .... DEER
Roentgen's discovery .... XRAY
rogation .... PRAYER
rogatory ...... QUESTIONING
Roger ..... RECEIVED, RIGHT, OK, OVER
Rogers, ___ ..... WILL, ROY
rogue .... PICAROON, SCAPEGRACE, BEGGAR, SCOUNDREL, KITE, KNAVE, VAGABOND, RASCAL
animal .... ELEPHANT
rogues, of .... PICARESQUE
gallery item .. ALIAS, MUG
roguish ... FUN-LOVING, ARCH
roi's heir .... DAUPHIN
realm .... FRANCE
wife .... REINE
roil ..... MUDDY, VEX, RILE, DISPLEASE, IRRITATE, IRK
roily .... MUDDY, TURBID, ANGRY
roister ..... REVEL, SWAGGER
Roland's magic possession .... HORN, OLIVANT
role .... FUNCTION, OFFICE, PART, CHARACTER, PERSON
without speech .... WALK-ON
roll .... BRIOCHE, ELAPSE, SCROLL, CATALOG(UE), CAKE, DRUMBEAT, PEAL, TRUNDLE, LIST, WRAP, ENFOLD, REGISTER, BUN, ROSTER, LURCH
about .... WELTER, WALLOW
along .... TRUNDLE
back .... REPULSE
hard .... BAGEL
of bills .... WAD
of bread .... MANCHET
of cloth .... BOLT
of coins ...... ROULEAU
of paper ..... WEB, BOLT
of something .. ROULEAU
out ... SPREAD, FLATTEN
parchment ..... SCROLL
prevent .... TRIG
slang ..... ROB, MONEY, WAD
the eyes .... GOGGLE
Rolland, Fr. novelist .. ROMAIN
rolled backward ... REVOLUTE
roller .... WHEEL, SKATE, CYLINDER, WAVE, CANARY, WINCE, BRAYER, PIGEON
coaster .... SWITCHBACK
rollick ...... ROMP, GAMBOL, CAPER, FRISK
rollicking .. LIVELY, CAREFREE
rolling stock ... LOCOMOTIVES
Stones member .. JAGGER, WATTS, WYMAN
sound .... RUMBLE
sudden .... LURCH
Rollo .... VIKING
rolltop .... DESK
rollway .... CHUTE
roly-poly .... PUDGY, DUMPY, PUDDING
rom .... GYPSY
romaine .... COS, LETTUCE
Romains, Fr. novelist .. JULES
Roman ..... LATIN, ITALIAN, QUIRITE
actor's boot .... BUSKIN
administrator .... PATRICIAN
agreement .... PACTA
apostle .... NERI
assembly .... FORUM, COMITIA
awning .... VELARIUM
basilica .... LATERAN
bathhouses ... THERMAE
bishop .... POPE
bottle .... AMPULLA
boxer's strap .... CESTUS
boxing-wrestling contest .. PANCRATIUM
bronze .... AES
buckle .... FIBULA
building for musical performances .. ODEUM
cap .... PILEUS
Catholic .... PAPIST, LATIN
Catholic Church .. ROME
Catholic festival .... LAMMAS
Catholic, French .... GALLICAN
census taker ..... CENSOR
chariot .... ESSED
circus arena .... HIPPODROME
circus fighter .... GLADIATOR
citizens .... EQUITES
civil law digest .. PANDECT
civilian .... QUIRITE
clan .... GENS
clasp .... FIBULA
cloak ... SAGUM, ABOLLA
coin ...... AES, AUREUS, SESTERCE, DENARIUS, TRIENS, SEMIS, SOLIDUS, BEZANT

commander .. CENTURION
commoner .... PLEBEIAN
corselet .. LORICA, LORLEA
court(s) .. ATRIA, ATRIUM
cuirass .. LORICA, LORLEA
date .... NONES, IDES
deity .... LAR
dictator .... SULLA
diviner .... AUSPEX
emperor .... TITUS, NERVA, OTHO, HADRIAN, GALBA, PROBUS, CARUS, OTTO, TRAJAN, CALIGULA
emperor's bodyguard ... PRETORIAN
emperor's decree .... RESCRIPT
emperor's standard ..... LABARUM
Empire part .... HISPANIA
empire founder .... AUGUSTUS
entrance .... ATRIUM
epigrammatist .. MARTIAL
fable writer .. PHAEDRUS
farce .... MIME
farewell .... ADDIO
fates .... PARCAE
festival ... LUPERCAL(IA), SATURNALIA, OPALIA
fiddler .... NERO
foot soldiers .... VELITES
fountain, famed ... TREVI
frontier fortification ..... LIMES
galley .. BIREME, TRIREME
games .... LUDI
games official .. (A)EDILE
garment .. TOGA, STOLE, TUNIC
general ... TITUS, SCIPIO, MARIUS, LUCULLUS, CASSIUS, AGRICOLA, SULLA, DRUSUS, AGRIPPA
girdle .... CESTUS
girl traitor ..... TARPEIA
gladiator ..... RETIARIUS
god, agriculture ... PICUS, SATURN
  chief ... JOVE, JUPITER
  festivity ...... COMUS
  fire .... VULCAN
  gates .... JANUS
  Hades..... DIS, ORCUS, PLUTO
  herds .... PAN
  household .... LAR, PENATES
  lightning .... JUPITER
  love ..... CUPID, AMOR
  lower world .. SERAPIS
  night .... SOMNUS
  pastoral ... LUPERCUS, FAUNUS
  patron ..... MERCURY
  rain .... JUPITER
  sea .... NEPTUNE
  season .... VERTUMNUS
  sleep ...... MORPHEUS, SOMNUS
  sun .... SOL
  thievery ..... MERCURY
  tutelary .... LAR
  underworld ...... DIS, ORCUS, PLUTO
  wine .... BACCHUS
  woods ...... SYLVANUS
  war ... MARS, QUIRINUS
goddess .... DEA
  agriculture ...... OPS
  beauty .... VENUS
  birth .... PARCA, LUCINA, MATUTA
  crops .... ANNONA
  crossroads .... TRIVIA
  dawn .... AURORA, MATUTA
  earth .... TELLUS, TERRA
  faith .... FIDES
  fates .... PARCAE
  fertility .... FAUNA
  fields .... TELLUS
  fire .... VESTA
  flowers .... FLORA
  fountain ..... FERONIA
  fruits .... POMONA
  harvest .... OPS
  health .... SALUS
  hearth .... VESTA
  herds .... PALES
  hope .... SPES
  horses .... EPONA
  hunting ...... DIANA, VACUNA
  light .... LUCINA
  love .... VENUS
  marriage .... JUNO
  moon .... LUNA
  night .... NOX
  peace ... PAX, MINERVA
  plenty .... OPS
  sea .... MARE
  summer ...... AESTAS
  underworld .... PROSERPINA
  vegetation ..... CERES
  virtue .... FIDES
  war .... MINERVA, BELLONA
  wisdom ..... MINERVA
governor.... PROCONSUL, PILATE, LEGATE
guard .... LICTOR
guardian spirits ... LARES, PENATES
Hades .... AVERNUS
half boot .... CALIGA
hall ...... ATRIUM, OECUS
harvest festival ... OPALIA
headband .... VITTA
hell .... AVERNUS
helmet .... GALEA
highway ...... ITER, VIA
hill .... (See Rome)
historian ...... TACITUS, NEPOS, LIVY
holiday .... FERIA
household gods ... LARES, PENATES
jar .... AMPHORA
judge .... (A)EDILE, QU(A)ESTOR
law .... LEX
lawmaker ..... SENATOR
legion commander ...... TRIBUNE
list .... ALBE
lower world ..... ORCUS, HADES
magistrate ...... CONSUL, PREFECT, DUUMVIR, CENSOR, TRIBUNE, PR(A)ETOR
magistrate's symbol ..... FASCES
maiden traitor .. TARPEIA
marble .... CIPOLIN
masses .... PLEBS
matron's garment .. STOLE
meal .... CENA, GENA
military unit .... LEGION, COHORT
monster: myth. .... TYPHON, LAMIA
month's first day .... CALENDS
name .... NOMEN
naturalist .... PLINY
noble .... PATRICIAN
nose .... NASUS
nymph: myth. .. EGERIA, M(A)ENAD
officer for 10 men .... DECURION
official .... EDILE, PREFECT
official with the fasces ... LICTOR
Optimus Princeps .... TRAJAN
orator ... CATO, CICERO, CAESAR
palace .... LATERAN
patron of literature ...... MAECENAS
people .... SABINES
philosopher .... SENECA
pin .... ACUS
plain .... CAMPAGNA
playwright ..... TERENCE
poet .....VERGIL, VIRGIL, JUVENAL, LUCRETIUS, CINNA, LUCAN, OVID
pontiff .... CAESAR
port .... OSTIA
portrait, wax ..... IMAGO
pound .... LIBRA
priest ... AUSPEX, AUGUR, FLAMEN
procession .... TRIUMPH
province .... DACIA, PANNONIA, PISIDIA, MOESIA, NUMIDIA
public land .... AGER
racing course .... HIPPODROME
river ...... TIBER, LETHE
road .... ITER, VIA
road, famous ... APPIAN
robe .... TOGA
room(s) .... ATRIUM, ATRIA
royal standard .... LABARUM
senator .... CATO, CICERO, PUBLIUS

serf .... COLONUS, COLONA
shield(s) ...... SCUTUM, EGIS, SCUTA, CLIPEUS
soldier .... VELITE, LEGIONARY
soldier's covering .... TESTUDO
soothsayer ... HARUSPEX
spirits .... LEMURES, MANES, LARES
standard ..... LABARUM
street .... CORSO
tablet .... TESSERA
taxman .... PUBLICAN
temple .... NAOS, CELLA
theater awning .... VELARIUM
theater's stage .... PROSCENIUM
ticket/token .... TESSERA
tragedian ...... SENECA
traitors' cliff .. TARPEIAN
treasurer ... QU(A)ESTOR
unit of weight .... LIBRA
urn .... CAPANNA
vase .... PYXIS
vestment ... TOGA, ROBE
war trumpet ...... TUBA
warrior ..... GLADIATOR
way .... VIA
weight ... SCRUPLE, BES, LIBRA
writer .... VARRO, TERENCE, LIVY, PLINY
writing tablet .. DIPTYCH

romance .... NOVEL, FICTION, (LOVE)AFFAIR, WOO, COURT
language ...... SPANISH, FRENCH, ITALIAN, PROVENCAL, ROMANIAN, CATALAN, LADIN

Romanian (see Rumanian)
capital .... BUCHAREST

Romanov, Russ. czar .... MIKHAIL

Romansh .... LADIN

romantic .... FANCIFUL, FABULOUS, VISIONARY, QUIXOTIC, SENTIMENTAL, BYRONIC

Romany .... GYPSY

Rome .... ROMA, RUM, ETERNAL CITY
conqueror of ... ALARIC
first emperor of .... AUGUSTUS
founder of ... ROMULUS
grandeur of ..... EMPIRE
hill of .... CAELIAN, AVENTINE, VIMINAL, PALATINE, QUIRINAL, CAPITOLINE
"pest" of ... PAPPAGALLO
port .... OSTIA
rebel against .. SPARTACUS

Romeo .... LOVER
and Juliet character ..... ESCALUS, TYBALT, PARIS, MERCUTIO, CAPULET, ABRAM, MONTAGUE, LAURENCE
enemy of .... TYBALT
father of ..... MONTAGUE
kinsman of ... MERCUTIO
love of .... JULIET, ROSALINE
rival of .... PARIS

Rommel, Ger. marshal .... ERWIN

romp .... PLAY, ROLLICK, FROLIC

rompers .... JUMPERS

Romulus .... QUIRINUS
brother of .... REMUS
parent of .... MARS, RHEA
saver of ..... (SHE)WOLF

Ronald ___, actor .. REAGAN, COLMAN

rondeau .. POEM, RO(U)NDEL, RONDO

rondure ..... CIRCLE, SPHERE

ronin ..... OUTCAST, OUTLAW

rood .... CROSS, CRUCIFIX

roof .... CUPOLA, DOME, GAMBREL, TOP, SHELTER, LEANTO, MANSARD
arched .... VAULT
coach's .... IMPERIAL
covering ...... SHINGLE, SLATE, THATCH
drain .... GUTTER
edge .... EAVE
feature .... EAVES
figuratively ...... HOME, HOUSE
glass for light .... BULL'S-EYE
lantern .... LOUVER
of the World ..... PAMIR, TIBET
opening ..... SKYLIGHT, LUNET(TE), SCUTTLE
point finial .... EPI
raise the ..... COMPLAIN
raised border .. COAMING
rounded .. CUPOLA, DOME
sloped ... LEANTO, SHED
support .. TRUSS, RAFTER, SPRAG, PURLIN(E)
trough .... GUTTER
two-sloped .... MANSARD
window .... DORMER, SKYLIGHT
woven work ... WATTLE

roofing slate .... RAG
slate trimmer .... ZAX
tile ..... PANTILE, SLATE

roofless .... HOMELESS, HYPETHRAL

rooflike covering ..... CANOPY

rooftree .... RIDGEPOLE, HOME, SHELTER

rook ..... CROW, SWINDLE(R), CASTLE, CHEAT
cry of .... CAW

rookery .... TENEMENT
inhabitant of .. PENGUIN, CROW, SEAL

rookie ...... RECRUIT, NOVICE

room ..... SALA, HALL, SALLE, CELL, CLOSET, STUDY, LODGE, QUARTER, SPACE, LEEWAY, CUDDY, ROTUNDA
band, ornamental .... FRIEZE
beneath roof ...... LOFT, ATTIC
conversation .. LOCUTORY
dressing ...... BOUDOIR
perfumer ...... INCENSE
harem .... ADA, ODA
hot bath .... CALDARIUM
inner .... BEN
private .... DEN, CLOSET, STUDY, SANCTUM
Pueblo Indian ..... KIVA
wine .... CELLAR
woman's sitting .... BOUDOIR

roomer .... LODGER

rooming house .... KIP
housekeeper .. LANDLORD

rooms .... QUARTERS, LODGINGS

roomy .... SPACIOUS

roorback .... LIE, LIBEL

roose .... PRAISE

Roosevelt, Mrs. .... (ANNA)ELEANOR, SARA
President .. FDR, TEDDY

roost .... PERCH, SIT

rooster .... COCK, BANTAM, CHANTICLEER
castrated .... CAPON
comb of ..... CARUNCLE
cry of .... CROW
fattened .... CAPON
feathers of ..... HACKLE
leg outgrowth ..... SPUR
young .... COCKEREL

root .... RADIX, RHIZOME, ORIGIN, SOURCE, BASE, CORE, PLUG, CHEER
aromatic ...... GINSENG, ORRICE
combining form .... RHIZ(O)
diuretic .... PAREIRA
dried .... RHATANY
dye .... CHOY, CHAY
edible ... TARO, RADISH, POTATO, YAM, PARSNIP, MANIOC, GIRASOL(E), EDDO, CASSAVA
emetic .... MANDRAKE
expectorant .... SENEGA
flavoring .. SARSAPARILLA
for planting .... SLIP
garlic .... RAMSON(S)
growth ...... TUBERCLE
hair ... FIBRIL, TRICHOME
medicinal ..... GINSENG, RHATANY
narcotic ..... MANDRAKE
of the .... RADICAL
part of .... RADICLE
perfume making .. ORRIS, ORRICE
purgative .... JALAP
relish .... RADISH
salad .... RAMSON(S), RAMPION
seasoning .... TURMERIC
shoot ... SUCKER, TILLER
small .... RADICEL
stock .... GINGER
substance ..... ZEDOARY
tip tissue ..... MERISTEM

U.S. statesman ... ELIHU
word .. ETYMON, RADICAL
rooting out .... EVULSION
rootlet .... RADICEL
rootlike .... RHIZOID
rootstalk .. RHIZOME, GINGER
rootstock ... RHIZOME, ORRIS, PIP, ORIGIN, TARO, GINGER, ORRICE
rope ... CORD, LASSO, STRAND, TIE, FASTEN, MARLIN, CABLE
and pulley block .... TACKLE
cattle catcher's .... BOLA
cord tied to .... MARLINE
cowboy's .... RIATA, LASSO, LARIAT
dancer .... FUNAMBULIST
dancer's .... POY
fiber ...... IXTLE, ABACA, HEMP, JUTE, MAGUEY, GOMUTI, COIR, ISTLE, BAST, SISAL
flag .... LANYARD
for cable's end .. MARLINE, MARLING
for hanging .... HALTER, HEMP, NOOSE
frayed end of .. FAG END
gaff to deck .... VANG
guiding ... LONGE, GUY, LUNGE, DRAGLINE
guy .... VANG
horse trainer's ... LONGE
in .... LURE, ENTICE
knotted at end ..... COLT
lead .... LONGE
loop ... BIGHT, FRAP, LAP
mooring .... PAINTER
old .... JUNK
pulling .... TUG
ship's .... SHROUD, LANYARD, RATLINE, PAINTER, VANG, GUY, STAY, TYE, EARING
steadying ... GUY, VANG
tether .... LARIAT
thin ..... STRING, CORD
thread a .... REEVE
towing .... CORDELLE
walker ... FUNAMBULIST
wire .... CABLE
roped .... TETHERED, LASSOED
Roper, Elmo .... POLLSTER
ropy .... GLUTINOUS
roque .... CROQUET
Roquefort .... CHEESE
rorqual ..... FINBACK, WHALE, RAZORBACK
rosaceous .... ROSY
plant ..... STRAWBERRY, AGRIMONY
rosary ...... BEADS, CHAPLET, GARDEN
prayer ... PATERNOSTER, AVE, GLORIA PATRI
subject .... MYSTERY
rose .... RHODA, FLOWER ERYSIPELAS, PERFUME, NOZZLE, RAMBLER, DAMASK
aborigine boxing champ LIONEL
apple .... POMAROSA
Bowl players ...... UCLA
bush .... SHADBLOW, SASKATOON
extract .... ATTAR
garden .... ROSARY
mallow .... HIBISCUS, HOLLYHOCK
moss .... PORTULACA
of Sharon ...... ALTHEA
plant .... AVENS
petal oil .... ATTAR
rash .... ROSEOLA, RUBELLA, MEASLES
straggling ..... RAMBLER
time .... JUNE, SPRING
under the ..... SECRETLY, SUB ROSA
wild .. EGLANTINE, BRIER
roseate .... ROSY, BRIGHT
rosebay .... RHODODENDRON, OLEANDER
rosebush fruit .... HIP
roseola ...... MEASLES, RASH, RUBELLA
rosette .... COCKADE
rosin ..... RESIN, FLUX, ROZET
Rosinante ...... HORSE, JADE
master of ..... QUIXOTE
rosolio .... CORDIAL
Ross, flag-maker ...... BETSY
U.S. woman governor ... NELLIE
Rossetti, poet ..... CHRISTINA, DANTE
Rossini's opera .... OTELLO
Rossiya .... RUSSIA
roster .... LIST, ROLL
rostrum .... DAIS, BEAK, TRIBUNE, PLATFORM, PULPIT, STAGE
rosy .... BRIGHT, RUDDY ROSACEOUS, PINK(Y)
fingered goddess .... AURORA
rot .... DECAY, PUTREFY, DECOMPOSE, SPOIL, RET
slang ... BOSH, NONSENSE, RUBBISH
rota .... LIST, COURT, ROUTINE, ROUND, ROSTER, CLASSIS
member ...... AUDITOR
Rotarian, female .... ANN
rotate ... SPIN, TWIRL, WHEEL, GYRATE, ROLL, PAN, TURN, REVOLVE
unevenly .... WOBBLE
rotating device .... CAM, AXIS, SPINDLE, ROTOR, AXLE, REEL, DASHER
rotation .... REVOLUTION
rotch(e) .... DOVEKIE, AUK, GUILLEMOT, DOVEKEY
rote .. ROUTINE, MECHANICAL
by .... MEMORY
rotenone source .... DERRIS
rotgut .... WHISKY
rotifer .... ANIMALCULE
rotisserie .... GRILL
pin .... SKEWER
rotor .... STATOR
rotl .... WEIGHT
plural of .... ARTAL
rotten ...... DECAYED, FOUL, SPOILED, TAINTED, PUTRID, BAD, NASTY, FETID, RANK, ADDLE
rottenstone .... TRIPOLI
rotund ..... PLUMP, SONOROUS
roturier .... COMMONER
roue .... LIBERTINE, RAKE, DEBAUCHEE, RAKEHELL
rouge .... COSMETIC
rough ...... UNEVEN, SHAGGY, STORMY, RIOTOUS, CRUDE, VIOLENT, RAGGED, RUGGED, AGRESTIC, HARSH, RUDE, COARSE, JAGGED, HUBBLY
and disorderly .... LARRIKIN
and-tumble .. DISORDERLY
and-tumble fight .. MELEE, BRAWL
cloth .... TERRY, DENIM, SHAG, DUFFEL, DUFFLE
combining form .... TRACHY
edged .... EROSE
in speech .... GRUFF
make .... FRET, FRAY
manner .... GRUFF
skin .... SHAGREEN
sounding ..... RAUCOUS
water .... SEA
roughen ... FRET, CHAP, FRAY
roughly .... ABOUT
roughneck ...... GOON, HOOD, THUG, BULLY, ROWDY
roughness .... ASPERITY
roughshod, go .... TRAMPLE
rouleau .... ROLL
roulette color ... RED, BLACK
man .... CROUPIER
term ..... NOIR, ROUGE, MANQUE, BAS, PASSE
round .... COURSE, TOUR, SPHERICAL, GLOBULAR, CIRCULAR, PLUMP, ANNULAR, SALVO, GLOBOID
and plump ..... CHUBBY
make .... CIRCINATE
of applause ..... PLAUDIT
of duty ...... BEAT, TOUR
of play .... INNING
protuberance ..... UMBO, KNOB
Table knight .. LANCELOT, GAWAIN, BORS, KAY, BORT, BALIN, BALAN, GARETH, GERAINT, GALAHAD, MO(R)DRED, MORGA(I)N, TRISTRAM, TRISTAN, BEDIVERE, PERCIVAL, PARSIFAL, PELLEAS
trip .... EXCURSION
up .... RODEO, COLLECT, GATHER, RUSTLE, CORRAL
watchman's ...... TOUR
roundabout .... DEVIOUS, INDIRECT, CIRCUITOUS, JACKET, AMBAGIOUS
expression ..... AMBAGE, PERIPHRASIS

way ... AMBAGE, DETOUR
rounded ... FUSIFORM, GIBBOUS
projection .. LOBE, KNOB
rounder .... WATCHMAN, POLICEMAN, GUARD, SENTINEL, DRUNKARD
Roundhead .... PURITAN
roundly .... SEVERELY
roundup .... RODEO
roundworm .... LUMBRICOID, NEMATODE, ASCARID, PARASITE, STRONGYL(E)
roupy .... HOARSE
rouse ... WAKE, EXCITE, HAUL, REVEILLE, ROUST, STIR (UP)
rousing ...... STIRRING, BRISK
Rousseau, work by .... EMILE
roust ...... STIR (UP), ROUT, DRIVE (OUT)
roustabout ...... DECK HAND, LABORER
rout ... DEBACLE, ROUST, MOB, RABBLE, FLIGHT, DEFEAT
in a way .... SKUNK
route .... COURSE, WAY, FORWARD, ITINERARY, RUN
shortest .... BEELINE
routine ...... REGULAR, ROTA, ROT(T)E, CUSTOMARY, HUMDRUM
task ...... CHORE, CHARE
rove .... WANDER, ROAM, RAMBLE, GAD, CARD, RANGE
for plunder .... MARAUD, FORAGE
rover .... WANDERER, PIRATE, NOMAD, TARGET
roving for adventure .. ERRANT
row ..... LINE, OAR, PADDLE, SHINDY, SQUABBLE, FILE, BRAWL, DISPUTE, NOISE, QUARREL, CLAMOR, RUCKUS, KICK-UP
form in a .... ALINE, ALIGN
of cut grass ..... SWATH
of planted seeds .. DRILL
rowan .... ASH
rowboat .. CANOE, COBLE, GIG, GONDOLA, WHERRY, SKIFF, SCULL, SHELL, BANCA, CAIQUE
racing ..... GIG, SCULL, SHELL
warship's .... GALLEY
rowdy .... HOOD(LUM), PLUG-UGLY, LARRIKIN, ROUGH(NECK)
young .... HOOLIGAN
Rowe's (N.) rake ... LOTHARIO
rowel .... PRICK, SPUR
rowen .... GRASS, AFTERMATH, HAY
rower .... OAR(SMAN), GONDOLIER
seat of .... THWART
rowing contest ..... REGATTA
rowlock ..... POPPET, THOLE
Roxas, Philippine president ... MANUEL
Roy Rogers' horse ... TRIGGER
royal ..... KINGLY, IMPERIAL, NOBLE, AUGUST, REGIUS, PRINCELY, REGAL, MAJESTIC
authority ...... SCEPTER, SCEPTRE
color .... PURPLE
council, Oriental .. DIVAN
crown .. TIARA, DIADEM, CORONET
domain/realm .. KINGDOM
flush, part of .... ACE, KING, QUEEN, JACK, TEN
house .... TUDOR, PLANTAGENET, WINDSOR, STUART, HAPSBURG
initials .... HRH
palace .... COURT
residence .... PALACE, BALMORAL
seat .... THRONE
staff ...... SCEPTER, ROD
title .. DAUPHIN, ROI, REY, SIRE, EMPEROR, CZAR, TSAR, KING, PRINCE, INFANTA
royalist ..... CAVALIER, TORY
royalty .... SOVEREIGNTY
RSVP, part of ... REPONDEZ, S'IL, VOUS, PLAIT
rub ...... MASSAGE, ABRADE, POLISH, SCOUR, RASP, GRATE, GRIND, SAND
a-dub .... DRUMBEAT
out ..... EXPUNGE, KILL, ERASE, SCRAPE, MURDER
the wrong way .... IRRITATE, DISPLEASE
to brightness .... POLISH, FURBISH
with nose ...... NUZZLE
with oil/liniment .... EMBROCATE
"Rubaiyat" author .... OMAR (KHAYYAM)
rhyming .... AABA
rubasse .... QUARTZ
rubber ... PARA, CAOUTCHOUC, GUMS, MASSEUR, MASSAGIST, ERASER, GUAYULE, EBONITE
band .... ELASTIC
boot .... WADER
City .... AKRON
filler in ...... KAOLIN(E)
game, first .... LEG
hard .... EBONITE, VULCANITE
necking vehicle ... STAGE
plant ...... CAUCHO, ULE
product basis .... LATEX
ring .... GASKET
roller .... SQUEEGEE
sap .... LATEX
sheeting .... PLIOFILM
shrub .... GUAYULE
shoe .... GALOSH(E), GOLOSH(E)
stamp... APPROVE, DATER
stamp inker .... PAD
substance like .... GUTTA-PERCHA
synthetic ..... NEOPRENE, BUNA, BUTYLE, CARIFLEX
thread wound with cotton LASTEX
tree ...... ULE, SERINGA
rubberneck ...... SIGHTSEER, GAZE(R), CRANE
rubbers .... GUMSHOE, OVERSHOE, GALOSHES
rubbery .... ELASTIC
rubbing tool .... FILE
rubbish ... DEBRIS, DUST, JUNK, TRUMPERY, RAFF, DROSS, TRIPE, (TOMMY)ROT, TRUCK, REFUSE, TRASH, NONSENSE
collect .... SCAVENGE
mine .... STENT
pile .... DUMP
slang .... ROT
rubble .... DEBRIS, SCREE
rubdown .... MASSAGE
rube .... RUSTIC, YOKEL
rubefacient .. SALVE, PLASTER
rubella ...... MEASLES, RASH, RUBEOLA, ROSEOLA
rubellite .... TOURMALINE
rubeola ... MEASLES, RUBELLA
rubiaceous plant ..... COFFEE, GARDENIA, IPECAC, CINCHONA
Rubicon, he crossed the ...... CAESAR
rubicund .... RUDDY, FLORID, REDDISH, ROSY
Rubinstein opera ... DEMONIO
pianist ... ARTUR, ANTON
rubious .... RED
ruble, 1/100 of a ... KOPE(C)K
rubric ...... TITLE, HEADING, RED(DISH)
ruby ..... CORUNDUM, STONE, RED, SARDIUS
spinel .... BALAS
ruche ...... FRILL, TRIMMING
ruck ... STACK, HEAP, CREASE, PUCKER, FOLD, WRINKLE
ruckus ..... UPROAR, BRAWL, ROW, MELEE, FRAY, HASSLE
ruction ... UPROAR, QUARREL
rudbeckia ..... (CONE)FLOWER
rudd ... CARP, RED-EYE, FISH, VIREO
rudder .... HELM
guide with .... STEER
handle ... TILLER, WHEEL
ruddle .... KEEL
ruddock .... ROBIN
ruddy ...... RUBICUND, ROSY, SANGUINE, RED(DISH), FLUSH(ED), FLORID
rude ..... CRUDE, UNCIVIL, COARSE, BOORISH, GROSS, UNCOUTH, ROUGH, SAUCY, HARSH, IMPOLITE, GRUFF
dwelling ... HOVEL, HUT
rudimentary ...... VESTIGIAL, INCHOATE
rudiment(s) ... ABC, ELEMENTS, BEGINNINGS, VESTIGE, FIRST
rue .... DEPLORE, HERB, REGRET, REPENT, GRIEVE, LAMENT, BEWAIL

plant ..... LEMON, LIME, ORANGE
rueful ..... SORRY, PENITENT
rufescent .... REDDISH
ruff ..... COLLAR, SANDPIPER, PIGEON, FRAISE
female .... REEVE
turned down ...... FALL
ruff(e) .... FISH, PERCH
ruffian ... PLUG UGLY, BRAVO, HIGHBINDER, THUG, TOUGH(IE), GOON, HOODLUM, HOOLIGAN
ruffle .... DISTURB, FRILL, FURBELOW, DERANGE, RIPPLE, WRINKLE, SHUFFLE, PLEAT, FLOUNCE
rufous ...... REDDISH, RUSTY
rug .. MAT, RUNNER, DRUGGET, FOOTCLOTH, MAUD, CARPET, TOUPEE, WILTON
ruga .. FOLD, CREASE, WRINKLE
rugate ..... FOLDED, CREASED
rugby .... FOOTBALL
football .... RUGGER
formation .. SCRUM(MAGE)
rival .... ETON
rugged ..... UNEVEN, STORMY, RUDE, STURDY, CRAGGY, HARDY, ROUGH, HARD, ROBUST
rugose/rugous ...... RIDGED, CORRUGATED
ruin ..... WRECK(AGE), BANE, SPOIL, HAVOC, DIDDLE, LOUSE UP, DOWNFALL, DESTROY
ruinous .... HARMFUL
ruins .... DEBRIS
rule ...... PRECEPT, DECISION, ORDER, NORM, REIGN, LAW, MAXIM, REGULATION, CUSTOM, PRESCRIPT, LINE, GOVERN, HABIT, STANDARD, CRITERION, REGIME(N), SWAY
as a .... USUALLY
book ... HOYLE, MANUAL
Britannia composer ..... ARNE
of thumb basis .... PRACTICE, EXPERIENCE
out ..... EXCLUDE, OMIT
ruler .... FERULE, EMIR, PRINCE, KING, MONARCH, GERENT, EMEER, QUEEN, POTENTATE, REGENT, TSAR, CZAR, RAJAH, GOVERNOR
absolute .. SHAH, TYRANT, DESPOT
amuser of a ..... CLOWN, JESTER
cruel .... DESPOT
hereditary ...... DYNAST
length of a .... FOOT
wife of .... EMPRESS, RANEE, QUEEN, TSARINA, CZARINA, REINA
rules of conduct .... CODE
Order author ... ROBERT
ruling .... PREVALENT, DECISION, LINE
party .... MAJORITY

Rum .... ROME, BAD, LIQUOR, TAF(F)IA, POOR, BACARDI
dessert .... BABA
source .... MOLASSES, SUGAR CANE
Rumanian .... MAGYAR
capital ..... BUCHAREST
city ...... BRASOV, CLUJ, PLOESTI, ARAD, IASI, ORADEA, YASSY, JASSY, TIMISOARA, LASI, GALATI
coin ..... LEU, LEY, BAN
composer .... ENESCO
district .... DOBRUJA
dramatist ...... IONESCO
folk dance .... HORA
king .... CAROL, (MIHAI) MICHAEL
monetary unit .. LEI, LEU, LEY
native .... MAGYAR, MOLDAVIAN
part of .... WALACHIA
premier........ MAURER, CEAUSESCU, ANTONESCU
river ..... ALUTA, ARGES, SERETH, CERNA
rumba .... DANCE
exponent .. CUBAN, CUGAT
rumble .... FREE-FOR-ALL, MELEE, LUMBER, ROLL
seat .... DICKEY
rumdinger .... ONER
rumen .... GULLET, CUD, PAUNCH
ruminant .. MEDITATIVE, GOAT, LLAMA, CATTLE, BISON, DEER, GIRAFFE, ALPACA, YAK, SHEEP, ANTELOPE, CAMEL
chew of .... CUD
stomach .... RUMEN, (AB)OMASUM, RETICULUM
ruminate .... PONDER, CHEW, MUSE, MEDITATE, REFLECT
rummage .. RANSACK, SEARCH, SALE, GRUB
rummer .... CUP, GLASS
rummy ..... GIN, ODD, QUEER, STRANGE, DRUNKARD, SOT, TOPER
bonus, sometimes .... ROODLES
game like .... COONCAN
slang .... DRUNK
strategy .... KNOCK
rumor ..... GOSSIP, HEARSAY, BRUIT, NOISE, REPORT, ONDIT, GRAPEVINE
rump .. ARSE, CROUP, BREECH, BUTTOCKS, CUT, FAG END
Rumpelstiltskin ..... DWARF
rumple .... MUSS, TOUSLE, DISHEVEL, CREASE, WRINKLE
rumpus .. DISTURBANCE, ROW, UPROAR, POTHER, STIR
rumrunner .... SMUGGLER, BOOTLEGGER
run ...... RACE, SCUD, LOPE, TRIP, SPRINT, OPERATE, SPEED, INCUR, LEAK, SPREAD, CREEP, PUBLISH, SMUGGLE, VIE WITH, TROT, FLOW, HIE, SCORE, ROUTE
across .... MEET, ENCOUNTER
after ..... CHASE, PURSUE
away .... ABSCOND, FLEE, ELOPE, DECAMP, BOLT
baseball .... HOME
cricket .... BYE
down .... SUMMARY, OUTLINE
in .... INSERT, FIGHT, INCLUDE, ARREST
in the long .. ULTIMATELY, EVENTUALLY
of-the-mill .. ORDINARY, AVERAGE, SO-SO
off the tracks ... DERAIL
over .... SPILL
through .... PIERCE, REEVE
runabout .... ROADSTER
runagate ..... DESERTER, RAT, VAGABOND, FUGITIVE, DRIFTER
runaround .... EXCUSES
runaway .... DESERTER, FUGITIVE
slave .... MAROON
runcible spoon .... FORK
runcinate ...... SAWTOOTHED
rundle .... RUNG
rundlet .... CASK, BARREL
rune ..... SONG, VERSE, POEM
rung .. RUNDLE, SPOKE, STAVE, CROSSBAR, STEP
runic alphabet ..... FUTHARK
runnel ..... BROOK, RIVULET, RUNLET, CHANNEL
runner .... AGENT, STOLON, COURIER, SMUGGLER, GATE, BLADE, FLAGELLUM, SKI, SKATE, CONTENDER, MESSENGER, RACER, SKEE, ERRAND BOY
way of .... LANE
running ... MELTING, LINEAR, CONTINUOUS, CURRENT, EASY, FLOWING, CURSIVE, CREEPING, CLIMBING
knot .... NOOSE
runt ... DWARF, PYGMY, CHIT
runway .... PATH, RAMP, (AIR)STRIP, TRACK, CHUTE, TROUGH, CHANNEL
rupee, newly minted ... SICCA
weight of .... TOLA
rupees, 15 .... MOHUR
rupture ...... BREAK, HERNIA, BREACH, BURST
support .... TRUSS
"Rur" characters .... ROBOTS
rural ...... RUSTIC, GEOPONIC, BUCOLIC, PASTORAL, AGRESTIC, ARCADIAN
abode ... BOWER, VILLA, HACIENDA
building .... BARN
opposed to ...... URBAN
poem .... ECLOGUE, PASTORAL
sound .. MOO, LOW, BAA,

BLEAT, CROW
ruse ... STRATEGEM, ARTIFICE, TRICK, DODGE
rush ... SURGE, DASH, CHARGE, DRIVE, HURRY, RACE, HASTE, SPATE, ONSLAUGHT, PRESS, TORRENT, CANDLE, REED, SCRIMMAGE, SPEED, HIE, HIGHTAIL, COURT, GUST
furiously .... RAMP
hour usually ... NINE(AM), NOON, FIVE(PM)
line (football) member ... GUARD, TACKLE, CENTER
of water .... WASH
violently ..... RAMP(AGE)
rusk .... BREAD, CAKE, BISCUIT, ZWIEBACK
Russ .... RUSSIAN, NIEMEN
Russell, Miss .... CONNIE, ROSALIND, GAIL, LILLIAN, JANE
philosopher .. BERTRAND
russet .. CLOTH, BROWN, APPLE
Russia ... ROSSIYA, MUSCOVY, RUTHENIA
capital ..... PETROGRAD
founder of .... IVAN
Russian ... RED, COMMUNIST, COMMIE, MUSCOVITE
administrative body ..... ZEMSTVO
airline ...... AEROFLOT
alcoholic drink .. KVASS, VODKA
anarchist ... KROPOTKIN
antelope .... SAIGA
aristocrat .... BOYAR(D)
assembly .... RADA
astronaut ..... GAGARIN
ballet dancer .. MASSINE, NUREYEV, PAVLOVA
capital .... MOSCOW, NOVGOROD, PETROGRAD
carriage ... TARANTAS(S), TROIKA, DROS(H)KY
cart .... TELEGA
cathedral .... SOBOR
cereal .... EMMER
chalet .... DACHA
chess champion .... ALEKHINE, BOTVINNIK, TAL, PETROSIAN, SMYSLOV, SPASSKY
choreographer .. MASSINE
citadel .... KREMLIN
city ..... OREL, MOSCOW, KIEV, OMSK, TASHKENT, SAMARKAND, BOKHARA, GOMEL, PSKOV, KIEV
coin ...... CHERVONETS, IMPERIAL, POLTINA, RUBLE, KOPE(C)K
collective farm .... KOLKHOZ
comedian ...... RAIKIN
community .... MIR
composer ..... BORODIN, STRAVINSKY, PROKOFIEV
cooperative ...... ARTEL
Cossack .... TATAR
council ... SOVIET, DUMA
country estate ... DACHA
dancer .... DANILOVA, PAVLOVA
dandelion .. KOK-SAGYZ
dramatist .... GOGOL
drink .. VODKA, KVAS(S), QUASS
dwelling .... ISBA
edict .... UKASE
empress .... TSARINA
exile's place .... SIBERIA
farmer .... KULAK
fur .. KARAKUL, CARACUL
greeting ...... BEAR HUG
guitar ...... BALALAIKA
guild .... ARTEL
gulf .... AZOV
hemp ... RINE, KONOPEL
holy picture .. IKON, ICON
hood .... BASHLYK
horse team ..... TROIKA
horseman ...... COSSACK
hut .... ISBA
ibex .... TEK
imperial order ... UKASE
inland sea .. ARAL, AZOF
James Bond .... ZAKHOV
lake ..... BAIKAL, ARAL, NEVA, LADOGA, ONEGA, LACHA, TOPO, ILMEN
leather ..... YUFT, JUPTI
Little .... UKRAINIAN
log hut ...... ISPA, ISBA
mammal........ DESMAN
marshal ...... ZHUKOV, KUTUZOV
measure .... VERST, ARSHIN, ARCHINE, LOF
mister .... GOSPODIN
monarchy founder ...... RURIK
monetary unit .... RUBLE
"mother of cities" .. KIEV
mountain .. ALAI, URAL
museum .... HERMITAGE
musical instrument ..... BALALAIKA
name for Russia .... ROSSIYA
negative/no .... NYET
news agency .... NOVOSTI, TASS
novelist .... TOLSTOI, TOLSTOY, GORKI, GORKY
oboe .... SZOPELKA
oil center .... BAKU
operatic singer .... CHALIAPIN
painter .... CHAGALL
parliament .... D(O)UMA
peasant .... KULAK, MUZHIK, MUZJIK
peasant cap ...... ASKA
peasants' district .... VOLOST
peninsula .... CRIMEA
physiologist ..... PAVLOV
pianist ..... RACHMANN
plain ... STEPPE, TUNDRA
plane .... MIG, ILYUSHIN
poet .... PUSHKIN
pound .... POOD
premier ...... KOSYGIN, STALIN, BULGANIN, KHRUSCHEV, MALENKOV
president ..... SHVERNIK
prison .... ETAPE
region ..... MARI, SIBERIA
resort ... YALTA, ODESSA, SOCHI
revolutionary leader ..... LENIN, KERENSKY, TROTSKY
river ...... VOLGA, NEVA, ONEGA, DONETS, OREL, LENA, URAL, DVINA, UFA
ruling family .... ROMANOFF, ROMANOV
saint .... OLGA
scarf .... BABUSHKA
sea .... ARAL
seaport .... PETSAMO
secret service .... CHEKA, KGB, GAY-PAY-OO, OGPU, NKVD, MVD
slang .... COMMIE
soup .... BORSCH
soviet, rural ..... VOLOST
spacecraft ..... SPUTNIK, VOYUZ
squadron ..... ESKADRA
stockade .... ETAPE
teapot .... SAMOVAR
trade union ...... ARTEL
urn .... SAMOVAR
vehicle .... TROIKA
villa .... DACHA
village .... MIR
violinist......... ELMAN, ZIMBALIST
wagon .... TELEGA
weight .. DOLA, POOD, PUD
wheat .... EMMER
whip .... KNOUT
windstorm .... BURAN
wolfhound .... ALAN, BORZOI
yes .... DA
youth organization .... KOMSOMOL
Russo-Japanese warship ...... MIKASA
rust .... OXIDE, ERODE, VERDIGRIS, FUNGUS, CORRODE, AERUGO
colored .... RUFOUS
fungus .... AECIA
life cycle of ..... TELIAL
on bronze .... PATINA
plant .... FERRUGO
sorus .... TELIUM
rustic ... YOKEL, CHURL, RUBE, BUCOLIC, GEOPONIC, CLOD, BOOR(ISH), HIND, RURAL, BUM(P)KIN, ARTLESS, ARCADIAN, HAYSEED, HICK, HOBNAIL
lover .... SWAIN
peasant ...... AGRESTIAN
pipe .... REED, CORN
rustle ..... SWISH, SUSURRATE

of silk skirt .. FROUFROU
up ... COLLECT, FORAGE
rustler .... THIEF, ROBBER
object of .... CATTLE
rustling .... SUSURRANT, SWISHING, FROUFROU
sound ..... SUSURROUS, SOUGH, SWISH
Rustum's son .... SOHRAB
rusty .... SHABBY
rut ...... GROOVE, FURROW, TRACK, HEAT, ROUTINE
rutabaga ..... TURNIP, SWEDE
rutaceous plant .... RUE, ORANGE, LEMON, LIME
Ruth, husband of ...... BOAZ
mother-in-law of .. NAOMI
sister of .... EILEEN
son of .... OBED
Ruthenia .... RUSSIA
Ruthenian .... UKRAINIAN
ruthless ...... PITILESS, CRUEL
rutilate ..... GLOW, GLITTER, GLEAM
Ruy Diaz de Bivar .. (EL) CID
Rwanda capital ...... KIGALI
neighbor ...... BURUNDI
people .... HUTU
president ...... KAYIBANDA
rye .... RIE, GYPSY, GRASS, CEREAL, WHISKY, GENTLEMAN
disease .... BLACKRUST, ERGOT
grass .... DARNEL
liquor .... WHISK(E)Y
ryot .... PEASANT
Ryukyu island ..... OKINAWA

S

S-curve .... OGEE, ESS
Greek .... SIGMA
Hebrew .... SIN
letter .... ESS
mark .... POTHOOK
shaped .... SIGMATE, SIGMOID, ESS
shaped molding .... OGEE
shaped seat .... TETE-A-TETE, VIS-A-VIS
shaped worm .... ESS
sound .... HISS
Sa, in chemistry .. SAMARIUM
Saar capital ... SAARBRUCKEN
Saarinen, architect ..... EERO
Saba .... SHEBA
Sabah capital ...... JESSELTON, KOTA KINABALU
part of .... LABUAN
peak .... KINABALU
sabadilla alkaloid .. VERATRIA, VERATRIN(E)
Sabaist's object of worship .... STARS
sabalo .... MILKFISH
Sabatini, novelist ..... RAFAEL
Sabbath .. SATURDAY, SUNDAY
Sabbatical privilege ..... REST, LEAVE
saber ... SWORD, YATAG(H)AN
toothed animal .... TIGER
sable ...... BLACK, FUR, FELT, DARK, MUSTELINE, SKUNK, SOBOL, LEMMING
animal like ..... MARTEN, WEASEL
fur .... ZIBEL(L)INE
imitation ..... KOLINSKY
sablefish .... BESHOW
sabot .... (WOODEN)SHOE, PATTEN, CLOG, DINGHY
Sabrina river .... SEVERN
sabulous ..... SANDY, GRITTY
Sac ... INDIAN, SAUK, POUCH, VENTER, BURSA, CYST, VESICLE, ASCUS
cavity like ...... BLISTER
part of ... STRATEGIC, AIR, COMMAND
small .... SACCULE
spore .... ASCUS
sacaton .... GRASS, HAY
saccate .... POUCHLIKE
saccharine .. SWEET, HONEYED, SIRUPY, SUGARY
saccharize .... FERMENT
saccharose ... SUCROSE, SUGAR
saccule .... SAC, BOSS
sacerdotal .... PRIESTLY, HIERATIC
sachem .... CHIEF, SAGAMORE
sachet ... PAD, BAG, POWDER
Sacs, Ger. playwright .. HANS
trade of .... COBBLER
Sachsen .... SAXONY
sack ... BAG, JACKET, SACQUE, DISMISS(AL), DISCHARGE, PLUNDER, RAVAGE, POKE, LOOT, BED, BASE, WINE, POUCH, GUNNY, PILLAGE
making cloth .. OSNABURG
sackbut-like instrument ...... LYRE, TROMBONE
sackcloth and ____ .... ASHES
symbol of .... PENITENCE, MOURNING, REMORSE
sacking .... BURLAP
sacque .... JACKET, SACK
sacrament .... BAPTISM, PENANCE, MATRIMONY, CONFIRMATION, EUCHARIST, MASS
sacrarium .. CHANCEL, SHRINE, SANCTUARY
sacred ..... HOLY, HALLOWED, VENERATED, INVIOLATE, DIVINE, SACROSANCT, INVIOLABLE, PIOUS, BLESSED, SAINT
beetle .... SCARAB
bird .... IBIS
book ...... BIBLE, KORAN
bull .... APIS, HAPI
chest .... CIST
city ..... MEDINA, MECCA, JERUSALEM, BENARES
College member .... CARDINAL
combining form .. HIERO, HAGI(O)
container ..... PYX, CIST, AMA
cord .... KUSTI
cow ...... UNTOUCHABLE
fig tree .... PIPAL
food .... MANNA
fountain ... HIPPOCRENE
hymn........... PSALM
image ..... PIETA, ICON, IKON
language .... PALI
literature .... VEDA
make .... SANCTIFY, CONSECRATE, BLESS, HALLOW
melody .... CHORALE
music .... MOTET
object .... RELIC
ode .... HYMN
opposed to .... PROFANE, SECULAR
picture .... ICON
place .. SHRINE, SANCTUM
plant .... RAGTREE
poem ..... PSLAM, HYMN
prohibition .... TABU, TABOO
relic .... HALIDOM
scriptures .... KORAN, BIBLE
shield .... ANCILE
song ..... MOTET, PSALM
things, traffic in .. SIMONY
tree ..... PIPAL, BO(TREE)
wine vessel .... AMA
word .... LOGOS, OM
writer .. HAGIOGRAPHER
writing ..... SCRIPTURE, AVESTA
sacredness .... SANCTITY
sacrifice .... OFFERING, OBLATION, COST
burning place of .... PILE
by killing ..... IMMOLATE
god demanding .... MOLOCH, MOLECH
human .... SUTTEE
object of .... HOMAGE, APPEASEMENT, ATONEMENT, EXPIATION
place of .... ALTAR
play, in baseball ... BUNT, FLY
sacrificial animal ...... LAMB
block .... ALTAR
fire .... IGNI
offering .... IMMOLATION, HIERA, LAMB
rite .... LIBATION
table .... ALTAR
sacrilege .... DESECRATION, PROFANATION
sacrilegious .... PROFANE, IRREVERENT, BLASPHEMOUS
sacrist(an) .... SEXTON

sacristy .... VESTRY
sacrosanct ..... DIVINE, HOLY, SACRED, INVIOLABLE
sad .... BAD, DEJECTED, DOLEFUL, TRISTE, DOLOROUS, BLUE, DOLENT, DISMAL
  sack .... BOLO
saddle ..... LOAD, ENCUMBER, SEAT, PAD, PANEL
  attachment ..... HOLSTER
  bag .... ALFORJA
  band .... GIRTH
  blanket .... TILPAH
  bow .... POMMEL
  cloth ..... PANEL, MANTA
  colloquial ..... PIGSKIN
  cover for ..... MOCHILA
  footrest .... STIRRUP
  front part ..... POMMEL
  gaiter .... GAMBADO
  girth .... CINCH
  gun case .... HOLSTER
  horse .... NAG, PALFREY, REMUDA, HACK
  legging .... GAMBADO
  lining .... PANEL
  pack .... APAREJO
  pad .... CORONA
  part ... GIRTH, POMMEL, CINCH, STIRRUP, CANTLE, LATIGO, PAD
  rear part .... CANTLE
  seat behind ..... PILLION
  stirrup .... GAMBADO
  strap ..... GIRTH, CINCH
Sadducee, opposite of .... PHARISEE
sadness ... PATHOS, DOLENTE, DOLOR
sadhi .... TSADI
sadiron .... FLATIRON
sadism .... MALTREATMENT
sadistic .... CRUEL
safari ...... JOURNEY, TREK, EXPEDITION, CARAVAN
safe ... PRUDENT, CAUTIOUS, VAULT, SECURE
  conduct .. PASS, CONVOY, PASSPORT
  cracker ..... YEGG(MAN)
safeblower .. PETERMAN, YEGG
safeguard ... PROTECT, PASS, CONVOY, GUARD
safekeeping .... CUSTODY, STORAGE
safety .... SECURITY
  device .... FENDER, MAE WEST, BUMPER, ARMOR, CATCH, VALVE
  lamp .... DAVY
  place of .... HAVEN, REFUGE, SANCTUARY, HARBOR, ISLAND
saffron .... DYE, PLANT, SEASONING, YELLOW, CROCUS
safrol(e) .... OIL
sag .... SINK, DROOP, CURVE, HANG, WILT, DECLINE, DRIFT, LEEWAY
saga ...... EPIC, EDDA, TALE, LEGEND, ILIAD
sagacious .... PERCEPTIVE, SHREWD, DISCERNING, ASTUTE, WISE, SAPIENT
sagacity ... ACUMEN, WISDOM
sagamore .... SACHEM
sage ... WISE, SOLON, NESTOR, PLANT, MINT, SCHOLAR, SEER, SAPIENT, HERB
  scarlet .... SALVIA
  hen .... GROUSE
  of Emporia ...... WHITE
Sagebrush State ..... NEVADA
sagger .... (FIRE)CLAY
Sagitta ... ARROW, KEYSTONE, CONSTELLATION
sagittary .... CENTAUR
sago .... STARCH, PALM, GOMUTI
saguaro .... CACTUS
Sahara ... DESERT, WASTELAND
  fertile area ...... FEZZAN
  like the .... ARID
  wind .... LESTE
sahib .... SIR, MASTER
saiga .... ANTELOPE
Saigon Chinese district .... CHOLON
sail .... CANVAS, GLIDE, FLOAT, NAVIGATE, CRUISE, LUG, KITE, VELA, VOYAGE, SPANKER, JIGGER
  around the world .... CIRCUMNAVIGATE
  bellying part of ... BUNT
  close to the wind ... LUFF, POINT
  corner .... CLEW
  edge of .... LUFF
  fastener .... CLEW
  fore-and-aft ... SPANKER, MIZ(Z)EN
  free edge of ...... LEECH
  furl .... REEF
  haul up .... TRICE
  hoist .... CLUE-UP
  ice .... SCOOTER
  kind of .. JIB, FOREROYAL, MAIN, ROYAL, LATEEN
  loop .... CRINGLE
  near the wind ..... LUFF
  out to sea ..... OUTSTAND
  part of .... REEF
  poetic .... SHEET
  reduce .... REEF
  ring .... CRINGLE
  rope ..... HALYARD, TYE
  specified distance ... LOG
  square .... LUG
  tackle .... HALYARD
  tapering cloth .... GORE
  triangular .. LATEEN, JIB
sailboat ... VINTA, SAIC, SLOOP, CAIQUE, SMACK, DHOW, BARK, BARQUE, SKIFF, YACHT, KUMPIT, YAWL, KETCH
sailfish ...... (BASKING)SHARK
  kin of .... MARLIN
sailing, oblique .. LOXODROMICS
  race .... REGATTA
  raft .... BALSA
  vessel .... SCHOONER, GALLEON, FRIGATE, KETCH, SLOOP, YAWL
sailor ... MARINER, GOB, TAR, SALT, LASCAR, NAVYMAN, JACK, SEADOG, DECK HAND, SHIPMAN, SEAMAN, HAT, SARTOR
  bed of .... HAMMOCK
  clumsy .... LUBBER
  contentious .. SEA LAWYER
  drink of .... GROG
  experienced .. SHELLBACK
  jersey .... FROCK
  kidnap .... SHANGHAI
  inexperienced, new ...... LANDSMAN, LUBBER
  prospeotive ..... MIDDY
sailor's bad luck ..... JONAH, JONAS
  biscuit .... TACK
  call .... AHOY
  choice .. PORGY, PIGFISH
  church .... BETHEL
  cord .. LANYARD, LANIARD
  dish .... SCOUSE
  handicraft ... SCRIMSHAW
  hat ...... SOU(TH)WESTER
  jumper .... BLOUSE
  leave ..... FURLOUGH
  mess tub .... KID
  patron saint ...... ELMO
  patroness ...... EULALIA
  quarters .... FO(RE)C(A)S(T)LE
  rebellion .... MUTINY
  social call .... GAM
  song .... SHANT(E)Y, CHANTEY
  sword .... CUTLAS(S)
  underwear .... SKIVY
  work song ... SHANT(E)Y, CHANTEY
  "yes" .... AYE-AYE
sain .... CROSS, BLESS
saint (see patron)..... SACRED, CANONIZE, HOLY, BLESSED, SAN(TA)
  Anthony's fire .... ERYSIPELAS
  Bernard .... DOG
  Andrew's Cross .... SATIRE, SALTIER
  Bernard monk's concern .. TRAVELER, WAYFARER
  declare person a .... CANONIZE
  Elmo's fire ... CORPOSANT
  homage to a ...... DULIA
  Joan character .. DAUPHIN
  John's bread ..... CAROB, ALGAROBA
  John's evil .... EPILEPSY
  Laurent, fashion stylist .. YVES
  memorial of .... RELIC
  Patrick's Day celebrant .. IRISH
  sacred image of .... ICON, (E)IKON
  tomb of .... SHRINE
  worshiper ... HAGIOLATER
  Vitus' dance .... CHOREA
Saint's day .... FIESTA

saintly .... PIOUS
saints, author of lives of ...... HAGIOGRAPHER
catalogue/list of .... DIPTYCH, HAGIOLOGY, CANON
register ...... MENOLOGY
rule by ... HAGIOCRACY, HAGIARCHY, THEOCRACY
worship of .. HAGIOLATRY
sake ... PURPOSE, END, CAUSE, BEHALF, BENEFIT, MOTIVE, ACCOUNT
saker .... FALCON
Sakhalin .... KARAFUTO
Saki .... MUNRO
Sakti .... MAYA
sal volatile ...... HARTSHORN
salaam .... OBEISANCE, GREETING, BOW
salable .... VENDIBLE, MARKETABLE
salacious .... OBSCENE, LUSTFUL
salad ... LETTUCE, (COLD)DISH, (COLE)SLAW
days .... TEENS
dressing ... MAYONNAISE, REMO(U)LADE
fruit .... MACEDOINE
green .... DANDELION, UDO, CRESS(E), ENDIVE
herb ..... CRESS, ENDIVE
kind of .... TOSSED
leaves .... ESCAROLE, SORREL
vegetable .... ENDIVE, CHICORY, SUCCORY
Saladin's foes .... CRUSADERS
salamander .... REPTILE, EFT, NEWT, TRITON, POKER, HELLBENDER, MUD PUPPY, LIZARD, WATER DOG, AXOLTL
Salambria .... PENEUS
salami .... SAUSAGE
salary ... EMOLUMENT, WAGE, COMPENSATION, PAY, STIPEND, SCREW
additional to .. PERQUISITE
increase .... RAISE
sale .... SELLING, DEAL, VENDITION, MARKET, BARTER
incentive .... REBATE
kind of .... AUCTION, INVENTORY, CLEARANCE, CASH, RUMMAGE, FIRE
Salem witchcraft trial judge .. SEWALL
salep .... TUBER
drink from ...... SALOOP
source of .... ORCHID
saleratus ...... BAKING SODA
sales talk .... PATTER, PITCH, LINE, SPIEL
salesman ... CLERK, DRUMMER
salicaceous tree ..... WILLOW, POPLAR
salicin .... GLUCOSIDE
saliferous ..... SALINE, SALTY
salient ... CAPERING, LEAPING, PROMINENT
salientian .... TOAD, FROG
salina ... POND, LAKE, MARSH
saline ...... SALTY, MARINAL
solution .... BRINE
Salish .... INDIAN, FLATHEAD
saliva ..... SPIT(TLE), SPUTUM
enzyme .... PTYALIN, AMYLASE
excessive secretion of .... PTYALISM
resembling ..... SIALOID
running from mouth .... SLAVER, DRIVEL, DROOL
wet/smear with .. SLOBBER
salix ... ITEA, OSIER, WILLOW
salle .... ROOM
sallet .... HELMET
sallow .... PASTY, PALE, PARLOUS, WILLOW, OSIER
sally ... SORTIE, QUIP, RETORT, JAUNT, EXCURSION, WITTICISM, RIPOSTE, ISSUE, RUSH OUT, JEST, JOKE
Lunn .... TEACAKE
with the fan ...... RAND
salmacis .... NYMPH
salmagundi ...... POTPOURRI, MEDLEY, OLIO, MIXTURE
salmon .... GRILSE, MORT, CHINOOK, JACK, QUINNAT, SPROD, COHO, SOCKEYE, HOLIA, CHINUCK, OUANANICHE
chinook ...... QUINNAT
color .... PINK
dog .... CHUM, KETA
eggs .... ROE
eggs relish .... CAVIAR(E)
female ... BAGGIT, RAUN
gristle .... GIB
hook .... KIP, GIB
humpback ...... HADDO, HOLIA
male ..... COCK, KIPPER
net .... MAUD
one year old ... BLUECAP
quinnat ...... CHINOOK
red .... SOCKEYE
running up river .... ANADROMOUS
salted .... LOX
silver .... COHO
smoked .... LOX
trout ...... NAMAYCUSH, STEELHEAD, HARDHEAD
young ..... SMOLT, PARR, GRILSE, SAMLET
salmonoid ...... STEELHEAD, TROUT, NAMAYCUSH
Salome's parent ... HEROD(IAS)
salon .... GALLERY, HALL, LEVEE, DRAWING ROOM, ART SHOW, SHOP
Salonika .... THERMA
saloon .... BAR, HALL, SEDAN, GINMILL, BARRELHOUSE, DIVE, DRAMSHOP, GROGGERY, HONKY-TONK, TAVERN, CANTINA, OASIS, GROGSHOP
keeper .... PUBLICAN
saloop .... DRINK
Salop .... SHROPSHIRE
salpa .... TUNICATE
salt ..... SAL, HUMOR, SAILOR, SEASON, TAR, BRINE, BORAX, PICRATE, WIT, NACL
away ...... STORE, SAVE
acid .... OLEATE
alkaline .... BORAX
bed .... VAT
bottle .... CRUET, CASTER, CASTOR
chemical .... ESTER
crystalline ...... NITER, NITRE
deposit .... LICK
factory .... SALTERN
lake .... SINK
malic acid ...... MALATE
marsh .... SALINA
meat .... SALAMI
organic .... ESTER
pertaining to .... SALINE
pond .... SALINA
pork .... SOWBELLY
preserve with ..... CORN
resembling ..... HALOID
rheum .... ECZEMA
rock .... HALITE
soluble .... SALAR
spring ..... LICK, SALINA
tax .... GABELLE
tree .... ATLE, TAMARISK
water .... BRINE
saltant ... LEAPING, DANCING, JUMPING
saltation .... PALPITATION, MUTATION, LEAP(ING), BEATING, DANCING
salted .... CORNED
saltpeter .... NITER, NITRE
saltworks ...... SALTERN, SALINA
saltwort ...... BARILLA, KALI
salty ...... PUNGENT, WITTY, PIQUANT, SHARP, BRINY SALINE
salubrious .... SALUTARY
Salus .... HYGEIA
concern of ...... HEALTH, PROSPERITY
salutary .... SALUBRIOUS, HEALTHFUL, BENEFICIAL, WHOLESOME, HEALTHY
salutation .... GREETING, WELCOME, SALAAM, AVE, HAIL, BOW, ALOHA
salute ..... GREET, WELCOME, BOW, TIP, HAIL, KISS, CURTSY
flag .... DIP
gun .... SALVO
salvage .... SAVE, RESCUE
salvation .... RESCUE, REDEMPTION
Army founder ... BOOTH
salve ...... SOOTHE, PLASTER, BALM, UNGUENT, DEMULCENT, NARD, CHRISM, LOTION, HAIL, ASSUAGE, SMOOTH, OINTMENT, POMADE
salver .... TRAY, WAITER
salvia .... PLANT, SAGE
salvo .... BROADSIDE, FUSILLADE, VOLLEY, SALUTE,

EVASION, EXCUSE
Samantha, actress .... EGGAR
samara .... KEY FRUIT, CHAT
tree bearing .... ASH, ELM
Samaritan magician ... MAGUS
sambar ... DEER, RUSA, MAHA
sambuke-like instrument ..... HARP
same .... DITTO, ALIKE, IDENTICAL, EQUAL, IDEM, SIMILAR
combining form ... HOMO
Samedi .... SATURDAY
samiel .... SIMOOM
samisen-like instrument ...... BANJO
samite .... LAME
samlet .... PARR, SALMON
Samoa .... NAVIGATORS
Samoan .... POLYNESIAN
bird .... IAO
capital .... TUTUILA
city .... APIA
cloth .... TAPA
clothes .... PAREUS
costume ...... PULETASI
council .... FONO
island ... SAVAII, UPOLU, TUTUILA
loincloth ..... LAVA-LAVA
maiden .... TAUPO
mollusk .... ASI
seaport .... APIA
waist cloth ... LAVA-LAVA
warrior .... TOA
samovar .... TEAPOT, URN
samp .... GRITS, HOMINY, PORRIDGE, (CORN)MEAL
sampan .... BOAT
samphire .... GLASSWORT
sample ... SPECIMEN, PATTERN, EXAMPLE, TASTE, TEST
cloth .... SWATCH
sampler .... TASTER
sampler item .... MOTTO
"Samson and Delilah" composer ... SAINT SAENS
Samson's deathplace .... GAZA
mistress .... DELILAH
vulnerable part ..... HAIR
Samuel .... PROPHET
parent of ..... HANNAH, ELKANAH
son of .... ABIA
teacher .... ELI
samurai ..... WARRIOR, RONIN
San .... SAINT
Antonio shrine ... ALAMO
Francisco .... FRISCO
Marino mount ... TITANO
Marino rulers ... REGENTS
sanatory .... CURATIVE
sanbenito wearer .. PENITENT, HERETIC
Sancho Panza's master .... (DON) QUIXOTE
sanctify .... PURIFY, CONSECRATE, HALLOW, BLESS
sanctimonious .... DEVOUT
sanction .... APPROVAL, LAW, SUPPORT, FIAT, DECREE, RATIFY, AMEN, IMPRIMATUR, APPROVE, PERMIT, FIRMAN, ENDORSE
sanctity ... HOLINESS, PURITY
sanctuary ... CHURCH, REFUGE, HAVEN, TEMPLE, SHELTER, BEMA, ASYLUM, FANE, SHRINE, GRIT, HALIDOM(E)
animal/bird .... RESERVATION
portable ... TABERNACLE
sanctum .... STUDY, DEN, ADYTUM, SMOOTH, POLISH
sand .... GRIT, COURAGE, POLISH, SMOOTH, BEACH
bank ...... CAY, SHOAL
bar .... SHOAL, SPIT, SHELF, REEF
dab .... FLATFISH
deposit .... ESKER
dollar ..... SEA URCHIN
eel .... LA(U)NCE
flea ... CHIGOE, CHIGGER
George ..... DUDEVANT, DUPIN
hill .... DUNE, DENE
launce .... EEL
lily .... SOAPROOT
lot game ..... BASEBALL
living in .. ARENICOLOUS
mound ..... DENE, DUNE
particles ..... SILT, GRIT
ridge .... ESKER, ESKAR, DUNE, OSAR
slang ... GRIT, COURAGE
snake .... ERYX
trotter .... CAMEL
viper .... HOGNOSE
sandal .... (OVER)SHOE, SLIPPER, HUARACHE
fastener ...... LATCHET, LACET
wooden .... PATTEN
sandals, winged ..... TALARIA
sandalwood .... INCENSE, SANTAL, ALGUM, ALMUG, LABURNUM
Island .. SUMBA, SOEMBA
sandarac ..... RESIN, INCENSE, ADAR, REALGAR, ARAR, ALERSE, MOROCCO
sandbank .... CAY, SPIT
channel .... GAT
sandbar .. SHELF, SHOAL, SPIT
Sandburg, poet .... CARL
sander .. POLISHER, SMOOTHER
sandglass .... HOURGLASS
what it tells ...... TIME
sandhog .... DIGGER
sandpaper .... ABRASIVE
sandpiper ...... YELLOWLEGS, BIRD, KNOT, STINT, GREENSHANK, JACKSNIPE, DUNLIN, TATTLER, RUFF, REE, STILT, PLOVER, STIB, TEREK
Arctic .... PECTORAL
beach ..... SANDERLING
female .... REEVE
relative ... PLOVER, SNIPE
spotted .... PEETWEET
sands ...... BEACH, MOMENTS
sandstone .... MEDINA, PSAMMITE, BEREA, PAAR, ITACOLUMITE, ARKOSE
sandstorm ... SIMOOM, SAMIEL
sandwich bread .... RYE
filling ..... HAM, CHEESE, SALAMI
island .... HAWAII
sandy .... ARENACEOUS, SHIFTING, SABULOUS, GRITTY, ARENOSE
color .... GINGER
mound .... DOWN
soil .... LOAM, LOESS
waste .... DESERT
sane ...... RATIONAL, SOBER, SENSIBLE, WISE, REASONABLE, LUCID, SOUND
sanforize .... PRESHRINK
sang froid ...... COMPOSURE, INSOUCIANCE, COOL, POISE
Sangraal ...... (HOLY)GRAIL
sanguinaria ... POPPY, PLANT, BLOODROOT
sanguine ...... RED, RUDDY, CONFIDENT, HOPEFUL, OPTIMISTIC
person .... OPTIMIST
Sanhedrin .. COURT, COUNCIL
sanicle .... PARSLEY
sanies ...... PUS, DISCHARGE
sanitarium .... RESORT
building ...... PAVILION
sanitary .... HYGIENIC
sannup .... INDIAN, ALGONQUIAN
sans .... WITHOUT
culotte .... REVOLUTIONARY, RADICAL
pareil .... PEERLESS
souci ...... GAY, CASTLE
Souci site ...... POTSDAM
Sanskrit .... VEDIC, INDIC
dialect .... PALI
epic .... RAMAYANA
god .... INDRA, VAYU
Santa .... HOLY, SAINT
____ .... FE, ANITA, CLAUS, BARBARA
Claus ... KRISS, KRINGLE
Claus' sled runner ...... REINDEER
Claus' vehicle ..... SLED
Claus' way .... CHIMNEY
stand-in of .. PAPA, POP, DAD(DY)
Santiago de Cuba ... ORIENTE
santon .... HERMIT, MONK
santonica .... WORMWOOD, WORMSEED
Sao Salvador .... BAHIA
sap ... JUICE, TRENCH, FLUID, VIGOR, FOOL, DRAIN, UNDERMINE, DIG, EXHAUST, WEAKEN
drain .. SPILE, TAP, SPOUT
flow of .... LACTESCENCE
tree .... LATEX, MILK, BALATA
sapajou .... CAPUCHIN, MONKEY, GRISON
saphead .... FOOL, DOLT
sapid .... SAVORY, TASTY, TASTEFUL

sapience .... WISDOM, SAGACITY
sapient ... WISE, DISCERNING, SAGE
sapindaceous plant .... SOAPBERRY
sapless .... DRY, INSIPID
sapling .... YOUTH
sapodilla ..... CHICO, SAPOTA, PLUM, ACANA, BUSTIC, MAMMEE, MAMEY, MARMALADE
saponaceous .... SOAPY
saponin .... GLUCOSIDE
sapor .... SAVOR, FLAVOR, RELISH, TASTE, TANG
saporous ...... TASTY, SAVORY
sapota .... MARMALADE, SAPODILLA
sapper ... DIGGER, TRENCHER
Sapphira's husband .. ANANIAS
  weakness .... LYING
sapphire ... BLUE, CORUNDUM, STONE, GEM
sapphirine .... SPINEL
Sappho's home .... LESBOS
  work .... POETRY
sappy .... JUICY
  slang ... SILLY, FATUOUS, FOOLISH, INANE
saprophyte .... FUNGUS
sapsago .... CHEESE
sapsucker ..... WOODPECKER
sapwood .... ALBURNUM
saraband .... DANCE
Saracen ...... ARAB, MOSLEM, MOOR
  foe of .... CRUSADER
  leader .... SALADIN
Sarah, diminutive of ... SADIE, SAL, SALLY
  handmaid of ..... HAGAR
  husband of ... ABRAHAM
  son .... ISAAC
saran .... RESIN
Sarawak rajah ...... BROOKE
sarcasm ... JEER, GIBE, IRONY, SATIRE
sarcastic .... IRONIC(AL), SATIRIC(AL), MORDANT, CAUSTIC, SARDONIC, VITRIOLIC
sarcoma .... TUMOR
sarcophagus ... TOMB, COFFIN
sard .... CHALCEDONY
sardine .. PILCHARD, HERRING, LOUR
  fish like .... BRISLING
Sardinian city ..... CAGLIARI
  coin .... CARLINE
  duchy .... SAVOIE
  language ...... CATALAN
  ruling house ..... SAVOY
  seaport .... BOSA
  sheep ..... MOUF(F)LON
sardius .... RUBY, SARD
sardonic .... SARCASTIC, IRONIC(AL), SATIRIC(AL)
sardonyx product ..... CAMEO
Sarg, U.S. puppeteer ... TONY
sargasso .... (GULF)WEED, SEAWEED
sark .... CHEMISE, SHIRT
sarmentose plant .... STRAWBERRY
sarong .... WAISTCLOTH, PAREUS, LOINCLOTH
Sarpedon's parent ...... ZEUS, EUROPA
sarsaparilla .... BEVERAGE, SMILAX, MEAD
sartor .... TAILOR
sash .... WAISTBAND, CUMMERBUND, FRAME, SCARF, TOBE, GIRDLE, OBI, BELT
  pane holder ...... SPRIG
sashay .... GAD, GLIDE
sasin ...... BUCK, ANTELOPE
Saskatchewan capital .. REGINA
saskatoon .... (SHAD)BUSH, SHADBLOW
sass ... DESSERT, PRESERVES, VEGETABLE, TALK
sassaby .... ANTELOPE
sassafras drink ..... SALOOP, ROOT BEER
  oil .... SAFROL(E)
Sassenach .... SAXON, ENGLISHMAN, LOWLANDER
Sassoon, poet ...... SIEGFRIED
sassy ..... IMPUDENT, SAUCY, TREE
Satan .... DEVIL, DEIL, LUCIFER, BELIAL, EBLIS, MEPHISTO, APOLLYON, ABADDON, (OLD)HARRY, (OLD)NICK, SHAITAN, HORNIE
  co-rebel of ...... AZAZEL
satanic .... DIABOLICAL, INFERNAL, WICKED
satchel .... ETUI, SCRIP, ETWEE, VALISE, (HAND)BAG
sate ...... GRATIFY, SATIATE, SATISFY, GLUT, SURFEIT, FILL
satellite .... FOLLOWER, DEPENDENT, MOON, PLANET
  artificial .... SPUTNIK, PLANETOID, LUNIK, ECHO, EXPLORER, PIONEER
  path of .... ORBIT
  shadow of ...... UMBRA
satiate ...... GRATIFY, GLUT, SURFEIT, SATE, CLOY, SATISFY, JADE
satin, adjective for ... SMOOTH, SOFT, GLOSSY
  fabric ...... RAYON, SILK, NYLON, CYPRUS, CYPRESS
  fabric smooth like ...... VELVET
  flower .... LUNARIA
  imitation .... SATEEN, SATINET(TE)
satiny .... LUSTROUS
satire .. IRONY, WIT, SARCASM, PASQUINADE
Satirical .... IRONIC(AL), SARCASTIC, CAUSTIC
  work .... SKIT, BURLESQUE, PARODY, CARICATURE, LAMPOON
satirist .... JUVENAL
satirize .. RIDICULE, LAMPOON
  in verse .... BERIME
satisfaction ..... ATONEMENT, REPARATION, PAYMENT
  for a killing .... CRO
  for injuries .... DAMAGES, GREE
satisfactory .... JAKE
satisfy .... GRATIFY, FULFILL, ANSWER, MEASURE UP, SOLVE, PLEASE
satisfying .... HUNKY
satrap ... GOVERNOR, TYRANT, SUBORDINATE
saturate .... SOAK, STEEP, SODDEN, SEETHE, DRENCH, SOP, IMBUE
saturaged state .. WET, SOGGY, SODDEN, SOAKED
Saturn ..... CRONUS, PLANET
  in alchemy .... LEAD
  wife of .... OPS
saturnalia ... ORGY, REVELRY
saturniid .... MOTH
saturnine .... TACITURN, GLOOMY, GRAVE, MOROSE, GLUM
satyr ..... BUTTERFLY, DEITY, LECHER, FAUN, SILENUS
  deity resembling a ...... SILENUS
  god attended by .... BACCHUS
  staff of .... THYRSUS
Sau .... SAVA
sauce ..... DRESSING, SEASON, RELISH, SOY, CHILI, MELBA, SOUBISE, MORNAY, WORCESTER, MATELOTE, VELOUTE, CURRY, FLAVOR
  and liqueurs .... CREMES
  bean .... SOJA, SOY(A)
  colloquial ... IMPUDENCE
  flavoring material .... CAPERS
  fish .... ALEC
  pepper .... TABASCO
  spicy ..... REMO(U)LADE
  thickener .... ROUX
  tomato .... CATSUP, KETCHUP
saucepan ...... POT, POSNET, CASSEROLE
saucer .... DISH
  flying .... UFO
  object likened to .... EYE
saucy ..... MALAPERT, RUDE, IMPUDENT, PERT, BOLD, INSOLENT, SASSY, PERKY, FRESH, COCKY, IMPERTINENT, BRASH, FLIP(PANT), ARCH
  girl ... MINX, MALAPERT, CHIT
  talk .... LIP
Saudi Arabian capital .... MECCA, RIYADH
  city .... MEDINA
  desert .... RED, NEFUD
  inhabitant ..... BEDOUIN
  monetary unit ..... RIYAL
  port .... JIDDA

province ..... HE(D)JAZ
principality .... ASIR
religious center .. MECCA, MEDINA
ruler ..... KING, FEISAL, (IBN)SAUD
state .... NEJD
sauger .... PERCH
Sauk .... SAC
Saul's father .... KISH
general .... ABNER
grandfather ... ABIEL, NER
kingdom .... ISRAEL
shepherd .... DOEG
son .... JONATHAN
successor .... DAVID
Sault Ste. Marie canals .. SOO
sauna .... BATH(HOUSE)
saunter ..... STROLL, LOITER, WALK, AMBLE, GAIT
across street ... JAYWALK
saurel .... SCAD, SKATE
saurian .... LIZARD, CROCODILE, DINOSAUR, REPTILE, ALLIGATOR
sauropod .... DINOSAUR
saury ... SKIPPER, LIZARDFISH
sausage ..... WEINER, WEENY, WEENIE, FRANKFURTER, SALAMI, PUDDING, (LIVER)WURST, BOLOGNA, SAVELOY
cover .... INTESTINE
shaped ...... ALLANTOID
saute .... FRY
sauterne .... YQUEM, WINE
Sava .... SAVE, SAU
savage ...... WILD, RUGGED, UNTAMED, FIERCE, FERAL, FEROCIOUS, HUN, FERINE, CRUEL, BARBARIAN, FELL, BESTIAL
Island .... NIUE
state .... FERITY
savanna(h) .... PLAIN, GRASSLAND
plain like .... PAMPAS, LLANO, STEPPE
savant .... SCHOLAR, SAGE, PUNDIT, PANDIT
save .... EXCEPT, RESCUE, SPARE, PRESERVE, BUT, SALVAGE, LAY BY, HOARD
all .... PINAFORE, OVERALLS
saveloy .... SAUSAGE
savin(e) ..... CEDAR, JUNIPER
saving ...... EXCEPT, FRUGAL
clause .... SALVO
in law .... EXCEPTION
savings bank .... SAVE-ALL
investments ..... LEGALS
savior .... REDEEMER, RESCUER, JESUS
savoir-faire .... TACT, DIPLOMACY
Savonarola, Ital. reformer .... GIROLAMO
savor ... SMACK, TASTE, SMELL, AROMA, TINGE, SEASON, FLAVOR, RELISH, SAPOR
savory ... SAPID, TOOTHSOME, MINT, SIPID, PIQUANT, YUMMY, TASTY, APPETIZING, SALTY, PALATABLE
smell .... AROMA
savoy .... CABBAGE
Savoyard show(man) ... RAREE
savvy .. UNDERSTAND, SHREWD, WISE, WISDOM
saw .... CUT, MOTTO, SAYING, MAXIM, PROVERB, ADAGE, REDE
blade .... WEB
cut of .... KERF
kind of ...... RIP, EDGER
notch .... KERF
sawfish's .... SERRA
surgical .... TREPAN, TREPHINE
toothed .... SERRATE
sawbones: sl. .... SURGEON
sawbuck: sl. .... TEN(SPOT)
sawdust .... COOM, SCOBS
sawfish .... RAY
snout .... SERRA
sawfly .... HORNTAIL
sawhorse ..... BUCK, TRESTLE
sawing frame .... HORSE
sawtooth .... SERRA
ridge .... SIERRA
sawtoothed ...... RUNCINATE
sawyer .. WOODCUTTER, BEETLE
Saxony's capital .... DRESDEN
Saxe ____.......... COBURG
Coburg and Gotha ...... WINDSOR
saxhorn .... TUBA
saxifrage ... SESELI, ROCKFOIL
Saxon ... SASSENACH, ENGLISH
Saxony ..... SACHSEN, YARN
capital of ...... DRESDEN, MAGDEBURG
city .... ERFURT
say .. AVER, UTTER, DECLARE, STATE, ALLEGE, REPORT, DICTUM, CHANCE, MOUTH
again ... ITERATE, REPEAT
repetitiously ..... CHANT, HARP
sayid .... SAID, FATIMID
saying .... ADAGE, SAW, PROVERB, MOTTO, EPIGRAM, MOT, MAXIM, DICTUM, APHORISM, AXIOM, GNOME
sayings attributed to Jesus .... LOGIA
Sb in chemistry ..... STIBIUM, ANTIMONY
scab .... CRUST, MANGE, SCOUNDREL, BLACKLEG, ESCHAR
scabbard ... CASE, SHEATH(E), PILCHER
plate .... CHAPE
what it sheathes .. SWORD, DAGGER, BAYONET, BOLO, SCIMITAR
scabby ... MANGY, MEAN, LOW, BASE, SCURVY, SCALY
scabbies .. ITCH, MANGE, PSORA
scabrous ..... MANGY, SCALY, RISQUE, SALACIOUS
scad .... SAUREL, SKATE
scads .... OODLES
scaffolding timber ... PUTLOG
scaffold ... GIBBET, PLATFORM, STAGE, GALLOWS, RIGGER
scalawag ..... RASCAL, SCAMP
scald .... BURN, HEAT
scale ..... CLIMB, ESCALADE, CLAMBER, GO UP, GAMUT, LAMELLA, PLATE, FLAKE, LAMINA
animal .... SQUAMA
chaffy .... PALEA
charges .... TARIFF
horny .... SCUTUM
insect's secretion .... LAC
measuring ..... VERNIER
model .... MOCK-UP
musical .... GAMUT
plant .... SQUAMA
pointer .... TONGUE
skin off .... BLANCH
weighing .... STEELYARD
scalelike part of animal/plant .. SQUAMA
scales .... BALANCE
covered with .. SQUAMATE, SQUAMOSE, SQUAMOUS, LEPIDOTE
the .... LIBRA
scaling ladder .... SCALOSE
of wall .... ESCALADE
scall .... SCURF
scallion ..... ONION, SHALLOT, LEEK
scallop ..... MOLLUSK, BADGE, CRENULATION, QUIN, CRENA, PINK
scalloped .... CRENATE
scalp ... CHEAT, ROB, DEFEAT
disease ... SCALL, FAVUS
to an Indian ..... TROPHY
tumor .... WEN
scalpel ... LANCET, BISTOURY, KNIFE
scalper ... PROFITEER, INDIAN
scaly ..... LEPROSE, SCURFY, SCABROUS, SCABBY, MANGY, BASE, LOW, MEAN, SQUAMATE, SQUARROSE
bark .... PSOROSIS
coating .... SCURF
combining form .... LEPID(O)
Scamander .... MENDERES
scammony .... RESIN
scamp ... SCALAWAG, ROGUE, RASCAL, SCOUNDREL, SCAPEGRACE, SPALPEEN
scamper ...... BRATTLE, SCUD, SCURRY
scampi .... PRAWN
scan ...... ANALYZE, STUDY, GLANCE, RECITE, SCRUTINIZE
scandal .. DISGRACE, OUTRAGE, SHAME
scandalize .... OFFEND, OUTRAGE, SHOCK, MALIGN
scandalmonger ... GOSSIP(ER), TALEBEARER
scandalous .... LIBELOUS, SHAMEFUL, OFFENSIVE
scandent plant .... VINE
Scandinavian .... NORSE(MAN), LAPP, DANE, SWEDE,

NORTHMAN, NORDIC, SQUAREHEAD, FINN
chieftain ... JARL, RURIK
coin .... ORE
country ...... NORWAY, SWEDEN, DENMARK, ICELAND
explorer .... ERIC
folklore being ..... TROLL
giantess ... URTH, WYRD
goblin .... NIS
god .... THOR, LOKI, ALFADIR
heaven: myth. .. ASGARD, ASGARTH
legend ...... SAGA, EDDA
legislature ..... T(H)ING
measure .... ALEN
monster .... KRAKEN
musician .... SKALD
name ...... SVEN, OLAF, NILS, ERIC
nation .... GEATAS
navigator .... ERIC
pirate sea rover .. VIKING
plateau .... FJELD
poem .... RUNE
poet .... SKALD
settler .... VARANGIAN
territorial division .. AMT
weight .... LOD
scant .... MEAGER, EXIGUOUS, SLIGHT, STINT, FEW, INADEQUATE, SHORT, SPARSE
scantling .. TIMBER, BEAM, STUD
scanty ...... MEAGER, SPARSE, SHORT, SMALL, SPARING, SCARCE
scape .... STALK
bearing .... SCAPOSE
scapegoat ..... BUTT, VICTIM, WHIPPING BOY, PATSY, FALL GUY
scapegrace .. RASCAL, ROGUE, SCAMP
scaphoid .... BOAT-SHAPED
scapolite .... SILICATE, WERNERITE
scar .... MARK, CICATRIX, NAVEL, BLEMISH, CICATRICE, CLIFF
scarab .... BEETLE, CHARM
Scaramouche ..... POLTROON, RASCAL, BRAGGART
author .... SABATINI
scarce ..... RARE, UNCOMMON
scarcely .... HARDLY
scarcity ..... PAUCITY, LACK, RARITY, SHORTAGE, DEARTH
scare ... STARTLE, FRIGHT(EN), FEAR, PANIC, ALARM
up .... PRODUCE
scarecrow .. MALKIN, MAUKIN, MAWKIN, JACKSTRAW, STRAW MAN, BUGABOO
stuffing .... STRAW
scarehead .... STREAMER, BANNER
scaremonger ..... ALARMIST, TERRORIST
scarf ...... ASCOT, NECKTIE, (NEC)KERCHIEF, SASH, TAPALO, MANTILLA, MUFFLER, FOULARD, BABUSHKA, SAREE, SARI, TIPPET
clerical ... TIPPET, STOLE
cloth .... LUNGI, LUNGEE
pope's .... ORALE
shoulder .... SASH
sun helmet ..... PUGGRY, PUG(G)REE
woman's .... STOLE, MANTILLA, PEPLOS, BOA
scarlatina .... FEVER
scarfskin .... CUTICLE, EPIDERMIS
scarlet .... RED
bird .... TANAGER
fever .... SCARLATINA
Scarlett O'Hara's home ...... TARA
scarp ..... SLOPE, DECLIVITY
scat .... TAX, SCRAM
scathing .... SEARING
scatter .... LITTER, SPRINKLE, STREW, DISPERSE, DISPEL, SHED, STUD, SOW, DISSIPATE
by blowing ..... WINNOW
for lost scent ...... CAST
grass .... TED
scatterbrained .... GIDDY, FLIGHTY, FRIVOLOUS
scattered .... SPORADIC, STUDDED, STREWN
scattergood .... SPENDTHRIFT, WASTREL, PRODIGAL
scattering of Jews .. DIASPORA
scaup ... DUCK, CANVASBACK, REDHEAD, SHUFFLER, DOGS, GRAYBACK
scavenger .... HYENA
scenario ... SCRIPT, OUTLINE, LIBRETTO
scend .... HEAVE, PITCH
scene .... LOCALE, SITE, TABLEAU, SETTING, VIEW, SPECTACLE
scenery .... DIORAMA, PANORAMA, PICTURE, VIEW, LANDSCAPE, VISTA
chewer: sl. .... HAM
mover ..... PROP(MAN)
natural .... LANDSCAPE
scenic .... PICTURESQUE, DRAMATIC
view .... SCAPE, PANORAMA, VISTA
scent ...... SMELL, PERFUME, TRACK, FRAGRANCE, CLUE, AROMA, NOSE, ODOR
animal's .... FOIL
kitchen .. AROMA, NIDOR
left by animal .... DRAG
of wine .... BOUQUET
subtle .... AURA
scented .... OLENT
water .... COLOGNE, BAY RUM
scepter .... FERULA, TRIDENT, ROD, WAND, STAFF, MACE
Schacht, Ger. financier .... HJALMAR
Scharre, mimist .... ROLF
schedule .... SLATE, LIST, CATALOGUE, BOOK, CALENDAR, INVENTORY, (TIME,)TABLE, AGENDA
Scheherazade's life-saver ..... TALES
Scheldt .... ESCAUT
schema ... OUTLINE, DIAGRAM PLAN
scheme .... SYSTEM, PLOT, INTRIGUE, PROJECT, CABAL, OUTLINE, PLAN, PURPOSE, DEVICE, PROJECT
utopian .... BUBBLE
scheming ... CRAFTY, TRICKY
Schick, pediatrician .... BELA
Schicklgruber's son .... (ADOLF) HITLER
schipperke .... DOG
schism ...... DIVISION, SPLIT, SEPARATION, SECESSION, CONCISION, SECT
schist .... ROCK, SLATE
schistosome .... FLUKE
schizocarp ..... REGMA, MAPLE
schizophrenia treatment ...... PHENIGAMA
schizophrenic syndrome ...... CATATONIA
Schlesien .... SILESIA
Schleswig-Holstein capital .... KIEL
schnapps .... GIN
schnauzer ... PINSCHER, DOG, TERRIER
schnozzle .... NOSE
Schnozzola .... DURANTE
scholar ... SAVANT, STUDENT, PUPIL, CLASSICIST, PUNDIT, PANDIT
assistant attendant ..... FAMULUS
inferior .... PEDANT
literary ...... HARMONIST
Moslem .... ULEM
scholarly .... STUDIOUS, ERUDITE, LEARNED
paper .... THESIS
people .... LITERATI
scholars' association .... ACADEMY
scholarship ...... LEARNING, BURSE, PEDANTRY, PHILOLOGY, ERUDITION
scholastic .... ACADEMIC, DOGMATIC, PEDANT(IC)
scholiast .... ANNOTATOR
school .... TRAIN, TEACH, COLLEGE, UNIVERSITY, EDUCATE, ACADEMY, LYCEE, ECOLE, SECT, ACADEME, LYCEUM
assignment ..... LESSON
banner .... PENNANT
book ..... PRIMER, TEXT, READER
boy, new .... SCUM
children's .... KINDERGARTEN, NURSERY
for training horses ...... MANEGE
grounds .... CAMPUS

group .... PTA
headmaster ..... RECTOR
honor society .... ARISTA
kind of .. PREP(ARATORY), ELEMENTARY, COLLEGE, MILITARY, SEMINARY
of birds .... POD
of fish ...... SHOAL, POD
of thought .... ISM
of whales ..... POD, GAM
official ...... PRINCIPAL
principal ... HEADMASTER
riding .... MANEGE
teacher .... MASTER
term .... SEMESTER
young women's .... SEMINARY
schooling .... EDUCATION
schoolmaster .... PEDANT, TEACHER, SNAPPER, PEDAGOGUE, DOMINIE
rod of .... FERULE
schooner ...... WAGON, SHIP
schorl .... T(O)URMALINE
schottish, dance like ... POLKA
Schranz, Austrian skier .. KARL
Schubert, composer ... FRANZ
classic .... AVE MARIA
Schumann Heink, singer ..... ERNESTINE
Schweiz .... SWITZERLAND
sciatic area .... HIP
science ... ART, SKILL, OLOGY, TECHNICS
applied .... TECHNOLOGY
combining form .. TECHNO
fiction writer ... ASIMOV, VERNE
of boxing .... FISTICUFFS
causes ...... ETIOLOGY
crop production ...... AGRONOMY
deciphering documents DIPLOMATICS
fruit cultivation ...... POMOLOGY
government .. POLITICS
heard sound .... ACOUSTIC(S)
human behavior ...... PSYCHOLOGY
law-making .... NOMOLOGY
medicine .. IATROLOGY
motion ..... KINETICS, DYNAMICS, KINEMATICS
mountains .. OROLOGY
musical sounds .... HARMONICS
origins ..... ETIOLOGY
plants .... BOTANY
public worship .... LITURGICS
soils ...... AGROLOGY
versification .. PROSODY
vital statistics .... DEMOGRAPHY
words ..... SEMANTICS
on freezing points .... CRYOSCOPY
on races ..... EUGENICS EUTHENICS
scientific quack ..... EMPIRIC
research animal .... HAMSTER
study of trees .... DENDROLOGY
scientist .... SAVANT
scilicet ..... NAMELY, TO WIT
scimitar .. SWORD, SAX, TURK
scincoid .... SKINK
scintilla ... SPARK, PARTICLE, WHIT, IOTA, TRACE, BIT
scintillate ... SPARKLE, FLASH, TWINKLE
sciolist .. QUACK, CHARLATAN, PEDANT
scion .... SHOOT, BUD, DESCENDANT, SPROUT, SON, GRAFT, HEIR, SLIP, SPRIG
Scipio, Roman general ...... AFRICANUS
victim of ..... CARTHAGE, HANNIBAL
scirrhus ..... TUMOR, CANCER
scission .... DIVISION, FISSION
scissorbill .... SKIMMER
scissors-like instrument ...... SHEARS
scissortail .... FLYCATCHER
sciurine animal ..... RODENT, MARMOT, SQUIRREL
sclerite .... SPICULE
scoff ... SNEER, GIBE, FLOUT, JEER, DERIDE, TAUNT, MOCK, RAIL, FLEER, JIBE, GIRD
scold .... (BE)RATE, REPROVE, REBUKE, RAIL, DERIDE, UPBRAID, REVILE, CHIDE, NAG, LAMBASTE, JAW, FLITE, FLAY
scolder ... NAG(GER), MAGPIE, BERATER
scolding .... EARFUL
scombroid .... MACKEREL
sconce .... SHED, HUT, SHELTER, HEAD, HELMET, SKULL, BULWARK, FORTIFY, BRAINS, FORT, SCREEN
scone .... (TEA)CAKE
scoop ... LADLE, SHOVEL, BEAT, DIG(OUT), GOUGE, TROWEL, ROUT, DREDGE
scoot .... DART, SCURRY, HIE
scooter .... SAILBOAT, MOTORBOAT
scop .... POET, BARD
scope .... AREA, RANGE, EXTENT, AMBIT, LATITUDE
limited .... LOCAL
scopoline .... NARCOTIC
scopulate .... BRUSHLIKE
scorch ...... BURN, SHRIVEL, SINGE, CHAR, SERE, SEAR, PARCH, BLISTER
score .... SCRATCH, DEBT, ACCOUNT, GRUDGE, RATING, TALLY, CHALK, TWENTY, MARK, NOTCH, CRITICIZE, TAB
scoreless, hold .... BLANK
scoria .... DROSS, SLAG, LAVA, AA
scorn ... DISDAIN, CONTEMPT, SPURN, DESPISE, MOCK, DERISION, CONTEMN
scorpine .... HOGFISH
Scorpio's brightest star .... ANTARES
scorpion .... ARACHNID, SCOURGE, WHIP, VINEGARROON
claw .... CHELA
fish .... LAPON
Scot .... KILTIE, GAEL, SCOTCHMAN, TAX, LEVY
Scotch ..... STINGY, WHISKY, SCORE, CUT, NOTCH, MAIM, CRUSH, STIFLE, BLOCK, WEDGE
scoter ... DUCK, EIDER, COOT
Scotia .... SCOTLAND
Scotland ... SCOTIA, MOLDING
capital ..... EDINBURGH
scotoma .... BLIND SPOT
Scotsman ... BLUECAP, SANDY
Scott novel .... IVANHOE
poem .... MARMION
Scottish .... CALEDONIAN
absent .... AWA
ache .... WARK, STOUND
active .... YAULD
ago .... SYNE
alas .... OCHONE
alder tree .... ARN
alderman .... BAILIE
ale .... YILL, NAPPY
alley .... WYND
assembly signal .. SLOGAN
attendant ..... GILLIE, GILLY
awl .... ELSEN
awry .... AGL(E)Y
bagpipe music .. PIBROCH, CORONACH
bailiff .... REEVE
bank .... BRAE
barren .... YELD
barter .... TROKE
beer .... YILL, NAPPY
beef cut .... SEY
beg .... SORN
beggar .... RANDY
belly .... WAME
biscuit .... SCONE
blaze .... INGLE
bold .... CROUSE
boor .... TYKE
bound .... STEND
boundary .... MEAR
box .... KIST
boy .... LOON
brandy .... ATHOLE
breeches .... TREWS
broadsword .. CLAYMORE
brook .... SIKE
broth ...... BROO, BREE
brow of hill .... SNAB
bucket .... STOOP, STOUP
burden .... BIRN
burn .... STREAM
bushel .... FOU
buxom .... SONSIE
cake ... SCONE, BANNOCK
cap .... BALMORAL, GLENGARRY, TAM(-O-SHANTER)
cat .... MALKIN

catch .... KEP
cattle .... NOWT
charm .... CANTRIP
cheese .... KEBBOK
chemise .... SARK
chest .... KIST
chief .... THANE
child ...... BAIRN, WEAN
church .... KIRK
churl .... CARLE
city ..... AYRS, GLASGOW
clan chief .... THANE
clothe .... CLEAD
codfish .... GLASHAN
coin .... BAWBEE, BAUBEE, DEMY, LION
comb .... KAME
congress .... MOD
corner .... NEUK
corpse .... LICH
countrified ..... HODDEN
county .... PEEBLES, ARGYLL, BUTE, AYR, BANFF, FIFE, ORKNEY
court officer ..... MACER
cow .... RUNT, CRUMMIE
crab .... PARTAN
cravat .... OVERLAY
craw .... CRAG
crowd ... MEINIE, MEINY
cry of blame ... DIRDUM
cuckoo .... GOWK
cup .... TASS
curlew .... WHAUP
cut .... SNEG
dagger .... SKEAN
dairymaid .... DEY
daisy .... GOWAN
deception .... BROGUE
dell .... SLACK
devil ... DEIL, MOHOUND
dining room .... SPENCE
dirge .... CORONACH
dish .... HAGGIS
do .... DAE
dog .... SEALYHAM
dolt ... GOMERAL, GOWK
donkey .... CUDDY
dramatist ...... BARRIE
dwarf .... BLASTIE
ear .... LUG
earnest money ... ARLES
earth .... YIRD
else .... ENSE
empty .... TOOM
endure .... DREE
explorer .... RAE
extent .... STENT
extra .... ORRA
fair .... TRYST
faithful .... LEAL
fall of rain .... ON-DING
farm worker ...... HIND, ORRAMAN
farmer .... CROFTER, COTTAR, COTTER
fellow .... CARL(E)
festivity .... KIRN
few .... WHEEN
fine .... WALLY
fireplace .... INGLE
first rate .... WALLY
firth .... KYLE
fold .... WIMPLE
fool .... GOMERAL
fox .... TOD
friend .... EME
game .... SHINTY
garment .... SARK
girl .... CUMMER, LASSIE, QUEAN
go .... GAE, GANG
goblet .... TASS
godmother .... CUMMER
goldsmith .... GED
good .... GUDE
good-for-nothing .. ORRA
gooseberry ..... THAPRES
guillotine ...... MAIDEN
gulf .... BISM
gypsy .... CAIRD
hag .... CARLINE
haggle .... PRIG
hamlet .... CLACHAN
handsome .... SONSY, SONSIE
hare ... MAUKIN, MALKIN
hawk .... ALLAN
head .... POW
heir .... TEIND
Highlander .. GAEL, CELT
hill ...... DOD(D), INCH
hill(side) .... BRAE
hellside hollow .. CORRIE
historian .... HUME
hoe .... PADLE
hut .... BOTHY
inlet .... GIO
inventor .... WATT
island ..... ARRAN, BUTE, INCH, IONA, HEBRIDES, UIST, HARRIS
jackdaw .... KAE
jade .... YAUD
jail .... TOLBOOTH
keen .... GLEG
kilt .... FILIBEG
kindle ..... LUNT, TIND
kindred .... SIB
king .... BRUCE
kiss .... PREE
knowledge .... KENNING
laborer .... HIND
lake .... LIN, LOCH, KATRINE
lake dwelling .. CRANNOG
land, flat .... LINKS
land tax .... CESS
landholder ...... LIARD, THANE, THEGN
lark .... LAVEROCK
light .... LICHT
little .... SMA
lively .... CROUSE
locker .... KIST
lord .... THANE
love .... LOE
lowlander ... SASSENACH
Lowlands ...... LALLAN
lucky .... SONSIE
magic spell ..... CANTRIP
magistrate ..... PROVOST, BAILIE
marauder .... MOSS TROOPER, CATERAN
mare .... YAUD
market .... TRYST
match .... LUNT
mathe ... GRUB, MAGGOT
mathematician .. NAPIER
Mayday .... BELTANE
measure .... CRAN
men's undergarment .... TREWS
miscellaneous ..... ORRA
mist .... DROW
money .... SILLER
more .... MAIR
mortgage ...... WADSET
mountain ... BEN, NEVIS
much ... MICKLE, MUCKLE
mud .... GLAR
municipal official .. BAILIE
musical instrument ...... BAGPIPE
must .... MAUN
myself .... MASEL
national emblem .... THISTLE
native ..... CALEDONIAN
neck .... CRAG
negative ..... DINNA, NAE
New Year's eve .... HOGMANAY
nimble .... YAULD
no .... NAE
once .... ANES
one ...... AIN, ANE, YIN
odd .... ORRA
outcry of blame .. DIRDUM
own .... AIN, ANE
ox .... NOWT, RUNT
oxter .... ARMPIT
pail ..... COGGIE, STOUP
pain ..... WARK, STANG, STOUND
parlor .... BEN
pay for a killing .... CRO
peak .... NEVIS
peasant .... COTTAR, CROFTER, COTTER
peep .... KEEK
pert .... CROUSE
philosopher ...... HUME, CAIRD
physicist .... BAIRD
pig .... GRICE
pipe .... CUTTY
pirate .... KIDD
plaid .... TARTAN, MAUD
plait .... WIMPLE
pleasant .... DOUCE
pocket .... POUCH
poet ..... BURNS, EDINA, HOGG, DUNBAR
pole .... CABER
poll .... POW, HEAD
pool .... LINN, CARR
porridge .... BROSE, SOWENS
port .... OBAN
pottage .... BROSE
pouch .... SPORRAN, SPLEUCHAN
praise .... ROOSE
prank .... CANTRIP
precipitation .... SNA
prefix to names ..... MAC
prison .... TOLBOOTH

privateer .... KIDD
pronunciation ..... BURR
pudding .... SAUSAGE
puzzle .... KITTLE
ragged .. DUDDY, DUDDIE
reef .... SKERRY
relish .... GUST
require .... NEID
resort .... OBAN
river ... ESK, DEE, DEVON, AYR, CLYDE, TAY, AFTON, DOON
river land .... CARSE
rivulet .... RINDLE
robber .... CATERAN
robbery .... REIF
rock .... SKERRY
rope .... WANTY
rosin .... ROZET
rowboat .... COBLE
rug .... MAUD
Satan ..... DEIL, HORNIE
scholarship ...... BURSE
schoolmaster .. DOMINIE
scold .... THREAP
scone .... FARL(E)
scratch .... RIT
seaport .... DUNDEE, GREENOCK
seize .... VANG
seldom .... SINDLE
self .... SEL
servant .... GILLY, GILLIE
sharp ..... GLEG, SNELLY
shawl .... MAUD
shelter .... BIELD
shirt .... SARK
silver .... SILLER
simpleton .... GOWK
since .... SYNE
sister ...... TITTY, TITTIE
skirt .... KILT
small .... SMA
smart .... STOUND
smoke .... LUNT
snow .... SNA
snow fall ...... ON-DING
soldier .... KERN(E)
spell .... CANTRIP
spirit .... BANSHEE
sponge .... SORN
squall .... BLEFFERT
stomach .... KYTE
stream .... BURN
student scholar .. BURSAR
suffer .... DREE
supple .... WANDLE
sweetheart .... JO(E)
sword .... SKEAN, CLAYMORE
tap .... TUCK
tartan pattern ..... SETT, PLAID
taste .... PREE, GUST
tatter .... TAVER
tea cake .... SCONE
tedious .... DREE
tenant .... CROFTER, COTTER, COTTAR
tern .... TARRET
terrier .... SEALYHAM, SKYE, CAIRN
theologian .... DUNS
thicket .... RONE
throat .... CRAG
thumb .... THOOM
tickle .... KITTLE
tinker .... CAIRD
toad .... TADE
tobacco pouch .... SPLEUCHAN
topper .... TAM
torch .... LUNT
tower .... PEEL
town .... BUR(G)H
toy .... WALLY
trade .... TROKE
tribal payment ..... CRO
trick .... BROGUE
trousers .... TREWS
true .... LEAL
turnip .... NEEP
tuyere .... TEW
twang .... TIRL
uncanny .... UNCO
uncle ...... EAM, (Y)EME
university scholar .... BURSAR
vagabond .... WAFF
vagrant .... CAIRD
valley ... SLACK, STRATH
vex .... FASH
vigor .... VIR
village .... REW
violet .... BLAVER
vulgar .... RANDY
walk .... GO
water spirit ..... KELPIE, KELPY
waterfall ... LIN(N), LYN
wear under kilts .. TREWS
weeds .... WRACK
weighing machine .... TRONE
weight .... TRONE
whaup .... CURLEW
whether .... GIN
whirlpool .... WEEL
whiskey ... USQUEBAUGH, ATHOL(E), MOUNTAIN DEW
witch .... CARLINE
woman .... CUMMER, RANDY, CARLINE
woman, unmarried ...... QUEAN
womb .... WAME
world .... WARL
worse .... WAUR
worthless .... WAFF
wrap .... MAUD
wrestle ...... WARS(T)LE
yawn .... GANT
yell .... GOWL

scoundrel .. VILLAIN, RASCAL, SCAMP, BASE, ROGUE, CAD, VARLET, KNAVE, BEGGAR, SCAB, REPROBATE
scour .... FLUSH, PURGE, LOOK OVER, SEARCH, SAND, POLISH, SCRAPE, SCRUB, FURBISH, RAKE, RUB, SKIRR
scourer .... CATHARTIC
scourge .... BANE, WHIP, SCORPION, AFFLICTION, LASH, FLOG, TORMENT, PLAGUE
of God .... ATTILA
scouring rush ..... HORSETAIL
scout ..... SPY, RECONNOITER, SCOFF, REJECT, RIDICULE, FELLOW, GUY, DO-GOODER, TENDERFOOT
boat .... VEDETTE
group ..... TROOP, DEN, PATROL, PACK
scow ..... BARGE, FLATBOAT, LIGHTER
puller .... TOWBOAT, TUG(BOAT)
scowl .... (G)LOWER, FROWN, MOUE, GRIMACE, LOUR
scrabble .... PAW, SCRAPE, SCRAWL, DOODLE
scrag .... NECK, HANG, THROTTLE, GARROTE
scraggly .. UNKEMPT, JAGGED
scraggy .... BONY, LEAN, SKINNY
scram ..... VAMO(O)SE, SCAT, SHOO, BEAT IT, GET LOST, LAM
scramble ... CLIMB, CLAMBER, SCUFFLE, MIX UP, TEAR, RAT RACE
scrambled .... PIED
scrap ..... TATTER, BIT, PIECE, DISCARD, ORT, LEFTOVER, ARGUMENT, SHRED, FRAGMENT, MAMMOCK, QUARREL, END, JUNK(RAG), FRACTION, FIGHT, MORSEL, ODDMENT
glass .... CULLET
hunt for ..... SCAVENGE
of paper only, sometimes.. TREATY, PACT
scrape .... ABRADE, RUB, SCOUR, GRIDE, PREDICAMENT, SCRATCH, SCUFF, RAKE, RASP, GRAZE, SHAVE, FIX
bottom ... DREDGE, SOUR
ground in golf ... SCLAFF
scraped linen .... LINT
metal .... FILING
scraper, water ..... SQUEEGEE
scrapings .... SHAVINGS
scrappy ... PUGNACIOUS, GAME
scraps .... SOUVENIRS, CLIPPINGS, MEMENTOS
literary .... ANA
scratch ..... GRATE, SCRAPE, CHAFE, RUB, SCRIBBLE
Old .... DEVIL
scratching ground for food .... RASORIAL
scratchy .... ITCHY
scrawl .... DOODLE, SCRIBBLE
scrawny .... LEAN, THIN, SCRAGGY
screak .... SCREECH
scream ..... SHRIEK, SQUALL, YELL, CATERWAUL, SCREECH
screamer .... HEADLINE
bird .... CHAJA
scree .... TALUS, STONE, PEBBLE, RUBBLE

screech .... SHRIEK, CRY, SCREAM
screechy .... SHRILL
screed .... HARANGUE, TIRADE, SPEECH
screen ... SCONCE, PARTITION, CURTAIN, PAVIS, SHIELD, SIFT, BLIND, GRILLE, MOVIES, SHADE, SHROUD, SECLUDE, PARAVENT
altar .... REREDOS
bar .... MULLION
bulletproof .. MANT(E)LET
canvas .... PAVESADE
chancel .... REREDOS
chimney .... BONNET
for concealment protection .. BLINDAGE
making material .... VETIVER
mesh .... SIEVE
wind .... PARAVENT
screw ..... PROPELLER, MISER SALARY, TURN, TWIST, TIGHTEN
part .... THREAD
pine tree ..... PANDANUS
thread .... HELIX
threader .... CHASER
screwball .... NUT
screwy ..... ODD, PECULIAR, ECCENTRIC
scribble .... SCRAWL, WRITE, DASH, DOODLE
scribbler .... HACK
scribe ..... WRITER, AUTHOR, PENMAN, CLERK, SECRETARY, AMANUENSIS, SCRIVENER
Biblical .... BARUCH
scrimmage .... MELEE, FIGHT, TUSSLE, AFFRAY
scrimp .... SKIMP, STINT, SCANTY, ECONOMIZE
scrip ..... SATCHEL, WALLET, LIST, BAG, WRITING, CERTIFICATE
script .... HANDWRITING, SCENARIO, PENMANSHIP, LIBRETTO, RONDE, SERTA
scriptural .... BIBLICAL
analysis .... EXEGESIS
interpreter ..... EXEGETE
scripture(s) ... BIBLE, KORAN, ALCORAN, BOOK, TORAH, SUTRA, ITALA
interpretation of .... ANAGOGE
passage .... TEXT
reader .... LECTOR
scrivener ... NOTARY, SCRIBE, COPYIST, AMANUENSIS
scrobiculate .... PITTED
scrod .... CODFISH
scrofula .... KING'S EVIL, STRUMA
scroll .... LIST, ROLL, SCHEDULE
of Ionic capitals .. VOLUTE
shaped ...... TURBINATE
tablet like .. CARTOUCH(E)
scromboid fish .... CERO
Scrooge .... MISER
scrouge ...... CROWD, PRESS, SQUEEZE
scrounge .... PILFER
scrub ... MEAN, POOR, SMALL, RUB, BRUSH, SCOUR, MOP
scrubber ...... CHARWOMAN
scrubbing implement .... MOP
scruff .. NAPE, NUQUE, NUBIA
scrunch .... CRUSH, CHEW
scruple ... QUALM, MISGIVING
scrupulous ... EXACT, HONEST, UPRIGHT, CAREFUL, PRECISE, CORRECT, FINICAL, RELIGIOUS
scrutinize ..... INSPECT, SCAN, EXAMINE, CON, EYE, PROBE
scud ...... SKIM, GLIDE, RUN
scuff .... SCRAPE, BRUSH, SHUFFLE, SLIPPER
scuffle ..... SHUFFLE, BRAWL, FRAY, MELEE, TUSSLE, FIGHT
scull .... PADDLE, SHELL, OAR, (RACING)BOAT, WHERRY
sculler ... BOATMAN, OARSMAN
scullery, content of ... POTS, PANS
scullion ... SERVANT, WRETCH
sculpin .... BULLHEAD, SEA RAVEN, HARDHEAD
sculptor .... CARVER, STATUARY
framework of .... ARMATURE
tool of .... CHISEL, GRAVER, CALIPER
sculpture head to chest .. BUST
medium .. CLAY, BRONZE, MARBLE
style of ...... GROTESQUE
sculptured .... GRAVEN, GLYPHIC
scum .... DROSS, REFUSE, SKIM, SPUME, PELLICLE
rid of .... DESPUMATE
scup .... PORGY, BURGOO, BREAM, FISH, SPAROID
kin of ... SNAPPER, GRUNT
scuppernong ... GRAPE, WINE, MUSCADINE
scurf .... SCALL, FURFUR, DANDRUFF
scurfy .... MANGY, LEPIDOTE, LEPROSE
scurrilous ... VULGAR, COARSE, THERSITICAL, ABUSIVE
scurry .. SCAMPER, RUN, DART, SCOOT, RACE, HIGHTAIL
scurvy ...... VILE, LOW, MEAN
scut .... TAIL
scutage .... TAX
Scutari .. USKUDAR, SHKODER, LAKE
scute .... SCUTUM
scutellate .... ROUND
scutter .... BUSTLE
scuttle ..... BASKET, BUCKET, SCURRY, SCAMPER, HATCHWAY, HOD, SINK
scuttlebut .... RUMOR, GOSSIP
scutum .... SHIELD, PLATELET
Scylla .... ROCK
whirlpool opposite ...... CHARYBDIS
scye .... ARMHOLE
scyphozoan .... JELLYFISH
scythe bearer .... DEATH
cut, one stroke ... SWATH
handle .... SNATH(E), SNEAD, NIB
sharpener ..... STRICKLE
sweep of .... SWATH
sea ..... WAVE, SWELL, MAIN, OCEAN, DEEP, MARE
anemone ...... ACTINIA, POLYP
animal, fishlike .... LANCELET, AMPHIOXUS
arm ... GULF, BAY, FIORD, FRITH, LOCH, LOUGH
bass .... JEWFISH
bat .... DEVILFISH
bird ..... ERN(E), GULL, ALBATROSS, SHAG, CORMORANT, PETREL, TERN, SOLAN, SCOTER, KESTREL, PUFFIN, MEW, FULMAR, EIDER, GANNET, NODDY, SKUA, SCAUP
biscuit .... HARDTACK
born goddess .... APHRODITE
borne .... AFLOAT
bread .... HARDTACK
calf .... SEAL
coast .... SHORE, STRAND
cow .... DUGONG, SIRENIAN, MANATEE, WALRUS, HIPPOPOTAMUS
creature, legendary ...... MERMAID, MERMAN
cucumber .... TREPANG, HOLOTHURIAN
devil .... ANGELFISH, SHARK, OCTOPUS, RAY
disaster aid device ...... SOFAR
dog ...... GOB, MARINER, TAR, SEAL, SAILOR
duck ..... SCAUP, COOT, SCO(O)TER, EIDER
eagle .... ERN(E), OSPREY, TERN
ear .... ABALONE
elephant .... SEAL
fan .... CORAL
farer ... MARINER, MAORI, SAILOR
foam ..... MEERSCHAUM, SPUME
fox .... SHARK
god ..... LER, NEPTUNE, NEREUS, TRITON, POSEIDON, AEGIR, PROTEUS
grave .... LOCKER
gull .... MEW, COB(B), KITTIWAKE
hog .... PORPOISE
holly .... ERYNGO, ERINGO
horse .... WALRUS, HIPPOCAMPUS
inhabitant: myth. ....

MERMAN, MERMAID
inlet .. FIORD, FJORD, RIA
lands beyond the .... OUTREMER
lawyer .... SAILOR
lettuce ..... LAVER, ULUA
lily .... CRINOID
lion .... SEAL
marker ..... BUOY, DAN
mew .... GULL
mile .... KNOT, NAUT
monster .... KRAKEN, LEVIATHAN
near the .... MARITIME
needle .... GAR(FISH)
nettle .... MEDUSA, ACALEPH, JELLYFISH
nymph .... NEREID, THETIS, SIREN, NAIAD, CALYPSO
of the .... PELAGIC, THALASSIC, NAVAL, MARINE, NAUTICAL, MARITIME
on the .... MARITIME
onion .... SQUILL(A)
pen .... POLYP
personified .... NEPTUNE
poetic .... FOAM
prefix .... MARI
put to .... SAIL
raven .... SCULPIN
robber .... PIRATE, BUCCANEER, FOMOR
robin .... GURNARD
rover .... PIRATE
serpent .... ELOPS
shell .... MOLLUSK
slug .... TREPANG
snail .... W(H)ELK
soldier .... MARINE
spot at .... ISLE(T)
spray .... SPINDRIFT
squirt .... TUNICATE, ASCIDIAN
surface movement ...... LIPPER
swallow .... TERN, PETREL
tangle .... SEAWEED
unicorn....... NARWHAL
urchin .... ECHINUS, ECHINOID
wall .... JETTY, BREAKWATER
water .... BRINE
with many islands .... ARCHIPELAGO
wolf ... BLENNY, PIRATE
worm .... LURG, SAO
worthy .... STANCH

seabat .... DEVILFIHS
Seabee's concern ... AIRFIELD, HARBOR
seaboard .... COAST
seacoast .... SHORE
seaflower ... POLYP, ANEMONE
seagull .... KITTIWAKE, MEW, COB
seahorse .... HIPPOCAMPUS
seal ...... PINNIPED, INITIAL, BULLA, BLADDERNOSE, STAMP, RATIFY, CLOSE, CACHET, SIGIL, SIGNET
bottle .... CAPSULE
cut skin of ...... FLENSE
eared ... SEA LION, OTARY
fur .... SEECATCH, URSAL
hooded ... BLADDERNOSE
hunter .... SWILER
kind of .... WAFER
large .... SEA LION
letter .... CACHET
male .... SEECATCH
off .... TRAP
Pope's .... BULL
rawhide ...... SHAGREEN
sound of .... BARK
tube .... CAPSULE
tusked .... WALRUS
with lead .... PLUMB
young .. PUP, HARP, CALF

sealed completely .. HERMETIC
sealer ..... SWILER, CALKER, PUTTY
sealing material ... MUCILAGE, PASTE, GLUE, TAPE, WAX(WAFER)
agent .... LUTE
seals, breeding place of ...... ROOKERY
flock of .... POD
pertaining to .... PHOCINE
seam ... WRINKLE, LINE, PURL, SUTURE, JUNCTURE
fill up .... CALK
filling material .. OAKUM, TAR
tapered .... DART
seamaid .... SIREN, MERMAID, NYMPH
seaman ... SAILOR, MARINER, GOB, RATING, JACKY, SALT, TAR
rating of .... ABLE
seamark .... LIGHTHOUSE, PHAROS, BEACON, BUOY, DAN
seamen's chapel ...... BETHEL
seamstress ...... SEMPTRESS, SEWER
seance ..... SESSION, MEETING, SITTING
noise .... RAP
participant .... MEDIUM, SPIRITUALIST
recording device .. OUIJA
seaplane stabilizer ... SPONSON
sear ...... WITHER, DRY(UP), BRAND, HARDEN, BURN, SERE, SCATHE
search ... EXPLORE, RUMMAGE, PROBE, SEEK, DELVE, GROPE, FORAGE, FERRET, QUEST, RANSACK, HUNT
for food .... FORAGE
for Holy Grail ... QUEST
for mineral .... PROSPECT
for talent .... SCOUT
party of a sort .... POSSE
person's person ... FRISK
steadily .... MOUSE
thoroughly ...... COMB
with divining rod .... DOWSE
searching ...... KEEN, SHARP
searing .... BURNING

seashore ..... COAST, BEACH, STRAND
of the .... LITTORAL
seasickness ..... MAL DE MER
seaside strip .... BOARDWALK
season ...... FALL, WINTER, SUMMER, SPRING, FLAVOR, SPICE, CURE, INURE, TEMPER, CORN, DEVIL, SALT
yield of .... VINTAGE
seasonable .... TIMELY, OPPORTUNE
seasonal .... PERIODIC
symbol .... HOLLY, PUMPKIN, SWALLOW, SNOW
seasoning ..... SPICE, GARLIC, SALT, CONDIMENT, MUSTARD
leaf .... BAY, LAUREL
pod .... CHILI
seasons .... HORAE
seat ... CHAIR, BENCH, STOOL, BUTTOCKS, CENTER, OTTOMAN, SEDILIA, PERCH, SOFA, SEDILE, GRADIN, VIS-A-VIS, SETTEE, INSTALL
bishop's .... METROPOLIS
chair's .... BOTTOM
coach .... DICKY
high .... ROOST
mobile .... WHEELCHAIR
of government .. CAPITAL
of judgment .. TRIBUNAL
on camel/elephant ...... HOWDAH, HOUDAH
royal .... THRONE
seats, church .... PEW, SEDILIA
se(a)wan .... WAMPUM
seaward .... OFF
seaweed ... TANGLE, SARGASSO, SARGASSUM, VAREC, NULLIPORE, ALGA, KELP, LAVER, AGAR, REDWARE, FUCUS, FUCOID
edible ..... DULSE, LIMU, CARRAG(H)EEN, AGAR, TANGLE
extract .... AGAR
genus .... ALARIA
leaflike part ...... FROND
product .... AGAR(AGAR)
purple .... SION
soda ash .... BARILLA
washed ashore .... SEAWARE, WRACK
seaworm .... LURG, SAO
seaworthy .... STANCH
sebaceous .... OILY
matter ... TALLOW, FAT, SEBUM
sec ...... BRUT, DRY, INSTANT
secede .... WITHDRAW, SEPARATE
secern .... SECRETE
secesh ... REB(EL), WITHDRAW
Seckel .... PEAR
seclude .... ISOLATE, IMMURE, SCREEN
secluded .... REMOTE,

SHUT OFF, ISOLATED, HERMITIC
spot .... NOOK
valley .... GLEN
seclusion .... PRIVACY, SOLITUDE, ISOLATION
second .... AID, MOMENT, INSTANT, TRICE, JIFFY, ASSISTANT, ABET, BACK
best .... RUNNER-UP
childhood ...... DOTAGE, SENILITY
estate .... NOBILITY
growth crop ..... ROWEN
hand dealer ... JUNKMAN, RAGMAN, SCRAPMAN
lieutenant: sl. .... SHAVETAIL
mentioned ..... LATTER
nature .... HABIT
placer ...... RUNNER-UP, ALSO-RAN
rate .... INFERIOR, MEDIOCRE
self .... ALTER EGO
story man ..... BURGLAR
team .... SCRUB
secondary .... MINOR, INFERIOR, BYE
secondhand ..... USED, WORN
secrecy .... PRIVACY
secret .... HIDDEN, MYSTERY, ARCANUM, ARCANE, OCCULT, COVERT, UNDERHAND, CRYPTIC, PRIVATE
action .... STEALTH
advisers' group .... CAMARILIA
agent .... SPY
agent's work .. ESPIONAGE
discussion ...... HUDDLE
meeting ...... CONCLAVE
most .... INMOST
place .... SANCTUM, HIDEOUT
remedy .... ELIXIR
service ... INTELLIGENCE
society .... CAMORRA, MAF(F)IA, TONG, KU KLUX, KLAN(KKK), PORO, BLACKHAND
watch .... ESPIONAGE, SPYING
writing .... CODE
secretary ...... AMANUENSIS, DESK, ESCRITOIRE
abbreviation .... SECY
public .... SCRIBE
secrete ... SECERN, CONCEAL, HIDE, STASH, CACHE
secretion .... SWEAT, SALIVA, SAP, MUCUS, LATEX, BILE SUDOR, EXUDATION, CHALONE
secretive ..... SLY, STEALTHY, RETICENT
secretly ..... SUBROSA, SLYLY, UNDERHAND
secrets .... PENETRALIA
sect .... FOLLOWING, DENOMINATION, CULT, FACTION, PARTY, SCHOOL
sectarian .... BIGOTED, APOSTATE
sectary .... DISSENTER
section ..... PART, SEGMENT, DIVISION
secular .... WORLDLY, TEMPORAL, LAIC(AL), LAY
secund .... UNILATERAL
secundine .... AFTERBIRTH
secure ... SAFE, FIRM, STABLE, SURE, GUARD, GET, ACQUIRE, FAST(EN), MOOR, BELAY, ANCHOR
place ... FASTNESS, FORT, STRONGHOLD
security .... SAFETY, SAFEGUARD, BOND, PLEDGE, GUARANTEE, SURETY, GRITH, GAGE
for payment .... LIEN, COLLATERAL, BOND
sedan .... AUTOMOBILE, (CLOSED)CAR, CHAIR, LITTER, LIMOUSINE
sedate .... QUIET, SERIOUS, CALM, GRAVE, SOBER, STAID, DEMURE
sedative .... URETHAN(E), DEMEROL, NEMBUTAL, CODEIN(E), AMYTAL, BARBITAL, BROMIDE, ANODYNE, LUMINAL, OPIATE, CALMATIVE
Seder, event commemorated by EXODUS
sedge clump .... TUSSOCK
sediment ...... SILT, MAGMA, SLUDGE, LEES, DREGS, DRAFF, GROUT, FOOTS, OOZE
sedimentary deposit layer ..... VARVE
sedition .... TREASON
seduce .... PERSUADE, TEMPT, LURE
seducer .... SIREN, VAMP, LOTHARIO, CASANOVA, ENTICER
seductive .... CHARMING
sedulous ..... BUSY, DILIGENT
sedum .... STONECROP
see .... DISCERN, ESPY, VISIT, DESCRY, BEHOLD, DIOCESE, PERCEIVE, VIEW, WITNESS, MEET, COMPREHEND
bishop's .... METROPOLIS
head of a .... BISHOP
slow to .... PURBLIND
seed .... SOW, GERM, OVULE, SPERM, PIP(PIN), BEAN
aromatic .... ANISE(ED), CUM(M)IN, GUAIAC, TONKA
bearing organ .... PISTIL
bud .... PLUMULE
case .... POD, BUR(R), CYPSELA
coat .... BRAN, ARIL, TESTA, HULL, TEG(U)MEN, HUSK
combining form .. SPERM, SPERMAT(O)
container ... PIT, STONE, POD
cover, false .... ARILLODE
edible .... PEA, BEAN, LENTIL, PULSE, SOY(BEAN), PISTACHIO, PINON
flavoring ..... CARAWAY, ANISE, CUM(M)IN
food ...... PEA, LENTIL, SOY, BEAN, LEGUME, SESAME, COQUITO
hole-making tool .... DIBBLE
immature .... OVULE
leaf .... COTYLEDON
lense-shaped ... LENTIGO
like .... SEMINAL
oil ...... CHAULMOOGRA, SESAME, GINGILI
oil-yielding ..... SESAME, TILL, BENNE, GINGILI, GINGELI
one-celled .... CARPEL
oyster .... SPAT
pear .... PIP
plant .... HERB, EXOGEN
pod .... CYPSELA
poisonous .. NUX VOMICA
prematurely produce .... BOLT
remove .... GIN
remover .... GIN, RIPPLE
rudimentary ..... OVULE
scar .... HILUM
spice .... NUTMEG, CARDAMON
stalk .... FUNICULUS
strong-smelling .... CARAWAY
vessel .... PERICARP, CAPSULE, BUR, POD, SILICLE
seedless .... AGAMOUS
plant .... FERN
seedling .... SAPLING
seeds: combining form .. CARPO
row of planted ... DRILL
study of ..... CARPOLOGY
seedsman .... SOWER
seedy .... SHABBY, TACKY
seeing .... VISION, SIGHT
seek ...... EXPLORE, SEARCH, INQUIRE, PURSUE
seel ...... HOODWINK, BLIND
seeled bird ... HAWK, FALCON
seem .... APPEAR, LOOK
seeming ... APPARENT, SHOW, QUASI, OSTENSIBLE
seemingly .... QUASI
seemly .... FAIR, COMELY, SUITABLE, FITTING, PROPER, MEET, DECENT
seen, can be .... VISIBLE, DISCERNIBLE, PERCEPTIBLE
seep .... LEAK, PERCOLATE, OOZE, PERMEATE
seer .... SOOTHSAYER, PROPHET, ARUSPEX
seeress .... SIBYL, CASSANDRA
seersucker .... FABRIC, LINEN
seesaw ... FLAP, TESTER, TILT, WAG, VACILLATE,

CROSSRUFF, BASCULE
seethe .... BOIL, BUBBLE, SIMMER, STEW, FERMENT
seething .... ABOIL
segment .... SECTION, DIVISION, PART, PORTION, SECTOR
of crustacean ... TELSON
sego .... PLANT, LILY
segregate .... ISOLATE, SEPARATE, SET APART
seidel .... MUG
seigneur .... LORD, NOBLE
seine .... NET, RIVER
city on the ...... ROUEN, TROYES
tributary .... EURE, OISE, MARNE
seism .... EARTHQUAKE
seismograph subject .. TREMOR, TEMBLOR, QUAKE
seize .... GRAB, ATTACK, ARREST, NAB, GRASP, LASH, TAKE, CONFISCATE, COLLAR
first .... PREEMPT
for debt .... DISTRAIN, GARNISH
for official use .... COMMANDEER
in law .... LEVY
power, etc. .... USURP
seizure .... ATTACK, FIT
selachian ...... RAY, SHARK, DOGFISH
Selassie, Emperor ..... HAILE
seldom .... RARELY
select ..... CHOICE, PICK(ED), EXCLUSIVE, WALE, CULL, ELITE, CHOOSE
selected .... INDUCTEE, DRAFTEE
selection .... CHOICE
selective service ...... DRAFT
Selene .... LUNA, MOON, ARTEMIS, HECATE
love of .... ENDYMION
selenite .... GYPSUM
self .... EGO
assurance .. CONFIDENCE, POISE, APLOMB
centered ... EGOCENTRIC, SELFISH
combining form ... AUTO
conceit ... VANITY, PRIDE, EGOTISM
confidence ..... PANACHE
confident ..... ASSURED, POISED, COCKSURE, COCKY
conscious ... SHY, TIMID
control, power of .. WILL
cremation ...... SUTTEE
defense art ..... JUJUTSU, KARATE, JUDO
denial .... SACRIFICE
denying ...... MONASTIC
destruction .... SUICIDE, IMMOLATION
determination .... FREE WILL
esteem ... PRIDE, VANITY, EGOISM
evident ...... AXIOMATIC
explanatory .... OBVIOUS
fertilization .... ORTHOGAMY
government .. HOME RULE
immolation ..... SUICIDE
important .... BUMBLING, POMPOUS
important person .. NIBS
love ...... NARC(ISS)ISM
possessed ... COOL, CALM, COMPOSED
propelled .. AUTOMOTIVE
protection ..... DEFENSE
reliant ...... DEPENDABLE
reproach ... REPENTANCE, REMORSE
restraint .. MODERATION, TEMPERANCE
righteous .... SMUG
satisfied .... SMUG
selfheal .... SANICLE
sell ... BETRAY, DUPE, TRADE, AUCTION, VEND, PEDDLE, BARTER, MARKET, HAWK
for .... FETCH
out sign .... SRO
seller .... VENDOR, PEDDLER, RETAILER, COSTER
on installment .... TALLYMAN
Selm .... LAGERLOF
selvage .... LIST
semantics, concern of .... MEANING
semasiology ...... SEMANTICS
semblance .... PRETENSE, LIKENESS, IMAGE, GUISE
seme .... DOTTED
Semele's father ..... CADMUS
son .... DIONYSUS
semester ... TERM, HALF YEAR
Seminole chief ...... OSCEOLA
semiology, subject of .. SIGNS, SYMPTOMS
Semiramis' husband ... NINUS
kingdom .... BABYLON
semisolid substance .. GELATIN
Semite .. HEBREW, JEW, ARAB, BABYLONIAN, PHOENICIAN
god .... STERAPH
Semitic language ..... PUNIC, ARAMAIC, HEBREW, ARABIC, AMHARIC
people ....CHALDEAN, BABYLONIAN
tribe .... AMMON
vampire .... LILITH
semolina .... MEAL
semper .... ALWAYS
sempstress .... SEAMSTRESS, SEWER
sen, 1/10 of a .... RIN
senate house .... CURIA
send ... DISPATCH, TRANSMIT, REMIT, FORWARD
back .. REMAND, RETURN, REMIT, REPATRIATE
flying .... ROUT
for .... SUMMON
forth .... EMIT
out ..... ISSUE, DESPATCH
packing .... DISMISS, DRIVE
Seneca .. IROQUOIAN, INDIAN, CAYUGA
senega .... MILKWORT
Senegal, capital of ... DAKAR
city ... THIES, KAOLOCK, DAKAR
ethnic group .... WOLOF, PEUL, SERERE
president ..... SENGHOR
senescent .... AGING
seneschal .. MAJOR DOMO, KAY
senhor .... SIR, (GENTLE)MAN
senile ..... DOITED, ELDERLY, AGED
senility ... DOTAGE, OLD AGE
senior .... OLDER, ELDER
class publication .... ANNUAL, YEARBOOK
member of group .. DEAN, DOYEN
seniorita .... MISS, LADY
seniority .... PRECEDENCE
senna .. PLANT, PEA, LAXATIVE
source of .... CASSIA
sennet .... FLOURISH
sennight .... WEEK
sensate .. CONSCIOUS, ESTHESIA
sensation ...... FEELING, HIT, EXCITEMENT, PERCEPTION
of smell ..... OLFACTION
of taste ..... GUSTATION
sensational .... LURID, STARTLING, EXCITING, SHOCKING
sense ... MEANING, FEEL(ING), PERCEIVE, SIGHT, TASTE, TOUCH, SAPIENCE, INTUIT, SMELL, HEARING
of sight, of the .... OPTIC
of smell ..... OLFACTION
of taste ..... GUSTATION
organ ... EYE, RECEPTOR, TASTE BUD, ANTENNA, FEELER, NOSE, EAR, PALP(US)
sixth .... INTUITION
sound .... LOGIC
senseless .... ABSURD, INEPT, INANE, FOOLISH, STUPID, FATUOUS, UNCONSCIOUS, IRRATIONAL, WANTON
senses, one of the ..... SIGHT, TASTE, SMELL, TOUCH, HEARING, INTUITION
sensible ... SANE, REASONABLE, RATIONAL, AWARE, WISE, PASSIBLE, LEVEL-HEADED
sensitive .... TE(T)CHY, RAW, TOUCHY, TENSE, TENDER, SORE
plant .... MIMOSA
sensitivity .... ERETHISM
sensual .... CARNAL, LUSTFUL, LYDIAN
sensualist .... SYBARITE
sensuous .... EPICURIAN
sentence .... DECISION, OPINION, JUDGMENT, DOOM
break down ..... PARSE
mark ... COLON, COMMA
part .... VERB, NOUN, PREDICATE

reading same backward .. PALINDROME
slang .... RAP
structure .... SYNTAX
sententious .... PITHY, TERSE, POINTED
sentient .... CONSCIOUS
sentiment .... ATTITUDE, FEELING, OPINION, EMOTION
sentimental .... MAWKISH, MAUDLIN, GUSHY, ROMANTIC, SOPPY, MUSHY, SPOONY, NAMBY-PAMBY
sentimentalism .... SCHMALTZ
sentimentality .... MUSH
sentinel .... SENTRY, WATCH(DOG), GUARD, PICKET
mounted ..... VEDETTE, VIDETTE, LOOKOUT
sentry ..... SENTINEL, WATCH, GUARD, BIVOUAC
box .... BOOTH
challenge of .... WHO GOES THERE
challenge of French ..... QUI VA LA
order of .... HALT
Seoul .... KEIJO
sepal .... LEAF, CALYX
separate .... (SET)APART, DIVIDE, SEGREGATE, SECEDE, SEVERAL, DISCRETE, ISOLATE, ALIENATE, SEVER, PART, SORT, DISTINCT, SPLIT, SECERN
forcibly .. REND, WRENCH
in botany .... SOLUTE
into parts ... DISMEMBER
separation ... BREAK, DIVORCE, SCHISM, SECESSION, AVULSION
in chemistry ... DIALYSIS
separatist .... DISSENTER
separator .... SEPTUM
Sephardic dialect .... LADINO
Sephardim .... JEWS
sepia ...... DUN, CUTTLEFISH, PIGMENT
sepiolite .... MEERSCHAUM
seppuku .. HARAKIRI, SUICIDE
seps .... SKINK, SNAKE
sept .... CLAN, TRIBE
September 13, Roman calendar IDES
septic .... INFECTIVE
septicemia .... SEPSIS
septime .... PARRY
septum .... PARTITION
septuple .... SEVENFOLD
sepulcher ...... TOMB, GRAVE, BURY, RELIQUARY, VAULT, CRYPT, SEPULTURE
sepulchral ... DISMAL, GLOOMY, TOMBLIKE
sepulture .. BURIAL, INTERMENT
sequel ... AFTERMATH, EFFECT, UPSHOT
sequence ...... RUN, SEQUEL, SUCCESSION, SERIES
sequester .... ISOLATE, SET APART, SEGREGATE, SEPARATE, SEIZE, CONFISCATE, ENISLE, SECLUDE
sequestered .... RETIRED, SECLUDED
sequin .... SPANGLE, ZECCHIN(O)
sequoia .... REDWOOD
seraglio ..... HAREM, PALACE, SERAI, ZENANA
serai .. CARAVANSARY, IMARET, INN, SERAGLIO
Serang .... CERAM
serape ...... BLANKET, SKAWL
seraph .... ANGEL, CHERUB
seraphic .... ANGELIC
Serb .... SLAV
Serbian guerrilla ... CHETNIK
sere ..... DRIED, WITHER(ED), DRY
serein .... RAIN
serenade .... NOCTURNE
mock .... SHIVAREE, CHARIVARI
serene ...... CALM, EQUABLE, TRANQUIL, IMPASSIVE, QUIET, COMPOSED
serenity ... REPOSE, CALMNESS
serf .... ESNE, SLAVE, THRALL, BONDMAN, HELOT, VILLEIN, LITUS
female .... NEIF
liberate a ..... MANUMIT
serfdom .. BONDAGE, HELOTRY, SLAVERY
sergeant .... TOPKICK, SARGE, NCO
at-law's cap ..... BIGGIN
fish ..... ROBALO, COBIA
seric .... SILKEN
sericeous ...... DOWNY, SILKY
series .... SET, SEQUENCE, SUCCESSION, CHAIN
of columns .. COLONNADE
of links .... CHAIN
of six .... HEXAD
of stairs .... FLIGHT
of steps .... SCALE
of trouble ... GA(U)NTLET
serin .... FINCH
serious ..... GRAVE, EARNEST, SOLEMN, GRIM, SOBER, SINCERE, CRITICAL, SEDATE
sermon .... LECTURE, SPEECH, DISCOURSE, HOMILY
sermonize .... PREACH
sermons, study of .... HOMILETICS
serous .... WATERY
membrane .. PERITONEUM
serow ...... JAGIA, ANTELOPE
serpent ... FIREWORK, SATAN, COCKATRICE, DRAGON, OPHIDIAN, BASILISK, SNAKE, SEPS, (A)BOMA, BOA, ELOPS
monster .... HYDRA, LAMIA, ELOPS
nine-headed ..... HYDRA
worship .... OPHISM
serpentine .... WINDING, CUNNING, COILED, OPHIDIAN, OPHITE, SINUOUS
serpigo .... RINGWORM
serranoid fish ..... CABRILLA, REDHIND
serried .... COMPACT
serum ..... ANTITOXIN, WHEY
serval .... WILDCAT
servant .... SLAVE, MAN, ANCILLARY, (BAT)MAN, HIND, DOMESTIC, MAID, MENIAL, GILLY, GILLIE
boy .... PAGE, GOSSOON, GARCON
college .... GYP
devoted .... FRIDAY
female ... SLAVEY, WENCH
feudal .... SERGEANT
head .... BUTLER
house of .... LODGE
liveried .... FLUNKY, LACKEY
male ... LACKEY, VALET, BUTLER
man's .... VALET
personal .... VALET, EQUERRY
seat in carriage .. RUMBLE
uniformed .... CHASSEUR
serve .... WAIT, SUPPLY, DELIVER, (AT)TEND, SATISFY
food ...... CATER, WAIT
server .... WAITER, TRAY, SALVER, ATTENDANT
alcoholic drinks .... BARTENDER
service .. EMPLOYMENT, WORK, MASS, RITE, USE, SHADBUSH
club ... ROTARY, KIWANIS, LIONS, JAYCEE
stripe, military .... HASH MARK
tree .... SORB
serviceable ... USEFUL, USABLE, UTILE
serviceman .... SOLDIER
services, one of the .. ARMY, NAVY, AIR FORCE
serviette .... NAPKIN
servile .... TAME, SLAVISH, MENIAL, FAWNING, ABJECT
serving .... PORTION
boy .... KNAVE
man .... POTMAN
stand ..... DUMB WAITER
servite .... MENDICANT
servitor .... ATTENDANT, ADHERENT, FOLLOWER, SERVANT
servitude .... BONDAGE, SLAVERY, YOKE, EASEMENT
symbol of .... YOKE
sesame .. TIL, BENNE, SEMSEM, TEEL, GINGILI
grass .... GAMA
oil .... BENI, GINGILI
seed ... GINGILI, GENGELI, GINGELLY
sess .... TAX
sessile .... IMMOBILE
session ... ASSEMBLY, SEANCE, MEETING, SITTING

discontinue ... ADJOURN, PROROGUE
sestet .... SEXTET(TE)
set ...... BATCH, JELLY, SEAT, RECORD, FIX, WANE, DECLINE, SCENERY, LAY, POST, EMBED, PRESCRIBE, RIGID, RESOLUTE, CLIQUE, COLLECTION, COTERIE, KIT
afloat .... LAUNCH
all ... PREPARED, READY
apart .... ISOLATE, SEGREGATE, RESERVE
aside .... ANNUL, DISCARD, REJECT, DEFER, PEND, QUASH, EARMARK
down ..... RECORD, LAY
down as a fact .... POSIT
firmly .... INFIX
forth ..... START, STATE, THETIC
free .... LIBERATE, DELIVER, EXTRICATE
in competition ...... PIT, MATCH
in motion ..... ACTIVATE, EXCITE
in operation .. LAUNCH
in type .... COMPOSE
of clothes ..... COSTUME, SUIT
of nine .... ENNEAD
of players .... TEAM
of rules .... CODE
of three .... TERNION
off ... EXPLODE, DETONATE
on fire ... KINDLE, IGNITE
on horse .... MOUNT
out .... DEFINE, PLAN, LEAVE, DEPART, GO
playing cards ..... DECK, PACK
right ..... REPAIR, ALIGN, AMEND, CORRECT
sail .... CAST OFF
thickly .... STUD
to .... BOUT, FIGHT, CONTEST
up ... FOUND, ESTABLISH, PITCH, ERECT
upon ... ATTACK, SIC(K)
value on .... PRICE, APPRAISE
seta .... BRISTLE, CHAETA
setback ..... UPSET, RELAPSE, EDDY, REVERSE, REVERSAL
Seth's brother ..... CAIN, ABEL
parent ..... ADAM, EVE
son .... ENOS
setoff .... OFFSET
seton .... DISCHARGE
setose .... BRISTLY
settee .... SEAT, BENCH, SOFA, LOUNGE
setter ... (GUN)DOG, RETRIEVER
setting ...... SCENE, MOUNT, LOCALE, MILIEU
jewels' .... PAVE
scheme .... DECOR
settle ...... BENCH, ARRANGE, COLONIZE, DECIDE, PAY, FIX, ALIGHT, SINK, REST, SOFA, LIQUIDATE, COUCH, CONCLUDE, END
argument ...... CLINCH
down ... ABATE, SUBSIDE
for the night .. BED DOWN
on land illegally .. SQUAT
settlement .... COLONY, VILLAGE, AGREEMENT, PAYMENT, PLANTATION
settled, in law .... VESTED
settler .... SOONER, HOMESTEADER, COLONIST, BOOMER
land .... HOMESTEAD
settlers led by Kok ... GRIQUA
settlings .... DREGS, LEES, SEDIMENT, DRAFF
Sevastapol is in ...... CRIMEA
seven ...... HEPTAD, VII, SEPT
against Thebes, one of ... TYDEUS
combining form .... HEPT(A)
days .... HEBDOMAD
deadly sins, one of the ... SLOTH, ENVY, LUST, ANGER, PRIDE, GLUTTONY
Dwarfs, one of ..... DOC, DOPEY, BASHFUL, HAPPY, SLEEPY, SNEEZY, GRUMPY
group of .... HEPTAD
Hills of Rome, one of the CAELIAN, PALATINE, AVENTINE, QUIRINAL, VIMINAL, CAPITOLINE
of number .... SEPTIMAL, SEPTENARY
series of .... HEPTAD
Wonders of the World ... COLOSSUS, PYRAMIDS, MAUSOLEUM, PHAROS
year period ..... TEENS
sevenfold .... SEPTUPLE
seventeen XVII
year locust ...... CICADA
seventh son .... SEER
sever .... SEPARATE, CUT, DIVIDE, BREAK(OFF)
several .... FEW, SEPARATE, DIVERS(E)
severe ..... ACUTE, DRASTIC, HARSH, SERIOUS, STERN, RIGOROUS
not .... BENIGN, LENIENT
Severn river .... USK
severity ... RIGOR, HARSHNESS, AUSTERITY
sew ... STITCH, BASTE, SUTURE, SEAM, FELL, QUILT, TACK
up ... MONOPOLIZE, CLOSE
sewage disposal ... SANITATION
hole .... CESSPOOL
Seward's "folly" .... ALASKA
sewan .... SHELLS
sewer .... DRAIN, PIPE, SEAMSTRESS, GUTTER, KENNEL
entrance ..... MANHOLE
sewing .... NEEDLEWORK
case .... ETUI, ETWEE
kit ... HUSSY, HOUSEWIFE
machine inventor .. HOWE
part .... LOOPER
sex appeal ... OOMPH, CHARM
hormone ...... STEROID
of a ... MASCULINE, MALE FEMALE, FEMININE
sexes, common to both .... EPICENE
sexless .... FRIGID
sext .... HOUR
sextant .... QUADRANT, ALTIMETER
sextet .... HEXAD
sexton .... GRAVEDIGGER, BELLRINGER, SACRIST(AN)
sextuple .... SIXFOLD
sexual ...... CARNAL, GAMIC
continence .... CHASTITY
desire, of .... EROTIC
excitement .... HEAT, (O)ESTRUS, RUT
inclination/urge .. LIBIDO
pervert .... DEVIATE
sexually cold .... FRIGID
sexy .... EROTIC
picture .... PINUP
Seychelles, capital of .... VICTORIA
island .... MAHE
Sforza, Ital. statesman .... CARLO
shabby ... UNKEMPT, RAGGED, SEEDY, DOWDY, WORN, MEAN, DINGY, MANGY, TACKY, RATTY, THREADBARE, DISGRACEFUL, CRUMMY
woman ...... SLATTERN, DOWD, SLOVEN
shack .... SHANTY, HOVEL, CABIN, HUT
shackle .. MANACLE, TRAMMEL, FETTER, GYVE, PINION, BILBO, RESTRAIN, HAMPER, LEG-IRON, IRON(S), CHAIN
shad .... ALEWIFE, ALOSE, ALOSA, ALLIS
fish like ..... MENHADEN
running upriver .... ANADROMOUS
shadbush .... SERVICE, SASKATOON, JUNEBERRY, ROSE
shaddock .... POMELO
shade .... UMBER, UMBRA, TRACE, TOUCH, SCREEN, COLOR, TONE, HUE, TINGE, BLIND, TINT, SHADOW
blue .... ALICE
cap's .... VISOR
lines .... HATCH
of difference ... NUANCE
of meaning ..... NUANCE
tree .... ELM, LIN
shaded walk ... MALL, ARBOR, ALAMEDA, CLOISTER
shades, the .... HADES
shadow .. DOG, GLOOM, OMEN, TAIL, TRAIL, GHOST, TRACE, VESTIGE, SHADE, UMBER,

UMBRA, SPY, CLOUD
astronomer's ... UMBRA
fighting ..... SCIAMACHY
man without .... ASCIAN
The .. (LAMONT) CRANSTON
shadowbox .... SPAR
Shadrach's fellow-captive ..... MESHACH, ABEDNEGO
shady .... DOUBTFUL, DISHONEST, DUBIOUS
retreat ... KIOSK, ARBOR, NOOK
SHAEF commander .... (IKE) EISENHOWER
theater ..... ETO, EUROPE
shaft .... ARBOR, HANDLE, SPEAR, BOLT, BEAM, OBELISK, SHANK, SPINDLE, ARROW, FLAGPOLE, SPIRE, POLE, THILL, CONDUIT, MISSILE, FLUE, PILLAR, COLUMN, JAVELIN, ARROYO
bearing .... HOTBOX
column's .. VERGE, SCAPE, FUST, TRUNK
feather's .... SCAPE
handle .... HELVE
mine .... PIT
part of .... JOURNAL, BOSS, GUDGEON, TRUNNION
shag ... NAP, MAT, TOBACCO, CORMORANT
shagbark .... WALNUT, HICKORY
shaggy ...... HIRSUTE, NAPPY, UNKEMPT, THRUMMY, HAIRY, SCRUBBY, BUSHY
shagreen ..... RAWHIDE, SKIN
Shah Jahan's masterpiece .... TAJ MAHAL
of Iran .... PAHLEVI
shaitan .. DEVIL, FIEND, SATAN
shake ...... WOBBLE, QUIVER, TREMBLE, VIBRATE, QUAKE, TREMOR, THRILL, SHIVER, JOLT, UNNERVE, WAVE, RID, JAR, MOMENT, SUCCUSS, ROCK, CONVULSE
down ...... EXTORT(ION), BLACKMAIL, BOGUS
due to cold ..... SHIVER
due to horror, fear ...... SHUDDER
up .... REVAMP
Shakespearean actor .... GIELGUD, OLIVIER, WILLIAMSON
Athenian .... TIMON
character .... ROMEO, TYBALT, CASSIUS, OTHELLO, IAGO, ORLANDO, LEAR, MERCUTIO, SHYLOCK, SOLINUS, BENVOLIO, BRUTUS, HAMLET, PORTIA, KATE
clown .. GOBBY, COSTARD, FESTE
elf .... PUCK
forest ...... SHERWOOD, ARDEN
king ..... LEAR, HAMLET
seven .... AGES
songwriter .... ARNE
theatre .... GLOBE
villain .... IAGO
witch .... CYCORAX
shaking ...... ASPEN, PALSIED
shako decoration ... POMPON
shakti .... DEVI, POWER
shaky .... WEAK, DOTTY, UNSOUND, CRANKY, UNCERTAIN, QUAKY, RICKETY
shale .... ROCK, PELITE
product .... TARE
shall .... MUST
shallop .... DINGHY, BOAT
shallot ..... ONION, SCALLION, ESCHALOT, BULB
kin .... LEEK
shallow .... SUPERFICIAL, SHOAL
lake ... LAGOON, LAGUNE
sham ... BASTARD, IMITATION, FALSE, HUMBUG, FAKE, FEIGN, COUNTERFEIT, ARTIFICIAL, PHON(E)Y
fight .... SCIAMACHY
shaman .... PRIEST, MEDICINE MAN
Shamash .... SUN GOD
shamble ... SHUFFLE, LUMBER, WALK, GAIT
shambles .... ABATTOIR, DISORDER
shame ... MORTIFY, DISGRACE, FIE, DISHONOR, ABASH, BLACKEYE
shamefaced ... SHY, BASHFUL
shameful .... INDECENT, OFFENSIVE
shameless .... BRAZEN
shammy .... CHAMOIS
Shamo .... GOBI
shampoo .... MASSAGE, WASH, SOAP, LOMILOMI
shamrock .... CLOVER
country .... IRELAND, ERIN, EIRE
Shan .... T(H)AI
shandrydan ..... CHAISE, CART
Shanghai .... SEAPORT, CHICKEN, KIDNAP
Shangri-la .... UTOPIA, PARADISE
shank .... CRUS, LEG, SHAFT, GAMB(E)
in botany ... FOOTSTALK
shanny .... BLENNY
Shantung .... TUSSA(H)
capital of .... TSINAN
city .... CHEFOO
shanty ... HOVEL, HUT, SHACK
shantytown .... SLUM
shape .... FIGURE, GUISE, PHANTON, FORM, STATE, CONDITION, MO(U)LD, MODEL
bust's .... TAILLE
shapeless .... AMORPHOUS
shapely .... SVELT, NEAT
shaping machine ..... EDGER, LATHE
shard ..... POTSHERD, SHEEL, PLATE, FRAGMENT
share .. (AP)PORTION, PARTAKE, PART, RATION, BIT, LOT, CUT, MOIETY, STAKE
in common ...... JOINT, MUTUAL
slang .... DIVVY
shark ... THRESHER, SWINDLER, CHEAT, TOPE, MAKO, SHOVELHEAD, GATA, HAMMERHEAD, MAN-EATER, DOGFISH, ANGELFISH, PORBEAGLE
eating fish .... PEGA
loan .... USURER
nurse .... GATA
rider/sucker .... REMORA
skin .... SHAGREEN
young .... PUPPY
sharp .. KEEN, PEAKED, ACUTE, CLEAR, DISTINCT, VITRIOLIC, CLEVER, SMART, PIERCING, PUNGENT, SEVERE, CUTTING, GLEG, PUNGENT, TRENCHANT, HANDSOME, EDGED, ACERB, ACIFORM, NIPPY, NIPPING, INCISIVE
at the end ...... ACUATE
blade .... RAZOR
colloquial ...... ADEPT, EXPERT
combining form .... ACET(O)
cry .... YELP
edged .... KEEN
end .... POINT
eyed one ... LYNX, EAGLE
in phonetics .. VOICELESS
northern seas .... PORBEAGLE
pain .... STING
reply .... RETORT
taste ...... TANG, TART
turn .... ZIG
witted .... KEEN
sharpen .... WHET, STROP, EDGE, HONE, GRIND
sharpening device .... WHETSTONE, STROP, HONE, GRINDSTONE, STRAP, GRINDER
sharper ..... SWINDLER, KITE, GYP, CHEAT
sharpness ... EDGE, ACERBITY, BARB
of temper ...... ASPERITY
Shasta ...... VOLCANO, DAISY
sharpshooter .... SHOT, MARKSMAN, SNIPER, RIFLEMAN
shatter .... BREAK, WRECK, BURST, SHIVER, DASH, SMASH
shave .... SCRAPE, GRAZE, TRIM, SKIVE, PLANE, SHEAR, PARE, WHITTLE, CUT
shaver ..... BOY, RAZOR, LAD, YOUTH, YOUNGSTER
shaveling ..... MONK, PRIEST
shavetail ... MULE, LIEUTENANT
Shavian forte .... WIT
shaw .... COPSE, THICKET

shawl .... MANTA, MAUD, PAISLEY, SERAPE, PEPLOS, WRAP, TALLITH, CASHMERE, MUFFLER
shawn .... OBOE
Shawnee .... INDIAN
bread .... PONE, JOHNNYCAKE
chief .... TECUMSEH, TECUMTHA
shay ..... CHAISE, CARRIAGE, STANHOPE, BUGGY
she .... FEMALE, FEMININE
carved it .... SCULPSIT
died .... OBIT
painted it ... PNXT, PINXIT
speaks .... LOQUITUR
wrote it .... SCRIPSIT
sheaf .... BUNDLE, BALE, BUNCH
shear ..... CLIP, CUT, FLEECE, POLL, TRIM, STRIP, SHAVE, CROP
shearing tool .... CLIPPER
Shearer, ____ .... NORMA, MOIRA
shearing machine ... CROPPER
shears .... SCISSORS
sheatfish .... CATFISH
sheath .. CAPSULE, SCABBARD, STALL, DRESS, OCREA, (EN)CASE, COT, SLEEVE, THECA, SPATHE
metalplate on .... CHAPE
sheathe ...... RETRACT, COVER
sheathed ...THECATE, OCREATE
sheaves of grain ...... STOCK, SHOCK
Sheba .... SABA
people .... SAB(A)EAN
queen of .... BALKIS
shebang ... BUSINESS, AFFAIR, THING, MATTER
shed ...... SCONCE, LEANTO, RADIATE, DISCARD, COTE, MOLT, CAST(OFF), DIFFUSE, DROP, FALL OUT
aircraft ..... AIRDROME, HANGAR
animal .... HOVEL
chicken .... COTE
sheep .... COTE
skin/feathers ... MO(U)LT, PEEL, MEW
shedding leaves annually ...... DECIDUOUS
Sheean, writer ...... VINCENT
sheen .... POLISH, GLOSS, LUSTRE, LUSTER, SHINE
Bishop .... FULTON
Sheena's domain .... JUNGLE
sheep ... CARACUL, KARAKUL, MERINO, SHA, OORIAL, URIAL, CHEVIOT, NAHOOR, LEICESTER, BROADTAIL, ARUI
brain ailment ...... GID
caretaker .... SHEPHERD
castrated ...... WETHER
cry of .... BAA, BLAT, BLEAT, MAA
descriptive of .... MEEK, TIMID
disease ... LOCO, SCRAPIE, SHAKES, ROT, COE, STAGGERS, WILDFIRE, GID, STURDY, ANTHRAX
dog ... COLLIE, SHEPHERD, SHELTIE, SHELTY
enclosure .... KRAAL
fat .... SUET, TALLOW
female .... EWE
flesh .... MUTTON, VEAL, LAMB
flock ... FOLD, DRYBAND
flock leader .... BELLWETHER
foot of .... TROTTER
fur .... CARACUL, KARAKUL, MOUTON
genus .... BOS, OVIS
grease .... SUINT
group of ... FOLD, FLOCK
head .... JEMMY
intestinal disorder ...... BRAXY
kept together ..... FOLD
killing bird .... KEA
like .... OVINE
like animal ...... SAIGA
male .... RAM, TUP, WETHER
mountain .... IBEX
mutton .... SUFFOLK
neck growth of .... POKE
parasite ..... COENURUS, FLUKE
pen .... FOLD, KRAAL
pertaining to ..... OVINE
sexual excitement ... RUT, HEAT, EBTRUS
shelter ...... COTE, FOLD
skin cap .... KALPAK, CALPAC(K)
skin dealer .. FELLMONGER
skin disease .... SCAB, MANGE
sound ..... BL(E)AT, BAA
stomach trouble .. BRAXY
tender .... SHEPHERD
unshorn .... HOG
walk .... SLAITH
white .... WILTSHIRE
white-faced .. CORRIEDALE
wild ... URIAL, ARUI, SHA, RASSE, OORIAL, MOUF(F)LON, AOUDAD, ARGALI, UDAD, SNA, NAHOOR
wool .... FLEECE
wool secretion .... YOLK
young .... HOG, (Y)EANLING, LAMB, TEG
sheepfold ...... COTE, KRAAL, REE, PEN
sheeplike ...... OVINE, MEEK, DOCILE
sheepshank .... KNOT
sheepshead .... SPAROID
sheepskin ......PARCHMENT, ROAN, SKIVER, DIPLOMA
cap .. CALPAC(K), KALPAK
sheepwalk .. PASTURE, SLAITH
sheer .... VEER, SWERVE, DEVIATE, TURN, STEEP, STARK, PURE, THIN, UTTER, ABSOLUTE
delight .... RAPTURE, ECSTASY
legs .... SHEARS
sheet ..... SAIL, NEWSPAPER, EXPANSE
bend .... KNOT
blurred .... MACKLE
metal(piece) ..... PLATE, LATH, LEAF
metal cutter .... SNIP
of lava .... COULEE
sheeting material ... PERCALE
shekel .... MONEY
sheldrake .... DUCK, MERGANSER
shelf .... REEF, LEDGE, MANTEL, BERM(E), GRADIN(E), RETABLE, SANDBAR, BEDROCK
drapery ... LAMBREQUIN, VALANCE
shell ..... CARAPACE, MISSILE, MOLLUSK, BOMBARD, COVER, BIELD, LORICA, CONCH, TUNICA, SHARD, RACING BOAT, CARTRIDGE, INTEGUMENT, POD, SHUCK
abalone .... ORMER
artillery ..... SHRAPNEL, OBUS
bean .... LIMA
boat .... HULL
corn .... HUSK
crab, clam, etc. ..... TEST
defective .... DUD
dish, baking ... SCALLOP
ear .... ORMER, ABALONE
enclosed in a .. OBTECTED
explosive .... BOMB, SHRAPNEL, GRENADE
failing to explode .. DUD
fish ... BARNACLE, NACRE, COCKLE
fragments .... SHRAPNEL
fruit .... RIND, PEEL
game ...... THIMBLERIG
hole .... CRATER
hurling device ... MORTAR
invertebrate's ...... TEST
mollusk's .... CONCH
money .. COWRIE, COWRY, PEAG(E), SE(A)WAN, WAMPUM
of .... TESTACEOUS
1/20 of .... GERAH
out .... PAY, GIVE
pastry .... TART
seed ..... TEST(A), HUSK
spiral .... CONCH
that doesn't explode ..... DUD
tip of .... WARNOSE
trumpet .... CONCH
turtle/tortoise .... PLASTRON
shellac(k) ... RESIN, VARNISH, BEAT, DRUB, LAC(QUER)
shellacking .... BEATING, WHIPPING
shellback .... SAILOR
shellbark .. WALNUT, HICKORY, SHAGBARK

Shelley, poet ... PERCY, ARIEL
elegy by .... ADONAIS
shellfish ..... CLAM, LOBSTER, SHRIMP, CRAB, MOLLUSK, SCALLOP, ABALONE, MOSSBACK, NACRE, BARNACLE, COCKLE
spawn .... SPAT
trap .... CREEL
shelter ..... COVER(T), HAVEN, REFUGE, RETREAT, SHED, SCONCE, NESTLE, CABANA, BIELD, ROOF
aircraft .... HANGAR, AIRDROME
airraid ... ABRI, DUGOUT
auto .... CARPORT
canvas .... TENT
cattle ... KRAAL, CORRAL
collapsible .... TENT
decorative ..... PAVILION
dove's .... COTE
hillside .... ABRI
movable ... MANT(E)LET
overhanging .... CANOPY
rain .... UMBRELLA
refugee's .... ASYLUM, SANCTUARY
ship's .... HARBOR
small .... COT
soldier's ..... (PUP)TENT
sheltered side .... LEE
shelty ..... PONY, (SHEEP)DOG
shelve ..... DEFER, LAY ASIDE, RETIRE
Shem's descendants .... S(H)EMITES
father .... NOAH
son ... ELAM, ARAM, LUD, AS(S)HUR
shenanigan .... MISCHIEF, NONSENSE, TRICK(ERY)
Shensi, capital of .... SIAN
sheol ... UNDERWORLD, HELL, HADES
shepherd .... PASTOR, MINISTER, SHEEP DOG, LEAD, TEND, DAPHNIS, ENDYMION, CORYDON
concern of .... SHEEP
dog .... COLLIE
kings .... HYKSOS
pipe .... OAT, REED
plaid .... MAUD
staff of ... CROOK, KENT, PEDA
shepherdess ...... AMARYLLIS
shepherds, god of .... PAN, FAUNUS
pertaining to .. PASTORAL, BUCOLIC
sherbet ... BEVERAGE, DESSERT, DRINK, ICE
Sheridan, Union general ...... PHILIP
sherif .... EMIR
ancestor of ..... FATIMA, MOHAMMED
sheriff ...... VISCOUNT, REEVE
aide of .... BULLDOG, CATCHPOLL, BAILIFF, YEOMAN
armed group of ... POSSE
badge of .... STAR
deputy .... BAILIFF
Sherlock Holmes, creator of .. DOYLE
man of .... WATSON
sherry ..... JEREZ, OLOROSO, AMONTILLADO, WINE
Sherwood Forest hero .... ROBIN HOOD
Shetland ....PONY, WOOL
fishing grounds ... HAAF
island .... MAINLAND
island tax .... SCAT(T)
pony ... SHELTIE, SHELTY
sheep dog ...... SHELTIE, SHELTY
shibboleth .... SLOGAN, PASSWORD, TEST WORD
shield ..... SCUTUM, (A)EGIS, PAVIS, TARGE, ARMOR, MANT(E)LET, DEFEND, PROTECT, SCUTA, ECU, BUCKLER, COVER, MULGA
arm .... BUCKLER
Athena's .... (A)EGIS
band across .... FESS
bar, heraldic ..... GEMEL
bearer .... ARMIGER, SQUIRE
boss/knob of ..... UMBO
bulletproof .. MANT(E)LET
center point .... FESS
hand .... BUCKLER
of shields ...... TESTUDO
rawhide ..... PARFLECHE
Roman .... TESTUDO
shaped .... SCUTATE, PELTATE, CLYPEATE, CLYPEIFORM
spike of .... UMBO
Zeus' .... (A)EGIS
shift ..... CHANGE, TRANSFER, MOVE, SHUNT, ASSIGNMENT, HAUL, VEER, DEVIATE, SWITCH, CHEMISE, TRICK
shifty ..... EVASIVE, TRICKY, FURTIVE
Shiite .... SHIAH, MOSLEM
opposed to .... SUNNITE
shikar .... HUNT(ING)
shikari ...... HUNTER, GUIDE
shill .... ACCOMPLICE, CONFEDERATE
confederate of a .... BARKER, GAMBLER
shillelagh ..... CUDGEL, CLUB
shillings, 21 .... GUINEA
shilly-shally .... HESITATE, WAVER, VACILLATE, HEDGE
shimmer ..... GLIMMER, FLASH
shimmy .... WOBBLE, DANCE, CHEMISE
shin .... CLIMB, SHANK
Shinar ... SUMER, BABYLONIA
shinbone .... TIBIA
shindig .... PARTY, DANCE
shindy ... ROW, DISTURBANCE, RIOT, COMMOTION
shine .... LIGHT, GLEAM, GLOW, EXCEL, GLOSS, POLISH, LUSTER, FLICKER, TWINKLE, RADIATE, GLITTER
shiner ... BLACKEYE, MINNOW
shingle .... SIGN(BOARD), GRAVEL, CLIP, SLAT, FACIA, SIDING, SHIM
man with ...... LAWYER, DOCTOR
shingles ...... HERPES, ZONA
shining ..... RADIANT, BRIGHT, EMINENT, LUCENT, NITID, LUCID, LUSTROUS
shinleaf ...... WINTERGREEN
shinny .... HOCKEY
shinplaster ... POULTICE, SCRIP
Shinto .... SINTU
deity .... KAMI
temple .... SHA
temple gate .... TORII
text .... KOJIKI, NOHONGI
ship .... VESSEL, AIRCRAFT, EMBARK, BRIG, BILANDER, LINER, CARRACK, HULK, DHOW, DROMON(D), TARTAN, GALLEON, CLIPPER, PINKIE, PINKY, YACHT, HOOKER
abandoned .... DERELICT
afterpart of .... QUARTER
anchor rope ... HAWSER
anchorage .... ROAD(STEAD), MARINA
balance of .... TRIM
ballast .... LASTAGE, KENTLEDGE
beak .... ROSTRUM
biscuit .... (HARD)TACK, PATILE
boat on ..... GIG, JOLLY, YAWL, PINNACE, DINGHY, LAUNCH
body of .... HULK, HULL
boom .... BUMPKIN
bow flag .... JACK
breadth .... BEAM
cabin .... CUDDY
canvas .... SAIL
capacity ...... TONNAGE
captain .... MASTER, SKIPPER
captive .... PRIZE
carpenter .... CHIPS
chains .... TYES
change course of ... TACK
channel .... GAT
clean bottom of .. BREAM
clean hull of ..... GRAVE
cleaning tool .... HOG
clumsy ...... TUB, ARK, DROGHER
coal .... COLLIER
coal bin .... BUNKER
crane .... DAVIT
crew member .... HAND, MATE, YEOMAN, STOKER
crosspiece .... BEAM
device for raising sunken CAMEL, CAISSON
direct a .... NAVIGATE
drain hole ..... SCUPPER
fender .... SKID
fictional .... CAINE
flag ...... BURGEE, JACK
flat-bottomed ..... KEEL
forward part ...... BOW, PROW, STEM

framework ...... HULL, CARCASS
fraud .... BARRATRY
fuel tank of ..... BUNKER
galley .. CABOOSE, CUDDY, KITCHEN
gun platform .. SPONSON
heave of .... SCEND
hold .... BULK
hospital .... SICK BAY
hunting .... RAIDER, SEALER, WHALER, WHALEBOAT
jail .... BRIG, HULK
kitchen .... GALLEY, CABOOSE
ladder .... RATLINE
land from ...... DEBARK
lateen-sailed .... TARTAN
left-side ..... LARBOARD, PORT
line on side ... PLIMSOLL
list .... MANIFEST
load ...... CARGO, BULK
logbook .... JOURNAL
lowest deck ...... ORLOP
made smaller ..... RAZEE
master .... CAPTAIN, SKIPPER
master's declaration .... PROTEST
merchant .... GAL(L)IOT, TRADER, GALLEON, ARGOSY
metal plating .... STRAKE
mooring place .... ANCHORAGE, MARINA, DOCK, BERTH
mythical .... ARGO
not seagoing ...... HULK
of the desert ..... CAMEL
of 1492 ..... NINA, PINTA
officer .... PURSER, MATE, MASTER, SKIPPER, BOS'N, CAPTAIN
opening .... HATCH(WAY)
part of .... DECK, SALON, POOP, GALLEY, STEERAGE, STERN, BOW, KEEL, RUDDER, PROMENADE
passage ... GAT, STEERAGE
passenger accommodation PASSAGE
passenger, clandestine ... STOWAWAY
path of .... LANE
peg .... KEVEL
permit .... PRATIQUE
personnel .... CREW, COMPLEMENT
petty officer .... BOS(U)N
pirate .... CORSAIR, FRIGATE, PRIVATEER
place for sick .... BAY
planking .... STRAKE
platform ...... SPONSON
poetic ...... KEEL, BARK
position finder ... LORAN
prison ...... HULK, BRIG
provisioner ... CHANDLER
prow's front .. CUTWATER
pull .... KEDGE
rear of .... AFT
record .... LOG
rib .... FUTTOCK
rigging ... GEAR, TACKLE
rope .... TYE
sailing .... TARTAN, SCHOONER, GALLEON, CLIPPER
sails .... KITES
scout .... PINNACE
side opening ... PORTHOLE
side scaffold ..... FLAKE
single-masted ... TARTAN
sink a .... SCUTTLE
skipper .... MASTER, CAPTAIN
slow .... BUCKET, TUB
smoke pipe ...... STACK, FUNNEL
space for provisions ..... LAZARETTO
speed measuring device .. LOG
square-masted ..... BRIG
square-rigged .. CLIPPER
steer a .. NAVIGATE, CONN
stern section ..... POOP, BUTTOCKS
supplier ..... CHANDLER
supply .... TENDER, TRANSPORT, COLLIER
table railing ...... FIDDLE
tender ...... COCKBOAT, PINNACE
tax on .... TONNAGE
timber ... KEELSON, SNY, CARLING, BITT, STEMSON, FUTTOCK
torpedoed May 1915 ... LUSITANIA
track .... WAKE
trading .... ARGOSY, GALLEON, GAL(L)IOT
troop .... TRANSPORT
two-masted .. BRIG, GRAB
water in the hold .. BILGE
waterline ...... PLIMSOLL
wheel .... HELM
whistle .... HORN, BLAST
widest breadth .... BEAM
windlass .... CAPSTAN
"window" ... PORTHOLE
worm ... TEREDO, BORER
wrecked .... WRACK

shipbuilding peg .. TRE(E)NAIL, TRUNNEL
shipjack .... SHAD
shipping hazard ... REEF, FOG
list .... MANIFEST
news .... SAILINGS
ships, collectively ...... CRAFT
group of .... FLEET, FLOTILLA
shipshape ... ORDERLY, NEAT, TRIM, TIDY
shipside scaffold .... FLAKE
shipworm .... TEREDO, BORER
shipwreck goods ... FLOTSAM, JETSAM
shipwrecked person .... CASTAWAY
shire .... COUNTY
shirk ...... NEGLECT, EVADE, SKULK, FUNK, GOLDBRICK, DODGE, SHUN, MALINGER
shirker ... TRUANT, SLACKER, DODGER, EVADER
shirt .... CHEMISE, CAMISE, SKIVVY, JERSEY, SARK, GUERNSEY, PARKA
broadcloth .... PIMA
collar stiffener ..... STAY
front .... DICK(E)Y, PLASTRON
front ornament .... STUD
sleeve ...... HOMESPUN, PLAIN, SIMPLE
sleeve button .. CUFFLINK
shittah .... ACACIA
shivaree .... SERENADE, CHARIVARI
shive .... SPLINTER, CORK
shiver .... SHAKE, QUAKE, BREAK, SHATTER, QUIVER, TREMBLE, SPLINTER, FRAGMENT, SHUDDER, CHITTER
shivery ..... BRITTLE, CHILLY, CHILLING
Shkoder .... SCUTARI
shoal ...... SHALLOW, MASS, SPIT, BANK, REEF, BAR, SCHOOL, RIFFLE
shoat .... PIG(LET), SHOTE
shock ... IMPACT, BLOW, STUN, APPAL(L), CONCUSSION, JOLT, JAR, BRUNT, STROKE, STARTLE, PARALYZE, TRAUMA
absorber ...... CUSHION, SNUBBER
dog .... POODLE
gather into a ...... STOOK
main .... BRUNT
tactics ..... BLITZKRIEG
therapy drug ... INSULIN, METRAZOL
to action ..... GALVANIZE
shod .... CALCED
shoddy .... SHAM, CHEAP
shoe ... FOOTWEAR, BROGAN, BOOT, BROGUE, GALOSH(E), PUMP, OXFORD, STOG(E)Y, CLOG, GAITER, LOAFER, CLODHOPPER
armor .... SOLLERET
canvas .... SNEAKER
cloglike .... PATTEN
fastener .... LATCHET
flap .... TONGUE
form .... LAST
front .... VAMP
heavy .... GALOSH(E)
house ..... MULE, SLIPPER
lace tag .... AGLET
leather .... SUEDE, FOXING
low ...... PUMP, SANDAL, SLIPPER
maker ..... CORDWAINER
mender .... COBBLER
moccasin-like ...... PAC
model .... LAST
ornament ...... BUCKLE
oxford .... BROGAN
part .... (IN)SOLE, RAND,

INSTEP, UPPER, HEEL, LAST, VAMP, EYELET, WELT
plate .... CALK, CREEPER, CRAMPON, CLAMPER, TRAMP
repair .... COBBLE
shape of .... LAST
sole addition ... HOBNAIL
sole part .... SHANK
spike .... CLIMBER
sport .... LOAFER
style .... PLATFORM
tennis .... SNEAKER
uppers material .... PRUNELLA, FOXING, LASTING
walking ...... BALMORAL
woman's .... CHOPINE
wooden .. CLOG, PATTEN, SABOT, GETA
wooden-soled .... CLOG, SABOT
shoebill ...... STORK, HERON
shoelace tip .... TAG
shoemaker .. COBBLER, SUTOR, SNOB, CORDWAINER
awl of .... ELSEN
block of .... LAST
patron saint of .. CRISPIN
shoes, brown .... TANS
open-heeled ... STEP-INS
work .... BROGAN
shoestring .... LACE(T)
shogun ... GOVERNOR, TYCOON
Sholem, author .... ASCH
shoo .. SCAT, GET OUT, SCRAM, DRIVE
shooi .... JAEGER
shoot ... ROD, CAST, TWINGE, BUD, SPRIG, TWIG, HURL, FIRE, FILM, THROW, DART, PLUG, FLAGELLUM, CHIT, SPROUT, PROJECT
firearm .... FIRE
forth .... BURGEON
from cover .... SNIPE, AMBUSH
game for food ..... POT
grafting .... (S)CION
lichen .... FROND
plant ... STOLON, (S)CION, VIMEN, RAT(T)OON
root/stem ..... TILLER, RAT(T)OON
scene again ..... RETAKE
seaweed .... FROND
shooter ...... MARBLE, ALLEY, TAW
shooting iron ... PISTOL, GUN, FIREARM
match .... SKEET, TIR
star ... METEOR, LEONID, BOLIDE, FIREBALL
shoots .... BROWSE
shop ...... STORE, BOUTIQUE, FACTORY, PARLOR
girl .... GRISETTE
nameplate of ..... FACIA
shophar .... HORN
shoplifter .... STEALER, BOOSTER
shopman .... CLERK
shoptalk .... SLANG
shoran .... RADAR
part of ... SHORT, RANGE, NAVIGATION
shore ... COAST, BEACH, PROP, RIVAGE, SAND, BANK, WATERSIDE
along .... LITTORAL
bird .... CURLEW, RUFF, SNIPE, AVOCET, SANDPIPER, STILT, PLOVER, RAIL, DOWITCHER, DOTT(E)REL
of the .... LITTORAL, COASTAL
poetic .... STRAND
short .... BRIEF, LOW, CONCISE, CURT, ABRUPT, SCANT, FRIABLE, LACKING, SHY
and fat ... TUBBY, PODGY, PUDGY, SQUAT
and stout .... SQUAB
and thick .... PODGY, CHUNKY, SQUAB
branch .... SNAG
cake .... BISCUIT
combining form .... BRACHY
comedy ... SKIT, SKETCH
fall .... LACK
for .... IN BRIEF
in .... BRIEFLY
in loan money .... STRINGENT
lived ...... TRANSIENT, EPHEMERAL, TRANSITORY, DECIDUOUS
musical passage .... MORCEAU
of .... LACKING
race .... DASH, SPRINT
rest .... NAP, SIESTA
ride .... SPIN
seller .... BEAR
shrift .... ABRUPT
skirt .... MINI
slang .... SHY
sighted .... MYOPIC
snort .... SHOT
song ...... ODE, DITTY, ARIETTA
sound .... SNAP
spoken .... LACONIC, CURT, BRIEF, TERSE
story .... CONTE
supply, in .... SCARCE
tail .... SCUT
tempered .... TESTY
visit .... CALL
winded ... PURSY, PUFFY
shortage ..... DEFICIT, LACK, DEFICIENCY, NEED
shortchange .... CHEAT
shortcoming .. FAULT, DEFECT
shorten .... REDUCE, ABBREVIATE, ABRIDGE, CROP, CUT, DOCK, LOP, REEVE, ELIDE, CONDENSE
mast/bowsprit ..... REEF
shortened ..... CURTATE, CUT
shortening .... LARD, FAT, OIL, OLEO
shorthand ... GREGG, PITMAN, STENOTYPE
character .... POT, HOOK
girl .... STENO
sign .... PHONOGRAM
shortly .... SOON, ANON, RUDELY
shorts .... TROUSERS, LEFT-OVERS
shortsighted .. MYOPIC, MYOPY
person .... MYOPE
shorty .... RUNT
Shoshonean Indian ..... OTOE, UTE, P(A)IUTE, HOPI, COMANCHE
Shostakovich, composer ...... DMITRI
shot ...... TRY, GUESS, SCOPE, RANGE, PELLET, MARKSMAN, DOSE, FLECKED, SHELL, LANGRAGE, LANGREL
and shell .... AMMO, AMMUNITION
that hits target ... CLOUT
shote .... SHOAT, PIG(LET)
shoulder .... CARRY, PUSH, EPAUL
armor .... PAULDRON
belt .... BALDRIC
blade .... SCAPULA
blade part ... ACROMION
bone .... HUMERUS
combining form .... OMO
muscle .... DELTOID
of the .... SCAPULAR
ornament .. EPAULET(TE)
pack .... KNAPSACK
protection for .... PAULDRON
road's .... BERM(E)
wrap ..... SHAWL, SCARF, STOLE
shoulders, covering for .... NUBIA
draw up .... SHRUG
fur piece ...... PALATINE
of the .... HUMERAL
shout ..... WHOOP, YELL, CRY, CALL, HOLLER
down .... SILENCE
of joy/approval .... OLE, HURRAH, VIVA, HEAR, HUZZA, BRAVO
shove .... BUNT, JOG, THRUST, NUDGE, PUSH, JOSTLE
off ...... LEAVE, DEPART
shovel ... SCOOP, SPADE, VAN, PEEL
shovelhead .... SHARK, STURGEON
show ...... EVINCE, EXHIBIT, DISPLAY, REVEAL, GUIDE, MANIFEST, PROVE, APPEAR, FLASH, PARADE, PAGEANT, EXPOSE, SIGHT, PRETENSE, MUMMERY
anger .... FUME
bill .... PLACARD
empty .... FARCE
hypocritical .. MUMMERY
in .... USHER
indecision ..... WAVER, FALTER, VACILLATE

in law ... PLEAD, ALLEGE
likeness .... MIRROR
of embarrassment .... SQUIRM
off ..... PARADE, FLAUNT
peep .... RAREE
stage ... REVUE, FOLLIES
up ...... ARRIVE, COME, APPEAR
vain .... POMP
water .... AQUACADE
shower ... SLEET, HAIL, SPRAY, SPRINKLE, SCATTER, POUR, BATH, PARTY, FALLOUT, RAIN(FALL), PEPPER
fall in a .... CASCADE
of meteors .. ANDROMID, LEONID
rain .... BRASH
showing good taste .... DECOROUS
showman, famous ...... FLO, ZIEGFELD, BARNUM, RINGLING, CARROLL, ROSE
showpiece .. EXAMPLE, EXHIBIT, SAMPLE
showy .... FLASHY, OSTENTATIOUS, ARTY, FLAMBOYANT, GAUDY, SWANKY, LOUD, GARISH, ORNATE, TAWDRY
display .... BLAZON, SPLURGE
display in dress .... FRIPPERY
gaieties .... GAUDS
show ..... PAGEANT(RY), EXTRAVAGANZA, SPECTACLE
thing, worthless .... TRUMPERY
shrapnel .... SHELL
shred .... WISP, VESTIGE, FRAZZLE, TATTER, FRAGMENT, RAG, SNIP, PARTICLE, DAG, MAMMOCK
shrew .... SORICINE, TERMAGANT, ERD, SCOLD, VIXEN, HARPY, VIRAGO, NAG
like .... SORICINE
mouse .... HYRAX
name of Shakespeare's ... KATE
sister of Shakespeare's ... BIANCA
shrewd ..... CLEVER, ARTFUL, SAGACIOUS, FOXY, CANNY, WILY, ASTUTE, CAGEY, CUNNING, SMART, SLY, KEEN
person ... FOX, SMOOTHIE
shrewish .... NAGGING, TERMAGANT
shrews of .... SORICINE
shriek .... CRY, SCREAM, YELL, SCREECH
shrieve .... SHERIFF
shrift .... ABSOLUTION
shrike ..... WOODCHAT, BIRD, OSCINE
shrill .... HIGH-PITCHED, STRIDENT, PIPY
sound/voice .... TREBLE, PIPING, REEDY, SKIRL, SHRIEK, SCREAM
shrimp .... CRUSTACEAN, MALACOSTRACAN, MACRURAN
appendage ..... UROPOD
covering .... MAIL
kin .... GRIBBLE
like crustacean .. PRAWN
shrine .... TABERNACLE, DAGOBA, ALTAR, MARTYRY, GROTTO
for relics ...... FERETORY
visitor .... PILGRIM
shrink .... CONTRACT, COWER, CRINGE, RECOIL, SHRIVEL, WIZEN
from .... FUNK
shrinking .... TIMID, SHY
shrive .... ABSOLVE
shrivel ...... CURL, WITHER, WRINKLE, WIZEN, MUMMIFY
shroff .... BANKER, MONEYCHANGER
Shropshire .... SALOP
river .... SEVERN
shroud .... VEIL, PALL, COVER, CEREMENT, SCREEN, SHEET
Shrove Tuesday .. MARDI GRAS
shrub ... BUSH, LILAC, SALAL, ELDER, PLANT, OLEASTER, LAUREL, SMILAX, ALTHEA, BRAMBLE, GORSE, SENNA, SUMAC, ALDER, SPIREA, MISTLETOE, MAGNOLIA, CASCARILLA, RHODORA
aromatic ..... LAVENDER, MINT, BERGAMOT, ROSEMARY
bean family ..... RETEM, BROOM
berry .... CURRANT
birch family ...... HAZEL
bushy ...... CADE, TOD, SAVIN
climbing .... AMPELOPSIS, CLEMATIS, LIANA
dwarfed .... BONSAI
evergreen .... LAUREL, ERICA, LAURUSTINE, OLEASTER, TOYON, SAVIN, HEATH, MYRTLE, JASMINE, TITI, YEW, SALAL, JUNIPER, FURZE, CAMELLIA, ILEX, OLEANDER
fence ...... HEDGE(ROW)
flowering ...... AZALEA, JASMINE, SYRINGA
genus ...... OLEA, ITEA, RHUS, LANTANA, SPIREA, SYRINGA, ERICA, EVEA
grape family .... AMPELOPSIS
grown flat ..... ESPALIER
heath family .... KALMIA
holly family .... ILEX
honeysuckle .. WEIGELA, VIBURNUM
mallow family .. HIBISCUS, ALTH(A)EA
mint family ... ROSEMARY
olive ..... OLEA, PRIVET, JASMIN(E)
Pacific coast ..... SALAL
pea family .. MESQUIT(E), CASSIA, LOTUS, MIMOSA, LABURNUM, LOTOS, WISTERIA
pepper family ... CUBEB, KAVA
poisonous .... SUMAC(H), OLEANDER
prickly .... BRAMBLE, CAPER, CHICO
rose family .. HARDHACK, SPIR(A)EA
rubber source .. GUAYULE
spiny ..... CHICO, FURZE, GORSE
spurge family .... CASCARILLA
stunted ... SCRUB, BONSAI
tea family .... CAMELLIA
tropical ... INGA, ABELIA, LANTANA, JASMIN(E), JESSAMINE, HENNA
shrubbery ..... BOSCAGE, TOD, COPPICE
shrubby .... FRUTESCENT, FRUTICOSE
shrubs, clump of ...... SCRUB
shuck ...... POD, HUSK, SHELL
shudder ..... QUAKE, TREMOR, SHAKE, TREMBLE
shuffle .... SHIFT, SCUFF, DECEIVE, MIX, RIFFLE, TRICK, SHAMBLE
shuffler .... COOT, DUCK
Shufu .... KASHGAR
shun .... EVADE, DODGE, AVOID
shunt ...... TURN OFF, SHIFT, DIVERT, SWITCH, SIDETRACK
shush ... HIST, HUSH, SILENCE, QUIET
Shushan .... SUSA
shut .... CLOSE, BAR, SECURED
eye: sl. .... SLEEP
in ... CONFINE, INVALID, PENT(UP)
out ..... BAN, EXCLUDE, OSTRACIZE
up ... IMPRISON, CLOSET, IMMURE
with force .... SLAM
shutter .... BLIND, SLIDE, PERSIENNE
shuttle, bobbin/spool .... PIRN
shuttlecock .... BIRD
shy ... COY, BASHFUL, WARY, SHORT, DIFFIDENT, DEMURE, BALK, RESERVED, RETIRING, MIM, TIMID, MODEST, RECOIL, START, CHARY, TIMOROUS, VERECUND, JIB
Shylock .... USURER, MONEYLENDER
daughter of ..... JESSICA
money of ..... DUCATS
shyster .... PETTIFOGGER
si: Sp. .... YES
sialid .... INSECT, DOBSON FLY
Siam .... THAILAND (see)
siamang .... GIBBON

Siamese (see Thailand)
capital .... BANGKOK, THONBURI, AYUDHYA
coin ... BAHT, ATT, TICAL
dynasty......... CHAKRI
isthmus .... KRA
king........ ADULYADEJ, MONGKUT, CHULALONGKORN, PRACHATIPOK, MAHIDOL
kingdom capital .... CHIENGMAI
measure ...... SOK, KUP, SISTI
monetary unit .....BAHT, TICAL
premier ...... THANARAT
queen .... SIRIKIT
river .... MENAM, CHAUPAYA
tongue .... LAO, TAI
tribe .... MEO
twins, one of ... CHANG, ENG
weight .... PAI, TICAL
Sian .... SINGAN
sib ..... KIN(SMAN), RELATIVE, BROTHER, SISTER
Sibelius, composer ..... JEAN
work .... FINLANDIA
Siberian .. VOGUL, SAMOYED(E)
antelope .... SAIGA
city .... OMSK, TOMSK
forests .... TAIGA
fur ... CALABAR, CALABER
ibex .... TEK
leopard .... OUNCE
mountains .... ALTAI
native ... TATAR, YAKUT, YUIT, KIRGIZ
peninsula .. KAMCHATKA, TAIMIR
plain .... STEPPE
region .. OMSK, TA(R)TARY
river ... AMUR, LENA, OB, IRTISH, YENISEI, KOLIMA, TOBOL
sheep .... ARGALI
squirrel .... CALABER, CALABAR, MINIVER
tent .... YURT
warehouse .... ETAPE
wasteland .... STEPPE
wild cat .... MANUL
wild sheep ...... ARGALI
windstorm .... BURAN
sibilance .... HISS
sibilate .... HISS
sibling ... SIS(TER), BROTHER, KIN
sibyl .... SEERESS, ORACLE, SORCERESS, WITCH, FORTUNETELLER
sibylline .... ORACULAR
sign .... OMEN
sic ... THUS, SO, SUCH, ATTACK
sicca .... SEAL
siccative ..... DRIER, DRYING
Sicilian .... TRINACRIAN, SICANIAN
capital .... PALERMO
city .... ENNA, GELA, RAGUSA, MAZZARO, PALERMO, CATANIA, TRAPANI
evergreen .... MAQUIS
hero .... ENTELLUS
inhabitant, legendary .... CYCLOPS
king .... RENE
landmark .... ETNA
resort .... ENNA
river .... ACIS
seaport ...... PALERMO, MARSALA, MILAZZO, MESSINA, MESSENE
secret society ..... MAFIA
shotgun .... LUPARA
volcano .... (A)ETNA
whirlpool ... CHARYBDIS
wine .... MARSALA
sick ... INDISPOSED, UNWELL, ILL, UNSOUND, SURFEITED, AILING, ATTACK
person .... INVALID, PATIENT
sickbed, of a ...... CLINICAL
sicken .... AIL, NAUSEATE
sickle ... HOOK, SIVE, SCYTHE, BUSHWHACKER
shaped .... FALCATE
sickness ... MALADY, DISEASE, NAUSEA
Sid ____ .... CAESAR
Siddhartha .... BUDDHA
side ...... ASPECT, FACTION, MINOR, FACET, FLANK
arm .... PISTOL, SWORD, BAYONET, REVOLVER
by side ...... ABREAST, COLLATERAL
dish .... ENTREE, ENTREMETS, SALAD, SLAW, TRIMMING
interest .... HOBBY, AVOCATION
kick .... ALTER EGO, CONFEDERATE, PARTNER, PAL, FRIEND
meat .... BACON
of a .... LATERAL
pain .... STITCH
portion .... RASHER
road .... BYWAY
step ...... AVOID, EVADE, DODGE
trip .... SALLY
view .... PROFILE
sideboard .... CREDENZA
sideburns ... MUTTON CHOPS, WHISKERS
sideline .... BENCH, BY-WORK
sidelong look .... SQUINT
sidereal .... STARRY, STELLAR
siderite .... METEORITE, IRON(ORE)
sidero, as combining form ... IRON, STAR
sides, unequal ...... SCALENE
sideslip .... SKID
sidesplitting .... CONVULSIVE, HEARTY
sidestep .... AVOID, EVADE
sidetrack ... SHUNT, SWITCH, DIVERT, TURN, SIDING, AVERT
sidewalk .... PAVEMENT, BANQUETTE
entrepreneur ... BEGGAR, HAWKER, PEDDLER, ARTIST, NEWSBOY
sideways, move .... SIDLE, EDGE, SKID
walker .... CRAB
sidewinder ..... RATTLESNAKE, CROTALUS
sidewise .... LATERAL
move .... SKEW, SIDLE
siding .. CLAPBOARD, SHINGLE, SPUR
sidle .... EDGE, SKEW, JIB
Sidon's name now ..... SAIDA
siecle .... AGE, CENTURY, PERIOD
siege .... INVESTMENT
lay ...... INVEST, BESET
siegers' shelter .... CAT, MANTLET
Siegfried .... SIGURD
follower ...... NIBELUNG
Line .. WESTWALL, LIMES
sword of ...... BALMUNG
wife of .... KRIEMHILD
sienna .... PIGMENT
Sierra ..... RANGE, PINTADO, KINGFISH, MADRE, LEONE, NEVADA
fish resembling .... MACKEREL
Leone capital .... FREETOWN
mountain .... DANA
Nevada fog ..... POGONIP
Nevada lake ..... TAHOE
Nevada peak .. WHITNEY, MULHACEN
siesta .... NAP, REST
sieur .... SIR
sieve .... SIFTER, STRAINER, SCREEN, FILTER, LAUN, TROMMEL, RIDDLE, BOLTER, CRIBBLE
like a .... ETHMOID
sift .... WINNOW, SIEVE, WEIGH, SCREEN, FILTER, BOLT
sifter ..... SIEVE, STRAINER, BOLTER
siftings .... RESIDUE
sigh ... YEARN, SUSPIRE, MOAN, SOUGH, SOB, SOUF
sight ...... VIEW, SPECTACLE, LOOK, GLIMPSE, VISION, EYE, AIM, SCENE, PICTURE, ESPY
by .... VISUAL(LY)
colloquial .... UGLY
come into .... LOOM
gun .... BEAD
of ..... VISUAL, OCULAR
sightless .... BLIND
sightly .... COMELY
sigil .... SIGNET, SEAL
sigmoid .... ESS, SIGMATE
sign(s) ... TOKEN, INDICATION, GESTURE, SYMPTOM, BADGE, EVIDENCE, INDEX, INDICIA, OMEN, SYMBOL, MARK,

VESTIGE, PORTENT, INDEX, EARMARK
affirmative .... NOD
arithmetical .... PLUS, MINUS
away .... CONVEY
Blue Eagle .... NRA
display .... PLACARD, SHINGLE
homage ... BOW, KNEEL, CURTSY, GENUFLECTION, SALAAM
in magic .... SIGIL
in music .... SEGNO, NEUM(E), CLEF, STAFF, PRESA
language science .... SEMIOLOGY
omission .... CARET
road/street ...... ARROW
up ... ENLIST, JOIN, HIRE, ENGAGE, EMPLOY, ENROL(L)
signal .. SIGN, TOKEN, NOTABLE, STRIKING, CUE, ALARM, BUZZ, WARN, FLAG
actor's .... CUE
assembly ...... REVEILLE
board .... SHINGLE
danger ...... RED FLAG, RED LIGHT, SIREN, SYMPTOM
entrance/exit ... SENNET
eye .... WINK
flag ...... ENSIGN, WAIF, JACK
for parley ..... CHAMADE, WHITE FLAG
Indian .... SMOKE
light .... FLARE, BEACON
lights out .... TAPS
parley .... CHAMADE
railroad .... FUSEE
retirement ..... CURFEW, TAPS
retreat .... CHAMADE
seance .... TAP
set ...... CODE, LORAN
stage ...... CUE, SENNET
warning ... ALARM, SIREN, WINK, RED LIGHT, ALERT, CAUTION
signaling apparatus .... SEMAPHORE, BEACON, HOWLER, FOGHORN, BLINKER
signature .... HAND, SEAL
flourish .... SCROLL, PARAPH
in radio .... THEME
of a sort .... THUMBMARK, CRISS-CROSS
musical .... THEME
signboard .... SHINGLE
signet .... SIGIL, SEAL
significance .... MEANING, MOMENT, IMPORT
significant ..... MEANINGFUL, IMPORTANT, MOMENTOUS
signify ..... MEAN, INDICATE, DENOTE, IMPLY, BODE
Signoret, actress ..... SIMONE
signpost .. CLUE, HERMA, GUIDE
signs, of .... SEMIOTIC
Sigurd .... SIEGFRIED
father of .... REGIN
victim of .... FAFNIR
Sikh religion founder .. NANAK
Sikkim capital ..... GANGTOK
inhabitants .... NEPALESE
king .... CHOGYAL
queen .... GYALMO
woman's dress ...... KHO
Sikorsky, airplane builder .... IGOR
silage .... FODDER
Silas Marner author ... ELIOT
ward of .... EPPIE
silence ... STILLNESS, REPRESS, THROTTLE, MUTE, (S)HUSH, HIST, QUIET(UDE), GAG, OYEZ, LULL, WHIST
silencer ... MUFFLER, HUSHER
silent ..... QUIET, STILL, MUM, MUTE, TACIT, INACTIVE, WHIST, NOISELESS
habitually ..... TACITURN
it is .... TACET
Silenus .... DEITY, SATYR
foster son of ... BACCHUS
Silesia .... SLASK, LINEN
silex ... SILICA, FLINT, QUARTZ
silhouette .... OUTLINE, PORTRAIT
silica .... SILEX, MINERAL, QUARTZ, SAND, MICA
deposit .... SINTER
silicate ... TREMOLITE, ESTER, MICA, CERITE, EPIDOTE
silique .... POD
silk .... ALAMODE, TULLE
and cotton cloth EOLIENNE
and wool cloth .... BARATHEA, EOLIENNE
cloth, damasklike ...... LAMPAS
cloth for ribbons, etc. .... SARCENET
cloth, striped .. TABARET
coarse .... TUSSA(H), TUSSAR, TUSSER
cocoon .... BAVE
corded .... FAILLE, PADUASOY, REP(S), REPP, OTTOMAN
cotton (tree) ..... CEIBA, KAPOK
damask-like ..... LAMPAS
fabric ...... SHANTUNG, SURAH, VOILE, PEKIN, PONGEE, CHARMEUSE, CAFFA, MOIRE, SATIN, SENDAL, BAREGE, GROS, MADRAS, MESSALINE, VELVET, VELOUR(S), SAMITE, TAFFETA
fiber .... FLOSS
filament .... BRIN
finely woven .... LANSDOWNE
for mourning ..... ALMAS
for ribbons .... SARCENET
glossy .... LUSTRING, LUTESTRING
hat .... TILE, TOPPER
heavy .... GROS
hit the ...... PARACHUTE
knitted .... JERSEY
like .... SERICEOUS
lining material .... SARCENET
net .... MALINE(S)
netting .... TULLE
producing moth .... AILANTHUS
raw ... GREGE, MARABOU
ribbed ... REP(S), FAILLE, REPP
ribbonlike .... GIMP
rough .... RAJAH
screen print ... SERIGRAPH
sheer .... VOILE
shreds .... NOIL
source of ..... COCOON, AILANTHUS, ERIA
stocking ...... ELEGANT, WEALTHY, WHIG
synthetic .... NYLON, ORLON, RAYON, DACRON
taffeta .... TABBY
thread ... TRAM, SLEAVE, FLOSS
threadmaker .... THROWSTER
twilled ... ALMA, SERGE, SURAH
twisted .... ROVE
veil .... TULLE
waste ..... NOIL, FLOSS, KNUB, FRISON
watered .... MOIRE, TABBY, MOREEN
weight .... PARI
silken .... SOFT, SMOOTH, GLOSSY, SERIC
silky .... SMOOTH, SATINY
silkworm ..... ERI(A), TUSSA(H), TUSSER, BOMBYX, TUSSORE
cocoon covering .. FLOSS
covering ...... COCOON
disease .... UJI
food .... MULBERRY
leaves .... MULBERRY, AILANTHUS
moth .... BOMBYCID, CECROPIA
raising .... SERICULTURE
silky .... SERICEOUS, SOFT, LUSTROUS
furred animal .. TAMARIN, MARMOSET
sill .... LEDGE
counterpart ..... LINTEL
projection .... DRIP
sillabub ... DESSERT, BEVERAGE
siller .... MONEY
Sills, singer .... BEVERLY
silly ...... ASININE, IMBECILE, INANE, FATUOUS, SAPPY, ABSURD, SLAP-HAPPY, DAFFY, DAFT, PUERILE, KOOKIE, KOOKY
language ....BOMBAST
one .... GOOSE
silo .... PIT, TOWER
silt......... WASH, SEDIMENT, ALLUVIUM

silurid .... CATFISH
silva .... WOODS
silver ... SILLER, COIN, MONEY, ARGENT(UM), SYCEE
Age writer ..... TACITUS, JUVENAL, MARTIAL
alloy ... BILLON, ALBATA
containing .... LUNAR
dollar: sl. ... CARTWHEEL
fluoride .... TACHIOL
fox fur .... PLATINA
gilded .... VERMEIL
in alchemy .... LUNA
ingot .... SYCEE, BULLION
lacework ...... FILIGREE
like/of ...... ARGENTINE
screen .. MOVIES, CINEMA
State ....NEVADA
telluride .... HESSITE
tongued ..... ELOQUENT
tongued person .. ORATOR
unminted ...... BULLION, SYCEE
wire work ..... FILIGREE
silverfish .... TARPON, SARGO
silverside(s) .... MINNOW, TINKER, GRUNION
silverware decoration .... GADROON
silvery .... ARGENT(INE)
silviculture .... FORESTRY
simar .... JACKET, ROBE
Simenon, author ... GEORGES
detective .... MAIGRET
novel .... MAIGRET
simian .... APE, MONKEY
astronaut .... BONNY, ASTROMONK
similar... AKIN, LIKE, AGNATE, ANALOGOUS, SUCH
combining form .. HOMEO
similarity .... LIKENESS
similarly .... LIKEWISE
simile .... METAPHOR
similitude .... FACSIMILE, IMAGE, LIKENESS
simmer ... BOIL, SEETHE, STEW
down ..... COOL, SUBSIDE
simnel ... FRUITCAKE, BISCUIT
simoleon .... DOLLAR
Simon ...... APOSTLE, PETER
pure ..... REAL, GENUINE, AMATEUR
the overseer .... LEGREE
simoon .... TEBBAD, WIND, SAMIEL
simp ...... DOLT, SIMPLETON
simper .... SMIRK, SMILE
simple ... MERE, SNAP, SINGLE, PLAIN, EASY, BARE, ARTLESS, GREEN, STUPID, COMMON, LOWLY, NATURAL
in law .... ABSOLUTE
machine ... LEVER, AXLE, WHEEL, PULLEY, SCREW
minded .... STUPID, FOOLISH
organism ...... AMOEBA, MONAD
simpleton ... MORON, IMBECILE, GOOSE, NITWIT, SAP, OAF, NINCOMPOOP, FOOL, DOLT, BOOBY, DIMWIT, COOT, DAW, GAUP, SOFTHEAD, NINNY, NODDY, DOODLE, GOMERAL, GOWK, GAWK, GABY, ZANY
Simplon ____ .... PASS
simply ... MERELY, ONLY, JUST
simulacrum .... IMAGE, TRAVESTY, SHAM
simular .... FEIGNED
simulate .... FEIGN, ACT, PRETEND, ASSUME, FAKE, SHAM, IMITATE, AFFECT, APE
simulation ... FEINT, PRETENSE, FEIGNING
simurgh .... ROC
sin .... FAULT, OFFENSE, INIQUITY, TRESPASS, ENVY, SLOTH, GREED, VICE, TRANSGRESS, EVIL, GUILT
capable of .... PECCABLE
petty ...... PECCADILLO
repentance for .... CONTRITION, ATTRITION, PENITENCE, REMORSE
Sinai .... MOUNT, HOREB
sinalbin .... GLUCOSIDE
Sinaloa capital ..... CULIACAN
sinapism .... PLASTER
Sinatra, former Mrs. ... AVA, MIA
Sinbad the ____ ...... SAILOR
transport of .... ROC
since ...... SITH, AGO, HENCE, INASMUCH AS, BEFORE NOW
sincere ... FAITHFUL, HONEST, EARNEST, OPEN, FRANK, CANDID
sinciput .... FOREHEAD
Sinclair, novelist ..... UPTON, MAY, CATHERINE, LEWIS
character .... DOREMUS, CASS, BABBITT
Sind, capital of ..... KARACHI
sine .... WITHOUT
prole .... CHILDLESS
qua ____ .... NON
sinecure .... SNAP
sinew(s) ..... TENDON, FORCE, THEWS, MUSCLE
sinewy ... TOUGH, MUSCULAR, BRAWNY, WIRY
sinful ..... WICKED, IMMORAL, EVIL, PECCANT
sing ..... BUZZ, HUM, CHANT, WARBLE, CAROL
in certain way ... CROON, YODEL, HUM
slang .. CONFESS, SQUEAL
Singapore founder ... RAFFLES
garment .... SAMFOO, KEBAYA, SARI, CHEONGSAM
old name ...... TEMASEK
president .... YUSOF
prime minister ...... LEE
soup .... SOTO
singe .... BURN
singer ... CAROLER, VOCALIST, CHORIST(ER), YODELER, BIRD, POET, CANTOR, MINSTREL
choir .... ALTO
female ... DIVA, SOPRANO, CHANTEUSE, CANTATRICE, COLORATURA, LIND, CHANTRESS, PRICE, STEVENS
male ... TENOR, BARITONE, MINSTREL, LANZA
opera ... MELBA, CALLAS, ALDA, PONS, PATTI, TAUBER, CARUSO, TIBBET, GLUCK, NILSSON, PINZA, TUCKER, TEBALDI, TRAUBEL
stock of ..... REPERTOIRE, REPERTORY
wandering ..... BUSKER, MINSTREL
singers' group .... CHOIR, TROUPE, ENSEMBLE
singing voice .... SOPRANO, TENOR, BARITONE, ALTO, FALSETTO, COLORATURA, BASSO
single .... INDIVIDUAL, SOLITARY, UNMARRIED, SOLE, (A)LONE, ACE, SOLO, UNWED
combining form .. MONO, UNI, HAPLO
file .... TANDEM
foot .... RACK
footed ...... MONOPODE
handed .... UNAIDED
in biology ... UNIVALENT
in telegraphy ... SIMPLEX
man .... BACHELOR
out ...... PICK, SELECT, CHOOSE
point .... ACE
sticker .. SAILBOAT, SLOOP
thing .... UNIT
track railway .. MONORAIL
singlet ... JERSEY, UNDERSHIRT
singly .... SOLO, ALONE, UNAIDED, ONE BY ONE
singsong recitation .... CHIME
singular ...... SOLE, UNIQUE, INDIVIDUAL, STRANGE, QUEER, UNUSUAL, ODD, RARE
opposed to ...... PLURAL
sinigrin .... GLUCOSIDE
sinister .... EVIL, OMINOUS, WICKED, BALEFUL, LEFT(SIDE), PORTENTOUS, GRIM
opposed to ..... DEXTER
sink .... FALL, SUBSIDE, RECEDE, DECLINE, LOWER, SEWER, CESSPOOL, BASIN, DIP, DESCEND, SETTLE, SAG, BOWL, SLUMP
ship deliberately .... SCUTTLE
sinker .... DOUGHNUT
Sinkiang capital .... URUMCHI
Sinn ____, Irish society .. FEIN
sinople .... CINNABAR
sinuate .... WAVY, SINUOUS
sinuous ..... WAVY, WINDING, DEVIOUS, SLITHERY, SERPENTINE

sinus ... CAVITY, BEND, CURVE, ANTRA, ANTRUM
Sioux .. CROW, OSAGE, PONCA, TETON, MANDAN, IOWA, CATAWBA, DAKOTA, OTO(E)
chief ...... SITTING BULL
sip ... DRINK, NIP, TASTE, TIFF
siphon .... DRAW, STRAW
sipid .... SAVORY
sipper .... STRAW
sippet ...... TOAST, CROUTON, FRAGMENT
sipping tube .... STRAW
sir ..... SEIGNOR, (MON)SIEUR, SAHIB, SENOR, EFFENDI, TUAN, SRI
sire .... BEGET, (FORE)FATHER
siren .. WITCH, CIRCE, NYMPH, ENCHANTRESS, CHARMER, LORELEI, (FOG)HORN, WHISTLE, VAMP, PARTHENOPE
Rhine ... LORELEI, LURLEI
sirenian ... MANATEE, SEA COW, DUGONG
Sirius ... CANICULA, DOG STAR
of .... SOTHIC
sirloin, beef .... BARON
sirocco .... WIND
Madeira Island .... LESTE
sirup (see syrup) .... TREACLE, ORGEAT, GRENADINE, SORGHUM, MOLASSES
sirupy .... SACCHARINE
sisal .... FIBER, HEMP, AGAVE, HENEQUIN
Sisera's enemy .... BARAK
murderer .... JAEL
soldiers ..... CANAANITES
siskin .... FINCH, TARIN
sissy ... PANTYWAIST, MILKSOP
like a .... EFFEMINATE
sister .... TITTY, TITTIE, NUN, SOROR, WOMAN, NURSE, SIB
British .... NURSE
fictional .... CARRIE
headdress of a ... CORNET
Sistine Chapel feature .... FRESCOES
Madonna painter .... RAPHAEL
sistrum .... RATTLE
sit ...... ROOST, POSE, PERCH, BROOD
in .... ATTEND
on .... REPRESS
site .... SEAT, SCENE, LOCALE, LOCATION, STEAD
sitology .... DIETETICS
Sitsang .... TIBET
sitter .... BROODER, NURSE
sitting ..... SESSION, MEETING, SEATED
Bull's antagonist .... CUSTER
room .... PARLOR, SALA, BOUDOIR
spiritual .... SEANCE
situate ...... LOCATE, POSIT, PLACE
situation .... STATE, POSITION, PLACE

difficult .... JAM, STRAIT, PLIGHT, FIX
situs ..... LOCATION, POSITION
Sitwell, poet .... EDITH, OSBERT
Siva's wife .... DEVI, MAYA, SA(K)TI
six .... HEXAD, SESTET
combining form ... HEXA
footed .... HEXAPOD
group of .... HEXAD, SEXTET(TE), SESTET, SEXTUPLET, SENARY
in dice game .. SICE, SISE
of .... SENARY
pointed figure ..... STAR
prefix .... HEXA
shooter .... REVOLVER
years, lasting .. SEXENNIAL
16 1/2 feet .. ROD, POLE, PERCH
sixth day, occurring every .... SEXTAN
sense .... INTUITION
sizable ... BIG, SUBSTANTIAL, HUGE
size .... MAGNITUDE, BULK
of hole .... BORE
of paper .... DEMY, FOOLSCAP, ROYAL
sizy ..... GLUTINOUS, VISCOUS
sizzle .... HISS, FRIZZ(LE)
sizzling .... (RED)HOT
skate ..... RAY, HORSE, CHAP, ROCKER
blade .... RUNNER
skating arena .... RINK
sign .... REDBALL
skean ...... DAGGER, SWORD
skedaddle .... BOLT, DECAMP, BLOW
skee .... SKI
skein ...... HANK, MESH, RAP
of yarn .... HASP
skeletal disease ..... RICKETS, RACHITIS
skeleton ...... FRAME(WORK), ATOMY, CARCASS, BONES
copy in printing .. DUMMY
force .... CADRE
hiding place of .. CLOSET
sea animal .... CORAL
Skelton, comedian ...... RED
skep .... BASKET, BEEHIVE
skeptic .. DOUBTER, AGNOSTIC, CYNIC, PYRRHO, LUCIAN
Biblical .... THOMAS
skeptical .... DUBIOUS
skerry .... REEF
sketch ... DESIGN, DRAW(ING), OUTLINE, DRAFT, SKIT, MAP, PLAYLET, AFTERPIECE
out .... DELINEATE
skete member .. MONK, HERMIT
skew .... SIDLE, SWERVE, SQUINT, OBLIQUE, TWIST
skewer .... PIN, SKIVER, SPIT, BROACH, BROCHETTE, TRUSS
ski .... RUNNER
run ..... SCHUSS, SLALOM, DOWNHILL, JUMP
skid ..... (SIDE)SLIP, RUNNER, BRAKE, SLIDE, TRIG
row character ....

VAGRANT, HOBO, DERELICT
skiddoo ..... LEAVE, DEPART
skiff ...... CAIQUE, ROWBOAT
skiing race .... SLALOM
skill .... TALENT, GIFT, PROFICIENCY, CRAFT, DEXTERITY, KNOW-HOW, PROWESS, FINESSE, SCIENCE, ADROIT, EXPERTISE
combining form .... TECHNO
manual ..... HANDICRAFT
skillet .... (FRYING)PAN, SPIDER
skillful .... EXPERT, DEFT, APT, DEXT(E)ROUS, ADROIT, HANDY, HABILE, ADEPT, ABLE, ACCOMPLISHED
one .... PRO
workmanship .. D(A)EDAL
skim ..... SCUD, SCUM, COAT, GLANCE, GLIDE, FLIT
skimmer .... SCISSORBILL
skimp ..... SCANTY, SCRIMP, ECONOMIZE
skimpy ... STINGY, NIGGARDLY
skin ..... CUTIS, (EPI)DERMIS, BARK, COAT, DERM(A), SHELL, STRIP
abscess ...... FURUNCLE
animal ...... PELT, HIDE, FUR, SUEDE, KID, PELLAGE, FELL
blemish .... WART, FRECKLE, MOLE
bulge .... INION
cast off .... SLOUGH
colloquial .... CHEAT, SWINDLE, DEFRAUD
coloration .... CYANOSIS
combining form .... DERMAT(O), DERM(O), DERMA
condition .... RASH, URTICARIA, HIVES, UREDO, LENTIGO
container .... KENCH
covering ...... HAIR, FUR
cut away .... PEEL, PARE
dark .... MELANIC
decoration ..... TATTOO
deep ...... SUPERFICIAL, SHALLOW
deer antler's .... VELVET
design on ..... TATTOO
discoloration ..... BRUISE
disease .... TINEA, TETTER, LEPROSY, PURPURA, PRURIGO, ARAKIS, ERYSIPELAS, ACNE, ECZEMA, RINGWORM, PSORA, MANGE, HIVES, PINTA, PSORIASIS, SCABIES, IMPETIGO, ITCH, SERPIGO, YAWS, MILIARIA, LICHEN, LUPUS, HUMOR, HERPES, SCALL, SCURF, FAVUS, VITILIGO
disease drug .. NEOMYCIN
disease, oil for .. CAJUPUT

diver's aid .... SCUBA
diving device .... AQUALUNG
drying frame ..... HERSE
dryness .... XEROSIS
duct dirt .... COMEDO
elevation ...... BLISTER, PAPULE, PIMPLE, PUSTULE, WHEAL, WALE, WELT
eruption ... EXANTHEMA
flaw .... WRINKLE
fold .... PLICA
fruit ... RIND, PEEL, ZEST
horny growth ..... CORN, KERATOSIS
inflammation ... PIMPLE, PAPULE, PUSTULE, BOIL, CARBUNCLE
injury .... CONTUSION, BRUISE
Latin .... CUTIS
layer .... DERMIS, DERM(A), CUTIS
like .... DERMATOID, DERMOID
lotion .... CALAMINE
nodule .... MILIUM
of the .. DERMIC, DERMAL, CUTANEOUS
oil .... SEBUM
opening .... PORE
outer layer ..... EPICARP
peel off ...... EXCORIATE
person with abnormal white .... ALBINO
pertaining to .... CUTANEOUS
redness .... RUBOR, ERYTHEMA
scales .... SCURF
scar ...... VACCINATION, BRAND
shed .... MOLT
shed by snake ... SLOUGH
ship's ... PLATE, ARMOR, SHELL
sore .... GALL
specialist .... DERMATOLOGIST
spot .... N(A)EVUS
strip the .... FLAY
swelling .... BLEB
treat .... TAW, TAN
tree .... BARK, RIND
tumor .... WEN
untanned ... SHAGREEN, KIP
whip mark .. WELT, WALE, STRIPE, WHEAL

skinflint ..... MISER, NIGGARD, TIGHTWAD
skink ... SEPS, LIZARD, ADDA
like/of the ..... SCINCOID
skinless .... APELLOUS
skinner .... SWINDLER, (MULE)DRIVER, STRIPPER
actress/writer .... CORNELIA (OTIS)
skinny .... SCRAGGY, EMACIATED, THIN, LEAN
skip ...... SPRING, RICOCHET, ABSCOND, DECAMP, PASS OVER, CAPER, DAP, OMIT, LEAP, JUMP, HOP, SKITTER
skipjack .... BEETLE, FISH, ELATER
skipper .... SAURY, RAIS, RAS, CAPTAIN, MASTER, BUTTERFLY
skirmish ...... BRUSH, MELEE, BATTLE, (AF)FRAY
skirr .... SCOUR, GLIDE
skirt .... BORDER, FRINGE, DIRNDL, PANNIER, KIRTLE, CHOGORI, HOBBLE, PETTICOAT
armor .... TASSE
ballet dancer's ..... TUTU
he wears one ...... SCOT
men's .... KILT
slang ..... WOMAN, GIRL
slit .... PLACKET
swish of silk ... FROUFROU
triangular part ..... GORE
waist .... PEPLUM

skit .... GIBE, SKETCH, SLAPSTICK, PARODY, PLAY(LET)
skitter .... SKIP, SCAMPER
skittish ..... NERVOUS, JUMPY, FICKLE, PLAYFUL
skivvy .... SHIRT
skittle(s) .... BOWLS, PIN, NINEPINS
skive ..... SHAVE, PARE, SLICE
skivvy .... UNDERWEAR, UNDERSHIRT
skoal .... TOAST
skua .... JAEGER, GULL
skulduggery .... TRICKERY
skulk ... LURK, MICHE, SLINK, SHIRK, MALINGER, PROWL
skull .... HEAD, CRANIUM, SCONCE, MAZARD
back part ..... OCCIPUT
bulge .... INION
cavity .... FOSSA, SINUS
domed part .... CALVARIA
of the ... CRANIAL, INIAL, CEPHALIC
part of ...... BRAINPAN, CRANIUM, BREGMA, CALVARIA
protuberance ..... INION
study of the .... CRANIOLOGY
surgical saw for .. TREPAN, TREPHINE

skullcap ... CALOT(TE), PILEUS, IVETTA, BEANIE, COIF, ZUCCHETTO
skunk ... CONEPATE, POLECAT, MEPHITIS, STINKER, CHINCHE, TELEDU
animal resembling ...... ZORIL(A), TELEDU
kin of ..... MINK, OTTER
spray of .... MUSK

sky ..... FIRMAMENT, HEAVEN, CLIMATE, VAULT, OLYMPUS, EMPYREAN, COPE
bear .... URSA
blue ... AZURE, CERULEAN
curved vault of .. WELKIN
highest point .... ZENITH
of the .... CELESTIAL
pilot .... AVIATOR, CHAPLAIN, CLERGYMAN
prefix .... SCIO

skylark .... FROLIC
genus .... ALAUDA
skylight .... DORMER
skyline .... HORIZON
skyways .... AIR LANES
slab ..... CHUNK, TILE, STELE, PIECE, VISCID, SLICE, DALLE, TABLE(T)
atop column .... ABACUS
slack ..... IDLE, LOOSE, SLOW, SLUGGISH, DULL, REMISS, MORASS, LAZE, RELAXED, LAX, WEAK, LULL, DELL, DUFF
slacken .... SLOW DOWN, LOOSEN, EASE, ABATE, LET UP, RELAX
slacker ... TRUANT, SHIRKER, SPIV, IDLER, LOAFER
slacks .... TROUSERS
slag ... DROSS, LAVA, SCORIA, CINDER
slake ..... QUENCH, SATISFY, HYDRATE
slalom .... SKI
slam ... SHUT, HIT, PAN, VOLE, BANG
slander ..... DEFAME, ASPERSE, TRADUCE, LIBEL, SMEAR, REVILE, MALEDICTION, MALIGN, CALUMNY, MUD
slanderous story ... ROORBACK
slang .. CANT, ARGOT, JARGON, PATOIS, SHOPTALK, DIALECT, LINGO
suffix .... EROO
slant .... TILT, INCLINE, OPINION, KEEL, CANT, RAKE, SLOPE, SKEW, BIAS, ANGLE, GLANCE, HEEL
combining form .. CLINO
line .... SOLIDUS
slanted edge .... BEVEL
slanting ..... OBLIQUE, ATILT, ASKEW
type .... ITALIC
slap ..... SPAT, CUFF, WHACK, BIFF, THWACK, RAP, SMACK, BLOW, REBUFF, SPANK
happy ... SILLY, FOOLISH
slapdash .... OFFHAND
slapjack .... PANCAKE
slapstick .... COMEDY, HORSEPLAY
slash .... CUT, GASH, JAG, SCOURGE, SLIT, LASH
Slask .... SILESIA
slat ...... STRIP, LATH, FLAP, BEAT, SPLINE
barrel .... STAVE
movable .... LOUVER
slate ...... TABLET, BALLOT, TICKET, LIST, ABUSE, ENROLL, BOOK, SCOLD, RAKE
ax/trimmer .... ZAX, SAX
excavation site .. QUARRY
roofing .... RAG

slater .... WOOD LOUSE
slattern ...... TROLLOP, SLUT, SLOVEN, DRAB
slaughter .... BUTCHER(Y), MASSACRE, CARNAGE, POGROM, HECATOMB
slaughterhouse ..... ABATTOIR, SHAMBLES
waste .... TANKAGE
Slav .... CROAT, VENED, BULGAR, SLOVENE, POLE, SLOVAK, CZECH, SERB(IAN)
slave .... BONDMAN, SERVANT, TOIL, HELOT, DRUDGE, SERF, THRALL, VASSAL
Biblical .... HAGAR
block .... CATASTA
driver ..... TASKMASTER
educated ...... HETAERA
female .... ODALISK, ODALISQUE, HETAERA, HETAIRA
liberate .... MANUMIT
mark of .... STIGMA, BRAND
Moslem ..... MAMELUKE
runaway ...... MAROON
ship .... SLAVER
soldier ...... MAMELUKE
temple .... HIERODULE
slaver .... DRIVEL, DROOL, SLOBBER, HUMBUG, NONSENSE
slavery .... BONDAGE, THRAL(L)DOM, SERVITUDE, SERFDOM, HELOTRY, DRUDGERY
free from .... MANUMIT, EMANCIPATE
slaves, dealer in ..... MANGO
tied together .... COFFLE
slavish .... SERVILE
slaw .... SALAD
slay .. DESTROY, MURDER, KILL
sleave .... THREAD, FLOSS, TANGLE
sleazy ..... TAWDRY, FLIMSY
sled ..... SLEIGH, TOBOGGAN, SLEDGE, BOBSLED, LUGE, DOUBLE-RIPPER, JUMPER, HURDLE, TRAVOIS(E), PUNG, TODE, GO-DEVIL
dog .... HUSKY
dog, command to .. MUSH
logging .... TODE
slider .... RUNNER
sledge .... HAMMER, DRAG, TRAVOIS(E), SLED, SLEIGH
sleek .. GLOSSY, OILY, SMOOTH, POLISH, UNCTUOUS, SLICK
sleep .... REST, REPOSE, SLUMBER, NOD, DOSS, BUNK, SHUTEYE
combining form .. HYPNO
deep .... STUPOR, SOPOR
drugged ...... NARCOSIS
god of .... SOMNUS, HYPNOS, HYPNUS
inability to ... INSOMNIA
inducing drug .... NARCOTIC, OPIATE
last .... DEATH
lightly .... DOSE
midday .... SIESTA
short .. (CAT)NAP, WINK, DOZE, SIESTA, SNOOZE, SNATCH
unnatural .. SOPOR, COMA, LETHARGY, STUPOR, TRANCE
winter ..... HIBERNATION
sleeper ... RACE HORSE, BEAM, TIE
long .... RIP, SLUGABED
sleepiness ...... SOMNOLENCE
sleeping bag .... SACK
car part .... BERTH
compartment ... CUBICLE
dress ...... NIGHTGOWN, PAJAMAS
pill .... VERONAL, BARBITAL, GOOFBALL
place .. DOSS, PAD, BUNK, COT, BERTH, BED, FLOP, LODGING
sickness carrier .. TSETSE
sickness cause .... TRYPANOSOME
sickness remedy .... SURAMIN
sleepless one ...... INSOMNIAC
sleeplike state .... COMA, TRANCE
sleepwalker .. SOMNAMBULIST
sleepy .... DROWSY, SOMNOLENT, OSCITANT, DOZY
sleet ... HAIL, RAIN, GRAUPEL
sleety .... BRUMAL
sleeve .... ARM, GIGOT
bar on .... CHEVRON
end of .... CUFF
hole .... SKYE, SCYE
kind of .... DOLMAN
sleeveless garment ..... CAPE, CLOAK, ABA, MANTLE
sleigh .... SLEDGE, SLED, CUTTER
boxlike .... PUNG
puller .... REINDEER
rider .... SANTA
slider .... RUNNER
sleight ..... SKILL, TRICK(ERY)
of hand .. LEGERDEMAIN, HOCUS-POCUS, MAGIC
of hand artist .. JUGGLER, MAGICIAN
slender .... WISPY, TENUOUS, FEEBLE, SLIGHT, LANK, LEAN, FRAIL, SVELT, SLIM, MEAGER, THIN, LITHE, WILLOWY, GRACILE
finial .... EPI
in phonetics ...... CLOSE
waisted .... WASPISH
sleuth ...... DETECTIVE, TEC, HAWKSHAW, PRIVATE EYE
fictional .... NERO, CHAN, HERCULE, TRENT, MOTO, HOLMES
slew ... SWAMP, SLOUGH, SLUE, LOT
Slezsko .... SILESIA
slice ..... SKIVE, GASH, PIECE, PORTION, SPATULA, HUNK, LAYER, SHAVE, CHUNK, CUT, SLAB, CANTLE, COLLOP, CHIP
bacon .... RASHER
slick .... SLEEK, GLOSSY, SMOOTH, OILY, UNCTUOUS, CLEVER, SMART, SUAVE
slang .... MAGAZINE
slicker .... COAT
slide ..... GLIDE, SLIP, CHUTE, PLATE, SLUE, COAST, LAWINE, SKID, SLIPSTICK, AVALANCHE
fastener .... ZIPPER
slight ...... WISPY, TENUOUS, SNUB, SLIM, FAINT, IGNORE, AFFRONT, GO-BY, CUT, NEGLECT, FRAIL, FRAGILE, THIN
slightest .... LEAST
amount .... GRAIN
slim .... SLENDER, SLIGHT, MEAGER, SCANT, THIN, SVELTE, SPARE, GRACILE
slime .... MUD, SLUDGE, SEDIMENT, OOZE, MUCK
combining form .. MYX(O)
slimsy ...... FLIMSY, SLIGHT, SLENDER
slimy .... VISCID, VISCOUS
matter .... GLEET, OOZE, SLUDGE, GOB
sling ..... CAST, FLING, HURL, DRINK
barrel/log ... PARBUCKLE
slingshot .... CATAPULT
killer with .... DAVID
slink ... SNEAK, LURK, SKULK, CREEP, STEAL
slinky ... SINUOUS, STEALTHY
slip ..... ERR(OR), MISTAKE, LAPSE, SCION, GAFFE, LEASH, SLIDE, CUTTING, TRIP, PETTICOAT, FAULT, SKID, BONER, LAPSUS, REEVE, TUMBLE
away .... ELAPSE
back .... RELAPSE
knot .... NOOSE
on garment ... SWEATER
out of place ... PROLAPSE
stream ..... RACE, WASH
up .... OVERSIGHT, ERROR
slipcase, book .... FOREL
slipover .... SWEATER
slipper ...... SCUFF, STEP-IN, PANTOF(F)LE, MULE
flat-heeled ... MARY JANE
strap .... SANDAL
slippery .... EELY, SLICK, SHIFTY, EVASIVE, SLIMY, GREASY, ELUSIVE
customer ... EEL, DEBTOR
slipshod ..... WISHY-WASHY, CARELESS, SLOVENLY, SLOPPY
slipstream ...... (PROP)WASH
slit ... SLASH, CUT, SPLIT, GASH
slither ..... SLIDE, SLIP, GLIDE
sliver .... SPLINTER, FIBER
slobber .... DROOL, SLAVER
sloe ...... HAW, BLACKTHORN, PLUM, GIN
slog ...... SLUG, TOIL, PLOD
slogan .... SHIBBOLETH,

CATCHWORD, MOTTO, (BATTLE)CRY, CATCH PHRASE
sloop ..... SAILBOAT, DANDY, CUTTER
of war .... FRIGATE
vessel like a .... HOY
slop ..... SLUSH, MUD, SNOW, SWILL, SPILL, SLOSH
over .... SPILL, GUSH
slope .. SCARP, TALUS, SLANT, INCLINE, DECLIVITY GRADE, BRAE, GRADIENT, SPLAY, GLACIS
combining form .. CLINO
sloping edge ..... BEZEL, BEZIL
sloppy ...... MUDDY, UNTIDY, MESSY, CARELESS, SLIPSHOD
slops ... TROUSERS, BREECHES
slosh .... WADE, SLOP
slot .... GROOVE, TRACK, KEYWAY, TRAIL
machine coin ...... SLUG
machine windfall .... JACKPOT
sloth .... INDOLENCE, LAZINESS, INERTIA, SLOWNESS, EDENTATE
three-toed .... AI
two-toed .... UNAU
slouch .... DROOP(ING), HULK
slough .... SHED, DISCARD, CAST OFF, SWAMP, MARSH
Slovakian city .... KOSICE
slovenly .... SLOPPY, UNTIDY, SLIPSHOD, FROWZY, UNKEMPT, DOWDY
Slovensko .... SLOVAKIA
slow ...... SLACK, SLUGGISH, GRADUAL, RETARD
footed creature .. TURTLE, SLOTH, UNAU, SLUG, LAGGARD, LORIS
in music .... LENTO, TARDO, LARGO, ANDANTE
leak .... DRIP
learner .... DUNCE
paced ...... TARDIGRADE
train .... LOCAL
witted ..... DULL, DENSE
witted person ... DUNCE, DOLT, DOPE
slowpoke ..... SNAIL, SLOTH, SLUGGARD
slubber .... SMEAR, STAIN, DAUB, BOTCH
sludge ...... MIRE, MUD, OOZE, SLEET, (DRIFT)ICE, SEDIMENT, SLUSH, FLOE
slue ... PIVOT, SLEW, SLOUGH, LOT
slug ... TOKEN, BLOW, SNAIL, HIT, BULLET, TREPANG, MOLLUSK, CATERPILLAR, PELLET, SWAT, GASTROPOD
genus .... LIMAX
sluggard ..... DRONE, IDLE(R), LOAFER, LAZY
slugger ... PRIZE FIGHTER, PUG
sluggish ... LETHARGIC, LAZY, DULL, TORPID, LANGUID, INERT, SLOW, LEADEN, LOGY, TARDIGRADE
slugs, of or like .... LIMACINE
sluice .... CHANNEL, (FLOOD)GATE, FLUME, PENSTOCK, SOW
slum .... GHETTO
kid .... GUTTERSNIPE
slumber ...... SLEEP, REPOSE
slump ... FALL, SINK, DECLINE
business ..... RECESSION
slur .... BLUR, DISCREDIT, DISPARAGE, ASPERSE, ELIDE, SMEAR, STAIN, SULLY, SMIRCH
slush ..... MIRE, MUD, DRIVEL, SLOP, PATCH
fund's use ..... BRIBE(RY)
slut ...... BITCH, DOG, DRAB, JADE, TROLLOP, QUEAN, SLATTERN
sly .... CAGEY, TRICKY, INSIDIOUS, FURTIVE, WILY, CRAFTY, FOXY, CUNNING
on the .... SECRETLY, COVERTLY
Slye, pathologist .... MAUD
smack ... SAILBOAT, FLAVOR, TRACE, SAVOR, SLAP, BLOW, BUSS, TASTE, KISS, WHACK, THWACK, PLAP
slang .... HEROIN
small ... LITTLE, LOW, TRIVIAL, PETTY, MEAN, MINIATURE, LIL, MINUTE, MINUSCULE, DINKY, WEE, PETIT(E), BANTAM, TINY, TEENY, PUNY
allowance .... PITTANCE
and active .... DAPPER
animal .... RUNT
amount ...... FRACTION, MITE, MODICUM, IOTA, MORSEL, GRAIN, MINIM, PINCH, DRAM
anything .... PINHEAD
arms .... PISTOLS, RIFLES, CARBINES, REVOLVERS
bite .... NIP
bottle .... VIAL, PHIAL
bright object ... SPANGLE
bunch .... WISP
car .... COMPACT
change .... COIN(S)
combining form .... MICR(O), STENO, LEPTO
cube .... DICE
fish .... FRY, MINNOW, SARDINE, ID(E), SMELT, FINGERLING
flag ... FANION, PENNANT
fry .... CHILDREN, YOUNGSTERS, KIDS
handbills ...... DODGER, FLYER
hollow .... AREOLA
horse ..... PONY, BIDET, SHETLAND
in law .... PETIT
man ..... BANTAM, RUNT
minded ... PETTY, MEAN
part .. DETAIL, FRACTION, BIT
person .... MIDGE, DWARF, RUNT, BANTAM, SHRIMP
pest .... GNAT, IMP
piece .... SNIP(PET)
point .... DOT
portion .... MODICUM
quantity ... SPOT, IOTA, BIT
role in movie/play .. BIT
shield .... ECU
space .... AREOLA
talk .... CHITCHAT
time ..... PETTY, MINOR
town .... BURGH
town paper ..... WEEKLY
violin .... KIT
smallage .... CELERY
smallest ...... TINIEST, LEAST, MINIM
liquid measure .. MINIMUM
planet .... MERCURY
smallpox .... VARIOLA, VARICELLA
disease of ..... ZYMOTIC
mark .... POCK
resembling ... VARIOLOID
smalt ...... PIGMENT, GLASS, BLUE, BICE
smalto .... ENAMEL
smaragd .... EMERALD
smart .. STING, SUFFER, SHARP, BRISK, CLEVER, NEAT, CHIC, APT, STYLISH, SLICK, DASHING, NIFTY, DAPPER, CLEAN, QUICK, WITTY, SPRUCE, SWANKY
aleck .. WISE GUY, QUACK
alecky .... FLIP
as a ____ .... WHIP
blow .... RAP
guy .... SLICK
set ..... ELITE, LITERATI
slang .... SPIFFY
smartly dressed ...... NATTY
phrased .... NEAT
smash ......SHATTER, WRECK, BREAK, CRASH, ROUT, DEFEAT, DASH,
smashup .. COLLISION, WRECK, RUIN, DISASTER
smaze, relative of ...... SMOG
smear .... SLUBBER, SOIL, SLANDER, SPOT, DAUB, MALIGN, DEFAME
smearcase .... CHEESE
smee .... POCHARD
smell ... SCENT, SENSE, SNIFF, FLAVOR, ODO(U)R, WHIFF, NOSE
fats' .... RANCID
goatlike .... HIRCINE
loss of .... ANOSMIA
of the sense of .... OLFACTORY
offensive .... STENCH, OLID, FETOR, RANK, FOUL, STINK, REEK, ODOR
organ of .... NOSE, OLFACTORY
pleasant .... AROMA
savory .... AROMA
stale ...... MUSTY, FUSTY

smeller .... FEELER, NOSE, ANTENNA
smelling .... REDOLENT
salts .... INHALANT
smelt ..... FISH, REFINE, FUSE, CAP(E)LIN, SPARLING
fish like .... TROUT
smelter .... FURNACE, FORGE, BLAST
smelting by-product .. SPEISS, SLAG, DROSS
waste .... TUTTY
smew ..... DUCK, MERGANSER, SCOTER
smidgen .... BIT, IOTA
smilax ... VINE, SARSAPARILLA
smile ... LAUGH, GRIN, SMIRK, SIMPER, SNEER, BEAM, GRIMACE
Mona Lisa ... ENIGMATIC, CRYPTIC
smiling ...... RIDENT, RIANT
smirch ..... DIRTY, DISCOLOR, SMEAR, STAIN, SULLY, SMUDGE, BLOT, SMUT(CH), TARNISH
smirk ..... SMILE, GRIN, LEER, SIMPER
smite .. HIT, DEFEAT, DISTRESS, STRIKE, ENAMOR, AFFLICT
smith .... METALWORKER, FORGE, VULCAN
block of .... ANVIL
furnace of .... FORGE
invisible ...... WAYLAND
smithereens ..... BITS, PIECES, FRAGMENTS
smithsonite .... CALAMINE
smithy .... FORGE, STITHY
smitten .... STRICKEN, AFFLICTED, ENAMORED
smock .... FROCK, CAMISE, CHEMISE
smog .... MIST, SMAZE
ingredient .... SMOKE, SOOT
smoke ... VAPOR, FUME, MIST, CIGAR(ETTE), REEK, SMOG, LUNT, FLOC, CURE
a pipe .... WHIFF
and mist ... SMOG, SMAZE
country boy's .. CORNSILK
fragrant .... INCENSE
good .... CIGAR
meat .... REEST
out .... FLUSH
pipe ..... STACK, FUNNEL
screen ..... CAMOUFLAGE
tree ..... YELLOWWOOD
smokeless power ..... FILITE, CORDITE
smoker .... PARTY, STAG
smokestack .... FUNNEL, CHIMNEY, FLUE
worker .... STEEPLEJACK
smoking pipe ...... HOOKAH, BRIAR, NARGHILE, CALUMET
room .... DIVAN
smoky quartz .... CAIRNGORM
smolder .... BURN
Smollett, novelist .... TOBIAS
smolt .... SALMON
smooch .... SMUTCH
smooth ...... VELVETY, SAND, BLAND, EVEN, CALM, SERENE, POLISH(ED), SUAVE, SOOTHE, OILY, SLEEK, SLICK, IRON, GLABROUS, URBANE, REFINE, SOFT, GRIND
and white .... ALABASTER
consonant .... LENE
feathers .... PREEN
in mechanics .... FRICTIONLESS
in music .... LEGATO
in performance .. DOLCE
in phonetics ..... LENE
over .... GLOSS
pated .... BALD
tongued ..... GLIB, OILY
with beak .... PREEN
smoothing rock ...... PUMICE
smorgasbord treat ...... EELS
smother .... SUFFOCATE, WELTER, STIFLE, CHOKE
smudge ... STAIN, SPOT, BLUR, SOIL, SMUTCH, SMEAR, SMOKE, BLOT, SLUR
smug .... TRIM, NEAT, COMPLACENT
smuggle ... SNEAK IN, BOOTLEG
smuggled goods .... CONTRABAND
whisky ..... MOONSHINE
smuggler .... GUNRUNNER, BOOTLEGGER, (RUM)RUNNER
ship of .... RUNNER
smut .... SOOT, CROCK, OBSCENITY, BUNT, FUNGUS
Smuts, S. African statesman .. JAN
smutty .... OBSCENE
Smyrna .... IZMIR
fig .... ELEME
snack ... TIFFIN, BITE, LUNCH, CANAPE
snaffle .... BIT, CURB
snafu ...... BOOBOO, MUDDLE, MIXED UP
snag .... TOOTH, TEAR, OBSTACLE, HITCH
snail .... HELIX, WHELK, NERITA, ESCARGOT, GASTROPOD, MOLLUSK, SLUG(GARD),
genus .... NERITA, OLEACINA
oyster-killer ...... DRILL
shell .... PERIWINKLE, CARACOLE
snails, of or like ... LIMACINE
snake ..... REPTILE, SERPENT (A)BOMA, VIPER, LORA, PYTHON, OPHIDIAN
big .... BOA, PYTHON, CONSTRICTOR, ANACONDA
bird .... DARTER
bite remedy ..... GUACO, CEDRON
black .... RACER
burrowing ..... GOPHER
castoff of .... SLOUGH
charmer's flute .... PUNGI
common .... ADDER
crusher .... BOA, CONSTRICTOR, PYTHON
deity .... ZOMBI
eyes .... AMBSACE
fish like .... EEL, LAMPREY
garter .... ELAP
haired woman .. MEDUSA, GORGON
hooded .... COBRA
horned ..... SAND VIPER
like .... SINUOUS, COLUBRINE, ANGUINE, APADAL
movement ..... SLITHER
poison ... VENOM, VIRUS
poisonous ... MOCCASIN, SEPS, KRAIT, COBRA, ASP, BONGAR, HABU, VIPER, CERASTES, MAMBA, COTTONMOUTH, ADDER
root .... STEVIA, SANICLE
sand .... ERYX
sea .... KERRIL
skin shedding .. ECDYSIS
sound ..... HISS, RATTLE
space on head of ... LORE
warning of .... HISS, RATTLE
water .... MOCCASIN
snakebird .... WRYNECK, DARTER, PLOTUS
snakehead .... FIGWORT
snakemouth .... ORCHID
snakes, study of .. OPHIOLOGY
snakestone .... AMMONITE
snaky ... ANGUINE, WINDING, SERPENTINE
snap ... BITE, SNATCH, BREAK, SPELL, COOKY, SINECURE, EASY, SIMPLE, FLIP, FLICK, KNAP, CLIP, FASTENER, WAFER, CRACK, FILLIP
snapdragon .... FIGWORT
snapper .... TURTLE, SESI, BEETLE, TAMURE
kin of .... SCUP
snappish ..... CROSS, UNCIVIL, RUDE, IRRITABLE, TESTY, EDGY
snappy .. BRISK, SHARP, SMART, STYLISH, CROSS
make it .... HURRY
snare .... CATCH, (DRAG)NET, GIN, WEB, RATTRAP, PIT(FALL), MESH, SPRINGE, BENET, (EN)TRAP
snark .... BOOJUM
snarl ..... COMPLICATE, KNOT, GIRN, TANGLE, GNAR(L), GROWL
snatch .... GRASP, GRAB, KIDNAP(PING), WREST, SEIZE, SPELL, BIT, TAKE, SWIPE
sneak .... STEAL, SKULK, MOOCH, LURK, SLINK
sneakers ..... (CANVAS)SHOES, GUMSHOES
sneaking .... COWARDLY, FURTIVE
snee .... DIRK
sneer .... SMILE, SCOFF, FLEER, SCORN, MOCK

sneering .. DERISIVE, SCORNFUL
sneeze .... SNUFF
sound .... ACHOO
sneezewort .... YARROW
snell .... LEADER, ACUTE, SMART, SEVERE, QUICK, KEEN, HARSH, SNOOD, GUT
Snerd, dummy ..... MORTIMER
snick ..... NICK, NOTCH, CUT, CLICK
and ____ .... SNEE
snicker .... NEIGH, TEHEE, TITTER, LAUGH, GIGGLE
snickersnee .... KNIFE
snide .... SLY, MALICIOUS, MEAN
sniff .... INHALE, SMELL, SCENT, SNORT, NOSE
sniffles .... (HEAD)COLD
sniffy .. SCORNFUL, DISDAINFUL
snifter ...... DRINK, SIP, NIP
snigger .... SNICKER
snip .... SHEAR, CUT, SHRIMP, BIT, PIECE, CLIP
snipe .... CIGAR, BIRD, WOODCOCK, GODWIT
sniper .... AMBUSHER
snippet ... SCRAP, FRAGMENT, TAC
snit .... TIZZY
snitch .... STEAL, PILFER, TELL, PEACH, INFORMER, SQUEAL
snivel .... SNIFF, SNUFFLE, FRET, WHINE, COMPLAIN
snob .... HIGH-HAT, PRIG, PARVENU, PRUDE
snobbery .... HAUTEUR
snobbish ..... RITZY, UPPISH, HIGH-HAT, STUCK-UP, PROUD, UPPITY, SNOOTY
snood .... RIBBON, SNELL, (HAIR)NET, FILLET
snook .... ROBALO
snoop .... PRY, SKULK, LURK, PROWL
snoot ... FACE, NOSE, GRIMACE
snooty .... SNOBBISH, HAUGHTY, PROUD
snooze ... NAP, DOZE, DROWSE
snore ... STERTOR, RHONCHUS, SNIFF
snorer, loud .... GRAMPUS
snort ... LAUGH, DRINK, SNIFF, SNUFF, NIP
snorter .... HUMDINGER
snotty .. OFFENSIVE, IMPUDENT
snout ... NEB, NOSE, NOZZLE, MUZZLE, ROSTRUM, JAWS, BEAK, SERRA
dig with ..... ROOT, ROUT
elephant's .... TRUNK
push/rub with ... NUZZLE
tapir's .... PROBOSCIS
snouted creature ...... TAPIR, DESMAN, PIG, ELEPHANT, ECHIDNA, ANTEATER, AARDVARK
snow .. FIRN, SLEET, SNA, PASH
bird ...... JUNCO, LERWA
briefly .... SPIT
bunting .... FINCH
field .... NEVE
granular ..... FIRN, NEVE
growing under .... NIVAL
gust of .... FLURRY
house ..... VOLE, IGLOO, IGLU
leopard .... OUNCE
of .... NIVAL
on a glacier .... NEVE
runner .... SKI, SKEE, (BOB)SLED, TOBOGGAN
shoe .... SKI
slang ... HEROIN, COCAINE
slide, mass ... AVALANCHE
travel over .... MUSH
watery .... SLOP
White's friends .. DWARFS
snowbird ..... JUNCO, LERWA, FINCH, ADDICT
snowbird's need ..... HEROIN, COCAINE, DOPE, DRUG
snowdrop .... ANEMONE
snowfall .... SLEET, HAIL
snowflake ... BUNTING, FINCH
snowlike .... NIVEOUS
snowshoe ... PAC, RACKET, SKI
snowstorm .... BLIZZARD
snowy .... NIVEOUS, SPOTLESS, WINTRY, WHITE, BRUMAL
weather need ... MUFFLER, OVERSHOES, EARMUFF
snub .... HIGH-HAT, CUT, SLIGHT, SCORN, AFFRONT, TURNED-UP, REBUFF, UPSTAGE
nose(d) .... PUG
snubber .... SNOB
snuff ... SMELL, SNIFF, SNORT, SCENT, ODOR, RAPPEE, PINCH, PUT OUT, MACCOBOY
out .. EXTINGUISH, DOUSE
snuffle .... SNIFF, TWANG, SNIVEL
snug ..... TAUT, WARM, COZY, SECURE, TRIM, NEAT, COSY, COMFORTABLE
as a bug ____ .. IN A RUG
retreat ...... NEST, DEN
snuggle ..... NESTLE, CUDDLE
so .... ERGO, THEREFORE, SIC, HENCE, VERY, THUS, LIKEWISE, THEN, TRUE
and so .... SOMEONE, SOMEBODY
be it ... AMEN, ALTERCATE
Big author ...... FERBER
Big heroine ...... SELINA
long .... GOOD-BY
Red the ____ ...... ROSE
so .... AVERAGE
soak .... SATURATE, WET, MACERATE, DRENCH, STEEP, SOG, SOP, SODDEN, SOUSE, RET, IMBRUE
colloquial .... DRINK
fiber .... RET
flax .... RET
in brine/vinegar .... MARINATE
slang ... HIT, BOX, PAWN, DRUNKARD
to soften .... RET, MACERATE, STEEP
up .... SORB
soaked .... SODDEN, SOGGY
soap .... DETERGENT, SAPO, CLEANSER, CASTILE
convert into .... SAPONIFY
cresol mixture .... LYSOL
foam .... SUDS
frame bar .... SESS
ingredient .... LYE
material .... TALLOW
oil .... CITRONELLA
olive oil .... CASTILE
opera .... MELODRAMA
plant .... AMOLE
slang .... MONEY
substitute ...... QUILIAI
vine .... GOGO
soapbark .... QUILIAI, MIMOSA
glucoside ... SAPONIN(E)
soapberry ... LICHEE, LITCHI, RAMBUTAN
soapbox character .. AGITATOR, ORATOR, DEMAGOGUE, QUACK
soapstone ..... TALC, STEATITE
soapsuds ...... FOAM, BUCK, LATHER
bleach in .... BUCK
soapy .... SAPONACEOUS, OILY, SUAVE, UNCTUOUS
water .... SUDS
soar .... FLY, RISE, TOWER
soaring .... HIGH, TOWERING
sob .... WEEP, CRY, SIGH
sober ... TEMPERATE, SOLEMN, SERIOUS, GRAVE, SEDATE, PLAIN, QUIET, STAID
sobriety .... TEMPERANCE, MODERATION
sobriquet .... AGNAME, NICKNAME, ALIAS
soccer .... FOOTBALL
player, famed ..... PELE, CHARLTON
Soche .... YARKAND
sociable .... FRIENDLY, OUTGOING, AFFABLE, NICE, FOLKSY
social ... PARTY, GATHERING, CIVIC, BEE
affair ..... SHINDIG, TEA, MUSICALE, SOIREE
appointment .... DATE
asset .. TACT, DIPLOMACY, GRACE
call .... GAM
class .... CASTE
climber ... TUFTHUNTER, UPSTART, SNOB
Contract author .... ROUSSEAU
contract theorist .. LOCKE, HOBBS, ROUSSEAU
disease in short ...... VD
error .... SOLECISM, FAUX PAS
finesse .... TACT
gathering for men .... SMOKER, STAG
grace, lacking .. GAUCHEE
insect .. ANT, BEE, VESPID, WASP, TERMITE
order .... REGIME
outcast ... PARIAH, LEPER

outdoors .... FRY
reformer, American ..... MOTT
register .... BLUEBOOK
science ..... SOCIOLOGY
standing .... STATION
system ... CASTE, REGIME
unit .... FAMILY
virtue .... TACT
visit .... GAM, CALL
wasp .... VESPID
socialist ..... MARX, FOURIER, ENGELS
society .... COMPANY, ASSOCIATION, COMMUNITY, VEREIN
bigwig .... NOB
bud .... (SUB)DEB, DEBUTANTE
combining form ... SOCIO
doings .... SOCIALS
entrance into ..... DEBUT
fashionable .... BONTON
for animals .... SPCA
Islands' capital .. PAPEETE
Islands, one of the ...... TAHITI
of Friends .... QUAKERS
of Friends founder .. FOX
of Jesus founder .... IGNATIUS (OF LOYOLA)
of the learned .. ACADEMY
with government .... POLITY
socials .... PARTIES
sociology .... DEMOTICS
sock ..... WALLOP, COMEDY, SHOE, STOCKING, BOX, BLOW
sockdolager .. FINISHER, ONER
socket .... MORTISE, PAN
bit .... POD
roof beam .... OPA
sockeye .... SALMON
socks .... SOX, HOSE
Socrates' disciple ..... PLATO
wife .... XANTHIPPE
sod ..... TURF, SWARD, GLEBE, PEAT, DIRT, EARTH, SOIL
soda ____ .... JERK, POP, FOUNTAIN
ash ..... BARILLA, ALKALI
ash source .... SEAWEED
caustic .... LYE
fountain order .... MALT, SHAKE, SUNDAE
water .... FIZZ
sodality .... FELLOWSHIP
sodden ..... SOAKED, SOGGY, STEEP, POACHY
sodium .... NATRUM
carbonate ...... NATRON, TRONA, SODA(ASH), SAL SODA
combining form .. NATRO
hydroxide .... LYE, CAUSTIC SODA
nitrate .... SALTPETER, CALICHE, SALTPETRE, NITER
oxide .... SODA
thiosulfate .... HYPO
Sodom's neighbor .. GOMORRAH
sodomite .... BUGGER
sodomy, form of ... PEDERASTY
sofa .... COUCH, SETTLE, LOUNGE, CHESTERFIELD, DAYBED, SQUAB, SETTEE, DIVAN, DAVENPORT, VIS-A-VIS
covering .... TIDY
soft ...... VELVETY, SMOOTH, BLAND, MILD, TEMPERATE, WEAK, EASY, PAPPY, GENTLE, HUSH, SUBDUED, LOW, TENDER, SMOOTH, FOOLISH
and limp .... FLABBY
drink ... ADE, POP, MEAD, COLA, SODA
fabric ..... SILK, PANNE, VELVET
feathers ... DOWN, EIDER
food .... PAP, SOUP
hair .... VILLUS
ice .... LOLLY
in music .... PIANO
in phonetics .... SIBILANT
job ..... SINECURE, SNAP
mass .... PULP
metal .... TIN, LEAD
mineral .... TALC
palate .... VELUM, UVULA
pedal ...... TONE DOWN, EASE, MODERATE, PLAYDOWN
roll .... BUN
saddle .... PANEL
shoulder .... BERM(E)
soap .... FLATTER, BLARNEY, CAJOLE
spoken .... SUAVE
sound .... SIGN, MURMUR
sweet and .... DOLCE
tissue .... BREI
toned organ stop .. DOLCE
soften ..... MITIGATE, TEMPER, RELENT, EASE, LOOSEN
by soaking .... RET, MACERATE, STEEP
softening .... LENITIVE
of the brain.... DEMENTIA
softhead .... SIMPLETON
softie .... SISSY, WEAKLING
softly .... LOW
Sogdian .... IRANIAN
soggy .... WET, SOAKED, SODDEN, POACHY
Soho feature ... RESTAURANTS
soigne .... TIDY, NEAT
soil ... LAND, SULLY, DEFILE, PURGE, CLAY, LOESS, MARL, SOD, GLEBE, GUMBO, LOAM, COUNTRY, EARTH, GROUND, DIRTY, SMIRCH
hard layer of .... PAN
hole-making tool .... DIBBLE
in combination ... AGRO
infertile .... PODZOL
organic part of ... HUMUS
poetic .... GLEBE
restorer .... VETCH
unfruitful .... BARREN
wind-deposited ... LOESS
soja .... SOY(BEAN), SAUCE
sojourn ... STAY, VISIT, TARRY
sojourner .... PILGRIM, TRUTH
Sol ... SUN(GOD), GOLD, NOTE
impresario ...... HUROK
sola .... ALONE
solace ..... COMFORT, RELIEF, ALLAY, CONSOLE, CHEER
solan goose .... GANNET
solanum .... NIGHTSHADE
solar .... HELIACAL
deity ...... HELIOS, SOL, LLEU
disk .... ATEN
furnace site .... ODEILLO
phenomenon ... ECLIPSE, CORONA
spot/streak ..... FACULA
system model ... ORRERY
solarium .... SUNROOM
solder ... BORAX, BOND, ROSIN, JOIN, PATCH, FUSE, BRAZE, CEMENT
soldier ...... WARRIOR, POILU, MAN-AT-ARMS, TERMITE
bag of ..... HAVERSACK, KNAPSACK, MUSETTE
brutal .... PANDOUR
call to quarters .. TATTOO
cap of .... SHAKO
cavalry ... UHLAN, SPAHI
fellow .... BUDDY
food of ..... CHOW, MESS, K-RATION
freebooting ... RAPPAREE
from Down Under ...... ANZAC
headgear ...... HELMET, CAP, BERET
killed .... CASUALTY
kind of ..... MERCENARY, LANCE(R), LEGIONARY, TERRITORIAL
Korean .... ROK
mercenary ..... HESSIAN, SWISSER, SWITZER
mounted ..... CAVALRY, SPAHI
of fortune .. ADVENTURER
old .... VET(ERAN)
pack of .... KIT
shelter of ...... FOXHOLE
slang ...... DOUGHBOY, DOGFACE, SADSACK
trainee .... CADET
with musket .. DRAG(O)ON
wounded in battle .... CASUALTY
soldierly .... MARTIAL
soldiers, collectively .... MILITARY, ARMED FORCES
rebellion of .... MUTINY
Three author .... KIPLING
sole ...... SINGLE, ONLY, ONE, (FLAT)FISH, PLAICE, HALIBUT, MERE, ALONE, SOLITARY
foot's .... PLANTAR, VOLA
of the foot's ...... VOLAR
plow's .... SLADE
solecism .... IMPROPRIETY, BARBARISM
solely .. MERELY, ONLY, ALONE
solemn ..... SACRED, FORMAL,

SERIOUS, SOBER, GRAVE, SOMBER
wonder .... AWE
looking .... OWLISH
word .... OATH, VOW, PLEDGE, TROTH, PAROL(E)
solemnity .... FORMALITY, GRAVITY
solemnize .... CELEBRATE
solfatara emission ...... GAS, VAPOR
solferino .... FUCHSIN, DYE
solicit ...... ENTREAT, APPLY, ASK, BEG, SEEK, BID
customers .... TOUT
solicitation .... ENTREATY, PETITION
solicitor .... LAWYER
solicitude ... CARE, CONCERN
solid ..... COMPACT, SOUND, FIRM, GENUINE, THICK, HARD, MASSIVE, MASSY
ground ... TERRA FIRMA
six-sided .... CUBE
solidago .... GOLDENROD
solidarity .... UNITY
solidified lava .... COULEE
solidify ...... GEL, SET, JELL, CONGEAL, HARDEN, CAKE
solidity .... FIRMNESS
solidus ... BEZANT, SLANT LINE
soliloquy .... MONOLOGUE
solitaire .... RECLUSE, PATIENCE, HERMIT, CANFIELD, GEM, CARD GAME
solitary .... SINGLE, ONLY, LONE(LY), REMOTE, HERMIT, ALONE, CONFINEMENT, HERMITIC
solitude .... ISOLATION, SECLUSION
sollar ... BRATTICE, GALLERY
solo ... (A)LONE, SURAKARTA, ARIA
Solomon .... SAGE, KING, WISEMAN
father of .... DAVID
island .... MALAITA, CHOISEUL, GUADALCANAL
Islands' capital .. HONIARA
Islands' city ...... KIETA, AUKI, SOHANO
sayings of ...... MAXIMS, PROVERBS
solon ... LEGISLATOR, SENATOR, LAWGIVER, LAWMAKER, SAGE, WISEMAN
soluble salt .... SALAR
solus .... ALONE
solution .... EXPLANATION, ANSWER, SEPARATION, BREAK
in pharmacy ...... AQUA
part of .... SOLUTE, SOLVENT
strength of .. TITER, TITRE
solve ..... UNRAVEL, EXPLAIN
solvent ..... DILUENT, WATER, ACETONE, MENSTRUUM, HEXONE
wood tar ..... FURAN(E)
soma .... TRUNK, BODY
Somalia capital .. MOGADISHU
city .... HARGEISA, BERBERA
monetary unit .. SOMALO
premier .... EGAL
Somaliland antelope ... BEIRA
somatic .... PHYSICAL, CORPOREAL, BODILY, PARIETAL
somber ..... SOLEMN, GLOOMY, SAD, DISMAL, GRAVE
sombrero .... HAT
some .... ANY, ABOUT
time ... LATER, ONE DAY
somersault .... TUMBLE, SOMERSET, FLIP(FLOP)
something done for effect .... EYEWASH
easy .... PIE
imagined .... FIGMENT
monstrous ..... PRODIGY, FREAK
notable/outstanding .... DAISY
that links .... COPULA
to stand on ..... FOOTING
sometime .... ONCE, FORMER, ERST(WHILE)
sometimes ..... OCCASIONALLY
somewhat .... RATHER
suffix .... ISH
somite ... TELSON, MATAMERE, SEGMENT
somnambulist .. SLEEPWALKER
somniferous ...... SOPORIFIC
somnolence ...... SLEEPINESS, DROWSINESS
somnolent ... SLEEPY, DROWSY
son .. HEIR, PROGENY, SCION, JUNIOR
favorite .... BENJAMIN
in law .... GENER
of: prefix ..... FITZ, MAC
of a .... FILIAL
rey's .... INFANTE
roi's .... DAUPHIN
younger .... CADET
sonance .... SOUND, TUNE
sonant ... VOICED, SOUNDING
opposed to .... SURD, VOICELESS
sonata, part of .... CODA, RONDO, MOVEMENT, SCHERZO
sonderclass .... YACHT
song .... DITTY, MELODY, CHANSON, CHANT, CANTICLE, POETRY, VERSE, LYRIC, BALLAD, RUNE, CANZONE, LIED(ER)
accompaniment ... VAMP
after .... EPODE
and-dance performer .... DISEUSE
baby's .... LULLABY
Christmas .. CAROL, NOEL
combining form .... MALACO
dirgelike ...... REQUIEM
evening .... VESPERS
flourish .... CADENZA
gay .... LILT
identification .... THEME, SIGNATURE
improvisation .... VAMP
joyful .... P(A)EAN
kind of ... BLUES, TORCH, SOUL, FOLK
last words .... TAG
like .... ARIOSE, CANOROUS, CANTABILE
lively .... CANZONET
love ... SERENADE, SERENA
merry .... GLEE, LILT
minstrel's .. LAY, BALLAD
morning .... MATIN
of .... MELIC
of joy .... CAROL
of lamentation .... THRENODY, DIRGE
of praise ... (H)ALLELUIA, PAEAN, HALLELUJAH, HYMN, LAUD, MANIFICAT
of Solomon .. CANTICLES
of Songs ..... CANTICLES
of triumph ...... PAEAN
operatic .... ARIA
part .... MADRIGAL
poetic .... RUNE
prefix .... MELO
radio program ... THEME, SIGNATURE
refrain .... BURDEN, CHORUS, FALLA
sacred ... MOTET, PSALM, HYMN, ANTHEM
sad .... BLUES, DIRGE
sailor's ...... CHANT(E)Y
section .... FIT
set of verses of ... STAVE
short .... DITTY, ODE, CAVATINA, ARIETTA, CANZONET
thrush .... MAVIS, MAVIE
words of .... LYRICS
writer .... LYRICIST
songbird .... MAVIS, LARK, THRUSH, CANARY, ORIOLE, PIPIT, WHINCHAT, WREN, REDWING, BULBUL, VIREO, VEERIE, ROBIN(ET), NIGHTINGALE, LINNET, REDSTART, BOBOLINK, THRASHER, SPARROW, BUNTING, GOLDFINCH, CARDINAL, TANAGER
mewing .... CATBIRD
of the .... TURDINE
vocal organ ..... SYRINX
songlike ...... MELIC, ARIOSE, CANOROUS, LYRIC, CANTABILE
songs, anthology of .. GARLAND,
songster ... SINGER, WARBLER
sonnet's last six lines .. SESTET
Sonora, capital of .... HERMOSILLO
Indian .... YAQUI
sonority .... RESONANCE
sonorous .... RESONANT, ROTUND
sonsy .... BUXOM, LUCKY, HANDSOME
soon .... ANON, ERELONG, PRONTO, QUICKLY,

EARLY, READILY, SHORTLY, BETIME, ENOW
afterward .... THEN
sooner .... HOMESTEADER, OKLAHOMAN, RATHER
than .... ERE
soosoo .... DOLPHIN
soot ... CROCK, GRIME, SMUT, COOM, CARBON, BISTRE, BISTER, COLLY, LAMPBLACK
full of .... FULIGINOUS
pigment .. BISTRE, BISTER
sooth ... FACT, REAL, SMOOTH, TRUTH
soothe .... SALVE, CALM, APPEASE, MOLLIFY, EASE, ALLAY, RELIEVE, COMFORT, LULL, PLACATE, PACIFY
soother .... ANODYNE, CONSOLER, SOLACER
soothing ... EASING, CALMING, LENITIVE
soothsay .. FORETELL, PREDICT
soothsayer ..... (H)ARUSPEX, PROPHET, AUGUR, SEER, MANTIS, ORACLE, DIVINER, TIRESIAS
brew of a ... HELLBROTH
soothsaying .... AUGURY
sooty .. DARK, DUSKY, BLACK
matter .... SMUT
sop ..... BRIBE, SOAK, STEEP, OOZE, MORSEL, CONCESSION
Sophia Scicolone ...... LOREN
sophism ... IDOLISM, FALLACY
sophist .... CASUIST
sophisticate .... CORRUPT, ADULTERATE, FALSIFY
sophisticated ... HEP, REFINED, HIP, SUBTLE, COMPLEX, BLASE, INTELLECTUAL
sophistry .. IDOLISM, FALLACY, CHICANERY
sopor .... STUPOR, LETHARGY
soporific ... SOMNIFIC, OPIATE, SULFONAL
sopping ...... WET, DRENCHED
soppy ... RAINY, SENTIMENTAL
soprano .... VOICE, TREBLE, PONS, ALBANESE, FARRAR, NILSSON
Sopwith plane ...... TABLOID
sora .... RAIL, ORTOLAN, CRAKE, BIRD
Sorata .... ILLAMPU
Sorb .... SLAV, APPLE
descendants .... WENDS
Sorbonne, the .... PARISU
sorcerer .... WARLOCK, MAGICIAN, WIZARD, CONJURER, MAGUS, CHALDEAN, HEX
attendant ..... FAMULUS
sorceress ..... SYBIL, WITCH, CIRCE, LAMIA, MEDEA
sorcery .... WITCHCRAFT, THEURGY, MAGIC, OBE, VOODOO, SORTILEGE, DIABLERIE, DIABOLISM, CONJURATION, WIZARDRY
sordid .. FILTHY, DIRTY, MEAN, BASE, SQUALID, WRETCHED, IGNOBLE
sordino .... MUTE
sore .... TENDER, PUSTULE, PAINFUL, FESTER, ACHING, TOUCHY, ANGRY, RESENTFUL, LESION
dressing .. PATCH, GAUZE
inflamed .... BLAIN
mustard application on .. POULTICE
open .... ULCER
ulcer-like .... CANCER
sorehead ..... LOSER, GRIPER, MALCONTENT
sorghum ...... GRASS, SIRUP, FODDER, MILO, FETERITA, KAF(F)IR
grain .... SORGO, KAOLIANG, DURRA, MILLET, DOURA(H)
millet-like .... MILO
soricine animal .... SHREW
sorority .... SOROSIS
sorosis .... SORORITY, MULBERRY, FRUIT
sorrel .... PLANT, HORSE
wood .... OCA
sorrow .... GRIEF, WOE, SADNESS, GRIEVE, ANGUISH, DOLOR
sorrowful expression ... ALAS, ALACK(ADAY), WOE IS ME
sinner .... PENITENT
sorry .... POOR, INFERIOR, MISERABLE, DISMAL, REGRETFUL, PENITENT, REMORSEFUL, SAD, CONTRITE
sort ...... KIND, CLASS, TYPE, NATURE, ILK, CLASSIFY, KIDNEY
of .... SOMEWHAT
sortie ... RAID, SALLY, FORAY
sortilege .... SORCERY, DIVINATION, PROPHECY
sorts, out of ...... CROSS, ILL, INDISPOSED
sotol, plant like ..... YUCCA
sot .... DRUNKARD, TOPER, SOUSE, BLOAT, RUMMY
soubise .... SAUCE
soubrette .... MAID(SERVANT)
soucar .... BANKER
souchong .... TEA
souffle .. PUFFY, SPOONBREAD
sough .... RUSTLE, SIGH, MURMUR, MOAN
soul .... EMBODIMENT, ATMAN, SPIRIT, AME, ANIMA, ESPRIT, ESSENCE, PNEUMA
dead person's ..... MANES
dwelling place .... TABERNACLE
personified ..... PSYCHE
singer .... (ARETHA) FRANKLIN
timid .... LAMB
sound ... NOISE, SEEM, APPEAR, SANE, WELL, TRIG, SOLID, SAFE, SECURE, FATHOM, HEALTHY, STABLE, RELIABLE, VALID, STRAIT, INLET, PLUMB, AUDIO, PURL, HONK, STRIDOR
amplifier ..... RESONATOR
auto horn .... HONK
bee's ...... DRONE, HUM
bell's .. DING, PEAL, TOLL, CLANG, JINGLE
bird ...... TWEET, CHIRP, PEEP, TWITTER
bomb .... WHINE
breathing ...... STRIDOR
bullet .... ZIP, PING
buzzing .... WHIR(R)
cat's ...... PURR, MEOW, MEWL
chuckling ..... CHORTLE
combining form .... PHON(O)
cooing .... CURR
deep ...... CAVERNOUS, BOOM, RUMBLE
depth .... PLUMB
discordant ...... JANGLE
donkey's .... BRAY, HEEHAW
dove's .... COO, CURR
dull .... THUD
elephant's .... ROAR, TRUMPET
from cold ...... CHATTER
gleeful .... CHORTLE
grating .... SCROOP, JAR
guttural .... GRUNT, GRATE
harsh .. GRIDE, JAR, RASP
heard .... ACOUSTIC
hissing ..... ZIP, SIZZLE, FIZZLE, FIZ(Z), SIBILATION, SIBILANCE, SWISH
hog's .... GRUNT
in harmony ...... CHIME
insect .... CHIRRUP, DRONE, HUM
lung .... RALE
menacing ...... GROWL, SNARL, GR-R-R
mournful .... KNELL
murmuring .... SOUGH, COO, CURR, HUM
of ...... SONIC, SONANT, TONAL, PHONIC
of contentment ... PURR
of delight .... SQUEAL
of disapproval .... HOOT, HISS, BOO, CATCALL
of footsteps ..... TRAMP, CLUMP
of goose .... HISS
of gunfire .... PEAL
of laughter .... PEAL
of pain ... GROAN, MOAN, OUCH, SHRIEK, YELL
of surprise .... GASP
of warning ...... TOCSIN, ALARM, HISS, SIREN, RATTLE
of whale .... SQUEAL, CLICK, MEW, CHIRRUP
of yearning .... SIGH
off .... SPEAK, ORATE
pensive .... SIGH
proofing material .. PUG
reverberating ..... ROLL
ringing .... TANG
rolling .... RUMBLE

rooster's .... CROW
rustling .... SWISH
science of ... ACOUSTIC(S)
shrill ...... SKIRL, ZING
sleeper's .... SNORE
snake ..... HISS, RATTLE
soft, rubbing ..... SWISH
steam .... HISS
strident .... SCROOP
surf .... ROTE
thin, sharp ...... SQUEAK, SQUEAL
thunder ..... (G)RUMBLE, ROLL, PEAL
trumpet .... BLARE
unit of measurement .... MACH, DECIBEL
voiceless ...... CEDILLA
warbling .... CHIRM
wave, bend ..... REFRACT
whiplash .... WHISH
whirring .... BURR, BIRR, ZIZZ

soundless .... ASONANT, SILENT, MUTE, STILL
soundproof, make ... DEAFEN, PUG
sounds in ear .... TINNITUS
soup ...... BISQUE, JULIENNE, CONSOMME, POT(T)AGE, GUMBO, CHOWDER, STEW, BOUILLON, BORSCHT
bread .... CROUTON
content .... NOODLE
dish .... TUREEN
flavor .... CHIVE
ingredient .... LENTIL, NOODLE, MACARONI
meat ... BISQUE, BURGOO
plant .... LEEK
slang ... NITROGLYCERIN, OVERCAST
spoon .... LADLE
thick .... PUREE, BISQUE, GUMBO, POTTAGE
thickening mixture ...... ROUX
thin .... BROTH
to ___ .... NUTS
to nuts ..... MEAL, MENU
vegetable .... OKRA, BISQUE, BURGOO, MINESTRONE

soupcon ... SUSPICION, TRACE
sour .... TART, ACID(ULOUS), ACETOUS, RANK, RANCID, CROSS, BITTER, ACETOSE, ACIDIC
ale ... VINEGAR, ALEGAR
disposition, of ... GROSS, TESTY, PEEVISH, LIVERISH
gourd .... BAOBAB
grass .... SORREL
gum .... TUPELO, NYSSA
milk drink .... LEBAN
puss .... PRUNE

source ...... SPRING, ORIGIN, ROOT, FOUNT(AIN), HEADSPRING
of genius/inspiration .... MUSE

sourdine .... MUTE
sourdough .... LEAVEN, SETTLER, PROSPECTOR
sourpuss .... CRAB
Sousa's employment .. MARINE, BANDLEADER
soubriquet .. MARCH KING
souse ..... BRINE, DRUNKARD, PICKLE, SOAK, STEEP, INTOXICATE, SWOOP
soused .... DRUNK, TIPSY
soutache .... BRAID
soutane ..... CASSOCK, TUNIC
South Africa, foreigner in .... UITLANDER
South African .... BOER, AFRIKANER
animal ...... SURICATE, QUAGGA
antelope .... GNU, BUSHBUCK, SASSABY
assembly .... RAAD
beverage .... MATE
camp .... LAAGER
capital ..... CAPE TOWN, PRETORIA
city .... CAPE TOWN, DURBAN
dialect ..... AFRIKAANS
district .... RAND
Dutch ...... BOER, TAAL
farmer .... BOER
fox .... ASSE
golfer .... PLAYER, SEWGOLUM
grassland .... VELD(T)
hill .... KOP
javelin .... ASSAGAI
legislature .... RAAD
monetary unit ..... RAND
monkey .... VERVET
mountain .... KOP
mulatto .... GRIQUA
native ... BANTU, KAFFIR, ZULU
plain .... VELD(T)
plateau .... KAROO
polecat .... MUSANG
policeman .... ZARP
policy ...... APARTHEID
president .... DONGES
prime minister .. VORSTER, VERWOERD, SMUTS, HERTZOG
province ... NATAL, CAPE, TRANSVAAL
racial policy .. APARTHEID
republic .... TRANSVAAL
river ..... VAAL, ORANGE, KUBANGO, OKAVANGO
road .... KLIP
settler .... BOER
spear .... ASSAGAI
swamp .... VLEI
tableland ..... KAR(R)OO
thong .... RIEM
town .... STAD
tribal council .... INDABA
valley ...... KLOOP, VAAL
village .... KRAAL
weapon ..... KNOBKERPIE
workmen .... VOLK

South American animal ...... VICUNA, ALPACA, LLAMA, TAYRA, TAPIR
alligator .... CAIMAN, CAYMAN
arid ground .... ESPINAL
armadillo ..... TATOUAY, MATACO, POYOU
bean .... TONKA
bird .... SERIEMA, TINAM(O)U, AGAMI, RHEA, SCREAMER, TURCO, JACU, TOPAZ, MANAKIN, HOA(C)TZIN, JACANA, GUACHARO, CURASSOW, ARACARI, GUAN
butternut .... SOUARI
city .... LIMA
coin .... CONDOR
crocodile ...... YACARE
dance .... BEGUINE, CARIOCA, SAMBA, TANGO
deer .... GEMUL
desolate region ... PUNA
duck .... PATO
fish .... CHARACIN, ARAPAIMA, PIRANHA
guinea pig .... PACA
hare .... TAPETI
hat .... JIPIJAPA
hawk .... CARACARA
herdsman ..... LLANERO
hog .... TAPIR
hummingbird .. WARRIOR
Indian ..... CARIB, INCA, MAYAN, ONA, GUARANI, PATAGONIAN, TEHUELCHE
knife .... MACHETE
laborer .... PEON, BRACERO
lapwing ..... TREUTERO
lizard .... TEJU
mammal ..... KINKAJOU, GRISON
missile weapon .... BOLA
monkey ...... SAPAJOU, CAPUCHIN, MARMOSET, ARABA, ACARI, TITI, TETEE
nightbird .... GUACHARO
opossum ..... YAPO(C)K, QUICA
ostrich .... RHEA
palm ...... GRUGRU, ITA
parrot .... MACAW, AMAZON
plain ... PAMPA(S), LLANO, PARAMO, CAMPO
plant .... PAREIRA, COPAIBA, RHATANY, GUACO, JABORANDI, JIPIJAPA
raccoon .... COATI
river ... AMAZON, PLATA, PARA, ORINOCO
rock .... TALPATATE
rodent ... TAPETI, PACA, TAPIR, RATEL, GUINEA PIG, NUTRIA, AGOUTI, CAPYBARA, COYPU, AGOUTY
ruminant .... LLAMA

seed ..... GUAIAC, TONKA
snake ..... ABOMA, BOA, BUSHMASTER
tanager ..... YENI, LINDO
tea leaf .... MATE
tick .... CARAPATO
tortoise ..... MATAMATA
toucan .... ARACARI
tree ...... CAROB, CEBIL, BALSA, MORA, BEBEERU, TOLU
trumpeter .... AGAMI
tuber .... OCA
turtle .... MATAMATA
ungulate .... TAPIR
weapon .... BOLAS
wild cat .. MARGAY, EYRA
wind .... PAMPERO
wood sorrel .... OCA
South Carolina capital ...... COLUMBIA
county .... JASPER, HORRY
river .... PEE, DEE SANTEE, CATAWBA
South Dakota capital .. PIERRE
city ... ABERDEEN, HURO
state animal .... COYOTE
state flower ..... PASQUE
"South Pacific" star ... PINZA
South Pole explorer .... AMUNDSEN
South Sea canoe .. PROA, PRAU
garment .... SARONG
island ...... BALI, SAMOA, TA(H)TI, ARU, OTAHEITE
island drink .... KAVA(KAVA)
loincloth ..... LAVA-LAVA
native ..... POLYNESIAN, KANAKA, BALINESE, SAMOAN, TAHITIAN
novel .... OMOO
shrub ...... KAVA(KAVA)
South wind .... NOTUS, AUSTER
southerly .... AUSTRAL
southern .... AUSTRAL
Cross .... CRUX
France .... MIDI
States .... DIXIE
southpaw ..... LEFT-HANDED, LEFTY
souvenir .... MEMENTO, KEEPSAKE, FAVOR, RELIC, SCRAP
sovereign ... SUPREME, CHIEF, MONARCH, RULER, KING, EMPEROR, PRINCE, LIEGE, SOVRAN, ROYAL, POUND, QUID
dignity .... MAJESTY
female .... QUEEN, EMPRESS, TSARINA
of a .... REGNAL
power .... SWAY
sovereignty ...... DOMINION, RULE, THRONE, EMPERY, SCEPTRE, ROYALTY
Soviet (see Russian) .. COUNCIL
administrative body ..... PRESIDIUM
government ... KREMLIN
news agency .... TASS
newspaper ...... PRAVDA
poet ...... YEVTUSHENKO
president ..... MIKOYAN, PODGORNY, KALININ
republic .... UZBEK, KAZAKH, LATVIA, TADZHIK, KIRGHIZ, UKRAINE, MOLDAVIA, TURKMEN
Russia .... USSR
Union founder ... LENIN
sovran .... SOVEREIGN
sow ..... PIG, SLUICE, PLANT, PROPAGATE, SEED, SWINE, SCATTER, BROADCAST, DISSEMINATE, STREW
bug .... SLATER, WOOD LOUSE, ISOPOD
young .... GILT
sowens .... PORRIDGE
sox .... SOCKS
soy(a) ..... SOJA, SAUCE, BEAN
soybean enzyme ...... URASE
cake .... TAHURE
product ... MISO, NAT(T)O, SUFU, TAHO, TOKUA, TAUSI, TEMPLA
sauce .... SOJA, TOYO
spa ... SPRING, BATH, RESORT
space .... ROOM, EXPANSE, EXTENT, AREA, GAP
Age initials .... NASA
Age launcher ... SPUTNIK
agency: abbr. ..... NASA
beacon .... QUASAR, PULSAR
between .... DISTANCE
between bird's eye and bill LORE
blank .... LACUNA
craft capsule ...... SPECS
craft part .... MODULE
craft to moon ... APOLLO
craft to Venus .. MARINER
dog .... STREIKA
empty ... VOID, VACUUM, BLANK
filled with matter .... PLENUM
filler .... SHIM
in biology ...... LACUNA
in from margin .. INDENT
monkey .... ENOS, ASTROMONK
of time .. SPAN, INTERVAL
pertaining to ... SPATIAL
ship blister .... MODULE
traveler .... ASTRONAUT, COSMONAUT
vehicle .... SPUTNIK, APOLLO, SATELLITE, EXPLORER
void .... VACUUM
spacious ...... ROOMY, VAST, LARGE
spade ...... SCOOP, SAM, DIG
tool like .... SPUD, SHOVEL
spadefoot .... TOAD
spades .... SUIT
spaghetti, food like .... MACARONI
ingredient ..... DURUM
spahi, spahee ... CAVALRYMAN
Spain .... ESPANA, IBERIA, HESPERIA
capital of .... MADRID
district of .... GRANADA, ASTURIAS, GALICIA, NAVARRE, ANDALUSIA
kingdom of ... ARAGON, CASTILE, LEON
Spalato .... SPLIT
spale .... LATH
spall .... GALLET, CHIP, FLAKE, SPLIT
spalpeen ..... SCAMP, RASCAL
span ... WINGSPREAD, BRIDGE, TEAM, CROSS, PAIR, PERIOD, QUARTER
in inches .... NINE
spang ... DIRECTLY, ABRUPTLY
spangle ... PAILLETTE, SEQUIN, GLITTER
Spaniard .... IBERIAN, CASTILIAN, SENOR
spaniel .... DOG, SPRINGER, PAPILLON, CLUMBER, COCKER
kind of ... TOY, WATER
Spanish abbot .... ABAD
afternoon .... TARDE
almond .... JORDAN
America mestizo .... LADINO
American country ...... MEXICO
American town .. PUEBLO
American War soldier ... ROUGHRIDER
another .... OTRO
apron .... DELANTAL
article ... EL, LAS, LA, LOS
as .... COMO
asphalt .... BREA
aunt .... TIA
baby .... NINA, NENA
barrel .... TONEL
bayonet .... YUCCA
bear .... OSO
berry, dried ...... PASA
blanket .... PONCHO, SERAPE, MANTA
blind .... CIEGO
blue .... AZUL
bonnet .... GORRA
booth ... CASILLA, TIENDA
botanist ..... MONARDES
boy .... NIÑO
breech .... BRAGA
brush .... CEPILLO
buffoon ...... GRACIOSO, COMICO
bull .... TORO
business firm ..... CASA
cape .... TRAFALGAR
capital .... MADRID
card game .... OMBRE, MONTE, OMBER
castle .... ALCAZAR, ALHAMBRA, TORRE
cathedral city ..... AVILA, SEVILLA
cellist .... CASALS
chaperon ..... DUEN(N)A
cheer ...... OLE, BRAVO

cigar ROPO
city CADIZ, CIUDAD, LEON, IRUN, CORUNNA, ALMERIA, JEREZ, MURCIA, GUERNICA, BILBAO, LORCA, MADRID, TOLEDO, PAMPLONA, SEGOVIA, CORDOVA, BADAJOZ, CARTAGENA, OVIEDO, VITORIA, ZARAGOZA
cloak CAPA, MANTA
clothing ROPA
clown GRACIOSO
club(house) CASINO
coffeepot CAFETERA
coin DOUBLOON, CENTAVO, PESETA, PESO, DOBLA, CENTEN, REAL, MARAVEDI, PISTOLE
collar CUELLO
colony in Africa IFNI
composer FALLA
conquistador CORTEZ, PIZARRO
cot CATRE
cough TOS
council JUNTA
court PATIO, JUZGADO
cow VACA
cowboy GAUCHO, VAQUERO
cup TAZA
cupid AMORINO, AMORETTO
dance FLAMENCO, TANGO, VALSE, SARABAND, JOTA, CARIOCA, PAVIN, BOLERO, DANZA, BAILE, GUARACHA, PAVAN(E), CANARY, CACHUCHA
daughter-in-law NUERA
Davis Cupper SANTANA, GISBERT, ARILLA, GIMENO
day DIA
dear CARO
dialect ARAGONESE, CASTILIAN, ASTURIAN, ANDALUSIAN
dictator FRANCO
dish OLLA, BACALAO, PAELLA
district GRANADA
dollar PIASTRE, DURO, PESO, PIASTER
dramatist TELLEZ
dress TRAJE
dressing gown BATA
drink VINO
each CADA
east ESTE
event CASO
execution GARROTE
expensive CARO
explorer MAGELLAN, BALBOA, DESOTO, CORONADO, MENENDEZ
face CARA
farm HACIENDA, RANCHO, GRANJA
fascist FALANGIST
feast FIESTA
fleet ARMADA, FLOTA
flesh CARNE
fly CANTHARIS
forest MONTE
fortress official ALCAIDE
friend AMIGO
game PELOTA, JAI ALAI
general ALVA
gentleman CABALLERO, GRENDEE, SEÑOR, DON, CAVALI(E)RO
girl NIÑA, CHICA
god of love AMADIS
governess DUENNA
grape MALAGA
grass ESPARTO
guitarist SEGOVIA
gypsy dance FLAMENCO
habit SIESTA, MANANA
half-breed LADINO
hall SALA
hamlet ALDEA
harbor PUERTO, ASILO
hard DURO
hat SOMBRERO
headdress MANTILLA
Hebrew dialect LADINO
herdsman PASTORES
hero (EL) CID, AMADIS
hill ALCOR, ALTO
holiday FIESTA
horse CABALLO, GENET, JENNET
horseman JINETE, CAVAL(I)ERO
hour HORA
house CASA
housecoat BATA
hunter's cap MONTERO
Inquisition prey HERETIC
island CANARY
inn POSADA, MESON, FONDA, VENTA
jacket CHAQUETA
jail CALABOZO
jar TARRO, JARRO, OLLA, TINAJA
kettle CALDERA, OLLA
kettledrum TIMPANO
king REY, ALFONSO, MILESIAN, JUAN
kingdom ARAGON, LEON, CASTILE, NAVARRE
knapsack MOCHILA
knife CUCHILLO
knight CABALLERO
lady DOÑA, SEÑORITA, SEÑORA
lame COJO
landlady DUENA
landmark ALHAMBRA, ESCORIAL
lasso REATO, RIATA
legislature CORTES
letter CARTA
lighthouse FARO
linen CREA, HILO
little POCO
lounging robe BATA
love AMOR
lover AMADOR
mackerel SIERRA
Madrid boulevard PRADO
Main CARIBBEAN
man HOMBRE
manager GERENTE
mantle CAPA
marry CASAR
matter CASO
mattress COLCHON
mayor ALCALDE
measure VARA, CANTARA, LINEA
meat CARNE
merchantship GALLEON
mestizo LADINO
mole TOPO
monetary unit PESETA
Moorish capital CORDOBA
Morocco seaport TETUAN
moss TILLANDSIA
mother MADRE
mountain MONTANA, MONTE, GUARA, MULHACEN
mountain pass ABRA
mountain range SIERRA
mounted soldier JINETE
moviehouse CINE
muffler BUFANDA
muralist SERT
my MIO
nobleman HIDALGO, GRANDEE, DON, CONDE, DUQUE
none NADA
nothing NADA
novelist CERVANTES, IBANEZ, BAROJA
now AHORA
pack saddle ALBARDA
painter DALI, PICASSO, SERT, MIRO, GOYA, MURILLO
palace ESCORIAL
paprika PIMIENTO
park ALAMEDA
peak MULHACEN
pedestal BASA
penal colony PRESIDIO
peninsula IBERIA
pianist ITURBI
pitch BREA
plantation HACIENDA
plowed land ARADA
poem ODA
police RURALE
porridge ATOLE
port CADIZ, PALOS
post office CORREO
pot OLIA
prefix HISPANO
pretty LINDO
priest PADRE, CURA
prince PRINCIPE
princess INFANTA
prison CALABOZO

promenade ...... PASEO
province ... AVILA, YESTA, LERIDA, CATALUNA, CATALONIA, ASTURIAS, MALAGA, LEON, JAEN
purse .... BOLSA
queen .... ELENA, REINA
rabbi ...... MAIMONIDES
raisin .... PASA
region .... ASTURIAS
ribbon .... CINTA
river ...... EBRO, TAGUS, MINO, DUERA, RIO, DOURO, ARGA, ADAJA, TAJO
robber .... LADRON
rubber .... CAUCHO
ruler .... FRANCO
ruling house ... BOURBON
Sahara ..... RIO DE ORO
sailing vessel .. GALLEON, CARVEL, CARAVEL(LE)
sale .... VENTA
saltwort .... BARILLA
seaport .... PALOS, ALMERIA, ADRA, BILBAO, MALAGA, ALGECIRAS, VIGO
seaport in Africa .. CEUTA
shawl .... MANTA, SERAPE, MANTILLA
she .... ELLA
sheep ... MERINO, OVEJA
sheepfold .... REDIL
sheepskin .... ZALEA
sheet ..... SABANA, HOJA, PLIEGO
shepherd ...... PASTORES
sherry .... JEREZ
ship .... BARCO
shirt .... CAMISA
shirtwaist .... BLUSA
shoe ..... ZAPATO, BOTIN
shoot .... TIRAR
shop ... TALLER, TIENDA
shrimp .... CAMARON
shy .... TIMIDO
sick ..... MALO, ENFERMO
sickle .... HOZ
side .... LADO, CARA
sidewalk .... ACERA
sign(al) ..... SENAL, SENA
signature .... FIRMA
silk .... SEDA
silly ...... TONTO, BOBO
silver .... PLATA
sitting room .. (ANTE)SALA
skin .... CUTIS
skipper .... PATRON, CAPITAN
skirt .... FALDA
sky .... CIELO
smoke .... FUMAR
snow .... NIEVE
some .... UNOS
something .... ALGO
song .... FLAMENCO
statesman ...... AZANA
steel .... ACERO
stock farm ..... RANCHO
stopover .... PARADA
stopper .... TAPON
storeroom ..... BODEGA
strawberry .... FRESA
street .... CALLE
streetcar .... TRANVIA
sun .... SOL
sweet .... DULCE
sword .. ESPADA, TOLEDO
tablecloth ...... MANTEL
teakettle .... TETERA
tennis star ...... GIMENO, SANTANA, ARILIA, GISBERT
thank you ...... GRACIAS
the .. EL, LA, LO, LOS, LAS
they .... ELLAS
thick .... ESPESO
thief .... LADRON
thimble .... DEDAL
thin .... FINO
thirst ...... SED, ANSIA
this .... ESTE, ESTA, ESTO
title .... DON, DOÑA, SEÑOR(A), CONDE, DUQUE
tomorrow ...... MAÑANA
tower .... TORRE, MIRADOR, MINARETE
town ... PUEBLO, ALDEA, CIUDAD
town official ... ALCALDE
ugly .... FEO
uncle .... TIO
until .... HASTA
vessel .... GALLEON
walking cane ... BASTON
warehouse ..... BODEGA
watch .... RELOJ
watchman ...... SERENO
watchtower ... MIRADOR
watchword .... LEMA
water .... AGUA
waterfall ...... CASCADA, CATARATA
watermelon ..... SANDIA
wave .... OLA
wax .... CERA
wealthy .... RICO
weapon ..... ARMA, BOLA
weather .... TIEMPO
web .... TELA
wedding .... BODA
weight .... PESO, PESA, CARGA, ARROBA, MARCO, TONELADA
well .... BIEN, POZO
whale .... BALLENA
wheat .... TRIGO
wheel .... DISCO
white .... PURO, BLANCO
who .... QUIEN
who knows ... QUIEN SABE
wine ... MALAGA, TINTO, VINO, SHERRY
wine-making center ..... JEREZ
woman .. MUJER, SEÑORA
wool .... LANA
work ... OBRA, TRABAJO
writer .... IBAÑEZ, ALARCON

spank ...... SMACK, PADDLE, SLAP, CUFF
spanker .... SAIL, DRIVER
spanking .... RAPID, BRISK, QUICK
spanner .... WRENCH
spar ...... POLE, YARD, GAFF, SPRIT, BEAM, RAFTER, BARITE, (SHADOW)BOX, MAST, BOOM, DISPUTE, WRANGLE, LONGERON
branch of service .. USCG, COAST GUARD
for stowing ..... STEEVE
lower a .... REEF
part of .... SEMPER, PARATUS
spare .... SAVE, RESERVE, EXTRA, SCANT(Y), MEAGER, THIN, LANKY, LEAN
sparge ..... SPLASH, SPRINKLE
sparing ... FRUGAL, THRIFTY, SCANTY, MEAGER
spark .... WOO, BEAU, COURT, ACTIVATE, ARC, TRACE, SCINTILLA, PARTICLE, KINDLE, LOVER
gives off ...... IGNESCENT
stream .... ARC
sparked .... ARCED
sparkle ... GLITTER, GLISTEN, FLASH, VIVACITY, GLEAM, EFFERVESCE, BRILLIANCE, CORUSCATE
sparkler .... DIAMOND, FIREWORK, EYE, BRILLIANT
sparkling water .. SODA WATER, FIZZ
Sparky, baseballer ...... LYLE
sparling ..... SMELT, HERRING
sparoid .... GILTHEAD, (SEA)BREAM, GAR, TAI, SCUP, PORGY
sparrow .... DONEY, WEAVERBIRD, FINCH, PASSERINE, RICEBIRD, CHIPPY
sparry .... SPATHIC, SPATHOSE
sparrowgrass ..... ASPARAGUS
sparse ..... SCANTY, MEAGER, SCARCE
opposite of ...... DENSE, CROWDED
Sparta .... LACEDAEMON
Spartan ... HARDY, WARLIKE, STOIC(AL), SEVERE, BRAVE, HEROIC
admiral .... LYSANDER
bondman .... HELOT
king ...... TYNDAREUS, LEONIDAS, CLEOMENES, AGESILAUS
lawgiver ..... LYCURGUS
magistrate ...... EPHOR
queen .... LEDA
serf/slave .... HELOT
spasm .... TIC, CONVULSION, THROE, CHOREA, FIT, KINK
muscle .... CRICK, CRAMP
of distress .... PANG
of pain .... SHOOT
twitch .... TIC
spasmodic .... FITFUL, INTERMITTENT
spasms, series of ..... CLONOS
Spassky, chess champ .. BORIS

spat .... GAITER, SLAP, DISPUTE, ROW, TIFF, QUARREL, OYSTER, SPAWN
spate .... FLOOD, DOWNPOUR, OUTPOURING, FLOOD, FRESHET, DELUGE, INUNDATION
spathe .... GLUME
enclosure .... SPADIX
spathic .... SPARRY
spatter ... SCATTER, SPRINKLE, SPRAY, SPLASH, DEFAME
spatterdash .... LEGGING
spatterdock .... LILY
spatula ..... SLICE, BLUNGER
spavined .... LAME
spawn ... PRODUCE, EGGS, ROE, SPAT
spay ..... STERILIZE, CASTRATE
spayed hen .... FOULARD
speak .... UTTER, TALK, DISCOURSE, ADDRESS, ORATE
angrily .... SNARL
at length ..... EXPATIATE
evasively .. HEDGE, STALL
imperfectly .... LISP, STUTTER, STAMMER
in silly way ..... DROOL, SLOBBER
inability to ...... ALALIA
incoherently .... GIBBER
irreverently .. BLASPHEME
lengthily ...... PERORATE
loudly .... EXCLAIM
noisily ...... RANT, RAVE, BLUSTER
of .... MENTION
sharply ..... SNAP, SNARL
softly .... WHISPER, MURMUR
unable to ... DUMB, MUTE
under the breath .... MUTTER
speakeasy .... BLINDPIG, BLIND TIGER
speaker, bete noire of .... HECKLER
loud .... STENTOR
speaking many tongues ...... POLYGLOT
style .... PARLANCE, PERSIFLAGE, DELIVERY
spear .. ASSAGAI, PIERCE, STAB, DART, PIKE, GAFF, JAVELIN, HARPOON, SHAFT, LANCE, BLADE, SHOOT
body of a .... SHAFT
fish .. GIG, GAFF, LEISTER
Neptune's ..... TRIDENT
of grass .... BLADE
point .... PIKE
shaped .... HASTATE
three-pronged .. TRIDENT, LEISTER
thrower .... WOMERA
spearfish .... MARLIN
spearhead .. VANGUARD, LEAD, VAN
spearwort ...... CROWFOOT
special ... UNIQUE, PECULIAR, UNUSUAL, SPECIFIC, PARTICULAR
specialist, foot diseases .... PODIATRIST
specialized ...... TECHNICAL
specialty .... FORTE, LINE, METIER
specie .... COIN
factory .... MINT
species ...... VARIETY, CLASS, SORT, KIND
specific ... PRECISE, DEFINITE, EXPLICIT, SPECIAL, CONCRETE
specify ...... DEFINE, DETAIL, STIPULATE, NAME
specimen ... EXAMPLE, SAMPLE, MODEL
specious .... PLAUSIBLE
reasoning ...... IDOLISM, SPHISM, SYLLOGISM
speck ... MOTE, BIT, SPOT, JOT, STAIN, MARK, PARTICLE, FLECK
speckle .... DOT, MOTTLE, DAPPLE, FLECK, SPOT, MACULATE
specs .... EYEGLASSES
spectacle ...... SIGHT, SHOW, EXHIBITION, SCENE, VIEW, PAGEANT
spectacles ..... SPECS, LENSES, SUNGLASSES
part ..... RIM, ARM, LENS
spectacular .... STRIKING
spectator .... ONLOOKER, WATCHER, OBSERVER, LOOKER-ON
specter .... APPARITION, GHOST, WRAITH, SHADOW, BOGEY, SPIRIT, SPOOK, PHANTOM, PHANTASM(A), FANTASM
spectral .. PHANTOM, GHOSTLY, EERY
speculate .. PONDER, MEDITATE, CONJECTURE, GUESS, GAMBLE, THINK
speculation reckless ... FLIER, FLYER
speculative ..... THEORETICAL
speculator .... PLUNGER, GUESSER, GAMBLER
inexperienced ..... LAMB
welshing ..... LAME DUCK
speculum .... MIRROR
speech .... TONGUE, TALK, EXPRESSION, UTTERANCE, OENOMEL, EPILOGUE, DIALECT, LIP, SERMON, ORATION, DECLAMATION, WHISPER
abusive .... TIRADE
art .... ORATORY, RHETORIC
blustering .... HARANGUE
brevity of ... LACONISM
combining form .. LOG(O)
defect ... LISP, STUTTER, APHASIA, STAMMER, ALOGIA, DYSPHONIA, DYSPHASIA, IMPEDIMENT
delirious .... RAVING
ecstatic ..... RHAPSODY
emphatic .... BIRR
exalted to trivial .. BATHOS
farewell ... VALEDICTORY
figure of .... LITOTES, SIMILE, METAPHOR, TROPE
formal .... ADDRESS, ORATION
graduation .... VALEDICTORY
human ...... LANGUAGE
incoherent .. GIBBERISH, JARGON
ill-tempered ... VINEGAR
last words .... TAG
loss of .... APHASIA, ALALIA, ANEPIA
loud, wild .... RANT
manner of .... DRAWL
narrative part .... CATASTASIS
noisy, blustering .... TIRADE, HARANGUE
opening part .. EXORDIUM
of praise .... PANEGYRIC
ornamental ending .. TAG
part of ..... (PRO)NOUN, (AD)VERB, ADJECTIVE
pompous ...... BOMBAST
slang .... SPIEL
sound ..... PHONE, LENIS, FORTIS, PHONEME
style of ...... LOCUTION, EUPHUISM
surplusage ..... PADDING
tiresome .... SCREED
wild .... RANT
speechless .... SILENT, VOICELESS, SURD, DUMB, MUTE, TONGUE-TIED, APHONIC, APHASIC
speed ..... VELOCITY, HASTE, REV, TEAR, RATE, FLY, RUSH, HIE
drug ...... METHEDRINE, AMPHETAMINE
full .... AMAIN
measuring device .... TACHOMETER
of sound .... MACH
unit, proposed ..... VELO
up .... ACCELERATE, HASTEN, HURRY
writing ..... SHORTHAND
speedily ... APACE, POSTHASTE
speedwell ... VERONICA, PLANT
speedy .. SWIFT, RAPID, QUICK, APACE, PROMPT, FAST
spelean .... CAVE-LIKE
speleology, subject of .. CAVES
spell .... CHARM, TRANCE, MEAN, SIGNIFY, PERIOD, HEX, FIT, TURN, STREAK
of activity ...... SPRINT, SPURT
out .... READ, INTERPRET
spellbind .... ENCHANT, ENTRANCE, HOLD, FASCINATE, CHARM
spellbinder .... ORATOR
spelling —— .... BEE
incorrect ... CACOGRAPHY
spelt .... WHEAT
spelter .... ZINC, INGOTS

spence ..... LARDER, PANTRY
spencer .... JACKET, TRYSAIL
spend ... CONSUME, WEAR OUT, EXHAUST, DISBURSE, PASS, LOSE
lavishly .... DISPEND, SQUANDER
the night ..... SHACK UP
the summer ... ESTIVATE
spendthrift ... SCATTERGOOD, ROUNDER, WASTREL, PRODIGAL, SQUANDERER, WASTEFUL
Spengler, philosopher .... OSWALD
Spenser, poet .... EDMUND
spent ..... WORN, EXHAUSTED, ALL IN, WEARY, TIRED, FAGGED, CONSUMED
sperm .. SEMEN, WHALE, SEED, MILT
whale .... CACHALOT
spermary ..... GONAD, TESTIS
spermatozoid .... GAMETE
spermophile .... SUSLIK, GOPHER, CHIPMUNK
spew ..... THROW UP, VOMIT, EJECT, SPUE
Speyer .... SPIRES
sphacelate .... MORTIFY
sphagnum .... (PEAT)MOSS
sphene .... TITANITE
sphere ... ORBIT, BALL, GLOBE, STAR, PLANET, SKY, FIELD, PROVINCE, DOMAIN, REALM, RONDURE
spherical .. GLOBULAR, ROUND, GLOBOUS, GLOBOSE, OVOID, GLOBATE, GLOBOID
spheroid, example of a .... EARTH, BALL
spherule .... GLOBULE
sphery ... STARLIKE, CELESTIAL
sphincter .... CONSTRICTOR
sphinx ...... MOTH, MONSTER
head of ..... RAM, HAWK
query of .... RIDDLE
site of ..... GIZA, GIZEH, THEBES
sphragistics' subject .... SEALS
sphygmus .... PULSE
spica .... STAR, SPIKE
spice ..... CINNAMON, AROMA, FLAVOR, MULL, CHILE, TURMERIC, GINGER, SASSAFRAS, CHIL(L)I, SPEARMINT, STACTE, SEASON, CLOVE, MACE, PEPPER, NUTMEG, CANELLA
bud ..... CLOVE, CAPER, SAFFRON
Island(s) ...... TERNATE, MOLUCCAS
leaf ... ANGELICA, BASIL, BORAGE, BURNET, CHERVIL, CHIVES, MINT, PARSLEY, SORREL, SAGE, THYME, TARRAGON, SAVORY, ROSEMARY
seed ... ANISE, CARAWAY, CUMIN, DILL, SESAME, MACE, FENNELL, POPPY, CORIANDER, CARDAMON, CELERY
spiceberry .... WINTERGREEN
spiced ale .... WASSAIL
dish .... SALMI, CHILI CON CARNE, TAMALE, OLLA
spick and span .... NEAT, TRIM, FRESH, CLEAN
spiculate .... NEEDLELIKE
spicule ..... SPIKE, SCLERITE, ACTINE
spicy ... AROMATIC, PUNGENT, PIQUANT, FRAGRANT, RACY, RISQUE, GINGERY, JUICY
sensation .... HEAT
spider ... TRIVET, ARACHNID, MITE, ARTHROPOD, SKILLET, (FRYING)PAN
class .... ARACHNIDA
crab .... MAJA, MAIA, THORNBACK
girl turned into .... ARACHNE
job of .... WEAVING, SPINNING
monkey .. ATELES, QUATA
nest of .... NIDUS
poison .... VENOM
poisonous .. TARANTULA
trap of .... WEB
spiegel .... PIG IRON
spiel .... SPEECH, TALK
spiffy ... NEAT, SMART, SPRUCE
spigot ..... SPILE, TAP, PLUG, PEG, FAUCET, VALVE
spike .... NAIL, ANTLER, MACKEREL, PIERCE, TINE, IMPALE, FOIL, BROB, THWART, SPINE, GAD
cereal .... EAR
fork's ..... PRONG, TINE
lavender .... MINT
like .... SPINATE
mountain climber's ..... PITON
of flowers ...... SPADIX, AMENT
of plantain ...... CHAT
shield's .... UMBO
spikelet .... SPINULE
spikenard ... OINTMENT, PLANT
spile ..... SPIGOT, PLUG, TAP, STAKE, SPOUT
spill ...... SLOP, OVERFLOW, FALL, SPILE, SPLINTER, PEG, PLUG, TUMBLE, ROD, PIN
the beans .... TELL, DIVULGE, SQUEAL, DISCLOSE, CONFESS, SING
Spillane's hero ...... HAMMER
spin ... ROTATE, BIRL, WHIRL, RIDE, TURN, GYRATE, WEAVE, REVOLVE, REEL, TWIRL
a —— ...... YARN, TALE, WEB
spinaceous plant .... SPINACH
spinach .... ORACH(E), GOOSEFOOT, GREENS, TALINUM
spinal .... RACHIDIAN
column .... SPINE, BACKBONE, R(H)ACHIS
column, having .... VERTEBRATE
cord .... MYELON
cord cut .... PITH
cord inflammation ...... MYELITIS, RACHITIS
cord membrane .... EPENDYMA
cord sheath .. MYELIN(E), MATER
cord tumor ..... GLIOMA
marrow .... NUCHA
spindle .. ARBOR, HYDROMETER, DISTAFF, BUFF, TRIBLET, MANDREL, ROD, PIN, SHAFT, AXIS, AXLE
flywheel .... WHARVE
shaped like ... FUSIFORM
weaver's .... QUILL
spindling .... GANGLING, GANGLY, LANKY
spindrift ... (SEA)SPRAY, SCUD, FOAM
spine ... THORN, SPIKE, QUILL, RAY, CHAETA, NEEDLE, BACKBONE, CHINE, RACHIS, PRICKLE
curvature of .. KYPHOS(IS), LORDOSIS
spinel ..... SAPPHIRINE, STONE, BALAS
ruby .... BALAS
spines, covered with ... HISPID
spinet ..... PIANO, VIRGINAL, HARPSICHORD
spinnaker .... SAIL
spinner ... LURE, TOP, SPIDER, WEAVER, SILKWORM
of life's thread ... CLOTHO
spinney ..... GROVE, THICKET
spinning machine ..... JENNY, MULE, THROSTLE
mule inventor .... CROMPTON
toy .... TOP
wheel .... CHARK(H)A
wheel part .... TREADLE, DISTAFF
spinster .... (OLD) MAID, FEME SOLE, FILLE
spiny .... SPINOSE, ACICULAR, THORNY, ACANTHOID, PRICKLY, HISPID
spiracle .. BLOWHOLE, AIR HOLE
spiraea .... HARDHACK, MEADOWSWEET
spiral .... HELICAL, HELIX
combining form .. HELICO
like a .... SPIROID
motion .... GYRE
of wire .... COIL
shaped .... HELICOID, TURBINATE
shell whorl ..... VOLUTE
spiraled .... VOLUTE
spirant .... FRICATIVE
spire .... STEEPLE, COIL, SPROUT, STALK, PEAK, FLECHE, SHAFT
ornament .... FINIAL
spirit ..... SOUL, MIND, LIFE,

WILL, GHOST, VIVACITY, MORALE, HEART, VIM, SPUNK, ARDOR, BOGEY, BOGIE, VIGOR, VERVE, COURAGE, PEP, DEVA, BANSHEE, ELAN, AHRIMAN, METTLE, MARA
heralding death .... BANSHEE, BANSHIE
living in fire .... SALAMANDER
mischievous ... ERLKING, GOBLIN
of chivalry .... ERRANTRY
of the sea ... DAVY JONES
presiding .... NUMEN
the .... GOD, HOLY GHOST
spirited ... ANIMATED, LIVELY, VIGOROUS, ENERGETIC, SPUNKY, ARDENT, FIERY, BRISK, PERKY
spiritless .... LISTLESS, DEPRESSED, DULL, COLD, LACKADAISICAL
spirits .... MOOD, TEMPER, DISPOSITION, LIQUOR, ETHANOL, LIQUEURS
believer .... ANIMIST
night-walking .. LEMURES
of the dead ...... MANES
of hartshorn ... AMMONIA
of wine .... ALCOHOL
out of .... SAD
spiritual .... FOLK SONG
being .... ENS, ANGEL
guide .. PRIEST, CONFESSOR
knowledge ...... GNOSIS
mother .... AMMA
opposite of .. CORPOREAL
sitting .... SEANCE
spiritualism, third party in .... MEDIUM
spiritualist's equipment .. OUIJA
spirituous drink .... WINE
spiritus frumenti ..... WHISKY
spirochete .... TREPONEMA
disease .... YAWS
spirogyra .... ALGA
spirt .... SPURT, GUSH
spirula .... MOLLUSK
kin of .... SQUID, CUTTLEFISH
spiry .... CURLED, COILED
spit .... SKEWER, BROACH, SHOAL, SANDBANK, IMPALE, EMIT, EXPECTORATE, RAIN, SNOW, SALIVA
spital ..... HOSPITAL, SHELTER
spitchcock .... EEL
spite ...... MALICE, ILL WILL, RANCOR, VENOM, GRUDGE, SPLEEN
spiteful ... VIPERINE, VIPEROUS, VENOMOUS, VINDICTIVE, MALICIOUS, SPLENETIC, CATTY, SNIDE
woman .... CAT
spitefulness .... SPLEEN
spitfire, Mexican .... (LUPE)VELEZ
spitter .. BROCK, SPITBALL, DEER
spitting image ...... LIKENESS
spittle .... SALIVA
insect ..... FROGHOPPER
spittoon .... CUSPIDOR
spitz dog .... POMERANIAN
spiv .... IDLER
splanchnic .... VISCERAL
splash ... DAUB, SPARGE, LAP, SPRINKLE, SPLATTER, SPLOTCH, SPATTER, DASH, SWASH
splashboard ...... MUDGUARD
splat .... SLAT
splatter ... SPLASH, SPRINKLE, SPATTER, DAB
splay ... BEVEL, AWRY, FLAN, AWKWARD, DISLOCATE, SPREAD(ING)
spleen .... SPITE, MALICE, MELANCHOLY, WHIM, MILT
surgery ..... LIENECTOMY, SPLENECTOMY
splendid .... LUSTROUS, GORGEOUS, GRAND, GLORIOUS, SUPERB, FINE, EXCELLENT, RIPPING
splendor ... BRILLIANCE, POMP, GLORY, ECLAT, GLITTER, GRANDEUR, LUSTER
splenetic ... PEEVISH, SPITEFUL, IRRITABLE
splice .. WED, MARRY, JOIN(T), UNITE
splint .... LATH
splinter ...... SHIVER, SLIVER, FLINDER, SPILL, SPLIT
splinters .... MATCHWOOD
split ...... SEPARATE, DIVIDE, BURST, RIVE, REND, CLEAVE, RIFT, CHAP, SCHISM, SPALATO, BREAK, BREACH, SLIVER, CLEFT
capable of being . FISSILE
open .... DEHISCE, BREAK
pulse .... DAL
rattan .... CANE
slang ... PEACH, SQUEAL, SHARE
splitting ..... ACHING, SEVERE
apart .... FISSION
splotch .. BLOT, STAIN, SPLASH, SPOT
splurge .... OSTENTATION
spode .... PORCELAIN, CHINAWARE
Spohr, composer ..... LOUIS
opera by ...... JESSONDA
spoil .... TAINT, DAMAGE, IMPAIR, ROT, VITIATE, DECAY, INDULGE, LOOT, MESS, ROB, SACK, PILLAGE, PLUNDER, SWIZE, MAR, LOUSE UP
liable to .... PERISHABLE
spoilation .... RAPINE
spoiled ... PAMPERED, WASTED
spoils ... BOOTY, LOOT, PRIZE, TROPHY
spoilsport .... MARPLOT, KILLJOY, WETBLANKET
spoke .... RUNG, BAR, PIN
spoken ..... UTTERED, ORAL, VOCAL
merely .... LIP
spokes .... RADII
spokeshave .... PLANE
spokesman ..... MOUTHPIECE
spoliate .... ROB, PLUNDER, DESPOIL
sponge ...... PARASITE, BUM, CAKE, ASCON, TRENCHER, PUDDING, MOOCH, SWAB, CADGE, PORIFERAN
cake .... JELLYROLL
gourd .. LOOF(A), LOOFAH
opening .... OSCULUM
slang .... DEAD BEAT
spicule .... ACTINE, OXEA, TOXA
substitute .... LOOFAH
throw the .... YIELD, SUBMIT, SURRENDER, GIVE UP
sponger .. CADGER, MOOCHER, LEECH, PARASITE
spongy ... ABSORBENT, ELASTIC, POROUS
sponsor .. SURETY, GODFATHER, PATRON, BACKER, ANGEL
beneficiary of .. PROTEGE
slang .... ANGEL
sponsorship .... AUSPICES, (A)EGIS
spontaneous ..... IMPULSIVE, AUTOMATIC
spontoon ..... PIKE, HALBERD
spoof ..... HOAX, JOKE, FOOL, TRICK, DECEIVE
spook .... GHOST, SPECTER
spooky .... WEIRD, EERIE, GHOSTLY, SPECTRAL
spool .... BOBBIN, REEL, COP, PIRN
spoon ... SCOOP, PET, CARESS, NECK
large .... LADLE
like implement .... OAR, PADDLE, SPATULA
shaped ...... SPATULATE
spoonbill .... PADDLEFISH, AJAJA, AIAIAI
spoonfed .... PAMPERED, CODDLED
spoony ..... MAWKISH, SILLY, FOOLISH, SENTIMENTAL, AMOROUS
spoor .... TRAIL, TRACK
Sporades island .... SAMOS
sporadic .... OCCASIONAL, DESULTORY, IRREGULAR
sporangium ..... SPORE CASE
spore ... GERM, SEED, ZYGOTE
case .... SPORANGIUM, ASCI, THECA, SORI, ASCUS
cluster(s) ... SORUS, SORI
producer .... FERN, MOSS
sac .... ASCUS, THECA
small .... SPORULE
sporran ...... PURSE, POUCH
sport .... PASTIME, DIVERSION, PLAY, FUN, DISPLAY, WEAR, FROLIC, JEST, MUTANT, GAME, PLAY, TRIFLE
group .... TEAM
official .. UMPIRE, REFEREE
shirt .... TEE
shoe .... LOAFER
team .... FIVE, NINE,

ELEVEN, CREW, FOURSOME, SQUAD
sporting .... FAIR
house ... CASINO, ALLEY, HALL
sports attendance ...... GATE
meet .... GYMKHANA, OLYMPICS
site .... RINK, OVAL, ARENA, LINKS, FIELD, COURSE, TRACK, STADIUM, COLISEUM, GRID, DIAMOND, COURT, GREEN
sportscaster .. COSELL, GOWDY, GIFFORD
sportsman's vest .. TATTERSALL
sporty .... FLASHY, SHOWY
spot .... STAIN, MARK, BLEMISH, BIT, SMUT(CH), FLECK, (FLY)SPECK, MACULA(TE)
colloquial .... JAM, TROUBLE
in mineral .... MACLE
on animal's face .. BLAZE
on lunar halo .... PARASELENE
on solar halo .... PARHELION
playing card .... PIP
skin ... STIGMA, MACULA
small .... FLECK, (PIN)POINT, PRICK, DOT
spotless ..... PURE, INNOCENT, CLEAN
spotlight .... FOCUS
spotted .... MACULATE, DAPPLE(D), MOTTLED, PIED, EYED
animal ..... (LEO)PARD, DAPPLE, CHEETAH, CAVY, GENET(TE), OCELOT, CHITAL, PACA
fever ...... TICK, TYPHUS
with drops ..... GUTTATE
spotter .. DETECTIVE, LOOKOUT
spotty ... IRREGULAR, UNEVEN
spousal .... NUPTIAL
spouse ..... WIFE, HUSBAND, CONSORT, MATE
spout .... NOZZLE, SPILE, SNOUT, STREAM, ELEVATOR, JET, GUSH
slang .... PAWN(SHOP)
steam .... JET
water .... GARGOYLE
whale's ...... BLOWHOLE
spraddle .... SPAN
sprag .... TRIG, WEDGE, CHOCK, BLOCK
sprain ...... WRICK, WRENCH
sprat .... HERRING, BRIT, BRISLING
sprawl ..... SPREAD, LOLL, LIE, CRAWL
spray ... ATOMIZE(R), SHOWER, SPRINKLE, SPRIG, MIST, BOUQUET, LIPPER, SPUME, NEBULIZE, TWIG
spread .... OLEO, SPLAY, UNFOLD, UNFURL, EXHIBIT, EXTEND, DISPERSE, SCATTER, COVER, FEAST, STRETCH, PROPAGATE, BRUIT, JAM, BUTTER, FAN, JELLY, OVERLAY
awkwardly ...... SPRAWL
colloquial .... MEAL, DISPLAY
false rumors ..... ASPERSE
for drying .... TED
grass .... TED
here and there .. SCATTER, STREW
out .... FAN, DEPLOY, EFFUSE, FLARE
rapidly ..... MUSHROOM
rumors .... HAWK
thick .... SLATHER
thin .... BRAY
troops .... DEPLOY
spreading .... PATULOUS
from the center .. RADIAL
implement .... MULCHER, SPATULA, TEDDER
spree .... BINGE, FROLIC, CAROUSAL, BUM, LARK, WASSAIL, BAT, TEAR, JAG, (HELL)BENDER, TOOT, FROLIC, ORGY, BUST(ER)
sprig ... TWIG, BRAD, SPRAY, STRIPLING, FELLOW
sprightly ...... GAY, LIVELY, BRISK, BLITHE, TID, CHIPPER, AGILE, ANIMATED, PERT, JAUNTY
spring .... LEAP, BOUND, DART(LE), VAULT, SOURCE, (A)RISE, SEASON, STEM, BOLT, WELL, JUMP, FOUNT(AIN)
Apollo's ..... CASTALIA
artificial ...... FOUNTAIN
back .. RECOIL, REBOUND, RESILE
Biblical .... AIN
chicken .... BROILER, FRYER
deposit ... TRONA, TUFA, TRAVERTIN
festival .... MAYDAY
flower ... CROCUS, TULIP
guard .... MIMIR
holiday .... EASTER
like .... VERNAL
mineral .... SPA
month ..... APRIL, MAY, MARCH
of .... FONTAL
poet's .... CASTALIA
poetic .... FONT
sign of .. BUDS, SWALLOW
slang ..... FREE, RELEASE
small .... GEYSER
tide .... FLOOD
water ... SELTZER, LYMPH
springboard .... BATULE
springbok .... GAZELLE, SPRINGER
springe .... SNARE, TRAP
springer ... SPANIEL, GRAMPUS, IMPOST
springhead .... SOURCE
springing back ..... RESILIENT, ELASTIC
springs .. THERMAE, SPA, BATHS
springtime .... MAY
springy .... ELASTIC, FLEXIBLE
sprinkle ... SHOWER, SPARGE, STREW, SCATTER, SPLASH, DUST, DEG, DREDGE, RAIN, SPRAY
water to purify .. BAPTIZE
with flour .... DREDGE
with sieve .... SIFT
sprinkling .... ASPERSION
with holy water .... ASPERGES
sprint ...... DASH, RACE, RUN
sprinter .. DASHER, TRACKMAN
sprit .... SPAR, BOOM
sprite ..... ELF, FAIRY, GHOST, PIXIE, PIXY, NIX, ARIEL, FAY, HOB, BROWNIE
helpful .... KOBOLD
mischievous .. PUCK, IMP, GOBLIN, KOBOLD
water ... NIX, UNDINE, NIS
sprout .... GERMINATE, GROW, SHOOT, (S)CION, BURGEON, CHIT, BUD, PULLULATE
root/stem .... TILLER, RAT(T)OON
spruce ... TRIG, LARCH, TRIM, NEAT, NATTY, EPINETTE, DAPPER, SMART, CONIFER
fruit .... CONE
slang .... SPIFFY
up .... TITIVATE
sprue .... PSILOSIS
spry .... AGILE, NIMBLE, ACTIVE, BRISK
spud .... POTATO
tool like .. SPADE, CHISEL
spue .... SPEW
spume ... FOAM, FROTH, SCUM
spun .... WOVE(N)
spunk ...... AMADOU, PUNK, SPARK, KINDLE, TINDER, GRIT, SPIRIT, PLUCK, METTLE, COURAGE
spunky .... GAME, BRAVE, SPIRITED
spur .... STIMULUS, ERGOT, RIDGE, GRIFFE, PRICK, SIDING, GOAD, ROWEL, STRUT, BRACE, INCITE, URGE, HURRY, CALCAR
gamecock's .... GAFF
mountain .... ARETE
spurge .... MILKWEED, EUPHORBIA
spurious .... FAKE, FALSE, COUNTERFEIT, ARTIFICIAL, SHAM, BASTARD, TIN, FORGED, BOGUS, PHON(E)Y
spurn .... REJECT, REFUSE, SCORN, DECLINE, KICK
spurr(e)y ...... (CHICK)WEED
spurt ...... JET, SPOUT, GUSH, STREAM, SQUIRT, BURST, DART
of energy .... LICK
sputnik .... SATELLITE
sputter ... SPLUTTER, JABBER, SPIT

sputum .... SPIT(TLE), SALIVA
spy .... FINK, OPERATIVE, PRY, SEE, PERCEIVE, WATCH, AGENT, UNDERCOVERMAN, KEEK, NOSE, PRIVATE EYE, SCOUT, FUCHS, (MATA)HARI, ARNOLD, ANDRE, CAVELL, ROSENBERG, INFORMER, STEIBER, CICERO, GEISLER, RINTELEN
spying .... ESPIONAGE
Spyri's heroine .... HEIDI
squab .... PIPER, PIGEON, COUCH, SOFA, CUSHION
squabble .... WRANGLE, QUARREL, ROW, DISPUTE, SPAT, MUSS, HASSLE, HASSEL
squad leader .... SERGEANT
squadron of airplanes .... ESCADRILLE
squalid ... SORDID, UNCLEAN, FOUL, FILTHY, MANGY
squall ... SCREAM, CRY, GUST, GALE, (WIND)STORM, TROUBLE, FLAW, WAUL, WAWL
squally ...... GUSTY, STORMY
squalor .... FILTH
squama .... SCALE
squamate .... SCALY
squander .... WASTE, DISSIPATE, (DI)SPEND
square .. PLAZA, PARK, SETTLE, RECONCILE, HONEST, FAIR, BALANCED, FORUM, QUADRATE, EVEN (UP), TALLY, AGREE, FIT, CUBICAL, PIAZZA
column .... PILASTER
dance .... HOEDOWN, QUADRILLE, REEL, LANC(I)ERS
dance need ...... CALLER
root of nine ..... THREE
shooter ..... FAIR DEALER
slang ..... BRIBE, HUNKY, WHITE
squared circle .... ARENA, (PRIZE)RING
squarehead .... GERMAN, SCANDINAVIAN, BOCHE
squaring circle .. CYCLOMETRY, CYCLOTOMY
squarrose .... SCALY
squash ... PEPO, PRESS, CRUSH, SILENCE, GOURD, SQUISH, FLATTEN, SPORT, QUELL, CASHAW, ZUCCHINI, CUSHAW
winter .... HUBBARD
squashy .... MUSHY
squat .... DUMPY, FUBSY, TUBBY, CROUCH, PUDGY
squatter .... SETTLER
squaw ..... WOMAN, MAHALA
Indian .... WIFE
squawbush .... SUMAC
squawk ..... CRY, COMPLAIN, PROTEST, HERON
squeak .... CREAK, CRY
squeal .... INFORM, SING, CRY, PEACH
squeamish .... QUEASY, FASTIDIOUS, DAINTY, FINICAL
person .... PRUDE
squeeze ...... SQUASH, WRING, CRUSH, JAM, NIP, EKE, EXTORT, (COM)PRESS, EXTRACT, HUG
chin .... CHUCK
squeezer, juice ...... REAMER
squelch .... CRUSH, (S)QUASH, KIBOSH, SUPPRESS, SUBDUE, SILENCE
squeteague .... CROAKER, GRUNT(ER)
squib .... FIRECRACKER, LAMPOON, DETONATOR, PASQUINADE
squid .... MOLLUSK, CUTTLEFISH, CALAMARY
arm of .... TENTACLE
relative .... SPIRULA
shell of .... PEN
squilgee .... SQUEEGEE
squill .... SEA ONION, LILY
squilla .. CRUSTACEAN, PRAWN, SHRIMP, MANTIS CRAB, STOMATOPOD
squinch ... CORBELING, LINTEL
squint .... SKEW, STRABISMUS, GLANCE, PEER
eyed .... CROSS-EYED
squire .. ARMIGER, ATTENDANT, GENTLEMAN, ESCORT, GALLANT, ARMOR-BEARER, DONZEL, HENCHMAN
squirm ... WIGGLE, WRIGGLE, WRITHE
squirrel .... MARMOSET, TAMARIN, RODENT, CHIPMUNK, WOODCHUCK, PHALANGER, SPERMOPHILE, CHICKAREE, PENTAIL, CALABAR, CALABER, XERUS
burrowing ..... GOPHER
flying .... ASSAPAN
flying aid ..... PATAGIUM
fur ... CALABAR, CALABER, VAIR
ground .... GOPHER, SUSLIK, SISEL
like rodent ... DORMOUSE
nest .... DREY, DRAY
parasite of ..... WABBLE
shrew .... TANA
skin .... CALABER, VAIR, CALABAR
skin fold ... PARACHUTE, PATAGIUM
squirt ... SPURT, SPIRT, SHOOT, JET, STREAM
gun .... SPRAY
sri .... MISTER
SRO, part of ..... STANDING, ROOM, ONLY
charge ...... STANDAGE
sign .... SOLDOUT
SS, Nazi .... BLACK SHIRTS
head .... HIMMLER
St. (see Saint) .... SAINT
Anthony's fire .... ERYSIPELAS
Elmo's fire ... CORPOSANT
Francis' birthplace ...... ASSISI
John's bread ..... CAROB
Laurence river discoverer CARTIER
stab ..... SPIT, PIERCE, GORE, WOUND, THRUST, PUNCH, PINK
colloquial .... TRY, ATTEMPT
stabile .... STATIONARY
opposite of ..... LABILE
stabilize(r) .... BALLAST
stable .... STEADY, FIRM, FIXED, CONSTANT, STEADFAST, SECURE, BARN, ENDURING, PADDOCK, MEW, LODGE
compartment ..... STALL
field .... PADDOCK
member .... BOXER, FIGHTER, RACEHORSE
part .... HAYMOW, HAYLOFT
sound ... NEIGH, SNORT, (W)HINNY
stableman .... (H)OSTLER, GROOM, CURRIER
stables, royal .... MEWS
staccato, opposed to .. LEGATO
stack ...... RICK, PILE, HEAP, CHIMNEY, SCINTLE, MOW, RUCK
base of .... STADDLE
stacte .... SPICE
staddle .... SUPPORT, BASE, CRUTCH, FRAME
stadia .... TRANSIT, ROD, RANGEFINDER
stadium .... BOWL, ARENA, PARK
passageway .... RAMP
staff ...... TRUNCHEON, ROD, POLE, STICK, CLUB, WAND, BATON, STAVE, RETINUE, CUDGEL, ANKUS, CANE, OFFICE, VERGE
bearer .... VERGER
bishop's ... ROD, CROSIER, CROOK
in music .... STAVE
member .... AIDE
metal cap .... SHOE
mountain climber's ..... ALPENSTOCK
officer, in short ..... ADC
officer's .... CADRE
plural of .... STAVES
shepherd's ...... CROOK
symbol .... CLEF
symbol of authority ..... WARDER, MACE
teaching .... FACULTY
winged .... CADUCEUS
Stafford, singer .... JO
stag ...... HART, (RED)DEER, POLLARD
horn's tine ..... BROCKET
mate of .... HIND
party .... SMOKER
stage ...... DOCK, PLATFORM, SCAFFOLD, PRESENT, DAIS, SHOW, LEGIT, PRODUCE,

PHASE, STEP, FOOTLIGHTS, (THE) BOARDS, THEATER, DRAMA
assignment .. PART, ROLE
assistant ..... PROMPTER
call, trumpet .... SENNET
curtain ...... BACKDROP
device .... SLOTE
direction ... EXIT, SENNET, ENTER, EXEUNT, MANET
extra .... SUPE(R)
footlights ...... FLOAT(S)
front .... APRON, ORCHESTRA
group: abbr. ...... ANTA
name ..... DUSE, COHEN
overact on .... HAM
part .... ROLE, LEAD
part of .... WING, PODIUM, PROSCENIUM, BOARDS, COULISSE, APRON
players .... CAST
profession ...... ACTING
prop ... CURTAIN, DROP, FOOTLIGHTS
remark ... ASIDE, AD LIB
settings .... SCENERY
show ...... VAUDEVILLE, REVUE, MUSICAL
side scene ..... COULISSE
slang .... LEGIT
trumpet call .... SENNET
whisper .... AD LIB, ASIDE

stagecoach .... CONCORD
stagehand ... GRIP, CALLBOY
stager ... VETERAN, OLD HAND
Stagg, Amos ___ ... ALONZO
stagger ..... WAMBLE, LURCH, STARTLE, TOTTER, REEL, SWAY, OVERWHELM
staggered arrangement .... ZIGZAG
staggering condition ...... GID
stagger(s) ...... GID, (A)REEL, VACILLATE
cause of ..... COENURUS
Stagirite .... ARISTOTLE
stagnant .... DULL, STANDING, SLUGGISH, TORPID, FOUL, STALE
stagnation .... STASIS
stagy .... THEATRICAL, AFFECTED
staid .... SOBER, FIXED, SETTLED, SEDATE, STEADY
stain ..... TARNISH, SLUBBER, SPLOTCH, TAINT, DISCOLOR, DYE, TINGE, SULLY, MACULA(TE), BLOT, SMUDGE, SPOT, SPOIL, CORRUPT, TINT, IMB(R)UE, DISHONOR
remover .... PUMICE
stainer for microscope .... SAFRANIN(E)
staining art .... MARBLING
stair .... STEP, STILE
face .... RISER
post .... NEWEL
staircase .... PERRON
bend .... RAMP
guard .... HANDRAIL
landing ...... HALFPACE
post ... BALUSTER, NEWEL
spiral .... CARACOLE
step .... WINDER

stairs pillar .... NEWEL
plane .... RAMP
set of .... FLIGHT
shaft .... WELL
stairway, mechanical .... ESCALATOR
step .... FLIER
stake ... SPILE, POST, INTEREST, SHARE, GAMBLE, FINANCE, ANTE, POT, PALE, PICKET, HITCH, PILE, TETHER, BET, WAGER, RISK, IMPONE
fence .... WEIR
for foundation .... SPILE
played for .... MAIN
wooden .... TREE
stakes .... BETS, WAGERS, PRIZE, KITTY
driver .... MAUL
fence of .... PALISADE
stalag inmate .. POW, PRISONER
stale .... VAPID, FLAT, BANAL, DRAB, MUSTY, HACK, HOAR, STAGNANT, TASTELESS, TRITE, HACKNEYED, FUSTY
stalemate .... DEADLOCK, CHECK, DRAW, IMPASSE, TIE
Stalin's daughter .... (SVETLANA) ALLILUYEVA
Stalinabad .... DUSHANBE
Stalingrad .... VOLGOGRAD
Stalino, former .... DONETSK
stalk ...... SCAPE, FILAMENT, HAULM, STEM, PEDICEL, CULM, PEDICLE, STRIPE(S), PETIOLE, STOVER, CAULIS
eyed crustacean .. PRAWN, LOBSTER, SHRIMP
flower .... PEDUNCLE
grass ... HA(U)LM, STRAW, CULM
having a ..... PETIOLATE
leaf .... PETIOLE
like structure ... PEDICEL
stalking horse .... BLIND, PRETEXT, DECOY
stall .. STABLE, COMPARTMENT, COT, CRIB, SEAT, STAND, MANGER, BOOTH, LOGE, TEMPORIZE, HEDGE, PUT OFF, DELAY
covering .... TILT
shop's front .... BULK
stallion .... (STUD)HORSE, STEED, ENTIRE, MORGAN
stalwart ...... FIRM, ROBUST, SUPPORTER
Stamboul .... ISTANBUL
stamen, part of ..... ANTHER, FILAMENT, STALK, POLLEN SAC
stamina .... ENDURANCE
stammer ...... STUTTER, HEM
stamp .... IMPRINT, MARK, CACHET, BRAND, DIE, SIGN, SIGIL, TAMP, IMPRESS
Chinese .... CHOP
mail .... POSTAGE
official/ornamental ..... SEAL
on coin .... MINTAGE
out .... SCOTCH

stampede .. FLIGHT, ROUT, RUN
stamper .... DATER
stamping ground .... HAUNT, HANG OUT
device .... DATER, PUNCHEON
stamps, substitute for .. INDICIA
Stan, the Man .... MUSIAL
stance .... POSTURE, POSITION
stanch .... STEM, CHECK, WATERTIGHT, FAITHFUL, LOYAL, TRUE, FIRM, STOP
stanchion .... BRACE, POST
stand ... POSITION, ATTITUDE, BOOTH, STALL, FACE, TANTALUS, CASTER, BEAR, RESIST, RACK, HALT, ENDURE, TOLERATE, UNDERGO, STATION, VIEW, OPINION
against .... OPPOSE
artist's .... EASEL
by .... MAINTAIN
conductor's ..... PODIUM
for ... REPRESENT, MEAN
for election .... RUN
high .... TOWER
in .... SUBSTITUTE
kind of .... LAST, ONE NIGHT, NEWS
on hind legs ..... RAMP, REAR
orator's .... SOAPBOX
ornamental ... PEDESTAL, TABORET
out .... PROJECT, DISSENTER
painter's .... EASEL
priest's .... PULPIT
sacrificial .... ALTAR
stockstill .... FREEZE
three-legged .... TRIPOD, TRIVET, TEAPOY
two-legged ...... BIPOD
standard ... BANNER, ENSIGN, CRITERION, REGULAR, ORDINARY, UNIFORM, NORMAL, GONFALON, FLAG, COLORS, MODEL, EXAMPLE, TYPICAL, YARDSTICK, CLASSIC
battle .... ORIFLAME
bearer ...... CANDIDATE, CHAMPION, LEADER, CHIEF, ENSIGN, VEXILLARY
of excellence ...... IDEAL
pasha's ..... HORSETAIL
standee, subway, etc. .... STRAPHANGER
standing .... STATUS, POSITION, RANK, REPUTATION, STAGNANT, PRESTIGE, ERECT, UPRIGHT
order .... SOP
out .... SALIENT
room area .... AISLES
room charge .. STANDAGE
with feet on ground ..... STATENT

Standish, colonist ..... MILES
standoffish .. ALOOF, RESERVED, WITHDRAWN
standoff .... TIE, DRAW
standpat(ter) .. CONSERVATIVE, TORY, DIEHARD
standstill .... HALT, STOP, CESSATION, DEADLOCK
stang .... PAIN
stanhope .... CARRIAGE, SHAY
stannum .... TIN
Stanovoi mountain ... KOLYMA, YABLONOI, ANADYR
stanza .... VERSE, STAVE, STROPE, ENVOI, STROPHE, DISTICH, (L)ENVOY
eight-line ...... TRIOLET, OCTAVE, OCTONARY
four-line ... TETRASTICH, QUATRAIN
seven-line ... HEPTASTICH
six-line .... SEXTAIN, HEXASTICH
stapelia .... MILKWEED
stapes .... (STIRRUP)BONE
staple ... FLOUR, SALT, SUGAR, PRINCIPAL, FIBER, CHIEF, COMMODITY
star .... SUN, ASTERISK, PLANET, ACE, EXCEL, LEADING, RIGEL, MIRA, NOVA
apple .... CAIMITO
binary .. ANTARES, ALGOL, ALBIREO
blue .... VEGA
brightest ... COR, LUCIDA, SIRIUS
Chamber ...... COURT, TRIBUNAL
cluster ...... ASTERISM, GALAXY, MILKY WAY
combining form .. ASTRO, SIDER(O)
Cygnus .... DENEB
Draconis' tail ..... JUZA
evening ..... HESPER(US), VESPER, VENUS
fallen .... ALGA
five-pointed ... PENTACLE
group .... DIPPER, CONSTELLATION
like a ... ASTRAL, STELLAR
Lyra .... VEGA
morning ..... PHOSPHOR, VENUS
neutron .... PULSAR
new .... NOVA
of a .... STELLAR
of David .... HEXAGRAM
Orion .... RIGEL
path of .... ORBIT
pertaining to a .. SIDEREAL
poetic .... LAMP
pulsing .... PULSAR
red .... ANTARES, RUSSIA
Scorpio .... ANTARES
shaped .... STELLATE, ASTERIATED, ASTEROID, ASTROSE
shell .... FLARE
shooting .... METEOR
six-pointed ... HEXAGRAM

spangled, in heraldry .... SEME
sports ... ACE, CHAMPION
thistle .... CALTRAP, CALTROP, WEED
yellow .... CAPELIA
starch .... AMYLUM, CARBOHYDRATE, AMYLOSE, ARROWROOT, CASSAVA, SAGO, TAPIOCA, GLYCOGEN, AMIDINE, MANIOC
food .... FARINA
grain nucleus .... HILUM
grain part ... GRANULOSE
like .... AMYLOID
pudding .... SAGO
source ... TARO, CASSAVA, SAGO, MANIOC, ARUM, COONTIE, CURCUMA, CANNA
starchy .... FORMAL, STIFF
food .... AMYLOID
plant .... AROID
root .... TARO
substance ...... AMYLOID
stare ..... GAZE, LOOK, GAPE, GLARE, OGLE, GAWK, GOGGLE
down .... OUTFACE
starfish ... ASTEROID, SUNSTAR, FIVE-FINGER
limb of .... RAY
relative ...... COMATULID
starflower .... PRIMROSE
stargazer ...... ASTRONOMER, ASTROLOGER
stark ... STIFF, RIGID, BARREN, BLEAK, DESOLATE, SHEER, UTTER(LY)
mad .... RAVING
starlet .... INGENUE
starlike .... ASTEROID, ASTRAL, STELLAR
starling .... MINO, BIRD, OXPECKER
kin of .. MYNA(H), ORIOLE
starnose .... MOLE
Starr of comic strips .. BRENDA
starry .... SIDEREAL, STELLAR
stars .... FATE, DESTINY, FORTUNE
dotted with .... SEME
group of .... CONSTELLATION
of the .. ASTRAL, SIDEREAL, STELLAR
worshiper of .... SABAIST
start ...... SHY, JERK, ROUSE, LAUNCH, OPEN, SHOCK, FRIGHT, COMMENCE(MENT), LEAD, EDGE, ONSET, INCEPTION, JIB
card game .... DEAL
starting point .. GATE, SCRATCH
startle ...... ALARM, SHOCK, SURPRISE, AFFRIGHT, SCARE, GALVANIZE
starvation, widespread .... FAMINE
starve ...... FAMISH, HUNGER
starved .. HUNGRY, FAMISHED
starwort .... ASTER, ALGA

stash ... HOARD, HIDE, CACHE, SECRETE
state .... CONDITION, STATUS, SPECIFY, FETTLE, ETAT, AVER, SITUATION, DECLARE, SAY, MOOD, POLITY
attorney .... DA
Beaver .... OREGON
Beehive .... UTAH
Cornhusk ..... NEBRASKA
Cotton .... ALABAMA
council .... SENATE
dependent ..... SATELLITE
Fair author ..... STONG
Hawkeye .... IOWA
Hen .... DELAWARE
house .... CAPITOL
Lone Star .... TEXAS
Mountain .... MONTANA
of affairs .... CASE
of balance .... EQUIPOISE
of excitement ... FERMENT
of mind ... MORALE, MOOD
of suspended animation .. ANABIOSIS
treasure .... MONTANA
treasury .... FISC
troops .... MILITIA
under oath ...... SWEAR, DEPOSE
without proof .. ALLEGE, CLAIM
statehouse .... CAPITOL
stately .... MAJESTIC, DIGNIFIED, GRAND, ROYAL, AUGUST, REGAL, IMPOSING
house ... MANSION, DOME, PALACE
music .... LARGO
statement .... ACCOUNT, DECLARATION, TESTIMONY, BILL, BULLETIN, PRECIS, ASSERTION
authoritative ... DICTUM
ex-employer's .... REFERENCE
formal .... AFFIDAVIT, DEPOSITION, COMMUNIQUE
in belief .. CREDO, CREED
of facts .... CASE
preliminary .... PREFACE
unsupported .... SAY-SO
stater .... COIN
stateroom .... CABIN
static .... STATIONARY, INACTIVE, STRAYS
opposed to ..... KINETIC, DYNAMIC
station .... DEPOT, POST, POSITION, LOCATION, RANK, STATUS, STOP, TERMINUS, TERMINAL, PLACE
stationary ... STABILE, STATIC, FIXED, AT REST, IMMOBILE
combining form ... STAT
stationer .... BOOKSELLER
stationery .. PAPETERIE, LINEN
item ... PAPER, ENVELOPE
statistician .... STATIST
statoscope .... BAROMETER

statuary .... STATUES, SCULPTOR
statue ... CARVING, ACROLITH, SCULPTURE, NIKE, EFFIGY, FIGULINE, FIGURINE
base of .... PEDESTAL, PLINTH
gigantic ...... COLOSSUS
ledgelike foundation .... SOCLE
London .... GOG, MAGOG
mold ..... (PLASTER)CAST
of ____ .... LIBERTY
of Liberty poetess .... LAZARUS
of Liberty sculptor ...... BARTHOLD
of Mary ...... MADONNA
statuesque .... STATELY, GRACEFUL
woman .... JUNO
statuette .... FIGURINE
award .... OSCAR
stature .... HEIGHT
status .... CONDITION, STATE, STANDING, RANK, POSITION
symbol ... MINK, YACHT, ROLLS ROYCE, DIAMOND
statute ... RULE, LAW, EDICT, ACT
part of .. TITLE, ARTICLE
stave ... STAFF, STICK, RUNG, STAP, LAG, VERSES, STANZA, PUNCTURE
off ... WARD, HOLD OFF, FEND, AVERT, STALL
staves, bundle of ..... SHOOK
hold .... HOOP
stavesacre .... LARKSPUR
stay .... (A)BIDE, REMAIN, RESIDE, HALT, TARRY, CHECK, STOP, DELAY, WAIT, GUY, TACK, PROP, SUPPORT, KEEP, DWELL, LIVE, LINGER, BRACE
longer .... TARRY
staying power ...... STAMINA, ENDURANCE
staylace .... A(I)GLET
stays .... CORSET, ABIDES
Ste. (see Saint) ...... SAINT(E)
stead .... LIEU, SERVICE, PLACE, SITE
steadfast .. STABLE, CONSTANT, FIRM, FIXED
steady .... FIRM, STABLE, FIXED, CONSTANT, EQUABLE, REGULAR, STAID, UNIFORM, CALM, EVEN
colloquial .... BEAU, SWEETHEART, BOY FRIEND
opposite of ..... ASTATIC, JERKY, UNSTABLE
steak .... T-BONE, PORTERHOUSE, SIRLOIN
steal ... PINCH, THIEVE, PILFER, NIM, FILCH, PURLOIN, LOOT, ROB, HOOK, SNITCH, CRIB, BURGLE, MOOCH, PRIG
cattle, etc. ...... RUSTLE
colloquial ..... BARGAIN, CRIB
ideas, writings .... CRIB, PLAGIARIZE, PIRATE
slang .... SWIPE, LIFT
trust money ... PECULATE
stealer .... THIEF, ROBBER, BURGLAR
stealthy .... SECRET, SURREPTITIOUS, FURTIVE, SLY, CLANDESTINE, SNEAKY, FELINE
steam ..... VAPOR, GAS, FUME
boiler safety device ...... HYDROSTAT
burn with .... SCALD
colloquial .... FORCE, ENERGY, POWER
engine ..... LOCOMOTIVE
give off .... REEK
roll ... CRUSH, OVERRIDE
steamboat stateroom ... TEXAS
steamer .... SHIP, LINER, WHALEBACK
steamship .... LINER, GREYHOUND
smokestack of ... FUNNEL
stearin .... SUET, TALLOW
steatite .... TALC, SOAPSTONE
steed .... HORSE, CHARGER, STALLION
steel ...... TOUGHEN, METAL
alloy .... INVAR
beam/bar .... IBAR, IRAIL, GIRDER
change to ..... ACIERATE
kind of .... TOLEDO, DAMASK, TEMPERED
making plant .... (RE)FINERY
making process .... DUPLEX, CEMENTATION
poetic .. SWORD, DAGGER
with inlaid gold .. DAMASK
steelhead .... TROUT, SALMONOID
steelyard ... SCALE, BALANCE
Steen, painter .... JAN
steenbok .... ANTELOPE
steep .... PRECIPITOUS, EXCESSIVE, LOFTY, ABRUPT, SOAK, MACERATE, IMBUE, SOP, SHEER, RET, SATURATE, IMMERSE
slope .... SCARP
steeple ...... TOWER, BELFRY, MINARET, FLECHE
part of ... BELFRY, SPIRE, EPI
steeplebush .... HARDHACK
steeplechase ..... HORSERACE
steer .... DIRECT, GUIDE, CATTLE, OX, YAK, HELM, BEEF, BULLOCK, BOVINE, PILOT, STIRK, STOT
clear off .... AVOID
ship .... CONN
slang .... TIP
zigzag course .. PLY, YAW
steering gear .... WHEEL, RUDDER, HELM, TILLER
steersman .. PILOT, HELMSMAN, WHEELER, COX(SWAIN), NAVIGATOR
steeve ... STOW, SPAR, DERRICK
stegomyia .... MOSQUITO
stein .... MUG
writer .... GERTRUDE
steinbok .... ANTELOPE
stele .... HEADSTONE, LAT, PILLAR, MONUMENT
stella .... STAR
stellar .... CHIEF, LEADING, SIDEREAL, ASTRAL
stellate .... STARRY
stem .... STALK, PETIOLE, PEDICEL, PEDUNCLE, CHECK, STOP, AXIS, ARISE, BINE, SPRING
angle .... AXIL
climbing .... BINE
covering .... OCREA
fleshy .... TUBER
for grafting .... SLIP
hollow .... CANE
joint .... NODE
leaf's .... FOOTSTALK
main .... TRUNK
of arrow .... STELE
palm .... CAUDEX
plant ..... AXIS, CAULIS
raceme's ...... R(H)ACHIS
rootlike ...... RHIZOME
rudimentary .. CAULICLE
ship's........BOW, PROW
shoot .... TILLER
trailing .... RUNNER
twining .... BIND
underground ..... TUBER, CORM
stench .... ODOR, SMELL, F(O)ETOR, STINK, REEK, MEPHITIS
Stendhal hero .... SOREL
Stengel, baseball's ..... CASEY
steno, combining form .. THIN, NARROW, SMALL
stenosis .... STRICTURE
stenography .... SHORTHAND
Stentor .... HERALD
stentorian .... LOUD
step .... GAIT, TREAD, FOOTBALL, FOOTPRINT, RUNG, PACE, STAIR, STRIDE, GRADIN, STAGE, RANK, WALK
dance .... PAS, CHASSE
down .... RESIGN, ABDICATE, REDUCE
fence .... STILE
in .... INTERVENE
ins .... UNDERPANTS, SLIPPERS
ladder .... RUNG
lightly .... TRIP
mincingly .... SASHAY
on heavily ..... TRAMPLE, PLOD
on it .... HURRY, HASTEN
projecting part .. NOSING
softly .... PAD, TIPTOE
up .... INCREASE, ACCELERATE
stepmother, of/like a .... NOVERCAL
steppe .... PLAIN, WASTELAND
plain like a ..... PAMPAS, LLANO, SAVANNA(H)

stepper .... DANCER
steps, outdoor ...... PERRON, STILE
sterculiaceous tree ... CACAO, KOLA
stere .... CUBIC METER
stereo .... BINAURAL
stereotype plate ..... CLICHE
stereotyped .... TRITE, HACKNEYED
sterile ... BARREN, INFERTILE, UNFRUITFUL, ACARPOUS, MULISH, OTIOSE, EFFETE
in botany ..... ACARPOUS
sterilize .... GELD, CASTRATE, EMASCULATE
sterlet .... STURGEON
sterling .. PENNY, EXCELLENT
stern ... FIRM, SEVERE, HARD, GRIM, REAR, DOUR, STRICT, FORBIDDING, AUSTERE, HARSH, AFT
toward the ...... ABAFT, AFT, REAR
wheeler ..... STEAMBOAT
sternum .... BREASTBONE
attachment .... RIB
sternutation .... SNEEZING, SNEEZE
sternutatory .... ERRHINE
substance .... SNUFF
stertor .... SNORE
stet .... LET IT STAND
Stettin river .... ODER
stevedore ... DOCKER, LUMPER, DOCK WORKER, STOWER, (UN)LOADER, LONGSHOREMAN
Stevens, singer .... RISE
Stevenson, statesman .. ADLAI
stew .... SIMMER, DISH, BOIL, POTPIE, HARICOT, TANK, OLIO, FRET, TERRINE, HODGEPODGE, POTPOURRI, OLLA, RAGOUT, HASH, GOULASH, BURGOO, POTTAGE, CURRY
colloquial ...... WORRY, MULLIGAN
flavor .... CHIVE
pan .... SKILLET
sailors' ... LOBSCOU(R)SE
steward .... MAJOR DOMO, SENESCHAL, REEVE, BUTLER, BAILIFF, MAITRE D'HOTEL, MANAGER, FACTOR
college/monastery ...... MANCIPLE
stewardess, airplane .. HOSTESS
stewardship .... MANAGEMENT
stewed .... DRUNK
fruit .... FOOL
stibium .... ANTIMONY
stich .... LINE, VERSE
stick .. WAND, STAFF, BATON, ROD, CANE, CLUB, STAB, ADHERE, PUNCTURE, PIERCE, POKE, COHERE, CLING, ABIDE, CLEAVE, IMPALE, FAGOT, PADDLE, PASTE, BAT, FERULE
around .... STAY
celery .... STALK
conductor's ...... BATON
fairy's .... WAND
for leveling grain .... STRICKLE
insect .... EMESA
jumping .... POGO
match .... LINSTOCK
metal cap ...... FERRULE
out ..... EXTRUDE, JUT, PROJECT, PROTRUDE
pointer .... FESCUE
policeman's .... TRUNCHEON, BILLY
sharp-pointed .... GOAD
slang ... GREAT, DEFRAUD
stirring .... MUDDLER
throwing ...... DINGBAT
up for .... DEFEND
sticker ...... BUR(R), THORN, LABEL
stickler ..... DISCIPLINARIAN, MARTINET
stickpin's place ..... NECKTIE, CRAVAT
sticks, the .... COUNTRY, BOONDOCKS
sticktight (fruit) .... (COCKLE)BUR
stickum .... GLUE
sticky .... TACKY, VISCID, TREACLY, ADHESIVE, GOOEY, GLUEY, HUMID, GUMMY, GLUTINOUS
substance ... GOO, GLUE, PASTE, GUM
stiff ...... WIRY, RIGID, FIRM, TAUT, TENSE, TIGHT, HARSH, HIGH, FORMAL, WOODEN
necked ...... STUBBORN, OBSTINATE
slang ..... HOBO, CORPSE
stiffen .... BRACE, TAUTEN
stiffening material ..... STAY
stifle .... SMOTHER, SUFFOCATE, SUPPRESS, REPRESS, CHECK, SCOTCH, CHOKE
stigma ... BRAND, SCAR, STAIN, BLOT, PORE, MARK
stigmatize ..... BRAND, MARK
stile .... STEP(S)
stiletto ...... STYLET, DAGGER
still ... WITHAL, QUIET, SILENT, STATIONARY, HUSHED, DISTILLERY, PLACID, WHIST, YET, INERT, MOTIONLESS, EVEN, SERENE, CALM, PHOTO, ALEMBIC
existing .... EXTANT
"Stillenacht" composer ...... GRUBER
stillness ...... SILENCE, HUSH, QUIETUDE
stilt .... PLOVER, BIRD, POLE, POST, SANDPIPER
stilted .... POMPOUS, BOMBASTIC, PEDANTIC
stiltlike toy ..... POGO STICK
stilton .... CHEESE
Stilwell's nickname .... VINEGAR JOE
stimulant ... EXCITANT, COFFEE
stimulate ..... WHET, EXCITE, (A)ROUSE, SPUR, FAN, ANIMATE
by electric shock .... GALVANIZE
stimulus ... INCENTIVE, SPUR, MOTIVE, DRIVE, IMPULSE, INDUCEMENT, FILLIP, STING, GOAD, INCITEMENT
sting .... PAIN, STIMULUS, BITE, SMART, PRICK, NETTLE, URTICATE
in zoology ..... ACULEUS
ray .... STINGAREE, BATFISH
slang ...... CHEAT, DUPE
stinger .... WASP, HORNET, GNAT, BEE, GADFLY
stinging ...... CAUSTIC, NIPPY
ant .... KELEP
creature ...... RAY, BEE, WASP, HORNET, ANT
hair .... NETTLE
sensation ... URTICATION
taste .... PUNGENT
stingaree .... RAY
stinger .... WASP, HORNET, VESPID, YELLOW JACKET, NETTLE, HIGHBALL
stingo ... ALE, BEER, ZEST, VIM, ENERGY
stingy ...... MISERLY, CLOSE, NIGGARDLY, PENURIOUS, SKIMPY, NEAR
stink .... STENCH, ODOR, SMELL, REEK
stinker .... PETREL
stinking ..... BAD-SMELLING, SMELLY, MALODOROUS, PUTRID, RANK, RANCID, MUSTY, FETID, NOISOME, FOUL
smut .... BUNT
stint .... DUTY, RESTRICT, LIMIT(ATION), SANDPIPER, ASSIGNMENT, BOUT, CHORE, TASK
stipe ... STEM, PETIOLE, STALK
stipel .... STIPULE
stipend ...... SALARY, WAGE, PENSION, ALLOWANCE, PREBEND
stipes ...... STALK, PEDUNCLE
stipulate ... SPECIFY, DEMAND, ARRANGE, PROVIDE
stipulation ...... AGREEMENT, CONDITION, PROVISION, CLAUSE, PROVISO
stipule, secondary .... STIPEL
stir .... AGITATE, SHAKE, (A)ROUSE, EXCITE, INCITE, ADO, PROVOKE, FUSS, MOVE(MENT), INFLAME, ROIL, ROUST, (A)WAKEN, TUMULT, TO-DO, CHURN
slang ...... PRISON, JAIL
up ... FOMENT, ROIL, RILE
stirabout .... PORRIDGE
stirk ...... HEIFER, BULLOCK
stirps ... RACE, STOCK, FAMILY
stirring ... MOVING, ROUSING, BUSY, ACTIVE
stirrup ... FOOTREST, GAMBADO
bone .... STAPES

cup ...... TOAST, DRINK
stitch ... SEW, CRICK, FASTEN, PAIN, ACHE, SUTURE, QUILT, TACK, BASTE, BIT
bird .... IHI
colloquial .... BIT
line .... SEAM
stitching material .... GUT, THREAD, WIRE, STAPLE
stitchwort ...... CHICKWEED
stithy .. SMITHY, FORGE, ANVIL
stoa .... PORTICO, WALK
stoat .... ERMINE
like animal .... MINK, WEASEL, MARTEN, OTTER
stoccado .... STAB, THRUST
stock .... STIRPS, TRUNK, RHIZOME, LINEAGE, ANCESTRY, RACE, BUTT, SUPPLY, STORE, CAPITAL, BREED, PROVIDE, TRITE, ORDINARY, GOODS, INVENTORY, REPERTORY, PLENISH, FUND
exchange .... BOURSE
dealer ... JOBBER, BEAR, BULL, BROKER
member(SHIP) ... SEAT, TRADER
speculator .. LAMEDUCK
telegraphic device ..... TICKER
trick ...... WASH SALE
farm ...... STUD, RANCH
in .... ON HAND
in trade ... LINE, STAPLE
keep in .... CARRY
market ..... EXCHANGE, BOURSE, CURB
market event .... CRASH, PANIC
market gamble ... FLYER
market maneuver .. RAID
of inferior ..... LOWBRED
replace ...... REPLENISH
still .... MOTIONLESS
take .... INVENTORY, APPRAISE
stockade .... ENCLOSURE, CORRAL, PEN, ETAPE, BARRIER, BOMA
stockfish .... HADDOCK, COD
stocking .. HOSE, SOCK, NYLON
stockish .... DULL
stockman .... RANCHER
stockpile ..... SUPPLY, STORE, RESERVE, HOARD
stockroom .... STORAGE
stocky ..... PLUMP, THICKSET, CHUNKY, STURDY, STOUT, STUBBED, STUBBY, DUMPY
stodgy .... DULL, TEDIOUS, BULKY
stogie ..... CIGAR, BOOT, SHOE
stoic ... IMPASSIVE, SPARTAN, PATIENT, EPICTETUS
first .... ZENO
philosopher .... SENECA
stoker ...... FIREMAN, TEASER
Stokowski, conductor .... LEOPOLD
stola .... PALLA
stole .... SCARF, ROBBED, BOA
stolen goods buyer .... FENCE
property ... LOOT, SWAG, PELF
stolid .... PHLEGMATIC, IMPASSIVE, WOODEN, DULL
stolon ..... RHIZOME, RUNNER
stoma .. PORE, MOUTH, ORIFICE
stomach .... CRAW, ABDOMEN, BELLY, APPETITE, DESIRE, TOLERATE, BEAR, CROP
ache .... GASTRALGIA, CARDIALGIA
animal's .... PAUNCH, CRAW, OMASUM, MAW
colloquial .... TUMMY, GIZZARD
disorder .... NAUSEA, BRASH, PYROSIS
gas .... FLATUS, FLATULENCE
inflammation .. GASTRITIS
opening .... PYLORUS
pertaining to ... GASTRIC
protruding .. BAYWINDOW
ruminants' .. PSALTERIUM, TRIPE, OMASUM, PAUNCH, MAW
stony concretion .... GASTROLITH
upset .... DYSPEPSIA, INDIGESTION
wall movement .... PERISTALSIS
washing out of ... LAVAGE
stomachache reliever .... ANTACID, ASPIRIN
stomatic .... ORAL
stomatopod .... SQUILLA, CRUSTACEAN
stomp .... STAMP
stone ..... ROCK, GEM, PELT, DENTRITE, DORNICK, LAPIS, PEBBLE
Age human .... CAVEMAN
Age period ... EOLITHIC, NEOLITHIC
Age tools .... (N)EOLITH
author .... IRVING
azure-blue .. LAPIS LAZULI
bladder ...... CALCULUS
broke .... PENNILESS
cameo .... ONYX
carver .... GRAVER
carved in relief .. CAMEO
cavity .... GEODE
change into .... PETRIFY
cherry .... PIT
Chief Justice ... HARLAN
chip ...... SPALL, GALLET
chisel .... CELT
clay .... SHALE
combining form .... LITH(O), PETR(O), LITE, LYTE
crop ..... ORPIN, SEDUM
cubic measure for ...... PERCH
cutter .... MASON
cutter's disease .... CHALICOSIS, SILICOSIS
cutter's chisel ..... DROVE
dress .... NIG, SCABBLE, TRIM
dressing tool .... ADZ(E), HACKHAMMER
drupe .... NUTLET
engraved on ... LAPIDARY
engraving ..... INTAGLIO
excavation site .. QUARRY
fire-starting ...... FLINT
flake .... SPALL
flint-like ... HORNSTONE
for throwing .. DORNICK, DINGBAT
fragments ...... BRASH, DEBRIS
fruit ... DRUPE, CHERRY, PUTAMEN, PLUM, PIT, PYRENE, PIP, SEED
gall .... CALCULUS
green .... OLIVINE
grinding .... MANO
hammer .... MASH
hard ... FLINT, ADAMANT
headed ax ... TOMAHAWK
heap ... CAIRN(E), SCREE, CARN(E)
huge .... MENHIR, MEGALITH, BOULDER
hurling apparatus .... ONAGER, CATAPULT, MANGONEL, TREBUCHET
implement ...... EOLITH, MANO
jar .... CROCK
kidney .... CALCULUS
Latin .... LAPIS
lifting device .. LEWIS(SON)
like .... LITHOID(AL)
measure .... PERCH
monument ..... MENHIR, DOLMEN, CROMLECH, STELE, CAIRN
ornamental .... JADE, SODALITE
parsley ..... HONEWORT
particles .... GRIT
paving .... SLAB, MACADAM, SETT, FLAG
peach .... PIT
pertaining to .... LITHIC
pestle .... MULLER
philosopher's ... CARMOT
piece(s) .. RUBBLE, SPALL, GALLET
pile .... TALUS
pillar .... STELE
precious .... GEM, DIAMOND, JEWEL, RUBY, PEARL, OPAL, EMERALD, SAPPHIRE
prefix .... LITHO
red .... SPINEL
roller ..... CARP, TOTER, DACE
roller, eternal .. SISYPHUS
semi-precious .. PERIDOT, TOPAZ, CHRYSOLITE, CHRYSOPRASE, ZIRCON, CORAL, ONYX, AGATE, OLIVIN, SARD, GARNET, TOURMALINE, AMETHYST
sharpening .. HONE, WHET
slab .... STELA, STELE, TABLET
spark-producing .. FLINT

square hewn .... ASHLAR, ASHLER
tablet .... STELE
throwing device .... ONAGER, CATAPULT, SLING(SHOT), MANGONEL
to death ...... LAPIDATE
tool .... NEOLITH, PALEOLITH
trim .... NIG, DRESS
turn to .... LAPIDIFY, PETRIFY
upright prehistoric ...... MENHIR
wall-facing ..... ASHLER, ASHLAR
with lined cavity .. GEODE
woman turned to .. NIOBE
stonechat ..... THRUSH, BIRD
stonecrop .... SEDUM, PLANT, ORPIN(E)
stonecutter .... MASON, LAPIDARY, LAPICIDE
stones, heap of .... SCREE, CAIRN, TALUS
roadbuilding .. MACADAM
"Stonewall ____," general .... JACKSON
stoneware ..... POTTERY, GRES
stonework .... MASONRY
stony .... PITILESS, HARD, PETROUS, PETROSAL
deposit in body .... CALCULUS
stooge .... HECKLER, FOIL, UNDERLING, TOOL, PAWN, DUMMY, MOE
stook .... SHOCK
stool ..... TABO(U)RET, STUMP, FOOTREST, PRIVY, LURE, DECOY
foot .. CRICKET, OTTOMAN
pigeon ...... INFORMER, PEACHER, NARK, DECOY, SPY
stoop ... DEIGN, CONDESCEND, SWOOP, BEND, PORCH, VERANDA(H), STOUP, LOUT
stop ... STANCH, BLOCK, PLUG, CLOSE, INTERCEPT, CEASE, END, PULL UP, DESIST, ARREST, WHOA, HALT, CHECK, DEFEAT, LET UP, BELAY
football carrier .. TACKLE
hole .... PLUG
legally .... ESTOP
nautical .... AVAST
resisting .... YIELD, SURRENDER, CAPITULATE
short .... BALK
talking .. DRY UP, SHUT UP
temporarily ..... PAUSE
watch .... TIMER
stopcock ..... FAUCET, VALVE
stopgap .... MAKESHIFT, SUBSTITUTE
stoppage of body fluid .. STASIS
debate .... CLOTURE, CLOSURE
hostilities ..... RESPITE, TRUCE, ARMISTICE
operation ... SHUTDOWN
stopped diapason .... MELODIA
stopper .... TAP, SPILE, CORK, PLUG, BUNG, SHIVE, STOPPLE, TAMPION, TOMPION
stopple .... STOPPER
storage place ..... STOREROOM, CRIB, CELLAR, ARSENAL, LOFT, BIN, DEPOT, HUTCH, CACHE, SILO, GRANARY, BARN, MAGAZINE
storax .. STYRENE, GUMRESIN, BALSAM
store .... STOCK, RESERVE, SUPPLY, HOARD, CACHE, STOW, DEPOSIT, BOUTIQUE, SHOP, WAREHOUSE, SAVE, LAY-UP, OUTLET, FUND, GARNER
army ...... CANTEEN, PX, COMMISSARY
fodder .... ENSILE
helper .... CLERK
kind of .... DRUG, GROCERY, FIVE-AND-TEN
small articles .... NOTIONS
storehouse .. ETAPE, GRANARY, DEPOT, BARN, REPERTORY
weapons ..... ARSENAL, ARMORY, MAGAZINE
storekeeper .... GROCER
storeroom .. BUTTERY, CELLAR, CLOSET
storied ... FAMOUS, LEGENDARY
stork .. ADJUTANT, MARABOU, JABIRU, AYAYA
delivery of .... BABY
kin of ...... HERON, IBIS, HAMMERHEAD
stork's bill ...... GERANIUM
storm .... RACE, ASSAULT, RANT, ATTACK, OUTBURST, FUME, TEMPEST, RIPSNORTER, STOUR
accompaniment .. SNOW, SLEET, HAIL, RAIN, THUNDER
center .... EYE
cloud formation .... WATERSPOUT
Country girl .... TESS
cyclonic ...... TYPHOON, HURRICANE
with rotating winds ..... CYCLONE, TORNADO
stormy .... WILD, RAGING, VIOLENT, INCLEMENT
Storting .... PARLIAMENT
sits in ____ .... OSLO
story .. ACCOUNT, NARRATION, NARRATIVE, RUMOR, REPORT, FLOOR, FABLE, MARCHEN, TALE, REDE
animal .... FABLE
bedtime .... YARN
colloquial .... FIB
complication in a .. NODE, NODUS
correspondent's .... DISPATCH
exaggerated ...... YARN
exclusive ... SCOOP, BEAT
false .... HOAX, CANARD, FABLE
heroic .... SAGA
long .... NOVEL
part of .... PASSUS
romantic .... GEST(E)
short .. CONTE, PARABLE
tell a .... SPIN
teller ...... RACONTEUR, SCHEHERAZADE, MUNCHAUSEN
traditional ...... MYTH, LEGEND
with moral lesson .... PARABLE, FABLE, ALLEGORY
storyteller: colloq. ... FIBBER, LIAR
stoss, opposite of .... ALEE
stound .... PAIN, ACHE, SMART
stoup .... TANKARD, PAIL, BUCKET, FONT
stour .... STORM, TURMOIL, COMBAT
stout ... BRAVE, STURDY, FAT, CORPULENT, OBESE, PORTER, BEER, ALE, THICKSET, STOCKY, PORTLY, HUSKY, BOCK
hero .... NERO(WOLFE)
novelist .... REX
stouthearted .... BRAVE
stove .... ETNA, HEATER, RANGE, OVEN, CHAUFFER, KITCHENER
stovepipe ... FLUE, (SILK)HAT
stover ... FODDER, CORNSTALKS
stow ... STORE, PACK, STEEVE
cargo .... STEEVE
Stowe, author .... HARRIET
character .... TOPSY, EVA, LEGREE
strabismic .... CROSS-EYED
strabismus .... SQUINT, CROSS-EYE
"Strad" .... VIOLIN
straddle .... BESTRIDE
colloquial .... HEDGE
Stradivarius .... VIOLIN
strafe ...... BOMBARD, RAKE
straggle .... STRAY, WANDER, RAMBLE, TRAIL
straggler .. STRAY, WANDERER
straight ... (UP)RIGHT, ERECT, DIRECT, HONEST, FRANK, PURE, UNMIXED, ALIGNED
away .... AT ONCE
combining form .. RECT(I)
edge ...... RULER, LINER
faced .... IMPASSIVE
jacket .... CAMISOLE
liner .... BEE, RULER
man .... FOIL, STOOGE
man's companion ...... COMEDIAN
out .... DIRECT
passage ...... ENFILADE
route .... BEELINE
row .... RANK
up .... VERTICAL
straightforward .... OPEN, FRANK, CANDID, HONEST
strain .... STRIVE, PULL, TENSION, HEAVE, PRESS, BREED, TAX, STRETCH,

FILTER, LINEAGE, FILTRATE, RACE, SIFT, SIEVE, TRACE, STOCK, LINE
strained .... TENSE
strainer .... SIEVE, SIFTER, FILTER, COLANDER, TAMIS, STRUM
strains .... TUNE, AIR
strait ... LEPANTO, MALACCA, MAGELLAN, MACKINAC, MESSINA, MENAI, EURIPUS, NECK, ISTHMUS, GIBRALTAR, NARROW, TIGHT, CHANNEL, KERCH
laced .... PRIGGISH, STUFFY
straiten .... CONTRACT, LIMIT, DISTRESS
straits .... DIFFICULTY, DISTRESS
of Messina rock .. SCYLLA
Settlement, part of ...... PENANG, MALACCA
Settlement weight .... CATTY, CHEE
strand .... SHORE, BEACH, GROUND, THREAD, STRING, ROPE, MAROON, NECKLACE
strange .... UNCANNY, UNKNOWN, ODD, EXOTIC, UNCO, NOVEL, UNUSUAL, OUTRE, FREMD, ALIEN, PECULIAR, QUEER, QUAINT, SINGULAR
strangely beautiful ... EXOTIC
stranger .... EMIGRE, TRAMONTANE, ALIEN, NEWCOMER, OUTSIDER, FOREIGNER, GUEST, NOVICE, OUTLANDER
strangle .... THROTTLE, SUFFOCATE, CHOKE, STIFLE, REPRESS, GARROTE, SMOTHER, SCRAG, JUGULATE
hold .... DEATH GRIP
strangler .... THUG
strangulate .... CHOKE, THROTTLE, GARROTE
strangury .... URINATION
strap ... TAB, LEASH, THONG, FASTEN(ER), REIN, BELT
falcon's .... JESS
for leading animal ...... HALTER
shaped ...... LIGULATE, LORATE
shoulder .... HALTER
straphanger .... STANDEE
strapping ...... WELL-BUILT, ROBUST
strass .... PASTE, (LEAD)GLASS
strategem ... TRICK, TREPAN, TRAPAN, SCHEME, DECEPTION, RUSE, MANEUVER, TACTIC, PLOY
strategic position .. VANTAGE
strategy .... TACTICS, MANEUVER, PLAN, ARTIFICE
stratified .... LAMINATED, LAYERED
stratum .... LAYER, LEVEL
horizontal, in geology ... TABLE
of mineral ...... STREAK
soft, crumbly ...... MARL
Straus, composer ..... OSKAR
Strauss work .... SALOME
Stravinsky, composer ... IGOR
work .... FIREBIRD
straw ... CULM, STALK, STEM, TRIFLE, FODDER
bale of .... TRUSS
bed .... PALLET
boss .... ASSISTANT
bunch of ... WHISK, WISP, TRUSS
coat .... MINO
colored .. FLAXEN, BLOND
cover around plant ..... MULCH
fine-cut .... CHAFF
for fodder .... CHAFF
for pointing ..... FESCUE
hat .... PANAMA, SAILOR
in the wind .... OMEN, SIGN, PORTENT
like .... STRAMINEOUS
man .... SCARECROW, JACKSTRAW, NONENTITY, DUMMY
plaited .... SENNIT
stack .... RICK, MOW
thatching ..... HA(U)LM
vote .... POLL
vote man .... GALLUP, HARRIS, ROPER, POLLSTER
vote objective .... CONSENSUS
worm .... CADDIS
strawberry bush ..... WAHOO
like fruit .... ETAERIO
stray ... WANDER, STRAGGLE, ROAM, ROVE, DEVIATE, MEANDER, ERR, DIGRESS, LOST
animal .. WAIF, MAVERICK
animal's place ... PINFOLD
strays .... STATIC
streak ...... STRIPE, STRAIN, TRAIT, SPELL, HURRY, VEIN, TEAR, STRIA, FREAK, MOTTLE
streaked .... STRIGOSE, LINEATE
streaks, full of .... LIN(E)Y
stream ... RIVER, FLOW, RUSH, BROOK, POUR, TORRENT, RUNNEL, BECK, CREEK, ARROYO, BOURNE, KILL, RILL
bed .. CHANNEL, RUNWAY
fence .... WEIR
limestone deposit .. TUFA
of lava .... COULEE
overflow .... FRESHET
rocky obstruction .... RIFFLE
sound ... PURL, MURMUR
source .. FOUNTAIN, HEAD
swift, violent ... TORRENT
streamer ..... FLAG, BANNER, HEADLINE, SCAREHEAD, PENNANT
streamlet .. RUNNEL, RIVULET
street .... CALLE, ROAD, AVENUE, RUE, VIA, LANE
Arab ... GAMIN, URCHIN, WAIF, MUDLARK
designating a .. DEAD END, ONE-WAY, EASY, MAIN
ditch .... GUTTER
hydrant .... FIREPLUG
market .... CURB
musicians' employer .... PADRONE
musicians' organ .... HURDY-GURDY
of shops ...... BAZ(A)AR
short .... COURT
show .... RAREE
stray ..... URCHIN, ARAB, GAMIN, WAIF
urchin ...... MUDLARK, GAMIN, ARAB, WAIF, GUTTERSNIPE
with houses both sides ... ROW
streetcar ... TRAM, TROLL(E)Y
cowcatcher ..... FENDER
driver .... MOTORMAN
streetwalker ... URCHIN, ARAB, GAMIN, PEDESTRIAN
Streisand, Miss ..... BARBRA
sister of ...... (ROZ)KIND
strength ...... POWER, VIGOR, MIGHT, MAIN, ENERGY, POTENCY, FORCE
source of .... SINEW
strengthen .... FORTIFY, PROP, BRACE
with alcohol ..... NEEDLE
strenuous .... VIGOROUS
streptomycin discoverer ...... WAKSMAN
stress .... STRAIN, PRESSURE, EMPHASIS, URGENCY, TENSION, ACCENT, EMPHASIZE
in music ... ACCENT, ARSIS
metrical .... ICTUS
stretch ...... TRACT, EXTEND, SPREAD, STRAIN, EXAGGERATE, EXPANSE, SWEEP
of water .... RIFFLE
stretched out .... PROLATE
stretcher .... LITTER, CROSSPIECE, TENTER
stretching muscle .... TENSOR
strew ...... SPREAD, SCATTER, SPRINKLE
stria .... GROOVE, FILLET, RIDGE, STREAK
stricken .. STRUCK, AFFLICTED
strict ...... RIGOROUS, RIGID, STRINGENT, PUNCTILIOUS, STERN, EXACT, ACCURATE, PRECISE
adherence to law .... LEGALISM
stricture .... CENSURE, CRITICISM, STENOSIS
stride .... PACE, STEP, STRADDLE, LOPE
strides .... PROGRESS, ADVANCEMENT

strident ..... SHRILL, GRATING
sound .... STRIDOR
strife .... WAR, CONFLICT, DISCORD, FEUD, CONTENTION, STRUGGLE, CONTEST, QUARREL
strigil .... FLUTING
strigose .... HISPID
strike ...... SMITE, BITE, HIT, BLOW, HUELGA, IMPRESS, HOOK, DAB, IGNITE, ATTACK, LASH, FIND, OCCUR, HAULDOWN, DISMANTLE
demonstrator, etc. ...... PICKET
dumb .. AMAZE, ASTOUND
feature .... LOCKOUT
gently .... PAT, TAP
kind of .. SIT-IN, HUNGER, SYMPATHY, SLOW-DOWN
of a sort .... BOYCOTT
off ..... ERASE, EXPUNGE, DELETE
out ...... FAN, CANCEL, EXPUNGE, DELETE
weapon .... PICKET
with closed fist ... PUNCH
with open palm .... SLAP
strikebreaker ... GOON, FINK, SCAB, BLACKLEG
strikebreakers' leader .. NOBLE
striker .... HARPOONER, CLAPPER, HAMMER, MALLET, BAT
striking .. REMARKABLE, VIVID
string .... CORD, THREAD, ROPE, TWINE, LINE, HANG, LACE, HOAX, JOSH, FOOL, CATGUT
attached: colloq. .... CONDITION
in horse racing .. STABLE
of beads .... CHAPLET, STRAND
quartet member .. VIOLA, VIOLONCELLO
up .... HANG
tipped end .... TAG, A(I)GLET
stringed instrument .... LYRE, MANDOLIN, VIOL(A), GUITAR, ZITHER, PANDORA, CELLO, HARP, SAMISEN, LUTE, KOTO, CITHARA, CITHER(N), REBEC, PSALTERY, DULCIMER, BANJO, CITOLE, CLAVICHORD, CITTERN, UKE(LELE)
instrument player ...... LUTANIST
instrument ridge ... NUT
toy .... YOYO
stringency .... SCARCITY
stringent ..... STRICT, SEVERE, TIGHT
stringy ...... LONG, FIBROUS, ROPY, VISCOUS
strip .... UNDRESS, SPOIL, BARE, DISMANTLE, TAB, FASCIA, DIVEST, DENUDE, SWATH, BATTEN, DISARRAY, FLENSE, LATH
from tree trunk .. FLITCH
landing .... RUNWAY
metal/wood ... SLAT, LIST
of land .... NECK
of leaves ..... DEFOLIATE
skin .... EXCORIATE, FLAY
stripe ... CHEVRON, BAND, BAR, FILLET, TYPE, SORT, STREAK
of color .... LIST
on skin ... WHEAL, WALE, WELT
striped ..... STRIATE, ZONATE
animal ... ZEBRA, BONGO
cloth .... MADRAS
lengthwise ..... VITTATE
squirrel ...... CHIPMUNK
stripling ... SPRIG, YOUTH, LAD
stripped ... SHORN, DEPRIVED, DIVESTED
stripteaser .... ECDYSIAST, (SALLY) RAND
covering for ...... FAN, G-STRING
strive .... STRUGGLE, ENDEAVOR, TRY, FIGHT, VIE, COPE
strobil(e) .... CONE
stroke ... STRIPE, BLOW, MARK, CARESS, PET, SHOT, FIT, FONDLE, ICTUS
brilliant ..... COUP, ACE
cutting ..... CHOP, SLICE
finishing .... COUP DE GRACE, COPESTONE
indirect .... BRICOLE
lucky ..... COUP, FLUKE
oblique .... BRICOLE
of luck .... WINDFALL
on hand's palm .. PANDY
tender .... CARESS
stroll .. WANDER, PROMENADE, SAUNTER, WALK
stroller .... VAGRANT
Stromboli .. ISLAND, VOLCANO
strong ...... INTENSE, STOUT, STURDY, VIRILE, FORCEFUL, ATHLETIC, PUISSANT, LUSTY, POWERFUL, ROBUST, HALE, TOUGH, FIRM
arm man .... GOON, GANGSTER, BOUNCER
articulation ...... FORTIS
current .... RIPTIDE, UNDERTOW
drink ... SPIRITS, LIQUOR
feeling ... PASSION, FIRE, HATRED
man ... ATLAS, HERCULES, SAMSON, TITAN, DICTATOR
muscled .... THEWY, BRAWNY, HERCULEAN
passion .... FLAME
point .... FORTE
scented .... OLID
strongbox ...... SAFE, VAULT, CHEST, COFFER
stronghold .... CITADEL, CASTLE, REDOUBT, FORT, FORT(RESS), AERIE, FASTNESS, KEEP
strongroom .... VAULT
strongyl(e) .... ROUNDWORM
strontium sulfite .. CELESTITE
strop .... STRAP, SHARPEN
strophe .... STANZA
strophulus .... MILIARIA
struck .... SMOKE, SMIT, SHUTDOWN
structural .... TECTONIC
order .... TEXTURE
structure ... BUILDING, EDIFICE
strudel .... PASTRY
struggle ...... STRIVE, LABOR, CONTEST, WRESTLE, EXERTION, TUSSLE, STRIFE, CONFLICT, TRY
strum ... TIRL, PLUCK, FINGER, THRUM
struma .... GOITER, SCROFULA
strummer .... GUITARIST
strumpet .... HARLOT
strut .... SPUR, SWAGGER, BRACE, GAIT
struthious bird .. RHEAL, EMU, OSTRICH
struts .... CABANE
strychnine source .... NUX VOMICA
stub .... STUMP, UPROOT, BUTT
stubble .... BEARD, STUMP
stubborn .... ORNERY, OBSTINATE, WILLFUL, OBDURATE, DOGGED, HARDHEADED, MULISH, FROWARD
animal .... ASS, MULE
hair tuft .... COWLICK
stubby .... STOCKY
stuckup .... SNOBBISH, HAUGHTY, MIRED, ARROGANT
stud ... BOSS, KNOB, NAILHEAD, PAVE, BUTTON, ADORN
horse .... STALLION
shoe .... HOBNAIL
student ..... PUPIL, DISCIPLE, TRAINEE, COLLEGIAN, COED, SCHOLAR
Annapolis .. MIDSHIPMAN
first year ..... FRESHMAN, PLEBE
former .... DROPOUT
group ... CLASS, SEMINAR
in charge ...... MONITOR
initiate .... HAZE
international law .... PUBLICIST
military school ... CADET
population .. ENROLMENT
second year .. SOPHOMORE
third year ..... JUNIOR
university .. VARSITARIAN
West Point ...... CADET
students' scrimmage .... RUSH
studies .... EDUCATION, SCHOOLING
studio ... ATELIER, WORKSHOP
study .. READ, EXAMINE, PORE, WEIGH, ESSAY, CON, CONSIDER, SCRUTINIZE, PONDER, DEN, ROOM
assignment ..... LESSON

by candlelight .... LUCUBRATE
group ... SEMINAR, CLASS
hard ...... BONE, CRAM
layout of .... CASE
musical .... ETUDE
of the Bible ... ISAGOGICS
private .. DEN, SANCTUM
superficially ... SMATTER
stuff .... ESSENCE, THINGS, JUNK, PACK, FILL, SATIATE, CRAM, PLUG
stuffed ... REPLETE, CRAMMED
stuffing ...... COTTON, KAPOK, WAD
stuffy .... CLOSE, DULL, PRIM, STRAIT-LACED
Stuka .... (DIVE)BOMBER
stulm .... ADIT
stum .... GRAPE, JUICE, MUST
stumble .. TRIP, BLUNDER, SLIP
stumbling block .. HINDRANCE, OBSTACLE
stump ... STUB, BUTT, STUBBLE, LOP, PUZZLE, PERPLEX, BAFFLE, FOIL, NONPLUS, ZUCHE
stumps: sl. .... LEGS
stun .... DAZE, STUPEFY, SHOCK, ASTOUND
stunning .... REMARKABLE
stunt ... FEAT, DWARF, TRICK
flying tour .. BARNSTORM
stunted tree ... SCRUB, SCRAG, BONSAI
stuntman .... ACROBAT, DAREDEVIL
stupa .... MOUND
stupe .... COMPRESS
stupefacient .... NARCOTIC
stupefy ... STUN, AMAZE, PALL, DAZE, ASTONISH, DOPE, ASTOUND, BEWILDER, OBFUSCATE
stupendous ... OVERWHELMING, IMMENSE
stupid ...... TOMFOOL, DULL, FOOLISH, INEPT, DENSE, SILLY, TIRESOME, ASININE, DOPEY, CRASS, DUMB, INSIPIENT
from overdrinking ...... SOTTISH
person ..... GOOSE, IDIOT, ASS, COOT, FATHEAD, LOON, DOLT, MORON, DUNCE, CLOD
stupor .... TRANCE, NARCOSIS, TORPOR, SOPOR, COMA, LETHARGY, OSCITANCY
combining form .. NARCO
in a .... DOPEY
sturdy ... FIRM, STOUT, HARDY, STRONG, GID
sturgeon ...... SHOVELHEAD, HAUSEN, STERLET, BELUGA, GANOID
eggs .... ROE
eggs relish ..... CAVIAR(E)
roe .... CAVIAR(E)
stutter .... STAMMER
sty .... PEN, HAW, BOIL
Stygian ..... HELLISH, DARK, INFERNAL, GLOOMY

style .... STYLUS, NEEDLE, POINTER, DESIGN, MANNER, FASHION, MODE, FAD, BRAND, MAKE, TON, VOGUE, ENTITLE, GENRE, TECHNIQUE, NAME, CALL
architectural .... ROCOCO
artistic .... GUSTO
bombastic .... TUMID
dress .... COSTUME
furniture .... EMPIRE
literary .... ROCOCO
out of ..... PASSE, DATED
painting ... GENRE, DADA, CUBISM
type ..... ROMAN, IONIC, ITALIC, GOTHIC
styled ...... YCLEPT, CALLED, NAMED
stylet ...... STILETTO, PROBE, LANCET, DAGGER
surgical .... PROBE, TROCAR
stylish ... DRESSY, TONY, CHIC, NIFTY, JAUNTY, NOBBY, MODISH, SMART, FASHIONABLE, A LA MODE
dresser ... FOP, BRUMMEL, TOFF, DUDE, SWELL, DANDY
ostentatiously .... SWANK(Y)
stylist .. DESIGNER, MANNERIST
stylite .... ASCETIC
stylized flower .... LIS
stylograph .... PEN
stylus ... SCRIBER, NEEDLE, PEN
stymie (stymy) .... OBSTRUCT, HINDER, IMPEDE, BLOCK, BALK, FOIL
styptic .... ASTRINGENT, AMADOU, ALUM
action of .... STYPSIS
substance .... ALUM
Styx .... LETHE, RIVER
ferryman of .... CHARON
suave ..... GRACIOUS, POLITE, POLISHED, SOAPY, URBANE, BLAND, AULIC, COURTLY, SMOOTH
subaltern .. AIDE, SUBORDINATE
subaqueous .... UNDERWATER
subcontinent .... INDIA
subcontract .... SUBLET, SUBLEASE
suberose .... CORKLIKE, SUBEROUS
subdue .. CONQUER, VANQUISH, TAME, OVERCOME, SOFTEN, SUBJUGATE, OVERPOWER, QUELL, CALM
subgum dish ..... CHOW MEIN
subject .... TEXT, LIABLE, CONTINGENT, OCCASION, VASSAL, NOUN, LIEGE, THEME, TOPIC, SERVANT, TRIBUTARY
change to another .... METASTASIS
main .... MOTIF
to discussion ..... MOOT, DEBATABLE
to third degree ... SWEAT

subjoin .. APPEND, ADD, ANNEX
subjugate .... CONQUER, VANQUISH, OVERCOME, TAME
subjugation .... CONQUEST
sublimate ..... REFINE, PURIFY
sublime ..... NOBLE, EXALTED, HIGH, MAJESTIC, LOFTY
submachine gun .... THOMPSON
submarine .... PIGBOAT, TUB, U-BOAT, SUBMERSIBLE
chaser ..... CORVET(TE)
device against .... PARAVANE
"eye" of ...... PERISCOPE
locator .... SONAR
nuclear .... GATO
submaxilla .... JAW(BONE)
submerge ... HIDE, SINK, DIP, SUBMERSE, SWAMP, WHELM
submerged continent .... ATLANTIS
submersible ...... SUBMARINE, U-BOAT
submission ...... SURRENDER, RESIGNATION
sign/act of .... VAIL, KNEEL, BOW, CURTSY
submissive .. TAME, OBEDIENT, PASSIVE, DOCILE, PROSTRATE, MEEK
submit .... SURRENDER, PROPOSE, SUCCUMB, OBEY, YIELD, BOW, GIVE IN
subordinate ..... SECONDARY, INFERIOR, AIDE, ASSISTANT, MYRMIDON
suborn ...... BRIBE, CORRUPT
subpoena ..... SUMMON, WRIT
subrogate .... SUBSTITUTE
subrosa .... SECRETLY
subscribe .... SIGN, SUPPORT, PLEDGE, AGREE, CONSENT
subsequently ... AFTERWARD, LATER
subservience ...... SERVILITY
subservient .... SERVILE
subside ... ABATE, SINK, WANE, FALL, SETTLE, EBB
subsidiary ...... TRIBUTARY, AUXILIARY, SUCCURSAL,
subsidy .. GRANT, SUBVENTION, AID, PENSION, SUPPORT
subsist .... LIVE, FARE, EXIST, ABIDE, FEED
subsistence ..... LIVELIHOOD, BEING
substance ..... GIST, ESSENCE, MATTER, MATERIAL, REALITY, PITH, MEANING, PURPORT, STUFF, WEALTH
drying .... DESSICANT
substandard .... POOR, INFERIOR
substantial ..... REAL, SOLID, AMPLE
substantiate .... CONFIRM, PROVE, VERIFY
substantive ... ACTUAL, NOUN, SOLID
substitute .... VICE, REPLACE, ALTERNATE, SUPPLANT, PROXY, SUBROGATE, EXCHANGE, FILL-IN

food .... ERSATZ
for .... PINCHHIT
for a name ..... DINGUS
temporary ..... STOPGAP
substitution of obligation ..... NOVATION
subterfuge .... ARTIFICE, DECEPTION, BLIND, DEVICE, EVASION, TRICK, PRETENSE
subterranean .. UNDERGROUND, HIDDEN, SECRET
subtile ... SUBTLE, THIN, RARE, TENUOUS, KEEN
subtitle .... SUBHEAD
subtle .... RARE, THIN, ACUTE, KEEN, DEFT, SLY, (SUPER)FINE, NICE, FINESPUN, ARTFUL, DELICATE, WILY, ARTFUL, SUBTILE
emanation .... AURA, ATMOSPHERE
variation ...... NUANCE, SHADE
subtlety ...... FINESSE, CRAFT, ART, QUILLET
subtract ... DEDUCT, DETRACT, LESSEN
suburb ..... TOWN, OUTSKIRT, BARRIO, ENVIRON, FAUBOURG
suburban residence .... VILLA
society .... VILLADOM
subvention ..... AID, GRANT, SUBSIDY
subversive .... DISSIDENT, REBEL, RED
subvert .... UNDERMINE, CORRUPT, RUIN
subway .... TUBE, METRO, TUNNEL
entrance .... KIOSK, COVER, TURNSTILE
stairway .... ESCALATOR
succeed ..... FOLLOW, ENSUE, PROSPER, FLOURISH, THRIVE, SUPERSEDE, SUPPLANT
success ... TRIUMPH, VICTORY
colloquial .... HIT
succession ... SEQUENCE, SERIES
of rulers .... DYNASTY
successive ...... CONSECUTIVE
successor .... HERES, HEIR, HERITOR
succinct ..... CONCISE, BRIEF, TERSE, PITHY, LACONIC, SHORT
succor .... HELP, AID, RELIEF, ASSIST(ANCE)
succory .... CHICORY
succubus .... DEMONESS
succulent .... JUICY
succumb ... SUBMIT, FALL, DIE, YIELD
succursal .... SUBSIDIARY
succuss .... SHAKE
such .... SIC
suck .. DRAW, ABSORB, INHALE, SIP
sucker ...... DUPE, LOLLIPOP, ALL-DAY, MUG, BABY, LEECK
suckers, having .... SURCULOSE
suckfish .... REMORA
suckle .... NURSE, REAR, FOSTER, LACTATE
suckler .... MAMMAL, NURSE, BABY, BOB
suckling .... CHILD, BOB, MAMMAL
sucrose ... SUGAR, SACCHAROSE
suction device .... LEECH
sud .... LATHER
Sudan, capital of .. KHARTOUM
chief of state .... AZHARI
city .... OMDURMAN, ELOBEID
lake ..... CHAD, T(S)ANA
prime minister .... MAHGOUB, SADIG, KHALIL
province .... DARFUR
region .... GEZIRA, SEGU
river .... ATBARA
town ... KODOK, FASHODA
Sudanese ..... MOSSI, FULAH, HAUSSA
antelope .... OTEROP
medicine man .... MUMBO JUMBO
Negros, of the .. NILOTIC
sultanate .... WADAI
Sudanic language ...... TOSHI, YORUBA, MANDINGO
sudarium/sudary ... VERONICA, HANDKERCHIEF
sudden .. ABRUPT, PRECIPITATE, HASTY
sudor ... SWEAT, PERSPIRATION
sudorific .. SWEATER, HIDROTIC
suds ..... FOAM, FROTH, BEER
sue .... WOO, APPEAL, PETITION, PLEAD, LITIGATE
____ Langdon ...... ANE
suede .... LEATHER
source .... CALF, KID
suet .... FAT, TALLOW
Suez Canal builder ... LESSEPS
suffer ...... DREE, UNDERGO, BEAR, ENDURE, EXPERIENCE, LET, ALLOW, TOLERATE, PERMIT
sufferance .... TOLERATION
suffering ..... DISTRESS, PAIN
martyr's .... PASSION
suffice .. SERVE, DO, SATISFY
sufficient .... ADEQUATE, ENOUGH, ENOW, AMPLE
suffix .... POSTFIX, SUBINDEX, DESINENCE
action .... ANCE
adjective ..... ENT, IAL, ISH, IST, OUS
carbohydrate .... OSE
chemical ...... ANE, ENE, OLE, ENOL, OLIC, ITOL
condition ... SION, STER, ANCE, EMIA
comparative ... IER, IOR
diminutive ... ULE, ETTE
follower .... ITE, IST
inflammation ...... ITIS
inhabitant of .... ITE
lacking .... LESS
one who ...... IST, STER
skin .... DERM
superlative .... EST
suffocate ... SMOTHER, CHOKE, STIFLE, ASPHYXIATE
suffocation, temporary .... APN(O)EA
suffragan .. BISHOP, AUXILIARY
suffrage .... VOTE, FRANCHISE, VOTING
suffragist, U.S. .... CATT
suffuse ... BATHE, OVERSPREAD, COLOR
suffusion ..... BLUSH, FLUSH, TINT
Sufi disciple .... MURID
wandering dervish ...... CALENDER
sugar .... SACCHAROSE, (LACT)OSE, MALTOSE, GLUCOSE, FLATTERY, SWEETEN, MANNOSE, MUSCOVADO, ARABINOSE, HEXOSE, DEXTROSE, FRUCTOSE
alcohol .... SORBITOL
beets .... SUCROSE
beets refuse .... BAGASSE
burnt .... CARAMEL
cane .... SUCROSE
cane, crushed .. MEGASS(E)
cane cutting tool .... MACHETE
cane disease ...... ILIAU
cane refuse .... BAGASSE, TRASH
cane sprout ..... RATOON
combining form .... SACCHAR(O)
convert into .... SACCHARIZE
crude .... GUR
crystalline .... FRUCTOSE, MALTOSE, GLUCOSE, LACTOSE
cube .... LUMP
flavoring ...... CARAMEL
foundation for candy .... FONDANT
fruit .... KETOSE, LEVULOSE, FRUCTOSE
lump .... LOAF
milk .... LACTOSE
mushroom ... TREHALOSE
palm sap .... JAGGERY
pentose .... RIBOSE
plum .... BONBON
raw .... MUSCOVADO, CASSONADE
slang .... MONEY
solution ... SYRUP, SIRUP
source of ... CANE, MAPLE, BEET
sprinkler .... DUSTER
substitute ... SACCHARIN
yeast .... TREHALOSE
sugarplum ..... BONBON, KISS
sugary ..... HONEYED, SWEET
suggest ... PROPOSE, INTIMATE, HINT, IMPLY, INSINUATE
suggestion .. PROPOSAL, HINT, TRACE, INDICATION
open to ...... AMENABLE, PERVIOUS
sui ____ ..... GENERIS, JURIS
suicidal charge ...... BANZAI

dive, bomber's .... KAMIKAZE
suicide .... HARA-KIRI, HARA-KARI, SEPPUKU
in law ...... FELO-DE-SE
Hindu widow's ... SUTTEE
sacrificial ... IMMOLATION
suint .... GREASE
derivative ...... POTASH
Suisse .... SWITZERLAND
suit .... AGREE, PETITION, WOOING, (BE)FIT, ADAPT, PLEASE, SATISFY
bring .... SUE
court ..... ACTION, CASE
of armor ...... PANOPLY
of mail .... ARMOR
playing card .... SPADES, DIAMONDS, HEARTS, CLUBS
tarot card ...... SWORDS, WANDS, CUPS, PENTACLES
to a ____ .... TEE
suitable .... MEET, APT, FIT(TING), APPROPRIATE, BECOMING, PROPER
suitcase .... VALISE, GRIP
suite .... RETINUE, TRAIN, STAFF, FLAT
suited to ____ .... A TEE
suitor ..... WOOER, ADMIRER, PETITIONER, SUER, FELLOW
Sulawesi .... CELEBES
sulcate ... GROOVED, FLUTED, FURROWED
sulcus ...... FURROW, GROOVE
Suleiman soubriquet .... MAGNIFICENT
sulfate ..... COPPERAS, ALUM
sulfide mixture .... MATTE
sulfonal .... SOPORIFIC
sulfur .... BRIMSTONE
alloy .... NIELLO
combining form ... THI(O)
sulfuric acid .... VITRIOL
sulk .... MOPE, POUT, PET, GROUCH
sulky ..... SULLEN, CARRIAGE, GLUM, GIG
sullage .... SILT, SEWAGE
sullen .... GLUM, SURLY, MOROSE, SULKY, DULL, BALEFUL, DOUR, MOODY, DORTY
Sullivan, ____ ..... ED, BARRY
Sullivan brothers .... FIVE, SAILORS
Sullivan's collaborator .... GILBERT
forte .... COMIC OPERA
sully ... TARNISH, SOIL, STAIN, BLEMISH, BLOT
sulphate, barium .... BARYTE
calcium .... GYPSUM
double .... ALUM
sulphide, arsenic ... ORPIMENT
lead .... GALENA
zinc .... BLENDE
sulphur .... BUTTERFLY
alloy .... NIELLO
bottom .... WHALE
sulphuric acid ...... VITRIOL
sulphurous ... FIERY, HEATED, HELLISH, INFERNAL, PASSIONATE
sultan ... CHICKEN, SULEIMAN, SALADIN, SELIM, MURAD, PADISHAH
chamberlain of .. EUNUCH
decree of .... IRADE
of Swat .... BABE (RUTH)
palace .... SERAI
wives' apartment .. HAREM
sultana .... GRAPE, RAISIN
sultanate ..... KUWAIT, OMAN, MUSCAT
sultry ..... HOT, CLOSE, FIERY, PASSIONATE, MUGGY, TORRID, HUMID, SWELTERING, TROPICAL
Sulu capital .... JOLO
Moslem .... MORO
sum ... AMOUNT, AGGREGATE, ADD, TOTAL, GIST, SUBSTANCE
subtracted ... DEDUCTION
up a speech .... PERORATE
sumac ..... RHUS, TEREBINTH
Sumatra burrowing animal ... TELEDU
city .... PADANG, MEDAN, PALEMBANG
deerlike animal ... NAPU, CHEVROTAIN
gibbon .... SIAMANG
gutta .... SIAK
island near .... NIAS
native of ...... MALAYAN, BAT(T)AK
shrew/squirrel .... TANA
volcano .... MERAPI
wild cat .... BALU
Sumbara volcano .. TAMBORA
Sumerian god .... ABU
summary ...... GIST, DIGEST, RESUME, EPITOME, RUN-DOWN, PRECIS, BRIEF, COMPEND(IUM), ABRIDGMENT, SYNOPSIS
of main points .... SYLLABUS
summer ailment .... HEATRASH
beverage .... ADE
French .... ETE
headliner .... HEATWAVE
house .... COTTAGE, BELVEDERE, CASINO, ALCOVE, PAVILION, KIOSK, MAHAL, GROTTO
insect .... GNAT
pertaining to .. (A)ESTIVAL
suit fabric .. PALM BEACH
theater .... STOCK
time .... DST
summit .... APEX, PEAK, PINNACLE, ACME, TOP, KNAP, ZENITH
summon ... CALL, SUBPOENA, SEND FOR, EVOKE, ROUSE, CONVENE, BID, CITE
by calling name ... PAGE
by incantation .. INVOKE
by magic .... CONJURE
demon .... CONJURE
for roll call ...... MUSTER
spirit .... CONJURE
to a meeting ... CONVOKE
summons ... EVOCATION, CALL, WRIT, CITAL, MONITION
sump ...... (CESS)POOL, PIT, WELL, OIL
sumpter ... PACKHORSE, MULE
sumptuous ... LAVISH, COSTLY, SPLENDID, RICH, DE LUXE
sun ... STAR, TAN, DRY, SOL, LUMINARY
bittern .... HELIAS
bow ...... RAINBOW, IRIS
burn .... TAN
Chinese president .... YAT-SEN
combining form .. HELI(O)
darkening of the .. ECLIPSE
disk .... ATEN
dried brick ..... (A)DOBE, DOBIE
dog .... PARHELION
fish .... OPAH, BREAM
for drying ..... INSOLATE
god ..... APOLLO, HELIOS, RA, HYPERION, PHOEBUS, AMON, VARUNA, MARDUK, SOL, MITHRA(S), HORUS, SHU, ATEN, TUM, SHAMASH, TITAN
greatest distance from ... APSIS
halo of .... CORONA
helmet ..... TOPI, TOPEE
helmet scarf .. PUGGREE, PUGGRY
mirror ...... HELIOSTAT
mock .... PARHELION
of the ... SOLAR, HELIACAL
orbit/path .... ECLIPTIC
personification of .. TITAN
pertaining to the .. SOLAR, HELIACAL
poetic ... PHOEBUS, LAMP
point farthest from ...... APHELION
radiation .... INSOLATION
room/porch ... SOLARIUM
shadow .... UMBRA
shield ... PARASOL, VISOR
spot ... FACULA, MACULA, FRECKLE
spurge .... TURNSOLE
streak .... FACULA
vitamin, so-called .... (COD) LIVER OIL
worship .... HELIOLATRY
Sun Yat-sen's party .... KUOMINTANG
sunbeam .... RAY
sunburn .... TAN
sunburnt .... ADUST
Sunda island .... BALI, JAVA, SUMATRA, FLORES, LOMBOK
sundae .... ICE-CREAM
Sunday .... SABBATH, LORD'S DAY
evangelist .... BILLY
supper treat ... MEATPIE
sunder .... PART, SEVER, SEPARATE, SPLIT, RIVE, CLEAVE, DIVIDE
sundial .... HOROLOGE
pointer .... GNOMON

sundog .... PARHELION
sundry ..... MISCELLANEOUS, DIVERS
sunfish ..... BREAM, CRAPPIE, ROACH, BLUEGILL, MOLA, CROPPIE, CICHLID
sunflower .... GIRASOL(E), HELIOTROPE, TURNSOLE, HELIANTHUS
state .... KANSAS
sunken .... HOLLOW
fence .... HAHA
place .... SAG
Sunkiang capital .... HARBIN
sunn .... HEMP
sunny ...... CHEERFUL, WARM
sunrise ... DAWN, DAYBREAK, AURORA
sunroom .... SOLARIUM
sunset, occurring at .... ACRONICAL
sunshade .... PARASOL, UMBRELLA, AWNING, VISOR
sunshine, bit of .... RAY
sunspot .... MACULA, FACULA
dark part .... UMBRA
sunstroke .. ICTUS, INSOLATION
sunwise .... CLOCKWISE
Suomi .... FINLAND
sup ... DINE, DRINK, SIP, EAT
super .... ACTOR, EXTRA
patriot .... JINGO, NATIONALIST
superabundance .... PLETHORA
superannuate .... RETIRE
superannuated .. ANILE, AGED, RETIRED, OBSOLETE, OUTDATED
superb ..... GRAND, ELEGANT, EXCELLENT, RICH
supercilious .... PROUD, HAUGHTY, SNOOTY, ARROGANT, SCORNFUL
superficial ...... SQUARE, LIP, SHALLOW, CURSORY, EXTERNAL, SKIN-DEEP
polish .... VENEER
superfine ... OVERNICE, SUBTLE, DELICATE, DE LUXE
superfluous .... SURPLUS, EXCESSIVE, DE TROP, REDUNDANT, OTIOSE
superhighway ..... AUTOBAHN, FREEWAY, SPEEDWAY
superhuman .... DIVINE
superintend .... OVERSEE, SUPERVISE, MANAGE, DIRECT
superintendent ... SURVEYOR, MANAGER
superior ...... HIGHER, BOSS, BETTER, UPPER, EXCELLENT
superiors ... BETTERS, CHIEFS, MASTERS
superlative .... EXTREME, SUPREME, ACME, EXCESSIVE, ULTRA
absolute .... ELATIVE
ending .... EST
supernal .... HEAVENLY, CELESTIAL, DIVINE, ETHEREAL
supernatural .... OCCULT, DIVINE, MIRACULOUS, UNEARTHLY, MAGIC
force .... MANA
happening ..... MIRACLE
supernumerary .... EXTRA, FIGURANT(E), ACTOR
superpower, a ..... USA, USSR
superscribe .... ADDRESS
supersede .... SUCCEED, SUPPLANT, REPLACE
supersensitive .... SORE, THIN-SKINNED
supersonic noise .... BOOM
supervene .... ENSUE, HAPPEN
supervise ... OVERSEE, DIRECT, MANAGE
supervisor .... DIRECTOR, OVERSEER, MANAGER
college .... PROCTOR
morals .... CENSOR
supine ..... LISTLESS, PASSIVE, INACTIVE
opposite of ...... PRONE
supper .... DINNER, MEAL
supplant .... REPLACE, SUPERSEDE, DISPLACE, OUST
supple ..... LITHE, LISSOM(E), LIMBER, PLIANT, FLEXIBLE
supplement .... ADD
in law .... CODICIL
supplicate .... PETITION, APPEAL, PLEAD, PRAY, REQUEST, ENTREAT
supplicant .... PLEADER, BEGGAR
supplication .... PETITION, PRAYER, PLEA, REQUEST, ROGATION, ENTREATY
supplies ..... STORES, ISSUES, PROVISIONS
supply ..... STOCK, FURNISH, PROVIDE, EQUIP, STORE
food .... CATER, PURVEY, PROVISION
ship ..... OILER, TENDER, VICTUAL(L)ER
support .... BUTTRESS, SHORE, BACK(UP), UPHOLD, BEAR, MAINTAIN, SUSTAIN, ABET, KEEP, SECOND
chief .... MAINSTAY
idea/cause ..... ESPOUSE
kind of ...... LEG, PROP, LIMB, PEDESTAL, PEG, BASE, MORAL, FINANCIAL, PILLAR, UNIPOD
main .... PILLAR
supporter .... PARTISAN, ABETTOR, SECOND, FOLLOWER, ROOTER, FAN, PATRON, ADHERENT, BACKER
supporting framework .... TRESTLE, TRELLIS, SKELETON, EASEL
member ..... LEG, MAST
suppose ...... TROW, ASSUME, IMAGINE, PRESUME, THINK, WEEN, OPINE, CONJECTURE, SURMISE, RECKON
supposed .... REPUTED, PUTATIVE
supposition .... THEORY, HYPOTHESIS, IF
suppository .... PESSARY
suppress .... QUELL, SUBDUE, CHECK, QUASH, CRUSH, CONCEAL, STOP, THROTTLE
news story .... KILL
suppurate .. FESTER, MATURATE
suppuration ..... PUS, PYOSIS
supra .... ABOVE
supreme .... DOMINANT, ULTIMATE, CHIEF, FINAL, UTMOST, HIGHEST
being .... GOD
Court nickname .... NINE OLD MEN
power .... IMPERIUM
Surakarta .... SOLO
Surat river .... TAPTI
surcease .... STOP, END
surcingle .... GIRDLE
surcoat .. JUPON, GIPON, CLOAK
surd ... IRRATIONAL, RADICAL, VOICELESS
sure ... POSITIVE, CONFIDENT, CERTAIN, UNERRING
grip .... CINCH
thing: sl. ... IN THE BAG, CINCH, PIPE
surely .... OF COURSE, YES, CERTAINLY
surety .... ASSURANCE, BOND, SECURITY, HOSTAGE, BAIL, SPONSOR, GUARANTEE
surf .... WAVES, SWELLS
duck .... SCOTER
noise .... ROTE, THUNDER
surface .... EXTERIOR
antique .... PATINA
curve .... CAMBER
front .... OBVERSE
gem's .... FACET
in aeronautics ... AIRFOIL
main .... OBVERSE
slanting/sloping ... CANT
surfbird .... PLOVER
surfeit .... SATE, SATIATE, CLOY, JADE, SATIETY, GLUT, EXCESS
surfeited ..... FED-UP, SATED, BLASE
surge .... SWELL, BILLOW, HEAVE, WAVE
of water/wave .... WASH
surgeon: colloq. .... SAWBONES, MEDICO
hammer of ..... PLESSOR
knife of .... LANCET, SCALPEL, BISTOURY
probe of .... STYLET
saw of .... TREPAN, TREPHINE
surgery .... OPERATION, NEOPLASTY
lip defect ... CHILOPLASTY
surgical compress ...... STUPE
instrument .. OSTEOTOME, TREPAN, BISTOURY, TROCAR, LEVATOR, SCALPEL, LANCET
knife .... BISTOURY, SCALPEL, LANCET, FLEAM, PHLEBOTOME
operation .... RESECT, LOBOTOMY

operation: comb. form .. TOMY
pad .... SPONGE
pincers .... FORCEPS
removal of body part .... ABLATION
removal of breast .... MASTECTOMY
sewing .... SUTURE
thread ... SETON, CATGUT
treatment ... OPERATION
Suribachi, site of .... IWO JIMA
suricate, kin of .... MONGOOSE, CIVET
Surinam capital .. PARAMARIBO
governor of ..... VRIES
prime minister ... PENGEL
toad .... PIPA
tree .... BALATA
surly ... GRUFF, SULKY, RUDE, SULLEN, CRUSTY, GRUMPY, ARROGANT, UNCIVIL, CROSS, BOORISH, CHURLISH
surmise .... OPINE, GUESS, CONJECTURE, IMAGINE, INFER
surmount .... OVERCOME, CONQUER, GET OVER, EXCEED, HURDLE, TOP
surname .... AGNOMEN, PATRONYMIC, COGNOMEN
surpass ...... EXCEED, EXCEL, TOP, ECLIPSE, BEST, OUTDO, CAP, TRANSCEND
surplice .... COTTA
vestment like ... ROCHET
surplus .... EXTRA, SPARE, EXCESS, OVERAGE
surprise .. ASTOUND, ASTONISH, AMAZE, STARTLE, JOLT
surrealist painter .... DALI
surrender ...... YIELD, CEDE, CESSION, REMISE, GIVE UP, SUBMIT, SUBMISSION, RESIGN
conditionally .... CAPITULATE
sign of ... WHITE FLAG, HANDS UP
surreptituous .. CLANDESTINE, SLY, SECRET, STEALTHY, FURTIVE, SNEAKY
surrey .... CARRIAGE
village .... KEW
surrogate ... DEPUTY, JUDGE, SUBSTITUTE
concern of .... WILLS
surround .... ENCOMPASS, (EN)CIRCLE, ENCLOSE, INVEST, BESET, GIRD, RING, ENVELOP, HEM, ENVIRON, BELEAGUER
surrounding .... MILIEU, ENVIRONMENT, AMBIENT
surtout .... (OVER)COAT
surveillance .... WATCH, OBSERVATION
survey ... INSPECT, VIEW, POLL, LOOK AT, CANVASS
surveying instrument .... ALIDADE, TRANSIT, LEVEL, STADIA, VERNIER, THEODOLITE, CALIPER, TACHYMETER
method .. DIALING, STADIA
surveyor's assistant .. RODMAN, LINEMAN
transit .... STADIA
survive .... (OUT)LIVE, WEATHER
survivor .... RELICT
Susa, location of .. IRAN, ELAM
Susan, diminutive of ... SUE, SUSIE, SUZY
susceptibilities ...... FEELINGS
susceptible ..... RESPONSIVE, LIABLE, SOFT, RECEPTIVE
to mistake ..... FALLIBLE
suslik ...... SISEL, SQUIRREL, GOPHER, SPERMOPHILE
suspect ... DISTRUST, PRESUME, IMAGINE, SURMISE
suspend ... HANG, HALT, STOP, HOLD, DEFER, EXCLUDE, ADJOURN
suspended .... PENSILE, PENDENT, HANGING, PENDANT
suspenders .... GARTERS, BRACES, GALLUSES
suspension .... DELAY, STOPPAGE, PENDENCY
of court sentence .... PROBATION
of hostilities ..... TRUCE, ARMISTICE
of proceedings .... ADJOURNMENT, RECESS
suspicion ...... TRACE, HINT, INKLING, MISTRUST, FEAR, HUNCH
suspicious .... LEERY, SKEPTICAL
suspiration .... SIGH
Susskind, TV man .... DAVID
sustain ... MAINTAIN, SUFFER, UPHOLD, CONFIRM, SUPPORT
sustenance ... FOOD, SUPPORT, BREAD
susu .... DOLPHIN
susurrant .... RUSTLING, MURMURING, WHISPERING
susurration .... MURMUR, RUSTLE, WHISPER
sutler .... VICTUAL(L)ER
customer of .... SOLDIER
sutor .... COBBLER, SYRUP
suttee ... SUICIDE, IMMOLATION
suture ... STITCH, SEW, SEAM, JUNCTION, RAPHE
suzerain ...... RULER, LIEGE, LORD
svelte ...... LITHE, LISSOM(E), SLENDER
Sverige .... SWEDEN
neighbor of ..... NORGE
swab ..... MOP, WIPE, BRUSH, SPONGE, MALKIN
swaddle ..... SWATHE, WRAP
swaddling clothes .... DUDS
swag .... SWAY, LURCH
slang .... LOOT, PLUNDER, BOOTY
swage ... DIE, STAMP, DOLLY, UPSET
swagger ...... STRUT, BLUFF, BLUSTER, RUFFLE, ROISTER
swaggering .... SWASH
Swahili cheer word .... HARAMBEE
swain .... SUITOR, LOVER, YOUTH, GALLANT
swallow .... ABSORB, GULP, RETRACT, BEAR, TAKE IN, BIRD, TERN, BOLT, QUAFF, INGEST
bird like a .... SWIFT, MARTIN, CRAN
greedily .... GORGE
like .... HIRUNDINE
swallowing, difficulty in ...... DYSPHAGIA
swallowtail .. BUTTERFLY, COAT
swallowwort ...... CELANDINE
swami ... LORD, MASTER, FAKIR
swamp ... INUNDATE, MARSH, SLOUGH, FEN, MORASS, BOG, OVERWHELM, FLOOD, MARISH
air .... MALARIA
fever .... MALARIA
Fox, soubriquet .. MARION
plant .... COWSLIP, SOLA, MARIGOLD
trees .... MANGROVE
vapor .... MIASM(A)
swampland ...... EVERGLADE
swamps ..... WETLAND, SLEW
swampy ... PALUDAL, MARSHY
area .... SLASH
swan ... WHOOPER, POET, BIRD, SWEAR, TRUMPETER, ANSA
constellation ... CYGNUS
female .... PEN
genus .... OLOR
lover .... LEDA
male .... COB
song ...... VALEDICTORY
young .... CYGNET
swanky .... STYLISH, POSH, SHOWY, PLUSH
swap .... BARTER, TRADE, EXCHANGE
swaraj .... HOME RULE
sward ..... SOD, LAWN, TURF
swarm .... TEEM, THRONG, CROWD, NEST, INVEST, OVERRUN, HIVE, SHIN, HORDE, MULTITUDE
swarmer ... BEE, LOCUST, ANT, INSECT
swarming .... TEEMING
swart(hy) ...... DARK, DUN, DUSKY
swash .... SPLASH, DASH
swastika .... FLYFOT
swat ...... BLOW, CLOUT, RAP
king of .... (BABE) RUTH
swath ..... ROW, TRACK, STRIP
swathe ..... BANDAGE, BIND, WARP(PING), ENVELOP
sway ..... OSCILLATE, SWING, ROCK, RULE, VEER, FLUCTUATE, DOMINION, CONTROL, POWER, LURCH
swear .. VOW, DEPOSE, CURSE, CUSS, PLEDGE, AFFIRM
falsely .... PERJURE
off .... RENOUNCE
word ...... PROFANITY,

CURSE, OATH
swearing .... JURANT
sweat ..... EXUDE, PERSPIRE, PERSPIRATION, FERMENT, SUDOR, TRANSUDE, EXPLOIT, HEAT, EXERCISE, SWELTER, OVERWORK, LATHER, OOZE, EGESTA
causing .... HIDROTIC
shirt .... JERSEY
sweater .... PULL-OVER, SUDORIFIC, JERSEY, SLIP-ON, CARDIGAN, GUERNSEY
Sweden .... SVERIGE
Swedish capital ... STOCKHOLM
city .. GOTEBORG, MALMO, UP(P)SALA
clover .... ALSIKE
coin .... KRONA, KRONE, ORE, CROWN
district .... LA(E)N
dwelling .... CHALET
explorer .... HEDIN
hero .... WASA
hut .... CHALET
island .. GOTLAND, OLAND
king ..... ERIC, GUSTAV, BERNADOTTE
lake .... MALAR
manual training .. SLOYD
measure .... STANG
monetary unit ... KRONA
mountain range .. KJOLEN
name .. NILS, SVEN, GRETA
native .... LAPP
"nightingale" .... (JENNY) LIND
Nobel Prize winner ..... LAGERLOF
noble's title .... GRAF
novelist ..... LAGERLOF
painter .... ZORN
parliament .... RIKSDAG
prime minister .... ERLANDER
seaport .... KALMAR, HALSINBORG, MALMO, VISBY, GOTEBORG
singer ...... YODEL(L)ER, YODLER
soprano .... LIND
turnip ...... RUTABAGA
sweeny .... ATROPHY
sweep ... BROOM, DUST, BRUSH, CLEAR, OAR, DRAG, RAKE, TRAIL, RANGE, STRETCH
sweeping .... EXTENSIVE
blow .... SWIPE
movement .... SWOOP
sweepstakes .... LOTTERY, (HORSE)RACE
sweet ..... PLEASANT, CANDY, LUSCIOUS, HONEY, DULCET, SUGARY
actress .... BLANCHE
and soft .... DOLCE
bay .... MAGNOLIA
cicely ... MYRRH, PARSLEY
clover .... MELILOT
drink .... NECTAR
flag ... CALAMUS, SEDGE
gum .... COPALM, LIQUIDAMBAR, BILSTED
liqueur .... RATAFIA, CORDIAL
natured .... DOUCE
pepper .... PIMIENTO, PAPRIKA
potato ... YAM, OCARINA, BATATA, CAMOTE
sap source ..... GOMUTI
smelling .... OLENT, FRAGRANT, ODOROUS
sound ... MUSIC, MELODY
sounding .... DULCET, MELODIOUS
tempered .... AMIABLE
sweetbread .. RUSK, PANCREAS
sweetbriar ... EGLANTINE, ROSE
sweeten .... DULCIFY
and spice .... MULL
sweetened drink .... FLIP
sweetener .... CYCLAMATE, SUCARYL, SUGAR, SACCHARIN, SYRUP,
sweetening ..... SUGAR, SIRUP, HONEY
sweetheart .... JILL, LASS(IE), LADYLOVE, VALENTINE, LOVER, BEAU, LEMAN, JO(E), PHILLIS, PHYLLIS, AMOUR, POPSY, GILL
colloquial ..... STEADY, BOY FRIEND, SWEETIE, FLAME
idealized ..... DULCINEA
sweetmeat ...... CONFECTION, CAKE, CANDY, PRESERVE, NOUGAT, DRAGEE, CARAMEL
sweetsop .... ATES, ATTA
swell .... DILATE, BULGE, SURGE, WAVE, PUFF(UP), TUMEFY, INFLATE, DISTEND, EXPAND, BLOAT, HUFF, HEAVE, INTUMESCE
colloquial ..... STYLISH, EXCELLENT, FOP
dresser ...... TOFF, FOP, DANDY, BRUMMEL, DUDE
in the ground ...... LIFT
sea .... SURF
with water .... BLOAT
swelled ..... TUMID, TURGID
swellfish .... PUFFER
swellhead .... BRAGGART
swellheaded ..... CONCEITED, BOASTFUL
swelling .... BLEB, NODE, TUMESCENT, TURGESCENCE, BULGE, PUFF, LUMP, EDEMA, TORUS, BUMP, GOITER
armpit/groin ..... BUBO
combining form .. C(O)ELE
foot .... CHILBLAIN
harmony ...... DIAPASON
wave .... ROLLER
swelter ...... PEBSPIRE, HEAT, ROAST, SWEAT
sweltering ..... SULTRY, HOT
swerve .... SHIFT, SKEW, DEVIATE, SHEER, VEER, CAREEN, DEFLECT
swift ... TANTIVY, FLEET, FAST, RAPID, BIRD, TOM
combining form .. TACHY
footed animal .... DEER, GAZELLE
footed maiden .... ATALANTA
Swift's "flying island" .... LAPUTA
hero .... GULLIVER
pen name ...... DRAPIER
swiftness ... SPEED, VELOCITY
swig .... DRINK, GULP
swiler .... SEALER
swill ... SLOP, DRINK, QUAFF, GULP, (HOG)WASH, GARBAGE
swim .... DIP, DIZZY
swimmer ...... FISH, MERMAN, NAIAD, MERMAID
swimming ... NATANT, CTENE
act of .... NATATION
bird .. SWAN, DUCK, LOON
pool ...... NATATORIUM, TANK
stroke/style ..... CRAWL, BREAST
suit .... MAILLOT
Swinburne, poet ... ALGERNON
swindle ... CHEAT, (DE)FRAUD, TRICK, SKIN, BILK, GIP, GYP, COZEN, GOUGE, WELSH, DIDDLE, BUNCO, CON, BUNKO, FLEECE, CLIP, HORNSWOGGLE
swindler ... TREPAN, SHARPER, CONMAN, FORGER, COZENER, GOUGE, JACKAL, HAWK, SHARK, CHEAT, GYP, GIP, SKIN(NER), (C)ROOK
swindling scheme ..... PLANT
swine .... HOG, PIG, PORCINE
breed .... DUROC
disease .... ROUGET, GARGET
feeding of ..... PANNAGE
female .... SOW
flesh .... PORK
genus .... SUS
male .... BOAR
young ... PORKER, PIGLET
swinelike .... PORCINE
swing ..... OSCILLATE, SWAY, HANG, STRETCH, BRANDISH, RHYTHM, SWITCH
fan .... HEPCAT
music .... JAZZ, JIVE
swinging .... PENDULOUS
swingle .... SWIP(P)LE
swink .. DRUDGE, LABOR, TOIL
swipe ... BLOW, STEAL, PILFER, HANDLE, LEVER
swipes .... BEER
swip(p)le .... FLAIL, SWINGLE
swirl ... EDDY, WHIRL, TWIST, CURL, WHORL
swirly ... TANGLED, KNOTTED
swish ... RUSTLE, FLOG, WHIP, CANE
Swiss architect .... (LE) CORBUSIER
army .... LANDWEHR
canton .... LUCERNE, TICINO, BASEL, BERN, ANE, ZURICH, VALAIS, URI, VAUD, GRISONS,

SCHWYZ, LUZERN, THURGAU, FRIBOURG
capital .... BERN(E)
castle .... CHILLON
cheese .... GRUYERE
city ..... ZURICH, BASEL, BASLE, THUN, GENEVA, BERN, LAUSSANNE, GENEVE
cottage .... CHALET
district .... CANTON, OBERLAND
Family Robinson author .. WYSS
federal council .... BUNDESRAT
herdsman .... SENN
Italian enclave .... CAMPIONE
Italian-speaking canton .. TICINO
lake .... LEMAN, ZUG, ZURICH, NEUCHATEL, LUCERNE, MAGGIORE, GENEVA, THUN, BRIENZ, BIENNE
language ... ROMANS(C)H
man of story .... TELL
mathematician .... EULER
measure ... ELLE, IM(M)I
mercenary soldier .... SWITZER, SWISSER
mountain .... RIGI, JURA, JUNGFRAU, WETTERHORN
mountain pass .. SIMPLON, BERNINA, GEMMI, KINZIG
mountaineer's horn ..... ALP(EN)HORN
native .... BRISON, VAUDOIS
painter .... KLEE
pass ... SIMPLON, GEMMI, BERNINA
patriot .... ZWINGLI
plant .... EDELWEISS
political division .... CANTON
president .... BONVIN
Protestant .... HELVETIC
psychologist ...... JUNG
resort ..... INTERLAKEN
Rhine port .. BASEL, BASLE
river .. REUSS, TICINO, AAR
scientist .... HALLER
shepherd .... SENN
sled .... LUGE
song .... YODEL
state .... CANTON
state council .. STANDERAT
town ... THUN, LOCARNO
union ...... SONDERBUND
wind .... BISE

Swisser .... SWITZER
switch .... SHUNT, ROD, TWIG, STICK, SHIFT, LASH, DIVERT, TRANSFER, (EX)CHANGE, HICKORY, RAT(T)AN, TOGGLE
blade knife .... SHIV
switchback .. ROLLER COASTER
switchman .... SHUNTER
Switzerland ...... HELVETIA, SUISSE
swivet, in a .... AGOG
swollen ..... TOROSE, TOROUS, BULGING, EDEMIC, TUMID, BOLLEN, VARICOSE, BLOATED, TURGID, TURGENT, BLOWN, DISTENDED
swoon .. FAINT(ING), SYNCOPE
swoop .... POUNCE, DESCENT, DESCEND
sword ..... RAPIER, SCIMITAR, BLADE, CUTLAS(S), ESTOC, ATAGHAN, SKEAN, GLA(I)VE, FALCHION
Archaic .... TUCK, BILBO
belt .... BALDRIC
blade, weaker part of .... FOIBLE
bulfighter's .... ESTOQUE
cavalry ... SABER, SABRE
curved .. SCIMITAR, SABER, CUTLASS, SCIMITER
fencing ...... EPEE, FOIL
fine-tempered ... TOLEDO
grass .... SEDGE
handle .... HAFT, HILT
Highlander's .. CLAYMORE
hilt's knob ..... POMMEL
knob .... POMMEL
legendary ..... BALMUNG, EXCALIBUR
lily .... GLADIOLUS
poetic .... STEEL
put to the .... KILL, SLAUGHTER
short .... SKEAN
shaped .... ENSATE, ENSIFORM, XIPHOID, GLADIATE
Siegfried's .... BALMUNG
St. George's .... ASCALON
strongest part of .. FORTE
thin .... RAPIER, TUCK
swordfish ...... DORADO, AUS
saw of .... SERRA
swordplay .... FENCING
swords, cross ... FIGHT, DUEL
swordsman ... FENCER, BLADE
sworn ..... PLEDGED, BOUND, PROMISED
word .... VOW, OATH
swound ...... FAINT, SWOON
sybarite .... EPICURE, SENSUALIST, VOLUPTUARY
sycamine .... MULBERRY
sycamore ..... BUTTON WOOD
syce .... GROOM
syconium .... FIG
sycophant ...... BOOTLICKER, FLUNK(E)Y, TOADY, YES-MAN, HANGER-ON, TOADEATER, PARASITE, FLATTERER, SPANIEL
sycosis victim .... BEARD
Syene .... ASWAN
syllabic .... SONANT
syllable, accented/unaccented THESIS, TONIC
contraction of a .... SYNALEPHA
last .... ULTIMA
metrical stress on .. ICTUS
musical .... TRA, LA
omission of last .... APOCOPE
short .... MORA
shortening of a .. SYSTOL
syllables, contraction of ...... SYNERESIS
syllabus .... SUMMARY, ABSTRACT
syllogism .... LOGIC, REASONING
middle term of .... MEAN
syllogisms, elliptical series of .. SORITES
sylph .... UNDINE, FAIRY
sylphlike .... GRACEFUL, SLENDER
sylvan .... WOODED
area .... WOODS, FOREST
diety .... SATYR, PAN, FAUN(US)
symbol (see emblem) .... EMBLEM, TOKEN, SIGN, TOTEM, MARK
American ... UNCLE SAM, EAGLE
bad luck .... OPAL
British .. JOHN BULL, LION
of achievement .. RIBBON
authority .... ROD, STAFF, SCEPTER, MACE, CROWN, BADGE, ENSIGN, GLOBE, FASCES
birth .... STORK
bondage .... YOKE
comedy .... SOCK
death ..... CROSS BONES
fortune ..... RAINBOW
grief .... RUE
hardness .... NAIL
immortality .... PH(O)ENIX
mourning ..... CREPE, CYPRESS
office .... VERGE
peace .... DOVE
plain speaking .. SPADE
purity .... LILY
royal power ..... ORB, SCEPTER
saintliness .... HALO
servitude .... YOKE
sovereignty .... MOUND
strength .... ATLAS, SINEW
success ..... RAINBOW
sun .... ATEN
universe ... MANDALGA
victory .... PALM, LAUREL
war .... MARS, ARES
wisdom .... OWL
phallic .... LINGA(M)
remembrance .... ROSEMARY
status ..... MINK, YACHT
symbolic .... TYPICAL
light .... HALO
representation .... ICONOLOGY
symbolize .... TYPIFY
symmetrical .... SPHERAL, BALANCED

symmetry ...... PROPORTION, HARMONY, BALANCE
sympathetic ...... CONGENIAL, TENDER, AGREEABLE
response .... ECHO
sympathize ..... COMMISERATE, CONDOLE
sympathy ..... CONSENT, PITY, AFFINITY, HARMONY, ACCORD, COMPASSION
expression of .... CONDOLENCE, CLEMENCY
symphonic jazz leader .... WHITEMAN
symphony form ..... SONATA
division of ... MOVEMENT
intended for Napoleon .. EROICA
third section of .. SCHERZO
symposium, kind of .... CONSENSUS
symptom ... INDICATION, SIGN, PRODROME, WARNING, FEVER, TEMPERATURE
symptoms appearing together SYNDROME
pertaining to .... SEMIOLOGY, SEMIOTIC
synagogue ..... SHUL, TEMPLE, CONGREGATION
figure .... RABBI
officer .... PARNAS
singer .... CANTOR
syncope ..... SWOON, ELISION, FAINT
syncretize .... RECONCILE, COMBINE
syncrisis .... CONTRAST
syndic .... MANAGER, MAGISTRATE
syne .... AGO, SINCE
synod ... COUNCIL, ASSEMBLY
synopsis .... SUMMARY, GIST, ABSTRACT, DIGEST, RESUME, BRIEF
synthetic ... ARTIFICIAL, SHAM
fabric .. DACRON, RAYON, ORLON, NYLON, ACETATE
rubber ...... NEOPREME, BUNA
silk ..... RAYON, NYLON
syntony .... RESONANCE
syphilis .... POX, LUES
lesion .... CHANCRE
remedy ..... SALVARSAN
test for .... HAHN
syphilitic .... LUETIO
Syria .... ARAM
Syrian .... ALAWITE, LEVANTINE, HITTITE
antelope .... ADDAX
bear .... DUBB
capital ...... DAMASCUS, ANTIOCH
city ...... ALEPPO, HOMS, PALMYRA, KADESH, HELIOPOLIS, SELEUCIA
goddess .... ASHTORETH
head of state .. AL-ATASSI
king .... ANTIOCHUS
mountain ...... HERMON
political party ... BAATII
premier .... ZAEYEN
religious follower .. DRUSE
river .... ORONTES
ruler .... ATASSI
seaport .... TRIPOLI
sect member ..... SUNNI, SHIITE
tribe ... AMALEK, SARACEN
tribesman .... DRUSE, SARACEN
weight .... COLA
syringa .... LILAC, MOCK ORANGE
syringe .... INJECTOR
syrinx .... PANPIPE
syrphus fly .... GNAT
syrup ..... SORGHUM, MAPLE, TREACLE, ORGEAT, MOLASSES
system .... METHOD, ARRANGEMENT, ORDER, ISM
betting .... PARIMUTUEL
of rule .... REGIME
of weights .... TROY
of worship ...... CULT
orderly .... COSMOS
political/social .... REGIME(N)
signals .... CODE
voting .... BALLOT
systematic .... ORDERLY, REGULAR, METHODICAL
arrangement ... SCHEMA
systematics .... TAXONOMY
systematize .... ARRANGE, ORGANIZE
syzygy .... DIPODY
Szczecin .... STETTIN
Szechwan capital ... CHENGTU
szopelka .... OBOE

T

T-bone steak .. PORTERHOUSE
Greek .... TAU
Hebrew ..... TAW, TETH, TAV, TAU
letter .... TEE
shaped .... TAU
ta, in chemistry .. TANTALUM
taa .... PAGODA
Taal .... AFRIKAANS
tab .. FLAP, LABEL, TAG, LOOP, STRAP, ACCOUNT, PAN, CHECK, BILL
colloquial ...... RECORD, RECKONING
in aeronautics ... AIRFOIL
shoe .... LATCHET, STRAP
tabanid .. (HORSE)FLY, GADFLY
tabard ...... JACKET, CLOAK, CAPE, MANTLE
tabaret ...... CLOTH, TABBY
tabasco .... SAUCE
capital of .... VILLAHERMOSA
tabby ..... MOREEN, TAFFETA, MOIRE, CAT, GOSSIP(ER), BRINDLED, SILK
taberna .. HUT, SHED, TAVERN
tabernacle .. TENT, DWELLING, SANCTUARY, SHRINE, HILET, TEMPLE, NICHE
tabes .... PHTHISIS, CONSUMPTION, ATROPHY, TUBERCULOSIS, EMACIATION
tabescent .... WASTING, WITHERING
tabetic .. CONSUMPTIVE, TABID
Tabitha .... DORCAS
table .... FURNITURE, BOARD, FOOD, POSTPONE, SHELVE, PEND, LIST(ING), DEFER, FARE, COMPILATION, FREEZE
centerpiece ... EPERGNE
cloth ... TAPIS, RUNNER, SPREAD
communion .... ALTAR, CREDENCE
companion .. MESSMATE
cover .... SCARF, BAIZE, SPREAD
decoration .... EPERGNE, DOILY, PLACEMAT
decorative cloth .... RUNNER
d'hote .... MEAL
game .. POOL, PINGPONG
in architecture .... CORNICE, MOLDING, PANEL
linen .. NAPERY, NAPKIN, DAMASK
napkin ...... SERVIETTE
of content .... INDEX
of the .... MENSAL
on wheels .. TEA WAGON
scrap .... ORT
server .... WAITER
subject with junior ..... SPINACH
tennis .... PINGPONG
three-legged .... TRIVET
top's section ..... LEAF
with drawers ...... DESK
writing .... ESCRITOIRE, SECRETARY
tableau ..... PICTURE, SCENE
tableland ... KAR(R)OO, MESA, PLATEAU, PUNA
tablet .... PAD, SLAB, TESSERA, STELE, FACIA, PILL, SLATE
blank ..... TABULA RASA
medicinal ..... TABLOID, TROCHE, LOZENGE, COUGH DROP
religious .... PAX
reused ...... PALIMPSEST
scroll-like .. CARTOUCH(E)
writing .. TRIPTYCH, SLATE
tableware item .. DISH, KNIFE, FORK, SPOON
tabloid .. TROCHE, NEWSPAPER
taboo .. BAN, TABU, VERBOTEN, PROHIBITION, PROHIBITED, FORBID(DEN)

opposite of .... NOA
tabor ...... DRUM, TIMBREL, TABOURET, AT(T)ABAL
taboret .... STOOL, STAND
Tabriz native ..... IRANI(AN)
tabu ...... TABOO, VERBOTEN, FORBIDDEN
tabular .... FLAT
tabulate .... LIST
tacamahac ...... GUM RESIN, POPLAR
tache .... BUCKLE, HOOK
tachina .... FLY
tacit ...... STILL, SOUNDLESS, UNSPOKEN, IMPLIED, IMPLICIT
taciturn ... SILENT, RETICENT, RESERVED, SATURNINE
one ...... INDIAN, CLAM
opposite of .... GARRULOUS, TALKATIVE, LOQUACIOUS
tack ...... NAIL, PIN, STITCH, ZIGZAG, FOOD, ATTACH, ADD, JIBE, SEW, BASTE, BRAD
room item .... SPUR SADDLE, STIRRUP
tackle .... GEAR, APPARATUS, SEIZE, UNDERTAKE, CAT, GRASP, LUFF, RIG
hoisting .. CAT, GARNET
in football ..... THROW, STOP
ship's .... JEERS
small .... JIGGER
tacky ...... DOWDY, SHABBY, SEEDY, STICKY,
Tacoma mount ..... RAINIER
tact ...... POISE, DIPLOMACY, SAVOIR-FAIRE, DELICACY, FINESSE
tactics .... MANEUVERS, STRATEGEM, STRATEGY, PLOY
tactile .... TANGIBLE
taction .... TOUCH, CONTACT
tactless ..... RUDE, IMPOLITE, GAUCHE
act .... GAUCHERIE, FAUX PAS
tad .. CHILD, TOT, YOUNGSTER
Tadmor .... PALMYRA
tadpole .. POLLIWOG, LARVA, POLLYWOG
Tadzhik's capital .... STALINABAD
taels, 16 .... CATTY
taenia .... FILLET, HEADBAND, TAPEWORM
taffarel .... TAFFRAIL
taffeta .... TABBY, FLORID, DAINTY, GAUDY, SAMITE
taffrail .... TAFFEREL
taffy .... CANDY, TOFFEE
colloquial .... FLATTERY
tafia .... RUM
Taft, sculptor ...... LORADO
tag .... LABEL, A(I)GLET, QUOTATION, TAIL END, LOCK, FOLLOW, TALLY, APPEND
end .... REMNANT
game chaser .... IT
Tagalog (see Philippines) ..... MALAYAN, FILIPINO
Tagore's forte ...... POETRY
Tagus .... TEJO, TAJO
city on the ..... TOLEDO
Tahiti, capital of ... PAPEETE
former name .. OTAHEITE
god .... ORO
Tahitian .... POLYNESIAN
canoe .... PAHI
god .... TAAROA, ORO
peaks .... MOOREA
people ..... POLYNESIAN
seaport .... PAPEETE
Tai .... THAI
taiga .... FORESTS
Taihoku .... TAIPEH
tail .. BUSH, SCUT, FLEE, HIND, REAR END, CUE, BUNT, QUEUE, RETINUE, SHADOW, FOLLOW, TAG
bushy .... BRUSH
coin's .... VERSO
colloquial ... DETECTIVE, SHADOWER
combining form .... URO
deer's/hare's .... SCUT
docked .... BOB
end .... TAG, REAR
ender .... LAST
feathers .... TRAIN
having .... CAUDATE
hood .... LIRIPIPE
like .... CAUDAL
pertaining to a .. CAUDAL
plane ...... STABILIZER
rabbit's .... SCUT
solid part .... DOCK
turn .... FLEE, RETREAT
word with ... BOB, HIGH, CAT
tailing ...... WASTE, REFUSE
tailless .. ACAUDAL, ANUROUS, ACAUDATE
amphibian .. TOAD, FROG, BATRACHIIA
tailor .... FIT, FASHION, BUSHELMAN, CLOTHIER, SNYDER, SARTOR
concern of .. FIT, STYLE
pattern of .. DELINEATOR
pressing iron of .. GOOSE
vent of .... SLIT
work of ...... SARTORIAL
tailors, of .... SARTORIAL
tain .... (TIN)FOIL, TIN PLATE
taint .... INFECT, SPOIL, STAIN, INFECT(ION), SULLY, COLOR, DYE, CONTAMINATE, TINGE, POLLUTE
Taipeh .... TAIHOKU
Taisho emperor .. YOSHIHITO
Taiwan .... FORMOSA
capital of ...... TAIPEH, TAIPEI
city .... TAINAN
deer .... SIKA
government .... KUOMINTANG
islands ...... PESCADORES
legislature .... YUAN
port .... KEELUNG
premier .... YEN
president ...... CHIANG
tea .... OOLONG
Taj Mahal ..... MAUSOLEUM
builder .... (SHAH) JAHAN
site of .... AGRA
take .. OCCUPY, WIN, GRASP, CHARM, OBTAIN, ACQUIRE, ASSUME, EAT, DRINK, BUY, ABSORB, RENT, LEASE, USE, ADOPT, ACCEPT, RECEIVE, PRESUME
a breather .... REST
a liking to ...... COTTON
amiss .. MISTAKE, RESENT
as one's own ..... ADOPT
back .. RETRACT, RECANT, RETURN
by force ...... CAPTURE, GRAB, USURP, WREST, COMMANDEER, SEIZE, CATCH, SNATCH
down .... NOTE, RECORD, WRITE
edge off .. DULL, BLUNT, OBTUND
effect .... INURE
exception .... DEMUR
forcibly .. WREST, REAVE
in ...... ADMIT, CHEAT, RECEIVE
into custody .. IMPOUND
it on the lam ... ESCAPE, FLEE
off ...... DEDUCT, FLEE, START, LEAVE, DOFF, REMOVE, DEPART
offense .... RESENT
on .... ASSUME, EMPLOY, OPPOSE, HIRE
out .. EXTRACT, REMOVE, ABSTRACT, DELE(TE), EXPUNGE, ELIDE
over .... ASSUME
part ...... PARTICIPATE
place ... OCCUR, HAPPEN, SUPERVENE
potshot at .... SNIPE
shape .... LOOM
slang .... CHEAT, TRICK, RECEIPT, PROFIT
the character of .... IMPERSONATE
time .... DELAY, LINGER, LOAF
to ____ .... TASK
umbrage .... RESENT
unfair share .... HOG
up again .... RESUME
up dare .. CONTEND, VIE, FIGHT, DEFY
taken aback ...... STARTLED, SURPRISED, DUMBFOUNDED
taking .. WINNING, INFECTIOUS
takings ... PROFITS, RECEIPTS
talapoin ... GUENON, MONKEY, MONK
talaria, location of ... ANKLES
of Hermes .... SANDALS, WINGS
talc ...... STEATITE, POWDER, SOAPSTONE, AGALITE
talcum ...... POWDER, TALC
tale ..... NARRATIVE, GOSSIP, FICTION, MARCHEN, REDE, FALSEHOOD, YARN, LEGEND

adventure ...... CONTE, GEST(E)
bearer ...... GOSSIP(ER), BUSYBODY, SCANDALMONGER
epic .... SAGA, ILIAD, AENEID
medieval .... LAI
of lamentation/woe ..... JEREMIAD
of Two Cities heroine ... LUCIE
tall ... FISH STORY, YARN
talent .... GIFT, GENIUS, ABILITY, ENDOWMENT, APTITUDE, KNACK, SKILL, FACULTY, FLAIR
natural .. DOWER, DOWRY
talented ...... GIFTED, ABLE
tales .. WRIT, JUROR(S), VENIRE
talesman .... JUROR
Talien(wan) .. DAIREN, DALNY
taliera .... TARA
talion .... REVENGE, PUNISHMENT
taliped .... CLUBFOOTED
talipes .... CLUBFOOT
talipot .... PALM
talisman .... OBEAH, OBI, AMULET, CHARM, FETISH, GRIGRI
beetle .... SCARAB
talk .. CONVERSATION, UTTER, CONSULT, DISCUSS, YABBER, CONFER(ENCE), JAW, CHIN, SPEECH, BLAT, PALAVER, SPEAK, LECTURE
abusive .... JAW
back ..... SASS, RETORT, RIPOSTE, COMEBACK, REJOINDER
big .... BRAG, BOAST
boastful .... GAS, BRAG, BLUSTER, CRACK, GASCONADE
chatty ..... GOSSIP, GAB
childishly .... DROLL, SLOBBER
down .... SILENCE
effusively .... GUSH
empty .. CHATTER, CANT, PATTER, BUNCOMBE, BULL, HUMBUG, GAS, HOGWASH, MOONSHINE, CLAPTRAP, FUDGE
evil ...... MALEDICTION, CURSE
excited ..... RANT, RAVE
flippant ..... PERSIFLAGE
foolish .. TATTLE, BABBLE, BLAB(BER), DROOL, BLATHER, GAB, DRIVEL, TWADDLE, PRATTLE, BULL, CHATTER, TWATTLE, FAPDOODLE, MOONSHINE, PRATE, POPPYCOCK
fresh .... LIP
friendly ..... COSE, COZE
from pulpit .... SERMON, HOMILY
glib .. PALAVER, PATTER
hearsay .. GOSSIP, RUMOR
impudent ..... SASS, LIP
incoherent(ly) .... GIBBER(ISH), JABBER, MAUNDER
informal .... (CHIT)CHAT, CAUSERIE
insincere .... BUNCOMBE
insincerely ...... PALTER
light .... CHAFF, BANTER, RAILLERY, PERSIFLAGE
made for effect .... BUNCOMBE
meaningless ...... CANT, MALARK(E)Y, PATTER, PIFFLE
melodramatic ... HEROICS
moral .. SERMON, HOMILY
noisily .... YAUP, YAWP, YAP
noisy .. YAP, RANT, BLAT, JANGLE
nonsensical ..... PIFFLE, JABBER
offensive .... JAW
out of .... PERSUADE, DISSUADE
over .... DISCUSS
peevishly .... CARP
persistently on something HARP
pert .... LIP
pointless .... TWADDLE, SLIPSLOP
pompous ..... FUSTIAN, BOMBAST
quiet(ly) ..... WHISPER, MURMUR
rapid .. CHATTER, PATTER
sales ..... SPIEL, PATTER
senseless ... BALDERDASH
sentimental ...... SLUSH
silly ..... CACKLE, BULL, DROOL, FLUMMERY
small ... PATTER, GOSSIP
solemn .... SERMON, HOMILY
stupid .... DROOL
to oneself .. SOLILOQUIZE
vernacular .... CANT, JARGON, LINGO
while crying .. BLUBBER
with another .. CONVERSE, CONVERSATION, DIALOGUE
talkative .... GARRULOUS, LOQUACIOUS, VOLUBLE, MOUTHY, GASSY, GABBY
bird .. MAGPIE, (BLUE)JAY
person .... JAY, MAGPIE, CHATTERBOX
talked about .... NOTORIOUS
talker, incessant .... GASBAG, CHATTERBOX, MAGPIE
talking dummy ...... SNERD
fond of .... LOQUACIOUS, GARRULOUS
picture .... TALKIE
to ... SCOLDING, REBUKE
tall .... HIGH, EXAGGERATED, HUGE, HIGHFLOWN, LOFTY, TAUNT
and lean .. LANKY, LATHY
chest .... HIGHBOY
tale .... YARN
tallboy .... CHEST
Tallchief, ballerina ... MARIA
tallest animal .... GIRAFFE
tallier .. SCORER, SCOREKEEPER
Tallinn .... REVEL, REVAL
tallith .... SHAWL, SCARF
tallow .... FAT, SUET, STEARIN
product .. CANDLE, SOAP
tree .... CERA, ROKA
tally ...... SCORE, ACCOUNT, LABEL, TAG, AGREE, JIBE, CORRESPOND, NOTCH, TAB, SQUARE, MATCH, REGISTER, CHALK UP
tallyho .... COACH, CRY
crier .... HUNTER
Talmud, part of .... GEMARA, MISHNA(H), HALAKAH, HALACHA, HAGGADA(H)
Talmudic anecdote/parable .. HAGGADA(H)
talon .. OGEE, POUNCE, CLAW, NAIL, STOCK, FANG, ZIPPER, HALLUX
Talos ... WATCHMAN, MISSILE
killer of ..... DAEDALUS
make of .... BRASS
talus .... SCREE, ANKLE(BONE), ASTRAGALUS, SLOPE, HUCKLEBONE
tam-o'-shanter .... CAP
tam .... GONG
tamandu(a) .... ANTEATER
tamarack ...... LARCH, TREE
tamarau .. BUFFALO, CARABAO
tamarin .... MARMOSET
tamarind, Philippine .... SAMPALOC
tamarisk salt tree ... ATLE(E)
tambour ... DRUM, TABORET, EMBROIDERY
tambourine .... DRUM, DAIRA, TABOR, TIMBREL, RIKK, DAIRE, TAAR
tame .. BREAK, DOMESTICATE, DOCILE, GENTLE, SERVILE, DULL, SUBDUE, BUST
tameness ...... MANSUETUDE, GENTLENESS, DOCILITY
tamer, wild horse .. COWBOY, BRONC(H)OBUSTER
Tamerlane ...... TIMURLENK
author of book ..... POE
Tamil .... DRAVIDIAN
Tamiroff, actor .... AKIM
Tammany Society official .... SACHEM
tamp .. PACK, POUND, THUMP
tamper .... PLOT, BRIBE, CHANGE, TINKER, MEDDLE, POUNDER, ALTER, CORRUPT
Tampico man .... SENOR
tampion ..... STOPPER, PLUG
tampon .... PLUG
tan .... BARK, TANNIN, FLOG, WHIP, BEIGE, DUN, TAW, ROSS, TAWNY, (EM)BROWN, SUNBURN, ECRU, BUFF
believe it or not! .... LUGGAGE
tanager .. SONGBIRD, REDBIRD
tanbark .... NAPA, ROSS

tandem .. BICYCLE, CARRIAGE
tang ...... TASTE, GUST, NIP, ODOR, TOUCH, TRACE, FLAVOR
Tanganyika merged with Zanzibar .. TANZANIA
mountain .. KILIMANJARO
town .... UJIJI
tangent .... TOUCHING, ADJACENT
tangerine.......... ORANGE, MANDARIN
crossed with grapefruit/pomelo .... TANGELO
tangible .. TACTILE, DEFINITE, PERCEPTIBLE, PALPABLE
tangle .. TRAP, SNARL, SLEAVE, KNOT, MUDDLE, WEAVE, INTERTWINE, SEAWEED, EMBROIL, MIX-UP
tangled mass .... SHAG, MAT, RAVEL
Tanis .... ZOAN
tank ...... POOL, STEW, VAT, POND, CISTERN
destroyer .... BAZOOKA, HALF-TRACK
farming ... HYDROPONICS
fish .... AQUARIUM
gunner's place .. TURRET
hot water .... BOILER
military .... MARK, SHERMAN
oil .... BUNKER
rainwater ...... CISTERN
tankard .. CUP, MUG, POTTLE, STOUP
tanker .... OILER, BUNKER
tanned hide .. LEATHER, CROP
tanning bark .... ALDER, KOA
material ..... SUMAC(H), CATECHU, CATECHIN, CASHOO, KINO, FURAN, QUEBRACHO, GAMBIER
powdered leaves .... SUMAC(H)
tantalize .. TITILLATE, TEASE, BEWITCH
Tantalus .... STAND
daughter of ...... NIOBE
father of .... ZEUS
punishment of .. THIRST, HUNGER
son of .... PELOPS
tantamount ..... EQUIVALENT
tantara .. FANFARE, FLOURISH, BLAST
tantivy .. SWIFT, FAST, GALLOP, HEADLONG
tantrum ..... OUTBURST, FIT, RAVE, CONNIPTION, RAGE, HUFF
Tanzania capital .... DAR ES SALAAM
city/seaport .. ZANZIBAR
island .... PEMBA
part of .... TANGANYIKA, ZANZIBAR
president ...... NYERERE
tap .... PLUG, CORK, BAR, BROACH, SPILE, RAP, KNOCK, FAUCET, STOPPER, LIQUOR, DRAW, TIT, COCK, SPIGOT, DECANT, DRAFT, FLIP
chin .... CHUCK
dancer .. HOOFER, ASTAIRE
tapa cloth source .. MULBERRY
wearer .... POLYNESIAN
tape ..... BAND, STRIP, DEMO
braided .... INKLE
taper .. CANDLE, WANE, WICK, LIGHT, DECREASE, LESSEN
tapered ..... TERETE, CONOID
tapering object .... CONE, PYRAMID, SPIRE, VOLCANO, SHIM
to a point .... SUBULATE
tapestry .... DOSSEL, DOSSAL, GOBELIN, ARRAS, TAPIS, DOSSER
tapeworm .. CESTODE, CESTOID, T(A)ENIA
drug .... TENIACIDE, TENIAFUGE
head of .... SCOLEX
infestation .. T(A)ENIASIS
larva .... COENURUS, CYSTICERCUS, MEASLES
sucker .... OSCULUM
taphouse ... INN, BAR(ROOM), TAVERN
tapioca source .... CAS(S)AVA, MANIOC, MANIHOT
tapir ..... UNGULATE, DANTA
animal resembling .. HOG
pride of a .... SNOUT
tapis .... TAPESTRY
tapper .... TELEGRAPHER
tappet .... CAM
tapping sound .. TICK, DRUM
tappings .... SAP
taproom .... BAR, SALOON
taps instrument ...... BUGLE, DRUM
series of .... PATTER
tapster .. BARMAID, BARTENDER
Tapuyan .... INDIAN, GES
tar .... SAILOR, BREA, PITCH, MALTHA, GOB, MARINER, SALT, ALCHITRAN
tarantas(s) .... CARRIAGE
tarantula .... SPIDER
tarboosh .... CAP, FEZ
tardy .. BELATED, LATE, SLOW, OVERDUE, DELAYED
tare ..... DEDUCTION, VETCH, WEED
allowance additional to .. TRET
Tarentum .... TARANTO
targe ...... BUCKLER, SHIELD
target ..... AIM, MARK, BUTT, CLOUT, OBJECTIVE, GOAL
center of .... BLANK, EYE
circle .... INNER
easy ...... SITTING DUCK
finder .... RADAR, SONAR
get on .... ZERO
knight's ...... QUINTAIN
mound behind .... BUTT
of blame .... SCAPEGOAT
practice place ... RANGE
range .... BUTTS
shooting gallery .. DUCK
shooting post .... MANT(E)LET
towed .... DROGUE
white cloth ...... CLOUT
Tarheel .... CAROLINIAN
tariff .... TAX, LIST, DUTY
Tarkington, novelist .. BOOTH
tarlatan .... MUSLIN
tarn .... LAKE, LOCH
location ..... MOUNTAIN
tarnation .... DAMNED, DAMNATION
tarnish .... DULL, SULLY, BESMIRCH, STAIN, BLEMISH, SOIL
taro dish .... POI
fermented in pit .... MOD
root ..... ED(D)O, GABI, KALO
sprouts .... DASHEEN
tarot .... CARD
tarpaulin .... CANVAS
tarpon .. MILKFISH, GAMEFISH, SABALO, SILVERFISH
Tarquin's avenger ... PORSENA
tarradiddle .... FIB
tarry .. LOITER, LINGER, WAIT, STAY, SOJOURN, BIDE
tarsal bone .... CALCANEUS
tarsus .... ANKLE, HOCK
tart ..... FLAN, SOUR, SHARP, HUSSY, KEEN, ACID(ULOUS), CUTTING, (FRUIT)PIE, PASTRY, WANTON, TRAMP
tartan .... PLAID, SHIP, HIGHLANDER
trousers .... TREWS
Tartar .... TATAR, TURK
emetic ...... MORDANT, EXPECTORANT
wine cask .... ARGAL, ARGOL
Tartarus .... HADES, HELL
Tartuf(f)e ...... HYPOCRITE, COMEDY
author .... MOLIERE
Tarzan's mate .... JANE
task ...... JOB, STINT, ONUS, ASSIGNMENT, DUTY
force .... COMMANDO
menial ...... DRUDGERY
routine .... CHORE
take to ... SCOLD, REBUKE
tedious .... GRIND
taskmaster .... OVERSEER SLAVE DRIVER, LEGREE
Tasman, Dutch navigator .... ABEL
Tasmanian capital ... HOBART
devil .... DASYURE
discoverer ...... TASMAN
phalanger .... TAPOA
pine .... HUON
river .... DERWENT
tiger/wolf ... THYLACINE
tass .... GOBLET, CUP, DRAFT
tassel ...... TUFT, CORNSILK, TERCEL, ZIZITH
taste ... PALATE, EXPERIENCE, FLAVOR, BENT, SAPO(U)R, GUSTO, TANG, DEGUST, SAVOR, LIKING, PREFERENCE, PENCHANT
daintily .... SIP
distinctive .... TANG,

SMACK, FLAVOR
for something ... TOOTH
having ...... SAPOROUS
kind of ... SOUR, SWEET, BITTER, SALTY
offensive .... RANK
try the .... SAMPLE
tasteful ..... REFINED, SAPID, TASTY, DISCRIMINATING, ELEGANT
luxury ...... ELEGANCE
tasteless ...... FLAT, INSIPID, STALE, VAPID
taster ...... SAMPLER, SIPPER STATE, VAPID
taster ...... SAMPLER, SIPPER
tasty ..... LUSCIOUS, SAVORY, PALATABLE, SAPID, TOOTHSOME, FLAVORFUL, DELICIOUS
colloquial ...... YUMMY
Tatar .. TARTAR, MONGOLIAN, TURK
capital .... KAZAN
drink .... KUMISS, KOUMIS(S)
ruler .... CHAM
tater .... POTATO
tatouay .... ARMADILLO
tatter ... RAG, SCRAP, SHRED, DAG, TAG
tattered .... DUDDY, DUDDIE, RAGGED
tatterdemalion .. RAGAMUFFIN
tattersall .... CHECKERED
tatters .... RAGS, RIBBONS
tattle ...... CHATTER, GOSSIP, BLAB, PEACH
tattler .... SANDPIPER, GOSSIP
tattoo .. DOT, MARK, SIGNAL, SUMMON, PINK
tau .... TEE, TAV
cross ...... ANKH, CRUX
taunt .... TALL, MOCK, SCOFF, RIDICULE, NEEDLE, GIBE, TWIT, JEER, REPROACH, JEST, JAPE
taupe .... GRAY
taurine animal .... BULL
Taurus .... BULL, CONSTELLATION
cluster .... HYAD(E)S
taut ..... FIRM, SNUG, TENSE, TIDY, TIGHT, TRIM, EDGY, STIFF, NERVOUS
tautog .... BLACKFISH, CHUB, MOLL
tautology .... PLEONASM, REDUNDANCE
tav .... TEE, TAU
tavern .... SALOON, INN, PUB, HOSTEL, BISTRO, KHAN, TAPROOM, ALEHOUSE, ROADHOUSE, ORDINARY, POTHOUSE
character .. BARFLY, SOT, TOPER
server .... POTBOY, BARMAID
taw .... MIB, AGATE, MARBLE, ALLEY
tawdry ..... SLEAZY, GAUDY, SHOWY, CHEAP, RAFFISH, GINGERBREAD
tawny .. TAN, DUSKY, SWART, RUBIATE
tax .... TITHE, LEVY, IMPOST, CESS, SCOT, SCAT(T), ASSESS, EXCISE, SESS
church .... TITHE
collector ...... OCTROI, CATCHPOLL, CATCHPOLE
commodity ..... OCTROI, DUTY, TARIFF, EXCISE
evader's nemesis .. TMAN
export/import ... TARIFF
feudal .... TALLAGE
man .... PUBLICAN
municipal .... OCTROI
official .... ASSESSOR
on ship ...... TONNAGE
privilege .... TOLL
protection ..... TRIBUTE
schedule .... TARIFF
substitute ..... SCUTAGE
taxable .... RAT(E)ABLE
taxi .... CAB, HACK
driver .. HACK, CABMAN, CABETTE
2-wheeled ...... HANSOM
taxicab .... HACK
parking space .... STAND
taxman .... PUBLICAN
taximeter for one .... ODOGRAPH, ODOMETER
taxonomy subject .... CLASSIFICATION, SYSTEMATICS
Taygeta ...... PLEIAD, STAR
Taylor, actress .... LIZ
composer, critic .. DEEMS
poet, writer .... BAYARD
U.S. president .... ZACHARY
tazza ..... CUP, VASE, BOWL
Tchaikovsky opus .... PATHETIQUE
Te Deum .... HYMN
hee .... TITTER, SNICKER, GIGGLE
tea ...... RECEPTION, PEKOE, PARTY, PARAGUAY, HOLLY, MATE, CHA(A), LAPSANG, TSIA, TCHA, LEDUM, YERBA, PTISAN, OSWEGO, CAMBRIC
add liquor to ...... LACE
alkaloid .... CAFFEIN(E)
beverage like .... CAMOMILE, BEEF
bitter principle .. THEINE
black .... PEKOE, BOHEA, CONGO(U), OOLONG, OOPAK, SOUCHONG
bowl .... CHAWAN
box ... CANISTER, CADDY
brand .. LIPTON, TETLEY, SALADA
caffeine .... THEINE
cake .... SCONE
container .... CADDY
decoction ...... TISANE
drink .... CAMBRIC
green .... HYSON
plant .... THEA
pot ...... URN, SAMOVAR, KETTLE
serve .... POUR
substitute ...... YAUPON
table .... TEAPOY
waterboiler for .... POT, URN, KETTLE, SAMOVAR
teaberry .... WINTERGREEN
teacake .... SCONE
teach ..... TRAIN, INSTRUCT, EDUCATE, DRILL, COACH, SCHOOL, TUTOR, DRILL, EDIFY
Edward ... BLACKBEARD, PRIVATEER, PIRATE
teacher .. TUTOR, PROFESSOR, MENTOR, INSTRUCTOR, RABBI, MULLA(H), PUNDIT, PEDAGOG(UE), DON, GURU, PRECEPTOR
bird .... WARBLER, VIREO
gift to .... APPLE
movie ...... (MR.) CHIPS
narrow-minded .. PEDANT
of music, great .... MAESTRO
of the deaf ..... ORALIST
pointer of .... FESCUE
unattached ..... DOCENT
teachers' group .... NEA
teaching .. TUITION, TUTELAGE, INSTRUCTION, PEDAGOGY
science of ... DIDACTICS, PEDAGOGY
teachings .... PRECEPT, DOCTRINE
teak ..... TREE, WOOD, TEGA
teakettle spout ...... NOZZLE
teal .... DUCK, BLUE
team (see baseball, football) ... JOIN, PAIR
athletic .... SQUAD
baseball .... NINE
basketball .. FIVE, QUINTET
cricket .... ELEVEN
football .... ELEVEN
of two animals ... SPAN, YOKE
rowing .... CREW
second placer .... RUNNER-UP
working ... CREW, GANG
teamster .... DRIVER, CARTER, CARRIER
teapot .... SAMOVAR, KETTLE
cover .... COS(E)Y
tear .. REND, RIP, LACERATE, SPLIT, DISRUPT, RIVE, RENT, TATTER, JAG, LANCINATE
down .... WRECK, DEMOLISH, DISMANTLE, RAZE
gas ...... LAC(H)RIMATOR
into ...... ATTACK, RIP
jerker .... SAD, SENTIMENTAL
limb from limb .... DISMEMBER
slang .. SPREE, CAROUSAL
teardrop diamond cut .... BRIOLETTE
tearful .... SAD, CRYING, WEEPING, LAC(H)RYMOSE
mother .... NIOBE
tearing apart .... DIVULSION

for .... LANIARY
tears, of .... LACHRIMAL, LACHRYMAL
teary lady .... NIOBE
Teasdale, poetess ...... SARA
tease ..... TANTALIZE, COMB, CARD, ANNOY, MOCK, RIDE, NEEDLE, HECTOR, RIB, HARASS, IMPORTUNE, VEX, TWIT, KID
teasel .... FLOWER, BURR, BONESET, HERB
teaser ..... PUZZLE(R), POSER
teasing, good-natured .. CHAFF
teat .. NIPPLE, TIT, MAMMILLA, PAP, DUG
Tebaldi, Met star ... RENATA
technetium .... MASARIUM
technical .... SPECIALIZED
technician .... EXPERT
technique ..... METHOD, ART, PROCEDURE
techy .... PEEVISH, IRRITABLE, SENSITIVE, TOUCHY
ted .... SPREAD, SCATTER
teddy .... BEAR
tedious ... BORING, TIRESOME, MONOTONOUS, HUMDRUM, IRKSOME, DREARY, WEARISOME
tedium .... BOREDOM, ENNUI, MONOTONY
tee .... TAU, MOUND
hee .... TITTER, SNICKER, GIGGLE
shaped thing .... ANKH, CRUX
to green .... HOLE
teem ...... ABOUND, SWARM, EMPTY, POUR
teenager ...... BOBBY SOXER, YOUTH
favorite record of .... TOP TEN
teeny .... TINY, WEE
teepee .... LODGE, WIGWAM, WICKIUP
teeter ...... SEESAW, WAVER, WOBBLE, VACILLATE, SWAY
teeth (see tooth) .... INCISORS, MOLARS, CUSPIDS, GRINDERS
arrangement .. DENTITION
artificial..... DENTURE, PLATE
cleaning substance ...... DENTIFRICE
click of .... CHATTER
coating .... ENAMEL
colloquial .... GRINDERS
combining form .... DENT(I), ODONT(O)
decay .... CARIES
deposit .... TARTAR
doctor .... DENTIST
extraction .. EXODONTIA
hard part of .. DENTIN(E), IVORY
having .... DENTATE, TOOTHED
having large .... MACRODONT
having small .... MICRODONT
long pointed ... TUSHES, TUSKS, FANGS
of .... DENTAL
science dealing with .... DENTISTRY, ODONTOLOGY
set of .... DENTURE
shaped ..... DENTIFORM, DENTOID
sharp .... FANGS
slang .... IVORIES
small .... DENTICLES
sockets .... ALVEOLI
sound .. GNASH, CHATTER
tearing .... LANIARY
without ..... EDENTATE
teething process .. DENTITION
toy .... CORAL
teethridge .... ALVEOLUS
teetotaler .... NON-DRINKER, ABSTAINER, DRY, NAZARITE
teetotalism .... TEMPERANCE, ABSTINENCE
teetotum .... TOP
tegmen .... COVERING, TEGUMENT
Tegucigalpa is capital of ..... HONDURAS
tegula .... ALULA, TILE
tegular .... TILE-LIKE
tegument ..... TEGMEN, SKIN, ARIL
Tehuelche ...... PATAGONIAN
teil .... LINDEN
Tejo .... TAGUS
Tel Aviv greeting ... SHALOM
tela .. MEMBRANE, TISSUE, WEB
telar .... WEBLIKE
telamon .. ATLANTES, BEARER
son of .... AJAX
telecast .... TELEVISE
telegram ..... MESSAGE, WIRE
slower ...... DAYLETTER
telegraph .... CABLE
code .... MORSE
jungle .... TOM-TOM
kind of ...... GRAPEVINE
lever ..... KEY, TAPPER
part .... KEY, TAPPER
signal .... DOT, DASH
wire support .... PYLON
telegraphic device for quotations TICKER
Telemachus' parent .... PENELOPE, ODYSSEUS/ULYSSES
telemeter ..... RANGE FINDER
teleost fish .... EEL
telephone ... CALL, RING(UP)
diaphragm .. TYMPANUM
exchange ..... CENTRAL, SWITCHBOARD
inventor .... BELL
main line ...... TRUNK
operator .... CENTRAL
wire .... LINE
telescope .... FIELD GLASS, BINOCLE, BINOCULAR, TUBE, SPYGLASS
attached to another ..... FINDER
measuring device ...... MICROMETER
opening ...... APERTURE
telescopic .... FARSEEING
telestic(h) .. ACROSTIC, POEM
television (see TV) ... VIDEO, TELLY
ad .... COMMERCIAL
"magic" .... COLOR
radar air navigation .... TELERAN
tube .... ICONOSCOPE
tell .... RELATE, RECOUNT, NARRATE, REPORT, REVEAL, RECITE, INFORM, ORDER
it to ____ ..... SWEENEY
it to the ____ .. MARINES, JUDGE
off ..... REBUKE, SCOLD
on .... INFORM TIRE, PEACH, SQUEAL
privately ...... WHISPER
slang .... RAT
teller ..... NARRATOR, CLERK, CASHIER
place of .... CAGE
window of ..... WICKET
telling .. STRIKING, FORCEFUL, COGENT, EFFECTIVE
telltale .. TATTLER, INDICATOR
tellurian .... EARTHMAN, EARTHLY, TERRESTIAL
telluride .... HESSITE
Tellus' domain .... EARTH
telson ...... SOMITE, SEGMENT
Telugu .... DRAVIDIAN
temblor ...... (EARTH)QUAKE, TREMOR
temerarious .. RASH, RECKLESS
temerity .. AUDACITY, NERVE, GALL, EFFRONTERY, CHEEK, RASHNESS, BOLDNESS
temper .... MODERATE, MOOD, DISPOSITION, COMPOSURE, RAGE, DANDER, (AN)NEAL, PET, SPIRIT, TANTRUM, QUALITY, CHARACTER, TONE
bad .... SPLEEN
kind of .... IRISH
of ugly .... ORNERY
tempera painting ...... SECCO
temperament .... DISPOSITION, NATURE, MOOD
condition of .. CHOLERIC, SANGUINE, BILIOUS, PHLEGMATIC, MELANCHOLIC
temperamental ... EXCITABLE, MOODY, TESTY
temperance ..... MODERATION, ABSTINENCE, SOBRIETY
temperate .. MODERATE, MILD, ABSTEMIOUS, SOBER
temperature regulator .... THERMOSTAT, CRYOSTAT
tempest ..... STORM, TUMULT
tempestuous .... VIOLENT, TURBULENT, STORMY
Templar .. CRUSADER, KNIGHT
temple ..... CHURCH, CELLA, NAOS, FANE, SANCTUARY, PAGODA, RATH(A), MOSQUE, BASILICA, TABERNACLE, JOSS HOUSE
Aztec .... TEOPAN

chamber .... NAOS, CELLA
Chinese .... PAGODA
for all gods .. PANTHEON
gateway .... TORII
girl .... BAYADERE, BAYADEER
Jupiter's ...... CAPITOL
innermost parts .... PENETRALIA
shrine .... ADYTUM
tempo .... PACE, SPEED, RATE, RHYTHM, TIME, BEAT, TAKT
temporal .. CIVIL, TRANSITORY, TRANSIENT, WORLDLY, SECULAR, MUNDANE
temporary .. INTERIM, ACTING, PROVISIONAL
amnesia .... FUGUE
temporize ...... STALL, HEDGE
tempt .... LURE, ENTICE, INDUCE, PROVOKE, SEDUCE
tempter .... DEVIL, SATAN
tempting .... SEDUCTIVE, ATTRACTIVE
temptress .. EVE, SIREN, CIRCE, LORELEI, ENCHANTRESS, DELILAH
ten .... 10, DECAD(E)
ares .... DECARE
cents .... DIME
combining form .... DEC(A), DEKA
Commandments .... DECALOG(UE)
cubic meters .. DECASTERE
decibels .... BEL
dollar gold piece .. EAGLE
gallon hat .... SOMBRERO
group of .... DECADE
legged crustacean .... LOBSTER, PRAWN, MACRURAN, SHRIMP
per center ...... AGENT
pfennig coin .. GROSCHEN
rins .... SEN
sided ...... DECAGONAL
square meters .. DECIARE
thousand ...... MYRIAD
times as large .. DECUPLE
year period ... DECADE, DECENNIAL, DECENNIUM, DECEN(N)ARY
tenace .... QUEENLACE, KING-JACK
tenacious .... RETENTIVE, PERSISTENT, STUBBORN, CLINGY
animal .... BULLDOG
follower .. TAIL, SHADOW
tenancy .... OCCUPANCY
tenant .. VILLEIN, OCCUPANT, INHABITANT, VASSAL, LESSEE, RENTER, INMATE, RESIDENT
tench .... CARP
tend ..... MINISTER, OPERATE, CARE, MIND, MANAGE, SERVE, INCLINE, BE APT
tendency .. BIAS, PROPENSITY, BENT, TREND, TENOR, DRIFT, INCLINATION, DISPOSITION
tender ...... DELICATE, SOFT, FRAGILE, FEBBLE, FRAIL, YOUNG, BID, PRESENT, BOAT, SHIP, OFFER, SORE, PROFFER, LIGHT, GENTLE, SENSITIVE
feeling ...... SENTIMENT
ship's .... PINNACE, COCKBOAT
yacht .... DINGHY
tenderfoot .... NEWCOMER, NOVICE, BOY SCOUT
tenderloin .... STEAK
tenderness of mood .... LANGUOR
tending .... APT
tendon ...... SINEW, MUSCLE, TISSUE, THEW, LEADER, HAMSTRING
division of ... TENOTOMY
nodule .... SESAMOID
tendrac .... TENREC
tendril .. STIPULE, BINE, CURL
having ..... CAPREOLATE
tenebrous ..... SAD, GLOOMY
tenement ..... HOUSE, ADOBE, APARTMENT, FLAT
district/house .. ROOKERY
Tenerife mountain .... TEYDE
tenet ... PRINCIPLE, OPINION, DOCTRINE, MAXIM, DOGMA, CREED, ISM
tenfold .... DECUPLE, DENARY
Tennessee capital .. NASHVILLE
city .. MEMPHIS, JACKSON, CHATTANOOGA, KNOXVILLE
federal agency in ... TVA
Indian ...... CHICKASAW
mountain inhabitant .... MELUNGEON
state flower .... IRIS
tennis .... RACKETS
champ ...... ROSEWALL, PERRY, BUDGE, BETZ, MARBLE, BUENO, KRAMER, SANTANA, ASHE, GONZALEZ, WILLS, HOAD, LAVER, GIMENO, STOLLE, TRABERT, GIBSON, JEAN, BOROTRA, LACOSTE, RIGGS, TILDEN
competition .... TOURNAMENT
equipment ..... RACKET, PADDLE, NET, BAT, RACQUET
first ball .... SERVICE
ground .... COURT
handicap .... BISQUE
modified .... HANDBALL, SQUASH
racket string .... CATGUT
scoring system .... VASS
stroke .... LOB, CUT, VOLLEY, SMASH, SERVICE, DRIVE, BAT, SLICE, CHOP
table .... PINGPONG
term .... DEUCE, SET, MATCH, ADVANTAGE, SERVICE, LINER, SINGLES, DOUBLES, BYE, LOVE SET, LET, ACE FAULT, VANTAGE
uncounted service ... LET
world championship cup DAVIS
Tennyson heroine ..... ISOLT, ENID, ELAINE
heroine's home .... ASTOLAT
tenon, companion of .... MORTISE
tenor ..... DRIFT, TENDENCY, MEANING, GIST
great .... CARUSO, MELCHIOR
kind of ...... FALSETTO
violin ...... ALTO, VIOLA
tenpins .... BOWLING, BOWLS
tenrec .... TENDRAC
habitat ... MADAGASCAR
tense .. TIGHT, STRAINED, FLEX, TAUT, DRAWN, RIGID, STIFF, ELECTRIC
oppostie of .. LAX, SLACK, LOOSE
tensile .... DUCTILE, PLASTIC, FLEXIBLE
tensimeter ...... MANOMETER
tension ...... STRAIN, STRESS
tent .. TABERNACLE, SHELTER, MARQUEE, YURT, ENCAMP
circus .... BIGTOP
dweller .. INDIAN, ARAB, BEDOUIN, SCENITE, KEDAR, NOMAD
flap .... FLY
Indian .... LODGE, TE(E)PEE, WIGWAM
large .... PAVILION
maker .... OMAR
show .. CIRCUS, MARQUEE
show man ...... CARNIE
surgical .. PLUG, DOSSIL
tentacle ...... FEELER, PALP, ANTENNA
feature .... SUCKER
tentacles, creature with ...... OCTOPUS, CEPHALOPOD, CUTTLE(FISH), SQUID
tentative .... PROVISIONAL
tenterhook .... NAIL
tenterhooks, on ..... ANXIOUS, TENSE
tenth muse .... SAPPHO
part .... TITHE
wave .... DECUMAN
tenths, pertaining to .... DECIMAL
tentmaker .. OMAR (KHAYYAM)
tenuity .. THINNESS, FINENESS, FAINTNESS, RARITY
tenuous ..... SLIGHT, FLIMSY, THIN, SLENDER, RARE
tenure ...... HOLDING, TERM
land .... SOCAGE
of office .... INCUMBENCY
teocalli .... TEMPLE
teonsinte .... GRASS
tepee .. TENT, WIGWAM, LODGE
tepid .... (LUKE)WARM
tequilla ..... MESCAL, AGAVE, PULQUE, LIQUOR
drinker ..... MEXICAN(O)
teraphim .... IDOLS

teratism ...... FETUS, FREAK, MONSTROSITY
teratoid .... MONSTER, MONSTROUS
tercel ..... HAWK, PEREGRINE
tercet .... TRIPLET
terebinth .. SUMAC, TEIL, TREE, LINDEN
yield ...... TURPENTINE
teredo .. SHIPWORM, MOLLUSK, BORER
tergal .... BACK, DORSAL
tergiversate ..... APOSTATIZE, HEDGE, LIE, EQUIVOCATE
tergiversation .... APOSTASY, EVASION
tergum .... BACK
term .. DURATION, EXPRESSION, PERIOD, NAME
of endearment .... HON(EY), DEARIE, TOOTS
of office .... TENURE
plural ...... CONDITIONS, STIPULATIONS
school .... SEMESTER
termagant .. SHREW, HELLCAT, VIXEN
termer .... PRISONER
terminal .... FINAL, STATION, LAST, DEPOT, EXTREMITY, END
negative .... CATHODE
positive .... ANODE
terminate .. CONCLUDE, STOP, CEASE, END, CLOSE
termination ..... FINISH, END, CONCLUSION, EXPIRY, EXPIRATION
in grammar .. DESINENCE
of right .... LAPSE
terminology ...... WORDING
termite .... ANAY, WHITE ANT
terms .... CONDITIONS, STIPULATIONS
come to .... AGREE
make .... TREAT, NEGOTIATE
tern ...... (SEA)BIRD, NODDY, (LOTTERY)PRIZE, MEDRICK
ternary .... THIRD, TRIAD, THREEFOLD, TRIPLE
terpene alcohol ... LINALOOL
derivative .... CAMPHOR
isomeric ..... LIMONENE
Terpsichore .... MUSE
concern of ..... DANCE, DANCING
terra .... EARTH
alba .. KAOLIN, GYPSUM, MAGNESIA
cotta .... CLAY
firma .... EARTH
terrace .. GALLERY, PLATEAU, PORTICO, PATIO, BALCONY, BERM(E)
staircase .... PERRON
terrain .... GROUND
terramycin ...... ANTIBIOTIC
terrapin ...... TURTLE, EMYD, CHELONIAN
terrene ..... EARTH(Y), LAND, MUNDANE, WORLDLY
terrestrial .... EARTHLY, WORLDLY, MUNDANE, GEAL
terret .... RING
terrible .... DIRE, SEVERE, DREADFUL, FEARFUL, AWFUL, INTENSE
terribly: colloq. .... VERY, EXTREMELY
terrier ...... AIREDALE, DOG, SCHNAUZER, WIREHAIR
kind of ..... FOX, BULL, BOSTON, IRISH, SKYE, SCOTCH, SEALYHAM
terrific: colloq. ... EXCELLENT, GREAT
terrify .... APPAL(L), DAUNT, ALARM, FRIGHTEN, DISMAY
terrifying .... GRIS(T)LY, DREADFUL, HORRID
terrigenous ...... EARTHBORN
terrine .... STEW
territorial division ...... AMT
territory .. TERRENE, DOMAIN, REGION, DISTRICT
disputed ..... KASHMIR, CHENPAO, DAMANSKY, SABAH
terror .. FEAR, PANIC, DREAD
colloquial .... PEST, NUISANCE
terrorist .... OGRE, ALARMIST, GOON, NIGHTRIDER, VIGILANTE
terrorize ... FRIGHTEN, SCARE
terse .... CONCISE, SUCCINCT, CRISP, PITHY, LACONIC
tertiary .... THIRD
tessellate .... INLAY, TILE, MOSAIC, CHECKER
tessellation .... MOSAIC
tessera .... TILE
test .... TRIAL, TRY(OUT), WORKOUT, CHECK, PROVE, EXAMINE
colloquial .... EXAM, MIDTERM
clam/crab's ...... SHELL
flight .... TRIAL RUN
operation ... SHAKEDOWN
ore .... ASSAY
paper .... LITMUS
print .... PROOF
quality of .... SAMPLE
severe .... ORDEAL, CRUCIBLE
vessel .... CRUCIBLE, CUPEL
testa .... INTEGUMENT, SHELL
testacean .... RHIZOPOD
testament .. COVENANT, WILL
testator .... LEGATOR
beneficiary of .... HEIR(ESS), (IN)HERITOR
tester .... CANOPY, CIEL, ASSAYER, SIPPER
testifier .. WITNESS, DEPONENT
statement of .. AFFIDAVIT, DEPOSITION
testify ...... DEPOSE, SWEAR, DEPONE, AFFIRM, MANIFEST
testimonial ...... CERTIFICATE, REFERENCE, COMPLIMENT, TRIBUTE
testimony .... DECLARATION, PROOF, EVIDENCE
testis .... GONAD
teston .... COIN
testudinate .... TORTOISE
testudo .... TORTOISE, SHIELD
testy .... TOUCHY, IRRITABLE, PEEVISH, PEPPERY, WASPISH, HOTHEADED
tetanus .. LOCKJAW, TRISMUS
tetched .... LOCO, DEMENTED
tetchy .... PEEVISH, IRRITABLE
tete-a-tete .... SEAT, CONVERSATION, FACE TO FACE
teth .... TEE
tether .... LEASH, FASTEN, LONGE, ROPE, LARIAT
Tethys .... TITANESS
father of ...... URANUS
husband of ... OCEANUS
tetrachord .... MESON
tetrad .... FOUR
tetragon ...... QUADRANGLE
Tetragrammaton ... YAHWEH, JEHOVAH, ADONAI
tetrarch .... HEROD
tetter ...... ECZEMA, HERPES, LICHEN
Teucrian .... TROJAN
Teuton(ic) .. DUTCH, ENGLISH, NORDIC, GERMAN(IC)
god .. WODEN, ODIN, ULL, AESIR, TYR, THOR, BALDER
goddess .... MERTHUS
hero .... OFFA
metal collar ..... TORQUE
Tevere .... TIBER
tewel .. BORE, FUNNEL, TUYERE
Texas .. CADDOAN, LONE STAR
capital .... AUSTIN
city .. DALLAS, HOUSTON, LAREDO, EL PASO, WACO, ARLINGTON, ABILENE, AMARILLO, PASADENA, TYLER, LUBBOCK, ODESSA
fever victim .... CATTLE
leaguer .. HIT, FLY BALL
mission .... ALAMO
mounted police .... RANGER
nickname .... LONE STAR
plant .... LOCO
river .. NECHES, BRAZOS, NUECES, PECOS
seaport ...... GALVESTON
shrine .... ALAMO
shrub .... GUAYULE
state flower .... BLUEBONNET
state tree .... PECAN
strip of land .... PANHANDLE
university ...... BAYLOR, BAYARD
winter wind ... NORTHER
text .. WORDING, LETTERPRESS, TOPIC, BOOK, SUBJECT
textile ...... WOVEN, CLOTH, FABRIC, FLAX, LINEN, WOOL, COTTON, DRAPERY
dealer .... MERCER
goods .... MERCERY

making apparatus .. LOOM
printing material .... CATECHIN
shop .... MERCERY
worker .... DYER
textual .... LITERAL
texture ...... FABRIC, WOOF, WEAVE, COMPOSITION, WEB, GRAIN, WALE
kind of .. PINE, COARSE, TWILLED, RIBBED
TFR, part of ...... TERRAIN, RADAR, FOLLOWING
Thai(land) .. SIAM(ESE), SHAN
airbase .... KORAT
canal .... KLONG
capital .... BANGKOK
city .... THONBURI, AYUTHIA
coin ...... BAHT, TICAL, ANNA, SATANG
king .... ANANDA, BHUMIBOL, NARESUAN
language .... LAO, SHAN
monetary unit .... BAHT
native .... LAO
palace ..... OHITRA LADA
premier .. KITTIKACHORN, THANARAT
queen .... SIRIKIT
resort .... HUA, HIN, PATTAYA
river .... (ME)NAM
state guesthouse .... BOROMABIMAN
temple .... WAT
throne room .... CHAKRI
weight .... KATI, CATTY
Thais ..... OPERA, COURTESAN
composer of .. MASSENET
thalamus .... TORUS
thalassic .... MARINE
Thalia .... MUSE, GRACE
sister of ..... ERATO, CLIO, EUTERPE, URANIA, POLYMNIA, CALLIOPE, AGLAIA
sphere of ..... COMEDY, POETRY, BLOOM
thallophyte .. ALGA, FUNGUS, LICHEN, BACTERIA
Thames landmark ..... ETON, BRIDGE
Thanatos personified .. DEATH
thane ..... FREEMAN, THEGN
latter-day equivalent of .. BARON, KNIGHT
thankless .... UNGRATEFUL
person .... INGRATE
Thant, U .... SITHU
nationality .... BURMESE
Thapsus, victor at .... CAESAR
that ... WHICH, WHO, WHOM, WHEN
is .... ID EST, VIZ
place .... THERE
thatch ..... ROOF(ING), PALM, HAIR
thatching material ... STRAW, PALM, RUSHES, NIPA, GRASS, COGON, HA(U)LM
thaumatology subject .... MIRACLE(S)
thaumaturge's working .... MIRACLE
thaumaturgy .... MAGIC
thaw .... MELT, DISSOLVE, LIQUEFY, SOFTEN, RELENT, EASE
subject of a .. SNOW, ICE, RESERVE, BERG
the Book .... BIBLE
"Enlightened One" ..... BUDDHA
Fair Penitent author .... ROWE
king .... LE ROI
same .... IDEM
seducer ...... LOTHARIO
Word .... LOGOS
theaceous tree .... TEA
thearchy .... THEOCRACY
theater .. STAGE, MOVIEHOUSE, PLAYHOUSE, OPERA(HOUSE), DRAMA, BOARDS
audience .... HOUSE
awning .... MARQUEE
box/compartment .. LOGE
call .... CURTAIN
central stage .... ARENA
cheapest seat .. GALLERY
cheap .... GAFF
club .... LAMBS
curtain ... TEASER, DROP
district ... RIALTO, SOHO, BROADWAY
entrance hall ... LOBBY, FOYER
fixture .... MARQUEE, CALLBOARD
goer on free ticket ...... DEADHEAD
ground floor ...... PIT, PARQUET, ORCHESTRA
group .... ASCAP
lobby .... FOYER
of war, 1945 .... ETO
part below balcony ..... PARTERRE
presentation ... CONCERT, PLAY, DRAMA, MUSICAL, REVUE, LECTURE, MOVIE
program .... BILL
seat .... LOGE, GALLERY, STALL
sign .... SRO, EXIT
slang .... LEGIT, GAFF
stage scenery .. COULISSE
street .... BROADWAY
the ..... STAGE, BOARDS, FOOTLIGHTS
theatrical .... HISTRIONIC, DRAMATIC, POMPOUS, AFFECTED, STAGY
company .... STOCK
curtain .... DROP
employee .... STAGEHAND
extra .... SUPER
financier: colloq. .... ANGEL
group .... TROUPE, CAST, ANTA
itinerary ... TOUR, TRIP, ROAD
nickname .... FLO, BILLY
producer .. ROSE, COHAN, ZIEGFELD
production ...... PLAY, REVUE, EXTRAVAGANZA
profession .... STAGE
role .... INGENUE, LEAD, HEAVY, STAR
show .... REVUE, EXTRAVAGANZA
sketch .... SKIT
Theban blind soothsayer ..... TIRESIAS
deities .... CABIRI
general ..... PELOPIDAS
god .... AMUN-RE
goddess .... MUT
king ...... CREON, LAIUS
poet .... PINDAR
queen .... JOCASTA
town .... LUXOR
Thebes .... LUXOR
founder of .... CADMUS
one of 7 against .... TYDUES
site of .... KARNAK
theca .... SAC, COCOON, CASE, CAPSULE
content .... SPORE, PUPA
thecate .... SHEATHE
Theda, actress .... BARA
theelin ... ESTRONE, HORMONE
theelol .... ESTRIOL, HORMONE
theft ..... ROBBERY, LARCENY, BURGLARY, THIEVERY
describing one .. GRAND, QUALIFIED
theine .... CAFFEINE
theme .. SUBJECT, ESSAY, TEXT, TOPIC, (LEIT)MOTIF
in a design ...... MOTIF
in art/music, etc. .. MOTIF
in radio .... SIGNATURE
Themis .... GODDESS
concern of .... JUSTICE, LAW
parent of .... GAEA, URANUS
what she holds .. SCALE
thenar .... PALM, SOLE
then ...... ALORS, THEREFORE
thence .... THEREFROM
thenceforth ...... THEREAFTER
theodolite .... TRANSIT
user of a .... SURVEYOR
theologian .... AQUINAS, LUTHER, CALVIN, ORIGEN, DIVINE, BEDE
theorbo .... LUTE
theorem .... PROPOSITION
expression of a .... FORMULA, EQUATION
theoretical ...... ACADEMIC, HYPOTHETICAL, SPECULATIVE, ABSTRACT
force .. OD(YLE), ODYL(E)
opposed to .. PRACTICAL, APPLIED
theorize ... GUESS, SPECULATE
theory ... IDEA, CONJECTURE, LAW, ISM, THESIS, HYPOTHESIS, SUPPOSITION, DOCTRINE
Darwin's .... EVOLUTION

Einstein's .. RELATIVITY
Malthusian .... POPULATION
Newton's ...... GRAVITY
therapeutic .... CURATIVE
therapy ... CURE, TREATMENT
there .... YON(DER), AT, TOWARD, THITHER, THEN
thereafter .... THENCEFORTH, SINCE
therefore ..... ERGO, HENCE, THEN, CONSEQUENTLY, ARGAL
therefrom .... THENCE
theriac(a) .... TREACLE, ANTIDOTE
theranthropic being .... CENTAUR, HARPY, MERMAID, THOTH, TRITON
therm .... CALORIE
Therma .... SALONIKA
thermae .... BATHS
thermion .... ELECTRODE
thermometer, type of .... CENTIGRADE, FAHRENHEIT, REAUMUR, CELSIUS, CRYOMETER
Thermopylae protagonist(s) ... PERSIANS, SPARTANS, XERXES, LEONIDAS
thermos .... JUG, FLASK
theroid .... BEASTLIKE
thersitical ... ABUSIVE, LOUD, SCURRILOUS
thesaurus .... TREASURY, LEXICON, DICTIONARY, STOREHOUSE
compiler .... ROGET
Theseus' father ...... AEGEUS
friend .... PIRITHOUS
mother .... AETHRA
victim .... MINOTAUR
wife .... PHAEDRA
thesis .. THEORY, PROPOSITION, DISSERTATION, POSTULATE, TREATISE, ESSAY, MONOGRAPH
Thespian .... ACTOR, PLAYER, TRAGEDIAN, PERFORMER
Thespis' forte ..... TRAGEDY
Thessalian city ...... LARISSA
mountain .. OSSA, PELION
river .... SALAMBRIA
tribe .... MYRMIDON
valley .... TEMPE
warrior ..... MYRMIDON
thetic .... PRESCRIBED
Thetis .... NEREID
husband of ..... PELEUS
son of .... ACHILLES
theurgist .... MAGICIAN
theurgy .... MAGIC
thews ..... MUSCLES, SINEWS
thewy .... MUSCULAR
they speak for themselves .... FACTS
thiamine deficiency disease ... BERIBERI
thick ...... DENSE, COMPACT, LUXURIANT, DULL, STUPID, CRASS, TURBID, CROSS, FAT
as thieves .... CLOSE
colloquial ... FRIENDLY, INTIMATE
end .... BUTT
headed .... DENSE, HEBETATE
lay .... EXAGGERATE
lipped .... LABROSE
skinned .... SHAMELESS, CALLOUS
slice .... SLAB
soup .... PUREE
sticky fluid ...... GRUME
thicken .. COAGULATE, DEEPEN, CURDLE, SOLIDIFY, INSPISSATE
thicket ..... SPINNEY, BRAKE, (UNDER)BRUSH, TOD, RONE, BUSH, BOSCAGE, COPPICE, CHAPARRAL, SHAW, COPSE, BOSK
thickhead .... DUNCE, IDIOT, FOOL
thickheaded .... STUPID, FOOLISH
thickness .. LAYER, STRATUM, PLY
thickset ..... STOUT, STOCKY, BEEFY, CHUNKY
thief ..... STEALER, PILFERER, FILCHER, GANEF, GANOV, GONOF, GONOPH, LURCHER, PICAROON, PRIG, LARCENER
buyer of his loot .. FENCE
cattle .... RUSTLER
compulsive .... KLEPTO(MANIAC)
discards of a ..... WAIF
literary ..... PLAGIARIST, PIRATE, LIFTER
store .... SHOPLIFTER
trainer .... FAGIN
wallet ...... PICKPOCKET
thieve .. STEAL, PILFER, SWIPE, FILCH
thieves' language ..... SLANG, ARGOT, CANT, JARGON
thigh, animal's .... HAM
and buttock .... HAM
armor plate ..... TUILLE
back of .... HAM
bone .... FEMUR
muscle ...... SARTORIUS
of the .... FEMORAL
part .... FLANK
pains .... SCIATICA
upper .... HIP
thill .... SHAFT, POLE
thimble .... THUMBSTALL
thimblerig ...... SHELL GAME
bettor .... SUCKER
thimblerigger .... CHEAT, SWINDLER
thimbleweed ...... ANEMONE, RUDBECKIA, CONEFLOWER
thin ... TENUOUS, LEAN, SLIM, SLENDER, SPARSE, RARE, SLIGHT, MEAGER, SCANT, LANKY, SHEER, SPARE, FINE, FLIMSY, SUBTLE, LIN(E)Y, REEDY, HAIRLINE
cake .... WAFER
coating ... FILM, VENEER
combining form .. STENO
glue .... SIZE
layer ...... VENEER, FILM
man .... SLATS
Man's dog .... ASTA
man's nickname .. SLIM, SLATS, LANKY
paper .... TISSUE
skinned ...... SENSITIVE
soup .... BROTH
thine .... YOUR(S)
thing .. ENTITY, BEING, OBJECT, ITEM, MATTER, AFFAIR, CONCERN
easy to do ...... CINCH
emitted ..... EMANATION
hard to handle .... HOT POTATO
imaginary .... MYTH
ineffectual .... DUD
in law .... RES
of same class .... CONGENER
of small value ... STIVE, TRIFLE
of value .... ASSET
out of place .... ESTRAY
worthless .... CHIP
things, one thousand .... CHILIAD
to be done ..... AGENDA
to be sold .... WARES
thingumajig .... THINGUMBOB, GADGET, CONTRIVANCE, DEVICE
thingumbob .. DEVICE, GADGET
think ..... CONCEIVE, IDEATE, JUDGE, CEREBRATE, TROW, RECKON, WEEN, DEEM, BROOD, SURMISE, REFLECT, OPINE, COGITATE, REASON
of ... CONSIDER, RECALL, RECOLLECT
over ..... PONDER, MULL
up .... INVENT
thinness .... RARITY, TENUITY
thiol .... MERCAPTAN
thiosulfate .... HYPO
third .... TERNARY, TERTIARY
degree user .... INVESTIGATOR, POLICE, INTERROGATOR
estate .... COMMONS, BOURGEOISIE
every .... TERTIAN
in music .... TIERCE
International .... COMINTERN
man, the ..... REF(EREE)
power .... CUBE
rate ..... POOR, INFERIOR
widow's .... DOWER
thirl .... PIERCE, THRILL
thirst ...... CRAVING, DESIRE
quencher .... POP
relieve .... SLAKE
Thirkell, writer ..... ANGELA
thirteen ... LONG DOZEN, XIII
"30" on copy .... END
this minute .... NOW, AT ONCE, PRONTO
Thisbe's love ...... PYRAMUS
thistle .. ARNICA, BURR, ASTER, COSMOS, HYSSOP
like plant ... ARTICHOKE, CARDOON

plant .... SAFLOWER
thistledown .... PAPPUS
thither .... THERE, YON
thole .... PIN, OARLOCK
purpose of ... FULCRUM
Thomas, Fr. composer ...... AMBROISE
opera by ...... MIGNON
thong ... WHIP(LASH), STRAP, RIEM, KNOUT, LEASH
strangling .... GAROTTE, GARROTE
Thor .... SISECH
Thor's father .... ODIN
noise .... THUNDER
sphere .... WAR
weapon .... HAMMER
wife .... SIF
thorax .... CHEST
insect's .... TRUNK
thorn .. TORUN, TREE, NETTLE, STOB, SPINE, PRICKLE, BRIAR, BRIER
apple .... DATURA, HAW, METEL
thornback .. RAY, SPIDER CRAB
Thorne novel .... TOPPER
thorny ...... SPINATE, SPINY, PRICKLY, BRAMBLY, SPINOSE
plant ...... BRIAR, BRIER
thorough .... COMPLETE, OUT-AND-OUT, ABSOLUTE
thoroughbred ... PEDIGREED, BLUEBLOOD, HIGHBORN
thoroughfare .. (PASSAGE)WAY, STREET, HIGHWAY, AVENUE, CONCOURSE
thoroughwort ...... BONESET, PLANT
thorp(e) ... HAMLET, VILLAGE
those in office .... INS
Thoth, representation of ..... IBIS
thou .... YOU
though .. NOTWITHSTANDING, HOWEVER
thought .... INTELLECT, IDEA, CONCEPT, HEED
transference of .... TELEPATHY
thoughtless .. RASH, RECKLESS, STUPID
act .... FOLLY
thousand dollars: sl. .. GRAND
prefix .... MILLI
years ..... MILLENNIUM, CHILIAD
thousandth ..... MILLESIMAL
anniversary .. MILLENARY
of an inch .... MIL
Thracian king .... TEREUS
slave .... SPARTACUS
soldier .... MYRMIDON
thrall ...... (EN)SLAVE, ESNE, SERF, BONDMAN
thralldom .... SLAVERY, SERVITUDE, BONDAGE
thrash ..... WALLOP, WHALE, FLOG, CANE, TAN, BEAT, ROUT, DEFEAT, LASH, DRUB, LAM, TROUNCE, BELABOR, WHIP, FLAIL, HIDE, LACE, LAMBAST(E), LARRUP

thrasher .... (SONG)BIRD
thrasonical .... BOASTFUL
thread .... INKLE, CORD, LINEN, LISLE, STRAND, FILAMENT, STRING, FILUM
a needle .... REEVE
appendage like ... CIRRUS
ball of .... CLEW
bits .... LINT
combining form .... NEMAT(O)
cotton .... LISLE
cutters, screws ..... TAP
discharge ....SETON
end .... THRUM
fine .... FILM
holder .... SPOOL, SHUTTLE, BOBBIN
knot .... BURL
like ...... FILOSE, FILAR, FIBROID
like part .... FILUM, FILAMENT
linen .... INKLE
lump ...... KNOT, BURL
material .. COTTON, FLAX, YARN, LINEN, SILK
metal .... WIRE
quantity .... SKEIN
rubber .... LASTEX
separate .... SLEAVE
silk .... TRAM
skein of .... HASP
surgical .... CATGUT, SETON
thick .... STRING
use of .... SEWING, SUTURE, WEAVING
used in labyrinth .. CLEW
weight .... DENIER
threadbare .... WORN, STALE, TRITE, SHABBY, RAGGED, SEEDY
threadworm ...... NEMATODE, FILARIA
thready ... STRINGY, FIBROUS
threap .. ARGUE, CHIDE, SCOLD
threat ... WARNING, MENACE
empty ... BLUSTER, BLUFF
threaten ... MENACE, HECTOR
threatening .... MINATORY, MINACIOUS, OMINOUS, MENACING, SULLEN
three ...... TRIO, TRIAD, TER, THRIN
angled .... TRIGONOUS
banded armadillo .. APAR
base hit .... TRIPLE
card's .... TREY
cut into .... TRISECT
cornered .... TRIGONOUS, TRIGONAL, TRIANGULAR
decker .... TRIREME
dimensional ...... CUBIC, STEREO
feet .... YARD
group of .... TRINE, TRINARY, TRIAD, TRINITY, TRIPLE(T), TRIPLEX, TRIPLICATE, TRIO
hand card game ... SKAT
in dice/domino .... TREY

in one .. TRIUNE, TRINITY
in sequence, same suit ... TIERCE
leafed .... TRIFOLIATE
leafed clover ... TREFOIL
legged seat .... STOOL
legged stand ... TEAPOY, TRIPOD, EASEL
legged table ..... TRIVET
lobbed .... TRIFID
month period .... TRIMESTER, QUARTER
prefix .... TRI
pronged ...... TRIDENT, TRIDENTATE
pronged spear .. TRIDENT, LEISTER
ribbed ..... TRICOSTATE
seeded ..... TRISPERMOUS
set of .... TERNION
shakes .... SECS
song for .... TRIO
times ... TRIPLE, TREBLE, THRICE
toed sloth .... AI
threefold .... TERNARY, TREBLE, TRIPLE, THRICE, TRINE, TRINAL, TRIPARTITE, TRIPLEX
threes, arranged in .. TERNATE
threescore .... SIXTY
threnody .. CORONACH, DIRGE, SONG, REQUIEM
thresh ...... BEAT(OUT), FLOG
out .... DISCUSS
thresher ...... SHARK, FLAIL
shark .... SEAFOX
threshing implement ... FLAIL, COMBINE
threshold .... LIMEN, (DOOR)SILL, ENTRANCE, EVE
threw ... TOSSED, CAST, FLUNG, HURLED
thrice ..... THREEFOLD, VERY
thrift ... ECONOMY, FRUGALITY
thrifty ..... FRUGAL, SPARING, PROVIDENT, ECONOMICAL
person .... HOARDER, MISER, NIGGARD, PENNY-PINCHER, SKINFLINT
thrill ... EXHILARATE, FLUSH, THIRL, ELECTRIFY, KICK, EXCITE, QUIVER, VIBRATE, TREMOR
thrilling .. ELECTRIC, EXCITING
thrips .... WOODWORM
thrive .... FLOURISH, PROSPER, GROW, SUCCEED, WAX, ADDLE, FATTEN, BATTEN
throat ... WEASAND, GULLET, CRAG, GORGE, MAW, THROTTLE, FAUCES
armor .... GORGET
clearing ..... HAWK, HEM
condition ...... GOITER
cut the .... JUGULATE
disease .. CROUP, ANGINA, THRUSH, GARGET
lozenge .... PASTIL(E)
of the ...... (JU)GULAR, GUTTURAL
part .... ESOPHAGUS,

LARYNX, TRACHEA, PHARYNX
skin, animal .... DEWLAP, WATTLE
sore .... PHARYNGITIS
sound .... CROAK
wrapper ...... MUFFLER
throaty ... HOARSE, GUTTURAL
throb .... PULSATE, BEAT, VIBRATE, PALPITATE, THUMP, POUND, PUMP, PULSATION
throbber .... HEART
throbbing .... PALPITANT, SALTATION, BEATING
throe(s) ..... SPASM, AGONY, (LABOR)PAINS, PANG, RACK
thrombosis ..... COAGULATION
thrombus ...... CLOT, FIBRIN
throne .... SOVEREIGN(TY), CHAIR, RULER
bishop's ..... CATHEDRA
covering .... CANOPY
seat of a .... TRANSOM
sitter ... EMPEROR, TSAR, POPE, CARDINAL, QUEEN
throng ... CROWD, MULTITUDE, PRESS, HORDE, SWARM, HOST, CONCOURSE
throstle .... THRUSH
throttle .... VALVE, STRANGLE, CHOKE, SUPPRESS, SILENCE, GAG, SCRAG
engine .... GUN
through .. PER, VIA, BY WAY OF, AMONG, FINISH, OVER, DONE
throw .... HURL, DASH, UPSET, SHED, FLING, TOSS, PITCH, CAST, HEAVE
at a mark ..... COCKSHY
away .... DISCARD
dice .. ROLL, CAST, MAIN
football opponent ...... TACKLE
into confusion .... DEMORALIZE
lava .... ERUPT
light back ...... REFLECT
of ball .... DELIVERY
out ... REJECT, DISCARD, EJECT, OUST, BOUNCE
over ..... JILT, ABANDON
overboard ..... JETTISON
stones at ...... LAPIDATE
the towel ... QUIT, YIELD
together .... ASSEMBLE
up .. VOMIT, SPEW, RETCH, PUKE, REJECT, REGORGE
throwaway .... LEAFLET, HANDBILL
throwback .... ATAVISM
thrown ... PITCHED, UNSEATED
thrum .... FRINGE, STRUM, DRUM, TIRL
thrummy .... SHAGGY
thrush .... OUZEL, ROBIN, APHTHA, MAVIS, THROSTLE, (SONG)BIRD, BLUEBIRD, VEERY, MISSEL, REDWING, NIGHTINGALE, PITTA
disease .... APHTHA
of the .... TURDINE
water .... WAGTAIL

thrust ... JAB, LUNGE, SHOVE, DRIVE, STAB, PIERCE, PUSH, TILT, FOIN, EXSERT, DARTLE, POKE
aside ..... SHOVE, BRUSH
down .... DETRUDE
fencing .... PASSADO
out lips .... POUT
Thsombe, Congo premier ..... MOISE
thud .... BLOW, THUMP
thug ... CUTTHROAT, ASSASSIN, DACOIT, TOUGH, GORILLA, STRANGLER, GOON, RUFFIAN
thuja ... CEDAR, ARBORVITAE, PINE
Thule, part of .... NORWAY, ICELAND
thumb .... POLLEX, DIGIT
a ride .... HITCHHIKE
fleshy bulge of .. THENAR
in architecture ... OVOLO
index .... TAB
protector ...... THIMBLE, STALL
thumbnail ..... BRIEF, SMALL
thumbstall .... THIMBLE
thump .... POUND, THUD, CUDGEL, THRASH, POMMEL, BEAT, THROB
thumping: colloq. .. WHOPPING, LARGE
thunder .... PEAL
at the beach .... SURF
forth .... FULMINATE
god .... THOR
sound ... CLAP, RUMBLE, CRASH, ROLL, PEAL, MUTTER
thunderbolt ...... LIGHTNING
thunderer ..... ZEUS, JUPITER
thunderfish .... LOACH, RAAD
thunderstone ...... BELEMITE, CUTTLEFISH
thurible .... CENSER
thurifer .... ACOLYTE, ALTAR BOY
thurify .... CENSE
Thuringian capital ... WEIMAR
castle .... WARTBURG
city .... GOTHA, JENA
thus ..... HENCE, THEREFORE, SIC, SO, ERGO
far .... YET
thwack ...... WHACK, SLAP, SMACK
thwart .... OBLIQUE, FRUSTRATE, DEFEAT, FOIL, HINDER, BALK, BAFFLE
Thyestes' brother .... ATREUS
parent .... PELOPS
thyme .... MINT, HERB
thymus .. GLAND, SWEETBREAD
thyroid disease ...... GOITER, CRETINISM, GOITRE
thysanuran ..... BRISTLE TAIL
ti, in chemistry .... TITANIUM
tiara .... HEADDRESS, CROWN, CORONET, DIADEM
wearer ... PEERESS, QUEEN, DUCHESS, PRINCESS
Tiber .... TEVERE
Tiberias Sea .... GALILEE

Tibet .... SITSANG
mountain pass ..... NITI, LIPU LEKH, MANA
Tibetan antelope ... SUS, GOA, CHIRU
capital .... LHASA
chief lama ...... DALAI, PANCHEN
deer .... SHOU
gazelle .... GOA
general .... CHANG
goat wool ... CASHMERE
high priest ...... BLAMA
monastery .... LAMASERY
monetary unit ..... SANG
monk .... LAMA
mountain ..... NANSHAN
ox .... YAK
oxlike animal ..... ZEBU
priest .... LAMA
religion .... LAMAISM
river .... SUTLEJ
wild sheep .... SHA, NAHOOR, BHARAL
zoo animal .... PANDA
tibia ..... SHIN(BONE), FLUTE, CNEMIS
Tibur .... TIVOLI
tic .. LATA(H), SPASM, TWITCH
tical's replacement ..... BAHT
Ticino .... TESSIN
tick ...... ACARID, PARASITE, MITE, CLICK, CHECK, MARK, MOMENT, INSECT, PILLOW CASE, ARACHNID, JIGGER
British ... CREDIT, TRUST
host of ... CATTLE, MAN, SHEEP
off ... COUNT, ENUMERATE
ticker .... TAPPER
slang .... HEART, CLOCK, WATCH, TIMEPIECE
tape figures .. QUOTATIONS
ticket ...... LICENSE, LABEL, TAG, PASS, DOCKET
candidates' ...... SLATE, BALLOT
free .. ANNIE OAKLEY, PASS
losing .... BLANK
of leave .... PAROLE
part .... STUB
slang ... DUCAT, DUCKET, PASTEBOARD
stub .... RAIN CHECK
tickle .... GRATIFY, AMUSE, STIR, TINGLE, TITILIATE, EXCITE
tickler ... PUZZLE, REMINDER
ticklish ... TOUCHY, DELICATE, FICKLE
tickseed ... DAISY, COREOPSIS
tid plus two .... BITS
tidal flow .... EBB, NEAP
wave ... TSUNAMI, EAGRE, BORE
tidbit ..... MORSEL, GOSSIP, CANAPE, CATE, KICKSHAW
tide, designation of a .. EBB, NEAP, FLOOD, SPRING, RIP
tidings .. NEWS, INFORMATION, REPORT, EVANGEL, WORD, GOSPEL

tidy ... TAUT, ORDERLY, TRIM, NEAT, SPRUCE, SHIPSHAPE, CONSIDERABLE, LARGE, TRIG
tie ...... BIND, FASTEN, KNOT, EQUAL, LINK, BOND, CRAVAT, BEAM, STATEMATE, NEXUS, FOUR-IN-HAND, UNION, TACH(E), ASCOT, LASH, TRUSS, STANDOFF, HITCH
beam .... BALK
boat .... MOOR
connecting ... LIGAMENT
contest .... DRAW
down ... CONFINE, HOLD
fabric .... REP
game to break .. RUBBER
in a race .... DEAD HEAT
up .... STOP, HINDER, CONNECTION
tieback .... SASH
Tientsin river .... HAI
tier ... ROW, RANK, PINAFORE, LACER, BANK
tierce .... HOUR, CASK
Tierra del Fuego Indian .. ONA
ties .... OXFORDS
support .... ROADBED
tiff .... HUFF, QUARREL, LIQUOR, SPAT, ARGUMENT, MIFF
tiffany ...... GAUZE, MUSLIN
tiffin .... LUNCH, TEA, SNACK
tiger ...... JAGUAR, LEOPARD, SABERTOOTH
cat ... OCELOT, MARGAY, SERVAL, CHATI
of Malaya, so-called ..... YAMASHITA
Persian ..... SHER, SHIR
young ..... CUB, WHELP
tigerish ... FEROCIOUS, CRUEL, FIERCE
colloquial ...... STINGY, MISERLY
place .... JAM, FIX, SPOT
slang .... DRUNK, TIPSY
tight .... TAUT, COMPACT, SEVERE, TENSE, CLOSE, SNUG, STINGY, MISERLY
place ..... JAM, FIX, SPOT
slang ..... TIPSY, DRUNK
tighten .... FRAP, TAUTEN, STRAITEN, SCREW
tightfisted ... STINGY, MISERLY
tightlipped .... SECRETIVE, TACITURN
tightrope walker .... ACROBAT, EQUILIBRIST, AERIALIST, FUNAMBULIST
tightwad ...... MISER, PIKER, SKINFLINT, NIGGARD, HUNKS
til .... SESAME
tilbury ..... CARRIAGE, COACH
tile ...... PANTILE, QUARRY, TESSERA, DALLE, BRICK, TEGULA, CERAMIC
like .... TEGULAR
making art .. CERAMICS
tiler .... DOORKEEPER
tiles, pertaining to ... TEGULAR
till .... UNTIL, UNTO, CULTIVATE, FARM, CASH (REGISTER), PLOW
land .... SUBDUE
tilled land ..... ARADA, FARM, TILTH
tiller .... HELM, FARMER, CULTIVATOR, PLOWMAN, SHOOT
Tillie the ____ .... TOILER
tilt ... SLANT, INCLINE, SLOPE, LIST, JOUST, HEEL, DEBATE, SEESAW, CANOPY, TIP, TOURNAMENT, TOURNEY
tilted .... ACOCK
tilth .... ARADA, FARM
tilting arena .... LISTS
target .... QUINTAIN
tournament .... CAR(R)OUSEL
timarau .... BUFFALO
timbal .... KETTLEDRUM
timber ...... WOOD, LUMBER, TREES, LOG, BITT
above keel ... DEADWOOD
arched .... CAMBER
borer .... GRIBBLE
crack .... ANEMOSIS
deciduous ... HARDWOOD
down bend .... SNY
dressed ...... PUNCHEON
foundation .... SPILE
grooved ...... COULISSE
heartwood ..... DURAMEN
hewn piece .... BALK
hitch .... KNOT
joining peg .. TRE(E)NAIL, TRUNNEL
rot .... DOAT
sawn .... LUMBER
small .... SCANTLING
soak .... RET
standing ..... STUMPAGE
state .... OREGON
support .... CORBEL
tree .... YEW
wolf .... LOBO
Timberlane, Judge ..... CASS
timbre .... TONE
timbrel ... TAMBOURINE, TABOR
time ...... PERIOD, INTERVAL, OCCASION, MOMENT, DATE, CLOCK, INSTANT, DURATION, ERA, EPOCH
beating device .... METRONOME
between ...... INTERIM, INTERVAL
combining form .... CHRON(O)
extension .... GRACE
free .... LEISURE, BREAK
honored .. TRADITIONAL
in music ... TEMPO, BEAT, VOLTA
incalculable .... EON
indicating device .... SUNDIAL, CLOCK, WATCH, HOURGLASS, CLEPSYDRA
limit .... DEADLINE
of day .... MORNING, (AFTER)NOON
of greatest vigor .... HEYDAY
of imprisonment .. TERM
of life ... TEENS, NONAGE, DOTAGE
of rejoicing .... JUBILEE
out ...... REST, RECESS, BREAK
pass the .... WHILE
pertaining to .... HORAL
poetic .... EVENTIDE
prosperous .... HEYDAY
science of .... HOROLOGY
spend .... WHILE
waster ... LOAFER, IDLER, SLACKER
timely .... OPPORTUNE, SEASONABLE, PROMPT
timepiece ... CLOCK, WATCH, HOROLOGE
art of making .... HOROLOGY
timer .... STOP WATCH
timeserver .... TRIMMER, OPPORTUNIST
timetable .... SCHEDULE
timid .... SHY, TIMOROUS, SHEEPISH, RESERVED, RETIRING, CHICKEN, PAVID
timidity, symbol of ... MOUSE
timing .... PACE
device ..... METRONOME, STOPWATCH
timon .... HELM, TILLER
Timor Archipelago, part ..... SUMBA, SUMBAWA, FLORES
capital ... KUPANG, DILI
coin .... AVO
timorous .... TIMID, FEARFUL, SHY, TREPID
Timoshenko, Soviet Marshal .. SEMYON
timothy .... GRASS, HAY
timpani .... KETTLEDRUMS
tin .... CAN, STANNUM, PRESERVE
alloy .... PEWTER
and lead alloy .... TERNE
box .... TRUMMEL
coated sheet metal ...... TAGGER
fish .... TORPEDO
foil .... TAIN
hat .... HELMET
metal sheet ..... LATTEN
mine .... STANNARY
of .... STANNOUS
Pan Alley character ..... COMPOSER, PROMOTER
Pan Alley group .. ASCAP
plate .... FOIL, TAIN
pyrite .... STANNITE
sheet .... LATTEN
slang .... MONEY
smeltery ..... STANNARY
strips .... TINSEL
threads, decorative ...... TINSEL
tinamou-like bird ..... QUAIL
tincal .... BORAX
tinct ...... TINGED, TINT(ED), COLOR
tincture .. TINT, TINGE, SHADE, VESTIGE, TRACE, COLOR,

VERT, ELIXIR
tind .... KINDLE
tinder .... AMADOU, PUNK
tinderbox, like a .... POWDER KEG
tine ... PRONG, SPIKE, ANTLER, TYND, BIT
tinea ...... RINGWORM, MOTH, LARVA
tinge ... TAINT, TOUCH, COLOR, TRACE, SHADE, DYE, TINT, FLAVOR, DASH
tinged .... TINCT
tingle ... NIP, PRICKLE, THIRL, DIRL, DINDLE
tiniest .... MINIM
tinker ...... BUNGLER, CAIRD, SILVERSIDES, MACKEREL, PUTTER, FUSS, MENDER
jargon of .... SHELTA
Shakespearean ... SNOUT
tinkle .... CLINK, JINGLE
tinkling .... GRACKLE
tin(s)man .... SMITH
tinsel .... SHOWY, GAUDY
tinseled .... CLINQUANT
tinstone .... CASSITERITE
tint ...... COLOR, TINGE, HUE, SHADE, STAIN, DYE
Tintagel Head's famous son ... ARTHUR
tinted .... TINCT
tintinnabula .... BELLS
tinware .... POTS, PANS
tiny .... MINUTE, SMALL, DIMINUTIVE, WEE, PETITE, TEENY, MINUSCLE
bit .... MORSEL
creature .... ATOMY. DWARF, RUNT
gold particles ...... DUST
opening .... PORE
tip ..... APEX, FEE, LIST, TOP, TAP, UPSET, NEB, CANT, HEEL, VAIL, GRATUITY, CUMSHAW, POINT(ER), TILT, HINT, SLANT, TOPPLE, STEER, GREASE
pen's .... NEB, NIB
off .... WARNING, HINT
tippet .... LIRIPIPE, FUR, AMICE, ALMUCE, SCARF, CAMAIL
tipple ... DRINK, LIQUOR, BIB
tippler .... TOPER, SOT
tips seller .... TOUT
tipstaff .... BAILIFF, CONSTABLE
tipster .... TOUT(ER)
tipsy .... AWRY, DRUNK, INTOXICATED, CROOKED, HIGH, LOADED, GROGGY
tiptop .... FIT, AONE, SHIPSHAPE
tirade .... HARANGUE, PHILIPPIC, SPEECH, DIATRIBE, SPATE
tirailleur .... MARKSMAN, SHARPSHOOTER
tire ...... WEARY, FAG, PNEU, JADE, CLOY, BORE
burst .... BLOWOUT
casing .... SHOE
iron .... STRAKE
out .... EXHAUST
part of .... CASING, SHOE, TUBE, TREAD, RIM
puncturer .... CALTRAP, CALTROP
tread mold .... MOULAGE
tired .... JADED, WEARY
feeling .... ENNUI, WEARINESS, FATIGUE
very .... ALL IN
Tiresias .... SOOTHSAYER
tiresome ... TEDIOUS, BORING, DREARY, DULL
person .... BORE
tirl .... THRUM, STRUM
tisane .... PTISAN, TEA, DECOCTION
Tisiphone .... FURY
tissue ... CLOTH, GAUZE, MESH, NETWORK, TELA, BAST, WEB, PAPER, PHLOEM, GRISTLE
animal .... CARTILAGE
area of dead .... INFARCT
cavity .... LOCULUS, VACUOLE
change in ... CATAPLASIA
combining form .. HIST(O)
connecting ..... TENDON, PONS
cutting instrument ...... MICROTOME
decay .... CARIES, GANGRENE
hardening .... SCLEROMA, SCLERIASIS
inflammation .... CELLULITIS
like .... HISTOID
nerve .... ALBA
plant .... PHLOEM, BAST
study of ...... HISTOLOGY
under epidermis .... HYPODERMA
Tisza .... THEISS
tit ...... BIRD, TEAT, NIPPLE, BREAST, HORSE, NAG, BLOW, GIRL, JADE, TAP
Titan .... HELIOS, ZEUS, CREUS, COEUS, CRONUS, ATLAS, EPIMETHEUS, IAPETUS, HYPERION, OCEANUS, PROMETHEUS, GIANT
female ..... DIONE, LETO, TETHYS, RHEA, THEIA, MAIA, EURYNOME, PHOEBE
parent of .... GAEA, URANUS, GAIA
place of consignment .... TARTARUS
Titania .... FAIRY, QUEEN
husband of ..... OBERON
titanic .... GIGANTIC
titanium dioxide ..... RUTILE
titanite .... SPHENE, MINERAL
Titans' war with Olympians ... TITANOMACHY
tithe ...... LEVY, TENTH, TAX
tithing .... DECENARY
Tithonus' love .... EOS
parent ...... LAOMEDON
transformation .... GRASSHOPPER
titi .... MONKEY, TREE, IRONWOOD
titian .... AUBURN
titillate ... EXCITE, TANTALIZE, STIMULATE, TICKLE
titivate ... SPURCE, DRESS(UP)
titlark .... PIPIT
title .... PARENT, LEGEND, CLAIM, RIGHT, NAME, CAPTION, APPELLATION, MUNIMENT, HEADING, DESIGNATION
descriptive ..... EPITHET
holder .. TITLIST, OWNER, CHAMPION
sports ... CHAMPION(SHIP)
of a noble .... RAS, LORD, EARL, COUNT, DUKE, BARON, MARQUISE, PRINCE
ownership .... DEED
pages .... ODDMENTE
surbordinate .. SUBHEAD
to property ... MUNIMENT, DEED
transfer .... CEDE
titled person .... NOBLE
titmouse ... CHICKADEE, NUN, TAT, PARUS, VERDIN, BLUECAP, MAG
Tito, Marshal .. (JOSIP) BROZ
resistance followers ..... PARTISANS
titter .... TEHEE, SNICKER, LAUGH, GIGGLE
tittie .... SISTER
tittle ... IOTA, DOT, JOT, WHIT, PARTICLE
tattle .. GOSSIP, CHATTER
tittup ... FRISK, FROLIC, CAPER, PRANCE
titular .... NOMINAL
Tiu .... TYR
Tivoli .... TIBUR
tizzy .... EXCITEMENT, DISTRACTION, DITHER, SNIT
Tlingit .... TONGA, INDIAN
tmesis .... DIACOPE
TNT .... TROTYL
to .... WITH, THITHER, AS FAR AS, UNTIL
do .... STIR, FUSS, COMMOTION
the point that ..... UNTIL
the point ..... PERTINENT, RELEVANT, GERMANE, APT, RELATED
wit .... NAMELY, SCILICET
your health ..... PROSIT, SKOAL
toad .... FROG, PEEPER, NATTERJACK, PADDOCK, ANURAN, BUFO, SALIENTIAN, SPADEFOOT, AGUA, PIPA, BATRACHIA, HYLA
back "wart" of .... VERRUCA
larva .... TADPOLE
sound .... CROAK

toadeater ...... SYCOPHANT, PARASITE
toadfish .... SAPO
toadflax .... WEED
toadstone's use .... CHARM
toadstool .... MUSHROOM, FUNGUS, BOLETUS, AGARIC
toady .. TRUCKLE, FLATTERER, SYCOPHANT, PARASITE, FLUNK(E)Y, LACKEY, LICKSPIT(TLE)
toast ..... COMPLIMENT, LEEP, SIPPET, BROWN, WARM, DRINK, SALUTE
British .... CHEERS
German .... PROSIT
Norwegian ...... SKOAL
object of a ..... HONOREE, CELEBRANT, LION, CELEBRITY, BELLE, AWARDEE, HERO
Spanish .... SALUD
type of .... MELBA
toastmaster ..... EMCEE, MC, SYMPOSIARCH
tobacco ... BROADLEAF, WEED, SHAG, BURLEY, PERIQUE, LATAKIA, MUNDUNGO, DACCHA, MUNDUNGUS
and paper ...... MAKING
bit of .... SCREW
box .... HUMIDOR
cake of .... PLUG
chewing ..... QUID, PLUG
corporal's ..... CAPORAL
Cuban .... VUELTA, CAPA
kiln .... OAST
leaf alkaloid .. NICOTINE
leaf bundle ...... HAND
left in pipe ...... DOTTEL, DOTTLE
odor .... FUNK
pipe .. DUDEEN, CHIBOUK, CHIBOURUE, MEERCHAUM, CORNCOB
plant pest .... THRIPS
pouch .... SPLEUCHAN
product .... CIGAR(ETTE), SNUFF, PLUG
rolled, twisted .. PIGTAIL
shredded .... SHAG
smoke .... WHIFF
snuff .... RAPPEE
soldier's ...... CAPORAL
Turkish .... LATAKIA
use of .... CHEWING, SMOKE, SNUFF
toboggan ..... SLED, COASTER, DECLINE
like vehicle ..... BOBSLED
runway of .... CHUTE
toby ...... CIGAR, MUG, JUG
content of .... ALE
tock .... HORNBILL
tocology .... OBSTETRICS, MIDWIFERY
tocsin .... BELL, ALARM
tod .... CLUMP, BUSH, FOX
toddle ..... WADDLE, TOTTER, PADDLE
toddler .... CHILD, BABY, TOT
toddy .. SAP, DRINK, BEVERAGE
toe ...... DIGIT, DACTYL(US)
bird's .... HALLUX
dance .... PIROUETTE
dancer .... BALLERINA
hold .... FOOTING
infection .... FELON, WHITLOW
membrane ... WEB(BING)
sore .... AGNAIL
the line ... BEHAVE, OBEY, CONFORM
toenails, work on ... PEDICURE
toes, on one's .... ALERT
whirling on the .... PIROUETTE
toffee/toffy .... CANDY, TAFFY
toft .. HOMESTEAD, MESSUAGE, KNOLL, HILLOCK
tog(s) ...... COAT, CLOTHES, DUDS, DRESS
toga .... ROBE, GOWN
together .... ASSOCIATED
toggery .. CLOTHES, CLOTHING, HABERDASHERY
toggle ... PIN, COTTER, BOLT, ROD
Togo, capital of .... LOME
language .... EVHE
president ..... EYADEMA, OLYMPIO
tribe .... MINA, EWE
Togoland plus Gold Coast .... GHANA
toil ... SNARE, LABOR, WORK, TRAVAIL, SLOG, DRUDGE
toile .... CLOTH, LINEN, CRETONNE
toilet ... COMMODE, LAVATORY, JOHN
case .... ETUI, ETWEE, MUSETTE
outdoor .... JAKES
water .... COLOGNE, BAYRUM, LAVENDER
toiletry item .. SOAP, COLOGNE, POWDER, COSMETICS
toils ..... SNARES, TRAPS, GIN
toilsome .... LABORIOUS
Tojo, Japan premier .. HIDEKI
tokay .... WINE, GRAPE
token ..... KEEPSAKE, PLEDGE, SCRIP, SLUG, SYMBOL, INDICATION, INDEX, SIGN, EARNEST
of servitude ...... YOKE
payment ...... ADVANCE, EARNEST, ARLES
tokens .... INDICIA
Tokyo .... YEDO, EDO
center .... SHIMBASI
Fifth Avenue of .. GINZA
tole .... ALLURE, ENTICE
Toledo .... SWORD, BLADE
tol(l)booth ..... JAIL, PRISON
tolerable .... BEARABLE, ENDURABLE, PASSABLE, SOSO
tolerably .... FAIRLY, MODERATELY
tolerance .... MARGIN, ALLOWANCE
tolerate ..... STAND, BROOK, ALLOW, PERMIT, BEAR, ENDURE, SUFFER
toll .. TAX, CHARGE, EXACTION, KNELL, RING
collector ..... PUBLICAN
road .... (TURN)PIKE
toller ..... BELL RINGER, DOG
German poet ..... ERNST
Tolstoy, Russian novelist ..... LEO, LEV
Toltec .... NAHUATL(AN)
tom ...... MALE, CAT, TURKEY
Dick and Harry .... ANYONE, EVERYONE
Thumb .... DWARF
tom .... DRUM
tomahawk .... HATCHET, (BATTLE)AX
tomalley .... LIVER
tomato ...... BERRY, WOMAN, GIRL, FRUIT, LOVE APPLE
juice jelly .... ASPIC
sauce .. CATSUP, KETCHUP
tomb .... SARCOPHAGUS, SEPULCHER, MASTABA(H), VAULT, GRAVE, CIST, OSSUARY, DOLMEN, CROMLECH, TAJ MAHAL, CRYPT
commemorative .... CENOTAPH
cover .... PALL
empty ...... CENOTAPH
flag .... BANDEROL(E)
for absent dead .... CENOTAPH
heroes' .... PANTHEON
imposing ... MAUSOLEUM
inscription on .. EPITAPH, IN MEMORIAM, HERE LIES, HIC JACET
mummy's ... MASTABA(H)
rock .... CIST
royal .... PYRAMID
saint's .... SHRINE
stone over ...... LEDGER, MEGALITH
tomboy ..... HOYDEN, HOIDEN
tombstone .... STELE
marshal ... (WYATT)EARP
tomcat .... GIB
tome .... BOOK, VOLUME
tomentose .... MATTED
tomfool .... STUPID, SILLY
tomfoolery .... NONSENSE, SILLINESS
Tommy, Brit. soldier .. ATKINS
tommyrot .... RUBBISH, NONSENSE
tomorrow .... MANANA
tomtit ... WREN, CHICKADEE, BIRD
ton .... STYLE, VOGUE
toncan .. ARACARI, TEAN, TOCO
tone ... SOUND, PITCH, STYLE, TINT, HUE, KEY
arm .... PICKUP
color .... TIMBRE
down .... SOFTEN
lack of .... ATONY
shade of .... NUANCE
toneless .... ATONY
tong member .... CHINESE
Tonga capital ... NUKUALOFA
king .... TUPOU

tongs .... CLAMP, FORCEPS, PINCERS
tongue .. SPEECH, LANGUAGE, GLOSSA, IDIOM, TAB, DIALECT, LINGUA
bell's .... CLAPPER
bone of .... HYOID
buckle's .... PIN
coating .... FUR(RING)
combining form .. .. GLOSS(O)
curbing device .. BRANKS
elevation on .... PAPILLA
inflammation .. GLOSSITIS
lashing ..... REPRIMAND, REPROOF
like organ ...... LINGUA, PROBOSCIS
of the .... GLOSSAL, LINGUAL
part of .... BLADE
shaped .... LANGUET(TE), LINGULATE
shoe's .... TAB
tied .... SPEECHLESS
use of .... TASTE, ARTICULATION, INGESTION
wagon's ..... POLE, NEAP
tongueless ...... MUTE, DUMB
tonic .... INVIGORATING, BEVERAGE, MEDICINE, PICKUP, FILLIP, ROBORANT, BRACER, BRACING, ELIXIR
bark .... CANELLA
in medicine ...... IRON
tonka bean .... GUAIAC
flavor .... COUMARIN
tonkin .... BAMBOO
capital .... HANOI
tonneau, later .... CHASSIS
tonsil .... AMYGDALA
inflammation ... QUINSY
instrument for .... GUILLOTINE
tonsorial artist ...... BARBER
tonsured person ...... PRIEST, MONK
tontine .... ANNUITY
tonus .... TONICITY
tony ..... STYLISH, LUXURIOUS
too .... ALSO, BESIDES, AS WELL, OVERLY, VERY, EXTREMELY, LIKEWISE
large .... OUTSIZE
many/much .... DE TROP
much, in music ... TANTO
tool .... IMPLEMENT, INSTRUMENT, UTENSIL, MEANS, DEVICE, GADGET
adz-shaped .... MATTOCK
bookbinding .... GOUGE
boring .. TREPAN, AUGER, DRILL, GIMLET, JUMPER, AWL
carpenter's .... SAW, BEVEL, PLANE
case .... KIT
cobbler's .... AWL
cutting ... BOLO, ADZ(E), MACHETE, SAW, SHEARS, SCISSORS, KNIFE, SICKLE, SCYTHE
engraver's .... BURIN
garden .... TROWEL, RAKE, HOE, SPADE
handle .... HELVE
hole enlarging .. REAMER
hole-making ..... DIBBLE
mason's .... CHISEL
molding .... DIE
person as a .... DUPE, PAWN, STOOGE, FRONT, DUMMY, PUPPET
pipe-bending .... HICKEY
pruning ...... BILLHOOK, SHEARS
reaper's .... FLAIL
set .... KIT
shaving .... RAZOR
toothed .... SAW
trimming .... SHEAR, SCISSOR
toolmaker .... MACHINIST
tools, set of .... KIT
toon .... TREE, WOOD
toot .... WHISTLE, HORN
sound ... BLAST, WHISTLE, HONK
tooth .... IVORY, TUSK, TUSH, INCISOR, CUSPID, MOLAR, GAM, PEG, TASTE, APPETITE
ache .... ODONTALGIA
and .... NAIL
boar's .... TUSK
canine .... FANG, CUSPID, LANIARY
combining form .... ODONT(O), DENT(I)
crooked .... SNAG
crust .... CEMENT
decay .... CARIES
deposit .. TOPHUS, CRUST
doctor .... DENTIST
dog's .... FANG
elephant .... TUSK
filler .... CEMENT
for a tooth ...... TALION
gear .... COG
growth on .... EXOSTOSIS
hollow in .... CAVITY
horse canine ...... TUSH
like .... ODONTOID
long, projecting ... TUSK
long, sharp .... FANG
of the .... DENTAL
part .... DENTIN(E), CROWN, PULP, CEMENT
paste .... DENTRIFICE, ZIRCATE
puller .... DENTIST
shaped .... DENTOID, DENTIFORM
small .... DENTIL, DENTICLE
snake's .... FANG
socket .... ALVEOLUS
substance .... PULP
use of ..... GNAW, BITE, PIERCE
walrus .... TUSK
wheel .... COG, GEAR
toothache ...... ODONTALGIA
toothed .... DENTATE, DENTED
wheel .... GEAR
toothlike part ..... TINE, COG, PRONG
projection ...... DENTIL, DENTICLE, DENT(ATION)
toothless .... EDENTATE
toothpaste .... ZIRCATE, DENTRIFICE
toothsome .... TASTY, PALATABLE, SAVORY
tootle .... WHISTLE
toots .... DEAR, DARLING
tootsy .... FOOT
top ... ROOF, LID, COP, COVER, ZENITH, HIGHEST, OUTDO, TOY, APEX, HEAD, LEAD, EXCEL, SURPASS
altar .... MENSA
blow one's .... ERUPT
bottle ..... CROWN, CAP
carriage's .... CAPOTE
cover .... LID, CAP
flight .... BEST, AONE, FIRST RATE
hat .... GIBUS
hill .... COP, BROW
hole .... FIRSTRATE
kick: sl. ...... SERGEANT
of head .... CROWN
of mountain ..... CREST, SUMMIT
of wave .... CREST
secret .... CLASSIFIED
shaped .... TURBINATE
spun with the fingers .... TEETOTUM
topaz .... GEM, QUARTZ, HUMMINGBIRD
author of .... URIS
topazolite .... GARNET
topcoat .... RAGLAN
tope .. SHARK, SHRINE, DRINK
topee ..... CAP, HELMET, HAT
toper .... DRUNK(ARD), RUMMY, TOSSPOT, SOT, SOUSE, BIBBER
tophat .... GIBUS
toph(e) .... TUFA, TUFF
Tophet(h) .... HELL
topi .... HELMET, CAP
topic .... SUBJECT, THEME, HEAD(ING), TEXT
topical .... LOCAL
topkick .... SARGE, SERGEANT
topknot ... HEADDRESS, TUFT
topnotch ... BEST, AONE, ONER
toponym .... NAME
topper .... COAT
topping .... CRUST
topple ...... FALL, OVERTURN, TOTTER
topsail .... RAFFE
topside .... DECK
topsy-turvy .... INVERTED, DISORDERLY
toque .... HAT
tor .... CRAG, HILL
tora(h) .... TETEL, PENTATEUCH
torch .... FLAMBEAU, FLASHLIGHT, LUNT, CRESSET, LINK
bearer .... LINKBOY, LINKMAN

for lure .... JACK
material ... TOW, PITCH, TALLOW
tore .... TORUS
toreador .... BULLFIGHTER
assistant of .... PICADOR
torero .... BULLFIGHTER
queue of .... COLETA
torii .... GATEWAY
Torino .... TURIN
Torme, singer .... MEL
torment .... AGONY, RACK, SUFFERING, PAIN, ANGUISH, ANNOY, TEASE, BADGER, BAIT, VEX, PLAGUE, HARASS, TORTURE, HAGRIDE
torn .. RENT, RIVEN, TATTERED, REFT
tornado .... WHIRLWIND, HURRICANE, CYCLONE, TWISTER
tore .... COWFISH, BULL, TRUNKFISH
torose ... SWOLLEN, KNOBBED, BULGING, CYLINDRICAL
torpedo ... PROJECTILE, RAY, NUMBFISH, CRAMPFISH
colloquial ... SABOTAGE, EGG
part of ..... WAR HEAD, PROPELLER, TRIGGER, FIN, RUDDER
slang .... FISH, BODYGUARD, GUNMAN
torpid ... DORMANT, SLUGGISH, DULL, NUMB, INERT
torpor ... STUPOR, LETHARGY, APATHY
torquate .... COLLARED
torque .... TWIST, COLLAR, NECKLACE
torques .... RUFF
torrefy .... PARCH, DRY
torrent .. RAPID, RUSH, FLOOD, SPATE, DOWNPOUR
torrid ..... ARID, SCORCHING, PARCHED, PASSIONATE, HOT, ARDENT, SULTRY, TROPICAL
torsion .... TWISTING
torsk .... CUSK, CODFISH
torso .... TRUNK
tort .... WRONG, DAMAGE
torte .... CAKE
torticollis .... WRYNECK
tortile ..... COILED, TWISTED
tortilla ... CORN CAKE, BREAD, FLAT
tortoise ...... EMYD, TESTUTO, TESTUDINATE, GALAPAGO, HICATEE, CHELONIAN, TURTLE
burrowing land .. GOPHER
of .... CHELONIAN
shell .... CARAPACE, BUTTERFLY
tortoises, of ..... TESTUDINAL, TESTUDINATE
Tortue .... TORTUGA
tortuous .. CROOKED, DEVIOUS, WINDING
torture ..... AGONY, ANGUISH, TORMENT, RACK, PAIN, THIRD DEGREE
for information .. SWEAT
instrument of ..... RACK
method of ... KEELHAUL, WATERCURE
torus ... THALAMUS, MOLDING, TORE
Tory .... CONSERVATIVE, REACTIONARY
Tosca's love .... MARIO
Toscana .... TUSCANY
Toscanini, conductor .... ARTURO
toss ..... CAST, FLING, PITCH, THROW, BUFFET, FLIP, HURL, SNAP, LOB
about .... BANDY
side to side ..... CAREEN
tossing expert ..... JUGGLER
tosspot ... DRUNKARD, TOPER, DRINKER, SOT
tot ... CHILD, TOTAL, ADD UP, DRINK
total ..... UTTER, COMPLETE, ENTIRE, WHOLE, SUM, ADD, AMOUNT, OUTRIGHT
totalitarian ruler ... DICTATOR
totality .... ENTIRETY
totalizator ..... PARI-MUTUEL, TOTE BOARD
tote ..... HAUL, CARRY, LOAD
totem .... XAT, POLE
toter .... LUGGER
totipalmate bird ..... GOOSE, DUCK, PELICAN, CORMORANT
totter ..... STAGGER, TODDLE, ROCK, SHAKE
toucan ...... ARACARI, TOCO
touch .... TINGE, ADJOIN, CONTACT, TINT, MENTION, PAT, TAP, FINGER, AFFECT, LOAN, FEEL, TRACE, ABUT
and go .... HASTY, UNCERTAIN, CASUAL
at .... STOP
closely .... OSCULATE
clumsily .... PAW
doctor's ...... PALPATE
examine by .... FEEL
for medical diagnosis .... PALPATE
ground with forehead ... KOWTOW
having sense of .. TACTILE
light, passing .... BRUSH
lightly .... KISS
me-not ..... IMPATIENS, JEWELWEED
of .... TANG, TACTILE, TACTIC, HAPTIC
off .... START, FIRE
perceptible by .. TACTILE
system worker ... STENO, TYPIST, TYPER
the feelings .... MOVE
touchable .... TACTILE
touchdown ..... GOAL, SCORE
touched ... MOVED, AFFECTED, DEMENTED
touching ... TACTION, MOVING, TANGENT
touchstone .. TEST, CRITERION
touchwood ... AMADOU, PUNK, TINDER
touchy .. TICKLISH, IRRITABLE, SENSITIVE, SORE, HUFFY
tough ...... COHESIVE, ROUGH, THUG, RUFFIAN, GLUTINOUS, STICKY, VISCOUS, HARDY, HARDBOILED, WIRY
guy ...... BUTCH, GOON
street .... HOODLUM
toughen .... ANNEAL
Toulouse, painter ... LAUTREC
toupee ...... WIG, HAIRPIECE, PERUKE, RUG
slang .... RUG
tour ... SHIFT, TRIP, CIRCUIT, ROUND, EYRE
de force .... FEAT
touraco kin .... CUCKOO
tourbillion .... FIREWORK, WHIRLWIND
tourist .... SIGHTSEER, TRAVELER, TRIPPER
guide of ..... CICERONE, DRAGOMAN
stopping place ... MOTEL, INN, HOSTELRY, HOTEL
travel schedule .... ITINERARY
tourmaline .... GEM, SCHORL, RUBELLITE
tournament .... CONTEST, TOURNEY, COMPETITION, JOUST
kind of ...... OPEN, PRO, AMATEUR, CAROUSEL
knights' ..... TILT, JOUST
tourney .... TOURNAMENT, JOUST
tourniquet ... BANDAGE, PAD, GARROT
tousle .... DISHEVEL, RUMPLE, MUSS
tout ... SOLICITOR, BALLYHOO, TIP(STER), PUFF, SPY, PRAISE
tovarisch .... COMRADE
tow ..... PULL, DRAG, FIBER, HARDS, HURDS
and pitch torch ... LINK
toward ...... FACING, ABOUT
center .... ENTAD
exterior .... ECTAD
mouth .... ORAD
towboat .... TUG, MULE
towel .... DRY, WIPE(R), ABSORBENT, DIAPER, NAPKIN
church service ... LAVABO
small .... SERVIETTE
tower ..... BASTIL(L)E, SOAR, REAR, SPIRE, TURRET, TOURELLE, PULLER, DRAGGER, ZIGGURAT
a kind of .... IVORY
bell .... BELFRY, CAMPANILE
Biblical ... BABEL, EDAR
bridge ...... BARBICAN
canal boat's ...... MULE
castle .... DONJON, BARBICAN
church .... STEEPLE
fodder .... SILO

fortified .... DONJON, DUNGEON, PEEL
gate .... BARBICAN
mosque .... MINARET
of Babel ..... MADHOUSE
of confusion ..... BABEL
pointed .... SPIRE
portable .... TURRET, BASTIL(LE)
signal .... BEACON
tapering ... SPIRE, STEEPLE
towering .... HIGH
towhead .... BLOND
towhee ..... CHEWINK, FINCH
kin .. BUNTING, SPARROW
town ..... HAMLET, VILLAGE, CITY, BOROUGH, BURG(H), PUEBLO, WICK
fortified/walled ... BURG, BURH
imaginary ..... PODUNK
league .... HANSEATIC
magistrate .... REEVE
map .... PLAT
near castle .... BOURG
section .... WARD
square ... PLAZA, CAMPO
street .... MAINDRAG
"Too Tough to Die" .... TOMBSTONE
township .... DEME
townsman .... CIT(IZEN), RESIDENT, OPPIDAN
Towser's treat .... BONE
toxic .... POISONOUS
toxicant .... POISON(OUS)
toxin .... VENOM, POISON
canned food ... BOTULIN
toxophilite .... ARCHER
toy .... PLAYTHING, FLIRT, DALLY, TEETOTUM, TRIFLE, TRINKET, BAUBLE, PLAY
bear .... TEDDY
dog .... TERRIER, CHIHUAHUA, PEKE
musical instrument ...... KAZOO
stilt-like ..... POGO STICK
stringed .... YOYO
with string ... TOP, YOYO, DIABOLO
tra la la .... REFRAIN
trace ... TANG, TINGE, TOUCH, MARK, SIGN, ENGRAM, TRACK, VESTIGE, TRAIL, FOLLOW, DELINEATE, DRAW, SLOT
trachea .... WINDPIPE, WEASAND
trachoma ... CONJUNCTIVITIS
track .... TRACE, VESTIGE, TRAIL, PATH, ROUTE, COURSE, WAY, CIRCUIT, FOLLOW, RUNWAY
circuit .... LAP
down .... HUNT, SEARCH
game ...... SPOOR, PUG
horse racing ...... TURF
mark .. RUT, FOOTPRINT, SPOOR, SLOT, SPUR
racing ...... SPEEDWAY, CINDER PATH
ship's .... WAKE
train .... RAILS
tracker .... HUNTER, HOUND, TAIL, DETECTIVE
tract ...... STRETCH, STEPPE, AREA, EXTENT, LEAFLET, PAMPHLET, TREATISE, ENTERON
tractable ..... EASY, DOCILE, COMPLIANT, OBEDIENT
tractate .... TREATISE
tractile .... DUCTILE, TENSILE
traction ... DRAWING, PULLING
tractor .... BULLDOZER, AIRPLANE, MULE
and trailer .... SEMI
caterpillar .... CAT
trade .. DEAL, SWAP, BUSINESS, SELL, CLIENTELE, EXCHANGE, METIER, CRAFT, WORK, OCCUPATION, BARTER, COMMERCE, CUSTOMERS
agreement ...... CARTEL
association ..... CARTEL, SYNDICATE
center ... MART, MARKET, EXCHANGE, PIT
of .... MERCANTILE
questionable .... TRAFFIC
union strategy .. RATTEN
unlawful .. CONTRABAND
wind .... MONSOON
trademark .... BRAND
trader ... MONGER, MERCHANT, SHIP
unauthorized .... INTERLOPER
tradesman .... HUCKSTER, ARTISAN, STOREKEEPER
trading .... COMMERCE, COMMERCIAL
center ..... RIALTO, PIT, EXCHANGE, EMPORIUM
grains .... PIT
place, stocks .. EXCHANGE
settlement ..... FACTORY
ship .... CRAY
stamp .... PREMIUM
tradition .. CUSTOM, PRACTICE, USAGE, (FOLK)LORE
traditional ...... CUSTOMARY, CONVENTIONAL, LEGENDARY
traduce .... VILIFY, SLUR, DEFAME, SLANDER, MALIGN, REVILE
traffic .... COMMERCE, TRADE, BUSINESS
direction ...... UTURN, ONEWAY
light ...... BLINKER, RED, GREEN, AMBER
stopper .... SIREN
violator .... JAYWALKER
trafficker ... TRADER, DEALER, MERCHANT
tragacanth .... GUM
tragedian ... ACTOR, THESPIAN, SHAKESPEARE
tragedy ...... DRAMA, PLAY, DISASTER, CATASTROPHE
tragic .... SAD, FATAL, CALAMITOUS, PATHETIC
tragopan .... PHEASANT
trail ... DRAG, TRACK, HUNT, PATH, TRAIPSE, HOUND, HEEL
along .... TAG, FOLLOW
animal ... SPOOR, SCENT, SLOT, PUG, FOIL
behind ... LAG, STRAGGLE
blazer .... PIONEER
of scent .... DRAG
secretly ... SHADOW, TAIL
thru mud .... DAGGLE
trailer .... TAIL, TRACKER, VAN, WAGON, TRACER
arbutus ..... MAYFLOWER
branch .... STOLON, RHIZOME, RUNNER
trailing .... DECUMBENT
train ..... SUITE, PROCESSION, SERIES, INSTRUCT, AIM, TEACH, DRILL, CHAIN, JERKWATER, RETINUE
designating a .. SPECIAL, LOCAL, EXPRESS, FREIGHT, FLIER, LIMITED
for position ..... GROOM
of attendants ... CORTEGE, SUITE, RETINUE, ENTOURAGE
overhead ..... MONORAIL, EL
rider with free ticket ..... DEADHEAD
trainee .... APPRENTICE, PUPIL, NOVITIATE
trainer .. COACH, INSTRUCTOR, TEACHER, HANDLER, GYMNAST
trainmen's car ...... CABOOSE
traipse ... GAD, TRAMP, TRAIL, WANDER
trait .... QUALITY, CHARACTERISTIC
traitor .... BETRAYER, APOSTATE, RENEGADE, RECREANT
American .... HISS, CHAMBERS
Austrian .... REDL
Czechoslovak .... GOTTWALD
Finnish ...... KUSIINEN
French ..... ESTERHAZY, LAVAL, PETAIN
Hungarian ...... RAKOSI
Norwegian ... QUISLING
Romanian ..... PAUKER
traject .... CAST, THROW
trajectory .... ARC
tram ... STREETCAR, TROLLEY
coal mine .... TUB
trammel .. POTHOOK, HAMPER, CONFINE, RESTRAIN, SHACKLE
tramontane ..... FOREIGNER, STRANGER, ALIEN
tramp .... HOBO, BUM, VAGABOND, VAGRANT, HIKE, RAMBLE, PLOD, TART, TRUDGE, HOOF, YEGG, CLUMP
identification mark ...... MONI(C)KER
offering to .... HANDOUT

trampolin(e) .... NET
user .... ACROBAT, TUMBLER
trance .... SPELL, DAZE, STUPOR, HYPNOSIS
tranquil .... CALM, PLACID, QUIET, SERENE, STILL
tranquility ..... POISE, PEACE
Base site .... MOON
of the spirit ... QUIETISM
tranquilize ..... CALM, QUIET, SOOTHE, RESERPINE, DEPRESSANT, SEDATIVE, OPIATE, ATARAXIC
transact ... DEAL, NEGOTIATE, TREAT
transaction ... DEAL, BUSINESS, SALE
transcend .... OVERSTEP, EXCEED, EXCEL, SURPASS
transcribe .... COPY
transcriber .... STENO, COPIER, COPYIST
transcript(ion) .... COPY, REPRODUCTION
transeunt, opposed to .... IMMANENT
transfer .... SEND, PASS, CEDE, REMOVE
blood .... TRANSFUSE
by will .... DEMISE
of court suit ... REMOVER
of lands, etc. .. MORTMAIN
property .... DEED, CONVEY, GRANT
residence .... MOVE
sovereignty ..... DEMISE
transference .... SWITCH
transfix .... NAIL, PIERCE, PIN, IMMOBILIZE, IMPALE
transform .... CONVERT, CHANGE, METAMORPHOSE, TRANSMUTE, TRANSFIGURE
transformation ..... CHANGE, METASTASIS, TRANSITION, METAMORPHOSIS
transformer, type of .... STEP-UP, STEP-DOWN
transfuse ..... INSTILL, IMBUE
transgress ...... SIN, VIOLATE, INFRACT, OVERSTEP, TRESPASS
transgression ... SIN, TRESPASS, VIOLATION, OFFENSE
transgressor ...... OFFENDER, SINNER
transient .... TEMPORARY, MOMENTARY, FLEETING, EPHEMERAL
laborer .... FLOATER
transit ...... PASSAGE, RAPID, THEODOLITE, CONVEYANCE
transition .. PASSAGE, PASSING, TRANSFER, CHANGE
transitive .... TRANSEUNT
transitory .... FLEETING, EPHEMERAL, TEMPORARY, BRIEF, MOMENTARY
translate .... INTERPRET, CHANGE, TRANSFER, DECODE, RENDER, METAPHRASE
translation ... VERSION, PONY, PARAPHRASE, RENDITION, INTERPRETATION
translator .... INTERPRETER
translucent .... CLEAR, TRANSPARENT, PELLUCID
transmit ..... SEND, FORWARD, CONVEY, CARRY
transmute .... CONVERT
transom .. LINTEL, CROSSPIECE, LOUVER, SLAT, TRAVE
transparent ..... DIAPHANOUS, SHEER, GAUZY, OPEN, CANDID, OBVIOUS, CLEAR, LIQUID, PELLUCID, HYALINE, TRANSLUCENT, HYALOID, LUCID, LIMPID
combining form .... HYAL(O)
not .... OPAQUE
transpire ... HAPPEN, OCCUR, LEAK OUT, PASS
transplant .... RESETTLE, RELOCATE, GRAFT
transport .... BANISH, (TROOP)SHIP, CARRY, ENTRANCE, ENRAPTURE, AIRPLANE
transporting, act of .. PORTAGE
transportation .... FARE, DEPORTATION, CONVEYANCE
charge .... FARE
route .... LINE, AIRLANE
service/system .... LINE
transported .... RAPT, CARRIED, ENTRANCED
transpose ...... INTERCHANGE, REVERSE, INVERT
transposition .... METATHESIS
transude .... SWEAT, OOZE, EXUDE
Transvaal capital .. PRETORIA
city .... BENONI
gold region .... RAND
transverse .... CROSSWISE
Transylvania city .... CLUJ
trap .... NET, SNARE, CATCH, GIN, NAIL, TREPAN, TOIL, PIT(FALL), CARRIAGE, CAPARISON, WHIN, LUGGAGE
fish .... WEIR, GIN
game .... GIN
kind of .... AMBUSH
slang .... MOUTH
trapan .... TRICK
trapdoor .... HATCH, DROP
trapper ..... SNARER, TREPAN
trappings .. DUDS, CAPARISON, ADORNMENTS, REGALIA
Trappist .... MONK
monk .... MERTON
traps, orchestra ..... DRUMS, CYMBALS, BELLS
trapshooting .... SKEET
target .... (CLAY)PIGEON
trash ..... REFUSE, RUBBISH, NONSENSE, COLLAR, RESTRAIN(T), TRIPE, (RIFF)RAFF, JUNK
gaudy .... KITSCH
receptable ... (DUST)BIN
trashy .... WORTHLESS
trauma ..... WOUND, INJURY, SHOCK
travail ... TOIL, PAIN, AGONY, WORK, ANGUISH
trave .... CROSSBEAM
travel .... TOUR, JOURNEY, TRIP, TRAFFIC, PAD
by car .... MOTOR
by ox wagon ...... TREK
in circle .... ORBIT
of .... VIATIC
on foot over snow .. MUSH
to holy place .... PILGRIMAGE
what it does .. BROADENS, EDUCATES
traveler .... TOURIST, VOYAGE(U)R, WAYFARER, VIATOR, TRIPPER
aid of .... COURIER, CICERONE
guidebook for .... BAEDEKER
kind of .... HOBO, VAGABOND, SALESMAN, TRAMP, NOMAD, PILGRIM
refuge ... OASIS, HOSPICE
stopping place of .... INN, SERAI, HOSPICE
travelers, company of .... CARAVAN
traveling bag .... VALISE, HOLDALL, GRIP(SACK)
actors' group ... TROUPE
companion ... CHAPERON, COURIER, ESCORT
show .... CIRCUS
yen for .... WANDERLUST
traverse ...... PIVOT, SWIVEL, COURSE, CROSS(PIECE)
travertine .... LIMESTONE
travesty ... MOCKERY, PARODY, BURLESQUE, CARICATURE, SATIRE
travois .... SLEDGE
trawl .... (DRAG)NET
trawler .... BOAT
tray .... SERVER, SALVER, COASTER, TILL
agriculture .... HYDROPONICS
dish ..... WAITER, SALVER
for types .... GALLEY
liquids .... CAPSULE
treacherous ..... PERFIDIOUS, DISLOYAL, FAITHLESS, DECEITFUL
person .... TRAITOR, RENEGADE, TURNCOAT, BETRAYER
treachery ... DECEIT, PERFIDY, BETRAYAL
treacle .. MOLASSES, ANTIDOTE, REMEDY
treacly .... STICKY
tread ... STEP, WALK, TRAMPLE, CHALAZA, PAD, CICATRICLE
sound .... CRUNCH
treadle .... PEDAL, LEVER
treadmill .... WHEEL
treason .... TREACHERY, SEDITION
kind of .... LESE MAJESTE

treasure ..... HOARD, VALUE, TROVE, CHERISH, PRIZE, WEALTH, APPRECIATE
container .... CHEST
isle of fiction .... MONTE CRISTO
state .... MONTANA
treasurer ... BURSAR, PURSER
treasury ... VAULT, BURSARY, FISC, COFFERS, THESAURUS, EXCHEQUER
agent .... TMAN
treat .... USE, BARGAIN, NEGOTIATE, DEAL, DELIGHT, ENTERTAIN, HANDLE, REGALE
badly ..... ABUSE, SCORN, INSULT, ILL USE
insolently ... ABUSE, HUFF
lightly .... PALTER
tenderly ... PET, CODDLE
with contempt .. CONTEMN
with warm application ... FOMENT
treatise ... DISCOURSE, PAPER, MONOGRAPH, THESIS, ESSAY, DISSERTATION
opening part .. EXORDIUM
treatment ...... USAGE, CARE, HANDLING, MANAGEMENT, APPROACH, USE
before doctor's arrival ... FIRST AID
sprain .... ARNICA
treaty .... AGREEMENT, PACT, MISE, PROTOCOL, COVENANT, COMPACT, CONCORDAT
kind of .... PEACE, ALLIANCE, ENTENTE, CONCORD
Trebizond .... TRABZON, SEAPORT
treble .. SOPRANO, THREEFOLD, TRIPLE, SHRILL
trebuchet's kin .... CATAPULT
missile .... STONE
tree ...... STAKE, POST, POLE, GALLOWS, HATRACK, CORNER, ARBOR, GALLOWS
balsam .... TOLU
bark .... CORTEX
bark remover .. SPUDDER
beech .... ROBLE
betelnut .... ARECA
biblical ...... OLIVE, FIG
birch family .. HORNBEAM, HAZEL
boxwood .... SERON
branch(es) ..... RAMAGE, SPRAY, SPRIG, TWIG
buckwheat .... TITI
bully .... BALATA
butter .... SHEA
coffee .... CHICOT
combining form .... DENDR(I), DENDR(O)
cone-bearing ...... FIR, CEDAR, YEW, PINE, SPRUCE
cottonwood ..... ALAMO, POPLAR
covering .... BARK
crook .... KNEE
custard apple .. SWEETSOP, SOURSOP
cutting ...... LOP(PING)
decay .... NECROSIS
disease ... KNOT, MOSAIC
dogwood .... TUPELO, ASSAGAI
dwarf(ing) ...... BONSAI
dwelling creature .... OPOSSUM
ebony family ...... KAKI
evergreen .... FIR, EUCALYPTUS, CAROB, THUJA, OLIVE, YEW, PINE, BAY
exudation ...... BALATA, GUM, COPAL, LATEX, ROSIN, RESIN, SAP, MILK
fiber .... BAST, BASS, BAOBAB
flowering ...... CATALPA, TITI, MAGNOLIA
fragrant wood .... BASSWOOD
fraxinus .... ASH
frog ...... TOAD, PEEPER, HYLA
fustic .... MORA
gamboge family .. CALABA
giant .... SEQUOIA, REDWOOD
gingko .... ICHO
grown flat ..... ESPALIER
gum ... ACACIA, BALATA, EUCALYPTUS, ICICA, CHICLE, BUMBO, SAPOTA, XYLAN, RUBBER, SAPODILLA, TUPELO, PEPPERIDGE
gum resin .... ANTRA
hardwood ... TEAK, OAK, MOLAVE, ASH, IPIL
head of .... CROWN
heart-shape leafed ...... CATALPA
hive .... BEEGUM
holly family .... ILEX
icy coating of ..... SLEET
iron .... ACLE
ironwood .... TITI
juice .... CHICLE, MANNA
kapok .... CEIBA
knot .... BURL
lemon .... CITRUS
light wood .... BALSA
like a .... ARBOREAL, DENDROID, DENDRITIC
lime .... CITRUS
linden .. BASSWOOD, LIME, LINN, TEIL
lily family ... DRACAENA
locust .... ACACIA
lotus .... SADR
madder family .. BANCAL
magnolia .... CHAMPAK, CHAMPAC, TULIP, WHITEWOOD
marmalade ...... MAMEY, SAPODILLA, CHICO, MAMMEE
mark on .... BLAZE
Mediterranean ... CAROB
mimosa family .. ACACIA
moss .... USNEA
mulberry family .. FUSTIC
myrtle family ... CAJEPUT, CAJUPUT, LEHUA
oak ...... ENCINA, ROBLE
oil .... BEN
of a .... CEDARN
of heaven ... AILANTHUS
of life ...... ARBORVITAE
olive .... OLEA
palm .... CALAMUS
palm-like .... ZAMIA
pea family ...... CASSIA, DIVI-DIVI, MIMOSA, LABURNUM
pear .... NOPAL
Philippine ...... YAKAL, MOLAVE, IPIL, SANTOL, SAMPALOC
pine .... PINON, CYPRESS, HEMLOCK, JUNIPER, LARCH
plum .... DAMSON
poisonous .... SASSY, UPAS
pomegranate .. BLAUSTINE
powder .... ARAROBA
pulse family ..... LOCUST
rain ..... SAMAN, ZAMIA
remnant ... STUB, STUMP
resin ... PINE, BALSAM, FIR
rose family .... LOQUAT, MEDLAR
sapodilla .... BUSTIC
screw pine ... PANDANUS
shade ... ASH, ELM, LINN
shaped ... DENDRIFORM, DENDROID
shoots .... BROWSE, TWIGS
silk .... SIRIS
silk-cotton .... CEIBA
soapberry .... LITCHI
source of balsam ... TOLU
stock ...... STEM, TRUNK
stump .... SNAG, RUNT, STOOL
stub .... STUMP
stunted .... SCRAG
stunting .... BONSAI
sumac ...... TEREBINTH
toad .... PEEPER
toad genus .... HYLA
top .... CROWN
"trembling" ..... ASPEN
trimmings ...... BRASH
tropical .... LEHUA, TAMARISK, PAPAYA, PALM, CINCHONA
trunk ...... BOLE, STOCK
trunk, growth on .... LICHEN
trunk knot .... BURL
trunk protuberance ..... KNAR
trunk ring ...... GIRDLE
trunk strip ...... FLITCH
trunk wood ... DURAMEN
walnut family .. HICKORY
wide-spreading .. CEDAR, JUNIPER

with applelike fruit ...... MEDLAR
with plumlike fruit ...... LOQUAT
with striped wood .... ARAROBA
with winged fruit ... ASH, ELM, MAPLE, SAMARA
young .... SAPLING, SEEDLING
treeless plain .... WOLD, SAVANNA, PAMPAS, TUNDRA, STEPPE
treelike .... DENDRITIC
in form ...... DENDROID
treenail .... PEG, TRUNNEL, SPIKE, PIN
trees .... FOREST, WOODS, TIMBER
book on .... SILVA, SYLVA
clump of ... TUFT, GROVE, BOSK, SCRUB
grove of pine ... PINETUM
of .... ARBOROUS
of a region .... SILVA
pertaining to .. ARBOREAL
place where sold .... NURSERY
study of ... DENDROLOGY
stunted .... SCRUB
treatise on .... SILVA
trefoil .... CLOVER, TRIFOLIUM, SHAMROCK
trek ...... TRAVEL, JOURNEY, MIGRATION
trellis ..... LATTICE, BOWER, ARBOR, ESPALIER
part .... LATH
trelliswork .... PERGOLA, LATTICEWORK
trematode .... FLATWORM, FLUKE
larva .... CERCARIA
tremble ...... SHIVER, QUIVER, TOTTER, VIBRATE, SHUDDER, WOBBLE, QUAKE, SHAKE
trembling .... PALPITANT
tremendous .... GREAT, ENORMOUS, EXTRAORDINARY
tremolite .... AMPHIBOLE
tremolo ..... QUAVER, TRILL, VIBRATO
tremor ..... QUAKE, SHAKING, THRILL, TREPIDATION, SHIVER
tremulous .... QUIVERING, FEARFUL, SHAKY, ASPEN, TREMULANT, QUAVERY
trenail .... TREENAIL
trench .... CUT, FURROW, DITCH, SAP, FOSSE
embankment ... PARADOS
knife .... BAYONET
moon .... RILL(E)
strengthener ... FASCINE
trenchant ..... SHARP, KEEN, INCISIVE, PENETRATING, FORCEFUL, CLEAR-CUT
trencher .... PLATTER, BOARD, SAPPER, DIGGER
trencherman .... EATER, PARASITE, SPONGER, HANGER-ON, GLUTTON
trend ..... DRIFT, TENDENCY, TENOR, COURSE
trepan ..... TREPHINE, AUGER, TRICK(STER)
trepang ..... SEA CUCUMBER, ECHINODERM
trephine .... TREPAN, SAW
trepidation ... ALARM, DREAD, FEAR, TREMOR
treponema .... SPIROCHETE
trespass .... SIN, TRANSGRESS, OFFEND, OFFENSE, INVADE, INFRINGE, ENCROACH, POACH
trespasser .... POACHER, INTRUDER, INVADER
tres ____ .... BIEN, CHIC
tress ... LOCK, PLAIT, BRAID, CURL, PIGTAIL, QUEUE, RINGLET
Treves .... TRIER
trews .... TROUSERS
trey, thing with .... DIE, DICE, CARD, DOMINO
triad .... TRINITY, TRINE, TRIUNE
trial ...... AFFLICTION, ESSAY, TEST, PROBATION, EXPERIMENT, HEARING, INQUEST
ancient method of ...... ORDEAL
balloon ... FEELER, KITE
by ____ .... COMBAT, JURY, FIRE
performance .... PROLUSION, REHEARSAL
scene of .... COURT
severe .... ORDEAL, CRUCIBLE
site .... VENUE
trials and ____ .. TRIBULATIONS
triangle .... TRIGON, SCALENE
for example .. IDIOPHONE
kind of ...... ISOSCELES, ETERNAL
part .... SIDE, BASE, HYPOTENUSE
side of .... LEG
word for a love .. ETERNAL
triangular .. THREE-CORNERED, TRIGONAL, TRIGONOUS, DELTOID, TRIQUETROUS
brace .... GUSSET
flag ... PENNANT, PENNON, BUNTING
insert in seam .... GUSSET
muscle of shoulder ...... DELTOID
piece in a sail ...... GORE
piece of land ...... GORE
sail .... LATEEN, SPINNAKER, JIB
triarchy .... TRIUMVIRATE
tribe ... CLAN, GENE, FAMILY, FOLK
leader ...... CHIEFTAIN, PATRIARCH
wandering ...... HORDE
tribal sign .... TOTEM
tribulation .... DISTRESS, SORROW, MISERY, AFFLICTION, TRIAL, WOE
tribunal ... BENCH, ROTA, BAR, SEAT, FORUM, COURT
tribune ... MAGISTRATE, DAIS, PLATFORM
tributary .... SUBJECT, SUBSIDIARY, RIVER, STREAM
tribute ..... HOMAGE, PRAISE, EULOGY, GIFT, TAX, OFFERING, OVATION
to dead person .. EULOGY, EPITAPH
trice ...... INSTANT, MOMENT, SEC(OND), TIE
tricentennial .... TERCENTARY
trichoid .... HAIRLIKE
trichome ... PRICKLE, BRISTLE, ROOT HAIR
trichord .... LYRE
trick ..... ENTRAP, FUB, FOB, (FLIM)FLAM, GULL, CHEAT, STUNT, GAFF, ARTIFICE, TREPAN, DUPE, DIDO, DODGE, HOODWINK, JAPE, DECEPTION, FRAUD, RUSE, GAG, PRANK, JOKE, CHICANE(RY), WILE, KNACK, STRATEGEM, HOAX, ASSIGNMENT, SHIFT, GIMMICK, DEVICE, NICK
device .... GIMMICK
easy to .... GULLIBLE
person easy to .... GULL, DUPE, CULLY, GOOF
trickery .... ARTIFICE, FRAUD, DECEPTION, ART, CRAFT, CHICANE(RY)
trickle ..... DRIP, SEEP, DROP, FLOW
tricks, win all .... CAPOT
trickster .... TREPAN, MAGICIAN, PRANKSTER, JOKER, CHEAT, SWINDLER
tricktrack .... BACKGAMMON
tricky ... DECEITFUL, CRAFTY, INTRICATE, SLY, CATCHY, SMART, DECEPTIVE
and sly .... DEEP
condition .... CATCH
tricolor .... FLAG
tricorn .... HAT
tricycle .... VELOCIPEDE, IRON HORSE
trident ...... SPEAR, LEISTER
bearer .... NEPTUNE, POSEIDON
warrior with ... RETIARUS
tridentate .... TRIFID
Tridentum .... TRENT
tried ..... TESTED, RELIABLE, PROVED
trierarch's command .. GALLEY, TRIREME
trifid .... TRIDENTATE
trifle .... LITTLE, DESSERT, PEWTER, TOY, DALLY, PLAY, FLIRT, DOIT, FICO, KICKSHAW, DIDDLE, PALTER, FALDERAL, FOLDEROL
trifles .... TRIVIA
trifling .... PALTRY, TRIVIAL, PETTY, PIDDLING, FRIVOLOUS
amount ... PEANUTS, FIG

objection .... CAVIL, QUIBBLE
trifoliate .... TERNATE, THREE-LEAFED
plant .... SHAMROCK, CLOVER, TRIFOLIUM, TREFOIL, TRILLIUM
trifolium .... CLOVER, SHAMROCK, TREFOIL
trig ..... NEAT, SMART, WELL, SPRUCE, SOUND, FIT, TRIM, PROP, WEDGE, CHOKE
trigeminal .... TRIFACIAL
trigger .... INITIATE, LAUNCH, FIRE, TRIP
triggerfish .... OLDWIFE
trigo .... WHEAT
trigon ..... TRIANGLE, LYRE, TRINE, HARP
trigonal .... TRIANGULAR
trigonometric function .... (CO)SINE, SECANT
line .. SECANT, TANGENT
trigonous ...... TRIANGULAR, THREE-CORNERED
trilateral .... THREE-SIDED
trill ...... VIBRATO, WARBLE, TIRALEE, ROLL, TREMOLO, MORDENT
trilogy writer .... ASCH, GALSWORTHY
trim ... TIDY, TRIG, TAUT, CUT, DECORATE, CLIP, DEFEAT, LOP, CHEAT, ORDERLY, NEAT, NIFTY, PRUNE, DAPPER, NATTY, DRESS, SCOLD, CHIDE, DOCK, PARE, FETTLE, DECK
beard/hair ..... BARBER, CLIP
coin .... NIG
feathers .... PREEN
in curves ...... SCALLOP, ESCALOP
lumber .... DRESS
shrubbery/wool .. SHEAR
trimmer .... TIMESERVER, OPPORTUNIST
trimming .... DEFEAT, RICKRACK, GIMP, BEATING, RUCHE, DECORATION, EDGING, ORNAMENT, GUIPURE,
braid/ribbon .. GALLOON
tool ... SHEARS, CLIP(PER), SCISSORS, ZAX
Trimurti .... TRINITY
Trinacrian .... SICILIAN
trinal .... TRIPLE, THREEFOLD
trinary .. TERNARY, THREEFOLD
trine ... TRIGON, THREEFOLD, TRIPLE, TRIAD, FAVORABLE, TRINITY
Trinidad city .... ARIMA
dance .... CALYPSO
fish .... GUPPY
music .... CALYPSO
of Hindu gods .. TRIMURTI
partner of ...... TOBACO
Trinity College scholar .... SIZER, SIZAR
trinitrotoluene .... TNT, EXPLOSIVE, TROTYL
trinket .... TRIFLE, TOY, ORNAMENT, JEWELRY, GEWGAW, KNICKNACK, GIMCRACK, KICKSHAW, BIJOU, GAUD
seller .... FAKER
trio, mythical .. FATES, GRACES, FURIES
of fiction ... MUSKETEERS
one of a ... HOPE, FAITH, CHARITY, CALM, COOL, COLLECTED, LACHESIS, ATHOS, PORTHOS, ARAMIS, TOM, DICK, HARRY, CLOTHO, ATROPOS
trioxide, of arsenic .. RATSBANE
trip ... STUMBLE, CAPER, SKIP, ERR, JOURNEY, TILT, OUTING, ERR, EXCURSION, JAUNT, VOYAGE, TUMBLE
tripartite .... THREEFOLD
tripe .... RUBBISH, TRASH
triple ... THREEFOLD, TERNARY, TREBLE, TRIAD, TRINAL, TRINE, TRIPLICATE
alliance .... AXIS, DREIBUND
crown .... TIARA
crown winner .... SECRETARIAT
time .... TRIPLEX
triplet .... TRISTICH
in music .... TERCET
tripod .... TRIPOS, CAT, TRIVET, SPIDER
part .... LEG
tripoli ..... ABRASIVE, ROCK, ROTTENSTONE
badmen, former .... PIRATES
ruler .... DEY, PASHA
where it is .... LIBYA, LEBANON
tripos .... TRIPOD
tripper .. PAWL, CAM, TOURIST, DETENT
trippet .... CAM
triptych .... TABLET
triquetrous ...... TRIHEDRAL, TRIANGULAR
trireme .... GALLEY
commander .. TRIERARCH
Tris, baseball player .. SPEAKER
trisaccharide .... TRIOSE
trismus .... LOCKJAW, TETANUS
triste .... SAD
tristesse .... SADNESS
tristful .... SAD, SORROWFUL
tristich .... TRIPLET
Tristram's beloved ... ISEULT, ISOLDE
trite .... HACK(NEYED), STALE, COMMONPLACE, CORNY, JEJUNE, STOCK, MUSTY
expression ...... CLICHE, BANALITY, PLATITUDE, CORN
triton .... NEWT, SNAIL, (SEA)GOD, SALAMANDER, EFT
lower extremity of .. TAIL
parent of ..... POSEIDON, AMPHITRITE
trumpet .... CONCH
triturate ... CRUSH, RUB, BRAY, GRIND, PULVERIZE
triumph ... SUCCESS, PREVAIL, VICTORY, EXULT(ATION), REJOICE, WIN
triumphant ...... EXULTANT, JUBILANT
triumvirate .... TRIARCHY
triume .... TRINITY, TRIAD
trivet .... TRIPOD, SPIDER
trivia .... TRIFLES
trivial ..... TRIFLING, PETTY, UNIMPORTANT, PALTRY, LITTLE, SLIGHT, BANAL, FLIMSY
objection .... CAVIL
trivium, part of .... LOGIC, GRAMMAR, RHETORIC, MUSIC, GEOMETRY, ARITHMETIC, ASTRONOMY
troche .... LOZENGE, COUGH DROP, PASTIL(LE), ROTULA
trochee .... TROCHAIC
and iamb ..... CHORIAMB
trochilus .... SCOTIA, HUMMINGBIRD, WARBLER
troglodyte .... CAVE MAN, RECLUSE, HERMIT, GORILLA, APE, CHIMPANZEE
trogon ...... QUE(T)ZAL, BIRD
troika .... VEHICLE
Troilus' father .... PRIAM
killer .... ACHILLES
love .... CRESSIDA
mother .... HECUBA
Trojan ..... ILIAN, TEUCRIAN, DARDAN(IAN)
commander ... ANTENOR
country .... TROY
epic .... ILIAD
hero .... (A)ENEAS
horse builder .... EPEUS
king .... PRIAM
peace offering .... (WOODEN)HORSE
War allies ...... DARDAN
War cause .... HELEN
War hero ...... MEMNON
War protagonist .. PARIS, HECTOR, AGENOR, ACHILLES, (A)ENEAS, DARDAN
War warriors .... MYRMIDONS
troll .. GNOME, GIANT, DWARF, IMP, ROLL, SING, CHANT, FISH, SPIN
trolley ..... CART, STREETCAR, TRAM
car .... DINKEY
trollop ...... SLATTERN, SLUT
trombone ... HORN, SAMBUKE
forerunner of .. SACKBUT
mouthpiece ..... BOCAL
part .... SLIDE
trommel ...... SIEVE, SCREEN
trona .... URAO
Trondheim .... NIDAROS
troop .... BAND, COMPANY, TROUPE, FLOCK, GROUP
barracks ..... CASERN(E)

disposition .. DEPLOYMENT
formation .... ECHELON, HERSE
member .... SOLDIER, BOY SCOUT
quarters ..... BARRACKS, BILLET, CANTON(MENT), CASERN
trooper .... CAVALRYMAN, POLICEMAN, MOUNTIE
troops' halting place .. ETAPE
quarters .... CANTON, BILLET
screen .... BLINDAGE
spread .... DEPLOY
station .. POST, GARRISON
stationed in a fort .... GARRISON
temporary encampment .. BIVOUAC
turning movement ...... WHEEL
troopship .... TRANSPORT
trop ...... MANY, TOO (MUCH)
trope .... METAPHOR
trophy ... MEMORIAL, AWARD, MEMENTO, PALM, LAUREL, PRIZE, SPOILS, (LOVING)CUP
athletic contest ... MEDAL
Indian .... SCALP
matador's .... EARS
war ..... ARMS, BANNER, FLAG
tropic .... CIRCLE, SOLAR
circle .... CAPRICORN, CANCER
tropical .... TORRID, HOT, SULTRY, FIGURATIVE, WARM
animal .... TAPIR
disease .... AGUE, MALARIA, BERIBERI, BUBA, DENGUE, SPRUE, PSILOSIS, YAWS, FRAMB(O)ESIA,
evergreen ..... CASHEW
fever .... CALENTURE
fish .... OPAH
fruit .. PAPAYA, PAWPAW, TAMARIND, DATE, MANGO, GUAVA
herb .... LOOFA
lizard .... SKINK, SCINCOID
snake ..... FER DE LANCE
tree ... CASSIA, CASHEW, PALM, GUAVA, TAMARIND, PAPAYA, BALSA, SAPOTA, COLIMA
trot .. JOG, RUN, AMBLE, GAIT, CANTER
troth .... PLEDGE, FAITH
Trotsky, Russian revolutionist LEON
trotter .... MORGAN
trotyl .... TNT
troubadour ...... BALLADEER, JONGLEUR, MINNESINGER, (LYRIC)POET, MUSICIAN, MINSTREL
song ....SERENADE
theme of .... LOVE, CHIVALRY
traveling ..... JONGLEUR
trouble .... ILL, VEX, ANNOY, DISTURB, WORRY, HARASS, AFFLICT, BOTHER, PAINS, FASH, OBSESS, IRK, INCOMMODE, PESTER, DISORDER, AILMENT
troublemaker ..... PEST, IMP, AGITATOR, PROVOCATEUR, ERIS, HELLION
trough ... BOSH, HOD, GUTTER, CHUTE, VALLEY, SLUICE, MANGER, SHOOT, DRAIN, RUNWAY
fodder .... CRIB
for logs .... FLUME
mining .... HUTCH
ore washing ... LAUNDER
washing ore .... BUDDLE
water wheel .. PENSTOCK
trounce .... BEAT, FLOG, THRASH, DEFEAT
troupe .... BAND, GROUP
trouper .... ACTOR
troupial ... ORIOLE, COWBIRD, GRACKLE, CACIQUE
trousers ..... PEGTOPS, PANTS, SLACKS, PAJAMAS, SLOPS, JEANS
bottom fold .... CUFF
cotton .... DUCKS
leather .... CHAPS, CHAPARAJOS
trousseau .... BUNDLE
item .... LINGERIE
trout ... STEELHEAD, CHAR(R), NAMAYCUSH, DOLLY VARDEN, BLUEBACK, SALMONOID, OQUASSA
family .... SALMON
fish like .... SMELT
flap .... FLY
sea .... KIPPER
trowel .. DARBY, FLOAT, PLANE
Troy ... ILIUM, ILION, WEIGHT
founder of .... ILUS, LAOMEDON
tale of .... ILIAD
truant .... SHIRKER, SLACKER, ERRANT, TRIVANT, VAGRANT
play .... MICHE
truce .... ARMISTICE, RESPITE, CEASEFIRE
signal ..... WHITE FLAG
Trucial Coast region ... OMAN
truck ...... BARROW, BARTER, EXCHANGE, TRUNDLE, CAMION, VAN, LORRY, DEALINGS, RUBBISH, BOGIE, BOGY
army ...... HALF-TRACK
artillery .... CAMION
dump .... TILLER
farm product .... VEGETABLES
rail .... LORRY
Truckee City .... RENO
truckle ...... CASTER, TOADY, CRINGE, YIELD, SUBMIT, TRUNDLE
truculent .... CRUEL, SAVAGE, HARSH, MEAN, RUDE, FIERCE, BELLIGERENT
trudge .... PLOD, ANKLE, WALK, TRAMP, SLOG, TRAIPSE
true .... RIGHT, CORRECT, EXACT, LAWFUL, RIGHTFUL, REAL, GENUINE, ALINE, ACTUAL
blue ..... LOYAL, STANCH
copy .... ESTREAT
level .... GEOID
love .... SWEETHEART
truffle ... MUSHROOM, FUNGUS, TUCKAHOE, EARTHNUT
Truk island .... TOL
truism ..... FACT, PLATITUDE, COMMONPLACE, AXIOM
trull .... TART, TROLLOP
truly .... REALLY, INDEED, IN FACT, SOOTH, QUITE, FAITHFULLY, ACTUALLY
Truman, cabinet member .... ACHESON, STIMSON, SNYDER, KIMBALL
playwright ...... CAPOTE
president .... HARRY
trump in card game ..... RUFF
trumpery .... NONSENSE, RUBBISH, PALTRY
trumpet ... HORN, PROCLAIM, CLARION
belt .... BALDRIC
blast ...... BLARE, FANFARE
call ... REVEILLE, SENNET, TAPS
caller .... GABRIEL
flourish .... FANFARE, TUCKET, TANTARA
muffler .... MUTE
shell ..... TRITON, CONCH
signal .... CHAMADE, FLOURISH
sound .... BLARE
trumpeter .... HERALD, ELEPHANT, SWAN, PIGEON, BUGLER, AGAMI, GABRIEL
trumps, five of .... PEDRO
truncate ... LOP, TRIM, STUMP
truncheon ..... CUDGEL, CLUB, STAFF, BATON, MACE
trundle ...... CASTER, CART, WHEEL, ROLL, RULL
trunk ... STEM, SNOUT, COFFER, PROBOSCIS, BOX, CHEST, COMPARTMENT, MAIN LINE STOCK
animal's .... SOMA
human .... TORSO
insect's .... THORAX
knot .... BURL
tree .... BOLE, BURL
trunkfish ..... TORO, COWFISH, CHAPIN
trunks .... BREECHES, SHORTS
trunnel .... TRE(E)NAIL
trunnion .... GUDGEON, JOURNAL
truss ..... BUNDLE, PACK, TIE, PROP, BRACE, BIND
trust .... RELY, CUSTODY, DUTY, CHARGE, CREDIT, CARTEL, MONOPOLY, HOPE, FAITH, RELIANCE, CONFIDENCE
betrayal of ..... PERFIDY

of/like a ...... FIDUCIAL, FIDUCIARY
territory .... MANDATE
to the British ...... TICK
trustee .... GARNISHEE, WARDEN, CUSTODIAN
trustworthy ... TESTED, TRIED, RELIABLE, STA(U)NCH, SAFE
trusty .... CONVICT
truth .... REALITY, FACT, ACTUALITY, VERACITY, VERITY, VERITAS, FACT
assumed in theology ..... MYSTERY
drug .... PENTOTHAL
personified .... UNA
truthful .... HONEST, VERACIOUS
boy .... WASHINGTON
try ...... TEST, MELT, REFINE, AFFLICT, EXPERIMENT, ATTEMPT, STRIVE, STAB, ESSAY
to do .... TACKLE
trying .... IRKSOME, PAINFUL, ANNOYING
experience ..... ORDEAL
tryma ...... DRUPELET, NUT, HICKORY
tryout .... TEST, TRIAL, AUDITION
trypsin .... ENZYME
trysail .... SPENCER
tryst .... DATE, MEETING, RENDEZVOUS
Tsaritsyn ...... STALINGRAD
tsaritza ... CZARINA, TSARINA
Tschaikowsky, composer ..... PET(E)R
tsetse ... FLY, KIVU, MUSCID, MAU
caused disease .. NAGANA, SLEEPING SICKNESS
Tse-tung, Chinese leader .. MAO
tsine .... OX, BANTENG
Tuareg .... BERBER
tub .... CASK, TRAM, BUCKET, FIRKIN, VAT, KID, BATH, KEELER, DAN, KIT, GYLE, KEEVE, KNOP, HOD, SKEEL, HOGSHEAD
2-handled .... COWL
tuba .... SAXHORN, BOMBARDON
instrument resembling ... EUPHONIUM
mouthpiece ..... BOCAL
tubby .... SQUAT
tube .... DUCT, PIPE, CYLINDER, HOSE, (ELECTRIC)RAILROAD, TELESCOPE, HUMIDOR
cannon/gun ..... BARREL
draining ..... CATHETER
electric wires' .. CONDUIT
for gas, smoke, etc. .... FLUE
glass .... PIPET(TE)
graduated .. HYDROMETER
joint of .... ELL
tapering .... BURETTE
underground ... TUNNEL, SUBWAY

vacuum .... DIODE
tuber ..... CASSAVA, MANIOC, RHIZOME, ONION, TARO, OCA, YAM, JALAP, CORM, BULB, EDDO, POTATO
dried orchid ..... SALEP
tubercle .... PROCESS, PROJECTION
tubercular .... LUNGER, CONSUMPTIVE
tuberculosis .... PHTHISIS, CONSUMPTION, WHITE PLAGUE
bovine .... GRAPE
lymphatic gland .... SCROFULA
tuberculous ... CONSUMPTIVE, PHTHISIC
tuberous .... KNOBBY
tubular .... FISTULOUS
tuck .... FOLD, WRAP, COVER, CRAM, PUCKER, SWORD, RUCHE, PLEAT, TAP, LAP
companion of ...... NIP
tuckahoe .... PORIA, TRUFFLE, FUNGUS
tucker .. COLLAR, CHEMISETTE, WEARY, TIRE
companion of ...... BIB
tucket ... TANTARA, FLOURISH
tufa ...... LIMESTONE, TUFF, TOPH(E)
tuff .... ROCK, TUFA
tuft .... CLUSTER, CLUMP
having a .... COMOSE
of feathers ...... PLUME, CREST, COP, TOPKNOT
of grass, etc. ..... TUSSOCK
of seed hairs ...... COMA
of threads, etc. .. TASSEL
on woman's hat .. POMPON
tufted ..... COMOSE, COMATE
tufthunter .... SNOB, SYCOPHANT, TOADY, SOCIAL CLIMBER
tug ..... DRAG, PULL, HAUL, STRAIN, TOW(BOAT), TOIL
boat pulled by ... BARGE, SCOW, SHIP
Tuileries .... PALACE
tuition ..... INSTRUCTION, FEE
tule .... BULRUSH
tulip .... FLOWER, BULB
tree .... POPLAR
tulle .... LACE, NET(TING), ILLUSION
tullibee .... WHITEFISH
Tully .... CICERO
tumble ... TRIP, SOMERSAULT, FALL, FLOP, SPILL, PLASH
tumbler ...... ACROBAT, DOG, PIGEON, (DRINKING)GLASS, TURNER, DOVE
net of ..... TRAMPOLIN(E)
tumbleweed .... THISTLE, AMARANTH
tumbling box ..... RUMBLE(R)
tumbrel .... (DUMP)CART, WAGON, CAISSON
tumefy .... SWELL
tumescence .... SWELLING
tumid ... SWOLLEN, BULGING, BOMBASTIC, POMPOUS

tummy .... STOMACH
ache .... COLIC
tumor .. SWELLING, NEOPLASM, MELANOMA, HEMATOMA, ANGIOMA, CYST, YAW, GUMMA, SCIRRHUS, NEUROMA
anal .. PILES, HEMORRHOID
benign ... ADENOMA, WEN
blood vessel ... ANGIOMA
bony tissue ..... OSTEOMA
brain .... GLIOMA
cartilaginous .... CHONDROMA
classification .... BENIGN, MALIGNANT
combining form .... C(O)ELE
epithelial ... CARCINOMA
fat tissue .... LIPOMA
fibrous .... FIBROMA, FIBROID, KELOID, CHELOID
glandular ..... ADENOMA
malignant ..... CANCER, EPITHELIOMA, SARCOMA
not malignant ... BENIGN
scar tissue ..... CHELOID, KELOID
skin ... PAPILLOMA, WEN
tendon .... GANGLION
tumult .... COMMOTION, UPROAR, CONFUSION, RIOT, TURMOIL, BABEL, DIN, STIR, HUBBUB
tumultous .... RIOTOUS, TURBULENT
tumulus ... BARROW, MOUND
tun .... CASK, VAT
tuna .... TUNNY, CACTUS, MACKEREL, PEAR, OPUNTIA
like fish ...... ALBACORE, BONITO
tundra ... PLAIN, WASTELAND
dweller .... LAPP
like wasteland ... STEPPE, PAMPAS
tune .... LILT, ARIA, TONE, MELODY, AIR, HARMONY, CONCORD
tunesmith .... COMPOSER, SONGWRITER
tungsten .... WOLFRAM, CARBOLOY
mineral ..... SCHEELITE, WOLFRAMITE
tungstite .... OCHER
Tungus .... MANCHU, MONGOLIAN
tunic ... COAT, ROBE, CHITON, STOLE, TOGA, GIPON, JUPON, KIRTLE, JAMA, BASQUE, FROCK
tunicate .... ASCIDIAN, SALPA
bulb .... ONION
tunicle .... VESTMENT
tuning fork .... DIAPASON
Tunisian capital ...... TUNIS
Berber .... KABYLE
city ...... SFAX, SOUSSE, KAIROUAN, BIZERTE
diplomat .. (MONGI) SLIM
measure .... SAA(H)

money .... DINAR
oasis .... GAFSA
president ... BOURGUIBA
ruler ... BEY, PASHA, DEY
tunnel ... FLUE, BURROW, SAP, DIG, TUBE, SIMPLON, SUBWAY
tunneler .... SAPPER, BURROWER, ANT
tunny ..... MACKEREL, TUNA, ALBACORE, AMIA
tup .... RAM, SHEEP
tupelo .... DOGWOOD, PEPPERIDGE, NYSSA, WATER GUM, LIME(TREE)
Tupi .... INDIAN, GUARANI
tuque .... CAP
turban ...... HEADDRESS, HAT, MANDIL
cloth ... LUNGEE, LUNGI
turbid ... CLOUDY, MUDDLED, MUDDY, ROILY
turbine ...... MOTOR, ENGINE
turbit .... PIGEON
turbot .. FLATFISH, BRILL, BUTT
flatfish like .... SOLE, HALIBUT, FLOUNDER
turbulence .... DISORDER, TUMULT, COMMOTION
turbulent ..... WILD, UNRULY, AGITATED
Turco .... TURK
turdine bird .... THRUSH
tureen .... (SOUP)DISH
turf ...... SOD, PEAT, SWARD, TRACK
of/like .... CEPITOSE
piece of .... DIVOT
turfy .... GRASSY
turgid ..... SWOLLEN, TOROSE, TOROUS, TUMID, BLOATED, BOMBASTIC
Turin .... TORINO
Turk ... OSMANLI, OTTOMAN, TATAR, TURCO, MOSLEM, HORSE, TA(R)TAR
Turkestan inhabitant ... SART
Moslem .... SALAR
mountain .... PAMIRS, ALAI
river ILI
tribe ... KIRGHIZ, USBEG
Turkey, Asiatic ... ANATOLIA
bird like ..... CURASSOW
buzzard .... VULTURE, AURA
capital of ...... ANKARA, ANGORA
chin adornment of ...... WATTLE, CARUNCLE
cock .... TOM
male .... TOM, GOBBLER
red dye ...... ALIZARIN, MADDER
slang .... FAILURE
sound .... GOBBLE
trot .... DANCE
wild .... BUSTARD
young .... POULT
Turki .... TURKOMAN, OSMANLI
Turkic people .... UZBEG, UZBEK

Turkish bathhouse .. BAGNIO
cab .... ARABA
cap ...... FEZ, KALPAK, CALPAC
capital .... ANKARA, ANGORA
caravansary .... IMARET
cavalryman ..... SPAHI, SPAHEE
chamber .... ODA(H)
chieftain .... ZAIM
city ... ISTANBUL, IZMIR, SMYRNA, ADANA, BURSA, EDIRNE, TARSUS, GALLIPOLI, AYADIN, AIDIN, AINTAB, EDESSA, KONIA, SIVAS, EBZURUM, GAZIANTEP, CAESAREA, KAYSERI, MANIS(S)A, URFA
coin .. LIRA, PARA, ASPER, ALTUN, PIASTER, PIASTRE, YUZLUK
college .... ULEMA
commander ...... SIRDAR
confection ..... HALVAH
court .... PORTE
decree .... IRADE
delight .... CANDY
dialect .... JAGATAI
dispute with Greece .... CYPRUS
district .... VILAYET
dulcimer .... CANUN
dynasty .... SELJUK
emblem .... CRESCENT
emissary .... CHIAUS
ensign .... HORSETAIL, CRESCENT
father .... BABA
flag ..... ALEM, CRESCENT
float .... KALAK
foreign quarter .... PERA, BEYOGLU
garment .... CAFTAN, KAFTAN
general .. KEMAL, INONU
government ..... PORTE
governor ... MALI, PASHA, WALI, BEY
harem resident .. KADEIN
hat .... FEZ
hell .... DAGH
house for men .... SELAM LIK
inn ...... IMARET, KHAN, SERAI
island .... TENEDOS
javelin ...... JER(R)EED, JER(R)ID
judge ...... CADI, KADI
liquor .... MASTIC
magistrate .... CADI
master .... EFFENDI
measure .... ARSHIN, DRA(H), KHAT, ALMUD, PIK, KILE
messenger ...... CHIAUS
military district ... ORDO
milk food .... YOG(H)URT
minister .... VIZI(E)R
mock battle .... JER(R)ID, JER(R)EED

monetary unit ... PIASTER, PIASTRE
money of account .. ASPER
monk .... DERVISH
mountain ...... ARARAT, TAURUS
non-Moslem .... GIAOUR, RAYAH, RAIA
oak .... CERRIS
official .... BASHAW, EMEER, EMIR, PASHA, PACHA
opium .... AFYON
oxcart .... ARABA
palace .... SERAI, SERAGLIO
parade .... ALAI
pasha's standard .... HORSETAIL
pavilion .... KIOSK
peasant .... RAYA
peninsula .... GALLIPOLI
people .... OSMANLI, KURD, TURKI
policeman ..... ZAPTIAH
pound .... LIRA
prayer rug .... MELAS
premier .... DEMIREL
president .... ATATURK, INONU, BAYAR, SUNAY
province .... VILAYET
regiment .... ALAI
region .... EREGLI, ESKISEHIR, KURDISTAN
rice dish ... PILAU, PILAW
river .... MARITSA, ARAS, TIGRIS, ZAB, MESTA, SARUS
robe .. DOLMAN, KAFTAN, CAFTAN
ruler ... SULTAN, CALIPH
saber .... YATAG(H)AN
scholar .... ULEMA
school .... ULEMA
sea .... MARMARA, BOSPORUS
seaport .... TRABZON, TREBIZOND
sergeant .... CHIAUS
sir .... EFFENDI
slave .... MAMELUKE, JANIZARY, JANISSARY
soldier .... NIZAM, JANIZARY, JANISSARY
standard .... ALEM, HORSETAIL
strait ...... DARDANELLES
sultan .... PADISHAH, SELIM, CALIF, CALIPH
sultan's guard .. JANIZARY
sultan's palace .. SERAGLIO
sultan's visit to mosque .. SELAM LIK
summerhouse .... KIOSK
sword ...... YATAGHAN, SCIMITAR
teacher ...... MULLA(H)
title .... GHAZI, EFFENDI, EMIR, EMEER, AG(H)A, PACHA, PASHA, BEY
tobacco .... LATAKIA
tower .... MANARAT
tribesman .... TATAR

veil .... YASHMAK, YASHMAC
viceroy .... KHEDIVE
"victorious warrior" .... GHAZI
vilayet subdivision ...... SANJAK
weight .. ROTL, OKE, OKA, MAUND
whip .... KURBASH
zither .... CANUM
Turko-Tartar tribe .. BASHKIR
turmeric ..... CURCUMA, REA
turmoil ... TUMULT, UPROAR, COMMOTION, STOUR, HUBBUB, WELTER
turn .... BEND, CURVE, REVOLVE, CANT, ROTATE, AVERT, BLUNT, DIVERT, SPIN, TREND, REPEL, PIVOT, DEVIATE, VOLUTE, SCREW, SWITCH
a new leaf ...... CHANGE, REFORM
around ..... SLUE, PIVOT
aside ...... BRUSH, FEND, SWERVE, SHUNT, BLANCH, DEFLECT, DAFF
away ... ESTRANGE, SHOO
back ... REPEL, REPULSE, PUSH, REFLEX
combining form .. TROPO
course .... YAW
down ..... REJECT, VETO, SPURN
equestrian .... CARACOLE
horsemanship .... CARACOLE
in ...... DELIVER, ENTER
in music .... VOLTA
inside out .... EVERT
into money ... (EN)CASH
left .... HAW
loose .... LIBERATE, RELEASE, FREE
of mind .... CAPRICE
off course .... YAW
on an axis .... ROLL
one side .... DEFLECT
out ..... BECOME, DISMISS, GATHERING, OUTPUT, EQUIPAGE, ARRAY
outward .... EVERT
over .... TRANSFER, CAPSIZE, KEEL
over a new leaf .. REFORM
over by tossing .... FLAP
page over .... LEAF
right .... JEE, GEE
ship's ...... YAW, TACK
single .... WINDING
to .... CONSULT
unfriendly .... ESTRANGE, ANTAGONIZE
up .... APPEAR
white .... PALE, BLANCH
turnabout ...... VOLTE-FACE, REVERSAL
turncoat ... TRAITOR, BOLTER, DESERTER, RENEGADE, RUNAGATE, APOSTATE, BAT
turned back piece ... REVERSE
in mathematics .. VERSED
up .... SNUB, ACOCK, TILTED
turner ... TUMBLER, GYMNAST, ACROBAT
actress .... LANA
turning joint .... HINGE
machine .... LATHE, SPANNER
point ..... PIVOT, CRUX, CRISIS, CLIMAX, SOLSTICE
turnip .... ROOT, SWEDE, RUTABAGA, NEEP
shaped .... NAPIFORM
turnix .... (GAME)BIRD
turnkey ..... JAILER, WARDER
turnout .... ATTENDANCE
turnover .... TART, PIE, UPSET
turnsole .... HELIOTROPE, SUNFLOWER, DYE
turnpike .. TOLLGATE, HIGHWAY
turnstile .... GATE
turntable operator .... DISC JOCKEY
Turnverein member .. TURNER, GYMNAST, TUMBLER
turpentine .... OLEORESIN, OIL, GAL(L)IPOT
substance like .... ELEMI
tree ... PINE, TEREBINTH, TARATA
turpeth .... EMETIC
turquoise .... GEM
turret ...... TOWER, BARTIZAN
gun .... CUPOLA
opening .... LOUVER
tower .... BARTISAN, BARTIZAN
viewing .... GAZEBO
turtle .... SNAPPER, HAWK(S)BILL, ARRAU, JURARA, TERRAPIN, CHELONIAN, REPTILE, EMYD, LEATHERNECK, MOSSBACK, LOGGERHEAD
descriptive of a .... SLOW(FOOT)
enclosure for ...... CRAWL
genus ...... CARETTA, EMYS
land .... TORTOISE, TESTUDO
of the ...... CHELONIAN
old .... MOSSBACK
protective covering ...... MAIL
shell .... CARAPACE, PLASTRON, PEE
shell substance .. CALIPEE, CALIPASH
turn .... CAPSIZE
Tuscan city .... FLORENCE, TOSCANA
wine .... CHIANTI
Tuscany island .... ELBA
river .... ORCIA
wine .... CHIANTI
tush .... CANINE, TOOTH
tusk .... FANG, IVORY, TOOTH
tusker ..... ELEPHANT, BOAR, WALRUS, WARTHOG, NARWHAL, PECCARY
tussah .... SHANTUNG, SILKWORM
tussis .... COUGH
tussle ... GRAPPLE, WRESTLE, SCUFFLE, FIGHT, STRUGGLE
tussock ..... THICKET, CLUMP, TUFT
tut .... TSK
tutelage .. CARE, PROTECTION, TEACHING, INSTRUCTION, GUARDIANSHIP
tutelary deity .... LAR(ES), PENATES, GENIUS
tutor .... TEACH(ER), DISCIPLINE, INSTRUCT(OR), MENTOR, COACH, MASTER
tutto .... ALL, ENTIRE
Tutuila city ...... PAGO PAGO
tux(edo) .... JACKET
tuyere ... NOZZLE, PIPE, TEW, TEWEL
TV (see television) ..... TELLY, VIDEO
award .... EMMY
broadcast ..... TELECAST
cabinet .... CONSOLE
camera move .... PAN
camera plate .... MOSAIC
camera platform .. DOLLY
commercial cat .. MORRIS
dragon .... OLLIE
emcee .... COMPERE
gossip columnist .... RONA (BARRET)
horse .... MISTER ED
interference ...... SNOW
lines on tube .... RASTER
name .... IMOGENE
pickup tube .. ORTHICON
plug .... COMMERCIAL
producer ..... SUSSKIND
room .... DEN
show, kind of .... QUIZ, PANEL, LIVE, GIVEAWAY, RERUN, MOVIE
stand .... ROLLAWAY
street for tots .... SESAME
time .... SLOT
Tver .... KALININ
twaddle ... BUNK, NONSENSE, PRATTLE, ROT, DRIVEL, FUSTIAN
twain .... TWO
character .... SAWYER
humorist .... MARK
twang .... PLUNK, TANG
tweak .... PINCH, PLUCK, TWIST, TWITCH
Tweeddale .... PEEBLES
tweeg .... HELLBENDER
tweet .... CHIRP
tweeter .... LOUDSPEAKER
tweeze .... PLUCK
tweezers .... PINCERS
Twelfth Night ..... EPIPHANY
character .... VIOLA, ORSINO, FESTE, MALVOLIO
composer ...... AMRAM
twelve .... DOZEN, XII
Biblical .... APOSTLES
by twelve .... GROSS

dozen .... GROSS
twelvemo .... DUODECIMO
twentieth .... VIGESIMAL
twenty .... SCORE
combining form ... ICOS, VIGINTI
dinars .... BISTI
fifth anniversary .... JUBILEE
five pounds .... PONY
minute walk ...... MILE
of .... VICENARY, VIGESIMAL
one .... BLACK JACK
one merit badge wearer .. EAGLE SCOUT
quires .... REAM
twibill .... MATTOCK, (BATTLE)AX
twice ... DOUBLY, TWO TIMES, BIS
prefix .... BI, DI
twiddle ... TWIRL, TOY, TRIFLE
twig ... ROD, SHOOT, BRANCH, SPRIG, (S)CION, LAYER
and branch angle .. AXIL
Brit. slang ...... NOTICE, OBSERVE
broom .... BARSOM
flexible ... OSIER, WICKER, WILLOW, SWITCH, WITHE
for grafting .... SLIP
willow .... SALLOW
twiggy ... SLENDER, DELICATE, VIRGATE
Britain's .... MODEL
twigs, bunch of ...... WHISK, FAGOT
clump of .... TUSSOCK
having .... VIRGATE
of .... VIMINAL
twilight .... DUSK, GLOAM, EVENTIDE, EVE, EVENFALL, CREPUSCLE
of the Gods .. RAGNAROK
sleep inducer .... SCOPOLAMIN
twill .... PRUNELLA
twilled fabric .... SERGE, DENIM, REP
twin .... DOUBLE, COUPLE, PAIR(ED), TWO, DIDYMOUS, GEMEL
Biblical .... ESAU
crystal .... MACLE
twinberry ...... HONEYSUCKLE
twine .... CORD, WREATHE, STRING, THREAD, SNARL, INTERLACE
material ... ABACA, HEMP, MAGUEY
twinge ...... SHOOT, QUALM, TWITCH, PAIN, PANG
of conscience .... COMPUNCTION, SCRUPLE, QUALM
twining stem .... BINE
twinkle ... SPARKLE, GLIMMER, FLICKER, WINK, GLINT, BLINK
twinkling .... INSTANT
twins .... GEMINI

twirl .... SPIN, ROTATE, WHIRL, FLOURISH
twist ...... WRICK, WRENCH, TWINE, WIND, SPRAIN, SKEW, CONTORT, SCREW, TIC, WRITHE, SQUIRM, TURN, CURVE, WARP
and turn ..... W(R)IGGLE
around ...... CURL, COIL
given to a ball ...... SPIN
in a tree .... GNARL
into thread ...... THROW
twisted ... CONTORTED, WRY, SKEW, AWRY, TORTILE
roll of cotton ...... SLUB
roll of tobacco .. PIGTAIL
thread .... LISLE
twister ... TORNADO, CYCLONE
twisting .... SPIRAL
pinch/pluck ..... TWEAK
twit .... UPBRAID, TAUNT, TEASE, RIB, JOSH, REPROACH, MOCK, RIDICULE
twitch .. JERK, PLUCK, SNATCH, PULL, TWEAK, TIC, TWINGE, VELLICATE
twitter ... CHATTER, FLUTTER, CHIRRUP, TITTER, CHIRP(ING)
two ... BRACE, TWAIN, COUPLE, PAIR, DUO
aces in dice ...... CRAPS, CRABS
base hit .... DOUBLE
bells .... ONE O'CLOCK
bit: sl. .... CHEAP, WORTHLESS
by two .... BINAL
celled .... BILOCULAR
consisting of .. DYAD(IC)
cups .... PINT
edged .... ANCIPITAL
faced .... BIFACIAL
faced being .. HYPOCRITE, JANUS
fisted .... VIRILE, VIGOROUS
footed animal .. BIPED(AL)
forked .... BIFURCATE
handed .. AMBIDEXTROUS, BIMANOUS
handed animal .. BIMANE
horned .... BICORN
horse chariot ...... BIGA
hundred milligrams ..... CARAT
leaf paper sheet ... FOLIO
legged .... BIPED
month period .. BIMESTER
of .... DUAL
plus tid .... BITS
seater .... TANDEM, ROADSTER
shillings .... FLORIN
sided .... BILATERAL
song for .... DUET
spot .... DEUCE
step .... DANCE
thousand pounds .... NETTON
toed sloth .... UNAU
together .... DUAD
week period .. FORTNIGHT

wheeled cab .... HANSOM
wheeled carriage .... CALECHE, TILBURY, HANSOM, GIG, CALASH, CART
year-old sheep .... TEG(G)
twofold ..... BINAL, DUPLE(X), BINARY, DOUBLE
twosome .... COUPLE
Ty, baseball great ..... COBB
Tyburn event .... EXECUTION, HANGING
Tyche ... FORTUNA, GODDESS
tycoon ... SHOGUN, FINANCIER, BARON, MOGUL
tyke ... MONGREL, CUR, DOG, BOOR, CHILD
Tyler, English rebel ..... WAT
tympan .... DRUM
tympanic membrane .... EARDRUM
tympanist .... DRUMMER
tympanum .... EARDRUM
tympany .... CONCEIT
Tyndareus .... SPARTAN
wife of .... LEDA
Tyne river city ...... JARROW
type ... TOKEN, EMBLEM, SIGN, CLASS, MODEL, CLASSIFY, SORT, KIND, BREED, VARIETY
assortment of .. FO(U)NT
blank .... QUAD(RAT)
body measure .... POINT
break in .... BATTER
case ...... UPPER, LOWER
disarrange ... SQUABBLE
face like writing .... CURSIVE
face projection .... KERN
jumbled .... PI(E)
kind of ... ITALIC, ROMAN, BOLDFACE, CONDENSED
line of .... SLUG
measure .... EM, EN
metal .... QUAD
mixed .... PI(E)
mold .... MATRIX
ornamental line .... SERIF
part .... KERN
set .... COMPOSE
size .. PICA, AGATE, FONT, ROMAN, BREVIER, ELITE, NONPAREIL, MINION
slanting .... ITALIC
style ... BODONI, CASLON, GARAMOND, CLOISTER, GOTHIC, ROMAN
tray .... GALLEY
typescript .... COPY
typesetter ...... LINOTYPIST, PRINTER, COMPOSITOR
typesetting .... COMPOSING
machine: colloq. ... LINO
typewriter, kind of .. TELETYPE, TELEX
part ...... ROLLER, KEY, SPACER, PLATEN, CARRIAGE
type .... PICA, ELITE
typhlosis .... BLINDNESS
typhoon ... STORM, HURRICANE

typhus carrier ... LOUSE, FLEA
cause of ..... RICKETTSIA
typical ..... CHARACTERISTIC, SYMBOLIC
typify .... EXEMPLIFY
typographer .... PRINTER
typographical error .. ERRATUM
Tyr .... TIU
parent of .... ODIN
tyrannical .... DESPOTIC, CRUEL, OPPRESSIVE
tyrannize .... OPPRESS
tyranny .. DESPOTISM, CRUELTY
tyrant .. DESPOT, OPPRESSOR
Tyre, king of .... HIRAM
princess of .... DIDO
tyro ... AMATEUR, BEGINNER, NOVICE
Tyrolean city .... INNSBRUCK
patriot .... HOFER
river .... ISAR
singer .... YOD(E)LER
tzigane .... GYPSY

U

U-boat .... SUBMARINE
boat locator ..... SONAR
Greek .... UPSILON
in chemistry .. URANIUM
letter .... EU
shaped bone ..... HYOID
turn, describing a .... HAIRPIN
Ubangi tributary ..... UELE
Ubermensch ...... SUPERMAN, OVERMAN
ubique .... EVERYWHERE
ubiquity ...... OMNIPRESENCE
Ucayali tributary ... APURIMAC
udder inflammation .. GARGET
product .... MILK
protuberance ..... TEAT, NIPPLE
Uganda capital ..... KAMPALA
city .... JINJA
kingdom ..... BUGANDA
president .... OBOTE
ugly ..... CROSS, UNGAINLY, HIDEOUS, UNSIGHTLY, VILE, REPULSIVE, OMINOUS, DANGEROUS
duckling once ..... SWAN
sight .... EYESORE
uhlan .... SOLDIER, CAVALRYMAN, GERMAN
uintaite .... ASPHALT, GILSONITE
uitlander .... FOREIGNER
ukase .... DECREE
Ukrainian capital ...... KIEV
city .... KHARKOV, KHERSON
farmer .... KULAK
holy city .... KLEV
legislature .... RADA
money of account ..... GRIVNA
native .... COSSACK
ukelele .... UKE
instrument like .. GUITAR
player .... HAWAIIAN
Ulan Bator ... KULUN, URGA, KHOTO
ulcer .... SORE, CANKER
discharge ... ICHOR, PUS, SANIES
venereal ...... CHANCRE
ulcerate .... FESTER
ule .... CAUCHO
fluid .... LATEX
ulema .... MUFTI
Ulianov, Vladimir ..... LENIN
ulmaceous tree .... ELM
ulmus .... ELM
ulna projection ... OLECRANON
Ulster .... OVERCOAT
lake .... ERNE
ult. ...... ULTIMATE, ULTIMO
Ultima Thule .... ICELAND
ultimate .... FARTHEST, EVENTUAL, FINAL, PRIMARY, MAXIMUM
ultimatum ...... LAST OFFER, DEMAND
ultra .... EXCESSIVE, RADICAL, EXTREME
modern ... AVANT GARDE
nationalist ...... JINGO, CHAUVINIST
ultramarine .... PIGMENT
ulu .... KNIFE
ululant .... HOWLING
ululate .... HOWL, WAIL, LAMENT, BAY, CRY, PULE
Ulysses .... ODYSSEUS
author of .... JOYCE
country of ...... ITHACA
father of .... LAERTES
kingdom of ...... ITHACA
name given to Cyclops ... NOMAN
son of ..... TELEMACHUS
wife of .... PENELOPE
umbelliferous plant .. CARROT, PARSLEY
umber ..... PIGMENT, SHADE, SHADOW, GRAYLING
bird .... UMBRETTE
umbilical cord ..... FUNICULUS
umbilicus .... NAVEL
umbles .... ENTRAILS
umbo ..... BEAK, BOSS, KNOB
umbra ...... SHADOW, SHADE
umbrage ... OFFENSE, FOLIAGE, RESENTMENT, SHADOW
umbrella .... COVER, PARASOL, (SUN)SHADE, GAMP, CHATTA
cloth for .... GLORIA
like flower .... UMBEL
like fungus .. MUSHROOM
part .... RIB
of leaves .... TALIPOT
style .... BUBBLE
thing like ...... CANOPY, (PARA)CHUTE
tree .... MAGNOLIA
umbrette .... UMBER, HAMMERHEAD
Umbria town .... ASSISI
umiak .... CANOE, KAYAK
umlaut .... DIERESIS
in linguistics .. MUTATION
umpire ..... ARBITER, JUDGE, REFEREE, DAYSMAN
UN agency .... WHO, UNESCO, FAO, IDA, ICAO, GATT, UNRRA
president .... SPAAK, ARANHA, ARCE, EVATT, ROMULO, NERVO, PANDIT, MAZA, MUNRO, MALIK, MANESCU, SLIM
secretary-general .... LIE, (U)THANT
una .... CATBOAT
unaccented .... ATONIC, STRESSLESS
vowel sound ..... SCHWA
unadorned ..... PLAIN, STARK, BALD, BARE
unadulterated .... NEAT, PURE
unaffected .... NATURAL, SIMPLE, NAIVE, SINCERE, ARTLESS
Unalaskan .... ALEUT
unalloyed .... PURE
unanimous .... SOLID
opinion ..... CONSENSUS
unapproachable .... ALOOF, DISTANT, INACCESSIBLE
unarmed .... DEFENSELESS
unassuming ..... MODEST, SHY, RETIRING, NATURAL
unattached ..... SINGLE, FREE, LOOSE, LONE, VAGILE
unau .... SLOTH
unavailing .... FUTILE
unavoidable ..... INEVITABLE
unawares, take .... SURPRISE
unbalanced .... DERANGED, LOPSIDED, UNEVEN
unbecoming .... IMPROPER, INDECOROUS
unbeliever .... DOUBTER, ATHEIST, PAGAN, SKEPTIC, AGNOSTIC, HERETIC, INFIDEL, MISCREANT
unbelieving .... INCREDULOUS
unbend ...... YIELD, RELENT, RELAX, STRAIGHTEN
unbending ..... RIGID, STIFF, FIRM, RESOLUTE, SET, ADAMANT
unbiased .... OBJECTIVE, IMPARTIAL
unbleached .... ECRU
fabric .... BEIGE
unblemished ...... SPOTLESS, CLEAN, STAINLESS
unborn young in uterus .. FETUS
unbosom ...... TELL, REVEAL
unbounded .... LIMITLESS
unbranded cow .... MAVERICK
unbroken ..... INTACT, WILD, WHOLE, CONTINUOUS

unburden .... RELIEVE, RID
unburnt brick .... ADOBE
uncalled for .... IMPERTINENT, GRATUITOUS, UNNECESSARY
uncanny .... WEIRD, EERIE, STRANGE, MYSTERIOUS, UNCO, EERY
unceasing ...... CONTINUOUS, ENDLESS, PERPETUAL
unceremonious ...... ABRUPT, INFORMAL, CURT
uncertain ... DOUBTFUL, VAGUE
uncertainty .. DUBIETY, DOUBT
unchaste .... WANTON
unchecked ...... LOOSE, RIFE, RAMPANT
unchristian .... WICKED
unciform ..... HOOK-SHAPED
uncinate .... HOOKLIKE, HAMATE, HOOKED
uncle .... NUNCLE, NUNKS, OOM, EAM
  American .... SAM
  cry .. YIELD, SURRENDER
  of fiction .... REMUS
  pertaining to .... AVUNCULAR
  Remus' author ... HARRIS
  Remus' rabbit ..... BRE'R
  slang ..... PAWNBROKER
  Tom's ___ ...... CABIN
unclean .... DIRTY, FOUL, FILTHY, OBSCENE, VILE, SQUALID, LEPROUS
  one, biblical ...... LEPER
unclose .... REVEAL, OPE(N)
unclothe ... UNCOVER, DIVEST, STRIP, UNDRESS
unclothed partially .... DISHABILLE
unco ...... WEIRD, NOTABLE, NEWS, UNCANNY, STRANGE, UNKNOWN, VERY
uncoil .... UNWIND
uncoined metal ..... BULLION
uncombed .... UNKEMPT
uncommitted .... UNPLEDGED, FREE
uncommon .... RARE, ODD, SINGULAR, SCARCE, STRANGE, UNUSUAL, EXOTIC
uncommunicative ..... SILENT, RESERVE, TACITURN, RETICENT
uncompromising .... SET, DETERMINED, ADAMANT
unconcerned ..... INSOUCIANT, INDIFFERENT, ALOOF
unconditional ..... ABSOLUTE, TOTAL, TERMLESS
unconfined ...... FREE, LOOSE
unconfirmed news .. HEARSAY, RUMOR, GOSSIP, REPORT
unconnected .... DISCRETE
unconquerable .... INVINCIBLE
unconscious ...... MINDLESS, UNAWARE, UNWITTING, BLOTTO
  state ... COMA, NARCOSIS, SWOON, TRANCE, HYPNOSIS, SYNCOPE
unconstrained .... DEGAGE, FREE
unconventional .... UNUSUAL, INFORMAL, OUTRE
  one .... REBEL
uncooked .... RAW
uncouth .... VULGAR, GAUCHE, AWKWARD, GAWKY, CRUDE, CLUMSY, AGRESTIC
  person ..... BUM(P)KIN, LOUT, CODGER, RUSTIC, GAWK, YOKEL, BOOR
uncover ...... REVEAL, BARE, OPEN, EXPOSE
  hat .... DOFF
uncovered .... NUDE, EXPOSED, NAKED, BARE
unction ...... OINTMENT, OIL, UNGUENT
  give extreme ..... ANELE
unctuous ..... OILY, PLASTIC, SMOOTH, SUAVE, GREASY, PINGUID, SLEEK, SOAPY
  substance ...... CERATE, GREASE, OINTMENT, UNGUENT, LANOLIN
uncultivated .... VIRGIN, FALLOW, WILD, COARSE
uncultured .... ILL-BRED, COARSE
und so weiter .. ETC, ET CETERA
undaunted .... INTREPID, FEARLESS, UNDISMAYED
unde, in heraldry ...... WAVY
undecided .... HESITANT, PENDENT, PENDING, IRRESOLUTE, WAVERING, UNCERTAIN
undeniable .... TRUE, IRREFUTABLE
under ..... (BE)NEATH, BELOW, LOWER, NETHER
  obligation ...... OWING, INDEBTED, BOUND
  par .... ILL, SICK
  prefix .... SUB, HYP
underage ... MINOR, IMMATURE
underbrush .... THICKET
undercover man .... SPY, SLEUTH, DETECTIVE
undercroft .... CRYPT
underdone .... RARE
undergarment .... SLIP, CHEMISE, SHIRT
undergo .... EXPERIENCE, ENDURE, SUFFER
undergraduate .... FROSH, SOPHOMORE, JUNIOR, PLEBE
underground .. SECRET, HIDDEN
  being ... TROLL, GNOME, DWARF
  burial place ...... CRYPT, CATACOMB
  drain .... SEWER
  fighter ...... PARTISAN, ELAS, MAQUI, EDES
  fungus ...... TUCKAHOE, EARTHNUT, TRUFFLE
  organization ..... MAFIA
  passage .... TUNNEL, BURROW, TUBE, SAP
  railway .... SUBWAY, TUBE, METRO
  resident .... GNOME, DWARF, TROLL
  stem .... TUBER, POTATO, CASSAVA, MANIOC, SALEP, ONION, STOCK, RHIZOME
  worker .... MINER, SANDHOG
underhand ..... SLY, COVERT, SECRET, CLANDESTINE
underhanded ... SLY, TRICKY, DECEITFUL
underline .. STRESS, EMPHASIZE
underling ...... SUBORDINATE, AIDE, SUBALTERN, SLAVE
underlying .... BASIC, FUNDAMENTAL
  principle .... ELIXIR
undermine .. SAP, WEAR AWAY, ERODE, WEAKEN, SUBVERT
undernourish .... FAMISH, STARVE
underpin .... PROP
underpinning .... SUPPORT
  colloquial .... LEGS
underrate .... BELITTLE
underscore .... STRESS, EMPHASIZE
undersea craft ... SUBMARINE, UBOAT
  explorer .... PICARD
undershirt ...... VEST, JERSEY, SKIVVY, PETTICOAT, SINGLET
undersigned, the ..... WRITER
undersized .... SMALL, SCRUBBY, RUNTY
  being .... DWARF, RUNT, PIGMY
understand .... PERCEIVE, COMPREHEND, SEE, KEN, INFER, ASSUME, GRASP, APPRECIATE
  colloquial ...... SAVVY, DIG, GET
understanding .... NOUS, AGREEMENT, DISCERNMENT, SENSE, ACCORD
  between nations, etc. ..... ENTENTE
understood ... TACIT, AGREED, SENSED, PRESUMED, ASSUMED, IMPLIED
  readily ... CLEAR, LUCID, LUCULENT
understrapper .. SUBORDINATE
understudy ...... SUBSTITUTE, APPRENTICE
undertake .... PROMISE, PLEDGE, CONTRACT, OFFER, VOLUNTEER, TRY, ASSUME, TACKLE
undertaker .... MORTICIAN
undertaking .... TASK, ENTERPRISE, PROMISE, GUARANTEE, JOB, VENTURE, PROJECT
undertow .... RIPTIDE
underwaist .... BRA
underwater ...... SUBMARINE
  apparatus .... SCUBA, SNORKEL, BATHYSPHERE, CAISSON, BATHYSCAPH
  craft .... SUBMARINE, UBOAT, PIGBOAT
  eye of sort .. HYDROSCOPE

ledge .... REEF
plant .... BENTHOS
prefix .... HYP(O)
projectile ...... TORPEDO
sound detection device ... SOFAR, SONAR
swimmer ..... FROGMAN, (SKIN)DIVER
worker .... SANDHOG
underwear ... LINGERIE, SLIP, SHORTS, PANTY, UNDIES, SCANTY, FLANNELS
underworld ... EARTH, HADES, SHEOL, HEL, EREBUS, ANTIPODES, GANGLAND
king .... YAMA
queen .... HEL
underwrite .... SUBSCRIBE, AGREE(TO), ASSUME, FINANCE, INSURE
underwriter .... INSURER, INSURANCEMAN
undeserving .... INDIGN
undesirable ... OBJECTIONABLE
person ...... BORE, BOOR, LOUT, LEPER, FELON
undeveloped .... LATENT
quality .... POTENTIAL
undies ... PANTIES, LINGERIE, UNDERWEAR
undiluted .... NEAT, SHEER, STRAIGHT, PURE
undine ..... NYMPH, SEAMAID, SYLPH
undisguised .... OPEN, OVERT, FRANK
undivided ... WHOLE, ENTIRE, INTACT
undomesticated .... WILD, UNTAMED, FERAL
undone .... UNFINISHED
undoubtedly ..... CERTAINLY, ADMITTEDLY
undraped .... BARE, NUDE
undress ..... STRIP, DISARRAY
stage of ..... DISHABILLE
undressed skin ...... PELT, KIP
Undset, Norwegian novelist ... SIGRID
undue .... IMPROPER, EXCESSIVE, INORDINATE
undulant fever ... BRUCELLOSIS
undulate ...... WAVE, RIPPLE
undulating .... WAVY
object ... WAVE, RIPPLE, SNAKE, WORM
undulation ...... PULSATION, SURGE, WAVE, HEAVE, RIPPLE
unduly .... UNJUSTLY, IMPROPERLY, EXCESSIVELY
undued ...... PLAIN, TINTLESS
undying .... ETERNAL, IMMORTAL, ABIDING
unearth ... DIG UP, DISCLOSE, DISCOVER, EXHUME
unearthly ..... EERIE, WEIRD, GHOSTLY
uneasy ..... FRETFUL, RESTIVE, ANXIOUS, RESTLESS, CONCERNED, FIDGETY, NERVOUS
feeling .... MALAISE
uneasiness .. MALAISE, UNREST, DISCOMFORT, ANXIETY
uneducated .... UNLETTERED, UNLEARNED, ILLITERATE
unemployed .... IDLE, AVAILABLE
unending ...... CONTINUOUS, CEASELESS
unenthusiastic ... COOL, COLD, INDIFFERENT
unequal .. UNEVEN, IRREGULAR, INADEQUATE
angled .... SCALENE
unequalled .... MATCHLESS, SUPREME, PEERLESS, NONPAREIL
unequivocal ... CLEAR, PLAIN
unerring .... EXACT, SURE, CERTAIN, ACCURATE
uneven .... EROSE, ROUGH, IRREGULAR, CROOKED, UNEQUAL, ODD, RUGGED, RAGGED, SPOTTY, HUBBLY
contest .... LOPSIDED
unexciting ..... TAME, DULL, VAPID
unexpected .... SUDDEN, UNFORESEEN
meeting ..... ENCOUNTER
unexploded .... LIVE
unexpressive .... DULL, BLAND
unfading .... FAST
flower ..... AMARANTH, EVERLASTING
unfailing ..... REGULAR, SURE, CERTAIN
unfair ...... PARTIAL, BIASED, DISHONEST, FOUL
unfaithful .... DISLOYAL, UNTRUE
unfavorable .... ADVERSE, CONTRARY, BAD, ILL, INIMICAL
unfeeling .... INSENSATE, INSENSIBLE, NUMB, CALLOUS, CRUEL, STONY
unfermented grape juice ...... STUM
unfit .... INEPT, INAPT
to eat .... INEDIBLE
unfix ...... DETACH, LOOSEN
unflattering ... FRANK, BLUNT, DEROGATORY
unfledged .... CALLOW
bird ..... EYAS, NESTLING
unflinching ... FIRM, RESOLUTE
unfold ..... REVEAL, DISCLOSE, EVOLVE, UNFURL, OPEN, SPREAD
unforeseen ..... UNEXPECTED, SUDDEN
unfortunate .... HAPLESS, LUCKLESS
unfounded .... BASELESS, IDLE
unfrequented ..... SOLITARY, LONELY
unfriendly ... ANTAGONISTIC, ILL, COLD, HOSTILE, INIMICAL
unfruitful .... BARREN, STERILE
unfurl ...... UNFOLD, SPREAD, UNROLL
ungainly ..... UGLY, CLUMSY, AWKWARD
ungodly ... IMPIOUS, WICKED, DREADFUL
ungovernable .. UNRULY, WILD, REBELLIOUS
ungracious .. RUDE, IMPOLITE, AWKWARD
ungual growth ... NAIL, HOOF, CLAW, TALON
unguent .... BALM, SALVE, OINTMENT, POMADE, CHRISM
unguis ... NAIL, HOOF, CLAW, TALON, UNGULA
ungula ... CLAW, NAIL, TALON, UNGUIS, HOOF
ungulate ...... TAPIR, HORSE, COW, CATTLE, HOOFED
unhappy .... ILL-CHOSEN, UNFORTUNATE, SAD, BLUE, MOROSE
unharmed .... SAFE
unhealthy ... SICKLY, MORBID
unhitch ... DETACH, UNFASTEN, RELEASE
unholy ..... WICKED, IMPIOUS, PROFANE
unhorse ...... OVERTHROW, SPILL, UPSET
unicellular animal .. AM(O)EBA, PROTOZOAN
unicorn ... MONOCERO, REEM, LIN
fish .... UNIE
whale .... NARWHAL
unidentified flying object .. UFO
uniform ... EVEN, UNVARYING, STANDARD, OUTFIT, STEADY, EQUABLE
servant's .... LIVERY
shoulder ornament ...... EPAULET(TE)
unify ... UNITE, CONSOLIDATE, WELD, INTEGRATE
unilateral .... ONE-SIDED
unimpeachable .... CLEAN, BLAMELESS, RELIABLE
unimportant .... PETTY, TRIVIAL
things .... TRIVIA
uninhabited .... DESOLATE, TENANTLESS
unintelligible chatter .... GIBBER(ISH)
unintentional .... UNWITTING
union ..... FUSION, JUNCTION, MARRIAGE, LIAISON, MERGER, ALLIANCE, LEAGUE, COALITION
business .... CARTEL, SYNDICATE
dues deduction .... CHECKOFF
from birth .. CONNATION
jack .... FLAG
labor .... ARTEL
member ... CARDHOLDER
merchants' ...... HANSE
of South Africa town .... MAFEKING
political .... BLOC, COALITION
soldier .... YANKEE

trade .... GUILD
unionist .... TORY, CONSERVATIVE, FEDERALIST
unique ..... SINGULAR, RARE, SOLE, SINGLE, UNUSUAL, PECULIAR
unisexual .... DECLINOUS
unison .. CONCORD, HARMONY, AGREEMENT
utter in .... CHORUS
Unisphere, part of ...... ASIA
unit .... ONE, STANDARD, ITEM, PIECE
caloric .... THERM
charge .... RATE
electrical ... VOLT, WATT, AMPERE
factor .... GENE
in medicine ...... DOSE, DOSAGE
of astronomical distance LIGHT YEAR, SECPAR, PARSEC
of brightness, c g s .... LAMBERT
of capacity .... LITER, LITRE
of electrical resistance ... OHM
of energy ... ERG, JOULE
of force .. DENE, DYNE, OD
of heat .. CALORIE, THERM
of instruction .... LESSON
of length ..... ANGSTROM, MICRON, CUBIT, METER
of light ..... LUMEN, LUX
of magnetic intensity .... OERSTED
of metrical time ... MORA
of pressure .... BARAD
of reluctance .... REL
of value .... POINT
of weight ... TON, GRAM, BUSHEL, KEEL, KEG, MAUND, CARAT
of work .... ERG(ON), JOULE, KILERG
of work energy ... JOULE
ultimate .... MONAD
wire .... MIL
unite ... COMBINE, COALESCE, FEDERATE, FUSE, WELD, JOIN, PIECE
United Arab Republic .. EGYPT
Kingdom national flag .. UNION JACK
Nations (see UN)
United States (see American /US) .... UNCLE SAM, AMERICA, USA
unity ..... ONENESS, CONCORD, HARMONY, SOLIDARITY
univalent .. SINGLE, UNPAIRED
univalve ...... SNAIL, MOLLUSK
shell's edge ..... LABRUM
universal .... PANDEMIC, ENTIRE, GENERIC, GENERAL, GLOBAL, CATHOLIC, ECUMENIC(AL)
language .... ESPERANTO, IDO, VOLAPUK
remedy .... AZOTH
universe ... COSMOS, CREATION, WORLD, EARTH, MACROCOSM
of the .... COSMIC
university business agent ..... SYNDIC
composition of .... SCHOOLS, COLLEGES
grounds .... CAMPUS
group .... FRAT(ERNITY), SORORITY
lecturer ..... PRELECTOR
official .... DEAN, REGISTRAR, RECTOR, TRUSTEE, REGENT, BURSAR, BEADLE, PROCTOR, PROVOST
professorship .... CHAIR
program of studies ...... CURRICULUM
rank .... DEGREE
teacher ...... PROFESSOR, INSTRUCTOR
team .... VARSITY
unjust ...... PARTIAL, UNFAIR, BIASED
unjustly .... UNDULY
unkempt ... MESSY, SLOVENLY, UNTIDY, SHAGGY, SHABBY, UNCOMBED, CRUDE, ROUGH
unkind .... CRUEL, HARSH
unknown ... UNCO, STRANGE, OBSCURE
person .... JOHN DOE
unlace .... LOOSEN, UNTIE, UNFASTEN
unlawful ... ILLICIT, ILLEGAL
goods/trade .... CONTRABAND
hunting ...... POACHING
importation .. SMUGGLING
intrusion ...... TRESPASS
liquor .... BOOTLEG
unlearned .... IGNORANT, ILLITERATE
unleash ...... RELEASE, LOOSE, SET FREE
unleavened .... AZYMOUS
unless .... SAVE, EXCEPT
unlettered .... IGNORANT, ILLITERATE, UNEDUCATED
unlike .... DIFFERENT, DISSIMILAR
unload ... UNBURDEN, DUMP, REMOVE, RID
unlock .... OPEN, REVEAL
unloose ...... UNDO, RELEASE, UNTIE
unlucky .. ILL-FATED, HAPLESS, ILL-STARRED
unman ... UNNERVE, CASTRATE
unmannerly .... RUDE, DISCOURTEOUS, IMPOLITE
unmarried .... CELIBATE, SINGLE, UNWED
in law .... SOLE
man .... BACHELOR, CELIBATE
state .... CELIBACY, MAIDENHOOD
woman .... SPINSTER, MAIDEN
unmentionables .. UNDERWEAR
unmistakable .... CLEAR, OBVIOUS, APPARENT
unmitigated .... ARRANT
unmoved ...... UNAFFECTED, INSENSATE
unnatural .... ARTIFICIAL, AFFECTED
unnerve ...... UNMAN, SHAKE, SHOCK
unoccupied ... VACANT, IDLE, EMPTY
unorganized ..... DISORDERLY
unpaid .... OWING, DUE
unpaired .... UNIVALENT, SINGLE, ODD
unpleasant .... OFFENSIVE, DISAGREEABLE, UNSAVORY, DISTASTEFUL
unpleasantness .... SPAT, QUARREL
unplowed .. UNTILLED, FALLOW
unpolished .... AGRESTIC, CRUDE, COARSE
unprecedented ... NOVEL, NEW
unpredictable .... CASUAL, CAPRICIOUS
unprejudiced ..... IMPARTIAL, FAIR, UNBIASED
unpremeditated .... SPONTANEOUS
unpressed ..... BAGGY, SEEDY, RUMPLED
unprincipled .... IMMORAL, UNSCRUPULOUS
unprintable usually .. OBSCENE, OBSCENITY, VULGAR(ITY)
unpropitious ... INOPPORTUNE
unqualified .... ABSOLUTE, COMPLETE, SHEER
unravel .... FEAZE, SOLVE, UNTANGLE, TEASE
unreadable .... ILLEGIBLE
unreal . FANCIFUL, IMAGINARY
unreasonable .... UNDUE, SENSELESS, INANE, IRRATIONAL
unreasoning devotion .. FETISH
unredeemed territory .... IRREDENTA
unreel .... UNWIND
unrefined .... CRUDE, COARSE, CRASS, GROSS
unrelenting .... STERN, ADAMANT
unremitting ...... INCESSANT, NON-STOP, PERSISTENT
unrest .... FERMENT, DISQUIET, AGITATION
unripe ..... GREEN, IMMATURE
unrivaled .... PEERLESS, MATCHLESS, NONPAREIL
unroll ..... DISPLAY, UNFURL
unroot .... STUB
unruffled ..... COOL, SMOOTH, UNFAZED, SERENE, CALM
unruly .... DISORDERLY, WILD, INTRACTABLE, FRACTIOUS, RESTIVE
child .... BRAT
hair .... COWLICK
unsavory .... TASTELESS, OFFENSIVE, DISAGREEABLE, UNPLEASANT
unsay .... RETRACT

unscramble ...... UNRAVEL, SOLVE, STRAIGHTEN, CLEAR UP
unscrupulous ..... DISHONEST, UNPRINCIPLED
person .... CHEAT(ER), SWINDLER
unseal .... OPEN
unseat ..... DISLODGE, OUST, UNHORSE
unseemly ...... INDECOROUS, IMPROPER, UNDUE
unsettle ... DISTURB, DISTRESS
unsettled .... UNCERTAIN, UNSTABLE
unsheathe .... DRAW
unsightly ... UGLY, UNGAINLY
unskilled .... INEPT, CLUMSY, AWKWARD
unsophisticated ..... ARTLESS, NAIVE, SIMPLE, INGENIOUS, SQUARE
unsparing ... LAVISH, LIBERAL, PROFUSE, SEVERE
unspoiled .... FRESH
unspeakable ... WICKED, VILE
unspoken ...... TACIT, SILENT, UNSAID
unstable .... FICKLE, CHANGEABLE, ERRATIC, ASTATIC, INCONSTANT, VARIABLE, LABILE
unsteady ... SHAKY, UNSTABLE, WAVERING, ERRATIC
unsuccessful ...... ABORTIVE
unsuitable ..... INAPT, UNFIT
untamed ...... FERAL, WILD, UNRULY, FERINE
state .... FERITY
untangle .... (UN)RAVEL
untanned hide .... KIP, SHAGREEN, PELT
untenanted .... VACANT
untended .... UNCARED, NEGLECTED
unterseeboot ..... SUBMARINE, U-BOAT
untidy .... SLOVENLY, UNKEMPT, SLOPPY, SLIPSHOD, DOWDY, MESSY, LITTERY, MUSSY
animal .... PIG
person ... SLOVEN, SLOB, SLATTERN
place .... (PIG)STY
untie ... LOOSE(N), UNDO, FREE
until ... BEFORE, UNTO, UP TO, PENDING, TILL
untimely .... PREMATURE, INOPPORTUNE
unto .... TILL, UNTIL
untold .... COUNTLESS, INCALCULABLE, INDESCRIBABLE
untouchable ...... BRAHMAN, LEPER, SACRED COW
untouched ... PURE, PRISTINE, VIRGIN
untoward ..... UNFORTUNATE
untreated .... RAW
untrue ..... DISLOYAL, FALSE, UNFAITHFUL
untruth .. LIE, FIB, FALSEHOOD, CANARD, MENDACITY
untwine .... (UN)RAVEL
untwist ... FEAZE, (UN)RAVEL, STRAIGHTEN
unusual .. UNIQUE, RARE, ODD, NOVEL, OUTRE, UNCOMMON, SINGULAR
unvarnished ... PLAIN, SIMPLE, LITERAL
unvarying sound ... MONOTONE, DRONE
unveil ...... REVEAL, UNMASK
unvoiced ..... SURD, ELIDED, MUTED
unwary .... CARELESS
unwholesome ...... NOXIOUS, UNHEALTHY, DISTASTEFUL, HARMFUL
unwieldy .... AWKWARD, CLUMSY, HULKING
ship .... HULK, ARK
unwilling .... LOATH, RELUCTANT, AVERSE
unwind ..... UNREEL, UNCOIL
unwise .... IMPOLITIC, FOOLISH, UNSOUND, TACTLESS
unwitting ...... UNCONSCIOUS, INNOCENT
unwonted .... RARE, UNACCUSTOMED, UNUSUAL
unworthy ..... UNDESERVING, UNDESERVED, INDIGN
unwrinkled .... SMOOTH
unwritten .... BLANK
but understood ... TACIT
law .... TRADITION, CUSTOM
unyielding ... ADAMANT, FIRM, SET, GRIM, OBDURATE, HARD, IRON
up .... ABOVE, OVER, ALOFT
and about .... ASTIR
and-coming ... PROMISING
in arms ... ANGRY, IRATE
prefix .... ANA
to-the-minute .. RED HOT
Upanishad .... ISHA
upas tree/poison ..... ANTIAR
upbeat .... ARSIS
upbraid ...... SCOLD, CHIDE, REPROVE, REBUKE, SCORE, TWIT, CENSURE, REPROACH
upbringing .... BREEDING
upcountry .... INLAND
Updike novel .... COUPLES, RABBIT REDUX
upend .... INVERT
upheaval .... STORM, CONVULSION
uphold ... SUPPORT, SUSTAIN, BACK
upholstery ... DOSSEL, DOSSAL, GOBELIN
material ..... MOQUETTE, VALANCE, TABARET, FRISE, MOREEN, VELOUR(S), MOHAIR, LAMPAS, SCRIM, VELURE
stuffing .... FLOCK
upkeep ...... MAINTENANCE, REPAIR
upland ...... PLATEAU, MESA
country .... TIBET
plover ...... SANDPIPER
uplift .... RAISE, ELEVATE, BRASSIERE
Upolu town/seaport .... APIA
upon .. ATOP, UP AND ON, OVER
upper .... VAMP, BERTH, HIGHER
air ...... OZONE, ETHER
Amazon ..... MARANON
case .... CAPITAL
class ... JUNIOR, SENIOR, ELITE
crust .... ELITE
hand ...... ADVANTAGE, LEAD, MASTERY
house .... SENATE
limit .... CEILING
Volta president .... LAMIZANE, YAMEOGO
uppermost .... FIRST
uppish/uppity .... PROUD, SNOBBISH, ARROGANT, HAUGHTY
upright ..... ERECT, HONEST, JUST, HONORABLE, VERTICAL
uprise .... ASCEND, SWELL, REBEL
uprising ... REVOLT, (E)MEUTE, REBELLION, PUTSCH, MUTINY
uproar .... COMMOTION, DISTURBANCE, TUMULT, RIOT, BABEL, HUBBUB, RUCKUS, DIN, NOISE, BROUHAHA, RACKET, TURMOIL, CLAMOR
uproot ..... STUB, ERADICATE, SUPPLANT, GRUB, DERACINATE
upset ... CAPSIZE, OVERTURN, DISTURB, TOPPLE, TOP OVER, DEFEAT, DISTRESS, DISORDER, SWAGE
upshot .... OUTCOME, RESULT
upside down .... TOPSY-TURVY
upsilon-shaped bone ... HYOID
upstage ...... SNOOTY, ALOOF, CONCEITED, SNUB
upstart ...... PARVENU, SNOB, WHIPPERSNAPPER
upturned nose .... SNUB, PUG
upward movement .... SCEND, LIFT
Uracus .... ASP, COBRA
place of an ... HEADDRESS
symbol .... ASP
Ural Altaic branch .... TATAR
Urania .... APHRODITE, MUSE
sphere of .... ASTRONOMY
uranic .... CELESTIAL
Uranus' discoverer .. HEBSCHEL
mother ...... GAIA, GAEA
offspring .... TITANS, FURIES, CYCLOPES, CRONUS, RHEA, SATURN
satellite .... ARIEL
wife .... GAEA
urban .... OPPIDAN
urbane ... POLISHED, SMOOTH, AFFABLE, SUAVE
urbanize ...... CITIFY, REFINE, POLISH
urchin ...... HEDGEHOG, IMP,

GAMIN, MUDLARK, (STREET)ARAB
urd .... PYROL
urde .... CLECHE
Urdu .... HINDUSTANI
uredo ...... HIVES, URTICARIA
urethane .... SEDATIVE, HYPNOTIC
uretic ... URINARY, DIURETIC
Urfa .... EDESSA
Urga .... ULAN BATOR
urge ... INCITE, PRESS, ALLEGE, PLEAD, EXHORT, EGG, GOAD, IMPORTUNE, COAX, PROD, SPUR, ENTREAT, YEN
urgency .... EXIGENCY
urgent ..... GRAVE, PRESSING, INSISTENT
Uriah .... HEEP
  wife of .... BATHSHEBA
urial .... CORIAL, SHA
Uriel .... ARCHANGEL
urinate .... PIDDLE
urination, difficult .... STRANGURY, DYSURIA
  excessive ..... POLYURIA
  involuntary ... ENURESIS
urinary ... URETIC, DIURETIC, URIC, URINOUS
  calculus .... UROLITH
  duct ... URETER, URETHRA
  inflammation .. CYSTITIS
urine .... PISS
Uris, author .... LEON
urn .... KIST, STEEN, VASE, VESSEL
  figurative .... GRAVE
  for bones ..... OSSUARY
  shaped ..... URCEOLATE
uroxanthin .... INDICAN
Ursa .... BEAR
ursine animal .... BEAR
  howler .... MONKEY, ARAGUATO
Urth .... NORN
urticaria ...... HIVES, UREDO
urticate .... STING
Uruguay's capital .... MONTEVIDEO
  city ... PAYSANDU, SALTO
  cowboy .... GAUCHO
  discoverer .... DIAZ
  first colony .... COLONIA
  language ...... SPANISH
  monetary unit ..... PESO
  president ...... GESTIDO
urus ...... AUROCHS, TUR, OX
US (see American) .... UNITED STATES, AMERICA
  capitol lobbyist .... RAINMAKER
  coin .... DIME, CENT, NICKEL, QUARTER, EAGLE
  expatriate in Paris .. STEIN
  flag .... OLD GLORY
  Great White Father ..... PRESIDENT
  imaginary town .... PODUNK
  insurance capital .... HARTFORD
  marine .... GYRENE, LEATHERNECK
  marines' slogan .... GUNG HO
  national military park ... SHILOH
  newspaper, oldest .... COURANT
  paper money .... GREENBACK, LONG GREEN
  patron saint (humorously) TAMMANY
  president's wife .... FIRST LADY
  soldier, WWI ... SAMMY, DOUGHBOY
  volcano .... SHASTA, LASSEN
  winter fog ...... POGONIP
usage .... TREATMENT, CUSTOM, PRACTICE, HABIT
usance .... USAGE, USE
use .... AVAIL, UTILITY, HABIT, EMPLOY, PURPOSE, WORTH, FUNCTION, UTILIZE, EXERCISE, CONSUME, SERVICE, TREAT
  as example .... CITE
  divining rod ..... DOWSE
  efforts .... EXERT, STRIVE
  of another's property .... USUFRUCT
  up .... EXPEND
  wastefully .... SQUANDER
used .... SECONDHAND
  up ... SPENT, EXHAUSTED, DEPLETED
useful .... UTILE, SERVICEABLE, HELPFUL, PRACTICAL
useless ... FUTILE, WORTHLESS, VAIN, IDLE, NEEDLESS, OTIOSE, INUTILE
user .... CONSUMER, UTILIZER
usher ... ESCORT, DOORKEEPER, FORERUN, INTRODUCE, HERALD
Uskudar .... SCUTARI
Usnach, son of .... NOISE
Uspallata Pass ... LA CUMBRE
  location .... ANDES
usquebaugh .... WHISKY
USSR (see Russian/Soviet)
ustulate .... BLACKENED, DISCOLORED
usual .... CUSTOMARY, HABITUAL, WONTED, NORMAL
usually .... COMMONLY, GENERALLY, ORDINARILY, AS A RULE, NORMALLY
usurer .... MONEYLENDER, SHYLOCK, VAMPIRE
usurp .... ASSUME, SEIZE, ARROGATE
Utah .... BEEHIVE (STATE)
  asphalt .... UINTA(H)ITE, GILSONITE
  city ...... PROVO, OREM, OGDEN, LOGAN
  Indian .... NAVAJO, PAIUTE, NAVAHO
  mountain .... UINTA, PEALE
  natives .... MORMONS
  nickname ...... BEEHIVE
  river .... WEBER, PROVO
  state bird ..... SEAGULL
  state emblem ... BEEHIVE
  state flower .... SEGO
  state tree .... SPRUCE
utensil ..... TOOL, IMPLEMENT
  maker .... COPPERSMITH
uterus .... WOMB, MATRIX
  growth .... MOLE
  inflammation .. METRITIS
  pain .... METRALGIA
  part .... CERVIX
  swelling .... MOLE
Uther's son .... ARTHUR
utile .... PRACTICAL
utilize .... USE
utmost ...... EXTREME, BEST, VERIEST, MAXIMUM, REMOTEST, GREATEST
Uto Aztecan Indian ... YAQUI
"Utopia" author .... MORE
  imaginary .. SHANGRI-LA
Utopian .... EDENIC, IDEALIST(IC), VISIONARY
  scheme .... BUBBLE
utricle .... SAC, VESICLE
Uttar Pradesh capital .... LUCKNOW
  city .... MEERUT
  part of .... OUDH
utter ...... SHEER, COMPLETE, TOTAL, VOICE, BROACH, EXPRESS, SPEAK, STARK, ABSOLUTE, EMIT, RANK
  defeat .... ROUT
  in unison ...... CHORUS
utterance .... EXPRESSION
utterly .... COMPLETELY, ENTIRELY, FULLY
uvarovite .... GARNET
uxorial .... WIFELY
Uzbek capital ..... TASHKENT
  city .... KHIVA

V

V, author of ...... PYNCHON
  formation flyers ... GEESE
  Greek .... UPSILON
  Hebrew .... VAV
  letter/shaped ...... VEE
  shaped cut .... NOTCH
  shaped piece .. WEDGE, PIE
  symbol .... VICTORY
vaca .... COW
vacancy ...... GAP, OPENING, EMPTINESS, BLANK, BREAK, VACUITY

vacant . . . FREE, HOLLOW, VOID, EMPTY, IDLE, UNOCCUPIED
vacate . . . LEAVE, VOID, ANNUL, QUIT
vacation . . . . RECESS, RESPITE, REST, HOLIDAY
vaccinate . . . . INOCULATE
vaccination pioneer . . . . JENNER
vaccine . . . . VIRUS
vaccinia . . . . COWPOX
vaccillate . . . . HESITATE, WAVER, TEETER, FALTER
vacuity . . INANITY, EMPTINESS, VOID, VACUUM
vacuous . . . . . . EMPTY, INANE, STUPID, IDLE
vacuum . . . . VOID
opposed to . . . . PLENUM
tube . . . . DIODE, ELECTRODE
vade mecum . . . . MANUAL
vagabond . . . . BUM, DRIFTER, TRAMP, WANDERER, WANDERING, VAGRANT, RASCAL, VAG, LOREL, TRUANT, (HO)BO, WAFF, LANDLO(U)PER, RUNAGATE
vagabondage . . . . . . VAGRANTS
vagary . . . . . ODDITY, CAPRICE, WHIM, FANCY
vagrant . . . WAYWARD, ROVER, WANDERER, VAGABOND, BEGGAR, NOMAD(IC), TRAMP, CAIRD, BUM, HOBO, SPIV
greeting of . . . . HOBO, HOBEAU
jargon of . . . . SHELTA
place in city . . SKID ROW
vague . . . . HAZY, OBSCURE, NEBULOUS, INDEFINITE, UNCERTAIN, SKETCHY, LOOSE
vail . . . . . TIP, GRATUITY, DOFF
vain . . . EMPTY, IDLE, USELESS, FUTILE, FRUITLESS, CONCEITED, PROUD, SMUG, OTIOSE
and affected . . . . . FOPPISH
bird . . . . PEACOCK
manners . . . . AIRS
person . . . . . DANDY, FOP, COXCOMB, COCKSCOMB
quest . . . . WILD GOOSE CHASE
vainglory . . . . . VANITY, PRIDE
vair . . . . FUR
valance . . . DRAPERY, CURTAIN
vale . . . . DALE, DINGLE, GLEN, VALLEY, FAREWELL, ADIEU
valediction . . . . FAREWELL, GOODBY, ADIEU
valedictory . . . . ORATION
Valence's river . . . . . . RHONE
valentine . . . . . . SWEETHEART, GREETING CARD
figure on a . . CUPID, EROS
Valera (Eamon de) nickname . . DEV
valerian . . . . BENNET, ALLHEAL, HEMLOCK, PLANT
valet . . . MANSERVANT, DRESSER
valetudinarian . . . . . INVALID, SICKLY, HYPOCHONDRIAC
Valetta native . . . . MALTESE
valgus . . . . KNOCK-KNEE(D)
Valhalla maiden . . VALKYR(IE)
presider at . . . . ODIN
valid . . . . SOUND, COGENT, DEFENSIBLE, LEGAL
not . . . . NULL, VOID
validate . . . CONFIRM, ATTEST, SEAL
validity . . . . SOUNDNESS
valise . . . . SUITCASE, PORTMANTEAU, GRIP(SACK)
Valkyrie . . . BRUN(N)HILD(E), BRYNHILD
love of . . . . SIGURD
vallancy . . . . WIG
vallation . . . . RAMPART, EARTHWORK, WALL
valley . . . . VALE, CANYON, KLOOF, DALE, GLADE, SWALE, WADI, DINGLE, DELL, GUTTER, GLEN, COMB(E), COOMB, BOLSON, GULCH, STRATH, HOLLOW
Apollo's . . . . TEMPE
Argolis . . . . NEMEA
between cliffs . . . . CAN(Y)ON
entrance of . . . . JAWS
moon . . . . RILL(E)
valor . . . . HEROISM
valorous . . . . BRAVE
valse . . . . WALTZ, TRISTE
valuable . . . . DEAR, PRIZED
discovery . . . . FIND
valuation . . . . APPRAISAL
value . . . ESTEEM, APPRECIATE, ADMIRE, ASSESS, WORTH, PRIZE, TREASURE
beyond amount owed . . . EQUITY
highly . . . . CHERISH
more . . . . PREFER
of little . . . . TRIFLING, TRIFLE, TRIVIAL
valve . . . . . FLOODGATE, SPIGOT, PLUG, COCK, DAMPER, POPPET, STOPCOCK, PETCOCK
engine . . . . CHOKE, THROTTLE
sliding . . . . PISTON
vamo(o)se . . . DEPART, LEAVE, GO, SCRAM, DECAMP, LAM
vamp . . . . FLIRT, SEDUCE, BEGUILE, UPPER, PATCH(WORK), REPAIR, ACCOMPANIMENT
vampire . . . . SIREN, LAMIA, FLIRT, BAT, BLOODSUCKER, LILITH
kind of . . . . USURER, BLACKMAILER
van . . . FRONT, WING, WAGON, TRUCK, TRAILER, FORE, LORRY
Diemen's land . . . . TASMANIA
Doren, critic . . . . . MARK, CARL
man . . . . MOVER
Vance, sleuth . . . . PHILO
vandal . . . . HUN
Vandyke . . . BEARD, COLLAR, GOATEE
forte of . . . . PORTRAITS
vane . . . . WEATHERCOCK
of feather . . . . . VEXILLUM
vanguard . . . . FRONT
vanilla . . . ORCHID, FLAVORING
vanish . . . . MELT, FADE, DISAPPEAR, EVANESCE
vanity . . . CONCEIT, EGO(T)ISM, FUTILITY, VAINGLORY, PRIDE
case . . . . ETUI
vanquish . . . DEFEAT, CONQUER, SUBDUE, OVERCOME, BEAT, SUBJUGATE, LICK, BEST
vantage point . . . . COIGN
vapid . . . . . . LIFELESS, INSIPID, STALE, FLAT, INANE, TASTELESS, DULL
vapor . . . SMOKE, HALITUS, FOG, REEK, MIST, STEAM, FUME, BRAG, BLUSTER, BRUME, CLOUD
aircraft's . . . . . . CONTRAIL
combining form . . . ATMO
in air . . . MIST, FOG, HAZE, SMOG
mass of . . . . WRACK
pressure measuring device TONOMETER
vaporizer . . . . ETNA
vaporous . . . . . FOGGY, MISTY, HALITOUS, FUMY
vaquero . . . . COWBOY
Varangian . . . SCANDINAVIAN
Vargas, Brazilian president . . . GETULIO
variable . . . MUTABLE, FICKLE, ABERRANT, PROTEAN, VOLATILE, CHANGEABLE
variation . . CHANGE, DEVIATION
slight . . . NUANCE, SHADE
varicella . . . . CHICKEN FOX
varicolored . . . . MOTLEY
phenomenon . . RAINBOW
varicose . . . . . VARIX, SWOLLEN, CIRSOID
varied . . . . D(A)EDAL
variegate . . . . DIVERSIFY
variegated . . . . . . PIED, DAPPLE
variety . . . SORT, KIND, CLASS
act . . . . TURN
show . . . . VAUDEVILLE
variola . . . . SMALLPOX
scar . . . . POCKMARK
variole . . . . FOVEOLA
various . . . . . . SEVERAL, MANY, DIFFERENT
varlet . . . . KNAVE, RASCAL, SCOUNDREL, PAGE, COISTREL
varmint . . . . VERMIN
varnish . . . ENAMEL, LACQUER, SHELLAC(K), JAPAN, GLOSS, EMBELLISH
and linseed oil mix . . . . . . MEGILP
material . . . . COPAL, TURPENTINE, OLEORESIN, SHELLAC, ELEMI, RESIN, MASTIC, TUNG(OIL)
varsity . . . . TEAM, COLLEGIATE

eight member ... STROKE
varus .... BOWLEG(GED)
opposite of ..... VALGUS
vary .... DIFFER, MODIFY, ALTER, DIVERSIFY, DIVERGE
vas .... DUCT, VESSEL
vascular organ ..... PLACENTA
vase .... TAZZA, POTICHE, JAR, URN, AMPHORA, LACRIMAL, JARDINIERE
making material .... MURRHINE
support .... PEDESTAL
vaseline ... JELLY, OINTMENT, PETROLATUM, LUBRICANT
vassal .... SUBJECT, SERVANT, LIEGE(MAN), BONDMAN, SLAVE
tax paid by ... TRIBUTE
vassalage ... FIEF, SERVITUDE
Vassar's pride .... MILLAY
vast ..... HUGE, ENORMOUS, IMMENSE, COSMIC, OCEANIC
vat .... TUB, CASK, TUN, BAC, TANK, KIER, KEEVE, CISTERN
vatic .... PROPHETIC
Vatican art gallery .... BELVEDERE
chapel .... SISTINE
guard's nationality ...... SWISS
vaticinate .... PROPHESY, FORETELL, PREDICT
vaticinator ..... ORACLE, SEER, PROPHET
Vaud .... CANTON
capital of ..... LAUSANNE
vaudeville .... BURLESQUE, VARIETY(SHOW)
vault ..... LEAP, COPE, SPRING, CATACOMB, BOUND, ARCH, SAFE
burial ..... TOMB, CRYPT
concave .... COVE
for bones ...... OSSUARY
horse's .... CURVET
inside curve/surface ..... INTRADOS
underground ... DONJON, DUNGEON
vaulted .... ARCHED
roof .... DOME
vaunt .... BRAG, BOAST, CROW
vavasor .... VASSAL
veal .... GIGOT
of/like .... VITULINE
neck .... SCRAG
sausage .... BOLOGNA
slice .... SCHNITZEL
stew .... GOULASH
Veda, part of .. YAJUR, SAMA, ATHARVA, RIG
vedette .... SENTINEL, SCOUT(BOAT)
Vedic .... SANSKRIT, PALI
god .... DYAUS, AGNI
goddess .... USHAS
sky serpent .... AHI
vee .... FIVER, FIN
veer .... SHIFT, DEVIATE, SWERVE, TURN, SLUE, SHEER
veery .... THRUSH
Vega, for one .... STAR

constellation ...... LYRA
vegetable ... PLANT, LETTUCE, CABBAGE, TOMATO, OKRA, BEET, SASS, SAUCE, POTATO, CARROT, LEEK, PEA, BEAN, LEGUME, ENDIVE
basket .... SCUTTLE
boiled, buttered .. VICHY
decaying matter ... DUFF
farmer .... TRUCKER
garden .... TRUCK, KALEYARD, KAILYARD
gas .... METHANE
growing art .... HORTICULTURE
leafstalk .... CHARD
marrow .... SQUASH
oyster .... SALSIFY
poison ...... PTOMAIN(E)
root ... TURNIP, PARSNIP
vegetables grown for sale ..... TRUCK
vegetarian .... VEGAN
sea mammal ... SEACOW, DUGONG, MANATEE
vegetation, covered with green VERDANT
green .... VERDURE
luxuriant .... LUSH
vehemence ... FERVOR, FORCE, PASSION, ARDOR, FIRE, FURY
vehement .... FERVENT, PASSIONATE, ARDENT
vehemently .... EARNESTLY
vehicle .... CART, SLED(GE), CONVEYANCE, CARRIAGE, CAR, VAN, TRAIN, WAGON
armored ... HALF-TRACK
covered ...... CARAVAN, SCHOONER, SEDAN
decrepit ... SHANDRYDAN
hospital .... AMBULANCE
"last ride" ..... HURDLE, TUMBRIL, TUMBREL
man-drawn .... (JIN)RICKSHA
on runners ..... SLED(GE), SLEIGH, TOBOGGAN
parade .... FLOAT
slow moving ...... SLUG
veil .... MANTILLA, CLOAK, MASK, SCREEN, YAS(H)MAK, CURTAIN, CAUL, CONCEAL
having a .... VELATE
in botany .... VELUM
material .... TULLE, ILLUSION, BAREGE
papal .... ORALE
veiled ... DISGUISED, HIDDEN, COVERED, VELATE
veiling .... CURTAIN
vein ... MOOD, BLOOD VESSEL, TENOR, VENA, STREAK, INTIMA
branch .... VENULE
heart .... VENA CAVA
inflammation .. PHLEBITIS
kind of .... JUGULAR
leaf .... RIB
mine ...... LEDGE, LODE, REEF
mineral .... LODE

rich ore .... BONANZA
swollen .... VARIX
varicose .... VARIX
veining, art of ..... MARBLING
veinless .... AVENOUS
veins collectively ... VENATION
having .... VENOSE, VENOUS, NERVATE
veinstone .... GANGUE
velamen .... MEMBRANE
velar .... GUTTURAL
veld(t) .... GRASSLAND
Velez, actress .... LUPE
velleity .... DESIRE, VOLITION, WISH
vellicate ..... TWITCH, PLUCK
vellication .. TWITCH(ING), TIC
vellum .... PARCHMENT
velocipede .... BICYCLE, TRICYCLE, HANDCAR
velocity ..... SPEED, RAPIDITY, SWIFTNESS, RATE
measuring device .... TACHOMETER
velum .... SOFT PALATE
velure .... VELVET, PAD
velutinous .... VELVETY
velvet ...... WINNINGS, GAIN, PROFIT, VELOUR, SILK, PANNE
velveteen .... FUSTIAN
velvety ..... SMOOTH, MELLOW, SOFT
vena .... VEIN
venal .... CORRUPT, MERCENARY, VENDIBLE
vend .... SELL, PUBLISH
vendace .... WHITEFISH
vendee .... BUYER
vender ..... ALIENOR, SELLER
vendetta .... FEUD
vendible ... VENAL, SAL(E)ABLE
vendition .... SALE
vendor ...... SELLER, PEDDLER
route of a .... WALK
vendue .... AUCTION
veneer .... ENAMEL, OVERLAY, LAYER, BURL, VARNISH, COATING
venerable .. OLD, HOARY, AGED
man ... SAGE, PATRIARCH
monk .... BEDE
venerate ..... REVERE, ADORE, WORSHIP, HALLOW
venerated .... SACRED
veneration .. AWE, ADORATION, HOMAGE, REVERENCE, WORSHIP
venereal infection: sl. ... DOSE, CLAP
sore/ulcer ..... CHANCRE
venery ...... CHASE, HUNTING
venesection ..... PHLEBOTOMY
Venetia .... VENETO
Venetian barge .. BUCENTAUR
boat .... GONDOLA
boatman .... GONDOLIER
bridge .... RIALTO
business center .. RIALTO
canals .... RII
chief magistrate ... DOGE
gondolier's song .... BARCAROLE

island .... RIALTO
magistrate .... DOGE
nobleman ... MAGNIFICO
painter .... TITIAN, TINTORETTO, VERONESE, TIEPOLO
red .... SIENA
resort .... LIDO
ruler .... DOGE
song ...... BARCAROL(L)E
state barge .. BUCENTAUR
street .... CANAL
traveler ... (MARCO) POLO
Venezia .... VENICE
Venezuela capital ... CARACAS
city ... MARACAIBO, CORO, VALENCIA
dam .... GURI
discoverer of .. COLUMBUS
fish .... GUPPY
Indian ... CARIB, TIMOTE
language .... SPANISH
mining town ...... AROA
monetary unit .. BOLIVAR
patriot .... BOLIVAR
plain .... LLANO
president .... LEONI, CALDERA
river ..... PAO, ORINOCO, APURE, CARONI
seaport ...... MARACAIBO
snake .... LORA
state .... LARA
tree .... BALATA
Venezuelan god ...... TSUMA
vengeance .... REPRISAL, REQUITAL, REVENGE, TALION, WANION
vengeful .... VINDICTIVE, SPITEFUL
veni, vidi, ____ VICI
venial .... PARDONABLE, EXCUSABLE
opposed to ..... MORTAL
Venice, "Little" .. VENEZUELA
race in .... REGATTA
state barge .. BUCENTAUR
venireman .... JUROR
Venite ..... PSALM, CANTICLE
venom .... MALICE, VIRUS, GALL, POISON, SPITE, BANE
venomous .... BANEFUL, POISONOUS, MALIGNANT, VIPERINE, VIPERISH, VIPEROUS, VIRULENT
venous .... VEINY
vent .... HOLE, ISSUE, OUTLET, PASSAGE, ESCAPE, EXPRESSION, FLUE, ORIFICE, APERTURE, OPENING
in earth's crust .... VOLCANO, GEYSER
tailor's .... SLIT
whale's .... SPIRACLE, BLOWHOLE
ventage ...... (FINGER) HOLE
venter ...... BELLY, ABDOMEN, WOMB, WAME
ventilate .... AIR, AERATE, FAN, EXPOSE
ventilating shaft .. DOWNCAST
ventilation .... AIRING
opening .... LOUVER
ventilator ..... FAN, BLOWER
ventral .... ABDOMINAL, STERNAL, H(A)EMAD
opposite of ..... DORSAL
ventriloquist .... BERGEN
Bergen's dummy .. SNERD, CHARLIE
medium of ...... DUMMY, PUPPET
venture .. BRAVE, ENTERPRISE, CHANCE, RISK, DARE(SAY), HAZARD
Venus .... PLANET, PHOSPHOR, APHRODITE, CYTHEREA
as morning star .. LUCIFER
beloved of ...... ADONIS
flytrap .... DIONAEA
girdle .... CESTUS
in alchemy ...... COPPER
island .... MELOS
Milo's .... STATUE
planet .... VESPER
poetical .... LUCIFER, HESPERUS
son of .... CUPID
tree sacred to ... MYRTLE
Venus's flytrap ...... DIONAEA
veracious .... HONEST, ACCURATE, TRUTHFUL, TRUE
veracity ..... TRUTH, HONESTY
veranda(h) .... LANAI, PORCH, PORTICO, PIAZZA, BALCONY, LOGGIA
in Dixie .... GALLERY
verb, expression of a .. ACTION, EXISTENCE, OCCURRENCE
verbal .... ORAL, SPOKEN, VOCAL
attack .... TIRADE, INVECTIVE, OBLOQUY
noun .... GERUND, INFINITIVE, PARTICIPLE
thrust .... DIG
verbatim ... WORD FOR WORD, LITERAL
verbenaceous plant .. LANTANA, VERBENA, VERVAIN
tree .... TEAK
verbiage .... PROLIXITY, WORDINESS
verbose ..... PROLIX, WORDY, WINDY
verboten .... FORBIDDEN, TABOO, TABU
verbs, derived from .... RHEMATIC
verd .... GREEN
antique ...... VERDIGRIS, MARBLE, PATINA
verdancy .... GREENNESS, INEXPERIENCE, VIRIDITY
verdant .... GREEN
Verdi, composer .... GUISEPPE
work ..... OTELLO, AIDA, ERNANI, (IL)TROVATORE, NABUCCO, DON CARLO, FALSTAFF
verdict .... JUDGMENT, DECISION, FINDING
verdigris ...... RUST, PATINA, VERD ANTIQUE
verdin .... TITMOUSE, BIRD
verditer .... BICE
verdure .... GREENERY, GREENNESS
verecund ...... MODEST, SHY, BASHFUL
verein .... SOCIETY
verge .... BRINK, EDGE, MARGIN, STAFF, ROD, MARGE
Vergil's birthplace ... MANTUA
hero .... (A)ENEAS
queen .... DIDO
work .... (A)ENEID
variest ... UTMOST, GREATEST
verify ...... CONFIRM, CHECK, AFFIRM, ATTEST
verily ..... REALLY, IN FACT, TRULY, INDEED, CERTES
veritable ...... ACTUAL, REAL
veritas .... TRUTH
verity .... FACT, TRUTH, REALITY
vermeil .... VERMILION
vermiform ..... WORM-SHAPED
process .... APPENDIX
vermilion ..... VERMEIL, RED, PIGMENT, CINNABAR, MINIUM
vermin ... VARMINT, VARMENT, LICE, BEDBUG, RAT, WEASEL, PEST
Vermont capital .. MONTPELIER
city ... BARRE, RUTLAND, BURLINGTON
vermouth .... WINE
vernacular ... DIALECT, IDIOM
vernal .... SPRINGLIKE, YOUTHFUL
Verne, author .... JULES
character .... NEMO
submarine .... NAUTILUS
veronal .... BARBITAL
veronica .... SUDARIUM, SPEEDWELL, FIGWORT, SUDARY
verruca .... WART
verrucose .... WARTY
versant .... SLOPE
versatile .... MANY-SIDED, TALENTED
verse ..... ALBA, LINE, POEM, TROCHEE, OCTAMETER, TRIPODY, DIMETER, STANZA, RUNE, (MON)STICH
accented .... ARSIS
analysis .... SCANSION
comic .... DOGGEREL
form .... COUPLET, DIMETER, IAMB, (DI)STICH, SONNET, PANTOUM, PANTUN, ANAPEST, VIRELAY, SPONDEE
free .... VERS LIBRE
half line of ... HEMISTICH
inside ring .... POSY
kind of .... DOGGEREL, LIMERICK, JINGLE
musical .... STAFF
satirical .... IAMBIC
set to music ..... LYRICS
two-feet .... DIMETER, DIPODY, SYZYGY
two-line .... DISTICH, COUPLET

unit .... FOOT
with nosegay ...... POSY
versed .... LEARNED, PROFICIENT, ADEPT, SKILLED, TURNED, FAMILIAR
verses, set of .... STAVE, STANZA, STROPHE, PANTUN
versifier .... POET(ASTER), RHYMER, RHYMESTER
versify ...... METRIFY, RHYME
version .... TRANSLATION, ACCOUNT, RENDITION
of Bible .... VULGATE, DOUAY
verso, opposed to ... OBVERSE, RECTO
versus .... AGAINST
vertebra: comb. form .... SPONDYL(O)
body of .... CENTRUM
top .... ATLAS
vertebral bone .... SACRUM, COCCYX
vertebrate ..... FISH, REPTILE, AVIS, MAMMAL
vertex .... APEX, TOP, ZENITH, SUMMIT
vertical .... UPRIGHT, PERPENDICULAR, PLUMB
verticil .... WHORL
vertiginous .... DIZZY
vertigo .... DIZZINESS, GIDDINESS, MEGRIM, DINUS, GID, STAGGERS
Vertumnus' wife .... POMONA
verve .... VIGOR, ELAN, ENTHUSIASM, PEP, SPIRIT
vervet .... MONKEY
relative .... GRIVET
very .... REAL, EVEN, ACTUAL, TRULY, SAME, GENUINE, TRES, QUITE
colloquial ..... TERRIBLY
in English slang .. BALLY
large .... DECUMAN
light ...... FLARE, SIGNAL
new .... REDHOT
well .... FINE, FIRST RATE
visica .... BLADDER
vesicant ...... MUSTARD GAS, EPISPASTIC
vesicate .... BLISTER
vesicle ...... CYST, BLEB, SAC, CAVITY, BLISTER, BULLA, UTRICLE
vespa ... WASP, YELLOWJACKET
vesper .... STAR, EVENING, EVENTIDE, HESPERUS, VENUS, EVE
vespers ... CANONICAL HOUR, EVENSONG
vespertilione .... BAT
vespiary inhabitant ..... WASP, HORNET, VESPID
vespid .... HORNET, WASP, YELLOWJACKET
vespine insect .... WASP
vessel .... UTENSIL, CASK, CANAL, VAS, BOWL, DUCT, SHIP, CRAFT, FRIGATE, GALLEON, GALLEY, AIRSHIP, DUCT, TUBE, PAN, LATEEN, LUGGER, (CAT)BOAT, CAR(R)ACK
anti-smuggling .. CUTTER
assayer's .... CUPEL
cargo .... OILER, FREIGHTER, TANKER, BARGE
Chinese .... JUNK, SAMPAN
clumsy ... ARK, DROGHER
combining form ... VASO
cooking .... PAN
Ecclesiastical .. AMA, PYX
fishing .... TRAWLER, SEALER, SMACK
Levantine ...... KETCH, SAIC
Malay ..... PRAU, PROA
merchant ...... ARGOSY
supply .... TENDER, COALER
three-masted ..... BARK, ZEBEC
vessels, having ..... VASCULAR
vest .... WAISTCOAT, UNDERSHIRT, CLOTHE, EMPOWER, ENDOW, BOLERO, TATTERSALL
pocket .... SMALL
Vesta .... HESTIA, MATCH
vestal ...... VIRGIN(AL) PURE, CHASTE, NUN
virgin .... TUCCIA, PRIESTESS
vested .... ROBED, FIXED, ABSOLUTE, SETTLED
vestibule ...... HALL, LOBBY, FOYER, HALL(WAY)
vestige(s) .. MARK, BIT, TRACK, RELIC, NARTHEX, SIGN, TRACE, SHRED, REMAINS, SHADOW
of burn .... ESCHAR
vestment .... GARMENT, ROBE, GOWN, TUNICLE
clerical ..... ALB, TIPPET, AMICE, CASSOCK, SURPLICE, CHASUBLE, COPE
eucharistic .... MANIPLE
Jewish priest's ... EPHOD
papal .... FANON
place for .... AMBRY
vestry .... SACRISTY
Vesuvian .... VOLCANIC, FUSEE, MATCH
vesuvianite .... IDOCRASE, EGERAN
Vesuvius .... VOLCANO
city destroyed by .... POMPEII
vetch .... TARE, AKRA, SATIVA, ERS
vet(eran) .... TROUPER, STAGER, OLD HAND, OLDTIMER
of battles ... WAR HORSE
veterinarian .... DOCTOR, FARRIER, LEECH, VET
vetiver .... GRASS, BENA
veto .... PROHIBIT, FORBID, KIBOSH, DISAPPROVE
vex .... ANNOY, DISTURB, IRRITATE, TORMENT, TROUBLE, GALL, ROIL, ACERBATE, FASH, HARASS, IRK, NETTLE, NEEDLE, CARK, RILE
vexatious .... ANNOYING, TROUBLESOME, IRRITABLE, PESKY
via ... BY WAY OF, THROUGH
viaduct ..... BRIDGE, TRESTLE
vial .... PHIAL, BOTTLE, AMP(O)ULE
viand(s) ... DISH, FOOD, FARE, VICTUALS
viaticum .... EUCHARIST
viator .... TRAVELER, WAYFARER
Viaud's pseudonym ..... LOTI
vibrant .... QUIVERING, RESONANT, PULSING, ENERGETIC
vibrate .... QUIVER, OSCILLATE, RESOUND, THRILL, JAR, TIRL, TREMBLE, FLUTTER, THROB, DINDLE, SHIMMY, RESONATE
vibration ..... QUIVER, THRILL, TREMOLO, FREMITUS
check .... DAMP
vibrator .... OSCILLATOR
vibrissa .... WHISKERS
viburnum .... SHRUB, HONEYSUCKLE, LANTANA, LIANA, LIANE
vicar .... DEPUTY, PRIEST, MINISTER, VICEGERENT
assistant of ..... CURATE
Christ's .... POPE
vicarious .... DEPUTY, SUBSTITUTE, DELEGATED
vice ...... SIN, STEAD, FAULT, ADDICTION, INSTEAD(OF), WEAKNESS
chairman, public dinner .. CROUPIER
president .... VEEP
versa .... CONVERSELY
vicegerent ..... VICAR, DEPUTY
vicenary number ..... TWENTY
viceroy .... BUTTERFLY, VICEGERENT, REGENT
of a .... VICEREGAL
wife of a ..... VICEREINE
Vichy and others ... WATERS, EAUX, SPAS
vicinage ..... NEIGHBORHOOD, VICINITY
vicinal .... LOCAL
vicinity ..... NEIGHBORHOOD, ENVIRONS
vicious ..... WICKED, UNRULY, MEAN, MALICIOUS
act .... OUTRAGE
vicissitude .... CHANGE
victim .... PREY, QUARRY, MARK, DUPE, LAMB
accident ..... CASUALTY
of Bellerphon ... CHINERA
of Cain .... ABEL
victor ... CONQUEROR, WINNER
actor ..... JORY, MATURE

character .... LENA, AXEL HEYST
victoria ... WATERLILY, QUEEN, EMPRESS, CARRIAGE, AUTO(MOBILE)
capital (Australia) ...... MELBOURNE
goddess .... NIKE
Victorian vice ...... PRUDERY, BIGOTRY
victorious .... PALMARY, TRIUMPHANT
victory ...... LAUREL, PALM, TRIUMPH, CONQUEST, SUCCESS
author of ...... CONRAD
costly .... PYRRHIC
crown of .... LAUREL, ANADEM
easy .... WALKAWAY, RUNAWAY
goddess of .... NIKE, ATHENA
kind of .... CADMEAN, PYRRHIC LANDSLIDE, ROUT
symbol of .... PALM, CHAPLET, LAUREL
Victrola ...... PHONOGRAPH
kin of .... GRAMOPHONE
victual(s) .... EAT, FEED, FOOD, VIAND, VITTLE, PROVISIONS
victualer .... SUTLER, INNKEEPER, CATERER
vicuna .... ALPACA
vide .... SEE
videliet .... NAMELY
video .... TELEVISION, TV
vie ... COMPETE, CONTEND, LIFE
Vienna .... WIEN
park .... PRATER
Woods composer .... STRAUSS
Viennese dress ...... DIRNDL, LEDERHOSEN
Vietnam (North) capital ...... HANOI
city .... HAIPHONG
monetary unit ..... DONG
native .... MEO
newspaper .... NHANDAN
premiér .... (PHAM VAN) DONG
president .... (HO CHI) MINH
Vietnam (South) Buddhist sect CAO DAI, HOA, HAO
capital .... SAIGON
city ....DANANG, DALAT, HUE
guerrillas ..... VIETCONG
holiday .... TET
monetary unit ... PIASTRE
New Year .... TET
premier .... KHANH, CAO KY
president .. THIEU, DIEM
view ... VISION, SIGHT, VISTA, SCENE, OPINION, GOAL, PANORAMA, SCAPE, NOTION, GLIMPSE, PROSPECT, SURVEY
viewpoint .... OPINION OUTLOOK
vigesimal .... TWENTIETH
vigil ..... WATCH, EVE, WAKE
vigilance, in medicine .... INSOMNIA
vigilant .... ALERT, WARY, WATCHFUL
vigilante .... NIGHTRIDER
vigor ... VITALITY, INTENSITY, ENERGY, SNAP, DASH, FORCE
vigorous .... ROBUST, STRONG, FORCEFUL, ENERGETIC
Viking ...... PIRATE, ROVER, NORSEMAN
famed ..... ERIC, ROLLO, OLAF
poet .... SKALD
vilayet .... EYALET
subdivision of .. SANJAK
vile .... MEAN, WICKED, DEPRAVED, BASE, EVIL, SCURVY
vilify .... DEFAME, ABUSE, SLANDER, ASPERSE, REVILE, TRADUCE, MALIGN, CALUMNIATE, LIBEL
vilipend .... VILIFY, BELITTLE, DISPARAGE, REVILE
Villa, Mexican leader .... PANCHO
village .... MUNICIPALITY, BARRIO, HAMLET, CASALE, KAIK, STAD, WICK, DORP, THROP(E), KRAAL, BURG, BURH, TOWN, CLACHAN
Biblical .... CANA
near castle .... BOURG
villain ... SCOUNDREL, ROGUE, CRIMINAL, MEANIE, MISCREANT, KNAVE, FELON
movie .... HEAVY
of story .... LEGREE, RASSENDALE
villainy .... CRIME
villatic ...... RURAL, RUSTIC
villein .... PEASANT, CARL(E), ESNE, SERF, TENANT
Villon, Fr. poet .... FRANCOIS
Vilnius .... VILNA, WILNO
vim .... PEP, ZIP, ELAN, ENERGY, VIGOR, SPIRIT, STINGO
vimen .... SHOOT
vin .... WINE
vina .... ZITHER
vinaceous ...... VINOUS, RED
fruit .... GRAPE
Vinci's patron .... SFORZA
vincible .... BEATABLE
vincit omnia ____ .... VERITAS
vindicate .... CLEAR, JUSTIFY, ABSOLVE
vindictive ..... (RE)VENGEFUL, SPITEFUL, MALICIOUS
vine ..... LIANA, GRAPE, BINE, CREEPER, LIANE, IVY, WISTERIA, PEA, HOP, ANGLEPOD, COW(H)AGE
coil of .... TENDRIL
gourd ..... COLOCYNTH
support .... RISEL, TENDRIL, TRELLIS
tuberous .... TAMUS
woody .... SMILAX
vinegar ...... ACETUM, EISEL, ALEGAR
bottle .... CRUET, CASTER, CASTOR
change to ...... ACETIFY
dregs .... MOTHER
eel .... NEMATODE
formation in ...... ROPE, MOTHER
from ale .... ALEGAR
kind of ..... PALM, CIDER
like/of .... ACETIC, ACETOUS, ACETOSE
pickling ...... MARINADE
preserve in .... MARINATE
producing ..... ACETOUS
spiced .... MARINADE
stringy substance .... MOTHER
worm .... EEL
vinegarroon .... SCORPION
vinegary .... SOUR, ILL-TEMPERED
vinery .... GREENHOUSE
vineyard .... CLOS
vingt et un ...... BLACKJACK, TWENTY-ONE
vinous ..... VINACEOUS, WINY
vintage .... WINE, MODEL, CHOICE, CROP
vintner's assistant .. GOURMET
viol .... SARINDA
viola ... VIOLET, PANSY, PLANT
clef .... ALTO
violate .... BREAK, RAPE, RAVISH, DESECRATE, PROFANE, ABUSE, INFRACT, INFRINGE
trust .... BETRAY
violation .... BREACH, DESECRATION, INFRACTION
violator .... LAWBREAKER
violence ..... SEVERITY, FORCE
violent ...... ROUGH, FURIOUS, STRONG, FORCEFUL, TEARING
anger .... FURY
blow .... BASH
contact .... IMPACT, COLLISION
violet ...... MAUVE, PURPLE, FLOWER
blue .... INDIGO
violin .... FIDDLE, CELLO, VIOLA, VIOL(ONCELLO)
border .... PURFLING
bow .... ARCO, FIDDLESTICK
bow's knob .... NUT
companion of ..... BOW
E-string .... QUINT
famous ... AMATI, STRAD, CREMONA
forerunner of the .... REBEC(K)
inlaid border .. PURFLING
instrument resembling ... REBEC(K)
part of ... NECK, SCROLL, PEG, NUT, BRIDGE, PEG(BOX), WAIST, BUTTON
piano piece ..... SONATA

player .... FIDDLER
rare ... KIT, STRAD, AMATI
small .... KIT
stroke .... UPBOW
violinist .... ELMAN, AUER, KREISLER, YSAYE, STERN, HEIFETZ, MENUHIN
comedian .... BENNY
direction to .... SPICCATO
Roman .... NERO
so-called .. (JACK) BENNY
violone .... CONTRABASS
VIP ..... TOPBRASS, BIGSHOT, CELEBRITY
viper .... ADDER, ASP, FER-DE-LANCE, SNAKE, REPTILE, COPPERHEAD, RATTLESNAKE, BUSHMASTER
horned .... CERASTES
viper's bugloss .... BUGWEED
viperine .... VENOMOUS
viperous .... VENOMOUS, MALICIOUS, SPITEFUL
virago ... TERMAGANT, VIXEN, FURY, SCOLD, AMAZON, HELLCAT
virelay .... VERSE, POEM
vireo .... GREENLET, (SONG)BIRD, REDEYE, RUDD
virescent .... GREENISH
virgate .... TWIGGY, ROD-SHAPED
Virgil (see Vergil)
virgin .. VESTAL, VIRGO, NUN, CHASTE, UNTOUCHED, PURE, PARTHENOS, MAID(EN), INITIAL, MADONNA
Islands' discoverer ...... COLUMBUS
queen .... ELIZABETH
the .... MARY
unblemished ... CAMILLA
vestal .... RHEA
virgin's-bower ..... CLEMATIS
virginal ...... HARPSICHORD, MAIDENLY, PURE
membrane .... HYMEN
Virginia capital .... RICHMOND
city .... ROANOKE, PORT NEWS, NORFOLK
cowslip .... BLUEBELL
creeper .... IVY, WOODBINE, VINE
dance .... REEL
mount .... VERNON
pine .... LOBLOLLY
river .... JAMES, RAPIDAN
seaport .... NORFOLK
settlement .. JAMESTOWN
state bird ..... CARDINAL
truffle ...... TUCKAHOE
virginity .... MAIDENHOOD
Virgo .... VIRGIN, CONSTELLATION
star .... SPICA
virgulate .... ROD-SHAPED, VIRGATE
viridian .... PIGMENT
viridity .... VERDANCY, GREENNESS
virile .... MANLY, MASCULINE, MALE

virtu .... CURIO, BIBELOT, RARITY
virtual .... LITERAL
virtually .... ALMOST, NEARLY, LITERALLY
virtue .... CHASTITY, EXCELLENCE, MERIT, QUALITY
virtues, one of the .. PRUDENCE, JUSTICE, HOPE, FAITH, CHARITY
virtuosity .... SKILL
virtuoso .... MAESTRO, CONNOISSEUR, ARTIST, AESTHETE
virtuous ..... CHASTE, MORAL
virulence .... DEADLINESS, VENOM, MALIGNANCY
virulent .... DEADLY, VENOMOUS, RABID, MALIGNANT, INFECTIOUS
virus .... POISON, VENOM, VACCINE, PATHOGEN
disease .... MEASLES, SMALLPOX, CHICKEN POX, VARICELLA, HERPES, VIROSIS, VARIOLA, RABIES, FLU, GRIP(PE), INFLUENZA, SHINGLES, POLIO, COLD
vis .... POWER, FORCE, STRENGTH
a-vis ...... FACE TO FACE
visage .... FACE, MAP, COUNTENANCE
viscera .... INTESTINES, INNARDS, VITALS, GUTS, ENTRAILS
viscid ..... VISCOUS, STICKY, SIRUPY, VISCOSE, GUMMY
viscount .... SHERIFF
heir of .... MASTER
viscous ...... VISCID, STICKY, SYRUPY, GLUEY, PASTY, SIZY
product ... PASTE, GLUE, GUM
substance ... PITCH, TAR, RESIN, SLIME, MOLASSES, SYRUP
vise ..... CLAMP, CLAM, DIAL
part of .... JAW
Vishinsky, Soviet diplomat .... ANDREI
Vishnu ...... (THE) PRESERVER
avatar of .... KRISHNA
incarnation of .. KRISHNA, RAMA
wife of .... SRI
visible .... PERCEPTIBLE, EVIDENT, DISCERNIBLE, IN SIGHT, VISUAL
to naked eye .... MACROSCOPIC
Visigoth .... TEUTON
king .... ALARIC
vision ...... IMAGE, DREAM, FANCY, PICTURE, (EYE)SIGHT
defect .... MYOPIA, DIPLOPIA, ANOPIA
double .... DIPLOPIA
pertaining to .. OPTIC(AL)

range .... EYESIGHT, EYESHOT
scope .... SCAN
tri-dimensional .... STEREOPSIS
visionary .... ILLUSIONIST, DREAMER, IMAGINARY, IMPRACTICAL, UTOPIAN, IDEALIST, QUIXOTIC, FANTAST
visit ... CALL, STAY, SOJOURN, GO TO, INFLICT
between whalers .... GAM
kind of .... SOCIAL, PROFESSIONAL, OFFICIAL
short ..... CALL, LOOK-IN
social .... GAM
visitant ...... VISITOR, GUEST
visitation .... DISASTER, AFFLICTION
visitor ..... VISITANT, GUEST, CALLER, COMPANY
visor .... MASK, VIZARD, BRIM, EYE-SHADE, VISARD
vista ... VIEW, OUTLOOK, SCENE
Vistula River .... WISLA
city on .... TORUN
tributary .... SAN
visual ...... VISIBLE, OPTICAL, OCULAR
disorder ... STRABISMUS, SQUINT, SCOTOMA
purple ...... RHODOPSIN
yellow .... RETINENE
visualize .... IMAGINE
vita .... LIFE
Nuova author .... DANTE
vital .... FATAL, DEADLY, ESSENTIAL, IMPORTANT, MORTAL
fluid .... BLOOD, SAP
organ .... HEART, LUNG, LIVER
principle .... SOUL
statistics of beauty contestant .... MEASUREMENTS
vitality ... ZEST, VIGOR, LIFE, ZING, ENERGY
vitalize .... ANIMATE
vitamin B .... CHOLINE
H .... BIOTIN
vitelline .... EGG YOLK
vitellus .... YOLK
vitiate ...... SPOIL, CORRUPT, PERVERT, INVALIDATE, TAINT, DEBASE
vitreous ... GLASSY, HYALINE, HYALOID
vitrics .... GLASSWARE
vitrify .... BAKE
vitrine .... SHOWCASE
vitriol .... SULFATE, SORY, BLUEJACK, BLUESTONE
vitriolic ..... SHARP, CAUSTIC, SARCASTIC, BITING
vitta ...... HEADBAND, RIBBON
vittle .... VICTUAL, FOOD
vituline animal .... CALF
vituperate ..... ABUSE, SCOLD, REVILE, BERATE
vituperation ...... INVECTIVE, ABUSE

viva .. ACCLAIM, EXCLAMATION, CHEER
voce .... ORALLY
vivacious .... GAY, LIVELY, SPIRITED
vivacity ... ELAN, DASH, VERVE, ANIMATION, GAIETY, BRIO
vivandiere .... SUTLER
vivarium .... HOTHOUSE, GREENHOUSE
vive le .... ROI
vivid .... LIVE(LY), BRIGHT, GRAPHIC, STRIKING
vivify .... ANIMATE
vixen .... SCOLD, VIRAGO, TERMAGANT, HELLCAT, SHREW, FOX
viz. ..... VIDELICET, NAMELY
vizard .... VISOR, MASK
Vladimir Ilich Ulianov .. LENIN
pianist ...... HOROWITZ
vocabulary .... GLOSSARY, DICTIONARY, LEXICON, ARGOT, JARGON, SLANG
of a .... LEXICAL
vocal ...... VERBAL, SONANT, ORAL, SPOKEN, UTTERED, SUNG, VOICED, ARTICULATE
chords site ..... LARYNX
composition ...... SONG
ornament ..... ROULADE
solo ...... ARIA, ARIOSO
vocalist .... SINGER
vocalize .... PHONATE
vocation .... TRADE, OCCUPATION, PROFESSION, CAREER, WORK, CALLING
voces .... VOX, VOICE
vociferation ... CLAMOR, RANT
vociferous ...... CLAMOROUS, BLATANT, BOISTEROUS
vodka mixture .. SCREWDRIVER
vogue ... MODE, FAD, FASHION, STYLE, TON
voice .... ARTICULATE, UTTER, SAY, VOX
colloquial ... SPOKESMAN, MOUTHPIECE
female ... ALTO, SOPRANO
impairment .. DYSPHONIA
kind of ..... BASS, ALTO, BASS(O), TENOR, SOPRANO, BARITONE, FALSETTO
loss of .... APHONIA
loud, strident .. FOGHORN
male ..... TENOR, BASSO
objection .... DEMUR, PROTEST, COMPLAIN
organ .... LARYNX
person with loud .... STENTOR
pertaining to .... VOCAL, PHONETIC
practice ...... SOLFEGGIO
quality .... TIMBRE
range .... DIAPASON
roaming .... VAGANS
voiced sound .... VIBRANT, SPEECH, SONG, SONANT, UTTERANCE
stop .... MEDIA
voiceless .. SURD, DUMB, MUTE, SILENT, SPEECHLESS, SPIRATE
sound ..... SURD, TENUIS
sound sign ..... CEDILLA
voices, for all .... TUTTI
void ...... VACATE, VACANT, EMPTY, LACKING, VACUUM, INVALID, CANCEL, ANNUL, NULLIFY, NULL, NULLITY
of infinite space .. INANE
voidance .... ANNULMENT
voided escutcheon ...... ORLE
voila .... BEHOLD, LO, SEE
voile .... FABRIC
voiture ... CARRIAGE, WAGON
volant .... FLYING, NIMBLE, QUICK, AGILE
Volapuk, inventor of .... SCHLEYER
volatile .... MUTABLE, MERCURIAL, FICKLE
liquid ... ETHER, ALCOHOL
volcanic .... VESUVIAN, EXPLOSIVE, EXTRUSIVE
activity ...... ERUPTION, BELCHING
ash .... TUFF
cinder .... SCORIA
dust .... TUFF
earth .... TRASS
ejection .... BELCH, LAPILLUS, LAVA, PUMICE, SCORIA, COULEE
glass .... OBSIDIAN
island .... LIPARI, IWO(JIMA), FAROE
mud .... SALSE
opening ..... FUMAROLE
rock .... PERLITE, RHYOLITE, TUFF, LAPILLUS, WACK, OBSIDIAN, TALPATATE, TAXITE, PROPYLITE, TEPHRITE, TRACHYTE, PUMICE, BASALT, LATITE
rock cavity ..... VESICLE
slag .... SCORIA, CINDER
soil .... TALPATATE
vent .... CRATER, SOLFATARA
volcano, cone of ... MONTICULE
crater-like basic .... CALDERA
island .... IWO JIMA
kind of .... ACTIVE, DORMANT, EXTINCT
molten rock ..... LAVA, MAGMA
mouth of .... FUMAROLE, CRATER
well known ...... PELEE, TAAL, ETNA, VESUVIUS, ASAMA, FUJI
vole .... RODENT, MOUSE, RAT, SLAM
volery .... AVIARY
Volga figure ...... BOATMAN
tributary .... KAMA
volition ...... VELLEITY, WILL
volk .... NATION, PEOPLE
volley ..... SALVO, FUSILLADE, BURST, BROADSIDE
volplane ...... GLIDE, COAST
Volstead Act dissenters .. WETS
supporters .... DRYS
Volsunga Saga dwarf .... NIBELUNG
hero .... SIGURD, SIEGFRIED
king .... ATLI
volt-ampere .... WATT
volta, in music ... TURN, TIME
Voltaire .... AROUET
character ..... PANGLOSS
novel by ...... CANDIDE
volte-face ...... ABOUT-FACE, REVERSAL
voluble ..... TALKATIVE, GLIB, GARRULOUS
volume .... BOOK, BULK, CUBAGE, MASS, QUANTITY, TOME, CUBATURE
of sound unit .. DECIBEL
voluminous ..... BULKY, FULL, LARGE
voluntarily .... FREELY
voluntary .... WILLFUL
volunteer ...... ENLIST, OFFER
opposed to .... DRAFTEE, CONSCRIPT
voluptuary .... SYBARITE, SENSUALIST, HEDONIST
voluptuous .... SENSUAL, SENSUOUS, LYDIAN
volute .... WHORL, TURN, SPIRALED
volution ...... COIL, ROLLING
vomica .... PUS
vomit ..... REGORGE, EMETIC, THROW UP, PUKE, BELCH, SPEW, REJECT
effort to .... RETCH
vomiting .... EMESIS
voodoo ... WITCHCRAFT, OBI, BEAH, HOODOO
deity .... ZOMBI(E)
voracious .... EDACIOUS, GREEDY, RAVENOUS, INSATIABLE, RAPACIOUS, ESURIENT
voracity ..... GREED, EDACITY, RAPACITY
Voroshilov, USSR president .. KLEMENTI
vortex .... EDDY, WHIRLPOOL, WHIRLWIND, GYRE
votary .... NUN, MONK, CELIBATE, FAN, DEVOTEE
vote ...... SUFFRAGE, BALLOT
by gesture .. THUMBS-UP, THUMBSDOWN
counting .... POLL
in .... ELECT
in opposition ...... CON
kind of .. STRAW, HAND, PROXY, SECRET, CON
non-candidate's .... WRITE-IN
of assent ... PLACET, AYE
presiding officer's .... CASTING
right to ...... SUFFRAGE, FRANCHISE
solicitation for a bill ..... LOBBY

survey .... POLL
voiced ... YEA, AYE, NAY
voter .... ELECTOR
voting method .... BALLOT, VOICE
vouch ... ATTEST, GUARANTEE, AFFIRM, SPONSOR, ASSURE
voucher .... CHIT, DEBENTURE
vouchsafe .... BESTOW, CONCEDE, DEIGN, GUARANTEE
vow .... OATH, PROMISE, PLEDGE, SWEAR
taker .... MONK, CELIBATE, NUN, VOTARY, WITNESS
vowel .... LETTER
change in sound .... UMLAUT
contraction of .... SYNERESIS
gradation ...... ABLAUT
mark ... MACRON, BREVE, TILDE, DI(A)ERESIS, UMLAUT, CIRCUMFLEX
slurring .... ELISION
vox .... VOICE
voyage ... JOURNEY, PASSAGE, TRIP
pleasure .... CRUISE
voyager .... SAILOR
voyageur .... TRAVELER, BOATMAN
voyeur .... PEEPING TOM
vrouw ... HOUSEWIFE, WOMAN
vs. .... VERSUS
Vulcan .... HEPHAESTUS, HEPHAISTOS
Star Trek .... (MR) SPOCK
vulcanite ... EBONITE, RUBBER
vulgar ..... COMMON, COARSE, CRUDE, LOW-BRED, RANDY, BOORISH, PLEBEIAN, GROSS, OBSCENE
Vulgate, author of the .... JEROME
vulnerable .... ASSAILABLE, WEAK
Vulpecula ...... LITTLE FOX, CONSTELLATION
vulpine .... FOXY, TRICKY, VULPECULAR, CUNNING
vulture ...... CONDOR, URUBU, LAMMERGEI(E)R, ATRATA
food .... CARRION
hawk resembling .... CARACARA

W

W, Arabic .... WAW
in chemistry ... TUNGSTEN
old English .... WEN
Waadt .... VAUD
Wabash River city .... TERRE HAUTE
tributary ... TIPPECANOE
wabble ...... LARVA, WOBBLE
wacker .... QUAKER
wacky .. ERRATIC, ECCENTRIC, ODD, QUEER
wad ..... MASS, CRAM, LUMP, STUFF, BUNDLE, PLUG, PLEDGET, BAT, DOSSIL, PAD
of paper money .... ROLL
wadding material .... COTTON, KAPOK, HEMP
waddle .... TODDLE, WAG, WOBBLE
waddler ...... DUCK, GOOSE, TODDLER, BABY
waddy .... CANE, WALKING STICK, CLUB
wade ..... FORD, SLOSH, SLOG, PADDLE
wader ... HERON, EGRET, IBIS, CRANE, RAIL, COOT, SNIPE
waders .... BOOTS
wadi ..... CHANNEL, RAVINE, VALLEY, OASIS, WATERCOURSE
wading bird (see bird) ... IBIS
wadset .... MORTGAGE
wafer .... CRACKER, CAKE, CANDY, DISK, SNAP
container ..... PYX, PIX
waff ..... GUST, PUFF, WAVE, WHIFF, GHOST, SOLITARY, VAGABOND
waffle .... (BATTER) CAKE
waft ..... WAIF, CARRY OVER, TRANSPORT, FLOAT, BREATH, GUST
wag ...... FARCEUR, JESTER, SHAKE, WIT, WAVE, JOKER, PUNSTER, WAGGLE, WIGGLE
wage .... HIRE, STIPEND, CARRY ON, PAY, ENGAGE, SALARY, EMOLUMENT
boost .... RAISE
deduct from ...... DOCK
earners collectively .... LABOR
war .... LEVY
wager ... BET, ANTE, PARLAY, VIE, IMPONE, GAMBLE, GAGE, STAKE, HAZARD
wages .... REWARD, RECOMPENSE, EMOLUMENT, STIPEND
after deductions .... TAKE-HOME
describing some .. LIVING, STARVATION
payment in kind .. TRUCK
wagged, thing that's .. FINGER, TAIL, TONGUE, FLAG, HEAD
wagger .... DOG, PIPIT
waggery .... JEST, WIT, JOKE
waggish .... JOCULAR, SPORTIVE, PLAYFUL, MERRY, ROGUISH
waggle .... TOTTER
dancer .... BEE
Wagner, composer .. RICHARD
father-in-law of ... LISZT
forte of .... OPERA
wife of .... COSIMA
Wagnerian earth goddess ..... ERDA
music festival city .... BAYREUTH
opus .... RIENZI, PARSIFAL, LOHENGRIN
role .... WOTAN, ELSA, ISOLDE, TRISTAN, SENTA, HAGEN
soprano .... NILSSON
wagon .... TRAM, TRAILER, DRAY, WAIN, VOITURE, CAMION, (T)CART, TUMBREL, TUMBRIL
ammunitions ... CAISSON
baggage ...... FOURGON
battle ... DREADNAUGHT
builder .... WAINWRIGHT
Charlemagne's .... WAIN
driver .... CARTER
freight charge .. CARTAGE
horse .... POLER
oriental .... ARABA
pin .... CLEVIS
police ..... BLACK MARIA
prairie .... SCHOONER
repairer ... WAINWRIGHT
shaft .... THILL
tongue .... NEAP
track .... RUT
yoke .... INSPAN
wagoner .... AURIGA
wagtail ... PIPIT, LARK, BIRD
wahoo ...... BURNING BUSH, SHRUB, ELM, BASSWOOD
fish .... ONO, PETO
waif ... GAMIN, ARAB, STRAY, FOUNDLING, WAFT, SIGNAL, MAVERICK
wail ... HOWL, (CATER)WAUL, YOWL, ULULATE, CRY, MOURN, LAMENT, WAWL, SOB
Wailing Wall chore .. PRAYER, LAMENTATION
devotee .... JEW
site .... JERUSALEM
wain .... WAGON, CART
wainscot .. CEIL, PANEL(ING), WALLBOARD, LINING
waist ...... BODICE, BLOUSE, BASQUE
circumference .... GIRTH
garment .... SARONG, LOINCLOTH
molding garment .... GIRDLE
of dress .... TAILLE
waistband .... BELT, SASH, GIRDLE, CINCTURE, OBI
waistcloth ... SARONG, PAREUS, LAVA-LAVA
waistcoat .... VEST, GILET, JACKET
waistline .... GIRTH
wait ... STAY, TARRY, REMAIN, BIDE, ATTEND
in ambush ...... COUCH
lie in .... AMBUSH, TRAP

on ..... SERVE, ATTEND, VISIT
waiter .... TRAY, SALVER, SERVER, GARCON, STEWARD, POTMAN
drive-in .... CARHOP
female .... WAITRESS
portable .... DUMB
waiting line ..... QUEUE, CUE
waitresses, chief of .. HOSTESS
waive ... RELINQUISH, GIVE UP, DEFER, FOR(E)GO, RENOUNCE
wake ... VIGIL, WATCH, TRACK
Island .... OTORI
periscope's ..... FEATHER
robin ..... PLANT, SARAH, ARUM, CUCKOOPINT, TRILLIUM, JACK-IN-THE-PULPIT
submarine's .... FEATHER
up from this ...... SLEEP, TRANCE, DREAM, COMA, STUPOR
wakeful .... SLEEPLESS
waken .... STIR, ROUSE
Waldorf .... SALAD
room .... SERT
wale ..... RIB, WELT, WHEAL, TEXTURE, SELECT, CHOICE, BLOW
Waler .... HORSE
Wales city .... SWANSEA, CARDIFF
floral emblem ..... LEEK
mountain ..... SNOWDON
patron saint ..... DAVID
poetic name ... CAMBRIA
river .. SEVERN, USK, WYE
seaport .... SWANSEA
walk ... TRAMP, TREAD, PLOD, HIKE, AMBLE, STOA, ALLEY, HOOF
about .... AMBULATE
baby's .... WADDLE, TODDLE
beach .... ESPLANADE
clumsily .... LUMBER
coating .... PARGET, PLASTER
covered ...... CLOISTER, ARCADE, STOA, PORTICO
daintily .... MINCE
kind of .... WADDLE, PRANCE, LIMP, TRAMP, STRUT, TODDLE, LAMBETH, STRIDE, LUMBER, WOBBLE, SWAGGER, MINCE
leisurely .... STROLL, PROMENADE, TRAIPSE, TRUDGE, SAUNTER
long ...... MARCH, HIKE
off .... LEAVE
on stilts ..... TRAMPOLIO
out on ... DESERT, LEAVE
public .... PARADE, PROMENADE
shaded .... MALL, ALAMEDA
softly ...... TIPTOE, PAD
through mud ..... SLOSH, SQUELCH
through water .... WADE
to and fro .... PACE
vain ... STRUT, SWAGGER, PEACOCK
walker .... PEDESTRIAN, AMBULANT
idle .... FLANEUR
walking .... AMBULANT, GRADIENT, PEDESTRIAN,
adapted for .. GRESSORIAL
idle .... FLANERIE
papers .... DISMISSAL
shoes .... BALMORAL
stick ... CANE, MALAGA, STILT, RATTAN, STAFF, POGO, SUPPLEJACK, MALACCA, WADDY
vendor .... PEDDLER
walkout .... STRIKE
wall ...... PARAPET, PARIES, SEPTUM, BULKHEAD, BARRIER
band .... CORDON
bench .... PODIUM
binder .... PERPEND
border .... DADO
bracket .... SCONCE
coating .... PLASTER
column .... PILASTER
cover .... KEIL, LAG(GING), MANTLE
dividing .... SEPTUM
end of .... ANTA
eyed fish ... PIKE, DORY, DORE
facing .... VENEER, REVETMENT
garden .... HAHA
hanging cloth .... ARRAS, TAPESTRY
indentation .. CRENEL(LE)
inscription .... GRAFFITO
kind of ... JETTY, RIPRAP
lining .... STEEN, WAINSCOT
lizard .... GECKO
loophole .... CRENEL(LE)
mine .... BRATTICE
opening ... BAY, SCUTTLE, CRENEL(LE), EMBRASURE
painter .... MURALIST
park .... HAHA
pertaining to .... MURAL
pier .... ANTA
recess .... BAY
river .... LEVEE, EMBANKMENT
sea .... MOLE, PIER, BREAKWATER
section .... PANEL
step .... STILE
stone .... ASHLAR
Street operator .... BEAR, BULL, BROKER, SPECULATOR
tapestry .... ARRAS
top layer .... COPING
top slab ...... CAPSTONE
wood lining .. WAINSCOT
wooden pin .... NOG
writing .... GRAFFITO
wallaba ... APA, ARAWAK, TREE
wallaby .... KANGAROO
Wallace, novelist .... LEW, IRVING
work .... BEN HUR, THE WORD
Wallach, actor .... ELI
wallaroo .... KANGAROO
wallboard .... WAINSCOT
walled town .... BURG
wallet .... POCKETBOOK, BILLFOLD, KNAPSACK, SCRIP
walleye .... ALEWIFE
walleyed .... DRUNK
fish .... PIKE, PERCH, POLLACK, ALEWIFE
slang .... DRUNK
wallflower .... HEARTSEASE
walloper .... WHOPPER
wallow .... FLOUNDER, PUDDLE, ROLL ABOUT, LUXURIATE, MUDHOLE, WELTER
walls, behind the .. IN PRISON
dividing .... SEPTA
wally ... FIRSTRATE, FINE, TOY
walnut .. HICKORY, SHAGBARK, TREE, BROWN, WOOD, TRYMA
Walpurgis Night revelers ..... WITCHES
walrus ... BRUT, SEAL, MORSE, SEACOW, SEAHORSE, PINNIPED, TUSKER
herd .... POD
male .... BULL
tooth .... TUSK
tusk .... IVORY
Walrus' list item ..... SHIP(S)
Walton, fisherman .... IZAAK
waltz .... DANCE, MUSIC, VALSE, BOSTON
dance like ..... REDOWA
king .... STRAUSS
wamble .... REEL, STAGGER
wame .... BELLY, WOMB, VENTER
wampum ... BEADS, SE(A)WAN, PEAG(E), MONEY
wamus ... CARDIGAN, JACKET
wan .... PALLID, PALE, COLORLESS, ASHEN
wand .... STAFF, SCEPTER, BATON, WITHE, ROD, VERGE, SHOOT, SWITCH, WATTLE, MACE
shaped like a ... VIRGATE
wander .... STROLL, STRAY, MEANDER, DRIFT, ROVE, STRAGGLE, GAD, TRAIPSE, RAMBLE, ROAM, DIGRESS, DIVAGATE
wanderer .... PILGRIM, LANDLO(U)PER, ARAB, ROVER, GYPSY, HOBO, VAGABOND, BEDOUIN, ITINERANT, VAGRANT, NOMAD, TRAMP
wandering .... ERRATIC, VAGRANT, NOMADIC, FOOTLOOSE, ERRANT, ODYSSEY
beggar .... FAKIR, VAGABOND, ROGUE
dervish .... CALENDER
extended .... ODYSSEY
minstrel .... GOLIARD

student .... GOLIARD
tribe .... GYPSY
wanderings .... ODYSSEY, TRAVELS
wanderoo .... MACAQUE, MONKEY, LANGUR
wandle .. SUPPLE, AGILE, LITHE
wane .... ABATE, EBB, DECLINE, SUBSIDE
wangle .... GET, JUGGLE, OBTAIN, FINAGLE, FALSIFY, W(R)IGGLE, WHEEDLE
wanigan .... ARK
want ... LACK, CRAVE, NEED, DESIRE, WISH, REQUIRE(MENT), DESTITUTION, POVERTY, SCARCITY, SHORTAGE
wanted man ..... DESPERADO, OUTLAW, ESCAPEE
wanton ... TRAMP, TART, RASH, WILD, LEWD, UNCHASTE, PLAYFUL, FROLICSOME, RECKLESS, SENSELESS
destroyer ...... VANDAL
wapiti .... DEER, ELK
war .... STRIFE, CONFLICT, BELLIGERENCE, HOSTILITY
acquisitions ...... SPOILS
against abuse .. CRUSADE
agency .... OSS
agreement .... CARTEL TRUCE, CEASEFIRE
and Peace author .... TOLSTOI
and Peace heroine .... NATASHA
at .... BELLIGERENT
bonnet wearer ... INDIAN
chariot .... ESSED
chief, name meaning .... CEDRIC
cry .... WHOOP, YELL, BANZAI, SLOGAN, AMORT, ALALA
dance .... PYRRHIC
engine, stone-throwing .. CATAPULT, TREBUCHET
fleet .... ARMADA
galley beak .... ROSTRUM
games .... MANEUVERS
gas .... MUSTARD, YPERITE, ADAMSITE
god ... MARS, ARES, TYR, IRRA
holy .... JIHAD, CRUSADE
horse .... CHARGER, VET(ERAN), COURSER, DESTRIER
horse head armor .... CHAMFRON, CHAMFRAIN
operation ..... CAMPAIGN
paint: sl. .... COSMETICS, REGALIA
participant .... ANTAGONIST, BELLIGERENT
pertaining to ... MARTIAL
preparation .... MOBILIZATION
pretext for .. CASUS BELLI
provoking event .... CASUS BELLI
religious ...... CRUSADE
symbol of .... MARS
vessel .... CORVETTE, PTBOAT, UBOAT, CRUISER, FLATTOP, DESTROYER, SUB, TRIREME, DREADNAUGHT
word .... DEBATE
warble .... YODEL, CAROL, SING, TRILL, BABBLE, LARVA, TUMOR
warbler (see songbird) .... BECCAFICO, SONGSTER, REDSTART, TROCHILUS
warbling .... CHIRM
ward .... FEND, GUARD, DISTRICT, AVERT, PARRY, CHARGE, PROTEGE(E)
kind of .... MINOR, INCOMPETENT
part of a ...... PRECINCT
person (entrusted) with a TRUSTEE, GUARDIAN, PATRON
politician ...... HEELER
warden .... PEAR, KEEPER, CUSTODIAN, TRUSTEE, GATEKEEPER, GUARDIAN, CONSTABLE, ALCAIDE, JAILER, JAILOR
forest .... RANGER
kind of ... GAME, FOREST, AIR-RAID, FIRE, PRISON
warder .... TURNKEY, WATCHMAN, CUSTODIAN, ROD, STAFF, GUARD
wardrobe ... CLOTHES, CLOSET, TROUSEAU
wardship .... CUSTODY
ware ..... CONSCIOUS, READY, PRUDENT, MERCHANDISE, DISHES, POTTERY
warehouse ... STORE, BODEGA, DEPOT, GODOWN, CAMARIN, ELEVATOR, ETAPE, HONG, ENTREPOT, MAGAZINE
for candles .. CHANDLERY
platform .... PALLET
receipt .... QUEDAN, WARRANT
weapons .... ARSENAL
wares ... MERCHANDISE, GOODS
warfare ... STRIFE, STRUGGLE, POLEMY, CONFLICT
temporary stoppage of ... TRUCE, ARMISTICE, CEASE-FIRE
Warfield, now a duchess ...... WALLIS
warhead of missile .. PAYLOAD
warlike .... BELLICOSE, BELLIGERENT, MARTIAL, MILITANT, HOSTILE
warlock .... SORCERER, CONJURER, MAGICIAN
warm ...... ARDENT, LIVELY, HEAT(ED), CORDIAL, SUNNY, THERMAL, FRESH
baths .... THERMAE
compress .... STUPE
make moderately .... TEPEFY
moderately ...... TEPID
springs .... THERMAE
warmonger .... JINGO, MILITARIST
warmth .... ARDOR, ENTHUSIASM, ZEAL
increasing in .. CALESCENT
warn ...... ADVISE, CAUTION, ADMONISH, FLAG, SIGNAL, ALERT, PORTEND
warning ...... OMEN, ALARM, PORTENT, PRESAGE, AUGURY, TIP-OFF
in law .... CAVEAT
signal ... ALAR(U)M, HISS, TOCSIN, SIREN, BEACON, ALERT
signal device .. FOGHORN, SIREN
snake's .... HISS, RATTLE
system, for short .. DEWS
weather ...... ADVISORY
word of .... FORE, BEWARE, LOOK OUT, OFF LIMIT
warp .. DEFORM, DISTORT(ION), ABERRATION, BIAS, SILT, MUD, CONTORT, PERVERT
thread ends ...... THRUM
warplane ..... SPAD, SPITFIRE, ZERO, FLYING FORTRESS, STUKA
warplanes, fleet of .. ARMADA
warrant ..... JUSTIFY, PLEVIN, AUTHORIZATION, GUARANTEE, MERIT, PRECEPT, VOUCHER, WRIT, ORDER
convict's ..... MITTIMUS
officer .... BOSUN
royal .... BERAT
warren .... RABBITRY, HUTCH
Chief Justice ...... EARL
inhabitant ..... RABBIT, GAME
warrigal .... DINGO
warring nations' agreement ... CARTEL, TRUCE, ARMISTICE
warrior .... FIGHTER, SOLDIER, COMBATANT, KURIPAN, SINGH, JINGO
arena .... GLADIATOR
Algerian .... SPAHI
female .... AMAZON
frenzied for battle .... BERSERK(ER)
Indian .... BRAVE
Japanese ...... SAMURAI
Philippine .. MAHARLIKA
warsaw .... FISH, GROUPER
warship .... MAN O'WAR, CRUISER, DREADNOUGHT, GALLEON, DESTROYER, FRIGATE, RAZEE, TRIREME, GALLEY, BATTLEWAGON, FLATTOP, IRONCLAD
armored .... IRONCLAD, MERRIMAC, MONITOR
boat on .... DINGHY, LAUNCH
convoy ..... CORVET(TE)
deck, lowest ..... ORLOP
eating quarters .... WARDROOM

gun emplacement .... TURRET
gun shield ..... CUPOLA
kitchen .... GALLEY
prison .... BRIG
ram .... BEAK
station for wounded ..... COCKPIT
tower .... TURRET
warships, fleet of .... ARMADA
wart .... TUMOR, PAPILLOMA, VERRUCA, KERATOSIS
Wartburg's important resident LUTHER
wartime detainee ... INTERNEE
detention ... INTERNMENT
warts, covered with .... VERRUCOSE
wary ... CANNY, LEERY, ALERT, CAG(E)Y, CHARY, SHY, CAUTIOUS, CAREFUL, SUSPICIOUS, CIRCUMSPECT
wash .... BATHE, DRIFT, ELUTE, SLOP, SWILL, LAVE, PURIFY, MOISTEN, RINSE
and iron ...... LAUNDER
basin/bowl ...... LAVER, LAVATORY, LAVABO
by rubbing .... SCRUB
hair/scalp ..... SHAMPOO
kind ... LOTION, MOUTH, HAIR
out with water ... FLUSH
washbowl in church .. LAVABO
washerwoman .... LAUNDRESS
washing ... LAVAGE, LAVATION
board .... DOLLY
out of an organ .. LAVAGE
lye/soapsuds ..... BUCK
water for ..... LAVATION
Washington art gallery .. FREER
bloomer .... CHAT
capital of ..... OLYMPIA
city .... YAKIMA, SEATTLE, TACOMA, SPOKANE, EVERETT
dam ... GRAND COULEE, WANAPUM
educator ..... BOOKER (T)
football team .. REDSKINS
hostess .. HOWAR, MESTA
Moscow telephone ...... HOTLINE
motto .... AL-KI
peak .... ALTA
river .... COLUMBIA
seeress .... DIXON
washout ..... FAILURE, FIASCO
washroom .... LAVATORY
washstand .... COMMODE
wasp .... HORNET, DIGGER, MUDDAUBER, WHAMP, VESPID, YELLOW JACKET, STINGER, COW KILLER
like a .... VESPINE
nest .... VESPIARY
prick of .... STING
waspish ...... BAD-TEMPERED, TESTY, IRRITABLE, SLIM-WAISTED
wassail .... CAROUSE, TOAST, REVELRY, CAROUSAL, DRINKING SONG
Wasserman test subject ...... SYPHILIS
waste .... FRITTER, OCEAN, CHAFF, DESERT, SPOIL, WILD(ERNESS), RUIN, WEAR AWAY, DECAY, EXCRETION, LEFTOVER, SQUANDER, BARREN, REFUSE
allowance .... TRET
arctic .... TUNDRA
away .... PEAK, EMACIATE, ROT, DECAY, GNAW, MO(U)LDER, MACERATE
cause of .... HASTE
deposit .... SLUDGE
drain .... SEWER
fiber .... NOIL, FLOSS
glass .... CULLET
lay .... RAVAGE, RAZE
maker .... HASTE
matter ... REFUSE, EJECT
metal ...... SLAG, DROSS
pipe ..... SEWER, DRAIN
product .... RUN-OFF
sugar cane/beets .... BAGASSE, MEGASS(E)
time .... IDLE, LOAF, LOITER, DAWDLE, FIDDLE, DIDDLE, FRIBBLE, FRIVOL
wasted ... GAUNT, EMACIATED
wasteful .... PRODIGAL, SPENDTHRIFT, EXTRAVAGANT
wasteland ... TUNDRA, STEPPE, DUST BOWL, DESERT, WILDERNESS, FOREST, MOOR, HEATH
reclamation .... INNING
wasting away .... MARASMUS, TABETIC, TABID, TABESCENT, EMACIATION, ATROPHY
disease .... TABES, CONSUMPTION, TUBERCULOSIS, TB, LEUKEMIA
disease, pertaining to .... HECTIC
wastrel .... PRODIGAL, SPENDTHRIFT, GOOD-FOR-NOTHING
wat .... HARE, HOT
watch .... LOOK, OBSERVE, TEND, GUARD(ING), LOOKOUT, SENTRY, EYE, VIGIL, HOROLOGE, TIMEPIECE
bearing .... JEWEL
chain .... FOB
covering ...... CRYSTAL
death ...... VIGIL, WAKE
during exams .... INVIGILATE
duty ..... PATROL, VIGIL
kind of .... REPEATER
mounted ...... VEDETTE
night .. NEW YEAR'S EVE
part ..... DETENT, HAND, DIAL, STUD, CLICK, PAWL, PALLET, STEM
pawl .... JUMPER
pocket .... FOB
secretly .... SPY
slang .... TICKER
soldier on ...... SENTRY, SENTINEL
sound .... TICK
time .... HOROLOGE
undercover .. ESPIONAGE, SPYING
watchdog .... GUARDIAN, MASTIFF, CERBERUS, DANDOG
watcher ... SPOTTER, LOOKOUT
ballroom .. WALLFLOWER
secret .... TAIL, SHADOW
watchful ... ALERT, VIGILANT, OBSERVANT, ATTENTIVE, OPEN-EYED
man .... IRA
watchmaker .... HOROLOGIST
watchman .. GUARD, SENTRY, SENTINEL, WARDER, WARDEN, LOOKOUT, VEDETTE
mythological .. HEIMDALL, ARGUS, TALOS
watchtower ...... BARBICAN, BEACON, MIRADOR
watchword ... SLOGAN, MOTTO, SHIBBOLETH, BATTLECRY, PASSWORD, CRY
person concerned with ... SENTRY, GUARD, SENTINEL
water ...... AQUA, SPRINKLE, IRRIGATE, DILUTE, EAU
animal ... POLYP, HYDRA, SEA ANEMONE, POLYZOAN ROTIFER, BRYOZOAN
as source of power ...... WHITE COAL
baptismal .... LAVER
barely above .... AWASH
barrier ..... DAM, DIKE, LEVEE, BOOM, WEIR, MOLE, EMBANKMENT
bearer, in astronomy .... AQUARIUS
borne .... AFLOAT, FLOATING
bottle .... CARAFE, DECANTER
brain in sheep ...... GID
brash .... PYROSIS, HEARTBURN
buffalo .. CARABAO, ARNEE
bug .... COCKROACH, BEETLE
carrier bird .. ALBATROSS
channel .... FLUME, SLUICE, DRAIN, GUTTER, AQUEDUCT, RACEWAY, GULLY, GULLET
chestnut ..... CALTRAP, CALTROP, LING
chinquapin ...... LOTUS
clock .... CLEPSYDRA
closet ... TOILET, STOOL, CLOACA
cloud .... RAIN
color ...... AQUARELLE, PAINTING
color painting ... FRESCO
combining form .... HYDR(O)

conduit ..... AQUEDUCT
container .... BREAKER, CISTERN, GOGLET, GURGLET
containing ..... HYDROUS
corral .... CRAWL
crake .... OUZEL
cress .... POTHERB, MUSTARD
cure ...... HYDROPATHY, HYDROTHERAPY, TORTURE
current .... RACE
deposit ... SILT, SEDIMENT
dog .... SPANIEL, SALAMANDER
excursion .... CRUISE
exhibition ... AQUACADE
fairy .... NIX
floating on .... AWASH
gate .... SLUICE, WICKET
gauge .... UDOMETER
glass .... GOBLET, TUMBLER
gum .... TUPELO
heater .... SAMOVAR
hemlock ...... COWBANE
hen .... COOT
hole .... POOL, POND
hunger for .... THIRST
ice .... SHERBET
jar ...... BANGA, OLLA, EWER, HYDRIA
jet, revolving .... GIRANDOLE
journey .... PASSAGE, VOYAGE
jug .... OLLA, EWER
keg .... BREAKER
like .... AQUEOUS
lily ...... LOTUS, LOTOS, NELUMBO, VICTORIA, WOCAS, FANWORT
lily leaf .... PAD
living in .... AQUATIC
logged .... SWAMPY, SOGGY
marker ..... DANDY ROLL
mill .... CLOW
moccasin .... SNAKE, VIPER, COTTONMOUTH
movement ... EBB, TIDE, SEICHE
nymph .... NAIAD, NEREID, OCEANID
of .... AQUEOUS
opossum .... YAPOK
ouzel ... DIPPER, THRUSH, PIET
parting .... DIVIDE
passage .... SLUICE, STRAIT, CHANNEL
pepper ..... SMARTWEED
pimpernel .. BROOKWEED
pipe ... HOSE, AQUEDUCT, HOOKA(H), NARGHILE, MAIN, DRAIN
plant ..... CHINQUAPIN, CALTROP, LOTUS
plant leaf .... PAD
plant leaf walker .... JACANA
pump .... RAM
raising device ...... RAM, NORIA, TABUT
rat .... THIEF, VOLE, MUSKRAT
rodent .... NUTRIA
sapphire .... IOLITE
scented ...... COLOGNE, BAYRUM
science of .. HYDROLOGY
search for .... DOWSE
snake .... MOCCASIN
soak .... SATURATE
soluble stuff .. HYDROGEL
sound .... (S)PLASH
spirit ... ARIEL, UNDINE, NIX(IE), KELPIE, KELPY
sports .... AQUATICS
spout .... SPATE, GARGOYLE, GEYSER, GUSH
spring .... LYMPH
sprite .... KELPIE, NIX(IE), KELPY, NYMPH, NAIAD, NEREID
storage .... CISTERN, TANK, RESERVOIR
surface .... RYME
thrush .... OUZEL
transportation .... FERRY
trough, mining .... LAUNDER
tube .... HOSE
vessel .... LOTA
washing ..... LAVATION
wave .... BILLOW
wheel ... TURBINE, NORIA
witch ... DOWSER, GREBE
without ... ANHYDROUS, DRY, ARID, PARCHED
worm .... NAID
waterbuck ... ANTELOPE, KOB
watercourse .... CANAL, CAN(Y)ON, FIORD, GORGE, RAVINE, CHANNEL, DIKE, NULLA, RUNNEL, BROOK, GULLY
watercraft ...... BOAT, SHIP, RAFT
watercress .... POTHERB
watered .... INFLATED, DILUTED, SPRINKLED
fabric .... MOIRE, TABBY
Wateree .... CAWTABA
waterfall ... CASCADE, LIN(N), CATARACT, CHIGNON, FOSS, CHUTE
waterfinder .... DOWSER, DIVINING ROD, DOWSING ROD
waterfront laborer .... ROUSTABOUT, STEVEDORE
watering place ... OASIS, SPA, WELL, SPRING
waterless ... ANHYDROUS, DRY, ARID, BARREN
Waterloo, victor of .... WELLINGTON
waterproof covering .... RAINCOAT, TARP(AULIN), GOSSAMER, PONCHO
to .... CALK, PAY
watershed .... DIVIDE
waterside ..... COAST, SHORE, BEACH
watertight box ...... CAISSON, COFFERDAM
make .... CA(U)LK
waterworks: sl. .... TEARS
waterwort .... ELATINE
watery ..... WASHY, AQUEOUS, THIN, SEROUS, HYDROUS, SOGGY
discharge .... RHEUM
grave .... SEA
wattle .... GILL, DEWLAP, LAPPET, WAND, TWIG, ROD
birds' .... CARUNCLE, GILL(S), JOWL
fish .... BARBEL
tree .... BOREE
Waugh, novelist ..... EVELYN
waul .... SQUALL, WAIL
waur .... WORSE
wave .. RIPPLE, FLAP, FLUTTER, SURF, FLOURISH, WAFF, UNDULATION, BRANDISH, CURVE, ROLLER, SWELL, SURGE, SEESAW, BILLOW, BREAKER, COMBER
back and forth .... WAG
channel .... BORE, EAGRE
heave of a .... SCEND
hollow of ...... VALLEY
large .. DECUMAN, SWELL, SEA, ROLLER
little .... RIPPLE
movement .... CHOP, UNDULATION
signaling .... WAFF
tidal .... EAGRE, BORE
to and fro ... WAG, FLAP
top of .... CREST
with foamy crest .... WHITECAP
wavelet .... RIPPLE
Wavell, Earl .... ARCHIBALD
waver .... TEETER, SWAY, FLUTTER, VACILLATE, FALTER, QUAVER, TREMBLE, HESITATE
wavering sound .... TREMOLO
waves breaking on shore ..... SURF
move in ..... UNDULATE, RIPPLE
sound of .... ROAR
space between .. TROUGH
tossing and tumbling .... WELTER
wavy .... UNDATE, SINUOUS, SINUATE
edged .... REPAND, UNDULATE
form ...... UNDULATION
in heraldry .... UNDE(E)
wax ...... GROW, PARAFFIN, CERA, CERE, PELA, CERESIN, CERUMEN, CERATE
and pitch mixture .... MALTHA
candle ...... PARAFFIN, CIERGE, TAPER
cloth treated with .... CERECLOTH, CEREMENT

cobbler's .... CODE
combining form .. CER(O)
covered with .. CERATED
figure .... CEROPLAST
like secretion .. CERUMEN
match .... VESTA
mineral ...... OZOCERITE
modeled in .. CEROPLASTIC
myrtle ...... BAYBERRY
ointment .... CERATE
palm .... CARNAUBA
producing ... CERIFEROUS
source ...... CARNAUBA
waxbill .... WEAVERBIRD
waxed runner .... SKI
waxwing .... CEDARBIRD
waxwork artist ...... TUSSAUD
waxy .... CERACEOUS
substance .... CUTIN, SUBERIN
way ..... PATH, MODE, ROAD, STREET, LANE, ROUTE, COURSE, METHOD, WONT
easy/direct ... HIGHROAD
give .... YIELD
of walking/running ..... GAIT
on the .... MOVING, PROCEEDING
out ...... EGRESS, EXIT
under .... MOVING, PROCEEDING
station town .... WHISTLE STOP
train .... LOCAL
up .... STAIRS
waybill .... MANIFEST
wayfarer ... VIATOR, TRAVELER
shelter for .. SPITAL, INN
wayfaring tree ... VIBURNUM, HOBBLEBUSH
waylay .... AMBUSH, AMBUSCADE
wayward ...... HEADSTRONG, WILLFUL, ERRATIC, CAPRICIOUS, VAGRANT
weaverbird .... WAXBILL
weak .... DECREPIT, FRAGILE, DELICATE, VULNERABLE, INEFFECTIVE, PUNY, ANILE, WAN, FEEBLE, INFIRM, FAINT, FLACCID, FLABBY, FRAIL, EFFETE
drink .... TIFF
kneed ...... TIMID, SOFT
minded ... DAFT, STUPID, IMBECILE, FOOLISH, INDECISIVE
morally .... FRAIL
point ..... DEFECT, FAULT
weaken .. UNDERMINE, DILUTE, ENERVATE, ATTENUATE, VITIATE, FLAG, DEBILITATE, SAP, ABATE, ENFEEBLE
morally .... VITIATE
spirit of .... DEMORALIZE
weakening .... SAPPING
weakfish ... TOTUAVA, ACOUPA
weakling ...... WALLYDRAG, SISSY, CRYBABY, PANTYWAIST, SOFTIE
weakness .... DEFECT, LIKING, FETISH, FONDNESS, FRAILTY, DELICACY, INFIRMITY, FAULT
bodily .... ASTHENIA, ATONY
in character ..... FOIBLE
moral .... FRAILTY
of an organ ..... ATONY
small ... FOIBLE, FRAILTY
weal ...... STRIPE, WELFARE, WALE, WELT, WHEAL, WELL-BEING
weald .... FOREST
wealth ...... ASSETS, RICHES, MEANS, ABUNDANCE, ASSET, OPULENCE, AFFLUENCE, FORTUNE
benefits from ... USANCE
god of .... PLUTUS
income from .... USANCE
mere .... PELF
personified .... MAMMON, CROESUS
wealthy ..... RICH, MONEYED, PROSPEROUS, OPULENT, WELL-TO-DO
government by .... PLUTOCRACY
person ..... PLUTOCRAT, CROESUS, NABOB, MIDAS
wean .... CHILD, BABY, WITHDRAW
weapon ...... CLUB, SWORD, ARQUEBUS, CROSSBOW, ARM, SLINGSHOT, LANCE, MACE
animal's ... TUSK, HORN
bird's ..... TALON, BEAK, CLAW
gaucho's .... BOLA(s)
hoplite .... SPEAR
Indian ..... TOMAHAWK
medieval ...... GISARME, HALBERD, CATAPULT
pampas .... BOLAS
plant's .... SPINE
war ..... CANNON, GUN
weaponry .... ORDNANCE
weapons: colloq. .. HARDWARE
wear .... CHAFE, DON, CLOTHES, ERODE, SPORT
away ... ABRADE, ERODE, CORRODE, FRET
down ..... EXHAUST, TIRE
out .... HACK
ragged ... FRAY, FRAZZLE
to tatters ...... FRAZZLE
well .... LAST
wearied .... TIRED, JADED, FAGGED
weariness ... ENNUI, FATIGUE, TEDIUM, BOREDOM, LASSITUDE
wearing apparel .... CLOTHES, GARMENTS, CLOTHING
away .... EROSION, ATTRITION
wearisome .... TEDIOUS, TOILSOME, BORING
grow .... PALL, BORE
person .... BORE
weary .. TIRE(D), CHAPFALLEN, FAG, JADE, WORNOUT, BORE(D), TEDIOUS, IRKSOME, TUCKER
weasand .... TRACHEA, WINDPIPE, THROAT, ESOPHAGUS
weasel ...... ERMINE, STOAT, VARE, MUSTELINE, PEKAN, SABLE, FERRET, ZORIL(A), VERMIN
family .... MUSTELA
like animal .... SABLE, MARTEN
relative .. STOAT, MARTEN, OTTER, MINK, FERRET
words ..... AMBIGUITIES, EQUIVOCATIONS
weather ... SURVIVE, SEASON, SKY
condition ..... CLIMATE
indicator .... BAROMETER
item .... MOISTURE, TEMPERATURE
map line ...... ISALLOBAR
personified .. JACKFROST
phenomenon ..... SMOG, SLEET, SMAZE, HAIL(STONE)
prolonged dry .... DROU(G)HT
report .... ADVISORY
study of ... METEOROLOGY
under the ..... ILL, SICK, AILING, TIPSY
warning .... ADVISORY
word ..... WARM, SLEET, WINDY, RAIN, STORMY
weathercock ..... VANE, FANE
weathered .... SURVIVED
weatherglass ..... BAROMETER
weathervane figure ..... COCK
weave .... ENTWINE, INTERLACE, TWIST, KNIT, PLAIT, MAT, BRAID
kind of .... LENO
weaver .... WEBSTER
bobbin of .... PIRN
girl .... IRENE
material of .... REED, WICKER, FIBER, YARN, SLEY
weaverbird .... WAXBILL, WHIDAH, TAHA, MAYA, SPARROW
weaving art .... LOOM
contestant .... ARACHNE
frame .... LOOM
machine .... LOOM
occupation .. HANDICRAFT
reed .... SLEY
yarn .... WEFT, WARP, WOOF
web ..... TISSUE, NET(WORK), TRAP, SNARE, GOSSAMER
feather's ...... VEXILLUM
footed .... PALMATE
footed bird ...... SWAN, AVOCET, DUCK, GOOSE
footed creature .. OTTER, BEAVER, TOAD, FROG, MUSKRAT
in anatomy ..... TISSUE, MEMBRANE
like membrane ..... TELA

pertaining to ... RETIARY
spinner .... SPINER, ARACHNE
toed .... PALMATE
webbed .... PALMATF
weber .... MAXWELL
wed .... ESPOUSE, MARRY, UNITE, WIVE
wedding .... MARRIAGE, NUPTIALS, BRIDAL
announcement .. BAN(N)S
day designation .... (1st YEAR) PAPER; (25th) SILVER; (30th) PEARL; (50th) GOLDEN; (75th) DIAMOND
March bride ...... ELSA
party member .. RINGBOY, BRIDESMAID, BESTMAN, SPONSOR
song .... OH PROMISE ME, HYMEN(EAL)
wedge .... COTTER, KEY, JAM, TRIG, SHIM, QUOIN, COIGN(E), CLEAT
driver .... MAUL, BEETLE
shaped ..... CUNEIFORM, CUNEATE, SPHENOID, SPHENIC, CUNEAL
shaped piece ... PIE, VEE, CHOCK, QUOIN
to prevent rolling .... SCOTCH, CHOCK, SPRAG
wedlock .... MATRIMONY, MARRIAGE
Wednesday .... MIDWEEK
Wednesday's god ...... ODIN
wee .... LITTLE
hours .... DAWN
weed .... BUR, COCKLE, SANDBUR(R), SPURR(E)Y, NETTLE, PLANTAIN, REMOVE, RID, TOADFLAX, PURSLANE, DOCK, CHARLOCK, QUITCH, DANDELION, BROME
Biblical .... TARE
buckwheat .... DOCK
colloquial .... CIGAR, TOBACCO
digging tool .... SPUD
herbicide ..... DOWPON
mourning .... CRAPE, WEEDER
narcotic .... MARIJUANA, MARIHUANA
noxious .... TARE
out .... UPROOT
poison(ous) ...... LOCO, DARNEL, HEMLOCK JIMSON
roadside ... DOGFENNEL
weeding tool ...... SPUD, HOE
weeds ...... CRAPE, WEEPER, WRACK
wearer .... WIDOW
weedy plant ..... CELANDINE
week .... HEBDOMAD, SENNIGHT
weekday .... FERIA
weekly .... HEBDOMADAL, PERIODICAL

newsmagazine .... NEWSWEEK, TIME
weeks, 52 .... YEAR
two .... FORTNIGHT
Weems, preacher .... PARSON
ween .... THINK, SUPPOSE, IMAGINE
weenie/weeny ...... SAUSAGE, WIENER(WURST)
weep ..... LAMENT, LAPWING, BLUBBER, CRY, MOURN, BEWAIL, SOB, BAWL
weeping goddess ...... NIOBE
philosopher .. HERACLITES
weevil .... CURCULIO, KIS, BEETLE, BORER, BOLL
larva .... GRUGRU
wing cover ...... SHARD
weft .... WOOF, YARN, FILLING
Weichsel .... VISTULA
weigh ...... CONSIDER, HOIST, PONDER, BEAR, BURDEN, HEFT, POISE, REFLECT, RAISE
down .... BURDEN
weighing device .... TRONE, SCALE, BALANCE, STEELYARD, FAIRBANKS
weight .. ROTL, OBOLUS, LOAD, HEFT, TON, STRESS, HEAVINESS, BURDEN, VALUE, EMPHASIS, IMPORTANCE, INFLUENCE, POWER
allowance ... TRET, TARE
balance .... RIDER
balloon's ...... BALLAST
boxer's .... FEATHER, LIGHT, BANTAM, MIDDLE, HEAVY
clock .... PEISE
coal .... KEEL
colloquial .... HEFT
deduction .... TARE
diamond .... CARAT
for wool .... TOD
4,000-pound .... LAST
hundred pounds .... CENTAL, CENTNER
leaden .... PLUMB
leg .... CLOG
lifting machine .. CRANE
measure .. TON, METAGE, KILO
metric ... KILO, CENTNER, QUINTAL
on animal's leg .... CLOG
pertaining to ..... BARIC
stabilizer .... BALLAST
system .... TROY, AVOIRDUPOIS, METRIC
3.17 grains .... CARAT
200 milligrams ... CARAT
unit ...... SHEKEL, TON, ROTL
watcher .... DIETER, MILADY, BOXER
with lead .... PLUMB
wool .... TOD
weights and measures, science of .... METROLOGY
weighty ... ONEROUS, SERIOUS, MOMENTOUS, BURDENSOME, OPPRESSIVE, HEAVY

weir .... BARRIER, FENCE, GARTH, TRAP, (MILL)DAM
weird ...... QUEER, SPOOKY, UNCO, EERIE, EERY, MYSTERIOUS, UNCANNY, ELDRITCH, ODD, UNEARTHLY
sister ..... FATE, CLOTHO, LACHESIS, TROPOS
wejack ...... PEKAN, WEASEL
weka .... RAIL
welcome .... GREET(ING), AGREEABLE, RECEIVE, HAIL
weld .... FUSS, UNITE, MIGNONETTE, SOLDER
welding material ... THERMIT, SOLDER
welfare ... WEAL, WELLBEING, PROSPERITY
organization .. RED CROSS, CARE, YMCA, YWCA
welkin .... HEAVEN, SKY
well ..... SPRING, HALE, TRIG, FOUNT(AIN), FIT, SHAFT, FLOW, GUSH, SUMP, EXPERTLY, PROPER, HEALTHY
along .... FAR
balanced .... POISED, SANE, SENSIBLE
being ... WELFARE, WEAL
bred .... GENTEEL, EDUCATED
doer ...... (BOY) SCOUT
done ..... BRAVO, BULLY
favored ..... HANDSOME, PRETTY
fed .... PLUMP, FAT
feeling .... EUPHORIA
groomed .... SLEEK, SOIGNE, SLICK
grounded ..... INFORMED
heeled ... RICH, WEALTHY, MONEYED
known .... FAMOUS, NOTORIOUS, FAMILIAR
lining ..... STEAN, STEEN
mannered .. COURTEOUS, POLITE
nigh ... ALMOST, NEARLY
off ... PROSPEROUS, RICH
ordered .... NEAT
pit .... SUMP
proportioned ..... TRIM
read person .. BOOKWORM
supplied with money .... LOADED
thought of .... ESTEEMED, REPUTABLE
timed ...... OPPORTUNE, AUSPICIOUS, SEASONABLE
to-do .... RICH, WEALTHY
watered ..... IRRIGUOUS
worn ... TRITE, OVERUSED
Welland .... CANAL
wellaway ...... ALAS, ALACK
Welle river .... UELE
Welles, actor .... ORSON
diplomat ...... SUMNER
Wellington's soubriquet ...... IRONDUKE, OLD NOSY
wellspring .... FOUNTAINHEAD

Welsh ...... CYMRIC, CYMRY, CAMBRIAN, TAFFY, CELT(IC)
astronomer .... MEE
boat .... CORACLE
buccaneer ...... MORGAN
cheese dish ..... RABBIT
dog .... CORGI
god of sea .... DYLAN
onion .... CIBOL
rabbit .... RAREBIT
slang .. CHEAT, SWINDLE
welsher ... CHEAT, DEADBEAT, SWINDLER
Welshman .... CAMBRIAN, CELT
welt ... LASH, WALE, W(H)EAL, THRASH, BEAT
welter .... ROLL, WALLOW, SOAKED, TURMOIL, CONFUSION
wen ... TALPA, TUMOR, CYST, MOLE
wench ...... MAID, SERVANT, WANTON, WOMAN, HUSSY, DOXY
wend ..... JOURNEY, TRAVEL, GO, PROCEED
Wendell, presidential candidate WILLKIE
Wendy's dog .... NANA
wer(e)gild .... BLOOD MONEY, CRO
werewolf .... LOUP-GAROU, LYCANTHROPE
wernard .... LIAR
wernerite .... SCAPOLITE
Wesley, (John) follower ...... METHODIST
West .... OCCIDENT
West African .... ASHANTI
baboon ..... (MAN)DRILL
fetish .... JUJU
Gold Coast city .... ACCRA, AKKRA
magic .... JUJU
taboo .... JUJU
tribe .... IBO
weaverbird ..... WHIDAH
West Bengal capital .... CALCUTTA
West, English novelist .... REBECCA
West Flanders capital .. BRUGES
West German capital ... BONN
chancellor .... ADENAUER, KIESINGER, BRANDT
president .... LUBKE
West Indies bird .... TODY, COURLAN, LIMPKIN
capital .... ROSEAU (DOMINICA), CASTRIES (ST. LUCIA), KINGSTOWN (ST. VINCENT)
coin .... PISTAREEN
egret .... GAULIN
fish .... BACALAO, TESTAR, PEGA, BANG, CABRILLA, CERO, BOGA, SESI
flea .... CHIGOE, CHIGGER
grouper .... BONACI
heron .... GAULIN
hog plum .... AMRA, JOBO
Indian .... TAINO, CARIB, ESTERON
island .... BAHAMA(S), HISPANIOLA, ANTILLES, JAMAICA, NEVIS, CURACAO, TRINIDAD, CAICOS, CUBA, HAITI, BARBUDA, LEEWARD, TOBAGO
liquor ...... MOBBY, RUM
lizard .... ARBALO, GALLIWASP
magic ...... OBEAH, OBI
mahogany .... CAOBA
music .... CALYPSO
native .... CARIB, CREOLE
native chief .... CACIQUE
Negro .... EBO(E), MAROON
patois .... GUMBO
plant .... ANIL
rodent .... AGOUTI
rum .... TAF(F)IA
sailboat ...... DROGHER
shark .... GATA
shrub .... ANIL, CASCARILLA
state .... ANTIGUA, GRENADA, DOMINICA, (ST.) LUCIA, (ST.) VINCENT
talisman .... OBEAH
taro .... TANIA
tree .... CALABA, GENIP(AP), ARALIE, BONACE, BALATA, GREENHEART
vessel .... DROGHER
volcano .... PELEE
"white man" .... BUCKRA
witchcraft ...... OBEAH, OBI
West Irian capital .... KATABARU, HOLLANDIA
West, newcomer to the .... TENDERFOOT
West, of Broadway ..... MAE
West Pointer ...... YEARLING, PLEB(E), CADET
West Virginia capital .... CHARLESTON
city .... WHEELING, WEIRTON
state bird .... CARDINAL
state nickname .... PANHANDLE
West wind .... ZEPHYR
of the .... FAVONIAN
western .... OCCIDENTAL, HESPERIAN, MOVIE
Australia capital .. PERTH
Dvina .... RIVER
Islands .... HEBRIDES
land .... HESPERIA
lawman .... SHERIFF, MARSHAL
movie character .... COWBOY, DESPERADO, FRONTIERSMAN, INDIAN, SCOUT
ocean .... ATLANTIC
soil .... GUMBO
Westerner ...... PLAINSMAN
Westminster Abbey .... PANTHEON
landmark .... ABBEY
rite .... CORONATION
street .... WHITEHALL
wet ..... DAMP, DANK, BATHE, SOAK, RET, RAINY, FOGGY, MOIST, SOPPING, ASOP, EMBRUE
all .... WRONG, MISTAKEN
blanket .... KILLJOY, SPOILSPORT
combining form .. HYGRO
plaster painting .. FRESCO
wetback ..... BRACERO, PEON
nationality of .. MEXICAN
wether .... SHEEP
wetland(s) .... MARSHES, SWAMPS
wetter .... CHILD, BABY
Weygand, Fr. general .... MAXIME
whack .... BEAT, WHANG, SLAP, BLOW, THWACK, SMACK
slang ...... SHARE, TRIAL, ATTEMPT, TRY
whacky ... WILD, ECCENTRIC, FOOLISH, MADCAP
whale ... CETE, THRASH, WHIP, SPERM, CACHALOT, CETACEAN, FINBACK, BOWHEAD
Arctic .... NARWHAL
baby .... CALF
biggest .... BLUE
blowhole ...... SPIRACLE
carcass .... KRENG
cut blubber of ... FLENSE
dolphin .... ORCA
fat .... BLUBBER
female .... COW
finback ...... RORQUAL, PORPOISE
food ...... BRIT, SHRIMP
food strainer ... BALEEN
grampus .... ORC
growth on jaw .. BALEEN
hunter of fiction ... AHAB
killer .. GRAMPUS, ORC(A), DOLPHIN
kind of ...... FIN(BACK), BLUE, SEI, HUMPBACK
male .... BULL
mammal resembling ..... DUGONG, MANATEE
Melville's ... MOBY DICK
morbid secretion .... AMBERGRIS
river .... DOLPHIN
shark .... MHOR
small .... PORPOISE, HOGFISH, DOLPHIN, BLACKFISH
sound ...... BARK, MEW, SQUEAL, CLICK, WHISTLE, CHIRRUP, WHINE

sperm .... CACHALOT
strip blubber from ...... FLENSE
tail part .... FLUKE
tusked .... NARWHAL
white ... BELUGA, HUSO, HUSE
young .... CALF
whaleback .... FREIGHTER
whalebone .... BALEEN
decorative article .... SCRIMSHAW
whaleman ...... HARPOONER
whaler's spear ...... HARPOON
whales, pertaining to .. CETIC, CETACEAN
school/herd of ..... GAM, POD
skin .... SCULP
whaling ship .... PEQUOD
post ...... LOGGERHEAD
whammy ..... JINX, EVIL EYE
whang ...... STRIKE, WHACK, THRASH
whangee ...... BAMBOO, CANE, WALKING STICK
wharf ... DOCK, JETTY, QUAY, PIER, LANDING, QUAI
loafer .... RAT
Wharton, novelist ..... EDITH
whatnot .... ETAGERE, CABINET
whaup .... CURLEW
wheal ... WELT, STRIPE, WALE, PUSTULE, PIMPLE
wheat .... CORN, DURUM, CEREAL, GRASS, GRAIN, SPELT, TRIGO, DURRA
beard ..... AWN, ARISTA
beer .... WEISS
coat .... BRAN
cracked .... GROATS
disease ... ERGOT, BUNT, AECIA, SMUT, RUST
flour foodstuff .... MACARONI, SPAGHETTI
flour substance .. GLUTEN
grass resembling .. CHEAT, CHESS
ground .... FLOUR, MEAL
hard-grained ..... SPELT, DURUM
head .... EAR
hulled .... GROATS
liquor ...... WHISK(E)Y
meal .... SEMOLINA
milling by-product ...... SHORTS
wheatear ...... CHACK, CHAT, WHITETAIL
wheedle ... WANGLE, CAJOLE, COAX, BLARNEY
wheel .... TURN, ROTATE, REVOLVE, PIVOT, PULLEY RUNDLE, HELM
animalcule .... ROTIFER
band .... STRAKE
block ... SPRAG, WEDGE, TRIG
break .. SKID, TRIG, DRAG
center of ..... HUB, NAVE
collar .... FLANGE
furniture .... CASTER
grooved .... SHEAVE
horse .... POLER
hub .... NAVE
like .... TROCHAL
little .... CASTER
motion ..... ROTATION, ROLL
part ... HUB, SPOKE, RIM, CAM, HOB, FELLY, AXLE, TIRE
projection .... CAM
pulley .... SHEAVE
resembling a ... TROCHAL
rim ...... FELLY, FELLOE, FLANGE
shaft .... AXLE
shaped .... ROTATE, ROTIFORM
small .... TRUCKLE, TRUNDLE, CASTER
spindle ..... AXLE, ARBOR
spoke .... RADIUS, RUNG
spur .... ROWEL
swivel .... CASTER
tire .... STRAKE
tooth .... SPROCKET
toothed .... COG
turner in Hades ... IXION
water .... NORIA
wheeler ... PILOT, STEERSMAN
wheelman .... CYCLIST, PILOT
wheels, move on .... ROLL
set of swiveled .. CASTER
shoe with .... SKATE
wheen .... FEW
wheeze ..... GAG, JOKE, GASP
wheezy breather .. ASTHMATIC
whelk ...... MUREX, PAPULE, PIMPLE, PUSTULE, GASTROPOD, SNAIL
whelp ... PUPPY, CHIT, YOUTH, BEAR
when ...... WHEREAS, WHILE, MOMENT, TIME
whenever .... ANYTIME
whereabouts .... LOCATION
whereas .... WHILE
wherefrom .... WHENCE
whereness .... UBIETY
wherewithal .... MEANS, RESOURCES, MONEY, CASH
wherry ..... ROWBOAT, SCULL, BARGE, LIGHTER
whet .... SHARPEN, HONE, STIMULATE, GRIND
whetstone .... HONE, BURR, BUHR
whether ... EITHER, IF, IN CASE
whey of milk .... SERUM
which .... WHATEVER
whichever .... ANYONE
whidah .... WEAVERBIRD, WIDOW BIRD
whiff .... BREATH, SMELL, PUFF, GUST, WAFT, SMOKE, WAFF
whiffet .... DOG, PUFF
whiffle ... VEER, SHIFT, BLOW, VACILLATE
Whig, opposed to .... TORY
while .... AS, UNTIL, YET, OCCUPY, ALBEIT
whilom .... FORMER(LY), ERST(WHILE), ONCE, QUONDAM
whim ...... CAPRICE, CRANK, KINK, CAPRICCIO, VAGARY, FANCY, NOTION
wham ...... GIMCRACK, TRINKET
whimper ...... MEWL, WHINE, YAMMER, PULE
whimsical .... FLIGHTY, FANTASTIC, FREAKISH, CAPRICIOUS, QUAINT
whimsicality .... CAPRICE, ODDITY
whimsy .... NOTION, CAPRICE, HUMOR, FANCY
whin ..... FURZE, ROCK, TRAP, GORSE, GREENSTONE
whinchat .... SONGBIRD
whine ...... PULE, WHIMPER, COMPLAIN, MEWL, YAMMER
whinny .... HINNY, NEIGH, FURZY
whip ...... WHALE, PULLOUT, BEAT, FLAY, DEFEAT, WHISK, WALE, LASH, FLAP, FLOG, KURBASH, COWHIDE, SCOURGE, FLAIL, SWISH, KNOUT, LARRUP, LICK, LACE, BELABOR, FLAGELLATE
Biblical .... SCORPION
blow .... FLICK
handle ... CROP, STOCK, BUTT
leather .... KURBASH, KNOUT
mark ...... WELT, WALE, STRIPE, W(H)EAL
riding ..... QUIRT, CROP
severely ...... TAN, FLOG
stroke .... FLICK
to a froth .... MILL
up ...... EXCITE, ROUSE
whipcord .... CATGUT
whiplash ...... FLOG, THRASH, THONG
snapper .... COSAQUE
sound .... WHISH
whippersnapper ..... UPSTART, SQUIRT
whippet ... GREYHOUND, DOG
whipping boy ..... SCAPEGOAT
stick ...... ROD, SWITCH, CANE
whippoorwill .... GOATSUCKER
feathers .... VIBRISSA
whir .... BUZZ, VIBRATE, BIRR
whirl .... GYRATE, EDDY, CIRCLE, ROTATE, SPIN, STIR, UPROAR, REEL, PIROUETTE, SWIRL, GYRE
whirler and howler ... DERVISH
whirilgig ... MERRY-GO-ROUND, CAROUSEL, BEETLE
whirling ____ ...... DERVISH
man .... DERVISH
motion .... SWIRL
on toes .... PIROUETTE
wind .... CYCLONE, TORNADO
whirlpool ..... EDDY, VORTEX,

MAELSTROM, WEEL, CHARYBDIS, GULF
whirlwind .... CYCLONE, TORNADO, HURRICANE, EDDY, TOURBILLION
Faroes .... OES
whirlybird .... HELICOPTER, AUTOGYRO, CHOPPER
whirr .... BIRR
whish .... SWISH, WHIZ
whisk ... WHIP, BEAT, BROOM, EGG-BEATER, CARRY, BRUSH
broom ..... RINGE, WISP
whiskers .... MUSTACHE, BEARD, SIDEBURNS, BURNSIDES
cat's .... VIBRISSA
chin .... GOATEE
side ..... CHOPS, MUTTON
whisk(e)y .... MOONSHINE, HOOCH, POT(H)EEN, ROTGUT, SCOTCH, REDEYE, RYE, MOUNTAIN DEW
storeroom ..... BUTTERY
to an Indian .. FIREWATER
whisper .... MURMUR, BREATH(E)
actor's .... ASIDE
whispered, something .... RUMOR, SECRET, HINT, CONFIDENCE
whist .... SILENT, STILL, SILENCE, CARD GAME
game series ...... RUBBER
game similar to .. BRIDGE RUFF
term .... SLAM, MORT, MISERE, VOLE
whistle ...... FOGHORN, TOOT, PIPE, TOTTLE
whistler ..... MARMOT, OUSEL, GOLDENEYE
whistling sound ..... STRIDOR, WHIZZ
in the ears ..... TINNITUS
whit .... BIT, IOTA, JOT, PARTICLE, DOIT, TITTLE
white ...... SILVER, HOAR(Y), PALE, WAN, ASHEN, SNOWY
admiral ...... BUTTERFLY
alkali .... SODA ASH
animal .... ALBINO
ant ...... ANAY, TERMITE
bait .... BRIT, SPRAT, HERRING
bear .... POLAR
cedar .... ARBORVITAE
cliffs site .... DOVER
clouds .... CERRI
coal .... WATER
collar employe ... CLERK
colored person .... CAUCASIAN
combining form .... LEUK(O)
creamy .... IVORY
earth .... GYPSUM, MAGNESIA, KAOLIN, TERRA ALBA
egg's ... ALBUMEN, GLAIR
eye .... SONGBIRD
fish .... ATINGA, MENHADEN, BELUGA, CISCO, POLLAN, TULLIBEE
flag signal .... TRUCE, SURRENDER
Friar .... CARMELITE, ALSATIAN
gum .... EUCALYPTUS
haired .... HOARY
Hart .... INN
hot ..... INCANDESCENT
House resident .... PRESIDENT
lead .... CERUSE, CERUSSITE
lie .... FIB
livered person .. COWARD
make ... BLANCH, BLEACH
man .... BUCKRA
man's burden .... IMPERIALISM
meat .... VEAL
men in .... DOCTORS
oak .... ROBLE
person ...... CAUCASIAN, PALEFACE
plague ... TUBERCULOSIS
race .... CAUCASIAN
Rose house .... YORK
Sea gulf ..... ARCHANGEL
slang ..... HONEST, FAIR
spruce .... EPINETTE
thorn .... MAYFLOWER
turning ..... ALBESCENT
whale .... BELUGA
women in .... NURSES, NUNS
whitebait .... BRIT
whitecap .... WAVE
whitefish ... VENDACE, BELUGA, POLLAN, MENHADEN, CISCO, TULLIBEE, ATINGA
whiten ... ETIOLATE, BLEACH, BLANCH
whitening .... CANESCENT
whitetail .... DEER, WHEATER
whitewall .... TIRE
whitewash .. PLASTER, PARGET
whitewood .... LINDEN, TULIP
whither .... WHERE, WHEREVER
whiting .... WEAKFISH, DRUMFISH, MENHADEN, HAKE, COD, CHALK
whitlow ..... AGNAIL, FELON
Whitman, poet .... WALT(ER)
Whitney, cotton gin inventor .. ELI
Whitsunday ..... PENTECOST
Whitsuntide .... PINKSTER
whittle ... PARE, CUT, REDUCE, SHAVE
whittling refuse ..... SHAVINGS
whiz(z) ...... WHIR(R), HISS, SPEED BY, BARGAIN, EXPERT
kid .... PRODIGY
kin .... LULU
who goes there? .. CHALLENGE, QUI VA LA
whoa .... STOP, HOLLA
whodunit .... MYSTERY
character .... DICK, SLEUTH, DETECTIVE, BUTLER, VICTIM
coiner of .... GORDON
movie .... CHILLER
staple ... MURDER, CLUES, CRIME
whoever .... ANYONE
whole .... UNCUT, TOTO, INTACT, ENTIRE, COMPLETE, TOTAL(ITY)
as a .... ALTOGETHER
combining form ... HOLO
costume .... ENSEMBLE
note .... SEMIBREVE
number .... INTEGER
wholesale .... GROSS
opposed to ...... RETAIL
wholesome .... HEALTHY, SALUTARY, SOUND
wholly .... ALL, ENTIRELY, PLUMB
whoop ... CALL, SHOUT, CRY, HOOT
whooper .... SWAN
whooping cough ... PERTUSSIS, CHINCOUGH
whop .... BEAT, THRASH, STRIKE, FLOP
whopper .... (BIG)LIE
whore .... HARLOT
whorehouse .... BROTHEL
whorl ... VERTICIL, VOLUTION, FLYWHEEL, VOLUTE
fingerprint ...... RIDGE
wicked ..... EVIL, NAUGHTY, SINFUL, IMPIOUS, GODLESS
act .... MISDEED, SIN
city .... SODOM, GOMORRAH, BABYLON
wicker .... WITHE, TWIG
basket .... SKEP, HAMPER, KIPSEY, PANNIER, KISH, CREEL, CRATE, CORF
cradle .... BASSINET
tree ..... OSIER, WILLOW
wickerwork material ... OSIER, WITHE, RAT(T)AN, WILLOW
wicket .... DOOR, GATE, WINDOW, ARCH, HOOP
in cricket .... INNING
in croquet ... HOOP, ARCH
part .... BAIL
wickiup ..... TEPEE, WIGWAM
wicopy .... BASSWOOD
wide .... BROAD, ROOMY, AMPLE
eyed .... ASTARE
open .... AGAPE
widen ..... SPREAD, BROADEN
widespread ..... PREVALENT, RIFE, RAMPANT, REGNANT
disease .... EPIDEMIC
fear .... PANIC
widgeon ... GOOSE, BALDPATE, DUCK, SMEW, SMEE, ZUISIN, MARECA
kin .. REDHEAD, POCHARD
widow ...... RELICT, BEREAVE, SUTTEE, FEME SOLE, MATRON
bird .... WHIDAH
inheritance of ... DOWER
titled, wealthy .... DOWAGER

widowhood .... VIDUAGE
widow's mites .... LEPTA
third ... DOWER, DOWRY
width ... BREADTH, BROADNESS, WIDENESS, LATITUDE
wield ...... HANDLE, EXERCISE
Wien .... VIENNA
wiener .... SAUSAGE, FRANKFURTER, HOTDOG
wienerschnitzel .... VEAL
Wiesbaden's location .. HESSE
wife .... FERE, BRIDE, SPOUSE, RIB, BETTER HALF, BALL AND CHAIN, MRS., FEME, YOKEFELLOW, MISSIS, MISSUS, MATRON, FROW, HELPMEET, HELPMATE
bequest to .... DOS
common-law .. MISTRESS
dowry of .... DOT
German .... FRAU
in law .... FEME
Indian .... SQUAW
killer .... UXORICIDE
king's ... CONSORT, QUEEN
knight's .... DAME
man's prospective .... INTENDED
of a .... UXORIAL
one .... MONOGAMY
rajah's ..... RANI, RANEE
submissive to one's ...... UXORIOUS
take to .... MARRY
wig ...... PERUKE, TO(U)PEE, TETE, GRIZZLE, GIZZ, PERIWIG
wigeon .... WIDGEON
wiggle ...... WAG, WANGLE, WRIGGLE
wiggler ... LARVA, WRIGGLER
wigwag ...... CODE, SIGNAL
wigwam ..... LODGE, TE(E)PEE, WICKIUP
wild .... PRIMITIVE, LICENTIOUS, UNBRIDLED, STORMY, DISORDERLY, RECKLESS, UNTAMED, GAGA, FERAL, FERINE, WASTE, DESOLATE, SAVAGE, FIERCE, PHRENETIC, HARUM-SCARUM, RIOTOUS
animal .... BEAST
apple ... CRAB, CREEPER
ass .... ONAGER
Bill ____ .... HICKOK
brier .... DOG ROSE
cat .... EYRA, LYNX, BOBCAT, OCELOT, SERVAL, MARGAY, MARGOT
cattle .. GAUR, BANTENG
celery .... SMALLAGE
country .... WEALD
cry .... EVOE, WHOOP, SCREAM, SHRIEK, SCREECH
dog ..... DHOLE, DINGO, CUON
duck .. MALLARD, SCAUP, REDHEAD, CANVASBACK, GOLDENEYE, GADWALL
Duck author ...... IBSEN
eyed .... HAGGARD
fowl ... PHEASANT, QUAIL, PARTRIDGE, DUCK
fowl flock .... SKEIN
goat ... IBEX, TAHR, TAIR
goose .... BRANT
goose's call ...... HONK
guess .... STAB
hog .... BENE, BOAR, PECCARY
honey source ... BEETREE
horse .... MUSTANG, BRONC(H)O, CAYUSE, TARPAN, BRUMBIE
Huntsman .... ODIN
hyacinth ..... BLUEBELL
life .... GAME
life preserve ... WETLAND
madder ...... BEDSTRAW
mustard ..... CHARLOCK
olive .... OLEASTER
ox ..... ANOA, BANTENG, REEM
ox hunter ... BUCCANEER
parsley .... LOVAGE
pig .... BOAR
plum .... SLOE
revelry .... ORGY
rose ...... (SWEET)BRIER, EGLANTINE
sheep ..... ARGALI, SHA, ARUI, URIAL, UDAD, MOUFLON, NAHOOR, AOUDAD, BIGHORN
sown .... OATS
state of being .... FERITY
swan .... ELKE
the .... NATURE
West show ...... RODEO
wildcat ...... LYNX, OCELOT, MARGAY, MARGOT, SERVAL
Wilde, dramatist ..... OSCAR
ballad's subject ... GAOL
play .... SALOME
wildebeest ... GNU, ANTELOPE
wilderness .. JUNGLE, TUNDRA, WASTE(LAND), STEPPE, WILD(S), BOONDOCKS, DESERT
wildfire .... LIGHTNING, ERYSIPELAS
wildlife preserve .. WETLAND, SANCTUARY
wildness .... FERITY
wile .... ART, ARTIFICE, TRICK(ERY), DECEIT, LURE, BEGUILE
wiles .... CHARM
will .... BEQUEATH, VOLITION, WISH, DESIRE, POWER, DECREE
addition to a ... CODICIL
bequeathed by .... TESTAMENTARY
convey by .... DEMISE
exercise of the .. VOLITION
handwritten .... HOLOGRAPH
having made a .. TESTATE
having no ... INTESTATE
in law ...... TESTAMENT
maker .... TESTATOR, DEVISOR
o'-the-wisp ... WILDFIRE, IGNIS FATUUS
power .... SELF-CONTROL
power, loss of ... ABULIA
Willard, boxing champion ... JESS
organization of Mrs. .... WCTU
temperance leader ...... FRANCES
Williams, ballplayer ..... TED
Williamson, Shakespearean actor .... NICOL
willful .... HEADSTRONG, WAYWARD, STUBBORN, OBSTINATE
willies .... JITTERS, NERVOUSNESS, CREEPS
willing .... BAIN, MINDED, DISPOSED, CONSENTING, LIEF
reluctantly .... FAIN
willingly ...... GLADLY, LIEF, READILY
Willkie, presidential candidate WENDELL
utopian dream of .... ONE WORLD
willow .... OSIER, SALLOW, ITEA, SALIX
ament .... CHAT
bark, glucoside from .... SALICIN
basket .... PRICKLE
catkin .... CHAT
herb .... ROSEBAY
of the ...... SALICACEOUS
shoot .... WAND
spike .... CHAT, CATKIN, AMENT
twig .... WITHE, SALLOW, OSIER
twigs, woven ... WICKER
willowy .... SVELT, SLIM, SLENDER
willy-nilly .... INDECISIVE, IRRESOLUTE
Wilson, President .. WOODROW
Wilson's thrush .... VEERY
wilt .... DROOP, LANGUISH, WITHER, SHRIVEL
Wilt the ____ .... STILT
wily ...... SLY, CRAFTY, FOXY, SUBTLE, ASTUTE, ARTFUL, INSIDIOUS
wimble ...... GIMLET, AUGER
Wimbledon event ..... TENNIS
wimple .... RIPPLE
wearer of .... NUN
win .. TRIUMPH, PREVAIL, EARN
all games .... SWEEP
all tricks .... VOLE, SLAM
wince ...... FLINCH, GRIMACE, RECOIL, REEL, ROLLER
winch .... CRANK, WINDLASS, HOIST, WHIM
Winchester .... RIFLE
wind .. ZEPHYR, STORM, GALE, HINT, NONSENSE, SCENT, COIL, LEVANTER, BUSTER, NOSER, BLAST, DUSTER, PAMPERO, REEL, SIMOOM, SAMIEL

away from .... ALEE
breath of .. WAFT, FLATUS
combining form .. ANEMO
cone .... SLEEVE
crack in timber made by ANEMOSIS
deposit .... LOESS, SEDIMENT
desert .... SIROCCO, SAMIEL, SIMOON
direction recorder .... ANEMOGRAPH, ANEMOSCOPE
driven clouds ..... SCUD
dry .... FOEHN
east .... EURUS
equatorial .... TRADE
gauge ..... ANEMOMETER
gentle .... ZEPHYR, BREEZE, AURA
gust of ...... PUFF, WAFT
high, strong ...... GALE
Indian Ocean .. MONSOON
indicator ... CONE, SOCK, (WEATHER) VANE, SLEEVE
instrument .. HORN, REED, SHAWN, PIPE, OCARINA, BASSOON, TROMBONE, CORNET, FLUTE, CLARINET, OBOE, TUBA, HARMONICA, BUGLE, SACKBUT
instrument finger hole ... VENTAGE
instrument mouthpiece .. LIP
mythical .... SANSAR
north ... BOREAS, AQUILO
northeast .... EURAQUILO, EUROCLYDON
puff .... FLATUS
Rocky Mountain .... CHINOOK
run before the ..... SCUD
scale .... BEAUFORT
science of the .... ANEMOLOGY
shake .... ANEMOSIS
shifting ...... VARIABLE
side away from ...... LEE
side toward ... WEATHER
sound ...... SOB, SOUGH, ROAR
south .... AUSTER
strong .... TEMPEST, STORM, GALE, PAMPERO
sudden, brief .... FLURRY, FLAW
up ..... END, CONCLUDE, FINISH
warm .... FOEHN
wave .... RIPPLE
west ...... ZEPHYR(US), FAVONIAN
whirling ..... CYCLONE, TORNADO
with snow/rain .... FLAW

windbag .... BRAGGART
windblown dust .... STOUR
windbreaker .... JACKET
winder pear .... WARDEN
windfall ..... VAIL, BONANZA, BOON, FORTUNE
windflower .... ANEMONE
windhover .... KESTREL, FALCON
winding .... MEANDROUS, AMBAGE, SPIRAL, MAZY, LABYRINTHINE, TORTUOUS
pathway .... AMBAGE
sheet .... SHROUD, CEREMENT
staircase ...... CARACOLE
windjammer .... SAILBOAT, SAILING SHIP
windlass .... CAPSTAN, WINCH, HOIST, REEL
cylinder .... BARREL
windmill fighter .... (DON) QUIXOTE
part .... SAIL, VANE
pump .... GIN
window bar .... MULLION
bay .... ORIEL
cleaned ...... SQUEEGEED
door .... TRANSOM
dormer .... LUTHERN
drapery ...... VALANCE, LAMBREQUIN
dressing .... TRIM
fastener ... HASP, LATCH
frame .... CASEMENT
frame piece .... STILE
of a .... FENESTRAL
part ..... PANE, JAMB(E), SILL, SASH, LINTEL, GRILL(E), GRATING
roof .... DORMER, SKYLIGHT
round .... ROUNDEL
shade ... BLIND, SHUTTER
ship's ...... DEADLIGHT
small ...... FENESTELLA, WICKET
trellised .... LATTICE
windpipe .... WEASAND, TRACHEA, THROTTLE
part of .... LARYNX
windrow ... FURROW, SWATH
winds, annual ...... ETESIAN
god of .... AEOLUS
study of ... ANEMOLOGY
windshake .... ANEMOSIS
windstorm .... BLIZZARD, BLOW, GALE, TYPHOON, BURAN, SQUALL, TWISTER
Windward Island ... GRENADA, MARTINIQUE, (ST.) LUCIA, DOMINICA, (ST.) VINCENT
opposed to .... LEEWARD
windy ...... STORMY, GUSTY, VERBOSE, AIRY, BOASTFUL, BLOWY
wine .... VINTAGE, PORT, CATAWBA, MUSCATEL, SHERRY, CANARY, MADEIRA, YQUEM, MUSCADEL
addicted to ...... VINOUS
addiction to ... VINOSITY
age of .... VINTAGE
and dine .... TREAT, ENTERTAIN
beverage .... NEGUS, SILLABUB
bottle .... DECANTER, MAGNUM
bottle indentation .. KICK
Burgundy ..... CHABLIS
burning of .. USTULATION
cask ... BUTT, PIPE, TUN, BOSS, PUNCHEON
cask deposit ..... ARGOL, ARGAL, TARTAR
choice .... VINTAGE
colored ...... VINACEOUS
combining form ... BINI, OENO
cup .... BEAKER
deposit .... GRIFFE, LEES
disorder .... CASSE
distillate .... COGNAC, BRANDY
drink, cold .. SANGAREE, COBBLER, SILLABUB
dry ... SEC, SACK, BRUT, VERMOUTH, CHIANTI, CHABLIS, CLARET, TUSCANY
effervescent .... CHAMPAGNE
film on .... BEESWING
flavor .... MULL
flavoring ...... DOSAGE, DOSE
formation in ...... ROPE
fragrance of ... BOUQUET
glass .... RUMMER
god .... BACCHUS
grapes harvester .... VINTAGER
grower's patron .... VINCENT
jug .... OLPE
kind of .. BRANDY, CIDER, CORDIAL, PORT, VERMOUTH, PERRY, MUSCATEL
like .... VINACEOUS
loss of color ..... CASSE
merchant ..... VINTNER
mixture .... NEGUS
new .... MUST
of .... VINOUS, VINACEOUS, VINIC
pitcher .... OLPE
receptacle .... AMA
red ..... CLARET, MEDOC, PORT, TINTA, CHIANTI, BURGUNDY, DUBONNET, TUSCANY
refuse ...... LEES, DREGS
revived .... STUM
Rhine ... MOSELLE, HOCK
sauterne .... YQUEM
seller .. VINTNER, BISTRO
sherry .. OLOROSO, JEREZ
shop .... BISTRO, ESTAMINET, TABERNA
spiced .... BISHOP, SANGAREE, NEGUS, HIPPOCRAS, MARINADE
stock .... CELLAR
storage place .... CELLAR, BUTTERY
strength .... SEVE
strengthen .... DOSE
sweet ...... MUSCATEL, TOKAY, CANARY, MADEIRA, PORT,

VERMOUTH, ALICANTE, MALMSEY, SAUTERNE
sweeten .... MULL
taster .... GOURMET
term ... BODY, BOUQUET, DRY, SEC, BRUT, VINTAGE, FLINTY
unfermented ...... MUST,
vessel .... TUN, AMA CHALICE, AMPULLA
white .... MOSELLE MALAGA, VERMOUTH, SAUTERNE, MADEIRA, MALMSEY, HOCK, CHABLIS, SACK, BARSAC, BURGUNDY, MARSALA
with honey ..... MULSE
wines, study of .... OENOLOGY
winesap ...... (WINTER)APPLE
wing .... PINNA, PINION, PENNON, ALA
bastard .... ALULA
bind the .... PINION
building .... BAY
combining form .. PTERO
cover .... ELYTRUM, ELYTRON, SHARD
footed ... ALIPED, SWIFT
footed creature ..... BAT, LEMUR
feather .... PINION
furnish with .... IMP
in anatomy .... ALA
length .... SPAN
movement .. BEAT, FLAP, FLUTTER
of building .. ELL, ALETTE, ANNEX
protuberance ... CALCAR
shaped .... ALAR(Y), ALIFORM
small .... ALULA
span of airplane .. SPREAD
support of airplane ...... CABANE
three-quilled ..... ALULA
winged .... ALATE(D), PENNATE, FEATHERED, FLEW, ALAR
being .... ANGEL, SERAPH(IM), AMOR
figure .... ICARUS, IDOLON, IDOLUM
goddess .... NIKE
fruit .... SAMARA
hat ... PETASUS, PETASOS
hat wearer .... HERMES (MERCURY)
horse .... PEGASUS
monster: myth. ... HARPY
sandals .... TALARIA
sandals wearer .... MERCURY (HERMES)
staff .... CADUCEUS
two .... DIPTERAL, DIPTEROUS
wingless .... APTEROUS, APTERAL
bird .... APTERYX, KIWI, EMU
winglet .... ALULA
winglike .... ALA(R), PTERYGOID
wings, flap the ...... WINNOW
furnish .... IMP
having .... ALATE(D)
having two ... BIPENNATE
wingspread .... SPAN
wink .... BAT, BLINK, INSTANT, SIGNAL, HINT, TWINKLE, NICTATE
winker .... EYE(LASH), BLINDER
winkle .... SNAIL
winks, forty .... NAP, DOZE
winner .... VICTOR
longshot/surprise .... SLEEPER
Winnie was his nickname ..... CHURCHILL
the Pooh author .. MILNE
winning .... CHARMING, ATTRACTIVE, TAKING
disposition ...... SWEET
lottery combination ..... TERN
point .... ACE
winnings: sl. .... VELVET
winnow ... SIFT, FAN, SCATTER
winsome .... ENGAGING, BONNY, CHARMING
winter ... SEASON, HIBERNATE
apple .... DELICIOUS, RUSSET
cap .... TUQUE
festival ...... POTLATCH
fodder .... SILAGE
of/like .... HIEMAL, BRUMAL, HIBERNAL
product ... FROST, SNOW
sleep ..... HIBERNATION
solstice festival .... SATURNALIA
spend the .... HIBERNATE
sport .... SKIING, SLALOM
squash .... CUSHAW
torpid in ...... DORMANT
vehicle .... SLEIGH, TOBOGGAN, SLED(GE)
wear .... EARMUFF, SNOWSHOES
weather .... SLEETY
winterberry .... HOLLY
wintergreen ... SHINLEAF, OIL, TEABERRY
false .... PYROLA
"Winter's Tale" shepherdess .. MOPSA, DORCAS
wintry ..... BRUMAL, HIEMAL, HIBERNAL, COLD, SNOWY
winze .... SHAFT
wipe ..... MOP, DRY, EFFACE, SWAB, JEER
out .... ELIMINATE, LIQUIDATE, ERASE, KILL, REMOVE, EXTERMINATE, ERADICATE
wiper ...... TOWEL, DUSTER, DISHRAG, CAM
finger/lip ...... NAPKIN, SERVIETTE
wire .... TELEGRAM, TELEGRAPH, CABLE(GRAM)
brush .... CARD
coil .... SPRING
cutting tool ...... PLIERS
drum's .... SNARE
light bulb .... FILAMENT
measure ..... MIL, STONE
nail .... BRAD
pen .... CAGE
rope .... CABLE
service .... UPI, INS, REUTERS
spiral of .... COIL
tapper ... BUGGER, TOUT
wiredancer .... AERIALIST
wirehair ...... (FOX) TERRIER
wireless .... RADIO
adjunct ...... ANTENNA, AERIAL
wirepuller .... PUPPETEER
wirework .... GRILLAGE
wireworm .... MILLIPEDE
wiry .... STIFF, SINEWY
Wisconsin capital .. MADISON
city .... MILWAUKEE, RACINE, KENOSHA, OSHKOSH, WAUSAU, APPLETON
footballers .... BADGERS
Indian .. SAC, WINNEBAGO
lake .... WINNEBAGO
motto .... FORWARD
native .... BADGER
state animal .... BADGER
state bird .... ROBIN
state fish .... MUSKY
state flower ..... VIOLET
wisdom .... SAPIENCE, SAGACITY, LEARNING, LORE, WIT, ERUDITION, KNOWLEDGE
goddess of .... MINERVA, ATHENA
source of .... LAMP
symbol of .... OWL
tooth .... MOLAR
universal .... PANSOPHY
wise ..... SAPIENT, JUDICIOUS, INFORMED, SHREWD, CUNNING, SAGE, DEEP, ERUDITE, SAGACIOUS, LEARNED
adviser .... MENTOR
and pithy ...... GNOMIC
guy .... SMARK ALECK
leader ...... STATESMAN
man .. NESTOR, SOLOMAN, MENTOR, SAVANT, SAGE, SOLON, MAHATMA
men, Biblical ..... MAGI
saying .... ADAGE, SAW, REDE, PROVERB, MAXIM
slang .... CONCEITED, KNOWING, FRESH, SAVVY
wiseacre .... QUACK, SMART ALECK, KNOW-IT-ALL
wisecrack ..... GIBE, RETORT, JOKE, GAG, QUIP
wish ..... DESIRE, CRAVE, BID, BEHEST
mere .... VELLEITY
wishbone .... FURCULUM, FOURCHETTE
wishy-washy ...... SLOVENLY,

SLIPSHOD, WEAK, THIN, INSIPID, WATERY, NAMPY-PAMBY
Wisla .... VISTULA
wisp .... BUNCH, SHRED, BUNDLE, TATE
wispy ...... SLIGHT, SLENDER
wisteria .... SHRUB, PEA, FLOWER, VIOLET
wit .... SENSE, WAG, MIND, HUMOR(IST)
descriptive of .... QUICK, NIMBLE
graceful, piercing .... ATTIC SALT
lively .... ESPRIT
lowest form of ..... PUN
sharp .... SALT
soul of .... BREVITY
sting of .... BARB
witch .... SORCERESS, HEX, HAG, CRONE, ENCHANTRESS, HARPY, WARLOCK, HELLCAT, SIREN, LAMIA, CARLINE, BELDAM(E), SYBIL
brew of ...... HELLBROTH
city .... SALEM
doctor ... MEDICINE MAN
folklore .... LILITH
Homer's .... CIRCE
means of transportation .. BROOM
Shakespeare's ... DUESSA
witchcraft ... SORCERY, MAGIC, WIZARDRY
talisman ..... OBI, OBEAH
witchery ... SORCERY, CHARM, FASCINATION
witches' broom .. HEXENBESEN
with .... AMONG, CUM
cruel tendencies .... SADISTIC
force .... AMAIN
spirit, in music .. CON BRIO
withal ... STILL, BESIDES, ALSO
withdraw ... SECEDE, RECANT, RETRACT, QUIT, WEAN, PULLOUT, EVACUATE, RETIRE, RETREAT, RECALL
withdrawn ..... RESERVED, SHY
withe .... WICKER, OSIER
wither .. FADE, SHRIVEL, WILT, DRY UP, DECAY, WIZEN, SCATHE
withering away ... TABESCENT
withhold .... RESTRAIN, KEEP(BACK), REFUSE, CHECK, DENY
within ..... INNER, BEN, INSIDE
without ..... LACKING, SANS, BEREFT, OUTSIDE, SINE, EX
charge ..... GRATIS, FREE
combining form ... ECTO
delay .... FORTHWITH, IMMEDIATELY
feet .... APOD
fluid .... DRY, ANEROID, DEHYDRATED
legal force .... NULL
life .... AZOIC
passengers: colloq. ...... DEADHEAD
preparation .. EXTEMPORE, IMPROMPTU
sound .... MUTE, SILENT
teeth .... EDENTATE
withstand .... ENDURE, RESIST, OPPOSE, BEAR
witless ..... FOOLISH, STUPID
witness ...... TESTIFY, ATTEST, TESTIFIER, OBSERVE(R), SEE, TESTE, ONLOOKER
bear ... TESTIFY, ATTEST
perjured ..... STRAWMAN
place in court .... STAND
witticism .... JOKE, GAG, WISECRACK, (BON)MOT, SALLY, QUIP, PUN
Witt's planetoid .... EROS
witty .... DROLL, JOCOSE, FACETIOUS, HUMOROUS, JOCULAR, SALTY
exchange ..... REPARTEE
poem .... EPIGRAM
reply .... RETORT, SALLY
wive .... MARRY
wivern .... DRAGON
wizard ..... SAGE, MAGICIAN, CONJURER, SHAMAN, SORCERER, PELLAR, ARCHIMAGE, MAGIAN, MAGE
of Menlo .... EDISON
wizardry ... SORCERY, MAGIC
wizen ..... WITHER, SHRIVEL, DRY(UP)
woad .... DYE, MUSTARD, PASTEL
woald .... WELD
wobble .... WADDLE, SHIMMY, SHAKE, VACILLATE
"Wobblies" of 1905 ..... IWW
wobbly .... SHAKY
Woden .... ODIN, OTHIN
woe ...... AFFLICTION, GRIEF, MISERY, SORROW, TROUBLE, DOLOR
woebegone ... SAD, DESOLATE
wolaba .... KANGAROO
wold ... MIGNONETTE, PLAIN, FLOWER
wolf ... PHILANDERER, LARVA, LUPUS
bound with magic rope .. FENRIR
cry of .... HOWL
female .... BITCH
foot(print) .... PAD
male .... DOG
of a .... LUPINE
prairie .... COYOTE
timber .... LOBO
young .... WHELP
Wolfe, fiction detective .. NERO
victim of .... MONTCALM
Wolfert, writer .... IRA
wolfhound ..... BORZOI, ALAN
wolfish .... RAPACIOUS, RAVENOUS
wolflike ..... THOOID, LUPINE, RAVENOUS
wolfram(ite) .. TUNGSTEN, CAL
wolfsbane .... ACONITE, MONKSHOOD
wolverine .... CARCAJOU, GLUTTON
woman .... CARLINE, EVE, DISTAFF, FROW, FEMALE, WIFE, LADY, SHE, MULIER, MUJER, SQUAW, JILL
adviser .... EGERIA
annoyer .... MASHER, OGLER
attendant ...... MATRON
bad-tempered .. VIRAGO, SHREW, BITCH, HELLCAT, VIXEN, SPITFIRE, FRUMP, TERMAGANT
bearing second child .... MULTIPARA
beautiful .. VENUS, SIREN, VISION, HOURI, BELLE, STUNNER, HELEN
birth control advocate ... SANGER
blouse .... BASQUE
bold .... QUEAN
bonnet .... CAPOTE
British sl. .... BIRD
cape of .... BERTHA, MANTEAU, PELERINE
chaste ... VIRGIN, VESTAL
childless ..... NULLIFARA
cloak .... CARDINAL, MANTEAU, MANTUA, CAPUCHIN
coat ... MANDARIN, MINK
collar .... BERTHA
colloquial (see slang) .... PETTICOAT, HEN, FILLY, FRAIL, BROAD
combining form ... GYN
companion .... CUMMER
conductor ...... QUACH
country ...... GAMMER, GAFFER
dirty ... SLUT, SLATTERN, TROLLOP, DRAB, MALKIN
domineering .. BATTLE-AX
dowdy .... FRUMP, SLATTERN, TROLLOP
dowry .... DOT
drawers .. PANTALET(TES)
dressing gown .... CAMISOLE, KIMONO
elderly .... MATRON, DOWAGER
escort of ..... (E)SQUIRE, CHAPERON
evening dress .... FORMAL
evil ..... HAG, HELLCAT, JEZEBEL
fairest .... HELEN
fascinating ...... WITCH
flyer .... AVIATRIX
frenzied ...... M(A)ENAD
graceful .... SYLPH
guard .... MATRON
haircut style .... BOB, BANGS, SHINGLES
hat of ... TOQUE, TURBAN, PILLBOX, BRETON, CLOCHE
hater ...... MYSOGINIST

head and shoulder covering ...... NUBIA
headdress ...... PINNER, FRET, POUF
hideous .... BELDAME, WITCH, MEDUSA
homosexual ..... LESBIAN
houseworker .... MARTHA
in uniform .. WAC, WREN, WAVE, SPAR, NURSE
jacket of .. SACK, SACQUE, SIMAR, CAMISOLE, PALETOT
killing .... FEMICIDE
loose ...... JADE, TART, WENCH, QUEAN, WANTON, HUSSY, TRULL
mantle .... MANTEAU
married .... MATRON, MADAM(E), MISSUS, MRS.
masculine traits of ...... VIRILISM
meek .... GRISELDA
model .... MANNEKIN, MANNEQUIN
nagging .... SHREW
neck wear .... STOLE
noble .... COUNTESS, DUCHESS, BARONESS
of poor repute .. DEMIREP
old ..... HAG, GRANDAM, GAMMER, WITCH, CRONE, CARLINE, GAFFER, HARRIDAN
old, unmarried .. SPINSTER
opera comic ..... BUFFA
origin of .... RIB
pants .... CULOTTES
patient .... GRISELDA
performer ...... DISEUSE, ACTRESS, ARTISTE
pert ...... MINX, HUSSY, TART
popular .... BELLE
pretty .. LOOKER, STUNNER
promiscuous ... CHIPPY, COCOTTE
quarrelsome .... VIRAGO, SHREW, RANDY, HARRIDAN, XANTHIPPE, TERMAGANT
repulsive .... GORGON
Reserve, USN ... WAVES
riding costume ... HABIT, JOSEPH
robe .... SIMAR
ruler ...... MATRIARCH, QUEEN, EMPRESS
scarf .... MANTILLA
scolding .... VIRAGO, SHREW, NAG, XANTHIPPE, TERMAGANT, FISHWIFE
seducer .... VAMPIRE, SIREN
shameless ..... JEZEBEL
shoe of .... CHOPINE
shoe style of .... WEDGIE
singer .... SOPRANO, CHANTEUSE, CHANTRESS, CANTATRICE
skirt .... KIRTLE
slang .... TIT, SKIRT, FLOSSIE, FLOSSY, BABE, BROAD, SQUAW
soothsayer ..... SEERESS, PYTHONESS
spiteful .... CAT
spy .... MATA HARI
stately .... JUNO
suckling baby .... WET NURSE
tongue's curb ... BRANKS
ugly ... BELDAM(E), HAG, WITCH, GORGON
unfruitful .... BARREN
untidy .. SLUT, SLATTERN, TROLLOP, DRAB, MALKIN
vest of .... JERKIN
violent .... FURY
warrior .... CAMILLA, AMAZON
wicked .... JEZEBEL
womb of ... WAME, BELLY MATRIX, UTERUS, VENTER
work of a .... DISTAFF
wrap of .. NUBIA, DOLMAN
writer .... SOB SISTER
yellow-haired ... BLONDE
young .... MISS, PUSS, BABE, NYMPH

womanhood ..... MULIEBRITY
womb .... WAME, MATRIX, BELLY, VENTER, UTERUS
women, club of ...... SOROSIS, SORORITY
government by .... MATRIARCHY
preoccupation of .. DIET, WEIGHT, STYLE, PRICES, MAKE-UP
reformatory .... MAGDALENE
seclusion of .... PURDAH
undergarment ...... BRA, SLIP, BLOOMERS, TEDDY, UNDIES, LINGERIE, CHEMISE, KNICKERS
underpants ..... STEP-INS
vest .... JERKIN

wombat .. BADGER, MARSUPIAL
wonder .... MIRACLE, AMAZEMENT, MUSE, MARVEL
boy .... PRODIGY
world's .... PHAROS, PYRAMID

wonderwork .... MIRACLE
Wanson, in Japanese .. GENSAN
wont .... ACCUSTOMED, CUSTOM, HABIT
wonted .... USUAL
woo .... COURT, SUE, SEEK, ENTREAT, SPARK
wood .... FOREST, GROVE, XYLEM, LUMBER, TIMBER, MAHOGANY
alcohol ...... METHANOL
anemone .. THIMBLEWEED
aromatic .... LINALOA
ash oxide .... POTASH
ashes extract .... LYE
axe breaker .. QUEBRACHO
bar .... FID
batted for distance ...... TIPCAT
bend in ..... SNY, WARP
betony ...... LOUSEWORT
bits .... KINDLING
black ...... TEAK, EBONY, DOOK
block ...... NOG, SPRAG, TRIG, WEDGE
borer .... TOREDO
burning piece .... FIREBRAND
charred .... BRAY
coal .... LIGNITE, CHARCOAL
combining form .... LIGN(O), XYL(O), HYL(O), LIGNI
cutter .... RIPSAW
cutting .... HAG
destroying insect .... TERMITE, ANAY
destroying mollusk ...... TEREDO
dressed .... TIMBER
dresser .... ADZ(E)
drug .... QUASSIA
dust .... COOM(B)
easily burned .... SPUNK
eater .... ANAY, TERMITE
elastic .... YEW
engraving ... XYLOGRAPH
flat piece .... SPLAT
fluting .... CHAMFER
for bows .... YEW
for bridges/piles .. ALDER
for dagger hilt .... DUDGEON
for furniture ...... EBONY, WALNUT, CALAMANDER
fragrant .... CEDAR, ALOES
groove .... CHAMFER
gum .... XYLAN
hard .... NARRA, MAHOGANY, EBONY, LOCUST, HICKORY, MOLAVE
hyacinth .... BLUEBELL, HAREBELL
ibis .... JABIRU
inlaid .... BUHL
knot .... KNAR
layer .... VENEER
light .... BALSA
louse .. SLATER, SOW BUG
made of .... XYLOID
make into ..... LIGNIFY
mark .... ROE
measure .... CORD, FOOT
nymph ... HUMMINGBIRD, MOTH, BUTTERFLY, (HAMA)DRYAD
of ... LIGNEOUS, XYLOID
oil .... TUNG
partially burned .. CINDER
piece of .... BOARD, PLANK, SLAT, STAVE, BILLET
pigeon .... RINGDOVE, CUSHAT, CULVER
pin ..... NOG, FID, PEG

pin in boat .... THOLE
preservative .. CREOSOTE
resinous ..... LIGNALOES
shoe .... PATTEN, SABOT, CLOG
small .... GROVE
sorrel ..... OXALIS, OCA
stand, top of ..... CRISS
strip ..... BATTEN, SLAT, LATH, SPLINT, SPLIT, SLIP, STAVE, LIST
striped .... ARAROBA
tar distillate ... CREOSOTE, PITCH
twist in .... WARP
veneer .... BURL
warbler .... WAGTAIL
wheel brake ..... SPRAG, TRIG, NOG, WEDGE
winds .... OBOE, FLUTE, CLARINET, BASSOON
worker ..... CARPENTER
worm .... THRIPS
woodbine ...... IVY, CREEPER, HONEYSUCKLE, PERIDOT
woodchat .... SHRIKE
woodchuck .... MARMOT, GROUNDHOG, WEJACK
woodcock relative .... SNIPE, SANDPIPER, PEWEE
woodcraft .... HUNTING, TRAPPING
woodcutter .... LUMBERJACK, LOGGER, SAWYER
wooded .... SYLVAN
area .... BOONDOCKS, WEALD
hill .... HOLT
wooden ...... STOLID, DULL, STIFF, INSENSITIVE, TREEN
bar .... TREE
bench .... SETTLE
board for meat-carving .. TRENCHER
bowl ..... KITTY, MAZER, MAZARD
brick .... DOOK
bucket .... CANNIKIN
club .... BILLET
collar .... CANGUE
hammer .... MALLET
horse giver ..... TROJAN
Indian's place .... CIGAR STORE
limb .... PEG LEG
pail .... PIGGIN
peg/pin ... THOLE, SPILE, NOG, FID, TRE(E)NAIL, DOWEL
pole/post .... TREE
seat .... BENCH
shoe ..... CLOG, SABOT, PATTEN
spool toy ..... DIABOLO
stake .... TREE
time-beaters .. CASTANETS
woodland ..... FOREST, GROVE
clearing .... GLADE
deity ...... PAN, SATYR, FAUN, SILENUS, SILVANUS
woodluck .... ARI SPONSA, DUCK
woodman .. FORESTER, RANGER
woodpecker .... FLICKER, YELLOWHAMMER, CHAB, SAPSUCKER, HIGH-HOLE, POPINJAY, COLY, REDHEAD
genus .... YUNX
woods .... GROVE, SILVA, FOREST
diety of the ..... SYLVAN
out of the .. SAFE, CLEAR
woodsia .... FERN
woodsman .... TRAPPER, HUNTER, VOYAGEUR
woodbine .... IVY
woodwaxen .... DYEWEED
woodwind .... OBOE, BASSOON, CLARINET, FLUTE
woodworm .... THRIPS
woody .... LIGNEOUS, XYLOID
fiber .... BAST
fiber substance .. LIGNIN
plant ..... SHRUB, TREE
tissue .... XYLEM
vine .... CLEMATIS
wooer .... SUITOR
woof ..... WEFT, BARK, ABB, FILLING, FABRIC, TEXTURE, CLOTH
woofer ... LOUD-SPEAKER, DOG
wooing ..... SUIT, COURTSHIP
wool .... ALPACA, MERINO, PILE, LANA, ANGORA, FLEECE
and cashmere .... CASHA
and silk cloth .. CAMLET, EOLIENNE
animal with ...... SHEEP, ALPACA, GOAT, VICUNA, MERINO
bearing ..... LANIFEROUS
blanket .... SERAPE
blemish .... MOTE
cleaning machine .... WILLOW(ER)
cloth .... FRIEZE
cluster .... NEP
coarse .... SHAG
comb .... CARD
combed knot of .... NOIL
combining form .... LANI
covered with .. FLOCCOSE, LANATE
fabric ... DELAINE, CASHA, ETAMINE, BEIGE, LANSDOWNE, FRISCA, VELOUR(S), REPP, REP(S), STAMMEL, CHALLIS, CHALLIE, FRIEZE, BEAVER, HODDEN, TARTAN
fat .... LANOLIN(E)
felted .... CASHA
fiber .. NOIL, SLIVER, PILE, FLOCK
fiber, batted ... BATTING
goat's .... CASHMERE
grease .... SUINT
knitted .... JERSEY
knot .... NOIL, BURL
like fabric ..... LANITAL
lock of .... TAG
matted .... DAGLOCK
measure .... HEER
oily substance ... GREASE
particles .... DOWN
piece of .... NOIL
produced one year .. CLIP
roll of .... SLUB
rug fibers .... NAP, PILE
salvage .... MUNGO
sheared at one time ..... CLIP, FLEECE
sheep .... MERINO
sheer .... VOILE
shreds of .... NOIL
spinning machine .... THROSTLE
synthetic .... LANITAL
thread .. WORSTED, YARN
tuft .... FLOCCUS, FLOCCULE, LOCK
twisted .... ROVE
unravel ... TEASE, CARD
waste ... MUNGO, FLOCK, FUD
watered .... MOREEN
weight .... TOD
yarn .... WORSTED
woolen cloth .... TARTAN, ETAMINE, JERSEY, CASHA, MOREEN, WORSTED, FRIEZE, MUNGO, CAMLET, SHODDY, HODDEN, MELTON, DOESKIN, KERSEY, RATINE, RATTEEN, TRICOT(INE), MERINO, PETERSHAM, DUFFLE, DUFFEL, CASIMIRE, CALAMANCO
jacket .... CARDIGAN
material .... CADDIS
shawl .... PAISLEY
twilled fabric .... SHALLOON, SERGE, CAS(S)IMERE
woolly ..... FLEECY, LANOSE, LANATE, FLOCCULENT
bear .... CATERPILLAR
haired people .... ULOTRICHI
tuft .... FLOCCULUS
woorali ..... CURARE, URARI
woozy .. MUDDLED, BEFUDDLED
word ...... REMARK, PLEDGE, PROMISE, NEWS, TIDINGS, PAROLE, SIGNAL, TALK, ORDER, INFORMATION, LOCUTION
action .... VERB
addition to end of .... PARAGOGE
airmail envelop .... PAR AVION
appropriate .. MOT JUSTE
blindness .... ALEXIA
book .... LEXICON, DICTIONARY, THESAURUS, LIBRETTO
change in a .. METAPLASM
derivation .... PARONYM
dropping of middle sound of .... SYNCOPE
dropping of last sound/ letter of ..... APOCOPE
exact .... MOT JUSTE
figurative .... TROPE, METAPHOR, SIMILE
final .. AMEN, ULTIMATUM

first of doxology .... GLORIA
for word .... LITERAL, VERBAL, VERBATIM, TEXTUAL, METAPHRASE
formative ending .... DESINENCE
four-letter .. TETRAGRAM
game .... ANAGRAM, CHARADE, ACROSTIC, CONUNDRUM
hard to pronounce ...... JAWBREAKER
in a ... BRIEFLY, IN SHORT
inventor ..... NEOLOGIST
inversion .. ANASTROPHE
last .... AMEN
last syllable of .. ULTIMA
long: colloq. .. MOUTHFUL
meaning, study of .... SEMANTICS, SEMASIOLOGY
misused ..... BARBARITY
new .... NEOLOGISM
new meaning of .... NEOLOGISM
of assent ..... YES, YEA, AMEN
of honor .... PLEDGE, PAROLE, PROMISE
of mouth .... ORAL
of only one .. MONOMIAL
of opposite meaning .... ANTONYM
of similar meaning ...... SYNONYM
of warning ... CAUTION, BEWARE
ordinary meaning .... LITERAL
origin of a .. ETYMOLOGY
original form ... ETYMON
prisoner's ...... PAROLE
puzzle ..... LOGOGRIPH, ACROSTIC, CHARADE, CROSSWORD, REBUS
reading same backward .. PALINDROME
same pronunciation, different meaning ..... HOMONYM, HOMOPHONE
same spelling, different meaning .... HOMOGRAPH, HETERONYM
shorten a ...... SYNCOPE
square .... PALINDROME
substitute .... METONYM
symbol ...... LOGOGRAM
the .... BIBLE, LOGOS
unprintable, usually ..... FOUR-LETTER
vowel omission .. APHESIS
with tail .. CAT, BOB, HIGH

wordiness .... PLEONISM, PROLIXITY, VERBIAGE, VERBOSITY
wording .... PHRASING, PHRASEOLOGY, DICTION, TEXT
words .... TEXT, LYRICS, DISPUTE
argument about .... LOGOMACHY
attack with ...... BASTE, ABUSE
author's .... TEXT
battle of .... LOGOMACHY
choice or .... DICTION
clever exchange of ...... REPARTEE
doctrine of ... NEOLOGY
eat one's .... RETRACT
few of .... LACONIC
incorrect use of .... CATACHRESIS
manner of expression .... ENUNCIATION, DICTION
misuse of .. MALAPROPISM
of .... VERBAL
of few .... LACONIC, TERSE, CURT
play on .... PUN
prefix .... LOGO
ridiculous user of .... (MRS.) MALAPROP

wordy ..... PROLIX, VERBOSE, WINDY, REDUNDANT
work ... JOB, EFFORT, LABOR, TOIL, EMPLOYMENT, OCCUPATION, CRAFT, BUSINESS, TASK, OPUS, GRIND, ERGON
against .... MILITATE
aimlessly .... PUTTER, POTTER
amount of .... LOAD
art .... PAINTING, SCULPTURE, MUSIC, CARVING, ETCHING, OIL, OPUS, COMPOSITION
artist's .... MASTER
assignment ...... SHIFT, BEAT, STINT, TASK, JOB, TRICK
at .... PLY
avoid .... SHIRK, SKULK, MALINGER
clothes cloth .. OSNABURG, DRILE, DENIM
energetically .... HUSTLE
evade .... MALINGER
fussily .... NIGGLE
great .... MASTER
group .... CREW, GANG, TEAM, DETAIL
hard .... TOIL, SWEAT, GRUB, PLUG, HUSTLE
in .... INSERT
incentive .... BONUS, TIP
life .... CAREER
of wonder .... MIRACLE
out .... SOLVE, DEVELOP, EVOLVE, EXERCISE, PRACTICE
pants .... LEVIS
patiently ... PLOD, TOIL, PLUG, PLY
shift .... TRICK
shoes .... BROGAN
suitable .... METIER
tedious ... CHORE, GRIND, TRAVAIL, DRUDGERY
time-out from ... BREAK, RECESS
trainee ..... APPRENTICE
trousers .... DUNGAREES
together: slogan .... GUNG HO
unit of .... ERG(ON)
unskillfully ..... DABBLE
with lead .... PLUMB

workable .... FEASIBLE
workaday .... COMMONPLACE, ORDINARY, PROSAIC, DRAB
workbag .... KIT
workbook .... MANUAL
workbox .... (TOOL)KIT, ETUI
worker .... LABORER, EMPLOYE, WAGE-EARNER, HAND
agricultural ... FARMER, OKIE
class ..... PROLETARIAT
coal mine ..... COLLIER
farm .... PEON, HIND
gem .... JEWELER
hard .... SCRUB
menial .... SERVANT, DRUDGE, DOMESTIC
migratory ... HOBO, PEON, BRACERO, OKIE
odd job .... JACK
restless .... FLOATER
skilled .... ARTISAN, CRAFTSMAN
stone ... MASON, JEWELER
transient ...... FLOATER, HOBO, OKIE
unskilled .... TINKER, COBBLER
white collar ...... CLERK
who replaces striker ..... RAT, SCAB

working .... RUNNING, OPERATING
workhorse ... SLAVE, DRUDGE, TOILER
Workman, explorer ... FANNY
workmanship ...... ARTISTRY
works .... OEUVRES
workshop ..... LAB, ATELIER, STUDIO
workout ..... PRACTICE, TEST, EXERCISE
world .... COSMOS, UNIVERSE, EARTH, GLOBE, MANKIND, DOMAIN, REALM
bearer of the ..... ATLAS
domain .... ANIMAL, VEGETABLE, MINERAL
of the .... TERRESTIAL, TEMPORAL, SECULAR, MUNDANE
out of this .... OUTRE
War I machinegun ...... POMPOM
War I plane ..... TAUBE, NIEUPORT, SPAD
War II title .... SCAP
wide .... UNIVERSAL, PANDEMIC, CATHOLIC, ECUMENIC, GLOBAL
wonder .... PYRAMID, PHAROS, COLOSSUS

worldly .... MUNDANE, SECULAR, TERRENE, TERRESTIAL, EARTHLY, TEMPORAL

wise .... SOPHISTICATED, KNOWING
worm ... NAID, ESS, ANNELID, ASCARID, HELMINTH, NEMATODE, WRETCH, TINEA, LOA
bait .... LURG
bloodsucking .... LEECH
combining form .. VERMI
drug .... VERMICIDE
eaten .... RAGGED, WORN-OUT
feeler of a .... PALP(US)
flat .... TREMATODE, FLUKE
in zoology ...... LYTTA
larva ..... CATERPILLAR, MAGGOT, GRUB, CERCARIA
marine .... NEMERTEAN
move like a ..... CREEP, CRAWL
out .... EXTRACT
parasitic ...... CESTODE, CESTOID, FLUKE
round .... ASCARID
sand .... NEMERTEAN
sea .... SAO
segment .... SOMITE, METAMERE
shaped ...... VERMIFORM
ship ..... BORER, TEREDO
silk .... ERIA
snail resembling .. SLUG
sucker .... LEECH
sucking organ of .... PROBOSCIS
threadlike ...... FILARIA
track .... NEREITE
water .... LEECH, TEREDO
worms .... medicine for intestinal .... SANTONINE(E)
of the Nile .... ASPS
parasitic .... FILARIA
wormseed .... SANTONICA
wormwood .... MOXA, MORTIFICATION, BITTERNESS, ABSINTH(E)
worn ..... TATTERED, SHABBY, SPENT, RAGGED, EROSE, JADED
by friction ..... ATTRITE
clothes .... RAGS
end .... FRAZZLE
look .... HAGGARD
out .... EXHAUSTED, TIRED, SPENT, DECREPIT, JADED, SEEDY, EFFETE
worried .... CAREWORN, ANXIOUS
worrier's crop .... ULCERS, WRINKLES
worry ...... HARASS, PESTER, ANNOY, DISTRESS, ANXIETY, CARE, FRET, STEW, GRIZZLE
colloquial ..... LOOKOUT, CONCERN
worship .... VENERATE, IDOLIZE, ADORE, REVERE, HOMAGE, ADORATION, DEIFY
animal .... ZOOLATRY
combining form .. LATRY
due God alone .. LATRIA
object of ... IDOL, HERO, SWEETHEART
of all gods ... PANTHEISM
of idols .... IDOLISM
of saints ... HAGIOLATRY
place of .. ALTAR, SHRINE, TEMPLE, SYNAGOGUE, CHAPEL, PAGODA
system of .. FETISH, CULT
worshipper .... ADORER, ADMIRER, VENERATOR, IDOLIST, IDOLATER
stars .... SABAIST
worst .... BEAT, DEFEAT, POOREST
Dressed Woman Awards creator .... BLACKWELL
worsted cloth .... SERGE, ETAMINE, WOOL
ribbon/yarn ..... CADDIS
wort .... HERB, PLANT
worth ... MERIT, PRICE, VALUE, IMPORTANCE
having ...... DESIRABLE, ASSET
of little .... TRIFLE, TRIFLING
worthless .... USELESS, GOOD-FOR-NOTHING, VAIN, NUGATORY, LOSEL, RIP
almost .... PALTRY, PETTY, PIDDLE
fellow ...... BUM, IDLER, LOSEL
horse ...... NAG, JADE, PLATER
ideas .... BILGE,
remains .... CARCASS, CARCASE, DREGS, SCRAPS
scrap .... ORT
thing .... TRIPE, FICO, CHIP
worthwhile .... OF VALUE
worthy .... DESERVING, MERITORIOUS, VALUABLE
Wouk, author ...... HERMAN
ship .... CAINE
wound ...... LESION, PIERCE, GASH, TRAUMA, INJURY, SORE, STAB, HURT
blood shed from ... GORE, SANIES
discharge from a .. ICHOR, PUS, SANIES
dressing .... PATCH
edge of .... LIP
jagged ..... LACERATION
mark .... SCAR
plug .... TENT, DOSSIL
woven double ..... TWO-PLY
goods dealer .... HOSIER
with raised design .... BROCHE
wow ..... INTERJECTION, HIT, AMUSE
wowser .... PRUDE
wrack ...... SEAWEED, RUIN, WRECKAGE, CLOUDS
wraith ... GHOST, APPARITION, SPECTRE, FETCH
wrangle ... QUARREL, ARGUE, BICKER, DISPUTE, ROW, HIGGLE
wrangler ... COWBOY, ARGUER
wrap .... SWATHE, COVER, ENVELOP, CLOAK, PELISSE, SWADDLE, NUBIA
around .... LOINCLOTH, SARONG
in burial cloth ..... CERE
shoulder ... CAPE, SHAWL
snugly .... TUCK
to deaden sound .... MUFFLE
up ..... FINISH, ENFOLD, ENVELOP
woman's ...... DOLMAN
wrapper .... VESTURE
book's .... JACKET
candy's .... TINFOIL
wrapping material .... CELLOPHANE, PAPER, LEAF, KRAFT, MATTING
wrasse .... CUNNER, FISHES
wrath .... ANGER, FURY, CHOLER, RAGE, IRE
wreak .... INFLICT, EXACT
wreath .... ANADEM, LEI, CHAPLET, GARLAND, ORLE, TORSE
bridal .... SPIREA
for achievement .... CORONA
for head .... ANADEM, CHAPLET, LAUREL
hanging .... FESTOON
victor's .... LAUREL, CROWN
wreathe .... COIL, TWIST, ENCIRCLE, ENVELOP
wreck ... RUIN, DESTRUCTION, DESTROY, DAMAGE, RAZE, SMASH(UP)
building ... TEAR DOWN
wreckage .... FLOTSAM, JETSAM, (W)RACK
wren ..... SONGBIRD, TOMTIT, JENNY
wrench .... SPRAIN, SPANNER, TWIST, JERK, WREST, WRICK
kind of ..... STILLSON, MONKEY
wrest ...... WRENCH, TWIST, USURP, WRING, EXTRACT, EXTORT
wrestle .... CONTEND, TUSSLE, GRAPPLE
wrestler ... MATMAN, MAULER, GRAPPLER
wrestling hold .... (HALF) NELSON, WRISTLOCK, (HEAD)LOCK, SCISSORS
match division .... FALL
oriental .... SUMO
place/school .... PAL(A)ESTRA
score .... FALL
sound .... THUD, GRUNT, GROAN
trick throw .... CHIP
wretch .... PARIAH, OUTCAST, MISER, WORM, HILDING, CAITIFF, SCULLION

wretched .... MISERABLE, WOEFUL, SAD, DISMAL, MEAN, FORLORN, ABJECT
wriggle ... WANGLE, WIGGLE, SQUIRM, DODGE
wriggler .... LARVA, HULA DANCER
Wright, airplane inventor ..... ORVILLE, WILBUR
wring ...... WREST, WRENCH, SQUEEZE, TWIST, EXTRACT, EXTORT, PRESS
neck of .... SCRAG
wrinkle .... RIMPLE, FURROW, RIDGE, CREASE, TWIST, CRIMP, SEAM, COCKLE, FOLD, RUCK, RUGA, RUMPLE, SHRIVEL, PUCKER, NOVELTY
wrinkled .... LINED, RUGATE, RUGOSE
wrist ..... CARPUS, CARPAL(E)
bone .... CARPAL(E), TRAPEZOID
bone, of a .... SCAPHOLD
guard .... BRACER
wristband ..... CUFF, BRACER
wristlet .... BRACELET, HANDCUFF
writ .... PROCESS, VENIRE, WARRANT, DOCUMENT, OYER BREVE, INJUNCTION, PRECEPT
Holy .... BIBLE
judicial .... TALES
of ____ ...... EXECUTION, PROHIBITION, CERTIORARI, VENIRE, RIGHT, MANDAMUS
of execution ..... ELEGIT
of right's issue ..... MISE
order of arrest ... CAPIAS
to serve in court .... SUBPOENA, SUMMONS, VENIRE
write ...... SCRAWL, INDITE, PEN, SCRIBBLE, COMPOSE, INSCRIBE, SCRIVE, LUCUBRATE
at length ...... EXPATIATE
effusively .... GUSH
hurriedly ..... DASH(OFF)
into law .... ENACT
one's name .... SIGN
up ...... SKETCH, REPORT
writer ..... SCRIBE, AUTHOR, PENMAN, AMANUENSIS, CLERK, COPYIST, POET, JOURNALIST
inferior .... HACK, POETASTER, SCRIBBLER
kind of ... GHOST, COPY, COPYIST
of trilogies .... ASCH
play .... DRAMATIST
unscrupulous .... PLAGIARIST
verse ..... POET, RHYMER
writers' group .... PEN
writhe ..... SQUIRM, CONTORT, TWIST
writing .... BOOK, POEM, DOCUMENT, LETTER, ARTICLE, DIARY, MONOGRAPH, TREATISE
as a profession ...... PEN
cipher ... CRYPTOGRAPHY
combining form .... LOG(UE)
desk .... SECRETARY, ESCRITOIRE, BUREAU
exalted to trivial .. BATHOS
flippant style of .... PERSIFLAGE
flourish ...... CURLICUE, TAG, CURLYCUE
foolish ...... TWADDLE, HOGWASH
implement .. PEN, STYLUS, QUILL, CHALK, BRUSH, PENCIL
mark .... CHARACTER
material, box for .... PAPETERIE
mystic .... RUNE
paper ..... STATIONERY, TALIPOT, PAPYRUS
paper size .... DEMY, IMPERIAL
parchment ..... VELLUM
pompous ...... FUSTIAN
preliminary ...... DRAFT
pretentious ..... KITSCH
secret ..... CIPHER, CODE
senseless ... BALDERDASH
sentimental ...... SLUSH
stroke .... SERIF
table .... ESCRITOIRE, DESK, BUREAU
tablet .... DIPTYCH
wall .... GRAFFITO
wedge-shaped .... CUNEI
writings .... LITERATURE
collection of ..... PAPERS
unpublished ... REMAINS
written, not ... ORAL, VERBAL, TACIT
order .... PRECEPT
plans, for short ... SKEDS
wrong .... EVIL, AMISS, ERRONEOUS, ABUSE, WICKED, IMMORAL, INCORRECT
act .... MISDEED, MISCONDUCT
civil .... TORT
do woman ..... SEDUCE, ABUSE
name .... MISNOMER
prefix .... MIS, MAL
wroth ..... IRATE, INCENSED, ANGRY
wrought .... FASHIONED, SHAPED, DECORATED, D(A)EDAL
up ..... EXCITED, TENSE, DISTURBED
wry .... TWISTED, DISTORTED, CONTRARY, PERVERSE
wryneck .... LOXIA, WEET, (SNAKE)BIRD
Wyandot .... HURON
Wycliffe disciple .... LOLLARD
Wylie, novelist ...... ELINOR
Wyoming capital ... CHEYENNE
cavern .... SHOSHONE
city ... LARAMIE, CASPER, SHERIDAN
mountain .... TETON, MORAN, LARAMIE
peak .... GANNETT
state tree .. COTTONWOOD
Wystan Hugh ____ ... AUDEN
wyvern .... DRAGON

X

X ..... TEN, MARK, SIGNATURE
Greek XI
letter .... EX
marker, usually .... ILLITERATE
marks the ____ .... SPOT
shaped .... EX
xanthic .... YELLOW
Xanthippe's husband .... SOCRATES
prototype ...... NAGGER, TERMAGANT, SHREW, VIRAGO
xanthous .... YELLOW
Xavier, saint .... FRANCIS
Xe, in chemistry ..... XENON
xebec .... SHIP
common users .. CORSAIRS
xema .... GULL
xeno .... GUEST
as prefix .... FOREIGN, STRANGE
Xeres .... JEREZ
xerophilous plant/animal ..... CACTUS, CAMEL, XEROPHTYE
xerotic .... DRY
Xerxes I, father of .... DARIUS
wife .... ESTHER
xiphoid .... ENSIFORM, SWORD-SHAPED
xiphosuran ...... KING CRAB, ARACHNID
Xmas .... YULE(TIDE), CHRISTMAS
Xtian. .... CHRISTIAN
xylan .... PENTOSAN
xylem ...... WOOD, HADROME
xyloid .... WOODY, LIGNEOUS
xylonite .... CELLULOID
xylophone-like instrument .... MARIMBA, SARON
xylotomous insect ... TERMITE, ANAY
xyst .... PORTICO
xyster .... (BONE)SCRAPER

Y

Y, Greek .... UPSILON
Hebrew .... YOD(H)
in mathematics .... ORDINATE
letter .... WYE
men .... ELIS
yabber ...... TALK, CHATTER, GIBBER
yacht .... CRUISE(R), KNOCKABOUT, CUTTER
club president .... COMMODORE
flag .... BURGEE
racing .... SONDERCLASS
racing champion .... INTREPID
sail .... SPINNAKER
tender .... DINGHY
yachting center ...... COWES
yachtsman .... LIPTON, CORINTHIAN
Yadkin .... PEEDEE, RIVER
yaffle .... WOODPECKER
yager .... RIFLEMAN
yahoo ..... BRUTE, BUMPKIN, LOUT
creator .... SWIFT
Yahwe(h) ..... GOD, JEHOVAH
yak .... SARLAK, OK
where found ...... TIBET
yaki .... CAYMAN
Yakutsk river .... LENA
Yale .... ELI, UNIVERSITY, LOCK
Bowl sound ...... BOOLA
Mr. .... (ELIHU) ROOT
Yalta conference member .... STALIN
native .... CRIMEAN
yam ..... ROOT, POTATO, UBE, UBI, HOI
bean .... BONIATA, KAMA
Yamashita, Jap. general ...... TOMOYUKI
sobriquet .... TIGER
yamen resident ... MANDARIN
yammer ... WHINE, COMPLAIN, YELL, WHIMPER, CLAMOR
Yangtze River city .... WUHU, NANKING
Yank ...... AMERICAN, JERK
Yankee .... AMERICAN, NORTHERNER
yap ..... YELP, JABBER, TALK, YAWP, YIP, BARK
slang .... MOUTH, ROWDY, HOODLUM
Yaqui .... RIVER, INDIAN
yard .... SPAR, GROUNDS
enclosed .... GARTH
in law .... CURTILAGE
kind of ... PATIO, COURT, QUAD
yards, 220 .... FURLONG
yarn ..... STORY, TALE, SLUB, MERINO, THREAD, FIBER, SPINEL, INKLE, GARN, BOUCLE, ANGORA
ball of .... CLEW
count .... TYPP
560 yards .... HANK
flax .... LINEN
knot .... BURL
knitting .... SAXONY
machine .... MULE
measure .... CLUE, CLEW, LEA, SPINDLE, COP, HANK, SKEIN
quantity .... SKEIN
roll of .... COP
skein of .... HASP
teller ..... MUNCHAUSEN, ANGLER
twilled .... CREWEL
twisted .... CREWEL
warp .... ABB
waste .... THRUM
winder .... PIRNER
woolen, inferior .... SHODDY
worsted .... CADDIS
yardstick .... STANDARD, CRITERION
yarrow .... MILFOIL, HERB
yashmak .... VEIL
yatag(h)an .... SABER
yaud .... MARE, JADE
yaupon ..... CASSINE, HOLLY, CASSENA
use of .... TEA
yaw .... TUMOR, DEVIATE, VEER
yawl .... JOLLYBOAT, SAILBOAT, KETCH, DANDY
yawn .... GAPE, CHASM, OSCITATE
aloud ..... YAWP, YAUP
meaning of, usually ..... FATIGUE, BOREDOM, DROWSINESS, ENNUI
yawner .... SLEEPYHEAD
yawning, fit of .... GAPES
yawp ...... YAP, GAPE, CRY, YAWN
yaws .... FRAMB(O)ESIA
cause of ..... SPIROCHETE
Yb, in chemistry .. YTTERBIUM
yclept ...... CALLED, NAMED, KNOWN (AS)
ye .... THEE, THOU
yea(h) ... YES, INDEED, TRULY
yean .... REAR, BRING FORTH
yeanling .... LAMB, KID, NEWBORN
year .... AGE, TIME, ANNO
designating a .... LUNAR, SOLAR, NATURAL, TROPICAL, SIDEREAL, LEAP, FISCAL, CALENDAR
every .... ANNUALLY, PER ANNUM
half .... SEMESTER
of plenary indulgence .... JUBILEE
yearbook .... ANNUAL, ALMANAC, ANNAL
yearling ...... LEVERET, COLT
yearly .... ANNUALLY, ETESIAN
calendar ...... ALMANAC
yearn .... HANKER, LONG, ACHE, SIGH, CRAVE, PINE
years, 1000 .... CHILIAD
yeast .... BARM, LEAVEN, FERMENT, FOAM, FROTH, ANAMITE, BEES
enzyme .... ZYMASE
Yed(d)o .... EDO, TOKYO
yegg .... CRIMINAL, SAFECRACKER, BURGLAR, TRAMP
yell .... YAMMER, SHOUT, SCREAM, SHRIEK, OUTCRY, CHEER, HOLLER, HALLOO
college ..... CHEER, RAH
ending cheers ..... TIGER
yellow .... CHROME, DYE, PIGMENT, MELINE, ECRU, XANTHOUS, GAMBOGE
bird .... FOLDFINCH, WARBLER, CANARY, MELINE, ORIOLE
brown ..... DUN, SORREL
bugle .... IVA
calla .... AROID
clay ..... OCHER, OCHRE
colloquial ... COWARDLY
color .. XANTHIC, ALOMA, AMBER, GOLD, OCHER, SAFFRON
colored fruit .... MANGO, LEMON, AZAROLE
combining form .... CHRYS(O), XANTH(O), LUTEO
compound ... LUTEOLIN
daisy .. BLACK-EYED SUSAN
dark .... OCHRE
dye stuff .... MORIN
egg's .... YOLK
fever .... VOMITO
fever carrier ..... AEDES, MOSQUITO
fever mosquito .... STEGOMYIA
flag signal .. QUARANTINE
gum resin .... CAMBOGIA
jacket .... WASP, VESPID, HORNET
journalism staple .... SCANDAL
lead ore ..... WULFENITE
metal ...... GOLD, BRASS
orange .... SAFFRON
pale ..... FLAXEN, BUFF
Peril harbinger .. CHINESE, MONGOLIANS
pigment .... FLAVIN, QUERCETIN, ORPIMENT, OCHRE, OCHER, ETIOLIN, SIL
quartz .... CITRINE
race .... CHINESE, MONGOL(IAN)
red .... CORAL
reddish .... SANDY
river .... HWANG HO
Sea .... HWANG HAI
Sea gulf .... POHAI

Sea port ...... TSINGTAO
Sea, river into ..... YALU
skin, cause of .. JAUNDICE
turning .... FLAVESCENT
yellowbird .... WARBLER, GOLDFINCH
tree, per song ... BANANA
yellowhammer .... BIRD, FLICKER, WOODPECKER, YITE, VERDIN
state .... ALABAMA
yellowish brown .. CINNAMON, HAZEL, DRAB, KHAKI, FAWN
complexion .... SALLOW
red .... RUFOUS
yellowlegs .... SANDPIPER
Yellowstone sight ...... FALLS, LAKE, PARK
yellowtail ...... CARANGOID, ROCKFISH, MENHADEN
relative .... CAVALLA, POMPANO
yellowthroat .... WARBLER, BIRD
yellowweed ..... GOLDENROD, RAGWORT, CROWFOOT
yelp .... BARK, YAP, CRY, YAWP, YIP
Yemen capital .... SANA
city .... TAIZ, SANA
dynasty .... RASSITE
king ... (AL)BADR, IMAM
monetary unit .... RIYAL
neighbor of .... OMAN
president/premier ...... (AL)SALAL
seaport .... MOCHA
seat of government .. TAIZ
sect .... ZAIDI
town .... DAMAR
Yemenite .... ARAB
yen ... DESIRE, URGE, YEARN, LONG(ING), LIKING
where used .... JAPAN
yenite .... LIVAITE
yeoman .... MANSERVANT, ASSISTANT, FREEHOLDER
yep .... YES
opposite of .... NOPE
yes .... AYE, YEP, YUP, AGREEMENT, YEA(H)
man .... SYCOPHANT
yeso .... GYPSUM
yet ... STILL, NOW, HOWEVER
yeti .. (ABOMINABLE) SNOWMAN
yew .... CONIFER, TREE
fruit .... BERRY, CONE
Yezd is in .... IRAN
Yiddish .... JEWISH, LANGUAGE
noodles .... FERFEL, FARFEL
synagogue .... SHUL
thief ..... GANEF, GANOF
yield .... GRANT, SUBMIT, PRODUCT, RELENT, CAPITULATE, DEFER, GIVE(IN), SUCCUMB, RETURN, PRODUCE, SURRENDER, (CON)CEDE
farm .... CROP
gold .... PAN OUT
point .... CONCEDE

yill .... ALE
yip .... YELP, BARK
Ymir .... GIANT
yo-heave-ho, for example ..... CHANT
yodel .... WARBLE
yodeler .... SWISS, TYROLEAN
yoga need .... CONCENTRATION
yogi .... ASCETIC, MYSTIC, SWAMI
ballplayer .... BERRA
yoke ..... CANGUE, HARNESS, BONDAGE, SERVITUDE, INSPAN, ENSLAVE, COUPLE, HALTER
part of .... OXBOW
yokefellow .... PARTNER, ASSOCIATE, HUSBAND, WIFE
yokel ..... RUSTIC, BUMPKIN, HICK, RUBE
Yokum's creator .... CAPP
yolk, egg .... YELLOW, VITELLUS
of the egg ..... VITELLINE
protein .... VITELLIN
yolked .... LECITHAL
yom .... DAY
Jewish holiday ... KIPPUR
yon(der) .... THERE
yore .... ELD, LONG AGO
yorker, game associated with .. CRICKET
Yorkshire native ... DALESMAN
port ..... HULL, WHITBY
river .... AIRE
Yoruba .... NEGRO
Yosemite sight .... PARK, CLIFFS, FALLS, REDWOOD
Yoshihito's empire ..... JAPAN
reign .... TAISHO
son .... HIROHITO
title .... EMPEROR
young .... YOUTHFUL, GREEN, RAW, IMMATURE, ADOLESCENT, JUVENILE
animal .... SUCKLING, TOTO
cat .... KITTEN, PUSSY, KITTY
bird .... FLEDGLING, NESTLING, OWLET
blood .... YOUTH
branch .... SHOOT
bull .... CALF
chicken .... FRYER
cod .... SCROD
cow .... CALF, HEIFER
deer .... DOE, FAWN
dog .... PUP(PY), WHELP
eel .... ELVER
fish ... PRY, FINGERLING, PARR, SMELT, GRILSE
fowl .... POULT
fox .... CUB
frog .... TADPOLE
girl ...... MISS, MOPPET, LASS, MAIDEN
goat .... KID
goose .... GOSLING
hare .... LEVERET
hawk ...... EYAS, EYRIE, AERIE
hen ... PULLET, POULARD

herring .... BRIT, SARDINE
hog .... GILT, SHOAT, PORKER, SHOTE
horse ...... COLT, FILLY, FOAL
kangaroo .... JOEY
lion ...... WHELP, CUB, LIONET
male .... BUCK
man ..... MASTER, YOUTH
Mormon church head ... BRIGHAM
oyster .... SPAT
ox .... STEER
pigeon .... SQUAB
salmon ... PARR, GRILSE
seal .... PUP
sheep .... LAMB
squab .... PIPER
swan .... CYGNET
tiger ...... CUB, WHELP
Turks, so-called .. REBELS
whale .... CUB
with .... PREGNANT, ON THE WAY
wolf .... WHELP
younger son .... CADET
youngster .... SHAVER, BANTLING, SMALL FRY, TOT, TAD, LAD, YOUTH, KID, MINOR, URCHIN, TEENAGER
yours truly .... ME
youth .... LAD, STRIPLING, SHAVER, SHAVELING, SAPLING, CHIEL(D), TEENAGER, YOUNGSTER, ADOLESCENCE, WHELP, MINOR
beautiful .... NARCISSUS
group: abbr. ... BSA, GSA
of a .... MINOR
youthful ... JUVENILE, VERNAL
works .... JUVENALIA
yow .... OUCH
yowl ...... WAIL, CRY, YELL
yperite .... MUSTARD GAS
where used in battle ..... YPRES
Yquem ... WINE, SAUTERNE(S)
Yseult .... ISOLDE
Yuan .... TAEL, DYNASTY
yuca .... MANIOC, CASSAVA
Yucatan capital ..... MERIDA
Indian .... MAYA
leaf fiber .... SISAL
Mayan city ..... USMAL
yucca ...... LILY, FLAT, PITA
fiber .... ISOTE
plant like .... SOTOL
Yuga .... ERA, AGE
period ..... TRETA, KALI, KRITA, DVAPARA
Yugoslav(ia) capital .... BELGRADE, BEOGRAD
city .... SENTA, ZAGREB, SKOPJE, SARAJEVO, NOVI SAD, NIS, AGRAM, SERAJEVO
coin .... DINAR, PARA
Commune .... STIP
district ... YUPA, BANAT

guerrillas .... CHETNIKS, PARTISANS
language .... SLOVENE
monetary unit ... DINAR
native .. CROAT, SLOVENE, SERB
news agency ..... TANJUG
part of .... CROATIA, BOSNIA, MONTENEGRO, MACEDONIA, SLOVENIA
peninsula .... ISTRIA
port .... RIJEKA
premier .... SPILJAK
president .... TITO (BROZ)
region .... DALMATIA, BANAT
republic .. MONTENEGRO, SERBIA, CROATIA
river ..... DRAU, DRINA, SAVA, DRAVA, PULJ, MORAVA, USKUB, TISZA
seaport ..... POLA, PULJ, ZARA, SPALATO
town .... CETINJE, CAPORETTO
Yukon capital .. WHITEHORSE
mining town .. SKAGWAY
mountain .... LOGAN, LUCANIA
peak .... LOGAN
region ...... KLONDIKE
tributary .... TANANA
yule .... CHRISTMAS
short for .... XMAS
symbol .. LOG, MISTLETOE
Yum yum's friend ..... KOKO
Yuma ...... MOHAVE, INDIAN, MOJAVE
yummy ... TASTY, DELECTABLE
Yunnan capital .... KUNMING
Yutang, writer .... LIN

Z

Z, Arabic .... ZE
English .... ZED
Greek .... ZETA
Hebrew .... ZAYIN
letter .. IZZARD, ZEE, ZED
Zabrze is in .... POLAND
zac .... IBEX
Starr father of .... RINGO
zacaton .... GRASS
Zaccur's father .... IMRI
Zambal .... MALAY
Zambezi tributary ..... SHIRE
Zamenhof's invention .... ESPERANTO
Zambia capital ...... LUSAKA
city .... LUSAKA, KITWE, NDOLA
language ...... BAMBA, TONGA, LOZI
president ...... KAUNDA
river .... ZAMBEZI
zany ..... BUFFOON, CLOWN, DOLT, SIMPLETON, FOOL
Zanzibar island ...... PEMBA
Zarathustra ...... ZOROASTER
zarf .... CUP
Zasu ____, comedienne .. PITTS
Zea .... KEOS, ISLAND
zeal .... ARDOR, FERVOR, PASSION, ENTHUSIASM, ELAN, VERVE
Zealand city .... COPENHAGEN
fiord .... ISSE
zealot ...... DEVOTEE, BIGOT, FAN, PARTISAN, FANATIC, ENTHUSIAST
zealotry .... FANATICISM
Zealots' conqueror .... TITUS, VESPASIAN
zealous ... FERVENT, ARDENT, RABID
zebec(k) .... SHIP
Zebedee's son .. JOHN, JAMES
zebra and horse offspring ..... ZEBRULA
and ass offspring .... ZEBRASS
animal resembling .. ASS, HORSE, QUAGGA
extinct .... QUAGGA
of the .... ZEBRINE
wood .... ARAROBA
young .... COLT
zebu .... BRAHMA
and yak offspring .. ZOBO, BO(H)
zebuder .... IBEX, ZAC
zecchin(o) ...... COIN, SEQUIN
zed, equivalent of .... ZEE, IZZARD
zee .... IZZARD
Zeeland, capital of .... MIDDELBURG
island ...... WALCHEREN
zenana ..... HAREM, SERAGLIO
factotum ...... EUNUCH
resident .... ODALISK, ODALISQUE, CONCUBINE
zenith .. APEX, PEAK, SUMMIT, TOP, ACME, HEIGHT, VERTEX
opposed to ...... NADIR
sun's .... NOON
Zeno philosophy ... STOICISM
follower ... STOIC, CYNIC
Zenobia .... QUEEN
domain of ..... PALMYRA
zephyr ...... BREEZE, WIND
Zephyrus ...... WEST, WIND, DEITY
zeppelin .... DIRIGIBLE, BLIMP
zero .... CIPHER, NIL, (N)AUGHT, NOTHING, (N)OUGHT, NULLITY
on a compass .... NORTH
Zerulah's son .... ABISHAI
zest ... BRIO, STINGO, FLAVOR, RELISH, PEEL, ZING, GUSTO, VITALITY, TASTE, PIQUANCY, ZEAL
zestful ...... SAPID, PIQUANT
zeta .... ZEE, ZED, IZZARD
Zeus .... JUPITER
attendant of .... NIKE
beloved to .... IO, EUROPA, LEDA
breastplate of ... (A)EGIS
brother of .... HADES
changed her to stone .... NIOBE
daughter of .. IRENE, HEBE
disguise of .... SWAN
Egyptian's ..... AMMON
epithet ... SOTER, AMMON
festival .... NEMEAN
gift to Minos ..... TALOS
messenger of .... IRIS
monster killed by .... TYPHOEUS
nurse of .... GOAT
oracle seat ..... DODONA
parent of .. RHEA, CRONUS
punishment to mankind of PANDORA
shield of .... (A)EGIS
sister of .... HERA
son of .... AMPHION, HEPHAESTUS, TANTALUS, SARPEDON, ARES, AEACUS, APOLLO, PERSEUS, HERMES, ARGUS, MINOS, ARCAS
surname of ..... ALASTOR
wife/lover of ... DEMETER, JUNO, CERES, LATONA, CALLISTO, THEMIS, AEGLE, LEDA, DANAE, HERA, LETO, DIONE, METIS, EUROPA, SEMELE, ALCMENE, AEGINA, EURYNOME, ANTIOPE, MAIA
Zhukov, marshal ..... GRIGORI
Zibeline .... (SABLE)FUR
Ziegfeld show ..... RIO RITA, SHOWGIRL
theatrical producer ...... FLO(RENZ)
ziggurat .... PYRAMID
zigzag .... CRANK(LE), TACK, STAGGER, FORKED
course .... TACK, PLY
road ..... SWITCHBACK
skiing race ...... SLALOM
what it has plenty of ..... ANGLES
Zilpah's son ..... GAD, ASHER
Zimbalist, violinist .... EFREM
zinc .... SPELTER
alloy ..... BIDRI, OROIDE, TOMBAK, TOMBAC(K)
blende ..... SPHALERITE
carbonate .... CALAMINE, SMITHSONITE
ingots .... SPELTER
oxide .... TUTTY
ore .... BLENDE
silicate .... CALAMINE
zing ..... ZEST, VITALITY, PEP
zingara, zingaro ...... GYPSY
zingel .... PERCH
zinnia .... ASTER
Zion ..... HILL, HEAVEN, JEW

site of .... JERUSALEM
Zionism, founder of ... HERZL
zip .. HISS, VIM, ENERGY, WHIZZ
and ____ .... ZING
Zipangu ..... CIPANGO, JAPAN
namer of .. (MARCO) POLO
zipper ..... (SLIDE) FASTENER, BOOT, OVERSHOE, TALON
zircon ..... AZORITE, JACINTH
zither, instrument like .. LYRE, ROTA, CITHARA, VINA
zizany .... COCKLE, TARES
zizith .... TASSELS
zloty is money of ..... POLAND
zoa, singular of .... ZOON
Zoan .... TANIS
zodiac .... GIRDLE, CIRCLE
sign ... CRAB, LEO, LIBRA, PISCES, GEMINI, ARIES, RAM, VIRGO
zodiacal chart .... HOROSCOPE
Zola, ____ .... EMILE
defender of ..... DREYFUS
heroine .... NANA
novel ..... NANA, VERITE GERMINAL
zombi(e) .... COCKTAIL, PYTHON, SNAKE
subject of ...... CORPSE
zone .... BELT, AREA, GIRDLE, CLIME
designation ..... TORRID, TEMPERATE, FRIGID
zoo .... MENAGERIE
floating .... ARK
zooid ..... CORAL, POLYPITE, HYDRANTH
zoological region ... NOTOGAEA
zoologist's concern .... ANIMAL(IA)
zoology branch on shells ...... CONCHOLOGY
zoophyte .... SPONGE, CORAL, RETEPORE
zoot ____ .... SUIT
"Zorba the Greek" composer .. THEODORAKIS
zoril(a) ... POLECAT, MARIPUT, WEASEL
animal like a .... SKUNK
Zoroaster ..... ZARATHUSTRA
Zoroastra's birthplace ...... AZERBAIJAN
Zoroastrian ... PARSEE, PARSI, YEMA
demon .... DEVA
evil spirit ...... AHRIMAN
fire worshipper .. CHEBER, PARSI
god ...... AHURA, MAZDA
sacred writings .... (ZEND)-AVESTA
supreme deity .. ORMAZD, ORMUZD
teaching ...... HUMATA, HUKHATA, HUVARSHTA
Zoroastrianism, commentary on ZEND
zoster .... BELT, GIRDLE
zuccetto .... SKULLCAP
zucchini .... SQUASH
Zug .... CANTON
Zuider ____ .... ZEE
zuisin .... WIDGEON
Zulu ..... MATABELE, BANTU, KAFFIR, ISLAND
band of warriors ... IMPI
headman .... INDUNA
language .... BANTU
native, Philippines ...... MUSLIM, MORO, BADJAO
spear ... ASSAGAI, ASSEGAI
Zululand capital .... ESHOWE
Zuni .... PUEBLO
Zweig, novelist ...... ARNOLD, STEFAN
zygodactyl bird .... PARROT
zygote .... OOSPERM
zymase .... ENZYME
zymone .... GLUTEN
zythepsary .... BREWER

Notes

Notes

Notes

Notes

About the Authors

Redentor Ma. Tuazon, a Philippine native, was about twelve years old when he first saw a crossword puzzle. That was back in 1923. He immediately became a devoted enthusiast and began collecting puzzle clues into notebooks. *The New Comprehensive A–Z Crossword Dictionary* is the result of those painstakingly kept notebooks, compiled over almost fifty years. Mr. Tuazon has been Director of Public Relations for the Boy Scouts of the Philippines, Public Information Officer of the Philippine National Red Cross and a newspaper reporter for the *Manila Daily Bulletin*. Now retired, he lives in Quezon City, Philippines.

Edy Garcia Schaffer was Mr. Tuazon's valuable co-researcher during many of the later years this dictionary was compiled. Mrs. Schaffer now resides in California.